Point / Counterpoint

Binding arbitration clauses are often included in consumer contracts and even in consumer bills. For example, if you open a credit card account, the terms and conditions of the credit application will likely require that you submit any dispute you have to binding arbitration.

Should Companies Be Permitted to Include Binding Arbitration Clauses In Consumer Contracts?

Yes	No
Arbitration is a much faster way to resolve a likely small dispute. Through the discovery process, a defendant could draw out a case for two to three years before the case would actually go to trial. Thus, the consumer benefits from the binding arbitration clause by forcing the defendant to resolve the dispute quickly. According to a recent study by Ernst & Young, 55 percent of consumer arbitrations were resolved in the consumer's favor.* Another study suggested that 93 percent of people who participated in arbitration thought that they were treated fairly.** Consumers receive fair and fast treatment through mandatory arbitration. Consumers have a choice as to whether to purchase a good or service, and in some cases the purchase may include a requirement on how disputes will be resolved. If a consumer is opposed to a mandatory arbitration clause, the consumer can purchase the good or service from another provider. In conclusion, companies should be permitted to include binding arbitration clauses in their consumer contracts.	Arbitration may require that the consumer pay more up-front costs to begin the dispute resolution process. For example, the consumer may have to pay for the costs of the arbitrator. To file a complaint, a consumer has to pay filing fees only, which cost around $150. To file a claim through the American Arbitration Association, a consumer has to pay between $500 and $1,000, and the consumer is required to advance the arbitrator's fees. Many consumers are not likely to read all the fine print when applying for a credit card or purchasing a service. A consumer has no bargaining power to remove a mandatory arbitration clause from the contract; consequently, the consumer has no choice. It is unfair to force a consumer to submit a dispute to arbitration when she or he has no power to bargain regarding that aspect of the sales or service contract. Finally, because arbitration is secret, a company can "hide" its disputes from the general public. The public exposure associated with lawsuits encourages companies to better respond to and resolve disputes. In conclusion, consumers are harmed more than helped by binding arbitration clauses in consumer contracts.

*Ernst & Young, Outcomes of Arbitration: An Empirical Study of Consumer Lending Cases, *available at* http://www.adrforum.com/rcontrol/documents/ResearchStudiesAndStatistics/2005ErnstAndYoung.pdf.

**Report To The Securities And Exchange Commission Regarding Arbitrator Conflict Disclosure Requirements In NASD And NYSE Securities Arbitrations, *available at* http://www.nyse.com/pdfs/arbconflict.pdf.

Point/Counterpoint: Along with the other helpful review material, at the end of the chapter the student is offered a Point/Counterpoint problem that encourages the reader to evaluate the conflicting reasoning surrounding a key issue in the chapter.

You Be The Judge Online: (www.mhhe.com/ybtj)
This interactive product includes 18 hypothetical business law cases. All of the cases are based on real cases within our Business Law texts. Each case allows you to watch interviews of the plaintiff and defendant before the courtroom argument, see the courtroom proceedings, view relevant evidence, read other actual cases relating to the issues in the case, and then create your own ruling. After your verdict is generated, view what an actual judge ruled (unscripted) in the case and then get the chance to defend or change your ruling. Topics include:

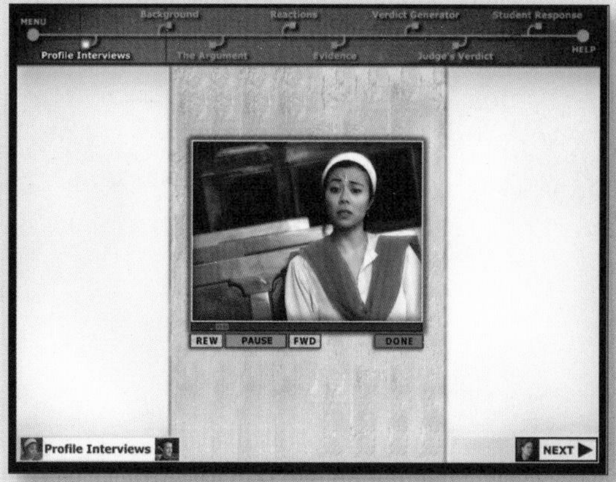

1. **Sexual harassment:** Did Sexy Prank Kill Promotion?
2. **Religious discrimination:** Dress Code Flips Burger Joint
3. **Fraud:** Blind Dates Go Bust
4. **Defamation:** Trashing the French Maid
5. **Partnership:** You Sunk My Partnership
6. **Warranty:** Who Is Distorting What?
7. **Verbal agreement:** Recording Studio Blues
8. **Liability:** Office Party Blame Game
9. **Property:** Subtracting the Addition
10. **Privacy/employment at will:** Fired for Whistling?
11. **Environmental law:** Digging Dogs Find Deadly Dirt
12. **Consumer law:** Misleading Menu Misery
13. **Tenant rights:** When the Lessee Leaves
14. **Consumer law:** The Not-So-Captive Audience
15. **Intellectual property:** Click Here, Get Sued
16. **Debt collection:** Overdue or Overdone?
17. **Intellectual property:** The Yoga Posture Puzzle
18. **Agency:** Duped by Duplication

Dynamic Business Law

Dynamic Business Law

NANCY KUBASEK
Bowling Green State University
M. NEIL BROWNE
Bowling Green State University
DANIEL J. HERRON
Miami University
ANDREA GIAMPETRO-MEYER
Loyola College
LINDA BARKACS
University of San Diego
LUCIEN DHOOGE
University of the Pacific
CARRIE WILLIAMSON
DLA Piper US LLP

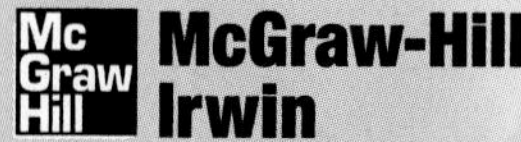

Boston Burr Ridge, IL Dubuque, IA New York San Francisco St. Louis
Bangkok Bogotá Caracas Kuala Lumpur Lisbon London Madrid Mexico City
Milan Montreal New Delhi Santiago Seoul Singapore Sydney Taipei Toronto

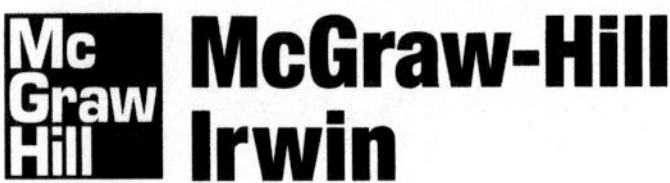

DYNAMIC BUSINESS LAW

Published by McGraw-Hill/Irwin, a business unit of The McGraw-Hill Companies, Inc., 1221 Avenue of the Americas, New York, NY, 10020.

Some ancillaries, including electronic and print components, may not be available to customers outside the United States.

This book is printed on acid-free paper.

1 2 3 4 5 6 7 8 9 0 DOW/DOW 0 9 8

ISBN 978-0-07-352491-7
MHID 0-07-352491-3

Editorial director: *Brent Gordon*
Publisher: *Paul Ducham*
Sponsoring editor: *Dana L. Woo*
Senior developmental editor: *Christine Scheid*
Editorial coordinator: *Megan Richter*
Marketing manager: *Sarah Schuessler*
Project manager: *Bruce Gin*
Senior production supervisor: *Debra R. Sylvester*
Design manager: *Kami Carter*
Senior photo research coordinator: *Jeremy Cheshareck*
Lead media project manager: *Brian Nacik*
Cover design: *Kami Carter*
Interior design: *Kami Carter*
Typeface: *10/12 Times New Roman*
Compositor: *Laserwords Private Limited*
Printer: *R. R. Donnelley*

Library of Congress Cataloging-in-Publication Data

Dynamic business law / Nancy Kubasek . . . [et al.]. — 1st ed.
p. cm.
Includes index.
ISBN-13: 978-0-07-352491-7 (alk. paper)
ISBN-10: 0-07-352491-3 (alk. paper)
1. Business law—United States. I. Kubasek, Nancy.
KF390.B84D96 2009
346.7307—dc22

2007031157

www.mhhe.com

About the Authors

Nancy K. Kubasek received her J.D. from the University of Toledo College of Law in 1981, and her B.A. from Bowling Green State University in 1978. She joined the BGSU faculty in 1982, became an associate professor in 1988, and a full professor in 1993.

During her tenure at Bowling Green State University, she has primarily taught courses in business law, legal environment of business, environmental law, health care law, and moral principles. She has published over 75 articles, primarily in law reviews and business journals. Most of her substantive articles focus on environmental questions, and she writes a quarterly column about environmental issues for the *Real Estate Law Journal.* She has helped get students involved in legal research, and a number of her articles are co-authored with students. She has also published a number of pedagogical articles in teaching journals, focusing primarily on the teaching of critical thinking and ethics.

She wrote the first environmental law text for undergraduate students, *Environmental Law,* and co-authored *The Legal Environment of Business: A Critical Thinking Approach.* She has written supplemental materials, such as study guides, test banks, and instructors' manuals.

Active in many professional organizations, she has served as President of the Academy of Legal Studies in Business, the national organization for professors of legal studies in colleges of business. She has served as President of the Tri-State Academy of Legal Studies in Business, her regional professional association.

In her leisure time, she and her husband, Neil Browne, fish for halibut and salmon in Alaska, as well as large-mouth bass in Florida. In addition, they are regular participants in polka, waltz, zydeco, and Cajun dance festivals in Europe and the United States. For almost 30 years, they have been successful tournament blackjack players. Both are avid exercisers—lifting weights, doing yoga, and running almost every day.

M. Neil Browne is Senior Lecturer and Research Associate, and a Distinguished Teaching Professor Emeritus at Bowling Green State University. He received his B.A. in History and Economics at the University of Houston, his Ph.D. in Economics at the University of Texas, and his J.D. from the University of Toledo. He has been a professor at Bowling Green for more than four decades.

Professor Browne teaches courses in jurisprudence, ethical reasoning, critical thinking, and economics at both the undergraduate and graduate levels. He has received recognition as the Silver Medalist National Professor of the Year, the Ohio Professor of the Year, Distinguished Teacher and Master Teacher at Bowling Green State University, as well as numerous research awards from his university and from professional organizations. His consulting activities with corporate, governmental, and educational institutions focus on improving the quality of critical thinking in those organizations. In addition, he serves as a Rule 26 expert with respect to the quality of the reasoning used by expert witnesses called by the party opponent in legal actions.

Professor Browne has published 20 books and over 130 professional journal articles in law journals, as well as economics, sociology, and higher education journals. His current research interests focus on the relationship between orthodox economic thinking and legal policy. In addition, he is in the midst of writing books about the power of questionable assumptions in economics, the usefulness of asking questions as a learning strategy, and the importance of critical thinking in environmental arguments.

Professor Browne tries to find time for a broad array of outside activities. He and his wife, Nancy Kubasek, fish for halibut and salmon in Alaska, as well as large-mouth bass in Florida, as frequently as possible. In addition, they are regular participants in polka, waltz, zydeco, and Cajun dance festivals in Europe and the United States. For almost 30 years, they have been successful tournament blackjack players. Both are avid exercisers—lifting weights, doing yoga, and running almost every day.

Daniel J. Herron is a professor of business legal studies at Miami University in Oxford, Ohio. He received his law degree from Case Western Reserve University School of Law in 1978 and is a member of the Ohio and federal bars. He has taught at Miami University, his alma mater, since 1992, having previously taught at the University of Wyoming, Western Carolina University, the University of North Carolina–Wilmington, and

Bowling Green State University. He has been a member of the Academy of Legal Studies in Business for nearly twenty-five years and has served as its executive secretary since 1991. His research interests focus on law and ethics, employment law, and legal history.

He has been married for over thirty years to his wife, Deborah, and they have two children, Elisabeth and Christopher, a daughter-in-law, Amanda, and one grandchild, Jack. Herron and his wife reside in Oxford, Ohio, with their two beagles, Max and Missy.

Andrea Giampetro-Meyer is chair of the Law & Social Responsibility Department in the Sellinger School of Business & Management at Loyola College in Maryland. She received her B.S. in business administration from Bowling Green State University and J.D. from the Marshall-Wythe School of Law at the College of William & Mary.

Professor Giampetro's research focuses primarily on legal responses to race and gender discrimination in employment. Her teaching interests are wide-ranging. She teaches at all levels of higher education, from courses designed especially for first year college students, to courses designed for high-level business executives. Professor Giampetro's preferred courses are the undergraduate legal environment of business course, and the graduate ethics & corporate social responsibility course.

Professor Giampetro has earned both national and local awards for teaching, including the Charles M. Hewitt Teaching Award from the Academy of Legal Studies in Business, and the Henry W. Rodgers III Distinguished Teacher of the Year Award from Loyola College. She has experience helping new teachers understand how to work toward teaching excellence. At Loyola College, she serves as a faculty mentor, especially to teachers struggling with how to encourage students to engage in high-level discussion in class. Professor Giampetro has also written several instructors' manuals for textbooks. In these manuals, she strives to provide practical information that gives teachers ideas about how to engage students in meaningful ways.

Professor Giampetro has also received the Holmes-Cardozo Award from the Academy of Legal Studies in Business in recognition of excellence in legal scholarship. She has published numerous articles, and they have appeared in leading journals. In keeping with Loyola College's Jesuit mission, her favorite articles pursue themes related to social justice, especially as it relates to eliminating discrimination and oppression.

Linda L. Barkacs received her J.D. from the University of San Diego in 1993. She also has a B.A. in political science from San Diego State University and an A.A. in accounting from Irvine Valley College.

Upon graduating from law school and passing the California bar exam, Professor Barkacs became an associate at a downtown San Diego law firm. During that time, she was involved in a number of high profile trials, including a sexual harassment case against the City of Oceanside that resulted in a $1.2 million verdict. In 1997, Professor Barkacs and her husband Craig (also a professor at USD), started their own law firm specializing in business and civil litigation (in both federal and state court), employment law cases, and appeals. They were also involved in numerous mediations and arbitrations.

Professor Barkacs began teaching at USD in 1997, and went full-time in Spring-2002. As an educator, she has designed and taught numerous courses on law, ethics, and negotiation. She teaches in USD's undergraduate and graduate programs, including the Master of Science in Executive Leadership (a Ken Blanchard program), the Master of Science in Global Leadership, and the Master of Science in Supply Chain Management. Professor Barkacs often teaches in USD's study-abroad classes and has traveled extensively throughout Europe, Asia, and South America.

Professor Barkacs has received numerous awards for her teaching at USD, including 2007 Professor of the Year, USD Senior Class (university-wide); and 2006–2007 Top Three Finalist, USD Outstanding Undergraduate Business Educator. She and her husband are principals in The Barkacs Group (www.tbgexecutivetraining.com), a consulting firm that provides negotiation, ethics, and teams training for the private sector. Professor Barkacs has published numerous journal articles in the areas of law, ethics, and negotiation. She and her husband are co-authoring a book on negotiation. She has been the president, vice president, conference chair, and treasurer for the Pacific Southwest Academy of Legal Studies in Business (www.pswalsb.net).

Professor Barkacs currently spends her time teaching, publishing, consulting for The Barkacs Group, and doing volunteer work for various civic causes. She enjoys walking, weight lifting, and spending her free time with her husband and their three cats, Crystal, Caspar, and Phoenix.

Lucien J. Dhooge is a professor of Business Law at the Eberhardt School of Business, University of the Pacific. He teaches international trade and commercial law, real estate law, and the legal and ethical environment of business.

After completing an undergraduate degree in history at the University of Colorado, Professor Dhooge attended the University of Denver College of Law, where he received his J.D. in 1983. He received his LL.M. in 1995 from the Georgetown University Law Center, where he specialized in international and comparative law. Prior to coming to the University of the Pacific, Professor Dhooge spent eleven years in the practice of law in Washington, D.C., and Denver.

Professor Dhooge is the author of three books and more than forty law review articles and has presented research papers and courses throughout the United States as well as in Europe and Asia. Professor Dhooge is the recipient of numerous research awards given by the Academy of Legal Studies in Business, including six Ralph C. Hoeber Awards granted annually for excellence in research. He was designated the outstanding junior business law faculty member in the United States by the Academy in 2002 and received the Kay Duffy Award for outstanding service in 2005. In 2003, the University of the Pacific designated him as an Eberhardt Teacher-Scholar. He was designated as an International Scholar by the Soros Foundation in 2006. Professor Dhooge currently serves on the Executive Committee of the Academy of Legal Studies in Business and is a past editor-in-chief of the *American Business Law Journal* and the *Journal of Legal Studies Education.*

A native of Chicago but raised in Denver, Professor Dhooge enjoys spending time with his family and following the fortunes of the Chicago Cubs and the Colorado Rockies professional baseball teams.

Carrie Williamson is an associate in the intellectual property litigation group at DLA Piper US LLP. She has participated in three patent infringement trials. She earned her J.D. from Boalt Hall, University of California at Berkeley, and her B.A. from Bowling Green State University. She has co-authored another book, *Practical Business Ethics: A Guide for a Busy Manager,* and six legal journal articles. Her research interests include critical thinking, ethics, the use of expert testimony, women's legal issues, and patent litigation issues.

Preface

We wrote this book because our primary sense of who we are as professionals is that we are teachers. We play various roles in our careers, but we are especially dedicated to our students. We want them to listen, read, create, and evaluate more effectively as a result of their experience in a business law class.

We tried to construct a book that is both comprehensive and readable. But the features integrated into the chapters provide its distinctive worth. Each feature stands by itself as an aid to the kind of learning we hope to encourage. Yet the features are also a cohesive unit, contributing both to the liberal education of the students who read it and to their skills as decision makers in a market economy.

Specifically, we provide what competing texts deliver, a comprehensive examination of all the relevant questions, concepts, and legal rules of business law. Our text must address the power and authority of constitutions, statutes, case law, and treaties as sources of law. Together the various elements of what we call "the law" make up the foundation and structure of the market exchange process.

Decisions to trade and produce require trust—trust that consumers, firms, workers, financial institutions, and asset owners will do as they promise and that violations of such promises will be unacceptable in the marketplace. Without guarantees that promises will be kept, market exchanges would grind to a halt. Business law provides these guarantees and the boundaries within which certain promises can be made and enforced.

Market decisions are made in a context—a persistently changing context. The law, in turn, is dynamic in response. New technologies and business practices bring new disputes over rights and responsibilities in a business setting. Future business leaders need knowledge of existing business law, as well as a set of skills permitting them to adjust efficiently and effectively to new legal issues as they arise over the course of their careers.

We are excited about the contents of our features and want to explain the function of each of them in preparing our students for leadership in business.

global context

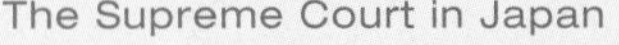

The Supreme Court in Japan

The supreme court of Japan, located in Tokyo, consists of 15 justices, including one chief justice. Because the justices ascend from lower courts, they are usually at least 60 years old. The full bench of the supreme court does not hear every appealed case. Rather, a petit (small) bench of five justices first hears each case to determine whether to transfer the case to a hearing before the full bench. The petit court transfers a case to the full bench if it believes that the appellant can prove that the law or decision in question is unconstitutional. Because proving the unconstitutionality of a law is extremely difficult, the full bench generally hears fewer than 10 cases annually.

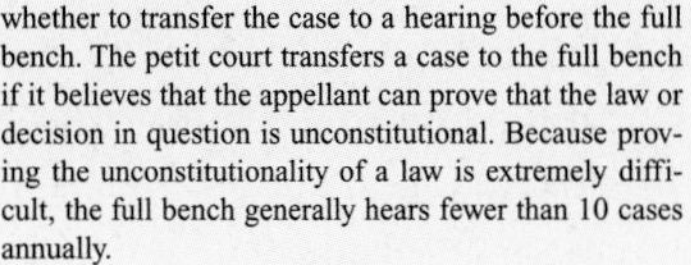

A. GLOBAL BOXES

This first feature highlights the emerging, interconnected market. Each chapter contains multiple Global Context boxes. Because so many market decisions are made in an international context, learners need to familiarize themselves with the likelihood that a particular legal principle essential to doing business in one country may not be appropriate in other countries. The Global Context boxes provide heightened awareness of this likelihood by illustrating how unique the law in a certain country often is. After reading dozens of these "stories of difference," readers will certainly better understand the need to discover relevant law in all jurisdictions where their market decisions have legal implications.

We believe that students learn innumerable valuable lessons about American business law by contrasting the concepts of our business law system with those of our primary trading partners. We typically use Canada, Japan, China, Russia, Mexico, and the European Union for our comparisons because modern business managers will more likely be interacting with the law in those particular jurisdictions.

B. E-COMMERCE BOXES

A central feature of modern business decisions is new technology, specifically the rapid spread of electronic commerce. This development has created new challenges and opportunities that were unforeseeable until very recently.

Our initial approach was to construct an e-commerce chapter that stood by itself. But the more we thought about that approach and listened to our reviewers, we decided to place E-Commerce boxes in most of our chapters, as well as integrate the e-commerce material throughout relevant chapters. By this infusion approach, we think we can best convince students of the pervasive influence of this new, complicating aspect of business decisions.

> **e-commerce AND THE LAW**
>
> **The Sliding Scale Standard for Internet Transactions**
>
> Does a business that has Internet contact with a plaintiff in a different state satisfy the minimum-contacts standard? Anyone who engages in transactions over the Internet should be concerned about this question.
>
> A federal district court established the following "sliding-scale" standard in the 1997 case *Zippo Mfg. Co. v. Zippo Dot Com, Inc.*: *
>
> [T]he likelihood that personal jurisdiction can be constitutionally exercised is directly proportionate to the nature and quality of commercial activity that an entity conducts over the Internet. This sliding scale is consistent with well developed personal jurisdiction principles.
>
> At one end of the spectrum are situations where a defendant clearly does business over the Internet. If the defendant enters into contracts with residents of a foreign jurisdiction that involve the knowing and repeated transmission of computer files over the Internet, personal jurisdiction is proper.
>
> At the opposite end are situations where a defendant has simply posted information on an Internet website which is accessible to users in foreign jurisdictions. A passive website that does little more than make information available to those who are interested in it is not grounds for the exercise of personal jurisdiction.
>
> The middle ground is occupied by interactive websites where a user can exchange information with the host computer. In these cases, the exercise of jurisdiction is determined by examining the level of interactivity and commercial nature of the exchange of information that occurs on the website.
>
> *952 F. Supp. 1119, 1124 (W.D. Pa. 1997)

C. CONNECTING TO THE CORE

The business curriculum, as experienced by students, can easily be seen as a collection of silos, with each silo, or academic department, walled off from the others with its own special language and issues. But successful business decisions start with recognition that decision makers should take advantage of the interrelatedness of the various subject areas.

To encourage the habit of seeing business decision making as connected and cohesive, most chapters contain a feature entitled "Connecting to the Core." The purpose of that section is to drive home the point that concepts from finance, accounting, marketing, management, and economics are closely linked to concepts and dilemmas in business law. The study of business law is best seen as a foundational component of the larger study of business administration.

> **connecting to the core**
>
> **Management: Creating Constructive Conflict**
>
> As discussed in the text, one of the benefits of mediation is that there is a greater likelihood that opposing parties will maintain relationships when they cooperatively seek a solution to the issues in conflict. While alternative dispute resolution involves a more formal forum for discussing conflict, business managers must frequently undertake the management of conflict in their workplace. As with the ideals of ADR, managers hope to preserve workplace relationships when resolving conflict among employees or between management and employees.
>
> Sometimes, however, it is important for managers to create *constructive conflict* within their organization, as certain kinds of conflict may advance organizational goals while presenting only nominal harm to employee relationships. For instance, managers could offer competitive incentives to employees who consistently exceed performance standards (e.g., providing a vacation to the highest-performing salespersons), reward cost-saving proposals from employees with bonuses, hire consultants or outside advisers to stimulate change, or use programmed conflict (i.e., role-playing exercises) to evaluate different positions on certain issues. Although it is at times damaging to workplace relationships and contrary to organizational objectives, conflict can be used, when properly managed, to stimulate change and the advancement of organizational objectives.
>
> Source: K. Williams, *Management: A Practical Introduction* (New York: McGraw-Hill/Irwin, 2006), pp. 412, 416–417.

D. CRITICAL THINKING

After each case in the book, we have provided critical thinking questions to highlight the need to think critically about the reasoning used by the court. In addition, we include in

> **CASE 3-2** J.E.B. v. ALABAMA, EX. REL. T.B.
> UNITED STATES SUPREME COURT
> 114 S. CT. 1419 (1994)
>
> 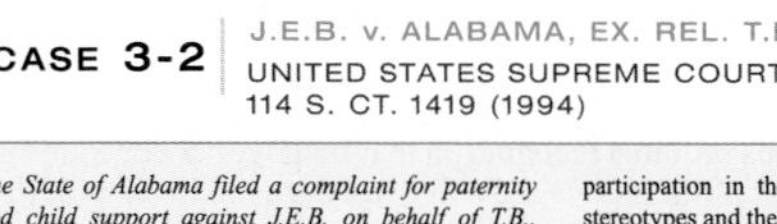
>
> *The State of Alabama filed a complaint for paternity and child support against J.E.B. on behalf of T.B., the unwed mother of a minor child. The court called a panel of twelve males and twenty-four females as potential jurors. Only ten males remained after three individuals were removed for cause. The state used its* proceedings. The community is harmed by the State's participation in the perpetuation of invidious group stereotypes and the inevitable loss of confidence in our judicial system that state-sanctioned discrimination in the courtroom engenders.
>
> As with race-based *Batson* claims, a party alleging gender discrimination must make a prima facie
>
> **REVERSED AND REMANDED in favor of JEB.**
>
> CRITICAL THINKING
>
> The defendant was contesting the removal of males from the jury. Does this fact weaken the court's reasoning? Explain.

Point / Counterpoint

Sarbanes-Oxley Act of 2002

Are the Costs Associated with the Sarbanes-Oxley Act Reason for Reform?	
No	**Yes**
Corporate and accounting scandals, such as Enron, were the reason the Sarbanes-Oxley Act of 2002 was drafted. The act promotes honesty and accountability in financial reporting, thus bringing increased security to investors. For example, corporations must now ensure the segregation of all duties related to accounting procedures. Although critics assert that the financial burden associated with the act is reason for reform, the compliance costs about which they speak are beginning to fall as individuals become familiar with the new systems. In addition, the Dow Jones Industrial Average is rising as a result of increased investor confidence. This confidence is the direct result of the requirement that corporations disclose information and allow for investigations by the Public Company Accounting Oversight Board.	Corporations need incentives to remain or go public. The Sarbanes-Oxley Act of 2002 is not an incentive. Although there may have been ample motivation for the development of an act that addresses accounting scandals, the costs associated with Sarbanes-Oxley are much too high. Simply purchasing and learning to use the materials needed for compliance with the act would cost approximately $3.5 million. Those who argue that the act should not be reformed often focus on the idea that every corporation is now being held to the same standards. However, as a result of the substantial economic costs associated with implementation of the guidelines, smaller businesses that would like to go public are forced to remain private to avoid the costs. Among small businesses that are already public, many are not able to gather the resources necessary to comply with the act.

every chapter a Point/Counterpoint problem that encourages the reader to evaluate the conflicting reasoning surrounding a key issue in the chapter.

But we do much more than just ask a lot of critical thinking questions at particular locations throughout the chapters. We encourage the use of a step-by-step critical thinking approach that has been developed and used in classrooms in many countries. We do not just repeatedly urge students to "think critically." Instead, we describe for them what is meant by that phrase in the context of business law. We include this step-by-step approach in Appendix A-1 at the end of Chapter 1. Instructors who wish to emphasize critical thinking can use that appendix as a structured approach for learning how to evaluate legal reasoning.

E. ETHICAL REASONING

Our book emphasizes consideration of all stakeholder interests in every market decision. Business ethics should never be an afterthought or something firms consider because they think they must.

Instead, business ethics is what provides the social legitimacy for markets, what distinguishes markets from the life of the jungle. While market decisions are calculating and purposeful, they must at the same time reflect awareness that the good and the right provide social borders that elevate those decisions above simple greed and egoism.

Ethical discussion focuses on the basic observation that we are socially and globally interdependent as entrepreneurs, asset owners, workers, businesspeople, and consumers. Our inescapable contact with one another requires that our aspirations be defined, at least in part, by their impact on others.

Our text has several ethical reasoning possibilities in each chapter. But for the reader to make use of this emphasis requires a practical step-by-step approach. In other words, our students need more than just a discussion about values or ethics. They need to have some sense that the discussion is headed somewhere. They want to know, "How will my behavior be any more ethical after I have read the chapter and participated in the class discussions?" Our text answers their question.

Chapter 2 provides a clear explanation of our approach—an approach that students can use on a regular basis.

The WPH Framework for Business Ethics

A useful set of ethical guidelines requires recognition that managerial decisions must meet the following primary criteria:

- The decisions affect particular groups of stakeholders in the operations of the firm. The pertinent question is thus, *Whom* would this decision affect?
- The decisions are made in pursuit of a particular *purpose.* Business decisions are instruments toward an ethical end.
- The decisions must meet the standards of action-oriented business behavior. Managers need a doable set of guidelines for *how* to make ethical decisions.

The language and organization of our model of ethical reasoning leans implicitly on standard ethical theories. But it meets the challenge of a fast-paced business world. It pushes stakeholders to the forefront of market decisions, where they belong, and does so in a manner that is both powerful and doable without becoming tedious.

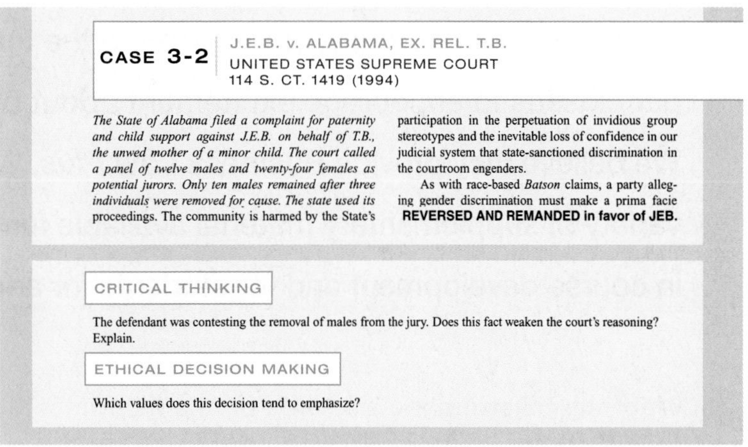

CASE 3-2 | J.E.B. v. ALABAMA, EX. REL. T.B.
UNITED STATES SUPREME COURT
114 S. CT. 1419 (1994)

The State of Alabama filed a complaint for paternity and child support against J.E.B. on behalf of T.B., the unwed mother of a minor child. The court called a panel of twelve males and twenty-four females as potential jurors. Only ten males remained after three individuals were removed for cause. The state used its proceedings. The community is harmed by the State's participation in the perpetuation of invidious group stereotypes and the inevitable loss of confidence in our judicial system that state-sanctioned discrimination in the courtroom engenders.

As with race-based *Batson* claims, a party alleging gender discrimination must make a prima facie

REVERSED AND REMANDED in favor of JEB.

CRITICAL THINKING

The defendant was contesting the removal of males from the jury. Does this fact weaken the court's reasoning? Explain.

ETHICAL DECISION MAKING

Which values does this decision tend to emphasize?

Business ethics are the guidelines we use to shape the world we wish to create. As such, they provide guidance for the kind of business behavior we want to reinforce. After each case excerpt, we pause to think about the ethics of business law by asking a question derived from the practical approach to business ethics developed in Chapter 2. Because we want students to see stakeholder interests as having numerous ethical dimensions, we have included frequent references to the ethical questions arising in modern business enterprises.

We have designed our features around the things we do in our classes to encourage excitement about business law. We believe they provide Business Law *Plus*. We also have a variety of supplementary material available for instructors to aid in course development and for students for additional study.

All of the following are available on the Instructor's CD-Rom, ISBN 978-0-07-326225-3, MHID 0-07-326225-0.

Instructor's Manual Written by our fellow coauthor Andrea Giampetro-Meyer, this resource includes lecture notes, case briefs, answers to all questions in each chapter, assignment ideas, teaching assistance (emphasizing practical tips new or part-time teachers can try right away), and suggested handouts.

Testbank Prepared by Vonda Laughlin of Carson-Newman College, our Testbank contains a variety of true/false, multiple-choice, and essay questions, as well as "scenario-based" questions, which are application-based and use a situation described in a narrative, with three to five multiple-choice test questions based on the situation. We've aligned our Testbank with new AACSB guidelines, tagging each question according to its knowledge and skill areas. Categories include Global, Ethics and Social Responsibility, Legal and Other External Environment, Communication, Diversity, Group Dynamics, Individual Dynamics, Production, and IT. Designations aligning questions with learning objectives exist as well.

EZ Test Online McGraw-Hill's EZ Test Online is a flexible and easy-to-use electronic testing program. The program allows instructors to create tests from book-specific items, accommodates a wide range of question types, and enables instructors to add their own questions. Multiple versions of the test can be created, and any test can be exported for use with course management systems such as WebCT, Blackboard, or any other course management system. EZ Test Online is accessible to busy instructors virtually anywhere via the Web, and the program eliminates the need for them to install test software. Utilizing EZ Test Online also allows instructors to create and deliver multiple-choice or true/false quiz questions using iQuiz for iPod. For more information about EZ Test Online, please see the Web site at **www.eztestonline.com**.

PowerPoint Presentation Slides Developed by Jeff Penley at Catawba Valley Community College, two different sets of slides are available for instructors. The Basic set consists of an outline of each chapter. The Premium set expands on this outline to include hypotheticals and ethical dilemmas, allowing the instructor to incorporate application into the lecture.

Instructor Video DVD (ISBN: 978-0-07-326223-9 / MHID: 0-07-326223-4)

The Instructor Video DVD contains clips from NBC and PBS that highlight current legal issues, with titles such as:

- Viacom Sues YouTube for Copyright Infringement (PBS)
- America's Number One Retailer, Wal-Mart, Faces the Biggest Civil Rights Case Ever against a U.S. Company (NBC)
- Courtroom or Circus? The Controversial Judge in Anna Nicole Smith's Courtroom Battle over Her Body Behaves Oddly (NBC)
- Government vs. Google (PBS)

Instructor notes, written by Linda Fried of the University of Colorado-Denver, located on the Web site give insight into how to incorporate segments into the classroom and offer questions to stimulate discussion.

You Be the Judge Online (www.mhhe.com/ybtj)

This interactive product includes 18 hypothetical business law cases. All of the cases are based on real cases within our business law texts. Each case allows you to watch interviews of the plaintiff and defendant before the courtroom argument, see the courtroom proceedings, view relevant evidence, read other actual cases relating to the issues in the case, and then create your own ruling. After your verdict is generated, view what an actual judge ruled (unscripted) in the case and then get the chance to defend or change your ruling. Topics include:

1. *Sexual harassment*: Did Sexy Prank Kill Promotion?
2. *Religious discrimination*: Dress Code Flips Burger Joint
3. *Fraud*: Blind Dates Go Bust
4. *Defamation*: Trashing the French Maid
5. *Partnership*: You Sunk My Partnership
6. *Warranty*: Who Is Distorting What?
7. *Verbal agreement*: Recording Studio Blues
8. *Liability*: Office Party Blame Game
9. *Property*: Subtracting the Addition
10. *Privacy/employment at will*: Fired for Whistling?
11. *Environmental law*: Digging Dogs Find Deadly Dirt
12. *Consumer law*: Misleading Menu Misery
13. *Tenant rights*: When the Lessee Leaves
14. *Consumer law*: The Not-So-Captive Audience
15. *Intellectual property*: Click Here, Get Sued
16. *Debt collection*: Overdue or Overdone?
17. *Intellectual property*: The Yoga Posture Puzzle
18. *Agency*: Duped by Duplication

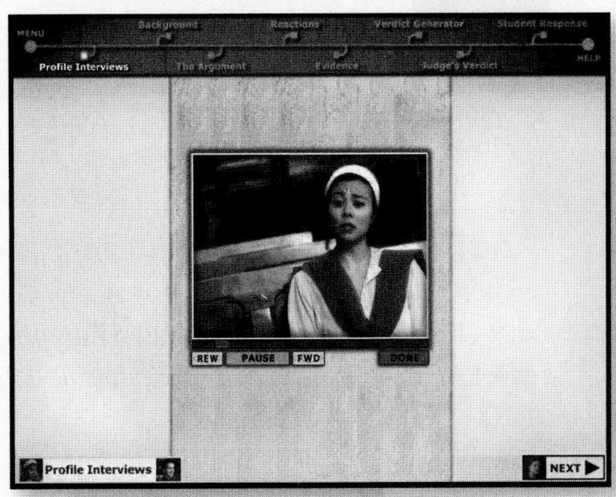

Online Learning Center **(www.mhhe.com/kubasek1e)**

With all of the possibilities that technology can offer, we've organized our Online Learning Center for ease of use for both instructor and student. Password-protected instructor materials can be found in the *Instructor Center*, including additional resources for classroom exercises and notes on how to incorporate all into the classroom. *You Be the Judge Online* (detailed above) is linked for accessibility and convenience. The *Student Center* offers opportunities for independent study, such as chapter quizzes and additional cases. In the Premium Content, students can also find narrated PowerPoint slides and other iPod content.

Enhanced Cartridge

Do you already use WebCT or Blackboard? Or are you hoping to put more of your course materials online? Are you looking for an easy way to assign more materials to your students and manage a gradebook? *Dynamic Business Law* comes with McGraw-Hill's new, enhanced cartridge, which will help you get your course up and running with much less time and effort. The content, enhanced with more assignments and more study materials than a standard cartridge, is *prepopulated* into appropriate chapters and content categories. Now there's no need to cut and paste our content into your course—it's already there! (But you can still choose to hide content we provide and add your own—just as you have before in WebCT and Blackboard.)

***Dynamic Business Law*'s enhanced-cartridge content includes:**

- iPod/MP3 content.
- Chapter pretests and posttests.
- Gradebook functionality.
- Discussion boards.
- Additional assignments.
- Personalized graphics, banners, and icons for your school.

And much more is also included! You can choose to package a password card with your text, or students can buy access via e-commerce through the book's Web site—for $10. Ask your McGraw-Hill sales representative about how to get the enhanced cartridge to accompany *Dynamic Business Law* for your course.

Acknowledgments

This final element of the Preface contains a palpable tone of gratitude and humility. Any project the scope of *Dynamic Business Law* is a collective activity; the authors are but the visible component of a remarkably large joint effort. We want to thank several contributors by name, but there are doubtlessly many other students, colleagues, and friends who made essential contributions to these pages.

Our largest gratitude goes to the dozens of business law colleagues who saved us from many embarrassing errors, while tolerating our stubborn reluctance to adhere to certain of their suggestions. Many thanks go to our manuscript reviewers and focus group participants:

Robert Bennett	Butler University
Jon Bible	Texas State University
Robert Bing	William Patterson University
Norman Bishara	University of Michigan
Joyce Boland-Devito	St. John's University
Michael Botello	El Camino College
Dan Cahoy	Penn State University
Jeanne Calderon	New York University
David Cooper	Fullerton College
Angelo Corpora	Palomar College
Angela Crossin	Purdue University–Calumet
Peter Dawson	Colin County Community College
Vince Enslein	Clinton Community College
Edward Gac	University of Colorado
Robert Gonzalez	American River College
Michelle Grunsted	University of Oklahoma
Howard Hammer	Ball State University
Dave Hanson	Duquesne University
Aubrey Helvey	Cameron University
Andy Hendrick	Coastal Carolina University
Georgia Holmes	Minnesota State University–Mankato
Russ Holmes	Des Moines Area Community College
Thomas Hughes	University of South Carolina
Lisa Johnson	University of Puget Sound
Steven Kaber	Baldwin-Wallace University
Cheryl Kirschner	Babson College
Paul Klein	Duquesne University
Rachel Kowal	New York University
Alan Lawson	Mt. San Antonio Community College
Mike Magasin	Pepperdine University
Bruce Mather	State University of New York–New Paltz
Jim Morgan	California State University–Chico

Tonia Murphy	University of Notre Dame
Steve Noel	Smith Knowles
Carol Nowicki	California State University–East Bay
Gary Patterson	University of California–Riverside and California State University–San Bernardino
Dirk Potter	California State University–Chico
Lisa Reed	University of Portland
Keith Roberts	University of Redlands
John Ruhnka	University of Colorado–Denver
Robert Sarachan	Cortland Community College
Steve Schamber	St. Louis Community College
Francine Segars Guice	Indiana University and Purdue University–Indianapolis
Craig Stilwell	Michigan State University
Dawn Swink	University of Saint Thomas
William Volz	Wayne State University
John Williams	Northwestern State University
Norman Greg Young	California State University–Pomona
Mary Kathryn Zachary	University of West Georgia

We'd also like to thank our Instructor's manual survey respondents:

Maria Defilippis	Raritan Valley Community College
Michelle Grunsted	University of Oklahoma
Alan Lawson	Mt. San Antonio Community College
Christine Mooney	Queensborough Community College
Jim Morgan	California State University–Chico
Tonia Murphy	Notre Dame
Bridget Petzall	Fayetteville Technical Community College
Francine Segars Guice	Indiana University and Purdue University–Indianapolis
Scott Taylor	Moberly Area Community College
Carol Vance	University of South Florida–Tampa

In addition, the book could not have been written without the competent and dedicated research assistance we received from Dan Tagliarina, Steve Weigand, Garrett Coyle, Allison Smith, Amanda Valentine, Steve Ruble, and Chad Puterbaugh.

Finally, a book is but a raw, unsold manuscript until the talent team at a publishing house starts to refine it. Our manuscript benefited immeasurably from the guidance of the multiple levels of skill provided to us by McGraw-Hill/Irwin. We respect and honor our Sponsoring Editor, Dana Woo; our Senior Development Editor, Christine Scheid; the book's Marketing Manager, Sarah Schuessler; its Project Manager, Bruce Gin; and our Editorial Coordinator, Megan Richter.

Brief Contents

Part Five
CREDITOR'S RIGHTS AND BANKRUPTCY

Part Six
AGENCY

Part Seven
BUSINESS ORGANIZATIONS

Part Eight
EMPLOYMENT AND LABOR RELATIONS

Part Nine
GOVERNMENT REGULATION

Part Ten
PROPERTY

Appendixes

Contents

Part One
THE LEGAL ENVIRONMENT OF BUSINESS

List of Cases

Chapter 2: Business Ethics

Chapter 3: The U.S. Legal System

Chapter 4: Alternative Dispute Resolution

Chapter 5: Constitutional Principles

Chapter 6: International and Comparative Law

Chapter 7: Crime and the Business Community

Chapter 8: Tort Law

Chapter 9: Negligence and Strict Liability

Chapter 10: Product Liability

Chapter 11: Liability of Accountants and Other Professionals

Chapter 12: Intellectual Property

Chapter 13: Introduction to Contracts

Chapter 14: Agreement

Chapter 15: Consideration

Chapter 16: Capacity and Legality

Chapter 17: Legal Assent

Chapter 18: Contracts in Writing

Chapter 19: Third-Party Rights to Contracts

Chapter 20: Discharge and Remedies

Chapter 21: Introduction to Sales and Lease Contracts

Chapter 22: Title, Risk of Loss, and Insurable Interest

Chapter 23: Performance and Obligations Under Sales and Leases

Chapter 24: Remedies for Breach of Sales and Lease Contracts

Chapter 25: Warranties

Chapter 26: Negotiable Instruments: Negotiability and Transferability

Chapter 27: Negotiation, Holder in Due Course, and Defenses

Chapter 28: Liability, Defenses, and Discharge

Chapter 29: Checks and Electronic Fund Transfers

Chapter 30: Secured Transactions

Chapter 31: Other Creditors' Remedies and Suretyship

Chapter 32: Bankruptcy and Reorganization

Chapter 33: Agency Formation and Duties

Chapter 34: Liability to Third Parties and Termination

Chapter 35: Forms of Business Organizations

Chapter 36: Partnerships: Nature, Formation, and Operation

Chapter 37: Partnerships: Termination and Limited Partnerships

Chapter 38: Corporations: Formation and Financing

Chapter 39: Corporations: Directors, Officers, and Shareholders

Chapter 40: Corporations: Mergers, Consolidations, Terminations

Chapter 41: Corporations: Securities and Investor Protection

Chapter 42: Employment and Labor Law

Chapter 43: Employment Discrimination

Chapter 44: Administrative Law

Chapter 45: Consumer Law

Chapter 46: Environmental Law

Chapter 47: Antitrust Law

Chapter 48: The Nature of Property, Personal Property, and Bailments

Chapter 49: Real Property

Chapter 50: Landlord-Tenant Law

Chapter 51: Insurance Law

Chapter 52: Wills and Trusts

An Introduction to Dynamic Business Law

Learning Objectives

After reading this chapter, you will be able to answer the following questions:

1. What is business law?
2. How does business law relate to business education?
3. What are the purposes of law?
4. What are alternative ways to classify the law?
5. What are the sources of the law?
6. What are the various schools of jurisprudence?

CHAPTER 1

This book is for future business managers, especially those who wish to be leaders. The preparation for that career requires, in part, an awareness of the legal issues arising in business. Businesses need to finance capital growth, purchase inputs, and hire and develop employees. In addition, they must sell to consumers, please owners, and comply with government rules. All these activities are full of potential legal conflicts.

Business law consists of the enforceable rules of conduct that govern commercial relationships. In other words, buyers and sellers interact in market exchanges within the rules that specify the boundaries of legal business behavior. Constitutions, legislatures, regulatory bodies, and courts spell out what market participants may or may not legally do.

Understanding business law is necessary for future businesspeople because there simply is no market transaction that occurs without legal guidelines. All contracts, employment decisions, and payments to a supplier are constrained and protected by business law. Each of the six functional areas of business—management, production and transportation, marketing, research and development, accounting and finance, and human resource management—sits on a foundation of business law. Exhibit 1-1 provides illustrations of areas of business law that apply to each of the six functional areas of business.

Exhibit 1-1
Business Law and the Six Functional Areas of Business

FUNCTIONAL AREA OF BUSINESS	RELEVANT AREAS OF BUSINESS LAW
Corporate management	International and comparative law White-collar crime Contracts Corporate law Antitrust law Administrative law Insurance law Employment law
Production and transportation	Tort law Contracts Environmental law Consumer law
Marketing	Tort law Contracts Antitrust law Consumer law Intellectual property
Research and development	Product liability Intellectual property Property law Consumer law
Accounting and finance	Liability of accountants Contracts Negotiable instruments and banking Bankruptcy White-collar crime
Human resource management	Contracts Employment and labor law Employment discrimination

Law and Its Purposes

Many of us might like to impose rules on others, defining their rights and responsibilities. Few of us can do this as individuals, but a majority of citizens in a democracy can agree to permit certain authorities to make and enforce rules describing what behavior is permitted and encouraged in their community. These rules are what we refer to as the **law**, and they are enforceable in the courts maintained by that community. Exhibit 1-2 provides a list of just a few of the numerous purposes fulfilled by the law.

Exhibit 1-2 Purposes of the Law

- Providing order such that one can depend on a promise or an expectation of obligations.
- Serving as an alternative to fighting.
- Facilitating a sense that change is possible, but only after a rational consideration of options.
- Encouraging social justice.
- Guaranteeing personal freedoms.
- Serving as a moral guide by indicating minimal expectations of citizens and organizations.

Each purpose of the law is important, but taken as a unit, Exhibit 1-2 is a reminder of why we are very proud when we say we are a society of laws. The respect we give to the law as a source of authority is in part a recognition of the fact that in the absence of law, we would rely solely on the goodwill and dependability of one another. Most of us greatly prefer the law to that option.

Classification of the Law

There are many ways of dividing laws into different groups. Classifying laws in this manner is a necessary process because we have many different laws that cover a wide range of subjects. Some of the classifications include national versus international law, federal versus state law, and public versus private law. **Private law** involves disputes between private individuals or groups. As an illustration, if a businessperson who owns a computer equipment store is delinquent in paying rent to the landlord, the resulting dispute entails private law. **Public law** involves disputes between private individuals or groups and their government. For instance, if a computer store dumps waste behind its building in violation of local, state, or federal environmental regulations, the resulting dispute focuses on public law.

Another distinction among types of laws is civil law versus criminal law. **Civil law** involves the rights and responsibilities involved in relationships between persons and between persons and their government. It also involves the remedies available when someone's rights are violated. One example of a civil law case involving a large business organization occurred in 1993. The restaurant chain Jack-In-the-Box was ordered to pay damages after a two-year-old child died of food poisoning from *E. coli* and several other people became ill from eating the tainted meat.

In contrast to civil law, **criminal law** involves incidents in which someone commits an act against the public as a unit. These crimes are prosecuted not by individuals but by the state or federal government. One example of a criminal law is the prohibition against insider trading on the stock exchange. Insider trading occurs when an individual uses insider, or secret, company information to increase her or his own finances or those of family or friends. For example, several years ago an IBM secretary allegedly told her husband, who told several other people, that the company was going to take over operations of

Lotus Development. This information was spread among a number of individuals before it was publicly announced. On the basis of this leak, 25 people bought stock that increased greatly in value following IBM's public announcement of the takeover. The Securities and Exchange Commission filed charges against the 25 stock purchasers because they were creating an unfair trading environment for the public.

One emerging category of the law is **cyberlaw.** While some new laws have been adopted to regulate the kinds of business activities that can now be conducted online, cyberlaw is primarily based on existing laws. Some laws need to be slightly adjusted, however, so that they can be applied in the realm of cyberspace. Laws involving contracts, for instance, are essentially the same in all situations, and yet certain adaptations are necessary because contracts can be made and signed online through retailers such as Amazon.com and eBay. Companies such as Napster and YouTube have called into question the issue of when the copying of certain intellectual property materials, such as music and video, does or does not constitute the theft of those materials.

Sources of Business Law

How is law created, and where do we look to find the laws?

CONSTITUTIONS

The United States Constitution and the constitution of each state establish the fundamental principles and rules by which the United States and the individual states are governed. The term **constitutional law** refers to the general limits and powers of these governments as stated in their written constitutions. The U.S. Constitution is the supreme law of the land, the foundation for all laws in the United States. It is the primary authority to study when trying to identify the relationship between business organizations and government.

STATUTES

Legislative actions, called *statutes,* provide another important source of law. The assortment of rules and regulations put forth by legislatures is what we call **statutory law.** These legislative acts can be found in the United States Code when they are passed by Congress or in the various state codes when they are enacted by state legislatures. The codes are a collection of all the laws in one convenient location.

Because so much business activity occurs within the jurisdiction of state courts, business managers must be familiar with the local city and county ordinances that govern matters not covered by federal or state codes. These ordinances address important business considerations such as local taxes, environmental standards, zoning, and building codes. For example, if you wish to open a Krispy Kreme franchise in Santa Fe, New Mexico, you must follow local guidelines regarding the area where you may build your store, the materials that you may use to build, and the state minimum wage that you must pay to employees making donuts. The regulations will be different if you wished to open your franchise in Toledo, Ohio, or Seattle, Washington.

While they are not a source of law in the same sense as constitutions and statutory law, **model** or **uniform laws** serve as a basis for some statutory law at the state level. Business activity is made more difficult when state laws vary. To prevent such problems, a group of legal scholars and lawyers formed the National Conference of Commissioners on Uniform State Laws (NCC). The NCC regularly urges states to enact model laws to provide greater uniformity of law. The response is entirely in the hands of the state legislatures. They can ignore a suggestion or adopt part or all of the proposed model law.

The proposals of the NCC, while not laws themselves, have been adopted on more than 200 occasions by state legislatures. The NCC is an especially important influence on business law. Paired with the publications of the American Law Institute, the NCC became the source of the *Uniform Commercial Code (UCC)*. The UCC is a body of law so significant for business activities that it will be the focus of intensive study in several chapters of this text. The UCC laws include sales laws and other regulations affecting commerce, such as bank deposits and collections, title documents, and warranties. For example, these laws govern the different types of warranties that companies such as Microsoft, Sony, and Honda provide with their products.

CASES

Constitutions, legislatures, and administrative agencies encourage certain behavior and prevent other actions. But the boundaries of these laws are seldom self-explanatory. Consequently, law must be interpreted.

Case law is the collection of legal interpretations made by judges. An alternative name for case law is **common law**. These interpretations are law unless they are revoked later by new statutory law.

Case law is especially significant for businesses because a modern business often operates in multiple legal jurisdictions. Because statutory laws are subject to interpretation, one court may have interpreted particular laws one way at one business location and a second court may interpret a similarly worded statute differently in a second business location.

Courts issue judicial decisions that often include interpretations of statutes and administrative regulations. These decisions contain the reasoning used by the courts to arrive at their decision. The reasoning depends heavily on **precedent**, the use of past decisions to guide future decisions. An earlier decision in a similar fact pattern is a precedent that guides later decisions, thereby providing greater stability and predictability to the law.

It is crucial that business managers pay attention to changes in the law and cases in which new precedents are set. These precedents must be taken into account when making future business decisions. For instance, courts sometimes make new rulings regarding the kinds of warnings companies should be required to provide to consumers about potential harm that could result from their products. One example was a case filed against McDonald's. After a woman was severely burned by very hot coffee, the company was found negligent for failing to provide a warning label on its hot-beverage cups. Now many retailers of hot beverages provide warning labels on their beverage cups because of the precedent that was set by this case.

Courts in one jurisdiction need not obey precedents in other jurisdictions, but they may be influenced by them. At least two current Supreme Court justices, for example, are using law in other countries as a basis for rethinking certain laws in the United States. The logic of this reliance on precedent is based on respect for those who have already wrestled with the issue and provided us guidance with their earlier decision.

When courts rely on precedent, they are obeying **stare decisis** ("standing by their decision"). This adherence to stare decisis creates greater predictability for both businesses and individuals who look to the courts for the rules on which they should rely when they engage in market exchanges. In accordance with stare decisis, rulings that are made in higher courts become binding precedent for lower courts. If an issue is brought before a state court, the court will ascertain whether the state supreme court has made a decision on a similar issue, which would have then set a binding precedent that the lower court would need to follow.

Even though this practice is meant to create a justice system that is consistent and reliable, different judges may view the facts of a case in different ways. Other times, courts are presented with a new issue and do not have a binding decision to follow. In such instances, they may look to decisions made in similar cases by nonbinding courts in other states or jurisdictions.

If a new issue comes before two state courts and there is no binding decision from the state supreme court, both state courts need to look for other rulings on similar cases. They are not bound by each other's decision, and so they might have different decisions on the same subject. The decisions in these lower courts can be appealed to the state appeals court however, and the appeals court's decision can be appealed to the state supreme court. If the state supreme court rules on the case, its decision is binding for the state but does not affect earlier decisions made by state courts. The state supreme court's decision affects only the decision being appealed and any future cases brought in the state on that particular subject.

One example of a case that has been used in accordance with stare decisis as a binding precedent is *Brown v. Board of Education,*[1] which abolished discriminatory policies for individuals of different racial backgrounds. For instance, in *Regents of the University of California v. Bakke,*[2] the plaintiff, a white male, had applied to the University of California at Davis medical school two years in a row and been denied admittance. He alleged that the admissions process was discriminatory, because out of 100 slots, 16 were reserved for members of minority races. The U.S. Supreme Court found that the school's admissions policy was not lawful, referencing *Brown* and stating that the basic principle behind it and similar cases was that individuals could not be excluded on the basis of race or ethnicity. The Court wrote, "Preferring members of any one group for no reason other than race or ethnic origin is discrimination for its own sake."

Another U.S. Supreme Court case that relied in part on *Brown v. Board of Education* was *Wygant et al. v. Jackson Board of Education et al.*[3] The Board of Education and teachers' union in Jackson, Michigan, had agreed that if teachers were laid off, the ones with more seniority would be retained and the minority teachers' percentage of the layoffs would not be higher than their percentage of all teachers employed by the school district at the time of the layoffs. When layoffs did occur, nonminority teachers were laid off and minority teachers with less seniority were retained. The nonminority teachers sued. When the case was brought before the Supreme Court, the Court ruled that the layoff policy was not lawful because "[c]arried to the logical extreme, the idea that black students are better off with black teachers could lead to the very system the Court rejected in *Brown v. Board of Education.*" Again in accordance with *Brown,* the Court ruled that singling people out on the basis of race was not lawful.

Just as state statutes have been strongly influenced by the suggestions of the NCC, common law evolves with the assistance of a mechanism called **Restatements of the Law.** These Restatements are summaries of the common law rules in a particular area of the law that have been enacted by most states. The American Law Institute prepares these Restatements for contracts, agency, property, torts, and many other areas of law that affect business decisions. While the Restatements are not themselves a source of business law, judges frequently use them to guide their interpretations in a particular case.

In addition to the Restatements, many influences are at work in the minds of judges when they interpret constitutions, statutes, and regulations. For example, the values and

[1] 347 U.S. 483 (1954).

[2] 438 U.S. 265 (1978).

[3] 476 U.S. 267 (1986).

social backgrounds of the judges function as lights and shadows, moving the judges toward particular legal decisions.

ADMINISTRATIVE LAW

Constitutions and statutes are never complete in the sense of covering all the detailed rules that affect government and business relations. The federal government, as well as state and local governments, has dozens of administrative agencies, whose task is to perform a particular government function. For example, the Environmental Protection Agency (EPA) has broad responsibilities to enforce federal statutes in the area of environmental protection.

Administrative law is the collection of rules and decisions made by all these administrative agencies. Just glance at Exhibit 1-3 to get a sense of the scope of a few of the major federal administrative agencies.

Businesses function within a framework of rules established by agencies like these. For example, the Occupational Safety and Health Administration (OSHA) oversees health and workplace safety and makes sure that employees will be working in conditions that are not hazardous. One instance in which OSHA exercised its authority occurred in 1994, when OSHA settled a complaint with United Parcel Service (UPS). The company was not providing adequate safety measures and equipment for workers who handled hazardous waste, and OSHA was responsible for making sure that UPS adapted its practices to follow federal safety guidelines.

TREATIES

A **treaty** is a binding agreement between two states or international organizations. Treaties may be called several things: international agreements, covenants, exchanges of letters, conventions, or protocols. In the United States, a treaty is generally negotiated by the executive branch. To be binding, it must then be approved by two-thirds of the Senate.

A treaty is similar to a contract in two important ways. Both treaties and contracts are attempts by parties to determine rights and obligations among themselves. In addition, when a party fails to obey a treaty or a contract, international law imposes liability on the party who failed to obey the agreement.

Exhibit 1-3 Major Federal Administrative Agencies

INDEPENDENT AGENCIES	EXECUTIVE AGENCIES
Commodity Futures Trading Commission (CFTC)	Federal Deposit Insurance Corporation (FDIC)
Consumer Product Safety Commission (CPSC)	Occupational Safety and Health Administration (OSHA)
Equal Employment Opportunity Commission (EEOC)	General Services Administration (GSA)
Federal Trade Commission (FTC)	National Aeronautics and Space Administration (NASA)
Federal Communications Commission (FCC)	Small Business Administration (SBA)
Interstate Commerce Commission (ICC)	International Development Cooperative Agency (IDCA)
National Labor Relations Board (NLRB)	National Science Foundation (NSF)
National Transportation Safety Board (NTSB)	Veterans Administration (VA)
Nuclear Regulatory Commission (NRC)	Office of Personnel Management (OPM)
Securities and Exchange Commission (SEC)	

EXECUTIVE ORDERS

The president and state governors can issue directives requiring that officials in the executive branch perform their functions in a particular manner. The Code of Federal Regulations (CFR) contains all the executive orders created by the president. (The CFR is online at www.gpoaccess.gov/cfr/index.html.) Presidents claim the power to issue such orders on the basis of their Article II, Section 1 constitutional power to "take care that the laws be faithfully executed."

An illustration of an especially controversial executive order is Order 9066, issued by President Franklin Roosevelt during World War II. On the basis of this order, Japanese-Americans on the West Coast, as well as thousands of Italian-American and German-American families, were sent to internment camps for the duration of the war.

SCHOOLS OF JURISPRUDENCE

When legislators or courts make law, they do so guided by certain habits of mind and specific beliefs about human nature. These views guide them toward particular legal solutions and away from others. This section briefly describes several of the more common guides to legal interpretation.

Natural law. The term **natural law** refers to the idea that there are certain ethical laws and principles that are morally right and "above" the laws devised by humans. This concept suggests that individuals should have the freedom to disobey a law enacted by people if their conscience goes against the law and they believe the law is wrong. The idea that people have basic human rights is rooted in the concept of natural law. For instance, Dow Chemical wants its suppliers to conform to U.S. environmental and labor laws, not just the local laws in the supplier's country, where regulations may not be as stringent. This reflects the beliefs that people have a right to be treated fairly in their jobs and that they have a right as human beings to a clean environment.

Legal positivism. The concept of **legal positivism** urges us to design our legal system on the basis of the belief that legitimate political authority deserves our obedience when it issues a rule. This idea stresses that society requires authority and the hierarchy that such authority demands. When a duly authorized branch of government issues a law, positivism would urge us to see our proper role as obedience. The law is then a set of appropriate commands.

This view sees law as something quite distinct from morality. Moral questions about the law should not interfere with our inclination to obey it. A judge with leanings in the direction of legal positivism, for example, might write that she is deciding to enforce the law in question but that her decision does not necessarily mean that she sees the law as the morally correct rule.

Identification with the vulnerable. Closely linked to pursuing legal change through natural law is pursuing change through **identification with the vulnerable**. Some members of our society are able to take care of themselves in terms of most life situations. Others, especially the ill, children, the aged, the disabled, and the poor, require assistance to meet their fundamental needs of life, health, and education.

This guide to legal change is tied closely to the pursuit of fairness in our society. The metaphor of a level playing field is linked with some higher law or body of moral principles that connects all of us in the human community. We might look at a particular employment contract, for example, and react by observing that "it is just not fair." Our caring impulse as a human feels outrage at that legal arrangement. That outrage can be a stimulus for legal change. One example of identification with the vulnerable is minimum-wage laws. They reflect the beliefs that workers should receive a minimum hourly wage and that employers should not be allowed to pay them less.

Historical school: tradition. One of the most often used guidelines for shaping the law is **tradition**, or **custom**, which is also called the *historical school*. Stare decisis is rooted in this perspective. When we follow tradition, we attempt to link our future behavior to the behavior of those who faced similar problems in earlier historical periods. The logic of the approach is that we need not reinvent the wheel each time a legal problem arises. Past practice is assumed to have been the product of careful thought.

Legal realism. **Legal realism** is based on the idea that, when ruling on a case, judges need to consider more than just the law. This school of thought dictates that they also take factors such as social and economic conditions into consideration when making a judgment. Followers of legal realism argue that the law must not be the sole factor in deciding a case, since legal guidelines were designed by humans and exist in an ever-changing society. Judges who follow this school of thought are more likely to depart from past court decisions to account for the fact that our society is constantly shifting and evolving. Those who subscribe to legal realism also believe that the law can never be enforced with complete consistency. They argue that because judges are human, they will bring different methods of reasoning to very similar cases.

One example of a law that has been enacted to reflect changes in our society is the Family and Medical Leave Act. This act mandates that businesses employing more than 50 people must provide their workers with up to 12 weeks' unpaid leave every year to take care of family-related affairs. This includes caring for ill parents, caring for oneself if one has an illness, adopting a child, or having a child. This law also protects pregnant women who take time off work, as their employers must provide them with the same pay and the same or an equivalent job when they return to work. This act reflects the fact that more mothers are working outside the home and more women are returning to work soon after they have a child. The act protects them against some types of employer discrimination that might occur after they return.

Cost-benefit analysis. Suppose that we could attach a monetary figure to the benefits of a particular law or legal decision. From this perspective, we would next need to examine all the costs of that same law or decision and place a monetary value on it. If we possessed those calculations, we could use **cost-benefit analysis** as a guide to legal change, choosing the legal alternatives that maximized the ratio of benefits to costs. For instance, in a contract dispute someone using this approach would attempt to attach responsibility for the problem in such a way that total benefit is maximized in relation to costs.

This approach to legal change is tied closely to the pursuit of efficiency. If the law to be applied yields more benefits than costs, then we have saved resources. Those resources can, in turn, be used to provide us with more goods and services. Our economy is thus more efficient in the sense of producing more for less.

For example, regulations enacted by the EPA can affect costs and benefits in the national economy. Polluted land is an economic loss as it cannot be used for farming or recreation. Polluted water can be toxic for fish and cannot be used for drinking. Polluted air can cause health problems and result in higher health care costs. While EPA regulations may end up costing companies more initially in order to control pollutants, the cost of environmental cleanup, and the loss of productivity in the economy as a whole, may be greater than the resources companies expend to control pollution.

GLOBAL AND COMPARATIVE LAW

Comparative and international law is extremely important for future business managers to study. Because of advances in technology and transportation, trade with other countries is far easier today than it was in past years. Now it is possible to make different components for the same product in various countries all over the world and then assemble them in another country. It is possible to operate an antique store in Poughkeepsie but sell to customers in Moscow or Taipei through a Web site.

As a result of this ease in trade, business managers must be familiar with global trade laws between nations that regulate business practices. For instance, the United States and other countries have entered into agreements such as the North American Free Trade Agreement (NAFTA) and the General Agreement on Tariffs and Trade (GATT). These agreements help establish the conditions of trade between countries.

It is also important that future business managers understand comparative law, which involves comparing and studying the laws in different countries. Business managers need to be aware of various trade laws and restrictions in different countries so that they can act accordingly when they set out to do business in those countries. The European Union, for example, has laws that differ from ours in terms of regulating the taxes on Internet sales and the amount of pollution that can be released into the environment. Companies doing business in the EU must take these standards into account.

Another example of a company conforming to different laws is the search engine company Google, which has agreed to restrict the content of searches performed on Google.cn, the Chinese version of the company's search engine. Google took this action to satisfy regulations set by the Chinese government, which did not want its citizens to have access to certain Web sites or pieces of information. To do business in China, Google had to conform to these standards. This loss of freedom of information or access to information was considered by some an "evil" such that they felt Google had violated its own mission statement to "do no evil."

Modern business managers must have an ongoing fascination with the law to function effectively. Business law tells business managers the basic rules of the business game. Play any game without having first studied the rules, and you will probably fail.

But, unlike an ordinary game, the business game has a rule book that is changing dynamically. In addition, increased globalization requires that business leaders be alert to legal differences among national jurisdictions.

Looking for more review material?

The Online Learning Center at **www.mhhe.com/kubasek1e** contains this chapter's "Assignment on the Internet" and also a list of URLs for more information, entitled "On the Internet." Find both of them in the Student Center portion of the OLC, along with quizzes and other helpful materials.

Appendix A-1 Critical Thinking and Business Law

Success in the modern business firm requires the development of **critical thinking skills**—the ability to understand the structure of what someone is saying and then to apply a set of evaluative criteria to determine the worth of what was said. In other words, businesspeople need to be able to sort sense from nonsense by developing attitudes and abilities that help them evaluate arguments about relevant business law.

Any critical thinking includes the application of evaluative standards to assess the quality of the reasoning being offered to support the conclusion. And there is no better context in which to develop critical thinking skills than in the study of the laws that affect business. Critical thinking skills learned in the study of business law will be easily transferred to the decisions of business stakeholders.

Legal reasoning is like other reasoning in some ways and different in others. When people, including lawyers and judges, reason, they do so for a purpose. Some problem or dilemma bothers them. The stimulus that gets them thinking is an *issue*. It is stated as a question because it is a call for action. It requires us to *do* something, to think about answers.

For instance, we may be interested in such issues as the following:

- When are union organizers permitted under the National Labor Relations Act to trespass on an employer's property?
- Do tobacco manufacturers have liability for the deaths of smokers?
- Must a business fulfill a contract when the contract is made with an unlicensed contractor in a state requiring that all contractors be licensed?

These questions have several potential answers. Which answer best accomplishes a particular business objective? Which answers are consistent with the law? Here is where critical thinking is essential to business success. Some answers can get the decision maker into trouble; others will advance the intended purpose. Each answer is called a *conclusion*.

Business firms often come into contact with such conclusions in the form of laws or court decisions. Business managers are therefore both consumers of and contributors to these legal conclusions. As businesspeople learn about and react to decisions or conclusions made by courts, they have two primary methods of response:

1. Memorizing and understanding the conclusions or rules of law as a guide for future business decisions.
2. Making judgments about the quality of the conclusions.

This book encourages you to do both. There are many forms of critical thinking, but they all share one characteristic: They focus on the quality of someone's reasoning. Critical thinking is active; it challenges each of us to form judgments about the quality of the link between a set of reasons and the conclusion supposedly derived from them. In particular, we will be focusing on the link between a court's reasons and its conclusions.

Our reactions to legal arguments shape our efforts to either support the status quo in the legal environment of business or offer support for particular changes.

The following structure for critical thinking is a thoroughly tested method used by successful market decision makers. Every time you read a case, try to follow this pattern of careful thinking.

1. Find the facts.

   Facts: Here we are looking for the most basic building blocks in a legal decision or argument. These building blocks, or facts, provide the environment or context in which the legal issue is to be resolved. Certain events occurred; certain actions were or were not taken; particular persons behaved or failed to behave in specific ways. All of these and many more possibilities together make up the intricate setting for the playing out of the issue in question. We always wonder, What happened in this case?

2. Look for the issue.

   Issue: In almost any legal conflict, finding and expressing the issue is an important step in forming our reaction. The issue is the question that caused the lawyers and their clients to enter the legal system. Usually, there are several reasonable perspectives concerning the correct way to word the issue in dispute. Don't let the possibility of *multiple* useful ways to word the issue cause you any confusion. The issue is certainly not just anything that we say it is.

3. Identify the judge's reasons and conclusion.

   Reasons and conclusion: Judges do not form legal conclusions on the basis of whim. They have support for their decisions. That support consists of their reasons. When we ask someone *why* a judge formed a particular conclusion, we are showing our respect for reasons as the proper basis for any assertion. We want a world rich with opinions so that we can have a broad field of choice. But we should agree with only those legal opinions that have convincing reasons supporting the conclusion. Asking "Why?" is our way of saying, "I want to believe you, but you have an obligation to help me by sharing the reasons for your conclusion."

4. Locate in the decision the rules of law that govern the judge's reasoning.

   Rules of law: Judges cannot offer just any reasoning that they please. They must always look back over their shoulders at the laws and previous court decisions that together provide an anchor for current and future decisions. What makes legal reasoning so complex is that statutes and legal findings are never *crystal* clear. They may seem very clear, but judges and businesspeople have room for interpretive flexibility in their reasoning.

5. Apply critical thinking to the reasoning.

   Evaluation of the reasoning: A judge's reasoning, once it has been laid before us by following the steps discussed here, is a message that we may either accept or reject. One of the most exciting things about our legal system is its potential for change. **Critical thinking in the legal context** consists of examining the legal opinion in search of potential problems in the reasoning.

Here is a small sample of some especially useful critical thinking tools for business managers when thinking about business law:

- Look for potential ambiguity in the reasoning. *Ambiguity* refers to a lack of clarity in a word or phrase in the reasoning. Many words have multiple meanings; until the intended meaning is discovered, we cannot tell whether we wish to agree or disagree with the reasoning.
- Ask whether the analogies used in the decision are strong. When judges follow particular precedents, they are saying that the key similarities between the facts in the precedent and those in the case at hand are so similar that it makes sense to apply the

same rule of law in both. Are there key differences in the factual situations that raise questions about the quality of that analogy?

- Check the quality of the judge's reasoning. Does the judge use evidence to support the opinion that is both abundant enough and reliable enough that we should agree with the reasoning?
- Think about the extent to which important missing information prevents you from being totally confident about the judge's reasoning. Is there important missing information that you would need to have before making up your mind?
- Consider the possibility of rival causes. When the judge claims that one action caused another, think about whether some alternative cause may have been responsible.

Business Ethics

CASE OPENER

Nike and "Sweatshop Labor"

Nike and other shoe manufacturers can reduce costs by having their shoes made in countries where wages are lower than they are in the United States. Workers in Indonesia and Vietnam are willing to work long hours for significantly less than is demanded by American workers. For example, after a recent wage increase, Indonesian workers in Nike plants made the rough equivalent of 20 cents per hour.

In one sense, what Nike wants to do is just smart business. By reducing labor costs, they can make more profits. In addition, Nike, by employing these workers, is giving them employment opportunities that would otherwise not be available.

Yet this situation is even more complicated than it first appears. In the late 1990s Nike's profits dropped by as much as 40 percent. Why? According to industry leaders, a major cause was the negative publicity shoe companies received from the production of their shoes in foreign "sweatshops." Typical of the criticisms was a student letter in the Brown University *Daily Herald:*

> [S]weatshops do not exist to promote economic development. They exist to *maximize profits* at the expense of human dignity. What little investments that companies do put into the local economy do not even come close to compensating for what they reap through disgustingly low wages and slave-like working conditions. The bottom line is that it is in the companies' best interests to keep workers poor and powerless. . . . Ending sweatshop labor will not solve the problem of poverty overnight, but it is an important step in the right direction.

In addition, UNITE, an organization that includes union, church, and college student groups, reports that Nike is rapidly moving its production facilities to China, where in

CHAPTER 2

factory-dormitory complexes, labor is regulated in military fashion. For example, young migrant women who work for Nike in China are allegedly restricted from leaving company grounds or quitting their jobs.

1. What would you do if you were in a position at Nike to decide whether to continue or revise your labor practices in foreign countries?
2. Since 1992, Nike has been implementing a code of conduct that mandates the enforcement of all child labor, fair wage, and health laws in its foreign plants. In doing so, is Nike moving toward improved ethics?

The Wrap-Up at the end of the chapter will answer these questions.

Learning Objectives

After reading this chapter, you will be able to answer the following questions:

1. What are business ethics and the social responsibility of business?
2. How are business law and business ethics related?
3. How can we use the WPH framework for ethical business decisions?

What a business manager in the situation described in the opening scenario should do is not altogether clear. Ethical conversation is less about finding the one and only right thing to do than it is about finding the better thing to do. Whatever you choose to do, some stakeholders will be hurt and others will benefit.

This chapter provides some assistance for thinking systematically about issues of right and wrong in business conduct. Initially, we need to sort through the meaning of key terms like *business ethics* and *social responsibility.* Then, because it is helpful to have a useful approach to ethical decision making, we provide a practical method by which future business managers can think more carefully about the ethical dilemmas they will face during their careers.

Business Ethics and Social Responsibility

Ethics is the study and practice of decisions about what is good, or right. Ethics guides us when we are wondering what we should be doing in a particular situation. **Business ethics** is the application of ethics to the special problems and opportunities experienced by businesspeople. For example, as a business manager, you might someday decide what is best for Nike and the various people affected by decisions at Nike. Is the company doing the right thing when it attempts to reduce costs of production by having its shoes assembled in countries where the working conditions are very substandard compared to those in the United States?

Such questions present businesses with ethical choices, each of which has advantages and disadvantages. An **ethical dilemma** is a problem about what a firm should do for which no clear, right decision is available. Reasonable people can expect to disagree about optimal solutions to ethical dilemmas.

For example, imagine yourself in the position of a business manager at Wells Fargo Bank. You know that providing bank accounts for customers has costs attached to it. You want to cover those costs by charging the customers the cost of their checking accounts. By doing so, you can preserve the bank's revenue for shareholders and employees of Wells Fargo. So far, the decision seems simple. But an ethical dilemma soon appears.

You learn from recent government reports that 12 million families cannot afford to have bank accounts when they are charged a fee to maintain one. You want to do the right thing in this situation. But what would that be? The study of business ethics can help you resolve this dilemma by suggesting approaches you can use that will show respect for others while maintaining a healthy business enterprise.

Making these decisions would be much easier if managers could focus only on the impact of decisions on the firm. If, for example, a firm had as its only objective the maximization of profits, the "right thing" to do would be the option that had the largest positive impact on the firm's profits.

But businesses operate in a community. Communities have expectations for behavior of individuals, groups, and businesses. Different communities have different expectations of businesses. Trying to identify what those expectations are and deciding whether to fulfill them complicate business ethics. The community often expects firms to do much more for it than just provide a useful good or service at a reasonable price. For example, a community may expect firms to resist paying bribes, even when the payment of such fees is an ordinary cost of doing business in certain global settings.

The **social responsibility of business** consists of the expectations that the community imposes on firms doing business inside its borders. These expectations must be honored to a certain extent, even when a firm wishes to ignore them, because firms are always subject to the implicit threat that legislation will impose social obligations on them. So, if the community expects businesses to obey certain standards of fairness even when the standards

connecting to the core

Accounting

One of the core areas of business that is increasingly devoting attention to ethics is accounting. Your accounting book may have even discussed ethics as a key concept of accounting. Ethics is a key concept for accounting because the goal of accounting is to provide useful information to decision makers. If information is to be useful, it must be trusted; the information can be trusted only when accountants are ethical. To encourage ethical behavior on the part of accountants, many texts remind future business leaders of the impact their preparation of financial statements can have. For instance, misleading information could lead to the wrongful closing of a plant with consequent harm to workers, consumers, and suppliers.

Source: J. J. Larson, K. D. Wild, and B. Chiappetta, *Principles of Financial Accounting,* 17th ed. (New York: McGraw-Hill, 2005), pp. 8–9.

interfere with profit maximization, firms that choose to ignore that expectation do so at their peril. See Exhibit 2-1 for a brief look at General Electric's approach to social responsibility.

Business Law and Business Ethics

Before business managers consider the social responsibilities of firms in their communities, they need to gather all the relevant facts. Nike's decision about where and how to manufacture their shoes depends on a huge array of facts: alternative costs, the legal framework in each relevant country, the social responsibilities of firms in the various jurisdictions, unemployment rates, and levels of literacy among potential workers, just to name a few. But experienced managers know that assembling the facts is just the beginning of a thoughtful business decision. Next, it makes sense to ask, *Is it legal to go forward with this decision?*

Exhibit 2-1
Good Citizenship and Profits

Given the number of corporate accounting scandals that have been revealed in the past few years, many corporations are making a point of assuring their investors that their corporate goals are not focused solely on profit. As investors lost millions of dollars during the collapse of companies such as WorldCom and Enron, some corporations have been placing increased emphasis on promoting themselves not only as profitable but as conscientious and ethical.

For example, the following three statements that compose GE's Citizenship Framework seek to assure current and potential investors that the company is dedicated to both stock performance and company integrity.

GE's Citizenship Framework

1. Strong economic performance and stakeholder impact.
2. Rigorous compliance with fundamental accounting and legal requirements.
3. Going beyond compliance by supporting ethical actions.

In linking *performance* and *integrity,* the company endeavors to pair high profits and compliance with government ethics regulations, promoting itself as a company worthy of investment that will be honest with shareholders. Whereas in years past companies may have focused solely on their profitability in an attempt to gain new investors, today many business managers realize that corporate honesty has become just as important to those who are seeking to buy stock.

The legality of the decision is the minimal standard that must be met. But the existence of that minimum standard is essential for the development of business ethics. To make this point, let's take a look at the growing practice of bribery in the absence of such legal standards. In some countries businesses must pay bribes to receive legitimate supplies. Though the businessperson may be morally opposed to paying the bribes, the supplies are necessary to stay in business and there may be no other means of obtaining them.

Thus, foreign companies face an ethical dilemma: They must decide whether to pay bribes or find alternative sources of supplies. For instance, when McDonald's opened its doors in Moscow, it made arrangements to receive its supplies from foreign providers. These arrangements ensured that the franchise did not have to engage in questionable business practices.

Look at Case 2-1 as an exercise in comparing what is legal with what is ethical. Business law affects ethics because it provides a floor for managerial ethics. At a minimum, ethics requires a presumption in favor of obedience to law. As you review the *Kipps* case, consider the relationship between law and ethics.

CASE 2-1 REXFORD KIPPS ET AL. v. JAMES CAILLER ET AL.

U.S. COURT OF APPEALS, FIFTH CIRCUIT, 1999
197 F.3D 765

Several universities actively recruited Kyle Kipps, a talented football player in southern Louisiana, in 1996 and 1997. Kyle's father, Rexford Kipps, was an assistant football coach at the University of Southwestern Louisiana (USL) for eleven years. In March 1996, Nelson Stokley, USL's head football coach, told Rexford Kipps that Kyle was to attend either USL or a college or university outside of Louisiana. When Kyle notified Stokley that he had orally committed to play at Louisiana State University (LSU) on a football scholarship, Stokley told Rexford Kipps to forbid his son to play football for LSU. Rexford Kipps argued that he could not and would not force his son to refuse to play for LSU. Consequently, Stokley terminated Kipps's employment with LSU. Both Nelson Schexnayder, Jr., USL Director of Athletics, and Ray Authement, President of USL, approved Kipps's termination. The President of the Board of Trustees, James Caillier, also approved Kipps's termination.

Rexford Kipps brought constitutional and state law claims against defendants Caillier, Schexnayder, Authement, and Stokley. These defendants filed for summary judgment, arguing that the at-will employment status of Kipps precluded any wrongful termination action. Furthermore, they claimed that they were entitled to qualified immunity and Kipps's termination was justified because Kyle's choice would affect USL's ability to recruit athletes. The district court granted Stokley, Schexnayder and Authement's motion for summary judgment on qualified immunity grounds. Kipps appealed to the U. S. Court of Appeals, 5th District.

JUDGE PARKER: Public officials acting within the scope of their official duties are shielded from civil liability by the qualified immunity doctrine. Government officials are entitled to qualified immunity "insofar as their conduct does not violate clearly established statutory or constitutional rights of which a reasonable person would have known."

In order to establish that the defendants are not entitled to qualified immunity, plaintiffs must satisfy a three-part test. First, "[a] court evaluating a claim of qualified immunity must first determine whether the plaintiff has alleged the deprivation of a constitutional right at all." Second, the court must "determine whether that right was clearly established at the time of the alleged violation." Finally, the court "must determine whether the record shows that the violation occurred, or at least gives rise to a genuine issue of material fact as to whether the defendant actually engaged in the conduct that violated the clearly-established right." If it is determined that the official's conduct was unconstitutional, then the court must decide whether the conduct was nonetheless "objectively reasonable."

Assuming arguendo that defendants violated Kipps's clearly established constitutional liberty interest in familial association, the resolution of this issue turns on whether the defendants' actions were "objectively reasonable." Because we find that defendants' actions were objectively reasonable, we affirm the district court's dismissal of Kipps's 1983 claim on the basis of qualified immunity.

Even if defendants violated Kipps's clearly established constitutional right, they are still entitled to qualified immunity if their actions were objectively reasonable. . . . The record indicates that Kipps was fired because his son chose to play football for a Louisiana school other than USL. Notwithstanding the defendants' subjective motivation and belief as to the lawfulness of their conduct, we find the defendants' motivation for terminating Kipps was objectively reasonable. Defendants' motivation, according to the record in this case, was to mitigate the damage that Kyle's attendance at LSU as opposed to USL would have on alumni relations and recruiting efforts.

The summary judgment record of this appeal contains no facts upon which we could find that defendants' actions were objectively unreasonable.

AFFIRMED.

CRITICAL THINKING

What reasons did the judge offer to support his decision that Kipps's termination was legal? Which facts in the case are most important in your mind when evaluating the reasoning?

Identify various meanings of the phrase "objectively reasonable." Which meaning do you think the court is using? Is it clear? How does this affect the validity of the argument given by Judge Parker?

ETHICAL DECISION MAKING

The *Kipps* case provides a snapshot of the complexity of the link between ethics and the law. Do you believe that some view of what it means to do the right thing is responsible for the legal decision in this case?

As the *Kipps* case demonstrates, business managers must sometimes decide whether to hire and fire particular employees. Their decisions will be guided by legal rules that have both ethical foundations and implications for needed legal reform.

In addition, the definition of business ethics refers to *standards* of business conduct. *It does not result in a set of correct decisions.* Business ethics can improve business decisions by serving as a reminder not to choose the first business option that comes to mind or the one that enriches us in the short run. But business ethics can never produce a list of correct business decisions that all ethical businesses will make.

Well-managed firms try to provide ethical leadership by establishing codes of ethics for the firm. For example, Exhibit 2-2 addresses the attempt by General Motors, a major automobile maker, to make a statement about the importance of business ethics to its firm. Notice, however, that this corporate code can never do more than provide guidance. The complications associated with managerial decisions do not permit any ethical guide to provide definitive lists of right and wrong decisions.

Exhibit 2-2
Ethical Business Practices

GENERAL MOTORS' CODE OF BUSINESS CONDUCT

The foundation for all conduct by GM and its employees is one of our core values: Integrity. Integrity is essential to achieving our vision of becoming the world leader in transportation products and services, earning the enthusiasm of our customers, working together as a team, innovating, and continuously improving. We call this Winning With Integrity.

These Guidelines are designed to help GM and its employees understand and meet fundamental obligations that are vital to our success. Some of those obligations are legal duties. They are established by the laws, regulations, and court rulings applicable to our business. Other obligations result from policies GM establishes to make sure our actions align with our core values and cultural priorities. Compliance with both types of obligation—our legal duties and our internal policies—is vital to our goal of winning with integrity.

Employees who violate these guidelines may be subject to disciplinary action which, in the judgment of management, is appropriate to the nature of the violation and which may include termination of employment. Employees may also be subject to civil and criminal penalties if the law has been violated.

Exhibit 2-3
Enron, WorldCom, and Shifts in Business Regulation

During the past several years, ethics violations have been uncovered in the accounting practices of a number of large companies. Enron and WorldCom were two of the perpetrators in these scandals. Both companies failed to report or record billions of dollars in profit losses, which resulted in stockholders believing that the companies were in a much better financial state than actually existed.

Enron's tangled web involved the company's creating multiple subsidiaries and related companies. These businesses were often treated as companies independent of Enron and not shown on the accounting books. Enron used the subsidiaries to conceal debts and losses in a very complex fraud scheme. When the company went bankrupt, employees who had based their retirement plans around Enron stock lost almost everything. Additionally, Enron auditor Arthur Andersen was found guilty of shredding documents about Enron's audits.

In June 2002, shortly after the Enron bankruptcy was announced, WorldCom revealed that it also had engaged in unethical accounting practices. WorldCom's violations included counting profits twice and concealing billions of dollars in expenses when making reports to the SEC. The company thereby made itself appear profitable when it was actually losing money. In total, WorldCom had more than $7 billion in misreported debt.

These two cases, among others, left investors understandably concerned about the truthfulness of individuals who were in charge of operating large corporations. Those in charge of these companies had been awarded million-dollar bonuses while completely disregarding stockholders and employees, who lost millions of dollars when the companies collapsed.

The revelations of Enron and WorldCom suggested quite blatantly that the business world could not be allowed to regulate itself ethically. Their downfall in part led to many federal regulations designed to promote truthfulness and ethical practices among business managers. In this new business environment, there is a much greater degree of government oversight to ensure that companies maintain high standards of ethical behavior. Companies are required to make their accounting records far more transparent, to satisfy not only the federal government but their understandably wary investors.

global context

Contractual Relationships and Ethics in Japan

In the United States, business contracts are extensive and lengthy. They stipulate action for nearly every possible situation that may arise between parties. Lawyers direct the process of creating and agreeing to a contract. Most American businesspersons would not think of drawing up a contract without legal assistance.

In Japan, however, the idea of involving lawyers in contractual relationships is quite upsetting. The Japanese are disturbed that American contracts discuss what would happen if one party in the contract cheated, lied, or wished to terminate. Such discussion is seen as a sign of distrust between the parties. Japanese contracts are based on trust. Often the relationship is finalized verbally rather than by a signature. These verbal agreements are called *yakusoku.*

Because contracts are founded on mutual trust between parties, the contents are open and flexible in comparison to the painstakingly rigid American contracts. This structure allows Japanese businesspersons to deal with problematic issues between the parties as they arise. The Japanese also prefer to solve contract problems through arbitration or compromise rather than through litigation. Executives will go to great lengths to avoid involving lawyers and the court system with their business. Japanese contractual relationships are shaped by the dominant sense of ethics in Japanese culture.

At the same time that business ethics guides decisions within firms, ethics helps guide the law. Law and business ethics serve as an interactive system—informing and assessing each other. For example, our ethical inclination to encourage trust, dependability, and efficiency in market exchanges shapes many of our business laws. See Exhibit 2-3 for instance. The principles of contract law, for instance, facilitate market exchanges and trade because the parties to an exchange can count on the enforceability of agreements. Legal rules that govern the exchange have been shaped in large part by our sense of commercial ethics.

Of course, different ethical understandings prevail in different countries. Thus, ethical conceptions shape business law and business relationships uniquely in each country. Increasingly, business leaders require sensitivity to the differences in legal guidelines in the various countries in which they operate. These differences are based on somewhat different understandings of ethical behavior among businesspeople in diverse countries.

As we mentioned above, business ethics does not yield one "correct" decision. So how are business managers to chart their way through the ethical decision-making process? One source of assistance consists of the general theories and schools of thought about ethics. Each ethical system provides a method for resolving ethical dilemmas by examining duties, consequences, virtues, justice, and so on. A detailed look at each of these ethical systems can be found in Appendix A-2.

In the interest of providing future business managers with a practical approach to business ethics *that they can use,* we suggest a three-step process: **the WPH approach**. This approach offers future business managers some **ethical guidelines**, or practical steps, that provide a dependable stimulus to ethical reasoning in a business context. Appendix A-2 provides the theoretical basis for the WPH approach used in this book.

The WPH Framework for Business Ethics

A useful set of ethical guidelines requires recognition that managerial decisions must meet the following primary criteria:

- The decisions affect particular groups of stakeholders in the operations of the firm. The pertinent question is thus, *Whom* would this decision affect?

global context

Business Ethics and Italian Taxes

When Italian corporations file their tax returns, the tax authorities assume that the corporations are underestimating their profits by 30 to 70 percent. Although this assumption has proved to be true, the Italian Revenue Service does not press charges. In fact, purposely understating profits is the accepted practice within Italy.

Knowing the faulty nature of the tax return, the Revenue Service sends an "invitation to discuss" about six months after a corporation has filed. The parties agree on a meeting date. At the meeting the corporation's executives do not attend. Instead, they send a *commercialista* whose "function exists for the primary purpose of negotiating corporation tax payments."

Several rounds of bargaining take place between the *commercialista* and the tax authorities. On the basis of the corporation's taxes the previous year and the estimation of the current return, the two parties agree on a payment that is usually much higher than the original estimation but is still less than face value.

This negotiating process, while it may seem foreign to Americans, is a common business practice in Italy. In the early 1980s an American banker learned the difficult lesson that, for a firm doing business in a foreign country, local custom has a significant impact on ethical practice. The banker refused, on ethical grounds, to underestimate profits on the tax return. The Italian Revenue Service suggested several times that he hire a *commercialista* and resubmit his tax return.

The American banker refused all such suggestions. Finally, the Revenue Service sent the American a notice that demanded payments 15 times larger than what he owed. The banker immediately arranged an appointment to express his outrage. When he arrived at the meeting, the Italian tax authorities were pleased to see him and said, "Now we can begin our negotiations."

Exhibit 2-4

The WPH Process of Ethical Decision Making

1. W—WHO (Stakeholders):
- Consumers
- Owners or investors
- Management
- Employees
- Community
- Future generations

2. P—PURPOSE (Values):
- Freedom
- Security
- Justice
- Efficiency

3. H—HOW (Guidelines):
- Public disclosure
- Universalization
- Golden Rule

- The decisions are made in pursuit of a particular *purpose.* Business decisions are instruments toward an ethical end.
- The decisions must meet the standards of action-oriented business behavior. Managers need a doable set of guidelines for *how* to make ethical decisions.

The remainder of this chapter explains and illustrates this framework. See Exhibit 2-4 for a summary of the key WPH elements.

WHO ARE THE RELEVANT STAKEHOLDERS?

The **stakeholders** of a firm are the many groups of people affected by the firm's decisions. Any given managerial decision affects, in varying degrees, the following stakeholders:

1. Owners or shareholders.
2. Employees.
3. Customers.
4. Management.
5. The general community where the firm operates.
6. Future generations.

Exhibit 2-5 gives a portrait of Nortel Networks' commitments to its primary stakeholders and demonstrates that Nortel is aware of the people involved in its various decisions.

When you consider the relevant stakeholders, try to go beyond the obvious. In the Case Nugget, Maria's encounter with her company's vice president clearly highlights certain common interests of management and its employees. However, a useful exercise for all of us is to force ourselves to think more broadly about additional stakeholders who may be affected just as much in the long run. Then we will be less likely to make decisions that have unintended negative ethical impacts.

Hypothetical Case Nugget — The Many Stakeholders in a Business Decision

Maria Lopez

Maria recently became the purchasing manager of a small lawn-mower manufacturing firm. She is excited about the opportunity to demonstrate her abilities in this new responsibility. She is very aware that several others in the firm are watching her closely because they do not believe she deserves the purchasing manager position.

Her new job at the firm requires that she interact with several senior managers and leaders. One vice president in particular, Brian O'Malley, is someone she admires because he has earned the respect of the CEO on the basis of his success at making profits for the firm. Again and again, he just seems to know how to discover and take advantage of competitive opportunities that end up paying off royally for the firm.

Maria's first responsibility is to buy the motors for the assembly line. The motors constitute 30 percent of the total construction cost of the lawn mowers. Consequently, even a small error on Maria's part would have huge implications for the firm's profitability. The bids from the motor suppliers are required to be secret in order to maximize competition among the suppliers. The bids are due at 5 p.m. today.

At 3 p.m., Maria accidentally sees Brian returning the submitted bids to the locked safe where they are to be stored, according to company policy, until all bids have been submitted at 5 p.m. Then at 4:45 p.m., she notices a postal delivery of a bid from Stein's Motor Company. Her head buzzes as it hits her that Stein's president is one of Brian O'Malley's cousins.

She has no idea what to do. However, she knows she has to decide quickly.

Maria's ethical dilemma is complex. Many of the issues in the dilemma pertain to her career and the welfare of her firm. But consider the many stakeholders whose interests were not introduced into the conversation. When we overlook important, relevant stakeholders, we are ignoring a significant component of ethical reasoning.

Consider the negative impact that results when a firm fails to show adequate respect for a major stakeholder. On December 3, 1984, a horrible catastrophe occurred at a chemical plant in Bhopal, India. The plant was a subsidiary of Union Carbide. Damage to some equipment resulted in the emission of a deadly gas, methyl isocyanate, into the atmosphere. The emission of the gas caused injuries to more than 200,000 workers and other people in the neighborhood of the chemical plant. Several thousand people died.

Exhibit 2-5
Commitments to Nortel Networks' Stakeholders

- *To Employees*

Nortel Networks commits to treating individuals with respect, following fair and equitable employment practices, and protecting and enhancing employee health and safety.

- *To Shareholders*

Nortel Networks seeks to provide value to shareholders, while maintaining financial prudence.

- *To Customers*

Nortel Networks maintains high ethical standards in all its customer relationships, and upholds the Core Value: "We fulfill our commitments and act with integrity."

- *To Suppliers*

Nortel Networks is fair in its choice of suppliers and honest in all business interactions with them.

Many factors, including worker error, faulty management decisions, equipment failures, and poor safety standards combined to cause the accident. Union Carbide was accused of not demanding the same rigorous safety standards in India as it had in the United States. Citizens of both India and the United States demanded the corporation be held responsible for its evident neglect of safety. Union Carbide argued that it could not operate the plant if it were required to obey rigid Indian safety standards and that the economic benefits of the plant to India outweighed the risks of not following these standards. After years of litigation in both U.S. and Indian courts, Union Carbide was eventually ordered to monetarily compensate the victims of the accident. Among other factors, Union Carbide's failure to respect the interests of a major stakeholder resulted in a disaster for the firm and for the community.

After we consider stakeholders, the next step in the WPH framework is to consider the purpose of business decisions. In the next section, we look first at the parties involved, and then we explore the purposes that bring these various parties together in a common effort.

WHAT ARE THE ULTIMATE *PURPOSES* OF THE DECISION?

When we think about the ultimate reason or purpose for why we make decisions in a business firm, we turn to the basic unit of business ethics—values. **Values** are positive abstractions that capture our sense of what is good or desirable. They are *ideas* that underlie conversations about business ethics. We derive our ethics from the interplay of values. Values represent our understanding of the purposes we will fulfill by making particular decisions.

For example, we value honesty. We want to live in communities where the trust that we associate with honesty prevails in our negotiations with one another. Business depends on the maintenance of a high degree of trust. No contract can protect us completely against every possible contingency. So we need some element of trust in one another when we buy and sell.

If we think about the definition of values for a moment, we realize two things immediately. First, there are a huge number of values that pull and push our decisions. Second, to state that a value is important in a particular situation is to start a conversation about what is meant by that particular value.

To help make WPH useful to you as a manager, Exhibit 2-6 outlines an efficient way to apply this second step in the WPH framework. The exhibit identifies four of the most

Exhibit 2-6
Primary Values and Business Ethics

VALUE	ALTERNATIVE MEANINGS
Freedom	**1.** To act without restriction from rules imposed by others.
	2. To possess the capacity or resources to act as one wishes.
	3. To escape the cares and demands of this world entirely.
Security	**1.** To possess a large enough supply of goods and services to meet basic needs.
	2. To be safe from those wising to interfere with your property rights.
	3. To achieve the psychological condition of self-confidence to such an extent that risks are welcome.
Justice	**1.** To receive the products of your labor.
	2. To treat all humans identically, regardless of race, class, gender, age, and sexual preference.
	3. To provide resources in proportion to need.
	4. To possess anything that someone else is willing to grant you.
Efficiency	**1.** To maximize the amount of wealth in society.
	2. To get the most from a particular output.
	3. To minimize costs.

important values influencing business ethics and presents alternative meanings for each. Exhibit 2-6 should not only help clarify the importance of values in your own mind but also enable you to question others who claim to be acting in an ethical fashion.

For instance, a manager might be deciding whether to fire an employee whose performance is less than impressive. In making this decision, the manager explores alternative visions of key values such as justice and efficiency and then makes choices about which action to take. Values and their alternative meanings are often the foundation for different ethical decisions.

To avoid ambiguity, many companies summarize their values in brief statements. Nortel Networks' statement of core values, shown in Exhibit 2-7, identifies for Nortel's stakeholders which positive abstractions guide its business decisions.

HOW DO WE MAKE ETHICAL DECISIONS?

Making ethical decisions has always been one of our most confusing *and* important human challenges. In the process of meeting this challenge, we have discovered a few general, ethical guidelines to assist us. An *ethical guideline* provides one path to ethical conduct. Notice that all three ethical guidelines below reflect a central principle of business ethics: consideration for stakeholders.

The Golden Rule. The idea that we should interact with other people in a manner consistent with the way we would like them to interact with us has deep historical roots. Both Confucius and Aristotle suggested versions of that identical guideline. One scholar has identified six ways the Golden Rule can be interpreted:

1. Do to others as you want them to gratify you.
2. Be considerate of others' feelings as you want them to be considerate of yours.
3. Treat others as persons of rational dignity like you.

Exhibit 2-7
Core Values: A Guide to Ethical Business Practice

NORTEL NETWORKS' CORE VALUES

1. We create superior value for our customers.
2. We work to provide shareholder value.
3. Our people are our strength.
4. We share one vision. We are one team.
5. We have only one standard—excellence.
6. We embrace change and reward innovation.
7. We fulfill our commitments and act with integrity.

New ways of organizing people and work within the corporation are giving each of us more decision-making responsibility. Given the complexity and constantly changing nature of our work and our world, no book of hard-and-fast rules—however long and detailed—could ever adequately cover all the dilemmas people face. In this context, every Nortel Networks' employee is asked to take leadership in ethical decision making.

In most situations, our personal values and honesty will guide us to the right decision. But in our capacity as employees and representatives of Nortel Networks, we must also always consider how our actions affect the integrity and credibility of the corporation as a whole. Our business ethics must reflect the standard of conduct outlined in this document—a standard grounded in the corporation's values and governing Nortel Networks' relationships with all stakeholders.

4. Extend brotherly or sisterly love to others, as you would want them to do to you.
5. Treat others according to moral insight, as you would have others treat you.
6. Do to others as God wants you to do to them.

Regardless of the version of the Golden Rule we use, this guideline urges us to be aware that other people—their rights and needs—matter.

Let's return to the ethical problem outlined at the beginning of this chapter. Using the Golden Rule as your ethical guideline, how you would you behave? Would you hide the information about where your company's shoes are manufactured, or would you disclose the information? Put yourself into the consumer's position. As a consumer, would you want to know that a shoe was manufactured in another country? Are there other stakeholders in the organization whose interests should be the focus of your application of the Golden Rule? The focus on others that is the foundation of the Golden Rule is also clearly reflected in a second ethical guideline: the public disclosure test.

Public disclosure test. Applying what you have learned to the ethical dilemma faced by Nike, suppose you decide to ignore the complaints about working conditions in your plants in foreign countries. Now suppose that your decision to ignore the complaints is printed in the newspaper. How would the public react? How would you feel about the public's having full knowledge of what you intend to do?

We tend to care about what others think about us as ethical agents. Stop for a moment and think of corporations that failed to apply the public disclosure test and generated negative reactions as a result. For example, Dr. Hugh Davis, a professor at Johns Hopkins University, invented the Dalkon Shield birth control device. In the late 1960s and early

1970s, Dr. Davis was considered a rising star in the field of women's health and family planning. By the mid-1980s, Dr. Davis was known as a dishonest man. A. H. Robins, the company that sold the Dalkon Shield, was bankrupt.

What caused the change in public opinion? Many women became infertile because of the device, and a few women died. The public learned that Dr. Davis—the man who was performing the apparently objective medical studies of the Dalkon Shield's safety—had a financial interest in the Dalkon Shield. Because of Dr. Davis's failure to disclose this interest, the birth control device was not tested appropriately, and many women were harmed as a result.

Dr. Davis is likely to have behaved differently if he had realized that the public would eventually know of his financial interest in the Dalkon Shield. Presumably, he would have made sure that he took actions to protect his reputation and ensure the safety of women who used the Dalkon Shield.

Another way to think of the public disclosure test is to view it as a ray of sunlight that makes our actions visible, rather than obscured. As Exhibit 2-8 suggests, the issue of transparency of behavior is often seen as a method of improving ethical behavior. The public disclosure test is sometimes called the "television test," for it requires us to imagine that our actions are being broadcast on national television. The premise behind the public disclosure test is that ethics is hard work, labor that we might resist if we did not have frequent reminders that we live in a community. As a member of a community, our self-concept is tied, at least in part, to how that community perceives us.

Universalization test. A third general guideline shares with the other two a focus on the "other"—the stakeholders whom our actions affect. Before we act, the universalization test asks us to consider what the world would be like were our decision copied by everyone else. Applying the universalization test causes us to wonder aloud: "Is what I am about to

Exhibit 2-8
A Mandate for Ethical Behavior

THE SARBANES-OXLEY ACT

The Corporate and Criminal Fraud Accountability Act, also known as the Sarbanes-Oxley Act, was signed by President Bush in 2002 in the wake of several corporate accounting scandals. The act is intended to promote high ethical standards among business managers and employees through a series of stringent requirements and controls that regulate several different facets of corporate operation.

Among other things, the act created the Public Company Accounting Oversight Board. This board is responsible for ensuring that auditors and public accounting firms compile accurate and truthful financial reports for the companies they audit. The act also requires that companies devise a system that allows employees to report suspicions of unethical behavior within the company. The act also protects these whistle-blowers from being fired or from retaliation by their employer for reporting a possible problem within the company.

Additionally, the chief executive officer (CEO) or chief financial officer (CFO) must personally vouch that the company's financial statements are correct, meet all SEC requirements for disclosure, and represent company finances accurately. The act provides for very harsh penalties in the case of violations. If the CEO or CFO knows that the company's financial reports are incorrect but claims they are truthful, or if he or she destroys or changes financial documents, the imposed fine can run into the millions of dollars.

e-commerce AND THE LAW

Computer Use and Ethics

The use of computers to store and transfer important business information has resulted in a new set of ethical concerns. How private is the computer screen? Are companies allowed to collect information about their customers? Who owns the information customers give to e-businesses? E-commerce law is gradually adjusting to such questions. But as the beginning of this chapter pointed out, knowing the law is just the first step in discovering ethical business decisions.

One case that considered questions related to e-commerce and privacy involved Toysmart.com and its privacy policy. In 2000, the Federal Trade Commission (FTC) filed a complaint against Toysmart.com, charging the online retailer with selling customer lists despite earlier privacy statements that its customers' personal data would never be shared with a third party. The customer lists were included as assets to be sold as part of the company's bankruptcy proceedings. The FTC issued a settlement with Toysmart.com allowing the lists to be sold as long as (1) the sale occurred before July 2001, (2) the lists would be sold to a family-oriented company, and (3) the buyer would agree to abide by the original Toysmart.com privacy policy. After the FTC imposed these restrictions, the end result was that customers' personal information was not sold.

The Toysmart.com case makes it clear that, for both ethical and legal reasons, companies that adopt a privacy policy need to think that policy through before announcing it to customers.

do the kind of action that, *were others to follow my example,* makes the world a better place for me and those I love?"

In summary, business managers can apply the WPH approach to most ethical dilemmas. The WPH framework provides a practical process suited to the frequently complex ethical dilemmas that business managers must address quickly in today's society.

CASE OPENER WRAP-UP

Nike

Nike, as well as other firms, affects the lives of many stakeholders in many countries. Nike's owners, workers, and customers are perhaps the most obvious stakeholders in decisions Nike makes about its production, marketing, and human relations policies. But the scope of Nike's activities is much broader than is suggested by that list of stakeholders. The company's activities also influence the lives of future generations, competing local businesses, and international relations among diverse trading partners. All of Nike's decisions have ethical implications.

What those decisions are can be guided by an appreciation of the conflicting values that lie under the surface when we make decisions that affect others. The WPH system of ethical decision making stimulates Nike and similar companies to ask questions about their behavior that highlight their possible effects on the community.

All of us would probably agree that Nike has a responsibility to try to be a sustainable business enterprise. Toward that end, profits are essential. But labor practices that cut costs may not be an effective way to make long-run profits because the multiple Nike stakeholders disagree about the benefits of such practices. Some argue that more humane labor and environmental policies would better support the firm's long-range goals of being a competitive and successful business firm.

Summary

Business Ethics and Social Responsibility

Business ethics is the application of ethics to the special problems and opportunities experienced by businesspeople.

The *social responsibility of business* consists of the expectations that the community imposes on firms doing business with its citizens.

Business Law and Business Ethics

Business ethics builds on business law. The law both affects and is affected by evolving ethical patterns. But business law provides only a floor for business ethics, telling business leaders the minimally acceptable course of action.

The WPH Framework for Business Ethics

Who are the relevant stakeholders? This question determines which interests (consumers, employees, managers, owners) are being pushed and prodded.

What are the ultimate purposes of the decision? This question determines which values (freedom, efficiency, security, and justice) are being upheld by the decision.

How do we make ethical decisions? This question leads us to apply general ethical guidelines:

- *Golden Rule:* Do unto others as you would have them do unto you.
- *Public disclosure test:* If the public knew about this decision, how would you decide?
- *Universalization test:* What would the world be like were our decision copied by everyone else.

Point / Counterpoint

Sarbanes-Oxley Act of 2002

Are the Costs Associated with the Sarbanes-Oxley Act Reason for Reform?	
No	**Yes**
Corporate and accounting scandals, such as Enron, were the reason the Sarbanes-Oxley Act of 2002 was drafted. The act promotes honesty and accountability in financial reporting, thus bringing increased security to investors. For example, corporations must now ensure the segregation of all duties related to accounting procedures. Although critics assert that the financial burden associated with the act is reason for reform, the compliance costs about which they speak are beginning to fall as individuals become familiar with the new systems. In addition, the Dow Jones Industrial Average is rising as a result of increased investor confidence. This confidence is the direct result of the requirement that corporations disclose information and allow for investigations by the Public Company Accounting Oversight Board.	Corporations need incentives to remain or go public. The Sarbanes-Oxley Act of 2002 is not an incentive. Although there may have been ample motivation for the development of an act that addresses accounting scandals, the costs associated with Sarbanes-Oxley are much too high. Simply purchasing and learning to use the materials needed for compliance with the act would cost approximately $3.5 million. Those who argue that the act should not be reformed often focus on the idea that every corporation is now being held to the same standards. However, as a result of the substantial economic costs associated with implementation of the guidelines, smaller businesses that would like to go public are forced to remain private to avoid the costs. Among small businesses that are already public, many are not able to gather the resources necessary to comply with the act.

Since the passing of the Sarbanes-Oxley Act, there have not been any known major accounting scandals. Without public disclosure, corporations would have little incentive to engage in rigorous evaluation of their own accounting practices. By forcing the corporations to disclose information, they are being held to higher ethical standards than they were previously.

In addition to the costs associated with the act, corporations are now monitored by commissions that are appointed rather than elected. These commissions lack the accountability that is necessary to make decisions about how to regulate, tax, and punish companies and individuals that may violate the provisions of the act. Thus, the act as it is currently written does not provide an equal opportunity to all corporations and businesses.

Questions & Problems

1. How do business ethics and business law interact with each other? Is one highly ethical and the other less ethical?
2. If business ethics does not offer guidance about what is always the right thing to do, is one behavior as good as the next?
3. How does the WPH approach to ethics approach an ethical problem?
4. Jarold Daniel Friedman worked as a temporary computer contractor for a pharmaceutical warehouse. The warehouse offered him a permanent position, but the warehouse required him to get a mumps vaccine, grown in chicken embryos, as a condition of his permanent employment. Friedman, a vegan, believed that the vaccination would violate his religious beliefs and declined to be vaccinated. As a result, the warehouse withdrew its offer of employment. Friedman claimed that the warehouse discriminated against him on the basis of religion. Do you agree with Friedman? Do employers have a duty to respect the beliefs of their employees? If so, what happens when that duty conflicts with employers' duty to provide a safe and healthy work environment? [*Friedman v. Southern California Permanente Medical Group,* 102 Cal. App. 4th 39 (2002).]
5. John Bigan owned a strip-mining operation in which he dug trenches to remove coal deposits. One of these trenches was nearly 20 feet deep and contained water about 10 feet deep. Bigan installed a pump in the trench to remove the water and asked Joseph Yania, the owner of another strip-mining operation, to help him start the pump. Bigan urged and taunted Yania, who could not swim, to jump from the edge of the trench into the water, where Bigan was working on the pump. Yania jumped and drowned. Yania's widow sued Bigan, alleging that he failed to rescue her husband. Do you think Bigan should have rescued Yania? Do you think the law should require that Bigan rescue Yania? Why or why not? What values are you employing in your argument? [*Yania v. Bigan,* 397 Pa. 316 (1959).]
6. Jennifer Erickson sued her employer, Bartell Drug Company, contending that its decision not to cover prescription contraceptives under its employee prescription drug plan constituted sex discrimination. Bartell argued that its decision was not sex discrimination because contraceptives were preventive, were voluntary, and did not treat an illness. With whom do you agree? Why? What values did you use to reach your conclusion? [*Erickson v. Bartell Drug Co.,* 141 F. Supp. 2d 1266 (2001).]
7. Entertainment Network, Inc. (ENI), a business that provided news, entertainment, and information via the Internet, sued government officials who prohibited the company

from filming the execution of Oklahoma City bomber Timothy McVeigh and selling the footage of the execution online. The government officials argued that a Justice Department regulation prohibiting audio and visual recording devices at federal executions applied in the case at hand. ENI, however, argued that the regulation violated the company's First Amendment right to free speech. How do you think the court should have ruled in this case? Do you think ENI might have altered its decision to broadcast the execution if it had applied the Golden Rule? [*Entm't Network, Inc. v. Lappin,* 134 F. Supp. 2d 1002 (2001).]

8. Heather Reider, a student at McNeese State University, was purchasing a ticket for a university baseball game at the ballpark ticket booth when a foul ball struck her in the eye, shattering her eye socket and causing permanent blindness in her right eye. Reider sued the university, claiming that because the ticket booth was not adequately protected from foul balls, the ballpark had an unreasonable defect that created the risk of substantial harm to patrons. Who do you think won the suit? What ethical issues does this case raise? [*Reider v. State of Louisiana,* 897 So. 2d 893 (2005).]

9. Javier Galindo, the husband of Richard Clark's housekeeper, was sitting in his car, parked in the driveway of Clark's house, waiting to pick up his wife. While he was waiting, a leaning 80-foot tree located on an adjacent property fell on Galindo's car and killed him. Galindo's wife sued Clark, alleging that Clark was liable for failing to notify Galindo about the danger posed by the leaning tree. Do you think that Clark had a legal responsibility to tell Galindo about the tree? Do you think Clark had an ethical responsibility to tell Galindo about the tree? Why might the answer to these questions be different? [*Galindo v. Town of Clarkstown,* 2 N.Y. 3d 633 (2004).]

10. The decedent in the case became very sick and sent a messenger to his longtime family physician, Dr. Eddingfield. The messenger told Eddingfield about the decedent's dangerous illness, told him that no other doctor could be reached in time to save the decedent, and paid Eddingfield up front for medical services for the decedent. Eddingfield refused to tender his services to the decedent without reason. When the decedent died, the administrator of his estate brought suit against Eddingfield, contending that Eddingfield wrongfully refused to enter into an employment contract with the decedent. How do you think the court should have ruled in this case? Does a doctor have a legal or ethical responsibility to help individuals against his or her will? [*Hurley v. Eddingfield,* 156 Ind. 416 (1901).]

11. Aileen Morris was an employee at a Kauszer's convenience store. Convenience Management Services, Inc. (CMSI), own Krauszer's. While working at the store, Aileen, a mother of nine children, was shot to death by a robber. The store was located in a dangerous area and had a history of robberies and criminal attacks. Despite the dangerous location, the store did not have an alarm, a security camera, or an immediate connection to the police. According to the plaintiffs, the absence of these security precautions created a dangerous environment. CMSI argued that it had no duty to protect Morris because the robbery and shooting were unforeseeable. How far do you think a company should go to protect employees? Do you think that CMSI was responsible for the shooting? Why or why not? [*Morris v. Krauszer's Food Stores,* 693 A.2d 510 (1997).]

12. Deborah Vargo-Adams was employed as a distribution clerk for the U.S. Postal Service. Adams was regularly absent from work and had been reprimanded and suspended several times. After receiving a notice of removal, Adams filed a grievance claiming that she suffered from migraine headaches and was frequently unable to go to work. The Postal Service reinstated Adams under the condition that she provide them with medical documentation of her illness and acceptable evidence for future absences when required. At first, Adams complied with the conditions. During an eight-month period, Adams was absent without leave more than two days, was late to work seven times, and was absent nine days. On each of these occasions she provided notice and excuses for her absences. Seven of her notices were rejected because her supervisor claimed that they lacked the proper documentation. After receiving the rejections, Adams stopped submitting her written excuses, but continued to verbally notify her supervisor that the absences were related to her illness. She continued to have an attendance problem and was terminated in 1995. Do you think the Postal Service should have made a better attempt to accommodate her "serious health condition"? Did the termination constitute a "wrongful discharge"? [*Vargo-Adams v. U.S. Postal Service,* 992 F. Supp. 939 (1998).]

13. Grand Central Partnership Social Services Corporation is a not-for-profit organization. The organization provides counseling, referrals, clothing, showers, and mail access for the homeless. Additionally, the organization implemented a program known as Pathways to Employment (PTE), designed to assist in the development of vocational skills. The program provided workshops covering topics such as interviewing skills and résumé writing. Participants in the PTE program were assigned to five areas: maintenance, food services, administration, outreach, and recycling. Each of these tasks related to the overall operation and goals of the center. Individuals participating in the PTE program were required to participate 40 hours per week and were paid between $40 and $60 per week. The plaintiffs, predominantly homeless and jobless individuals, alleged that the wages paid by Grand Central were below minimum wage and therefore unlawful. Grand Central argued that participants in the PTE program were trainees, not employees, and that the participants were learning valuable job readiness skills. Do you think that this is an appropriate distinction? What ethical issues should be considered? [*Archie v. Grand Central Partnership,* 997 F. Supp. 504 (1998).]

14. Doctors diagnosed Leo Guilbeault with lung cancer. He had been smoking the same brand, Camel cigarettes, since 1951. Guilbeault filed a complaint against the manufacturer of Camel cigarettes, R. J. Reynolds Tobacco Co. According to Guilbeault, Reynolds failed to adequately warn consumers about the dangers of smoking. Prior to 1970, Camel cigarettes were sold without a warning label. After the Labeling Act of 1966, Reynolds began to put warning labels on packages of cigarettes. Guilbeault believes that Reynolds knew about the adverse health consequences of smoking before 1970 and, therefore, that Reynolds had a duty to warn consumers of these consequences. Do you agree with his argument? Should Reynolds have warned consumers earlier? [*Guilbeault v. R. J. Reynolds Tobacco Co.,* 44 Fed. R. Serv. 3d 124 (1999).]

Looking for more review material?

The Online Learning Center at **www.mhhe.com/kubasek1e** contains this chapter's "Assignment on the Internet" and also a list of URLs for more information, entitled "On the Internet." Find both of them in the Student Center portion of the OLC, along with quizzes and other helpful materials.

Appendix A-2 Theories of Business Ethics

Ethical Relativism and Situational Ethics

An ethical school of thought that may seem appealing on the surface is ethical relativism. **Ethical relativism** is a theory of ethics that denies the existence of objective moral standards. Rather, according to ethical relativism, individuals must evaluate actions on the basis of what they feel is best for themselves. Ethical relativism holds that when two individuals disagree over a question about morality, both individuals are correct because no objective standard exists to evaluate their actions. Instead, morality is relative, and thus no one can criticize another's behavior as immoral. Many people find ethical relativism attractive because it promotes tolerance.

Ethical relativism may appear attractive at first glance, but very few people are willing to accept the logical conclusions of this theory. For example, ethical relativism requires us to see murder as a moral action as long as the murderer believes that the action is best for himself or herself. Once a person accepts the appropriateness of criticizing behavior in some situations, the person has rejected ethical relativism and must develop a more complex ethical theory.

Situational ethics is a theory that at first appears similar to ethical relativism but is actually substantially different. Like ethical relativism, **situational ethics** requires that we evaluate the morality of an action by imagining ourselves in the position of the person facing the ethical dilemma. But unlike ethical relativism, situational ethics allows us to judge other people's actions. In other words, situational ethics holds that once we put ourselves in another person's shoes, we can evaluate whether that person's action was ethical.

While situational ethics provides a useful rule of thumb to use when thinking about the ethical decision-making process, it does not offer specific-enough criteria to be useful in many real-world situations. Once we imagine ourselves in the position of a person facing an ethical dilemma, situational ethics does not tell us *how* to evaluate that person's actions. An alternative school of ethical thought, however, provides a much more judgmental approach to ethical dilemmas.

Absolutism

Absolutism, or *ethical fundamentalism,* requires that individuals defer to a set of rules to guide them in the ethical decision-making process. Unlike ethical relativism and situational ethics, absolutism holds that whether an action is moral does not depend on the perspective of the person facing the ethical dilemma. Rather, whether an action is moral depends on whether the action conforms to the given set of ethical rules.

Of course, people disagree about which set of rules to follow. Why should we accept and act on any one absolutist set of rules? Absolutism cannot tell us, for example, why we ought to follow the doctrines set forth in the Koran and not Hindu doctrines.

Moreover, the unquestionable nature of the rules in most absolutist repositories seems overly inflexible when applied to different situations. For instance, "Thou shalt not kill" seems to be an absolute rule, but, in practice, killing in self-defense seems to be an acceptable exception to this rule.

Consequentialism

In contrast to absolutism, consequentialism does not provide a rigid set of rules to follow regardless of the situation. Rather, as the word *consequentialism* suggests, this ethical approach "depends on the consequences." **Consequentialism** is a general approach to ethical dilemmas that requires that we inquire about the consequences to relevant people of our making a particular decision.

Utilitarianism is one form of consequentialism that business managers may find useful. Like many consequentialist theories of ethics, **utilitarianism** urges managers to take those actions that provide the greatest pleasure after having subtracted the pain or harm associated with the action in question.

Utilitarianism has two main branches: act utilitarianism and rule utilitarianism. **Act utilitarianism** tells business managers to examine all the potential actions in each situation and choose the action that yields the greatest amount of pleasure over pain for all involved. For example, according to act utilitarianism, a business manager who deceives an employee may be acting morally if the act of deception maximizes pleasure over pain for everyone involved.

Rule utilitarians, on the other hand, see great potential for the abuse of act utilitarianism. Instead of advocating the maximization of pleasure over pain in each individual situation, **rule utilitarianism** holds that general rules that *on balance* produce the greatest amount of pleasure for all involved should be established and followed in each situation. Thus, even if the business manager's decision to deceive an employee maximizes pleasure over pain in a given situation, the act probably would not be consistent with rule utilitarianism because deception does not generally produce the greatest satisfaction.

Rule utilitarianism underlies many laws in the United States. For example, labor laws prohibit employers from hiring children to do manufacturing work, even though in some situations the transaction would maximize pleasure over pain.

One form of utilitarianism commonly applied by firms and government is **cost-benefit analysis.** When a business makes decisions based on cost-benefit analysis, it is comparing the pleasure and pain of its optional choices, as that pleasure and pain are measured in monetary terms.

As we have shown, consequentialism is not altogether helpful because of the extreme difficulty in making the required calculations about consequences. Another issue raises an important additional objection to consequentialist thinking: Where does the important social value of justice fit into consequentialist reasoning? Many business decisions could be beneficial in their consequences for a majority of the population, but is it fair to require that a few be harmed so that the majority can be improved? Consequentialism does not provide definite answers to these questions, but an alternative ethical theory does.

Deontology

Deontology is an alternative theoretical approach to consequentialism. When you see references to **Kantian ethics,** the analysis that follows the reference will be a discussion of the most famous of the deontological approaches to business ethics. Unlike a person espousing consequentialism, a person using a deontological approach will not see the relevance of making a list of harms and benefits that result from a particular decision. Instead, **deontology** consists of acting on the basis of the recognition that certain actions are right or wrong, regardless of their consequences. For example, a business leader might consider it wrong to terminate a person whose spouse has terminal cancer because a firm has an obligation to support its employees when they are vulnerable, *period.*

But how are business managers to decide whether an action is right or wrong? The German deontological philosopher Immanuel Kant proposed the categorical imperative to determine whether an action is right. According to the **categorical imperative,** an action is moral only if it would be consistent for everyone in society to act in the same way. Thus, for example, applying the categorical imperative would lead you to conclude that you should not cheat on a drug test, because if everyone acted in the same way, the drug test would be meaningless.

From the deontological viewpoint, the duties or obligations that we owe one another as humans are much more ethically significant than are measurements of the impacts of business decisions. For example, a person using a deontological theory of ethics may see any business behavior that violates our duty of trust as being wrong. To sell a car that one knows will probably not be usable after four years is, from this perspective, unethical. No set of positive consequences that might flow from the production decision can overcome the certainty of the deontological recognition that the sale is wrong.

The duties that we owe others imply that human beings have fundamental rights based on the dignity of each individual. This **principle of rights** asserts that whether a business decision is ethical depends on how the decision affects the rights of all involved. This principle is foundational to Western culture: the Declaration of Independence, for example, asserts that everyone has the right to "life, liberty, and the pursuit of happiness."

But just as consequentialism is incredibly complicated, deontology is difficult to apply because people disagree about what duties we owe to one another and which duties are more important than others when they conflict. For example, imagine the dilemma of a scientist working for a tobacco firm who discovers that cigarettes are carcinogenic. She owes a duty of trust to her employer, but she also has a conflicting duty to the community to do no harm. Where would a business manager find a list of relevant duties under the deontological framework, and why should we accept and act on any particular list?

In addition, as with absolutism, the absolute nature of many deontological lists of duties and rights seems overly rigid when applied to a wide variety of contexts. For instance, saying that we owe a duty to respect human life sounds absolute. In application, however, we might be forced to harm one life to preserve other life. An alternative theory of ethics, called *virtue ethics,* avoids this rigidity problem by providing us with abstract goals to pursue continually.

Virtue Ethics

Virtue ethics is an ethical system in which the development of virtues, or positive character traits such as courage, justice, and truthfulness, is the basis for morality. A morally excellent (and thus good) person develops virtues and distinguishes them from vices, or negative character traits such as cowardice and vanity. This development of virtues occurs through practice. Virtues are the habits of mind that move us toward excellence, the good life, or human flourishing.

As a guide to business ethics, virtue ethics requires that managers act in such a way that they will increase their contributions to the good life. Virtue ethics tells them to follow the character traits that, upon introspective reflection, they see as consistent with virtue. Identifying the relevant virtues and vices requires reasoning about the kind of human behavior that moves us toward the good, successful, or happy life.

A difficulty with the application of virtue ethics is the lack of agreement about the meaning of "the good life." Without that agreement, we are not able to agree about what types of behavior are consistent with our achievement of that goal. Even so, virtue ethics is useful in reminding us that ethics is grounded in a sense of what it means to be virtuous—we need some moral beacon to call us toward a more morally excellent condition. An alternative theory of business ethics, the ethics of care, offers a clear conception of what is virtuous.

Ethics of Care

The **ethics of care** holds that the right course of action is the option most consistent with the building and maintaining of human relationships. Those who adhere to an ethic of care argue that traditional moral hierarchies ignore an important element of life: relationships. Care for the nurturing of our many relationships serves as a reminder of the importance of responsibility to others.

According to someone who adheres to an ethic of care, when one person cares for another person, the first person is acting morally. When other ethical theories emphasize different moral dimensions as a basis for resolving ethical dilemmas, they rarely consider the harm they might do to relationships; thus, from the perspective of the ethics of care, alternative theories of business ethics often encourage unethical behavior.

Ethics-of-care theorists argue that when one individual, the *caregiver,* meets the needs of one other person, the *cared-for* party, the caregiver is actually helping to meet the needs of all the individuals who fall within the cared-for party's *web of care.* Thus, by specifically helping one other individual, the caregiver is assisting numerous people.

The strength of this theoretical approach is that it focuses on the basis of ethics in general: the significance of the interests of other people. The urging to care for relationships speaks to the fundamental basis of why we are concerned about ethics in the first place. Most of us do not need any encouragement to think about how a decision will affect us personally. But ethical reasoning requires that we weigh the impact of decisions on the larger community.

Let's examine how these ethical theories are applied in real-world firms. Exhibit A-2.1 is an abridged version of the Johnson & Johnson Credo, or statement of shared corporate values. General Robert Wood Johnson, who guided Johnson & Johnson from a small, family-owned business to a worldwide enterprise, believed the corporation had social responsibilities beyond the manufacturing and marketing of products. In 1943, he wrote and published the Johnson & Johnson Credo, a document outlining those responsibilities. Does the credo depend more on ethical relativism, situational ethics, absolutism, consequentialism, deontology, virtue ethics, or the ethics of care for its ethical vision?

Exhibit A-2.1 Johnson & Johnson's Credo

THE CREDO

We believe our first responsibility is to the doctors, nurses and patients, to mothers and fathers and all others who use our products and services. In meeting their needs everything we do must be of high quality. We must constantly strive to reduce our costs in order to maintain reasonable prices. Customers' orders must be serviced promptly and accurately. Our suppliers and distributors must have an opportunity to make a fair profit.

We are responsible to our employees, the men and women who work with us throughout the world. Everyone must be considered as an individual. We must respect their dignity and recognize their merit. They must have a sense of security in their jobs. Compensation must be fair and adequate, and working conditions clean, orderly and safe. We must be mindful of ways to help our employees fulfill their family responsibilities. Employees must feel free to make suggestions and complaints. There must be equal opportunity for employment, development and advancement for those qualified. We must provide competent management, and their actions must be just and ethical.

Exhibit A-2.1 Johnson & Johnson's Credo (*continued*)

We are responsible to the communities in which we live and work and to the world community as well. We must be good citizens—support good works and charities and bear our fair share of taxes. We must encourage civic improvements and better health and education. We must maintain in good order the property we are privileged to use, protecting the environment and natural resources.

Our final responsibility is to our stockholders. Business must make a sound profit. We must experiment with new ideas. Research must be carried on, innovative programs developed and mistakes paid for. New equipment must be purchased, new facilities provided and new products launched. Reserves must be created to provide for adverse times. When we operate according to these principles, the stockholders should realize a fair return.

At a Glance

THEORIES OF BUSINESS ETHICS

Ethical approach	Description
Ethical relativism	Asserts that morality is relative.
Situational ethics	Requires that when we evaluate whether an action is ethical, we imagine ourselves in the position of the person facing an ethical dilemma.
Consequentialism	Considers the consequences (i.e., harms and benefits) of making a particular decision.
Deontology	Recognizes certain actions as right or wrong regardless of the consequences.
Virtue ethics	Encourages individuals to develop virtues (e.g., courage and truthfulness) that guide behavior.
Ethics of care	Holds that ethical behavior is determined by actions that care for and maintain human relationships.

The U.S. Legal System

CASE OPENER

Questionable Jurisdiction over Caterpillar

James Lewis, a resident of Kentucky, sustained an injury while operating a Caterpillar bulldozer. He filed suit against Caterpillar, a company incorporated in Delaware but with its principal place of business in Illinois. Lewis also filed suit against the supplier of the bulldozer, Whayne Supply Company, whose principal place of business was Kentucky. Lewis filed his case in a Kentucky state court, alleging defective manufacture, negligence, failure to warn, and breach of warranty. Lewis and Whayne Supply Company agreed to settle out of court. Caterpillar then filed a motion to exercise its right of removal (its right to move the case from the state to the federal court system), arguing that the federal court had jurisdiction over the case because Caterpillar and Lewis were from different states. Lewis disagreed with Caterpillar's contention, claiming that because he had not completed his settlement with Whayne, the case still included a defendant (Whayne) from Lewis's state, Kentucky. Thus, Lewis argued, federal courts did not have jurisdiction over the case.

The court agreed with Caterpillar's argument and moved the case to a federal district court. Shortly thereafter, Lewis and Whayne finalized their settlement agreement, and the district court dismissed Whayne from the lawsuit. The federal district court granted Caterpillar a favorable judgment. Lewis, however, appealed the district court's decision, renewing his argument that the district court did not have jurisdiction over the case. The court of appeals agreed with Lewis, holding that because Whayne was a defendant in the case at the time that Caterpillar moved the case from state to federal court, the diversity of citizenship necessary to give the federal court jurisdiction over the case was absent. Thus, a

CHAPTER 3

state court should have resolved the dispute. Consequently, the appellate court vacated the district court's decision. Caterpillar then appealed to the U.S. Supreme Court.

1. What factors determine whether the state or federal court system hears a case?
2. If you were a businessperson with Caterpillar, why might you prefer a federal court to hear the dispute with Lewis instead of a state court?

The Wrap-Up at the end of the chapter will answer these questions.

Learning Objectives

After reading this chapter, you will be able to answer the following questions:

1. What are the different types of jurisdiction a court must have before it can render a binding decision in a case?
2. What is venue?
3. What are the threshold requirements that must be met before a court will hear a case?
4. How is our dual court system structured?
5. What are the steps in civil litigation?

As the opening scenario illustrates, when a dispute arises, parties in this country do not simply "go to court." They often must choose between federal and state court systems. This chapter examines these systems, as well as the trial procedures that apply in civil cases.

Jurisdiction

The word *jurisdiction* comes from the Latin terms *juris,* meaning "law," and *diction,* meaning "to speak." A useful way to understand jurisdiction is to think of it as referring to courts' power to hear cases and render decisions that bind the parties before them. A court must have several types of jurisdiction to decide any particular case.

ORIGINAL VERSUS APPELLATE JURISDICTION

Trial courts, or **courts of original jurisdiction,** have the power to hear and decide cases when they first enter the legal system. In these courts, the parties present evidence and call witnesses to testify. Most state court systems refer to trial courts as *courts of common pleas* or *county courts.* The federal system calls them *district courts.*

Courts of appellate jurisdiction, or **appellate courts,** have the power to review previous judicial decisions to determine whether trial courts erred in their decisions. Appellate courts do not hold trials. Rather, appellate judges review transcripts of trial court proceedings and occasionally consider additional oral and written arguments from each party.

Appellate courts handle primarily questions of law, not questions of fact. A **question of law** is an issue concerning the interpretation or application of a law. In contrast, a **question of fact** is a question about an event or characteristic in the case. For example, whether a student yelled racial slurs on a college campus is a question of fact. On the other hand, whether the First Amendment protects the student's right to utter racial slurs is a question of law.

Only judges can decide questions of law. Questions of fact are determined in the trial court. In a *bench trial* (a trial with no jury), the judge decides questions of fact; in a *jury trial,* the jury decides questions of fact. Appellate courts can, however, overrule trial courts' decisions on questions of fact, but only when the trial court's finding was clearly erroneous or when no trial evidence supports the trial court's finding.

JURISDICTION OVER PERSONS AND PROPERTY

***In personam* jurisdiction** (literally, "jurisdiction over the person"), is a court's power to render a decision affecting the rights of the specific persons before the court. Generally, a court's power to exercise *in personam* jurisdiction extends only over a specific geographic region. In the state court system, a court's *in personam* jurisdiction usually extends to the state's borders. In the federal system, on the other hand, each court's jurisdiction extends across its geographic district.

A court acquires *in personam* jurisdiction over a person (the **plaintiff**) when she files a lawsuit with the court. The court acquires jurisdiction over the person the plaintiff is suing (the **defendant**) when it gives him a copy of the complaint and a summons. The **complaint** specifies the factual and legal basis for the lawsuit and the relief the plaintiff seeks. The **summons** is a court order that notifies the defendant of the lawsuit and explains how and when to respond to the complaint.

Service of process is the procedure by which courts present these documents to defendants. Traditionally, courts use **personal service:** An officer of the court hands the summons and complaint to the defendant. Recently, however, courts have employed other methods of service, including *residential service,* in which a court representative leaves the summons and complaint with a responsible adult at the defendant's home, and *service by certified* or *ordinary mail.*

connecting to the core

Finance

Individuals who are interested in starting a corporation must prepare the articles of incorporation, including the corporation's name, its purpose, and the number of shares to be issued. These individuals must also choose the state in which to incorporate, which is a decision that is highly relevant to where the corporation should reasonably expect to be sued. As this chapter explains, a state court may have *in personam* jurisdiction over a corporation that was incorporated within that state. Arguably, corporations prefer to be sued within their states of incorporation rather than in other states, perhaps due to their familiarity with the state's laws or their hope of having a more favorable jury in their "home" state. To increase the likelihood of being sued within its state of incorporation, a corporation may opt to include a choice-of-forum clause in its business agreements, which could require that all suits related to particular business agreements be filed within the company's state of incorporation. However, a choice-of-forum clause would be relevant only in business-to-business transactions, not with consumers who use the corporation's products or services.

Source: S. Ross, R. W. Westerfield, B. D. Jordan, *Fundamentals of Corporate Finance* (New York: McGraw-Hill/Irwin, 2006), p. 6.

If the defendant is a corporation, courts generally serve either the president of the corporation or an agent that the corporation has appointed to receive service. Most states require that corporations appoint an agent for service when they incorporate. Corporations are subject to *in personam* jurisdiction in three locations: the state of their incorporation, the location of their main offices, and the geographic areas in which they conduct business.

Courts have *in personam* jurisdiction only over persons within a specific geographic region. In the past, a state court could not acquire *in personam* jurisdiction over out-of-state defendants unless it served the defendants within the court's home state. Thus, defendants who injured plaintiffs could evade legal action by leaving the state and remaining outside its borders. To alleviate this problem, most states have enacted **long-arm statutes,** which enable the court to serve defendants outside the state as long as the defendant has sufficient minimum contacts within the state and it seems fair to assert long-arm jurisdiction over him or her. The U.S. Supreme Court established this "minimum-contacts" standard in the 1945 case *International Shoe Co. v. State of Washington.*[1]

Each state has its own minimum-contact requirements, but most state statutes hold that acts like committing a tort or doing business in the state are sufficient to allow the state to serve a defendant. In the opening scenario, the company sold products in Kentucky, and its products caused an injury in that state. These two facts were sufficient minimum contacts to allow the Kentucky court to serve Caterpillar, even though it was an out-of-state company. Compare the facts of the Caterpillar case to those in the Case Nugget, where the court found that the contacts were insufficient to give the court jurisdiction over the out-of-state resident.

If a defendant has property in a state, a plaintiff may file suit against the defendant's property instead of the owner. For example, suppose a Utah resident had not paid property taxes on a piece of land she owned in Idaho. Idaho courts have ***in rem* jurisdiction** (Latin for "jurisdiction over the thing") over the property. Thus, an Idaho state court has the power to seize the property and sell it to pay the property taxes in an *in rem* proceeding.

Courts can also gain **quasi *in rem* jurisdiction,** or *attachment jurisdiction,* over a defendant's property *unrelated* to the plaintiff's claim. For example, suppose Charlie, a Massachusetts resident, ran a red light while he was vacationing in California and collided

[1] 326 U.S. 310.

e-commerce AND THE LAW

The Sliding Scale Standard for Internet Transactions

Does a business that has Internet contact with a plaintiff in a different state satisfy the minimum-contacts standard? Anyone who engages in transactions over the Internet should be concerned about this question.

A federal district court established the following "sliding-scale" standard in the 1997 case *Zippo Mfg. Co. v. Zippo Dot Com, Inc.*: *

> [T]he likelihood that personal jurisdiction can be constitutionally exercised is directly proportionate to the nature and quality of commercial activity that an entity conducts over the Internet. This sliding scale is consistent with well developed personal jurisdiction principles.

At one end of the spectrum are situations where a defendant clearly does business over the Internet. If the defendant enters into contracts with residents of a foreign jurisdiction that involve the knowing and repeated transmission of computer files over the Internet, personal jurisdiction is proper.

At the opposite end are situations where a defendant has simply posted information on an Internet Web site which is accessible to users in foreign jurisdictions. A passive Web site that does little more than make information available to those who are interested in it is not grounds for the exercise of personal jurisdiction.

The middle ground is occupied by interactive Web sites where a user can exchange information with the host computer. In these cases, the exercise of jurisdiction is determined by examining the level of interactivity and commercial nature of the exchange of information that occurs on the Web site.

*952 F. Supp. 1119, 1124 (W.D. Pa. 1997)

Case Nugget A Question of Minimum Contacts

Hagan v. Field
Court of Appeals of Texas, Fifth District, Dallas
2006 Tex. App. LEXIS 393

The plaintiff, a Texas resident, and the defendants, Colorado residents, were cat breeders who met at a cat show in Colorado. Subsequently, plaintiff sent two cats to the defendants in Colorado for breeding and sent a third cat to them to be sold. A dispute over the return of the two breeding cats arose, and plaintiff filed suit against the defendants in Texas. Defendants alleged that the Texas court lacked personal jurisdiction over them because they did not have minimum contacts with the state of Texas. The trial court disagreed, and the defendants appealed. The court of appeals reversed the decision of the trial court, finding that under the Texas long-arm statute, the Texas court could exercise jurisdiction over an out-of-state defendant only if (1) the defendant has purposefully established minimum contacts with the forum state, and (2) the exercise of jurisdiction comports with traditional notions of fair play and substantial justice.

In this case, the defendants were not residents of Texas and had no business in Texas. The only contact defendants had with Texas was a single trip they made to Texas to pick up two other cats, not related to the litigation, that they were going to take to a cat show. During that same visit, defendants took a cat unrelated to the lawsuit to see a Texas veterinarian, and plaintiff's husband assisted the defendants with a Web page for their business. These actions, even in combination with the defendants' sending the plaintiff a check for the proceeds from the breeding, were not found to constitute sufficient minimum contacts to give the Texas court jurisdiction. The defendants were not availing themselves of the benefits of the state of Texas, nor were their contacts sufficient to put them on notice that they could be subject to the court's jurisdiction.

with Jessica's car. Suppose further that Jessica suffered extensive injuries from the accident and successfully sued Charlie for $200,000 in a California state court. The California court can exercise quasi *in rem* jurisdiction over Charlie's California vacation home by seizing it, selling it, and transferring $200,000 to Jessica to satisfy her judgment against Charlie. If Charlie's vacation home is worth more than $200,000, however, the court must return the excess proceeds to Charlie.

SUBJECT-MATTER JURISDICTION

Subject-matter jurisdiction is a court's power to hear certain kinds of cases. Most industrialized countries have a single court system, with courts that have the power to hear both national law cases and local law cases. In contrast, the United States has both a state and a federal court system. Subject-matter jurisdiction determines which court system may hear a particular case. Cases may fall under state jurisdiction, exclusive federal jurisdiction, or concurrent jurisdiction. Figure 3-1 illustrates the subject-matter-jurisdiction divisions.

Exclusive federal jurisdiction. The federal court system has exclusive jurisdiction over very few cases: admiralty cases, bankruptcy cases, federal criminal prosecutions, lawsuits in which one state sues another state, claims against the United States, and cases involving federal copyrights, patents, or trademarks. Additionally, federal courts have exclusive jurisdiction over claims arising under federal statutes that specify exclusive federal jurisdiction.

State jurisdiction. The state court system has a broad range of jurisdiction; state courts have the power to hear all cases not within the exclusive jurisdiction of the federal court system. State courts also have exclusive jurisdiction over certain cases, such as cases concerning adoption and divorce. Most cases, therefore, fall under state court jurisdiction.

The Caterpillar case fell under state court jurisdiction because its subject matter—product liability and negligence—did not place the case under the exclusive jurisdiction of the federal court system.

Figure 3-1 Subject-Matter-Jurisdiction Divisions

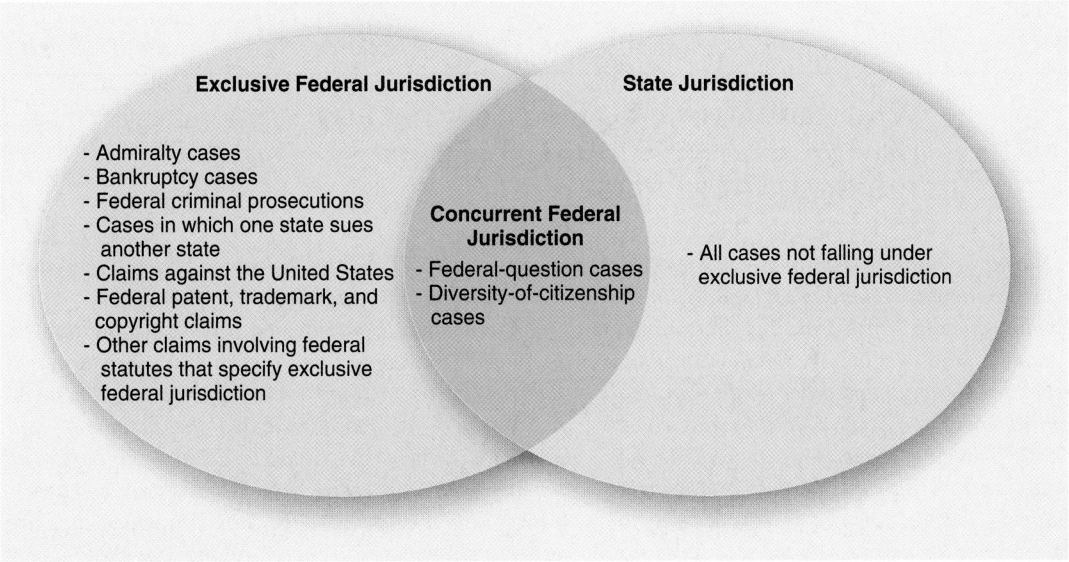

Concurrent federal jurisdiction. Concurrent federal jurisdiction means that both state and federal courts have jurisdiction over a case. Concurrent jurisdiction covers two types of cases: federal-question and diversity-of-citizenship cases. *Federal-question* cases require an interpretation of the United States Constitution, a federal statute, or a federal treaty. For example, suppose a plaintiff alleges that a Florida campaign financing law violates his First Amendment free speech rights. Because this case raises a federal question, it falls under concurrent jurisdiction, and both state and federal courts have the power to hear it.

A *diversity-of-citizenship* case must satisfy two conditions: (1) The plaintiff(s) does (do) not reside in the same state as the defendant(s), and (2) the controversy concerns an amount in excess of $75,000. Courts use the location of a party's residence to determine whether diversity of citizenship exists. Most federal court cases are based on diversity of citizenship.

A business may reside in two states: the state of its incorporation and the state of its principal place of business. Thus, in the opening scenario, Caterpillar was a resident of Delaware, the state where it incorporated, and of Illinois, the state of its primary place of business.

Diversity must be complete, however, for a case to fall under concurrent jurisdiction. In the Caterpillar case, Lewis argued that diversity was not complete because both he and the supply company, the second defendant he originally sued, were residents of Kentucky. The appellate court agreed with his argument and overturned the district court's decision because the district court lacked subject-matter jurisdiction.

When a plaintiff files a case involving concurrent jurisdiction in a state court, the defendant has a *right of removal.* This right entitles the defendant to transfer the case to the federal court system. Thus, either party to a case involving concurrent jurisdiction has the ability to ensure that the case will be heard in the federal court system: The plaintiff can file the case in state court initially, and the defendant can transfer the case to federal court by exercising her right of removal. In the opening scenario, Caterpillar exercised its right of removal, and the state trial court moved the case to a federal district court.

The issue of subject-matter jurisdiction often arises when the parties to a lawsuit disagree about whether to try the case in state or federal court, as Case 3-1 illustrates.

CASE 3-1

WACHOVIA BANK, N. A. v. SCHMIDT
UNITED STATES SUPREME COURT
126 S. CT. 941 (2006)

Petitioner Wachovia Bank, National Association (Wachovia), is a national banking association with its designated main office in North Carolina and branch offices in many states, including South Carolina. Plaintiff-respondent Schmidt and other South Carolina citizens sued Wachovia in a South Carolina state court for fraudulently inducing them to participate in an illegitimate tax shelter. Shortly thereafter, Wachovia filed a petition in Federal District Court, seeking to compel arbitration of the dispute. As the sole basis for federal-court jurisdiction, Wachovia claimed there was diversity of citizenship between the parties.

The District Court denied Wachovia's petition on the merits. On appeal, the Fourth Circuit determined that the District Court lacked subject-matter jurisdiction over the action, vacated the judgment, and instructed the District Court to dismiss the case. The appeals court observed that for diversity purposes, Wachovia is a citizen of "the States in which they are respectively located." Therefore the appellate court found Wachovia to be "located" in, and therefore a "citizen" of, every State in which it maintains a branch office. Thus, Wachovia's South Carolina branch operations rendered it a citizen of that State. Given the South Carolina citizenship of the opposing parties, the court concluded that the matter could not be adjudicated in federal court.

Wachovia appealed to the United States Supreme Court.

JUSTICE GINSBURG: This case concerns the citizenship, for purposes of federal-court diversity jurisdiction, of national banks, i.e., corporate entities chartered not by any State, but by the Comptroller of the Currency of the U.S. Treasury. Congress empowered federal district courts to adjudicate civil actions between citizens of different States where the amount in controversy exceeds $75,000. A business organized as a corporation, for diversity jurisdiction purposes, is deemed to be a citizen of any State by which it has been incorporated and, since 1958, also of the State where it has its principal place of business. State banks, usually chartered as corporate bodies by a particular State, ordinarily fit comfortably within this prescription. Federally chartered national banks do not, for they are not incorporated by "any State." For diversity jurisdiction purposes, therefore, Congress has discretely provided that national banks "shall . . . be deemed citizens of the States in which they are respectively located."

The question presented turns on the meaning, in §1348's context, of the word "located." Does it signal, as the petitioning national bank and the United States, as *amicus curiae,* urge, that the bank's citizenship is determined by the place designated in the bank's articles of association as the location of its main office? Or does it mean, in addition, as respondents urge and the Court of Appeals held, that a national bank is a citizen of every State in which it maintains a branch

Recognizing that "located" is not a word of enduring rigidity, but one that gains its precise meaning from context, we hold that a national bank, for § 1348 purposes, is a citizen of the State in which its main office, as set forth in its articles of association, is located. Were we to hold, as the Court of Appeals did, that a national bank is additionally a citizen of every State in which it has established a branch, the access of a federally chartered bank to a federal forum would be drastically curtailed in comparison to the access afforded state banks and other state-incorporated entities. Congress, we are satisfied, created no such anomaly.

REVERSED in favor of Wachovia.

CRITICAL THINKING

What guideline does Justice Ginsburg provide for determining which alternative interpretation of a word is the most appropriate in a certain context? In other words, what did she suggest as a guideline for sorting out solutions to ambiguity?

ETHICAL DECISION MAKING

What is the ethical problem suggested by this case?
Why does it matter who has jurisdiction in a case like this one?

Venue

Once a case is in the proper court system, **venue** determines which trial court in the system will hear the case. Venue is a matter of geographic location determined by each state's statutes. Usually, the trial court where the defendant resides is the appropriate venue. If a case involves property, the trial court where the property is located is also an appropriate venue. Finally, if the focus of the case is a particular incident, the trial court where the dispute occurred is an appropriate venue. The plaintiff initially chooses from among the appropriate venues when she files the case.

If the location of the court where the plaintiff filed the case is an inconvenience to the defendant or if the defendant believes it will be difficult to select an unbiased jury in that venue, he may request that the judge move the case by filing a motion for a change of venue. The judge has the discretion to grant or deny the motion.

The Structure of the Court System

The U.S. legal system has two parallel court structures: a federal system and a state system. Once a plaintiff files a case in one of the systems, the case remains in that system throughout the appeals process. The only exception to this rule occurs when a party to a lawsuit appeals the decision of a state supreme court to the U.S. Supreme Court.

THE FEDERAL COURT SYSTEM

The federal court system derives its power from Article III, Section 2, of the U.S. Constitution and consists of three main levels: trial courts, intermediate appellate courts, and the court of last resort. Figure 3-2 illustrates this system.

Federal trial courts. In the federal court system, the trial courts, or courts of original jurisdiction, are U.S. district courts. The United States has 94 districts; each district has at least one trial court of general jurisdiction. Courts of general jurisdiction have the power to hear a wide range of cases and can grant almost any type of remedy. Almost every case in the federal system begins in one of these courts.

A small number of cases, however, do not begin in trial courts of general jurisdiction. For cases concerning certain subject matter, Congress has established special trial courts of limited jurisdiction. The types of cases for which Congress has established these special trial courts include bankruptcy cases, claims against the U.S. government, international trade and customs cases, and disputes over certain tax deficiencies.

In an extremely limited number of cases, the U.S. Supreme Court functions as a trial court of limited jurisdiction. These cases include controversies between states and lawsuits against foreign ambassadors.

Figure 3-2 The Federal Court System

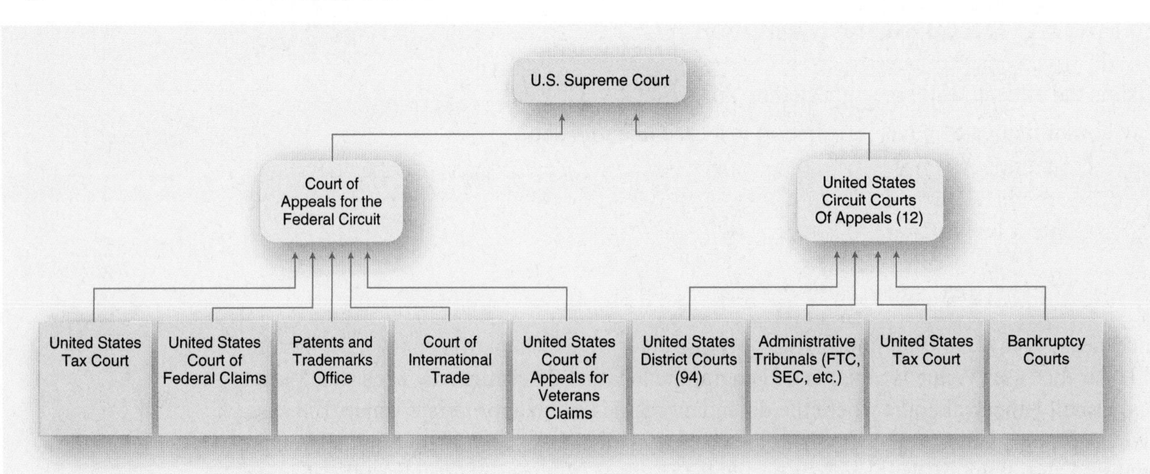

Figure 3-3 The Circuits of the Federal Court System

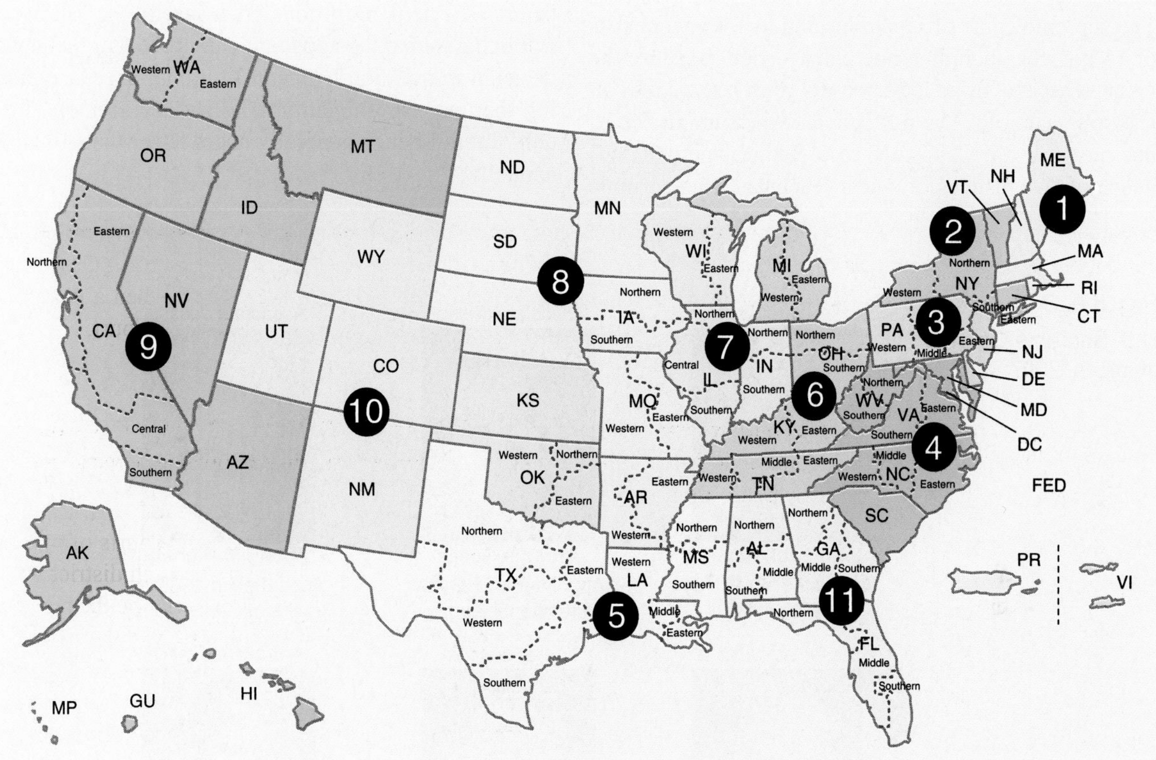

Intermediate courts of appeal. The U.S. circuit courts of appeal make up the second level of courts in the federal system. The United States has 12 circuits, including a circuit for the District of Columbia. Each circuit court hears appeals from district courts in its geographic area. Additionally, a federal circuit court of appeals hears appeals from government administrative agencies. Figure 3-3 illustrates the geographic circuit divisions.

The court of last resort. The U.S. Supreme Court is the final appellate court in the federal system. Nine justices, who have lifetime appointments, make up the high court. Figure 3-4 shows the nine justices on the U.S. Supreme Court in 2007.

The U.S. Supreme Court hears appeals of cases from the court of last resort in a state system. The Court will not, however, hear cases considering questions of pure state law. The Court also functions as a trial court in rare occasions. The structure and functioning of the U.S. Supreme Court system differ from those of similar courts in other countries, as the Global Context box illustrates.

STATE COURT SYSTEMS

No uniform state court structure exists because each state has devised its own court system. Most states, however, have a structure similar to the federal court system's structure.

State trial courts. In state court systems, most cases begin in a trial court of general jurisdiction. As in the federal system, state trial courts of general jurisdiction have the power to hear all cases over which the state court system has jurisdiction except those cases

global context

The Supreme Court in Japan

The supreme court of Japan, located in Tokyo, consists of 15 justices, including one chief justice. Because the justices ascend from lower courts, they are usually at least 60 years old. The full bench of the supreme court does not hear every appealed case. Rather, a petit (small) bench of five justices first hears each case to determine whether to transfer the case to a hearing before the full bench. The petit court transfers a case to the full bench if it believes that the appellant can prove that the law or decision in question is unconstitutional. Because proving the unconstitutionality of a law is extremely difficult, the full bench generally hears fewer than 10 cases annually.

Figure 3-4

U.S. Supreme Court Justices, 2007

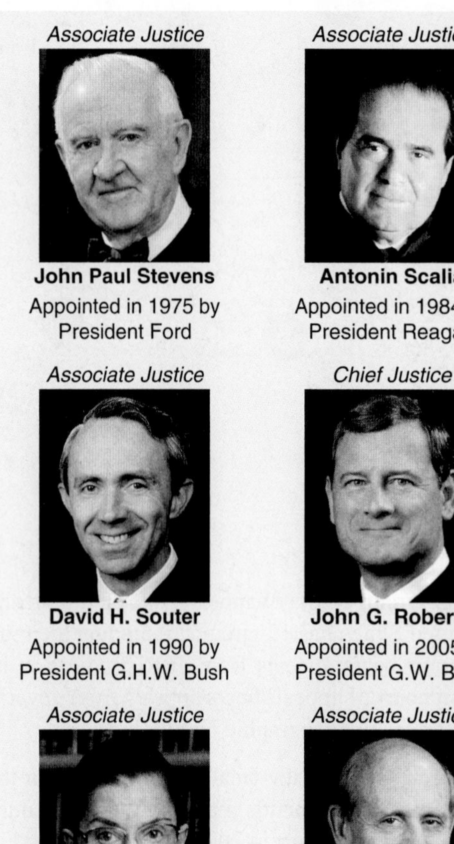

for which the state has established special trial courts of limited jurisdiction. Most states have a trial court of general jurisdiction in each county. The names of these courts vary by state, but most states refer to them as *courts of common pleas* or *county courts.* In some states, these courts have specialized divisions: domestic relations, probate, and so on.

global context

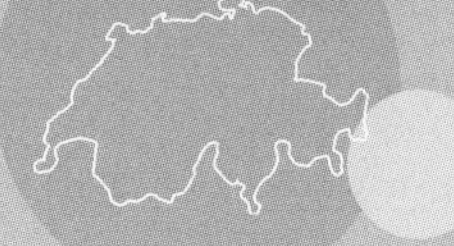

Federal and Cantonal Law in Switzerland

Unlike the United States, Switzerland has a unitary, rather than a dual, court system. Switzerland is a confederation of 23 individual entities, like states, called *cantons.* Each canton applies its own cantonal law, but all cantons also apply federal laws and codes.

Swiss cantons differ not only in the local laws they apply but also in the official language of their courts. Sixteen are predominantly German-speaking; six others are French-speaking; and one speaks mostly Italian. Each canton has its own judicial structure and procedures.

The German-speaking cantons have extensive court structures. Justices of the peace preside with limited jurisdiction. Five judges oversee each court in the canton, including the one appellate court in each canton. These cantons also have commercial courts with two professional judges and three "business" judges (government-selected individuals with professional business careers). Finally, the court of cassation's seven judges hear appeals from all 16 German cantons.

The French- and Italian-speaking court structures are simpler. In both, each canton has a justice of the peace, a court of first instance with a single judge and general jurisdiction, and one court of appeals. French-speaking cantons have a court of cassation; the Italian canton does not. An appeal in the Italian-speaking canton returns to the appellate court, where a different panel of judges tries the case.

Most states also have trial courts of limited jurisdiction. Usually, these courts can grant only certain remedies. For example, small-claims courts, a common type of court of limited jurisdiction in most states, may not grant damage awards larger than a specified amount. Other courts of limited jurisdiction have the power to hear only certain types of cases. For example, probate courts hear only cases about asset and obligation transfers after an individual's death.

Intermediate courts of appeal. Intermediate courts of appeal, analogous to federal circuit courts of appeal, exist in approximately half the states. These courts usually have broad jurisdiction, hearing appeals from courts of general and limited jurisdictions, as well as from state administrative agencies. The names of these courts also vary by state, but most states call them *courts of appeal* or *superior courts.*

Courts of last resort. Appeals from the state intermediate courts of appeal lead cases to the state court of last resort. Most states call this court the *supreme court,* although some states refer to it as the *court of appeals.* Because approximately half of the states lack intermediate courts of appeal, appeals from trial courts in these states go directly to the state court of last resort.

Threshold Requirements

Before a case makes it to court, however, it must meet three *threshold requirements.* These requirements ensure that courts hear only cases that genuinely require adjudication. The three requirements are standing, case or controversy, and ripeness.

STANDING

A person who has the legal right to bring an action in court has **standing** (or *standing to sue*). For a person to have standing, the outcome of a case must personally affect him or her. For example, if you hire a landscaper to mow your lawn every week and she fails to show up every other week, you have standing to sue your landscaper. But if your friend hired the landscaper to mow his lawn, you lack the standing to sue on your friend's behalf because you do not have a personal stake in the outcome of the case. The American legal system requires that a plaintiff have a personal stake in the outcome of the case because, the theory goes, the plaintiff's personal stake stimulates her to present the best possible case.

Standing requirements are subject to frequent litigation when citizen groups sue to enforce environmental laws. For example, the standing of the plaintiff, Friends of the Earth (FOE), was a central issue in the 2000 U.S. Supreme Court case *FOE v. Laidlaw Environmental Services.*[2] In the case, FOE filed a lawsuit against Laidlaw, alleging that it had violated the Clean Water Act by discharging excessive amounts of pollutants into a river.

Writing for the majority, Justice Ginsburg cited three factors plaintiffs need for standing: (1) The plaintiff must have an injury in fact that is concrete and actual or imminent; (2) the injury must be fairly traceable to the challenged action of the defendant; and (3) it must be likely that the injury will be redressed by a favorable decision.[3] In applying those criteria to the Laidlaw case, the Supreme Court found that FOE members' testimony that they were afraid to fish and swim in a river they previously enjoyed satisfied the first two criteria. The Court held that although the FOE members would not directly receive money from a penalty against Laidlaw, they would benefit because the penalties would deter Laidlaw and other companies from polluting the river in the future.[4] The Court ruled in FOE's favor and assessed Laidlaw a $405,800 penalty payable to the U.S. Treasury.

CASE OR CONTROVERSY

The **case or controversy** (or *justiciable controversy*) requirement ensures that courts do not render advisory opinions. Three criteria are necessary for a case or controversy to exist. First, the relationship between the plaintiff and the defendant must be adverse. Second, actual or threatened actions of at least one of the parties must give rise to an actual legal dispute. Third, courts must have the ability to render a decision that will resolve the dispute. In other words, courts can give final judgments that solve existing problems; they cannot provide rulings about hypothetical situations.

RIPENESS

The case or controversy requirement is closely linked to the **ripeness** requirement. A case is *ripe* if a judge's decision is capable of affecting the parties immediately. Usually the issue of ripeness arises when one party claims that the case is moot—in other words, there is no point in the court's hearing the case because no judgment can affect the situation between the parties.

In the Laidlaw case cited previously, Laidlaw also argued that the case was moot because by the time the case went to trial, the company had complied with the requirements of its discharge permits. Thus, Laidlaw argued, the only remedy left to the courts—a penalty Laidlaw must pay to the government—would not affect the plaintiffs. The Supreme Court disagreed, ruling that the fact that a defendant voluntarily ceases a practice once litigation has commenced does not deprive a federal court of its power to determine the legality of the practice, because such a ruling would leave the defendant free to return to

[2] 120 S. Ct. 923 (2000).

[3] Ibid.

[4] Ibid.

his old unlawful practices. Thus, the Court found the case was not moot because imposing a penalty on the defendant would have an important deterrent effect.[5]

Steps in Civil Litigation

The U.S. litigation system is an adversary system: a neutral fact finder—a judge or jury—hears evidence and arguments that opposing sides present and then decides the case on the basis of the facts and law. Strict rules govern the types of evidence fact finders may consider. Theoretically, fact finders make informed and impartial rulings because each party has an incentive to find all relevant evidence and make the strongest possible arguments on behalf of her or his position.

Critics of the adversary system, however, point out several drawbacks: the time and expense each lawsuit requires, the damage a suit may cause to the litigating parties' relationship, and the unfair advantage to those with wealth and experience using the court system.

THE PRETRIAL STAGE

The *rules of civil procedure* govern civil case proceedings. The Federal Rules of Civil Procedure apply in all federal courts. Each state has its own set of rules, but most states' rules are very similar to the Federal Rules of Civil Procedure. In addition, each court usually has its own set of local court rules.

Informal negotiations. The initial attempt to resolve a business dispute is usually informal: a discussion or negotiation among the parties to try to find a solution. If the parties are unable to resolve their dispute, one party often seeks an attorney's advice. Together, the attorney and client may be able to resolve the dispute informally with the other party.

Pleadings. The first formal stage of a lawsuit is the *pleading stage.* The plaintiff's attorney initiates a lawsuit by filing a *complaint* in the appropriate court. The complaint states the names of the parties to the action, the basis for the court's subject-matter jurisdiction, the facts on which the plaintiff bases his claim, and the relief the plaintiff seeks. The pleadings prevent surprises at trial; they allow attorneys to prepare arguments to counter the other side's claims. Exhibit 3-1 shows a typical complaint.

Service of process. To obtain *in personam* jurisdiction over a defendant and to satisfy due process, a court must notify the defendant of the pending lawsuit. Service of process occurs when the party's attorney serves (delivers) a copy of the complaint and a summons to the opposing counsel.

The complaint explains the basis of the lawsuit to the defendant. The summons tells the defendant that if he or she does not respond to the lawsuit within a certain period of time, the plaintiff will receive a default judgment. A **default judgment** is a judgment in favor of the plaintiff that occurs when the defendant fails to answer the complaint and the plaintiff's complaint alleges facts that would support such a judgment.

Defendant's response. The defendant responds to the complaint with an **answer.** In this document, the defendant denies, affirms, or claims no knowledge of the accuracy of the plaintiff's allegations.

A defendant uses an *affirmative defense* when her or his answer admits that the facts contained in the complaint are accurate but also includes additional facts that justify the

[5] Ibid.

Exhibit 3-1 Typical Complaint

THE COURT OF COMMON PLEAS OF CLARK COUNTY, NEVADA

Bob Lyons and Sue Lyons, Plaintiffs

v.

Christine Collins, Defendant

COMPLAINT FOR NEGLIGENCE

Case No. ______

Now come the plaintiffs, Bob Lyons and Sue Lyons, and, for their complaint, allege as follows:

1. Plaintiffs, Bob Lyons and Sue Lyons, both of 825 Havercamp Street, are citizens of Clark County, in the state of Nevada, and defendant, Christine Collins, 947 Rainbow Ave., is a citizen of Clark County in the state of Nevada.
2. On May 1, 2001, the Defendant built a wooden hanging bridge across a stream that runs through the plaintiffs' property at 825 Havercamp Street.
3. Defendant negligently used ropes in the construction of the bridge that were not thick enough to sustain human traffic on the bridge.
4. At approximately 4:00 p.m., on May 20, 2001, the plaintiffs were attempting to carry a box of landscaping stones across the bridge when the ropes broke, and the bridge collapsed, causing plaintiffs to fall seven feet into the stream.
5. As a result of the fall, plaintiff, Bob Lyons, suffered a broken arm, a broken leg, and a skull fracture, incurring $160,000 in medical expenses.
6. As a result of the fall, plaintiff, Sue Lyons, suffered two broken cervical vertebrae, and a skull fracture, incurring $300,000 in medical expenses.
7. As a result of the fall, the landscaping stones, which had cost $1,200, were destroyed.
8. As a result of the foregoing injuries, plaintiff, Bob Lyons, was required to miss eight weeks of work, resulting in a loss of $2,400 in wages.
9. As a result of the foregoing injuries, plaintiff, Sue Lyons, was required to miss twelve weeks of work, resulting in a loss of $3,600 in wages.

WHEREFORE, Plaintiffs demand judgment in the amount of $467,200, plus costs of this action.

Harlon Elliot
Attorney for Plaintiff
824 Sahara Ave.
Las Vegas, Nevada 89117

JURY DEMAND

Plaintiff demands a trial by jury in this matter.

defendant's actions and provide a legally sound reason to deny relief to the plaintiff. For example, if a woman sued a man for battery because he punched her in the face, he might claim that he hit her only because she aimed a gun at him and threatened to shoot. His claim that he was acting in self-defense is an affirmative defense.

If the defendant plans to raise an affirmative defense, he must raise it in his answer to give the plaintiff adequate notice. If he fails to raise an affirmative defense in the answer, the judge will likely not allow him to raise it during the trial.

Upon receiving the complaint, if the defendant believes that even though all the plaintiff's factual allegations are true, the law does not entitle the plaintiff to a favorable judgment, the defendant may file a **motion to dismiss**, or *demurrer.* (A **motion** is a request by a party for the court to do something; in this instance, the request is to dismiss the case.) In deciding whether to grant a motion to dismiss, a judge accepts the facts as stated by the plaintiff and rules on the legal issues in the case. Judges generally grant motions to dismiss only when it appears beyond a doubt that the plaintiff cannot prove any set of facts to justify granting the judgment she seeks.

If the defendant believes he has a claim against the plaintiff, he includes this **counterclaim** with the answer. As Exhibit 3-2 shows, the form of a counterclaim is identical to the form of a complaint. The defendant states the facts supporting his claim and asks for relief.

If the defendant files a counterclaim, the plaintiff generally files a reply. A **reply** is an answer to a counterclaim. In the reply, the plaintiff admits, denies, or claims a lack of knowledge as to the accuracy of the facts of the defendant's counterclaim. If the plaintiff plans to use an affirmative defense, she must raise it in the reply.

Pretrial motions. The early pleadings establish the legal and factual issues of the case. After the pleadings, the plaintiff or defendant may file a motion to conclude the case early, eliminate some claims, or gain some advantage. A party may move, or request, that the court do almost anything pertaining to the case. For example, if the plaintiff files a suit about the right to a piece of property, she may move that the court prohibit the current possessor of the land from selling it. Courts may grant or deny such motions at their discretion.

When a party files a motion with the court, the court sends a copy to the opposing attorney, who may respond to the motion, usually by requesting that the judge deny the motion. In many cases, the judge rules on the motion immediately. In other cases, the judge holds a hearing at which the attorneys for both sides argue how the judge should decide the motion.

Two primary pretrial motions are a motion for judgment on the pleadings and a motion for summary judgment. Once the parties file the pleadings, either party can file a **motion for judgment on the pleadings.** The motion is a request for the court to consider that all the facts in the pleadings are true and to apply the law to those facts. The court grants the motion if, after this process, it finds that the only reasonable decision is in favor of the moving party.

Either party can file a **motion for summary judgment** after the discovery process (described below). The motion asserts that no factual disputes exist and that if the judge applied the law to the undisputed facts, her only reasonable decision would be in favor of the moving party. The difference between this motion and a motion for judgment on the pleadings is that in a motion for summary judgment, the moving party may use affidavits (sworn statements from the parties or witnesses), relevant documents, and depositions or interrogatories (a party's sworn answers to written questions) to support his motion. The judge grants the motion if, after examining the evidence, she finds no factual disputes. If, however, she finds any factual issues about which the parties disagree, she denies the motion and sends the case to trial.

Discovery. After filing the initial pleadings and motions, the parties gather information from each other through **discovery.** The discovery process enables the parties to learn about facts surrounding the case so that they are not surprised in the courtroom. Three common discovery tools are interrogatories, requests to produce documents, and depositions.

Interrogatories are written questions that one party sends to the other to answer under oath. Frequently, a *request to admit certain facts* accompanies interrogatories. Attorneys work with their clients to answer interrogatories and requested admissions of facts.

Exhibit 3-2 Defendant's Answer and Counterclaim

THE COURT OF COMMON PLEAS OF CLARK COUNTY, NEVADA

Bob Lyons and Sue Lyons, Plaintiffs v. Christine Collins, Defendant ANSWER AND COUNTERCLAIM FOR BREACH OF CONTRACT Case No. _____

Now comes the defendant, Christine Collins, and answers the complaint of plaintiff herein as follows:

First Defense

1. Admits the allegations in paragraphs 1 and 2.
2. Denies the allegation in paragraph 3.
3. Is without knowledge as to the truth or falsity of the allegations contained in paragraphs 4, 5, 6, 7, 8, and 9.

Second Defense

4. If the court believes the allegations contained in paragraph 3, which the defendant expressly denies, plaintiffs should still be denied recovery because they were informed prior to the construction of the bridge that there should be no more than one person on the bridge at one time and that no individual weighing more than 200 pounds should be allowed to walk on the bridge.

Counterclaim

5. On April 15, the parties agreed that Defendant would build a wooden hanging bridge across a stream that runs through the defendants' property at 825 Havercamp Street, in exchange for which plaintiffs would pay defendant $2,000 upon completion of construction.
6. On May 1, 2001, the Defendant built the agreed upon ornament, wooden, hanging bridge across a stream that runs through the defendants' property at 825 Havercamp Street, but Plaintiffs failed to pay the agreed upon price for the bridge.
7. By their failure to pay, plaintiffs breached their contract and are liable to defendant for the contract price of $2,000.

WHEREFORE, defendant prays for a judgment dismissing the plaintiffs' complaint, and granting the defendant a judgment against plaintiff in the amount of $2,000 plus costs of this action.

____

Melissa Davenport

Attorney for Defendant

777 Decatur Ave.

Las Vegas, Nevada 89117

A **request to produce documents** (or other items) forces the opposing party to produce (turn over) certain information unless it is privileged or irrelevant to the case. Parties may request documents such as photographs, contracts, written estimates, medical records, tax forms, and other government documents. In tort cases, the defendant frequently asks the plaintiff to submit a mental- or physical-examination report.

Finally, the parties may obtain testimony from a witness before trial through a deposition. At a **deposition**, attorneys examine a witness under oath. A court reporter (stenographer) records every word the witnesses and attorneys speak. Both parties receive a copy of the testimony in document form. Depositions provide information and may also set up inconsistencies between a witness's testimony at the deposition and his testimony at trial. If a party discovers an inconsistency in the testimony of one of the other party's witnesses, she can bring the inconsistency to the fact finder's attention to diminish the witness's credibility.

The parties may also use depositions when a witness is elderly, moving, or ill such that he may be unavailable at the time of the trial.

If a party does not comply with requests for discovery, the court may admit the facts the other party sought to discover. Attorneys who feel that certain material is outside the scope of the case often argue that the material is irrelevant to the case. If the court disagrees, however, the party must supply the requested information. Although these discovery tools are important in the United States, not all countries have a discovery process.

In discovery, as in other areas, technology is having an impact. It is estimated that 90 percent of all documents and communications are created and maintained in electronic formats. In December 2006, the Federal Rules of Civil Procedure were amended to reflect changes in technology. Parties are now required to "make provisions for disclosure or discovery of electronically stored information"[6] at the start of the litigation process, and they must develop a discovery plan during their pretrial conferences. Once it appears that litigation is imminent, litigants have an obligation not to delete or destroy electronic files that may be discoverable. However, "absent exceptional circumstances, a court may not impose sanctions . . . on a party for failing to provide electronically stored information lost as a result of the routine, good-faith operation of an electronic information system."[7]

Parties who might become embroiled in litigation, however, probably should not count on using the good-faith exception because the consequences of destroying electronic data can be significant. For example, in the sex discrimination case of *Zubulake v. UBS Warburg LLC,*[8] the judge found that the company's employees had intentionally deleted e-mail messages, lost a number of backup tapes, and failed to produce files as requested. As a sanction, she issued an *adverse-inference* instruction to the jury, basically telling them that they could assume that any documents not produced would have been harmful to the company's case. The jury ultimately awarded the woman $29.3 million in damages.

Morgan Stanley had to pay an even bigger price for its failure to meet its obligations for electronic discovery of relevant e-mail messages and documents. In *Coleman Holdings Inc. v. Morgan Stanley & Co.,*[9] the firm produced more than 1,300 pages of e-mail messages but failed to reveal in a timely fashion the existence of 1,423 backup tapes. In that case, the court also issued an adverse-inference instruction, stating that Morgan Stanley would have to bear the burden of proving that it lacked knowledge of the fraud. The jury found in favor of the plaintiff and awarded damages in the amount of $1.6 billion. Morgan Stanley also had to pay the U.S. Securities and Exchange Commission $15 million in fines for failure to comply with discovery requirements in a related commission investigation.

What organizations can learn from these cases is that as soon as they reasonably anticipate that litigation will occur, they must suspend their routine policy for retaining and destroying documents and put in place a "litigation hold" to make sure that documents that might be relevant to the lawsuit are preserved. Some plaintiffs' lawyers are now sending *litigation-hold demand* letters to potential defendants, making it almost impossible for a firm to claim that relevant documents were innocently deleted.

Pretrial conference. A pretrial conference precedes the trial. A **pretrial conference** is an informal meeting of the judge with the attorneys representing the parties. During this conference, the parties try to narrow the legal and factual issues and possibly work out a settlement. If the parties cannot reach a settlement, the attorneys and the judge discuss the

[6] Rule 16(B), Federal Rules of Civil Procedure.

[7] Rule 37(F), Federal Rules of Civil Procedure.

[8] 231 F.R.D. 159, 2005 U.S. Dist. LEXIS 1525 (S.D.N.Y., Feb. 2, 2005).

[9] 2005 WL 679071 (Fla. Cir. Ct., Mar. 1, 2005).

administrative details of the trial: its length, witnesses, and any pretrial stipulations of fact or law to which the parties agree.

THE TRIAL

If a plaintiff seeks at least $20 in monetary damages, the Seventh Amendment to the U.S. Constitution entitles the parties to a jury trial. The plaintiff must, however, demand a jury trial in his or her complaint. Following the English tradition, most civil trials have 12 jurors; however, in many jurisdictions the number of required jurors has been reduced by the legislature. In some jurisdictions, fewer than 12 jurors may be allowed if both parties consent. If the plaintiff seeks an equitable remedy (an injunction or other court order) or if the parties have waived their right to a jury, a judge serves as the fact finder in the case.

Trials have six stages: jury selection, opening statements, examination of witnesses, closing arguments, conference on jury instructions, and posttrial motions. The following sections describe these stages.

Jury selection. The jury selection process begins when the clerk of the courts randomly selects a number of potential jurors from the citizens within the court's jurisdiction. Once the potential jurors have reported for jury duty, the **voir dire,** or jury selection, process begins. The voir dire process selects the jurors who will decide the case, as well as two or three "alternate jurors" who will watch the trial and be available to replace any juror who, for some legitimate reason, must leave jury duty before the trial ends.

During voir dire, the judge and/or attorneys question potential jurors to determine whether they are able to render an unbiased opinion in the case. If a potential juror's response to a question indicates that she or he may be biased, either attorney may challenge, or ask the court to remove, that potential juror "for cause." For example, a lawyer could challenge for cause a potential juror who was a college roommate of the defendant. In most states, each party has a certain number of **peremptory challenges.** These peremptory challenges allow a party to challenge a certain number of potential jurors without giving a reason.

Peremptory challenges, however, may lead to abuse. For example, in the past, attorneys have used peremptory challenges to eliminate a certain class, ethnic group, or gender from the jury. In the 1986 case *Batson v. Kentucky,*[10] the U.S. Supreme Court ruled that race-based peremptory challenges in criminal cases violate the equal protection clause of the Fourteenth Amendment to the U.S. Constitution. (Chapter 5 discusses the amendments to the Constitution in more detail.) The Supreme Court later extended the ban on race-based challenges to civil cases. In Case 3-2, the U.S. Supreme Court addressed the issue of whether the equal protection clause covers gender-based challenges.

The voir dire process has become more sophisticated over time. In cases involving significant amounts of money, rather than relying on their instinct or experience during jury selection, attorneys use professional jury selection services to identify demographic data to help select ideal jurors.

Jury selection firms also provide additional services, including mock trials and shadow juries. Jury selection firms set up **mock trials** by recruiting individuals who match the demographics of the real jury to listen to attorneys' arguments and witnesses' testimony. These mock trials give attorneys a sense of how their approach to the case will appear to the actual jurors. If the mock jury is not receptive to a particular argument or witness's testimony, the attorneys can modify their approach before trial.

Parties also often hire jury selection firms to provide shadow juries. Like a mock trial, a **shadow jury** uses individuals whose demographics match the demographics of a trial's

[10] 476 U.S. 79 (1986).

CASE 3-2 J.E.B. v. ALABAMA, EX. REL. T.B.
UNITED STATES SUPREME COURT
114 S. CT. 1419 (1994)

The State of Alabama filed a complaint for paternity and child support against J.E.B. on behalf of T.B., the unwed mother of a minor child. The court called a panel of twelve males and twenty-four females as potential jurors. Only ten males remained after three individuals were removed for cause. The state used its peremptory challenges to remove nine male jurors, and J.E.B. removed the tenth, resulting in an all female jury. The trial court rejected J.E.B.'s objection to the gender-based challenges, and the jury found J.E.B. to be the father. J.E.B. appealed, and the court of appeals affirmed the trial court's ruling that the Equal Protection Clause does not prohibit gender-based challenges. The Alabama Supreme Court declined to hear the appeal, and J.E.B. appealed to the U.S. Supreme Court.

JUSTICE BLACKMUN: Discrimination in jury selection, whether based on race or on gender, causes harm to the litigants, the community, and the individual jurors who are wrongfully excluded from participation in the judicial process. The litigants are harmed by the risk that the prejudice which motivated the discriminatory selection of the jury will infect the entire proceedings. The community is harmed by the State's participation in the perpetuation of invidious group stereotypes and the inevitable loss of confidence in our judicial system that state-sanctioned discrimination in the courtroom engenders.

As with race-based *Batson* claims, a party alleging gender discrimination must make a prima facie showing of intentional discrimination before the party exercising the challenge is required to explain the basis for the strike. When an explanation is required, it need not rise to the level of a "for cause" challenge; rather, it merely must be based on a juror characteristic other than gender and the proffered explanation may not be pretextual.

Equal opportunity to participate in the fair administration of justice is fundamental to our democratic system. It reaffirms the promise of equality under the law—that all citizens, regardless of race, ethnicity, or gender, have the chance to take part directly in our democracy. When persons are excluded from participation in our democratic processes solely because of race or gender, this promise of equality dims, and the integrity of our judicial system is jeopardized.

REVERSED AND REMANDED in favor of JEB.

CRITICAL THINKING

The defendant was contesting the removal of males from the jury. Does this fact weaken the court's reasoning? Explain.

ETHICAL DECISION MAKING

Which values does this decision tend to emphasize?

real jurors. A shadow jury, however, sits inside the courtroom to watch the actual trial. At the end of each day of the trial, the shadow jury deliberates, giving the attorneys an idea of how the real jurors are reacting to the case. If the shadow jury finds the opposing side to be winning, the attorneys can modify their strategy.

Many attorneys believe that these services increase their clients' chances of winning cases. Critics argue, however, that jury selection services give an unfair advantage to one side when only one party can afford these services.

Opening statements. Once the attorneys have impaneled, or selected, a jury, the case begins with opening statements. Each party's attorney explains to the judge and jury which facts he or she intends to prove, the legal conclusions to which these facts lead, and how the fact finder should decide the case based on those facts.

The examination of witnesses and presentation of evidence. Following opening statements, the plaintiff and defendant, in turn, present their cases-in-chief by examining witnesses and presenting evidence. The plaintiff has the burden of proving the case, meaning that if neither side presents a convincing case, the fact finder must rule in favor of the defendant. Thus, the plaintiff presents her case first.

The procedure for each witness is the same. First, the plaintiff's attorney questions the witness in *direct examination.* The plaintiff's attorney asks the witness questions to elicit facts that support the plaintiff's case-in-chief. Questions must relate to matters about which the witness has direct knowledge. Attorneys cannot elicit "hearsay" from the witnesses. *Hearsay* is testimony about what a witness heard another person say. Hearsay is impermissible because the opposing attorney cannot question the person who made the original statement to determine the statement's veracity.

The federal rules of evidence also prohibit attorneys from asking leading questions. Leading questions are questions that imply a specific answer. For example, an attorney cannot ask a witness, "Did the defendant come to your office and ask you to purchase stock from him?" Instead, attorneys must ask questions such as, "When did you first encounter the defendant?"

After direct examination, opposing counsel may *cross-examine* the witness. Opposing counsel, however, may ask only questions related to the witness's direct examination. On cross-examination, attorneys can ask leading questions. Attorneys try to show inconsistencies in the witness's testimony, cast doubt on the claims of the plaintiff's case, and elicit information to support the defendant's case.

After cross-examination, the plaintiff's attorney may conduct a *redirect examination,* a series of questions to repair damage done by the cross-examination. At the judge's discretion, opposing counsel has an opportunity to *re-cross* the witness to question his testimony on redirect examination. The parties follow this procedure for each of the plaintiff's witnesses.

Immediately following the plaintiff's presentation of her case, the defendant may move for a **directed verdict.** This motion is a request for the court to direct a verdict for the defendant because even if the jury accepted all the evidence and testimony presented by the plaintiff as true, the jury would still have no legal basis for a decision in favor of the plaintiff. The federal court system refers to a motion for a directed verdict as a *motion for a judgment as a matter of law.* Courts rarely grant motions for a directed verdict because plaintiffs almost always present at least *some* evidence to support each element of the cause of action.

If the court denies the defendant's motion for a directed verdict, the defendant then presents his case. The parties question the defendant's witnesses in the same manner as they questioned the plaintiff's witnesses, except that the defendant's attorney conducts direct and redirect examination and the plaintiff's attorney conducts cross-examination and re-cross-examination.

Closing arguments. After the defendant's case, the attorneys present closing arguments. In the *closing argument,* each attorney summarizes evidence from the trial in a

global context

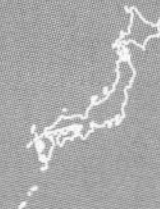

Trials in Japan

Civil procedure in Japan differs significantly from American civil procedure. The Japanese legal system has no juries and no distinct pretrial stage. Instead, a trial is a series of discrete meetings between the parties and the judge. At the first meeting, the parties identify the most critical and contested issues. They choose one and recess to gather evidence and marshal arguments on the issue.

At the next meeting, the judge rules on the chosen issue. If the judge decides against the plaintiff, the case is over. If the plaintiff wins, the process continues with the next issue. The process continues until the plaintiff loses an issue or until the judge decides all issues in the plaintiff's favor, resulting in a verdict for the plaintiff.

In addition, the discovery process in the Japanese court system is not as simple as it is in the United States. To obtain evidence, parties must convince the judge to order others to testify or produce documents. The judge can fine or jail parties who refuse to comply with such orders. Additionally, if a party does not comply with the judge's requests for discovery, the judge may admit the facts the other party sought to discover.

manner consistent with his or her client's case. The plaintiff's attorney presents her closing argument first, followed by the defendant's attorney, and the plaintiff has the option to present a rebuttal of the defendant's closing argument.

Jury instructions. In a jury trial, the judge "charges the jury" by instructing the jurors how the law applies to the facts of the case. Both sides' attorneys submit statements to the judge explaining how they believe he should charge the jury. The judge's instructions are usually a combination of both sides' suggestions.

Different types of cases require different standards of proof. In most civil cases, the plaintiff must prove her case by a *preponderance of the evidence;* in other words, she must show that her claim is more likely to be true than the defendant's claim. In some civil cases, particularly cases involving fraud or oral contracts, the plaintiff must prove her case by *clear and convincing evidence,* a higher standard of proof. Criminal cases have an even higher burden of proof: The prosecution must prove its case *beyond a reasonable doubt.*

After the judge charges the jury, the jurors retire to the jury room to deliberate. Once they reach a decision, they return to the courtroom, where the judge reads their verdict and discharges them from their duty.

Trial procedures in the United States are quite different from trial procedures in other countries, as the Global Context box illustrates.

Posttrial motions. Once the trial ends, the party who received the favorable verdict files a *motion for a judgment in accordance with the verdict.* Until the judge enters the judgment, the court has not issued a legally binding decision for the case.

The party who loses at trial has a number of available options. One option is to file a *motion for a judgment notwithstanding the verdict,* or *judgment non obstante verdicto,* asking the judge to issue a judgment contrary to the jury's verdict. To grant the motion, the judge must find that, when viewing the evidence in the light most favorable to the nonmoving party, a reasonable jury could not have found in favor of that party. In other words, as a matter of law, the judge must determine that the trial did not produce sufficient evidence to support the jury's verdict. This motion is similar to a motion for a directed verdict, except the parties cannot make this motion until *after* the jury issues a verdict. The federal court system refers to this motion as a *motion for judgment as a matter of law.*

The losing party can also file a *motion for a new trial.* Judges grant motions for a new trial only if they believe the jury's decision was clearly erroneous but they are not sure that the other side should necessarily have won the case. A judge often grants a motion for a new trial when the parties discover new evidence, when the judge made an erroneous ruling, or when misconduct during the trial may have prevented the jury from reaching a fair decision.

APPELLATE PROCEDURE

Either party may appeal the judge's decision on posttrial motions or on her or his final judgment. Sometimes, both parties appeal the same decision. For example, if a jury awarded the plaintiff $10,000 in damages, the plaintiff and the defendant may both appeal the amount of the judgment. Appellate courts, however, reverse only about 1 out of every 10 trial court decisions on appeal.

To be eligible for appeal, the losing party must argue that a prejudicial error of law occurred during the trial. A **prejudicial error of law** is a mistake so significant that it likely affected the outcome of the case. For example, a prejudicial error could occur if the judge improperly admitted hearsay evidence that allowed the plaintiff to prove an element of her case.

To appeal a case, the attorney for the appealing party (the appellant) files a notice of appeal with the clerk of the trial court within a prescribed time. The clerk then forwards the record of appeal to the appeals court. The record of appeal typically contains a number of items: the pleadings, a trial transcript, copies of the trial exhibits, copies of the judge's rulings on the parties' motions, the attorneys' arguments, jury instructions, the jury's verdict, posttrial motions, and the judgment order.

The appellant then files a **brief,** or written argument, with the court. Appellants file briefs to explain why the judgment in the lower court was erroneous and why the appeals court should reverse it. The attorney for the party who won in the lower court (the appellee) files an answering brief. The appellant may then file a reply brief in response to the appellee's brief. Generally, however, appellants do not file reply briefs.

The appeals court then usually allows the attorneys to present oral arguments before the court. The court considers these arguments, reviews the record of the case, and renders a decision.

An appellate court may render four basic decisions. The court can accept the lower court's judgment by *affirming* the decision of the lower court. Alternatively, if the appellate court concludes that the lower court's decision was correct but the remedy was inappropriate, it *modifies* the remedy. If the appellate court decides that the lower court was incorrect in its decision, it *reverses* the lower court's decision. Finally, if the appeals court thinks the lower court committed an error but does not know how that error affected the outcome of the case, it *remands* the case to the lower court for a new trial.

An appellate court usually has a bench with at least three judges. Appellate courts do not have juries; rather, the judges decide the case by majority vote. One of the judges who votes with the majority records the court's decision and its reasons in the *majority opinion.* These decisions have precedential value—that is, judges use these prior appellate court decisions to make decisions in future cases. Also, these decisions establish new guidelines in the law that all citizens must follow. If a judge agrees with the majority's decision, but for different reasons, she may write a *concurring opinion,* stating the reasons she used to reach the majority's conclusion. Finally, judges disagreeing with the majority may write a *dissenting opinion,* giving their reasons for reaching a contrary conclusion. Attorneys arguing that a court should change the law frequently cite dissenting opinions from previous cases in their briefs. Likewise, appellate judges who change the law often cite dissenting opinions from past cases.

For most cases, only one appeal is available. In states with both an intermediate and a final court of appeals, a losing party may appeal from the intermediate appellate court to the state supreme court. In a limited number of cases, the losing party can appeal the decision of a state supreme court or a federal circuit court of appeals to the U.S. Supreme Court.

Appeal to the U.S. Supreme Court. Every year thousands of individuals file appeals with the U.S. Supreme Court. The Court, however, hears, on average, only 80 to 90 cases every year. To file an appeal to the U.S. Supreme Court, a party files a petition asking the Court to issue a **writ of certiorari,** an order to the lower court to send to the Supreme Court the record of the case. The Court issues very few writs.

The justices review petitions and issue a writ only when at least four justices vote to hear the case (the *rule of four*). The court is most likely to issue a writ in four instances: (1) The case presents a substantial federal question that the Supreme Court has not yet addressed; (2) multiple circuit courts of appeal have decided the issue of the case in different ways; (3) a state court of last resort has ruled that a federal law is invalid or has upheld a state law that may violate federal law; or (4) a federal court has ruled that an act of Congress is unconstitutional. If the Supreme Court does not issue a writ of certiorari, the lower court's decision stands.

CASE OPENER WRAP-UP

Caterpillar

The timing of events was crucial to the outcome of the Caterpillar case. At the time Lewis filed the case in the state court system, one of the defendants and the plaintiff were from the same state, so the state court system had jurisdiction. Once the supply company reached an agreement with Lewis, the other defendant, Caterpillar, filed a motion to exercise its right of removal because diversity of citizenship existed in the absence of the Kentucky defendant. But the agreement was not final at the time of the motion because the agreement was subject to the insurer's approval. Thus, the appellate court ruled that because the supply company was still a party to the agreement, the federal court system could not exercise jurisdiction over the case.

The U.S. Supreme Court, however, overruled the appellate court. The Supreme Court ruled that the state court should not have granted Caterpillar's initial motion to remove the case because at the time of removal, the insurer had not accepted the settlement agreement, the supply company remained a party in the case, and, therefore, the diversity of citizenship was not complete. The Supreme Court held further, however, that the district court's error in hearing the case was not fatal because the settlement agreement was approved and the case satisfied the jurisdictional requirements by the time the federal court issued its decision. The Court ruled that to require the district court to send the case back to the state system would be an undue waste of judicial resources.

Why might Caterpillar have wanted to move the case to the federal court system? First, the case involved product liability claims. Data suggest that average damage awards in product liability cases tend to be higher in state courts than in federal courts. Second, Caterpillar may have feared local prejudice. While all judges must strive for neutrality, out-of-state defendants may fear that state judges are slightly biased in favor of in-state parties.

Summary

Jurisdiction	*In personam jurisdiction* is the power of a court to render a decision affecting a person's legal rights. *Subject-matter jurisdiction* is the power of a court to render a decision in a particular type of case. The three forms of subject-matter jurisdiction are state, exclusive federal, and concurrent.
Venue	*Venue* is the geographic location of the trial.
Structure of the Court System	The U.S. has two parallel court structures: the state and federal systems. The federal structure has *district courts* (trial courts), *circuit courts of appeal,* and the *U.S. Supreme Court.* The state court structure varies by state, but generally includes courts of common pleas (trial courts), state courts of appeal, and a state supreme court.
Threshold Requirements	*Standing:* For a person to have the legal right to file a case, the outcome of the case must personally affect that person. *Case or controversy:* There must be an issue before the court that a judicial decision is capable of resolving. Parties cannot ask the judge for an "advisory opinion." *Ripeness:* The case cannot be moot; it must be ready for a decision to be made.
Steps in Civil Litigation	The stages of a civil trial include pretrial, trial, posttrial, and appellate stages. *Pretrial* includes consultation with attorneys, pleadings, the discovery process, and the pretrial conference. The *trial* begins with jury selection, followed by opening statements, the plaintiff's case, the defendant's case, closing arguments, jury instructions, jury deliberations, the jury's verdict, and the judgment. After the trial, parties may file *posttrial motions.* The parties may then file *appeals* to the appropriate appellate court and, in some cases, to the U.S. Supreme Court.

Point / Counterpoint

Who Should Decide Questions of Fact in Our Legal System?	
Judges	**Juries**
Those who believe judges should decide questions of fact often argue that judges are more competent than juries. Judges spend their careers in the legal world, which enables them to develop considerable expertise in evaluating evidence. In contrast, many jurors have little experience in evaluating evidence. Indeed, social science research suggests that jurors are often influenced by legally and logically irrelevant factors.	Scholars who believe that juries should decide questions of fact argue that jury competence is only half the story. To make intelligent policy decisions, we should consider juror competence *in light of available alternatives,* and, they argue, judges are far from perfect. Like jurors, judges have personal biases that affect the way they view evidence. Moreover, it is not clear at all that judges are more competent than juries

This problem is exacerbated because the potential jurors most likely to have experience in evaluating evidence—professionals such as doctors and lawyers—are often able to escape jury duty. Justice should be immune to flashy smiles and expensive suits.

Many proponents of this view also emphasize the importance of uniformity. Each jury is composed of different individuals with different beliefs and backgrounds. Judges, on the other hand, remain more consistent from trial to trial. Thus, by placing questions of fact in judges' hands, the legal system will decide similar questions of fact similarly. This uniformity increases the predictability of the legal system, enabling individuals to conform their behavior more easily to the law's requirements.

This predictability tends to increase the efficiency of the legal system. As noted in the chapter, jury selection has become an enormously important and frequently expensive element in the litigation process. Litigants concerned with potentially unpredictable jury verdicts expend significant resources on mock trials and shadow juries to determine the likely outcome of their cases. More predictable judge-made decisions on questions of fact would permit litigants to save these resources.

in evaluating certain kinds of evidence—witnesses' credibility, for example.

Proponents of this view also highlight the democratic injection into the legal system that juries provide. Judges tend to be white, male, and upper-class. Jurors, in contrast, are drawn from a much more diverse pool of citizens. Their methods of analyzing questions of fact, therefore, are more likely to reflect the beliefs and experiences of the entire political community, not just an elite cross section of that community. Thus, allowing juries to decide questions of fact tends to promote popular sovereignty in the judicial branch.

Questions & Problems

1. Explain the two types of jurisdiction that a court must have to hear a case and render a binding decision over the parties.
2. Explain the differences between trial courts and appellate courts.
3. Identify and define the alternative tools of discovery.
4. Explain the three threshold requirements a plaintiff must meet before he or she can file a lawsuit.
5. Missouri was International Shoe Corporation's principal place of business, but the company employed between 11 and 13 salespersons in the state of Washington who exhibited samples and solicited orders for shoes from prospective buyers in Washington. The state of Washington assessed the company for contributions to a state unemployment fund. The state served the assessment on one of International Shoe Corporation's sales representatives in Washington and sent a copy by registered mail to the company's Missouri headquarters. International Shoe's representative challenged the assessment on numerous grounds, arguing that the state had not properly served the corporation. Is the corporation's defense valid? Why or why not? [*International Shoe Co. v. Washington,* 326 U.S. 310 (1945).]
6. The Robinsons, residents of New York, bought a new Audi car from Seaway Volkswagen Corp., a retailer incorporated in New York and with its principal place of business

there. World-Wide Volkswagen, a company incorporated in New York and doing business in New York, New Jersey, and Connecticut, distributed the car to Seaway. Neither Seaway nor World-Wide did business in Oklahoma, and neither company shipped cars there. The Robinsons were driving through Oklahoma when another vehicle struck their Audi in the rear. The gas tank of the Audi exploded, injuring several members of the family. The Robinsons brought a product liability suit against the manufacturer, distributor, and retailer of the car in an Oklahoma state court. Seaway and World-Wide argued that the Oklahoma state court did not have *in personam* jurisdiction over them. After the state's trial court and supreme court held that the state did have *in personam* jurisdiction over Seaway and World-Wide, the companies appealed to the U.S. Supreme Court. How do you think the Court decided in this case? Why? [*World-Wide Volkswagen Corp. v. Woodson,* 444 U.S. 286 (1980).]

7. Flanagan's, a New Jersey irrigation system installation company, ordered an irrigation pump from another New Jersey corporation, Aquarius, and paid a $3,500 down payment for the product. Watertronics, a Wisconsin corporation, manufactured the pump. Flanagan's had no direct contact with Watertronics other than a four-minute telephone conversation in which Flanagan's unsuccessfully attempted to get a better price on a pump. After receiving and installing the pump, Flanagan's was unhappy with its performance, so the company refused to pay the $34,000 balance due on the pump. Watertronics sued Flanagan's in Wisconsin state court. Flanagan's argued that the court could not exercise *in personam* jurisdiction over it. Do you think the Wisconsin state court had *in personam* jurisdiction over Flanagan's? Why or why not? [*Watertronics, Inc. v. Flanagan's Inc.,* 635 N.W.2d 27 (2001).]

8. Le Cabaret 481, Inc., an adult entertainment corporation, wanted to open a strip club in the city of Kingston. Kingston, however, passed an ordinance prohibiting adult businesses from operating within 300 feet of any church, school, nursery, public park, or residential property. Le Cabaret 481 filed a suit against the city, arguing that the ordinance left no feasible locations in the city for an adult business and thus violated the company's First Amendment right to free expression. The city, on the other hand, argued that Le Cabaret 481 did not present a ripe case to the court because the company had not applied for a building permit for its adult business. The company argued that it could not find a location for which it could apply for a permit. Do you think Le Cabaret 481 satisfied the ripeness requirement for its suit against the city? Why or why not? [*Le Cabaret 481, Inc. v. Municipality of Kingston,* 2005 U.S. Dist. LEXIS 706 (2005).]

9. Thirteen record labels filed a copyright violation suit against Hummer Winblad Venture Partners (Hummer), an owner of Napster, a peer-to-peer file-sharing network for online distribution of music. Hummer filed a counterclaim alleging antitrust violations against the record labels because they conspired to exclude independent music distributors like Napster from the online music distribution market. The record labels argued that Hummer lacked standing to make its counterclaims because Hummer, not Napster, made the counterclaims and Hummer never competed directly with the record labels. Hummer, on the other hand, argued that it had standing because it financed Napster, a participant in the online music distribution market. How do you think the court ruled in this case? Why? [*In re Napster Copyright Litig. v. Hummer Winblad Venture Partners,* 354 F. Supp. 2d 1113 (2005).]

10. Athena Automotive, Inc., a Georgia corporation, conducted an automobile repair business under the trade name "Brakes for Less" in Silver Spring, Maryland, until August 10, 1994. Although it ceased business operations in 1994, Athena continued to maintain its corporate charter in good standing with the Georgia secretary of state.

On August 8, 1997, Athena filed an action in federal court in Maryland against John DiGregorio and J&D Automotive, Inc., a Maryland corporation. Athena alleged that J&D breached its agreement to purchase Athena's assets and that, through fraud, both DiGregorio and J&D obtained and converted the assets to their own use. Athena demanded $270,000 in compensatory damages and $1 million in punitive damages. DiGregorio and J&D filed a motion to dismiss, claiming a lack of subject-matter jurisdiction because Athena was a citizen of Georgia; thus, diversity of citizenship did not exist. The district court denied the defendants' motion, reasoning that diversity of citizenship existed because the three years between Athena's last business activity in Maryland and the date it filed suit was "sufficient to shed Athena Automotive of its local character." How do you think the appellate court ruled in this case? Why? [*Athena Automotive, Inc. v. John J. DiGregorio; J & D Automotive, Inc.,* 166 F.3d 288 (1999).]

11. The Fish and Wildlife Service (FWS) proposed limiting the release of water from an irrigation project to protect two endangered species of fish. The proposed action reduced some ranchers' access to water. These ranchers filed a lawsuit challenging the restriction, but the district court dismissed their case for lack of standing. The ranchers appealed on grounds that they would suffer direct economic loss from the enforcement of the FWS action; hence, they had standing to challenge the action. How do you think the U.S. Supreme Court ruled in this case? Why? [*Bennett v. Spear,* 115 S. Ct. 1154 (1997).]

Looking for more review material?

The Online Learning Center at **www.mhhe.com/kubasek1e** contains this chapter's "Assignment on the Internet" and also a list of URLs for more information entitled "On the Internet." Find both of them in the Student Center portion of the OLC, along with quizzes and other helpful materials.

Alternative Dispute Resolution

CASE OPENER

Mandatory Arbitration at Hooters

In 1994, Hooters Restaurant in Myrtle Beach, South Carolina, began systematically using an alternative dispute resolution program, a program to resolve disputes outside the traditional court system. Employees of Hooters had to sign an "agreement to arbitrate employment-related disputes" to be eligible for raises, transfers, and promotions. Under the agreement, both Hooters and the employee agreed to resolve all disputes arising out of employment, including "any claim of discrimination, sexual harassment, retaliation, or wrongful discharge, whether arising under federal or state law," through arbitration. *Arbitration* is a type of alternative dispute resolution where a neutral third party makes a decision that resolves the dispute.

In a separate policy document not shared with employees until after they had signed the agreement, Hooters set forth the rules and procedures of its arbitration program:

- The employee had to provide notice of the specifics of the claim, but Hooters did not need to file any type of response to these specifics or notify the employee of what kinds of defenses the company planned to raise.
- Only the employee had to provide a list of all fact witnesses and a brief summary of the facts known to each.
- While the employee and Hooters could each choose an arbitrator from a list, and the two arbitrators chosen would then select a third to create the arbitration panel that would hear the dispute, Hooters alone selected the arbitrators on the list.
- Only Hooters had the right to widen the scope of arbitration to include any matter, whereas the employee was limited to the matters raised in his or her notice.
- Only Hooters had the right to record the arbitration.
- Only Hooters had the right to sue to vacate or modify an arbitration award if the arbitration panel exceeded its authority.
- Only Hooters could cancel the agreement to arbitrate or change the arbitration rules.

CHAPTER 4

Annette Phillips had been a bartender at Hooters restaurant in Myrtle Beach since 1989. When Hooters adopted its new arbitration policy, she was given a copy of the agreement to review for five days and then sign. In June 1996, a Hooters official grabbed and slapped her buttocks. After appealing to her manager for help and being told to "let it go," she quit her job. When she threatened to file a lawsuit for sexual harassment, Hooters filed an action in federal district court to compel arbitration of Phillips's claims.[1]

1. Should Phillips be forced to settle her claim through arbitration?
2. Assume your company's arbitration policy was exactly like Hooters'. Which aspects would you retain, and which might you change?

The Wrap-Up at the end of the chapter will answer these questions using the legal principles discussed in this chapter.

Learning Objectives

After reading this chapter, you will be able to answer the following questions:

1. What are the primary forms of alternative dispute resolution?
2. What are other ADR methods?
3. What is court-annexed ADR?
4. How is ADR used in international disputes?

[1] *Hooters of America, Inc. v. Phillips,* 173 F.3d 933 (4th Cir.1999).

Many companies, like Hooters Restaurant, are finding that using **alternative dispute resolution (ADR)** to resolve their legal problems offers many benefits. The term *ADR* refers to the resolution of legal disputes through methods other than litigation, such as negotiation, mediation, arbitration, summary jury trials, minitrials, neutral case evaluations, and private trials. Organizations often use ADR to resolve disputes involving contracts, insurance, labor, the environment, securities, technology, and international trade.

Some organizations have created internal mediation systems for resolving disputes within the organization. For example, United Parcel Service (UPS) has a five-step dispute resolution program:

1. *Open door:* The employees are encouraged to bring their problems to their supervisors.
2. *Facilitation:* The regional managers ensure that the open-door options are explored.
3. *Peer review:* The employee and the company representative communicate the differing perspectives of the dispute before a panel of three employees (two selected by the complainant and one by the employer), which recommends a nonbinding solution.
4. *Mandatory mediation.*
5. *Optional binding arbitration.*[2]

Why might a business prefer to resolve a dispute through ADR rather than litigation? First, ADR methods are generally faster and cheaper than litigation. According to the National Arbitration Forum, the average time from filing a complaint to receiving a judgment through litigation is 25 months.[3] Because ADR is faster, it is usually cheaper. According to the American Intellectual Property Law Association, for litigation of patent cases valued in the $1 million to $25 million range, the average cost to each party from the filing of the complaint through the close of discovery is $1.9 million.[4] Through the end of trial, the average cost to each party is $3.5 million. Thus, if a party can resolve a dispute in the early stages of the case through alternative dispute resolution, this may save significant money. Second, a business may wish to avoid the uncertainty associated with a jury decision; many forms of ADR give the participants more control over the resolution of the dispute. Specifically, the parties can select a neutral third party, frequently a person with expertise in the area of the dispute, to help facilitate resolution of the case. Third, a business may wish to avoid setting a precedent through a court decision. Thus, many businesses prefer ADR because of its confidential nature. Fourth, because many forms of ADR are less adversarial than litigation, the parties are able to preserve a business relationship.

Not only are businesses increasingly turning to ADR, but courts are generally quite supportive of ADR methods, which alleviate some of the pressure on the overwhelming court dockets. Congress has recognized the benefits of ADR methods through its enactment of the Alternative Dispute Resolution Act of 1998. This act requires that federal district courts have an ADR program along with a set of rules regarding the program. Congress also passed the Administrative Dispute Resolution Act, which mandates that federal agencies create internal ADR programs.

[2] F. Peter Phillips, "Mediation Is Alternative to Adjudicating Disputes: Internal Employment Dispute Management Programs Are New Trend," *National Law Journal,* June 14, 2004, p. S4.

[3] National Arbitration Forum, *Business-to-Business Mediation/Arbitration vs. Litigation: What Courts, Statistics, & Public Perceptions Show about How Commercial Mediation and Commercial Arbitration Compare to the Litigation System,* January 2005, p. 3.

[4] AIPLA, *Report of the Economic Survey,* 2005, pp. 1-109–1-110.

This chapter explains the various ADR methods, as well as the advantages and disadvantages of each. Because ADR is becoming more favored internationally, the latter portion of this chapter discusses its use in other countries.

Primary Forms of Alternative Dispute Resolution

NEGOTIATION

Many business managers make frequent use of **negotiation**, a bargaining process in which disputing parties interact informally, either with or without lawyers, to attempt to resolve their dispute. A neutral third party, such as a judge or jury, is not involved. Thus, negotiation differs from other methods of dispute resolution because the parties maintain high levels of autonomy. Some courts require that parties negotiate before they bring their dispute to trial.

Before negotiation begins, each side must determine its goals for the negotiation. Moreover, each side must identify the information it is willing to give the other party. A party can enter negotiations with one of two approaches: adversarial or problem solving. In **adversarial negotiation**, each party seeks to maximize its own gain. In contrast, in **problem-solving negotiation**, the parties seek joint gain. Typically, however, to reach a successful settlement, each party must give up something in exchange for getting something from the other side. Because negotiation generally occurs in every case before a more formal dispute resolution method is chosen, negotiation is not necessarily considered an alternative to litigation.

MEDIATION

An extension of negotiation is mediation. In **mediation**, the disputing parties select a neutral party to help facilitate communication and suggest ways for the parties to solve their dispute. Therefore, the distinguishing feature of mediation is that the parties voluntarily select a neutral third party to help them work together to resolve the dispute. The neutral third party frequently has expertise in the area of the dispute.

Mediation begins when parties select a mediator. Typically, a week before the mediation, each party provides the mediator with a short brief explaining why it should win. Attorneys, along with client representatives, then meet with the mediator. The mediator first assures the parties that the proceedings are confidential, and the parties take turns explaining the dispute to the mediator.

One of the mediator's main goals is to help each party listen carefully to the opposing party's concerns. The mediator asks the parties to identify any additional concerns. This discussion is an attempt to identify underlying circumstances that might have contributed to the dispute. A dispute typically arises after various problematic incidents; mediation permits the parties to address the various incidents, as well as the underlying circumstances leading to those incidents. After concerns have been highlighted, the mediator emphasizes areas of agreement and reframes the disputed points.

The parties then begin generating alternatives or solutions for the disputed points. The mediator helps the parties evaluate the alternatives by comparing the alternatives with the disputed points and interests identified earlier. Finally, the mediator helps the parties create a solution. Because the mediator's role is to facilitate an agreement, the mediator will often need to be persuasive to help the parties concede certain points so that agreement can be reached.

global context

Mediation in Sweden

In the 1960s, Sweden began expanding urban housing with the construction of large-scale, multiple-occupant buildings with individual units (commonly known as "flats"). The flats fell into disrepair, and only those without the means to choose their housing occupied the rather unpleasant flats. Tenants, desperate to have rent lowered, utilities fixed, and defacing of the property stopped, began bringing suits against the housing companies.

Recognizing that the courts could become overloaded with tenants suing the housing companies, the government took action. It ordered housing companies to alter the structure of their companies so that greater attention could be given to the upkeep of the flats. The housing companies responded by using the concept of mediation. One particular company, SABO, divided its flats geographically into areas of about 1,000 residents and named a local mediator to each area. The mediator's duties primarily involve keeping the lines of communication open between the tenants, the employees, and the superiors. While the area mediators have not eliminated the problems with the flats completely, tenants now have more direct and personable access to the housing companies.

The mediation concludes when an agreement between the parties is reached. The agreement is then usually put into the form of a contract and signed by the parties. The mediator may participate in the drafting of the contract. If one of the parties does not follow the agreement, that party can be sued for breach of contract. However, parties typically abide by the agreement because they helped to create it.

If mediation is not successful, the parties can turn to litigation or arbitration to resolve their dispute. However, nothing said during the mediation can be used in another dispute resolution method; the mediation process is confidential.

There are more than 2,500 state and federal rules regarding mediation. Lawmakers have recognized that with such a large number of different laws governing ADR, conducting business in different states is difficult and unduly complicated. In an attempt to create uniformity in mediation procedures, the American Bar Association committee helped draft the Uniform Mediation Act (UMA), which provides for a mediation privilege, which protects communications made during mediation as privileged, and requires that mediators identify any conflicts of interest. Thus far, nine states have enacted the UMA.[5]

Selecting a mediator. Mediators are available through nonprofit sources as well as private companies, such as Judicial Arbitration and Mediation Services (JAMS). JAMS has more than 200 full-time neutrals specializing in complex, multiparty business cases.[6] When selecting a mediator, parties should be aware that mediators come from a variety of backgrounds: experts in the area of the dispute, lawyers, judges, psychologists, and sociologists.

Advantages and disadvantages of mediation. For those disputes in which the parties must maintain a working relationship, mediation is popular because it allows parties to preserve their relationship throughout the dispute. Mediation helps parties work together to reach a consensus. Because parties are encouraged to communicate openly, they usually do not experience bitterness toward the opposing parties. Furthermore, each party typically leaves mediation with a better understanding of the opposing party; consequently, this understanding may actually facilitate a better working relationship between the parties. Therefore, the first advantage of mediation is that it helps disputing parties preserve their relationships.

[5] "A Few Facts about the Uniform Mediation Act," www.nccusl.org/Update/uniformact_factsheets/uniformacts-fs-uma2001.asp.

[6] "JAMS: The Resolution Experts: Fact Sheet," www.jamsadr.com/press/kit.asp.

connecting to the core

Management: Creating Constructive Conflict

As discussed in the text, one of the benefits of mediation is that there is a greater likelihood that opposing parties will maintain relationships when they cooperatively seek a solution to the issues in conflict. While alternative dispute resolution involves a more formal forum for discussing conflict, business managers must frequently undertake the management of conflict in their workplace. As with the ideals of ADR, managers hope to preserve workplace relationships when resolving conflict among employees or between management and employees.

Sometimes, however, it is important for managers to create *constructive conflict* within their organization, as certain kinds of conflict may advance organizational goals while presenting only nominal harm to employee relationships. For instance, managers could offer competitive incentives to employees who consistently exceed performance standards (e.g., providing a vacation to the highest-performing salespersons), reward cost-saving proposals from employees with bonuses, hire consultants or outside advisers to stimulate change, or use programmed conflict (i.e., role-playing exercises) to evaluate different positions on certain issues. Although it is at times damaging to workplace relationships and contrary to organizational objectives, conflict can be used, when properly managed, to stimulate change and the advancement of organizational objectives.

Source: A. Kinicki and B. Williams, *Management: A Practical Introduction* (New York: McGraw-Hill/Irwin, 2006), pp. 412, 416–417.

The second advantage to mediation is the potential for creative solutions. The parties are responsible for offering alternatives to solve problems. A party to mediation is often not necessarily looking for a money award. Instead, that party may be trying to find a solution so that both parties can benefit from the resolution of the dispute.

In addition, parties to mediation have a high level of autonomy. Unlike litigation or arbitration, where a neutral third party makes a decision that resolves the dispute, mediation allows parties to take control of the process and resolve the dispute together. The parties generally have more dedication to the agreement because they helped make the decision. Finally, mediation, like other methods of alternative dispute resolution, is less costly, less time-consuming, and less complicated than litigation.

These benefits can obviously be very worthwhile. However, critics of mediation argue that its informal process improperly creates an image of equality between the parties. Consequently, we improperly assume that the resulting agreement between the parties is also equal. However, if one party has more power than the other, the agreement is not necessarily fair or equal. Thus, the image of equality in mediation can be misleading. Furthermore, a party who knows that he or she has no chance of winning a case could enter the mediation process in bad faith, with no intention of making an agreement. Therefore, some people may abuse the mediation process in an attempt to simply draw out the dispute.

Uses of mediation. Mediation is used to resolve collective bargaining disputes. Because workers and employers must continue to work together, mediation typically helps preserve the relationship between the workers and the employers. Under the National Labor Relations Act (NLRA), a union must contact the Federal Mediation and Conciliation Services to attempt to mediate its demands before beginning a strike to achieve higher wages or better working hours.

Similarly, the Equal Employment Opportunity Commission (EEOC) encourages the mediation of employment discrimination claims. The EEOC has a mediation program that uses mediators employed by the EEOC, as well as external mediators trained in mediation and discrimination law. Between 1999 and 2003, the EEOC mediation program held over 52,400 mediations.[7] Approximately 69 percent of these mediations (more than 35,100 charges) were successfully resolved in an average of 85 days.[8]

Mediation is also commonly used in environmental disputes. For example, Japan has created a committee, the Environmental Pollution Disputes Committee, devoted solely to the resolution of environmental disputes. This committee may use mediation or arbitration. Why is mediation particularly useful for environmental disputes? First, mediation allows for creative solutions and compromises, which are often needed in environmental disputes. Suppose an endangered species makes its home on land that an entrepreneur recently purchased with the intention of building a bed-and-breakfast facility. Because the Endangered Species Act prohibits landowners from destroying an endangered species' habitat, the entrepreneur cannot build on the land. Mediation can help the landowner come to some kind of compromise to use the land. For example, there might be a way to preserve a portion of the land so that the species may thrive while the landowner can operate the bed-and-breakfast in perhaps a smaller facility.

Second, multiple parties are often involved in environmental disputes. While most dispute resolution methods limit the participation of parties, numerous parties can participate in mediation. Third, those involved in environmental disputes will often become involved in future disputes. Thus, it is important that the parties maintain a good relationship, and mediation helps them do so.

In Germany, mediation has a special use by the parliamentary groups, the Bundestag and the Bundesrat, similar to Congress. These two groups must reach a majority consensus on all pieces of federal legislation in Germany. The Mediation Committee was formed for the purpose of reaching such consensus on bills being debated by the two groups. The Mediation Committee is composed of 16 members from each group. The meetings of the committee are confidential to prevent outside political pressures from barring consensus. Free of unwanted pressures, the committee creates a proposal for the disputed bill. The frequency of the meetings of the Mediation Committee depends on the political atmosphere of the time. Between 1972 and 1976, when rival majorities held the Bundestag and the Bundesrat, the Mediation Committee convened 96 times. Yet between 1983 and 1987, the committee met only six times.

Mediation and litigation. While mediation is one of the more common alternatives to litigation, a primary purpose of mediation is to keep disputes out of the court system. However, sometimes litigation results from mediation. In one of the most important mediation-related cases, the *Folb* decision held that there is a mediation privilege under the Federal Rules of Evidence (see Case 4-1).

ARBITRATION

One of the most frequently used methods of dispute resolution is **arbitration**, the resolution of a dispute by a neutral third party outside the judicial setting. Arbitration is often a voluntary process in that parties typically have a contractual agreement to arbitrate any disputes. This agreement may stipulate how the arbitrator will be selected and how the hearing will be administered.

If a party wants to begin arbitration, it sends the other party a written demand for arbitration. This demand identifies the parties involved, the dispute issue, and the type of

7 "History of the EEOC Mediation Program," www.eeoc.gov/mediate/history.html.

8 Ibid.

CASE 4-1 SCOTT FOLB v. MOTION PICTURE INDUSTRY PENSION & HEALTH PLANS ET AL.

DISTRICT COURT FOR THE CENTRAL DISTRICT OF CALIFORNIA
16 F. SUPP. 2D 1164 (C.D. CAL. 1998)

Scott Folb was fired from his position as Administrative Director at the Motion Picture Industry Pension & Health Plans (the "Plans"). Folb argued that he was fired in retaliation for various whistle-blowing activities in which he was involved. Folb objected to and reported various misbehaviors by the Plans. The Plans argued that Folb was fired for sexually harassing another employee, Vivian Vasquez.

Earlier, Vasquez had filed a sexual harassment complaint against Folb, her manager. In February 1997, Vasquez and the Plans engaged in formal mediation to settle Vasquez's sexual harassment claims. Vasquez and the Plans signed an agreement ensuring the confidentiality of the mediation. Vasquez's counsel prepared a mediation brief and provided copies of this brief to the Plans' attorney as well as the mediator. The Plans had hired an outside attorney to investigate Vasquez's sexual harassment claim. At some point, the lawyer for the Plans gave the outside attorney a copy of the mediation brief prepared by Vasquez's attorney, who did not authorize the Plans to give this brief to the outside attorney.

Folb, in his own claim against the Plans, wanted the Plans to produce (1) Vasquez's mediation brief; (2) correspondence between Vasquez's attorney and counsel for the Plans regarding mediation or other settlement discussions; and (3) notes prepared by Vasquez's attorney regarding settlement communications. Folb argued that the Plans claimed that they legitimately fired Folb because of the sexual harassment. Yet, Folb argued that in the mediation and negotiations, the Plans may have argued that Vasquez was never sexually harassed at all. The Plans refused to produce the information because they asserted that the documents were confidential. Magistrate Judge Woehrle denied Folb's motion to compel production of the documents, and Folb filed objections.

JUDGE PAEZ: [T]he Court must decide whether to adopt a federal mediation privilege under FED. R. EVID. 501. . . . To determine whether an asserted privilege constitutes such a public good, in light of reason and experience, the Court must consider (1) whether the asserted privilege is "rooted in the imperative need for confidence and trust[;]" (2) whether the privilege would serve public ends; (3) whether the evidentiary detriment caused by exercise of the privilege is modest; and (4) whether denial of the federal privilege would frustrate a parallel privilege adopted by the states.

a. Need for Confidence and Trust

The proliferation of federal district court rules purporting to protect the confidentiality of mediation and the ADR Bill now pending before the United States Senate indicate a commitment to encouraging confidential mediation as an alternative means of resolving disputes that would otherwise result in protracted litigation. . . . [M]ost federal courts considering the issue have protected confidential settlement negotiations and mediation proceedings, either by relying on state law or by applying the confidentiality provisions of federal court ADR programs. . . . [T]he Court concludes that the proposed blanket mediation privilege is rooted in the imperative need for confidence and trust among participants.

b. Public Ends

A new privilege must serve a public good sufficiently important to justify creating an exception to the "general rule disfavoring testimonial privileges." . . . The proposed blanket mediation privilege would serve public ends by encouraging prompt, consensual resolution of disputes, minimizing the social and individual costs of litigation, and markedly reducing the size of state and federal court dockets.

c. Evidentiary Detriment

. . . [T]here is very little evidentiary benefit to be gained by refusing to recognize a mediation privilege.

d. Mediation Privilege in the 50 States

. . . [S]tate legislatures and state courts have overwhelmingly chosen to protect confidential communications in mediation proceedings in order to facilitate settlement of disputes through alternative dispute resolution. "Denial of the federal privilege . . . would frustrate the purposes of the state legislation that was enacted to foster these (*sic*) confidential communication." Accordingly, this Court finds it is appropriate, in light of reason and experience, to adopt a federal mediation privilege applicable to all communications made in conjunction with a formal mediation.

e. Contours of the Privilege

The mediation underlying the instant dispute was a formal mediation with a neutral mediator, not a private settlement discussion between the parties. Accordingly, the mediation privilege adopted today applies only to information disclosed in conjunction with mediation proceedings with a neutral.

On the facts presented here, the Court concludes that communications to the mediator and communications between parties during the mediation are protected. In addition, communications in preparation for and during the course of mediation with a neutral must be protected. Subsequent negotiations between the parties, however, are not protected even if they include information initially disclosed in the mediation. To protect additional communications, the parties are required to return to mediation. A contrary rule would permit a party to claim the privilege with respect to any settlement negotiations, so long as the communications took place following an attempt to mediate the dispute.

CRITICAL THINKING

What was the judge's logic in distinguishing between facts discussed during the mediation and facts discussed in negotiations outside mediation? Do you agree with his reasoning?

ETHICAL DECISION MAKING

Which of the two primary parties in this case might have behaved differently if the parties' actions had been subjected to the public disclosure test? Explain.

relief claimed. The opposing party typically responds to the demand in writing, indicating agreement or disagreement with the claim that the dispute is arbitrable.

Selecting an arbitrator. If the contract does not specify how the parties will select an arbitrator, they typically use either the Federal Mediation and Conciliation Services (FMCS), a government agency, or the American Arbitration Association (AAA), a private, nonprofit organization. The AAA has more than 8,000 arbitrators and mediators worldwide, over 1,000 of whom are bilingual or multilingual.[9] In 2005, more than 142,000 cases were filed with the AAA.[10]

When a party contacts one of the agencies, the party receives a list of potential arbitrators. This list includes biographical information about the potential arbitrators, and both parties examine the list and agree on an arbitrator. While most arbitrations are conducted by one arbitrator, panels of three arbitrators are becoming more frequent. Typically, each party chooses one arbitrator, and then those two arbitrators select an additional arbitrator.

Lawyers, professors, or other professionals typically serve as arbitrators. The general qualifications for being an arbitrator are honesty, impartiality, and subject-matter competence. Additionally, arbitrators are expected to follow the Arbitrator's Code of Ethics.

[9] American Arbitration Association, "Fast Facts," www.adr.org/FastFacts.

[10] "AAA and Cybersettle Join Forces," *Dispute Resolution Journal* 61 (November 2006–January 2006), p. 5.

Once the parties agree on an arbitrator, the parties and arbitrator agree on the location and time of the arbitration. The parties may or may not have a discovery period. Additionally, they determine which procedural and substantive rules will be followed during the arbitration.

The arbitration hearing. The arbitration hearing is quite similar to a trial. Both parties present their case to a neutral third party; they may represent themselves or use legal counsel. During this presentation, the parties may introduce witnesses and documentation, may cross-examine the witnesses, and may offer closing statements. The fact finder offers a legally binding decision. In these ways, a trial and an arbitration hearing are similar.

However, arbitration is also different in several ways. First, the arbitrator often takes a much more active role in an arbitration hearing, in the sense that the arbitrator is more likely than a judge to question a witness. Second, no official written record of the hearing is kept. Third, the rules of evidence applicable in a trial are typically relaxed in arbitration. Fourth, the arbitrator is not as constrained by precedent as are judges.

The arbitrator's award. The arbitrator typically provides a decision within 30 days of the arbitration hearing. The arbitrator's decision is called an *award,* even if no monetary compensation is awarded. The arbitrator's decision differs from a judge's decision in several ways. The arbitrator does not have to state any findings of fact, conclusions of law, or reasons to support the award, and he or she is not as bound by precedent as a judge. Also, because the arbitrator was hired to resolve a dispute between two parties, the arbitrator is more likely to make a compromise ruling instead of a win-lose ruling. After all, if the parties are satisfied with the ruling, they will probably be more likely to use that arbitrator again to resolve future disputes.

The arbitrator's decision is legally binding. In certain cases, a decision may be appealed to the district court. However, few of these cases are appealed. The courts give extreme deference to arbitrators' decisions. Unless a party can clearly demonstrate that an arbitrator's decision was contrary to law or that there was a defect in the arbitration process, the decision will be upheld. The Federal Arbitration Act (FAA), the federal law enacted to encourage the use of arbitration, explicitly lists four grounds on which an arbitrator's award may be set aside:

1. The award was the result of corruption, fraud, or other undue means.
2. The arbitrator displayed bias or corruption.
3. The arbitrator refused to postpone the hearing despite sufficient cause, refused to hear relevant evidence, or otherwise misbehaved to prejudice the rights of one of the parties.
4. The arbitrator exceeded his or her authority or failed to use that authority to make a mutual, final, and definite award.

Consequently, in the United States, arbitration decisions are generally upheld. In fact, the Fifth Circuit recently held that "manifest disregard of the law and contrary to public policy are the only nonstatutory bases recognized by this circuit for the vacatur of an arbitration award."[11] Other countries are taking actions to increase the number of arbitrations, while reducing the need to appeal the arbitration decisions. For example, Brazilian lawmakers reformed several articles in the Brazilian Civil Code to increase the practice of

[11] *Kergosien et al. v. Ocean Energy, Inc.*, 390 F.3d 346 (5th Cir. 2004).

arbitration. These reforms mandate that parties sign an "arbitration commitment" during arbitration proceedings. This commitment states the disputed issue, the venue of the arbitration, and the parties involved. The arbitration commitment renders the outcome of the arbitration comparable to a decision handed down by the judiciary branch. Consequently, parties no longer need to appeal to the judiciary branch after an arbitration hearing.

Advantages and disadvantages of arbitration. Arbitration may be preferable to litigation for several reasons. First, arbitration is more efficient and less expensive than litigation. For example, on May 11, 2005, Google filed a complaint with the National Arbitration Forum because another party had registered the following Internet domain names: googkle.com, ghoogle.com, gfoogle.com, and gooigle.com.[12] Less than two months later, an arbitration panel concluded that these domain names were confusingly similar to the google.com trademark and that they had been registered in bad faith. Consequently, the panel determined that the googkle.com, ghoogle.com, gfoogle.com, and gooigle.com domain names be transferred to Google.

Second, parties have more control over the process of dispute resolution through arbitration. They choose the arbitrator and determine how formal the process will be. Third, the parties can choose someone to serve as the arbitrator who has expertise in the specific subject matter. Because the arbitrator has expertise, the parties believe that the arbitrator will be able to make a better decision. Fourth, the arbitrator has greater flexibility in decision making than a judge has. Unlike judges, who are bound by precedent, arbitrators generally do not have to offer reasons for their decisions.

However, arbitration is not without its critics. First, arbitration panels are being used more frequently, resulting in a loss of some of the prior advantages of arbitration. For example, using a panel, as opposed to one arbitrator, causes greater scheduling difficulties because of the number of people involved, consequently negating some of the efficiency associated with arbitration. Along the same lines, paying an arbitration panel is more costly than paying one arbitrator.

Second, because appealing an arbitration award is so difficult, some scholars argue that injustice is more likely to occur. Third, some individuals are concerned that by agreeing to give up one's right to litigate, one may be losing important civil rights or giving up important potential remedies without really understanding which rights are being given up. Especially in an employment context, people may not really want to give up such rights, but they have no choice if they want the job.

Fourth, some scholars are afraid that if more and more employers and institutions turn to mandatory arbitration, it will become more like litigation. An increasing number of people will be forced to arbitrate their disputes; consequently, the efficiency associated with arbitration will start to erode.

Fifth, some scholars are concerned about the privacy associated with arbitration. Companies and employers are able to "hide" their disputes through arbitration. Suppose a credit card company is charging greater amounts of money than its posted finance charge. If an individual arbitrates her claim, other customers might not learn about the problem and therefore won't know to check their credit card statements to ensure that they are being charged the correct amount. If the claim went to court, the publicity surrounding the case would probably better educate people to pay more attention to their statements. Thus, the confidentiality associated with an arbitration proceeding may be harmful in some cases.

[12] *Google Inc. v. Sergey Gridasov,* Claim Number: FA0505000474816, National Arbitration Forum (2005), www.arb-forum.com/domains/decisions /4_7_4816.htm.

Any controversy, dispute, or claim of whatever nature arising out of, in connection with, or in relation to the interpretation, performance, or breach of this agreement, including any claim based on contract, tort, or statute, shall be resolved, at the request of any party to this agreement, by final and binding arbitration conducted at a location determined by the arbitrator in (City, State) administered by and in accordance with the existing Rules of Practice and Procedure of Judicial Arbitration and Mediation Services (JAMS), Inc., and judgment upon any award rendered by the arbitrator may be entered by any state or federal court having jurisdiction thereof.

Exhibit 4-1
Sample Binding Arbitration Clause

If you applied the ethical principle of universalization to arbitration, would you be able to justify its use in spite of these disadvantages? Why might the application of the universalization principle cause one to become hesitant to use arbitration?

Methods of securing arbitration. Given the benefits associated with arbitration, parties may voluntarily submit their cases to arbitration. The primary method of securing arbitration is through a **binding arbitration clause**, a provision in a contract that mandates that all disputes arising under the contract must be settled by arbitration. The clause also typically states how the arbitrator will be selected. Exhibit 4-1 shows an example of a binding arbitration clause that could be included in almost any business contract.

If a contract does not contain a binding arbitration clause, parties may secure arbitration by entering into a **submission agreement**, a contract providing that a specific dispute will be resolved through arbitration. The submission agreement typically states the following: the nature of the dispute; how the arbitrator will be selected; the place of the arbitration; and any limitations on the arbitrator's authority to remedy the dispute.

If parties have a binding arbitration agreement or have entered into a submission agreement, the parties *must* resolve the dispute through arbitration. Both federal and state courts must uphold agreements to arbitrate. In 2003, the Ninth Circuit joined all other circuits in concluding that Title VII does not bar compulsory arbitration of claims.[13]

Like the law in general, however, the law governing arbitration agreements is not a fixed set of rules or precedents. Rather, it changes as new and unforeseen issues arise. In many cases, lawmakers and courts do not fully understand the consequences of the laws they enact and the decisions they issue. Thus, although federal and state courts originally upheld all arbitration agreements, more recently they have not upheld certain types of arbitration clauses. For example, as Case 4-2 illustrates, courts do not uphold arbitration agreements when federal statutory rights are at issue if the agreement is not "clear and unmistakable."

The Supreme Court recently considered whether a broad arbitration clause in individual consumers' contracts would apply to class actions by the consumers. In *Green Tree Financial Corp. v. Bazzle,* the Court concluded that the Federal Arbitration Act did not preclude class arbitration; thus, the case would be decided on the basis of the interpretation of the arbitration clause in the context of state law.[14] Similarly, in *James v. McDonald's Corp.,* the Seventh Circuit agreed that a McDonald's customer could be compelled to arbitrate a dispute over a prize in McDonald's "Who Wants To Be a Millionaire?" sweepstakes when the arbitration clause was included in the official rules posted in participating McDonald's restaurants.[15]

[13] *EEOC v. Luce, Forward, Hamilton, & Scripps,* 345 F.3d 742 (9th Cir. 2003).

[14] 539 U.S. 444 (2003).

[15] 417 F.3d 672 (7th Cir. 2005).

CASE 4-2 JEROME BROWN v. ABF FREIGHT SYSTEMS, INC.
U.S. COURT OF APPEALS, FOURTH CIRCUIT
183 F.3D 319 (1999)

Jerome Brown, a diabetic commercial truck driver, claimed that ABF Freight Systems violated the Americans with Disabilities Act and the Virginians with Disabilities Act when it informed him that ABF would no longer accept his bids for yard and dock jobs. He filed his claim in a district court in Virginia. However, ABF argued that its collective bargaining agreement ("CBA") with Brown's union, the International Brotherhood of Teamsters, required Brown to submit his ADA claim to arbitration in accordance with the agreement. The District Court ruled that Brown would have to submit his claim to arbitration, and Brown appealed.

CIRCUIT JUDGE LUTTIG: Because we conclude that the collective bargaining agreement in question does not clearly and unmistakably require the arbitration of statutory discrimination claims, we reverse the judgment of the district court.

In reviewing Brown's claims, we write on a slate that is far from clean. In *Wright v. Universal Maritime Serv. Corp.,* the Court established that a union-negotiated waiver of employees' right to a federal judicial forum for statutory employment-discrimination claims must be clear and unmistakable. Because the asserted waiver did not meet that standard, the Court expressly declined to reach the question whether even a waiver that did would be enforceable. In addition, . . . we applied the *Universal Maritime* standard in *Carson v. Giant Food, Inc.* . . . concluding that under the Supreme Court's newly announced standard, the CBA in question did not compel arbitration of appellee's statutory discrimination claims. It is with the benefit of the decisions in these two recent cases, *Universal Maritime* and *Carson,* that we consider this appeal.

. . . The question whether the parties to a CBA agreed to arbitrate discrimination claims arising under the ADA—or any other federal statutory antidiscrimination law—is one of contract interpretation. In making that determination, however, we do not apply the usual interpretive presumption in favor of arbitration. . . . Rather, under the rule of *Universal Maritime,* we will not find an intent to arbitrate statutory claims absent a "clear and unmistakable" waiver of an employee's "statutory right to a judicial forum for claims of employment discrimination."

In *Carson,* a panel of this court explained that the requirement of a "clear and unmistakable" waiver can be satisfied through two possible means. First, and most obviously, such intent can be demonstrated through the drafting of an "explicit arbitration clause" pursuant to which the union agrees to submit all statutory employment-discrimination claims to arbitration. Second, where the arbitration clause is "not so clear," employees might yet be bound to arbitrate their federal claims if "another provision, like a nondiscrimination clause, makes it unmistakably clear that the discrimination statutes at issue are part of the agreement."

With respect to the first of these means, there is no doubt that the arbitration clause contained in Article 37 of the CBA in this case is insufficiently explicit to pass muster under *Universal Maritime.* The clause is a standard one, submitting to arbitration "all grievances or questions of interpretation arising under . . . this Agreement." Because the arbitration clause refers only to grievances arising under the Agreement, it cannot be read to require arbitration of those grievances arising out of alleged statutory violations.

Under *Carson*'s second means, however, even such a "broad but nonspecific" arbitration clause may, nonetheless, require arbitration of statutory discrimination claims if another provision of the agreement has . . . established with the "requisite degree of clarity" that the "discrimination statute[ ] at issue is part of the agreement." Because the only provision that might even arguably qualify—Article 37, the nondiscrimination clause—does not make it "unmistakably clear" that it is incorporating federal statutory employment discrimination law, we hold that the argument grounded in this alternative of *Carson* is also unavailing.

Article 37 begins with an explicit agreement between the Employer and the Union that neither will discriminate against any individual "with respect to hiring, compensation, terms or conditions of employment" or "limit, segregate or classify employees in any way to deprive any individual employee of employment opportunities" because of that individual's "race, color,

[CONTINUED]

religion, sex, age, or national origin." While the language of this contractual agreement not to discriminate on certain specified bases in certain specified ways may parallel, or even parrot, the language of federal antidiscrimination statutes and prohibit some of the same conduct, none of those statutes is thereby explicitly incorporated into the agreement, by reference or otherwise. As a result, the contractual rights the agreement creates "cannot be said to be congruent with," those established by statute or common law, and an arbitrator in interpreting the scope of those rights pursuant to the general arbitration clause will be bound to interpret the explicit terms of the agreement rather than of any federal statutory antidiscrimination law.

ABF argues that the catch-all concluding clause of the first sentence of Article 37, by which the Employer and Union agree not to "engage in any other discriminatory acts prohibited by law," constitutes the explicit incorporation of federal statutory discrimination law contemplated by *Carson.* We disagree. There is a significant difference between an agreement not to commit discriminatory acts that are prohibited by law and an agreement to incorporate the antidiscrimination statutes that prohibit those acts. . . . Rather, the parties must make "unmistakably clear" their intent to incorporate in their entirety the "discrimination statutes at issue," as we said in *Carson.* This, these parties have not done.

Accordingly, because we cannot say that the intent of the union to waive its employees' statutory right to a federal forum has been clearly and unmistakably established, we reverse the district court's order dismissing Brown's ADA claim.

REVERSED.

CRITICAL THINKING

What reasoning is used to come to the conclusion that Brown did not have to submit his claim to arbitration?

ETHICAL DECISION MAKING

What values are being advanced by this decision?

Another constraint on binding arbitration clauses is that they must be drafted in such a way as to ensure that the courts do not see them as being unconscionable. An *unconscionable contract provision* has been defined as one in which the terms are "manifestly unfair or oppressive and are dictated by a dominant party."[16] The doctrine has been used most often to strike down binding arbitration clauses in consumer and employment contracts.

For example, in the Hooters illustration at the beginning of the chapter, the court refused to uphold the contract because of a number of provisions it found to be unconscionable, including requiring that employees provide notice of the specifics of the claim but not making the company file any type of response to these specifics or notify the employee of what kinds of defenses the company planned to raise; making only the employee provide a list of all fact witnesses and a brief summary of the facts known to each; allowing the company to widen the scope of arbitration to include any matter, whereas the employee was limited to those raised in his or her notice; giving only the company the right to record the arbitration; allowing only the company to sue to vacate or modify an arbitration award because the arbitration panel exceeded its authority; and allowing only the company to

[16] *Farris v. County of Camden,* 61 F. Supp. 2d 307, 341 (D. N.J. 1999).

cancel the agreement to arbitrate or change the arbitration rules. Provisions found to be unconscionable in other binding arbitration clauses included provisions that mandated cost sharing for hiring a three-member arbitration panel,[17] limited available damages,[18] adopted unreasonably short time periods for filing claims, and limited the amount of discovery available.[19]

Exhibit 4-2 offers tips on creating a binding arbitration clause.

Common uses of arbitration. Arbitration is used in a variety of situations. It is commonly used in labor disputes. And just like the management of Hooters, employers are often eager to resolve all employment-related disputes through arbitration. However, before *Gilmer,* discussed in Case 4-3, employers and employees were extremely uncertain as to whether employees could be required to resolve all employment disputes through arbitration, especially those involving discrimination claims.

Exhibit 4-2
Tips for Creating a Binding Arbitration Clause

Overall, make sure the clause treats both parties fairly.

1. *Be clear and unmistakable.* If you wish to arbitrate employment disputes or discrimination claims, make sure that you explicitly state "employment disputes and discrimination claims" in the binding arbitration clause.
2. *The arbitration clause must be bilateral.* If the arbitration clause requires one party only to arbitrate but does not spell out the same requirement for the other party, the clause will probably not be upheld. This agreement would be asking one party to give up its right to have a claim before a jury while the other party retains that right. The courts are concerned about fairness. This bilateral consideration must extend to damages. For example, both parties must be able to get the same damages.
3. *State explicitly which party will pay the arbitrator's fees, and make sure that it will not cost the employee more to arbitrate than it would have cost to litigate.* Courts have refused to enforce arbitration agreements that require that the plaintiff pay the costs of the arbitration. Some courts have refused to enforce agreements requiring that the employee pay a pro rata share of arbitration expenses.[20] Furthermore, a court recently refused to enforce an agreement that did not specify who would pay the arbitrator's fees along with other costs. For ease and assurance that the agreement will be enforced, companies might consider stating that they will pay the costs of the arbitration.
4. *Specify how the arbitrator will be selected.*
5. *Spell out the costs associated with the arbitration.*
6. *Avoid limitations on the remedies available to the parties.* Limitations on punitive damages or attorney fees are likely to be causes for refusing to uphold cases.
7. *Consider other potential parties when determining where to hold the arbitration.* If a credit card company states in its arbitration clause that all disputes will be arbitrated in its state of incorporation, a court might be more likely to not enforce the agreement. Requiring that consumers travel far distances may be perceived as an unfair burden on the consumer.

[17] *Maciejewski v. Alpha Systems Lab Inc.,* 87 Cal. Rptr. 2d 390 (Cal. Ct. App. 1999).

[18] *Johnson v. Circuit City Stores, Inc.* 203 F.3d 821 (4th Cir. 2000).

[19] *Geiger v. Ryan's Family Steak House and Employment Dispute Services Inc.,* 2001 WL 278120 (S.D. Ind. 2001).

[20] See, e.g., *Shubin v. William Lyon Homes, Inc.,* 84 Cal. App. 4th 1041 (2000) and *Cole v. Burns Internal Security Services,* 105 F.3d 1465 (D.C. Cir. 1997).

CASE 4-3 ROBERT GILMER v. INTERSTATE/JOHNSON LANE CORPORATION

UNITED STATES SUPREME COURT
500 U.S. 20 (1991)

Plaintiff Robert Gilmer filed a charge with the Equal Employment Opportunity Commission (EEOC) and sued his employer, defendant Interstate/Johnson Lane Corporation. Gilmer alleged that his employer violated the Age Discrimination in Employment Act (ADEA). When the defendant hired him as a registered securities dealer, Gilmer had signed an agreement to settle by arbitration any disputes arising out of that employment. The employer therefore filed a motion to compel arbitration. The trial court denied the defendant's motion and defendant appealed to the circuit court. The circuit court reversed in favor of the defendant and the plaintiff appealed to the U.S. Supreme Court.

JUSTICE WHITE: The question presented in this case is whether a claim under the Age Discrimination in Employment Act of 1967 (ADEA) can be subjected to compulsory arbitration pursuant to an arbitration agreement in a securities registration application.

. . . It is by now clear that statutory claims may be the subject of an arbitration agreement, enforceable pursuant to the FAA. . . . In [recent] cases we recognized that "by agreeing to arbitrate a statutory claim, a party does not forgo the substantive rights afforded by the statute; it only submits to their resolution in an arbitral, rather than a judicial, forum."

Although all statutory claims may not be appropriate for arbitration, "[h]aving made the bargain to arbitrate, the party should be held to it unless Congress itself has evinced an intention to preclude a waiver of judicial remedies for the statutory rights at issue." The burden is on Gilmer to show that Congress intended to preclude a waiver of a judicial forum for ADEA claims. . . . Throughout such an inquiry, it should be kept in mind that "questions of arbitrability must be addressed with a healthy regard for the federal policy favoring arbitration."

Gilmer concedes that nothing in the text of the ADEA or its legislative history explicitly precludes arbitration. He argues, however, that compulsory arbitration of ADEA claims pursuant to arbitration agreements would be inconsistent with the statutory framework and purposes of the ADEA. Like the Court of Appeals, we disagree.

We also are unpersuaded by the argument that arbitration will undermine the role of the EEOC in enforcing the ADEA. An individual ADEA claimant subject to an arbitration agreement will still be free to file a charge with the EEOC, even though the claimant is not able to institute a private judicial action. Indeed, Gilmer filed a charge with the EEOC in this case.

Gilmer also argues that compulsory arbitration is improper because it deprives claimants of the judicial forum provided for by the ADEA. Congress, however, did not explicitly preclude arbitration or other nonjudicial resolution of claims, even in its recent amendments to the ADEA. Moreover, Gilmer's argument ignores the ADEA's flexible approach to resolution of claims. The EEOC, for example, is directed to pursue "informal methods of conciliation, conference, and persuasion," which suggests that out-of-court dispute resolution, such as arbitration, is consistent with the statutory scheme established by Congress.

In arguing that arbitration is inconsistent with the ADEA, Gilmer also raises a host of challenges to the adequacy of arbitration procedures. Such generalized attacks on arbitration "res[t] on suspicion of arbitration as a method of weakening the protections afforded in the substantive law to would-be complainants," and as such, they are "far out of step with our current strong endorsement of the federal statutes favoring this method of resolving disputes."

Gilmer also complains that the discovery allowed in arbitration is more limited than in the federal courts, which he contends will make it difficult to prove discrimination. It is unlikely, however, that age discrimination claims require more extensive discovery than other claims that we have found to be arbitrable, such as RICO and antitrust claims. Although those procedures might not be as extensive as in the federal courts, by agreeing to arbitrate, a party "trades the procedures and opportunity for review of the courtroom for the simplicity, informality, and expedition of arbitration."

[CONTINUED]

It is also argued that arbitration procedures cannot adequately further the purposes of the ADEA because they do not provide for broad equitable relief and class actions. As the court below noted, however, arbitrators do have the power to fashion equitable relief. Indeed, the NYSE rules applicable here do not restrict the types of relief an arbitrator may award, but merely refer to "damages and/or other relief."

AFFIRMED in favor of Defendant, Johnson/ Lane Interstate Corp.

CRITICAL THINKING

What are the primary facts in *Gilmer v. Interstate/Johnson Lane Corporation?* What missing facts should be called for when evaluating the judge's reasoning? What ambiguities are present in the reasoning?

ETHICAL DECISION MAKING

What group of stakeholders would be most happy with the outcome of this case? Which would be the least happy?

Gilmer upheld the validity of the National Association of Securities Dealers' policy of requiring all employees who execute, buy, or sell orders at brokerages or investment banks to arbitrate all employment disputes as a condition of their employment. Immediately following this case, the use of mandatory arbitration agreements in employment contracts increased significantly.

However, the EEOC became concerned about whether arbitration agreements that had to be accepted as a condition of employment were actually voluntary. In July 1997, the EEOC issued a statement regarding arbitration agreements; the statement indicated that arbitration of discrimination claims as a condition of employment was in conflict with the fundamental principles of employment laws. What values are involved in the EEOC's protection of workers against employers forcing employees into arbitration?

While the EEOC strongly supported agreements to arbitrate once a dispute has arisen, they did not support inclusion of arbitration agreements as an unconditional element of employment. In response to the EEOC's statement, the National Association of Securities Dealers created a policy that allowed employees to choose between entering into a private arbitration agreement with the employer and reserving the right to file suit in a federal or state court for discrimination claims.

Gilmer did not end the questions about whether binding arbitration contracts in the employment area should be enforced. Two subsequent U.S. Supreme Court decisions, however, have clarified the impact of the Federal Arbitration Act on binding arbitration clauses in employment contracts. Perhaps the most significant ruling was that in the 2001 case of *Circuit City v. Saint Clair Adams.*[21] In that case, the plaintiff, an employee of Circuit City,

[21] 532 U.S. 105 (2001).

had signed a binding arbitration agreement that had specifically included claims based on discrimination, but two years later he brought an employment discrimination case against his employer in state court. Circuit City filed suit in federal district court to enjoin the state case and compel arbitration. The district court issued the order.

On appeal of the district court's order, the circuit court of appeals held that the Federal Arbitration Act did not apply to employment contracts. This ruling was contrary to all other appellate rulings, and the U.S. Supreme Court heard the case. The high court overruled the circuit court's ruling, clearly setting forth the rule that the Federal Arbitration Act does apply to employment contracts, thereby making binding arbitration agreements in employment contracts enforceable, a decision giving much relief to employers. Many commentators forecast that this decision will lead to an even greater number of employers putting binding arbitration clauses in their employment contracts.

A subsequent decision by the high court, however, was not viewed quite so favorably by many employers. As discussed in Case 4-4, the court went back to a situation similar to that in *Gilmer,* but in this case, it was not the employee seeking to bring a discrimination claim—it was the EEOC. While this case involved the ADA, the high court stated that the analysis was applicable to all the civil rights statutes used to eradicate discrimination in the workplace.

CASE 4-4 EQUAL EMPLOYMENT OPPORTUNITY COMMISSION v. WAFFLE HOUSE, INC.

UNITED STATES SUPREME COURT
534 U.S. 279 (2002)

All employees of respondent Waffle House had to sign an agreement requiring employment disputes to be settled by binding arbitration. After Eric Baker suffered a seizure and was fired by Waffle House, he filed a discrimination charge with the Equal Employment Opportunity Commission (EEOC) alleging that his discharge violated the Americans with Disabilities Act of 1990 (ADA) under Title VII. The EEOC subsequently filed an enforcement suit, to which Baker is not a party, alleging that Waffle House's employment practices, including Baker's discharge "because of his disability," violated the ADA. The EEOC sought the following: an injunction to "eradicate the effects of [respondent's] past and present unlawful employment practices"; specific relief designed to make Baker whole, including back pay, reinstatement, and compensatory damages; and punitive damages for malicious and reckless conduct.

Waffle House sought to dismiss the EEOC's suit and compel arbitration because of the binding arbitration clause signed by Baker. The District Court denied Waffle House's motion to dismiss. The Fourth Circuit agreed with the District Court that the arbitration agreement between Baker and respondent did not foreclose the enforcement action because the EEOC was not a party to the contract, but had independent statutory authority to bring an action to enforce the statute. However, the appellate court held that the EEOC was limited to injunctive relief and precluded from seeking victim-specific relief because the FAA policy favoring enforcement of private arbitration agreements outweighs the EEOC's right to proceed in federal court when it seeks primarily to vindicate private, rather than public, interests. EEOC appealed to the United States Supreme Court.

JUSTICE STEVENS: When Title VII was enacted in 1964, it authorized private actions by individual employees and public actions by the Attorney General in cases involving a "pattern or practice" of discrimination. . . .

In 1972, Congress amended Title VII to authorize the EEOC to bring its own enforcement actions; indeed, we have observed that the 1972 amendments created a system in which the EEOC was intended "to bear the primary burden of litigation. . . ."

In 1991, Congress again amended Title VII to allow the recovery of compensatory and punitive damages by a "complaining party." The term includes both private plaintiffs and the EEOC. . . . Thus, these statutes unambiguously authorize the EEOC to obtain the relief that it seeks in its complaint if it can prove its case against respondent.

The Court of Appeals based its decision on its evaluation of the "competing policies" implemented by the ADA and the FAA . . . It recognized that the EEOC never agreed to arbitrate its statutory claim . . . and that the EEOC has "independent statutory authority" to vindicate the public interest, but opined that permitting the EEOC to prosecute Baker's claim in court "would significantly trample" the strong federal policy favoring arbitration, because Baker had agreed to submit his claim to arbitration. To effectuate this policy, the court distinguished between injunctive and victim-specific relief, and held that the EEOC is barred from obtaining the latter, because any public interest served when the EEOC pursues "make whole" relief is outweighed by the policy goals favoring arbitration. Only when the EEOC seeks broad injunctive relief, in the Court of Appeals' view, does the public interest overcome the goals underpinning the FAA.

If it were true that the EEOC could prosecute its claim only with Baker's consent, or if its prayer for relief could be dictated by Baker, the court's analysis might be persuasive. But once a charge is filed, the exact opposite is true under the statute—the EEOC is in command of the process. The EEOC has exclusive jurisdiction over the claim for 180 days. During that time, the employee must obtain a right-to-sue letter from the agency before prosecuting the claim. If, however, the EEOC files suit on its own, the employee has no independent cause of action, although the employee may intervene in the EEOC's suit. In fact, the EEOC takes the position that it may pursue a claim on the employee's behalf even after the employee has disavowed any desire to seek relief. The statute makes the EEOC the master of its own case and confers on the agency the authority to evaluate the strength of the public interest at stake. Absent textual support for a contrary view, it is the public agency's province—not that of the court—to determine whether public resources should be committed to the recovery of victim-specific relief. And if the agency makes that determination, the statutory text unambiguously authorizes it to proceed in a judicial forum.

The Court of Appeals . . . simply sought to balance the policy goals of the FAA against the clear language of Title VII and the agreement. While this may be a more coherent approach, it is inconsistent with our recent arbitration cases. The FAA directs courts to place arbitration agreements on equal footing with other contracts, but it "does not require parties to arbitrate when they have not agreed to do so." . . . Here there is no ambiguity. No one asserts that the EEOC is a party to the contract, or that it agreed to arbitrate its claims. It goes without saying that a contract cannot bind a nonparty. Accordingly, the proarbitration policy goals of the FAA do not require the agency to relinquish its statutory authority if it has not agreed to do so.

[T]he statutory language is clear; the EEOC has the authority to pursue victim-specific relief regardless of the forum that the employer and employee have chosen to resolve their disputes. Rather than attempt to split the difference, we are persuaded that, pursuant to Title VII and the ADA, whenever the EEOC chooses from among the many charges filed each year to bring an enforcement action in a particular case, the agency may be seeking to vindicate a public interest, not simply provide make-whole relief for the employee, even when it pursues entirely victim-specific relief. To hold otherwise would undermine the detailed enforcement scheme created by Congress simply to give greater effect to an agreement between private parties that does not even contemplate the EEOC's statutory function.

The only issue before this Court is whether the fact that Baker has signed a mandatory arbitration agreement limits the remedies available to the EEOC. The text of the relevant statutes provides a clear answer to that question. They do not authorize the courts to balance the competing policies of the ADA and the FAA, or to second-guess the agency's judgment concerning which of the remedies authorized by law that it shall seek in any given case.

REVERSED in favor of petitioner, EEOC.

[CONTINUED]

CRITICAL THINKING

How are previous rules of law and precedents used in Justice Stevens' reasoning? Is sufficient evidence provided to support the extension of these precedents to this case?

The EEOC filed the claim because of the damages suffered by Baker as a result of Waffle House's actions. Are there potential alternative causes for the damages suffered by Baker?

ETHICAL DECISION MAKING

What is the purpose of the decision that Waffle House made in the facts leading to this case?

Arbitration is also used in medical malpractice cases, environmental disputes, commercial contract disputes, and insurance liability claims. However, no area uses arbitration in as great a percentage of cases as does the employment area.

Other ADR Methods

Several other methods of ADR are used less frequently than those discussed above. Some of these methods are similar to negotiation, involving the assistance of a neutral third party. It will be clear after finishing this section that today's manager really does have a variety of options to choose from when a dispute arises. Exhibit 4-3 provides some key questions for a manager to consider when choosing from among this array of dispute resolution options.

MED-ARB

Med-arb is a dispute resolution process in which the parties agree to start out in mediation and, if the mediation is unsuccessful on one or more points, also agree to move on to arbitration. In some cases, the same neutral third party may participate in both the mediation and the arbitration. However, some critics argue that if parties know that the mediator may become the ultimate decision maker, they will be less likely to disclose information during

Exhibit 4-3
Questions to Ask When Selecting a Dispute Resolution Method

If you are a party in a dispute, ask yourself the following questions to determine which dispute resolution method would be best.

1. How concerned am I about keeping costs low?
2. How quickly do I want to resolve the dispute?
3. Do I want to keep the dispute private?
4. Do I want to protect the relationship between the disputing parties?
5. Am I concerned about vindication?
6. Do I want to set a precedent with the resolution of my dispute?

e-commerce AND THE LAW

ADR in Cyberspace

Increasingly, litigants are using arbitration and mediation to resolve disputes in e-commerce cases. The National Arbitration Forum (www.arbitration-forum.com) is one of the world's most active organizations in the ADR field, and it is helping more and more litigants resolve e-commerce disputes. This chapter has already discussed one example of the National Arbitration Forum's work: the conflict involving Google and which domain names rightfully belong to that company. Another example highlights Hillary Clinton's right to use the domain name hillaryclinton.com.

Recently, a National Arbitration Forum arbitrator resolved a dispute between Hillary Clinton and Michele Dinoia. In 2001, Dinoia registered the domain name hillaryclinton.com and then used it for a Web site to profit from Senator Clinton's name. When an individual went to hillaryclinton.com, the individual was directed to commercial sites and pop-up ads. Dinoia profited from pay-per-click results. When considering the dispute between Clinton and Dinoia, the arbitrator highlighted the facts that Dinoia was using the domain name in bad faith and that Clinton had trademark rights to her name. The use of "Hillary Clinton" in the domain name was likely to confuse individuals clicking on hillaryclinton.com.

The National Arbitration Forum issued the Hillary Clinton decision based on its authority under the Uniform Domain Name Dispute Resolution Policy of the Internet Corporation for Assigned Names and Numbers, known as ICANN. An important advantage to using the ADR policy outlined in ICANN is that it is faster and cheaper than pursuing litigation based on trademark law.

Source: "National Arbitration Forum Issues Decision on Hillary Clinton Web Address," *Business Wire,* March 21, 2005.

the mediation stage. In contrast, others argue that having the same neutral mediator-arbitrator offers faster resolution because the third party is familiar with the facts of the case.[22]

SUMMARY JURY TRIAL

The summary jury trial began in 1983 when a court in Cleveland attempted to relieve pressure on an overloaded docket. A **summary jury trial** is an abbreviated trial that leads to a nonbinding jury verdict. Two advantages are inherent in this method of dispute resolution. First, it is quick; a summary jury trial lasts only a day. Second, because the jury offers a verdict, both parties get a chance to see how their case would fare before a jury of their peers.

The process of the summary jury trial is similar to that of a regular trial, but there are some important differences. Each judge can set his or her own rules. At the start of the summary trial, the judge advises the jury on the law. Then, each party's lawyer presents an opening statement along with a limited amount of evidence before the jury. Two key differences here are that the lawyers have a limited amount of time for this presentation, and there are generally no witnesses. All the evidence is presented by the lawyers. The jury then reaches a verdict. Although this verdict is only advisory, the jury is not aware that the verdict is not binding. After the jury provides the verdict, the parties participate in a settlement conference, where they decide either to accept the jury verdict, to reject the verdict, or to settle on some compromise. Approximately 95 percent of cases are settled at this time. However, if the case is not settled, it will go to a regular trial. At that trial, nothing from the summary jury trial is admissible as evidence.

MINITRIAL

A **minitrial** is similar to arbitration and mediation because it involves a neutral third party. Disputing businesses generally use minitrials. Business representatives of the disputing businesses participate and have settlement authority. Lawyers for each side present their

[22] See Gerald F. Phillips, "Same Neutral Med-Arb: What Does the Future Hold?"*Dispute Resolution Journal* 60 (May–July 2005), p. 24.

global context

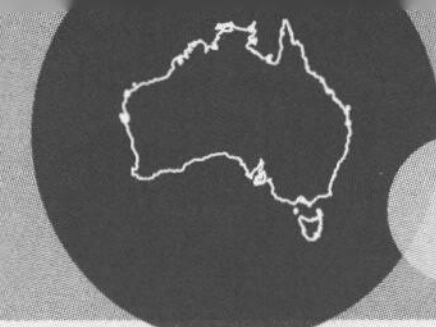

Arbitration in Australia

In preparation for the 2000 Olympics in Sydney, Australia established a unique forum of arbitration: the Court of Arbitration for Sport (CAS). CAS was created in 1996 to assist individuals and sporting associations involved in sport-related disputes ranging from disciplinary measures to endorsement contracts. CAS is accessible to any individual or sporting association capable of entering into a legal transaction.

There are two divisions within CAS. The first division, Ordinary Arbitration, focuses on disputes arising from legal relations. For example, two television stations vying for coverage of the Indy 500 could settle the matter in the Ordinary Arbitration Division. The second division is the Appeals Arbitration Division, which handles disputes over qualifications and disciplinary decisions of sports federations or associations. A swimmer who tests positive for steroids, but denies the charge, could bring suit against the federation for the accusation in the Appeals Arbitration Division.

Athletes and sports federations may find several advantages to using CAS over a traditional court system. CAS is suitable for international disputes because it allows the parties to choose the applicable law. The Code of Sports-Related Arbitration, which governs CAS, is a flexible code designed to be expeditious and efficient.

arguments before these representatives and the neutral adviser, who then offers an opinion as to what the verdict would be if the case went to trial. The neutral adviser's opinion, like the jury's verdict in the summary jury trial, is not binding. Next, the business representatives discuss settlement options. If they reach an agreement, they enter into a contract that reflects the terms of the settlement.

A minitrial may be preferred to arbitration for three reasons. First, a minitrial is less costly than arbitration. Second, in the typical minitrial, the business representatives, who presumably understand the complex matters of the dispute better than an outside arbitrator, have settlement authority. Third, the procedures of the minitrial can be modified to meet more precisely the needs of the parties. For example, parties may give the neutral adviser the authority to settle the case if the representatives cannot come to a settlement agreement after a certain period of time.

EARLY NEUTRAL CASE EVALUATION

With *early neutral case evaluation,* the parties select a neutral third party and explain their respective positions to this neutral, who then evaluates the strengths and weaknesses of the case. The parties use this evaluation to reach a settlement. Eighteen federal district courts currently use early neutral case evaluation.[23]

PRIVATE TRIALS

Several states now allow **private trials,** an ADR method in which a referee is selected and paid by the disputing parties to offer a legally binding judgment in a dispute. The referees do not have to have any specific training; however, because retired judges often serve as referees, this method is often referred to as "rent-a-judge."

Generally, a private trial occurs after a case has been filed in district or state court. After the parties have engaged in discovery and developed their positions, the parties may choose to participate in a private trial. The parties would typically notify the trial judge overseeing their case that they are participating in a private trial. The disputing parties determine the time and place of the trial and conduct the trial in private to ensure confidentiality. The referee writes a report stating the findings of fact and the conclusions of the law. This

[23] Michael H. Diamant et al., "Strategies for Mediation, Arbitration, and Other Forms of Alternative Dispute Resolution," SK074 ALI-ABA 205 (2005), citing the CPR Institute for Dispute Resolution, www.cprador.org.

global context

ADR in Japan

Some judges, lawyers, and politicians in the United States advocate the adoption of Japan's ADR techniques into the U.S. judiciary system. The techniques come in three forms: compromise, conciliation, and arbitration.

Compromise (wakai) is defined as a contractual agreement between parties that becomes the basis for a voluntary settlement. Due to the voluntary nature, no compromise is possible if one party does not wish to settle. Compromise may be proposed at three distinct times. First, a simple compromise may be reached before the initiation of a suit. Second, after initiation, but before litigation, the parties may appear in court and present a compromise. Such a compromise is legally binding on both parties. Third, parties may compromise during litigation, which is when most compromises occur. It has been estimated that nearly one-third of all disputes are settled using compromise.

The second ADR technique used in Japan is *conciliation (chotei)*. Conciliation, reaching compromise through a third party's intervention, has been a part of Japanese culture for hundreds of years. In modern times, conciliation committees consist of one judge and two appointed members of the community. Acceptance of the committee's recommendation is not necessary, but if the parties wish to concede, the recommendation has the force of a judgment.

The final type of ADR is *arbitration (chusai)*. The arbitration procedure in Japan is markedly similar to that in the United States. A two or three judge panel reaches a recommendation that is a binding decision.

The success and popularity of all three types of ADR in Japan is attributed to the attitudes of citizens. People in Japan are reluctant to bring a lawsuit against a fellow citizen. To them, using ADR is a less brash way to resolve a dispute than suing someone outright. Obviously, this attitude is quite distinct from that of the American legal culture.

report is filed with the trial judge; however, if any party is dissatisfied with the resolution of the case, the party can request a trial before a trial court judge. If this request is denied, the party can appeal the decision of the referee.

Recently, private firms have started to offer private jury trials. The jurors are hired by the private firms and are often better educated than typical jurors and have served in multiple private jury trials. Many scholars criticize the typical jury because they believe that such a jury is unable to accurately fulfill its role as fact finder. Thus, offering a better-educated, experienced jury helps assuage criticisms of the jury yet offers the advantage of judgment by a jury of peers.

The private trial has been criticized for several reasons. First, scholars argue that use of the private trial could lead to a two-tiered system of justice. Those who have financial resources can afford a private trial that is much faster and cheaper than litigation, while those who are lacking resources are forced to use the slower public system. Second, private trials, like arbitration, have been criticized because they allow disputing parties to "hide" the dispute from the public.

Court-Annexed ADR

The 1998 Alternative Dispute Resolution Act required that in all district courts, civil litigants must "consider the use of an alternative dispute resolution process at an appropriate stage in the litigation." However, each district court can decide whether to *require* ADR. Some courts mandate certain forms of ADR, while other courts make ADR completely voluntary. Some simply mandate that all potential litigants be informed about alternatives to litigation. Some courts refer almost all civil cases to ADR, while others refer cases according to subject matter.

Mediation is the primary ADR process used in federal district courts. In the federal system, most of the district courts and almost all the circuit courts have mediation programs using judges or lawyers as mediators. Mediation programs are also under way in more than one-third of the state courts and in many bankruptcy courts. However, the "mandatory" component is not necessary to move cases to arbitration or mediation; 580 cases were voluntarily mediated in the Northern District of Texas in 1996.[24] Between 1995 and 2005, mediators for the Third Circuit conducted mediations in 3,316 cases and settled 1,240 cases.[25]

The district courts vary greatly in terms of which ADR methods are approved. For example, in the Northern District Court of Alabama, each judge conducts an ADR evaluation conference to determine whether a case would be appropriate for ADR. The case could be either arbitrated or mediated. In contrast, in the Northern District of California, arbitration, mediation, early neutral evaluation, and settlement conferences have been approved for use, and approximately 43 percent of parties choose mediation.[26] The ADR staff of the Northern District of California also works with parties to structure a nonbinding summary bench or jury trial. The judicial officer may order a nonbinding arbitration to all simple contract and tort cases under $100,000.

Moreover, some courts use ADR to resolve particular disputes within a case. For example, some judges appoint special masters or discovery masters to assist in resolving complex disputes. The special master may mediate discovery disputes within the case and make discovery rulings if the parties cannot resolve the disputes. A judge may also be creative in employing ADR methods to resolve discovery disputes. When the parties could not agree to a location for a deposition, a Florida district court judge created a new form of ADR technique by ordering the parties to "convene at a neutral site agreeable to both parties. If counsel cannot agree on a neutral site, they shall meet on the front steps of the [courthouse]. Each lawyer shall be entitled to be accompanied by one paralegal who shall act as an attendant and witness. At that time and location, counsel shall engage in one (1) game of 'rock, paper, scissors.' The winner of this engagement shall be entitled to select the location for the 30(b)(6) deposition. . . ."[27]

Appellate courts also use ADR techniques. All 13 appellate courts have created programs to help parties resolve issues on appeal. These programs typically encourage mediation. For example, the Tenth Circuit's mediation office may schedule a mandatory settlement conference for any civil case on its docket. Once the conference is scheduled, the parties are required to participate. The purpose of the conference is to explore the possibility of settlement.

Use of ADR in International Disputes

Think, for a moment, how difficult litigation would be for an international dispute. Where would the case be heard? Who would decide the case? What kinds of awards would be offered? Because these questions are difficult to answer in the global context, ADR is favored over litigation. For example, the European Union has been considering a directive that would offer mediation as a dispute resolution option for companies doing business in Europe.[28]

[24] Elizabeth Plapinger and Donna Steinstra, *ADR and Settlement in the Federal District Courts: A Sourcebook for Judges and Lawyers* (Federal Judicial Center and CPR Institute for Dispute Resolution, 1996), p. 6.

[25] William F. James, "Alternate Dispute Resolution and Mediation Resolves Disputes More Effectively and Efficiently," *Missouri Lawyers Weekly,* July 3, 2006.

[26] Justin Scheck, "The Option to Be Heard," *The Recorder,* January 2, 2007, p. 7.

[27] *Avista Management, Inc. v. Wausau Underwriters Ins. Co.,* Case No. 6:05-cv-1430-Orl-31JGG, District Court for the Middle District of Florida, (Order of June 6, 2006).

[28] C. Mark Baker and Aníbal M. Sabater, "Continental Drift: The European Union Tries to Warm Up to ADR, but Its Embrace Is Tentative, at Best," *National Law Journal.,* November 27, 2006, p. 14.

Over 100 countries now belong to the United Nations Convention on the Recognition and Enforcement of Foreign Arbitral Awards, otherwise known as the New York Convention. This treaty ensures that an arbitration award will be enforced by countries that are parties to the treaty. There are three defenses to lack of enforcement of the arbitration award. First, the arbitrator acted outside the scope of her or his authority when making the decision. Second, one of the parties to the agreement did not have the authority to enter into a legal contract. Third, the losing party did not receive notice of the arbitration.

Various organizations offer dispute resolution methods for international companies. These organizations include the American Arbitration Association, the International Chamber of Commerce, the United Nations Commission of International Trade Law, and the London Court of International Arbitration. The number of arbitration cases they hear each year is not insubstantial; the Arbitration Court of the International Chamber of Commerce alone heard 541 arbitration cases in 2000.[29]

The United States favors arbitration for resolution of international disputes. The *Mitsubishi* case illustrates this U.S. policy (see the Case Nugget). Similarly, given that

Case Nugget Preference for Arbitration

Mitsubishi Motors Corp. v. Soler Chrysler-Plymouth 473 U.S. 614 (1985)

Plaintiff Mitsubishi Motors was a joint-venture company formed by a Swiss and a Japanese firm to engage in the worldwide distribution of motor vehicles manufactured in the United States and bearing Mitsubishi and Chrysler trademarks. Defendant Soler Chrysler-Plymouth, a dealership incorporated in Puerto Rico, entered into a distributorship agreement with Mitsubishi that included a binding arbitration clause. Defendant Soler began to have difficulty selling the requisite number of cars, so it asked Mitsubishi to delay shipment of several orders. Defendant refused to accept liability for its failure to sell vehicles under the contract. In accordance with a binding arbitration clause in the distribution agreement, plaintiff Mitsubishi filed an action to compel arbitration. The district court ordered arbitration of all claims, including defendant's allegations of antitrust violations. The court of appeals reversed in favor of the Soler Chrysler-Plymouth. Plaintiff Mitsubishi appealed to the U.S. Supreme Court.

The Supreme Court considered whether an American court could enforce an agreement to resolve antitrust claims by arbitration when that agreement arises from an international transaction. The Supreme Court found that the liberal policy favoring arbitration agreements in the Arbitration Act "creates a body of federal substantive law establishing and regulating the duty to honor an agreement to arbitrate." The Supreme Court concluded that "concerns of international comity, respect for the capacities of foreign and transnational tribunals, and sensitivity to the need of the international commercial system for predictability in the resolution of dispute" required that the Court enforce the parties' agreement.

The Supreme Court decided in favor of Mitsubishi, requiring "this representative of the American business community to honor its bargain" by holding the agreement to arbitrate enforceable.

[29] Emmanuel Gaillard, "The New ADR Rules of the International Chamber of Commerce," *New York University Law Journal*, October 10, 2001, p. 3.

arbitration in Japan and China has become increasingly popular, the Japan Commercial Arbitration Association (JCAA) and the China International Economic and Trade Arbitration Commission (CIETAC) have revised their rules to encourage the filing of international arbitration cases in Japan.[30]

CASE OPENER WRAP-UP

Hooters

The District Court of Virginia denied Hooters' petition to compel arbitration. Hooters appealed to the Fourth Circuit Court of Appeals, which likewise refused to enforce the arbitration agreement. The court held that although an agreement to arbitrate sexual harassment claims is generally enforceable, the employer in this particular case promulgated "egregiously unfair" arbitration rules that called into question its contractual obligation to draft the arbitration rules in good faith.[31] The court found the arbitration rules so one-sided that it concluded, "Their only possible purpose is to undermine the neutrality of the proceeding." Thus, when employers create mandatory arbitration agreements, they should consider the principles of fairness when drafting these agreements.

Although the procedures that turned the arbitration proceeding into a one-sided affair clearly need to be redrafted, Hooters did do some things well. For example, it clearly stipulated in the agreement exactly which claims were going to be arbitrated, thereby giving employees full notice of the rights they were giving up. It also gave employees five days to think about signing the agreement. Had they provided full details of the arbitration procedures, employees would have had time to review and consider the contents of the agreement.

Summary

Primary Forms of Alternative Dispute Resolution	*Negotiation:* An informal bargaining process, with or without lawyers, to try to solve a dispute. *Arbitration:* An ADR method in which a neutral third party (known as the arbitrator) hears both parties' cases and renders a binding decision. *Summary jury trial:* An abbreviated trial that leads to a nonbinding jury verdict. *Minitrial:* An ADR method in which a neutral adviser oversees presentation of the dispute, with the settlement authority residing with the senior executives of the disputing corporations.
Other ADR Methods	*Early neutral case evaluation:* An ADR method in which parties independently explain their positions to a neutral third party who evaluates the strengths and weaknesses of the case. This evaluation guides them in their settlement. *Private trial:* A trial in which the disputing parties select and pay a referee to provide a legally binding judgment in a dispute.
Court-Annexed ADR	Programs whereby courts encourage or mandate that parties use some form of ADR before they bring a dispute to trial.
Use of ADR in International Disputes	ADR is favored in international disputes.

[30] Melanie Ries and Bryant Woo, "International Arbitration in Japan & China: A Review of the Revised Arbitration Rules of the JCAA and CIETAC," *Dispute Resolution Journal* 61 (November 2006–January 2007), p. 63.

[31] *Hooters of America, Inc. v. Phillips,* 173 F.3d 933 (4th Cir.1999).

Point / Counterpoint

Binding arbitration clauses are often included in consumer contracts and even in consumer bills. For example, if you open a credit card account, the terms and conditions of the credit application will likely require that you submit any dispute you have to binding arbitration.

Should Companies Be Permitted to Include Binding Arbitration Clauses In Consumer Contracts?

Yes	No
Arbitration is a much faster way to resolve a likely small dispute. Through the discovery process, a defendant could draw out a case for two to three years before the case would actually go to trial. Thus, the consumer benefits from the binding arbitration clause by forcing the defendant to resolve the dispute quickly. According to a recent study by Ernst & Young, 55 percent of consumer arbitrations were resolved in the consumer's favor.* Another study suggested that 93 percent of people who participated in arbitration thought that they were treated fairly.** Consumers receive fair and fast treatment through mandatory arbitration. Consumers have a choice as to whether to purchase a good or service, and in some cases the purchase may include a requirement on how disputes will be resolved. If a consumer is opposed to a mandatory arbitration clause, the consumer can purchase the good or service from another provider. In conclusion, companies should be permitted to include binding arbitration clauses in their consumer contracts.	Arbitration may require that the consumer pay more up-front costs to begin the dispute resolution process. For example, the consumer may have to pay for the costs of the arbitrator. To file a complaint, a consumer has to pay filing fees only, which cost around $150. To file a claim through the American Arbitration Association, a consumer has to pay between $500 and $1,000, and the consumer is required to advance the arbitrator's fees. Many consumers are not likely to read all the fine print when applying for a credit card or purchasing a service. A consumer has no bargaining power to remove a mandatory arbitration clause from the contract; consequently, the consumer has no choice. It is unfair to force a consumer to submit a dispute to arbitration when she or he has no power to bargain regarding that aspect of the sales or service contract. Finally, because arbitration is secret, a company can "hide" its disputes from the general public. The public exposure associated with lawsuits encourages companies to better respond to and resolve disputes. In conclusion, consumers are harmed more than helped by binding arbitration clauses in consumer contracts.

*Ernst & Young, Outcomes of Arbitration: An Empirical Study of Consumer Lending Cases, *available at* http://www.adrforum.com/rcontrol/documents/ResearchStudiesAndStatistics/2005ErnstAndYoung.pdf.

**Report To The Securities And Exchange Commission Regarding Arbitrator Conflict Disclosure Requirements In NASD And NYSE Securities Arbitrations, *available at* http://www.nyse.com/pdfs/arbconflict.pdf.

Questions & Problems

1. What are the advantages and disadvantages of ADR?
2. How is mediation similar to arbitration?
3. When will a court overturn an arbitrator's decision?

4. How do you secure arbitration as a means of resolving a dispute?
5. Why is a minitrial sometimes described as a combination of other forms of ADR?
6. What type of ADR is preferred for resolving international disputes?
7. General Dynamics sent out a companywide e-mail to its employees announcing a policy requiring arbitration of employment disputes. Some time after the e-mail was sent, an employee filed a lawsuit arguing that he was fired because of a disability. General Dynamics argued that the employee should be required to arbitrate his claim under the new company policy. Do you think the court required that the employee arbitrate his claim? Why? [*Campbell v. General Dynamics* (D. Mass. 2004).]
8. Plaintiffs, members of the International Brotherhood of Teamsters, Local 30, sued the Turnpike Commission, arguing that the commission was violating the Fair Labor Standards Act (FLSA), by imposing a fluctuating-hours method of compensation on the plaintiffs. The grievance first went to mediation; when this process was unsuccessful, the lawsuit was filed. Plaintiffs sought to introduce evidence of statements made by one of the commission's attorneys during depositions taken for and introduced in the mediation. Plaintiffs sought to introduce the evidence on the grounds that it was necessary for them to establish their retaliation claim under the FLSA. Defendants argued that the statements, which were made for the purpose of furthering the mediation process, should not be admissible in court. How do you believe the court ruled in this case, and why? [*Patsy B. Sheldone et al. v. Pennsylvania Turnpike Commission,* 48 Fed. R. Serv. 3d 943 (2001).]
9. Adams, an African-American, applied for a position with Frank's as an executive assistant in the company's Detroit, Michigan, facility. Before it would consider Adams for the position, however, Frank's required that Adams complete and sign an application form that provided for compulsory arbitration of any and all employment claims. Specifically, by signing the form, applicants averred:

   > I understand and agree that any claim I may wish to file against the Company or any of its employees or agents relative to my employment or termination of employment (including but not limited to any claim for any tort, discrimination, breach of contract, violation of public policy or statutory claim) must be filed no more than six months after either occurrence of which I am complaining or the termination of my employment, whichever occurs first. I specifically agree not to commence any claim more than six months after the date of termination of my employment and waive any statutes of limitation to the contrary. Any and all claims will be submitted for binding and final arbitration before the American Arbitration Association; arbitration will be the exclusive remedy for any and all claims unless prohibited by applicable law.

   Frank's hired Adams as an executive assistant to Cohen. Five months later Frank's replaced Cohen with Carol Cox, who is white. Cox created an executive administrative assistant position and did not hire Adams for the position, claiming that she needed to hire a more highly qualified individual for the job. Cox hired Lorraine Kryszak, an outside applicant, who is also white. Adams filed a complaint with the EEOC alleging that Frank's bypassed her for promotion to executive administrative assistant because of her race. She subsequently resigned.

   The EEOC investigated the matter and issued a determination that concluded that Frank's had bypassed Adams for promotion because of her race. The EEOC subsequently filed suit in the district court, alleging that Frank's had engaged in unlawful employment practices by (1) bypassing Adams for promotion to executive administrative assistant because of her race and (2) requiring that Adams and other applicants sign and comply with an application for employment that requires arbitration of statutory rights afforded them by Title VII.

In its complaint, the EEOC requested (1) a permanent injunction enjoining Frank's from engaging in employment discrimination on the basis of race; (2) a permanent injunction enjoining Frank's from requiring that prospective applicants or employees sign an arbitration agreement limiting the right to sue under Title VII; (3) an order requiring that Frank's institute and carry out policies, practices, and programs providing equal employment opportunities to African-Americans.

The district court declared the arbitration provision in the employment application enforceable, in light of *Gilmer v. Interstate/Johnson Lane Corp.;* held that the EEOC was bound by Adams's agreement to arbitrate in its effort to bring an employment discrimination claim on her behalf; and concluded that while, as a general principle, the EEOC could sue for injunctive relief on behalf of a class of individuals, it could not do so in this case because it had not identified a class of individuals that suffered discrimination on the basis of race under Frank's employment. The EEOC appealed. What do you think the outcome of the appeal was, and why? [*EEOC v. Frank's Nursery & Crafts,* 79 Fair Emp. Cases (BNA) (1999).]

10. The Sacharow brothers were the executors of their deceased father's estate. The brothers filed a statement of claim with the National Association of Securities Dealers (NASD) against Smith Barney in 1994. They alleged that Smith Barney, through one of its brokers, made risky and speculative investments that resulted in significant losses in their father's investment account. The brothers argued that their father was unable to monitor his account because of his health status.

The father's customer agreement with Smith Barney contained a clause that mandated arbitration. While Smith Barney agreed that there originally was an agreement to arbitrate, the company argued that because the transactions that the Sacharow brothers disputed occurred six years prior to the filing of the claim, their claim was ineligible according to the six-year eligibility provision of the arbitration codes of the National Association of Securities Dealers and the New York Stock Exchange. The brothers argued that arbitrators, instead of courts, should determine whether potential claims are eligible for arbitration. Smith Barney highlighted the fact that many securities firms have been receiving injunctions to prevent customers from arbitrating claims older than six years from the date of filling. Why did the New York Court of Appeals rule in favor of the brothers? [*In the Matter of Smith Barney Shearson Inc. et al. v. Jeffrey S. Sacharow et al.,* 91 N.Y.2d 39 (1997).]

11. Miller injured her arm while at work at Public Storage Management. She took a medical leave for eight months. At the end of the leave, she was unable to return to work and was fired. Miller filed suit against Public Storage Management for violation of the Americans with Disabilities Act. Miller's employment contract included an arbitration clause mandating that any controversy over employment discrimination be resolved through arbitration. How did the court of appeals rule? Why? [*Miller v. Public Storage Management, Inc.,* 121 F.3d 215 (5th Cir. 1997).]

12. When Matthew Shankle was hired by B-G Maintenance Management (B-G), he signed an employment agreement that included a binding arbitration clause. This clause stated that any disputes between Shankle and B-G were to be resolved through arbitration and that Shankle would "be responsible for one-half of the arbitrator's fees, and the company is responsible for the remaining half." Shankle was fired, and he brought suit against B-G for employment discrimination. B-G moved to mandate arbitration. The arbitrator required a $6,000 deposit. The district court ruled in Shankle's favor by refusing to compel arbitration because the fee-splitting requirement was held to be unenforceable. B-G appealed. Did the appellate court agree with Shankle? Why or why not? [*Shankle v. B-G Maintenance Management of Colorado,* 163 F.3d 1230 (10th Cir. 1999).]

13. The Fair Labor Standards Act (FLSA) requires payment of overtime to employees who work more than 40 hours a week unless the employee is in an "administrative" or "executive" position. Delfina Montes worked more than 40 hours a week for Shearson Lehman, and the firm did not pay her overtime on the grounds that she held an administrative position that was exempt from the FLSA overtime requirement. An arbitrator hearing this case decided in favor of Shearson Lehman. Montes petitioned the district court to vacate the arbitration board's decision because Shearson's attorney made the following statements before the arbitration board: "[Y]ou as an arbitrator are not guided strictly to follow case precedent"; "You have to decide whether you're going to follow the statutes that have been presented to you, or whether you will do . . . what is right and just and equitable in this case." Montes argued that the arbitrator could not simply ignore the law when arbitrating a case, which was what she felt Shearson's attorneys had asked the arbitrator to do.

Montes's petition was denied by the district court. How do you believe the court of appeals ruled in this case? Why? [*Delfina Montes v. Shearson Lehman Brothers, Inc.,* 128 F.3d 1456 (11th Cir. 1997).]

14. Plaintiffs Armendariz and Olague-Rodgers were employed by defendant Foundation Health Psychcare Services, Inc. On June 20, 1996, they were told they were being terminated because their positions were being eliminated. They sued the defendant for wrongful termination, arguing that they had been fired because of their perceived and/or actual sexual orientation.

Both had signed employment agreements that contained binding arbitration clauses requiring that they submit all employment disputes to binding arbitration and limiting their remedies related to employment claims to "a sum equal to the wages I would have earned from the date of any discharge until the date of the arbitration award." The agreement further provided that the plaintiff would not be entitled to any other remedy at law or equity.

On what grounds do you believe that the California State Supreme Court ultimately refused to enforce the binding arbitration clause? [*Marybeth Armendariz et al. v. Foundation Health Psychcare Services, Inc.,* 6 P.3d 669 (2000).]

15. Mr. Gwin, a homeowner, and Allied-Bruce-Termix, a termite exterminator, entered into a lifetime termite control contract regarding protection of Mr. Gwin's house from termites. In the contract, they agreed that all disputes would be settled by arbitration. Mr. Dobson, another individual, purchased Mr. Gibbs' house and took over the contract with the exterminator. When Allied-Bruce-Termix did not meet the terms of the contract, Dobson filed suit in court. The state supreme court ruled in favor of Dobson, stating that the Federal Arbitration Act did not apply to the contract because the contract did not involve an interstate transaction. The case was appealed to the U.S. Supreme Court. Why did the Court overrule the state supreme court? [*Allied-Bruce-Termix Cos. v. Dobson,* 513 U.S. 265 (1995).]

16. Correll entered into an employment agreement with Distinctive Dental Service (DDS). This agreement stated that Correll could not directly or indirectly engage in business with any competitor located within 7 miles of DDS. Furthermore, the employment agreement included a clause providing that any dispute between Correll and DDS should be settled by arbitration. When Correll's wife, who was also a dentist, went to work for a competitor within 7 miles of DDS, Correll was fired. Correll filed a suit against DDS for marital-status discrimination, but DDS demanded arbitration. The district court ruled in Correll's favor by refusing to enforce the arbitration clause. DDS appealed. What did the appellate court decide? [*Correll v. Distinctive Dental Services,* 594 N.W.2d 222 (Minn. Ct. App. 1999).]

Looking for more review material?

The Online Learning Center at **www.mhhe.com/kubasek1e** contains this chapter's "Assignment on the Internet" and also a list of URLs for more information entitled "On the Internet." Find both of them in the Student Center portion of the OLC, along with quizzes and other helpful materials.

Constitutional Principles

CASE OPENER

Regulations on Interstate Wine Sales: A Violation of the Commerce Clause?

Michigan and New York passed state statutes allowing in-state, but not out-of-state, wineries to sell wine directly to state residents. The statutes permitted out-of-state wine wholesalers, on the other hand, to sell to state residents. Thus, out-of-state wineries wishing to sell wine to Michigan and New York residents had to sell through a wholesaler. Because many small wineries produce insufficient quantities of wine to sell via wholesaler, however, the statutes effectively prohibited them from selling to Michigan and New York residents.

Michigan residents and an out-of-state winery challenged the statutes as violating the commerce clause of the U.S. Constitution. Michigan and New York argued that the Twenty-First Amendment protected the statutes. The Twenty-First Amendment states that "[t]he transportation or importation [of intoxicating liquors] into any state . . . for delivery or use therein, in violation of the laws thereof, is . . . prohibited." Moreover, the states argued that the statutes advanced legitimate public purposes: curbing wine sales to minors via the Internet, stemming tax evasion on wine sales, protecting public health and safety, and ensuring regulatory accountability.

The district court agreed with the states' argument, but on appeal, the appellate court ruled that the statutes violated the commerce clause. Michigan and New York then appealed the case to the U.S. Supreme Court.[1]

[1] *Granholm v. Heald,* 125 S. Ct. 1885 (2005).

CHAPTER 5

1. Do you think the Michigan and New York statutes violate the commerce clause? Why?
2. Would your answer to the previous question change if the state statutes regulated the sale of corn instead of wine? Why or why not?

The Wrap-Up at the end of the chapter will answer these questions.

Learning Objectives

After reading this chapter, you will be able to answer the following questions:

1. What is federalism?
2. How does the U.S. government's system of checks and balances operate?
3. What effects does the commerce clause have on the government's regulation of business?
4. How does the Bill of Rights protect the citizens of the United States?

The U.S. Constitution sets forth the framework of our nation's government; it establishes a system of government that divides power between the federal government and the states. This system of government provides the focus for this chapter.

In this chapter we examine the constitutional provisions that affect business. Then we turn our focus to the primary source of the federal government's authority to regulate business: the commerce clause. We next examine the federal government's authority to tax and spend. Finally, in the last part of the chapter, we focus on how several amendments to the Constitution affect business.

The U.S. Constitution

The U.S. Constitution establishes a system of government based on the principle of **federalism,** according to which the authority to govern is divided between federal and state governments. According to the Tenth Amendment to the Constitution, all powers that the Constitution neither gives exclusively to the federal government nor takes from the states are reserved for the states. Because the federal government has only those powers granted to it by the Constitution, federal legislation that affects business must be based on an expressed constitutional grant of authority.

In addition to allocating authority between state and federal governments, the Constitution allocates the power of the federal government among the three branches of government. The first three articles of the Constitution establish three independent branches of the federal government: the legislative, executive, and judicial branches. The Constitution ensures that each branch maintains a separate sphere of power to prevent any one branch from obtaining undue power and monopolizing control of government.

The Constitution also establishes a system of *checks and balances.* Each branch's powers keep the other branches from dominating the government. For example, Congress, the legislative or lawmaking branch, has the power to enact legislation, but the president can veto a law that Congress passes. The legislature, however, can overturn a presidential veto with a two-thirds vote of the members of Congress. And if Congress passes a bill and the president signs it, the judiciary can strike it down as unconstitutional. Figure 5-1 illustrates the system of checks and balances in more detail.

JUDICIAL REVIEW

Although the Constitution does not explicitly allow courts to review legislative and executive actions to determine whether they are constitutional, early common law established this process, which is known as **judicial review.** In the landmark 1803 U.S. Supreme Court case *Marbury v. Madison,*[2] Chief Justice John Marshall wrote for the majority:

> [I]f a law be in opposition to the constitution; if both the law and the constitution apply to a particular case, so that the court must either decide that case [conforms] to the law, disregarding the constitution; or [conforms] to the constitution, disregarding the law; the court must determine which of these conflicting rules governs the case. This is of the very essence of judicial duty.

Judicial review also allows courts to review the constitutionality of lower courts' decisions.

[2] 5 U.S. 137 (1803).

connecting to the core

Accounting

The concept of separation of powers in the federal government can be analogized to a concept taught in accounting: internal controls. Internal controls are the policies and procedures used to increase the likelihood that the organization's objectives will be met. Internal controls, like our system of checks and balances, require a separation of duties, with the functions of authorizing, recording, and custody to be performed by different individuals. This separation of duties minimizes the likelihood that an illegal action will occur because there is more than one individual responsible for carrying out a transaction. Each party's behavior is checked by that of the other employees.

Source: T. Edmonds, F. McNair, E. Milam, and P. Olds, *Fundamental Financial Accounting Concepts* (New York: McGraw Hill, 2000), pp. 259–260.

The Supremacy Clause and Federal Preemption

The **supremacy clause,** located in Article V of the Constitution, provides that the Constitution, laws, and treaties of the United States constitute the supreme law of the land, "any Thing in the Constitution or Laws of any State to the Contrary notwithstanding." Any state or local law that directly conflicts with the Constitution, federal laws, or treaties is void.

Figure 5-1 The System of Checks and Balances

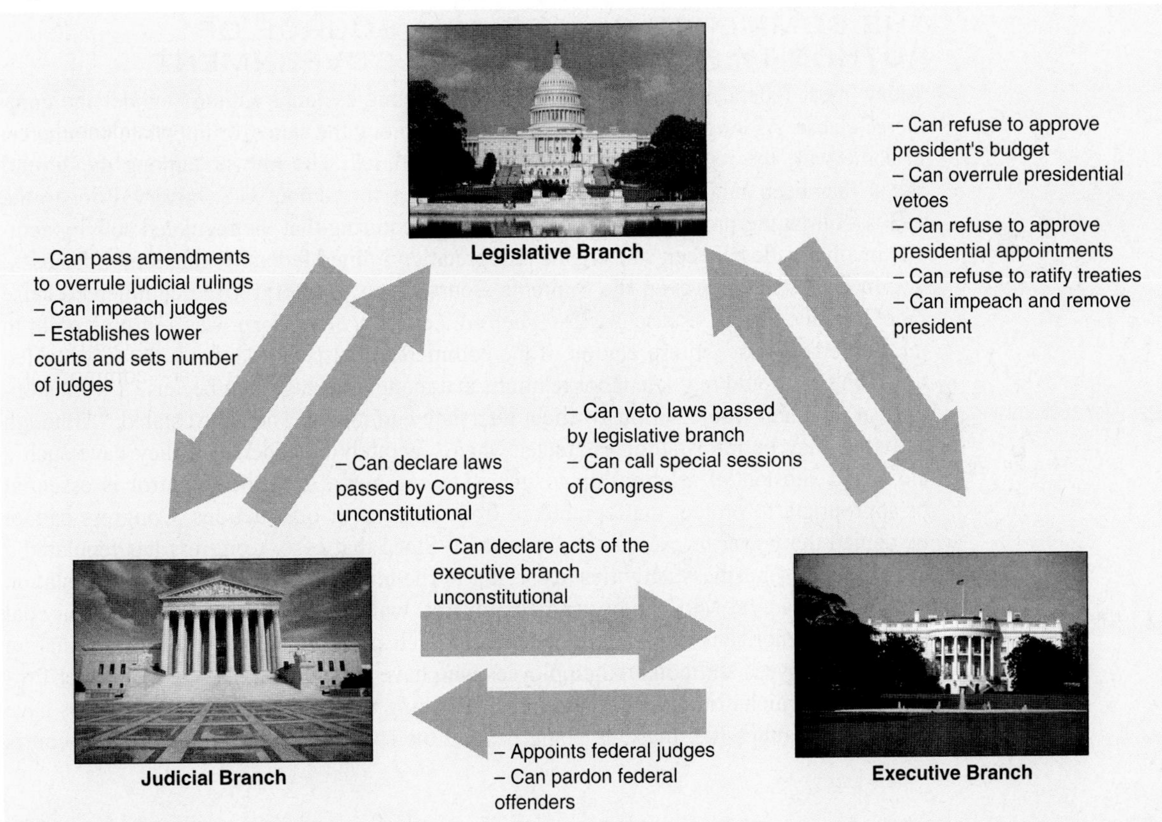
Legislative Branch
– Can refuse to approve president's budget
– Can overrule presidential vetoes
– Can refuse to approve presidential appointments
– Can refuse to ratify treaties
– Can impeach and remove president
– Can pass amendments to overrule judicial rulings
– Can impeach judges
– Establishes lower courts and sets number of judges
– Can veto laws passed by legislative branch
– Can call special sessions of Congress
– Can declare laws passed by Congress unconstitutional
– Can declare acts of the executive branch unconstitutional
Judicial Branch
Executive Branch
– Appoints federal judges
– Can pardon federal offenders

Federal laws include rules passed by federal administrative agencies. For example, the Federal Aviation Administration has banned the use of cell phones on airplanes. If a Missouri law permitted cell phone usage on airplanes, it would be unconstitutional according to the supremacy clause.

In some areas, the state and federal governments have **concurrent authority**; that is, both governments have the power to regulate the same subject matter. In such cases, the states may regulate in the area as long as a person's compliance with the state regulation would not cause him or her to be in violation of a federal regulation. For example, Congress has established a number of environmental standards, but some states have passed even more protective standards.

Sometimes, however, in areas where the state and federal governments have concurrent authority, the federal government can decide to regulate that area exclusively. In such a situation, according to the doctrine of **federal preemption,** the state law is unconstitutional. To determine whether Congress intended to provide exclusive regulation, courts look to the language of the statute and transcripts of congressional hearings.

The Commerce Clause

The primary source of authority for federal regulation of business is the **commerce clause,** located in Article I, Section 8, of the Constitution. This clause states that the U.S. Congress has the power to "regulate Commerce with foreign Nations, and among the several States, and with the Indian Tribes." This allocation of authority simultaneously empowers the federal government and restricts the power of state governments.

THE COMMERCE CLAUSE AS A SOURCE OF AUTHORITY FOR THE FEDERAL GOVERNMENT

Today, most federal regulations are exercises of congressional authority under the commerce clause. As long as a law affects commerce among the states, or interstate commerce, in some way, the regulation is generally constitutional. The phrase "among the several states" has been subject to changing interpretations throughout U.S. history. Prior to the 1930s, courts interpreted the clause very strictly, requiring that the regulated activity actually involve trade between states. This interpretation limited federal regulation of business.

In the 1930s, however, the Supreme Court began to interpret the commerce clause more broadly. The 1937 case *NLRB v. Jones & Laughlin Steel Corp.* was a turning point in the Supreme Court's interpretation of the commerce clause. In that case, the Court ruled that Congress could regulate labor relations at a manufacturing plant because a work stoppage at the plant would seriously affect interstate commerce. The Court stated, "Although activities may be intrastate in character when separately considered, if they have such a close and substantial relationship to interstate commerce that their control is essential or appropriate to protect that commerce from burdens or obstructions, Congress cannot be denied the power to exercise that control."[3] Since that case, Congress has regulated a broad range of business activities according to the commerce clause, through legislation such as the Federal Mine Safety and Health Act, which sets standards for safety in coal mines; the Americans with Disabilities Act, which prohibits firms from discriminating against employees and potential employees who have disabilities; and the Consumer Protection Act, which criminalizes certain loan-sharking activities. Although businesses have challenged statutes like these as being beyond the scope of congressional power, courts

[3] *NLRB v. Jones & Laughlin Steel Corp.*, 301 U.S. 1 (1937).

have upheld the statutes as valid exercises of congressional authority according to the commerce clause.[4]

The 1995 case *United States v. Lopez,*[5] however, marked another significant change in the Supreme Court's interpretation of the commerce clause. In *Lopez,* the Court ruled that Congress had exceeded its commerce clause authority when it passed the Gun-Free School Zone Act, a law banning the possession of guns within 1,000 feet of any school. In its ruling, the Court said that Congress could not regulate in an area that had "nothing to do with commerce, or any sort of economic enterprise."

Case 5-1 illustrates how the Supreme Court applies the commerce clause to determine the constitutionality of congressional regulations.

THE COMMERCE CLAUSE AS A RESTRICTION ON STATE AUTHORITY

The federal government's authority to regulate interstate commerce sometimes conflicts with the states' authority to regulate intrastate commerce. Courts have attempted to resolve this conflict by distinguishing between regulations of commerce and regulations under states' police power. **Police power** consists of the residual powers retained by each state to safeguard the health and welfare of its citizenry. Typical exercises of a state's police power include state criminal laws, building codes, zoning laws, sanitation standards for restaurants, and regulations for the practice of medicine.

Sometimes a state's use of its police power affects interstate commerce. If the purpose of a state law is to regulate interstate commerce or to discriminate against interstate commerce, the law is usually unconstitutional. Likewise, if a law substantially interferes with interstate commerce, it is generally unconstitutional. This restriction on states' authority to pass laws that substantially affect interstate commerce is called the **dormant commerce clause.**

Most cases are not so simple, however, and courts must balance the states' interest in protecting their citizens against the impact on interstate commerce. In balancing these competing interests, a court generally asks whether the state regulation is rationally related to a legitimate state end. If it is, the court then asks whether the regulatory burden imposed on interstate commerce is outweighed by the state's interest in enforcing the legislation. The court may also inquire whether there is a less drastic alternative available to attain the legitimate state purpose. In the opening vignette, it is difficult to see how the state's interest in protecting the public's health is rationally related to a regulatory scheme banning direct sales of wine from out of state. There is nothing inherently more harmful about wine produced out of state, and there is no reason why more wine would be purchased from out-of-state venders.

Although the supremacy clause establishes the sovereignty of federal law, courts generally presume that laws passed in accordance with states' police power are valid. For example, the city of Chicago passed an ordinance banning spray paint in the city as a means to reduce graffiti. Paint manufacturers challenged the legislation as a violation of the dormant commerce clause, but the U.S. court of appeals upheld the legislation.[6] The legislation did not treat paint from out-of-state manufacturers any differently than paint from in-state manufacturers; it had been demonstrated that limiting the availability of

[4] See *U.S. v. Lake,* 985 F.2d 265 (1995); *International House of Pancakes v. Theodore Pinnock,* 844 F. Supp. 574 (1993); and *Perez v. United States,* 402 U.S. 146 (1971).

[5] 514 U.S. 549 (1995).

[6] *Nat'l Paint & Coatings Ass'n v. Chi.,* 803 F. Supp. 135 (1992).

CASE 5-1 CHRISTY BRZONKALA v. ANTONIO J. MORRISON ET AL.

UNITED STATES SUPREME COURT
120 S. CT. 1740 (2000)

Petitioner Christy Brzonkala met respondents Antonio Morrison and James Crawford at a campus party at Virginia Polytechnic Institute (Virginia Tech), where they were all students. At the party, the respondents allegedly assaulted and raped her. According to Brzonkala, during the months following the rape, Morrison made boasting, debasing, and vulgar remarks in the dormitory's dining room about what he would do to women. Brzonkala alleged she become severely emotionally disturbed and depressed as a result of this attack and Morrison's subsequent behavior. Consequently, she had to seek assistance from a university psychiatrist, who prescribed antidepressant medication. Shortly thereafter, she stopped attending classes and withdrew from the university.

Brzonkala filed a complaint against the respondents under the university's Sexual Assault Policy. Morrison was initially found guilty and suspended for two semesters, but his punishment was ultimately set aside.

She then sued Morrison, Crawford, and Virginia Tech in federal court, alleging, among other claims, that Morrison's and Crawford's attack violated the Violence Against Women Act. The respondents moved to dismiss the complaint on the grounds that it failed to state a claim and that the Act's (§ 13981's) civil remedy was unconstitutional.

The District Court found that Brzonkala's complaint stated a claim against the respondents under § 13981, but dismissed the complaint because it concluded that Congress lacked constitutional authority to enact § 13981's civil remedy. The United States Court of Appeals, by a divided vote, affirmed the District Court's conclusion. Brzonkala appealed.

CHIEF JUSTICE REHNQUIST: . . . Section 13981 was part of the Violence Against Women Act of 1994. . . . It states that "[a]ll persons within the United States shall have the right to be free from crimes of violence motivated by gender." To enforce that right, subsection (c) declares:

"A person . . . who commits a crime of violence motivated by gender and thus deprives another of the right declared in subsection (b) of this section shall be liable to the party injured, in an action for the recovery of compensatory and punitive damages, injunctive and declaratory relief, and such other relief as a court may deem appropriate." . . .

Every law enacted by Congress must be based on one or more of its powers enumerated in the Constitution. . . . [W]e turn to the question whether § 13981 falls within Congress' power under Article I, § 8, of the Constitution. Brzonkala and the United States rely upon the third clause of the Article, which gives Congress power "[t]o regulate Commerce with foreign Nations, and among the several States, and with the Indian Tribes."

As we discussed at length in Lopez, our interpretation of the Commerce Clause has changed as our Nation has developed. . . . Lopez emphasized, however, that even under our modern, expansive interpretation of the Commerce Clause, Congress' regulatory authority is not without effective bounds.

. . . [M]odern Commerce Clause jurisprudence has "identified three broad categories of activity that Congress may regulate under its commerce power." . . . "First, Congress may regulate the use of the channels of interstate commerce." . . . "Second, Congress is empowered to regulate and protect the instrumentalities of interstate commerce, or persons or things in interstate commerce, even though the threat may come only from intrastate activities." . . . "Finally, Congress' commerce authority includes the power to regulate those activities having a substantial relation to interstate commerce, . . . i.e., those activities that substantially affect interstate commerce."

Petitioners . . . seek to sustain § 13981 as a regulation of activity that substantially affects interstate commerce. Given § 13981's focus on gender-motivated violence wherever it occurs . . . we agree that this is the proper inquiry.

Since Lopez most recently canvassed and clarified our case law governing this third category of Commerce Clause regulation, it provides the proper framework for conducting the required analysis of § 13981. In Lopez, we held that the Gun-Free School Zones Act of 1990, which made it a federal crime to knowingly possess a firearm in a school zone, exceeded Congress' authority under the Commerce Clause. Several significant considerations contributed to our decision.

First, we observed that § 922(q) was "a criminal statute that by its terms has nothing to do with 'commerce' or any sort of economic enterprise, however broadly one might define those terms." . . . [T]he pattern of analysis is clear. "Where economic activity substantially affects interstate commerce, legislation regulating that activity will be sustained."

Both petitioners and Justice Souter's dissent downplay the role that the economic nature of the regulated activity plays in our Commerce Clause analysis. But a fair reading of Lopez shows that the noneconomic, criminal nature of the conduct at issue was central to our decision in that case. . . . Lopez's review of Commerce Clause case law demonstrates that in those cases where we have sustained federal regulation of intrastate activity based upon the activity's substantial effects on interstate commerce, the activity in question has been some sort of economic endeavor.

The second consideration that we found important in analyzing § 922(q) was that

> the statute contained "no express jurisdictional element which might limit its reach to a discrete set of firearm possessions that additionally have an explicit connection with or effect on interstate commerce." Such a jurisdictional element may establish that the enactment is in pursuance of Congress' regulation of interstate commerce.

Third, we noted that neither § 922(q) " 'nor its legislative history contain[s] express congressional findings regarding the effects upon interstate commerce of gun possession in a school zone.' " . . . While "Congress normally is not required to make formal findings as to the substantial burdens that an activity has on interstate commerce," the existence of such findings may "enable us to evaluate the legislative judgment that the activity in question substantially affect[s] interstate commerce, even though no such substantial effect [is] visible to the naked eye."

Finally, our decision in Lopez rested in part on the fact that the link between gun possession and a substantial effect on interstate commerce was attenuated. The United States argued that the possession of guns may lead to violent crime, and that violent crime "can be expected to affect the functioning of the national economy in two ways. First, the costs of violent crime are substantial, and, through the mechanism of insurance, those costs are spread throughout the population. Second, violent crime reduces the willingness of individuals to travel to areas within the country that are perceived to be unsafe." The Government also argued that the presence of guns at schools poses a threat to the educational process, which in turn threatens to produce a less efficient and productive workforce, which will negatively affect national productivity and thus interstate commerce.

We rejected these "costs of crime" and "national productivity" arguments because they would permit Congress to "regulate not only all violent crime, but all activities that might lead to violent crime, regardless of how tenuously they relate to interstate commerce." We noted that, under this but-for reasoning: "Congress could regulate any activity that it found was related to the economic productivity of individual citizens: family law (including marriage, divorce, and child custody), for example. Under the[se] theories . . . , it is difficult to perceive any limitation on federal power, even in areas such as criminal law enforcement or education where States historically have been sovereign. Thus, if we were to accept the Government's arguments, we are hard pressed to posit any activity by an individual that Congress is without power to regulate."

With these principles underlying our Commerce Clause jurisprudence as reference points, the proper resolution of the present cases is clear. Gender-motivated crimes of violence are not, in any sense of the phrase, economic activity. While we need not adopt a categorical rule against aggregating the effects of any noneconomic activity in order to decide these cases, thus far in our Nation's history our cases have upheld Commerce Clause regulation of intrastate activity only where that activity is economic in nature.

Like the Gun-Free School Zones Act at issue in Lopez, § 13981 contains no jurisdictional element establishing that the federal cause of action is in pursuance of Congress' power to regulate interstate commerce.

In contrast with the lack of congressional findings that we faced in Lopez, § 13981 is supported by numerous findings regarding the serious impact that gender-motivated violence has on victims and their families. . . . But the existence of congressional findings is not sufficient, by itself, to sustain the constitutionality of Commerce Clause legislation. As we stated in Lopez, " '[S]imply because Congress may conclude that a particular activity substantially affects interstate commerce does not necessarily make it so.' " . . . Rather, "'[w]hether particular operations affect interstate commerce sufficiently to come under the constitutional power of Congress to regulate them is ultimately a judicial rather than a legislative question, and can be settled finally only by this Court.'"

In these cases, Congress' findings are substantially weakened by the fact that they rely so heavily on a method of reasoning that we have already rejected as unworkable if we are to maintain the Constitution's enumeration of powers. Congress found that gender-motivated violence affects interstate commerce "by deterring potential victims from traveling interstate, from engaging in employment in interstate business, and from transacting with business, and in places involved in interstate commerce; . . . by diminishing national productivity, increasing medical and other costs, and decreasing the supply of and the demand for interstate products." Given these findings and petitioners' arguments, the concern that we expressed in Lopez that Congress might use the Commerce Clause to completely obliterate the Constitution's distinction between national and local authority seems well founded.

The reasoning that petitioners advance seeks to follow the but-for causal chain from the initial occurrence of violent crime (the suppression of which has always been the prime object of the States' police power) to every attenuated effect upon interstate commerce. If accepted, petitioners' reasoning would allow Congress to regulate any crime as long as the nationwide, aggregated impact of that crime has substantial effects on employment, production, transit, or consumption. Indeed, if Congress may regulate gender-motivated violence, it would be able to regulate murder or any other type of violence since gender-motivated violence, as a subset of all violent crime, is certain to have lesser economic impacts than the larger class of which it is a part.

We accordingly reject the argument that Congress may regulate noneconomic, violent criminal conduct based solely on that conduct's aggregate effect on interstate commerce. The Constitution requires a distinction between what is truly national and what is truly local. . . . In recognizing this fact we preserve one of the few principles that has been consistent since the Clause was adopted. The regulation and punishment of intrastate violence that is not directed at the instrumentalities, channels, or goods involved in interstate commerce has always been the province of the States.

AFFIRMED in favor of respondents.

Dissent

JUSTICE SOUTER, with whom Justice Stevens, Justice Ginsberg, and Justice Breyer join

. . . Congress has the power to legislate with regard to activity that, in the aggregate, has a substantial effect on interstate commerce. The fact of such a substantial effect is not an issue for the courts in the first instance, but for the Congress, whose institutional capacity for gathering evidence and taking testimony far exceeds ours. By passing legislation, Congress indicates its conclusion, whether explicitly or not, that facts support its exercise of the commerce power. The business of the courts is to review the congressional assessment, not for soundness but simply for the rationality of concluding that a jurisdictional basis exists in fact. Any explicit findings that Congress chooses to make, though not dispositive of the question of rationality, may advance judicial review by identifying factual authority on which Congress relied.

One obvious difference from United States v. Lopez is the mountain of data assembled by Congress, here showing the effects of violence against women on interstate commerce. Passage of the Act in 1994 was preceded by four years of hearings, which included testimony from physicians and law professors; from survivors of rape and domestic violence; and from representatives of state law enforcement and private business. The record includes reports on gender bias from task forces in twenty-one states, and we have the benefit of specific factual findings of the eight separate Reports issued by Congress and its committees over the long course leading to enactment.

Having identified the problem of violence against women, Congress may address what it sees as the most threatening manifestation. . . . Congress found that "crimes of violence motivated by gender have a substantial adverse effect on interstate commerce, by deterring potential victims from traveling interstate, from engaging in employment in interstate business, and from transacting with business, and in places involved, in interstate commerce . . . [,] by diminishing national productivity, increasing medical and other costs, and decreasing the supply of and the demand for interstate products. . . ."

Congress thereby explicitly stated the predicate for the exercise of its Commerce Clause power. Is its conclusion irrational in view of the data amassed? True, the methodology of particular studies may be challenged, and some of the figures arrived at may be disputed. But the sufficiency of the evidence before Congress to provide a rational basis for the finding cannot seriously be questioned. . . . Indeed, the legislative record here is far more voluminous than the record compiled by Congress and found sufficient in two prior cases upholding Title II of the Civil Rights Act of 1964 against Commerce Clause challenges.

The fact that the Act does not pass muster before the Court today is therefore proof, to a degree that Lopez was not, that the Court's nominal adherence to the substantial effects test is merely that. Although a new jurisprudence has not emerged with any distinctness, it is clear that some congressional conclusions about obviously substantial, cumulative effects on commerce are being assigned lesser values than the once-stable doctrine would assign them. These devaluations are accomplished not by any express repudiation of the substantial effects test or its application through the aggregation of individual conduct, but by supplanting rational basis scrutiny with a new criterion of review.

Thus the elusive heart of the majority's analysis in these cases is its statement that Congress's findings of fact are "weakened" by the presence of a disfavored "method of reasoning." This seems to suggest that the "substantial effects" analysis is not a factual enquiry, for Congress in the first instance with subsequent judicial review looking only to the rationality of the congressional conclusion, but one of a rather different sort, dependent upon a uniquely judicial competence.

This new characterization of substantial effects has no support in our cases (the self-fulfilling prophecies of Lopez aside), least of all those the majority cites.

ETHICAL DECISION MAKING

Explain how different stakeholders would be the primary beneficiaries of the majority and minority decisions.

spray paint would decrease the amount of graffiti; and it is within the states' police power to determine that graffiti is not good for the public welfare.

Case 5-2 illustrates an attempt to challenge a state regulation on grounds that it places an undue burden on interstate commerce.

CASE 5-2 NATIONAL ELECTRICAL MANUFACTURERS ASSOCIATION v. WILLIAM H. SORRELL, ATTORNEY GENERAL OF THE STATE OF VERMONT, JOHN KASSEL ET AL.

SECOND CIRCUIT COURT OF APPEALS
53 ERC 1385 (2001)

In 1998, the Vermont Legislature enacted a statute requiring manufacturers of certain mercury-containing products (including thermostats, batteries, and lamps) to label their products and packaging to inform consumers that the products (1) contain mercury and (2) on disposal, should be recycled or disposed of as hazardous waste. The trade association of manufacturers of mercury-containing light bulbs (NEMA) brought action against state officials, seeking to have the law declared unconstitutional, and asking for a preliminary injunction to prohibit enforcement of the law. The United States District Court granted the preliminary injunction, and officials appealed.

CHIEF JUDGE JOHN M. WALKER, JR.: [1] A statute may violate the well-established "dormant" aspect of the Commerce Clause in one of two ways: it may clearly discriminate against interstate commerce, in which case it is virtually invalid per se, or even if it does not evince such discriminatory effect, it may still be unconstitutional if it imposes a burden on interstate commerce incommensurate with the local benefits secured. . . .

[2] NEMA argues that section 6621d violates the Commerce Clause in the latter manner. We disagree and thus conclude that NEMA cannot show likely success on the merits of its Commerce Clause claim.

In *Pike,* the Supreme Court adopted a balancing test to determine whether state statutes that incidentally burden interstate commerce violate the Commerce Clause. The Court held that [w]here the statute regulates even-handedly to effectuate a legitimate local public interest, and its effects on interstate commerce are only incidental, it will be upheld unless the burden imposed on such commerce is clearly excessive in relation to the putative local benefits. If a legitimate local purpose is found, then the question becomes one of degree. And the extent of the burden that will be tolerated will of course depend on the nature of the local interest involved, and on whether it could be promoted as well with a lesser impact on interstate activities.

For a state statute to run afoul of the Pike standard, the statute, at a minimum, must impose a burden on interstate commerce that is qualitatively or quantitatively different from that imposed on intrastate commerce. Under Pike, if no such unequal burden be shown, a reviewing court need not proceed further.

[3] The focus of our disparate burden analysis is a state's shifting the costs of regulation to other states. . . . Such circumstances raise the risk that state policymakers will not bear the true political costs of their decisions, because those costs will fall in some measure on the residents of other political jurisdictions. . . .

While several types of burdens on interstate commerce would qualify as "disparate" to trigger Pike balancing, NEMA cites two in particular in this case: (1) control of commerce that occurs wholly beyond the state's borders and (2) risk of imposing regulatory requirements inconsistent with those of other states. Regulations that fall into the first category may be said to have extraterritorial operation, while those in the second may be said to create interstate regulatory conflicts.

[4] A regulation may disproportionately burden interstate commerce if it has the practical effect of requiring out-of-state commerce to be conducted at the regulating state's direction.

[5] Given the manufacturing and distribution systems used by its members, NEMA argues that, if its members continue selling in Vermont, they would also be forced as a practical matter to label lamps sold in every other state. . . . We disagree. . . .

NEMA's extraterritoriality contention fails because the statute does not inescapably require manufacturers to label all lamps wherever distributed. . . . To the extent the statute may be said to "require" labels on lamps sold outside Vermont, then, it is only because the manufacturers are unwilling to modify their production and distribution systems to differentiate between Vermont-bound and non-Vermont-bound lamps. To avoid the statute's alleged impact on other states, lamp manufacturers could arrange their production and distribution processes to produce labeled lamps solely for the Vermont market and then pass much of the increased costs along to Vermont consumers in the form of higher prices. . . . To be sure, manufacturers will rarely be able to fully pass through to consumers the costs of a new tax or regulation. . . . But that manufacturers must bear some of the costs of the Vermont regulation in the form of lower profits does not cause the statute to violate the Commerce Clause. Such a burden is simply attributable to legitimate intrastate regulation.

NEMA's lament that Vermont's labeling requirement violates the Commerce Clause because it effectively forces manufacturers not to sell lamps in Vermont is nonetheless unpersuasive for three reasons. First, it is axiomatic that the increased cost of complying with a regulation may drive up the sales price of the product and thus erode demand for the product such that production becomes unprofitable. Consequently, any regulation may drive some or all producers or distributors from the regulating state. But in every such case, a decision to abandon the state's market rests entirely with individual manufacturers based on the opportunity cost of capital, their individual production costs, and what the demand in the state will bear. Because none of these variables is controlled by the state in this case, we cannot say that the choice to stay or leave has been made for manufacturers by the state legislature, as the Commerce Clause would prohibit. Although a regulation might violate the Commerce Clause by creating market incentives that encourage out-of-state manufacturers to abandon a state market while encouraging in-state manufacturers to pick up the slack, the instant regulation is evenhanded such that lamp producers both inside and outside Vermont would face the same putative need to develop separate production and distribution systems to accommodate simultaneously the Vermont market and other state markets.

Second, the manufacturers' choice to discontinue Vermont sales would not amount to a special, disproportionate injury to interstate commerce of the sort required by our precedents. If lamp manufacturers were to withdraw from the Vermont market, only Vermont residents would feel any appreciable effect, in the lost utility of mercury-bearing bulbs. Any loss felt by residents of other states would be minor by comparison.

NEMA also contends that the statute burdens interstate commerce by exposing its members to the possibility of multiple, inconsistent labeling requirements imposed by other states. A state regulation might impose a disproportionate burden on interstate commerce if the regulation is in substantial conflict with a common regulatory scheme in place in other states. . . . It is not enough to point to a risk of conflicting regulatory regimes in multiple states; there must be an actual conflict between the challenged regulation and those in place in other states. . . . No such conflict has been shown here. NEMA concedes that no other state even regulates the labeling of mercury-bearing bulbs. . . . Indeed, there is record evidence that the Vermont statute is consistent with regimes under consideration by other states. While the scope of conflict required to state a dormant Commerce Clause claim is somewhat unclear, it is clear that the present case involves no conflict whatsoever.

REVERSED in favor of Defendant, State of Vermont.

CRITICAL THINKING

Explain why you agree or disagree with the reasoning of the court in this case.

ETHICAL DECISION MAKING

Identify the primary stakeholders helped and hurt by the outcome of this case.

Taxing and Spending Powers of the Federal Government

No government can function without a source of revenue. Article I, Section 8, of the Constitution gives the federal government the "Power to lay and collect Taxes, Duties, Imports and Excises." The taxes laid by Congress, however, must be uniform across the states. In other words, the government cannot impose higher taxes on residents of one state than another.

Although tax collection allows the government to provide essential services, the government can also use taxes for other purposes. For example, to encourage the development of certain industries and discourage the development of others, the government can provide tax credits for firms entering favored industries. As long as the "motive of Congress and the effect of its legislative action are to secure revenue for the benefit of the general government,"[7] the tax is constitutional. The fact that it also has a regulatory impact does not affect the constitutionality of the tax.

[7] *J. W. Hampton Co. v. United States*, 276 U.S. 394 (1928).

e-commerce AND THE LAW

Sales Taxes on Internet Transactions?

Due to the rapid rise in Internet commerce in recent years, many states have become concerned about their ability to collect sales tax on Internet transactions. Sales taxes are a large source of revenue for state governments, but states can require that a business submit sales tax payments only if the business has a store or distribution center in the state. Otherwise, states cannot collect sales taxes, although residents are supposed to self-report the taxes.

Increased access to the Internet has led some to argue for a tax on Internet access and a sales tax on Internet purchases. Due to myriad state tax jurisdictions, however, the federal government passed a moratorium on Internet taxes until October 21, 2001, while a panel discussed the best approach to Internet tax policy.

In April 2000, the Advisory Commission on Electronic Commerce submitted its recommendations to Congress. One recommendation was to examine the "digital divide," that is, the difference in computer access between the rich and the poor. The commission also recommended an examination of the privacy implications of Internet taxation. Finally, the commission recommended that Congress implement a moratorium on international taxes and tariffs. The commission also listed its majority policy proposals. These proposals included extending the sales tax moratorium for five years to allow states to collaborate further on implementing a sales tax regime, implementing a permanent moratorium on Internet access taxes, and eliminating the 3 percent federal excise tax on communications.

On December 3, 2004, Congress extended the moratorium until 2007. Nevertheless, the debate continues over how to resolve the question of Internet taxation.

Article I, Section 8, also grants Congress spending power by authorizing it to "pay the Debts and provide for the common Defence and general Welfare of the United States." As with its power to tax, Congress can use its spending power to achieve social welfare objectives. For example, in the 1987 case *South Dakota v. Dole,*[8] the Supreme Court upheld a federal statute that grants federal funds for state highways to only those states in which 21 is the legal drinking age.

Other Constitutional Restrictions on Government

THE PRIVILEGES AND IMMUNITIES CLAUSE

Article IV, Section 2, of the Constitution states that "Citizens of each State shall be entitled to all Privileges and Immunities of Citizens in the several States." This provision, called the **privileges and immunities clause,** prohibits states from discriminating against citizens of other states when those nonresidents engage in ordinary and essential activities. These activities include buying and selling property, seeking employment, and using the court system. States may treat residents and nonresidents differently only when they have substantial reason for doing so.

For example, according to the privileges and immunities clause, a state cannot prohibit nonresidents from opening restaurants in the state. States can, however, allow state universities to charge higher tuition to out-of-state students because residents pay taxes that fund state universities, while out-of-state students do not.

THE FULL FAITH AND CREDIT CLAUSE

Article IV, Section 1, of the Constitution contains the **full faith and credit clause.** This clause states, "Full Faith and Credit shall be given in each State to the public Acts, Records,

[8] 483 U.S. 203 (1987).

and judicial Proceedings of every other State." This provision requires that courts in all states uphold contracts and public acts established in other states. For example, this clause protects wills, marriage and divorce decrees, and judgments in civil courts. Courts have held, however, that states do not have to give full faith and credit to laws that violate their "public policy." Thus, for example, although Massachusetts permits same-sex marriage, the full faith and credit clause does not require that other states recognize such marriages.

THE CONTRACT CLAUSE

Article I, Section 9, contains the **contract clause,** which states that government may not pass any "Law impairing the Obligation of Contract." In application, courts interpret this clause to mean that no law can be passed that will unreasonably interfere with existing contracts. For example, in the 1934 U.S. Supreme Court case *Home Building & Loan Association v. Blaisdell,*[9] the Home Building & Loan Association challenged Minnesota's Mortgage Moratorium Act as a violation of the contract clause. The act, implemented temporarily during the Great Depression, authorized courts to extend the redemption periods of mortgages to delay foreclosures of mortgages on real estate. The Court ruled that the act's provisions were within the state's police power to protect its citizens and did not violate the contract clause. Although the act impaired contractual obligations between lenders and borrowers, the Court held that courts must balance even substantial contractual impairments against states' interest in protecting the welfare of their citizens.

The Amendments to the Constitution

The first 10 amendments to the U.S. Constitution, known as the *Bill of Rights,* substantially affect government regulation of business. These amendments prohibit the federal government from infringing on individual freedoms. Moreover, the Fourteenth Amendment extends most of the provisions in the Bill of Rights to the states, prohibiting state interference in citizens' exercise of their rights. Thus, the federal and state governments cannot deprive individuals of the freedoms protected by the Bill of Rights.

Many other countries do not have constitutional provisions to protect citizens from the government. The Australian constitution, for example, creates the framework for government in Australia. In many of the countries that do have individual protections in their constitutions, these protections have emerged recently, as the Global Context box on Canada's constitution illustrates. Some other countries' constitutions provide rights that American citizens do not have. The constitution of Belarus, for example, featured later in this chapter, guarantees citizens' right to health care.

Courts apply many amendments to corporations because corporations are treated, in most cases, as "artificial persons." The remainder of this chapter describes the amendments that most significantly affect the regulatory environment of business. Exhibit 5-1 summarizes the first 10 amendments.

THE FIRST AMENDMENT

Freedom of speech and assembly. The First Amendment guarantees freedom of speech, including gestures and other forms of expression, and of the press. It prohibits abridgment of the right to assemble peacefully and to petition the government for redress

[9] 290 U.S. 398.

Exhibit 5-1
Summary of the Bill of Rights

AMENDMENT	PROVISIONS
First	• Protects freedom of religion, press, speech, and peaceable assembly. • Ensures that citizens have the right to ask the government to redress grievances.
Second	• Finds that in light of the need for a well regulated militia for security, government cannot infringe on citizens' right to bear arms.
Third	• Provides that government cannot house soldiers in private residences during peacetime, or during war except for provisions in the law.
Fourth	• Protects citizens from unreasonable search and seizure. • Ensures that government issues warrants only with probable cause.
Fifth	• Ensures that government does not put citizens on trial except by the indictment of a grand jury. • Gives citizens the right to not testify against themselves. • Prevents government from trying citizens twice for the same crime. • Creates the right to due process. • Provides that government cannot take private property for public use without just compensation.
Sixth	• Provides the right to a speedy public trial with an impartial jury, the right to know what criminal accusations a citizen faces, the right to have witnesses both against and for the accused, and the right to have an attorney.
Seventh	• States that in common law suits where the monetary value exceeds $20, citizens have the right to a trial by jury.
Eighth	• Provides that government will not set bail at excessive levels. • Prohibits government imposition of excessive fines. • Prohibits cruel and unusual punishment.
Ninth	• Provides that although the Bill of Rights names certain rights, such naming does not remove other rights retained by citizens.
Tenth	• Provides that powers that the Constitution does not give to the federal government are reserved to the states.

of grievances. Finally, it prohibits the government from aiding the establishment of religion and from interfering with the free exercise of religion.

Like other rights, First Amendment rights are not absolute. For example, a person does not have the right to yell "Fire!" in a crowded theater. Nor does the First Amendment protect false statements about another that are injurious to that person's reputation. Due to the difficulty of determining the boundaries of individual rights, courts hear a large number of First Amendment cases.

global context

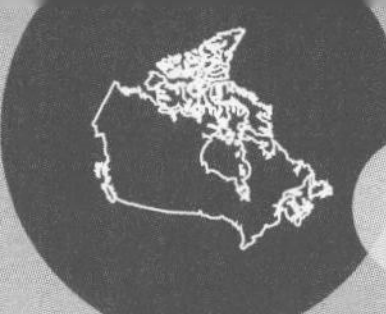

Constitution Act of Canada

The United States is not the only country to hold that a national constitution is the supreme law of the land. Section 52(1) of the Constitution Act of Canada, passed in 1982, states, "[T]he Constitution of Canada is the supreme law of Canada, and any law that is inconsistent with the provisions of the Constitution is, to the extent of the inconsistency, of no force or effect."

The Constitution Act established the Canadian Charter of Rights and Freedoms, which superseded the 1960 Canadian Bill of Rights. The Bill of Rights had applied only to the Canadian national government, not to the provincial governments. Like the Fourteenth Amendment of the U.S. Constitution, Section 32(1) of the Canadian Charter states that the charter applies to Canada's Parliament and national government and to the legislature and government of each province of Canada. Like the U.S. Bill of Rights, the Canadian Charter protects rights and fundamental freedoms, including freedom of conscience and religion, freedom of peaceful assembly and association, freedom from unreasonable searches and seizures, and the right to equal protection of the law. These rights and freedoms, however, are qualified. The charter states, in Section 1, "The Canadian Charter of Rights and Freedoms guarantees the rights and freedoms set out in the subject only to such reasonable limits prescribed by law as can be demonstrably justified in a free and democratic society."

Political speech. The First Amendment protections also apply to corporations. Courts do not, however, treat all corporate speech the same. Sometimes corporations engage in **political speech**; that is, they support political candidates or referenda. At one time, states restricted firms' political advertising because they feared that corporations, with their large assets, would drown out other voices. In the 1978 case *First National Bank of Boston* v. *Bellotti,*[10] however, the U.S. Supreme Court considered the constitutionality of a Massachusetts law that prohibited certain corporations from spending money to influence voters on issues that did not materially affect the corporation. The Court held that the law was unconstitutional, stating, "The concept that the government may restrict speech of some elements of our society in order to enhance the relative voice of others is wholly foreign to the First Amendment." The Court ruled that the First Amendment protects corporate political speech to the same extent as ordinary citizens' political speech.

Commercial speech. Not all corporate speech is political speech. **Commercial speech** is speech that conveys information related to the sale of goods and services. Courts analyze government restrictions on commercial speech according to a four-part test established in *Central Hudson Gas & Electric Corp. v. Public Service Commission of New York.*[11] The Central Hudson test is illustrated in Figure 5-2.

In Case 5-3, the Supreme Court applied this test to several New York regulations.

Unprotected speech. The First Amendment right to free speech is not absolute. In the 1942 case *Chaplinsky v. New Hampshire,*[12] the U.S. Supreme Court held:

> There are certain well-defined and narrowly limited classes of speech, the prevention and punishment of which have never been thought to raise any Constitutional problem. These include the lewd and obscene, the profane, the libelous, and the insulting or fighting words—those which by their very utterance inflict injury or tend to incite an immediate breach of the peace.

[10] 435 U.S. 765 (1978).
[11] 447 U.S. 557 (1980).
[12] 315 U.S. 568 (1942).

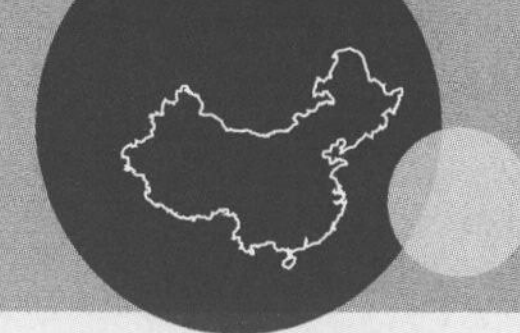

global context

Free Speech in China

The Chinese constitution does not guarantee freedom of speech or assembly, nor does it recognize any form of natural rights or human rights. Instead, it recognizes citizens' rights, which are specifically enumerated in the Chinese constitution or laws. Not only does the Chinese constitution not provide protections for expressive activity, but numerous Chinese laws prohibit citizens from engaging in political acts directed against the regime—acts that are protected in the United States. For example, Article 25 of China's Publishing Control Act prohibits the publication of any material that opposes the basic rules of the constitution. Articles 7 and 12 of the Law on Assemblies, Processions, and Demonstrations prohibit assemblies, processions, and demonstrations that oppose these basic rules.

Figure 5-2

The Central Hudson Test for Commercial Speech

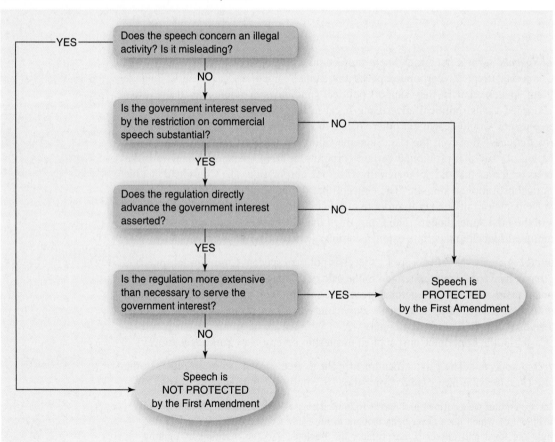

Does the speech concern an illegal activity? Is it misleading?
YES
NO
Is the government interest served by the restriction on commercial speech substantial?
NO
YES
Does the regulation directly advance the government interest asserted?
NO
YES
Is the regulation more extensive than necessary to serve the government interest?
YES
NO
Speech is PROTECTED by the First Amendment
Speech is NOT PROTECTED by the First Amendment

CASE 5-3 BAD FROG BREWERY v. NEW YORK STATE LIQUOR AUTH.

U.S. COURT OF APPEALS FOR THE SECOND CIRCUIT 134 F.3D 87 (1998)

Bad Frog, a Michigan corporation, manufactures and markets alcoholic beverages under its "Bad Frog" trademark. Each label prominently features an artist's rendering of a frog holding up its middle "finger." Versions of the label feature slogans such as "He just don't care," "An amphibian with an attitude," "Turning bad into good," and "The beer so good . . . it's bad."

In May 1996, Bad Frog's New York distributor applied to the New York State Liquor Authority for brand label approval and registration pursuant to section 107-a(4)(a) of New York's Alcoholic Beverage Control Law. NYSLA denied the application in July. Explaining its rationale for the rejection, the Authority found that the label "encourages combative behavior" and that the gesture and the slogan, "He just don't care," placed close to and in larger type than a warning concerning potential health problems, foster a defiance to the health warning on the label, entice underage drinkers, and invite the public not to heed conventional wisdom and to disobey standards of decorum.

In addition, the Authority said that it considered that approval of this label means that the label could appear in grocery and convenience stores, with obvious exposure on the shelf to children of tender age, and that it is sensitive to the label's adverse effects on a youthful audience.

Bad Frog filed the suit against the NYSLA in October 1996 and sought a preliminary injunction barring NYSLA from taking any steps to prohibit the sale of beer by Bad Frog under the controversial labels.

JON O. NEWMAN, CIRCUIT JUDGE: Bad Frog's label attempts to function, like a trademark, to identify the source of the product. The picture on a beer bottle of a frog behaving badly is reasonably to be understood as attempting to identify to consumers a product of the Bad Frog Brewery. In addition, the label serves to propose a commercial transaction. Though the label communicates no information beyond the source of the product, we think that minimal information, conveyed in the context of a proposal of a commercial transaction, suffices to invoke the protections for commercial speech, articulated in Central Hudson. We thus assess the prohibition of Bad Frog's labels under the commercial speech standards outlined in Central Hudson.

Central Hudson sets forth the analytical framework for assessing governmental restrictions on commercial speech:

> At the outset, we must determine whether the expression is protected by the First Amendment. For commercial speech to come within that provision, it at least must concern lawful activity and not be misleading. Next, we ask whether the asserted government interest is substantial. If both inquiries yield positive answers, we must determine whether the regulation directly advances the government interest asserted, and whether it is not more extensive than is necessary to serve that interest.

The last two steps in the analysis have been considered, somewhat in tandem, to determine if there is a sufficient "'fit' between the [regulator's] ends and the means chosen to accomplish those ends." The burden to establish that "reasonable fit" is on the governmental agency defending its regulation, though the fit need not satisfy a least-restrictive-means standard.

A. Lawful Activity and Not Deceptive

We agree with the District Court that Bad Frog's labels pass Central Hudson's threshold requirement that the speech "must concern lawful activity and not be misleading." The consumption of beer (at least by adults) is legal in New York, and the labels cannot be said to be deceptive, even if they are offensive.

B. Substantial State Interests

NYSLA advances two interests to support its asserted power to ban Bad Frog's labels: (i) the State's interest in "protecting children from vulgar and profane advertising," and (ii) the State's interest "in acting consistently to promote temperance, i.e., the moderate and responsible use of alcohol among those above the legal drinking age and abstention among those below the legal drinking age."

Both of the asserted interests are "substantial" within the meaning of Central Hudson. States have "a compelling interest in protecting the physical and psychological well-being of minors," and "this interest extends to shielding minors from the influence of literature that is not obscene by adult standards."

The Supreme Court also has recognized that states have a substantial interest in regulating alcohol consumption. We agree with the District Court that New York's asserted concern for "temperance" is also a substantial state interest.

C. Direct Advancement of the State Interest

To meet the "direct advancement" requirement, a state must demonstrate that "the harms it recites are real and that its restriction will in fact alleviate them to a material degree." A restriction will fail this third part of the Central Hudson test if it "provides only ineffective or remote support for the government's purpose."

(1) Advancing the interest in protecting children from vulgarity.

A prohibition that makes only a minute contribution to the advancement of a state interest can hardly be considered to have advanced the interest "to a material degree."

NYSLA endeavors to advance the state interest in preventing exposure of children to vulgar displays by taking only the limited step of barring such displays from the labels of alcoholic beverages. In view of the wide currency of vulgar displays throughout contemporary society, including comic books targeted directly at children, barring such displays from labels for alcoholic beverages cannot realistically be expected to reduce children's exposure to such displays to any significant degree.

We appreciate that NYSLA has no authority to prohibit vulgar displays appearing beyond the marketing of alcoholic beverages, but a state may not avoid the criterion of materially advancing its interest by authorizing only one component of its regulatory machinery to attack a narrow manifestation of a perceived problem. If New York decides to make a substantial effort to insulate children from vulgar displays in some significant sphere of activity, at least with respect to materials likely to be seen by children, NYSLA's label prohibition might well be found to make a justifiable contribution to the material advancement of such an effort, but its currently isolated response to the perceived problem, applicable only to labels on a product that children cannot purchase, does not suffice. We do not mean that a state must attack a problem with a total effort or fail the third criterion of a valid commercial speech limitation. Our point is that a state must demonstrate that its commercial speech limitation is part of a substantial effort to advance a valid state interest, not merely the removal of a few grains of offensive sand from a beach of vulgarity.

The valid state interest here is not insulating children from these labels, or even insulating them from vulgar displays on labels for alcoholic beverages; it is insulating children from displays of vulgarity.

(2) Advancing the state interest in temperance.

We agree with the District Court that NYSLA has not established that its rejection of Bad Frog's application directly advances the state's interest in "temperance."

NYSLA maintains that the raised finger gesture and the slogan "He just don't care" urge consumers generally to defy authority and particularly to disregard the Surgeon General's warning, which appears on the label next to the gesturing frog. NYSLA also contends that the frog appeals to youngsters and promotes underage drinking.

The truth of these propositions is not so self-evident as to relieve the state of the burden of marshalling some empirical evidence to support its assumptions. All that is clear is that the gesture of "giving the finger" is offensive. Whether viewing that gesture on a beer label will encourage disregard of health warnings or encourage underage drinking remain matters of speculation.

NYSLA has not shown that its denial of Bad Frog's application directly and materially advances either of its asserted state interests.

D. Narrow Tailoring

Central Hudson's fourth criterion, sometimes referred to as "narrow tailoring," requires consideration of whether the prohibition is more extensive than necessary to serve the asserted state interest. Since NYSLA's prohibition of Bad Frog's labels has not been shown to make even an arguable advancement of the state interest in temperance, we consider here only whether the prohibition is more extensive than necessary to serve the asserted interest in insulating children from vulgarity.

In this case, Bad Frog has suggested numerous less intrusive alternatives to advance the asserted State interest in protecting children from vulgarity, short of a complete statewide ban on its labels. Appellant suggests "the restriction of advertising to point-of-sale locations; limitations on billboard advertising; restrictions on over-the-air-advertising; and segregation of the product in the store." Even if we were to assume that the state materially advances its asserted interest by shielding children from viewing the Bad Frog labels, it is plainly excessive to prohibit the labels from all use, including placement on bottles displayed in bars and taverns where parental supervision of children is to be expected. Moreover, to whatever extent NYSLA is concerned that children will be harmfully exposed to the Bad Frog labels when wandering without parental supervision around grocery and convenience stores where beer is sold, that concern could be less intrusively dealt with by placing restrictions on the permissible locations where the appellant's products may be displayed within such stores. Or, with the labels permitted, restrictions might be imposed on placement of the frog illustration on the outside of six-packs or cases, sold in such stores.

NYSLA's complete statewide ban on the use of Bad Frog's labels lacks a "reasonable fit" with the state's asserted interest in shielding minors from vulgarity, and NYSLA gave inadequate consideration to alternatives to this blanket suppression of commercial speech.

REVERSED and REMANDED.

CRITICAL THINKING

Suppose an editorial writer read the Bad Frog case and concluded that the Supreme Court is apparently uninterested in temperance. Explain how the editorial writer has misunderstood the Court's reasoning.

ETHICAL DECISION MAKING

What values are competing with freedom of speech in this case?

How do the standards in the *Central Hudson* decision give us a strong sense about how important freedom of speech is to the Court as a value?

Thus, for example, the First Amendment does not protect *defamation,* or speech that harms the reputation of another. As you will learn in Chapter 6, moreover, courts may require that an individual who uses such speech compensate the person whose reputation was harmed by the speech.

The First Amendment does not protect *obscenity,* either, although in many cases courts find it difficult to determine whether particular speech constitutes obscenity. In the 1973 case *Miller v. California,*[13] the U.S. Supreme Court established a three-part standard to determine whether speech is obscene:

1. Would the average person, applying contemporary community standards, find that the speech, taken as a whole, appeals to the prurient (marked by or arousing an immoderate or unwholesome interest or desire) interest?
2. Does the speech depict or describe, in a patently offensive way, sexual conduct specifically defined by law?
3. Does the speech, taken as a whole, lack serious literary, artistic, political, or scientific value?

If the answer to all three questions is yes, then the First Amendment does not protect the speech in question. Can you identify any significant ambiguities in the Miller standard?

[13] 413 U.S. 15 (1973).

Case Nugget **How Do Courts Balance the Government's Interest in Protecting Children from Exposure to Sexually Oriented Programming with Upholding Basic Free-Speech Principles?**

U.S. v. Playboy
529 U.S. 803 (2000)

Congress passed the Communications Decency Act (CDA) to regulate speech or expression that is harmful to minors. An adult-oriented cable television operator, Playboy Entertainment Group, Inc. (Playboy), challenged the filtering provision of the CDA, which aimed to scramble or block channels during hours when children are likely to be viewing.

Playboy won the case. The Court stated:

> The history of the law of free expression is one of vindication in cases involving speech that many citizens may find shabby, offensive, or even ugly. It follows that all content-based restrictions on speech must give us more than a moment's pause. If television broadcasts can expose children to the real risk of harmful exposure to indecent materials, even in their own home and without parental consent, there is a problem the Government can address. It must do so, however, in a way consistent with First Amendment principles. Here the Government has not met the burden the First Amendment imposes. The Government has failed to show that [the section of the CDA Playboy has challenged] is the least restrictive means for addressing a real problem; and the District Court did not err in holding the statute violative of the First Amendment.

Fighting words are a third class of unprotected speech. In *Chaplinsky v. New Hampshire,* a man protesting the government called the city marshal a "damned racketeer" and a "damned Fascist." The city arrested him for violating a statute prohibiting the use of offensive, derisive, or annoying words toward another in a public place. The U.S. Supreme Court held: "The English language has a number of words and expressions which by general consent are 'fighting words' when said without a disarming smile. . . . Such words, as ordinary men know, are likely to cause a fight." The Court further held that "'damned racketeer' and 'damned Fascist' are epithets likely to provoke the average person to retaliation, and thereby cause a breach of the peace."[14] Thus, the Court determined that the First Amendment did not protect the man's speech.

Many universities believe that "hate speech," or derogatory speech directed at members of another group, such as another race, satisfies the definition of fighting words. Thus, 60 percent of universities have banned verbal abuse and verbal harassment, and 28 percent of universities have banned advocacy of an offensive viewpoint.[15] State and federal appellate courts have struck down many of these hate-speech codes, but no cases have reached the Supreme Court yet. The international community, however, is less protective of hate speech. For example, a United Nations declaration and a number of foreign laws state that hate speech is not a protected form of expression.[16]

Freedom of religion. The First Amendment contains two provisions that protect citizens' freedom of religion. The **establishment clause** maintains that government

[14] See note 12.

[15] Timothy C. Shiell, *Campus Hate Speech on Trial* (Lawrence: University Press of Kansas, 1998), pp. 2, 49.

[16] Ibid., p. 32.

e-commerce AND THE LAW

Is Computer Code Speech

In fall 1999, Eric Corley, publisher of the online journal *2600: The Hacker Quarterly,* posted DeCSS (De-Content Scramble System) to the journal. This program allows individuals with technological expertise to decipher CSS (Content Scrambling System), the code the film industry has developed to prevent people from making copies of DVD movies. In addition to posting DeCSS, Corley included links that led site visitors to other sites that posted DeCSS (hyperlinks).

Soon after Corley posted DeCSS and the hyperlinks, he found himself in trouble with the Hollywood studios that are members of the Motion Picture Association of America (MPAA). They sued Corley, asking a judge to issue an injunction prohibiting both the initial posting and the hyperlinks.

The Hollywood studios were trying to protect their property rights. Congress had passed a statute, the Digital Millennium Copyright Act (DMCA), to help artists and other copyright holders curb piracy. The DMCA prohibits the use of, or trafficking in, computer code that circumvents the encryption scheme that protects certain digital content. The DMCA makes it clear that the entertainment industry has the right to put copyright protection codes on a range of digital media, including DVD movies. The Hollywood studios are trying to stop pirates from making it possible for people to have access to films that are being shown in theaters. If piracy is allowed, who will purchase movie tickets or DVDs?

Corley asserted that he is not a pirate. Instead, he and his company are protectors of free speech. Corley argued that the DMCA violates the rights of programmers and scientists to share software programs and computer code. He believes the First Amendment guarantees him the right to post DeCSS and the hyperlinks. Corley maintains that journalists, programmers, and scientists should be free to share information on the Web and should not be responsible if people use the information to engage in piracy. In August 2000, New York District Judge Lewis Kaplan issued a permanent injunction prohibiting Corley from posting DeCSS on his Web site or knowingly linking via a hyperlink to any other Web site containing DeCSS. This injunction enforced the DMCA's anticircumvention provisions. Judge Kaplan ruled that the DMCA was a valid exercise of the government's power and that the law did not violate Corley's First Amendment rights.

On November 28, 2001, a three-judge panel of the U.S. Court of Appeals for the Second Circuit, in Manhattan, affirmed Kaplan's decision and reasoning.* The appellate court panel agreed with Judge Kaplan's decision that computer code is content-neutral speech and that a narrowly tailored injunction did not burden substantially more speech than necessary to further the government's interest in preventing unauthorized access to copyrighted materials.

* 273 F.3d 429 (2d Cir. 2001).

"shall make no law respecting an establishment of religion." In the 1971 case *Lemon v. Kurtzman,*[17] the U.S. Supreme Court codified the following three tests to determine whether a particular government statute violates the establishment clause:

1. Does the statute have a secular legislative purpose?
2. Does the statute's principal or primary effect either advance or inhibit religion?
3. Does the statute foster an excessive government entanglement with religion?

To determine whether the statute fosters an excessive government entanglement with religion, courts examine the character and purposes of the institutions benefited, the nature of the aid that the government provides, and the resulting relationship between the government and the religious authority.

The **free-exercise clause** states that government cannot make a law "prohibiting the free exercise" of religion. Although government must remain neutral in matters of religion, determining whether a government action advances religion or merely allows free exercise

[17] 403 U.S. 602 (1971).

of religion is often difficult. Likewise, determining whether a government action establishes religion or simply avoids interference with free exercise of religion is also difficult.

Issues concerning the establishment clause and the free-exercise clause often arise in workplace settings. In government workplaces, this conflict sometimes raises difficult issues. For example, in 1966, Tucker, an employee of the California Department of Education, insisted on signing office memos with his name and the letters "SOTLJC," an abbreviation for "Servant of the Lord Jesus Christ." In an attempt to avoid workplace disruptions and the appearance of government support for religion, Tucker's supervisor prohibited all displays of religious symbols in the workplace. The supervisor suspended Tucker for refusing to comply with the restrictions. When Tucker challenged the suspension on grounds that the rules interfered with his free exercise of religion, the appellate court agreed.[18]

In private workplaces, issues related to free exercise of religion most often arise under Title VII, the federal law prohibiting employment discrimination. We discuss this important legislation in greater detail in Chapter 42.

THE FOURTH AMENDMENT

Freedom from unreasonable searches and seizures. The Fourth Amendment guarantees citizens the right to be "secure in their persons, their homes, and their personal property." Thus, it prohibits government from conducting unreasonable searches of individuals and seizing their property to use as evidence against them.

A search is unreasonable if the government official conducting the search does not first obtain a search warrant from a court. A **search warrant** is a court order that authorizes law enforcement agents to search for or seize items specifically described in the warrant. Government officials can obtain search warrants only if they can show *probable cause* to believe that the search will uncover specific evidence of criminal activity. In other words, the government officials must have a sufficient reason based on known facts to obtain a warrant.

The Supreme Court has ruled, however, that in certain circumstances, government officials do not need a search warrant. For example, when law enforcement officials believe it is likely that the items sought will be removed before they can obtain a warrant, they may conduct a search without a warrant. Law enforcement officials frequently conduct automobile searches without a warrant according to this rule.

In most other cases, though, law enforcement officials must obtain a warrant before conducting a search. For example, an Ohio law required that buyers of five or more beer kegs provide the beer distributor with the address of the party where the kegs would be consumed. Additionally, the law required that the buyers sign a form allowing police and liquor agents to enter their property without a warrant to search the premises to enforce state liquor laws. In 2001, a college professor challenged the law on grounds that it infringed on citizens' Fourth Amendment rights.[19] Before the court decided the case, Ohio repealed the law.[20]

In addition to protecting individuals and their homes, the Fourth Amendment also protects corporations and places of business. This protection generally applies in criminal cases, but Fourth Amendment issues also arise when government regulations authorize administrative agencies to conduct warrantless searches.

[18] *Tucker v. State of Cal. Dep't of Ed.*, 97 F.3d 1204 (9th Cir. 1996).

[19] Robert Ruth, "Lawsuit Challenges Restrictions on Beer Buyers," *Columbus Dispatch*, May 26, 2001, p. 1B.

[20] *Hooper v. Morkle*, 219 F.R.D. 120 (2003).

e-commerce AND THE LAW

Technology and the Fourth Amendment

Technological improvements have raised new issues in the application of the Fourth Amendment. New technologies have made eavesdropping and other covert activities easier. For example, in a 2001 U.S. Supreme Court case, police had information suggesting that Danny Kyllo grew marijuana in his home. Growing marijuana indoors requires heat lamps that use large amounts of electricity, and Kyllo had unusually high electric bills. The police used a thermal imager, an instrument that detects heat emissions, to provide them with the evidence necessary to obtain a warrant to physically search his house.

The Court addressed the issue of whether the use of thermal-imaging instruments on private property constituted a "search." Judges analyze cases by comparing them to past cases to see how other judges determined similar cases. Thus, in this case, the Court asked whether using thermal-imaging instruments is more like going through someone's garbage or more like using a high-powered telescope to look through someone's window. Previous Supreme Court cases held that the former behavior does not constitute a search but the latter scenario does constitute a search and therefore requires a warrant. The appellate court, examining the use of this technology for the first time, ruled that using thermal imaging was not a search prohibited by the Fourth Amendment without a warrant.

On appeal, however, the U.S. Supreme Court ruled that police use of thermal-imaging devices to detect heat patterns emanating from private homes constitutes a search that requires a warrant. The Court held, further, that the warrant requirement applies not only to the relatively crude thermal-imaging device but also to any "more sophisticated systems" that give the police knowledge that in the past would have required physical entry into the home. In explaining the Court's decision, Justice Scalia wrote that in the home, "all details are intimate details, because the entire area is held safe from prying government eyes." He added that the Court's precedents "draw a firm line at the entrance to one's house."

This case, however, is not necessarily the final word on the use of technology. The Court relied heavily on the fact that police used thermal imaging to see inside Kyllo's home. Thus, courts may in the future uphold thermal imaging of other locations.

Although administrative searches usually require search warrants, courts have established an exception to this rule: If an industry has a long history of pervasive regulation, a warrantless search is not unreasonable. In such industries, administrative agencies can use warrantless searches to ensure that firms uphold regulations.

This *pervasive-regulation exception,* however, is not always easy to interpret. Courts have ruled that warrantless searches authorized by the Federal Mine Safety and Health Act are legal because the federal regulatory presence is comprehensive and well defined. Thus, reasonable commercial-property owners ought to know that their property is subject to periodic inspections.[21] A warrantless search based on the Occupational Safety and Health Act, however, may violate the Fourth Amendment because no significant legislation of working conditions existed before Congress passed that act in 1970. Hence, businesspeople covered by the law cannot reasonably anticipate warrantless searches. Case 5-4 illustrates how the supreme court of Michigan treated one city's attempt to authorize warrantless administrative searches.

THE FIFTH AMENDMENT

The Fifth Amendment protects individuals in several important ways. First, it protects against *self-incrimination,* meaning that in a criminal case, the defendant does not have to testify in court as a witness against herself or himself. The Fifth Amendment also protects against *double jeopardy.* Thus, government cannot try a person more than once for the same crime.

[21] *Raymond J. Donovan, Secretary of Labor, United States Department of Labor v. Douglas Dewey et al.,* 452 U.S. 594, 101 S. Ct. 2534 (1981).

CASE 5-4 HILDEGARD GORA ET AL. v. CITY OF FERNDALE
SUPREME COURT OF MICHIGAN
551 N.W.2D 454 (1998)

In November 1990, the city of Ferndale enacted a comprehensive ordinance regulating massage parlors. The regulations, among other things, established the procedures and educational requirements for obtaining a city license or permit to own, operate, or work in a massage parlor, and prescribed necessary facilities, hours of operation, and employee conduct and dress. The ordinance also provided for periodic inspections of massage parlor establishments by the chief of police or other authorized inspectors. The failure of any licensee to allow an inspection officer access to the premises, or hinder such officer in any manner, was designated as a misdemeanor punishable by a fine of up to $500 or ninety days in jail.

The plaintiffs challenged the constitutionality of a number of the provisions of the ordinance, including the provision for searches without a warrant. Initially, the court found that several sections of the ordinance violated the state and federal constitutions. The Court of Appeals eventually found that two provisions were unconstitutional, including the provision for a search without a warrant. The court reasoned that the administrative search exception to the warrant requirement was inapplicable because the State of Michigan did not pervasively regulate the massage parlor industry. The city appealed.

JUSTICE TAYLOR: While it is well established that the Fourth Amendment's prohibition of unreasonable searches and seizures applies to administrative inspections of private commercial property, an exemption from the search warrant requirement exists for administrative inspections of closely regulated industries. Whether the exemption applies is primarily determined by " 'the pervasiveness and regularity of the . . . regulation' and the effect of such regulation upon an owner's expectation of privacy." When a person chooses to engage in a "pervasively regulated business . . . he does so with the knowledge that his business . . . will be subject to effective inspection." . . . In part, the justification for this is that, unlike under general inspection schemes, the person in the pervasively regulated business "is not left to wonder about the purposes of the inspector or the limits of his task" as long as the regulations provide notice of and implicitly restrict the scope of the inspection to those areas of the business that must be examined to enforce the regulations. . . .

We are unpersuaded by plaintiffs' contention that there can be no finding that the massage parlor trade is a pervasively regulated industry in the absence of a history of regulation by the City of Ferndale. The United States Supreme Court expressly rejected an approach that relied exclusively on historical factors . . . stating that "if the length of regulation were the only criterion, absurd results would occur." Rather, "it is the pervasiveness and regularity of the . . . regulation that ultimately determines whether a warrant is necessary to render an inspection program reasonable under the Fourth Amendment." . . . Moreover, the goal of the ordinance is primarily to prevent massage establishments from being used as a front for prostitution, which, as "the oldest profession," historically has been subject to pervasive regulation for perhaps longer than any other industry.

While regulation of massage parlors has not been as extensive as that of some other enterprises, such as the liquor or firearms industries, it has nonetheless been held to be a pervasively regulated industry. . . . [I]n Indianapolis v. Wright . . . the Indiana Supreme Court upheld a local massage parlor inspection ordinance similar to the one at issue in this case. . . . [T]he court concluded that this was a pervasively regulated enterprise and that the massage parlor inspection scheme authorized by the ordinance was reasonable and permissible under the administrative search exception to the warrant requirement. When appealed, the U.S. Supreme Court dismissed the appeal for want of a substantial federal question. . . . [T]he Supreme Court's disposition of a case in this manner is a decision on the merits that is *stare decisis* with regard to the issues presented, including, of course, the question of pervasive

[CONTINUED]

regulation. . . . Thus, we conclude that the U.S. Supreme Court has determined that the massage parlor industry is a pervasively regulated business and that inspections of massage parlors conducted without warrants pursuant to a comprehensive licensing and regulation ordinance are permissible under the administrative search exception to the warrant requirement of the Fourth Amendment.

REVERSED in favor of defendant.

CRITICAL THINKING

What ambiguous term is the focus of the court's opinion? Why do you believe the court does or does not satisfactorily resolve the ambiguity of the term?

ETHICAL DECISION MAKING

Even if an agency is not successful, as the City of Ferndale was, in arguing that a warrant is unnecessary, it is still easier to obtain a warrant in a commercial context because the courts require a slightly lower standard of probable cause in a business context. An agency can generally obtain a search warrant by demonstrating that it wishes to search a business under a general and neutral enforcement plan. Should the city have been required to obtain a search warrant on ethical grounds? Why or why not?

Due process. For businesspeople and corporations, the Fifth Amendment's **due process clause** provides extensive protection. This clause states that government cannot deprive a person of life, liberty, or property without *due process* of law.

The due process clause guarantees two types of due process: procedural and substantive. **Procedural due process** requires that the government use fair procedures when taking the life, liberty, or property of an individual or corporation. At a minimum, procedural due process entitles a person to notice of any legal action against her and to a hearing before an impartial tribunal. Originally, courts interpreted the due process clause as protecting an individual's right of procedural due process only in federal criminal proceedings. The subsequent passage of the Fourteenth Amendment extended the requirement of due process to criminal proceedings by state governments. Today, courts apply the due process clause to diverse situations, including the termination of welfare benefits, food stamps, or Social Security benefits, the suspension of a driver's license, the discharge of a public employee from his job, and the suspension of a student from school.

The procedures that government must follow when taking an individual's life, liberty, or property vary according to the nature of the taking. Generally, more procedures are necessary as the magnitude of potential deprivation increases.

Substantive due process refers to the basic fairness of laws that may deprive an individual of her life, liberty, or property. To satisfy the substantive due process requirement, government must have a proper purpose for enacting laws that restrict individuals' liberty or the use of their property. The standard for determining whether a law violates substantive due process depends on the nature of the potential deprivation. Laws affecting fundamental rights must bear a substantial relationship to a compelling government purpose. These fundamental rights generally include the rights protected in the Constitution: the right to vote, the right to travel freely from state to state, the right to privacy, and so on. Compelling state interests include, for example, public safety and national security.

Not all laws, however, affect fundamental rights. To show that laws that do not affect fundamental rights satisfy the substantive due process requirement, government must prove only that the law bears a rational relationship to a legitimate state interest. Courts uphold most government regulations according to this *rational-basis test.* For example, courts have upheld minimum-wage laws, rent control laws, banking regulations, environmental laws, and regulations prohibiting unfair trade practices according to the rational-basis test.

The prohibition against uncompensated takings. The Fifth Amendment also provides that when government takes private property for public use, it must pay the owner *just compensation,* or fair market value, for his property. This provision is called the **takings clause,** and it applies to corporations. Several significant issues have arisen with respect to the takings clause. For example, what constitutes a "public use" for which government can take private property? We discuss this issue in greater detail in Chapter 48.

The takings clause has prompted other issues as well. What happens, for instance, when a government regulation interferes so substantially with an individual's use of her property that it effectively "takes" her property? For example, environmental regulations often affect the way landowners can use their property. In many cases, property owners have challenged the constitutionality of these regulations, as Case 5-5 illustrates.

The privilege against self-incrimination. Although most provisions of the Fifth Amendment apply to corporations, corporations do not enjoy the Fifth Amendment's protection against self-incrimination. Sole proprietors, however, are entitled to this protection. Thus, different businesses have different constitutional rights depending on their form of business organization.

CASE 5-5

LUCAS v. SOUTH CAROLINA COASTAL COMMISSION
UNITED STATES SUPREME COURT
112 U.S. 2886 (1992)

In 1986, David Lucas purchased two beachfront lots on the South Carolina coast. He paid $975,000 for the lots, intending to build a home for himself on one and sell the other to a wealthy buyer. Nineteen months after his purchase, South Carolina passed a Beachfront Management Act, which banned construction close to the shore to prevent flying debris and other environmental damage from Atlantic storms. The new law prevented Lucas from constructing either house, which he believed rendered his land "valueless." Lucas sued the state, seeking "just compensation" under the Takings Clause of the Fifth Amendment. The trial court found in favor of Lucas and awarded him $1.2 million. On appeal, the state argued successfully that a landowner had no right to harm his land, which Lucas would be doing by constructing the homes, and reversed the trial court's decision. Lucas appealed to the U.S. Supreme Court.

JUSTICE SCALIA: Prior to Justice Holmes' exposition in *Pennsylvania Coal Co. v. Mahon,* it was generally thought that the Takings Clause reached only a "direct appropriation" of property, or the functional equivalent of a "practical ouster of [the owner's] possession."

We have, however, described at least two discrete categories of regulatory action as compensable without case-specific inquiry into the public interest advanced in support of the restraint. The first encompasses regulations that compel the property owner to suffer a physical "invasion" of his property. In general (at least with regard to permanent invasions), no matter how minute the intrusion, and no matter how weighty the public purpose behind it, we have required compensation.

The second situation in which we have found categorical treatment appropriate is where regulation denies all economically beneficial or productive use of land. As we have said on numerous occasions, the Fifth Amendment is violated when land-use regulation "does not substantially advance legitimate state interests or *denies an owner economically viable use of his land.*"

Affirmatively supporting a compensation requirement is the fact that regulations that leave the owner of land without economically beneficial or productive options for its use—typically, as here, by requiring land to be left substantially in its natural state—carry with them a heightened risk that private property is being pressed into some form of public service under the guise of mitigating serious public harm. . . .

[P]etitioner "concede[d] that the beach/dune area of South Carolina's shores is an extremely valuable public resource; that the erection of new construction contributes to the erosion and destruction of this public resource; and that discouraging new construction in close proximity to the beach/dune area is necessary to prevent a great public harm." In the [state] court's view, these concessions brought petitioner's challenge within a long line of this Court's cases, sustaining against Due Process and Takings Clause challenges against the State's use of its "police powers" to enjoin a property owner from activities akin to public nuisances [e.g., order to destroy diseased cedar trees to prevent infection of nearby orchards].

It is correct that many of our prior opinions have suggested that "harmful or noxious uses" of property may be proscribed by government regulation without the requirement of compensation. For a number of reasons, however, we think the South Carolina Supreme Court was too quick to conclude that principle decides the present case. The "harmful or noxious uses" principle was the Court's early attempt to describe in theoretical terms why government may, consistent with the Takings Clause, affect property values by regulation without incurring an obligation to compensate—a reality we nowadays acknowledge explicitly with respect to the full scope of the State's police power. . . .

Where the State seeks to sustain regulation that deprives land of all economically beneficial use, we think it may resist compensation only if the logically antecedent inquiry into the nature of the owner's estate shows that the proscribed use interests were not part of his title to begin with. . . .

The "total taking" inquiry we require today will ordinarily entail analysis of, among other things, the degree of harm to public lands and resources, or adjacent private property, posed by the claimant's proposed activities, the social value of the claimant's activities and their suitability to the locality in question, and the relative ease with which the alleged harm can be avoided through measures taken by the claimant and the government (or adjacent private landowners) alike. The fact that a particular use has long been engaged in by similarly situated owners ordinarily imports a lack of any common-law prohibition (though changed circumstances or new knowledge may make what was previously permissible no longer so). So also does the fact that other landowners, similarly situated, are permitted to continue the use denied to the claimant.

It seems unlikely that common-law principles would have prevented the erection of any habitable or productive improvements on petitioner's land. We emphasize that to win its case . . . South Carolina must identify background principles of nuisance and property law that prohibit the uses he now intends in the circumstances in which the property is presently found. Only on this showing can the State fairly claim that, in proscribing all such beneficial uses, the Beachfront Management Act is taking nothing.

REVERSED and REMANDED in favor of plaintiff.

CRITICAL THINKING

The Court outlines two instances in which compensation is required, one being that the landowner has lost all economically beneficial productive use of the land. What are the descriptive assumptions underlying the decision to require compensation in this instance?

[CONTINUED]

ETHICAL DECISION MAKING

Many people very passionately support expanding the concept of regulatory takings to a multitude of laws. Opponents of this group feel equally as strong that the use of the concept of regulatory takings should be extremely limited. The strong feelings of both groups have been influenced by the conflicting value preferences of those in each group. Can you identify which strongly held values would be influencing each group's positions?

For example, in the 1988 U.S. Supreme Court case *Braswell v. United States,*[22] the Court distinguished between the rights of corporate-record custodians and sole proprietors. Braswell was both the operator and the sole shareholder of his business. When a grand jury issued a subpoena requiring that he produce corporate books and records, Braswell argued that the subpoena violated his Fifth Amendment privilege against self-incrimination. The Court denied Braswell's claim, writing that "subpoenaed business records are not privileged, and as a custodian for the records, the act of producing the records is in a representative capacity, not a personal one, so the records must be produced."[23] The Court held that the subpoena would have violated Braswell's privilege against self-incrimination if his business had been a sole proprietorship.

THE NINTH AMENDMENT

Privacy rights. The Ninth Amendment states, "The enumeration in the Constitution, of certain rights, shall not be construed to deny or disparage others retained by the people." Although this amendment does not expressly guarantee the right to privacy, courts have interpreted the Ninth Amendment, together with the First, Third, Fourth, and Fifth Amendments, as providing individuals with a right to privacy.

In the 1965 case *Griswold v. Connecticut,*[24] the Supreme Court ruled that a Connecticut law prohibiting the use of contraceptives was unconstitutional because it violated individuals' right to privacy. Justice Douglas wrote:

> [S]pecific guarantees in the Bill of Rights have penumbras [fringes]. . . . Various guarantees create zones of privacy. The right of association contained in the penumbra of the First Amendment is one. . . . The Third Amendment in its prohibition against the quartering of soldiers 'in any house' in time of peace without the consent of the owner is another facet of that privacy. The Fourth Amendment explicitly affirms the 'right of the people to be secure in their persons, houses, papers, and effects, against unreasonable searches and seizures.' The Fifth Amendment in its Self-Incrimination Clause enables the citizen to create a zone of privacy which government may not force him to surrender to his detriment.

The right to privacy has since been used in a broad variety of contexts.

[22] 487 U.S. 99 (1988).

[23] Ibid.

[24] 381 U.S. 479 (1965).

THE FOURTEENTH AMENDMENT

Equal protection. The Fourteenth Amendment contains the **equal protection clause,** which prevents states from denying "the equal protection of the laws" to any citizen. This clause combats discrimination because it applies whenever government treats certain individuals differently than other similarly situated individuals, usually through a classification scheme.

As with the due process clause, to determine whether a law violates the equal protection clause, courts use different standards based on the nature of the rights the classification affects. Three different standards of scrutiny apply: strict scrutiny, intermediate scrutiny, and the rational-basis test.

If a law prevents individuals from exercising a fundamental right, or if the law's classification scheme involves suspect classifications, the action will be subject to **strict scrutiny.** *Suspect classifications* include classifications based on race, national origin, and citizenship. Courts uphold suspect classifications only if they are necessary to promote a compelling state interest. In cases involving suspect classifications, courts do not begin their analysis with a presumption that the classification is constitutional, so few laws pass the strict-scrutiny standard. For example, in the 1954 case *Brown v. Board of Education,*[25] the U.S. Supreme Court ruled that the classification scheme used to racially segregate public schools violated the equal protection clause.

Several courts have held, however, that in some cases, remedying past discrimination against a group is a compelling state interest. Chapter 42 discusses this issue in greater detail.

If the law's classification scheme is based on gender or on the legitimacy of children, courts use **intermediate scrutiny.** According to this standard, the law is constitutional only if it is substantially related to an important government objective.

When a classification scheme involves other matters, courts apply a **rational-basis test.** According to this test, courts ask whether there is any justifiable reason to believe that the classification scheme advances a legitimate government interest. Because courts begin their analysis with a strong presumption that the government action is constitutional, almost all laws pass this test.

CASE OPENER WRAP-UP

Wine Sales Regulation

The Supreme Court ruled that "in all but the narrowest circumstances, state laws violate the Commerce Clause if they mandate 'differential treatment of in-state and out-of-state economic interests that benefits the former and burdens the latter.'" The Michigan and New York statutes deprived citizens of their right to "have access to other states' markets on equal terms." The Court determined that the statutes violated the commerce clause and were unconstitutional because the states could achieve their goals without discriminating against interstate commerce. The same reasoning would apply if the state were attempting to regulate corn; in fact, the state would have even less of an argument for regulating corn because corn would not be subject to abuse by the citizens the way alcohol might be.

[25] 347 U.S. 483 (1954).

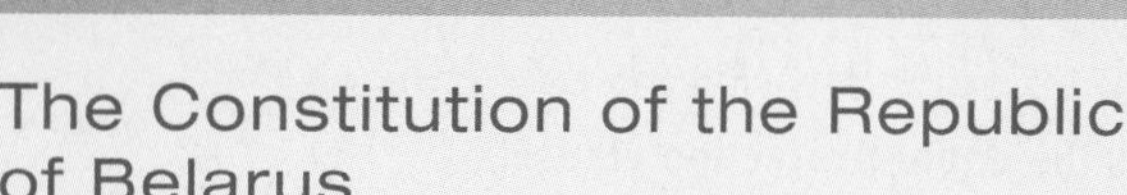

global context

The Constitution of the Republic of Belarus

The constitution of Belarus, adopted in 1994, provides Belarusian citizens with an exhaustive set of rights that surpasses most other nations' constitutions. The Belarusian constitution guarantees the following rights to citizens:

- Citizens accused of crimes are presumed innocent until proven guilty (Article 26).
- The defendant in a criminal case enjoys protection from providing evidence against herself or close family relations (Article 27).
- Citizens can move freely and choose their place of residence within the Republic of Belarus. They can leave Belarus and return without hindrance (Article 30).
- Citizens have the right to profess any religion individually or jointly with others or to profess none at all. They also have the right to express and spread beliefs connected with their attitudes toward religion and to participate in religious rituals (Article 31).
- Citizens have freedom of thought and belief and may freely express their thoughts and beliefs (Article 33).
- Citizens may organize assemblies, rallies, street marches, demonstrations, and pickets that do not disturb law and order or violate other citizens' rights (Article 35).
- Citizens have the right to choose a profession, type of occupation, and work in accordance with their capabilities, education, and vocational training. Moreover, they have the right to healthy and safe working conditions.
- The constitution binds the Belarusian government to create the conditions necessary for full employment of the population. For citizens who are unemployed for reasons beyond their control, the constitution guarantees training in new specializations, an upgrade of their qualifications, and unemployment benefits (Article 41).
- The constitution limits the workweek to 40 hours. It guarantees annual paid leave, weekly rest days, and shorter working hours for citizens who work at night (Article 43).
- Citizens have the right to health care, including free treatment at all government health care establishments (Article 45).

Summary

The U.S. Constitution	*Federalism:* The authority to govern is divided between two sovereigns, or supreme lawmakers: the federal government and the states. *Checks and balances:* The Constitution divides power among the legislative, executive, and judicial branches of government. The system of checks and balances allocates specific powers to each branch to keep the other branches from dominating government.
The Supremacy Clause and Federal Preemption	*Federal supremacy:* Any state or local law that directly conflicts with the U.S. Constitution or federal laws or treaties is void. *Concurrent authority:* Both state and federal governments have the power to regulate certain matters; generally, the federal government defers to the state. *Federal preemption:* The federal government uses this doctrine to strike down laws that do not directly conflict with a federal law but attempt to regulate an area within federal legislative jurisdiction.
The Commerce Clause	This clause grants the federal government the authority to pass regulations that significantly affect interstate commerce. Today, it provides the basis for most federal government regulations.

Police powers are the residual powers retained by states to pass laws to safeguard the health and welfare of their citizens.

The *dormant commerce clause* prohibits states from passing laws that significantly interfere with interstate commerce.

Taxing and Spending Powers of the Federal Government

Congressional taxes must be uniform across all states. Congress can use taxes and spending for purposes other than generating revenue; e.g., it can use them to indirectly promote social goals.

Other Constitutional Restrictions on Government

The *privileges and immunities clause* prohibits states from discriminating against citizens of other states.

The *full faith and credit clause* states that in civil matters, courts in all states must uphold rights established by legal documents.

The *contract clause* states that Congress cannot pass laws that unreasonably interfere with existing contracts.

The Amendments to the Constitution

First Amendment

- Protects corporate speech in certain circumstances. It protects corporate political speech to the same extent that it protects individuals' political speech. The Central Hudson test determines whether the First Amendment protects particular corporate commercial speech.
- Contains the *establishment clause,* which states that Congress may not make laws respecting an establishment of religion, and the *free-exercise clause,* which states that Congress may not make laws prohibiting the free exercise of religion.

Fourth Amendment

- Protects both corporations and individuals from unreasonable government searches and seizures. Although administrative searches generally require a warrant, administrative agencies may inspect some industries without a warrant to ensure compliance with industry regulations.

Fifth Amendment

- States that government cannot take an individual's life, liberty, or property without due process of law. There are two types of due process: *procedural due process,* which focuses on rules for enforcing laws and entitles individuals to notice of legal action against them, and *substantive due process,* which requires that government have a proper purpose for enacting laws that restrict individuals' liberty or the use of their property.
- States that if government takes private property for public use, it must compensate the owner. The extent to which some government regulations constitute takings, however, generates much litigation.
- Includes a privilege against self-incrimination, although the provision does not apply to corporations. Only individual citizens and sole proprietorships may exercise this right.
- Guarantees individuals equal protection under the law. Courts use three different standards of scrutiny in equal protection cases: (1) *strict scrutiny,* to analyze government actions that abridge fundamental rights or that include suspect classifications; (2) *intermediate scrutiny,* to analyze classifications based on gender or on legitimacy of children; (3) the *rational-basis test,* to analyze classifications involving other matters.

Fourteenth Amendment

- Applies the Due Process Clause, except parts of the Fifth Amendment, to the states and contains the Equal Protection Clause.

Point / Counterpoint

The Countermajoritarian Difficulty

Is Judicial Review Consistent with Our System of Democracy?	
No	**Yes**
Our system of government is one of popular sovereignty: Voters have the liberty to make the laws under which they will live. As established in *Marbury v. Madison,* judicial review permits the Supreme Court to strike down laws passed by Congress—laws that ostensibly represent the will of a majority of Americans. The Supreme Court, however, is not politically accountable. By declaring a law unconstitutional, the Supreme Court makes it enormously difficult for voters to overturn that decision; only an amendment to the Constitution (requiring approval of two-thirds of Congress and three-quarters of the state legislatures) can override it. Judicial review stymies voters' liberty to govern themselves. Proponents of judicial review argue that it is necessary to protect the ideals in the Constitution. But the Constitution represents the values a majority of Americans held more than two centuries ago. The acts of the political branches of government, on the other hand, are more likely to accurately reflect the values of a majority of Americans today. Thus, to promote the values of a majority of Americans, the Supreme Court should refrain from judicial review. Judicial review is especially problematic because the nine unelected justices of the Supreme Court are not likely to reflect the views of the nation as a whole. A vast majority of the justices throughout American history have been white, male, and wealthy. Thus, the values they promote when they strike down legislative acts are likely to differ from the values of a majority of Americans.	Judicial review has an important role to play in ensuring that our democracy functions. Without the possibility for judicial review, elected representatives could pass laws to insulate themselves from political pressure. For example, Congress could pass a law making it a crime to criticize congresspersons. Such laws inhibit democracy from functioning well. The Supreme Court, insulated from political pressure, should exercise its power of judicial review to ensure participation and reinforce representation in the political process. Judicial review also allows the Supreme Court to transcend legislative preoccupation with immediate results and protect values at the center of our political system (e.g., protection of minority rights). Our system, moreover, has many countermajoritarian features. The Constitution established the Senate, in which Wyoming and California are on equal footing; and the electoral college, not a popular majority, elects the president. Senate rules permit *filibustering,* allowing one senator to obstruct a proposed piece of legislation unless a supermajority of senators overrides the filibuster. In short, our system is *republican,* not majority rule. Judicial review is not inconsistent with this form of government. Additionally, the Supreme Court has a high turnover rate. On average, a Supreme Court vacancy opens up every 22 months, so a one-term president can expect to fill two Supreme Court seats. This high turnover rate tends to ensure that the Court stays in step with the national pulse. And the political branches of government are not exactly the paradigms of deliberative democracy that high school textbooks make them out to be.

Questions & Problems

1. Explain how each branch of the government checks the power of the other branches.
2. How can both Sue and Sam be correct when Sue claims the commerce clause increases government's power and Sam claims the commerce clause reduces government's power?
3. What is the purpose of the contract clause?
4. How does the contract clause affect state regulation?
5. How does the First Amendment protection of corporate political speech differ from the protection of corporate commercial speech?
6. The state of Oklahoma required that all coal-burning power plants in the state purchase at least 10 percent of the coal they burned from Oklahoma coal mines. The state of Wyoming challenged the legislation. On what constitutional basis do you think Wyoming brought its action? Do you believe Wyoming's challenge was successful? Why or why not? [*Wyoming v. Oklahoma,* 502 U.S. 437 (1992).]
7. During a legal search of Alvin Smith's house, police discovered a large amount of child pornography. A subsequent police investigation revealed that Smith had taken 1,768 sexually explicit pictures of girls below the age of 18. The investigation also revealed that the children depicted in the pictures were Florida residents and that Smith, a Florida resident, took the pictures in his house. The paper on which the photographs were printed, however, came from Rochester, New York, and the photographs were processed by equipment made in California. The government prosecuted Smith for violating a federal statute prohibiting child pornography. Smith challenged his conviction on grounds that Congress overstepped its commerce clause authority because his production of child pornography did not involve or substantially affect interstate commerce. Do you think the court agreed with Smith's argument? Why or why not? [*United States v. Smith,* 402 F.3d 1303 (2005).]
8. Deputy Catherine Hedges stopped Allan Hollowell for driving his truck 56 mph in a 35-mph zone. Hedges called for backup, and when other officers arrived, they discovered that Hollowell's license was suspended. The officers placed him under arrest, searched his person, and found marijuana and crack cocaine. Upon searching the truck, the officers discovered a set of scales, plastic bags, a laptop computer, and a large quantity of cocaine. The trial court found Hollowell guilty of two felonies and misdemeanors. Hollowell appealed, contending that the trial court erred by including the evidence police discovered searching his person and his truck. How do you think the supreme court of Indiana ruled in this case? [*Hollowell v. Indiana,* 753 N.E.2d. 612 (2001).]
9. An interstate trucking company filed suit against the state of Michigan, alleging that Michigan's $100 annual fee on trucks involved in intrastate commerce violates the dormant commerce clause. The trucking company argued that the fee discriminates against trucks involved in both intrastate and interstate commerce because they spend less time carrying cargo in Michigan than do trucks involved with solely intrastate commerce. The state argued that the fee is a valid exercise of its police power, intending to defray the costs of regulating the size and weight of trucks in Michigan. With whom do you think the U.S. Supreme Court sided in this case? Why? [*Am. Trucking Ass'ns v. Mich. PSC,* 125 S. Ct. 2419 (2005).]

10. The city of Dallas passed a local ordinance restricting admission to "Class E" dance halls to individuals between the ages of 14 and 18. The ordinance, however, did not impose age restrictions at other establishments where teenagers congregated. Charles Stanglin operated both a Class E dance hall and a roller-skating rink in the same building. He sued to have the ordinance struck down as an unconstitutional violation of the equal protection clause. The trial court upheld the ordinance, but a higher Texas court overturned the decision. The city appealed to the U.S. Supreme Court. What standard do you think the Supreme Court applied to the case? Why? What do you think was the result of an equal protection analysis according to that standard? [*City of Dallas v. Stanglin,* 490 U.S. 19 (1989).]
11. The Federal Alcohol Administration Act prohibited beer labels from disclosing the alcohol content of the beer. Coors Brewing Company challenged the regulation. The government argued that it had a substantial interest in preventing "strength wars" among beer producers. Moreover, the government argued, the act was narrowly tailored to further that interest. Apply the Central Hudson test to explain how you believe the U.S. Supreme Court ruled in this case. [*Rubin v. Coors Brewing Co.,* 115 S. Ct. 1585 (1995).]
12. Harris County arrested Carl Pruett for violating a law prohibiting bail-bond businesses from soliciting individuals with outstanding arrest warrants. The purpose of the law, according to the county, was to prevent individuals from fleeing the county when notified of their outstanding arrest warrants by bail-bonding companies. Pruett argued that the law was an unconstitutional restriction of his right to free speech. How do you think the court ruled in this case? Why? [*Harris County Bail Bond Bd. v. Pruett,* 2005 Tex. App. LEXIS 1912 (2005).]
13. In April 1986 the FBI arrested Larry Dean Dusenbery in his home. After the FBI removed Dusenbery from the premises and placed him in custody, it obtained and executed a search warrant for his property. During the search, FBI agents seized drugs, drug paraphernalia, weapons, an automobile, and $21,939 in currency. Dusenbery pleaded guilty to a charge of possession with intent to distribute. The trial court sentenced him to 12 years in prison and a 6-year special parole. Two years later, the FBI began to administratively forfeit the seized possessions. This process required that the FBI send written notice of the forfeiture procedures to Dusenbery. The FBI, in accordance with this policy, sent letters to Dusenbery by certified mail to the federal corrections institution where he was incarcerated. The FBI sent identical letters to his home address and his mother's address. The FBI received no response, but nevertheless it proceeded with the forfeiture of his assets. Five years later, Dusenbery filed a motion requesting that the FBI return his property to him. He received a response from the United States government informing him that the FBI had returned all property not used in the drug business and had forfeited the rest of it. Dusenbery filed a civil suit claiming that the FBI denied his right of due process when it forfeited his property because he had never received the letter from the FBI. The district court ruled that the FBI had not violated his due process rights; the FBI satisfied his rights when it sent the notice. How do you think the appellate court ruled in this case? Why? [*Dusenbery v. United States,* 534 U.S. 161 (2002).]
14. In 1996 Congress passed the Telecommunications Act. This legislation addressed growing public concern that children could access, at least in part, sexually explicit programming through a phenomenon called "signal bleed." Signal bleed occurs when visual or audio portions of programs can be seen or heard despite cable providers' attempt to scramble the programs. The act required that cable providers fully scramble

or otherwise fully block those channels or that they limit transmission to hours when children are unlikely to watch television. Most cable operators adopted the latter approach, broadcasting programs only during an eight-hour period at night. Playboy Entertainment Group, a firm that transmitted sexually explicit programming to cable television operators, filed suit against the federal government. The suit claimed that the Telecommunications Act violated the First Amendment, and it asked for an injunction prohibiting the act's enforcement. The district court ruled that the act imposed a content-based restriction on speech; the court concluded that although the government interests were compelling, the government could further those interests in a less restrictive way. How do you think the U.S. Supreme Court ruled in this case? Why? [*United States v. Playboy Entertainment Group,* 529 U.S. 803 (2000).]

15. The Bloomington City Council passed a zoning ordinance limiting occupancy of dwellings in certain neighborhoods to a maximum of three unrelated adults. A grandfather clause in the ordinance protected property rented to more than three unrelated adults at the time the ordinance was passed. (*Grandfather clauses* state that when ordinances are passed, uses of land that existed before the new ordinance may continue even though the use is forbidden in the new ordinance.) After the passage of the ordinance, Jack Leisz bought some grandfathered rental property that lost its protection because it had not been properly registered with the city. Thus, the ordinance limited the number of renters permitted on the property. A trial court convicted Leisz for violating the ordinance. Leisz contested the ordinance as an uncompensated regulatory taking of his property. How do you think the supreme court of Indiana ruled in this case? [*Board of Zoning Appeals v. Leisz,* 702 N.E.2d 1026 (1998).]

Looking for more review material?

The Online Learning Center at **www.mhhe.com/kubasek1e** contains this chapter's "Assignment on the Internet" and also a list of URLs for more information entitled "On the Internet." Find both of them in the Student Center portion of the OLC, along with quizzes and other helpful materials.

International and Comparative Law

CASE OPENER

Unocal and Myanmar

In 1993, Unocal Corporation invested in the Moattama Gas Transportation Company (MGTC) with Total Petroleum of France and the Myanma Oil and Gas Enterprise, a company owned by the government of Myanmar. MGTC was to construct and operate a natural gas pipeline from the Yadana gas field, located in the Andaman Sea off the coast of Myanmar, to Thailand. Agreements among the MGTC partners appointed the military to provide security for the portion of the project passing through Myanmar's territory.

The military allegedly engaged in numerous human rights violations in its provision of security for the pipeline project. The military was accused of confiscating personal property and food from villagers, forcibly relocating people in the path of the pipeline, and utilizing forced labor for pipeline-related construction projects. Laborers who failed to adequately perform their duties or attempted to escape were allegedly subject to beatings, torture, and, in some instances, summary execution.

For its part, Unocal claimed that only paid voluntary labor recruited from local villages was utilized to construct the pipeline. Workers were compensated in amounts above the prevailing wage and were provided with appropriate training and health care. Unocal further noted that forced labor is expressly prohibited by its code of conduct and U.S. law and is strictly limited pursuant to the laws of Myanmar.

In 1996, as a result of the alleged abuses, 14 villagers initiated litigation against the participants in MGTC in the U.S. District Court for the Central District of California. The plaintiffs alleged that the defendants engaged in arbitrary arrest; false imprisonment; torture; cruel, inhuman, and degrading treatment; battery; assault; and intentional infliction of emotional distress. It was additionally alleged that the defendants failed to exercise reasonable care in selecting the military to provide security for the project. The plaintiffs

CHAPTER

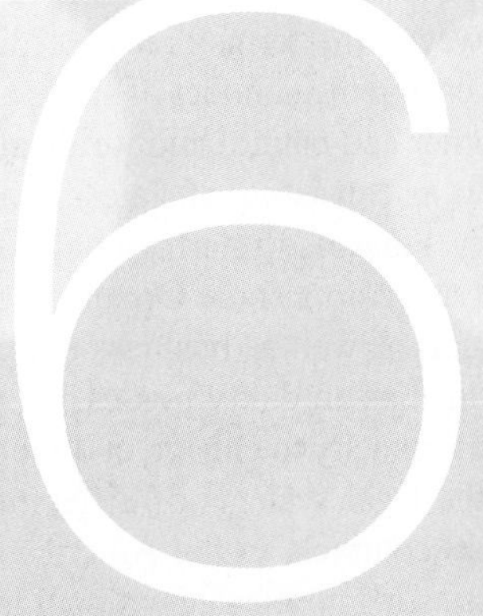

maintained that such actions violated federal and state law, international treaties, and customary international law.

1. Could Unocal have done anything different to avoid the outcome of its investment in Myanmar?

The Wrap-Up at the end of this chapter will answer this question.

Learning Objectives

After reading this chapter, you will be able to answer the following questions:

1. What is international law?
2. How is business transacted in the international marketplace?
3. What ethical considerations impact business in the international marketplace?
4. What is the General Agreement on Tariffs and Trade, and what are its important provisions?
5. What are regional trade agreements?
6. What is comparative law?
7. How does contract law differ among states?
8. How does employment law differ among states?
9. How are disputes settled in the international marketplace?

The terms *international law* and *comparative law* are often used interchangeably. However, the terms are quite different. **International law** has been defined as the laws governing the conduct of states and international organizations and their relations with one another and natural and juridical persons.[1] We generally think of **international organizations** as consisting of states. Examples include the United Nations, the International Monetary Fund, the International Bank for Reconstruction and Development (World Bank), and the World Trade Organization. The term *natural and juridical persons* refers to individuals as well as business organizations. *Statehood,* for purposes of international law, is defined as an entity possessing territory, a permanent population, a government, and the legal capacity to engage in diplomatic relations.[2] In contrast, **comparative law** is the study of the legal systems of different states. For example, a comparative legal theorist might study contracts in the American, Chinese, and French legal systems by identifying and contrasting applicable national laws.

Comparative legal studies start with the examination of national sources of law embodied in constitutions, legislative enactments, administrative rules and regulations, and the decisions of judicial bodies. But where does one find principles of international law? Article 38 of the Statute of the International Court of Justice, a part of the United Nations system, identifies four sources of international law. These sources are customs, international agreements, general principles of law recognized by legal systems throughout the world (such as equity and elementary considerations of humanity), and secondary sources (such as decisions of the International Court of Justice, resolutions of the U.N. General Assembly, and scholarly writings).[3]

Most important for our purposes are customs and international agreements. *Customary international law* consists of two elements. First, in order to be deemed a custom, there must be a general and consistent practice by states. Second, states must accept this general and consistent practice as binding law. In the *Paquete Habana* case, the U.S. Supreme Court held that in the absence of a governing international agreement or controlling executive or legislative act or judicial decision, U.S. courts must rely on customary international law.[4]

By contrast, an *international agreement* is defined as a written agreement that is made between states governed by international law and that relates to an international subject matter.[5] International agreements may be bilateral (between two states) or multilateral (between three or more states). Regardless of their form, international agreements do not take effect in the signatory states until they have been ratified. Ratification occurs in many different ways throughout the world. In the United States, ratification requires the advice and consent of two-thirds of the Senate after the president's submission of the international agreement for consideration.[6] Most international agreements do not take effect until a designated number of states have ratified their obligations.

Doing Business Internationally

A company seeking to enter a foreign market has a number of options. The simplest method of doing so is through the **export** of the company's product to the foreign marketplace. A **foreign sales representative** is an agent who distributes, represents, or sells goods on

[1] Restatement (Third) of the Foreign Relations Law of the United States, §101 (1987).

[2] Montevideo Convention on the Rights and Duties of States, December 26, 1933, art. 1, 165 L.N.T.S. 19, reprinted in *American Journal of International Law* 28 (Supp. 1934), p. 75.

[3] Statute of the International Court of Justice, June 26, 1945, art. 38, 59 Stat. 1055, 1060.

[4] 175 U.S. 677, 700 (1900).

[5] Vienna Convention on the Law of Treaties, May 23, 1969, art. 2, 1155 U.N.T.S. 331.

[6] U.S. Const., art. II, §2, cl. 2.

connecting to the core

Economics

While exports provide a means by which a business can enter a foreign market, as you may have learned in your economics class, an overemphasis on exporting can create tension among trading countries. For instance, if one country imports more than it exports, thereby having a trade deficit, other countries necessarily have a trade surplus. When the United States has a trade deficit, for example, U.S. citizens are consuming more than the country is producing, meaning that the trade deficit allows U.S. consumers to live at a higher standard of living than would likely be possible if they had to depend only on domestic goods. Consequently, other countries' exports to the United States serve as somewhat of a "free lunch." In addition to allowing a higher standard of living, a trade deficit may mitigate inflationary pressures. Trade deficits have certain drawbacks, however, such as potential difficulty in reaching full employment. Also, countries that operate at a trade surplus might adopt different trade initiatives to discontinue contributing to another nation's proverbial "free lunch." Nevertheless, from the perspective of the individual businessperson, the more that the businessperson can export, the more likely that the businessperson will be able to increase her or his "bottom line."

Source: Bradley Schiller, *The Economy Today* (New York: McGraw-Hill/Irwin, 2006), pp. 377–378.

behalf of a foreign seller. The representative uses materials provided by the company to market its product to potential buyers and forwards orders directly to the company. The representative is usually compensated through the payment of commissions on completed transactions. Companies may also engage **distributors** for their products in foreign marketplaces. A distributor is a merchant that purchases goods from a seller for resale in a foreign market. The distributor is responsible for supporting and servicing the products it sells. Unlike the foreign sales representative, the distributor takes title to the goods and assumes the risk of being unable to resell them at a profit.

Companies seeking to enter foreign markets may also do so through franchise and licensing agreements. A **franchise agreement** is a contract whereby a company (known as the *franchisor*) grants permission (a license) to a foreign entity (known as a *franchisee*) to utilize the franchisor's name, trademark, or copyright in the operation of a business and associated sale of goods in a foreign state. In return for this license, the franchisee remits payments to the franchisor, usually based on a percentage of the franchisee's gross or net sales. In a **licensing agreement,** the foreign company (known as the *licensor*) grants permission to a company in the targeted market (known as the *licensee*) to utilize the licensor's intellectual property, consisting of patents, trademarks, copyrights, or trade secrets. In return, the licensor receives royalty payments from the licensee, usually based on the licensee's gross or net sales. Some of the difficulties and risks associated with franchising in the international marketplace are discussed in the Case Nugget.

Companies seeking a more permanent presence in a foreign jurisdiction have several different options. A company may establish a **representative office** for limited purposes such as market analysis or product promotion. A company seeking a more significant presence may form a **joint venture** with a company located in the host state. A joint venture is an association between two or more parties wherein the parties share profits and management responsibilities with respect to a specific project. Companies may also establish a **foreign subsidiary,** or **affiliate.** An affiliate is a business enterprise located in one state that is directly or indirectly owned and controlled by a company located in another state. The affiliate is usually established in conformity with the laws of the foreign state and is subject to that state's regulation. However, as was demonstrated in the Unocal case at the

Case Nugget Franchising

Dymocks Franchise Systems (NSW) Pty Ltd. v. Todd
Judicial Committee of the Privy Council, 1 NZLR 289 (2004)

Dymocks was a group of companies that operated retail bookstores in Australia and franchises in New Zealand through Dymocks Franchise System (DFS). DFS entered into three contracts with Bilgola Enterprises and Lambton Quay Books Ltd., owned by the Todds, for the operation of bookstores in New Zealand. DFS subsequently terminated the agreements on the basis that the Todds breached the contracts by inefficiently managing the businesses, failing to maintain adequate sales, and sharing financial information with a third party. The Todds claimed that the termination was a breach of contract by DFS.

In proceedings spanning seven weeks, the trial judge held that DFS could terminate the franchise agreements on the sole basis of the disclosure of the financial information, which violated an obligation of good faith and confidentiality implied in all such agreements. This conclusion was based on sources from North American and Australian law. The court of appeal reversed this decision with respect to the obligation of good faith and confidentiality in U.S. and Australian law. The court also held that imposition of such an obligation conflicted with certainty in commercial contracts and was reserved solely for employment contracts. The Judicial Committee of the Privy Council agreed with the court of appeal's holding on the lack of expert testimony. However, the Judicial Committee refused to endorse the court of appeal's conclusion that the imposition of an implied obligation of good faith and confidentiality in franchise agreements was an undesirable result. Rather, the Judicial Committee reserved the issue of the desirability of such an obligation for decision at a later date.

beginning of the chapter, participants in collaborative investments may find themselves liable for actions of their business partners even if they did not participate in such actions or expressly disapproved of their commission.

Ethical Considerations

International businesspersons must take ethical considerations into account in the decision-making process. For example, if a company is considering the export of its product for ultimate consumption by overseas consumers, it must resolve issues relating to proper usage and safety. Such consumers may not fully understand risks associated with use of the product, or national safety standards may offer less protection than those applicable to the product in the United States. An example in this regard is tobacco products. Although these products are subject to stringent regulation in the United States with respect to advertising, health warnings, and availability to minors, this regulation is the exception rather than the global norm. U.S. tobacco companies may find it prudent to attempt to minimize the negative impact of the absence of stringent regulation, realizing that such controls are within the exclusive jurisdiction of national governments.

A related question is whether companies have an ethical obligation to provide beneficial products at reduced or no cost to consumers who cannot otherwise afford them.

For example, there are currently more than 25 million people who are HIV-positive in sub-Saharan Africa, and more than 20 million people have died of AIDS. HIV/AIDS is the leading cause of death in the region. Drug therapy to assist those infected with HIV is beyond the financial reach of these victims as well as their national governments. As such, do pharmaceutical companies have an ethical duty to reduce the cost of their drugs or give drugs away free of charge? Should the pharmaceutical companies permit the manufacture of generic copies of their drugs for treatment of those infected with HIV in sub-Saharan Africa? Are there other, less drastic alternatives available that would be effective in combating the epidemic while preserving and protecting the rights of the pharmaceutical companies to their products?

Ethical considerations are not limited to the products a company places in the international stream of commerce. Companies must also carefully consider the location of their operations. For example, although many states offer the benefit of lower labor costs than those in the United States, companies employing workers in these states must be careful to avoid the perception or reality of exploiting the workers. An example is Nike, Inc. In an effort to lower its labor costs, Nike entered into contracts with factories in Vietnam and Indonesia to produce Nike apparel. Although these operations were successful to the extent they lowered Nike's cost of doing business and helped the company achieve greater prosperity, consumers, foreign employees, and human rights groups criticized the working conditions in the factories. Nike was alleged to be making enormous profits, while its foreign workers suffered unfair wages, unreasonable hours, and unsafe working conditions. However, even though the working conditions may be considered poor by Western standards, they are equal to or better than the conditions prevalent in the host states. Nike may also be defended on the ground that it must remain competitive as other manufacturers have factories with similar working conditions. Nevertheless, Nike's decision to operate factories in such locations resulted in the expenditure of capital and time defending the company's reputation and preventing permanent harm to its profitability.

A related question is whether companies have the obligation to refrain from conducting business in states with repressive forms of government. The Unocal case is an example in this regard. Despite its knowledge of the brutality of the military dictatorship in power in Myanmar, Unocal chose to enter into a partnership with other private interests for the exploitation of offshore natural gas deposits. Unocal's investment may be defended on the basis that companies in the natural resource industry make investment decisions based on the location of resources rather than political considerations. Nevertheless, as with Nike, Unocal's decision to invest in Myanmar resulted in the expenditure of capital and time defending the company's reputation.

Ethical considerations also arise from how a company does business overseas. For example, the **Foreign Corrupt Practices Act (FCPA)** prohibits U.S. companies from offering or paying bribes to foreign government officials, political parties, and candidates for office for the purpose of obtaining or retaining business.[7] This act arose from the payment of bribes by Lockheed to politicians in Japan and the Netherlands for the purpose of securing government contracts in the 1970s. Four hundred companies subsequently admitted to the payment of hundreds of millions of dollars in bribes all over the world. Violations may be punished by the imposition of significant fines, as well as imprisonment, on companies and individuals. The FCPA also requires the maintenance of records that fairly and accurately reflect company transactions and the disposition of assets.

[7] 15 U.S.C. §§ 78dd-1–78ff (2000).

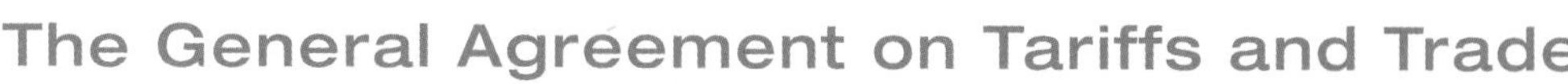

The General Agreement on Tariffs and Trade

There are two primary types of barriers to international trade. **Tariffs** are taxes levied on imported goods. Tariffs may be calculated as a percentage of the value of the imported good *(ad valorem tariff),* on the basis of the number or weight of the imported units or a flat per-unit charge *(specific tariff),* or as a combination of the two *(compound tariff).* A **nontariff barrier** is any impediment to trade other than tariffs. Examples of nontariff barriers include quotas, embargoes, and indirect barriers. *Quotas* are limits on imported goods, usually imposed for national economic reasons or for the protection of domestic industry. An *embargo* is a ban on trade with a particular state or on the sale of specific products, usually on the basis of foreign policy or national security. *Indirect barriers* are laws, practices, customs, and traditions that have the effect of limiting or discouraging the sale and purchase of imported goods.

The **General Agreement on Tariffs and Trade (GATT)** is a comprehensive multilateral trading system designed to achieve distortion-free international trade through the minimization of tariffs and removal of artificial barriers. GATT is a legacy of the Great Depression and World War II. Originally conceived as a temporary measure, GATT became effective on January 1, 1948. The United States was one of the 23 signatories to what was referred to as *GATT 1947.* In the intervening years, GATT has undergone numerous changes as a result of eight different negotiating rounds. The most recently completed round is the Uruguay Round, whose 1994 agreement took effect on January 1, 1995. Thus, the most recent version of the GATT is known as *GATT 1994.*

The Uruguay Round established the **World Trade Organization (WTO).** The WTO facilitates international cooperation in opening markets and provides a forum for future trade negotiations and the settlement of international trade disputes. WTO membership presently consists of 147 states, thereby making GATT the most comprehensive trading system in world history.

GATT established several general principles of trade law. Article I addresses the principle of **most favored nation,** a principle now known as **normal trade relations.** This principle requires that WTO member states treat like goods coming from other WTO member states on an equal basis. WTO member states are specifically prohibited from discriminating against like products on the basis of their country of origin. **National treatment** is set forth in Article III. National treatment prohibits WTO member states from regulating, taxing, or otherwise treating imported products any differently than domestically produced products. Article XI prohibits **quantitative restrictions** on imports. These restrictions impose limits on the importation of certain products, on the basis of number of units, weight, or value, for national economic reasons or the protection of domestic industry.

Article VI relates to dumping and subsidies. **Dumping** is the practice wherein an exporter sells products in a foreign state for less than the price charged for the same or comparable goods in the exporter's home market. Article VI condemns dumping if it causes or threatens to cause material injury to an established industry. This determination is usually made by examination of the volume of imports, their effect on prices, and the impact on the affected industry. The remedy for dumping is the assessment of antidumping duties. *Antidumping duties* are tariffs imposed on dumped products equal to the margin of dumping, specifically, the difference between the export and domestic prices. Antidumping duties may be imposed only after the completion of an investigation by appropriate government authorities.

A **subsidy** is a government financial contribution that confers a benefit on a specific industry or enterprise. Examples of subsidies include direct transfers of funds, such as loans and grants; loan guarantees; tax credits; government procurement; and price supports.

There are three basic types of subsidies. *Actionable subsidies* are illegal under Article VI. Actionable subsidies include subsidies payable to domestic manufacturers either on the basis of export performance or for the use of domestic, rather than imported, input in the manufacturing process. Actionable subsidies are remedied through the imposition of countervailing duties. Countervailing duties are special tariffs imposed on subsidized goods in order to offset the beneficial effect of the illegal subsidy. *Nonactionable subsidies* consist of expenditures on research and development, aid to underdeveloped regions within a state, and aid to foster compliance with environmental standards. *Domestic subsidies* are generally not actionable unless they are not part of the government's legitimate responsibility of directing industrial growth and funding social programs and they cause material injury to benefits conferred by the GATT on other WTO member states.

Disputes between WTO member states are governed by GATT's dispute settlement procedures. The **Dispute Settlement Understanding** allows recognized governments of WTO member states to bring an action alleging a violation of the GATT. After an aggrieved state files a complaint, the process commences with consultation in an attempt to resolve the dispute. The states may also utilize mediation involving a trade expert. If such efforts are unsuccessful, a panel is established by the WTO Secretariat to hear the dispute. This panel, consisting of three to five trade experts, hears oral arguments and reviews the written submissions of the parties. The panel then drafts and ultimately adopts a report determining the merits of the claims. Aggrieved states have the right to contest the panel's decision before the WTO's appellate body. The panel and the appellate body may only recommend that a state found to be in violation of its obligations cease and desist from such practices within a reasonable time. Failure of a state to comply may lead to the imposition of sanctions, usually consisting of the suspension of concessions by the injured state. Such sanctions may impose only an equivalent burden on the noncomplying state and can be imposed only for as long as the trade barrier remains in place.

Regional Trade Agreements

There are two basic types of regional trade agreements: free trade and bilateral trade. In a **free trade agreement,** two or more states agree to reduce and gradually eliminate tariffs and other trade barriers. The **North American Free Trade Agreement (NAFTA)** between the United States, Canada, and Mexico is an example of a regional free trade agreement. In effect since January 1, 1994, NAFTA mirrors many of the provisions set forth in GATT but accords favorable treatment only to goods of "North American origin." NAFTA also reduces barriers to direct foreign investment and ensures the free flow of capital. Disputes between NAFTA members are resolved through a dispute resolution process coordinated by the Free Trade Commission. This process involves attempts to reach a negotiated settlement, the convocation of dispute resolution panels to hear evidence and determine the existence of a violation, and enforcement of orders through the authorization of retaliation in the event of noncompliance. In addition, unlike GATT, NAFTA addresses environmental and workers' rights issues. NAFTA members pledge to cooperate in protecting the environment and developing common environmental standards. NAFTA members also recognize basic labor rights, including freedom of association, the right to engage in collective bargaining and strikes, prohibitions on forced labor and child labor, freedom from employment discrimination, the right to receive equal pay for work of equal value, and the right to minimum acceptable working conditions and occupational safety and health. The United States is also a party to the Central American Free Trade Agreement (CAFTA) with El Salvador, Guatemala, Nicaragua, Honduras, Costa Rica, and the Dominican Republic.

A *customs union* is a free trade area with the additional feature of a common external tariff on products originating from outside the union. The European Union (EU) is an example of a customs union. The EU is a loose association of states with a basis in international law formed for the purpose of forging closer ties among the peoples of Europe. The modern EU had its inception in three treaties between Belgium, France, Italy, Luxembourg, the Netherlands, and West Germany (now Germany) in the 1950s. These treaties integrated industrial sectors within the states, eradicated internal tariffs, created a common external tariff for goods originating in nonmember states, and strove to create a common market through the free movement of people, services, goods, and capital. Subsequent rounds of expansion added Austria, Denmark, Finland, Greece, Ireland, Portugal, Spain, Sweden, and the United Kingdom. Expansion in 2004 added 10 more member states, specifically, Cyprus, the Czech Republic, Estonia, Hungary, Latvia, Lithuania, Malta, Poland, Slovakia, and Slovenia. This expansion created the largest regional trading bloc in the world, containing more than 440 million people. The most recent expansion occurred in January 2007 with the addition of Bulgaria and Romania.

The EU is primarily governed by four institutions: the Council of Ministers, the European Commission, the European Parliament, and the European Court of Justice. These institutions create, enforce, and interpret EU law. EU law is found in the primary source, the treaties themselves, and in secondary sources of law consisting of legislation designed to implement the treaties. The supremacy doctrine provides that EU law preempts inconsistent national laws in fields where a transfer of power and integration have occurred. National law governs in fields where no transfer of authority has occurred.

States may also enter into **bilateral trade agreements,** which relate to trade between two states. For example, the United States has several bilateral free trade agreements, including agreements with Australia, Bahrain, Chile, Israel, Jordan, Morocco, and Singapore.

Comparative Law

As previously defined, comparative law is the study of the legal systems of different states. Why would someone wish to study comparative law? What are the benefits of comparing the laws and legal systems of different states? First, one may gain a better understanding of the general purpose of law through the study of other legal systems. Second, the study of other legal systems assists in the development of a critical viewpoint of one's own legal system.

Studying a variety of legal systems demonstrates that one's own legal system is only one of many alternatives. After thinking critically about alternative laws, one might decide that one's own state should adopt the other state's law or method of resolving a dispute. Central and Eastern European states benefited from the study of comparative law while rebuilding their own systems after the collapse of their totalitarian political systems and communist economic systems in the 1990s. The rapidly evolving economic transformation of the People's Republic of China is a more recent example of a state benefiting from comparative legal studies. Future business managers can benefit from comparative law study as the laws they will encounter will likely be different from American laws. Moreover, different cultures and legal systems have different expectations regarding business transactions. Punctuality, dress, language, gestures, and negotiating styles vary throughout the world. Learning about these variations could mean the difference between cementing a transaction and losing a deal to a competitor.

What do comparative legal scholars actually study? In other words, what kinds of questions do they ask? Comparative legal scholars can ask a broad range of questions. These questions are generally classified into two categories: questions about the system and its procedures and questions about substantive law. In the discussion below, initial consideration is given to different legal systems and procedures. This is followed by consideration of substantive law through a comparison of contract law and employment law in a variety of states. The chapter concludes with considerations relevant to private dispute resolution.

Legal Systems and Procedures

CIVIL LAW SYSTEMS

Although legal codes date as far back as the Code of Hammurabi, **civil law systems** are derived from Roman law. Many modern civil law systems were strongly influenced by the French Civil Code of 1804 and the German Civil Code of 1896. Other legal systems fashioned their own laws around a mixture of these codes. The codes generally covered areas of private law such as property, contracts, torts, and family law. The codes tended to reflect preferences for the protection of private property, individual freedom, and freedom of contract.

Today, codes in civil law systems serve as the sole official source of law. Secondary sources of law include custom and general principles of law. Precedent is not an important source of law in the civil law system. The civil law system is the most common legal system in the world. Examples of civil law systems can be found in most European nations, the People's Republic of China, and Japan. Furthermore, the state of Louisiana, because of its French roots, is classified as having a "mixed" legal system.

Civil law systems use a system of separation of powers. However, this system is unlike the U.S. system of checks and balances. In civil law systems, the legislative branch has ultimate authority, and the judicial branch is often mistrusted. Why? Remember, the ultimate source of law in civil law systems is the codes. Consequently, the judicial branch interprets the code and applies the code to resolve disputes. However, the judicial branch cannot create its own law. Thus, the separation of powers refers to the limitations on the judicial branch and superiority of the codes.

Judges in the civil law system typically become judges early in their careers. They complete a training period, take an examination, and become judges. Judges at the highest judicial levels are typically professors or experienced practitioners. Because the judges cannot "create" new law and are required to interpret and apply the code to the facts of the case, the public does not often know the identity and record of judges in a civil case.

After the pleadings have entered the legal system, the evidence period begins. This period is characterized by a series of meetings and hearings. The primary responsibility for the development of evidence rests with the judge. Consequently, the judge asks witnesses questions and introduces legal theories. Neither the parties nor the judge is required to formally admit evidence to the court, and hearsay and opinion are considered acceptable forms of evidence.

Judges in the civil law system have primary responsibility for determining and applying the correct legal principles. However, the judge responsible for deciding the case may be a different judge than the one who helped gather evidence. In fact, several judges might serve on a panel to decide the case.

COMMON LAW SYSTEMS

Common law systems originated from the English legal system. English common law began in 1066, when William the Conqueror assumed the English throne. The centralization of government paved the way for a centralized court system.

In the common law system, the courts develop rules governing areas of law. In addition to relying on constitutions, legislation, and regulations, courts are guided by precedent, or *stare decisis;* thus, if a higher court has created a precedent, a lower court is bound by that precedent. However, if a court cannot find a precedent to guide its reasoning, the court may offer its own rule. Both the emphasis on precedent and the judge's ability to create rules are important characteristics of common law systems. Examples of common law systems are seen in Australia, India, the United Kingdom, and the United States.

Unlike judges in the civil law system, judges in the common law system are typically appointed. In the United States, certain judges are elected, while others are appointed. The training and examination required to become a civil law judge helps ensure that such judges are qualified; the fact that a person is capable of being elected does not necessarily mean that the person is also qualified to be a judge.

How are judges in the common law system perceived? Because common law judges have opportunities to make law through their decisions, common law judges are relatively well known and the public perceives them as powerful individuals who shape the law. This status has resulted in recent criticism of judges in the United States as "activist" and going beyond the bounds of existing constitutional and statutory restraints. Clearly, common law judges have much more public visibility associated with their jobs than do civil law judges.

There are numerous procedural differences between the common law system and the civil law system. The common law system is an *adversarial system,* a system in which two opposing sides present their arguments before a neutral fact finder who determines which side has presented the most credible evidence or met its burden of proof. The use of the adversarial method in common law systems leads to procedures that differ from those in civil law systems. First, after the advocates enter pleadings in the common law system, there is a period of pretrial discovery. Second, the judge typically does not become significantly involved in the case until trial. Third, in the common law system, the judge is not responsible for gathering any evidence; the parties themselves bear this responsibility. Fourth, common law systems rely on juries as fact finders; civil law systems do not use juries. Fifth, as a consequence of the use of juries, common law systems have extensive rules governing admissibility of evidence.

OTHER LEGAL SYSTEMS

Although the civil and common law systems are predominant, there are other legal systems worthy of mention. *Socialist legal systems,* such as exist in Cuba and North Korea, are based on the premise that the rights of society as a whole outweigh the rights of the individual. In such systems, law does not act as a limit on the exercise of government power. Traditionally, the state owns the means of production and property in a socialist legal system.

An *Islamic legal system* is based on the fundamental tenet that law is derived from and interpreted in harmony with *Shari'a* ("God's law") and the Koran. The preeminent concern is moral conduct, such as honoring agreements and acting in good faith. However, there are many interpretations of Islamic law, as evidenced by the differences between legal systems in Iran, Pakistan, and Saudi Arabia and as practiced by the former Taliban regime in Afghanistan.

Substantive Law

COMPARATIVE CONTRACT LAW

The U.S. businessperson in the global marketplace should give careful thought to the question of what law may be applicable to the interpretation and enforcement of his or her contracts. Although this issue may be resolved by using a choice-of-law clause (discussed later in the chapter), the absence of such a clause may result in the contract being subject to either of the parties' national laws or the lex mercatoria. In addition, if the contract is for the sale of goods, it may be subject to the Convention on the International Sale of Goods (CISG). Thus, it is imperative that the international businessperson be aware of the provisions of each of these laws. While many provisions of national laws, the lex mercatoria, and the CISG are closely related to principles of U.S. contract law, the businessperson who assumes that these laws are identical, or similar enough that any differences are inconsequential to contract interpretation and enforcement, is likely to be unpleasantly surprised. This section reviews the sources of contract law in the international marketplace and notes some of the similarities and differences between these sources.

The lex mercatoria and national contract codes. One potential source of contract law is the lex mercatoria. The **lex mercatoria,** literally the "law of merchants," is defined as the body of customs or trade usages developed by merchants to facilitate business transactions. The lex mercatoria has its sources in public international law, uniform laws, general principles of contract law, rules of international organizations, custom and usage, standard form contracts, and arbitral decisions.

Another source of law applicable to international contracts is *national laws.* In the United States, these laws are embodied in the common law of contracts and, for contracts relating to the sale of goods, in the Uniform Commercial Code. Given the predominance of the civil law system, most nations' contract laws are set forth in codes. These codes have many similarities to U.S. law. For example, Section 2-615 of the Uniform Commercial Code excuses delays in the delivery of goods or nondelivery in the event performance has been rendered "impracticable by the occurrence of a contingency the nonoccurrence of which was a basic assumption on which the contract was made." In a similar fashion, the Civil Code of the Russian Federation excuses nonperformance if it is the result of an unanticipated "material change of circumstances" that could not be avoided through the exercise of reasonable care. A similar excuse for nonperformance exists in the Unified Contract Law of the People's Republic of China and the Principles of European Contract Law. Under China's national contract code, a nonperforming party is excused from liability if its inability to perform was the result of *force majeure* ("superior force"). Force majeure is a "situation which, on an objective view, is unforeseeable, unavoidable and is not able to be overcome." The Principles of European Contract Law excuse nonperformance if it is due to an impediment that is not "reasonably expected" and is beyond the control of the nonperforming party.

Despite their similarities, the differences between U.S. law and national contract codes may be very pronounced. The Principles of European Contract Law contain several examples of such differences. The Principles state that circulars, advertisements, or proposals to supply goods or services at stated prices made by a professional supplier are presumed to be standing offers to sell or supply at the stated price until the stock of goods, or the supplier's capacity to supply the service, is exhausted. With respect to acceptance, the European Principles provide a contract is concluded only when the acceptance reaches the offeror. The Principles further require that the parties negotiate in good faith, and parties are required to give reasons for terminating contract negotiations. This is a considerable difference from the U.S. approach, in which parties do not owe one another a duty to negotiate in good faith and a party may terminate negotiations in bad faith without liability unless the other party relied on the likelihood of conclusion of a final agreement. Furthermore, the European Principles do not contain a statute of frauds, and a contract can be proved by any means. Contracts are subject to interpretation utilizing the totality of the circumstances surrounding the transaction, including statements of the parties prior to entering into the contract.

Even in the areas where U.S. law and national contract codes converge, there are differences of which the international businessperson must be aware. For example, despite the presence of writing requirements as in the United States, the Russian Civil Code further declares foreign economic transactions invalid unless expressed in writing. The code places strong emphasis on formalities, including the written form, certification by a notary, and, in some cases, government registration. Similar formality is required by China's Unified Contract Law, which provides that all written contracts must state the name and residence of each party, subject matter of the contract, quantity and quality of the subject matter, price, period, place and methods of contractual performance, liability for breach, and methods of dispute resolution.

The Convention on the International Sale of Goods. The **Convention on the International Sale of Goods (CISG)** applies to transactions involving the commercial sale of goods. A *commercial sale of goods* is defined as the exchange of tangible personal property between merchants in return for consideration. A *merchant* is a person engaged in the transfer of goods in the ordinary course of business. National contract law applies in areas not covered by the CISG, such as services, real estate, and intellectual property. The CISG was adopted in 1980 and has been ratified by the majority of states in the developed world. States adopting the CISG include Australia, Canada, China, Korea, Mexico, Russia, most nations of Western Europe, and the United States, where it became effective in 1988. Notable states that have not adopted the CISG include Brazil, Japan, Ireland, India, Pakistan, Saudi Arabia, and the United Kingdom.

As a result of its adoption, there are two sets of laws governing the sale of goods in the United States, the CISG and the Uniform Commercial Code (UCC). The UCC applies if both parties to the sales transaction are residents of the United States. However, the CISG is applicable if one party is a U.S. resident and the other party is a resident of a jurisdiction that has ratified the CISG. Nevertheless, the parties are always free to opt out of the CISG and select another law to apply to their transaction. In the absence of a choice-of-law clause, the CISG applies to the sale of goods between merchants residing in different states that have ratified the CISG. The CISG also applies if national conflict-of-law rules direct the court or arbitral body to apply the law of a state that has ratified the CISG. Finally, the CISG may serve as evidence of trade usage and customs.

The U.S. businessperson must be aware of the similarities and differences between the UCC and the CISG in order to determine which set of rules they wish to have apply to their international contracts. There are numerous similarities between the UCC and CISG. For example, both recognize express warranties and implied warranties of merchantability and fitness for a particular purpose arising from the sale of goods.[8] Another similarity is in the area of damages. The UCC and the CISG limit damages to those that were foreseeable at the time of the formation of the contract. Furthermore, only damages that may be proved with some degree of certainty may be awarded. The nonbreaching party has a duty to mitigate damages, and damage awards may be reduced to the extent that the loss could have been prevented or minimized through mitigation.

However, the differences between the UCC and CISG are substantial in many areas. For example, the UCC adheres to the mailbox rule with respect to the effective time of acceptance; the CISG rejects the mailbox rule and provides that acceptance becomes effective only on its receipt by the offeror. The UCC also adheres to the statute of frauds and the parol evidence rule. As a result, contracts in excess of $500 in value must be in writing.[9]

[8] Compare UCC §§ 2-313–316 with CISG art. 35.

[9] UCC, § 2-201.

Such contracts are not subject to interpretation through prior or contemporaneous oral statements or writings if they are unambiguous in their terms.[10] By contrast, Article 11 of the CISG abolishes the statute of frauds and further provides that a contract may be proved by any means. The CISG also requires that the buyer inspect the goods on receipt, inform the seller of any nonconformity within a reasonable time, and provide notice to the seller specifying the nature of the nonconformity.[11] By comparison, under the UCC, the buyer need only state in general terms the nature of the nonconformity except in cases where the defect could have been corrected by the seller before the deadline for completion of performance.[12] Unlike the UCC, the CISG provides that the right to correct defective performances may extend beyond the deadline established by the contract.[13] The CISG also recognizes the concept of *nachfrist.* This concept allows the buyer to give notice to the seller that delivery will be accepted beyond the time prescribed in the contract. The buyer must accept any proper tender of performance during such time. The seller may also use nachfrist to request additional time to perform from the buyer. The buyer must respond to this request, or it is deemed automatically granted.[14] The UCC does not recognize nachfrist in its provisions. The Case Nugget exemplifies one of the differences between the CISG and the UCC: the requirement of specificity with respect to identifying nonconformities in performance.

Case Nugget — The Convention on the International Sale of Goods

P. v. I. Kantonsgericht Nidwalden, Switzerland (1997)

A company based in Italy delivered furniture to a Swiss company, which resold the goods in Asia. The Swiss buyer subsequently refused to pay for the furniture on the basis that it was defective. Specifically, the buyer advised the seller that the shipment contained "wrong parts" and the furniture was "full of breakages." The buyer did not identify specific defects in the furniture and accompanying parts sufficiently enough for the seller to remedy its allegedly defective performance. The seller subsequently initiated litigation against the buyer to recover the purchase price in the Kantonsgericht (district court) for the Nidwalden Canton in Switzerland.

The Kantonsgericht ruled in favor of the seller. Applying the CISG, the court held that the buyer could not rely on the alleged nonconformities in the parts and furniture. The court noted that Article 39(1) of the CISG required that a party alleging a defective tender of goods must specify the nature of the lack of conformity. The descriptions provided by the buyer were too general, and the buyer did not give the seller adequate notice of the nonconformities so that it could correct its allegedly defective performance. As a result, the court held that the seller was entitled to recover the purchase price in its entirety from the buyer.

[10] Ibid. § 2-202.

[11] CISG, art. 38.

[12] UCC, § 2-605.

[13] Compare UCC § 2-508 with CISG art. 48.

[14] CISG, arts. 47–49, 63.

COMPARATIVE EMPLOYMENT LAW

The employment relationship in the United States is governed by the *employment-at-will standard.* Under this standard, either the employer or the employee may terminate the employment relationship at any time. Furthermore, the employer and employee are free to determine the conditions of employment.

However, although the employment-at-will doctrine remains predominant in the United States, the nature of the employment relationship has changed as federal, state, and local governments have imposed various restrictions. These restrictions provide protection for workers and relate to such topics as minimum wages, unemployment and workers' compensation, occupational health and safety, employment discrimination, and termination. An employer will find that these restrictions vary significantly when it seeks to hire employees outside the United States. These differences may be acute given the rejection of the employment-at-will standard outside the United States. This section discusses two differences, specifically, minimum-wage laws and termination. The section concludes with a look at the effect of international labor standards on the employment relationship.

National regulation of the employment relationship

Minimum-wage laws. Under the Fair Labor Standards Act (FLSA), all U.S. employers are required to pay a minimum wage to employees.[15] The current minimum wage under the act is $5.15 per hour but is scheduled to increase to $7.25 per hour by the summer of 2009. The federal minimum wage is a floor below which states are not authorized to legislate with respect to employment within the scope of the FLSA. States are free to adopt minimum-wage laws in excess of the federal rate, and the majority of states have done so to date.[16]

The U.S. businessperson seeking to hire employees overseas will find a wide variety of laws relating to the payment of minimum wages. Some states, such as the People's Republic of China and Hong Kong, have no national minimum-wage laws. Under the Labor Code adopted by China in 1995, minimum wages are established by local government officials. A similar method of regulation is found in Canada, which also lacks a national minimum-wage law: Minimum wages are established individually by the provinces. Thus, the minimum wage is C$8 (Canadian dollars) in British Columbia but only C$5.90 in Alberta. In other states that lack national minimum-wage laws, minimum wages are established by industrial collective agreements. Examples of states subscribing to this approach include Austria, Denmark, Finland, Germany, Italy, Sweden, and Switzerland.

There is considerable variety among states with national minimum-wage laws. Some states establish different minimum wages depending on the age of the worker. For example, in the United Kingdom, workers 16 and 17 years old are entitled to £3 per hour. Workers between the ages of 18 and 21 years are entitled to £4.10 per hour. Workers over the age of 22 years receive £4.85 per hour.

There are also wide differences among states that do not distinguish between workers on the basis of age. Some states establish a minimum wage based on an hourly rate. For example, in Ireland, employers are required to pay no less than €7 (euros) per hour. Other states calculate minimum wages on the basis of weekly earnings. Australia, for example, requires that employers pay A$467.40 (Australian dollars) per week. States may also require the payment of minimum wages calculated on the basis of monthly earnings. In the Russian Federation, national law establishes the minimum wage as R300 (rubles) per

[15] 29 U.S.C. § 206(a)(1) (2000).

[16] The states are Alaska, Arizona, Arkansas, California, Colorado, Connecticut, Delaware, Florida, Hawaii, Illinois, Maine, Maryland, Massachusetts, Michigan, Minnesota, Missouri, Montana, Nevada, New Jersey, New York, North Carolina, Ohio, Oregon, Pennsylvania, Rhode Island, Vermont, Washington and West Virginia. Washington currently has the highest minimum wage in the United States at $7.93 per hour.

month. Other examples in this regard include Greece, Poland, Portugal, the Netherlands, Spain, and Turkey. However, there is great disparity in established rates in these states. For example, the Netherlands sets the minimum monthly wage at €1349.14; Greece, at €605; and Poland, at €180. Finally, some states have a combination of minimum-wage requirements. For example, France requires that employers meet two minimum wage standards, specifically, €7.61 per hour and €1154.18 per month. Another example is Taiwan, which adopted a law effective in July 2007 raising the minimum monthly wage to U.S. $576 and the minimum hourly wage to U.S. $3.17.

Employment termination laws. As previously noted, the employment relationship in the United States has traditionally been based on the employment-at-will doctrine. The relationship may be terminated at the will of the employer or the employee except in the case of express employment agreements, the premature termination of which could lead to a breach-of-contract claim. This doctrine has been modified over the years by the adoption of federal and state laws prohibiting the termination of employment on the basis of certain statuses such as race, gender, age, and disability.[17] In addition, termination of employment on the basis of "whistle-blowing" is also prohibited.[18] Finally, the employment contract has been expanded in certain circumstances to include statements contained within employment manuals.[19]

By contrast, the employment-at-will doctrine has been rejected in most of the world. In many states, employment is viewed as a property right or a lifetime entitlement. Many states require that employers provide their workers with a written employment agreement. For example, French, German, and Italian laws require that employees have a written contract setting forth the work to be performed, salary and benefits, vacation, starting date, place of performance of the work, and notification periods. The Labor Code of the Russian Federation requires that a written contract must be executed with an employee no later than three days after the employee begins work. Similarly, the Labor Code of the People's Republic of China requires a written contract specifying its term, the conditions under which the labor is to be performed, salary, disciplinary procedures, termination, and liability for breach of contract. Some of these states prohibit the use of temporary employees. German law prohibits temporary employment arrangements in excess of two years without a showing of good cause. Failure to show good cause converts a temporary arrangement into permanent employment with all applicable protections. By contrast, China's Labor Code allows the term of employment to be "fixed, flexible or set according to a certain amount of work to be fulfilled." Nevertheless, based upon a recent law adopted by China in June 2007, fixed term contracts are discouraged, and severance pay must be given if a fixed term contract expires and is not renewed without cause.

These jurisdictions also sharply restrict the ability of the employer to terminate the relationship. The German Termination Protection Act of 2004 provides that, in the absence of detrimental behavior, employees of "works" with more than 10 employees can be terminated only if the termination is "socially justified." Social justification depends on the worker's age, years of service, disability, and number of dependents. The employer must provide notice of four weeks to seven months, depending on the employee's years of service. Termination also must be coordinated with the appropriate works councils. Employers must pay severance equal to one-half month's gross salary for every year of service.

[17] 29 U.S.C. § 623(a)(1) (2000) (age discrimination); 42 U.S.C. § 2000e-2(a)(1) (2000) (race, national origin, gender, and religion); Americans with Disabilities Act of 1990, Pub. L. No. 101-336, 104 Stat. 327.

[18] Whistleblower Protection Act of 1989, Pub. L. No. 101-12, 103 Stat. 16.

[19] See, e.g., *Litton v. Maverick Paper Co.*, 354 F. Supp. 2d 1209 (D. Kan. 2005); *Continental Airlines, Inc. v. Keenan*, 731 P.2d 708 (Colo. 1987); *Gaudio v. Griffin Health Servs. Corp.*, 733 A.2d 197 (Conn. 1999); *O'Brien v. New England Tel. & Tel. Co.*, 664 N.E.2d 843 (Mass. 1996); *Bobbitt v. The Orchard, Ltd.*, 603 So. 2d 356 (Miss. 1992); *Wuchte v. McNeil*, 505 S.E.2d 142 (N.C. App. 1998); *Thompson v. St. Regis Paper Co.*, 685 P.2d 1081 (Wash. 1984).

Termination laws are similar in other jurisdictions. France's Labor Code states that termination of employment by companies with more than 20 employees on grounds other than *faute grave* requires written notice in French, a pretermination meeting with the employee, and a required waiting period. Redundancies (layoffs for economic reasons) require the existence of severe economic constraints and notice to the government. China's Labor Code allows for termination for serious violations of applicable rules or dereliction of duty, accusations of criminal conduct, inability to perform the job, or a "genuine need to reduce staff" as a result of "being on the verge of bankruptcy or due to major difficulties in production and business operations."

International labor standards. Employers must exercise care in order to ensure that their employment practices conform to international labor standards. This concern is particularly acute in the developing world, where national labor protections are lax or nonexistent, enforcement attitudes vary widely, and the temptation to exploit local populations is significant.

International labor standards arise from general human rights instruments that apply across a broad spectrum of areas and from specialized documents that focus exclusively on labor. There are numerous general international human rights instruments that address labor issues. For example, the Universal Declaration of Human Rights of 1948, often referred to as the basis for modern human rights law, prohibits slavery and grants everyone the right to free choice of employment, just and favorable conditions of work, reasonable limitation of working hours, and compensation adequate to provide for the worker's health and that of his or her family.[20] The International Covenant on Economic, Social and Cultural Rights also recognizes these rights, as well as fair wages and safe and healthy working conditions.[21]

Many of the specialized instruments that focus exclusively on labor rights arise from norms developed by the International Labor Organization (ILO). Established in 1919 by the Treaty of Versailles, the ILO operates under the principle that "labor should not be regarded merely as a commodity or article of commerce." In 1998, the ILO issued its Declaration on Fundamental Principles and Rights at Work. This declaration enumerated a number of "core labor standards," including freedom of association, the right to engage in collective bargaining, and the elimination of all forms of forced or compulsory labor, child labor, and employment discrimination.[22] Many of the ILO's instruments relate to specific labor practices. For example, the Convention Concerning Forced or Compulsory Labor and the Abolition of Forced Labor Convention obligate states to prohibit the utilization of forced or compulsory labor, including labor for the benefit of private individuals, companies, or associations.[23]

Violation of standards established by general human rights instruments and ILO documents served as the basis for the allegations brought against Unocal that arose from its investment in the Yadana natural gas field in Myanmar. The claimants alleged that the military, acting as Unocal's agent in providing security for the pipeline project, violated labor rights established by the Universal Declaration of Human Rights, the International Covenant on Civil and Political Rights, the Convention Concerning Forced or Compulsory Labor, and conventions abolishing slavery. Unocal's experience in Myanmar, as demonstrated in Case 6-1, serves as an example of the risks associated with employing local

[20] Universal Declaration of Human Rights, G.A. Res. 217A (III), U.N. GAOR, 3d Sess., at 71, arts. 4, 23–25, U.N. Doc. A/810 (1948).

[21] International Covenant on Economic, Social and Cultural Rights, G.A. Res. 2200A (XXI), 21 U.N. GAOR, 21st Sess., Supp. No. 16, arts. 6–7, 11, U.N. Doc. A/6316 (1966).

[22] ILO, Declaration on Fundamental Principles and Rights at Work, art. 2(a–d) (1998).

[23] Abolition of Forced Labor Convention (ILO No. 105), art. 1, 320 U.N.T.S. 291 (1957); Convention Concerning Forced or Compulsory Labor (ILO No. 29), arts. 1–2, 4–5, 39 U.N.T.S. 55 (1930).

CASE 6-1 | DOE v. UNOCAL CORPORATION
UNITED STATES DISTRICT COURT FOR THE CENTRAL DISTRICT OF CALIFORNIA
963 F. SUPP. 880 (C.D. CAL. 1997)

Doe plaintiffs, farmers from the Tenasserim region of Burma, bring this class action against defendants Unocal Corporation (Unocal), Total, S.A. (Total), the Myanma Oil and Gas Enterprise (MOGE), the State Law and Order Restoration Council (SLORC), and individuals John Imle, President of Unocal, and Roger C. Beach, Chairman and Chief Executive Officer of Unocal. According to plaintiffs' complaint, SLORC is a military junta that seized control in Burma in 1988, and MOGE is a state-owned company controlled by SLORC that produces and sells energy products.

DISTRICT JUDGE PAEZ: Plaintiffs contend that in or before 1991, several international oil companies, including Unocal and Total, began negotiating with SLORC regarding oil and gas exploration in Burma. As a result of these negotiations, the Yadana gas pipeline project was established to obtain natural gas and oil from the Andaman Sea and transport it, via a pipeline, across the Tenasserim region of Burma. In July of 1992, Total and MOGE signed a production-sharing contract for a joint venture gas drilling project in the Yadana natural gas field. In early 1993, Unocal formally agreed to participate in the joint venture drilling project.

Plaintiffs allege on information and belief that the parties agreed that SLORC, acting as an agent for the joint venture, would clear forest, level ground, and provide labor, materials and security for the Yadana pipeline project. Plaintiffs also contend, on information and belief, that Unocal and Total subsidized SLORC activities in the region. According to plaintiffs, when Unocal and Total entered into the agreement by which SLORC undertook to clear the pipeline route and provide security for the pipeline, defendants knew or should have known that SLORC had a history of human rights abuses violative of customary international law, including the use of forced relocation and forced labor. Plaintiffs assert, on information and belief, that defendants Unocal and Total were aware of and benefited from, and continue to be aware of and benefit from, the use of forced labor to support the Yadana gas pipeline project.

Unocal moves to dismiss plaintiffs' complaint for lack of subject-matter jurisdiction.

Jurisdiction may be premised on the Alien Tort Claims Act (ATCA) which provides that the district courts shall have original jurisdiction of any civil action by an alien for a tort only, committed in violation of the law of nations or a treaty of the United States. 28 U.S.C. §1350. Thus, the ATCA requires (1) a claim by an alien, (2) alleging a tort, and (3) a violation of international law. Here, plaintiffs are aliens, and they assert tort claims. However, the parties dispute whether plaintiffs may assert claims based on violations of international law against the private defendants.

To the extent a state action requirement is incorporated into the ATCA, courts look to the standards developed under 42 U.S.C. §1983. "A private individual acts under color of law within the meaning of section 1983 when he acts together with state officials or with significant state aid." Under the joint action approach, private actors can be state actors if they are "willful participants in joint action with the state or its agents." An agreement between government and a private party can create joint action. Here, plaintiffs allege that SLORC and MOGE are agents of the private defendants; that the defendants are joint venturers, working in concert with one another; and that the defendants have conspired to commit the violations of international law alleged in the complaint in order to further the interests of the Yadana gas pipeline project. Additional factual inquiry is not necessary. Plaintiffs have alleged that the private plaintiffs were and are jointly engaged with the state officials in the challenged activity, namely forced labor and other human rights violations in furtherance of the pipeline project. These allegations are sufficient to support subject-matter jurisdiction under the ATCA.

Moreover, the private actors may be liable for violations of international law even absent state action. Individual liability remained available, in the face of the 19th century trend toward statism, for a handful of private acts, including piracy and slave trading. The allegations of forced labor in this case are sufficient to constitute an allegation of participation in slave trading. Although there is no allegation that SLORC

[CONTINUED]

is physically selling Burmese citizens to the private defendants, plaintiffs allege that, despite their knowledge of SLORC's practice of forced labor, both in general and with respect to the pipeline project, the private defendants have paid and continue to pay SLORC to provide labor and security for the pipeline, essentially treating SLORC as an overseer, accepting the benefit of and approving the use of forced labor. These allegations are sufficient to establish subject-matter jurisdiction under the ATCA.

FINDING FOR PLAINTIFF.

CRITICAL THINKING

Before you could be convinced that Judge Paez was correct in his decision, what additional information would you like to have? In other words, what factual matters that do not appear in the decision itself would be highly relevant?

ETHICAL DECISION MAKING

This case explicitly involves a very wide range of stakeholders. What other stakeholders are affected by the actions described in this case? How might their inclusion in the thinking of the court have altered or strengthened the decision?

populations, especially in states with poor human rights records and inadequate or poorly enforced labor protections.

Dispute Settlement in an International Context

Disputes between parties to international transactions may be resolved through two primary means. Assuming the parties are unable to resolve their dispute through settlement negotiations, mediation, conciliation, or some other form of nonadversarial dispute resolution, the parties may utilize litigation or arbitration to resolve their differences. However, each of these forms of dispute resolution has disadvantages of which an international businessperson must be aware.

LITIGATION

The first determination that must be made before a party to an international dispute avails itself of litigation is whether the selected court has **jurisdiction,** specifically, the power to hear the case and resolve the dispute. Judgments entered by a court without jurisdiction are null and void. There are two primary types of jurisdiction. A court must possess **subject-matter jurisdiction,** which is the power of the court over the type of case presented to it. In the United States, subject-matter jurisdiction is based on the type of case (such as civil, criminal, probate, or domestic relations) or the amount of money at issue.

By contrast, **personal jurisdiction** is the power of the court over the persons appearing before it. **General personal jurisdiction** permits adjudication of any claims against a defendant regardless of whether the claim has anything to do with the forum. In order to obtain general personal jurisdiction, the defendant must maintain some presence in the forum. **Specific personal jurisdiction** permits adjudication of claims arising from or relating to the defendant's activities in the forum. In order for a court to exercise specific personal jurisdiction, the defendant must have purposefully availed itself of the protections of the forum, and the selected forum must be reasonable.[24] Merely placing a product into the stream of commerce is not sufficient to meet the purposeful availment prong unless the product was designed specifically for the forum or the defendant provided regular advice to customers or maintained a distributor in the forum. The reasonableness of the selected forum is determined by balancing the burden on the defendant, the interest of the forum in resolving the dispute, the plaintiff's interest in obtaining relief in the forum, and foreign policy concerns. The Case Nugget addresses the issue of asserting personal jurisdiction over a foreign defendant on the basis of the defendant's presence in the jurisdiction through the Internet.

Case Nugget — Personal Jurisdiction and the Internet

Hy Cite Corporation v. badbusinessbureau.com
297 F. Supp. 2d 1154 (W.D. Wis. 2004)

Hy Cite, a Wisconsin corporation, marketed and sold china, glassware, cookware, and related products under the trademark "Royal Prestige." Badbusinessbureau.com was a limited liability company organized and existing under the laws of St. Kitts/Nevis, West Indies. Badbusinessbureau owned and operated a Web site, "The Rip-Off Report," which served as a forum for the posting of consumer complaints. Hy Cite's products were subject to 30 to 40 of these complaints. Hy Cite filed a lawsuit against badbusinessbureau claiming that the postings were false and damaged Hy Cite's reputation.

The U.S. district court dismissed Hy Cite's complaint for lack of personal jurisdiction. With respect to general personal jurisdiction, the court held that badbusinessbureau did not have "continuous and systematic general business contracts" with Wisconsin due to the absence of an office, agents and employees, and a substantial amount of business in the forum. The court also found the lack of targeting of Wisconsin Internet users to be indicative of a lack of general personal jurisdiction. The court also rejected the exercise of specific personal jurisdiction. The court held that badbusinessbureau did not purposefully avail itself of the benefits and protections of Wisconsin's laws as it received no donations or advertisements from Wisconsin residents and did not advertise in Wisconsin or target its residents. Furthermore, badbusinessbureau did not engage in intentionally harmful behavior expressly directed at Wisconsin residents. Rather, the harmful conduct, if any, was the complaints written by consumers and posted by them on the Web site.

Some of the uncertainties associated with personal jurisdiction may be minimized through the use of forum selection and choice-of-law clauses in international agreements. A **forum selection agreement** is a clause contained within a contract wherein the parties choose the location where disputes between them will be resolved. In the United States, such clauses are presumptively valid and will be disregarded only if they are unreasonable.[25]

[24] *Asahi Metal Indus. v. Superior Court,* 480 U.S. 102, 109, 113 (1987).
[25] *M/S Bremen v. Zapata Off-Shore Co.,* 407 U.S. 1, 15 (1972).

Grounds for ignoring a forum selection clause include fraud or coercion in its procurement, unconscionability, lack of notice, or serious inconvenience posed by the selected forum. A **choice-of-law clause** is a clause contained in a contract wherein the parties choose the law of a certain state to apply to the interpretation of the contract or in the event of a dispute. Choice-of-law clauses are generally enforceable as long as there is a reasonable relation between the transaction and the law of the selected jurisdiction.

The plaintiff must also select the proper **venue** for the litigation. Proper venue is the court possessing subject-matter and personal jurisdiction that is the most appropriate geographic location for the resolution of the dispute. With respect to federal litigation in the United States, the Alien Venue Statute provides that aliens may be sued in any federal judicial district but makes an exception for suits against foreign sovereigns, which may be initiated only in U.S. District Court for the District of Columbia.[26]

There are other problems associated with the use of litigation as a method of international dispute resolution. Methods of discovery used in civil litigation in the United States may be ineffective if used to obtain evidence located abroad. Although the **Hague Evidence Convention,** a multilateral convention establishing procedures for transnational discovery between private persons in different states, attempts to resolve such problems, it has been ratified by only 35 states. Furthermore, judgments obtained in foreign courts may not be enforceable in other states. For example, in the United States, foreign judgments are not entitled to full faith and credit but are only evidence of the justice of the plaintiff's claims.[27] U.S. courts may ignore the results of foreign proceedings under numerous circumstances, including lack of fairness, jurisdiction, or timely notice; fraud; and inconsistency with U.S. public policy. Foreign states take similar views with respect to U.S. judgments. Courts in such states may refuse to enforce U.S. civil judgments deemed to be criminal or penal in nature (such as taxes and fines) and awards of punitive damages.

ARBITRATION

Arbitration is a type of alternative dispute resolution wherein disputes are submitted for resolution to private, nonofficial persons selected in a manner provided by law or the agreement of the parties. The **New York Convention** has been of significant benefit in the use of arbitration to resolve private international disputes.[28] The New York Convention is an international agreement governing the arbitration of such disputes. It has been ratified by 134 states to date, including the United States. The convention applies to the recognition and enforcement of arbitral awards made in one state and sought to be enforced in another state. It applies when the award is made and enforcement is sought in the territories of contracting states. The convention requires that each state recognize written arbitration agreements concerning a subject matter capable of settlement by arbitration. Furthermore, each state must recognize arbitral awards as enforceable in their national courts. These provisions thus eliminate concerns regarding the enforcement of judicial decisions of national courts. Case 6-2 summarizes the approach of U.S. courts to the enforcement of arbitration clauses in accordance with the New York Convention.

[26] 28 U.S.C. § 1391(d) (2000).

[27] Restatement (Third) of the Foreign Relations Law of the United States, § 481 (1987).

[28] Convention on the Recognition and Enforcement of Foreign Arbitral Awards, June 10, 1958, 21 U.S.T. 2517, 330 U.N.T.S. 38.

CASE 6-2 BEST CONCRETE MIX CORP. v. LLOYD'S OF LONDON UNDERWRITERS

2006 U.S. DIST. LEXIS 5015 (W.D.N.Y., FEB. 8, 2006)

BLOCK, SENIOR DISTRICT JUDGE: Best Concrete Mix Corp. ("Best") and Dame Realty, LLC ("Dame") (collectively, "plaintiffs"), filed suit in state court against Lloyd's of London Underwriters, Lloyd's of London (collectively, "Underwriters"), VIP Marine Services, Inc. ("VIP"), Julian Trifan ("Trifan"), and Tilcon New York, Inc. ("Tilcon"), seeking a declaratory judgment that plaintiffs are entitled to coverage under an insurance policy (the "policy") issued by Underwriters to VIP, under which Best was an additional insured. Plaintiffs' state court action arose out of a suit filed by Trifan against plaintiffs seeking damages for injuries sustained by Trifan while performing construction work for Best. The policy contains an arbitration clause providing for arbitration in London, United Kingdom, of all disputes arising in connection with the policy. On June 1, 2004, Underwriters removed plaintiffs' action to this court pursuant to the United Nations Convention on the Recognition and Enforcement of Foreign Arbitral Awards ("the Convention"), which gives district courts jurisdiction over actions relating to certain commercial arbitration agreements that are not entirely domestic in scope. Underwriters now move for an order staying the litigation and compelling arbitration in London pursuant to the terms of this arbitration clause.

Best, Dame and VIP are corporations organized under the laws of New York, with their principal place of business in New York. Best hired VIP to build a dock at premises owned by Dame in Queens, New York; VIP agreed with Best that VIP would obtain an insurance policy to cover VIP for any injuries or accidents occurring during the course of the construction and that Best would be an additional insured under the policy.

The Second Circuit has held that an arbitration agreement exists within the meaning of the Convention if (1) there is a written agreement; (2) the writing provides for arbitration in the territory of a signatory of the convention; (3) the subject matter is commercial; and (4) the subject matter is not entirely domestic in scope. Upon finding that such an agreement exists, a federal court must compel arbitration of any dispute falling within the scope of the agreement pursuant to the terms of the agreement.

[P]laintiffs argue that the policy, although in writing, cannot constitute a "written agreement" within the meaning of the Convention as applied to them because they were not signatories to the policy. The Court disagrees. While arbitration is a matter of contract and a party cannot be required to submit to arbitration any dispute which he has not agreed to so submit, it does not follow that an obligation to arbitrate attaches only to one who has personally signed the written arbitration provision. Under the theory of estoppel, a company knowingly exploiting an agreement with an arbitration clause can be estopped from avoiding arbitration despite having never signed the agreement. By seeking to enforce its indemnification rights as an additional insured under the policy, Best must also be bound by its arbitration clause because it wishes to avail itself of the protection and direct benefits afforded by the policy.

With respect to the second and third criteria, the parties do not dispute that the United Kingdom, the location for arbitration designated by the policy, is a signatory to the Convention, nor that the subject matter of the agreement, an insurance contract, is commercial. With respect to the fourth criterion, an agreement is "entirely domestic in scope" only if it "aris[es] out of . . . a [legal] relationship which is entirely between citizens of the United States." 9 U.S.C. § 202. Here, although plaintiffs are U.S. corporations seeking coverage for an accident occurring in the U.S., the individuals from whom they seek the coverage—Underwriters—are in the U.K.

The indemnification dispute falls within the scope of the arbitration clause. In light of the strong federal policy in favor of arbitration, the existence of a broad agreement to arbitrate creates a presumption of arbitrability which is only overcome if it may be said with positive assurance that the arbitration clause is not susceptible of an interpretation that covers the dispute. Doubts should be resolved in favor of coverage.

The present arbitration clause is broad, providing for arbitration of "any dispute under or in connection with this insurance," and a dispute over plaintiffs' entitlement to indemnification as an additional insured under the terms of the policy is clearly a dispute "under or in connection with" that policy.

Defendants' motion to compel arbitration is granted and the litigation is stayed pending its outcome.

CRITICAL THINKING

Are you convinced that Judge Block was correct in requiring the plaintiffs to submit their dispute to arbitration despite the fact they were not signatories to the policy containing the arbitration provision? How far does the theory of estoppel extend to prevent a party from litigating a case involving a contract containing an arbitration provision? What actions might constitute an availment by a party of the protections and benefits of such a contract as to impose an obligation to arbitrate disputes?

Arbitration as a means of dispute resolution has many advantages over litigation. Arbitration is cheaper and faster, and it is a nonpublic procedure. Arbitration also permits the parties to select the forum and the presiding party. Enforceability concerns arising from judicial decisions are also minimized. However, international businesspersons should be aware of some of the disadvantages to the use of arbitration as a means of dispute resolution. The ability of the parties to conduct discovery of the opposing party's case may be limited, as well as the ability to appeal an adverse decision. Furthermore, arbitrators' decisions may not serve as precedent in future cases. Any company contemplating the use of arbitration as a means of dispute resolution must carefully balance these disadvantages with the benefits of the arbitral process.

CASE OPENER WRAP-UP

Unocal

Unocal aggressively pursued its defense of the litigation initiated by the villagers. The litigation continued for a period of eight years and generated numerous court opinions. Finally, in December 2004, Unocal entered into a settlement agreement resolving the claims against it. Although the terms of the settlement were confidential, news reports suggested Unocal compensated the plaintiffs for their losses and provided funds to enable them to develop programs to improve living conditions, health care, and educational opportunities for people located in the pipeline area. Four months later, ChevronTexaco Corporation acquired Unocal for $16.4 billion in stock and cash.

Summary

Doing Business Internationally

International law refers to the laws governing the conduct of states and international organizations and their relations with one another and natural and juridical persons.

Ethical Considerations

Firms participating in international markets have special ethical considerations, including whether to do business with repressive governments, whether to provide products for the poor at reduced prices, and whether to treat workers according to local custom or to international standards of humane treatment.

The General Agreement on Tariffs and Trade

GATT is a comprehensive multilateral trading system designed to achieve distortion-free international trade through the minimization of tariffs and removal of artificial barriers. It established several general principles of trade law:

- *Article I:* Addresses the principle of *most favored nation,* now known as *normal trade relations;* requires that WTO member states treat like goods coming from other WTO member states on an equal basis, specifically prohibiting member states from discriminating against like products on the basis of their country of origin.
- *Article III:* Sets forth the principle of *national treatment,* which prohibits WTO member states from regulating, taxing or otherwise treating imported products any differently than domestically produced products.
- *Article VI:* Prohibits certain types of *dumping* and *subsidies.*
- *Article XI:* Prohibits *quantitative restrictions* on imports (e.g., limits on importation of certain products on the basis of number of units, weight, or value for national economic reasons or the protection of domestic industry).

Regional Trade Agreements

Free trade agreement: Two or more states agree to reduce and gradually eliminate tariffs and other trade barriers [e.g., North American Free Trade Agreement (NAFTA)].

Bilateral trade agreement: Two states agree on issues relating to trade between them (e.g., United States–Australia agreement).

Comparative Law

Comparative law is the study of the legal systems of different states. This study provides a better understanding of the general purpose of law, assists in the development of a critical viewpoint of one's own legal system, and demonstrates that one's own legal system is only one of many alternatives. After thinking critically about alternative laws, one might decide that one's own state should adopt the other state's law or method of resolving a dispute.

Legal Systems and Procedures

Civil law systems constitute the majority of the world's legal systems and are based on detailed national legal codes, which serve as the sole official source of law. *Common law* systems derive from the British and American models and are based upon constitutions, legislation, regulations, and their interpretation by courts of law. *Socialist law* systems are based on the premises that the rights of society as a whole outweigh individual rights and that the state owns the means of production and property. *Islamic law* systems are based on the tenet that law is derived from and interpreted in conformance with *Shari'a* (God's Law) and the Koran.

Dispute Settlement in an International Context

If the parties to international transactions are unable to resolve their dispute through nonadversarial methods, the parties may use litigation or arbitration to resolve their differences.

Point / Counterpoint

Could Unocal Have Done Anything Different to Avoid the Outcome of Its Investment in Myanmar?	
No	**Yes**
Unocal had no choice with respect to where it invested as the natural resource at issue, specifically, the Yadana natural gas field, is located in Myanmar, and the company must pursue resources where they are located, without regard to political and human rights considerations. Another oil and gas company would have become involved in the development of the Yadana natural gas field in Unocal's absence. Furthermore, Unocal could not successfully resist the demands of Myanmar's military dictatorship to provide security for the project without jeopardizing its permission to conduct business operations in the country. Unocal complied with Myanmar's laws and its own code of conduct with respect to its construction and operation of the pipeline and should not be held accountable for the actions of the military, which operated entirely independent of Unocal's control. Finally, Unocal did not favor the dictatorship or violate its pledge of political neutrality by retaining the military to provide security for the project.	Unocal could have refrained from investing in Myanmar. This course of action had considerable precedent as a number of companies left Myanmar in the mid-1990s, including Apple Computer, Eddie Bauer, Hewlett-Packard, Levi Strauss and Company, Liz Claiborne, Macy's, and PepsiCo. Another course of action would have been to proceed with the investment but resist the appointment of the military to provide security for the project. Such a course would be consistent with Unocal's code of conduct providing for respect for human rights, compliance with the "highest ethical standards" in the retention and supervision of contractors, and maintenance of neutrality in Myanmar's internal political affairs.

Questions & Problems

1. Google launched its Chinese Internet search engine google.cn in 2005. In order to gain access to China's 103 million Internet users, the second-largest number in the world (only the United States has more), Google censored access to Web sites deemed offensive to the Chinese government, such as Web sites regarding democracy, the Falun Gong religious group, the Tibetan freedom movement, and the suppression of antigovernment protesters in Tiananmen Square in 1989. In so doing, google.cn became the first search engine to self-censor access to Web sites. In its defense, Google claimed that it was required to obey Chinese law in order to offer its search engine to Chinese citizens. Critics claimed that Google's self-censorship violated its corporate mission statement of "Don't Be Evil." Is Google's self-censorship of Web sites on google.cn ethical? Should Google have refused to offer its search engine to Chinese citizens until such time as it could do so without having to engage in censorship? Does censorship violate Google's corporate mission statement? Why or why not?
2. Spain divided unroasted nondecaffeinated coffee into five separate classifications. A 7 percent tariff was imposed on three of these classifications. The other two

classifications were duty-free. Brazil, the principal supplier of the coffee subject to the tariff, alleged that the Spanish classification regime failed to extend most-favored-nation treatment to like products originating from Brazil, thus violating GATT. Spain defended the classifications on the basis that the products were not like products due to differences resulting from geographic factors, cultivation methods, processing, and genetics. The GATT panel rejected these arguments. The panel noted that most coffees are blends, coffee is universally regarded as a well-defined and single product intended for drinking, and no other state maintained a similar classification scheme. The panel thus concluded that the classification system discriminated against like products in violation of GATT's most-favored-nation requirement. Do you agree with this decision? Is coffee a single universal product regardless of where it is grown, how it is processed, or what the cost is to consumers? [*Spain—Tariff Treatment of Unroasted Coffee,* 1981 GATTPD LEXIS 5 (1981).]

3. Italy adopted a law that permitted the government to extend credit to Italian farmers in order to finance the purchase of agricultural machinery. Farmers purchasing machinery manufactured in Italy were entitled to a loan up to 75 percent of the value of the machinery for a term of five years at a 3 percent interest rate. Farmers purchasing machinery not manufactured in Italy were also entitled to loans but at an interest rate of 10 percent. The United Kingdom claimed that the Italian loan program violated GATT's national treatment obligation by modifying the conditions of sale between imported and domestically produced machinery. Italy defended the loan program on the basis that national treatment applied only to sales in the context of international trade and not to internal conditions of sale. Italy also claimed that national treatment was not applicable to economic development initiatives such as the loan program. The GATT panel disagreed and held that the national treatment requirement applied to internal conditions impacting domestic sales. The panel also concluded that economic development initiatives were required to be consistent with the principle of national treatment. Based on this decision, are there any limits to the concept of national treatment? How might a state undertake an economic development initiative without violating national treatment? [*Italy—Imported Agricultural Machinery,* GATT Report L/833-7S/60 (1958).]

4. A Canadian winery entered into a contract to purchase corks from the U.S. subsidiary of a French company. The parties reached an agreement on quantity, price, payment, and shipping terms during a telephone conversation. The corks were sent to the winery in 11 separate shipments accompanied by invoices providing that "[a]ny dispute arising under the present contract is under the sole jurisdiction of the Court of Commerce of the City of Perpignan." The winery never objected to the language contained in the invoices. The winery subsequently filed a lawsuit in U.S. district court in California against the U.S. subsidiary and its French parent as a result of the tainting of its wine by the corks. The sellers moved to dismiss the litigation on the basis of the forum selection agreement. The district court enforced the clause and dismissed the litigation, but the U.S. Court of Appeals for the Ninth Circuit reversed this decision. Applying the CISG, the Ninth Circuit held that the forum selection clause was a material alteration of the parties' oral agreement. As such, the winery's failure to object to the inclusion of the clause was irrelevant. Do you agree? How would you define the term *material alteration?* Should parties in international commercial transactions be penalized for their failure to adequately review documents? Why or why not? [*Chateau des Charmes Wines Ltd. v. Sabate USA, Inc.,* 328 F.3d 528 (9th Cir. 2003).]

5. The European labor market has been criticized as inefficient due to the many benefits and high degree of job security provided to workers. In contrast, the labor market in the United States has been criticized for the opposite reasons, specifically, for providing too few benefits to workers and providing little job security. What are the advantages and disadvantages of each model? Which model is preferable? Why? Is there a compromise that combines the strengths of both models? What would be the features of such a compromise?
6. In *Asahi Metal Industries v. Superior Court,* the U.S. Supreme Court held that the mere placement of a product in the stream of commerce is not sufficient to subject the manufacturer to the personal jurisdiction of a California state court in the absence of "purposeful availment," such as designing a product specifically for the forum, maintaining a distributor in the forum, or providing regular advice to customers in the forum. Is this reasoning still valid in the modern global marketplace where goods routinely cross international boundaries? Why or why not?
7. A U.S. company entered into a contract with an Italian company. The contract stated that any dispute arising related to the contract was to be resolved in the Arbitration Court of the Chamber of Commerce of Venice, Italy. The U.S. company subsequently brought an action in U.S. federal court alleging breach of contract and tortious interference with contractual relations. The U.S. company contended that the forum selection clause was inoperative as it would result in substantial inconvenience and was not applicable to the tort claim. The court rejected these arguments. The court held that (a) a forum selection agreement encompassing claims arising from a contract includes contract-based tort claims; (b) the contract was the result of arm's-length negotiations between experienced business entities; and (c) the forum selection agreement was not so one-sided as to be characterized as unconscionable. How would you draft a forum selection clause to avoid the arguments advanced by the U.S. company yet not be so one-sided as to be deemed unconscionable? Would the result be different if one of the parties was not a merchant or if the clause had been concealed in the small print "boilerplate" of a standard form agreement? [*Tennessee Imports, Inc. v. Pier Paulo,* 745 F. Supp. 1314 (M.D. Tenn. 1990).]
8. A U.S.-based Internet service provider that operated an auction site was sued in a French court by two nonprofit organizations dedicated to the elimination of anti-Semitism. The basis of the lawsuit was the availability of Nazi-related propaganda and Third Reich memorabilia on the auction site. The French Criminal Code prohibits the exhibition of Nazi propaganda and the offering of artifacts for sale. The French court ordered the Internet service provider to eliminate the access of French citizens to its auction site and other sites containing Nazi propaganda and post warnings to French citizens with respect to the French Criminal Code. A daily penalty of €100,000 was to be assessed for every day that the service provider failed to comply with the order. Although the service provider did implement part of the court's order, it claimed that it did not have the technology to block French citizens from accessing prohibited Web sites unless it removed all Nazi-related material. Such removal would conflict with the service provider's First Amendment rights under the U.S. Constitution. As a result, the service provider filed a lawsuit in the United States seeking a declaration that the French court's order was not enforceable. How should the U.S. court decide this case? Should the U.S. court enforce the order of the French court? Why or why not? Should an Internet service provider be responsible for all material accessible through use of its service? If the answer to this question is no, should there be an exception for extremely offensive materials such as those

relating to Nazism? How would you assess the Internet service provider's business practices relating to respect for the social policies and cultural sensitivities of the locations where it transacts business? [*Yahoo!, Inc. v. La Ligue Contre Le Racisme et L'Antisemitisme,* 169 F. Supp. 2d 1181 (N.D. Cal. 2001).]

9. The operator of several restaurants in Paris, France, initiated litigation against a franchisor seeking to prevent it from terminating the franchise. The Master License Agreement governing the franchise provided that failure of the franchisee to meet quality, safety and cleanliness (QSC) standards for its operations would harm the successful operation of restaurants around the world and injure the value of the franchisor's trade name. The failure to meet QSC was defined as a substantial breach of the Master License Agreement and a basis for its termination. The franchisee failed to maintain the restaurants in compliance with the QSC. Conditions at the franchisee's restaurants were described by witnesses as "filthy," "grimy," "unsanitary," and "disgusting." After consultations with the franchisee failed to result in improvement of the conditions, the franchisor declared the Master License Agreement to be in default and gave the franchisee six months to take corrective action. The franchisor subsequently terminated the franchise. The court upheld the termination and found that the franchisor satisfied its duties of good faith and fair dealing with the franchisee. What do "good faith" and "fair dealing" mean? What actions must a franchisor take to satisfy these duties? [*Dayan v. McDonald's Corp.,* 466 N.E.2d 958 (Ill. App. 1984).]

10. The defendant, a vice president of a U.S. military equipment supplier, purchased two airline tickets for the cousin of the chief of maintenance of the Niger air force. The airline tickets were used by the cousin and his wife to honeymoon in Europe after their wedding in Niger. The cousin testified that the tickets were a personal gift. However, the defendant was indicted for bribery in violation of the FCPA after his company received contracts with Niger's air force and the company failed to report its purchase of the airline tickets. Despite the defendant's claim that he did not act with corrupt intent and the ticket was a gift rather than a bribe, he was convicted by the district court. His conviction was upheld on appeal. Do you agree? Are there differences between a bribe and a gift? If so, what are these differences? [*United States v. Liebo,* 923 F.2d 1308 (8th Cir. 1991).]

11. A construction company submitted a bid to build a municipal swimming pool in the Netherlands. The mayor and his municipal councilors found this bid to be the best and to be within the municipality's budget for the project. However, the town council rejected the bid and awarded the contract to another firm. The construction company sued the town for expenses incurred in preparing the bid and damages suffered as a result of loss of the contract. The court held that, under Dutch law, there are three stages of contract negotiation. In the initial stage, either party may break off negotiations without incurring liability. In the second or continuing stage, either party may break off the negotiations but is liable to the other party for expenses. In the final stage, the parties are prohibited from terminating negotiations without incurring liability for damages resulting from loss of the contract. Parties enter the third stage of negotiations when they have a mutual and reasonable expectation that a contract will result from the negotiations. In this case, the court concluded the parties were in the continuing-negotiation stage and awarded the construction company the expenses incurred in preparing its bid proposal. Is such an approach to contract negotiations realistic? How would you define the different stages of negotiation created by the court? [*Plas v. Valburg,* 18-6 Netherlandse Jurisprudentie 723 (1983).]

12. The plaintiff, a financial institution organized under the laws of Latvia, filed a lawsuit against a bank organized under the laws of the Russian Federation. The lawsuit alleged breach of a foreign currency exchange contract negotiated in Riga and Moscow but involving a deposit of funds to be made in New York. The Russian bank moved to dismiss on the basis of FSIA. The court held that, although the Russian bank was a foreign state according to FSIA, it did not qualify for immunity. Specifically, the court concluded that the Russian bank engaged in a commercial activity having a significant direct effect in the United States. As such, the court could exercise jurisdiction over the dispute and the Russian bank. Do you agree that a U.S. court should exercise jurisdiction over a dispute between two foreign entities regarding a contract negotiated entirely outside the United States when the only connection is a deposit to be made in a bank account in New York? How would you define "significant direct effect" for purposes of applying the commercial activity exception to FSIA? [*Parex Bank v. Russian Savings Bank,* 116 F. Supp. 2d 415 (S.D.N.Y. 2000).]
13. A financial company organized under the laws of the Netherlands Antilles sought a money transmission license from the state of New York on behalf of a third party. The financial company arranged to obtain security for the bond it was required to post for this application from the U.S. branch of a British bank. The British bank subsequently withdrew from negotiations, and the financial company was unable to obtain an alternative source of security. The financial company brought an action in U.S. court alleging the existence of a conspiracy to drive it out of the money transfer business by depriving it of banking services, thus violating U.S. antitrust laws. The court dismissed the case on the basis of *forum non conveniens.* The court specifically disregarded the financial company's contention that the alternative forum in the United Kingdom was inadequate because the U.S. remedy of treble damages was unavailable. Should the available remedies and the size of the potential recovery determine whether a foreign jurisdiction is an adequate alternative forum? Why or why not? [*Capital Currency Exchange v. National Westminster Bank,* 155 F.3d 603 (2d Cir. 1998).]
14. A U.S. citizen was injured on a cruise ship operated by an Italian company. The passenger filed suit in a U.S. federal court one year and two months later. The Italian company claimed that the provisions of the cruise ticket barred civil actions alleging personal injury filed more than one year after the injury. The passenger claimed that this provision was invalid under Italian law, which was designated in another portion of the ticket as the "ruling law of the contract." The court applied this choice-of-law clause despite the fact that this was a consumer transaction rather than a commercial transaction between merchants. The court found there was no fraud, injustice, or public policy that prevented the enforcement of the choice-of-law clause against its own drafter. As the one-year statute of limitations was unenforceable under Italian law, the passenger's claims were not time-barred. Should choice-of-law provisions be limited to commercial transactions rather than consumer transactions such as cruises? If you have ever taken a cruise, did you read the ticket prior to your departure? If your ticket contained a choice of law, do you believe that you had any ability to successfully negotiate its provisions with the cruise line? [*Milanovich v. Costa Crociere, S.p.A.,* 954 F.2d 763 (D.C. Cir. 1992).]
15. The U.S. Court of Appeals for the Second Circuit refused to enforce an award of the Iran–United States Claims Tribunal in favor of several Iranian parties and against a U.S. company in an amount in excess of $3.5 million. The court found that the U.S. company was not informed that the tribunal required original documentation

to substantiate its claims. The U.S. company thus proceeded to present its case without such documentation, only to have the case rejected for lack of proof. The court concluded that the resulting judgment was unenforceable under the New York Convention as the U.S. company was unable to present its case and was denied due process of law. Under what circumstances should a court refuse to enforce an arbitration award under the New York Convention? What process is due to the parties in the context of an arbitration proceeding? [*Iran Aircraft Indus. v. Avco Corp.*, 980 F.2d 141 (2d Cir. 1992).]

Looking for more review material?

The Online Learning Center at **www.mhhe.com/kubasek1e** contains this chapter's "Assignment on the Internet" and also a list of URLs for more information, entitled "On the Internet." Find both of them in the Student Center portion of the OLC, along with quizzes and other helpful materials.

Crime and the Business Community

CASE OPENER

Untenable Trading

In late 1997, John Freeman, employed at Goldman Sachs & Co., Inc., began misappropriating nonpublic information concerning impending mergers and acquisitions. Rather than using that information to make trades himself, Freeman began disclosing the insider information to James Cooper and Benton Erskine, with the understanding and agreement that they would share a portion of their trading profits with him.

During the course of the scheme, Cooper received Freeman's permission to tip other individuals who might be able to assist them. Freemen knew of two people to whom Cooper gave the tips. Cooper, however, also tipped certain individuals without Freeman's knowledge or consent, including Chad Conner, a stockbroker. Cooper began regularly tipping Conner, who, in turn, tipped numerous other brokerage clients.

In the early fall of 1998, Freeman left Goldman Sachs to work part-time for Credit Suisse First Boston (CSFB), another investment bank. While Freeman continued to misappropriate information from CSFB, Conner and his clients believed the information they were now receiving was not as profitable as it had been in the past. Conner told Cooper that one of his clients was willing to pay the "New York source" $100,000 to return to Goldman Sachs. Cooper communicated this offer to Freeman.

Prior to receiving this offer, Freeman had been apprehended by the FBI and had agreed to assist them. On February 23, 2000, Conner and Cooper participated in a three-way telephone and online conversation with an FBI agent posing as Freeman. During this telephone conversation, Conner reiterated his offer to pay Freeman $100,000 to return to Goldman Sachs. The agent posing as Freeman asked Conner to personally deliver $5,000 to Atlantic City, and Conner agreed. On March 4, 2000, FBI agents arrested Conner in Atlantic City and seized an envelope containing $5,000. Conner was subsequently charged with commercial bribery and 81 counts of insider trading.[1]

[1] *United States v. Geibel,* 369 F.3d 682 (2004).

CHAPTER 7

1. Do you believe Conner did anything illegal?
2. If a person has inside information and does not trade on it himself but passes it on to another who uses it to trade, is the person who passed on the information guilty of insider trading?

The Wrap-Up at the end of the chapter will answer these questions.

Learning Objectives

After reading this chapter, you will be able to answer the following questions:

1. What are the basic elements of a crime?
2. What are some of the common crimes affecting businesses, and how do you prove those crimes?
3. When a crime is committed to benefit a corporation, who can be held liable for the crime?
4. What are the basic constitutional safeguards for a person accused of a crime?
5. What are the basic steps of a criminal proceeding?
6. How do we attempt to prevent the commission of white-collar crimes?

As the opening scenario illustrates, crime can come in many forms and affect large numbers of people. Also, crimes can quickly grow with respect to the number of people involved. It is important to note that Freeman, Cooper, Conner, and everyone Conner told made large sums of money, but at the expense of other investors. Although the crime might seem like a victimless one at first, it is important to remember that crime always has a victim, even if the victim is not readily identifiable.

In this chapter, we introduce the elements of criminal law and discuss some common crimes occurring in the business context. We discuss how liability can be assessed to corporations and corporate executives, as well as discuss common defenses to criminal charges. We then move on to discuss several important constitutional safeguards that arise in the criminal context. Next, we explain the process of criminal procedure, and we conclude with a discussion of some of the primary laws used to combat business crime.

Elements of a Crime

The purpose of criminal law is to punish an offender for causing harm to public health, safety, or morals. Note that in a criminal proceeding, the *government* files the charges against the defendant. Thus, the government is always a party to a criminal action. Government involvement distinguishes criminal trials from civil proceedings. For civil actions, an individual person or corporation can file a suit. The difference exists because in a criminal trial society is seen as the victim, whereas in a civil trial there is an individual victim or victims.

Criminal laws usually define criminal behavior and set guidelines for punishment. To punish an individual for criminal behavior, the government must demonstrate the two elements of a crime:

1. Wrongful behavior, that is, ***actus reus*** (guilty act).
2. Wrongful state of mind, also known as ***mens rea*** (guilty mind).

The government thus must show that a defendant committed a prohibited act with a wrongful intent.

To prove the first element, *actus reus* (guilty act), the government must establish the nonmental elements of the crime. That is, the government must demonstrate that a prohibited act or a prohibited consequence resulted because of the actions of the defendant.

To prove the second element, *mens rea* (guilty state of mind), the government must prove that the defendant acted with purpose, knowledge, recklessness, or negligence, depending on which of these states of mind is required by the law defining the relevant offense. The defendant's type of wrongful state of mind helps determine the seriousness of the punishment for the crime. First, a defendant can *purposefully* commit a crime by engaging in a specific wrongful behavior to bring about a specific wrongful result. Second, a defendant can *knowingly* commit a wrongful act if the person knows the act is wrongful or believes that an act is wrongful yet does nothing to confirm or disconfirm this belief. Third, a defendant is *reckless* if a criminal act occurs when the individual consciously ignores substantial risk. Finally, a defendant is *negligent* if he or she does not meet a standard of care that the reasonable person would use in the context that led to the criminal act.

In certain cases, liability may be assessed even without establishing the guilty-mind criterion discussed above. Only certain crimes, typically violations of regulatory statutes, allow punishment to be assessed without having to prove guilty mind. When liability is assessed without the guilty-mind criterion, it is known as **liability without fault**, or **strict liability**. Liability without fault involves actions that, regardless of the care taken, are deemed illegal to engage in; such acts are specifically prohibited or bring about a specifically prohibited result. Liability without fault would apply, for example, if a business were to sell cigarettes or alcohol to a minor. Although the business might not have intended to sell cigarettes or alcohol to a minor (thus lacking a guilty mind), the statutory violation still allows liability to be assessed.

In the recent case *Meyer v. Holley,*[2] the Supreme Court held a corporation liable without fault when an interracial couple sued because a salesperson for the corporation allegedly prevented the couple from buying a house due to racial discrimination. The Fair Housing Act expressly prohibits racial discrimination with respect to the sale of a dwelling. The alleged discriminatory act violated the Fair Housing Act, and thus the corporation was found to be liable without fault. That is, the federal statute was violated, and the corporation was held legally accountable regardless of the mental state *(mens rea)* of the salesperson at the time of the wrong.

Classification of Crimes

Crimes are divided into categories based on the seriousness of the offense. Today, the categories used are felonies, misdemeanors, or petty crimes. **Felonies** include serious crimes, such as murder, that are punishable by imprisonment for more than one year or death. **Misdemeanors** are less serious crimes punishable by fines or imprisonment for less than one year. **Petty offenses,** such as violating a building code, are minor misdemeanors and are usually punishable by a jail sentence of less than six months or a small fine. The statute defining the crime usually establishes whether the crime is a felony, misdemeanor, or petty offense.

Crimes may also be federal or state, depending on whether they are enacted by the state or federal legislature.

Common Crimes Affecting Business

When people hear the word *crime,* they often think of homicide. In this section, however, we do not examine violent crimes; instead, we focus on the crimes that occur in a business context. As a future business manager, you should become familiar with the following crimes, which could affect your company.

PROPERTY CRIMES AGAINST BUSINESS

We now examine four criminal acts: robbery, burglary, larceny, and arson. Certainly, these crimes do not occur solely in the business context; however, they are crimes that could be committed against your future business. We distinguish these crimes from white-collar crimes for three reasons. First, individuals who are not employees often commit these crimes, while employees often commit white-collar crimes. Second, these crimes are committed against the business, while white-collar crimes are usually committed against society. Third, these crimes may involve violence, while white-collar crimes usually do not involve violence.

Robbery. **Robbery** is defined by most states as the forceful and unlawful taking of personal property. If force or fear is absent, the crime is not robbery; it is theft. For example, if someone stole your wallet undetected while you were walking down the street, the person committed theft. However, if that person tackled you, pinned you down, and wrested your wallet from you, he or she committed robbery. If someone threatened you with a deadly weapon while taking your property, that person would likely be charged with *aggravated robbery,* which carries a more severe penalty.

[2] 537 U.S. 280 (2003).

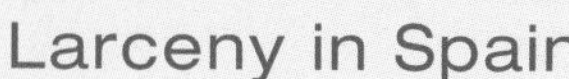

Larceny in Spain

Laws governing the crime of larceny in Spain differ from U.S laws in several ways. The frequent legal definition of larceny in the United States is the fraudulent intent to deprive an owner *permanently* of property without threat or force. Therefore, if one's intent is to return the property, one cannot be convicted of larceny. In Spain, an individual can be convicted of this crime despite intent to return the property. Spanish laws lack specification about the time period that the defendant may keep the property before becoming criminally liable. The crime constitutes larceny if the property is taken without the owner's consent.

Once a person is convicted, the punishment for larceny in Spain is relatively minor with one exception. If the stolen property is something (1) used in religious services, (2) stolen during a religious service, or (3) stolen from a religious building, the fine and potential jail time immediately increase. This concern about the location of the larceny differs from U.S. law, in which location is immaterial for the conviction of larceny. While location of the crime in the United States may dictate whether the crime is tried in federal or state court, a crucifix stolen from a Catholic church and a rake stolen from someone's garage would be treated equally under the law.

Burglary. A **burglary** occurs when someone unlawfully enters a building with the intent to commit a felony. Although the words *breaking and entering* usually come to mind, an individual does not have to break anything. If the person enters the building unlawfully with intent to commit a wrongful act, the requirement for burglary is met.

Larceny. Although the definition may vary slightly state by state, **larceny** is the secretive and wrongful taking and carrying away of the personal property of another with the intent to permanently deprive the rightful owner of its use or possession. Unlike robbery, larceny does not require force or fear. In the business context, larceny occurs, for example, when an employee takes office supplies, such as paper or CDs, for personal use.

States generally make a distinction between *grand larceny* and *petty larceny.* Grand larceny involves items of greater value; thus, it is a felony and carries more severe penalties. As the Global Context reveals, other nations distinguish between different degrees of larceny in different ways, and sometimes these distinctions reflect a particular aspect of a nation's culture.

Arson. **Arson** is the intentional burning of another's dwelling. The definition of arson is typically expanded to include other real property beyond dwellings, as well as destruction by means other than burning, such as the use of explosive devices. While not common, arson is a problem that could potentially befall businesses.

WHITE-COLLAR CRIME

Originally, white-collar crimes were distinguished from other crimes because of the social status of the offender. The more modern approach is to define **white-collar crime** as a variety of nonviolent illegal acts against society that occur most frequently in the business context. Clearly, the crimes described in the opening scenario fall under this broad definition of white-collar crime.

Mail fraud, bribery, embezzlement, and computer crimes are examples of offenses typically classified as white-collar crimes. These crimes occur more frequently than you might think. According to some estimates, one in three American households is the victim of white-collar crime every year.

The consequences of white-collar crimes are far-reaching. First, the cost of white-collar crimes can be tremendous. It is estimated that fraud in the health care industry alone costs society over $100 billion each year. Second, in cases where company employees commit the crime, many companies fail to report the crime to avoid publicity. Third, white-collar crimes can be costly to the environment. For example, improper disposal of chemicals, such as dumping chemicals in a stream, has long-term repercussions for marine life, the surrounding ecosystem, and any humans who may come in contact with the contaminated water source.

Of course, the amount of money collected in fines from corporate executives engaged in criminal activity has not been insignificant either. For example, in 1999, the government won over $490 million in fines, judgments, and settlements from health care fraud cases alone. Fines, however, are only one way that those found guilty of fraud and other white-collar crimes might be punished.

There are at least four alternative ways to punish white-collar criminals. First, confinement has been mandated for certain types of white-collar crimes. As the prevalence of white-collar crime has increased, so too has the number of white-collar offenders who are in jail. A second type of punishment that white-collar criminals receive is mandated community service, such as giving speeches about business crime. For instance, junk-bond king Michael Milliken was compelled to give speeches on corporate crime after he was convicted of insider trading. Third, judges may disqualify the individual from employment. For instance, the judge may prohibit the offender from engaging in an occupation where the same or a similar criminal act could occur again. Fourth, the offender can be placed under house arrest. Individuals must wear a sensor so that the government can monitor whether they have left their houses.

Bribery. One of the better known white-collar crimes is bribery. **Bribery** is the offering, giving, soliciting, or receiving of money or any object of value for the purpose of influencing the judgment or conduct of a person in a position of trust. *Bribery of a public official* is a statutory offense under federal law. The purpose of this law against bribery is to maintain the integrity of the government. This statute also covers bribes offered to witnesses in exchange for testimony. Perhaps one of the most publicized recent examples of bribery was the 2002 Winter Olympics bribery scandal in Salt Lake City, Utah. The Salt Lake City Olympics Bid Committee allegedly gave International Olympic Committee members between $4 million and $7 million in cash and other benefits. These benefits included college tuition assistance payments, shopping trips for bathroom fixtures and doorknobs, and trips to the Super Bowl.

To demonstrate bribery under this statute, the government must show three elements: (1) Something of value was offered, given, or promised to (2) a federal public official with (3) intent to influence that person's judgment or conduct. The "thing of value" element has been construed very liberally; actual commercial value is not necessary. For instance, had the Salt Lake City Olympics Bid Committee given a member of the International Olympic Committee shares of stock in a new Silicon Valley start-up called BellyUp.com but the shares turned out to be worthless because the start-up was never established, this act may constitute bribery even though the stock is commercially worthless. Ultimately, the Dept. of Justice was unable to prove any of the 15 charges of bribery that it had filed against two members of the Salt Lake City Olympics Bid Committee. Several members of the committee resigned, however. As a result of investigations into the matter, ten members of the International Olympics Committee were fired and another ten were sanctioned.

Additionally, the definition of a "public official" is also expansive. The statute defines *public officials* as members of Congress, government officers and employees, and anyone "acting for or on behalf of" the federal government "in any official function, under or by authority of" a federal government department or agency. For example, individuals who work for private corporations that have some degree of responsibility for carrying out federal programs or policies are considered public officials. The Case Nugget provides an interesting twist on the crime of bribery.

Case Nugget A Question of Bribery?

United States of America, Plaintiff-Appellee, v. Sonya Evette Singleton, Defendant-Appellant
Circuit Court of Appeals for the Tenth Circuit
165 F.3d 1297 (1999)

Often, when two defendants are charged with a crime, a prosecutor might offer to give one defendant leniency in exchange for truthful testimony against the other. Are such prosecutor plea deals really bribes and thus violative of federal bribery law, which prohibits the exchange of anything of value for testimony? The Tenth Circuit did not think so in this case.

Sonya Singleton was charged with money laundering and conspiring to distribute cocaine. Her co-conspirator, Napoleon Douglas, entered into a plea agreement with the prosecuting attorney under which he agreed to testify truthfully. In exchange, the prosecuting attorney promised leniency; the government would not prosecute him for related offenses, and the attorney would advise the sentencing court of Douglas's cooperation. Singleton argued that such an agreement violated the "anti-gratuity" statute, U.S.C. § 201(c)(2). The district court allowed Douglas's testimony and convicted Singleton. A panel of the Tenth Circuit Court reversed the conviction, arguing that the attorney's promise for leniency did violate federal bribery law. The full circuit voted to rehear the case.

On rehearing, the court reinstated the defendant's conviction, noting that to hold otherwise would "deprive the sovereign of a recognized or established prerogative, title, or interest." The court held that from the common law, we have a long-standing practice sanctioning the testimony of accomplices against their confederates in exchange for leniency, and this long-standing practice created a vested sovereign prerogative in the government. In light of the long-standing practice of leniency for testimony, the court had to presume that if Congress had intended to overturn this ingrained aspect of American legal culture, it would have done so in clear, unmistakable, and unarguable language.

Another type of bribery is *commercial bribery,* which includes a bribe in exchange for new information or payoffs. For example, suppose Comdac Computers. is looking for a company that manufactures a certain type of computer part. Jane Devlon owns such a company, and realizes that if Comdac gets the computer parts from her, she will potentially make a lot of money. When Comdac sends its contractor to the Devlon factory, Devlon offers the contractor $500,000 in exchange for the contractor's promise that Comdac will buy all such parts from only her factory for the next year. Alternatively, she might offer the contractor $5,000 to disclose the dollar amounts of the competing bids so that she can offer a better bid to earn the contract. The opening to this chapter also involves commercial bribery. Conner's offer of money to Freeman to return to his old job, so that he could provide better tips, is a commercial bribe.

One final type of bribery is the *bribery of foreign officials.* The purpose of the Foreign Corrupt Practices Act (FCPA) serves to combat such bribery. The FCPA prohibits payments to foreign officials to corruptly influence an official act or decision or to influence a foreign government. You might think of the FCPA as an extension of the law to prevent bribery of a public official. The FCPA allows the government to prosecute those who bribe foreign officials.

But Congress does not pass laws affecting foreign affairs in a vacuum. Laws governing white-collar crime, like all laws, are dynamic, and one source of change in these laws is international law. Multinational organizations in which the United States is a member often pressure the United States to alter American law so that it conforms to certain international standards. Thus, for example, Congress amended the FCPA in 1998 to conform to the antibribery convention adopted by the Organization for Economic Cooperation and Development (OECD). The amendments broaden the scope of actions covered by the FCPA and the definition of a public official. As of this writing, it is expected that 30 OECD countries—such as Japan, South Korea, and Brazil—will adopt similar antibribery statutes. Before the amendment, U.S. companies complained that antibribery laws disadvantaged them because many European and Asian competitors were not subject to similar laws. Between May 1994 and April 1998, bribes were allegedly used to influence the outcomes of 239 international contract competitions.

Extortion. Often confused with bribery, but completely different, is the crime of extortion. **Extortion,** otherwise known as *blackmail,* is the making of threats for the purpose of obtaining money or property. Whereas bribery is offering someone something to obtain a desired result, extortion involves the threat of doing something if the target of the extortion does not relinquish money or a specific piece of property. For example, if Connors in the opening scenario threatened to tell the government about Freeman's actions if he did not return to Goldman Sachs, then Connors would have committed extortion. Connors's actions would have been extortion because he would have issued a threat (to tell the government about Freeman's insider trading) for the purpose of obtaining money (to get Freeman to behave in a way that would enable Connors to make more money by receiving the more profitable tips from Goldman Sachs).

Fraud. Criminal **fraud** encompasses a variety of means by which an individual intentionally uses some sort of misrepresentation to gain an advantage over another person. Fraud generally requires the following three elements: (1) a material false representation made with intent to deceive *(scienter),* (2) a victim's reasonable reliance on the false representation, and (3) damages. Both the federal and the state governments have passed a number of statutes listing specific types of fraudulent schemes. These schemes to defraud include a multitude of frauds, such as credit card fraud, insurance fraud, and securities fraud. Exhibit 7-1 summarizes the fraudulent acts that might occur in the corporate setting, many of which are discussed below.

In June 2000, the FBI achieved its largest *securities fraud* crackdown in history when it arrested a group of Mafia leaders for a series of scams that cost investors an estimated $25 million. Government officials claimed that the Mob bought large stakes in small companies and then bribed and coerced brokers to promote the stocks to other investors at inflated prices.

The Enron scandal also involves securities fraud, with Enron's top executives allegedly overstating its earnings to maintain high stock prices. Complex accounting methods were used to hide the corporation's debt. Enron's top executives and big investors sold their stock, while encouraging employees to continue buying company stock. With the drastic decline in the company's stock value, many Enron employees lost much of their 401(k) investments.

Another specific type of securities fraud involved in the Enron case, as well as in the opening scenario to this chapter, is insider trading. Illegal **insider trading** is generally a person's buying or selling of a security, in breach of a fiduciary duty or other relationship of trust and confidence, while in possession of material, nonpublic information about the security. Insider-trading violations may also include "tipping" such information, securities trading by the person "tipped," and securities trading by those who misappropriate such

Exhibit 7-1
Selected Types of Fraudulent Crimes

1. *Forgery:* The fraudulent making or altering of any writing in a way that changes the legal rights and liabilities of another.
2. *Defalcation:* The misappropriation of trust funds or money held in a fiduciary capacity.
3. *False entries:* The making of an entry into the books of a bank or corporation that is designed to represent the existence of funds that do not exist.
4. *False token:* A false document or sign of existence used to perpetrate a fraud, such as making counterfeit money.
5. *False pretenses:* A designed misrepresentation of existing facts or conditions by which a person obtains another's money or goods, such as the writing of a worthless check.
6. *Fraudulent concealment:* The suppression of a material fact that a person is legally bound to disclose.
7. *Mail fraud:* The use of mails to defraud the public.
8. *Health care fraud:* Any fraudulent act committed in the provision of health care products or services.
9. *Telemarketing fraud:* Any scheme, including cramming and slamming, using the telephone to commit a fraudulent act.
10. *Ponzi scheme:* An investment swindle in which high profits are promised from fictitious sources and early investors are paid off with funds raised from later ones.
11. *Check kiting:* Drawing checks on an account in one bank and depositing them in an account in a second bank when neither account has sufficient funds to cover the amounts drawn. Just before the checks are returned for payment to the first bank, the kiter covers them by depositing checks drawn on the account in the second bank. Due to the delay created by the collection of funds by one bank from the other, known as the "float" time, an artificial balance is created.
12. *Pretexting:* Using fraudulent means to obtain information about someone's phone use.

information.[3] Enron's big investors and top executives knew the stock prices were overinflated due to the overstated earnings. They then used their knowledge, which was not public knowledge, to decide to sell off their stock before the price lowered drastically, thus engaging in insider trading. How might insider trading violate each of the ethical norms we have previously discussed?

Another example of insider trading involves Qwest Communications, a Denver-based local phone provider in 14 western and midwestern states. Qwest has been under investigation over the past few years for various white-collar crimes, including insider trading. Robin Szeliga, Qwest's former chief financial officer, is the highest-ranking official at Qwest to admit wrongdoing in the scandal. She admits to selling 10,000 shares of Qwest stock in 2001 for a net profit of $125,000. Szeliga knew some of Qwest's business units would not meet their targets. She also knew Qwest had illegally used nonrecurring revenue to try to meet its goals. Because the information Robin acted on was not public, and because she gained substantially by acting on the private information, Szeliga recently pleaded guilty to a single count of insider trading.

Stock-option backdating is yet another type of securities fraud that the SEC has been increasingly cracking down on. Backdating occurs when an employee falsifies documents

[3] U.S. Securities and Exchange Commission, www.sec.gov/answers/insider.htm.

to make it appear as if the company had granted options on certain dates, but the dates are selected after the fact by looking backward for dates on which the stock price was low, thereby falsely inflating the net profits of the company. In 2007, Myron F. Olesnyckyj, the former general counsel of Monster Worldwide, Inc., pleaded guilty to securities fraud for participating in a multiyear scheme with other Monster executives to secretly backdate stock options granted to thousands of Monster officers, directors, and employees, including himself. By backdating and improperly accounting for options, Monster granted undisclosed compensation to its employees, failed to recognize compensation expenses, and overstated its net income by $340 million from 1997 through 2005. Olesnyckyj personally made $381,000 from the scheme, which he agreed to forfeit.

An additional type of fraud is false pretenses. **False pretenses** is the illegal obtainment of property belonging to another through materially false representations of an existing fact, with knowledge of the falsity of the representations and with the interest to defraud. For example, Jim goes door-to-door selling vacuum cleaners at an amazing discount. To obtain the discount, the customers must pay immediately, and the vacuum cleaner will be delivered in three to five business days. However, Jim possesses no vacuum cleaners and does not plan on delivering any. Jim has committed the crime of false pretenses, as he illegally obtained another's property (the money he received as payment) by making false representations (telling the "customers" they would be receiving a vacuum) with the knowledge of the falsity (he knew there were no vacuum cleaners) and the intent to defraud (he did not plan on delivering any vacuum cleaners).

Forgery, the fraudulent making or altering of any writing in a way that changes the legal rights and liabilities of another, is another type of fraud. If you sign your colleague's name to the back of a check made out to your colleague, you have committed forgery.

One of the most frequently prosecuted frauds is *mail fraud,* which is the use of mails to defraud the public. The Mail Fraud Act of 1990 makes mail fraud a federal crime. To prove mail fraud, the government must demonstrate two elements: (1) an intent to defraud, and (2) the use of or causing the use of mails to further the fraudulent scheme. Case 7-1 demonstrates the consideration of these two elements.

Congress amended the mail fraud statute in 1994 to include commercial carriers and courier services as substitutes for the U.S. mail. In other words, using FedEx or UPS to further a fraudulent scheme can be prosecuted as mail fraud. Similarly, the wire fraud statute attempts to prevent the use of wire, radio, or television transmissions to defraud the public.

Other types of fraud include health care fraud, telemarketing fraud, and bankruptcy fraud. The Department of Justice recently named *health care fraud* its top priority after violent crime. An example of health care fraud is the submission of false claims to insurance plans such as Medicare or Medicaid. Additionally, some doctors prescribe unneeded equipment to patients and then receive kickbacks from the manufacturers of the equipment.

Telemarketing fraud has also gained much attention recently. The National Fraud Information Center reported that telephone cramming was the top telemarketing fraud of 1998. *Cramming* is a scheme in which companies bill consumers for optional services that the consumers did not order. Another frequent telemarketing scheme is *slamming,* in which consumers are tricked into changing their phone service to another carrier without their consent.

The elderly, who have been more susceptible to telemarketing fraud, are often the specific targets of telemarketing schemes. Thus, the Department of Justice and the FBI have been collaborating on various undercover operations, such as Operation Senior Sentinel, to investigate and prosecute fraudulent telemarketers.

CASE 7-1 UNITED STATES OF AMERICA v. GERSON COHEN
COURT OF APPEALS FOR THE THIRD CIRCUIT
171 F.3d 796 (1999)

Gerson Cohen, a meat salesperson for Butler Foods, made illegal cash payments to supermarkets' meat managers in an attempt to persuade them to buy their meat from Butler Foods. If the customer bought at least 10,000 pounds of meat per week, the cash payments usually amounted to one penny per pound of meat purchased. After a customer made the minimum purchase, Larry Lipoff, part owner of Butler Foods, would give the cash payment to the salespeople, who then gave the cash to the customer. Over a period of three years, Cohen made payments totaling $111,548.21 to managers for Thriftway Food Stores. The District Court convicted Cohen on twenty-five counts of mail fraud, in violation of 18 U.S.C. § 1341. Cohen appealed his conviction.

JUDGE NYGAARD: Cohen argues that the Government's evidence was insufficient to prove that he used the U.S. mail. We disagree. An essential element of mail fraud is "the use of the United States mails in furtherance of the fraudulent scheme"—*United States v. Hannigan,* 27 F.3d 890, 892 (3d Cir. 1994). This element requires some competent evidence that, as a routine business practice or office custom, the type of document at issue in the case was sent through the U.S. mail. As we indicated in Hannigan, "[T]he prosecution need not affirmatively disprove every conceivable alternative theory as to how the specific correspondence was delivered," but "some reference to the correspondence in question is required."

Cohen himself need not have placed the particular documents into the U.S. mail. A mailing is knowingly caused within the terms of the statute where one does an act with knowledge that the use of the mails will follow in the ordinary course of business. . . . Here, the bookkeeper for Butler Foods, who supervised the clerical workers who were responsible for generating and mailing invoices, testified extensively about the company's standard business practice for billing its customers. She testified that after the meat invoices were prepared, they were placed in envelopes, run through the postal meter, and put in a U.S. mail bin which Lipoff took to the post office in his car. She testified that Butler Foods never used any delivery method other than the U.S. mail for any of its invoices, and that the Thriftway invoices at issue in this case were handled in the normal manner.

A manager at the company testified that it was standard practice to pick up the invoices in the U.S. mail bin and drop them off at the post office, and that he himself did this on occasion. Finally, an accountant for the Thriftway stores testified that it was normal business practice for his company to receive Butler Foods' invoices through the U.S. mail. This testimony provides sufficient evidence that Butler routinely delivered its invoices through the U.S. mails.

AFFIRMED.

CRITICAL THINKING

Are you persuaded that Thriftway was using the mails to perpetuate a fraudulent scheme? Why or why not? What part of the opinion supports your conclusion?

ETHICAL DECISION MAKING

Return to the WPH process of ethical decision making. Whom does this decision affect? In other words, who are the stakeholders in this decision?

Another type of fraud involves bankruptcies. In 2004, more than 1.6 million bankruptcy filings occurred. An individual can file for bankruptcy to be relieved of oppressive debt. Yet claims need to be carefully reviewed to prevent *bankruptcy fraud.* For example, an individual might hide some assets so that they will not be considered during the proceedings. Conversely, a creditor (a party to whom another owes money) might file a false claim against a debtor (the party who owes money to a creditor). Thus, bankruptcy fraud can occur on the part of the debtor or the creditor. The U.S. Department of Justice estimates that 10 percent of all bankruptcy petitions contain some elements of fraud. However, between the year 2000 and the year 2005, only a few more than 1,000 defendants have faced bankruptcy fraud charges.

Expect the number of defendants facing bankruptcy fraud to be on the rise with the culmination of the Justice Department's Operation Truth or Consequences. In October 2006, the Justice Department created an Internet hotline for the public to report suspected bankruptcy fraud to the U.S. Trustee Program. This hotline is just one aspect of the Department of Justice's revitalized commitment to combating bankruptcy fraud and protecting the integrity of the bankruptcy system.

Sometimes fraud cases can be very complex and involve multiple types of fraud. For example, in one case, a Beverly Hills lawyer was recently convicted of three counts of mail fraud, seven counts of wire fraud, and five counts of lying to a court hearing. In an elaborate fraudulent scheme, the lawyer had purchased a yacht for $1.9 million, sold it to two other partners to drive up its insurance value, and then had a company he owned repurchase the yacht and insure it for $3.5 million. Finally, he and his partners sunk the yacht and tried to collect the insurance.

A fraudulent crime that has recently come into the public eye is pretexting. *Pretexting* can be defined as using or causing others to use false pretenses, fraudulent statements, fraudulent or stolen documents, or other misrepresentations, including posing as an account holder or employee of a telecommunications carrier, to obtain telephone records of another. Pretexting entered the national lexicon in 2006 when news broke that the investigators Hewlett-Packard's board of directors had hired to locate the source of several leaks to the media were engaging in this practice. Under the federal Telephone Records and Privacy Protection Act of 2006, anyone convicted of employing fraudulent tactics to persuade phone companies to hand over confidential data about a customer's calling habits can be sent to prison for up to 10 years. Some states also have statutes outlawing pretexting.

Both individuals and businesses can be victims of fraud. To minimize the chances that your firm will be a victim of fraud, review Exhibit 7-2, "Fraud Prevention Tips," very carefully.

Embezzlement. Joe is Kathleen's attorney. Kathleen gave Joe $5,000 to put in escrow, an account where Joe will have access to the money, although the money is not his to use as he pleases. Suppose Joe takes some of that money out of the account and uses it to gamble, and he "fixes" the records to cover up the fact that he has used some of the money for his personal use. He has committed the crime of **embezzlement,** the wrongful conversion of another's property by one who is lawfully in possession of that property. Embezzlement is distinguished from larceny because the individual did not take the property from another; he was already in possession of the property.

Embezzlement usually occurs when an employee steals money. Thus, it is often employees in banks who commit the crime. However, as the recent embezzlement of $6.9 million from the American Cancer Society demonstrates, even nonprofit organizations are vulnerable to the crime of embezzlement. White-collar crimes such as embezzlement are a problem in many countries. For example, the Chinese government, which has been focusing on economic crimes, caught employees in two major Chinese banks altering deposit slips and

Exhibit 7-2 Fraud Prevention Tips

RED FLAGS SUGGESTING POSSIBLE FRAUD

When looking at a brochure offering an investment opportunity that seems almost too good to be true, it may indeed not be as good as it seems, especially if it contains these red flags of fraud:

- *No independent proof of profitability:* The brochure provides the investment strategy but includes no details that can be verified, such as names and addresses of specific companies in which it invests.
- *Control by a single person.*
- *No audited financial statements and no evidence of internal controls.*
- *Unusually high rates of return:* Rates of return are significantly higher than those for other funds with a similar investment strategy.
- *New investors' reliance primarily on existing investors in deciding to invest.*

False "Assurances" That an Investment Opportunity Is Not Fraudulent

- *Long-time existence of investment opportunity:* A Ponzi scheme can operate for a long time. As long as the company keeps getting new investors, it can continue to use the new investors to pay off the few who insist on collecting their returns. Many investors may be content to accumulate paper profits, especially if there is a financial incentive for reinvestment of profits. For example, the Financial Advisory Fund had been in business for almost 20 years before its fraudulent foundation was uncovered.
- *A list of names and addresses of satisfied investors you can contact:* All such schemes will have some satisfied investors who have received payments from the new investment money.
- *Membership in the Better Business Bureau:* Any company can pay to join. If most of the investors had not attempted to withdraw their funds and the company was still getting new investments, there would have been be no disgruntled investors to complain to the BBB.
- *A report of profitability from Dun & Bradstreet:* Dun & Bradstreet does not do an independent financial audit of a company's profits. As stated on its Web site, Dun & Bradstreet simply provides the information regarding profits that it receives from companies.
- *Acceptance of money rolled over from IRAs:* There is no government check on the soundness of firms that roll over IRAs.
- *Bank references:* If a firm simply has a large amount of money in a checking account in a bank and has never sought a loan from the bank, the bank would have no reason to do any due diligence on the firm. Also, if the owner of the firm is personable and the account has never been overdrawn, the bank personnel may well give the firm a good reference.
- *Glossy brochures and television ads:* All you need for both is some money and the knowledge that many people may be overly impressed by a fancy brochure or ad campaign.

These tips come from Barry Minkow, who went from starting his own carpet cleaning business at the age of 16, to taking this multimillion-dollar company public at the age 20, to facing a 23-year prison sentence and $26 million victim restitution payment at the age of 21 for massive fraud and theft perpetuated on behalf of his company, to now being a pastor and the cofounder of the Fraud Discovery Institute.

The fascinating story of how Barry Minkow, through fraudulent Ponzi schemes, check kiting, and theft, managed to build the multimillion-dollar ZZZZ Best Carpet Cleaning Company by the age of 20 is contained in his book, *Cleaning Up.* The book also provides insights into why some people may commit white-collar crimes, and it describes many of the long-running frauds Minkow has helped to uncover since deciding to use his understanding of the perpetuation of fraud to help uncover and prevent it.

global context

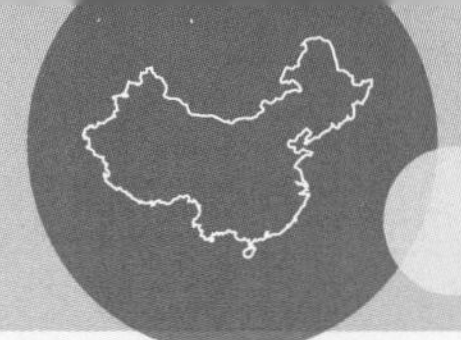

Embezzlement and Bribery in China

Between 1981 and 1982, the People's Republic of China witnessed a dramatic rise in white-collar crimes, including embezzlement, extortion, and bribery. Chinese officials were alarmed by the increase and sought to severely punish all economic offenders regardless of political or social rank. On March 8, 1982, a resolution entitled "Severely Punishing Criminals Who Do Great Damage to the Economy" was added to the Chinese Criminal Code. The provision targeted top-ranking officials by stating that any state functionaries who extort, accept bribes, or exploit their office would no longer receive the fixed-term punishment (usually 10 years) allocated for bribery and extortion. Instead, those officials found guilty of extortion and accepting bribes would be sentenced to life imprisonment or possibly put to death.

Bank fraud is another white-collar crime that may be punishable by death. In 2004, China executed four people, including employees of two of its Big Four state banks, for fraud totaling $15 million. Three of the cases involved China Construction Bank.

A former accounting officer at this bank worked with others to steal 20 million yuan ($2.4 million) from the bank using fake papers. He and an accomplice were executed, along with another Construction Bank employee who was found to have taken 20 million yuan from the bank in an unrelated case. Additionally, an official employed by the Bank of China was executed for cheating.

The precise number of people executed in China is a secret. Estimates range from 5,000 to 10,000 a year, for crimes including murder, corruption, and on occasion even bottom-pinching. Most are executed by a single shot in the back of the head.

Such punishments may seem extreme, but the reaction of the Chinese to this increase in white-collar crime reflects the culture's unusually great concern for social harmony.

bank orders to direct the money to personal accounts throughout China. Those employees received death sentences for embezzlement, as discussed in the Global Context box.

Computer crimes. The term **computer crime** refers broadly to any wrongful act that (1) is directed against computers, (2) uses computers to commit a crime, or (3) involves computers. Computer crime is not necessarily a new kind of crime but is, instead, a new way of committing traditional crimes. Consider fraud, a crime that has existed for centuries. Today, online auctions, such as eBay, are a common source of fraud in the United States. Indeed, some statistics suggest that, compared with nonelectronic methods, using computers is a more profitable method of committing crimes. According to federal officials, the average loss in a nonelectronic embezzlement is $23,500; in contrast, in a computer fraud case, the average loss is almost $500,000.[4]

Computer crimes are often difficult to prosecute, in large part because they are difficult to detect. A computer crime could be committed by an insider, such as an employee, or by an outsider, such as a **hacker**—a person who illegally accesses or enters another person's or a company's computer system to obtain information or to steal money. In addition, computer systems are quite open to attack. The American Society for Industrial Security has reported that the losses from computer crimes in a single year were more than $250 billion for U.S. companies. Furthermore, the attacks are frequent. The IRS alone detects 800 to 1,200 cases of computer system misuse annually.

[4] Charles Alexander, The Wells Fargo Stickup, Time.Com. http://www.time.com/time/magazine/article/0,9171,954673-3,00.html (accessed 054/01/07)

A **cyber terrorist** is a hacker whose intention is the exploitation of a target computer or network to create a serious impact, such as the crippling of a communications network or the sabotage of a business or organization. The activity of a cyber terrorist can have an impact on millions of citizens if the terrorist's attack is successful, particularly if it involved the computer systems of a major stock exchange, any bank, or any federal agency or government.

In an attempt to aid prosecutions of computer crimes, Congress passed the Counterfeit Access Device and Computer Fraud and Abuse Act of 1984 (also know as the Computer Fraud and Abuse Act, or CFAA). The act prohibits six broad categories of computer crimes:

1. Unauthorized use of or access to a computer to obtain classified military or foreign policy information with the intent to harm the United States or to benefit a foreign country.
2. Unauthorized use of a computer to collect financial or credit information protected under federal privacy law.
3. Unauthorized access to a federal computer and the use, modification, destruction, or disclosure of data it contains or the prevention of authorized persons' use of such data.
4. Alteration or modification of data in financial computers causing a loss of $1,000 or more.
5. Modification of data that impedes medical treatment to individuals.
6. Fraudulent transfer of computer passwords or other similar data that could aid unauthorized access that either (a) affects interstate commerce or (b) permits access to a government computer.

Computer crimes falling into the first category are felonies, whereas the others are misdemeanors.

The National Information Infrastructure Protection Act of 1996 amended the Computer Fraud and Abuse Act. One of the major changes to the CFFA is the substitution of the term *protected computers* for *federal interest computers* so that the statute now protects any computer attached to the Internet.

In a further attempt to aid prosecution of computer crimes, the U.S. Department of Justice formed the Computer Crime and Intellectual Property Section (CCIPS) in its Criminal Division. Attorneys in this division prosecute only federal computer crimes. They also coordinate their activities with numerous government entities, the private sector, scholars, and foreign representatives in an attempt to develop a global response to computer crime.

Destruction of computer data. Destruction of data is one of the most serious problems facing companies today. A **virus** is a computer program that rearranges, damages, destroys, or replaces computer data. Thus, if an employee or a hacker creates and releases a virus, a company can easily lose vital information.

The most economically destructive computer crime to date was the creation of the "love bug" virus. In May 2000, the virus spread rapidly throughout the world by e-mail. Once the e-mail was opened, it destroyed files on the user's computer, and then the virus sent itself to every address in that computer's e-mail address book. In the end, the virus caused over $10 billion in damages and halted computers in major companies and government agencies worldwide.

Companies can try to prevent the destruction of data by installing virus detection programs on their computers. However, the detection programs recognize only previously existing harmful files. As a result, if someone creates a new virus, the detection program is useless.

Unlawful appropriation of data or services. When an employee uses his or her computer in a manner not authorized by the employer, the employee has committed a crime. Employers, then, must clearly communicate with employees about authorized versus unauthorized behavior. For example, if an employee uses her work computer to run her own personal business on the side, her employer may argue that she is engaging in theft because she is not using her computer in an authorized manner. Thus, when you become a business manager, you will want to make sure that you explicitly list acceptable computer uses, along with the penalties associated with unauthorized use.

Liability for Crimes

An individual or a corporation can be charged with and convicted of a crime. However, there has been much debate over whether corporations should be held criminally responsible.

CORPORATE CRIMINAL LIABILITY

Under the common law, a corporation could not be considered a criminal because it was not an actual person and thus did not have a "mind." Consequently, it could not meet the *mens rea* (guilty-mind) requirement for a crime. Slowly, however, courts began to impose liability on corporations for **strict-liability offenses,** those offenses that do not require state of mind. Next, courts imposed liability on corporations by imputing the state of mind of the employee to the corporation. Currently, corporations can be held criminally accountable for almost any crime. However, they cannot be held liable for crimes that are punishable only by a prison sentence.

The first case in which criminal liability was assigned to a corporation for a crime other than a strict-liability offense was decided by the United States Supreme Court in 1909.[5] Over the years, the courts have refined the standards required for finding a corporation criminally liable for the acts of one of its employees or agents. Today, for a corporation to be held criminally liable for the acts of an agent, it must be shown that (1) the individual was acting within the scope of her or his employment; (2) the individual was acting with the purpose of benefiting the corporation; and (3) the act was imputed to the corporation.

LIABILITY OF CORPORATE EXECUTIVES

In addition to corporations having criminal liability, corporate executives may also be personally liable for a business crime. The beneficiary of the crime can be irrelevant, as corporate executives and officers can be found to be personally liable regardless of whether the crimes were committed for their personal benefit or for the benefit of the corporation. Also, under the "responsible corporate officer" doctrine, a court may assess criminal liability on a corporate executive or officer even if he or she did not engage in, direct, or even know about a specific criminal violation. As Case 7-2 demonstrates, corporate executives sometimes have the responsibility and power to ensure the company's compliance with the law. If the executive fails to meet this responsibility, the executive can be held criminally liable.

Since *United States v. Park* (Case 7-2), the general rule that corporate executives may be held accountable for the crimes arising from their failure to meet their responsibility has remained intact. The rule has, in fact, broadened so that now executives can be held criminally liable for offenses that we generally do not think of as crimes. For example, in *United States v. Iverson,*[6] a corporate officer of a waste treatment facility was convicted

[5] *New York Central & Hudson River Railroad Company v. United States,* 212 U.S. 481 (1909).

[6] 162 F.3d 1015 (1998).

CASE 7-2 UNITED STATES v. PARK
UNITED STATES SUPREME COURT
421 U.S. 658 (1975)

Defendant Park, the president of a national food-chain corporation, was charged, along with the corporation, with violating the Federal Food, Drug, and Cosmetic Act by allowing food in the warehouse to be exposed to rodent contamination. Park had conceded that his responsibility for the "entire operation" included warehouse sanitation, but claimed that he had delegated the responsibility for sanitation to dependable subordinates. He admitted at trial that he had received a warning letter from the Food and Drug Administration regarding the unsanitary conditions at one of the company's warehouses. The trial court found the defendant guilty. The court of appeals reversed. The case was appealed to the U.S. Supreme Court.

CHIEF JUSTICE BURGER: The question presented was whether "the manager of a corporation, as well as the corporation itself, may be prosecuted under the Federal Food, Drug, and Cosmetic Act of 1938 for the introduction of misbranded and adulterated articles into interstate commerce." In Dotterweich, a jury had disagreed as to the corporation, a jobber purchasing drugs from manufacturers and shipping them in interstate commerce under its own label, but had convicted Dotterweich, the corporation's president and general manager.

Central to the Court's conclusion that individuals other than proprietors are subject to the criminal provisions of the Act was the reality that "the only way in which a corporation can act is through the individuals who act on its behalf." The Court also noted that corporate officers had been subject to criminal liability under the Federal Food and Drugs Act of 1906, and it observed that a contrary result under the 1938 legislation would have been incompatible with the expressed intent of Congress to "enlarge and stiffen the penal net" and to discourage a view of the act's criminal penalties as a "license for the conduct of illegitimate business."

The rationale of the interpretation given the Act in Dotterweich, as holding criminally accountable the persons whose failure to exercise the authority and supervisory responsibility reposed in them by the business organization, resulted in the violation complained of, has been confirmed in our subsequent cases. Thus, the Court has reaffirmed the proposition that "the public interest in the purity of its food is so great as to warrant the imposition of the highest standard of care on distributors." In order to make "distributors of food the strictest censors of their merchandise," the Act punishes "neglect where the law requires care, and inaction where it imposes a duty." The accused, if he does not will the violation, usually is in a position to prevent it with no more care than society might reasonably expect and no more exertion than it might reasonably extract from one who assumed his responsibilities."

Thus, Dotterweich and the cases which have followed reveal that in providing sanctions which reach and touch the individuals who execute the corporate mission—and this by no means necessarily confined to a single corporate agent or employee—the Act imposes not only a positive duty to seek out and remedy violations when they occur, but also, and primarily, a duty to implement measures that will insure that violations will not occur. The requirements of foresight and vigilance imposed on responsible corporate agents are beyond question, demanding, and perhaps onerous, but they are not more stringent than the public has a right to expect of those who voluntarily assume positions of authority in business enterprises whose services and products affect the health and well-being of the public that supports them.

The Act does not, as we observed in Dotterweich, make criminal liability turn on "awareness of some wrongdoing" or "conscious fraud." The duty imposed by Congress on responsible corporate agents is, we emphasize, one that requires the highest standard of foresight and vigilance, but the Act, in its criminal aspect, does not require that which is objectively impossible. The theory upon which responsible corporate agents are held criminally accountable for "causing" violations of the Act permits a claim that a defendant was "powerless" to prevent or correct the violation to "be raised defensively at a trial on the merits."

. . . [I]t is equally clear that the Government established a prima facie case when it introduced evidence sufficient to warrant a finding by the trier of the facts that the defendant had, by reason of his position in the corporation, responsibility and authority either to prevent in the first instance, or promptly to correct, the violation complained of, and that he failed

[CONTINUED]

to do so. The failure thus to fulfill the duty imposed by the interaction of the corporate agent's authority and that statute furnishes a sufficient causal link. The considerations, which prompted the imposition of this duty, and the scope of the duty, provide the measure of culpability.

REVERSED in favor of the Government.

CRITICAL THINKING

The Court relies heavily on the *Dotterweich* decision in coming to its present conclusion. Why does the Court use *Dotterweich* to reach its conclusion? Do you think the Court should have relied so heavily on *Dotterweich?*

ETHICAL DECISION MAKING

Suppose you were in Park's position in this case. You allegedly allowed food in your warehouse to be exposed to rodent contamination. If you were guided by the public disclosure test, what would you decide to do?

and sentenced for violating the Clean Water Act after he ordered employees to illegally dispose of wastewater. This case demonstrates that corporate executives can be sentenced not only for committing the common law crimes that we have traditionally understood to be criminal offenses but also for violating provisions of regulatory statutes that permit criminal sanctions. In such cases, **vicarious liability,** or liability imposed on one person for the acts of another, is assessed to the corporate executive. In fact, courts have held that employers are vicariously liable for the wrongful acts of their employees if the employer directed, partook in, or authorized the wrongful act.

Defenses to Crimes

In addition to claiming that the defendant is innocent or that the prosecution did not follow proper procedures, the defense may use several **affirmative defenses,** which are excuses for unlawful behavior. Some of the most common defenses include mistake of fact, intoxication, insanity, duress, and entrapment.

INFANCY

Under the law, persons who are under the age of majority (the age at which one is considered a legal adult) are considered to be **infants.** Those who have not reached the age of majority typically are considered to lack the mental capabilities of an adult, and thus infancy can be used as a partial defense to defuse the guilty-mind requirement of a crime. However, it should be noted that for some offenses, people who have not reached the age of majority can be determined by a judge to be a legal adult and can then be tried as such.

MISTAKE

With a **mistake-of-fact** defense, the defense tries to prove that a defendant made an honest and reasonable mistake that negates the guilty-mind element of a crime. For example, in the case at the start of this chapter, if Connors thought the information provided by Freeman was public knowledge, they could not have committed insider trading.

In contrast, *mistake of law* is generally not a legitimate defense. For example, Connors could not escape conviction by claiming he did not know insider trading is against the law. While initially these two rules may seem contradictory (because in both cases, the defendant seems to lack a guilty mind), the mistake-of-law rule serves a policy goal. Courts have refused to recognize mistake of law as a defense because they fear that doing so would create a disincentive for people to learn basic tenets of law.

INTOXICATION

If a person has been forced to ingest an intoxicating substance or involuntarily ingests an intoxicating agent, that person can claim **involuntary intoxication.** This defense applies only if the intoxication left the person unable to understand that the act committed was wrong. In most states, a defendant cannot claim intoxication as a defense when the defendant knowingly chose to become intoxicated.

INSANITY

Although a claim of insanity is a well-known criminal defense, it is not used as often as the public believes. A person cannot simply claim he or she is or was crazy; psychiatrists usually testify to the defendant's mental state at the time of the crime. Although the standards vary from state to state, in general defendants can claim **insanity** when their mental condition at the time the crime was committed was so impaired that they could not (1) understand the wrongful nature of the specific act or (2) distinguish between right and wrong in a general sense.

When the insanity defense is used, there is often a "battle of the experts." The psychiatrist testifying on behalf of the defense claims the accused was insane, and the psychiatrist for the prosecution refutes the defense psychiatrist's diagnosis. Furthermore, legal scholars debate whether psychiatrists who apply the tests of legal insanity are able to determine whether an individual is or was insane at the time of the criminal act. The complexity of the insanity standards almost guarantees that psychiatric experts will disagree about the application of the standards.

Adding to the complexity of the insanity standards is the fact that the test used to establish one's mental state varies depending on the jurisdiction. Approximately one-third of the states still apply the M'Naghten test. The *M'Naghten test,* also known as the "right-wrong test," allows a defendant to be found not guilty if he or she did not understand the nature of the act.

Another test used when the insanity defense is employed is the irresistible-impulse test. The *irresistible-impulse test* holds that a person may be deemed not guilty by reason of insanity even if he or she knew a criminal act was wrong, as long as some "irresistible impulse" resulting from a mental deficiency drove the person to commit the crime.

A third test used for establishing criminal insanity is the test recognized in the Model Penal Code. Section 4.01 of the code states, "A person is not responsible for criminal conduct if at the time of such conduct as a result of mental disease or defect he lacks substantial capacity either to appreciate the wrongfulness of his conduct or to conform his conduct to the requirements of the law." While the standard set forth in the Model Penal Code is easier to meet than the standard set forth in either the M'Naghten or the irresistible-impulse test, it is still extremely difficult to prove criminal insanity.

Most people have become very aware of the defense of insanity because of its use in the highly publicized case brought against Andrea Yates for the murder of her five children.

In raising the insanity defense, Andrea's lawyer argued that his client believed killing her children was the right thing to do. In support of this claim, he offered evidence that she had said that her children were "going to be tormented the rest of their lives, and they were going to perish in the fires of hell," and so she killed them to save them. This defense was not successful in her first trial. However, that verdict was overturned on appeal due to erroneous testimony, and in the retrial the defense was successful.

DURESS

If Greg threatened Bill with immediate bodily harm or loss of life unless Bill performed a wrongful act, Bill can use the **duress** defense. However, to claim duress, Bill must establish the following three elements:

1. Greg threatened Bill with *serious bodily harm or loss of life.* Threatening to take Bill's money would not be considered duress.
2. Greg's threat of harm must be *more serious* than the harm caused by Bill's crime. If Greg threatened to injure Bill's daughter seriously unless Bill handed over the $5,000 in the company cash register, duress would apply.
3. Greg's threat of harm must be *immediate* and *inescapable.* If Greg threatened to kill Bill in a year if Bill did not comply with Greg's order, Bill could not use the duress defense.

ENTRAPMENT

A relatively common defense for white-collar crime is entrapment. A defendant can use the **entrapment** defense if the idea for a crime originated not with the defendant but with a police officer or other government official who suggested it to the defendant, who would not otherwise have committed the crime. The purpose of this defense is to prevent law enforcement officials from instigating crime.

Typically, a defendant claims an undercover government official suggested that a crime be committed and pressured the defendant into performing that crime. To refute the defense, the prosecution must demonstrate either that the defendant was not induced by government agents to commit the crime or that the defendant was predisposed to commit the crime. In other words, a long-term drug dealer could not use the entrapment defense to claim that the undercover agent who offered to buy the dealer's drugs was the one who gave the dealer the idea to sell drugs.

NECESSITY

One possible defense of a crime is to argue that the commission of the crime was necessary to prevent a more severe crime from occurring. Section 3.01 of the Model Penal Code allows for the **necessity defense** when "the harm or evil sought to be avoided by such conduct is greater than that sought to be prevented by the law defining the offense charged." For example, a person could use the necessity defense if he or she broke into a store to prevent arson from occurring at night. While breaking into a store is a crime, it was a necessary action in order to prevent the more severe crime of arson.

JUSTIFIABLE USE OF FORCE

Although not typically used in white-collar crime cases, one defense that can be used in cases involving physical violence to another is **justifiable use of force.** The most well-known justifiable use of force is self-defense in protection of one's life. However, there are other examples of a justifiable use of force. In many jurisdictions, the affirmative defense of justifiable use of force can be used for defense of one's dwelling, defense of other property, and prevention of a crime, in addition to defense of self. The force used must be reasonable. That is, the force must be nonexcessive, which is understood in the law to be enough force to make an adequate defense but not more than is necessary for protection. Deadly force (force that is sufficient to kill or cause seriously bodily harm) is unjustifiable in cases where the threat of deadly force does not exist. In other words, deadly force cannot be used when there is no reasonable apprehension of suffering serious bodily harm or death. Deadly force can never be used to protect property, as the law values life over property.

Constitutional Safeguards

As stated previously, the state is always the party bringing charges in a criminal trial. The state obviously has vast amounts of resources at its disposal that it can use to try to obtain a guilty verdict. In an attempt to stabilize the imbalance of power in criminal proceedings, certain constitutional safeguards have been built into the system to ensure that defendants are protected during criminal proceedings. The vast majority, but not all, of the safeguards are contained within the Bill of Rights, the first 10 amendments to the Constitution.

FOURTH AMENDMENT PROTECTIONS

The right of the people to be secure in their persons, houses, papers, and effects, against unreasonable searches and seizures, shall not be violated, and no warrants shall issue, but upon probable cause, supported by oath or affirmation, and particularly describing the place to be searched, and the persons or things to be seized.

The Fourth Amendment contains two important safeguards: protection from unreasonable search and seizure, and restrictions placed on warrants.

The prohibition against unreasonable search and seizure is fairly straightforward. Government officials are not allowed to perform any searches without a proper warrant or without probable cause for a search. The Fourth Amendment therefore serves to protect an individual's privacy.

The restrictions on warrants contained in the Fourth Amendment are less straightforward than is the protection against unreasonable search and seizures. The Fourth Amendment requires that a person or his or her property may not be searched without a warrant or probable cause. The protection also extends to the issuance of arrest warrants. Furthermore, the Fourth Amendment requires that warrants be specific in regard to who is to be arrested, or what objects are to be sought, and in which locations the search is to be conducted. Accordingly, the Fourth Amendment prevents law enforcement officials from receiving general warrants allowing them to search anywhere for anything illegal they might find.

The protections of the Fourth Amendment are extended to businesses as well. Thus, government inspectors may not legally enter a business to conduct an inspection without a warrant. However, there are a few exceptions to the rule. No warrant is necessary to search highly regulated industries, such as those involving food, liquor, or firearms. It is important to note that general manufacturing is *not* included in the list of highly regulated industries, and thus a warrant is required for an agent to inspect a manufacturing plant.

FIFTH AMENDMENT PROTECTIONS

. . . nor shall any person be subject for the same offense to be twice put in jeopardy of life or limb; nor shall be compelled in any criminal case to be a witness against himself, nor be deprived of life, liberty, or property, without due process of law.

The three main provisions of the Fifth Amendment are the prohibition on double jeopardy, the right not to incriminate oneself, and the right to due process.

Double jeopardy occurs when one person is retried for the same criminal offense after being declared not guilty. The Constitution expressly forbids the government from recharging anyone with the same criminal offense after the person has been adjudicated not guilty. However, it is worth mentioning that double jeopardy applies only to criminal offenses. Therefore, although a person may be found not guilty of a criminal offense, the same person might still face a civil charge, which is decided independently of the verdict in the criminal case and entails a lower burden of proof.

Whenever anyone says, "I take the fifth," the person is referring to his constitutional right to not testify against himself. That is, in a criminal trial, a defendant does not have to testify, and cannot be forced by the state to testify, against herself. It is paramount for businesspersons to note that the right not to engage in self-incrimination does *not* apply to corporations but, rather, applies only to natural persons (corporations are legal entities, not natural persons, in the eyes of the law). Nonetheless, sole proprietorships that have not been incorporated may be considered as natural persons embodied in the person of the sole proprietor, and therefore they may use the Fifth Amendment protection against self-incrimination.

The guarantee of due process of law ensures that a defendant may not be stricken of life, liberty, or property without first going through the appropriate legal actions (typically a trial or plea bargaining). Unlike the right not to incriminate oneself, the guarantee of due process of law does extend to corporations.

SIXTH AMENDMENT PROTECTIONS

In all criminal prosecutions, the accused shall enjoy the right to a speedy and public trial, by an impartial jury . . . and to be informed of the nature and cause of the accusation; to be confronted with the witnesses against him; to have compulsory process for obtaining witnesses in his favor, and to have the assistance of counsel for his defense.

The Sixth Amendment protections are crucial to ensuring fair proceedings in a criminal trial. The rights contained in the Sixth Amendment are clearly spelled out as:

1. The right to a speedy and public trial.
2. The right to a trial by an impartial jury of one's peers.
3. The right to be informed of the accusations against oneself.
4. The right to confront witnesses.
5. The right to have witnesses on one's side.
6. The right to counsel at various stages of the proceedings.

EIGHTH AMENDMENT PROTECTIONS

Excessive bail shall not be required, nor excessive fines imposed, nor cruel and unusual punishments inflicted.

While the explicit meaning of "excessive bail," "excessive fines," and "cruel and unusual punishment" is ambiguous and open to judicial interpretation, the protections embodied in the Eighth Amendment are easy to grasp.

FOURTEENTH AMENDMENT PROTECTIONS

No state shall make or enforce any law which shall abridge the privileges or immunities of citizens of the United States; nor shall any state deprive any person of life, liberty, or property, without due process of law; nor deny to any person within its jurisdiction the equal protection of the laws.

While not part of the Bill of Rights, the Fourteenth Amendment does contain important constitutional safeguards. These safeguards include the extension of the guarantee to due process to all states, no longer guaranteeing due process solely at the federal level. Accordingly, the Fourteenth Amendment serves as an extension of the Fifth Amendment in the protection of due process. The Fourteenth Amendment also extends most of the constitutional protections down to defendants at the state level.

THE EXCLUSIONARY RULE

The exclusionary rule is not directly stated in any specific amendment. The *exclusionary rule* holds that all evidence obtained in violation of the constitutional rights spelled out in the Fourth, Fifth, and Sixth amendments is normally not admissible at trial. That is, evidence that was illegally obtained because it violates a constitutional safeguard may not be used as evidence in trial. Such evidence is considered "fruit of the poisonous tree," as it is the result of an illegal procedure, and thus is tainted evidence.

However, there are some exceptions to the exclusionary rule. One of them is the *good-faith exception.* Under this exception, evidence found when an official acts in good faith is admissible at trial. Thus, if a law enforcement official uses an incorrect search warrant to obtain evidence but, in so doing, the official acted in good faith, believing the search warrant to be correct and thus valid, the evidence is admissible.

Another exception is the *inevitability exception.* The inevitability exception holds that illegally obtained evidence may legally be used at trial if the evidence would have been obtained "inevitably" by law enforcement officials using lawful means.

Criminal Procedure

Criminal procedure differs from civil procedure in several key ways. First, the government, referred to as the *prosecutor,* always brings the criminal case, whereas in a civil case, the plaintiff filing the case can be an individual, business, or government entity. Second, the outcome of each is different. In a criminal case, the objective is punishment, so the defendant may be fined or imprisoned; in a civil case, the objective is to remedy a wrong done to the plaintiff, so the defendant either will have to provide compensation to the plaintiff or may be subject to an equitable remedy such as an injunction or order for specific performance. Other differences will become clear as you read the following sections describing the pretrial, trial, and posttrial procedures in a criminal case. The complete criminal procedure is illustrated in Figure 7-1.

PRETRIAL PROCEDURE

Prior to an arrest, grand juries may conduct criminal investigatory proceedings or issue a grand jury subpoena for company records. Criminal proceedings generally begin when an individual is **arrested** for a crime. A law enforcement officer must perform the arrest. This officer is often a police officer but may also be an agent of another government agency, such as the Bureau of Alcohol, Tobacco and Firearms; the Federal Bureau of Investigation; or the Immigration and Naturalization Service. A law enforcement officer should obtain an arrest warrant before an individual is taken into custody. Ordinarily, to obtain an arrest warrant, the law enforcement agent must demonstrate that there is **probable cause,** or a likelihood, that a suspect committed or is planning to commit a crime. A *magistrate,* the lowest-ranking judicial official, issues the arrest warrant. In certain circumstances, however, courts have recognized that law enforcement agents can arrest a suspect without a warrant if the officer believes there is probable cause but not enough time to obtain the warrant.

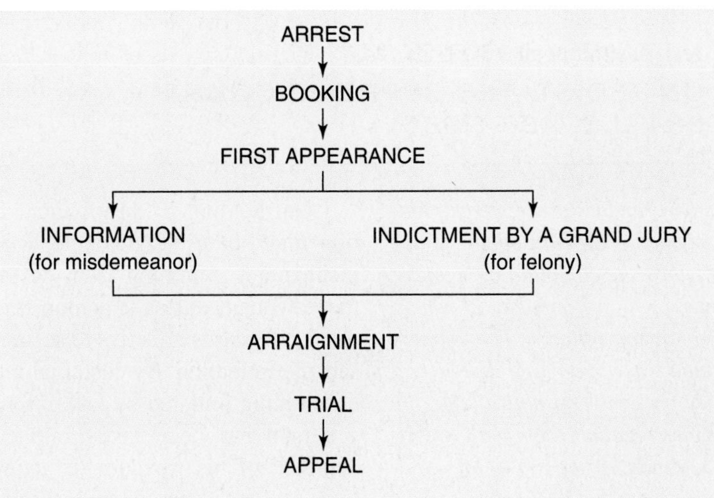

Figure 7-1
Steps in a Criminal Procedure

When law enforcement agents arrest individuals, the officers must inform the individuals of their **Miranda rights.** If they fail to do so, any information a defendant offers at the time of the arrest is not admissible at trial. To comply with the Supreme Court's requirements for protecting a citizen's rights, a law enforcement officer must inform the defendant of the following facts before questioning:

1. "You have the right to remain silent and refuse to answer any questions."
2. "Anything you say may be used against you in a court of law."
3. "You have the right to consult an attorney before speaking to the police and have an attorney present during any questioning now or in the future."
4. "If you cannot afford an attorney, one will be appointed for you before the questioning begins."
5. "If you do not have an attorney available, you have the right to remain silent until you have had an opportunity to consult with one."
6. "Now that I have advised you of your rights, are you willing to answer any questions without an attorney present?"

Case 7-3 presents the seminal case in which it was ruled that police officers must inform people they arrest of their rights. Notice the points of law from which the Miranda rights are derived.

The Miranda rights are not absolute. In fact, the Supreme Court has several times allowed for exceptions to the Miranda rights. For example, in *New York v. Quarles,*[7] the Court created a "public safety" exception to the Miranda rights. This exception allows statements to be used at trial, even if a person was not informed of his or her Miranda rights, if the need to protect the public is served by the admissibility of the statements in question.

In *Arizona v. Fulminante,*[8] the Court held that a coerced confession can be ignored and treated as nonprejudicial at trial if the other evidence is sufficient to obtain a conviction. That is, when a person can be found guilty beyond a reasonable doubt without the evidence of a coerced confession, it does not matter that the defendant's Miranda rights were violated in obtaining the confession.

[7] 467 U.S. 649 (1984).
[8] 499 U.S. 279 (1991).

CASE 7-3 MIRANDA v. ARIZONA
UNITED STATES SUPREME COURT
384 U.S. 436 (1966)

On March 13, 1963, Ernesto Miranda was arrested for kidnapping and rape and taken in custody to a Phoenix police station. After being identified by the complaining witness, the police took him to "Interrogation Room No. 2" where he was questioned by two police officers. The officers admitted at trial that Miranda was not advised that he had a right to have an attorney present. Two hours later, the officers emerged from the interrogation room with a written confession signed by Miranda. At the top of the statement was a typed paragraph stating that the confession was made voluntarily, without threats or promises of immunity and "with full knowledge of my legal rights, understanding any statement I make may be used against me."

At his trial, the written confession was admitted into evidence over the objection of defense counsel, and the officers testified to the prior oral confession made by Miranda during the interrogation. Miranda was found guilty and sentenced to 20 to 30 years' imprisonment. On appeal, the Supreme Court of Arizona held that Miranda's constitutional rights were not violated and affirmed the conviction. Miranda appealed to the Supreme Court, which joined his case with the cases of three other defendants making similar constitutional arguments regarding a violation of rights.

JUSTICE WARREN: The cases before us raise questions which go to the roots of our concepts of American criminal jurisprudence: the restraints society must observe consistent with the Federal Constitution in prosecuting individuals for crime. More specifically, we deal with the admissibility of statements obtained from an individual who is subjected to custodial police interrogation and the necessity for procedures which assure that the individual is accorded his privilege under the Fifth Amendment to the Constitution not to be compelled to incriminate himself.

This case is but an explication of basic rights enshrined in our Constitution—that "No person . . . shall be compelled in any criminal case to be a witness against himself," and that "the accused shall . . . have the Assistance of Counsel"—rights which were put in jeopardy in this case through official overbearing. These precious rights were fixed in our Constitution only after centuries of persecution and struggle. And in the words of Chief Justice Marshall, they were secured "for ages to come, and . . . designed to approach immortality as nearly as human institutions can approach it."

Our holding . . . briefly stated is this: the prosecution may not use statements, whether exculpatory or inculpatory, stemming from custodial interrogation of the defendant unless it demonstrates the use of procedural safeguards effective to secure the privilege against self-incrimination. By custodial interrogation, we mean questioning initiated by law enforcement officers after a person has been taken into custody or otherwise deprived of his freedom of action in any significant way. As for the procedural safeguards to be employed, unless other fully effective means are devised to inform accused persons of their right of silence and to assure a continuous opportunity to exercise it, the following measures are required.

Prior to any questioning, the person must be warned that he has a right to remain silent, that any statement he does make may be used as evidence against him, and that he has a right to the presence of an attorney, either retained or appointed. The defendant may waive effectuation of these rights, provided the waiver is made voluntarily, knowingly and intelligently. If, however, he indicates in any manner and at any stage of the process that he wishes to consult with an attorney before speaking there can be no questioning. Likewise, if the individual is alone and indicates in any manner that he does not wish to be interrogated, the police may not question him. The mere fact that he may have answered some questions or volunteered some statements on his own does not deprive him of the right to refrain from answering any further inquiries until he has consulted with an attorney and thereafter consents to be questioned.

From the testimony of the officers and by the admission of respondent, it is clear that Miranda was not in any way apprised of his right to consult with an attorney and to have one present during the interrogation, nor was his right not to be compelled to incriminate himself effectively protected in any other manner. Without these warnings the statements were inadmissible. The mere fact that he signed a statement which contained a typed-in clause stating that he had "full knowledge" of his "legal rights" does not approach the knowing and intelligent waiver required to relinquish constitutional rights.

Therefore, in accordance with the foregoing, the judgment of the Supreme Court of Arizona is reversed.

REVERSED.

[CONTINUED]

CRITICAL THINKING

What is the reasoning structure in the *Miranda* case?

Does Justice Warren offer a logically powerful argument for why defendants should have a greater protection of their rights than was currently practiced at the time?

ETHICAL DECISION MAKING

In arguing for greater protection of the rights of the accused, what values is Justice Warren holding?

With what values might Justice Warren's values be in contention?

A third exception to the Miranda rights involves interrogation and the right to counsel. *Davis v. United States*[9] held that defendants must "unequivocally and assertively" state their right to counsel in order to activate their rights. The phrase, "Maybe I should talk to a lawyer," or a similar utterance made during an interrogation does not affirmatively signal that an accused desires to activate his or her right to counsel.

Despite the fact that the Miranda rights have been recognized for over 40 years, the parameters of their application are still frequently limited, with a ruling by the U.S. Supreme Court often being necessitated. For example, in the second term of 2004 alone, there were three rulings by the high court clarifying applications of the warnings. In *Missouri v. Seibert,*[10] the high court held that a confession made after receipt of the Miranda warnings was not admissible if the police had initially asked for the confession before giving the warnings. In *United States v. Patane,*[11] the Court ruled that physical evidence discovered as a result of statements made without the Miranda warnings was admissible in court as long as the statements were not forced by police, even though the statements themselves were not admissible. In the third case, *Yarborough v. Alvarado,*[12] the court clarified when a person was "in custody" and therefore entitled to receive the Miranda warnings. The Court held that a person was in custody when a reasonable person of the defendant's age and educational background would not feel free to leave or terminate the questioning.

After being arrested and read their Miranda rights, defendants are taken to the police station for **booking,** a procedure during which the name of the defendant and the alleged crime are recorded in the investigating agency's or police department's records. After the prosecutor files the complaint, the defendant makes the **first appearance,** which is the appearance before a magistrate who determines whether there was probable cause for the arrest. If the magistrate ascertains that probable cause did not exist, the individual is freed.

If the defendant committed a minor offense and pleads guilty, the magistrate sentences the individual. However, if the defendant claims innocence, the magistrate ensures that the defendant has a lawyer, or appoints one, if necessary, for an indigent defendant, and sets bail. **Bail** is the amount of money defendants pay to the court on release from custody as security that they will return for trial.

[9] 512 U.S. 452 (1994).

[10] 542 U.S. 600 (2004).

[11] 542 U.S. 630 (2004).

[12] 541 U.S. 652 (2004).

Next, the prosecutor has a choice: Should the case be prosecuted? The *Principles of Federal Prosecution,* established by the U.S. Department of Justice, suggest that at the federal level the decision to prosecute depends on two primary factors: (1) whether the evidence is sufficient to obtain a conviction, and (2) whether prosecuting the case serves a federal interest. If the prosecutor decides not to go forward with the case, the defendant may still be liable for his or her actions in civil court.

If the prosecutor chooses to proceed with a criminal action, the prosecutor must demonstrate the likelihood that the defendant's actions and intent meet the elements of a crime by charging the defendant with a crime through an *information* or an *indictment.* For a misdemeanor, the prosecutor must present to the magistrate evidence sufficient to justify prosecution of the defendant. This is done through a written document called an **information,** a formal accusation stating the facts and specifying the violation of criminal law. However, for a felony, the prosecutor must present a grand jury with evidence adequate to justify bringing the defendant to trial. If the grand jury agrees that the evidence is adequate, it issues an **indictment,** a written accusation of the crime allegedly committed by the defendant.

Note that the grand jury does not determine guilt. It is simply a group of citizens who consider evidence of criminal conduct presented by the prosecutor and then determine whether there is enough evidence to try the defendant for the crime.

For example, on March 14, 2002, the U.S. Justice Department issued an indictment against Arthur Andersen, the accounting firm that was accused of obstruction of justice in Enron's collapse. Enron, once a multibillion-dollar corporation involved in energy trading, had filed for bankruptcy in early December 2001. Following Enron's collapse, the U.S. Securities and Exchange Commission stated that it would widen its investigation into Enron by considering whether Arthur Andersen, Enron's chief auditor, destroyed documents while an investigation was under way. Allegedly, the massive shredding stopped around November 8, 2001, after the SEC issued Andersen a subpoena. The grand jury indicted Andersen for ordering its employees to intentionally destroy documents that included information about official proceedings and criminal investigations.

In federal cases, a defendant accused of a felony has a constitutional right to a grand jury indictment. However, a felony prosecution may proceed by information if the defendant waives that right. For instance, in a high-profile case in which the defense attorney is trying to work out a deal with the prosecution, the defendant may ask that the case proceed by information. Federal misdemeanor cases may proceed by indictment or information.

If the criminal trial takes place in state court, the defendant may or may not have access to a grand jury. The U.S. Supreme Court has held that a grand jury trial is not a fundamental right, and thus states are not required to offer grand juries. About half the states still require that felony prosecutions be initiated by grand jury indictments; most of the rest use information as the method for commencing prosecution.

If the grand jury issues an indictment, the defendant appears in court to answer the indictment. This postindictment appearance in court is called the **arraignment.** At this time, the defendant enters a plea of guilty or not guilty. A defendant may also enter a plea of **nolo contendere,** a plea in which the defendant does not admit guilt but agrees not to contest the charges. The advantage of a nolo contendere plea over a plea of guilty is that the former cannot be used against the defendant in a civil suit. If the defendant pleads not guilty, his case will be heard before a **petit jury,** which is a fact-finding jury.

At any time, the prosecutor and defendant can make a **plea bargain,** an agreement in which the prosecutor agrees to reduce charges, drop charges, or recommend a certain sentence if the defendant pleads guilty. Plea bargaining benefits both parties: The defendant gets a lesser sentence, and the prosecution saves time and resources by not trying the case.

Businesspeople who commit crimes that affect business often engage in plea bargaining to avoid the publicity associated with a trial and the risk of a severe sentence.

TRIAL PROCEDURE

If the case goes to trial and the crime is a felony or a misdemeanor punishable by six months or more in prison, the defendant has a constitutional right to a jury trial. In most states, if the defendant waives the right to a jury trial, the judge will hear the case. When a judge is the fact finder in a case, the trial is called a **bench trial.**

In a criminal trial, the prosecutor has the burden of proof and the defendant does not have to prove anything. The **burden of proof** has two elements: the burden of production of evidence and the burden of persuasion. To meet the *burden of production of evidence,* the prosecution must produce any tangible evidence and testimony that prove the elements of the crime that the defendant allegedly committed. Along with producing evidence, the prosecution also has the *burden of persuasion:* The prosecutor must persuade the jury *beyond reasonable doubt* that the defendant committed the crime. The burden of proof, then, is higher in a criminal case than in a civil case, because in a civil case the burden of persuasion requires only that the claim be supported by a preponderance of the evidence.

In a criminal case, unlike a civil case, a defendant cannot be forced to testify at a criminal trial. The Fifth Amendment guarantees the defendant freedom from self-incrimination.

After the jury hears the case, it deliberates and tries to reach a verdict. A jury that is unable to reach a verdict is known as a "hung jury." If the jury finds the defendant not guilty, the accused is acquitted and released. If the jury returns a guilty verdict, the judge will set a date for sentencing the criminal.

POSTTRIAL PROCEDURE

If the petit jury returns a verdict of not guilty, the government cannot appeal the acquittal. However, if the verdict is guilty, the defendant may appeal the verdict by claiming that a prejudicial error of law occurred at the original trial.

If there is no appeal, the defendant will be sentenced after the judge has received additional information relevant to sentencing. Prior to 1991, sentencing was *indeterminate,* with judges allowed, but not required, to engage in free-form fact finding before selecting the appropriate punishment within broad statutory ranges. In 1991, however, there was a shift to *determinate sentencing,* under which federal sentences are determined largely by the guidelines set forth by the 1991 Sentencing Guidelines. These guidelines shifted much of the authority to sentence away from the judges by prescribing a specific range of possible penalties for each crime.

In determining the precise sentence within that range, judges are given certain factors to consider, such as the defendant's criminal record. Guidelines have also been established for white-collar crimes, once again allowing judges to consider individual factors such as the company's history of past violations and the firm's cooperation with federal investigators. Many states have adopted similar state sentencing guidelines. Although some people have criticized the federal Sentencing Guidelines for being too harsh, the Global Context box demonstrates that they are rather tame compared to some of the punishments handed down in Dubai.

The role of the federal Sentencing Guidelines has been sharply curtailed by two significant Supreme Court cases. The first case is *Blakely v. Washington,*[13] a case involving a Sixth Amendment challenge to the procedure followed under the Washington sentencing guidelines for imposing an aggravated penalty above the standard range set by the guidelines. In *Blakely,* the Court held that in cases involving state laws for determinate

[13] 124 S. Ct. 2531 (2004).

global context

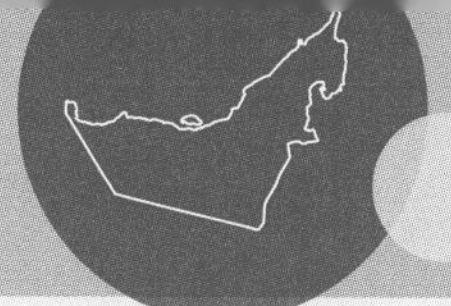

First-Class Jails in Dubai

Dubai, the second-largest emirate in the United Arab Emirates (UAE), takes a novel approach to criminals convicted of business crimes. In 1998 Dubai began construction on a multimillion-dollar jail for elite white-collar criminals. Prisoners will have double rooms with air-conditioning, television, and beds. Along with having Internet access, the inmates will have access to secretarial services.

In sharp contrast, consider how Dubai punishes other criminals. In 1997 two individuals were crucified as punishment for their crimes. Why is there such a distinction between the treatment of "common" criminals and that of white-collar criminals? Dubai is trying to attract global business and is thus willing to accommodate criminal businesspeople to prevent financial losses.

Source: "Executive-Class Jail Cells," *The New York Times,* October 11, 1998, sec. 6, p. 21.

sentencing, judges are bound by facts consistent with the verdict or those admitted by the defendant. Blakely pleaded guilty to a lower offense than the one with which he was originally charged. The prosecutor recommended that Blakely be sentenced to the statutorily mandated maximum of 53 months, but the judge expanded his sentence to three years beyond that recommendation. The Court found the extension violated Blakely's Sixth Amendment rights because he did not admit to the facts the judge took into consideration nor did a jury find the facts relevant to a verdict. It should be noted that the *Blakely* decision does not hold determinate sentencing to be unconstitutional but, rather, requires that determinate sentencing comply with Sixth Amendment protections.

The second case is *U.S. v. Booker,*[14] which had far more radical effects than the *Blakely* case. *Booker* extended the *Blakely* holding and applied it to the federal Sentencing Guidelines. Moreover, *Booker* found that the two sections of the federal law mandating determinate sentences were unconstitutional and struck them from the statute, effectively making the act advisory. Once the sentencing is no longer mandatory, judicial fact-finding is not "legally essential to punishment" and does not pose any Sixth Amendment problem.

Tools for Fighting Business Crime

While there are clearly a significant number of business-related crimes that can be committed, there are certain federal laws that help fight such crime. Three federal laws that have been somewhat successful in this battle are RICO, the False Claims Act, and the Sarbanes-Oxley Act of 2002. While these laws are currently extremely powerful white-collar crime laws, RICO and the False Claims Act were created with different purposes in mind. Sarbanes-Oxley, however, was created to specifically combat white-collar crime.

THE RACKETEER INFLUENCED AND CORRUPT ORGANIZATIONS ACT

One of the most important tools for fighting white-collar crime is in Title IX of the Organized Crime Control Act of 1970: the *Racketeer Influenced and Corrupt Organizations Act (RICO).* Although the statute was originally enacted to combat organized crime, in effect it prevents legitimate businesses from serving as covers for racketeering. This statute prohibits persons employed by or associated with an enterprise from engaging in a

[14] 125 S. Ct. 738 (2005).

pattern of racketeering activity. Anyone whose business or property has been damaged by this pattern of racketeering activity can sue to recover treble damages and attorney fees in a civil action.

Demonstrating a claim under RICO requires proof of a pattern of racketeering. Courts have defined a pattern as more than one action. Thus, a one-time violator could not be prosecuted under RICO because there could be no pattern as yet. Some courts additionally have found that a pattern requires continued criminal activity over a "substantial" period of time. Although *pattern* is restricted to more than one act, racketeering has been defined broadly to include almost all criminal actions, such as acts of violence, fraud, bribery, securities fraud, and the provision of illegal goods and services. Therefore, RICO is an extremely effective tool in combating white-collar crimes.

In addition to being held civilly liable under RICO, a violator may also be subject to RICO's criminal penalties. A person found to have violated the act may be subject to a fine of up to $25,000 per violation, imprisonment for up to 20 years, or both.

THE FALSE CLAIMS ACT

Since 1986 private citizens have been using the *False Claims Act* to sue employers on behalf of the government for fraud against the government. For example, an employee in a health care facility might realize that his employer is submitting fraudulent claims to Medicare. The employee can bring a suit against the employer on behalf of the government for fraud against the government.

If an employee realizes that her employer is committing fraud against the government, she must first notify the government of her intent to file the case on behalf of the government. If the government chooses to intervene and prosecute the case itself, with the help of the employee, the citizen would receive 25 percent of the amount recovered. If the government opts to not get involved, and the citizen continues with the case on behalf of the government, she receives 30 percent.

Certainly, an employee who brings a suit against his employer might be worried about retaliation, such as being fired or demoted. Thus, the act provides protection for those employees who use the law. If an employer is found guilty of retaliation, the employer may be forced to pay the employee twice the amount of back pay plus special damages.

The biggest reward thus far under the act was the approximately $51 million share that four whistle-blowers and their attorneys received for blowing the whistle on a Swiss drug company, Serono, for participating in a marketing scheme that resulted in physicians' illegally prescribing over $11.5 million worth of a drug that was paid for by Medicaid. The government settled the case against the company for $704 million. The reward in this case, however, was far above the norm. The Justice Department estimates that the median award in all the 425 cases settled between the act's inception and July 2001 was around $150,000. Between 1986 and the first quarter of 2006, the total amount of money recovered by the government was over $17 billion.

Despite the fact that some of these cases might not have been pursued had it not been for the False Claims Act, there are many who are opposed to the act. Some argue that the whistle-blowers are receiving money that should belong to the taxpayers, while others say that the act prompts people to not report fraud right away but wait until the value of the case grows. Still others complain that the act results in frivolous lawsuits as employees try to find an "easy" way to make money.

Defenders of the False Claims Act point out that the act has led to some significant cases of fraud being reported that otherwise might have cost the government millions of dollars. They also point out that when an employee does report a fraudulent employer, it is going to be very difficult for that employee to get a job in that field in the future, and thus a significant incentive needs to be offered to get employees to report such fraud.

A number of False Claims Act cases have been filed against universities, including an interesting case filed in 2006 against Chapman University. In this case, three faculty members alleged that the institution for years encouraged early dismissals, resulting in many students' not getting the minimum classroom training required in several subjects. If the college had admitted that it had engaged in this practice, it would never have been accredited and thus never have received millions of dollars in federal grants and student aid, which the lawsuit claimed it took under false pretenses.[15] The case had not been resolved at the time this book went to press.

THE SARBANES-OXLEY ACT

Unlike RICO and the False Claims Act, the *Sarbanes-Oxley Act* of 2002 was intended to curb white-collar crime. Congress passed Sarbanes-Oxley largely in response to the business scandals of the early 2000s, such as Enron, WorldCom, and Global Crossing, as well as the accounting firm Arthur Andersen. While much of the act consists of new rules and regulations for accounting firms, part of the act specifically addresses the issue of white-collar crime.

Sarbanes-Oxley makes it illegal for registered public accounting firms to provide non-audit services to an audit client. The Section 201 of the act specifically names as illegal:

1. Bookkeeping or other services related to the accounting records or financial statements of the audit client.
2. Financial information systems design and implementation.
3. Appraisal or valuation services, fairness opinions, or contribution-in-kind reports.
4. Actuarial services.
5. Internal audit outsourcing services.
6. Management functions or human resources.
7. Broker or dealer, investment adviser, or investment banking services.
8. Legal services and expert services unrelated to the audit.
9. Any other service that the Board determines, by regulation, is impermissible (Sarbanes-Oxley § 201).

In addition to criminalizing the activities listed above, Sarbanes-Oxley has amended the penalties associated with other white-collar crimes. Under Sarbanes-Oxley, it is now a felony to willfully fail to maintain proper records of audits and work papers for at least five years, and the punishment for not maintaining these records is up to 10 years' imprisonment. Also, the destruction of documents received updated punishments. The destruction of documents involved in a federal bankruptcy investigation is now a felony with possible sentences of up to 20 years' imprisonment. Similarly, the punishment for securities fraud has been increased to 25 years' imprisonment.

In addition, Sarbanes-Oxley has extended the statute of limitations regarding the discovery of fraud. The statute of limitations now extends to two years from the date of discovery of the fraud and five years from the criminal act. The old statute was one year from discovery and three from the act. Also, much like the False Claims Act, Sarbanes-Oxley has taken affirmative steps toward further protecting whistle-blowers.

[15] Martin Van Der Werf, "Lawsuit U.: The Growing Reach of the False Claims Act Has Lawyers Fearing Trouble Everywhere," *Chronicle of Higher Education,* August 4, 2006, available at http://chronicle.com/weekly/v52/i48/48a02301.htm

connecting to the core

Income Taxation Accounting

In one of your tax or accounting courses, you probably learned about disallowance provisions of the IRS*. An important disallowance in the tax code is the one for payments considered to be in violation of public policy, such as bribes or fines. Initially the courts developed the principle that a payment that is in violation of public policy is not a necessary expense and therefore should not be deductible. While allowing deductions for fines or bribes might help a business's bottom line, it would clearly dilute the effect of any criminal penalty and would be, in effect, subsidizing a taxpayer's wrongdoing. So, when you think about it, you really learned about one of the tools for fighting white-collar crime in your tax or accounting class: the disallowance provision of the tax code that fights white-collar crime by not allowing criminals to deduct the amount they must pay for fines from their tax liability.

*William Hoffman, Jr., et al., *Individual Income Taxes 2006* (Thomson, 2006), pp. 6–11.

CASE OPENER WRAP-UP

Untenable Trading

Cooper ended up being convicted of commercial bribery, based on the jury's finding that he had caused approximately $4,000 in cash to be mailed to John Freeman as payment for information Freeman was misappropriating from his employment.

If you were asked by a friend for privileged information regarding stocks, how would you respond? If you do pass on the information and your friend uses it to trade in stocks, you may both be liable for insider trading.

Summary

Elements of a Crime

Actus reus: Wrongful behavior (guilty act).
Mens rea: Wrongful state of mind or intent (guilty mind).

Classification of Crimes

Felonies: Serious crimes punishable by imprisonment for more than one year or death.
Misdemeanors: Less serious crimes punishable by fines or imprisonment for less than one year.
Petty offenses: Minor misdemeanors punishable by small fines or short jail sentences.

Common Crimes Affecting Business

Property crimes against business:

1. Robbery
2. Burglary
3. Larceny
4. Arson

White-collar crime:

1. Bribery
2. Extortion

3. Fraud
4. Embezzlement
5. Computer crimes

   a. Destruction of computer data
   b. Unlawful appropriation of data or services

Liability for Crimes Both corporations, as legal entities, and the corporate officers and managers can be held liable for crimes committed on behalf of the corporation.

Defenses to Crimes
Infancy
Mistake
Intoxication
Insanity
Duress
Entrapment
Necessity
Justifiable use of force

Constitutional Safeguards

Fourth Amendment:

1. Protection from unreasonable search and seizure.
2. Restrictions on warrants.

Fifth Amendment:

1. Prohibition of double jeopardy.
2. Right not to incriminate oneself.
3. Right to due process.

Sixth Amendment:

1. Right to a speedy and public trial.
2. Right to a trial by an impartial jury of one's peers.
3. Right to be informed of the accusations against oneself.
4. Right to confront witnesses.
5. Right to have witnesses on one's side.
6. Right to counsel at various stages of the proceedings.

Eighth Amendment:

1. Freedom from excessive bail.
2. Freedom from excessive fines.
3. Freedom from cruel and unusual punishment.

Fourteenth Amendment:

1. Extension of the right to due process to all state matters.
2. Extension of most constitutional rights to defendants at the state level.

Exclusionary rule:

1. Illegally obtained evidence is inadmissible in court.

Criminal Procedure	*Pretrial procedure:* The arrest, booking, first appearance, indictment, and arraignment. *Trial procedure:* Jury selection, trial with burden of proof on prosecution, jury deliberations, jury verdict, and (if guilty) sentencing hearing. *Posttrial procedure:* Appeal.
Tools for Fighting Business Crime	*RICO:* Prohibits persons employed by or associated with an enterprise from engaging in a pattern of racketeering activity. Anyone whose business or property has been damaged by this pattern of activity can sue under RICO to recover treble damages and attorney fees in a civil action. *False Claims Act:* Allows employees to sue employers on behalf of the federal government for fraud against the government. The employee retains a share of the recovery as a reward for his or her efforts. *Sarbanes-Oxley Act:* Criminalizes specific nonaudit services when provided by a registered accounting firm to an audit client; also increases the punishment for a number of white-collar offenses.

Point / Counterpoint

How Severely Should the Law Punish Individuals Convicted of White-Collar Crime?

As you are considering this issue, you might want to think about statistics that would help you resolve it.

Less Severely than Violent Criminals

Street crimes are different in kind than white-collar crimes. Whereas white-collar crime affects only individuals' property, street crime threatens individuals' lives and health. The law ought to recognize that protecting lives is more important than protecting property.

Moreover, white-collar crime tends to affect higher-income individuals, whereas street crime tends to affect lower-income individuals who lack the resources to protect themselves. Street crime disproportionately affects lower-income individuals who cannot afford the private security measures that higher-income individuals use to protect their persons and their property. The law ought to protect those who lack the power to protect themselves.

A third reason to punish white-collar crime less heavily than street crime is that white-collar criminals are more likely to engage in careful cost-benefit analysis when determining whether to commit white-collar crime. If the severity of the punishment, discounted by the chance they will get caught, is less than the expected payoff from the white-collar crime, rational individuals won't see the crime as a profitable enterprise. It seems less

More Severely than Violent Criminals

It is far from clear that white-collar crime has less serious consequences than street crime. For example, individuals who defraud the government in effect steal taxes paid by all members of society, whereas individuals in possession of small amounts of marijuana may never adversely affect other members of society.

Indeed, white-collar crime affects all groups in society in both direct and indirect ways. Companies victimized by white-collar crime often must raise the prices of their goods to recoup the costs of the crime. Everyone in society feels the effects of the higher prices. Street crime, while by no means negligible, tends to affect smaller circles of people. Thus, to get the biggest bang for our buck, we should punish white-collar crime more heavily than street crime.

Another reason to punish white-collar crime more heavily than street crime focuses on the underlying causes of crime. Much street crime has its roots in other social problems. Often, individuals commit street crime because of the poor environments in which they were raised. Much white-collar crime, however, is committed by well-off individuals out of avarice. The law ought to dole out more severe punishments for crimes caused by individual responsibility, and society ought to likely that street criminals engage in the same kind of careful cost-benefit analysis before deciding, for example, whether to use illegal drugs. Thus, the most effective punishment for undeterrable street crime is likely to be severe punishment that incapacitates the criminals so that they are unable to commit more street crime. White-collar crime, on the other hand, can effectively be curbed by setting the punishment just high enough to make the crime unprofitable.

use other mechanisms to address crime caused by aleatory factors.

Questions & Problems

1. How does criminal law differ from civil law, both in terms of their purposes and in terms of the procedures used in each type of case.
2. Explain how crimes are classified.
3. List and define the primary affirmative defenses used in criminal cases.
4. Explain the federal laws that are currently being used to try to fight white-collar crime.
5. Robert Morris, a PhD student in computer science at Cornell University, designed a computer program known as a "worm" and released it onto the Internet. The worm spread and multiplied and eventually caused computers at various educational and military institutions to crash. Morris argued that he released the worm to demonstrate to fellow graduate students the lack of security protecting computer networks. With what crime was he most likely charged? Was this prosecution successful? [*United States v. Robert Tappen Morris,* 928 F.2d 504 (1991).]
6. Wayne T. Schmuck was a used-car distributor who purchased used cars, rolled back their odometers, and sold them to Wisconsin retail dealers at prices artificially inflated by the low-mileage readings. Those dealers, not knowing about the false odometers and inflated prices, resold the cars to customers and finished the transactions by mailing title application forms to the state on behalf of the customers. Schmuck was charged with 12 counts of mail fraud. The district court convicted and the circuit court affirmed. How did the Supreme Court rule? Why? [*Schmuck v. United States,* 109 S. Ct. 1443 (1989).]
7. The Pasquantinos, while in New York, ordered liquor over the telephone from discount package stores in Maryland. They employed Hilts and others to drive the liquor over the Canadian border, without paying the required excise taxes. The drivers avoided paying taxes by hiding the liquor in their vehicles and failing to declare the goods to Canadian customs officials. During the time of the Pasquantinos' smuggling operation, between 1996 and 2000, Canada heavily taxed the importation of alcoholic beverages. The Pasquantinos and Hilts were indicted for charges of federal wire fraud. They contest no wire fraud existed because the federal government cannot enforce the revenue laws of Canada, and this therefore prevents the existence in the United States of a fraud charge. How did the Supreme Court rule? Should the Pasquantinos and Hilts be able to succeed in their legal argument? [*Pasquantino v. United States,* 125 S. Ct. 1766 (2005).]
8. Thomas Faulkner, a truck driver for North American Van Lines, was supposed to transport 105 refrigerators from San Diego to Hartford, Connecticut. Faulkner stopped

in Las Vegas, Nevada, to call appliance store owner Richard Urbauer, to whom he offered to sell the refrigerators. After Faulkner and Urbauer debated the sale of the refrigerators, Faulkner broke the truck's seals and opened two cartons to show Urbauer the refrigerators. While Urbauer examined the refrigerators, Faulkner began to rearrange the cartons. They began to discuss the deal again but could not reach an agreement. When Faulkner left the store, he was arrested. He was prosecuted and convicted of embezzlement. Faulkner appealed, arguing that the evidence failed to establish embezzlement because he never physically removed goods from the truck and never sold the goods. What did the appellate court decide? [*United States v. Faulkner,* 638 F.2d 129 (9th Cir. 1981).]

9. Two campus security officers questioned Michael Jensen when they saw him walking across campus with a dormitory lounge chair propped on his head at 3:13 a.m. Jensen refused to identify himself to the officers but claimed he was simply playing a prank by carrying the chair from one residence hall to another residence hall across campus. The officers repeatedly asked him for identification, which he repeatedly refused to provide. When the officers told him that they would remove his identification from his jeans pocket, he began to comply. When the officers told Jensen that he was under arrest, Jensen ran away. Later, he was caught and indicted by a grand jury for petit larceny. Jensen claimed that there was no evidence that he did not intend to return the chair, so the indictment was flawed. Why did the court of appeals affirm the indictment? [*People of New York v. Jensen,* 86 N.Y.2d 248 (1995); 1995 N.Y. LEXIS 2230.]

10. Dotterweich, the general manager of a pharmaceutical company, was charged with violating the Food, Drug, and Cosmetics Act because he shipped misbranded drugs to a physician. Dotterweich argued that he had no personal contact with the shipments, so he should not be held responsible. However, he was responsible for overseeing the company's business and instructed employees to fill orders received by physicians. Was he held criminally responsible for violating the act? [*United States v. Dotterweich,* 320 U.S. 277 (1943); 1943 U.S. LEXIS 1100.]

11. Bernadette Sablan was fired from her job at the Bank of Hawaii for circumventing security procedures when retrieving files. One night after drinking at a bar with a friend, she entered an unlocked door at the bank. She went to her old workstation and logged on to the mainframe by using an old password. She contends that she simply accessed several files and logged out. The government argued that she changed and deleted several files. Regardless, her actions damaged several bank files.

Sablan was charged with computer fraud. She argued that the government had to establish the *mens rea* element of the crime—that is, the government had to prove she intentionally tried to damage the files. The district court ruled that the intention element applied only to accessing the files. Sablan argued that the legislation in question was intended to apply only to those who intentionally damage computer data, and she appealed. How did the court of appeals rule? Why? [*United States v. Sablan,* 92 F.3d 865, 866 (9th Cir. 1996).]

Looking for more review material?

The Online Learning Center at **www.mhhe.com/kubasek1e** contains this chapter's "Assignment on the Internet" and also a list of URLs for more information, entitled "On the Internet." Find both of them in the Student Center portion of the OLC, along with quizzes and other helpful materials.

Tort Law

CASE OPENER

Rubin v. U.S. News

Richard Rubin, chief executive of Republic Metals, a gold-refining company, agreed to be interviewed and photographed for a *U.S. News & World Report* article.[1] Rubin argued that he had been told the article was about the Peruvian value tax, a rebate given to those who export gold from Peru. However, when the article appeared in the magazine, it was titled "The Golden Age of Crime: Why International Drug Traffickers Are Invading the Global Gold Trade." The author of the article explained how the gold trade is used as a tool for money laundering, and Rubin, also pictured, was quoted as saying, "There's a dual economic system. There's on the books and there's off the books."

When Rubin discovered that the article was about money laundering, he brought suit against *U.S. News & World Report.* Rubin argued that the story implied he is or has been involved in money laundering through his gold-refining business and that this implication hurt his reputation. *U.S. News* issued a clarification stating that the purpose of the article was not to imply Rubin was involved in illegal activity.

[1] See Susan R. Miller, "*U.S. News* Sued by Gold Trader," quoted in "Money Laundering Story," *Broward Daily Business Review,* May 25, 2000, p. A1; "News Magazine Sued," *National Law Journal,* June 12, 2000, p. B2.

CHAPTER 8

1. Suppose you are Rubin. You are concerned that the article has damaged your gold-refining business. What do you do? Why?
2. Now suppose you are a manager at a company that does business with Rubin's refining company. You read the story in *U.S. News*. Does the story lead to any change in your business with Rubin? Why?

The Wrap-Up at the end of the chapter will answer these questions using the legal principles discussed in this chapter.

Learning Objectives

After reading this chapter, you will be able to answer the following questions:

1 How are torts classified?

2 What are some of the most common intentional torts, and what are the elements needed to prove these torts?

3 What types of damages are available in tort cases?

As a future business manager, you will likely be involved in a situation where one party believes he or she has been injured by the actions of another party, in the same way Rubin believed he had been injured by the *U.S. News & World Report* article. The purpose of this chapter is to examine common, intentional wrongs that might occur in the workplace. A **tort** is commonly defined as a wrong or injury to another, other than a breach of contract. In fact, *tort* is a French word meaning "wrong." This chapter first examines the goals of tort law and the three primary classifications of torts. Next, the chapter explains a variety of intentional torts one might encounter. It concludes by discussing damages that may be available in tort cases.

Introduction to Tort Law

The previous chapter focused on criminal law and the punishment individuals may receive for committing crimes. When a person commits a crime, the victim of that crime will frequently be able to bring a tort action against the criminal, because the same actions that constitute a criminal offense often constitute a tort.

While the primary objectives of criminal law are to punish wrongdoers and preserve order in society, tort law's primary objective is to provide compensation for injured parties. It also contributes to maintaining order in society because it discourages private retaliation by injured persons and their friends. After all, we do not want to live in a community where vigilantes with tempers are roaming about righting some harm they believe has occurred to them.

A third objective of tort law is to give citizens a sense that they live in a just society. Our collective sense of right and wrong suggests that someone who creates harm should make things right by compensating those who were harmed. The recognition that one will have to pay for the personal injuries she or he causes may also serve to deter the commission of torts.

Although this chapter discusses torts as if they were the same everywhere, tort law is primarily state law, so states may have slightly different definitions of each tort. In describing torts, this chapter uses the definitions common in most states, noting the instances where there seems to be a significant difference in the way certain states define the tort.

Despite the public impression of a litigation explosion, tort litigation has been declining slightly since 1990.[2] The National Center for State Courts compiled statistics on tort filings in 15 states. From 1995 to 2004, there has been a general downward trend in the overall number of tort filings each year. In 2003, the last year for which detailed data are available, there were 198,377 tort filings in the 15 studied states.[3] The number of tort cases being heard in the federal system is also falling; the number of tort cases resolved in U.S. district courts fell 79 percent between 1985 and 2003.[4] However, even when the number of tort cases is not increasing, there are still enough cases filed each year that potential tort liability should concern a competent business manager.

Classification of Torts

Torts are most commonly classified as intentional, negligent, or strict-liability torts. Each category differs in terms of the elements needed to prove the tort, the available damages,

[2] National Center for State Courts, www.ncsconline.org/D_Research/csp/2002_Files/2002_Tables_10-16.pdf (accessed September 9, 2005).

[3] *Examining the Work of State Courts, 2005: A National Perspective from the Court Statistics Project* (2006) p. 27. (The Court Statistics Project is a joint project of the National Center for State Courts, the State Justice Institute, and the Bureau of Justice Statistics of the Department of Justice.)

[4] Thomas H. Cohen, *Federal Tort Trials and Verdicts, 2002–03,* Bureau of Justice Statistics, August 17, 2005.

the available defenses, and the degree of willfulness of the actor. **Intentional torts** occur when the defendant takes an action intending certain consequences will result or knowing certain consequences are likely to result. **Negligent torts** occur when the defendant acts in a way that subjects other people to an unreasonable risk of harm. In other words, the defendant is careless to someone else's detriment. Finally, **strict-liability torts** occur when the defendant takes an action that is inherently dangerous and cannot ever be undertaken safely, no matter what precautions the defendant takes. It is important to remember that when we discuss these classifications we are referring to their use in the United States. The Chinese legal system, for example, narrowly defines the activities actionable under tort law.

In this chapter, we focus on intentional torts. Negligence and strict liability will be discussed in greater detail in Chapter 9.

Intentional Torts

Intentional torts are the most "willful" of torts. Intentional torts are predicated on the common element of intent. The intent at issue is not intent to harm but, rather, is intent to engage in a specific act, which ultimately results in an injury, physical or economic, to another. In fact, one does not need to establish a motive when proving liability in an intentional tort case. Moreover, in tort law it is assumed people intend what could be considered the normal consequences of their actions. For example, were Rob to throw a rock toward a group of people, it would be assumed under the law that he intended to hit someone with the rock and that the person hit would be hurt, regardless of Rob's intention merely to scare the group of people.

Not all harms intentionally committed will fall neatly into an existing category of torts. Therefore, a general theory of intentional tort liability has been created to aid judges in their decision making. In Section 870 of the Restatement (Second) of Torts, the general theory is explained as:

> One who intentionally causes injury to another is subject to liability to the other for that injury, if his conduct is generally culpable and not justifiable under the circumstances. This liability may be imposed although the actor's conduct does not come within a traditional category of tort liability.

Intentional torts are divided into the following three categories: (1) torts against persons, (2) torts against property, and (3) torts against economic interests. The following sections discuss a number of specific torts that fall into each category, along with the defenses for each.

INTENTIONAL TORTS AGAINST PERSONS

Torts against persons are intentional acts that harm an individual's physical or mental integrity. As you might imagine, there are a significant number of these torts. In this section, we explore the intentional torts against persons that a businessperson is most likely to either commit or be a victim of: assault and battery, defamation, privacy torts, false imprisonment, intentional infliction of emotional distress, and misuse of legal procedure.

Assault and battery. Assault and battery are two of the most common torts. Imagine, after searching for a parking space for 20 minutes, that you finally pull into a spot. However, as soon as you turn off your car, a man who looks like Mike Tyson pounds on your car window, claiming you took his spot. He angrily yells, "You just took my spot! If you don't move your car now, I'm going to hit you so hard you won't remember what your car looks like!" The man has just assaulted you.

An **assault** occurs when one person places another in fear or apprehension of an immediate, offensive bodily contact. Therefore, in the above example, if you think the man is just joking and you start laughing, no assault has taken place. There is no assault because the element of apprehension is missing. However, apprehension and fear are not the same thing when it comes to assault. A person may be in apprehension of physical harm, but the same person might be too courageous to be afraid of that physical harm. An assault occurs if apprehension exists, regardless of fear. However, someone who is overly fearful is not assaulted whenever he or she experiences apprehension. The test for assault involves *reasonable* apprehension. In other words, if a reasonable person would experience apprehension in a given situation, and the person in that situation does experience apprehension (not necessarily fear), an assault occurs.

Likewise, if a man called you on the telephone and threatened to come over and break your nose, this is not an assault because there is no question of *immediate* bodily harm. Immediacy is also the reason that words, however violent, are not typically considered enough to establish an assault. Words without a sign of action do not usually imply immediacy. Moreover, words, in most situations, are not enough to create reasonable apprehension of harm. Without immediacy or reasonable apprehension, words do not constitute an assault.

Regardless, if words are enough to establish a reasonable apprehension of immediate harm, the words would constitute an assault. Typically, words convey an assault when combined with what might be an otherwise innocent movement. For example, Patrick and Sam are drinking at a bar. Patrick has had a few too many beers and starts an argument with Sam. Sam tries to calm Patrick down, at which point Patrick screams, "I'm going to cut you." While screaming, Patrick starts to reach toward his pocket, causing Sam to become apprehensive. Together, Patrick's words and actions would constitute an assault, as reasonable apprehension of immediate physical bodily harm has been established by a threat and what can be construed as a motion toward grabbing a knife.

An assault is often, but not always, followed by a **battery**, an intentional, unwanted, offensive bodily contact. Almost any unwanted, intentional contact constitutes a battery. Even contacts that are harmless, if unwanted, are batteries. The intent of a person in making a contact is irrelevant for establishing liability. That is, a plaintiff may prove liability without having to demonstrate that the defendant intended to be offensive with his or her contact. Even if a touch was intended as a joke, if the reasonable person would be offended, the contact is deemed "offensive."[5] To return to the example of the parking-space incident, if the man actually hit you, his action would constitute a battery. In contrast, if you both happened to be getting out of your respective cars at the same time and consequently bumped into each other, no battery would have occurred because there was no *intentional* bodily contact.

There are a limited number of defenses available to an action for a battery. A party charged with a battery may argue that the offended party consented to the contact. *Consent,* as a defense, mitigates the element of unwanted. A person cannot commit a battery if the contact was consented to and therefore wanted.

The most common defense to battery is *self-defense,* responding to the force of another with comparable force in order to defend oneself. In our parking-space example, suppose the man took a swing at you and, to try to keep him from hitting you, you shoved him, causing him to fall backward and hit his head on the street. When he sues you for battery and attempts to get compensation for the concussion you gave him, you would be able to escape liability by arguing that you were acting in self-defense. In terms of the degree of

[5] Restatement (Second) of Torts, sec. 19.

force you may use, you cannot respond with greater force than is being used against you. You may use deadly force but only to defend against another's deadly force.

A third defense, *defense of others,* is just what it sounds like. If a large man is pummeling you, your brother could use his fists and try to hit the man in an attempt to make him stop hitting you. The degree of force your brother can use in defending you is limited to the degree of force you could use yourself.

A final defense to a claim of battery is *defense of property.* You can use *reasonable force* to defend your property from an intruder. The use of deadly force in defense of property is rarely, if ever, considered justified.

Defamation. The tort alleged in this chapter's opening case was **defamation,** which is the intentional publication (communication to a third party) of a false statement harmful to an individual's reputation.[6] In addition to the person who publishes a false statement, anyone who republishes, or in any manner repeats, a defamatory statement is also liable for defamation, even if he or she cites the original source of the defamation.

If the defamation is published in a permanent form, such as printed in a magazine or newspaper, it is known as *libel.*[7] Television and radio broadcasts are also considered libel, since they are permanently recorded. In the case of libel, "general damages" are presumed. Thus, the victim would be entitled to compensation for the damages that are presumed to flow from defamation yet are hard to prove, such as the humiliation the victim would feel.

If the defamation is made orally, then it is *slander.*[8] In order to recover damages in a case of slander, the plaintiff must prove "special damages"; that is, the plaintiff must show specific monetary loss that resulted from the defamatory statements. While libel is contained in a permanent form, slander, by virtue of being spoken, is not. It is the lack of permanence that gives way to the special damages involved with slander. If the people who heard the slander do not act in a way to cause harm to the slandered person, there is no cause for compensation, which is one of the main goals of tort law.

One exception to the requirement of special damages occurs if the false statements constitute *slander per se.* Slander per se statements are considered to be so inherently harmful that general damages are presumed. The kinds of statements considered slander per se are claims that the plaintiff (1) has a loathsome, communicable disease (traditionally venereal disease or leprosy); (2) has committed a crime for which imprisonment is a possibility; (3) is professionally incompetent; or (4) if a woman, has engaged in sexual misconduct.

Chinese law treats defamation in a similar manner. First, the Chinese courts determine whether there is a defamatory statement (i.e., if derogatory words have been used to insult another person). Second, the statement must be published in writing, orally, or by gestures or signs. Third, the statement must clearly identify a particular person. However, in China, defamation can be a civil or criminal action.

If you say your boss is a tyrant, or your roommate is a slob, are you in danger of being sued for defamation? You probably are not because such statements are not really statements of fact; rather, they are opinions, and subjective opinions that are not capable of being proved are generally not actionable.

One of the important elements of defamation is that the defamatory statement must be damaging to someone's reputation, as the Case Nugget illustrates.

[6] Restatement (Second) of Torts, sec. 558.

[7] Restatement (Second) of Torts, sec. 568.

[8] Restatement (Second) of Torts, sec. 568A.

Case Nugget — Can You Defame a Person Who Has No Good Reputation to Be Harmed?

Thomas P. Lamb v. Tony Rizzo
United States Court of Appeals for the Tenth Circuit
391 F.3d 1133 (2004)

The state of Kansas incarcerated Thomas P. Lamb over 30 years ago. He is serving three consecutive life sentences for two counts of first-degree kidnapping and one count of first-degree murder. In July 2001, newspaper reporter Tony Rizzo wrote two articles about Lamb's convictions and upcoming parole hearing. When Lamb's request for parole was subsequently denied, he sued Rizzo in Kansas state court, asserting, among other things, that Rizzo's articles contained "lies and false information" that caused Lamb to be denied parole.

Rizzo filed a motion to dismiss, attaching to it numerous newspaper articles chronicling Lamb's criminal history. In the motion, Rizzo contended that Lamb was libel-proof as a matter of law; in other words, Lamb's public reputation at the time the articles were published was so diminished with respect to a specific subject (his kidnapping and murder convictions) that he could not be further injured by allegedly false statements on that subject. Because damage to one's reputation is the heart of a defamation action in Kansas, argued Rizzo, Lamb's claims must be dismissed.

The district court dismissed Lamb's complaint for failure to state a claim on which relief could be granted. Lamb appealed.

In upholding the dismissal, the appellate court said:

> [T]he facts surrounding Mr. Lamb's case fit within the Kansas Supreme Court's description of when the [libel-proof] doctrine might apply. Mr. Lamb . . . was convicted long before Mr. Rizzo's allegedly defamatory articles were published. Thus, Mr. Lamb had already suffered from a lowered reputation in the community due to his prior convictions for the crime alleged in the publication or for a similar crime.

Clearly, a plaintiff's reputation is an important factor in determining whether a defamation case will be successful.

The increase in communication over the Internet has presented new questions for the law of defamation to answer. First, does a false statement made over this information network constitute defamation? Second, who can be held liable if defamation does exist?

The court first attempted to answer these issues in the case of *Cubby v. CompuServ.*[9] In that case, CompuServ was sued because of defamatory statements published on one of the forums available through its online information service. In holding that CompuServ could not be held liable, the court made an analogy between an online information service provider such as CompuServ and bookstores, saying, "CompuServ's CIS product is in essence an electronic, for profit library." The court went on to say that once CompuServ decides to carry a given publication such as a news forum, it has little or no editorial control over that forum. It would therefore be no more feasible for CompuServ to examine every publication it carries for defamatory material than it would be for libraries or booksellers to do so.

[9] 77b F. Supp. 135 (1991).

global context

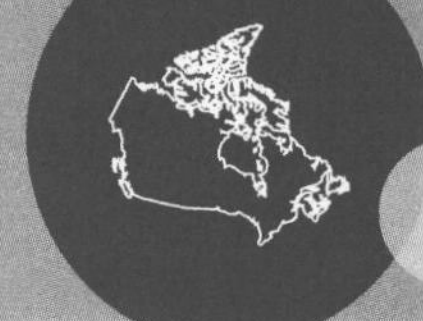

Liability of Online Service Providers in Canada

In Canada, there have not yet been any landmark cases or any legislation to clearly establish the liability of online service providers (OSPs) for content they disseminated but did not originate. Currently, an OSP being sued under such circumstances in Canada would have to rely on the existing Canadian libel code's defense of innocent dissemination, which will succeed if the defendant demonstrates all of the following:

a. The defendant does not know of the libel contained in the work published or authored by him or her.
b. There was no reason for the defendant to suppose the work he or she authored or published would be libelous.
c. It was not negligence on the defendant's part that he or she did not know the work contained libelous material.

Since *Cubby* was decided, the Communications Decency Act of 1996[10] was passed. One section of this act gives immunity to providers of interactive computer services for liability they might otherwise incur on account of material disseminated by them but created by others. This immunity is illustrated in the E-Commerce box later in this chapter.

A person who is accused of defamation can raise two defenses: truth and privilege. *Truth* is frequently considered to be an absolute defense. That is, one cannot be held liable for defamation, regardless of whether damages result, if the statement made was the truth. If I say Bill is a convicted felon, and he is, I have not committed defamation. Under ordinary circumstances, the fact that you thought a statement was true is not a defense. So if I honestly believe Bill is a convicted felon and I tell others he is, but he is not, then I have committed slander, despite my sincere belief in the truth of what I have said.

Privilege is an affirmative defense in a defamation action. An affirmative defense, as you may recall from Chapter 7, occurs when the defendant admits to the accusation but argues that there is a reason why he should not be held liable.

A privilege is either absolute or conditional. When an **absolute privilege** exists, one cannot be sued for defamation for any false statements made, regardless of intent or knowledge of the falsity of the claim. Absolute privilege arises in only a limited number of circumstances. The speech and debate clause of the U.S. Constitution gives an absolute privilege to individuals speaking on the House and Senate floors during congressional debate. This privilege exists because the House wants to get to the truth of matters before it, and if people testifying before Congress had to fear they might be sued, they might be afraid to testify. Therefore, the law protects them from being sued for defamation because of anything they say on the floor of the House or Senate.

Absolute privilege also arises in the courtroom during a trial. Again, we do not want people to be afraid to testify in court, so we prohibit their being sued for whatever occurs within the courtroom.

Conditional privilege is the second type. Under a conditional privilege, a party will not be held liable for defamation unless the false statement was made with **actual malice.**[11] A statement is made with actual malice if it is made with *either* knowledge of its falsity or reckless disregard for its truth.[12]

Businesspersons should be most concerned about the conditional privilege that arises with respect to job recommendations. To encourage employers to give honest assessments

[10] 47 U.S.C. § 230.

[11] Restatement (Second) of Torts, sec. 580A.

[12] *New York Times, Co. v. Sullivan,* 376 U.S. 254 (1964).

of their former employees, this privilege protects an employer who makes a false statement about a former worker: The employer will not be held liable as long as the statement was made in good faith and was made only to those who had a legitimate interest in the information being communicated.

Another conditional privilege is the **public figure privilege.** Public figures are individuals who are in the public eye, typically politicians and entertainers. Because these individuals have a significant impact on our lives, we want to encourage free discussion about them, so we do not hold people liable for making false statements about them as long as the statements were not made with malice. This privilege does not seem to place an unfair burden on the public figure because such an individual can easily respond publicly to any false claims given that he or she is already in the public eye and has appropriate outlets available to give his or her opinion.

There are those who believe a conditional privilege should apply when the defamatory statement is posted somewhere on the Internet. The reasoning behind application of the privilege in this context is that the person who has been defamed over the Internet can respond to the defamatory remarks in the same forum with minimal effort. Thus, there is less need for the stronger legal protection we ordinarily give to private parties who are defamed.

In addition, we want to encourage free expression and the exchange of ideas on the Internet. One way to do so is to allow people to openly respond to criticisms on the Internet. When people are overly concerned about making errors, free exchange is hindered. Relaxing defamation standards in regard to the Internet can encourage people to speak their minds freely.

Thus far, however, no such privilege has been established. And when a person is found to have committed defamation on an online bulletin board or Web site, the damages can be significant. For example, a jury awarded $3 million to a university professor who sued a former student who had accused him of being a pedophile on a Web site she maintained.[13]

Privacy torts. The fact that truth is an absolute defense to a defamation action does not mean people are free to reveal everything they know. Four distinct torts, collectively referred to as *invasion of privacy,* protect the individual's right to keep certain things out of the public view, even if they are true. Each of the four privacy torts protects a slightly different aspect of one's right to privacy. The four privacy torts are (1) false light, (2) public disclosure of private facts, (3) appropriation for commercial gain, and (4) intrusion on an individual's affairs or seclusion.

False light is closely related to defamation and occurs when publicity about a person creates an impression about that individual that is not valid. It could involve attributing characteristics or beliefs to a person that she does not possess or creating the impression that an individual has taken certain actions he has not taken. Sometimes tabloids publish articles that may lead to false-light claims, as Case 8-1 illustrates.

Public disclosure of private facts about a person occurs when someone publicizes a private fact about an individual and that fact is something a reasonable person would find highly offensive.[14] The individual must have not waived his or her right to privacy. Publication of information about someone's sex life or failure to pay debts would fall under this tort.

Appropriation for commercial gain occurs when someone uses another person's name, likeness, voice, or other identifying characteristic for commercial gain without that person's permission.[15] If a company hired someone who sounded like former President

[13] See Paul J. Martin, "North Dakota Jury Awards $3M for Internet Defamation," *Lawyers Weekly USA,* www.lawyersweeklyusa.com/usanews040802a.cfm (accessed April 8, 2002).

[14] Restatement (Second) of Torts, sec. 652D.

[15] Restatement (Second) of Torts, sec. 652C.

global context

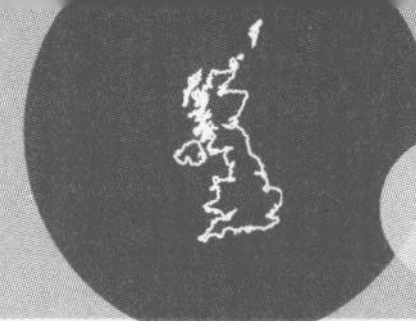

Defamation of Public Figures in the United Kingdom

As you know from your reading, the media in the United States have the ability to print false information about public figures without being liable if they can demonstrate they did so without malice. In the United Kingdom, public figures about whom false statements have been made have a much easier time winning a libel case.

All a public figure, or any other libel plaintiff, must do to win a case against the media is demonstrate that the defamatory statement was communicated in the United Kingdom and his or her reputation was damaged as a result. The only defenses available to the defendant media are either (1) the statements made were true or (2) the statements were made in Parliament or court. The burden of proving the truth of the alleged defamatory statement is thus on the defendant.

If a statement was originally broadcast by a company in the United States and was rebroadcast in the United Kingdom without the consent of the originator of the broadcast, the U.S. company may still be held liable in the U.K. court.

CASE 8-1 | NELLIE MITCHELL v. GLOBE INC. D/B/A "SUN" UNITED STATES DISTRICT COURT, W.D. ARKANSAS 786 F. SUPP. 791 (1992)

Ninety-six-year-old Nellie Mitchell had operated a newsstand on the Mountain Home, Arkansas, town square since 1963. Known to almost everyone in this small Ozark Mountain town, she cared for herself and raised a family as a single parent for all of these years on what must have been the meager earnings of a "paper girl."

The October 2 edition of the Sun contained a photograph of the plaintiff, Mrs. Mitchell, in conjunction with a story entitled:

SPECIAL DELIVERY
World's oldest newspaper carrier, 101, quits because she's pregnant!

"I guess walking all those miles kept me young"

The "story" purported to be about "papergal Audrey Wiles" in Stirling, Australia, who had been delivering papers for ninety-four years. Readers were told Ms. Wiles became pregnant by "Will" a "reclusive millionaire" she met on her newspaper route. "I used to put Will's paper in the door when it rained, and one thing just kind of led to another."

In words that could certainly have described Nellie Mitchell, the article, which was in the form and style of a factual newspaper account, said: "[S]he's become like a city landmark because nearly everyone at one time or another has seen her trudging down the road with a large stack of papers under her arm."

A photograph of Nellie, apparently "trudging down the road with a large stack of papers under her arm," was used in conjunction with the story. The picture used in the October 2 edition of the Sun had been used by the defendant in a reasonably factual and accurate article about Mrs. Mitchell published in another of the defendant's publications, the Examiner, *in 1980.*

The case was tried before a jury that found the defendant's conduct had invaded Mrs. Mitchell's privacy by placing her in a false light and had amounted to an intentional infliction of emotional distress. The jury awarded the plaintiff $650,000 in compensatory damages and $850,000 in punitive damages.

Defendant filed a motion for judgment as a matter of law or, alternatively, for remittitur of the jury award, or alternatively for new trial.

CHIEF JUDGE H. FRANKLIN WATERS: Testimony at trial indicated most of the defendant's articles are created "TOH" or "top of the head," in the words of John Vadar, editor of the *Sun.* That is, the authors, none of whom use their real name, are given a headline and a picture and then "make up" the accompanying stories. In fact, according to the evidence, the editor, and perhaps others, "make up" a series of headlines for stories to appear in each issue, and they are placed on a table. The "reporters" or perhaps, according to defendant's contentions at the trial, the "authors of fiction" select from this list the stories they wish to write. . . .

[CONTINUED]

In order to prevail on this claim [of false light], the plaintiff has the burden of proving by clear and convincing evidence the following:

One, the false light in which she was placed by the publicity would be highly offensive to a reasonable person, and

Two, the defendant acted with actual malice in publishing the statements at issue in this case. Actual malice means Globe International intended, or recklessly failed to anticipate, readers would construe the publicized matter as conveying actual facts or events concerning Mrs. Mitchell. . . .

Defendant argues there was no evidence of intentional conduct on the part of Globe. It is further argued no one understood the story to state actual facts about Mrs. Mitchell. . . .

The court cannot say as a matter of law the article is incapable of being interpreted as portraying actual events or facts regarding the plaintiff. The "facts" conveyed are not so inherently impossible or fantastic they could not be understood to convey actual facts. Nor can we say no person could take them seriously. Moreover, even if the headline and certain facts contained in the article could not be reasonably believed, other facts, e.g., the implication of sexual promiscuity, could reasonably be believed. . . .

In making this determination we "consider the surrounding circumstances in which the statements were made, the medium by which they were published and the audience for which they were intended." . . . No distinction is made between those articles that are wholly fictional and the articles that are intended to be factual. Fictional articles are not denoted as such. The *Sun* apparently intends for the readers to determine which articles are fact and which are fiction or what percentage of a given article is fact or fiction. . . .

[T]he court believes the jury could have, and apparently did, find the defendant intended their readers to construe the article in question as conveying actual facts or events concerning Mrs. Mitchell, or at the very least the defendant recklessly failed to anticipate the article would be so construed. The court believes the publication methods utilized by the defendant make it reasonable for the jury to draw such a conclusion.

MOTION DENIED.

CRITICAL THINKING

Why did the court conclude the jury's award would stand? Do you agree with the reasons that led to the court's ruling? Why or why not?

What is the fundamental issue being addressed by this case? Can the decision be seen as a preference for one value over another? If so, do you see this value preference as justified? Why or why not?

ETHICAL DECISION MAKING

Various stakeholders would be affected by the court's ruling in this decision. Which set of stakeholders would you weigh the heaviest in deciding a case of this type? On what grounds would you raise their interests above those of other relevant parties?

Bill Clinton to endorse a product on the radio, the company could be found liable for this tort.

The final privacy tort is **intrusion on an individual's affairs or seclusion,** which occurs when someone invades a person's solitude, seclusion, or personal affairs when the

connecting to the core

Marketing: Use of a Celebrity's Likeness

In your marketing class, you may have learned about the role of celebrities in advertising. Although appropriation for commercial gain—a company's use of a celebrity's name, likeness, or voice without the celebrity's permission—would subject the company to liability, a company could choose to use a celebrity's name, likeness, or voice *with* the celebrity's permission in the hope of increasing sales. However, one risk of using celebrities in advertisements is that the image of the celebrity may change over time to one that is inconsistent with the product's image. For instance, Kobe Bryant's court appearances altered his usual image as merely a basketball star. Nevertheless, some business managers may believe that celebrities will enhance the image of their products and, consequently, may choose to use a celebrity's name, likeness, or voice with permission to hopefully influence company sales.

Source: R. Kerin, S. Hartley, E. Berkowitz, and W. Rudelius, *Marketing* (New York: McGraw-Hill/Irwin, 2005), pp. 502–503.

person has the right to expect privacy.[16] Some examples of invasion of privacy include wiretapping and using people's passwords to gain access to their e-mail messages. Likewise, if someone operated an ice skating rink and installed two-way mirrors in the women's dressing room, this action would constitute an invasion of privacy because the skaters should be able to expect a certain degree of privacy in a dressing room.

Entertainers often allege invasion-of-privacy claims. For example, Joan Collins recently sued the *Globe* for invasion of privacy when it took pictures of her and a male friend. However, editors and owners often claim that the public "demands" these invasions of privacy. As evidence of this "demand," they point out the higher circulation they have when they print sensational pictures.

False imprisonment. **False imprisonment** occurs when an individual is confined or restrained against his or her will for an appreciable period of time. The imprisonment may occur by a number of different means: (1) physical restraint, such as tying someone to a chair, (2) physical force, such as forcibly pinning someone against a wall, (3) threatening to use immediate physical force, or (4) refusal to release the plaintiff's property. The use of moral pressure is not enough to establish a false imprisonment. For example, the Pushy Toy Company is holding a "training session" for new moms, which is really a thinly veiled demonstration of new products in a conference room. People are told they are free to leave at any time. Once Hillary realizes what is going on, she decides to leave. As she approaches the exit, the CEO of Pushy Toys tells Hillary that only a terrible mother would leave early but she is free to leave if she wants to be a terrible mother. The moral pressure the CEO is using, although ethically repugnant, does not constitute a false imprisonment as Hillary is still free to leave.

Given retailers' efforts to crack down on shoplifters, sometimes stores find it necessary to detain a suspected shoplifter. Because retailers and security guards are the usual defendants in false-imprisonment cases, this tort is known as the "shopkeeper's tort." Whenever a retailer has a reason to believe that a person is guilty of shoplifting, the store may question the person about said shoplifting. The suspect cannot be held for an unreasonable length of time, and the questioning itself must be reasonable. Retailers who question suspected shoplifters are protected under what is commonly called the "shopkeeper's privilege." Case 8-2 examines what constitutes a reasonable detention.

[16] Restatement (Second) of Torts, sec. 652B.

global context

Privacy in China

China's Civil Code recognizes that a citizen has a right to definite remedies when a privacy violation occurs. While they constitute a small portion of the civil docket, defamation and invasion-of-privacy claims have been increasing in China. Unlike the case in the United States, civil or criminal liability may be imposed for defamation or invasion of privacy in China. Plaintiffs may recover actual damages (i.e., lost income) or damages for emotional distress.

CASE 8-2 | WAL-MART STORES, INC. v. MARTIN RODRIGUEZ
SUPREME COURT OF TEXAS
92 S.W.3D 502 (2002)

Martin Rodriguez was employed by R & C Enterprises, where he purchased supplies for R & C at the local Wal-Mart, paying by company check. Because Rodriguez was the first employee to present an R & C check there, Wal-Mart's register prompted the cashier to request personal identification. Rodriguez offered his driver's license and the cashier entered his license number into Wal-Mart's check identification system. Under that system, any R & C check presented thereafter would be approved without a prompt for further identification, and Wal-Mart's register would automatically print Rodriguez's driver's license number on the back of the presented R & C check.

In July 1998, after Rodriguez had left the company's employ, Long purchased goods at the same Wal-Mart with an R & C check. Long signed the check illegibly, but his name was not printed under the illegible signature as required by store policy. Although the check contained R & C's address and business phone number, its only legible personal identification was Rodriguez's license number, which Wal-Mart's register automatically imprinted on the check's back.

Long's R & C check was returned for insufficient funds. Following the store's usual procedure, Wal-Mart employees called the phone number printed on the check and sent three letters to the address it listed for R & C. The third letter, sent certified mail, was returned as undeliverable. An employee then filled out a preprinted hot check complaint form and delivered that form and the returned check to the District Attorney's Office. The complaint listed "R & C Enterprises" as the check's "maker," and Rodriguez's driver's license number was written in the space provided for the "maker's" number. The form stated: "I understand that if charges are filed a warrant will be issued for the Maker who may be placed in jail." Wal-Mart had nothing further to do with processing its complaint or filing the criminal charge.

Rodriguez was eventually handcuffed and taken to jail, where he remained from Saturday afternoon until he made bail Sunday evening. The next day Rodriguez spoke with an assistant district attorney, and the charges against him were dismissed. He then sued Wal-Mart for false imprisonment, as well as several other claims. Wal-Mart filed a motion requesting summary judgment. The trial court granted Wal-Mart summary judgment on all of Rodriguez's claims. The court of appeals affirmed the trial court's summary judgment on all but the false imprisonment claim. Wal-Mart appealed regarding the false imprisonment claim.

JUSTICE ENOCH: The court of appeals noted, in the complaint delivered to the district attorney, Wal-Mart failed to disclose it "knew that its check identification system could provide an erroneous driver's license number in relation to a company check." Failure to disclose this possibility, according to the court of appeals, raised a fact issue about whether Wal-Mart could be liable for Rodriguez's alleged false imprisonment. We disagree.

No Wal-Mart employee participated in Rodriguez's arrest and detention. Wal-Mart's only connection to the imprisonment was delivering the returned check and complaint to the district attorney's office. But in Texas, as both parties concede, liability for false imprisonment extends beyond those who willfully participate in detaining the complaining party to those who request or direct the detention. False imprisonment's first element may thus be satisfied by conduct intended to cause one to be detained, and in fact causes the detention, even when the actor does not participate in the detention. We have sometimes referred to this causation standard as "instigation" of the false imprisonment.

When the alleged detention results from an unlawful arrest, to prove instigation a plaintiff must show the defendant clearly directed or requested the arrest. As the Restatement explains, "[I]n the case of an arrest, [instigation] is the equivalent, in words or conduct, of 'Officer, arrest that man!'" To hold a third party liable for instigating the detention, then, "the act of arrest [must be] made by the officer, not of his or her own volition, but to carry out the request of the defendant."

The complaint form Wal-Mart filled out alleged the commission of a crime and provided information the district attorney's office could use to identify the suspect. By signing the complaint, Wal-Mart certified it knew the information provided could lead to an arrest. But the form contained no explicit request or direction to have any particular person arrested. Ordinarily then, Wal-Mart's act of filing this complaint would not, by itself, make it liable for Rodriguez's subsequent detention.

But Rodriguez asserts, and the court of appeals held, a party providing information to legal authorities may nevertheless be liable for false imprisonment when it fails to disclose potentially exculpatory facts in its report. Rodriguez argues a person who supplies incomplete information renders the authorities' reasonable exercise of discretion impossible, so the law may justly charge that person with directing the false imprisonment no matter who actually made the decision to arrest. Thus, according to Rodriguez, Wal-Mart can be liable for his alleged false imprisonment because it failed to inform the district attorney it "knew that its check identification system could provide an erroneous driver's license number in relation to a company check."

In *Schnaufer v. Price,* we held, while a simple mistake in identification would not make a reporting party liable, "if a person should willfully identify the wrong man as being the criminal, for the purpose of having him arrested," that person could be liable for false imprisonment. This language is consistent with the prevailing majority rule a third party will not be liable for instigating a false imprisonment unless the third party knowingly provides false information resulting in the arrest.

Following *Schnaufer* and our reasoning in *Lieck,* we agree a defendant may be liable for instigating an unlawful arrest if he knowingly provides false information to law enforcement authorities resulting in the arrest. Applying that principle here, we see Rodriguez has alleged Wal-Mart failed to disclose its identification system was unreliable, but not that it knowingly provided false information. As we noted in *Lieck,* failing to make a full and fair disclosure is not the equivalent of knowingly providing false information. All citizens have a clear legal right to report criminal misconduct to law enforcement authorities. In fact, the law encourages such communication. Although a private citizen may be liable for directing an arrest that results in a false imprisonment, the law will not generally permit inferring such direction simply from a report of crime made to the authorities. Such an inference is justified when a party provides information in its report it knows is false. Merely providing inaccurate or incomplete information, however, will not make a party liable for instigating a subsequent false imprisonment.

False imprisonment is an intentional tort, requiring a willful detention by the defendant. We recognize here it is unlikely Rodriguez would have been arrested had Wal-Mart's employees followed Wal-Mart's policies, or had Wal-Mart more carefully designed its check identification system. His arrest was unfortunate, unnecessary, and embarrassing. But we decline to hold negligently providing inaccurate or incomplete information to legal authorities will make a reporting party liable for false imprisonment.

The claim here is false imprisonment. And false imprisonment requires knowingly providing false information. Ultimately, Rodriguez's evidence shows only Wal-Mart's employees could not have been certain the driver's license number printed on the returned check belonged to the check's drawer, but it might have. It does not show Wal-Mart knew the information it provided was false.

REVERSED.

[CONTINUED]

CRITICAL THINKING

What do you see as the fundamental issue being considered in this decision? Does the opinion take a desirable stance on this issue, and thereby serve to create an acceptable precedent for subsequent cases?

ETHICAL DECISION MAKING

How could the court have used the universalization principle to demonstrate the importance of following the logic it used? In other words, what does the community gain by always following the logic in this case?

While many false-imprisonment cases arise in conjunction with claims of shoplifting, cases of false imprisonment are not limited to suits against retailers or security guards. For example, three ambulance drivers recently filed a false-imprisonment suit against a local psychiatric center because the crisis center locked them in and would not allow them to leave. The crisis center claimed the drivers had committed certain improprieties when delivering a violent girl to the crisis center.

Proving damages in a false-imprisonment case is not easy. If the physical restraint caused harm requiring medical treatment, such damages would be clear, but most cases of false imprisonment do not involve physical harm. Typically, plaintiffs request compensation for lost time from work and for pain and suffering from the mental distress and humiliation.

Intentional infliction of emotional distress. Sometimes called the "tort of outrage," **intentional infliction of emotional distress** occurs when someone engages in outrageous, intentional conduct likely to cause extreme emotional distress to the party toward whom the conduct is directed. For example, if a person calls his former employer and falsely tells her that her son was just arrested for a double homicide after a botched robbery attempt, most courts would find that behavior to be outrageous enough to satisfy the first element of the tort.

Before damages are awarded in some jurisdictions, the plaintiff must demonstrate injury through physical symptoms directly related to the emotional distress. For instance, in the above example, if the employer had fainted upon hearing the news, hitting her head on the table and cutting it as she passed out, she would have physical symptoms sufficient to justify a recovery. Other physical symptoms commonly arising from emotional distress include headaches, a sudden onset of high blood pressure, hives, chills, inability to sleep, or inability to get out of bed.

Case 8-3 provides an illustration of this tort.

Misuse of legal procedure. A group of three separate torts has developed to protect those who are unreasonably subjected to litigation. These three torts are malicious prosecution, wrongful civil proceedings, and abuse of process. These torts are intended to serve two functions. First, they are an attempt to proactively limit frivolous litigation. Second, they try to rectify harm done to a party through inappropriate litigation.

CASE 8-3 CINDY R. LOURCEY ET AL. v. ESTATE OF CHARLES SCARLETT

SUPREME COURT OF TENNESSEE, AT NASHVILLE
146 S.W.3D 48 (2004)

On February 5, 2001, Cindy Lourcey was working as a postal carrier for the United States Postal Service. While delivering mail by postal vehicle, Lourcey encountered Charles Scarlett and his wife, Joanne Scarlett, who was nude from the waist up, in the middle of the street. When Lourcey stopped her vehicle to provide assistance, Charles Scarlett told her his wife was having a seizure. As Lourcey used her cell phone to call emergency 911 to request help, Charles Scarlett pulled out a pistol and shot his wife in the head. He then turned and faced Lourcey, pointed the pistol at his head, pulled the trigger, and killed himself.

As a result of Charles Scarlett's conduct, Cindy Lourcey alleges she suffered from post-traumatic stress disorder and major depression following the incident and was unable to return to work. In addition, she suffered physical injury and impairment, mental injury and impairment, pain and suffering, medical expenses, lost wages, and lost earning capacity. Lourcey accordingly brought suit against Scarlett's estate for an intentional infliction of emotional distress.

The Estate of Charles Scarlett moved to dismiss the complaint. The motion stated the claim for intentional infliction of emotional distress should be dismissed because Charles Scarlett's conduct was not outrageous. The plaintiffs responded Scarlett's intentional acts of attempted murder and suicide were sufficiently outrageous to support the intentional infliction of emotional distress claim.

Following a hearing, the trial court granted the defendant's motion and dismissed the complaint. The Court of Appeals reversed the trial court's judgment, however, and remanded the case to the trial court for further proceedings on the claims for intentional infliction of emotional distress. The Estate subsequently appealed.

JUDGE ANDERSON: When reviewing the trial court's dismissal of a complaint, we accept the factual allegations contained in the complaint as true. The issue presents a question of law, which we review de novo without according a presumption of correctness to the conclusions reached below. If the factual allegations state a claim upon which damages can be awarded, dismissal is inappropriate.

The defendant first argues the trial court properly dismissed the complaint for failure to state a claim for intentional infliction of emotional distress because the conduct of Charles Scarlett was not "outrageous" as a matter of law. The defendant asserts "life is full of scenes of tragedy" and argues "there was no outrageous conduct directed towards Lourcey."

The plaintiffs respond the complaint states a claim for intentional infliction of emotional distress based on the actions of Charles Scarlett, which were outrageous.

We begin the analysis of these issues by first examining the elements required for intentional infliction of emotional distress. To state a claim for intentional infliction of emotional distress, a plaintiff must establish: (1) the defendant's conduct was intentional or reckless; (2) the defendant's conduct was so outrageous it cannot be tolerated by civilized society; and (3) the defendant's conduct resulted in serious mental injury to the plaintiff.

In describing these elements, we have emphasized it is not sufficient that a defendant "has acted with an intent which is tortious or even criminal, or he has intended to inflict emotional distress." A plaintiff must in addition show the defendant's conduct was "so outrageous in character, and so extreme in degree, as to go beyond all possible bounds of decency and to be regarded as atrocious, and utterly intolerable in a civilized community."

Applying the foregoing principles, we conclude the allegations in the plaintiffs' complaint, when accepted as true, state a claim for intentional infliction of emotional distress. The complaint alleges Charles Scarlett's conduct was intentional and it caused Cindy Lourcey serious mental injury in the form of post-traumatic stress disorder, depression, and related problems. Moreover, the complaint describes conduct that is "outrageous" under the standards discussed in *Bain* and *Miller*. This conduct, which occurred in Lourcey's immediate presence and involved her as a participant, was not simply a tragedy common to daily life as asserted by the defendant. Indeed, the complaint clearly alleges conduct that was outrageous in character, extreme in degree, beyond all possible bounds of decency, and utterly intolerable in a civilized society.

[CONTINUED]

In reaching this conclusion, we need not address the defendant's argument that a claim for intentional infliction of emotional distress under Tennessee law requires the alleged outrageous conduct be "directed at" the plaintiff. Assuming there is such a requirement, a question we do not decide today, the allegations in the plaintiffs' complaint, when accepted as true, demonstrate Scarlett's conduct was directed at Cindy Lourcey. The complaint states Charles Scarlett told Lourcey his wife was having a seizure and he knew Lourcey was seeking help in response to his statement. The complaint further states Lourcey was in close proximity when Scarlett shot his wife and Scarlett turned to face Lourcey before shooting himself in the head. Accordingly, we conclude the plaintiffs' complaint states a claim upon which relief could be granted pursuant to Tennessee law for intentional infliction of emotional distress.

AFFIRMED.

CRITICAL THINKING

How is this case largely dependent on the use of specific definitions of particular terms? How good are the definitions used?

What is the nature of the assumption that allows for existing entities to be held responsible for the actions of deceased individuals? Especially in a case such as this, in which the involvement of the plaintiff was more or less a matter of random chance (an "act of God," if you will)—a situation out of the control of those now held responsible—what reasoning allows for justification of this assignment of culpability?

ETHICAL DECISION MAKING

What values are responsible for permitting a person to recover damages from a dead person?

The first two of these torts, **malicious prosecution** and **wrongful civil proceedings,** serve very similar functions. Both torts seek to compensate people wrongfully charged with either criminal or civil matters. Plaintiffs successful with misuse-of-legal-procedure torts are entitled to damages for legal fees related to the improperly brought litigation; harm to reputation, credit, or standing caused by the false claims; and any emotional distress caused by the improper litigation.

Abuse of process is more general than malicious prosecution and wrongful civil actions. Abuse of process applies to both criminal and civil matters in which a legal procedure is misused to achieve a different goal than the procedure intends. For example, Ben and Jennifer are recently divorced. Ben owes Jennifer alimony as part of the divorce settlement. As a form of retaliation, Ben sues Jennifer for slandering him to his business partners. Ben's attorney offers Jennifer the option of settling out of court if she will simply drop the alimony requirement from the divorce settlement. Regardless of whether Ben would (or does) win in court, Jennifer can file abuse-of-process charges against Ben in civil court because legal proceedings for slander are not intended to be used as mitigating devices for divorce disputes.

e-commerce AND THE LAW

Tort Law versus Criminal Law to Improve the Online Personals Industry

Suppose your ex-boyfriend posed as you on a number of online personals sites, such as iwantu.com. He posted what he describes as your rape fantasies. In addition, he posted your name and address. He then encouraged men to act out your fantasies in person. Would you be afraid? How might criminal law respond? Could tort law also help you?

In a real case, Gary Dellapenta, the ex-boyfriend, was sentenced to six years in prison for violating California's cyberstalking law. Dellapenta was convicted in 1999, a time when California's cyberstalking law was new.

If someone were threatening you as Dellapenta threatened his ex-girlfriend, you might want the creator of the Web site and/or an Internet service provider to assist you in pulling the posts before harm occurs.

Unfortunately, Internet service providers are exempt from liability under tort law if they fail to respond to your concerns. The Communications Decency Act of 1996 outlined this exemption.

You might be able to pursue the creator of the Web site, depending on how the facts play out, and your state's law. You might be able to sue for defamation, false-light invasion of privacy, negligence, and/or intentional infliction of emotional distress. You will face an uphill battle, though, in meeting your burden of proof. In the mid-1990s, Ken Zeran was unable to prove tort claims against a radio station that broadcast untrue information that suggested Zeran was selling T-shirts and other items with insensitive remarks about the Oklahoma City bombing of a federal building. In Zeran's case, he was unable to prove any of the torts he alleged.

Perhaps as cyberstalking becomes more prevalent, and more frightening, tort law will change to provide more protection to victims of cyberstalking.

INTENTIONAL TORTS AGAINST PROPERTY

Trespass to realty. The tort of **trespass to realty,** also called *trespass to real property,* occurs when a person intentionally (1) enters the land of another without permission; (2) causes an object to be placed on the land of another without the landowner's permission; (3) stays on the land of another when the owner tells him to depart; or (4) refuses to remove something he placed on the property that the landowner asked him to remove.[17]

It is no defense for a person to argue that she thought she had a legal right to be on the property or she thought the land belonged to someone else. The intent refers to intentionally being on that particular piece of land.[18] In a recent, unusual case heard in a small claims court in Westchester County, a plaintiff sued the defendant for trespass to realty when the defendant entered the plaintiff's property to serve the plaintiff with a reply affidavit for another legal action. The defendant had previously been barred from entering the plaintiff's property. The plaintiff argued that the defendant could not dictate how legal papers are served. The plaintiff sued for $3,000 in compensatory, nominal, and punitive damages. While the court ruled that the defendant committed trespass to realty, it awarded only nominal damages in the sum of $1.

Because guests are welcomed onto one's property, they are not considered trespassers. However, if a guest is asked to leave and he or she refuses, the person immediately becomes a trespasser and no longer maintains a right to be on the property in question. If charges were brought against such a person, the person cannot raise the defense that he or she was a guest.

[17] Restatement (Second) of Torts, sec. 158.

[18] Restatement (Second) of Torts, sec. 164.

Also, when a trespasser is on someone's property, the trespasser is liable for damages she or he might cause to the property. Furthermore, under common law, a trespasser cannot hold an owner of property liable for damages the trespasser sustains while on the property. However, as of late, courts have been shifting away from this common law rule. Now, courts typically maintain that owners owe a reasonable duty to anyone who may end up on their property. The specifics of the duty vary by jurisdiction, as well as by the status of the parties. In some jurisdictions, it is possible, although rare, for owners to be liable for trespassers who were injured while trying to steal property from the owners.

Private nuisance. A **private nuisance** occurs when a person uses her property in an unreasonable manner that harms a neighbor's use or enjoyment of his property.[19] Using one's property in a manner that caused the neighbor to be subjected to flooding, vibrations, excessive noise, or smoke could lead to a nuisance claim.

Trespass to personal property. A person commits trespass to personal property, also called **trespass to personalty,** by temporarily exerting control over another's personal property or interfering with the true owner's right to use the property. Under trespass to personal property, the trespasser is responsible for damages caused to the property, as well as for damages caused to the owner related to the trespasser's wrongful possession of the property.[20] For example, if I take someone's bike from their garage and use it for a week, I have committed trespass to personalty. If I return the bike after it has a flat tire, I will have to compensate the owner for the cost of repairing the tire and any other expenses that resulted from my having the bike for a week. Also, if the bike was the only way the person had to get to work, I would be responsible for the person's lost wages resulting from the missed work, because I took the person's means of transportation.

Conversion. **Conversion** occurs when a person permanently removes personal property from the owner's possession and control.[21] When conversion occurs, the true owner can no longer regain the property. The owner usually recovers damages for the full value of the converted item, plus any additional damages that resulted from the loss.

It is not a defense to conversion for a person to argue that she believed she had a legal claim to the goods. For example, if Brittany accidentally takes Melvin's suitcase believing it to be hers and then loses it, she is still liable for conversion. Moreover, the possession of stolen goods also makes a person liable for conversion. Therefore, buying goods in good faith without knowledge of any impropriety also is not a defense to conversion. Even if a person bought the goods believing the purchase was legal, the person with the stolen goods is liable to the legal owner of the goods.

An illustration of conversion comes from a recent case heard in the Westchester County Supreme Court. An amateur race-car driver left her race car at a service station. While the car was in the possession of the service station, an employee of the station, with a known drinking problem, apparently drove the car, wrecked it, and totally destroyed it. The car could never be returned in the condition it was in when brought to the station. The owner sued for conversion and recovered the value of the car in damages.

[19] Restatement (Second) of Torts, sec. 821D.

[20] Restatement (Second) of Torts, sec. 218.

[21] Restatement (Second) of Torts, sec. 222A.

INTENTIONAL TORTS AGAINST ECONOMIC INTERESTS

All businesspersons should be familiar with the torts against economic interest. The five most common torts against economic interests, frequently referred to as "business torts," are disparagement, intentional interference with contract, unfair competition, misappropriation, and fraudulent misrepresentation. The first tort, **disparagement,** is most easily understood as a form of defamation. It is the defamation of a business product or service.

The plaintiff in a disparagement case must prove that the defendant published a false statement of a material fact about the plaintiff's product or service that resulted in a loss of sales. When such statements are criticisms of the quality, honesty, or reputation of the business or product, the tort is sometimes called **slander of quality** (if spoken) or **trade libel** (if in printed form). If the statements relate to the ownership of the business property, the term **slander of title** is used.

Damages for disparaging are ordinarily based on a decrease in profits that can be linked to the publication of the false statement. An alternative, although less common, way to prove damages is to demonstrate that the plaintiff had been negotiating a contract with a third party but the third party lost interest shortly after the publication of the false statement. The profits the plaintiff would have made on the contract would be the damages.

Some interesting variations of the tort of disparagement have developed. For example, in 2007, California became the thirteenth state to recognize the tort of **food disparagement,** which critics call "veggie libel." Such laws provide ranchers and farmers with a cause of action when someone knowingly makes false, damaging statements about a food product. The California law was drafted in response to an incident during 2006 in which Taco Bell executives wrongly identified green onions grown at Boskovich Farms in Oxnard as the source of an E. coli outbreak that sickened 70 of the fast-food chain's customers.

The most famous "veggie libel" lawsuit was one filed by a cattle rancher against talk-show host Oprah Winfrey and one of her guests. Oprah had said, during the broadcast at issue in the case, that the conversation they were having about the possibility of contracting disease from meat had caused her to give up eating hamburgers. Shortly after the show aired, the price of cattle futures fell.

Oprah and her guest were sued under the Texas veggie libel law, which says anyone who knowingly makes a false claim that a perishable food product is unsafe may be required to pay damages to the producer of the product. The jury in the case decided there was no liability, because the statements were merely the parties' opinions, not knowingly false statements of fact.

With the growing use of technology, it seems almost inevitable a computer-related disparagement tort would evolve, and it has. *Disparagement by computer* occurs when (1) erroneous information from a computer about a business's credit standing or reputation impairs the business's ability to obtain credit and (2) the computer information's owner fails to correct the incorrect information in a timely manner.

Intentional interference with contract. Another tort against economic interests is the tort of **intentional interference with contract.** To successfully bring a claim of intentional interference with contract, the plaintiff must prove (1) a valid and enforceable contract between the two parties existed; (2) the defendant party knew of the existence of the contract and its terms; (3) the defendant intentionally undertook steps to cause one of the parties to breach the contract; and (4) the plaintiff was injured as a result of the breach.[22]

[22] Restatement (Second) of Torts, sec. 766.

When a contract exists, clear liability is placed on third parties for inducing a party to the contract to breach the contract. However, when a prospective contract exists, a third party might be liable for inducing a party to pull out of the contract before it is formed. Because the essence of business involves competition, simply offering a better deal is not enough to create liability when a prospective contract exists. However, if a party uses illegal means to cause another party not to enter into a contract, the party who acted illegally is liable for interfering with contractual relations.[23]

The most common situation involving intentional interference with a contract in the business context is a situation in which one employer tries to lure an employee away from another employer. Liability in such a situation, however, is limited to the case where the employee has a contract for a set period of time and the prospective employer actually knows of the contract.

Several damage remedies are available when a third party interferes with a contract. Injured parties may recover for what was directly lost through the breached contract. Injured parties may also recover any losses suffered related to the breached contract, in addition to damages for emotional distress and harm to reputation.[24]

Unfair competition. The tort of **unfair competition** exists because of American views toward business. Americans believe business is intended to make a profit, and the law protects businesses acting on this profit motive. Therefore, when someone enters a business with the sole intent of driving another firm out of business, the law punishes this act as unfair competition. For example, if there is only one jewelry store in town, Mark cannot come in and set up a store where he makes no profits, just to drive the other store out of business, so that an acquaintance of his can then move in and open up a legitimate jewelry store once the competition has been eliminated.

Fraudulent misrepresentation. **Fraudulent misrepresentation** occurs when a party uses intentional deceit to facilitate personal gain. To establish that a fraudulent misrepresentation exists, a party must demonstrate all the following:

1. A party knowingly, or with reckless disregard for the truth, misrepresented material facts and conditions.
2. The party intended to have other parties rely on the misrepresentations.
3. The injured party reasonably relied on the misrepresentations.
4. The injured party suffered damages because of a reliance on the misrepresentations.
5. A direct link exists between the injuries suffered and a reliance on the misrepresentations.[25]

Similar to the criminal act of fraud, in the civil act of fraudulent misrepresentation, a party materially misrepresents something and thereby causes another party to suffer damages. Typically, fraudulent misrepresentation applies only to the misrepresentation of material facts. However, when a party with expert knowledge regarding a specific matter states an opinion, any party reasonably relying on the statement, although it is an opinion and not fact, may recover damages under the tort of fraudulent misrepresentation.

[23] Restatement (Second) of Torts, sec. 766B.

[24] Restatement (Second) of Torts, sec. 774A.

[25] Restatement (Second) of Torts, sec. 525.

TYPE	PURPOSE	AMOUNT
Compensatory	To make the plaintiff whole again.	An amount equivalent to all losses caused by the tort, including compensation for pain and suffering, but not attorney fees.
Nominal	To recognize that the defendant committed a tort against the plaintiff.	A trivial amount, typically $1–$5.
Punitive	To punish the defendant and deter future wrongdoers.	Based on two factors: the severity of the wrongful conduct and the wealth of the defendant.

Exhibit 8-1 Types of Tort Damages

Damages Available in Tort Cases

There are three types of damages available in tort cases: compensatory, nominal, and punitive (see Exhibit 8-1). You will see this system of classifying damages again when we talk about damages in other contexts, such as in cases involving the breach of a contract.

COMPENSATORY DAMAGES

As the primary objective of tort law is to compensate victims, the primary type of damages are **compensatory damages,** damages designed to compensate the victim for all the harm caused by the person who committed the tort, often referred to as the **tortfeasor.** While we seem to hear a lot about "runaway jury" awards, the overall median jury award for personal injury cases from 1998 to 2004 was $35,298. And that amount actually fell from $37,086 in 2003 to $35,000 in 2004.[26]

Compensatory damages are typically rewarded for pain and suffering, costs to repair damaged property, medical expenses, and lost wages. For example, suppose Rubin could demonstrate he and his company lost money because of the *U.S. News & World Report* article. He might be able to recover those losses from *U.S. News.* Surprisingly, attorney fees are *not* recoverable as compensatory damages, despite the fact that most plaintiffs could not bring an action against the tortfeasor without hiring an attorney. Because the plaintiffs in personal injury cases must usually pay their attorneys anywhere from one-third to one-half of their recovery, some argue that compensatory damages fail to meet the intended goal of properly compensating victims. Others point out that one of the ways plaintiffs can, in essence, recover their attorney fees is by increasing their pain and suffering damages enough to cover these expenses.

NOMINAL DAMAGES

Nominal damages are a small amount of money given to recognize that a defendant did indeed commit a tort in a case where there were no compensable damages suffered by the plaintiff. A plaintiff may receive nominal damages by simply failing to prove actual damages.

[26] JVR news release, www.juryverdictresearch.com/Press_Room/Press_releases/Verdict_study/verdict_study41.html (accessed October 10, 2006).

PUNITIVE DAMAGES

Punitive damages are damages awarded to punish the defendant. They are given only when the defendant's conduct is extremely outrageous. The purposes of punitive damages are both to punish the defendant and to deter him and others who are similarly situated from engaging in that kind of activity again. In awarding punitive damages, juries usually consider the egregiousness or willfulness of the tort and the wealth of the defendant. Obviously, the more wrongful the nature of the defendant, the greater the desire to send a message that such behavior will not be tolerated; and the greater the wealth of the defendant, the higher the damages must be in order to be significant.

While the threat of large punitive damages is seen by many groups, including consumer advocates, as a good method for encouraging manufacturers to produce the safest possible products, others disagree. They believe that no threat beyond compensatory damages is required; and they argue that the main effect of punitive damages is the discouraging of innovation, because manufacturers will be afraid of the risk of producing a defective product, which could cost them millions in punitive damages.

Since the late 1970s, insurance companies and "tort reform" groups have been trying to limit the amount of punitive damages that can be assessed. These advocates of tort reform have tried repeatedly to get the courts to strike down punitive damages as unconstitutional violations of the due process rights of defendants.

The 1994 case of *Honda Motor Company v. Oberg*[27] provided tort reformists with their first judicial victory. In this case, the U.S. Supreme Court finally struck down a punitive-damage award as being a violation of due process. *Oberg,* however, was a limited victory because of two unique aspects of the case. First, the punitive damages were over 500 times the amount of the compensatory damages, which is extraordinarily rare. Second, the state law under which the damages were awarded was the only state law in the country that had no provision for judicial review of the amount of punitive-damage awards, and it was the denial of this safeguard that violated the due process clause. Because of its unusual facts, *Oberg* did not provide much guidance as to when punitive damages were so excessive as to violate due process.

A few years later, however, in *BMW v. Gore,*[28] the Supreme Court set forth a test that a number of commentators thought would substantially curb punitive-damage awards. The Court said three factors should be considered in determining whether an award was grossly excessive: "the degree of reprehensibility of the nondisclosure; the disparity between the harm or potential harm suffered by [the plaintiff] and his punitive damages award; and the difference between this remedy and the civil penalties authorized or imposed in comparable cases." However, a 1999 study found that the year after *BMW v. Gore,* punitive-damage awards across the country were not reduced any more frequently than they had been the year before the decision.[29] (Exhibit 8-2 lists several cases that resulted in major punitive-damage awards.)

Since *BMW v. Gore,* the Supreme Court has continued to encourage the courts to carefully scrutinize punitive-damage awards. In the 2001 case of *Cooper Industries, Inc. v. Leatherman Tool Group, Inc.,*[30] the high court ruled that appellate courts must review the trial court's decision on the constitutionality of an award *de novo,* meaning they should no longer give deference to the trial court's determination that the jury award was not

[27] 114 S. Ct. 2331 (1994).

[28] *BMW of North America v. Ira Gore, Jr.,* 116 S. Ct. 1589 (1995).

[29] James Dam, "Large Punitives Mostly Upheld, but $5B Award Overturned," *Lawyer's Weekly USA,* November 12, 2001, p. A1.

[30] 532 U.S. 424 (2001).

Exhibit 8-2 Some Major Punitive-Damage Awards in Recent Years

CASE	JURY AWARD	ULTIMATE RESOLUTION
Romo v. Ford Motor Co., 99 Cal. App. 4th 1115 (2002)	The Romo family was in an accident in which their 1978 Ford Bronco rolled over. The top of the Bronco collapsed and shattered, killing three of the family members and seriously injuring the other three. The jury awarded the Romos more than $6 million in compensatory damages and $290 million in punitive damages.	After several appeals, the jury verdict was lowered to under $3 million.
Liebeck v. McDonald's, 787 A2d 443 (1994)	A jury awarded Stella Liebeck $2.9 million in damages, including $2.7 million in punitive damages for extensive burns she received when she spilled 170-degree coffee on her legs. Part of the reason for the high punitive-damage award was the fact that McDonald's had prior knowledge of other customers receiving burns from the excessively hot coffee.	The trial court reduced the original jury award to $640,000. Subsequently, the parties settled out of court for an undisclosed amount.
Gober v. Ralphs Grocery Company, 128 Cal. App. 4th 648 (2005)	In the largest sexual harassment jury verdict in the United States, the jury awarded six plaintiffs $30.6 million dollars in damages, approximately $30 million of which was punitive damages.	The judge reduced the verdict to approximately $8 million, in light of *State Farm v. Campbell.* Both parties appealed and the case is now awaiting retrial.
Robinson v. State Farm Idaho, 2000 WL 1877745	A plaintiff's insurance company, State Farm, was found to have acted in bad faith when it refused to cover the injuries she sustained in an auto accident by claiming her injuries must have been caused by something other than the accident. The company's refusal had ostensibly been based on a recommendation from an independent company that had reviewed her medical records, but she demonstrated State Farm had a practice of referring claims to that company knowing no payment would be recommended. The jury awarded her punitive damages of $9.5 million, which was 95 times the amount of the compensatory damages.	The award was appealed and subsequently upheld by the Idaho Supreme Court.
Williams v. Phillip Morris, Inc., 2002 U.S. Dist. LEXIS 13522 (2002)	Williams's estate brought a fraud and negligence suit against Philip Morris after Williams died of lung cancer. The jury awarded Williams's estate $820,000 in compensatory damages and $79.5 million in punitive damages.	The trial judge reduced the damages to $32 million. The Oregon court of appeals affirmed the original $79.5 million verdict. The state supreme court vacated the decision and remanded the case to be decided in light of *State Farm v. Campbell.* The Oregon court of appeals subsequently ruled the $79.5 million award was lawful under *State Farm.*
Anderson, et al. v. Islamic Republic of Iran, 90 F. Supp. 107 (D.C. May 2001)	Anderson filed suit against Iderzbollah, and the nation of Iran that funded the group, for damages suffered during his captivity of slightly less than seven years. The jury awarded him $41.7 million in compensatory damages and $300 million in punitives.	Anderson settled for the award of $41 million compensatory, plus an additional $4.1 million for agreeing not to attempt to collect the punitive-damage award. He was able to collect this award from Iranian assets frozen in the U.S. by a special act of Congress.

unconstitutionally excessive and uphold it, unless there was a clear abuse of discretion on the part of the trial court judge.

In the 2003 case *State Farm v. Campbell,*[31] the Supreme Court once again addressed the issue of how to properly determine punitive damages. The Campbells had won a jury verdict for $1 million in compensatory damages and $145 million in punitive damages after State Farm failed to settle what was clearly a valid claim. The high court ruled that punitive-damage awards should bear some relationship to the actual harm caused and should not focus on the wealth of the defendants. While refusing to draw a firm line as to what ratio of compensatories to punitives was acceptable, the Court did say that "in practice, few awards exceeding a single-digit ratio between punitive and compensatory damages, to a significant degree, will satisfy due process."[32] The Court also stated that damages should not focus on deterrence based on wealth, or actions unrelated to the case at hand. Case 8-4 demonstrates how the courts are applying these guidelines today.

[31] 123 S. Ct. 1513 (2003).

[32] Ibid., p. 1524.

CASE 8-4 CLARK v. CHRYSLER CORPORATION
UNITED STATES COURT OF APPEALS FOR THE SIXTH CIRCUIT
2006 U.S. APP. LEXIS 2435

Charles Clark was fatally injured in an automobile accident when he pulled into an intersection in front of an oncoming vehicle and collided with it. He was not wearing a seat belt and was consequently ejected from his vehicle. His wife sued Chrysler, claiming that its pickup truck was defectively and negligently designed.

After a three-day trial, the jury rendered a unanimous verdict in favor of Mrs. Clark on claims of strict liability, negligence, and failure to warn. The jury found Chrysler and Mr. Clark each 50% at fault, returning a verdict of $471,258.26 in compensatory damages and $3,000,000 in punitive damages. The court entered a judgment against Chrysler for $3,235,629.13, reflecting 50% of the compensatory damages plus the $3 million punitive damages award. After a series of appeals, the last being an appeal of the trial court's motion to deny the defendant's motion for remittitur, the case finally landed at the Circuit Court of Appeals on the issue of whether the jury verdict was constitutionally excessive.

JUDGE JANE A. RESTANI: . . . The Court in *State Farm* elaborated on the three *Gore* guideposts that courts must consider when reviewing punitive damage awards. Namely, (1) the degree of reprehensibility of the defendant's misconduct; (2) the disparity between the actual or potential harm suffered by the plaintiff and the punitive damage award; and (3) the difference between the punitive damages awarded by the jury and the civil penalties authorized or imposed in comparable cases. . . . In light of *State Farm* . . . we conclude that the $3 million award here is constitutionally excessive. An application of the *Gore* guideposts to the facts of this case reveals that a punitive damage award approximately equal to twice the amount of compensatory damages, or $471,258.26, would comport with the requirements of due process.

With respect to the first *Gore* guidepost, *State Farm* emphasized that the degree of reprehensibility is the most important indicium of the reasonableness of a punitive damages award. . . .The Court laid out a list of five criteria that lower courts must consider in determining the reprehensibility of a defendant's conduct: the harm caused was physical as opposed to economic; the tortious conduct evinced an indifference to or a reckless disregard of the health or safety of others; the target of the conduct had financial vulnerability; the conduct involved repeated actions or was an isolated incident; and the harm was the result of intentional malice, trickery, or deceit, or mere accident. The existence of any one of these factors weighing in favor of a plaintiff may not be sufficient to sustain a punitive damages award; and the absence of all of them renders any award suspect. . . .[T]he physical harm suffered by Mr. Clark weighs strongly in favor of finding Chrysler's conduct reprehensible. After considering the four other factors, however, we conclude that the factors as a whole show that Chrysler's conduct was not sufficiently reprehensible to warrant a $3 million punishment.

. . . The second guidepost is the disparity between the actual or potential harm inflicted on the plaintiff and the punitive damage award. . . . [B]ecause the compensatory damage award here is not particularly large, a 1:1 ratio is inappropriate. . . . But due to the lack of several of the reprehensibility factors, any ratio higher than 2:1 is unwarranted. Accordingly, we conclude that a ratio of approximately 2:1 would comport with the requirements of due process.

The third guidepost is the difference between the punitive damage award and the civil or criminal penalties that could be imposed for comparable misconduct. . . . Given *State Farm's* focus on civil penalties, however, we now conclude that a $3 million punitive damage award is excessive in light of comparable civil penalties.

DENIAL OF CHRYSLER'S MOTION FOR REMITTITUR REVERSED AND REMANDED WITH INSTRUCTIONS TO ENTER A PUNITIVE DAMAGE AWARD OF $471,258.26,

CRITICAL THINKING

The decision that the punitive damage award was excessive in this case was primarily based on the interpretation of several ambiguous words. What words in the judge's opinion are ambiguous? Would different interpretations of these words change the court's ruling?

ETHICAL DECISION MAKING

What values are guiding the judge's decision that the punitive damage award was excessive? Do you think that the values promoted by the decision are appropriate for the situation? Why or why not?

Even though we now have more guidance from the Court as to when punitive damages will be allowed, it is not always easy to predict what a court will do in any given case. For example, the appellate court in California upheld a $28 million punitive-damage award against Philip Morris in a case where the compensatory damages were only $850,000. The court acknowledged that under *State Farm,* there is a presumption that a ratio significantly greater than 9 to1 of punitives to compensatories violates due process, but in this case the "extreme reprehensibility" of Philip Morris's conduct in marketing its cigarettes and the "scale and profitability" of its misconduct justified the 33-to-1 ratio.[33]

Attempts to curb punitive-damage awards are being made not only in the courts but also in the legislatures with so-called tort reform legislation. The one successful piece of tort reform legislation at the national level is the Class Action Fairness Act (CAFA), signed into law by President Bush in February 2005. After many unsuccessful attempts, Congress

[33] "$28M Punitive Award Upheld in Cigarette Smoker, Recent Decisions," *Lawyer's Weekly USA,* May 8, 2006, p. 6.

finally passed CAFA, which is designed to function as a tort reform limiting the conditions under which class action suits can be brought, as opposed to limiting the damage awards under such suits. CAFA grants original jurisdiction to the federal courts over any civil action where (1) the amount in controversy is in excess of $5 million, (2) the action is brought as a "class action" with at least 100 class members, and (3) any one of the plaintiffs is a citizen of a state different from that of any defendant, and two-thirds or more of the class members and the primary defendant are not citizens of the state in which the action was filed.

Therefore, even actions originated as state actions will fall into the original jurisdiction of the federal courts if all the above criteria are met. Once in the federal courts, CAFA deems that all cases failing to meet federal requirements for class action suits will be immediately dismissed, even if previously accepted under state law. As such, CAFA is designed to limit the number of large, interstate class action suits.

Whether CAFA will fulfill this purpose is not yet certain. According to the Federal Judicial Courts Center, as recently as four months after the Class Action Fairness Act went into force, there was a sharp increase in the number of federal tort and contract class actions. After the act went into force, the number of cases removed from state court increased from 18 percent of all class actions to 23 percent. Prior to CAFA, the average number of class actions filed in federal courts was 10.48 per day; after CAFA, the number was 11.96 per day.[34]

Case Nugget — An Unusual Limitation on Punitive Damages

Crabtree v. Estate of Crabtree
837 N.E.2d 135 (Sup. Ct., Ind., 2005)

Two girls were riding with their drunken father in an automobile when he caused an accident, injuring them. A year after the accident, he died, and the girls sued his estate, seeking compensatory and punitive damages. They were awarded compensatory damages of $1,100 each, minus the amount they had received from insurance claims filed previously. The trial court judge ruled that they could not collect punitive damages from the estate because the tortfeasor was dead. The court of appeals upheld the verdict on grounds that the state legislature prohibits recovery from the estate of a deceased tortfeasor. The rationale for this rule is that the purpose of punitive damages is to punish the wrongdoer and deter similar conduct in the future, and because the tortfeasor was no longer alive, the purpose of punitive damages cannot be served. Thus, when a person has a claim against the estate of a tortfeasor, it is important to check state law to see whether punitive damages are available in such cases.

CASE OPENER WRAP-UP

The Resolution of *Rubins v. U.S. News*

Rubin is continuing with his suit against *U.S. News*. Will Rubin be able to demonstrate the elements of defamation? Under the elements of defamation, he must be able to demonstrate that he suffered financial loss because of the story.

[34] Marcia Coyle, "Class Action Changes Bring Quick Impact," *National Law Journal*, October 2, 2006, p. 6.

global context

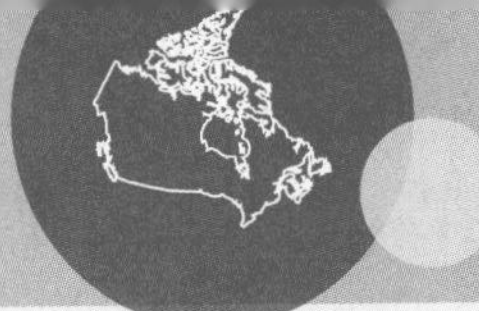

Punitive Damages in Canada

Those who believe the United States tort system is in need of reform with respect to its treatment of punitive damages may look to their Canadian neighbors with envy. Punitive-damage awards in Canada are both rare and small.

A study in 1990 reported on punitive-damage awards in Ontario. The researchers found that the highest award was $50,000. The majority of punitive-damage awards were for less than $25,000; the median award was approximately 20 percent of the compensatory-damage award in the particular case.

Following English common law, Canadian courts have traditionally restricted punitive damages to two situations: cases involving oppressive, arbitrary, or unconstitutional actions by government servants and cases in which the defendant's conduct was calculated to have made a profit in excess of compensatory damages. In 1989, the Canadian Supreme Court recognized that punitive damages could also be awarded for conduct deserving punishment because of its "harsh, vindictive, reprehensible, and malicious manner."

Two reasons seem to explain the differences in Canadian and American treatment of punitive damages. First, Canadians see something undignified about the flamboyant punitive-damage awards in the United States. Second, civil juries are much less common in Canada, and, in general, judges tend to be much more conservative than juries in making punitive-damage awards.

Perhaps when the case is decided, we will know more about whether the reporter really told Rubin he was writing an article about the Peruvian value tax or about money laundering in the gold trade. However, both parties could have worked to prevent the lawsuit by communicating more clearly. Perhaps Rubin and the author could have avoided this dispute if they had learned a little more about tort law.

Summary

Introduction to Tort Law

Tort: A civil wrong giving the injured party the right to bring a lawsuit against the wrongdoer to recover compensation for the injuries.

Goals of tort law:

1. Compensate innocent persons who are injured.
2. Prevent private retaliation by injured parties.
3. Reinforce a vision of a just society.
4. Deter future wrongs.

Classification of Torts

Intentional torts occur when the defendant takes an action intending that certain consequences will result or knowing they are likely to result.

Negligent torts occur when the defendant fails to act in a responsible way and thereby subjects other people to an unreasonable risk of harm.

Strict-liability torts occur when the defendant takes an action that is inherently dangerous and cannot ever be undertaken safely.

Intentional Torts

Intentional torts against persons:

Assault and battery
Defamation
Privacy torts
False imprisonment

Intentional infliction of emotional distress
Misuse of legal procedure

Intentional torts against property:
Trespass to realty
Private nuisance
Trespass to personalty
Conversion

Intentional torts against economic interest:
Disparagement
Intentional interference with contract
Unfair competition
Misappropriation
Fraudulent misrepresentation

Damages Available in Tort Cases

Compensatory damages: An award that puts the plaintiff in the position he or she would have been in had the tort not occurred.

Nominal damages: A minimal amount that signifies the defendant's behavior was wrongful but caused no harm.

Punitive damages: Damages that punish the defendant and deter such conduct in the future.

Point / Counterpoint

Should Punitive Damages Be More Strictly Limited?

Yes

Excessive punitive damages are fundamentally unfair.

Punitive damages are not a normal part of the tort system. Tort law is supposed to be a way to compensate victims. Punitive damages are almost quasi-criminal in nature; they are designed to punish the defendant. And they reward a plaintiff with, in some cases, riches far beyond what any reasonable person would see as compensation. Tort cases, with the possibility of huge punitive-damage awards, have turned into nothing but litigation lotteries, which have nothing to do with the purposes of our tort system.

The possibility of a huge punitive-damage award causes people to bring all sorts of loony lawsuits in hopes of striking it rich. If punitive damages were more reasonable, you would not see people, for example, suing the phone company for publishing false information about a physician that led to a botched liposuction or suing NBC for millions because a *Fear Factor* episode that involved eating rats made a viewer "dizzy and lightheaded and caused him to vomit and run into a doorway."

No

The BMW standard for excessive punitive damages strikes a fair balance, protecting the interests of both consumers and firms.

In the 20 years prior to the BMW case, courts handed down a number of huge punitive-damage awards, some even exceeding $100 million. However, in the years since the BMW case, we have seen that the court's three-pronged test has resulted in punitive-damage awards being much lower, generally staying below a 9-to-1 ratio of punitive to compensatory damages. They now appear to be much more reasonable and to fulfill their necessary function. If we examine the top 10 jury verdicts of 2005, the awards are significantly lower than those of 2004 and previous years. There is no longer any need to further limit punitive damages, as they are now reasonably related to the harm the defendant has caused and they are still large enough to deter behavior.

Punitive damages, in their current manifestation, fulfill two important functions. First, they represent an important way for a significantly harmed plaintiff to recover costs and attorney fees. Without the possibility

Besides, unfair punitive-damage awards can ruin a defendant's good name and, in some cases, run target companies out of business. We must bring fairness back to our tort system by limiting punitive damages. Sure, damage awards have fallen since the BMW and State Farm cases, but they were so exorbitant that they could hardly have gone any higher! Besides, the fact that they have fallen does not mean that they have fallen to reasonable levels.

We need more stringent standards for punitive damages to bring predictability, efficiency, and fairness to our civil justice system. We must all work together for these necessary changes.

of large punitive-damage awards, the plaintiff may not actually be compensated for his or her losses because so much of the recovery goes to the attorneys and costs of litigation.

Second, punitive damages perform a necessary deterrence function. If corporations no longer have to fear punitive-damage awards that will hurt them, they will lose some of their motivation to produce safe products and behave as responsible citizens.

With the BMW rule, as clarified by *State Farm,* we now have a system in which punitive damages can serve their intended purpose without posing an unreasonable risk to potential defendants.

Questions & Problems

1. Distinguish the three types of damages available in tort cases.
2. Explain why some people see punitive damages as a necessary aspect of our tort system, while others want to restrict their availability.
3. List five intentional torts, and explain the elements needed to prove each.
4. Thomas Gottier was a regular patron at his local Denny's restaurant, typically spending long hours drinking coffee or tea and reading. On the day in question, Gottier became impatient with the service he was receiving. Gottier searched for a manager to convey his complaint. Unable to locate a manager, Gottier saw his waiter (Bruner) and approached him. Witnesses report that Gottier approached Bruner in a rude manner, instructing him to get out of his way. When Bruner did not comply, Gottier pushed him and "kind of slapped" him in the face. Bruner responded by striking Gottier across the head with a coffee pot, causing lacerations. Gottier sued Bruner and Denny's for negligence and battery. Bruner defended his actions by claiming self-defense. Explain why you do or do not believe this defense will be successful. [*Gottier v. Denny's Restaurant,* 2001 Cal. App. LEXIS 2880.]
5. Erica Aponte, age seven, attended Thanksgiving dinner at the home of Michael and Deborah Castor, her aunt and uncle. Following dinner, Erica, accompanied by her cousin, went outside and crawled under/through an electric wire fence that enclosed Castor's horse paddock area. Erica was subsequently kicked in the face by Castor's horse, sustaining injury. Teresa Aponte, Erica's mother, filed suit against Castor, seeking damages for Erica's injuries. Castor filed a motion for summary judgment, arguing that because Erica did not have permission to leave the house or enter the paddock area, and did so without her parents' or Castor's knowledge, Erica was a trespasser and, therefore, he should not be held liable for her injuries. Aponte responded that Erica was a social guest, not a trespasser; Castor should have warned Aponte regarding the dangerous nature of the horse; and genuine issues of material fact existed that would preclude the granting of summary judgment. The trial court granted summary judgment. Aponte appealed. How did the court rule on appeal? Why? [*Aponte v. Castor,* 155 Ohio App. 3d 553 (2003).]

6. Anthony Caruso lived in Mohican Historic Housing from 1998 to 2001, when he died. Mohican Historic Housing Association was aware Margherita Del Core was Caruso's next of kin, his sister. Although Mohican had been informed Del Core was Caruso's next of kin, it did not respond to efforts by the hospital to obtain that information after his death. In the absence of that information, the hospital arranged for Caruso's burial in a pauper's grave. Four months later, Mohican informed Del Core of the death. Del Core filed suit against Mohican for, among other things, inflicting extreme emotional distress upon her by not informing her in a timely manner about her brother's death, so that she could have arranged a proper funeral. The trial court granted Mohican's motion to dismiss, and Del Core appealed. Is Mohican liable for an intentional infliction of emotional distress? Should Mohican have informed Del Core sooner regarding her brother's death? [*Del Core v. Mohican Historic Housing Assocs.*, 81 Conn. App. 120 (2004).]

7. Jamie Messenger was an aspiring 14-year-old model. *Young and Modern* magazine hired Messenger for a shoot in New York. At the shoot, she took a variety of photographs and gave consent for *YM* to use the photos, but she never obtained written consent from a parent or guardian. *YM* used the photos of Messenger to illustrate a Love Crisis column. Her pictures were next to an article describing a young woman's sexual misfortunes. The article detailed an event in which a 14-year-old got drunk and had sex with her boyfriend and two of his friends. Captions reading, "I got trashed and had sex with three guys" and "Afraid you are pregnant" accompanied her pictures. Messenger brought suit against *YM* for invasion of privacy, specifically false light. Does she have a compelling case? Why or why not? [*Messenger v. Gruner,* 94 N.Y.2d 436, 727 N.E.2d 549 (2000).]

8. South Carolina's General Assembly, in an effort to control credit fraud, passed a bill allowing the Department of Public Safety (DPS) to sell electronically stored information and photographs from driver's licenses to private companies for the limited purpose of identity verification. DPS agreed to make available to Image Data the information and photograph appearing on the face of South Carolina driver's licenses and state-issued personal identification cards. In return, Image Data agreed to pay DPS for the information and photographs. The system was to work as follows: Image Data would electronically provide an image (i.e., photograph) corresponding to the identification provided by a customer to a merchant at the point of sale; the merchant could then use the image to verify the customer's identification. Image Data operated a pilot test program of its True I.D. system, in which approximately 2,000 transactions occurred. Sloan's image was not displayed during the pilot program. Afterward, DPS terminated its contract with Image Data. The General Assembly subsequently passed another act prohibiting DPS from selling or providing a private party with Social Security numbers, photographs, or signatures taken for purposes of a driver's license or personal identification card. Mary Sloan filed suit alleging invasion of privacy through the unlawful appropriation of her driver's license information and photograph by DPS and Image Data. She also argued that DPS disclosed Social Security numbers to Image Data, as well as information from personal identification cards in addition to driver's licenses, and that Image Data intended to use the information not simply to prevent fraud but to accumulate and sell information concerning consumers' buying habits. The trial court granted DPS's motion to dismiss, and Sloan appealed. Did DPS's and Image Data's actions constitute an invasion of privacy by misappropriation of personality? Why? [*Sloan v. S.C. Dep't of Pub. Safety,* 355 S.C. 321 (2003).]

9. Mathis entered into a contract with Pacific Cornetta under which he undertook to solicit orders for Pacific Cornetta's products from retailers in return for a 5 percent commission. This contract was terminable at will by either party. The next year, Mathis entered into a one-year contract with John Evans under which Evans agreed to serve as his subagent and to solicit orders for the various products Mathis handled, including those of Pacific Cornetta, in return for a commission of 1 percent on net sales. This agreement specified that either party could terminate it only on written notice of six months. A few months after Mathis's arrangement with Evans commenced, Pacific Cornetta began to criticize Mathis to Evans and initiated efforts to persuade Evans to break his contract with Mathis. Evans ultimately entered into a contract with Pacific Cornetta to act as its sales representative, and the following day Evans terminated his contract with Mathis without having given him the required notice. Two days later, Pacific Cornetta terminated its contract with Mathis. Mathis then filed an action against Pacific Cornetta for tortious interference with contractual relations. Was Mathis successful in his suit? Why? [*Mathis v. Liu,* 276 F.3d 1027 (2002).]

10. Neurotron Inc. manufactures a medical testing device known as the Neurometer CPT. This device tests the patient's ability to feel electrical shocks delivered through the skin at a decreasing rate. Neurotron filed suit against Highmark, an operator of nonprofit health care plans. The suit alleged disparagement of its Neurometer in Highmark's company newsletter. The newsletter provides information about experimental services Highmark will, or will not, cover for its members. Neurotron requested that Highmark review Neurotron's CPT. On the basis of this review, Highmark concluded, "CPT was investigational and therefore not covered." Highmark wrote, "The neuro-selective current perception threshold test is performed to provide an objective measure of subjective sensation. It requires the patient's conscious perception of the stimulation applied. The neuro-selective current perception threshold test has no proven clinical utility and is not eligible for payment, since it is considered to be investigational." On the basis of this statement, Neurotron filed a disparagement suit. Though the company was not specifically named in the review, Neurotron claimed that the reasonable reader would know Highmark was referring to its CPT. Using your knowledge of what constitutes a tort of disparagement, predict the outcome of this case and explain your reasoning. [*Neurotron v. Medical Service Assoc.,* 254 F.3d 44, 2001 U.S. App. LEXIS 13757.]

11. In 1997 an Alaskan citizen contacted the Alaska Department of Health to inquire about the health implications of ozone-generating air purifiers. The Health Department asked Dr. Lori Feyk to investigate the possible health risks and report back. After researching the topic, she was asked to prepare a report of her findings as a health bulletin to distribute. The bulletin, entitled "Ozone Generators—Warning—Not for Occupied Spaces," stated that ozone "is a potent lung irritant that can cause respiratory distress, and levels of ozone that clean air effectively are unsafe to human health." Further, the bulletin cited a Minnesota case in which the state found Alpine Industries, an ozone-generator producer, "guilty of fraud and antitrust laws by making false and misleading claims about the efficacy and safety of ozone-generating Alpine purifiers." Alpine Industries filed suit against Feyk for libel. Create a defense for Feyk in this suit. [*Alpine Industries v. Feyk,* 22 P.3d 445 (2001).]

12. Katherina LeDoux was an EMT for the Tess Corners Volunteer Fire Department, which responded to an emergency 911 call at the Pachowitz residence regarding

an overdose or possible overdose. After completing the EMT response, LeDoux returned home and later spoke to a friend, Sally Slocomb, to discuss the fact that she had assisted in transporting Pachowitz to the hospital emergency room for a possible overdose. While LeDoux had never met Pachowitz before the EMT response, LeDoux had learned about Pachowitz and her medical condition from a conversation with Slocomb and another woman. LeDoux had also learned that Slocomb worked with Pachowitz and that Slocomb and Pachowitz were very close friends. LeDoux placed the telephone call to Slocomb after the EMT emergency response because she was concerned about Pachowitz and thought Slocomb could possibly be of assistance to Pachowitz. Following LeDoux's telephone call, Slocomb drove to the hospital, where she revealed the EMT response to the Pachowitz home and discussed Pachowitz's situation with other staff. Pachowitz filed suit against LeDoux, alleging LeDoux had defamed her and violated her privacy by publicizing information concerning her medical condition and making untrue statements indicating she had attempted suicide. The matter proceeded to trial, and the jury held LeDoux liable for violating Pachowitz's right of privacy by publicizing a matter concerning her private life. LeDoux appealed. Should LeDoux be held liable for her comments? Why? [*Pachowitz v. LeDoux,* 2003 WI App. 120 (2003).]

13. Michael Buchanan went shopping in Maxfield Enterprises Inc.'s store, which is located on Melrose Avenue in Los Angeles. Buchanan did not know, at the time he entered the store, that celebrities Jennifer Lopez and Ben Affleck were also in the store, shopping. Less than 20 minutes after Buchanan entered the store, Maxfield store manager Jacqueline Sassoon asked Buchanan to leave the store. When Buchanan asked Sassoon for an explanation, she refused to give a reason. When Buchanan became angered, Maxfield store security placed him under a citizen's arrest. Two local sheriff's deputies, on hand because of Affleck and Lopez, handcuffed Buchanan and escorted him into the Maxfield parking lot. Because of the presence of Lopez and Affleck, the parking lot was "thronged" with TV and other media reporters and film crews. Buchanan was led, handcuffed, straight into the media circus. After Buchanan was walked around the store parking lot, Sassoon told the deputies she did not want Buchanan arrested after all. The deputies removed the handcuffs and Buchanan was free to leave. Excerpts from television and print media purported to report that a stalker had shadowed Lopez and Affleck in the Maxfield store and the stalker was removed from the scene by police officers who had responded to a call from the store about the stalker. Buchanan sued Maxfield for invasion of privacy, alleging that the defendant invaded his right to privacy by parading him, handcuffed, before the media and, as a result of this, that he suffered injury to his reputation, as well as mental anguish and emotional distress. Buchanan also sued for false imprisonment and intentional infliction of emotional distress. Maxfield filed a motion to dismiss, which was granted by the trial court. Buchanan appealed. Was Buchanan successful on appeal? What must he prove to be successful in his claims? [*Buchanan v. Maxfield Enterprises, Inc.,* 130 Cal. App. 4th 418 (2005).]

Looking for more review material?

The Online Learning Center at **www.mhhe.com/kubasek1e** contains this chapter's "Assignment on the Internet" and also a list of URLs for more information, entitled "On the Internet." Find both of them in the Student Center portion of the OLC, along with quizzes and other helpful materials.

Negligence and Strict Liability

CASE OPENER

Tort Liability for the Boy Scouts of America?

Numerous boys have brought suits against the Boy Scouts of America.[1] These boys were sexually molested by their respective scout masters. These molestations occurred on officially sanctioned scouting events, such as on overnight camping trips or at week-long Boy Scout camps.

The boys argue that the Boy Scouts had a duty of care to protect its members from being molested by scout leaders. In other words, they argue that the Boy Scouts, as an organization, should have been aware that young scouts are vulnerable to molestation and that it should have taken steps to protect the scouts. The boys see the organization's failure to do so as negligence.

In response, the Boy Scouts of America argues that molestation by particular scout leaders was not foreseeable; thus, the organization believes it did not have a duty of care to protect scouts from molestation.

[1] Kevin Livingston, "Panel OKs Boy Scout Molest Suit," *The Recorder,* May 15, 2000, p.1; Theodore Postel, "Boy Scout Alleges Molestation," *Chicago Daily Law Bulletin,* February 7, 2000, p.1; and *"Doe v. Boy Scouts of America," Connecticut Law Tribune,* February 15, 1999.

CHAPTER 9

1. Suppose you are the judge in this case. Do you think that the Boy Scouts has a duty of care to protect its scouts from molestation by scout leaders? Why or why not?
2. Now suppose you are the manager of a day care facility. You hear about the cases against the Boy Scouts. Do you need to be concerned about similar charges against your day care facility? Why or why not?

The Wrap-Up at the end of the chapter will answer these questions.

Learning Objectives

After reading this chapter, you will be able to answer the following questions:

1 What are the elements of negligence?

2 What are the doctrines that help a plaintiff establish a case of negligence?

3 What are the defenses to a claim of negligence?

4 What are the elements of strict liability?

Introduction to Negligence and Strict Liability

In the previous chapter we discussed intentional torts, wrongs in which an individual took an action that he or she should have known would harm another person. In this chapter, we consider two other types of torts: negligent and strict-liability torts. These torts are generally committed when an individual fails to maintain a duty of care to another individual. Thus, the Boy Scouts could potentially be held liable if the organization owed the boys a duty of care that it failed to meet.

Suppose Ross uses a piece of wood to smack Joey, the mailman, on the face. Ross has committed battery. If Ross is building a tree house in his yard, however, and accidentally drops a piece of wood on Joey, who is delivering Ross's mail, Ross's action lacks intent, so there is no battery. Yet he might be negligent.

Allegations of negligence are made in a wide variety of circumstances. For example, people have alleged negligence when incidents of teenage violence occurred. The parents of Marcos Delgado, Jr., filed a claim of negligence against a movie theater when it admitted 13-year-old Raymond Aiolentuna without an adult to the R-rated movie *Dead Presidents.* After the movie, Aiolentuna emerged from the theater, walked one block, and shot Delgado. Delgado's parents argued that the movie theater was negligent because it did not enforce the movie ratings system. The court, however, ruled in favor of the movie theater.[2] In another instance, the families of the victims of the 1999 Columbine school shootings in Colorado sued the two alleged shooters and the gun manufacturer for negligence. What exactly is required to establish a successful negligence claim?

In this chapter, we begin by examining the elements of negligence. Then we consider the methods that courts have adopted to help plaintiffs make successful negligence claims. Next, we examine the defenses that defendants to negligence claims can raise. Finally, we consider strict-liability torts.

Elements of Negligence

Negligence is behavior that creates an unreasonable risk of harm to others. In contrast to intentional torts, which result from a person's willfully taking actions that are likely to cause injury, negligent torts involve the failure to exercise reasonable care to protect another's person or property.

Sometimes, however, harm occurs because an individual suffers an **unfortunate accident,** an incident that simply could not be avoided, even with reasonable care. For example, suppose Jonathan is driving on the highway when he suffers a stroke. Because of the stroke, he crashes into two other vehicles. He is not, however, liable for damages caused by the accident. Yet if Jonathan had some type of warning that the stroke was going to occur, he might be liable for the accident.

To win a negligence case, the plaintiff must prove four elements: (1) duty, (2) breach of duty, (3) causation, and (4) damages. (See Exhibit 9-1.) A plaintiff who cannot establish all four of these elements will be denied recovery.

Exhibit 9-1
Elements of Negligence

To prove negligence, a plaintiff must demonstrate:

1. Duty
2. Breach of duty
3. Causation
4. Damages

[2] *Delgado v. American Multi-Cinema Inc.*, 99 C.D.O.S. 4772, Los Angeles Superior Court (1999).

DUTY

The plaintiff must first establish that the defendant owes a *duty* to the plaintiff. In some particular situations, the law specifies the duty of care one individual owes to another. In most cases, however, the courts use the reasonable person standard to determine the defendant's duty of care. The **reasonable person standard** is a measurement of the way members of society expect an individual to act in a given situation. To determine the defendant's duty of care, the judge or jury must determine the degree of care and skill that a reasonable person would exercise under similar circumstances. The judge or jury then uses this standard to evaluate the actions of the individual in the case.

Let's return to the Boy Scouts of America case in the opening scenario. Do you think a reasonable person owed the boys a duty of care?

When courts attempt to determine whether a reasonable person would have owed a duty to others, they consider four questions:

1. How likely was it that the harm would occur?
2. How serious was the harm?
3. How socially beneficial was the defendant's conduct that posed the risk of harm?
4. What costs would have been necessary to reduce the risk of harm?

In many situations, it is far from clear what a reasonable person would do. For example, if a reasonable person saw an infant drowning in a shallow swimming pool, what would she do? In most situations like this one, the law holds that individuals have no duty to rescue strangers from perilous situations.

In some cases, however, the courts hold that individuals have a duty to aid strangers in certain types of peril. For example, if Sam negligently hits Janice with his car and, as a result, Janice is lying in the street, Sam has a duty to remove her from that dangerous position. Similarly, employers have a special duty to protect their employees from dangerous situations.

The courts generally hold that landowners have a duty of care to protect individuals on their property. Similarly, businesses have a duty of care to customers who enter business property. It is important, therefore, for future business managers to be knowledgeable about this duty. Businesses should warn customers about risks they may encounter on business property. Some risks, however, are obvious, and businesses need not warn customers about them. For example, a business need not inform customers that they could get a paper cut from the pages of a book.

The courts generally hold that businesses have a duty of care to protect their customers against foreseeable risks about which the owner knew or reasonably should have known. For example, in *Haywood v. Baseline Construction Company,* a woman who tripped over lumber on the front porch of the House of Blues restaurant in Los Angeles sued for negligence. The business's attempt to warn customers by marking the lumber with yellow construction tape was insufficient to avoid the determination of negligence; the woman was awarded $91,366 in damages.

Case 9-1 considers the issue of when a person owes a duty to another.

Professionals have more training than ordinary people. Thus, when professionals are serving in their professional capacity, courts generally hold that they have a higher duty of care to clients than does the ordinary person. A professional cannot defend against a negligence suit by claiming ignorance of generally accepted principles in her or his field of expertise. Clients who feel that they have suffered damages as a result of a professional's breach of her duty of care can bring a negligence case against her. These actions are referred to as *malpractice cases,* and they are discussed in greater detail in Chapter 11.

CASE 9-1 ROLAND C. FEICHTNER v. CITY OF CLEVELAND ET AL.

COURT OF APPEALS OF OHIO, EIGHTH APPELLATE DISTRICT, CUYAHOGA COUNTY
95 OHIO APP. 3D 388 (1994)

On April 13, 1991, Roland Feichtner was driving south on Interstate 77 in Cleveland, Ohio. A portion of I-77 was being resurfaced by Kenmore Construction Company. Traffic on I-77 South was diverted to the extreme right lane and the berm of the highway. Feichtner was driving on the berm. When he passed under an overpass on I-77, a fourteen pound sandstone rock crashed through the windshield on the passenger side of the vehicle. Feichtner's wife was killed. When the police investigated the death, they discovered that Ronald Jackson had thrown a rock that he had obtained from a nearby construction site off the bridge, and this rock was the one that crashed through Feichtner's window. Jackson was indicted for the murder of Feichtner's wife.

During Jackson's pending hearings, Feichtner filed a negligence claim against Cleveland and five construction companies. He argued that their negligence was the proximate cause of his wife's death. Feichtner claimed that the construction companies "knew or should have known" of the hazard of leaving debris near the bridge. The construction companies denied liability and filed a motion for summary judgment. They argued that Feichtner could not demonstrate the element of duty. The trial court granted the construction company's motions for summary judgment, stating that Feichtner failed to establish a duty toward Feichtner's wife. Feichtner appealed.

JUDGE NAHRA: When the defendants furnish evidence which demonstrates the plaintiff has not established the elements necessary to maintain his negligence action, summary judgment is properly granted in favor of defendants.

As to the elements of a cause of action in negligence it can be said that "[i]t is rudimentary that in order to establish actionable negligence, one must show the existence of a duty, a breach of the duty, and an injury resulting proximately therefrom." Thus, the existence of a duty is fundamental to establishing actionable negligence. If there is no duty, then no legal liability can arise on account of negligence. Where there is no obligation of care or caution, there can be no actionable negligence. Only when one fails to discharge an existing duty can there be liability for negligence.

A review of the evidence before the trial court in this case leads to the conclusion appellant did not establish the elements necessary to maintain his negligence action. The evidence reveals appellees owed no special duty toward appellant's wife and, furthermore, any negligence on their part was not the proximate cause of her death.

That conclusion is supported by a review of the Ohio Supreme Court's opinion in *Fed. Steel & Wire Corp. v. Ruhlin Constr. Co.* (1989). Ruhlin is particularly applicable to this case because of the similarity of certain facts.

In Ruhlin, a construction company had undertaken repairs of the Lorain-Carnegie bridge in Cleveland. The court noted that "[f]rom the very beginning of the project," Ruhlin was aware of "severe theft and vandalism problems," including specific instances of vandals throwing construction materials off the bridge. . . . When work on the project was shut down for the winter, . . . Ruhlin left a quantity of construction materials on the bridge, stopped posting security guards, and replaced the barbed wire fencing with a simple barricade and a snow fence.

Over the winter, Federal, which occupied a building directly beneath the construction area, suffered significant damage to its building from vandals throwing Ruhlin's construction materials off the bridge. Federal instituted an action against Ruhlin; however, eventually, the trial court granted Ruhlin's motion for a directed verdict with a finding that Ruhlin owed no duty to Federal.

> Ordinarily, there is no duty to control the conduct of a third person by preventing him or her from causing harm to another, except in cases where there exists a special relationship between the actor and the third person which gives rise to a duty to control, or between the actor and another which gives the other the right to protection. Thus, liability in negligence will not lie in the absence of a special duty owed by a particular defendant.

. . . We recognize that there is no common-law duty to anticipate or foresee criminal activity. Thus, the law usually does not require the prudent person to expect the criminal activity of others. As a result, the duty to protect against injury caused by third parties, which may be imposed where a special relationship exists, is expressed as an exception to the general rule of no liability.

The existence of such a "special" duty depends on the foreseeability of the injury. . . . This court has held the foreseeability of criminal acts will depend upon the knowledge of the defendant-business, which must be determined from the totality of the circumstances. Only when the totality of the circumstances are "somewhat overwhelming" will a defendant-business be held liable for the criminal acts of a third party. The rationale for this rule is stated thus:

> In delimiting the scope of duty to exercise care, regard must be had for the probability that injury may result from the act complained of. No one is bound to take care to prevent consequences, which, in the light of human experience, are beyond the range of probability.

It was this standard which led the Supreme Court in Ruhlin to conclude a special duty was owed by Ruhlin to Federal under the circumstances of that case. The court stated the rationale of its decision thus:

> [I]f a person exercises control over real or personal property and such person is aware that the property is subject to repeated third-party vandalism, causing injury to or affecting parties off the controller's premises, then a special duty may arise to those parties whose injuries are reasonably foreseeable, to take adequate measures under the circumstances to prevent future vandalism.

In this case, however, no such "overwhelming" circumstances exist. Appellant presented no evidence from which to conclude that an exception to the general rule of no liability had been established which created a special duty on the part of appellees.

The evidence demonstrated the construction debris generated by the companies was not on the Fleet Avenue bridge as alleged in appellant's complaint. Rather, it was on a site at least twenty-five to thirty yards away from the bridge. The evidence further demonstrated that, contrary to the allegations of the complaint, prior to the incident there were no documented reports that persons were taking the construction debris and then transporting it to the bridge to throw it off. The only evidence on this point was a statement made in his deposition by one of the company owners that such a thing occurring was within the realm of possibility. This was insufficient to create a special duty on appellee's part.

Furthermore, there was no evidence that any of the appellees failed to comply with any safety regulations. Therefore, no liability in tort on this basis was established.

Accordingly, appellant's assignment of error is overruled. The judgment of the trial court is affirmed.

AFFIRMED.

CRITICAL THINKING

The court uses an analogy in this case to reach its conclusion. It compares the current case to the case of *Federal Steel & Wire Corp. v. Ruhlin Construction Company.* How strong is this analogy?

Do you think there are any differences in the two cases that the court is ignoring? If so, why are these differences important?

ETHICAL DECISION MAKING

Return to the WPH process of ethical decision making. Identify the purpose of the court's decision.

What value is the court particularly upholding in its decision that the City of Cleveland was not negligent?

e-commerce AND THE LAW

Negligence on the Internet

A commonly offered explanation for the increasing occurrence of violence is the increased violence portrayed in the media. Some plaintiffs try to hold owners of certain Web sites liable under negligence theories for violent acts committed by teenagers. For example, in *James v. Meow Media,* a 14-year-old boy took six guns to school and shot three of his classmates to death. The parents of the deceased classmates brought suit against several Internet Web sites and the creators and distributors of various video games. The parents argued that these defendants had a duty of ordinary care to the slain girls.

The courts have been consistent, however, in finding that it was not foreseeable that a boy who played certain video games and viewed certain Web sites would murder three of his classmates. In similar cases, courts have ruled that defendants (such as Web-site owners, creators and distributors of video games, and directors and producers of movies) do not have a duty to protect a person from the criminal acts of a third party unless there is a special relationship that requires that the defendant act with that duty.

Although it appears that Web-site owners, manufacturers, and producers will not be held liable, plaintiffs continue to bring suits against these groups of people. Can you think of an argument for why these groups of people might owe a duty of care to these plaintiffs?

BREACH OF DUTY

Once the plaintiff has established that the defendant owes her a duty of care, she must prove that the defendant's conduct violated that duty. This violation is called a *breach of duty.* For example, the driver of an automobile owes the other passengers in his car a duty of care to obey traffic signs. If he fails to stop at a stop sign, he has violated his duty to follow traffic signs and has therefore breached his duty of care.

CAUSATION

Causation is the third element of a successful negligence claim, and it has two separate elements: actual cause and proximate cause. The plaintiff must prove both elements of causation to be able to recover damages.

The first element, **actual cause** (also known as *cause in fact*) is the determination that the defendant's breach of duty resulted directly in the plaintiff's injury. The courts commonly determine whether a breach of duty actually caused the plaintiff's injury by asking whether the plaintiff would have been injured if the defendant had fulfilled his or her duty. If the answer is no, then the actual cause of the plaintiff's injury was the defendant's breach. Actual cause is sometimes referred to as "but-for" causation because the plaintiff argues that the damages she suffered would not have occurred *but for* (except because of) the actions of the defendant.

Proximate cause, sometimes referred to as *legal cause,* refers to the extent to which, as a matter of policy, a defendant may be held liable for the consequences of his actions. In most states, proximate cause is determined by foreseeability. Proximate cause is said to exist only when both the plaintiff and the plaintiff's damages were reasonably foreseeable at the time the defendant breached his duty to the plaintiff. Thus, if the defendant could not reasonably foresee the damages that the plaintiff suffered as a result of his action, the plaintiff's negligence claim will not be sustained because it lacks the element of proximate causation.

For example, if a defective tire on a vehicle blows out, it is foreseeable that the driver may lose control and hit a pedestrian. It is not foreseeable, however, that the pedestrian may be a scientist carrying a briefcase full of chemicals that may explode on impact, causing a third-floor window to shatter, injuring an accountant at his desk. In most states, the accountant would not succeed if he sued the tire manufacturer for negligence. The tire failure is not considered a proximate cause of the accountant's injury because the contents of the pedestrian's briefcase were highly unusual. The pedestrian, however, would be eligible to recover damages from the tire manufacturer because hitting a pedestrian is a foreseeable consequence of tire failure. Thus, the defect in the tire is a proximate cause of the pedestrian's injury.

Let's return to the Boy Scout scenario from the beginning of this chapter. The Boy Scouts of America argued that specific cases of molestation are not foreseeable. Do you think a scout's molestation is foreseeable?

Palsgraf v. Long Island Railroad Company is one of the most well-known cases addressing the issue of proximate cause (see Case 9-2).

CASE 9-2 PALSGRAF v. LONG ISLAND RAILROAD COMPANY
NEW YORK COURT OF APPEALS
248 N.Y. 33 (1928)

Mrs. Palsgraf was waiting for a train on a platform of a railroad. When a different train came into the station, two men ran to get on that train before it left the station. While one of the men safely reached the train, the other man, who was carrying a package, jumped on the already moving train but seemed as though he was going to fall off the train. The guard on the moving train tried to help pull the man on the train, while another guard off of the train pushed the man from behind. Consequently, his small package wrapped in newspaper, which contained fireworks, fell upon the rails, causing the fireworks to explode. The shock of the explosion dislodged scales at the other end of the platform, and the falling scales hit Mrs. Palsgraf, causing injuries for which she brought suit against the railroad.

JUDGE CARDOZO: Nothing in the situation gave notice that the falling package had in it the potency of peril to persons thus removed. Negligence is not actionable unless it involves the invasion of a legally protected interest, the violation of a right. "Proof of negligence in the air, so to speak, will not do." If no hazard was apparent to the eye of ordinary vigilance, an act innocent and harmless, at least to outward seeming, with reference to her, did not take to itself the quality of a tort because it happened to be a wrong, though apparently not one involving the risk of bodily insecurity, with reference to someone else. "In every instance, before negligence can be predicated of a given act, back of the act must be sought and found a duty to the individual complaining, the observance of which would have averted or avoided the injury." "The ideas of negligence and duty are strictly correlative" (Bowen, L. J., in *Thomas v. Quartermaine,* 18 Q. B. D. 685, 694).

The argument for the plaintiff is built upon the shifting meanings of such words as "wrong" and "wrongful," and shares their instability. What the plaintiff must show is "a wrong" to herself, i.e., a violation of her own right, and not merely a wrong to someone else, nor conduct "wrongful" because unsocial, but not "a wrong" to any one. We are told that one who drives at reckless speed through a crowded city street is guilty of a negligent act and, therefore, of a wrongful one irrespective of the consequences. Negligent the act is, and wrongful in the sense that it is unsocial, but wrongful and unsocial in relation to other travelers, only because the eye of vigilance perceives the risk of damage. If the same act were to be committed on a speedway or a race course, it would lose its wrongful quality. . . . [W]rong is defined in terms of the natural or probable, at least when unintentional (*Parrot v. Wells-Fargo Co.* [The Nitro-Glycerine Case], 15 Wall. [U.S.] 524). . . . Here, by concession, there was nothing in the situation to suggest to the most cautious mind that the parcel wrapped in newspaper would spread wreckage through the station. If the guard had thrown it down knowingly and willfully, he would not have threatened the plaintiff's safety, so far as appearances could warn him. His conduct would not have involved, even then, an unreasonable probability of invasion of her bodily security. Liability can be no greater where the act is inadvertent.

Negligence, like risk, is thus a term of relation. Negligence in the abstract, apart from things related, is surely not a tort, if indeed it is understandable at all. . . .

[CONTINUED]

Negligence is not a tort unless it results in the commission of a wrong, and the commission of a wrong imports the violation of a right, in this case, we are told, the right to be protected against interference with one's bodily security. But bodily security is protected, not against all forms of interference or aggression, but only against some. One who seeks redress at law does not make out a cause of action by showing without more, that there has been damage to his person. If the harm was not willful, he must show that the act as to him had possibilities of danger so many and apparent as to entitle him to be protected against the doing of it, though the harm was unintended. Affront to personalty is still the keynote of the wrong.

The law of causation, remote or proximate, is thus foreign to the case before us. The question of liability is always anterior to the question of the measure of the consequences that go with liability. If there is no tort to be redressed, there is no occasion to consider what damage might be recovered if there were a finding of a tort.

REVERSED AND COMPLAINT DISMISSED.

CRITICAL THINKING

Why does the court believe that Mrs. Palsgraf should not be awarded damages? Are you persuaded by these reasons? Why or why not?

ETHICAL DECISION MAKING

Think about the WPH process of ethical decision making. It may seem unfair that Mrs. Palsgraf was unable to collect damages for her injuries. Study the list of values or purposes for a decision. Which value do you think the court was upholding through its decision? Which value is in conflict with this favored value? With which value do you most agree?

The decision in *Palsgraf* set out the rule of foreseeability that is followed by most states today. However, a different definition of proximate cause is followed in a small minority of states. Courts in a few states do not distinguish actual cause from proximate cause. In these states, if the defendant's action constitutes an actual cause, it is also considered the proximate cause. Therefore, in these few states, both the pedestrian-scientist and the third-floor accountant would be able to recover damages from the tire manufacturer in the previous example.

DAMAGES

Damages are the final required element of a negligence action. The plaintiff must have sustained compensable injury as a result of the defendant's actions. Because the purpose of tort law is to compensate individuals who suffer injuries as a result of another's action or inaction, a person cannot bring an action in negligence seeking only nominal damages. Rather, a person must seek **compensatory damages,** or damages intended to reimburse a plaintiff for her or his losses.

In typical negligence cases, courts rarely award **punitive damages,** or *exemplary damages,* which are imposed to punish the offender and deter others from committing similar offenses. Instead, courts usually award punitive damages in cases in which the offender has committed **gross negligence,** an action committed with extreme reckless disregard for the property or life of another person.

global context

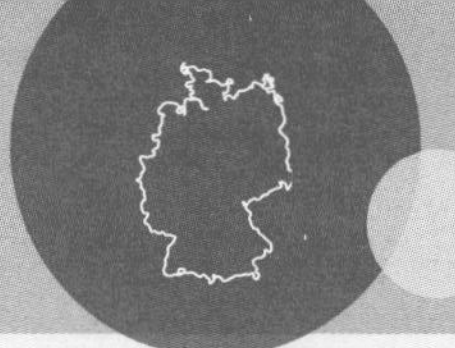

Negligence in Germany

German law is concerned with the defendant's ability to foresee, understand, and avoid danger. Both mental and physical capabilities are taken into account. For example, the duty-of-care standard stipulates that "physical and mental disabilities or defects, panic, or confusion" exempt the defendant from being found negligent. Also, though the distinction is not recognized by a statute, the courts distinguish between conscious and unconscious negligence. *Conscious negligence* requires knowledge that the offense is about to occur and that it is an actual offense. *Unconscious negligence* occurs when the defendant is either unaware that the act constitutes an offense or unaware that the act is occurring at all. In such cases, the defendant is found not guilty by reason of unconscious negligence.

Plaintiff's Doctrines

The plaintiff has the burden of proving all four elements of a negligence case. Direct evidence of negligence by the defendant, however, is not always available. For example, there may have been no witnesses to the negligent conduct and other evidence may have been destroyed. Therefore, two doctrines have been adopted by courts to aid plaintiffs in establishing negligence claims: *res ipsa loquitur* and negligence per se.

RES IPSA LOQUITUR

Res ipsa loquitur literally means "the thing speaks for itself." The plaintiff uses this doctrine to allow the judge or jury to infer that more likely than not, the defendant's negligence was the cause of the plaintiff's harm, even though there is no direct evidence of the defendant's lack of due care. To establish *res ipsa loquitur* in most states, the plaintiff must demonstrate that:

1. The event was a kind that ordinarily does not occur in the absence of negligence.
2. Other responsible causes, including the conduct of third parties and the plaintiff, have been sufficiently eliminated.
3. The indicated negligence is within the scope of the defendant's duty to the plaintiff.

Proof of these three elements does not require a finding of negligence, however; it merely permits it. Once the plaintiff has demonstrated these three elements, the burden of proof shifts to the defendant, who must prove that he was not negligent to avoid liability.

One of the earliest uses of *res ipsa loquitur* was the case of *Escola v. Coca Cola.*[3] In that case, the plaintiff, a waitress, was injured when a bottle of Coca-Cola that she was removing from a case exploded in her hand. From the facts that (1) bottled soft drinks ordinarily do not spontaneously explode and (2) the bottles had been sitting in a case, undisturbed, in the restaurant for approximately 36 hours before the plaintiff simply removed the bottle from the case, the jury reasonably inferred that the defendant's negligence in the filling of the bottle resulted in its explosion. The plaintiff therefore recovered damages without direct proof of the defendant's negligence. Plaintiffs in numerous accident cases have subsequently used the doctrine where there has been no direct evidence of negligence. The defendant's best response to this doctrine is to demonstrate other possible causes of the accident.

Case 9-3 illustrates a plaintiff's attempt to use *res ipsa loquitur.*

[3] 24 Cal. 2d 453 , 150 P.2d 436 (1944).

CASE 9-3 JANET KAMBAT v. ST. FRANCIS HOSPITAL ET AL.
COURT OF APPEALS OF NEW YORK
89 N.Y.2D 489 (1997)

In August 1986, at St. Francis Hospital, Dr. Ralph Sperrazza performed an abdominal hysterectomy on Florence Fenzel. During the operation, ten laparotomy pads were available for use. Dr. Sperrazza placed several of these pads inside the defendant, next to the bowel. A few months following the operation, Fenzel began to complain of stomach pain. Approximately three months after the operation, x-rays of Fenzel's abdomen revealed a foreign object in her abdomen. A few days later, Dr. Robert Barone discovered that the foreign object partially or fully inside her bowel was an 18-by-18-inch laparotomy pad similar to the one used during Fenzel's hysterectomy. Barone removed the object. Fenzel's condition continued to worsen, and she died later that month due to infection-related illness.

Fenzel's family sued the hospital for negligence in leaving the laparotomy pad inside Fenzel. During the trial, Fenzel's family produced evidence that the abdominal pads were available only in operating rooms, where patients could not access them. Three experts testified for Fenzel's family, arguing about the precise location of the pad inside the bowel. In contrast, the hospital argued that standard procedures were followed during the operation and all pads and medical instruments were counted after the operation. Furthermore, the hospital argued that laparotomy pads were left in places accessible to plaintiffs. Thus, the hospital claimed that the plaintiff swallowed the pad.

The trial court refused to allow Fenzel's family to use res ipsa loquitur during the trial, and the jury ruled in favor of the hospital. The trial court argued that res ipsa loquitur was not applicable because lengthy and inconsistent expert testimony was not within the experience of a layperson. The appellate court agreed with the trial court's refusal to allow res ipsa loquitur.

JUDGE KAYE: Where the actual or specific cause of an accident is unknown, under the doctrine of *res ipsa loquitur* a jury may in certain circumstances infer negligence merely from the happening of an event and the defendant's relation to it. *Res ipsa loquitur* "simply recognizes what we know from our everyday experience: that some accidents by their very nature would ordinarily not happen without negligence." . . .

Once a plaintiff's proof establishes the following three conditions, a prima facie case of negligence exists and plaintiff is entitled to have *res ipsa loquitur* charged to the jury. First, the event must be of a kind that ordinarily does not occur in the absence of someone's negligence; second, it must be caused by an agency or instrumentality within the exclusive control of the defendant; and third, it must not have been due to any voluntary action or contribution on the part of the plaintiff.

To rely on *res ipsa loquitur,* a plaintiff need not conclusively eliminate the possibility of all other causes of the injury. It is enough that the evidence supporting the three conditions afford a rational basis for concluding that "it is more likely than not" that the injury was caused by defendant's negligence; otherwise, all that is required is that the likelihood of other possible causes of the injury "be so reduced that the greater probability lies at defendant's door." . . . *Res ipsa loquitur* thus involves little more than application of the ordinary rules of circumstantial evidence to certain unusual events, and it is appropriately charged when, "upon 'a commonsense appraisal of the probative value' of the circumstantial evidence, . . . [the] inference of negligence is justified."

Submission of *res ipsa loquitur,* moreover, merely permits the jury to infer negligence from the circumstances of the occurrence. The jury is thus allowed—but not compelled—to draw the permissible inference. In those cases where "conflicting inferences may be drawn, choice of inference must be made by the jury." . . .

In the typical *res ipsa loquitur* case, the jury can reasonably draw upon past experience common to the community for the conclusion that the adverse event generally would not occur absent negligent conduct. In medical malpractice cases, however, the common knowledge and everyday experience of lay jurors may be inadequate to support this inference. . . . Courts in this State have differed as to whether expert testimony can supply the necessary foundation for consideration of *res ipsa loquitur* by a jury.

Widespread consensus exists, however, that a narrow category of factually simple medical malpractice cases requires no expert to enable the jury reasonably to conclude that the accident would not happen without negligence. Not surprisingly, the oft-cited example is where a surgeon leaves a sponge or foreign object inside the plaintiff's body. As explained by Prosser and Keeton in their classic treatise:

> There are, however, some medical and surgical errors on which any layman is competent to pass judgment and conclude from common experience that such things do not happen if there has been proper skill and care. When an operation leaves a sponge or implement in the patient's interior, . . . the thing speaks for itself without the aid of any expert's advice.

Manifestly, the lay jury here did not require expert testimony to conclude that an 18-by-18-inch laparotomy pad is not ordinarily discovered inside a patient's abdomen following a hysterectomy in the absence of negligence. Thus, plaintiffs' undisputed proof that this occurred satisfied the first requirement of *res ipsa loquitur.*

Turning to these remaining *res ipsa loquitur* conditions, plaintiffs' evidence that similar pads were used during decedent's surgery, that decedent was unconscious throughout the operation, that laparotomy pads are not accessible to patients, and that it would be anatomically impossible to swallow such pads sufficed to allow the jury to conclude that defendants had exclusive control of the laparotomy pad "at the time of the alleged act of negligence" and that it did not result from any voluntary action by the patient.

We agree with the Appellate Division dissenters, moreover, that defendants' evidence tending to rebut the three conditions did not disqualify this case from consideration under *res ipsa loquitur.* Plaintiffs were not obligated to eliminate every alternative explanation for the event. Defendants' evidence that they used due care and expert testimony supporting their competing theory that decedent might have had access to laparotomy pads and inflicted the injury upon herself by swallowing the pad merely raised alternative inferences to be evaluated by the jury in determining liability. The undisputed fact remained in evidence that a laparotomy pad measuring 18 inches square was discovered in decedent's abdomen: "From this the jury may still be permitted to infer that the defendants' witnesses are not to be believed, that something went wrong with the precautions described, that the full truth has not been told." Thus, the inference of negligence could reasonably have been drawn "upon 'a commonsense appraisal of the probative value' of the circumstantial evidence," and it was error to refuse plaintiffs' request to charge *res ipsa loquitur.*

REVERSED.

CRITICAL THINKING

What evidence does the court give for its conclusion that the plaintiffs could have used *res ipsa loquitur?* Are you persuaded by this evidence? Why or why not?

ETHICAL DECISION MAKING

Suppose you were a business manager for the hospital when this case was first brought to the hospital's attention. The plaintiffs' attorney has contacted you, claiming that the doctor in this case was negligent. The attorney argues that the hospital should pay the plaintiff family in an attempt to compensate for the doctor's negligence. Suppose your actions are guided by the public disclosure test. What would your response to the plaintiff family be?

connecting to the core

Personal Taxation and Accounting

One topic discussed in personal income tax and some accounting classes is the tax consequences of getting a damages award. These consequences depend on the type of damages received. The damages a plaintiff receives as compensation for loss of income are generally taxed as ordinary income. The damages a plaintiff receives as compensation for damaged or destroyed property are taxed as if the amount were received in a sale or exchange of the property, and thus the recipient realizes a gain if the damage payments received exceed the property's basis. Punitive damages are always treated as ordinary income because they are not designed to compensate the plaintiff for any loss but, rather, will put the victim in a better economic position than he or she was in before the tort occurred.

Compensatory damages for physical personal injury or physical sickness, however, can be excluded from gross income, including amounts received for loss of income associated with the injury or sickness. However, compensatory damages awarded because of emotional distress are not considered to be in that category, and so they cannot be excluded.

Source: William Hoffman, Jr., et al., *Individual Income Taxes 2006* (Thomson, 2006), pp. 6–11.

NEGLIGENCE PER SE

Negligence per se (literally, "negligence in or of itself") is another doctrine that helps plaintiffs succeed in negligence cases. Negligence per se applies to cases in which the defendant has violated a statute enacted to prevent a certain type of harm from befalling a specific group to which the plaintiff belongs. If the defendant's violation causes the plaintiff to suffer from the type of harm that the statute intends to prevent, the violation is deemed negligence per se. The plaintiff does not have to show that a reasonable person would exercise a certain duty of care toward the plaintiff. Instead, the plaintiff can offer evidence of the defendant's violation of the statute to establish proof of the negligence.

For example, if Ohio passes a statute prohibiting the sale of alcohol to minors, and a minor runs a red light and kills two pedestrians while driving under the influence of alcohol sold to him illegally, the liquor store's violation of the statute prohibiting the sale of alcohol to minors establishes negligence per se on the part of the store. The families of the pedestrians do not need to establish that a reasonable person would have a duty not to sell alcohol to a minor. The Case Nugget provides another illustration of negligence per se.

Case Nugget — A Clear Illustration of Negligence Per Se

O'Guin v. Bingham County
122 P.3d 308 (Sup. Ct., Id., 2005)

Shaun and Alex O'Guin cut across a field on their way home from school and entered the back of a landfill that was not fenced off, despite a law that required it to be fenced. A portion of a wall of the landfill collapsed, killing the boys. The boys' parents sued the county that operated the landfill, alleging that failure to have the landfill properly fenced constituted negligence per se.

The court agreed, explaining that the following four elements of negligence per se had been met: (1) The statute or regulation clearly defines the required standard of conduct, (2) the statute or regulation must have been intended to prevent the type of harm the defendant's act or omission caused, (3) the plaintiff must be a member of the class of persons the statute or regulation was designed to protect, and (4) the violation must have been the proximate cause of death.

global context

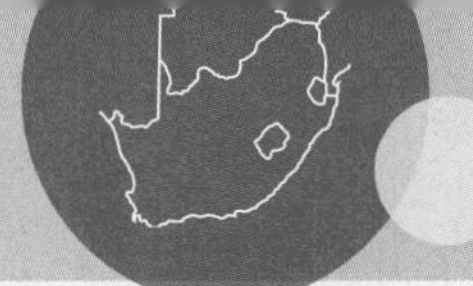

Negligence in South African Law

South Africa's legal system is a combination of selected legal traditions—from Roman to Dutch to German. The Roman *actiones legis Aquiliae* influences South Africa's statutes concerning liability. Under this Roman tradition, certain cases concerning liability mandate the presence of *culpa,* or negligence. South African law dictates that individuals can be found negligent in three different ways.

Negligence is first defined as failure to observe an accepted standard of conduct. In other words, individuals must exercise care and foresight with regard to others. A failure to do so indicates negligent behavior. Second, negligence is determined by whether the defendant could have prevented the consequent damages. The law expects individuals to take precautions to avoid harm or damage. Finally, South African law outlines the extent to which one can be found negligent in a crisis situation. In such instances, individuals have a duty to do what is "reasonably" expected. Because of the obvious ambiguity associated with this definition, South African law cites the American "doctrine of sudden emergency" as a standard for determining negligence in crisis situations. Encompassing all three of these definitions is an implicit duty of the individual to take precautions to prevent harm.

A defendant who complies with legislative statutes, however, can still be held liable if a reasonable person would have exercised a more stringent duty of care toward the plaintiff. The legislative statutes are minimum, not sufficient, standards for behavior.

Before examining the defenses against negligence claims, compare the definition of negligence in the United States with its definition in South Africa, as described in the Global Context box.

SPECIAL PLAINTIFF'S DOCTRINES AND STATUTES

In addition to recognizing *res ipsa loquitur* and negligence per se, some states have established other doctrines or statutes to aid plaintiffs in negligence suits. For example, suppose an airplane taxiing at Reagan National Airport in the winter runs off the runway and into the Potomac River due to the negligence of the airline. Some bystanders observe the crash and jump into the water to rescue the crash survivors. If any of the bystanders are injured while attempting to rescue the survivors, many courts will hold the airline liable for their injuries under what is known as the *danger invites rescue* doctrine.

Many states have also enacted statutes to aid plaintiffs in successfully establishing specific kinds of negligence claims. For instance, many states have **dram shop acts,** which allow bartenders and bar owners to be held liable for injuries caused by individuals who become intoxicated at the bar. Other states have passed laws that hold hosts liable for injuries caused by individuals who became intoxicated at the hosts' homes.

Defenses to Negligence

The courts' doctrines of *res ipsa loquitur* and negligence per se help the plaintiff in a negligence case, but the courts permit certain defenses that relieve the defendant from liability even when the plaintiff has proved all four elements of negligence. Defendants can successfully rebut negligence claims with contributory negligence, comparative negligence, assumption of the risk, and other special negligence defenses.

CONTRIBUTORY NEGLIGENCE

Contributory negligence, a defense once available in all states but replaced today in some states by the defense of comparative negligence (discussed in the next section), applies in cases in which the defendant and the plaintiff were both negligent. The defendant must prove that (1) the plaintiff's conduct fell below the standard of care needed to prevent unreasonable risk of harm and (2) the plaintiff's failure was a contributing cause to the plaintiff's injury. How can defendants use contributory negligence in a case? Some defense lawyers argue that if a plaintiff involved in a car accident failed to wear her seatbelt, that failure constitutes contributory negligence because her action contributed to her injuries.

If the defendant successfully proves contributory negligence, no matter how slight the plaintiff's negligence, the plaintiff will be denied any recovery of damages. Because this defense seems unfair, many states have adopted the **last-clear-chance doctrine.** This doctrine allows the plaintiff to recover damages despite proof of contributory negligence as long as the defendant had a final clear opportunity to avoid the action that injured the plaintiff.

For example, suppose that Samantha and Nicole, in their cars, are facing each other while stopped at a red light. The light turns green, and Nicole starts to turn left at the intersection. Samantha sees Nicole start to turn, but she still continues to travel straight through the intersection and crashes into Nicole's car. Although Samantha had the right-of-way at the intersection, she could have avoided hitting Nicole's car by braking or swerving. Thus, according to the last-clear-chance doctrine, Nicole could recover damages.

COMPARATIVE NEGLIGENCE

The adoption of the last-clear-chance doctrine, however, leaves many situations in which an extremely careless defendant can cause a great deal of harm to a plaintiff who is barred from recovery due to minimal contributory negligence. Thus, most states have replaced the contributory negligence defense with either pure or modified comparative negligence.

According to a **pure comparative negligence** defense, the court determines the percentage of fault of the defendant. The defendant is then liable for that percentage of the plaintiff's damages.

Courts calculate damages according to **modified comparative negligence** in the same manner, except that the defendant must be more than 50 percent at fault before the plaintiff can recover.

Twenty-eight states have adopted modified comparative negligence, thirteen have adopted pure comparative negligence, and nine have adopted contributory negligence. Every state has adopted one of these three defenses. Thus, the parties to a negligence suit cannot choose among them.

ASSUMPTION OF THE RISK

Another defense available to defendants facing negligence claims is called **assumption of the risk.** To use this defense successfully, a defendant must prove that the plaintiff voluntarily and unreasonably encountered the risk of the actual harm the defendant caused. In other words, the plaintiff willingly assumed as a risk the harm she suffered. There are two types of this defense. *Express assumption of the risk* occurs when the plaintiff expressly agrees (usually in a written contract) to assume the risk posed by the defendant's behavior. In contrast, *implied assumption of the risk* means that the plaintiff implicitly assumed a known risk.

The most difficult part of establishing this defense is showing that the plaintiff assumed the risk of the *actual* harm she suffered. A 1998 case against the Family Fitness Center illustrates an unsuccessful attempt to use assumption of the risk as a defense against a negligence claim.[4] In that case, the plaintiff was injured when a sauna bench on which he was lying collapsed beneath him at the defendant's facility. The trial court granted summary

[4] *Leon v. Family Fitness Center, Inc.*, 61 Cal. App. 4th 1227 (1998).

judgment in favor of the defendant on the basis of assumption of the risk. The plaintiff had signed a contract that included the following provision: "Buyer is aware that participation in a sport or physical exercise may result in accidents or injury, and Buyer assumes the risk connected with the participation in a sport or exercise and represents that Member is in good health and suffers from no physical impairment which would limit their use of FFC's facilities." The appellate court overturned the trial court's decision because the type of injury the plaintiff suffered was not the type of risk he had assumed. The court held that anyone signing a membership agreement could be deemed to have waived any hazard known to relate to the use of the health club facilities, such as the risk of a sprained ankle due to improper exercise or overexertion, a broken toe from a dropped weight, injuries due to malfunctioning exercise or sports equipment, or injuries from slipping in the locker-room shower. No patron, however, could be charged with realistically appreciating the risk of injury from simply reclining on a sauna bench. Because the collapse of a sauna bench, when properly used, is not a "known risk," the court concluded that the plaintiff did not assume the risk of this incident as a matter of law.

Case 9-4 illustrates the successful use of assumption of the risk as a defense. Compare this case to the action against the Family Fitness Center to see whether you agree with the different outcomes in the two cases.

CASE 9-4 | EX PARTE EMMETTE L. BARRAN III
SUPREME COURT OF ALABAMA
730 SO. 2D 203 (1998)

When Jason Jones enrolled at Auburn University in 1993, he chose to become a pledge of the Kappa Alpha fraternity. Within two days, Jones began to experience hazing by fraternity members. Hazing activities included the following: (1) digging a ditch and jumping into it after it was filled with water, urine, feces, dinner leftovers, and vomit; (2) receiving paddlings to his buttocks; (3) eating foods such as peppers, hot sauce, and butter; (4) being pushed and kicked; (5) doing chores for fraternity members; (6) appearing at 2 a.m. "meetings" where pledges would be hazed for several hours; and (7) "running the gauntlet," in which pledges would run down a hallway and flight of stairs while fraternity members would push, kick, and hit them. Although Jones was aware that 20–40% of the pledges dropped out of the pledge program, Jones remained in the program until he was suspended from the university for poor academic performance. In 1995, Jones sued the national and local Kappa Alpha organization, alleging negligence, assault and battery, negligent supervision, and various other claims. He argued that he suffered "mental and physical injuries" as a result of the hazing. For the negligence claims, the trial court granted summary judgment for Kappa Alpha. The trial court argued that Jones assumed the risk of hazing because he voluntarily entered the organization and could have quit at any time. Jones appealed, and the Court of Civil Appeals reversed the negligence ruling, reasoning that the peer pressure associated with fraternity life prevented Jones from voluntarily withdrawing from the pledge class. Kappa Alpha appealed.

JUSTICE SEE: Assumption of the risk has two subjective elements: (1) the plaintiff's knowledge and appreciation of the risk; and (2) the plaintiff's voluntary exposure to that risk. . . . [I]n order to find, as a matter of law, that Jones assumed the risk, this Court must determine that reasonable persons would agree that Jones knew and appreciated the risks of hazing and that he voluntarily exposed himself to those risks.

First, KA and its members argue that Jones knew and appreciated the risks inherent in hazing. . . . Jones's deposition indicates that before he became a KA pledge he was unfamiliar with the specific hazing practices engaged in at KA, but that the hazing began within two days of his becoming a pledge; that despite the severe and continuing nature of the hazing, Jones remained a pledge and continued to participate in the hazing activities for a full academic year; that Jones knew and appreciated that hazing was both illegal and against school rules; and that he repeatedly helped KA cover up the hazing by lying about its occurrence to school officials, his doctor, and even his own family. Given Jones's early introduction to the practice of hazing and its hazards, and in light of his own admission that he realized that hazing would continue to occur, the trial court correctly determined that reasonable people would conclude that Jones knew of and appreciated the risks of hazing.

Second, in addition to establishing that Jones both knew of and appreciated the risk, KA and the individual defendants argue that Jones voluntarily exposed himself to the hazing. Jones responds by arguing that a coercive environment hampered his free will to the extent that he could not voluntarily choose to leave the fraternity. The Court of Civil Appeals, in reversing the summary judgment as to KA and the individual defendants, stated that it was not clear that Jones voluntarily assumed the risk of hazing, because, that court stated:

> In today's society, numerous college students are confronted with the great pressures associated with fraternity life and . . . compliance with the initiation requirements places the students in a position of functioning in what may be construed as a coercive environment.

With respect to the facts in this case, we disagree. . . . The record indicates that Jones voluntarily chose to continue his participation in the hazing activities. After numerous hazing events, Jones continued to come back for more two o'clock meetings, more paddlings, and more gauntlet runs, and did so for a full academic year. Auburn University officials, in an effort to help him, asked him if he was being subjected to hazing activities, but he chose not to ask the officials to intervene. Jones's parents, likewise acting in an effort to help him, asked him if he was being subjected to hazing activities, but he chose not to ask his parents for help.

Moreover, we are not convinced by Jones's argument that peer pressure created a coercive environment that prevented him from exercising free choice. Jones had reached the age of majority when he enrolled at Auburn University and pledged the KA fraternity. We have previously noted: "College students and fraternity members are not children. Save for very few legal exceptions, they are adult citizens, ready, able, and willing to be responsible for their own actions." Thus, even for college students, the privileges of liberty are wrapped in the obligations of responsibility.

Jones realized that between 20% and 40% of his fellow pledges voluntarily chose to leave the fraternity and the hazing, but he chose to stay. See Prosser & Keeton, The Law of Torts 491 ("Where there is a reasonably safe alternative open, the plaintiff's choice of the dangerous way is a free one, and may amount to assumption of the risk. . . ."). As a responsible adult in the eyes of the law, Jones cannot be heard to argue that peer pressure prevented him from leaving the very hazing activities that, he admits, several of his peers left.

Jones's own deposition testimony indicates that he believed he was free to leave the hazing activities:

> *Q:* You didn't have to let this [hazing] happen to you, did you?
>
> *A:* No.
>
> *Q:* And you could have quit at any time?
>
> *A:* Yes.
>
> *Q:* But yet you chose to go through with what you have described here in your complaint with the aspirations that you were going to become a brother in the Kappa Alpha Order? You were willing to subject yourself to this for the chance to become a member of the brotherhood . . . were you not?
>
> *A:* Yes.

We conclude that Jones's participation in the hazing activities was of his own volition. The trial court correctly determined that reasonable people could reach no conclusion other than that Jones voluntarily exposed himself to the hazing.

REVERSED AND REMANDED.

CRITICAL THINKING

Is there any important missing information that might influence your thinking about the court's conclusion that Jones participated in the hazing activities of his own volition? Why is this missing information important?

[CONTINUED]

ETHICAL DECISION MAKING

Return to the WPH process of ethical decision making. Which stakeholders are affected by the court's decision? Why are these people affected?

SPECIAL DEFENSES TO NEGLIGENCE

Many states have additional ways to defend against a claim of negligence. For example, laws in some states hold that people in peril who receive voluntary aid from others cannot hold those offering aid liable for negligence. These laws, commonly called **Good Samaritan statutes,** attempt to encourage selfless and courageous behavior by removing the threat of liability.

The defendant in a negligence suit can also avoid liability by establishing a superseding cause. A *superseding cause* is an unforeseeable event that interrupts the causal chain between the defendant's breach of duty and the damages the plaintiff suffered. For example, suppose Jennifer is improperly storing ammonia in her garage when a meteor strikes her garage, spilling the ammonia into a stream nearby. Will, living downstream, drinks water from the stream and becomes dangerously ill. Because the meteor was unforeseeable, Jennifer is not liable for Will's injuries, even though she breached her duty of care to Will.

Superseding causes allow the defendant to avoid liability because they are evidence that the defendant's breach of duty was not the proximate cause of the plaintiff's injuries. In other words, superseding causes disprove the causation element necessary to sustain a negligence claim.

STRICT LIABILITY

Strict liability is liability without fault. The law holds an individual liable without fault when the activity in which she engages satisfies three conditions: (1) It involves a risk of serious harm to people or property; (2) it is so inherently dangerous that it cannot ever be safely undertaken; and (3) it is not usually performed in the immediate community. Instead of banning these activities, the law allows people to engage in such activities but holds them liable for all resulting harm.

Inherently dangerous activities include dynamite blasting in a populated area and keeping animals that have not been domesticated. If an animal has shown a "vicious propensity," strict liability applies and the owner of the animal is responsible for any injuries suffered in an attack by the animal.[5] If an individual keeps an animal that has not shown vicious propensity, he has a duty to warn and protect individuals who come into contact with the animal. Case 9-5 illustrates an application of strict liability in regard to injuries caused by animals.

As you will see in the next chapter, in today's society, strict liability has had an enormous impact on cases involving unreasonably dangerous products.

[5] *Schwartz v. Armand ERPF Estate,* 688 N.Y.S.2d 55 (Sup. Ct., App. Div., N.Y., 1999).

CASE 9-5 GREGORY SCORZA v. ALFREDO MARTINEZ AND WORLDWIDE PRIMATES, INC.

COURT OF APPEAL OF FLORIDA, FOURTH DISTRICT
683 SO. 2D 1115 (1996)

When Hurricane Andrew hit South Florida in August 1992, a number of primates whose cages were damaged escaped from Worldwide Primates, a breeder of monkeys and other primates. One of the escaped primates, a macaque monkey, was captured by Mr. Gomez, who then sold the monkey to Alfredo Martinez. Martinez sold the monkey to Gregory Scorza, who purchased the monkey for use in his business, which entailed photographing people with exotic animals. Martinez told Scorza that the monkey was a capuchin monkey and "a sweetheart." Scorza paid Martinez $500 and took the monkey home. When Scorza tried to remove the monkey from its cage, however, the monkey bit him. Scorza then took the monkey to a veterinarian, who told Scorza that the monkey was a macaque monkey, a breed of monkey known for carrying the hepatitis-B virus. The veterinarian notified the Florida Game and Fresh Water Fish Commission about the monkey. Later, the Commission returned the monkey to Worldwide.

Scorza brought a claim of negligence and strict liability against Worldwide. Scorza argued that Worldwide, as the owner of the monkey, was strictly liable for any injuries caused by the monkey. Worldwide argued that because Scorza purchased the monkey from Martinez, it was no longer the owner of the animal and thus not strictly liable for injuries. The trial judge ordered summary judgment in Worldwide's favor.

JUDGE STEVENSON: The owner, keeper, or possessor of a wild animal is strictly liable if the animal injures another. Furthermore, "if the animal is one of a class that is not indigenous to the locality, its escape does not prevent its possessor from being liable for the harm done by the animal no matter how long after its escape; in this case the risk of liability continues until some third person takes possession of the animal." Scorza had taken possession of the monkey at the time of the injury, and for the purposes of strict liability, Worldwide was not responsible for the monkey at that time. Therefore, the trial court was correct in granting summary judgment in favor of Worldwide on the strict liability count.

AFFIRMED.

CRITICAL THINKING

Are there any potentially ambiguous words or phrases used in the court's reasoning? How do these words or phrases affect the court's conclusion?

ETHICAL DECISION MAKING

If you were a business manager at Worldwide Primates, you would be very happy with this decision. Which other stakeholders would be happy with this decision? Which stakeholders might be unhappy? Why?

Defendants in strict-liability suits have several defenses available to them. Although contributory negligence is not available to defendants in strict-liability claims, defendants in some states can argue that the plaintiff was comparatively negligent and thus reduce their liability. Moreover, assumption of the risk is also an allowable defense.

CASE OPENER WRAP-UP

Boy Scouts of America

The courts have been divided in deciding whether the Boy Scouts organization has a duty of care to its scouts. At least two courts have ruled that Boy Scouts owes a duty of care to protect its scouts from sexual molestation. One of these courts cited the high incidence of sexual abuse in scouting as evidence for its conclusion that Boy Scouts has a duty of care. At least one court, however, has disagreed, holding that there is no duty of care because the molestation was not foreseeable. Which court is correct? Remember that tort law is basically state law, and so it is possible that we will never have agreement among all the states on this issue. Whatever each state's supreme court holds in response to the issue determines the law in that state.

What can the Boy Scouts and similar groups do to protect themselves from liability? First, the Boy Scouts can conduct better screenings of those who wish to serve as scout leaders. If a scout leader had a history of sexual misconduct and the Boy Scouts did not look at his background, the courts would be more likely to hold the Boy Scouts liable. Until the courts reach a consensus as to whether the Boy Scouts owes a duty of care to protect its scouts from sexual molestation, the organization may wish to behave as though there is a duty of care.

Summary

Introduction to Negligence and Strict Liability	When an individual fails to maintain a duty of care to protect other individuals, negligence and strict liability may occur.
Elements of Negligence	*Duty:* The standard of care that the defendant (i.e., a reasonable person) owes the plaintiff.
	Breach of duty: The defendant's lack of maintaining the standard of care a reasonable person would owe the plaintiff.
	Causation: The defendant's conduct (breach of duty) led to the plaintiff's injury.
	Damages: The plaintiff suffered compensable injuries.
Plaintiff's Doctrines	*Res ipsa loquitur:* Doctrine that permits the judge or jury to *infer* that the defendant's negligence was the cause of the plaintiff's harm in cases in which there is no direct evidence of the defendant's lack of due care.
	Negligence per se: Doctrine that permits a plaintiff to prove negligence by offering evidence of the defendant's violation of a statute that has been enacted to prevent a certain type of harm.
Defenses to Negligence	*Contributory negligence;* A defense that allows the defendant to entirely escape liability by demonstrating any degree of negligence on the part of the plaintiff that contributed to the plaintiff's harm.
	Comparative negligence; A defense that allows the liability to be apportioned between plaintiff and defendant in accordance with the degree of responsibility each bears for the harm suffered by the plaintiff.
	Assumption of the risk: A defense that allows the defendant to escape liability by establishing that the plaintiff engaged in an activity fully aware that the type of harm he or she suffered was a possible consequence of engaging in that activity.

Strict Liability Persons who engage in activities that are so inherently dangerous that no amount of due care can make them safe are strictly liable, regardless of the degree of care they used when undertaking the activity.

Point / Counterpoint

Should Negligence Law Hold All Individuals to the "Reasonable Person" Standard?

No

One major problem with the reasonable person standard is that it fails to set up clear rules to which individuals can conform their behavior. "Reasonableness" varies tremendously from one person to another; what one person considers reasonable, another considers unnecessary. Unclear laws also discourage efficiency because both the plaintiff and the defendant may believe they are likely to be victorious in court and thus have little incentive to settle. When the law is clear, individuals have a better idea of the strength of their case, and those with poor chances of victory have an incentive to settle and thereby avoid costly litigation expenses.

In addition, the reasonable person standard holds all individuals to the same duty of care, regardless of their individual characteristics. This standard is unfair to individuals who exercise all the possible care of which they are capable yet whose level of care still does not meet the reasonable person standard. Alternatively, individuals can exercise levels of care that they know create a substantial likelihood of harm to others yet the care satisfies the reasonable person standard. Thus, the reasonable person standard functions like a regressive tax. To promote fairness to all defendants, tort law ought to take into account individualized factors. Instead of asking whether the defendant has behaved reasonably, the law ought to ask whether the defendant has behaved reasonably given his or her individual characteristics, including age, education, gender, wealth, and so on.

Yes

The law should certainly concern itself with fairness to defendants, but that concern is only half the story. The law also ought to concern itself with fairness to plaintiffs. A plaintiff who gets run over by a high school dropout is no less injured than a plaintiff who gets run over by a professor. Yet an individualized negligence standard might allow the second plaintiff to recover but not the first. Civil society requires a certain absolute level of care from all its members, regardless of their individual predispositions.

Moreover, a more individualized standard in negligence law would tend to decrease, not increase, the clarity of the law. An injured defendant would have to ascertain the plaintiff's individual characteristics to determine the likelihood of victory in court, and more variables mean more uncertainty. Who owes a higher standard of care: a college-educated yet poor defendant or a high school–educated yet rich defendant? If the law wants to promote uniformity, consistency, and stability, it ought to use a uniform standard, not a more individualized one.

Finally, it is not clear how individualized characteristics of a defendant would count. How does a defendant's gender affect the standard of care to which the law will hold him or her? If females are held to a different standard of care than men, is the law making a statement about the relative reasonableness of men and women?

Questions & Problems

1. List and define the elements that are necessary to prove a case of negligence.
2. Explain the differences between contributory and comparative negligence.
3. Explain the relationship between negligence per se and *res ipsa loquitur.*
4. What are dram shop statutes?
5. Explain the purpose of Good Samaritan statutes.
6. List and describe the elements that must be proved for a successful strict-liability claim.
7. James Napoli and Kurt Buckholz were both attending Camp Alvernia. The two boys were preparing for a game of baseball, and Buckholz was swinging a bat on the sidelines to warm up. He accidentally hit Napoli in the jaw with the bat. Napoli's mother brought an action against the camp to recover damages for Napoli's injuries. The defendants argued that by voluntarily allowing her son to participate in the camp's sporting activities, Napoli's mother assumed the risk of Napoli's incurring an injury. Do you think that danger is inherent in the game of baseball? How would this affect the court's decision? [*Napoli v. Mount Alvernia, Inc.*, 657 N.Y.S.2d 197 (1997).]
8. Dr. Robert Lee Berry worked for Lakeview Anesthesia Associates but was fired when Lakeview discovered that he was practicing medicine under the influence of narcotics. Berry sought employment elsewhere and obtained a job as an anesthesiologist at Kadlec Medical Center. Kadlec hired Berry in part due to positive written employment references from Lakeview, which did not disclose Berry's drug problem. Then, while under the influence of narcotics, Berry improperly administered an anesthetic to a patient, causing her to suffer extensive brain damage. The patient's family brought a successful malpractice suit against Kadlec. Kadlec, in turn, brought a negligence suit against Lakeview, alleging that Lakeview breached its duty to disclose Berry's prior adverse employment history. How do you think the court ruled in this case? Why? [*Kadlec Med. Ctr. v. Lakeview Anesthesia Assocs.*, 2005 U.S. Dist. LEXIS 9221 (2005).]
9. Eileen Hennessey resided in a condominium that bordered the Louisquisset Golf Club. Hennessey reported that golf balls pelted her home every year when the golf season resumed. On a Sunday afternoon, Hennessey was in her garden reading and enjoying the outdoors when a stray golf ball struck her in the side of her head, causing injury. Pyne, the golfer who hit the ball, was fully aware of the proximity of Hennessey's home to the course, as well as her usual presence on her property. Hennessey filed suit, claiming negligence on Pyne's behalf for failure to yell "fore," or give any other warning, after seeing his ball veer off course. Pyne filed a motion for summary judgment. Why is the defense of assumption of the risk relevant or irrelevant to this case? [*Hennessey v. Pyne,* 694 A.2d 691 (Sup. Ct. R.I., 1997).]
10. While visiting a horse ranch with his parents, a four-year-old boy crawled under an electric fence to see the horses. Once the boy was in the enclosure, one of the horses kicked the boy in the head, causing severe brain damage. The boy's parents filed a negligence action against the owners of the horse and ranch. What rules of liability

are applicable to this case? Construct arguments for both the plaintiff and the defendants in this case. [*Schwartz v. Armand ERPF Estate,* 255 A.D.3d 35, 688 N.Y.S.2d 55 (1999).]

11. At 7:30 p.m. on February 3, 1995, Mary Ann Eckstein was driving her vehicle along a windy, unlit stretch of road. Ahead of her, Joan Sandow had parked her car on the left side of the street to distribute materials into the mailboxes on the right. Sandow was wearing dark clothes and a black raincoat. Eckstein was driving down the roadway using her high beams and slowed down when she saw Sandow's car on the side of the road. Eckstein then felt her car hit something and stopped to investigate. After she exited the car, she saw Sandow in the road. Sandow filed a negligence claim against Eckstein, seeking compensatory damages. Eckstein responded to the suit by alleging contributory negligence. The plaintiff responded by arguing that motorists have an added duty of care for pedestrians. The trial court found for Sandow. How do you think the appellate court found? What is the basis for your decision? [*Sandow v. Eckstein,* 67 Conn. App. 243 (2001).]

12. David Burton smoked Camel cigarettes for 43 years, and, in 1993, he developed serious circulatory problems in his legs. His doctor informed him that smoking was causing his circulatory problems. Two other doctors confirmed his doctor's diagnosis and recommended vascular bypass surgery, which Burton underwent unsuccessfully. After the operation, Burton had both of his legs amputated below the knee. Burton brought suit against the R. J. Reynolds Tobacco Company, alleging that the company negligently failed to warn him of the health hazards caused by smoking. R. J. Reynolds argued that it did not have a duty to warn Burton of the hazards that smoking posed to his health. What do you think? Should R. J. Reynolds be found negligent? Why? [*Burton v. R. J. Reynolds Tobacco Co.,* 397 F.3d 906 (2005).]

13. Plaintiff Artlip was using the pool facility at her apartment. She was drinking a glass of wine when she noticed that a bee was flying too close to her. When Artlip tried to avoid the bee by stepping back, her foot was caught in a hole on the deck. The hole was intentionally made and allowed for a tree to grow through the deck. Artlip argued that the hole was a result of poor maintenance of the pool area and brought a suit against her landlord. She alleged that the landlord was negligent because the deck was not properly maintained and the hole was not clearly marked. The landlord demonstrated that Artlip was very familiar with the pool area. His maintenance supervisor testified that the deck was in good condition and had been inspected on many occasions by the county inspector. Do you think the court found the landlord's behavior to be negligent? [*Artlip v. Queler,* 470 S.E.2d 260 (1996).]

14. Ginger Klostermeier was a regular customer of the In & Out Mart in Lucas County, Ohio. On May 29, 1998, she went to the store to purchase lottery tickets but fell immediately upon entering the door. The clerk helped Klostermeier up, and Klostermeier made her purchase. Klostermeier was later treated for injuries sustained to her upper body, including a broken left arm. Klostermeier suffered from multiple sclerosis, although it was in remission at the time of her fall. Examination of and research into the door revealed that the closer had been replaced on November 3, 1997, and that the door Klostermeier had used to enter the store took an average of 1.602 seconds to close. This is in noncompliance with the Americans with Disabilities Act, which states that doors must have a minimum closing time of three seconds to accommodate persons with disabilities. Klostermeier sued the store and the installer of the door closer. One of Klostermeier's claims was negligence per se, because the door violated the Americans with Disabilities Act. The trial court and the court of

appeals both ruled that the store was not guilty of negligence per se, though for different reasons. Can you articulate possible reasons why violation of the Americans with Disabilities Act does not constitute negligence per se? [*Ginger R. Klostermeier v. In & Out Mart, Inc., et al.*, 2001 Ohio App. LEXIS 1499 (2001).]

15. Paula Baddeaux was riding in a pickup truck with her fiancé Dave Zeringue. The rear tire on Zeringue's pickup truck blew out, and the poor road conditions resulted in the truck's flipping over. Both Baddeaux and Zeringue were seriously injured. They filed suit against the Department of Transportation and Development (DOTD), and a trial judge found the DOTD 75 percent responsible for the accident. Baddeaux was awarded $308,825.85. The DOTD appealed the trial judge's decision, arguing that Baddeaux's overweight condition contributed to the costliness of her recovery. Baddeaux had a history of weight problems, and at the time of the accident she weighed over 200 pounds. She sustained serious knee injuries, and in failing to follow her doctor's recommendation to lose weight, Baddeaux made the knee injuries difficult and costly to treat. Do you think this was sufficient to warrant comparative negligence? Why or why not? [*Baddeaux v. State of Louisiana Department of Transportation and Development,* 690 So. 2d 203 (1997).]

Looking for more review material?

The Online Learning Center at **www.mhhe.com/kubasek1e** contains this chapter's "Assignment on the Internet" and also a list of URLs for more information entitled "On the Internet." Find both of them in the Student Center portion of the OLC, along with quizzes and other helpful materials.

Product Liability

CASE OPENER

Ford and Bridgestone/Firestone

Donna Bailey was paralyzed from the neck down after her friend's Ford Explorer, in which she was a passenger, rolled over. The tread on one of the tires on the Explorer, a Firestone tire, had separated. Bailey brought suit against both Ford and Bridgestone/Firestone after the March 2000 accident. In August 2000, Bridgestone/Firestone recalled millions of its tires due to concerns about deaths following tread separations. The Firestone tire on Bailey's friend's Explorer was not one of the tires named in the original Firestone recall.

Bailey was not the only injured party to file suit against Ford or Bridgestone/Firestone. In fact, several lawsuits against those companies are pending. One of Bailey's attorneys characterized the highly publicized problems as the "largest vehicular product liability crisis in the history of this country." In June 2001, a motion in a class action case filed by a number of owners of Explorers asked the judge to order a recall of all Explorers made between 1990, the first year that the model was produced, and the end of 2000.

1. What do you think the outcome of Bailey's case was?
2. What can Ford and Bridgestone/Firestone do about the other pending lawsuits?
3. How do product liability issues affect you?

The Wrap-Up at the end of the chapter will answer these questions.

Learning Objectives

After reading this chapter, you will be able to answer the following questions:

1. What are the theories of liability in product liability cases?
2. What is market share liability?

CHAPTER 10

PART ONE

The Legal Environment of Business

Breast implants, Fen-Phen, Ford Explorers, cigarettes, fast food, fingers in fast food—all of these topics have been the subject of product liability suits. According to the National Center for State Courts, about 40,000 product liability cases are filed annually in state courts. Moreover, Jury Verdict Research reported that the overall median compensatory award for product liability cases tried before juries between 1993 and 2002 was $700,000. If a company manufactures or sells a product, it should expect to be a party to a product liability lawsuit.

In this chapter, we examine the legal theories commonly used by plaintiffs in product liability cases, along with some of the defenses that are used against these cases. By understanding the law of product liability, you may be less likely to take actions that would lead you and your company into costly litigation.

Theories of Liability for Defective Products

Product liability law is based primarily on tort law. There are three commonly used theories of recovery in product liability cases: negligence, strict product liability, and breach of warranty. A plaintiff may bring a lawsuit based on as many of these theories of liability as apply to the plaintiff's factual situation. However, under any of these theories, the plaintiff must generally show two common elements: (1) that the product is defective, and (2) that the defect existed when the product left the defendant's control.

How might a product be defective? Suppose you select a glass bottle of Diet Coke at the grocery store. When you grab the bottle, it shatters in your hand and severely cuts your thumb. Most bottles of soda do not shatter when touched; thus, there must have been a problem in the manufacture of this particular bottle. When an individual product (e.g., the shattered Diet Coke bottle) has a defect making it more dangerous than the other identical products (the 200 other Diet Coke bottles at the grocery store), this individual product has a **manufacturing defect.**

Given your severe cut from the Diet Coke bottle, you get into your car to drive to the hospital. Unfortunately, someone rear-ends your car; the crash causes your driver's seat to bend backward such that you hit your head on the backseat and suffer a serious neck injury. The design of the driver's seat allowed the seat to bend backward, and all driver's seats in this type of car have the same design. When all products of a particular design are defective and dangerous, these products have a **design defect.**

Because of the pain associated with your neck injury and lacerated thumb, you take a new over-the-counter pain reliever. You follow the instructions on the box and take two pills. However, you begin to feel incredibly ill. You rush to the hospital to discover that you are experiencing negative side effects from the pain reliever because it has interacted with some of your other medications. You had carefully read the instructions and warnings, but you did not see anything about drug interactions. A product may be defective if a manufacturer **fails to provide adequate warnings** about potential dangers associated with the product.

In summary, a product may be defective because of a manufacturing defect, a design defect, or inadequate warnings. As you read the chapter, think about how these types of defects fit in with the theories of liability.

NEGLIGENCE

To win a case based on negligence, the plaintiff must prove the four elements of negligence explained in Chapter 9: (1) The defendant manufacturer or seller owed a duty of care to the plaintiff; (2) the defendant breached that duty of care by supplying a defective product; (3) this breach of duty caused the plaintiff's injury; and (4) the plaintiff suffered actual injury.

Prior to the landmark 1916 case of *MacPherson v. Buick Motor Co.*, negligence was rarely used as a theory of recovery for an injury caused by a defective product because

Case Nugget The Famous Case of the McDonald's Coffee Spill

Liebeck v. McDonald's Corp.

One of the most famous product liability cases is the McDonald's coffee-cup case. Stella Liebeck, a 79-year-old woman, spilled a cup of McDonald's coffee in her lap. She sued McDonald's, and in 1994, a jury awarded her almost $3 million in damages. Many people cite the case as an example of the need for product liability law reform; however, they either intentionally or inadvertently omit a discussion of the facts of the case:

- Liebeck spilled the entire cup of coffee in her lap. McDonald's required that its franchises serve coffee at 180 to 190 degrees Fahrenheit. Liquid at this high temperature causes third-degree burns in two to seven seconds. Liebeck suffered third-degree burns on her skin that required skin grafting. She was in the hospital for eight days and required two years of treatment for the burns.
- Liebeck asked McDonald's to cover her medical costs of $20,000; McDonald's offered to settle for $800. She filed the lawsuit after McDonald's refused to raise its offer from $800.
- Through documents produced by McDonald's, Liebeck discovered that between 1982 and 1992, McDonald's had received over 700 complaints about the temperature of the coffee. Some of these complaints discussed burns in varying degrees of severity.
- While the jury awarded Liebeck $200,000 in compensatory damages and $2,700,000 in punitive damages, the court reduced the damages award to $160,000 in compensatory damages and $480,000 in punitive damages.

How do these facts affect your thinking about product liability law?

of the difficulty of establishing the element of duty. Until that case, the courts said that a plaintiff who was not the purchaser of the defective product could not establish a duty of care, because one could not owe a duty to someone with whom one was not "in privity of contract." Being *in privity of contract* means being a party to a contract. Because most consumers do not purchase goods directly from the manufacturers, product liability cases against manufacturers were rare before the *MacPherson* case.

Following *MacPherson,* any foreseeable plaintiff can sue a manufacturer for its breach of duty of care. Foreseeable plaintiffs include users, consumers, and bystanders. Moreover, foreseeable plaintiffs can bring a case against retailers, wholesalers, and manufacturers. However, retailers and wholesalers can satisfy their duty of care by making a cursory reasonable inspection of a product when they receive it from the manufacturer.

Negligent failure to warn. To bring a successful case based on negligent failure to warn, the plaintiff must demonstrate that the defendant knew or should have known that without a warning, the product would be dangerous in its ordinary use, or in any *reasonably foreseeable* use, yet the defendant still failed to provide a warning. For example, the Tenth Circuit recently affirmed a trial court decision in which a smoker was awarded approximately $200,000 from R. J. Reynolds Tobacco, which before 1969 had negligently failed to warn smokers of the harm associated with smoking cigarettes. No duty to warn exists for dangers arising either from unforeseeable misuses of a product or from obvious dangers. A producer

global context

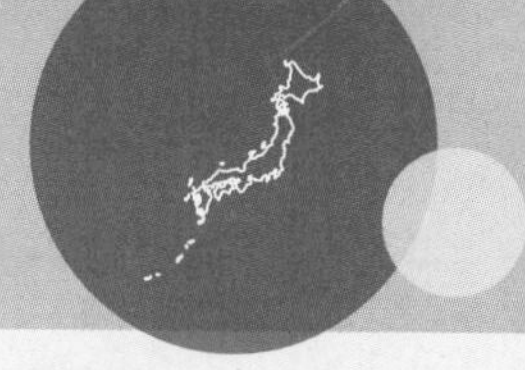

Negligence in Japan

Proving a manufacturer's negligence in Japan sounds similar to proving negligence in the United States. In Japan, the burden of proof is on the consumer, who must show that the manufacturer violated the "duty of care, which is the duty to foresee harmful results and the duty to avoid their occurrence." However, courts or arbitration committees (the preferred forum for settling a product liability dispute in Japan) favor settling on the manufacturer's behalf. Therefore, proving that a manufacturer could foresee the results is especially difficult.

of razor blades, for example, need not give a warning that a razor blade may cut someone. Courts often consider the likelihood of the injury, the seriousness of the injury, and the ease of warning when deciding whether a manufacturer was negligent in failing to warn.

When providing a warning, the manufacturer must ensure that the warning will reach those who are intended to use the product. For example, if parties other than the original purchaser will be likely to use the product, the warning should be placed directly on the product itself, not just in a manual that comes with the product. Picture warnings may be

Case Nugget — Failure to Warn about Food

Pelman v. McDonald's

Consumers have recently been bringing cases that attempt to hold others liable for their health problems allegedly caused by unhealthy food. In *Pelman v. McDonald's,** the plaintiffs alleged that McDonald's failed to warn customers of the "ingredients, quantity, qualities and levels of cholesterol, fat, salt and sugar content and other ingredients in those products, and that a diet high in fat, salt, sugar and cholesterol could lead to obesity and health problems." Judge Sweet originally dismissed the plaintiffs' claims, stating his decision was guided by the principle that legal consequences should not attach to the consumption of hamburgers and other fast-food fare unless consumers are unaware of the dangers of eating such food. He determined that consumers know, or should reasonably know, the potential negative health effects associated with eating fast food. The plaintiffs filed an amended complaint, asserting that McDonald's engaged in a scheme of deceptive advertising that in effect created the impression that McDonald's' food products were nutritionally beneficial and part of a healthy lifestyle. In September 2006, Judge Sweet refused to dismiss the plaintiffs' claims, and the case was moving forward.

Similarly, in *Gorran v. Atkins Nutritionals, Inc.,* Jody Gorran argued that he developed heart disease by following the Atkins diet, which encourages dieters to limit carbohydrates such as bread, rice, and pasta while increasing meat, cheese, eggs, and other high-protein (and high-fat) foods.† According to Gorran's complaint, Atkins Nutritionals promoted the health benefits of its diet while knowing that some people were "fat-sensitive" and subject to adverse health effects, yet Atkins failed to warn the public. The judge denied Atkins Nutritionals' motion to dismiss, and the case moved on to the discovery phase.

* 237 F. Supp. 2d 512 (S.D.N.Y 2003).

† "Judge Rebuffs Atkins' Second Bid to Dismiss Dieter's Lawsuit," *Andrews Product Liability Litigation Reporter* 16, no. 1 (2005), p. 2.

required if children, or those who are illiterate, are likely to come into contact with the product and risk harm from its use.

Products such as drugs and cosmetics are often the basis for actions based on negligent failure to warn because the use of these products frequently causes adverse reactions. When the user of a cosmetic or an over-the-counter drug has a reaction to that product, many courts find that there is no duty to warn unless the plaintiff proves that (1) the product contained an ingredient to which an appreciable number of people would have an adverse reaction; (2) the defendant knew or should have known, in the exercise of ordinary care, about the existence of this group; and (3) the plaintiff's reaction was due to his or her membership in this abnormal group.

Other courts, however, use a balancing test to determine negligence in such cases. They weigh the degree of danger to be avoided with the ease of warning. For example, in 1994, a jury awarded over $8.8 million to a man who suffered permanent liver damage as a result of drinking a glass of wine with a Tylenol capsule (the award was reduced to $350,000 due to a statutory cap). As early as 1977, the company knew that combining a normal dose of Tylenol with a small amount of wine could cause massive liver damage in some people, but the company failed to put a warning to that effect on the label because such a reaction was rare. Through the balancing test, the court found that the degree of potential harm was substantial and that it would have been relatively easy to place a warning on the product label. Other product liability cases involving pharmaceuticals are discussed in Exhibit 10-1.

Negligence per se. As you know from Chapter 9, a statute violation that causes the harm that the statute was enacted to prevent constitutes *negligence per se.* This doctrine is also applicable to product liability cases based on negligence. When a law establishes labeling, design, or content requirements for products, the manufacturer has a duty to meet these requirements. Failure by the manufacturer to meet those standards means that the manufacturer has breached its duty of reasonable care. If the plaintiff can establish that the failure to meet such a standard caused injury, the plaintiff can recover under negligence per se.

Damages. Damages that are recoverable in negligence-based product liability cases are the same as those in any action based on negligence: compensatory damages and punitive damages. As you should recall from Chapter 8, compensatory damages are those designed to make the plaintiff whole again; they cover items such as medical bills, lost wages, and compensation for pain and suffering. While this list of recoverable harms may seem "obvious" to us, not all countries allow such extensive recovery. For example, in German product liability cases, consumers do not have a right to recover damages for pain and suffering or for emotional distress. Punitive damages are meant to punish the defendant for extremely harmful conduct. The amount of the punitive-damage award is determined by the wealth of the defendant and the maliciousness of the action.

Defenses to a negligence-based product liability action. The defenses to negligence discussed in the previous chapter are available in product liability cases based on negligence. A common defense in such cases is that the plaintiff's own failure to act reasonably contributed to the plaintiff's own harm. This negligence on the part of the plaintiff allows the defendant to raise the defense of *contributory, comparative,* or *modified comparative negligence,* depending on which defense is accepted by the state where the case arose. Remember, in a state that allows the contributory negligence defense, proof of any negligence by the plaintiff is an absolute bar to recovery. In a state where the defense of pure comparative negligence is allowed, the plaintiff can recover for only that portion of the harm attributable to the defendant's negligence. In a modified comparative negligence state, the plaintiff can recover the percentage of harm caused by the defendant as long as the jury finds the plaintiff's negligence responsible for less than 50 percent of the harm.

Exhibit 10-1 Recent Pharmaceutical Litigation

Accutane (cystic acne medication)

Some people taking Accutane have experienced depression, and some have even committed suicide. Parents of a 14-year-old boy who committed suicide while taking Accutane have sued the manufacturer for negligence. In April 2002, another teenage boy taking Accutane was killed after he flew a small plane into a Florida office building; his mother is suing the manufacturer for wrongful death.

Hoffmann–La Roche is the manufacturer of Accutane, which is exclusively manufactured in the United States, in New Jersey. Many plaintiffs have sued Hoffmann–La Roche in New Jersey, but most of the plaintiffs live in other states. In 2006 in *Rowe v. Hoffmann–La Roche,* the New Jersey appellate court considered whether to apply Michigan law or New Jersey law when the plaintiff was a Michigan resident. This decision was particularly important because under product liability law in Michigan, FDA approval of a warning of a drug's side effects is a complete defense. However, in New Jersey, FDA approval simply provides a rebuttable presumption of the adequacy of the warning. Thus, New Jersey law is more favorable to plaintiffs than Michigan law. The New Jersey appellate court determined that New Jersey law would apply, concluding that New Jersey has a public policy interest in ensuring that drugs manufactured there are subject to the state's product liability laws. In January 2007, the New Jersey Supreme Court heard oral arguments on appeal. This case provides an important example of why manufacturers should consider state law when they select manufacturing locations.

Baycol (drug to lower cholesterol)

Bayer, the manufacturer of Baycol, voluntarily removed the drug from the market in 2001 after some patients developed rhabdomyolysis, a kidney disorder in which toxic muscle cells are released into the bloodstream. Patients can then develop fatal organ failure. As of January 2004, Bayer estimated that it had settled approximately 2,000 Baycol cases but still faced approximately 10,000 more. In January 2007, Bayer entered into an $8 million settlement in a 30-state consumer enforcement action against Bayer for failure to warn.

Paxil (antidepressant)

Patients taking Paxil reportedly experienced a variety of side effects: anxiety, agitation, confusion, dizziness, fatigue, headache, insomnia, irritability, nausea, palpitations, sweating, sleep disturbances, sensory disturbances, tremor, and vision distortion. Some Paxil patents committed suicide. As of April 2004, there were about 1,500 Paxil-withdrawal plaintiffs in over 30 states. Plaintiffs frequently bring the following claims: intentional misrepresentation, fraud, negligence, strict liability, and warranty claims. A class action lawsuit claimed GlaxoSmithKline promoted Paxil to children under eighteen and concealed information about the medication's safety and effectiveness. In April 2007, the class action settled after GlaxoSmithKline agreed to pay $63.8 million.

A closely related defense is *assumption of the risk.* This defense arises when a consumer knows that a defect exists but still proceeds unreasonably to make use of the product, creating a situation in which the consumer has voluntarily assumed the risk of injury from the defect and thus cannot recover. To decide whether the plaintiff did indeed assume the risk, the trier of fact may consider such factors as the plaintiff's age, experience, knowledge, and understanding, as well as the obviousness of the defect and the danger it poses. When a plaintiff knows of a danger but does not fully appreciate the magnitude of the risk, the applicability of the defense is a question for the jury to determine.

Another common defense is *misuse* of the product. The misuse must be unreasonable or unforeseeable. When a defendant raises the defense of product misuse, the defendant is really arguing that the harm was caused not by the defendant's negligence but by the plaintiff's failure to properly use the product.

The *state-of-the-art defense* is used by a defendant to demonstrate that his alleged negligent behavior was reasonable, given the available scientific knowledge existing at the time the product was sold or produced. If a case is based on the defendant's negligent

global context

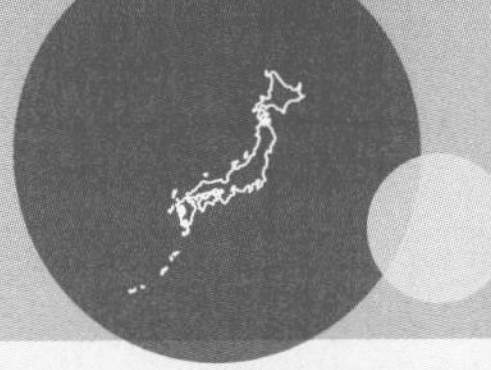

Product Misuse in Japan

Like the United States, Japan also addresses situations in which the consumer misuses a defective product. In Japan, such a situation is called *comparative negligence.* The negligence of both the defendant and the plaintiff is taken into account when determining the distribution of damages. The leading case of comparative negligence is that of *Miyahara v. Matsumoto Gas Company.* In this case, the defendant purchased a gas stove from Matsumoto. A faulty rubber nose valve caused the stove to start a fire, resulting in extensive damage to Miyahara's home. An investigation after the fire, however, showed that Miyahara had failed to close the valve before going to sleep the evening of the fire. Consequently, both he and the gas company were found negligent. The cost of the damages was split between the two parties.

defective design of a product, the state-of-the-art defense refers to the technological feasibility of producing a safer product at the time the product was manufactured. In cases of negligent failure to warn, the state-of-the-art defense refers to the scientific knowability of a risk associated with a product at the time of its production. This is a valid defense in a negligence case because the focus is on the reasonableness of the defendant's conduct. However, the state of scientific knowledge at the time of production, and the lack of a feasible way to make a safer product, does not always preclude liability. The court may find that the defendant's conduct was still unreasonable because even in its technologically safest form, the risks posed by the defect in the design so outweighed the benefits of the product that the reasonable person would not have produced a product of that design.

Does compliance with safety regulations constitute a defense? Sometimes. *Compliance with federal laws* may lead to the defense that use of state tort law is preempted by a federal statute designed to ensure the safety of a particular class of products. Case 10-1 illustrates one situation in which the court accepted the preemption argument and found that compliance with a federal statute designed to regulate cigarette lighters relieved a manufacturer from potential tort liability.

CASE 10-1 BILLY WAYNE FRITH AND WANDA FRITH AS PARENTS AND NATURAL GUARDIANS OF JOSHUA BRENT FRITH, A MINOR v. BIC CORPORATION

SUPREME COURT OF MISSISSIPPI
JAN. 15, 2004

In December 1994, Josh Frith, a ten-year-old, found a disposable cigarette lighter in the ditch behind his house. He attempted to light the lighter, which did not light but produced sparks. Unfortunately, Josh was walking past a gasoline container when the lighter produced some sparks. The sparks caused an explosion, which severely burned Josh.

Josh's parents filed suit against BIC, the manufacturer of the cigarette lighter, as well as the manufacturer of the gasoline container. Josh identified the lighter as a BIC J-26 Model Child Guard cigarette lighter. BIC filed a motion for summary judgment, arguing that the Friths' state law product liability claims were preempted by federal law. The trial court granted summary judgment in favor of BIC.

JUSTICE CARLSON: [T]he crucial claim asserted against BIC is that of a design defect in a disposable lighter resulting in an allegedly insufficient child resistant product which enabled a ten-year-old boy to use the lighter in such a way as to produce sparks which ignited fumes from a nearby gasoline container.

When determining whether a cause of action has been preempted by federal law, "the purpose of

Congress is the ultimate touchstone." *Cipollone v. Liggett Group,* 505 U.S. 504, 516, 112 S.Ct. 2608, 2619, 120 L.Ed.2d 407 (1992) [quoting Retail Clerks v. Schermerhorn, 375 U.S. 96, 103, 84 S.Ct. 219, 222, 11 L.Ed.2d 179 (1963)]. The intent of Congress may be "explicitly stated in the statute's language or implicitly contained in its structure and purpose." In the absence of an express congressional command, state law is preempted if that law actually conflicts with federal law, or if federal law so thoroughly occupies a legislative field "as to make reasonable the inference that Congress left no room for the States to supplement it."

The Consumer Product Safety Commission (CPSC), a federal commission, previously underwent a comprehensive process to establish uniform child resistance standards for disposable lighters which would most effectively and feasibly achieve the federal safety objectives of reducing fire-related injuries and deaths involving children. After considering many alternatives, the CPSC made an obviously knowing and conscious regulatory decision intended to encourage public acceptance and use of child resistance lighters by adult consumers.

The Court notes that Defendants have alleged, and Plaintiffs have not rebutted, that the design of the J-26 Model Child Guard cigarette lighter at issue in this lawsuit is in full compliance with the child resistance safety standards of the CPSC regulations for cigarette lighters enacted by the CPSC. To apply state or common law standards to the design of this cigarette lighter could subject BIC to two different regulations of the same subject: the federal regulations of the CPSC and the higher common law standard urged by the Plaintiff. Clearly, this was not what Congress intended when it passed the CPSA.

A review of the record in this case, including the pleadings, reveals that the standard which the Friths would have us apply to BIC is a higher standard than that established by federal law. In essence the Friths argue that BIC should be held to the standard of producing a lighter which a 10-year-old child cannot use. The Friths assert that while the States are no doubt obligated to apply what the Friths perceive to be the minimum standard established by federal law, the States are not prohibited from establishing a higher standard which would further protect their consumer-citizens. The applicable federal safety standard is that lighter companies are to implement safety devices on the lighters so that they cannot be successfully used by children five years of age. 16 C.F.R. §1210.1. The standard proposed by the Friths is a higher standard than that established by federal law.

The record before us unequivocally reveals a genuine effort by Congress and federal regulators to reach a balance by sanctioning child-resistant lighters not too difficult for adult operation. A more stringent standard would no doubt frustrate the objective of the disposable lighter regulations. In today's case, the federal standards applicable to lighters were intended to make it as difficult as feasibly possible for a five-year-old child to use. If a state law claim succeeded in imposing stricter child-resistant requirements for disposable lighters such that a ten-year-old child could not operate the lighter to produce a flame or sparks, then the lighter would be sufficiently difficult for an adult to operate, thus causing adults to resort to less safe methods of producing fire, such as matches. The end result would be that the more stringent state standard would stand as an obstacle to the accomplishment of the federal objective of producing for the adult consumer a usable lighter which was yet as child-resistant as feasible for children five years of age and younger. If we were to adopt the Friths' standard of requiring lighters to be designed in such a way as to prevent even so much as a spark from being produced by the lighter when in the hands of a ten-year-old child, we would be adopting a state law which would no doubt undermine and frustrate the federal objective and thus conflict with federal law. This we refuse to do.

SUMMARY JUDGMENT AFFIRMED

CRITICAL THINKING

Consider the judge's reasoning that led to the summary judgment's being affirmed. Is there any additional information that you would like to know that would help you decide whether BIC should be held responsible?

[CONTINUED]

ETHICAL DECISION MAKING

Recall the WPH process for ethical decision making. Who are the relevant stakeholders affected by this decision?

Each preemption case requires careful scrutiny of the purpose of the statute. For example, in *Tebbetts v. Ford Motor Co.,* the plaintiff argued that the 1988 Ford Escort was defectively designed because it did not have a driver's side air bag. Ford raised the preemption defense, arguing that it had complied with federal safety regulations under the National Traffic and Motor Vehicle Safety Act (NTMVSA). Consequently, Ford argued that its compliance preempted recovery under state product liability laws. After considering the legislative history and the law, the court discovered a clause in the law stating that "[c]ompliance with any Federal motor vehicle safety standard issued under this act does not exempt any person from any liability under common law." Thus, the court ruled that the Tebbetts were not preempted from bringing their product liability action.

Similarly, oil companies have argued that their compliance with the Clean Air Act should not subject them to tort liability for MTBE contamination in groundwater. Through the Clean Air Act, Congress required that oil companies include an oxygenate in gasoline to allow the gasoline to burn more cleanly and thus to improve air quality. MTBE, or methyl tertiary butyl ether, is one type of oxygenate. While everyone expected MTBE to help improve air quality, widespread use of this oxygenate had a negative consequence: It contaminated water. A very small amount of MTBE affects the smell and taste of water. Given these extreme negative consequences, numerous states banned MTBE. Moreover, cities and individuals have sued oil companies to pay for the costs, in the millions of dollars, that will be incurred to clean the drinking water. While a few courts have agreed with the oil companies, most cases have held that the Clean Air Act does not preempt tort cases because the oil companies had a choice of oxygenates to use. Moreover, the courts state that the problem of water contamination is too far removed from the problem that Congress was trying to address through the Clean Air Act regulations; thus, there is no preemption.

Certain statutory defenses are also available in negligence-based product liability cases. To ensure that there will be sufficient evidence from which a trier of fact can make a decision, states have *statutes of limitations* that limit the time within which all types of civil actions may be brought. In most states, the statute of limitations for tort actions, and thus for negligence-based product liability cases, varies between one and four years from the date of injury.

Statutes of repose provide an additional statutory defense by barring actions arising more than a specified number of years after the product was purchased. Statutes of repose are usually much longer than statutes of limitations, generally running at least 10 years.

STRICT PRODUCT LIABILITY

The requirements for proving strict product liability can be found in Section 402A of the Restatement (Second) of Torts. This section reads as follows:

(1) One who sells any product in a defective condition, unreasonably dangerous to the user or consumer or his family is subject to liability for physical harm, thereby, caused to the ultimate user or consumer, or to this property, if

(a) the seller is engaged in the business of selling such a product, and

(b) it is expected to and does reach the consumer or user without substantial change in the condition in which it was sold.

(2) The rule stated in Subsection (1) applies although

(a) the seller has exercised all possible care in the preparation and sale of his product, and

(b) the user or consumer has not bought the product from or entered into any contractual relation with the seller.

Under **strict product liability**, courts may hold liable the manufacturer, distributor, or retailer to any reasonably foreseeable injured party. Any reasonably foreseeable injured party includes the buyer; the buyer's family, guests, and friends; and foreseeable bystanders. The actions of the manufacturer or seller are not relevant; rather, strict product liability focuses on the *product.* Thus, duty is irrelevant. Courts focus on whether the product was in a "defective condition, unreasonably dangerous" when sold. To succeed in a strict liability action, the plaintiff must prove three things:

1. The product was defective when sold.
2. The product was so defective that the product was unreasonably dangerous.
3. The product was the cause of the plaintiff's injury.

Exhibit 10-2 The Battle of the Experts

EXPERT OPINION IN PRODUCT LIABILITY CASES

Plaintiffs use experts in product liability cases to show the existence of a flaw or to show that a flaw caused the plaintiff's injuries. To rebut the plaintiff's expert opinion, the defense usually hires an expert to show that there is no defect or that the product did not cause the plaintiff's injuries. These experts frequently battle over the scientific evidence regarding causation.

Expert testimony is used in various types of litigation: drugs, breast implants, automobile accidents, and pollution. Expert opinion is generally admissible in a trial if two conditions are met:

1. The subject matter is one in which scientific, technical, or other specialized knowledge would help the finder of fact, and the knowledge is relevant and reliable.
2. The expert offering the testimony is qualified as an expert.

Juries, or even judges, have sometimes been persuaded by an "expert" advocating "junk science." Junk science may be "biased data, spurious inferences, and logical legerdemain, patched together by researchers whose enthusiasm for discovery and diagnosis outstrips their skill. It is a catalog of every conceivable kind of error: data dredging, wishful thinking, truculent dogmatism, and now and again, outright fraud."* In an attempt to reduce the use of junk science in the courtroom, the Supreme Court, in *Daubert v. Merrell Dow Pharmaceutical,* determined that judges are responsible for assessing expert opinion. It identified four considerations for relevant and reliable opinions:

1. Did the expert use the scientific method?
2. Has the expert's theory or technique been subjected to peer review and publication?
3. Does the particular technique have a significant rate of error?
4. Is the methodology generally accepted in the scientific community?

Expert-witness fees may range from $100 to $1,000 an hour. Experts are usually deposed during litigation, so their time preparing for depositions and trial can easily run into hundreds of hours, which can be quite costly for clients.

*Peter Huber, *Galileo's Revenge: Junk Science in the Courtroom,* New York, Basic Books (1991).

As stated earlier, a product may be defective because of (1) a flaw in its manufacturing that led to its being more dangerous; (2) a defective design; or (3) missing or inadequate instructions or warnings that could have reduced or eliminated foreseeable risks posed by the product.

Plaintiffs usually prove that a defect exists by means of (1) experts who testify as to the type of flaw in the product that led to the plaintiff's injury and/or (2) evidence of the circumstances surrounding the accident that would lead the jury to infer that the accident must have been caused by a defect in the product. Exhibit 10-2 describes how expert opinion is used in product liability cases. Case 10-2 illustrates how circumstances can provide a reasonable basis for such an inference.

CASE 10-2

WELGE v. PLANTERS LIFESAVERS CO.
COURT OF APPEALS FOR THE SEVENTH CIRCUIT
17 F.3D 209 (7TH CIR.1994)

Richard Welge, who boarded with Karen Godfrey, liked peanuts on his ice cream sundaes. Godfrey bought a 24-ounce vacuum-sealed plastic-capped jar of Planters peanuts for Welge at K-Mart. To obtain a $2 rebate, Godfrey needed proof of her purchase from the jar of peanuts. She used an Exacto knife to remove the part of the label that contained the bar code and placed the jar on top of the refrigerator for Welge. A week later, Welge removed the plastic seal from the jar, uncapped it, took some peanuts, replaced the cap, and returned the jar to the top of the refrigerator. A week after that, he took down the jar, removed the plastic cap, spilled some peanuts into his left hand to put on his sundae, and replaced the cap with his right hand. As he pushed the cap down on the open jar, the jar shattered. His hand was severely cut, and became permanently impaired.

Welge filed product liability actions against K-Mart, the seller of the product; Planters, the manufacturer of the peanuts; and Brockway, the manufacturer of the glass jar. Defendants filed a motion for summary judgment after discovery. The district judge granted the motion on the ground that the plaintiff had failed to exclude possible causes of the accident other than a defect introduced during the manufacturing process. The plaintiff appealed.

JUSTICE POSNER: No doubt there are men strong enough to shatter a thick glass jar with one blow. But Welge's testimony stands uncontradicted that he used no more than the normal force that one exerts in snapping a plastic lid onto a jar. So the jar must have been defective. No expert testimony and no fancy doctrine are required for such a conclusion. A nondefective jar does not shatter when normal force is used to clamp its plastic lid on. The question is when the defect was introduced. It could have been at any time from the manufacture of the glass jar by Brockway (for no one suggests that the defect might have been caused by something in the raw materials out of which the jar was made) to moments before the accident. But testimony by Welge and Godfrey . . . excludes all reasonable possibility that the defect was introduced into the jar after Godfrey plucked it from a shelf in the K-Mart store. From the shelf she put it in her shopping cart. The checker at the check out counter scanned the bar code without banging the jar. She then placed the jar in a plastic bag. Godfrey carried the bag to her car and put it on the floor. She drove directly home, without incident. After the bar code portion of the label was removed, the jar sat on top of the refrigerator except for the two times Welge removed it to take peanuts out of it. Throughout this process it was not, so far as anyone knows, jostled, dropped, bumped, or otherwise subjected to stress beyond what is to be expected in the ordinary use of the product. Chicago is not Los Angeles; there were no earthquakes. Chicago is not Amityville either; no supernatural interventions are alleged. So the defect must have been introduced earlier, when the jar was in the hands of the defendants.

. . . [I]t is always possible that the jar was damaged while it was sitting unattended on the top of the refrigerator, in which event they are not responsible. Only if it had been securely under lock and key when not being used could the plaintiff and Karen Godfrey be certain that nothing happened to damage it after she brought it home. That is true—there are no metaphysical certainties—but it leads nowhere. Elves may have played ninepins with the jar of peanuts while Welge and Godfrey were sleeping; but elves could remove a jar of peanuts from a locked cupboard. The plaintiff in a product liability suit is not required to exclude every possibility, however fantastic or remote, that the defect which led to the accident was caused by someone other than one of the defendants. The doctrine of *res ipsa loquitur* teaches that an accident that is unlikely to occur, unless the defendant was negligent, is itself circumstantial evidence that the defendant was negligent. The doctrine is not strictly applicable to a product liability case because, unlike an ordinary accident case, the defendant in a products case has parted with possession and control of the harmful object before the accident occurs. . . . But the doctrine merely instantiates the broader principle, which is as applicable to a products case as to any other tort case, that an accident can itself be evidence of liability. . . . If it is the kind of accident that would not have occurred but for a defect in the product, and if it is reasonably plain that the defect was not introduced after the product was sold, the accident is evidence that the product was defective when sold. The second condition (as well as the first) has been established here, at least to a probability sufficient to defeat a motion for summary judgment. Normal people do not lock up their jars and cans lest something happens to damage these containers while no one is looking. The probability of such damage is too remote. It is not only too remote to make a rational person take measures to prevent it; it is too remote to defeat a product liability suit should a container prove dangerously defective.

. . . [I]f the probability that the defect which caused the accident arose after Karen Godfrey bought the jar of Planters peanuts is very small—and on the present state of the record we are required to assume that it is—then the probability that the defect was introduced by one of the defendants is very high.

. . . The strict-liability element in modern product liability law comes precisely from the fact that a seller, subject to that law, is liable for defects in his product even if those defects were introduced, without the slightest fault of his own for failing to discover them, at some anterior stage of production. . . . So the fact that K-Mart sold a defective jar of peanuts to Karen Godfrey would be conclusive of K-Mart's liability, and since it is a large and solvent firm there would be no need for the plaintiff to look further for a tortfeasor.

. . . Here we know to a virtual certainty (always assuming that the plaintiff's evidence is believed, which is a matter for the jury) that the accident was not due to mishandling after purchase, but to a defect that had been introduced earlier.

REVERSED AND REMANDED in favor of the plaintiff.

CRITICAL THINKING

What are Justice Posner's reasons for reversing the decision? Do you find his reasons compelling?

ETHICAL DECISION MAKING

Suppose the defect had been introduced by Brockway and that corporate management had been aware of the defect but believed the chances of someone's being hurt were small enough as to be negligible. Therefore, Brockway did not inform Planters of the defect. Should it have informed Planters?

In Case 10-2, the product had a manufacturing defect, which was fairly straightforward to prove. However, it is sometimes more difficult to prove that a design is defective. States are not in agreement as to how to establish a design defect, and two different tests have evolved to determine when a product is so defective as to be unreasonably dangerous. The first test, set out in the Restatement (Second) of Torts, is the *consumer expectations test:* Did the product meet the standards that would be expected by the reasonable consumer? This test relies on the experiences and expectations of the ordinary consumer, and thus it is not answered by the use of expert testimony about the merits of the design.

The second is the *feasible alternatives test,* sometimes referred to as the *risk-utility test.* In applying this test, the court focuses on the usefulness and safety of the design and compares it to an alternative design. The exact factors that the court examines are detailed in Case 10-3, which makes explicit the differences between the two tests.

CASE 10-3 SPERRY–NEW HOLLAND, A DIVISION OF SPERRY CORPORATION v. JOHN PAUL PRESTAGE AND PAM PRESTAGE

SUPREME COURT OF MISSISSIPPI
617 SO. 2D 248 (1993)

Mr. Prestage's foot and lower leg were caught in a combine manufactured by defendant-appellant Sperry–New Holland. He and his wife sued defendant for damages arising out of the accident. Their first cause of action was based on the theory of strict product liability. A jury awarded John $1,425,000 for his injuries and Pam $218,750 for loss of consortium (the ability to engage in sexual relations with one's spouse). Defendant appealed.

JUDGE PRATHER: . . . Two competing theories of strict liability in tort can be extrapolated from our case law. While our older decisions applied a "consumer expectations" analysis in products cases, recent decisions have turned on an analysis under "risk-utility." We today apply a "risk-utility" analysis and write to clarify our reasons for the adoption for that test.

Section 402A is still the law in Mississippi. How this Court defines the phrases "defective conditions" and "unreasonably dangerous" used in 402A dictates whether a "consumer expectations" analysis or a "risk-utility" analysis will prevail. Problems have arisen because our past decisions have been unclear and have been misinterpreted in some instances.

"Consumer Expectations" Analysis

. . . In a "consumer expectations" analysis, "ordinarily the phrase 'defective condition' means that the article has something wrong with it, that it did not function as expected." Comment g of Section 402A defines "defective condition" as "a condition not contemplated by the ultimate consumer, which will be unreasonably dangerous to him." Thus, in a "consumer expectations" analysis, for a plaintiff to recover, the defect in a product which causes his injuries must not be one which the plaintiff, as an ordinary consumer, would know to be unreasonably dangerous to him. In other words, if the plaintiff, applying the knowledge of an ordinary consumer, sees a danger and can appreciate that danger, then he cannot recover for any injury resulting from that appreciated danger.

"Risk-Utility" Analysis

In a "risk-utility" analysis, a product is "unreasonably dangerous" if a reasonable person would conclude that the danger-in-fact, whether foreseeable or not, outweighs the utility of the product. Thus, even if a plaintiff appreciates the danger of a product, he can still recover for any injury resulting from the danger, provided that the utility of the product is outweighed by the danger that the product creates. Under the "risk-utility" test, either the judge or the jury can balance the utility and danger-in-fact, or risk, of the product.

A "risk-utility" analysis best protects both the manufacturer and the consumer. It does not create a duty on the manufacturer to create a completely safe product. Creating such a product is often impossible or prohibitively expensive. Instead, a manufacturer is charged with the duty to make its product reasonably safe, regardless of whether the plaintiff is aware of the product's dangerousness. . . . In balancing the utility of the product against the risk it creates, an ordinary person's ability to avoid the danger by exercising care is also weighed.

Having here reiterated this Court's adoption of a "risk-utility" analysis for product liability cases, we hold, necessarily, that the "patent danger" bar is no longer applicable in Mississippi. Under a "risk-utility" analysis, the "patent danger" rule does not apply. In "risk-utility," the openness and obviousness of a product's design is simply a factor to consider in determining whether a product is unreasonably dangerous.

There is sufficient evidence to show that Prestage tried his case under a "risk-utility" analysis. It is also clear from the record that the trial court understood "risk-utility" to be the law in Mississippi and applied that test correctly.

AFFIRMED in favor of plaintiff.

CRITICAL THINKING

Why was the risk-utility test viewed as the best method of evaluating this case?

ETHICAL DECISION MAKING

The risk-utility test allows products to pose a danger to consumers as long as they are reasonably safe. Under which ethical theory would producing such a product be ethical? Under which theory would such production not be ethical?

Exhibit 10-3 Impact of the Restatement (Third) of Torts

Section 402A of the Restatement (Second) of Torts is generally the foundation of modern product liability law, but that section has been subject to considerable criticism. In 1998, these criticisms led the American Law Institute to adopt the"Restatement of the Law (Third), Torts: Product Liability," which is intended to replace Section 402A.

Under the Restatement (Third):

> [O]ne engaged in the business of selling or otherwise distributing products who sells or distributes a defective product is subject to liability for harm to persons or property caused by the defect.

The section departs from the Restatement (Second) by holding the seller to a different standard of liability, depending on whether the defect in question is a manufacturing defect, a design defect, or a defective warning.

It is only a manufacturing defect that results in strict liability. A manufacturing defect arises when "the product departs from its intended design," and liability is imposed regardless of the care taken by the manufacturer.

The Restatement (Third) applies a reasonableness standard to design defects, stating:

> [A] product is defective in design when the foreseeable risks of the harm posed by the product could have been reduced or avoided by the adoption of a reasonable alternative design by the seller . . . and the omission of the alternative design renders the product not reasonably safe.

Continued

e-commerce AND THE LAW

In a footnote in the Sperry–New Holland case, the court relied on Professor John Wade's article "On the Nature of Strict Tort Liability for Products"* to list seven factors a trial court may find helpful when balancing a product's utility against the risk the product creates:

1. The usefulness and desirability of the product—its utility to the user and to the public as a whole.
2. The safety aspects of the product—the likelihood that it will cause injury and the probable seriousness of the injury.
3. The availability of a substitute product that would meet the same need and not be as unsafe.
4. The manufacturer's ability to eliminate the unsafe character of the product without impairing its usefulness or making it too expensive to maintain its utility.
5. The user's ability to avoid danger by the exercise of care in the use of the product.
6. The user's anticipated awareness of the dangers inherent in the product and their avoidability, because of general public knowledge of the obvious condition of the product or of the existence of suitable warnings or instructions.
7. The feasibility, on the part of the manufacturer, of spreading the loss by setting the price of the product or carrying liability insurance.

With regard to factor 6, the court's analysis considered whether warnings included in an owner's manual were suitable to warn Prestage of the danger of the combine. One of Sperry's expert witnesses testified: "Warnings are a third-rate way of preventing accidents. . . . [W]arnings are something that . . . operators read once, and forget."

Query: Is it possible that as owner's and user's manuals become available online, judges and experts will be less sympathetic to the owner or user who says he read the warnings once but then forgot about them? Have you ever misplaced an owner's or user's manual and later looked for it online when you needed information about a product? If so, are you more likely to review safety information than you may have been in the past, when it was easy to misplace manuals?

* *Mississippi Law Journal* 44 (1973), p. 825.

Exhibit 10-3 *Continued*

Comments in the Restatement (Third) list a number of factors the court can use to determine whether a reasonable alternative design renders the product not reasonably safe, including:

> the magnitude and probability of the foreseeable risks of harm, the instructions and warnings accompanying the product, and the nature and strength of consumer expectations regarding the product, including expectations arising from product portrayal and marketing, . . . the relative advantage and disadvantages of the product as designed and as it alternatively could have been designed, . . . the likely effects of the alternative design on product longevity, maintenance, repair and esthetics, and the range of consumer choice among products.

Thus, the Restatement (Third) has in effect shifted to a risk-utility test.

The Restatement (Third) has likewise adopted a reasonableness standard for defective warnings:

> A product is defective because of inadequate instructions or warnings when the foreseeable risks of harm posed by the product could have been reduced or avoided by the provision of reasonable instructions or warnings by the seller . . . and the omission of the warnings renders the product not reasonably safe.

The potential effects of changes brought about by the newest Restatement have yet to be fully felt. As of 2001, the Restatement (Third) had not been widely adopted by the states.

Liability to bystanders. We have been looking thus far at liability to those who are in lawful possession of the defective product. The question arises as to whether strict product liability can be used by someone other than the owner or user of the product. Note that in the case described in the beginning of this chapter, Donna Bailey was a passenger in the car and therefore a bystander. Case 10-4 provides the rationale of one court that chose to allow recovery by a bystander.

CASE 10-4 JAMES A. PETERSON, ADM'R OF THE ESTATE OF MARADEAN PETERSON ET AL. v. LOU BACKRODT CHEVROLET CO.

APPELLATE COURT OF ILLINOIS
307 N.E.2D 729 (1974)

Defendant Lou Backrodt Chevrolet sold an automobile with a defective brake system. The defective brakes failed, causing the driver to strike two minors, killing one and injuring the other. The deceased minor's estate brought this product liability action against the seller of the defective automobile. The trial court dismissed the action against the defendant on the grounds that bystanders did not have a cause of action. The plaintiff appealed.

JUSTICE GUILD: The question of whether a bystander can employ the doctrine of strict liability in a lawsuit has been thoroughly considered by reviewing courts and legal commentators. These authorities indicate that permitting the bystander to maintain an action based on strict tort liability is the more enlightened approach. This has been the result when this issue has been considered in light of Illinois law.

The rationale behind this result is best expressed by this statement of the California Supreme court in *Elmore v. American Motors Corp.*

> If anything, bystanders should be entitled to greater protection than the consumer or user where injury to bystanders from the defect is reasonably foreseeable. Consumer and users, at least, have the opportunity to inspect for defects and to limit their purchases to articles manufactured by reputable manufacturers and sold by reputable retailers, whereas the bystander ordinarily has no such opportunities. In short, the bystander is in greater need of protection from defective products which are dangerous, and if any distinction should be made between bystanders and users, it should be made . . . to extend greater liability in favor of the bystanders.
>
> . . . [T]he doctrine of strict liability in tort is available in an action for personal injuries by a bystander against the manufacturer and the retailer.

We agree with the California Supreme Court's cogent reasoning and hold that it is equally applicable when directed to those in the business of selling used cars.

REVERSED AND REMANDED in favor of plaintiff.

CRITICAL THINKING

What reason does the California court give for affording bystanders more protection? Do you find this reason compelling? Why or why not?

ETHICAL DECISION MAKING

Might Lou Backrodt Chevrolet have acted differently in withholding information about the brakes if the corporation had applied the Golden Rule test to its actions?

connecting to the core

Total Quality Management

Even better than knowing how to defend your firm in a product liability case is being able to prevent the lawsuit from arising in the first place. One concept, introduced in your management class, that may reduce the number of defective products is *total quality management (TQM)*. TQM is a process by which all members of an organization function to achieve goals associated with producing a high-quality product.

Source: S. Certo, *Modern Management* (Upper Saddle River, NJ: Prentice Hall, 2000), pp. 504–505.

Defenses to a strict–product liability action. Most of the defenses to a negligence-based product liability claim are available in a strict–product liability case. These defenses include product misuse, assumption of the risk, and the lapse of time under statutes of limitations and statutes of repose.

One defense that may not be available in all states, however, is the state-of-the-art defense. Courts have rejected the use of this defense in most strict-liability cases, reasoning that the issue in such cases is not what the producers knew at the time the products were produced but whether the product was defective and whether the defect caused it to be unreasonably dangerous. For example, the supreme court of Missouri, in a case involving an asbestos claim, said that the state of the art has no bearing on the outcome of a strict-liability claim because the issue is the defective condition of the product, not the manufacturer's knowledge, negligence, or fault.

The refusal of most courts to allow the state-of-the-art defense in strict-liability cases is consistent with the social policy reasons for imposing strict liability. A reason for imposing strict liability is that the manufacturers or producers are best able to spread the cost of the risk; this risk-spreading function does not change with the availability of scientific knowledge. The counterargument is that if the manufacturer has indeed done everything as safely and carefully as available data allow, it seems unfair to impose liability on the defendant. After all, how else could the company have manufactured the product?

WARRANTY

Another theory of liability for defective products is *breach of warranty.* Unlike negligence and strict-liability theories, breach of warranty stems from contract theory rather than tort theory. This theory of liability is established through the Uniform Commercial Code (UCC). A **warranty** is a guarantee or a binding promise regarding a product. Generally, the product (or the product's performance) does not meet the manufacturer's or seller's promises.

Warranties may be either *express* (clearly stated by the seller or manufacturer) or *implied* (automatically arising out of a transaction). Either type may give rise to liability. Two types of implied warranties may provide the basis for a product liability action: warranty of merchantability and warranty of fitness for a particular purpose.

Express warranty. When a seller makes an affirmative representation about a product, this representation becomes part of the bargain. The representation may be a written or verbal guarantee about the product. For example, a car dealer may make an express statement that the car will work perfectly for the first 30,000 miles. In contrast, a car dealer may engage in vague sales talk (e.g., "This car runs well.") that does not constitute an express warranty.

Determining whether a statement is a warranty may be a difficult task. In one case, for example, the court considered whether advertising statements constituted a warranty: When a consumer was deciding whether to buy a luxury yacht, the seller gave him a brochure with a picture of the yacht along with the following caption: "Offering the best performance and cruising accommodations in its class, the 3375 Esprit offers a choice of either stern drive or inboard power, superb handling and sleeping accommodations for six." The buyer argued that on the basis of express representations about the yacht in this brochure, he chose to purchase the $150,000 yacht. Later, the yacht had mechanical and electrical problems. The supreme court of Utah concluded that an express warranty is a promise or affirmation of fact. "[T]he photograph and caption contained in Cruisers' brochure are not objective or specific enough to qualify as either facts or promises; the statements made in the caption are merely opinions, and the photograph makes no additional assertions with regard to the problems of which Boud has complained." Thus, the court ruled there was no express warranty.

To establish a claim for breach of express warranty, the plaintiff must show that (1) the representation was the basis of the bargain and (2) there was a breach of the representation. Generally, the plaintiff simply has to demonstrate a breach of warranty; she does not have to prove that the occurrence of the breach was the defendant's fault.

Implied warranty of merchantability. When a seller sells a particular kind of goods, there is an implied warranty of merchantability. *Merchantability* means that the particular goods would be accepted by others who deal in similar goods. Thus, an implied warranty of merchantability means that the goods are fit for the purpose for which they are sold and used.

Contracts for sales of goods frequently contain numerous disclaimers, and one of these disclaimers includes the implied warranty of merchantability. If the disclaimer uses the word *merchantability,* the disclaimer will be upheld for economic losses but not personal injuries.

Implied warranty of fitness for a particular purpose. When a customer purchases a product for a particular purpose and the seller is aware of this purpose, an implied warranty of fitness for a particular purpose arises. The buyer is relying on the seller's skill and judgment to select the particular goods.

Exhibit 10-4 summarizes the three theories of product liability.

Market Share Liability

In most cases, the plaintiff can identify the manufacturer of a defective product that caused the injury at issue. Sometimes, however, some plaintiffs may not learn of their injuries until years after the injury occurs. By this time, plaintiffs cannot trace the product to any particular manufacturer. Often, a number of manufacturers produced the same product, and the plaintiff would have no idea whose product had been used. A plaintiff may have even used more than one manufacturer's product.

Prior to the 1980s, plaintiffs in this situation would have been unable to gain any sort of recovery for their injuries. However, recovery may be possible today because of the **market share theory,** created by the California Supreme Court in the case of *Sindell v. Abbott Laboratories.*

In *Sindell,* the plaintiffs' mothers had all taken a drug known as diethylstilbestrol (DES) during pregnancies that had occurred before the drug was banned in 1973. Because DES had been produced 20 years before the plaintiffs suffered any effects from the drug their mothers had taken, it was impossible to trace the defective drug back to each manufacturer

Exhibit 10-4 Summary of Product Liability Theories

THEORIES OF LIABILITY	WHO CAN SUE	WHO CAN BE LIABLE	DEFENSES	DAMAGES
Negligence	Any foreseeable plaintiff	Any commercial supplier in the distribution chain (Retailers and sellers can satisfy their duty by a cursory reasonable inspection.)	Assumption of the risk Comparative/ contributory negligence	Personal injuries Property damages No recovery solely for economic damages
Strict liability	Anyone harmed (buyer, user, bystander)	Any commercial supplier in the distribution chain	Assumption of the risk Product misuse	Personal injuries Property damages No recovery solely for economic damages
Warranty	Privity required (Injured party must be the buyer, the buyer's family, or the buyer's guest.)	Any seller	Assumption of the risk Product misuse Disclaimer	Recovery solely for economic damage

that had produced the drug causing each individual's problems. To balance the competing interests of the victims, who had suffered injury from the drug, and the defendants, who did not want to be held liable for a drug they did not produce, the court allowed the plaintiffs to sue all the manufacturers that had produced the drug at the time that the plaintiffs' mothers had used the drug. Then the judge apportioned liability among the defendant-manufacturers on the basis of the share of the market they had held at the time that the drug had been produced.

This theory has since been used by some other courts, primarily in drug cases. Courts using the market share theory generally require that the plaintiff prove that (1) all defendants are tortfeasors; (2) the allegedly harmful products are identical and share the same defective qualities; (3) the plaintiff is unable to identify which defendant caused her injury, through no fault of her own; and (4) the manufacturers of substantially all the defective products in the relevant area and during the relevant time are named as defendants.

Some states have modified the approach of *Sindell.* At least one court has held that the plaintiff need sue only one maker of the allegedly defective drug. If the plaintiff can prove that the defendant manufactured a drug of the type taken by the plaintiff's mother at the time of the mother's pregnancy, that defendant can be held liable for all damages. However, the defendant may join other defendants, and the jury may apportion liability among all defendants.

While the utility of this theory for drug cases is evident, plaintiffs have not been as successful in extending the theory to products other than drugs. For example, in 2001, plaintiffs who were unable to identify the maker of the guns that were used to kill their family members were unsuccessful in their attempt to sue a group of manufacturers for negligent marketing under the theory of market share liability. However, at least one court has extended the theory to lead carbonate to permit market share liability for lead poisoning (see Case 10-5).

CASE 10-5

STEVEN THOMAS, A MINOR, BY HIS GUARDIAN AD LITEM, SUSAN M. GRAMLING, PLAINTIFF-APPELLANT-PETITIONER, v. CLINTON L. MALLETT, BILLIE R. MALLETT, & GERMANTOWN MUTUAL INS. CO., DEFENDANTS

SUPREME COURT OF WISCONSIN
2005 WI 129, 285 WIS. 2D 236, 701 N.W.2D 523 (2005)

Steven Thomas, a minor born in 1990, claimed that he ingested lead paint from two different houses he lived in during the early 1990s. He suffered serious neurological disorders that he claimed were caused by ingestion of paint containing white lead carbonate. His disorders require lifetime monitoring. He brought suit against his landlords, their insurers, and lead carbonate manufacturers to recover damages through claims of strict liability, negligence, civil conspiracy, and enterprise liability. The manufacturers moved for summary judgment, arguing that Thomas could not prove causation because he could not identify the specific manufacturer that produced the lead carbonate that caused his injuries. The lower court granted the manufacturers' summary judgment motion, and the court of appeals affirmed.

The Collins case was particularly important to the court's decision because it established the risk-contribution theory in Wisconsin. In Collins, the plaintiff's mother had ingested DES when pregnant to prevent miscarriage. Medical researchers established a link between fetal exposure to DES and adenosis of the vagina. The plaintiff developed adenocarcinoma and had most of her reproductive system removed. She later sued 12 drug companies that manufactured or marketed DES. The plaintiff's mother could not remember where she had purchased the DES, and the court had determined that plaintiff had to prove a particular drug company produced or marketed the particular DES her mother ingested. Because each drug company contributed to the risk of injury to the public and was in a better position than the plaintiff to absorb the cost of the injury, the court determined it was better for the companies to share the cost of the injury rather than place the burden on the innocent plaintiff.

JUSTICE BUTLER, JR. The main policy reasons identified by Collins warrant extension of the risk-contribution theory here. First, the record makes clear that the Pigment Manufacturers "contributed to the risk of injury to the public and, consequently, the risk of injury to individual plaintiffs such as" Thomas. Many of the individual defendants did more than simply contribute to a risk; they knew of the harm white lead carbonate pigments caused and continued production and promotion of the pigment notwithstanding that knowledge. Some manufacturers, paradoxically, even promoted their nonlead-based pigments as alternatives that were safe in that they did not pose the risk of lead poisoning. For those that did not have explicit knowledge of the harm they were engendering, given the growing medical literature in the early part of the century, Thomas's historical experts submit that by the 1920s the entire industry knew or should have known of the dangers of its products and should have ceased producing the lead pigments, including white lead carbonate. In short, we agree with Thomas that the record easily establishes the Pigment Manufacturers' culpability for, at a minimum, contributing to creating a risk of injury to the public.

Second, as compared to Thomas, the Pigment Manufacturers are in a better position to absorb the cost of the injury. They can insure themselves against liability, absorb the damage award, or pass the cost along to the consuming public as a cost of doing business. As we concluded in Collins, it is better to have the Pigment Manufacturers or consumers share the cost of the injury rather than place the burden on the innocent plaintiff.

Thomas is also unable to identify the precise manufacturer of the white lead carbonate that caused his injuries due to the number of manufacturers, the passage of time, and the loss of records. Additionally, he cannot identify which of the three types of white lead carbonate he ingested. On this failure of proof, the Pigment Manufacturers contend, Thomas's claim must fall. They argue that because white lead carbonate was not "fungible" or manufactured from a chemically identical formula, Collins' risk-contribution cannot be applied here. We disagree.

. . . [A] product can be fungible as it presents a "uniformity of risk." *Id.* at 165. Under this meaning, "[a]s a result of sharing an identical or virtually identical chemical formula, each manufacturer's product posed the same amount of risk as every other manufacturer's product. The products therefore were 'identically defective,' with none being more or less defective than the rest." *Id.* . . .

[W]e have already noted that white lead carbonates were produced utilizing "virtually identical chemical formulas" such that all white lead carbonates were "identically defective." It is the common denominator in the various white lead carbonate formulas that matters; namely, lead.

Thomas has brought claims for both negligence and strict product liability. Applying the risk-contribution theory to Thomas's negligence claim, he will have to prove the following elements to the satisfaction of the trier of fact:

(1) That he ingested white lead carbonate;

(2) That the white lead carbonate caused his injuries;

(3) That the Pigment Manufacturer produced or marketed the type of white lead carbonate he ingested; and

(4) That the Pigment Manufacturers' conduct in producing or marketing the white lead carbonate constituted a breach of a legally recognized duty to Thomas.

Because Thomas cannot prove the specific type of white lead carbonate he ingested, he need only prove that the Pigment Manufacturers produced or marketed white lead carbonate for use during the relevant time period: the duration of the houses' existence.

Applying the risk-contribution theory to Thomas's strict product liability claim, Thomas will have to prove the following elements to the satisfaction of the trier of fact:

(1) That the white lead carbonate was defective when it left the possession or control of the pigment manufacturers;

(2) That it was unreasonably dangerous to the user or consumer;

(3) That the defect was a cause of Thomas's injuries or damages;

(4) That the pigment manufacturer engaged in the business of producing or marketing white lead carbonate or, put negatively, that this is not an isolated or infrequent transaction not related to the principal business of the pigment manufacturer; and,

(5) That the product was one which the company expected to reach the user or consumer without substantial change in the condition it was in when sold.

Once Thomas makes a prima facie case under either claim, the burden of proof shifts to each defendant to prove by a preponderance of the evidence that it did not produce or market white lead carbonate either during the relevant time period or in the geographical market where the house is located. However, if relevant records do not exist that can substantiate either defense, "we believe that the equities of [white lead carbonate] cases favor placing the consequences on the [Pigment Manufacturers]." In addition to these specific defenses, and unlike in the DES cases, the Pigment Manufacturers here may have ample grounds to attack and eviscerate Thomas's prima facie case, with some of those grounds including that lead poisoning could stem from any number of substances (since lead itself is ubiquitous) and that it is difficult to know whether Thomas's injuries stem from lead poisoning as they are not signature injuries.

The procedure is not perfect and could result in drawing in some defendants who are actually innocent, particularly given the significantly larger time span at issue in this particular case. However, Collins declared that "we accept this as the price the defendants, and perhaps ultimately society, must pay to provide the plaintiff an adequate remedy under the law."

We further conclude that the risk-contribution theory applies to white lead carbonate cases.

REVERSED.

CRITICAL THINKING

What reasons did the court offer to support its conclusion to reverse summary judgment in this case? Are you persuaded by those reasons? Why or why not?

ETHICAL DECISION MAKING

What are the values associated with holding the lead carbonate manufacturers accountable? In other words, which values were guiding the judge's decision? Do you think the values promoted by the decision are appropriate for the situation?

global context

Collective Insurance in Scandinavia

The Scandinavian countries of Sweden, Finland, Denmark, and Norway share a unique feature: the role of collective insurance groups in product liability. Manufacturers, producers, and importers of similar products form cooperative groups and obtain an insurance policy. For example, in Finland, a voluntary insurance policy group headed by the Finnish Pharmaceutical Insurance Pool enlists pharmaceutical companies as members. To hear the appeals of those seeking damages, the pool appoints a board. The board follows the basic liability principle of insurance groups, which is that causation, rather than fault or defectiveness, determines compensation.

Pharmaceutical companies find this principle especially appealing because they can admit liability without damaging the name of their products as a whole. Supporters of the insurance system also point out that elimination of the defectiveness requirement enables product developers to concentrate on improving their products, as opposed to being tied up with product liability cases.

CASE OPENER WRAP-UP

Ford and Bridgestone/Firestone

Donna Bailey settled her case, with one of the stipulations being public disclosure of the documents involved with the Ford and Bridgestone/Firestone investigations. Any information from tire recalls has to be publicly disclosed as part of her settlement. By now, much of the personal injury litigation has been settled by the companies. However, the ramifications of product liability continue to be felt.

In May 2001, Ford announced that it was recalling even more Firestone tires, including those that were given to customers as replacements during the previous recall. Ford's CEO said that Ford did not have "enough confidence in the future performance" of the tires to continue to use them on Ford vehicles. Bridgestone/Firestone's CEO disputed the claim, noting that the real problem lay with the safety of the Ford Explorer. The replacements cost Ford about $3 billion and prompted further congressional investigations of Bridgestone/Firestone and Ford.

One day before Ford made its announcement, Bridgestone/Firestone announced that it would no longer sell tires to Ford. This left Bridgestone/Firestone free to call into question the safety of the Ford Explorer without fear of losing Ford as a customer. Soon after the announcement, Bridgestone/Firestone released evidence from Venezuela that Ford Explorers, equipped with Goodyear tires, had rolled over in that country.

Plaintiffs continue to bring suits against Firestone after tires detread. In February 2007, a Texas jury awarded $29.5 million to a teenager who was partially paralyzed after a rollover in a Ford-designed Mazda SUV. The jury had previously found that Ford was 75 percent at fault, Bridgestone/Firestone 15 percent, and Mazda 10 percent. The last of this story has probably not been heard, with several investigations pending.

Source: MSNBC staff and wire reporters, "Settlement Reached in Lawsuit against Ford and Bridgestone/Firestone," *Firestone Tires: In the News,* January 8, 2001, www.elslaw.com/firestone_news_settlement.htm (accessed May 23, 2001); Keith Bradsher, "Ford Intends to Replace 13 Million Firestone Wilderness Tires," *The New York Times,* May 23, 2001; "Teen Paralyzed in SUV Rollovers Awarded $29.5 Million," *Texas Lawyer,* February 19, 2007, p. 27.

Summary

Theories of liability for defective products	*Negligence:* Plaintiff must show that (1) the defendant manufacturer or seller owed a duty of care to the plaintiff; (2) the defendant breached that duty of care by supplying a defective product; (3) this breach of duty caused the plaintiff's injury; and (4) the plaintiff suffered actual injury. *Strict-product liability:* Plaintiff must show that (1) the product was defective when sold; (2) the product was so defective that the product was unreasonably dangerous; and (3) the product was the cause of the plaintiff's injury. *Warranty:* A guarantee or a binding promise regarding a product. *Express warranty:* The plaintiff must show that (1) the representation was the basis of the bargain and (2) there was a breach of the representation. *Implied Warranty of Merchantability:* Goods are fit for the purpose for which they are sold and used. *Implied Warranty of Fitness for a Particular Purpose:* A customer purchases a product for a particular purpose and the seller is aware of this purpose.
Market Share Liability	When plaintiffs cannot trace a product to any particular manufacturer and a number of manufacturers produced the same product, a court may use the theory of market share liability to impose a portion of fault on a number of manufacturers.

Point / Counterpoint

Many smokers are now bringing lawsuits against tobacco companies. Their theories of the case range from failure to warn to fraud.

Should Smokers Be Permitted to Recover Money from Tobacco Companies?	
Yes	**No**
Cigarette companies made misrepresentations to consumers to get them to smoke or continue smoking. Moreover, cigarette companies developed "light" cigarettes, and some evidence suggests that cigarette companies made light cigarettes more addictive. Smoking should not be treated any differently than other products in liability cases. As long as the consumer establishes the elements, the consumer should be permitted to recover damages. Tobacco companies are in a much better position than individual consumers to bear the load of	Smokers use products that they know or should know are harmful. Any individuals who started smoking in the last 10 years clearly had knowledge that cigarettes were harmful, yet they chose to use a harmful product. Smokers should not now be permitted to collect money for committing an act that they knew or should have known would be detrimental to their health. Several well-known cases have awarded plaintiffs tens of millions of dollars, but this should not have been allowed to happen. A smoker should not be permitted to get a "lottery ticket" on the basis of his or her unhealthy behavior.

the financial costs of smoking. These companies benefit from cigarette sales. Thus, they should be required to pay for the harm that their product imposed, and consumers should be permitted to recover damages for their cigarette smoking.	Furthermore, smokers face the problem of trying to tie liability to one particular cigarette manufacturer. A smoker may have smoked numerous cigarette brands. Thus, it would be unfair to require one cigarette manufacturer to pay on behalf of all. In short, consumers should not be permitted to recover damages through tobacco litigation.

Questions & Problems

1. Explain what privity is and what impact it had on the development of product liability law.
2. Explain the elements one would have to prove to bring a successful product liability case based on negligence.
3. Explain the defenses one can raise in a product liability case based on negligence.
4. Why would a defendant prefer to be found to have produced a product that was defectively manufactured rather than defectively designed?
5. How does the consumer expectations test differ from the feasible alternatives test?
6. Explain the defenses available in a case based on a theory of strict-product liability.
7. Boutte fell asleep at the wheel while driving his car, struck a cement wall, and broke both of his ankles. He sued Nissan Motor Corp., alleging that the improper placement of the lap belt constituted negligent design. In testimony, the plaintiff's expert explained that a proper seat belt is positioned over the pelvis. Boutte's seat belt was positioned over his thighs, and the improper placement allowed him to slide forward and injure his ankles. The expert also explained that a passive restraint system, which was used by other manufacturers, would have kept the lap belt in the correct position. The expert for the manufacturer disagreed and argued that even with a passive restraint system Boutte would have sustained the same injuries. Initially, the jury attributed 84 percent of the fault to the plaintiff. On appeal, the defendant argued that Boutte's injuries were not a result of the seat belt placement and that the plaintiff's expert testimony should not have been considered in the trial court. How do you think the appellate court ruled in this case and why? [*Boutte v. Nissan Motor Corp.,* 3d Cir. (1995) 48 ALR 5th 86.]
8. Douglas Martin had been drinking when he went to see his friend Marcel Nadeau. As the two were leaving to get more beer, Martin saw Nadeau's .38 Colt Mustang pistol. Nadeau removed the magazine and handed the gun to Martin. Nadeau turned away briefly, and when he turned back around, Martin had the gun in his hand, pointed toward his head. Nadeau heard the gun discharge, and Martin died not long after. Valerie-Ann Bolduc, acting as administrator of Martin's estate, sued Colt's Manufacturing Company, Inc., for negligent design. In Massachusetts, for a plaintiff to prevail in a negligent design case, she must show both that the defendant failed to exercise reasonable care to eliminate avoidable or foreseeable dangers to the user and that there is a functional alternative design that would reduce the product's risk. Bolduc alleged that neither Martin nor Nadeau knew that the gun would fire with the

magazine removed. She also alleged that there is an alternative design that includes a feature to stop the gun from firing when the magazine is disconnected. Thus, it appears that Bolduc satisfied both prongs of the Massachusetts test. Yet the district court ruled that Bolduc could not prevail on the claim and dismissed the case. What are possible reasons the district court used to find that Colt had not negligently designed the product? [*Valerie-Ann Bolduc v. Colt's Manufacturing Company, Inc.,* 968 F. Supp. 16 (1997).]

9. National Fulfillment Services was a tenant in an office building owned by Holmes Corporate Center. A fire in the building on February 4, 1992, damaged National Fulfillment's offices. National Fulfillment filed suit against the providers of fire and burglar alarm services, referred to as ADT, to recover uninsured losses. Among other claims, National Fulfillment alleged strict liability and negligence, claiming that ADT's alarm failed to alert firefighters in a timely manner; thus, more damage was sustained than National Fulfillment had insurance for. ADT noted that its contract was with Holmes Corporate Center, not with National Fulfillment, and that Holmes had a duty to defend ADT against any lawsuit filed by a nonparty to the agreement. The district court granted summary judgment for ADT. National Fulfillment appealed. Did the court of appeals grant National Fulfillment's claims of strict liability and negligence, or did it affirm the decision of the district court? Why? [*Krueger Associates, Inc., Individually and Trading as National Fulfillment Services v. The American District Telegraph Company of Pennsylvania and ADT Security Systems, Inc.,* 247 F.3d 61 (2001).]

10. Finley, an office worker, sued NCR Corporation after she developed carpal tunnel syndrome. Arguing that the defectively designed keyboard caused her injury, Finley claimed that NCR had a duty to warn her about the possibility of carpal tunnel syndrome. The defendants argued that carpal tunnel syndrome is developed through overuse and depends on personal characteristics, not the characteristics of the keyboard. Further, NCR claimed that it did not have a duty to warn since a computer keyboard is safe for its intended use without a warning. The court granted the defendant's request for summary judgment. Do you think NCR was negligent in failing to provide an adequate warning about carpal tunnel syndrome? Why or why not? [*Finley v. NCR Corp.,* 964 F. Supp. 882 (1996) 59 ALR 5th 479.]

11. Plaintiff's son was given St. Joseph's Aspirin for Children when he had the flu. The aspirin triggered Reye's syndrome, leaving the child a quadriplegic, blind, and mentally retarded. The aspirin contained a warning, approved by the Food and Drug Administration, about the dangers of giving aspirin to children with the flu. The product was advertised in Spanish in the Los Angeles area, but the warning was not in Spanish. The child's guardians could not read English. Do you believe the court imposed liability on the company for failure of its duty to warn? Why or why not? [*Ramirez v. Plough, Inc.,* 25 Cal. Rptr. 2d (1993).]

12. Plaintiff Darren Traub was playing basketball and tried to dunk the ball, but his hand hit the rim and he fell down, hurting both wrists. He sued the manufacturer and the university, claiming that the rigid rim caused his injury or made it worse. The defendants filed a motion for summary judgment. Do you think it should have been granted? [*Traub v. Cornell,* 1998 WL 187401 (N.D. N.Y.) (1998).]

13. In 1991, three-year-old Douglas Moore was playing with one of BIC's lighters. While playing with the lighter, he started a fire that severely injured his 17-month-old brother. BIC Manufacturers Inc. placed several child-safety warning labels on their lighters. These labels identified the risk of fire or injury as a result of misusing the

product. The lighter provided warnings to adults to "keep out of reach of children" or "keep away from children." The BIC Corporation had knowledge that its lighters could be manipulated by children, but it felt that including safety features would significantly increase the cost of the lighter. The Moore family brought a strict-liability suit against BIC. Explain why strict liability should or should not be applicable in this case. [*Price v. BIC Corp.,* 702 A.2d 330 (Sup. Ct., N.H.1997).]

14. Claude Swope was employed by Columbian Chemical Company as a maintenance worker. Columbian produced a product that required the use of ozone in its manufacturing. For this manufacturing, Columbian used ozone generators purchased from Emory Inc. Swope brought a product liability suit against these two companies, claiming he was completely and permanently disabled as a result of the ozone generators. He claimed "that Columbian knew to a substantial certainty that its continual exposures of Mr. Swope to harmful amounts of ozone without providing him with any respiratory protection would cause repeated damage to his lungs." He alleged that the companies should be liable due to the inherently dangerous design and failure to warn of that danger. Construct an argument for the defense or plaintiff in this case. [*Swope v. Columbian,* 2002 U.S. App. LEXIS 934.]
15. McClaran was severely burned and injured when a steel-melting furnace he was stationed at exploded. Union Carbide manufactured the furnace. McClaran brought suit against Union Carbide for product liability. In the suit, the cause of the explosion was examined. The investigation revealed that water leaked from the roof of the furnace into the molten steel, causing the explosion. Union Carbide designed the roof to be sprayed when necessary to reduce the temperature. The system had a vacuum to remove the water once dispensed and a backup drain on one side in case the vacuum failed. In addition to these features, the system had visual inspection points from which water could drain. At the time of the explosion, the vacuum line had a hole that prevented it from working, and the unit was tilted to the opposite side of the drain. The inspection hatches were covered with dust and debris that prevented any drainage. McClaran did not make connections or allegations to the defective nature of the product when it left Union Carbide. How do you believe the court ruled? Explain your reasoning. [*McClaran v. Union Carbide,* 2002 U.S. App. LEXIS 942.]

Looking for more review material?

The Online Learning Center at **www.mhhe.com/kubasek1e** contains this chapter's "Assignment on the Internet" and also a list of URLs for more information entitled "On the Internet." Find both of them in the Student Center portion of the OLC, along with quizzes and other helpful materials.

Liability of Accountants and Other Professionals

CASE OPENER

Questionable Accounting at WorldCom

Bert C. Roberts, Jr., was chairman of WorldCom's board of directors. Immediately prior to his service as chairman of WorldCom, Roberts was chairman of the board of MCI. WorldCom acquired MCI on September 14, 1998, in a transaction valued at $40 billion. The acquisition made WorldCom the second-largest telecommunications company in the world.

Roberts signed a number of documents filed by WorldCom with the Securities and Exchange Commission. These documents included Form 10-K for 1999, 2000, and 2001 and the registration statements for the 2000 and 2001 offerings, as well as registration statements filed in connection with WorldCom's acquisition of SkyTel Communications, Inc., in 1999 and of Intermedia Communications, Inc., in 2001.

On June 25, 2002, WorldCom announced a massive restatement of its financial statements for 2001 and the first quarter of 2002. Several weeks later, the company entered bankruptcy. WorldCom ultimately made approximately $76 billion in financial adjustments for 2000 and 2001, reducing the company's net equity from approximately $50 billion to approximately minus $20 billion. It is undisputed that beginning at least as early as 2001, WorldCom executives engaged in a secretive scheme to misrepresent WorldCom's financial condition in the company's filings with the SEC.

The facts underlying WorldCom's June 25 announcement spurred numerous lawsuits. A consolidated class action was brought on behalf of a class of all persons and entities, excluding defendants and certain others affiliated with them or with WorldCom, who were financially injured after they acquired publicly traded WorldCom securities between April 29, 1999, and June 25, 2002. Roberts faces charges under a number of different federal acts regulating securities.[1]

[1] *In re WorldCom, Inc., Sec. Litig.*, 2005 U.S. Dist. LEXIS 4193 (2005).

CHAPTER 11

1. Who should be liable for the massive loss the investors suffered due to the restatement of WorldCom's financial records?
2. What could Roberts have done to have avoided the catastrophe that ensued when WorldCom had to restate its financial statements?

The Wrap-Up at the end of the chapter will answer these questions.

Learning Objectives

After reading this chapter, you will be able to answer the following questions:

1. Under common law, what is the duty of an accountant to his or her clients?
2. Under common law, what is the duty of an accountant to third parties?
3. What are the rights of accountants and their clients?
4. What is the impact of federal securities law on accountant liability?
5. What is the extent of liability of professionals other than accountants?

Just as the manufacturers and sellers of defective products may be liable for harm caused by their products, professionals who provide substandard services may likewise be liable for the harm they cause. Actions brought against attorneys, lawyers, real estate brokers, doctors, architects, and other professionals are referred to as **malpractice actions.** Just as product liability cases are based on different legal theories, so are malpractice actions. Most malpractice cases are based on theories of negligence, breach of contract, or fraud.

Because most businesspersons require accounting services, they are more likely to encounter malpractice by an accountant than by other professionals, and so we focus here on accountant liability. Prior to February 2002, most people had probably not given much thought to questions about the extent to which accountants should be held liable for their failure to properly perform their professional responsibilities. However, after a significant amount of the responsibility for the bankruptcy of the Enron Corporation was placed on the firms that provided accounting services for the corporation, the role of these professionals and their accountability became a question of significant public interest.

Common Law Accountant Liability to Clients

Three primary types of liability are assessed to accountants under the common law: negligence, breach of contract, and fraud.

ACCOUNTANT LIABILITY FOR NEGLIGENCE

An accountant is liable to his or her client for negligence if he or she fails to exercise the care of a competent, reasonable professional and that failure causes loss or injury to the client. To prove negligence on the part of the accountant, the plaintiff establishes the basic elements of negligence as discussed in Chapter 9: duty, breach of duty, causation, and damages.

At minimum, the duty of care of the accountant entails compliance with the *generally accepted accounting principles (GAAP),* established by the Financial Accounting Standards Board (FASB), and the *generally accepted auditing standards (GAAS),* established by the American Institute of Certified Public Accountants (AICPA). While failure to comply with GAAP and GAAS will almost certainly constitute a breach of duty, compliance does not automatically mean the duty of care has been met. In some circumstances, a reasonable, competent accountant would do more than GAAP or GAAS requires. Also, sometimes a state statute or judicial opinion may impose additional legal requirements on accountants beyond GAAP and GAAS.

Generally, unless engaged to detect fraud, an accountant is not a fraud detector unless the fraud is uncovered in the course of exercising reasonable care and skill. An accountant is, likewise, not required to have perfect judgment; she or he will not be held liable simply for errors in judgment that were made in good faith while operating in accordance with GAAP and GAAS. Nonetheless, when an accountant fails to meet these standards or fails to detect fraud or misconduct that a normal audit would uncover, he or she may be held liable for negligence.

A failure to adhere to GAAS can have serious professional repercussions for accountants. For example, John Goldberger, an accountant in Pennsylvania, lost the privilege of appearing and practicing before the SEC because he had negligently performed an audit, failing to live up to professional standards and identify fraud while conducting the audit. The SEC argued that Goldberger (1) failed to obtain sufficient competent evidence to afford a reasonable basis for his firm's opinion on the issuer's financial statements; (2) failed to properly assess whether the issuer's financial statements were fairly presented

connecting to the core

Accounting

In addition to relying on independent accountants to review its financial information, a company may rely on its internal control system to monitor business activities, in the hope of reducing the likelihood of error and instances of fraudulent behavior. An effective internal control system should incorporate the following principles:

1. An internal control system should clearly identify the individuals responsible for performing particular tasks, thereby increasing the degree of accountability for employees.
2. A company should maintain adequate records.
3. Expensive assets should be insured, and employees who transfer large amounts of cash should be bonded, so that an insurance policy would cover losses from theft by those employees.
4. The responsibility of handling assets should be separated from the responsibility of record keeping for those assets.
5. Responsibility for transactions or a series of transactions should be divided among several individuals or departments.
6. Technological controls should be implemented, hopefully reducing the likelihood of mechanical and mathematical errors.
7. Regular reviews by internal auditors, along with external auditors, can increase the likelihood that financial statements accurately present company information.

In sum, while independent auditors or accountants may reduce the likelihood of error or fraud, an effective internal control system may also promote accuracy and ethical behavior, both for the company's employees and the independent auditors conducting their own review.

Source: K. Larson, J. Wild, and B. Chiappetta, *Principles of Financial Accounting* (New York: McGraw-Hill/Irwin, 2005), pp. 308–310.

in conformity to generally accepted accounting principles; and (3) failed to exercise due professional care in the performance of an audit.[2]

When faced with a charge of negligence, an accountant has several defenses available. First, the accountant can simply argue that he or she did not fail to meet the professional standards. Second, the accountant can argue, regardless of a failure to meet the professional standard of care, that the alleged failure is not the cause of the client's loss. In other words, the accountant can argue that he or she should not be held liable because he or she did not cause the client's damages. Third, an accountant may argue the defense of contributory or comparative negligence. However, only a few states recognize contributory or comparative negligence as a valid defense for accountant negligence.

In addition to asserting a defense to a charge of negligence, accountants can attempt to proactively limit their liability. When an audit is complete, the accountant issues an opinion letter stating his or her assessment of the company that was audited. Usually, an *unqualified* opinion letter is issued. To avoid potential liability, the accountant may make a qualification or issue a disclaimer as part of the opinion letter.

Any qualifications or disclaimers made must be specific, because broad, general qualifications or disclaimers do not grant protection. An example of a qualification is a statement, included in the opinion letter, declaring the accountant's doubt about the accuracy of the papers presented by a client. However, including a qualification or a disclaimer does not protect an accountant from liability based on the failure to discover fraudulent financial transactions that an accountant properly applying GAAP and GAAS would have discovered.

[2] *Golderberger v. State Board of Accountancy,* 833 A.2d 815 (2003).

connecting to the core

State Codes of Ethics for CPAs

Remember from your accounting class that many state ethics codes require that CPAs who audit financial statements must disclose areas in which those statements fail to comply with GAAP. Thus, one way accountants can reduce their chance of being found negligent is by making sure they are in compliance with their state code of ethics.

Another area in which accountants may not be liable for their work product involves unaudited financial statements. On occasion, a business may hire an accountant to create an unaudited financial statement for some purpose. A financial statement is considered unaudited if no, or insubstantial, accounting procedures were used in the compilation of the document. Accountants are not liable for the contents of an unaudited financial statement. Nonetheless, an accountant can still be held liable if he or she fails to clearly mark the financial statement as being unaudited.

ACCOUNTANT LIABILITY FOR BREACH OF CONTRACT

Whenever an accountant is hired to perform a task, the accountant enters into a contract with his or her client. The contract is frequently referred to as an *engagement letter* between the parties. In entering into the contract, the accountant makes certain explicit and implicit promises.

Explicitly, the accountant agrees to perform the contractual agreed-on tasks. Implicitly, the accountant agrees to complete the work in a competent and professional manner according to professional standards (GAAP and GAAS). Failure to fulfill these explicit and implicit agreements can subject an accountant to liability based on a breach of contract. An accountant liability for a breach of contract is similar to that of anyone else involved in a contractual dispute. (See Chapter 20 for further discussion regarding breach of contracts.)

When an accountant breaches a contract, the client is entitled to recovery for certain damages. First, the client is entitled to recovery for the cost of obtaining a different accountant to perform the breached contractual duties. Second, the client is entitled to any reasonable and foreseeable damages related to the accountant's breach. Suppose, for example, that Collin, an accountant, is performing an audit for Isis. Collin breaches his contract with Isis, and, as a result, her business's assets drop in value. Isis is entitled to recovery for the cost of hiring another accountant as well as for the loss in value of her assets, which occurred because Collin breached his contract with Isis.

When an accountant engages in a material breach of contract, he or she is not entitled to compensation for work completed. However, if the contract is substantially performed, the accountant may be entitled to partial compensation. In the instance of substantial performance, the accountant is entitled to the full amount of the contractually agreed-on fee minus the amount of damages caused by the accountant. Therefore, in the event of an immaterial breach, the accountant may still recover something for services rendered.

ACCOUNTANT LIABILITY FOR FRAUD

An accountant is liable to his or her client for fraud when all of the following have occurred:

1. The accountant misrepresented a material fact.
2. The accountant acted with the intent to deceive.
3. The client justifiably relied on the misrepresentation.
4. The client suffered an injury by relying on the fraudulent information.

An accountant who commits fraud is liable to those parties he or she reasonably should have foreseen would be injured through a justifiable reliance on the fraudulent information.

Accountants may be held liable for actual fraud or constructive fraud, depending on the circumstances. *Actual fraud* exists when the accountant's actions meet the above enumerated criteria. *Constructive fraud* is fraud without fraudulent intent. To establish constructive fraud, a plaintiff must prove that the accountant was grossly negligent in performing his or her duties. Evidence of a reckless disregard for duty and professional standards can help establish gross negligence and, thus, constructive fraud. When accountants are found liable for fraud, they can be assessed compensatory, as well as punitive, damages.

A new trend has arisen in civil suits seeking damages for accountant fraud. Over the last few years, plaintiffs have been successful in bringing fraud suits against accountants under the Racketeer Influenced and Corrupt Organizations Act (RICO) discussed in Chapter 7.

global context

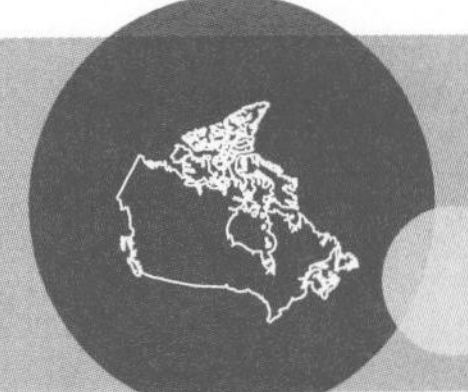

Liability of Accountants to Third Parties in Canada

As in the United States, in Canada the common law provides that accountants can be held liable on the basis of negligence in carrying out their duties. The accountant's duty of care to clients is established by the contractual relationship. What the duty of care to nonclients should be has been a controversial issue, especially with respect to the duty that arises in conjunction with a nonclient's reliance on an auditor's report.

Under common law in Canada, plaintiffs must prove that they reasonably relied on an auditor's report to their detriment. However, provincial securities laws are now, in some provinces, providing an important exception to the need to prove reliance for misrepresentations made in a prospectus distributed by the issuer of securities. For example, the Ontario Securities Act gives purchasers of securities in the primary market a right of action for damages against auditors. The right of action relates to misrepresentations in auditors' reports, opinions, or statements included or referred to in the prospectus with the auditors' filed consent. It is not necessary for purchasers to prove that they relied on the misrepresentation. In 2005, the Ontario Securities Act was amended to expand auditors' statutory liability to misrepresentations in secondary-market disclosures made with the auditors' written consent.

In Quebec, if a plaintiff can prove fault, damage, and a causal link between the two, these are sufficient grounds for a court to hold the accountant liable.

Common Law Accountant Liability to Third Parties

An important issue in accountant liability that has not been decided in the same way by all states is whether third parties have any claim against an accountant on the basis of their reliance on negligently prepared financial statements. Third-party liability, as decided by the states, falls into three general groupings: (1) privity or near privity (the Ultramares rule), (2) foreseen users and classes of users (the Restatement rule), and (3) reasonably foreseeable users. Third-party liability was the focus of the most famous case involving accountant legal liability, *Ultramares v. Touche,*[3] discussed below.

[3] 255 N.Y. 170 (1931).

LIABILITY BASED ON PRIVITY OR NEAR-PRIVITY (THE ULTRAMARES RULE)

In *Ultramares v. Touche,* Justice Benjamin Cardozo, writing for the highest state court in New York, took a narrow view of which third parties were permissible plaintiffs. Because of concern that a more liberal rule would subject accountants to a liability of "an indeterminate amount, for an indeterminate time, to an indeterminate class," Cardozo held an accountant liable in negligence only to those with whom he or she had *privity of contract,* meaning the client and anyone for whose "primary benefit" the accounting statements were prepared.

The New York courts have fundamentally continued the *Ultramares* approach by requiring that the accountant be aware of the particular use for his or her work product, that there be known reliance on the work product by an identified third party, and that there be conduct by the accountant recognizing his or her awareness of such reliance. This has been referred to as the *near-privity,* or *primary-benefit, test* and only a few states utilize it because it is viewed as too restrictive. The near-privity requirement was appended to the original privity requirement in the 1985 New York case *Credit Alliance Corp. v. Arthur Andersen & Co.* (see Case 11-1).

CASE 11-1 CREDIT ALLIANCE CORP. v. ARTHUR ANDERSEN & CO.

COURT OF APPEALS FOR NEW YORK

65 N.Y.2D 536; 483 N.E.2D 110; 493 N.Y.S.2D 435; 1985 N.Y. LEXIS 15157 (1985)

Prior to 1978, Credit Alliance had provided financing to L. B. Smith, Inc. of Virginia, a capital intensive enterprise that regularly required financing. During 1978, Credit Alliance advised Smith that as a condition to extending additional major financing, they would insist upon examining an audited financial statement. Accordingly, Smith, on two separate occasions, provided Credit Alliance with its consolidated financial statements, covering itself and its subsidiaries. These statements contained an auditor's report prepared by Arthur Andersen stating it had examined the statements in accordance with generally accepted auditing standards ("GAAS") and found them to reflect fairly the financial position of Smith in conformity with generally accepted accounting principles ("GAAP"). In reliance upon the statements, Credit Alliance provided substantial amounts in financing to Smith.

In 1980, Smith filed a petition for bankruptcy. By that time, Smith had already defaulted on several millions of dollars of obligations to Credit Alliance. In August 1981, Credit Alliance sued for damages lost on its outstanding loans to Smith, claiming both negligence and fraud by Andersen in the preparation of its audit reports. The complaint alleges Andersen knew, should have known or was on notice that the certified statements were being utilized by Smith to induce companies such as Credit Alliance to make credit available to Smith. It is also alleged Andersen knew or recklessly disregarded facts which indicated the certified statements were misleading.

Andersen filed a motion to dismiss the complaint. The court concluded Credit Alliance fell within the exception to the general rule that requires privity to maintain an action against an accountant for negligence. Andersen appealed.

JUDGE JASEN: In the seminal case of *Ultramares Corp. v Touche* (255 NY 170), this court, speaking through the opinion of Chief Judge Cardozo more than 50 years ago, disallowed a cause of action in negligence against a public accounting firm for inaccurately prepared financial statements which were relied upon by a plaintiff having no contractual privity with the accountants. This court distinguished its holding from *Glanzer v Shepard* (233 NY 236), a case decided in an opinion also written by Cardozo nine years earlier.

We explained that in *Glanzer,* an action in negligence against public weighers had been permitted, despite the absence of a contract between the parties, because the plaintiff's intended reliance, on the information *directly transmitted* by the weighers, created a bond so closely approaching privity it was, in practical effect, virtually indistinguishable there from. This court has subsequently reaffirmed its holding in *Ultramares* which has been, and continues to be, much discussed and analyzed by the commentators and by the courts of other jurisdictions. This appeal now provides us with the opportunity to re-examine and delineate the principles enunciated in both *Ultramares* and *Glanzer.* Inasmuch as we believe a relationship "so close as to approach that of privity" (255 NY, at pp 182–183) remains valid as the predicate for imposing liability upon accountants to noncontractual parties for the negligent preparation of financial reports, we restate and elaborate upon our adherence to that standard today.

The critical distinctions between the two cases were highlighted in *Ultramares* where we explained:

> In *Glanzer v. Shepard* . . . [the certificate of weight], which was made out in duplicate, one copy to the seller and the other to the buyer, *recites that it was made by order of the former for the use of the latter.* . . . Here was something more than the rendition of a service in the expectation that the one who ordered the certificate would use it thereafter in the operations of his business as occasion might require. Here was a case where *the transmission of the certificate to another was* not merely one possibility among many, but *the 'end and aim of the transaction,'* as certain and immediate and deliberately willed as if a husband were to order a gown to be delivered to his wife, or a telegraph company, contracting with the sender of a message, were to telegraph it wrongly to the damage of the person expected to receive it. . . . The *intimacy of the resulting nexus* is attested by the fact that after stating the case in terms of legal duty, we went on to point out that . . . we could reach the same result by stating it in terms of contract. . . . The bond was *so close as to approach that of privity, if not completely one with it.* Not so in the case at hand [i.e., *Ultramares*]. No one would be likely to urge that there was a contractual relation, *or even one approaching it,* at the root of any duty that was owing from the [accountants] now before us to the indeterminate class of persons who, presently or in the future, might deal with the [accountants' client] in reliance on the audit. In a word, the service rendered by the defendant in *Glanzer v. Shepard* was primarily for the information of a third person, *in effect, if not in name, a party to the contract,* and only incidentally for that of the formal promisee. (*Ultramares Corp. v Touche, supra,* at pp 182–183 [emphasis added].)

Upon examination of *Ultramares* and *Glanzer* and our recent affirmation of their holdings in *White,* certain criteria may be gleaned. Before accountants may be held liable in negligence to noncontractual parties who rely to their detriment on inaccurate financial reports, certain prerequisites must be satisfied: (1) the accountants must have been aware that the financial reports were to be used for a particular purpose or purposes; (2) in the furtherance of which a known party or parties was intended to rely; and (3) there must have been some conduct on the part of the accountants linking them to that party or parties, which evinces the accountants' understanding of that party or parties' reliance. While these criteria permit some flexibility in the application of the doctrine of privity to accountant liability, they do not represent a departure from the principles articulated in *Ultramares, Glanzer* and *White,* but, rather, they are intended to preserve the wisdom and policy set forth therein.

In the appeals we decide today, application of the foregoing principles presents little difficulty. The facts as alleged by Credit Alliance fail to demonstrate the existence of a relationship between the parties sufficiently approaching privity. Though the complaint and supporting affidavit do allege Andersen specifically knew, should have known or was on notice that Credit Alliance was being shown the reports by Smith, Andersen's client, in order to induce their reliance thereon, nevertheless, there is no adequate allegation of either a particular purpose for the reports' preparation or the prerequisite conduct on the part of the accountants. While the allegations state Smith sought to induce plaintiffs to extend credit, no claim is made Andersen was being employed to prepare the reports with that particular purpose in mind. Moreover, there is no allegation Andersen had any direct dealings with Credit Alliance, had specifically agreed with Smith to prepare the report for Credit Alliance's use or according to Credit Alliance's requirements, or had specifically agreed with Smith to provide Credit Alliance with a copy or actually did so. Indeed, there is simply no allegation of any word or action on the part of Andersen directed to Credit Alliance, or anything contained in Andersen's retainer agreement with Smith which provided the necessary link between them. We therefore dismiss the charges against Arthur Andersen.

REVERSED.

[CONTINUED]

CRITICAL THINKING

Think about the judge's reasoning that led to the conclusion that the relationship between Arthur Andersen & Co. and Credit Alliance was not enough to establish privity. Is there any additional information that you would have liked to know that would help decide whether Andersen acted negligently?

ETHICAL DECISION MAKING

What are the values associated with requiring that the relationship between Andersen and Credit Alliance be enough to establish privity? What values would have been in conflict when making the decision?

Do you think the values promoted by the decision are appropriate for the situation? Why or why not?

LIABILITY TO FORESEEN USERS AND FORESEEN CLASS OF USERS (THE RESTATEMENT RULE)

About half the states have adopted a somewhat more expansive approach to accountant liability for negligence to third parties. This test is referred to as the *Restatement test* because it was codified in the Restatement (Second) of Torts. It holds an accountant liable to known third-party users of the accountant's work product and also to those in the limited class whose reliance on the work was specifically foreseen by the accountant.

The rationale behind the Restatement test is simple: Much of what accountants do is prepare work for parties that are not their clients; therefore, it makes sense for accountants to owe a duty to these intended receivers. The test extends liability to those people, or the class of people, the accountant foresaw or should have foreseen as being the recipients of and relying on his or her work. Despite the expansion, as Section 552 of the Restatement of Torts explains, accountant liability is not extended to potential investors and the general public.

For example, assume that a client has an accountant certify financial statements as part of a loan application of Third State Bank. The accountant, who is aware of this purpose, negligently audits the statements, which overvalue inventory and undervalue liabilities. The client not only uses the financials at Third State Bank but also uses them in a loan application at Federal State Bank, which makes the loan. When the client defaults on the loan because of too much indebtedness, Federal State can properly sue the accountant for negligence because the bank's use of the financial statements for loan considerations was foreseeable, even if the specific institution was not. The Restatement test requires that the user be specifically known to the accountant or be of the limited class of foreseen users who utilize the accountant's work product in the contemplated manner. It is viewed as a middle-ground test between the very restrictive, pro-accountant primary-benefit test represented by *Ultramares* and the liability-expanding reasonably foreseeable users test discussed next.

LIABILITY TO REASONABLY FORESEEABLE USERS

Very few states have adopted the general negligence standard of accountant third-party liability called the *reasonably foreseeable users test.* This test holds an accountant liable to any third party that was or should have been foreseen as a possible user of the accountant's work product and that, in fact, did use and rely on that work product for a proper business purpose. The justification for this expanded accountant liability was succinctly stated by the New Jersey Supreme Court in a case subsequently overruled by statute:

> The responsibility of a public accountant is not only to the client who pays his fee, but also to investors, creditors, and others who may rely on the financial statements which he certifies. . . . The auditor's function has expanded from that of a watchdog for management to an independent evaluator of the adequacy and fairness of financial statements issued by management to stockholders, creditors and others.[4]

The court justified its protection of reasonably foreseeable users on the policy grounds that this approach would encourage accountants to be more careful and thorough and the cost of the increased liability risk, through insurance or otherwise, could be spread among all the accountant's clients. Courts used similar reasoning as justification for imposing strict product liability.

The *Bily* decision excerpted in Case 11-2 contains a good discussion of the three theories of the accountant's legal liability to third parties.

[4] *Rosenbloom, Inc. v Adler,* 461 A.2d 138 (1983).

CASE 11-2

BILY v. ARTHUR YOUNG & CO.
SUPREME COURT OF CALIFORNIA
834 P. 24, 745 (1992)

Plaintiffs purchased stock warrants (rights to purchase) for blocks of Osborne Computer Corp., the manufacturer of the first mass market portable personal computer. Because of an inability to produce a new product line with sufficient speed and the entry of IBM-compatible software into the personal computer market, Osborne filed for bankruptcy shortly after the warrants were issued. Plaintiffs, thus, received nothing for their investment.

Arthur Young had audited Osborne's financial statements for the two years preceding the issuance of the warrants and had issued unqualified opinions on their fairness and compliance with Generally Accepted Accounting Principles. Plaintiffs sued Arthur Young for fraud, negligence, and negligent misrepresentation. After a thirteen week trial in which the plaintiff's expert witness alleged forty deficiencies in Arthur Young's audit and its noncompliance with Generally Accepted Auditing Standards, the jury found Arthur Young liable for professional negligence. Arthur Young appealed based on the jury instructions regarding its liability to third parties.

CHIEF JUSTICE LUCAS: The AICPA's professional standards refer to the public responsibility of auditors:

> A distinguishing mark of a profession is acceptance of its responsibility to the public. The accounting profession's public consists of clients, credit grantors, governments, employers, investors, the business and financial community, and others who rely on the objectivity and integrity of certified public accountants to maintain the orderly functions of commerce. This reliance imposes a public interest responsibility on certified public accountants. [2 AICPA Professional Standards (CCH 1988) §53.01]

[The court then discussed different states' approaches to the issue of accountant liability to third parties.]

A. Privity of Relationship

The New York Court of Appeals restated the law in light of *Ultramares, White v. Guarente,* and other cases in *Credit Alliance v. Arthur Andersen & Co.* (1985) 65 N.Y. 2d 536 [493 N.Y.S. 2d 435, 483 N.E. 2d 110]. *Credit Alliance* subsumed two cases with different factual postures: in the first case, plaintiff alleged it loaned funds to the auditor's client in reliance on audited financial statements which overstated the client's assets and net worth; in the second, the same scenario occurred, but plaintiff also alleged the auditor knew plaintiff was the client's principal lender and communicated directly and frequently with plaintiff regarding its continuing audit reports. The court dismissed plaintiff's negligence claim in the first case, but sustained the claim in the second.

The New York court promulgated the following rule for determining auditor liability to third parties for negligence:

> Before accountants may be held liable in negligence to noncontractual parties who rely to their detriment on inaccurate financial reports, certain prerequisites must be satisfied: (1) the accountant must have been aware that the financial reports were to be used for a particular purpose or purposes; (2) in the furtherance of which a known party or parties was intended to rely; and (3) there must have been some conduct on the part of the accountants linking them to party or parties, which evinces the accountants' understanding of that party or parties reliance. (*Credit Alliance v. Arthur Andersen & Co.,* supra, 483 N.E. 2d at p. 118)

Discussing the application of its rule to the cases at hand, the court observed the primary, if not exclusive, "end and aim" of the audits in the second case was to satisfy the lender. The auditor's "direct communications and personal meetings [with the lender] result[ed] in a nexus between them sufficiently approaching privity. In contrast, in the first case, although the complaint did not allege the auditor knew or should have known of the lender's reliance on its reports: "There was no allegation of either a particular purpose for the reports' preparation or the prerequisite conduct on the part of the accountants . . . [nor] any allegation [the auditor] had any direct dealings with plaintiffs, and agreed with [the client] to prepare the report for plaintiffs' use or according to plaintiffs' requirements, or had specifically agreed with [the client] to provide plaintiffs with a copy [of the report] or actually did so."

B. Foreseeability

Arguing that accountants should be subject to liability to third persons on the same basis as other tortfeasors, Justice Howard Wiener advocated rejection of the rule of *Ultramares* in a 1983 law review article. In its place, he proposed a rule based on foreseeability of injury to third persons. Criticizing what he called the "anachronistic protection" given to accountants by the traditional rules limiting third person liability, he concluded:

> Accountant liability based on foreseeable injury would serve the dual functions of compensation for injury and deterrence of negligent conduct. Moreover, it is a just and rational judicial policy that the same criteria govern the imposition of negligence liability, regardless of the context in which it arises. The accountant, the investor, and the general public will in the long run benefit when the liability of the certified public accountant for negligent misrepresentation is measured by the foreseeability standard.

Under the rule proposed by Justice Wiener, "[f]oreseeability of the risk would be a question of fact for the jury to be disturbed on appeal only where there is insufficient evidence to support the finding."

C. The Restatement: Intent to Benefit Third Persons

Section 552 of the Restatement Second of Torts covers "Information Negligently Supplied for the Guidance of Others." It states a general principle that one who negligently supplies false information "for the guidance of others in their business transactions" is liable for economic loss suffered by the recipients in justifiable reliance on the information. But the liability created by the general principle is expressly limited to loss suffered: "(a) by the person or one of a limited group of persons for whose benefit and guidance he intends to supply the information or knows that the recipient intends to supply it, and (b) through reliance upon it in a transaction that he intends the information to influence or knows that the recipient so intends or in a substantially similar transaction." To paraphrase, a supplier of information is liable for negligence to a third party only if he or she indents to supply the information for the benefit of one or more third parties in a specific transaction or type of transaction identified to the supplier.

The authors of the Restatement Second of Torts offer several variations on the problem before us as illustrations of section 552. For example, the auditor may be held liable to a third party lender if the auditor is informed by the client that the audit will be used to obtain a $50,000 loan, even if the specific lender remains unnamed or the client names one lender then borrows from another. However, there is no liability where the auditor agrees to conduct the audit with the express understanding the report will be transmitted only to a specified bank and it is then transmitted to other lenders. Similarly, there is no liability when the client's transaction (as represented to the auditor) changes so as to increase materially the audit risk, e.g., a third person originally considers selling goods to the client on credit and later buys a controlling interest in the client's stock, both in reliance on the auditor's report.

Under the Restatement rule, an auditor retained to conduct an annual audit and to furnish an opinion for no particular purpose generally undertakes no duty to third parties. Such an auditor is not informed

> of any intended use of the financial statements; but . . . knows that the financial statements, accompanied by an auditor's opinion, are customarily used in a wide variety of financial transactions by the [client] corporation, and that they may be relied upon by lenders, investors, shareholders, creditors, purchasers, and the like, in numerous possible kinds of transactions. [The client corporation] uses the financial statements and accompanying auditor's opinion to obtain a loan from [a particular] bank. Because of [the auditor's] negligence, he issues an unqualifiedly favourable opinion upon a balance sheet that materially misstates the financial position of [the corporation] and through reliance upon it [the bank] suffers pecuniary loss.

Consistent with the text of section 552, the authors conclude: "[The auditor] is not liable to [the bank]."

Analysis of Auditor's Liability to Third Persons for Audit Opinions

A. Negligence

In permitting negligence liability to be imposed in the absence of privity, we outlined the factors to be considered in making such a decision: "The determination whether in a specific case the defendant will be held liable to a third person not in privity is a matter of policy and involves the balancing of various factors, among which are the extent to which the transaction was intended to affect the plaintiff, the foreseeability of harm to him, the degree of certainty that the plaintiff suffered injury, the moral blame attached to the defendant's conduct, and the policy of preventing future harm."

Viewing the problem before us in light of the factors set forth above, we decline to permit all merely foreseeable third party users of audit reports to sue the auditor on a theory of professional negligence. Our holding is premised on three central concerns: (1) Given the secondary "watchdog" role of the auditor, the complexity of the professional opinions rendered in audit reports, and the difficult and potentially tenuous causal relationships between audit reports and economic losses from investment and credit decisions, the auditor exposed to negligence claims from all foreseeable third parties faces potential liability far out of proportion to its fault; (2) the generally more sophisticated class of plaintiffs in auditor liability classes (e.g., business lenders and investors) permits the effective use of contract rather than tort liability to control and adjust the relevant risks through "private ordering"; and (3) the asserted advantages of more accurate auditing and more efficient loss spreading relied upon by those who advocate a pure foreseeability approach are unlikely to occur; indeed, dislocations of resources, including increased expense and decreased availability of auditing services in some sectors of the economy, are more probable consequences of expanded liability.

For the reasons stated above, we hold that an auditor's liability for general negligence in the conduct of an audit of its client's financial statements is confined to the client, i.e., the person who contracts for or engages the audit services. Other persons may not recover on a pure negligence theory.

There is, however, a further narrow class of persons who, although not clients, may reasonably come to receive and rely on audit reports and whose existence constitutes a risk of audit reporting that may fairly be imposed on the auditor. Such persons are specifically intended beneficiaries of the audit report who are known to the auditor and for whose benefit it renders the audit report. While such persons may not recover on a general negligence theory, we hold they may, . . . recover on a theory of negligent misrepresentation.

REVERSED.

[CONTINUED]

CRITICAL THINKING

If you were a justice sitting on the supreme court of a state that had yet to decide which of the three rules to follow in determining the extent of auditors' liability to third parties, which of the rules would you adopt? Why?

ETHICAL DECISION MAKING

Which stakeholders would primarily benefit from each of the three alternatives?

Accountants' and Clients' Rights

As with most professional exchanges, when an accountant and a client are engaged in a contract, certain legal issues and rights arise from the contract. Two of the most salient rights issues involved in the accountant-client relationship are working papers and accountant-client privilege.

WORKING PAPERS

Working papers are the various documents used and developed during an audit, including notes, calculations, copies, memorandums, and other papers constituting the accountant's work product. Legal issues involving rights arise when the audit is complete and a new set of documents, the working papers, has been created.

After an audit, the accountant is the legal owner of the working papers. Accountants are advised to maintain all working papers because they can be used as evidence in negligence cases (to show competency of work product). Not only is it wise for accountants to keep their working papers, but the Sarbanes-Oxley Act of 2002 requires it. According to Section 802(a)(1) of the act, accountants must maintain working papers for five years, starting with the end of the fiscal period in which the audit was conducted. Under Sarbanes-Oxley Section 802(b), willful violation of Section 802(a)(1) will result in a fine, imprisonment up to 10 years, or both.

Although the accountant is the legal owner of the working papers, the information contained within is that of the client. Accordingly, the client has a right to access working papers on request. Also, because of the sensitive nature of the material contained within the working papers, an accountant may not disclose working papers unless (1) the client consents or (2) the court orders the documents. Improper disclosure of a client's working papers is considered to be professionally unethical.

ACCOUNTANT-CLIENT PRIVILEGE

Another rights issue involved in accountant-client interactions is the question of the existence of an accountant-client privilege. Accountant-client privilege is not recognized by the common law or by federal law. In contrast, a number of states have adopted statutes granting some form of accountant-client privilege. It is important to mention, however, that when a federal law is at issue, state protection of an accountant-client privilege does not apply.

When the privilege is granted, it is typically granted to the client, although it has been extended to the accountant in some states. Also, accountants are sometimes granted privilege that does not quite amount to an accountant-client privilege. For example, under the IRS Restructuring and Reform Act, accountants who are authorized by federal law to practice before the IRS have privilege of confidentiality when giving tax advice to clients with respect to the Internal Revenue Code.

Even where privilege does not exist, it is professionally unethical for an accountant to willfully disclose the contents of confidential communications with a client. Such disclosure is ethical only when it occurs in accordance with the American Institute of Certified Public Accountants (AICPA) or GAAS requirements, as part of a court order, or on the client's request.

Federal Securities Law and Accountant Liability

Several federal acts have been critical in assessing criminal and civil liability to accountants. Among these acts are the Securities Act of 1933, the Securities Exchange Act of 1934, the Private Securities Litigation Reform Act of 1995, and the Sarbanes-Oxley Act of 2002. Also, as mentioned in Chapter 7 and earlier in this chapter, RICO has been useful in bringing suits against accountants for their wrongdoings.

THE SECURITIES ACT OF 1933

Under Section 11 of the Securities Act of 1933, accountants are civilly liable for misstatements and omissions of material facts made in registration statements the SEC requires. When a person buys a security covered by a registration statement that contains false information or is missing information, the accountant who helped prepare and file the statement may be liable for damages.

In order to recover damages, a plaintiff—in this case, someone who purchased a security covered by a registration statement containing false information or missing information—does not need to prove reliance on the statement to recover damages, nor does he or she need to establish privity. In other words, the purchaser may recover damages even if he or she did not know about or rely on the false or missing information in the registration statement. Also, the purchaser of a security may recover damages even if he or she was not a party to the contractual agreement. Originally, courts held accountants liable only to those who purchased securities in an initial public offering (IPO). The courts have since expanded liability to subsequent purchasers as well, as the Case Nugget illustrates.

Accountants are liable when they do not perform their jobs according to the generally accepted standards and practices of their profession. Under Section 11 of the Securities Act, accountants have a duty to perform their tasks with due diligence. This includes the creation of financial statements filed with the SEC as part of registration statements.

Under Section 11, an accountant is not liable if "after reasonable investigation, [he or she has] reasonable ground to believe and did believe, at the time such part of the registration statement became effective, that the statements therein were true and that there was no omission to state a material fact required to be stated therein or necessary to make the statements therein not misleading."[5] An accountant's failure to fulfill obligations under GAAP and GAAS is prima facie evidence of a failure of due diligence.

[5] U.S.C. § 77(b)(3).

Case Nugget — The Expansion of Liability to Subsequent Purchasers

Lee v. Ernst & Young, L.L.P
294 F.3d 969 (2002)

In *Lee v. Ernst & Young, L.L.P,* plaintiffs brought a class action suit against Ernst & Young for its alleged filing of a materially false and misleading statement with the SEC. The district court initially dismissed the class of plaintiffs who did not partake in the IPO. However, the Eighth Circuit ruled that "aftermarket purchasers of Summit stock who can make a prima facie showing that the Summit shares they purchased can be traced to the registration statement alleged to be false and misleading" are entitled to recovery of damages. Thus the ruling expanded liability to subsequent purchasers. In explaining its holding, the court said that the language of Section 11 of the statute, providing recovery for "any person acquiring such security," clearly contains no words limiting recovery to initial purchasers.

In an effort to avoid liability, an accountant can prove due diligence by showing evidence that he or she did not act fraudulently or negligently in preparing the registration statements in question. In addition, an accountant has other defenses to liability under the Securities Act. An accountant can argue that no misstatements or omissions exist; therefore, he or she is not liable. An accountant may acknowledge the existence of misstatements or omissions but contest that he or she is not liable because the misstatements or omissions do not involve material facts. An accountant may also claim as a defense that the misstatements or omissions had no causal connection to the purchaser's loss or that the purchaser invested in the securities knowing of the misstatement or omission.

The final defense available to an accountant is to argue that the misstatement or omission did not occur as a result of the financial statement created by the accountant. That is, the accountant can acknowledge a misstatement or omission but assert that it was made by another party. An accountant cannot be held liable for something he or she did not do. For example, if two accounting firms both provided information to the SEC about the same public company and one of the sets of paperwork contained misstatements, the firm that did not file the false paperwork would not be liable. Only the firm that filed the paperwork with the misstatements would be liable.

Returning to the WorldCom case in the opening scenario, Roberts was charged with, among other things, violation of Section 11 of the Securities Act for the statements he filed with the SEC. In his case, he asserted the affirmative defense of due diligence. Roberts argued that he "relied and was entitled to rely on the integrity of WorldCom's officers and the work of WorldCom's auditor in connection with the contents of the Registration Statements."[6] Should Roberts's alleged reliance on his employees enable him to claim that he acted with due diligence? According to the SEC, directors must perform "a due diligence inquiry," regardless of whether another expert is used to compile the statement.[7] Furthermore, courts have held that a director may not rely on a defense of reliance when "red flags" warning of the questionable quality of an audit exist.[8]

[6] See footnote 1.

[7] "New High Risk Ventures," SEC Release No. 5275, 1972 WL 125474, p. 6.

[8] *WorldCom,* 346 F. Supp. 2d, p. 672.

The Securities Act carries with it certain penalties for violation of the act. For willful violations, the U.S. Department of Justice can seek fines up to $10,000, imprisonment up to five years, or both. In addition, as a proactive effort to prevent future fraud, the SEC may seek an injunction against willful violators to prevent them from engaging in similar practices in the future. The SEC can also ask the court to impose other forms of relief on the liable accountant.

Another relevant, and related section of the Securities Act is Section 15. Under Section 15, "[E]very person who, by or through stock ownership, agency, or otherwise . . . controls any person liable under section 11 or 12, shall also be liable jointly and severally with and to the same extent as such controlled person to any person to whom such controlled person is liable."[9] Section 15 is typically used to charge executive board members or other high-level officials who fail to use a reasonable standard of care when running their business. To establish liability under Section 15, a plaintiff must prove control on the part of the defendant and an underlying claim under Section 11 or 12 of the Securities Act.

Section 15 does contain an affirmative defense. Under Section 15, a controlling person will not be liable if he or she "had no knowledge of or reasonable ground to believe in the existence of the facts by reason of which the liability of the controlled person is alleged to exist."[10] In the opening scenario, Roberts was charged with violations under Section 15 as well as Section 11. He asserted the affirmative defense available to him. However, the court determined that as the chairman of the board of directors for WorldCom, he clearly was a controlling person. The question remains, Did Roberts have reasonable ground to believe in the financial statements he signed? If Roberts did believe he signed accurate documents, should he still be held liable for his failure to review the documents thoroughly?

THE SECURITIES EXCHANGE ACT OF 1934

Liability under Section 18 of the Securities Exchange Act of 1934. The Securities Exchange Act of 1934, Section 18, states:

> Any person who shall make or cause to be made any statement in any application, report, or document . . . , which statement was at the time and in the light of the circumstances under which it was made false or misleading with respect to any material fact, shall be liable to any person (not knowing that such statement was false or misleading) who, in reliance upon such statement, shall have purchased or sold a security at a price which was affected by such statement, for damages caused by such reliance, unless the person sued shall prove that he acted in good faith and had no knowledge that such statement was false or misleading.

According to Section 18, accountants are liable for fraudulent statements made to the SEC in documents filed with the SEC. Section 18 contains a built-in statute of limitations requiring for recovery that the action be brought within one year of discovering the fraud and within three years of the fraud's occurrence.

Whereas the Securities Act imposes liability for negligence in performing an audit or in the construction of a financial statement, the Securities Exchange Act imposes liability for fraudulent statements made to the SEC. Also, the Securities Exchange Act requires a higher burden of proof for the plaintiff to recover than does the Securities Act.

[9] 15 U.S.C. §770.

[10] Ibid.

To recover damages under Section 18 of the Securities Exchange Act, a plaintiff must prove two things. First, the false or misleading statement in question actually affected the price of the security. Second, reliance was placed on the false or misleading statement without knowledge of its inaccuracy. Like the Securities Act, the Securities Exchange Act does not require privity, but it now requires demonstration of reliance on the false or misleading statement. The Securities Act did not require demonstration of reliance.

Another difference between the Securities Act and the Securities Exchange Act is the duty imposed on accountants. Instead of requiring due diligence, the Securities Exchange Act uses a "good-faith" requirement. Under Section 18, an accountant is not liable if he or she acted in good faith. *Good faith* involves the accountant's lack of knowledge that the financial statement was false or misleading, as well as lack of intent to use the falsity to gain an unfair advantage over another person. Without knowledge and intent, the accountant cannot be found liable.

For a plaintiff to prove the absence of good faith on the part of the accountant, he or she must establish three things. First, the plaintiff must prove *scienter,* knowledge of the wrong committed at the time of the act. Thus, the plaintiff must establish that the accountant knowingly committed an illegal act. Second, he or she must show reckless conduct by the accountant. Third, the plaintiff must demonstrate gross negligence in the accountant's actions. Without all three elements, a plaintiff will not succeed with a claim under the Securities Exchange Act.

In addition to good faith, a second defense available to accountants under the act is the buyer's or seller's knowledge of the falsity. If the accountant can prove that the plaintiff knew the statements in question were false, the accountant is not liable. The reasoning behind this defense is that the act aims to impose liability in order to create fair dealings and well-informed consumers in regard to the securities they are trading. If the plaintiff knows a statement is false, she or he places no reliance on the statement, and reliance must be proved to establish a claim. Therefore, without reliance on the falsity, the accountant would not be liable to the plaintiff.

Liability under Section 10(b) of the Securities Exchange Act and SEC Rule 10b-5. An accountant may face liability not only under Section 18 of the Securities Exchange Act but also under Section 10(b) of that act and the corresponding SEC Rule 10b-5. Both Section 10(b) and Rule 10b-5 are antifraud provisions. Section 10(b) makes it unlawful for accountants, or anyone, to use "any manipulative or deceptive device or contrivance in contravention of such rules and regulations as the [SEC] may prescribe as necessary or appropriate in the public interest or for the protection of investors." Under this provision, accountants are liable to buyers and sellers for fraudulent statements made to the SEC, as well as written or oral fraudulent statements made in the process of selling any security.

For a buyer or seller of a security to recover under Section 10(b) and Rule 10b-5, she or he must prove each of the following six elements:

1. Status as purchaser or seller (privity not required).
2. Scienter.
3. Fraudulent act or deception.
4. Reliance on the fraudulent statement.
5. Statement in regard to a material fact.
6. Reliance on the statement as the cause of the plaintiff's (buyer's or seller's) loss.

Once the buyer or seller establishes all six elements, he or she is eligible for recovery of damages from the liable accountant. Case 11-3 discusses the circumstances under which an accounting firm is liable under Section 10(b) and Rule 10b-5.

CASE 11-3 GREAT NECK CAPITAL APPRECIATION INV. P'SHIP, L.L.P. v. PRICEWATERHOUSECOOPERS, L.L.P.

UNITED STATES DISTRICT COURT FOR THE EASTERN DISTRICT OF WISCONSIN
137 F. SUPP. 2D 1114; 2001 U.S. DIST. LEXIS 5235; FED. SEC. L. REP. (CCH) P91,435 (2001)

Harnischfeger is a holding company for subsidiaries involved in the manufacture of machinery. PricewaterhouseCoopers, L.L.P. ("PwC") was Harnischfeger's outside auditor. As Harnischfeger's accountant, PwC prepared and audited Harnischfeger's financial statements. PwC filed the necessary statements with the SEC stating Harnischfeger's 1997 financial statements were fairly presented in accordance with Generally Accepted Accounting Principles (GAAP), and PwC had performed its audit in accordance with General Accepted Auditing Standards (GAAS). On November 20, 1997, Harnischfeger issued a press release about its financial condition, and PwC reviewed it and advised Harnischfeger the financial information in the release conformed with GAAP.

In 1996, the Beloit Company, a Harnischfeger subsidiary, entered into contracts with Asia Pulp and Paper Company ("APP"), which required Beloit to construct and install fine paper machines in Indonesia. The four APP projects represented the largest order in Beloit's history and involved a total value of about $600 million. As the result of financial difficulties related in part to these projects, Harnischfeger's earnings dropped dramatically in 1998, and by June 1999 the company was in bankruptcy.

On May 29, 1999, plaintiffs commenced this securities fraud class action on behalf of themselves and others who purchased the stock of Harnischfeger Industries, during the period November 20, 1997, through August 26, 1998. Plaintiffs allege PwC violated Section 10(b) of the Securities Exchange Act of 1934 and Rule 10b.

JUDGE ADELMAN: The substantive elements of a securities fraud claim are provided in §10(b) of the Exchange Act, which states it is unlawful for any person "to use or employ, in connection with the purchase or sale of any security . . . any manipulative or deceptive device or contrivance in contravention of such rules and regulations as the [SEC] may prescribe." 15 U.S.C. § 78j(b). One such rule is Rule 10b-5, which prohibits the making of any untrue statement of material fact or the omission of a material fact that would render statements made misleading in connection with the purchase or sale of any security. 17 C.F.R. § 240.10b-5. To state a valid Rule 10b-5 claim a plaintiff must allege the defendant: (1) made a misstatement or omission (2) of material fact (3) with scienter, (4) in connection with the purchase or sale of securities, (5) upon which the plaintiff relied, and (6) that reliance proximately caused the plaintiff's injury.

Scienter is a "mental state embracing intent to deceive, manipulate or defraud." The Seventh Circuit has interpreted *Ernst & Ernst v. Hochfelder,* 425 U.S. 185, as establishing "reckless disregard of the truth counts as intent" for the purpose of the 10b-5 scienter requirement. "Reckless conduct is, at the least, conduct which is highly unreasonable and which represents an extreme departure from the standards of ordinary care . . . to the extent that the danger was either known to the defendant or so obvious that the defendant must have been aware of it." An egregious refusal to see the obvious, or to investigate the doubtful, may in some cases give rise to an inference of . . . recklessness."

Before addressing the question of whether plaintiffs have adequately pleaded PwC knowingly made misstatements, I need to determine what statements may be attributed to PwC for purposes of §10(b).

A party who aids and abets a misrepresentation may not be held liable under §10(b). Rather, the statute "prohibits only the making of a material misstatement (or omission) or the commission of a manipulative act. The proscription does not include giving aid to a person who commits a manipulative or deceptive act." In *Central Bank of Denver, N.A. v. First Interstate Bank of Denver, N.A.,* 511 U.S. 164, the Supreme Court stated such "secondary" liability would "circumvent the reliance requirement" of §10(b) by allowing a plaintiff to recover "without any showing that [he] relied upon the [defendant's] statements or actions." Plaintiffs argue, however, even though PwC may not be held liable as an aider and abettor, its participation in the press release was extensive enough for it to be considered a primary violator of §10(b) and Rule 10b-5.

Since the Supreme Court decided *Central Bank,* the Seventh Circuit has not had occasion to address the question of what degree of participation in the commission of a deceptive act is sufficient to hold a secondary actor such as an accountant liable for securities fraud as a primary violator. However, a number of points with respect to this issue are clear. First, an accountant liability for aiding and abetting is hard to distinguish from primary liability. Second, based on the decisions of those circuits that have addressed the issue, a general rule can be said to have emerged: a secondary actor must actually make, author, publicly adopt or allow its name to be associated with a misleading statement in order for it to be held liable as a primary violator of §10(b) and Rule 10b-5.

In the present case plaintiffs allege PwC assisted with the press release by reviewing it and advising Harnischfeger that it conformed with GAAP. Plaintiffs do not allege PwC drafted the release, publicly adopted it, or allowed its name to be associated with it. Thus, based on the facts alleged in the complaint, I conclude PwC cannot be held liable under §10(b) as a primary violator for misstatements in the release. The facts alleged suggest PwC's actions with respect to the release more closely approximate aiding and abetting Harnischfeger's misstatements than making misstatements itself. Thus, it would be inconsistent with *Central Bank* to hold PwC liable for the statements in the release, and I decline to do so.

PwC may, however, be held liable for statements in the audit report. PwC's report was first disseminated to investors on January 29, 1998 when it was filed with the SEC. It follows, therefore, plaintiffs cannot state a claim against PwC based on purchases of Harnischfeger stock made prior to that date.

PwC's motion to dismiss is granted in part and denied in part. Plaintiffs' charges are denied where they apply to the statement released by Harnischfeger. PwC's motion to dismiss is denied where it goes towards plaintiffs' contention of statements filed with the SEC.

MOTION TO DISMISS GRANTED IN PART AND DENIED IN PART.

CRITICAL THINKING

What words or phrases in this decision could be considered ambiguous? How may the outcome of this case change if different meanings were given to those words or phrases?

ETHICAL DECISION MAKING

How would the judge's ruling be different than above if his decision were guided by the Golden Rule?

Section 32 of the Securities and Exchange Act identifies the penalties for violations of the act. Accordingly, an accountant guilty of violating the Securities Exchange Act can be punished with a fine of not more than $5 million, imprisonment for not more than 20 years, or both. An accounting firm (and not an individual) may be fined up to $25 million.

Liability under Section 20(a) of the Securities Exchange Act. Similar to Section 15 of the Securities Act, Section 20(a) of the Securities Exchange Act is a controlling-person provision. Section 20(a) states:

> Every person who, directly or indirectly, controls any person liable under any provision of this chapter or of any rule or regulation thereunder shall also be liable jointly and severally with and to the same extent as such controlled person to any person to whom such controlled person is liable, unless the controlling person acted in good faith and did not directly or indirectly induce the act or acts constituting the violation or cause of action.[11]

[11] 15 U.S.C. § 78t.

Similarities between Section 15 of the Securities Act, discussed above, and Section 20(a) of the Securities Exchange Act should be immediately obvious. Both provisions seek to apply liability to high-level officials for their direct misdeeds or their negligence in running their corporations.

Also similar in both sections is the method of proving liability. Under Section 20(a), to establish liability, the plaintiff must show that (1) there was a primary violation by a controlled person; (2) the defendant controlled the primary violator; and (3) the defendant in a meaningful way participated in the primary violation. The first two requirements directly echo Section 15 of the Securities Act, but the third provides an additional step to be achieved by a plaintiff in a case.

Another similarity is that both Section 20(a) of the Securities Exchange Act and Section 15 of the Securities Act provide defendants with an affirmative defense. The affirmative defense under Section 20(a) allows defendants to avoid liability when "the controlling person acted in good faith and did not directly or indirectly induce the act or acts constituting the [underlying] violation or cause of action."[12]

Roberts, from the opening scenario, also faced charges under Section 20(a). Once again, he asserted his affirmative defense. Since the Second Circuit held in *Marbury Mgmt. v. Kohn*[13] that Section 20(a) of the Securities Exchange Act parallels Section 15 of the Securities Act, we know Roberts meets the first two criteria for establishing liability. If Roberts were not at all involved in the primary act, or were he to establish that he acted in good faith, he would not be held liable for the losses suffered by the crash of WorldCom's stock.

THE PRIVATE SECURITIES LITIGATION REFORM ACT OF 1995

The Private Securities Litigation Reform Act (PSLRA) placed new statutory obligations on accountants. PSLRA requires that, when performing an audit, accountants use adequate procedures so that they can detect any illegal acts committed by the audited company. Also under PSLRA is a specific set of actions and guidelines an accountant must follow after identifying a potentially illegal activity when conducting an audit. Depending on the circumstances, upon detection an accountant must immediately notify the board of directors, the audit committee, or the SEC.[14]

PSLRA states that accountants are liable for the portion of the damages for which they are responsible.[15] Furthermore, PSLRA amended the Securities Exchange Act of 1934 by making it a violation of the Securities Exchange Act to in any way aid and abet a violation of the Securities and Exchange Act. In the event of a willful violation of PSLRA, the SEC can seek an injunction against the accountant and/or monetary fines. It is important to note that, under PSLRA, an accountant's silence when the accountant thinks he or she might have discovered fraud is enough to constitute aiding and abetting.

THE SARBANES-OXLEY ACT OF 2002

As explained in Chapter 7, the Sarbanes-Oxley Act was enacted in 2002 by Congress as a response to the business scandals of the early 2000s. The act consists largely of new rules and regulations for public accounting firms in an attempt to reduce fraud in accounting practices. One way the act aims to limit fraud is through its creation of the Public Company

[12] 15 U.S.C. § 78t(a).
[13] 629 F.2d 705 (1980).
[14] 15 U.S.C. § 78j-1.
[15] 15 U.S.C. § 78-4(g).

Accounting Oversight Board. The board consists of five members, one chair and four additional members, and reports to the SEC. Titles I and II, the key provisions of the act, outline the duties of the board, as well as establish the new requirements for public accounting firms.

The board was created by Sarbanes-Oxley to obtain greater government oversight of public accounting firms and thus protect investors from another Enron- and Arthur Andersen–style scandal. The board has the power to oversee the audit procedures used for public companies and to ensure compliance with securities law, including the new provisions in Sarbanes-Oxley.

The board also has several other duties it is to fulfill under Sarbanes-Oxley. First, the board is responsible for registering public accounting firms that prepare audit reports for issuers. Second, the board establishes standards and rules for audit reports, as well as quality control and ethics standards for registered public accounting firms. Third, the board is responsible for inspecting, investigating, and enforcing compliance on registered public accounting firms and anyone associated with the firms.

In addition to establishing the duties of the public accounting oversight board, Sarbanes-Oxley also establishes rules for auditor independence. One of the key ways it encourages auditor independence is by prohibiting registered public accounting firms (RPAFs) from engaging in the following nonauditing acts:

- Bookkeeping.
- Financial information systems design and implementation.
- Appraisal or valuation services.
- Actuarial services.
- Internal-audit outsourcing services.
- Management functions or human resources.
- Broker or dealer, investment adviser, or investment banking services.
- Legal or expert services unrelated to the audit.
- Any additional service the board deems impermissible.

Three additional rules provided by Title II of the act help ensure auditor independence: (1) The lead or coordinating partners of audits of issuers may not provide audit services for more than five consecutive years to one particular issuer; (2) any audit service provided by an RPAF to an issuer must go through a preapproval process, and any nonaudit function performed by the auditor for the issuer must be disclosed in financial statements; and (3) an RPAF may not perform audit services for an issuer if the issuer's CEO, controller, CFO, chief accounting officer, or equivalent executive was employed by that RPAF and participated in any capacity in the audit of that issuer during the one-year period preceding the date of the initiation of the (current) audit.

The act also prohibits the destruction or falsification of records with the intent to obstruct or influence federal investigations or bankruptcy proceedings. The consequences of violating this prohibition can be either a fine, imprisonment for up to 20 years, or both.

Liability of Other Professionals

By no stretch of the imagination are accountants the only professionals who are likely to be sued for malpractice. As people become more aware of the legal requirements placed on professionals, they also become increasingly aware of a lack of quality in some services. With this awareness comes an increase in lawsuits against injurious professionals to hold them accountable for their substandard work.

Frequently doctors and other health practitioners are faced with malpractice suits. Most people have heard horror stories of doctors' failing to notice what should have been an obvious, suspicious lump or amputating the wrong limb. It is over incidents like these that patients may sue doctors and other health practitioners for malpractice. In essence, malpractice suits serve to award the victim just compensation, as well as to deter professionals from failing to perform to the standards of their profession.

Many people in the business context who provide professional services are potential targets of liability suits. These people include attorneys, lawyers, real estate brokers, architects, and other professionals. Much like accountants, these professionals may be liable for negligence or breach of contract. Whenever professionals do not perform their duty according to the standards of their professions and another person is harmed, the professionals may be liable for negligence. Also, when professionals breach their contractual obligations and cause harm to another, the professionals may be sued for breach of either explicit or implicit contractual agreements. Some professionals may also be held liable for fraud if their actions were intentional and another was harmed through reliance on the professional.

Furthermore, professionals not only are potential targets of malpractice suits but also might be on the receiving end of malpractice. For instance, if an accountant misleads an attorney by providing fraudulent information, the attorney is the victim of malpractice. However, if the same attorney provides fraudulent information to a client, the attorney could face a malpractice suit. Thus the attorney could be a plaintiff in one malpractice case and the defendant in another.

An example of an attorney malpractice suit is *Gulf Ins. Co. v. Jones.*[16] In *Gulf,* we see an attorney malpractice suit arising out of a medical malpractice suit. Donald R. Blum, a podiatrist, performed a procedure on Sonia Y. Jones. After her surgery, Jones suffered from excruciating pain in her feet and required corrective surgery to cure the pain. Jones sued Blum for malpractice, claiming he was negligent in the performance of his surgery. Blum's insurer, Gulf Insurance, retained Cowles & Thompson, PC, to represent him. Due to conflicts at the law firm, a less experienced associate named Paula Shiroma-Bender represented Blum. After being found liable, Blum sued Cowles & Thompson, as well as Shiorma-Bender, for legal malpractice. Blum also sued his insurer for failing to settle out of court. The court determined that Blum did not meet his burden of proof. Nonetheless, the case serves as an example of how insurers, doctors, and attorneys all may end up being the target of malpractice suits.

CASE OPENER WRAP-UP

WorldCom

Roberts faced charges of liability under Sections 11 and 15 of the Securities Act and Sections 10(b) and 20(a) of the Securities Exchange Act. He raised an affirmative defense against all the claims against him. On the basis of his argument for the affirmative defenses, Roberts moved for summary judgment. In March 2005, Judge Cote denied Roberts's motion for summary judgment on all counts, claiming Roberts did not meet his burden of proof as to any of the affirmative defenses. After the failed motion for summary judgment, Roberts was scheduled to go to trial. No ruling has yet been given in the trial. However, WorldCom's former CEO, Bernard J. Ebbers, was convicted approximately at the start of Roberts's trial, in the same district in which Roberts is being tried.

[16] 2005 U.S. App. LEXIS 16228 (2005).

Summary

Common Law Accountant Liability to Clients

There are three primary types of common law accountant liability to clients:

1. *Accountant liability for negligence:* An accountant is liable to his or her client for negligence if the accountant fails to exercise the care of a competent, reasonable professional and that failure causes loss or injury to the client. At a minimum, an accountant has a duty to perform his or her task according to generally accepted accounting principles (GAAP) and generally accepted auditing standards (GAAS).
2. *Accountant liability for breach of contract:* Whenever an accountant is hired to perform a specific task, he or she enters into a contract with the client. Explicitly, the accountant agrees to perform the contractual agreed-on tasks. Implicitly, the accountant agrees to complete the work in a competent and professional manner according to professional standards (GAAP and GAAS). Accountants may be held liable for violating their explicit or implicit agreements.
3. *Accountant liability for fraud:* Accountants who commit fraud are liable to those parties the accountant reasonably should have foreseen as being injured through a justifiable reliance on the fraudulent information. Accountants may be held liable for two types of fraud: actual or constructive. Actual fraud exists when the accountant's actions meet the criteria necessary to prove fraud. Constructive fraud is fraud without fraudulent intent. To establish constructive fraud, a plaintiff must prove that the accountant was grossly negligent in performing his or her duties.

Common Law Accountant Liability to Third Parties

Third-party liability, as decided by the states, falls into three general groupings:

1. *Privity or near-privity (the Ultramares rule):* Requires that the third party be in privity of contract with the accountant or be substantially close enough to the accountant to constitute near-privity.
2. *Foreseen users and class of users (the Restatement rule):* Requires that third party be a known recipient or be of a class of known recipients of the accountant's work for liability to be established.
3. *Reasonably foreseeable users:* Allows any third party that should have been reasonably foreseen as using the product of an accountant's work to bring suit against the accountant for liability.

Accountants' and Clients' Rights

Working papers are the various documents used and developed during an audit, including notes, calculations, copies, memorandums, and other papers constituting the accountant's work product. The accountant is the legal owner of the working papers, but the material is the data of the client, and therefore the client may access the working papers at any time upon request.

Accountant-client privilege does not exist under the federal law. However, some states have granted this right. Typically, when granted, the client has the right to privilege, whereas the accountant has fewer protections.

Federal Securities Law and Accountant Liability

Securities Act of 1933:

- Under Section11, accountants are civilly liable for misstatements and omissions of material facts made in registration statements filed with the SEC.
- Section 15 applies liability to controlling persons when a violation under Section 11 occurs.

Securities Exchange Act of 1934:

- According to Section 18, accountants are liable for fraudulent statements made to the SEC in documents filed with the SEC.
- Section 10(b) and SEC Rule 10b-5 make it unlawful for accountants, or anyone, to use, "any manipulative or deceptive device or contrivance in contravention of such rules and regulations as the [SEC] may prescribe as necessary or appropriate in the public interest or for the protection of investors."
- Section 20(a) (similar to Section 15 of the Securities Act) is a controlling-person provision. When a person is in control of a primary violator of the act and the person significantly partook in the illegal activity, he or she may be liable.

Private Securities Litigation Reform Act of 1995:

- The act requires that accountants use adequate procedures when performing an audit so that they can detect any illegal acts of the company being audited. Also under the act is a specific set of actions and guidelines an accountant must follow after identifying a potentially illegal activity when conducting an audit.

Sarbanes-Oxley Act of 2002:

- The act consists largely of new rules and regulations for public accountant firms in an attempt to reduce fraud in accounting practices. To limit fraud, the act created the Public Company Accounting Oversight Board. Titles I and II outline the duties of the board, as well as establish the new requirements for public accounting firms.

Liability of Other Professionals

Many professionals who provide services, including attorneys, lawyers, real estate brokers, doctors, architects, and other professionals, are potential targets for professional liability. These professionals are liable under the same theories as accountants.

Point / Counterpoint

Is Sarbanes-Oxley Helping or Harming the Business Climate?	
Harming	**Helping**
While Congress may have had the best of intentions in passing Sarbanes-Oxley, the law has failed because of unintended consequences. The act has seriously hurt American corporations and financial markets without increasing investor confidence. One important unintended consequence may be a significant increase in the number of companies that remain private, rather than going public, and consequently are subject to much less regulation than public companies. Some small public companies have gone back to being privately held. In a 2003 survey of CEO readers of *Chief Executive Magazine,* 82 percent of the respondents revealed that they believe it is better to remain a private company than to go public.[a]	Sarbanes-Oxley, like any law, could perhaps be improved by some minor tinkering, but basically it is a sound piece of legislation that should not be rolled back. Just think about what the law does. It forces companies to implement tough internal controls to ensure that the financial information they provide investors is honest and accurate, not false information as occurred in the Enron and WorldCom cases. It eliminates many of the Wall Street conflicts of interest that previously led major Wall Street firms to recommend that their clients buy stocks that the firms themselves thought were worthless. Opponents of Sarbanes-Oxley argue that the law should be abolished because the percentage of IPOs

The law disproportionately affects small businesses, imposing unfair costs on them. According to California congressman Brad Sherman, "The Government Accountability Office found that, proportionately, small public companies were spending considerably more on implementing Sarbanes-Oxley than large companies. Firms with less than $75 million in market capitalization were spending $1.14 in audit fees per $100 of revenue, the congressional researchers calculated, compared to just 13 cents per $100 of revenue for firms with greater than $1 billion in market capitalization."[b] A law that imposes such disparate costs clearly is not working.

Also, while the act was supposed to eliminate conflicts of interest by prohibiting the firm doing the company's auditing from doing a number of other, non-auditing functions, the act did not abolish what many consider the major conflict-of-interest problem. A conflict of interest still exists because auditing firms are paid by the companies they audit.

What are we getting for these increased negative consequences? According to an editorial in the *New York Times,* we are not even getting increased consumer confidence. The editorial writer argues: "[T]he best measure of investor confidence is the price-earnings ratio—the price that investors are willing to pay for each dollar of a company's reported earnings. The overall price-earnings ratio for the Standard & Poor's 500 stock index, however, has declined continuously since the Sarbanes-Oxley Act was being drafted in the spring of 2002."[c]

One last piece of evidence that supports the need to significantly roll back this onerous regulation is the fact that foreign firms may be reluctant to make initial public offerings in the U.S. markets because they are fearful of Sarbanes-Oxley requirements. In 2005, 23 of 24 firms that had raised more than $1 billion in capital chose not to register their security offerings in U.S. markets, according to the New York Stock Exchange.[d]

Given all the negative consequences of the act, and its limited benefits, the law should be abolished or significantly reformed.

filed in the United States has fallen since Sarbanes-Oxley's enactment. However, that claim is really misleading because, in fact, the U.S. share of IPOs actually began falling six years before Sarbanes-Oxley was passed, declining from approximately 60 percent in 1996 to 8 percent in 2001. And the U.S. share of IPOs was approximately 15 percent in 2005, which is actually higher than it was in 2001.[e]

Also, the U.S. markets still attract more money than any other markets in the world. Why? Primarily because of a reputation for fairness and transparency, which has been strengthened by Sarbanes-Oxley.

Look at the two main groups that are behind the movement to roll back the law—the Chamber of Commerce and Wall Street insiders. Those whose behavior is being scrutinized are the ones who have a problem with the scrutiny.

We should not let time cause our memories of Enron to fade. The public needs to retain the protections we have from Sarbanes-Oxley. The act may impose some costs, but it is better that the costs be imposed on the firms that are making the profits than on innocent members of the investing public.

[a] "Getting Real about Sarbanes-Oxley," Editorial, *Chief Executive Magazine,* July 2003, available at http://findarticles.com/p/articles/mi_m4070/is_190/ai_107204657.

[b] Brad Sherman, "Making Sarbanes-Oxley Work Better for Small Public Companies," October 18, 2006, available at www.house.gov/list/speech/ca27_sherman/op_061018.html.

[c] William A. Niskanen, "Enron's Latest Victims—American Markets," *The New York Times,* January 3, 2007, available at www.nytimes.com/2007/01/03/opinion/03niskanen.html?ex=1325480400&en=5b590f938ab3ba85&ei=5088&partner=rssnyt&emc=rss.

[d] Mallory Factor, "Cox and Sarbox:For the Good of Business and the American Shareholder, Sarbanes-Oxley Must Be Repealed or Radically Reformed," *National Review Online,* available at http://article.nationalreview.com/?q=OTllNGE4MjMxYmRiMGQ1ZGU4Y2U2MDZlZDczNTY3M2E=.

[e] Reynolds Holding, "Plugging the IPO Drain," *Time Magazine,* March 19, 2007, available at www.time.com/time/magazine/article/0,9171,1587282,00.html.

Questions & Problems

1. What are the fundamental differences between the three theories of third-party accountant negligence?
2. When would an accountant-client privilege arise?
3. For what do *GAAP* and *GAAS* stand, and what function do they serve in the accounting profession?
4. Coopers & Lybrand, LLP, provide accounting and auditing services to Oregon Steel Mills, Inc. In 1994, Coopers & Lybrand advised Oregon to report a stock transaction as a $12.3 million gain on Oregon's financial statements and reports. When Coopers & Lybrand audited Oregon's financial statements, Coopers & Lybrand gave its opinion that the statements fairly represented Oregon's financial position in accordance with GAAP. Shortly before the initial SEC filing for Oregon's planned public offering, Coopers & Lybrand informed Oregon that the 1994 transaction might have been reported incorrectly. The SEC concluded that the accounting treatment for the 1994 transaction was incorrect, and it required that Oregon restate its financial statements. Because of the time required to change the financial statements as well as other documents related to the planned offering, Oregon's initial filing with the SEC was delayed. Oregon eventually sold $80 million of newly issued stock and $235 million of debt. Although the price of Oregon's stock was the same when Coopers & Lybrand discovered the accounting error as when Oregon issued the stock, the stock price had risen and fallen between those dates. Oregon alleged that on the date it would have issued the stock but for Coopers & Lybrand's negligence, its stock sold for $16 per share. Oregon brought action, claiming Coopers & Lybrand's negligent conduct caused the delay that resulted in the stock being offered for less than $16 a share. Oregon therefore sought as damages the difference between what Oregon actually received for its stock and debt and what it alleged it would have received if the securities offering had occurred on time, approximately $35 million. Should Coopers & Lybrand be liable for Oregon's losses? What did the court decide? [*Oregon Steel Mills, Inc. v. Coopers and Lybrand, L.L.P.,* 336 Ore. 329 (2004).]
5. The Board of Trustees of Community College District No. 508 operates and manages City Colleges of Chicago. City Colleges is a public agency, and its investment policies must comply with the Public Funds Investment Act. Accordingly, in 1988, 1990, and 1992, the board adopted resolutions authorizing its treasurer, Phillip Luhmann, to invest City Colleges' funds only in instruments permitted by the Investment Act. The investment policy directed that securities should generally be purchased with the intent of holding to maturity so as to minimize interest rate risk. Despite this clear mandate, Luhmann invested in securities not authorized by the resolutions. Further, he repeatedly engaged in a practice known as "pairing off" securities, buying a security and expecting to sell it for a profit before he was required to pay for it. In February 1994, the board learned that Luhmann had violated City Colleges' investment policy. Luhmann was terminated. The board then brought suit against Coopers & Lybrand, the firm that conducted an audit of the board in 1993 and failed to identify Luhmann's indiscretions. The board sought more than $50 million in compensatory damages, allegedly resulting from the failure of Coopers to discover and report to the board inappropriate investments made by Luhmann. Was the board successful in its claim? Why or why not? [*The Board of Trustees of Community College District No. 508 v. Coopers & Lybrand,* 208 Ill. 2d 259 (2003).]

6. Jeffrey Canty formed Canty Roofing and Sheetmetal (CRS), Inc. Contractors working on public construction projects in Massachusetts are required by statute to post payment and performance bonds on a project-by-project basis. CRS routinely bid on public works jobs and, thus, from time to time required bonds. North American Specialty Insurance (NASI) Co. entered into a bonding relationship with CRS. Once this relationship commenced, NASI told Canty that CRS would be required to provide updated financial statements, prepared by an independent certified public accountant, for each succeeding calendar year. In late 1995, Canty agreed to sell CRS, structured as a sale of stock. Shortly thereafter, Dias & Lapalme (D&L) prepared an independent, review-level financial statement for CRS with respect to calendar year 1995. This statement, issued by D&L, lacked specific information regarding the change in ownership. To make matters worse, the notes to the financial statement contained three arguably misleading comments that implied Canty's continuing participation as CRS's sole shareholder. CRS thereafter obtained new contracts for work on public buildings. To facilitate these engagements, NASI wrote bonds (relying, it claims, on the 1995 financial statement) totaling $847,630 and $874,500. CRS eventually defaulted on these bonds. This calamity forced NASI, as a surety, to step into the breach, costing it nearly $2 million. NASI sued D&L and Lapalme for negligent misrepresentation and deceptive trade practices. NASI grounded its complaint on the assertion that but for the accountants' omission of accurate ownership information in the 1995 financial statement, it would not have continued furnishing bonds for CRS (and, therefore, would have avoided the ensuing losses). The district court granted summary judgment for D&L and Lapalme, and NASI appealed. How did the court rule on appeal? Why? [*North Am. Specialty Ins. Co. v. Lapalme,* 258 F.3d 35 (2001).]
7. Allwaste Inc. engaged Morgan Stanley to evaluate the possible sale of Allwaste. Morgan Stanley would provide advice to the Allwaste board of directors. The agreement provided that Morgan Stanley had "duties solely to Allwaste" and that any advice or opinions provided by Morgan Stanley could not be disclosed or referred to publicly without Morgan Stanley's consent. Under the proposed merger, Allwaste and Philip would be merged into a new company to be owned by Philip, and each share of Allwaste common stock would be converted into 0.611 share of Philip common stock. Morgan Stanley provided the board with a written fairness opinion stating, based on the information it had reviewed, that Morgan Stanley believed the number of shares of Philip stock to be received for each share of Allwaste stock was "fair from a financial point of view to the holders of Allwaste Common Stock." Morgan Stanley, however, "expressed no opinion or recommendation as to how the holders of Allwaste Common Stock should vote at the stockholders' meeting held in connection with the Merger." The fairness opinion stated that Morgan Stanley had "assumed and relied upon without independent verification the accuracy and completeness of the information supplied or otherwise made available to us by [Allwaste] and Philip for the purposes of this opinion" and that it was written "for the information of the Board of Directors of the Company only and may not be used for any other purpose without [Morgan Stanley's] prior consent," except for filings with the Securities and Exchange Commission. The shareholders approved the merger. Subsequently, Philip disclosed that it had filed inaccurate financial statements for several years. This revelation led to a sharp decrease in the price of Philip common stock. Option holders of former Allwaste stock brought suit against Morgan Stanley. The complaint alleged that Morgan Stanley had failed to conduct adequate investigation of Philip or to inform the board of the problems that ultimately led to the decline in Philip's stock

price and the value of plaintiffs' options. Is Morgan Stanley liable to the option holders for its failure to detect Philip's inaccurate financial statements? Does the decision depend on which theory of liability is used? [*Collins v. Morgan Stanley Dean Witter,* 224 F.3d 496 (2000).]

8. KGA is a public accounting firm that performed audits for Webb Cooley Company. KGA performed its audits after the calendar year in question. Thus, KGA issued its report on the 1998 financial statement in May 1999; KGA issued its report on the 1999 financial statement in April 2000. Compass Bank was Webb Cooley's lender. In April 1999, before KGA completed the 1998 audit, Compass loaned Webb Cooley $1.5 million pursuant to a term loan and extended Webb Cooley an additional $3.5 million revolving credit line. Compass increased Webb Cooley's credit line by $1 million in March 2000 and by an additional $500,000 in May 2000. Shortly after the May 2000 credit-line increase, Webb Cooley defaulted on its loans, and it eventually filed for bankruptcy. Compass then filed an action against KGA, claiming that KGA negligently misrepresented Webb Cooley's finances in the 1998 and 1999 audits, causing Compass to extend additional credit to Webb Cooley. Is KGA liable to Compass for the losses suffered by Webb Cooley's defaulting on its loans, and if so, for how much is KGA liable? [*Compass Bank v. King Griffin & Adamson P.C.,* 2004 U.S. App. LEXIS 21593 (2004).]

9. The Manhattan Investment Fund began trading U.S. securities in 1996. When the fund began losing money, the fund's manager, Michael Berger, hid losses from investors by manufacturing false monthly account statements. Deloitte & Touche Bermuda (DTB) became the fund's auditor in 1997 and issued its first audit, for the 1996 fiscal year, on May 27, 1997. The 1996 audit is addressed to "the Shareholders of Manhattan Investment Fund Ltd.," and the cover letter for the audit represents that the audit was conducted "in accordance with auditing standards generally accepted in the United States of America." Audits for the fiscal years 1997 and 1998, with similar cover letters, were issued on March 20, 1998, and March 16, 1999, respectively. All three of DTB's audits were "clean" audits. DTB withdrew its three audits in January 2000, after the Securities and Exchange Commission initiated an investigation of the fund. The plaintiffs, who generally contended that DTB ignored evidence of Berger's fraud and failed its responsibilities as auditor, asserted seven causes of action against DTB: violation of Section 10(b) of the Securities Exchange Act and Rule 10b-5 promulgated thereunder, aiding and abetting common law fraud, aiding and abetting breach of fiduciary duty, common law fraud, gross negligence, negligence, and professional malpractice. How did the court rule? Why? [*Cromer Fin. Ltd. v. Berger,* 2003 U.S. Dist. LEXIS 10554 (2004).]

10. CUC International, Inc., acquired HFS in a stock-for-stock merger. CUC was the surviving corporation and was renamed Cendant. Ernst & Young (E&Y) had audited CUC's financial statements for years, as well as worked with CUC and HFS during the merger. Cendant alleges its former senior management caused the company's operating income to be inflated by approximately $500 million. It alleges the "entire senior management of CUC, including but not limited to IRS former chairman and chief executive officer Walter Forbes, its former president Kirk Shelton, and two of its former chief financial officers, Stuart Bell and his successor Cosmo Corigliano," were involved in the illegal scheme. It states the purpose of the fraud was to report sufficient income to meet Wall Street targets and to keep the price of the company's stock inflated. According to Cendant, CUC targeted HFS as a merger partner and victim of the fraudulent scheme. Cendant alleges Ernst & Young was either negligent in failing to discover the fraud or knowingly or recklessly facilitated it. It alleges E&Y participated in the fraud by creating false documents to reverse excess merger reserves into operating income. Cendant also claims E&Y had a duty to report the information to board and audit committee members who were not involved in the fraud and could have ended it. Moreover, E&Y represented to HFS representatives in comfort letters and oral reassurances before the merger that CUC's financial statements were accurate. Is Ernst & Young liable for its failure to detect the alleged fraud? [*In re Cendant Corp. Secs. Litig.,* 139 F. Supp. 2d 585 (2001).]

11. PricewaterhouseCoopers was hired by JTD Health Systems, Inc., to perform an audit of the financial statements for 1995. In 1995, JTD hired Tammy Heiby as accounting coordinator. Heiby was overwhelmed by the position and failed to make payroll tax deposits. She then hid these failures by falsifying journal entries. During Coopers' audit, Coopers was unable to reconcile the cash account or explain the approximately $30,000 surplus funds in the account. Coopers reported to JTD that the surplus was due to changes in Medicaid/Medicare direct-deposit procedures. Coopers determined no investigation was needed because the cash account was reconciled to within "an immaterial difference." JTD received a call from the IRS concerning the missed payments for 1995, and eventually for 1996 as well. The IRS waived penalties and interest for the 1995 taxes, but it declined to do so for the 1996 taxes. JTD did not request that Coopers investigate the payment of the taxes for either 1995 or 1996. On January 19, 1999, JTD filed a complaint against Coopers alleging professional negligence for failure to discover the lack of tax payments. The case went to trial, and the jury returned a verdict in favor of JTD, with damages set at $389,333. The jury then found that JTD was 38 percent comparatively negligent, thus reducing the damages to $241,861. On May 9, 2000, Coopers filed a motion for a judgment notwithstanding the verdict or a new trial. The trial court denied the motion. Coopers again appealed. How did the court rule on appeal? Why? [*JTD Health Sys., Inc., v. Pricewaterhouse-Coopers, L.L.P.,* 141 Ohio App. 3d 280 (2001).]

12. Equisure, Inc., was required to file audited financial statements when it applied to have its stock listed on the American Stock Exchange. It retained an accounting firm, Stirtz Bernards Boyden Surdel & Larter, P.A. Stirtz issued a favorable interim audit report, which Equisure used to gain listing on the stock exchange. Equisure later retained Stirtz to audit the financial statements required for Equisure's Form 10 filing with the Securities and Exchange Commission. Stirtz's auditor knew the audit was for the SEC reports. Stirtz issued a "clean" audit opinion, which, with the audited financial statements, was included in Equisure's SEC filing and made available to the public. NorAm Investment Services, a securities broker, began lending margin credit to purchasers of Equisure stock. These purchasers advanced only a portion of the purchase price; NorAm extended credit (a margin loan) for the balance and held the stock as collateral for the loan, charging interest on the balance. When NorAm had loaned approximately $900,000 in margin credit, its president, Nathan Newman, reviewed Stirtz's audit report and the audited financial statements. On the basis of his review, NorAm extended over $1.6 million of additional margin credit to purchase Equisure shares. When AmEx stopped trading Equisure stock due to allegations of insider trading and possible stock manipulation, the stock became worthless. NorAm was left without collateral for over $2.5 million in margin loans. Stirtz resigned as auditor of Equisure and warned that its audit report might be misleading and should no longer be relied on. NorAm sued Stirtz for negligent misrepresentation, negligence, and violation of the Minnesota Consumer Fraud Act. The district court granted

Stirtz's motion for summary judgment, ruling under the Restatement (Second) of Torts, Section 552, that Stirtz was not liable to NorAm. NorAm appealed. Is Stirtz liable to NorAm for the losses suffered? Why? [*NorAm Inv. Servs. v. Stirtz, Bernard, Boyden, Surdel, & Larter, P.A.*, 611 N.W.2d 372 (2000).]

13. AOP provided mortgage loans to prospective homeowners. To fund these loans, "warehouse funders" such as HSA advanced monies to AOP under mortgage purchase agreements. After the closing of a mortgage loan, AOP sold the loan to financial institutions on the secondary mortgage market and used the proceeds from those sales to repay the warehouse funders. AOP's revenues consisted primarily of the points and other fees borrowers paid in connection with obtaining the mortgage loans. In 1997, AOP's common stock began trading publicly, and the company expanded its operations through various acquisitions. During this time, AOP began losing money because the mortgage fees generated from those acquisitions did not cover its increased operating expenses. AOP used later funds received from warehouse funders—designated to fund specific mortgage loans—to fund earlier mortgage loans. AOP also used any available funds to repay the warehouse funders, including funds provided for other mortgage loans, when a specific mortgage loan did not close and funds had to be returned to a warehouse funder. In its internal and financial books, AOP recorded the amount wrongfully diverted from mortgage loan funds as a liability to certain escrow agents involved in the transfer of the mortgage loan funds, when AOP, in fact, owed the diverted funds to the warehouse funders. In its financial statements, AOP also disguised its growing liability to the warehouse funders by creating a "phantom" payable to The Skulsky Trust, which was a related party controlled by Paul Skulsky and Jeffrey Skulsky. The Werblin Firm and Casuccio audited and approved the 1997 and 1998 annual reports and financial statements. Citrin audited and approved the 1999 reports and financial statements. On March 22, 2002, HSA filed a complaint against Werblin and Citrin. The claim alleged fraud on the ground they engaged in a fraudulent scheme to conceal AOP's true financial condition and made material misrepresentations and omissions in AOP's Form 10-K for the years 1997, 1998, and 1999. The defendants moved to dismiss the complaint. How did the court decide? Why? [*HSA Residential Mortg. Servs. v. Casuccio,* 350 F. Supp. 2d 352 (2003).]

14. Davis, Sita & Company is a professional association organized under the laws of Maryland and having its principal place of business in Maryland. The Gourmet Source, Inc., first retained Davis in June 1997 to perform an audit and to report on its financial condition as of June 1, 1997. On March 31, 1998, Gourmet again retained Davis to prepare an audit report of its 1997 year-end financial statements. Gerber Trade Finance, Inc., is a trade finance company, which financed Gourmet's inventory purchases. Claiming to be one of Gourmet's principal secured creditors, Gerber alleged it relied on the 1997 year-end audit report in its decision to make additional extensions of credit to Gourmet. Gerber claimed losses of $682,500 due to misleading and false information in the 1997 year-end financial statements. Specifically, Gerber alleged the financial statements overstated Gourmet's accounts receivable by more than $200,000 and stated that Gourmet had paid a liability of $167,500, when in fact it was in default. Gerber claimed Davis was negligent in that it should have detected the errors in the financial statements and it knew or should have known that Gerber, as Gourmet's primary secured lender, would rely on the accuracy of the financial statements to its detriment. Was Gerber successful in establishing itself as a third party with a right to recover? Under which theories of liability may Gerber recover? [*Gerber Trade Fin., Inc. v. Davis, Sita & Co., P.A.*, 128 F. Supp. 2d 86 (2001).]

15. GWAM retained BDO to audit its financial statements in preparation for an initial public offering of notes. BDO issued audit opinions on GWAM's financial statements for the fiscal years 1992 through 1995. The audit opinions did not endorse GWAM or otherwise express an opinion regarding the quality of the investment. BDO represented only GWAM's financial statements, which always revealed GWAM was losing money and which fairly and accurately reflected GWAM's financial condition. Consequently, BDO's audit opinion was meaningful to an investor only when read in conjunction with GWAM's financial statements. BDO's audit opinion for the year ending in 1995 also included a "going-concern" qualification expressing doubt about GWAM's continued financial viability. In the summer of 1996, GWAM defaulted on its securities and shortly thereafter filed for bankruptcy. Investors who purchased high-risk, publicly offered GWAM securities through their own stockbrokers sued BDO in a class action suit alleging BDO was negligent for not stating concerns over the soundness of GWAM's finances. Most of the appellants admit they did not review GWAM's financial statements nor did they see or hear BDO's audit opinion with respect to those financial statements prior to making their investment. Many of the appellants contended they relied either solely or primarily on their broker's recommendation to buy the securities. Several of the appellants contended they would not have invested in GWAM had their broker shared what the audited financial statements actually showed—that GWAM was losing money and had never been profitable. None of the appellants asserted that they actually relied on any representation in BDO's audit opinions in making their decision to invest in the securities. BDO moved for summary judgment. The court ruled in BDO's favor, and the plaintiffs appealed. Were the plaintiffs successful in asserting a claim on appeal? Why? [*White v. BDO Seidman, L.L.P.,* 249 Ga. App. 668 (2001).]

Looking for more review material?

The Online Learning Center at **www.mhhe.com/kubasek1e** contains this chapter's "Assignment on the Internet" and also a list of URLs for more information, entitled "On the Internet." Find both of them in the Student Center portion of the OLC, along with quizzes and other helpful materials.

Intellectual Property

CASE OPENER

Owning Ideas: A Question of Intellectual Property

Papa John's International, Inc., is a chain restaurant that manages a series of franchises throughout this country and other countries. Of Papa John's 3,000 restaurants, 80 percent are franchises. When a corporation franchises, it issues licenses allowing a business owner to use its name, recipes, and other forms of intellectual property in exchange for a recurring payment as well as a percentage of the profits. When a franchise does not fulfill the terms of this agreement, the corporation has the right to terminate the franchise.

On May 3, 2004, Papa John's exercised this ability when it terminated a number of Papa John's franchises in Illinois and Michigan. Papa John's sent notices to the terminated franchises ordering them to cease operation of the restaurants and to comply with the post-termination obligations in their contract. These obligations included posting signs that were to state the restaurants were no longer affiliated with Papa John's and answering the telephone in a manner that would not affiliate the restaurants with Papa John's. Additionally, the former franchises were expected to immediately return confidential information and any Papa John's property, as well as discontinue using Papa John's trademarks.

Papa John's sued these former franchises, claiming that they continued to use Papa John's registered copyrights, trademarks, and trade secrets in violation of the posttermination agreement. Papa John's claimed that the restaurants continued to operate under the name "Papa Tony's."

Antoin Rezko, the chief executive officer (CEO) of the former franchises, was the named defendant in this civil suit. Rezko argued to have the Papa John's suit dismissed on the grounds that Papa John's had not sufficiently made a legal case proving the alleged violations of copyrights, trademarks, and trade secrets.[1]

[1] *Papa John's Int'l, Inc. v. Rezko,* 446 F. Supp. 2d 801 (N.D. Ill. 2006).

CHAPTER 12

1. What argument must Papa John's make to prove that Rezko and the former franchises violated copyright laws?
2. What are the elements of trademark infringement that Papa John's must argue to prove that Rezko and the former franchises violated the law?
3. What argument must Papa John's make to prove that Rezko and the former franchises illegally used a trade secret?

The Wrap-Up at the end of the chapter will answer these questions.

Learning Objectives

After reading this chapter, you will be able to answer the following questions:

1 What are trademarks, and how do we protect them?

2 What are copyrights, and how do we protect them?

3 What are patents, and how do we protect them?

4 What are trade secrets, and how do we protect them?

5 How do treaties expand protection of intellectual property?

Intellectual Property

Intellectual property consists of the fruits of one's mind. The laws of intellectual property protect property that is primarily the result of mental creativity rather than physical effort. In the opening scenario, Papa John's recipes, training software, and slogans and the designs on its boxes, restaurants, and advertisements are all the result of a person's or group's creative labor, rather than physical effort. Protection for various forms of intellectual property comes from trademarks, trade secret protection, patents, and copyrights, all of which are discussed in this chapter.

Trademarks

A **trademark** is a distinctive mark, word, design, picture, or arrangement that is used by a producer in conjunction with a product and tends to cause consumers to identify the product with the producer. Even the shape of a product or package may be a trademark if it is nonfunctional. Papa John's, the plaintiff in the opening scenario, has registered trademarks such as the name "Papa John's," as well as "Papa John's Pizza," and the phrase "Better Ingredients. Better Pizza."

Even though the description of a trademark is very broad, there has still been substantial litigation over precisely what features can and cannot serve as a trademark. In one case, discussed in the Case Nugget, the U.S. Supreme Court grappled with the issue of whether a color can be a trademark.

Case Nugget Color as a Trademark?

Qualitex Co. v. Jacobson Products Co.
514 U.S. 159 (1995)

For years, the plaintiff, Qualitex Co., had colored the dry-cleaning press pads it manufactured a special shade of green-gold. When Jacobson Products, a competitor, started coloring its pads the same shade of green-gold, Qualitex sued Jacobson Products for trademark infringement. The defendant challenged the legitimacy of the trademark, arguing that color alone should not qualify for registration as a trademark.

The district court found in favor of the plaintiff, but the Ninth Circuit reversed, holding that color alone could not be registered as a trademark. The plaintiff appealed to the U.S. Supreme Court.

In writing for the majority that a color could constitute a trademark, Justice Breyer said that both the language of the Lanham Act and the basic underlying principles of trademark law would seem to include color within the universe of things that could qualify as a trademark. He noted that the broad language used to describe trademarks included "any word, name, symbol, or device, or any combination thereof." Human beings might use as a "symbol" or "device" almost anything at all that is capable of carrying meaning. Justice Breyer noted that a particular shape (of a Coca-Cola bottle), a particular sound (of NBC's three chimes), and even a particular scent (of plumeria blossoms on sewing thread), could be trademarked, and he reasoned that if a shape, a sound, and a fragrance can act as symbols, it made sense that so could a color.

He also noted that a color, if unusual enough in the context, could in fact come to identify goods with their source, just as descriptive words on a product could. The Court concluded that the green-gold color acts as a symbol that has developed secondary meaning (i.e., customers identified the green-gold color as Qualitex's) and identifies the press pads' source. The high court therefore reversed the decision in favor of the plaintiff.

connecting to the core

Marketing: The Benefits of Trademarks

As you may have learned in your marketing class, trademarks arguably benefit both consumers and companies. A registered brand name, design, or picture provides consumers with a familiar symbol by which they can identify desirable products. Were companies permitted to copy images or names from other brands, consumers would likely be confused about which brand they were actually purchasing; consequently, they might purchase products that they were previously dissatisfied with or had no intention to purchase.

Trademarks benefit companies by building brand equity, in the sense that certain trademarks convey value that does not relate to a product's functionality. In other words, consumers might be willing to pay more for a particular brand even though there may be alternative products of comparable quality. For example, consumers are often willing to pay higher prices for Duracell batteries, Bose entertainment systems, and Microsoft software even though identically functional products are available at a lower price. Hence, trademarks benefit consumers by distinguishing products that they are purchasing, and they also allow companies to reap the benefits of brand equity—the higher prices that consumers are willing to pay for a particular brand.

Source: R. Kerin, S. Hartley, E. Berkowitz, and W. Rudelius, *Marketing* (New York: McGraw-Hill/Irwin, 2006), pp. 300–301.

A trademark used *intrastate* is protected under state common law. To be protected in *interstate* use, the trademark must be registered with the U.S. Patent Office under the Lanham Act of 1947. Several types of marks are protected under this act (see Exhibit 12-1 for a list).

If a mark is registered, the holder of the mark may recover damages from an infringer who uses it to pass off goods as being those of the mark owner. The owner may also obtain an injunction prohibiting the infringer from using the mark. (Only the latter remedy is available for an unregistered mark.) Therefore, if the defendant in the Papa John's case was found to have committed trademark infringement against Papa John's, Papa John's can receive damages as well as obtain an injunction to keep the trademark violation from occurring in the future.

Once the mark is registered, the registration must be renewed between the fifth and sixth years. After that initial renewal, the mark holder must renew the registration every 10 years. (If the mark was initially registered before 1990, however, renewal is necessary only every 20 years.)

To register a mark with the Patent Office, one must submit a drawing of the mark and indicate when it was first used in interstate commerce and how it is used. The Patent Office conducts an investigation to verify those facts and will register a trademark as long as it is not generic, descriptive, immoral, deceptive, the name of a person whose permission has not been obtained, or substantially similar to another's trademark.

Exhibit 12-1
Types of Marks

1. *Service mark:* A mark used in conjunction with a service.
2. *Product trademark:* A mark affixed to a good, its packaging, or its labeling.
3. *Collective mark:* A mark identifying the producers as belonging to a larger group, such as a trade union.
4. *Certification mark:* A mark licensed by a group that has established certain criteria for use of the mark, such as "U.L. Tested" or "Good Housekeeping Seal of Approval."

Determining whether a mark is generic has become more difficult in this era of increasing globalization. For example, can a foreign word that would be generic in its country of origin be used as a trademark in this country? The court's decision on that issue is presented in Case 12-1.

CASE 12-1 OTOKOYAMA CO. LTD., A JAPANESE CORPORATION v. WINE OF JAPAN IMPORT, INC.

UNITED STATES COURT OF APPEALS, SECOND CIRCUIT
175 F.3D 783 (1999)

Otokoyoma Co. Ltd, a Japanese brewer that imported its "Otokoyama" sake into the United States, brought a trademark infringement action against a competitor, Wine of Japan Import, Inc., which imported "Mutsu Otokoyama" sake, claiming that the defendant had infringed on its trademark "Otokoyama." The plaintiff sought an injunction prohibiting the defendant from using the term.

The defendant counterclaimed, seeking to cancel the plaintiff's trademarks. The United States District Court for the Southern District of New York granted preliminary injunction for the plaintiff, and the defendant appealed.

CIRCUIT JUDGE LEVAL: . . . Generic terms are not eligible for protection as trademarks; everyone may use them to refer to the goods they designate. . . . This rule protects the interest of the consuming public in understanding the nature of goods offered for sale, as well as a fair marketplace among competitors by insuring that every provider may refer to his goods as what they are. . . .

The same rule applies when the word designates the product in a language other than English. This extension rests on the assumption that there are (or someday will be) customers in the United States who speak that foreign language. Because of the diversity of the population of the United States, coupled with temporary visitors, all of whom are part of the United States marketplace, commerce in the United States utilizes innumerable foreign languages. No merchant may obtain the exclusive right over a trademark designation if that exclusivity would prevent competitors from designating a product as what it is in the foreign language their customers know best. Courts and the USPTO apply this policy, known as the doctrine of "foreign equivalents" . . . to make generic foreign words ineligible for private ownership as trademarks. This rule, furthermore, does not apply only to words that designate an entire species. Generic words for sub-classifications or varieties of a good are similarly ineligible for trademark protection. See, e.g., . . . "fontina" held generic for a type of cheese ". . . bundt" held generic for a variety of ring-shaped coffee cake. A word may also be generic by virtue of its association with a particular region, cultural movement, or legend.

The defendant contended in the district court that the word "otokoyama" falls within the generic category. It claimed that in Japanese, otokoyama has long been understood as designating a variety of dry, manly sake that originated more than 300 years ago. . . . If otokoyama in Japanese signifies a type of sake, and one United States merchant were given the exclusive right to use that word to designate its brand of sake, competing merchants would be prevented from calling their product by the word which designates that product in Japanese. Any Japanese-speaking customers and others who are familiar with the Japanese terminology would be misled to believe that there is only one brand of otokoyama available in the United States. . . . Consumers would be forced either to spend additional time and money investigating the characteristics of competing goods or to pay a premium price to the seller with trademark rights in the accepted generic term.

The meaning of otokoyama in Japanese, and particularly whether it designates sake, or a type or category of sake, was therefore highly relevant to whether plaintiff may assert the exclusive right to use that word as a mark applied to sake. Defendant should have been allowed to introduce evidence of otokoyama's meaning and usage in Japan to support its claim that the mark is generic and therefore ineligible for protection as a trademark. In light of this error, the district court's finding that plaintiff is likely to succeed on the merits cannot be sustained.

REVERSED in favor of the Defendant.

[CONTINUED]

CRITICAL THINKING

What evidence did the Court use to support its conclusion that Wine of Japan, Inc., should have been allowed to discuss the meaning of *otokoyama* during the trial? Can you think of any reason why the other courts did not allow a discussion about the meaning of *otokoyama*?

ETHICAL DECISION MAKING

Suppose you were the judge hearing this case, trying to decide how to rule. If your decision were guided by the universalization test, how would you decide the case? Why?

It is sometimes difficult to determine whether a trademark will be protected. Also, once a trademark is registered, it is not always easy to predict whether a similar mark will be found to infringe on the registered trademark. For instance, in our original case, "Papa John's" and "Papa Tony's"—the name taken by the former Papa John's franchises—are not identical names. But the legal question is more complicated. The judge has to decide whether the "defendant's use of the mark is likely to cause confusion among consumers." This decision is based on factors such as "the similarity of the marks; the similarity of the products or services in issue; . . . the sophistication of consumers"; and even the "intent of the defendant to palm off its product as that of another."[2]

Case 12-2 demonstrates a typical analysis used in a trademark infringement suit.

[2] *Papa John's Int'l, Inc. v. Rezko,* 446 F. Supp. 2d 801 (N.D. Ill. 2006).

CASE 12-2

TOYS "R" US, INC. v. CANARSIE KIDDIE SHOP, INC.
DISTRICT COURT OF THE EASTERN DISTRICT OF NEW YORK
559 F. SUPP. 1189 (1983)

Beginning in 1960, plaintiff Toys-R-Us, Inc., sold children's clothes in stores across the country. The firm obtained a registered trademark and service mark for Toys "R" Us *in 1961 and aggressively advertised and promoted their products using these marks. In the late 1970s, defendant Canarsie Kiddie Shop, Inc., opened two kids' clothing stores within two miles of a Toys "R" Us Shop, and contemplated opening a third. The owner of Canarsie Kiddie Shop, Inc., called the stores Kids "r" Us. He never attempted to register the name. Toys "R" Us sued for trademark infringement in the federal district court.*

JUDGE GLASSER: In assessing the likelihood of confusion and in balancing the equities, this Court must consider the now classic factors. . . .

1. Strength of the Senior User's Mark

. . . "The term 'strength' as applied to trademarks refers to the distinctiveness of the mark, or more precisely, its tendency to identify goods sold under the mark as emanating from the particular, although possibly anonymous, source." A mark can fall into one of four general categories which, in order of ascending strength, are: (1) generic; (2) descriptive; (3) suggestive;

and (4) arbitrary or fanciful. The strength of a mark is generally dependent both on its place upon the scale and on whether it has acquired secondary meaning.

A generic term "refers, or has come to be understood as referring to the genus of which the particular product is a species." A generic term is entitled to no trademark protection whatsoever, since any manufacturer or seller has the right to call a product by its name.

A descriptive mark identifies a significant characteristic of the product, but is not the common name of the product. A mark is descriptive if it "informs the purchasing public of the characteristics, quality, functions, uses, ingredients, components, or other properties of a product, or conveys comparable information about a service." To achieve trademark protection a descriptive term must have attained secondary meaning, that is, it must have "become distinctive of the applicant's goods in commerce."

A suggestive mark is one that "requires imagination, thought and perception to reach a conclusion as to the nature of the goods." These marks fall short of directly describing the qualities or functions of a particular product or service, but merely suggest such qualities. If a term is suggestive, it is entitled to protection without proof of secondary meaning.

Arbitrary or fanciful marks require no extended definition. They are marks which in no way describe or suggest the qualities of the product.

. . . Because I find that through the plaintiff's advertising and marketing efforts the plaintiff's mark has developed strong secondary meaning as a source of children's products, it is sufficient for purposes of this decision to note merely that the plaintiff's mark is one of medium strength, clearly entitled to protection, but falling short of the protection afforded an arbitrary or fanciful mark.

2. Degree of Similarity between the Two Marks

. . . [T]he key inquiry is . . . whether a similarity exists which is likely to cause confusion. This test must be applied from the perspective of prospective purchasers. Thus, it must be determined whether "the *impression* which the infringing [mark] makes upon the consumer is such that he is likely to believe the product is from the same source as the one he knows under the trade-mark." In making this determination, it is the overall impression of the mark as a whole that must be considered.

Turning to the two marks involved here, various similarities and differences are readily apparent. The patent similarity between the marks is that they both employ the phrase, "R Us." Further, both marks employee the letter "R" in place of the word "are," although the plaintiff's mark uses an inverted capitalized "R," while the defendants generally use a non-inverted lower case "r" for their mark.

The most glaring difference between the marks is that in one the phrase "R Us" is preceded by the word "Toys," while in the other it is preceded by the word "Kids." Other differences include the following: plaintiff's mark ends with an exclamation point, plaintiff frequently utilizes the image of a giraffe alongside its mark, plaintiff's mark is set forth in stylized lettering, usually multi-colored, and plaintiff frequently utilizes the words, "a children's bargain basement" under the logo in its advertising.

. . . While the marks are clearly distinguishable when placed side by side, there are sufficiently strong similarities to create the possibility that some consumers might believe that the two marks emanated from the same source. The similarities in sound and association also create the possibility that some consumers might mistake one mark for the other when seeing or hearing the mark alone

3. Proximity of the Products

Where the products in question are competitive, the likelihood of consumer confusion increases.

. . . [B]oth plaintiff and defendants sell children's clothing; . . . the plaintiff and defendants currently are direct product competitors.

4. The Likelihood That Plaintiff Will "Bridge the Gap"

. . . "[B]ridging the gap" refers to two distinct possibilities; first, that the senior user presently intends to expand his sales efforts to compete directly with the junior user, thus creating the likelihood that the two products will be directly competitive; second, that while there is no present intention to bridge the gap, consumers will assume otherwise and conclude, in this era of corporate diversification, that the parties are related companies. . . . I find both possibilities present here.

5. Evidence of Actual Confusion

Evidence of actual confusion is a strong indication that there is a likelihood of confusion. It is not, however, a prerequisite for the plaintiff to recover.

6. Junior User's Good Faith

The state of mind of the junior user is an important factor in striking the balance of the equities. In the instant case, Mr. Pomeranc asserted at trial that he did not recall whether he was aware of the plaintiff's mark when he chose to name his store Kids 'r' Us in 1977.

I do not find this testimony to be credible. In view of the proximity of the stores, the overlapping of their products, and the strong advertising and marketing effort conducted by the plaintiff for a considerable amount of time prior to the defendants' adoption of the name Kids 'r' Us, it is difficult to believe that the defendants were unaware of the plaintiff's use of the Toys "R" Us mark.

The defendants adopted the Kids 'r' Us mark with knowledge of plaintiff's mark. A lack of good faith is relevant not only in balancing the equities, but also is a factor supporting a finding of a likelihood of confusion.

7. Quality of the Junior User's Product

If the junior user's product is of a low quality, the senior user's interest in avoiding any confusion is heightened. In the instant case, there is no suggestion that the defendants' products are inferior, and this factor therefore is not relevant.

8. Sophistication of the Purchasers

The level of sophistication of the average purchaser also bears on the likelihood of confusion. Every product, because of the type of buyer that it attracts, has its own distinct threshold for confusion of the source or origin.

The goods sold by both plaintiff and defendants are moderately priced clothing articles, which are not major expenditures for most purchasers. Consumers of such goods, therefore, do not exercise the same degree of care in buying as when purchasing more expensive items. Further, it may be that the consumers purchasing from the plaintiff and defendants are influenced in part by the desires of their children, for whom the products offered by plaintiff and defendants are meant.

9. Junior User's Goodwill

[A] powerful equitable argument against finding infringement is created when the junior user, through concurrent use of an identical trademark, develops goodwill in their mark. Defendants have not expended large sums advertising their store or promoting its name. Further, it appears that most of the defendants' customers are local "repeat shoppers," who come to the Kids 'r' Us store primarily because of their own past experiences with it. In light of this lack of development of goodwill, I find that the defendants do not have a strong equitable interest in retaining the Kids 'r' Us mark.

Conclusion on Likelihood of Confusion

[T]he defendants use of the Kids 'r' Us mark does create a likelihood of confusion for an appreciable number of consumers.

In reaching this determination, I place primary importance on the strong secondary meaning that the plaintiff has developed in its mark, the directly competitive nature of the products offered by the plaintiff and defendants, the plaintiff's substantially developed plans to open stores similar in format to those of the defendants', the lack of sophistication of the purchasers, the similarities between the marks, the defendants' lack of good faith in adopting the mark, and the limited goodwill the defendants have developed in their mark.

Judgment for the plaintiff.

CRITICAL THINKING

How does this depend to a large extent on the definitions of a few particular terms? How good are the definitions used? What standard are you using in determining whether the definitions are good?

ETHICAL DECISION MAKING

If you were the owner of Canarsie Kiddie Shop, Inc., how would your decision to refer to your store as Kids "r" Us change if you were to act in accordance with the Golden Rule?

What values are in conflict when considering the decisions of the owner of Canarsie Kiddie Shop, Inc, and one who follows the Golden Rule?

e-commerce AND THE LAW

TRADEMARKS AND DOMAIN NAMES

If you have a very strong trademark, what better domain name to have than that trademark? Unfortunately, the same trademark may be owned by two companies selling noncompeting goods, yet there can be only one user of any single domain name. For example, *Apple* is a trademark owned by both a computer company and the company that produces the Beatles' records. Both cannot establish a Web site identified as apple.com.

Domain names are important because they are the way people and businesses are located on the Web. A domain name is made up of a series of domains separated by periods. Most Web sites have two domains. The first-level domain, the one that the address ends with, generally identifies the type of site. For example, if it is a government site, it will end in *gov.* An educational site will end in *edu,* a network site in *net,* an organization in *org,* and a business in *com.* These top-level domain names are the same worldwide.

The second-level domain is usually the name of whoever maintains the site. For a college, for example, it would be an abbreviation of the college name, as in *bgsu.* Businesses generally want to use their company name or some other trademark associated with their product, because that name will obviously make it easiest for their customers to find them.

So how does a company go about securing a domain name that reflects its trademark? Network Solutions, Inc. (NSI), which is funded by the National Science Foundation, is responsible for registering domain names. This entity acts on behalf of the Internet Network Information Center, which handles the daily administration of the domain-name system in the United States.

Before 1995, a company or person would apply to the NSI to use a specific domain name, and as long as no one else held that name, registration was granted. Since 1995, however, the NSI has been a little more careful in handing out names. Anyone seeking to register a domain name must now state in the application that the name will not infringe on anyone else's intellectual property rights and that the registrant intends to use the name on a regular basis on the Internet.

A registrant may lose registration of a domain name by not using it for more than 90 days, or the domain name may be canceled if the registrant lied on the registration application. If you have a registered trademark and find that someone is using your trademark as a domain name, and that person does not also have ownership of that mark, you may give written notice to the NSI; under its Domain Dispute Policy, the NSI will most likely put the name "on hold," meaning that no one can use that name until the dispute is resolved. Of course, if that person had registered the domain name before you had obtained the trademark, there is probably nothing you can do. The person will be entitled to retain the domain name.

Some firms have tried to get the domain name they desire by going to another country. That alternative is certainly a possibility. However, many countries require that a firm be incorporated within their borders before it can gain the right to the domain name there. An additional problem is that trademark law relating to domain names is even more unclear abroad than it is in the United States.

For the new entrepreneur, the best advice is to try to simultaneously apply for federal trademark protection and register the domain name. For those not yet on the Web, the sooner you register your domain name, the more likely you are to get the name you want. If you feel that your mark is being violated by someone else's domain name, you may want to sue the person for infringement, because the unauthorized use of another's trademark in a domain name has been found to be illegal. You may be in for quite a fight, however, because this is a new area of the law.

TRADE DRESS

The term **trade dress** refers to the overall appearance and image of a product. Trade dress is entitled to the same protection as a trademark. To succeed on a claim of trade-dress infringement, a party must prove three elements: (1) The trade dress is primarily nonfunctional; (2) the trade dress is inherently distinctive or has acquired a secondary meaning; and (3) the alleged infringement creates a likelihood of confusion.

The main focus of a case of trade-dress infringement is usually on whether or not there is likely to be consumer confusion. For example, in a recent case,[3] Tour 18, Ltd., a golf course, copied golf holes from famous golf courses without permission of the course owners. In copying a hole from one of the most famous courses in the country, Harbour Town Hole 19, Tour 18 even copied the Harbour Town lighthouse, which is the distinctive feature of that hole. In its advertising, Tour 18 prominently featured pictures of this hole, including the lighthouse. The operator of the Harbour Town course sued Tour 18 for trade-dress infringement. The court found that there was infringement and made Tour 18 remove the lighthouse and disclaim in its advertising any affiliation with the owner of the Harbour Town course.

Trade-dress violations occur over a wide range of products. Two very different examples of trade-dress infringement were at issue in *Bubba's Bar-B-Q Oven v. The Holland Company*[4] and *Two Pesos v. Taco Cabana.*[5] In the first case, Bubba had copied almost exactly the physical appearance of Holland Company's very successful gas-fired barbecue grill, and the court found the copy to be trade-dress infringement. In the second case, Taco Cabana's trade dress consisted of "a festive eating atmosphere having interior dining and patio areas decorated with artifacts, bright colors, paintings and murals; . . . a patio that has interior and exterior areas with the interior patio capable of being sealed off from the outside patio by overhead garage doors;" a stepped exterior of the building that has "a festive and vivid color scheme using top border paint and neon stripes;" and "bright awnings and umbrellas." When Two Pesos opened a series of competing Mexican restaurants that mimicked those features almost perfectly, the court found the company guilty of trade-dress infringement.

Federal Trademark Dilution Act Of 1995

Under the Lanham Act, trademark owners were protected from the unauthorized use of their marks on only competing goods or related goods, where the use might lead to consumer confusion. Consequently, a mark might be used without permission on completely unrelated goods, thereby potentially diminishing the value of the mark. In response to this problem, a number of states passed *trademark dilution laws,* which prohibited the use of "distinctive" or "famous" trademarks, such as "McDonald's," even without a showing of consumer confusion.

In 1995, Congress made similar protection available at the federal level by passing the Federal Trademark Dilution Act. In one of the first cases decided under this law, the court said that the protection available under this act extended not just to identical marks but also to similar marks. In that case, Ringling Brothers–Barnum & Bailey was challenging Utah's use of the slogan "The Greatest Snow on Earth" as diluting the circus's famous "The Greatest Show on Earth." In denying Utah's motion to dismiss on the ground that the slogans were not identical, the court said that the marks need not be identical.

Copyrights

Copyrights protect the *expression* of creative ideas. That is, they do not protect the ideas themselves but protect only the fixed form of expressing the ideas. Copyrights protect a

[3] *Pebble Beach Co. v. Tour 18 Ltd.*, 942 F. Supp. 1513.

[4] 175 F.3d 1013 (1999).

[5] 112 S. Ct. 2753 (1994).

Exhibit 12-2
Criteria for a Copyright

Fixed form
Original
Creative

diverse range of creative works, such as books, periodicals, musical compositions, plays, motion pictures, sound recordings, lectures, works of art, and computer programs. Titles and short phrases may not be copyrighted. When Papa John's sued Rezko, Papa John's also included a copyright claim that was dismissed because it was not clear from the complaint whether Papa John's was alleging that Rezko was actually misusing the copyrighted works themselves or the ideas contained in the works. It is only the expression of the idea that is protected by copyright law, and not the underlying idea.

There are three criteria for a work to be copyrightable. First, it must be *fixed,* which means set out in a tangible medium of expression. Second, it must be *original.* Third, it must be *creative.* (See Exhibit 12-2.)

A copyright automatically arises under common law when the idea is expressed in tangible form. However, if the work is freely distributed without notice of copyright, the work falls into the public domain. A copyrighted work that is reproduced with the appropriate notice affixed is protected for the life of its creator plus 70 years.

Under the common law of copyright, an infringer may be enjoined only from reproducing a copyrighted work. For the creator to be able to not only seek an injunction but also recover damages arising from the infringement, the copyrighted work must be registered. One may register a work by filing a form with the Register of Copyright and providing two copies of the copyrighted materials to the Library of Congress. Whenever the work is reproduced, the appropriate notice of copyright *should* accompany it, although such notice is no longer required by law. Printed works, for example, should be published with the word *copyright* and the symbol © or the abbreviation *copr.,* followed by the first date of publication and the name of the copyright owner. Once the work is registered, as long as it is always accompanied by the notice of copyright when reproduced, the holder of the copyright has the additional right to sue an infringer for damages caused by the infringer's use of the copyrighted material and to recover any profits made by the infringer on the copyrighted material.

It is not always easy to determine whether a copyright has been infringed, even when two works are similar. After all, if we are talking about creative works, such as photographs of a famous scene, two people might independently take very similar pictures at completely different times and without even knowing of each other's work. Case 12-3 illustrates the court's reasoning in a successful copyright infringement case.

CASE 12-3

TY INC. v. GMA ACCESSORIES INC.
U.S. COURT OF APPEALS SEVENTH CIRCUIT
45 U.S.P.Q. 1519 (1998)

Ty began selling the popular "Beanie Babies" line of miniature stuffed bean-bag animals, including Squealer, the pig, in 1993. The popularity of this line led GMA to bring out its own line of bean-bag stuffed animals three years later.

Ty filed an action to obtain a preliminary injunction under the Copyright Act against the sale by GMA of "Preston the Pig" and "Louie the Cow." These are bean-bag animals manufactured by GMA that Ty contends are copies of its copyrighted pig ("Squealer") and cow ("Daisy").

The district court granted the injunction. GMA appealed the part of the injunction that enjoined the sale of Preston.

JUSTICE RICHARD POSNER: We have appended to our opinion five pictures found in the appellate record. The first shows Squealer (the darker pig, actually pink) and Preston (white). The second is a picture of two real pigs. The third and fourth are different views of the design for Preston that Janet Salmon submitted to GMA several months before Preston went into production. The fifth is a picture of the two bean-bag cows; they are nearly identical. A glance at the first picture shows a striking similarity between the two bean-bag pigs as well. . . .

The two pigs are so nearly identical that if the second is a copy of the first, the second clearly infringes Ty's copyright. But identity is not infringement. The Copyright Act forbids only copying; if independent creation results in an identical work, the creator of that work is free to sell it. . . . The practical basis for this rule is that unlike the case of patents and trademarks, the creator of an expressive work—an author or sculptor or composer—cannot canvass the entire universe of copyrighted works to discover whether his poem or song or, as in this case, "soft sculpture" is identical to some work in which copyright subsists, especially since unpublished, unregistered works are copyrightable. . . . But identity can be powerful evidence of copying. . . . The more a work is both like an already copyrighted work and—for this is equally important—unlike anything that is in the public domain, the less likely it is to be an independent creation. As is generally true in the law, circumstantial evidence—evidence merely probabilistic rather than certain—can confer sufficient confidence on an inference, here of copying, to warrant a legal finding.

The issue of copying can be broken down into two subissues. The first is whether the alleged copier had access to the work that he is claimed to have copied; the second is whether, if so, he used his access to copy. . . .

Obviously, access does not entail copying. . . . But copying entails access. If, therefore, two works are so similar as to make it highly probable that the later one is a copy of the earlier one, the issue of access need not be addressed separately, since if the later work was a copy its creator must have had access to the original. . . .

What . . . is not a factor here is that two works may be strikingly similar—may in fact be identical—not because one is copied from the other but because both are copies of the same thing in the public domain. . . . A similarity may be striking without being suspicious.

But here it is both. GMA's pig is strikingly similar to Ty's pig but not to anything in the public domain—a real pig, for example. . . . The parties' bean-bag pigs bear little resemblance to real pigs even if we overlook the striking anatomical anomaly of Preston—he has three toes, whereas real pigs have cloven hooves. . . .

Real pigs are not the only pigs in the public domain. But GMA has not pointed to any fictional pig in the public domain that Preston resembles. Preston resembles only Squealer, and resembles him so closely as to warrant an inference that GMA copied Squealer. In rebuttal all that GMA presented was the affidavit of the designer, Salmon, who swears . . . that she never looked at a Squealer before submitting her design. But it is not her design drawing that is alleged to infringe the copyright on Squealer; it is the manufactured Preston, the soft sculpture itself, which, as a comparison of the first with the third and fourth pictures in the appendix is much more like Squealer than Salmon's drawing is.

. . . A glance at the last picture in the appendix shows an identity between Louie the Cow and Ty's Daisy that is so complete (and also not explainable by reference to resemblance to a real cow or other public domain figure) as to compel an inference of copying. If GMA thus must have had access to Louie, it is probable, quite apart from any inference from the evidence of similarity, that it had access to Squealer as well.

Access (and copying) may be inferred when two works are so similar to each other and not to anything in the public domain that it is likely that the creator of the second work copied the first, but the inference can be rebutted by disproving access or otherwise showing independent creation. . . .

The granting of a preliminary injunction depends on proof of irreparable harm if the injunction is withheld as well as on the likelihood of success on the merits when the case is fully tried. . . .

We may assume that if Ty licensed all who want to make Beanie Babies, appropriate compensatory relief in this case would be to make GMA pay for the license at Ty's standard rate retroactive to the date on which GMA began selling Preston. . . . GMA's infringement is not only depriving Ty of the income on some number of pigs but also disrupting its scheme of distribution. The harm to its marketing plan cannot readily be monetized and so is appropriately described as irreparable. . . . The harm is aggravated by differences in appearance and quality control (remember the defective Preston) that while not big enough to rebut an inference of copying could impair Ty's goodwill if customers buy Preston thinking it is a Beanie Baby rather than a knockoff. This is a type of loss more commonly associated with trademark cases, but it is applicable to copyright as well.

AFFIRMED in favor of the plaintiff.

[CONTINUED]

CRITICAL THINKING

What type of information could the defendant, GMA, have submitted in the district court case that might have kept the court from issuing the injunction?

ETHICAL DECISION MAKING

As an executive at GMA, how would you have responded to this case if your actions were guided by the Golden Rule? What values would be important in making your decision?

A source of controversy involving copyrighted works is the application of the **fair-use doctrine.** This doctrine provides that a portion of a copyrighted work may be reproduced for purposes of "criticism, comment, news reporting, teaching (including multiple copies for classroom use), scholarship, and research."

In determining whether the fair-use doctrine provides a valid defense to a claim of copyright infringement, Section 107 of the Copyright Act requires that the court weigh the following four factors:

1. The purpose and character of the use, including whether such use is of a commercial nature or is for nonprofit educational purposes.
2. The nature of the copyrighted work.
3. The amount and substantiality of the portion used in relation to the copyrighted work as a whole.
4. The effect of the use on the potential market for or value of the copyrighted work.

Case 12-4 examines a typical situation where the issue of fair use arises: the college classroom.

CASE 12-4 PRINCETON UNIVERSITY PRESS v. MICHIGAN DOCUMENT SERVICES, INC.

UNITED STATES COURT OF APPEALS, SIXTH CIRCUIT
93 F.3D 1381 (1996)

Defendant Michigan Document Services, Inc., is a commercial copyshop that reproduced substantial segments of copyrighted works of scholarship, bound the copies into "coursepacks," and sold the coursepacks to students for use in fulfilling reading assignments given by professors at the University of Michigan. The copyshop did not obtain copyright owners' permission to duplicate their copyrighted works.

Princeton University Press and two other publishers whose works had been used without permission sued MDS for copyright infringement. The trial court ruled in favor of the copyright holders, and MDS appealed.

CIRCUIT JUDGE DAVID A. NELSON: . . . "[T]o negate fair use," the Supreme Court has said "one need only show that if the challenged use 'should become widespread, it would adversely affect the potential market for the copyrighted work.' " . . . Under this test, we believe, it is reasonably clear that the plaintiff publishers have succeeded in negating fair use.

. . . [M]ost of the copyshops that compete with MDS in the sale of coursepacks pay permission fees for the privilege of duplicating and selling excerpts from copyrighted works. The three plaintiffs together have been collecting permission fees at a rate approaching

$500,000 a year. If copyshops across the nation were to start doing what the defendants have been doing here, this revenue stream would shrivel and the potential value of the copyrighted works of scholarship published by the plaintiffs would be diminished accordingly.

. . . Although [the federal] Classroom Guidelines purport to "state the minimum and not the maximum standards of educational fair use," they do evoke a general idea, at least, of the type of educational copying Congress had in mind. The guidelines allow multiple copies for classroom use provided that (1) the copying meets the test of brevity (1,000 words, in the present context); (2) the copying meets the test of spontaneity, under which "[t]he inspiration and decision to use the work and the moment of its use for maximum teaching effectiveness [must be] so close in time that it would be unreasonable to expect a timely reply to a request for permission"; (3) no more than nine instances of multiple copying take place during a term, and only a limited number of copies are made from the works of any one author or from any one collective work; (4) each copy contains a notice of copyright; (5) the copying does not substitute for the purchase of "books, publishers' reprints or periodicals"; and (6) the student is not charged any more than the actual cost of copying. The Classroom Guidelines also make clear that unauthorized copying to create "anthologies, compilations or collective works" is prohibited.

In its systematic and premeditated character, its magnitude, its anthological content, and its commercial motivation, the copying done by MDS goes well beyond anything envisioned by the Congress that chose to incorporate the guidelines in the legislative history. Although the guidelines do not purport to be a complete and definitive statement of fair use law for educational copying, and although they do not have the force of law, they do provide us general guidance. The fact that the MDS copying is light years away from the safe harbor of the guidelines weighs against a finding of fair use.

Judgment on issue of fair use affirmed in favor of Plaintiff, but damages award vacated and case remanded for reconsideration of damages.

CRITICAL THINKING

What do you see as the fundamental issue being addressed in this case?
Does the decision of the court create a desirable precedent?

ETHICAL DECISION MAKING

What ethical issue did the managers of Michigan Document Service need to consider when they were deciding whether to require permissions for the materials they were copying? How would the application of the universalization test affect the way they would think about this decision?

Patents

A **patent** protects a product, process, invention, machine, or plant produced by asexual reproduction. For this protection to be granted, three criteria must be satisfied. First, the object of the patent must be *novel,* or new. No one else must have previously made or published the plans for this object. Second, the object must be *useful,* unless it is a design. It must provide some utility to society. Third, the object must be *nonobvious.* (See Exhibit 12-3.) The invention must not be one that a person of ordinary skill in the trade

global context

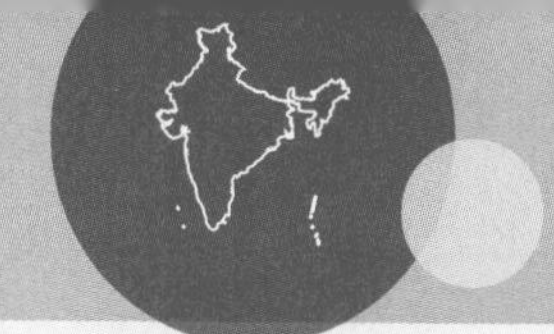

Computer Program Protection in the EU

In May 1991, the Council of European Communities implemented a directive for the purpose of protecting computer programs. The directive equated the protection of computer programs with the protection of literary works under the Berne Convention standards. The protection is inclusive of all "preparatory design material," and the only parameter necessary for a program to be eligible is that it must be the intellectual creation of the author. If a program is developed by a group of individuals, the rights are jointly held. If an employee creates a program while fulfilling an employer's instructions, the employer has exclusive rights over the program. These protections are guaranteed for life and 70 years after the author's death. The specific remedies against violators of the directive are left to the jurisdiction of each member state.

In October 1998, the Data Protection Directive enhanced the above directive. The Data Protection Directive requires each member state to legally regulate the processing of personal data within the European Union. Most importantly, the directive stated that personal data would be permitted to travel outside the EU only if the destination country had an adequate level of protection for the subject of the data. This stipulation may affect the EU's trading relations. The U.S., Canada, Japan and Australia, for example, do not have comprehensive statutes that regulate information within the private sector. Other countries have even less adequate protection for certain data. If these countries wish to receive the same amount of information from European countries as they have in the past, they may have to consider altering their regulations.

Exhibit 12-3
Criteria for a Patent

- Novel
- Useful
- Nonobvious

could have easily discovered. When a patent is issued for an object, it gives its holder the exclusive right to produce, sell, and use the object of the patent for 20 years from the date of application. The holder of the patent may *license,* or allow others to manufacture and sell, the patented object. In most cases, patents are licensed in exchange for the payment of *royalties,* a sum of money paid for each use of the patented process.

The only restrictions on the patent holder are that he or she may not use the patent for an illegal purpose. The two most common illegal purposes would by tying arrangements and cross-licensing. A **tying arrangement** occurs when the holder issues a license to use the patented object *only* if the licensee agrees to buy some nonpatented product from the holder. **Cross-licensing** occurs when two patent holders license each other to use their patents *only* on the condition that neither licenses anyone else to use his or her patent without the other's consent. Both of these activities are unlawful because they tend to reduce competition.

To obtain a patent, one generally contacts an attorney licensed to practice before the U.S. Patent Office. The attorney does a *patent search* to make sure that no other similar patent exists. If none exist, the attorney fills out a patent application and files it with the Patent Office. The Patent Office evaluates the application, and if the object meets the criteria already described, a patent is issued within approximately two years. While two years may seem like a long time, it is short compared to the six years it typically takes to secure a patent in Japan.

Once the patent is issued, the holder may bring a patent infringement suit in a federal court against anyone who uses, sells, or manufactures the patented invention without the permission of the patent holder. A successful action may result in an injunction prohibiting further use of the patented item by the infringer and also an award of damages. Sometimes, however, the result of the case is that the holder loses the patent. This loss would occur if the infringer is able to prove that the Patent Office should not have issued the patent in the first place.

Trade Secrets

A **trade secret** is a process, product, method of operation, or compilation of information that gives a businessperson an advantage over his or her competitors. Inventions and designs may also be considered trade secrets. For instance, Papa John's dough and sauce recipes might be considered trade secrets, as might the number of pepperoni slices Papa John's chefs are trained to put on its pizzas. A trade secret is protected by the common law from unlawful appropriation by competitors as long as it is kept secret and consists of elements not generally known in the trade.

Competitors may discover a "secret" by any lawful means, such as by doing reverse engineering or by going on public tours of plants and observing the use of trade secrets. Lawful discovery of a secret means there is no longer a trade secret to be protected.

If a competitor acquires a trade secret by unlawful means, the originator of the secret can take legal action. In order to enjoin such a competitor from continuing to use a trade secret and/or to recover damages caused by the use of the secret, a plaintiff must prove that:

1. A trade secret actually existed.
2. The defendant acquired it through unlawful means, such as breaking into the plaintiff's business and stealing it or securing it through misuse of a confidential relationship with the plaintiff or one of the plaintiff's present or former employees.
3. The defendant used the trade secret without the plaintiff's permission.

A common dilemma facing an inventor is whether to protect an invention through patent or trade-secret law. If the inventor successfully patents the invention and defends the patent, the inventor has a guaranteed exclusive monopoly on the use of the invention for 20 years, a substantial period of time. The problem is that once this period is over, the patented good goes into the public domain and everyone has access to it. There is also the risk that the patent may be successfully challenged and the protection lost prematurely.

Trade secret law, on the other hand, could protect the invention in perpetuity. The problem is that once someone discovers the secret lawfully, the protection is lost.

International Protection of Intellectual Property

Because many American companies operate worldwide, they need to be able to protect their intellectual property abroad as well as at home. The primary international protection for intellectual property is offered through multilateral conventions. These treaties are generally administered by the World Intellectual Property Organization, a specialized agency of the United Nations.

THE BERNE CONVENTION OF 1886

The Berne Convention of 1886, to which 81 countries are now signatories, is the oldest treaty designed to protect artistic rights. Four basic principles underlie the obligations of signatories to the treaty:

1. The *national treatment principle,* which requires that each member nation protect artists of all signatory nations equally.
2. The *nonconditional protection principle,* which requires that protection not be conditioned on the use of formalities, although the country of origin may require registration or a similar formality.

3. The *protection independent of protection in the country of origin principle,* which allows nationals of nonsignatory countries to protect works if they are created in a member country.
4. The *common rules principle,* which establishes minimum standards for granting copyrights that all nations must meet.

THE UNIVERSAL COPYRIGHT CONVENTION OF 1952, AS REVISED IN 1971

The Universal Copyright Convention (UCC) is one of the two treaties that protect copyrights. The treaty was developed by the United Nations as an alternative for countries that wanted to participate in some form of multilateral protection of copyrights, but did not want to agree to the terms of the Berne Convention. The United States, China, and the Soviet Union are among the nations that are now signatories, but had initially refused to enter the convention. Today, 93 nations have signed either the 1952 or the 1971 version.

The primary way the UCC differs from the Berne Convention is that the UCC allows members to establish formalities for protection and making exceptions to common rules as long as the exceptions are not inconsistent with the essence of the treaty. An additional difference is that it does not require signatory countries to protect author's rights.

THE PARIS CONVENTION OF 1883

The Paris Convention now has 101 members that have agreed to protect so-called industrial rights, such as inventions and trademarks. Unfair competition is also restricted under this treaty.

The treaty has been revised several times, and not all members have signed all versions. While the treaty is highly complex, it has three basic principles: (1) *national treatment,* as defined under the Berne Convention; (2) *the right of priority,* which allows a national of a member state 12 months after filing in his or her home nation to file an application in any other member state and have the date of application be the date of the filing in the home nation; and (3) *common rules,* which set out minimum standards of protection in all states. These common rules include such items as outlawing false labeling and protecting trade names of companies from member states even without registration.

The Patent Cooperation Treaty of 1970, was open to signatories of the Paris Convention. It contains a provision for making a patent application filed in any member state an international application that is as effective as individually filed applications in all member states. When the application is filed in any member state, the application is then forwarded to an international search authority.

Despite the existence of such agreements, enforcement in foreign countries is often very lax. In 1994, problems with blatant trademark infringement in China were so severe that President Clinton threatened to impose trade sanctions if enforcement were not improved.

THE 1994 AGREEMENT ON TRADE-RELATED ASPECTS OF INTELLECTUAL PROPERTY RIGHTS

Over 100 nations are signatories to the 1994 Agreement on Trade-Related Aspects of Intellectual Property Rights (TRIPP). The primary benefit of this agreement is that it mandates that each signatory nation establish broad intellectual property protections and effective means for enforcing these protections. It also provides that no country can give its own citizens better intellectual property protections than it grants to citizens of other nations that are signatories to the agreement.

global context

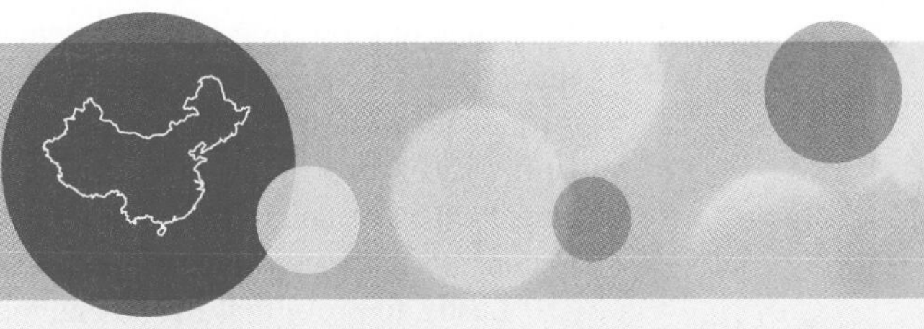

Software Piracy in China

An ongoing source of tension between the United States and China has been China's lax enforcement of intellectual property laws. A study released in July 1999 found that 95 percent of the business software installed in China during 1998 was pirated. Software piracy was estimated to have cost China $1.2 billion that year, more than in any other Asian nation, according to one study.*

The first indication that China is attempting to crack down on the piracy of software occurred in July 1999, when China handed down its first criminal sentence for software piracy. Wang Antao was sentenced to four years in prison, fined 20,000 yuan ($2,400), and required to pay the software owner 280,000 yuan ($33,800) for selling a slightly modified version of the company's software without permission.

Since then, progress has been made, albeit slowly. According to the Business Software Alliance, the percentage of pirated software in computers in 2005 in China was 86%, down from 93% in 2003. And in April of 2007, a senior vice president and general counsel for Microsoft reported that the previous year had been the most encouraging one for more personal computers were being sold in the country with legitimate software installed. He expressed a belief that the Chinese government had indeed taken action to curb software piracy in the region, although the Chinese remain one of the biggest pirates of the company's software.

However, the improvements did not prevent President Bush, that same month, from putting China on its "priority watch list," which will subject them to extra scrutiny and could eventually lead to economic sanctions if the administration decides to bring trade cases before the World Trade Organization. The list is included in an annual report the administration is required to provide to Congress each year that highlights the problems U.S. companies are facing around the world with copyright piracy.

* The study was conducted by the U.S. Business Software Alliance and the Software and Information Industry Association.

CASE OPENER WRAP-UP

Owning Ideas: A Question Of Intellectual Property

The defendant in the case of *Papa John's v. Rezko* sought to have the suit dismissed because, as he argued, the plaintiff had not sufficiently proved the legal elements of copyright violation, trademark infringement, and illegal acquisition of a trade secret.

Remember: This case did not decide whether the plaintiff should receive damages or other legal remedies. Rather, it decided whether the plaintiff's case should continue to trial or should be dropped, as the defendant sought in his motion to dismiss.

Let's look at the legal requirements that must be met under state and federal laws to argue the plaintiff's case.

To argue that Rezko and the former franchises violated a registered copyright, the plaintiff needed to be able to successfully state that (1) they had ownership of a copyright and (2) Rezko had made unauthorized copies or derivative works based on the original, registered materials.

To argue that the defendant committed a trademark infringement, the plaintiff needed to be able to prove that (1) its trademarks were protectable and (2) the use of these trademarks by Rezko and the former franchises was likely to cause confusion among consumers. As mentioned earlier in this chapter, the court would base its decision on factors such as the similarity of the marks, the similarity of the products or services, the sophistication of consumers, the strength of the Papa John's trademarks, and the intent of the former franchises to convince their consumers that their product was a Papa John's product.

Lastly, to prove that Rezko and the former franchises violated the trade-secret laws in their state, the plaintiff needed to be able to prove that the information in question was in fact a trade secret, that Rezko and the former franchises misappropriated this information, and that the restaurants actually used this information in their business.

The court denied the defendant's motion to dismiss with respect to all claims except the copyright claim. The court believed that the plaintiff could prove its case, or at least should have the opportunity to argue its case, in a court of law. The copyright claim was dismissed, but with leave to replead the copyright claim in a matter that clearly aligned the plaintiff's allegation with the legal requirements for copyright violation.

Summary

Intellectual Property

Intellectual property is property that is the result of one's intellectual and creative efforts, rather than physical efforts.

Trademarks

A *trademark* is a distinctive mark, word, design, picture, or arrangement that is used by a producer in conjunction with a product and that tends to cause the consumer to identify the product with the producer. Trademarks used in interstate commerce can be protected under the Lanham Act.

Copyrights

A *copyright* protects the fixed form of the *expression* of an original, creative idea. The most common defense to an allegation of copyright infringement is the *fair-use doctrine,* which provides that a portion of a copyrighted work may be reproduced for purposes of "criticism, comment, news reporting, teaching (including multiple copies for classroom use), scholarship, and research."

Patents

A *patent* protects a product, process, invention, machine, or plant that is produced by asexual reproduction and that meets the criteria of being novel, useful, and nonobvious. Obtaining a patent under the Lanham Act allows the holder to license the use of his or her patented idea for royalties as long as the holder does not enter into a tying arrangement or engage in cross-licensing.

Trade Secrets

An alternative to using a patent is to protect information as a trade secret, which allows the holder of a trade secret to sue one who illegally takes a person's trade secret if the owner of the secret can prove that:

1. A trade secret actually existed.
2. The defendant acquired it through unlawful means, such as breaking into the plaintiff's business and stealing it or securing it through misuse of a confidential relationship with the plaintiff or one of the plaintiff's present or former employees.
3. The defendant used the trade secret without the plaintiff's permission.

International Protection of Intellectual Property

Intellectual property is protected internationally primarily by the use of treaties. Such treaties include the Universal Copyright Convention, the Berne Convention, the Paris Convention of 1883, and the TRIPPS agreement.

Point / Counterpoint

The process of applying for a patent and keeping a patent can be difficult and costly. As you know, an alternative to patenting an invention is to protect it through trade-secret law.

Should Inventors Avoid the Hassles of Patent Protection and Protect Their Inventions through Trade-Secret Law?	
Yes	**No**
Inventors should choose to protect their inventions through trade-secret law. Trade-secret protection does not require registration with government agencies. Unlike patent protection, whereby the owner of the patent has exclusive rights to produce, sell, and use the object of the patent only for a limited time, trade-secret protection offers the owner of the trade secret exclusive rights indefinitely. For example, the unique process by which Coca-Cola makes its soft drink has been protected as a trade secret for over 100 years. This approach has prevented competitors from duplicating Coca-Cola's product. Patent holders also risk the chance of losing their patent if a challenger is able to show that the patent should not have been issued. Because trade-secret protection is not limited by registration requirements, inventors should use trade-secret law to protect their products.	Inventors should not choose to protect their inventions through trade-secret law. Protection through trade-secret law is risky. It is the responsibility of the owner of the trade secret to take precautionary measures to maintain the privacy of the secret. With technological advances, the chance of competitors' using legal methods such as reverse engineering to discover the trade secret is likely. An owner of a patent may bring a patent infringement suit if the patent has been used without permission. If a trade secret is discovered through lawful means, it is no longer a secret and the owner cannot bring actions against those using the product or process. Through patent protection the owner can decide whether to license the patent and can earn a profit from those who choose to use the product. The risks associated with trade-secret protection are too great to make it a desirable choice.

Questions & Problems

1. Identify the four primary kinds of trademarks, and explain what makes each distinct.
2. List and define the classic factors that a court must weigh when determining whether there has been trademark infringement that warrants an award of damages and an injunction.
3. Explain how trademarks and domain names are related.
4. What is the relationship between copyright infringement and the fair-use doctrine?
5. Explain two common illegal ways patents can be used.
6. Identify the factors one would look at when deciding whether to protect intellectual property with either a patent or a trade-secret law.
7. Miller Brewing produced a reduced-calorie beer called "Miller Lite," which it began selling in the 1970s and spent millions of dollars advertising. In 1980, Falstaff Brewing Corporation started marketing a reduced-calorie beer called "Falstaff Lite." Miller filed an action seeking an injunction against Falstaff to prevent it from using the term

Lite. What was the outcome of the case? [*Miller Brewing Co. v. Falstaff Brewing Corporation,* 655 F.2d 5 (1987).]

8. CMM brought suit against Ocean Coast Properties, alleging federal copyright, trademark, and trade-dress infringement. CMM ran radio promotional contests entitled "Payroll Payoff" and "Paycheck Payoff." Both were registered as service marks in 1991. The radio station announces a name, and if the person announced calls the station, she or he is "on the payroll" until replaced by the next listener. The promotion was not original to CMM; rather, the idea for the promotion came from another station's promotion called "Working Women's Wednesday." After learning that the promotion was not original, another station, WPOR, began to run a promotion entitled "Payday Contest." Both WPOR and CMM used direct mail to advertise their promotions. The brochures for the stations contained similar graphics and phrases. In arguing that the two promotions could create confusion, CMM testified that it was contacted several times by listeners asking if its promotion was connected to WPOR's promotion. Do you think the court ruled in favor of CMM? [*CMM Cable Rep, Inc. v. Ocean Coast Properties Inc.,* 888 F. Supp 192 (1995).]

9. Plaintiff Columbia Pictures Industries Inc. brought a copyright infringement action against Miramax Films Corp. The successful motion picture *Men in Black,* produced by Columbia Pictures, grossed over $250 million at the box office in 1997. In advertising the film, Columbia produced a copyrighted MIB poster and two copyrighted MIB trailers shown in theaters. The poster shows Will Smith and Tommy Lee Jones standing in front of the New York City skyline. They hold oversized weapons, and the copy reads "Protecting the Earth from the Scum of the Universe." The movie trailers use the same slogan and show a shadow of Smith and Jones superimposed over the letters MIB.

   In 1998, Miramax Films Corporation produced the film *The Big One.* This was a documentary concerning corporate America's quest for profits at the expense of jobs and plant closings. Prior to the release, Miramax also produced posters and movie trailers. The posters featured Michael Moore, the writer and director of the film, standing in front of the New York City skyline with an oversized microphone. The copy reads "Protecting the Earth from the Scum of Corporate America." The slogan is used again in the movie trailer, and the trailer ends with a picture of Moore superimposed over the letters TBO.

   The promotions for *The Big One* were pulled after Miramax received complaints from Columbia Pictures. Columbia argued that Miramax used copyrighted material to generate profits for the film. Miramax contended that it was protected under the fair-use doctrine, and it argued that the films were not similar in nature. Whom do you think the court decided in favor of? Why? [*Columbia Pictures Industries Inc. v. Miramax Films Corp.,* 11 F. Supp. 1179 (57).]

10. The plaintiff, Lone Star Steakhouse, operates over 30 Lone Star Steakhouse & Saloon restaurants in the United States. The trademarks "Lone Star Café" and "Lone Star Steakhouse & Saloon" are owned by Lone Star Steakhouse. Clothing and accessories with the logo are also sold in the restaurant. In 1991 the defendant, Alpha, opened a restaurant named "Lone Star Grill" in Arlington, Virginia. Alpha conducted extensive advertising in the Virginia and Washington, D.C., area. The advertisements featured coupons with the words *Lone Star* and a five-pointed star similar to the one used by Lone Star Steakhouse. Lone Star Steakhouse operates four restaurants in Virginia and one restaurant in Washington, D.C. They testified that on several occasions customers presented coupons for Lone Star Grill. To prevent customer dissatisfaction, Lone Star Steakhouse would give customers free drinks, coupons, or meal discounts. Lone

Star Steakhouse & Saloon brought a trademark infringement action against Lone Star Grill. How do you think the court decided, and why? [*Lone Star Steakhouse & Saloon v. Alpha of Virginia,* 43 F.3d 922 (1995).]

11. The Stop & Shop Supermarket and Big Y Foods are supermarkets offering the same services and competing for the same customers. In an advertisement introducing their new, easy-to-use scan saver cards, Stop & Shop Supermarket used the slogan "It's that Simple." The supermarket used the slogan in radio, television, and print advertisements. The service mark was licensed to the supermarket by plaintiff Fullerton, who owns the right to the service mark. After Stop & Shop started using the slogan, Big Y Foods began to use a similar slogan, "We Make Life Simple." Both service marks are always accompanied by the name of the store. Fullerton and Stop & Shop Supermarket brought an action alleging infringement of the service mark. Do you think that the court granted the injunction? Why or why not? [*The Stop & Shop Supermarket Company and Fullerton Corp. v. Big Y Foods Inc.,* 943 F. Supp. 120 (1996).]

12. Nike, Inc., has trademarks for its name, a "swoosh" design, and the phrase "just do it." These marks appear on Nike clothing, hats, shoes, and other athletic products. Mike and his daughter started, for a summer project, Just Did it Enterprises, to manufacture and sell, through mail order, T-shirts and sweatshirts that had the name Mike and the swoosh emblazoned on them. The project lost money, and Nike sued them for trademark infringement. Discuss the likely outcome of Nike's suit. [*Nike, Inc. v. Just Did It Enterprises,* 6 F.3d 1225 (1993).]

13. Superior Form Builders held a copyright for animal mannequins. The sculpted animal forms were used to mount animal skins. The owner of Superior Form Builders, Tommy Knight, considers the mannequins to be a form of artistic expression. The defendant, Dan Chase Taxidermy Supply Company, ordered four of Knight's mannequins from the Superior Form catalog. Chase, a competitor of Superior Form, ordered under a fictitious name. He used the mannequins to mount animal skins and made few changes to the forms. When Knight realized that Chase was using the Superior Form mannequins, he sued for copyright infringement. Chase argued that the copyright should never have been granted because the mannequins were useful and unoriginal. How do you think the court decided? [*Superior Form Builders, Inc v. Chase Taxidermy Supply Co.,* 74 F.3d 488 (4th Cir. 1996).]

14. GoTo.Com's logo features a green circle surrounded by a yellow background, with the words *Go* and *To* printed in the circle. Disney Corp. started to use its logo, a green circle surrounded by a yellow background with the word *Go* printed inside, on its GoNetwork's page. GoTo.Com filed suit against Disney Corporation, seeking an injunction. Do you think the court granted the injunction? What factors would it have considered in making its decision? [*GoTo.com, Inc. v. Walt Disney Co.,* 202 F.3d 1199, 1207 (9th Cir. 2000).]

Looking for more review material?

The Online Learning Center at **www.mhhe.com/kubasek1e** contains this chapter's "Assignment on the Internet" and also a list of URLs for more information, entitled "On the Internet." Find both of them in the Student Center portion of the OLC, along with quizzes and other helpful materials.

Introduction to Contracts

CASE OPENER

A Questionable Contract

Caro Davis was the niece of Blanche Whitehead, who was married to Rupert Whitehead. Before marrying Frank Davis, Caro lived for many years with the Whiteheads, who were childless and extremely fond of Caro. After their marriage, Caro and Frank moved to Canada, but for the next 18 years, they continued to have a close and loving relationship with the Whiteheads, regularly corresponding and frequently visiting them.

Then Mrs. Whitehead had a series of strokes and was placed in a private hospital; Mr. Whitehead's health also began to fail. He wrote Mr. Davis, telling him that Mrs. Whitehead, more than anything else, wanted to spend her last remaining days with Caro. Mr. Whitehead also expressed concern that his health was failing and that people were taking advantage of his failing health and skimming money from him. He detailed all the property he owned, and said that he thought his total worth was around $150,000. He said that if Frank and Caro would come immediately and stay with him and his wife, helping him manage his affairs and care for Mrs. Whitehead, he and his wife would leave all their property to the couple. Mr. Whitehead wrote in the letter, "The next attack will be my end, I am 65 and my health has been bad for years, so, the Drs. don't give me much longer to live. So if you can come, Caro will inherit everything and you will make our lives happier and see Blanche is provided for to the end." He asked Frank to let him know as soon as possible whether they could come.

Mr. Davis wrote Mr. Whitehead that they would come by train as soon as he could wind up his affairs, and he also confirmed his intentions by a telegram. The Davises began making preparations to move to California, but before they could wind up all Mr. Davis's business affairs, Mr. Whitehead committed suicide. The Davises immediately went to California, where Caro remained with Mrs. Whitehead, caring for her, for the next three weeks, until she died.

CHAPTER 13

Upon her death, it was discovered that both the Whiteheads had bequeathed their estates to two nephews. Mr. and Mrs. Davis sued for specific performance, to have the court enforce the contract under which the Whiteheads were to bequeath their estate to Caro Davis.[1]

1. Was there an offer to make a unilateral or bilateral contract?
2. Why would it matter whether this was a unilateral or bilateral offer?
3. By what standard would the courts determine whether a contract existed?

The Wrap-Up at the end of the chapter will answer these questions.

Learning Objectives

After reading this chapter, you will be able to answer the following questions:

1. What is a contract?
2. What are the sources of contract law?
3. How can contracts be classified?
4. What are the rules that guide the interpretation of contracts?

[1] *Davis v. Jacoby,* 1 Cal. 2d 370, 34 P.2d 1026.

The Definition of a Contract

This part of the text focuses on contracts, but what is a contract? The definition provided by the Restatement (Second) of Contracts is that a **contract** "is a promise or set of promises for the breach of which the law gives a remedy or the performance of which the law in some way recognizes a duty."[2] Another, perhaps simpler, way to think of a contract is that it is a set of legally enforceable promises. Business students should be especially interested in contract law because of the fundamental role contracts play in business. After all, almost all business relationships are created by contracts.

ELEMENTS OF A CONTRACT

The definition of a contract can be fleshed out by examining the four elements that are necessary for a contract to exist. These elements are the agreement, the consideration, contractual capacity, and a legal object. The **agreement** consists of an **offer** by one party, called the *offeror,* to enter into a contract, and an **acceptance** of the terms of the offer by the other party, called the *offeree.* This first element is discussed in detail in Chapter 14.

The second element of the contract is the **consideration,** which is defined as the bargained-for exchange. Another way to think of the consideration is that it is what each party gets in exchange for his or her promise under the contract. Consideration is further discussed in Chapter 15.

The third element is **contractual capacity.** Capacity is the legal ability to enter into a binding agreement. Most adults over the age of majority have the legal ability to enter into binding contracts, but Chapter 16 explains when people have either limited or no capacity to enter into these agreements. Persons who do not have the capacity to enter into legally binding contracts include those under the age of majority, people suffering from mental illness, and intoxicated persons.

Chapter 16 also discusses the fourth element of a binding, legal contract, **legal object.** The contract cannot be either illegal or against public policy.

DEFENSES TO THE ENFORCEMENT OF A CONTRACT

Sometimes the parties may enter into what appears to be a legally binding contract because all four elements of a contract are present, but one of the parties may have a defense to the contract's enforcement. Such defenses fall into two categories. The first, discussed in Chapter 17, is a **lack of genuine assent.** A contract is supposed to be entered into freely by both parties, but sometimes the offeror secures the acceptance of the agreement through improper means, such as fraud, duress, undue influence, or misrepresentation. In these situations, there really is no genuine assent to the contract, and the offeree may be able to raise the lack of genuine assent as a defense to enforcement of the agreement.

The second defense, discussed in Chapter 18, is that the contract lacks the *proper form,* which typically means it lacks a writing. Certain contracts require a writing, and if there is none, the agreement will not be enforced.

THE OBJECTIVE THEORY OF CONTRACTS

Contract law is said to be based on an *objective theory of contracts,* which means that the existence and interpretation of a contract is based on the outward manifestations of intent by the parties. The focus is on the outward behaviors of the parties as they would be

[2] Restatement (Second) of Contracts, sec. 1.

interpreted by the reasonable person viewing them. Thus, as a general rule, the subjective intent of the parties is not relevant; rather, what is relevant is how they represented their intent through their actions and words.

The subjective intent may be relevant, however, under a limited number of circumstances. For example, as Chapter 17 explains in its discussion of mistake, if a mutual misunderstanding between the parties exists, and as a result of that misunderstanding the parties did not really come to a meeting of the minds, there is no contract. In such a situation, the courts may look at how each party subjectively interpreted the situation to determine whether the parties had really reached an agreement.

Sources of Contract Law

The two most important sources of contract law are case law and the Uniform Commercial code (UCC). A third source of law, which has become more important with increasing globalization, is the Convention on Contracts for International Sales of Goods (CISG). This part of the book focuses primarily on the law of contracts as established by the common law. Part Three of this book, "Domestic and International Sales Law," focuses more on the law as set out by the UCC and CISG.

COMMON LAW

Today's law of contracts actually originated from judicial decisions in England; based on these English decisions, early courts in the United States modified the basic law of contracts. Since then, contract law has been modified by our legislatures and by rulings of our courts. The law of contracts is primarily common law. Therefore, to find out what the law is, one could go to the Reporters and read the decisions, but an easier way to know the law would be to go to the Restatement (Second) of the Law of Contracts. Prominent legal scholars, recruited by the American Law Institute, organized the principles of the common law of contracts into the original *Restatement of the Law, Contracts.* The compilation has subsequently been revised and published as *Restatement of the Law Second, Contracts.*

The Restatement (Second) is not actually the law itself, although judges frequently cite it in cases because it is an authoritative statement of what the law is. As the common law of contracts evolved in the various states, not all states interpreted all aspects of the law in the same way, so that while we can make generalizations about the law of contracts, one would of course always want to know exactly what the law at issue in one's own state is. In the Restatement (Second), the drafters often explain what the law about a particular matter is in the majority of states and then provide alternative approaches that other states have adopted.

UNIFORM COMMERCIAL CODE

Having different laws governing contracts in different states did not make interstate commerce flow smoothly. To remedy some of the difficulties created by a patchwork of different laws governing commercial transactions, the National Conference of Commissioners on Uniform State Laws and the American Law Institute drafted a set of commercial laws that could be applicable to all states. This effort was called the **Uniform Commercial Code (UCC).** The UCC became law in each state that adopted it in whole or part as an element of its state code. Thus, for example, if a firm enters into a contract governed by the Uniform Commercial Code in Ohio, it would be operating under the Ohio Uniform Commercial Code.

global context

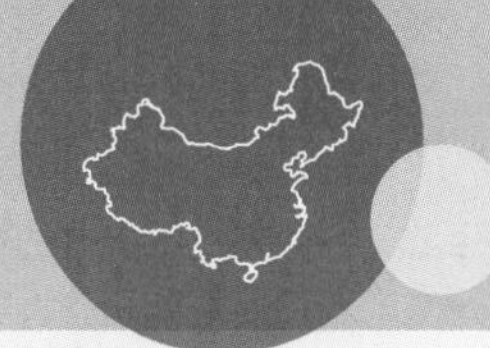

China

Compared to the United States, other countries have slightly different laws for different types of contracts. China, for example, not only has seven chapters of general provisions for contracts but also has chapters with special provisions for 15 different types of contracts. Some of the types of contracts for which special provisions have been drafted are contracts for sales, leases, loans, donations, construction projects, storage, and transportation.

The part of the Uniform Commercial Code that is relevant to contracts is Article 2, which governs contracts for the sale (exchange for a price) of goods (tangible, movable objects). This part of the book will sometimes point out important differences between the UCC and the common law, but contracts governed by the UCC are discussed primarily in Part Three of this text.

Also relevant to contract law is UCC Article 2A, which governs contracts for the lease of goods. For instance, if a person leased a car from a dealership, the lease contract would be governed by Article 2A. In contrast, if the person purchased the car, the purchase contract would be governed by Article 2 of the UCC.

Classification of Contracts

Contracts are classified in a number of different ways. Different classifications are useful for different purposes. This section describes the primary ways by which we classify contracts.

BILATERAL VERSUS UNILATERAL CONTRACTS

All contracts can be categorized as either unilateral or bilateral. Knowing whether a contract is unilateral or bilateral is important because that classification determines when the offeree is legally bound to perform, Thus, whether a contract is bilateral or unilateral depends on what response the offeror (the party proposing the contract) expects from the offeree (the person agreeing to or accepting the contract).

If the offeror wants a promise from the offeree to form a binding contract, the contract is a **bilateral contract.** A bilateral contract is commonly defined as a promise in exchange for a promise. As soon as the promises are exchanged, a contract is formed and the parties' legal obligations arise. For example, when Shannon promises to pay Gary $1,000 in exchange for his promise to paint her car on July 1, they have a bilateral contract. If either party fails to perform, the other may sue for breach.

In a **unilateral contract,** the offeror wants a performance to form the contract. The offeror wants the offeree to do something, not promise to do something. Perhaps the most common kind of unilateral offer is a reward. If Jim loses his dog, he may post a sign saying "$50 reward for the safe return of my Poodle, Frenchie." If Rita calls Jim and says, "Don't worry, I'll find your dog," she is not making a contract because the unilateral offer calls for an action, not a promise.

Just as the offeree is under no obligation to actually do the act called for by the offeror, the offeror may revoke the offer at any time before performance. Initially this situation created problems because a person could be halfway through the performance and then the offeror could revoke the offer. Because of the unfairness of such a scenario, today the courts hold that once an offeree begins performance, the offeror must hold the offer open for a reasonable time to allow the offeree to complete the performance.

Sometimes the key issue in a case may be whether the offer is for a unilateral or bilateral contract. That issue was central to the outcome of the case in the opening scenario. If Mr. Davis had been made an offer for a unilateral contract, which could be accepted only by performance, there could have been no contract because the offeror, Mr. Whitehead, killed himself before the contract could be accepted by performance. Because the death of the offeror terminates the offer, the offer would have been closed before Davis could have accepted it.

Case 13-1 provides another illustration of the importance of distinguishing between a unilateral and a bilateral contract.

CASE 13-1

D.L. PEOPLES GROUP, INC. v. HAWLEY
COURT OF APPEAL OF FLORIDA, FIRST DISTRICT
804 SO. 2D 561, FLA. APP. 1 DIST (2002)

Hawley responded to an ad in a Missouri newspaper designed to recruit Admissions Representatives to recruit Missouri residents to attend Appellant's college in Florida. The Appellant's representative interviewed Hawley in Missouri and recommended that Hawley be hired as a recruiter to recruit students from Missouri. An Admissions Representative Agreement (agreement) was mailed to Hawley, who signed it on November 16, 1996, in Missouri. The agreement was subsequently mailed to Appellant's President, for the "final say," and he executed the agreement on December 2, 1996, in his office in Kissimmee, Florida. Hawley was then trained exclusively in Missouri. Hawley was shot and killed in Missouri while attempting to make one of his first calls.

The agreement provided that Appellant was to pay Hawley a commission if Hawley successfully recruited students for Appellant's school, to provide Hawley with an opportunity to participate in Appellant's health and life insurance plans, and to provide appropriate payroll taxes for social security, unemployment and workers' compensation. Hawley agreed, among other things, to devote exclusive time and effort to Appellant's business, to operate in the territory assigned by Appellant, to maintain a certain level of liability and property damage insurance, to maintain certain licenses and levels of expertise in applicable areas, and to attend and complete Appellant's training program.

The heirs of Hawley argued that they should be entitled to workers' compensation from the state of Florida for his death. The trial court, however, denied their claim because the Florida statute provided that workers' compensation would be paid only when the contract of employment was formed in Florida, and Hawley's employment contract was a unilateral contract that could be formed solely by employee's performance in Missouri. Thus, because the contract was not formed in Florida, he was not covered by workers' compensation. Hawley's heirs appealed on grounds that the contract was in fact a bilateral contract formed in Florida when executed by the Appellant's President.

JUDGE BROWNING: . . . These mutual responsibilities constitute a bilateral contract. To form a bilateral contract, there must be mutuality of obligation. . . . Thus, the agreement is a bilateral contract, and Chapter 440 must be examined to determine the resulting consequences.

Section 440.09(1)(d), Florida Statutes (1999), provides in pertinent part, that:

> [I]f an accident happens while the employee is employed elsewhere than in this state, which would entitle the employee or his or her dependents to compensation if it had happened in this state, the employee or his or her dependents are entitled to compensation *if the contract of employment was made in this state,* or the employment was principally localized in this state.

Thus, based on the plain language of the statute, if a contract is formed in Florida, the accident is compensable under Florida workers' compensation law. . . . The employment contract between Appellant and Hawley was executed in Florida. A contract is created where the last act necessary to make a binding agreement

[CONTINUED]

takes place. . . . Where one contracting party signs the contract, and the other party accepts and signs the contract, a binding contract results. . . . It is undisputed that Hawley signed the agreement then sent it to Appellant in Kissimmee, Florida, where it was signed and executed by Appellant's President. Because the last act necessary to complete the agreement, i.e., Appellant's President's signature, was performed in Florida, the contract was made in Florida. Accordingly, Florida workers' compensation law applies. The JCC erred by finding the agreement was a unilateral contract and Florida workers' compensation law inapplicable. . . .

REVERSED.

CRITICAL THINKING

Give an example of a realistically possible piece of missing information that could change the acceptability of Judge Browning's reasoning. What effect would this new information have?

In what way is the case especially subject to the proper definition of pertinent terms? What words or phrases are particularly crucial? Are alternate definitions possible, and if so, how could the use of one of these alternatives affect the acceptability of the conclusion?

ETHICAL DECISION MAKING

Who are the stakeholders primarily affected by this ruling? What ethical theory might be used to justify the consequences imposed on the relevant parties? How so?

What do you think a public disclosure test of this ruling would yield? How might the outcome vary between regions or countries? What differences in individuals and populations could cause such variation?

EXPRESS VERSUS IMPLIED CONTRACTS

Contracts are classified as express or implied, depending on how they are created. **Express contracts** have all their terms clearly set forth in either written or spoken words. The contract in the opening scenario was an express contract, as Mr. Whitehead clearly laid out the terms for the contract in his telephone conversation with Mr. Davis. **Implied contracts,** in contrast, arise not from words but from the conduct of the parties. For instance, when you have a dental emergency and the dentist pulls your severely infected tooth without prior negotiation about payment, or even any mention of payment, you have an implied contract for payment for his services. However, if you go to the dentist's office and ask him how much it will cost to have him whiten your teeth, and you sign a written agreement that stipulates exactly what the process will entail and how much you will pay, you have an express contract.

As a general rule, three conditions must be met for the courts to find an implied, or as it is sometimes called, an *implied-in-fact,* contract. First, the plaintiff provided some property or service to the defendant. Second, the plaintiff expected to be paid for such property or service, and a reasonable person in the position of the defendant would have expected to pay for such property or services. Third, the defendant had an opportunity to reject the property or services, but did not. In Case 13-2, the court had to decide whether the facts gave rise to an implied-in-fact contract.

CASE 13-2 PACHE v. AVIATION VOLUNTEER FIRE CO.
20 A.D.3D 731, 800 N.Y.S.2D 228
N.Y.A.D. 3 DEPT. (2005)

Mr. Pache was the fire chief of the Aviation Volunteer Fire Company, which serves several neighborhoods in the Bronx. Mr. Pache suffered a fatal heart attack at the scene of a fire. His widow applied for Worker's Compensation, and was ultimately granted benefits by the Worker's Compensation Board. The decision was based on a finding that there was an implied contract between Aviation and the City of New York giving rise to the City's liability pursuant to the Volunteer Fireman's Benefit Law. The City appealed.

MERCURE, J.: . . . The City initially contended that claimant was not a covered employee within the meaning of Volunteer Firefighters' Benefit Law because the City had no written contract with Aviation. In relevant part, Volunteer Firefighters' Benefit Law § 30(2) provides:

> If at the time of injury the volunteer fire[fighter] was a member of [an incorporated] fire company . . . and located in a city, . . . protected under a contract by the fire department or fire company of which the volunteer fire[fighter] was a member, any benefit under this chapter shall be a city . . . charge.

Having conceded at oral argument that an implied contract against the City is a legal possibility, the City argues that it was error to find an implied contract in this case because there was no evidence that the Commissioner of the Fire Department of the City of New York (hereinafter FDNY) ever approved such a contract and there was insufficient proof of the elements of formation of an implied contract. We find both contentions to be unavailing.

In general, "it is well settled that a contract may be implied in fact where inferences may be drawn from the facts and circumstances of the case and the intention of the parties as indicated by their conduct." . . . However, there cannot be a valid implied contract with a municipality when the Legislature has assigned the authority to enter into contracts to a specific municipal officer or body or has prescribed the manner in which the contract must be approved, and there is no proof that the statutory requirements have been satisfied.

Here, the City relies on several provisions of the City Charter for the proposition that the Commissioner of the FDNY has the exclusive authority to enter into contracts on behalf of the FDNY (New York City Charter §§ 16-389, 17-394, 19-487). To the extent that this argument—explicitly asserted for the first time before this Court—is properly before us, it is unpersuasive because these provisions, individually and in conjunction, do not include an express assignment of exclusive contracting authority to the Commissioner.

The City further contends that there was insufficient evidence to support the Board's finding of an implied-in-fact contract because there was no evidence of assent by the City to the alleged contract. While acknowledging the absence of direct evidence on the issue of assent, we conclude that the Board's finding of an implied contract between the City and Aviation should not be disturbed. The Board was presented with evidence that Aviation had been in existence since 1923, and that it worked "hand in hand" with the local FDNY company to fight fires. There was evidence that the local fire company occasionally called Aviation to request its assistance. A representative of the City provided evidence that the City was aware of Aviation, and knew that it fought fires in conjunction with the FDNY. If Aviation arrived at the scene of a fire before the local FDNY company, Aviation would be in charge of a fire scene until the FDNY company arrived and would thereafter continue working under its supervision. There was no evidence that City officials or the local fire company ever objected to or rejected the services of Aviation. Moreover, although the City was directed to produce an employee from the local FDNY company with knowledge of the relationship between the local fire company and Aviation as well as other facts relevant to the implied contract issue, it failed to do so. . . . Inasmuch as the Board was entitled to draw reasonable and adverse inferences from the City's failure to produce a knowledgeable employee, we are satisfied that substantial evidence supports the Board's determination that an implied-in-fact contract existed between the City and Aviation.

Affirmed in favor of Plaintiff.

[CONTINUED]

CRITICAL THINKING

Do you agree that enough evidence has been considered in establishing an implied-in-fact contract? If so, what makes the evidence strong; and if not, what further evidence do you feel would be necessary to make a confident claim?

Could an appreciable body of evidence be found in this case in support of an opposite contention? What would this evidence look like?

ETHICAL DECISION MAKING

Attempt to justify the decision reached by the court in terms of different guidelines for ethical decision making. Which fits strongest and which weakest with the case data? Why?

What values might the court be attempting to uphold with this ruling? What values are necessarily sacrificed to these interests? How would this preference be justified?

QUASI-CONTRACTS

Quasi-contracts are sometimes called *implied-in-law contracts,* but they are not actually contracts. Rather, in order to prevent one party from being unjustly enriched at the expense of another, the courts impose contractual obligations on one of the parties, as if that party had entered into a contract.

For example, assume Jones hears a noise out in his driveway. He looks out and sees a group of workers apparently getting ready to resurface his driveway. The doorbell rings, and he does not answer it. He goes down into his basement office and stays there until the workers have gone and he has a resurfaced driveway. When he receives a bill from the paving company, he refuses to pay on grounds that he did not ask to have the driveway paved. In such a case, where Jones knew that the company was getting ready to bestow on him a benefit to which he was not entitled, the court will probably impose a quasi-contract, requiring that Jones pay the paving company the fair market value of the resurfacing. Imposing such a duty prevents Jones from being unjustly enriched at the expense of the paving company.

There are limits to the doctrine, however; specifically, the enrichment must be unjust. Sometimes a benefit may simply be conferred on you because of a mistake by the other party, and the courts will not make people pay for others' mistakes. To go back to our previous example, had Jones been out of town when his driveway was repaved, he would have just gotten lucky. The courts are not going to make him pay for the pavers' mistake when he could have done nothing to prevent the benefit from being bestowed on him. Case 13-3 illustrates a situation in which it may have initially appeared as if recovery in quasi-contract would be possible, but on further review the court found that the doctrine was not applicable.

CASE 13-3 DCB CONST. CO., INC. v. CENTRAL CITY DEVELOPMENT CO.

COLORADO COURT OF APPEALS
940 P.2D 958 (COLO. APP. 1996)

DCB Construction Co. was hired by a lessee of Central City Development Co. (CCD) to make improvements to the property the lessee was leasing that would enable the property to be used as a casino. The lessee had previously assumed all responsibility for repairing and maintaining the property, and was authorized to make alterations and additions of a nature that would not ruin the historic character of the building, provided Development Co. gave consent to any such alterations or additions, which consent Development Co. agreed would not be unreasonably withheld.

Prior to DCB's and the lessee's signing the contract, Central City Development approved the lessee's plans to enter into the agreement with DCB. Also prior to the execution of the agreement, CCD posted a written notice notifying all contractors, subcontractors, and suppliers that CCD was not liable for any costs associated with the work and that CCD's interest in the property would not be subject to any lien for such costs.

DCB began work under the agreement, but ceased work in November 1992 because of the lessee's nonpayment. In early 1993, CCD evicted the lessee because of its failure to make rental payments under the leases. Shortly thereafter, DCB sued Central City Development Co. for payments due from the lessee. After a bench trial of DCB's unjust enrichment claim, the trial court determined that Development Co. had been unjustly enriched by DCB's work and entered judgment against CCD for $279,652.94, representing the amount not paid by the lessee under the construction contract, plus prejudgment interest on that sum and costs, for a total judgment of $333,191.

JUDGE CRISWELL: . . . [S]uch a claim is not one based upon any contract, as such; the obligation under that type of claim arises, "not from consent of the parties, as in the case of contracts, express or implied in fact, but from the law of natural immutable justice and equity." . . . The sole claim is based upon a contract implied in law, or unjust enrichment.

To recover under a claim for unjust enrichment, it must be established that:

1. A benefit was conferred upon the defendant;
2. The defendant appreciated the benefit; and
3. "[T]he benefit was accepted by the defendant under such circumstances that it would be inequitable for it to be retained without payment of its value." . . .

[T]he mere fact that a benefit has been bestowed and is appreciated is not sufficient to give rise to a claim for unjust enrichment. Even where a person has received a benefit from another, he is liable to pay therefor only if the circumstances of its receipt or retention are such that, as between the two persons, it is unjust for him to retain it. The mere fact that a person benefits another is not itself sufficient to require the other to make restitution therefor. . . .

What circumstances, then, give rise to such an injustice that requiring restitution would be appropriate? According to the *Restatement,* the conferring of a benefit does not give rise to such a claim unless the benefit was conferred as a result of mistake or coercion, was bestowed pursuant to a request from the party to be charged, or was conferred to protect the interest of that party or some third party. While this list of circumstances may not be exclusive, nevertheless, prior Colorado jurisprudence confirms that something more than the conferral of a benefit alone is required. . . .

Here, DCB makes no claim that its work was undertaken as a result of any mistaken belief that Development Co. would be liable therefor; nor is there any claim that its work resulted from some fraud, coercion, or other malefaction either by Development Co. or by some other person. Its sole assertion of injustice, aside from the conferral of the benefit itself, appears to be based upon what it considers to be the inordinate value of that benefit. However, DCB has referred us to no court opinion, and we are aware of none, which measures injustice solely on the basis of quantitative monetary enhancement.

Further, the benefit conferred upon Development Co.'s property here resulted from the performance of the obligation assumed by DCB in its contract with the lessee, a third party. And, absent special and unique circumstances, a benefit conferred upon a defendant by the performance of such an obligation cannot form the basis for a claim of unjust enrichment against that defendant. ("A person who has conferred a benefit upon another as the performance of a contract with a third party is not entitled to restitution from the other merely because of a failure of performance by the third person.").

Hence, unless the contract with the third party is "rescindable because of fraud, mistake or duress," the fact that that third party fails to deliver to a plaintiff the consideration called for by the contract provides no proper basis for a claim of unjust enrichment against a person who may have benefited from that plaintiff's performance of its contractual obligation. This is so, "because a payment made freely and with a knowledge of the facts cannot be recovered unless made in anticipation of a promise" made or implied *by the party benefited.*

There are several bases for the rule adopted by *Restatement* §110. One is that no person should be called upon to pay the debt of another without his or her prior assent. And, in the case of a lessor, if, as here, the lease calls for any improvements made by the lessee to become the lessor's property, the lessor has not been enriched at all. That provision of the lease is simply a part of the consideration that the lessee agreed to provide to the lessor in return for the creation of a leasehold in the property by the lessor. . . .

Here, then, the benefit, if any, bestowed upon Development Co. resulted from DCB's performance of a contractual obligation owed by it to the lessee. Further, there was no allegation or proof that such performance resulted from some mistake or from fraud, duress, or other improper conduct by Development Co. On the contrary, the undisputed evidence is that Development Co. gave actual notice to DCB before any work commenced that it would not be liable for any work performed. DCB performed its work placing sole reliance upon the lessee and upon its financial condition. The fact that such reliance was apparently misplaced, and DCB has not received the consideration promised by the lessee, does not render Development Co.'s retention of any benefits bestowed inequitable . . . it does not, as a matter of law, support the conclusion that such benefit was bestowed or retained unjustly. Hence, the judgment based on unjust enrichment cannot stand.

Judgment in favor of DCB reversed.

CRITICAL THINKING

What words or phrases important to the reasoning of this decision might be ambiguous? What alternate definitions for these terms are possible? How does the ruling appear to be defining the words or phrases? Would another choice affect the acceptability of the conclusion?

Provide an example of one piece of new evidence that might lead Judge Criswell to a different conclusion, and explain how this information changes the consideration.

ETHICAL DECISION MAKING

Which stakeholders are affected by this ruling, and in what ways? Who benefits and who suffers? Does this ruling establish a positive precedent in terms of the potential effect on future participants in disputes of this sort?

Does this decision appear to follow the Golden Rule guideline? Why or why not? How is this question particularly relative to the person making the judgment, and what sorts of interpersonal differences might lead to a variety of responses?

While the court failed to find a quasi-contract in Case 13-3, sometimes the doctrine is used by the court to provide recovery. The Case Nugget illustrates the successful use of this concept.

Case Nugget A Quasi-Contract

Contship Containerlines, Inc. v. Howard Industries
309 F.3d 910 (6th Cir. 2002)

Defendant Howard produces laundry detergent and is in the business of compounding or blending certain chemical products. Plaintiff Contship is a maritime shipper that filed an action against Howard for payment of freight charges for shipping products from Howard's plant in Houston, Texas, to the nation of Syria in February and March 1999.

Howard had contacted Transworld Freight Forwarding, Inc., to act as a freight forwarder for it, that is, to assist it in booking and preparing cargo for shipment. According to Howard, it paid Transworld for all the payments alleged to be due to Contship. Further, Howard contended that Transworld was not its agent and had no authority to incur a debt on its behalf with Contship. Finally, Howard claims that it at no time signed any documents obligating it to pay Contship.

Contship argued that Howard was billed directly with the export invoices and that all documents associated with the shipping listed Howard as liable for the payment of shipping costs. Howard actually delivered the goods to Contship's vessels in Houston, Texas. Contship did not dispute that Howard paid Transworld fees that were supposed to include the freight charges, but Contship argued that Howard did so at its own peril and was obligated to ensure payment to the actual shipper of the goods.

In examining the facts of this case, the court of appeals found that the undisputed facts were sufficient to establish the necessary elements of a quasi-contract. The court noted that Howard delivered its goods to Contship and that Contship transported those goods exactly as Howard wished and, by doing so, conferred a benefit on Howard. Plaintiff Contship did not behave opportunistically or trick Howard into using its services but, rather, behaved as any carrier would if a shipper delivered goods to it. Defendant Howard's payments to Transworld were undertaken at its own risk, and the court did not view the transactions between those two parties as relevant to whether a quasi-contract should be imposed between Howard and Contship. To not do so, the court held, would to be to allow the unjust enrichment of Howard at the expense of plaintiff Contship.

VALID, VOID, VOIDABLE, AND UNENFORCEABLE CONTRACTS

What everyone hopes to enter into, of course, is a **valid** contract. A valid contract is one that contains all the legal elements of a contract, as set forth in the beginning of this chapter. As a general rule, a valid contract is one that will be enforced. However, sometimes a contract may be valid, yet unenforceable.

A valid contract may be **unenforceable** when there is some law that prohibits the courts from enforcing it. For example, the statute of frauds, discussed in Chapter 18, requires that certain contracts must be evidenced by a writing before they can be enforced. Similarly, the statute of limitations mandates that an action for breach of contract must be brought within a set period of time, thereby limiting the enforceability of the contract.

A **void** contract is in effect not a contract at all. Either its object is illegal or it has some defect that is so serious that it is not a contract. If you entered into a contract with an assassin to kill your business law professor, that would be a void contract because it is obviously illegal to carry out the terms of the agreement.

A contract is **voidable** if one or both of the parties has the ability to either withdraw from the contract or enforce it. If the parties discover that the contract is voidable after one or both have partially performed, and one party chooses to have the contract terminated, both parties must return anything they had already exchanged under the agreement so that they will be returned to the condition they were in at the time they entered into the agreement.

Certain types of errors in the formation of a contract lead to its being voidable. Typically, the person who can void the contract is the person whom the court is attempting to protect, or the party the court believes might be taken advantage of by the other party. For example, contracts by minors are usually voidable by the minor, as discussed in Chapter 16. Contracts entered into as a result of fraud, duress, or undue influence—a problem with the validity of the acceptance, as described in Chapter 17— may be voided by the innocent party.

EXECUTED VERSUS EXECUTORY CONTRACTS

Once all the terms of the contract have been fully performed, the contract is said to have been **executed.** As long as some of the duties under the contract have not yet been performed, the contract is considered **executory.** For example, if Randolph hires Carmine to paint his garage on Saturday for $800, with $200 paid as a down payment and the balance due on completion of the job, the contract becomes executory as soon as the agreement is reached. When the down payment has been made and the painting is halfway completed, it is still executory. Once the painting has been finished and the final payment made, the contract is an executed contract.

FORMAL VERSUS INFORMAL CONTRACTS

Contracts may also be classified as formal or informal. **Formal contracts** are those that have a special form or must be created in a specific manner. The Restatement (Second) of Contracts identifies the following four types of formal contracts: (1) contracts under seal, (2) recognizances, (3) letters of credit, and (4) negotiable instruments.

When people hear the term *formal contract,* what often comes to mind is a **contract under seal.** The term *under seal* comes from the days when the contract was literally sealed by a piece of soft wax into which an impression was made. Today, sealed contracts may still be literally sealed with wax or some other soft substance, but they are more likely to be simply identified with the word *seal* or the letters *L.S.* (an abbreviation for *locus sigilli,* which means "the place for the seal") at the end of the document. Preprinted contract forms with a seal printed on them can be purchased today, and parties using such documents are presumed, without evidence to the contrary, to be adopting the seal for the contract.

States today do not require that contracts be under seal. However, 10 states still allow a contract without consideration to be enforced if it is under seal.

A **recognizance** arises when a person acknowledges in court that he or she will perform some specified act or pay a price upon failure to do so. An example of a recognizance is a bond used as bail in a criminal case. The person agrees to return to court for trial or forfeit the bond.

A **letter of credit** is an agreement by the person who issues the letter to pay a sum of money on receipt of an invoice and other documents. The Uniform Commercial Code governs letters of credit.

Negotiable instruments are written documents, signed by a party that makes an unconditional promise to pay a specific sum of money on demand or at a certain time to the holder of the instrument. The most common forms of negotiable instruments are checks, notes, drafts, and certificates of deposit. They are governed primarily by the UCC. (Negotiable instruments are discussed in detail in Chapters 26 and 27.)

Any contract that is not a formal contract is an **informal contract,** also called a **simple contract.** Informal contracts may in fact be quite complex, but they are called "simple" because no formalities are required in making them.

global context

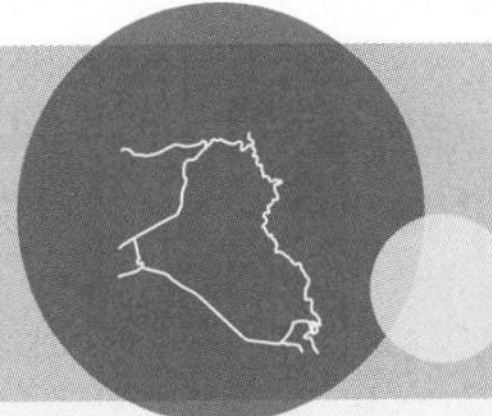

A Special Kind of Contract in Iraq

While most states basically recognize the marriage contract, a different kind of marriage contract, sanctioned by Shiite clerics, is legal in Iraq. Called *muta'a* ("contract for a pleasure marriage"), such agreements can last anywhere from an hour to 10 years and can be renewed. The male can usually void the contract earlier than agreed on, but the female can do so only if such a provision is negotiated when the contract is formed. Under the contract, the male typically receives sexual intimacy, in exchange for which the woman receives money. For a one-hour contract, she can generally expect the equivalent of $100; for a longer-term arrangement, $200 a month is typical, although she might receive more. The couple agree to not have children, and if the woman does get pregnant, she can have an abortion but then must pay a fine to a cleric. *Muta'as* originally developed as a way for widows and divorced women to earn a living and for couples whose parents would not allow a permanent marriage to be together. Many women's rights advocates, however, see these contracts as exploiting women and are opposed to their increased popularity after the fall of Saddam.

Source: Rick Jervic, "'Pleasure Marriages' Regain Popularity in Iraq," *USA Today,* May 5, 2005, p. 8A.

Interpretation of Contracts

Perhaps the most well-known rule of interpretation is the plain-meaning rule. The **plain-meaning rule** states that if a writing, or a term in question, appears to be plain and unambiguous on its face, its meaning must be determined from the four corners of the instrument, without resort to extrinsic evidence, with the words given their ordinary meaning.

Although parties try to draft contracts as clearly as possible, sometimes parties disagree about exactly what their obligations are under the agreement. Over time, the courts have developed some general guidelines to aid them in interpreting contracts. The rules help judges ascertain the intentions of the parties:

- A contract will be interpreted so as to give effect to the parties' intentions at the time they entered into the contract. If possible, the parties' intentions should be ascertained from the writing. The contract should also be interpreted in such a way as to give effect to the contract as a whole. In other words, each part should be interpreted so that the contract as a whole makes sense.

- If multiple interpretations are possible, the interpretation that would allow the contract to be carried out should be adopted. In other words, the contract should be interpreted in a way that makes it lawful, operative, definite, reasonable, and capable of being carried into effect.
- If the contract contains ambiguity, the ambiguity should be interpreted against the interests of the drafter. After all, the drafter is the one who could have prevented the ambiguity in the first place.
- If there is a conflict in the contract between preprinted terms and handwritten ones, the handwritten ones prevail. If there is a conflict between numerals and numbers that are written out in words, the written words will prevail. If there is a conflict between general terms and specific ones, the specific terms will apply.
- Technical words in a contract must be interpreted as usually understood by persons in the profession or business to which they relate, unless clearly used in a different sense.

CASE OPENER WRAP-UP

The Questionable Contract

The main issue in the Caro case was whether a valid contract existed. The nephews argued that if Mr. Whitehead had made an offer, it was for a unilateral contract, and because he died before Caro and Frank could perform the services necessary to accept the contract, there could be no acceptance by performance. The trial court agreed with the nephews.

The supreme court of the state, however, using the objective standard for determining whether a contract existed, found that there was in fact an offer for a bilateral contract, which Mr. Davis accepted by his letter in which he agreed to come. While no services could be rendered to Mr. Whitehead due to his death, Caro did in fact render care for Mrs. Whitehead, as required by the contract, until her death. Therefore, the contract was fully performed by the Whiteheads.

Because Mr. Davis had relinquished his business so that the couple could move to California to live with the Whiteheads, no remedy other than enforcement of the contract would be adequate.

Summary

The Definition of a Contract Contracts at their simplest level are legally enforceable agreements. A *valid contract* is generally viewed as one that has the following elements: agreement, consideration, legal object, and parties with legal capacity.

Sources of Contract Law The two most important sources of contract law are the Uniform Commercial Code and state common law. The Uniform Commercial Code, in Article 2, governs contracts for the sale of goods. All other contracts are also governed by the UCC.

Classification of Contracts Contracts may be classified in a number of ways. Every contract is either unilateral or bilateral; express or implied; valid, voidable, void, or enforceable; executed or executory; and formal or informal.

Interpretation of Contracts Courts have established rules to help interpret contracts so that the intent of the agreements can be ascertained and enforced.

Point / Counterpoint

Recovery based on quasi-contract allows the court to impose liability on a party that did not enter into a contract; three conditions must exist: (1) A benefit was conferred on the defendant; (2) the defendant appreciated the benefit; and (3) because of the circumstances under which the defendant received the benefit, it would be unjust to allow the defendant to retain the benefit without compensating the party that conferred it.

Does the Third Condition of the Test for Imposition of Recovery in Quasi-Contract Unjustifiably Limit the Court's Ability to Impose Relief Where It Is Needed?	
Yes	**No**
Limiting the application of the doctrine to circumstances in which the imposition of liability is required to prevent unjust enrichment is unfair. Looking at the case law, the "circumstances" that justify imposition of liability all focus on what the recipient of the benefit did. If he did not in some way acquiesce to the imposition of the benefit, no liability can be imposed. Such a limitation makes an artificial distinction based on the point in time at which the recipient discovers the conferral of the benefit. If there was some possible way for the recipient to have prevented the conferral, he has to pay; but if he had no way to prevent it, he does not have to pay. This distinction sounds fair enough at first glance, but it overlooks the fact that in either situation the recipient gets something he did not pay for and the other party conferred a benefit for no compensation. What if the benefit is really significant? What if ABC Construction builds a new garage for the Smiths, who were on vacation, instead of for their neighbors, who ordered the garage? Is it really fair for the Smiths to get that garage for free?	The limitation is a necessary one, preventing those knowledgeable about the law from taking unfair advantage of those with less knowledge. While it may seem unfair for someone to receive a benefit from another party when she did not pay any price for that benefit, if she did not ask for the benefit and did not encourage the other party to provide it, there is no justification for making her pay for what is essentially the acting party's mistake. If we presume that neither party is acting with the intent of getting something undeserved, the recipient is still most innocent in the situation and, as such, should not be required to pay for the other party's mistake. Further, while we say that one party is receiving a benefit, that recipient may be receiving a legal "benefit" that is of no value to her. It seems especially unfair to make someone pay for a benefit that she had no desire to obtain in the first place, even though many others may find that benefit highly desirable.

Questions & Problems

1. Explain why the first question a person should ask when getting ready to analyze a contract problem is this: "Is the alleged contract a contract for the sale of a good?"
2. What is the difference between an offer for a unilateral contract and an offer for a bilateral contract? Why might that difference be important to understand?
3. Explain how a valid contract differs from one that is void or voidable.

4. Explain what is meant by the objective theory of contracts.
5. What must a party prove to recover under the theory of quasi-contract?
6. What is the difference between a formal and an informal contract?
7. Fourteen individuals sued the City of Providence after they applied for positions as police officers and sought admission to the Academy, from which each individual was required to graduate, to obtain a position as a police officer. However, the city, following the replacement of its police chief, barred the 14 individuals from attending the Academy on the basis of new selection criteria. Before the replacement of the city's police chief, each recruit had received a letter dated October 15 that stated that the individual had successfully passed an oral evaluation and that the letter was a "conditional offer of employment," requiring the successful passing of medical and psychological examinations prior to admittance to the Academy. In response, most recruits informed their employers at the time that they expected to leave soon and removed their names from other employment opportunities. Most recruits passed both the medical and psychological examinations and argued that they should be entitled to a slot at the Academy, as the letter constituted a unilateral offer. The city argued, however, that the letter did not constitute an offer because the third paragraph stated that "an actual offer of employment" would not be made until all results were known, as the number of qualified applicants exceeded the number of available slots at the Academy. Does the letter of October 15 constitute an offer to enter a unilateral contract or merely express the possibility of an offer to enter a bilateral contract in the future? Under either response, what would be required for the contract to become enforceable? [*Ardito v. City of Providence,* 2003 U.S. Dist. LEXIS 8858.]
8. Anthony Maglica and Claire Halasz, as boyfriend and girlfriend, lived together, held themselves out as a married couple, and acted as companions toward each other. In fact, Claire changed her last name to "Maglica," even though the couple never married. Together, the couple worked in a business owned solely by Anthony, although Claire participated in a substantial part of the work. The company, Mag Instrument, was incorporated in 1974, and all shares went to Anthony. However, both Anthony and Claire were paid equal salaries. After the company began manufacturing flashlights, the company grew rapidly, now exceeding hundreds of millions of dollars in net worth. In 1992, Claire and Anthony separated, and subsequently Claire filed suit against Anthony for breach of contract and claimed damages under a theory of quasi-contract. No contract existed between Anthony and Claire. Does Claire have any remedy under a theory of quasi-contract? If so, what must she prove? [*Maglica v. Maglica,* 1998 Cal. App. LEXIS 750.]
9. Barry Pucello was injured in an automobile accident in 1979. One of Pucello's coworkers placed Pucello in contact with an attorney, Allen Feingold. Feingold called Pucello to recommend a doctor, and the next day Feingold and Pucello discussed the possibility of Feingold's representation. Although they did not discuss contingency-fee arrangements, Pucello gave Feingold some information about the accident. Immediately, Feingold began work on the case, inspecting the accident site, taking pictures, and obtaining a police report. Feingold also succeeded in obtaining an admission from the other driver. Less than one month later, Feingold mailed Pucello a copy of his contingency-fee agreement, which provided for a 50-50 split in any remedy that might be obtained. Concerned by this high attorney fee, Pucello sought counsel from another attorney, who succeeded in obtaining recovery for Pucello for his injuries. Pucello also

told Feingold to keep the pictures, reports, and admissions. Feingold, acknowledging that no express agreement existed with Pucello, argued that Pucello still benefited from his work, in that the other driver would be much more unlikely to alter his story after already admitting liability to Feingold. Does Feingold have a valid quasi-contract claim? Why or why not? [*Feingold v. Pucello,* 1995 Pa. Super. LEXIS 26.]

Looking for more review material?

The Online Learning Center at **www.mhhe.com/kubasek1e** contains this chapter's "Assignment on the Internet" and also a list of URLs for more information entitled "On the Internet." Find both of them in the Student Center portion of the OLC, along with quizzes and other helpful materials.

Agreement

CASE OPENER

The Problematic Promotion

Pepsi had a promotion whereby consumers were encouraged to collect "Pepsi points" by consuming Pepsi products. They could then redeem the points for merchandise. If they did not have quite enough points for the prize they wanted, they could buy the needed additional points for 10 cents each; however, at least 15 original Pepsi points had to accompany each order.

At the climax of an early commercial for the promotion, three young boys are sitting in front of a high school building, one reading his Pepsi Stuff catalog, while the others drink Pepsi, all gazing in awe at an object rushing overhead as the military march in the background builds to a crescendo. A Harrier Jet swings into view and lands by the side of the school building, next to a bicycle rack. Several students run for cover, and the velocity of the wind strips one hapless faculty member down to his underwear. While the faculty member is being deprived of his dignity, the voice-over announces: "Now the more Pepsi you drink, the more great stuff you're gonna get."

A teenager opens the cockpit of the fighter and can be seen, without a helmet, holding a Pepsi. He exclaims, "Sure beats the bus," and chortles. The military drumroll sounds a final time as the following words appear: "Harrier Fighter 7,000,000 Pepsi Points." A few seconds later, the following appears in more stylized script: "Drink Pepsi—Get Stuff."

John Leonard decided to accept Pepsi's offer of the Harrier fighter jet for 7 million Pepsi points. He quickly realized that it would be easier to raise the money to buy points

CHAPTER 14

than to collect the 7 million points. In early March 1996, he filled out an order form requesting the jet and submitted it to Pepsi, along with 15 Pepsi points and a check for $700,000.

In response, Pepsi sent him a letter saying, "The item that you have requested is not part of the Pepsi Stuff collection. It is not included in the catalogue or on the order form, and only catalogue merchandise can be redeemed under this program." John then sued for breach of contract.

1. Did Pepsi offer to sell the Harrier jet for 7 million points?
2. Did Leonard's submission of the order form constitute an acceptance?

The Wrap-Up at the end of the chapter will answer these questions.

Learning Objectives

After reading this chapter, you will be able to answer the following questions:

1. What are the elements of a valid offer?
2. How may an offer terminate?
3. What are the elements of an acceptance?

Elements of the Offer

The first element of a contract is the agreement. Formation of the agreement begins when the party that is initiating the contract, the offeror, makes an offer to another party, the offeree. Remember, this chapter is focusing on the elements of a contract under the common law. Some of these elements have been modified under the UCC for contracts for the sale of goods, and these changes are discussed in Chapter 21.

INTENT

The first element of the offer is intent. The offeror must manifest intent to be bound by the offeree's acceptance. As explained in Chapter 13, contracts are interpreted using an objective standard. Application of that standard means that the courts are concerned with only the party's outward manifestations of intent, not internal thought processes. The courts interpret the words and actions of the parties the way a reasonable person would interpret them.

Thus, if an individual is clearly joking or speaking out in anger, the reasonable person would not think that the individual seriously intended to make an offer and the courts will consequently not treat the words as an offer. If someone attempts to accept such an offer, the courts will not find that a contract has been made.

Sometimes an offeror may try to avoid being bound to a contract by later claiming that he was only joking when he made the offer, but the courts are not interested in his hidden intent. As Case 14-1 demonstrates, if you joke too well, you may find yourself in an unwanted contract.

CASE 14-1

LUCY v. ZEHMER
SUPREME COURT OF APPEALS OF VIRGINIA
196 VA. 493, 84 S.E.2D 516 (1954)

Plaintiffs W. O. and J. C. Lucy had wanted to purchase Ferguson Farm from the Zehmers for at least eight years. One night, Lucy stopped by the establishment the Zehmers operated and said that he bet Zehmer wouldn't accept $50,000 for the place. Zehmer replied that he would, but he bet that Lucy wouldn't pay $50,000 for it. Over the course of the evening, the parties drank whiskey and engaged in casual conversation, with the talk repeatedly returning to the sale of Ferguson Farm. Eventually Lucy got Zehmer to draw up a contract for the sale of the farm for $50,000.

When Lucy later attempted to enforce the agreement, Zehmer refused to complete the sale, arguing that he had been drunk, and that the agreement to sell the property had been made in jest. Lucy sued to enforce the agreement. The trial court found for the defendants and the plaintiff appealed.

JUSTICE BUCHANAN: If it be assumed, contrary to what we think the evidence shows, that Zehmer was jesting about selling his farm to Lucy and that the transaction was intended by him to be a joke, nevertheless the evidence shows that Lucy did not so understand it but considered it to be a serious business transaction and the contract to be binding on the Zehmers as well as on himself. The very next day he arranged with his brother to put up half the money and take a half interest in the land. The day after that he employed an attorney to examine the title. The next night, Tuesday, he was back at Zehmer's place and there Zehmer told him for the first time, Lucy said, that he wasn't going to sell, and he told Zehmer, "You know you sold that place fair and square." After receiving the report from his attorney that the title was good, he wrote to Zehmer that he was ready to close the deal.

Not only did Lucy actually believe, but the evidence shows he was warranted in believing, that the contract represented a serious business transaction and a good faith sale and purchase of the farm.

In the field of contracts, as generally elsewhere, "We must look to the outward expression of a person as manifesting his intention rather than to his secret and unexpressed intention. 'The law imputes to a person an intention corresponding to the reasonable meaning of his words and acts.'"

At no time prior to the execution of the contract had Zehmer indicated to Lucy by word or act that he was not in earnest about selling the farm. They had argued about it and discussed its terms, as Zehmer admitted, for a long time. Lucy testified that if there was any jesting it was about paying $50,000 that night. The contract and the evidence show that he was not expected to pay the money that night. Zehmer said that after the writing was signed he laid it down on the counter in front of Lucy. Lucy said Zehmer handed it to him. In any event there had been what appeared to be a good faith offer and a good faith acceptance, followed by the execution and apparent delivery of a written contract. Both said that Lucy put the writing in his pocket and then offered Zehmer $5 to seal the bargain. Not until then, even under the defendants' evidence, was anything said or done to indicate that the matter was a joke. Both of the Zehmers testified that when Zehmer asked his wife to sign he whispered that it was a joke so Lucy wouldn't hear and that it was not intended that he should hear.

The mental assent of the parties is not requisite for the formation of a contract. If the words or other acts of one of the parties have but one reasonable meaning, his undisclosed intention is immaterial except when an unreasonable meaning which he attaches to his manifestations is known to the other party.

The law, therefore, judges of an agreement between two persons exclusively from those expressions of their intentions which are communicated between them.

An agreement or mutual assent is of course essential to a valid contract but the law imputes to a person an intention corresponding to the reasonable meaning of his words and acts. If his words and acts, judged by a reasonable standard, manifest an intention to agree, it is immaterial what may be the real but unexpressed state of his mind.

So a person cannot set up that he was merely jesting when his conduct and words would warrant a reasonable person in believing that he intended a real agreement. . . .

Whether the writing signed by the defendants and now sought to be enforced by the complainants was the result of a serious offer by Lucy and a serious acceptance by the defendants, or was a serious offer by Lucy and an acceptance in secret jest by the defendants, in either event it constituted a binding contract of sale between the parties.

Defendants contend further, however, that even though a contract was made, equity should decline to enforce it under the circumstances. These circumstances have been set forth in detail above. They disclose some drinking by the two parties but not to an extent that they were unable to understand fully what they were doing. There was no fraud, no misrepresentation, no sharp practice and no dealing between unequal parties. The farm had been bought for $11,000 and was assessed for taxation at $6,300. The purchase price was $50,000. Zehmer admitted that it was a good price. There is in fact present in this case none of the grounds usually urged against specific performance.

REVERSED AND REMANDED in favor of Plaintiff.

CRITICAL THINKING

How can one be held to have made a contract when the necessary acceptance was "in secret jest"? In other words, why must a joke be visibly a joke to a reasonable observer for there to be no acceptance?

ETHICAL DECISION MAKING

What stakeholders are being protected by this ruling? What value is playing the largest role in shaping this ruling?

Preliminary negotiations. An invitation to negotiate or an expression of possible interest in an exchange is not an offer because it does not express any willingness to be bound by an acceptance. For example, if Rachael asked Bill whether he would sell his car for $5,000, she is not making an offer; she is just inquiring about his potential willingness to sell. Likewise, when a firm or government entity requests bids for a construction project, the request is just an invitation for contractors to make offers. Thus, the bids would be the offers.

While this discussion of preliminary negotiations and the examples may make it seem as if it is easy to distinguish an offer from an invitation to negotiate, whether an offer in fact existed is a question of fact and sometimes ends up being litigated. It is therefore important that when you are either making an offer or attempting to begin negotiations about a possible contract, you use very precise language that clearly expresses your intent.

Advertisements. Another illustration of the offer to make an offer is the advertisement. If a custom furniture maker places an advertisement in the paper that reads, "Old-fashioned, hand-crafted cedar rocking chairs only $250 the first week in May," the store is merely inviting potential customers to come to the store and offer $250 for a rocker. Because no reasonable person would expect the store to be able to sell a rocking chair to every person who might see the ad, the court would interpret the intent of the store as being to invite readers to make an offer.

Under limited circumstances, however, an ad can be treated as an offer. If it appears from the wording of the ad that the store did, in fact, intend to make an offer, the courts will treat it as an offer. In general, when the ad specifies a limited quantity and provides a specific means by which the offer can be accepted, the courts will treat the ad as an offer, as demonstrated by the Case Nugget.

Case Nugget — When Is an Ad an Offer?

Lefkowitz v. Great Minneapolis Surplus Store, Inc.
251 Minn.188, 86 N.W.2d 689 (1957)

In this case, the defendant had published a newspaper announcement stating: "Saturday 9 AM Sharp, 3 Brand New Fur Coats, Worth up to $1,000.00, First Come First Served $1 Each." Morris Lefkowitz arrived at the store, dollar in hand, but was informed that under the defendant's "house rules," the offer was open to ladies but not gentlemen. The court ruled that because the plaintiff had fulfilled all the terms of the advertisement, and the advertisement was specific and left nothing open for negotiation, a contract had been formed.

From this case came the often-quoted exception to the rule that advertisements do not create any power of acceptance in potential offerees: an advertisement that is "clear, definite, and explicit, and leaves nothing open for negotiation." In that circumstance, "it constitutes an offer, acceptance of which will complete the contract."

The plaintiff in the case described in the opening scenario tried to rely on the *Lefkowitz* decision to argue that the commercial was an offer because it was "clear, definite, explicit, and left nothing to negotiation." After all, the commercial clearly stated that 7 million points earned a Harrier jet, and the catalog provided an additional means of buying the points for cash.

The court, however, found that the commercial could not be regarded as sufficiently definite because it specifically reserved the details of the offer to a separate writing, the catalog. Also, the commercial itself made no mention of the steps a potential offeree would be required to take to accept the alleged offer of a Harrier jet.

The court further found that the only offer in this scenario was the plaintiff's letter of March 27, 1996, along with the order form and the appropriate number of Pepsi points. As Pepsi rejected this offer with its letter, there is no contract.

To prevent possible "bait-and-switch" advertising that would appear as offers, some states have consumer protection laws requiring that advertisers state in their ads either that quantities of the item are limited to the first *X* number of people or that rain checks will be available if the item sells out.

Auctions. Another situation in which what seems to be an offer may not be is the auction. When a person places a good with an auctioneer for sale by auction, is the seller making an offer or is the bidder? It depends on what kind of auction is taking place.

If nothing is stated to the contrary in the terms of the auction, an auction is presumed to be *with reserve.* In an auction with reserve, the seller is merely expressing intent to receive offers. The auctioneer may withdraw the item from auction at any time before the auctioneer's hammer falls, signaling the acceptance of the bid. Similarly, at any time before the hammer falls, the bidder may also revoke the bid.

In an auction *without reserve,* the seller is treated as making an offer to accept the highest bid. Thus, the seller must accept the highest bid. Not surprisingly, very few auctions are without reserve.

DEFINITE AND CERTAIN TERMS

Under the common law, the terms of the offer must be definite and certain. In other words, all the material terms must be included. The *material terms* are those terms that would allow a court to determine what the damages would be in the event that one of the parties was to breach the contract. These terms include the subject matter, price, quantity, quality, and parties.

Sometimes an offer contains not the material term itself but a method for determining the term. For example, Guy's Sailboats is building Sara a sailboat, and the parties want to make it possible for her to pay one-third of the price of the boat in advance, one-third on delivery, and one-third in 12 monthly payments, with interest, beginning a month after delivery. Rather than stipulating an interest rate to be charged on the monthly payments, the contract might specify an external standard according to which the interest rate would be set through the course of the 12-month payment period.

The question of whether the terms of an alleged offer were adequate for the formation of a valid contract often arises in cases where one party believes that a contract had been formed and the other believes there had been no contract because the terms of the alleged offer were not definite enough. That issue is the focus of Case 14-2.

COMMUNICATION TO THE OFFEREE

The offer must be communicated to the offeree or to the offeree's agent. Only the offeree to whom the offer was directed can accept the offer. If Bill overhears Sam offer to sell his car to Helen for $5,000, he cannot walk over and form a contract by accepting the offer. If he says to Sam, "I'll give you $5,000 for your car," he is not accepting the offer but, rather, is making a new offer.

CASE 14-2 ANDRUS v. STATE, DEPARTMENT OF TRANSPORTATION, AND CITY OF OLYMPIA

WASHINGTON STATE APPELLATE COURT
117 P.3D 1152 (WASH. APP. 2005)

Scott Andrus applied for a position as a building inspector with the city of Olympia. He received a call from Tom Hill, an engineering supervisor with the city. Hill stated, "You're our number one choice, and I'm offering you the job." Andrus responded "Great" and "Yes." Hill did not discuss the specifics of the job, so Andrus asked Hill to fax him those details. The city never sent such a fax or a written job offer and request for acceptance.

On the same day that Andrus received the call from Hill, the city checked Andrus's employment references, including his current employer (the Washington Department of Transportation), which proved unsatisfactory. Hill called Andrus the next day, informing him that the city had withdrawn the job offer because of further reference checks.

Andrus sued the city and the DOT, claiming wrongful discharge and arguing that the phone call from Hill offering the position was an employment contract. He also alleged that the DOT was liable for defamation for providing a bad employment reference to the city. The superior court granted the city's request to dismiss his claims without a trial, and he appealed only the breach of contract claim against the city.

JUSTICE QUINN-BRINTNALL: An enforceable contract requires, among other things, an offer with *reasonably certain* terms. Restatement (Second) of Contracts §33 (1979) ("The fact that one or more terms of a proposed bargain are left open or uncertain may show that a manifestation of intention is not intended to be understood as an offer or as an acceptance"). Hill's "job offer" contained no starting date, salary, or benefit information. Moreover, it was to be followed by a written offer and request for acceptance. Under these facts, the July 13 phone conversation did not form an employment contract.

AFFIRMED in favor of the city.

CRITICAL THINKING

How could the original phone call from Hill be considered an employment contract? What would have to be included in the conversation? What could be left out? How different do you think the call would have needed to be in order to qualify as an employment contract between the plaintiff and the city? Why?

ETHICAL DECISION MAKING

How well does this decision hold up under examinations of ethicality, such as the public disclosure test and the universalization test? Do you think Justice Quinn-Brintall took such examinations into account in reaching this decision? Why or why not?

Termination of the Offer

Offers, once made, do not last forever. At some point in time they terminate. When an offer is said to be terminated, it can no longer be accepted to form a binding contract. Another way of looking at the termination of an offer is that it is the termination of the offeree's power to form a legally binding contract by accepting the offer. An offer can terminate in one of five ways: revocation by the offeror, rejection or counteroffer by the offeree, death or incapacity of the offeror, destruction or subsequent illegality of the subject matter of the offer, or lapse of time or failure of other conditions stated in the offer.

connecting to the core

Marketing

You may have learned in a marketing class about the six components of the communication process, usually including the following:

1. *Source:* The company or business that produces the information conveyed to the buyer.
2. *Message:* The information sent by the source.
3. *Channel of communication:* The means by which the message is conveyed, such as a letter or a salesperson.
4. *Receivers:* The consumers or prospective purchasers who read or see the message.
5. *Encoding:* The process by which a source transforms its ideas into a set of symbols.
6. *Decoding:* The process whereby the receiver evaluates the symbols and transforms them back into an idea.

This communication process is also relevant to the contractual agreement between an offeror and an offeree. An offeror, for example, may want to sell a house, and the communication to a prospective buyer is crucial. The offeror should be very clear about the terms and conditions of the intended sale so that the encoding and decoding processes involve very little ambiguity when certain words of the offer are translated by the offeree. By avoiding ambiguity in the terms of an offer, the offeror and offeree are less likely to find themselves in court for disputes about the terms of a contract or even about whether a contract exists.

Source: R. Kerin, S. Hartley, E. Berkowitz, and W. Rudelius, *Marketing* (New York: McGraw-Hill/Irwin, 2006), pp. 470–472.

REVOCATION BY THE OFFEROR

The offeror is said to be the "master of his offer" and, as such, can revoke it at any time, even if he says he will hold the offer open for a stated period of time. If Jim sends Carol a letter offering to mow her yard every week during the summer for the price of $20 per week as long as she responds to his offer within the next month, he can still change his mind and tell her at any time before she responds that he is no longer interested in working for her, thereby revoking his offer.

If a person wishes to ensure that an offer will in fact be held open for a set period of time, the person may do so by entering into an option contract with the offeror. An **option contract** is an agreement whereby the offeree gives the offeror a piece of consideration in exchange for the offeror's agreement to hold the offer open for the specified period of time.

There is no requirement as to the value of the consideration. If the consideration is money, the parties may agree that if the offer is eventually accepted and a contract is formed, the consideration for the option contract will become part of the offeree's payment under the contract. This situation frequently arises in contracts involving real estate. Jones may be considering opening a restaurant and would like to have the option of purchasing a lot owned by Smith, so he gives Smith $1,000 for a 30-day option to purchase the lot, with the provision that the $1,000 will be deducted from the purchase price if Jones purchases the property. In the event that Jones does not buy the property, Smith will keep the $1,000.

Under the UCC, there is an additional limitation on the offeror's ability to revoke the offer. A promise to hold an offer for the sale of a good open for a specified period cannot be revoked if it is made in writing and signed by a merchant.

As a general rule, the revocation is effective when it is received by the offeree. Because of this rule, if it is really important to the offeror that the offeree knows that the offer has been revoked, he should personally deliver the revocation to the offeree.

REJECTION OR COUNTEROFFER BY THE OFFEREE

The second means by which an offer can be terminated is rejection by the offeree. Regardless of how long the offer was stated to be open, once the offeree rejects it, it is terminated. In our earlier example, if Carol calls Jim and says that she is not interested in his working for her this summer or any summer because of the poor quality of the work he has done for her in the past but then she calls him back an hour later to say she has changed her mind and would like to hire him in accordance with his proposed terms, it is too late. There is no offer for her to accept because her rejection terminated the offer.

In the same illustration, if Carol tells Jim she would indeed like him to cut her grass every week this summer but she will pay him only $15 each week, she has made a *counteroffer,* which is defined by the Restatement as "an offer made by an offeree to his offeror relating to the same matter as the original offer and proposing a substituted bargain differing from that proposed by the original offer."[1] A counteroffer terminates the original offer, and so Carol's counteroffer terminated Jim's original offer. Thus, if you receive an offer that you might want to accept but you are wondering whether you can get better terms, you should inquire about how set the offeror is on the terms proposed before you make a counteroffer. For example, Carol might have simply asked Jim whether he would consider doing the job at any other price.

DEATH OR INCAPACITY OF THE OFFEROR

An offer terminates immediately if the offeror dies or loses the legal capacity to enter into the contract. This termination occurs even if the offeree does not know of the terminating event. The exception to this rule occurs when the parties had already entered into an option contract to hold the offer open for a set period of time. If an option contract exists, the administrator of the offeror's estate or the guardian of the offeror must hold the offer open until it expires in accordance with the option contract.

DESTRUCTION OR SUBSEQUENT ILLEGALITY OF THE SUBJECT MATTER

If the subject matter of the offer is destroyed or becomes illegal, the offer immediately terminates. For example, if Jamie offers Bill a job managing the riverboat casino he plans to open on January 1 but, before Bill accepts the offer, the state decides to no longer allow riverboat casinos to operate in the state, the offer of employment terminates.

LAPSE OF TIME OR FAILURE OF ANOTHER CONDITION SPECIFIED IN THE OFFER

As noted earlier, the offeror has the power to revoke the offer at any time, even if the offer states that it will be held open a set amount of time. But if the offer states that it will be held open for only a certain time, the offer will terminate when that time expires. In the absence of a time condition in the offer, the offer will expire after the lapse of a reasonable amount of time. What constitutes a reasonable amount of time varies, depending on the

[1] Restatement (Second) of Contracts, sec. 39 (1981).

Case Nugget The Importance of Conditions in Offers

Adone v. Paletto
2005 NY Slip Op 50196U; 6 Misc. 3d 1026A; 800 N.Y.S.2d 341

On July 26, 2004, the defendants' counsel made an "Offer to Compromise" and settle the action in the amount of $500,000, plus costs accrued to that date, which represented the entire available coverage under the defendants' insurance policy. Part of the offer stated:

> If within ten days thereafter the claimant serves a written notice that he accepts the offer, either party may file the summons, complaint, and offer, with proof of acceptance, and thereupon the clerk shall enter judgment accordingly. If the offer is not accepted and the claimant fails to obtain a more favorable judgment, he shall not recover costs from the time of the offer, but shall pay costs from that time. An offer of judgment shall not be made known to the jury.

On August 9, 2004, the parties appeared before the court for a settlement conference. At that conference, the plaintiffs' counsel rejected the defendants' offer of $500,000 and made a demand of $700,000 to settle the case. The demand for $700,000 was clearly not an acceptance of the offer of compromise of $500,000; instead, it was a counteroffer that rejected the $500,000 offer of compromise.

The plaintiffs' $700,000 demand was not acceptable to the defendants and the case was not settled. On September 24, 2004, the plaintiffs' counsel sent a letter to the defendants accepting the entry of a $500,000 judgment, which would include interest from the date of the summary judgment and costs that were offered two months before, on July 26, 2004. On September 28, 2004, that acceptance was rejected by the defendants in writing because it was not within 10 days of the offer.

The plaintiffs' motion for a judgment to enforce the offer to compromise was denied because the acceptance was not within the 10-day time frame.

subject matter of the offer. For example, an offer by a retailer to purchase seasonal goods from a wholesaler would lapse before an offer to purchase goods that could be easily sold all year long. The Case Nugget illustrates the consequences of not paying attention to the time or other limiting conditions specified in an offer.

The Acceptance

Once an offer has been made, the offeree has the power to accept that offer and form a contract. Examining acceptance under the common law, the basic requirements for a valid acceptance parallel those for a valid offer. There should be a manifestation of intent to be bound by the acceptance to the contract, agreement to the definite and certain terms of the offer, and communication to the offeror.

MANIFESTATION OF INTENT TO BE BOUND TO THE CONTRACT

In general, there are two ways an offeree can manifest intent to enter into the contract: by performance or by a return promise. The offeree must either do or say something to form the contract.

Recall, from Chapter 12, the distinction between a bilateral and a unilateral contract. If the offer is for a unilateral contract, the offeree can accept only by providing the requested

global context

Contracts in Japan

The Japanese tend to view contracts as ongoing relationships in which parties work with each other to smooth out any problems that arise in performance of the contract. The Japanese tend to be suspicious of long, detailed contracts. They have a distinct preference for short, flexible contracts that leave a number of terms to be decided later.

performance. If Bill offered to pay $500 to anyone who returned his lost dog to him, Mary could accept the offer only by returning the dog. Bill did not want her promise, and if she called and promised to return the dog to him, that promise would have no legal effect because the only way to accept a unilateral offer is by performance.

Remember from the previous section that the offeror has the right to revoke the offer at any time before it has been accepted. This rule is slightly modified with respect to unilateral offers. When a party has made a unilateral offer and another party has begun performance, the offeror must give the offeree a reasonable time to complete the performance.

With a bilateral contract, what the offeror wants to form the contract is not performance but, rather, a return promise. Sometimes, however, it is not clear whether the offeror wants performance or a return promise. In such a case, the offeree has the option of either performing or making a return promise.

Silence as a form of acceptance. Silence, as a general rule, cannot be used to form a contract. For example, Lisa and Marie both work at a local diner where the manager is very flexible about the waitresses' hours and lets them trade shifts. Marie calls Lisa and leaves her a voice-mail message saying, "I can't work my three night shifts this week. If you can cover them for me, I'll pay you an extra $40 on top of the money you'll receive from the boss for working my shifts. If I don't hear from you by 7 p.m. tomorrow, I'll assume we have a deal and you will work for me. Thanks so much!" If Lisa does not call back, no contract has been formed because silence under these circumstances would not constitute acceptance.

There are, however, a limited number of circumstances under which silence can be an acceptance. In the most common situation, the parties, by their previous course of dealing with each other, have established a pattern of behavior whereby it would be reasonable to assume that silence was intended to communicate acceptance. For example, a wholesaler and a retailer have a long-standing relationship in which the wholesaler routinely ships a certain type of merchandise to the retailer, who would reject the shipment if it did not meet his needs. After such a pattern of behavior has been established, it is reasonable for the wholesaler to assume that when a shipment is not sent back, the retailer means to accept it.

Silence can also be acceptance when the offeree receives the benefits of the offered services with reasonable opportunity to reject them and knowledge that some form of compensation is expected yet remains silent. In this case, an implied-in-fact contract would be created. Because many unscrupulous businesspersons once took advantage of this rule and sent unordered merchandise to people, stating that the goods could be returned or be kept on payment of a set price, most states have passed laws providing that unsolicited merchandise does not have to be returned and may be kept by the recipient as a gift, with no contract being formed.

A third situation occurs when the parties agree that silence will be an acceptance. For example, a person may join a book club, and the contract provides that a new book will be sent every month if the party does not send in a notification card rejecting the month's selection.

ACCEPTANCE OF DEFINITE AND CERTAIN TERMS: THE MIRROR-IMAGE RULE

When a bilateral contract is being formed under the common law, the mirror-image rule applies to the acceptance. The **mirror-image rule** says that the terms of the acceptance must mirror the terms of the offer. If the terms of the acceptance do not mirror the terms of the offer, no contract is formed. Instead, the attempted acceptance is a counteroffer.

The mirror-image rule has caused a significant amount of trouble for businesses, because often buyers would make an offer on one form that contained not only the essential terms of the contract but also a number of additional, somewhat minor terms. Generally, the offer was on a standard form that had a place where the essential terms were written in. The seller would often return his standard form with its preprinted terms, along with the essential terms written in to match the terms of the offer. The problem was that because these preprinted forms did not match, there was legally no contract. If both parties performed their contracts, there were no problems, but the fact that there was no contract meant that on occasion one party could decide to simply not perform, leaving the other party with no remedy. Or, if the parties did perform, the buyer might perform according to the terms on the buyer form and be sued for breach by the seller, who believed that the terms on the seller form were the terms of the agreement.

To eliminate this problem of the "battle of the forms," UCC Section 2-207 significantly modified the mirror-image rule by providing that, as a general rule, an offeree may include in the acceptance terms that are additional to or different from the terms of the offer as long as (1) the offeror did not explicitly state in the offer that all terms of the offer must be accepted exactly as proposed; (2) the offeror does not promptly reject the new terms on receipt of the acceptance; and (3) the new terms do not materially change the terms of the original offer.

In the case of additional terms related to issues not addressed in the original offer, if none of the foregoing conditions occur, then a contract is formed and the terms of the agreement are those of the acceptance, as long as the parties are merchants. If the parties are not merchants, the additional terms are merely proposals for addition to the contract and must be accepted by the offeror.

If the terms of the acceptance are different from those in the offer, various states treat the terms differently. In most states, the terms are said to cancel each other out, and the court will then look to the UCC for neutral terms to insert into the contract.

COMMUNICATION TO THE OFFEROR

An offeror has the power to control the means by which the acceptance is communicated, and if the offeror specifies that only a certain means of communication will be accepted, then only that method of communication forms a valid offer. Suppose, for example, that Jennifer offers to paint Bill's car for $500 but says that he must accept the offer by telephone before midnight on Thursday. If he sends her an e-mail Thursday morning accepting her offer, there is no valid contract. Even though e-mail might be a valid means of accepting a contract offer if no means is specified, when the offer is limited to a specific means of communicating the acceptance, only that means results in a valid contract. Thus, Bill's attempted acceptance was simply a new offer.

If no means of communicating the acceptance is specified, any reasonable means is generally acceptable. Telephone, mail, fax, and e-mail are all valid means of accepting an offer. When drafting an offer, if a person wishes acceptance to be only by a particular means, the offer must make it clear that only certain means are allowed. As Case 14-3 illustrates, courts will carefully interpret provisions specifying the means of acceptance.

CASE 14-3 OSPREY L.L.C. v. KELLY-MOORE PAINT CO.
SUPREME COURT OF OKLAHOMA
984 P.2D 194, 1999 OKLA. LEXIS 64

The plaintiff leased commercial premises to the defendant. The lease required that defendant provide notice of its intent to renew the lease at least six months prior to the lease's expiration, and notice was to be given in writing and delivered personally or through registered first class mail. Defendant attempted to extend the lease by faxing a renewal letter on the last day of the six-month notification period. Although fax and telephone records confirmed that the fax was transmitted, the plaintiff denied receiving the fax.

The plaintiff refused to renew the lease and demanded that the defendant vacate the premises at the end of the current lease term. The defendant refused to vacate the premises, so the plaintiff filed an action for forcible entry and detainer.

The trial court found that the faxed notice effectively renewed the lease, and the appeals court reversed. The supreme court granted certiorari.

JUDGE KAUGER: . . . The precise issue of whether a faxed or facsimile delivery of a written notice to renew a commercial lease is sufficient to exercise timely the renewal option of the lease is one of first impression in Oklahoma. Neither party has cited to a case from another jurisdiction which has decided this question, or to any case which has specifically defined "personal delivery" as including facsimile delivery.

Osprey argues that: 1) the lease specifically prescribed limited means of acceptance of the option, and it required that the notice of renewal be delivered either personally or sent by United States mail, registered or certified; 2) Kelly-Moore failed to follow the contractual requirements of the lease when it delivered its notice by fax; and 3) because the terms for extending the lease specified in the contract were not met, the notice was invalid and the lease expired on August 31, 1997. Kelly-Moore counters that: 1) the lease by the use of the word "shall" mandates that the notice be written, but the use of the word "may" is permissive; and 2) although the notice provision of the lease permits delivery personally or by United States mail, it does not exclude other modes of delivery or transmission which would include delivery by facsimile. Kelly-Moore also asserts that the lease specified that time was of the essence and that faxing the notice was the functional equivalent of personal delivery because it provided virtually instantaneous communication.

Although the question tendered is novel in Oklahoma, the sufficiency of the notice given when exercising an option contract or an option to renew or extend a lease has been considered by several jurisdictions. A few have found that delivery of notice by means other than hand delivery or by certified or registered mail was insufficient if the terms of the contract specifically referred to the method of delivery. However, the majority have reached the opposite conclusion. These courts generally recognize that, despite the contention that there must be strict compliance with the notice terms of a lease option agreement, use of an alternative method does not render the notice defective if the substituted method performed the same function or served the same purpose as the authorized method.

Language in a contract is given its plain and ordinary meaning, unless some technical term is used in a manner meant to convey a specific technical concept. . . . The lease does not appear to be ambiguous. "Shall" is ordinarily construed as mandatory and "may" is ordinarily construed as permissive. The contract clearly requires that notice "shall" be in writing. The provision for delivery, either personally or by certified or registered mail, uses the permissive "may" and it does not bar other modes of transmission which are just as effective.

The purpose of providing notice by personal delivery or registered mail is to insure the delivery of the notice, and to settle any dispute which might arise between the parties concerning whether the notice was received. A substituted method of notice which performs the same function and serves the same purpose as an authorized method of notice is not defective. Here, the contract provided that time was of the essence. Although Osprey denies that it ever received the fax, the fax activity report and telephone company records confirm that the fax was transmitted successfully, and that it was sent to Osprey's correct facsimile number on the last day of the deadline to extend the lease. The fax provided immediate written communication similar to personal delivery and, like a telegram, would be timely if it were properly transmitted before

[CONTINUED]

the expiration of the deadline to renew. Kelly-Moore's use of the fax served the same function and the same purpose as the two methods suggested by the lease and it was transmitted before the expiration of the deadline to renew. Under these facts, we hold that the faxed or facsimile delivery of the written notice to renew the commercial lease was sufficient to exercise timely the renewal option of the lease.

REVERSED in favor of Defendant.

CRITICAL THINKING

Could the information provided in this case lead to a different conclusion than that reached by the court? Would some elements need to be considered differently? How would their interpretation need to be changed?

Alternatively, might a different court have viewed this dispute differently? Come up with a short list of personal characteristics that might lead the deciding body to rule in this way and a contrasting list of characteristics that might have facilitated the court's coming to an opposite conclusion.

ETHICAL DECISION MAKING

Consider Osprey's denial of receiving the fax in question from Kelly-Moore. If this denial does amount to a false claim, what is the motivation for the commission of this falsehood? What is its ultimate purpose?

How might different ethical perspectives lead to contradictory opinions regarding this behavior? Does it necessarily amount to a blameworthy action? Why or why not?

The mailbox rule. Because not all acceptances are made in person, a rule needed to be developed to determine the point at which an acceptance made through the mail became effective. The courts settled on the **mailbox rule,** which provides that an acceptance is valid when it is placed in the mailbox, whereas a revocation is effective only when received by the offeree.

Today, the mailbox rule has been expanded to apply to faxes in some jurisdictions. Case 14-4 provides the rationale for that extension.

CASE 14-4 | TRINITY HOMES, L.L.C. v. FANG
VIRGINIA CIRCUIT COURT
63 VA. CIR. 409, 2003 VA. CIR. LEXIS 349

Stewart, the Plaintiffs' agent, alleges that he placed the Agreement to purchase Defendants' property in his facsimile machine, dialed the number for Nicholson, pushed the button to start the facsimile, and then went on an errand. The facsimile machine utilized by Stewart was not a modern version and did not provide any verification that a facsimile was being transmitted and/or that such facsimile was received. There are no phone records relative to the alleged transmission of the facsimile by Stewart. Shortly after the time Stewart alleged he forwarded the facsimile to Nicholson, he received a phone call from Nicholson indicating that Defendants did not wish to sell the property nor enter into a contract with Plaintiffs for that purpose.

Plaintiffs sued to enforce the contract they believed was formed by the sending of the facsimile.

JUDGE MARC JACOBSON: Initially, it is necessary to consider whether facsimile (fax) transmissions are similar to or should be treated the same as the Mailbox Rule in regard to the acceptance of a contract.

The Mailbox Rule states that, once an offeree has dispatched his acceptance, it is too late for the offeror to revoke the offer. The Mailbox Rule has been accepted in most American jurisdictions and by the Restatement of Contracts. . . . The Restatement addresses the issue of the application of the Mailbox Rule to electronic communication in §64, which states: "Acceptance given by telephone or other medium of substantially instantaneous two-way communication is governed by the principles applicable to acceptances where the parties are in the presence of each other." This is, therefore, a two-prong test: (1) the communication must be "substantially instantaneous"; and (2) the communication must be two-way. "The rationale of the Restatement's position is that when parties are conversing using 'substantially instantaneous two-way communication,' they are, in essence, in each other's presence."

To be substantially instantaneous, the transmission must occur within a few seconds, or, at most, within a minute or two. . . . For a communication to be two-way, one party must be able to "determine readily whether the other party is aware of the first party's communications, through immediate verbal response or, when the communication is face-to-face, through nonverbal cues." . . . Further, if a communication is not two-way, "the offeror will not know exactly when the offeree accepts and may attempt to revoke the offer after the offeree has already sent his instantaneous acceptance to the offeror. . . . In such a situation, the Mailbox Rule should continue to apply and the contract should be considered accepted upon dispatch of the offeree's acceptance."

This Court concludes that the Mailbox Rule is applicable in the instant cause and thus the issue is one of fact, whether or not the facsimile transmission of Plaintiff's Exhibit 4 was actually forwarded or transmitted by Stewart to Nicholson. The Court in considering the totality of the evidence and the totality of the circumstances, finds and concludes that the burden has not been met nor satisfied and finds for the Defendants.

Judgment in favor of Defendants.

CRITICAL THINKING

What are some of the larger implications of the mailbox rule? When would it be beneficial, and when might it be harmful?

How does the rule affect this case? Do you see its effect as desirable or undesirable? Why? How might its role in this case be related to its role in other cases, as you considered above?

ETHICAL DECISION MAKING

What do you see as the purpose of the court's ruling in this case? Is a desire to protect a particular value or set of values apparent? Why or why not?

How else might you formulate the purpose of this decision? Are any groups of stakeholders provided special consideration or benefit? Defend your response.

e-commerce AND THE LAW

The Mailbox Rule and E-Commerce

The future of the mailbox rule is in question, at least as it applies to electronic acceptances. In the case of computer information transactions, such as acceptances via e-mail, the law is clear: Electronic acceptance is effective when received. For all other transactions, though, the law is unclear.

In a recent article,* Valerie Watnick, a professor of business law at Baruch College, offered reasons why the mailbox rule should apply as a default rule in e-commerce cases in which the law is unclear. She offers justifications for her view:

1. The mailbox rule fosters certainty and helps courts avoid complex factual inquiries that are likely in electronic acceptance cases.
2. The mailbox rule is practical in that it supplies the date the contract was formed without sorting out circular communications.
3. Electronic communication is very much like mail, only faster. It is not instantaneous. Messages are broken into "packets" of information, which are sent along different routes to a final destination. Sometimes, it takes hours for a complete message to reach its final destination.

Watnick concludes: "[A] dispatch rule in electronic contracting will allow parties to freely contract through electronic means, without regard to whether both parties have knowledge of the existence of the contract at the moment of its formation."

Do you agree with Watnick?

* Information for this text box comes from Valerie Watnick, "The Electronic Formation of Contracts and the Common Law 'Mailbox Rule,'" 56 BAYLOR L. REV. 175 (2004).

Authorized means of acceptance. The means by which the acceptance can be communicated to the offeror may either be expressly stated in the offer, which is called an *express authorization,* or be implied from the facts and circumstances surrounding the communication of the offer to the offeree. If the offer specifies that acceptance must be communicated by a specific mode, that mode is the only means for accepting the offer, and once the acceptance is dispatched, the contract has been formed. If any other attempted means of acceptance is used, there is no valid contract. For example, if the offer says acceptance must be by certified mail, then as soon as the acceptance is taken to the post office, there is a valid contract. If the offeree instead faxes an acceptance, there is no contract.

According to the Restatement, if no mode of communication is specified in the offer, any reasonable means of acceptance is valid. To determine the reasonableness of the means, courts look at such factors as the means by which the offer was communicated and the surrounding circumstances.

Effect of an unauthorized means of acceptance. As noted above, when an offer specifies that acceptance must be communicated by a particular mode, no other form of acceptance is valid. However, if the offer merely authorizes certain modes of acceptance but does not condition acceptance on the use of those modes, use of an unauthorized means of acceptance is acceptable but the contract is not formed until the acceptance is received by the offeror. For example, if Beth sends an offer to Joe via a fax, saying in the offer that acceptance may be via fax or e-mail, and Joe accepts her offer by overnight mail, his acceptance is valid but it is effective only on receipt.

Similarly, if the offeree makes a mistake and sends the acceptance to the wrong address, there is no acceptance on dispatch. However, if a correction is made and the letter eventually reaches the offeror, the acceptance is valid on receipt, assuming the offer was still open.

The effect of an acceptance after a rejection. As previously stated, if an acceptance is received after a rejection is received, the acceptance is not valid because the rejection terminated the offer. However, sometimes a rejection is dispatched, but before it is received, the acceptance is communicated to the offeror. In that case, a valid contract has been formed because the rejection is not effective until it is received. Suppose Brenda e-mails an offer to Harry, and he puts a rejection in the mail; then, before it is received, Harry calls Brenda and tells her he accepts. A valid contract has been formed, and the rejection will have no effect when it is received. However, if the telephone call had been made after Brenda had received the rejection, there could be no contract.

CASE OPENER WRAP-UP

Harrier Jet

Much to the plaintiff's dismay, the court in the Pepsi case found that the commercial could not be regarded as sufficiently definite to be an offer, because it specifically reserved the details of the offer to a separate writing, the catalog.[2] Also, the commercial itself made no mention of the steps a potential offeree would be required to take to accept the alleged offer of a Harrier jet. As in most cases where a consumer attempts to place an order for an advertised item, the court regarded the plaintiff's purported acceptance as an offer. And it was an offer that Pepsi obviously rejected.

[2] *Leonard v. Pepsico,* 210 F.3d 88, 2000 U.S. App. LEXIS 6855.

Summary

Elements of the Offer	A valid offer requires (1) the manifestation of the offeror's intent to be bound, (2) definite and certain terms, and (3) communication to an offeree.
Termination of the Offer	An offer can be terminated by revocation by the offeror; rejection or counteroffer by the offeree; death or incapacity of the offeror; destruction or subsequent illegality of the subject matter of the offer; or lapse of time or failure of other conditions stated in the offer.
The Acceptance	An acceptance is valid when a manifestation of intent to be bound to the terms of the offer is communicated to the offeror by the offeree.

Point / Counterpoint

Should the Mailbox Rule Mean That Acceptance Is Effective on Deposit or on Receipt?

On Receipt

Mailing a letter has been a customary way of accepting an offer. Businesses may send offers via mail, expecting responses in the form of acceptance or rejection also through the mail. But when businesses send offers, the offers do not create a power of acceptance in the offeree until the notice is received. Why then should the timing of acceptance be any different?

If acceptance were effective at the time of deposit, businesses or other individuals making the offers would be at a distinct disadvantage, as they would not know when the offers were actually accepted. For example, if an individual wants to purchase real estate and he makes an offer to buy a tract of land, he would then have to wait until he receives a definite response from the offeree before he makes any other offers to buy. In other words, if the letter of acceptance was mailed a week ago, he would be legally bound to a contract for the seven days that the letter was in transit. Acceptance on deposit promotes inefficiency in business transactions, as offerors are inhibited in their efforts to create contracts.

Furthermore, a person who mails a letter has the power to intercept the letter from the postal service before the letter is delivered. Because individuals have this power to intercept letters, acceptance cannot occur at the time of deposit, as one cannot be said to be bound by contract for properly recalling a letter that had previously been mailed.

Finally, acceptance on deposit would suggest that the letter would not even need to arrive at the intended destination for the contract to be binding. If an offeree misspells the street name, the offeror may never receive the acceptance, so binding the offeror would be extremely inequitable in such situations.

On Deposit

Lines must be drawn somewhere. In the context of acceptance by mail, the line must be either at the time of deposit or at the time of receipt. Regardless of which time courts choose as the time of acceptance, one of the parties will bear more of the risk, as she or he will be bound for a period of time without actual knowledge that the contract has been created. However, the offeror is generally in a better position to bear the risk, particularly when the offeror is a large company or a merchant that is very familiar with the creation of contracts by mail.

With regard to the time lag between mailing and receipt, modern-day mail makes the time lag almost negligible, as mail is delivered very quickly. Offerees even have the option of sending letters overnight. Businesses and other individuals, therefore, are unlikely to realize any kind of inefficiency in their operations due to the practically unnoticeable time lag between deposit and receipt. Although the time lag may have been an important factor for the mailbox rule at one point, this reason is virtually inapplicable today.

The power to intercept a letter does not suggest that the offeree has the right to intercept the letter. This issue still begs the question as to when the moment of acceptance is effective. If the mailbox rule continues to hold that acceptance is effective at the time of deposit, the offeree thereafter does not have the right to intercept the letter before it reaches the offeror, even though the offeree could physically obtain the letter.

Additionally, the mailbox rule that holds that acceptance is effective on deposit has been followed for years. The rule has been upheld in many jurisdictions and has gained considerable support in treatises and scholarly journals. Thus, the line has been drawn, and few compelling reasons exist to warrant a different line that would suggest acceptance is effective on receipt.

Questions & Problems

1. How do the elements of an offer differ between the common law and the UCC?
2. How do the elements of an acceptance differ between the common law and the UCC?
3. What is the mirror-image rule?
4. What is the mailbox rule?
5. In response to an excessive supply of 1954 Ford models, Capital City Ford heavily advertised in newspapers and on the radio the following message:

   TWO FOR ONE . . . For two weeks BUY A NEW '54 FORD NOW TRADE EVEN FOR A '55 FORD. Don't Wait—Buy a 1954 Ford now, when the 1955 models come out we'll trade even for your '54. You pay only sales tax and license fee. Your '55 Ford will be the same model, same body style, accessory group, etc. A sure thing for you—a gamble for us, but we'll take it. Hurry, though, this offer good only for the remainder of September. The 1954 car must be returned with only normal wear and tear. Physical damage, such as dented fenders, torn upholstery, etc. must be charged to owner or repaired at owner's expense. No convertibles or Skyliners on this basis.

   In response to the advertisement, Leland Johnson purchased a 1954 Ford and later requested that Capital City Ford accept his 1954 as an even trade for the new 1955 model. However, Capital City Ford refused, claiming that the advertisement was merely an invitation to bargain. In response, Johnson sued for specific performance of the contract, claiming that the advertisement was an offer and that his purchasing of the 1954 model operated as an acceptance. Which argument do you find most persuasive? Why? What did the court hold? [*Johnson v. Capital City Ford Co.,* 85 So. 2d 75, 79 (La. Ct. App.1955).]
6. Michael and Laurie Montgomery negotiated with Norma English with regard to the potential sale of the Montgomerys' home. English submitted a bid for $272,000, but she included a request to purchase some of the Montgomerys' personal property and expressed that an "as-is" provision was not applicable to the sale. When the Montgomerys received the offer, they deleted the personal property provision, deleted provisions related to latent defects and a building inspection, and added a specific as-is rider. English's agent then delivered the counteroffer to English, who initialed many, but not all, of the Montgomerys' modifications, such as the deletion of the personal property provision. The Montgomerys refused to proceed with the sale, so English filed suit for specific performance of the contract. Under the mirror-image rule, did a contract exist between the Montgomerys and English? Why or why not? [*Montgomery v. English,* 2005 Fla. App. LEXIS 4704.]
7. Wilbert Heikkila, wanting to sell eight of his parcels of land, signed an agreement with Kangas Realty. Thereafter, David McLaughlin met with a Kangas representative, who created a handwritten offer to purchase three of the parcels. McLaughlin signed the offer and provided the Kangas agent with three earnest-money checks for each parcel. The agent then created three separate purchase agreements, which McLaughlin did not sign, but his wife did sign and initial all three agreements. Two days later, Heikkila met with the Kangas agent, changing the price on all three parcels by writing on the purchase agreements. Heikkila also altered the closing dates for the parcels and reserved mineral rights for each parcel. The McLaughlins did not make any additional marks or signings on the purchase agreements. However, the Kangas agent returned

the checks to the McLaughlins, indicating that Heikkila had withdrawn his offer to sell the parcels. The court held that this transaction was subject to the statute of frauds, which requires that a contract for the sale of land be in writing. Were there an offer and an acceptance, thereby creating an enforceable contract? Why or why not? [*McLaughlin v. Heikkila,* 2005 Minn. App. LEXIS 591.]

8. Frank Scheck offered to sell a piece of real estate to a specified prospective buyer, agreeing also to pay a broker, A. A. Marchiondo, a percentage of the sale price. Scheck fixed a six-day period during which the offer would be left open. However, Scheck changed his mind, and sent a letter to Marchiondo in which Scheck said that he had revoked the offer. After Marchiondo's work in attempting to obtain the offeree's acceptance, Marchiondo received the letter on the morning of the sixth day, and later that day the offeree contacted Marchiondo and accepted the offer to purchase the real estate. Marchiondo claimed that Scheck could not terminate the offer, as a contract had been created, and that Scheck's failure to pay Marchiondo's commission constituted a breach of contract. The trial court dismissed Marchiondo's complaint, and Marchiondo appealed. Was Scheck's letter a proper termination of the offer? Why or why not? What was the appellate court's reasoning? [*Marchiondo v. Scheck,* 1967 N.M. LEXIS 2815.]
9. Marilyn Bouchard opened a restaurant called "Castle Garden Café" in Rhode Island in 2002, hiring Denise Raab. Bouchard and Raab began negotiating a transfer of real estate and ownership from Bouchard to Raab. Raab's attorney drafted a letter, outlining that the sale price of $180,000 would include the real estate, building, inventory, and equipment with equal monthly payments at a 5 percent interest rate to be paid over a period of 10 years. Neither party signed this document, and no other written documents were included as part of the potential sale. The letter also provided that Raab would obtain a life insurance policy of $150,000. Thereafter, Raab obtained a life insurance policy for only $117,000, but she allowed the policy to lapse after three months. In 2003, Raab controlled the complete operation of the restaurant. Raab also occupied a garage on the premises as a temporary residence, making improvements valued at $20,800 to the garage and restaurant. Raab applied to have the liquor license transferred, as mentioned in the letter for transfer, but the city council never made a decision on the application, although Bouchard asked the city council to renew her own license. In 2004, Bouchard learned that real estate and personal property taxes were unpaid, along with the beverage and meal tax and corporate tax. Subsequently, Bouchard decided to close the restaurant, notifying Raab of the closure. Although the statute of frauds would have required the alleged contract to be in writing, the court held that Bouchard's admission that there was an oral agreement removed the application of the statute of frauds. Raab sued for specific performance of the contract. Were the terms of the agreement definite and certain enough to create an enforceable contract? Why or why not? [*Raab v. Bouchard,* 2005 R.I. Super. LEXIS 96.]
10. Hazelton Manufacturing is a wholesale supplier of heating and cooling equipment, including boilers manufactured by H. B. Smith. In 2000, Hazelton received an unsolicited facsimile from Smith, quoting prices for three "Mills" boilers. Smith had sent the facsimile to a number of distributors, on the basis of his understanding that the three boilers were needed for a construction project at Dartmouth High School. Although Smith would usually quote a "retail" price that distributors would later increase before resale, Smith indicated that the "net" price for all three boilers would not be discounted on sale to the distributor. Not realizing this refusal to discount, Hazelton considered the quoted price of $131,711 to be the retail price and reduced it

to a "dealer" price of $88,200. Hazelton forwarded the dealer quotation, unsolicited, to numerous businesses, including I&R, as Hazelton believed these companies might be interested in the Dartmouth project. I&R considered Hazelton's quotation in its calculations for a subcontractor bid on the Dartmouth project. After I&R received the subcontractor bid, I&R contacted Hazelton to purchase the boilers at the quoted cost of $88,200. By this time, Hazelton recognized the error in the quotation and refused to sell the boilers to I&R. Subsequently, I&R purchased boilers from another company for $144,000 and sued Hazelton for the difference under a breach-of-contract theory. Was Hazelton's mistaken quotation an offer? Did I&R's contacting Hazelton to purchase the boilers for $88,200 constitute an acceptance? [*I&R Mech. Inc. v. Hazelton Mfg. Co.,* 2004 Mass. App. LEXIS 1276.]

11. Jane Shaw permitted Hudson & Marshall to auction a 775-acre farm at a public auction. Shaw's agreement with Hudson & Marshall indicated that the auction was "subject to a reserve price of $750,000." Larry Moss attended the auction and was the highest bidder. Hudson & Marshall drafted a memorandum of sale to memorialize the agreement, but Shaw did not sign the memorandum. She later sold the property to another party. Although the material advertising the auction did not mention that the auction was with reserve, the parties disputed whether the auctioneer stated that the sale was subject to Shaw's approval. Moss sued to enforce the alleged contract for sale of a portion of Shaw's property. The trial court held that sufficient evidence established that the auctioneer had stated that the sale was subject to the Shaw's approval. Could Moss successfully enforce the alleged contract? Why or why not? [*Moss v. Hudson & Marshall, Inc.,* 2004 Ga. App. LEXIS 615.]

12. Sarah and Eddie Hogan wanted to sell 2.5 acres of land through their real estate agent, Darita Richardson. On December 10, 2001, Warren Kent offered to purchase the land for $52,500. An "Agreement to Buy or Sell" was created, which Kent signed right away. One term of the agreement was that the offer would expire on December 11, 2001, at 3 p.m., and it stated additionally, "Time is of the essence and all deadlines are final except where modifications, changes, or extensions are made in writing and signed by all parties." Although Richardson scheduled a meeting on December 11, 2001, at 2 p.m. with the Hogans, the Hogans failed to appear. However, the parties agreed to a two-day extension, lasting until December 13, 2001, at 3 p.m., and the extension was binding and irrevocable according to the "Addendum to Agreement to Purchase or Sell." The Hogans signed both documents at 9 a.m. on December 13, 2001. At about 11 a.m., Kent also signed the addendum. However, neither Kent's agent nor Richardson contacted the Hogans prior to 3 p.m. about Kent's acceptance. After 3 p.m., Richardson realized that the Hogans had not placed the date and time next to their signatures. When she met with the Hogans, the Hogans placed the date and the time as 4:48 p.m., informing Richardson that they, the Hogans, had changed their minds about the sale. Kent sued for specific performance of the contract. What effect, if any, did the failure to communicate the acceptance of the offer prior to 3 p.m. have in terms of whether a contract was formed? What was the appellate court's reasoning? [*Kent v. Hogan,* 2004 La. App. LEXIS 2539.]

Looking for more review material?

The Online Learning Center at **www.mhhe.com/kubasek1e** contains this chapter's "Assignment on the Internet" and also a list of URLs for more information, entitled "On the Internet." Find both of them in the Student Center portion of the OLC, along with quizzes and other helpful materials.

Consideration

CASE OPENER

Upper Deck—Contract Liability or Gift?

In 1988 the Upper Deck Company was a baseball card company with an idea for a better baseball card: one that had a hologram on it. By the 1990s Upper Deck was a major corporation whose value was at least a quarter of a billion dollars. In 1988, however, the outlook wasn't bright for Upper Deck, which lacked the funds for a $100,000 deposit it needed to buy some special paper by August 1. Without that deposit its contract with the Major League Baseball Players Association would have been jeopardized.

Upper Deck's corporate attorney, Anthony Passante, Jr., found the money. That evening, the directors of the company accepted the loan and, in gratitude, agreed that Passante should have 3 percent of the firm's stock. Passante never sought to collect the stock, and later the company reneged on its promise. Passante sued for breach of oral contract.[1]

1. If you were on the jury, how would you decide the case? Was the offer of 3 percent of the firm's stock legal consideration for the loan? Or was it a mere gift?
2. Does Upper Deck have a moral obligation to give Passante the stock? If so, is this legally enforceable?

The Wrap-Up at the end of the chapter will answer these questions.

Learning Objectives

After reading this chapter, you will be able to answer the following questions:

1 What is consideration?

2 What are the rules regarding consideration?

[1] *Passante v. McWilliam,* 53 Cal. App. 4th 1240 (1997).

CHAPTER 15

3 What is promissory estoppel and when can it be used?

4 What is an illusory promise?

5 How are the UCC rules regarding consideration different from the common law rules regarding consideration?

6 What is the difference between a liquidated debt and an unliquidated debt?

7 What is an accord and satisfaction?

What Is Consideration?

Consideration is required in every contract. It is what a person will receive in return for performing a contract obligation. Suppose, for example, that Dan agrees to purchase Mary's car for $1,000. Dan's payment of $1,000 is the consideration Mary will receive for Dan's car. Mary's turning over ownership of the car to Dan is the consideration Dan will receive in exchange. In the business context, consideration is usually money. Consideration can be anything, however, as long as it is the product of a bargained-for exchange. It consists of something of value given to another party in exchange for something else of value. The following are examples of consideration:

- A benefit to the promisor (e.g., a promise to stay in a job until a particular project is completed—this is a benefit to the employer).
- A detriment to the promisee (e.g., a promise to your football coach to refrain from riding your motorcycle during football season even though you love riding it).
- A promise to do something (e.g., a promise to cook dinner for your roommate for the next six months).
- A promise to refrain from doing something (e.g., a promise to stop drinking alcohol during exam week).

Rules of Consideration

As in any area of law, there are a number of rules governing consideration, as well as exceptions to the rules. The trick to understanding consideration is simply to understand the various rules and their exceptions. We explore these principles below.

LACK OF CONSIDERATION

Rule: *For a promise to be enforced by the courts, there must be consideration.*

A court will enforce one party's promise only if the other party promised something (an act, money, etc.) in exchange. For example, in a bilateral contract (a promise for a promise), the consideration for each promise is a return promise. Consider this example: Sue promises to pay Mike $2,000 for his car. Mike promises to sell Sue his car for $2,000. The exchange will be done tomorrow. There is an oral contract. Sue's promise to pay Mike $2,000 for the car is her consideration to Mike. Mike's promise to sell Sue the car for $2,000 is his consideration to Sue. There has been a mutual exchange of something of value—a promise to pay $2,000, and a promise to sell the car for $2,000. In a unilateral contract (a promise for an act), one party's consideration is the promise and the other party's consideration is the act. Suppose your professor made the following statement in class: "If any student shows up at my house on Saturday and does the gardening, I will pay that student $100." You show up and do the gardening. The professor's consideration to you is the promise of the payment of $100 on completion of the gardening, and your consideration to the professor is the act of completing the gardening. Once again, there has been a mutual exchange of something of value. In Case 15-1, the court must decide whether continued employment is consideration for signing a noncompete agreement.

The exception to the rule requiring consideration is **promissory estoppel.** Promissory estoppel occurs when one party makes a promise knowing the other party will rely on it, the other party does rely on it, and the only way to avoid injustice is to enforce the promise.

CASE 15-1 ANTHONY A. LABRIOLA v. POLLARD GROUP, INC.
SUPREME COURT OF WASHINGTON
100 P.3D 791 (SUP. CT. WASH. 2004)

In 1997, Employer hired Employee to work as a commercial print salesperson, and the parties entered into an employment agreement. Under the agreement, Employer could terminate Employee without cause. Employee's compensation consisted of a base salary and commission from sales. The agreement also contained a restrictive covenant not to compete in the custom printing business for a period of three years after employment ended. The agreement had no geographical limitations.

Nearly five years later, in April 2002, Employer requested and Employee executed a "Noncompetition and Confidentiality Agreement" (noncompete agreement). The noncompete agreement required Employee to refrain from accepting employment with a competitor for a period of three years within 75 miles of Employer's business in Tacoma, Washington. Employee remained an "at-will" employee and received no additional benefits. Employer incurred no additional obligations from the noncompete agreement. The noncompete agreement also contained clauses for confidentiality, severability, and an award of attorneys' fees and costs.

A few months later, in July 2002, Employer announced a new commission sales compensation schedule. The new schedule raised the threshold sales level required for commissions to be paid. The old schedule's threshold paid commission when an employee generated sales of at least $25,000 for the month, while the new schedule paid commission to an employee only after sales for the month exceeded $60,000. Employee determined that the new schedule would reduce his income by about 25 percent and sought employment for a similar position elsewhere. On November 12, 2002, Employer discovered Employee's intention to seek employment with a competitor and terminated Employee. Employer sent a letter to the competitor interested in hiring Employee, stating its intent to enforce Employee's noncompete agreement. The competitor did not hire Employee. Employee remains unemployed despite actively seeking a position similar to the one he had held with Employer.

The Employee sued the Employer. The trial court ruled against the employee and the employee appealed to the state supreme court.

JUDGE IRELAND: . . . Issue 1. Is there consideration for the formation of a contract when an employee, already employed by the employer, executes a noncompete agreement but receives no new benefit and the employer incurs no further obligations?

Employee claims that the noncompete agreement fails for lack of consideration; in other words, a contract was not formed. Employer contends that the noncompete agreement is enforceable because future and continued employment and/or job training served as the Employer's consideration in exchange for Employee's execution of the noncompete agreement. . . . The general rule in Washington is that consideration exists if the employee enters into a noncompete agreement when he or she is first hired. . . . A noncompete agreement entered into after employment will be enforced if it is supported by independent consideration. . . . Independent, additional consideration is required for the valid formation of a modification or subsequent agreement. There is no consideration when "one party is to perform some additional obligation while the other party is simply to perform that which he promised in the original contract." [Citations omitted]. Independent consideration may include increased wages, a promotion, a bonus, a fixed term of employment, or perhaps access to protected information. . . . Independent consideration involves new promises or obligations previously not required of the parties. . . .

In the present case, Employer contends that continued employment served as consideration for the 2002 noncompete agreement . . . [but] Employee's noncompete agreement made no promises as to future employment and wages. Further, during deposition, Robin Pollard, Employer's president, conceded that "no extra benefits or consideration or promises [were] made to [Employee] if he signed the noncompete."

Consideration is a bargained-for exchange of promises. A comparison of the status of the employer before and after the noncompete agreement confirms that the 2002 noncompete agreement was entered into without consideration. Employer did not incur additional duties or obligations from the noncompete agreement. Prior to execution of the 2002 noncompete agreement,

[CONTINUED]

Employee was an "at will" Employee. After Employee executed the noncompete agreement, he still remained an "at will" employee terminable at Employer's pleasure. We hold that continued employment in this case did not serve as consideration by Employer in exchange for Employee's promise not to compete.

We hold that the 2002 noncompete agreement lacked independent consideration and is not enforceable against the Employee.

REVERSED in favor of Employee.

CRITICAL THINKING

What is the reasoning used by the court to support its decision? Are there any ambiguous words or phrases in that reasoning that you would want defined before you decided whether to agree with the court's ruling?

ETHICAL DECISION MAKING

Return to the WPH framework. Who are the stakeholders in this case? Is the decision of the employer consistent with how one would act when using the Golden Rule as one's guide?

How does promissory estoppel work? Suppose that upon graduation from college, Amanda receives a job offer across the country. She gives up her apartment, cancels all her other job interviews, and moves all her possessions. After arriving, she rents a new apartment and shows up for work. The only problem is, Amanda is told there is no job! May Amanda sue the employer? The answer in most states is yes, under the theory of promissory estoppel. She spent a lot of money in reliance on the job offer. She also moved across country. Amanda may be able to recover her *reliance damages* (i.e., money she spent in "reliance" on the job offer). Promissory estoppel is not awarded regularly, but in the right case it can provide a remedy where no other remedy exists. The Case Nugget provides an illustration of the successful use of promissory estoppel.

ADEQUACY OF CONSIDERATION

Rule: *The court seldom considers adequacy of consideration.*

What this rule means is that the court does not weigh whether you made a good bargain. Example: Donna purchases a stereo from Celia, a friend in her business law class. Donna pays $500 for the stereo, but later realizes that the stereo is not worth $100! May Donna sue Celia? Typically, the answer is no. It is Donna's responsibility to do her research and determine what price she should pay. The court will not set aside the sale because she made a bad deal.

There is an exception to this rule. Suppose that you are on the verge of bankruptcy and your creditors are threatening legal action. You know that if you default on your mortgage,

Case Nugget Promissory Estoppel

Double AA Builders, Ltd. v. Grand State Construction L.L.C. 114 P.3d 835 (Ariz. Ct. App. 2005)

In anticipation of submitting a bid for the construction of a Home Depot Store in Mesa, Arizona, Double AA solicited bids from subcontractors for various portions of the work. Grand State faxed a written but unsigned bid to Double AA in the amount of $115,000 for installation of the exterior insulation finish system (EIFS) on the project. The proposal stated: "Our price is good for 30 days." Double AA relied on several subcontractor bids, including Grand State's, in preparing its overall price for the project.

On December 21, 2001, Home Depot advised Double AA that it was the successful bidder for the project. On January 11, 2002, within the 30-day "price is good" period, Double AA sent a subcontract for the EIFS work to Grand State to be signed and returned. Grand State advised Double AA that it would not sign the subcontract or perform on the project. Double AA subsequently entered into a subcontract with a replacement subcontractor to install the EIFS at a cost of $131,449, which exceeded Grand State's quoted price by $16,449. Double AA demanded that Grand State pay the difference between its bid and Double AA's ultimate cost to perform the same work. After Grand State refused, Double AA filed suit based on promissory estoppel.

When a general contractor prepares an overall bid for a competitively bid construction project, it receives bids and quotes from subcontractors for portions of the work. The general contractor uses the bids in preparing its overall price for the project. A subcontractor's refusal to honor its bid can be financially disastrous for the general contractor, because the general contractor will typically be bound by the bid price it submitted to the project owner.

Promissory estoppel may be used to require that the subcontractor perform according to the terms of its bid to the contractor if the contractor receives the contract award, because the contractor has relied on the subcontractor's bid and must perform for a price based on that reliance. Double AA prevailed. Nonperformance by the subcontractor resulted in damages equal to the difference between what the contractor had to pay and what the contractor would have paid had the subcontractor performed.

car payment, bank loans, credit card payments, and other bills, the court may order your assets sold to pay the creditors. Instead of risking this result, you decide to "sell" your assets. You sell your BMW to your best friend for $50 and your vacation house to your sister for $500. Now asset-free, you declare bankruptcy, knowing that your creditors will be able to collect nothing! Is this permissible? The answer, of course, is no. In such a case, the court will look at "adequacy of consideration." If it appears that the "sale" of the assets was done to avoid payment to creditors, the court may set aside each sale and sell the assets to pay your creditors. In Case 15-2, the court had to consider whether $1 plus "love and affection" was adequate consideration for the transfer of property.

CASE 15-2

THELMA AGNES SMITH v. DAVID PHILLIP RILEY

COURT OF APPEALS OF TENNESSEE, EASTERN SECTION, AT KNOXVILLE

2002 TENN. APP. LEXIS 65 (2002)

The plaintiff, Thelma Agnes Smith, lived with the defendant out of wedlock for several years. When the relationship ended, she sued the defendant, seeking to enforce two written agreements with him regarding the sale and assignment of property to her. The trial court enforced the agreements and divided the parties' property. The defendant appealed, arguing that the agreements lacked consideration and were void as against public policy.

JUDGE CHARLES D. SUSANO: . . . Thelma Agnes Smith and David Phillip Riley, both of whom then resided in Florida, separated from their respective spouses in 1997 and began a romantic relationship. In early 1998, the two moved to Tennessee and began cohabitating. . . . Smith and Riley opened a joint checking account in March, 1998. Over time, Smith deposited into that account $9,500—the proceeds from an insurance settlement and monies received when her divorce later became final; she also deposited her monthly social security check of $337 into the same account. Smith continued to deposit her social security check in the joint account until December, 1998, when she opened her own checking account. Riley also contributed to the joint account. He placed a settlement of $84,000 from the Veteran's Administration into the account. In addition, he deposited his monthly pension check of $ 2,036 into the same account. . . .

On July 31, 1998, Riley entered into a lease with Jerry Strickland and Wanda Strickland with respect to a residence owned by them; the lease was accompanied by an option to purchase. Almost four months later, on November 20, 1998, Smith and Riley returned to their attorney's office, at which time the attorney prepared a bill of sale and an assignment. In the bill of sale, Riley transferred [to Smith] a one-half undivided interest in seven items of personal property. . . . Riley also assigned to Smith a one-half undivided interest in the lease and option to purchase with the Stricklands, which interest included a right of survivorship in the one-half interest retained by Riley as well. The property Riley sold and assigned to Smith in the two agreements was stated in each to be "for and in consideration of the sum of One Dollar ($1.00) and other and good and valuable consideration, the sufficiency of which is hereby acknowledged. . . ."

When Smith and Riley separated in April, 1999, Smith filed suit against Riley in the trial court, seeking the dissolution of their "domestic partnership." Smith alleged that she and Riley had been living together for several years without the benefit of marriage and had acquired both real and personal property, some of which Riley had assigned to her. As a result, she asked the court to award her 50 percent of the "partnership" assets, leaving the other 50 percent to Riley. . . . [The trial court ruled in favor of Smith and Riley appealed].

Riley first argues that the trial court erred in finding that the bill of sale and assignment are supported by valid consideration. Specifically, Riley relies on Smith's statements at trial that she considered their pending engagement and the funds she deposited into their joint account to be consideration for their agreements.

It is a well-settled principle of contract law that in order for a contract to be binding, it must, among other things, be supported by sufficient consideration. [Citations omitted]. In expounding on the adequacy of consideration, the Tennessee Supreme Court has stated that it is not necessary that the benefit conferred or the detriment suffered by the promisee shall be equal to the responsibility assumed. Any consideration, however small, will support a promise. In the absence of fraud, the courts will not undertake to regulate the amount of the consideration. The parties are left to contract for themselves, taking for granted that the consideration is one valuable in the eyes of the law. . . .

Quoting the United States Supreme Court, the Tennessee Supreme Court went on to state that "[a] stipulation in consideration of $1 is just as effectual and valuable a consideration as a larger sum stipulated for or paid." [Citations omitted]. Indeed, the consideration of love and affection has been deemed sufficient to support a conveyance. . . .

Both the bill of sale and the assignment recite that they are undertaken "for and in consideration of the sum of One Dollar ($1.00) and other and good and valuable consideration, the sufficiency of which is hereby acknowledged. . . ." Facially, the documents are therefore supported by sufficient consideration, as clearly recognized by the Supreme Court. . . . Moreover,

Smith's "society and consortium"—a concept comparable to the love and affection . . . is further evidence of sufficient consideration to support these conveyances.

Riley calls our attention to Smith's statement at trial that she considered the funds she deposited into their joint account to be consideration for the conveyances. If this were the only consideration involved in this case, Riley's argument regarding past consideration supporting a present transaction might have some merit. However, the recitals of nominal consideration that are present in both agreements, as well as the consideration of Smith's love and affection, are adequate consideration and will support the conveyances represented by the assignment and bill of sale. . . .

Judgment affirmed in favor of Plaintiff.

CRITICAL THINKING

What is the reasoning of the appellant in terms of why the consideration was not adequate to cause the contracts to be enforceable? What key rule of law did this reasoning overlook?

ETHICAL DECISION MAKING

What values are being advanced by the logic of the relevant rule of law in this case? In other words, what values prevent the rule of law from being that "consideration must be in an amount similar in value to the item or services being transferred in order for the contract to be enforceable"?

global context

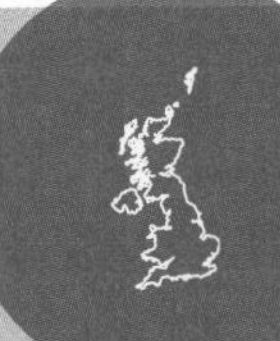

Deeds in England

England has the same requirement for consideration as the United States and even shares the exception of promissory estoppel. However, England has an additional exception to the requirement for consideration: specialty contracts or deeds. In England, a *deed* is a document that creates a binding obligation between parties without consideration when certain formalities are honored. These formalities include a written document signed by the person making it, a witness to the maker's signature, and delivery of the document to the other party with a statement or an accompanying act indicating the maker's intention to be bound by the deed. Deeds are used in England to create enforceable promises of gifts to charity. This exception to the requirement for consideration is also found in Canadian law.

ILLUSORY PROMISE

Rule: *An illusory promise is not consideration.*

What is an illusory promise? Suppose Shawn offers to sell Molly his skis for $300. Molly responds, "I'll look at them in the morning, and if I like them, I'll pay you." At this point,

Molly has not committed to doing anything. The law considers this an illusory promise (i.e., it is not a promise at all). Moreover, an illusory promise is not consideration.

PAST CONSIDERATION

Rule: *Past consideration is no consideration at all.*

Consideration is an essential element of a contract. For a court to enforce a promise, both sides must offer consideration. Imagine that you have graduated from college and gotten a great job. After working at the company for five years, your boss says to you, "Because you have done such a great job the last five years, I am going to give you 5 percent of the company stock." Six months later, you still have not received the stock. May you sue your boss to enforce the promise? The answer is no. For a promise to be enforceable, there must be bargaining and an exchange. In this example, there was no exchange. Work done in the past, by definition, has already been performed. As such, you have given nothing in exchange, and the court will not enforce the promise. You are at the mercy of your boss's goodwill to keep her promise. A promise cannot be based on consideration that was provided before the promise was made.

As you have probably guessed by now, there is an exception to this rule. Under the Restatement (Second) of Contracts (a persuasive, though not binding, authority), promises based on past consideration may be enforceable "to the extent necessary to avoid injustice." In some cases, if past consideration was given with expectation of future payment, the court may enforce the promise.

PREEXISTING DUTY

Rule: *A promise to do something that you are already obligated to do is not valid consideration.*

There are actually two parts to this rule. First, *performance of a duty you are obligated to do under the law is not good consideration.* For example, a police officer is sworn to uphold the law. Part of that public duty involves catching suspected criminals. If someone offers a reward for the capture of a suspected criminal, the police officer may not collect the reward, as he or she was already obligated to apprehend the suspect. Second, *performance of an existing contractual duty is not good consideration.* Gene decides to have a pool built in his backyard. Under the existing contract, the pool is to be completed by June 1, just in time for summer. The pool contractor comes to Gene and explains that due to a shortage of workers, the completion date cannot be met; however, if Gene were to pay an extra $5,000, additional workers could be hired and the pool would be completed on time. Gene tells the contractor that he will pay the $5,000. On June 1, the pool is completed and the contractor asks for the additional $5,000 payment. Is Gene legally obligated to pay? The answer is no. The pool contractor had a preexisting contractual duty to complete the pool by June 1. Gene is under no obligation to pay the additional money.

Exceptions to the preexisting-duty rule. There are exceptions to the preexisting-duty rule: unforeseen circumstances, additional work, and UCC—sale of goods

If **unforeseen circumstances** cause a party to make a promise regarding an unfinished project, that promise is valid consideration. Let's once again consider the pool example. Suppose that Gene's pool contractor has been building pools in Gene's neighborhood for the last 20 years. During all that time, the contractor has never had any problem with rocks—until now. While bulldozing the hole for the pool in Gene's backyard, the pool contractor hits solid rock. It is estimated that it will cost an additional $5,000 to clear the rock by using jackhammers and possibly even dynamite! The contractor explains that he is sorry, but unless Gene agrees to pay the additional money, he will not be able to finish the pool. Gene agrees to pay. When the pool is completed, the contractor asks for the additional $5,000. Will a court enforce this promise? The answer is yes. Even though the contractor is completing only what he was obligated to do under the contract, neither party knew of the solid rock. The contractor has given additional consideration (removal of the rock) and Gene will be held to his promise to pay the additional money.

If a party to a contract agrees to do **additional work** (i.e., more than she is obligated to do under the contract), the promise is valid consideration. Using the pool example, if the contractor asks Gene for an additional $10,000 but agrees to add a waterfall and a deck to the pool, the promise to do the additional work is consideration. If Gene agrees to pay the $10,000, that is his consideration. Both parties are now bound.

The rules and exceptions we have been discussing fall under the common law of contracts. The Uniform Commercial Code (UCC) has changed the common law in significant ways. Under Article 2 of the UCC (sale of goods), *an agreement modifying a contract needs no consideration to be binding.* This is an exception to the preexisting-duty rule. Under UCC 2-209:[2]

1. An agreement modifying a contract within this Article needs no consideration to be binding.
2. A signed agreement which excludes modification or rescission except by a signed writing cannot be otherwise modified or rescinded, but except as between merchants such a requirement on a form supplied by the merchant must be separately signed by the other party.

Gary is a manufacturer of blow dryers. He sends a purchase order for 10,000 white on/off switches from a switch manufacturer. Later, Gary telephones the switch manufacturer and changes his order to 5,000 white switches and 5,000 red switches. Under the UCC, no additional consideration is required for the modification of the agreement to be binding. Moreover, unless stated otherwise, such an agreement need not be in writing. In Case 15-3, the court had to decide whether the parties had entered an agreement stating that all modifications to the contract must be in writing. The court then had to determine whether there was consent to a modification of the agreement.

[2] www.law.cornell.edu/ucc/2/article2.htm#s2-209.

CASE 15-3

CLOUD CORPORATION v. HASBRO, INC.
UNITED STATES COURT OF APPEALS FOR THE SEVENTH CIRCUIT
314 F.3D 289 (7TH CIR. 2002)

"Wonder World Aquarium" is a toy that defendant Hasbro, Inc., sold for a brief period in the mid-1990s. The toy comes as a package that contained the aquarium itself, some plastic fish, and large or small packets of a powder that when dissolved in distilled water forms a transparent gelatinous filling for the aquarium that simulates water. The plastic fish can be inserted into the gel to create the illusion of a real fish tank.

Plaintiff Cloud Corporation made the powder for the defendant. Mistakenly believing the market for the toy was going to expand, the plaintiff manufactured a great number of packets of powder in advance of receiving formal purchase orders. Hasbro refused to accept delivery of the additional packets or pay for them. Plaintiff sued for breach of contract, and the trial court found in favor of the defendant. The plaintiff appealed.

JUDGE POSNER: Hasbro contracted out the manufacture of this remarkable product. Southern Clay Products Company was to sell and ship Laponite HB, a patented synthetic clay, to Cloud Corporation, which was to mix the Laponite with a preservative according to a formula supplied by Hasbro, pack the mixture in the packets that we mentioned, and ship them to affiliates of Hasbro in East Asia. The affiliates would prepare and package the final product—that is, the aquarium, the packet of gel, and the plastic fish (and "pretend blood")—and ship it back to Hasbro in the United States for distribution to retailers.

The project was in operation by the middle of 1995. Hasbro would from time to time issue purchase orders for a specified number of large and small packets to Cloud, which would in turn order the quantity of Laponite from Southern Clay Products that it needed in order to manufacture the specified number of packets. The required quantity of Laponite depended not only on the number of large and small packets ordered by Hasbro but also on the formula that Hasbro supplied to Cloud specifying the proportion of Laponite in each packet. The formula was changed frequently. The less Laponite per packet specified in the formula, the more packets could be manufactured for a given quantity of the ingredient.

Early in 1997 Hasbro discovered that its East Asian affiliates, the assemblers of the final package, had more than enough powder on hand to supply Hasbro's needs, which were diminishing, no doubt because Wonder World Aquarium was losing market appeal. Mistakenly believing that Hasbro's market was expanding rather than contracting, Cloud had manufactured a great many packets of powder in advance of receiving formal purchase orders for them from Hasbro. Hasbro refused to accept delivery of these packets or to pay for them. Contending that this refusal was a breach of contract, Cloud sued Hasbro in federal district court in Chicago, seeking more than $600,000 in damages based mainly on the price of the packets that it had manufactured and not delivered to Hasbro and now was stuck with—for the packets, being usable only in Wonder World Aquaria, had no resale value. After a bench trial, the district judge ruled in favor of Hasbro. The case was appealed. The governing law is the Uniform Commercial Code as interpreted in Illinois.

In October 1995, Hasbro had sent a letter to all its suppliers, including Cloud, that contained a "terms and conditions" form to govern future purchase orders. One of the terms was that a supplier could not deviate from a purchase order without Hasbro's written consent. As requested, Cloud signed the form and returned it to Hasbro. Nevertheless, to make assurance doubly sure, every time Hasbro sent a purchase order to Cloud it would include an acknowledgment form for Cloud to sign that contained the same terms and conditions that were in the October letter. Cloud did not sign any of these acknowledgment forms. The order acknowledgments that it sent Hasbro in response to Hasbro's purchase orders contained on the back of each acknowledgment Cloud's own set of terms and conditions—and the provision in Hasbro's letter and forms requiring Hasbro's written consent to any modification of the purchase order was not among them. There was a space for Hasbro to sign Cloud's acknowledgment form but it never did so. . . .

In June 1996, Hasbro notified Cloud that it was to use a new formula in manufacturing the powder, a formula that required so much less Laponite that the same quantity would enable Cloud to produce a third again as many packets. Cloud determined that by using the new formula it could produce from the quantity of Laponite that it had on hand 4.5 million small and 5 million large packets, compared to the 3.8 and 3.9 million called for by the February and April orders but not yet delivered. Although it had received no additional purchase orders, Cloud sent Hasbro an order acknowledgment for 4.5 million small and 5 million large packets with a delivery date similar to that for the April order, but at a lower price per packet, reflecting the smaller quantity of Laponite, the expensive ingredient in the powder, in each packet.

Cloud's acknowledgment was sent in June. Hasbro did not respond to it—at least not explicitly. It did receive it, however. And Hasbro's representative continued having e-mail exchanges and phone conversations with Cloud. These focused on delivery dates and, importantly, on the quantities to be delivered on those dates. Importantly because some very large numbers—much larger than the February and April numbers, numbers consistent however with Cloud's order acknowledgment sent to Hasbro in June—appear in these and other e-mails written by her. In two of the e-mails the quantity Cloud is to ship is described as "more or less depending on the formula," consistent with Cloud's understanding that if the formula reduced the amount of Laponite per packet Cloud should increase the number of packets it made rather than return unused Laponite to Southern Clay Products.

Was Cloud commercially unreasonable in producing the additional quantity without a purchase order? If not, should the Uniform Commercial Code, which was intended to conform sales law to the customs and usages of business people, nevertheless condemn Cloud for failing to request written purchase orders for the additional quantity that the change in formula enabled it to manufacture? Or was Hasbro contractually obligated to pay for that additional quantity?

The answer to these questions depends on whether there was a valid modification of the quantity specifications in the February and April purchase orders (obviously Hasbro cannot complain about the price modification!). The October letter provided that purchase orders could not be modified without Hasbro's written consent. Cloud signed the letter and so became bound by it, consideration being furnished by Hasbro's continuing to do business with Cloud. Hasbro's order acknowledgments accompanying its February and April purchase orders also provided that the orders could not be modified without Hasbro's written consent.

In the case of discrepant order and acceptance forms, if the acceptance merely adds a term, that term binds the offeror . . . this modification of the common law's "mirror image" rule minimizes transaction costs by eliminating a negotiation over the additional term unless the offeror is unwilling to accede to the offeree's desire for it. But what if term added by the acceptance contradicts a term in the offer? Then it doesn't become a part of the contract—that much is clear. But is there a contract, and if so what are its terms? The UCC doesn't say, but the majority rule, and the rule in Illinois, is that the inconsistent terms cancel each other out and the court fills the resulting void with a term of its own devising. In this case, however, there was neither a supplemental nor an inconsistent term in the acceptance; there was *no* term concerning modification, and in such a situation Hasbro's term is enforceable. The offeree's silence is not interpreted as rejection in this situation because transaction costs would again be higher if the offeror had to quiz the offeree on whether every term in the offer not mentioned in the acceptance was acceptable to the offeree. Cloud, the offeree, knew that Hasbro wanted the modification provision and if this was unacceptable it should have said so.

The quantity term in a contract for the sale of goods for more than $500 must be memorialized in a writing signed by the party sought to be held to that term and so must a modification of that term. However—and here we part company with the district judge—Kathy Esposito's e-mails, plus the notation that we quoted earlier signed by Maryann Ricci, another member of Hasbro's purchasing department, satisfy the statutory requirement. The UCC does not require that the contract itself be in writing, only that there be adequate documentary evidence of its existence and essential terms, which there was here . . . between merchants . . . if within a reasonable time a writing in confirmation of the contract and sufficient against the sender is received and the party receiving it has reason to know its contents, it satisfies the requirements of subsection 1 [the statute of frauds] . . . unless written notice of objection to its contents is given within 10 days after it is received." . . . Cloud sent an order acknowledgment, reciting the increased quantity, shortly after the oral modification, and Hasbro did not object within ten days. . . . Cloud could have been more careful. But a failure to insist that every i be dotted and t crossed is not the same thing as being unreasonable. In any event . . . Hasbro did give its written consent to the modification.

REVERSED in favor of Defendant.

CRITICAL THINKING

What evidence does the court use to establish Hasbro's written consent to the modification? How strong is this evidence? Does it indisputably lead to the conclusion reached by the court?

What other conclusions might be possible, and how would different interpretations of the evidence lead to these alternatives?

[CONTINUED]

ETHICAL DECISION MAKING

Can the actions of the parties involved in this dispute be tied to their support of certain values? What values might each side be seeking to protect?

On the basis of the above ruling, what values does the court appear to be interested in preserving? What ethical guideline(s) might have been followed in choosing these values? Support your answer.

Uniform Commercial Code: Requirement and Output Contracts

Rule: *Under UCC Section 2-306, requirement and output contracts are permitted for the sale of goods.*

A **requirement contract** is an agreement whereby the buyer agrees to purchase all his goods from one seller. No quantity is stated in the contract. Under common law, such a contract would be void because the buyer has made no commitment and, therefore, there is no consideration. An **output contract** is an agreement whereby the seller guarantees to sell

Case Nugget Requirement Contracts

Mast Long Term Care v. Forest Hills Rest Home et al.
156 N.C. App. 556 (N.C. Ct. App. 2003)

Mast Long Term Care and Forest Hills Rest Home entered into an agreement whereby the rest home was to buy from Mast all the drugs needed for its patients that were not commonly stocked at the rest home. The rest home argued that the agreement was not a valid contract since it contained vague purchasing terms, obligating it to buy only those drugs not commonly stocked.

At the hearing, Forest Hills Rest Home argued that the vendor-pharmacist agreement between the parties lacked consideration. The agreement did not state any price terms with respect to the pharmaceuticals to be supplied. The court ruled that North Carolina law permitted requirement contracts and that the sale of drugs was governed by the North Carolina Uniform Commercial Code (UCC). Under the UCC, the failure to omit certain material terms did not invalidate the contract, as courts were permitted to read into a contract good-faith requirements. No definite amount needed to be stated in the agreement. Moreover, consideration need not consist of a promise to pay money for goods or services. Instead, it can take the shape of mutual promises to perform some act or to forbear from taking some action.

In this case, the consideration for the parties' agreement consisted of the plaintiff's promise to supply the defendant with certain pharmaceuticals and the defendant's counterpromise to stock the plaintiff's products at its pharmacy and to sell them to its patients. Accordingly, the agreement does not fail for either lack of consideration or lack of specificity.

everything she produces to one buyer. Once again, no quantity is stated, and under common law, there is lack of consideration. Because such contracts are valued by merchants, under the UCC both requirement and output contracts are valid with the limitation that the output or requirement must be made in "good faith." The consideration, then, is that the party act in good faith. Neither party may take advantage of the other party either by requiring more than was expected when the deal was signed or by producing more than was expected when the deal was signed.

Partial Payment of a Debt

Partial payment of a debt may or may not be valid consideration, depending on whether the debt is liquidated or unliquidated. In a **liquidated debt,** there is no dispute about the fact that money is owed and the amount of money owed. Example: Natalie owes $3,000 on her credit card. She calls the credit card company and explains that she is a poor student and cannot afford to pay the entire $3,000. The credit card company agrees to accept $2,000 as payment in full. The following month, Natalie receives her new credit card statement showing that she owes the remaining $1,000. May the credit card company collect the additional $1,000? Yes! A creditor's promise to accept less than owed, when the debtor is already obligated to pay the full amount, is not binding.

The exception to the rule regarding liquidated debt occurs when the debtor offers different performance. Suppose Natalie offered the credit card company her car in full settlement of the $3,000 debt. If the credit card company accepts, regardless of the value of the car, the debt is paid in full and the credit card company may not sue Natalie for any additional money.

In an **unliquidated debt,** the parties either dispute the fact that any money is owed or agree that some money is owed but dispute the amount. A dispute over an unliquidated debt may be settled for less than the full amount if the parties enter into an **accord and satisfaction.** For an accord and satisfaction to be enforceable, three requirements must be met:

1. The debt is unliquidated (i.e., the amount or existence of the debt is in dispute).
2. The creditor agrees to accept as full payment less than the creditor claims is owed.
3. The debtor pays the amount they have agree on.

Under such circumstances, the debt is fully discharged. The *accord* is the new agreement to pay less than the creditor claims is owed. The *satisfaction* is the payment, by the debtor, of the reduced amount. If the debtor fails to pay the new amount, the creditor may then sue for the full amount of the original debt. It pays to keep your word. In the following case, the court had to determine whether there was consideration in an accord and satisfaction.

One way that people sometimes attempt to create an accord and satisfaction is by sending a check to the creditor and writing "paid in full" on the check. Under the common law, in many states this did create an accord and satisfaction, and if the creditor cashed the check, he or she was bound to accept the lesser amount as payment in full. The UCC, however, has changed the scope of this rule. Under UCC Section 3-311, effective in 30 states, the rule remains in place but has two major exceptions.

First, in cases of business organizations, thousands of checks may be received each day. To protect themselves, businesses may notify their debtors that any offer to settle a claim for less than the amount owed must be sent to a particular address and/or person. If you check the terms printed on your credit card statement, you will likely find language directing you to send such payments to a different address and person than regular

Case Nugget Accord and Satisfaction

Thomas v. CitiMortgage, Inc.
2005 U.S. Dist. LEXIS 14641 (Dist. Ct. Ill. 2005)

In November 1979, Thomas assumed a previously existing mortgage, which CitiMortgage now holds. Under the terms of the mortgage, Thomas was required to make a monthly payment on the first day of each month. Beginning in April 1996, Thomas's payments on the mortgage became sporadic. On December 16, 1996, Thomas sent a letter to Lee Hilliard of CitiMortgage, stating that he had sent check 2279 to CitiMortgage on May 22, 1996, but that the check had apparently been lost. In the letter, Thomas also wrote:

> My primary concern is the effect on my credit rating and the fact that I have an application to refinace [*sic*] the mortgage which cannot be finalized, at great cost to me, unless this matter is resolved and my credit cleared up. I have enclosed a check in the amount of the monthly payment on condition that it be applied to tha [*sic*] May payment and that it will allow you to remove the negative material relative to my credit rating. I will put a stop payment on check # 2279, or if it has already been processed somehow, I can be given a credit at the closing of the new mortgage.

CitiMortgage never received or deposited check 2279, but it did cash the check enclosed with the December 16, 1996, letter and credited it to Thomas's account. At CitiMortgage as of 1996, mail was sorted in a central mail room. The persons processing checks lacked the authority either to accept conditions on payments or to change credit reports, as did Hilliard. In his breach-of-contract claim, Thomas asserted that he and CitiMortgage had entered an agreement whereby he would make a payment on his mortgage in exchange for CitiMortgage's agreement to "remove the negative material" from his credit rating. He further claimed that CitiMortgage accepted the contract when it cashed the check he enclosed with the December 16, 1996, letter. Whether Thomas's claim was considered an accord and satisfaction or a simple contract, he could not prevail unless he established that consideration supported the agreement.

Consideration can consist of a promise, an act, or a forbearance. Something one is already legally obligated to do, however, cannot constitute consideration. The pre-existing-duty rule provides that where a party does what it is already legally obligated to do, there is no consideration because there has been no detriment. Thomas claimed that the payment he made with his December 16, 1996, letter constituted consideration for the agreement. As of December 16, 1996, however, Thomas was already two months in arrears on his mortgage payment. He had not made the payments due November 1, 1996, and December 1, 1996. Thus, he was already legally obligated—under the terms of the mortgage—to make the payment he enclosed with the December 16, 1996, letter. Accordingly, that payment could not be consideration for an additional agreement to "remove the negative material" from his credit rating.

payments are sent to. This safeguard protects businesses from inadvertently creating accord and satisfaction agreements. Below is an example:

> *Conditional Payments:* Any payment check or other form of payment that you send us for less than the full balance that is marked "paid in full" or contains a similar notation, or that you otherwise tender in full satisfaction of a disputed amount, must be sent to [address

omitted]. We reserve all rights regarding these payments (e.g., if it is determined that there is no valid dispute or if any such check is received at any other address, we may accept the check and you will still owe any remaining balance).[3]

Second, if a business does inadvertently cash a "paid-in-full" check, the business has 90 days from the date it cashed that check to offer repayment in the same amount to the debtor. For example, if John owed $3,000 to his credit card company and sent the company a $2,000 check marked "paid in full" and mailed to the correct address and person, the credit card company has 90 days to offer to repay John the $2,000. Once the offer has been made by the business, no accord and satisfaction exists.

connecting to the core

Finance

Students usually learn in their finance class that business owners and individuals must pay taxes on income. According to the IRS, whenever a bank or other creditor discharges a loan obligation by accepting a lower amount as full payment of the debt, the difference is income on which the borrower must pay taxes.

For example, if a small business owner borrows $100,000 from a bank but cannot repay the full $100,000, the bank might agree to accept only $80,000 as full payment of the debt. As mentioned in the text, the bank may be entitled to the unpaid $20,000 and could sue for the difference, as the bank received no additional consideration in exchange for its accepting the lower amount. But assuming the bank does not sue and fully intends to accept the $80,000 as full payment of the $100,000 loan, the business owner would then have an obligation to the IRS, namely, recognizing the unpaid $20,000 as taxable income. Because the business owner received $100,000 and repaid only $80,000 for the amount borrowed, the owner is financially in a better position, having $20,000 more than what he had prior to the loan transaction. Consequently, the IRS requires that the business owner report the $20,000 as income, on which he must pay taxes at the applicable rate.

Hence, although a bank may accept a lower amount as full payment of a liquidated debt, the owner would still have an obligation to the IRS to pay taxes on the difference between the amount initially owed to the bank and the amount repaid in full satisfaction of the debt.

CASE OPENER WRAP-UP

Upper Deck

As you know from the Case Opener, Passante sued Upper Deck for breach of oral contract. At trial, the jury awarded him close to $33 million—the value of 3 percent of Upper Deck's stock at the time of the trial in 1993. Upper Deck appealed.

As a matter of law, any claim by Passante for breach of contract is necessarily based on the rule that consideration must result from a bargained-for exchange. In this case, the

[3] From Chase Visa statement.

appellate court held that if the stock promised was truly bargained for, then Passante had an obligation to Upper Deck, as its counsel, to give the firm the opportunity to have separate counsel represent it in the course of that bargaining. The legal profession has certain rules regarding business transactions with clients. Bargaining between the parties might have resulted in Passante's settling for just a reasonable finder's fee.

Passante had already arranged the loan (even though the loan had not been formally accepted by the board) before the idea of giving him stock was ever brought up. There was no evidence that Passante had any expectation that he be given stock in return for arranging the $100,000 loan. All of Passante's services had already been rendered by the time the idea of giving him some stock was proposed. If there was no expectation of payment by either party when the services were rendered, the promise was a mere promise to make a gift and not enforceable. The promise of 3 percent of the stock was simply a gift—that is, an unenforceable promise from a grateful corporate board. It represented a moral obligation but was legally unenforceable.

Summary

Consideration

Consideration is something of value given in exchange for something else of value; it must be the product of a mutually bargained-for exchange.

Rules of Consideration

The key to understanding consideration is understanding the various rules:

- For a promise to be enforced by the courts, there must be consideration.
- *Exception: Promissory estoppel* occurs when one party makes a promise knowing the other party will rely on it, the other party does rely on it, and the only way to avoid injustice is to enforce the promise even though it is not supported by consideration.
- The court seldom considers adequacy of consideration.
- An illusory promise is not consideration.
- Past consideration is no consideration at all.
- A promise to do something that you are already obligated to do is not valid consideration. (This rule is also known as the *preexisting-duty rule.*) Understanding this rule's application is assisted by understanding the difference between a liquidated and an unliquidated debt.

Uniform Commercial Code: Requirement and Output Contracts

A *requirement contract* is an agreement whereby the buyer agrees to purchase all his goods from one seller. No quantity is stated in the contract.

An *output contract* is an agreement whereby the seller guarantees to sell everything she produces to one buyer. Once again, no quantity is stated.

Partial Payment of a Debt

In a *liquidated debt,* there is no dispute about the fact that money is owed and the amount of money owed. In an *unliquidated debt,* the parties either dispute the fact that any money is owed or agree that some money is owed but dispute the amount.

For an *accord and satisfaction* to be enforceable, three requirements must be met: (1) The debt is unliquidated (i.e., the amount or existence of the debt is in dispute); (2) the creditor agrees to accept as full payment less than the creditor claims is owed; and (3) the debtor pays the amount they have agree on. The accord is the agreement, and the satisfaction is the payment.

Point / Counterpoint

Should the Courts Require Consideration to Create a Binding Contract?	
Yes	**No**
The rules of consideration have been established for many years and precedent should be followed. Requiring consideration gives the court a way to distinguish binding promises from nonbinding promises. Without a requirement of consideration, there would be no way to distinguish between a promise made as a gift and a promise made as part of a contract. We have enough exceptions to the rule requiring consideration to make enforcement of the rule fair. For example, if a promise was made and there was expectation of economic benefit, some courts will permit enforcement of the promise under the moral-obligation exception. If we suddenly did not require consideration to create binding contracts, the courts would fill with civil cases of people trying to fulfill all kind of promises.	All promises should be enforced. There is no need to distinguish between binding promises and nonbinding promises if all promises are enforced. If a person makes a promise, the timing of the promise should not make a difference. For example, if Barbara's grandmother promises her $50,000 for "all you have done for me these last five years," why should Barbara be denied the $50,000 because it was based on acts she had done in the past (i.e., past consideration)? The right thing to do, both ethically and morally, would be to enforce this promise whether or not Barbara did the acts with expectation of payment. Under the current exception, if an act was done with expectation of payment, it meets the moral-obligation exception in some states. This exception rewards those who expect something when they do something good and punishes those who do the right thing with no expectation of reward.

Questions & Problems

1. List the four types of consideration described in the text.
2. What is required to prove promissory estoppel when consideration is missing?
3. Can $1 be adequate consideration? Why or why not?
4. List and describe the three exceptions to the preexisting-duty rule.
5. List the three elements of accord and satisfaction.
6. When Holloman applied for a job at Circuit City, she signed a "Dispute Resolution Agreement" (DRA) that stated: "This agreement requires you and Circuit City to arbitrate certain legal disputes related to your application for employment or employment with Circuit City." The job application then added, "Circuit City will consider your application only if this agreement is signed." Finally, the DRA contained this statement: "I understand that my employment, compensation and terms and conditions of employment can be altered or terminated, with or without cause, and with or without notice, at any time, at the option of either Circuit City or myself. "Holloman was hired, but later quit and sued Circuit City, claiming she had been discriminated against

and constructively discharged. Holloman argued that the arbitration agreement was illusory and not supported by consideration because of Circuit City's unilateral ability to terminate or modify the agreement. How should the court rule? Explain your reasoning. [*Holloman v. Circuit City Stores,* 162 Md. App. 332 (Md. Ct. App. 2005).]

7. On October 10, 2000, the Snoebergers transferred 2 acres of realty to their daughter and her husband, the Prendergasts. The only restriction in the deed, recorded the next day, was a denial of the right to maintain a mobile home or scrap yard on the property. The Prendergasts then began construction of a house on the site. On June 19, 2001, a "Memorandum" was executed by the four parties, notarized, and recorded. This memorandum stated, in pertinent part: "The parties agree the following described premises shall not be sold during the life of James Snoeberger and Barbara Snoeberger." On July 22, 2002, the Prendergasts filed a complaint asking the court to declare the memorandum unenforceable. They alleged that they wished to sell the house and property but the Snoebergers were trying to enforce the memorandum to prevent the sale. The question before the court was whether there was consideration to enforce the promise not to sell the premises. How should the court decide? Why? [*Prendergast et al. v James Snoeberger et al.,* 154 Ohio App. 3d 162 (Ohio Ct. App. 2003).]

8. On February 1, 2004, Zhang entered into a contract to buy former realtor Frank Sorichetti's Las Vegas home for $532,500. The contract listed a March closing date and a few household furnishings as part of the sale. On February 3, Sorichetti told Zhang that he was terminating the sale "to stay in the house a little longer" and that Nevada law allows the rescission of real property purchase agreements within three days of contracting. Sorichetti stated that he would sell the home, however, if Zhang paid more money. Zhang agreed. Another contract was drafted, reciting a new sales price, $578,000. This contract added to the included household furnishings drapes that were not listed in the February 1 agreement, and it set an April, rather than March, closing date. The primary issue before the court was whether a real property purchase agreement is enforceable when it is executed by the buyer only because the seller would not perform under an earlier purchase agreement for a lesser price. Should the court enforce the second contract? Why or why not? [*Zhang v. The Eighth Judicial District Court of the State of Nevada,* 103 P.3d 20 (Sup. Ct. Nev. 2004).]

9. Drexel University sued to enforce a pledge agreement executed by Wirth less than two months before his death. The agreement stated that in consideration of the decedent's interest in education, and "intending to be legally bound," the decedent "irrevocably pledged and promised to pay" Drexel the sum of $150,000. The pledge agreement, which also was executed by representatives of Drexel, provided that the pledged sum "shall be used by" Drexel to create an endowed scholarship fund in the decedent's name, "per the terms of the attached Letter of Understanding." The letter of understanding, which also was executed by the decedent and representatives of Drexel, provided, inter alia, that the scholarship fund would become effective immediately on the transfer of the initial $50,000, which was to take place on or before December 31, 2000. The pledge agreement further stated: "I acknowledge that [Drexel's] promise to use the amount pledged by me shall constitute full and adequate consideration for this pledge." Was there consideration for the agreement? Explain your decision. [*Drexel University v. Wirth,* 14 A.D.3d 572 (Sup. Ct. N.Y. 2003).]

10. Five employees of American Electric Power (AEP) Service Corp. invented a new product. "In consideration of the sum of One Dollar (1.00), and of other good and valuable consideration paid to the undersigned Assignor," each employee signed an agreement giving AEP exclusive patent rights to the invention. Some of the employees sued, alleging that there was no contract because AEP never paid the one dollar. How do you think the court ruled? Explain your reasoning. [*Bennett et al. v. American Electric Power Service Corporation,* 2001 Ohio App. LEXIS 4357 (Ohio Ct. App. 2001).]

11. Between 1993 and 2002, defendant Apex Media Sales (AMS), Inc., was plaintiff Adell Broadcasting's exclusive media representative for national religious and secular broadcast spot and program sales. Several months before the parties ended their relationship, Kevin Adell, the plaintiff's president, expressed dissatisfaction with the representation by AMS. He believed that the AMS sales staff was not selling available air time for full value and that AMS's personnel, including its president, defendant Dennis Hart, were not available and responsive to the plaintiff's needs. AMS and Hart were also dissatisfied with the relationship because the plaintiff owed them outstanding commission payments. On February 26, 2002, the parties amended their agreement in an attempt to save the relationship. The parties agreed that the plaintiff owed $568,461 in commissions but that AMS would consider an immediate payment of $370,000 as full satisfaction of all commissions owed through December 2001. The parties also agreed that the commission rate for AMS would decrease from 15 to 10 percent, that there would be a 30-day termination provision to end the business relationship, and that Adell Broadcasting would pay commissions to AMS on 30-day terms. The parties thereafter continued dealing with each other, but their problems did not abate. In April 2002, they severed the relationship. The plaintiff filed suit against AMS and Hart, alleging several causes of action. The defendants filed a counter-complaint seeking, among other things, rescission of the amended agreement. The plaintiff sought partial summary disposition on that claim, arguing that the defendants were barred from seeking rescission because they did not tender back the $370,000. On appeal, the court had to decide whether there was consideration for the amended agreement. How would you decide? Why? [*Adell Broadcasting Corp. et al. v. Apex Media Sales, Inc., et al.,* 708 N.W.2d 778 (2005).]

12. Arnone sued Deutsche Bank for a breach of oral contract after his termination from employment at the bank. Arnone claims that the bank refused to pay him a bonus for securing certain business for the bank, "despite the promises and assurances" of his supervisors that he had earned the bonus and that it would be paid to him in the amount of $825,000. Arnone led a formal presentation in September 1998 on behalf of the bank to bid for a potentially lucrative investment management appointment. By December 1998, the bank was awarded an account worth approximately $9 billion. In early December 1998, Arnone confirmed with his supervisor his expectation of a bonus of at least $800,000 based on the $9 billion in business brought into the bank. The bank ultimately was forced to forgo the account, due to no fault of Arnone. Arnone, however, maintains that the bank made a separate and distinct promise to pay him a bonus as if the business had been retained. He and his supervisors had several conversations regarding his bonus after the bank resigned from the account. According to Arnone, his supervisor said to him, "You know, Jerry, we're going to pay you as if the . . . business came in." Should the court enforce the supervisor's promise? Why or why not? [*Arnone v. Deutsche Bank et al.,* 2003 U.S. Dist. LEXIS 7941 (Dist. Ct. N.Y. 2003).]

13. ASAL Products, Inc., an office supply wholesaler, sued appellant, Office Pavilion, an office supply company, for breach of a contract to supply chairs. Office Pavilion contended that the contract was unenforceable because it was not supported by consideration and was indefinite. The parties agreed that the purpose of entering into this agreement was for Pavilion to supply and ASAL to purchase from Pavilion products known as keyboard trays and accessories for those keyboard trays. ASAL agreed to order a minimum of 1,000 units per year. Pavilion agreed to supply ASAL with up to a maximum of 2,000 units per month plus the accessories for the ordered units. Approximately a month after the contract was signed, ASAL became interested in expanding its contract to include Herman Miller's Aeron chair, and ASAL commenced negotiations with Kemp, ASAL's sales manager, for this modification. While these negotiations were proceeding, ASAL marketed the chair in January and February, in addition to the keyboard tray, to determine demand for the chair. On March 11, 1999, Kemp forwarded ASAL a letter regarding amending the parties' contract for the keyboard trays to include the Aeron chairs. After the letter regarding the chairs was sent, ASAL purchased six chairs from Pavilion to display at a trade show in Germany. The show was such a success that ASAL immediately reevaluated its sales forecast and requested a meeting with Kemp, ASAL wanted 2,450 chairs to cover sales orders from the show plus 30 chairs to use as samples. However, while ASAL wanted the chairs, it did not include a deposit with its order or specify model numbers for the chairs. Kemp replied that it could not fill the order. ASAL filed a breach-of-contract action, claiming as damages its lost profits for all expected sales under the contract for its two-year duration. While Pavilion admitted the existence of the keyboard contract, it defended against the much larger chair contract, contending that the agreement lacked consideration. Was there consideration for the modification? Why or why not? [*Office Pavilion South Florida, Inc., v. ASAL Products, Inc.,* 849 So. 2d 367 (2003).]

14. In February 2000, CNS International Ministries, Inc., signed a contract with Eiman Brothers Roofing Systems. Under the contract, Eiman would provide CNS with a clay tile roof for one of its properties. Based on the size of the roof provided in CNS's plans, the total amount of the contract was $52,731. In May 2000, Eiman realized that the plan provided by CNS underestimated the roof's actual size, requiring an additional 20 to 25 squares. Eiman, demanding a second contract, recalculated and rebid the project. In May 2000, CNS signed a contract modification proposal sent by Eiman, adding $23,000 in costs. With the work substantially complete, CNS noted problems in Eiman's performance and its alleged failure to deliver on assurances to correct those problems. Consequently, CNS ordered Eiman to stop working on the roof. Eiman then brought a breach-of-contract action. At the time of the alleged breach, CNS had paid a total of $29,000 on the contract. CNS claimed that the contract was unenforceable for lack of consideration, in that Eiman had a preexisting duty to CNS. Specifically, CNS argued that the May 2000 proposal called for Eiman to perform in exactly the same manner as specified in the original contract. Did Eiman have a preexisting duty to CNS? Why or why not? [*Eiman Brothers Roofing Systems, Inc. v. CNS International Ministries, Inc.,* 158 S.W.3d 920 (2005).]

Looking for more review material?

The Online Learning Center at **www.mhhe.com/kubasek1e** contains this chapter's "Assignment on the Internet" and also a list of URLs for more information, entitled "On the Internet." Find both of them in the Student Center portion of the OLC, along with quizzes and other helpful materials.

Capacity and Legality

CASE OPENER

A Wasted Education

Ten months before he attained the age of majority, John Adamowski paid for and received a course in elementary aviation from Curtiss-Wright Flying Service. Five months later, he purchased and received a limited commercial pilot's course from the same company. Two months after receiving the commercial pilot's license, he entered into a contract with Curtiss-Wright for an advanced course of instruction to become a transport pilot, but he withdrew from the course within the month and paid nothing.

Six months after reaching the age of majority, Adamowski received a bill from Curtiss-Wright for the balance due on his course. He visited Curtiss-Wright's attorney and denied liability but said nothing about disaffirmance. He took no further action until a few days shy of a year from the date on which he had attained the age of majority. At that time, he filed suit against Curtiss-Wright, seeking to disaffirm his contracts for the aviation courses and recover the money he had paid for them on grounds that he had entered into the contracts as a minor and thus had the right to disaffirm them and receive back what he had given up under the contracts. Curtiss-Wright argued that the courses were necessaries and, as such, that Adamowski was not entitled to disaffirm the contracts for them.[1]

1. Were the contracts for necessaries and, as such, not subject to being disaffirmed?
2. Even if the plaintiff had the right to disaffirm the contracts, was almost a year too long to wait to disaffirm them?

The Wrap-Up at the end of the chapter will answer these questions.

[1] *John P. Adamowski v. The Curtiss-Wright Flying Service, Inc.*, 300 Mass. 281, 15 N.E.2d 467, 1938 Mass. LEXIS 942.

CHAPTER 16

Learning Objectives

After reading this chapter, you will be able to answer the following questions:

1. Under what circumstances would a party have limited capacity to enter into a contract?
2. What is the legal effect of a lack of capacity on a person's ability to enter into a contract?
3. What is the legal effect of entering into a contract for an illegal purpose?

Capacity

Capacity is the third element of a legally binding contract. A person who has legal capacity to contract is one who has the mental ability to understand his or her rights and obligations under a contract and therefore will presumably be able to understand how to comply with the terms of the agreement. *Incapacity,* or *incompetence,* as it is sometimes called, is some sort of mental or physical defect that prevents a natural person from being able to enter into a legally binding contract. Depending on the nature and extent of the defect, a person may have either no capacity, therefore voiding any attempted contract, or limited capacity, resulting in the ability to form only voidable contracts.

Historically, people with limited or no capacity included married women, minors, and insane persons. Other categories were added by statutes, such as people for whom guardians had been appointed, including habitual drunkards, narcotic addicts, spendthrifts, the elderly, and convicts. Today, married women have been removed from the category of those lacking contractual capacity, although in a few states their capacity to enter into certain kinds of contracts is still limited. In this section of the chapter, we explain the current law limiting the capacity of some categories of persons to enter into legally binding agreements.

MINORS

One of the oldest limitations on capacity is the ability of minors to enter into only voidable contracts. Today, in all but three states, a minor is someone under the age of 18.[2] In most states, however, a person is given full legal capacity to enter into contracts when he or she becomes emancipated before reaching the age of majority. *Emancipation* occurs when a minor's parents or legal guardians give up their right to exercise legal control over the minor, typically when the minor moves out of the parents' house and begins supporting himself or herself. Often the minor will petition the court for a declaration of emancipation. In most cases, when a minor marries, she or he is considered emancipated.

Disaffirmance of the contract. Because their contracts are voidable, minors have the right, until a reasonable time after reaching the age of majority, to disaffirm or void their contracts. Note that it is only the minor who has the right to disaffirm, never the adult with whom the minor entered into the agreement. There are no formalities required to disaffirm the contract; the minor need only manifest an intention to rescind the contract, either by words or by actions. However, the minor must avoid the entire contract; he or she cannot choose to disaffirm only a portion of it.

The obligations of the minor on disaffirmance vary from state to state. Traditionally, most states simply required the minor to notify the competent party of the intent to disaffirm and to return to the competent party any consideration received under the contract that was still under the minor's control, regardless of the condition of the consideration. If the consideration has been destroyed or damaged, the minor returns whatever is left of it, and the other party has no recourse against the minor under most circumstances. For instance, if William, a minor, purchased a stereo receiver from Sound Systems, Inc., under a six-month contract and dropped it a week after he took it home, he could return it to the store in its broken condition and tell the owner that he wished to rescind the contract. He would be entitled to the return of his down payment and would owe no further obligations to the store.

[2] In Alabama, Nebraska, and Wyoming, full capacity to contract does not arise until the person reaches the age of 19, which is the age of majority in those states. In Mississippi, the age of majority is still 21.

global context

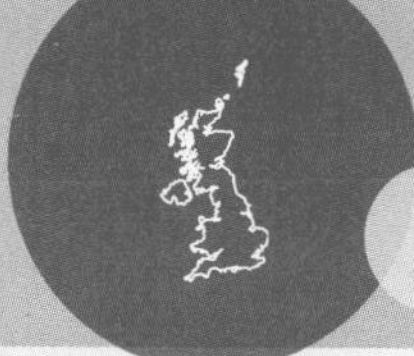

The Age of Majority in Great Britain

People in the United States take the idea of an "age of majority" for granted. The only debate seems to be over whether that age should be 18, 19, or 21. Yet in Great Britain there is no magical age at which a young person suddenly acquires the legal capacity to enter into a contract. British courts will not enforce contracts with immature minors. However, the determination of whether a person is too immature to enter into a contract is made on a case-by-case basis. If a person under the age of 18 is considered by the courts to be able to look out for his or her own interests, then the contract will be enforced. If not, the contract will be void. In determining whether the young person was mature enough to enter into the contract, a key factor is often the fairness of the agreement. The assumption is that if the agreement is one-sided and favors the adult, the young person probably lacked the maturity to enter into the contract.

Such a rule makes sense if you view minors as innocents in need of protection from competent adults who would otherwise take advantage of them. However, the rule is not going to encourage competent parties to enter into contracts with minors, and some argue that it allows a knowledgeable and unethical minor to take advantage of a competent party. Consequently, a number of states have modified the duty of the minor on disaffirmance, holding that the minor has a duty of restitution that requires that she or he place the competent party back in the position that party was in at the time that the contract was made. Thus, continuing with the receiver example, in some states, William would have a duty of restoration that would require that he compensate the store owner for the difference between the value of the receiver in the condition it was in when given to William and its value in the condition it was in when returned. Case 16-1 illustrates the application of the majority rule for return of consideration on disaffirmance.

CASE 16-1

SWALBERG v. HANNEGAN
UTAH COURT OF APPEALS
883 P.2D 931 (UTAH APP. 1994)

The parties entered into a contract for the sale and purchase of the automobile. The minor's age was not discussed and there was no allegation that the minor misrepresented his age. The minor made a down payment and promised to pay the remaining balance three months later. Thereafter, the minor disaffirmed the contract on the basis of his minority. The seller filed the complaint asking for enforcement of the contract or to be put back into his pre-contractual state. The seller argued that the minor did not properly restore the automobile under Utah Code Ann. § 15-2-2 (1986) because it was returned in a condition that was worth substantially less than the purchase price. The trial court awarded a sum to the seller representing the remaining balance owed minus the value of the automobile when it was returned. The plaintiff appealed.

JUDGE BENCH: The dispositive issue on appeal is whether a minor who disaffirms a contract is required to restore the full value of the property received under the contract. Defendant argues that Utah law does not require a disaffirming minor to restore the other party to his or her precontractual status.

Utah Code Ann. § 15-2-2 (1986) provides:

> A minor is bound not only for the reasonable value of necessities but also for his contracts, unless he disaffirms them before or within a reasonable time after he obtains his majority and restores to the other party all money or property received by him by virtue of said contracts and remaining within his control at any time after attaining his majority.

. . . This statute requires only that the property remaining within the minor's control be returned to the other party. The trial court held, however, that defendant was required to return the property in its original condition or be liable for the difference in value. This holding is clearly contrary to the provisions of this unamended nineteenth century statute, as interpreted by controlling Utah case law.

In Blake v. Harding . . . , a minor sold a pony, harness, and buggy to an adult at an agreed value of $150, for which the adult delivered 3,000 shares of stock in a mining company. The minor later disaffirmed the contract and returned the stock to the adult. The minor sued to recover $150 since the adult had sold the pony, harness, and buggy. The jury was instructed that "if you believe that the contract in evidence was fair and reasonable, and was free from any fraud or bad faith on the part of the [adult], and if you further find that the mining stock traded to the [minor] by the [adult] is now worthless, the [minor] is not entitled to recover in this action." A jury returned a verdict in favor of the adult. The Utah Supreme Court reversed the verdict and held that the jury instruction was in "direct conflict with our statute." The Supreme Court stated that this jury instruction would require the minor to place the adult in his precontractual status, which would "disregard and misapply the purpose of the law. The law is intended for the benefit and protection of the minor; and hence an adult, in dealing with a minor, assumes all the risk of loss." Id.

Further, in Harvey v. Hadfield, . . . (1962), a minor contracted with an adult to buy a house-trailer. The minor paid $1,000 as a down payment without selecting a trailer. The minor later disaffirmed the contract, requesting the return of his money. When the adult refused to return the money, the minor brought an action against the adult. . . . The supreme court stated that section 15-2-2 "cannot be tortured to support the adult's contention that the disaffirming minor must compensate the adult for damages the adult may have incurred" so long as the property is returned to the adult.

In view of these Utah cases interpreting the language of section 15-2-2, the trial court erred in requiring defendant to restore plaintiff to his precontractual status. . . .

Section 15-2-2 requires that a disaffirming minor must only return the property remaining within his or her control. The Utah Supreme Court has interpreted this statute to allow a minor to effectively disaffirm the underlying contract without restoring the full value of the property received under the contract. Although we do not necessarily believe in the wisdom of this approach, we are not in a position to hold contrary to controlling case law under the doctrine of stare decisis. If a contracting and disaffirming minor is to be held responsible for waste of property received under a contract, it is for the legislature to so provide. Alternatively, the Supreme Court might . . . overrule existing case law.

REVERSED in favor of defendant.

CRITICAL THINKING

How does the explicitly stated reliance on legal precedent affect the acceptability of the reasoning of this ruling? Is the conclusion reached the result of fair consideration of all available evidence? What issues are raised by this question regarding the workings of the U.S. legal system at large? How do you think these problems would best be resolved?

ETHICAL DECISION MAKING

Does this decision maintain an awareness of the interests of all relevant stakeholders? Are these interests properly weighted? Does any party receive unequal or unjustified treatment? Why or why not?

Can a larger purpose be deciphered from the ruling of the court in this case? Does Judge Bench appear to be acting out of any value preferences?

The disaffirmance must occur before or within a reasonable time of the minor's reaching the age of majority. What constitutes a reasonable time is determined on a case-by-case basis. For example, in the situation described in the opening scenario, the court found that it was not unreasonable for the defendant to disaffirm his contract almost a year after attaining the age of majority. In deciding to allow the disaffirmance, the court explained that the contracts were wholly executed and that there was no evidence that an earlier disaffirmance would have benefited the defendant or saved it from any harm. The court further noted that the plaintiff had made no use of his education in aviation, which had been of no apparent benefit to him. Under such circumstances, the court felt that a year was a reasonable time period within which to disaffirm a contract.

Exceptions to the minor's right to disaffirm the contract. The minor's right to disaffirm is designed to protect the minor from competent parties that might otherwise take advantage of him or her. But there are certain situations in which, primarily for public policy reasons, either the courts or state legislatures have determined that the minor should not have the right to disaffirm the contract. As a general rule, most states will not allow a minor to disaffirm contracts for life insurance, health insurance, psychological counseling, the performance of duties related to stock and bond transfers and bank accounts, education loan contracts, child support contracts, marriage contracts, and contracts to enlist in the armed services.

Most of these exceptions apply in most, but not all, states. Another issue on which the states disagree is the minor's misrepresentation of his or her age. While the majority rule is that misrepresentation does not affect the minor's right to disaffirm the contract, some states hold that when a minor who appears to be of the age of majority misrepresents his or her age and a competent party relies on that misrepresentation in good faith, the minor gives up the right to disaffirm the agreement. Thus, a minor who misrepresents his age in those states is treated as an adult. One justification for this rule is that any minor who is going to misrepresent his or her age does not need the protection that disaffirmance is designed to provide.

Other states have found a compromise between the two extreme positions either by requiring that the minor restore the competent party to that party's precontract position before allowing the disaffirmance or by allowing the minor to disaffirm but then giving the competent party the right to sue the minor in tort and recover damages for fraud.

Liability of minors for necessaries. Contracts for necessaries are sometimes considered an exception to the rule that minors can disaffirm their contracts. Technically, however, the minor can disaffirm contracts for necessaries. However, the minor will still be held liable for the reasonable value of the necessary. The purpose of this limitation on the minor's right to disaffirm contracts for necessaries is to ensure that minors are able to obtain the basic necessities of life when their parents will not provide them.

A *contract for a necessary* is a contract that supplies the minor with the basic necessities of life, generally thought of as food, clothing, shelter, and basic medical services. It is sometimes difficult, however, to determine whether something is in fact a necessary. Some courts define a necessary as what is needed for the minor to maintain his or her standard of living and financial and social status, but this can lead to a problem when an item that may be considered a necessary for a child of upper-income parents might be considered a luxury to a child of lower-income parents.

Whether an item is considered a necessary is also related to whether the minor's parents are willing to provide the item in question for the minor. For example, while shelter is clearly a necessary, Case 16-2 demonstrates that even rent for an apartment may not be considered a necessary.

connecting to the core

Marketing

Although minors may lack the capacity to enter certain legally binding contracts, this lack of capacity has not deterred companies from heavily marketing their products to minors. Marketing experts understand very well the impact that sociocultural influences, such as family relationships, can have on consumer behavior. For instance, some research suggests that children develop strong brand preferences at age two, frequently maintaining these preferences for decades.

In response to such findings, some companies have been marketing products specifically for young children. Sony, for example, introduced "My First Sony" to children, hoping that this type of audio equipment would affect the children's purchasing decisions when they reached the age of majority. In addition, brand preferences in children may influence purchasing decisions of parents. According to one study, children under the age of 12 annually influence more than $300 billion in family purchases, and teenagers are responsible for influencing about $500 billion in family purchases, spending $175 million of their own money. On the basis of these large figures, perhaps it comes as little surprise that companies spend approximately $32 billion every year to reach preteens and teens, even if some of these children do not possess the capacity to make many of the purchases themselves.

Source: R. Kerin, S. Hartley, E. Berkowitz, and W. Rudelius, *Marketing* (New York: McGraw-Hill/Irwin, 2005), pp. 136–138 (citing "Get 'Em While They're Young," *Marketing News,* November 10, 1997, p. 2; and "Kids Gaining Voice in How Home Looks," *Advertising Age,* March 29, 2004, p. S4).

CASE 16-2

KIM YOUNG v. PHILLIP WEAVER
COURT OF APPEALS OF ALABAMA
883 SO. 2D 234 (ALA. CIV. APP. 2003)

Eighteen year old Kim Young, who had a full-time job, had been living with her parents all of her life, and decided she wanted to move out. She and a friend, who was also a minor, signed a contract for the lease of an apartment with Weaver. No adult signed the lease as a guarantor. Ms. Young paid a security deposit and entered a lease set to expire about 10 months later. Her parents did not want her to move out, and kept her room waiting at their home so that she could return at any time. Ms. Young lived in the apartment for approximately two months before returning to live with her parents. She stopped paying the apartment rent. The landlord sued her for her share of the rent still owed. The trial court entered a judgment for the landlord, and Ms. Young appealed.*

JUDGE MURDOCK: . . . Determining whether the subject of a contract is a necessity to a minor entails a two-step analysis:

. . . [F]irst a court must determine whether the subject of the contract is generally considered a necessity. If the subject is so considered, then it is for the fact-finder to determine, on the particular facts and circumstances of the case, whether the subject of the contract is, in fact, a necessity to that minor. The first inquiry is a question of law; the second inquiry entails a factual determination.

There is little question that, in general, lodging is considered a necessity. . . . [T]ypical necessities include "things for bodily need—food, support and maintenance, clothing, medicine and medical attention, and lodging." Thus, the question in this case is whether the trial court erred in concluding as a factual matter that the apartment leased by Young was a necessity for her.

. . . Young contends that the apartment was not a necessity to her because, she argues, her parents did not "kick" her out of their house and they kept her room waiting so that she could return to their home at any time. Young's father testified that every time he talked to his daughter on the telephone while she lived in the apartment he asked her to move back in with them; he also testified that he was willing to take Young back at any time. In essence, because Young's parents were able

* Nineteen is the age of majority in Alabama.

and willing to house Young at the same time she contracted to lease the apartment, Young argues that in this case the particular lodging at issue was not a necessity.

In support of this contention, Young cites Harris v. Raughton, a case in which:

> Bremman R. Raughton, a minor, bought an automobile from the appellants. He paid $90 cash as the down payment. . . . [T]he car would not operate satisfactorily, so about two days after the sale he returned it to the appellants and demanded a refund of the initial payment. This was refused, and the automobile was left at appellants' place of business.

Raughton sued Harris and the other appellants to recover his down payment. The evidence showed that Raughton was married and had bought the automobile to use as transportation to and from his place of employment. However, the evidence also showed that Raughton already owned a truck that he had been using for the same purpose and that he had not disposed of at the time he purchased the new automobile. The court determined that, because Raughton had another vehicle available to him, the automobile in question was not a necessity, and thus, Raughton was at liberty to void the contract for the purchase of the automobile.

By analogy, Young argues that because she had a place to live provided by her parents still available to her at the time she signed the lease agreement and during the time she lived in the apartment, the apartment was not a necessity. In other words, she argues that the apartment was not "necessary to [Young's] position and condition as a minor" at the time she signed the lease.

Several authorities from other states support this position, in situations which involved facts similar to those in this case. . . . "To enable an infant to contract for articles as necessaries, he must have been in actual need of them, and obliged to procure them for himself. They are not necessaries as to him, however necessary they may be in their nature, if he was already supplied with sufficient articles of the kind, or if he had a parent or guardian who was able and willing to supply them."

Given the authorities cited above and the particular facts of this case, we conclude that the trial court erred in its determination that the apartment in question was a necessity for Young. Therefore, as a minor, Young is not legally bound under the lease agreement. . . .

The above rule may, at times, work a hardship. The law must, however, have a definite policy, and its rules must be fixed. The law has fixed its policy with reference to the protection of infants with regard to their contracts, and those who deal with them, except when actually supplying them with necessaries, deal with them at their peril.

OVERRULED in favor of Defendant.

CRITICAL THINKING

What critical thinking concerns raised by this case are similar to those produced by Case16-1? How is this example different? Can any common statements be made about the reasoning used in these two decisions?

How does this ruling hinge on the definition of key terms? What are the relevant words or phrases, and are they inherently ambiguous? If so, do you think the court selected the best possible definition? Why or why not? What other definitions are possible? How could the use of one of these alternatives affect the acceptability of the conclusion?

ETHICAL DECISION MAKING

What sort of stance on ethical issues is reflected by this decision, as made especially clear by the final paragraph? How does this represent a desirable approach to ethics in legal reasoning? What might its drawbacks be? Can you come up with a more ethically defensible way to look at these sorts of questions? If so, what does your approach entail, and if not, why is the stance taken by the court best for these situations?

One of the issues raised in the opening scenario was whether the classes constituted a necessity. The court found that, given the defendant's social class, it would be difficult to find that instruction in aviation was really a necessary. Although perhaps some forms of education might constitute a necessary under certain circumstances, the defendant's circumstances did not merit such a finding.

Ratification. Once a person reaches the age of majority, he or she may ratify, or legally affirm, contracts made as a minor. Once ratified, the contract is no longer voidable. Ratification may be either express or implied.

An *express ratification* occurs when, after reaching the age of majority, the person states, either orally or in writing, that he or she intends to be bound by the contract entered into as a minor. For example, when she is 17, Marcy enters into an agreement to purchase an automobile from Sam for 10 monthly payments of $1,000. After making the fifth payment, Marcy turns 18 and decides to move out of state. She e-mails Sam and tells him not to worry because even though she is moving, she still intends to make her monthly payments to purchase the car. She has expressly ratified the contract.

An *implied ratification* occurs when the former minor takes some action after reaching the age of majority that is consistent with intent to ratify the contract. Going back to the previous example, if the day after she turns 18, Marcy enters into an agreement with Joe to sell him the car in six months, that action is obviously consistent with intent to finish purchasing the car, so she has impliedly ratified the contract. Most courts find that continuing to act in accordance with the contract, such as continuing to make regular payments under a contract after reaching the age of majority, constitutes ratification. For instance, if Marcy continued using the car and making payments on it for several months after reaching the age of majority, the courts would probably find that she had ratified the contract.

Parents' liability for their children's contracts, necessaries, and torts. As a general rule, parents are not liable for contracts entered into by their minor children. Because of this rule, merchants are often reluctant to enter into contracts with minors unless some competent person is willing to agree to cosign the contract. In that way, the competent person will be legally bound to perform the obligations undertaken by the minor if the minor no longer wishes to live up to the terms of the contract.

Parents do, however, have a legal duty to provide their children with the basic necessities of life, such as food, clothing, and shelter. Thus, they may be held liable in some states for the reasonable value of necessaries for which their children enter into contracts.

In most states, parents are not liable for the torts of their minor children; minors are liable for their own personal torts. In many states, however, parents may be liable in cases where a child causes harm because the parent failed to properly supervise the child, thereby subjecting others to an unreasonable risk of harm from the child.

MENTALLY INCAPACITATED PERSONS

Persons suffering from a mental illness or deficiency may have full, limited, or no legal capacity to enter into a binding contract, depending on the nature and extent of their mental deficiency. If a person suffers from mental problems yet still understands the nature of the contract and the obligations imposed by it, then the person may enter into a binding, legal agreement. Suppose, for example, that Gina suffers from the delusion that she is a rock star. When an encyclopedia salesperson comes to her door, she buys a set of encyclopedias from him because she believes that it is important that she be knowledgeable to set a good example for her fans. As long as she understands that she is binding herself through a contract to make monthly payments for two years to pay for the encyclopedias, then she is bound to the contract. If, after making a year of payments, she no longer suffers from her delusions and wishes to disaffirm the contract, she will not be able to do so because her delusions did not affect her understanding of what she was legally agreeing to do.

However, a person has only limited capacity to enter into a contract if she suffers from a mental illness or deficiency that prevents her from understanding the nature and obligations of the transaction she is entering into. If, in the above scenario, Gina's delusions prevented her from understanding that she was signing a contract and she thought she was giving the salesperson her autograph when she signed the contract, the contract is voidable. She may disaffirm it at any time until a reasonable time after she no longer suffers from the mental deficiency. Once the mental deficiency has been removed, she may also choose to ratify the contract.

As with contracts of minors, a contract of a person suffering from a mental deficiency that is for necessaries can be enforced for the reasonable value of the necessary.

If a person's mental deficiencies have resulted in his being adjudicated insane and a guardian has been appointed for him, he has no capacity to enter into contracts and any contract he attempts to enter into is void. Guardians may be appointed not only for those who are adjudicated insane but also for those who are adjudicated habitual drunkards and those whose judgment has been impaired because of a condition such as Alzheimer's. In any case, although the person for whom the guardian has been appointed no longer has the legal capacity to enter into contracts, the guardian has the legal capacity to enter into contracts on that person's behalf.

INTOXICATED PERSONS

For purposes of determining capacity, intoxicated persons include those under the influence of alcohol or drugs. There is some variation among states in the treatment of the capacity of intoxicated persons to enter into contracts. As a general rule, most states follow the Restatement of Contracts, Section 16, which provides that contracts of an intoxicated person are voidable if the other party had reason to know that because of the intoxicated person's condition, that person was unable to understand the nature and consequences of the transaction or is unable to act in a reasonable manner in relation to the transaction. If the intoxication merely causes someone to exercise poor judgment, the person's capacity to enter into a legally binding contract is not affected unless the other party unfairly capitalizes on this impaired judgment.

Likewise, if one party had no way of knowing that the other was intoxicated at the time the agreement was made, and the agreement is a fair one, it will be upheld by most courts. For example, Lisa e-mails Rob and offers to buy his antique car from him for $8,000. Rob has just broken up with his girlfriend and has been drinking nonstop all day. He gets the e-mail message and immediately responds in the affirmative. Lisa had no way of knowing Rob was intoxicated, and so they would have a valid contract in most states.

Once sober, the previously intoxicated person has the ability to either ratify or disaffirm the contract. Because public policy does not favor intoxication, the courts tend to not be sympathetic to intoxicated parties and will fairly liberally interpret behavior that seems like ratification as ratifying the contract. If Jim became intoxicated at a bar one evening, and Randi took advantage of the situation by getting him to sign a contract to sell her his 2004 SUV for $8,000, any act Jim takes consistent with ratification after becoming sober will result in a binding contract. If Randi appears at his house the next morning with the cash, shows him the contract drafted on a napkin that he signed, and asks for the keys and the title, then by giving her the keys and saying, "I knew I shouldn't have drunk that much," Jim has entered into a binding contract.

If the contract is disaffirmed on the basis of intoxication, each party to the contract must return the other to the condition he or she was in at the time the contract was entered into. Also, as with contracts of other persons who have limited capacity, a contract of an intoxicated person for necessaries will be enforced for the reasonable value of the necessaries.

Legality

To be enforceable, contracts must have legal subject matter and must be able to be performed legally. They cannot violate either state or federal law. When a contract is overturned due to having illegal subject matter or being illegal to perform, the attempted contract is generally declared void.

To be considered an illegal contract, a contract need not be in violation of a statute. When contracts are against generally accepted public policy, these agreements are determined to be illegal and therefore unenforceable. Agreements are ruled illegal or unenforceable for two main reasons: First, doing so openly states that agreements of the kind deemed unenforceable are undesirable in our society, and, second, doing so prevents the legal system's being used to promote agreements against society.

CONTRACTS THAT VIOLATE STATE OR FEDERAL STATUTES

As previously stated, certain agreements are illegal because either the subject matter or the performance of the agreement violates a state or federal statute. Given the various state and federal statutes, there are a large number of possible ways in which contracts can violate a statute. Some of the more common ways are discussed below.

Agreements to commit a crime or tort. Again, contracts cannot be for illegal purposes or require illegal acts for performance. Therefore, any agreement to commit a crime or tort is illegal and unenforceable. However, should a legal contract be formed and the subject of the contract then becomes illegal under a new statute, the contract is considered to be discharged by law. For example, Jim agrees to paint Heather's house green. After Jim and Heather enter into their agreement, the town government passes a law saying nonbrick houses cannot be any color other than white, blue, or gray. Because it would now be illegal for Jim to paint Heather's house green, the contract is discharged by law. While the example is silly, sometimes laws are passed that render the subject of a contract illegal.

Licensing statutes. All 50 states have statutes requiring that people working in certain professions obtain a license before practicing their craft. For example, doctors of all varieties, plumbers, cosmetologists, lawyers, electricians, teachers, and stockbrokers are all required to obtain a license before practicing. While this list of professions is far from exhaustive, it demonstrates how widespread the licensing requirement can be in various states.

When licensing is required by law, people in certain fields must obtain a license before they can legally enter into an agreement to perform the restricted service. Frequently, such licenses can be obtained only after extensive schooling or training. The requirement of schooling and licensing demonstrates the concern society places on proper performance of duties in the designated professions.

Licensing statutes have two main purposes in addition to indicating concern with proper performance. The first is to give the government an avenue by which to regulate the specific industries. By requiring that professionals obtain a license, the government has some control over who can perform which jobs, as well as how many people can perform these jobs. Furthermore, by charging for licenses, the government can regulate an industry. When licensing preconditions are established to advance public purposes, they thereby create incentives for improved public performance. However, in certain situations, it would seem that the main reason for licensing a specific group is to obtain additional revenue.

The second main purpose of licensing statutes, the protection of the public's health, safety, and welfare, is more closely related to the public interest. By imposing legal standards on a profession, the government is attempting to prevent people from being harmed due to substandard work. For example, surgery is a delicate, complicated process. It is not in the public's best interest to allow an unqualified person to perform surgery. Therefore, to limit the number of people who might be harmed during surgery, the government steps in and requires that prospective surgeons, even after extensive schooling, obtain a license.

Given the different reasons for licensing various professionals, there are different outcomes when someone enters into an agreement with a person who is unlawfully unlicensed. The state in which the unlicensed person is practicing is relevant because many licensing statutes occur at the state level and thus vary from state to state. For example, in some states, the statutes set out "no license, no contract." These states will not enforce any agreement with an unlawfully unlicensed professional.

However, in states that do not explicitly bar the enforcement of all contracts with unlicensed professionals, the courts typically consider the profession in question and examine why professionals in that field are required to be licensed. If the purpose of licensing is to provide government control over the profession, most states allow enforcement of the contract. Although the unlicensed professional is acting in violation of the law, there are no grave reasons that the contract should not be carried out. Nonetheless, because the professional is in violation of the law, he or she is usually required to pay a fine for working without the necessary license.

Conversely, if the licensing statute is intended to protect the public's health, safety, and welfare, the agreement is typically deemed illegal and unenforceable. Licensing statutes do not protect the public if people without the necessary licenses are allowed to practice the restricted professions. Returning to the example of the surgeon, the public would not be made safer if the government allowed unlicensed people to perform surgery. Therefore, a person cannot enter into a contract for professional service with an unlicensed professional when the law requires a license out of intent to protect the public.

Usury. Almost as widespread as licensing statutes, statutes prohibiting usury are found on the books of nearly every state. **Usury** occurs when a party gives a loan at an interest rate exceeding the legal maximum. The legal maximum interest rate varies from state to state, but it is easy to determine the rate of any given state.

While usury statutes act as a ceiling in terms of setting a maximum possible rate, there are a few legal exceptions whereby loans may exceed the predetermined maximum. One exception relates to corporate loans. Most states with usury statutes allow corporations to lend and borrow at rates exceeding the maximum. The rationale behind the corporation exception is that if a business needs money to expand and is willing to pay the higher interest rate, the corporation should be afforded the opportunity to borrow. The converse is that if a corporation is willing to borrow at a high interest rate, parties should be allowed to lend at that rate for corporations only. The intent is to facilitate business transactions in order to keep the economy in a healthy state.

Another exception to usury statutes applies to smaller loans. Many states allow parties to make small loans at rates above the maximum to parties that cannot obtain a needed loan at the statutory maximum. The belief is that if people need money and the statutory maximum is not inducing others to lend, certain parties will make the necessary loans at a higher rate as long as the loan is "small," a caveat defined however the state sees fit. This exception is the principle that allows cash advance institutions to operate.

In the event there is no exception allowing a usurious loan, the legal outcome varies by state. A minority of states declare all usurious loans void, which means the lending party is not entitled to any recovery. Thus, the lending party can recover neither the interest nor the principal from the lendee. A larger number of states allow lenders to recover the principal amount they loaned but not any interest on the loan. States most favorable toward lenders allow recovery of the principal as well as an amount of interest up to, but not exceeding, the statutory maximum. In essence, these states allow lenders to recover all but the excess interest, as if the loan were given at the statutory maximum rate.

Gambling. As with licensing statutes, all states engage in at least some regulation of gambling. As used in this chapter, the term **gambling** refers to agreements in which parties pay consideration (money placed during bets) for the chance, or opportunity, to obtain an amount of money or property.

While gambling is illegal in the vast majority of states, some states allow casino gambling. The states most notable for casino gambling are Nevada, New Jersey, and Louisiana. Some states allow certain other types of gambling, either intentionally or through legal loopholes. For example, given California's definition of gambling, betting on draw poker is legal. Some states make other exceptions, such as for horse tracks, casinos located on Native American reservations, or legal state-run lotteries, which, although most people do not consider them to be such, are a form of gambling.

Sabbath laws. A large number of states still have what are known as *Sabbath, Sunday,* or *blue* laws on the books. **Sabbath laws** limit the types of business activities in which parties can legally engage on Sundays.

For most states with Sabbath law restrictions, these laws date back to Colonial times, when many such laws prohibited shops from being opened and prohibited all work on the "Lord's day" (Sunday). The activities restricted today by Sabbath laws vary from state to state. Most Sabbath laws pertain to the sale of alcoholic beverages. These laws tend to prohibit the sale of all alcohol, or at least of specific types, either all day or at particular times on Sundays. Some Sabbath laws go as far as to make it illegal to enter into any contractual relationship on a Sunday. However, an executed, or fully performed, contract created on a Sunday cannot be rescinded.

There are exceptions to Sabbath laws. Most states with Sabbath laws allow the performance of charity work on Sundays. In addition, Sabbath laws do not typically apply to contracts involving the obtaining of "necessities," typically defined as prescription medication, food, or anything else related to health or survival.

Regardless of how widespread Sabbath laws are, the vast majority of states do not enforce some or all of their Sabbath laws. In fact, some Sabbath laws have in the past been deemed unconstitutional according to the First Amendment. Regardless, if Sabbath laws are on the books, they can be applied despite convention to the contrary, and some states do apply such laws. Prudent businesspersons should always find out whether Sabbath laws exist in their state and, if they do, whether authorities enforce these laws.

AGREEMENTS IN CONTRADICTION TO PUBLIC POLICY

Unlike agreements that are precluded by statute, some types of agreements are not illegal per se, as they are not in violation of any statute or legal code. Rather, they are unenforceable because courts have deemed these types of contracts to be against commonly held public policy. Public policy involves both the government's concern for its citizens and the beliefs people hold regarding the proper subject of business transactions. The focus is what is "in society's best interest."

Contracts in restraint of trade. It is a widely held belief in economics, as well as in America in general, that competition drives down prices, which is good for consumers. Accordingly, agreements that restrain trade are viewed as being harmful to consumers, and thus against public policy. These restraints on trade are also known as *anticompetitive agreements.* Not only are anticompetitive agreements against public policy, but they also frequently violate antitrust laws. See Chapter 47 for an in-depth discussion of antitrust law.

There is an exception that allows specific types of restraints on trade. When a restraint on trade is reasonable, as determined by the courts, and the restraint is part of a subordinate, or ancillary, clause, the restraint is typically allowed. Such restraints are known as **covenants not to compete,** or *restrictive covenants.* Covenants not to compete tend to come in two varieties. The first involves noncompetition in the sale of an ongoing business, and the second involves noncompetition in employment, both of which are discussed below.

The first category of permissible restraints on trade is covenants not to compete that involve the sale of an ongoing business. *Ongoing* refers to the status of the business being sold: The business is still running and will still run on its own; it is not being merged and is not closing down.

The public policy argument in favor of supporting restrictions regarding the sale of a business involves the fairness of the sale. Let us examine a hypothetical situation to see why this restraint on trade is allowed. Suppose you purchase a jewelry store from Ann Smith. Ann is a well-respected member of the community, and her business has been around for many years. The people in the community know the store, and they trust Ann to provide fair exchanges. As a well-informed businessperson, you know about Ann's reputation. In fact, her good reputation made the purchase more appealing.

Now suppose Ann turns around and opens another jewelry store a block away one month later. Ann's loyal customers are likely to go to her new store because they still trust her. In the meantime, Ann's good name is no longer associated with your store, and your business suffers accordingly. You entered into the sales agreement thinking you would benefit from Ann's good name, but in the end you overpaid for a business that lacks the benefit of Ann's name because Ann took her name with her when she went into competition with your store. In the interest of self-proclaimed fairness, courts are willing to impose restrictions preventing Ann, or others in her position, from going into immediate competition with you, or others in your position. Public policy requests fairness in business transactions, and this fairness does not occur when people profit from a business transaction and then start a new business that destroys the business they just sold.

Consequently, the restraints to trade being discussed with the sale of an ongoing business involve the seller's ability to open up another business within a certain geographic location within a designated time period. As mentioned in the beginning of this section, to be enforceable, a covenant not to compete needs to be in a subordinate clause in the contract. If the covenant not to compete is a part of the main agreement, and therefore not subordinate, the agreement is typically considered unenforceable and void as it goes against public policy by creating unreasonable restraints on trade. The unreasonableness arises because when the covenant is an integral part of the contract, it cannot be objected to. In contrast, when the covenant is subordinate, the specific noncompetition clause can be removed and the agreement can go forward as planned. In Case 16-3, the court had to determine the reasonableness of a covenant not to compete signed in conjunction with the sale of a business.

CASE 16-3 ALFRED W. GANN AND CONNIE A. GANN, HUSBAND AND WIFE, PLAINTIFFS-APPELLEES, v. GERRY MORRIS, DEFENDANT-APPELLANT

COURT OF APPEALS OF ARIZONA, DIVISION 2
122 ARIZ. 517, 596 P.2D 43 (1979)

Defendant entered into an agreement to sell his silk screening business or lettering shop to plaintiffs. The agreement provided in part that defendant would not enter into silk screening or lettering shop business within a geographic radius for a period of ten years, would not compete in any manner whatsoever with plaintiffs, and would refer all business contacts to plaintiffs. The trial court found that seller breached the contract by competing with buyers and failing to refer all business under the terms of that contract. On appeal, defendant argued that the contract, including the covenant not to compete, was unenforceable as a restraint of trade, which violated public policy.

JUSTICE RICHMOND: Covenants not to compete, although amounting to partial restraints of trade, will be enforced where they are ancillary to contracts for employment or sale of a business and are reasonably limited as to time and territory. . . . What is reasonable depends on the whole subject matter of the contract, the kind and character of the business, its location, the purpose to be accomplished by the restriction, and all the circumstances which show the intention of the parties.

Courts distinguish between covenants incidental to employment contracts and those incidental to sales of businesses because the policy considerations necessarily differ. In the case of employment contracts, an employee is restricted from using his personal skills and experience, which may seriously impair his ability to earn a living. In light of the potential hardship and uneven bargaining position of the parties, courts scrutinize employer-employee agreements closely. . . . Courts have shown greater reluctance to interfere where the contract involves the sale of a business.

Where limited as to time and space, the covenant is ordinarily valid unless it is to refrain from all business whatsoever. Here, the seller agreed not to enter into the silk screening or lettering shop business within Tucson and a 100-mile radius of Tucson for 10 years. Although the covenant goes on to say that seller will not compete in any manner whatsoever, that language is clearly limited by the subject matter of the entire contract to the kind and character of the business sold.

The rationale for enforcing covenants not to compete is particularly valid in the case of a small business, operated by an individual who had developed a clientele and a reputation in a specialized business area. The sale of such a business necessarily includes the sale of good will and the purchaser has the right to assure himself as best he can of the transfer of the good will.

At the time of the sale in this case, one of the customers of the business had offices in Benson, Phoenix and San Manuel, an area extending beyond the 100-mile restriction in the agreement. Restrictions for 10 years or more have been upheld where it was determined that the covenant was reasonable under all the circumstances.

From the foregoing, we conclude the scope of the covenant in this case is not unreasonable as broader than necessary to protect the interest of the buyers of a small silk screening business. The seller offered no evidence to the contrary. Under the circumstances the buyers are "entitled to enforcement of the covenant as written, it having been entered into voluntarily and for a consideration."

On the question of damages, the trial court's findings are supported by invoices for sales made in violation of the agreement, and testimony of both buyer and seller as to average cost and profits per sale. The trial court limited its award to the lost profits specifically established by such evidence. We find no error in its computation.

AFFIRMED in favor of Plaintiffs.

[CONTINUED]

CRITICAL THINKING

Provide an example of a piece of evidence that the seller could have provided to indicate the unreasonableness of the scope of the covenant in this case. How does your example weigh in comparison to the evidence provided to the contrary? Do you think it would or should be sufficient to change the conclusion of the court? Defend your answer.

ETHICAL DECISION MAKING

What values are in conflict in this case? Which are supported by the ruling, and which are not? How well can the ethical stance taken by the court in this area be defended, and what ethical guidelines might be used in the effort to do so?

The second category of permissible restraints on trade is covenants not to compete that involve employment contracts. The covenants in employment contracts are similar to those in sales contracts. However, with employment, the employee is agreeing, in the event of her leaving, not to compete with her boss for a designated period of time within a designated geographic area.

These covenants in employment contracts are not unusual. In fact, many middle or upper-level managers enter into agreements not to compete with their employers. In such a covenant, the employee is agreeing not to work for competitors or to start his own competing business. The noncompetition comes into effect after the employee stops working for his current employer.

Covenants not to compete in employment contracts are legal in most states. However, to be legal, the covenant needs to protect a legitimate business interest. Furthermore, the covenant needs to be for a reasonable period of time and geographic area so that it does not unlawfully impinge on the employee's rights. The agreement must not be for a longer period of time or larger geographic region than is necessary to protect the business interest. In other words, protecting a business interest can allow a covenant to be considered legal *only* if the restrictions on trade in the covenant are no more than what is necessary to protect the legitimate business interest.

Given the variations from state to state, it should come as no surprise that the enforceability of covenants not to compete also varies from state to state. For example, California does not allow any covenants not to compete. On a different note, Texas requires that the employee gain a specific benefit from a contract beyond employment before its courts will enforce a covenant not to compete. The employee must be given, or gain, something even if the covenant not to compete is for a reasonable period of time and geographic region.

Unconscionable contracts or clauses. When courts are asked to review contracts, fairness is not usually high on their lists of things for which to look. Instead, courts typically assume that the contracting parties are intelligent, responsible adults. The belief is, barring proof of coercion, that parties enter into contracts because they want to do so. Nevertheless, there are times when agreements are so one-sided that the courts will not make the harmed, innocent person fulfill his or her contractual duties. These heavily one-sided agreements are known as **unconscionable** agreements. The term *unconscionable* refers to the fact that the agreement in question is so unfair that it is void of conscience.

Rules against unconscionable contracts exist in both the Restatement (Second) of Contracts and the Uniform Commercial Code. However, before the Restatement and the UCC existed, the common law would not enforce contracts the courts deemed too unfair, or unconscionable. Now UCC Section 2-302 states:

> (1) If the court as a matter of law finds the contract or any clause of the contract to have been unconscionable at the time it was made, the court may refuse to enforce the contract, or it may enforce the remainder of the contract without the clause, or it may so limit the application of any unconscionable clause as to avoid any unconscionable result; (2) When it is claimed or appears to the court that the contract or any clause thereof may be unconscionable, the parties shall be afforded a reasonable opportunity to present evidence as to its commercial setting, purpose, and effect to aid the court in making the determination.

Every state, with the exception of California and Louisiana, has incorporated this UCC section into its state's UCC. Section 208 of the Restatement also incorporates the above section from the UCC.

There are two main types of unconscionable agreements, procedural and substantive. **Procedural unconscionability** relates to conditions that would impair one party's understanding of a contract, as well as to the integration of terms into a contract. Regarding impaired understanding of contractual terms, the factors can be anything from tiny, hard-to-read print on the back of an agreement to excessive use of legalese (unnecessarily technical legal language) or even the inability of a person to fully read a contract and ask any questions before he or she was required to sign.

Most frequently, procedural unconscionability arises when one party presents the other with an adhesion contract. An **adhesion contract** is a contract created by a party to an agreement that is presented to the other party on a take-it-or-leave-it basis. That is, the contract is presented as complete, as well as given as the only chance the presented party (known as the *adhering party*) will have to enter into the agreement. While adhesion contracts are themselves legal, the presence of one does raise some potential problem indicators for courts. Given that adhesion contracts usually do not allow for debate regarding the agreement, courts tend to examine adhesion contracts to see if they can determine how voluntary the agreement really was.

Conversely, **substantive unconscionability** involves overly harsh or lopsided substance in an agreement. That is, if an agreement is terribly one-sided, it is probably invalid on the basis of substantive notions of fairness and just dealing. Courts would find the following, for example, to be substantively unconscionable: high differences between cost and price in a sales agreement; agreements in which one party gains vastly more than the other; agreements in which one party is prevented from having any sort of equal benefit; agreements in which one party has little to no legal recourse, according to the agreement; and portions of an agreement that are completely unrelated to anything having to do with either party's business risk.

Exculpatory clauses. An **exculpatory clause** is a statement releasing one of the parties to an agreement from all liability, regardless of who is at fault or what the injury suffered is. Because tort law attempts to return the wronged party to a state he or she was in before the wrong occurred, anything preventing this corrective mechanism is against public policy. It does not benefit society to allow some parties to get away with not having to pay for wrongs they commit simply because they state they will not be liable in various contracts. In fact, the patently unfair nature of an exculpatory clause is closely tied to the idea of unconscionable contracts.

Exculpatory clauses frequently show up in rental agreements for commercial or residential property. These clauses are often found to be against public policy because sometimes people are injured while on property they are renting from another and sometimes these injuries are due to the carelessness, negligence, or other wrongdoings of the owner. Once again, it does not serve the public's interest to allow landlords, especially when it comes to residential property, to simply disavow all liabilities in advance. Were they allowed to do so, there would be nothing requiring that landlords fix problems with their rental units, including potentially lethal problems, such as faulty electric wiring or the presence of lead-based paint.

A basic test to determine whether an exculpatory clause is unenforceable is to see if the enforcing party engages in a business directly related to the public interest. Examples of such businesses include banks, transportation providers, and public utilities. Courts believe it is against the public interest to allow businesses engaging in work in the public's interest to not be held accountable to the public they are serving.

Another concern with large businesses that are serving the public interest is the unfair bargaining power they can possess in negotiating a contract. Given the power these businesses have, they could simply demand that all customers accept the exculpatory clause, thus escaping all possible liability. While the idea of these businesses' not being liable is bad, what is worse is that there would be no punitive financial motive for them to carefully conduct their business operations, or so the argument goes. As a result, the potential for increased accidents would be large. Obviously, it is not in the public's interest to have unsafe businesses that are not accountable to the public. Thus, these businesses cannot enforce exculpatory clauses.

Case 16-4 details a court's determination that an illegal exculpatory clause existed.

CASE 16-4

ERIC LUCIER AND KAREN A. HALEY v. ANGELA AND JAMES WILLIAMS, CAMBRIDGE ASSOCIATES, LTD., AND AL VASYS

SUPERIOR COURT OF NEW JERSEY, APPELLATE DIVISION
841 A.2D 907 (2004)

Eric Lucier and Karen A. Haley, a young married couple, were first-time home buyers. They contracted with the Williams to purchase a single-family residence. Lucier and Haley engaged the services of Cambridge Associates, Ltd. (CAL) to perform a home inspection. Al Vasys had formed CAL and was its president. Lucier dealt directly with Vasys, and Vasys performed the inspection and issued the home inspection report on behalf of CAL.

The home inspection agreement contains a provision limiting CAL's liability to "$500, or 50% of fees actually paid to CAL by Client, whichever sum is smaller." This provision, as several others in the form agreement prepared by CAL, was followed by a line for placement of the clients' initials. Lucier initialed this provision. The fee for the home inspection contract was $385, which Lucier paid to CAL.

Lucier claims when he began to read the agreement, in Vasys' presence, he felt some of the language was unfair and confusing. According to Lucier, Vasys stated he would not change any provisions, that it was a standard contract based upon home inspections done in New Jersey, and Lucier would have to sign the agreement "as-is" or not at all. Vasys does not dispute this, but relies upon Lucier's signing the agreement and initialing the limitation of liability clause. Likewise, Lucier does not deny signing the contract or initialing that clause.

Lucier and Haley obtained title to the property from the Williams. Shortly after, they noticed leaks in the house. They engaged the services of a roofing *contractor and found out the roof was defective. Lucier and Haley argue Vasys should have observed and reported the problem to them. The cost of repair was about $8,000 to $10,000.*

Lucier and Haley brought suit against the Williams, CAL, and Vasys, seeking damages to compensate them for the loss occasioned by the alleged defect. CAL and Vasys moved for partial summary judgment seeking a declaration that the limit of their liability in the action, if any, was one-half the contract price, or $192.50. The motion for partial summary judgment was granted. Lucier and Haley then filed this appeal, seeking review of the partial summary judgment order.

JUDGE LISA: There is no hard and fast definition of unconscionability. As the Supreme Court explained in *Kugler v. Romain,* unconscionability is "an amorphous concept obviously designed to establish a broad business ethic." The standard of conduct that the term implies is a lack of "good faith, honesty in fact and observance of fair dealing."

In determining whether to enforce the terms of a contract, we look not only to its adhesive nature, but also to "the subject matter of the contract, the parties' relative bargaining positions, the degree of economic compulsion motivating the 'adhering' party, and the public interests affected by the contract." Where the provision limits a party's liability, we pay particular attention to any inequality in the bargaining power and status of the parties, as well as the substance of the contract.

We also focus our inquiry on whether the limitation is a reasonable allocation of risk between the parties or whether it runs afoul of the public policy disfavoring clauses which effectively immunize parties from liability for their own negligent actions. To be enforceable, the amount of the cap on a party's liability must be sufficient to provide a realistic incentive to act diligently.

Applying these principles to the home inspection contract before us, we find the limitation of liability provision unconscionable. We do not hesitate to hold it unenforceable for the following reasons: (1) the contract, prepared by the home inspector, is one of adhesion; (2) the parties, one a consumer and the other a professional expert, have grossly unequal bargaining status; and (3) the substance of the provision eviscerates the contract and its fundamental purpose because the potential damage level is so nominal that it has the practical effect of avoiding almost all responsibility for the professional's negligence. Additionally, the provision is contrary to our state's public policy of effectuating the purpose of a home inspection contract to render reliable evaluation of a home's fitness for purchase and holding professionals to certain industry standards.

This is a classic contract of adhesion. There were no negotiations leading up to its preparation. The contract was presented to Lucier on a standardized preprinted form, prepared by CAL, on a take-it-or-leave-it basis, without any opportunity for him to negotiate or modify any of its terms.

The bargaining position between the parties was grossly disparate. Vasys has been in the home inspection business for twenty years. He has inspected thousands of homes. He has an engineering degree. He has served as an expert witness in construction matters. He holds various designations in the building and construction field. He advertises his company and holds it and himself out as possessing expertise in the home inspection field. Lucier and Haley, on the other hand, are unknowledgeable and unsophisticated in matters of home construction. They are consumers. They placed their trust in this expert. They had every reason to expect he would act with diligence and competence in inspecting the home they desired to purchase and discover and report major defects. The disparity in the positions of these parties is clear and substantial.

The foisting of a contract of this type in this setting on an inexperienced consumer clearly demonstrates a lack of fair dealing by the professional. The cost of homes in New Jersey is substantial.

The limitation of liability clause here is also against public policy. First, it allows the home inspector to circumvent the state's public policy of holding professional service providers to certain industry standards. Second, it contravenes the stated public policy of New Jersey regarding home inspectors.

With professional services, exculpation clauses are particularly disfavored. The very nature of a professional service is one in which the person receiving the service relies upon the expertise, training, knowledge and stature of the professional. Exculpation provisions are antithetical to such a relationship.

In summary, the limitation of liability provision in this contract is unconscionable and violates the public policy of our State. The contract is one of adhesion, the bargaining power of the parties is unequal, the impact of the liability clause is negligible to the home inspector while potentially severe to the home buyer, and the provision conflicts with the purpose of home inspection contracts and our Legislature's requirement of accountability by home inspectors for their errors and omissions.

REVERSED AND REMANDED.

CRITICAL THINKING

In this decision, does Judge Lisa make any assumptions regarding the facts of the case without proper evidence to support their inclusion as a reasoning step? For instance, what evidence supports her characterization of Lucier? Is it possible that, given the supplied information, Lucier is actually significantly different from the way he has been presented? How might such differences affect the acceptability of the conclusion? Can you locate any other assumptions in this ruling? How do they affect the reasoning?

ETHICAL DECISION MAKING

Examine the ethicality of the actions of each party leading up to this dispute. Who behaved in a blameworthy fashion, and who in a praiseworthy fashion? What facts from the case and what ethical theories or guidelines can be used to support your claim?

Now consider each party's stance in the legal dispute. Does either one appear more or less ethical, relative to that party's earlier actions? Why or why not?

While businesses closely linked to the public interest cannot enforce exculpatory clauses, not all exculpatory clauses are unlawful. To be able to enforce an exculpatory clause, the party seeking enforcement must be a private business or an individual and must *not* be important to the public interest. These private businesses or individuals provide nonessential services, and thus do not have the same bargaining power as the previously discussed groups, such as banks, utilities, or airlines. Given their lack of huge bargaining power, it is assumed that private businesses and individuals will enter on relatively equal terms and will voluntarily agree on or decline the final contract.

Examples of private businesses that can enforce exculpatory clauses include skiing facilities such as resorts or rental places, private gyms or health clubs, any business offering sky diving or bungee jumping, and amusement parks, to name a few. Because the services provided by all these businesses, as well as others in this category, are not something related to the public interest and not something in which people must engage, these parties are allowed to deny liability if the party with which they are contracting agrees to the exculpatory clause. Just because these parties *might* be able to enforce an exculpatory clause, however, does not mean the clause is always automatically enforceable.

EFFECT OF ILLEGAL AGREEMENTS

Generally speaking, when an agreement is deemed illegal, courts will label the contract void. The reason most illegal agreements are void is that, in most cases, both parties are equally responsible for the illegal agreement. In the law, when both parties are equally responsible for an illegal agreement, it is known as ***in pari delicto.***

When both parties are at fault, it does not make sense for the courts to attempt to salvage the agreement or reward either party. Therefore, most illegal agreements are void, meaning neither party can enforce the agreement and neither is entitled to recovery.

However, it is not always the case that both parties are at fault. In the event that one party is not responsible for an illegal agreement or that there are special circumstances forgiving the illegality, it makes sense sometimes to allow one party to an illegal agreement to recover various damages.

The first exception to the general rule occurs when a member of a protected class is involved in an agreement that contradicts a statute intended to protect the specific class. In the event of such a contradiction, the member of the protected class is allowed to sue for performance. The reasoning is that if a statute is intended to protect a specific class, the statute should not be allowed to be used by people outside the class to harm those inside the class.

For example, a work agreement between a truck driver and his or her employer may specify that the driver gets paid for the number of hours worked. Yet certain statutes limit the number of hours truck drivers may drive in a given time period. If the truck driver accidentally drives more than the allowable hours, the driver has technically violated a statute. However, this violation does not allow the employer to refuse to pay the driver for the extra hours. Rather, the driver may sue the employer to enforce the work agreement.

The second exception to the voiding of illegal agreements occurs when there is a justifiable ignorance of facts. A *justifiable ignorance of facts* is one party's lack of knowledge regarding a provision of the agreement that would make it illegal. While ignorance of the law does not excuse illegal behavior, not knowing that the other party to a contract intended to fulfill the agreement through illegal means does function as an excuse.

When one of the parties is relatively innocent in the whole deal, the court may give back any consideration the innocent party gave or may require exchange for partial performance such that both parties can be returned to the positions they were in before they entered into the agreement. Conversely, if one party is completely innocent of any illegality and has completed his or her portion of the contract, then—depending on the reason the contract is considered illegal and depending on which state's laws are in question—the court might enforce the entire agreement.

A third exception to the general rule occurs when one of the parties withdraws from an illegal agreement. The key to any recovery is that the party must have withdrawn before any illegality occurred. If this is the case and if part or full performance has occurred, the party may recover value for whatever portion has been completed. However, if the party is involved in any way in the illegal activity, the party cannot recover at all.

Severable contracts. **Severable contracts,** also known as *divisible contracts,* are those that contain multiple parts which can each be performed separately. In addition, separate consideration is offered for each individual part. In essence, a severable contract is like numerous contracts in one. Conversely, an **indivisible contract** is one requiring complete performance by both parties, even if it appears as if the contract contains multiple parts, similar to a severable contract.

With respect to illegality, severable contracts have a huge advantage over indivisible contracts: If the severable contract has both legal and illegal portions, the court has the option of declaring void only those sections of the agreement that are illegal. The court can then enforce the remaining, legal portions of the contract. Indivisible contracts must be enforced or rejected in their entirety. For a court to be able to enforce part of a severable contract, the parts that are enforced must still represent the main purpose of the original agreement. If declaring parts of a contract void substantially alters the contract, the court is not likely to enforce the remaining portions of the agreement. Courts ultimately want to facilitate business transactions and enforce the legal wishes of parties, and severable contracts enable them to do so.

Case Nugget — Determining the Legality of an Arbitration Clause

Buckeye Check Cashing, Inc. v. Cardegna et al.
United States Supreme Court
126 S. Ct. 1204, 163 L. Ed. 2d 1038 (2006)

The respondents, Cardegna et al., entered into a number of deferred-payment transactions with Buckeye Check Cashing. Each agreement they signed contained a provision requiring binding arbitration to resolve disputes arising out of the agreement. The respondents filed a class action suit against Buckeye Check Cashing in Florida state court, alleging that Buckeye charged usurious interest rates and that the agreement violated various Florida laws, rendering it illegal on its face. The trial court denied Buckeye's motion to compel arbitration, holding that a court rather than an arbitrator should resolve a claim that a contract is illegal and void *ab initio.* A state appellate court reversed, but its decision was in turn reversed by the Florida Supreme Court, which reasoned that enforcing an arbitration agreement in a contract challenged as unlawful would violate state public policy and contract law. The case was appealed to the United States Supreme Court to determine whether the courts or an arbitrator should determine the legality of a potentially illegal contract containing a binding arbitration clause.

The Court answered this question by relying on three established propositions. First, as a matter of substantive federal arbitration law, an arbitration provision is severable from the remainder of the contract. Second, unless the challenge is to the arbitration clause itself, the issue of the contract's validity is considered by the arbitrator in the first instance. Third, this arbitration law applies in state as well as federal courts. Applying these propositions to the case, the high court concluded that when an agreement as a whole, but not specifically its arbitration provisions, is challenged, the arbitration provisions are enforceable apart from the remainder of the contract. The challenge to the legality of the contract itself should therefore be considered by an arbitrator, not a court.

CASE OPENER WRAP-UP

A Wasted Education

On appeal, the judge agreed with the trial court judge that education in aviation was not a necessary.

The court further found that the delay in disaffirming the contracts for nearly a year after reaching the age of majority did not, as a matter of law, constitute a ratification of them. The court reasoned that the contracts were wholly executed and that there was no evidence that an earlier disaffirmance would have benefited the defendant or saved it from harm. In addition, the plaintiff had not made use of his education in aviation during that time, or at any other time, so the plaintiff received no benefit from the delay.

Summary

Capacity

Natural persons over the age of majority are presumed to have the full legal capacity to enter into binding legal contracts.

A person has only limited capacity to enter into a legally binding contract if the person is:

- A minor.
- Suffering from a mental deficiency that prevents the person from understanding the nature and obligations of contracts.
- Intoxicated.

A person has no capacity to enter into a contract if the person:

- Has been adjudicated insane.
- Has been adjudicated a habitual drunkard.
- Has had a legal guardian appointed to enter into contracts on his or her behalf.

Legality

Contracts that do not have a legal object are not valid.

Contracts may lack a legal object because they violate a statute or violate public policy.

Point / Counterpoint

Should the Law Bind Mentally Incompetent Individuals to Their Contracts?

No

Binding mentally incompetent individuals to their contracts sharply increases the likelihood of fraud. If contract law bound such individuals to their contracts, unscrupulous sellers could legally induce mentally incompetent individuals to enter into extortionist or fraudulent contracts, and courts, bound to apply the law, would enforce those contracts. If, however, the law did not enforce contracts made with mentally incompetent individuals, opportunists could not use the law to prey on these people. Hence, permitting mentally incompetent individuals to escape their contracts sends a message to opportunistic individuals that the law will not sanction their fraudulent practices.

In addition to discouraging fraud, contract laws that permit mentally incompetent individuals to void their contracts protect the most vulnerable members of society. The law binds mentally *competent* individuals to their contracts under the assumption that they are capable of looking out for their best interests. But mentally *incompetent* individuals lack the ability to protect their best interests. Critics call these types of

Yes

Allowing mentally incompetent individuals to void their contracts is paternalistic. The great majority of mentally incompetent individuals live with mentally competent relatives, friends, or guardians who watch out for their best interests. Compared to judges, these guardians are much more likely to be able to act in the best interests of the mentally incompetent.

Moreover, this paternalism hurts mentally incompetent individuals more than it helps them. If mentally incompetent individuals can legally void their contracts, competent individuals will be less willing to enter into evenhanded contracts with them. As a result, mentally incompetent individuals will have fewer opportunities to enter into contracts consistent with their best interests. Hence, although the purpose of allowing mentally incompetent individuals to escape their contracts is well meaning, the result is malicious to the very individuals the law intends to help.

Proponents of allowing mentally incompetent individuals to void their contracts argue that doing so would discourage fraud. But their position encourages laws paternalistic, but a major function of the law is to protect individuals such as the mentally incompetent who cannot protect themselves.

Indeed, if the justification for contract law is rooted in our desire for individuals to be able to enter into mutually beneficial exchanges, allowing mentally incompetent individuals, who by definition cannot determine what is in their self-interest, to void their contracts is consistent with this justification.

fraud against mentally competent individuals. If these individuals can escape their contracts, they have an incentive to enter risky contracts with mentally competent individuals. If the gamble pays off, they can adhere to the contract; if not, they can void the contract and return to the position they were in before entering it. Thus, binding mentally incompetent individuals to their contracts actually *decreases* the prevalence of one type of fraud.

Finally, courts lack the institutional competence to determine mental competence. How can courts reliably determine which individuals lack the mental competence to look out for their own interests?

Questions & Problems

1. How does the concept of the age of majority differ in Great Britain from that in the United States?
2. Explain the obligations of a minor who chooses to disaffirm a contract.
3. Go back to the discussion of contracts that cannot be disaffirmed by minors, and explain the policy reasons that support each of the exceptions. Can you make an argument for any additional kinds of contracts that should not be subject to disaffirmance by minors?
4. If all you know about a man is that his neighbors think he is crazy, you do not know whether the contract he entered into was valid, voidable, or void. Why not?
5. What factors determine whether a covenant not to compete is legal or illegal?
6. What is the relationship between contracts in restraint of trade and unconscionable contracts?
7. Two minor boys signed a lease with a real estate company for an apartment in mid-September 1982 and moved into the apartment soon afterward. The lease was to last through mid-August 1983. The boys paid the required rent for September and October, but in mid-November they found themselves financially unable to make that month's rental payment. Because they were unable to pay, the boys vacated the premises and returned home to their parents. In January 1983, the real estate company sued the boys to obtain damages for unpaid rent and expenses for November and December of the previous year. The boys denied any liability on the basis of their status as minors. The trial court found that housing was a necessary and, therefore, that the boys should be held liable to the leasor, Webster Street Partnership, Ltd. On appeal, the district court overturned the lower court's decision on grounds that the lease did not prove a necessary because the minors had the ability at any time to return home. Webster appealed. How do you think the supreme court of Nebraska ruled, and why? [*Webster Street Partnership, Ltd. v. Sheridan,* 220 Neb. 9, 368 N.W.2d 439 (1985).]
8. Sixteen-year-old Joseph Dodson bought a used pickup truck from Shrader's Auto for $4,900. Nine months later, the truck began malfunctioning, so Dodson took it to a mechanic, who informed Dodson that the truck might have a burnt valve. Dodson did

not repair the truck but continued to drive it. A month later, the engine burned out and the truck would no longer run. Dodson disaffirmed the contract and returned the truck to Shrader's Auto, asking for a return of the purchase price. The Shraders refused to return the purchase price to him and would not take possession of the truck. Dodson then left the truck in his front yard, where it was hit by an unknown driver. Dodson sued the Shraders, seeking restitution of his purchase price. The trial court granted restitution of the purchase price to the plaintiff, and the defendants appealed. Why do you think the judgment of the trial court was either upheld or reversed on appeal? [*Dodson v. Shrader, et al.*, 824 S.W.2d 545 (1992).]

9. Seigneur joined NFI, a health and fitness facility, to lose weight and become fit. She was in poor physical condition and had back problems that she discussed with NFI prior to signing a contract with the facility. The contract she ultimately signed contained a clause that said NFI was not responsible for injuries sustained during exercise. Seigneur claimed that she tore a muscle in her shoulder while doing a series of tests to evaluate her physical condition. The tear required surgery to be repaired, and her surgeon stated that he believed the injury was caused by her using an upper-torso weight machine during her fitness evaluation. She sued NFI for negligence. NFI filed a motion for summary judgment on the basis of the exculpatory clause. The trial court granted NFI's motion, and Seigneur appealed. Do you believe the appellate court upheld the motion for summary judgment? Why or why not? [*Seigneur v. National Fitness Institute, Inc.*, 752 A.2d 631 (Ct. App. Md. 2000).]

10. On July 16, 1997, Chicago Steel entered into a contract with ADT in which ADT agreed to design, sell, install, and/or maintain a fire alarm system and provide fire alarm monitoring and reporting services for Chicago Steel's plant at 6630 W. Wrightwood Avenue in Chicago. Under the terms of the contract, ADT was to maintain the fire alarm system and inspect it four times a year. Chicago Steel was to pay ADT $3,472 annually.

The contract stated that ADT was not an insurer and would be exempt from liability for damage to property, whether based on breach of contract, negligence, or strict liability. The contract also contained a limitation-of-damages clause limiting any liability on ADT's part to the greater of 10 percent of the annual service charge or $1,000. The contract, however, gave Chicago Steel the option to pay for an allocation of additional liability to ADT. The record reflects that Chicago Steel did not exercise that option.

On January 2, 1999, after the alarm system's installation, a fire occurred at the Wrightwood plant, causing substantial damage to property located there. The plaintiffs sued ADT, alleging that the failure of the alarm system and/or ADT's failure to maintain and monitor the system caused a delay in notification to the Chicago fire department and resulted in substantial property damage. Their complaint included four counts: (1) strict product liability, (2) breach of contract, (3) negligence, and (4) gross negligence.

ADT filed a motion to dismiss the plaintiffs' complaint, based in part on the exculpatory clause contained in its fire alarm installation and maintenance contract with Chicago Steel, which released ADT from future negligence, breach of contract, and strict liability claims. The trial court granted the motion. On appeal, do you think the exculpatory clause was enforced by the appellate court? Why or why not? [*Chicago Steel Rule and Die Fabricators Company and Travelers Indemnity Company of Illinois v. ADT Security Systems, Inc., ADT Security Services, Inc.*, 327 Ill. App. 3d 642, 763 N.E.2d 839 (2002).]

Looking for more review material?

The Online Learning Center at **www.mhhe.com/kubasek1e** contains this chapter's "Assignment on the Internet" and also a list of URLs for more information, entitled "On the Internet." Find both of them in the Student Center portion of the OLC, along with quizzes and other helpful materials.

Legal Assent

CASE OPENER

A Disagreement over an Agreement

Patricia and Billy Welkener sought a divorce.[1] The two parties, having reached an agreement for the division of their property, appeared in court to recite into the record their agreement. In court, Patricia agreed, among other things, to receive $1,098.84 per month from Billy's retirement account.

At the conclusion of the hearing, the judge decreed the settlement to be final. Subsequently, Patricia asked the court to enter judgment that she receive 32.7 percent of Billy's retirement account, which is the percentage version of the amount she was previously awarded. Patricia argued that stating the award in terms of a percentage, rather than a specific amount, was important as this would allow her to share in any future increase in Billy's monthly retirement benefit.

Patricia further argued that when the agreement was announced in open court, she had described the agreement in terms of dollars and cents as a means of describing the percentage she would be entitled to receive. She claimed that listing the amount in terms of a sum, as opposed to a percentage, was a mistake in the contract and, therefore, that the terms to which she agreed were not accurately reflected in the court's final decision.

1. Imagine you were the judge in this case. Do you think the agreement reached in court between the Welkeners accurately reflects what the parties intended?
2. Under which ethical system would Patricia Welkener be entitled to the change in terms? Why?

The Wrap-Up at the end of the chapter will answer these questions.

[1] *Welkener v. Welkener,* 71 S.W.3d 364 (2001).

CHAPTER 17

Learning Objectives

After reading this chapter, you will be able to answer the following questions:

1 Why is legal assent important?

2 What are the elements of mistake?

3 What are the elements of misrepresentation?

4 What are the elements of undue influence?

5 What are the elements of duress?

6 What are the elements of unconscionability?

The Importance of Legal Assent

When two people talk to each other in the hope that an exchange will take place, all kinds of things can go wrong. Global business needs dependability. Just imagine what it would be like if "Yes" meant "Maybe"! Deals would be closed only to be reopened again and again. The costs of all purchases would soar. Businesses would be forced to charge extra to pay for all the extra time they had to spend to finally get to the point where "Yes" really meant "Yes."

To make business transactions smoother and more dependable, the law has developed rules about when an assent to buy or sell is a **legal assent,** that is, a promise to buy or sell that the courts will require the parties to obey. The reason there needs to be such a concept is to distinguish legal assent from other kinds of assent that courts see as not reaching the level of legal assent. Something is wrong with those other kinds of assent such that courts do not require parties to follow through on them. The point here is that courts see some forms of assent as more genuine or real than others.

It is important for businesspeople to know the differences among the various kinds of assent. Why do the differences matter? One person may think he has sold his boat to another, but without legal assent the contract may be **voidable,** a circumstance that can cost businesses major profits when the sale is of a much larger scope than a single boat. When a contract is voidable, it may be **rescinded,** or canceled. All the work in making the original deal would be wasted.

The cancellation of a contract permits the person who canceled it to require the return of everything she gave the other party. At the same time, the person who rescinds the contract must herself return whatever she has received from the other party. An enormous waste of time and an unnecessary cost of doing business may be the result. The major theme of this chapter is that *best-practice firms aim for legal assent in their contracts.* This chapter shows you how to achieve legal assent. It explains the major obstacles to legal assent: mistake, misrepresentation, undue influence, duress, and unconscionability. By knowing about these potential problems, you will be in a good position to avoid them.

Mistake

When people agree to buy or sell, they do so with a particular understanding about the nature of the good or service they are about to exchange. However, one or both parties may think they consented to exchange a particular thing only to find out later that no meeting of the minds had occurred. People may misunderstand either some fact about the deal or the value of what is being exchanged. We focus on misunderstandings about facts because they are the only issues that raise the potential of rescission in American courts.

But European courts take a different approach to mistakes about *the value of performance* of the contract. In general, they agree with the reluctance of American courts to interfere with a contract just because the value of the item in question has changed since the agreement. The parties are assumed to have accepted the risk that the value might change later when they made the contract. However, European courts permit rescission of the contract for a mistake of value when the mistake involves more than 50 percent of the value at the time of the contract.

Legal assent is absent when a legal mistake occurs. The term *mistake* in contract law has a special meaning that deserves special attention because it is not quite the same as the ordinary use of the term. A **mistake** is an erroneous belief about the facts of the contract *at the time the contract is concluded.*

There is one more important aspect of the definition of mistake. Later in this chapter, when we discuss misrepresentation, our focus will be on incorrect beliefs about the facts of the contract caused by the other party's untrue statements. Mistakes in contract law do not result from the untrue statements of the other party to the contract.

Mistakes may be **unilateral,** the result of an error by *one* party about a material fact, that is, a fact that is important in the context of the particular contract. Alternatively, they may be **mutual,** shared by both parties to the agreement. This distinction is important in determining which contracts are voidable.

UNILATERAL MISTAKE

In general, a unilateral mistake does not void a contract. Courts are hesitant to interfere with a contract in a situation where one of the parties has a correct understanding of the material facts of the agreement. For instance, a widow seeking to rescind her and her husband's election to have his retirement benefits paid out over *his life* was not permitted to receive survivor's pension benefits. The court held that representatives of the retirement system had provided sufficient information to the plaintiff and her husband before they elected that particular form of payout.[2]

But sometimes, rescission is permitted for even unilateral mistakes. Because our economic well-being depends so heavily on reliable contracts, we want to be fully aware of the circumstances under which unilateral mistakes permit rescission. Any of the following conditions would permit a court to invalidate a contract on grounds of unilateral mistake:

1. One party made a mistake about a material fact, and the other party either knew or had reason to know about the mistake.
2. The mistake was caused by a clerical error that did not result from gross negligence.
3. The mistake was so serious that the contract is unconscionable, that is, so unreasonable that it is outrageous.

These situations are rare, but it is important to be aware of them because any rescission can be costly in terms of time and lost opportunities.

Returning to the case in the opening scenario, suppose Patricia Welkener committed a unilateral mistake when she agreed to the terms of the division of property. What would she have to prove to demonstrate that a unilateral mistake was made such that the decision should be corrected? Did Patricia Welkener's supposed misunderstanding amount to a unilateral mistake?

MUTUAL MISTAKE

In cases where both parties to a contract are mistaken about either a current or a past material fact, either can choose to rescind the contract. Rescinding such a contract is fair because any agreement between the parties was an illusion: An ambiguity in some key fact prevented the parties from being in actual agreement.

The famous story of the ship *Peerless*[3] has taught generations of students the importance of being very clear in defining material facts in any contract. The parties to the contract that led to the contract disagreement had agreed that the vessel *Peerless* would deliver the cotton they were exchanging. Unfortunately for them, there were two ships named *Peerless.* So when the deal was made, one party had one *Peerless* in mind while the other meant the second *Peerless.* The times the ships sailed were materially different, so the

[2] *Ricks v. Missouri Local Government Employees Retirement System,* 1999 WL 663217 (MO. App. WD).

[3] *Raffles v. Wichelhaus,* 159 Eng. Rep. 375 (1864).

court rescinded the contract. *Warning:* Anticipate ambiguity in material facts, and clarify them in advance to save yourself headaches later.

Case Nugget A Questionable "Mistake"

Mary W. Scott (Respondent-Appellant) v. Mid-Carolina Homes, Inc. (Appellant-Respondent)
Court of Appeals of South Carolina
293 S.C. 191(1987)

Mary Scott signed a contract to purchase a repossessed 1984 mobile home from Mid-Carolina Homes, Inc., for $5,644, to be paid in full before delivery. She gave the salesperson a check for $2,913.71, and agreed to pay the balance before the end of the month. Within the next week, the salesman called and told her he could not sell her the home because it had a bent frame, and the South Carolina Manufactured Housing Board would not permit him to sell a home with a bent frame. She offered to buy it as is and sign a waiver, but the salesman said that would not be legal. A few weeks later, Mid-Carolina sold the mobile home to another couple for $9,220. Scott sued and was awarded $3,600 actual damages and $6,400 punitive damages for breach of contract accompanied by a fraudulent act and $3,000 actual damages for violation of a state consumer protection law. The appeals court upheld the award.

On appeal, Mid-Carolina argued that it was entitled to rescind the contract because the salesperson was acting under a mistake of fact when he gave Scott the sales price. In upholding the award, the state supreme court explained that a contract may be rescinded for unilateral mistake only when the mistake has been induced by fraud, deceit, misrepresentation, concealment, or imposition of the party opposed to the rescission, without negligence on the part of the party claiming rescission, or when the mistake is accompanied by very strong and extraordinary circumstances that would make it a great wrong to enforce the agreement. Mid-Carolina had not demonstrated the presence of any of the circumstances that would justify a rescission. The salesperson was in the superior bargaining position to know the price, and the buyer's reliance on a salesperson's representation of the price was reasonable.

For a mutual mistake to interfere with legal consent it must involve all the following:

1. A basic assumption about the subject matter of the contract.
2. A material effect on the agreement.
3. An adverse effect on a party who did not agree to bear the risk of mistake at the time of the agreement.

Courts will not void contracts for reason of mutual mistake if even one of the preceding attributes is missing.

For instance, to rise to the level of a basic assumption, the mistake would need to be about the existence, quality, or quantity of the items to be exchanged. To meet the second condition, the mistake must involve the essence of the agreement. A fact is material when it provides a basis for a person's agreeing to enter into the contract. The second element is not satisfied when the person attempting to avoid the contract simply claims that the item to be exchanged is not the one he had intended to exchange.

The third condition is necessary to protect those who bargain with someone who agreed, at the time of the agreement, to bear the risk of mistake but then later wishes to avoid that risk when the contract does not work out as well as he or she had planned. This situation might arise, for instance, if the adversely affected party had agreed in the contract to accept the items "as is" but later felt they were not worth the price paid. Case 17-1 offers you the opportunity to see the elements of mutual mistake analyzed in the sale of a business.

CASE 17-1 RONALD JACKSON AND WILLA JACKSON, APPELLANT v. ROBERT R. BLANCHARD, HELEN M. BLANCHARD, MAYNARD L. SHELLHAMER, AND PHILIP SCHLEMMER, APPELLEE

COURT OF APPEALS OF INDIANA, FOURTH DISTRICT
601 N.E.2D 411 (1992)

The Blanchards owned the Corner Cupboard Restaurant until 1985, when they sold it on contract. Schlemmer and Shellhammer became the new assignees under the contract and took over operations of the Corner Cupboard.

In late 1988, Schlemmer and Shellhammer sold the Corner Cupboard to the Jacksons. Prior to finalizing the sale, Jackson and Schlemmer discussed the septic system and a certain well located on the restaurant property. Schlemmer told Jackson that he had been told there was a workable well located on the property, but neither he nor the previous owners before him had ever used it; they had always purchased their water from the filling station across the street. Schlemmer also told Jackson that the septic system had backed up on occasion, but he thought this problem had been fixed.

At the closing, the Jacksons met the Blanchards, who were there to give the Jacksons a warranty deed to the restaurant. Prior to executing the deed, Jackson and Blanchard discussed the well. Blanchard explained to Jackson that there was a working well on the property, but that neither he nor any of the previous owners had utilized it.

Soon after the sale, Mr. Jackson attempted to supply the restaurant with water from the well, and realized it was plugged and that his only recourse was to drill a new well. Then he discovered that two other landowners were hooked into the septic discharge line, and that the discharge line was illegally dumping into a lake, thus subjecting him to penalties of up to $25,000 per day. Finally, Jackson further discovered that numerous underground petroleum storage tanks had been buried on the restaurant property.

The Jacksons sued the defendants, seeking, among other claims, rescission of the assignment contract from Schlemmer and Shellhammer based on mutual mistake of fact. Defendants filed a motion for summary judgment, which was granted by the court. The Jacksons appealed.

JUDGE MILLER: Mutual assent is a prerequisite to the creation of a contract. However, "where both parties share a common assumption about a vital fact upon which they based their bargain, and that assumption is false, the transaction may be voided if because of the mistake a quite different exchange of values occurs from the exchange of values contemplated by the parties." It is not enough that both parties are mistaken about any fact; rather, the mistaken fact complained of must be one that is "of the essence of the agreement. . . ."

The Jacksons argue that the existence of a working well was a material fact going to the heart of the agreement. Our review of the designated materials shows that this is not the case. It was only several months after purchasing the restaurant and purchasing their water from the filling station that the Jacksons attempted to supply the restaurant with well water. Thus, the Jacksons knew at the time they purchased the restaurant that the well was unusable without a new pump and piping, and that until such work, they would have to purchase their water from another source. We cannot conclude that an operable well was an essential factor in the Jacksons' decision to purchase the restaurant. . . . The fact that the well was actually unable to provide water, while contrary to the assumptions of both parties, was not a mistake of material fact.

The Jacksons next argue that because they and Schlemmer and Shellhammer were unaware of the existence of the underground storage tanks, this constituted grounds for rescinding the contract. . . . While the discovery of the underground storage tanks might have been an unfortunate surprise . . . [i]t does not affect the suitability of the premises for the purpose of operating a restaurant—the very thing bought by the Jacksons. . . . We cannot say that ignorance of the existence of the underground storage tanks constituted a mutual mistake.

Finally, the Jacksons contend that there was no meeting of the minds because neither party was aware of the problems with the septic system. . . . We conclude that what the Jacksons bargained for was a functioning restaurant, not necessarily one that would avoid all infringements of the law. Thus, in order to qualify as a material mistake, the Jacksons must prove that any subsequently discovered conditions regarding the septic system rendered it, and the restaurant, inoperable.

The Jacksons do not dispute that the restaurant's septic system is functional; their sole complaint is that the current method of discharge may subject them to civil penalties. From this alone, we could determine that the subsequently discovered problems were not material. As we stated earlier, it is only those mistakes which are material or essential to the parties' agreement that properly fall within the definition of mutual mistake.

AFFIRMED.

CRITICAL THINKING

What is fundamentally at issue in this dispute? That is, what basic question do the two sides disagree on? What evidence does each use to defend their position?

Do you agree with the court's finding of which side's argument was superior? Why or why not?

How might key pieces of evidence have been interpreted differently? Have they been considered in the most appropriate way? Should this change the outcome of the case?

ETHICAL DECISION MAKING

On the basis of the provided information, do your best to sketch the ethical considerations taken into account by each side in this dispute before the lawsuit. Does your projection paint either as approaching matters from the ethical high ground?

What facts of the case led you to your stance, and what ethical guidelines did you use to reach your conclusion?

Did you find yourself making any assumptions about behaviors not justified in terms of available information? If so, what do you think caused you to make these assumptions? Why is this sort of phenomenon important to consider in thinking critically about the court's decision?

connecting to the core

Marketing

Marketing courses teach students that the packaging and labeling of a product are important elements in sales. The term *packaging* refers to the container in which a product is sold, while *labeling* refers to the information on the package that describes how the product is to be used, what the package contains, and who made the product. While packaging and labeling may be important for protecting the product being shipped and sold, they also differentiate one company's products from competitors' products. Coca-Cola's easily recognizable contour-shaped bottle, for example, distinguishes its soda from other soft drinks.

Packaging and labeling are also relevant in our discussion of legal assent, in the sense that a label provides information that is important to a potential buyer, who may decide to either accept or reject the product on the basis of the information contained in the label. For instance, a person who wants to purchase a microwave would likely look at the description of the product on the label. If for some reason the box pictures a white microwave but contains a black one, the purchaser would likely not be bound to the sales agreement, as no "meeting of the minds" existed at the time of the purchase between the seller and the consumer. In other words, a mutual mistake may exist, as the seller was likely mistaken about the product being sold in the "white microwave" package, and the purchaser was mistaken about the color of the microwave based on the information in the label. In addition to describing the product or the color, a label may contain terms of a warranty that could entice consumers to purchase one microwave over another. A label, for example, that states that a consumer is entitled to a complete two-year replacement warranty would be binding on both parties at the time the purchase is made. Hence, the packaging and labeling of a product contain information about the product and its use, possibly including information about any warranties, that binds the seller and purchaser to the terms of the information on the label once the purchaser tenders payment for the product.

Source: R. Kerin, S. Hartley, E. Berkowitz, and W. Rudelius, *Marketing* (New York: McGraw-Hill/Irwin, 2005), pp. 307–308.

Misrepresentation

Misrepresentations are similar to mistakes. In both cases, at least one of the parties is in error about a fact material to the agreement. But a **misrepresentation** is an untruthful assertion by one of the parties about a material fact. One party said something that prevented the parties from having the mental agreement necessary for a legal contract. The parties only appeared to agree, so their contract lacked legal assent.

The courts are insistent that there must be a meeting of the minds for a valid contract. Thus, they might rescind a contract even though the person making the false assertion was entirely innocent of any intentional deception.

INNOCENT MISREPRESENTATION

An **innocent misrepresentation** results from a false statement about a fact material to an agreement that the person making the statement believed to be true. The person who made the false statement had no knowledge of the falsity of the claim. We say the person lacked **scienter.**

Innocent misrepresentations permit the party that was misled by the false statement to rescind the contract. However, because the party that made the false statement had no intent to mislead, the aggrieved party cannot sue for damages. The reasoning in these cases has the appearance of the arguments in a mutual mistake case, as you might expect.

In Case 17-2, you can get a clear sense of the various elements the plaintiff must prove when trying to rescind a sales contract on grounds of innocent misrepresentation. The case should increase your awareness of the businessperson's need to pay attention to and explain material facts *while the terms of the contract are being created.*

CASE 17-2 MARK SIECH AND PAM SIECH, PLAINTIFFS-RESPONDENTS v. ERV'S SALES & SERVICE, DEFENDANT-APPELLANT

COURT OF APPEALS OF WISCONSIN
1998 WESTLAW 866091 (DEC. 15, 1998)

The Sieches ordered a custom-made boat from Erv's Sales and Service after the sales agent had represented that, after delivery, they could add at least a forty-five-inch live well to the boat. The Sieches ordered the boat based upon this representation. They subsequently discovered that the live well could not be added because it would substantially compromise the boat's structural integrity, as well as void the manufacturer's warranty on the boat. After making this discovery, the Sieches refused delivery of the boat, and asked for their deposit to be returned. When the defendant refused to return their deposit, the plaintiffs sued in small claims court. The small claims court held that a rescission of the contract was appropriate and ordered the defendant to return the $2,000 down payment. Defendant appealed.

JUDGE ROBERT O. WEISEL: Rescission of a contract is an appropriate remedy when a person's manifestation of assent to the contract is induced by a fraudulent or material misrepresentation made by another person which the recipient is justified in relying upon. An innocent misrepresentation can form the basis for contract rescission. A non-fraudulent misrepresentation does not make a contract voidable unless it is material. Therefore, to demonstrate a claim for rescission of the sales contract based upon an innocent misrepresentation, the Sieches must show that: (1) Erv's made a misrepresentation of fact; (2) the misrepresentation was material; (3) the Sieches' reliance on the misrepresentation induced them to enter the contract; and (4) the Sieches were justified in relying on the representation.

A misrepresentation of fact is an assertion that is not in accordance with the facts as they exist. In this instance, the trial court found that the representation of fact Erv's agent made was that at least a forty-five-inch live well could be added to the boat the Sieches ordered. The evidence reflects that, in fact, this representation was untrue. The trial court found that the proposed modification would significantly compromise the boat's structural integrity [and thus] voided the manufacturer's warranty for the boat. The representation that the modification was a feasible alternative to meet the Sieches' desires was erroneous because the modification would have voided the warranty.

The trial court concluded that the installation of the well was material to the purchasers at the time of the order. A misrepresentation is material if it is likely to induce a reasonable person to manifest his assent by the misrepresentation or if the maker knows that it is likely that the recipient will be induced to manifest his assent by the misrepresentation. Because Siech intended to use the boat for muskie tournament fishing, the lack of a sufficiently-sized live well rendered the boat unfit for his intended use. The necessity of the live well was fully disclosed to the sales agent, who fully understood that such a well was of critical importance to the Sieches. Notwithstanding such information the agent represented that post-manufacturer modification creating a forty-five-inch live well was possible when, in fact, such modification ultimately turned out to be unfeasible. The trial court therefore properly concluded that the existence of at least a forty-five-inch live well was material to the purchaser entering into a contract for the purchase of this custom boat.

The trial court concluded that [Siech] was induced to enter into the contract for the purchase of the boat based upon the representation that a post-sales modification of the boat was possible. Siech testified that he wanted the boat for a particular purpose and that the representation that the boat could be modified to meet that purpose substantially contributed to his decision to make the contract. The evidence is sufficient to support the element of reliance required for the rescission of the contract.

Finally, there is no basis in the record establishing that the Sieches' reliance on the agent's misrepresentation was unjustified. The agent's assertion was not of peripheral importance but rather was directed at the core issue of the sale, purchasing a boat conducive to muskie fishing. Further, there are no factual circumstances evident in the record indicating that the Sieches should not have taken this representation seriously.

Erv's contends that it is entitled to retain the $2,000 deposit because the Sieches breached the contract without justification, resulting in damages to Erv's despite Erv's efforts to mitigate. We have determined that the trial court correctly concluded that the Sieches did not breach but were justified in rescinding the contract.

AFFIRMED.

CRITICAL THINKING

What information might be useful to know that is not included in this decision? Try to come up with at least one piece of missing information that would support the conclusion reached on appeal and one that would call the reasoning of the decision into question.

Can you think of a single piece of information that might have caused the court to reach the opposite conclusion? If so, what is the nature of this information, and what makes it so influential?

ETHICAL DECISION MAKING

Who are the main stakeholders in this case? Who experiences costs and benefits that immediately follow from the ruling, and how might these costs and benefits break down in terms of future parties?

In terms of effect on stakeholders, could a more ethically defensible conclusion reasonably have been reached? If so, how would you ethically justify the superiority of the new conclusion; if not, what makes the court's decision so desirable?

NEGLIGENT MISREPRESENTATION

In some contract negotiations, one party makes a statement of material fact that he thinks is true, but he is negligent in making the assertion. Such a **negligent misrepresentation** results when the party making the statement would have known the truth about the fact had he used reasonable care to discover or reveal it.

Even though there was no actual intent to deceive, the party making the false statement is treated in contract law as if the intent were present. If this standard seems unfair to you, remember that the courts find negligent misrepresentation only when the party making the false statement should have known the truth had she used the skills and competence required of a person in her position or profession. The impact of negligent misrepresentation is identical to that of fraudulent misrepresentation, discussed next.

FRAUDULENT MISREPRESENTATION

Any fraud on the part of a party to a contract provides a basis for rescission. The parties cannot be said to have assented when one of the parties was tricked into the "agreement" by a fraudulent misrepresentation. Thus, the agreement was not voluntary and can be rescinded on the grounds that there was no meeting of the minds.

Even in countries that are trying to encourage joint ventures and global commercial activity, such as the People's Republic of China, fraudulent claims can end the country's hospitality to agreements with outsiders.[4] In China, accusations of outsiders' fraudulent misrepresentation have resulted in heavy fines and even refusals to allow the fraudulent party to enter into any more agreements with Chinese firms. The point is that in most, if not all, cultures, there is little judicial sympathy for those who consciously mislead others in commercial activities.

A **fraudulent misrepresentation** is a false representation of a material fact that is consciously false and intended to mislead the other party. Fraudulent misrepresentation is **intentional misrepresentation.** Here scienter is clear. The party making the misrepresentation either knows or believes that the factual claim is false or knows that there is no basis for the assertion.

To understand the requirements for a finding of fraudulent misrepresentation, start with the two elements from the definition:

1. *A false statement about a past or existing fact that is material to the contract and*
2. *Intent to deceive:* Intent can be inferred from the particular circumstances.

Then add a third necessary element:

3. *Justifiable reliance on the false statement by the innocent party to the agreement:* Justifiable reliance is generally present unless the injured party knew, or should have known by the extravagance of the claim, that the false statement was indeed false. For example, a person could not justifiably rely on a claim by another that a hair on her head, while worth $1,000, was available for $10.

Finally, if damages are sought, the defrauded party must have been injured by the misrepresentation.

Each of these elements can become a source of debate in any attempt to rescind a contract on grounds of fraudulent misrepresentation. Thus, it is your responsibility as a person who will be involved with dozens of contracts in your business activities to know these elements. A rescinded contract is a time-consuming and expensive business opportunity that has gone wrong. And don't forget that you can collect damages only from parties you can locate.

Before we go into greater detail about the elements of fraudulent misrepresentation, please consider Case 17-3. Follow the court's reasoning as it thinks through the elements of the attempt to rescind a contract.

[4] Charles D. Paglee, "Contracts and Agreements in the People's Republic of China," www.qis.net/chinalaw/explan1.htm, updated March 6, 1998.

CASE 17-3

GARY W. CRUSE AND VENITA R. CRUSE v. COLDWELL BANKER/GRABEN REAL ESTATE, INC.

SUPREME COURT OF ALABAMA
667 SO. 2D 714 (1995)

Mr. and Mrs. Cruse sued Mr. and Mrs. Harris, Coldwell Banker, and Graben Real Estate, Inc., alleging defective workmanship in the construction of a house that they had bought from the Harrises, and alleging that the defendants had fraudulently misrepresented and/or suppressed material facts about the condition of the house.

When the Cruses began looking for a home, they contacted Graben Real Estate, and a Graben Real

Estate agent took them to see the Harrises' house. Randy Harris, a building contractor, had built the house for sale, and he and his wife were occupying it at that time. Graben Real Estate listed that house as "new" in its real estate advertisements, and the agent told the Cruses that it was new. She also told the Cruses that the house was comparable to, or even better than, the other houses in the neighborhood, that it was a good buy, and that if they purchased the house they could look forward to years of convenient, trouble-free living.

The Cruses signed a contract on November 11, 1992, to purchase the house from the Harrises. When they told the agent they wanted to hire an independent contractor to assess its condition, she told them that it was not really necessary to do so because Randy Harris was a contractor and because the house was well-built.

The Cruses signed an "Acceptance Inspection Contract," which stated that they had inspected the property or waived the right to do so and accepted it in "as-is" condition, and that they based their decision to purchase on their own inspection and not on any representations by the broker.

Plaintiffs took possession of the residence in mid-December 1992 and, soon thereafter, they began noticing many defects in the structure and in its electrical wiring. They contacted Graben Real Estate, who sent an agent to remedy the problems. The defects continued and multiplied, so they sued. At the trial, defendants moved for summary judgment, which was granted. Plaintiffs appealed.

JUSTICE BUTTS: To establish fraudulent misrepresentations, the Cruses are required to show that Graben Real Estate made a false representation concerning a material fact and that they relied upon that representation, to their detriment. The Cruses contend that Graben Real Estate represented to them that the house was new; that, in reliance on that representation, they decided not to hire a contractor to inspect the house and discover its defects; and that reliance resulted in damage to them.

The unequivocal term "new," when applied to real estate, is not merely descriptive. It is a definite legal term that carries with it the implied warranty of habitability and prevents the realtor from invoking the protection of the doctrine of caveat emptor. Graben Real Estate marketed the house as "new," both in print and in direct response to the Cruses' queries. In so doing, Graben Real Estate made statements that went beyond the patter of sales talk and became representations of material fact. Moreover, Gary Cruse testified . . . that he relied upon this representation in failing to hire a contractor to inspect the house before he bought it.

Graben Real Estate argues that even if it did misrepresent the newness of the house, the Cruses could not have justifiably believed the misrepresentation and relied upon it to the point that they would not closely inspect the house before buying it. Graben Real Estate relies heavily on the fact that the Cruses knew that the house was being occupied by the Harrises at the time of the sale, and concludes that this alone should have proved to the Cruses that the house was not actually new. . . . We do not agree that the mere knowledge of the Harrises' prior occupancy so wholly contradicted the printed and spoken representations of Graben Real Estate that the Cruses could not, as a matter of law, have justifiably relied upon them.

Graben Real Estate also argues that, regardless of whether the house was new or was used, the Cruses cannot recover because they signed an "as-is" agreement at the time of the sale, thereby, Graben Real Estate says, accepting the condition of the house without a prior inspection. Graben Real Estate relies on Hope v. Brannan, wherein this Court held that buyers of a 58-year-old house who signed a statement accepting the house "as-is," without independently inspecting it for defects, could not maintain an action for fraud arising from the seller's statements concerning the condition of the house.

Graben Real Estate's reliance on Hope is misplaced; in Hope, the house was not new, nor was it represented to be new. A buyer's failure to inspect the premises of a 58-year-old house before signing an "as-is" agreement is hardly the equivalent of the Cruses' failure to inspect the premises of a house that their realtor had represented to be new.

The evidence establishes that Graben Real Estate misrepresented a material fact and creates a jury question as to whether the Cruses could have justifiably relied upon this misrepresentation in deciding not to closely inspect the house before buying it. The fact that the Cruses knew the house was occupied by a third party before they bought it, along with the fact that they signed an "as-is" agreement, separate from the purchase contract, for a house they claim to have regarded as new, are elements for the jury to consider.

REVERSED AND REMANDED.

[CONTINUED]

CRITICAL THINKING

Several key points in the reasoning of this decision rely on personal testimony. On the basis of your life experience and any knowledge you may have accumulated through your educational career, how reliable do you think witness testimony is as a form of evidence in legal disputes? What are some of the ways that this testimonial evidence might be flawed? What are its particular strengths? In this case, do you think the testimonies are valid? Why or why not?

ETHICAL DECISION MAKING

What general values might the court be seen as interested in protecting in this ruling? How are these similar to values upheld by earlier cases in this chapter? How are they different? What opposing values are seen as less important in these rulings?

Let's now revisit each of the elements of fraudulent misrepresentation. While the elements may have seemed relatively straightforward when they were presented, they become more complicated in the context of actual disagreements among parties to a contract.

False assertion of fact. For fraudulent misrepresentation to be the basis for a contract rescission, the statement of fact need not be an actual assertion. Either concealment or nondisclosure can be treated as the equivalent of an actual assertion. **Concealment** involves the *active* hiding of the truth about a material fact, for example, removing 20,000 miles from the odometer on your car before selling it to me. **Nondisclosure** is different because it refers to a failure to provide pertinent information about the projected contract. The courts have until recently been hesitant to use nondisclosure as a basis for rescinding a contract because it is a passive form of misleading conduct. Under ordinary situations associated with a legal bargain, it is not the obligation of one party to bring up any and all facts he or she might possess. Each individual is, to a large extent, treated as a responsible decision maker.

However, courts will now find nondisclosure as having the same legal effect as an actual false assertion under certain conditions:

1. *A relationship of trust exists between the parties to the contract.* In this situation the relationship provides a reasonable basis for one person's expectation that the other would never act to defraud him or her.
2. *There is failure to correct assertions of fact that are no longer true in light of events that have occurred since the initial consent to the terms of the agreement.* An illustration is my failing to inform you of the recent outbreak of rust on my "rust-free" car that you have agreed to purchase next month.

Nondisclosure is especially likely to provide the basis for rescission when one party has information about a basic assumption of the deal that is unavailable to the other party. As a result of this logic, sellers have a special duty to disclose because they know more about the structural makeup of the item being purchased.

Intent to deceive. *Scienter* is present when the party accused of making the fraudulent assertion believed that the assertion was false or made the claim without any regard for whether it was true or false. Alternatively, *intent to deceive* is present when the party making the false statement claims or implies that he or she has personal knowledge of the accuracy of the assertion. Any resulting assent is not legal because the injured party was not allowed to join the mind of the deceiving party. The party with scienter or intent to deceive wanted the contract to be fulfilled on the basis of a falsehood.

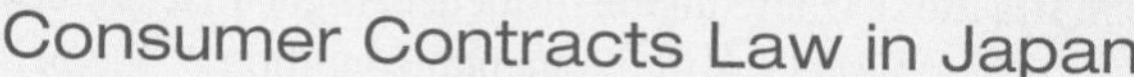

global context

Consumer Contracts Law in Japan

In 1997, after studying the application of civil law in the country, the Japanese Social Policy Council, an advisory body to the prime minister, recognized that the environment surrounding consumers was growing more diversified and that there was a significant gap between consumers and businesses in their access to information and knowledge as well as in their negotiating power. Because it cannot honestly be said that consumers and businesses are equal, as contracting parties are presumed to be under the country's Civil Code, the council developed a special Consumer Contracts Law. This legislation is considered to place consumers and businesses on a more equal footing in transactions.

Under the Consumer Contracts Law, if a business fails to provide a consumer with information or makes misrepresentations concerning basic or other important contractual matters that are necessary for the consumer to make a judgment about the contract, and if the consumer would not have entered into the contract had the information been provided or the misrepresentation not been made, the consumer may cancel the contract. This provision is applicable whenever a business, in trying to induce a consumer to enter into a contract, (1) fails to provide information about the contents of the contract, (2) fails to provide important information necessary for the consumer to make the decision to enter into the contract, or (3) makes misrepresentations. In many of these cases, the consumer would not have been entitled to relief under the Civil Code because of its strict requirements for the application of fraud.

Justifiable reliance on the false assertion. What responsibilities does the injured party have in instances where a false assertion was made by the other party? As we said earlier, the injured party has no justifiable claim of fraud when he or she relied on assertions that should have been obviously false. Anyone who pays for a house in reliance on the claim that it was "built before the founding of our country" cannot then later try to rescind the contract on grounds of fraudulent misrepresentation.

In addition, parties to contracts cannot successfully claim they justifiably relied on a false assertion of fact when the error in the statement would have been clear to anyone who had inspected the item being exchanged. However, even this duty to inspect is declining in modern contract law. Increasing responsibility is being placed on the person who made the erroneous assertion.

Before leaving this section about misrepresentation, consider what would have happened if Billy Welkener, in the opening scenario, had known he was going to receive a dramatic increase in his retirement benefits in a few years but failed to tell his then wife, Patricia? Would she be able to claim that the contract lacked assent because of Billy's misrepresentation? Although no evidence was presented to show Billy knew of such an increase in benefits, it is important to consider all possible situations in determining whether a contract truly did contain assent.

Undue Influence

When legal assent is present, both parties to the agreement are assumed to have made their own choices based on complete freedom to consent to or reject the terms of the bargain. However, many factors in our lives can work together to make our choices anything but free. **Undue influence** refers to those special relationships in which one person has taken advantage of his or her dominant position in a relationship to unduly persuade the other person. The persuasive efforts of the dominant person must have interfered with the ability of the other person to make his or her own decision. When people are bargaining with their attorney, doctor, guardian, relative, or anyone else in a relationship involving a high degree of trust, they can be persuaded by unusual pressures unique to that relationship.

The assent that results may not be legal consent. The courts may see the undue influence of the relationship as interfering with the free choice required for an enforceable contract. Whatever contracts result from undue influence can be voided.

Are all contracts among parties in situations where undue influence might arise thereby likely to be rescinded? Not necessarily. The courts look to the mental condition of the person who would ordinarily rely on the guidance of the dominant person. Courts look to the extent to which the dominant person used the persuasive powers of his or her dominance to "produce" the assent of the other person.

Factors that enter into the finding of undue influence are the following:

1. Was the dominant party rushing the other party to consent?
2. Did the dominant party gain undue enrichment from the agreement?
3. Was the nondominant party isolated from other advisers at the time of the agreement?
4. Is the contract unreasonable in the sense that the results of the exchange overwhelmingly benefit the dominant party?

The more of these factors present, the more likely a court is to rescind the contract on grounds of undue influence.

For example, a recent undue-influence case against Disney will eventually be decided on the basis of the set of circumstances that led to a dying Disney executive's surrendering $2 million in benefits on his deathbed.[5] The Ninth Circuit Court of Appeals reinstated the lawsuit based on the circumstances of a hospital meeting in which a Disney financial officer obtained the signed waiver of benefits. The plaintiff's illness, plus the $2 million that Disney and its insurer stood to gain, was enough to take the case to a jury. The following Case Nugget provides another illustration of undue influence.

Case Nugget A Case of Undue Influence

In re Cheryl E.
Court of Appeals of California, Second Appellate District, Division Six
161 Cal. App. 3d 587 (1984)

At the time the plaintiff entered into an agreement to give her child up for adoption, she was 41 years old, had eight children, had never worked outside the home, had only a ninth-grade education, and had been receiving aid to dependent children. She had discussed the possibility of giving her baby up for adoption with a caseworker shortly before the child was born. She was evicted from her home the day before the child was born. The caseworker came to the hospital and told her she had to sign forms that would allow the baby, Cheryl, to receive medical care and be removed from the hospital. Shortly thereafter, an adoption worker (AW) met with the plaintiff in the parking lot of the Public Social Services Agency (PSSA) and told her that she could get her child back within a year if she changed her mind but said that if she did not sign the papers, the child might be given to her husband and his girlfriend. The AW told the plaintiff she did not need to read the document because it just contained everything they had discussed.

Several months later, the plaintiff met with the AW and her supervisor and told them she was ready to take her daughter back, but they told her she could no longer do that because the child had bonded with her foster preadoptive parents, with whom the child had been living. The court found that the plaintiff had indeed relinquished her child as a result of fraud and undue influence. The appellate court agreed, finding that the following elements characterized the persuasion of the AW as sufficiently excessive to be indicative of undue influence: (1) discussion and consummation of the transaction in an unusual place, (2) insistent demand that the business be finished at once, (3) extreme emphasis on untoward consequences of delay, and (4) absence of third-party advisers to the subservient party.

[5] Bob Egelko, "$2 M Suit Reinstated against Disney," 1999 WL 9736736.

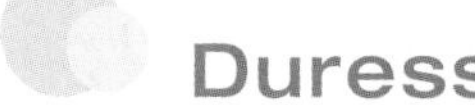

Duress

Duress is a much more visible and active interference with free will than is undue influence. **Duress** is found when one party was forced into the agreement by the wrongful act of another.

The wrongful act may come in various forms. Any of the following would trigger a successful request for rescission on grounds of duress:

- One party threatens physical harm or extortion to gain consent to a contract.
- One party threatens to file a criminal lawsuit unless consent is given to the terms of the contract. (Threats to bring civil cases against a party to a lawsuit do not constitute duress unless the suit is frivolous.)
- One party threatens the other's economic interests (this is known as *economic duress*). For instance, a person refuses to perform according to a contract unless the other person either signs another contract with the one making the threat or pays that person a higher price than was specified in the original agreement.

The injured party makes the case for duress by demonstrating that the threat left him or her no reasonable alternatives. The point is that the free will necessary for legal consent had been removed by the specifics of the threat.

Consider the extent to which the threat in Case 17-4 left the plaintiff no reasonable options other than signing the agreement.

CASE 17-4

ELIZABETH CURRAN v. HO SUNG KWON
UNITED STATES SEVENTH CIRCUIT COURT OF APPEALS
153 F.3D 481 (7TH CIR. 1998)

In 1982, Ho Sung Kwon tried to develop a relationship with Elizabeth Curran, a professional model who was not interested in Kwon. In an attempt to gain Curran's interest, Kwon fabricated a modeling contest sponsored by Revlon. After Curran won the fabricated contest in New York, Kwon, the "supervisor" of the contest, accompanied her to Paris for the next stage of the contest. However, when Curran discovered she was supposed to share a hotel room with Kwon, she refused to stay in the room. Kwon left the room, but he left his passport and $1,200 in cash with Curran.

The next morning, Curran tried to fly back to New York. When Kwon discovered that his passport and money were missing, he reported the theft. Curran was arrested at the airport and held overnight. Although Kwon did not want to press charges, the French prosecutor set a trial for two days later. Curran sought the advice of legal counsel in Paris, and her father also flew to Paris for support. Curran was acquitted, and one day later she signed a release in which she was paid $10,260 so that Kwon and Revlon could be released from any claim which might be brought by Curran regarding the fabricated modeling contest. She left Paris the same day she signed the release.

However, soon after she returned to the United States, Curran disavowed the release and returned payment to Kwon. Approximately one year later she filed suit against Kwon and Revlon, alleging negligence, fraudulent misrepresentation, and false arrest. Kwon filed for summary judgment, citing the release Curran signed in Paris. However, Curran claimed she signed the release under duress; thus, the release was voidable. She stated that she was "tired, confused, and fearful during her stay in Paris," and she argued that she was afraid that she would not be able to leave the country if she did not sign the release. The District Court ruled that the release was not signed under duress and was not voidable.

[CONTINUED]

JUDGE RIPPLE: Curran makes no claim that she can meet the high standard of proof required under French law to prove the "violence" that would justify vitiating the contract. Nor, assuming Illinois law did apply, do we believe that she could show the type of coercion contemplated by the governing Illinois cases . . . (defining duress as "a condition where one is induced by a wrongful act or threat of another to make a contract under circumstances which deprive him of the exercise of his free will, and it may be conceded that a contract executed under duress is voidable"). Put simply, she cannot, on this record, demonstrate that her execution of the release was not the product of her free will.

As the district court noted, Curran had endured some difficult circumstances in the days before the execution of the release. Nevertheless, it is undisputed that, at the time she executed the document, she had been exonerated of any criminal charges under French law and had been assured that she was free to leave France. The claim that her freedom was contingent on her signing the release is simply not supported by the record. Indeed, she had rejected a settlement offer prior to the disposition of those charges. Moreover, at the time that she executed the release, she had the advice of both her French and American counsel and had familial support through the presence of her father. Under these circumstances, the record simply would not support a determination by the trier of fact that she executed the release under duress. She was not "bereft of the quality of mind essential to the making of a contract."

AFFIRMED.

CRITICAL THINKING

Why does Judge Ripple interpret the facts of this case as not logically leading to the plaintiff's being "bereft of the quality of mind essential to the making of a contract"? Are there any key assumptions in this reasoning process? What models of psychological thought might lead to the conclusion that this situation would produce such a state in the plaintiff? Is Judge Ripple's stance adequately justified? Why or why not?

ETHICAL DECISION MAKING

The ethics of the individual parties directly involved in the relevant circumstances are questionable and interesting. Formulate an argument for whichever party you feel acted in a more ethically acceptable fashion, from the beginning of the provided information up to and including the original lawsuit. Justify your stance in terms of at least one ethical theory.

Unconscionability

A final way to question the appropriateness of consent arises when one of the parties has so much more bargaining power than the other that he or she dictates the terms of the agreement. Such an agreement can be rescinded on grounds of **unconscionability.** The disproportionate amount of power possessed by one party to the contract has made a mockery of the idea of free will, a necessity for legal consent. The resulting contract is called an **adhesion contract.**

Although unconscionability has traditionally been limited to the sale of goods under the Uniform Commercial Code, many courts have not followed that tradition. When they see contracts written by one party and then presented to the other party with the threat to "take it or leave it," they sometimes extend the idea of unconscionability beyond the sale of goods.

global context

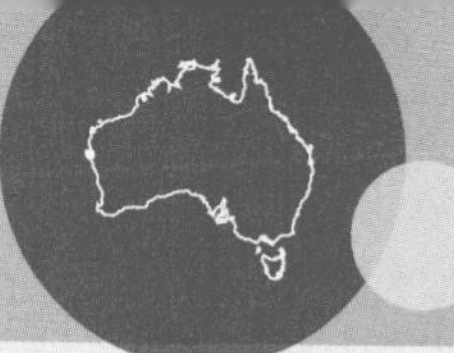

Duress in Australia

Australia recognizes a special category of duress that is not set aside for special treatment in the United States: duress of goods. *Duress of goods* occurs whenever an illegitimate threat is made to hold on to goods unless a payment is made or an agreement is entered into. This situation can be contrasted to a situation in which someone legitimately holds on to goods when money is owed on them or the goods have been used as security for a loan.

Australia also recognizes economic duress, which is the unacceptable use of economic power to place the victim in a situation where he or she has no practical alternative but to submit to the accompanying demand.

To prove economic duress, a plaintiff must establish that (1) pressure was used to procure his or her assent to an agreement or to the payment of money, (2) the pressure was illegitimate in the circumstance, (3) the pressure in fact contributed to the person's assenting to the transaction, and (4) the person's assent to the transaction was reasonable in the circumstances.

Just as with economic duress in the United States, it is often unclear when pressure is illegitimate. A threat to do something unlawful is almost always undue pressure. A threat to use the civil legal process is usually considered lawful, unless the contemplated legal action would clearly be an abuse of process. "Driving a hard bargain" or refusing to do any more business with someone in the future is generally not regarded as economic duress, however.

In arguing for a switch from a dollar amount to a percentage, Patricia Welkener, in the opening scenario, claims that the contract she entered into was unconscionable. Her argument is that the mistake of using an amount and not a percentage precludes her award from ever increasing. As such, each month she would be cheated out of money to which she is entitled. As the months go by, the unfairness is compounded, ultimately making the enforcement of the contract unconscionable. Do you think the court agrees with Patricia Welkener's logic?

Follow the judge's reasoning in Case 17-5 to review the type of reasoning that makes up a claim for unconscionability.

CASE 17-5

ORVILLE ARNOLD AND MAXINE ARNOLD, PLAINTIFFS v. UNITED COMPANIES LENDING CORPORATION, A CORPORATION, AND MICHAEL T. SEARLS, AN INDIVIDUAL, DEFENDANTS
SUPREME COURT OF APPEALS OF WEST VIRGINIA
1998 WL 8651015

On September 17, 1996, Michael Searls came to the residence of Orville and Maxine Arnold, an elderly couple. He offered to arrange a loan for the Arnolds, acting as a loan broker. He procured a loan for them. Out of the loan proceeds, a mortgage broker fee of $940.00 was paid to Searls and/or Accent Financial Services, with which Searls is affiliated.

At the loan closing, United Lending had the benefit of legal counsel, while the Arnolds apparently did not. During the course of the transaction, the Arnolds were presented with more than twenty-five documents to sign. Among these documents were a promissory note, reflecting a principal sum of $19,300.00 and a yearly interest rate of 12.990%; a Deed of Trust, giving United Lending a security interest in the Arnolds' real estate; and a two-page form labeled "Acknowledgment and Agreement to Mediate or Arbitrate," which stated that all legal controversies arising out of the loan would be resolved through nonappealable, confidential arbitration, and that all damages would be direct damages, with no punitive damages available. However, this agreement to not arbitrate did not limit the lender's right to pursue legal actions in a court of law relating to collection of the loan.

On July 10, 1997, the Arnolds filed suit against United Lending and Searls, seeking a declaratory judgment adjudging the arbitration agreement to be void and unenforceable. On August 11, 1997, United Lending moved to dismiss the entire action on the basis of the compulsory arbitration agreement. The circuit court certified three questions to the state supreme court.

JUSTICE McCUSKEY: We reformulate the question as follows: Whether an arbitration agreement entered into as part of a consumer loan transaction containing a substantial waiver of the consumer's rights, including access to the courts, while preserving for all practical purposes the lender's right to a judicial forum, is void as a matter of law.

The drafters of the Uniform Consumer Credit Code explained that the [basic test] of unconscionability is whether . . . the conduct involved is, or the contract or clauses involved are, so one-sided as to be unconscionable under the circumstances existing at the time the conduct occurs or is threatened or at the time of the making of the contract. . . . [T]his Court stated:

> ["W]here a party alleges that the arbitration provision was unconscionable, or was thrust upon him because he was unwary and taken advantage of, or that the contract was one of adhesion, the question of whether an arbitration provision was bargained for and valid is a matter of law for the court to determine by reference to the entire contract. . . ." A determination of unconscionability must focus on the relative positions of the parties, the adequacy of the bargaining position, the meaningful alternatives available to the plaintiff, and "the existence of unfair terms in the contract."

Applying the rule . . . leads us to the inescapable conclusion that the arbitration agreement between the Arnolds and United Lending is "void for unconscionability" as a matter of law. . . . The relative positions of the parties, a national corporate lender on one side and elderly, unsophisticated consumers on the other, were "grossly unequal." In addition, there is no evidence that the loan broker made any other loan option available to the Arnolds. In fact, the record does not indicate that the Arnolds were seeking a loan, but rather were solicited by defendant Searls. Thus, the element of "a comparable, meaningful alternative" to the loan from United Lending is lacking. Because the Arnolds had no meaningful alternative to obtaining the loan from United Lending, and also did not have the benefit of legal counsel during the transaction, their bargaining position was clearly inadequate when compared to that of United Lending.

Given the nature of this arbitration agreement, combined with the great disparity in bargaining power, one can safely infer that the terms were not bargained for and that allowing such a one-sided agreement to stand would unfairly defeat the Arnolds' legitimate expectations.

Finally, the terms of the agreement are "unreasonably favorable" to United Lending. United Lending's acts or omissions could seriously damage the Arnolds, yet the Arnolds' only recourse would be to submit the matter to binding arbitration. At the same time, United Lending's access to the courts is wholly preserved in every conceivable situation where United Lending would want to secure judicial relief against the Arnolds. The wholesale waiver of the Arnolds' rights together with the complete preservation of United Lending's rights "is inherently inequitable and unconscionable because in a way it nullifies all the other provisions of the contract."

Judgment in favor of Plaintiffs.

CRITICAL THINKING

Cases like this highlight the importance of language in the legal system. Phrases quoted from the law are subject to significant judicial discretion, and it is indeed the construction of particular definitions for these phrases that allows rulings like this to be possible. Using the contextual clues found in the information in the passage, choose two of the descriptions in quotes and write your idea of how the judge must be defining the relevant phrase. Then come up with some other ways these phrases could have been defined. Would the use of your alternatives significantly affect the reasonableness of the conclusion?

ETHICAL DECISION MAKING

How does this issue lend itself very well to considerations of ethicality? What sort of theoretical approach do you see the court taking with this ruling? On the basis of other decisions you have encountered in this book, what do you think is probably the most common ethical framework U.S. courts use in guiding their rulings? How well does this case fit with larger trends? Support your answer.

global context

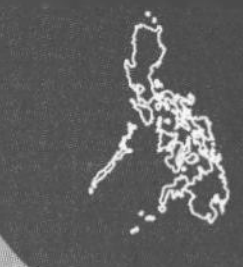

Defects in Assent in the Philippines

The law in the Philippines is somewhat unusual in the way it limits the time for rescinding a contract. In the Philippines, if consent is given through mistake, violence, intimidation, undue influence, or fraud, contracts are valid until they are annulled. The period within which to annul such a contract is four years. In cases of intimidation, violence, or undue influence, the time period is measured from the time the defect in the assent ceases. In cases of mistake or fraud, it is measured from the time of the discovery of the defect.

CASE OPENER WRAP-UP

A Disagreement over an Agreement

The trial court did not agree with Patricia Welkener's argument regarding a mistake in the contract. Patricia appealed, and the court affirmed the lower court's decision. The court held that Patricia failed to present evidence at trial amounting to proof that the award she was granted was unreasonable. At the time, the award represented the percentage Patricia and her counsel sought. Furthermore, no evidence was presented regarding the likelihood of Billy Welkener's benefits increasing. Accordingly, the court found the award to be reasonable and, in so doing, rejected Patricia's argument that the contract was unconscionable. Without proof of unconscionability or sufficient evidence showing a genuine issue created by Patricia's supposed unilateral mistake, the court affirmed the decision that upheld the contract as agreed to in court by both parties.

Summary

The Importance of Legal Assent — If assent is not genuine, or legal, a contract may be voidable. For purposes of planning, it is important for people to understand the circumstances under which failure of assent may render their contracts voidable.

Mistake — *Mistakes* are erroneous beliefs about the material facts of a contract at the time the agreement is made. They may be either unilateral or mutual. Only under certain rare conditions are unilateral mistakes a basis for rescinding a contract. However, if both parties to a contract are mistaken about a material fact, either can opt to rescind the contract. In cases of mutual mistake, the agreement was not based on a meeting of the minds, a basic criterion for a legal assent.

Misrepresentation — *Misrepresentation* is an intentional untruthful assertion by one of the parties about a material fact. An innocent misrepresentation occurs when the party making the false assertion believes it to be true. The misled party may rescind the contract. When a misrepresentation is fraudulent, any assent that is given is gained by deceit. The courts permit rescission for fraudulent misrepresentation. In addition to requiring false assertion and intent to deceive, fraudulent misrepresentation also requires justifiable reliance on the assertion by the innocent party.

Undue Influence — *Undue influence* refers to the persuasive efforts of a dominant party who uses a special relationship with another party to interfere with the other's free choice of the terms of a contract. Any relationship in which one party has an unusual degree of trust in the other can trigger concern about undue influence in gaining the assent of the more dependent party.

Duress *Duress* occurs when one party threatens the other with a wrongful act unless assent is given. Such assent is not legal assent because coercion interferes with the party's free will. For the courts to rescind the agreement, the injured party must demonstrate that the duress left no reasonable alternatives to agreeing to the contract.

Unconscionability *Unconscionability* may be a basis for avoiding a contract if one party has so much relative bargaining power that he or she, in effect, dictates the terms of the contract. The resulting agreement is an adhesion contract.

Point / Counterpoint

The principles of legal assent are based on the belief that, in the main, each person can look out for himself or herself. Thus, parties are usually held to the agreements they make on the grounds that the terms were reached by decisions guided by the free wills of both parties. But we live in a world of rapid technological change, where chemicals, fibers, and services come in a blinding array of complexity that could make decision making more difficult for some people.

<table>
<tr><th colspan="2">Should Courts Provide More Protection from Agreements Based on Lack of Knowledge on the Part of the Buyer?</th></tr>
<tr><th>Yes</th><th>No</th></tr>
<tr><td>Courts should protect buyers from assent that is based on ignorance. For an assent to be worthy of legal protection, the buyer must appreciate what he or she has agreed to purchase. Otherwise contract law protects the strong from the weak.
For assent to be a cornerstone of a fair legal framework, it must flow from something other than large-scale misunderstanding about the safety, composition, and longevity of what we purchase.
Just go to any grocery store and ask yourself, "How much do I know about what I am about to assent to purchase?"</td><td>Existing contract law already contains adequate protection against severe cases of buyer confusion. Much of this chapter contains reasoning that buyers could use in certain instances to rescind an agreement.
What is especially disturbing about the suggestion that courts should provide more protection for parties to a contract is the danger the suggestion poses for personal liberty and independence. What will happen to our incentive to learn and grow as individuals if we know that the local judge and jury are ready to protect us from our own failure to discover more about goods and services that we plan to purchase?</td></tr>
</table>

Questions & Problems

1. Explain the difference between a unilateral mistake and a mutual mistake.

2. Explain when a unilateral mistake can lead to a contract's being voidable.

3. Distinguish innocent misrepresentation from fraudulent misrepresentation.

4. Explain how nondisclosure can be treated as misrepresentation.
5. Explain the primary differences between duress and undue influence.
6. Olga Mestrovic, the wife of an internationally known sculptor and artist, died owning a number of his works of art. Her will directed that all the artwork be sold, with the proceeds split among the surviving family members. She also owned real estate that, likewise, was to be sold. The executor, 1st Source Bank, sold the real estate to Wilkins, along with specified pieces of personal property that were in the house, such as the refrigerator, stove, and French sconces. When Wilkins took possession of the property, he complained to the bank that the property was a mess. The bank said it would either hire a rubbish removal service or allow Wilkins to clean it up and pay him for doing so.

   In the process of cleaning up, Wilkins discovered eight drawings and one sculpture done by the artist. Wilkins claimed that he owned these items under his agreement with the bank, but the bank sought to recover them. The probate court ruled that there was no contract for the sale of the works of art. What argument do you think Wilkins made on appeal? How do you think the court ruled? Why? [*Wilkins v. 1st Source Bank,* 548 N.E.2d 170 (Ind. Ct. App. 1990).]
7. The appellant, Independent School District No. 622, in preparing to move into a new building one block away, called three movers to get bids for the cost of moving the school's property. The school district received bids for $19,854, $59,880, and $83,972. Because appellee Metcalf's bid was so low, an employee of the school district contacted the company to make sure the bid was correct. The appellee assured him that the company was "comfortable with the bid."

   Prior to the move, the parties discussed the terms of the agreement and the dates. In January 1997, the contract was issued. The parties discussed various details of the move on six additional occasions. On the first day of the move, the appellant received a requested invoice for the move, on which the estimate of $20,000 was listed. Midway through the move, appellant school district was presented with an invoice for $16,686, which it paid. At the end of the move, the school district received a second invoice for $49,854. It paid $3,168, which was the amount remaining on the original bid. The respondent sued for breach of contract, and sought damages of $45,991, the unpaid portion of the second invoice.

   At the trial court, summary judgment was given to the school district. What argument do you think the appellant made as to why he was entitled to the full amount of his second invoice? Look carefully at the facts surrounding the making of the contract. Why do you think the respondent was or was not successful? [*A.A. Metcalf v. North St. Paul–Maplewood-Oakdale Schools,* 587 N.W.2d 311 (1998).]
8. In December 1992, Koontz entered into an agreement with Tatum & Denziger (T & D), an architectural firm, whereby the firm was to design a residence for Koontz at a price of 10 percent of the actual cost of construction. When the parties entered into the agreement, T & D estimated that the entire process, from design through final construction, should be able to be completed in less than 24 months. Koontz received the first plans in January 1993, sent them back for modification, and got the second set back on June 10, 1994. At that time, T & D estimated that the cost of construction would be $800,000. Koontz took bids for construction from three preselected contractors, and the bids he received ranged from $983,000 to $1,200,000. Koontz immediately terminated his contract with T & D and asked that all architectural fees paid through the date of the termination be returned. T & D offered to continue working on the project and suggested revisions to lower costs, but Koontz refused. He

ultimately hired a different architect, who designed a house that Koontz constructed for $870,000.

After the house was completed in 1996, Koontz sued T & D for, among other claims, negligent misrepresentation, alleging that T & D negligently represented that the cost of the construction phase of the project would be significantly lower, that the design phase could be completed in a reasonable time, and that the architect's fees would be reasonable. T & D filed a motion for summary judgment, which was granted. What do you believe the outcome of Koontz's appeal was? Why? [*Koontz v. Thomas and Denzinger,* 1999 WL 31459 (S.C. App.).]

9. Audrey Vokes was a 51-year-old widow who wanted to become an "accomplished dancer." She was invited to attend a "dance party" at J. P. Davenports' School of Dancing, an Arthur Murray franchise. She subsequently signed up for dance classes, at which she received elaborate praise. Her instructor initially sold her eight half-hour dance lessons for $14.50 each, to be used one each month. Eventually, after being continually told that she had excellent potential and that she was developing into a beautiful dancer—when in fact she was not developing her dance ability and had no aptitude for dance—she ended up purchasing a total of 2,302 hours' worth of dance lessons for a total of $31,090.45. When it finally became clear to Vokes that she was not developing her dance skills, in part because she had trouble even hearing the musical beat, she sued Arthur Murray. What would be the basis of her argument? Her case was initially dismissed by the trial court. What do you think the result of her appeal was? [*Okes v. Arthur Murray,* 212 So. 2d 906 (1968).]

10. Arnold Olson and his now-deceased spouse deeded their property to their six children in perpetuity until they die. During a subsequent conversation with his son and daughter-in-law, held in the presence of two of the other children, he granted his son part of that property, which included the home and several buildings. He told the son and his wife that he would give him the part of the property with the buildings on it as long as they did not sell the property while he was alive, because he wanted to live in a trailer on the property. He then executed a second deed conveying the property but failed to include the life estate in this second deed.

    The father lived in his trailer on the property for four years. Then the son told him that he would have to move because they were selling the property. The father and the other children sued to have the contract reformed on the grounds of mistake. The trial court agreed and reformed the contract to include the provision for the father's life estate. Why do you think the appellate court either affirmed or reversed the lower court's decision? [*Olson v. Olson,* 1998 WL 170111.]

11. The Winklers were interested in purchasing a home in the Valleyview Farms housing development. They contacted the developer, Galehouse, and selected a lot that cost $57,000. They asked the developer to show them plans for houses for which the construction costs would range from $180,000 to $190,000, indicating that this was the price they would be willing to spend for construction only and wasn't to include the lot price. The developer gave them several books and plans to look at.

    After the Winklers had several conversations with Galehouse, the developer drafted plans for a 2,261-square-foot house and gave the Winklers a quote of $198,000 for construction. The lot price was not included. After several months of adding options and upgrades to the plan, the cost rose to $242,000, excluding the lot. The parties then engaged in a couple of weeks of negotiations regarding the price of the construction and lot. Eventually they reached a compromise of a total price of $291,000 ($243,000 for the construction and $48,000 for the lot).

Galehouse prepared a written contract to reflect the parties' agreement, but the developer forgot to include the lot price. The Winklers paid Galehouse $48,000, the lot price, as a deposit on the contract. When the construction was completed, and the Winklers were finalizing their loan from the bank, the parties discovered the drafting error. Galehouse sued to have the contract reformed to reflect the agreed-on price. Should the contract be reformed? Why or why not? [*Galehouse v. Winkler,* 1998 WL 312527.]

12. Plaintiff Stirlen was the chief financial officer for Supercuts. On numerous occasions, he informed Lipson, to whom he reported directly, and other corporate officers of various operating problems he felt contributed to the general decline in Supercuts' retail profits and of "accounting irregularities" he feared might be in violation of state and federal statutes and regulations. After Stirlen brought his concerns to the company's auditor, Lipson allegedly reprimanded him, accused him of being a "troublemaker," and told him that if he did not reverse his position on the issues taken to the auditor he would no longer be considered a "member of the team." Stirlen was terminated the following month, and he subsequently filed suit for wrongful discharge. Supercuts' general counsel moved to compel arbitration under the compulsory arbitration provision of the employment contract between the parties.

The contract provided that all claims arising out of an individual's employment, including civil rights actions and tort claims, must be submitted to arbitration within one year of the date on which the dispute arose, or the employee waives his right to pursue the claim. Damages that could be awarded through arbitration were limited to "a money award not to exceed the amount of actual damages for breach of contract, less any proper offset for mitigation of such damages, and the parties shall not be entitled to any other remedy at law or in equity, including but not limited to other money damages, punitive damages, specific performance, and/or injunctive relief." In the event that an employee did submit a dispute to arbitration, the employee's employment would immediately cease, as would any claims he had to unpaid benefits, without any penalty to the company, pending the outcome of the arbitration.

The agreement did not totally prevent the use of the courts, however. It provided that the following need not be submitted to arbitration: "Any action initiated by the Company seeking specific performance or injunctive or other equitable relief in connection with any breach . . . of this Agreement."

The trial court found that this agreement was unconscionable. How do you believe the appellate court ruled on this case? Why? [*Stirlen v. Supercuts, Inc., et al.,* 51 Cal. App. 1519 (1997).]

Looking for more review material?

The Online Learning Center at **www.mhhe.com/kubasek1e** contains this chapter's "Assignment on the Internet" and also a list of URLs for more information, entitled "On the Internet." Find both of them in the Student Center portion of the OLC, along with quizzes and other helpful materials.

Contracts in Writing

CASE OPENER

Dairy Farm Dispute

Carlin Krieg owned a dairy farm that was appraised at $154,000. Krieg informed Donald Hieber he intended to sell the farm at a price of $106,000, with an additional $24,000 for the machinery and $1,000 per cow for the cattle. Hieber told Krieg he was interested in purchasing the farm, machinery, and cattle.

Krieg orally informed Hieber that he wanted to retain a "right of residency" in the farm. Krieg executed a handwritten statement, which Hieber signed. The statement provides, in part: "I [Krieg] have the privilege of living in home for life time."

Krieg and Hieber executed a purchase agreement. The purchase agreement contained an integration clause stating that the agreement was to be considered whole and there were no other agreements, outside of that writing, between the parties.

At closing, Krieg canceled insurance coverage on the farm in the amount of $189,000, and retained insurance coverage only in the amount of $5,000 for his personal property. Hieber purchased insurance coverage on the farm.

Approximately one year later, the house located on the farm was partially burned in an accidental fire, rendering it uninhabitable. Because the fire loss was covered by Hieber's insurance policy, Hieber filed an insurance claim and received the insurance proceeds. Hieber did not repair the house but, rather, used the proceeds to reduce his mortgage debt on the farm.

Krieg filed a complaint for right of residency against Hieber, alleging estoppel and breach of contract. In his complaint, Krieg argued that his right of residency served as consideration for the reduced purchase price in the purchase agreement between himself and Hieber and, thus, that Hieber breached the contract by not using the fire insurance proceeds to reconstruct the house in which Krieg resided. The court ruled in favor of Hieber. In

CHAPTER 18

particular, Krieg challenged the trial court's consideration of evidence regarding the "negotiations" between the contracting parties on the purchase price of the farm.[1]

1. If you were an attorney representing Krieg, what information would you include regarding the negotiations in the writing to ensure your client's house is protected?
2. Under which, if any, ethical theories should Hieber be held responsible for repairing Krieg's house?

The Wrap-Up at the end of the chapter will answer these questions.

Learning Objectives

After reading this chapter, you will be able to answer the following questions:

1. What is the purpose of the statute of frauds?
2. Which kinds of contracts require a writing to satisfy the statute of frauds?
3. What must a writing contain to be sufficient to satisfy the statute of frauds?
4. What is the purpose of the parol evidence rule?

[1] *Krieg v. Hieber,* 802 N.E.2d 938 (2004).

Written contracts provide certain advantages oral contracts lack. Where disputes may arise regarding the specifics of the terms of an oral contract, such disputes are easier to settle when the contractual terms are solidified in writing. In addition, when parties to a contract write down their terms, the moment of writing allows both parties to reconsider their terms and ensure that the parties are advocating what they desire in the contract. In general, written contracts aid in the conduct of smooth business transactions. Accordingly, some contracts are required to be in writing.

While the American statute of frauds outlines which contracts must be in writing, the idea of requiring that certain contracts be in writing actually comes from an English act. In 1677, the English Parliament passed the Act for the Prevention of Frauds and Perjuries. This act was intended to correct a problem in the common law that arose when parties were in dispute over the existence of a contract. Consequently, the act required that specific types of contracts be in writing to ensure their enforceability. Such a contract must have been written and signed by the party denying the existence of the contract.

Although the law frequently references the *statute of frauds,* the term is somewhat misleading. There is no federal legislation entitled "Statute of Frauds." Rather, the statute exists as legislation at the state level. In fact, almost every state has created its own version of the 1677 English act, adopting all or part of that act. The exceptions are Louisiana, which has not passed such legislation, and New Mexico and Maryland, which follow statutes of frauds created by judicial decision and not the legislature. Interestingly enough, the English have repealed almost all their requirements for writing, while American states and courts are still expanding the requirements for what falls within the statute of frauds.

In addition to the statute's not being a unitary government act, the name "statute of frauds" is misleading in another way. The statute of frauds does not relate to fraudulent contracts, nor does it address the issue of illegal contracts. Rather, the statute addresses the enforceability of contracts that fail to meet the requirements set forth in the statute. Furthermore, the statute serves to protect promisors from poorly considered oral contracts by requiring that certain contracts be in writing.

This chapter addresses some commonalities of the statutes of frauds of different states, while referring simply to the "statute of frauds" as if it were a unitary law. The chapter examines which contracts need to be in writing, as well as exceptions to the rule. Then the chapter examines the parol evidence rule, which discusses which types of oral evidence are admissible, and when, as related to contracts within the scope of the statute of frauds.

Statute of Frauds

The **statute of frauds** has three main purposes. First, the statute attempts to ease contractual negotiations by requiring sufficiently reliable evidence to prove the existence and specific terms of a contract. When a contract is deemed important enough to be required to be in writing under the statute of frauds, the statute specifies what is considered reliable evidence.

The second main purpose of the statute of frauds is to prevent unreliable oral evidence from interfering with a contractual relationship. By requiring that a contract be in writing, the statute precludes the admittance of oral evidence denying the existence of a contract or claiming additional terms that would substantially alter the contract from its agreed-on written form. This chapter further discusses the admissibility or denial of oral evidence later, in the section on the parol evidence rule.

The third main purpose of the statute of frauds is to prevent parties from entering into contracts with which they do not agree. That is, the statute provides some degree of cautionary protection for parties by requiring a written and signed contract. The parties must carefully consider the terms, agree to them, write them out, and finally sign the contract. It is the law's assumption that the aforementioned steps will allow parties time for careful consideration. Accordingly, the statute works to prevent hasty, improperly considered contracts.

Contracts Falling within the Statute of Frauds

As previously mentioned, only specific types of contracts are within the scope of the statute of frauds and thus required to be evidenced in writing. These types of contracts are (1) contracts whose terms prevent possible performance within one year, (2) promises made in consideration of marriage, (3) contracts for one party to pay the debt of another if the initial party fails to pay, and (4) contracts related to an interest in land. Although required to be in writing under the Uniform Commercial Code (UCC), and not the statute of frauds, a related fifth category is contracts for the sale of goods totaling more than \$500.[2]

CONTRACTS WHOSE TERMS PREVENT POSSIBLE PERFORMANCE WITHIN ONE YEAR

Contracts whose performance, based on the terms of the contract, could not possibly occur within one year fall within the statute of frauds and, therefore, must be in writing.[3] It is important to realize that the one-year period begins to run the day after the contract is created, *not* when the contract is scheduled to begin.

For example, Robert enters into a contract with Elise to work for her for one year starting on October 1. If the contract was created on the prior September 15, it is impossible for the contract to be completed in one year from September 16; therefore, the contract must be in writing. However, if the contract is scheduled to start immediately, it can be completed in one year and need not be in writing as it is not within the statute of frauds.

The test for compliance with the one-year rule is not related to the likelihood of the completion of the contract within one year. Rather, the test considers the *possibility* of completing the contract in one year. While the above example is within the statute because, according to the contract terms, it cannot be performed within one year, a contract for lifetime employment does not need to be in writing.

If Robert contracts with Elise for lifetime employment, they do not have to write and sign the agreement because it is possible for the contract to be completed within one year: Robert *could* die after two days of work. Moreover, Robert and Elise's contract, if oral, would be enforceable, as it is not within the statute of frauds. The possibility that a contract's terms could be performed within one year removes the contract from the statute's written requirements.

Similarly, contracts for complex construction projects need not be in writing because, theoretically, they can be completed within one year if a sufficiently large crew works around the clock every day, even if the scenario is highly unlikely.

PROMISES MADE IN CONSIDERATION OF MARRIAGE

Agreements regarding marriage in which one party is gaining something other than a return on his or her promise to marry is within the statute of frauds and must be in writing.[4] In other words, when one party promises something to the other as part of an offer of marriage, the contract must be in writing to be enforceable.

[2] UCC § 2-201.

[3] Restatement (Second) of Contracts, sec. 130.

[4] Ibid, sec. 124.

For example, Ed and Jeanie want to get married. Ed promises Jeanie that he will buy her a new car every other year if she will marry him. To be enforceable, Ed and Jeanie's agreement must be in writing because Jeanie stands to benefit, by way of new cars, if she marries Ed.

It is important to realize that mutual promises to marry do not fall within the statute of frauds. If Ed and Jeanie promise each other they will get married, this agreement does not need to be in writing because neither party is gaining anything other than a return on his or her promise to marry and, therefore, the agreement does not fall within the statute.

While a mutual promise to marry does not fall within the statute of frauds, prenuptial agreements do. A **prenuptial agreement** is an agreement two parties enter into before marriage that clearly states the ownership rights each party enjoys in the other party's property. To be enforceable, prenuptial agreements must be in writing. Furthermore, although consideration is not legally required, courts tend to privilege prenuptial agreements that involve consideration. A prenuptial agreement is not automatically enforceable just because it is in writing. Although writing is required, it is not sufficient to establish enforceability. Consideration as one of the terms offers evidence that both parties understand and agree to all the terms of the agreement and that the agreement is not biased in favor of one of the parties.

CONTRACTS FOR ONE PARTY TO PAY THE DEBT OF ANOTHER IF THE INITIAL PARTY FAILS TO PAY

The contracts within the statute of frauds involving promises to pay a debt are of a very limited kind. Called **secondary obligations,** these promises are also referred to as *secondary promises, collateral promises,* or *suretyship promises.* A secondary obligation occurs when a party outside a primary agreement promises to fulfill one of the original party's (primary debtor's) obligations if the original party fails to fulfill his or her obligation. For example, Helen enters into a contract with Tom to sell Tom her car. Subsequently, Diana agrees to pay Tom's debt if he fails to pay Helen the money he owes her. To be enforceable, Diana's promise needs to be in writing because it is a secondary obligation and therefore falls within the statute.

It is important to understand the distinction between primary and secondary obligations to know when the statute requires a written agreement. **Primary obligations** are debts incurred in an initial contract. Using our car-sale example, the primary obligation is Tom's promise to pay Helen for the car. Primary obligations are not within the statute of frauds and, therefore, need not be in writing to be enforceable. Secondary obligations, as explained above, are within the statute and need to be in writing.

A specific instance of a secondary obligation involves the administrator or executor of an estate. Administrators and executors of estates are responsible for paying off the debts of an estate and then dividing the remaining assets appropriately among the heirs. While an agreement to pay the estate's debts with the estate's funds need not be in writing, promises the administrator or executor makes to pay these debts personally are within the statute of frauds and must be in writing. Because the administrator or executor is promising to pay with his or her own money, and not the estate's, the promise must be in writing to be enforceable; the administrator or executor has assumed a secondary obligation.

There is an exception as to when a secondary obligation needs to be in writing: the *main-purpose rule.* If the main purpose for incurring a secondary obligation is to obtain a personal benefit, the promise does not fall within the statute and does not have to be in writing.[5] The assumption is that a party attempting to achieve a personal benefit will not

[5] Ibid., sec. 116.

back out of the promise, therefore eliminating the need of a written record of the promise. The court's job is to use the context surrounding the agreement to determine the third party's main purpose for entering the agreement; this will determine whether a writing is required for the agreement to be enforceable.

Case 18-1 is an example of a court's consideration of a suretyship promise to attempt to determine whether the promise falls within the statute of frauds.

CASE 18-1

POWER ENTERTAINMENT, INC., ET AL. v. NATIONAL FOOTBALL LEAGUE PROPERTIES, INC.

UNITED STATES COURT OF APPEALS FOR THE FIFTH CIRCUIT
151 F.3D 247 (1998)

Pro Set had a licensing agreement with NFLP, which allowed Pro Set to market NFL cards bearing the statement "official card of the National Football League." Pro Set filed for bankruptcy owing NFLP approximately $800,000 in unpaid royalties from card sales. Representatives of Power Entertainment met with NFLP to discuss taking over the licensing agreement between NFLP and Pro Set. Power Entertainment alleges NFLP orally agreed to transfer Pro Set's license to Power Entertainment in return for Power Entertainment's agreement to assume Pro Set's debt to NFLP. NFLP subsequently refused to transfer the licensing agreement to Power Entertainment.

Power Entertainment then brought a breach of contract suit against NFLP seeking damages for amounts spent in reliance on the alleged agreement and for lost profits. The district court granted NFLP's motion to dismiss, holding Power Entertainment's contract claim failed as a matter of law because it was not in writing and Power Entertainment had failed to plead facts sufficient to support an estoppel claim. Power Entertainment filed timely notice of appeal.

JUDGE BENAVIDES: In granting NFLP's motion to dismiss, the district court concluded the "suretyship" statute of frauds rendered the alleged oral agreement between NFLP and Power Entertainment unenforceable because Power Entertainment promised to assume Pro Set's debt to NFLP as part of the alleged oral agreement. The relevant statute of frauds provision under Texas law provides "a promise by one person to answer for the debt, default, or miscarriage of another person" must be in writing. As the Supreme Court of Texas has explained, the suretyship statute of frauds serves an evidentiary function:

> Probably the basic reason for requiring a promise to answer for the debt of another to be in writing is the promisor has received no direct benefit from the transaction. When the promisor receives something, this is subject to proof and tends to corroborate the making of the promise. Perjury is thus more likely in the case of a guaranty where nothing but the promise is of evidentiary value. The lack of any benefit received by the promisor not only increases the hardship of his being called upon to pay but also increases the importance of being sure that he is justly charged.

These evidentiary concerns do not pertain, however, if "the promise is made for the promisor's own benefit and not at all for the benefit of the third person. . . ." Consistent with this common-sense approach, the Texas courts have adopted the "main purpose doctrine," which, broadly speaking, removes an oral agreement to pay the debt of another from the statute of frauds "wherever the main purpose and object of the promisor is not to answer for another, but to subserve some purpose of his own. . . ."

In applying the main purpose doctrine under Texas law, this court has articulated the three factors used by Texas courts to determine whether the main purpose doctrine applies:

(1) [Whether the] promisor intended to become primarily liable for the debt, in effect making it his original obligation, rather than to become a surety for another;

(2) [Whether there] was consideration for the promise; and

(3) [Whether the r]eceipt of the consideration was the promisor's main purpose or leading object in making the promise; that is, the consideration given for the promise was primarily for the promisor's use and benefit.

Applying these factors to the facts alleged by Power Entertainment, it is apparent Power Entertainment may be able to show the alleged oral agreement falls outside of the statute of frauds. Consistent with the allegations in its complaint, Power Entertainment may be able to adduce facts that would prove Power Entertainment intended to create primary responsibility on its part to pay Pro Set's $800,000 debt to NFLP, rather than merely acting as a surety for Pro Set's obligation. According to Power Entertainment's complaint, Pro Set had already declared bankruptcy and defaulted on its royalty obligations to NFLP, and there is no indication Pro Set was involved in any way in the negotiations between NFLP and Power Entertainment.

Further, the licensing agreement constituted valuable consideration for Power Entertainment's agreement to pay Pro Set's debt. Finally, Power Entertainment apparently agreed to pay Pro Set's debt to NFLP not to aid Pro Set, but to induce NFLP to transfer Pro Set's licensing agreement to Power Entertainment for Power Entertainment's use and benefit. Under these circumstances, we conclude Power Entertainment may be able to prove a set of facts that would allow a jury to find the alleged oral agreement is not barred by the statute of frauds. Thus, the district court erred in dismissing Power Entertainment's complaint based on the statute of frauds.

REVERSED AND REMANDED.

CRITICAL THINKING

Why do you think that the judge describes a certain approach to verbal contracts as "common sense," and what is that approach? How strong is the argument for the commonsense approach? What assumptions are probably shared by most people who accept this argument as common sense?

ETHICAL DECISION MAKING

The judge seems to think that in some circumstances a verbal agreement could facilitate unethical behavior. What ethical theory does the judge seem to assume that most people use in ethical decision making? Why might it be wise to use the judge's assumption when making business decisions?

CONTRACTS RELATED TO AN INTEREST IN LAND

Within the statute of frauds, "land" encompasses not only the land and soil itself but anything attached to the land, such as trees or buildings. The statute is intended to prevent oral claims to the existence of a contract for the sale of land. That is, because the statute requires a writing as evidence of the contract, a claim to an oral contract for the sale of land is not enough to prove such a contract existed. Recall the opening scenario. Had Krieg and Hieber not put their agreement in writing, it would definitely be unenforceable.

In addition to contracts for the sale of land, contracts transferring other interests in land are also within the statute of frauds. Mortgages and leases are within the statute because they are considered transfers of interest in land.

global context

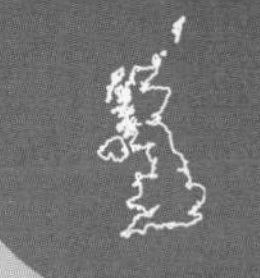

England and the Statute of Frauds

As stated in the text, England gave birth to the statute of frauds. While the United States, in addition to numerous other Western countries, has subsequently adopted versions of the 1677 English act, the English have gone in the opposite direction. Instead of expanding the powers and use of the 1677 act, the English have severely limited the number of cases falling within their statute of frauds.

Although formal complaints were levied against the English statute of frauds as early as 1937, no action was taken until 1953. In that year, the Law Reform Committee addressed numerous arguments that had been made in 1937 in favor of repeal of the statute of frauds. The 1953 committee recommended that Parliament repeal Section 4 of the 1677 act, which is where specific types of contracts are identified as required to be in writing. The Law Reform Act of 1954 subsequently repealed Section 4, with one cautionary exception. The 1954 act still required that promises to pay for the debt of others be in writing. In other words, the only provision still active (requiring a writing) under the statute of frauds in the country that invented the statute is what we would call *suretyship* or *collateral* promise.

Determining exactly what constitutes an "interest in land" within the statue of frauds is difficult. While the sale of land and the transfer of mortgages and leases all are within the statute, a number of things that seem as if they are interests in land do not fall within the statute. For example, promises to sell crops annually, agreements between parties for profit sharing from the sale of real property, and boundary disputes that have been settled through the use of land are all not within the statute of frauds and, therefore, do not require evidence in writing. The Case Nugget presents a case related to land in which the parties disagreed as to whether a writing was needed.

Case Nugget — What Is an "Interest in Land?"

Shelby's, Inc. v. Sierra Bravo, Inc.
68 S.W.3d 604 (2002)

Shelby's and Sierra entered into a written agreement in which Shelby's granted Sierra permission to use Shelby's land as a disposal site for waste and debris Sierra removed as part of the construction of a new highway. Shelby's claimed the parties also entered into an oral contract for Sierra to construct a waterway and building pad on Shelby's property. Sierra never completed the construction and denied an oral contract existed. Shelby's sued and the jury found in its favor.

Sierra appealed on the basis that the oral agreement was within the statute of frauds and therefore unenforceable. Sierra saw the alleged oral agreement as involving a sale of an interest in land, which is within the statute of frauds. Therefore, the agreement, to be enforceable, would have had to be in writing. The court firmly disagreed with Sierra's argument. The court stated:

> We agree with the well-reasoned argument of Respondent [Shelby's]. The contract in this case was not a "sale," much less a sale of an interest in lands. . . . Here, there was no transfer of ownership or title. The written agreement gave Appellant [Sierra] permission to deposit debris and soil on Respondent's land, not the right to do so. The oral contract was for the construction of a waterway and building pad and passed no interest in the land. . . . We decline to create a new category to which the statute of frauds applies, that of a contract for services for the deposit of dirt and soil on land. The trial court did not err in denying Appellant's motion for judgment notwithstanding the verdict. Appellant's point is denied and the judgment of the trial court is affirmed.

CONTRACTS FOR THE SALE OF GOODS TOTALING MORE THAN $500

Agreements in which the total price for a sale is $500 or more are required by the UCC, Section 2-201, to be recorded in a written contract or a memorandum. To satisfy the UCC's requirement for a written document, the contract or memorandum need only state the quantity to be sold. Buyer, seller, price, and method of payment do not need to be included in the writing according to the UCC. Contractual terms beyond quantity may be written, but they need not be. In fact, terms other than quantity can be inexact or left out of the writing as long as what is written does not contradict the parties' agreement. The contract will be enforceable for the stated quantity and not a unit more. Furthermore, for the contract to be enforceable, the party against whom action is sought must have signed the written document.

For example, Donnie and Gretchen enter into a sales contract. Donnie wrote the agreement, and Gretchen was the only party to sign the agreement. Later, Donnie attempts to enforce the agreement against Gretchen for the agreed-to quantity. Because Gretchen signed the agreement, Donnie can bring suit against her. However, because Donnie did not sign the agreement, Gretchen could not sue him in return nor could she do so if their roles were reversed. The UCC and the statute of frauds require that the party denying or in violation of the contract needs to have signed the written agreement, whereas the party bringing suit could have but need not have signed the writing.

In addition to sales contracts for $500 or more, there are other specific situations under the UCC for contracts that need to be in writing. These situations are contracts involving the sale of securities[6] and personal property[7] if the sale is greater than $5,000 in price.

FURTHER REQUIREMENTS SPECIFIC TO CERTAIN STATES

As discussed at the beginning of the chapter, the statute of frauds is actually state law. Consequently, certain states have various requirements not found in other states. While these requirements are not universal, it is important to note some of the distinctive elements of the statute of frauds in a minority of the states.

Some states require a writing within the statute of frauds under what is called the *equal dignity rule.* Under the **equal dignity rule,** contracts that would normally fall under the statute and need a writing if negotiated by the principal must be in writing even if negotiated by an agent. For example, Luke appoints Tony to act as his agent. Tony enters into an agreement for Luke with Carrie that cannot be completed within one year according to the contractual terms. Had Luke contracted directly with Carrie, the agreement would be within the statute and require a writing. Therefore, Tony's contract, which is on behalf of Luke, must also be in writing according to the equal dignity rule.

A minority of states have special provisions in matters related to promises to pay debt. One example is a promise to pay a debt that has already been discharged because of bankruptcy. For such an agreement to be enforceable, the agreement must be in writing to prevent the promisor from hiding behind the fact that the debt has been discharged. Another example is a promise to pay a debt where collection of the debt is barred by a statute of limitations. The logic here is the same as that in the first example. In both cases

[6] UCC § 8-319.
[7] UCC § 81-206.

the promisor, if the agreement is not in writing, can easily prove he or she does not need to pay. Therefore, the statute of frauds in certain states requires that both of these types of promises be in writing to be enforceable.

The last example of rules existing in a minority of states involves situations in which the contract cannot be performed in the promisor's lifetime. For example, Heather promises to give $10,000 to Michelle's charity on Heather's death. According to the terms of the promise, the agreement cannot be carried out within Heather's lifetime. In some states, Heather's promise would fall within the statute of frauds and would therefore have to be in writing. The intent here is to offer some protection to estates from claims made on the estate on the basis of alleged oral contracts. Requiring written evidence of a promise to pay after death limits the legal disputes concerning such a promise.

Exceptions to the Statute of Frauds

As with most legal rules, there are certain exceptions to which the statute of frauds does not apply, even though under normal circumstances it would. These exceptions are (1) admission, (2) partial performance, (3) promissory estoppel, and (4), although not under the statute of frauds, exceptions under the UCC.

ADMISSION

An **admission** is a statement made in court, under oath, or at some stage during a legal proceeding in which a party against whom charges have been brought admits that an oral contract existed, even though the contract was required to be in writing.[8]

For example, Sarah enters into an agreement with Jennifer for the sale of a plot of land. The parties fail to write down their agreement but proceed as if the agreement were finalized. Jennifer changes her mind and does not go through with the transaction. Sarah then sues Jennifer. If Jennifer admits during trial that there was an oral contract between herself and Sarah, the courts would uphold the contract for the sale of land. Without this admission, the agreement between Sarah and Jennifer for the sale of interest in land would need to be in writing to be enforceable.

All states except Louisiana and California adhere to the admission exception. To the extent that the statute of frauds is intended to require proper evidence of agreements, the admission exception is well reasoned. However, to the extent that the statute is intended to encourage care and caution in establishing the specific details of agreements, the admission exception seems to unnecessarily punish honest parties while rewarding dishonest ones.

Similar to the statute of frauds, the UCC makes a comparable exception in cases where parties admit to the existence of an oral contract. However, unlike the Statute of Frauds, the UCC provides that a contract required to be in writing but admitted to in court will be enforceable only for the quantity admitted.[9]

PARTIAL PERFORMANCE

Although the statute of frauds requires a writing for sales of interests in land, there is an exception based on the theory of partial performance. Under **partial performance,** if the

[8] Restatement (Second) of Contracts, sec. 133.
[9] UCC § 2-201(3)(b).

buyer in an alleged contract for the sale of land has paid any portion of the sale price, has begun to permanently improve the land, or has taken possession of the land, the courts will consider the contract partially performed, and this partial performance will amount to proof of the contract.

Accordingly, partial performance can override the statute's requirement for a written agreement. The logic here is that the actions of both parties demonstrate the existence of their agreement, so the agreement no longer needs to be in writing to be enforceable. Under similar sections of the UCC, an oral contract is enforceable by the buyer or seller to the extent that he or she accepts payment or delivery of the goods in question.[10]

PROMISSORY ESTOPPEL

Under certain circumstances, when a party relies on an oral contract that within the statute of frauds is required to be in writing, the reliance can create a situation in which the contract is nevertheless enforceable. **Promissory estoppel** is the legal enforcement of an otherwise unenforceable contract due to a party's detrimental reliance on the contract.

For promissory estoppel to be in effect, the party's reliance must be to his own detriment. Furthermore, the reliance must have been reasonably foreseeable; that is, the party who did not rely on the contract should have known that the other party was going to rely on it.[11]

Suppose you enter into a contract to buy a house after having accepted an offer on your current house. However, the new house costs more than your old house did, and the person from whom you are buying knows about the sale of your old house and the difference in the prices. To pay for the price difference, you sell your collection of rare coins. Unfortunately, during this whole process, you forgot to create a written contract for the purchase of the house. The other person now refuses to sell the house to you. You are now homeless and have sold off your only real assets. Because the other person reasonably should have known you were relying on the contract, and because you did so to your own detriment, under promissory estoppel you could win performance of the sales contract.

EXCEPTIONS UNDER THE UCC

In addition to the exceptions under the statute of frauds, exceptions also exist under the UCC as to when a contract ordinarily required to be in writing need not be in writing. For instance, under the UCC, oral contracts between merchants need not be in writing to be enforceable. Therefore, if one merchant agrees to sell goods to another, the contract is enforceable even if it is not in writing.

Likewise, oral contracts for customized goods are enforceable even if they would normally have to be in writing. The reasoning is that customized goods are not likely to be able to be sold to a general audience. Accordingly, if one party backs out of an oral arrangement for the sale of customized goods, the party that did not back out probably incurred unreasonable costs due to the negated contract. To prevent one party from bearing the cost of a canceled contract, the UCC allows oral agreements to be enforced when they are for customized goods.

In Case 18-2, notice the criteria the court sets forth when determining whether goods qualify as customized, or "specially manufactured," goods.

[10] UCC § 2-201(3)(c).

[11] Restatement (Second) of Contracts, sec. 139.

CASE 18-2 BARBARA H. KALAS v. EDWARD W. COOK, EXECUTOR (ESTATE OF ADELMA G. SIMMONS)

APPELLATE COURT OF CONNECTICUT
800 A.2D 553 (2002)

Clinton Press of Tolland operated a printing press and, for several decades, provided written materials, including books and pamphlets, for Adelma G. Simmons. Simmons ordered these materials for use and sale at her farm, known as Caprilands Herb Farm.

Due to limited space at Caprilands, the written materials would remain stored at the plaintiff's print shop until Simmons decided delivery was necessary. The materials were delivered either routinely, based on Simmons' ordinary need for materials, or upon her request for a special delivery. After each delivery, the plaintiff sent an invoice requesting payment by Simmons. These invoices were honored.

In 1991, the town of Tolland acquired the land on which the plaintiff resided. In early 1997, the plaintiff was notified she would have to vacate the property by the end of that calendar year. Upon receiving that notice, the plaintiff decided to close her business. The plaintiff and Simmons agreed the materials printed for Caprilands and stored at the plaintiff's print shop would be delivered on an accelerated basis.

On December 3, 1997, after several months of deterioration of her physical health, Simmons died. Simmons' will was admitted to probate, and the defendant was appointed executor of her estate. The plaintiff submitted a claim against the estate for $24,599.38 for unpaid deliveries to Caprilands. These deliveries took place from February 12, 1997, to December 11, 1997, with the last two deliveries occurring after Simmons' death. The defendant appealed, arguing there was no written agreement between the print shop and Caprilands.

JUDGE PETERS: On appeal, the defendant argues the oral contract was invalid because a writing was required by § 42a-2-201. This argument is unpersuasive.

The defendant's § 42a-2-201 argument fails as a matter of substance. While we agree § 42a-2-201 is the applicable statute, this section does not bar the enforcement of the plaintiff's oral agreement.

Under § 42a-2-201, oral agreements for the sale of goods at a price of $500 or more are presumptively unenforceable. The applicable provisions in this case, however, are other subsections of § 42a-2-201.

Under § 42a-2-201 (3) (a), an oral contract for the sale of goods is enforceable if the goods in question are "specially manufactured." In determining whether the specially manufactured goods exception applies, courts generally apply a four part standard:

> (1) the goods must be specially made for the buyer; (2) the goods must be unsuitable for sale to others in the ordinary course of the seller's business; (3) the seller must have substantially begun to have manufactured the goods or to have a commitment for their procurement; and (4) the manufacture or commitment must have been commenced under circumstances reasonably indicating the goods are for the buyer and prior to the seller's receipt of notification of contractual repudiation.

In applying this standard, "courts have traditionally looked to the goods themselves. The term 'specially manufactured,' therefore, refers to the nature of the particular goods in question and not to whether the goods were made in an unusual, as opposed to the regular, business operation or manufacturing process of the seller."

Printed material, particularly that, as in this case, names the buyer, has been deemed by both state and federal courts to fall within the exception set out for specially manufactured goods.

It is inherent in the court's findings the printed materials in the present case were specially manufactured goods. The materials were printed specifically for Caprilands. The materials included brochures and labels with the Caprilands name, as well as books that were written and designed by Simmons. The plaintiff testified the books were printed, as Simmons had requested, in a rustic style with typed inserts and hand-drawn pictures. Therefore, none of these materials was suitable for sale to others. It is undisputed, at the time of breach of the alleged contract, goods printed for Simmons already had been produced.

We conclude, in light of the nature of the goods at issue and the findings of the trial court, the oral

[CONTINUED]

agreement in this case falls within the exception for specially manufactured goods. To be enforceable, the agreement for their production was, therefore, not required to be in writing under § 42a-2-201 (3) (a). Accordingly, we affirm the judgment of the court on this issue because it reached the right result.

AFFIRMED.

CRITICAL THINKING

The judge's argument in this case seems to be simple and clear, but try to find all the assumptions and ambiguities the judge uses in this argument. Are there any assumptions that could reasonably be rejected? How would that rejection affect the judge's argument? Are there any ambiguities that could be resolved differently? How would it affect the argument if an ambiguity were resolved differently?

ETHICAL DECISION MAKING

The plaintiff probably was not thinking about the legal environment when the verbal agreement between Caprilands and the plaintiff was made. Imagine you are the plaintiff. Make an argument for the legitimacy of your claim against the Simmons estate using ethical rather than legal reasoning.

Sufficiency of the Writing

Although there are no specific requirements for the form of a written contract under the Statute of Frauds, certain elements need to be present for a writing to constitute proper evidence of a written contract under the statute. It is worth mentioning that a consequence of not having one standard form is that multiple documents can together evidence the existence of a written agreement under the statute.

Required elements in the writing include the identification of the parties to the contract, the subject of the agreement, the consideration (if any), and any pertinent terms of the contract. Furthermore, the contract must be signed. Although traditional, the signature does not need to be located at the end of the agreement. In fact, the signature does not need to be the full signature; a mark, such as an initial, is permissible as long as the mark is placed with the intent to function as a signature. While it is standard for both parties to sign the agreement, because the writing is being offered as proof of an agreement, only the party against whom action is sought needs to have signed the writing. If only one party signed, it is possible to have an agreement enforceable against one party (the signing party) but not the other (the nonsigning party). For example, Hieber signed the agreement mentioned in the opening scenario, and it is therefore enforceable against him. Even if Krieg did not sign the agreement, he can still bring actions against Hieber; however, Hieber could not file contractual claims against Krieg in return. The required elements in a writing can be contained in a memorandum, a document, or a compilation of several documents.

The requirements under the UCC for sales contracts vary slightly from those under the statute of frauds. The UCC does not require that the parties be named in the agreement.

connecting to the core

Management

As management classes stress, writing is an essential skill. One attribute of an effective business manager or lawyer is the ability to write well, and the more writing practice you have now, the more likely you are to be an effective writer in your professional career. Contracts under the statute of frauds are one example in which a business manager or lawyer is required to demonstrate his writing skills. But a business manager may engage frequently in other written communication, especially via e-mail, which tends to induce individuals to use a more relaxed, informal writing style, even though informalities via e-mail may not be appropriate in a professional setting.

Although this brief overview cannot provide an exhaustive list of writing principles, a few important principles you should keep in mind include knowing your purpose for the written communication, having a developed strategy for the writing (e.g., placing reasons in order from most important to least important or from least controversial to most controversial), avoiding ambiguity, using the active voice instead of the passive, and having a clear layout. These principles, if developed, will benefit a future business manager who drafts a contract under the statute of frauds or who merely engages regularly in written communications with a supervisor or client.

Source: Angelo Kinicki and Brian K. Williams, *Management: A Practical Introduction* (New York: McGraw-Hill/Irwin, 2006), p. 507.

Rather, the UCC requires that the writing clearly state the quantity to be sold. Similar to the statute of frauds, the UCC allows a variety of written documents to constitute a writing. Some documents that count include faxes, e-mails, invoices, bills of lading, sales slips, checks, or any combination of these documents.

Also noteworthy is the fact that oral testimony can be elicited that establishes the existence of a writing that would meet the requirements under the statute of frauds. For example, testimony regarding an invoice for products sold, when the actual invoice is not produced, is enough in certain states to meet the requirements under the statute.

Case 18-3 demonstrates how judges go about determining what constitutes a writing and when a writing is sufficient under the statute of frauds.

CASE 18-3

STEWART LAMLE v. MATTEL, INC.
UNITED STATES COURT OF APPEALS FOR THE FEDERAL CIRCUIT
394 F.3D 1355 (2005)

Steward Lamle is the inventor of Farook, a board game. Lamle obtained two patents for Farook from the United States Patent and Trademark Office and negotiated with Mattel, Inc., regarding the licensing of Farook by Mattel. Early in these negotiations, Lamle signed Mattel's standard Product Disclosure Form, which contained the following provision:

> *I understand that . . . no obligation is assumed by [Mattel] unless and until a formal written contract is agreed to and entered into, and then the obligation shall be only that which is expressed in the formal, written contract.*

The negotiations advanced, and a meeting was held on June 11 where the parties discussed the terms of a licensing agreement. At the meeting, Mattel and Lamle agreed on many terms of a license including a three-year term, the geographic scope, the schedule for payment, and the percentage royalty. Mattel asked

Lamle to "draft a formal document memorializing 'The Deal'" and "promised [that] it would sign a formal, written contract before January 1, 1998."

Mattel employee Mike Bucher subsequently sent Lamle an email entitled "Farook Deal" on June 26 that substantially repeated terms agreed to at the June 11 meeting. The email stated the terms "have been agreed in principal [sic] by . . . Mattel subject to contract." The salutation "Best regards Mike Bucher" appears at the end of the email.

On October 8, Mattel notified Lamle of its decision not to go ahead with the production of Farook. Lamle filed action asserting, inter alia, a claim of breach of contract. The district court granted summary judgment in favor of Mattel on all claims. The Court of Appeals vacated that grant of summary judgment and remanded the case to the district court. The district court on remand again granted summary judgment in favor of Mattel on all claims. Lamle appealed again.

JUDGE DYK: Mattel contends, and the district court held, any oral agreement made during the June 11 meeting cannot be enforced because of the California Statute of Frauds.

There is no question the alleged oral agreement for a three year license was one that, by its terms, could not be "performed within a year from the making thereof." The only question, therefore, is whether there is a writing to evidence the agreement or an applicable exception to the Statute of Frauds. To satisfy the Statute of Frauds, a writing must contain all the material terms of the contract. The writing must also be signed by the party against whom enforcement is sought. Lamle argues the June 26 email from Bucher satisfied both requirements.

The June 26 email specified the term of the license, the geographic scope, the percentage royalty, and the total advance and minimum amount to be paid under the contract. Bucher stated these terms had "been agreed in principal [sic] by [his] superiors at Mattel subject to contract" and the email message "covers the basic points."

California law is clear that "a note or memorandum under the statute of frauds need not contain all of the details of an agreement between the parties." Rather, the statute only requires "every material term of an agreement within its provisions be reduced to written form." "If the court, after acquiring knowledge of all the facts concerning the transaction which the parties themselves possessed at the time the agreement was made, can plainly determine from the memorandum the identity of the parties to the contract, the nature of its subject matter, and its essential terms, the memorandum will be held to be adequate." What is an essential term "depends on the agreement and its context and also on the subsequent conduct of the parties."

Mattel correctly points out the June 26 email does not contain all the terms that Lamle asserts are part of the oral contract. In particular, Mattel correctly notes Lamle alleges Mattel (1) guaranteed to sell 200,000 units of Farook each year; (2) promised to sell Farook units to Lamle at cost; and (3) promised Lamle the right to approve or disapprove the design and packaging of Farook units. None of these terms appears in the June 26 email. Again, we think there is a genuine issue of material fact as to the materiality of these terms. The Ninth Circuit, interpreting California law, has stated "the subject matter, the price, and the party against whom enforcement is sought" are the "few terms deemed essential as a matter of law by California courts." A jury could well conclude these omitted terms allegedly agreed to at the meeting but not reflected in the writing were not material.

There also remains the issue of whether an email is a writing "subscribed by the party to be charged or by the party's agent." The party to be charged in this case is Mattel, and the June 26 email was written by Bucher, an employee of Mattel, and his name appears at the end of the email, which concludes with "Best regards Mike Bucher." Mattel has not disputed the agency authority of Bucher to bind it. Therefore, the only question is whether Bucher's name on an email is a valid writing and signature to satisfy the Statute of Frauds.

California law does provide, however, typed names appearing on the end of telegrams are sufficient to be writings under the Statute of Frauds. California law also provides that a typewritten name is sufficient to be a signature. We can see no meaningful difference between a typewritten signature on a telegram and an email. Therefore, we conclude under California law the June 26 email satisfies the Statute of Frauds, assuming there was a binding oral agreement on June 11 and the email includes all the material terms of that agreement.

To prove a contract with Mattel, Lamle must prove the parties objectively intended to be immediately bound by an oral contract on June 11; the June 26 email contains the material terms of that oral contract; and Bucher had actual or apparent authority to sign for Mattel. Reviewing the record, Lamle has presented sufficient evidence to create genuine issues of material fact on these points. This is not to say Lamle should prevail at trial. Indeed, among other things, Lamle faces a difficult burden persuading the jury, despite Mattel's stating it would sign a formal contract later, the objective intention of both parties was to be immediately bound by the oral contract, and to abrogate a prior written agreement to the contrary.

Therefore, we vacate the grant of summary judgment with respect to the breach of contract claim and remand for further proceedings consistent with this opinion.

VACATED-IN-PART AND REMANDED.

CRITICAL THINKING

The judge makes an argument about what constitutes a signature by referring to precedent and drawing an analogy between e-mails and telegrams. How strong is the analogy the judge makes? Outline an argument against the judge's analogy. Explain.

ETHICAL DECISION MAKING

When Mattel's agents in charge of buying or rejecting games were negotiating with Lamle, they may have considered the ethical aspects of their decisions. If you were Mattel's agent, what ethical guidelines and values would you want to consider while evaluating the ethicality of terminating Mattel's relationship with Lamle? What ethical considerations would you find the most important?

Parol Evidence Rule

A problem arises with written contracts when a party asserts that the writing is in some way deficient. In order to smooth transactions by limiting the types of evidence admissible to address the written agreement, the courts rely heavily on the parol evidence rule. The **parol evidence rule** is a common law rule that specifically addresses the admissibility of oral evidence as it relates to written contracts. The parol evidence rule states that oral evidence of an agreement made prior to or contemporaneously with the written agreement is inadmissible when the parties intend to have a written agreement be the complete and final version of their agreement.[12] *Parol* in "parol evidence rule" means speech or words, specifically words outside the original writing.

The purpose of the parol evidence rule is to restrict evidence from being admitted that substantially contradicts the agreement in its written form. Therefore, evidence of prior agreements and negotiations, as well as contemporaneous agreements and negotiations, is typically excluded under the parol evidence rule. A written agreement is assumed to be complete, and evidence contradicting this final agreement usually impedes business transactions, which is why the parol evidence rule exists.

However, when a court determines that the written agreement does *not* represent a complete and final version of the agreement, evidence may be admissible to further the court's

[12] Restatement (Second) of Contracts, sec. 213.

understanding of the agreement. The admissible evidence is limited to additional elements, missing in the writing, that are consistent with the written agreement. These elements may be terms typically included in similar transactions that have been left out in the specific writing, or they may be separate agreements in which consideration had been offered.

A cautionary note is in order. "Parol evidence rule," on its face, is a misnomer. First and foremost, parol evidence applies to both parol, spoken words, and written speech. The parol evidence rule covers evidence extrinsic to the original writing and is not limited to spoken words. Second, the parol evidence rule is *not* a rule of evidence but, rather, relates to substantive legal issues; namely, what constitutes a legally binding agreement and how do we know what the agreement is. Third, the parol evidence rule is not a unitary concept or rule but an amalgamation of different rules and conditions.

Although the parol evidence rule applies to writings created at the same time as the written agreement, these writings tend to be treated differently than prior or contemporaneous oral agreements. That is, the writings are more readily admitted as part of the written agreement than is oral evidence regarding conditions or terms in the final agreement. The reasoning is that judges are allowed discretion in determining which documents constitute the final contract. As long as the contemporaneous written documents do not substantially contradict what is in the final writing, judges can deem these other writings to be part of the final written agreement. Consequently, the parol evidence rule does not usually exclude extrinsic written evidence.

Sometimes parties take the initiative and attempt to signal to judges that the written agreement is intended to be the final and complete statement of the agreement. A **merger clause** is a clause parties include in a written agreement within the statute of frauds that states that the written agreement accurately reflects the final, complete version of the agreement. Not all courts consider merger clauses to be conclusive proof of a contract. Nonetheless, where merger clauses are accepted, they greatly reduce the amount of guesswork courts must do in determining whether a written agreement was in fact intended to be the final statement of the agreement. Case 18-4 demonstrates how merger clauses can be used to defend against charges brought on the basis of a statement in a nonmerged oral agreement.

CASE 18-4

FIRST DATA POS, INC. v. JOSEPH WILLIS ET AL.
SUPREME COURT OF GEORGIA
273 GA. 792 (2001)

First Data POS, Inc., purchased COIN Banking Systems, a software development company, from the Willis Group. The parties executed a Stock Purchase Agreement in which First Data agreed to pay appellees $2.5 million in exchange for all of COIN's stock. The Agreement provided appellees might receive additional payments, so long as COIN's post-acquisition business generated certain levels of revenue over the three-year period following the Agreement's execution. The Agreement expressly stated First Data was under no obligation to carry on the current business of COIN, or even to maintain COIN as a business entity, but rather First Data was authorized "at any time without limitation and without notice to appellees to reorganize or merge COIN out of existence or cease the sale of any of the products or services of COIN." Finally, the Agreement contained a standard merger clause, which stated:

> *The Agreement . . . constitutes the entire agreement between the parties with respect to the subject matter contained herein and supersedes all prior agreements and understandings, both oral and written, by and between the parties hereto with respect to the subject matter hereof.*

Approximately three years after the Agreement's execution, appellees filed suit alleging during the pre-contractual negotiations, First Data had misrepresented its intention to increase COIN's business after it acquired the company, and those misrepresentations had induced appellees to enter into the Agreement and to sell COIN's stock for less than its then-current market value. Appellees' complaint against First Data alleged fraudulent misrepresentation, breach of contract, and violation of Georgia's Civil RICO Act. Appellees predicated their RICO count upon an allegation First Data's purported misrepresentations had amounted to criminal theft by deception under O.C.G.A. § 16-8-3.

The trial court granted summary judgment in favor of First Data on all three counts. The Court of Appeals reversed the trial court's grant of summary judgment as to appellees' civil RICO count, concluding the trial court erred by ruling the merger clause precluded appellees' claim First Data's pre-contractual representations amounted to criminal theft by deception.

JUSTICE SEARS: The Court of Appeals erred by concluding the Agreement's merger clause did not preclude appellees' claim First Data's pre-contractual representations amounted to theft by deception. The Agreement's unambiguous merger clause states it was the parties' intention the Agreement supersede all pre-contractual agreements and representations, both oral and written, concerning First Data's acquisition of COIN's stock.

It is axiomatic contracts must be construed to give effect to the parties' intentions, which must whenever possible be determined from a construction of the contract as a whole. Whenever the language of a contract is plain, unambiguous, and capable of only one reasonable interpretation, no construction is required or even permissible, and the contractual language used by the parties must be afforded its literal meaning. Where a conflict exists between oral and written representations, it has long been the law in Georgia if the parties have reduced their agreement to writing, all oral representations made antecedent to execution of the written contract are merged into and extinguished by the contract and are not binding upon the parties. In written contracts containing a merger clause, prior or contemporaneous representations that contradict the written contract "cannot be used to vary the terms of a valid written agreement purporting to contain the entire agreement of the parties, nor would the violation of any such alleged oral agreement amount to actionable fraud."

This Court has held "the rational basis for merger clauses is that where parties enter into a final contract all prior negotiations, understandings, and agreements on the same subject are merged into the final contract, and are accordingly extinguished." As recently noted by the United States Court of Appeals for the Seventh Circuit, merger clauses exist in written contracts specifically to "preclude any claim of deceit by prior representations. . . . A person who has received written disclosure of the truth may not claim to rely on contrary oral falsehoods." It is for this reason our own Court of Appeals has recently held a RICO count alleging theft by deception based upon pre-contractual representations is foreclosed by the written terms of a valid contractual merger clause.

It follows from these well established precepts of contract law and the precedent based thereon that any impressions held by appellees based upon First Data's purported pre-contractual representations that it would increase COIN's business after the acquisition were superseded by the merger clause contained in the parties' Agreement, which expressly put appellees on notice the Agreement's terms superseded any and all prior representations not contained therein.

Thus, appellees' claim they were deceived by First Data's pre-contractual misrepresentations, and their allegation First Data committed theft by such deception, have no basis. Under the express terms of the Agreement, appellees could not have reasonably placed their reliance upon any pre-contractual representation not also included in the Agreement's language, and thus appellees could not have been deceived by such pre-contractual representations. Without deception, of course, there can be neither theft by deception nor a valid RICO claim based upon theft by deception.

Accordingly, for the reasons explained above, we conclude the Court of Appeals erred in ruling the contractual merger clause did not preclude appellees' claim First Data had committed criminal theft by deception in making pre-contractual representations regarding the future business operations of COIN Banking Systems. As a matter of law, a valid merger clause executed by two or more parties in an arm's length transaction precludes any subsequent claim of deceit based upon pre-contractual representations. Therefore, this matter is reversed.

REVERSED.

[CONTINUED]

CRITICAL THINKING

The judge explains the reasoning behind the precedent of extinguishing all claims that might be based on negotiations or obsolete contracts made before a contract is agreed to. How does the judge apply that precedent to the case at hand?

If you represented the appellees, how would you try to defend your claim against the judge's analysis?

ETHICAL DECISION MAKING

If the appellees are correct in their claims about matters of fact, First Data POS, Inc., misrepresented its intentions by making statements during negotiations that did not match up to the final contract. These misrepresentations turned out to have no legal bearing on the case, but what do they say about the ethics and values of First Data POS, Inc.?

Is there an ethical theory that First Data POS, Inc., could use to justify its actions? How?

Exceptions to the Parol Evidence Rule

As with the statute of frauds, there are exceptions to the general applicability of the parol evidence rule. That is, there are situations where parol evidence, which is normally excluded, may be admissible in court. These exceptions are (1) contracts that have been subsequently modified, (2) contracts conditioned on orally agreed-on terms, (3) contracts that are not final as they are part written and part oral, (4) contracts with ambiguous terms, (5) incomplete contracts, (6) contracts with obvious typographical errors, (7) voidable or void contracts, and (8) evidence of prior dealings or usage of trade.

In the case discussed in the opening scenario, Krieg appealed on the basis of the court's admittance of parol evidence regarding the negotiation discussion. If Krieg is to have a valid point, there must not be an exception available to Hieber. Which of the following exceptions could Hieber use to justify the court's use of parol evidence in its decision?

CONTRACTS THAT HAVE BEEN SUBSEQUENTLY MODIFIED

Although parol evidence contradictory to the final terms is inadmissible, evidence regarding a contract's subsequent modification is admissible. To be admissible, the modification must have been made after the writing, and the evidence must clearly indicate this later modification.

Despite the allowance of evidence to demonstrate modifications, not all evidence of modification is admissible. If the agreement is required to be in writing as it is within the statute of frauds, oral modifications are unenforceable. However, oral evidence of a subsequent written agreement is admissible. In addition, if the contract's terms require that modification be in writing, oral modifications are inadmissible and unenforceable.[13]

[13] UCC § 2-209(2),(3).

global context

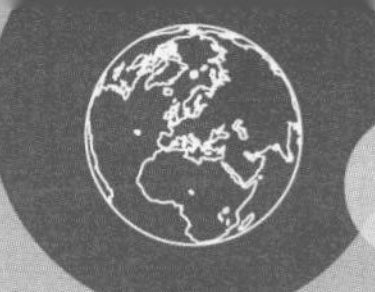

Civil Law Countries and the Parol Evidence Rule

A number of our European allies are civil law countries (e.g., Germany and France), as opposed to common law countries. As such, these countries have a different approach to many of the same legal doctrines the United States follows. For example, German law does not have a parol evidence rule. Instead, German courts tend to allow what American courts call *parol evidence.* The logic is that such information is important for knowing the parties' intent when they entered into the contracts.

Unlike Germany, France does have a parol evidence rule, albeit a very limited one. The French parol evidence rule, unlike the American version of the rule, does not apply to commercial contracts. Consequently, while parties to contracts in France have some protection from the consideration of parol evidence in trial, this protection does not exist when it comes to commercial contracts. The French court system is attempting to best facilitate business exchanges by allowing parol evidence to clarify all points related to terms of a contract or what a party thought he or she was agreeing to.

Interestingly enough, the parol evidence rule, a long-standing tradition in the common law, actually came to American law by way of French law. Similarly, the statute of frauds came to American law through English common law. Yet the United States applies the statute of frauds and the parol evidence rule to a larger number of cases than does either country where these ideas originated.

CONTRACTS CONDITIONED ON ORALLY AGREED-ON TERMS

The parol evidence rule does not prevent parties from introducing evidence proving the written agreement was conditioned on terms agreed to orally. The reason the parol evidence rule does not apply is that the evidence being elicited does not substantially modify the written agreement. Rather, what is at issue with such evidence is the enforceability of the contract as written. No terms are altered, so the parol evidence rule does not apply.

When an entire contract is conditioned on something occurring first, the first thing is known as a **condition precedent.** Evidence of the existence of a condition precedent agreed to orally is admissible, as stated previously, because the contract is not modified by such evidence; rather, its enforceability is called into question. Since the statute of frauds is concerned primarily with the enforceability of agreements, it logically follows that the parol evidence rule does not apply to evidence of condition precedents.

NONFINALIZED, PARTIALLY WRITTEN AND PARTIALLY ORAL, CONTRACTS

When a contract consists of both written and oral elements, judges tend to treat the agreement as nonfinalized. Accordingly, the judge makes the assumption that the parties do not intend to have the written agreement represent the entire agreement. Therefore, oral evidence related to the contract is admissible because the written document is not the complete and final representation of the agreement.

CONTRACTS CONTAINING AMBIGUOUS TERMS

When a contract contains what the court deems to be ambiguous terms, the court is faced with a dilemma in interpretation. To attempt to reach the most accurate interpretation of the original agreement, the court allows evidence, even if it is oral, for the sole purpose of clarifying ambiguous terms. As with the evidence regarding orally agreed-on condition precedents, evidence used to clarify ambiguity is believed not to modify the contract but, rather, to clarify. Accordingly, oral evidence related to ambiguity is admissible *only* to clarify, and not to change, any of the contractual terms.

INCOMPLETE CONTRACTS

When a contract is fundamentally flawed because it is missing critical information, courts can allow parol evidence to provide the missing information. Typically, the missing information is related to essential terms of the contract. Parol evidence will be admitted to clarify the contract by filling in the missing parts while not modifying, in any substantial way, the written agreement. Parol evidence is used to attempt to facilitate business transactions, as opposed to forcing the parties to enter into a new, complete agreement.

CONTRACTS WITH OBVIOUS TYPOGRAPHICAL ERRORS

Whenever a written agreement under the statute of frauds contains a serious, and obvious, typographical error (typo), parol evidence is admissible to demonstrate that the typo was a typo, as well as to set forth the proper term. Allowing parol evidence to correct typos does not fundamentally alter the written agreement because the typo is not an accurate reflection of the parties' agreement. The agreement is not altered by correcting a typo; rather, the agreement is granted better clarity.

VOID OR VOIDABLE CONTRACTS

Certain conditions can make an otherwise valid contract void or voidable. (Refer to Chapter 13 for an in-depth discussion of what makes a contract void or voidable.) While the contract does not list these conditions, the courts allow parol evidence to demonstrate that the contract is void or voidable. As with the vast majority of the exceptions to the parol evidence rule, allowing evidence proving a contract is void or voidable does not fundamentally alter the terms of the contract. Rather, the parol evidence would address the enforceability of the agreement, which is not the same as changing the terms of the agreement. Furthermore, evidence of a defense against a contract (discussed in Chapter 16), is admissible to prove a contract is void or voidable.

EVIDENCE OF PRIOR DEALINGS OR USAGE OF TRADE

This final exception, although directly related to those already mentioned, actually falls under the UCC and not the statute of frauds. Regardless, this exception also allows otherwise inadmissible parol evidence for a specific reason.

According to the UCC, parol evidence is admissible for the sake of clarification if the evidence addresses prior dealings between the parties or usages of trade in the same business field as the parties are in.[14] Evidence related to past dealings can help clarify missing or ambiguous terms by examining how the parties had previously interacted. The assumption is that parties will continue to interact in a similar manner, because repeated interactions tend to indicate pleasant interactions between the parties. Therefore, if a term is missing or ambiguous, the courts rely on evidence of what was done between the parties in the past to attempt to gauge what was intended in the contract in question.

Similarly, when a contract is ambiguous or incomplete, the courts examine the standard practices in the business. Here, the courts are assuming that businesses intend to engage in standard transactions. Furthermore, the courts believe common business practices might sometimes be overlooked and, therefore, not be included when these common practices accurately reflect the intentions of the parties involved. Once again, an exception to the applicability of the parol evidence rule is made to allow evidence to clarify a contract, as opposed to changing any material terms of the contract.

[14] UCC §§ 1-205 and 2-202.

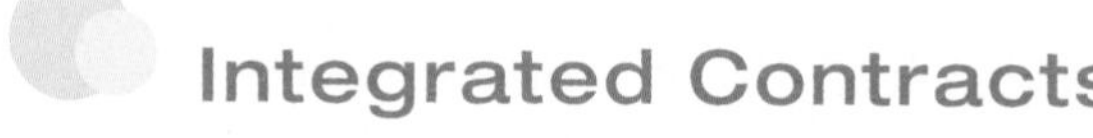

Integrated Contracts

Integrated contracts are written contracts intended to be the complete and final representation of the parties' agreement. When the courts deem a contract integrated, with the exception of the above exceptions, parol evidence is inadmissible. With partially integrated contracts, parol evidence is admissible to the extent it clarifies part of the contract or addresses the enforcement of the contract.[15] Therefore, the easiest test to determine the admissibility of parol evidence is to check whether the written contract, within the statute of frauds, is an integrated contract.

As previously discussed, one way parties can indicate their desire to create an integrated contract is through the use of a merger clause. A merger clause explicitly states that the written contract is intended to be the complete and final version of the contract between the parties and that other possible agreements between the parties, besides the one in question, are not part of the final written agreement. In essence, a merger clause seeks to blend other agreements either into the final agreement or into something explicitly stated as being outside the final agreement. Most states will allow a merger clause to constitute the stated intent of the parties involved unless proof of a personal defense against the contract is offered by one of the parties. However, it is worth mentioning that some states consider merger clauses to be recommendations, but not necessarily binding on the parties.

Krieg and Hieber included a merger clause in their case, discussed at the beginning of this chapter. Even so, the court considered parol evidence regarding the negotiation process. Do you think the court erred in including this evidence? Why? Alternatively, what are some possible reasons the court could give for admitting the parol evidence?

Case Nugget — A Clear Illustration of the Need for a Writing

Scalisi et al. v. New York University Medical Center
805 N.Y.S.2d 62 (N.Y. App. Div., 1st Dept., Dec. 6, 2005)

The plaintiffs in this breach-of-contract action learned the importance of getting guarantees in writing. The plaintiffs allegedly entered into an oral agreement with the Medical Center for an in vitro fertilization procedure that would not result in the birth of an autistic child. Subsequently, the parties signed a written contract that stated that a certain percentage of children are born with physical and mental defects and the occurrence of such defects is "beyond the control of the physician." The document also stated that the medical center and its physicians would not "assume responsibility for the physical and mental characteristic or hereditary tendencies" of any child born as a result of the in vitro procedure.

When one of the twins born as a result of the in vitro procedure was born with "autistic traits," the parents sued for breach of the oral agreement, alleging that they had entered into the oral agreement with the hospital for the purpose of having offspring free of autism. The lower court granted the hospital summary judgment, holding that the written agreement signed by the parents barred the admissibility of the oral agreement. The state court of appeals affirmed, finding that even if the alleged oral promises had been made, they were inadmissible in light of the existence of the subsequent written agreement that is directly contradictory to the oral agreement.

[15] Restatement (Second) of Contracts, sec. 216.

CASE OPENER WRAP-UP

Dairy Farm Dispute

After the bench trial, the court found in favor of Hieber, and Krieg appealed. On appeal, the court held that the use of parol evidence by the lower court was admissible. The appellate court determined that the parol evidence was used to clarify the agreement and in no way altered the agreement as stated. Accordingly, the parol evidence was admitted for clarification purposes only. The court acknowledged the merger agreement but stated that merger clauses do not preclude parol evidence used to clarify agreements.

Despite Krieg's loss on his point regarding the parol evidence, he did end up winning on appeal. The court, in reconsidering what the parol evidence entailed, stated that the trial court misconstrued the evidence. In the end, the appellate court ruled that Hieber was responsible for fixing Krieg's house. The most interesting part of the case is the fact that the appellate court made its decision for Krieg on the basis of the very evidence Krieg attempted to keep out.

Summary

Statute of Frauds

The term *statute of frauds* refers to various state laws modeled after the 1677 English Act for the Prevention of Frauds and Perjuries. These state laws are intended to (1) ease contractual negotiations by requiring sufficient reliable evidence to prove the existence and specific terms of a contract, (2) prevent unreliable oral evidence from interfering with a contractual relationship, and (3) prevent parties from entering into contracts with which they do not agree.

Contracts Falling within the Statute of Frauds

1. Contracts whose terms prevent possible performance within one year.
2. Promises made in consideration of marriage.
3. Contracts for one party to pay the debt of another if the initial party fails to pay.
4. Contracts related to an interest in land.
5. Under the Uniform Commercial Code, contracts for the sale of goods totaling more than $500.

Exceptions to the Statute of Frauds

1. Admission.
2. Partial performance.
3. Promissory estoppel.
4. Various exceptions under the UCC.

Sufficiency of the Writing

A sufficient writing under the statute of frauds must clearly indicate (1) the parties to the contract, (2) the subject of the agreement, (3) the consideration given for the contract, (4) all relevant contractual terms, and (5) at least the signature of the party against whom action is brought.

Under the UCC, a writing must clearly indicate (1) the quantity to be sold and (2) the signature of the party being sued.

Under neither the statute of frauds nor the UCC must the writing be contained within one document.

Parol Evidence Rule

The *parol evidence rule* is a common law rule stating that oral evidence of an agreement made prior to or contemporaneously with the written agreement is inadmissible when the parties intend to have a written agreement be the complete and final version of their agreement.

Exceptions to the Parol Evidence Rule

1. Contracts that are subsequently modified.
2. Contracts conditioned on orally agreed-on terms.
3. Contracts that are not final as they are part written and part oral.
4. Contracts with ambiguous terms.
5. Incomplete contracts.
6. Contracts with obvious typographical errors.
7. Voidable or void contracts.
8. Evidence of prior dealings or usage of trade.

Integrated Contracts

Integrated contracts are written contracts within the statute of frauds intended to be the complete and final representation of the parties' agreement, thus precluding the admissibility of parol evidence other than in the exceptions listed above.

Point / Counterpoint

Does the United States Still Benefit from Having a Statute of Frauds?

Yes

The statute of frauds provides great benefit to America. The rule serves as a social lubricant aiding business transactions. By requiring that certain types of contracts be in writing, we know that all these contracts either will have enough evidence to prove the existence and terms of the contract or will be unenforceable. Because only certain contracts are required to be in writing, the rule does not preclude oral contracts, but it ensures that the most important contracts can be enacted without complications.

Another way in which the statute of frauds benefits America is by preventing unreliable evidence from being used in court. Human memories are notoriously weak and faulty, and it does not make sense to base important legal decisions on what someone says he or she remembers. Furthermore, people with a vested interest can change their testimony on the basis of changed circumstances in order to gain personally from the changed circumstances. However, with the requirement that certain

No

The United States does not benefit from the statute of frauds, and the states should repeal the relevant sections of their laws.

One of the greatest problems with the statute of frauds is that it acts as an impediment to contractual agreements. When parties agree, why should they be subjected to unnecessary formalities? The written requirements of the statute of frauds get in the way of business transactions more often than they help.

Furthermore, the required writing frequently imposes additional costs on the parties to the agreement. When even simple agreements (although this applies to the more technical ones as well) must be written, parties have to spend more time with the agreements. The time spent writing down an agreement in which neither party contests any of the terms is time *not* spent conducting other business. Frequently, these parties have to hire attorneys to write their contracts. The attorney fees impose additional costs on the parties to the agreement, helping to decrease whatever contracts be in writing, the parties become bound to what they wrote and need not rely on faulty memory or biased testimony.

Finally, the act of writing gives people time to pause for reflection. No one benefits when parties hastily rush into an agreement they later regret. The problem of hasty agreements is lessened when the parties are required to take time to write out the terms of their agreement. Thoughtful reflection prevents parties from entering into contracts with which they do not agree, and this means fewer cases are brought due to one party's entering an unfair, or otherwise defective, agreement.

benefit might have been gained from the original agreement before the writing took place.

In addition, the statute of frauds provides unnecessary loopholes for unscrupulous people. Although most parties enter agreements in good faith, it is not uncommon for parties to seek a way out of contracts they cannot perform. The writing requirements are not always accurately fulfilled, and when this occurs, unethical parties can exploit minor technicalities to have a contract declared void. In the end, the innocent party is harmed by the writing requirement, and the unethical party escapes a bad situation with little to no harm. America is not served by a system that enables such behavior.

Questions & Problems

1. Explain the purpose of the statute of frauds.

2. Describe the contents of a writing that would be sufficient to satisfy the statute of frauds under the common law.

3. Explain how the requirements of the statute of frauds under the UCC are different from those under the common law.

4. List the kinds of contracts that require a writing under the statute of frauds.

5. Identify the exceptions to the parol evidence rule, and explain why some people might argue that the rule is not very effective.

6. Nate Crabtree entered into negotiations with Elizabeth Arden Sales Corporation, which manufactures and sells cosmetics. Crabtree requested a three-year contract at $25,000 per year. Ms. Elizabeth Arden indicated that she was willing to enter a two-year contract based on an annual salary of $20,000 for the first six months, increasing to $25,000 for the second six months and $30,000 for the second year, with $5,000 extra each year for expenses. Arden's secretary created a memorandum on a telephone order blank that included these provisions, stating at the bottom "2 year to make good," although the memorandum was not signed. Several days later, Crabtree accepted the invitation to join Arden's company. When Crabtree showed up for work, a payroll change card was created and initialed by the executive vice president, Mr. Johns, which included the names of the parties, Crabtree's job classification, and the same salary provisions as the memorandum but without any length-of-employment language. Crabtree received the scheduled salary increase after six months of employment, but he did not receive the additional increase at the end of the first year. Johns and Mr. Carstens, the comptroller of the corporation, said that they would straighten out the matter, preparing another payroll change card with the scheduled increase to $30,000 "per contractual arrangements with Miss Arden." But Arden refused to approve the increase. Crabtree quit and sued for breach of contract. Do the three writings—the memorandum and the two payroll cards—satisfy the requirement of a writing under the statute of frauds? How might Crabtree argue that parol evidence is admissible to explain the duration-of-employment provision of the memorandum? [*Crabtree v. Elizabeth Arden Sales Corp.,* 305 N.Y. 48 (1953).]

7. The Laths were the owners of a farm that they wished to sell. Mrs. Mitchell considered purchasing the land, but found that an ice house located across the road was objectionable. Mitchell argued that the Laths orally agreed to remove the ice house in consideration of her promise to purchase the property, which she agreed to purchase for $8,400 in a written contract. After Mitchell moved into her new home and made several improvements to the land, the Laths had not removed the ice house and expressly communicated their intention never to do so. Mitchell sued the Laths for breach of contract. What effect does the parol evidence rule have on the admissibility of the oral agreement to remove the ice house? Why this effect? [*Mitchill v. Lath,* 247 N.Y. 377 (1928).]

8. Betaco, owned by George Mikelsons, is a corporation that purchases aircraft for sale or lease to other companies. Mikelsons became interested in purchasing a Citation Jet, manufactured by Cessna, so he requested additional information about the Citation Jet from Cessna. In response, Cessna indicated in a cover letter to a packet of materials that the Citation Jet was "much faster, more efficient, and has more range than the popular Citation I." Mikelsons signed the purchase agreement and returned it to Cessna, along with the required deposit of $150,000 toward the final purchase price of $2.495 million. Paul Ruley and another Betaco employee evaluated the suitability of the Citation Jet and concluded that the Citation Jet would have no greater range than the Citation I and that the plane would not meet the full fuel range of 1,500 mentioned in the preliminary specifications. Learning about Ruley's findings, Mikelsons contacted Cessna and demanded a return of the deposit. However, Cessna refused to return the deposit, pointing to a clause in the purchase agreement that stated, "This agreement is the only agreement controlling this purchase and sale, express or implied, either verbal or in writing, and is binding on Purchaser and Seller." Is the express warranty in the cover letter admissible under the parol evidence rule? What effect, if any, does the purported integration clause have on the admissibility of the terms of the cover letter? [*Betaco, Inc. v. Cessna Aircraft Co.,* 32 F.3d 1126 (7th Cir. 1994).]

9. Harold and Henry Lee each owned 50 percent of Capitol City Liquor Company, a wholesale distributor of alcohol. Capitol City generated a large portion of its sales with Seagram, a distiller of alcoholic beverages. The Lees wanted to sell their interest in Capitol City, and, consequently, they discussed their plans to sell the company with Jack Yogman, the executive vice president of Seagram. However, Harold Lee offered to sell Capitol City to Seagram only on the condition that Seagram relocate Harold's sons to a new distributorship in another city. An officer of Seagram, John Barth, visited the Lees and negotiated the purchase of Capitol City's assets, recording the agreement to sell in writing, although no language of relocation was included in the purchase agreement. Prior to acquiring his half interest in Capitol City, Harold Lee served Seagram in a position of responsibility, namely, as the chief executive officer of one of the wholly-owned subsidiaries, while he also maintained friendships with the principals of Seagram. Nevertheless, Seagram did not relocate Harold's sons in accordance with the oral agreement, so the Lees sued Seagram for breach of contract. Should Harold be barred from submitting evidence about the oral agreement on the basis of the parol evidence rule? What reasoning could Harold submit about his relationship with Seagram to persuade the court to not apply the parol evidence rule? [*Lee v. Joseph Seagram & Sons,* 552 F.2d 447 (2nd Cir. 1977).]

10. R. E. Haase owned Whataburger franchise rights for the City of Longview, Texas. In 1992, Haase hired Joseph Glazer as a manager trainee; shortly thereafter, Haase promoted Glazer to supervisor for five of Haase's franchise restaurants. Glazer claimed that in 1994 Haase agreed to assist Glazer in his establishing a Whataburger franchise restaurant and that Glazer was to provide Haase with 2 percent of the net sales. Glazer claimed that this contract was evidenced by three letters from Haase to Whataburger and a cash flow statement Glazer had prepared that indicated a 2 percent payment of net sales to Haase. By 1995, Glazer had not received a franchise, and he quit working for Haase. After Haase opened another franchise, Glazer sued for breach of contract, fraud, and fraudulent inducement. Does Glazer have an enforceable contract claim under the statute of frauds? Should the claim for fraud or fraudulent inducement have any bearing on whether the court should enforce Glazer's contract? [*Haase v. Glazer,* 62 S.W.3d 795 (TX 2001).]

11. Wayne Wilson entered into a lease-purchase agreement with Maryl Morgan. Thereafter, Morgan told Wilson that he would purchase the property, but Morgan never proceeded with the purchase. Donald Burnett, the executor for Wilson's estate, filed suit against Morgan for specific performance of the contract. Although there was no written agreement to purchase the property, Burnett claimed the exception of promissory estoppel to the statute of frauds. Was the court convinced by Burnett's argument for the promissory estoppel exception to the statute of frauds? Why or why not? [*Burnett v. Morgan,* 1986 Kan. App. LEXIS 1031.]

12. Robert Reiss quit his job in Kansas and moved his family to Arkansas, where he began to work as a meat-cutter for Country Corner Food & Drug, Inc. Reiss's wife was pregnant at the time he began to work for Country Corner, so he discussed the provisions of family insurance with his employer, who allegedly agreed to provide insurance for all family members, including the baby. After Reiss's son was born, the child experienced health problems and spent some time in the hospital. After Reiss requested that his employer assume responsibility for the medical bills, Reiss was terminated. Reiss brought suit against Country Corner for breach of contract and compensation for medical expenses. Because the employment contract was never in writing, Country Corner claimed that the contract was unenforceable under the statute of frauds. In response, Reiss claimed that the statute of frauds did not apply because the employment was for an indefinite duration and that, even if the statute applied, the exception of promissory estoppel should apply because Reiss relied to his detriment on his employer's promises. According to the court, which argument was most consistent with the principles of the statute of frauds? [*Country Corner Food & Drug, Inc. v. Reiss,* 1987 Ark. App. LEXIS 2586.]

13. Henry Milgrom agreed to purchase all of Mr. Varnell's peanuts grown in one year under a federal quota program. The purchase price for the peanuts was $640 per ton. Varnell claims that Milgrom agreed through Milgrom's agent to purchase all other peanuts produced by Varnell, in addition to the quota peanuts, at $600 per ton. Milgrom thereafter refused to take delivery of any peanuts, and Varnell had to sell his peanuts elsewhere at a price below $600. Varnell sued for breach of the modified contract, requesting $60,000 in damages. Milgrom paid $16,000 for the quota peanuts but refused to pay for the additional peanuts. Varnell claimed that the statute of frauds did not apply, as the modified oral agreement constituted a waiver of the statute. Milgrom, however, never claimed that the oral agreement existed. Did Varnell succeed in his claim that the statute of frauds was "waived," or was Varnell required to show something more? [*Varnell v. Milgrom,* 1985 N.C. App. LEXIS 4286.]

14. Benito Brino owned real property that he leased to Salvatore and Linda Gabriele. During the lease, the Gabrieles attempted to purchase the property from Brino. Both parties agreed on a purchase price of $565,000 with a closing date of September 15, 2001. However, the Gabrieles were not able to obtain the full amount in loan financing from the bank, so they made a counteroffer to purchase for $450,000, which Brino rejected. The Gabrieles later obtained the full $565,000 from another lending institution and drafted an addendum to the July sales agreement that altered the closing date to May 5, 2002. Brino orally accepted the terms of the agreement, but the document was not signed until May 16, 2002, after the closing date. Consequently, the bank refused to acknowledge the addendum's validity. Thereafter, the Gabrieles drafted a second sales agreement with the same terms as the July agreement, except that the second agreement did not include a closing date but stated that the effective date would be the signing date. Both parties signed the agreement on June 16, 2002, and the bank accepted the agreement and agreed to provide the loan. The Gabrieles informed Brino that they were ready to close, but Brino did not convey title of the property to the Gabrieles. The Gabrieles brought suit against Brino, seeking specific performance, but Brino argued that the agreement was not enforceable as it did not satisfy the statute of frauds, primarily because the agreement did not designate the seller. In response, the Gabrieles claimed that their obtaining financing was partial performance of the agreement. How did the court resolve this issue with regard to the statute of frauds? [*Gabriele v. Brino,* 2004 Conn. App. LEXIS 428.]

Looking for more review material?

The Online Learning Center at **www.mhhe.com/kubasek1e** contains this chapter's "Assignment on the Internet" and also a list of URLs for more information entitled "On the Internet." Find both of them in the Student Center portion of the OLC, along with quizzes and other helpful materials.

Third-Party Rights to Contracts

CASE OPENER

Fallout from a Forgettable Fight

On June 28, 1997, in Las Vegas, Nevada, heavyweight boxers Mike Tyson and Evander Holyfield met for what was to be a night to remember. During the third round of the fight, a desperate Tyson bit off a piece of Holyfield's ear. The fight continued until moments later when Tyson bit Holyfield's other ear.[1] Tyson was disqualified, and numerous fans were unhappy with the outcome. Some fans were so outraged that they decided to sue Tyson, the fight promoters, and the telecasters, seeking a refund.[2] The fans sued on the basis of, among other theories, a claim to being third-party beneficiaries to various contracts into which the defendants had entered.

1. Are the fans entitled to refunds on the basis of a theory of third-party beneficiary rights? What type of beneficiaries would the fans have to be to be able to enforce contractual rights?
2. If you were one of the fight promoters, what sorts of contractual duties would you have to the viewers?

The Wrap-Up at the end of the chapter will answer these questions.

Learning Objectives

After reading this chapter, you will be able to answer the following questions:

1 What is an assignment?

2 What are the rights and duties of an assignor?

[1] CNN/SI, "Year in Review 1997," http://sportsillustrated.cnn.com/features/1997/yearinreview/topstories.
[2] *Castillo v. Tyson,* 268 A.D.2d 336 (2000).

CHAPTER 19

3 What are the rights and duties of an assignee?

4 What is a third-party beneficiary contract?

5 What are the differences among donee beneficiaries, creditor beneficiaries, and incidental beneficiaries?

As you read in Chapter 13, contracts involve agreements between two parties where both parties agree to give something to or do something for the other party. Contracts are typically private agreements, in the sense that the focus of the contract is the two parties involved and no one else. Accordingly, parties not in *privity of contract* (i.e., parties other than the contracting parties) usually do not have rights to a contract. However, as frequently is the case in the law, there are exceptions to the general rule.

There are two main situations in which a third party gains rights to a contract to which she or he is not a party. In the first, one of the contracting parties transfers rights or duties to a third party. In the second, the third party is a direct beneficiary of a contract involving two other parties. This chapter examines both of these situations.

Assignments and Delegations

Contracts typically involve an agreement between two parties where each party agrees to do something for the other. That is, both parties are **obligors** (contractual parties who agreed to do something for the other party) and **obligees** (contractual parties who agreed to receive something from the other party). Consequently, contracts create a situation in which both parties have a duty to perform the agreed-on action and a right to be the recipient of the other party's duty. These rights and duties can be transferred to *third parties*—parties not part of the original contract. This section discusses both the transfer of rights (assignment) and the transfer of duties (delegation) to third parties.

ASSIGNMENT

Assignment occurs when a party to a contract (an **assignor**) transfers her rights to a contract to a third party (an **assignee**). In other words, the assignor gives to an assignee the right to collect what was contractually agreed on in the first contract (see Figure 19-1). For example, Lisa agrees to sell her car to Luke for $8,000. Lisa then assigns her right to receive Luke's payment to Kelly. Kelly, who was not part of the original contract between Luke and Lisa, is an assignee and now has the right to receive payment from Luke for Lisa's car.

When an assignor transfers her rights to an assignee, the assignor legally gives up all rights she previously had to collect on the contract.[3] Now the assignee may legally demand

Figure 19-1 Assignment of Rights

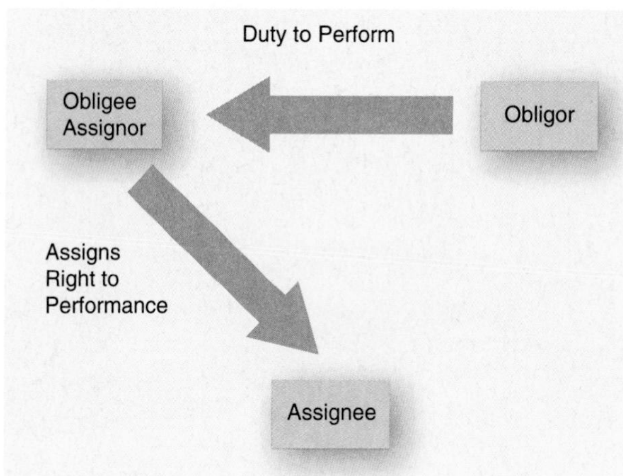

[3] Restatement (Second) of Contracts, sec. 317.

global context

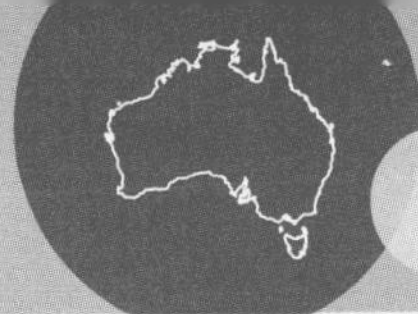

Expanding Third-Party Rights in Australia and the United Kingdom

Most countries do not grant third-party rights to contracts. Rather, most countries require that a party be a direct party to a contract before he or she can recover under the contract. The doctrine of privity requires that parties be a part of a contract before they can recover under the contract. The logic is that if a person is not a party to a contract, then he or she does not have the right to enforce the contract because no consideration was offered under the contract.

One notable exception is Australia, where a third party can sue for breach of contract. In most other countries, privity must be established before a party may sue.

However, privity requirements are beginning to be relaxed in the United Kingdom. In the United Kingdom, solicitors (lawyers) have been held liable to intended beneficiaries of wills when the solicitor was negligent in the creation of the will. Allowing third parties to sue on the basis of a tort theory of negligence demonstrates a movement away from a privity requirement and thus an expansion of third-party rights. Privity is still required in most situations in Australia and the United Kingdom, but the number of exceptions is continuing to grow.

performance from the other party to the original contract. Returning to our example, once Lisa transfers her right to Kelly, Lisa can no longer require that Luke pay her for her car; however, Kelly can request that Luke pay her for Lisa's car.

Assignees essentially fill in for the assignor as the legal recipient of the contractual duties. As such, the assignee acquires the same rights the assignor had. Assignees are offered no additional protections. Moreover, the obligor (the other party to the contract, who owes a duty to the assignee) may raise any of the same defenses for nonperformance to the assignee that he would have been able to raise against the assignor. Returning to our earlier example, if Lisa failed to deliver her car to Luke, he can legally refuse to pay Kelly on the basis of Lisa's breach of contract. It does not matter that Kelly had no duty in the original contract; she is subject to the same defense Luke has against Lisa, and therefore Kelly would not be paid in this situation.

Although there is no legally required wording to be used or forms to be filled out for assignments to be valid, certain restrictions exist. First, although assignments may be given orally or in writing,[4] the UCC requires that assignments be in writing when the amount being assigned is greater than $5,000.[5] Furthermore, assignments covered by the statute of frauds also must be in writing. Because it is difficult to prove the existence of assignments given orally, it is usually suggested that assignments be in writing.

Second, an assignee must agree to accept the assigned rights. An assignee may decline an assignment if he has not legally agreed to the assignment and if he declines in a timely fashion after learning about the assignment and its terms.[6] There is no protocol an assignee must follow to reject an assignment, but once the assignment is rejected, it is considered rejected from the time it was first offered. Third, in some situations contractual rights cannot be assigned.[7]

Rights that cannot be assigned. Exhibit 19-1 lists the four situations in which contractual rights cannot be assigned to a third party. We discuss each of them below.

[4] Restatement (Second) of Contracts, sec. 324.
[5] UCC §1-206.
[6] Restatement (Second) of Contracts, sec. 327.
[7] Ibid, sec. 317(2).

global context

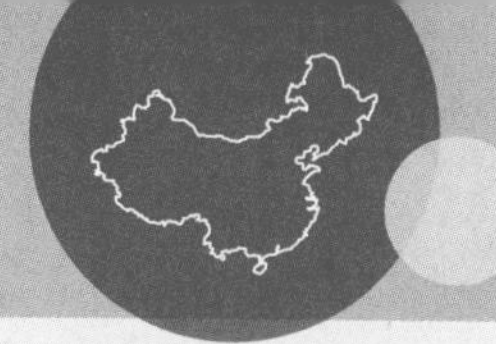

Assignment of Rights in China

Almost all developed market economies permit the free assignability of contract rights. Assignments are important because they play a crucial role in business financing. Banks and businesses make loans and pay debts through assignments. China, which has central planning rather than free-market planning, does not permit free assignment of contracts. Limited assignability is true of most centrally planned economies. When a contract is with the state, approval by the proper state authority must first be obtained, unless the contract allows for assignments. If the contract is with a private party, the assignor must first get the obligor's approval before an assignment can be made. While not prevented, assignments are limited in China.

Exhibit 19-1 Contractual Rights That Cannot Be Assigned

1. Rights that are personal in nature.
2. Rights whose assignment would increase the obligor's risk or duties.
3. Rights whose assignment is prohibited by contract.
4. Rights whose assignment is prohibited by law or public policy.

First, the rights to a contract cannot be assigned when the contract is personal in nature. For a contract to be personal in nature, the obligor must have promised something specific to the person receiving it. Because the subject matter of the contract is personal, third parties cannot legally become the recipient in such situations. The sole exception occurs when the only part of a contract left to be fulfilled is the payment,[8] because rights to payment can always be assigned.

Suppose you are offered several scholarships to different colleges. You cannot attend more than one school, so you cannot use all the different scholarships. Furthermore, because the scholarship offers are personal, that is, based on your unique skills and talents, you cannot transfer your right to the scholarships to a friend. In this sense, college scholarships demonstrate rights of a personal nature that cannot be assigned.

Case 19-1 demonstrates another situation in which a contractual duty cannot be assigned because the courts deemed it personal in nature.

[8] Ibid., secs. 317 and 318.

CASE 19-1 TRAFFIC CONTROL SERVICES v. UNITED RENTALS NORTHWEST, INC.

SUPREME COURT OF NEVADA
87 P.3D 1054 (2004)

Phillip A. Burkhardt, a former United employee, became dissatisfied with United's customer service and obtained a position in Las Vegas with NES.

As a condition of employment with NES, and in exchange for $10,000, he signed noncompetition and nondisclosure covenants. The covenants stipulated that if Burkhardt's employment with NES was terminated, Burkhardt would not, for a period of one year, engage in selling, leasing, marketing, distributing, or dealing with trench shoring equipment within a sixty-mile radius of his work location. Additionally, Burkhardt agreed, in perpetuity, to keep secret and not disclose *to any other party any information to include, but not be limited to, customer lists, employee lists, price lists, pricing strategies, training programs and manuals, trade manuals, and sales programs and materials.*

On June 30, 2002, United and NES entered into an asset purchase agreement. The purchase agreement was limited to certain assets, providing "all contracts and agreements that are not listed as 'Assumed Contracts' are 'Excluded Assets.'" While the agreement listed other noncompetition covenants as assumed contracts, Burkhardt's noncompetition covenant was not on the list. The purchase agreement also contained a recitation that "none of the Assumed Contracts requiring a consent to assignment have been obtained prior to the Closing Date."

A week before closure of the asset purchase, United requested or demanded Burkhardt and a number of other employees sign new one-year noncompetition and nondisclosure covenants. Burkhardt refused.

On August 5, 2002, Burkhardt accepted employment with Traffic Control. United terminated Burkhardt's employment on August 8, 2002, after which he returned all of his work-related items to company officials.

Burkhardt commenced his new position on August 10, 2002, after signing new noncompetition and nondisclosure covenants. He began contacting companies to solicit business on behalf of Traffic Control but was mostly unsuccessful in obtaining new business.

NES and United filed a complaint alleging Burkhardt obtained confidential information during his employment with them, and subsequently used and disclosed NES/United confidential information, contacted United's clients, and attempted to solicit United's customers. The district court ultimately ruled in favor of United, enforcing the noncompetition covenant. Burkhardt appealed.

PER CURIAM: Traffic Control and Burkhardt contend the purported assignment was invalid. We agree and hold, absent an agreement negotiated at arm's length, which explicitly permits assignment and which is supported by separate consideration, employee noncompetition covenants are not assignable.

Employers commonly rely upon restrictive covenants, primarily nondisclosure and noncompetition covenants, to safeguard important business interests.

"Because the loss of a person's livelihood is a very serious matter, post employment anti-competitive covenants are scrutinized with greater care than are similar covenants incident to the sale of a business." The question of whether noncompetition covenants may be assigned from one employer to another through the medium of an asset sale (or otherwise) is an issue of first impression for this court.

There is a distinct split among jurisdictions regarding whether noncompetition covenants are assignable absent an employee's consent.

We agree with those jurisdictions holding noncompetition covenants are personal in nature and, therefore, unassignable as a matter of law, absent the employee's express consent. When an employee enters into a covenant not to compete with his employer, he may consider the character and personality of his employer to determine whether he is willing to be held to a contract that will restrain him from future competition with his employer, even after termination of employment. This does not mean, however, the employee is willing to suffer the same restriction with a stranger to the original obligation. Certainly, the sale of a business fundamentally alters the nature of an employment relationship.

Burkhardt testified, by way of deposition, to his concern about working for a company other than NES, especially United. In this, he covenanted specifically with NES not to compete with NES. At the hearing on the motion for a preliminary injunction, the district court agreed with Burkhardt the noncompetition covenant was personal in nature but concluded, because the covenant held value, it was assignable. Testimony also established United enjoyed a much greater volume of business in the trench shoring business than NES. Therefore, Burkhardt's obligation materially changed when the covenant was assigned. Burkhardt was thus "foreclosed from competing on any level with a much larger business entity." This is, of course, specifically the risk an employee must consider when agreeing to assignability of a noncompetition covenant.

NES's attempted assignment to United of Burkhardt's covenant was invalid. Covenants not to compete are personal in nature and therefore are not assignable absent the employee's express consent. Further, an employer must obtain such consent through arm's-length negotiation with the employee, supported by valuable consideration beyond that necessary to support the underlying covenant. Accordingly, we reverse.

REVERSED.

[CONTINUED]

CRITICAL THINKING

What do you make of the fact that courts are extremely divided on issues of this sort? What differences do you think underlie this division? Are key terms defined differently, or are certain points relative to subjective interpretation by significantly different individuals?

What evidence does the court use to support its stance on the issue? How strong is its argument? Support your answer.

ETHICAL DECISION MAKING

Who are the stakeholders directly affected by this ruling? What might its impact be on future stakeholders involved in similar situations?

Does the court appear to you to be seeking to provide the most happiness to the most people possible, to be following its duty as an ethical entity, or to be acting in keeping with some other moral code? Why?

Second, rights cannot be assigned when the assignment would increase the risk or duties the obligor would face in fulfilling the original contract. For example, Ben agrees to replace the siding on Erin's two-bedroom ranch. Erin cannot assign her right to Ben's services to Chris, who lives in a three-story, five-bedroom house because Ben's (the obligor's) duties would be greatly increased from the work required in the original contract with Erin to the work required in the agreement with Chris.

Third, rights cannot be assigned when the contract expressly forbids assignments. When parties include an *antiassignment clause* in their contract, the parties are attempting to limit their ability to assign their rights under the contract. However, the wording of the antiassignment clause is determinative regarding the effectiveness of the clause. That is, if worded improperly or ambiguously, the clause does not effectively limit assignments.

Most courts consider contractual prohibitions against assignments as promises. Consequently, courts consider assignments made despite the clause to be effective, but the party who makes the assignment will still be liable for breaching the terms of the contract. Moreover, unless the clause is very specific in what it prohibits, courts generally consider the antiassignment clause to prevent delegation of duties, not assignment of rights.[9] A clause stating "All assignments are void under this contract" would be considered effective in prohibiting the assignment of rights. In contrast, when a contract includes a clause explicitly permitting assignments, the parties may assign rights, even when assignments would normally be considered improper because of an increased duty, risk, or burden to the obligor.[10]

Even in the presence of an anti-assignment clause, there are exceptions in which assignments can still be made. For instance, anti-assignment clauses do not affect assignments made by operation of law. That is, if a law necessitates an assignment, such as in bankruptcy cases, the assignment is effective regardless of any contractual agreement to the contrary.

Likewise, as previously stated, the right to assign monetary payments cannot be denied. Therefore, even when a contract has an antiassignment clause, either party may

[9] Ibid., sec. 322(1) and UCC § 2-210(3).

[10] Restatement (Second) of Contracts, sec. 323(1).

still assign his or her right to receive payment.[11] Part of the reason the law does not bar the right to receive payment is that too often businesses transfer rights to payments in the regular course of business. Allowing parties to prevent these transfers would have a negative impact on the business community. Also, one's duty to pay is not affected when the party to whom one must make a payment changes. That is, no added burden is placed on the obligor when the recipient of a payment changes, requiring that payment be sent to a different party.

In addition, assignments for the right to receive damages for a breach of contract to sell goods or services are unaffected by antiassignment clauses.[12] Therefore, if one party breaches the contract, the other party can sue the breaching party and transfer the right to recovery to a third party.

Finally, when law or public policy forbids assignments, the forbidden rights cannot be assigned. Various state and federal statutes prohibit the assigning of specific rights. Even when no statute prohibits an assignment, if the assignment is determined to be against public policy, the assignment is deemed ineffective. Except as outlined in this section, all other rights are presumed to be assignable. Once it has been established that an assignment is valid, notice should be given to the obligor regarding the assignment.

Notice of assignment. Although notice need not be given for a valid assignment, it is usually a good idea for the assignor or the assignee to notify the obligor of the assignment. Assignments are effective immediately, regardless of notice, but by providing notice the assignor can help avoid two serious complications with assignments.

The first complication involves the obligor's fulfilling of the contractual duty. Without notice of assignment, the obligor can discharge his contractual duties simply by fulfilling his duties to the assignor. Because fulfilling the contract discharges the obligor's duties, the act will also constitute a discharge of the assignee's claim on the assignor's right. However, after the obligor has been given notice, the obligor can discharge his contractual obligations only by fulfilling the contract for the assignee.

For example, Peter contracts with Lois to purchase her speedboat. Lois assigns her right to collect Peter's money to Meghan. Neither Lois nor Meghan notifies Peter of the assignment. Accordingly, Peter pays Lois for the boat. Peter's contractual duties have been discharged, and Meghan cannot request performance from Peter. Now, had Peter been notified about the assignment, the only way he could fulfill his contractual obligations would be to pay Meghan the money owed to Lois. If Peter pays Lois, Meghan may still legally request that Peter pay her. By giving the obligor proper notice, such problems with performance of the contract can be avoided.

Case 19-2 discusses what makes a proper notification of assignment.

The second complication regarding a lack of notice involves the granting of multiple assignments of the same right. When an assignor assigns two or more parties the same right, confusion arises as to which party has the right to the contract. Most states use the **first-assignment-in-time rule,** which states that the first party granted the assignment is the party correctly entitled to the contractual right. By giving proper notice, a party can ensure there is no confusion over when the assignment was made. Furthermore, a minority of states have adopted the **English rule,** which states that the first assignee to give notice of assignment to the obligor is the party with rights to the contract. Consequently, especially when living in a state using the English rule, parties are well advised to give notice of assignments to ensure they maintain their assigned rights.

[11] UCC § 9-318(4).

[12] UCC § 2-210(2).

CASE 19-2 FULTON COUNTY v. AMERICAN FACTORS OF NASHVILLE, INC.

COURT OF APPEALS OF GEORGIA, FOURTH DIVISION
250 GA. APP. 366 (2001)

American Factors of Nashville, Inc., and Total Quality Maintenance of Georgia (TQM) entered into an accounts receivable factoring agreement. In the agreement, TQM sold and assigned American Factors invoices for custodial services. Some of the invoices assigned to American Factors were from Fulton County. TQM sent a notice to Fulton County regarding the assignment. Fulton County erroneously paid TQM instead of American Factors. When they did not receive payment, American Factors brought suit against Fulton County. Fulton County claims the notice of assignment was improper, and therefore the payments to TQM were appropriate. Both parties filed for summary judgment. The court ruled in favor of American Factors. Fulton County appealed.

JUDGE SMITH: The record shows each invoice at issue was forwarded to the county with a form statement rubber-stamped on the face of the invoice. This statement, with the word "NOTICE" and the name, address, and telephone number of American Factors in capital letters and typeface approximately the same size as the largest typeface on the original invoice, states:

> NOTICE
>
> This account has been sold, assigned and is payable at Brentwood, Tennessee to
>
> AMERICAN FACTORS OF NASHVILLE, INC.
> P.O. BOX 954
> BRENTWOOD, TN 37024-0954
>
> Remittance to other than American Factors of Nashville, Inc. does not constitute payment of this Invoice. American Factors of Nashville, Inc. must be given notification of any claims agreements or merchandise returns which would affect the payment of all or part of this Invoice on the due date.

In addition, a cover sheet prepared by American Factors was attached to each invoice, identifying the relevant invoice by invoice number, date, and amount and including a notice and certification by TQM's president the invoice had been assigned to American Factors.

The county contends this notice was inadequate because it was not forwarded to the chairman of the Fulton County Board of Commissioners. To support its position, the county points to a provision in the contract between the county and TQM that the terms of the contract shall not be modified unless in writing "signed by the County's and Contractor's duly authorized representative." Although the contract does not expressly define "duly authorized representative," the county contends the chairman of the county commission is its only duly authorized representative and therefore the only person authorized to receive notice. But this is not so. The enabling legislation for the Fulton County Board of Commissioners authorizes the chairman among other duties to "sign all official papers and other instruments and documents on behalf of the Board of Commissioners as directed or authorized by ordinance, resolution, or policy of the Board of Commissioners." But others may be authorized to *receive notice* on the county's behalf. We therefore consider only whether the notice given the county was sufficient to amount to "notification."

The general definitions for the Uniform Commercial Code set forth in detail the manner in which notice or notification is given and received. O.C.G.A. § 11-1-201 (26) provides:

> A person "notifies" or "gives" a notice or notification to another by taking such steps as may be reasonably required to inform the other in ordinary course whether or not such other actually comes to know of it. A person "receives" a notice or notification when: (a) It comes to his attention; or (b) It is duly delivered at the place of business through which the contract was made or at any other place held out by him as the place for receipt of such communications.

The undisputed record shows adequate notification was received under O.C.G.A. § 11-9-318 (3). Steve Fullard was the building services manager for Fulton County and was in charge of overseeing custodial services for the county. He determined which services needed to be performed by a vendor rather than in-house, developed contract specifications, received the bids, and recommended selection of a vendor. After selection of TQM on this particular contract, he was responsible for supervising TQM's performance, receiving invoices, making sure they were processed, making biweekly written or oral reports to his superior, and resolving any complaints or problems with TQM. Fullard plainly was "the individual conducting that transaction" within the meaning of O.C.G.A. § 11-1-201 (27). Fullard is named as the addressee on each invoice, and his superior testified Fullard received the invoices and processed them for payment until the time of his termination. Adequate notification of the assignment, therefore, was received by the county in accordance with O.C.G.A. § 11-9-318 (3), and the trial court did not err in so holding.

AFFIRMED.

CRITICAL THINKING

Construct a reasonable definition of notice or notification that contrasts with that laid out by the UCC, as quoted above. What aspects of the UCC definition are strongest, and which are weakest? How does your definition compensate for these strengths and weaknesses?

Next, reexamine this case from the perspective of the court, using your new definition for notice. Is the acceptability of the conclusion affected? How so? Does this exercise lead you to any new understandings about the importance of terminology in legal disputes or about the costs and benefits of relying on external standards to dictate these important definitions?

ETHICAL DECISION MAKING

Examine the actions that led up to this dispute, and use the available information to make the best guesses you can in regard to the motivations and causations underlying the relevant acts. Can the behavior of one side or the other be deemed more ethically defensible? If so, which side, and why? What ethical theories or guidelines support your claim? Does the decision of the court reflect an agreement with your view?

Suppose Shelia assigns her contractual rights to Tony. Then, a week later, Shelia assigns the same rights to Christine. Under the first-assignment-in-time rule, Tony legally has Shelia's rights to the contract. However, if Christine gives notice first and the state in question uses the English rule, although Shelia assigned her rights to Tony first, legally Christine would possess Shelia's rights to the contract.

The Restatement (Second) of Contracts states a view in between the first-assignment-in-time rule and the English rule.[13] The Restatement grants legal right to the first assignee in most situations. However, if the first assignment is legally voidable or revocable by the assignor, subsequent assignments are considered evidence of the voiding or revocation of the first assignment. In such situations, the later assignee has legal right to the contract. Also, the later assignee is considered the legal owner of the contractual right if she offers something to the assignor as consideration and then obtains (1) performance by the obligor on his duty, (2) judgment requiring performance by the obligor, (3) a new contract with

[13] Sec. 342.

Figure 19-2 Delegation of Duties

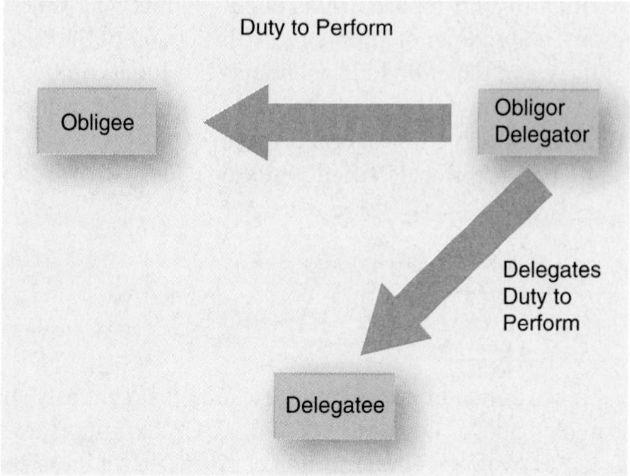

the obligor, or (4) evidence frequently used to signify a contractual right (e.g., a writing indicating a contractual obligation).

DELEGATION

A **delegation** occurs when a party to a contract (a **delegator**) transfers her duty to perform to a third party who is not part of the original contract (a **delegatee**). Whereas assignments transfer rights to a contract, delegations transfer duties. (See Figure 19-2.) Instead of receiving something, as in an assignment, delegations require that the delegatee fulfill the delegator's contractual obligation to the obligee—the party to the contract to whom a duty is owed. For example, John contracts with Teresa to have her deliver machinery to his factory. Teresa then delegates her duty to Bill, who delivers the machinery to John.

One important distinction between assignments and delegations involves the rights of the transferring party—the assignor or the delegator. In assignments, after the assignment is made, the assignor has no right left to the original contract. Conversely, with delegations, the delegator is not relieved of his duty to perform by making a delegation. If the delegatee fails to fulfill the contract, the delegator is still liable to the obligee for fulfillment of the contract. Using the previous example, if Bill fails to deliver the machinery to John, Teresa is liable to John for damages.

Duties that cannot be delegated. As with assignments, the starting assumption is that duties to a contract can be delegated. However, courts tend to examine delegations more closely than assignments. The reasoning is that assignments usually do not affect the party to the contract who is not involved in the assignment (the obligor), whereas a delegation forces the party to the contract who is not involved in the delegation (the obligee) to receive performance of the contract from a party with whom the obligee did not directly contract.

Also just as with assignments, there are certain situations in which duties cannot be delegated to a third party (see Exhibit 19-2).[14] The first type of duty that cannot be delegated, mirroring assignments, is any duty of a personal nature. A duty is personal in nature when it requires the specific talents, skills, or expertise of the obligor. For example,

[14] Restatement (Second) of Contracts, sec. 318, and UCC § 2-210.

connecting to the core

Management

Management classes teach that delegation is an important concept in a managerial environment. All forms of delegating need not take place in the context of a contract: Delegation in a general sense refers to one's authority and right to pass along certain responsibilities to another, such as a manager's delegating responsibility to an employee for the purpose of the employee's completing a particular task. The primary purpose of delegation in a business environment is efficiency, in the sense that tasks may be completed more quickly by delegatees (i.e., employees) while the delegators (i.e., managers) focus on supervising the quality of work of a larger number of delegatees.

Similar to delegation in a contractual context, delegation in a managerial context usually does not remove the manager's obligation to have the task completed in the event that a delegatee fails to perform his or her task. Often, an employee's inadequate performance reflects poorly on the manager who delegated the task, even though the duty to perform was transferred to the employee. Therefore, whether delegation takes place in the context of a contract or a managerial environment, the delegator should be relatively active (compared to an assignor) to ensure that the delegatee is performing as expected, thereby increasing the likelihood of recognizing efficiency in either context.

Source: Angelo Kinicki and Brian K. Williams, *Management: A Practical Introduction* (New York: McGraw-Hill/Irwin, 2006), p. 250.

Exhibit 19-2
Duties That Cannot Be Delegated

1. Duties that are personal in nature.
2. Duties for which the delegatee's performance will vary significantly from the delegator's.
3. Duties in contracts that forbid delegations.

Victoria contracts with Michael, a famous artist, to paint her portrait. Victoria contracted with Michael because of his skill and expertise. Therefore, Michael cannot delegate his duty to paint Victoria's portrait to anyone else, not even someone of equal skill or talent.

An interesting situation arises when the initial contract bears an implicit assumption that work will be performed by others. In such situations, if supervision is important to the task, the supervision could be considered to be a personal duty that the obligor may not delegate to others. Suppose you are planning to have a new office building built to specifications you have personally created. You contract with Ian, a well-respected manager of a construction firm. Both you and Ian know that Ian will not build the office building single-handedly, but because he was sought out for his management skills, his contractual duties would be considered personal and therefore cannot be delegated.

Delegation for personal duties is admissible where otherwise not allowed when there is an explicit or implicit contractual agreement to allow delegations. Usually, for a delegation of personal duties to be effective, the contract must state that delegations are permitted.

While personal duties typically cannot be delegated, any nonpersonal duties in a contract can be delegated. For example, the delivering of goods, mowing of one's lawn, paying of money, or painting of a house are all considered nonpersonal duties. These duties are nonpersonal because they do not require particular skill or expertise and therefore can be completed by most people. Accordingly, one can delegate these nonpersonal duties.

The second type of duty one cannot delegate is a duty whose performance by the delegatee would vary significantly from the performance by the delegator. To protect the obligee, who is a part of the original contract, when performance would differ substantially from what the obligee contractually has the right to, courts will rule that the delegation is ineffective. The focus here is the skill or abilities of the delegatee. If the delegatee cannot perform the contract to a level comparable to the performance of the delegator, the obligee would be unnecessarily harmed, and thus the delegation is deemed ineffective.

The third situation in which delegations are prohibited occurs when the contract prohibits them. When parties include agreements not to delegate, the courts typically treat these inclusions as indications of the parties' desire to consider the contractual obligations as personal. Consequently, the courts frequently find otherwise-allowable delegations to be inappropriate when an agreement not to delegate is in the contract. However, even if a clause prohibiting delegations exists, the courts will probably allow delegations to occur if they are impersonal. For example, courts consider the payment of money impersonal, and therefore delegable, even if a contract prohibits delegations.

Case 19-3 demonstrates the problems arising from a party's failure to acknowledge a nondelegation agreement. Although the case discusses assignments of obligations, the court is treating the term *assignment* as a synonym for *delegation of duties.* Some courts use the term *assignment* to refer to a transfer of either rights *or* duties, which sometimes confuses people.

CASE 19-3 FOREST COMMODITY CORP. v. LONE STAR INDUSTRIES, INC., ET AL.

COURT OF APPEALS OF GEORGIA, THIRD DIVISION
255 GA. APP. 244 (2002)

CAL and FCC entered into a three-year contract for the "thru-putting" of aggregate stone. In the contract, FCC agreed to provide terminal space for unloading aggregate stone, which FCC would then store, reload onto trucks and weigh for transshipment. CAL promised to unload a minimum of 150,000 tons per year, for a total of 450,000 tons over the three-year contract period. The agreement also contained a provision prohibiting the assignment or subcontracting of any portion of the obligations without the written consent of the other party.

During the contract period, CAL unloaded a total of 198,170 tons of aggregate. Soon thereafter, CAL entered into negotiations with Martin Marietta Materials, Inc., for the sale of CAL's assets. Martin Marietta agreed to accept CAL's rights and obligations under the agreement with FCC, and CAL requested FCC accept an assignment of the thru-put agreement to Martin Marietta. FCC refused to consent to the assignment. FCC and Martin Marietta eventually entered into a substantially similar contract for the thru-putting of aggregate. It is undisputed after Martin Marietta's acquisition of CAL and its assets, and pursuant to the new contract entered into with FCC, Martin Marietta thru-put 286,698 tons of aggregate stone at the FCC terminal during the remainder of the original contract period for the CAL thru-put agreement. When combined with the 198,170 tons shipped by CAL, a total of 484,868 tons of aggregate stone was shipped through the FCC facility, 34,868 tons more than the guaranteed minimum under the original agreement.

FCC sued CAL for breach of contract, alleging CAL failed to ship the minimum amount of aggregate stone under the contract. CAL filed a motion for summary judgment as to the breach of contract claim. The trial court granted the motion for summary judgment, finding that FCC was precluded from enforcing the contract because it failed to comply with the nonassignability clause. FCC appealed.

JUDGE JOHNSON: FCC contends the trial court erred in granting summary judgment to CAL because there are genuine issues of material fact regarding whether FCC assigned the contract. However, the irrefutable evidence, even when construed in a light most favorable to FCC, points inevitably to the conclusion an assignment of the CAL thru-put agreement was effected. The numerous items of undisputed facts in this case show FCC's interests and obligations in the

CAL thru-put agreement were transferred to Woodchips Export Corporation ("WEC") without the written consent of CAL, thereby violating the nonassignability clause of the agreement and extinguishing any right to recovery which FCC may have had.

The thru-put agreement obligated FCC to provide a marine terminal facility for the off-loading of aggregate and to perform both the reloading of the aggregate onto trucks and the weighing of such trucks. Yet, the evidence in the record shows the terminal facility where the CAL aggregate was off-loaded was leased by FCC to WEC. In addition, it is undisputed FCC had no employees and no equipment to perform the obligations under the CAL agreement. FCC's vice-president admits FCC had no employees and FCC entered into an unwritten agreement with WEC under which WEC agreed to perform FCC's obligations as its operations agent.

Moreover, FCC's tax returns for the years covered by the thru-put agreement show the only income received by FCC during this time period was rental income. These tax returns do not show any income for aggregate thru-putting, nor do they include any expenses for employee wages, equipment rental or maintenance, or fuel expenditures necessary to carry out its obligations under the CAL thru-put agreement. On the other hand, WEC's income statements and tax returns reveal WEC deducted the expenses incurred in conjunction with aggregate thru-putting and received income for the thru-put of aggregate in amounts that correspond to the amounts generated by the CAL thru-put agreement.

Indeed, FCC's own accountants testified such debiting and crediting could not have occurred between these two parties since FCC files separate tax returns from the tax returns of WEC and other related companies. Furthermore, the same accountants testified even if such funds had, in fact, been debited and credited between these two companies, the income would first have appeared on the company actually earning it, which in this case was WEC. As a final note, FCC has offered no documentary evidence supporting this accounting practice, such as documents memorializing such intercompany adjustments through debits and credits.

FCC next argues no assignment can be found in this case since there is no written assignment document or any other document indicating an intent to assign. However, an assignment can be inferred from the totality of the circumstances and need not be reduced to writing. In addition, Georgia courts may look to tax returns as probative evidence in ascertaining the existence of an assignment. The affirmative decision to declare the thru-put income on the tax returns of WEC and not on the tax returns of FCC is certainly evidence of an intent to assign. Moreover, FCC's vice-president testified oral agreements between FCC and WEC were entered into under his direction and supervision, showing yet another intent to assign. The trial court properly found FCC had assigned the CAL thru-put agreement to WEC.

AFFIRMED.

CRITICAL THINKING

Do you agree with the reasoning of this decision? Is the evidence as strongly in support of the court's conclusion as the judge states? Is unfair weight (or lack thereof) given to any pieces of evidence?

Further, what evidence might not be included in this decision that could affect the court's conclusion? Come up with at least one fact, not included in the ruling but possible given the information provided above, that would have a significant impact on the acceptability of this reasoning.

ETHICAL DECISION MAKING

How do you think this decision would hold up under the public disclosure test? Who might react favorably, and who unfavorably? What differences in ethical standards could explain contradictory reactions? Where do you think the majority of the U.S. public would fall? Why?

global context

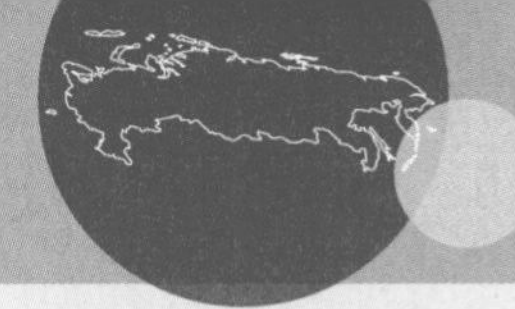

Reformation of Assignments and Delegations in Russia

Many of the advanced industrialized nations have fairly similar laws regarding assignments and delegations. Part of this similarity is attributable to the similarity of these market-based economies.

Russia, which was centrally planned under the Soviet Union, is attempting to join the industrialized nations with respect to a market-based economy. To aid this transition, the Russians have modified the Russian Civil Code to reflect the freedom of assignments found in the German code. This change to free assignment of rights and duties is critical to Russia's potential for success in switching to a market-based economy.

Assignment of the Contract

Frequently, contracts use ambiguous language that makes it unclear what is being assigned or delegated. Examples of ambiguous language are "I assign the contract" or "I assign all of my rights under the contract." When a court cannot clearly tell what the parties intended, the court usually considers the assignment to be of both rights and duties. In other words, when ambiguous language is used, the court considers that the assignor has assigned his rights as well as delegated any duties he had under the contract. (See Figure 19-3.) Doing so removes any right the assignor had to collect under the contract, but he is still liable to the obligee for any duties the delegatee, who is also the assignee, fails to perform.

Third-Party Beneficiary Contracts

We have thus far learned about one of the ways in which third parties may obtain rights or duties to a contract: through assignments or delegations. We now move on to the other

Figure 19-3 Assignment of the Contract

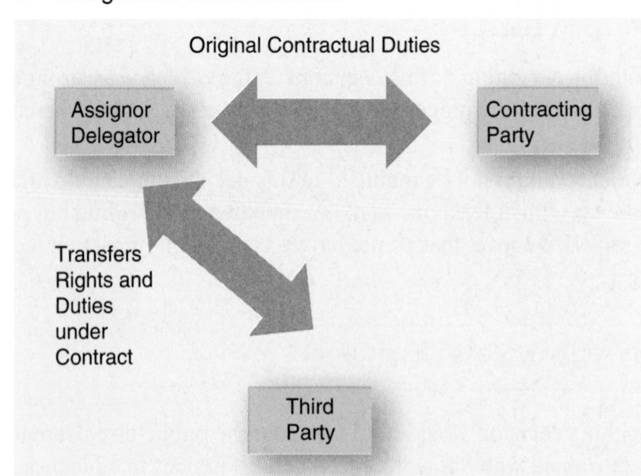

way, which is that the third party is an intended beneficiary to the contract. A **third-party beneficiary** is created when two parties enter into a contract with the intended end purpose of benefiting a third party. To be a third-party beneficiary, the third party does not need to be explicitly named in the contract, as long as the terms of the contract or events occurring after the creation of the contract make it clear who is the intended recipient of the contractual benefits.

INTENDED BENEFICIARIES

Early in the common law, courts had difficulty when contracts were written to benefit third parties. The courts were not sure how to treat these contracts, and usually deemed third parties to have no rights to contracts to which they were not in privity. Now, however, third parties who are intended beneficiaries have the right to enforce contracts. An **intended beneficiary** is a third party to a contract whom the contracting parties intended to benefit directly from their contract.

Intended beneficiaries may enforce their rights to a contract when both parties to the contract intended for the third party to benefit. In determining whether a third party is an intended beneficiary, courts ask whether the contracting parties intended that the third party be the "direct," "primary," or "express" beneficiary of the contract.

The **promisor** in a third-party beneficiary contract is the party to the contract who made the promise that benefits the third party. The **promisee** is the party to the contract who owes something to the promisor in exchange for the promise made to the third-party beneficiary. For example, Amanda contracts with Alex to clean his house. In exchange, Alex will pay Amanda's credit card debt. The credit card company is the third-party beneficiary, as the contract is created to benefit the company. Alex is the promisor, for he made the promise to pay the third-party beneficiary. Amanda is the promisee because she owes a duty to the promisor, Alex.

In a third-party beneficiary contract, the intended beneficiary may sue the promisor to enforce the contract Although the promisee typically owes something to the third-party beneficiary before the contract with the promisor exists, if the third party sues the promisee after the promisor does not fulfill his or her obligations, the promisee can then sue the promisor for breach of contract. Therefore, courts allow the third-party beneficiary to sue the promisor, thus eliminating the litigation that would ensue if the promisee sued the promisor. Returning to our earlier example, if Alex fails to pay the credit card company for Amanda's debt, the credit card company has the right to sue Alex, even though it is Amanda's debt.

Let us return to the opening scenario. The fans of the Tyson fight argued that they were third-party beneficiaries and therefore had rights under several contracts that were violated when Tyson was disqualified early in the fight. Boxing matches are widely viewed events, and one can argue that the fights are organized for the enjoyment of the fans. Does the idea of boxing matches' being organized for the fans make the fans the "direct," "primary," or "express" beneficiaries of contracts involved in the fight? In other words, are the fans of the Tyson fight intended beneficiaries to the contracts Tyson entered when agreeing to the fight? What else do we need to know before we can determine whether the fans have a legal right to a refund?

There are two types of intended beneficiaries: creditor beneficiaries and donee beneficiaries.

Creditor beneficiaries. A **creditor beneficiary** is a third party that benefits from a contract in which the promisor agrees to pay the promisee's debt. In our previous example, because Alex (the promisor) agreed to pay the debt of Amanda (the promisee), Amanda's credit card company is a creditor beneficiary.

Case 19-4 is a famous dispute in which the courts began to recognize the rights of third parties to sue promisors for performance.

CASE 19-4 | LAWRENCE v. FOX
COURT OF APPEALS OF NEW YORK
20 N.Y. 268 (1859)

In November of 1857, Holly, at the request of Fox, loaned him $300. Before loaning the money, Holly informed Fox that she owed Lawrence $300 due the next day. In consideration of the loan, at the time of the loan, Fox agreed to pay Lawrence for Holly the next day. Fox did not pay and Lawrence sued him. Fox sought to dismiss the charges because there was no proof tending to show Holly was indebted to Lawrence; the agreement by Fox with Holly to pay Lawrence was void for want of consideration, and there was no privity between Lawrence and Fox. Fox's motion to dismiss was denied. The jury ultimately found in favor of Lawrence for the sum of the loan plus interest. Fox appealed and the judgment was affirmed. Fox then appealed again.

JUDGE GRAY: But it is claimed notwithstanding this promise was established by competent evidence, it was void for the want of consideration. It is now more than a quarter of a century since it was settled by the Supreme Court of this State that a promise in all material respects like the one under consideration was valid; and the judgment of that court was unanimously affirmed by the Court for the Correction of Errors. In *Farley v. Cleaveland,* Moon owed Farley and sold to Cleaveland a quantity of hay, in consideration of which Cleaveland promised to pay Moon's debt to Farley. The decision in favor of Farley's right to recover was placed upon the ground the hay received by Cleaveland from Moon was a valid consideration for Cleaveland's promise to pay Farley, and the subsisting liability of Moon to pay Farley was no objection to the recovery.

The fact the money advanced by Holly to the defendant was a loan to him for a day, and it thereby became the property of the defendant, seemed to impress the defendant's counsel with the idea because the defendant's promise was not a trust fund placed by the plaintiff in the defendant's hands, out of which he was to realize money as from the sale of a chattel or the collection of a debt, the promise although made for the benefit of the plaintiff could not enure to his benefit. The hay which Cleaveland delivered to Moon was not to be paid to Farley, but the debt incurred by Cleaveland for the purchase of the hay, like the debt incurred by the defendant for money borrowed, was what was to be paid. That case has been often referred to by the courts of this State, and has never been doubted as sound authority for the principle upheld by it. It puts to rest the objection the defendant's promise was void for want of consideration.

The report of that case shows the promise was not only made to Moon but to the plaintiff Farley. In this case the promise was made to Holly and not expressly to the plaintiff; and this difference between the two cases presents the question, raised by the defendant's objection, as to the want of privity between the plaintiff and defendant. As early as 1806 it was announced by the Supreme Court of this State, upon what was then regarded as the settled law of England, "That where one person makes a promise to another for the benefit of a third person, that third person may maintain an action upon it."

The same principle is adjudged in several cases in Massachusetts. I will refer to but few of them. In *Hall* v. *Marston* the court says: "It seems to have been well settled if A promises B for a valuable consideration to pay C, the latter may maintain assumpsit for the money." In *Brewer* v. *Dyer,* the recovery was upheld, as the court said, "upon the principle of law *long recognized and clearly established,* when one person, for a valuable consideration, engages with another, by a simple contract, to do some act for the benefit of a third, the latter, who would enjoy the benefit of the act, may maintain an action for the breach of such engagement; that it does not rest upon the ground of any actual or supposed relationship between the parties as some of the earlier cases would seem to indicate, but upon the broader and more satisfactory basis, that the law operating on the act of the parties creates the duty, establishes a privity, and implies the promise and obligation on which the action is founded."

But it is urged, because the defendant was not in any sense a trustee of the property of Holly for the benefit of the plaintiff, the law will not imply a promise. I agree many of the cases where a promise was implied were cases of trusts, created for the benefit of the promiser. The case of *Felton* v. *Dickinson,* and others that might be cited, are of that class; but concede them all to have been cases of trusts, and it proves nothing against the application of the rule to this case.

In this case the defendant, upon ample consideration received from Holly, promised Holly to pay his debt to the plaintiff. The consideration received and the promise to Holly made it as plainly his duty to pay the plaintiff as if the money had been remitted to him for that purpose, and as well implied a promise to do so as if he had been made a trustee of property to be converted into cash with which to pay. The fact a breach of the duty imposed in the one case may be visited, and justly, with more serious consequences than in the other, by no means disproves the payment to be a duty in both.

The principle illustrated by the example so frequently quoted (which concisely states the case in hand) "that a promise made to one for the benefit of another, he for whose benefit it is made may bring an action for its breach," has been applied to trust cases, not because it was exclusively applicable to those cases, but because it was a principle of law, and as such applicable to those cases. It was also insisted Holly could have discharged the defendant from his promise, though it was intended by both parties for the benefit of the plaintiff, and therefore the plaintiff was not entitled to maintain this suit for the recovery of a demand over which he had no control. It is enough the plaintiff did not release the defendant from his promise, and whether he could or not is a question not now necessarily involved.

The cases cited, and especially that of *Farley* v. *Cleaveland,* establish the validity of a parol promise; it stands then upon the footing of a written one. Suppose the defendant had given his note in which, for value received of Holly, he had promised to pay the plaintiff and the plaintiff had accepted the promise, retaining Holly's liability. Very clearly Holly could not have discharged that promise, be the right to release the defendant as it may. No one can doubt he owes the sum of money demanded of him, or in accordance with his promise it was his duty to have paid it to the plaintiff. Nor can it be doubted, whatever may be the diversity of opinion elsewhere, the adjudications in this State, from a very early period, approved by experience, have established the defendant's liability; if, therefore, it could be shown a more strict and technically accurate application of the rules applied, would lead to a different result (which I by no means concede), the effort should not be made in the face of manifest justice.

AFFIRMED.

JUDGE COMSTOCK, DISSENTING: The plaintiff had nothing to do with the promise on which he brought this action. It was not made to him, nor did the consideration proceed from him. If he can maintain the suit, it is because an anomaly has found its way into the law on this subject. In general, there must be privity of contract. The party who sues upon a promise must be the promisee, or he must have some legal interest in the undertaking. In this case, it is plain that Holly, who loaned the money to the defendant, and to whom the promise in question was made, could at any time have claimed it should be performed to himself personally. He had lent the money to the defendant, and at the same time directed the latter to pay the sum to the plaintiff. This direction he could countermand, and if he had done so, manifestly the defendant's promise to pay according to the direction would have ceased to exist. The plaintiff would receive a benefit by a complete execution of the arrangement, but the arrangement itself was between other parties, and was under their exclusive control. If the defendant had paid the money to Holly, his debt would have been discharged thereby. Therefore, Holly might have released the demand or assigned it to another person, or the parties might have annulled the promise now in question, and designated some other creditor of Holly as the party to whom the money should be paid. It has never been claimed, in a case thus situated, the right of a third person to sue upon the promise rested on any sound principle of law. We are to inquire whether the rule has been so established by positive authority.

The cases in which some trust was involved are frequently referred to as authority for the doctrine now in question, but they do not sustain it. If A delivers money or property to B, which the latter accepts upon a trust for the benefit of C, the latter can enforce the trust by an appropriate action for that purpose. If the trust be of money, I think the beneficiary may assent to it and bring the action for money had and received to his use. If it be of something else than money, the trustee must account for it according to the terms of the trust, and upon principles of equity. There is some authority even for saying an express promise founded on the possession of a trust fund may be enforced by an action at law in the name of the beneficiary, although it was made to the creator of the trust.

Thus, in *Comyn's Digest,* it is laid down if a man promise a pig of lead to A, and his executor give lead to make a pig to B, who assumes to deliver it to A, an assumpsit lies by A against him. The case of *The Delaware and Hudson Canal Company* v. *The Westchester County Bank* involved a trust because the defendants had received from a third party a bill of exchange under an agreement they would endeavor to collect it, and would pay over the proceeds when collected to the plaintiffs. A fund received under such an agreement does not belong to the person who receives it. He must account for it specifically; and perhaps there is no gross violation of principle in permitting the equitable owner of it to sue upon an express promise to pay it over. Having a specific interest in the thing, the undertaking to account for it may be regarded as in some sense made with him through the author of the trust. But further than this we cannot go without violating plain rules of law. In the case before us there was nothing in the nature of a trust or agency. The defendant borrowed the money of Holly and received it as his own. The plaintiff had no right in the fund, legal or equitable. The promise to repay the money created an obligation in favor of the lender to whom it was made and not in favor of any one else.

The question was also involved in some confusion by the earlier cases in Massachusetts. Indeed, the Supreme Court of that State seem at one time to have made a nearer approach to the doctrine on which this action must rest, than the courts of this State have ever done. But in the recent case of *Mellen, Administratrix,* v. *Whipple,* the subject was carefully reviewed and the doctrine utterly overthrown. One Rollin was indebted to the plaintiff's testator, and had secured the debt by a mortgage on his land. He then conveyed the equity of redemption to the defendant, by a deed which contained a clause declaring the defendant was to assume and pay the mortgage. It was conceded the acceptance of the deed with such a clause in it was equivalent to an express promise to pay the mortgage debt; and the question was, whether the mortgagee or his representative could sue on that undertaking. It was held the suit could not be maintained. In the course of a very careful and discriminating opinion by Judge Metcalf, it was shown the cases which had been supposed to favor the action belonged to exceptional classes, none of which embraced the pure and simple case of an attempt by one person to enforce a promise made to another, from whom the consideration wholly proceeded. I am of that opinion.

CRITICAL THINKING

Form an opinion on the contemporary relevance of this ruling. Given the widespread and extremely significant changes in U.S. society and the world over the last 150 years, what is the justification for consideration of such an old case? How does this type of process aid our legal system, and how might it detract from the reasonableness of modern deliberations?

ETHICAL DECISION MAKING

Consider the actions of Fox, both leading up to and through the course of the described legal disputes. What do you see as the primary motivation for his behavior? Examine this from an ethical point of view. What stakeholders does Fox have in mind? What values might he be attempting to uphold through his actions? Try to see both sides of the issue; if you are inclined to see Fox as acting ethically, form an argument placing blame on him; if you are inclined to see him as acting unethically, form an argument attacking his actions. How do different ethical theories play into your considerations?

Donee beneficiaries. The other type of intended beneficiaries is donee beneficiaries. **Donee beneficiaries** are third parties who benefit from a contract in which a promisor agrees to give a gift to the third party. The most common form of donee beneficiary contracts is life insurance policies. Someone (the promisee) pays premiums on a life insurance plan to have the insurer (the promisor) agree to pay a third party (the donee beneficiary) on the promisee's death.

The fans in the Tyson case argued they are intended beneficiaries. If the fans are correct, and we know Tyson did not have a debt to the fans, then they must be donee beneficiaries. Does an agreement to perform create a situation in which the audience becomes the intended beneficiaries of the performance?

Vesting of rights. Although an intended beneficiary can enforce her rights to a contract, she cannot do so until her rights to the contract **vest**—the maturing of rights such that a party can legally act on the rights. Before a third party's rights have vested, the original contracting parties can make changes to the original contract without the permission of the third party. For example, third-party rights in a life insurance policy do not vest until the promisee's death. Consequently, Jane (the promisee) can change the intended beneficiary of her life insurance policy from Mary to Peter. Jane does not need Mary's permission, and Mary cannot sue Jane, because Mary's rights have not vested.

Generally, one of three things must occur for a third party's right to a contract to vest.[15] First, under certain circumstances, third-party rights vest immediately. When rights vest immediately, the third party can enforce the contract at any time. These rights take effect instantaneously, even if the beneficiary does not know about the contract.

Second, rights may vest when the beneficiary decides to accept the rights to the contract. Sometimes the beneficiary must positively accept the rights, such as by notifying the contracting parties of acceptance. However, in the absence of an overt act of rejecting the rights to a contract, acceptance is assumed when the beneficiary becomes aware of the contract.

Third, the beneficiary must change his position based on a reliance on the contractual rights. In other words, the beneficiary must take some action he would not have taken otherwise because he is expecting to benefit from the contract. For example, Vince is a third-party beneficiary to a contract. When he finds out about the contract, he decides to lease a new car because he is expecting to benefit from the contract. Obtaining the lease would cause his rights to the contract to vest because it demonstrates a change in position based on reliance on the contract.

If a contract specifies that the original contracting parties maintain the right to alter or rescind the contract, the vesting of the third party's rights does not preclude the promisor or the promisee from changing the original contract. Return to the earlier example of the life insurance policy. All life insurance policies allow the promisee to change the beneficiary. Therefore, as described earlier, there are situations where the vesting of rights does not prevent changes to the contractual obligations of the original contracting parties.

Many states hold that donee beneficiary rights vest before creditor beneficiary rights. The rationale is that even if the contract is altered when there is a creditor beneficiary, the creditor beneficiary still maintains her rights against the debtor (the promisee). Suppose your friend owes you $1,000. Your friend enters a contract in which you are a creditor beneficiary. If your friend and the other party change the contract before your rights vest, you still have a right to the money your friend owes you, even if you cannot enforce this right against the person with whom your friend contracted. Donee beneficiaries do not have the

[15] Restatement (Second) of Contracts, sec. 311.

Exhibit 19-3
Creditor versus Donee Beneficiaries

CREDITOR BENEFICIARY	DONEE BENEFICIARY
Purpose of the Contract	
Contractual performance fulfills an obligation to a third party.	Contractual performance gives a gift to a third party.
Enforcement of Rights	
Beneficiary can enforce rights to a contract if the contract is valid and the rights have vested.	Beneficiary has limited ability to enforce contracts, depending on the jurisdiction.
Beneficiary can enforce rights against the promisor or the promisee.	Beneficiary can enforce rights against the promisor.

same option as creditor beneficiaries, and thus many states allow their rights to vest more quickly than those of creditor beneficiaries.

Creditor versus donee beneficiaries. There are two main distinctions between creditor beneficiaries and donee beneficiaries (see Exhibit 19-3). The first distinction is based on the reason the third-party beneficiary contract was created. If the promise in the contract is intended to release a party from an obligation to a third party, such as the paying of one's debt, the contract involves a creditor beneficiary. Conversely, if the contract intends to grant a gift to a third party, the third party is a donee beneficiary.

The second distinction involves conditions under which an intended beneficiary can enforce his rights under a contract. Creditor beneficiaries can enforce their rights under a contract whenever the contract is valid. Donee beneficiaries can enforce their rights to most contracts. However, some jurisdictions do not allow donee beneficiaries to enforce their contractual rights in all situations. For example, the state of New York does not grant donee beneficiaries the right to enforce a contract unless the promisee is connected to the donee through a familial relationship.

When a donee beneficiary may enforce his rights under a contract, he may do so only against the promisor. The reason the donee beneficiary cannot sue the promisee is that the promisee had no duty to the donee beneficiary. Conversely, creditor beneficiaries may sue the promisor or the promisee for performance, as both parties owed a duty to the creditor beneficiary. However, if the creditor beneficiary wins a judgment against one party, she may not seek judgment against the other party. In addition, if a creditor beneficiary wins judgment against the promisee, the promisee may sue the promisor to recover under a theory of breach of contract.[16]

As you might have guessed, it is not always easy to determine when someone is a creditor or a donee beneficiary. Sometimes a contract is created for reasons that are intended both to be charitable and to pay a debt. Given the lack of clear distinction as to when someone is a creditor beneficiary and when he is a donee beneficiary, the Restatement (Second) of Contracts takes a different approach.[17] The Restatement focuses on the distinction between intended and incidental beneficiaries.

Creditor and donee beneficiaries are both intended beneficiaries, and according to the Restatement, intended beneficiaries have the right to enforce a contract. When it is

[16] Restatement (Second) of Contracts, sec. 310.

[17] Ibid., sec. 302.

clear that the contract was created for the benefit of a third party, and performance of the contractual duties will pay off the payee's debt or give a gift as the payee intended, then the third party is an intended beneficiary.

INCIDENTAL BENEFICIARIES

Similar to intended beneficiaries, incidental beneficiaries are third-party beneficiaries to contracts. However, unlike the case with intended beneficiaries, the contracting parties do not *intend* to benefit incidental beneficiaries. An **incidental beneficiary** is one who unintentionally gains a benefit from a contract between other parties. (See Exhibit 19-4.)

For example, Cassandra contracts with Garrett to have him build a well-financed private high school on property she owns. The new school will raise the property values of the houses surrounding it. Although neither Cassandra nor Garrett intended to benefit these local homeowners, the homeowners still benefited from the contract between Cassandra and Garrett. Accordingly, the local homeowners are incidental beneficiaries to Cassandra and Garrett's contract.

One significant difference between intended and incidental beneficiaries is that incidental beneficiaries cannot sue to enforce a contract. Going back to Cassandra and Garrett, if they decide to rescind their contract, the local homeowners cannot sue to enforce the contract because it was never Cassandra or Garrett's intent to benefit the homeowners. Incidental beneficiaries maintain no rights to enforce other people's contracts.

In determining whether a party is an incidental beneficiary, the courts will take a reasonable person approach. In this approach, the courts ask if a reasonable person in the position of the party in question would believe the contracting parties intended to benefit the party in question. If the reasonable person would believe that the contracting parties consciously intended to benefit him or her, the courts consider the party an intended beneficiary. If the reasonable person would not find such intent, the third party is an incidental beneficiary.

As a thought experiment, consider the reasonable person test in context of the Tyson case from the opening scenario. For the fans to be able to receive refunds, the reasonable person in the position of the fans would have to believe Tyson intended to benefit him or her with Tyson's performance. Do the fans meet the reasonable person test? Contrast the Tyson case with the one described in the Case Nugget, in which the court found that there was sufficient evidence that the plaintiff was an intended beneficiary.

The court considers other elements besides the reasonable person approach when determining whether a party is an intended or incidental beneficiary. One thing the court considers is whether performance of the contract is done directly to the third party. In the Cassandra and Garrett example, performance of the contract, that is, the payment and the building of the school, is contained wholly within the contracting parties. Nothing is explicitly done for or given to a third party, and therefore the homeowners are incidental beneficiaries.

The court also examines the third party's ability to control the specifics of performance of the contract. That is, if a third party has the ability to provide input regarding how the contractual duties are fulfilled, the third party is probably an intended beneficiary. For example, Dianne (the promisee) agrees to pay Charles (the promisor) to paint Henry's (the third party's) house. Henry tells Charles what color he wants the house, as well as when Charles should be there to paint. Henry's ability to control how Charles paints the house demonstrates his status as an intended beneficiary. In addition, note that Charles renders performance directly to Henry, so the test discussed in the previous paragraph also indicates Henry's status as an intended beneficiary.

Case Nugget Intended or Incidental Beneficiary?

Wesley Locke v. Ozark City Board of Education
910 So. 2d 1247 (Ala. 2005)

Wesley Locke, a physical education teacher employed by the Dale County Department of Education, served as an umpire for high school baseball games. Locke was a member of the Southeast Alabama Umpires Association, which provides officials to athletic events sponsored by the Alabama High School Athletic Association (AHSAA).

One evening, Locke was serving as the head umpire in a baseball game between Carroll High School and George W. Long High School. Carroll High School, where the game was being held, did not provide police protection or other security personnel for the game. After the baseball game, the parent of one of the baseball players for Carroll High School attacked Locke, punching him three times in the face and causing him to sustain physical injuries to his neck and face that subjected him to pain, discomfort, scarring, and blurred vision. Locke sued the Ozark City Board of Education, alleging that the board breached its contract with the AHSAA by failing to provide police protection at the baseball game and that Locke was an intended third-party beneficiary under the contract.

While the trial court found that Locke was not an intended beneficiary and awarded summary judgment to the Board of Education, the court of appeals disagreed It found evidence that the parties anticipated the existence of third parties by contract language stating that the purpose of the words "adequate police protection" was to provide good game administration and supervision. The court reasoned that game administration and supervision necessarily involved umpires. The court found further evidence of the AHSAA's and the board's intent for the police protection to directly benefit the umpires, who were involved in game administration and supervision, in a letter from the AHSAA sanctioning one of the high schools for the incident involving the injured party.

The state supreme court reiterated that to recover under a third-party beneficiary theory, a complainant must show (1) that the contracting parties intended, at the time the contract was created, to bestow a direct benefit on a third party; (2) that the complainant was the intended beneficiary of the contract; and (3) that the contract was breached. Applying this standard to the facts, the court found that Locke had presented substantial evidence indicating that the board and the AHSAA intended to provide a direct benefit to umpires, that he was an intended direct beneficiary of the contract, and that the board breached the contract. It therefore overturned the summary judgment and remanded the case to the trial court for hearing on the issue of whether the board had provided adequate protection at the game.

A third factor the courts examine in determining the type of third-party beneficiary is whether the contract directly states that the third party is the benefiting party. In the previous example, because Charles agreed in the contract to paint Henry's house, the contract lists Henry as the beneficiary. Consequently, Henry is an intended beneficiary. Although Henry meets all three additional tests, besides the reasonable person test, it is not necessary to meet all three. If a third party meets at least one of the last three tests, he is usually an intended beneficiary.

INTENDED BENEFICIARIES	INCIDENTAL BENEFICIARIES
Contracting parties intended to benefit the third party with their contract.	Contracting parties did not intend to benefit the third party with their contract.
Beneficiary has the right to enforce the contract.	Beneficiary does not have the right to enforce the contract.
Beneficiary benefits from direct reception of contractual performance.	Beneficiary benefits from indirect circumstances created by contractual performance.

Exhibit 19-4
Intended versus Incidental Beneficiaries

CASE OPENER WRAP-UP

Fallout from a Forgettable Fight

The court hearing the Tyson case quickly dismissed the claims. The court held the fans were in no way third-party beneficiaries to any contract into which Tyson, the promoters, or the telecasters had entered. The fans cannot meet any of the tests for determining that a party is an intended beneficiary. Simply put, the fans are incidental beneficiaries.

Summary

Assignments and Delegations

Contracts typically involve an agreement between two parties:

Obligor: Contractual party who owes a duty to the other party in privity of the contract.

Obligee: Contractual party who is owed a duty from the other party in privity of the contract.

An *assignment* is the transfer of rights under a contract to a third party.

Assignor: The party to a contract who transfers his or her rights to a third party.

Assignee: A party not in privity to a contract who is the recipient of a transfer of rights to a contract.

Contractual rights that cannot be assigned:

1. Rights personal in nature.
2. Rights that would increase the obligor's risks or duties.
3. Rights in a contract that expressly forbids assignment.

A *delegation* is the transfer of a duty under a contract to a third party.

Delegator: The party to a contract who transfers his or her duty to a third party.

Delegatee: A party not in privity to a contract who is the recipient of a transfer of duty to a contract.

Contractual duties that cannot be assigned:

1. Duties personal in nature.
2. Duties resulting in performance substantially different from that which the obligee originally contracted.
3. Duties in a contract that expressly forbids delegation.

Assignment of the Contract

When ambiguous language is used, courts interpret the transfer to consist of an assignment of rights and a delegation of duties.

Third-Party Beneficiary Contracts

An *intended beneficiary* is a third party to a contract whom the contracting parties intended to benefit directly from their contract.

Promisor: A third-party beneficiary to a contract who made the promise that benefits the third party.

Promisee: A party to the contract who owes something to the promisor in exchange for the promise made to the third-party beneficiary.

Creditor beneficiary: A third party who benefits from a contract in which the promisor agrees to pay the promisee's debt.

Donee beneficiary: A third party who benefits from a contract in which a promisor agrees to give a gift to the third party.

Vest: The maturing of rights such that a party can legally act on the rights.

An *incidental beneficiary* is a third party who unintentionally gains a benefit from a contract between other parties. That is, it was never the conscious objective of the contracting parties to benefit the third party.

Point / Counterpoint

Should Incidental Beneficiaries Be Allowed to Sue to Enforce a Contract?	
Yes	**No**
Suppose a major buyer places a large order for widgets from a manufacturer that employs its workers *at will* (at-will employment is discussed in Chapter 10). Suppose further that the buyer breaches its contract with the manufacturer before the manufacturer makes the widgets for the order. Because of the late notice of the buyer's breach, the manufacturer is unable to find a replacement buyer. As a result, the manufacturer is forced to lay off many of its workers, many of whom are unable to find replacement work. These workers are *incidental beneficiaries* of the manufacturer's contract with the buyer, and under current law they cannot sue to enforce the contract.	The difficulties facing the at-will employees in the widget manufacturing example may be compelling, but contract law is not the ideal way to address the problem. Such an approach would be expensive and slow because incidental beneficiaries could recover a remedy only after a series of lawsuits with many expensive lawyers. Instead, we ought to use the social welfare system—tax redistribution and unemployment benefits—to aid vulnerable workers. Moreover, it is not clear that at-will workers are enormously susceptible to exploitation. A number of econometric studies have attempted to determine whether at-will employees receive higher wages than those of "secure" employees who provide equivalent labor. Although the

A number of legal scholars find this result unfair. The manufacturer's workers relied on the promises of the buyer when they made important financial decisions, such as how many hours to work and whether to look for additional employment opportunities. Moreover, at-will workers tend to have very little bargaining power. They also usually lack the resources to relocate in response to job openings in other cities, states, or countries or to obtain additional training to prepare them for other job markets. As a result, at-will employees often have difficulty finding replacement employment when buyers breach contracts with their employer. In such cases, the law fails to help the most vulnerable.

studies are not entirely conclusive, a significant amount of the evidence suggests that at-will workers receive a "bonus" to take the risks of at-will employment (economists call these bonuses *compensating differentials*).

Permitting incidental beneficiaries to sue to enforce a contract would also establish perverse incentives for the incidental beneficiaries. At-will employees laid off when a third party breaches a contract with their employer would know that they can recover damages if they do not find replacement work. If they find replacement work, though, they can recover only the difference between what they would have earned if the breach had not occurred and what they actually earned in their replacement work. This incentive would encourage the laid-off workers to avoid finding replacement work. (Economists call perverse incentive structures like this one a *moral hazard.*)

Questions & Problems

1. Integrate the concept of assignments with the concept of delegations.
2. Why is it that incidental beneficiaries cannot enforce rights under a contract? Should they be able to enforce such rights?
3. Explain the conditions under which an intended beneficiary's rights vest. What might an intended beneficiary do to ensure her rights vest?
4. Explain the difference between an assignor's liability and a delegator's liability after rights have been transferred to a third party.
5. Why are courts stricter with interpretations of antidelegation clauses in contracts than with antiassignment clauses?
6. Explain the desirability to business of allowing a transfer of rights or duties to third parties.
7. California farmers and farming entities purchase water from Westlands Water District, which receives its water from the U.S. Bureau of Reclamation under a 1963 contract between Westlands and the bureau. In 1993, Westlands and other water districts sued the bureau for reducing their water supply. The farmers, though not parties to the 1963 contract, intervened as plaintiffs. After negotiations, all parties except the farmers stipulated to dismissal of the districts' complaint. The farmers pressed forward with, as relevant here, the claim that the United States had breached the contract. They contended they were third-party beneficiaries entitled to enforce the contract. The district court ultimately held that the farmers were neither contracting parties nor intended third-party beneficiaries of the contract. The Ninth Circuit affirmed. If you were on the Supreme Court, how would you rule on appeal? Justify your legal decision. [*Orff v. United States,* 125 S. Ct. 2606 (2005).]

8. As part of his employment with Hoaster, Hess executed an employment agreement in which he consented not to disclose proprietary information and covenanted not to compete with Hoaster within a 25 mile radius of the city of Lebanon for a period of five years after the termination of his employment. The restrictive covenants in the agent's agreement contained no language regarding assignability. Hoaster entered into a sales agreement with Gebhard & Co. to sell all the assets associated with the insurance portion of its business. The contract included the sale of all of Hoaster's then-existing contracts and agreements, including Hess's employment agreement containing the covenant not to compete. Hess did not consent to the assignment of the covenant to Gebhard, and no one ever discussed the covenant with him or asked him to agree to its assignment. Hess worked for Hoaster until Gebhard assumed control, when Hess's position was eliminated. Unbeknownst to Hoaster and Gebhard, before leaving, Hess began employment negotiations with Bowman's Insurance Agency, a competing firm. Less than one week after leaving Hoaster, Hess used information he had acquired while in Hoaster's employ and solicited one of Hoaster's major clients as a new client for Bowman's. Gebhard and Hoaster learned of this and sent Hess a letter, with a copy to Bowman's, reminding Hess of the covenant not to compete and threatening legal action if Hess refused to comply. As a result of the letter, Bowman's decided against hiring Hess. Shortly thereafter, Hess filed suit against Gebhard, who joined Hoaster as a party defendant. The court ruled in favor of the defendants. Hess appealed and the court affirmed. Hess appealed again. How did the court rule on appeal? Why? [*Hess v. Gebhard & Co.,* 570 Pa. 148 (2002).]
9. The farmers are former customers of Ron Kaufman, the owner and operator of Southeast Implements, Inc., a Case International Harvester equipment dealership. Between 1996 and 1998, they agreed to purchase or lease various items of farm equipment from Southeast. In each instance, the farmers and Kaufman orally negotiated the terms of the purchases/leases, and Kaufman then prepared written purchase agreements for each transaction, assigning his rights thereunder to Case. Case, in turn, after approving the assignments and agreeing to finance the purchases/leases, paid Kaufman for the equipment and looked to the farmers, as debtors, for payment. The written purchase agreements, however, were prepared and assigned without the farmers' knowledge and did not reflect the terms of the oral contracts. Kaufman inflated the purchase/lease prices and forged the farmers' signatures, thereby obtaining thousands of dollars in overpayments from Case. When Case became aware of Kaufman's fraud, it sent representatives to meet with the individual farmers. After verifying that the farmers were in possession of equipment covered by the forged purchase agreements, Case attempted to enforce the terms of the forged contracts. The farmers allege that Case's assignment was improper because the rights assigned were not the ones to which the farmers agreed. The farmers filed suit against Case and Southeast. The court found in favor of Case, and the farmers appealed. Is Kaufman's assignment made to Case binding? What defenses might the farmers have against Case? [*Day v. Case Credit Corp.,* 427 F.3d 1148 (2005).]
10. Action Steel entered into a contract with Systems Builders for the construction of an addition to a commercial building. Systems Builders was the general contractor and agreed to erect a building designed and manufactured by Varco-Pruden. Part of System Builders' contract with Action Steel included an agreement for the parties not to sue each other or any subcontractors or agents if another insurance plan was taken out on neighboring properties or the finished project. During the first winter after construction of the addition was complete, only a few months later, a portion of the

building collapsed. Midwestern insured Action Steel under a policy issued after completion of the construction. Subsequently, Midwestern sued Varco-Pruden to recover what Midwestern paid to Action Steel. Varco-Pruden moved for summary judgment and won. Midwestern appealed. Was Midwestern a third party to the contract such that it could sue Varco-Pruden? Does the agreement not to sue apply to Midwestern? [*Midwestern Indem. Co. v. Sys. Builders, Inc.,* 801 N.E.2d 661 (2004).]

11. Stine loaned her daughter and son-in-law Stewart $100,000 to purchase a home. In return, the Stewarts jointly executed a promissory note for $100,000, payable on demand to Stine. The Stewarts did not give a security interest or mortgage to secure the note. The Stewarts eventually paid $50,000 on the note, leaving $50,000, together with unpaid accrued interest, due. The Stewarts divorced and executed an Agreement Incident to Divorce, which disposed of marital property, including the home. The agreement provided that Stewart could lease the house, but if Stewart sold it, he agreed that "any monies owing to [Stine] are to be paid in the current principal sum of $50,000.00." The parties further agreed that if the proceeds from the sale of the house were not enough to cover the money owed to Stine, the Stewarts would split the difference equally. Stine did not sign the agreement. Stewart sold the property. Stewart did not pay the proceeds to Stine and did not make any further payments on the $50,000 principal. Consequently, Stine sued Stewart for breaching the agreement, claiming the agreement acknowledged the existing debt Stewart owed her under the note. The trial court found Stine to be an intended third-party beneficiary of the agreement and ordered Stewart to pay Stine. The appellate court held that the agreement does not clearly and unequivocally acknowledge the debt owed to Stine and, therefore, does not "express Stewart's willingness to pay any debt." Therefore, the court of appeals reversed the decision. Stine appealed. Was Stine an intended third-party beneficiary to the contract? Why? [*Stine v. Stewart,* 80 S.W.3d 586 (2002).]

12. CEI and NU were planning a multibillion-dollar merger. Among the terms and conditions of the underlying merger agreement, CEI agreed to purchase all of NU's outstanding shares for $3.6 billion to $1.2 billion over the prevailing market price. Shortly before the scheduled closing, CEI declared NU had suffered a material adverse change that "dramatically lowered" NU's valuation, and CEI declined to proceed with the merger unless NU would agree to a lower share price. NU rejected the share price reduction, treated CEI's demand as an anticipatory repudiation and breach of the agreement, and declared the merger was "effectively terminated." Both parties brought suit. The district court ruled NU could sue on behalf of its shareholders for the $1.2 billion. The court reasoned the merger agreement expressly designated NU's shareholders as intended third-party beneficiaries. Due to subsequent legal actions, both parties appealed. The appellate court then decided the issue of whether any of NU shareholders were intended third-party beneficiaries. If you were on the court, how would you have ruled? Why? [*Consol. Edison, Inc. v. Northeast Utils.,* 426 F.3d 524 (2005).]

13. Sevenarts and Chalk & Vermilion Fine Arts, Ltd., entered into an agreement under which Sevenarts licensed Chalk & Vermilion to cast and sell limited-edition sculptures from models created by an artist known as Erte. The license agreement contains a binding arbitration clause. Sevenarts and Chalk & Vermilion subsequently modified the agreement to reflect an agreement to create five more casts and distribute them to Ronald Borsack. Borsack did not sign either the license agreement or the addendum. Borsack claims he convinced Sevenarts to grant the exclusive licensing rights for the Erte sculptures to Chalk & Vermilion. Borsack asserts the addendum was evidence of

Chalk & Vermilion's oral agreement to pay him a "finder's fee" of five artist's proofs each time a new Erte sculpture was produced. Chalk & Vermilion denied having entered into any such agreement. Borsack contended that after approximately six and a half years of receiving his "finder's fee," the defendants ceased to deliver the five proofs each time a new sculpture was produced. Borsack brought suit asserting, among other things, that he had a right as a third-party beneficiary to his five sculptures. The defendants asserted that Borsack must submit his claim to arbitration according to the arbitration agreement in the licensing agreement. Is Borsack a third-party beneficiary, and if so, is he bound by the arbitration agreement? Why? [*Borsack v. Chalk & Vermilion Fine Arts,* 974 F.Supp. 293 (1997).]

14. The Vogans contracted with Markley to build a home for $169,633.59. The Vogans contacted MidAmerica for a mortgage. MidAmerica orally contracted with Hayes Appraisal to do the initial appraisal and make periodic appraisals of the progress of the construction. MidAmerica was to disburse progress payments to Markley on the basis of progress reports received from Hayes Appraisal. On March 20, Hayes Appraisal certified that the home was 60 percent complete. Only eight days later, Hayes Appraisal issued another progress report, indicating 90 percent of the work had been completed on the home. This was an inaccurate report, overstating the extent of the contractor's progress on the job. As late as October, substantial additional work was required on the house. At this point, Markley defaulted on the job after having been paid all the initial $170,000 and much of the additional monies raised by the Vogans. The Vogans filed a petition against Hayes Appraisal, contending it negligently certified the extent of the completed construction. The court denied Hayes Appraisal's motions for directed verdict in which it argued that the Vogans were not third-party beneficiaries of its contract with MidAmerica and that the March progress reports did not proximately cause the damages alleged. The jury returned a verdict for the Vogans. Hayes Appraisal appealed. It contended that the evidence was insufficient to prove the Vogans were third-party beneficiaries or to prove its conduct proximately caused any damage to the Vogans. The court of appeals reversed. The Vogans appealed. How did the court rule on appeal? Why? [*Vogan v. Hayes Appraisal Assoc.,* 588 N.W.2d 420 (1999).]

15. Thomas and Cohen entered into an agreement with Eugene Micci, setting forth the terms of the dissolution of their partnership with Eugene Micci concerning the law firm of Micci, Cohen and Thomas. Under the termination agreement, Cohen and Thomas would pay Eugene Micci $72,785 in installments as the firm settled any negligence and property damage suits. After Eugene Micci failed to pay his ex-wife, Dianne Micci, alimony and child support, Thomas and Cohen subsequently began sending the payments owed to Eugene Micci to Dianne Micci. Dianne Micci, however, stopped receiving payments from Thomas and Cohen in 1997. She then sued Thomas and Cohen. The court held that Dianne Micci was a third-party beneficiary to the termination agreement and therefore was entitled to payment by Thomas and Cohen. The trial court concluded the intent of the promisee, Eugene Micci, was crucial and the intent of the promisors, Thomas and Cohen, was irrelevant in deciding third-party beneficiary status. Thomas and Cohen appealed. If you heard the case, how would you decide? What factors were crucial in forming your decision? [*Micci v. Thomas,* 55 Conn.App. 14 (1999).]

16. Debbie Esquivel rented a hotel room at the Baytown La Quinta. She asked the clerk where she could park a rented U-Haul moving van containing personal property and towing her car. A clerk told her to park on the street adjacent to the hotel and assured

her the van would be safe "because of the security it [the hotel] provided." The next day, Esquivel's van and car were missing. Esquivel learned that Murray Guard provided security to the La Quinta in question. She sued Murray Guard, claiming she was an intended third-party beneficiary. The court granted Murray Guard's motion for summary judgment. Esquivel appealed. Does the contract between La Quinta and Murray Guard create intended third-party beneficiaries? Why? [*Esquivel v. Murray Guard, Inc.*, 992 S.W.2d 536 (1999).]

Looking for more review material?

The Online Learning Center at **www.mhhe.com/kubasek1e** contains this chapter's "Assignment on the Internet" and also a list of URLs for more information entitled "On the Internet." Find both of them in the Student Center portion of the OLC, along with quizzes and other helpful materials.

Discharge and Remedies

CASE OPENER

The Battle of the Pharmacies

Walgreen operated a pharmacy in a mall in Milwaukee, Wisconsin, owned by Sara Creek. Under Walgreen's lease, Sara Creek promised not to rent space in the mall to anyone else who wanted to operate a pharmacy. Several years into the lease, Sara Creek informed Walgreen that it intended to buy out the anchor tenant in the mall and install a Phar-Mor discount store in its place. This store would include a pharmacy the same size as Walgreen's and would be within 200 feet of Walgreen's store. The Phar-Mor pharmacy would sell pharmaceuticals at a deeper discount than that of Walgreen. Walgreen was granted an injunction against the new lease by the Seventh Circuit court. Sara Creek Property Co. appealed, claiming that monetary damages would be a more appropriate remedy and then the Phar-Mor pharmacy could be allowed to move in.[1]

1. Do you think monetary damages alone would be an adequate remedy for Walgreen?
2. What kind of remedy should the court grant Walgreen?

The Wrap-Up at the end of the chapter will answer these questions.

Learning Objectives

After reading this chapter, you will be able to answer the following questions:

1. What are the primary methods for discharging a contract?
2. What are the primary legal remedies available for a breach of contract?
3. What are the primary equitable remedies available for a breach of contract?

[1] *Walgreen Co. v. Sara Creek Property Co.*, U.S. Court of Appeals for the Seventh Circuit, 966 F.2d 273 (1992).

CHAPTER 20

PART TWO

Contracts

Methods of Discharging a Contract

The previous seven chapters focus primarily on how parties enter into a legally binding agreement. Once a party has entered into a binding agreement, how does the party terminate his or her obligation under the contract? That question is the focus of this chapter. When a party's obligations under a contract are terminated, the party is said to be discharged. There are a number of ways by which a party's contractual obligations can be terminated and the party thereby discharged. The first, and the one most parties hope to secure from the other when they enter into an agreement, is performance. The others are the happening of a condition or its failure to occur, material breach by one or both parties, agreement of the parties, and operation of law. This chapter explains each of these methods.

CONDITIONS

Under ordinary circumstances, a party's duty to perform the promise agreed to in a contract is absolute. Sometimes, however, a party's duty to perform may be affected by whether a certain condition occurs. Contracts containing conditions affecting the performance obligations of the parties are called *conditional contracts.* The conditions may be either implied by law or expressly inserted into the contract by the parties.

Discharge by conditions precedent, subsequent, and concurrent. There are three types of conditions: condition precedent, condition subsequent and concurrent conditions. A **condition precedent** is a particular event that must occur in order for a party's duty to arise. If the event does not occur, the party's duty to perform does not arise. Frequently, real estate contracts are conditioned on an event such as the buyer's being able to sell his current home by a certain date. If the home does not sell, the condition does not arise. Thus, the parties have no duty to perform and are discharged from the contract.

Another common example of a contract containing a condition precedent is an insurance contract. If Bill purchases a life insurance contract, he is obligated to pay the monthly premiums specified in the contract, but the insurance company's obligation to perform arises only when he dies. His death is the condition that triggers the company's duty to pay his beneficiary.

A **condition subsequent** is a future event that terminates the obligations of the parties when it occurs. For example, John may enter into an agreement to lease an apartment for five years, conditioned on his not being called to active duty in the National Guard. If he is called to serve, his obligation to be bound by the lease is discharged.

Concurrent conditions occur when each party's performance is conditioned on the performance of the other. They occur only when the parties are required to perform for each other simultaneously. For example, when a buyer is supposed to pay for goods on delivery, the buyer's duty to pay is impliedly conditioned on the seller's duty to deliver the goods, and the seller's duty to deliver the goods is impliedly conditioned on the buyer's duty to pay for the goods. The legal effect of a contract's being concurrently conditioned is that each party must offer to perform before being able to sue the other for nonperformance.

Express and implied conditions. Conditions in contracts are also described as being express or implied. **Express conditions** are explicitly stated in the contract and are usually preceded by words such as *conditioned on, if, provided that,* or *when.* For example, in a situation involving a potential sale of a house, the offer expressly required that the buyer make a deposit of $1,000 "on acceptance." The buyer wrote "accepted" on the offer and returned it but did not include the deposit. No deposit of money was ever made. The seller then canceled the transaction. Several weeks later, the buyer attempted to tender payment to the seller. The court found that under the terms of the contract, payment of the $1,000 was an express condition of acceptance and since the acceptance was incomplete, there was no contract.[2]

Implied conditions are those that are not explicitly stated but are inferred from the nature and language of the contract. For example, if one enters into a contract with a builder to replace the windows in one's house, there is an implied condition that the builder will be given access to the home so that she may fulfill her obligations under the contract.

DISCHARGE BY PERFORMANCE

In most situations, parties discharge their obligations by doing what they respectively agreed to do under the terms of the contract; this is called *discharge by performance.* Parties also discharge their duty by making an offer to perform and being ready, willing, and able to perform. This offer of performance is known as a **tender.** If a painter shows up at Sam's house with his paint and ladders and is ready to start painting the garage, he has tendered performance. If Sam refuses to let him start, the painter has now discharged his duties under the contract by his tender of performance and he may sue Sam for material breach (discussed later in this chapter).

Types of performance. There are two primary kinds of performance: complete performance and substantial performance. Performance may also be conditioned on the satisfaction of a party to the contract or of a third party.

Complete performance occurs when all aspects of the parties' duties under the contract are carried out perfectly. In many instances, complete performance is difficult, if not impossible, to attain, and courts today generally require only substantial performance.

Substantial performance occurs when the following conditions have been met: (1) completion of nearly all the terms of the agreement, (2) an honest effort to complete all the terms, and (3) no willful departure from the terms of the agreement. Substantial performance discharges the party's responsibilities under the contract, although the court may require that the party compensate the other party for any loss in value caused by the failure to meet all the standards set forth in the contract. For example, if a contract called for all bedrooms of a house to be painted blue but one was inadvertently painted green, the court may require that the contractor compensate the buyer by the amount that it will cost the buyer to have that room repainted. The difficulty of determining whether there has in fact been substantial performance is illustrated in the Case Nugget.

Performance subject to satisfaction of a contracting party. Sometimes the performance of the contract is subject to the satisfaction of one of the contracting parties. In such a case, a party is not discharged from the contract until the other party is satisfied. Satisfaction is considered an express condition that must be met before the other party's obligation to pay for the performance arises.

Satisfaction may be judged according to either a subjective or an objective standard. When the judgment involved is a matter of personal taste, such as when a person is having a dress custom made for her, the courts apply a subjective satisfaction standard. As long as the person, in good faith, is not satisfied, the other party is deemed to have not met the condition.

If the performance is one related to a mechanical or utility standard, the objective satisfaction standard applies. Also, if the contract does not clearly specify that the satisfaction

[2] *Smith v. Holmwood,* 231 Cal. App. 2d 549 (1965).

is to be personal, the objective standard applies. When an objective standard is used, the courts ask whether a reasonable person would be satisfied with the performance.

Sometimes the contract is conditioned on the satisfaction of a third party. Usually, such provisions arise in construction contracts specifying that before a buyer accepts a building, an architect must provide a certificate that the building was constructed according to the plans and specifications.

Case Nugget A Question of Substantial Performance

Ujdur v. Thompson
Court of Appeals of Idaho
126 Idaho 6, 878 P.2d 180 (1994)

On August 1, 1989, Richard Ujdur and Wesley Thompson entered into a sales contract to jointly purchase approximately 110 acres of land in Lemhi County, Idaho, from a bank. They agreed to purchase the land in equal, undivided shares, with Ujdur advancing the down payment to the bank. A dispute arose between Ujdur and Thompson over Thompson's failure to make equal payments on the contract. In October 1990, Ujdur filed an action for breach of contract, alleging that Thompson had failed to pay any portion of the annual contract payments to the bank.

On the eve of trial, scheduled for April 9, 1992, the parties reached a settlement. Their written settlement agreement, filed with the district court, stated, among other things, that:

1. Thompson must pay Ujdur $37,681.20 plus interest by April 9, 1992, with $9.29 accruing per day beginning April 10, 1992.
2. If Thompson does not pay said amount by or on the cutoff date, he would deliver to Ujdur his quitclaim deed to the property.
3. If Thompson delivered the payments on July 8, 1992, on July 9 Ujdur would sign a motion to dismiss the lawsuit with prejudice.

On July 8, 1992, Thompson delivered a letter to Udjur's attorney stating that he held "sufficient funds to pay out Mr. Ujdur pursuant to the settlement negotiation agreement" in the amount of $38,517.30, which, as he calculated, included the accumulated interest due. However, this sum was calculated in error and was $5,719.79 short of the amount actually required by the agreement. Ujdur did not accept the tender.

The next day, July 9, Thompson delivered the amount and asked for a quitclaim deed from Ujdur. Ujdur again refused to accept the payment, this time on the ground of untimeliness. Ujdur demanded that Thompson deliver a quitclaim deed for the property. When Thompson refused to deliver the deed, the parties brought the matter before the district court.

At the hearing before the district court, Thompson argued that his actions taken on July 8 and July 9 constituted substantial performance and that Ujdur was thus obligated to accept the July 9 payment and deliver a quitclaim deed. The district court was not persuaded by Thompson's argument because the parties had bargained for a strict construction of the timeliness requirement. The court further found that Ujdur had not accepted Thompson's deficient payment tendered on July 8 and that Thompson's late payment, although made in good faith, did not constitute substantial performance.

DISCHARGE BY MATERIAL BREACH

A *breach* occurs whenever a party fails to perform her obligations under the contract. If the breach is a minor one, it may entitle the nonbreaching party to damages but it does not discharge the nonbreaching party from the contract.

A **material breach,** however, discharges the nonbreaching party from his obligations under the contract. A material breach occurs when a party unjustifiably fails to substantially perform his obligations under the contract. It is often difficult to know when the court is going to determine that a breach is material. Case 20-1 demonstrates the analysis a court may use to determine whether a defendant's behavior constitutes material breach.

CASE 20-1 MILLER v. MILLS CONSTRUCTION, INC.
EIGHTH CIRCUIT COURT OF APPEALS
352 F.3D 1166 (8TH CIR. 2003)

Mills Construction, Inc., contracted with the City of Brookings, South Dakota, to construct a series of buildings. As one of the buildings required the erection of a steel clear span, Mills subcontracted the erection of this particular building to Wilma Miller, who conducted business under the name Double Diamond Construction. Under this contract, Double Diamond agreed to supply the labor and equipment, while Mills agreed to obtain prefabricated steel from American Buildings Company (ABC) for the construction.

When Double Diamond began construction of the building on April 15, 1998, the company recognized numerous problems with the materials supplied by ABC to Mills, and notified Mills of the problems. Mills recommended that Double Diamond contact ABC directly, but when Double Diamond notified ABC, ABC did not resolve the problems with the materials. Therefore, Double Diamond discontinued construction on May 12, 1998, claiming that construction could not continue until ABC or Mills fixed the problems with the materials. Wilma Miller specified her concerns in a letter to ABC, Mills, and the City of Brookings, dated May 14, 1998, in which she also questioned the structural integrity of the building.

On May 15, 1998, an ABC representative visited the site, and videotaped the building and documented the alleged structural problems. However, the representative concluded that no problems existed with the structure, unless the building was hit by a tornado. Nevertheless, the building collapsed later that evening with winds estimated at 35 miles-per-hour.

Following the collapse, Double Diamond requested payment from Mills for the work completed prior to the collapse. When Mills did not pay the full amount for the work, Double Diamond filed suit for damages. Mills counterclaimed for breach of contract and negligence. The trial court found in favor of Double Diamond, concluding that Mills failed to provide appropriate materials for the construction. Mills appealed, claiming that the trial court did not specify that there had been a material breach.

JUDGE LAY: On appeal, Mills argues that the district court erred because it did not find that Mills' failure to provide appropriate materials was a material breach of the contract. Mills suggests that without a finding of material breach, Double Diamond was not entitled to recover any damages.

A material breach of contract allows the aggrieved party to cancel the contract and recover damages for the breach. However, if the breach is not material, the aggrieved party may not cancel the contract but may recover damages for the nonmaterial breach. Under South Dakota law, a material breach is one that "would defeat the very object of the contract." Whether a party's conduct amounts to a material breach is a question of fact.

The district court found that Mills breached the contract by failing to provide appropriate materials, but it did not use the term "material" to describe Mills' breach. The object of the contract in this case was the construction of the arena by a specified date. Mills' failure to provide suitable building materials prevented proper construction of the building and made the structure vulnerable to collapse. As the district court noted, the record is replete with evidence of problems with the materials supplied by Mills prior to the collapse. These problems eventually required Double Diamond to stop working on the building because nothing more could be done until the problems were corrected. The sheer number of problems with the materials led the district court to find that it was impossible for Double Diamond to perform under the contract. The record also contains evidence that Double Diamond notified Mills and ABC of the problems on several occasions, thereby providing Mills with an opportunity to cure the deficiencies.

On these facts, we conclude that a finding of material breach is implicit in the district court's finding that Mills breached the contract by failing to provide appropriate materials.

Mills further argues on appeal that the district court erred by failing to find that Double Diamond was excused from performance of the contract. Mills asserts that absent a finding that Double Diamond was excused from performance, Double Diamond breached the contract by refusing to return to the project and is not entitled to recover. Material breach provides one basis for excusing Double Diamond's performance under the contract. Another basis for excusing Double Diamond's performance is the district court's recognition that Mills made Double Diamond's performance under the contract impossible.

As our prior discussion illustrates, the parties tried this case as a breach of contract case. The district court found Mills breached the contract, and we have concluded that implicit in its decision is a finding of material breach. Under South Dakota law, the plaintiff in an action for breach of contract "is entitled to recover all his detriment proximately caused by the breach, not exceeding the amount he would have gained by full performance." It is well-settled in this circuit that "the amount of damages in a nonjury case is within the discretion of the trial court and cannot be overturned unless clearly erroneous."

AFFIRMED in favor of plaintiff, Wilma Miller.

CRITICAL THINKING

How should this appeal finding be interpreted in terms of future implications? Is there anything undesirable or potentially dangerous about granting such wide discretion to appeals courts?

ETHICAL DECISION MAKING

Who are the stakeholders affected by this decision? What are the likely consequences for these parties? How would these consequences be ethically justified?

What stakeholders were affected by the actions of Mills examined in this case? Does the ruling protect values such as justice and fairness for the relevant parties? Why or why not?

In the Walgreen's case in the opening scenario, there was no question of whether the defendant had materially breached the contract. A key term of the 30-year lease between Walgreen's and the defendant was the exclusivity clause. Walgreen's would never have entered into the lease if it could not have been the only drugstore in the shopping center. To allow not just another discount drugstore in the shopping center but a deeper-discount drugstore that would open up right next door to Walgreen's was clearly a material breach of the agreement.

Anticipatory repudiation. Sometimes a contracting party may decide not to complete the contract before the actual time of performance. This situation often arises when market conditions change and one party realizes that it will not be profitable to carry out the terms of the contract. The breaching party may convey the anticipatory breach to the nonbreaching party either by making an express indication of her intent to no longer perform or by taking an action that would be inconsistent with her ability to carry out the contract when performance was due.

Once the contract has been anticipatorily repudiated, the nonbreaching party is discharged from his obligations under the contract. He is free to go ahead and sue for breach, as well as find another similar contract elsewhere. However, if the nonbreaching party wishes, he may decide to give the party who repudiated the opportunity to change her mind and still perform.

DISCHARGE BY MUTUAL AGREEMENT

Sometimes the parties to a contract agree to discharge each other from their obligations. They may do so through four primary means: discharge by mutual rescission, discharge by a substituted contract, discharge by accord and satisfaction, or discharge by novation.

Mutual recission. Parties may agree that they simply wish to discharge each other from their mutual obligations and therefore rescind or cancel the contract. For example, if James had agreed to cater a graduation reception for Bill's son but it appeared that the child was not going to graduate when planned, James could agree to no longer hold Bill responsible for paying him the agreed-on cost for the catering in exchange for Bill's agreement to no longer expect James to cater a reception.

Substituted contract. Sometimes, instead of canceling the contract and terminating their relationship, the parties wish to substitute a new agreement in place of the original. The substituted contract immediately discharges the parties from their obligations under the old contract and replaces those obligations with the new obligations imposed by the substituted contract.

Accord and satisfaction. An accord and satisfaction is used when one of the parties wishes to substitute a different performance for his original duty under the contract. The promise to perform the new duty is called the *accord,* and the actual performance of that new duty is called the *satisfaction.* The party's duty under the contract is not discharged until the new duty is actually performed. Thus it is the satisfaction that discharges the party.

Novation. Sometimes the parties to the agreement wish to replace one of the parties with a third party. This substitution of a party is called a **novation.** The original duties remain the same under the contract, but one party is discharged and the third party now takes that original party's place. All three parties must agree to the novation in order for it to be valid.

DISCHARGE BY OPERATION OF LAW

Sometimes a contract may be discharged not by anything the parties do but, rather, by operation of law. Alteration of the contract, bankruptcy, tolling of the statute of limitations, impossibility, commercial impracticability, and frustration of purpose are all situations in which a contract may be discharged by operation of law.

Alteration of the contract. The courts wish to uphold the sanctity of contracts. Therefore, if one of the parties materially alters a written contract without the knowledge of the other party, the courts have held that such alteration allows the innocent party to be discharged from the contract. For example, if a seller, without knowledge of the buyer, changes the price of the contract, the buyer can treat the contract as terminated.

connecting to the core

Management

As you may have learned in a management class, consensus is generally the goal when groups engage in some method of problem solving. Techniques for group problem solving include the use of interacting groups, nominal groups, and Delphi groups. *Interacting groups,* which are most commonly used, are groups in which the members deliberate, perhaps with much arguing and disagreement initially, until a consensus is reached. *Nominal groups* are those that involve no discussion at first, as group members are usually asked to write down as many ideas as possible and thereafter the ideas are written on a board and voted on by group members. *Delphi groups* involve the use of a diverse group of experts, who anonymously complete questionnaires to produce ideas, and their combined judgments are evaluated to hopefully find a consensus of expert opinion.

While these methods may be useful in certain business environments, the goal of consensus is nevertheless just as critical in the context of contracts, particularly after a contract has been formed. For instance, if a party realizes he cannot perform the contract and cannot claim that performance is impossible or impracticable, his only alternative to being sued by the other party is consensus, or mutual agreement, with the other party. If the nonperforming party is fortunate, the other party may agree to rescind the contract or create a substitute contract. The nonperforming party may choose to use the interacting-group problem-solving technique to hopefully reach a consensus.

Source: Angelo Kinicki and Brian K. Williams, *Management: A Practical Introduction* (New York: McGraw-Hill/Irwin, 2006), pp. 221–223.

Bankruptcy. When a party files bankruptcy, the court allocates the assets of the bankrupt among the bankrupt's creditors and then issues the party a discharge in bankruptcy. Once the assets have been distributed, all of the bankrupt's debts are discharged. (Bankruptcy is discussed in detail in Chapter 32).

Tolling of the statute of limitations. The tolling of the statute of limitations does not technically discharge a party's obligations under the contract. However, once the statute of limitations has tolled, neither party can any longer sue the other for breach, so for all practical purposes the parties are no longer bound to perform.

Impossibility of performance. Sometimes an unforeseen event occurs that makes it physically or legally impossible for a party to carry out the terms of the contract. In such a situation, the party will be discharged on grounds of impossibility of performance. Courts distinguish between *objective impossibility,* meaning it is in fact not possible to lawfully carry out one's contractual obligations, and *subjective impossibility,* meaning it would be very difficult to carry out the contract. Objective impossibility, but not subjective impossibility, discharges the parties' obligations under the contract.

For example, if farmer Gray has a contract with the Hunts Corporation to provide it with 100 bushels of tomatoes on August 30 and a flood wipes out Gray's crop, it is not physically impossible for him to comply with the agreement. He has to go out on the market and purchase 100 bushels of tomatoes to ship to the Hunts Corporation. It may be inconvenient, and perhaps subjectively impossible, but it is not objectively impossible.

In contrast, suppose farmer Jones owns a historic farmhouse built in 1827 and he agrees to sell it to Smith, but the night before the parties are to exchange money for the title, lightning strikes the farmhouse and the building burns to the ground. It is now objectively impossible to comply with the terms of the contract, so the parties are discharged from their obligations. The historic farmhouse is not like tomatoes; the subject matter of the contract is forever destroyed and cannot be re-created.

There are three main situations in which the courts find objective impossibility. The first is *destruction of the subject matter,* as in the example of the historic farmhouse destroyed by fire. If we go back to the example of the tomatoes, note that we said the farmer still had to perform because it was still possible for him to obtain tomatoes elsewhere. To protect himself in the event that his crop was destroyed, farmer Gray could have drafted the contract to identify the subject matter as 100 bushels of tomatoes grown on the Gray family farm. In that case, if Gray's fields were flooded, it would be objectively impossible to comply with the contract because there would be no tomatoes from the Gray farm in existence.

The second situation of objective impossibility is the *death or incapacity of a party whose personal services are necessary* to fulfill the terms of the contract. For example, if a famous artist is commissioned to paint a portrait and the artist dies, the contract is discharged. The artist's style is unique, and there is no way for anyone to take over the artist's role.

The third situation is *subsequent illegality.* If the law changes after the contract is made, rendering the performance of the contract illegal, then the contract is discharged. For example, Bill orders a case of a nutritional supplement from Osco Drugs and Supplements. Before his order can be filled, the nutritional supplement is banned because of recently discovered harmful side effects. The parties are now discharged from their duties because to sell the banned substance would be to violate the law.

Commercial impracticability. Commercial impracticability can be seen as a response to what some might interpret as a somewhat unfair harshness of the objective impossibility standard. Commercial impracticability is used when performance is still objectively possible but would be extraordinarily injurious or expensive to one party. Commercial impracticability arises when, because of an unforeseeable event, one party would incur unreasonable expense, injury, or loss if that party were forced to carry out the terms of the agreement.

According to the Restatement (Second) of Contracts, Section 261 (1981), discharge by reason of impracticability requires that the party claiming discharge prove the following three elements:

1. That an event occurred whose nonoccurrence was a basic assumption of the contract.
2. That there is commercial impracticability of continued performance.
3. That the party claiming discharge did not expressly or impliedly agree to performance in spite of impracticability that would otherwise justify his nonperformance.

It is sometimes difficult to know whether the potential harm to the party seeking to avoid the contract is sufficient to give rise to the use of commercial impracticability. The doctrine is most commonly used in situations in which raw materials needed for manufacturing goods under the contract become extraordinarily expensive or difficult to obtain because of an embargo, war, crop failure, or unexpected closure of a plant. Case 20-2 illustrates how the courts sometimes struggle to determine whether to apply the doctrine of commercial impracticability to discharge a contract.

Frustration of purpose. Closely related to impracticability is frustration of purpose. Sometimes, when a contract is entered into, both parties recognize that the contract is

CASE 20-2 THRIFTY RENT-A-CAR SYSTEM v. SOUTH FLORIDA TRANSPORT

UNITED STATES DISTRICT COURT FOR THE NORTHERN DISTRICT OF OKLAHOMA
2005 U.S. DIST. LEXIS 38489

The plaintiffs, Thrifty Rent-A-Car System and its affiliates DTG and Rental Car Finance Corp., allowed South Florida Transport (SFT), the defendant, to establish a Thrifty franchise. In 2003, Thrifty and SFT entered into four agreements, which provided SFT the right to use Thrifty's trademark and business methods in exchange for payment to Thrifty of licensing and administrative fees. The agreements also provided that SFT would maintain a fleet of automobiles for rental.

In July 2004, SFT provided DTG with a check as payment, but the check was returned for insufficient funds. SFT continued to make delinquent payments, and by August, SFT owed Thrifty and DTG $1,134,819.40. Due to SFT's failure to make payments, Thrifty and DTG informed SFT that they were going to terminate the licensing agreements and repossess the vehicles, to which DTG had legal title. However, DTG agreed to postpone repossession due to predictions of severe weather, and allowed SFT to continue renting vehicles until repossession was completed.

When DTG repossessed the vehicles, DTG noticed that numerous cars were missing. In response, SFT notified DTG that it had sold 51 vehicles without authorization. By August 2005, SFT owed Thrifty and DTG $4,238,249.53. SFT claimed that several hurricanes rendered their business operations commercially impracticable. The plaintiffs filed a motion for summary judgment, seeking full reimbursement for the debts owed by SFT.

JUDGE EAGAN: Performance may become impracticable due to extreme and unreasonable difficulty, expense, injury, or loss to one of the parties involved. Impracticability does not equate to impracticality, however. "A mere change in the degree of difficulty or expense . . . unless well beyond the normal range does not amount to impracticability since it is this sort of risk that a fixed-price contract is intended to cover." The law also imposes an objective standard on the duty to perform for those seeking to invoke the defense of impracticability. A party to a contract is not discharged from his duty to perform merely by demonstrating that a supervening event prevented him from performing; he must also demonstrate that similarly situated parties were also deprived of the ability to perform.

The undisputed facts relevant to Greenstein's claim of impracticability are as follows: In August and September 2004, Hurricanes Charley, Frances, Ivan, and Jeanne hit the state of Florida. One of those storms, Hurricane Ivan, also affected the state of Alabama. Although some of SFT's rental car business locations incurred damage during the course of the storm, it is undisputed that the locations remained substantially intact, and the vehicles leased from DTG were not destroyed.

The hurricanes in late summer 2004 clearly constitute supervening events for the purposes of impracticability doctrine. However, the record suggests that the nonoccurrence of those hurricanes was not an assumption upon which the parties grounded their agreement. Hardy testified that he lived in Florida approximately ten years, during which time severe weather, including hurricanes, had hit the coast of Florida.

The doctrine of commercial impracticability is typically invoked in cases involving the sale of goods. Codified in section 2-615 of the Uniform Commercial Code (UCC), which has been adopted by the Oklahoma legislature, the doctrine of commercial impracticability provides a defense to a seller for a delay in delivery or nondelivery of promised goods if performance has been made impracticable by a contingency, the non-occurrence of which is an assumption of the contract.

Commercial impracticability may excuse a party from performance of his obligations under a contract where performance has become commercially impracticable because of unforeseen supervening circumstances not within the contemplation of the parties at the time of contracting. UCC commentary provides that a party pleading commercial impracticability must demonstrate the "basic assumption" prong of the test also found in the impracticability of performance context, that is, that the non-occurrence of the supervening event was a basic assumption of the parties at the time of contracting. A rise or a collapse in the market standing alone does not constitute a justification for failure to perform. A contract is deemed commercially impracticable when, due to unforeseen events, performance may only be obtained at "an excessive and unreasonable cost . . . or when all means of performance are commercially senseless." In applying the doctrine of commercial impracticability, the crucial question is "whether the cost of performance has in fact become so excessive and unreasonable that failure to excuse performance would result in grave injustice."

For many of the reasons already discussed, defendant is not entitled to the defense of commercial impracticability. The evidence strongly suggests that the non-occurrence of hurricanes was not a basic assumption of the parties' agreements. Moreover, defendant provides no evidence to support a suggestion that the event of the hurricanes made the cost of performance of the terms of the agreements unduly burdensome, or even remotely more expensive. Finally, the Court observes, again, that SFT was behind on its payments to Thrifty and DTG before the arrival of the hurricanes in August 2004. No genuine issue of material fact exists, and the Court holds that the defense of commercial impracticability is unavailable to defendant.

Plaintiff's motion for summary judgment granted.

CRITICAL THINKING

What are the implications of the court's decision that commercial impracticability is not constituted by the significant hurricane damages imposed on Florida in 2004? Especially given the increased rates of severe weather and natural disasters witnessed recently around the world, to what extent can parties entering into contracts reasonably be expected to plan for the effects of a rapidly changing global climate?

ETHICAL DECISION MAKING

How might ethical theories founded in deontology and an ethics of care differ in their interpretation of the behaviors examined in this case? Which interpretation do you think is more ethically defendable? Which interpretation does Judge Eagan appear to favor? Justify your response.

What purpose does this ruling appear to support? Is there a larger ethical end implied by Judge Eagan's decision? Why or why not?

to fulfill a particular purpose, and the happening of that purpose is said to be a basic assumption on which the contract is made. If, due to factors beyond the control of the parties, the event does not occur, and neither party had assumed the risk of the event's nonoccurrence, the contract may be discharged.

This doctrine arose from the so-called coronation cases in England. Numerous parties had contracted for rooms along the parade route for the king's coronation, but the king became ill and the coronation was canceled. The courts held that the parties' duties under the room contracts should be discharged and that any payments made in advance should be returned as the essential purposes of the contracts could no longer be fulfilled, through no fault of any of the parties.

This doctrine is not frequently used. For example, if you contract for an organist to play at your daughter's wedding but the groom gets cold feet at the last moment and the wedding is canceled, you cannot use frustration of purpose to discharge the contract because the groom's changing his mind was a foreseeable event, even though it was unlikely.

Case Nugget An Unforeseeable Event?

Liggett Restaurant Group, Inc. v. City of Pontiac
260 Mich. App. 127, 676 N.W.2d 633 (Mich. App. 2003).

Elias Brothers Restaurants, Inc., had a contract with the defendant, City of Pontiac Stadium Building Authority, to provide concessions at the Silverdome until 2000. The parties renegotiated the contract in 1990, and Elias Brothers agreed to pay additional consideration for the option to extend the contract until 2005 to coordinate with the end of the Detroit Lions' sublease. The additional consideration involved paying the city a higher percentage on profits from sales. This option was exercised on December 1, 1998, and the Detroit Lions prematurely discontinued playing in the Silverdome after the 2001 football season.

The plaintiff sought to use the frustration-of-purpose doctrine to discharge its obligations under the contract extension and therefore have returned to it the additional consideration it had paid under the extension. The plaintiff argued that the contract was made on the assumption that the Lions would play in the Silverdome until their lease ran out and thus their early departure frustrated the purpose of the extension.

The court said the doctrine was inapplicable in this case. The court first set forth the conditions under which the doctrine applied: (1) the contract must be at least partially executory; (2) the frustrated party's purpose in making the contract must have been known to both parties when the contract was made; (3) this purpose must have been basically frustrated by an event not reasonably foreseeable at the time the contract was made, the occurrence of which has not been due to the fault of the frustrated party and the risk of which was not assumed by him. Then the court noted that the situation clearly did not meet the third criterion. Far from being an unforeseeable event, the Lions' leaving prematurely was expressly addressed in the original contract by a paragraph specifying a reduction in the guaranteed minimum annual payment for each year in which the Lions did not play a minimum of eight games in the stadium.

Remedies

The fact that one party has breached a contract does not necessarily mean that the nonbreaching party will sue. A number of factors go into the decision of whether or not it makes sense to file suit. Some of those considerations include (1) the likelihood of success, (2) the desire or need to maintain an ongoing relationship with the potential defendant, (3) the possibility of getting a better or faster resolution through some form of alternative dispute resolution, and (4) the cost of litigation or some form of ADR as compared to the value of the likely remedy.

The remedies the potential plaintiff will be thinking about can generally be classified as either *legal remedies* (also known as *monetary damages*) or *equitable remedies,* some form of court-ordered action. The distinction between legal and equitable remedies can be traced back to a time in our legal system's English roots when, instead of one unitary legal system, there were two separate courts, a court of law and a court of equity. When parties were seeking money damages, they went to the court of law; but when parties needed any remedy other than money damages, they went to the High Court of Chancery, which was a court of equity. When the United States was establishing its legal system, it combined both these types of powers in a unitary system. The reasons for this joinder are not known, but it seems likely that the primary reason was that the early colonists simply did not have the resources to support two separate systems. The courts did, however, still maintain the distinction between legal and equitable remedies. However, unlike judges in the old English courts, judges in the U.S. system have the power to award both legal and equitable remedies in the same case. This section discusses these various remedies.

LEGAL REMEDIES (MONETARY DAMAGES)

Monetary damages are also referred to as *legal damages,* and they include compensatory, punitive, nominal, and liquidated damages. Whenever possible, courts award monetary damages rather than some form of equitable relief.

Compensatory damages. The most frequently awarded damages are **compensatory damages,** damages designed to put the plaintiff in the position he would have been in had the contract been fully performed. These damages are said to compensate the plaintiff for his loss of the benefit of the bargain. He can recover, however, only for those provable losses that were foreseeable at the time the contract was entered into. Sometimes, the plaintiff actually may have no losses. Suppose, for example, that Dr. Wilcox hires Jeremy to work exclusively as his research assistant during the fall semester, for a salary of $2,000 per month. If Wilcox breaches the contract and terminates Jeremy for no reason with two months left on the contract, and the only job Jeremy can get as a substitute pays only $500 per month, Jeremy would be entitled to compensatory damages of $3,000. However, if Jeremy gets a new job that pays $2,500 per month, he is actually better off, so no compensatory damages would be awarded. Sometimes these damages are referred to as *expectation damages* because they compensate a person for the benefit she or he expected to gain as a result of entering into the contract.

In addition to losing the benefit of the bargain, the plaintiff may suffer other losses directly caused by the breach. These losses may be compensated for as *incidental damages.* For example, because Jeremy was unfairly terminated before his contractual term was over, he may have to spend money to find another job. His job search expenditures would be considered incidental damages.

Some kinds of contracts have special rules for determining compensatory damages, namely, contracts for the sale of goods or land and construction contracts. Each of these are discussed in a little more detail below.

Contracts for the sale of goods are governed today by the Uniform Commercial Code. If the seller breaches the contract, compensatory damages are generally calculated as the difference between the contract price and the market price on the day the goods were supposed to be delivered,[3] plus any incidental damages resulting from the breach. In other words, this measure of damages is the difference between what the buyer would have paid for the goods under the contract and what he or she is now going to have to pay to obtain the goods from another seller. Occasionally, however, the buyer may have no damages because the market price of the goods is lower than the parties had anticipated it would be at the date of delivery and so the buyer can now actually purchase the goods at a lower price than the contract price.

If the buyer breaches before accepting the goods, the seller would be able to resell the goods and recover as compensatory damages the difference between the price he sold the

[3] UCC §§ 2-708 and 2-713.

goods for and the contract price, plus any incidental expenses associated with the sale.[4] If the seller is unable to sell the goods to another buyer, as might be the case, for example, with shirts embroidered with a company's monogram, then the seller may be entitled to the contract price as damages. If the buyer breaches before the goods are even manufactured, the seller's damages would typically be based on the profits that would have been made from the sale.

In construction contracts, contracts whereby an owner enters into an agreement to have a building constructed, damages are calculated differently depending on who the breaching party is and what stage the construction is in when the breach occurs. If the contract is breached by the owner before the construction is begun, damages are simply lost profits, which are calculated by subtracting the projected costs of construction from the contract price. For example, if Cameron Construction Company anticipates building a warehouse for the Johnson Corporation with a contract price of $500,000 and the cost of raw materials and labor are $420,000, Cameron could recover $80,000 in lost profits if the Johnson Corporation were to breach the contract before performance had begun.

If, however, Cameron Construction had already expended $20,000 in materials and labor on the job when the breach occurred, the company would be able to recover $100,000 in damages because the amount of damages when construction is in progress is measured by the lost profits plus any money already invested in the project. If the breach by the owner had occurred after construction was completed, the construction company would be entitled to recover the entire contract price, plus interest from the time payment for the project was due.

If the construction company or contractor breaches the contract before or during the construction, the owner's damages are generally measured by the cost of hiring another company to complete the project, plus any incidental costs associated with obtaining a new contractor, as well as any costs arising from delays in the construction project. If the contractor completes the job but finishes after the date for completion, the owner is entitled to damages for the loss of the use of the building that she would have had if the contract had been completed in a timely manner.

Consequential damages. It should be apparent by now that contract law requires greater certainty in the proof of damages than does tort law. Damages are not recoverable for breach of contract unless they can be proved with a high degree of certainty. One type of damages in contract cases that is often especially difficult to prove is what are called **consequential** or **special damages.** Consequential damages are foreseeable damages that result from special facts and circumstances arising outside the contract itself. These damages must be within the contemplation of the parties at the time the breach occurs.

In Case 20-3, a classic case, the court distinguishes consequential damages from the damages that arise naturally from a breach of contract.

Punitive damages. Just as in tort law, **punitive damages** in contract law are designed to punish the defendant and deter him and others from engaging in similar behavior in the future. Because the primary objective of contract law, however, is to ensure that parties' expectations are met, punitive, or exemplary, damages are rarely awarded. Most jurisdictions award them only when the defendant has engaged in reprehensible conduct such as fraud. The primary factor in determining the amount of punitive damages is how much is necessary to "punish" the defendant; thus the amount depends on matters such as the wealth and income of the defendant.

[4] UCC §§ 2-706 and 2-710.

CASE 20-3 HADLEY v. BAXENDALE
COURT OF EXCHEQUER
156 ENG. REP. 145 (1854)

Plaintiffs were millers in Gloucester. On May 11, their mill was stopped when the crank shaft of the mill broke. They had to send the shaft to Greenwich to be used as a model for a new crank to be molded. The plaintiffs' servant took the shaft to the defendant, a common carrier, and told the defendant's clerk that the mill was stopped, and that the shaft must be sent immediately. The clerk said it would be delivered at Greenwich on the following day. The defendant's clerk was told that a special entry, if required, should be made to hasten the shaft's delivery. The delivery of the shaft at Greenwich was delayed by some neglect, and consequently, the plaintiffs did not receive the new shaft for several days after they would otherwise have received it. During that time the mill was shut down, and the plaintiffs thereby lost the profits they would otherwise have received had the shaft been delivered on time. They sought to recover damages for lost profits during that time. The defendant argued that the lost profits were "too remote." The court decided for the plaintiffs and allowed the jury to consider the lost profits in awarding damages. The defendant appealed.

JUSTICE ALDERSON: We think that there ought to be a new trial in this case; but, in so doing, we deem it to be expedient and necessary to state explicitly the rule which the Judge, at the next trial, ought, in our opinion, to direct the jury to be governed by when they estimate the damages. . . .

Now we think the proper rule in such a case as the present is this: Where two parties have made a contract which one of them has broken, the damages which the other party ought to receive in respect of such breach of contract should be such as may fairly and reasonably be considered either arising naturally, i.e., according to the usual course of things, from such breach of contract itself, or such as may reasonably be supposed to have been in the contemplation of both parties, at the time they made the contract, as the probable result of the breach of it. Now, if the special circumstances under which the contract was actually made were communicated by the plaintiffs to the defendants, and thus known to both parties, the damages resulting from the breach of such a contract, which they would reasonably contemplate, would be the amount of injury which would ordinarily follow from a breach of contract under these special circumstances so known and communicated. But, on the other hand, if these special circumstances were wholly unknown to the party breaking the contract, he, at the most, could only be supposed to have had in his contemplation the amount of injury which would arise generally, and in the great multitude of cases not affected by any special circumstances, from such a breach of contract. For, had the special circumstances been known, the parties might have specially provided for the breach of contract by special terms as to the damages in that case; and of this advantage it would be very unjust to deprive them. . . . Now, in the present case, if we are to apply the principles above laid down, we find that the only circumstances here communicated by the plaintiffs to the defendants at the time the contract was made, were, that the article to be carried was the broken shaft of a mill, and that the plaintiffs were the millers of the mill.

But how do these circumstances show reasonably that the profits of the mill must be stopped by an unreasonable delay in the delivery of the broken shaft by the carrier to the third person? . . . But it is obvious that, in the great multitude of cases of millers sending off broken shafts to third persons by a carrier under ordinary circumstances, such consequences would not, in all probability, have occurred; and these special circumstances were here never communicated by the plaintiffs to the defendants. It follows therefore, that the loss of profits here cannot reasonably be considered such a consequence of the breach of contract as could have been fairly and reasonably contemplated by both the parties when they made this contract. For such loss would neither have flowed naturally from the breach of this contract in the great multitude of such cases occurring under ordinary circumstances, nor were the special circumstances, which, perhaps, would have made it a reasonable and natural consequence of such breach of contract, communicated to or known by the defendants.

Judgment for defendant for a new trial.

[CONTINUED]

CRITICAL THINKING

What are the key terms essential to this argument? Are alternative definitions of important words or phrases possible? If so, how could the acceptability of this argument be affected by the use of these alternative meanings?

What additional information would be useful in deciding the acceptability of this argument? For instance, what do we really know about the proposed loss of profit? Does this missing information have a significant impact on the reasoning?

ETHICAL DECISION MAKING

What value preferences can be discovered in Judge Alderson's ruling? Are they properly justified? What ethical theories or guidelines might aid in their justification? Why?

Nominal damages. In a case where no actual damages resulted from the breach of contract, the court may award the plaintiff **nominal damages.** The award is typically for $1 or $5, but it serves to signify that the plaintiff has been wronged by the defendant.

Liquidated damages. Typically, the court determines the amount of damages to which a nonbreaching party is entitled. Sometimes, however, the parties recognize that if there is a breach of contract, it will probably be somewhat difficult for the court to determine exactly what the damages are. To prevent a difficult court battle, the parties specify in advance what the **liquidated damages** will be if there is a particular kind of breach. The parties specify these damages in what is called a *liquidated-* or *stipulated-damage clause* in the contract. The damages may be specified as either a fixed amount or a formula for determining how much money is due. Such clauses are frequently used in construction contracts when the buyer needs to know the property is going to be available by a specific date so that she can make her plans for moving in. In such a case, the parties may estimate in advance what it will cost the buyer for storage and temporary housing if the property is not ready by the specified date. The courts generally enforce these clauses as long as they appear to bear a reasonable relationship to what the actual costs will be. If the amount specified is so unreasonable as to not seem to bear any logical relationship to foreseeable costs, the courts declare the clause a penalty clause and do not enforce it.

Mitigation of damages. When a contract has been breached, the nonbreaching party is often angry at the breaching party and may wish to make the breaching party "pay through the nose." However, the courts do not allow a nonbreaching party to intentionally increase his damages. In fact, to recover damages in a breach-of-contract case, the plaintiff must demonstrate that he used reasonable efforts to minimize the damage resulting from the breach. This obligation is referred to as the *duty to mitigate one's damages.*

Thus, if you are the manager of a hotel and a person who had booked 10 rooms for the week calls to cancel all the reservations, you have a duty to attempt to rent the rooms to minimize the damages. The mitigation must be reasonable, however, and no one is expected to settle for something less than what was contemplated under the contract in order to mitigate the damages.

One area where interesting mitigation issues arise is cases in which an employee is wrongfully discharged and must seek new employment to mitigate her damages. If the

global context

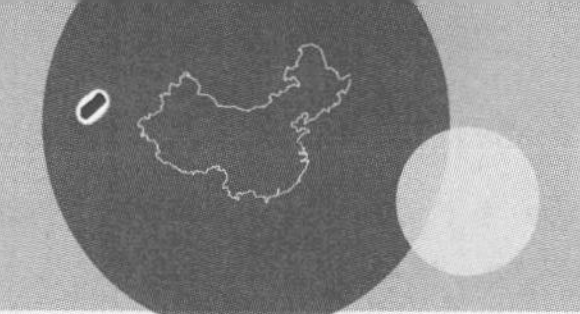

Liquidated Damages in China

Article 114 of Chapter 7, Liability for Breach of Contracts, of Contract Law of the People's Republic of China provides for the equivalent of the liquidated-damage clause recognized under U.S. law. The first part of the Chinese law is almost identical to our law. It provides that the parties to a contract may agree that one party shall, when violating the contract, pay breach-of-contract damages of a certain amount in light of the breach or they may agree on the calculating method of compensation for losses resulting from the breach of contract.

However, the Chinese law has an interesting twist for circumstances in which the projected damages end up being different from what the actual damages are. If the agreed breach-of-contract damages are lower than the losses caused, any party may request that the people's court or an arbitration institution increase it; if it is excessively higher than the losses caused, any party may request that the people's court or an arbitration institution make an appropriate reduction.

employee does not seek alternative employment, the amount of lost wages recovered as damages will be reduced by the amount the employee reasonably could have earned in another job. If the employee does not find another job, the court must decide whether the employee could have found comparable alternative employment with reasonable effort. A famous case, presented in Case 20-4, illustrates this dilemma that the courts sometimes face.

CASE 20-4

PARKER v. TWENTIETH CENTURY–FOX FILM CORP.
SUPREME COURT OF CALIFORNIA
3 CAL. 3D 176, 474 P.2D 689 (1970)

Plaintiff signed a contract to play the female lead in defendant's contemplated production of a musical motion picture entitled "Bloomer Girl." The contract provided that defendant would pay plaintiff a minimum "guaranteed compensation" of $53,571.42 per week for 14 weeks commencing May 23, 1966, for a total of $750,000. Prior to May 1966 the defendant notified the plaintiff that the firm was not going to produce the film, but to avoid damage to the plaintiff, the defendant would employ plaintiff as the leading actress in another film tentatively entitled "Big Country, Big Man" for identical compensation. But unlike "Bloomer Girl," "Big Country" was a dramatic western movie. "Bloomer Girl" was to have been filmed in California, while "Big Country" was to be produced in Australia. Also, certain terms in the proffered contract varied from those of the original. Plaintiff was given one week within which to accept the alternative film offer; she did not and the offer lapsed. Plaintiff then sued to recover the agreed guaranteed compensation. The defendant claimed that the plaintiff failed to mitigate her damages by refusing the role in the western, and since she would have had no damages had she taken the alternative role, she should not be entitled to any recovery. The court granted summary judgment to the plaintiff and the defendant appealed.

JUDGE BURKE: . . . The duty of mitigation of damages does not require the plaintiff to seek or to accept other employment of a different or inferior kind. . . . [I]t is clear that the trial court correctly ruled that plaintiff's failure to accept defendant's tendered substitute employment could not be applied in mitigation of damages because the offer of the 'Big Country' lead was of employment both different and inferior, and that no factual dispute was presented on that issue. The mere circumstance that 'Bloomer Girl' was to be a musical review calling upon plaintiff's talents as a dancer as well as an actress, and was to be produced in the City of Los Angeles, whereas 'Big Country' was a straight dramatic role in a 'Western Type' story taking place in an opal mine in Australia, demonstrates the difference in kind between the two employments; the female lead as a dramatic actress in a western style motion picture can by no stretch of imagination be considered the equivalent of or substantially similar to the lead in a song-and-dance production.

Additionally, the substitute 'Big Country' offer proposed to eliminate or impair the director and screenplay approvals accorded to plaintiff under the original 'Bloomer Girl' contract and thus constituted an offer of inferior employment. No expertise or judicial notice is required in order to hold that the deprivation or infringement of an employee's rights held under an original employment contract converts the available 'other employment' relied upon by the employer to mitigate damages into inferior employment which the employee need not seek or accept.

AFFIRMED in favor of plaintiff.

CRITICAL THINKING

Could the concept of commercial impracticability apply in this case? That is, could an argument be made on behalf of the defendant that continuing the production of "*Bloomer Girl*" would be commercially impracticable, thereby discharging the defendant from contractual obligations? If so, would this significantly affect the reasonableness of this finding? Why or why not?

ETHICAL DECISION MAKING

Do the arguments of the plaintiff and defendant reflect appropriate consideration of ethical guidelines? Has each given consideration to the interests and rights of all relevant stakeholders?

EQUITABLE REMEDIES

As noted earlier, equitable remedies grew out of the English court's authority to fashion remedies when the existing laws did not provide any adequate ones. These remedies were typically unique solutions specifically crafted to the demands of the situations. Today, the most common equitable remedies include rescission and restitution, orders for specific performance, and injunctions.

As a carryover from the days of the English courts of law and equity, a party seeking equitable relief must meet five requirements. The party must prove that (1) there is no adequate legal remedy available; (2) irreparable harm to the plaintiff may result if the equitable remedy is not granted; (3) the contract is legally valid (except when seeking relief in quasi-contract); (4) the contract terms are clear and unambiguous; and (5) the plaintiff has "clean hands," that is, has not been deceitful or done anything in breach of the contract.

Rescission and restitution. Sometimes the parties simply want to be returned to their precontract status; they want to have the contract terminated and to have any transferred property returned to its original owner. That is, they want rescission and restitution.

Rescission is the termination of the contract, and **restitution** is the return of any property given up under the contract.

Restitution and rescission are most frequently awarded in situations in which there is a lack of genuine assent (discussed in Chapter 17). When a party enters into a contract because of fraud, duress, undue influence, or a bilateral mistake, the contract is voidable and the party who wants out may seek to avoid the contract or, in other words, may seek rescission and restitution.

Specific performance. **Specific performance** is sometimes called *specific enforcement.* It is an order requiring that the breaching party fulfill the terms of the agreement. Courts are very reluctant to grant specific performance and will do so only when monetary damages simply are not adequate, typically because the subject matter of the contract is unique. If the subject matter is unique, then even if the nonbreaching party is given compensation, he cannot go elsewhere to buy the item from someone else, so this renders any kind of money damages inadequate.

Primarily for historical reasons, every piece of real property is considered unique. Therefore, an order for specific performance would often be the appropriate remedy for the breach of a contract for the sale of a piece of real estate.

Under the UCC, orders for specific performance of a contract for the sale of goods may be awarded "where the goods are unique or in other proper circumstances."[5] While the other circumstances have not been delineated by the UCC, the case law reveals that a commonly accepted circumstance is one in which the good is scarce or is no longer being produced and therefore would be difficult to obtain on the open market.

Injunction. An **injunction** is an order either forcing a person to do something or prohibiting a person from doing something. Most commonly, injunctions are prohibitions against actions. Such an injunction might be used, for example, as a remedy in a contract case involving a personal service. Mandy is a lounge singer, and she has a contract to perform at JZ's Lounge every weekend night from January through June. Two months into her contract she decides to work for Bally's Lounge instead because Bally's will pay her twice as much. There is no way to adequately calculate the damages that would arise from the singer's going over to the other club to perform, so money damages would not really be an adequate remedy. Instead, the owner of JZ's may obtain an injunction prohibiting Mandy from performing in any lounge until the end of June, when her term of performance under the contract will have been completed.

In the Walgreen's case in the opening scenario, the appellate court agreed with the trial court judge that it would be extremely difficult for the court to calculate how to adequately determine the damages that Walgreen's would sustain if Sara Creek were allowed to simply violate the contract's exclusivity clause and lease space to another drugstore. The court would have had to determine how much business the new store would take from Walgreen's over the course of the next 10 years, and it felt that such a calculation would be almost impossible to figure. Hence, the court agreed that money damages would not be adequate, and an injunction prohibiting the leasing of the space in violation of the exclusivity clause would be the only adequate remedy.

[5] UCC § 2-716.

Sometimes, when a party is suing another for breach of contract, one of the parties is concerned that before the court has had a chance to decide the case, the other party will do something to make it impossible for the concerned party to get the relief he would be entitled to. In such a situation, the concerned party may ask for a preliminary injunction to prohibit the other party from taking any action during the course of the lawsuit that would cause irreparable harm to any of the parties to the contract. For example, Jim agrees to sell Bob a very rare antique car for $15,000, but then says he is not going to comply with the terms of the agreement. Bob sues Jim for breach of contract, but before the case goes to trial, Bob finds out that Sara has told Jim that she would be willing to pay him $20,000 for the car. Bob may seek a preliminary injunction to prohibit Jim from selling the car to anyone else until the court decides whether Bob is entitled to an order for specific performance forcing Jim to sell the car to him. Thus, the preliminary injunction fulfills the purpose of maintaining the status quo until the case can be finally decided.

Reformation. Sometimes a written contract does not reflect the parties' actual agreement, or there are inconsistencies in the contract, such as the price being listed as "$200,000 (twenty thousand dollars)." In such a case, the written document may be rewritten to reflect what the parties had agreed on.

Recovery based on quasi-contract. When an enforceable contract does not in fact exist, the court may grant a recovery based on quasi-contract; that is, the court may impose a contractlike obligation on a party to prevent an injustice from occurring. Recovery in quasi-contract is often sought when a party thought a valid contract existed and thus gave up something of value in relying on the existence of a contract. To justify recovery under a theory of quasi-contract, sometimes referred to as recovery in quantum meriut, a plaintiff must prove that (1) the plaintiff conferred a benefit on the defendant; (2) the plaintiff had reasonably expected to be compensated for the benefit conferred on the defendant; and (3) the defendant would be unjustly enriched from receiving the benefit without compensating the plaintiff for it.

CASE OPENER WRAP-UP

Battle of the Pharmacies

The decision by Judge Posner found that the benefits of substituting an injunction for damages were inadequate. The damages resulting from the new drugstore's moving into the shopping center would be too uncertain to calculate for the 10 years remaining on the lease. In contrast, an injunction could be issued rather simply and would require no court follow-up, therefore making an injunction the better remedy when weighing the costs of the injunction against the costs of attempting to calculate damages. Nevertheless, even if it were true, as the defendant argued, that Walgreen's damages were smaller than Sara Creek's gain from allowing a second pharmacy into the shopping mall, there must be a price for dissolving the injunction that will make both parties better off, but determining that price would be nothing more than a "battle of experts." Judge Posner also found this situation an unworthy one in which to reward the breach of contract.

Summary

Discharge

Contracts may be discharged in a number of different ways, including:

- The occurrence or nonoccurrence of a condition.
- Complete or substantial performance.
- Material breach.
- Mutual agreement.
- Operation of law.

Remedies

Courts may grant parties in a breach-of-contract action legal or equitable remedies. Legal remedies, or money damages, include:

- Compensatory damages
- Nominal damages
- Punitive damages
- Liquidated damages

Equitable remedies, which will be granted only when legal remedies are inadequate, include:

- Restitution and recission
- Specific performance
- Injunction

Point / Counterpoint

Should Nonbreaching Parties Be Required to Mitigate Damages?

No

Courts' requiring nonbreaching parties to mitigate damages is unfair.

Contract law is designed to reward both parties for the agreement that they have reached. If one party is irresponsible and cannot perform as agreed, why should courts then punish the nonbreaching party by requiring him or her to mitigate damages? After all, the nonbreaching party likely made decisions subsequent to the contract on the assumption that the contract terms would be carried out, and mitigating damages introduces stress regarding those decisions. For instance, if a hotel owner entered a contract with a person who agreed to rent 50 hotel rooms and a

Yes

Courts' requiring nonbreaching parties to mitigate damages provides the most equitable solution when a contract is breached.

Although a nonbreaching party could understandably be frustrated with the breaching party, such a breach does not license the nonbreaching party to force the breaching party to provide full payment for the contract, especially when many costs could have been avoided. For example, if a city contracts with a company to construct a bridge across a river and the city later learns that the roads that would connect to the bridge would disrupt a nesting bald eagle, the company should not be permitted to still build the conference room for a weekend, the hotel owner would focus his time and energy on advertising for other weekends. But to require the hotel owner, after learning that the person no longer wanted the rooms, to mitigate damages places stress on the owner that he would not have otherwise experienced. Instead of completely focusing on booking rooms for other weekends, the hotel owner must now take time away from advertising those rooms so that he can try to fill the 50 vacant rooms and conference room, even if he wants to sue for breach of contract.

In addition, requiring nonbreaching parties to mitigate damages encourages irresponsible behavior on the part of contracting parties. If a party knows she can breach a contract as long as she provides enough notice, she may be able to avoid most, if not all, liability. Returning to the hotel example, if the person who contracted to rent the 50 rooms notifies the hotel owner of the breach two months before the weekend she contracted for, the hotel owner could fill the rooms and the breaching party would likely not be liable for any damages, even though the hotel owner incurred greater expense and spent additional time filling the rooms with other guests. "Mitigating damages," therefore, is just a fancy way of saying that the burden shifts back to the nonbreaching parties, rewarding the very people who should bear the costs of breaching contract.

bridge and demand full payment. The city would then have to pay for a useless bridge, even though the company could have avoided the costs of building the bridge.

In this example and similar contexts, the breaching parties would have an incentive to do nothing and still demand payment, even though damages could have been reduced. For instance, if a person entered a two-year employment contract to work for a company but the company could not honor the contract, the nonbreaching party should not be entitled to sit at home for two years and still receive compensation.

In other words, if nonbreaching parties were not required to mitigate damages—either by discontinuing performance, as in the bridge example, or by finding a reasonable replacement, such as a different job in the employment example—nonbreaching parties would run up the costs by completing performance under the contract or doing nothing. In the context of finding a reasonable alternative, nonbreaching parties would actually have an incentive to do nothing.

Finally, mitigating damages promotes better relationships between contracting parties, making both parties more willing to contract again in the future.

Questions & Problems

1. Explain the difference between legal and equitable remedies.
2. Explain how the existence of conditions subsequent and precedent affects the discharge of a contract.
3. Explain the relationship between commercial impracticability and frustration of purpose.
4. List the conditions that must be met for a court to impose a quasi-contract.
5. Robert Ewalt was hired by Coos-Curry Electric Cooperative as its chief accountant in May 1999 and fired on August 26, 2002. He filed suit and claimed, among other things, that his discharge violated an employment contract between him and his employer. Ewalt signed an at-will employment provision that noted, in part, "I may resign or be terminated, with or without cause or notice, at any time."

Coos-Curry's "Policy Bulletin No. 41," described enforcement of certain work rules by supervisors. The policy described a process of progressive discipline and included the statement that "violation of any of these rules will constitute just cause for disciplinary action up to and including discharge," along with a list of 22 different violations.

Ewalt argued that those guidelines created a contract under which his employment could be terminated only for just cause. Should the court decide in favor of Ewalt or Coos-Curry? Why? [*Ewalt v. Coos-Curry Electric Cooperative, Inc.,* 202 Ore. App. 257, 120 P.3d 1288 (2005).]

6. Andrew Finch, a stockbroker at Morgan Stanley Dean Witter & Co., assumed that his role in making Morgan Stanley the lead underwriter on the initial public offering (IPO) of Webmethods stock would allow him to allocate 75,000 shares of the stock to his clients. He prematurely acted on this belief by telling clients they could purchase the IPO shares through him. Several investors set up a vehicle at Morgan Stanley (Twin Fires) to purchase these funds through Finch.

   Before the IPO of Webmethods was issued, Finch learned that his allotment was only 225 shares. Too embarrassed to tell his clients, Finch pretended that trading of the stock had been delayed. As the price of the stock shot up from $35 to $212 on the first day, the clients were celebrating—until they realized that they had never purchased as much stock as Finch led them to believe they had. The clients argued that an equitable remedy would be for Morgan Stanley to compensate them for the gains they would have made (nearly $12 million) had they purchased the stock as they had intended. Should the courts grant the proposed equitable remedy? Why or why not? [*Twin Fires Inv., LLC v. Morgan Stanley Dean Witter & Co.,* 445 Mass. 411, 837 N.E.2d 1121 (Mass. 2005).]

7. Williams owns two trucks that he uses to transport, under contract, frozen produce. Williams drives one truck himself and employs a driver to drive the other one. He provides the driver with a CB radio, cell phone, and expense money so that the driver can stay in communication with him. As a carrier, Williams is subject to the rules of the Department of Transportation for common carriers. One of these rules requires that all drivers be tested for drug use. Williams hired Hall as a driver, but did not require that he take a drug test.

   Williams had a contract with Mountaire Farms to pick up frozen-chicken produce from suppliers and deliver it to specific locations in New York and New Jersey. Williams assigned the delivery to Hall, who picked up the poultry but failed to deliver it because he was high on illegal drugs. Hall was arrested and the poultry recovered, but by the time it was recovered, the produce had spoiled, a loss valued at $33,373.63. Williams argued that he should be excused from liability under the contract on the grounds of commercial impracticability; the unforeseen drug use of his driver was an intervening circumstance beyond his control that prevented the fulfillment of the contract. Do you agree or disagree with Williams' argument? Why or why not? [*Mountaire Farms, Inc. v. Williams,* Not Reported in A.2d, 2005 WL 1177569 (Del. Super. 2005).]

8. Shirley and Vince Ladner leased 10 acres of their land to J. D. Pigg, who used the land for his cattle farm. The Ladners and Pigg created a 10-year contract, providing that rent be paid annually on August 1. Pigg executed the lease with his first payment in cash in August 2000. On August 1, 2001, Mrs. Pigg attempted to mail the check for the second rent payment, but placed the incorrect address on the envelope. Consequently, the check was returned to the Pigg residence, and Mrs. Pigg then properly forwarded the check to the Ladners. However, the Ladners did not receive the check

until August 8, 2001, at which time they refused to accept payment and returned the check to Pigg. The Ladners claimed the lease had been terminated by Pigg's failure to submit timely payment, as this failure constituted a material breach. Is Pigg's failure to tender payment on August 1 a material breach of the lease? Why or why not? [*Ladner v. Pigg,* 2005 Miss. App. LEXIS 350.]

9. The Gentrys contracted with Squires Construction to build a house. The Gentrys showed Squires a photograph of a house that they wanted their home to look like but did not provide Squires with any blueprints. Squires suggested that it use some of its own drawings to construct the house, which would save the Gentrys some money, as the Gentrys were concerned largely with cost and even agreed to perform some of the work on the house themselves. After Squires completed much of the construction, the Gentrys refused to provide the final payment through a lender, claiming that Squires had made mistakes in the construction, such as building the first floor with 8- instead of 10-foot ceilings, failing to caulk the windows, and creating problems with the front porch. Squires sued for breach of contract and, alternatively, for equitable relief under quantum meruit. The Gentrys counterclaimed, arguing that Squires had breached the contract. The trial court concluded that Squires had not substantially performed. Did Squires successfully recover under the equitable remedy doctrine of quantum meruit? Why or why not? [*Gentry v. Squires Constr., Inc.,* 2006 Tex. App. LEXIS 2299.]

10. NW agreed to sell real property in Tacoma to O'Connor & Associates. The purchase agreement was created, but an addendum provided that the sale was subject to NW's obtaining "plat approval" from the city of Tacoma. After NW encountered financial problems, NW was unsuccessful in its attempts to obtain plat approval from the city. Thereafter, NW asked O'Connor whether O'Connor would be interested in purchasing the property "as is," after which O'Connor could seek plat approval. O'Connor declined this offer, and subsequently NW sold the property to Tacoma Northpark. Concerned that O'Connor might sue, Tacoma Northpark filed an action to quiet title (an action to establish ownership) to the land; unsurprisingly, O'Connor filed a counterclaim against Tacoma Northpark and a cross-claim against NW. With regard to O'Connor's claim against NW for breach of contract, what is NW's best argument that it is not liable? How did the court decide? [*Tacoma Northpark, LLC v. NW, LLC,* 2004 Wash. App. LEXIS 1932.]

11. Brad Gupta formed two companies, Ameriquest Holdings and Ananya Aviation, for which he purchased three airplanes that were in lease agreements with U.S. Airways and Continental Airlines. However, after the events of September 11, 2001, the two airlines did not renew their leases for the three planes now owned by Gupta. Consequently, Gupta could not continue his loan repayments, and U.S. Bancorp Equipment Finance foreclosed and sold the planes. U.S. Bancorp sought to enforce the loan agreements for the millions of dollars still owed for Gupta's debt after the proceeds from the sale of the airplanes had been deducted. Gupta, however, argued that the events of September 11, 2001, resulted in immense losses to the airline industry and that performance of the loan agreements (i.e., repayment) was impossible. Did Gupta properly raise the defense of impossibility? What was the court's reasoning? [*U.S. Bancorp Equip. Fin., Inc. v. Ameriquest Holdings,* 2004 U.S. Dist. LEXIS 24709.]

Looking for more review material?

The Online Learning Center at **www.mhhe.com/kubasek1e** contains this chapter's "Assignment on the Internet" and also a list of URLs for more information entitled "On the Internet." Find both of them in the Student Center portion of the OLC, along with quizzes and other helpful materials.

Introduction to Sales and Lease Contracts

CASE OPENER

Who Is Liable for Ears Falling Off: The Farmers, the Seed Company, or the Weather?

In the spring of 1981 Robert and Wiliam Peterson bought Migro Seed Company, Inc., corn seeds from John Sandall. Both Petersons were local farmers, and John Sandall, also a farmer, was Migro's area dealer. Migro produces hybrid seeds for sale, and the corn seeds bought by the Petersons were a "product of scientific genetic cross-breeding to produce a seed having desirable germination, growing, and production qualities."[1]

Around July 23, 1981, the Petersons discovered that nearly 70 percent of their corn, grown from the Migro seeds, had broken off at the ear level after a typical Nebraskan thunderstorm the evening before. However, corn growing from non-Migro seeds had not suffered such damage.

It turns out that silica in the sandy soil in this particular area of Nebraska had been absorbed by these plants, causing them to develop a brittle stalk and thus break at about the first ear-of-corn level. No other variety of corn seed had this problem. When John Sandall, the neighboring farmer and Migro dealer, sold the Petersons the 102 bags of seed, the literature accompanying the seed indicated that one of the Migro seed's attributes was "excellent stalk quality."

When the crop was harvested, the Petersons harvested approximately 19½ bushels per acre of the Migro corn while averaging 113¾ bushels per acre of corn grown from seed provided by other seed companies.

The Petersons brought a lawsuit for breach of contract. A number of initial questions present themselves.

[1] See *Peterson v. North American Plant Breeders,* 218 Neb. 258, 354 N.W.2d 625 (1984).

CHAPTER 21

1. Is the sale of seed a contract for the sale of goods when it was the resulting plant that may have been defective? Does this contract fall under UCC Article 2 or under common law?
2. Are the parties involved here merchants under the UCC and thus subject to a higher standard of care?

The Wrap-Up at the end of the chapter will answer these questions.

Learning Objectives

After reading this chapter, you will be able to answer the following questions:

1. What is the UCC?
2. What is a sales contract?
3. What kinds of contracts fall under the UCC interpretations?
4. What is a merchant, and why is that designation significant?
5. What is the CISG?
6. What is a lease contract?

Businesses and organizations that purchase products need to be aware of which laws govern their purchases because the laws can differ. Three sources of laws that interpret sales contracts exist: state common law, the Uniform Commercial Code, and state statutory law. There is very little, if any, federal law that governs contracts for the buying and selling of items, and when such law does exist, it is highly specialized (e.g., the buying and selling of stock under laws created by the Securities and Exchange Commission).

This chapter introduces the Uniform Commercial Code. It explains the scope and significance of the UCC, discusses sections of the UCC that govern both sales and lease contracts, reviews how these contracts are formed, and provides a summary of the legislation that governs international sales contracts.

The Uniform Commercial Code

THE SCOPE OF THE UCC

In some areas of law, federal statutes ensure that the same law applies to all the states. Federal statutes do not govern the formation of sales and lease contracts. Instead, each state passes its own laws to outline rules in this area. Consequently, laws vary from state to state. While all states (except Louisiana) follow the English common law, over 200 years of legal precedent that has developed in each separate state can create differences in contract interpretation and application. With the development of interstate commercial activities, these differences began to pose problems for parties from different states entering into a contract with each other. What was needed was some kind of uniform law for business transactions that all the states could adopt.

In some areas of law, lawyers and law school professors have worked together to pass *uniform,* or model, state laws, that states may consider adopting. Two important groups of lawyers and law school professors are the National Conference of Commissioners on Uniform State Laws (NCCUSL) and the American Law Institute (ALI), which worked together to create the **Uniform Commercial Code (UCC).** The UCC was created in 1952, and has been adopted by all 50 states, the District of Columbia, and the Virgin Islands. When a state adopts the UCC, that code becomes part of the law of that particular state; it becomes the commercial code for that state. Each state is allowed to rewrite parts of the UCC to reflect the wishes of its state legislature.

The UCC is divided into sections known as *articles.* These articles cover a wide range of topics, from sales contracts to secured transactions (see Exhibit 21-1). This book explains all the articles of the UCC, starting in this chapter and ending with Chapter 29, which explains the law that governs secured transactions. The NCCUSL and ALI work to revise the UCC as business practices change. For example, as lease contracts have become more common, the NCCUSL and ALI have worked to add an article that addresses lease contracts. The NCCUSL sometimes proposes new laws to address areas of the law not covered by the UCC. For instance, later in this chapter you will read about the Uniform Commercial Information Transactions Act (UCITA), which responds to issues related to software licenses, information purchases, and other e-commerce topics.

Exhibit 21-1 An Outline of the UCC

ARTICLE	TOPIC
1	General provisions
2	Sales
2(A)	Leases
3	Negotiable instruments
4	Bank deposits and collections
4(A)	Wire transfers
5	Letters of credit
6	Bulk transfers
7	Documents of title
8	Investment securities
9	Secured transactions

Exhibit 21-2
Common Law or UCC?

1. Does the transaction involve a sale or lease (as opposed to, let's say, a gift)?
   If yes → go to question 2.
   If "no" → apply the appropriate area of common or statutory law.
2. Is the transaction for the sale or lease of a good?
   If yes → go to question 3.
   If no → apply common law.
3. If the contract is for the sale or lease of both goods and nongoods, which type of item is predominant in the contract?
   If goods → UCC Article 2 applies; go to question 4.
   If nongoods (real estate or services) → common law applies.
4. If this is a UCC Article 2 transaction, is either party a merchant?
   If yes → pay close attention as to when the special rules on merchants apply.
   If no → then only "reasonable" care applies to the parties; no "special" or heightened duty of care will apply to a party deemed to be a merchant.

THE SIGNIFICANCE OF THE UCC

The UCC is significant because it clarifies sales law and makes this area of law more predictable to businesses that engage in transactions in more than one state. Essentially, the UCC facilitates commercial transactions.

However, it is important to emphasize that the UCC does not pertain to all business transactions. Under UCC Article 2, the subject matter of this chapter, the UCC explains the creation and interpretation of sales contracts

Articles 2 and 2(A) of the UCC

Article 2 of the UCC governs sales contracts, while Article 2(A) governs lease contracts. Specifically, Article 2 focuses on contracts for the sale of goods; Article 2(A) focuses on contracts for the lease of goods. For the purpose of "selling something," the UCC divides all the items that can be bought and sold into three categories: goods, realty, and services (including intangible goods such as securities). Article 2 pertains only to the sale of goods. Nonetheless, Article 2 is not a comprehensive guide to sales contract formation. When Article 2 is silent on an issue of sales contract formation or interpretation, the common law rules apply. Of course, if a state has passed statutory law regarding contracts, that law always supersedes the common law. Additionally, it is important to note that under the UCC the rules for transactions involving merchants differ from those for transactions involving regular buyers and sellers. Merchants will generally be held to a higher standard of care and behavior than nonmerchants. Every state except Louisiana[2] has adopted Article 2 of the UCC.

If you are not sure whether a contract falls under common law or under the UCC, the decision-tree rubric in Exhibit 21-2 can help you make a determination. To use this rubric, consider the following definitions of many of its terms.

[2] Louisiana's civil tradition is based on the Code Napoleon, or the French Civil Code.

ARTICLE 2 OF THE UCC

Sale. Section 2-106(1) of the UCC states that a **sale** "consists of the passing of title from the seller to the buyer for a price." Thus, in the transaction involving the Petersons and Migro Seed Company, the sale consisted of the passing of title (right of ownership) of the seeds themselves from Migro to the Petersons for a price.

Goods. Section 2-105 of the UCC defines **goods** as "all [tangible] things . . . which are movable at the time of identification to the contract for sale." Items are tangible if they exist physically. The issue in our opening case is whether the goods being bought are the seeds or the subsequent plants, which were defective. Note that Section 2-105 reads "at the time of identification to the contract." At the time that the contract was created by the Petersons, the items being sold were the seeds. Seeds are goods because they are tangible and can be moved. Some items are not goods under Article 2. For example, corporate stocks and copyrights are not tangible, so they are not goods. Real estate cannot be moved, so it is not a good. Yet items attached to real estate that are used for business activities are known as *trade fixtures* and are treated as goods under the UCC. Consider the Case Nugget.

Case Nugget The Difference between Realty and Personalty

J.K.S.P Restaurant v. County of Nassau
513 N.Y.S.2d 716 (N.Y. App. Div. 1987)

A creditor foreclosed on a diner in Hampstead, New York. Furthermore, the county stepped into the case as well in order to secure past-due taxes. The diner was on a piece of property, but the diner itself was a prefabricated home that was placed on the real estate. When the creditor and county began foreclosure proceedings, they sought to take title to the land from the diner's owners. They argued that the diner itself was part of the realty as it had been affixed to the realty with the intention that it was a permanent fixture; moreover, they argued that its removal would materially alter the realty to which it was attached. The diner's owner claimed that the diner itself was a trade fixture not subject to the foreclosure (the original agreement listed only the "real property" as security for the debt).

The court surveyed a long line of legal precedents, both from New York and from other jurisdictions, in attempting to answer the question of whether the diner was a trade fixture or part of the realty. The court focused first on the issue of whether removing the diner would materially alter the real estate. The court held that the diner was indeed a trade fixture but then concluded that it could be a trade fixture as part of the realty (and thus subject to the foreclosure) or a removable trade fixture and not subject to the foreclosure. In the end, the court ruled that two related questions needed answering: (1) Was the diner affixed to the realty in such a way as to indicate a permanent attachment? (2) Could the diner be moved without materially altering the realty? Since the record contained insufficient facts, the court sent the case back to the trial court for further review focusing on those two questions.

Items taken from real estate may be treated as goods. Minerals, clay, and soil can all be treated as goods, with their sales contract governed by Article 2, if the owner takes these

connecting to the core

Marketing

While the determination of whether something is a "good" is useful for knowing whether Article 2 applies to a transaction, the term *good* may also be divided into several categories for marketing purposes. For instance, consumer goods are often classified in one of four categories: (1) convenience goods, (2) shopping goods, (3) specialty goods, and (4) unsought goods. *Convenience goods* (e.g., toothpaste, groceries, and hand soap) are generally inexpensive and are often promoted by differentiation in prices and widespread availability. *Shopping goods* (e.g., cameras, televisions, and clothing) are more expensive than most convenience goods, and marketing focuses largely on differentiating one company's goods from a competitor's. *Specialty goods* (e.g., Rolex watches, Lexus vehicles) are typically very expensive, involving marketing that emphasizes the uniqueness of the brand and status. *Unsought goods* (e.g., burial insurance, thesauri, etc.) are usually not heavily marketed, as demand and distribution are relatively low.

Source: R. Kerin, S. Hartley, E. Berkowitz, and W. Rudelius, *Marketing* (New York: McGraw-Hill/Irwin, 2005), pp. 264–265.

items out of the ground and then sells them to the buyer. Should the owner sell the buyer the right to come and remove the items, the contract would be governed not by the UCC but by common law for the sale of an interest in realty, in this case, an interest known as a "profit." Crops that are sold while still growing in the field are also considered goods, and their sale contracts are subject to UCC interpretation.

Mixed goods and services contracts. Sometimes, it is not easy to tell whether something is a good because a tangible item is tied to or mixed with something intangible, such as a service. For instance, if Migro had sold not just the seeds but also seminars on efficient crop management and crop rotation and if the Petersons had bought a "package deal" that included the seeds and the seminars, it would not have been as clear that the contract was for the sale of a good. A contract that combines a good with a service is a **mixed sale.** Article 2 applies to mixed sales if the goods are the predominant part of the transaction.

In Case 21-1, the court had to decide whether a particular contract (a settlement agreement) was a contract for the sale of goods (foot-pump slippers) or a contract for something intangible (a settlement to resolve a lawsuit). The distinction was especially important to the plaintiff, Novamedix, because if the contract was for the sale of goods, the company could take advantage of other provisions of the UCC, especially implied warranties that the foot-pump slippers would serve the purpose for which they were designed.

To resolve contract issues in cases in which a tangible good is mixed with something intangible (e.g., a service or a legal settlement), most states employ some variation of the *predominant-purpose test* discussed in Case 21-1. In the Novamedix case, the court determined that the case should not be governed by Article 2 of the UCC because the settlement agreement was not predominantly a sale of goods. The predominant purpose of the agreement was to settle the patent infringement suit, not to transfer foot-pump slippers. The reader can infer from the court's analysis that the settlement agreement was more of a service contract than a goods contract, with the service component focusing on the terms of the settlement.

e-commerce AND THE LAW

The UCC and the Internet

The Uniform Commercial Code was designed to address the sale of tangible goods such as scooters, electric power tools, and jeans. Because the UCC was written long before the Internet and e-commerce boom, this legislation was not designed for transactions related to less tangible things, such as software and information. Not surprisingly, the UCC does not respond well to certain legal issues that arise in today's marketplace. For example, the UCC does not tell us the answers to these questions: What rules should govern computer software, which is likely to be licensed rather than sold as a good? What about downloadable software files? What rules should govern information providers like America Online (AOL), which provides a continuing service? What rules should govern the exchange of information, such as stock quotes? What rules cover travel reservations a person makes online?

The National Conference of Commissioners on Uniform State Laws (NCCUSL) has adopted the Uniform Commercial Information Transactions Act (UCITA), which answers the questions above and many more. This law promises to do for electronic contracting what the UCC did for transactions in physical goods: protect consumers by providing predictability, uniformity, and clear rules. As with the UCC, states will choose whether to adopt UCITA. In 2001, Virginia became the first state to enact UCITA, probably because major Internet-related companies (e.g., AOL, UUNET Technologies) are headquartered in northern Virginia.

Source: Robert Holleyman, "Updating Contract Law for the Digital Age," *USA Today* (magazine), March 1, 2000; and Scott W. Burt, "Controversial New Rules for Computer Contracts," *Metropolitan Corporate Counsel*/8 (June 2000), col. 1.

CASE 21-1 NOVAMEDIX, LIMITED, PLAINTIFF-APPELLANT, v. NDM ACQUISITION CORPORATION AND VESTA HEALTHCARE, INC., DEFENDANTS-APPELLEES

U.S. COURT OF APPEALS, FEDERAL CIRCUIT
166 F.3D 1177 (1999)

This case shows that even when a lawsuit ends through settlement, the dispute is not necessarily over. In this case, Novamedix and a competitor, NDM, resolved a patent infringement lawsuit by entering into a settlement agreement. At issue in the patent infringement lawsuit was a particular medical device—a foot-pump slipper, designed to aid in blood circulation from the feet to the heart of bedridden patients. Prior to the patent infringement lawsuit, both companies manufactured this particular foot-pump slipper. As a consequence of the patent infringement suit, NDM agreed to admit that it had infringed on Novamedix's patents, cease infringing on the patents, deliver its entire inventory of foot-pump slippers to Novamedix, grant Novamedix an exclusive license under NDM's own patents, and pay Novamedix $47,500.

When Novamedix received the inventory of foot-pump slippers, the company claimed that the slippers could not be sold because they did not meet FDA requirements for this particular medical device. Novamedix had wanted to sell NDM's inventory to NDM's former customers, but could not do so because the product failed to meet FDA requirements. Novamedix then filed suit against NDM, arguing that the settlement agreement was a contract for the sale of goods and therefore subject to the implied warranties of merchantability and fitness of New York's version of the UCC. In essence, Novamedix asked the court to declare the settlement agreement a contract for the sale of goods so it could take advantage of warranties outlined in the UCC. Novamedix asked the court to interpret the settlement agreement for NDM's inventory under Article 2 of the UCC because the foot-pump slippers were a "good" and title had passed for them from NDM to Novamedix. NDM contended that the agreement should not be interpreted under UCC Article 2. A lower court agreed with NDM, and Novamedix appealed.

SENIOR CIRCUIT JUDGE EDWARD S. SMITH: . . . Appellant [Novamedix] argues that under New York law, a "contract for the sale of goods" requires only that there be a sale (i.e., the "passing of title from the seller to the buyer for a price") . . . and that the subject of the sale be goods rather than services. Here, the argument goes, the settlement agreement was a contract for the sale of the defective slippers, because NDM passed title of the slippers (the goods) to Novamedix in exchange for a release for its patent infringement claim (the price).

We disagree. The world of commercial transactions is not limited to the binary world presented by Appellant, a world in which an agreement that passes title to Article 2 goods must either be a contract for the sale of goods or a contract for the sale of services. Many commercial transactions are not governed by Article 2 of the UCC: sale of land or securities, assignment of a contract right, or granting a license under a patent or copyright, just to name a few. The mere fact that title to Article 2 goods changed hands during one of these transactions does not by that fact alone make the transaction a sale of goods. . . . Here the mere fact that the parties' settlement agreement includes the transfer of personal property in its provisions does not make it a simple sale of goods (slippers) for a price (release of a legal claim). The settlement agreement between NDM and Novamedix is an agreement to release a legal claim for (1) binding admissions, (2) money damages of $47,500, (3) patent license rights, and (4) transfer of NDM's existing inventory to Novamedix. To elevate the inventory term over the other elements of consideration given by NDM is to distort the entire agreement through the lens of Novamedix's asserted purpose of selling the inventory when it entered into the agreement. The settlement agreement is no more a contract for the sale of slippers than it is a licensing agreement for NDM's patents. In fact, it is neither exclusively; it is a mixed contract, similar to a mixed contract for the provision of both goods and services. It should therefore be analyzed as a mixed contract.

To determine whether the UCC's implied warranties apply in a mixed goods/services contract, New York courts apply the "predominant purpose" test; if the predominant purpose of the contract was to sell goods, the contract falls within the UCC. However, "[i]f service predominates and the transfer of title to personal property is an incidental feature of the transaction, the contract does not fall within the ambit of the Code."

. . . Although the present settlement agreement is not a mixed goods/services contract, the same analysis is applicable to determine whether it should be treated as a contract for the sale of goods. Thus, the UCC's implied warranties of merchantability and fitness apply to the settlement agreement only if its predominant purpose was for the sale of slippers. We hold that it was not. The essential nature of the settlement agreement was to settle a patent infringement lawsuit. The agreement arose out of a patent infringement suit. The agreement contained multiple provisions relating to patent rights held by Novamedix and NDM. . . . Perhaps the inventory-related provisions were essential elements of the overall agreement, at least to Novamedix; perhaps they even support Novamedix's professed intent to sell the slippers to NDM's former customers. But those factors are simply not relevant to the question of whether the "essential nature" of the agreement was the exchange of slippers for the release of a legal claim. It was not, and cannot be construed as such with the benefit of hindsight. Therefore, the agreement was not a contract for the sale of goods, and the implied warranties of the UCC do not apply to it. . . .

AFFIRMED.

CRITICAL THINKING

Novamedix asks the court to simplify the case. How so? What rule does the court choose instead of a simple rule? Why do you suppose the court chooses a more complicated analysis than the one Novamedix prefers?

ETHICAL DECISION MAKING

In Chapter 2, you learned about the WPH framework for business ethics, which asks you to consider three questions: *Whom* would this decision affect? What is the *purpose* of the business decision? *How* should managers make decisions? When you are thinking about the purpose of a decision, it is helpful to consider values. Which value does this federal court show it prefers by ruling in NDM's favor?

Exhibit 21-3 Determining Merchant Status Under UCC Article 2

A buyer or seller is a merchant if the answer to any of these three questions is yes:

- Does the buyer or seller in question deal in goods of the kind involved in the sales contract?
- Does the buyer or seller in question, by occupation, hold himself or herself out as having knowledge and skill unique to the practices or goods involved in the transaction?
- Has the buyer or seller in question employed a merchant as a broker, agent, or other intermediary?

Merchants. UCC Article 2 pertains to anyone buying and selling goods. However, the UCC distinguishes merchants from regular buyers and sellers (see Exhibit 21-3); thus it contains provisions that either (1) apply only to merchants or (2) impose greater duties on merchants. The drafters of the UCC assumed that merchants have a greater ability to look out for themselves than do ordinary buyers and sellers.

UCC Section 2-104(1) defines a **merchant** as "a person who deals in goods of the kind, or otherwise by his occupation, holds himself out as having knowledge or skill peculiar to the practices or goods involved in the transaction, or to whom such knowledge or skill may be attributed by his employment of an agent or broker or other intermediary who, by his occupation, holds himself out as having such knowledge or skill."

Case 21-2 considers the questions of whether a particular person is a merchant and, if so, what impact this merchant status has on a dispute about who owns certain goods. In this case, the goods in question were paintings.

CASE 21-2 DEWELDON, LTD. v. MCKEAN

U.S. DISTRICT COURT FOR THE DISTRICT OF RHODE ISLAND

125 F.3D 24 (1997)

This case arose after Felix DeWeldon, a well-known sculptor and art collector, sold three paintings to Robert McKean in 1994.

Felix DeWeldon declared bankruptcy in 1991. In 1992, DeWeldon, Ltd., purchased all Felix DeWeldon's personal property from the bankruptcy trustee. After this purchase, the director of DeWeldon, Ltd., entrusted the paintings to Felix DeWeldon as custodian. DeWeldon, Ltd., did nothing to make it clear Felix DeWeldon did not own the paintings. For example, DeWeldon, Ltd., did not put a sign on the premises of Beacon Rock, Felix DeWeldon's home in Newport, Rhode Island, nor did DeWeldon, Ltd., tag or label the paintings themselves.

In 1993, Nancy Wardell, the sole shareholder of DeWeldon, Ltd., sold all of her DeWeldon, Ltd., stock to the Byron Preservation Trust. This trust sold Felix DeWeldon an option to repurchase the paintings and a contractual right to continue to retain possession of the paintings until the option expired.

In 1993, DeWeldon, Ltd., sued Felix DeWeldon, seeking possession of the paintings, but was unsuccessful because of the option to repurchase and right of possession. The court enjoined Felix DeWeldon from transferring or removing the paintings from Beacon Rock. The paintings that became the subject of this lawsuit never left Beacon Rock until McKean bought them in 1994.

The question in this case is whether DeWeldon, Ltd., can recover the three paintings it had entrusted to Felix DeWeldon, or, alternatively, whether the district court correctly ruled in favor of McKean, the buyer.

SENIOR CIRCUIT JUDGE HILL: As a general rule, a seller [in this case Felix DeWeldon] cannot pass better title than he has himself. Nevertheless, the Uniform Commercial Cole (UCC) as adopted by Rhode Island provides that an owner [in this case DeWeldon, Ltd.] who entrusts items to a merchant who deals in goods of that kind gives him or her the power to transfer all rights of the entruster to a buyer in the ordinary course of business. . . .

In order for McKean to be protected . . . , DeWeldon, Ltd. must have allowed Felix DeWeldon to retain possession of the paintings. McKean must have bought the paintings in the ordinary course of business. He must have given value for the paintings, without actual or constructive notice of DeWeldon Ltd.'s claim of ownership to them. Finally, Felix DeWeldon must have been a merchant as defined by R.I. Gen. Laws Sec. 6A-2-104. Under this section, a merchant is one who has special knowledge or skill and deals in goods of the kind or "otherwise by his or her occupation holds himself out as having knowledge or skill peculiar to the practices or goods involved in the transaction. . . ." . . . [The court then resolves the preceding factual issues in McKean's favor before looking at the merchant issue.]

. . . Felix DeWeldon acted as a merchant within the meaning of the Rhode Island Commercial Code. Under the Code, "merchant" is given an expansive definition. . . . The Code provides that a merchant is "one who . . . by his occupation holds himself out as having knowledge or skill peculiar to the practices . . . involved in the transaction . . ." R.I. Gen. Laws Sec. 6A-2-104. Comment 2 to this section notes that "almost every person in the business world would, therefore, be deemed to be a 'merchant.'" . . .

The entrustment provision of the UCC is designed to enhance the reliability of commercial sales by merchants who deal in the kind of goods sold. . . . It shifts the risk of resale to the one who leaves his property with the merchant. . . . The district court found that Felix DeWeldon was a "well-known" artist whose work was for sale commercially and a "collector." There was art work all over Felix DeWeldson's home. He had recently sold paintings to a European buyer. By his occupation he held himself out as having knowledge and skill peculiar to art and the art trade. McKean viewed him as an art dealer.

We conclude from these facts that Felix DeWeldon was a "merchant" within the meaning of the entrustment provision of the UCC as adopted by the Rhode Island Commercial Code.

When a person knowingly delivers his property into the possession of a merchant dealing in goods of that kind, that person assumes the risk of the merchant's acting unscrupulously by selling the property to an innocent purchaser. The entrustment provision places the loss upon the party who vested the merchant with the ability to transfer the property with apparently good title. The entrustor in this case, DeWeldon, Ltd., took that risk and bears the consequences.

DeWeldon, Ltd. entrusted three paintings to the care of Felix DeWeldon. Felix DeWeldon was a merchant who bought and sold paintings. Robert McKean was a purchaser in the ordinary course of business who paid value for the paintings without notice of any claim of ownership by another. Under the law of Rhode Island, McKean took good title to the paintings. . . .

AFFIRMED.

CRITICAL THINKING

In Chapter 1, you learned of the importance of a particular set of facts in determining the outcome of a case. If you could change one fact in this case to make it more likely that the judge would rule in favor of DeWeldon, Ltd., which fact would you change? Explain.

ETHICAL DECISION MAKING

Apply the universalization test to the outcome of this case. Does the universalization test support Judge Hill's decision?

In Case 21-2, we see another feature of merchant status. Felix DeWeldon was a merchant because, by his occupation as an artist, he held himself out as having knowledge or skill peculiar to the paintings. Under Rhode Island's commercial code, one who entrusts goods to a merchant (DeWeldon, Ltd., entrusted the paintings to Felix DeWeldon) assumes the risk that the merchant will act unscrupulously and sell the goods to an innocent third party (McKean). The result of this entrustment was that McKean got to keep the paintings. If Felix DeWeldon had not been a merchant, DeWeldon, Ltd., would have won the case.

At this point, be thinking of questions about merchants as they relate to the transaction between the Petersons, Migro Seed Company, and John Sandall. Specifically, can any part of UCC Section 2-104(1) be used to argue that John Sandall is a merchant; what about the Petersons? Also, consider the possibility that if the Petersons are merchants, a court will assume that the Petersons need less protection than they would if they had been nonmerchant buyers of the seeds. There is no question, it seems, that Migro Seed Company is a merchant. However, if the Petersons sue John Sandall as well, is he a merchant and subject to a higher standard of care? If the Petersons are merchants, then as merchants in the business of farming, should they have known that their sandy soil, rich in silica, could pose a problem? These are all questions whose answers could depend on whether merchant status is conferred on any of these parties.

ARTICLE 2(A) OF THE UCC

Every state except Louisiana has adopted Article 2 of the UCC. Article 2(A) covers contracts for the lease of goods. This section of the UCC is increasingly important, as consumers (both individuals and businesses) are more likely to lease goods today than ever before. Consumers lease cars, equipment, and machines. This article does not cover leases related to real property.

Leases. UCC Section 2A-103(j) defines a **lease** as "a transfer of the right to possession and use of goods for a term in return for consideration." A **lessor** is "a person who transfers the right to possession and use of goods under a lease."[3] A **lessee** is "a person who acquires the right to possession and use of goods under a lease."[4] Thus, if you lease a car, the company that leases the car to you (the lessor) transfers the right of possession and use of the car to you (the lessee) in return for consideration (money). If, as part of the contract with Migro Seed Company, the Petersons had leased a machine that plows the fields and plants the seeds, the Petersons would have been lessees for that equipment rather than purchasers.

Special kinds of leases. Two special kinds of leases are consumer and finance leases. A **consumer lease** is a lease (1) that has a value of $25,000 or less and (2) that exists between a lessor regularly engaged in the business of leasing or selling and a lessee who leases the goods primarily for a personal, family, or household purpose.[5] The UCC offers protections to consumers who sign lease agreements. For example, in some situations consumers may recover attorney fees if the lessor subjects them to an unconscionable lease.

A **finance lease** is complicated by the addition of a third person—a supplier or vendor who plays a separate role from that of the lessor. In a finance lease, the lessor does

[3] UCC § 2A-103(p).
[4] UCC § 2A-103(o).
[5] UCC § 2A-103(1)(e).

global context

Regulation of Leases in China

In recent years, China's legislators have worked to enhance and clarify the country's commercial code. Currently, China has legislation that covers the sale of goods and the supply of services. The country does not, however, have legislation that covers leases.

Recently, China's Law Reform Commission has recommended that China regulate leasing companies. This commission believes that a statute delineating the obligations of lessors and lessees involved in lease agreements will protect Chinese consumers, who currently seek remedies through the country's common law. Legal costs in China prohibit many consumers from filing complaints.

The proposed law covers a range of business services, including home decoration and rentals of videos, cars, dinner jackets, wedding dresses, and machinery. The committee is especially concerned about the number of consumer complaints related to home renovation and wedding dress rentals.

Source: Quinton Chan, "Increased Consumer Protection Considered," *South China Morning Post,* December 18, 2000.

not select, manufacture, or supply the goods. Rather, the lessor acquires title to the goods or the right to their possession and use in connection with the terms of the lease.[6] For example, suppose that, because of the particularly sandy soil, the Petersons needed a special type of machine to plow the fields and spread the seeds and they decided to lease the machine, rather than buy it from Migro. Further suppose that the Petersons asked Migro to design the machine and then asked the bank to buy the machine and subsequently lease it to them. The Petersons would be the lessees, the bank would be the lessor (also called the *financer*), and Migro Seed Company would be the supplier. The UCC outlines the specific duties and rights of all three parties to finance leases.

How Sales and Lease Contracts Are Formed under the UCC

In Part Two of this textbook, you studied the common law of contracts, from the rules for agreements to the remedies for breaches. Sales and lease contracts require the same components as general contracts, but some UCC provisions that govern contracts for the sale or lease of goods are not identical to the common law requirements you learned about in Part Two. This section highlights the most important provisions of the UCC with regard to the formation of sales and lease contracts.

FORMATION IN GENERAL

Contracts for the sale or lease of goods may be made in any manner sufficient to show agreement.[7] Courts are willing to consider the conduct of the parties to determine whether a contract exists. Contracts for the sale or lease of goods may also be formed even though some terms of the contract or lease are left open.[8] A court will uphold a contract for the sale or lease of goods as long as the parties intended to make a contract and there is a reasonably certain basis for giving an appropriate remedy.[9]

[6] UCC § 2A-103(1)(g).
[7] UCC §§ 2-204(1) and 2A-204(1).
[8] UCC §§ 2-204(3) and 2A-204(3).
[9] Ibid.

Exhibit 21-4 The UCC and Open Terms

TERM LEFT OPEN	INTERPRETATION UNDER UCC
Price	A "reasonable price" is supplied at the time of delivery.
Payment	Payment is due at the time and place at which the buyer is to receive the goods.
Delivery	The place for delivery is the seller's place of business.
Time	The contract must be performed within a reasonable time.
Duration	The party that wants to terminate an ongoing contract must use good faith and give reasonable notification.
Quantity	Courts generally have no basis for determining a remedy.

OFFER AND ACCEPTANCE

Offer. Under the UCC, if certain contract terms are left open, it is acceptable to fill them in. Exhibit 21-4 indicates what generally happens under the UCC when certain terms of a contract or lease are left open. The UCC also creates a new category of offers: the firm offer. Under UCC Section 2-205, offers made by merchants are considered **firm offers** if the offer (1) is made in writing and (2) gives assurances that it will be irrevocable for up to three months despite a lack of consideration for the irrevocability. If a firm offer is silent as to time, the UCC assumes a three-month irrevocability period. This contrasts sharply with the common law, under which an offer is revocable at any time prior to acceptance unless a period of irrevocability (also known as an *option*) is supported by some kind of consideration.

Acceptance. Under the UCC, an acceptance may be made by any reasonable means of communication,[10] and it is effective when dispatched. It is also important to note that the **mirror-image rule** that applies under common law does not apply under the UCC. Recall that the mirror-image rule states that an offeree's acceptance must be on the exact terms of the offer. If the acceptance includes additional terms, the acceptance becomes a counteroffer instead of an acceptance.

Under the UCC, additional terms are permitted in contracts for the sale or lease of goods. Under UCC Section 2-207(1), additional terms will not negate acceptance unless acceptance is made expressly conditional on assent to the additional terms.

In Case 21-3, the court considered a situation in which merchants disagreed about which terms were part of their contract. The court applied UCC 2-207, which states that if both parties are merchants, any additional terms contained in an acceptance become part of the sales contract unless (1) the offer expressly limits acceptance to the terms of the offer, (2) the additional terms materially alter the terms of the original contract, or (3) the offeror notifies the offeree that he or she objects to the additional terms within a reasonable time after receiving the offeree's modified acceptance. Pay particular attention to which part of UCC 2-207 the court applied.

In Case 21-3, the court focused on the materiality of additional terms and demonstrated how courts rule on a case-by-case basis. The court also focused on the precise relationship between the parties to the contract and on the way those parties interacted over time.

[10] UCC §§ 2-206(1) and 2A-206(1).

CASE 21-3 WAUKESHA FOUNDRY, INCORPORATED (PLAINTIFF-APPELLEE) v. INDUSTRIAL ENGINEERING, INCORPORATED (DEFENDANT-APPELLANT)

U.S. COURT OF APPEALS, SEVENTH CIRCUIT
91 F.3D 1002 (1996)

This lawsuit arose when Industrial Engineering, Inc. (Industrial), failed to pay Waukesha Foundry, Inc. (Waukesha), for metal castings Waukesha had supplied to Industrial and Waukesha sought a court's help in collecting the balance due. Industrial and Waukesha were in a business relationship from 1989 until 1993. In particular, Industrial regularly purchased metal castings from Waukesha as part of its manufacture of glass television picture tubes.

Typically, Industrial placed an order for each shipment of castings by placing an order over the telephone, which Waukesha then accepted. Industrial then faxed a confirming purchase order to Waukesha. Although precise facts were in dispute, it was clear that at some point the two made a contract of sale. Both parties behaved as if they were acting according to a series of contracts for the sale of metal castings.

On sixty occasions between 1989 and 1993, Industrial called Waukesha and ordered steel castings. Following each order, Waukesha manufactured and shipped the castings to Industrial. The key question in the case was what the parties agreed to under the contracts. The problem in the case was that the parties exchanged writings that contained different terms. A focal point in the litigation was a packing slip Waukesha enclosed with every shipment of castings. This packing slip outlined the terms and conditions of the sale. After each shipment, Waukesha sent an invoice, which included the same list of terms and conditions of sale as the packing slips.

The language on the packing slips and invoices became relevant because that language placed significant limitations on remedies Industrial could pursue if it was unsatisfied with the metal castings. For example, the packing slip and invoice informed Industrial that, among other things, it had only ten days to report any defects and that the damages that could be claimed were limited. Industrial was, in fact, unsatisfied with several shipments of castings, so it refused to pay Waukesha the full amount due. Industrial failed to report the defects within the time period outlined in the packing slips and invoices, but continued to refuse to pay, arguing that the limitations outlined in the packing slips and invoices were not binding. Waukesha sued to force Industrial to comply with the terms and conditions outlined in the packing slips and invoices.

The United States District Court for the Eastern District of Wisconsin entered summary judgment in favor of Waukesha, and Industrial appealed.

CIRCUIT JUDGE KANNE: . . . Industrial offers several arguments on appeal. It suggests that the circumstances attending the formation and execution of the contract for the sale of castings do not show that it consented to the limited remedies iterated on Waukesha's . . . packing slips, and invoices. Because it did not consent to these additional terms, argues Industrial, it retained default remedies available under the UCC. . . .

. . . Once a contract of sale is established, UCC sec. 2-207 determines whether additional terms are made a part of that contract. In cases involving merchants (such as this one), there are three circumstances that preclude the incorporation of additional terms contained in written confirmation into a contract of sale. It is the second of these three circumstances that is relevant to this appeal, namely, when the additional terms "materially alter" the contract. . . . The district court determined that "courts in Wisconsin and elsewhere generally consider . . . disclaimers and limitations of remedies to be 'material alterations.'" Although the district court cited two cases of potentially persuasive authority for this decision . . . we do not share its interpretation of the term "material."

The district court's analysis appears to assume that certain terms may be per se material without regard to the context in which they are proposed or the course of dealing between the parties. . . . [T]he thrust of our prior decisions analyzing the materiality of additional terms counsels against an across-the-board categorical approach to the materiality question. Instead, we have viewed the question of materiality as invoking an inquiry into the circumstances of the parties' relationship, expectations, and course of dealing. . . .

[CONTINUED]

... An alteration is material if the party against whom it is sought to be enforced would be ambushed by its addition to the contract. In such circumstances, consent to the alteration cannot be presumed.... [H]owever, consent may be presumed from something less than lack of surprise ... our determination of unfair surprise was favorably illuminated by consideration of UCC sec. 1-205, which addresses course of dealing and usages of trade. It is hardly earth shattering that this section should inform our approach to section 2-207 (2), for our discussion above should indicate that the rule of materiality is not ironclad. As we said ... [e]ven if the alteration is material, the other party can, of course, decide to accept it.... Put differently, consent can be inferred from other things besides the unsurprising character of the new term: even from silence, in the face of a course of dealings that makes it reasonable for the other party to infer consent from a failure to object.

The facts in this case that are undisputed lead to the ineluctable conclusion that Industrial consented to the terms and conditions contained in more than four hundred packing slips and invoices it received from Waukesha....

AFFIRMED.

CRITICAL THINKING

The phrase "unfair surprise" is a significant ambiguous phrase. Explain why this phrase matters. Has Judge Kanne defined the phrase well? Can you think of alternative definitions that, if adopted by Judge Kanne, would have led to a different outcome?

ETHICAL DECISION MAKING

By the court's ruling in favor of Waukesha, which ethical norm does the court show it prefers? Which ethical norm does Industrial Engineering, Inc., probably prefer?

CONSIDERATION

Sales and lease contracts require consideration. Under the common law, when a contract is modified, it must be supported by new consideration. The UCC eliminates that requirement for the modification of sales and lease contracts.[11] The UCC requires only that modifications be made in good faith.[12]

REQUIREMENTS UNDER THE STATUTE OF FRAUDS

Under common law, the statute of frauds requires that all material terms to a contract be in writing. Under the UCC, contracts for the sale of goods must be in writing if they are valued at $500 or more;[13] lease contracts that require payments of $1,000 or more must be in writing to be enforceable.[14] There is a significant difference between the statute of frauds and the UCC as to what constitutes a **writing** that satisfies the statute. Common law requires some kind of writing created or signed by the party who is contesting the enforceability of the contract. This rule holds true under the UCC unless the parties are merchants. If two merchants have an oral agreement, a written memo from either party to the other is deemed to satisfy the statute of frauds, even if it is not acknowledged by the receiving

[11] UCC §§ 2-209(1) and 2A-208(1).

[12] UCC § 1-203.

[13] UCC § 2-201(1).

[14] UCC § 2A-201(1).

party. If the memo is not objected to within 10 days of receipt, the oral agreement, memorialized by the memo, is binding.

The UCC outlines three exceptions to the statute of fraud's writing requirements.[15] First, the UCC recognizes an exception for *specifically manufactured* goods. If a buyer or lessee has ordered goods made to meet her specific needs, the buyer or lessee may not assert the statute of frauds if (1) the goods are not suitable for sale or lease to others in the ordinary course of the seller's or lessor's business and (2) the seller or lessor has either substantially begun the manufacture of the goods or made commitments for their procurement. Second, the UCC recognizes an exception when parties *admit* that a sales or lease contract was made. Specifically, if a party to an oral sales or lease contract admits in pleadings, testimony, or court that he agreed to a contract or lease, that party cannot assert the statute of frauds against the enforcement of the oral contract. The lease or sales contract is not enforceable beyond the quantity of goods admitted. Third, the UCC includes a *partial-performance* exception. An oral sales or lease contract is enforceable to the extent that payment has been made and accepted or goods have been received and accepted.

In Case 21-4, the court applied the partial-performance exception to the statute of frauds. When considering whether to enforce an oral contract, a court looks at the extent to which the parties have performed their obligations under that contract. In Case 21-4, the court wanted to protect the reliance of Monetti, the performing party. It did so by enforcing the oral contract.

[15] UCC §§ 2-201(3) and 2A-201(4).

CASE 21-4

MONETTI, S.P.A., AND MELFORM U.S.A., INC., PLAINTIFFS-APPELLANTS v. ANCHOR HOCKING CORPORATION, DEFENDANT-APPELLEE

U.S. DISTRICT COURT, E.D. PENNSYLVANIA
931 F.2D 1178 (1991)

The plaintiff, Monetti, is an Italian firm that makes decorative plastic trays and related products for the food service industry. It began negotiations with the Schneiders, a father and son who owned a U.S.-based company that was in the food products importing business. During the negotiations, the defendant in this case, the Anchor Hocking Corporation, bought out the Schneiders. The defendant employed the Schneiders for a while after the purchase and then fired them abruptly. Based on negotiations with the Schneiders and the subsequent negotiations with Anchor Hocking, Monetti claims, among other things, that it has a contract for the buying and selling of its products with Anchor Hocking. The claim is based upon the existence of certain memos sent by Monetti to the Schneiders and then to Anchor Hocking. At issue is the timing of the memos in relationship to the creation of the alleged contract, and whether those memos satisfy the UCC's Statute of Frauds provisions.

CIRCUIT JUDGE POSNER: . . . Can a memo that precedes the actual formation of the contract ever constitute the writing required by the statute of frauds? Under the Uniform Commercial Code, why not? Its statute of frauds does not require that any contracts "be in writing." All that is required is a document that provides solid evidence of the existence of a contract; the contract itself can be oral. Three cases should be distinguished. In the first, the precontractual writing is merely one party's offer. We have held, interpreting Illinois' version of the Uniform Commercial Code, that an offer won't do. Otherwise there would be an acute danger that a party whose offer had been rejected would nevertheless try to use it as the basis for a suit. The second case is that of notes made in preparation for a negotiating session, and this is another plausible case for holding the statute unsatisfied, lest a breakdown of contract negotiations become the launching pad for a suit on an alleged oral contract. Third is the case—arguably this case—where the precontractual writing—the Schneider memo and the attachment to it—indicates the promisor's (Anchor Hocking's) acceptance of the promisee's (Monetti's) offer; the case, in other words, where all the essential terms are stated in the writing and the only problem is that the writing was prepared before the contract became final. The only difficulty with holding that such a writing satisfies the statute of frauds is the use of the perfect tense by the draftsmen of the Uniform Commercial Code: the writing must be sufficient to demonstrate that "a contract for sale has been made. . . . The 'futuristic' nature of the writing disqualifies it." . . . Yet under a general statute of frauds, "it is well settled that a memorandum satisfying the Statute may be made before the contract is concluded." . . . And while merely because the UCC's draftsmen relaxed one requirement of the statute of frauds—that there be a writing containing all the essential terms of the contract—doesn't exclude the possibility that they wanted to stiffen another, by excluding writings made before the contract itself was made, the choice of tenses is weak evidence. No doubt they had in mind, as the typical case to be governed by section 2-201, a deal made over the phone and evidenced by a confirmation slip. They may not have foreseen a case like the present, or provided for it. The distinction between what is assumed and what is prescribed is critical in interpretation generally.

In both of the decisions that we cited for the narrow interpretation, the judges' concern was with our first two classes of case; and judicial language, like other language, should be read in context. . . .

. . . [S]hortly after the Schneider memo was prepared, Monetti gave dramatic evidence of the existence of a contract by turning over its entire distribution operation in the United States to Anchor Hocking. (In fact it had started to do this even earlier.) Monetti was hardly likely to do that without a contract—without in fact a contract requiring Anchor Hocking to purchase a minimum of $27 million worth of Monetti's products over the next ten years, for that was a provision to which Schneider in the memo had indicated agreement, and it is the only form of compensation to Monetti for abandoning its distribution business that the various drafts make reference to and apparently the only one the parties ever discussed.

This partial performance took the contract out of the general Illinois statute of frauds. Unilateral performance is pretty solid evidence that there really was a contract—for why else would the party have performed unilaterally? Almost the whole purpose of contracts is to protect the party who performs first from being taken advantage of by the other party, so if a party performs first there is some basis for inferring that he had a contract. The inference of contract from partial performance is especially powerful in a case such as this, since while the nonenforcement of an oral contract leaves the parties free to pursue their noncontractual remedies, such as a suit for *quantum meruit* (a form of restitution). . . . [O]nce Monetti turned over its trade secrets and other intangible assets to Anchor Hocking it had no way of recovering these things. (Of course, Monetti may just have been foolish.) The partial-performance exception to the statute of frauds is often explained (and its boundaries fixed accordingly) as necessary to protect the reliance of the performing party, so that if he can be made whole by restitution the oral contract will not be enforced. This is the Illinois rationale . . . and it is not limited to Illinois. . . . It supports enforcement of the oral contract in this case. . . .

REVERSED AND REMANDED.

CRITICAL THINKING

In this case, the judge chose carefully how to word the issue. Step into the plaintiff's shoes and write the issue as Monetti saw it. In other words, if Monetti, through its lawyers, were allowed to state the issue, how would the issue read?

ETHICAL DECISION MAKING

Which primary value does the court's decision show that the court prefers? Which primary value does Monetti probably prefer?

THE PAROL EVIDENCE RULE

The **parol evidence rule** is a legal concept that aims to protect sales or lease contracts that the parties intended to be the final expression of their agreement. The UCC states that when a written agreement exists that is intended to be a final expression, neither party can provide additional evidence that alters or contradicts the written contract.[16] Courts, however, allow the parties to explain or supplement the written contract with either (1) additional terms that are consistent with the terms in the agreement or (2) evidence that helps the court interpret the agreement, including previous conduct of the parties regarding the contract in question (course of performance),[17] the way the parties have interacted in past transactions (course of dealings),[18] and the way others in a specific place, vocation, trade, or industry usually conduct business (usage of trade).[19] Recall that the court in Case 21-3, *Waukesha Foundry, Inc. v. Industrial Engineering, Inc.*, looked at how the parties had interacted in the past when it was deciding which contract provisions to enforce.

When courts interpret sales and lease contracts, they look at a combination of four factors: (1) express terms, (2) course of performance, (3) course of dealing, and (4) usage of trade. If they must, courts prioritize these factors as listed. Consider the Case Nugget.

Case Nugget Course of Dealing and Usage of Trade

Loizeaux Builders Supply Co. v. Donald B. Ludwig Company
366 A.2d 721 (N.J. 1976)

When the defendant building contractor phoned the supply company about the stated price of concrete, the supply company informed the builder that the price would be "adhered to for the year." The builder then put a continuing order in that resulted in concrete being shipped to the builder from February of that year through March of the following year. The phone call had been placed in February. The supply company did not deny any of the facts stated by the builder.

On January 1 in this time period, the stated price of the concrete was increased; the builder was notified of this but did not believe the increase applied to it in light of the phone conversation from the previous February. The builder paid only the "phone call" price, and the supply company sued for the difference. The question was whether the higher price of January 1 applied to the transaction in light of the phone call stating that the lower price would be "adhered to for the year."

In finding for the supply house and awarding the higher price for deliveries after January 1, the court relied on (1) the plain meaning of "adhered to for *the* year" as opposed to "adhered to for *a* year"; (2) the customary practice in the trade for building supply products to be increased on January 1 if they were to be increased at all; and (3) the fact that the builder had had actual notice of the January 1 price increase prior to the deliveries after January 1.

[16] UCC §§ 2-202 and 2A-202.

[17] UCC §§ 2-208(10) and 2A-207(1).

[18] UCC § 1-205(1).

[19] UCC § 1-205(4).

global context

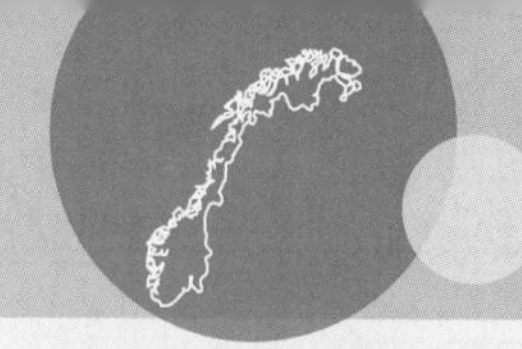

E-Start-Ups in Norway

Countries face different challenges with regard to e-start-ups. In Norway, e-businesses are starting up but not at the same rate as in other countries. E-start-ups from Norway have tended to incorporate outside the country.

One significant challenge e-start-ups face in Norway is that the country's stock market is not as advantageous as nearby stock markets, such as those in Stockholm and London. For example, it is difficult for a company to meet listing requirements for the Oslo Stock Exchange if the company has not yet generated profits. Norway recently relaxed the listing requirements but still requires a net-profit showing.

Another challenge is Norway's tax system. Although this country has one of the lowest corporate tax rates in Europe, certain tax liabilities are problematic for e-start-ups. For example, Norway taxes options to employees at a marginal tax rate of approximately 55 percent. Plus, the company pays a payroll tax of approximately 26 percent on the same benefit.

Finally, some of Norway's laws are not in line with the CISG. One important deviation relates to online agreements. While the CISG holds that an online agreement is binding when the seller has accepted the buyer's offer to buy, Norway's law states that agreement occurs when the buyer's acceptance has reached the knowledge of the seller. Norway is in the process of adopting CISG rules on the conclusion of agreements. By complying with the CISG, it is likely Norway will face fewer obstacles in promoting e-business.

Source: Oyvind Hovland, "Norway," *Corporate Finance,* April 1, 2000.

UNCONSCIONABILITY

You learned about the concept of unconscionability in Part Two. A contract or contract provision is *unconscionable* if it is so unfair that a court would be unreasonable if it enforced the contract. The UCC outlines actions a court can take if it discovers that a contract or lease provision or the contract or lease as a whole is unconscionable.[20] If a court finds that a contract or lease provision or the contract or lease as a whole was unconscionable when it was made, the court either can refuse to enforce the contract or lease or can enforce the parts of the contract or lease that are fair.

Contracts for the International Sale of Goods

THE SCOPE OF THE CISG

You read at the beginning of this chapter that lawyers and legal scholars drafted the UCC in part to facilitate increased commercial transactions across state lines. By the 1970s, it became clear that, increasingly, businesses planned to conduct commercial transactions not only across state lines but also across country borders. In 1980, the **United Nations Convention on Contracts for the International Sale of Goods (CISG)** was offered as a treaty that countries could sign, indicating their willingness to allow this treaty to govern international business-to-business sales contracts. The United Nations CISG treaty provides the legal structure for international sales. Many major trading nations, including the NAFTA[21] nations (Canada, the United States, and Mexico), have signed the CISG. Additionally, many South American and European countries have signed or are considering signing this treaty.

[20] UCC §§ 2-302 and 2A-108.

[21] North American Free Trade Agreement.

Exhibit 21-5
Conflict Avoidance in the Global Economy

Businesses that operate in the global economy try to avoid conflict by asking the following key questions as they form contracts:

- If our business ends up in a dispute with a trading partner, what *language* should govern the dispute?
- In what *forum* should our dispute be resolved?
- Which country's *laws* should apply to the dispute?

After thinking about these questions, businesses create what are known as choice-of-language, forum-selection, and choice-of-law clauses.

THE SIGNIFICANCE OF THE CISG

The CISG is important because if a problem arises with an international sale and a party to the transaction initiates litigation, the UCC does not provide guidance in the litigation; instead, the CISG preempts the UCC. The CISG covers the same general topics as the UCC. For instance, the CISG covers offers, acceptances, and other contract topics. However, specific provisions of the CISG differ from the UCC. For example, the CISG requirements related to the statute of frauds are more lenient than those under the UCC. In particular, the CISG does not require that contracts be in writing.

Businesses that have chosen to operate globally see the CISG as providing the same benefits as the UCC: clarity, predictability, and uniformity. Businesses that create international contracts are increasingly careful to consider the unique context in which they operate. Exhibit 21-5 lists key questions businesses ask as they try to minimize disputes when they transact business in the global economy.

CASE OPENER WRAP-UP

Petersons and Migro

This case illustrates two classic issues that one has to consider when first addressing a potential UCC Article 2 case. One issue is the type of item involved. First of all, is this a contract for the sale of goods? The key concept to remember when answering this question is whether, *at the time of the contract creation,* the items being bought and sold had physical or tangible properties and were able to be moved. Then the second question is, Is the contract *predominantly* for the sale of these goods, as opposed to services and/or real estate? If the answers to these questions are yes, the case falls under Article 2 of the Uniform Commercial Code as opposed to purely common law.

In this case, the answers to these two questions are fairly clear. Yes, the purchase of "seeds" constitutes a purchase of goods. Seeds have physical property and can be moved. Moreover, it is the seeds that were the item being bought and sold at the time that the contract was executed. Since the seeds were the only items bought and sold under the contract, it is a contract for the sale of goods, not real estate or services.

The other issue that this case illustrates is the merchant status of the parties involved. Clearly, since Migro was in the business of selling seeds, Migro was a merchant for UCC Article 2 purposes. But what about the middleman, John Sandall, whose primary business was farming? What of the plaintiffs, the Petersons, whose sole business was farming?

Though ultimately the case did not turn on this issue, the status of farmers poses a perplexing problem for the legal system, because it is one of the areas where the UCC does not fulfill its goals of uniformity and consistency. The 50 states are divided, with some states' courts holding that farmers are not merchants and other states' courts holding that they are. Not surprisingly, many states with strong agriculturally based economies find that farmers are not merchants and thus give a slight advantage to the farmer. How? Being a nonmerchant is an advantage because higher standards are imposed on merchants. The chapter illustrates this in a number of areas, the statute of frauds being one.

In the end, the court found that Migro was liable for the defective seeds. The Petersons were awarded damages determined by the difference between what they earned from the defective crop and what was reasonably expected. A subsequent chapter provides much more detail on the nature of damages and how they are computed.

Summary

The Uniform Commercial Code

Scope of the UCC: The UCC is a uniform or model law that governs commercial transactions, from the sale of goods to secured transactions.

Significance of the UCC: The UCC adds clarity and predictability to sales law.

Articles 2 and 2(A) of the UCC

Article 2 (Sales) covers contracts for the sale of goods.

- *Sale:* The passing of title from the seller to the buyer for a price.
- *Goods:* Tangible things that can be moved.
- *Mixed goods and services contracts:* Contracts that include both goods and services. Courts apply Article 2 if the goods are the predominant part of the transaction.
- *Merchants:* Buyers or sellers who (1) deal in goods of the kind, (2), by occupation, hold themselves out as having knowledge and skill unique to the practices or goods involved in the transaction, or (3) employ a merchant as a broker, agent, or other intermediary. Various provisions of the UCC distinguish merchants from ordinary buyers and sellers.

Article 2(A)(Leases) covers contracts for the lease of goods.

- *Leases:* Transfers of the right to possession and use of goods for a term in return for consideration.
- *Special kinds of leases:* Consumer leases and finance leases. The UCC outlines special rules and protections for each kind of lease.

How Sales and Lease Contracts Are Formed under the UCC

Formation in general: The UCC is more lenient than common law regarding contract formation. Courts look at the intent of the parties to a sales or lease contract.

Offer and acceptance: Offers are valid even if terms are left open. The common law mirror-image rule does not apply to contracts for the sale or lease of goods. Courts look on a case-by-case basis to determine whether to allow additional terms.

Consideration: When sales and lease contracts are modified, these modifications do not need to be supported by new consideration.

Statute of frauds: Contracts for the sale of goods must be in writing if the goods are valued at $500 or more. Lease contracts that require payments of $1,000 or more must be in writing. Exceptions exist for:

- Specifically manufactured goods.
- Contracts that parties admit exist.
- Situations in which partial performance has occurred.

Parol evidence: Courts try to enforce sales and lease contracts as written. Sometimes courts will allow parties to introduce:

- Additional terms that are consistent with contract terms.
- Information that helps interpret the agreement, including course of performance, course of dealing, and/or usage of trade.

Unconscionability: Under the UCC, a court can refuse to enforce the parts of a contract or lease that are unfair or one-sided.

Contracts for the International Sale of Goods

Scope of the CISG: The CISG is a treaty countries can sign to govern international business-to-business sales contracts. Many major trading nations have signed the CISG.

Significance of the CISG: The CISG is important because it, rather than the UCC, governs international sales contracts. The CISG provides clarity, predictability, and uniformity for businesses that operate in the global economy.

Point / Counterpoint

Should Farmers Be Treated as Merchants and Thus Be Held to Higher Standards of Care under the UCC?

Yes	No
The business fact of the matter is that farmers are businesspeople running a for-profit business. To treat them as anything other than merchants would be flying in the face of reality. Moreover, as businesspersons, they should be held to the higher standards the UCC may impose in order to protect nonmerchants with whom farmers may enter into contracts. Treating farmers as nonmerchants smacks of a paternalism arising from the antiquated notion that farmers are agrarian innocents who need government and legal protection from the "big bad corporations" that would otherwise take advantage of them. This view not only is antiquated but is demeaning to the agricultural industry.	A farmer is not the kind of "merchant" that the UCC had in mind at its creation. In defining a merchant as someone who deals in goods of a kind, the inference is that such a businessperson is dealing regularly with similar goods in the stream of commerce. Farming's main function is the growing of food, whether from the ground or from animals. Far more time, and far more time on a daily basis, is devoted to this activity than to the selling of these food products. In fact, most farmers sell crops and animals only at very specific times of the year, and the number of transactions are few. This is not the continuous activity that we think of when we think of merchant activities. Moreover, often the farmer is not selling directly to a nonmerchant consumer but is selling to some kind of

As the agricultural industry has developed, the profile of the farmer being a lone soul on the plains with his wife and family toiling to pull crops out of the ground is a romantic 19th-century fiction. Farming has developed into big business; as such, it should be treated accordingly by the UCC.	agricultural co-op, large distributor, or food manufacturing company. Such buyers are in the daily business of buying and selling and are clearly merchants. Farmers dealing only a couple of times a year with such businesses are not on the same playing field and should not be held to the same standards of care as the UCC identifies.

Questions & Problems

1. This text devotes a lot of attention to the Uniform Commercial Code. What is so significant about the UCC?

2. How are "goods" defined by Section 2-105 of the UCC ?

3. How does the United Nations Convention on Contracts for the International Sale of Goods differ from the UCC in terms of its significance?

4. Thomas Helvey is suing the Wabash County Rural Electrical Company for breach of contract. The electric company caused 135-volt electricity to enter Helvey's home, damaging 110-volt appliances. Helvey brought suit claiming his contract with the electric company falls under UCC Article 2 for the sale of a good. Construct an argument for the plaintiff positing that electricity is a good. Why would this position be beneficial to the plaintiff? Next, construct an argument on behalf of the defendant positing that electricity is not a good under UCC Article 2. Which argument seems more persuasive to you? [*Helvey v. Wabash County REMC,* 278 N.E.2d 608 (1972).]

5. The plaintiff, Betty Epstein, visited a beauty parlor to get her hair dyed. In the dying process, the beautician used a prebleach solution manufactured by Clairol, Inc., and then a commercial dye manufactured by Sales Affiliate, Inc. The treatment went awry, and the plaintiff suffered severe hair loss, injuries to both hair and scalp, and some disfigurement. She sued the beauty salon, Clairol, and Sales Affiliate under Article 2 of the UCC. The defendants claimed that the contract was predominantly for services rather than for the sale of a good. How would you construct arguments supporting each side? What difference does it make whether the beauty treatment is a good or a service? [*Epstein v. Giannattasio,* 197 A.2d 342 (1963).]

6. An agricultural cooperative sued Carroll Nelson for breach of contract under UCC Article 2. Nelson was a Texas wheat farmer and had an oral contract with the cooperative for the purchase of his wheat. The cooperative had forwarded to Nelson a written confirmation of the agreement, but Nelson did not acknowledge or sign any confirmation. When the cooperative initiated the lawsuit, Nelson raised the statute of frauds as a defense. He claimed that because he was not a merchant, a signed memorandum with his signature of some sort was needed for the contract to be enforceable. The cooperative claimed that because Nelson was a merchant, the unobjected-to memorandum satisfied the statute of frauds for agreements between merchants. Is farmer Nelson a merchant? [*Nelson v. Co-operative Exchange,* 548 S.W.2d 352 (1977).]

7. Anthony J. Ruzzo, Sr., entered into an agreement with LaRose Enterprises, which engages in business under the name Taylor Rental Center (Taylor), for the use of a plumbing tool known as a "power snake." While Ruzzo was using the power snake, it malfunctioned, and he was shocked severely and suffered serious personal injuries. What kind of agreement exists between Ruzzo and Taylor, and how might the kind of agreement affect the case? [*Ruzzo v. LaRose Enterprises,* 748 A.2d 261 (2000).]

8. Consider a transaction that has three parties: (1) J.W.C.J.R. Corp. (JWCJR) and its owner, John W. Cumberledge, Jr. (Cumberledge), (2) Bottomline Systems, Inc. (Bottomline), and (3) Colonial Pacific Leasing Corp. (Colonial Leasing). JWCJR/Cumberledge, an autobody shop and its owner, sought a computer and software package that would allow the shop to generate estimates for insurance companies and improve the way the shop was managed. Bottomline demonstrated a computer and software system to JWCJR/Cumberledge. JWCJR/Cumberledge decided to obtain the system Bottomline demonstrated and subsequently entered into an agreement with Colonial Leasing. Colonial Leasing then purchased equipment from Bottomline. JWCJR/Cumberledge agreed to make payments to Colonial Leasing. What kind of lease do these facts indicate? If the computer system does not work, why does it matter what kind of lease exists? [*Colonial Pacific Leasing Corp. v. JWCJR Corp.,* 977 P.2d 541 (1999).]

9. The purchaser, American Parts, Inc., negotiated with the seller, Deering Milliken, for the purchase of fabric. After oral negotiations, Deering Milliken forwarded to the purchaser a written confirmation of the order stating a price of $1.75 per yard. American Parts responded with a written memo stating that it could not agree to anything more than $1.50 per yard. The seller did not respond. The seller began shipping goods to the purchaser, who accepted them. The dispute in the case is whether the contract is for $1.75 or $1.50 per yard. How could you construct an argument for each party? [*American Parts, Inc., v. American Arbitration Association,* 154 N.W.2d 5 (1967).]

10. Wisconsin Knife Works, having some unused manufacturing capacity, decided to try to manufacture spade bits for sale to its parent, Black & Decker, a large producer of tools, including drills. A spade bit is made out of a chunk of metal called a *spade bit blank,* and Wisconsin Knife Works had to find a source of supply for these blanks. National Metal Crafters was eager to supply the spade bit blanks. After some negotiating, Wisconsin Knife Works sent National Metal Crafters a series of purchase orders. On the back of each purchase order was printed "Acceptance of this Order, either by acknowledgement or performance, constitutes an unqualified agreement to the following." A list of "Conditions of Purchase" followed, of which the first was "No modification of this contract shall be binding upon Buyer [Wisconsin Knife Works] unless made in writing and signed by Buyer's authorized representative. Buyer shall have the right to make changes in the Order by a notice, in writing, to Seller." The seller met the terms of the first two purchase orders from Wisconsin Knife Works. After the first two orders, National Metal Crafters was late with the deliveries. No delivery date had been specified on the purchase orders, but the delivery dates had been communicated orally between the two parties to the contract. Wisconsin Knife Works claimed that National Metal Crafters breached the contract. National Metal Crafters claimed that it had modified the dates for delivery and that Wisconsin had accepted these dates. What could constitute a binding modification after this contract was formed? [*Wisconsin Knife Works v. National Metal Crafters,* 781 F.2d 1280 (1986).]

11. Utah International, a mining company, entered into a 35-year requirements contract with Colorado-Ute Electric Association, Inc., for the sale of coal. Utah International was to provide all the coal that Colorado-Ute would need in the operation of new electricity generators. Utah International claims that Colorado-Ute built generators that will use far more coal than Utah International is willing to supply and that this breached the contract. Utah International is asking to be released from the contract due to Colorado-Ute's alleged breach. A requirements contract is a contract in which the buyer agrees to purchase and the seller agrees to sell all or up to a stated amount of what the buyer requires. What are the limits placed on a requirements contract? Should this contract be terminated? [*Utah International v. Colorado-Ute Electric Association, Inc.*, 426 F. Supp 1093 (1976).]

12. Edward J. Wagner entered into a contract with Graziano Construction Company to paint and supply materials in connection with the construction of a shopping center by the Graziano company as general contractors. The agreement between Wagner and Graziano provided, in part:

> Without invalidating this contract the Contractor may add to or reduce the work to be performed hereunder. No extra work or changes from plans and specifications under this contract will be recognized or paid for, unless agreed to in writing before the extra work is started or the changes made, in which written order shall be specified in detail the extra work or changes desired, the price to be paid or the amount to be deducted should said change decrease the amount to be paid hereunder.

Wagner claims that the defendant's general superintendent verbally requested that Wagner perform some extra work and supply additional material. The superintendent assured him that such orders did not need to be in writing, despite the provision in the written contract to the contrary. Wagner states that after he performed the new tasks, Graziano refused to pay for the supplemental work and additional materials. Wagner sued Graziano, claiming damages of $5,192.22 (the amount of the extra work and materials). Does the UCC's parol evidence rule apply in this situation? That is, can parol evidence establish the oral contract? [*Wagner v. Graziano Construction Company,* 136 A.2d 82 (1957).]

13. Mitchell Aircraft Spares, Inc. (Mitchell), has filed a lawsuit against European Aircraft Service AG (EAS) asserting claims for breach of contract and breach of warranty. Mitchell, an Illinois corporation, is a broker in the market for surplus aircraft parts. EAS is a Swedish corporation that buys parts from companies in Western Europe and the United States and sells these parts to a wide variety of purchasers. At issue is Mitchell's claim that he suffered damages in the amount of $120,000 because EAS sent him integrated drive generators (IDGs) with the wrong part numbers. In Mitchell's industry, specific part numbers are important. What law is likely to govern this dispute? Explain. [*Mitchell Aircraft Spares, Inc. v. European Aircraft Service AB,* 23 F. Supp. 2d 915 (1998).]

Looking for more review material?

The Online Learning Center at **www.mhhe.com/kubasek1e** contains this chapter's "Assignment on the Internet" and also a list of URLs for more information entitled "On the Internet." Find both of them in the Student Center portion of the OLC, along with quizzes and other helpful materials.

Title, Risk of Loss, and Insurable Interest

CASE OPENER

Diamonds in Bloom

Charles Bloom & Company of New York (Charles Bloom) was founded in 1979 to engage in diamond sales to retailers and individual customers. The company, which is located on Fifth Avenue in New York City, emphasizes customer service. The principles of knowledge, honesty, and cordial business underlie Charles Bloom's transactions with both retailers and individual customers.

Charles Bloom's logo is "a perfect rose blooming with a diamond in its center."[1] This logo, known as *Diamonds in Bloom,* is designed to create an image of delicate strength. The logo symbolizes "the Diamonds in Bloom philosophy: provide friendly, personalized service and offer solid experience and quality merchandise."[2] Hillary Rodham Clinton has worn Diamonds in Bloom to promote breast cancer awareness.[3]

Although Charles Bloom prides itself on customer service, some of its customers have not returned the courtesy. In the early 1990s, Charles Bloom was forced to sue one of its retail customers, Echo Jewelers, after Echo filed for bankruptcy without returning diamonds it had obtained from Charles Bloom and without compensating Charles Bloom for the diamonds.

Charles Bloom had entered into a business relationship with Mark LaMotta and Richard Giadosz, owners of Echo Jewelers. Charles Bloom would deliver diamonds to Echo via the use of a memorandum, which contained a description of each diamond, including each diamond's weight and price. The memorandum stated:

> The goods described and valued below are delivered to you for EXAMINATION AND INSPECTION ONLY and are the property of CHARLES BLOOM AND COMPANY and subject to their order and shall be returned to them on demand. Such merchandise, until

[1] www.diamondsinbloom.com.

[2] Ibid.

[3] Ibid.

CHAPTER 22

returned to them and actually received, are at your risk from all hazards. NO RIGHT OR POWER IS GIVEN TO YOU TO SELL, PLEDGE, HYPOTHECATE OR OTHERWISE DISPOSE OF THIS MERCHANDISE regardless of prior transactions. A sale of this merchandise can only be effected and title will pass only if, and when, the said CHARLES BLOOM AND COMPANY shall agree to such sale and a bill of sale rendered therefor.

Charles Bloom engaged in a course of dealings with Echo Jewelers beginning in 1985. Charles Bloom stopped delivering diamonds to Echo in 1990 and began assessing a finance charge against Echo's account. It turns out that Echo continually accepted diamonds from Charles Bloom, kept them, and incorporated them into jewelry without paying for the diamonds. By the time Echo filed for bankruptcy, it did not know where Charles Blooms' diamonds were located, and it stated that the diamonds "got eaten up in the course of doing business . . . over the years."[4] Charles Bloom sued LaMotta and Giadosz, claiming that the owners of Echo Jewelers had converted the diamonds in question. Charles Bloom asked the court for damages, including the finance charges in arrears.

1. What kind of sales contract had Charles Bloom established with LaMotta, Giadosz, and their company, Echo Jewelers?
2. In terms of the damages Charles Bloom is seeking, what is the significance of the sales contract between Charles Bloom and Echo Jewelers?
3. Did title to the diamonds remain with Charles Bloom, or had it passed to Echo Jewelers?

The Wrap-Up at the end of the chapter will answer these questions.

[4] 652 A.2d 1238, 1241.

Learning Objectives

After reading this chapter, you will be able to answer the following questions:

1 What is the concept of title? How does it pass?

2 What is risk of loss?

3 What is insurable interest?

4 What are the different kinds of sales contracts, and how does each type affect title passing, risk of loss, and insurable interest?

When Charles Bloom engages in business transactions with both retailers, such as Echo Jewelers, and individual customers, the company needs to know its rights and responsibilities. In particular, Charles Bloom needs to know the UCC's rules regarding title, risk of loss, and insurable interest. This chapter explains these three concepts. It does so in the context of different kinds of sales contracts, including simple delivery, common-carrier delivery, goods-in-bailment, and conditional sales contracts.

The Concept of Title

The UCC defines a **sale** as the passing of title from the seller to the buyer for a price. However, this definition does not indicate the relationship between *passing title* and *ownership.* Suppose, for example, that you are the owner of a jewelry store that wants to buy 20 diamonds from Charles Bloom & Company. The deal includes a list of diamonds, with descriptions and a price for each diamond. Delivery is to be within one month.

This looks like a pretty straightforward deal—description of goods, quantity, price, time of delivery—but it is not. It does not tell the parties:

- When the buyer can resell the goods to a third party.
- When insurance on the goods can be purchased.
- When the goods become part of the buyer's inventory and can serve as collateral for a loan.

In addition, there is no indication of who takes the loss if the goods are damaged before delivery, during possession by the seller, or in transit.

Each of these issues needs to be considered before the owner of the goods can be established. Generally, the party with "good title" to the goods has ownership: You cannot own goods unless you have good title to them. This chapter discusses acquiring good title as well as the other topics listed above.

THREE KINDS OF TITLE

There are three kinds of title: good title, void title, and voidable title. First, **good title** is title that is acquired from someone who already owns the goods free and clear. Next, **void title** is not true title. Someone who purchases stolen goods, knowingly or unknowingly, has void title. Finally, **voidable title** occurs in certain situations where the contract between the original parties would be void but the goods have already been sold to a third party. The next few sections of the chapter discuss these types of title in detail.

Acquiring Good Title

The most obvious way of attaining good title is acquiring it from someone who has good title, that is, the person who owns it free and clear, without any qualifications. In contrast, someone who has come into possession of stolen goods never has good title and can never pass a good title. A person in possession of stolen goods has void title.

However, problems may arise when someone thinks he or she has good title but actually has void title. Consider Case 22-1, which concerns the sale of a stolen vehicle and whether a car dealership's title was voidable or void.

The key point to remember, which many people misunderstand, is that good faith is actually irrelevant when passing a void title. If a person has a void title (as in the best, and most frequent, example: a person has possession of stolen goods), then no matter how honorable the intentions of the seller are, that good-faith seller cannot pass anything to the buyer but another void title. The only exception to this is the entrustment situation, which is discussed later in the chapter.

CASE 22-1 ALFONSO CANDELA, APPELLANT, v. PORT MOTORS, INC., RESPONDENT, ET AL., DEFENDANT

SUPREME COURT OF NEW YORK, APPELLATE DIVISION, SECOND DEPARTMENT
208 A.D.2D 486; 617 N.Y.S.2D 49 (1994)

Candela purchased a car for approximately $19,000 from Port Motors, Inc. The police later seized the car, claiming that it may have been stolen. Candela brought suit against Port Motors for breach of warranty of title. Port's defense was that it indeed passed a good title to Candela.

New York's Supreme Court, which is New York's trial court level, granted Port Motors' motion for summary judgment, agreeing with Port that the car dealer had "voidable" title. In the decision below, the appellate court decides whether Port Motors' title was merely voidable, or whether it was void. The significance of the decision is that if Port Motors purchased the vehicle from a thief, or from the successor to a thief, Port's title would be void, and it could not have conveyed good title to Candela.

MEMORANDUM BY JUDGES BRACKEN, BALLETTA, COPERTINO, AND HART: In his complaint, the plaintiff alleged that the defendant, Port Motors, Inc., (hereinafter Port) sold him a 1988 Lincoln Town Car for $19,067. The complaint further states that Port knew, or should have known, that it did not have valid title to the Lincoln Town Car, and that this car was later seized by officers of the Nassau County Police Department as a "suspected stolen vehicle."

In support of its motion for summary judgment, Port offered evidence which tended to show that it had no knowledge of the car's having been stolen prior to its purchase from a wholesaler, Joseph Scaffadi. The plaintiff, in opposing Port's motion, produced a "police investigative report" which details the circumstances which led police officers to suspect that the car was in fact stolen. The court granted Port's motion, and the instant appeal ensued. We reverse.

Contrary to Port's contention, the plaintiff would be entitled to recover damages based on Port's violation of his warranty of title if the subject vehicle is proved to have been stolen from its original owner. . . . For the purposes of applying UCC 2-403(1), a car thief is not a "purchaser," and if it is proven that Port purchased the vehicle from an actual car thief, or from the successor in interest to a car thief, then Port's title would be void, and not merely "voidable." Thus, if it were proven that Port purchased the vehicle from a thief, or from the successor of a thief, Port could not convey good title to a subsequent purchaser for value, pursuant to UCC 2-403(1). . . .

Whether the Lincoln Town Car purchased by the plaintiff was in fact a stolen vehicle is thus a material issue to be decided at trial. Port failed to adduce proof sufficient to warrant the conclusion that, as a mater of law, the subject vehicle had not been stolen, as alleged in the plaintiff's complaint. The Supreme Court therefore erred in granting summary judgment to Port.

REVERSED.

[CONTINUED]

CRITICAL THINKING

The appellate court reversed the trial court's decision to grant a summary judgment to Port. Candela is going to have the opportunity to have a court rule on whether Port Motors passed good title to him. What key facts will determine whether the title was void or voidable?

ETHICAL DECISION MAKING

Why would Port Motors, Inc., fight Candela in court? Shouldn't the car dealer want to make its customers happy? What ethical norm must be underlying Port Motors' behavior in contesting Candela's claim?

VOIDABLE TITLE

When a seller transfers goods to a buyer, normally the buyer gets good title. However, the buyer gets only voidable title if any of the following apply:

- The buyer has deceived the seller regarding his or her true identity.
- The buyer has written a bad check for the goods.
- The buyer has committed criminal fraud in securing the goods.
- The buyer and seller agreed that title would not pass until some later time.
- The buyer is a minor.

The first four of these situations that can create a voidable title are articulated in Section 2-403 of Article 2 of the UCC; the final one, the buyer is a minor, comes from common law. A seller who discovers any of these situations has the right to cancel the contract and reclaim the goods, even if they have already been delivered to the buyer. That is why the title is called *voidable.* The Case Nugget presents an example of a situation giving rise to a voidable title.

THIRD-PARTY PURCHASERS AND GOOD TITLE

Problems develop when a buyer with the voidable title turns around and sells the goods to a third-party purchaser. If that third-party purchaser made a good-faith purchase for value (as opposed to receiving the goods as a gift), he or she gets good title, not void or voidable title. See Exhibit 22-1 below.

Here is an example of how voidable title works: Suppose a seller sells a bicycle to a buyer and the buyer pays with a bad check. Before the seller can reclaim the bike, the buyer sells the bike to a third-party good-faith purchaser for value. The buyer then takes off, never to be seen again. The seller cannot reclaim the bike from the third-party purchaser because that party has good title. Although this result may seem unfair, it upholds the philosophy of the Uniform Commercial Code itself: the facilitation of commercial activity. The code believes that good-faith purchasers should not have to look over their shoulders to determine whether a commercial transaction is valid.

Case 22-2 deals with whether good title to a 1968 Chevrolet Camaro has been passed to a good-faith purchaser. The significance of the case is that the court's decision about what kind of title passed to a good-faith purchaser will determine who actually gets possession of the Camaro.

Case Nugget Voidable Title

Landshire Food Service, Inc. v. Coghill
709 S.W.2d 509 (Mo. App. 1986)

Coghill sold his Rolls Royce to Daniel Bellman, who paid him with a cashiers check for $94,500. Coghill transferred title over to Bellman. Bellman turned around and advertised the sale of the car and sold it to Barry Hyken for $62,000, transferring title to Hyken.

In the meantime, the cashiers check given by Bellman to Coghill turned out to be a forgery and was dishonored by the bank. Coghill then reported the car missing and stolen. Three weeks after Hyken took possession and title to the vehicle, the police arrived and seized the "stolen" car. Coghill and Hyken now both claim title to the car. The issue posed is, What kind of title did Bellman have? Did he have a good, voidable, or void title.

In answering this issue, the court ruled:

> [T]he initial question is whether a bona fide purchaser for value takes good title from one who procured the automobile by a fraudulent purchase? The answer is yes. Where the original owner, although induced by fraud, has voluntarily given to another apparent ownership in the motor vehicle, a bona fide purchaser, who has relied upon that person's possession of the certificate of title and of the vehicle, is protected. . . . The person who procures title through fraud receives voidable title and is able to transfer good title to a bona fide purchaser. Although the result may seem harsh, the purpose of this rule is to promote the free transferability of property in commerce.

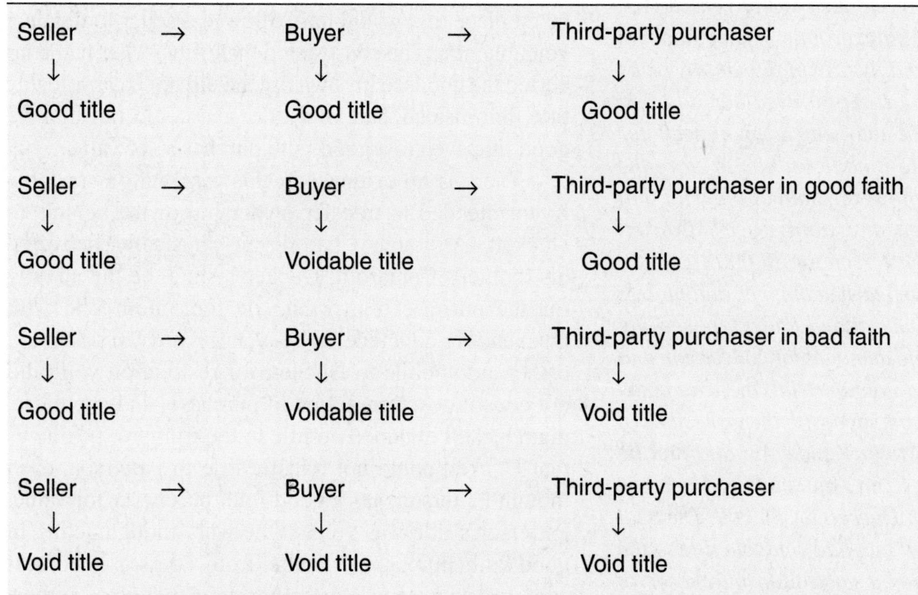

Exhibit 22-1
Who Gets What Kind of Title?

ENTRUSTMENT

If an owner *entrusts* the possession of goods to a merchant who deals in goods of that kind, the merchant can transfer all rights in the goods to a buyer in the ordinary course of business. Recall that in the previous chapter, the case of *DeWeldon v. McKean* presented an

CASE 22-2 GWENDOLYN V. RYAN v. PATTERSON AND SON MOTORS, AND JOE PATTERSON, INDIVIDUALLY

COURT OF CIVIL APPEALS OF ALABAMA
726 SO. 2D 667 (1998)

Gwendolyn Ryan purchased a 1968 Chevrolet Camaro in 1988 for $6,000. In the spring of 1995, with Gwendolyn Ryan's knowledge and consent, Ryan's son Chad and Ernie Duckett towed the automobile to Duckett's shop to perform restorative work on the vehicle. Chad Ryan and Duckett agreed that Duckett would assist Chad Ryan with the restoration of the automobile in exchange for Chad Ryan's assistance with repairs and renovations to Duckett's shop.

Duckett rented the shop premises from Patterson. After several months, Duckett left Patterson's premises and moved vehicles, including the Camaro, to property owned by his uncle. Chad Ryan repeatedly asked Duckett about returning the Camaro, but Duckett kept putting him off. Duckett's story was different. He said he repeatedly asked Chad Ryan to pick up the automobile, but that Chad kept delaying. The Camaro remained in Duckett's possession until June 1996.

In June 1996, Duckett attempted to sell the Camaro pursuant to the Alabama Abandoned Motor Vehicle Act. He published notice of the sale on June 13 and June 20, but he never notified Gwendolyn Ryan personally or by certified mail, nor did he attempt to find her address. On June 24, Duckett sold the vehicle to himself for $1,500, the amount he said it had cost him to store the Camaro. Duckett's uncle, however, said at the trial that he did not charge Duckett any storage fees. Duckett then sold the Camaro to Patterson for $4,000.

When Gwendolyn Ryan learned that her automobile had been sold, she sued Duckett and Patterson, seeking the return of the Camaro and damages for conversion and wrongful detention. After a nonjury trial, the trial court held that Duckett had not complied with the provisions of the Alabama Abandoned Motor Vehicle Act and that he had converted Gwendolyn Ryan's automobile. The court entered a judgment against Duckett for $6,000. The trial court also held that Duckett had had voidable title to the Camaro, that Patterson was a good faith purchaser of the automobile, and that Patterson was entitled to retain possession of the Camaro. Gwendolyn Ryan appeals only from that aspect of the judgment allowing Patterson to retain possession of the Camaro. She contends that delivery of the automobile to Duckett was not a transaction of purchase and that he was merely a bailee and had no title to the Camaro. Therefore, Ryan argues, he could not transfer title to Patterson, even though Patterson was a good faith purchaser for value.

RETIRED JUSTICE BEATTY: . . . A transaction of purchase occurs when there is a delivery of possession from a seller to a buyer with the intent that the buyer become the owner . . . a good faith purchaser of a stolen automobile did not acquire good title because the owner did not consent to the transfer of the automobile to the seller. . . .

[The Uniform Commercial Code] recognizes that a person with voidable title has power to transfer a good title to a good faith purchaser for value. Voidable title can only arise from a voluntary transfer, and the rightful owner must assent to the transfer. "A possessor of goods does not have voidable title unless the true owner has consented to the transfer of title to him." . . . In this case the rightful owner did not consent or assent to the transfer of the automobile . . . the owner's intent [is] critical in determining whether a transaction of purchase had taken place that would have allowed a seller to obtain a voidable title. The court stated that if the seller had converted the goods to his own use, he did not have voidable title, but instead, had void title, and could not transfer good title even to a good faith purchaser for value.

There is no evidence in this case that Gwendolyn Ryan intended to transfer ownership of the vehicle to Duckett. Although Chad Ryan physically delivered his mother's Camaro to Duckett's shop, he did so only for the purpose of working on the automobile with Duckett. We conclude that Gwendolyn Ryan's delivery of her automobile to Duckett for restoration work did not constitute a transaction of purchase, and, therefore, that Duckett obtained no title to the Camaro. It follows that Duckett could not transfer title to Patterson, even though Patterson was a good faith purchaser for value. Patterson's title was void. "One who, though acting in good faith, purchases a chattel from a person in possession, but without title or authority or indicia of authority, from the true owner to sell, acquires as against the true owner, no title, and the latter may maintain trover for its conversion." . . . Because Patterson obtained no title to the Camaro upon its sale to him, Gwendolyn Ryan is entitled to possession of her automobile.

REVERSED.

[CONTINUED]

CRITICAL THINKING

In Chapter 1, you learned of the importance of a particular set of facts in determining the outcome of a case. If you could change one fact in this case to make it more likely the judge would rule in favor of Patterson, which fact would you change? Explain.

ETHICAL DECISION MAKING

Apply the universalization test to the outcome of this case. Does the universalization test support Justice Beatty's decision?

example of **entrustment.** In that case, an owner had entrusted a merchant (a well-known artist) with possession of paintings.

One form of entrustment occurs when someone entrusts the possession of a good (e.g., a car) to a merchant and asks him to repair that good. Suppose the merchant fraudulently or accidentally sells the item as if it were part of his inventory. If the purchaser is a good-faith purchaser (i.e., did not know that the item belonged to someone else and paid a fair market value, not some unreasonable discounted value), then that purchaser gets a good title. The original owner's only recourse is to bring suit against the merchant. Again, the rationale behind this concept is the facilitation of commercial activity regarding good-faith purchasers in the marketplace.

Consider Case 22-3, which asks whether a bank can premise a claim of ownership to certain vehicles on the doctrine of entrustment. This doctrine is available only to buyers in the ordinary course of business. Therefore, key questions in this case are whether Bank One, Milwaukee, is a buyer in the ordinary course of business and whether Bank One meets the definition of good faith.

CASE 22-3 BANK ONE, MILWAUKEE, N.A., PLAINTIFF-APPELLANT v. LOEBER MOTORS, INC., ET AL., DEFENDANTS-APPELLEES

APPELLATE COURT OF ILLINOIS, FIRST DISTRICT, FIRST DIVISION

293 ILL. APP. 3D 14; 687 N.E.2D 1111 (1997)

Bank One engages in the business of leasing automobiles. Bank One has established a relationship with several automobile dealerships, including Loeber Motors, Inc. (the named defendant) and Valet Automobile Leasing, Inc.

Valet Automobile Leasing, Inc., had an oral arrangement with a company called Leased Car Sales (Leased Car) in which Leased Car, a used car dealer, performed Valet's duties under the Valet–Bank One dealer agreement, and Valet presented the lease package to Bank One as if Valet had organized it.

The real trouble in the lawsuit started when Leased Car wrote checks to defendant dealers that bounced. The defendant dealers moved to repossess certain cars that are the subject of this litigation, and Bank One filed suit to seek a declaration as to who rightfully owned the vehicles.

Bank One is claiming good title to the cars in dispute under the concept of "entrustment." To seek protection under the concept of entrustment, Bank One needs to establish itself as a buyer in the ordinary course, which requires Bank One to show it acted in good faith.

Bank One makes its claim of good faith even though it recognized that its leasing business procedures were suspect with respect to Valet.

JUSTICE GALLAGHER: Before the trial court, Bank One premised its claim to ownership of the vehicles on the entrustment doctrine as laid out in the Uniform Commercial Code, which states: "Any entrusting of possession of goods to a merchant who deals in goods of that kind gives him power to transfer all rights of the entruster to a buyer in ordinary course of business. . . . " The doctrine applies only where the following elements are met: (1) an actual entrustment of the goods by the delivery of a possession to a merchant; (2) the party that receives the goods must be a merchant who deals in goods of that kind; (3) the merchant must sell the entrusted goods; and (4) the purchaser must be a buyer in the ordinary course of business. . . . In its summary judgment motion, Bank One argued that the defendant dealers entrusted the automobiles to Leased Car by giving Leased Car possession of the vehicles, that Leased Car was a merchant dealing in goods of that kind, that Leased Car sold the automobiles to Bank One, and that Bank One bought the automobiles in the ordinary course of business. The dealers moved for summary judgment as well, asserting that Leased Car was not a merchant dealing in goods of the kind at issue here, because Leased Car was a used car dealer and not a new car dealer; the dealers also argued that Bank One was not a buyer in the ordinary course.

The trial court granted summary judgment in favor of the defendant dealers. It appeared to premise its holding on the fact that Leased Car was not a merchant that dealt in the sale of new cars, as Leased Car did not hold a state license to sell new cars. However, Bank One later filed a motion to reconsider, and in ruling on that motion the court stated that it had not buttressed its decision solely upon the licensing question. Instead, the trial court suggested that it had also found Bank One not to be a buyer of the vehicles in the ordinary course of business.

On appeal, Bank One contends that it was entitled to summary judgment because the trial court erred when it held that the entrustment doctrine did not apply to make Bank One the rightful owner of the ten vehicles at issue in this litigation. We confine our review to the issues of (1) whether Leased Car Sales was a merchant dealing in goods of the kind at issue in these transactions, and (2) whether Bank One purchased the subject vehicles from Leased Car (through Valet) in the ordinary course of business. . . .

In our opinion, even though Leased Car may have violated state law by selling new cars without a license to do so, it was licensed to sell "goods of the same fundamental nature." Furthermore, the entrustment statute provides that entrusting "includes any delivery and any acquiescence in retention of possession . . . regardless of whether the procurement of the entrusting or possessor's disposition of the goods has been such as to be larcenous under the criminal law." . . . [W]e disagree with the trial court's holding that the entrustment provision of the Uniform Commercial Code did not apply here simply because Leased Car was not a licensed new car dealer.

This court must now determine whether Bank One qualified as a buyer in the ordinary course of business when it purchased these vehicles through Valet from Leased Car. . . . [UCC] 1-201(9) . . . defines a "buyer in the ordinary course of business" as follows:

> [A] person who in good faith and without knowledge that the sale to him is in violation of the ownership rights or security interest of a third party in the goods, buys in [the] ordinary course from a person in the business of selling goods of that kind. . . .

The parties do not challenge this definition of a "buyer in the ordinary course." However, the parties offer competing definitions of "good faith" under the Code. Bank One asserts that "good faith" means honesty in fact in the conduct or transaction concerned. By contrast, the dealers urge that Bank One—itself a merchant—must be subject to the higher standard set forth in the sales article of the Uniform Commercial Code: "'Good Faith' in the case of a merchant means honesty in fact *and the observance of reasonable commercial standards of fair dealing in the trade.*" As an initial matter, then, we shall decide which "good faith" standard applies to the present case.

The Uniform Commercial Code offers the following definition of "merchant":

> [A] person who deals in goods of the kind or otherwise, by his occupation, holds himself out as having knowledge or skill peculiar to the practices or goods involved in the transaction or to whom such knowledge or skill may be attributed by his employment of an agent or broker or other intermediary who, by his occupation, holds himself out as having such knowledge or skill.

Bank One insists that it cannot be considered a merchant in this case because it never held itself out as a "dealer" of cars or as one "having knowledge or skill peculiar" to vehicles. We reject Bank One's position. The record unequivocally demonstrates that

Bank One indeed had "knowledge or skill peculiar to the practices . . . involved in the transactions" that form the basis of this litigation. By its own admission, Bank One has been engaged in the business of leasing automobiles for several years. . . . Having determined that Bank One acted as a "merchant" with respect to these transactions, we find instructive the Official Code Comment to 1-201 (19), which states:

> 'Good Faith' whenever it is used in the Code, means at least what is here stated. In certain Articles, by specific provision, additional requirements are made applicable . . . good faith is expressly defined as including in the case of a merchant observance of reasonable commercial standards of fair dealing in the trade. . . .

Because this case falls under the sales article of the Uniform Commercial Code, we hold that for Bank One to qualify as a buyer in the ordinary course, it must meet the heightened "good faith" standard of a merchant required under that article.

Assuming Bank One purchased these ten vehicles with honesty in fact, we next consider whether Bank One observed reasonable commercial standards of fair dealing in the trade. One aspect of these transactions that this court finds intriguing is that Bank One never paid the full price for the automobiles in question. . . . As aptly stated in a case frequently cited by Bank One, "the amount of consideration is significant evidence of good faith." . . .

We find that, under these facts, by engaging in these transactions Bank One did not observe reasonable commercial standards of fair dealing in the trade.

AFFIRMED.

CRITICAL THINKING

The court considers an ambiguous phrase, *good faith.* Did Bank One argue that it acted in good faith? Using what definition of good faith?

ETHICAL DECISION MAKING

Consider the concept of entrustment. Essentially, entrustment provides that the rightful owner cannot get back the goods if a merchant sells them to a good-faith purchaser. The code seems to be placing the facilitation of commerce above the property rights of an innocent and rightful owner. Is this a legitimate approach? Why or why not?

RECOURSE UNDER THE UCC

The determination of who has good title does not always result in the expected and equitable solution to a problem. For example, suppose you purchased a couch at a furniture store. It is pretty safe to say that once you identify the couch and pay for it, you have "title" to it. Now suppose that when the store attempts to deliver the couch to your home, lightning hits the store's delivery truck and destroys the couch. Is the store legally obligated to replace the couch? Most of us would intuitively answer that it is. After all, you never took possession of the couch. However, as previously noted, *you* have title. Under pre-UCC law, this loss could have fallen on whoever had title at that time—and that person would be you. Under the UCC, if the store is a merchant, the risk of loss remains with the seller until the couch is actually delivered to you.

As a result of these kinds of dilemmas, the UCC breaks up the various issues traditionally correlated with title and treats them separately. Several different issues normally are thought of under the concept of title:

- *Ownership:* When does title actually transfer from the seller to the buyer, since the right to transfer ownership of the goods, whether through a subsequent sale or gift, is tied to title?

- *Encumbrance:* The right to encumber goods as collateral for a debt is dependent on who is holding title. When title passes is important because having title means that one can then sell or encumber the goods. In other words, having title means that one can pass title.
- *Loss:* In regard to the right to indemnification if the goods are damaged, when the risk of loss attaches is important. This is because, regardless of title passing, we need to know the seller's and buyer's responsibility to each other in the event that the goods are damaged or destroyed prior to the buyer's taking complete possession of the goods.
- *Insurable interest:* An *insurable interest* is the right to insure the goods against any risk exposure such as damage or destruction. When an insurable interest is created in the goods is important. Both the buyer and the seller can insure themselves for potential loss, in the event the goods are damaged or destroyed at some point in the transaction. A key point is identifying the earliest time in the transaction that the buyer can claim an insurable interest. The Case Nugget addresses that issue.

Case Nugget — When Does Insurable Interest Arise?

National Compressor Corp. v. Carrow and McGee
417 F.2d 97 (1969)

National Compressor bought a large compressor from Davis, who had bought the compressor from Carrow and McGee. Title to the compressor was not to pass to National Compressor until the compressor was removed from Carrow and McGee's property. Prior to the compressor's being moved (and title passing to National Compressor) a fire broke out at the site, destroying the compressor. National Compressor had already paid the $12,000 purchase price. The issue before the court was whether National Compressor had any kind of insurable interest since clearly title had not yet passed. The defendants claimed that National Compressor had no standing to bring the lawsuit as it had no "interest" in the property since title had yet to pass.

The court ruled otherwise, stating that National Compressor had an insurable and special interest in the good, thus giving it standing to sue. The court ruled:

> Where a third party so deals with goods *which have been identified to a contract* for sale as to cause actionable injury to a party to that contract (a) a right of action against the third party is in either party to the contract for sale who has title to or a security interest or a special property or an insurable interest in the goods; and if the goods have been destroyed or converted a right of action is also in the party who either bore the risk of loss under the contract for sale or has since the injury assumed that risk as against the other. . . .

The buyer obtains a special property and an insurable interest in goods by identification of existing goods as goods to which the contract refers even though the goods so identified are noncomforming and he has an option to return or reject them. Such identification can be made at any time and in any manner explicitly agreed to by the parties. In the absence of explicit agreement identification occurs (a) when the contract is made if it is for the sale of goods already existing and identified. . . .

One very important point to note is that the parties are always free to create a contract that lays out and defines such issues as when title passes and when risk of loss passes. The UCC's rules are essentially the default rules for contracts that do not clearly spell out such provisions.

Let's look at each one of these issues within the context of the four kinds of sales contracts that Article 2 creates.

Types of Sales Contracts

The UCC lays out essentially four broad factual scenarios for the sale of goods:

1. *Simple delivery contract:* A simple delivery contract occurs when the purchased goods are transferred to the buyer from the seller at either the time of the sale or some time later by the seller's delivery.
2. *Common-carrier delivery contract:* This type of contract occurs when the goods are delivered to the buyer via a common carrier, such as a trucking line.
3. *Goods-in-bailment contract:* This type of contract occurs when the purchased goods are in some kind of storage under the control of a third party, such as a warehouseman.
4. *Conditional sales contract:* A conditional sales contract occurs when the sale itself is contingent on approval, for example.

In the sections that follow, this chapter answers questions about ownership, encumbrance, loss, and insurable interest as they relate to these four types of sales contracts.

SIMPLE DELIVERY CONTRACT

With a **simple delivery contract,** the buyer and seller typically execute an agreement, and the buyer leaves with the goods. To most of us, it appears that title, risk of loss, and insurable interest all pass to the buyer at the moment the transaction is consummated and the buyer walks out with the goods. However, under the UCC, there are three distinct steps: (1) Title transfers to the buyer on the goods' being identified to the contract, that is, when the contract is executed; (2) risk of loss transfers to the buyer when the buyer takes possession; and (3) insurable interest is created in the buyer when the goods are identified to the contract, in other words, at the same time that title passes.

But what happens if the buyer comes back later to pick up the goods or arranges to have the seller, or an agent of the seller, deliver the goods at a later time? For the purposes of title and insurable interest, nothing really changes. The dilemma occurs with risk of loss.

Let's suppose a buyer and seller execute a contract in which the seller is going to deliver a refrigerator later in the day to the buyer. Through no fault of the seller, the refrigerator is damaged in a fire at the seller's store. Who has the risk of loss if neither party is at fault? In this case, the issue rests on the seller's status. If the seller is a merchant, as in this instance, the risk of loss remains with the seller until the goods are actually delivered to the buyer. If the seller is not a merchant, the risk of loss remains with the buyer under the rule of **tender of delivery.** Simply put, tender of delivery is the moment the goods were available for the buyer to take. Consider this example: You purchase a dresser at a garage sale, but you want to go home and get your truck so that you can get it home easily. Unfortunately, a car hits the dresser and destroys it. You, the buyer, cannot get your money back because (1) the law does not consider the seller a merchant and (2) you could have taken the dresser with you when you bought it.

Note that the results are different if either party is at fault for the damage. In that case, the responsible person is liable under tort law for the damage caused. Case 22-4 considers who has the risk of loss between an innocent seller and an innocent buyer.

CASE 22-4

EMERY v. WEED
SUPERIOR COURT OF PENNSYLVANIA
343 PA. SUPER. 224; 494 A.2D 438 (1985)

In this case, Emery's son had been making down payments on a Pacer Corvette sports car sold by an automobile dealership owned by Weed Chevrolet (Weed). Emery's son died prior to paying off and taking possession of the car. In the meantime, through no negligence or fault of the automobile dealership, the car was stolen from the dealership. Emery is suing for the return of the monies paid and to cancel the contract. Weed is counterclaiming, stating that it is entitled to keep the down payments, and also to recover damages in the amount of the difference between the purchase price of the Pacer and its market value on the date Emery sought to cancel the agreement. The trial court ruled in favor of Emery, and Weed appeals.

JUDGE SPAETH: . . .With respect to several of these [UCC] provisions, there is no dispute. The parties agree that the Pacer Corvette "suffer[ed] casualty without the fault of either party," . . . and that the casualty was "total" and occurred "before the risk of loss [had] pass[ed] to the buyer." . . . We . . . agree with the trial court that risk of loss had not passed, but we base that conclusion on 13 Pa.C.S. § 2509(c) ("In any case not within subsection (a) or (b), the risk of loss passes to the buyer on his receipt of the goods if the seller is a merchant. . . .")

The item "identified when the contract was made" was the Pacer Corvette identified in the agreement of sale by its serial number. Appellant argues that it was not required by the agreement to deliver that very Pacer because, it asserts, "[e]ach such automobile was identical to all of the others manufactured, down to the details with respect to the paint job and extras." This assertion, however, is not supported by the record, which only shows that all Pacer Corvettes were painted black and silver; as will be recalled, the trial court disallowed testimony as to the effect that all Pacer Corvettes were identical. Quite apart from its identification in the agreement by serial number, the Pacer was identified by being removed from the display showroom, after the agreement was signed, and being covered and locked. From this it may be inferred that there was "a meeting of the minds as to the particular or actual goods designated." This agreement by [seller] and appellee's son that [seller] would deliver the Pacer identified in the contract was in no way affected by the seller's later apparent willingness to provide [buyer] with a different Pacer. [Seller] argues that "the parties . . . did not consider the particular automobile (the Pacer identified in the agreement by its serial number) to be unique. . . ." However, Section 2613 does not require such proof; it only requires that [buyer] establish that the "contract require[d] for its performance [the Pacer Corvette] identified when the contract [was] made." He has done so.

AFFIRMED.

CRITICAL THINKING

Is the court's decision consistent with your commonsense belief about whether risk of loss had passed? Explain how the court used the UCC to reach its conclusion.

ETHICAL DECISION MAKING

Which primary value does the court's decision show it prefers? Which primary value does Weed Chevrolet probably prefer?

global context

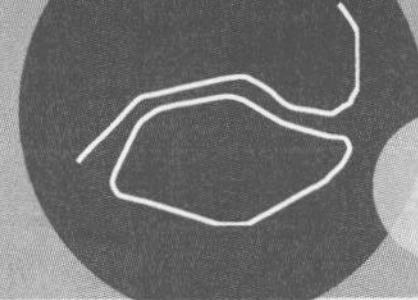

Singapore Takes Steps to Halt Piracy

Singapore and Indonesia recently signed an agreement that allows Singapore-registered ships to hire Indonesian sailors. The agreement will benefit both Indonesian sailors (approximately 10,000 are available for work) and Singapore ship owners, who need workers.

This agreement aims to halt piracy, which occurs when sailors are out of work in a deteriorating economy. Indonesian waters are especially crime-ridden. Last year, one-quarter of the 469 attacks on ships occurred in Indonesian waters. The agreement between Singapore and Indonesia will put Indonesian sailors on Singapore-flagged ships, where the sailors will have new, legal opportunities to support themselves.

Source: Susan Sim, "Maritime Deal Promises to Cut Piracy in Region," *The Straits Times* (Singapore), February 23, 2001.

With a simple delivery contract whereby a seller transfers goods to a buyer without the middle-delivery common carrier, the various interests transfer as shown below. (*Note:* Even if the seller has its agent deliver the goods to the buyer, this is still a simple delivery.)

Simple delivery: seller → buyer

1. Title transfers on identification of the goods to the contract.
2. If the seller is a merchant, risk of loss transfers on delivery of the goods to the buyer; if the seller is not a merchant, risk of loss transfers when the goods are made available for the buyer to possess (tender of delivery).
3. The parties may buy insurance on their goods if they hold title or have any risk of loss or other economic interest.

COMMON-CARRIER DELIVERY CONTRACT

If a buyer and seller execute a contract and the seller subsequently places the goods with a common carrier for delivery to the buyer, the parties have executed a **common-carrier delivery contract.** Note that a common carrier is an independent contractor and not an agent of the seller. What makes the common carrier an independent contractor, rather than an agent, is that the carrier controls the primary aspects of performance, such as how the goods are actually delivered.

The UCC names two kinds of delivery contracts in this category: origin or shipment contracts and destination contracts. *Shipment contracts* require that the seller ship the goods to the buyer via a common carrier. The seller is required to make proper shipping arrangements and deliver the goods into the common carrier's hands. Title passes to the buyer at the time and place of shipment. Thus, the buyer bears the risk of loss while the goods are in transit. *Destination contracts* require that the seller deliver the goods to the destination stipulated in the sales contract. This may be the buyer's place of business or some other location. The seller bears the risk of loss until that time. Case 22-5 discusses the issue of who bears the risk of loss in a case in which the parties disagreed about whether the contract was an origin/shipment contract or a destination contract. See also Exhibit 22-2 below which identifies shipping terms that create the conditions of transit and delivery.

Exhibit 22-2 Shipping Terms Specifying Requirements for Delivery

TERM	EXPLANATION
FOB (free on board)	The selling price includes transportation costs, and the seller carries the risk of loss to either the place of shipment or the place of destination.
FAS (free alongside)	The seller, at seller's expense, delivers the goods alongside the ship before the risk passes to the buyer.
CIF or C&F (cost, insurance and freight; cost and freight)	The seller puts the goods in possession of a carrier before the risk passes to the buyer . Contracts are usually shipment contracts rather than destination contracts.
Delivery ex-ship (delivery from the carrying vessel)	Risk of loss passes to the buyer when the goods leave the ship.

CASE 22-5 PILERI INDUSTRIES, INC. v. CONSOLIDATED INDUSTRIES, INC.

COURT OF CIVIL APPEALS OF ALABAMA
740 SO. 2D 1108 (1999)

In this case, Pileri Industries, the seller, shipped goods via a common carrier to Consolidated Industries, Inc., the buyer. The goods were subsequently lost prior to actual delivery. Pileri claimed the sales contract was a shipping contract and thus the risk of loss had passed to the buyer, Consolidated Industries.

Consolidated Industries disagreed. Consolidated claimed the sales contract was a destination contract, and that the risk of loss remained with Pileri Industries, the seller. The trial court, through a nonjury trial, held that Pileri could not support this assertion that there was a shipping contract and thus held for Consolidated Industries, Inc.

The Court of Civil Appeals held that Pileri, the seller, was not entitled to judgment in a breach-of-contract action, and that Pileri's delivery of goods to the carrier did not entitle Pileri to recover money for the goods shipped. What follows is a portion of the dissent in appellate case.

JUDGE: CRAWLEY, DISSENTING . . . I respectfully dissent because I believe that the trial court erred as a matter of law by entering judgment for Consolidated. . . . [E]ven if Consolidated had established that it never received the November 4 shipment, I would not thereby have proved that it was relieved of its contractual duty to pay for the goods. Under . . . the Uniform Commercial Code, a determination of whether the seller or buyer bears the risk of loss of goods in transit depends on whether the agreement of sale is a "shipment" contract or a "destination" contract.

Under [Article 2 of the Uniform Commercial Code] the "shipment" contract is regarded as the normal one and the "destination" contract as the variant type. . . . Both of these types of contracts usually employ mercantile terms or "trade symbols" specifying the requirements for delivery, such as "F.O.B. the place of shipment," . . . or "F.O.B. the place of destination." *Where no such term is employed and there has been no specific agreement otherwise, the contract for the transportation of goods by carrier will be presumed to be a shipping contract.*

Unlike the majority of this court, I believe that Pileri made a prima facie showing that the contract was a shipment contract and that Consolidated presented no evidence to the contrary. As the main opinion points out, I have, in the absence of Alabama case law on the subject, turned to the construction of the relevant UCC sections by some of our sister states.

In interpreting the UCC we must keep in mind the legislative mandate that is to be . . . applied to promote its underlying purposes and policies, one of which is to make uniform the law among various jurisdictions. . . .

At trial, Pileri introduced a bill of lading indicating that it delivered the goods on November 4, 1992, to Roadway Express for shipment to Consolidated. Mr. Pileri testified that the agreement was a "shipping contract" that required Consolidated to pay the shipping costs and to assume the risk of loss once Pileri had delivered the goods to a common carrier. Pileri stated that it made 14 shipments to Consolidated. It introduced 10 shipping invoices, 6 of which were marked "F.O.B. Farmingdale," Pileri's place of business. For the other four shipping invoices, the "F.O.B." term was left blank.

Although those invoices pertained to a prior agreement of the parties, rather than to the parties' new agreement made on March 30, 1992, they are relevant because they indicate a course of dealing between Pileri and Consolidated. . . . In the absence of any evidence from Consolidated indicating that the agreement was a "destination contract," Pileri was entitled to rely on the presumption established in § 7-2-503, Ala. Code 1975 (Comment 5), that the agreement was a "shipping contract." . . . Here, however, Pileri did more than merely rely on the presumption. Mr. Pileri testified that the "standard procedure" among Government contractors was that, unless otherwise agreed between the parties, the contract was "an F.O.B. contract." Consolidated did not object to Mr. Pileri's testimony on this point. . . . Pileri established Consolidated's liability on an account stated; it also established a breach of a shipment contract by Consolidated. . . . Consolidated presented no evidence either challenging the accuracy of the stated account or disputing Pileri's characterization of the agreement as a shipment contract. Consolidated neither pleaded nor proved the affirmative defense of failure of consideration. The judgment for Consolidated is erroneous as a matter of law and is due to be reversed.

The majority had affirmed; the dissent disagrees.

CRITICAL THINKING

From reading the dissent, can you make any inferences about why the majority must have ruled in favor of Consolidated? Does this case illustrate the significance of who bears the burden of proof?

ETHICAL DECISION MAKING

Which primary value does the dissent's argument show it prefers? Identify and explain a value that clashes with this value.

With a shipment contract whereby a seller transfers goods to a buyer with delivery of the goods effected by a common carrier, the various interests transfer as follows:

Shipment contract: seller → common carrier → buyer

1. If the shipment contract is an origin contract (if the contract is vague or ambiguous, an origin contract will be presumed), the title passes to the buyer when the goods are turned over by the seller to the common carrier.
2. If the shipment contract is a destination contract, the title transfers from the seller to the buyer when the common carrier delivers the goods to the buyer.
3. The risk of loss in either situation—origin or destination contract—transfers from the seller to the buyer simultaneously with the title.
4. An insurable interest is created when the buyer and/or seller holds title or retains a risk of loss.

e-commerce AND THE LAW

The Effect on Port Operators

Globalization and the development of information technology are changing the way port operators conduct their business. According to Ernst Frankel, a professor of ocean systems at the Massachusetts Institute of Technology, ports and terminals are streamlining their management, automating their business operations and production processes, and viewing themselves as part of an integrated system that includes carrier systems.

In the future, it is likely that changes in technology will include integrated ports and shipping lines that offer door-to-door service. Frankel believes that regional and global wireless networks will bring ports, carriers, and shippers together to "maximize operating efficiencies." He states that the factor driving this change is customer need. The bottom line is that the customer wants "knowledge, speed, innovation and quality," and changes in technology are making customer wishes come true.

Source: "Technology Carriers and Operators Learn Integration Lessons," *Lloyd's List International* 6 (March 2, 2001).

GOODS-IN-BAILMENT CONTRACT

Goods in bailment are simply goods that are in some kind of storage (e.g., in a warehouse or on board a ship), so the seller cannot transfer physical possession of them. Instead, the seller has one of three documents indicating ownership of the goods: a negotiable document of title, a nonnegotiable document of title, or a contract or other instrument showing ownership that is not a negotiable or nonnegotiable document of title. If the seller has a negotiable document (i.e., a document containing the words "deliver to the order of [seller]"), then both title and risk of loss transfer from the seller to the buyer as soon as that negotiable instrument is endorsed over to the buyer. On the other hand, if the document is nonnegotiable (i.e., a document lacking the words "to the order of"), then the title passes with the instrument of title but the risk of loss does not pass to the buyer until the bailee (the custodian of the goods) is notified of the transfer or a reasonable time has elapsed since the transaction. Finally, if there is neither a negotiable or nonnegotiable document of title, then the title passes at the time the sales contract is executed but the risk does not pass to the buyer until the bailee is notified of the transaction and acknowledges such notification.

With goods in bailment, the three interests—title, risk of loss, insurable interest—pass in the following way:

> Seller → buyer, but the goods are elsewhere in some kind of storage and in a third party's possession and care.

1. Title passes from the seller to the buyer when the document of title (e.g., a warehouse receipt or a bill of lading) is actually endorsed or signed over to the buyer. If there is no document of title, then title passes when the goods are identified to the contract and the contract is executed.
2. Risk of loss passes to the buyer simultaneously with the document of title provided that the document of title is a negotiable one. If it is nonnegotiable, the risk does not pass until the bailee (the possessor or custodian of the goods) is notified or a reasonable time elapses. If there is no document of title, risk passes to the buyer on notification and acknowledgment by the bailee.
3. Insurable interest is created when either party has title, risk of loss, or other economic interest attached to the goods (e.g., a creditor who secures a loan by taking the goods as collateral).

global context

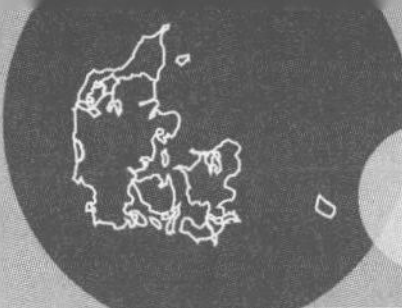

Merger of Denmark's Maersk Line with the United States' Sea-Land

The importance and significance of clear shipping terms in a contract is highlighted when one understands the magnitude of trans-global shipping. For example, Maersk Sealand acquired Sea-Land's international liner operations from CSX Corporation. The new company is now the largest maritime shipping firm in the world. It has a fleet of more than 250 vessels, making it twice as large as The Evergreen Group, the largest Asian carrier.

In spite of the size of Maersk Sealand, Asia is still considered the container shipping hub of the world. Of the top 20 carriers in the world, 11 carriers are Asian, and 6 of the top 10 carriers are Asian.

Some companies, such as The Evergreen Group, are growing on their own, while others, such as Maersk Sealand, are growing by acquiring other companies. It is possible that more container lines will merge in the near future. It remains to be seen which companies and regions of the world will win the battle for market share and position in this industry.

Source: Ira Lewis and Daniel Y. Coulter, "The Voluntary Intermodal Sealift Agreement: Strategic Transportation for National Defense," *Transportation* 40.

CONDITIONAL SALES CONTRACT

Conditional contracts are either sale-on-approval contracts or sale-or-return contracts. A contract is a **sale-on-approval contract** if the seller allows the buyer to take possession of the goods before deciding whether to complete the contract by making the purchase. Title and risk of loss remain with the seller until the buyer notifies the seller about the approval of the contract.

A **Sale-or-return contract** occurs when the seller and buyer agree that the buyer may return the goods at a later time. Such contracts usually occur when the buyer is buying inventory to resell. For example, suppose the seller is a dress wholesaler and the buyer is a retailer who is purchasing the dresses to sell in her store. In their sale-or-return agreement, the insurable interest is created in the buyer once the goods are identified in the contract. Title and risk of loss depend on whether the goods are in bailment, delivered by common carrier, or delivered by the seller himself. Without an agreement to the contrary, if the buyer subsequently returns the dresses, she does so at her own expense and risk.

Consider the Diamonds in Bloom scenario at the beginning of this chapter. The case explains how the relationship between Charles Bloom and Echo Jewelers would have been considered a bailment prior to the rights being refined and explained in the UCC.[5] Recall that Echo held diamonds that it had obtained from Bloom but not yet paid for. Under the UCC, this consignment agreement negotiated between Charles Bloom and Echo Jewelers was a conditional sales contract.

In *Bloom,* the court explained that it was difficult to tell whether the agreement is a sale-or-return or a sale-on-approval because it was difficult to determine what actually happened to the diamonds. The issue mattered because if title had passed to Echo Jewelers, Charles Bloom would not have a cause of action against LaMotta and Giadosz as individual tortfeasors who engaged in conversion. Instead, Charles Bloom would have merely accounts receivable, and its claim would fall under the jurisdiction of the bankruptcy court.

In particular, the court explained that if the goods were sale-on-approval, title would have passed to Echo Jewelers when Echo used any of the diamonds within each consignment. If the goods were sale-or-return, and diamonds were incorporated into settings, Echo Jewelers would have extinguished its option to return the diamonds and the transaction would have become a sale.

[5] *Charles Bloom v. Echo Jewelers,* 652 A.2d 1238, 1243.

However, as this chapter has noted, the parties are allowed to come up with their own terms; the UCC's rules are merely default rules. In the case of Charles Bloom and Echo Jewelers, the court noted that the agreement between the parties was a modified sale-on-approval. The agreement stated that the title to the diamonds would not pass until Charles Bloom agreed to a sale and delivered a bill of sale. The Wrap-Up at the end of the chapter covers the court's final questions.

Risk of Loss during a Breach of Contract

WHEN THE SELLER IS IN BREACH

The failure to deliver goods is the most common way a sales contract is breached. If the seller does not provide the goods that were described in the contract, the buyer may either (1) accept the nonconforming goods as is or (2) reject the goods subject to the seller's curing the deficiency in the goods. The buyer may reject the goods if no cure is possible or the seller fails to cure the deficiency within a reasonable time. In all these instances, the risk of loss remains with the seller until either the buyer accepts the goods or the seller cures the deficiency and provides the buyer with conforming goods.

If a cure is not possible or if the seller has failed to cure the deficiency within a reasonable time, the buyer has the option to revoke the contract. (The remedies will be discussed in subsequent chapters.) However, the UCC creates a disincentive for buyers who do so: If the risk of loss would have transferred to the buyer had there not been a breach, the risk transfers to the buyer to the extent of any insurance the buyer has. The loss reverts to the breaching seller only to the extent that the buyer's insurance does not cover it.

WHEN THE BUYER IS IN BREACH

Most buyer breaches occur when a buyer refuses to accept conforming goods from the seller and then the goods are subsequently lost or damaged. With an origin or shipment contract, the risk would have already transferred to the breaching buyer. However, if the contract is a destination contract, the risk remains with the seller. In order to encourage sellers to create origin contracts, the UCC requires that the risk of loss remain with the seller to the extent of the seller's insurance. If the seller does not have insurance or the loss exceeds the seller's insurance, the remainder transfers to the breaching buyer.

CASE OPENER WRAP-UP

Diamonds in Bloom

As this chapter has explained, the court determined that the agreement between Charles Bloom and Echo Jewelers was a modified sale-on-approval. The agreement said that title passes when Charles Bloom agrees to a sale and delivers a bill of sale.

From the evidence presented in the trial record, the court could not tell when the conversions occurred. When Charles Bloom refrained from asking for the diamonds and instead billed Echo Jewelers and assessed a finance charge, does that mean a sale had occurred, title passed, and Charles Bloom then had accounts receivable? Alternatively, is it possible Echo Jewelers had already converted the diamonds when Charles Bloom sent an invoice, that Charles Bloom did not know of the conversion, and consequently Charles Bloom had never given up its rights to the jewels? Thus, the key questions for the trial court to determine on remand were these: (1) When were the diamonds appropriated, and (2) when did Charles Bloom know the diamonds had been converted?

As in many cases, we do not know what the trial court ultimately ruled. After reading the Diamonds in Bloom Web site, it is likely your sympathies will be with Charles Bloom & Company. It is easy to root for the business that promises to "provide friendly, personalized service and offer solid experience and quality merchandise." Hopefully, the trial court determined that the modified sale-on-approval contract could be interpreted in a way that would make Charles Bloom the victim of conversion with a potential remedy against the tortfeasors, not just another business with accounts receivable it must try to collect from a bankrupt business.[6]

[6] www.diamondsinbloom.com.

Summary

The Concept of Title

There are three kinds of title: good title, void title, and voidable title.

- *Good title* is title that is acquired from someone who already owns the goods free and clear.
- *Void title* is not true title. Someone who purchases stolen goods has void title.
- *Voidable title* occurs in certain situations in which the contract between the original parties would be void but the goods have already been sold to a third party.

Acquiring Good Title

Article 2 of the Uniform Commercial Code covers issues related to acquiring good title.

- The most obvious way to attain *good title* is to acquire it from someone who has good title.
- Someone who has come into possession of stolen goods never has title and can pass only *void title.*
- A buyer gets *voidable title* if he or she has deceived the seller regarding his or her true identity, written a bad check for the goods, committed criminal fraud in securing the goods, or is a minor or if the buyer and seller agreed that title would not pass until some later time.

Third-party purchasers generally get good title. If an owner *entrusts* the possession of goods to a merchant who deals in goods of that kind, the merchant can transfer all rights in the goods to a buyer in the ordinary course of business.

The UCC provides recourse for situations in which good title may not be enough for an equitable result. The UCC responds to issues related to the following:

- *Ownership* refers to transfer of title.
- *Encumbrance* refers to when goods may be used as collateral for a debt.
- *Loss* refers to who has the risk of loss, which matters when someone is seeking indemnification for damaged goods.
- *Insurable interest* refers to the right to insure goods against any risk exposure.

Types of Sales Contracts

A *simple delivery contract* is formed when the buyer and seller execute an agreement and the buyer leaves with the goods. *Title* transfers to the buyer when the contract is executed. *Risk of loss* transfers to the buyer when the buyer takes possession. *Insurable interest* is created in the buyer at the same time title passes.

A *common-carrier delivery contract* exists when a buyer and seller execute a contract and the seller subsequently places the goods with a common carrier. There are two types of common-carrier delivery contracts: origin, or shipment, contracts and destination contracts.

- In *shipment contracts,* title transfers to the buyer at the time and place of shipment. The buyer bears the risk of loss while the goods are in transit.
- In *destination contracts,* the seller bears the risk of loss until the seller delivers the goods to the destination stipulated in the sales contract.

A *goods-in-bailment contract* is one that identifies goods that are in some kind of storage. Rules regarding passage of title, risk of loss, and insurable interest vary depending on whether the seller has a negotiable document of title, a nonnegotiable document of title, or a contract showing ownership that is neither a negotiable nor nonnegotiable document of title.

A *conditional sales contract* includes sale-on-approval or sale-or-return contracts.

- In a *sale-on-approval contract,* title and risk of loss remain with the seller until the buyer notifies the seller about the approval of the contract.
- In a *sale-or-return contract,* the insurable interest is created in the buyer once the goods are identified in the contract. Title and risk of loss depend on whether the goods are in bailment, delivered by common carrier, or delivered by the seller.

Risk of Loss during a Breach of Contract

When the seller is in breach by failing to deliver goods, the buyer may either accept the nonconforming goods as is or reject the goods subject to the seller's curing the deficiencies in the goods. Risk of loss remains with the seller until the buyer accepts the goods or the deficiencies are corrected.

When the buyer is in breach because he or she has refused to accept conforming goods and then the goods are subsequently lost or damaged, who bears the risk of loss depends on the type of contract that exists between the buyer and seller.

Point / Counterpoint

If a merchant (bailee) is holding goods for someone for repair or storage and sells those goods to a good-faith purchaser, that good-faith purchaser gets good title and the previous owner may recover the loss only from the bailee by suing in the tort of conversion.

Is It Right That a Bailee Who Has Only Possession, Not Title, Can Pass a Good Title to a Purchaser?

Yes	No
The primary purpose of the Uniform Commercial Code, in addition to attempting to "uniformize" manners and methods of commercial processes, is to facilitate and enable commercial activity. To put it succinctly, purchasers should not have to look over their shoulders, so to speak, regarding every transaction for fear that the title may not be valid. The facilitation of commercial activity requires	The entrustment rule is an example of the Uniform Commercial Code's taking a principle to an illogical and inequitable conclusion. There is no question that the focus of the Uniform Commercial Code is the facilitation of commerce, and the example of the buyer in the ordinary course of business that the opposing view makes is valid except that it is misplaced. A merchant who

that a good-faith purchaser can rely on the sale to validate his or her title to the goods.

We see such a perspective in other areas of the Uniform Commercial Code. As we see in Article 9, on secured transactions, if a buyer in the ordinary course of business purchases an item that is encumbered, the purchaser gets title over the creditor.

This philosophy puts the greater goal of the Uniform Commercial Code ahead of any individualized inconvenience of losing title to goods in entrustment. The focus of the code is the facilitation of commerce, and, as such, parties who put goods into entrustment must exercise due care in choosing a bailee.

has a voidable title can pass on a good title; a merchant who has a good title can obviously pass on a good title. But a merchant who has a void or bad title or no title at all cannot pass on a good title. This is a fundamental premise regarding the ability to pass title.

The entrustment rule is the exception to this title rule and it is misplaced. First, common sense tells us that this situation occurs so infrequently as to negate the need for a special rule. Second, when it does occur, often the goods may be unique or one of a kind and are not replaceable. As such, the inequity in denying possession to the true owner of unique goods truly outweighs the need to facilitate commercial activity.

Questions & Problems

1. How does the UCC define a "sale"?

2. What are the three kinds of title that one can have to goods?

3. What are the various ways that a buyer can acquire voidable title?

4. Mitchell Coach Manufacturing Company, Inc., produces motor homes and sells them to other retail dealers and directly to customers. Ronny Stephens was a customer. WW, Inc., bought and sold motor homes from Mitchell. Under their agreement, WW would pay Mitchell either a down payment on a motor home before the motor home was purchased or the entire amount due for the completed product. Under the agreement, the title of the motor home remained with WW until Stephens paid in full. WW paid Mitchell a down payment of $10,000 for the construction of the motor home. Upon completion, the motor home was to be picked up by Stephens at Mitchell. WW paid the remaining balance to Mitchell, but the check was returned for lack of sufficient funds. Stephens, through a loan, had paid for the motor home in full, but WW had not paid Mitchell. Both Mitchell and Stephens claim title to the motor home. Who does title belong to? [*Mitchell Coach Manufacturing Company, Inc. v. Ronny Stephens,* 19 F. Supp. 2d 1277 (1998).]

5. Sture Graffman entered into a contract with Miguel Espel whereby Espel and his company (MTS) became the exclusive agent for the promotion and sale of Graffman's Picasso painting. Espel asked his brother-in-law, Michael Delecea, to help in the sale of the painting. The painting was sent to Delecea in New York, and Delecea contacted the Avanti Gallery. The gallery owners found a buyer for the painting, and the painting was sold for $875,000. Delecea sent Espel $550,000 and used $200,000 of the proceeds to pay off Espel's debts. Graffman never received any of the money. Subsequently, Graffman brought an action seeking the recovery of the painting or sufficient compensatory damages. Is the entrustment rule applicable? Was the buyer's title to the painting void? How do you think the court handled the dispute? [*Graffman v. Espel,* 96 Civ. 8247 (1998).]

6. Marilyn Thomas purchased an installed pool heater from Sunkissed. The pool heater was delivered to Marilyn's residence, but the delivery slip was signed by Nancy Thomas. Marilyn did not know of anyone by that name. She called Sunkissed to advise them to move the heater. The neighborhood was not safe, and she was worried that the heater would be taken. The heater remained in her driveway for approximately four days. When Marilyn noticed that the heater was no longer in her driveway, she again contacted Sunkissed, but she was told "not to worry." Who was responsible for the loss of the heater? Did Sunkissed actually "deliver" the heater to Marilyn? How do you think the court decided? [*In re Marilyn Thomas,* 182 B.R. 347 (1995).]
7 In 1987 R.H. Love Gallery owned the title to a painting entitled *Marlton's Cove.* The gallery sold 50 percent of the painting to Altman Fine Arts, a New York art dealer, and 50 percent to Andre Lopoukhine, a Boston art dealer. In 1989, plaintiff Morgold, Inc., purchased Altman's 50 percent of the painting. Morgold and Lopoukhine decided to try to sell the painting. In 1990, Lopoukhine sold the painting to Mark Grossman. Lopoukhine did not pay Morgold the 50 percent due for the sale of the painting. Morgold argued that this lack of payment indicated that the title was never officially passed on to Grossman. Through an art dealer, Grossman sold the painting to Fred Keeler. In 1991, Morgold contacted Keeler and claimed to be the sole owner of the painting. Who do you believe owns title to the painting? [*Morgold, Inc. v. Keeler,* 891 F. Supp. 1361 (1995).]
8. MAN Roland agreed to sell Quantum Color Corporation a used press for $405,000. According to the contract, Quantum was supposed to pay $5,000 at the time of the contract, $265,000 at delivery, and the balance of $135,000 before the press was actually used. The first two payments were made, but MAN Roland did not receive the $135,000. MAN Roland alleged that Quantum had been using the press and, therefore, that Quantum was required to pay the balance. Quantum argued that MAN Roland breached the contract by delivering nonconforming goods. Part of the contract indicated that MAN Roland would provide standard equipment and installation, but MAN Roland did not install the equipment or provide Quantum with the standard equipment. How do you think the court settled this case? [*MAN Roland Inc. v. Quantum Color Corp.,* 57 F. Supp. 2d 576 (1999).]
9. William and Donna Hardy purchased a motor home in July 1993 for $38,989. The day after purchasing the motor home, the Hardys commenced a cross-country trip. The Hardys had noticed a small crack on the windshield, but the sellers of the motor home promised to fix the problem when the Hardys returned. Once on the road, the Hardys noticed a loud, clanking noise. They stopped at a dealership and were informed that the drive shaft needed to be replaced. The dealer told the Hardys that this replacement could be done after they completed the trip. The Hardys continued their trip but soon noticed a burning smell. They went to another dealership, and the mechanic worked on the drive shaft. The burning smell was no longer present, but the motor home continued to make loud noises. When the Hardys finally reached California, they took the Winnebago to a third dealer. The mechanic declined to perform any repairs on the motor home. The Hardys called the Winnebago hotline to see whether it was safe to continue driving the motor home. They were told that it was safe to drive the vehicle home. The Hardys returned home after putting 7,500 miles on the motor home. Hardy took the motor home to the original dealer, but he was told that it would take a few months to make the necessary repairs. Hardy demanded a refund from Winnebago. Did Hardy demonstrate revocation of

acceptance? How do you think the court decided? [*Hardy v. Winnebago Industries, Inc.,* 706 A.2d 1086 (1998).]

10. Joseph Perna purchased a 1981 Oldsmobile at a traffic auction from Alfred Locascio. He was told that the New York City Parking Violations Bureau had seized the car. Perna subsequently sold the car to a co-worker, Elio Marino. Marino registered and insured the vehicle and also spent several hundred dollars on necessary repairs. While driving the vehicle, Marino's son was pulled over by the police and arrested for driving a stolen vehicle. The charges were eventually dropped, but he spent the night in jail. Did Marino have title to the vehicle? How do you think the court resolved the conflict? [*Marino v. Perna,* 629 N.Y.S.2d 669 (1995).]

11. Amar entered into a sales contract with the defendant, Karinol, for the purchase of electronic watches. The contract was silent as to shipping terms. However, the contract did have a notation in it stating that the goods were to be delivered to a location in Mexico. Moreover, seller Karinol put the goods into the possession of a common carrier with the instructions to deliver the goods to the plaintiff-buyer in Mexico. When the goods arrived and were opened for customs, the watches were missing. Between the buyer and the seller, who has the risk of loss? In light of these facts, is this a destination or a shipment contract? [*Pestana v. Karinol,* 367 So. 2d 1096 (1979).]

12. Mr. and Mrs. Kahr donate clothing to Goodwill. Unbeknownst to them, there is a bag of antique sterling-silver silverware in the bag valued in excess of $3,000. When the Kahrs realize what they have done, they immediately call Goodwill. However, Goodwill has sold the silverware for $15 to a purchaser. The Kahrs bring suit against the purchaser for the return of the silverware. Do they get it back because the silver was "lost property," or is this a classic entrustment case? [*Kahr v. Markland,* 543 N.E.2d 579 (1989).]

13. Lumber Sales, Inc., contracted to sell five train carloads of lumber to Brown under a destination contract. Lumber delivered four carloads, which Brown received and paid for. However, the fifth carload was delivered to a railroad siding about ½ mile from the buyer's place of business (the usual point of delivery). The buyer was notified of the delivery. However, before the buyer could secure the goods, they were stolen. Who bears the risk of loss, the buyer or the seller? Had delivery been effected even though the buyer had not taken possession of the goods? [*Lumber Sales, Inc. v. Brown,* 469 S.W. 888 (1971).]

Looking for more review material?

The Online Learning Center at **www.mhhe.com/kubasek1e** contains this chapter's "Assignment on the Internet" and also a list of URLs for more information, entitled "On the Internet." Find both of them in the Student Center portion of the OLC, along with quizzes and other helpful materials.

Performance and Obligations under Sales and Leases

CASE OPENER

Will the Sun Shine for Alpha Chi Omega?

Alpha Chi Omega, like all sororities, is steeped in tradition. The organization was founded in 1885 to help its members "seek the heights."[1] At the first appearance of the seven founders of Alpha Chi Omega, the women attached scarlet and olive streamers to their dresses. From that moment on, Alpha Chi Omega included particular colors as part of its traditions. Examples of these traditions include a choice of a particular flower (the red carnation), a stick pin that includes the colors scarlet and olive green, a coat of arms that includes the colors scarlet and olive green, and a variety of toasts and songs. For instance, the song "We Believe" indicates that the sorority "believe[s] in sunshine [a]nd all the things it can do."

In 1992, the Bowling Green State University (BGSU) chapter of Alpha Chi Omega faced a challenge to its traditions when it became involved in a dispute with a clothing company over the purchase of 168 imprinted sweaters and masks from Johnathan James Furlong for the sorority's Midnight Masquerade party, scheduled for October 24, 1992.

Through an oral contract, and a subsequent written description of the sweaters, the sorority agreed to buy the sweaters from Furlong. The sorority gave him a $2,000 down payment and agreed to pay the remaining $1,612 balance when Furlong delivered the sweaters. Furlong had a two-year business relationship with the sorority, although he had never before interacted with the two sorority sisters who arranged for this particular deal, Emily Lieberman and Amy Altomondo.

Lieberman and Furlong agreed that the sweaters would include three colors—hunter green letters on top of maroon letters outlined in navy blue—and the masks would be hunter green. Furlong indicated that a third party would imprint the sweaters. Furlong also delivered to Lieberman a sample sweater with maroon letters so she could see the color. Furlong confirmed with Lieberman by sending a two-page written description of the sweaters.

[1] www.alphachiomega.org indicates that Alpha Chi Omega's open motto is "Together let us seek the heights."

CHAPTER 23

Furlong delivered the sweaters on October 23, 1992. On receipt of delivery, the sorority gave Furlong a check to pay off the balance of the purchase price. However, later that day, Lieberman inspected the sweaters and screamed in dismay when she discovered several unauthorized design changes. She asked the sorority's bank to stop payment on its check, and Altomondo called Furlong to tell him that the sweaters did not meet Alpha Chi Omega's agreement and that the sorority was rejecting the sweaters.

In particular, Furlong had authorized the following changes to the sweaters without the knowledge or consent of Lieberman, Altomondo, or anyone in the sorority: (1) The navy blue outline was eliminated, (2) each side of the sweater was printed with two rather than three colors, (3) the maroon color was changed to red, (4) the color scheme for the letters on the sweaters was changed from maroon and hunter green to navy blue, and (5) the masks were changed from hunter green to red. After rejecting the sweaters, Altomondo offered to return the sweaters and masks to Furlong, but Furlong said no.

Furlong believed that it was within his discretion to make these changes and that, due to time constraints, it would have been impossible for him to get approval from Lieberman or Altomondo prior to the printing. Furlong also believed the sorority should pay the remainder of the balance due and keep the sweaters and masks, but Alpha Chi Omega did not want the sweaters and masks and wanted its down payment back. At a minimum, Furlong wanted Alpha Chi Omega to compromise and pay a reduced price for the sweaters.

1. What are Alpha Chi Omega's obligations to Furlong? Should the sorority compromise? Is the sorority too particular about the colors?
2. What are Furlong's obligations to Alpha Chi Omega? Should he reorder the sweaters and masks and get them right? Should he accept his loss and seek business elsewhere?

The Wrap-Up at the end of the chapter will answer these questions.

Source: www.alphachiomega.org and *Furlong v. Alpha Chi Omega Sorority,* 657 N.E.2d 866 (1993).

Learning Objectives

After reading this chapter, you will be able to answer the following questions:

1 What is the difference between conforming and nonconforming goods?

2 What is the perfect tender rule?

3 What is the right to cure?

4 What is a revocation of the contract as compared to rejection of nonconforming goods?

5 What is commercial impracticability?

When individuals and/or organizations like Alpha Chi Omega enter into sales contracts or leases with others, they need to know their rights and obligations. Businesses like Furlong's also need to know their rights and obligations so that they can engage in efficient business transactions. This chapter explains the performance obligations of sellers and buyers. Additionally, it explains the performance obligations of lessors and lessees, which are similar to those of buyers and sellers. The chapter explains the perfect tender rule and exceptions to this rule. It also explains the buyer's general obligation to inspect, pay for, and accept goods, and it discusses exceptions to this general obligation.

The Basic Performance Obligation

The obligations of sellers/lessors and buyers/lessees are determined by (1) terms the parties outline in agreements, (2) custom, and (3) rules outlined by the Uniform Commercial Code (UCC). This chapter focuses on rules outlined by the UCC.

Under the UCC, sellers and lessors are *obligated to transfer and deliver conforming goods.* Buyers and lessees are *obligated to accept and pay for conforming goods in accordance with the contract.* Courts rely on UCC rules to clarify these obligations when the contract or lease the parties agreed to is unclear. In the case that opens the chapter, Furlong is obligated to transfer and deliver conforming goods to Alpha Chi Omega. Alpha Chi Omega is obligated to accept and pay for conforming goods in accordance with the contract. What is a "conforming good" in the context of the dispute between Alpha Chi Omega and Furlong? Does the UCC obligate Alpha Chi Omega to accept and pay for the sweaters and masks? The question of what constitutes conforming goods is significant. This chapter addresses that topic after explaining how the idea of good faith places transactions in a particular context. What if there was an issue of mistake? Remember that at common law a unilateral mistake may still constitute a binding contract whereas a bilateral mistake will not. Issues of mistake often raise the corollary issue of unconscionability. Consider the Case Nugget.

GOOD FAITH

UCC Section 1-203 requires **good faith** in the performance and enforcement of every contract. Good faith means *honesty in fact.* When the parties are merchants, the UCC imposes a higher standard. Between merchants, the UCC imposes not only honesty in fact but also reasonable commercial standards of fair dealing. This second requirement is often called **commercial reasonableness.** In the context of good faith, courts decide the specific obligations of sellers/lessors and buyers/lessees. The next few sections of the chapter discuss these specific obligations.

Case Nugget Mistake and Unconscionability

Donovan v. RRL Corporation
26 Cal. 4th 261 (2001)

The Donovans showed up at the defendant car dealership. After hearing the sales pitch, Mr. Donovan stated that he'd take the car at the price quoted in the newspaper, \$25,995. The horrified salesman said that he could go as low as \$37,995 but not \$25,995. At that point, Donovan showed the salesman a copy of an ad that had been running in the local newspaper identifying the very same automobile for \$25,995. The salesman responded that that advertisement had to be a mistake. Donovan said that he wanted the car at the \$25,995 price. He subsequently brought an action in the municipal court in Orange County. The trial court found for RRL Corp. on mistake. However, the California court of appeals reversed, stating that all the material elements of a contract were clearly stated in the advertisement and that Donovan's acceptance of those terms constituted a good contract.

The California Supreme Court heard the case, reversing it on a combination of mistake and unconscionability. The supreme court found that a contract was indeed created but that the contract could be rescinded since the evidence showed (1) the defendant's unilateral mistake was made in good faith; (2) the defendant did not bear the risk of the mistake; and (3) the enforcement of a contract with an erroneous price would be unconscionable as a matter of law.

Specific Obligations of Sellers and Lessors

THE PERFECT TENDER RULE

The UCC requires that sellers and lessors tender conforming goods to the buyer or lessee. UCC Sections 2-503(1) and 2A-508(1) state that **tender of delivery** requires that the seller/lessor have and hold conforming goods at the disposal of the buyer/lessee and give the buyer/lessee reasonable notification to enable him or her to take delivery. **Conforming goods** are goods that conform to contract specifications.

A common law rule known as the **perfect tender rule** required that the seller deliver goods in conformity with the terms of the contract, right down to the last detail. UCC Sections 2-601 and 2A-509 embrace the perfect tender rule. These sections indicate that if goods or tender of delivery fail *in any respect* to conform to the contract, the buyer/lessee has the right to accept the goods, reject the entire shipment, or accept part and reject part. Common law usually substitutes perfect tender with the doctrine of substantial performance. *Substantial performance* occurs when all the material elements of a contract are satisfied even if some nonmaterial requirements may not be satisfied. The perfect tender rule would not recognize the distinction between material and immaterial contractual requirements.

Consider Case 23-1, which provides an illustration of a situation in which UCC's version of the perfect tender rule was relevant when compared to the common law rule of material breach under the doctrine of substantial performance. As you read the case, think about Alpha Chi Omega's conflict over the sweaters and masks for the Midnight Masquerade party. Does Case 23-1 give you a hint about whether the sun will shine for the sisters of Alpha Chi?

connecting to the core

Marketing

Conforming goods are often customized purchases, similar to Alpha Chi Omega's request for customized sweaters and masks. To provide greater ease in consumers' purchasing of customized products, many companies' Web sites are very interactive and personalized to enhance transactions between buyers and sellers. As you may have learned in your marketing course, these individualized systems are referred to as *choiceboards.* For example, Nike designed a choiceboard, the Nike iD Customized Product, which consumers can access on the Internet, that allows consumers to design, view, and purchase customized shoes and backpacks. Similarly, Dell's choiceboard allows consumers to build their own computers.

One of the primary benefits of companies' using choiceboards is that these companies can easily acquire information about consumers' preferences, permitting the companies to more easily fulfill consumers' specific needs. As a future business manager, you may want to consider the benefits of your company's using a choiceboard to market products, thereby allowing consumers to make customized purchases.

Source: R. Kerin, S. Hartley, E. Berkowitz, and W. Rudelius, *Marketing* (New York: McGraw-Hill/Irwin, 2005), pp. 560–561.

CASE 23-1 ALASKA PACIFIC TRADING CO. v. EAGON FOREST PRODUCTS INC.

WASHINGTON APPELLATE DIVISION 1
933 P.2D 417 (1997)

Alaska Pacific Trading Company (ALPAC) and Eagon Forest Products, Inc. (Eagon) contracted to buy and sell raw logs. ALPAC and Eagon engaged in months of communications about a shipment of 15,000 cubic meters of logs from Argentina to Korea between the end of July and the end of August 1993. The delivery date passed without ALPAC shipping the logs. Eagon canceled the contract, alleging that ALPAC had breached the agreement by failing to deliver. ALPAC alleged that its failure to deliver was not a material breach and that the parties had modified the delivery date. Alternatively, ALPAC argued that Eagon breached the contract by failing to provide adequate assurances or repudiating the contract. The miscommunication between the parties occurred after the market for logs began to soften, making the contract less attractive to Eagon. ALPAC was reluctant to ship the goods because it was concerned that Eagon might not accept the shipment. However, Eagon never stated that it would not accept the cargo.

In the ruling below, the judge decides whether ALPAC breached the contract. ALPAC wants the court to rely on the common law doctrine of material breach under the doctrine of substantial performance, while Eagon wants the court to rely on the UCC's perfect tender rule. If the court decides to apply UCC rules, and if ALPAC failed to deliver, Eagon would be allowed to "reject the whole."

JUDGE AGID: ALPAC's first contention is that it did not breach the contract by failing to timely deliver the logs because time of delivery was not a material term of the contract. ALPAC relies on common law contract cases to support its position that, when the parties have not indicated that time is of the essence, late delivery is not a material breach which excuses the buyer's duty to accept the goods. . . . However, as a contract for the sale of goods, this contract is governed by the Uniform Commercial Code, Article II (UCC II) which replaced the common law of material breach, on which ALPAC relies, with the "perfect tender" rule. Under this rule, "If the goods or the tender of delivery fail in any respect to conform to the contract, the buyer may . . . reject the whole." . . . Both the plain language of the rule and the official comments clearly state that, if the tender of the goods differs from the terms of the contract in any way, the seller breaches the contract and

[CONTINUED]

the buyer is released from its duty to accept the goods. . . . ALPAC does not dispute that the contract specified a date for shipment or that the logs were not shipped by that date. Thus, under the perfect tender rule, ALPAC breached its duty under the contract and released Eagon from its duty to accept the logs.

AFFIRMED.

CRITICAL THINKING

Here, Eagon got lucky. The company got out of a contract that was unfavorable to it, given the softening market for logs. In what way did Judge Agid simplify the case? Is it fair to say the judge oversimplified the case?

ETHICAL DECISION MAKING

What ethical norm or value underlies Judge Agid's decision? Explain.

EXCEPTIONS TO THE PERFECT TENDER RULE

The perfect tender rule is not as inflexible as it appears. Although the rule itself demands perfection, both courts and UCC drafters have created exceptions that reduce the rule's rigidity. These exceptions limit the seller's obligation to deliver conforming goods and/or limit the buyer's power to reject goods that do not conform. This section of the chapter explains the six most important exceptions to the perfect tender rule. These exceptions allow sellers/lessors and buyers/lessees to ask questions such as:

- What are the norms in the particular industry and/or what past dealings have the parties had with one another?
- What does the parties' agreement say?
- Is it possible for the seller/lessor to cure or correct problems?
- What if the goods have been destroyed?
- What if nonconformity substantially impairs the value of goods?
- What if unforeseen circumstances make contract performance commercially impracticable?

Look again at these questions, and ask which might be relevant to Alpha Chi Omega's deal with Furlong. For example, we know Furlong had past dealings with Alpha Chi Omega. Had the sorority accepted and paid for nonconforming goods in the past? Could Furlong have corrected or "cured" the problems with the sweaters and masks? What would have happened if the sweaters and masks had met the agreement the parties outlined but then the goods were damaged in a flood? After reading the following subsections, determine whether these or any other exceptions might be relevant.

Norms in the industry and past dealings between the parties. When the buyer alleges that goods failed to conform to contract specifications, the buyer does not automatically have the right to reject the goods. The UCC requires that courts consider norms in a particular trade. Sometimes, the norms for a particular trade do not permit a buyer to reject goods with minor flaws. UCC Section 1-205(2) defines **usage of trade** as any practice that members of an industry expect to be part of their dealings.

e-commerce AND THE LAW

UCITA

The Uniform Computer Information Transactions Act (UCITA) is a proposed model law under review in several states. UCITA outlines a framework to govern software licenses. Software vendors such as Microsoft are generally in favor of UCITA because this model legislation protects software vendors.

One important way in which UCITA protects software vendors is that it makes sure perfect tender rules that generally apply to the sale of goods do not apply to software. UCITA's rules change when and why a consumer of software can reject a defective product. For example, if a software transaction involves a negotiated contract, UCITA eliminates customers' rights to inspect a product on delivery and reject it for any defects that do not conform to the requirements of the contract. Instead, a buyer of software must prove that the defect represents a material breach of the contract.

Source: Ed Foster, "The Gripe Line," *Info World,* July 3, 2000, and Jeff Moad, "If It Works for Microsoft, Does It Work For You?" *Eweek* (from ZD Wire), May 18, 2001.

In addition to its requirement on usage of trade, the UCC requires that courts consider the ideas of course of dealing and course of performance. UCC 1-205(1) defines **course of dealing** as previous commercial transactions between the same parties. Under UCC 208(1), **course of performance** refers to the history of dealings between the parties in the particular contract at issue. This rule states that when a contract for sale involves repeated occasions for performance by either party with the other's knowledge of the nature of the performance and opportunity for objection to it, any course of performance accepted or acquiesced to without objection is relevant to determine what the parties' agreement means.

For example, if Alpha Chi Omega had contracted with Furlong to provide sweaters, t-shirts, and other goods throughout the year, and if the sorority had recently accepted t-shirts and caps that were not quite what it had in mind, that fact would be relevant in deciding what to do about the disagreement over the sweaters and masks for the Midnight Masquerade party. If the sorority had allowed Furlong to use his discretion in the past, a court would consider that fact in determining whether Alpha Chi Omega could reject the nonconforming sweaters.

Exceptions outlined in the parties' agreement. Sometimes, language in the parties' agreement limits the rigidity of the perfect tender rule. For instance, parties may agree that the seller must have the opportunity to repair or replace nonconforming goods within a particular period of time. Alternatively, parties may agree with a level of performance that is less than perfect. They could indicate, by agreement, the expectation regarding performance. Alpha Chi Omega could have included language in the agreement suggesting that the sweaters and masks needed to be "reasonably close" to the description provided in the two-page confirmation document. In the best-case scenario for Furlong, the contract would have included a clause that allowed him to use his discretion to make changes in merchandise, especially when he was operating on a short deadline. Unfortunately, Furlong did not include this language in the agreement.

The seller's/lessor's right to cure. Under UCC Sections 2-508 and 2A-513, sellers and lessors have the right to **cure** or fix problems with nonconforming goods. In particular, sellers and lessors can repair, adjust, or replace defective or nonconforming goods as long as they give prompt notice of the intent to cure and go ahead and cure within the contract time for performance. For instance, in our Alpha Chi Omega example, Furlong could have notified the sorority that he would replace the sweaters and masks prior to the party. If he did so, the sorority could not have rejected the replacement sweaters and masks if they conformed to the parties' agreement. The problem for Furlong was that he did not have time to cure the defects because he delivered the sweaters and masks just one day before the Midnight Masquerade party.

global context

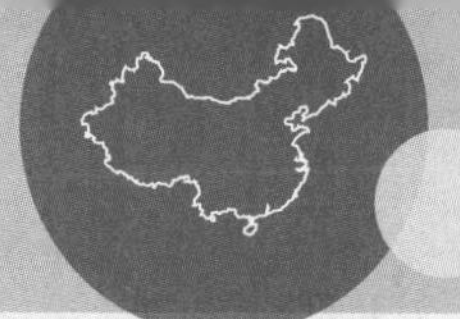

Nonconforming Goods in China and the CISG

The Uniform Commercial Code is not a model law that other countries have adopted. For example, China embraces the Convention on Contracts for the International Sale of Goods (CISG), not the UCC. Rules under the CISG differ from those under the UCC. Article 49(1) of the CISG allows *avoidance* (the term used for the buyer's refusing to accept nonconforming goods) only if there is substantial and foreseeable nonconformity of the goods. In other words, the CISG follows more closely the common law concept of substantial performance than it does the perfect tender rule.

Consider, for example, what would happen if an American company shipped nonconforming goods to another American company.* Under the UCC, the buyer could reject the nonconforming goods. If the American company* shipped nonconforming goods to a Chinese buyer, the result would be different.

It is likely a Chinese buyer would be permitted by the CISG to resort only to a remedy that included a reasonable price reduction for nonconforming goods. It is possible (but unlikely) that the Chinese buyer could pursue the issue of nonconforming goods as a criminal matter.

China is not the only country that does not apply the UCC. Hong Kong, Japan, and Indonesia are additional examples of Pacific Rim countries that do not apply UCC rules.

* Example from Jacques G. Boettcher, "The China Predicament," *Multinational Business Review* 9 (April 1, 2001).

Under UCC 2-508(2) and 2A-513(2), the seller or lessor can still exercise the right to cure once the contract time for performance has passed as long as the seller or lessor has reasonable grounds to believe that the nonconforming tender would be acceptable to the buyer or lessee. In the next case, Case 23-2, the court decides whether a seller should have been allowed the right to cure and what consequence the court should impose if a buyer fails to give the seller this opportunity.

CASE 23-2 | DEJESUS v. CAT AUTO TECH. CORP.

615 N.Y.S.2D 236
N.Y. CITY CIV. CT. (1994)

Cat Auto Tech. Corp. purchased 10,000 gift certificates from DeJesus. Cat Auto Tech Corp., an Amoco gasoline station operator, contracted with DeJesus to make 10,000 gift certificates of various denominations, with the Amoco gasoline name and logo on them, stapled together in booklets that included approximately eight gift certificates in each. Delivery was to be within two weeks. Montefiore Hospital had wanted to give these gift certificates to their employees as a Christmas gift.

Michael DiBarro, president of Cat Auto Tech. Corp., stated that the finished product differed from the sample DeJesus had provided in two respects: the paper was different, and the sample contained a decorative border, whereas the finished product did not. Additionally, DiBarro complained that the logo colors were not within the printed borders of the Amoco logo. When the court looked at the certificates, it noted that within a book of gift certificates, two of the eight certificates had colors immediately outside the borders. On one, the problem was slightly noticeable, and on the other, the court could notice the problem only when it inspected closely. DeJesus stated that DiBarro had accepted these minor changes, and that any minor defects were insignificant.

DeJesus delivered the goods to the Cat Auto Tech. Corp. approximately two weeks after the agreed upon delivery date. DiBarro accepted the delivery and paid by check. He did not inspect the certificates at the time of delivery or before he paid. He inspected the certificates a day later, placed a stop payment order on the check without notifying DeJesus, and did not let DeJesus know why he was stopping payment on the check. DeJesus did not know of the stop payment until she eventually received a notice from her bank that she had insufficient funds in her account.

DeJesus wants Cat Auto Tech. Corp. to pay the balance due on the contract, and asks the court to clarify the seller's right to cure defects in nonconforming goods.

JUDGE LUCINDO SUAREZ: . . . UCC 2-601 provides that "if the goods . . . fail in any respect to conform to the contract, the buyer may . . . reject the whole. . . ." . . . New York subscribe[s] to the perfect tender rule, which allows a buyer to reject goods that fail to conform to the contract. UCC 2-602(1) provides the manner to accomplish an effective rejection: Rejection of goods must be within a reasonable time after their delivery or tender. It is ineffective unless the buyer seasonably notifies the seller.

An effective rejection requires the buyer to seasonably notify the seller, even though the delivery is of wholly nonconforming goods. In the case at bar delivery was made two weeks after the date called for in the contract. Defendant buyer paid for the goods by check, inspected them the next day and issued a stop payment order on the check. The time to cure a defective tender, if at all, was immediate. The buyer's notification of its rejection by a stop payment order on its draft was not seasonable, nor within a reasonable time. . . . Indeed, no reasonable attempt on the part of the buyer to notify the seller was undertaken. . . .

The purpose of notification is to afford the seller the opportunity to cure, or to permit the seller to minimize her losses, such as providing a decrease in the price. This opportunity was never afforded to the seller. The perfect tender rule is limited by the seller's ability to cure, which is conditioned upon receipt of notice. UCC 2-508 provides: (1) Where . . . tender . . . by the seller is rejected because nonconforming and the time for performance has not yet expired, the seller may seasonably notify the buyer of his intention to cure and may then, within the contract time, make a conforming delivery. (2) Where the buyer rejects a nonconforming tender which the seller had reasonable grounds to believe would be acceptable with or without the money allowance, the seller may, if he seasonably notifies the buyer, have a further reasonable time to substitute a conforming tender.

Defendant's payment for the goods without inspection on the day of delivery, approximately two weeks after the time called for by the contract, effectively waived the performance provisions of the contract regarding the time of delivery. . . . Therefore, the time within which to perform having expired, subdivision (2) must be referenced. However, subdivision (2) by implication is only applicable if there has been an effective rejection, which is not the case herein.

Defendant's payment by check for the goods upon their delivery provided the plaintiff with a measure of reliance that the same would be acceptable. Defendant's failure to properly notify plaintiff of the nonconformity effectively prevented plaintiff from an opportunity to cure any defects, within the time limitations of this case, and therefore defendant's actions cannot be considered to have effectively rejected the goods herein.

Judgment is awarded in favor of plaintiff in the amount of $1,252.00, representing the balance due and owing under the contract with interest from December 7, 1993.

Judgment for plaintiff.

CRITICAL THINKING

In Chapter 1, you learned of the importance of a particular set of facts in determining the outcome of a case. If you could change one fact in this case to make it more likely the judge would rule in favor of Cat Auto Tech Corp., which fact would you change? Explain.

ETHICAL DECISION MAKING

Apply the universalization test to the outcome of this case. Does the universalization test support Justice Suarez's decision?

Destroyed goods. Under UCC Sections 2-613 and 2A-221, if goods are identified at the time the parties entered into a contract and these goods are destroyed through no fault of the parties before risk passes to the buyer or lessee, the parties are excused from performance. For instance, if a fire or some other natural disaster had destroyed the Alpha Chi Omega sweaters and masks prior to the Midnight Masquerade party, Furlong would have been excused from performance. If the goods are only partially destroyed, the buyer can inspect the goods and decide whether to (1) treat the contract as void or (2) ask the seller for a reduction of the contract price and then accept the damaged goods.

Case Nugget — Rejection or Acceptance of Nonconforming Goods

Clark v. Zaid, Inc.
263 Md. 127 (1971)

Arianna Clark wanted to redo her entire dining room, so she ordered from the Zaid, Inc., catalog four chairs, a table, a buffet, and a hutch. The total due was $2,500, of which she put $900 down. When the furniture was delivered, Clark immediately noticed that the furniture was severely damaged to the point of being unusable. She immediately notified the defendant, Zaid, Inc. A Zaid representative came to Clark's home, inspected the furniture, and offered to restore it. Clark refused, claiming that no degree of repair or restoration could restore it substantively. Clark then sued for her $900 payment to be returned, and Zaid countersued for the balance due of $1,600.

In the meantime, during the pendency of this lawsuit, Clark decided to have some linoleum work done in the dining room. In the course of that work, Clark's luck remained the same, and the linoleum workers badly damaged the buffet. After complaining to the linoleum company, Clark received a $515 settlement (the original purchase price for the buffet) from the linoleum company for the damage to the buffet. The linoleum company then took possession of the buffet.

In light of this turn of events, Zaid claimed that Clark had "accepted" the goods and thus that her rejection of nonconforming goods was no longer effective and Zaid was entitled to its $1,600 balance due. The trial judge awarded a summary judgment decision in favor of Zaid, Inc., and Clark appealed.

The Maryland Court of Appeals reversed, sending the case back to the trial court for the resolution of material facts (such as whether a cure could have been effected). On the specific issue of the damaged buffet, the court held for Clark in that:

> . . . the Code makes it plain that a buyer in possession who has rightfully and effectively rejected goods may resell the goods either for the account of the seller, with the right to reimbursement for expenses and commission, if the buyer has no security interest in the goods, or for the buyer's own account to the extent of his security interest, plus expenses; and his action in either case, if it is exercised in good faith and is reasonable under the circumstances *will not* constitute acceptance. . . . [emphasis added]

Substantial impairment. Two sections of the UCC use the concept of **substantial impairment** to modify the perfect tender rule. The first applies when a buyer *revokes acceptance of goods.* UCC Section 2-608 indicates that the buyer who has accepted goods may later revoke the acceptance only if the buyer can show that the defects substantially impair the value of the goods. The second applies when the buyer and seller have entered into an *installment contract.* UCC Sections 2-612(2) and 2A-510(1) indicate that if a buyer/lessee rejects an installment of a particular item, that buyer/lessee may do so only if the defects substantially impair the value of the goods and cannot be cured. In Case 23-3, the court considers the concept of substantial impairment in the context of an installment contract. A buyer wants to revoke an installment of a particular item, and the court must decide whether the buyer may do so. That means the buyer must show that defects substantially impair the value of the goods and cannot be cured.

CASE 23-3 MIDWEST MOBILE DIAGNOSTIC IMAGING v. DYNAMICS CORP. OF AMERICA

165 F.3D 27
C.A.6 (MICH.) 1998

Midwest Mobile Diagnostic Imaging (MMDI) brought suit against Ellis & Watts (E & W), a division of Dynamics Corporation of America, for breach of contract. The dispute arose when E & W delivered the first of four trailers equipped with magnetic resonance imaging (MRI) scanners that E & W had agreed to deliver pursuant to a Purchase Agreement. E & W designs and manufactures trailers for mobile medical uses. MMDI decided to buy the MRI scanners directly from the manufacturer, but it needed assistance from E & W. E & W needed to install the trailers subject to the manufacturer's specifications and approval. MMDI entered into an agreement with E & W for four mobile MRI units. Delivery of the MRI units was conditioned on the manufacturer's final approval that the trailers conformed to certain minimum specifications.

The manufacturer subsequently delivered the first scanner to E & W in September 1995. In November, MMDI paid E & W for the first trailer. The manufacturer then completed its testing of that trailer at the end of November. The first test found that the trailer complied with all technical specifications. A second test failed because it was a "road test," meaning the MRI failed to meet requirements after the trailer was moved and parked. The problem was that the unit's side walls flexed too much, causing unacceptable "ghosting" in the MRI scans. In December, E & W installed a reinforcing brace that solved the wall-flexing problem and satisfied all of the manufacturer's specifications.

MMDI then objected to the reinforcing brace because MMDI believed the brace created numerous problems, including that the brace impeded service access to the magnet, it affected the appearance of the trailer, and the brace could affect the resale value of the trailer. Consequently, MMDI refused to accept the trailer with the brace and demanded that E & W return the full purchase price. E & W believes the brace solves the problems with the MRI, the trailer passed the manufacturer's tests, and E & W had fulfilled its contractual obligations. MMDI and E & W tried to negotiate a compromise, but MMDI ultimately canceled the contract and contracted with another manufacturer. MMDI filed suit, seeking damages.

The district court ruled in favor of MMDI, holding that E & W was liable for tendering a nonconforming MRI unit and substantially impairing the remaining value of the contract to MMDI. On appeal, E & W asked the court to consider whether (1) E & W breached its Purchase Agreement by tendering a nonconforming good; (2) MMDI rightfully rejected E & W's tender of the first trailer with the reinforcing brace; (3) E & W adequately assured MMDI that it would cure within a reasonable time, and whether E & W did in fact cure; and (4) any nonconformity in the first trailer substantially impaired the value of the contract as a whole. The court first found that E & W had breached the purchase agreement. The court's response to issues 2, 3 and 4 appears in the opinion below.

JUSTICE GALLAGHER: . . . Pursuant to the perfect tender rule, a buyer may reject nonconforming goods if they fail in any respect to conform to the contract. The perfect tender rule, however, is relaxed in installment contracts. An installment sale is a contract for multiple items that permits delivery in separate groups and at different times. Although the MRI units

[CONTINUED]

were individual commercial units, the Purchase Agreement between MMDI and E & W was an installment contract, because it provided for delivery of individual units at different times. Moreover, a buyer may reject any nonconforming installment if the nonconformity substantially impairs the value of that installment and cannot be cured within a reasonable time. However, if the seller gives adequate assurance of curing the nonconformity, the buyer must accept that installment. After the first trailer failed its road test because of the wall-flexing problem, E & W promised to cure the defect and, therefore, was entitled under law to a reasonable amount of time in which to cure the defect. E & W tendered its attempted cure on December 13, 1995, by delivering the trailer with the reinforced brace. This attempted cure substantially breached the Purchase Agreement, because the reinforcing brace (1) was not included in the original structural design; (2) blocked access to the scanner for servicing; (3) was unsightly for use in a mobile medical unit; and (4) decreased the resale value of the unit. Accordingly, we find that MMDI rightfully rejected the attempted cure.

If the nonconformity in any given installment substantially impairs the value of the whole contract, then there is a breach of the whole. MMDI's purpose in entering into the Purchase Agreement was to obtain, in a timely fashion, the four mobile MRI units that it needed to serve its growing client demand. As the district court reasoned, by failing to cure the initial tender of November 28, 1995, E & W substantially delayed completion of the contract. In addition, loss of even one installment substantially impaired the value of the whole contract to MMDI, because it reduced MMDI's anticipated capacity by at least 25%. . . .

Because E & W tendered a nonconforming MRI unit, and thereby substantially impaired the remaining value of the contract to MMDI, E & W was liable for breach of contract. . . .

AFFIRMED.

CRITICAL THINKING

The court considered an ambiguous phrase, *substantially impairs.* Why is this ambiguity significant? What reasoning did the court use to decide that E & W's actions substantially impaired the value of the contract between the parties?

ETHICAL DECISION MAKING

The concept of substantial impairment is supposed to work to the advantage of the seller. Why didn't that happen in this case? What ethical norm underlies the court's decision?

Commercial impracticability. UCC Sections 2-615(a) and 2A-405(a) state that a delay in delivery or nondelivery, in whole or in part, is not a breach in circumstances in which performance has been made impracticable because a contingency has occurred that was not contemplated when the parties reached an agreement. For example, this rule would be relevant if a change in government regulation that neither party contemplated forbids the import or export of a particular item the parties had agreed would be shipped.

In our Alpha Chi Omega example, suppose a local florist had agreed to provide the sorority with red carnations (the sorority's flower) all year at a particular price but then a disease swept the country that wiped out all but 10 percent of the country's carnation supply. The florist could still get carnations but only at a significantly higher price than the agreement indicated. The florist would then assert the commercial-impracticability exception to the perfect tender rule, explaining that the parties did not contemplate the nationwide destruction of carnations when they reached their agreement.

Specific Obligations of Buyers and Lessees

THE BASIC OBLIGATION: INSPECTION, PAYMENT, AND ACCEPTANCE

Under UCC Sections 2-301 and 2A-516(1), buyers and lessees are obligated to accept and pay for conforming goods in accordance with the contract. Before paying for and accepting the goods, buyers/lessees ordinarily inspect the goods to make sure they conform to the specifications in the parties' agreement.

EXCEPTIONS TO THE BASIC OBLIGATION

Buyers/lessees do not always end up accepting and paying for goods. Sometimes, on inspection, the buyer or lessee decides to reject the goods and refrain from paying for them. We have already seen that happen in prior cases in the chapter. For example, Midwest Mobile Diagnostic Imaging ended up rejecting the MRI trailer supplied by Dynamics Corporation of America and finding another supplier. In this section, the chapter takes a look at exceptions to the buyer's/lessee's basic obligation. These exceptions allow sellers/lessors and buyers/lessees to ask questions such as:

- What forms of payment are allowed under the UCC?
- In what circumstances can a buyer reject goods?
- Is the buyer allowed to accept part but not all of the goods?
- In what circumstances can a buyer revoke acceptance of goods?
- How and when can a buyer reject nonconforming goods?
- Are installment contracts treated differently than other kinds of contracts?

Review these questions again, and ask yourself which are relevant to Alpha Chi Omega's deal with Furlong. For example: Under what circumstances is Alpha Chi Omega allowed to reject the sweaters and masks? Could the sorority have accepted the masks but not the sweaters? If Alpha Chi Omega had accepted the sweaters, under what circumstances could it revoke the acceptance? How could the sorority reject the goods when Furlong said he would not take them back? Would it have mattered if the deal had been an installment contract? This section of the chapter answers the questions listed above in three subsections that cover (1) problems on inspection, (2) problems with acceptance, and (3) rescission or revocation of acceptance by the buyer or lessee. Note that this section asks these questions from the buyer's perspective.

Problems on inspection. If all goes well in a transaction over the sale or lease of goods, the buyer or lessee inspects the goods and then pays by any means the parties have agreed on, including payment by cash, check, or credit card. Unless the parties have agreed otherwise, the buyer or lessee typically inspects the goods before paying. Under UCC Sections 2-513(1) and 2A-515(1), the seller or lessor must provide an opportunity for inspection before enforcing payment.

The concept of reasonableness governs the inspection process. For example, inspection must take place at a reasonable time and place, in a reasonable way. Once the buyer or lessee inspects the goods, he or she decides whether to accept the goods. Sometimes, on inspection, the buyer or lessee decides not to accept the goods. For instance, in Case 23-2, Cat Auto Tech. Corp. inspected the gift certificates and decided it did not want to accept the goods. In the case involving Alpha Chi Omega, the sorority inspected the goods and decided not to accept them. When, on inspection, the buyer or lessee determines that there may be a problem with the goods, he or she wants to know what circumstances allow a buyer or lessee to reject goods. Of course, if the goods are conforming, the buyer or lessee wants to know how to communicate acceptance.

Problems with acceptance. When all goes well, UCC Sections 2-606(1) and 2A-515(1)(a) indicate that the buyer or lessee, after inspecting, signifies agreement to the seller or lessor that the goods are either (1) conforming or (2) acceptable even though they are nonconforming. UCC Sections 2-602(1), 2-606(1), and 2A-515(1)(b) allow the seller or lessor to presume acceptance if the buyer or lessee fails to reject the goods within a reasonable period of time. Sometimes, there is confusion about whether the buyer or lessee has accepted the goods. Recall that in Case 23-2, DeJesus had assumed Cat. Auto Tech. Corp. had accepted the gift certificates because Cat. Auto had not communicated otherwise within a reasonable period of time.

UCC Sections 2-601(c) and 2A-509(1) allow the buyer or lessee to make a partial acceptance when the goods are nonconforming and the seller or lessor has failed to cure the defects. For instance, if Cat. Auto had immediately needed some of the gift certificates DeJesus printed, it could have accepted some of them and then asked DeJesus to reprint the rest. (Recall, however, that the court thought Cat. Auto's concerns were insignificant and ruled that Cat. Auto should have given DeJesus the opportunity to cure.)

When goods are nonconforming, the buyer or lessee is allowed to revoke or withdraw acceptance of the goods. The previous section on specific obligations of sellers/lessors discussed this concept under the topic of substantial impairment. From the buyer's/lessee's perspective, the buyer or lessee may revoke acceptance if the nonconformity substantially impairs the value of the goods but only if he or she had a legitimate reason for the initial acceptance. Case 23-3 presented a good example of a situation in which it was reasonable for the buyer to revoke acceptance. Initially, MMDI had thought E & W was going to be able to supply an appropriate MRI trailer unit. After unsuccessful negotiations and fix-it strategies, MMDI gave up and sought a new supplier. The nonconforming trailer substantially impaired the value of the MRI trailer unit. Ultimately, MMDI rejected the trailer. UCC Sections 2-601, 2-602, and 2A-509 allow the buyer or lessee to reject nonconforming goods by notifying the seller or lessor within a reasonable period of time. MMDI did issue reasonable notice to E & W.

Rescission or revocation of acceptance by buyer. Cases in which a buyer decides to assert his or her right to reject nonconforming goods are often categorized under the heading "rescission or revocation of acceptance by buyer." Case 23-4 is one in which a buyer with an installment contract decided to reject nonconforming goods. Rescission or revocation of acceptance by the buyer is the primary subject of the case. The case provides a good review of a wide range of topics that fall under the subject of performance and obligation. Note how the case includes the concept of good faith. This chapter started with the concept of good faith, and it will end with the same topic. It is always good to remember the context in which courts judge the extent to which a buyer or seller has met his or her contractual obligations.

Case Nugget **Perfect Tender, Rescission, and Good Faith**

Y&N Furniture Inc. v. Nwabuoku
734 N.Y.S.2d 392 (2001)

The defendant, Nwabuoku, purchased $1,500 worth of furniture from the plaintiff, Y&N Furniture. Through an arrangement with the plaintiff, the defendant financed the purchase through a financing company named Beneficial. On receipt of the furniture, the defendant was to notify Beneficial that receipt was effected, and Beneficial would pay Y&N the $1,500 purchase price. Nwabuoku would then begin paying Beneficial the amount due plus interest according to their financing agreement. Nwabuoku refused to acknowledge receipt to Beneficial and eventually rejected the goods, claiming that he did not want the furniture.

The Civil Court of the City of New York found that Nwabuoku had rejected the goods and the court cited the perfect tender rule as requiring "exact performance by the seller." Moreover, the court held that "rejection of goods must be within a reasonable time of their delivery or tender." The court indicated that Nwabuoku did indeed make a rightful rejection. However, the court noted that a rejection of goods must be based on some claim that the goods are in some way nonconforming. The defendant in this case had a disagreement over the terms of the financing (though the terms were clearly stated in the financing statements). The defendant made no claim of nonconforming goods. As such, the court found that "in this case, too, we have a rejection that is not only 'wrongful,' but also in bad faith." A wrongful rejection is not necessarily in bad faith; the buyer may honestly believe that the goods fail to conform but may simply be mistaken. But a rejection that does not even purport to rest on an honest assessment of conformity of the goods has "the effect of destroying or injuring the right of the seller to receive the fruits of the contract."

CASE 23-4 HUBBARD v. UTZ QUALITY FOODS, INC.
U.S. DISTRICT COURT (W.D. NEW YORK)
903 F. SUPP. 444 (1995)

In this case, a dispute arose between a potato farmer, David Hubbard (Hubbard), and UTZ Quality Foods, Inc. (UTZ), over whether UTZ was within its legal rights when it decided to rescind or revoke acceptance of potatoes supplied by Hubbard. UTZ claims that the potatoes Hubbard supplied failed to meet the quality standards outlined in the parties' agreement.

In particular, UTZ claimed the potatoes did not meet the color standards outlined in the agreement. UTZ did not want dark potato chips, so it demanded that the potatoes had to be the whitest or lightest possible color. Potato color is defined from designation No. 1 (best or lightest) to 5 (the darkest). UTZ's contract indicated that potatoes must meet at least the No. 2 color standards. UTZ contends that the potatoes do not meet this standard, while Hubbard contends that UTZ is arbitrarily refusing to accept his potatoes. The court states that "this case turns on matters of law relating to the rights of a buyer, such as UTZ, to reject a seller's goods that are deemed to be nonconforming." In the case below, the court explores UTZ's rights.

JUDGE SPAETH: . . . The primary legal issue in this matter is whether UTZ's rejection of Hubbard's potatoes was proper or wrongful. It is clear that this transaction is a sale of goods governed by New York Uniform Commercial Code (UCC) . . . both Hubbard and UTZ are "merchants." . . . It is also clear that the contract between the parties is an "installment contract." . . . [C]oncerning payment, [the contract] states that "[b]uyer agrees to pay for all potatoes accepted within 30 days of acceptance. . . ." This language suggests paying per shipment, since each shipment is subject to inspection (and acceptance). . . . Clearly this is an "installment" contract as defined in UCC 2-612(1).

As an installment contract, the question of whether UTZ's rejection was wrongful or proper is governed by UCC 2-612(2) and (3). UCC 2-612(2) states that a "buyer may reject any installment which is non-conforming if the non-conformity substantially impairs the value of that installment and cannot be cured. . . ." UCC 2-612(3) states that "whenever non-conformity or default with respect to one or more installments substantially impairs the value of the whole contract there is a breach of the whole."

The purpose of this "substantial impairment" requirement is "to preclude a party from canceling a contract for trivial defects." In this case, UTZ rejected Hubbard's potatoes based upon their failure to satisfy the color standard set forth in paragraph 3(c) of the contract. Thus, the issue for me to decide is whether the failure of Hubbard's potatoes to meet the required #1 or #2 color minimum constitutes a "substantial impairment" of the installments.

Whether goods conform to contract terms is a question of fact. Moreover, in determining whether goods conform to contract terms, a buyer is bound by the "good faith" requirements set forth in NYUCC 1-203—"Every . . . duty within this Act imposes an obligation of good faith in its enforcement or performance." Thus, UTZ's determination that Hubbard's potatoes failed to satisfy the contract terms must be fairly reached.

The UTZ-Hubbard contract contains many specific requirements regarding the quality of the potatoes. In paragraph 1 the contract states that "only specified varieties as stated in contract will be accepted. . . ." Paragraph 3(a) states that "All shipments shall meet the United States Standards for Grades of Potatoes for Chipping, USDA, January 1978 . . . , in addition to other provisions enumerated in this 'Section 3' loads that do not meet these standards may be subject to rejection. . . ." Paragraph 3(b) sets forth specific size requirements . . . ; paragraph 3(c) sets forth specific gravity requirements; paragraph 3(d) contains the color requirements at issue in this case; and paragraph 3(f) sets forth a number of other defects or incidents of improper treatment or handling of the potatoes that provide UTZ with the right to reject the potatoes.

Clearly, the quality standards are of great importance to UTZ. They are the most detailed aspect of the contract—far more so than timing or even quantity specifications.

In a contract of this type, where the quality standards are set forth with great specificity, the failure to satisfy one of the specifically enumerated standards is a "substantial impairment." UTZ obviously cares the most about the specific quality specifications, as is evident from the numerous references throughout the contact.

Additionally, I find that UTZ's determination that the potatoes did not meet the required #2 color standard was made in good faith, as required by UCC 1-203. As noted above, the manner of visual testing utilized by UTZ was reasonable and customary. Further, Smith and DeGroft, the UTZ testers who rejected Hubbard's potatoes, provided credible testimony about their respective experience (Smith—30 years, DeGroft—5–6 years) and method of making such determinations. Accordingly, I find that UTZ fairly and in good faith determined that Hubbard's potatoes were nonconforming.

Thus, I find that Hubbard's failure to meet the proper color standard amounted to a "substantial impairment" of the installments (2-612(2)), substantially impairing the whole contract (2-612(3)). Accordingly, I find that UTZ's rejection of Hubbard's potatoes was proper. . . .

Judgment for defendant.

CRITICAL THINKING

The court tells us that the purpose of the substantial-impairment requirement is to preclude a party from canceling a contract for trivial defects. Then the court considers whether UTZ canceled the contract for trivial defects. Explain the relationship between the court's explanation of the purpose of the substantial-impairment requirement and the concept of good faith.

[CONTINUED]

ETHICAL DECISION MAKING

Both parties probably prefer the ethical norm or value of security. How so? Which facts would each party highlight in explaining how a particular decision would enhance the value of security?

CASE OPENER WRAP-UP

Alpha Chi Omega

In *Furlong v. Alpha Chi Omega Sorority,*[2] the court ruled in favor of Alpha Chi Omega. The court analyzed the case from the perspective of the basic performance obligation and then looked at exceptions from both the seller's and the buyer's perspectives.

Furlong's basic obligation was to transfer and deliver conforming goods. Alpha Chi Omega was required to accept and pay for conforming goods in accordance with the contract.

Clearly, Furlong did not transfer and deliver "conforming goods." The court ruled that the design specifications for the sweaters and masks became part of the basis of the bargain and thus became an express warranty in the contract. The sweaters and masks failed to meet the requirements of the parties' agreement. None of the exceptions to the perfect tender rule helped Furlong. The one that had the most potential to help him was the seller's right to cure, but, unfortunately, he did not have time to cure the defects since he delivered the sweaters and masks just one day before the Midnight Masquerade party. Furlong learned an important lesson. He should have included language in the agreement that gave him discretion to make design changes without approval, especially in situations in which there was a short timeline for getting the merchandise to the buyers.

Alpha Chi Omega met all of its obligations. The sorority inspected the sweaters within a reasonable amount of time. It did not "accept" the goods simply by issuing a check. Instead, it clearly rejected the goods. Soon after inspection, Altomondo and Lieberman called Furlong to notify him that they were rejecting the goods. They were within their rights to reject the goods "in whole." That Furlong refused to acknowledge their rejection did not give him any increased power or rights.

Even though the sisters of Alpha Chi Omega did not get to wear the sweaters and masks they had ordered to the Midnight Masquerade party, in the end the sun did shine for Alpha Chi Omega. The court ruled that the sorority was entitled to cancel the contract and recover the partial payment of the purchase price. Unfortunately, the case does not tell us what the sisters wore to the party.

[2] 657 N.E.2d 866 (1993).

Summary

The Basic Performance Obligation

Under the UCC, sellers and lessors are obligated to *transfer and deliver conforming goods.*

Buyers and lessees are obligated to *accept and pay for conforming goods* in accordance with the contract.

The UCC requires *good faith* in the performance and enforcement of every contract.

Specific Obligations of Sellers and Lessors

The *perfect tender rule* indicates that if goods or tender of delivery fail in any respect to conform to the contract, the buyer/lessee has the right to accept the goods, reject the entire shipment, or accept part and reject part.

Exceptions to the perfect tender rule allow sellers/lessors and buyers/lessees to consider:

- Norms in the industry and past dealings between the parties.
- Exceptions outlined in the parties' agreement.
- The seller's/lessor's right to cure.
- Excuse from performance when identified goods are destroyed through no fault of the parties.
- The concept of substantial impairment as it relates to revocation of acceptance and installment contracts.
- The concept of commercial impracticability.

Specific Obligations of Buyers and Lessees

If all goes well in a transaction over the sale or lease of goods, the buyer or lessee inspects the goods and then *pays* according to the agreement.

The seller or lessor must provide an opportunity for *inspection.*

- The concept of reasonableness governs the inspection process.
- After inspection, the buyer or lessee decides whether to accept the goods.

After inspecting, the buyer/lessee signifies *acceptance* or partial acceptance.

- Sellers or lessors sometimes presume acceptance.
- Partial acceptance is allowed in some circumstances.
- Buyers or lessees are allowed to revoke or withdraw acceptance of nonconforming goods.
- Buyers or lessees must issue reasonable notice if they decide to reject goods.

Cases in which a buyer decides to assert his or her right to reject nonconforming goods are often categorized under the heading "rescission or revocation of acceptance by buyer."

Point / Counterpoint

According to its critics, the application of the perfect tender rule can be a hypertechnical application of contractual obligations that really have no bearing on the substance of the contract but allow a party to escape contractual obligations on second thought.

Should the Perfect Tender Rule Be Ignored by the Courts and Replaced with the Common Law and CISG Concept of Substantial Performance?	
Yes	**No**
Common law really got it right through its cases holding that only material obligations must be complied with and immaterial ones are just that—immaterial and inconsequential. Common law has perfected, so to speak, the substantial-performance rule to a very workable conclusion. It gives the trier of fact flexibility in determining the impact of nonperformance in the overall scheme of the contractual relationship while keeping the focus on the intent of the parties and the ultimate injury or harmlessness of the noncompliance. Further, as we see more and more countries adopting the CISG, UCC concepts such as the perfect tender rule are out of sync with the rest of the commercial world. In the ever-accelerating venue of international transactions, uniformity is clearly the order of the day. We all need to be on the same page with contract interpretation.	The underlying concept that is the foundation of contract law worldwide is the notion that the parties are free to negotiate the terms and conditions of their respective contracts. Nothing in the UCC prohibits the parties from negotiating a substantial-performance definition in the performance obligation of the contract. However, by creating something other than the perfect tender rule, the courts send the message that the will of the parties may be frustrated if the noncompliance is somehow lessened to some level of immateriality. But who is better to determine this immateriality: the parties or the courts? By including specific performance requirements in the contract, the parties indicate what is material and what is not material. This determination should be left undisturbed by the courts and common law.

Questions & Problems

1. What determines the obligations of sellers/lessors and buyers/lessees?
2. Explain what the "good faith" and "commercial reasonableness" obligations are.
3. Explain what the perfect tender rule is and how it can be modified.
4. Amboy Closeouts, Inc., agreed to purchase 25,000 Christmas ornaments from Polar Trading, Inc. Alcorn, president of Amboy, requested 14 cases of the ornaments as samples and agreed to purchase the samples if he was pleased with the quality. He received the samples and determined that they were in satisfactory condition, but the bill was never paid. Alcorn contacted Polar Trading to order more ornaments, but he was told that he needed to fax a copy of a deposit check in order to secure the shipment. Alcorn faxed a copy of the $2,000 deposit check to Polar Trading, but he did not mail the check. Polar Trading sent a total of 352 ornaments to Alcorn. After receiving the shipment, Alcorn contacted Polar Trading and reported that many of the cases were defective. He had already sold some of the ornaments, but the rest were sent back. Polar Trading sold some of the returned ornaments but was unable to sell the complete shipment. Amboy argued that, under the UCC, it had the right to reject all the goods, accept all the goods, or partially accept and reject some of the goods. Further, Amboy argued that Polar Trading breached the contract by delivering defective goods and, therefore, no payment was due. How did the court decide? [*Polar Trading, Inc. v. Amboy Closeouts, Inc.*, 899 S.W.2d 577 (1995).]

5. Allied and Pulsar are both companies in the business of selling computer component parts. Allied ordered 50,000 computer chips from Pulsar and sold the chips to Apple. After inspecting the chips, Apple found 35,000 of them to be defective and returned the chips to Allied. Allied contacted Pulsar, and although the 30-day return period had expired, Pulsar agreed to take back the defective chips. Pulsar never returned the chips, nor did it provide Allied with a refund for the 35,000 chips. Allied purchased new chips from an acceptable substitute and was able to refill Apple's request. Allied brought a suit against Pulsar, requesting a refund. Did Pulsar breach the contract? Did Pulsar cure the defective delivery? [*Allied Semi-Conductors International, Limited v. Pulsar Components International, Incorporated,* 907 F. Supp. 618 (1995).]

6. Wilbur Reed operated a small greenhouse in Montana. He ordered most of his plants from McCalif Grower Supplies. Reed often supplied local Kmart and Ernst stores with his products. During the holiday season, he agreed to provide them with poinsettia plants. Reed ordered the plants from McCalif, and McCalif had growers send the plants to Reed from Colorado. Reed's employee accepted the boxes at the airport and did not note any damages to the packaging. However, when the boxes were opened, the poinsettias appeared damaged. Reed contacted McCalif and notified it that the poinsettias were damaged as a result of poor packing. McCalif advised Reed to report the damages to the carrier, Delta Airlines. Delta paid Reed $924.66 in compensation. McCalif was not able to supply Reed with more poinsettias before the holiday season. As a result, Reed lost accounts to many of the stores. McCalif sued Reed for payment for the poinsettias, $3,223.56. Reed refused to pay and argued that McCalif had failed to deliver according to their contract. Who did the court agree with? [*McCalif Grower Supplies, Inc. v. Wilbur Reed,* 900 P.2d 880 (1995).]

7. Emanuel Law Outlines (ELO) is owned and operated by Steven Emanuel. The company provides study aids for law students. Multi-State Legal Studies, Inc., conducts bar review courses for law school graduates. Multi-State and ELO entered into a contractual relationship whereby ELO would provide Multi-State with 950 copies of subject summaries for the California bar exam. ELO provided each of the requested subjects on time and made the necessary changes that Multi-State requested. In February, Emanuel underwent quadruple bypass surgery and began to fall behind in his work. He had informed Multi-State in January about his surgery. The last set of subjects was due in May. According to Emanuel, ELO contacted Multi-State and explained that the deadline needed to be extended. Multi-State agreed that early June would be acceptable. Multi-State's president, Feinberg, denied ever agreeing to the change in deadline. ELO sent the supplement to Multi-State in June. Multi-State terminated the contract, stating that ELO's failure to meet the May deadline constituted a material breach of contract. Is Multi-State correct? Did ELO cure the breach by providing Multi-State with the material in June? [*Emanuel Law Outlines v. Multi-State Legal Studies, Inc.,* 899 F. Supp. 1081 (1995).]

8. Rockland Industries agreed to purchase three containers of antimony oxide at $1.80 per pound from Manley-Regan Chemicals. Rockland produces drapes, and antimony oxide is used to fireproof the drapes. A representative from Manley-Regan, David Hess, worked with Conrad Ailstock, Rockland's purchasing agent. Hess informed Ailstock of a slight delay, but he assured Ailstock that the product, which was coming from China, was "on the water." Three months after the two companies had made the agreement, Hess contacted Ailstock to report that the product was not coming. According to Hess, Manley-Regan was considering legal claims against the Chinese supplier or the Chinese government. Rockland was forced to find another supplier,

but the price was substantially higher. Rockland brought suit to recover the difference between Manley-Regan's quoted price and the price of the substitute antimony oxide. Is the commercial-impracticability defense appropriate? Explain. [*Rockland Industries, Inc. v. Manley-Regan Chemicals Division,* 991 F. Supp. 468 (1998).]

9. Alamance Board of Education accepted a bid from Bobby Murray Chevrolet, a General Motors franchisee, to provide approximately 1,200 school bus chassis. After the agreement, the EPA enacted changes in allowed emission levels. The engines described in the bid were not in compliance with the more stringent standards. The school system purchased the chassis from another store and informed Murray that it intended to hold him liable for any excess in costs. The difference between the bid price and the actual amount totaled $150,152.94. Bobby Murray Chevrolet subsequently claimed that GM had breached its contract with Murray and that it became commercially impracticable to deliver the product. Will the concept of commercial impracticability excuse Bobby Murray Chevrolet's failure to perform? [*Alamance Board of Education v. Bobby Murray Chevrolet, Inc., v. General Motors Corporation,* 465 S.E.2d 306 (1996).]

10. David Cooper purchased a computer and software for his supermarket business. He was using a software program recommended and installed by the seller, Contemporary Computer Systems, Inc. The sales contract had a clause that stated that no refunds would be given after the 90-day warranty period. Cooper initially had problems with both the hardware and the software. Contemporary Computer Systems tried to remedy these problems. A pattern of problems and attempts to fix went on for some time, far beyond the 90-day time period expressly described in the contract. When Cooper had had enough, he decided to revoke the contract and demand his money back. Contemporary Computer Systems said the 90-day express clause in the contract precludes this action. Who won? [*David Cooper, Inc. v. Contemporary Computer Systems, Inc.,* 846 S.W.2d 777 (1993).]

11. North American Lighting (NAL) purchased a headlight aiming system from Hopkins Manufacturing Corporation (Hopkins). NAL produces headlamps for most major automobile manufacturers. It is important that NAL produce headlamps that meet government safety requirements, which ensure that drivers can see what they need to see without blinding oncoming motorists. Hopkins tried to sell NAL its Machine Vision System (MVS), which Hopkins believed was appropriate for the kind of testing NAL had to undertake to comply with federal guidelines. NAL decided to purchase the MVS even though it saw problems from the start. NAL based its purchase decision on Hopkins' promises that software could be added to the system to make it meet NAL's needs. After approximately two years of working with Hopkins, and the MVS still failing to meet NAL's needs, NAL informed Hopkins that it was revoking acceptance. The issue in the case is whether NAL can recover the amount it tendered Hopkins in partial payment. Hopkins wants the unpaid purchase price, as well as an amount that approximates the reasonable rental value of the equipment Hopkins had loaned to NAL. Who gets what? [*North American Lighting, Inc. v. Hopkins Manufacturing Corp.,* 37 F.3d 1253 (1994).]

12. Aubrey Reeves purchased a computer system for his business from Radio Shack Computer Center. Radio Shack is the local retailer for products sold by Tandy, its parent company. During negotiations, it became clear that Reeves needed software that Radio Shack could not provide. A Radio Shack salesperson referred Reeves to a software source book, let Reeves know he could choose compatible software from the source book, and informed him that Tandy does not support or service software

from the source book. A disclaimer to this effect appears in the source book. Reeves eventually purchased computers from Tandy, some software from Tandy, and more specialized software from a company called Lizcon. The Lizcon software did not meet Reeves's needs. Reeves subsequently sent a letter to Tandy, asking for rescission of the contract and damages. Can Reeves rescind? [*Aubrey's R.V. Center, Inc. v. Tandy Corporation,* 731 P.2d 1124 (1987).]

13. Landrum sold Gappelberg a big-screen television. The television had many defects, some of which Landrum and his service representatives fixed. Three weeks after the sale, the television stopped working altogether, and Gappelberg let Landrum know. Landrum promised to fix the television, but he did not. Gappelberg then requested return of consideration and asked the service representative to pick up the set but not to repair it because he would not accept it or a replacement. The question in the case was whether Gappelberg was allowed to prevent Landrum from curing the nonconforming television by his refusal to accept a replacement set. What did the court decide? Are you more sympathetic to Landrum or Gappelberg? [*Leitchfield Development Corp. v. Clark,* 757 S.W.2d 207 (1988).]

Looking for more review material?

The Online Learning Center at **www.mhhe.com/kubasek1e** contains this chapter's "Assignment on the Internet" and also a list of URLs for more information, entitled "On the Internet." Find both of them in the Student Center portion of the OLC, along with quizzes and other helpful materials.

Remedies for Breach of Sales and Lease Contracts

CASE OPENER

Two All-Beef Patties, Special Sauce, Lettuce, Cheese . . .

When you bite into a Big Mac at McDonald's, savor the shredded lettuce on your taco at Taco Bell, or head to Pizza Hut to sample the offerings at the salad bar, do you ever stop and give serious thought to who supplies all the lettuce for these products? In May and June 1991, the fast-food industry faced a serious business challenge when the price of lettuce rose dramatically. The fallout from that price increase included a lawsuit between the companies that supply lettuce to McDonald's: KGM Harvesting Company; its parent, Coronet Foods; and Fresh Network, which serves as a lettuce broker to Castellini Company. Castellini sells the lettuce to Club Chef. Club Chef chops and shreds the lettuce and then supplies it to McDonald's, Taco Bell, and Pizza Hut.

KGM Harvesting Company, the seller, had a contract to deliver 14 loads of lettuce each week to lettuce broker Fresh Network, the buyer, for 9 cents a pound. When the price of lettuce rose, KGM refused to deliver the lettuce it had promised to Fresh Network and instead sold the lettuce to others and made a profit of between $800,000 and $1,100,000. Fresh Network was angry over KGM's breach and subsequently pursued two actions. First, Fresh Network refused to pay KGM $233,000, the amount it owed the supplier for lettuce it had already delivered. Second, Fresh Network purchased lettuce in the open market to fulfill its contractual obligation to Castellini/Club Chef. Fresh Network was forced to spend approximately $700,000 more for lettuce in the open market than it would have paid KGM. Castellini covered all but $70,000 of Fresh Network's extra expense. Castellini passed the extra cost along to Club Chef, which passed at least part of this cost along to its fast-food customers.

Both KGM and Fresh Network filed complaints under the Perishable Agricultural Commodities Act (PACA), which promotes fair trading practices in the fruit and vegetable

CHAPTER 24

industry.[1] KGM sought the balance due on its outstanding invoices ($233,000). Fresh Network sought damages for the difference between the price it was forced to pay to buy replacement lettuce and the price it had established through its contract with KGM ($700,000).

1. Can KGM, the seller, seek the balance due on its outstanding invoices? Will the court punish KGM for its refusal to honor its contract with Fresh Network?
2. Is Fresh Network, the buyer, allowed to buy lettuce on the open market and then seek damages against KGM? Does it matter that most of Fresh Network's additional cost was ultimately passed on to fast-food customers? What happens to the profit (between $800,000 and $1,100,000) KGM made by selling to other buyers the lettuce it was obligated to deliver to Fresh Network?

The Wrap-Up at the end of the chapter will answer these questions.

Source: Facts are from *KGM Harvesting Company v. Fresh Network,* 42 Cal. Rptr. 2d 286 (1995).

Learning Objectives

After reading this chapter, you will be able to answer the following questions:

1. What constitutes a breach of a sales contract?
2. What money damages are available for breach?
3. When is specific performance of the contract a remedy?
4. What is cover?

[1] One of PACA's features is that it provides procedures for resolving disputes, including disputes about remedies allowed under the UCC.

5 What is resale?

6 What are liquidated damages?

This chapter explains the remedies available to companies such as KGM and Fresh Network. The first section restates the primary goal of contract remedies. This section helps you understand the range of remedies available to sellers/lessors and buyers/lessees. The next two sections list and explain the remedies available to sellers/lessors and buyers/lessees. The first of these sections focuses on remedies available to sellers/lessors, from the right to cancel the contract to the right to reclaim goods. Then the next section looks at remedies available to buyers/lessees, from the right to recover goods to the right to accept nonconforming goods and then seek damages. The last section of the chapter provides examples of situations in which the parties' agreement modifies or limits remedies available under the UCC.

The Goal of Contract Remedies

The obligations of sellers/lessors and buyers/lessees are determined by (1) terms the parties outline in agreements, (2) custom, and (3) rules outlined by the Uniform Commercial Code (UCC). This chapter focuses primarily on rules outlined by the UCC.

The UCC adopts several common law principles, including principles that underlie remedies available under the UCC. In *KGM Harvesting Company v. Fresh Network,*[2] the court began its analysis with a reminder of the general purpose of remedies under common law contract rules and the UCC. The court said:

> The basic premise of contract law is to effectuate the expectations of the parties to the agreement, to give them the "benefit of the bargain" they struck when they entered into the agreement. In its basic premise, contract law therefore differs significantly from tort law. Contract actions are created to enforce the intentions of the parties to the agreement, while tort law is primarily designed to vindicate social policy. The basic object of damages is *compensation,* and in the law of contracts the theory is that the party injured by the breach should receive as nearly as possible the benefits of performance. A compensation system that gives the aggrieved party the benefit of the bargain, and no more, furthers the goal of predictability about the cost of contractual relationships in our commercial system.

Thus, as you think about the range of remedies available to sellers/lessors and buyers/lessees, think about what remedies would give the parties the benefit of the bargain they struck, and nothing more. Of course, the ultimate goal of contractual remedies is the possibility, if not probability, a system that provides compensation will also function as a system of deterrence in which parties do not breach contracts or, if they do, will be amenable to a mutually satisfied settlement. After all, remember the old adage that when disputes turn into litigation, the only winners are often the attorneys. The UCC creates a statute of limitations for bringing a lawsuit arising under a breach of contract for the sale of goods. UCC Section 2-725(1) states that four years is the time frame for a plaintiff to file suit once a cause of action accrues.

Remedies Available to Sellers and Lessors under the UCC

CANCEL THE CONTRACT

UCC Sections 2-703(f) and 2A-523(1)(a) allow a seller or lessor to cancel the contract if the buyer or lessee is in breach. The UCC requires that sellers/lessors notify buyers/lessees of the

[2] 42 Cal. Rptr. 2d 286, 289. Quotes from and citations to cases the court cites have been omitted from the extract.

cancellation. Then the seller or lessor pursues remedies available under the UCC. Remember, these remedies give the seller/lessor the benefit of the bargain, and nothing more.

Case Nugget Statute of Limitations

Troy Boiler Works, Inc. v. Sterile Technologies, Inc.
777 N.Y.S.2d 574 (2003)

The defendant, Sterile Technologies, Inc., purchased a sterilizer from the plaintiff, Troy Boiler Works, on an installment payment plan. The defendant was to make installment payments charged with 1.5 percent interest per month. The sterilizer was delivered on August 23,1996. The last payment was received on April 21, 1998. At the time of the last payment, the defendant still owed the plaintiff $112,615 as the balance due on the sterilizer; as of the time of the filing of the lawsuit, the defendant owed an additional $134,214 in finance charges. The plaintiff filed its lawsuit to collect on the account on November 20, 2002. The defendant moved to have the suit dismissed as it was filed after the four-year statute of limitations had run out (April 21,1998, to November 20, 2002, is four years, seven months, and one day).

The issue before the court was the determination of the appropriate statute of limitations to apply. UCC Section 2-725 places the statute of limitations on suing on a contract for the sale of goods at four years from the time the cause of action accrues (in this case April 21, 1998). However, the plaintiff argued that this lawsuit was a suit to collect money on account, rather than one for breach of a contract for the sale of goods, and thus that the six-year statute of limitations under New York's general contract statutes should prevail. The court had to decide whether the state's general statute of limitations for contract—the six years—or the UCC's specific statute of limitations on contracts for the sale of goods—the four years—applied.

The New York trial court dismissed the claim, stating that the four-year statute of limitations applied. The court cited an Oregon appellate case, *Moorman Manufacturing Co. of California v. Hall:**

> . . . although an account stated is based on a separate agreement between the parties, it relates and cannot be divorced from the underlying sales transaction. The UCC drafters intended one limitation to apply to all transactions involving the sale of goods, regardless of the theory of liability asserted. To hold that the UCC limitation period does not apply to actions on account, despite the underlying sale of goods, would run counter to the drafters' purpose of providing consistency and predictability in commercial transactions.

*113 Or. App 30 (1992).

WITHHOLD DELIVERY

Sometimes a buyer breaches the contract or lease before the seller has delivered the goods. For instance, the buyer or lessee might fail to pay according to the terms of the agreement. UCC Sections 2-703(a) and 2A-523(1)(c) allow sellers or lessors to withhold delivery of goods when the buyer or lessee is in breach.

RESELL OR DISPOSE OF THE GOODS

Sellers or lessors are allowed to sell the goods to another buyer or dispose of the goods when the buyer is in breach and the goods have not yet been delivered. The seller/lessor then holds the buyer/lessee liable for any loss. UCC Section 2-706 allows the seller to recover the difference between the resale price and the contract price, plus incidental damages and minus expenses saved. Although the buyer is liable for these damages, the seller gets to keep any profits it makes on the resale. UCC Section 2A-527(2) outlines a similar rule for lease agreements. The lessor is allowed to lease the goods to another party and recover unpaid lease payments and any deficiency between the lease payments due under the original lease contract and those due under the new contract. The lessor can also seek incidental damages.

SUE TO GET THE BENEFIT OF THE BARGAIN

In trying to give the seller or lessor the benefit of the bargain, and nothing more, courts often grant damages to recover the purchase price or lease payments due. In Case 24-1, the court grants a remedy it believes gives the seller the benefit of the bargain. This remedy includes compensation for lost profits.

CASE 24-1 KENCO HOMES, INC. v. WILLIAMS

COURT OF APPEALS OF WASHINGTON, DIVISION 2
972 P.2D 125 (1999)

On September 27, 1994, Kenco Homes, Inc. (Kenco), and Dale and Debi Williams (the Williams) entered into a written contract whereby Kenco agreed to sell, and Williams agreed to buy, a mobile home that Kenco had not yet ordered from the factory. The contract called for a price of $39,400, with $500 down. The parties agreed that (1) the contract was enforceable only if Williams obtained financing, (2) the contract would be enforceable only if Williams later approved a bid for site improvements, (3) the UCC governed the contract, although Kenco did not have the right to collect liquidated damages, and (4) the contract provided for reasonable attorney fees to the prevailing party.

After the first two conditions were met (financing and the approval of a bid for site improvements), the Williams repudiated the entire transaction because "[they] found a better deal elsewhere." Kenco did not place the order for the mobile home and sued the Williams for lost profits.

The trial court rejected Kenco's claim for lost profits. Instead, the court ruled that Kenco would be adequately compensated by retaining the Williams' $500 down payment. The court also ruled that the Williams were the prevailing party and should receive reasonable attorney fees.

Kenco appealed, asking the court to consider (1) whether the trial court used the correct measure of damages and (2) whether the trial court properly awarded attorney fees to the Williams.

J. MORGAN: . . . Under the Uniform Commercial Code (UCC), a nonbreaching seller may recover "damages for nonacceptance" from a breaching buyer. The measure of such damages is as follows: (1) Subject to subsection (2) and to the provisions of this Article with respect to proof of market price, the measure of damages for nonacceptance or repudiation by the buyer is the difference between the market price . . . at the time and place for tender and the unpaid contract price together with incidental damages provided in this Article . . . , but less expenses saved in consequence of the buyer's breach. (2) *If the measure of damages provided in subsection (1) is inadequate to put the seller in as good a position as performance would have done* then the measure of damages is the profit (including reasonable overhead) which the seller would have made from full performance by the buyer, together with any incidental damages provided in this Article . . . , due allowance for costs reasonably incurred and due credit for payments or proceeds of resale.

As the italicized words demonstrate, the statute's purpose is to put the nonbreaching seller in the position that he or she would have occupied if the breaching buyer had fully performed (or, in alternative terms, to give the nonbreaching seller the benefit of his or her bargain). A party claiming damages under subsection (2) bears the burden of showing that an award of damages under subsection (1) would be inadequate.

In general, the adequacy of damages under subsection (1) depends on whether the nonbreaching seller has a readily available market on which he or she can resell the goods that the breaching buyer should have taken. When a buyer breaches before either side has begun to perform, the amount needed to give the seller the benefit of his or her bargain is the difference between the contract price and the seller's expected cost of performance. Using market price, this difference can, in turn, be subdivided into two smaller differences: (a) the difference between the contract price and the market price, and (b) the difference between the market price and the seller's expected cost of performance. So long as a nonbreaching seller can reasonably resell the breached goods on the open market, he or she can recover the difference between contract price and market price by invoking subsection (1), and the difference between market price and his or her expected cost of performance by reselling the breached goods on the open market. Thus, he or she is made whole by subsection (1), and subsection (1) damages should be deemed "adequate." But if a nonbreaching seller cannot reasonably resell the breached goods on the open market, he or she cannot recover, merely by invoking subsection (1), the difference between market price and his or her expected cost of performance. Hence, he or she is not made whole by subsection (1); subsection (1) damages are "inadequate to put the seller in as good a position as performance would have done"; and subsection (2) comes into play.

The cases illustrate at least three specific situations in which a nonbreaching seller cannot reasonably resell on the open market. In the first, the seller never comes into possession of the breached goods; although he or she plans to acquire such goods before the buyer's breach, he or she rightfully elects not to acquire them after the buyer's breach. In the second, the seller possesses some or all of the breached goods, but they are of such an odd or peculiar nature that the seller lacks a post-breach market on which to sell them; they are, for example, unfinished, obsolete, or highly specialized. In the third situation, the seller again possesses some or all of the breached goods, but because the market is already oversupplied with such goods (i.e., the available supply exceeds demand), he or she cannot resell the breached goods without displacing another sale. . . .

. . . In this case, Kenco did not order the breached goods before Williams repudiated. After Williams repudiated, Kenco was not required to order the breached goods from the factory; it rightfully elected not to do so; and it could not resell the breached goods on the open market. Here, then, "the measure of damages provided in subsection (1) is inadequate to put [Kenco] in as good a position as [Williams'] performance would have done; subsection (2) states the applicable measure of damages;" and Kenco is entitled to lost profit of $11,133.

The second issue is whether Kenco is entitled to reasonable attorneys fees. The parties' contract provided that the prevailing party would be entitled to such fees. Kenco is the prevailing party. . . .

REVERSED.

CRITICAL THINKING

How could the trial court judge have reached the conclusion that the $500 down payment was adequate to put the seller in as good a position as it would have been in if performance had occurred? What different facts and/or reasoning allows the appellate court to reverse the trial court's decision?

ETHICAL DECISION MAKING

Is this court's decision consistent with the Golden Rule? Explain.

LIQUIDATED DAMAGES

The Kenco case above makes passing mention of liquidated damages. **Liquidated damages** are damages identified *before* the breach occurs. The parties are free to negotiate, as part of the contract, a liquidated-damage clause in which the parties agree in advance what the damages will be for each party should a breach occur. Generally speaking, a court will enforce a liquidated-damage clause as long as it is not so far out of reasonable range as to be punitive in nature. Liquidated-damage clauses that are deemed to be punitive in nature are not enforceable.

The code provides for liquidated damages if the parties have not expressly negotiated a liquidated-damage clause. UCC Section 2-718 pertains to liquidated damages and allows the nonbreaching seller to claim against a breaching buyer 20 percent of the purchase price or $500, whichever is less, as liquidated damages.

Likewise, though the UCC does not mention the availability of punitive damages, other than in its voiding of liquidated damages that are punitive in nature, an issue that remains unsettled is the awarding of punitive damages against a breaching party who intentionally or egregiously breaches the contract. You will remember from tort law that when a tort is committed either intentionally or recklessly, the court may infer legal malice and instruct a jury that it may consider the awarding of punitive damages in addition to compensatory damages. Although this concept is well settled in tort law, it has never been widely applied in contract law. Yet there are some who argue that it should be, especially to deter intentional breaches of contract.

STOP DELIVERY

UCC Sections 2-705(1) and 2A-526(1) allow a seller or lessor to stop delivery of goods that are in transit. *In transit* means that the seller or lessor has delivered the goods to a carrier or bailee but the carrier or bailee has not yet turned them over to the buyer. Of course, the seller/lessor must give timely notice to the carrier/bailee so that the carrier/bailee is able to stop delivery. Also, the rules are different for insolvent and solvent buyers and lessees. If the buyer/lessee is insolvent, the carrier/bailee can stop delivery regardless of the quantity shipped. If the buyer/lessee is solvent, however, the carrier or bailee can stop delivery only if the quantity shipped is a large shipment (e.g., a carload or truckload).

RECLAIM THE GOODS

Under UCC Sections 2-709(1) and 2A-529(1), if the buyer or lessee has possession of the goods and is in breach, the seller or lessor can sue for the purchase price of the goods or for the lease payments due, plus incidental damages. In some circumstances, the UCC allows the seller or lessee to reclaim the goods. UCC 2-702(2) allows a seller to reclaim goods when it discovers the buyer is insolvent. UCC 2A-525(2) allows a lessor to reclaim goods when the lessee fails to make payments according to the lease terms.

Remedies Available to Buyers and Lessees under the UCC

CANCEL THE CONTRACT

Sometimes, sellers or lessors fail to deliver the goods and thus are in breach. UCC Sections 2-711(1) and 2A-508(1)(a) allow buyers and lessees to cancel the contract and then seek remedies that give them the benefit of the bargain. In Case 24-2, a buyer of heating coils had the right to cancel a contract with the seller because the coils did not work according to the buyer's specifications. The buyer subsequently sued for damages.

OBTAIN COVER

Case 24-2 also explains the buyer's right to obtain cover. Under UCC Sections 2-712 and 2A-518, buyers and lessees are allowed to **cover,** or substitute, goods for those due under the sales or lease agreement. The "lettuce" case at the beginning of the chapter focuses on the issue of the buyer's ability to obtain cover and then seek damages. Think of the facts in that case as you read this subsection and the one below.

As you read Case 24-2, notice that, in obtaining cover, the buyer must (1) demonstrate good faith in obtaining the substitute goods, (2) pay a reasonable amount for the substitute goods, (3) act without unreasonable delay in purchasing the substitute goods, and (4) purchase goods that are reasonable substitutes.

CASE 24-2

U.S.A. COIL & AIR, INC. v. HODESS BUILDING CO.
WL 66582
R.I. SUPER. (1999)

U.S.A. Coil and Air, Inc. (USA) and Hodess Building Co. (Hodess) were involved in a legal dispute that arose after USA supplied cooling coils for an HVAC system, which was part of a "clean-room" project for Lockheed/Sanders. USA agreed to provide the needed coils to Hodess for $33,156.00. USA did provide the coils, but the coils failed to perform as specified.

USA subsequently sent Hodess replacement coils, but these, too, failed. USA believed the failure was related to Hodess' flawed system, not the coils. Hodess informed USA that it would replace the coils, using a different vendor to supply the coils.

USA requested to have its coils returned, and Hodess agreed, as long as USA paid for shipping or sent someone to pick up the coils. Communication between the parties broke down. Hodess never paid the contract price of $33,156.00. USA brought a breach of contract action to recover this amount. Hodess counterclaimed for breach of contract and asked for its $83,374.95 in replacement costs.

J. GIBNEY: . . . If a buyer rightfully rejects a tender of goods in a contract such as this one, he is entitled to cancel the contract. UCC 2-711(1). Once the contract is cancelled, the buyer's obligation to pay the purchase price is discharged. UCC 2-106(3).

USA does not dispute that both sets of coils it provided failed to conform to the performance specifications referenced in the contract purchase order. . . . USA blames the system design for the failure. . . . [T]his court finds that the plaintiff breached the contract purchase order when it failed to provide coils which met the performance specifications. Thus, Hodess was excused from paying the purchase price.

Moreover, with respect to USA's right to cure its breach, Hodess allowed USA the opportunity to do so. Hodess installed USA's replacement coils, carefully following USA's instructions and modifying the system at USA's suggestion. When the replacement coils failed, USA's attempts to cure the breach failed as well. . . . USA is not entitled to recover. . . .

The defendant counterclaims, arguing breach of contract and seeking recovery of the replacement costs incurred due to the breach. Generally, "where a right of action for breach exists, compensatory damages will be given for the net amount of the losses caused and gains prevented by the defendant's breach, in excess of savings made possible." The goal is to place the injured party in as good a position as he would have been if the contract had not been breached. . . . When a buyer justifiably revokes acceptance of goods, the measure of direct damages is the difference between the cost of cover and the contract price, less any expenses saved as a result of the seller's breach. UCC 2-711(1)(b). To cover, a buyer must "in good faith and without unreasonable delay" make a "reasonable purchase or contract to purchase . . . goods in substitution for those due from the seller." UCC 2-712(1). Whether the buyer acted in good faith and in a reasonable manner is determined with reference to the conditions at the time and place the buyer attempted to cover. UCC 2-712 at comment 2. It is irrelevant that hindsight may later suggest a cheaper or more effective method. The burden of proof is on the seller of goods to prove that cover was not reasonably obtained. . . .

Having found USA breached the contract, this court also concludes that USA is liable for the resulting damages incurred by Hodess. To replace the defective coils, Hodess incurred substantial expenses for engineering, supervision of, and replacement of the coils. Hodess documented its expenditures with receipts and project expense reports, demonstrating a total reasonable replacement cost of $83,734.95. USA did not present any evidence which would tend to dispute the reasonableness of cover costs. . . . Thus, using the damages formula enunciated in UCC 2-711(1)(b), Hodess is entitled to the replacement costs less the contract price [which was $33,156.00], or $50,578.95. . . .

Judgment for defendant.

CRITICAL THINKING

Hodess appears to have had an advantage in the case because it had better evidence. How so? How could USA have increased its chances of winning?

ETHICAL DECISION MAKING

Suppose Hodess later discovers that its system design was flawed and it was not really USA's fault that the coils did not work. Which ethical test or tests would encourage Hodess's executives to come forward with that information?

SUE TO RECOVER DAMAGES

In Case 24-2, although Hodess was able to cover, it still incurred damages. Buyers such as Hodess, and lessees, are entitled to incidental and consequential damages. **Consequential damages** include damages for lost profits as long as these damages are not too speculative. These monetary damages give the injured buyer or lessee the benefit of the bargain.

RECOVER THE GOODS

UCC Sections 2-502 and 2A-522 allow buyers and lessees to recover the goods identified in the contract if the seller or lessor becomes insolvent within 10 days after receiving the first payment due under the agreement. Buyers or lessees are obligated to pay the remaining balance according to the terms of the agreement.

OBTAIN SPECIFIC PERFORMANCE

UCC Sections 2-716(1) and 2A-521(1) allow buyers and lessees to seek the remedy of specific performance when either (1) the goods are unique or (2) a remedy at law is inadequate. **Specific performance** usually requires that the seller or lessor deliver the particular goods identified in the contract. Sometimes, however, doing so is not possible. In Case 24-3, the court decides what to do when it believes specific performance is the appropriate remedy but the goods identified in the contract have been sold to another buyer. Notice that cover is not a possible remedy for this buyer.

CASE 24-3 KING AIRCRAFT SALES, INC. v. LANE
COURT OF APPEALS OF WASHINGTON, DIVISION 1
846 P.2D 550 (1993)

In October 1988, King Aircraft Sales (King) entered into an agreement with Joe Lane and Lane Aviation, Inc. (Lane), to purchase two "quality, no damage" aircraft from Lane for $870,000. King made a $10,000 deposit. Before the expiration of the time to perform, Lane told King it was backing out of the agreement. Lane ultimately sold the planes to another buyer, Priester Aviation, for $870,000. Priester subsequently sold the planes. King sued Lane, seeking the remedy of specific performance.

The trial court found that the planes were "one of a kind" or "possibly the best" in the U.S. However, it did not find that the planes were "unique" because other planes of the same make and model were available. The planes Lane had initially offered King, however, were so rare in terms of their exceptional condition that King had no prospect to cover its anticipated resales by purchasing alternative planes. The trial court agreed with King that there was no possibility of finding similar or better planes.

The trial court ruled that King was entitled to specific performance and, because Lane had already sold the planes to someone else, awarded relief in the form of "value." The trial court determined value by using a lost expectation of profit approach. Lane appeals this outcome. The issue on appeal is whether the trial court erred when it granted monetary damages as a remedy in a claim for specific performance under Washington's version of the UCC, specifically RCW 62A.2-716.

ACTING CHIEF JUDGE PEKELIS: . . . Lane's principal claim on appeal is that because this was solely an action for specific performance under the UCC, and because the goods had been sold and thus inaccessible, no remedy was available to King. Lane contends the trial court had no authority to make a dollar value award. Its argument is as follows: Because King failed to plead a claim for monetary damages in its original complaint and had twice been denied permission by the court to add such a claim, no right to a damages remedy existed. However, because an adequate remedy at law existed, albeit not one available to King, specific performance was not proper here either.

We disagree and find that the remedy fashioned by the trial court was proper under the UCC and Washington common law.

The UCC, 2-716, codified in Washington as RCW 62A.2-716 provides:

> 62A.2-716 Buyer's right to specific performance or replevin.
>
> (1) *Specific performance may be decreed where the goods are unique or in other proper circumstances.*
>
> (2) The decree for specific performance may include such terms and conditions as to the payment of the price, *damages,* or other relief as the court may deem just. . . .
>
> (Emphasis added.)

The UCC . . . does not expressly require that the remedy at law be inadequate in order to invoke specific performance. However, the stated intent of the drafters of the UCC was to continue "in general prior policy as to specific performance and injunction against breach," and also "to further *a more liberal attitude* than some courts have shown" toward specific performance. (Emphasis added.)

Nevertheless, there is a split of authority among those jurisdictions which have considered whether a buyer's remedy at law must be inadequate before specific performance can be granted. . . .

We find the *Sedmak* case* particularly instructive on both its facts and the law. There, Mr. and Mrs. Sedmak were told they could buy a limited edition "pace car" when it arrived at the dealership for the suggested retail price of approximately $15,000. Factory changes were made to the car at the Sedmaks' request before delivery to the dealer. When the car arrived at the dealership the Sedmaks were told they could *bid* on the car, but its popularity had increased the price. The Sedmaks did not bid, but sued for specific performance. The court held that the pace car was not unique in the traditional legal sense; however, its "mileage,

* The court is referring to *Sedmak v. Charlie's Chevrolet, Inc.,* 622 S.W.2d 694 (Mo. App. 1981).

condition, ownership and appearance" did make it difficult, if not impossible, to obtain the replication without considerable expense, delay, and inconvenience. The court ordered specific performance even though the legal remedy of damages may have been available to make the Sedmaks "whole."

The *Sedmak* case also addressed the UCC's adoption of the term "in other proper circumstances" and Official Comment 2, RCW 62A.2-716 [FN2]: . . .

> In view of this Article's emphasis on the commercial feasibility of replacement, a new concept of what are "unique" goods is introduced in this section. Specific performance is no longer limited to goods which are already specified or ascertained at the time of contracting. The test of uniqueness under this section must be made in terms of the total situation which characterizes the contract. . . . [U]niqueness is not the sole basis of the remedy under this section for the relief may also be granted "in other proper circumstances" and inability to cover is strong evidence of "other proper circumstances."

The general term "in other circumstances" expresses the drafters' intent to "further a more liberal attitude than some courts have shown in connection with the specific performance of contracts of sale." Sec. 400.2-716, UCC, Comment 1. . . .

We agree with the *Sedmak* court's interpretation of 2-716 and, like that court, find the liberal interpretation urged by the UCC drafters to be entirely consistent with the common law of our state. . . .

We conclude that the trial court properly determined that specific performance was an appropriate remedy here. At the time King commenced its action for specific performance, Lane was still in possession of the planes; thus, the court properly acquired equity jurisdiction. The airplanes, although not necessarily "unique," were rare enough so as to make the ability to cover virtually impossible. Furthermore, Lane, by its own act of selling the planes, incapacitated itself from performance. Under these circumstances, the court of equity did not err in finding that "other proper circumstances" were present for issuance of relief under a claim of specific performance under the UCC. The trial court had the discretion to award the legal remedy of damages or other relief deemed just by the trial court. . . . *[W]e conclude that under RCW 62A.2-716 and Washington Common law the trial court's determination that "other proper circumstances" existed is correct and permitted it to fashion the relief it did.*

AFFIRMED.

CRITICAL THINKING

The court announced that it agreed with a liberal interpretation of UCC 2-716. Can you infer from the court's reasoning what it would have argued if it had agreed with a conservative interpretation of UCC 2-716?

ETHICAL DECISION MAKING

Explain what Lane wanted the court to decide. If the court had agreed with Lane, which ethical norm would have provided the most support for this decision?

REJECT NONCONFORMING GOODS

In Chapter 23, and this chapter, several of the cases have focused on what happens when the seller or lessor delivers nonconforming goods. This section and the next two review the buyer's/lessee's remedies when the seller/lessor delivers nonconforming goods. First, UCC Sections 2-601 and 2A-519 allow the buyer or lessee to reject the goods. The buyer or lessee may then obtain cover or cancel the contract.

REVOKE ACCEPTANCE OF NONCONFORMING GOODS

UCC Sections 2-608 and 2A-517 sometimes allow the buyer or lessee to revoke acceptance of nonconforming goods. For instance, in Case 24-2, Hodess rejected acceptance of the nonconforming coils USA provided. Hodess was allowed to reject acceptance because it had made a reasonable assumption that the nonconformity would be cured but then the nonconformity was not cured within a reasonable amount of time.

Case Nugget Right to Cure

Dunleavy v. Paris Ceramics USA, Inc.
47 Conn. Supp. 565 (2002)

Anne Dunleavy owned and operated an interior design business, Unique Interiors. She had contracted with Terry and Nancy McClinch to completely renovate their home, including retiling their swimming pool area and terrace with very expensive French limestone. Dunleavy purchased the limestone tiles from the defendant, Paris Ceramics, for a cost of $124,963. Of course, she turned around and sold them to the McClinches, along with installation, at a greatly marked-up price, but one that was well within commercial reasonableness.

Within a few months, in late October and early November (the tiles were installed in August 2001), the tiles began to flake and scale and most were breaking up. Dunleavy and representatives from the defendant company inspected the site in January, and all parties agreed that the limestone tiles were deficient. All agreed that the stone had to be taken up and replaced. The plaintiff, Dunleavy, wrote to the defendant asking for a refund of the $124,963. The McClinches had decided not to continue to use Unique Interiors and had refused to pay the portion of their bill referencing the installation and the limestone tile itself.

Paris Ceramics wrote to plaintiff Dunleavy offering to "cure" the defect by replacing the tile. The plaintiff never responded. Then Paris Ceramics demanded its right to cure the defect. The plaintiff then responded by filing suit for the $124,963. Defendant Paris Ceramics contended that the plaintiff was barred from recovering damages because she refused the defendant's offer to cure the breach. The defendant correctly cites the law as holding that when the buyer has rejected nonconforming goods, the seller has the right to effect a cure; the failure of the buyer to accept that cure precludes the buyer from suing for subsequent damages.

However, the court, though agreeing with the defendant's statement of law, held that the goods had already been accepted by Dunleavy and then resold to the McClinches. There is no right to cure once the goods have been accepted. The court then found for the plaintiff for $124,953 less a $49,000 salvage fee Dunleavy was able to procure from the salvage of the limestone.

ACCEPT THE NONCONFORMING GOODS AND SEEK DAMAGES

Under UCC Sections 2-607, 2-714, and 2A-519, buyers or lessees are allowed to accept nonconforming goods and then seek monetary damages to give them the benefit of the bargain. The buyer/lessee must give the seller/lessor reasonable notice of the defect.

connecting to the core

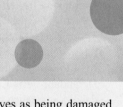

Economics

In your economics class, you may have discussed the government's role in the market through its taxing and spending powers, referred to as *fiscal policy.* The government may use these powers to affect market outcomes, particularly when the market does not self-adjust (via the "invisible hand") as desired. For example, the government could decrease taxes in the hope of stimulating investment and consumer spending. However, the government also plays a much more basic and essential role in the market: It lays the legal foundation on which market transactions may occur. This particular function of the government in the economy is intimately related with the subject matter of this textbook—the intersection of law and business.

Fundamentally, the government creates laws (e.g., states' adopting of the UCC) that protect parties on both sides of business transactions. For instance, as discussed in this chapter, the government creates laws that protect buyers and sellers in contractual relationships. If a seller fails to deliver a good for which a buyer has already tendered payment, the buyer can seek a remedy, either by suing for compensation or by obtaining specific performance for delivery of the goods. Had the government not created laws to enforce contractual agreements, buyers would be less willing to make payments prior to receiving goods and sellers would be less willing to deliver goods prior to receiving payments. Hence, the absence of business law would create strong disincentives to buy and sell. Therefore, the government plays a critical role in establishing the legal foundation on which buyers and sellers can form contractual agreements, and where one party fails to meet his or her obligations, the other party can seek redress for any damages.

global context

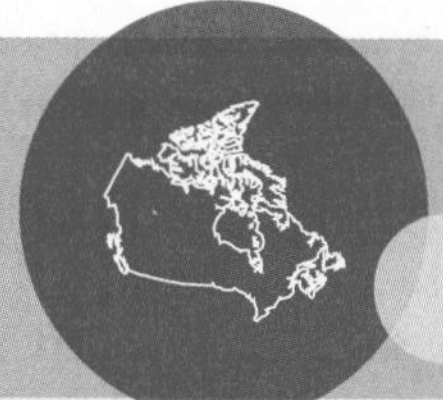

Canada Does Not Need "Lemon Laws"

In the United States, lemon laws exist to provide remedies for buyers of defective cars when sellers have limited the remedies otherwise provided by the UCC. Lemon laws allow buyers to get a new car, seek replacement of defective parts, or obtain a refund of the consideration they have paid in situations in which a buyer has repeatedly complained about car defects and the seller has been unable to correct the defects after numerous attempts. The buyer who gets a refund of consideration gives the lemon back.

Canada does not have lemon laws.* Instead, each province runs an arbitration program through which a buyer can lodge complaints against a carmaker for selling a car that the consumer perceives as being damaged goods. So far, Canadian carmakers have bought back only a few vehicles. For instance, DaimlerChrysler Canada buys "very, very few" lemons, while its U.S. parent has purchased approximately 58,000 in the past eight years.† Dennis DesRosiers, an independent Toronto analyst, says the Canadian car industry does not need a lemon law because "cars are so well built these days that the chances of getting a lemon [in Canada] are very low."‡

* David Steinhart, "'Lemon' Resales Not Happening in Canada," *National Post,* March 20, 2001.

† Ibid.

‡ Ibid.

Modifications or Limitations to Remedies Otherwise Provided by the UCC

Parties to sales and lease contracts are allowed to modify or limit remedies. Under UCC Sections 2-719 and 2A-503, parties are allowed to create agreements that make it clear the remedies outlined in the agreement are exclusive remedies. Courts uphold modifications or limitations to remedies unless the remedies fail in their essential purpose.

In Case 24-4, the court applies UCC 2-719 to rule on whether a seller could limit the buyer's remedies to repair, replace, or refund. These remedies are standard remedies in the bottling industry. Pay attention to the court's explanation of when remedies outlined in an agreement "failed of their essential purpose."

CASE 24-4 FIGGIE INTERNATIONAL, INC. v. DESTILERIA SERRALLES, INC.

U.S. COURT OF APPEALS, FOURTH CIRCUIT
190 F.3D 252 (1999)

In this case, a dispute arose between Figgie International, Inc. (Figgie), and Destileria Serralles, Inc. (Serralles), over bottle-labeling equipment Figgie sold to Serralles. Serralles is a distributor of rum and other products. It operates a bottling plant in Puerto Rico. When the bottle-labeling equipment failed to place a clear label on a clear bottle of "Cristal" Rum with a raised glass oval, Figgie attempted to repair the equipment. After several attempts to fix the equipment, Figgie returned the purchase price of the equipment and Serralles returned the equipment.

Serralles asked Figgie to pay for alleged losses caused by the equipment's failure to perform as expected. This failure caused a delay in Serralles' production of Cristal Rum. Figgie instituted a declaratory judgment action, asserting that Serralles' remedy for breach was limited to repair, replace, or refund under both the written terms and conditions of the sales agreement (which was lost) and pursuant to usage of trade in the bottle-labeling industry. In this case, the court considered the extent to which usage of trade in the bottling industry makes it clear that Serralles' remedy was limited to repair, replace, or refund. Serralles disputes that usage of trade imposes this limitation. Serralles also argues that because this limited remedy fails of its essential purpose, it is entitled to the full array of remedies the UCC provides.

CIRCUIT JUDGE TRAXLER: . . . Because the crux of this appeal centers on whether the agreement between the parties limited Serralles' remedy for breach to repair, replacement, or refund of the purchase price, we begin with the language of S.C.Code Sec. 36-2-719, which governs modifications or limitations to the remedies otherwise provided by the UCC for breach of a sales agreement. Section 36-2-719 provides that:

> (1) Subject to the provisions of subsections (2) and (3) of this section and of the preceding section (Sec. 36-2-318) on liquidation of damages,
>
> (a) the agreement may provide for remedies in addition to or in substitution for those provided in this chapter and may limit or alter the measure of damages recoverable under this chapter, as by limiting the buyer's remedies to return of the goods and repayment of the price, or to repair

and replacement of nonconforming goods or parts; and

(b) resort to a remedy as provided is optional unless the remedy is expressly agreed to be exclusive, in which case it is the sole remedy.

(2) Where circumstances cause an exclusive or limited remedy to fail of its essential purpose, remedy may be had as provided in this act.

(3) Consequential damages may be limited or excluded unless the limitation or exclusion is unconscionable. Limitation of consequential damages for injury to the person in the case of consumer goods is prima facie unconscionable, but limitation of damages where the loss is commercial is not.

Under these provisions, parties to a commercial sales agreement may provide for remedies in addition to those provided by the UCC, or limit themselves to specified remedies in lieu of those provided by the UCC. An "[a]greement" for purposes in the UCC is defined as "the bargain of the parties in fact as found in their language or by implication from other circumstances, *including course of dealing or usage of trade. . . .*" . . . (emphasis added). In turn, the Code provides that "[a] course of dealing between parties and any usage of trade in the vocation, or trade in which they are engaged or of which they are or should be aware give particular meaning to and supplement or qualify terms of an agreement." . . . "Usage of trade" is defined as "any practice or method of dealing having such regularity of observance in a place, vocation or trade as to justify an exception that it will be observed with respect to the transaction in question. . . ."

. . . Serralles contends that the district court erred in concluding that usage of trade in the bottle-labeling industry supplemented the agreement between the parties with the limited remedy of repair, replacement, or refund. We disagree.

. . . Figgie submitted several affidavits of persons with extensive experience in the bottle-labeling and packaging industry, attesting that sellers in the industry always limit the available remedies in the event of a breach to repair, replacement, or return, and specifically exclude consequential damages. . . . Serralles offered no evidence to contradict the affidavits submitted by Figgie. Accordingly, the district court correctly concluded that usage of trade would limit Serralles to the exclusive remedy of repair, replacement, or return.

. . . Serralles contends that a limited remedy imposed or implied by trade usage cannot be an exclusive remedy because it is neither "expressly agreed to" nor "explicit." We disagree.

Section 36-2-719 provides that the "agreement" between the parties may limit remedies. Section 36-1-201(3) defines "[a]greement" as including terms "impli[ed] from circumstances including course of dealing or usage of trade." . . . It seems clear to us that . . . usage of trade will supplement agreements and may indeed impose an exclusive remedy in the event of a breach. . . .

Having determined that usage of trade supplemented the agreement of the parties with the exclusive remedy of repair, replacement, or return, we turn to Serralles' contention that the limited remedy "fail[ed] of its essential purpose," entitling it to nevertheless pursue the full array of UCC remedies. *See* S.C.Code Ann. Sec. 36-2-719(2). We conclude that it did not.

Section 36-2-719(1)(a) specifically contemplates that the parties to an agreement may, as they did in this case, limit remedies in the event of a breach to "return of the goods and repayment of the price or to repair and replacement of nonconforming goods or parts." Section 36-2-719(2), however, provides that the general remedies of the UCC will apply, notwithstanding an agreed-upon exclusive remedy, if the "circumstances cause [the remedy] to fail of its essential purpose." Under this provision, "where an apparently fair and reasonable clause because of circumstances fails in its purpose or operates to deprive either party of substantial value of the bargain, it must give way to the general remedy provisions of [the Code]." . . . In the instant case, however, there is no evidence that the limited remedy of repair, replacement, or return has failed of its essential purpose or that the contracting parties have been deprived of the substantial value of the bargain.

Serralles argues that Figgie, by first attempting to repair the equipment, elected to pursue repair as the exclusive remedy and, thereby, forgo enforcement of the remedy and reimbursement. From this premise, Serralles contends that Figgie's failure to repair the machines resulted in the remedy failing of its essential purpose. We find no support in the language of the

[CONTINUED]

UCC or in the cases interpreting it for this novel argument, and no evidence that this contemplated remedy of return and refund, once invoked, failed of its essential purpose.

. . . The district court correctly concluded that a limited remedy of repair, replacement, or return did not fail of its essential purpose.

AFFIRMED.

CRITICAL THINKING

Identify a significant ambiguous phrase that affects your ability to accept the court's conclusion. Explain the ambiguity and why it matters.

ETHICAL DECISION MAKING

Both parties probably prefer the ethical norm or value of efficiency. How so? Which facts would each party highlight in explaining how a particular decision would enhance the value of efficiency?

e-commerce AND THE LAW

Computer Contracts

Sometimes, computer purchasers are surprised to find out they are bound to agreements that were created when sellers included contracts in the box in which the computer was delivered. Some of these agreements limit the purchaser's remedies. For instance, in *Hill v. Gateway 2000,** Hill purchased a computer from Gateway 2000 by placing a telephone order. The computer arrived through the mail. Gateway had placed a contract in the computer's shipping box that indicated that the terms sent in the box were binding on the buyer unless the buyer returned the computer within 30 days. One of the terms in this contract was a provision that stated that any disputes between the parties would be resolved through arbitration. The order taker had not read any of the terms of the contract over the telephone when Hill placed the order. When the computer arrived, Hill did not read the contract. In an effort to avoid the arbitration clause, Hill asked the court to determine that Gateway 2000 could not limit buyers' remedies or avenues through which they seek remedies (i.e., through arbitration) by bundling hardware and legal documents. The court ruled that the contract was binding on the parties. The court stated, "A contract need not be read to be effective; people who accept take the risk that the unread terms may in retrospect prove unwelcome."†

* 105 F.3d 1147 (1997).

† Ibid., at p. 1148.

global context

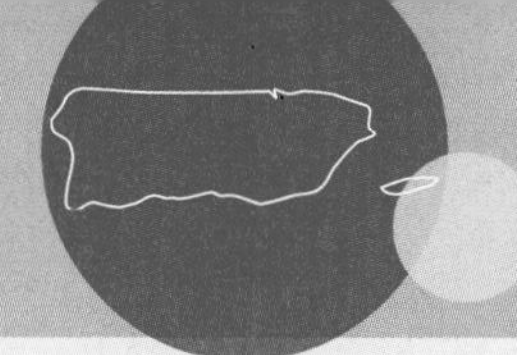

Puerto Rico, Rum, and Politics

Destileria Serralles, Inc., produces most of the rum sold on the island of Puerto Rico. In 1998, the company had annual sales totaling over $100 million. It produces and distributes more than 80 different product lines to countries throughout the world. Its flagship rum is sold under the Don Q label.

Destileria Serralles, other Puerto Rican rum producers, and the citizens of Puerto Rico found themselves in a political battle with the United States in 2001. U.S. lawmakers threatened to stop returning to Puerto Rico a portion of the taxes from rum sales after Puerto Rico demanded that the U.S. Navy stop conducting bombing exercises on Vieques, an island off Puerto Rico. By virtue of a century-old federal law, Puerto Rico receives approximately $250 million per year when the U.S. returns a portion of taxes from rum sales. The dispute hit a political low when Representative James Hansen, a Republican from Utah, called Puerto Rico "a welfare state."

President Bush decided to halt the bombing exercises in 2003. At this point, lawmakers have not decided whether to stop returning to Puerto Rico a portion of the taxes from rum sales.

* Data from http://www.serralles.com.

CASE OPENER WRAP-UP

Lettuce[3]

The chapter opener asks whether KGM, the seller, is allowed to seek the balance due on its outstanding invoices. The answer is clearly yes. Buyers are obligated to pay for conforming goods delivered according to the terms of the agreement. In fact, the parties agreed that Fresh Network owed KGM the outstanding balance of $233,000 at the beginning of the case, leaving Fresh Network's complaint against KGM as the focus of the judge's and jury's attention. It is also clear that the court will not punish KGM for its refusal to honor its contract with Fresh Network. Contract actions strive to enforce the intentions of the parties, not to punish sellers or buyers.

You learned in the chapter that buyers are allowed to obtain cover. In this case, KGM did not accuse Fresh Network of covering inappropriately. Often, cases that focus on issues related to cover accuse the buyer of (1) engaging in actions that show a lack of good faith in obtaining substitute goods, (2) paying too much for substitute goods, (3) unreasonably delaying its purchase of substitute goods, and/or (4) purchasing goods that are of a higher quality or grade and therefore not a reasonable substitute.[4] Instead, KGM argued that because Fresh Network was ultimately able to pass on the extra expense (except for $70,000) to Castellini Company,[5] and Castellini was able to pass this cost along to Club Chef, which passed the cost along to fast-food customers, Fresh Network should not recover the difference between the cover price and the contract price. KGM urged the court to refrain from allowing Fresh Network to obtain what it called a "windfall."[6]

The court did not agree with KGM. The court was aware of KGM's profit on the sale of the lettuce to other buyers.[7] The court's focus, however, was on the clear language of

[3] See *KGM Harvesting Company v. Fresh Network,* 42 Cal. Rptr. 2d 286 (1995).

[4] Ibid., p. 381.

[5] These parties had a "cost plus" contract that protected Fresh Network.

[6] Ibid., see footnote 3, at p. 382.

[7] Ibid., see footnote 3. The court said, "Seller, not surprisingly, does not focus on post-breach events impacting on *seller's* ultimate profit or loss. As noted earlier, seller made a profit of between $800,000 and $1,100,000 for selling the lettuce at the higher market price rather than the lower nine cents per pound contract price."

UCC 2-712, which allowed Fresh Network to recover the difference between the cover price and the contract price. KGM knew of Fresh Network's contract with Castellini and was aware of the possibility that the price of lettuce would fluctuate. The court also reminded KGM that the object of contract damages is to give Fresh Network, as nearly as possible, the equivalent of the benefits of performance. The court stated, "Only by reimbursing buyer for the additional costs above [the contract price], nine cents a pound, could the buyer truly receive the benefit of the bargain."[8] The court further stated, "What the buyer chooses to do with that bargain is not relevant to the determination of damages under section 2-712."[9]

Ultimately, the jury awarded Fresh Network $665,960.22, which represented the difference between the contract price of 9 cents a pound and the price Fresh Network paid to cover by purchasing substitute lettuce. The jury did not see this as a windfall to Fresh Network. The court subtracted the $233,000 that Fresh Network owed KGM on its invoices, leaving Fresh Network with a net award of $422,960.22.

[8] Ibid., at p. 383.

[9] Ibid., at p. 389.

Summary

The Goal of Contract Remedies

The goal of contract remedies is to give the parties the *benefit of the bargain they struck,* and nothing more.

Remedies Available to Sellers and Lessors under the UCC

When the buyer/lessee is in breach, the seller/lessor can:

- Cancel the contract.
- Withhold delivery.
- Sell or dispose of the goods.
- Sue to recover the purchase price, lease payments due, or some other measure of damages that give the seller or lessor the benefit of the bargain.
- Claim liquidated damages.
- Stop delivery.
- Reclaim the goods.

Remedies Available to Buyers and Lessees under the UCC

When the seller/lessor is in breach, the buyer/lessee can:

- Cancel the contract.
- Obtain cover.
- Sue to recover damages.
- Recover the goods.
- Obtain specific performance.
- Reject nonconforming goods.
- Revoke acceptance of nonconforming goods.
- Accept the nonconforming goods and seek damages.

Modifications or Limitations to Remedies Otherwise Provided by the UCC

Parties to sales and lease contracts are allowed to *modify or limit remedies.*

Courts uphold modifications or limitations to remedies unless the remedies fail in their *essential purpose.*

Point / Counterpoint

Generally speaking, punitive damages have not been a remedy applied to breach-of-contract cases. Usually, some kind of compensatory damages or specific performance are the most common remedies. However, tort law permits the awarding of punitive damages to deter legal malice, that is, intentional wrongdoing.

Shouldn't Such a Remedy Be Available in Contract Law to Deter Intentional or Egregious Breaches of Contract?	
Yes	**No**
The fundamental concept behind contract law is the integrity of the agreement, the integrity of the "meeting of the minds." When that integrity is wantonly disregarded, the law should have the discretion to impose sanctions that go beyond simply compensating for the injury caused to the opposing side. Contract law and the Uniform Commercial Code rest on the good faith and fair dealings of the parties. Intentional and egregious breaches cannot be ignored. If we permit intentional and egregious breaches of contract for economic gain, the underlying foundation of the "meeting of the minds" becomes irrelevant. What is to prevent a party from intentionally breaching if resale is possible to effect greater economic gain even after having to pay damages for the nonbreaching party's cover?	The hallmark nature of contract law is that the parties are free to negotiate and determine the material elements of their respective contracts. Nothing prohibits the parties from agreeing on liquidated-damage clauses within their contracts. To allow courts or juries the discretion to award punitive damages only creates a windfall opportunity for the nonbreaching party while serving no public good. The purpose of awarding of punitive damages in tort cases is to prevent such behavior from occurring in society. However, contracts are fundamentally different from torts in that contract law is purely private law between members of society for economic reasons. The public good is advanced when courts protect the integrity of the contractual agreement and permit the parties to recover only those losses actually incurred should a breach occur.

Questions & Problems

1. What options are available to a seller or lessor when the buyer or lessee is in breach?
2. Explain what consequential damages are and when they may be awarded.
3. Explain what the buyer's right to cover is.
4. A restaurant called "The Inn Between" entered into a contract to purchase a used restaurant computer system. The contract included installation and training from Remanco Metropolitan, Inc. The contract also required that Remanco keep the computer system in good operating order. The system was delivered and installed on March 29, 1995. The following day the computer malfunctioned and was down for three hours. Between March 30 and July 3, the restaurant contacted Remanco 48 times to report malfunctions. Though Remanco responded to each of the problems, the computer system continued to break down. Inn Between brought an action to

revoke its acceptance of the computer system. It viewed the system as a nonconforming good. Remanco counterclaimed, seeking the unpaid price under the system maintenance agreement and for nonreturn of the system. Which side gets the remedy it seeks? [*The Inn Between, Inc. v. Remanco Metropolitan, Inc.*, 662 N.Y.S.2d 1011 (1997).]

5. Gerado Dunham purchased a 1990 Chevrolet pickup truck for $12,945. The truck was in need of several repairs, but the dealer agreed to complete the repairs before delivering the vehicle. After the truck was delivered, Dunham noticed that the repairs had not been made. He returned the truck to the dealer to be repaired. The transmission was replaced three times, but the problem persisted. Dunham sought arbitration under the state's lemon laws. The truck was functional, but the problems were not fixable. The arbitrator ordered the dealer to refund the full purchase price of the vehicle. The dealer appealed the award. Does the buyer get the remedy he seeks? [*Royal Chrysler-Oneonta, Inc. v. Dunham,* 663 N.Y.S.2d 410 (1997).]

6. Charles Woods planned on opening a "Family Fun Center." The center would be an indoor recreational center with miniature golf, video games, and food services. Woods contacted Kenosha Associates to lease a building for the center. The lessor agreed to provide heat, ventilation, air-conditioning, bathrooms, and lighting for the building. After Woods signed the lease but before he was able to move into the building, Kenosha sent him a letter ending the agreement. Woods sued Kenosha for financial damages and lost profits he suffered as a result of the breach. The jury agreed with Woods and awarded him $1,033,124.32 in damages. Kenosha Associates appealed the decision, arguing that the jury should not have been able to provide damages for loss of profits because this measure of damages was too speculative. Does the appellate court agree with the trial court's award of damages for lost profit? [*T & HW Enterprises v. Kenosha Associates,* 557 N.W.2d 480 (1996).]

7. Duncan McCoy, owner of Alex-Duncan Shrimp Chef, Inc., hired Mitsuboshi Cutlery, Inc., to manufacture shrimp knives. These knives were covered by a patent and trademarks held by McCoy. Mitsuboshi produced 150,000 knives, but on delivery McCoy's separate marketing division refused to accept or pay for the knives. McCoy acknowledged that he was responsible for the division's failure to pay for the knives and purchased 20,000 of the knives. Mitsuboshi contacted McCoy to arrange payment and delivery of the 130,000 remaining knives, but McCoy refused to pay for them. Eventually, Mitsuboshi sold the knives to other restaurant wholesalers. McCoy sued Mitsuboshi for reselling the knives, but Mitsuboshi argued that it was entitled to resell them because McCoy had breached the contract. Was Mitsuboshi allowed to resell the knives? [*McCoy v. Mitsuboshi Cutlery, Inc.,* 67 F.3d 917 (1995).]

8. Andy and Melinda Meche purchased a car from Harvey, Inc. The Meches were interested in a low-priced car, and Harvey sold discounted program cars, which are vehicles that were previously owned by rental agencies. The sales representative explained to the Meches that program cars were usually under warranty and had relatively low mileage. The representative added that the cars were well maintained by the rental agencies and were "like new." After a short test drive, the Meches purchased a program car. The representative failed to tell them that the car had been previously wrecked and damaged. The Meches immediately noticed problems with the car and returned to Harvey to have the car inspected. On two occasions the representative told the Meches that the car had never been wrecked. A year later the Meches were involved in an accident, and the repairman noticed that the car had previously been wrecked and repaired. The Meches had put approximately 46,000 miles on the car.

They brought an action to demand full rescission of the sale. Harvey, Inc., believed the proper measure of damages should be reduction of the sales price. The company also believed the buyers should pay for their use of the automobile. Finally, Harvey, Inc., did not agree with the trial court's finding of bad faith and subsequent award of attorney fees to the Meches. What is the appropriate remedy? [*Meche v. Harvey, Inc.* 664 So. 2d 855 (1996).]

9. Bigelow-Sanford, Inc., contracted with the defendant, Gunny Corporation, for the purchase of 100,000 linear yards of jute at $.64/yard. Gunny made three of the scheduled deliveries, delivering a total of approximately 22,000 yards, but was then unable to make any more deliveries. Bigelow-Sanford was able to buy 78,000 yards on the open market for $1.21/yard, almost double its contract price with Gunny. Gunny claims that these purchases are commercially unreasonable and as such it should not be liable for the cover damages. Who gets what remedy? [*Bigelow-Sanford v. Gunny Corporation,* 649 F.2d 1060 (1981).]
10. Maria Palomo purchased a used car from LeBlanc Hyundai Partnership. She explained to the sales representative that she needed the car to go to work and to take care of her grandchildren. The representative told her that the car would be appropriate for those purposes and that, if she took care of the car, it "would last forever." Palomo believed that this comment meant that the car would last her the rest of her life. She kept up with regular maintenance, but she began to have problems with the car. Palomo's mechanic recommended that she replace the car's engine. Palomo wanted to return the car to LeBlanc and be refunded the purchase price. The trial court awarded her $1,000 for repairs and damages. She appealed the decision. Should Palomo be allowed to revoke acceptance? What is the appropriate remedy? [*Palomo v. LeBlanc,* 665 So. 2d 414 (1996).]
11. Lupofresh, Inc., agreed to sell hops to Pabst Brewing Company. When the hops were processed and ready to be shipped to Pabst, Pabst canceled the order, claiming that the contract's pricing mechanism violated federal antitrust laws. In the subsequent lawsuit by Lupofresh for breach of contract, Pabst claimed that before Lupofresh could maintain a claim for the price, it had to attempt to resell the hops on the market since the goods had not been accepted by Pabst and had been merely identified to the contract. Did Lupofresh make a reasonable effort to resell the goods? Can Lupofresh recover the full purchase price from Pabst? [*Lupofresh, Inc. v. Pabst Brewing Company, Inc.,* 505 A.2d 37 (1985).]
12. Sherman Burrus, a printer, purchased a printing press from Itek Corporation. Itek's salesperson knew that Burrus was a job printer and even suggested various features regarding the printer that would be pertinent to Burrus's business. Burrus had continuing problems with the printer that Itek never corrected. In the subsequent lawsuit, Burrus asked the court to award consequential damages, including an amount to compensate him for lost business. Itek claimed that the defects were due to Burrus's improper maintenance and operation of the machine, but the court disagreed and ruled in favor of Burrus. What is the appropriate measure of damages? [*Burrus v. Itek Corporation,* 360 N.E.2d 1168 (1977).]
13. New Pacific Overseas Group (USA) Inc. (New Pacific) alleged that Excal International Development Corp. (Excal) and its president, Kenneth Shin-Hai King (King), breached a series of contracts for the sale and installation of concrete-block manufacturing equipment to New Pacific. New Pacific asked a court to issue a preliminary injunction that would require specific performance of the contracts, including the return of a computer unit taken by King from the equipment. Excal claimed that none

of the goods identified in the contract were unique and that, subsequently, specific performance was an inappropriate remedy. Is Excal correct? [*New Pacific Overseas Group (USA) Inc. v. Excal International Development Corp.,* 2001 WL 40822 (2001).]

Looking for more review material?

The Online Learning Center at **www.mhhe.com/kubasek1e** contains this chapter's "Assignment on the Internet" and also a list of URLs for more information entitled "On the Internet." Find both of them in the Student Center portion of the OLC, along with quizzes and other helpful materials.

Warranties

CASE OPENER

The Aflatoxin Problem

Carl and Dorothy-Helen Huprich raise Arabian horses for breeding and selling. In 1989, they purchased corn from farmer David Bitto to feed to their horses after having it tested for aflatoxin, a toxin often present in horse feed. The sample tested negative, so the Huprichs purchased a large amount of feed. Soon after they began feeding their horses the corn, two died and a third soon fell ill and died as well. The Huprichs began to suspect that the corn was the culprit after another two horses died and a veterinarian confirmed that the horses had died from leukoencephalomalacia, a fatal brain disease that results from the toxin Fumonisin B-1. This toxin grows on mold known as *Fusarium Monoliforme,* a mold often present on feed corn. The Huprichs sued Bitto, alleging breach of implied warranty of merchantability[1]. You will learn more about implied warranty of merchantability in this chapter.

1. Suppose Bitto knew the toxin Fumonisin B-1 was frequently present on feed corn. Would it have been ethical to not inform the Huprichs of the need to also test for that toxin when they failed to do so?
2. Suppose the toxin was not present when Bitto sold the corn to the Huprichs but the mold was present. The mold by itself does not cause the disease from which the Huprichs' horses died. If the toxin grew on the mold after the Huprichs purchased the corn, has Bitto breached any warranties by selling them feed corn that had mold growing on it?

The Wrap-Up at the end of the chapter will answer these questions.

[1] *Huprich v. Bitto,* 667 So. 2d 685; 1995 Ala. LEXIS 307; CCH Prod. Liab. Rep. P14, 267; 28 U.C.C. Rep. Serv. 2d (Callaghan) 526.

CHAPTER 25

Learning Objectives

After reading this chapter, you will be able to answer the following questions:

1. What are express warranties?
2. What is the implied warranty of title?
3. What is the implied warranty of merchantability?
4. What is the implied warranty of particular purpose?
5. Do warranties apply to third parties?
6. Can warranties be disclaimed?

Introduction

Chapters 21 through 24 have illustrated how the Uniform Commercial Code modified common law contract formation and execution to facilitate the ease of contracts for the buying and selling of goods and to reflect certain generally accepted business practices.

This chapter focuses on how the UCC changed the common law of **warranties,** which are assurances by one party that the other party can rely on its representations of fact. The warranties discussed in this chapter include both express and implied warranties. *Express warranties* are explicitly stated, whereas *implied warranties* are automatically, as a matter of law, injected into the contract.

After reading this chapter, you will understand what types of warranties arise with the creation of a contract. You will also understand how these warranties can be limited, as well as what role warranty law plays in protecting consumers.

Types of Warranties

Warranties generally arise in conjunction with a sale or lease. They impose certain duties on the seller or lessor, and if the seller or lessor fails to live up to these duties, he or she may be sued for breach of warranty. There are three basic categories of warranties: warranties of title, express warranties, and implied warranties. Each will be discussed in the following sections.

WARRANTIES OF TITLE

While no warranties automatically arise under the common law, the UCC assumes that the seller:

1. Has good and valid title to the goods.
2. Has the right to transfer title free and clear of any liens, judgments, or infringements of intellectual property rights of which the buyer does not have knowledge.

The UCC specifically permits buyers to recover from sellers who have breached these **warranties of title.** The only exceptions to title warranties occur if they are disclaimed or modified by specific language in the contract or if the seller is obviously unable to guarantee title, as would be the case, for instance, at a sheriff's sale of seized goods. A buyer knows that goods repossessed and then resold and purchased through a sheriff's sale may have clouds on the title and unresolved liens that may surface.

Clearly, if the buyer is aware of any problem with the transfer of goods, the buyer is indeed purchasing them at her own risk. In contrast, if the buyer is unaware that the seller is transferring goods for which no good title passes or on which there are encumbrances or patent claims, the buyer may treat the contract as being in breach. Under such circumstances, the buyer may then avail himself of the remedies available under a breach situation. Consider Case 25-1, in which the seller has breached the implied warranty of title.

The warranty of title at issue in Case 25-1 arises automatically. Likewise, some warranties that relate to the nature of the goods also arise automatically, and they are generally referred to as the *implied warranties of quality* arising under the UCC. These warranties, discussed later in this chapter, include the implied warranty of merchantability, the implied warranty of fitness for a particular purpose, and the implied warranty of trade usage. Before we delve into the nature of these three UCC-created warranties, we will examine the common law concept of express warranties and the changes that the UCC has made to this concept.

CASE 25-1 JOHN COLTON AND PAMELA COLTON, PLAINTIFFS AND APPELLEES, v. LEE DECKER AND BETTY DECKER, DEFENDANTS AND APPELLANTS

SUPREME COURT OF SOUTH DAKOTA
540 N.W.2D 172; 1995 S.D. LEXIS 136;
47 A.L.R.5TH 951;
30 U.C.C. REP. SERV. 2D (CALLAGHAN) 206
NOVEMBER 15, 1995

Plaintiff John Colton was a truck driver who worked for a period of time for defendant Lee Decker in South Dakota. During this time Colton drove Decker's truck and subsequently purchased the truck from Decker. Decker affirmed during the sale that he had built the truck essentially himself as he had purchased the truck after its repossession from someone else. About a year and a half after the sale of the truck, Colton was stopped for speeding in Wyoming, where state troopers discovered that the vehicle identification numbers (VINs) on the truck did not match, often an indication of a stolen vehicle. The truck was confiscated, and after a nine-month investigation where several different VINs were discovered, it was determined that the truck did belong to Colton. However, the truck was inoperable because it had been dismantled and unsheltered during the winter and had to be towed back to South Dakota. Colton filed suit against Decker charging breach of warranty of title and warranty of merchantability, as well as breach of express warranty of description.

JUSTICE KONENKAMP: Wyoming authorities challenged the authenticity of Colton's title as the truck had three different VINs engraved at various points. Under these circumstances Colton [alleged] Decker breached the warranty of title under [appropriate provisions of South Dakota's UCC statutes]:

(1) Subject to subsection (2) [of South Dakota's UCC statutes] there is in a contract for sale a warranty by the seller. [T]hat

- (a) The title conveyed shall be good, and its transfer rightful; and
- (b) The goods shall be delivered free from any security interest or other lien or encumbrance of which the buyer at the time of contracting has no knowledge.

(2) A warranty under subsection (1) will be excluded or modified only by specific language or by circumstances which give the buyer reason to know that the person selling does not claim title in himself or that he is purporting to sell only such right or title as he or a third person may have.

Comment 1 to UCC § 2-312 states a buyer is entitled to "receive a good, clear title transferred . . . in a rightful manner so [the buyer] will not be exposed to a lawsuit in order to protect it." A split of authority persists on the scope of § 2-312. Decker relies on those cases which hold that a breach of warranty of title occurs only when an outstanding superior title exists. . . . Other courts hold that under § 2-312 mere initiation of a colorable challenge, one which is not spurious, regardless of the outcome, is sufficient to violate the warranty of title. . . . "Good title" typically means "the title which the seller gives to the buyer is 'free from reasonable doubt, that is, not only a valid title in fact, but [also] one that can again be sold to a reasonable purchaser. . . .'" . . . We find the latter to be the better rule.

Wyoming Highway Patrol officials questioned Colton's ownership due to contradictory VINs, thus casting a colorable challenge to its title. This was sufficient for a breach of title warranty claim. . . . Indeed, the majority view holds that a purchaser can recover for a breach of warranty of title by merely showing the existence of a cloud on the title. . . . Once breach of good title is established, good faith is not a defense, nor is a lack of knowledge of the defect. . . . Purchasers should not be required to enter into a contest on the validity of ownership over a titled motor vehicle. . . . As the undisputed facts reveal, Colton was forced into a contest over ownership because of conflicting VINs and an improper title. Thus, we uphold the circuit court's ruling that Decker breached the warranty of title.

AFFIRMED in favor of plaintiffs.

[CONTINUED]

CRITICAL THINKING

What is the main reason the court ruled in favor of Colton? Do you agree that this interpretation is better than the other?

ETHICAL DECISION MAKING

Did Decker act ethically in failing to tell Colton about the conflicting VINs? Why or why not?

Case Nugget — Third-Party Beneficiary to Express Warranty

Schaurer v. Mandarin Gems of California, Inc.
125 Cal. App. 4th 949 (2005)

Sarah Jane Schaurer not only had the misfortune of a very short-lived marriage to her husband Erstad but had the misfortune compounded when she learned that her supposed $45,000 engagement ring was actually worth only half of that amount. When she discovered this, after the divorce, she sued the defendant, Mandarin Gems of California, Inc., the company that sold the ring to her ex-husband and that had expressly warranted that the ring's value was $45,500.

The issue before the trial court was whether Sarah Jane had the rights that her ex-husband Erstad had regarding his sales contract with the defendant. As the court framed the issue:

> Plaintiff undoubtedly owns the ring. . . . But, ownership of gifted property, even if awarded in a divorce, does not automatically carry with it ownership of the rights of the person who bought the gift . . . contrary to the plaintiff's hypothesis, the divorce judgment did not give the plaintiff the ring embellished with Erstad's rights under the contract. . . .

The court of appeals held that indeed the plaintiff did not have Erstad's contractual rights. However, the court found that "the fact that Erstad did not assign or transfer his rights to the plaintiff does not mean she is without recourse. For although plaintiff does not have Erstad's rights by virtue of the divorce judgment, she nonetheless has standing in her own right to sue for breach of contract as a third party beneficiary under the [sales contract]."

The court held that Sarah Jane could indeed maintain her suit against Mandarin Gems of California under a breach of express warranty since she did qualify as a third-party beneficiary. The court wrote:

> We conclude the pleading here meets the test of demonstrating plaintiff's standing as a third party beneficiary to enforce the contract between Erstad and defendant. The couple went shopping for an engagement ring. They were together when plaintiff chose the ring she wanted or, as alleged in the complaint, she 'caused the ring to be purchased for her.' Erstad allegedly bought the ring for the sole and stated purpose of giving the ring to plaintiff . . . the jeweler must have understood Erstad's intent to enter into a sales contract for the plaintiff's benefit. Thus plaintiff has adequately pleaded her status as a third party beneficiary, and she is entitled to proceed with her contract claim against defendant. . . .

EXPRESS WARRANTIES

Although the common law does not use the term *express warranties,* the concept and application does exist in the common law. It seems only fair and equitable that promises made by a seller to induce a buyer to execute a sales contract should be enforceable. An **express warranty** is any description of the good's physical nature or its use, either in general or specific circumstances, that becomes part of the contract. To use common law language, an express warranty is a material term of the sale or lease contract.

Express warranties may be found in advertisements or brochures (e.g., "This electric saw comes with a lifetime guarantee"). Such a warranty may also be part of a written sales or lease contract; or it may be a salesperson's oral promise concerning the good, made while attempting to close a deal. A sample or model may also provide an express warranty. Generally speaking, if the buyer relies on representations, those representations become part of the contract in the form of express warranties. Consider Case 25-2, which arose over the issue of whether a federally mandated label constitutes an express warranty.

CASE 25-2

DONALD WELCHERT, RICK WELCHERT, JERRY WELCHERT, DEBORAH WELCHERT, APPELLEES, v. AMERICAN CYANAMID INC., APPELLANT

U.S. COURT OF APPEALS FOR THE EIGHTH CIRCUIT
59 F.3D 69; 1995 U.S. APP. LEXIS 15719; CCH PROD. LIAB. REP. P14,246; 1995

Deborah and Jerry Welchert began commercially growing vegetables in 1989. In 1990, they leased a tract of land southeast of Blair, Nebraska, for this purpose that was also to be farmed by Jerry's brother Rick Welchert. After they began planting vegetables, the Welcherts noticed that the vegetables were not growing properly. Deborah discovered that the herbicide Pursuit, manufactured by Cyanamid, had been applied to the land. Finding a label for Pursuit Plus, a different product, Deborah, Rick and Jerry reviewed the label. This label claimed that crops could be planted eighteen months after application of the herbicide. Crops were again planted on the land in 1991, but continued to experience growth problems.

Meanwhile, Rick and another brother, Donald, leased another property in 1991 that had been treated with Pursuit Plus in 1989. Rick never read the Pursuit Plus label, relying on Deborah's account. Donald also did not read the label. The vegetables planted on this land experienced growth problems as well. All four Welcherts filed a suit alleging breach of express warranty for damages caused to their crops by Pursuit and Pursuit Plus.

Pursuit and Pursuit Plus are regulated by the federal government under the Federal Insecticide, Fungicide, and Rodenticide Act (FIFRA), which has specific labeling requirements. The U.S. District Court for the District of Nebraska ruled that the Welcherts' express warranty claims were not preempted by FIFRA. Cyanamid appealed.

JUDGE McMILLIAN: Section 24 of FIFRA, as amended, provides in part:

(a) In general

A State may regulate the sale or use of any federally registered pesticide or device in the State, but only if and to the extent the regulation does not permit any sale or use prohibited by this subchapter.

(b) Uniformity

Such State shall not impose or continue in effect any requirements for labeling or packaging in addition to or different from those required under this subchapter.

At issue in the present case is the extent to which subsection (b) preempts a state law cause of action for breach of an express warranty. . . .

The express warranty claim of the Welcherts is based entirely on the label's statement with regard to the herbicide's carryover effect. They have not alleged that Cyanamid made any other statements with regard to the product which might serve as the basis for their express warranty claim. . . . [F]ederal regulation requires a pesticide manufacturer to provide labeling information about rotational crop restrictions. . . . Cyanamid's label statement on rotational crop use is thus a mandated disclosure, not a "voluntarily undertaken" promise. See Higgins v. Monsanto Co., 862 F. Supp. 751, 761 (N.D.N.Y. 1994) (Higgins) ("Express warranties have a voluntary quality, which is missing if they are mandated by EPA. The rationale that warrantors should be held to contracts that they voluntarily enter into does not apply when their actions are forced."). The determination that the challenged label statement was required by federal law was essential to the Worm court's [Worm v. American Cyanamid Co., 5 F.3d 744 (4th Cir. 1993)] decision on the preemption of the express warranty claim. The Worm court further rejected the plaintiff's argument that claims of breach of express warranty were not preempted because it "suggested that what was approved by the EPA was inadequate for purposes of establishing a state cause of action."

In the present case, like Worm, the Welcherts' express warranty claim arose solely on the bases of a labeling statement specifically required by federal law and approved by EPA. . . . Where Congress has so clearly put pesticide labeling requirements in the hands of the EPA, the Welcherts' claim challenging the accuracy of the herbicide label's federally-mandated and approved statement cannot survive. See Worm, 5 F.3d at 748 ("Because the language on the label was determined by the EPA to comply with the federal standards, to argue that the warnings on the label are inadequate is to seek to hold the label to a standard different from the federal one."). To hold otherwise would be to allow state courts to sit, in effect, as super-EPA review boards that could question the adequacy of the EPA's determination of whether a pesticide registrant successfully complied with the specific labeling requirements of its own regulations. In such case, state court consideration of the label statement would be an "additional requirement." In light of the extensive federal statutory and regulatory provisions on pesticide registration and labeling requirements, the preemptive language of §24(b) of FIFRA must be read to preclude the Welcherts' claim. Consequently, we hold that their state law claim for breach of an express warranty is preempted by FIFRA.

REVERSED in favor of defendant.

CRITICAL THINKING

If FIFRA did not regulate Pursuit and Pursuit Plus, and Cyanamid had put the label on voluntarily, would the label then have constituted an express warranty? Why or why not?

ETHICAL DECISION MAKING

The continued problems of the Welcherts with the land where Pursuit and Pursuit Plus had been applied perhaps indicate a problem with the pesticide or with the label. Although American Cyanamid won this case, as an ethical company, should it spend money to do more research on its products to determine whether the label should be changed?

Sometimes it is difficult to tell the difference between a statement of opinion and an express warranty. Statements of opinion are often salespersons' exaggerations and are known as "puffing." Puffing generally does not create an express warranty because it is not considered a representation of facts. Thus, if a salesperson says, "This is the finest piece

connecting to the core

Marketing

As you may have learned in your marketing class, *product positioning* refers to the value that consumers place on one product, on the basis of its attributes, relative to competitors' products. One important attribute that may influence consumers' purchasing decisions is the kind of warranty that is included with a particular company's product. Therefore, companies may choose to differentiate their products from competitors' products in part by offering better warranties. In other words, companies may position or reposition their products on the basis of product attributes that are important to consumers, including warranty provisions.

For example, E. Gluck Corp., which manufactures Anne Klein, Armitron, JLO, and, most recently, Donald J. Trump watches, provides a "limited-lifetime" warranty, meaning that the manufacturer guarantees the inner workings of the watch for the lifetime of the watch but does not guarantee normal wear and tear of the band and crystal. By providing a limited-lifetime warranty, E. Gluck Corp. distinguishes its products from those of other manufacturers, many of which offer only 10- or 11-year limited warranties. This difference in the duration of the limited warranty may influence consumers' purchasing decisions. Therefore, companies may be able to better position their products by offering better express warranties than their competitors.

Source: R. Kerin, S. Hartley, E. Berkowitz, and W. Rudelius, *Marketing* (New York: McGraw-Hill/Irwin, 2005), pp. 249–250.

of luggage I've ever seen," no one expects the buyer to rely on that as a promise. However, if the statement is "This suitcase is made of real crocodile," an express warranty may be created.

IMPLIED WARRANTIES OF QUALITY

Implied warranties arise by operation of law under certain circumstances. Earlier, you read about the implied warranties of title that arise under the UCC. This section focuses on the three warranties of quality that arise under the UCC.

Implied warranty of merchantability. Consider the following scenario: You purchase a toaster from a local discount store. When you use the toaster, all you get is either burnt toast or bread that is only slightly warm. You take the toaster back to the store and are met with this answer: "Well, we don't guarantee how well the toaster will work. After all, it does toast, either very, very lightly or very, very burnt." This answer, of course, is nonsense. There is a reasonable expectation of how a toaster will perform. That reasonable expectation is codified in the UCC **implied warranty of merchantability.**

To invoke this implied warranty, the purchaser must have purchased or leased the good from a merchant. Thus, a dirt bike purchased at a bicycle shop is covered by the warranty of merchantability, but a bike that is bought from a neighbor is not, unless the neighbor is a bicycle merchant.

Under the UCC, the goods must be *merchantable,* meaning that they must:

1. Be able to pass without objection in the trade or market for similar goods.
2. In the case of fungible goods, be of fair average quality within the description.
3. Be fit for the ordinary purposes for which such goods are used.
4. Be produced, within the variations permitted by the agreement, of even kind, quality, and quantity within each unit and among all units involved.
5. Be adequately contained, packaged, and labeled as the agreement may require.
6. Conform to the promises or affirmations made on the container or label, if any.

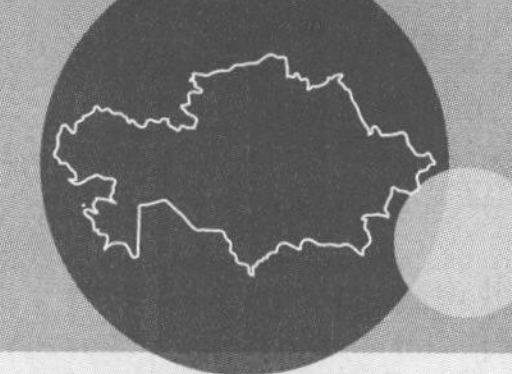

global context

Warranties in Kazakhstan

What Western law refers to as a *warranty* is called a *pledge* in Kazakhstan. Pledges serve the same function as warranties: They indicate the seller's confidence in the performance of a product and the buyer's right to compensation for nonperformance. Specifically, the Civil Code defines a pledge as "a means of securing the performance of an obligation by virtue of which the creditor (pledgeholder) has the right, in the event of the failure of the debtor to perform the obligation secured by the pledge, to receive satisfaction from the value of the pledged property preferentially before other creditors of the person to whom this property belongs." A pledge can be given in two instances. First, and most commonly, it can arise from a contract. Second, it can be given because the situation lends itself to legislation that demands a pledge be issued.

When a pledge is violated, the concept of penalties is employed. Penalties are similar to remedies in the U.S. law. Penalties are always issued in monetary form, the amount of which is usually determined by a court. Parties may stipulate penalties for failing to fulfill a pledge in the contract, but this is not necessary for compensation to be collected. Legislation does exist that specifies penalty amounts for particular situations in an attempt to avoid excessive payments.

Given the description of the warranty of merchantability, when Bitto sold the corn to the Huprichs, did the implied warranty of merchantability include a promise that the corn did not contain the toxin Fumonisin B-1? Did it include a promise that the corn did not contain *Fusarium monoliforme* mold, on which the toxin frequently grows?

The quintessential case defining and illustrating the implied warranty of merchantability is that of the Blue Ship Tearoom and Ms. Webster (see Case 25-3). The case concerned the merchantability of food.

CASE 25-3 | PRISCILLA D. WEBSTER v. BLUE SHIP TEA ROOM, INC.

SUPREME JUDICIAL COURT OF MASSACHUSETTS
347 MASS. 421, 198 N.E.2D 309 (1964)

A restaurant patron who ordered seafood chowder and choked on a fishbone brought this case. The plaintiff maintained that she would not have reasonably expected to find a bone in the chowder. At the trial, a jury found for Ms. Webster. The Blue Ship Tearoom, the defendant, appealed the case on the basis of the legal interpretation of the implied warranty of merchantability. The appellate decision below has become a classic in American jurisprudential reasoning.

JUDGE REARDON: . . . On Saturday, April 25, 1959, about 1 p.m., the plaintiff, accompanied by her sister and her aunt, entered the Blue Ship Tea Room operated by the defendant. The group was seated at a table and supplied with menus.

This restaurant, which the plaintiff characterized as "quaint," was located in Boston "on the third floor of an old building on T Wharf which overlooks the ocean."

The plaintiff, who had been born and brought up in New England (a fact of some consequence), ordered clam chowder and crabmeat salad. Within a few minutes she received tidings to the effect that "there was no more clam chowder," whereupon she ordered a cup of fish chowder. Presently, there was set before her "a small bowl of fish chowder." She had previously enjoyed a breakfast about 9 a.m. which had given her no difficulty. "The fish chowder contained haddock, potatoes, milk, water and seasoning. The chowder was milky in color and not clear. The haddock and potatoes were in chunks" (also a fact of consequence). "She agitated it a little with the spoon and observed that it was a fairly full bowl. . . . It was hot when she got it, but she did not tip it with her spoon because it was hot . . . but stirred it in an up and under motion. She denied that she did this because she was looking for something, but it was rather because she wanted an even distribution of fish and potatoes." "She started to eat it, alternating between the chowder and crackers which were on the table with . . . [some] rolls. She ate about 3 or 4 spoonfuls then stopped. She looked at the spoonfuls as she was eating. She saw equal parts of liquid, potato and fish as she spooned it into her mouth. She did not see anything unusual about it. After 3 or 4 spoonfuls she was aware that something had lodged in her throat because she couldn't swallow and couldn't clear her throat by gulping and she could feel it." This misadventure led to two esophagoscopies at the Massachusetts General Hospital, in the second of which, on April 27, 1959, a fish bone was found and removed. The sequence of events produced injury to the plaintiff which was not insubstantial.

We must decide whether a fish bone lurking in a fish chowder, about the ingredients of which there is no other complaint, constitutes a breach of implied warranty under applicable provisions of the Uniform Commercial Code, the annotations to which are not helpful on this point. As the judge put it in his charge, "Was the fish chowder fit to be eaten and wholesome? . . . [N]obody is claiming that the fish itself wasn't wholesome. . . . But the bone of contention here—I don't mean that for a pun—but was this fish bone a foreign substance that made the fish chowder unwholesome or not fit to be eaten?" The plaintiff has vigorously reminded us of the high standards imposed by this court where the sale of food is involved . . . and has made reference to cases involving stones in beans . . . , trichinae in pork . . . , and to certain other cases, here and elsewhere, serving to bolster her contention of breach of warranty.

The defendant asserts that here was a native New Englander eating fish chowder in a "quaint" Boston dining place where she had been before; that "[f]ish chowder, as it is served and enjoyed by New Englanders, is a hearty dish, originally designed to satisfy the appetites of our seamen and fishermen"; that "[t]his court knows well that we are not talking of some insipid broth as is customarily served to convalescents." We are asked to rule in such fashion that no chef is forced "to reduce the pieces of fish in the chowder to miniscule size in an effort to ascertain if they contained any pieces of bone." "In so ruling," we are told (in the defendant's brief), "the court will not only uphold its reputation for legal knowledge and acumen, but will, as loyal sons of Massachusetts, save our world-renowned fish chowder from degenerating into an insipid broth containing the mere essence of its former stature as a culinary masterpiece."

Notwithstanding these passionate entreaties we are bound to examine with detachment the nature of fish chowder and what might happen to it under varying interpretations of the Uniform Commercial Code.

Chowder is an ancient dish preexisting even "the appetites of our seamen and fishermen." It was perhaps the common ancestor of the "more refined cream soups, purees, and bisques." . . . The word "chowder" comes from the French "chaudiere," meaning a "cauldron" or "pot." "In the fishing villages of Brittany . . . 'faire la chaudiere' means to supply a cauldron in which is cooked a mess of fish and biscuit with some savoury condiments, a hodgepodge contributed by the fishermen themselves, each of whom in return receives his share of the prepared dish. The Breton fishermen probably carried the custom to Newfoundland, long famous for its chowder, whence it has spread to Nova Scotia, New Brunswick, and New England." A New English Dictionary (MacMillan and Co., 1893) p. 386. Our literature over the years abounds in references not only to the delights of chowder but also to its manufacture. A namesake of the plaintiff, Daniel Webster, had a recipe for fish chowder which has survived into a number of modern cookbooks and in which the removal of fish bones is not mentioned at all. One old time recipe recited in the New English Dictionary study defines chowder as "A dish made of fresh fish (esp. cod) or clams, stewed with slices of pork or bacon, onions, and biscuit. 'Cider and champagne are sometimes added.'" Hawthorne, in The House of the Seven Gables . . . , speaks of "[a] codfish of sixty pounds, caught in the bay, [which] had been dissolved into the rich liquid of a chowder."

A chowder variant, cod "Muddle," was made in Plymouth in the 1890s by taking "a three or four pound codfish, head added. Season with salt and pepper and boil in just enough water to keep from burning. When cooked, add milk and piece of butter." The recitation of these ancient formulae suffices to indicate that in the construction of chowders in these parts in other years, worries about fish bones played no role whatsoever. This broad outlook on chowders has persisted in more modern cookbooks. "The chowder of today is much the same as the old chowder. . . ." The American Woman's Cook Book, supra, p. 176. The all embracing Fannie Farmer states in a portion of her recipe, fish chowder is made with a "fish skinned, but head and tail left on. Cut off head and tail and remove fish from backbone. Cut fish in 2-inch pieces and set aside. Put head, tail, and backbone broken in pieces, in stewpan; add 2 cups cold water and bring slowly to boiling point. . . ." The liquor thus produced from the bones is added to the balance of the chowder. . . .

Thus, we consider a dish which for many long years, if well made, has been made generally as outlined above. It is not too much to say that a person sitting down in New England to consume a good New England fish chowder embarks on a gustatory adventure which may entail the removal of some fish bones from his bowl as he proceeds. We are not inclined to tamper with age old recipes by any amendment reflecting the plaintiff's view of the effect of the Uniform Commercial Code upon them. We are aware of the heavy body of case law involving foreign substances in food, but we sense a strong distinction between them and those relative to unwholesomeness of the food itself, e.g., tainted mackerel . . . and a fish bone in a fish chowder. Certain Massachusetts cooks might cavil at the ingredients contained in the chowder in this case in that it lacked the heartening lift of salt pork. In any event, we consider that the joys of life in New England include the ready availability of fresh fish chowder. We should be prepared to cope with the hazards of fish bones, the occasional presence of which in chowders is, it seems to us, to be anticipated, and which, in the light of a hallowed tradition, do not impair their fitness or merchantability. While we are buoyed up in this conclusion by Shapiro v. Hotel Statler Corp. 132 F. Supp. 891 (S. D. Cal.), in which the bone which afflicted the plaintiff appeared in "Hot Barquette of Seafood Mornay," we know that the United States District Court of Southern California, situated as are we upon a coast, might be expected to share our views. We are most impressed, however, by Allen v. Grafton, 170 Ohio St. 249, where in Ohio, the Midwest, in a case where the plaintiff was injured by a piece of oyster shell in an order of friend [sic] oysters, Mr. Justice Taft (now Chief Justice) in a majority opinion held that "the possible presence of a piece of oyster shell in or attached to an oyster is so well known to anyone who eats oysters that we can say as a matter of law that one who eats oysters can reasonably anticipate and guard against eating such a piece of shell. . . ."

Thus, while we sympathize with the plaintiff who has suffered a peculiarly New England injury, the order must be . . . judgment for the defendant.

REVERSED in favor of defendant.

CRITICAL THINKING

As with most legal decisions, the critical thinking activity that is most obvious is the need to reexamine the analogies used by the court in justifying its conclusion. The plaintiff wished the court to say that fish chowder was like what? What analogy did the defendant want the court to accept? Would the aptness of the analogy depend at all on the size of the bone in the fish chowder?

CRITICAL THINKING

The judge mainly used assumption of risk to rule against Webster, though she suffered an injury in fact. Should the restaurant have somehow compensated her? What would the WPH framework indicate should be done?

Case Nugget — Implied Warranty of Merchantability: Blue Ship Tea Room Follow-Up

Jackson v. Bumble Bee Seafoods, Inc.
2003 Mass. App. Div. 6 (2003)

Anthony Jackson ate tuna fish from two cans of tuna canned by the defendant, Bumble Bee Seafoods, Inc. The tuna had been purchased by Canteen Corporation. Small tuna fish bones were in the canned tuna and lodged in Jackson's mouth. Jackson sued Bumble Bee Seafoods, Inc., for breach of the implied warranty of merchantability (and apparently had a Massachusetts attorney who was unaware of Massachusetts case law on this issue).

The trial court granted summary judgment to the defendant, and the plaintiff appealed to the Massachusetts court of appeals.

The court of appeals cited *Phillips v. West Springfield,* which held that a cause of action would lie for the plaintiff if "the consumer reasonably should not have expected to find the injury-causing substance in the food." Yet, noting that *Phillips* goes on to cite the Blue Ship Tea Room case, the court of appeals stated:

> [A]s a matter of law, bones in fish chowder should reasonably be expected. . . . As the Supreme Judicial Court has determined as a matter of law consumers must reasonably expect to find small bones in their chowder, we must find that as a matter of law consumers must reasonably expect to find small ones in canned tuna. Therefore, there are no material facts at issue on plaintiff's claim arising out of the claimed breach of warranty of merchantability; and, the trial court was correct to grant Bumble Bee summary judgment on the portion of plaintiff's case sounding in breach of warranty.

* 405 Mass. 411 (1989).

Implied warranty of fitness for a particular purpose. Another important UCC implied warranty is the **implied warranty of fitness for a particular purpose.** This warranty comes about when a seller or lessor knows or has reason to know (1) why the buyer or lessee is purchasing or leasing the goods in question and (2) that the buyer or lessee is relying on him or her to make the selection. Under this warranty, the seller or lessor does not have to be a merchant.

An implied warranty of fitness for a particular purpose should not be confused with an express warranty. If the buyer walks into a store and the salesclerk says, "This saw will cut through metal," the seller has created an express warranty. However, if the buyer comes into the store and asks the salesclerk for a saw to cut through some copper tubing and the salesclerk refers the customer to a wall of different saws, it is reasonable for the buyer to assume that all the saws on the wall will satisfy the *particular purpose* that the buyer has indicated. Thus, an implied warranty of fitness for a particular purpose has been created.

Case 25-4 focuses on the nature of the knowledge the seller may have that gives rise to the implied warranty of fitness for a particular purpose.

Implied warranty of trade usage. The UCC, always diligent in its goal to facilitate the flow and ease of commercial activity, recognizes that a well-accepted course of dealing or trade usage may create implied warranties dependent on the circumstances. For example, if it is generally accepted in the trade that a certain product is always preassembled and shrink-wrapped, the failure of the seller to deliver the goods in that condition would be a breach of the **implied warranty of trade usage.**

CASE 25-4 JAMES BOYES AND ELEANOR CLOUSER, PLAINTIFFS, v. GREENWICH BOAT WORKS, INC., ALBEMARLE BOATS, GREGORY POOLE EQUIPMENT CO., A/K/A GREGORY POOLE POWER SYSTEMS, CATERPILLAR, INC., DEFENDANTS.

U.S. DISTRICT COURT FOR THE DISTRICT OF NEW JERSEY

27 F. SUPP. 2D 543, 1998 U.S. DIST. LEXIS 20585

The plaintiffs, Boyes and Clouser, in this case attended a boat show in Philadelphia at which they met a Marvin Hitchner, president of defendant Greenwich Boat Works, and an authorized dealer of Albemarle Boats. The plaintiffs contend that Hitchner made a number of representations to them regarding fuel consumption, speed, engine power, etc., of Albemarle boats. Moreover, the plaintiffs claim that the defendants knew the purpose for which the plaintiffs were purchasing the boat and recommended the boat in question pursuant to that knowledge. The plaintiffs subsequently bought an Albemarle boat for $175,000. Upon the boat's delivery, the plaintiffs began having difficulties with the boat specifically in the areas that Hitchner had made the alleged representations. The plaintiffs brought suit in part on breach of the warranty of merchantability, implied warranty of particular purpose, and breach of express warranties.

The question that the court is addressing below is whether the other defendants (such as the engine manufacturer) besides Greenwich may be held liable for the breach of the implied warranty of fitness for a particular purpose. Specifically, these defendants have asked the court to dismiss this claim.

JUDGE IRENAS: . . . The defendants have moved for summary judgment on the plaintiffs [*sic*] breach of the implied warranty of fitness for a particular purpose claim. The defendants contend that the plaintiffs are incapable as a matter of law of proving a breach of this claim. The defendants claim that Greenwich was the only party advised of the particular purpose for which the plaintiffs required the vessel and that this notice cannot be imputed to the other defendants. The defendants also maintain that Greenwich is not liable for the breach because it was not notified within a "reasonable time" as required by . . . the Uniform Commercial Code. . . .

The plaintiffs respond that since the advice given by Greenwich was based on advice they received from the other defendants, the other defendants are also liable for the breach of this implied warranty. They also deny that Greenwich was not given notice since they assert that they did complain to Greenwich upon receipt of the boat and satisfied the reasonable time requirement by making the other defendants aware of the breach. Since this Court finds that there are disputed facts which bear on these issues, this motion will be denied.

In New Jersey, "where a tender has been accepted, the buyer must, within a reasonable time after he discovers or should have discovered any breach, notify the seller of a breach or be barred from any remedy." . . . Under the U.C.C., "what is a reasonable time for taking any action depends on the nature, purpose, and circumstances of such action."

. . . This notice restriction "is designed to defeat commercial bad faith, not to deprive a good faith consumer of his remedy." . . . Courts have interpreted this section as implying a requirement that the defendant be prejudiced by the lack of notice. . . . While the plaintiffs claim that all of the defendants were aware of the problems, even if the plaintiffs failed to complain with a "reasonable time," the defendants have not alleged any prejudice from such delay. For this reason the claim that Greenwich is not liable is denied. . . . The defendants maintain that outside of Greenwich, the other defendants were not made aware of the particular purpose for which the plaintiffs intended to use the vessel. They allege that absent this knowledge, they are not liable for a breach of the implied warranty of fitness for a particular purpose. However, the plaintiffs maintain that the information used by Greenwich in creating the belief that the vessel would serve the purposes necessary for plaintiffs came directly from information relayed from the other defendants. In cases such as this it is possible that the other defendants will also be responsible for a breach of this implied warranty. . . . In this case the plaintiffs maintain that the information they received from Greenwich was passed on by the other defendants and this fact may entitle them to a claim against all of the defendants. Accordingly, the motion for summary judgment for this claim is denied.

MOTION DENIED.

CRITICAL THINKING

What facts were in dispute by the plaintiffs and defendants? How did the plaintiffs use the disputed facts against the defendants?

ETHICAL DECISION MAKING

How could an ethical manager avoid the problem that lies at the base of this case? What should the engine manufacturer, for instance, have done? How would use of the WPH model of ethics by the engine manufacturer have prevented this case from developing in the first place?

Warranty Rights of Third Parties

The idea of a seller's being in breach of an implied warranty raises an entirely new issue: Is the seller liable to anyone other than the buyer? This question may initially sound peculiar. After all, the seller and the buyer are bound together by contract, and if either breaches, then the breaching party is liable to the nonbreaching party.

Consider this possible scenario: Jane buys a blender from a local store. Prior to using the blender, she lends it to her cousin Valerie to use at a party. While Valerie is blending drinks at the party, the blades fly off the blender and injure her. What obligation, if any, does the seller have to the injured Valerie? No contractual relationship exists between Valerie and the seller. However, it seems to be patently unfair to conclude that Valerie has no cause of action against the seller. The UCC recognizes this unfairness, and clearly states that Valerie may indeed have a cause of action based on breach of warranty against the seller. The states are given the following three choices regarding *third-party beneficiaries of warranties*:

1. Seller's warranties extend to the buyer's household members and guests.
2. Seller's warranties extend to any reasonable and foreseeable user.
3. Seller's warranties extend to anyone injured by the good.

Most states have adopted the second option. Nevertheless, a number of questions remain concerning third-party rights, the nature of privity of contract, and the ability to maintain a lawsuit under the warranty rights of a UCC contract. Note these questions in Case 25-5.

CASE 25-5 SHELLEY JO BUETTNER, PLAINTIFF-APPELLANT, v. R. W. MARTIN & SONS, ET AL., DEFENDANTS

U.S. COURT OF APPEALS FOR THE FOURTH CIRCUIT
47 F.3D 116; 1995 U.S. APP. LEXIS 2801;
25 U.C.C. REP SERV. 2D (CALLAGHAN) 1086; CCH PROD. LIAB. REP. P14,149; (1995)

In December 1986, Shared Hospital Services purchased a used ironer from R. W. Martin & Sons. This ironer was inspected by Lawrence Leroy McClain, a laundry equipment mechanic, to ensure that the ironer was worth the amount Martin was asking for it. Martin sold the ironer to SHS with a specific "as is" clause in both the written sales proposal and the sales invoice. The ironer had a feed drive roll but no safety guard when it was originally produced in 1970, nor did SHS put a safety guard on the ironer subsequent to its purchase of the ironer. Even today, it is not custom to install a feed drive roll safety guard by industry standards.

Just four years after the purchase of the used ironer, Shelley Buettner, a supervisor in the flatwork division of SHS, was injured by the ironer. On October 31, 1990, Buettner's sweater got tied up in the ironer and amputation of her right arm below the elbow occurred as a result. Buettner sued both McClain and Martin, alleging negligent design, negligent failure to warn, negligent failure to install safety devices, and breach of implied warranty of merchantability. The district court granted summary judgment for both defendants; Buettner appealed the decision with respect to Martin.

CIRCUIT JUDGE WILKINSON: Buettner first argues that Virginia Code § 8.2-318 creates an implied warranty of merchantability for the benefit of remote users independent of any warranties to the purchaser created by the contract of sale. According to Buettner, because Martin did not deal directly with her in negotiating a disclaimer of warranties, the "as is" clause in the contract of sale, which disclaimed all implied warranties as to SHS, is not effective as to her.

We cannot agree. Under Virginia Code § 8.2-314, a warranty of merchantability is implied in every contract for the sale of goods unless the warranty is "excluded or modified" pursuant to § 8.2-316. Here Martin effectively disclaimed all warranties, including any implied warranty of merchantability, by selling the ironer "as is" to Buettner's employer; such a disclaimer is expressly authorized by Va. Code § 8.2-316(3)(a). Thus, no warranty arose under § 8.2-314 on which Buettner can now rely. Buettner insists, however, that as a foreseeable user of the ironer, she can rely on an implied warranty of merchantability running directly to her, independent of any warranties created by the contract between Martin and SHS. Buettner bases her interpretation on the text of § 8.2-318, which reads:

> **When lack of privity no defense in action against manufacturer or seller of goods.**—Lack of privity between plaintiff and defendant shall be no defense in any action brought against the manufacturer or seller of goods to recover damages for breach of warranty, express or implied, or for negligence, although the plaintiff did not purchase the goods from the defendant, if the plaintiff was a person whom the manufacturer or seller might reasonably have expected to use, consume, or be affected by the goods. . . .

As Buettner notes, the Virginia legislature chose to adopt this provision in place of the first alternative version of U.C.C. § 2-318, which simply extends warranties to certain third party beneficiaries. According to Buettner, the legislature, by "rejecting" the U.C.C.'s express reliance on a "third party beneficiary" theory, specifically intended to create an independent warranty for remote users.

Buettner misconceives the purpose of the Virginia statute. Rather than rejecting a third party beneficiary theory of warranty liability, the Virginia legislature simply chose to adopt a provision creating a broader class of beneficiaries than that created by the U.C.C. provision, which is limited to household guests and members. Such a broad statute was in keeping with the Virginia anti-privity statute that pre-dated the current § 8.2-318. See Va. Code § 8.2-318, Virginia Comment. Contrary to Buettner's contention, § 8.2-318 does not create for the benefit of nonpurchasing users an independent warranty of merchantability but rather simply preserves for remote users the warranties already enjoyed by an immediate purchaser. Moreover, the statute in no way purports to limit a seller's ability to disclaim warranties to foreseeable users.

The U.C.C. Official Comment is instructive in this regard. See In re Varney Wood Products, Inc., 458 F.2d 435, 437 (4th Cir. 1972) (although the Official Comments of the Uniform Commercial Code are not binding upon the court, they nonetheless provide valuable guidance). Although, as Buettner notes, the Virginia anti-privity statute differs from the U.C.C. model provision, the intent of both statutes is essentially the same: to confer on foreseeable users of a product both the benefits and limitations of warranties provided to the purchaser. The Official Comment provides: "To the extent that the contract of sale contains provisions under which warranties are excluded or modified, or remedies for breach are limited, such provisions are equally operative against beneficiaries of warranties under this section." U.C.C. § 2-318, Official Comment 1. According to this rationale, Buettner can enjoy no more contractual rights than are enjoyed by the purchaser, SHS. See, e.g., Goodbar v. Whitehead Bros., 591 F. Supp. 552, 567 (W.D. Va. 1984) (in general, a third party user "can rise no higher than [the] purchaser through which he obtained the implied warranty"), aff'd sub nom. Beale v. Hardy, 769 F.2d 213 (4th Cir. 1985).

The cases cited by Buettner for the contrary proposition are inapposite. For instance, Buettner cites Brockett v. Harrell Bros., Inc., 206 Va. 457, 143 S.E.2d 897 (Va. 1965), for the proposition that "the obvious purpose and effect of [the anti-privity statute that preceded § 8.2-318] . . . is to insure the implied warranty of fitness by the manufacturer to the consumer, despite the lack of privity between the two." Id. at 901. See also Swift & Co. v. Wells, 201 Va. 213, 110 S.E.2d 203, 208-09 (Va. 1959). Brockett, however, dealt with an implied warranty of fitness imposed by the common law on manufacturers of food. Brockett, 143 S.E.2d at 900 (an "implied warranty of fitness is imposed by operation of law [on sellers of food] as a matter of public policy for the protection of health and life"). See also Wells, 110 S.E.2d at 206 ("Since an early date, the courts have made a distinction with respect to warranties between the sale of food and other articles of commerce."). Neither Brockett nor Wells dealt with the question whether a seller could disclaim a warranty to the ultimate user by disclaiming the warranty to the purchaser. Moreover, both Brockett and Wells pre-dated the enactment of the current § 8.2-318 and thus have little bearing on our interpretation of that provision.

We likewise reject Buettner's suggestion that a seller must negotiate a warranty disclaimer with an individual foreseeable user despite the inclusion of an otherwise valid disclaimer in the contract of sale. Were we to hold otherwise, a seller would be virtually incapable of disclaiming any implied warranties as to all foreseeable users, contrary to the clear intent of § 8.2-316. Recognizing that any warranty runs through the purchaser to foreseeable users is sound policy: remote users enjoy no fewer contractual rights than do the purchasers, while employer-purchasers, who bear the major portion of costs of employee injuries and are in the best position to evaluate risks to employees who will be using the goods, are given appropriate incentives to negotiate warranties with vendors. See Reibold v. Simon Aerials, Inc., 859 F. Supp. 193, 199 (E.D. Va. 1994) ("Allowing employer-purchasers to receive the benefit of their bargain with the manufacturer should result in economically efficient transactions which account for the employees' potential injury costs.").

AFFIRMED in favor of defendants.

CRITICAL THINKING

The court rejects the case law Buettner cited in defense of her position. What was the court's reasoning for this rejection? Do you find the court's reasoning to be sound? Why or why not?

ETHICAL DECISION MAKING

The plaintiff in this case was badly injured by a product purchased by her employer and made by the defendant. Recalling the four theories of ethics from Chapter 2, how would SHS conduct itself with regard to Buettner under each of the four theories? Which theory do you feel is most appropriate in this case?

global context

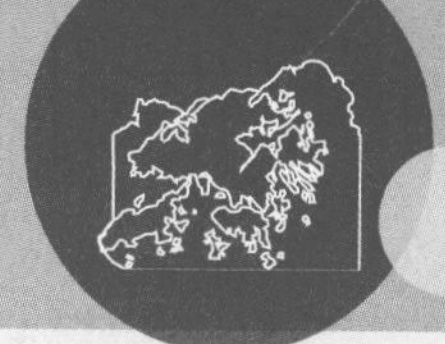

Warranties in Hong Kong.

An important distinction must be made between conditions and warranties in Hong Kong business contracts involving the sale of goods. In such contracts, time of payment and delivery are considered warranties unless otherwise specified. If the time of payment or delivery is not fulfilled, the procedures for breach of warranty are followed. These procedures differ from those that take place if a condition is violated. For example, if advance payment is considered a warranty and the payment is not made, the seller can sue for damages; but if the contract names payment as a condition, the seller can either recall the contract and resell the goods or sue for damages.

Warranty Disclaimers and Waivers

There really is no question as to whether an implied warranty may be disclaimed. The real question is *how* it is to be disclaimed. Generally speaking, if an implied warranty is to be disclaimed, the seller must do so in clear, unambiguous, conspicuous language. In order to disclaim the implied warranty of fitness for a particular purpose, the seller must disclaim the warranty in writing. The seller may disclaim the warranty of merchantability either orally or in writing; however, some states require that the term *merchantability* must be used in the disclaimer.

So, to avoid potential liability, a seller of corn for feed, for example, might decide to put in any sales contract for feed corn a clause that states, "No guarantees are made, either expressly or impliedly, that this feed corn has not been contaminated by mold or the toxin Fumonisin. Buyer is advised to test the corn to determine the presence of these potential contaminants." Of course, such a disclaimer might certainly have a negative impact on the sales of one's product!

The buyer may also waive both implied and express warranties. A buyer may waive these rights by (1) failing to examine goods for which an express warranty was created by a sample or model or (2) failing to comply with the seller's request to inspect the goods. For example, a printer requests that the buyer come into the shop to proof letterhead and envelopes. The buyer refuses, claiming that he is too busy, and tells the printer to go ahead and run the stationery. On receipt of the stationery, the buyer discovers that the numbers in the phone number are transposed, making the stationery useless. Unfortunately, the buyer has indeed waived his rights due to his failure to inspect.

A buyer may also waive her warranty rights under the contract by failing to comply with the statute of limitations. Under the UCC, the buyer or seller must bring a lawsuit on a breached contract within four years of when the breach occurred or when the nonbreaching party became aware of it. The buyer and seller are free to negotiate contractually a shorter time period (as long as it is not less than one year), but they are not free to negotiate a longer time period than the four years.

While the UCC remains the primary codification of both state and federal laws regarding sellers' warranties, there has been, in addition to the UCC, specific legislation pertaining to this issue. The 1975 federal law known as the Magnuson-Moss Act requires that if a seller decides to issue a written warranty for a consumer good (the seller is not required to do so), the seller must indicate whether that warranty is a *full* warranty or a

Case Nugget Disclaiming the Implied Warranty of Merchantability

LaBella v. Charlie Thomas, Inc., and Mercedes-Benz of North America, Inc.
942 S.W.2d 127

Joseph LaBella leased a Mercedes-Benz from the defendant Charlie Thomas, Inc. Forty-four thousand miles and approximately 18 months into the lease, the car began "running a little rough." LaBella took it to the dealership, which tore the engine apart only to find that some valves were bent due to some kind of misuse by LaBella. The bill was $514.44, which LaBella refused to pay, claiming that the work should be covered under the warranty. The defendant refused to release the car until LaBella paid the amount due, which he did. He then brought suit for recovering the $514.44 In his suit, he sued under breach of implied warranties.

The defendants claimed that the implied warranties had been disclaimed. The trial court granted the defendants summary judgment and the plaintiff appealed.

The court of appeals looked first at the language of the disclaimer. The language in the lease stated in part:

> Any warranties on the products sold hereby are those made by the manufacturer; the seller . . . hereby expressly disclaims all warranties, either express or implied, including any implied warranty of merchantability or fitness for a particular purpose. . . .

As the UCC requires, in Sections 2-316(b) and 2A-214(b), language disclaiming implied warranties must be conspicuous and language disclaiming merchantability must refer to *merchantability* by name. The appellate court noted that the above disclaimer satisfied these requirements. However, the language was not clear on whether the disclaimer applied to leases; the disclaimer referred only to "products *sold*."

As the court of appeals stated, "We hold that while the disclaimers relied upon by [defendants] may be sufficiently conspicuous as a matter of law in a sales transaction, there is a fact question whether these disclaimers, which clearly refer to a sale of a vehicle, effectively disclaimed all implied warranties, including the implied warranty of merchantability, when the car was leased. . . ." As such, the granting of summary judgment for the defendants was reversed, and the issue of fact regarding the application of the disclaimer to the lease was remanded back to the trial court for a factual determination.

limited warranty. This applies to any consumer good sold for more than $10. If the written warranty is silent, it is presumed to be a full warranty, which means that if the good fails or is defective, the good or its defective part will be replaced. If replacement cannot be timely effected, the buyer has the right to a refund or a full replacement.

If the good is sold for more than $15, the written warranty must disclose a number of items of information—names and addresses of the warrantors, any limitations on the warranty, and the procedures required to activate the warranty remedies—all in readable and easily understood language, in other words, not in *legalese!*

CASE OPENER WRAP-UP

Feed Corn

The Huprichs' claim against Bitto based on an implied warranty of merchantability was unsuccessful for a reason that may surprise you. The court found that Bitto was not a merchant under the Alabama state definition and could therefore not be sued for breach of warranty. A farmer is usually not a merchant because there is generally no evidence that by virtue of his occupation as a farmer, he holds himself out as a seller of the goods with the expertise and skills of a merchant. In this case, Bitto did not advertise his corn crop or solicit sales, relying instead on word of mouth to sell it.

Even if he had been a merchant, however, Bitto would most likely have still won this case, because the court found that while the mold may have been present when Bitto sold the corn, there was no evidence that the toxin was present. Therefore, the feed was nothing other than corn of average quality and fit for its ordinary purposes of consumption. In fact, there was evidence that Bitto stored his corn in such a way as to limit growth of the toxin, perhaps making his corn of even better quality than most corn on the market.

Summary

Introduction

A *warranty* is a promise on the part of the seller with respect to certain characteristics of the good.

Types of Warranties

Warranties of title:

1. Passage of good title.
2. Implied promise of no liens or judgments against title.
3. Implied promise that title is not subject to any copyright, patent, or trademark infringement.

Express warranties:

1. Description of the good's physical nature or its use.
2. Either general or specific.
3. Material term of the contract.
4. Reliance of buyer on representations.

Implied warranties:

Implied warranty of merchantability: A warranty based on a reasonable expectation of performance of the purchased good. The good must:

1. Pass without objection.
2. Be of fair quality within the description.
3. Be fit for ordinary uses.
4. Have even quality.
5. Be adequately packaged.
6. Conform to promises made on the label.

Implied warranty of fitness: A warranty that arises when the seller knows the purpose for which the buyer is purchasing goods and the buyer relies on the seller's judgment.

Implied warranty of trade usage: A warranty that arises as a result of generally accepted trade practices.

Warranty Rights of Third Parties

Third-party beneficiaries of warranties:

1. Seller's warranties may extend to the buyer's household members and guests.
2. Seller's warranties may extend to any reasonable and foreseeable user.
3. Seller's warranties may extend to anyone injured by the good.

Warranty Disclaimers and Waivers

Methods of waiving:

1. Seller does not make warranties in the first place (express).
2. Seller disclaims in clear, unambiguous, conspicuous language (implied).
3. Buyer fails or refuses to examine goods.
4. Buyer fails to file suit within the time of the statute of limitations.

Magnuson-Moss Act: If a seller decides to issue a written warranty for a consumer good, the seller must indicate whether the warranty is full or limited.

Point / Counterpoint

Should Merchants Be Able to Disclaim the Implied Warranty of Merchantability?

Yes

When there is a sale of any type of good, the seller has the right, under our broad concept of freedom of contract, to set whatever terms, conditions, or limitations she or he pleases as long as the market will bear it.

No one forces the buyer into an agreement, and as long as the terms, conditions, or limitations are clear and unambiguous, the buyer is free to accept or reject the terms offered. This is especially true with the implied warranties, particularly the implied warranty of merchantability.

If the implied warranties were not able to be disclaimed, the market would be severely limited. Goods would not be put into the stream of commerce for fear of creating additional liability for the seller. Often, the issue of merchantability is not within the seller's control, especially when the seller is a pass-through for a manufacturer or distributor.

Ultimately, not allowing a seller to disclaim the implied warranties infringes on one of the fundamental rights of a free market: the freedom to contract.

No

The 19th-century notion that all contractual parties are free to pick and choose their contracts is antiquated and flies in the face of modern reality. Consumer buyers have no more expertise in the marketplace than any nonexpert has in any field of expertise. Therefore, the UCC has an obligation to level the playing field, especially when the sale is between a merchant and a nonmerchant. The UCC already imposes higher standards of care on merchants and should do so in the area of implied warranties.

If a merchant, in the course of his or her business, regularly sells goods of a kind, then that merchant should have to put into the stream of commerce merchantable goods. If a merchant cannot put merchantable goods into the stream of commerce, then those goods should not be put into the stream of commerce.

A merchant disclaiming merchantability is akin to a tortfeasor disclaiming negligence liability: Such disclaiming simply can't be done, and it shouldn't be permitted to be done.

Questions & Problems

1. Differentiate between an implied warranty and an express warranty.
2. Is the implied warranty of title merely a codification of common law rules, or is it a new concept initiated by the UCC?
3. Differentiate between the implied warranties of merchantability and of particular purpose. Can these two warranties overlap?
4. Should the implied warranty of merchantability apply only when the seller is a merchant?
5. Does the Magnuson-Moss Act limit or enhance the UCC's concept of implied warranties?
6. Explain the statute of limitations and how it affects a buyer's rights under the UCC.
7. Duall Building Restoration, Inc., brought an action against the property owner of 1143 East Jersey, alleging that the owner had failed to make the necessary payments specified in the parties' painting contract. Duall had been contracted to restore the brick walls of the property. The painting job carried a five-year guarantee against peeling or flaking. The property owners counterclaimed, stating that the paint had been defectively applied. Duall had applied Modac paint to the walls, but the paint had peeled from the walls. A brochure for the paint indicated that it was fit for the specific purpose of waterproofing brick walls. The paint manufacturer had assured Duall that the paint would adhere to the brick walls. Who was responsible for the damage? Was this a breach of the implied warranty of merchantability? How do you think the court resolved the conflict? [*Duall Bldg. v. 1143 East Jersey and Monsey Products,* 652 A.2d 1225 (1995).]
8. Kevin Scott purchased a Ford van on credit on May 14, 1987. The total cost of the van was $18,399, and Scott made a down payment of $3,406. After the van was damaged in a traffic accident, Scott failed to make the necessary installment payments required by the contract. The van was repossessed in 1998 and sold at a public auction in 1989. The credit company advised Scott that there was a deficiency of $6,452.56 that he had to pay. Ford Motor Credit Company (FMCC) filed suit for the deficiency on April 16, 1992. Scott argued that the period of limitations for FMCC's claim had passed. Maryland code required that "[a] civil action at law shall be filed within three years from the date it accrues unless another provision of the Code provides a different period of time within which an action shall be commenced." Do you agree with Scott? Why or why not? [*Scott v. Ford Motor Credit Company,* 691 A.2d 1320 (1997).]
9. After living in their home for three years, Roger Nathaniel and Sharon Diamond sold the home to the plaintiffs, Marc Copland and Joan Lund. Nathaniel and Diamond hired a pest control company to inspect the home. The company reported that there was evidence of a previously treated infestation but that no evidence of active infestation was found. This report was provided to Copland and Lund prior to the sale of the home. The contract specified that the purchaser had inspected the premises and agreed to purchase it "as is." A year later, the plaintiffs discovered that levels of chlordane were present on the property. The plaintiffs discovered that the home had been treated 10 years prior for termites. At that time, chlordane was used to remove termites. Despite one toxicologist's report that the level of chlordane did not constitute a health concern, Copland and Lund spent $50,000 removing the contaminated soil from their property. They brought an action against the previous owners, Nathaniel

and Diamond. How do you think the court decided? [*Copland v. Nathaniel,* 624. N.Y.S.2d 514 (1995).]

10. Bishop Logging, a family-owned logging contractor, was planning on expanding hardwood production. Bishop planned on implementing a fully mechanized swamp-logging operation. No equipment was available that met the company's specifications, so it began to design a package that would meet its needs. Bishop contacted a representative from John Deere to see whether existing equipment could be modified. John Deere sold Bishop $608,899 in machinery. Under the John Deere "New Equipment Warranty," the equipment would be repaired or replaced only during the warranty period. Normally, the warranty excluded problems resulting from unusual use of the machinery, but John Deere waived this part of the warranty. After Bishop began logging, various mechanical problems occurred. John Deere made over $110,000 in warranty repairs. Despite the repairs, the logging system failed to operate as represented by John Deere, and Bishop sued to recover financial losses. Should Bishop recover lost profits and damages for breach of express warranty? What do you think the court decided? [*Bishop Logging v. John Deere Industries,* 455 S.E.2d 183 (1995).]

11. Knapp Shoes manufactures and distributes work shoes and sells and distributes shoes made by other shoe companies. One of Knapp's suppliers, Sylvania, produced several models of Knapp shoes. The leather Sylvania used to manufacture the soles tended to fall apart easily. There were additional problems with each line of shoe manufactured by Sylvania. Sylvania claimed that it "stood behind" its product and fully warranted its product against manufacturing defects. Knapp subsequently fell behind on its payments to Sylvania. Sylvania complained to Knapp, but Knapp contended that the defective shoes were jeopardizing important accounts. In 1990 Knapp tried to return two of the models of shoes Sylvania had produced for Knapp in 1988, but Sylvania would not accept the return. Knapp sued Sylvania for breach of express warranty and of implied warranties of merchantability and fitness for particular purpose. Sylvania countersued for the unpaid bills. How do you think the court decided? [*Knapp Shoes Inc. v. Sylvania Shoe Mfg. Corp.,* 72 F.3d 190 (1995).]

12. Mrs. Cipollone had been a lifetime smoker, starting back in the 1940s. She subsequently died in 1984 from lung cancer. Her husband brought suit against the cigarette companies of the Liggett Group and Philip Morris, citing breach of express warranty and fraud. Mr. Cipollone based these allegations on advertisements that the defendants ran on television, particularly during the *Arthur Godfrey Show.* At trial, the court did not permit the defendants to introduce evidence to show that Mrs. Cipollone did not rely on these advertising representations in deciding whether to continue smoking. Does the plaintiff have the burden to show that the express warranties were in fact relied on? Conversely, may the defense introduce evidence to show just the opposite? [*Cipollone v. Liggett Group Inc.,* 893 F.2d 541 (1992).]

13. Brown worked in the retail paint business. Catania, a customer, asked Brown for a recommendation for an exterior house paint specifically for stucco walls. Brown recommended a particular brand called Pierce's Shingle and Shake. Brown also explained how the stucco walls should be prepared and how the paint should be applied. After doing the painting, Catania noticed that the paint blistered and peeled within a very short time after application. Catania sued Brown, alleging breach of the implied warranty of fitness for a particular purpose. Should he prevail? [*Catania v. Brown,* 231 A.2d 668 (1964).]

14. The homeowners in a residential subdivision brought an action after their water pipes were damaged by corrosive water. They alleged breach of implied warranty. The

Municipal Utility District (MUD) and ECO Resources, a company retained by MUD to provide service, were named in the suit. ECO Resources was responsible only for servicing; it did not sell the water. MUD sold the water to the homeowners in the subdivision. Was ECO Resources a merchant for the purposes of this claim? How would the answer to this question affect the decision of whether an implied warranty of merchantability existed with ECO Resources? [*Loyd v. ECO Resources, Inc.*, 956 S.W.2d 110 (1997).]

15. Rodney Sullivan owned a 40-foot fiberglass lobster boat, *Sea Fever.* Sullivan purchased the boat new from Young Bros. & Co. The exhaust system was constructed with fiberglass tubing manufactured by Vernay Products. A year after Sullivan purchased the boat, a crack developed in the glass tubing. Young repaired the crack, but one year later more problems occurred with the glass tubing and the boat sank. The boat sank because there was a deficiency in the thickness of the glass. The quality of the tubing in *Sea Fever* did not conform to the manufacturer's brochure's representation. Sullivan alleged breach of express and implied warranty of merchantability. Was the tubing fit for the purposes for which the manufacturer knew it would be used? Who was at fault? [*Sullivan v. Young Bros. and Co. Inc.*, 893 F. Supp. 1148 (1995).]

Looking for more review material?

The Online Learning Center at **www.mhhe.com/kubasek1e** contains this chapter's "Assignment on the Internet" and also a list of URLs for more information, entitled "On the Internet." Find both of them in the Student Center portion of the OLC, along with quizzes and other helpful materials.

Negotiable Instruments: Negotiability and Transferability

CASE OPENER

Oral Agreements and Negotiable Instruments

As a gambling facility, MGM Desert Inn Inc. regularly holds and executes negotiable instruments. During a period of two months, patron William E. Shack, Jr., entered MGM and delivered eight checks to the casino in exchange for markers. These checks, which totaled $93,400, were signed by Shack and dated at the time of transfer. When MGM sent Shack's checks to the bank for payment, they were dishonored because the funds in Shack's account were insufficient.

MGM filed an action in district court to obtain the $93,400. Shack contended that a casino host had told him that he had sufficient remaining casino credit to receive the markers. The district court judge ruled in favor of MGM, affirming its argument that the checks were negotiable instruments and stating that no evidence of an oral agreement between the casino and Shack was provided. The checks contained Shack's signature, on a specified date, and were to be payable on demand from Shack's bank to MGM. Shack was ordered to pay MGM $5,000 for attorney fees in addition to the $93,400 originally owed on the checks.[1]

1. If you were employed at MGM, what would you do to avoid future disputes with your patrons about the nature of payment agreements?
2. Assuming that Shack's claims about an oral agreement with MGM were true, would this affect your decision as to whether the checks' payments were currently due?

The Wrap-Up at the end of the chapter will answer these questions.

[1] *MGM Desert Inn, Inc., dba Desert Inn Hotel & Casino v. William E. Shack,* U.S. District Court, District of Nevada, 809 F. Supp. 783 (1993).

CHAPTER 26

Learning Objectives

After reading this chapter, you will be able to answer the following questions:

1. Why is there a need for negotiable instruments?
2. What are the types of negotiable instruments recognized by the UCC?
3. What are the requirements of negotiability?
4. What are the words of negotiability?

Once a sales contract has been created and executed and the parties are aware of their respective obligations under the contract, the next phase is the *payment* by the buyer to the seller for the goods purchased. Payment is usually made in one of three ways: in cash, through credit arrangements (which will be discussed in the chapter on secured transactions), or with a *substitute for cash.* It is this substitute for cash that is the focus of this and the next three chapters.

A substitute for cash, or a **negotiable instrument,** is a written document containing the signature of the creator that makes an unconditional promise or order to pay a sum certain in money at either a time certain or on demand. Negotiable instruments are executed on a daily basis in the form of checks, certificates of deposit, drafts, and promissory notes in exchange for goods, services, or business financing.

Figure 26-1 illustrates where negotiable instruments fit in the process of market exchange for a good or service.

The Need for Negotiable Instruments

A currency or cash substitution has existed for centuries in Anglo-American law, predating much of the common law itself. The ancient lex mercatoria, or law of merchants, of England recognized that agreements could be paid for with documents that promised payment and that these documents themselves could then be circulated as a substitute for money. However, the English king's court did not at first accept the use of document paper as money. Therefore, merchants had to develop their own system and rules for using documents as payments.

It was not until 1882 that England codified the law of merchants in the Bill of Exchange Act. Fourteen years later, in the United States, the Uniform Negotiable Instruments Law was adopted; its form resembled the approach to negotiable instruments taken earlier by England. By 1920 all states had approved the law, which served as the precursor to Article 3 of the UCC, governing negotiable instruments.

It is easy to figure out why using documents as payments would greatly facilitate commercial transactions, especially in times when actual currency or cash was in short supply or when it was dangerous to transfer large amounts of currency or precious metals. These documents of payment were generically called *commercial paper* and under Article 3 of the UCC were specifically labeled *negotiable instruments.*

Figure 26-1

Negotiable Instruments and Market Exchange

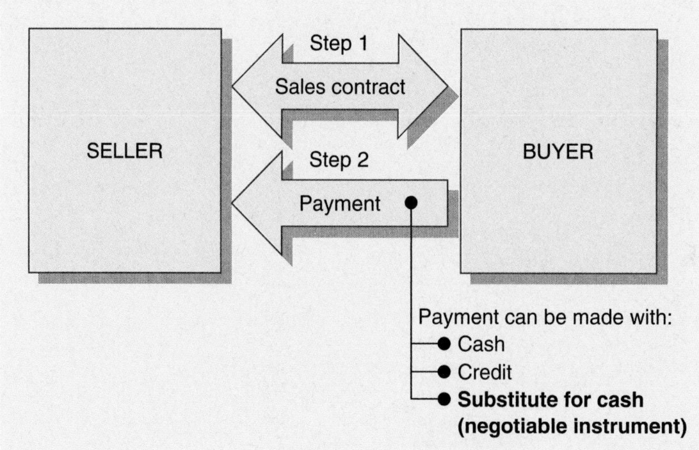

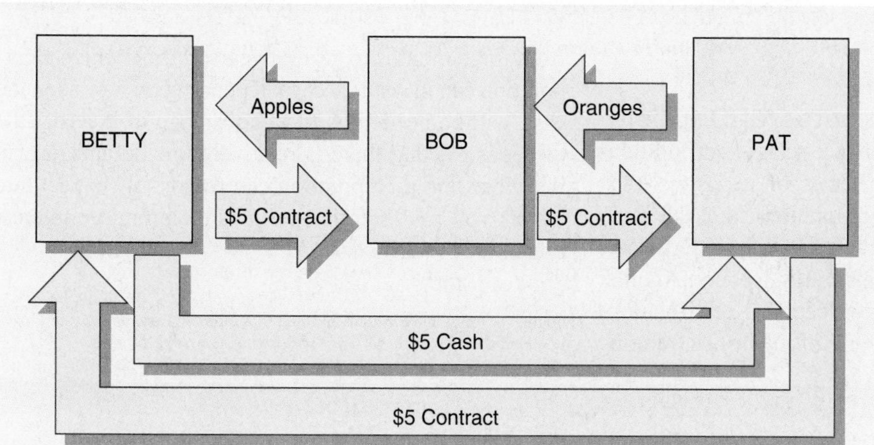

Figure 26-2
Negotiable-Instrument Assignment

CONTRACTS AS COMMERCIAL PAPER

We have already discussed one prevalent form of commercial paper: contracts. It does not matter whether the contract is a common law contract or a UCC Article 2 contract. Both kinds are examples of commercial paper. As such, through the process of assignment, these contracts may be circulated and transferred throughout the commercial world. The very simple visual in Figure 26-2 will help you understand the process of assignment. Follow the visual step-by-step as you read the following:

> Bob sells a bushel of apples to Betty; in exchange, Betty executes a contract to pay Bob $5 on demand. A few days later, Bob buys some oranges from Pat for $5. Instead of paying Pat the $5 cash, Bob *assigns* Betty's obligation to pay Bob the $5 to Pat. When Pat demands the money from Betty, Betty will pay Pat the $5 and everyone will be square.

Figure 26-2 is very simplistic. However, it demonstrates the point that any contractual obligation, except for personal ones and nonassignable ones, may be transferred and, as such, is classified as commercial paper.

PROBLEMS WITH COMMERCIAL PAPER

Even though the illustration with Bob, Betty, and Pat is a simple one, it still contains a potential problem. Consider that fact pattern again, only this time assume that the apples Bob sold to Betty were all rotten. Betty did not know the apples' condition at the time because they looked and felt fine. It was only after cutting into them that the problem became apparent.

When Pat demands the $5 from Betty, Betty naturally is going to refuse, claiming that Bob had breached their original contract by delivering to her defective apples. Betty would be justified and on legally safe ground to refuse to pay. Pat could do nothing against Betty and would have to go back and sue Bob. The commercial paper that Bob transferred to Pat was not acceptable. In other words, the whole reason for having the transferability of commercial paper as a substitute for currency is defeated under these circumstances.

Types of Negotiable Instruments

Under Article 3, the UCC recognizes four specific types of negotiable instruments: notes and certificates of deposits, a highly specialized type of note; and drafts and checks, a

connecting to the core

Finance

Advantages of Certificates of Deposit

As you learned in your finance class, corporations might opt to invest in certificates of deposit if they have idle cash. Cash that a corporation is not currently using would earn a higher interest rate in a certificate of deposit than in a corporate savings account. Another advantage of a corporation's selecting a certificate of deposit is that there are a variety of maturities, ranging from three months to several years, during which a corporation can invest idle cash depending on how soon the cash will be needed. A third advantage of a certificate of deposit is that there is relatively low default risk, in the sense that a corporation can reasonably expect that a bank will pay the principal plus the promised interest rate at the maturity date.

Source: S. Ross, R. W. Westerfield, and B. D. Jordan, *Fundamentals of Corporate Finance* (New York: McGraw-Hill/Irwin, 2006), pp. 654–655.

highly specialized type of draft (UCC Section 3-104). A **note** is a promise, by the *maker* of the note, to pay a payee [UCC 3-103(a)(9)]. A **draft** is an order by a *drawer* to a drawee to pay a payee [UCC 3-103(a)(6)]; in our example above, Bob could have drawn a draft ordering Betty to pay Pat $5 since Betty owed Bob $5. A note is a two-party instrument, while, by definition, a draft is a three-party instrument.

Notes and drafts can be either demand instruments or time instruments. With a **demand instrument,** the payee (or subsequent holder) can demand actual payment at any time. The UCC defines an instrument "payable on demand" as one that "(i) states that it is payable on demand or at sight, or otherwise indicates that it is payable at the will of the holder, or (ii) does not state any time of payment" [3-108(a)]. With a **time instrument,** payment can be made only at a specific time designated in the future. The UCC requires that an "instrument payable at a definite time" have a time easily determined from the document itself [3-108(b)].

Certificates of deposit and checks are specific illustrations of these distinctions. A **certificate of deposit** is a promise made by a bank to pay a payee a certain amount of money at a future time. The UCC defines a certificate of deposit as "an instrument containing an acknowledgment by a bank that a sum of money has been received by the bank and a promise by the bank to repay the sum of money. A certificate of deposit is a note of the bank" [3-104(j)]. Usually, a payee buys one of these instruments from a bank and then collects the principle plus a determined amount of interest in the future. However, because these instruments have a present value, even though they are not payable until some future time, the payee may transfer them or even sell them before the future date of payment.

A **check** is a specific draft, drawn by the owner of a checking account, ordering the bank to pay the payee from that drawer's account [UCC 3-104(f)]. A check is always a demand instrument and can never be a time instrument (postdating does not affect the ability of the holder to cash the check before the postdate). Types of checks include:

- *Cashier's check:* "[A] draft with respect to which the drawer and drawee are the same bank or branches of the same bank" [UCC 3-104(f)].
- *Traveler's check:* "[A]n instrument that (i) is payable on demand, (ii) is drawn on or payable at or through a bank, (iii) is designated by the term 'traveller's check' or by a substantially similar term, and (iv) requires, as a condition to payment, a countersignature by a person whose signature appears on the instrument" [UCC 3-104(i)].
- *Certified check:* "[A] check accepted by the bank on which it is drawn" [UCC 3-409(d)].

Figure 26-3 Potential Complexity of Negotiable Instruments

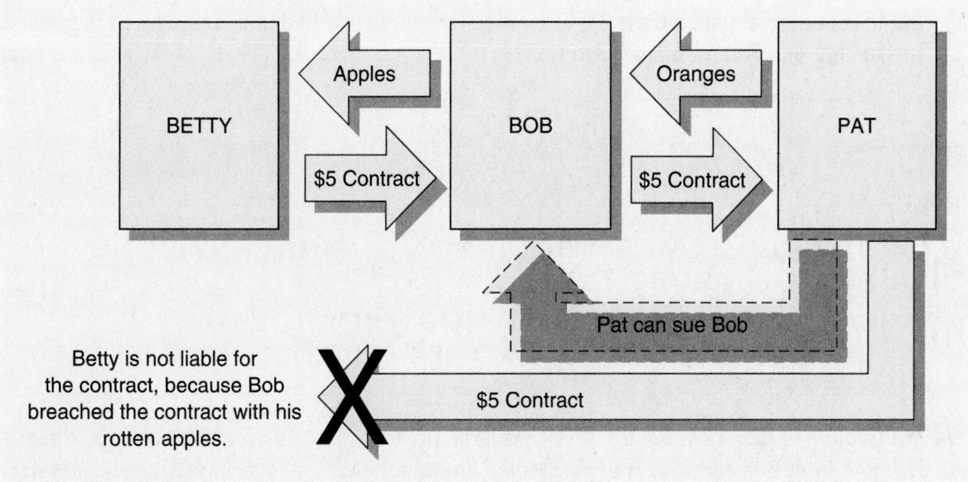

An Overview of the Law of Negotiable Instruments

To have a negotiable instrument, specific requirements of *negotiability* must be met. However—and this a very important concept that many students miss—if an instrument fails to qualify as a negotiable instrument, this does *not* mean that the instrument fails to be a perfectly good, perfectly enforceable contract. All it means is that the special rules regarding negotiable instruments do not apply. Once an instrument is a negotiable instrument, it has the potential of conferring on its possessor some special qualities. Let's go back to our example with Bob, Betty, and Pat. Use Figure 26-3 to follow the logic of the exchanges.

> Betty buys apples from Bob for $5 and gives Bob a negotiable note promising to pay the $5 on demand. Bob then buys oranges from Pat for $5 and properly transfers (or *negotiates*) the $5 negotiable note to Pat. Pat presents the note to Betty for payment after Betty has found out that the apples she bought from Bob were all bad. Betty refuses to pay Pat the $5. Bob, that shady apple dealer, has disappeared. Pat sues Betty for the $5. Under the rules of negotiable instruments, Pat could very well prevail, and Betty, regardless of the awful apples she got from Bob, might just have to pay Pat.

That's an awful lot of information to jump in with right away, so we need to break down the steps. The following are the issues that have to be explored to understand this chain of events:

1. What constitutes a negotiable instrument?
2. How does one transfer a negotiable instrument?
3. What is the status of a holder of a negotiable instrument?
4. What happens when the person who created a negotiable instrument has a good defense for not honoring his or her paying on the instrument?

Clearly, when the contracts for such transactions are not in breach, everything works out fine. Potential problems, however, led to the evolution of the law surrounding negotiable commercial paper. Case 26-1 discusses the issue of whether a contract is a negotiable instrument or a common law contract.

CASE 26-1 SAMUEL JAMES THOMPSON v. FIRST CITIZENS BANK & TRUST CO.

COURT OF APPEALS OF NORTH CAROLINA 151 N.C. APP., 567 S.E.2D 184 (2002)

On 5 November 1998, plaintiff [Samuel James Thompson] borrowed $10,500 from defendant [First Citizens Bank & Trust Co.]. As collateral for the loan, defendant required plaintiff to purchase a $10,000 certificate of deposit (CD). Plaintiff met with Catherine Huggins (Huggins), defendant's employee, to execute the documents associated with the loan and with the purchase of the CD. Huggins gave plaintiff a CD confirmation form with her signature, acknowledging that plaintiff had opened a CD account with an initial deposit of $10,000. On the same day, plaintiff executed an "Assignment of Deposit Account," assigning the CD to defendant as collateral for his loan. In November 1999, plaintiff paid off the $10,000 loan from defendant, and presented the CD confirmation for payment. Defendant refused to pay the amount due on the CD and claimed that, notwithstanding the signed CD confirmation, plaintiff had not deposited $10,000 to purchase a CD.

JUDGE BIGGS: . . . Defendant argues that the trial court erred in granting summary judgment for plaintiff, and contends that the evidence raised a genuine issue of material fact regarding whether there was consideration for the CD. The resolution of this issue requires us to examine several features of the commercial transaction at issue. First, plaintiff and defendant disagree about whether the CD is a negotiable instrument as defined by the Uniform Commercial Code (UCC). We conclude that the CD at issue in the present case is not a negotiable instrument, and therefore is not governed by the negotiable instrument provisions of the UCC. The UCC applies only to negotiable instruments.

A "negotiable instrument" is "an unconditional promise or order to pay a fixed amount of money[.]" Negotiable instruments, also called simply "instruments," may include, e.g., a personal check, cashier's check, traveler's check, or CD. N.C.G.S. 25-3-104, however, provides that a financial document such as a CD "is not an instrument if, at the time it is issued or first comes into possession of a holder, it contains a conspicuous statement, however expressed, to the effect that the promise or order is not negotiable or is not an instrument governed by this Article.

In the instant case, the CD confirmation clearly states, in upper case type, "NON-TRANSFERABLE." We conclude that this qualifies as "a conspicuous statement . . . that the promise or order is not negotiable," and, thus, that the CD does not fall within the purview of the negotiable instrument provisions of the UCC.

"Because the certificate of deposit at issue does not fall under the UCC, we must turn to the common law." Holloway at 100, 423 S.E.2d at 755. The CD confirmation is a contract between plaintiff and defendant, and its interpretation is governed by principles of contract law.

. . . Notwithstanding the language of the CD confirmation, defendant contends that language in its "Deposit Account Agreement" booklet establishes that the CD confirmation was issued subject to a condition precedent. This document states that an account "is not opened or valid until we receive . . . the initial deposit in cash or collectible funds." The CD confirmation is, however, the document that verifies or acknowledges that this condition precedent (deposit of money) has already occurred. Therefore, the bank booklet does not raise an issue of fact.

Nor is evidence of a unilateral mistake admissible to contradict the terms of a contract. Goodwin

[CONTINUED]

v. Cashwell, 102 N.C. App. 275, 277, 401 S.E.2d 840, 840 (1991) (parol evidence rule excludes consideration of unilateral error made by one party in calculations pertaining to settlement agreement; Court notes that a "unilateral mistake, unaccompanied by fraud, imposition, undue influence, or like oppressive circumstances, is not sufficient to void a contract").

AFFIRMED in favor of defendant.

Judges GREENE and HUDSON concur.

CRITICAL THINKING

Judge Biggs gives only one reason for ruling that the contract was not a negotiable instrument. What is the reason and the evidence to support it?

ETHICAL DECISION MAKING

Did First Citizens Bank & Trust Co. have an ethical obligation to provide further information about the negotiability of the contract? If so, what could the bank do to prevent similar cases in the future?

REQUIREMENTS FOR NEGOTIABILITY

The UCC requires that for an instrument to be negotiable (do *not* equate *negotiable* with *enforceable*), the instrument must satisfy the six requirements in the following definition: A negotiable instrument is a written document that is signed by the maker or drawer with an unconditional promise or order to pay a sum certain in money on demand or at a time certain to the order of bearer [UCC 3-104(a)].The six requirements are:

1. The instrument is a written document;
2. It is signed by the creator of the instrument;
3. The instrument has an unconditional promise or order to pay;
4. The amount to be paid is a sum certain in money;
5. Payment is to be made either on demand or at a fixed future time (a time *certain*);
6. The document must contain the words of negotiability "to the order of" or, in the alternative, words indicating that it is a bearer instrument.

Study the fascinating case in the Case Nugget. The courts made a ruling based on some of the requirements for negotiability. Does the contested instrument meet the other requirements?

As you read through the following explanations pertaining to the requirements of negotiability, use Figure 26-4 as an example of the requirements as they apply to personal checks.

Written document. The written-document requirement is not as simple at it may appear. Clearly, the law does not permit an *oral* negotiable instrument. Telling someone that you unconditionally promise to pay her $50 next Tuesday does not create a negotiable instrument. However, under the right factual circumstances and when the words are provable, such a statement may be a binding, enforceable contract.

Case Nugget Requirements for Negotiability

Andre Deeks, Plaintiff-Appellant, v. United States, Defendant-Appellee
U.S. Court of Appeals for the Federal Circuit
151 Fed. Appx. 936 (2005)

In 1792, Colonel Marinus Willett wrote a document, stating that in 1781 he had entered into an agreement with 60 members of the Oneida tribe. In return for their help in fighting during the Revolutionary War, the colonel promised each of the 60 members a blanket, but he later found himself without the means to fulfill his commitment. In 2004, Andre Deeks filed suit against the U.S. government, claiming that he, as the possessor of Colonel Willett's note, was owed $3 million because the government had never paid its debt to the Oneida tribe. The trial court dismissed Deeks's case, stating that the case was time-barred and should have been filed by 1866. In addition, the trial court found that Deeks lacked standing to bring suit against the government because he had not shown that he had any relation to the Oneida tribe or that he had suffered any injury due to the breach of contract.

Deeks appealed, claiming that the document written by Colonel Willet was a "Bill of Credit in bearer form," which had transferred to him, the current possessor, the standing to sue for the document's enforcement. Deeks also accused the trial court of "nullifying laws governing negotiable instruments." The appeals court affirmed the decision of the trial court, again finding that the suit had been filed long after any applicable statute of limitations. Additionally, the appeals court "reject[ed] Deeks' contention that the Willett Document is a 'bill of credit' or some negotiable instrument, as the text reveals neither an intent that it be circulated as money . . . , nor an unconditional promise to pay a certain sum."

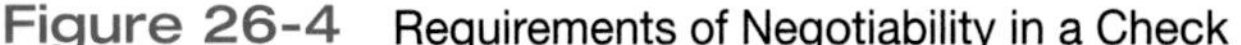

What makes the writing requirement a little complex is the mandate that the written document must have two characteristics: **relative permanence** and **movability.** Writing a negotiable instrument in the mud, for example, clearly lacks permanence; it will likely

Figure 26-4 Requirements of Negotiability in a Check

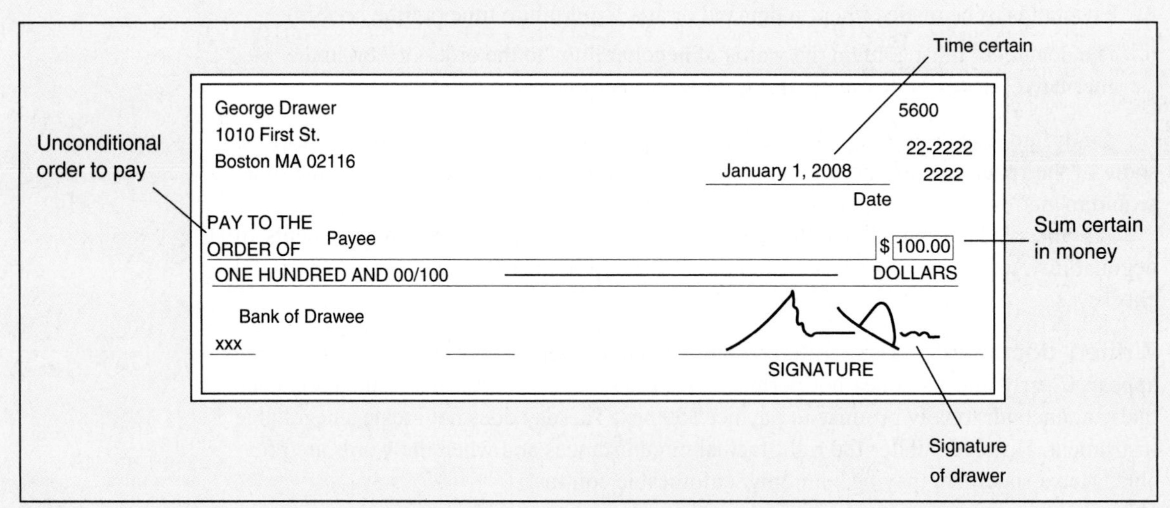

disappear as the mud dries. Thus, it is not a negotiable instrument. Likewise, the mud is something that one cannot move about in a commercially reasonable or expected manner. After all, one of the reasons for negotiable instruments is the ease with which they can be moved about.

Signature of the maker or drawer. The UCC and cases interpreting the signature requirement are fairly liberal in interpreting what constitutes a signature. Anyone's affirmative mark, from a full-blown *John Hancock* to an *X,* will suffice provided the party intended that the mark be placed on the instrument and uses that mark to identify himself [UCC 1-201(39)]. The UCC specifies that a signature "may be made (i) manually or by means of a device or machine, and (ii) by the use of any name, including a trade or assumed name, or by a word, mark, or symbol executed or adopted by a person with present intention to authenticate a writing" [3-401(b)].

Likewise, the signature of a duly authorized agent also satisfies this requirement. An agent's signature on behalf of her principal binds the principal and satisfies this signature requirement [UCC 3-401(b)].

A handwritten negotiable instrument satisfies the signature requirement even when no formal signature is present. The handwritten statement "I, John Smith, promise to pay Roberta Alexander or to bearer, the sum of $20 on Tuesday July 4, 2008" would satisfy the signature requirement because the handwriting affirms the maker's intent and, in that handwritten promise, the maker wrote his own name, John Smith.

Automated signatures, either by stamp or machine, satisfy the writing requirement as well. Even when the stamp or machine signature is fraudulently applied, such as by a person who had no authority to apply it, the signature may be valid if the maker or drawer intended that his or her name be affixed. Case 26-2 discusses the extent to which wire transfers and electronic signatures can be governed by the laws set forth by the Uniform Commercial Code.

CASE 26-2

STATE v. WARNER
SUPREME COURT OF OHIO
55 OHIO ST. 3D 31, 564 N.E.2D 18 (1990)

On December 13, 1985, defendant-appellant, Marvin L. Warner [controlling shareholder of Home State], and two former Home State Savings Bank ("Home State") presidents, David J. Schiebel and Burton M. Bongard, were indicted and charged with numerous felonies arising from Home State's dealings with ESM Government Securities, Inc. ("ESM"). The amended indictment charged Warner with forty-two counts of misapplication of funds and forty-one counts of unauthorized acts in violation of Ohio Revised Code 1153.01. Further, Warner was indicted on four counts of securities fraud. . . . The Ohio Revised Code makes it a crime to fraudulently transfer funds by means of a draft or other written instrument. Therefore, one issue before the court in this very complicated securities fraud case is whether an electronic transfer qualifies as a "draft" or "other written instrument." The Ohio Court of Appeals determined that an electronic transfer did not qualify as a "draft" or "other written instrument" and reversed.

JUSTICE HOLMES: Since this issue is one of first impression for this court, we will consider how other jurisdictions have applied laws drafted primarily to address traditional written documents, such as checks, but applied to modern wire transfers. In Richards v. Platte Valley Bank the United States Court of Appeals decided that the word "check" as used in the

Uniform Fiduciaries Act could be interpreted to include wire transfers of funds. The Richards court stated:

> We believe wire transfers are analogous to checks for application of the Uniform Fiduciaries Act. The transfer of funds by cable or telegraph is in law a check. Lourie v. Chase Nat'l Bank.
>
> The transfer item must be in some form of writing, such as letter, telegram or magnetic disc. . . . Wire transfers are considered irrevocable after transmission. Delbrueck, 609 F. 2d at 1051.
>
> The wire transfer requirements are similar to the definition of a check under the Uniform Commercial Code. A check is defined as a draft drawn upon a bank and payable on demand, signed by the maker or drawer, containing an unconditional promise to pay a sum certain in money to the order of the payee. A wire transfer is a written order to pay, drawn upon a bank containing an unconditional promise to pay a sum certain in money to the order of the beneficiary. The only element missing is the maker's signature. We do not consider this element significant for purposes of excluding wire transfers from the operation of the Uniform Fiduciaries Act.

Although the Uniform Commercial Code is not directly applicable to this case due to the nature of the transfer, analogous use of its concepts supports the proposition that wire transfers are written instruments for purposes of R.C. 1153.01. Delbrueck & Co. v. Mfrs. Hanover Trust Co. ("the Uniform Commercial Code ['UCC'] is not applicable to this case because the UCC does not specifically address the problems of electronic funds transfer. However, analogous use of concepts such as the finality of checks once 'accepted' support the irrevocability of these transfers").

In Illinois, ex rel. Lignoul, v. Continental Ill. Natl. Bank & Trust Co. of Chicago, certiorari denied (1976), the United States Court of Appeals, Seventh Circuit, decided that making an electronic transfer of funds through a computer terminal was essentially the same as issuing a check. The Lignoul court observed:

> The check is merely the means used by the bank to attain the desired objective, i.e., the payment of the money to its customer. The card serves the same purpose as the check. It is an order on the bank. Any order to pay which is properly executed by a customer, whether it be check, card or electronic device, must be recognized as a routine banking function when used as here. The relationship between the bank and its customer is the same. . . .

In today's modern banking environment, electronic transfers have become commonplace. On an average day, six hundred billion dollars in funds are transferred by wire or electronic means. . . . As noted in the discussion above, under modern day conditions, transferring assets of a savings and loan association over the Fedwire is the equivalent of sending a check or issuing a draft.

Through R.C. 1553.01, the General Assembly clearly intended to criminalize the unauthorized transfers of an association's assets regardless of form. Thus, the transfer of funds through the Fedwire system qualifies as a "draft" or other "written statement" as those terms are used in R.C. 1153.01. Accordingly, the court of appeals' conclusion that the authorized transfer of Home State's assets over the Fedwire did not constitute a "writing" within the meaning of R.C. 1153.01 was erroneous.

REVERSED in favor of plaintiff.

CRITICAL THINKING

What evidence might the court of appeals have used in its determination that an electronic transfer did not qualify as a draft?

ETHICAL DECISION MAKING

Home State Savings probably suffered negative publicity from this case. What types of policies might the company implement to prevent such fraudulent activity in the future? Would those policies assist the relevant stakeholders?

global context

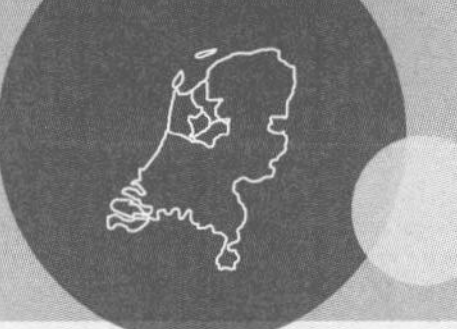

Formation of a Negotiable Instrument in Dutch Commercial Law

In the Netherlands, an acknowledgment of debt is made when a negotiable instrument is formed. Two examples of an acknowledgment of debt are the *wisselbrief,* or a bill of exchange, and the check. A bill of exchange is an instruction by the issuer of the bill (drawer) to the person responsible for payment (drawee) to pay a designated amount to a third party (payee). The bill of exchange does not bind the drawee to the payee automatically. The drawee must accept the acknowledgment of debt.

Once the bill of exchange has been accepted, a relationship is established between the drawee and the payee. What rights and privileges does the payee exercise in this relationship? If a person has sold a product and draws a bill of exchange, does that person still owe payment of the purchase price or is it replaced with claims arising from the bill of exchange? In regard to the unpaid purchase price, is the payee afforded the rights and privileges of the seller against the buyer that would enable him or her to collect?

The answers to these questions differ among various negotiable instruments. For a bill of exchange, though, the relationship that results from the bill does not alter any other relationship between the parties. Thus, the payee may exercise the rights and privileges of a seller.

Unconditional promise or order to pay. The promise or order to pay must be specific and not implied. The language must be affirmative in nature [UCC 3-103(a)(9)]. For example, simply acknowledging a debt does not create language for payment; therefore, a common IOU is not a promise or an order to pay and thus cannot be a negotiable instrument. Nevertheless, an IOU is a very strong piece of evidence for demonstrating the existence of a debt and, as such, will prove an enforceable contract of debt. However, an IOU can become a negotiable instrument if the language "payable on demand," or something expressing similar affirmative agreement to pay, is included.

The unconditional nature of the promise or order is often the controversial variable of this requirement of negotiability. Stated as simply as possible, the promise or order to pay cannot be contingent on something else happening. An instrument stating "I promise to pay if the following occurs" is not a negotiable instrument. Remember: It may be a perfectly enforceable contract, but it fails to satisfy the terms of negotiability.

The UCC further outlines what is enough to make a promise or order conditional. The UCC states, "[A] promise or order is unconditional *unless* it states (i) an express condition to payment, (ii) that the promise or order is subject to or governed by another writing, or (iii) that rights or obligations with respect to the promise or order are stated in another writing. A reference to another writing does not of itself make the promise or order conditional" [UCC 3-hol106(a)] (emphasis added). Note that the mere mentioning of another document does not make a promise or order conditional. A promise or order becomes conditional due to another document only if the other document directly creates a situation under which the promise or order may not be honored.

References to the reasons that an instrument is created normally do not cause the promise or order to pay to become conditional. For instance, stating "I promise to pay . . . as per the contract for the sale of goods between . . ." does not make this promise a conditional one. This kind of promise would be conditional, and thus not negotiable, only when the language of the instrument says that the promise or order is based on or subject to conditions, terms, circumstances, or contingencies stated in another document, such as a contract, mortgage, or bill of sale.

Likewise, identifying the source of the payment does not destroy negotiability. An instrument that states "I promise to pay from the corporate account" merely identifies the source of the funds; it does not impose a condition on the promise or order to pay.

Any of these references, while not affecting the negotiability of the instrument, naturally has an effect on its marketability. Because the point of negotiable instruments is the ease of transference within commercial society, anything that may cast questions or concerns could make the instrument less desirable to a purchaser. However, as Case 26-3 demonstrates, marketability should not be confused with negotiability.

CASE 26-3 AMERITRUST COMPANY, N.A. v. C. K. WHITE

U.S. COURT OF APPEALS, ELEVENTH CIRCUIT.
73 F.3D 1553 (1996)

This suit is based on a promissory note, and was brought by the owner of the note, plaintiff-appellant Ameritrust Company, N.A. ("Ameritrust"), against the maker, defendant-appellee C. K. White ("White"). White executed the note as part of the purchase price of a limited partner's share in a limited partnership known as Amberwood Apartments of Bartow County, II, Ltd. ("Amberwood"). White made the note payable to Amberwood. Thereafter, Amberwood's general partner, Cardinal Industries, Inc. ("Cardinal"), endorsed the note on behalf of Amberwood to one of Cardinal's affiliates, Cardinal Industries of Georgia Service Corporation ("CISC"). CISC subsequently endorsed the note to Ameritrust as security for a loan from Ameritrust to CISC.

The note contained a forfeiture clause providing that if payments were not timely made, White would lose his interest in the partnership and the partnership would have no obligation to account for any payments previously made. It is this clause that led the district court to its holding that the promissory note was not negotiable and thus not governed by Georgia's Uniform Commercial Code.

CLARK, SENIOR CIRCUIT JUDGE: ... We turn first to an examination of the note's negotiability, as the determination on this issue is potentially dispositive. If the note is negotiable, then Ameritrust may qualify as a holder in due course, in which case White's defense, the put option, is ineffectual. On the other hand, if the note is non-negotiable, then it is governed by Georgia common law relating to the assignment of a contractual right, rather than by Article Three of the Uniform Commercial Code, in which case Ameritrust took the note subject to any defenses that White could assert against the assignors, including the put option defense.

The district court determined that the note was not a negotiable instrument and, therefore, that Ameritrust was not a holder in due course. The court predicated its decision on the forfeiture clause contained in the note, which provides:

> The undersigned agrees that, in the event any payment due pursuant to the terms of this Note be not timely made, the undersigned shall retroactively lose any interest in the Partnership from the date hereof and the Partnership shall have no obligation to account for any payments theretofore made by the undersigned, and that this remedy is in addition to other remedies afforded by the Partnership Agreement.

In reaching its decision, the court relied on O.C.G.A. § 11-3-104(1), which reads: "Any writing to be a negotiable instrument within this article must: . . . (b) Contain an unconditional promise or order to pay a sum certain in money and no other promise, order, obligation, or power given by the maker or drawer except as authorized by this article." The court found that the forfeiture clause was an impermissible "other power" within the meaning of the statute.

Ameritrust argues that the forfeiture clause does not destroy negotiability because it is merely a provision regarding security and collateral. . . .

. . . In this case, Ameritrust is the holder of the note. Amberwood is the holder of the option to cause a forfeiture and the "would be" beneficiary of any forfeiture. The district court in *Signet Bank* further stated that "although the forfeiture provisions may not explicitly make the obligor's promise to pay less certain, the practical effect of the provision may cause this result." The court then quoted from an Ohio decision involving a virtually identical promissory note:

> A situation could develop, by mistake or otherwise, wherein the partnership exercises its option before the holder declares a default. In such case, the maker might well decline to cure an overdue payment or to make future payments because of the forfeiture. This exemplifies the reason why negotiable instruments may contain no other promise, order, obligation, or power except as authorized by the statute.

We agree with the reasoning of the district court in *Signet Bank* and the district court in this case. To be negotiable, a note must be a courier without luggage; it must move unencumbered. However unlikely the scenario described in the quotation above, this potential created by the forfeiture clause destroys the note's negotiability.

. . . As such, Ameritrust took the note subject to White's put option defense and any other defenses.

AFFIRMED IN PART in favor of defendant.

CRITICAL THINKING

Judge Clark found that the note did not meet the definition of negotiability. What were his reasons?

ETHICAL DECISION MAKING

Did any of the parties involved have an ethical obligation to warn Ameritrust that the note was not a negotiable instrument?

Sum certain in money. Negotiable instruments must promise or order that payment be made in a national currency [UCC 3-104(a)]. For example, U.S. dollars, English pounds, euros, and Japanese yen all satisfy the currency requirement. Bushels of apples, gold, shares of stock, diamonds and rare gems, and the like, are not currencies. While promises to pay in apples or gold or stock may form a perfectly enforceable contract, the resulting instrument is not a negotiable instrument. An instrument promising payment in "German marks and rare French wine" would not be negotiable. Even changing the *and* to an *or* would not salvage negotiability. Payment *must* be made in a currency. Case 26-4 establishes the idea that although the sum certain must be made in a currency, the specific type of currency is not relevant.

Payable at a time certain or on demand. A negotiable instrument must be payable on demand or at a specific time that can be computed from the instrument itself. Obviously, if the instrument states a specific date, the instrument has stated a time certain. If the instrument is dated and then states that "payment will be made 10 days after above date," the instrument is negotiable because the specific date can be calculated. A dated instrument that states "Payment is to be made at some future time after above date" is clearly nonnegotiable (though, again, it may be enforceable as a contract).

Likewise, an instrument that states that "payment will be made 10 days after delivery of the goods" but indicates nowhere in the instrument when delivery is to be made is not a

CASE 26-4 DIF BANK DEUTSCHE INVESTITIONS FINANZ GMBH v. FLUORMATIC CORPORATION OF AMERICA

U.S. DISTRICT COURT, NORTHERN DISTRICT OF ILLINOIS, EASTERN DIVISION
1991 U.S. DIST. LEXIS 520

DIF Bank is a company organized under the laws of the Federal Republic of Germany and is engaged in the business of banking. Fluormatic is a Delaware corporation with its principal place of business in Villa Park, Illinois. Multimatic Maschinen GmbH & Co. ("Multimatic") is a company organized under the laws of the Federal Republic of Germany and engaged in the manufacture of dry cleaning equipment. Fluormatic is in the business of distributing and servicing dry cleaning equipment. Multimatic and Fluormatic are both owned by Mr. H. F. Gustav Koetter ("Koetter").

Between May 9, 1981, and July 11, 1986, Fluormatic regularly purchased dry cleaning equipment from Multimatic. Fluormatic generally paid for the equipment either by promissory notes made payable to Multimatic in U.S. dollars or by endorsing drafts in deutsche marks drawn by Multimatic. Two promissory notes and six drafts are at controversy here. Multimatic received the notes and drafts from Fluormatic and discounted them to DIF Bank, which credited funds to Multimatic. DIF Bank presented the notes and drafts on their due dates and payment was not made. DIF Bank gave Fluormatic notice of the dishonor and the drafts were duly protested.

DIF Bank brought this two-count complaint against Fluormatic for recovery on the instruments.

JUDGE ALESIA: Fluormatic . . . argues that the drafts are not negotiable because they are not payable in a "sum certain" as required by paragraphs 3-104 and 3-106 of the Code. Ill. Rev. Stat. ch. 26, paras. 3-104 and 3-106 (1961). The drafts, while payable in German deutsche marks, do not specify an exchange rate. The failure to include an exchange rate, Fluormatic contends, requires the conclusion that the drafts are not payable in "a sum certain" as required under the Code. Fluormatic states that "various courts" have held this to be true, but cites only Northern Trust Co. v. E.T. Clancy Export Corp., 612 F.Supp. 712 (N.D. Ill. 1985). The Northern Trust Co. court addressed variable interest rates, not foreign currency exchange rates.

Section 3-107(2) of the Code provides:

> (2) A promise or order to pay a sum stated in a foreign currency is for a *sum certain in money* and, unless a different medium of payment is specified in the instrument, may be satisfied by payment of that number of dollars which the stated foreign currency will purchase at the buying sight rate for that currency on the day on which the instrument is payable or, if payable on demand, on the day of demand. If such an instrument specifies a foreign currency as the medium of payment the instrument is payable in that currency. Ill. Rev. Stat. ch. 26, para. 3-107(2) (1961) (emphasis supplied).

The clear import of this section is that an instrument may be made payable in a foreign currency without affecting that instrument's negotiability. *See also* Ill. Rev. Stat. ch. 26, para. 1-201(24) (1961) (defining "money" as a "medium of exchange authorized or adopted by a domestic or foreign government as part of its currency"). Accordingly, Fluormatic's objection . . . is overruled. . . .

The amount of money to be paid must be an amount which can be determined specifically from the instrument itself. Obviously, an amount of 48 dollars Canadian is specific and is a *sum certain.* What about 48 dollars Canadian plus 9% interest compounded quarterly? While the actual amount is not specifically stated, that amount can be computed exactly from the information found on the instrument itself.

Furthermore, even a negotiable instrument with a variable interest rate, such as a mortgage note, is acceptable. A 1990 revision of the U.C.C. accepts such a variance as long as the principle amount of the note is a sum certain in money.

Judgment in favor of plaintiff.

[CONTINUED]

CRITICAL THINKING

Why was the evidence provided by Fluormatic unacceptable? What conditions would the company have had to have met to have been seen as acceptable to the court?

ETHICAL DECISION MAKING

Fluormatic's defense in this case was not strong. What values would have led the company to have chosen to settle the matter with DIF Bank rather than trying the issue in court?

negotiable instrument. (It might also be nonnegotiable if such a reference is construed to be a condition of payment as well.)

There are two noteworthy exceptions to the time-certain requirement. First, an instrument that permits acceleration of payment does not violate this requirement as long as there is a fixed date of payment if the acceleration clause is not effected. Second, an instrument that permits an extension of the payment is still negotiable if there is a fixed time for payment provided that the maker does not have the right to extend the time of payment indefinitely [UCC 3-108(b)(ii),(iii),(iv)].

Demand instruments, such as checks, are payable as soon as they are issued. If an instrument is silent as to the time of payment, the UCC presumes that it is a demand instrument and thus retains its negotiable status [3-108(a)].

Words of negotiability. Finally, for an instrument to be negotiable, the instrument must indicate that it was created for the purpose of being transferred. How can an instrument, or better yet its maker or drawer, indicate this purpose? It can do so by having the phrase *to the order of* near the payee's name. When a specific payee is named, this is known as an *order instrument* [UCC 3-109(b)]. For the maker or drawer to indicate that she anticipates the instrument she is creating will be circulated, she writes "to the order of" and then the name of the payee, or some variation of that wording. Examples of order negotiable-instrument language are "Pay to the order of Jim Smith" and "Pay to Jim Smith on his order."

Negotiable instruments payable to whoever is bearing them are known as *bearer instruments* [UCC 3-109(a)]. Bearer instruments are treated like cash. Accordingly, one who comes into possession of a bearer instrument by any means, including theft, may claim the payment due on the instrument. Also, endorsing an order instrument, such as a check, converts the instrument into a bearer instrument that may be claimed by anyone in possession of it. Instruments payable to no one, to "X," or to "cash" are also considered bearer instruments.

The phrase *to the order of* is then necessary to create a negotiable instrument. Wordings such as "Pay to bearer," "Pay to Jim Smith or bearer," "Pay to cash," and "Pay to the order of cash [or bearer]" would all result in the paper being negotiable. Once the six elements of negotiability are satisfied, the instrument created is indeed negotiable.

Until the situation moves beyond the two contractual parties, it does not really matter whether an instrument is negotiable. Consider a contractual situation such as that in Figure 26-5.

Figure 26-5 Illustrative Contract Situation

Buyer<===>Seller

Sales Contract

Negotiable Instrument issued pursuant to that contract

Buyer is maker or drawer and seller is payee

Figure 26-6 Effect of a Third Party

Buyer<==============================>Seller===============================>Third party

Seller transfers the negotiable instrument to third party who will now either transfer it to yet another party or who will attempt to collect on it against the maker/drawer buyer.

The relationship between the buyer and the seller is controlled by the terms of the underlying contract. The status of the negotiable instrument is really irrelevant, as it is a matter between the buyer and the seller. The instrument's being negotiable, however, becomes important when a third party comes into the situation, as in the scenario in Figure 26-6.

This situation then leads us to the second stage of negotiable instruments: Once the negotiable instrument has been created, how is it transferred? That question will be answered in Chapter 27.

e-commerce AND THE LAW

The End of the Float?

Consumers who rely on "float" (the time it takes for a check to go through the traditional check-clearing process) have a limited amount of time to enjoy the delayed payment afforded by the process. Businesses in many parts of the country are testing new technology that speeds up the check-clearing process. Soon, float might be an outdated tradition.

In Nevada, for instance, Nevada State Bank allows businesses that purchase a special service to scan checks, send them electronically, and get money for checks drawn on other banks much more quickly; the delay in check processing is cut by 40 percent. Other banks are testing similar products and services. In some states, businesses can substitute electronic images of checks for the checks themselves. Here's how the process works: (1) A customer gives a business a check in payment for a product or service, (2) the business scans the check and sends it to the bank providing the new check-clearing products and services, (3) the bank sends the image to the customer's bank, (4) the customer's bank prints a substitute check, and, quickly, (5) the customer's payment is deposited in the business's account at that business's bank.

It remains to be seen what kinds of litigation will emerge from this expedited process.

global context

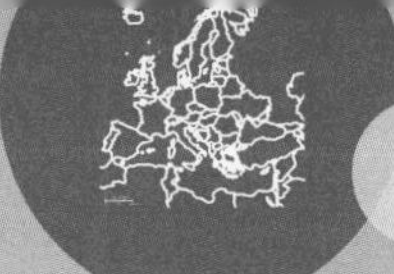

European Union: Negotiable Instruments as Defined by the EEC

At the European Economic Council's Contractual Obligations Convention, the issue of how to characterize negotiable instruments was addressed. Definitions of negotiable instruments differ among member countries. Rather than creating one encompassing definition, however, the EEC decided to defer characterization of negotiable instruments to each country. In other words, each member country of the EEC decides what types of documents are to be considered negotiable instruments. While this decision may prevent problems arising from altering definitions, it could also cause problems in cross-border transactions.

To thwart such complications, the convention decided to define a general concept of negotiability. Therefore, if a transaction is defined as a negotiable instrument within a certain country, it must conform to certain general characteristics as defined by the EEC. These general characteristics are intended to dilute the complexities of cross-border transactions.

CASE OPENER WRAP-UP

An Oral Agreement with MGM

Referring to the dispute between MGM Desert Inn Inc. and Shack, the court held that the potential oral agreement was irrelevant to the negotiability of the checks. Instead, the district court focused on the criteria established within the UCC for negotiability, and it concluded that the checks were negotiable instruments. The checks were written documents, were signed by the maker, contained an unconditional promise to pay, specified the sum of money to be paid, were payable on demand, and contained words of negotiability, so the checks were determined to be negotiable instruments. Hence, MGM was considered the holder of the instruments.

Summary

The Need for Negotiable Instruments

Contracts as commercial paper:

1. Any contractual obligations, except for personal ones and nonassignable ones, may be transferred and thus is a form of commercial paper.

Problems with commercial paper:

1. A breach of the contract invalidates the commercial paper.

Types of Negotiable Instruments

1. *Note:* Promise by maker to pay a payee (e.g., a certificate of deposit).
2. *Draft:* Order by a drawer to a drawee to pay a payee (e.g., a check).

Demand instrument: Payee can demand actual payment at any time.

Time instrument: Payment will be made only at a specific designated time.

An Overview of the Law of Negotiable Instruments

Requirements for negotiability:

1. Written document:
    - Relative permanence
    - Movability

2. Signature of the maker or drawer:
   - Affirmative mark
   - Duly authorized agent
   - Handwritten, even without signature
   - Automated signature
3. Unconditional promise or order to pay:
   - Must be specific, not implied
4. Sum certain in money:
   - Currency only, any currency acceptable
5. Payable at a time certain or on demand:
   - Acceleration of payment
   - Extension of payment
6. Words of negotiability:
   - To the order of
   - Order instrument

Significance of negotiability: More than a two-party transaction.

Point / Counterpoint

Should Payments Be Made in the Form of Conditional Contractual Agreements Rather Than in Unconditional Negotiable Agreements?

Yes	No
Conditional contractual agreements are preferred. Businesspeople would be wise to establish payment contracts primarily in the form of conditional contracts rather than unconditional negotiable instruments. Assuming both parties abide by the stipulations in the contract, payment is guaranteed. Payment will not get "lost" among many parties—each claiming that a previous party did not fulfill his obligations in the contract. The conditional aspect of the payment contract makes the sale more appealing to the buyer. The buyer feels safe in the knowledge that she will not have to pay for an item that does not fit the conditions agreed on in the payment contract. Plus, the buyer can feel confident that an unknown individual will not approach her to	Unconditional negotiable instruments are a superior form of payment. Businesspeople should prefer unconditional negotiable instruments rather than conditional contractual agreements. Unconditional negotiable instruments allow flexibility in payment and a much higher yield in profits. First, negotiable instruments allow only secure monetary payment. Payment must be presented in the form of a national currency. The restrictions on form of payment are ideal for large businesses because large businesses cannot calculate the exact worth of gold or diamonds at a future payment date. Businesses operate nationally

collect money for a debt the original seller transferred. Because the buyer's debt is conditional and payable to the seller *only,* the buyer will always know that her debt was paid properly and directly.

The conditional aspect of the contract also keeps all involved parties honest. The seller cannot secretly transfer the debt to another individual knowing full well that his product is poor. The seller is held directly accountable for his product and the buyer is held directly accountable for her payment.

Conditional agreements allow for more flexibility in payment than do unconditional negotiable instruments. Unconditional negotiable instruments can be paid in *only* a national currency. Under a conditional agreement, a wine connoisseur can arrange to be paid for his shipment of fine cheese with a bottle of extremely rare 1945 Fonseca—an item he considers a priceless acquisition.

and internationally with cash, not gems or bottles of fine wine.

Second, businesses can earn a high yield by investing excess cash in certificates of deposit. Idle cash becomes active in earning a higher interest than the cash would earn in a national savings bank. Also, the risk is relatively low. Businesses earn extra money using a negotiable instrument.

Negotiable instruments allow for flexibility in payment. With negotiable instruments, payment can be specified to be made "on demand" or "at time certain." Though these specifications seem rigid, payments can be accelerated or extended, provided a time is always set and the payment is not extended indefinitely. The flexibility in payment allows businesses to work well together.

Questions & Problems

1. Explain the reason behind the need for negotiable instruments.

2. Are negotiable instruments more similar to money or contracts? Explain.

3. Identify and define each of the elements of negotiability.

4. Dr. Linda Williamson owned a pediatric practice, "Albermarle Pediatrics." Her live-in boyfriend, Robert Holt, managed all financial aspects of the medical practice. Holt was an authorized signatory on the bank account of Albermarle Pediatrics. He used a signature stamp bearing Williamson's name for business purposes. However, Holt used the stamp for personal expenses. He used the stamp to write checks payable to himself, his business ventures, and his mother. Additionally, Williamson's stamped signature appeared on promissory notes totaling approximately $1.6 million. Williamson ended her personal and business relationship with Holt. Holt subsequently brought an action against Williamson, demanding payment of the promissory notes. Williamson maintained that she was unaware of her stamped signature's being used to secure the promissory notes and contracts. How do you think the court decided this case? [*Holt v. Williamson,* 481 S.E.2d 307 (1997).

5. On April 30, 1993, Joshua Leibowitz executed a promissory note for $100,000, effective as of October 12, 1989. The note was signed by the maker, Plitman, and the drawer, Leibowitz, and contained an order to pay a sum certain in money. Also under the terms of the note, Leibowitz was to pay the note on demand. However, when Plitman demanded payment on the note, Leibowitz did not make the payment. Plitman moved for partial summary judgment against Leibowitz on his claim for breach of a promissory note. Do you think the court granted the motion? Was the promissory note valid and enforceable? [*Plitman v. Leibowitz,* 1997 U.S. Dist. LEXIS 5813.]

6. Winthrop Southeast borrowed approximately $1,161,000 from Investors Savings bank to fund an acquisition. The terms of the promissory note executed by Winthrop to Investors bank stated that the loan would be repaid in undetermined installments beginning in February 1993. The note stated that "this Note may not be transferred or assigned by Noteholder without the prior written consent of Winthrop Southeast." As collateral for the loan, Winthrop pledged to Investors bank a security interest in the income, fees, and profits of the acquisition. However, no payments were ever made on the note or in regard to the security agreement. The Resolution Trust Corporation (RTC) was appointed receiver for Investors bank. RTC notified Winthrop in writing that the loan was in default in 1994. In 1995, RTC assigned its interest in the note and security agreement to RTC Commercial Loan Trust, a separate entity from RTC. The note was subsequently assigned to National Loan Investors (NLI). NLI brought an action against Winthrop, and the trial court found in favor of NLI. On appeal, Winthrop challenged the ruling, contending that because Winthrop failed to give prior written consent to the assignment, NLI was not a valid holder by assignment. How do you think the court decided. Was the promissory note a negotiable instrument? [*Apartment Investment and Management Company v. National Loan Investors,* 518 S.E.2d 627 (1999).]

7. On March 28, 1994, Brobeil Marine, Inc., executed a commercial purpose note from Fleet Bank. The note stated that "all principal and interest under this Note are payable on demand by Bank." In return, Brobeil agreed to unconditionally guarantee to Fleet Bank "the payment of all indebtedness, liabilities and obligations of Debtor to Bank of every kind and nature whether heretofore or hereafter created, arising or existing or at any time due or owing from Debtor to Bank." When Fleet Bank served Brobeil with demands for payment of the principal and interest owed on the note, Brobeil refused to make the necessary payment. Did the note meet the requirements for a negotiable instrument? Was Fleet Bank entitled to demand full payment of the note on any date after its execution? [*Fleet Bank v. Brobeil Marine, Inc.*, 236 A.D.2d 815 (1997).]

8. Doseung Chung, the plaintiff, a horse player, was at Belmont Park Racetrack, which is owned by the defendant, New York Racing Association. While at the track, Chung was using a voucher to place bets on the races through an automated betting machine. After placing a bet, Chung took his betting ticket but forgot his voucher, which had thousands of dollars left on it. A few minutes later, he returned to the machine, but the voucher was gone. Chung put an electronic stop on the voucher, but the voucher had been cashed out about one minute after it was left in the machine. Chung subsequently sued the racetrack, arguing that the track was negligent in not requiring proof of identity when patrons cash out their vouchers, which constitute negotiable instruments. How did the court rule? Why? [*Doseung Chung v. New York Racing Ass'n.,* 714 N.Y.S.2d 429 (2000).]

9. Regent Corporation imports finished textile products for resale in the United States. Regent contracted Azmat Bangladesh, Ltd., a textile company, for the purchase of sheets and pillowcases. The contract required payment by Regent by "100% confirmed irrevocable letter of credit, 90 days from bill of lading date." When the requested goods arrived in the United States, they were held for inspection. Regent had specified that the goods be manufactured in Bangladesh, but, instead, the goods had been manufactured in Pakistan. Regent sought to enjoin the bank from making any payment to Azmat. The court initially determined that the contract was not a negotiable instrument because it was not "payable on demand or

at a definite time." Do you agree with this conclusion? How do you think the court decided on appeal? [*Regent Corporation v. Azmat Bangladesh, Ltd.*, 253 A.D.2d 134 (1999).]

10. Anthony Bango needed several short-term loans to fund a real estate closing. He contacted Dennis Mulholland of Ohio Financial Mortgage Corp, (OFMC), and Mulholland located an interested investor, James Jarvis. Jarvis was faxed a note stating, "Upon the closing of this Real Estate Transaction the lender will be repaid the principal sum of $30,000 along with the closing costs agreed upon by all parties in full by the borrower." Jarvis transferred the money to Mulholland, and Mulholland delivered the money to Bango. Bango, who had a criminal record, requested that the money be delivered in cash. After receiving the money, Bango notified Mulholland that other investors had not come through with their loans and that an additional $20,000 was needed. Again, Jarvis transferred the money to Mulholland to give to Bango. Bango verbally agreed to pay $70,000 in return for the total loan of $50,000. When Bango did not make payment, Mulholland contacted him again. Bango revealed that the real estate transaction did not exist; instead, the money was needed for his personal debts. Jarvis collected only $8,500 of the loan. Jarvis filed a motion for summary judgment against Dennis Mulholland and OFMC. He claimed that the initial fax was a negotiable instrument. The trial court determined that Mulholland's fax did not constitute a promissory note or any other type of negotiable instrument. Do you agree? How does this determination affect the outcome of the case? [*Jarvis v. Silbert,* 1999 Ohio App. LEXIS 4828.]

11. Harold Heidingsfelder, the vice president of J.O.H. Construction Co., Inc., signed a credit agreement with Pelican Plumbing Supply. The agreement stated, "In consideration of an open account privilege, I hereby understand and agree to the above terms. Should it become necessary to place this account for collection I shall personally obligate myself and my corporation, if any, to pay the entire amount due including service charges, attorney's fees, and all costs of collection, including court costs." Heidingsfelder signed the agreement only as a credit application and did not intend to obligate himself personally for the debts of J.O.H. His signature was followed by the name "J.O.H. Construction Co." When J.O.H. failed to make the appropriate payment on its account, Pelican sued both J.O.H. and Heidingsfelder for payment. Heidingsfelder challenged Pelican's contentions, asserting that he did not intend to sign the agreement in his personal capacity. How do you think the court resolved this conflict? Examine the language of the agreement. Was the agreement a negotiable instrument? [*Pelican Plumbing Supply v. J.O.H. Construct*ion, 653 So. 2d 699 (1995).]

12. Sami and Jacqueline Tamman alleged that Isaac Schinazi asked them for a loan, stating that he intended to use the money for investment purposes. The Tammans and Schinazi drew up a document after the money was given to Schinazi. The document is entitled "Receipt of Monies Received." The typed portion of the entire document reads, "Receipt is hereby acknowledged of US $318.778 as full and final payment by Sami and/or Jacqueline Tamman to be invested by Sami and Isaac Schinazi. Sami and Isaac are fully responsible for the funds. At any end of month this amount can be reimbursed on request to the owner." The document was signed by the defendant and dated May 8, 1998. In the summer of 2000, plaintiff Sami Tamman made a demand for the return of the money, but the defendant did not make any payment. The Tammans sued, arguing that recovery was warranted because the undisputed evidence established the existence of a promissory note and that, after the plaintiffs demanded payment, the defendant and his father failed to pay in accordance with the note. The defendant denied that the subject document constituted a promissory note. Did the document constitute a promissory note? Why or why not? [*Tamman v. Schinazi,* 2004 U.S. Dist. LEXIS 13896.]

Looking for more review material?

The Online Learning Center at **www.mhhe.com/kubasek1e** contains this chapter's "Assignment on the Internet" and also a list of URLs for more information, entitled "On the Internet." Find both of them in the Student Center portion of the OLC, along with quizzes and other helpful materials.

Negotiation, Holder in Due Course, and Defenses

CASE OPENER

Stolen Money Orders and Holder in Due Course Status

In December 1990, Stacy Anne Dillabough presented two American Express money orders in the amounts of $550 and $650 to Chuckie's Enterprise, Inc., a check-cashing business in Pennsylvania.[1] Later, in February 1991, Robert Lynn presented an American Express money order in the amount of $200 to Chuckie's. All money orders were endorsed, and the payees showed photo identification when presenting the money orders. Consequently, Chuckie's cashed the money orders and gave the appropriate amounts of money to Dillabough and Lynn.

When Chuckie's presented these money orders for payment at the American Express bank, American Express refused to honor the money orders because it discovered that the numbers on the money orders had been logged as stolen.[2] Another individual, Robert Triffin, purchased the American Express money orders from Chuckie's and took assignment of all of Chuckie's rights in the money orders. Triffin thus brought suit against American Express, along with Dillabough and Lynn.

At trial, American Express argued that the money orders were nonnegotiable and that the language on the back of each money order stated that American Express would not pay if the money order was stolen. Triffin argued that by purchasing the money orders from Chuckie's, he gained a special legal status, called *holder in due course* status, and, therefore, American Express's defense was not applicable to him.

[1] "Digests of Recent Opinions: Superior Court," *Pennsylvania Law Weekly,* February 19, 1996, p.15.

[2] Michael A. Riccardi, "High Court to Decide Status of Money Orders; Is Amex Liable for Stolen Blank Papers?" *The Legal Intelligencer,* July 10, 1996, p. 1.

CHAPTER 27

1. Who do you think should bear the costs of the stolen money orders? In other words, should American Express be required to pay Triffin? Why or why not?
2. Suppose you are a business manager at Chuckie's. You learn that the court holds that American Express does not have to pay for the stolen money orders. Would you make any changes in your business? Would you be less likely to accept American Express money orders in the future?

The Wrap-Up at the end of the chapter will answer these questions.

Learning Objectives

After reading this chapter, you will be able to answer the following questions:

1 What is negotiation?

2 What is a holder in due course?

3 What requirements must be met to obtain holder in due course status?

4 What is the shelter principle?

5 In what ways has the holder in due course doctrine been abused?

As you can see in the American Express case, financial transactions with negotiable instruments can be risky. A **negotiable instrument,** as explained in the previous chapter, is a written document signed by the maker or drawer with an unconditional promise or order to pay a certain sum in money on demand or at a specified time to the order of bearer (UCC Section 3-104). An instrument must have these specific elements to be considered a negotiable instrument under the UCC.

One important characteristic of negotiable instruments is the ease associated with transferring the instrument to a third party. Once a negotiable instrument is created, it can be transferred to another party through negotiation. **Negotiation** is the transfer of possession to a third party who becomes the holder of the negotiable instrument (UCC 3-201). Thus, in the case above, Chuckie's transferred the money orders to Triffin through negotiation.

A party who possesses a negotiable instrument payable to the party or to the bearer of the instrument is a **holder** of the instrument [UCC 1-201(b)(21)]. A holder's right to an instrument may be limited, and the holder is subject to certain defenses. For example, when a party refuses to make payment on an instrument based on breach of contract, the holder may not be able to collect payment because of this defense.

In contrast, certain holders, **holders in due course,** have even more extensive legal rights to the negotiable instrument. In the same way that some credit card holders receive platinum credit cards, the holder in due course can be considered a "platinum holder." This special status is generated by the holder in due course's freedom from competing claims and defenses to the instrument.

Consequently, as a future business manager who may be involved in establishing the terms of negotiable instruments, you will want to know whether your business is a holder or a holder in due course because your legal rights will vary based on this status. Would Chuckie's or Triffin be considered a holder in due course of the American Express money orders and thus entitled to greater protection? Why should they receive greater legal protection?

In this chapter, first, we examine the characteristics of negotiation. Second, we consider the purpose of the holder in due course doctrine. Third, we examine the requirements for HDC status. We also briefly discuss the shelter principle and the HDC as well as various abuses and remedies of these abuses of the HDC doctrine.

Negotiation

When the rights to a negotiable instrument are transferred from one party to another, such a transfer is called a *negotiation.* In understanding the rules of negotiation, it is important to understand that the rules are slightly different depending on whether the instrument is an **order instrument** (i.e., an instrument payable to a specific, named payee) or a **bearer instrument** (an instrument payable to cash or whomever is in possession of the instrument) (UCC Section 3-109). Bearer paper requires only a delivery of the instrument to the holder by the payee. In contrast, order paper requires delivery *and* an endorsement.

DELIVERY

Delivery simply requires the physical handing of an instrument from one who is entitled to it to the person who is intended to receive it. Thus, a bearer instrument that falls out a window, blown off someone's desk by the wind, and lands in someone's hand has not been properly negotiated. This lucky person cannot legally demand payment of that instrument because she is not a proper holder. However, you could pass it on to someone who could legally collect on it.

Drawers must be careful when delivering an instrument because if the drawer is negligent in how he or she makes the delivery, the drawer may be liable for notes paid with forged or unauthorized endorsements. For example, in *Park State Bank v. Arena Auto Auction,*[3] an Illinois court held that the drawer (the party issuing the check), and not the payor bank (the bank issuing the funds for the check), was liable for a check cashed by an Illinois business. The problem with the check was that the drawer mailed the check to the wrong business. Instead of sending it to a business in Alabama, the drawer mailed the check to a business of the same name, but unassociated with the Alabama business, located in Illinois. The payor bank paid the check to the Illinois corporation, which was a client of the bank, because it had the same name as the Alabama corporation and thus was listed on the check as the payee (the party intended to receive the funds from the check). When the drawer tried to sue the payor bank, the court ruled that the drawer acted negligently in delivering the check to the wrong business (which acted in good faith in cashing the check) and therefore the drawer was liable for the amount of the check.

Case 27-1 considers whether proper delivery of a negotiable instrument had been made, thus meeting the delivery requirement.

[3] 207 N.E.2d 158 (Ill. App. Ct. 1965).

CASE 27-1

MARC A. STEFANO v. FIRST UNION NATIONAL BANK OF VIRGINIA

U.S. DISTRICT COURT FOR THE EASTERN DISTRICT OF VIRGINIA, ALEXANDRIA DIVISION

981 F. SUPP. 417 (1997)

In 1993, Anthony Stefano, father of Marc Stefano and Leo Stefano, learned that he was suffering from a terminal illness. A retired civil servant living in McLean, Virginia, Anthony, by prudent planning and management, had acquired a sizeable portfolio of bonds and certificates of deposit. After consultation with his sons, Anthony decided to avoid estate and probate taxes by ensuring that the bonds and certificates would not pass through his probate estate. To this end, he directed that various bonds and certificates be titled jointly in his name and that of one or the other, or both, of his sons. At his father's direction, plaintiff, who is a licensed attorney, took steps to accomplish the retitling of the bonds and certificates. As a result, interest and call checks were made payable jointly to the father and one or both sons and sent to the father's address in McLean, Virginia.

After Anthony's death on April 10, 1993, Leo, as executor, actively administered his father's estate. In this connection, Leo was charged with the management of several rental properties which Leo and Marc, through inheritance, now owned. Also, Leo moved into his father's McLean, Virginia, residence and therefore received all correspondence mailed to that address, including the periodic interest and call checks from the retitled bonds and certificates of deposit.

In November 1993, Leo established a Virginia Limited Partnership titled "II S Limited Partnership," and subsequently opened an account under the partnership name with Ameribanc, First Union's predecessor in interest. During the period from December 1993 through June 1994, Leo received in the mail delivered to the McLean residence twenty-three checks payable in part to plaintiff. Leo then placed the stamped endorsement of his II S partnership on the back of each check, and presented the checks to First Union for deposit into the II S partnership account. First Union accepted all twenty-three checks, and credited the proceeds to the account of II S Limited Partnership, an entity in which Marc Stefano has never had any interest. At no time did Marc Stefano personally endorse any of the checks.

One issue before the court is whether delivery of the checks had been made to the payee. If no delivery had been made to the payee, then the defendant bank claims that the payee plaintiff cannot claim that the bank wrongfully converted the checks since the payee never had them in the first place.

JUDGE T. S. ELLIS, III: Defendant further contends that the Code's delivery requirement bars plaintiff from recovering on the eighteen checks made payable to Marc and Anthony, jointly. None of the checks, the defendant contends, were delivered to either payee, Anthony having passed away and Marc residing in California. Instead, these checks were delivered to the McLean address, which had been Anthony's residence, but was now Leo's.

The so-called "delivery requirement," which precludes an action for conversion by a payee who did not "receive delivery of the instrument either directly or through delivery to an agent or a co-payee," was added by the 1993 revisions to resolve the question whether a payee who never received an instrument is a proper plaintiff in a conversion action. *See* Virginia Code § 8.3A-420, Official Comment 1. While answering the question in the negative, the Code clearly accepts certain forms of "constructive" delivery as sufficient. Moreover, the Code also makes clear that in cases of multiple payees, it is sufficient that delivery is made to any of the payees or agents of payees. Thus, as the Official Comment confirms, delivery in person is not necessary; proper delivery can be made to a mailbox or to an agent of any of the payees.

This constructive delivery principle, applied here, compels the conclusion that the requisite delivery occurred. Although plaintiff, a California resident, did not personally receive delivery of any of the checks, each was delivered to the residence of Anthony, a co-payee on eighteen of the remaining twenty checks. And, although Anthony was deceased, Leo was Anthony's executor who received each of the checks as an agent of the estate. Thus, each of the checks was properly delivered to an agent of one of the payees.

Seeking to avoid this conclusion, defendant argues that plaintiff's asserted 100% interest in all checks made payable to Marc and Anthony, jointly, dictates a finding that plaintiff did not receive delivery of any of these checks. Defendant reasons that if Anthony's estate had no actual interest in the checks, then delivery could not properly be made to the estate's agent. Under the defendant's rationale, delivery to one payee constitutes delivery to a co-payee only if both payees retain an interest in the check. Yet, the Code suggests otherwise; § 8.3A-420 clearly contemplates that payees eligible to sue may have little or no interest in a multiple payee check, and that a conversion claim may be maintained even where delivery is made to a payee with no actual interest in the check. Accordingly, defendant's attempt to limit the scope of delivery under § 8.3A-420 must fail.

In sum, then, checks made payable to Marc and Anthony jointly and received in the mail by Leo as Anthony's executor and agent, have been properly "delivered" under the Code.

Order issued for trial by jury.

Subsequent trial ruled in favor of Marc Stefano for $50,567.82

CRITICAL THINKING

Judge Ellis reaches his conclusion using reasons supported by several pieces of evidence. What do you think is one of the most compelling pieces of evidence? Why is that evidence particularly strong?

ETHICAL DECISION MAKING

Had Leo used the WPH framework, how would his behavior have differed from what he actually did in this case?

global context

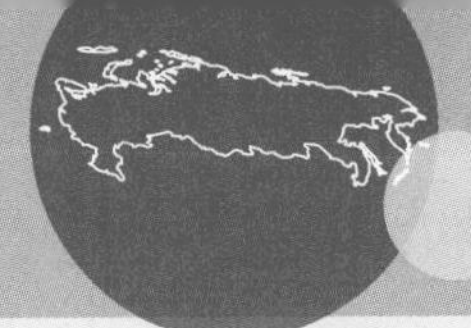

The Evolution of Bills of Exchange in Russia

The concept of bills of exchange has been present in Russian economic transactions since the late-17th century. The first statutes regulating bills of exchange were influenced by the German models and then later the French. In the 1930s, however, bills of exchange were outlawed. They were not considered legitimate documentary transactions in the USSR. It was not until the 1990s that bills of exchange reemerged in Russia, and even then they could be used only in foreign trade transactions. The Decree of the Presidium, adopted on June 24, 1991, declared that bills of exchange were again lawful but only to finance interenterprise indebtedness in regard to foreign transactions.

Eventually Russia recognized the benefits of lifting the ban on domestic bills of exchange. Thus, in March 1997, the Russian Federation reintroduced previously repealed legislation from 1937 that declares bills of exchange and promissory notes legitimate documentary transactions. The legislation was in accordance with the language of the 1930 Geneva Convention. The acceptance of previously repealed legislation is a rarity in the Russian legal system.

ENDORSEMENT

Order paper must be *endorsed* as well as *delivered* to be negotiated. The person creating the endorsement is the **endorser,** and the person receiving the endorsement is the **endorsee.** Normally, there is a place on the negotiable instrument for endorsements (such as on the back of a check). If there is no room on the instrument or if all the room has been taken by previous endorsements, an **allonge** may be attached. An allonge is simply an additional piece of paper with the endorsements. It must be firmly attached (staples usually work; paper clips do not) [UCC 3-204(a)]. There are three kinds of endorsements that will affect the legal status of the negotiable instrument in different ways: unqualified, qualified, and restrictive endorsements.

Unqualified endorsements: blank and special endorsements. There are two kinds of unqualified endorsements: blank and special. A **blank endorsement** is simply the payee's or last endorsee's signature, nothing else [UCC 3-205(b)]. See Figure 27-1 for an illustration. The effect of this unqualified, blank endorsement is that it turns the previous order paper into bearer paper. An instrument with an unqualified, blank endorsement may now be negotiated by delivery only.

A **special endorsement** is the endorser's signature along with a named endorsee [UCC 3-205(a)]. Figure 27-2 contains an illustration. For example, the words "Pay to Jackie Jones" followed by the endorser's signature create a special endorsement.

Note that in an endorsement, the words of negotiability, *to the order of,* are not needed. The instrument remains negotiable. The effect of this kind of endorsement is that it keeps order paper as order paper and thus continues to require an endorsement and delivery for further negotiation.

Hernando Cortez

Figure 27-1
Blank Endorsement

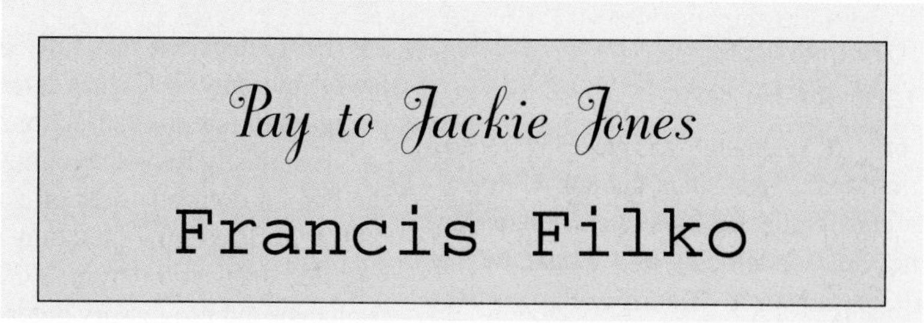

Figure 27-2
Special Endorsement

Pay to Jackie Jones
Francis Filko

Qualified endorsements. As with unqualified endorsements, there are two versions of qualified endorsements: **blank qualified endorsements** and **special qualified endorsements.** What makes them qualified is the addition of the words *without recourse.* When negotiable instruments are passed from one party to another, the person transferring the instrument is guaranteeing certain aspects of the instrument by virtue of his or her signature. When an endorser signs with a signature, the endorser is guaranteeing that he or she will pay a subsequent holder of the instrument in the event the instrument is not honored by the party that created it [UCC 3-415(a)]. Endorsing the instrument with the restrictive endorsement *without recourse* states that the endorser does not intend to be bound to this guarantee [UCC 3-415(b)].

For example, many times people mistakenly write checks to their insurance agent when the proper recipient is the insurance company. In these cases, the insurance agent can restrictively endorse the check, following his signature with the statement "without recourse," and hand the check over to the agency. Figure 27-3 shows an example. The agent, in this case, has effectively negotiated the check to the company and is not liable for the amount in the event there is a problem with the check.

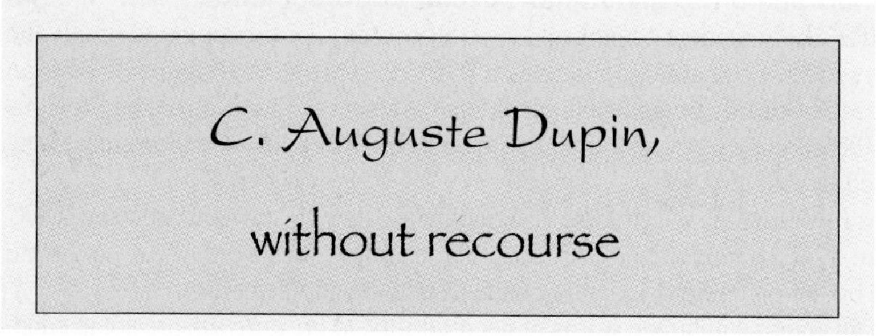

Figure 27-3
Blank Qualified Endorsement

C. Auguste Dupin,
without recourse

Special qualified endorsement. While any endorser is free to restrictively endorse, with either a blank or a special endorsement, the marketability and hence transferability of that instrument diminishes greatly. Who would accept an instrument from someone who will only restrictively endorse it? Such an endorsement is more or less a red flag that there may be a problem with the instrument. Needless to say, this kind of endorsement is not widely used, but it is an option for the endorser.

Restrictive endorsements. **Restrictive endorsements** attempt to either limit the transferability of the instrument or control the manner of payment under the instrument [UCC 3-206(a)]. Such an endorsement does not succeed in its attempt. No type of endorsement can prohibit further transfer; in other words, once an instrument is negotiable, it remains negotiable. However, a restrictive endorsement can limit what is done with the instrument.

The UCC gives four examples of restrictive endorsements:

1. The endorsement for deposit or collection only.
2. The endorsement to prohibit further endorsement.
3. The conditional endorsement.
4. The trust endorsement.

The most common restrictive endorsement is the **endorsement for deposit or collection only.** Signing the back of a check with an unqualified blank endorsement and then adding "for deposit only" turns that endorsement into a blank restrictive endorsement [UCC 3-206(c)]. That check cannot be cashed; it can only be deposited into an account—*any* account. To be perfectly safe, the restrictive endorsement should read "for deposit only into National Bank Account #12345" and be signed by the endorser. Case 27-2 discusses endorsement problems.

CASE 27-2

MID-ATLANTIC TENNIS COURTS, INC. v. CITIZENS BANK AND TRUST COMPANY OF MARYLAND

U.S. DISTRICT COURT FOR THE DISTRICT OF MARYLAND

658 F. SUPP. 140 (1987)

In early 1983, Mid-Atlantic Tennis Courts, a small family-held corporation, decided to expand its business. For this purpose, it hired Loy Smith (whose whereabouts are presently unknown) as a commission salesman. Smith was authorized to sell tennis court jobs and to deliver the executed contracts and any customer deposits received directly to the business office of Mid-Atlantic in Clifton, Virginia.

In early 1984, Smith devised a scheme to defraud Mid-Atlantic. Using customer leads from Mid-Atlantic, Smith entered into eight contracts with potential customers but did not inform Mid-Atlantic of them. In all cases, he accepted deposit checks from the customers made payable either to himself only, to Mid-Atlantic only, or to himself and Mid-Atlantic jointly, and in one case, to himself and an apparently fictitious corporation named SMD. In the summer of 1984, Smith opened two checking accounts with defendant Citizens' Bank in his own name, viz., Loy Thompson Smith, into which he deposited 23 checks, drawn by eight different drawers on a number of drawees, including some drawn on the defendant. As to all of these checks, the defendant was the depositary bank, as defined in Md. Comm. Law Code Ann. [UCC] § 4-105(a). Eventually, Smith disappeared, and the scheme became known to Mid-Atlantic when the would-be customers complained about the lack of progress on their tennis courts.

SMALKIN, DISTRICT JUDGE: In this suit, the plaintiff requests recovery "only for those checks improperly deposited with the endorsement 'for deposit only' or no endorsement" in either one of the two personal checking accounts Smith opened with the defendant. It is undisputed from the deposition of Citizens' Vice President, Mr. Haste, that these checks (the ones that were not endorsed in any fashion with the name Mid-Atlantic) should not have been accepted by defendant for deposit in *anyone's* account other than Mid-Atlantic's.

The defendant has not answered, in its opposition affidavits, the affidavit assertions of Jim Lieberton, President of Mid-Atlantic, to the effect that Smith deposited the checks in his own account and that Mid-Atlantic has not received the proceeds of the checks, to which it was entitled as payee. Thus, it is clear that the plaintiff was the payee and "owner" of the checks in question, and that they have been converted in the common law sense, *viz.*, that Mid-Atlantic, as the true owner, has been deprived of the checks or the proceeds thereof. The U.C.C., in § 3-419, applies conversion principles to negotiable instruments.

For commercial law analysis purposes, the form of the various instruments must be examined. There are 23 checks listed. Of those, plaintiff seeks recovery for only 13. Of those 13, two were deposited having no endorsement whatever, and the remaining 11 bore "endorsements" that consisted only of the words "for deposit only." The total amount of these 13 items was $72,158.45, which appears to be all the recovery the plaintiff seeks by this lawsuit.

It is utterly clear that the defendant did not act in conformity with the reasonable commercial standards of banking when it took in items with no endorsement at all or with no endorsement, save the restrictive language "for deposit only," that had been deposited in Smith's personal banking account, when the named payee was solely Mid-Atlantic. This was the case with every item for which the plaintiff now seeks compensation. An officer of the defendant has essentially admitted this lapse of conformity to banking standards, there is nothing disputing it in defendant's summary judgment opposition, and the legal conclusion is utterly clear. Thus, defendant, as a depositary bank, has conversion liability to plaintiff whether or not any proceeds of the checks remain in its hands.

It is axiomatic that an item is converted when it is paid on a forged endorsement, because the payment is made to one who has no good title. This is just as true in the case where an endorsement necessary to transfer title is missing, because, without the necessary endorsement, there can be no negotiation of the order paper (such as all this paper was). Although a bank is privileged in some circumstances to supply a missing endorsement, the only endorsement that it can supply is that of *its customer,* and it is clear Mid-Atlantic was not defendant's customer, because it had no account with defendant. Until the bank supplies the missing endorsement of its customer, usually with a rubber stamp, it is not a holder of the item. In this case, the missing endorsement was not that of defendant's customer, Smith, but that of the payee, Mid-Atlantic, who was not defendant's customer. Thus, the depositary bank never became the holder of the checks because of the absence of any endorsement whatever, a deficiency that it could not remedy by a stamp endorsement. Because the depositary bank never became a holder in its own right, and because it took items as to which there was no endorsement whatever, it did not have good title to these items, and, therefore, it converted them when it eventually paid the proceeds over to Smith. Although U.C.C. § 3-419(3) usually protects depositary banks which have no proceeds of the items remaining in their hands that protection is unavailable where, as here, the depositary bank has not adhered to reasonable commercial banking standards.

Thus, the Court concludes there is no genuine dispute of material fact, that plaintiff is entitled to summary judgment against the defendant for all the items deposited bearing no endorsement or the "endorsement" of "for deposit only." The damages are the face amounts of the items.

As an additional ground for recovery, the defendant is liable to the plaintiff for breach of the restrictive endorsement "for deposit only" on the items so marked, for the reason the items were never deposited to the account of Mid-Atlantic, which is the only treatment consistent with a "for deposit only" restrictive endorsement made by, or (even purportedly) on behalf of, a named payee. Thus, the plaintiff has two U.C.C. theories of recovery available with regard to the items that bore nothing more than the language "for deposit only," *i.e.,* conversion and breach of restriction, but either theory entitles it to summary judgment on these items, and the recovery is the same.

ORDER ISSUED in favor of plaintiff

CRITICAL THINKING

What is the reasoning used to support the district judge's decision? Are there missing facts in the case that, were they provided, would better enable you to evaluate this reasoning?

ETHICAL DECISION MAKING

What are the values being promoted in the court's decision? If the bank operated under the ethics-of-care philosophy, would it have forced Mid-Atlantic to court?

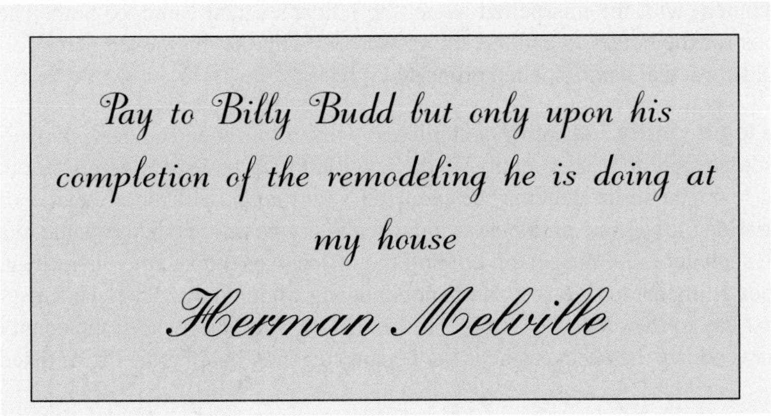

Pay to Billy Budd but only upon his completion of the remodeling he is doing at my house

Herman Melville

Figure 27-4
Conditional Endorsement

Endorsement to prohibit further endorsement. The second kind of restrictive endorsement, the **endorsement to prohibit further endorsement,** is used very rarely. "Pay to John Smith only" with the endorser's signature is an example of such an endorsement. The operative word in this special endorsement is the world *only.* While this endorsement does not prohibit further transfer, it does provide some protection to John Smith [UCC 3-206(a)]. Even if John Smith endorses this instrument over to someone, because of this restrictive endorsement, John Smith is not liable on the instrument until he is paid.

Conditional endorsement. The third kind of restrictive endorsement is a **conditional endorsement.** The endorser can put a condition on payment (one that if it were on the face of the instrument would destroy negotiability, but it does not affect negotiability here) [UCC 3-204(a)]. An example is "Pay to Billy Budd but only upon his completion of the remodeling he is doing at my house [signed] Herman Melville" (see Figure 27-4). In effect, such an endorsement serves to create a defense for the endorser against Billy Budd in the event that Billy Budd does not complete the job. However, it does not affect the ability of the instrument to be further negotiated.

Trust endorsement. The fourth kind of restrictive endorsement is the **trust endorsement.** This kind of endorsement is used when the instrument is being transferred to an agent or trustee for the benefit of either the endorser or a third party [UCC 3-206(d)]. It might read "Pay to Jill Rogers in trust for Billy Watkins" or "Pay to Jill Rogers as agent for Billy Watkins" and then have either Watkins' signature or another endorser's signature. Such an endorsement permits the endorser to have the rights of a holder by virtue of the trust endorsement.

Regardless of the type or kind of endorsement, if the instrument is indeed a negotiable one and if the transfer has been a proper negotiation, we would then go on to the third part of this process, covered in the next chapter: the status and rights of the third-party holder.

NONCRIMINAL ENDORSEMENT PROBLEMS

In situations involving fraud or forgery, it should come as no surprise that problems with endorsements exist. These criminal endorsement issues are examined in the next chapter. However, even in situations not involving criminal offenses, endorsement problems may also arise. We consider these problems below.

Misspelled name. One problem with endorsements occurs when a negotiable instrument contains a misspelled name. In the event of a misspelled name, the holder may endorse the document with the misspelled name, the holder's actual name, or both. The typical practice is for the holder to endorse the instrument with the misspelled name followed by the holder's actual name, spelled properly.

Payable to a legal entity. Another complication regarding endorsements involves instruments made payable to a legal entity. If the legal entity is an estate, organization, partnership, and so on, the instrument may be endorsed by any authorized representative of the entity. A variation of the same problem occurs when instruments are made payable to a public office. In such an event, the person holding the office may endorse the instrument. For example, upon filing her local taxes, Sarah, not knowing whom to make her check payable to, filled in "Pay to the order of County Tax Collector." Bill Deepockets, the county tax collector, may endorse the check, as he is the person currently holding the office listed on the check.

Alternative or joint payees. A third endorsement problem arises when a negotiable instrument has been made payable to more than one person. Two possibilities arise when the instrument is payable to more than one person. The first possibility is that there are *alternative payees.* When the instrument reads "Pay to the order of Jones *or* Smith," the instrument contains alternative payees. In the event of alternative payees, the endorsement of any one of the listed payees is sufficient.

The second possibility is that there are *joint payees.* Joint payees exist when an instrument lists more than one person as a payee and the instrument is to be payable to *all* the listed payees, typically indicated by the word *and.* In the event of joint payees, the instrument would read, "Pay to the order of Smith *and* Jones." An instrument bearing joint payees require the endorsement of all listed payees before the instrument may be negotiated.

Courts have held that when an instrument is silent as to the issue of whether the listed payees are joint or alternative, the instrument is to be interpreted as containing alternative payees. That is, when an instrument does not specify whether the payees are joint or alternative, the endorsement of only one listed payee is required to negotiate the instrument.

Holder in Due Course Doctrine

Suppose you want to purchase computers for your office building. You contract with a computer seller, Data Corp., to buy 50 computers. As partial payment, you give Data Corp. a note for $30,000. Data Corp. negotiates the note to Data Corp.'s landlord, Morgan, for payment of rent.

Suppose Morgan meets all the requirements (which you will soon learn) to be a holder in due course. You discover your computers are damaged, and you claim that Data Corp. breached its contract with you. If Data Corp. still held the $30,000 note, you could refuse to honor the note and claim as a defense that Data Corp. breached the contract. However, remember that Data Corp. negotiated the note to Morgan. Because Morgan is a holder in due course (HDC), you must pay Morgan because a holder in due course has higher rights to a negotiated instrument. If Morgan were simply a holder, you could use the defense of breach of contract against Morgan.

REASON FOR HOLDER IN DUE COURSE STATUS

Do you think the elevated holder in due course status is fair? The purpose of HDC status is to protect a financial intermediary. In other words, someone who processes a payment should not be required to shoulder the transaction risks. Thus, the legal system offers greater legal protection to certain parties to encourage them to engage in financial transactions.

For example, Chuckie's, the check-cashing company in the American Express case, should not be required to shoulder the transaction risks because it was simply a financial intermediary, and the law wants to encourage companies like Chuckie's to engage in financial interactions. As you read this chapter, keep in mind the purpose of HDC status.

Requirements for Holder in Due Course Status

To be considered a *holder in due course,* a party must meet four requirements regarding the taking of the instrument. These requirements are established in UCC Section 3-302.

1. The party must be a holder of a complete and authentic negotiable instrument.
2. The holder must take the instrument for value.
3. The holder must take the instrument in good faith.
4. The holder must take the instrument without notice of defects.

Meeting these requirements is very valuable, as the Case Nugget demonstrates.

Case Nugget HDC Status to the Rescue

Watson Coatings, Inc. v. American Express Travel Services, Inc.
436 F.3d 1036 (2006)

Christine Mayfield used to work for Watson Coatings, Inc., and part of her role there included that of company treasurer. During her time as treasurer, Mayfield wrote approximately 45 to 47 checks from Watson's account to American Express for personal debt totaling $745,969.39. With each check that was submitted, American Express credited Mayfield's personal account. After Mayfield was dismissed from Watson Coatings, the money she had taken was discovered and suit was filed against American Express for taking the money from Mayfield despite the checks' having been clearly labeled as belonging to Watson Coatings, Inc.

The district court granted American Express's motion for summary judgment, but Watson filed an appeal. In the opinion written by Judge Smith, the extent to which American Express can be considered a holder in due course of the checks written by Mayfield was considered. The judge explains that because a payee can be considered a holder in due course, American Express would qualify. However, the court also needed to decide whether holder in due course status would offer any protection to American Express.

The appeals court found that even though Watson had brought forth several common law claims against American Express, the fact that American Express is a holder in due course can serve as a defense. The checks had been accepted by American Express in good faith, making it the holder in due course of the documents. Thus, the court affirmed the district court's grant of summary judgment to American Express.

Case 27-3 examines the required elements of holder in due course status. We consider the required elements in closer detail below.

CASE 27-3 MICHAEL J. KANE, JR. v. GRACE KROLL
COURT OF APPEALS OF WISCONSIN
538 N.W.2D 605 (1995)

Michael Kane, Jr. (Kane), sold Gerald Kroll, Jr. (Gerald), some cows. Gerald could not pay for the cows, so he arranged for his mother, Grace Kroll (Grace), to pay Kane. In exchange for her payment to Kane, Gerald planned to repay his mother with $6,100, the proceeds from his expected sale of a load of hay. Grace issued a personal check to Kane in the amount of $6,100. However, the next day, Gerald told his mother he would not be able to repay her because the sale of hay fell through. Thus, she stopped payment on the check to Kane. When Kane presented the check to the bank, the bank refused to pay.

Kane filed suit against Grace to recover the $6,100. Grace argued that she had no legal obligation to repay Gerald's debt and thus no obligation to pay Kane. Kane argued that he was a holder in due course and was not subject to Grace's defense of failure of consideration. The trial court held that Kane was not a holder in due course because he did not prove he took the check in good faith and without notice of Grace's defenses. Kane appeals.

JUDGE MYSE: Whether Kane is a holder in due course is an issue involving application of § 403.302 STATS., to undisputed facts. A holder must meet three requirements to be a holder in due course under § 403.302, STATS. The holder must take the instrument (1) for value; (2) in good faith; and (3) without notice that it is overdue or has been dishonored or of any defense against or claim to it on the part of any person. We examine each of these elements in turn.

First, a holder must take the instrument for value. Section 403.302(1)(a), STATS. Under § 403.303(2), STATS., a holder takes for value when he takes an instrument in payment for an antecedent claim against *any person.* In this case, Kane took the instrument from Grace in payment of Gerald's debt and thereby satisfied the requirement of § 403.302(1)(a).

Second, a holder must take the instrument in good faith, defined in § 401.201(19), STATS., as "honesty in fact in the conduct or transaction concerned." The holder's initial burden on the issues of notice and good faith is a slight one. As one commentator has noted:

> The burden of proof of the allegations in the Complaint rests upon the plaintiff. It is not necessary, however, that the plaintiff allege in the complaint that good faith was an integral part of the transaction at each stage. That is an affirmative defense which must be raised by the defendant, if at all. [Russell A. Eisenberg, *Good Faith Under The Uniform Commercial Code—A New Look At An Old Problem,* 54 MARQ. L. REV. 1, 14 (1971) (emphasis and footnote omitted)].

In this case, Kane's affidavit supports his contention that he accepted the check in good faith for the payment of Gerald's antecedent debt. Moreover, none of the affidavits supplied by either party suggests evidence of bad faith on Kane's part. In the absence of such evidence, we conclude Kane took the check in good faith as a matter of law.

Finally, the last requirement to become a holder in due course is that the holder take the instrument without notice that it is overdue or has been dishonored or of any defense against it or claim to it on the part of any person. Section 403.302(1)(c), STATS. The knowledge of the defense for purposes of determining holder in due course status must exist at the time of issue. Therefore, we must examine whether Kane had knowledge of any defense at the time he took the check.

Because the requirement that a holder show that it did not have knowledge of a defense or claim to the instrument involves proof of a negative fact, the burden of proof is a slight one. In this case, the facts in Kane's affidavit suggest no knowledge of any claims or defenses, so the burden shifts to Grace to produce evidence that Kane had such knowledge. Grace argues that Kane was on notice that she had no pre-existing obligation to pay her son's debt and that this constitutes knowledge of a defense. We disagree. Section 403.303(2), STATS., clearly allows a holder in due course to accept payment from one person for payment of the debt of another. Additionally, the fact that Grace, like any drawer, had the power to stop payment on the check does not constitute a defense that would prevent Kane from being a holder in due course. If it did, no holder would be a holder in due course because any drawer has the power to issue a stop payment order. Since Grace has not alleged that Kane had knowledge of any defense at the time he took the check, we hold that Kane met the requirement of 403.302(1)(c), STATS.

Because Kane took for value, in good faith, without knowledge of claims or defenses to the check, we conclude he was a holder in due course. As a holder in due course, Kane is not subject to Grace's claimed failure of consideration. Therefore, the fact that Gerald broke his promise to repay Grace the day after the check was issued does not affect Kane's status as a holder in due course.

Based upon the foregoing, we conclude that Kane was a holder in due course of the check and therefore not subject to Grace's asserted defenses. Thus, the trial court erred by granting judgment dismissing Kane's complaint. We reverse the judgment and remand to the trial court with directions to enter judgment in Kane's favor.

REVERSED AND REMANDED.

CRITICAL THINKING

How do rules of law play into the court's reasoning? Are there ambiguities present in these rules of law?

ETHICAL DECISION MAKING

Think about the WPH process of ethical decision making. What is the ultimate purpose of the judge's decision that Kane was a holder in due course? In other words, what value was guiding the judge to conclude that Kane should receive holder in due course status?

BE A HOLDER OF A COMPLETE AND AUTHENTIC NEGOTIABLE INSTRUMENT

Party must be a holder. First, as we mentioned earlier in the chapter, to be a holder in due course, a party taking the instrument must be a *holder,* a party who is in possession of an instrument that is payable to the party or to the bearer of the instrument. [UCC 1-201(20)]. For example, if Adam Brewer possesses a check that states "Payable to Adam Brewer," Adam is a holder. However, suppose Adam asked his bank for a cashier's check to buy a boat from his friend, Corey Baum. (See Figure 27-5.) Even though Adam possesses the cashier's check and his name appears on the check, he is not a holder of the check because it is payable to his friend. When Adam gives the cashier's check to his friend, Corey, the friend becomes the first holder of the cashier's check.

Figure 27-5 Illustration of the Relationship between Being a Payee and Being a Holder

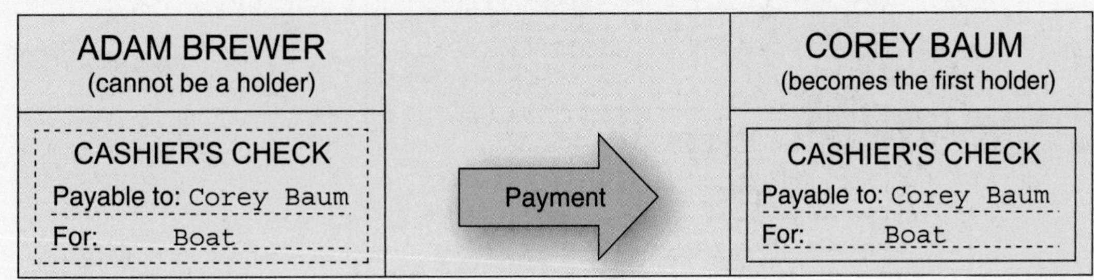

Similarly, if someone steals a check "Payable to Adam Brewer" and forges Adam's signature on the back of the check, this thief is not a holder of the check (see Figure 27-6). Because the check is payable to Adam Brewer and not the thief, the thief cannot be considered a holder, even if he forges Adam's name.

Instrument must be negotiable. Second, the instrument must be negotiable. A party cannot be a holder in due course of a nonnegotiable instrument. If an instrument lacks any of the requirements for negotiability as discussed in the previous chapter, the holder cannot be a holder in due course.

Instrument must be complete and authentic. Third, the negotiable instrument must be complete and authentic. [UCC 3-302(a)(1)]. When the instrument is issued or negotiated, the note must appear complete and authentic. What happens if the instrument is incomplete? For example, suppose that someone writing a check forgets to write the date on the check.

The UCC allows the holder to complete the check as long as the completion is consistent with the intent of the issuer (3-115). For example, suppose you write a check to a company to purchase some business supplies. Although you write the company's name, you forget to write the date. Under the UCC, the company may complete the instrument—in this instance, the check—by writing the date. However, if the person completes the instrument in a way that is inconsistent with the intent of the issuer, the instrument is considered materially altered.

If an instrument has been clearly materially altered or is so irregular or incomplete that its authenticity is called into question, the UCC bars a person taking this flawed instrument from becoming a holder in due course [3-302(a)(1)].

TAKE INSTRUMENT FOR VALUE

How an instrument is taken for value. The holder in due course must take the negotiable instrument "for value." In other areas of the law, taking something for value usually means taking something with consideration, a bargained-for promise. However, the for-value requirement is more stringent than consideration: The party must take the instrument in exchange for a promise that has already been performed. The UCC explicitly excludes promises that have not yet been performed as "value." In other words, the party must suffer

Figure 27-6
Illustration of a Failed Attempt to Become a Holder through Forgery

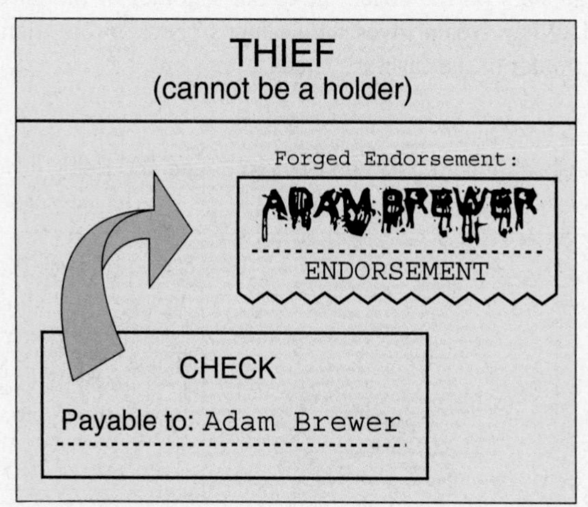

global context

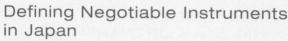

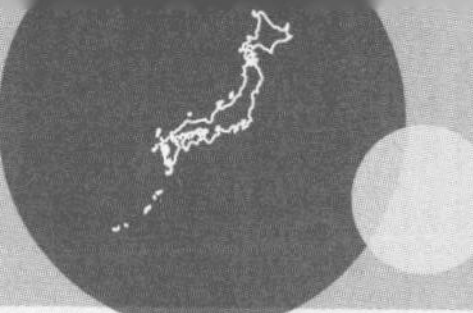

Defining Negotiable Instruments in Japan

The Japanese Commercial Code does not recognize the term *negotiable instruments.* In fact, the Japanese do not have any term to describe negotiable instruments. Instead, they recognize the concept of *yuka shoken,* which means "valuable securities." The concept is not defined in the law, and it is not restricted to a single statute. *Yuka shoken* is a legal concept integrated into various facets of the law. Documents usually considered negotiable instruments are encompassed by the concept of *yuka shoken,* including checks, drafts, bonds, and stocks.

Japan does have separate legislation governing the two general categories of negotiable instruments. These two categories are also recognized in the United States. The first is commercial paper, or bills, notes, and checks. The formation, transfer, and defense of these are provided for in the Bills Law and the Checks Law. The second category is investment securities, including stocks and bonds. There are several different statutes dealing with investment securities. It is important to note, however, that Japanese law does not define the categories of commercial paper or investment securities. Additionally, none of the documents under these categories are defined as negotiable instruments.

The ambiguity surrounding "valuable securities" has created problems. Because there is no single definition, judges and scholars interpret *yuka shoken* based on the definition they find most satisfactory at the time. The varying interpretations can lead to arbitrary exercise of judicial power.

an out-of-pocket loss (UCC 3-303). Why? If a party has not yet performed the promise, he or she has not completely committed financially to the transaction and thus should not receive special legal protection. Therefore, when a party receives a negotiable instrument as a gift or acquires it through mistake, the party will be a holder instead of an HDC.

Barbour v. Handlos Real Estate.[4] offers an example of a holder's meeting the holder in due course requirement of taking for value. Lucile and Alphonse Handlos accepted a note made out to their son as payment for a loan they had previously made to him. Having already given their son the loan, the Handloses had made an investment and thus had taken the note for value previously given. When the note was challenged, the Handloses were afforded holder in due course status.

A holder can take an instrument for value if the holder:

1. Performs the promise for which the instrument was issued.
2. Acquires a security interest or other lien in the instrument.
3. Takes the instrument for payment of a preceding claim.
4. Exchanges the instrument for another negotiable instrument.
5. Exchanges the instrument for an irrevocable obligation to a third party. [UCC 3-303(a)]

Banking transactions and value. Other sections of the UCC are relevant in determining whether a commercial bank has given value for a check. For example, Section 4-211 states that, in the context of determining a bank's status as an HDC, a bank has given value for the negotiable instrument to the extent that the bank has a security interest in the instrument. Section 4-210 specifically identifies circumstances in which a bank has acquired a security interest in a negotiable instrument. In some of these circumstances, although the bank gives value, the bank does not intend to become an HDC. Case 27-4 demonstrates how a bank can become an HDC by acquiring a security interest in a check.

[4] 393 N.W.2d 581 (Mich. Ct. App. 1986).

CASE 27-4 BRADEN CORP. & FRANK W. SPLITTORFF v. THE CITIZENS NATIONAL BANK OF EVANSVILLE

COURT OF APPEALS OF INDIANA, FIRST DISTRICT
661 N.E.2D 838 (1996)

Frank Splittorff was president of two corporations: Braden Corp. and Polymer Technology Corp. While Braden Corp. had a bank account at National Bank of Detroit (NBD), Polymer Corp. had an account at Citizens National Bank of Evansville (Citizens). Splittorff wrote a check from Braden Corp.'s NBD account for $5,000 payable to the order of Polymer Corp on December 3, 1993. Polymer Corp. presented the check for deposit at Citizens on the same day. Citizens gave Polymer a provisional credit for the amount of the check, and Polymer immediately used these funds to pay several checks that Polymer had previously written. Later that day, Citizens forwarded the check to NBD for collection. However, NBD refused to honor the check because of insufficient funds. Citizens presented the check to NBD for payment two more times; however, the check was refused both times. In response, Citizens notified Braden Corp. that there were insufficient funds in its account to cover the $5,000 check.

On January 3, 1994, Splittorff met with two Citizens employees to verify that Braden Corp.'s account had sufficient funds to cover the check. One of the Citizens employees confirmed the balance of Braden Corp.'s account and arranged to present the check to NBD for payment herself. However, on the same day, Splittorff's son, a Braden Corp. official, issued a stop payment order on the $5,000 check. When the Citizens employee personally presented the check at NBD on January 4, 1994, NBD informed her of the stop payment order. In response, Citizens sent a letter to Splittorff demanding payment of the $5,000. Approximately one month later, Citizens filed suit against Braden Corp. and Splittorff for check deception and fraud. The trial court held that Citizens was a holder in due course and was entitled to $5,000 in damages for the check, $15,000 in treble damages, $2,400 in collection costs, and court costs. Braden Corp. and Splittorff appealed.

JUDGE BAKER: First, the defendants contend that the trial court erred in concluding that Citizens was a holder in due course and, therefore, not subject to their defenses of bankruptcy, failure of consideration, and waiver. IND. CODE § 26-1-3-302 states:

> (1) A holder in due course is a holder who takes the instrument
> (a) For value; and
> (b) In good faith; and
> (c) Without notice that it is overdue or has been dishonored or of any defense against or claim to it on the part of any person.

Specifically, the defendants assert that Citizens is not a holder in due course because it did not give value for the check. The defendants are mistaken.

The record reveals that Citizens not only gave provisional credit for the check but also permitted Polymer to draw against that credit. IND. CODE § 26-1-4-209 provides:

> For purposes of determining its status as a holder in due course, the bank has given value to the extent that it has a security interest in an item, provided that the bank otherwise complies with the requirements of I.C. § 26-1-3-302 on what constitutes a holder in due course.

Further, IND. CODE § 26-1-4-208 provides:

> (1) A bank has a security interest in an item and any accompanying documents or the proceeds of either:
> (a) in case of an item deposited in an account, to the extent to which credit given for the item has been withdrawn or applied;

Thus, when Citizens allowed Polymer to draw against the credit given for the defendants' check it acquired a security interest in the proceeds of the check to the extent of the withdrawn funds. This security interest constituted value.

The defendants also assert that Citizens does not qualify as a holder in due course because "[It] had the responsibility to debit the $5,000.00 back out of [Polymer Corp.'s] account once it learned the Braden check had initially been dishonored," yet failed to do so. In addition, the defendants claim that Citizens' failure to immediately debit the account following dishonor demonstrates Citizens' failure to mitigate its loss, and, therefore, bars any recovery. However, the defendants

[CONTINUED]

fail to cite any authority, and we find none, establishing that a bank's failure to debit an account after an initial dishonor of a check prevents it from taking the check as a holder in due course or otherwise bars recovery. Accordingly, the trial court properly determined that Citizens was a holder in due course. Furthermore, because Citizens is a holder in due course, it is not subject to the defendants' defenses of bankruptcy, failure of consideration or waiver. See IND. CODE § 26-1-3-305(1) (a holder in due course takes the instrument free from all claims to it on the part of any person).

AFFIRMED.

CRITICAL THINKING

Why does the judge conclude that Citizens was a holder in due course? Is there any additional missing information that would help you evaluate the court's decision?

ETHICAL DECISION MAKING

Return to the WPH process of ethical decision making. According to the facts of the case, Splittorff's behavior, combined with his son's order to stop payment on the check, seems somewhat questionable. Following the universalization test, what would you have done in Splittorff's position? Why?

Exceptions to the value requirement. The UCC creates certain exemptions to the for-value requirement. In these cases, a holder may take an instrument for value, but the holder does not become a holder in due course. Section 3-303(3) states that a holder is not an HDC if he or she takes the negotiable instrument:

1. By purchasing it at judicial sale or by taking it under legal process.
2. By acquiring it through taking over an estate.
3. By purchasing it as part of a bulk transaction not in the regular course of business of the transferor.

TAKE INSTRUMENT IN GOOD FAITH

The HDC must take the negotiable instrument in good faith [UCC 3-302(a)(2)(ii)]. What exactly is good faith? Historically, there has been some debate about whether *good faith* had an objective or subjective definition. For example, when determining whether a holder took an instrument in good faith in the objective sense, some courts would decide whether the holder purchased the instrument with a proper degree of caution through a usual and ordinary manner of conducting business. Looking at good faith in an objective sense means considering what the reasonable holder would have done.

However, other courts looked at good faith in a subjective sense by asking whether the holder acted honestly when taking the instrument. To look at good faith in a subjective sense means considering the holder's actual behavior.

The UCC's definition of good faith is somewhere in the middle of the subjective and objective standard. The UCC defines good faith as "honesty in fact and the observance of

connecting to the core

Economics

Banks as HDC

As discussed in the text, the greater protection of a holder in due course encourages financial transactions while protecting financial intermediaries. As you read in Case 27-4, banks, which are financial intermediaries, may occupy the role of a holder in due course. By the law's extending greater protection for holders in due course, banks are entitled to liability protection when they acquire a security interest. This protection promotes the essential role that banks play in our economy, namely, banks' transferring large sums of money from savers to spenders. In other words, banks use the large sums of savings to provide entrepreneurs with loans needed to start or expand businesses, while also reducing the costs and time that individuals would spend looking for savings and investment opportunities were these individuals not able to rely on banks. By the law's providing greater protection in situations where banks function as holders in due course, banks are much more likely to continue processing payments when they are not responsible for the risks of such transactions.

Source: Bradley R. Schiller, *The Economy Today* (New York: McGraw-Hill/Irwin, 2006), pp. 269, 673.

reasonable commercial standards of fair dealing" [3-103(a)(4)]. Therefore, to act in good faith, a holder must not deviate from the reasonable commercial standards of fair dealing. The UCC drafters were most concerned with the fairness of the dealing.

Hartford Ins. Group v. Citizens Fidelity Bank & Trust Co.[5] offers an example of a bank's being considered an HDC because it acted in good faith and within reasonable commercial standards of fair dealing. In this case, a customer of Citizens Fidelity Bank deposited a check from his insurance company. The bank accepted the check, credited its customer's account, and sent the check to Hartford Ins. Group's bank. Apparently, the drawer of the check told Citizens' customer not to negotiate the check, but he did so without telling his bank about his notification. Before Citizens credited its customer's account, the bank manager, who had known the customer for four years, approved the check in accordance with standard Citizens Bank policy. Furthermore, there were no irregularities on the face of the check. Accordingly, the bank accepted what appeared to be a valid check from one of its longtime customers in accordance with standard, reasonable bank policy. As such, the court deemed Citizens a holder in due course and therefore not liable for the check.

When considering whether a holder took the negotiable instrument in good faith, the court looks at only the holder's state of mind. The transferor may have acted in bad faith. Case 27-5 provides an example of the process the court uses to determine whether a holder has taken an instrument in good faith.

TAKE INSTRUMENT WITHOUT NOTICE

Finally, a holder must take an instrument without notice of various claims to or defects of the negotiable instrument. If the holder has notice or is aware of any of the following defects, the holder cannot be an HDC [UCC 3-302(a)]:

1. The instrument is overdue.
2. The instrument has been dishonored.

[5] 579 S.W.2d 628 (Ky. Ct. App. 1979).

CASE 27-5 MAINE FAMILY FEDERAL CREDIT UNION v. SUN LIFE ASSURANCE COMPANY OF CANADA ET AL.

SUPREME JUDICIAL COURT OF MAINE
727 A.2D 335 (1999)

Elden Guerrette (Guerrette) purchased a life insurance policy from Steven Hall (Hall), an agent of Sun Life Assurance Company (Sun Life). Guerrette made his three adult children—Daniel, Joel, and Claire—his beneficiaries of this policy. When Guerrette died, Sun Life issued each child a check for $40,759.35. These checks were drawn on Sun Life's account at Chase Manhattan Bank. Hall was supposed to deliver the checks to the beneficiaries.

Instead, Hall and his associate, Paul Richard, fraudulently convinced the beneficiaries to endorse the checks and sign them over to him to allegedly be invested in Hall and Richard's corporation. Richard deposited the checks into his account at the Maine Family Federal Credit Union (Credit Union). The Credit Union permitted Richard to immediately access those funds.

However, the next day, the Guerrette beneficiaries regretted their decision to sign over the checks and asked Sun Life to stop payment on the checks. Sun Life ordered Chase Manhattan to stop payment; thus, when the Credit Union presented the beneficiary checks for payment, Chase refused payment. Because the Credit Union had already made the funds available to Richard, he had used approximately $42,000. The Credit Union then filed suit against Sun Life, the Guerrettes, and Richard in an attempt to recover those funds. The Credit Union argued that it was a holder in due course and thus not subject to the defenses raised by Sun Life and the Guerrettes. However, the trial court held that the credit union did not act in good faith and was thus not a holder in due course. The Credit Union appealed.

JUDGE SAUFLEY: We therefore turn to the definition of "good faith" contained in Article 3-A of the Maine U.C.C. [This] definition provides:

> "Good faith" means honesty in fact *and* the observance of reasonable commercial standards of fair dealing. 11 M.R.S.A. § 3-1103(1)(d) (1995).

Because the tests are presented in the conjunctive, a holder must now satisfy both a subjective and an objective test of "good faith."

1. Honesty in Fact

Prior to the changes adopted by the Legislature in 1993, the holder in due course doctrine turned on a subjective standard of good faith and was often referred to as the "pure heart and empty head" standard. That standard merely required a holder to take an instrument with "honesty in fact" to become a holder in due course.

It is undisputed that the Credit Union had no knowledge that Richard obtained the Sun Life checks by fraud. Nor was the Credit Union aware that a stop payment order had been placed on the Sun Life checks. The Credit Union expeditiously gave value on the checks, having no knowledge that they would be dishonored. In essence the Credit Union acted as banks have, for years, been allowed to act without risk to holder in due course status. The Credit Union acted with honesty in fact.

Thus, had the matter at bar been decided before the Legislature's addition of the objective component of "good faith," there can be little question that the Credit Union would have been determined to have been a holder in due course. Because it took the instruments without notice of any possible dishonor, defect, fraud, or illegality, it could have given value immediately and yet have been assured of holder in due course status. Today, however, something more than mere subjective good faith is required of a holder in due course.

2. Reasonable Commercial Standards of Fair Dealing

We turn then to the objective prong of the good faith analysis. The addition of the language requiring the holder to prove conduct meeting "reasonable commercial standards of fair dealing" signals a significant change in the definition of a holder in due course. The pure heart of the holder must now be accompanied by reasoning that assures conduct comporting with reasonable commercial standards of fair dealing.

The difficulty is [in] the lack of definition of the term "fair dealing" in the U.C.C. The most obvious question arising from the use of the term "fair" is: fairness to whom? Transactions involving negotiable instruments have traditionally required the detailed level of control and definition of roles set out in the U.C.C. precisely because there are so many parties who may be involved in a single transaction. If a holder is required to act "fairly," regarding all parties, it must engage in an almost impossible balancing of rights and interests. Accordingly, the drafters limited the requirement of fair dealing to conduct that is reasonable in the commercial context of the transaction at issue. In other words, the holder must act in a way that is fair according to commercial standards that are themselves reasonable.

[T]he jury's task here was to decide whether the Credit Union observed the banking industries' commercial standards relating to the giving of value on uncollected funds, and, if so, whether those standards are reasonably designed to result in fair dealing.

The evidence produced by the Credit Union in support of its position that it acted in accordance with objective good faith included the following: The Credit Union's internal policy was to make provisional credit available immediately upon the deposit of a check by one of its members. . . . The Credit Union also presented evidence that neither Regulation CC nor the Credit Union's internal policy required it to hold the checks or to investigate the genesis of checks before extending provisional credit. It asserted that it acted exactly as its policy and the law allowed when it immediately extended provisional credit on these checks, despite the fact that they were drawn for relatively large amounts on an out-of-state bank. Finally, the Credit Union presented expert testimony that most credit unions in Maine follow similar policies.

In urging the jury to find that the Credit Union had not acted in good faith, Sun Life and the Guerrettes argued that the Credit Union's conduct did not comport with reasonable commercial standards of fair dealing when it allowed its member access to provisional credit on checks totaling over $120,000 drawn on an out-of-state bank without either: (1) further investigation to assure that the deposited checks would be paid by the bank upon which they were drawn, or (2) holding the instruments to allow any irregularities to come to light.

The factfinder must consider all of the facts relevant to the transaction. The amount of the checks and the location of the payor bank, however, are relevant facts that a bank, observing reasonable commercial standards of fair dealing, takes into account when deciding whether to place such a hold on the account. The jury was entitled to consider that, under Regulation CC, when a check in an amount greater than $5,000 is deposited, or when a check is payable by a nonlocal bank, a credit union is permitted to withhold provisional credit for longer periods of time than it is allowed in other circumstances. Therefore, the size of the check and the location of the payor bank are, under the objective standard of good faith, factors which a jury may also consider when deciding whether a depositary bank is a holder in due course.

The Credit Union's President admitted the risks inherent in the Credit Union's policy and admitted that it would not have been difficult to place a hold on these funds for the few days that it would normally take for the payor bank to pay the checks. He conceded that the amount of the checks were relatively large, that they were drawn on an out-of-state bank, and that these circumstances "could have" presented the Credit Union with cause to place a hold on the account. He also testified to his understanding that some commercial banks followed a policy of holding nonlocal checks for three business days before giving provisional credit. Moreover, the Credit Union had no written policy explicitly guiding its staff regarding the placing of a hold on uncollected funds. Rather, the decision on whether to place a temporary hold on an account was left to the "comfort level" of the teller accepting the deposit. There was no dispute that the amount of the three checks far exceeded the $5,000 threshold for a discretionary hold established by the Credit Union's own policy.

On these facts the jury could rationally have concluded that the reasonable commercial standard of fair dealing would require the placing of a hold on the uncollected funds for a reasonable period of time and that, in giving value under these circumstances, the Credit Union did not act according to commercial standards that were reasonably structured to result in fair dealing.

We recognize that the Legislature's addition of an objective standard of conduct in this area of law may well have the effect of slowing the "wheels of commerce." . . . Notwithstanding society's oftcited need for certainty and speed in commercial transactions, however, the Legislature necessarily must have concluded that the addition of the objective requirement to the definition of "good faith" serves an important goal. The paramount necessity of unquestioned negotiability has given way, at least in part, to the desire for reasonable commercial fairness in negotiable transactions.

AFFIRMED.

[CONTINUED]

CRITICAL THINKING

What evidence does the court use to support its conclusion that Maine Family Federal Credit Union did not act in good faith? Do you think that any of the counterevidence offered by the president of the credit union was particularly persuasive?

ETHICAL DECISION MAKING

Judge Saufley was rather explicit in identifying the purposes behind the definition of good faith. What values support the UCC's definition of good faith? What values are in conflict with these preferred values?

3. The instrument was issued as part of a series that is in default.
4. The instrument has been altered or contains an unauthorized signature.
5. There is a claim to the instrument. (These claims are described in Section 3-306.)
6. Another party has a defense or claim in recoupment to the instrument.

What does it mean to have notice? According to the UCC, a person has notice of a fact in any one of the following circumstances:

1. She has actual knowledge of the fact.
2. She receives notice or notification of it.
3. The facts and circumstances known to the person at the time in question give the person reason to know that the fact exists. [UCC 1-201(25)]

For example, suppose that Chuckie's, the check-cashing company from the chapter opener, received a letter from American Express that listed the numbers of the American Express money orders that had been stolen. As long as Chuckie's received this letter *before* it accidentally accepted the stolen money orders, Chuckie's would have notice of a defect and thus could not be a holder in due course. The UCC states that "to be effective, notice must be received at a time and in a manner that gives a reasonable opportunity to act on it" [3-302(f)].

Suppose that a person receives an instrument that has clearly been altered; however, the person taking the instrument does not inspect the instrument and thus does not notice the obvious alteration. As stated earlier, one of the requirements of becoming a holder in due course is to accept a complete and authentic negotiable instrument [UCC 3-302(a)(1)]. Consequently, the question of a holder's awareness of such extreme irregularities does not matter; the very existence of such irregularities means that the holder cannot be a holder in due course.

If a person has notice of a defect before he or she gives value for the instrument but still gives value, the person will not be able to claim holder in due course status.

Overdue instruments. Suppose you accept a check from a business associate. Unfortunately, the check falls behind your desk and is lost for the next four months. If you try to negotiate this instrument to another party, this party will not be permitted to claim holder in due course status because the check is overdue. If a holder has notice that an instrument is overdue, the holder cannot claim holder in due course status. How does a holder know whether an instrument is overdue? Overdue status is dependent on the type of instrument. The UCC states how two types of instruments—demand or time instruments—may be overdue (3-304).

Demand instruments. First, a **demand instrument,** an instrument payable on demand, becomes overdue if it has been outstanding for an unreasonably long period of time after its date [UCC 3-304(a)(3)]. If the demand instrument is a check, the UCC states that the check is overdue 90 days after its date [UCC 3-304(a)(2)]. Thus, because your check has been outstanding for four months, it is overdue. The date on the check would give another party notice of its overdue status; thus, the party cannot claim HDC status.

Time instruments. Second, a **time instrument,** an instrument payable at a definite time, becomes overdue at any time after the expressed due date on the instrument. For example, suppose a customer tries to negotiate a promissory note to you on January 2, 2008. However, the note states that it is payable by January 1, 2008. You have notice that the promissory note is overdue; you must have acquired the note before January 1, 2008, for the note to be negotiable.

Most of the rules regarding whether a time instrument is overdue depend on the payment structure of the time instrument. For example, a time instrument may or may not be payable in installments. If the instrument requires that a party make payment on an instrument in a lump sum rather than in installments, the instrument is overdue if the party does not make the lump-sum payment by the due date [UCC 3-304(b)(2)]. However, how does nonpayment of installments affect whether the instrument is overdue? Overdue status depends on whether a late payment applies to the principal or the interest on the instrument. If a party misses payment of an installment on the principal of an instrument, the instrument is overdue until this installment is paid [UCC 3-304(b)(1)]. However, if a party misses a payment of interest on this instrument, the instrument is not overdue [UCC 3-304(c)].

Sometimes, parties agree to accelerate the due date of an instrument. Thus, if a party does not make payment on either the principal *or* the interest on the instrument by the accelerated due date, the instrument is overdue [UCC 3-304(b)(3) and 304(c)]. Because it may be difficult for a holder taking an instrument to determine whether there has been an accelerated due date, the UCC permits this holder to become an HDC if he or she had no reason to know about the accelerated due date.

Why might a party have reason to know that an installment payment on the principal was not made and thus the instrument is overdue? This information is usually included on a credit report. For example, if a bank is considering purchasing a consumer note from a retailer, the bank can determine whether all payments have been made on the note by looking at the consumer's credit report. If the credit report indicates that an installment had not been paid, the bank would have notice that the instrument was overdue.

Dishonored instruments. If a holder is aware that an instrument he or she is taking has been dishonored, the party cannot become a HDC. An instrument is **dishonored** when a party refuses to pay the instrument. For example, suppose you deposit a check from a customer into your company's account at a Wells Fargo bank. The customer has an account at Chase Manhattan. Wells Fargo credits your account and later presents the check for payment at Chase.

However, Chase refuses to pay because there are insufficient funds in your customer's account. Chase has dishonored the check and would likely stamp the phrase "insufficient funds" on your check. If you then tried to negotiate this check to another party, the party, seeing the words *insufficient funds,* would have notice that the check was dishonored.

However, if a party would have no reason to know that a note has been dishonored, the party can become an HDC. Thus, if Chase did not stamp the phrase "insufficient funds" on the check, the new party would likely not have notice that the check was dishonored. Consequently, this new party could become an HDC.

Claims or defenses. If a party is aware of any claim or defense to an instrument, that party has notice and can thus not become an HDC [UCC 3-302(a)(2)(v),(vi)]. However, if the party had no reason to know that various claims or defenses applied to an instrument even if the claims and defenses existed, the party would not be precluded from becoming an HDC.

In Case 27-6, George and Mary Lou Clark Hathorn tried to argue that the holder of their mortgage and promissory note took the instruments with the knowledge that they had a specific defense to the instrument.

CASE 27-6

GEORGE T. HATHORN v. WILLIAM R. LOFTUS
SUPREME COURT OF NEW HAMPSHIRE
726 A.2D 1278 (1999)

On September 24, 1987, George and Mary Lou Clark Hathorn purchased a group home for the elderly from Thomas and Jane Batchelder, who were represented by William Loftus. The purchase agreement stated that the sale of the home was contingent upon the parties' agreement to a management contract. Both parties agreed that the Batchelders would manage the home. As a result of the agreement, the Hathorns executed a $10,000 promissory note to the Batchelders. This note was secured by a mortgage. The first payment on this note was due in late September 1989. However, in 1988, because of a dispute regarding the Batchelders' performance as managers, the Hathorns elected to terminate the management contract. The Hathorns sought a declaratory judgment in June 1989 that they lawfully terminated the management contract.

In August 1989, the Batchelders transferred the promissory note and mortgage to Loftus as partial-payment for his attorney services. The Batchelders owed Loftus approximately $20,000. The Hathorns told Loftus that they would pay the September 1989 installment on the note in escrow until the declaratory judgment litigation was resolved.

In May 1992, the court ruled in the declaratory judgment action against the Batchelders, finding that the Batchelders had to pay the Hathorns' attorney fees and costs of approximately $11,000. The Hathorns petitioned the court to have this amount be set off against the mortgage and note. In June 1993, the trial court ruled that the Hathorns' promissory note was discharged in full "subject to the rights, if any, of third parties." Loftus, claiming to be a holder in due course of the note, refused to release the mortgage. The Hathorns filed a petition to quiet title in May 1994. Loftus counterclaimed, demanding payment on the note. The trial court ruled for Loftus. The Hathorns appealed.

JUDGE BRODERICK: The Hathorns argue that the trial court erred by concluding that Loftus acquired the note without notice of their *defense* of set-off. They contend that the court erred when it concluded that Loftus did not have notice of their *claim* of set-off to the note because the Hathorns' declaratory judgment petition was equitable in nature and Loftus subjectively believed that they were unlikely to prevail. The Hathorns assert that the court failed to recognize that their request for attorney's fees and costs in the declaratory judgment petition constituted a defense of set-off or "defense or claim in recoupment," preventing Loftus from becoming a holder in due course. We initially address the Hathorns' synonymous use of the terms "recoupment" and "set-off."

Recoupment may be used defensively or affirmatively and encompasses the right of a defendant to reduce or eliminate the plaintiff's demand either because (1) the plaintiff has not complied with some cross-obligation under the contract on which the plaintiff sues, or (2) the plaintiff has violated some legal duty in making or performing that contract. By its nature, a claim or defense in recoupment concerning a negotiable instrument must arise from the transaction that gave rise to the instrument itself. Set-off, however, applies when "there are mutual debts or demands between the plaintiff and defendant at the time of the commencement of the plaintiff's action," and unlike recoupment, the mutual debts arise out of separate transactions. Neither recoupment nor set-off helps the Hathorns in this case.

First, the Hathorns' request for attorney's fees and costs pursuant to the terms of the management contract in their petition for declaratory judgment cannot constitute a claim or defense in recoupment because it did not arise out of the transaction from which the note arose. The note arose from the purchase of the group home. The claim for attorney's fees and costs arose from the Batchelders' breach of the management contract. While the management contract originally stemmed from the property sale, fulfillment of the purchase and sale agreement was simply conditioned on the *execution* of the management contract, *not* on the parties' *performance* of their obligations under it. The parties satisfied this condition precedent, completed the sale, and thereafter executed the mortgage and promissory note. Subsequent performance under the management contract and the note were mutually exclusive; thus, non-performance of one did not affect the validity or enforcement of the other. Because the Hathorns' request for attorney's fees and costs arose from the Batchelders' breach of the management contract, a transaction separate from the note itself, it cannot be characterized as a claim or defense of recoupment.

Second, the Hathorns' request for attorney's fees and costs could not constitute a claim or defense of set-off at the time Loftus acquired the note because it was not liquidated.

Finally, even if the request for attorney's fees and costs constituted a claim or defense of set-off, it could not compromise Loftus' status as holder in due course because set-off, by its nature, does not arise from the transaction which gave rise to the note. See 6A W. Hawkland & L. Lawrence, Uniform Commercial Code Series § 3-302:18, at 130 (1993); RSA 382-A: 3-305(a)(3) comment 3 (resolving division in case law to clarify that transferee of instrument is protected from claims or defenses unrelated to transaction from which instrument arose).

AFFIRMED.

CRITICAL THINKING

What evidence does the judge offer to support his conclusion? Does this evidence persuade you? What additional evidence would you like to see?

ETHICAL DECISION MAKING

Does it seem fair to you that the court is offering protection to Loftus's claim? Think about the purpose of the decision. What value(s) is consistent with giving protection to Loftus? Which value(s) is consistent with giving greater protection to the Hathorns? Which value do you think carries more weight in this case?

Exhibit 27-1 Defenses and the Holder in Due Course

A holder in due course is generally free from personal defenses but is subject to real defenses. The holder in due course is *free* from the following personal defenses:

1. Lack or failure of consideration
2. Breach of contract
3. Fraud in the inducement in the underlying contract
4. Incapacity*
5. Illegality*
6. Duress*
7. Unauthorized completion or material alteration of the instrument
8. Unauthorized acquisition of the instrument

The HDC is *subject to* the following real defenses:

1. Fraud in the essence
2. Discharge of the party liable through bankruptcy
3. Forgery
4. Material alteration of a completed instrument
5. Infancy—when a party is below the legal age of consent

* Although an HDC cannot normally be submitted to the defenses of incapacity, illegality, or duress, these defenses do sometimes apply. If the incapacity, illegality, or duress was significant enough for a court to deem the original contract void, the HDC will be subject to these defenses. Once incapacity (or illegality or duress) is present to the extent that the contract is void, the defense of incapacity (or illegality or duress) is a real defense. In other words, if the contract is void due to incapacity, illegality, or duress, a party can use that defense against an HDC.

Exhibit 27-1 provides a summary of the defenses that do and do not apply to the holder in due course.

The Shelter Principle and HDC

Generally, if an item is transferred from one person to another, the transferee acquires all the rights that the transferor had in the item. This idea is called the **shelter principle** [UCC Section 3-203(b)]. Therefore, following the shelter principle, even if a holder cannot attain holder in due course status, the holder can acquire the rights and privileges of an HDC *if* the item is being transferred *from* an HDC. Note that the instrument does not need to be transferred directly from an HDC for the recipient to have the rights of an HDC. Under the shelter principle, as long as the holder of an instrument can demonstrate that someone through the line of transfers had obtained the rights of an HDC, then all subsequent holders have the rights of an HDC.

Therefore, in the chapter opener, plaintiff Triffin received the American Express money orders from Chuckie's, a holder in due course. If Triffin did not qualify for HDC status on his own, he would have received the rights that Chuckie's, the transferor, had. In other words, Triffin is taking "shelter" in Chuckie's status as an HDC.

One exception to the shelter principle involves cases of fraud or other illegal activities. If a person engages in fraud or other illegal interference with an instrument, he or she may not become an HDC, even if obtaining the instrument later from an HDC. For example, Chad and Dave devise a scheme to defraud Jenny. Jenny, unaware of the fraud, writes a check to Dave. Dave negotiates the check to Mandy. Mandy, through the negotiation, becomes an HDC. Mandy eventually negotiates the check to Chad. Although Chad should be an HDC under the shelter principle, because he was part of the original fraud against Jenny, he does not obtain the rights of an HDC.

The shelter principle may at first seem contrary to the idea of the HDC principle; however, the purpose of the shelter principle is to encourage the marketability of instruments. The greater protection offered to an HDC is very appealing; thus, allowing parties to achieve the rights of the HDC through the shelter principle encourages financial interactions.

Abuse of the Holder in Due Course Doctrine

While HDC status offers great protection to financial intermediaries, the intermediaries might attempt to abuse this protection. For example, suppose you are starting a small business and a salesman for a company called Office Supplies Made Easy comes to your new office and wants to sell you high-quality office supplies. You pay for the office supplies with a negotiable installment note on which you are supposed to pay three installments of $1,000. However, the next day, the Office Supplies Made Easy salesman negotiates the note to a finance company. When you receive your office supplies, you discover that the supplies are extremely low-quality and certainly not worth the $3,000 you agreed to pay. You call Office Supplies Made Easy, saying that you want to return the office supplies. However, an employee tells you that your installment note has been negotiated to the finance company, which became a holder in due course.

Consequently, the finance company calls your office every day because you have refused to pay for the low-quality supplies. You later discover that the finance company is in the practice of negotiating all notes from all salespersons of Office Supplies Made Easy. It appears to you that Office Supplies Made Easy and the finance company have some kind of arrangement so that the finance company can attain HDC status. Claims or defenses you have against Office Supplies Made Easy do not apply to the finance company.

When cases like this have arisen in court, judges have looked at the connection between the transferor and the transferee. If the companies are closely connected, as in the Office Supplies Made Easy example, some judges apply the salesperson's knowledge of your claims and defenses to the finance company. Consequently, this application prevents the finance company from achieving HDC status.

To ensure that companies could not abuse the HDC status, the FTC created several rules in the 1970s that helped to protect consumers against HDC abuse as in the Office Supplies Made Easy example. The FTC rule requires that every consumer credit contract or any purchase money loan contain the following statement in 10pt, boldface type:

> **ANY HOLDER OF THIS CONSUMER CREDIT CONTRACT IS SUBJECT TO ALL CLAIMS AND DEFENSES WHICH THE DEBTOR COULD ASSERT AGAINST THE SELLER OF GOODS OR SERVICES OBTAINED PURSUANT HERETO OR WITH THE PROCEEDS HEREOF. RECOVERY HEREUNDER BY THE DEBTOR SHALL NOT EXCEED AMOUNTS PAID BY THE DEBTOR HEREUNDER.**[6]

Consequently, no subsequent holder of the contract will have the rights of an HDC.

[6] FTC Holder in Due Course Regulations, 16 C.F.R. 433.2 (1978).

global context

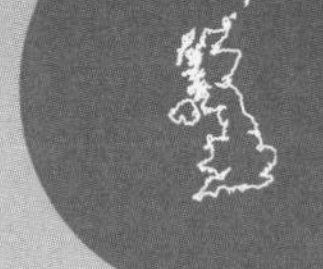

Negotiable Instruments in England and Similarities to the HDC Doctrine in the United States

In England, the doctrine of privity of contract declares that contracts are exclusive to those who created them. However, this doctrine often limits and complicates business transactions. The problems created by privity of contract in England can be countered by using a negotiable instrument. Unlike contracts, in England bills of exchange, promissory notes, and checks can be negotiated between parties.

Negotiable instruments are used in business, in England as in the United States, to facilitate business transactions. To ease the exchange and free flow of money in business transactions, businesses need to be able to transfer quickly money or other forms of payment. In the United States, companies can transfer their right to collect or their duty to perform under a contract. The English practice of privity prevents similar transfers. Accordingly, English businesses must be able to transfer money a different way in order to conduct regular business. It is the ease of transferability of negotiable instruments and the rights that come with a transferred negotiable instrument, as outlined in this chapter, that make negotiable instruments an ideal way for English businesses to avoid the problems created by the privity requirement.

CASE OPENER WRAP-UP

American Express

At the trial level, the court ruled that American Express did not have to pay for the stolen money orders. However, the superior court reversed this holding, stating that the money orders were negotiable instruments. The superior court ruled that American Express's arguments regarding why it was not required to pay did not apply to Chuckie's or Triffin because both were holders in due course. The Pennsylvania Supreme Court affirmed the superior court's holding that American Express, rather than Triffin, was required to bear the costs of the stolen money orders.[7]

As discussed earlier in the chapter, the purpose of the holder in due course doctrine is to protect financial intermediaries and encourage them to continue to engage in financial transactions. Thus, if you were a manager for Chuckie's and discovered that American Express would not be responsible for the stolen money orders, you would probably be less likely to accept American Express money orders. As discussed in the Global Context box, Indian law provides similar protection for holders in due course who unknowingly receive stolen instruments.

[7] "Digests of Recent Opinion: Supreme Court," *Pennsylvania Law Weekly,* September 14, 1998, p. 15.

global context

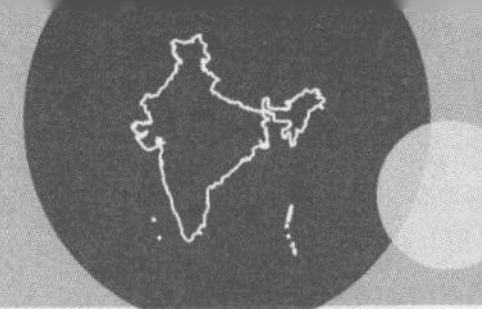

Holder in Due Course in India

In India, the holder in due course is the only person involved in a negotiable-instrument transaction who retains certain rights over an instrument obtained unlawfully. There are four ways an instrument can be obtained unlawfully: (1) The instrument stemmed from an illegal consideration; (2) consideration was totally absent; (3) the instrument was delivered with contingent conditions that have not been fulfilled; or (4) the instrument was obtained by fraud or theft.

In the instance of lost bills of exchange, holders may ask the drawer to issue another bill as long as the lost one has not been compensated. The drawer is required to reissue the lost instrument. The drawer can request that a security be given to him or her in the event that the lost bill is later claimed. Notice that these provisions are exclusive to bills of exchange and do not include promissory notes.

Summary

Negotiation

Delivery: The physical handing over of a negotiable instrument.

Endorsements:

1. Unqualified endorsements
2. Qualified endorsements

Holder in Due Course Doctrine

The HDC doctrine provides incentive for financial intermediaries to engage in transactions because they receive greater legal protection.

Requirements for Holder in Due Course Status

1. *Be a holder of a complete and authentic negotiable instrument.*
2. *Take instrument for value:* Holder must suffer an out-of-pocket loss.
3. *Take instrument in good faith:* Holder must take the instrument with "honesty in fact and the observance of reasonable commercial standards of fair dealing."
4. *Take instrument without notice:* Holder must take the instrument without notice of the following defects: It is overdue, dishonored, or part of a series in default; it has been altered or has an unauthorized signature; or it is subject to claims or defenses.

The Shelter Principle and HDC

Shelter principle: If a holder cannot attain HDC status, the holder can acquire the rights and privileges of an HDC *if* the item is being transferred *from* an HDC.

Abuse of the Holder in Due Course Doctrine

FTC rule: Negotiation of consumer notes may not be subject to HDC status.

Point / Counterpoint

Should Someone Who Commits an Illegal Activity to Obtain a Negotiable Instrument Still Be Considered a Holder in Due Course?

Yes

Someone who commits an illegal activity to obtain a negotiable instrument should still be considered an HDC.

Suppose a person took a misplaced betting ticket and cashed it (knowing full well the voucher was not his to cash). That person should still be awarded holder in due course status.

The UCC established four requirements a holder must fulfill to be considered a holder in due course. The first requirement is that "the party must be a holder of a complete and authentic negotiable instrument." Assuming the criminal was wise enough to ensure that his recently obtained negotiable instrument is complete and authentic, a criminal can fulfill the first requirement to qualify as a holder in due course.

Another requirement established by the UCC is that "the holder must take the instrument in good faith." Especially because the definition of "good faith" is unclear, a criminal could easily obtain an instrument in good faith. Some criminals may be lucky enough to *find* a misplaced voucher. The criminal has no reason to believe the voucher should belong to someone else. The "criminal" is fortunate, and he fulfills the good-faith requirement established by the UCC.

Additionally, to be a holder in due course, the holder "must take the instrument without notice of defects," including notice that the instrument is overdue, dishonored, or altered or has an unauthorized signature. As a criminal who does not know anything about the instrument's background, the criminal fulfills this requirement.

Meeting the requirements under the UCC should provide a holder the rights of HDC status.

No

A criminal action should prevent HDC status.

A person who obtains a negotiable instrument through an illegal activity does not deserve the status of holder in due course. The criminal does not fulfill all the requirements set by the UCC to become a holder in due course.

A criminal does not fulfill two of the four requirements set by the UCC to be deemed a holder in due course. While a criminal may be in possession of a complete and authentic negotiable instrument and the instrument may have been obtained without notice of defects, fulfilling two of the four requirements is not sufficient for the criminal to be considered a holder in due course.

If obtaining the negotiable instrument through thievery, the criminal does not fulfill the second UCC requirement. The second requirement is known as both "taking the instrument for value" and "suffering an out of pocket loss." A criminal may "happen upon" a negotiable instrument, but he does not pay anything for the instrument. Therefore, the criminal should not be considered a holder in due course.

A criminal should not be awarded the status of holder in due course for yet another reason. The holder in due course doctrine was created to provide incentive for financial intermediaries to engage in transactions without fear of liability. The holder in due course doctrine was *not* designed to encourage or provide incentives for thieves and criminals to dishonestly obtain negotiable instruments.

Providing incentives to financial intermediaries through the holder in due course doctrine is an excellent idea. A party that simply processes a payment should *not* be required to shoulder transaction risks. However, a thief or criminal does not simply process a payment. A criminal does not fulfill the role intended for the holder in due course. Therefore, a criminal should not receive the protections available to a holder in due course.

Questions & Problems

1. Evaluate the following statement: "Order paper and bearer paper must be delivered to be negotiated."
2. Explain the rationale for the following statement: "The purpose of holder in due course status is to encourage parties to engage in financial transactions."
3. What are the requirements of holder in due course status?
4. L&M had a checking account with Wells Fargo Bank. Gentner performed consulting services for L&M, and L&M paid Gentner with a $60,000 check. Eleven days after issuing the check, L&M orally instructed Gentner to stop payment on the check. When Gentner presented the check to Wells Fargo for payment, the bank issued a cashier's check, payable to Gentner, for $60,000. Wells Fargo later placed a stop-payment order on the cashier's check, and when Gentner deposited the cashier's check at another bank, it was not honored. Gentner claimed that the original stop payment was never made by L&M and that it was a holder in due course of the cashier's check. Wells Fargo argued that the holder in due course doctrine did not apply because Gentner purchased the cashier's check for payment to itself rather than the check's being purchased by another party for payment to Gentner. Gentner sued Wells Fargo for wrongful dishonor of a cashier's check. The trial court found for Gentner, determining that it was a holder in due course of a cashier's check. How do you think the case was decided on appeal? [*Gentner and Company, Inc. v. Wells Fargo Bank,* 76 Cal. App. 4th 1165 (1999).]
5. Bond issued a $300,000 note to Goss in 1988. The note was secured by a deed of land. Goss later entered into an agreement to purchase commercial property owned by RAM. In lieu of partial payment, Gaetani, general partner of RAM, accepted the $300,000 note. Supanich, a trustee for Goss, endorsed the note. The note endorsement read: "For value received, the undersigned hereby assigns and transfers all right, title and interest in and to within Note to Toney E. Gaetani, Sr." The endorsement did not contain the words *without recourse.* Bond paid no principal and only partial interest on the note. Gaetani brought an action against Goss, Supanich, and Bond. At issue was whether the endorsement language allowed Gaetani to recover directly against Goss. Despite the lack of the words *without recourse,* the trial court held that Gaetani could not recover from Goss. Do you think the court allowed Gaetani to recover from Goss on appeal? [*Gaetani v. Goss-Golden,* 84 Cal. App. 4th 1118 (2000).]
6. At the end of January 2001, while cleaning out his self-storage locker, Kim Griffith found a certificate of deposit purportedly issued by Mellon Bank, N.A., of Pittsburgh, Pennsylvania, on July 3, 1975, for the amount of $530,000 plus interest to be payable to bearer on August 4, 1975. The CD was in one of several books Griffith had purchased from an unnamed buyer. On its face, the certificate of deposit had not been marked paid. On August 15, 2002, more than a year after finding the certificate of deposit, Griffith presented it for payment in person at a Mellon Bank office in Pennsylvania. Mellon refused to honor the certificate of deposit, arguing that because the bearer certificate of deposit matured 27 years earlier, the certificate was questionable on its face and thus was not genuine. Based on Mellon's refusal to honor the certificate of deposit, Griffith filed suit against Mellon. Mellon argues that it has no records of the CD as not being paid and that under Pennsylvania law it falls to Griffith

to prove nonpayment. Griffith argues he is a holder in due course and is entitled to payment regardless of any possible defenses Mellon might raise. Is Griffith a holder in due course? Should he be able to collect on the CD? Why or why not? [*Griffith v. Mellon Bank, N.A.*, 328 F. Supp. 2d 536 (2004).]

7. Nickelson executed a note payable in the sum of $71,250 "to the order of Aaron Ziegelman and William K. Langfan." Ziegelman and Langfan used the note to secure a loan from NatWest for their business venture. Langfan transferred all of his rights, title, and interest in the note to Ziegelman in 1986. Langfan did not endorse the note. In 1994 Langfan executed an allonge, titled "corrective allonge to promissory note." It stated, "Pay to the order of Aaron Ziegelman, without recourse. This allonge is being made solely for the purposes of correcting transfer of Note(s) executed on or about January 16, 1986, by and between William K. Langfan to Aaron Ziegelman, and for such purposes only." Ziegelman subsequently defaulted with respect to his obligations under the credit agreement, and the note was assigned to NatWest. After obtaining the corrective allonge, NatWest transferred the note to Esca Enterprises. Esca then sold the note to the plaintiff in this case, Cadle Company. Cadle claims that, at the time the note was transferred by Esca to Cadle, the allonge and corrective allonge were attached to it. Nickelson refused to pay on the note, arguing that there was a defect in the chain of title. During discovery for the trial, the corrective allonge was not attached to the note. Cadle was eventually able to produce the corrective allonge, and it argued that it became separated during copying done in connection with the litigation. Who do you think has title to the note? Was Langfan's transfer legitimate? [*The Cadle Company v. Nickelson,* 1996 U.S. Dist. LEXIS 18665 (1996).]

8. Daniel DeMarais is the former chief financial officer (CFO) of Apex, IT. Through a Minnesota Department of Revenue investigation it came to light that DeMarais had embezzled well over $ 400,000 from the company. DeMarais embezzled funds from Apex in part by using Apex's corporate checks to pay the amounts due on a personal credit card account he maintained with Chase Manhattan Bank USA, N.A. According to Apex, Chase had notice of Apex's claims to these funds because the payments were "unusual, irregular, and large" and were made using business checks from Apex's corporate accounts. Apex demanded that Chase return all funds it received from DeMarais, which Chase refused to do. Apex then sued Chase, seeking equitable relief. Chase contends that Apex's claim must fail because Chase is a holder in due course. Does Chase meet the requirements for a holder in due course? Should Chase have taken more precautions given the unusual nature of the payments? [*Apex IT v. Chase Manhattan Bank USA, N.A.*, 2005 U.S. Dist. LEXIS 3917 (2005).]

9. James Mills received a draft in the amount of $484.12 from Cigna Insurance for workers' compensation benefits. He falsely told Cigna that he had failed to receive the check, and he requested that payment be stopped and a new draft issued. Before payment was stopped, Mills negotiated the initial draft to Sun Corp. Sun Corp., a holder in due course, presented the draft for payment, but it was dishonored. Robert Triffin then obtained an assignment of an interest in the negotiable instrument from Sun Corp. Triffin agreed that he was not a holder in due course of the instrument by virtue of its being negotiated to him for value, in good faith, or without notice of dishonor. However, he did argue that under the shelter provision Sun Corp.'s status as a holder in due course was vested in him. Was Triffin entitled to enforce the instrument? Did he become a holder in due course of the instrument? How do you think the court decided? [*Triffin v. Cigna Insurance Company,* 687 A.2d 1045 (1997).]

10. Gateway executed and delivered to Metro a promissory note for $1 million. David Wabick executed a guaranty to Metro in favor of the Gateway note. Wabick unconditionally guaranteed the "prompt and full payment to Metro when due of all of the indebtedness and liabilities of Gateway." Several months later, the FDIC was appointed receiver of Metro. The FDIC conveyed all of its rights, title, and interest in the Gateway loan to Missouri Bridge Bank by executing an "assignment of note and mortgages" and an allonge to the Gateway note. The allonge properly identified the bank for which the FDIC served as receiver and the date of the assignment, but it incorrectly listed the date of the note to which the allonge was fixed. In addition to executing the allonge, the FDIC endorsed the Gateway note with the same language. Handwritten changes were made to the allonge to correct mistakes regarding the date and the name of the parties, but the date listed was accurate. The Bridge Bank subsequently assigned its rights to the note to Boatmen's Bank. When Boatmen's made a demand to Wabick for the payment of the note, Wabick argued that Boatmen's was not a holder in due course of the guaranty. Wabick claimed that the defects in the allonge prevented the transfer of the note and guaranty to Bridge Bank and broke the chain of negotiation. Boatmen's argued that it was a holder in due course and entitled to the guaranty. It argued that the FDIC's endorsement on the note, which was legitimate, should control the court's decision. Do you think the court determined that Boatmen's was a holder in due course? Was the chain of negotiation broken? [*Boatmen's First National Bank of Kansas City v. Wabick,* 1996 U.S. Dist. LEXIS 10338 (1996).]
11. Sherri Spencer was appointed executrix for Max Wolf. She hired Angela Wallace to initiate probate proceedings. Wallace allegedly forged Wolf's signature and converted assets from his estate from three different banks. Wallace endorsed the checks by hand, writing "by Max Wolf, For Deposit Only." Each bank paid the full amount of the cashier's check to Sterling Bank. The checks did not indicate the person for whose benefit the check was to be deposited. The funds were deposited into Wallace's Sterling Bank client trust account. Spencer sued Sterling Bank for breach of a restrictive endorsement. Should Sterling be held responsible? Can a check endorsed, "for deposit only" without further limitation be deposited into any account? [*Spencer v. Sterling Bank,* 63 Cal. App. 4th 1055 (1998).]
12. Pershing & Co. discovered that five Royal Dutch certificates issued to Hilson & Co. were missing from its inventory. Pershing applied to its bank for replacements. The bank required that Pershing execute an "Affidavit for Lost Securities," stating that the certificates had been lost, stolen, or destroyed, and purchase an indemnity bond. Sixteen years later, Haber received four of the original missing stock certificates in a sealed envelope as a wedding present from his uncle. Haber's uncle did not take the certificates by endorsement and was not a holder in due course. Haber did not open the envelope until 1996. Haber sold the certificates, and the bank originally credited his account with $2.77 million. However, the bank later informed Haber that it was rescinding the sale, and it debited his account for the amount of the proceeds. Haber contended that he was a holder in due course of the certificates. Do you think Haber was a holder in due course of the stock certificates? Why or why not? [*Haber v. Fireman's Fund Insurance Surety Corp.,* 2000 U.S. Dist. LEXIS 9458 (2000).]

Looking for more review material?

The Online Learning Center at **www.mhhe.com/kubasek1e** contains this chapter's "Assignment on the Internet" and also a list of URLs for more information, entitled "On the Internet." Find both of them in the Student Center portion of the OLC, along with quizzes and other helpful materials.

Liability, Defenses, and Discharge

CASE OPENER

Citizens National Bank and the Forged Checks

Scott Rodgers Real Estate (Century 21) opened four checking accounts with Citizens National Bank. The president of Century 21 had sole signature authority for all accounts. A receptionist at Century 21 issued four checks and forged the president's signature on each of these checks. She then deposited these checks in her own bank account. Later, the receptionist concealed the bank statements from the company's controller so that the company could not immediately discover the stolen checks. When Century 21 finally discovered the stolen checks, it brought suit against Citizens for reimbursement of the amounts of the forged checks.

1. Who do you think should bear the liability for the forged checks—Century 21 or Citizens National Bank? What values are guiding your decision?
2. Does the fact that the receptionist had a history of embezzlement change your mind about which party should be liable?

The Wrap-Up at the end of the chapter will answer these questions.

Learning Objectives

After reading this chapter, you will be able to answer the following questions:

1. What information is needed to determine signature liability?
2. What is warranty liability?
3. How does one avoid liability for negotiable instruments?

CHAPTER 28

As you can see from the Century 21 opener, it is not always clear who should bear responsibility for the amount of a negotiable instrument. This chapter explains the various ways a party may be liable for a negotiable instrument. First, when a person signs a negotiable instrument, he or she is potentially liable for the instrument. This type of liability is called **signature liability.** In contrast, a party may be liable if the transfer of the instrument breaches a warranty associated with the instrument. This second type of liability is called **warranty liability.** After we consider both signature and warranty liability, we examine the defenses to these types of liability. Finally, we investigate how liability for a negotiable instrument may be discharged.

Signature Liability

UCC Section 3-401(a) imposes liability if the party or the party's agent signs the instrument. If a party does not sign, the party cannot be held liable. Thus, because the receptionist at Century 21 forged the president's name on the check, should Century 21 be liable?

Because the signature on an instrument leads to liability, it is important to know what counts as a signature. According to the UCC, a signature can be any name, word, mark, or symbol used by a party to authenticate a writing [3-401(b)]. Thus, if you wrote either your full name or an *X* with the intent to authenticate an instrument, either writing would constitute a signature.

When a party signs a negotiable instrument, he or she might be signing as a maker, acceptor, drawer, or endorser of the instrument. The signer's status as a maker, acceptor, drawer, or endorser of the note establishes the extent of the signer's liability. In other words, issuers and acceptors have a certain type of liability, while drawers and endorsers have another type of signature liability. Issuers and acceptors are primarily liable for a negotiable instrument, while drawers and endorsers are secondarily liable. If it is not possible to tell the status of the party, the general rule is that the party is considered an endorser (UCC 3-204, comment 1). Exhibit 28-1 provides a summary of the various endorsing parties and their roles.

PRIMARY LIABILITY OF MAKERS AND ACCEPTORS

A party who is **primarily liable** for an instrument must pay the stated amount on the instrument when it is presented for payment. This liability for the stated amount begins as soon as the instrument is issued. Moreover, the primarily liable party must pay without resorting to any other party. For example, suppose you own a business and write a check drawing on your funds in your business account at First National Bank. First National has

Exhibit 28-1 Parties Signing a Negotiable Instrument

ENDORSING PARTY	DESCRIPTION	ROLE
Maker	A person promising to pay a set sum to the holder of a promissory note or certificate of deposit	Promises to pay money
Acceptor	A person (drawee) who accepts and signs the draft to agree to pay the draft when it is presented	Pays the money, or is responsible for paying the money, when it is requested
Drawer	A person ordering the drawee to pay	Orders someone (the drawee) to pay
Endorser	A person who signs an instrument to restrict payment of it, negotiate it, or incur liability	Signs an instrument at some point during negotiation

e-commerce AND THE LAW

Signatures and the Internet

On June 30, 2000, the Electronic Signatures in Global and National Commerce Act (the *E-Sign Act*) became federal law. The E-Sign Act gives legal force to digital signatures and online contracts in financial, business, consumer, personal, and government contexts. For example, the act covers loan transactions made, insured, or guaranteed by the federal government. The act applies to "transferable records" and states that any instrument that is a loan relating to real property and that would be considered a note under Article 3 of the UCC is considered a transferable record. Thus, students can now electronically sign their student loans. Furthermore, citizens can file and digitally sign their tax returns.

What exactly is a digital signature? A *digital signature* is a personal identifier that can be broken into electronic code. In other words, the signer "stamps" a document with his or her "signature" by placing data unique to the signer on it. Currently, there are two types of digital signatures: biometric and key-based signatures. Biometric digital signatures stamp the document with unique physical characteristics such as a fingerprint. Key-based signatures use digital "keys." The signer has a public key and a private key. These keys scramble information so that only parties with appropriate keys may read the information. The signer can use the private key to sign documents.

Source: David M. Nadler & Valerie M. Furman, "Landmark Electronic Signatures Legislation Becomes Effective," *Derivatives Litigation Reporter*, February 26, 2001.

primary liability for the check; it must pay the stated amount when the check is presented for payment.

The UCC establishes that certain parties—makers and acceptors—are primarily liable. First, a **maker** is a party who has promised to pay. For example, the maker of a promissory note is primarily liable for the amount of the note because the party has promised to pay the amount of the instrument. Moreover, UCC Section 3-412 states that a party who signs as an issuer of an instrument is liable for the amount of the instrument as soon as it is issued. For example, a bank that issues a cashier's check is primarily liable for the amount of the check as soon as the cashier's check is created (UCC 4-412).

Second, an **acceptor**, a drawee of a draft who accepts and signs the draft to agree to pay the draft when it is presented, is primarily liable [UCC 3-413(a)]. A party who accepts a draft by signing on the face of the draft is primarily liable (UCC 3-413). For example, when a bank accepts a check, it is primarily liable for the amount of the check (UCC 3-409).

SECONDARY LIABILITY OF DRAWERS AND ENDORSERS

A party who is **secondarily liable** for an instrument must pay the amount on the instrument if the primarily liable party defaults. Return to the First National Bank example. First National has primary liability for the check; it must pay the stated amount when the check is presented for payment. However, suppose First National dishonors this check because of insufficient funds in your account. Because the primarily liable party, the bank, has defaulted, you, the issuer of the check, are now liable.

Drawers and endorsers are secondarily liable parties. An **endorser** is a party who signs an instrument to restrict payment of it, negotiate it, or incur liability [UCC 3-204(b)]. A **drawer** is a person who signs as a party ordering payment [UCC 3-103(a)(5)]. For example, if you write a check from your bank account that is payable to the electric company, you are the drawer of the check, the bank is the drawee, and the electric company is the holder of the check. The holder of the check (the electric company) presents the check to the drawee (the bank) for payment. **Presentment** is defined in the UCC as making a demand for the drawee to pay [UCC 3-501(a)]. The UCC creates specific rules that govern the time and manner of presentment.

Suppose the holder (the electric company) presented your check and the bank dishonored the check because of insufficient funds in your account. The UCC states that drawers of drafts are liable for an instrument only after it has been dishonored (3-414, 3-415). Thus, you (the drawer) are now liable for the check.

By adding a disclaimer to her or his signature on a draft, a drawer might avoid liability if the instrument is dishonored [UCC 3-414(e)]. However, a drawer of a check may not include such a disclaimer of liability.

Three conditions must be met for a drawer or endorser to become liable. First, the holder of the instrument must present the instrument in a proper and timely fashion. Second, the instrument must be dishonored. Third, notice of the dishonor must be given to the drawer.

Presentment. An instrument must be presented in a proper and timely manner. Exhibit 28-2 provides a summary of the requirements for presentment of a negotiable instrument. First, the instrument must be presented to the proper party. If the instrument is a note, the holder must present the note to the maker of the note. In contrast, if the instrument is a draft, the holder must present the instrument to drawee. Thus, continuing our electric company example, the electric company must present the check to the bank (the drawee).

Exhibit 28-2 Proper Presentment of a Negotiable Instrument

1. Presented to the proper party
2. Presented in a proper way
3. Presented in a timely manner

Second, the instrument must be presented to the proper party in a proper way. UCC Section 3-501(b) states that an instrument can be presented (1) by any commercially reasonable means, (2) through a clearinghouse procedure, or (3) at the place designated in the instrument.

Third, the instrument must be presented to the proper party in a timely manner. Thus, if the instrument is a note, the holder must present the note to the maker on the note's due date. If the instrument is a draft, such as a check, the holder must present the instrument within a *reasonable* time. The failure to present an instrument on time is the most common reason that improper presentment occurs, which ultimately discharges unqualified endorsers from secondary liability.

The UCC states a specific timeline for presentment. If a holder does not present the instrument within a reasonable time, the drawer or endorser may not be held secondarily liable. Therefore, if the electric company waited 60 days to present your check to the bank, it probably cannot hold you secondarily liable because the UCC states that a check must be presented within 30 days of its date to hold the drawer secondarily liable [3-414(f)]. Similarly, to hold an endorser secondarily liable, a holder must present a check within 30 days of the endorsement [UCC 3-415(e)].

Dishonor. When a holder presents an instrument within a timely and proper manner but acceptance or payment is refused, the instrument has been **dishonored.** The instrument must be explicitly dishonored; a refusal to pay does not necessarily mean that the instrument has been dishonored. For example, suppose you are a holder of a check that is payable to your business. You present this check for payment, but the bank refuses to pay the check because you cannot present identification [UCC 3-501(b)(2)]. Alternatively, a bank may refuse to pay on an instrument because the endorsement of the instrument is not proper. Again, this refusal to pay does not dishonor the instrument. Situations in which refusals to pay do not constitute dishonorment are found in UCC Section 3-501(b) and

Exhibit 28-3 Refusals to Pay That Do Not Dishonor an Instrument

REASON FOR REFUSAL	UCC TEXT
Holder's failure to comply with certain requests	Upon demand of the person to whom *presentment* is made, the person making presentment must (i) exhibit the *instrument,* (ii) give reasonable identification and, if presentment is made on behalf of another person, reasonable evidence of authority to do so, and (iii) sign a receipt on the instrument for any payment made or surrender the instrument if full payment is made. [3-501(b)(2)]
Lack of proper endorsement or failure to comply with terms of the instrument	Without dishonoring the *instrument,* the *party* to whom *presentment* is made may (i) return the instrument for lack of a necessary *endorsement,* or (ii) refuse payment or *acceptance* for failure of the presentment to comply with the terms of the instrument, an agreement of the parties, or other applicable law or rule. [3-501(b)(3)]
Presentment after an established cutoff hour	The *party* to whom *presentment* is made may treat presentment as occurring on the next business day after the day of presentment if the party to whom presentment is made has established a cut-off hour not earlier than 2 p.m. for the receipt and processing of *instruments* presented for payment or *acceptance* and presentment is made after the cut-off hour. [3-501(b)(4)]

are listed in Exhibit 28-3. Remember, a secondarily liable party becomes liable *only* if a primarily liable party dishonors the instrument.

Notice of dishonor. The UCC provides a specific timeline in which notice of dishonor of an instrument must be given to a secondarily liable party (3-503). (The process of determining secondary liability is summarized in Exhibit 28-4.) If the party that dishonors an instrument is a collection bank, it must give notice before midnight of the next day [UCC 3-503(c)]. Other parties must give notice of the dishonor within 30 days of the day on which they receive notice of dishonor. This notice can be given in any commercially reasonable manner: oral, written, or electronic communication [UCC 3-503(b)]. The notice must identify the instrument in question and state that this instrument has been dishonored. If the word *dishonored* appears on the instrument, this writing is enough to constitute notice. As long as the holder gives notice to the secondarily liable parties about the dishonor of the instrument, the holder can sue the other parties.

If all three of these conditions are met, the holder can bring suit against the secondarily liable party. However, in most cases, while a secondarily liable party may have to pay a holder the amount of the instrument, this secondarily liable party can then seek recourse against the primarily liable party. For example, suppose Angie issues a promissory note to Cesar. Cesar endorses the note on the back and transfers this note to Roopa. When the note is due, Roopa presents the note to Angie. However, Angie dishonors the note. Roopa gives notice of dishonor to Cesar and sues Cesar for the value of the instrument. Cesar will be liable; however, he can sue Angie because she was primarily liable for the amount of the promissory note.

In the event an instrument contains more than one endorsement, each endorser is liable for the full amount to any subsequent endorser or to any holder. For example, Ron issues a note to Jenna. Jenna endorses the note and transfers it to Sally, who endorses and transfers to Bill. Bill presents the note to Ron, who refuses to honor it. Bill can then receive payment from Sally, who transferred the note to him. However, Bill can also seek repayment from Jenna, who endorsed the note before Sally did. If Bill seeks repayment from Sally, Sally can seek repayment from Jenna, who endorsed the note prior to Sally. The secondary

Exhibit 28-4 Summary of Process of Determining Secondary Liability

	NOTE	DRAFT
Holder must present instrument to?	Maker	Drawee
When should the instrument be presented?	On due date	Reasonable time; if a check, 30 days within date of check or 30 days within time of endorsement
If the instrument is presented and dishonored, who is usually now liable for the instrument?	Any endorser	Drawer or endorser
What are the requirements for an instrument to be officially dishonored so that a holder may then turn to secondarily liable parties?	**1.** Present to maker for payment. **2.** Maker dishonors. **3.** Holder gives notice of dishonor to secondarily liable parties (endorsers).	**1.** Present to drawee for payment. **2.** Drawee dishonors. **3.** Holder gives timely notice of dishonor to drawer or endorsers.

liability established through endorsement requires that endorsers pay anyone who endorses the instrument after him or her.

ACCOMMODATION PARTIES

Suppose that, after you graduate from college, you decide to start your own business. You need to borrow a significant amount of money from the bank and you plan to create a promissory note. However, because you have never owned your own business and have little credit history, the bank is a little wary about whether you will be able to pay the note. Therefore, the bank decides to ask you to have a third party sign the note to ensure the bank will be paid. Consequently, your business law professor cosigns your note. This third party is called an **accommodation party**, a party who signs an instrument to provide credit for another party that has also signed the instrument [UCC 3-419(a)].

Accommodation parties may be primarily or secondarily liable for an instrument and can sign as makers, drawers, acceptors, or endorsers. However, accommodation parties more frequently sign as makers or endorsers. As a maker, an accommodation party has primary liability, but as an endorser, the party has secondary liability.

Suppose you, in the example above, cannot pay your note, and your business professor, as an accommodation party, pays the note instead. This professor has a right of reimbursement to recover the money from you, the accommodated party [UCC 3-419(e)]. If, however, you, the accommodated party, pay the note when it is due, you cannot force the professor to contribute to the amount due on the loan.

Case 28-1 considers whether a party was an accommodated party. As you will see, the court asks very specific questions regarding the intent of the parties, as well as the position of the signature on the instrument.

AGENTS' SIGNATURES

An **agent** is a party who has authority to act on behalf of and bind another party, the **principal.** The agent typically binds the principal through the agent's signature. (Agents'

CASE 28-1

STAR BANK v. THEODORE JACKSON, JR.
COURT OF APPEALS OF OHIO, FIRST APPELLATE DISTRICT, HAMILTON COUNTY
2000 OHIO APP. LEXIS 5567 (2000)

Limestone Development, Inc., made a promissory note with Star Bank to borrow money for the purposes of expanding business. Theodore Jackson and Douglas Hendrickson were Limestone's only shareholders. Both executed the note on behalf of the corporation in their corporate capacities, and they also acted individually as co-signers.

When Limestone, Hendrickson and Jackson defaulted on the note, Star Bank demanded payment, ultimately culminating in a case brought against Jackson to recover the balance on the promissory note.

Subsequently, Jackson filed a motion for relief from judgment. Jackson argued he had been led to believe the bank had no intention of ever seeking payment from him, and that his signature on the note was merely perfunctory. Jackson also claimed the bank had not requested any of his personal financial information, and he was never included in the negotiations. Further, in his business relationship with Hendrickson, Jackson had devoted his time, effort and skill, and Hendrickson had contributed his financial wherewithal. Hendrickson controlled all aspects of the loan, including the disbursements of the proceeds. The trial court overruled Jackson's motion for relief from judgment, and this appeal followed.

JUDGE DOAN: A "maker" of a note is "a person who signs or is identified in a note as a person undertaking to pay." A party's signature in the lower right corner of an instrument indicates that he or she intended to sign as a maker of the instrument. In this case, Jackson's signature appears in the lower right corner of the note. Thus, he is regarded as a maker and not as an endorser. An individual signing a note as a co-maker with another individual is jointly and severally liable for the debt, except as otherwise provided in the instrument.

In this case, the note states that "LIMESTONE DEVELOPMENT, INC. and all cosigners signing this Note (referred to in this Note individually and collectively as 'Borrower') jointly and severally promise to pay to [the bank], or order, the principal." Thus, under the note's clear and unambiguous language, Jackson is jointly and severally liable on the note.

A party's status as a maker of a note does not preclude that party from also being an accommodation party. A party signs as an accommodation party when "an instrument is issued for value given for the benefit of a party to the instrument and another party to the instrument signs the instrument for the purpose of incurring liability on the instrument without being a direct beneficiary of the value given for the instrument." An accommodation party may sign the instrument as maker, drawer, acceptor, or endorser and that party is liable to pay the instrument in the capacity in which he or she has signed.

Jackson correctly asserts that the issue of whether a party signs an instrument as an accommodation party generally presents a question of fact. However, even if Jackson is an accommodation party, as an accommodation maker, he is still obligated to pay the note according to its terms. He has only a few defenses against the holder, such as impairment of collateral, none of which he raised in the trial court.

As an accommodation party, Jackson may have a right to recover against the other co-makers of the note. However, that right would be relevant in an action for contribution and indemnity against Limestone and Hendrickson; it is not a valid defense in an action by the holder to enforce the note. Consequently, Jackson is not entitled to relief from judgment on this basis.

In sum, we hold that Jackson failed to present operative facts showing that he had a meritorious defense to present if relief from judgment were granted, and that the trial court did not abuse its discretion in overruling his motion. Consequently, we overrule his assignment of error and affirm the trial court's judgment.

JUDGMENT AFFIRMED.

[CONTINUED]

CRITICAL THINKING

The judge found the evidence persuasive enough to find Jackson an accommodation maker. What evidence seemed to convince the judge? Do you see any reason to suspect that this evidence may not be adequate to reach the judge's conclusion?

ETHICAL DECISION MAKING

Think about the WPH process of ethical decision making. What was the purpose of determining that Jackson was an accommodation party? In other words, which values were guiding the judge's decision?

signatures and liabilities are summarized in Figure 28-1.) The agent's binding power through signature similarly applies to negotiable instruments (UCC 3-402). As long as the agent is *authorized* to sign a negotiable instrument on behalf of a principal, the agent's signature can create liability for the principal.

Previously, the UCC required that the agent clearly identify the principal when signing. UCC Section 3-401, which states that a party cannot be liable unless his signature appears on the instrument, was interpreted to mean that if a principal's name was not on the instrument, he could not be held liable. This interpretation has changed. The UCC now states that if an agent signs an instrument truly on behalf of a principal, this principal *can* be held liable even if he or she is not "identified in the instrument" [3-402(a)]. This policy ensures that someone will always be held liable for the instrument. While this new interpretation serves its purpose, what values are in conflict between the old and the new interpretations? Would an ethical dilemma arise when determining whether one was "truly" signing on behalf of a principal?

Can an agent be personally liable for a negotiable instrument? Interpretation of the UCC has changed to make it easier to find that the agent was representing the principal when signing. Now it is a little more difficult to hold an agent personally liable for a negotiable instrument. The authorized agent cannot be liable if she did not sign her own name to the instrument (UCC 3-401). If the authorized agent simply signs her own name to the instrument, she might be liable. If the holder of the instrument is a holder in due course and is not aware and does not have reason to know that the agent has signed on behalf of a principal, the agent may be held personally liable. If the holder of the instrument is not a holder in due course, the agent can usually escape liability by demonstrating that it was not the intent of the principal to hold the agent personally responsible.

There is an exception to agent liability. Even if the holder is a holder in due course and the agent simply signed his name, the agent will not be liable under specific conditions. If the instrument is a check payable from the principal's account and the principal is clearly identified on the check, the agent will not be liable on the check [UCC 3-402(c)].

Finally, the agent can be personally liable if he was not authorized to sign on behalf of the principal. This unauthorized writing falls into a broader category of unauthorized signatures.

Unauthorized signatures and endorsements. As a general rule, if a signature to a negotiable instrument is unauthorized, this unauthorized signature will not impose liability to the named party. This rule applies to two cases: forgery and unauthorized agents.

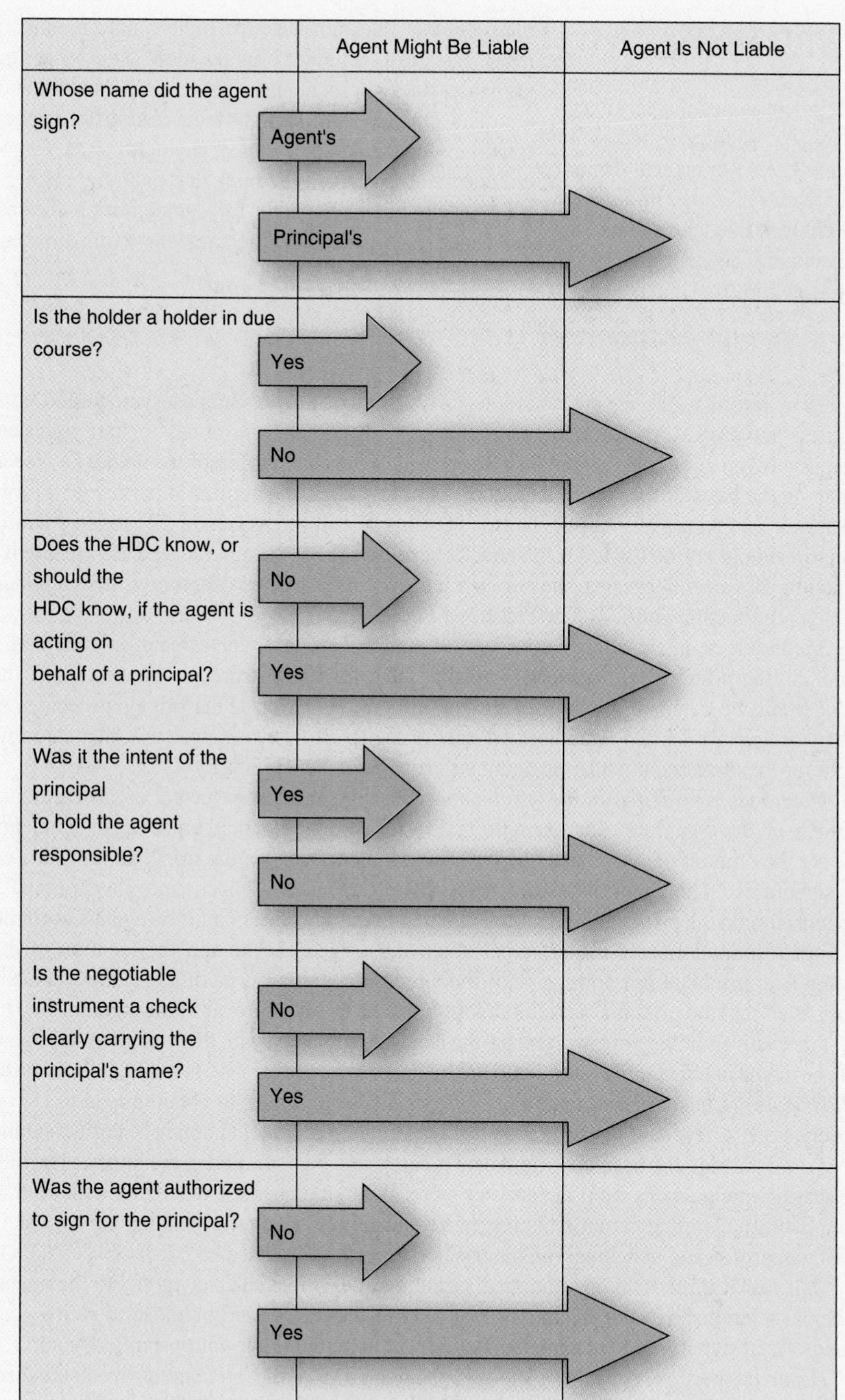

Figure 28-1
Agents' Signatures and Agents' Liability

global context

Negotiability and Forgery in Japan

The extent to which an instrument is negotiable affects how a jurisdiction regards forgery. If forgery occurs in Japan, the true purchaser is protected over the real owner, in the sense that the purchaser retains his or her rights over the instrument. Also, the purchaser's title is unaffected in the event of forgery. This retention of rights differs from U.S. law. If a bill or note is forged in the United States, the purchaser does not have the right to hold the instrument, release it, or enforce its payment. In essence, the purchaser does not retain any rights over the instrument.

The Japanese and U.S. systems also differ in their treatment of banks that make payment on a forged endorsement. In Japan, the bank that pays a check with a forgery is not responsible for compensating the real owner. Banks in the United States, however, do retain this liability.

First, return to the accommodation party example above. Suppose you forged your business law professor's name to ensure that you would get your money to start your new business. If you could not pay on the note, your business law professor would not be forced to pay on the basis of the forged signature. Similarly, this rule applies to parties who forge the drawer's signature on a check. Thus, under this rule, it seems Century 21 in the opening scenario should not be liable for the checks because the receptionist forged the president's signature. However, forgery in the employment context is treated differently, as we explain below in the section entitled "The Fictitious-Payee Rule."

Second, if an agent is not authorized to sign a negotiable instrument on behalf of a principal, the principal will generally not be liable for the instrument. Consequently, the agent would be personally liable for the instrument. However, if the principal decides to **ratify**, or approve of, the unauthorized agent's signature, the principal will then become liable for the instrument while the agent will escape personal liability [UCC 3-403(a)].

How does a principal ratify an unauthorized signature? A principal could explicitly approve of the signature. For example, a Florida court held that a principal could not recover the amount of two checks he gave to his agent because the principal had ratified the signatures.[1] The agent, who was supposed to deposit two checks into the principal's account, forged the principal's signature and deposited the checks into the agent's account. The agent ultimately told the principal about the forged checks and the location of the money. The principal did nothing until the agent later ran away with the money, and the court ruled that the principal's inaction was the same as his approval of his signature.

Alternatively, if the principal accepts the benefits associated with this unauthorized signature, he or she in effect ratifies the signature by his or her conduct. For example, in *Rakestraw v. Rodriguez,*[2] a husband had forged his wife's signature in order to obtain a loan to start a grocery store. A few days later, the wife discovered the forgery, did nothing to correct it, and even participated in the business over the next few years. Part of running the business including sharing in the profits from the grocery store. When the business failed, the wife tried to avoid liability, claiming her husband forged her signature. The court ruled that her actions in sharing in profits and in helping run the business effectively ratified her signature.

This ratification of an unauthorized signature does not exclusively apply to the agent-principal relationship. Your business law professor could similarly choose to ratify your unauthorized signature of his name so that he would be liable for your promissory note.

However, there are some exceptions to the general rule that an unauthorized signature is not enforceable. Generally, the policy behind these exceptions is that courts want to

[1] *Fulka v. Florida Commercial Banks, Inc.*, 371 So. 2d 521 (Fla. Dist. Ct. App. 1979).

[2] 500 P.2d 1401 (Cal. 1972).

place the burden on the parties who are in the best position to take a loss or take action to recover a loss. Moreover, particularly in regard to the last two rules that will be discussed here (the imposter rule and the fictitious-payee rule), the court focuses on the intent of the party who is issuing the instrument.

Negligence. In some cases, a party's negligence will not permit the party to escape liability for an unauthorized signature. If the party whose signature was forged behaved so negligently as to "substantially contribute to . . . the making of a forged signature," the party may be precluded from escaping liability (UCC 3-406).

For example, in *Thompson Maple Products v. Citizens National Bank,*[3] Thompson was a corporation that manufactured bowling pins from maple logs. Thompson would accept loads of logs from timber owners. When a load arrived at the mill, a Thompson employee filled out a scaling slip that listed the name of the owner, along with the quantity and grade of the logs. Thompson office employees then used these slips to prepare checks for the owner of the logs. A Thompson employee, Emery Albers, took blank scaling slips and filled them out for fictitious loads of logs. The office employees, thinking the slips represented real loads of wood, then prepared checks for payment. Albers then took the checks, forged the name of the owner of the logs, and cashed the checks or deposited them into his bank account at Citizens National Bank. The court ruled that Thompson "substantially contributed" to the forgeries because the blank scaling slips to record loads of logs were easily accessible. In fact, office employees gave Albers two entire pads of these slips. Moreover, even though it was company policy for the slips to be initialed by authorized employees who were accepting the loads, Thompson office employees created checks for slips that were not authorized. Thus, Thompson's negligence led to the conclusion that Thompson should be liable.

The imposter rule. Suppose that Jamaar, a business manager, has been communicating through e-mail with Carlie, a potential employee. Jamaar has scheduled a meeting with Carlie. However, Samantha, without Carlie's knowledge, decides to impersonate Carlie at the interview. Samantha (as Carlie) tells Jamaar she will strongly consider signing an employment agreement if Jamaar will issue her a $200 check as a presigning bonus. Jamaar agrees and issues the check to Carlie that day. Samantha forges Carlie's name and deposits the check into her own account. Will Jamaar be liable for the amount of the check?

Jamaar's signature has not been forged; he clearly signed the check with intent to transfer money to Carlie. But he did not know Carlie was actually Samantha. Is Samantha's signature considered a forgery? No. Under the UCC's **imposter rule,** if a maker or drawer issues a negotiable instrument to an imposter, the imposter's endorsement will be effective [3-404(a)]. The court considers the intent of the drawer or maker when issuing the instrument. Because Jamaar intended for Samantha (as Carlie) to have the instrument, her endorsement of the instrument is considered valid. Moreover, it is easier for Jamaar, as maker or drawer, to identify the true identity of Carlie than it would be for a later holder of the check to do so. Perhaps some of you are surprised by the imposter rule. The UCC, as stated, places an immense responsibility on Jamaar to ensure that he is not being duped. What values are in conflict here? Should Jamaar be forced to shoulder this responsibility?

The fictitious-payee rule. Suppose now that Jamaar, who has been authorized to write checks from the company account, draws bonus checks from the company account for five more potential employees. Unfortunately, Jamaar never actually interviewed these employees; thus, these people are not entitled to the bonuses. Jamaar takes these checks that are made out to the fictitious potential employees, endorses the checks in their names, and

[3] 234 A.2d 32 (Pa. Super. Ct. 1967).

connecting to the core

Management

As the "Signature Liability" section and the opening scenario have illustrated, employees of a company may engage in unethical behavior in their handling of checks. Therefore, employers have the important responsibility of hiring employees who will not engage in such questionable behavior. Employers' selecting the best candidates for hire typically involves three methods. First, employers request that candidates provide background information by submitting applications, résumés, and references. Second, employers often interview prospective employees to obtain more information from the candidates and, at times, evaluate their responses to hypothetical situations. Third, employers may require that candidates take ability tests, job performance tests, personality tests, and drug tests. These three methods of the employee selection process are designed not only to help employers hire the best employees but also to ensure that employers do not hire candidates who have previously participated in unethical behavior for other employers. These methods do not guarantee that employees will behave ethically, particularly when handling checks, but this selection process might reduce the likelihood that an employer will hire a questionable employee.

Source: Angelo Kinicki and Brian K. Williams, *Management: A Practical Introduction* (New York: McGraw-Hill/Irwin, 2006), pp. 286–289.

deposits these checks into his personal bank account. These potential employees have no interest (i.e., no right to payment) in the check and are thus called **fictitious payees** (UCC 3-404, 3-405). As with the endorsement in the imposter case, Jamaar's endorsement of the fictitious payees is not considered forgery [UCC 3-404(b)(2)]. Jamaar's company will be liable for the checks.

Why is the company liable? Courts view the company as being in a better position to bear the loss of the checks. The loss has occurred because Jamaar, a company employee, has acted wrongly. Although the company is liable for the amounts of the checks, the company can recover the money from Jamaar.

Consequently, if we apply this rule to the Century 21 opening case, it would seem that Century 21 should be held liable because it is in a better position to bear the loss of the checks. Its own employee acted wrongly, and the company is in a better position to monitor the employee's behavior.

Warranty Liability

In the previous section, we explained how a party might be liable for an instrument on the basis of his or her signature on the instrument. In this section, we consider another type of liability: warranty liability. A party may be liable for an instrument because of a breach of warranty. There are two relevant types of warranties here: transfer warranties and presentment warranties.

TRANSFER WARRANTY

A negotiable instrument can be transferred from one party to another. A party who transfers a negotiable instrument to another party in good faith for consideration creates *transfer warranties* regarding the instrument and the transfer itself [UCC 3-416(a)]. Transfer warranties always apply to the party to whom the instrument is transferred (the transferee).

When a party transfers an instrument for consideration, he or she warrants:

1. The transferor is entitled to enforce the negotiable instrument.
2. Signatures on the instrument are authentic and authorized.

3. The instrument has not been altered.
4. The instrument is not subject to a defense or claim in recoupment.
5. The transferor has no knowledge of insolvency proceedings against the maker, acceptor, or drawer of the instrument. [UCC 3-416(a)]

If the transfer is through endorsement, these warranties apply to any future holders. However, if the transfer does not occur through endorsement, the warranties apply only to the transferee. For example, suppose Lisa creates a note payable to Chris. Chris endorses the notes and transfers it for consideration to Yolanda. Because Chris has endorsed the instrument and transferred it for consideration, the warranties apply to Yolanda. Moreover, if Yolanda transfers the instrument to another party, the warranties Chris made would apply to this later holder.

These rules on whether the warranties apply to future holders or only to the immediate transferee are important because liability can be imposed for breach of warranty. If the warranties apply and there is a breach of one of the warranties, the parties can bring suit against the transferor, the warrantor, for damages suffered as a result of the breach [UCC 3-416(b)]. Thus, suppose Chris forges Lisa's signature on the note and then transfers the note to Yolanda, who later transfers the note to Gary. This forgery breaches one of the warranties on the instrument. Therefore, because Chris transferred the note through endorsement, Gary, the subsequent holder, can recover damages from Chris.

As soon as a transferee discovers a breach of warranty has occurred, he or she can bring suit against the transferor. However, the transferee must give notice of the breach of warranty claim to the transferor within 30 days of discovering the breach [UCC 3-416(c)]. If the transferee does not give notice within 30 days of discovering the breach, the warranty will be discharged to some extent. If the transferred instrument is a check, the warranties cannot be disclaimed [UCC 3-416(c)].

While warranties on checks cannot be disclaimed, they can be disclaimed on other instruments. When parties agree to a disclaimer, an endorser can disclaim warranties by including in the endorsement the phrase "without warranties." This endorsement is similar to the restrictive endorsement *without recourse,* which you learned about in the previous chapter. However, *without warranties* disclaims warranty liability, whereas *without recourse* disclaims contract liability.

PRESENTMENT WARRANTY

In the signature liability section, we discussed the requirements for a negotiable instrument to be properly presented for payment. Certain warranties are associated with the presentment of an instrument. Remember presentment occurs when a party properly presents an instrument for acceptance and the party to whom it was presented accepts the instrument or pays it in good faith.

Why are presentment warranties needed? Parties who accept or pay instruments may worry they are not paying the proper party. Thus, while transfer warranties apply to the transferee, presentment warranties cover parties who accept instruments for payment. The party presenting the instrument and any previous transferor of the instrument make these presentment warranties. Therefore, if there is a breach of presentment warranty, the acceptor can recover damages from the presenting party or previous transferors. As with the notice rule for transfer warranties, a party must give notice of a breach of presentment warranty within 30 days.

There are two types of presentment warranties. These types depend on what kind of instrument is being presented to a certain kind of party. When a party presents an unaccepted draft to a drawee, the holder guarantees:

1. The warrantor of the instrument is entitled to enforce the instrument.
2. The instrument has not been altered.
3. The warrantor has no knowledge that the drawer's signature or the draft is unauthorized. [UCC 3-417(a)]

These warranties apply only to the drawee who pays or accepts the drafts in good faith.

If the instrument is not an unaccepted draft presented to a drawee, only one presentment warranty applies. The party presenting the instrument guarantees that the warrantor is or was entitled to payment or authorized to obtain payment [UCC 3-417(d)(1)]. In other words, only warranty (1) listed above applies to presentments of instruments other than unaccepted drafts.

Case 28-2 considers whether a bank that cashed forged checks gives presentment and transfer warranties.

CASE 28-2 HALLIBURTON ENERGY SERVICES, INC. v. FLEET NATIONAL BANK

U.S. DISTRICT COURT FOR THE SOUTHERN DISTRICT OF TEXAS, HOUSTON DIVISION
334 F. SUPP. 2D 930 (2004)

On March 20, 2000, Halliburton issued a check, drawn on a Citibank account, to Arthur Andersen for $215,000.00. The check was deposited in the United States mail. An unknown person stole the check from the mail and then altered the payee to "Paul A. Schumacher."

On March 27, 2000, a person claiming to be "Paul A. Schumacher" opened a Fleet brokerage account from the bank's Internet site. The person posing as "Paul A. Schumacher" endorsed the altered check by signing the name "Paul A. Schumacher" on the back and presented it to Fleet, which honored it. Fleet then presented the check to Citibank, the drawee/payor bank. On March 30, 2000, Citibank charged Halliburton's checking account the sum of $215,000.00 because Citibank had paid the check in full.

On May 15, 2000, Arthur Andersen informed Halliburton it had not received the $215,000.00 check. A Halliburton employee working for Accounts Payable then contacted Citibank and learned that the check had been paid. On May 17, Halliburton requested the original check from Citibank. Upon receiving and examining the check, Halliburton saw that the payee's name had been altered and that the check had been endorsed by the fictitious payee, "Paul A. Schumacher" "for deposit only."

On June 26, 2000, Citibank notified Fleet that Fleet had honored a fraudulently altered check and asked for prompt reimbursement of what Citibank deemed a wrongful payment. The request was denied. Citibank then assigned any claim it may have against Fleet to Halliburton. Halliburton sued, and filed for summary judgment.

JUDGE LAKE: . . . Section 3.404 covers cases in which an instrument is payable to a fictitious or nonexistent person and in which the payee is a real person but the drawer or maker of the instrument did not intend the payee to have any interest in the instrument. The defense to which section 4.208(c) refers, by incorporating section 3.404(b), is known as the "fictitious payee" or "impostor" rule. An impostor is "one who pretends to be someone else to deceive others, esp. to receive the benefits of a negotiable instrument," or "a person who practices deception under an assumed character, identity or name."

The impostor rule applies when a bank has honored a check made out to a fictitious payee. If the impostor's endorsement is effective, the collecting bank then becomes a "holder in due course." A "holder in due course is one who takes an instrument (1) for value, (2) in good faith, and (3) without notice of any defense." Even a forger can effectively endorse an instrument. Unless the depository bank knew about the forgery, there is no breach of presentment warranty when the depository bank presents it to the drawee. Therefore, in such circumstances, the presenting bank is not liable for the drawer's or drawee's loss.

Under section 3.404(d) the drawee may override the depository/collecting/ presenting bank's affirmative defense only if the collecting bank failed "to exercise ordinary care in paying or taking the instrument and that failure contributed to loss resulting from the payment of the instrument." The "ordinary care" standard is just that: It does not mandate that a depository bank engage in peculiar vigilance. In fact, the comments accompanying section 3.404(d) suggest that a collecting bank is not liable for breaching its presentment warranties unless it knew the instrument had been altered when that bank accepted it.

If the drawee bank can establish that the collecting bank failed to exercise ordinary care, the drawee may recover from the presenting bank "to the extent the failure to exercise ordinary care contributed to the loss."

Halliburton has not presented evidence that Fleet was anything other than a holder in due course. In other words, Halliburton has not offered evidence of Fleet's bad faith, e.g., that Fleet's employees connived with the forger. Nor has Halliburton provided any evidence that Fleet had reason to believe the check had been fraudulently altered. Perhaps at trial Halliburton can convince the jury that Fleet, which dealt directly with the impostor, took the forged check with notice of the forgery or accepted the instrument by failing to exercise ordinary care, which would have exposed the forgery. But whether Fleet could have readily ascertained that the check had been fraudulently altered is a fact issue that precludes summary judgment for Halliburton. There are too many questions that need to be answered to support Halliburton's motion for summary judgment.

MOTION DENIED.

CRITICAL THINKING

The motion for summary judgment was denied because there is too much omitted information. As a judge, what information would you deem relevant that is missing from the case? Why is the missing information relevant to this case?

ETHICAL DECISION MAKING

Think about the ethical theories you were presented with earlier. Part of the above case, and the issue of presentment warranties, is who should bear the burden for a fraudulent check. Which party would a deontologist hold responsible for the cashing of a forged check? What about a consequentialist?

Avoiding Liability for Negotiable Instruments

If a party tries to enforce a negotiable instrument, a defendant can try to avoid liability in two ways. First, the defendant can try to claim a defense to liability. Second, the defendant can try to claim that the liability has been discharged.

DEFENSES TO LIABILITY

In the previous chapter, we listed defenses to liability that did or did not apply to a holder in due course. Here, we return to these defenses to liability. There are two categories of defenses: real defenses and personal defenses. **Real defenses,** also called *universal defenses,* apply to all parties. **Personal defenses** do not apply to holders in due course.

Real defenses. A party's right to enforce a negotiable instrument is subject to the following real defenses:

1. Infancy (being below the legal age of consent), to the extent that it makes a contract void.
2. Duress, to the extent that it makes a contract void.
3. Lack of legal capacity, to the extent that it makes a contract void.
4. Illegality of the transaction, to the extent that it makes a contract void.
5. Fraud in the factum.
6. Discharge through insolvency proceedings (bankruptcy).
7. Forgery.
8. Material alteration.

The first six defenses are stated explicitly in UCC Section 3-305. As we discussed earlier in this chapter, the UCC establishes forgery as a defense to liability because a party must have signed the instrument to be held liable. Finally, a material alteration of an instrument discharges a party of a liability [UCC 3-407(a)].

Fraud in the factum. When a party signs a negotiable instrument without knowing that it is, in fact, a negotiable instrument, the party can claim **fraud in the factum** (also called *fraud in the execution* and *fraud in the essence*) as a defense. For example, suppose Michael Jordan believes he is signing an autograph for a fan, but he is actually signing a promissory note. Because he did not intend to sign a negotiable instrument, he will not be held liable for the instrument.

Similarly, suppose you, a business manager, are negotiating with another company to purchase materials for your manufacturing business. After your negotiations, the company asks you to sign a document as a preorder for the materials. You hurriedly sign the document and leave. However, instead of signing a preorder, you have actually signed a note. Will you be held liable for this note? In this case, it depends.

For another illustration of these issues, see the Case Nugget.

Although fraud in the factum is a real defense, courts have held that the signer's experience may determine whether the signer should have known what he or she was actually signing. Recall the situation with Jamaar in which he was solely responsible for ensuring the identity of the individual he is signing a check to. However, that level of responsibility is not required of Michael Jordan in this situation. Can you account for the difference in the two situations, pointing out the differing values and ethical norms?

As another example, consider *Schaeffer v. United Bank & Trust Co.*[4] United Bank sued Schaeffer to collect on a promissory note Schaeffer had signed as an accommodation maker. However, the Maryland court ultimately ruled that Schaeffer was not liable due to fraud in the factum. It turns out Schaeffer barely knew how to read, did not understand the document he was signing, and was lied to by the note's maker who had told Schaeffer that

[4] 360 A.2d 461 (Md. Ct. Spec. App. 1976).

Case Nugget Defense of Ignorance?

Laborer's Pension Fund v. A & C Envtl., Inc.
301 F.3d 762 (2002)

A & C Environmental, Inc., is a corporation that transports and disposes of non-hazardous waste. In April 1999, A & C was asked to complete a job in Gary, Indiana, which prompted representatives from Laborer's Pension Fund to approach the company. Frattini of the fund asked Clark of A & C to sign a form that would guarantee the five individuals who would work in Gary, Indiana, the coverage of the local union. Clark was hesitant to sign the agreement because he feared that if someone within his company were covered under the union, the entire company would then be covered. It wasn't until after Frattini of the fund guaranteed Clark that the only employees of A & C who would be affected would be those working in Gary, Indiana, that the agreement was signed. When A & C did not pay dues for all of its employees, the fund brought suit for delinquent contributions.

The district court ruled against the fund as a result of the fraud-in-the-execution defense that was brought forth by A & C. The court had decided that any reasonable juror would believe that Clark did not know that he was agreeing to pay the fund dues for each employee of A & C. The fund appealed to the Seventh District of the U.S. Court of Appeals.

In the opinion written by Judge Ripple, the Seventh Circuit found that Clark may not have known what he was agreeing to. Unlike the district court, however, the appeals court found that Clark had a reasonable opportunity to review the document, which was written in English. Although Frattini of the fund had misrepresented the contents of the document to Clark, there was an opportunity to review the document, which established dues for all employees of A & C. Thus, the court of appeals reversed the decision of the district court.

Schaeffer's signature would serve as a character witness. The court ruled that United Bank was not a holder in due course and was subject to Schaeffer's defense even if the bank were a holder in due course as the note was void due to fraud in the factum.

Material alteration. The UCC defines a *material alteration* as "an unauthorized change in an instrument that purports to modify in any respect the obligation of a party, or an unauthorized addition of words or numbers or other change to an incomplete instrument relating to the obligation of a party" (3-407). Only unauthorized changes that affect the rights of the party are considered material alterations.

Suppose Hope creates a promissory note payable to Patrick. Patrick decides Hope should pay him $2 more. If Patrick changes the instrument to reflect the additional $2, he has made an unauthorized change that affects Hope's rights. Changes that typically fall under Section 3-407 include changes to the parties to the instrument, the amount of the instrument, the date the instrument is due, and the applicable interest rate.

If the material alteration is fraudulent, the party whose rights have been affected by the change is completely discharged from the instrument [UCC 3-407(b)]. However, if the material alteration is not fraudulent, the instrument will be enforced only under the original terms. Case 28-3 considers whether an addition to a note was a material and fraudulent alteration.

CASE 28-3 FIRST NATIONAL BANK v. REGINALD ROBERTSON, NANCY ROBERTSON, AND JAMES NELSON

SUPREME COURT OF NORTH DAKOTA
442 N.W.2D 430 (1989)

Reginald and Nancy Robertson and James Nelson executed a promissory note that was secured by a real estate mortgage. This note was renewed and signed by Reginald and Nancy. When the renewal note was delinquent, First National discovered James had not signed the renewal note and asked him to sign. Before he signed, First National added the dates of three security agreements on the note. The dates were added in the area of the note designated for security agreements that secure the note. The three security agreements had all been paid in full. The Bank told James the note was the same note as previously signed by Reginald and Nancy

Because the note was delinquent, First National brought suit, seeking to foreclose the real estate mortgage. The Robertsons argued the material and fraudulent alteration (the adding of the dates as security) of the renewal note was a defense to the foreclosure action. The trial court found the Bank materially and fraudulently altered the promissory note and thus discharged the Robertsons from the obligation on the note. First National appealed.

First National argues the alteration was not material because the addition of the dates of the three security agreements did not change the parties' contract. The Robertsons argue the note was to be secured only by the mortgage and thus the addition was fraudulent and materially altered the note.

JUDGE LEVINE: The issue is whether the trial court clearly erred in finding a material and fraudulent alteration.

1. *Material Alteration*

An alteration is material when it changes the contract of any party to the instrument, in any respect, including changes in:

> a. The number or relations of the parties;
>
> b. An incomplete instrument, by completing it otherwise than as authorized; or
>
> c. The writing as signed, by adding to it or by removing any part of it. NDCC § 41-03-44(1) [UCC 3-407].

In this case, whether there was a material alteration depends upon whether the addition of the security agreements to the face of the note, after it had been signed by Reginald and Nancy, changed the contract.

The trial court resorted to the parties' course of dealing to determine what they intended as security for the note. A course of dealing is "a sequence of previous conduct between the parties to a particular transaction which is fairly to be regarded as establishing a common basis of understanding for interpreting their expressions and other conduct." NDCC § 41-01-15(1) [UCC 1-205]. A course of dealing between parties may give particular meaning to and supplement or qualify the terms of an agreement. NDCC § 41-01-15(3) [UCC 1-205].

Reginald, Nancy and James presented evidence of a course of dealing over several years during which they received loans from the Bank and provided specific security for each loan. They presented evidence that in this instance, the parties intended the real estate mortgage to be the sole security for the note. The trial court determined from the evidence that the parties established a course of dealing in which they expressly agreed upon specific security to secure individual promissory notes.

The evidence supports the finding that the addition of the security agreements changed the contract, and constitutes a material alteration under NDCC § 41-03-44 [UCC 3-407].

2. *Fraud*

There can be no discharge unless the alteration was both material and fraudulent. NDCC § 41-03-44 [UCC 3-407]. Neither Title 41 of the North Dakota Century Code, nor the UCC defines "fraudulent." However, fraud, under the UCC § 3-407, has been defined as "requir[ing] a dishonest and deceitful purpose to acquire more than one was entitled to under the note as signed by the makers rather than only a misguided purpose."

There was evidence that when the promissory note was executed by Reginald and Nancy, no additional security was sought, other than the real estate mortgage listed on the promissory note. There was evidence that when the Bank requested James to sign the renewal note, the Bank misrepresented to James that it was the same note previously signed by Reginald and Nancy, when in fact, the note had been altered. In addition, after the note was delinquent, Reginald offered to convey title to the mortgaged property to the Bank, but the Bank refused, insisting that it receive payment for the difference between the sale price of the property and the debt. There were no discussions of any security agreements or reliance on any other collateral during these negotiations. Reginald testified that the security agreements were in the Bank's possession to be used only in the event the Bank granted him a working capital loan, but the loan was never granted. The evidence supports the trial court's finding that, by the alteration, the Bank fraudulently attempted to increase its security in order to increase its potential recovery on the delinquent note.

We conclude that the trial court did not clearly err in finding that the Bank materially and fraudulently altered the promissory note. We have considered the Bank's other arguments and are neither definitely nor firmly convinced that a mistake has been made.

AFFIRMED.

CRITICAL THINKING

Think about the judge's reasoning that leads to the conclusion that the bank materially and fraudulently altered the promissory note. Is there any additional information that you would have liked to know that would help decide whether the bank materially and fraudulently altered the note?

ETHICAL DECISION MAKING

Recall the WPH framework. Suppose that your decision is guided by the Golden Rule. Would you have changed your decision to add the information to the note? What values are in conflict when considering whether one should act according to the Golden Rule? What values conflict with the actions of the bank manager?

Personal defenses. Personal defenses apply to holders, not holders in due course. Personal defenses can be divided into two categories. First, there are general defenses that can be asserted against the defendant on general contract theory. These defenses include:

1. Breach of contract or warranty.
2. Lack or failure of consideration.
3. Fraud in the inducement.
4. Illegality.
5. Mental incapacity.

Second, the UCC lists specific personal defenses created by provisions of Article 3. These defenses, summarized in Exhibit 28-5, include the following:

1. Defense of nonissuance, conditional issuance, or issuance for a special purpose [3-105(b)].
2. Defense of modification or nullification of an obligation by a separate agreement (3-117).

Exhibit 28-5
Summary of Defenses to Liability for a Negotiable Instrument

Real (universal) defenses	Infancy (below the legal age of consent)*
	Duress*
	Lack of legal capacity*
	Illegality of the transaction*
	Fraud in the factum
	Discharge through insolvency proceedings
	Forgery
	Material alteration
Personal defenses	*Contract defenses:*
	Breach of contract or warranty
	Lack or failure of consideration
	Fraud in the inducement
	Illegality
	Mental incapacity
	Article 3 defenses:
	Nonissuance of an instrument
	Modification of obligation by separate agreement
	Nondelivery of the instrument
	Unauthorized, nonfraudulent completion of instrument

* To the extent that it makes a contract void.

3. Defense of nondelivery of the instrument [3-105(b)].
4. Defense of unauthorized, nonfraudulent completion of an instrument (3-115).

DISCHARGE OF LIABILITY ON INSTRUMENTS

When a party's liability for a negotiable instrument is terminated, this party's liability has been **discharged.** In other words, the party is released from liability. Discharge can occur through a variety of ways. For example, as stated earlier, discharge of endorsers can occur if a party who has a right to enforce the instrument has materially altered an instrument. Keep in mind discharge is not effective against a holder in due course (UCC 3-601).

Discharge through payment and tender of payment. Earlier in this chapter, we discussed how a party becomes liable for an instrument by signing the instrument. If a party (or another party on the first party's behalf) who has signed an instrument as an obligation to pay then pays the full amount due, all parties who are liable will be discharged (UCC 3-602).

For example, Stuart creates a note in which he promises to pay Vanessa $1,000. If Stuart pays the $1,000 on the due date, he will be discharged from liability on the note. However, if Stuart makes the payment on the note to John, knowing that John stole the note from Vanessa and is wrongfully possessing it, Stuart's obligation will not be discharged. Paying John does not discharge Stuart's liability because John, who stole the note, is not a holder and not entitled to the amount on the note [UCC 3-602(b)(2)].

Moreover, some parties' obligations on an instrument will be discharged if the obliged party tenders full payment on the due date but the holder of the instrument refuses to accept the money [UCC 3-603(b)]. If Stuart makes a proper tender of the full amount ($1,000) to Vanessa on the note's due date but she improperly refuses to accept the money, Stuart will still be liable for the $1,000 but will not have to pay interest on the amount. However, if any endorsers or accommodation parties are liable for Stuart's note, these parties' obligation will be discharged.

Discharge by cancellation or renunciation. A party who is entitled to enforce an instrument may decide to cancel the instrument with or without consideration. Canceling the instrument discharges the obligation of a party who must pay the instrument (UCC 3-604). The party who decides to cancel the instrument may engage in an intentional voluntary act to cancel the instrument. For example, the party might write "Paid" on the instrument, intentionally destroy or mutilate the instrument, or give the instrument to the obliged party.

Alternatively, a party may renounce an instrument by promising not to sue to enforce the instrument. Renunciation occurs when a party agrees, in writing, not to sue the obliged party.

Discharge by reacquisition. Reacquisition occurs when a former holder of an instrument has the instrument transferred back to him or her by negotiation or other means. When reacquisition occurs, anyone who endorsed the instrument in between the initial acquisition and the reacquisition by the holder has his or her endorsement canceled. When an endorsement is canceled, discharge occurs. The holder who reacquired the instrument can further negotiate the instrument, but the intermediate endorsers will not be held liable (UCC 3-207).

For example, suppose Gina acquires a note through negotiation. Gina endorses and transfers the note to Jeremy. Jeremy endorses and transfers to Amanda, who endorses and transfers to Ben. Ben then endorses the note and transfers it back to Gina. When Gina endorses the note, she cancels Jeremy's, Amanda's, and Ben's endorsements. Were the note to be dishonored, Jeremy, Amanda, and Ben would all not be liable on the amount of the instrument.

Discharge by impairment of recourse. A right to recourse is the ability of a party to seek reimbursement. Typically, when a holder presents an instrument to an endorser, the endorser presented with the instrument can seek recourse from prior endorsers, the maker, the drawer, or accommodating parties. However, if the holder has in some way impaired the endorsers' ability to seek recourse from any of these parties, the endorser is not liable on the instrument [UCC 3-605(i)].

For example, Mary is the holder of a promissory note. She presents the note to Peter, a previous endorser. Normally Peter would have to pay the note and would be entitled to collect from a number of other parties. However, Mary carelessly defaced the note in such a way as to make the note worthless. Since Peter cannot invoke his right to recourse because of Mary's actions, he is not liable on the note and does not have to pay Mary.

Discharge by impairment of collateral. If a party posts collateral to ensure his performance of the negotiable instrument and the holder of the collateral impairs the value of the collateral, the party to the instrument is discharged from the instrument to the extent of the damage to the collateral [UCC 3-605(d)].

CASE OPENER WRAP-UP

Citizens National Bank and the Forged Checks

The trial court ruled in favor of Citizens National Bank. The trial court concluded that if a party who fails to exercise ordinary care substantially contributes to a forgery, he or she is then precluded from asserting the forgery as a defense.

The court concluded that Century 21 failed to exercise ordinary care in hiring and supervising the receptionist, who had a criminal record of embezzlement. This fact seemed to be quite persuasive to the court. Did this fact affect your initial decision about the case?

Moreover, Century 21 failed to notify the bank with reasonable promptness. These facts, in addition to the court's ruling that the bank observed reasonable commercial standards when processing the forged checks, led to the conclusion that Century 21 should not be reimbursed.

Several lessons can be drawn from this case. First, it emphasizes that as a business manager, you will need to carefully select your employees because hiring decisions can have an enormous impact on the financial success of your company. Second, it emphasizes the importance of paying close attention to your financial accounts. Perhaps if Century 21 had notified the bank sooner, it might have been able to recover a portion of the money.

Summary

Signature Liability

A party can be held liable for an instrument only if the party has signed the instrument.

Primary liability of makers and acceptors: They must pay the stated amount on the instrument when it is presented for payment.

Secondary liability of drawers and endorsers: They must pay the amount on the instrument if the primarily liable party dishonors the instrument and the following three conditions are met:

1. Presentment
2. Dishonor
3. Notice of dishonor

Accommodation party: An accommodation party is one who signs an instrument to provide credit for another party who has also signed the instrument.

Agents' signature: As long as the agent is *authorized* to sign a negotiable instrument on behalf of a principal, the agent's signature can create liability for the principal.

Unauthorized signature: If a signature to a negotiable instrument is unauthorized, this unauthorized signature will not impose liability to the named party.

1. Negligence
2. Imposter rule
3. Fictitious-payee rule

Warranty Liability

Transfer warranty: When a party transfers an instrument to another party for consideration, the party makes certain promises or warranties regarding the instrument and the transfer itself.

Presentment warranty: When a party properly presents an instrument for acceptance, the party makes certain promises regarding the instrument and the party who is entitled to payment.

Avoiding Liability for Negotiable Instruments

1. *Defenses to liability:* The arguments as to why a party should not be held liable for an instrument include:

   a. Real defenses

   b. Personal defenses

2. *Discharge of liability:* Release from liability can occur through:

   a. Discharge by payment or tender of payment
   b. Discharge by cancellation or renunciation
   c. Discharge by reacquisition
   d. Discharge by impairment of recourse
   e. Discharge by impairment of collateral

Point / Counterpoint

Should a Company Be Held Liable When an Employee's Work-Related Illegal Actions Include the Endorsement of Fraudulent Checks?

Yes

A company should always be held liable for an employee's work-related illegal actions. The company hired the employee and put him in the position to commit an illegal action, so the company should be held responsible.

A company benefits from the work of each of its employees. If employees are profitable, company profits increase, shareholder stock increases, and salaries increase; everyone benefits. Thus, because the company *benefits* when the employee is *profitable,* the company should also experience *losses* when the employee is *unprofitable* or *harmful.*

One of the factors in assigning liability for fraudulent checks is the ability of a party to bear the loss of the checks. A company is better equipped to bear a loss of funds than an individual. The losses occurred because of the actions of a specific *company* employee. Therefore, a company should shoulder the blame and pay for the losses from the fraudulent checks. After the company bears the losses of the checks, the company can then assess how to penalize the employee who endorsed the fraudulent checks.

A company should be held liable for an employee's actions because the company has the ability to monitor employee activities and the company chose to use the employee to represent the company.

No

Companies should not be held liable for an employee's fraudulent checks. The employees, not the companies, should be held liable.

Every employee is an individual who controls his or her own actions. Though a company can try to monitor employee activities, if an employee wants to commit an illegal act, she will. Most companies hire smart, well-qualified people. Smart people can always find a way around even the best company security systems.

Employees also need to feel the consequences of their own actions. If a corporation always takes the hit for an employee's poor decision, the employee cannot learn to change his behavior.

Companies should not be blamed for an employee's fraudulent checks because, sometimes, the bank responsible for paying out the fraudulent checks should be held responsible. Banks are companies as well, and as such, they should be aware of suspicious activities. When cashing large checks, the bank could easily require a verification code that would be known only by someone authorized to give checks.

Employees make their own decisions and are not forced to act against the law. Therefore, the employees should be held personally accountable.

Questions & Problems

1. What is the distinction between primary and secondary liability for a signed negotiable instrument?
2. Evaluate the following statement: "A party can never be held liable for a negotiable instrument if he or she did not sign the check."
3. What are the similarities and differences between transfer and presentment warranties?
4. How are real defenses different from personal defenses to liability for a negotiable instrument?
5. Joshua Herrera found a purse in a dumpster. He contacted the owner of the purse, and it was returned to its owner. After returning the purse, Herrera returned to the dumpster. He found a check written out to "cash." Herrera testified that he thought that meant that he "could get money for the check." He presented the check at a bank, and the bank teller instructed him to put his name on the payee line next to cash. Herrera added the words "to Joshua Herrera" to the payee line and endorsed the check. The trial court found Herrera guilty of forgery. On appeal, Herrera argued that he did not alter the check because he did not change the legal efficacy of the check. Herrera claimed that the check was a bearer instrument and payable to anyone possessing the instrument. How do you think the court decided? [*State of New Mexico v. Joshua Herrera,* 2000 N.M. App. LEXIS 100 (2001).]
6. Jasmine Williams was the beneficiary of her mother's life insurance policy with defendant Metropolitan Life Insurance Company. Following Williams's mother's death, MetLife established a "Total Control Account" for her. This account was established by MetLife with PNC Banks, but Williams received a personalized checkbook for the account and successfully wrote at least one check on the account. At some point thereafter, a woman named Latshia Sneed allegedly gained access to Williams's checkbooks and financial information. She then contacted PNC Banks using Williams's name, had Williams's address changed to her own, and requested that a new checkbook be sent to her address. Sneed later proceeded to write and forge the plaintiff's signature on 12 checks, payable to herself, totaling $48,900. She then deposited the checks into her own account. Once she found out about the loss of the $48,900, Williams informed MetLife and PNC of the loss and attempted to recover the money. She claimed that, despite assurances by MetLife that the money in the account was "guaranteed" against fraud, MetLife refused to reimburse the money. PNC also refused to repay the account for the forged checks. MetLife and PNC based their refusals on Williams's alleged negligence in failing to properly monitor her account and detect Sneed's fraud before it reached the level that it did. Williams filed suit against MetLife and PNC. Was Williams successful in her claims? Why or why not? [*Williams v. Metro. Life Ins. Co.,* 367 F. Supp. 2d 844 (2005).]
7. TUSRIF agreed to loan $200,000 to NCI for the development of a saw-milling enterprise in Russia. NCI was to repay the loan in 28 monthly installments. The parties prior to the signing of the note discussed the fee schedule. When TUSRIF sent the completed loan documents to NCI for signature, it mistakenly omitted the fee schedule page. Realizing its mistake, TUSRIF later attached two schedule pages to the note after it was signed. Because of the omission, NCI refused to make any payments on

the note; instead, it claimed that the loan was not due until its maturity date. TUSRIF sued NCI for breach of the note. NCI claimed that its obligation under the note was discharged due to TUSRIF's material alteration of the note. Should the court accept NCI's defense? Why or why not? [*TUSRIF v. Neal & Company, Inc.,* 1998 U.S. Dist. LEXIS 13581 (1998).

8. In 1992, Eric M. Schmitz executed two "Limited Power of Attorney" forms with Georgetown Financial, a Wisconsin company that provided investment, insurance, and financial services. James O'Hearn was the sole owner and chief executive officer of Georgetown Financial. Georgetown Financial purchased mutual funds through Putnam Investments for Schmitz. Putnam issued two checks and mailed them to Schmitz, in care of Georgetown Financial, as designated in the account application. O'Hearn presented both checks to Firstar Bank for deposit into a Georgetown Financial account. The larger check did not include an endorsement by or on behalf of Schmitz. The smaller check included an endorsement bearing Schmitz's name that Schmitz claims is a forged signature. Both checks were stamped with a Georgetown Financial deposit stamp and marked "for deposit only." Firstar Bank deposited the face value of both checks into a Georgetown Financial account. Schmitz never received the funds deposited into the account. Schmitz argued that because Georgetown Financial did not have authority to endorse the check, Firstar Bank was liable as a matter of law for making payment on this check, which was presented by Georgetown Financial without his actual or purported signature. Should Firstar Bank be held liable for cashing the checks? How did the court decide? [*Schmitz v. Firstar Bank Milwaukee,* 2003 WI 21 (2003).]
9. Olga Ensenat, an 88-year-old woman, had substantial investment accounts. Eventually her niece, Diana Flores, moved in to take care of Ensenat. While living with her, Flores withdrew on Ensenat's accounts, forged Ensenat's signature, and deposited the money into Flores's accounts. In the end Flores embezzled $157,386.30, all of which was deposited at Hancock Bank, where Flores had an account. Ensenat alleged that she did not herself withdraw or authorize any other person to withdraw retirement funds from her accounts. Ensenat sued Hancock Bank, claiming it was responsible because it allowed the checks to be paid or deposited without her endorsement, signature, or authorization. Did the court agree with Ensenat and find Hancock Bank liable for the deposited checks? Why or why not? [*Hancock Bank v. Ensenat,* 819 So. 2d 3 (2001).]
10. Mark Weisman, an authorized agent of three insurance companies, submitted fraudulent payment requests to the insurance companies using various customers' names. Weisman forged endorsements on 91 checks and deposited them into his personal bank account. Weisman was arrested and is insolvent, and an action was brought against the drawee banks. The banks did not review every check to verify that the payee endorsement was legible and matched the named payee on the front of the check, but they did employ a random checking policy and an automated verification system. The district court determined that the banks maintaining the insurance companies' accounts did not conduct a review of the forged endorsements and failed to comply with reasonable commercial standards. Do you agree with this decision? How do you think the case was decided on appeal? [*The Guardian Life Insurance Company of America v. Weisman,* 223 F.3d 229 (2000).]
11. National Union insured Kaiser Foundation Health Plan. Steven Mack is a former employee of Kaiser. During a two-month period, Mack introduced into Kaiser's accounts-payable stream a series of fraudulent invoices with forged approvals for

payment. Kaiser issued 15 checks on these fraudulent invoices, totaling $985,867.94, which were then deposited into accounts opened by Mack and/or his accomplices. National Union alleged that each of these checks and the circumstances under which they were deposited presented sufficient irregularities and indications of fraud that Bank of America's acceptance of these checks constituted negligence. National Union sued Bank of America regarding a single check Bank of America accepted for $76,142. Bank of America has moved to dismiss the claims against it. Was Bank of America successful in its motion to dismiss? Is Bank of America liable for the check it cashed to a fictitious payee? [*National Union Fire Insurance Co. v. Bank of America,* 240 F. Supp. 2d 455 (2003).]

12. A thief stole checks from a customer of Decibel Credit Union. Over the next 40 days, the thief forged the signature on 14 of these stolen checks, stealing $2,350. All these checks were cashed at Pueblo Bank, where the thief had an account. On some days, the thief cashed two checks in one day. Pueblo Bank processed all 14 checks, and Decibel paid the checks. When Decibel's customer received his bank statement and learned that someone had been using his checks, he notified Decibel. Decibel demanded that Pueblo Bank reimburse it for the amounts of the stolen checks. Pueblo Bank declined. Decibel filed suit against Pueblo Bank. The trial court granted summary judgment for Decibel for the following reasons: (1) Decibel had given timely notice to Pueblo Bank as soon as the forgery was discovered by the customer; (2) by submitting the checks to Decibel for payment, Pueblo Bank triggered its responsibility for presentment and transfer warranties; and (3) because the warranties were triggered, Decibel was entitled to reimbursement. Pueblo Bank appealed. How did the judge rule on appeal? Who should be liable for the checks? [*Decibel Credit Union v. Pueblo Bank & Trust Company,* 996 P.2d 784 (2000).]

13. Michelle Campbell worked for Luiz Simmons as his secretary. After Campbell was hired, she formed an acquaintanceship with Simmons's outside bookkeeper, Denise Evans. Campbell began to forge Simmons's name to checks drawn on several of her employer's accounts. Because Evans was a participant in the scheme and because Simmons trusted his employees, Campbell's forgeries went undetected by Simmons for over two years. During this time, Michael Lennon sold Campbell his Chevrolet Blazer for $22,000. Campbell paid for the Blazer, in part, with a forged check from Simmons's account. Simmons and Lennon knew one another through a business relationship. Also, Lennon and Campbell were once romantically involved, during which time Campbell forged Lennon's name on credit card applications and accumulated $17,000 in credit card debt in Lennon's name. More than 15 months after the sale of the Chevrolet Blazer, Simmons discovered that Campbell, with the aid of Evans, had been embezzling funds from his accounts for over two years by forging his signature on checks. Simmons filed a complaint against Lennon to recover for the amount of the forged check he accepted as payment from Campbell. Simmons argued that Lennon should have known the check was a forgery because he knew Simmons, as well as had firsthand experience with Campbell's illegal actions. How did the court decide the case? Should Lennon have been more cautious in accepting a check from Campbell given their past interactions? [*Simmons v. Lennon,* 139 Md. App. 15 (2001).]

14. Cletus Onyekwere opened a checking account for his company, Weafri Well Services, with NatWest bank. Onyekwere and his wife were the only authorized signatories on the account. In January 1997, the bank received a letter requiring that Onyekwere's future statements be sent to an address in Nigeria. The bank claimed that this letter was suspicious, and it faxed a letter to Onyekwere to confirm the letter. Onyekwere never responded to the fax, and his address was never changed. Starting in February 1997, the bank paid seven allegedly forged checks bearing what was believed to be Onyekwere's signature. The bank claimed that the forged signatures were not obvious; even Onyekwere presented not admissible evidence that the employees should have discovered that the signature was forged. The last forged check, check number 120, was returned for insufficient funds. The check and a statement were mailed to Onyekwere in early March. Onyekwere did not respond to the bank until the end of June. The bank tried to recover the amounts paid on the seven checks, but no recovery was made. Onyekwere sued the bank to recover the amounts debited from its account under the allegedly forged checks. Do you think the bank acted in accordance with reasonable commercial standards when paying the checks? What other information might help you make this decision? [*Weafri Well Services, Co. v. Fleet Bank,* 2000 U.S. Dist. LEXIS 14394 (2000).]

Looking for more review material?

The Online Learning Center at **www.mhhe.com/kubasek1e** contains this chapter's "Assignment on the Internet" and also a list of URLs for more information, entitled "On the Internet." Find both of them in the Student Center portion of the OLC, along with quizzes and other helpful materials.

Checks and Electronic Fund Transfers

CASE OPENER

Posting Checks from Highest to Lowest Dollar Amount

Dana and Andrea Patterson were customers who had a checking account at a bank that was part of NationsBank. The Pattersons argued that their account was wrongly subject to insufficient-fund fees and overdraft fees because of NationsBank's policy of posting checks. If the bank received multiple checks to post to a customer's account, NationsBank, like other banks, had a policy of posting checks from highest to lowest dollar amount. In other words, the bank posted the largest check first, regardless of the check number.

The Pattersons argued that this policy generated greater fees for NationsBank because the bank could charge overdraft fees on a greater number of checks. Moreover, they argued that NationsBank did not disclose this policy to the customers and this nondisclosure violated the Truth in Savings Act. NationsBank, which became Bank of America after the Pattersons brought suit, argued that customers prefer this high-to-low payment policy because it ensures that the most important checks are paid first.

Customers at other banks have brought similar suits, arguing that the bank's high-to-low posting policy forces them into overdraft status. A group of customers in Alabama were recently granted class certification to bring a class action suit against Compass Bancshares. This group of customers argues that because the bank assessed overdraft and insufficient-fund fees on the smaller checks that were rejected because of the high-to-low policy, the bank fraudulently engaged in deliberate efforts to increase its revenue through these fees.

1. Suppose that you are a business manager at a new bank. You are determining bank policy regarding posting order. What additional information would you need to create a policy for your bank regarding posting order?
2. Now suppose that you have created a policy. How would you decide to communicate this policy to your customers?

CHAPTER 29

The Wrap-Up at the end of the chapter will answer these questions.

Learning Objectives

After reading this chapter, you will be able to answer the following questions:

1. What are the components of a check?
2. What are the differences among the various types of checks?
3. How and where are deposits accepted?
4. When may a bank charge a customer's account?
5. What are the different types of electronic fund transfers?
6. What is the Uniform Money Services Business Act?

As suggested in the NationsBank example, the relationship between the bank and its customers is quite complicated. When a customer opens an account at a bank, he or she creates a contractual relationship with the bank. Within this relationship, both the customer and the bank have certain rights and duties. This relationship is governed by Article 4 of the UCC. For example, the customer has the right to order a stop payment on a check for any or no reason. The corresponding duty of the bank is to follow this order.

As we explained in previous chapters, checks are considered negotiable instruments under Article 3 of the UCC. However, Article 4 of the UCC is also relevant; this section of the UCC governs the transfer of checks between banks. Thus, both Article 3 and Article 4 are relevant to this chapter.

Article 3 of the UCC outlines the requirements negotiable instruments, including checks, must meet. Article 3 also establishes the rights and responsibilities pertaining to parties to negotiable instruments. Article 4 creates a framework controlling deposit and checking agreements between banks and customers. In addition, Article 4 directs the relationships between banks as checks are processed among different banks. Moreover, according to UCC Section 4-102(a), when conflicts arise between rules in Articles 3 and 4, Article 4 is to take precedence.

In 2003, Americans wrote approximately 70 billion checks. Clearly, checks are an enormous part of the bank-customer relationship. In fact, of all the negotiable instruments regulated by the UCC, checks are the most common type used. Thus, we begin this chapter by taking a closer look at different types of checks. Then we examine the process of check collection: If the bank accepts a check, how is the money from one account actually transferred to another account? Next, we consider when a bank may charge a customer's account in the context of potential problems with checks, such as stale, postdated, and forged checks. Finally, we turn to an increasingly important element of the banking process: the electronic transfer of funds.

Checks

Although you have likely written a check, do you know what the actual characteristics of checks are? (The key terms and an illustration are provided in Exhibit 29-1 and Figure 29-1.) According to the UCC, a check is a special kind of draft. A **draft** is an instrument that is an order. Three parties are related to an order. First, a **drawer** is the party that gives the order. Second, a **drawee** is the party that must obey the order. Finally, the **payee** is the party that receives the benefit of the order. Thus, when you write a check at the grocery store, you are the drawer ordering the drawee (your bank) to make a payment to the payee (the grocery store).

A **check** is a special draft that orders the drawee, a bank, to pay a fixed amount of money on demand [UCC Section 3-104(f)]. The UCC defines a bank as "any business engaged in the business of banking" [4-105(1)]. Consequently, savings banks, savings and loans, credit unions, and trust companies are all considered banks. The drawer of a check writes the check and thus orders the bank to pay. The payee is that party to whom the check is written.

Exhibit 29-1 Key Terms for Checks

Term	Definition
Draft	An instrument whereby one party orders a second party to pay an amount of money to the party listed on the instrument
Drawer	The party giving the order to pay on a draft
Drawee	The party ordered to pay on a draft
Payee	The party receiving the money from the draft

Figure 29-1 A Check

Payee

MARY BROWN
123 MAIN STREET
MIDTOWN, ML 48729
PHONE #: 123-456-7890

4321

Date: 8/2/2007

PAY TO THE ORDER OF: Luke Paul Correl $ 130.00

one hundred and thirty and xx/100 DOLLARS

Ω Bank
Midtown USA

MEMO:

Mary Brown

3 1415 65 358 97932 38 46

Drawer's signature

CASHIER'S CHECKS

A **cashier's check** is a check for which both the drawer and the drawee are the same bank [UCC3-104(g)]. (See Figure 29-2 for an example.) The payee of the check is a specific person. In other words, the bank is drawing on itself and thus assumes the responsibility for paying the check to that specific person.

Figure 29-2 A Cashier's Check

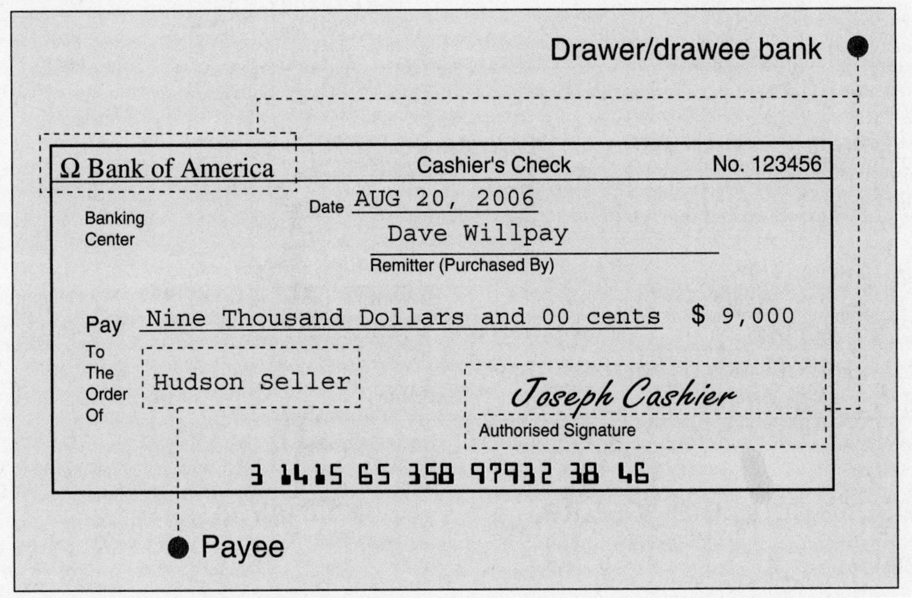

Customers often purchase cashier's checks to give to creditors who want to be sure the funds represented by the check are available. Cashier's checks are useful because they are considered by many in the business community to be the near equivalent of cash. For example, suppose Dave is buying a used car for $9,000 and wants to pay with a personal check. The seller of the car, Hudson, is not sure Dave actually has $9,000 in his checking account. Thus, Hudson asks Dave to pay for the car with a cashier's check. Dave goes to his bank and transfers the $9,000 to the bank. The bank then creates a check for $9,000 payable to Hudson.

TELLER'S CHECKS

A teller's check is similar to a cashier's check in that both the drawer and the drawee are banks. However, a **teller's check** is different because it is a check that is drawn by one bank and usually drawn on another bank [UCC 3-104(h)]. In other words, bank A is the drawer, while bank B is the drawee. In some cases, the drawee is a nonbank, but the check is payable at a bank.

TRAVELER'S CHECKS

A **traveler's check** is an instrument that must have the following characteristics (see Figure 29-3):

1. Is payable on demand.
2. Is drawn on or through a bank.
3. Is designated by the phrase *traveler's check.*
4. Requires a countersignature by a person whose signature appears on the instrument. [UCC 3-104(i)]

Figure 29-3 A Traveler's Check

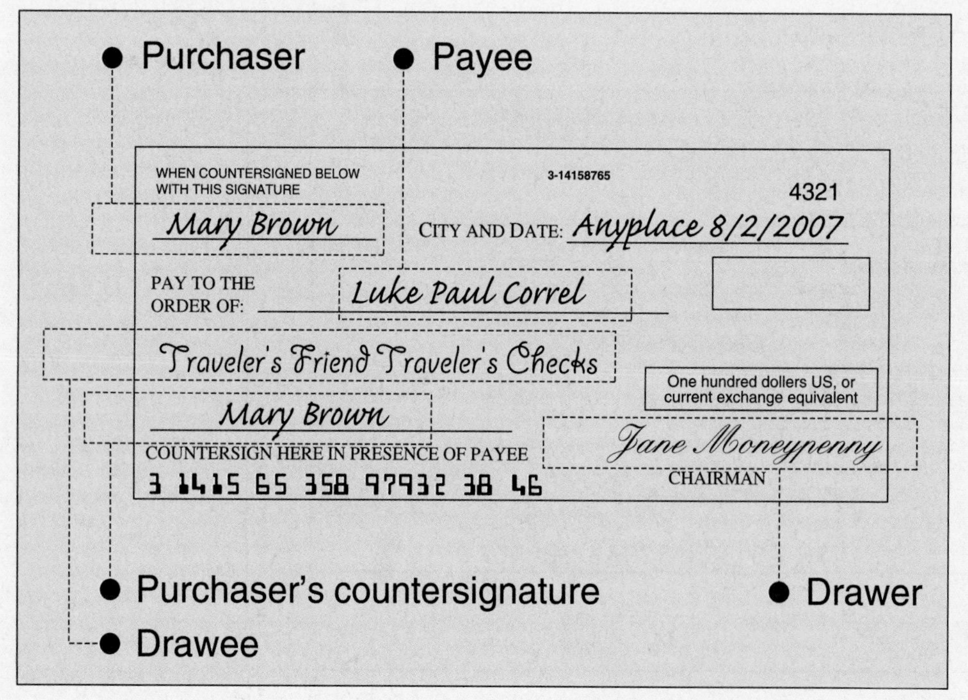

The drawer of a traveler's check is usually a large financial organization, such as American Express. The person who signs the traveler's check must sign it when she buys the checks. When the person is ready to use the traveler's check to make some kind of payment, the same person must sign the traveler's check in the presence of the acceptor.

MONEY ORDERS

Money orders (see Figure 29-4), particularly personal money orders, are usually in the same form as personal checks and are considered checks under UCC Section 3-104. Both banks and nonbanks sell money orders. The money order states that a certain amount of money is to be paid to a particular person. The amount of money to be paid is usually already imprinted on the money order. The person purchasing the money order signs the money order as the drawer and fills in the name of the person who is to receive the money.

CERTIFIED CHECKS

A **certified check** is a check that is accepted at the bank at which it is drawn [UCC 3-409(d)]. For example, suppose Hope writes a check to Jeremiah from her account at Citizens National Bank (CNB). Hope asks CNB to certify her check. CNB then accepts the check, withdraws the money from Hope's account, and places that money in its certified check account. CNB then signs or stamps the face of the check to indicate that it is certified. In other words, CNB is promising that funds are available to pay the check.

Banks are not required to certify checks [UCC 3-409(d)]. If a bank refuses to certify a check, the check is not considered dishonored; it merely lacks the extra protection of certification. However, once the bank does certify a check, the drawer of the check is no longer liable for the amount of the check [UCC 3-414(c)]. The bank has become primarily liable for the check.

WHY USE CASHIER'S, TELLER'S, OR CERTIFIED CHECKS?

There are a number of reasons to use a cashier's, teller's, or certified check as opposed to a regular check when conducting business exchanges. While all of these types of drafts are

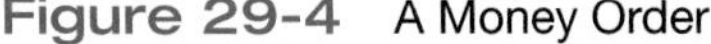
Figure 29-4 A Money Order

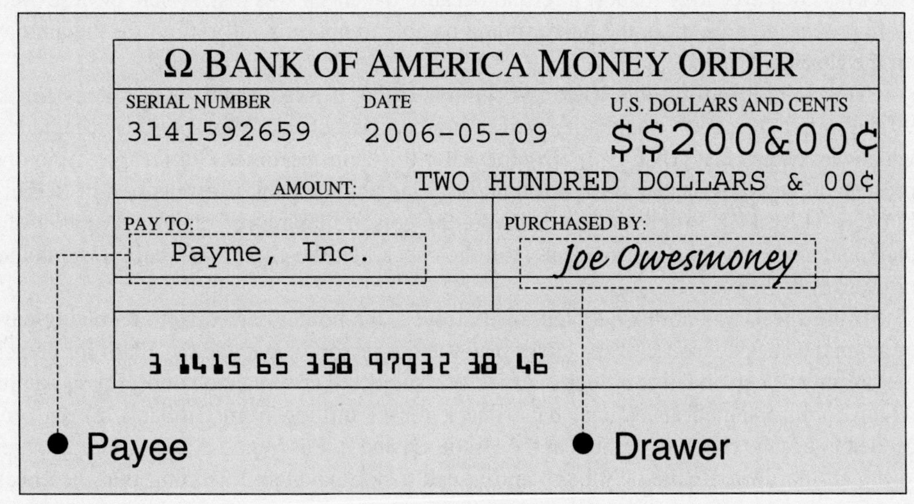

different, one thing they have in common is an increased guarantee of being paid. That is, a cashier's, teller's, or certified check is less likely to be denied by a bank.

Cashier's checks are a valuable business tool because the bank, and not the individual, is the drawer as well as the drawee. When the cashier's check is presented for payment, the bank, and not the individual, must pay for the cashier's check. The added guarantee of knowing the bank is paying for the cashier's check makes the cashier's check a veritable guarantee to pay. One downside of the cashier's check is that it must be paid for in advance, including a small fee. However, because the cashier's check is paid for first, it can be purchased at any bank, regardless of whether one has an account at the bank.

Teller's checks function like cashier's checks. Teller's checks tend to carry with them a similar guarantee to be paid. However, because the teller's check is drawn on a bank other than the one issuing the teller's check, the process is a step removed from the one regarding cashier's checks. That is, the bank ordering payment is not the bank making the payment, so the guarantee of sufficient funds is not as strong as it is with cashier's checks. Given the weaker guarantee, a teller's check is used primarily when a customer wants to buy a cashier's check from a bank that does not currently have the funds to cover the cashier's check and thus issues a teller's check. Consequently, although a cashier's check is preferred to a teller's check, the teller's check is almost as good as the cashier's check.

Certified checks are useful in business because when a bank certifies a check, it essentially says that it cannot refuse liability on the check. A certified check is one the bank sets aside money for and agrees to pay when the certified check is presented. Despite the added guarantee, there are two main drawbacks to a certified check. The first is one must have an account at a specific bank to obtain a certified check. That is, unlike cashier's or teller's checks, if a person does not have an account at a bank, he or she cannot obtain a certified check from the bank. The second drawback is that banks do not have to certify checks. Banks may refuse to certify any check for any reason. Refusing to certify is not the same as dishonoring a check, but it does not provide the same guarantee that a certified check has. While banks do not have to certify a check, they are not allowed to refuse to sell a cashier's or teller's check as long as the payment is valid.

LOST, STOLEN, OR DESTROYED CASHIER'S, TELLER'S, OR CERTIFIED CHECKS

In the event a cashier's, teller's, or certified check is lost, stolen, or destroyed, the UCC allows for recovery. According to UCC 3-312, the remitter (the party who purchased the check) or the payee may request a refund because the check was lost, stolen, or destroyed. With proper identification, the party should be able to obtain a full refund for the amount on the check.

The claim is enforceable when the claim is made; if it is a cashier's or teller's check, 90 days after the check was made; or if it is a certified check, 90 days after acceptance, whichever occurs last [UCC 3-312(b)(1)]. After the claim becomes enforceable, if no one presented the check for payment, a refund is issued and the bank is discharged of liability [UCC 3-312(b)(4)]. When a claim is made, the person making the claim warrants to the bank and any party who has an interest in the check that the check was really lost, stolen, or destroyed.

If the check was not lost, stolen, or destroyed, the holder barred from receiving payment on the check because of the claim may sue the person who made the claim for breach of warranty. A person filing a false claim is also subject to criminal penalties. For example, Allan Boren obtained an official bank check for $1 million from Citibank. Boren proceeded to use the check to gamble at the Hilton Casino in Las Vegas. After suffering losses at the casino, Boren called Citibank and issued a stop payment, claiming that the check was lost or stolen. Boren was indicted for bank fraud because he falsely claimed that his bank check was lost or stolen.

Accepting Deposits

Charging a customer's account is only part of the bank-customer relationship; the bank must also credit a customer's account when the customer makes cash and check deposits to her account. This section considers the check collection process (Figure 29-5) and examines several issues that focus on the availability of deposited money.

THE CHECK COLLECTION PROCESS

Suppose Jack Blackstone gives Molly Whetfield a check to pay her for her consulting services. When Molly deposits that check into her account, how does the money from Jack's account actually get transferred into Molly's account? This section examines several issues regarding deposits made to banks.

TYPES OF BANKS INVOLVED IN CHECK COLLECTION

The check collection process is established by Article 4 of the UCC. Section 4-105 of the UCC defines the four types of banks that may be involved in the check collection process. (See Exhibit 29-2 for a summary of the four types.) Return to the Jack and Molly example. First, suppose Molly presents Jack's check to her bank for deposit in her account. Molly's bank is called the **depositary bank,** the first bank that receives a check for payment. Second, Jack's bank is called the **payor bank,** the bank on which a check is drawn. NationsBank, as referred to in the chapter opener, is another example of a payor bank. Third, any

Figure 29-5 Illustration of the Check Collection Process

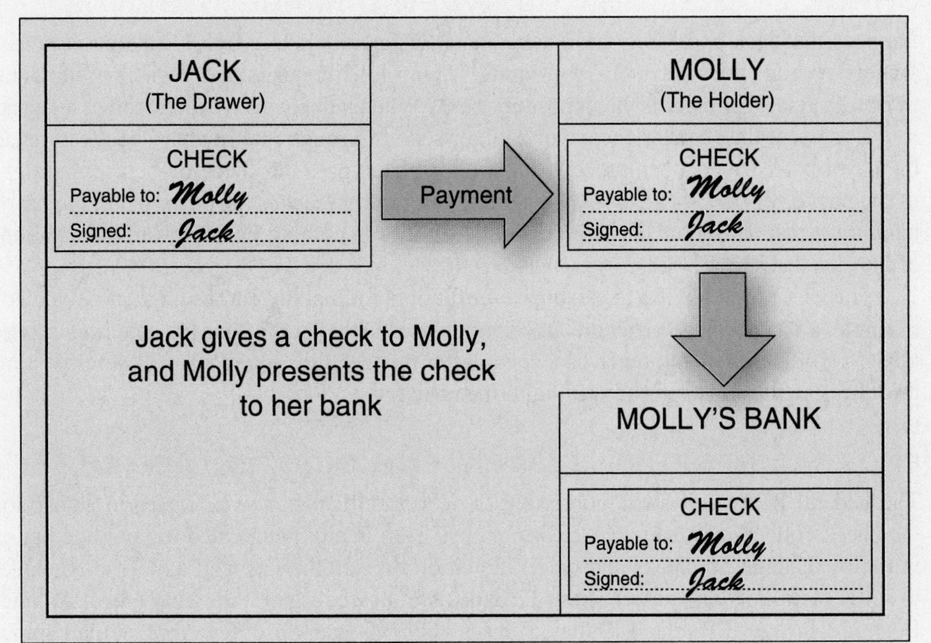

Exhibit 29-2
Type of Check-Collecting Bank

Depositary bank	The first bank accepting a check for payment
Payor bank	The bank ultimately responsible for granting funds for the check
Collecting bank	A bank, other than the payor bank, handling the check at any point from the time the check is deposited to the time it reaches the payor bank
Intermediary bank	A bank receiving a transferred check during the collection process [excluding the first bank (depositary) and the last bank (payor)]

kind of bank (besides the payor bank) that handles Jack's check during the collection process is called a **collecting bank.** Finally, any bank (besides the payor bank and depositary bank) to which the check is transferred is called the **intermediary bank.**

A bank involved in the check collection process may be classified as several of these types of banks at the same time. For example, when Molly deposits Jack's check at her bank, her bank is both the depositary bank and the collection bank.

CHECK COLLECTION WITHIN THE SAME BANK

Sometimes the depositary bank is the same bank as the payor bank. When the depositary bank is the same bank as the payor bank, the check is referred to as an "on-us item." For example, suppose Molly's and Jack's accounts are at the same bank. When Molly deposits Jack's check into her account, the check does not have to be sent to another bank because she and Jack share the same bank. Instead, the bank gives a "provisional" credit to Molly's account. If this bank does not dishonor the check on the second day, the check is paid [UCC 4-215(e)(2)]. Finally, on the third day, the provisional credit becomes an actual payment.

CHECK COLLECTION BETWEEN DIFFERENT BANKS

Suppose that Jack and Molly have accounts at different banks. Molly's account is in Los Angeles, while Jack's account is in Miami. When Molly deposits Jack's check at her bank in Los Angeles, her bank is the depositary bank. When a depositary bank receives a check, it must present the check at the payor bank or send it through intermediary banks to reach the payor bank. Once a bank receives a check, it must pass the check on before midnight of the next day [UCC 4-202(b)]. When the check finally reaches the payor bank, the payor bank must respond to the check by dishonoring it or becoming liable for the face amount of the check (UCC 4-302).

The UCC allows banks to establish cutoff hours for making entries on their books. For example, a bank may determine that 2 p.m. or later is the cutoff hour for handling checks (UCC 4-108). If the bank receives a check after this deadline, the bank will defer posting this check to its customer's account until the next day.

FEDERAL RESERVE SYSTEM FOR CLEARING CHECKS

The Federal Reserve System, consisting of 12 central banks, acts as a clearinghouse for the check collection process. (A clearinghouse is an institution created to facilitate banks in their exchange of checks and drafts drawn on one another, as well as to enable banks to settle their daily balances.) These 12 banks are located in the following cities: Atlanta, Boston, Chicago, Cleveland, Dallas, Kansas City, Minneapolis, New York, Philadelphia,

Richmond, Saint Louis, and San Francisco. Most banks have accounts with the Federal Reserve. Thus, when Molly deposits Jack's check at her bank in Los Angeles, this bank will deposit the check in the San Francisco Federal Reserve Bank. The San Francisco Federal Reserve Bank will transfer the check to the Atlanta Federal Reserve Bank, which serves Miami. Finally, the Atlanta Federal Reserve Bank will transfer the check to Jack's bank in Miami.

ELECTRONIC CHECK PRESENTMENT

In the past, checks were physically presented to each bank in the chain of collection. Now, checks are transmitted electronically from bank to bank (UCC 4-110). Through electronic check presentment, a check can be processed on the day on which it is deposited. An item is encoded with information that is transferred from one bank's computer to another bank's computer. The person who enters the information into the computer (i.e., encodes the information) warrants that the information is correct (UCC 4-209). Alternatively, the image of a check may be transmitted for payment to other banks.

Substitute checks. To further facilitate electronic presentment, in 2004 Congress passed the *Check Clearing for the 21st Century Act* (also known as *Check 21* or the *Check Truncation Act*). Check 21 allows banks to forgo sending original checks as part of the collection or return process and instead send a truncated version. In place of the original paper check, a bank may send (1) a substitute check or (2), by agreement, an electronic image of the check along with data from the magnetic ink character recognition (MICR) line on the original check.

A substitute check is similar to the electronic image that may be sent in lieu of the original paper check. Check 21 defines a substitute check as a paper reproduction of the original check that conforms to the following requirements:

1. Contains a clear replication of the front and back of the original paper check.
2. Bears an MICR line with all the information on the original check's MICR line.
3. Conforms with generally applicable industry standards for paper stock, dimensions, and other general qualities.
4. Is suitable for automated processing in the same manner as the original paper check.

Check 21 provides the guidelines for the issuance and use of substitute checks. The act also allows for the use of digital or paper substitutions for the original paper check.

AVAILABILITY SCHEDULE FOR DEPOSITED CHECKS

Once a check is considered deposited in a customer's account, when are the funds available to the customer? In the past, banks placed extended holds (e.g., 10 days) on deposited funds to ensure that the payor bank would not dishonor the check. If the check was from out of state, the bank might place a two-week hold on the check.

Because customers were frustrated with such extended holds on checks, Congress enacted the Expedited Funds Availability Act of 1987. This act created explicit timelines that mandate when banks must make deposited funds available to customers. If the risk of dishonor is low, the funds must be made available very quickly. For example, the first $100 of any amount deposited must be available to the depositor on the business day following the day of deposit [12 C.F.R. Section 229.10(a)–(c)]. The availability of the rest of the funds depends on whether the check is local, what the amount of the check is, and how the depositor wishes to withdraw the funds.

1. If the deposited check is drawn on a bank within the same Federal Reserve Bank area, the depositary bank must make the deposited funds available to the customer on the second business day following the deposit day [12 C.F.R. 229.10(b)].
2. If the deposited check is outside the same Federal Reserve Bank area, the depositary bank must make the funds available on the fifth business day following the day of deposit [12 C.F.R. 229.12(c)].

There are some exceptions to these rules. For example, if a customer makes a deposit at an ATM not owned by the bank that is receiving the deposit, the bank places a five-day hold on the deposit, including cash deposits. Moreover, if a customer makes a deposit over $5,000, the depositary bank may place an eight-day hold on the funds.

THE TRUTH-IN-SAVINGS ACT

In an effort to allow consumers to be better informed, Congress passed the Truth-in-Savings Act (TISA) in 1991. TISA requires that depositary institutions disclose, in great detail, the terms and conditions of their accounts. Depositary institutions include commercial banks, savings banks, credit unions, and savings and loan associations.

TISA requires that banks inform their customers of a number of specific pieces of information relevant to the bank's accounts. This information is to be handed to the customer as a pamphlet, brochure, or handout before the customer opens a deposit account. The information that must be given to the customer includes:

1. The minimum balance required to open an account and to be paid interest.
2. The manner in which the balance of the account will be calculated.
3. The annual percentage yield of interest for the account.
4. The way interest on the account will be calculated.
5. Notification of any fees, charges, and penalties the account may be assessed and how they are calculated.
6. Notification of any limitations on withdrawals or deposits.

Furthermore, TISA and Regulation DD, which serves as the act's implementing regulation, require that banks pay interest based on the full balance of interest-bearing accounts daily. The requirement prevents banks from calculating interest on accounts when the account is at its lowest balance. For example, say your account maintains a balance of $500. However, on the last day of the period you withdraw $400. The bank must pay interest on the entire sum of your balance on a daily basis as opposed to paying you interest on the $100 you left in your account at the end of the period.

Also, TISA and Regulation DD mandate requirements for the information that must be included on the account's monthly statement. The monthly statement must include the interest earned, a summation of fees charged, an explanation of how fees were calculated, and the number of days the statement covers.

When a Bank May Charge a Customer's Account

The following sections consider certain problems related to a bank's accepting and paying a customer's check.

WRONGFUL DISHONOR

When a customer opens a checking account, both the customer and the bank accept certain duties and rights. Generally, the customer assumes a duty to keep sufficient funds in her account to cover the checks written on her account. If the customer does not have enough funds to cover a check, the bank will dishonor the check, and the customer becomes liable for the amount of the check.

Similarly, under the *properly payable rule,* the bank has a duty to pay checks from the customer's account as long as the check is "properly payable" [UCC Section 4-401(a)]. In other words, the check must be authorized by the drawer and must not violate the agreement between the bank and the customer. Generally, for a check to be considered properly payable, it must:

1. Have the drawer's authorized signature on the check.
2. Be paid to a person entitled to enforce the check.
3. Not have been altered.
4. Not have been completed by addition of unauthorized terms if the check was incomplete.
5. Be paid on or after the date of the check.
6. Not be subject to a stop payment from the drawer.

If the bank wrongfully fails to pay a check—wrongfully dishonoring the check—the bank may be liable to the customer for damages. The UCC clearly states that banks can be held liable, but it does not cite a specific theory for recovery. Therefore, someone whose check was dishonored need prove only that the dishonoring was wrongful, and he or she will be entitled to recovery. Case 29-1 provides an example of the damages a customer may potentially recover from a bank for wrongful dishonor.

CASE 29-1

THE TWIN CITY BANK v. KENNETH ISAACS
SUPREME COURT OF ARKANSAS
672 S.W.2D 651 (1984)

The Issacs discovered their checkbook was missing on Sunday, May 13, 1979. They promptly reported the loss to Twin City Bank the next day. They learned that two checks totaling $2,050 had been forged and charged to their account. When they reported the lost checkbook, their account balance was approximately $2,000.

Because Mr. Issacs had been previously convicted of burglary, the bank thought he might be involved with the forgeries. Thus, the bank froze the Isaacs' account. However, the individual who forged the checks was discovered and convicted at the end of May 1979. The police notified the bank that there was no evidence to connect the Issacs to the forgeries. Yet the bank continued to keep the account frozen. The Issacs filed suit for wrongful dishonor in June 1979. Their account was kept frozen for the next four years.

At trial, the jury awarded the Issacs $18,500 in compensatory damages and $45,000 in punitive damages. The bank appealed.

JUDGE HAYS: On the issue of damages, the bank maintains there was insufficient evidence to support the $18,500 award for mental anguish, for loss of credit and loss of the bargain on a house, that the award of punitive damages should not have been given at all as there was not only insufficient proof of actual damages but insufficient evidence of malice or intent to oppress on the part of the bank. The bank does not challenge the sufficiency of the evidence of its wrongful dishonor, but contends only that there was no evidence to support an award of damages. These arguments cannot be sustained.

The statute upon which this suit was based is Ark. Stat. Ann. § 85-4-402:

> Bank's liability to customer for wrongful dishonor—A payor bank is liable to its customer for damages proximately caused by the wrongful dishonor of an item. When the dishonor occurs through mistake, liability is limited to actual damages proved. If so

proximately caused and proved damages may include damages for an arrest or prosecution of the customer or other consequential damages.

The jury was instructed that if they found the bank liable they were to fix the amount of money which would compensate the Isaacs "for any of the following elements of damage sustained which were proximately caused by the conduct of Twin City Bank: 1) Any amounts of money wrongfully held by the defendant and remaining unpaid 2) any mental anguish and embarrassment suffered by the plaintiffs 3) any financial losses sustained by the [Isaacs]."

Initially, there can be no serious question as to certain losses: the $2,000 wrongfully withheld by the bank for four years, and the value of two vehicles repossessed because the Isaacs' did not have access to their funds, resulting in a loss of approximately $2,200. Additionally, after the account was frozen the bank continued to charge the account a service charge and overdraft fees on checks written before the forgeries but presented after the account was frozen. The bank does not refute these damages but argues there is no showing of any financial deprivation from loss of credit or loss of the bargain on a house the Isaacs wanted to buy, and insufficient proof of mental anguish. We find, however, that in addition to the losses previously mentioned, there was sufficient evidence to sustain damages for mental suffering, loss of credit, and sufficient demonstration of some loss attributable to the inability to pursue the purchase of a home.

Decisions upholding recovery for mental suffering under the code have found injury resulting from circumstances comparable to this case. In *North Shore Bank* v. *Palmer* for example, a $275 forged check was paid from Palmer's account. After the bank knew or should have known the check was forged, it charged Palmer with the $275 check and later wrongfully dishonored other checks. Part of the actual damages awarded was attributed to mental suffering for the "embarrassment and humiliation Palmer suffered from having been turned down for credit for the first time in his life."

In *Morse* v. *Mutual Federal Savings and Loan,* $2,200 was awarded for "false defamatory implications arising from temporary financial embarrassment." And in *Farmers & Merchants State Bank of Krum* v. *Ferguson,* the plaintiff's account in the amount of $7,000 was frozen for apparently one month for reasons not stated. The plaintiff was awarded $25,000 for mental anguish, $3,000 for loss of credit based on a denial of a loan, $5,000 for loss of time spent making explanations to creditors, and $1,500 for loss of use of his money. The court justified the mental suffering award because the dishonor was found to be with malice—the bank had failed to notify Ferguson that the account was frozen, some checks were honored while others were not, and the bank continued to withdraw loan payments due it during the entire time.

In this case, prior to the forgery incident the Isaacs' credit reputation with Twin City Bank was described by the bank as "impeccable" and the freezing of their funds had a traumatic effect on their lives. They obviously lost their credit standing with Twin City, and were unable to secure credit commercially at other institutions because of their status at Twin City. The Isaacs had to borrow from friends and family, and were left in a precarious position financially. They did not have use of their $2,000 for four years. The allegation relative to the loss of a house resulted from the dishonor of an earnest money check for a home they were planning to buy, ending prospects for the purchase at that time. Though there may have been insufficient proof of loss of the bargain on the house, as the bank argues, nevertheless this evidence was admissible as an element of mental suffering. The denial of credit contributed to some monetary loss as occurred in *Ferguson,* in addition to its being a reasonable element of mental suffering as was found in *Palmer.* There was also testimony that the financial strain contributed to marital difficulties leading at one point to the filing of a divorce suit. The suit was dropped but there was testimony that the difficulties caused by the bank's action caused substantial problems in the marriage. Finally, the Isaacs lost equities in two vehicles repossessed as a result of the withholding of their funds. One of these, a new van, was repossessed by Twin City in June, 1979, before a five day grace period for a current installment had expired.

We believe there was substantial evidence to support the verdict. The jury heard the evidence of the amount wrongfully withheld, the loss of two vehicles, credit loss through loan denials, loss of the use of their money for four years, the suffering occasioned by marital difficulties, the inability to acquire a home they wanted, and the general anxieties which accompanied the financial strain.

AFFIRMED.

CRITICAL THINKING

Judge Hays uses several cases to make analogies with the Isaacs' case. Do you think these analogies are effective? Are there any differences between those cases and the facts in this case that suggest that Judge Hays should not have relied so heavily on them?

ETHICAL DECISION MAKING

Return to the WPH framework. Suppose you are the bank manager who decided to keep a freeze on the Isaacs' funds for four years. If your actions are guided by the public disclosure test, would you have behaved differently?

OVERDRAFTS

Suppose you write 10 checks on your company's account to pay your employees' salaries. Unfortunately, you do not have sufficient funds to cover the full amount of the last check; you are short $50. The bank has two options: (1) Dishonor the last check, or (2) create an **overdraft** by paying the check and charging the account the amount short [UCC 4-401(a)]. Thus, when you make your next deposit, $50 will be deducted from that deposit.

How frequently do banks have to dishonor checks because of insufficient funds? In Europe, less than 1 percent of personal checks are returned because of insufficient funds. Approximately 1 percent of checks are returned because of insufficient funds in the United States. In contrast, 9.5 percent of personal checks bounce in Qatar, while 3.4 percent are returned in Saudi Arabia.

Many banks offer overdraft protection to their customers. In other words, some banks will promise to credit their customers' accounts if there are insufficient funds. However, these banks may charge the customers for this service, just as the bank in the NationsBank opening example charged customers. Alternatively, banks may give several options to customers to prevent overdrafts. For example, the bank may link the checking account to the customer's savings account or credit card; thus, if a customer has insufficient funds in her checking account, the bank may draw on the savings account or credit card.

If the bank chooses to dishonor the check, the holder can attempt to resubmit the check at a later date. However, as we explained in Chapter 26, once the check has been dishonored, the holder must notify the endorsers of the check of the dishonor. If the holder does not give proper notice, the endorsers will not be responsible for the amount of the check.

STOP-PAYMENT ORDER

A customer can issue a **stop-payment order**, an order by a drawer to the drawee bank not to pay a check that has been drawn on the customer's account (UCC 4-403). A customer issues a stop-payment order when she has issued a check that has not yet been accepted and she wishes the check not to be accepted. For example, Angelina orders a pair of boots from her favorite store and writes a check to cover the cost in advance. Angelina is informed the next day that the boots have been discontinued and she will not be receiving the boots. Given that Angelina has already issued the check, she can issue a stop-payment order for her check because the check is no longer covering the purchase of her boots. If the bank pays a check in violation of a stop-payment order, the bank will incur liability for the damages suffered by the customer due to the stop payment [UCC 4-403(b)].

To be effective, the stop order must meet two requirements: (1) The customer must give the order in a reasonable time, and (2) the customer must describe the item with "reasonable certainty" [UCC 4-403(a)]. For example, the stop-payment order must be given so that the bank has enough time to instruct its tellers and other employees that they should not pay the check. Moreover, the UCC states that the stop-payment order must reach the bank by a certain cutoff time. Generally, the stop-payment order should list:

1. The date of the check
2. The name of the payee
3. The amount of the check
4. The number of the check
5. The checking account number

There are several issues regarding stop-payment orders. First, how is the stop-payment order given? A stop-payment order may be given orally or in writing. If it is an oral order, it is valid for just 14 days unless the order is later confirmed in writing. If the order is given through writing, the order is valid for six months and can be extended for another six months [UCC 4-403(b)]. Note that not all states allow stop-payment orders to be delivered orally. In the event that oral stop-payment orders are not allowed, they must be given in writing.

Second, if the customer issues a stop payment and does not have a valid legal ground for this order, the holder of the instrument will likely sue the customer. Not only will the customer be liable for the value of the check, but he will also probably be liable for any damages incurred by the payee of the check because of the stop-payment order. Even with a valid legal reason, if the holder of the check is a holder in due course, the drawer's defenses will not apply and he will still be liable for the check.

Finally, payment cannot be stopped on certified checks, cashier's checks, or teller's checks [UCC 3-411(b)].

POSTDATED CHECKS

Under previous versions of Articles 3 and 4 of the UCC, a check could not be charged to a customer's account until the date of the check. Thus, some customers attempted to hold off payment on a check by postdating the check and giving it to the payee. However, because banks generally use an automated system to process checks, checks are now frequently paid without regard to the date. If a bank pays a check before its date and thus depletes a customer's account, the bank could be liable to the customer for damages. Thus, some banks include certain clauses in their customer agreements that state they may pay checks regardless of the date.

The UCC presents a middle ground that protects a bank from liability while permitting customers to postdate checks. Section 4-401(c) states that customers can postdate checks but they must give the bank notice of the postdated check. Therefore, the bank can assume that it can pay all checks on presentment unless the bank has received notice. Most banks charge a processing fee for notice of a postdated check.

STALE CHECKS

If a check is not presented to a bank within six months of its date, the check is considered a **stale check.** As described in the Global Context box, a payee is required to present a check much more quickly in China. If a payee presents an uncertified stale check to a bank, the bank is not required to pay the amount of the check (UCC 4-404). However, if the bank pays the check in good faith, it may charge the drawer's account.

global context

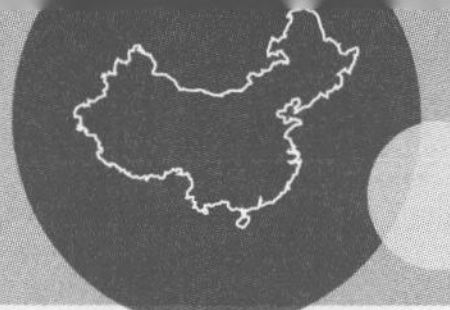

Checks in China

China adopted the Law of the People's Republic of China on Negotiable Instruments (Negotiable Instruments Law) on May 10, 1995. According to this law, when opening an account, the customer must demonstrate that she is financially creditworthy and must deposit a certain amount of money in the account. The bank determines whether the customer is financially creditworthy.

The Negotiable Instruments Law governs both deposits and payments from a checking account. This law states that the payee of a check must present the check for payment within 10 days of the date of the check's issuance. According to the Negotiable Instruments Law, this rule applies only when the payee and drawer are from the same "place." If this time limit expires, the drawee is discharged from his obligation to pay. However, the drawer is still liable for the amount of the check.

Source: Guiguo Wang, *Wang's Business Law of China,* 3d ed. (1999), pp. 494–498.

Case 29-2 combines questions regarding stale checks and stop-payment orders. In this case, the bank cashed a check dated 19 months earlier. Moreover, the check had been subject to an oral stop-payment order. Should the bank be liable for the amount of the check?

CASE 29-2

SCOTT D. LEIBLING, P.C. v. MELLON PSFS (NJ) NATIONAL ASSOCIATION

SUPERIOR COURT OF NEW JERSEY, LAW DIVISION, SPECIAL CIVIL PART, CAMDEN COUNTY
710 A.2D 1067 (1998)

Scott D. Liebling, P.C., an attorney, had an attorney trust account ("Account") at Mellon Bank (NJ) National Association. Mellon uses a computerized system to process checks for payment. Liebling represented Fredy Ramos in a personal injury case that led to a settlement.

In May 1995, Liebling issued check number 1031 for over $8000 to Ramos as a result of the settlement. However, a few days later, Liebling mistakenly issued check number 1043 in the same amount to Ramos. Mellon honored this first check on May 26, 1995. Around May 30, 1995, Liebling called Ramos and explained that check 1043 was issued in error and should be destroyed. Moreover, Liebling called the bank and ordered an oral stop payment on the second check. On December 21, 1996, Ramos cashed check number 1043.

Liebling filed a complaint against Mellon, arguing Mellon breached their duty of good faith, payment of a stale check, and breach of contract as a result of Mellon honoring the second check, check 1043.

JUDGE RAND

Issue

Whether the defendant bank acted in good faith when it honored a check that was presented for payment nineteen months after it was issued and subsequent to the expiration of an oral stop payment order?

Discussion

It is important to consider the relevant New Jersey statute sections before discussing what actions constitute "good faith." Under N.J.S.A. 12A:4-403(b):

> A stop payment order is effective for six months, but it lapses after 14 calendar days if the original order was oral and was not confirmed in writing within that period. A stop payment order may be renewed for additional six-month periods by a writing given to the bank within a period during which the stop-payment order is effective.

In addition, N.J.S.A. 12A:4-404 states:

> A bank is under no obligation to a customer having a checking account to pay a check . . . which is

> presented more than six months after its date, but it *may charge its customer's account for a payment made thereafter in good faith.*

Thus, the issue in the present case turns on whether Mellon acted in good faith when it honored Plaintiff's check. Good faith under N.J. Uniform Commercial Code has been defined in N.J.S.A. 12A:3-103(a)(4) as "honesty in fact and the observance of reasonable commercial standards of fair dealing." Since there is no New Jersey case law directly on point, it is necessary to consider alternate sources.

. . . Plaintiff's argument centers on the proposition that the bank's duty of good faith required it to inquire or consult with Plaintiff before honoring a stale check that had a previous oral stop payment order on it. This argument was upheld in the Pre-Code case of Goldberg v. Manufacturers Hanover Trust Co., 199 Misc. 167, 102 N.Y.S.2d 144 (NY Mun. Ct. 1951). In that case, the bank was held liable to the drawer for payment of a 27 month old check even though a stop payment order had expired. The Court predicated liability on the bank's payment of the check without inquiring into its own records which would have revealed the lapsed stop payment order and put the bank on notice. The [1962] N.J. Study Comment to N.J.S.A. 12A:4-404 cites Redfield, The Law of Commercial Paper § 584, noting that the "practical way out of this dilemma is the simple expedient of making inquiry."

However, in the Uniform Commercial Code Treatise, "Hawkland § 4-404:01", Mr. Hawkland stated that the above case [is] not consistent with the Uniform Commercial Code. Specifically, "the duty [of inquiry] is inconsistent with the provisions of subsection 4-403(2) on the expiration of the 'effectiveness' of stop orders. Such a duty is hardly practical today."

Plaintiff counters that . . . this Court should give total credence to the explanatory comments drafted many years before the most recent code § 4-404 revisions. Pursuant to § 4-404, the bank may charge the customer's account for a check presented more than six months after it is dated as long as the bank acts in good faith. N.J.S.A. § 12A:3-103(a)(4) defines good faith. The definition "honesty in fact and the observance of reasonable commercial standards of fair dealings" is a revision from the 1961 version of the Code. It interjects a subjective analysis into the concept of fair dealings.

In 1990, Articles III and IV of the Code were substantially revised relating to, among other things, bank deposits and collections to become effective on June 1, 1995. The Court is satisfied as pointed out by the Defendant that those Amendments were enacted in order to address the effect of automated systems utilized by banks with the substantial increase in check usage after the original enactment of the Code. The Official Code Comment to the 1995 Amendments for § 12A:4-101, states as follows:

> 2. . . . An important goal of the 1990 revision of Article 4 is to promote the efficiency of the check collection process by making the provisions of Article 4 more compatible with the needs of an automated system and, by doing so, increase the speed and lower the cost of check collection for those who write and receive checks. [Code Comment to N.J.S.A. § 12A:4-101 (1995) (Supp. p. 157).]

The 1995 Amendments to § 12A:4-404 New Jersey Study Comment include different language than that on which the Plaintiff totally relied. Plaintiff's reliance upon the 1962 Study Comment is misplaced and outdated. The more modern and up to date approach requires a rejection of the 1962 Study Comment upon which Plaintiff's argument solely rests.

Thus, in determining whether defendant bank in the present action acted in good faith, the above cited material must be analyzed and applied. First, it appears clear that the Uniform Commercial Code acknowledges that computerized check processing systems are common and accepted banking procedures in the United States. Therefore, it can not be said that defendant bank acted in bad faith by using a computerized system when it honored Plaintiff's "stale" check. Furthermore, it appears that the test for good faith is a subjective test. Thus, based on all of the foregoing material, as long as defendant bank used an adequate computer system for processing checks (here there is no proof to the contrary), it appears to have acted in good faith even though it did not consult the Plaintiff before it honored the "stale" check that had an expired oral stop-payment order on it. [T]he obligation of a bank to stop payment on a check does not continue in perpetuity once the stop payment order expires.

The bank's conduct was fair and in accordance with reasonable commercial standards.

Judgment for defendant Mellon.

[CONTINUED]

CRITICAL THINKING

What evidence does the judge rely on to come to the conclusion that the bank was not liable? Do you think the judge ignores any important evidence? Is there any missing information that would help you come to a conclusion regarding the bank's liability?

ETHICAL REASONING

What are the values associated with not holding the bank responsible to honor an expired stop-payment order? What values are in conflict? Do you think the values promoted by the decision are appropriate for the situation? Why or why not?

DEATH OR INCOMPETENCE OF A CUSTOMER

If the drawer of the check has died or is adjudicated incompetent, the bank, depending on its knowledge of the customer's death or incompetence, may be authorized to pay the check. If the bank is not aware or does not have a "reasonable opportunity to act on the knowledge," the bank is authorized to pay the check [UCC 4-405(a)].

In contrast, if the bank was aware of the death, the bank may pay the checks drawn on the account for 10 days after the date of death [UCC 4-405(b)]. If the bank, with notice of the customer's death, pays a check after the 10-day period, the bank may be liable. This 10-day period begins on the date of the customer's death. Thus, if the bank receives notice of the customer's death 12 days after the customer died, the bank cannot pay the checks. Moreover, this 10-day period is applicable only to the death of a customer; it does not apply when a customer has been adjudicated insane.

FORGERIES AND ALTERATIONS

In 1999, attempted check fraud in the United States rose to approximately $2.2 billion, while merchants and banks suffered actual losses approximating $679 million through check fraud. Thus, banks are clearly concerned about the acceptance of altered or forged checks.

Checks bearing forged signatures. Under the properly payable rule, the bank may pay a check only if it is authorized by the customer. Who is liable if a bank cashes a check signed by an unauthorized person? In other words, what happens when someone forges a drawer's signature on a check?

The UCC establishes that a forged signature has no legal effect as a signature of the drawer [3-403(a)]. Consequently, in most cases, if a bank pays a check when the drawer's signature has been forged, the bank will be liable for the amount of the check.

However, there are some exceptions to this rule. First, if the customer's negligence substantially contributed to a forged signature and the bank pays the check in good faith, the bank is not required to repay the customer [UCC 3-406(a)]. For example, if the customer is an employer who keeps a rubber stamp of his signature in an unlocked drawer, and an employee uses the signature stamp to create a check payable to employee, the customer has substantially contributed to the forged signature and will likely not be able to recover the amount of the check.

Yet, if the bank that pays the check is also negligent, the customer may be able to recover part of the money. For example, suppose the employer-customer notified the bank of the employee's unauthorized use of the signature stamp but the bank paid the check anyway. The customer's liability for the amount of the check may be reduced by the bank's negligence in paying the check when it had been notified that the check was unauthorized.

Another exception to the forgery liability rule is related to the customer's duty to examine the bank statement. Banks make a customer's statement available to the customer approximately once a month. This statement lists or includes all the checks that have been charged against the customer's account over that past month. A customer must examine her bank statement reasonably promptly for any forgeries or unauthorized payments. If the customer discovers a forgery or unauthorized payment, she must notify the bank promptly [UCC 4-406(c)]. Under the UCC, if the customer does not notify the bank of an unauthorized signature within 30 days after the statement has been made available, she cannot hold the bank liable for the payment [4-406(d)]. See the Case Nugget, where this rule is applied.

Case Nugget — Thirty Days to Report

Fernando Tatis v. US Bancorp
F.3d 672 (2007)

Plaintiff-appellant Fernando Tatis, a major-league baseball player, opened several banking accounts through US Bank. One of the many accounts Tatis opened was a personal checking account about which he received the terms of conditions before becoming the primary signatory for the account. When the account was initially established, Tatis asked that all bank statements be held in the bank's Professional Sports Division. The personal checks were then sent to Tatis's residence in Montreal, where an employee proceeded to take the checks and forge several of them between August and November 2001. Tatis later brought suit against the bank to recover his lost funds. The defendant contested Tatis's accusations and moved for summary judgment.

The district court granted the defendant's motion for summary judgment, and when Tatis moved for reconsideration with the district court, his motion was denied. Tatis then appealed the district court's decision to the Sixth Circuit of the U.S. Court of Appeals.

In the opinion written by Alan Sharp, the Sixth Circuit found that Tatis did not have the right to recover the funds from the bank. When the account was opened, Tatis was notified by the terms and conditions he received that he had only 30 days after the bank statements became available to report any unauthorized signatures or alterations. Although Tatis was not given the statements directly, they were made available to him and held at the location that he had requested.

By not reporting the first forgery that appeared on the first bank statement, Tatis lost rights to all subsequent funds that were taken. As a result of payments being made on the checks previously written by Tatis's employee, the bank could claim that Tatis had failed to report that the employee was not an authorized signatory on the account. Hence, even after Tatis noticed the forgeries, he was not able to recover any funds.

The duty to examine the bank statement is particularly important in cases where there have been multiple forgeries by the same forger, or "same wrongdoer." If a customer examines a statement and does not notify the bank of the first forgery within 30 days, the customer will be liable for future forgeries on the customer's account by the same wrongdoer. For example, in one case, a customer was not aware of 17 forged checks totaling $13,000 paid on his account over a period of four months. In the fifth month, he discovered five checks forged on his account and reported these to the bank. The customer discovered his grandson had been the forger on these checks. The customer asked the bank to credit his account for the five unauthorized payments in the fifth month. When the bank refused, the customer sued. The court held that because the customer did not review his statement in the first month and all unauthorized signatures were from the same forger, the customer could not recover any of the subsequent forgeries. Case 29-3 considers whether a customer has reasonably examined his statement.

CASE 29-3 | WEAFRI WELL SERVICES, CO., LTD. v. FLEET BANK, NATIONAL ASSOCIATION

U.S. DISTRICT COURT FOR THE SOUTHERN DISTRICT OF NEW YORK
87 F. SUPP. 2D 234 (2000)

Cletus Onyekwere was the principal shareholder and CEO of Weafri Well Services, a Nigerian corporation that services oil wells and rigs. Onyekwere opened a checking account by mail with National Westminster Bank (NatWest) in December 1993. Onyekwere and his wife were the only authorized signers for the checking account. In May 1996, NatWest merged with Fleet Bank.

In August 1996, Onyekwere ordered new checks for his account, and he left these checks in a locked briefcase at his brother's apartment in Houston, Texas. When Onyekwere made trips between Houston and Nigeria, he retrieved the new checks from the locked briefcase but always returned them to the locked case. Onyekwere wrote checks 114–118 and 143–150.

Starting in February 1997, Fleet paid seven checks that were allegedly forged. These were check numbers 120, 121, 135, 136, 138, 139, and 140. The amounts of the checks ranged from $2800 to $91,000. The first allegedly forged check was paid in February 1997, while the last check was paid in June 1997. These checks were processed for payment at the Fleet Bank in Melville, NY.

Onyekwere claimed he did not receive his February 1997 bank statement until June 20, 1997. Within three or four days, Onyekwere notified Fleet Bank check 120 was a forgery. Once Fleet was notified, it started actions to recover amounts on the seven allegedly forged checks, but no recovery was made. When Fleet Bank did not credit Onyekwere's account, Onyekwere brought suit. The following opinion considers both Onyekwere's and Fleet's motions for summary judgment. In response to Onyekwere's suit, Fleet claimed they were not liable because Onyekwere failed to examine his statement within a reasonable time.

JUDGE MARTIN: [A]lthough the risk of loss due to forgeries is initially on the bank, under U.C.C. § 4-406 when a bank "sends" an account statement to its customer, the customer must exercise reasonable care and promptness to examine its statement to discover forgeries and must notify the bank promptly of any discovered forgeries. If the customer fails to comply with this duty, under certain circumstances the customer may be precluded from asserting the forgeries against the bank, for in these circumstances the risk of loss shifts from bank to customer. See U.C.C. § 4-406(2). However, U.C.C. § 4-406(3) shifts the risk of loss back to the bank where the customer establishes that the bank failed to exercise ordinary care in paying the forged checks.

U.C.C. § 4-406(2) sets forth the conditions under which a customer will be precluded from asserting forgeries against the bank. Under this provision, if the bank demonstrates that the customer failed to fulfill its duty to examine its statements to discover forgeries with reasonable care and promptness and to notify the bank promptly, then the customer cannot recover for subsequent forgeries by the same wrongdoer paid after the first forged check and statement "was available" to the customer for at least fourteen days.

1. There Is No Question of Fact That Plaintiff Failed to Examine Its Statement with Reasonable Care and to Notify Defendant Bank of the Forgeries Promptly

Defendant Bank has established that there is no question of fact that with respect to checks 135, 136, 138, 139, and 140, Plaintiff failed to examine its February 1997 Statement with reasonable care and promptness and to notify the bank of these forgeries promptly, as required by U.C.C. § 4-406(1) and (2)(b). Under U.C.C. § 4-406(2)(b), a customer may not recover for subsequent forgeries by the same wrongdoer that are paid after the initial check and statement "was available" to the customer for a reasonable period not exceeding fourteen days. Here, the February 1997 Statement "was available" under section 4-406(2)(b) when Defendant Bank mailed it to Plaintiff on or about March 4, 1997. Thus, because Plaintiff did not notify Defendant Bank of the forgery of check 120, which was contained in the February 1997 Statement, Plaintiff failed to examine its statement with reasonable care and promptness and to notify Defendant Bank of the forgery promptly. See U.C.C. § 4-406(1), (2)(b). Accordingly, Plaintiff cannot recover for the subsequent forgeries by the same wrongdoer that were paid after approximately March 18—checks 135, 136, 138, 139, and 140—unless Plaintiff shows to the exclusion of a question of fact that the bank lacked ordinary care in paying these checks.

Summary judgment for plaintiff denied.

CRITICAL THINKING

The case was decided primarily around the interpretation of several ambiguous words. What words in the judge's opinion are ambiguous? How would different interpretations of these words change the outcome of the case?

ETHICAL DECISION MAKING

Consider the individuals who could potentially be affected by this decision. Do you think this decision is harmful to individuals who hold a banking account? Should they have been considered in this case? If yes, why? If no, return to the WPH framework and attempt to think of an ethical justification for this ruling.

Again, if the bank was negligent in paying the forged checks, the customer's liability for the checks may be diminished through comparative negligence [UCC 4-406(e)]. Regardless of the 30-day requirement for multiple forgeries or the care used in cashing a check, a customer must report a forgery within one year from the date the statement is available to the customer or he will lose the right to recover this money [UCC 4-406(f)].

Finally, because a drawer is generally not liable for a forged check, the bank must credit a drawer's account for a paid forged check. The bank would likely then try to recover the money from the forger; a forged signature is effective as the signature of the forger [UCC 3-403(a)]. In other words, if Christina Simpson forges Ricky McIntyre's signature on his check, forging "Ricky McIntyre" functions to make Christina liable for the amount of the check.

e-commerce AND THE LAW

Using Technology to Fight Check Fraud

Banks rely on advances in technology to try to stay ahead of thieves who use the new technology to forge or alter checks. In 1996, Keybank experienced new account fraud in 42 percent of its demand deposit accounts. In mid-1997, Keybank started using "Early Warning," a database that is a combination of commercially available databases. Early Warning compares Social Security numbers with birth dates and compares phone numbers with zip codes. In other words, Early Warning makes it easier for financial institutions to determine whether a customer is opening an account to perpetuate a fraud. The use of Early Warning has reduced check fraud in Keybank's demand deposit accounts from 42 to 13 percent.

Source: "Industry Focus: How Banks Are Using Technology to Help Control Check Fraud," *Preventing Business Fraud,* November 1999.

Checks bearing forged endorsements. If a bank pays a check that has been fraudulently endorsed, who is responsible? In the same way that a drawer is not responsible for a check that bear the drawer's forged signature, the drawer is similarly not responsible for a check that has been fraudulently endorsed. Generally, when an endorsement has been forged, the first party to accept the forged instrument is ultimately liable for the loss because a forged endorsement does not legally transfer title [UCC 4-207(a)(2)]. However, the drawer again has a duty to examine her statement for fraudulent endorsements and then notify the bank. As such, the drawer must report all forged endorsements within a three-year period after the customer was returned the forged items or given his or her statement containing the forged items. If the customer does not report the forgery within three years, the bank is no longer liable for the customer's loss (UCC 4-111).

Altered checks. Remember, under the properly payable rule, a bank is to pay only those checks that are authorized. When a party makes an unauthorized change or alteration to a check, the check becomes unauthorized. The UCC defines **alteration** as a change (without consent) that modifies the obligation of a party to the instrument. Generally, if a bank pays a check that has been altered, the bank will be liable for the alteration.

For example, suppose a drawer writes a check for $5. The payee changes the amount paid to $55 and presents the check for payment. The bank pays $55 to the payee. The drawer discovers the alteration on his statement and reports it to the bank. The bank will then credit the drawer's account with $50; the drawer remains liable for the original amount of the check. The bank is liable for the $50 (UCC 4-111).

Again, a customer's substantial contribution to the alteration will limit the customer's ability to require that the bank credit his or her account. In other words, if the customer leaves large blank spaces open on the check so that another party may easily alter the check, the customer will likely be liable for the altered amount of the check. Similarly, suppose you, as a business manager, send an employee to purchase some supplies for a company picnic. You give the employee a check payable to the store, but you do not fill in the dollar amount of the check. The employee then writes in an amount that is $20 more than the total cost of the goods and asks for $20 in cash back. You do not become aware of the employee's action until you receive your bank statement. Under the UCC, any drawer who leaves the dollar amount blank may not later protest paying whatever amount has been written on the check [4-401(d)(2)].

As in the case of forged signatures, the customer's duty to examine his bank statement also applies to looking for altered checks. Thus, if the customer does not discover the altered check or does not report the altered check within a reasonable time, the bank's liability for the altered check is reduced. Similarly, if both the customer and the bank are

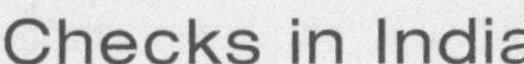

global context

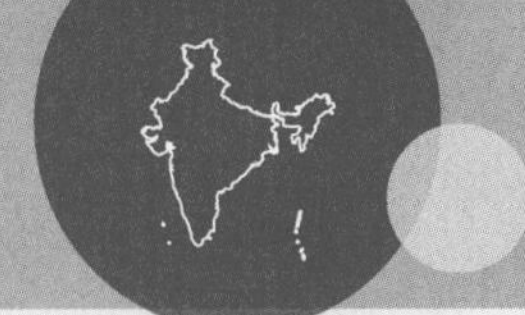

Checks in India

India, like Great Britain, has adopted the Negotiable Instruments Act of 1881. Most of the laws regarding negotiable instruments, particularly checks, are the same as or quite similar to the U.S. rules regarding checks.

First, a bank has a statutory obligation to honor checks drawn by its customers. If a banker dishonors a customer's check without justification, the banker makes himself potentially liable to the customer for injury. The customer is entitled to claim substantial damages even if she has suffered no actual loss. The customer has to simply show that her credit has suffered.

Second, if a customer's negligence contributes to an alteration or forgery, the customer will be potentially liable for this contribution. If a customer writes a check where the words and figures differ, it is not a valid check. The bank has a duty to ensure that the amount of the check has not been altered. If the amount of the check is given in words only, the check can be paid. However, if the amount is written in figures only, the check must usually be returned to the customer after being stamped with the following: "amount must be stated in words."

Source: M. L. Tannan, *Tannan's Banking Law and Practice in India,* 19th ed. (1998).

negligent in contributing to and paying an altered check, both parties will be responsible for a portion of the check.

Moreover, if a bank proves that losses from later altered checks occurred due to the customer's failure to identify and report the illegally altered checks, the bank will have a reduced liability due to the customer's contributory negligence (UCC 4-406). The bank may assert the defense of contributory negligence only if the bank exercised ordinary care (adherence to standard practices in the industry) when it cashed the altered check.

Electronic Fund Transfers

The application of technology to the banking system has made the banking process more efficient and less reliant on paperwork. When money is transferred by an electronic terminal, telephone, or computer, this transfer is called an **electronic fund transfer (EFT).** Consumer fund transfers are governed by the Electronic Fund Transfer Act of 1978, while commercial electronic fund transfers are governed by Article 4(A) of the UCC. By 1996, all 50 states had adopted Article 4(A).

TYPES OF EFT SYSTEMS

The most common types of electronic fund systems are automated teller machines, point-of-sale systems, direct deposits and withdrawals, and pay-by-telephone systems.

Automated teller machines. **Automated teller machines (ATMs),** machines connected to a bank's computer, are located in convenient places so that customers may conduct banking transactions without actually going into a bank. Customers may withdraw and deposit money, as well as check the balance of their savings and checking accounts. Customers use an ATM bank card and a personal identification number to access their accounts through the ATM.

Point-of-sale systems. A **point-of-sale system** allows a consumer to directly transfer funds from a banking account to a merchant. For example, Jay buys a CD from Best Buy and pays for the CD with his debit card. The Best Buy employee swipes Jay's debit card to determine whether there are enough funds in Jay's account to pay for the CD. Jay signs a receipt like a credit card receipt, and the amount of the sale is charged to Jay's bank account.

Direct deposits and withdrawals. A **direct deposit** or withdrawal is a preauthorized action performed on a customer's account through an electronic terminal. For example,

connecting to the core

Financial Accounting

Direct deposit is an attractive method for corporations to use in paying employees as companies can control the timing of withdrawals from company bank accounts. In other words, every payroll day would show withdrawals from a company's bank account for each employee paid by direct deposit. The alternative to direct deposit is that companies would have to more closely monitor their company bank accounts after every payroll day, as some employees may take several days longer to cash or deposit their paychecks, and the amount within a company bank account would not necessarily reflect the amount remaining after each employee is paid. However, direct deposit simplifies payroll procedures only for those employees who choose to be paid by direct deposit. But what if certain employees still prefer to receive traditional paychecks? To further simplify payroll procedures, larger companies may choose to create special payroll accounts, from which these companies would issue regular checks or directly deposit funds in employees' accounts, depending on employees' preferences. Regardless, larger companies often prefer using payroll bank accounts because these companies can essentially use one check or one electronic transfer of funds from regular company accounts to payroll bank accounts, from which each employee would be paid. This separate payroll account allows a company to more easily reconcile transactions in a regular company account, because each payroll day shows up as one withdrawal from the regular account that is deposited into a payroll account.

Source: K. Larson, J. Wild, and B. Chiappetta, *Principles of Financial Accounting* (New York: McGraw-Hill/Irwin, 2005), p. 446.

an employee may now choose to have her paycheck directly deposited into her checking account instead of receiving a check from the employer. A customer can similarly authorize a direct withdrawal. For instance, a customer might have her phone bill directly withdrawn from his bank account each month.

Pay-by-telephone systems. Some merchants allow customers to use the telephone to make payments or transfer funds. For example, a customer may transfer money from a savings account to a checking account over the phone. Moreover, the IRS permits taxpayers to file and pay over the telephone.

Online purchases and banking. Various banks and credit card companies allow customers to engage in banking transactions online. Customers may access their account statements and transfer funds online. Similarly, credit card companies allow customers to make monthly payments. Companies are moving toward offering more and more online services.

CONSUMER FUND TRANSFERS

Consumer fund transactions are governed by the *Electronic Fund Transfer Act of 1978 (EFTA)*. This act sets out the rights and liabilities of the parties involved in electronic fund transfers. Regulation E of the act allows the Federal Reserve Board to issue rules and regulations to enforce EFTA. The following transactions are considered consumer fund transactions: transactions in which a retail customer pays for an item with a debit card that allows the customer's bank account to be instantly charged, ATM transactions, and direct deposits of paychecks.

Customer and bank rights and responsibilities. EFTA requires that merchants inform customers of their rights regarding EFTs. First, if a customer's ATM card is lost or stolen, the customer must notify the bank within two days. The customer is then liable for only the first $50 stolen. If the customer does not notify the bank, the customer will then be held liable for up to $500 that is stolen. Second, the bank has a duty to provide

global context

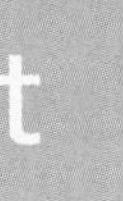

Electronic Fund Transfers in Australia

Customers in Australia make approximately 43,000 complaints about ATMs. The biggest complaint is that the machines are not reliable. In approximately 28,500 of those cases, the bank was found to be liable for the ATM problem. Overall, customers made about 70,000 complaints regarding some kind of electronic transfer.

Many customers have been confused about the fees generated by ATMs. Recently, banks agreed to spell out the fees imposed for ATM use by placing labels on the ATMs to educate consumers about the fees. A parliamentary report had earlier determined that banks were charging customers $2 more per transaction if the customer used another bank's ATM. This report suggested that the noncustomer fees be dropped completely. It is estimated that these fees generate approximately $600 million for big banks in Australia.

Source: Sherrill Nixon, "Banks Agree to Spell Out Confusing Bank Fees," *Sydney Morning Herald,* April 5, 2001, p. 4., and "Fed: ACCC Says Bank Fee Changes Could Hurt Country People," *AAP Newsfeed,* February 21, 2001.

a monthly statement that includes electronic fund transfers, and the customer has a duty to examine this bank statement for any unauthorized electronic fund transfers or errors. Third, the customer has a duty to notify the bank of any errors in the electronic transactions within 60 days of receiving the statement. Fourth, a bank is required to provide customers with receipts for electronic transactions. Finally, the bank must notify the customer that preauthorized payments may be stopped; however, the customer must stop the payment by notifying the bank at any time up to three days before the preauthorized payment is scheduled. While a customer may stop a preauthorized payment, a customer cannot order a stop payment on an EFT because such transfers occur instantaneously. The Case Nugget examines the relative responsibilities of the bank and customer.

Case Nugget — Overdraft Fees for Electronic Fund Transfers

Andrew Gale v. Hyde Park Bank
384 F.3d 451 (2004)

Andrew Gale made a purchase with his debit card in December 2001. When Gale overdrew his bank account in April 2002 because the funds from December had not been posted, he sued the bank. Gale claimed that he was entitled to losses because the bank had not made the electronic fund transfer in a timely manner. The bank's delay, Gale claimed, had led to his belief that there were more funds in the account than were actually available.

The district court dismissed Gale's claim, stating that the bank had actually posted the electronic fund transfer in a timely manner. The district court reported that the transfer had been posted within 48 hours of the bank's receiving notification. Gale then took the case to the Seventh Circuit of the U.S. Court of Appeals.

In the opinion written by Judge Easterbrook, the Seventh Circuit found that the bank had fulfilled its responsibilities. The bank had a responsibility to update the account statement as soon as it received notification of a withdrawal; no evidence was brought forth to the contrary. The bank, however, is not the only party to have responsibility; Gale has it as well. Gale's contract with the bank indicates that he has the responsibility to keep track of electronic fund transfers, just as he must when he writes a check. The Seventh Circuit found that the losses Gale experienced could be directly linked to Gale's failure to keep the account adequately funded. Thus, the court ruled that the bank was not liable for the losses accrued by Gale.

Unauthorized transfers. Under EFTA, an unauthorized electronic transfer is a federal felony punishable through criminal sanctions, such as a $10,000 fine or 10-year prison sentence. An electronic transfer is unauthorized if (1) it is initiated by a person who has no authority to transfer, (2) the customer receives no benefit from the transfer, and (3) the customer did not give his personal identification number to the unauthorized party.

When banks violate EFTA, consumers may recover actual and punitive damages, where the punitive damages total between $100 and $1,000. If the consumers are part of a class action suit, the punitive damages are capped at $500,000 or 1 percent of the institution's net worth.

COMMERCIAL FUND TRANSFERS

Because EFTA did not cover all situations where funds may be electronically transferred, Article 4(A) of the UCC was issued to address commercial fund transfers. An important type of commercial fund transfer is a wire transfer. Funds are "wired" between two commercial parties. There are two major payment systems that coordinate wire payments: the Federal Reserve wire transfer network (Fedwire) and the New York Clearing House Interbank Payments Systems (CHIPS). These two systems account for the transfer of more than $1 trillion daily. This sum is substantially more than is transferred by any other means.

E-Money and Online Banking

With the rapid advancements in technology, the banking system is also finding itself changing rapidly. Electronic payments, or e-payments, are becoming increasingly prevalent in daily life. Increasingly, bank transactions are being conducted electronically, marking a shift away from physical currency. In fact, it is possible for electronic forms of money to completely replace physical currency such as paper and coin money. **Digital cash,** money stored electronically on microchips, magnetic strips, or other computer media, would allow for the elimination of physical currency.

Helping to lead the digital banking revolution are the various forms of **e-money** (electronic money). The most common example of e-money is **stored-value cards.** Stored-value cards are typically plastic cards that contain magnetic strips. The magnetic strips, similar to those on credit cards or ATM cards, contain data regarding the value of the card. For example, suppose a new laundry facility opened up near your apartment. However, instead of your using quarters, the facility requires that you get a card and use a machine to put a balance on the card. Then, when you are ready to do your laundry, you insert the card into the washer and the cost of a load of laundry is deducted automatically from the card. Because the information regarding the amount on the card is stored in the magnetic strip on the card, the card is referred to as a *stored-value card.*

Another, newer, type of e-money is the **smart card.** Smart cards are the same size as regular check and ATM cards and look the same from the front. However, instead of having a magnetic strip, smart cards contain microchips for storing data. The advantage of the microchip over the magnetic strip is that the microchip can hold a far greater amount of data than a magnetic strip. However, because this is still a new technology, not all businesses are equipped to read smart cards yet. As the technology expands, expect to see a large influx in the use of smart cards.

Related to the expansion of technology in banking is the increase in use of online banking. With online banking, banks allow customers electronic access to their accounts so that they can check their accounts, transfer money, order payments, pay bills, check their investments, and, through some banks, even trade stock. While services vary from bank to bank, more banks are offering at least some form of online banking to their customers.

ONLINE BANKING SERVICES

Although online banking services vary among banks, as was previously stated, there are three services most banks with online banking offer. These three services are (1) bill consolidation and payment, (2) transfer of funds from one account to another, and (3) loan applications (an appearance at the bank to sign the loan is typically required to finalize the loan process). By offering the listed three services, banks help cut down on their own costs as well as allow customers greater control over their funds.

Despite the number of banking services offered online, not all banking services can be conducted over the Internet. For example, depositing and withdrawing funds are two services that cannot be conducted from a computer with an Internet connection. However, the smart-card technology might allow for withdrawals and deposits from home computers hooked up to the Internet. The microchips in the smart cards could be read by devices attached to a home computer, allowing for withdrawals or deposits; but this technology has not yet been developed and marketed to consumers.

REGULATORY COMPLIANCE

In the main, banks are in favor of the increased use of online banking. Part of the reason banks like online banking is it helps reduce the bank's operating cost and thus increase its profits. One way online banking reduces cost is through paperless billing. By not having to send paper statements to their customers, banks save on paper, ink, and envelopes, as well as postage. The bank posts all the information to the user's account online, which does not cost the bank much at all.

Another reason banks are in favor of online banking is that it decreases what is known as "float" time. *Float time* is the period between the time a check is written and the time it is presented for final payment, during which a customer can still use his or her funds. As the check does not have to transfer between banks, accounts can be credited or debited more quickly.

However, as with other areas of the Internet, it is not clear which laws apply to online banking. Part of the problem is related to the legal definition of *bank.* Banks are required by law to have a geographically defined market area, as well as to report to the proper authorities regarding their deposits and loans. The requirements just discussed are designed to ensure that all Americans have access to banks and that banks are not discriminating by choosing only certain locations for operation. The requirements are established primarily in two pieces of legislation: the Home Mortgage Disclosure Act, 12 U.S.C. Sections 2801–2810, and the Community Reinvestment Act (CRA) of 1977, 12 U.S.C. Sections 2901–2908. The CRA requires that a bank's market area surround the bank and be divided based on normal divisions, such as standard metropolitan areas or county lines.

The requirement of a defined market area poses a problem for cyberbanks. How exactly would a cyberbank establish a geographic market region? Consequently, banks with online services are in a bit of a gray area when it comes to legal compliance. Not only is it hard for banks to comply with the Home Mortgage Disclosure Act and the CRA, but it is not yet clear if the banks need to comply with these two laws.

PRIVACY PROTECTION

Are e-money institutions the same as traditional financial institutions? Do the same laws apply? These two questions hold the key to the question: How secure are e-payments and e-money? The answer is, We do not know.

E-money payment information. Which laws apply to e-money is still mostly untested legal ground. That is, there is little clarity regarding which laws do apply to e-money. The Federal Reserve has explicitly stated that Regulation E, which regulates traditional electronic fund transfers, does not apply to e-money transactions. Nonetheless, laws regarding computer files, not directly related to banking, might apply to e-money, such as laws against unauthorized access of electronic files or communication. There are several such laws regarding electronic files and communication, and it is not clear if they apply to e-money.

E-money issuer's financial records. In 1978 Congress passed the *Right to Financial Privacy Act* of 1978 [12 U.S.C. Section 3401 et seq]. Under the Right to Financial Privacy Act, financial institutions, such as banks, may not give a federal agency information regarding a person's finances without either that person's explicit consent or a warrant. The Right to Financial Privacy Act may apply to digital cash providers if the provider is considered a legal bank or credit provider that supplies customers with a card considered to be similar to a credit or debit card. However, given the lack of a physical location for the digital cash provider, it is also possible that the Right to Financial Privacy Act does not apply, in which case digital cash providers may release your financial information freely to any federal agency.

Consumer financial data. In an effort to further protect people's financial privacy, Congress passed the *Financial Services Modernization Act,* also known as the *Gramm-Leach-Bliley Act* (12 U.S.C. Sections 24a, 248b, 1820a, 1828b). The act's purpose is to control how financial institutions handle customer information, ultimately providing greater privacy protections to financial institution customers. Financial institutions are prohibited from disclosing personal information about their clients to third parties unless certain requirements set forth in the act are met. In addition, financial institutions are legally required to present customers with the institution's privacy policies and practices.

The Uniform Money Services Business Act

As online banking has been expanding over the last few years, state legislatures have been attempting to respond to the expansion with legislation. However, states have been sporadically and unpredictably passing regulations regarding money services. Given that e-money services operate in numerous states, the slapdash manner in which the laws have been passed makes conducting interstate business difficult for e-money businesses.

Due to the lack of uniformity, the National Conference of Commissioners on Uniform State Laws (NCCUSL) proposed a model state law regarding money transactions and financial transactions conducted by entities other than banks. A model state law does not have the force of law but is proposed as an example of a law that states can propose and adopt, hopefully creating symmetry among the various state laws. The proposed law, known as the *Uniform Money Services Business Act (UMSBA),* would affect online services and e-money services, as well as traditional money services.

TRADITIONAL MONEY SERVICES

Money service businesses do not face all the same regulations as those of traditional financial service businesses. The difference in regulations occurs because money service businesses do not engage in all the same services as do traditional financial service businesses. For example, money service businesses do not accept deposits. However, they do issue stored-value cards, money orders, and traveler's checks. In addition, money service businesses cash checks, exchange foreign currency, and transfer money, domestically and abroad. While the listed services prove helpful to a lot of people, the same services have been misused by a number of people. Customers do not typically have continuing relationships with the businesses and thus will use money service businesses to perpetrate money-based crimes, such as money laundering and financial terrorist activities.

The rules and restrictions set forth in UMSBA apply to persons or businesses that transfer money (such as wire transfers), cash checks, or exchange currency. In addition, UMSBA licenses businesses that engage in the three previously mentioned services. Furthermore, these licensed businesses are subject to state examinations and compliance with record-keeping requirements, as well as requirements that the business report all of its activities to the appropriate state board. Investment rules would also apply to these businesses under UMSBA. The impact of the investment rules means the licensed businesses would have to follow "safety and soundness rules" set forth in UMSBA to guarantee proper auditing and general financial soundness (UMSBA 2-204).

INTERNET-BASED MONEY SERVICES

Historically, Internet-based money services and e-money services have been treated differently than traditional money services, but UMSBA seeks to eliminate the differences. One way the law intends to accomplish this elimination of distinctions is by changing all references to "money" to "monetary value." The new term does not limit itself to traditional physical currency the way the old term does.

While the specific ramifications of the law are not clear, it would appear the following fall within UMSBA:

1. Stored-value cards, such as value-added cards, smart cards, and prepaid cards.
2. E-money systems to be used at home for payments over the Internet.
3. Internet scrip, which is the equivalent of money that is transferred electronically over the Internet but can still be redeemed for physical cash.

CASE OPENER WRAP-UP

Posting Checks from Highest to Lowest Dollar Amount

NationsBank, which became Bank of America, decided to settle the suit with the Pattersons, which had become a class action lawsuit. Bank of America agreed to pay a total of $5 million to customers who had an account that was subject to overdraft fees due to the high-to-low posting policy during the class period. However, each customer was permitted to collect only up to $50, the cost of fees for two bounced checks.

Other banks have agreed to settle class action suits. For example, CoreStates Bank agreed to a $2.2 million settlement in a high-to-low posting policy class action lawsuit. One court denied class certification to customers of an Alabama bank. Thus, as a bank manager, you should be aware of how many banks are settling these suits. Moreover, you should know whether the high-to-low posting policy is considered to be a reasonable commercial practice. How many banks actually use the high-to-low policy?

What kind of disclosure to the customers did you decide was adequate? Bank of America previously notified its customers of its high-to-low posting policy through a pamphlet it gave to the customers when they opened accounts. The pamphlet contained a notice similar to the following:

> If you make withdrawal requests which exceed the available funds in your account, we may honor any, all, or none of the amounts requested; and if we choose to honor any requests, we may pay the requests in any order we choose.

However, Bank of America changed its policy to give additional notification to customers by printing the policy on each monthly banking statement.

Summary

Checks

Draft: An instrument that is an order.

Drawer: The party that gives the order.

Drawee: The party that must obey the order.

Payee: The party that receives the benefit of the order.

Check: A special draft that orders the drawee, a bank, to pay a fixed amount of money on demand.

Cashier's check: A check in which both the drawer and the drawee of a check are the same bank.

Teller's check: A check that is drawn by one bank and usually drawn on another bank.

Traveler's check: An instrument that is payable on demand, is drawn on or through a bank, is designated by the phrase *traveler's check,* and requires a countersignature by a person whose signature appears on the instrument.

Money order: An instrument stating that a certain amount of money is to be paid to a particular person.

Certified check: A check that is accepted at the bank at which it is drawn.

Accepting Deposits

Depositary bank: The first bank that receives a check for payment.

Payor bank: The bank on which a check is drawn.

Collecting bank: Any kind of bank (besides the payor bank) that handles a check during the collection process.

Intermediary bank: Any bank (besides the payor bank and depositary bank) to which the check is transferred.

Truth-in-Savings Act: Federal act that requires that depositary institutions disclose, in great detail, the terms and conditions of their accounts.

When a Bank May Charge a Customer's Account

Properly payable rule: A bank may pay an instrument only when it is authorized by the drawer and does not violate the agreement between the bank and the customer.

Wrongful dishonor: A bank refuses to pay a properly payable check; the bank incurs liability.

Overdraft: If there are insufficient funds in the customer's account, the bank may (1) dishonor the check or (2) create an overdraft by paying the check and charging the account the amount short.

Stop-payment order: A drawer orders the drawee bank to not pay a check that has been drawn on the customer's account.

Postdated check: A customer can postdate a check but must give the bank notice of the postdated check.

Stale check: A check is not presented to a bank within six months of its date.

Death or incompetence of a customer: If the drawer of the check has died or is adjudicated incompetent, the bank, depending on its knowledge of the customer's death or incompetence, may or may not be authorized to pay the check.

Forgeries and alterations:

1. *Check bearing a forged signature:* Generally, the drawer is not liable for a forged check unless the drawer substantially contributed to the forgery.
2. *Check bearing a forged endorsement:* Neither the drawer nor the drawer's bank is liable for a forged endorsement.
3. *Altered check:* If an unauthorized change modifies the obligation of a party to the instrument, the drawer is generally not liable for the altered amount unless he or she negligently contributed to the alteration.

Electronic Fund Transfers

Money is transferred by an electronic terminal, telephone, or computer.

Types of EFT systems:

ATMs (automated teller machines): Machines connected to a bank's computer, located in convenient places, that allow customers to conduct banking transactions without actually going into a bank.

Point-of-sale system: System that allows a consumer to directly transfer funds from a bank account to a merchant.

Direct deposits and withdrawals: Preauthorized actions performed on a customer's account through an electronic terminal.

Pay-by-telephone system: System whereby merchants allow customers to use the telephone to make payments or transfer funds.

Online banking: System in which banks grant customers electronic access to account data to perform banking tasks, such as transferring funds between accounts, online.

E-Money and Online Banking

Digital cash: Money stored electronically on microchips, magnetic strips, or other computer media.

Stored-value cards: Plastic cards that contain magnetic strips, similar to those on credit cards or ATM cards, containing data regarding the value of the card.

Smart cards: Cards that are the same size as regular check and ATM cards but that contain microchips, instead of a magnetic strip, for storing larger amounts of data.

The Uniform Money Services Business Act

A model state law regarding money transactions and financial transactions conducted by entities other than banks; proposed by the National Conference of Commissioners on Uniform State Laws (NCCUSL) in an effort to create symmetry among the various state laws.

Point / Counterpoint

Should a Company Be Allowed to Require That Employees Receive Payment through Direct Deposit?

Yes

A company should be allowed to require that employees receive payment through direct deposit because direct-deposit payment is the most efficient form of payment for both employers and employees.

Direct deposit allows employers and employees security they would not have with mailed paychecks. Companies can keep track of employee payments more accurately when employees are paid through one payment method.

Through direct deposit, employers are assured that *all employees* are paid at the same time, on the same day. Neither employees nor employers need to be concerned with lost, stolen, delayed, or damaged paychecks.

Many people have already chosen the convenience of online banking for their other banking needs; adding direct deposit only simplifies their lives. In fact, studies show that the average worker spends between 8.5 and 24 hours each year cashing and depositing payroll checks.*

Direct deposit allows for a separate payroll account and more exact bookkeeping. The losses normally associated with stolen and doubled paychecks can be reinvested in the company, eventually allowing for potential salary/wage increases for all. Furthermore, a company saves a lot of money on paper costs alone by switching to direct deposit.

Many people willingly choose to directly deposit their paychecks. A company establishing a requirement of direct-deposit payment would only streamline and simplify the process for everyone involved.

*www.msmoney.com.

No

A company should not be allowed to require that its employees receive payment through direct deposit. While direct deposit is a good option for employers to provide to employees, the choice of payment form should be left to the employees.

First, very few guidelines have been established regarding direct-deposit procedures. Employees would not necessarily be provided an in-depth statement discussing the details of each pay period. With direct deposit, employees have more difficulty ensuring that pay statements are accurate.

Wage-based employees, for example, need to know exactly what they are paid per hour, for how many hours, so that the employees know whether they need to be paid overtime wages. Some direct-deposit statements list only the amount of money transferred to the employee's account.

Some employees simply prefer to literally hold and personally deposit a physical check. They also have a physical copy of their pay stub for paper records. The absence of a physical receipt creates "holes" in an individual's paper records. These holes can create problems when an individual gathers documents in preparation for tax season.

Direct deposit can also cause problems with an individual's banking practices. When money is automatically (though sometimes not regularly) deposited, the individual can have difficulty keeping track of deductions and bank account balances.

While companies can and should present to employees a list of the advantages of direct deposit, the ultimate decision should be left to the employees, because the employees are most heavily affected if their paychecks are not deposited properly.

Questions & Problems

1. Who are the three parties involved in the transfer of money through a check?
2. What types of banks are involved in the check collection process? How are these banks different?
3. Explain the difference between a stop payment and an overdraft.
4. Explain the reason for the following policy: A customer has a duty to examine his or her bank statement.
5. Evaluate the following statement: "If a signature on a check is forged, the customer will never be responsible for the amount on the check."
6. IBP, Inc., issued and delivered a check payable for $135,234.18 to Meyer Cattle Company and Sylvan State Bank. IBP wrote the check on its account at Mercantile Bank. Sylvan Bank was listed as a payee because it had a security interest in Meyer's cattle. Meyer subsequently lost the check. The check was found nine years later, and Tim Meyer endorsed the check for deposit at Sylvan Bank. Sylvan's vice president also endorsed the check. When Mercantile Bank received the check, it withdrew the money from IBP's account. After discovering that the bank had cashed the check, IBP contacted the bank and demanded reimbursement. It claimed that the bank had improperly honored the stale instrument and had an obligation to return the funds. IBP brought a lawsuit against Meyer, Sylvan Bank, and Mercantile Bank. How do you think the court decided? [*IBP, Inc. v. Mercantile Bank of Topeka,* 6 F. Supp. 2d 1258 (1998).]
7. Andrew Daniels issued a check in the amount of $575 to Advance America. Advance America apparently agreed to hold the check until a certain date, and if Daniels had not paid the amount of the check to Advance America by that date, it would present the check to Daniels's bank, Charter One, for payment. According to Daniels, he satisfied the obligation owed to Advance America, yet Advance America presented his check to Charter One for payment. Therefore, Daniels paid Charter One a fee to place a stop-payment order on his check to Advance America. Despite the stop-payment order, Daniels alleged that Charter One processed his check to Advance America. As a result of Charter One's failure to honor the stop-payment order, Daniels contended that he was charged additional fees by Charter One because his account did not contain sufficient funds to pay the amount of the check to Advance America. Daniels also contended that Charter One knew that negative information concerning the incident "would be reported to the credit bureau, put on the Internet, and placed on [his] driver's license." Daniels sued, and the district court dismissed his claims. Daniels appealed. Was Daniels successful on appeal? Why or why not? [*Daniels v. Charter One Bank,* 39 Fed. Appx. 223 (2002).]
8. Margaret Glodt died on February 26, 1996. Lisa S. Mac was appointed as administrator of her estate. James Glodt, Margaret's nephew, refused to turn over Margaret's checkbooks. Margaret had checking accounts at two banks. Mac closed the accounts on November 27, 1996. She received statements from both banks around February 1997. She realized that most of the funds had been withdrawn from the accounts around the time of Margaret's death. Mac obtained copies of the checks and learned they were forgeries. James had forged the checks before Margaret's death, but the banks did not make payment until shortly after her death. Mac sued both of the banks. The banks claimed that Mac's action was precluded by the one-year time limit for a

customer to discover and report a check with an unauthorized signature. How do you think the court decided? [*Mac v. Bank of America,* 76 Cal. App. 562 (1999).]

9. Speer and Ventura Classics sold used automobiles to each other. On receipt of five drafts paying for automobiles, totaling $87,750, Bank of Texas gave Speer immediate credit, and Speer withdrew the funds before the drafts were presented to State Bank for payment or collection. When State Bank received the forwarded drafts, it called Ventura's representative, who did not authorize payment. Accordingly, State Bank returned the drafts to Bank of Texas unpaid. On receipt of the returned drafts, Bank of Texas resubmitted the drafts to State Bank. In response to the second receipt of the drafts, an employee of State Bank, not authorized to do so, issued a cashier's check in the amount of $87,750 to pay for the drafts. The following day, State Bank informed Bank of Texas that the cashier's check had been issued mistakenly, without authorization. Consequently, a stop-payment order was placed on the check. Bank of Texas claimed to have received the check and submitted it for payment prior to receipt of notice of the stop-payment order. The district court ruled that State Bank was not liable on Bank of Texas's claims because State Bank was not a payor of the drafts but, rather, a collecting bank. Bank of Texas appealed. Was Bank of Texas successful on appeal? Was State Bank a payor or collecting bank? [*State Bank & Trust v. First State Bank,* 2000 U.S. App. LEXIS 33359 (2000).]

10. David Marx maintained a checking account with Whitney National Bank. Marx's January 1995 statement contained evidence of five forged checks totaling $2,373. Marx never reviewed the statement. He added his two children, Stanley Marx and Maxine Marx, to the account in April 1995. Stanley Marx reviewed the May 1995 bank statement and discovered 17 forged checks totaling almost $13,000. Five of these checks, totaling $10,000, appeared for the first time on the May statement. Joel Goodman, David Marx's grandson, was both the maker and the payee of the forged instruments. The Marxes admitted that Joel had access to his grandfather's checkbook whenever he visited Marx. Marx filed suit against Whitney, asserting that it was obligated to restore the $10,000 to his checking account. Marx admitted that he was negligent for not looking at his January through April statements; he asked only for recovery of the forged checks identified in the May statement. Whitney claimed that Marx failed to exercise reasonable care in the handling of his account. Do you think the court found for Marx? Why or why not? [*Marx v. Whitney National Bank,* 713 So. 2d 1142 (1998).]

11. Bruce Rickett presented a check to Commerce Bank issued to him on January 3, 1998, by DeSimone Auto in the amount of $12,000. The check was actually dated January 3, 1997. The check was for the sale of a car, and the two parties had an understanding that the check would not be presented for payment if the car was damaged. Shortly after writing the check, DeSimone found damage on the car. DeSimone returned the car to Rickett and issued a stop payment on the check. Rickett had already presented the check for payment on January 5, 1998, and had drawn against it. The bank argued that it was a holder in due course of the check and demanded payment from DeSimone. DeSimone contended that the date of "January 3, 1997," affected the validity of the check. The bank noted that, during the first few weeks of a new year, it is commonplace for customers to write the wrong year date. DeSimone argued that the check was overdue because it was not received 90 days after the date on the check. How do you think the court decided? [*Commerce Bank v. Rickett,* 748 A.2d 111 (2000).]

12. Two New Jersey casinos cashed checks totaling $143,000 drawn by Seigel, one of its patrons, on his cash management account at Merrill Lynch. Seigel placed a stop-payment order on the checks, but Merrill Lynch paid them by mistake. Merrill Lynch

argued that it "stood in the shoes" of the casinos to whom valid and enforceable checks were given and therefore Seigel had not suffered any actual loss as a result of the payment of the check. The trial court granted summary judgment for Merrill Lynch. How do you think the case was decided on appeal? [*Seigel v. Merrill Lynch,* 745 A.2d 301 (2000).]

13. On November 30, 2000, Wal-Mart issued a check made payable to Alcon Laboratories, Inc., in the amount of $563,288.95, written on a Wachovia Bank checking account. Wal-Mart mailed the check, but Alcon never received it. On December 7, 2000, an individual named Pit Foo Wong deposited the check in his account at Asia Bank. The payee on the check had been altered from "Alcon Laboratories, Inc." to "Pit Foo Wong." In accordance with Federal Reserve procedures, Asia Bank presented the check to the Federal Reserve Bank (FRB) of New York, which then presented the check to the FRB in Richmond. On December 8, 2000, the FRB presented the check to Wachovia, and Wachovia issued payment. Wachovia, in accordance with its internal policy, did not manually review the copy of the check presented by the FRB. However, it did review the check information through an electronic tracking system. No fraud was detected at this time. Although the employees at Asia Bank allowed Wong to deposit the check, their suspicions were aroused by his deposit of over $500,000 and a hold was placed on the funds. Asia Bank twice contacted Wal-Mart, which informed Asia Bank that the check was "good." After determining that Alcon had not received the check, Alcon called Wal-Mart. Wal-Mart indicated that the check had been paid and its policy was to wait 30 days before tracing missing checks. When Wal-Mart discovered the Alcon check had been altered, it notified Wachovia, which sought reimbursement from Asia Bank. By this time the hold expired and Wong wired the money out of his account. Asia Bank refused to reimburse Wachovia, and Wachovia brought suit against the FRB for breach of presentment and transfer warranties under the UCC and federal regulations. The FRB filed a third-party complaint against Wal-Mart, alleging that Wal-Mart's failure to exercise ordinary care substantially contributed to the alteration of the check. The district court granted summary judgment in favor of both Wachovia and Wal-Mart. The parties appealed. How do you think the court ruled on appeal? Should Wal-Mart have detected the alteration earlier? [*Wachovia Bank, N.A. v. FRB,* 338 F.3d 318 (2003).]

Looking for more review material?

The Online Learning Center at **www.mhhe.com/kubasek1e** contains this chapter's "Assignment on the Internet" and also a list of URLs for more information, entitled "On the Internet." Find both of them in the Student Center portion of the OLC, along with quizzes and other helpful materials.

Secured Transactions

CASE OPENER

The Underpriced Boat

Alan H. Terris purchased a powerboat from OxBow Marina, Inc., an affiliate of General Motors. Terris planned to pay for the boat in installments and signed an agreement stating he would pay the total amount of the boat, $109,090.91, in 83 monthly payments of $673.93 and one final payment of $53,154.52. Under this agreement, General Motors Acceptance Corporation (GMAC) had the right to repossess the boat if he did not make his monthly payments.

Almost three years later, Terris was unable to make his monthly payments, and General Motors Acceptance Corporation repossessed the boat. After advertising the sale, GMAC sold the boat for $26,000. At the time of the sale, the amount that Terris owed GMAC for the boat was $65,350.42, so GMAC sought to recover the balance of $39,350.42 in court. However, Terris argued that the boat was sold for a price much lower than it was worth. He noted that the *N.A.D.A. Large Boat Appraisal Guide* indicated that the plaintiff's boat had a high book value of $53,010, an average book value of $43,470, and a low book value of $33,930, and that his boat was in good condition.[1]

1. If you were the judge deciding this case, would you grant GMAC the full $39,350.42 deficiency?
2. Suppose that you were the manager of GMAC. How could you ensure that you would receive full reimbursement for this boat and for every other item you repossess and sell?

The Wrap-Up at the end of the chapter will answer these questions.

[1] *General Motors Acceptance Corp. v. Terris; Memorandum of Decision, Connecticut Law Tribune.*, October 31, 1994, at 1125.

CHAPTER 30

Learning Objectives

After reading this chapter, you will be able to answer the following questions:

1. What are the important definitions associated with secured transactions?
2. How are secured interests created?
3. How are secured interests perfected?
4. What is the scope of a security interest?
5. How are disputes regarding priority handled?
6. What is default?

The agreement made between GMAC and Terris before Terris purchased the boat is a common component of business transactions. Such agreements are called *secured transactions.* A **secured transaction** is a transaction in which the payment of a debt is guaranteed by personal property owned by the debtor. In the case of Terris, he guaranteed that he would pay his debt (the debt he owes for the boat) by giving GMAC rights to the boat. In other words, he said, "If I don't pay you everything, you can take the boat from me."

Put yourself in the position of a creditor. If you were making a loan to someone, you would want to somehow ensure that the person repays you. If he does not repay you, you can take the secured property or asset to defray the damages associated with the individual's nonpayment. In contrast, a creditor that does not have a secured interest must file a lawsuit, obtain a judgment, and execute on the judgment to recover money for the unpaid debt.

Article 9 of the Uniform Commercial Code (UCC) governs secured transactions in personal property (as opposed to real property). Thus, throughout the chapter, we will refer to Article 9 of the UCC. As you learned earlier in this book, the National Conference of Commissioners of Uniform State Laws (NCCUSL) is a group of lawyers that researches and drafts legislation to provide uniform law across states. In 1998, NCCUSL approved a new version of Article 9. This version was submitted to the states in 1999 and became effective in most states in 2001. As of June 30, 2006, with some variation, all states have enacted Article 9. Thus, while the law governing secured transactions is state law, the states' enactment of Article 9 permits us to summarize across all states to discuss laws regarding secured transactions.

In the first section of this chapter, we examine the concepts and terms associated with the secured transactions. Then, in the second section, we examine how secured transactions are created. In the third section, we consider how secured parties protect their interest in collateral through perfection, and, in the fourth section, we examine the types of collateral that can be used in secured transactions. In the fifth section, we examine the various conflicts that occur among parties who have interests in secured transactions. Finally, in the sixth section, we explain the remedies associated with a debtor's default of a loan.

Important Definitions Associated with Secured Transactions

It is important to understand the definitions of the terms used in secured transactions to understand how secured transactions are created. These definitions generally come from the UCC's definition of the terms:

1. A **secured interest** is an "interest in personal property or fixtures which secures payment or performance of an obligation" [UCC Section 1-201(37)]. Suppose Best Buy sells you a laptop on credit. Best Buy retains a secured interest in the laptop, which means that the store can repossess the laptop if you fail to make payments on the laptop.
2. A **secured party** is the person or party that holds the interest in the secured property. Thus, in the example above, Best Buy is the secured party. The secured party is also known as the *secured creditor.*
3. A **debtor** is the person or party that has an obligation to the secured party, the person who owns the interest in the secured property. You, the laptop owner, are the debtor because you have an obligation to make payments.

Exhibit 30-1
Collateral under the UCC

1. Goods (consumer goods, farm products, inventory, equipment, fixtures, and accessories)
2. Indispensable paper (documents of title, negotiable instruments, investment property, and chattel paper)
3. Intangibles (accounts, goodwill, literary rights)
4. Proceeds

4. A **security agreement** is the agreement in which the debtor gives the secured interest to the secured party. Thus, when you made the agreement with Best Buy, you created a security agreement.
5. **Collateral** is the property that is subject to the security interest. In the Best Buy example, the laptop is the collateral. Exhibit 30-1 lists different types of collateral under the UCC.

Creation of Secured Interests

How does a creditor become a secured party? To become a secured party, the creditor must gain a security interest in the collateral of the debtor. The secured party must take three steps to create the security interest:

1. The two parties create a security agreement and either (a) there is a record of the security agreement (usually a written agreement that describes the collateral and is signed by the debtor) or (b) the secured party is in possession of the collateral.
2. The secured party must give value to get the security agreement.
3. The debtor has a right in or to the collateral. [UCC 9-203(b)].

Once these three criteria are met, the secured party's rights attach to the collateral. When **attachment** occurs, the creditor becomes the secured party who has a security interest in the collateral. Let's examine these criteria a little more closely.

WRITTEN AGREEMENT

The written agreement, often referred to as the **security agreement,** must be signed by the debtor. Moreover, the agreement must describe the collateral. The description of the collateral must be accurate and detailed enough such that the description reasonably identifies the collateral. For example, in a description of a laptop that is serving as collateral, the serial number of the laptop might be listed in the written agreement. Let's go back to the GMAC case. The security agreement between Terris and GMAC/OxBow Marina, Inc., most likely included the following: (1) a statement that Terris was buying the boat on credit from GMAC/OxBow Marina; (2) a statement that GMAC/OxBow Marina is retaining a security interest in the boat; (3) a description of the boat as well as its serial number; (4) the price of the boat as well as the amount of the monthly payments due to GMAC/OxBow; and (5) a description of the process of GMAC/OxBow's repossessing the boat.

It is important that the collateral be described clearly in the written agreement because the creditor could lose its rights to the collateral if it is not described clearly. For example, Community First Bank gave a loan to Bakersfield Westar Ambulance, Inc. Bakersfield also happened to have an account with Community First Bank, so when Bakersfield fell behind on its loan, the bank took money from the account to satisfy the loan. Bakersfield sued on grounds that the bank did not have a right to "set off" these funds. Community First Bank argued that in its security agreement, the collateral was described as "all personal property of any kind which is delivered to or in the possession of the bank." The court found that this description was not clear enough because neither the specific account nor bank accounts in general were addressed; thus, the court ruled in favor of Bakersfield Westar Ambulance, Inc.[2]

VALUE

The secured party must give value. What exactly does it mean to "give value"? According to the UCC, value is consideration. Thus, in the boat example, the use of the boat was considered the value that GMAC gave to Terris. Alternatively, suppose you receive a loan from a company. The money is the value given by the company, the secured party.

DEBTOR RIGHTS IN THE COLLATERAL

The final criterion necessary for the attachment of the security interest is the debtor's rights in the collateral. Terris, the buyer of the boat, had a legal right to the boat (the collateral) after he signed his agreement.

PURCHASE-MONEY SECURITY INTEREST

Now that we have discussed the criteria necessary for the creation of a security interest, we briefly consider one specific type of security interest, the **purchase-money security interest (PMSI),** which is formed when a debtor uses borrowed money from the secured party to buy the collateral.

According to the UCC, a PMSI exists when a security interest is retained or taken by (1) the seller of the collateral to secure part or all of the purchase price *or* (2) a person who gives something of value to the debtor so the debtor can gain rights to or use of the collateral (9-103). In our laptop example, you bought the laptop on credit from Best Buy. Best Buy extended credit to you for the entire purchase price of the laptop. In other words, Best Buy is lending you the money to buy the laptop. Because the laptop is the collateral, the dealership has a PMSI.

The examples we have used in this chapter thus far have been examples of PMSIs. What is an example of a secured transaction in which the secured party does *not* have a PMSI? Suppose your company borrows money from the bank to purchase parts that will be placed into your company's product. As collateral, the bank takes a security interest in the company's deposit accounts, held at the bank. As you read the Global Context box on secured transactions in South Korea, consider the differences between the loans given in the United States and the loans given in South Korea.

Perfected Security Interest

Suppose that you borrow money from a bank and the bank has a secured interest in your wedding ring. You are supposed to make monthly payments to the bank, but you lose your job and suddenly cannot make the payments. When you fail to make these payments, you **default** on the loan. Because the bank has a secured interest in your ring, it can repossess your ring when you default on the loan.

But suppose you also borrowed money from another creditor, your boss, and you used your ring as collateral for that transaction. Your boss was unaware that you used the ring as

[2] "Security Agreement Did Not Assure Bank's Security Interest," *Commercial Lending Litigation News,* October 3, 1997.

global context

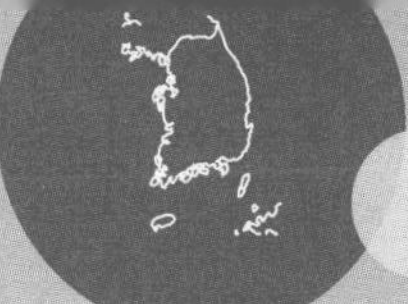

Secured Transactions in South Korea

South Korean law categorizes secured transactions as either personal security or real rights. Personal security is obtained when a surety, who acts as a third party, is designated as being liable for the fulfillment of contractual obligations when the debtor fails to act. If such a situation arises, the surety is responsible for compensation damages in addition to the original obligations.

The most popular type of secured transaction in South Korea is a *yangdo tambo,* which means "security by transfer of title." A *yangdo tambo* is appropriate when a debtor is seeking a loan. To receive the loan, the debtor must transfer the title of the collateral to the creditor. Once the loan has been paid in full, the title will be returned to the debtor. Throughout the transaction, the creditor retains control of the collateral. *Yangdo tambo,* despite its commonality, is not enumerated in South Korean law. Its use and acceptance arises from customary practices.

collateral for your bank loan. Both your boss and your bank have an interest in your ring. Who gets the ring? The party that *perfects* its interest in the ring will have first claim to the ring.

When a party perfects its interest in collateral, it is legally protecting its claim to the collateral. **Perfection** is defined as the series of legal steps a secured party takes to protect its right in the collateral from other creditors who wish to have their debts returned through the same collateral. We consider below the various methods of perfection.

PERFECTION BY FILING

The most common way to perfect an interest is to file a financing statement with a state agency. According to the UCC, a **financing statement** should list the names and addresses of all the parties involved, a description of the collateral, and the signature of the debtor (UCC Section 9-502). First, the names and addresses of the statement are important elements because someone looking for the financing statement may wish to contact the secured party or the debtor. Second, the financing statement must be filed under the name of the debtor whether the debtor is an individual, a partnership, or a corporation. If the statement is filed under an incorrect name, the perfection is likely not effective. Third, the financing statement must include a description of the collateral. The purpose of including a description of the collateral is to inform other potential parties who might wish to lend money to the debtor. The description of the collateral may be replicated from the description of the collateral in the security agreement.

Once the financing statement is filed, the statement becomes public knowledge. Parties considering making a loan to another party are expected to reasonably look for notification of secured interests. Consequently, if you asked to borrow money from your boss, your boss should check with state agencies to ensure that you have not already used your ring as collateral. If your boss discovered that your bank has perfected its interest in your ring, your boss should not agree to loan you money with the ring as your collateral because the bank's perfection of the security interest means that the ring will go directly to the bank. Your boss would have a claim against the ring only as an unsecured creditor.

Place and duration of filing. Suppose you need to file a financing statement. Where should you file? For how long is the filing effective? The place of filing depends on whether the debtor is an individual or a business. If the debtor is an individual, the secured party files the financing statement in the state in which the debtor resides. Prior to the 1998 Article 9 revision, the secured party was required to file the financing statement in the state in which the collateral was located. Alternatively, if the debtor is a registered business, the secured party files the financing statement in the state in which the business's certificate of organization was issued. If the debtor is an unregistered business, the secured party files the financing statement in the state where the chief executive office of the business is located. Finally, if the debtor is a foreign person or business, the secured party files the financing statement in Washington, D.C.

The actual place of filing changes from state to state. Sometimes the statements are filed with the secretary of state. Alternatively, the statements might be filed with the county clerk. Under the 1999 version of Article 9, each state must establish a central filing office.

Once you have filed the financing statement with the correct agency, for how long is the statement valid? Under the UCC, the statement is valid for five years (9-515). After the five years, the statement expires, and the security interest is not protected. However, within six months of the expiration date of the financing statement, the secured party can file a continuation statement, which is valid for another five years.

PERFECTION BY POSSESSION

Sometimes a debtor gives a creditor the collateral to hold until the loan is paid off. For example, suppose that you borrow money from a bank and give the bank your diamond necklace to hold until you pay back the loan. The transfer of the collateral to the secured party is called a **pledge.** When the bank takes possession of the necklace, it has perfected its interest without filing a financing statement. Once you pay off the loan, the necklace is returned to you.

There are several advantages associated with perfection by possession. First, a secured party does not have to go through the hassle of filing a financing statement. In fact, the parties do not have to even create a written security agreement. Second, there is little chance that another party will loan money to the debtor relying on the collateral that another secured party possesses. Third, if the debtor defaults on the loan, the secured party already has possession of the collateral, so there is no hassle in trying to repossess.

Despite the many advantages of perfection by possession, it is often impractical because the debtor cannot benefit from the use of the collateral. For example, if you get a loan from a bank to purchase farm equipment, you likely need the farm equipment to produce crops that will enable you to make payments on the loan. As you read the Global Context box on secured transactions in Indonesia, think about the relationship between U.S. laws with respect to perfection by possession and Indonesian practices of security by possession.

Certain types of collateral *must* be perfected through possession. These types of collateral include **instruments**—writings that serve as evidence of rights to payment of money, such as certificates of deposit—and stocks and bonds.

AUTOMATIC PERFECTION

If a retailer had to file a financing statement every time it sold on credit a laptop, a wide-screen television, or a washer and dryer, the retailer would do nothing but file statements. Moreover, it does not make sense for the retailer to possess the collateral. Thus, when a creditor sells a consumer good to a debtor on a credit basis or a creditor extends a loan to a debtor for the purchase of a consumer good, the security interest in the good perfects automatically. Under the UCC, a **consumer good** is a good used or bought for use primarily for personal, family, or household purposes [9-102(23)]. Thus, if an item is purchased for business use, the security interest would not perfect automatically; the secured party would have to file a financing statement.

global context

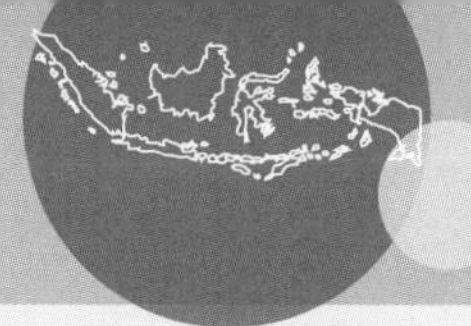

Secured Transactions in Indonesia

Rights governing secured transactions in Indonesia are subdivided into two categories. The first category includes security rights conferred by law. According to the Indonesian Civil Code, both movable and immovable assets belonging to the debtor constitute security. Thus, the creditors have equal preference over the debtor's assets unless otherwise specified in the contract.

The second category of security rights includes those created by private agreement. These include mortgages, pledges, and fiduciary transfers. Only mortgages and pledges are legally recognized for creating security interests over movable and immovable property. Mortgages govern immovable property, which is mostly land, while pledges act as security for tangible items, such as cars, and intangibles, such as patent rights. For a pledge to be legitimate, there must be physical transfer of the secured assets. The growing commercial market of Indonesia demanded a more flexible method of transfer for movable goods. In response to this need, fiduciary transfers have emerged. Fiduciary transfers require only a theoretical transfer of security rights, not a physical one as pledges do. Despite their commonality and popularity, these fiduciary transfers are not recognized in the Civil Code. This lack of recognition is in part explained by the novelty of this type of security.

The example of the sale of a consumer good in the previous paragraph is an example of a PMSI. When a PMSI in a consumer good is created, the security interest is automatically perfected; the creditor does not need to file a financing statement. However, if the PMSI is in a fixture or a motor vehicle, the security interest is *not* automatically perfected.

Clearly, the designation of property as a consumer good has important business ramifications. Case 30-1 considers whether a particular good should be classified as a consumer good or a motor vehicle.

CASE 30-1

GERALD GAUCHER v. COLD SPRINGS RV CORP.
SUPREME COURT OF NEW HAMPSHIRE
142 N.H. 299 (1997)

In May 1990, Gerald Gaucher entered into a "Retail Installment Contract and Security Agreement" with Cold Springs RV Corp. This agreement provided for the purchase of a travel trailer. In the agreement, Gaucher agreed to pay $320 a month for seven years and granted Cold Spring a security interest in the trailer.

The agreement also stated that Gaucher's failure to make a timely payment would be considered default and would result in Cold Springs' repossession of the trailer. Gaucher's payments were not timely, and he fell behind in the payments. After various payment failures for a year and a half, Cold Springs notified Gaucher that it was going to repossess the trailer unless they received full payment. Cold Spring repossessed the trailer and sold it without giving Gaucher notice of the sale. Gaucher brought a suit against Cold Springs for violating the Uniform Commercial Code. The trial court ruled in favor of Gaucher, ruling that the trailer was a consumer good. Cold Springs appealed.

JUDGE HORTON: The defendant argued below that its repossession and sale of the plaintiff's travel trailer was not governed by Article 9 of the Uniform Commercial Code because the travel trailer was a motor vehicle governed solely by RSA chapter 361-A (concerning retail installment sales of motor vehicles) and RSA 261:23-:29 (governing security interests in vehicles). The defendant also argued that the plaintiff was not entitled to the specific damages provided by RSA 382-A:9-507(1) for consumer goods because the travel trailer was not a consumer good. The superior court assumed without deciding that the travel trailer was a motor vehicle, but rejected the defendant's contention that the motor vehicle statutes rendered the default, repossession, and disposition provisions of Article 9 inapplicable. The superior court further concluded that the travel trailer was a consumer good because the plaintiff used it for personal purposes. Ruling that the defendant failed to provide the notice required by RSA 382-A:9-504(3), the court awarded the plaintiff the specific damages applicable to consumer goods under RSA 382-A:9-507(1).

Relying on Laro v. Leisure Acres Mobile Home Park Associates, 139 N.H. 545, 548, 659 A.2d 432, 435 (1995), the defendant now argues that the travel trailer was not a consumer good because it "functioned essentially as real estate," not personal property. Assuming without deciding that the defendant's general challenge below to the travel trailer's status as a consumer good is sufficient to preserve this new legal theory, cf. Riverwood Commercial Prop's v. Cole, 134 N.H. 487, 490, 593 A.2d 1153, 1155-56 (1991), we conclude that the defendant's reliance on Laro is misplaced. In Laro, the mobile home at issue was manufactured housing, which by statute was treated as real estate.

In this case, the defendant cites no persuasive legal authority to support its contention that a travel trailer is akin to real estate. Both the factual record and decisions from other jurisdictions support the superior court's conclusion that the travel trailer was a consumer good. The plaintiff submitted an affidavit stating that "at all times the Travel Trailer was used for personal, family and household purposes." We hold that the superior court properly focused on the travel trailer's use by the plaintiff and correctly characterized the travel trailer as a consumer good.

AFFIRMED.

CRITICAL THINKING

What was the primary issue in this case, and what reasons did the judge of this court use to support his conclusion? Would the judge have concluded differently if he found that the mobile home was *not* a consumer good? Why or why not?

ETHICAL DECISION MAKING

Return to the WPH process of ethical decision making. The public disclosure test is closely related to this case. The UCC requires that a creditor *notify* the debtor of the sale of repossessed goods, and Cold Springs RV Corp. did not do so. It is quite possible that the reason Cold Springs did not let Gaucher know about the sale of the RV was because it was doing something it did not want him to know about. Would this behavior pass the public disclosure test?

PERFECTION OF MOVABLE COLLATERAL

Suppose you borrow money from a bank in Ohio to buy farm equipment. This bank files a financing statement in Ohio and perfects its interest in the equipment. As collateral, you use your coin collection. However, after a year, you move to Indiana and bring your farm equipment with you. After you are in Indiana for a few months, you decide to take out a loan from a bank in Indiana, and you use your coin collection as collateral again. If the bank in Indiana tries to search for a financing statement in Indiana, it will obviously not find one. What happens if you default on your loans?

According to the UCC, a security interest in collateral that has been perfected in one state will generally transfer to another state for a period of four months from the date that

Exhibit 30-2
Summary of Methods of Perfection by Type of Collateral

Perfection by Filing

1. *Chattel paper:* Writing that indicates the debtor's monetary obligation as well as a secured interest
2. *Documents of title:* Papers that demonstrate the owner's possession of the goods (e.g., warehouse receipts)
3. *Accounts:* Rights to payments for goods sold or leased
4. *General intangibles:* Trademarks, copyrights, patents, etc.
5. *Equipment:* Goods purchased primarily for business use
6. *Farm products:* Products of livestock or crops
7. *Inventory:* Goods held for sale or lease
8. *Fixtures:* Goods that have become attached to real estate

Automatic Perfection

Purchase-money security interests in consumer goods

Perfection by Possession

1. Chattel paper
2. Documents of title
3. Instruments (stocks, bonds, checks, etc.)
4. Equipment

Perfection of Interests in Motor Vehicles

Notation of secured interest on certificate of title

the property is brought into the state. The secured party may reperfect the interest in the new state. However, if the interest is not reperfected, the secured party loses its protection.

For example, Versity Sodding Service, a landscaping and nursery business, borrowed $450,000 in 1990 from First Eastern Bank, N.A., of Wilkes Barre, Pennsylvania, to finance the purchase of landscaping equipment. The bank took as collateral security for its loan a lien on inventory, machinery, equipment, furniture, and fixtures. In accordance with Pennsylvania law, the bank filed its agreement with the secretary of state in Pennsylvania. After 1990, Versity moved the equipment first to Maryland and then to New Jersey. Versity eventually filed bankruptcy while in New Jersey. When the bank sought to collect its collateral, both the bankruptcy court and the district court held that the bank had lost its security interest in the equipment because it failed to perfect by the filing of financing statements in the state of New Jersey.[3]

PERFECTION OF SECURITY INTERESTS IN AUTOMOBILES AND BOATS

We have now discussed various methods of perfection: perfection by filing, perfection by possession, automatic possession, and perfection of movable collateral. Exhibit 30-2 provides a summary of the methods of perfection. None of these methods apply to perfection of automobiles and boats. Each state has created special laws that pertain to perfection of motor vehicles.

[3] Marvin Krasny and Kevin J. Carey, "Third Circuit Court Decides Issue of Moveable Goods under UCC," *Legal Intelligencer,* April 24, 1998, p. 5.

Almost every state requires a certificate of title for any motor vehicle. Perfection of a security interest in a motor vehicle occurs when the secured party makes a notation of this interest on the certificate of title. The rationale for noting the interest on the title is that the title will (theoretically) follow the car owner everywhere. Thus, the title would be the best place to note a secured interest. If a creditor examines a title and discovers no notation of a secured interest in the vehicle, the creditor can assume that no other creditors have a secured interest in the vehicle. Let's go back to the chapter opening case again. By noting the secured interest on the title of Terris's boat, GMAC is automatically preventing Terris from using the boat as collateral for another loan.

The Scope of a Security Interest

Generally, once a secured party perfects its interest in collateral, the perfection is effective until the collateral is sold, exchanged, or transferred. Our examination of security interests to this point has been concerned with property the debtor currently possesses. However, a security interest can also apply to personal property that is not yet in the debtor's possession.

AFTER-ACQUIRED PROPERTY

You borrow $60,000 from your bank to start an electronics store. However, you have recently graduated from college and have only your car, valued at $3,500, as collateral. The bank will take a security interest in your car, but it will also take a security interest in the materials that you will purchase to open your store. For example, you will need to create an inventory of televisions, computers, and stereos, which are **after-acquired property**, property acquired by the debtor after the security agreement is made. After-acquired property can be inventory, livestock, equipment, or almost any other kind of property. Under the UCC, a party may agree, through a clause in the security agreement, that the security interest will attach to after-acquired property. Whenever the debtor purchases new equipment or goods, the security interest is attached to the new good. Thus, whenever you buy a television to sell in your store, the bank's security interest in the television is attached.

PROCEEDS

When a debtor sells collateral, he or she receives **proceeds**, something that is exchanged for collateral. The secured party automatically has an interest in the proceeds. Why? If you use a good as collateral for a bank loan and then sell that good, the bank has nothing to secure its loan to you. Consequently, the security interest in the good also applies to the proceeds from the good.

Under the UCC, the secured party's interest in the proceeds lasts only 10 days after the debtor receives the proceeds. At that time, the secured party will typically need to file a new financing statement. The parties may also agree in the security agreement that there will be extended coverage of interest in the proceeds.

Termination of a Security Interest

Suppose that rather than defaulting on his loan payment, Terris paid GMAC the full amount for his boat as required under the agreement: $109,090.91. If a secured party has filed a financing statement and the debtor has repaid the secured party, the secured party must file a termination statement with the filing office. A **termination statement** is an amendment to a financing statement that states that the debtor has no obligation to the secured party [UCC Section 9-513(a)]. After repayment by the debtor, the secured party has one month to file the termination statement. However, if the debtor makes a written request to the secured party to file the termination statement, the secured party has 20 days to file the termination statement [UCC 9-513(b)]. If the secured party does not file a termination statement, the debtor may recover $500 from the secured party [UCC 9-625(e)].

Priority Disputes

We have spent much time discussing the perfection of a security interest. Why? Remember, perfection of an interest is supposed to serve as protection of the secured party's interest in collateral from other creditors. In this section, we consider various conflicts between creditors who claim interest in the same collateral. A conflict may arise with just a piece of property; however, priority disputes are most likely to arise when a debtor files for bankruptcy.

SECURED VERSUS UNSECURED CREDITORS

Generally, secured parties have priority over unsecured creditors. Thus, if two parties provide a loan based on the same collateral, the party with the secured interest will have priority in repossessing the collateral over the party with the unsecured interest. This priority to the collateral does not depend on the perfection of a secured interest. Rather, the priority depends on the *attachment* of the secured interest.

SECURED VERSUS SECURED CREDITORS

Who has priority to the collateral when both parties are secured creditors? If both parties are secured, the determination of priority for claim to collateral moves to considerations of time and perfection.

If there is a dispute between a perfected secured party and an unperfected secured party, the creditor with the perfected interest has priority over the unperfected interest. But what if the dispute is between two secured parties with perfected interests? The party that perfected its interest first will have priority in claim to the collateral (UCC 9-317). Finally, if neither party has perfected its security interest, the party that attached its security interest first will have first claim to the collateral.

Consider the following real-world example: On March 21, 1995, a debtor took out a loan from First State Bank of Newcastle, Wyoming, for the purchase of two trucks. The debtor executed a security agreement with the bank and described the two trucks as collateral. Two years earlier, the debtor had taken out a loan with Farm Credit Services of the Midlands, PCA, and signed a security agreement which gave Farm Credit Services rights to after-acquired property as collateral. The debtor eventually defaulted on his loans to both creditors. Which creditor had rights to the trucks as collateral?

At first it may seem that this is a priority dispute between two secured unperfected agreements. If that were the case, then Farm Credit Services would have the right to the two trucks because it was the first to attach its agreement. However, the courts in this case found that the written agreement with Farm Credit Services was not specific enough in describing the collateral to justify attachment. The description of "after-acquired property" was not specific enough to grant Farm Credit Services attachment rights to the specific trucks as collateral. Consequently, this dispute was between a secured unperfected agreement and an unsecured agreement, and the secured agreement of First State Bank won.[4] Exhibit 30-3 provides a summary of the priority of creditors' claims to collateral.

[4] "After-Acquired Property Clause Alone Is Insufficient for Attachment," *Commercial Lending Litigation News,* March 6, 1998.

Exhibit 30-3
Summary of Priority of Creditors' Claims to Collateral

DISPUTE	WINNER
Secured vs. unsecured	Secured
Secured perfected vs. secured unperfected	Secured perfected
Secured perfected vs. secured perfected	The party who perfected its interest first
Secured unperfected vs. secured unperfected	The party who attached its interest first

PMSI conflicts. There is an exception to these priority rules. Generally, if a purchase-money security interest is involved, the perfected PMSI will almost always have priority over other claims to collateral. The rules regarding PMSIs depend on whether the collateral is inventory or noninventory.

First, if the PMSI is in inventory, the perfected PMSI has priority over a previously perfected non-PMSI if the following two conditions are met: (1) The PMSI party perfects its interest before or at the same time that the debtor receives his inventory, and (2) the PMSI party checks for previous secured interests and gives written notice to the holders of the PMSI [UCC 9-324(b)]. For example, General Electric Capital Commercial Automotive Inc. (GECC) entered into a security agreement with Spartan Motors, Ltd. GECC loaned Spartan over $1 million and secured this loan by attaching its rights to Spartan's entire inventory as collateral. GECC filed this agreement in the office of the Dutchess County clerk with the New York secretary of state. A few years later, Spartan signed another security agreement, but this time it was with General Motors Acceptance Corporation (GMAC). This agreement, however, was an agreement that involved a PMSI. GMAC loaned money to Spartan so that Spartan could purchase its inventory. Realizing that this was a PMSI, GMAC filed its agreement *and* notified GECC of its competing security interest.

The next year, Spartan filed a bankruptcy petition and went out of business. GMAC repossessed two BMWs that were purchased with the money it had loaned to Spartan and sold them in an auction for $194,500. GECC brought an action against GMAC on grounds that GECC's security interest had priority. In the end, the court found that because GMAC had a PMSI in inventory *and* notified GECC of the competing agreement, GMAC had priority to the profits from the sale of the BMWs.[5]

What happens if the collateral is *not* inventory? If the PMSI is in noninventory collateral, the PMSI has priority over any other secured perfected interests as long as the PMSI is perfected within 20 days of the debtor's possession of the collateral [UCC 9-324(a)].

SECURED PARTY VERSUS BUYER

If a debtor sells collateral in which a secured party has an interest, the security interest generally remains in effect. Suppose you obtain a loan from a bank and use your boat as collateral. You need more money, so you sell your boat. The bank's secured interest in the boat remains with the boat. If you default on the loan, the bank can seize the boat from the buyer. However, the UCC provides some exceptions to this general rule.

Buyer in the ordinary course of business. A **buyer in the ordinary course of business** is a person who routinely buys goods in good faith from a person who routinely sells these goods. Under the UCC, a buyer in the ordinary course of business can take

[5] "Post-Purchase Advances Given Priority," *New York Law Journal,* July 24, 1998, p. 21.

the goods free of any security interest created by the seller of the good *even if* the security interest is perfected [9-320(a)]. What is the rationale for this rule? Asking buyers to determine whether a security interest in inventory exists is burdensome. Thus, the purpose of this rule is to encourage commerce. For example, if your company buys products from an electronics store in the ordinary course of business, you can take possession of these products free of any security interest created by the party who originally sold the products to the electronics store.

Buyers of consumer goods. Suppose you buy a digital camera for $800 on credit from Circuit City, an electronics store. Circuit City has a security agreement for a PMSI in the digital camera. (Remember, a PMSI in a consumer good perfects automatically.) However, you discover that you don't have enough money to pay for your rent. Consequently, you sell your digital camera to your neighbor, who is unaware of Circuit City's secured interest in the camera. Can Circuit City repossess the camera? Under the UCC, as long as the buyer is not aware of the security interest, purchases the good for his or her personal use, and purchases the good before the secured party files a financial statement, the buyer obtains the good free of the security interest [9-320(b)]. Even though the secured party's interest perfects automatically, the secured party must have filed a financial statement to repossess a consumer good from another buyer.

Consider Case 30-2, in which the court considers the sale of consumer goods to a third party.

CASE 30-2

IN RE CHARLES T. LAU, DEBTOR
U.S. BANKRUPTCY COURT FOR THE NORTHERN DISTRICT OF OHIO, WESTERN DIVISION
140 B.R. 172 (1992)

Charles Lau, the defendant, purchased a 45-inch TV, sleeper sofa, love seat, corner table, entertainment center, diamond ring, gold chain, and microwave. Lau charged all of these items to his Sears credit card. When he defaulted on his payment to the credit card, Sears tried to repossess the items. However, Lau claimed that he was no longer in possession of most of the items. The sleeper sofa, love seat, and corner table were at his former girlfriend's parents' home. Lau claimed that he demanded the return of these items when he and his girlfriend, Teresa Rierman, broke up, but her parents refused to return the items. Instead, they paid Lau $150 for these items. Lau sold the entertainment center to another party and gave the microwave to the Riermans. Lau gave Teresa Rierman the diamond ring. The only item Lau possessed at the time of the trial was the gold chain, which was broken.

Sears brought suit against Lau to protest the discharge of his debt in the bankruptcy proceeding. During the trial, Lau tried to argue that Sears could repossess the items from the Riermans.

JUDGE KRASNIEWSKI: Defendant's counsel [Lau's counsel] argued that defendant advised plaintiff [Sears] of the location of the items and that plaintiff may seek recourse and attempt to replevin the items from Ms. Rierman and her parents. Because it is not necessary for plaintiff to have filed a financing statement in order to perfect its security interest in the items, the court is not convinced that plaintiff has any recourse against Ms. Rierman and her parents. See O.R.C. § 1309.21(A)(4) (a financing statement must be filed to perfect a security interest except to perfect a purchase money security interest in consumer goods).

[CONTINUED]

A subsequent purchaser, for example Ms. Rierman and her parents, may take the items free of any security interest if they represent a buyer who buys without knowledge of the security interest. Ms. Rierman and her parents may not have known of the purchase money security interest extended by plaintiff to defendant in the items they currently possess. Even if the third parties were aware of the security interest, plaintiff may be unsuccessful in an attempt to repossess these items.

The debt owed plaintiff from defendant in the amount of $3,059.04 is nondischargeable.

Judgment for plaintiff.

CRITICAL THINKING

What is the issue and conclusion in this case? What reasons does the judge use to support his argument? How convincing are they? What evidence would be needed for the judge to conclude in the opposite way?

ETHICAL DECISION MAKING

Return to the WPH process of ethical decision making. Suppose you are the manager of Sears. Before you decide to take this case to court, you have seemingly two options: (1) Prevent the discharge of Lau's debt to you in his bankruptcy hearing, or (2) repossess the items that the Riermans supposedly bought from Lau. Both of these actions have consequences. Who would be affected by each of these decisions, and in what ways would they be affected? Which decision would harm the fewest individuals?

Buyers of chattel paper and instruments. If a buyer purchases **chattel paper**, a writing that indicates both a monetary obligation and a security interest in specific goods, or an *instrument,* a writing that demonstrates a right to payment of money, in the ordinary course of business, the buyer can obtain the good free of any security interest. The buyer must typically be unaware of the security interest in the good. Why is there an exception for buyers of chattel paper and instruments? Both chattel paper and instruments are easily transferable. Consequently, the UCC provides that these forms of collateral can be sold to a buyer free of the secured party's interest.

Default

Generally, when a debtor fails to make payments on a loan or declares bankruptcy, the debtor has **defaulted** on the loan. However, the UCC does not define default. Consequently, each security agreement provides the specific definition of what is considered defaulting on the loan. Moreover, each agreement determines the procedures and consequences that occur in the event of default. Because the creditor is usually in a better bargaining position, the creditor usually determines the definition of default.

What are a secured party's remedies to recover its money when a debtor defaults on a loan? The secured party can (1) take possession of the collateral or (2) ignore its rights in the collateral and proceed to judgment. However, the party is not limited to just one of these remedies. If one method is unsuccessful, the party can attempt to pursue the other method. Note that these remedies are limited if the debtor has filed for bankruptcy.

Case Nugget Rights of a Secured Party

In re Tower Air, Inc.
397 F.3d 191 (3d Cir. 2005)

May a secured party recover insurance proceeds for damage to collateral that had been repaired and returned to the lender? Tower, an airline, borrowed $21 million from Finova to purchase an aircraft and four aircraft engines. As part of the security agreement, Finova received a security interest in the aircraft and four engines (i.e., the collateral). Moreover, the security agreement also provided that Tower would insure the collateral and that Finova would also have a security interest in the insurance proceeds. The lender perfected its security interest in the planes, engines, and insurance.

In 1997, one of the engines was damaged. Using its own funds, Tower repaired the engine for $2.25 million (while $1.91 million was attributable to the accident). However, Tower did not submit an insurance claim.

Tower later filed for bankruptcy. Because Finova had a secured interest, all collateral, including the repaired engine, was returned to the lender. The bankruptcy trustee then discovered the insurance policy and filed a claim for $1.91 million in repairs. The insurance company settled the claim by paying approximately $950,000. Finova objected to the settlement and argued that it was entitled to the insurance proceeds pursuant to the security agreement. The bankruptcy court ruled that the insurance proceeds should be paid to Finova, and the district court agreed.

On appeal, the trustee argued that Finova should not recover the insurance proceeds because it had already recovered the fully repaired engine. Recovering both the insurance proceeds and the repaired engine would be unfair. The court ruled that Finova was permitted to recover the collateral and insurance money to the extent of the amount of the debt. Much of the collateral was damaged; thus, Finova was permitted to recover the full value of the insurance proceeds.

TAKING POSSESSION OF THE COLLATERAL

If a debtor defaults on a loan, the secured party can take possession of the collateral (UCC 9-609). While the secured party may act without any court order to retain possession of the property, the secured party may not "breach the peace" in repossessing the property. What exactly is *breaching the peace?* The UCC does not define the phrase. Generally, if the secured party can repossess the collateral without using force or committing trespass, the action is not a breach of the peace. If the secured party is unable to repossess the property without breaching the peace, the party will file suit against the debtor to obtain a court order for the debtor to turn over the property. Case 30-3 demonstrates the court's consideration of breach of peace in the repossession of a van.

Generally, the security agreement will state that if the debtor defaults on the loan, the debtor must turn over the collateral in a reasonable time and manner. If the debtor refuses to turn over the property, the secured party will typically hire a repossession company to obtain the collateral. Once the secured party has possession of the collateral, the party can choose to (1) dispose of the collateral or (2) retain the collateral.

Disposition of the collateral. Under the UCC, the secured party can sell, lease, or transfer the collateral in any commercially reasonable method (9-610). The secured party may sell the collateral in a private or public sale. As discussed in the E-Commerce box in

CASE 30-3 LESTER IVY v. GENERAL MOTORS ACCEPTANCE CORPORATION & AMERICAN LENDERS SERVICE COMPANY OF JACKSON, INC.

SUPREME COURT OF MISSISSIPPI
612 SO. 2D 1108 (1992)

Lester Ivy defaulted on his loan from General Motors Acceptance Corporation (GMAC). Consequently, GMAC hired American Lenders Service Company to repossess Ivy's van. In March 1988, two employees of American Lenders, Dax Freeman and Jonathan Baker, went to Ivy's home and discovered Ivy's van parked near Ivy's mobile home. After unsuccessfully attempting to start Ivy's van, they hitched the van to their tow truck and started to drive out of the driveway. Ivy thought that someone was trying to steal his van, so he "chased after" the tow truck and van. While driving his pickup truck, Ivy passed Freeman and Baker and pulled in front of them so they were forced to stop their tow truck. Freeman and Baker stated that they worked for American Lenders and were repossessing his truck. Ivy retrieved his personal belongings after Freeman and Baker showed him documents that seemed to validate the repossession. Freeman and Baker gave Ivy a telephone number to call to get his van back.

Seven months later, Ivy filed a complaint against GMAC and American Lenders, arguing that Freeman and Baker's repossession was invalid because they breached the peace. Ivy requested actual and punitive damages. At trial, a jury awarded Ivy $5,000 in actual damages and $100,000 in punitive damages. The trial judge disagreed with the jury and threw out the punitive damage award. Ivy appealed the overturning of the punitive damage award while GMAC appealed the finding that there was a breach of the peace.

JUSTICE PRATHER: GMAC contends that its agents did not breach the peace and, therefore, it should not have been held liable for actual damages. Ivy, of course, disagrees.

Mississippi law authorizes a creditor or secured party to repossess collateral without judicial process if he or she can do so without breaching the peace. The legislature did not define "breach of peace," but this Court has provided some indication. For example, this Court has held that entering a private driveway to repossess collateral without use of force does not constitute a breach of peace.

This Court has also held that a creditor who repossesses collateral despite the fact that the debtor has withheld his or her consent or has strongly objected, did not breach the peace. . . . Courts in other jurisdictions have generally held that the use of trickery or deceit to peaceably repossess collateral does not constitute a breach of peace. . . . A Florida Court of Appeal opined that a debtor's "physical objection"—"even from a public street"—bars repossession. . . . A Georgia Court of Appeal found a breach of peace in a case in which: (1) the creditor repossessed the debtor's automobile by blocking it with another automobile; (2) the creditor informed the debtor that he could just "walk his a** home"; and (3) the debtor "unequivocally protested" the manner of repossession. . . . The Ohio Supreme Court opined that the use of intimidation or acts "fraught with the likelihood of violence" constitutes a breach of peace.

In sum, much of the litigation involving self-help repossession statutes involves the issue of whether a breach of peace has occurred. Disposition of this issue is not a simple task:

> Since physical violence will ordinarily result in a breach of peace, the secured party's right to repossession will end if repossession evokes physical violence, either on the part of the debtor or the secured party. At the other extreme from physical violence, a secured party may peaceably persuade the debtor to give up the collateral so that no breach of peace occurs. Between those two extreme situations—one in which violence occurs and the other in which the debtor peaceably gives up the collateral—lies the line which divides those cases in which the secured party may exercise self-help repossession and those in which he must resort to the courts. As with most dividing lines, the line between those two extremes is sometimes hard to locate and, even if it is located, it sometimes moves.
>
> 9 W. Hawkland, Uniform Commercial Code Series, at § 9-503:03 (1991).

Application of the foregoing principles to the evidence viewed in a light most favorable to the verdict leads this

Court to conclude that a breach of peace did occur. This Court, therefore, affirms on this issue.

Ivy contends that his version of the facts . . . supports the jury award of punitive damages. Thus, Ivy concludes, the trial judge erred by overturning the verdict. GMAC counters that the evidence simply did not support the award and that this Court should affirm.

Mississippi law authorizes a creditor or secured party to repossess collateral without judicial process if he or she can do so without breaching the peace. . . . If the creditor breaches the peace, then "the repossession [will be deemed] wrongful, and the debtor may sue the [creditor] in conversion for return of the collateral or [actual and consequential] damages, plus punitive damages *in the proper case." See* 9 W. Hawkland, supra at § 9-503:03 (1991) (emphasis added).

In Mississippi, this Court has allowed an award of punitive damages in cases involving a repossession attended by "malice, fraud, oppression or willful wrong evincing a disregard of the rights" of the debtor. Thus, a creditor must do more than cause a mere breach of peace before he or she can be held liable for punitive damages. Restated, a breach of peace may be deemed tortious—for which the creditor will be held liable for actual and damages—but the tortiousness of the conduct must rise to a heightened level before punitive damages may be imposed.

In sum, Mississippi case law provides little guidance on determining whether a creditor or agent's conduct is so malicious, oppressive, or fraudulent that an award of punitive is warranted. Nonetheless, viewing the evidence in a light most favorable to the plaintiff and viewing Mississippi's allowance of "self-help" repossession, this Court concludes that Ivy has failed to prove by a preponderance that GMAC's agents' repossession of his van was attended by "malice, fraud, oppression or willful wrong evincing a disregard of [his] the rights." In other words, their conduct did not rise to the requisite heightened level of tortiousness to warrant imposition of punitive damages. This Court therefore affirms on this issue.

AFFIRMED on all issues.

CRITICAL THINKING

What is the argument that this judge is making? How good are his reasons? Is there any information that you feel he left out that would help you come to a conclusion on the issue presented in this case?

ETHICAL DECISION MAKING

Return to the WPH process of ethical decision making. Suppose you were Freeman or Baker in this situation. How might you have behaved differently if you were following the Golden Rule?

this chapter, one of the newest ways creditors sell collateral is online. Regardless of where the collateral is sold, however, the secured party must strive to receive the best price for the collateral. Striving to receive the best price is part of the requirement to make every aspect of the sale in a "commercially reasonable manner." There is some dispute over what is commercially reasonable. A clear example of a sale that is not reasonable is the following: Suppose you, as a secured party, repossess a diamond necklace worth $10,000 and attempt to sell this necklace to recover the funds for a $10,000 loan. You give very little notice of the sale; thus, you receive only one offer to buy the necklace. You reject the offer and decide to purchase the necklace yourself for $1,000. You apply the $1,000 to the debtor's loan; the debtor still owes you $9,000. If this example actually occurred, the debtor could bring a suit against you for failing to comply with the commercially reasonable requirement established in the UCC. Consider Case 30-4, in which a debtor argued that a disposition did not meet the commercially reasonable requirement.

CASE 30-4

ROC-CENTURY ASSOCIATES v. ANTHONY J. GIUNTA, PERSONAL REPRESENTATIVE OF THE ESTATE OF STELLA SALTONSTALL

SUPREME JUDICIAL COURT OF MAINE
658 A.2D 223 (1995)

ROC-Century Associates loaned $1,000,000 to Stella Saltonstall on December 30, 1986, and Saltonstall signed and delivered a promissory note ("Note") to ROC. As security for the loan, she assigned to ROC her interest as a general partner in CWM Equities ("Collateral"). The maturity date on the Note was January 1, 1988.

Unfortunately, Saltonstall died in May 1988, and she owed $909,017.83 in principal on the Note, plus accrued interest and late fees. After her death, ROC filed a claim against the estate for the amount owing on the note. ROC later sold the collateral, Saltonstall's interest as a general partner in CWM Equities, at auction after providing notice to the estate as well as publishing a notice of public sale in the New York Law Journal and the Wall Street Journal. When ROC sold the collateral for $45,000, the personal representative of Saltonstall's estate disallowed ROC's claim against the estate, arguing that the sale was not commercially reasonable because the value of the collateral far surpassed $45,000. At trial, the court decided that the sale was not commercially reasonable and the value of the collateral was $176,006.

JUDGE WATHEN: ROC argues that the court erred as a matter of law in finding that the sale was commercially unreasonable. We apply the clearly erroneous standard in reviewing a challenge to such a finding. Expert testimony at trial indicated that ROC's characterization of the asset as an interest in the partnership, rather than as a liquidating interest in a dissolved partnership, and its statement in the notice to bidders that claims against Saltonstall's estate could also be asserted against CWM Equities, could have significantly undercut its value. This evidence, coupled with the fact that the Collateral, that secured a debt in the amount of $1,000,000, was sold for $45,000, is sufficient, under the clearly erroneous standard, to support the court's factual finding that the sale was not accomplished in a commercially reasonable manner.

Under the rule that we adopt today for cases in which the sale of collateral is not conducted in a commercially reasonable manner, a rebuttable presumption is raised that the value of the collateral sold is equal to the amount of the indebtedness. To overcome the presumption and establish a right to a deficiency judgment, a creditor must present evidence of the fair and reasonable value of the collateral and must show that the value was less than the debt. This rule encourages loans, while at the same time it imposes liability on a creditor for the actual damages resulting from a failure to conduct a commercially reasonable sale.

[T]he Probate Court applied the rebuttable presumption rule correctly and found that the fair value of the Collateral is $176,006 and that ROC is entitled to the balance of the principal and interest due on the note, less $176,006.

AFFIRMED.

[CONTINUED]

CRITICAL THINKING

What was the judge's conclusion in this case? Was it supported with strong reasons? Was the argument clear, or were there some significantly ambiguous words within the argument that you would like to have clarified? How good was the evidence?

ETHICAL DECISION MAKING

How might adherence to the public disclosure test have changed the behavior of ROC in this case?

Suppose that in the diamond necklace example, you sold the necklace to a buyer for $7,500. Assuming that this sale meets the commercially reasonable requirement, the debtor would still owe you $2,500. The sale has amounted in a deficiency; consequently, the debtor is liable to the secured party for the deficiency. However, suppose that the sale of the necklace yielded $12,000. Do you, the secured party, get to keep the $2,000? If the sale of collateral leads to a surplus, the surplus must be returned to the debtor.

In 1980, the Federal Trade Commission investigated General Motors Acceptance Corporation for possible violation of UCC guidelines with respect to returning surpluses to the debtor. The FTC charged that for six years, GMAC had conducted "sham" sales of repossessed automobiles that deprived defaulted customers of their surplus. For example, it was charged that GMAC in some instances would sell the repossessed cars to itself at low prices so that there would be no surplus and then sell them again to make a profit. GMAC settled before the charge was taken to court and agreed to pay $2 million to customers whose cars it repossessed from 1974 to1980.[6] What you can learn from this is that it is important, as a manager of a corporation that repossesses merchandise, to ensure that all surpluses are returned to defaulted consumers.

In addition to adhering to the commercially reasonable–manner requirement, the secured party must also notify the debtor of the sale. Additionally, the secured party must notify any other parties who have secured interests in the collateral.

Once the collateral is sold, the proceeds must be paid in the following order: (1) paying the reasonable expenses of retaking and disposing of the collateral (including attorney fees), (2) satisfying the debt of the secured party, and (3) satisfying remaining holders of junior security interests [UCC 9-615(a)].

Retention of the collateral. Instead of disposing of the collateral, the secured party may choose to keep the collateral in full or partial satisfaction of the debt. However, the secured party must notify the debtor of this intent by sending written notice. The debtor has 21 days to object to the secured party's retention of the collateral. If the debtor does not object to the retention, the secured party may retain the collateral (UCC 9-620–9-622). By retaining the collateral for full satisfaction of debt, the secured party gives up any claim to the debt. In other words, the secured party cannot demand additional money from the debtor. Consequently, if the collateral is not valued at the full amount of the money due to the secured party, the secured party has no right to additional money from the debtor.

[6] Jane Seaberry, "GMAC to Pay $2 Million for Reclaimed Cars," *Washington Post,* March 5, 1980, p. D7.

e-commerce AND THE LAW

Online Auctions of Repossessed Collateral

Over the past few years, many creditors seeking to dispose of repossessed collateral have chosen to do so online. Watching the success of eBay.com, an Internet auction site, creditors began to realize that there were many advantages to auctioning off repossessed collateral over the Internet. For instance, the Internet allows for more auction participants, and in an auction this typically translates into a higher sale price.

Someday you, as a manager of a corporation, may be in possession of repossessed collateral you wish to dispose of. Consequently, it is important to know about the option of Internet auctions. More important, however, you should know that auctioning repossessed collateral online is not the same as auctioning consumer items on eBay. There are a couple of things to keep in mind when auctioning off your repossessed collateral over the Internet. First, consumers on eBay tend to be looking for new items at cheaper prices, not used items. Consequently, you may want to auction off your items through an Internet auction designed for repossessed collateral, such as www.bid4assets.com. Second, you should somehow incorporate a way to accept non-Internet bids. If you don't, it is possible that the borrower from whom you repossessed the collateral could argue that your auctioning of the item did not meet UCC standards because not everyone has Internet access. Consequently, look for a site that offers an easy way to incorporate off-line bids, or handle those bids yourself.

The 1999 version of Article 9 provides for the debtor and secured party to agree that the secured party retains the collateral for partial payment of the debt.

If the debtor objects to the secured party's retention of the collateral, the secured party must sell or dispose of the collateral. Why might a debtor want to object to a party's retention of the collateral? Suppose you use a Van Gogh painting as collateral for a $5,000 car loan. The Van Gogh painting could certainly be sold for more than $5,000; thus, you, the debtor, would want the sale to occur so that you can recover the surplus from the sale.

PROCEEDING TO JUDGMENT

Another remedy for a defaulted loan is the secured party's rejection of the right in the collateral and the party's filing of a suit against the debtor. The secured party can sue the debtor for the entire amount of the debt. Rather than taking the time to organize the sale of the collateral, the secured party may choose to file suit. In contrast, an unsecured creditor has just one option: to file suit and seek a judgment in the amount of the debt.

Could there be other reasons for rejecting the right in the collateral? Let's look at one final real-world example. Trans World Airlines Inc. (TWA), was having major financial trouble in 1991. In fact, it had defaulted on its loans to two major creditors. Both creditors had the opportunity to repossess 10 jets and 96 spare aircraft, but the creditors continued to consistently postpone repossessing the collateral. Their reason for doing so was that they knew that the value of the aircraft was far less than what was owed to them by TWA, and they were sure that TWA would seek protection in U.S. bankruptcy court. Consequently, they chose to stick out the situation in hopes that TWA would either solve its financial problems or sell to another carrier.[7]

[7] Christopher Carey, "Creditors Unlikely to Seize TWA Jets," *St. Louis Post-Dispatch,* July 30, 1991, p. 7B.

CASE OPENER WRAP-UP

General Motors Acceptance Corporation

At trial, the court found that the sale of the boat for $26,000 was unreasonable and that the fair market value of the boat was $40,000. Consequently, Terris had to pay GMAC a deficiency of $25,350.42. If you were the manager of General Motors Acceptance Corporation, how would you have avoided the loss of $14,000? Unfortunately, the answer is not simple. The law under the UCC tells you that if you, as a manager, ensure that repossessed collateral is sold in a "commercially reasonable manner," you will be entitled to the full deficiency minus the profit of the sale. However, different judges may find different behavior to be "commercially reasonable." Consequently, the best possible thing you can do, as a manager, is to put forth as much effort as possible to ensure that you are receiving the best offer available for the merchandise.

Summary

Important Definitions Associated with Secured Transactions

Secured interest: An interest in personal property or fixtures that secures payment or performance of an obligation.

Secured party: The person or party that holds the interest in the secured property.

Debtor: The person or party that has an obligation to the secured party, the person who owns interest in the property.

Security agreement: The agreement in which the debtor gives the secured interest to the secured party.

Collateral: The property that is subject to the security interest.

Creation of Secured Interests

Attachment of a security interest requires these three elements:

Written agreement: An agreement that describes the collateral and is signed by the debtor.

Value: An item of value given from the creditor to the debtor.

Debtor rights in the collateral: The rights of the debtor over the collateral.

A *purchase-money security interest* is formed when a debtor uses borrowed money (e.g., buying on credit) from the secured party to buy the collateral.

Perfected Security Interests

A *perfected security interest* is a security interest in which the creditor has legally protected his or her claim to the collateral. Methods of perfection include:

1. *Perfection by filing:* Perfection of an interest by filing a financing statement with a state agency.
   - *Place and duration of filing:* Generally, the financial statements for consumer goods must be filed with the county clerk, and the statement is valid for five years.
2. *Perfection by possession:* Perfection of an interest by holding the collateral of the debtor until the loan is paid off.

3. *Automatic perfection:* Perfection that automatically occurs when a retailer sells a consumer good.
4. *Perfection of movable collateral:* Collateral that moves to another state must be "reperfected" after four months.
5. *Perfection of security interests in automobiles and boats:* An interest in an automobile or boat is perfected by noting the interest on the certificate of title.

The Scope of a Security Interest

After-acquired property: A creditor has a security interest in property acquired by the debtor after the security agreement is made if a clause to this effect is included in the agreement.

Proceeds: A creditor automatically has rights to the proceeds from the sale of collateral for 10 days.

Termination of a Security Interest

Termination statement: An amending to a financing statement stating that the debtor has no obligation to the secured party.

Priority Disputes

Priority disputes occur when two corporations or individuals claim rights to the same collateral.

Secured versus unsecured: When an individual with a secured interest is disputing with an individual with an unsecured interest, the individual with the secured interest wins.

Secured versus secured: When two individuals with secured interests are disputing, the individual who perfected his or her interest first wins.

PMSI conflicts: If a party with a perfected purchase-money security interest disputes with another party, the PMSI party will almost always have a right to the collateral—regardless of when the agreement was perfected.

Secured party versus buyer: If a debtor sells his collateral, the creditor may dispute with the buyer over the collateral.

1. *Buyers in the ordinary course of business:* If a person buys the collateral in the ordinary course of business without realizing that it is collateral, she has a right to the good.
2. *Buyers of consumer goods:* As long as the consumer does not know that the product is secured, the buyer's new product is free of any security interest.
3. *Buyers of chattel paper and instruments:* If the buyer purchases chattel paper and instruments, he is free from any security interest.

Default

Default occurs when a debtor fails to pay back her or his loan. Remedies include:

1. *Taking possession of the collateral:* If a debtor defaults on a loan, the secured party can take possession of the collateral.

   Disposition of the collateral: The creditor may sell, lease, or transfer the collateral.

   Retention of the collateral: The creditor may choose to keep the collateral as payment of the debt.
2. *Proceeding to judgment:* A secured party may sue the debtor for the entire amount of the debt instead of dealing with the collateral.

Point / Counterpoint

Secured transactions give a creditor more security in ensuring that it will be repaid even if the debtor is unable to pay. As you learned in this chapter, when a debtor has both secured and unsecured creditors, the secured creditors will be paid first. Some scholars have argued that secured credit unfairly transfers risk to unsecured creditors.

Should Secured Credit Be Limited?	
Yes	**No**
Suppose an unsecured creditor extended a loan to a debtor years before a secured creditor makes a loan. Later, a secured creditor extends credit to the debtor and gains an interest in the debtor's property. The debtor's financial situation has changed since the unsecured loan. Because of the secured creditor's interest, the likelihood that the unsecured creditor will be paid in full is now lower. The unsecured creditor's only response is to increase its interest rate; however, the unsecured creditor does not necessarily know about the secured creditor's interest in the collateral. Consequently, when the debtor is unable to pay, the unsecured creditor may get nothing. Moreover, the availability of secured credit may force a debtor to encumber her assets to obtain credit. By limiting the availability of secured credit, both unsecured creditors and debtors will be treated more fairly.	Debtors and creditors are rational actors who have to make choices. An unsecured creditor makes a choice in extending credit to a debtor. The unsecured creditor makes money based on the interest it charges the debtor. Frequently, the interest rate on an unsecured loan is much higher than the interest rate on a secured loan. The unsecured creditor is compensated for the higher risk it may face. Moreover, a debtor has a choice as to whether he wants to give the creditor an interest in his property. The debtor may choose a secured loan because of the lower interest rate. We should not restrict the debtor's choice. Finally, many people who receive secured credit are economically disadvantaged. Limiting the availability of secured credit would harm these parties' ability to access credit.

Questions & Problems

1. Explain why a creditor would want a secured interest.
2. How is a security interest created?
3. What options does a secured party have if a debtor defaults?
4. TIFI and Verdigris, Inc., are both creditors of Precision, Inc. Both companies claim a prior perfected security interest in equipment, furniture, merchandise, and fixtures (the collateral), all of which were previously owned by Precision. The collateral was stored at a manufacturing facility leased from TIFI to Precision. TIFI subsequently went bankrupt and perfected its security interest in the collateral. The collateral was transferred, and TIFI perfected its security interest. TIFI knew that Verdigris had a prior security interest. Verdigris provided loans to Precision, and the loans were secured by a security interest in the collateral. The security interest was perfected. Verdigris's security agreement contained a future advance clause securing "a

promissory note . . . and all other indebtedness and liabilities of all kinds of Debtor to Secured Party (whether created directly or acquired by Secured Party indirectly by assignment or otherwise, and whatever now existing or hereafter arising, . . . due or to become due, primary or secondary, and all renewals and extensions thereof)." TIFI and Verdigris had competing secured claims to the collateral. How do you think the court resolved the conflict? [*In re Tulsa Industrial Facilities, Inc.,* 186 B.R. 517 (1995).]

5. Maureen Mauro purchased a car from GMAC. GMAC was a secured party under the contract, and Mauro was responsible for making monthly payments. After Mauro defaulted in making her monthly payments, GMAC contacted Tri-City Auto Recovery to repossess the car. Tri-City employees Anthony and Edward Russo went to the Mauro home to tow the vehicle at 8:30 p.m. Mauro noticed that her headlights had been turned on and ran outside with an unloaded shotgun. She pointed the gun at Anthony Russo and told him to get out of the car. He stepped out of the car and attempted to grab the shotgun from Mauro. After calling the police, Mauro's husband also struggled with Anthony Russo. Edward Russo joined in the fight. The Mauros filed an action alleging that the repossession constituted a breach of peace. GMAC sought summary judgment dismissing the Mauros' claims for lack of merit. How do you think the court decided? [*Mauro v. GMAC,* 626 N.Y.S.2d 374 (1995).]
6. Both Purina Mills and Mountain Farm Credit Service (MFCS) claimed to be entitled to the proceeds from the sale of the debtor's cattle. Purina Mills argued that it held a first-priority, perfected security interest in the proceeds. Purina Mills supplied Grey Dawn Farms with feed on credit. Purina Mills obtained a security agreement and filed the financing statements necessary to perfect its security interest in the cattle. Grey Dawn Farms and MFCS had also entered into several security agreements. Though the cattle were offered as collateral, MFCS never perfected its security interest. Grey Dawn Farms made plans to auction its cattle. After the auction, MFCS was paid in full. Purina Mills did not receive full compensation. Purina Mills subsequently demanded payment from MFCS. How do you think the court decided this case? [*Mountain Farm Credit Service v. Purina Mills, Inc.*, 459 S.E.2d 75 (1995).]
7. After Kelli Birrell defaulted on her car payments, Indiana Auto Sales & Repair paid an independent contractor $30 to repossess the car. The contractor's 15-year-old, unlicensed employee was directed to repossess the vehicle. During the repossession, the boy exceeded the speed limit and crashed into Birrell. She sustained serious, personal injuries as a result of the collision. Birrell brought a lawsuit against Indiana Auto Sales & Repair for the injuries she sustained during the repossession. The trial court found in favor of Indiana Auto Sales & Repair. Birrell appealed the decision. Do you think the court of appeals affirmed or reversed the decision? Why or why not? [*Birrell v. Indiana Auto Sales & Repair,* 698 N.E.2d 6 (1998).]
8. Century Energy is a partnership in the business of producing oil and gas. Century received a loan from the First Interstate Bank of Commerce. A security agreement was executed, and two of Century's oil pumps, the F pump and the E pump, served as the collateral. First Interstate Bank perfected its security interest by filing the appropriate financial statements. Century subsequently developed a second business entity, Limited. Limited became indebted to New Oil, Inc., and the F pump was transferred to New Oil to satisfy the debt. First Interstate Bank became aware that New Oil claimed ownership of the F pump. New Oil notified First Interstate Bank that it intended to sell the F pump. First Interstate Bank brought an action to have the rights of the F pump determined. The trial court found that First Interstate Bank had a

perfected security interest in the pumping unit that was superior to any interest of New Oil. New Oil appealed the decision. How do you think the court decided on appeal? [*New Oil, Inc. v. First Interstate Bank of Commerce,* 895 P.2d 871 (1995).]

9. James Koontz entered into an agreement with Chrysler to purchase a 1988 Plymouth Sundance. He was to make 60 monthly payments of $185.92. When Koontz defaulted on the loan, Chrysler notified him that the vehicle would be repossessed if the payments were not made. Koontz told Chrysler that he was planning on making up the payments, and he urged Chrysler not to repossess the car. Despite his urgings, Chrysler sent the M&M Agency to repossess the vehicle. When he heard the repossession in process, Koontz, who was in his underwear, ran outside and yelled, "Don't take it!" Chrysler subsequently sold the vehicle and filed a complaint against Koontz to retrieve the balance of the loan. Koontz filed an affirmative defense and alleged that Chrysler had breached the peace when repossessing the car. The trial court ruled in favor of Chrysler. How do you think the court decided the case on appeal? [*Chrysler Credit Corp. v. Koontz,* 661 N.E.2d 1171 (1996).]

10. For-Med, Inc., and David Anderson executed a loan and security agreement in the amount of $79,924.89 with First Westside Bank. Anderson offered his 1978 Blue Bird motor home as collateral. After Anderson and For-Med defaulted on the loan, First Westside repossessed the motor home and sold it for $60,000. The motor home was very large, and First Westside claimed that it could not be left on its parking lot for show. Therefore, First Westside did not officially advertise that the motor vehicle was for sale. Rather, bids were solicited by word of mouth from financial institutions, dealers, and customers. A customer purchased the motor home, and after making $22,000 worth of repairs, he was able to sell the vehicle for only $58,000. First Westside sued For-Med and David Anderson to collect the difference between the loan and the sale price of the motor home. The court found in favor of First Westside. On appeal, For-Med and Anderson argued that the sale of the collateral was not commercially reasonable because First Westside failed to adequately advertise the motor home. Therefore, For-Med and Anderson believed that First Westside failed to obtain the best price under the circumstances. How do you think the court decided on appeal? Was the sale price of the collateral commercially unreasonable? [*First Westside Bank v. For-Med, Inc.*, 529 N.W.2d 66 (1995).]

11. Kevin Scott purchased a new Ford van on credit from Koons Ford of Baltimore, Inc. He made a down payment of $3,406 and agreed to make 60 monthly payments of $403.93 to pay off the balance. The contract was assigned to Koons Ford by Ford Motor Credit Company (FMCC). Scott's van was subsequently wrecked, and the cost of repair exceeded the value of the van. FMCC was paid the insurance proceeds, but Scott did not continue to make the installment payments. The van was repossessed and sold. FMCC notified Scott that he was responsible for a difference of $6,452.56. Scott never paid the balance of the payments, and four years later FMCC brought an action to reclaim the balance. Did FMCC, as the assignee of Koons Ford's security interest in the van, have the right to receive the monthly payments provided for in the agreement between Scott and Koons Ford? How do you think the court decided? [*Scott v. Ford Motor Credit Company,* 691 A.2d 1320 (1997).]

12. Color Leasing leased to Con-Graph one Miller printing press. When the lease expired, Color Leasing sold the printing press to Con-Graph. Con-Graph signed a note agreeing to pay Color leasing in 36 equal, monthly installments. Con-Graph also executed a security agreement granting Color Leasing "a continuing security interest in all of [Con-Graph's] accounts receivables, contract rights, chattel paper, security agreements, documents, machinery, equipment, fixtures, general intangibles, goods, instruments, inventory, trademarks, patents, license rights and good will whether now owned or hereafter acquired." When Con-Graph defaulted on its loans from Old Stone Bank, the bank notified Color Leasing that the bank would be seizing and selling Con-Graph's collateral. Color Leasing informed the bank of its status as a purchase-money secured creditor and demanded the return of the printing press. The bank eventually sold the printing press at a private sale. Color Leasing then brought an action to recover its damages from the seizure and sale of the printing press. Color Leasing believed that it had perfected a purchase-money security interest in the printing press. How do you think the court decided? [*Color Leasing 3, L.P. v. Federal Deposit Insurance Corporation,* 975 F. Supp. 177 (1997).]

13. Bindley Western Industries sold Reliable Drug Stores more than $1 million worth of goods. Bindley did not demand payment in advance, arrange for a letter of credit, or take a purchase-money security interest under the UCC. Bindley's security interest was never perfected. Reliable Drug Stores subsequently filed for bankruptcy. Bindley immediately attempted to reclaim the goods. Reliable Drug Stores owed secured creditors approximately $79 million, but the total value of Reliable's assets was only $62 million. All of Reliable's assets, including the inventory in question, were transferred to the secured creditors. Bindley brought an action to recover all the unpaid inventory. Do you think Bindley was successful? Why or why not? [*In the Matter of: Reliable Drug Stores, Inc.*, 70 F.3d 948 (1995).]

Looking for more review material?

The Online Learning Center at **www.mhhe.com/kubasek1e** contains this chapter's "Assignment on the Internet" and also a list of URLs for more information, entitled "On the Internet." Find both of them in the Student Center portion of the OLC, along with quizzes and other helpful materials.

Other Creditors' Remedies and Suretyship

CASE OPENER

Liens and Payments for Remodeling

Cathy Watson contracted Tri-State Construction, Planners & Associates to build an extension on her dining and living rooms on her New York house and to construct a garage for $32,000. Tri-State hired another company, N.F. Waterproofing Company, to lay a concrete foundation for $9,500. N.F. Waterproofing never received payment for $8,000 of the original $9,500 and filed an $8,000 lien on Watson's property. Watson did not receive notice of the lien until she tried to refinance her house and found that the lien prohibited the refinancing. Watson insisted that N.F. Waterproofing should go after Tri-State, not her, for the payment. N.F. Waterproofing placed the $8,000 lien in mid-October, while the last work performed on the house was done in the previous April.

1. If you were N.F. Waterproofing, who would you pursue for your payment? Is it fair for you to file a lien against Watson, even though she did not directly hire you to lay the concrete foundation?
2. What procedures must be followed when placing a lien on property? Watson was never notified of the lien, and the lien was placed more than six months after the work was performed.

The Wrap-Up at the end of the chapter will answer these questions.

Creditors' Rights and Bankruptcy

PART FIVE

CHAPTER 31

Learning Objectives

After reading this chapter, you will be able to answer the following questions:

1. How can liens assist creditors?
2. How does mortgage foreclosure assist creditors?
3. What is a creditors' composition agreement for the benefit of creditors?
4. What is an assignment for the benefit of creditors?
5. What are suretyship and guaranty contracts?

The opening scenario presents a few of the many problems that a debtor and creditor may face when the creditor attempts to collect a debt. A debtor is a party that has an obligation to another party, while a creditor is a party that is entitled to the debtor's payment.

A creditor wants to ensure that it is repaid for money extended or work performed for its debtors. Creditors have a variety of tools available to ensure their repayment. Some of these tools are created at the time the creditor agrees to extend money to the debtor. An example is the secured transaction, which you learned about in the previous chapter. Through an agreement between the creditor and the debtor, a creditor may take a secured interest in a debtor's personal property. If the debtor does not repay the creditor, the creditor can take possession of the personal property as repayment. Similarly, a creditor may take a secured interest in a debtor's real property in the form of a mortgage.

Moreover, a creditor may believe that extending money to a debtor alone is too risky. If the risk is too high, a creditor may require that a third party agree to pay the creditor on behalf of or in place of the debtor. Again, all parties are making an agreement regarding the creditor's right to be repaid.

However, sometimes a creditor gains an interest in a debtor's property through statute or common law rather than agreement. For example, most state legislatures have recognized that a landlord has an interest in a tenant's furniture if the tenant fails to pay rent. When signing the lease, the tenant did not make an agreement that the landlord could take possession of the tenant's property; rather, the state legislature created a statute that gives the landlord the interest.

Generally, laws regarding debt collection are state laws. However, if the debtor is a consumer, federal laws such as the Fair Debt Collection Practices Act may restrict the creditor's activities. For example, under the Fair Debt Collection Practices Act, the creditor may not make false statements when collecting a debt.

The purpose of this chapter is to examine the tools available to creditors for satisfying a debtor's obligation. We first consider the laws creditors may use to obtain money to satisfy a debtor's obligation, including such remedies as liens, mortgage foreclosures, creditors' composition agreements, and assignments for the benefit of creditors. In the second half of the chapter, we discuss actions that a creditor can take *before* making a loan that will ensure that the debt will be repaid, including such third-party agreements as suretyship and guaranty contracts.

Laws Assisting Creditors

Generally, a **lien** is a claim to property. If you, as a creditor, have a lien on your debtor's property, you have a claim to the property or the proceeds of the sale of the property. More important, your claim to the property must be settled before the property (or proceeds) is distributed to other creditors. A person who holds a lien is called a *lienholder.*

In the previous chapter, you learned about secured interests. A lien and a secured interest are both claims to property. In short, a secured interest is a *consensual lien:* The parties agree to the secured party's claim to the debtor's property. There are three types of liens: consensual liens, statutory liens, and judgment liens.

STATUTORY LIENS

Consider the following example: Suppose that you purchase new office furniture on credit. You sign an agreement with the seller, giving the seller a secured interest in your new furniture to ensure that you will make your monthly payments. The agreement between you and the seller creates the seller's secured interest. Suppose that you hire an interior designer to reupholster your old furniture to match your new furniture. If he or she completes the job and you cannot pay, the interior designer can create a lien (and thus becomes a lienholder) on your old furniture. This lien arises under state law to ensure that the designer will be compensated for his or her work. A *statutory lien* is a lien that is created solely through statute, regardless of whether the debtor wishes the lien to be created.

Suppose that one creditor has a secured interest in your furniture while another creditor has a lien on your furniture. Who has priority in obtaining your property or the proceeds of the sale of your property? By comparing the time at which the lien was created to the time at which the secured interest was perfected, you can determine which creditor has priority. If the secured interest is perfected, generally the creditor with the perfected secured interest will have priority over the lien creditor. If the secured interest is unperfected, the lien creditor will have priority over the unsecured interest. However, if a creditor perfects a security interest after another creditor establishes a lien on the property, the creditor with the recently perfected secured interest will not have priority over the lien creditor.

We examine below two particular kinds of statutory liens: mechanic's lien and artisan's lien.

Mechanic's lien. When a person hires a worker to make improvements on real property but is later unable to pay the worker, the worker can create a **mechanic's lien** on the person's improved real property. What are the characteristics of the mechanic's lien? First, a mechanic's lien must be on real property, not personal property. For example, if a worker builds an addition to a house or remodels a room within the house, the worker can create a lien on the house, which is real property. Second, as stated earlier, the mechanic's lien is created by statute. Thus, when N.F. Waterproofing placed a lien on Watson's house in the opening scenario, the lien was a mechanic's lien.

Suppose that you hire a contractor to build a wall in your office. However, you cannot pay for the entire amount of the construction work. Consequently, under state law, the contractor can create a mechanic's lien on your office property. If you do not pay your debt to the contractor, he or she can foreclose on the property to force a sale of the property to cover your debt.

What procedures must the contractor follow to create a lien? The party filing the lien must follow the requirements under the state statute, and the requirements vary from state to state. However, generally, the contractor must file, with the county clerk, a written notice of the lien on the property within a specific time period. Usually, the lien must be filed within 60 to 120 days after the delivery of materials or the last work has been completed by the contractor.

If the contractor decides to foreclose on the lien, the contractor must give the debtor notice of the foreclosure. Generally, the lien foreclosure action must be filed within 90 days of filing the lien. The foreclosure leads to a sale of the improved property. The sale must be advertised and must take place within a certain time, usually around six months to two years. The proceeds of the sale will be used to pay the debt to the contractor. If the proceeds are greater than the debt owed to the contractor, the surplus proceeds will be returned to the debtor.

However, creating a lien on property does not automatically ensure that a contractor will receive money. If a contractor performs deficient work, the mechanic's lien may not be enforced.

Compare the Bend Tarp Case Nugget to the Bates County Redi-Mix Case Nugget. While a contractor may not be entitled to foreclose on a lien when the contractor performs negligently, a supplier of goods is entitled to a lien despite a negligent performance.

Case Nugget — Foreclosing on a Lien

Bend Tarp and Liner, Inc. v. William Bundy and The Whitcomb Group, Defendants, and Cascade Highlands, LLC, and United Pacific Insurance Co., a Pennsylvania Corporation
Court of Appeals of Oregon 154 Ore. App. 372 (1998)

Bundy hired Bend Tarp and Liner to install a liner in a pond on his golf course. The day after the liner had been installed, Bundy discovered that a section of the wall of the pond had collapsed. At the point of the collapse, the pond liner had torn and water escaped from the pond. Bundy believed that the water loss was due to the torn liner, while Bend Tarp argued that the collapse of the wall was responsible for the tear. Bundy refused to pay Bend unless Bend agreed to repair the lining. Bend refused and filed a lien on the amount of the contract for the pond work plus interest. When Bundy still did not pay, Bend began action to foreclose its lien.

As a defense against the foreclosure, Bundy argued that Bend breached its contract because Bundy received no benefit from the liner; thus, Bend could not foreclose. The trial court ruled that Bend's installation of the liner was defective and thus Bend was not entitled to foreclose its lien. Bend appealed. The appellate court reviewed all evidence and agreed with the trial court. Thus, Bend could not foreclose on its lien.

Case Nugget — Suppliers of Goods and Mechanic's Liens

Bates County Redi-Mix Inc. v. Windler et al.
Missouri Court of Appeals, Western District,
No. WD63152 (2005)

Bates County Redi-Mix supplied concrete to a subcontractor hired by a general contractor, who was hired by the owner. Because the subcontractor improperly installed the concrete, the concrete had to be removed and replaced. Bates sought a mechanic's lien for the concrete it supplied. The trial court concluded that Bates was not entitled to a lien because the concrete was not incorporated in the finished property. The appellate court argued that Bates, as a materialman, is in a special position in supplying goods to a contractor because it lost its interest in the concrete once it was delivered to the subcontractor. The court emphasized the purpose of the lien law was to encourage suppliers such as Bates to extend credit for land improvements. Moreover, Bates was not responsible for the defective installation of the concrete. Finally, the court held that the owner is in a better position, compared to the supplier, to oversee the contractor's work and ensure that the contractor properly installs the product. Thus, despite the improper installation, the court concluded that the supplier was entitled to a mechanic's lien for the concrete it supplied.

Artisan's lien. In contrast to a mechanic's lien, which is a claim on real property, an **artisan's lien** is a claim on personal property. Suppose that you take your television to a repair shop, and the repairman keeps your television to make extensive repairs. A week later, the repairman notifies you that the repairs are finished; unfortunately, you discover that you cannot pay for the repairs. Consequently, the repairman may keep your television until you can pay for the parts and labor used in repairing it. If you never make the payment, the repairman is permitted to foreclose and sell your television to satisfy your debt.

The artisan's lien is not automatically created whenever a party makes an improvement to personal property. Case 31-1 illustrates the elements necessary to give rise to an artisan's lien.

CASE 31-1

BRENT MARTIN v. OHIO CITIZENS BANK ET AL.
COURT OF APPEALS OF OHIO, SIXTH APPELLATE DISTRICT, LUCAS COUNTY
1999 OHIO APP. LEXIS 3034

In April 1996, Stuart Humason bought a boat from the estate of Joseph May. Humason then sold the boat to Brent Martin for $200. Martin immediately began to make repairs to the boat. However, approximately two weeks later, Martin was notified that the boat did not belong to the estate of Joseph May. Martin received his $200 back and was advised to stop working on the boat. At the time Martin purchased the boat, its owner sold the boat to Robert Nickles. Although Nickles knew that Martin had possession of the boat, the boat remained on Martin's property for several months. During this time, Martin made further repairs on the boat and protected it from the elements.

In July 1996, Martin filed a complaint for foreclosure on the boat against the previous owner and Ohio Citizens Bank, which had a secured interest in the boat. Martin argued that he had an artisan's lien on the boat for $5,171.98 for repairs and storage. He later amended this amount in January 1997 to $6,242.98 for additional repairs made on the boat. In August 1997, he amended the amount again to $15,000. At trial, Martin testified that he repaired the boat because he thought he would eventually own it. The trial court ruled that Martin was not entitled to an artisan's lien. Martin appealed.

JUDGE KNEPPER: It is well-settled that:

> An artisan who furnishes materials or performs labor for the building or repair of chattel property has a valid common-law lien upon such chattel property for the reasonable value of such labor and materials while he retains such chattel property in his possession. Metropolitan Securities Co. v. Orlow (1923), 107 Ohio St. 583, 140 N.E. 306, at paragraph one of the syllabus.

However, in order to assert such a common-law claim, the chattel upon which labor and skill was bestowed must have been bailed to the claimant for that particular purpose.

As stated above appellant, a floor installer by profession, testified at trial that he performed work on the boat in the belief that it would someday belong to him. No evidence was presented that appellee gave the boat to appellant for appellant to repair, or that appellee left the boat in appellant's keeping with the specific intention of having appellant repair the boat. Evidence was presented, however, that Netry told appellant to stop working on the boat in April 1996, approximately two weeks after appellant and Humason attempted to purchase the boat from May's estate.

This court has reviewed the entire record of proceedings before the trial court and, upon consideration thereof and the law, finds that appellant is not entitled to a common-law artisan's lien in this case.

AFFIRMED.

Clearly, if work is performed without an agreement between the appellant and the appellee, an artisan's lien may not be present.

[CONTINUED]

CRITICAL THINKING

Is there any important missing information that might influence your willingness to agree with the court's conclusion that Martin was not entitled to an artisan's lien?

Does the judge make a strong argument? What would you add to the judge's argument if you wanted to make it stronger?

ETHICAL DECISION MAKING

What was the purpose of the court's decision in this case? What values are being upheld in this opinion? Why do you think the judge upheld those values?

Now suppose the repairman gave you your television back and told you to pay the debt as soon as you could. Five months later, the repairman claims that he has an artisan's lien on your television and wants to sell your TV to cover the debt. The repairman will not be successful because an artisan's lien is possessory. As long as the repairman retains possession of the television, he or she will hold the lien. However, if the lienholder voluntarily surrenders possession, the lien is lost.

What kind of priority does the artisan's lien have in relation to other claims on property? Both artisan's and mechanic's liens have priority over other types of liens; thus, they are called *super-priority liens*. Exhibit 31-1 compares the two types of liens.

Exhibit 31-1 Comparison of Mechanic's and Artisan's Liens

	MECHANIC'S LIEN	ARTISAN'S LIEN
Type of property	Real property	Personal property
Possession required?	No	Yes
How is the lien created?	By common law	By statute

JUDICIAL LIENS

Once a debt is due but unpaid by the debtor, the creditor may bring legal action against the debtor. When a creditor, through legal action, seizes a debtor's property to satisfy the debt, the creditor has a **judicial lien**. There are three types of judicial liens: attachment, writ of execution, and garnishment. These judicial liens usually occur at different steps during the legal action against the debtor.

Attachment. **Attachment** is a court-ordered judgment permitting a local court officer, such as a sheriff, to seize a debtor's property. Under statute, a creditor who has an enforceable right of payment under law may obtain an attachment. A creditor typically seeks an attachment as a prejudgment remedy in legal action. The attachment brings the debtor's property under the court's control until the legal action is complete. Typically, a creditor may ask the court to attach the debtor's checking and savings accounts, certificates of deposit, or even personal or real property.

Why would a creditor want to attach property? An attachment can help to ensure that a debtor does not sell or hide property in an attempt to avoid paying his or her debt. An unsecured creditor typically uses attachment; secured creditors do not need to create an attachment because they usually already have the right to repossess the property. Before a creditor can attach, he or she must follow specific procedures:

1. The creditor must file a lawsuit against the debtor, alleging that the debtor owes the creditor. The creditor may then seek a right-to-attach order from the court. The process for seeking a right-to-attach order is usually very procedurally specific. The creditor must state that the debtor owes the creditor and list the grounds for the creditor's attachment.
2. Generally, the creditor must then post a bond with the court. This bond must cover the amount of the court costs associated with the attachment along with any damage associated with a wrongful attachment. The amount of the bond is usually established by statute.
3. Next, the court holds a hearing regarding the attachment. At the hearing, the debtor typically makes an argument that the creditor will not succeed on the underlying action or that the attached property is exempt or is needed to support the debtor or his or her family.
4. The court will then likely issue a right-to-attach order. The order directs the county clerk to issue a *writ of attachment,* a document authorizing a law officer to seize the debtor's nonexempt property.

After the law officer seizes the property, he or she must safely hold the property. Thus, the debtor is unable to sell or otherwise dispose of the property. The debtor may have an option to post a counterbond for the release of his property. If the creditor is successful in the legal action against the debtor, the creditor will likely be permitted to sell the property to satisfy the debt. However, if the debtor is successful in the legal action, the debtor can recover damages from the creditor for any losses he suffered while deprived of the property. Moreover, if the property was wrongfully attached, the debtor can recover punitive damages from the creditor.

Writ of execution. Suppose that as a creditor, you bring a legal action against a debtor who refuses to pay you. You successfully bring your action, yet the debtor still does not pay you. What can you do now? You can go back to the clerk of courts to ask for a **writ of execution**, a judicial order authorizing a local law officer to seize and sell any of the debtor's real or personal nonexempt property within the court's geographic jurisdiction. The purpose of this action is to enforce the judgment awarded by the court. This seized property will be sold, and you will receive the proceeds to satisfy the judgment from the legal action. If, however, the debtor pays the judgment before the sale, the court will return the property to the debtor. If there is a surplus in the sale proceeds, this money will be returned to the debtor.

Some states permit the debtor to designate which property will be seized under the writ of execution. However, if the debtor refuses to designate property, the law officer may take any nonexempt property.

Exempt property. We have been discussing creditor's actions to seize property to satisfy a debtor's obligation. Some of this property is exempt from seizure. Most states create exemptions for both real and personal property. These exemptions may provide protection for a certain type of property or a certain value. However, these exemptions generally apply only to individuals.

One of these exemptions is the **homestead exemption,** which permits a debtor to retain all or a portion of the family home so that the family will retain some form of shelter. If the debtor does not have a family, the exemption may not apply. The amount of the homestead exemption varies from state to state; a typical exemption is approximately $25,000. However, in Florida, the exemption is 100 percent of the value of the home.

The following items are also typically exempt from seizure:

1. Household goods, appliances, and furniture (usually up to $2,700).
2. Clothing.
3. Equity in a vehicle (usually up to $2,500).
4. Tools and instruments needed to carry on a trade.

The debtor has the responsibility to claim property as exempt by filing a list of exempt property with the court. Next, if the exemption is limited to a certain amount of money, an appraiser will assess the property claimed by the debtor as exempt.

Garnishment. Under state law, a creditor may also ask for a **garnishment order**, an order that satisfies a debt by seizing a debtor's property that is being held by a third party, typically a bank or an employer. The garnishment order is usually directed at a bank where the debtor has an account or at an employer who pays the debtor wages. Under a garnishment order, the bank or the employer takes part of the debtor's savings or wages and pays the creditor directly. Thus, any potential future employer should be particularly aware of garnishment procedures.

A creditor may obtain a garnishment order as a prejudgment or postjudgment remedy. If the creditor wants a prejudgment garnishment, he or she will have to successfully argue in a hearing that the garnishment is necessary. Typically, the third party will garnish the wages, money, or property until the entire debt is paid to the creditor.

How much money, property, or wages is garnished? Both federal and state laws restrict the amount of money that can be garnished. For example, some states do not allow wage garnishment for any claim except a child support claim. Furthermore, the Federal Consumer Credit Protection Act states that a debtor must be able to keep the greater of the following two options: 75 percent of his or her weekly net income or 30 times the federal minimum wage. However, these restrictions do not apply if the garnishment is for certain debts, such as child support. Similarly, state laws provide dollar restrictions on the amount garnished from an employee's wages. If the debtor does not make 30 times the federal minimum wage (or another dollar amount set through state law), the debtor's wages are exempt from garnishment.

Moreover, the debtor can stop the wage garnishment by filing a notice with the court that will lead to a hearing. At the hearing, the judge will decide whether the wages are exempt. Only one wage garnishment is permissible at a time; thus, if several creditors wish to garnish a debtor's wages, the first creditor to file will usually receive the garnished wages.

Recently, the courts have considered whether creditors can attach, through garnishment, a debtor's pension. Case 31-2 provides an illustration of such an attempt.

In addition, courts have ruled that creditors may not attach Social Security benefits.

Thus far we have discussed mechanic's liens, artisan's liens, and judicial liens. Exhibit 31-2 (page 816) lists other types of liens.

MORTGAGE FORECLOSURE

A creditor who holds an interest in real property usually has a mortgage. A mortgagee can foreclose on the property when the debtor (the mortgagor) defaults. Usually, the foreclosure leads to a sale of property. However, before foreclosure and sale of property can occur, the mortgagee must follow the state procedures for foreclosing a mortgage. Basically, the mortgagee must give the debtor notice of the foreclosure. At any time before the sale of

CASE 31-2 UNITED STATES OF AMERICA v. CHARLES SMITH
U.S. COURT OF APPEALS FOR THE FOURTH CIRCUIT
47 F.3D 681 (1995)

Over a period of nine years, Charles Smith promised to invest his friends' and acquaintances' money—approximately $350,000—in several business schemes. However, he actually used this money for his personal expenses. Smith was then indicted for criminal fraud. After he pled guilty, the judge ordered him to turn over his entire pension payment of $1,188 each month to repay his friends. Smith appealed, arguing that this ruling violated the Employee Retirement Income Security Act (ERISA), which prevented his pension fund from being transferred in any manner.

JUDGE ERVIN: The Employee Retirement Income Security Act (ERISA) provides that "each pension plan shall provide that benefits provided under the plan may not be assigned or alienated." . . .

This court has long recognized a "strong public policy against the alienability of an ERISA plan participant's benefits. The Supreme Court, as well, has found that it is not "appropriate to approve any generalized equitable exception—either for employee malfeasance or for criminal misconduct—to ERISA's prohibition on the assignment or alienation of pension benefits." Guidry v. Sheet Metal Workers Nat'l Pension Fund, 493 U.S. 365, 376 (1990) ("Guidry"). In Guidry, the Court was faced with the competing policies of ERISA and the Labor-Management Reporting and Disclosure Act of 1959 (LMRDA), which was designed to prevent the corruption of union officials. The Court refused to allow ERISA pension benefits to be used to effectuate the remedial goals of LMRDA because such use would imply that "ERISA's anti-alienation provision would be inapplicable whenever a judgment creditor relied on the remedial provisions of a federal statute. Such an approach would eviscerate the protections of [ERISA]."

The government urges that Guidry is inapplicable because that case prohibited alienation of funds that had not yet been disbursed to the beneficiary. The government's position is that once pension funds have been distributed, the anti-alienability statute no longer applies.

We believe there is a distinction between funds disbursed from an ERISA plan before an employee has retired and such funds paid as an annuity for retirement purposes. The Supreme Court has noted that the purpose of ERISA is to safeguard a stream of income for pensioners. Where an employee elects to draw on her ERISA plan prior to her retirement, she forfeits the protection provided by the Act. Where, however, the funds are paid pursuant to the terms of the plan as income during retirement years, ERISA prohibits their alienation.

In the case at hand, the government attempted to require Smith to draw down his benefits due under the plans as a lump sum and turn it over intact as restitution. Upon discovering that Smith was not eligible for lump sum distribution, the government agreed to the recovery of his benefits as they are paid to him. It is clear that the government would not have been successful in requiring Smith to request a lump sum distribution. As this court held in Tenneco, benefits in the hands of the fiduciary are beyond the reach of garnishment. The government should not be allowed to do indirectly what it cannot do directly; it cannot require Smith to turn over his pension benefits in a lump sum, nor can it require him to turn over his benefits as they are paid to him. "Understandably, there may be a natural distaste for the result we reach here. The statute, however, is clear." Guidry, 493 U.S. at 377. Congress has made a policy decision to protect the ERISA income of retirees, "even if that decision prevents others from securing relief for the wrongs done them."

On remand the court must determine an appropriate amount of restitution that Smith must pay based on his financial resources. Although the court cannot mechanically deprive Smith of his pension benefits, it can determine restitution based on a balance of the victims' interest in compensation and Smith's other financial resources. Although the district court may determine an appropriate amount of restitution based on its findings as required by Bruchey, it must make that determination while leaving Smith's ERISA-protected benefits in his possession. Congress requires that ERISA beneficiaries retain their pension benefits for retirement purposes.

VACATED AND REMANDED.

[CONTINUED]

CRITICAL THINKING

The judge argues that the purpose of ERISA is to provide an income to pensioners. What reasons does the judge give to support this argument? How does the judge's perception of the purpose of ERISA lead to the decision the judge makes?

ETHICAL DECISION MAKING

What values are reflected in the court's decision? What values would likely lead to a different decision? What values would the court be promoting if it made Smith use his pension funds to pay back his friends?

property, the debtor may recover the property by paying the debt along with additional costs and interest. In some cases, the debtor may even recover the property after the sale.

If the proceeds from the sale of the property are greater than the debt owed, the debtor retains the extra money. However, if the proceeds do not cover the debt, the mortgagee can seek a *deficiency judgment,* an order that permits the creditor to recover property beyond the foreclosed property.

CREDITORS' COMPOSITION AGREEMENTS

Thus far, we have discussed rights and remedies in situations in which creditors try to force debtors to pay. However, one remedy that is more voluntary for the debtor is a *composition agreement,* a contract between creditors and debtor in which the creditors agree to accept a lesser amount to satisfy the debts and discharge the rest of the debt. However, if the debtor does not pay his debt under the composition agreement, the creditors may collect on the

Exhibit 31-2 Other Types of Liens

- *Attorney's lien:* The right of an attorney to keep a client's money or possession until the client pays his or her debt.
- *Broker's lien:* A claim to property by a real estate broker for its commission.
- *Common law lien:* A claim to property by implication of the law rather than statute.
- *Consummate lien:* The lien of a judgment that arises when a motion for a new trial has been denied.
- *Equitable lien:* A claim on property either created by a sales contract or imposed by the court to be fair.
- *Innkeeper's lien:* A claim on the baggage of guests who stay at an inn and are unable to pay their bill.
- *Landlord's lien:* A claim on the furniture and property in an apartment by a landlord.
- *Maritime lien:* A claim on a vessel for some service made to the vessel.
- *Medicare lien:* A hospital's claim to medical benefits paid under the Medicare Act.
- *Possessory lien:* A claim to property in which the lienholder has the right to be in possession of the property until the debt is paid.
- *Tax lien:* A claim against a taxpayer's property for unpaid taxes.
- *Vendor's lien:* A vendor's claim to land for the unpaid purchase price of the land.

e-commerce AND THE LAW

Internet Assistance to Creditors

The Internet has opened the door to a plethora of companies offering online assistance to creditors. Naturally, the influence of these companies on the law is grand. For instance, the ability to download the filing forms and complete them on a computer greatly expedites the filing process.

Specifically, a useful site to browse is www.mechanicslien.com. This site specializes in providing lien and bond claim systems. Visitors to this site will find compliance regulations and management techniques, as well as credit professionals and in-house counsel to help resolve construction payment claims. The company that runs this site assists creditors in perfecting receivable claims, mechanic's liens, or bond claims. Furthermore, since state laws vary from state to state and change periodically, this company will help interpret a creditor's rights according to which state he or she lives in.

In the past, subcontractors and suppliers lost tens of millions of dollars because they did not know their rights as creditors and therefore forfeited their lien rights and other legal rights. Now, the Internet provides creditors with the most recent regulations and can save creditors lots of time and energy. What an advantage for creditors!

original debt or the debt under the composition agreement. Unless the agreement is formed under duress, the courts usually uphold such agreements.

Why would creditors agree to a composition agreement? Generally, creditors do not have an incentive to accept a lesser amount to satisfy a debt. However, if the creditors believe that a debtor, such as a small start-up business, could not cover the entire debt, even through bankruptcy, the creditor may agree to accept a smaller amount to permit the business to continue operating.

ASSIGNMENT FOR THE BENEFIT OF CREDITORS

Another voluntary action the debtor can make to pay his or her debts is to transfer, or assign, title of his or her property to a trustee or an assignee who sells the property to pay the creditors on a pro rata basis with the proceeds of the sale. This transfer of title is called *assignment for the benefit of creditors,* and it is permitted through state law. If a creditor chooses to accept the payment, this will usually discharge the debt. However, the creditor is not required to accept.

Why would a creditor accept this payment? Even though the creditor might not receive the full amount of the debt, the creditor is receiving at least part of the debt. Furthermore, the creditor is saving the time and expense of trying to force the debtor to pay through other remedies.

Suretyship and Guaranty Contracts

Suppose you are the business manager of a company that extends credit to consumers. You are going to sell a high-priced good to a buyer through a payment plan when you suddenly discover that the buyer has a bad credit history. You want to make the sale, yet you are worried that the debtor will default on the loan. What can you do?

One option is to have the debtor find a third party who agrees to be liable for the debt. When a third party agrees to be liable for a debtor's loan, the party creates either a *suretyship* or a *guaranty arrangement.* The third party's liability is your security in the loan, as it provides additional protection against loss, should the debtor default on his or her loan.

global context

The Guarantor in England and Wales

Suppose your brother has applied for a bank loan to start a business, and the bank demands that a guarantor exist on the loan for security. Your brother asks you to be the guarantor on his loan, but you have some doubts. He has always been irresponsible with his finances, and you have little faith that his business will flourish; however, you also feel obligated as his sibling to help him. He insists that you have nothing to worry about and his new idea for a business will surely succeed.

The courts in England and Wales have decided that a lender may *not* always be able to force a sale of the property to satisfy the debt. If the guarantor is in a relationship of trust with the debtor (husband/wife, parent/child, employer/employee, etc.) and enters the agreement because of misrepresentation or pressure from the debtor, the courts may be willing to discharge the guarantor's debt.

If it looks as though the agreement may not be to the borrower's and/or guarantor's advantage, the lender must take steps to ensure that the borrower and guarantor are aware of the risk involved. Typically, these steps involve the lender directing the borrower and guarantor to receive independent legal advice.

SURETYSHIP

A **suretyship** is a contract between a creditor and a third party who agrees to pay another person's debt. This third party, also known as the *surety* or *cosigner,* is primarily liable for the debt. In other words, as soon as the debt is due, the surety is responsible for the payment. The debtor does not have to be in default in order for the creditor to seek payment from the surety. Thus, the suretyship is not simply an agreement in which the surety agrees to cover the loan if the debtor cannot pay. The surety must pay even if the creditor has not asked the original debtor to pay. This agreement does not have to be in writing.

A suretyship contract is particularly common in loans to young adults. For example, suppose you are in college and decide that you want to buy a new car. However, you need a loan to pay for the car, and the bank will not give you a loan unless you have a cosigner. If one of your parents cosigns your loan, he or she is acting as a surety. That parent is responsible for the payment.

GUARANTY

A **guaranty** is distinct from the suretyship in terms of the liability to the creditor. As you just learned, the surety is *primarily liable* to the creditor for a debtor's debt. In contrast, the third party in a guaranty contract is *secondarily liable* for the debt. Thus, in a guaranty, the third party, usually called the *guarantor,* must pay the debt *only* after the debtor has defaulted. Typically, the guarantor is not responsible until the creditors have tried unsuccessfully to collect the debt from the debtor.

Suppose that you are starting your own business and need a loan to cover some expenses. You attempt to obtain a bank loan, but the bank believes that your business may not be successful and you may not be able to pay your loan. However, the bank will offer the loan if a third party will be a guarantor and thus agree to be responsible for your loan if you cannot pay it. In this situation, both parties benefit. You receive the loan necessary to start your business, while the bank gains the safety and security that it will not lose its loaned money.

Generally, this agreement must be made in writing. This contract establishes the terms of the guaranty agreement. Thus, it will state the length of time for which the guaranty will be liable if the debtor defaults. A guaranty may be a continuing agreement to cover numerous transactions. Alternatively, the contract can state a fixed amount of time.

Exhibit 31-3 Comparison of Suretyship and Guaranty

	SURETYSHIP	GUARANTY
Name of third party	Surety	Guarantor
Type of liability	Third party primarily liable	Third party secondarily liable
Agreement required in writing?	No	Yes

Because of the distinction in liability between a surety and a guarantor, both creditors and debtors must make sure that the contract among the three parties is clear in stating whether the third party is a guarantor or a surety. Exhibit 31-3 compares suretyship and guaranty.

In Case 31-3, the third party signed a car loan as "CoBuyer." As you will read, the court needed to determine whether he was a guarantor or a surety.

CASE 31-3 GENERAL MOTORS ACCEPTANCE CORPORATION v. SEYMOURE DANIELS

COURT OF APPEALS OF MARYLAND
303 MD. 254 (1985)

In June 1981, John Daniels wanted to purchase a used automobile from Lindsay Cadillac Company. However, John had a poor credit history. To enable John to purchase the automobile, John's brother, Seymoure Daniels, signed the contract on the line designated "CoBuyer." Lindsay Cadillac then assigned the contract to General Motors Acceptance Corp. (GMAC), a company that engages in the financing of vehicles. In May 1982, GMAC stated that Daniels' contract was in default. When GMAC finally recovered the vehicle, it was in a condition of total loss. Consequently, GMAC brought legal action against Seymoure Daniels. The court ruled that Seymoure was a guarantor of the contract; thus, GMAC first had to bring action against John. GMAC appealed.

JUDGE COLE

I.

A contract of suretyship is a tripartite agreement among a principal obligor, his obligee, and a surety. This contract is a direct and original undertaking under which the surety is primarily or jointly liable with the principal obligor and therefore is responsible at once if the principal obligor fails to perform. A surety is usually bound with his principal by the same instrument, executed at the same time, and on the same consideration.

Ultimate liability rests upon the principal obligor rather than the surety, but the obligee has remedy against both.

A contract of guaranty, similar to a contract of suretyship, is an accessory contract. Despite this similarity, a contract of guaranty has several distinguishing characteristics. First, this particular contract is collateral to and independent of the principal contract that is guaranteed and, as a result, the guarantor is not a party to the principal obligation. A guarantor is therefore secondarily liable to the creditor on his contract and his promise to answer for the debt, default, or miscarriage of another becomes absolute upon default of the principal debtor and the satisfaction of the conditions precedent to liability. Second, the original contract of the principal is not the guarantor's contract, and the guarantor is not bound to take notice of its nonperformance. Rather, the guarantor agrees that the principal is able to and will perform a contract that he has made or is about to make, and that if he defaults the guarantor will pay the resulting damages provided the guarantor is notified of the principal's default. As such, the guarantor insures the ability or solvency of the principal. [I]n sum, the guarantor promises to perform if the principal does not. By contrast, a surety promises to do the same thing that the principal undertakes.

II.

Our review of the evidence in this case convinces us that the District Court erred in finding that Seymoure was a guarantor rather than a surety with respect to the installment sales contract. In our judgment the indicia for determining whether a contract is one for suretyship or one for guaranty all point to the existence of a suretyship agreement.

Initially, we note that because the contractual language is clear and unambiguous on its face, we confine our review to the contract itself. Seymoure agreed to purchase the subject automobile by affixing his signature to the installment sales contract on the line designated "Buyer." The contract clearly stated that all buyers agreed to be jointly and severally liable for the purchase of that vehicle. Therefore, under the objective law of contracts, a reasonable person knew or should have known that he was subjecting himself to primary liability for the purchase of the automobile. In short, although uncompensated sureties are favorites of the law, Seymoure's careless indifference does not insulate him from primary liability on that agreement.

Seymoure executed the same contract as his brother, thereby making himself a party to the original contract. This fact, standing alone, ordinarily negates the existence of a guaranty. As one court observed, "It is certain that in most cases 'the joint execution of a contract by the principal and another operates to exclude the idea of a guaranty and that in all cases such fact is an index pointing to suretyship.'"

Both Seymoure and John signed the contract at the same time. Although not dispositive, this fact tends to establish the existence of a contract of suretyship rather than a contract of guaranty. Furthermore, there are no competent facts indicating that Seymoure expressly agreed to pay for the automobile only upon the default of John. Seymoure also did not qualify his signature in any manner. Thus, by the terms of the contract Seymoure agreed to be primarily and jointly liable with John for the purchase of the automobile. GMAC was therefore not required to proceed against John in the first instance, and the failure of GMAC promptly to notify Seymoure of the default in payments and of the lapse in physical damage insurance coverage does not constitute a discharge.

REVERSED.

CRITICAL THINKING

How did the judge arrive at definitions for *guarantor* and *surety?* How did the court decide which term to apply to Seymoure? Are there ambiguities in the judge's definitions of *guarantor* and *surety* that affect your confidence in the judge's decision?

ETHICAL DECISION MAKING

John and Seymoure seem to have made two different ethical decisions. Imagine that both brothers have read this book, and outline a conversation the two might have about the ethics of their respective actions.

DEFENSES OF THE SURETY AND THE GUARANTOR

If a creditor brings legal action against a surety or guarantor, the surety or guarantor may use several defenses to argue that he or she should not be required to pay a creditor. Generally, the defenses available to the debtor are also available to the surety and the guarantor.

As suggested in previous chapters, certain kinds of contracts must be in writing to be enforceable. An agreement to pay the debt of another is one type of contract that must be in writing. Because the third party may not receive a benefit in return for its promise to pay the debt of another, courts require the creditor to provide the writing itself when trying to enforce the agreement against the third party. If a guarantor's oral promise to pay a debt is not in writing, the guarantor can raise the statute of frauds defense. By requiring that the creditor produce the writing, courts provide greater protection to ensure that innocent third parties are not unfairly charged.

A surety or guarantor could argue that she has been discharged from the debt. The reasons for discharge can vary. If the debtor has paid the sum owed to the creditor, the debtor's liability, as well as the surety's or guarantor's liability, is discharged. Furthermore, if the debtor makes an agreement that materially alters the original contract without the consent of the surety or guarantor, the surety's or guarantor's liability is discharged.

While the surety or guarantor may assert that her bankruptcy or incapacity is a defense against paying the creditor, the surety or guarantor cannot use the debtor's bankruptcy or incapacity as a defense. However, if the debtor engaged in fraud to convince the surety or guarantor to enter the contract, the surety or guarantor may assert this fraud as a defense and will likely be discharged from liability.

RIGHTS OF THE SURETY AND THE GUARANTOR

If a surety or guarantor pays the debtor's obligation to the creditor, the surety or guarantor has certain rights. First, the surety or guarantor has a right to subrogation, which means that the surety or guarantor is entitled to all the rights that the creditor had against the debtor. If the surety or guarantor pays the debtor's loan, he or she has the right to reimbursement from the debtor. The surety or guarantor can recover the actual amount of the debt paid to the creditor as well as the expenses associated with taking legal action against the debtor for reimbursement.

If there are multiple cosureties or guarantors who pay the debtor's obligation to the creditor, one surety might have paid a greater proportion of the obligation. This surety or guarantor has the *right of contribution,* which means that the other sureties or guarantors must pay their equal shares; consequently, the surety who originally paid the large amount can recover this money.

CASE OPENER WRAP-UP

Tri-State

Legally, N.F. Waterproofing, as a subcontractor, has every right to file a mechanic's lien on Watson's property, despite the absence of an agreement between Watson and N.F. Waterproofing. If the subcontractor does not receive payment from the primary contractor, the subcontractor can seek payment directly from the property owner. However, N.F. Waterproofing filed the mechanic's lien over six months after the last date work was performed on the house, and according to New York state law, a lien on residential property must be filed within four months of the last date work was performed on the property. Thus, the lien was wrongful and defective, and Tri-State sought court action to have the mechanic's lien removed.

Clearly, had N.F. Waterproofing had a better understanding of mechanic's liens, it would have investigated state legislation regarding liens before filing the lien on Watson's property and would have timely filed its lien. Unfortunately, this situation resulted in many costly inconveniences for all parties involved. By further investigating the state legislation, Watson was able to clear herself from liability.

Summary

Laws Assisting Creditors

Lien: A claim to property.

Principal types include:

1. *Consensual lien:* A secured interest in property created by agreement of the parties.
2. *Statutory lien:* A claim to property created through statute.

   Mechanic's lien: A claim on real property.

   Artisan's lien: A claim on personal property.
3. *Judicial lien:* Legal action whereby a creditor seizes a debtor's property to satisfy the debt.

   Attachment: A court-ordered judgment permitting a local court officer to seize a debtor's property.

   Writ of execution: A document authorizing a law officer to seize the debtor's nonexempt property.

   Garnishment: An order that satisfies a debt by seizing a debtor's property that is being held by a third party, such as a bank or an employer.

Mortgage foreclosure: The foreclosure and sale of mortgaged property to pay a debt.

Creditors' composition agreement: A contract between creditors and debtor in which the creditors agree to accept a lesser amount to satisfy the debts and discharge the remainder of the debt.

Assignment for the benefit of creditors: The transfer of the title of property to a trustee who sells the property to pay the creditors on a pro rata basis with the proceeds of the sale.

Suretyship and Guaranty Contracts

Suretyship: A contract between a creditor and a third party who agrees to pay another person's debt and is thus primarily liable for that debt.

Guaranty: A third party, usually called the *guarantor,* who must pay the debt *only* after the debtor has defaulted and who is thus secondarily liable for that debt.

Defenses of the surety and guarantor:

1. Statute of frauds
2. Discharge from the debt
3. Bankruptcy
4. Debtor's engaging in fraud

Rights of the surety and guarantor:

1. *Right to subrogation:* Surety or guarantor is entitled to all the rights that the creditor had against the debtor.
2. *Right to reimbursement:* Surety or guarantor can recover the actual amount of the debt paid to the creditor as well as legal expenses against the debtor for reimbursement.
3. *Right of contribution:* Other sureties or guarantors must pay their equal shares.

Point / Counterpoint

As you learned in this chapter, the homestead exemption allows a debtor to retain a portion or all of the family home even though the debtor is unable to pay his or her debts. Each state has its own rules regarding the amount of the exemption. Some states, such as Florida and Texas, have no dollar limit on the homestead exemption. Thus, if a house is worth $1 million and a debtor is unable to pay his debt, he may be permitted to keep the home and still discharge other debts. In contrast, some states have homestead exemptions of $5,000.

Should Congress Create a Federal Homestead Exemption That Would Apply across All States?

Yes	No
Congress should create a federal homestead exemption. Because each state has its own exemption, a debtor is treated differently depending on the state laws. It seems unfair that a debtor in Texas can keep his entire home while a similar debtor in a different state may be forced to sell his home. When the homestead exemption is particularly high or unlimited, a debtor may be more likely to shield assets from creditors. For example, some of the Enron executives may be permitted to keep their luxurious homes because of Texas's generous homestead exemption. Under the new bankruptcy law, the federal government has limited the homestead exemption to $125,000 if the debtor acquired the property within 1,215 days before filing for bankruptcy. The federal government is willing to limit the homestead exemption in certain cases. Thus, the federal government could set both a floor and a ceiling for the homestead exemption to provide more certainty for both debtors and creditors across the country.	Each state should establish its own homestead exemption. The homestead exemptions are generally found in the state statutes and even in some state constitutions. The homestead exemption is like the sales tax: Each state should be free to determine how its citizens will be treated. If a citizen is unhappy with the protections she receives in one state, she can always move to another state. Moreover, imposing a federal exemption would fail to take into account varying property values. For example, the median house price in the San Francisco Bay area is approximately $550,000. However, the median house price in certain areas of Ohio is $93,000. Geography accounts for varying house values; consequently, the homestead exemption should not be uniform. Finally, unlimited homestead exemptions provide security and stability to families. Limiting the homestead exemptions would penalize and uproot children who should not be held responsible for debt problems.

Questions & Problems

1. What criterion must be satisfied for each type of lien to exist? What are the major differences between the mechanic's lien, artisan's lien, and judicial lien?
2. What is the difference between a surety and a guarantor? Why is this distinction important to business law?
3. A class action suit was filed against ARB, a company that repossesses motor vehicles on behalf of creditors with a secured interest in the vehicles. When a vehicle

contains personal property, ARB notifies the debtor by letter and informs the debtor that a $25 fee is required to reclaim the debtor's personal property from storage. If not reclaimed, the personal property will either be destroyed or be shipped back to the lender with the vehicle as collateral. Does ARB have a lien on this personal property? Is ARB entitled to compensation for expenses in taking care of the property? [*Nadalin v. Automobile Recovery Bureau, Inc.*, 169 F.3d 1084 (7th Cir. 1999).]

4. After a construction dispute regarding the construction of their home, the Johnstons sued Tri-State, the builder. Under a Washington state statute, they sued to attach Tri-State's real property without prior notice or hearing. They were granted a writ of attachment, and the property was attached. Instead of having a postattachment hearing, as allowed by the statute, Tri-State sued in federal court, contending that the statute violates the due process clause of the Fourteenth Amendment. How do the conditions of attachment affect this lawsuit? Must there be a hearing along with attachment? [*Tri-State Development, Inc. v. Johnston,* 160 F.3d 528 (9th Cir. 1998).]
5. Linden, a condo owners association, sued McKenna, owner of 12 condos in the association, to collect unpaid charges that were secured by a $75,000 lien. The trial court issued a strict foreclosure against McKenna. The mortgage holder on McKenna's condos took priority, redeemed the condo units, and paid Linden $15,000. Does the foreclosure process affect the lien? Does it affect Linden's options in recovering the debt? [*Linden Condominium Association, Inc. v. McKenna,* 726 A.2d 502 (Sup. Ct. Conn. 1999).]
6. Dowling hired a contractor to work on his home. The budget was $875,579. When the work was nearly completed, the parties signed a contract stating the final price as $835,579 with no changes. On completion, Dowling offered $67,474 as final payment. The contractor refused, saying that $141,275 was owed due to further changes after the contract was signed. The contractor sued, seeking foreclosure on the mechanic's lien filed on the property. Since the changes occurred after the contract was signed, is the mechanic's lien affected? Is foreclosure still an option for the contractor? [*Wright Brothers Builders, Inc. v. Dowling,* 720 A.2d 235 (Sup. Ct. Conn. 1998).]
7. A prime contractor to the army failed to pay a subcontractor for a construction project for the army. The contractor went bankrupt, so the subcontractor sued the army to assert an equitable lien on army funds for the construction project. Can the subcontractor foreclose on a lien against government property? [*Dept. of the Army v. Blue Fox, Inc.,* 119 S. Ct. 687 (1999).]
8. Creditors holding judgment liens covering certain property obtained against the owner of the property initiated a foreclosure process. KeyBank had a mortgage on the property and was served the complaint but did not respond. Even after a notice of foreclosure, the bank failed to respond. The sheriff, to compensate the judgment lienholders, then sold the property. Later, KeyBank appeared for the first time and moved to vacate the previous actions. Which do you think has priority in the property, KeyBank's mortgage lien or the judgment liens? [*Galt Alloys, Inc. v. KeyBank N.A.,* 708 N.E.2d 701 (Sup. Ct. Ohio 1999).]
9. Power entertainment sued National Football League Properties (NFLP), claiming that NFLP promised to transfer a license to sell NFL collectible cards in return for Power's promise to assume the debt owed to NFLP by Pro Set, a licensee of NFLP. Power claimed that NFLP breached the agreement by refusing to execute the deal. Do you feel that NFLP was fraudulent in persuading Power to assume the debt and act as a surety to Pro Set? Why? [*Power Entertainment, Inc. v. National Football League Properties, Inc.,* 151 F.3d 247 (5th Cir. 1998).]

10. Two livestock dealers applied to American to serve as a surety by issuing bonds to meet the Packers and Stockyard Act requirements. These requirements maintain that the dealer must have a reasonable bond to secure the performance of its obligations to protect farmers and ranchers in case their livestock is sold to insolvent or defaulting purchasers. American issued the bonds, relying on the information provided in the applications. When the dealers defaulted on payment owed to hog sellers, the sellers made claims against the surety bonds for the purchase money they were due. Then American found that the bond signatures were forged, and it refused to pay. Given the nature of the surety relationship of American, was American justified in its refusal to pay? Why? [*American Manufacturing Mutual Insurance Co. v. Tison Hog Market, Inc.,* 182 F.3d 1284 (11th Cir. 1999).]
11. Williams, Sandman, and Walker were partners in Pavilion. All three signed a letter of credit and a security agreement to obtain a bank loan for the Pavilion business. Besides each of them signing guaranty agreements, they all pledged their interest in another business they owned together as collateral. When Pavilion defaulted on payment to the bank, the bank demanded payment from the three partners. Of the three, Williams was the only one who would not pay. Therefore, Sandman and Walker foreclosed on Williams's interest in the other business and bought Williams's interest at a public sale. Williams sued Sandman and Walker for their actions. Were Sandman and Walker justified in foreclosing on Williams's interest in the other business, according to their guaranty agreement? Why? [*Williams v. Sandman,* 187 F.3d 379 (1999 WL 598213, 4th Cir.)]

Looking for more review material?

The Online Learning Center at **www.mhhe.com/kubasek1e** contains this chapter's "Assignment on the Internet" and also a list of URLs for more information, entitled "On the Internet." Find both of them in the Student Center portion of the OLC, along with quizzes and other helpful materials.

Bankruptcy and Reorganization

CASE OPENER

United Airlines Bankruptcy

After the September 11, 2001, terrorist attacks, many airlines suffered significant financial losses. The airline industry suffered a loss of more than $7 billion in 2001. The airline hit hardest by the decrease in passengers was United Airlines. In an attempt to reduce costs, United cut thousands of jobs and negotiated with employees to reduce wages. Despite these attempts, United expected to lose approximately $20 million per day.

In 2002, after the federal government refused to give United a $1.8 billion loan guarantee, United Airlines sought relief by filing for Chapter 11 bankruptcy. This type of bankruptcy allowed United to reorganize its structure and debt while continuing to operate flights during the reorganization.

1. Suppose you are one of the United employees. How would you feel about the reduction in wages? Does the fact that you would be permitted to continue working during the reorganization change your response?
2. How would you handle this situation if you were one of United's large creditors, or, alternatively, if you were one of the company's smaller creditors who worried about being shut out by the larger lenders?

The Wrap-Up at the end of the chapter will answer these questions.

CHAPTER 32

Learning Objectives

After reading this chapter, you will be able to answer the following questions:

1 What are the goals of the Bankruptcy Act?

2 What specific types of relief are available through bankruptcy?

3 What are the types of relief available?

When an entity is unable to pay its debts, bankruptcy law provides various options for the entity to resolve these debts. Bankruptcy remedies are available to individuals, partnerships, and corporations. In 2005, more than 1.7 million bankruptcies were filed, and 34,222 businesses, like United Airlines, filed for bankruptcy.[1]

Generally, a **debtor** is defined as an entity that owes money to another entity. The term *debtor* is defined differently under each type of bankruptcy remedy; thus, an individual or company that is eligible for one type of bankruptcy might not be eligible for another type of bankruptcy.

This chapter explains the various bankruptcy remedies available to debtors. We begin with a discussion of the goals of bankruptcy law and an overview of the Bankruptcy Code. We spend the rest of the chapter considering specific types of bankruptcy relief under the code.

The Bankruptcy Act and Its Goals

Suppose that in the opening scenario, United decides to use all of its assets to pay its entire debt to only two of its creditors, while all other creditors would receive nothing. The creditors who were not paid would have been treated unfairly; perhaps United, the debtor, could have paid each creditor half of the debt it owed them. This scenario highlights the two general goals of bankruptcy laws. First, bankruptcy laws provide protection to **creditors**—entities to whom a debtor owes money. Bankruptcy laws ensure that creditors competing for a debtor's assets are treated equally and receive a fair share of the debtor's assets. Second, bankruptcy laws provide opportunities for debtors to gain a fresh financial start. In summary, bankruptcy law provides an organized method by which **insolvent debtors**—debtors who cannot pay their debts in a timely fashion—respond to their debts.

Bankruptcy law is federal law. Article I, Section 8, of the Constitution states: "The Congress shall have the power . . . To establish an uniform rule of naturalization and uniform laws on the subject of bankruptcies throughout the United States." Congress first addressed bankruptcy relief in the Bankruptcy Act of 1898. This act was replaced by the 1978 Bankruptcy Code, which was amended in 1984, 1986, and 1994.

Congress recently revised the Bankruptcy Code through the **Bankruptcy Abuse Prevention and Consumer Protection Act of 2005 (BAPCPA).** This act, spanning over 500 pages, took effect in October 2005. Moreover, this revision includes the most comprehensive changes to bankruptcy law in over 25 years. Some of the reasons cited for these comprehensive changes include:

1. Increased numbers of bankruptcy filings. In 1998, the total number of bankruptcy filings surpassed 1 million filings for the first time. In 2004, the number increased to over 1.6 million filings.
2. Significant losses associated with bankruptcy filings. According to testimony given before Senate subcommittees, in 1997 debtors discharged more than $44 billion in debt through bankruptcy relief. Furthermore, the Credit Union National Association estimated that credit unions' bankruptcy-related losses in 2004 would total approximately $900 million.

[1] "Bankruptcy Filings in Federal Courts Hit New Record," *Daily Record* (New York), December 6, 2005.

3. "Loopholes and incentives that allow and—sometimes—even encourage opportunistic personal filings and abuse."
4. "The fact that some bankruptcy debtors are able to repay a significant portion of their debt."[2]

Exhibit 32-1 Types of Bankruptcy Relief by Chapter

Chapter 7	Sale of debtor's assets by trustee and the distribution of money to creditors
Chapter 9	Adjustment of a municipality's debts
Chapter 11	Reorganization of the debtor's financial affairs under supervision of the bankruptcy court
Chapter 12	Reorganization of family farmers' debts
Chapter 13	Reorganization of an individual's debts
Chapter 15	Recognition of insolvency proceedings pending in a foreign country and relief for foreign debtors

TITLE 11 OF THE UNITED STATES CODE

Title 11 of the United States Code (U.S.C.) contains the Bankruptcy Code, which is divided into chapters. Chapters 1, 3, and 5 provide the general definitions and provisions concerning bankruptcy case administration and debtors. These chapters apply to all types of bankruptcy relief. Chapters 7, 9, 11, 12, 13, and 15, briefly described in Exhibit 32-1, apply six specific types of bankruptcy relief.

In the following sections, we discuss bankruptcy relief under Chapters 7, 11, 12, and 13.

Exhibit 32-2 displays bankruptcy statistics in the United States for 2005. Notice the ratio between the number of filings under each chapter. What is it about Chapters 7 and 13 that render many more filings than do Chapters 11 and 12?

Exhibit 32-2 Bankruptcy Filing Statistics, Fiscal Year 2005

Total filings	1,782,643
Nonbusiness filings	1,748,421
Business filings	34,222
Chapter 7	1,346,201
Chapter 11	6,637
Chapter 12	364
Chapter 13	429,316

Source: American Bankruptcy Institute, "Bankruptcy Filings Set Record on Eve of New Law" (press release), December 15, 2005. Numbers of filings may be higher than normal because parties sought to file before the new bankruptcy laws went into effect.

While bankruptcy law is federal law, state law applies to bankruptcy cases in the sense that state laws regarding debtor's property and creditor claims may apply. For example, states may have different laws regarding what property is subject to collection and sale through bankruptcy. Federal law also addresses what property is subject to collection and sale through bankruptcy. As you learned in previous chapters, when there is a conflict between a federal and a state law, the federal law trumps the state law and is supreme.

[2] "Factors Supporting Bankruptcy Reform," U.S. House of Representatives Judiciary Committee Report 109-031, 109th Congress, 1st Sess., April 8, 2005. Bankruptcy Abuse Prevention and Consumer Protection Act of 2005 Report of the Committee on the Judiciary, House of Representatives, to accompany S. 256.

Attributes of Bankruptcy Cases

In what ways are bankruptcy cases similar to and different from other types of cases? First, while the Federal Rules of Civil Procedure set forth procedural rules for civil cases, the Bankruptcy Rules set forth procedures for bankruptcy cases. Second, like other federal cases, bankruptcy cases are filed in federal district courts. However, bankruptcy cases are then referred to bankruptcy judges, under the authority of the district courts. Bankruptcy judges are appointed to their positions, and they serve 14-year terms. These judges make decisions regarding the administration of the bankruptcy proceedings. For example, a bankruptcy judge can decide what the debtor's assets are, how the assets are to be sold, and what assets the debtor may keep. However, the judge cannot make decisions about state law claims.

As with other cases, a bankruptcy ruling can be appealed. The appeal goes to the district court judge. Moreover, a jury can hear a bankruptcy case if the district court as well as the interested parties approve.

PERCEPTIONS OF BANKRUPTCY

Historically, bankruptcy has had a negative connotation and was often associated with individuals who were not responsible with money. In the past, individuals who filed for bankruptcy were denied government licenses or permits. Moreover, creditors harassed bankrupt debtors.

During the congressional debates regarding the 2005 Bankruptcy Abuse Prevention and Consumer Protection Act, Congressman James Sensenbrenner argued: "Every day that goes by without these reforms, more abuse and fraud goes undetected. . . . America's economy should not suffer any longer from the billions of dollars in losses associated with the profligate and abusive bankruptcy filings."[3]

However, recent studies have suggested that most people, perhaps 80 percent, sought bankruptcy protection because an event outside their control occurred.[4] For example, an individual might file for bankruptcy because the family's home was destroyed by Hurricane Katrina, or because he suffers from cancer and his insurance company refuses to cover certain treatments. Financial problems after these types of disasters are understandable; thus, bankruptcy today does not carry such a negative connotation. Moreover, Congress has recognized that denial of licenses or creditor harassment hinders a debtor's fresh start; thus, Congress has passed laws that provide greater protection for debtors.[5] For example, government units are no longer permitted to deny licenses and permits to bankrupt debtors.

While debtors have enjoyed greater protections under the code, Case 32-1, that of Thomas and Kathaline Laws, demonstrates that the courts also restrict those protections at times.

[3] U.S. House Judiciary Committee, "Committee Approves Senate-Passed Bankruptcy Reform Legislation without Amendment" (press release), March 16, 2005, http://judiciary.house.gov/newscenter.aspx?A=461.

[4] See, e.g., National Association of Consumer Bankruptcy Attorneys, "Study: Controversial Bankruptcy Law Reforms Not Working" (press release), February 22, 2006, and Denise G. Callahan, "Survey Indicates New Law Punishes Debtors," *Wisconsin Law Journal,* March 15, 2006.

[5] Sec. 525(a).

CASE 32-1 IN THE MATTER OF: THOMAS AND KATHALINE LAWS, DEBTORS

U.S. BANKRUPTCY COURT FOR THE DISTRICT OF NEBRASKA
CASE NO. BK98-41336, CHAPTER 7

Thomas and Kathaline Laws petitioned the court to use their attorney's mailing address on their bankruptcy forms. They were seeking to avoid local publicity regarding their bankruptcy. Specifically, they wanted to hide the bankruptcy from one of their elderly parents as well as one of their employers.

JUDGE MINAHAN, JR.: Debtors' counsel and debtors do not reside in the same town. If the debtors are permitted to use their counsel's office address, it is unlikely that the filing of the debtors' bankruptcy petition will be publicized in newspapers distributed in the community in which the debtors reside.

Except in unusual circumstances, such as when a debtor is threatened by assault from a former spouse, it is not appropriate for the court to take any action which reduces or diminishes publicity about the filing of a bankruptcy case. The news media should be free, at their discretion, to report the filing of a bankruptcy case. A bankruptcy filing is highly pertinent information to commercial enterprises in the geographic area where the debtor resides. Businesses must make daily decisions about entering into credit transactions with members of the public. The legitimate financial interests of businesses will be frustrated if the filing of a bankruptcy case is maintained on a confidential basis. The need of the public to know of the filing of the bankruptcy case, and the right of the news media to obtain and publish this information outweighs the debtors' desire to avoid the embarrassment and difficulties attendant to the filing of bankruptcy. Bankruptcy debtors are not entitled to be protected from publicity about the filing of the bankruptcy case. Congress has, however, determined that bankruptcy debtors are entitled to be protected from certain actions of their creditors, and from certain discriminatory employment practices. I therefore conclude that the debtors' Motion to use their attorney's mailing address on their bankruptcy schedules and statement of financial affairs should be, and is hereby overruled.

Judgment against petitioners.

CRITICAL THINKING

What evidence did the judge use to support his ruling? Does the judge's reasoning convince you? Why or why not?

ETHICAL DECISION MAKING

The judge's ruling is a reflection of his values. What values underlie the ruling?

Bankruptcy Proceedings

Most bankruptcy cases share a set of procedures, or certain actions that must be taken in every bankruptcy case. These actions are as follows:

1. All bankruptcy cases begin with a filing of petition for bankruptcy.
2. Once the petition is filed, the court grants an automatic stay for creditor actions against the debtor's estate. In other words, creditors' legal actions against the debtor must cease.
3. The court determines whether an order of relief should be granted.

4. The creditors meet with the debtor.
5. Some type of payment plan is created and approved, usually by the creditors and the court.
6. The payment plan is carried out through actions of the trustee and the debtor.
7. Debts remaining after the plan is carried out are usually discharged.

We will discuss the particulars of this process as it applies to the different forms of bankruptcy throughout the chapter.

global context

Bankruptcy Law in Spain

In Spain, bankruptcy procedures differ between insolvent businesses and individuals. Procedures for the business bankruptcies follow statutes within both the civil and the commercial codes, while those for the individual bankruptcies adhere to the statutes of the civil code only. Statutes governing business bankruptcies are referred to as *business insolvency laws.*

When a business is beyond restoration, it must declare a state of *quiebra,* or definitive insolvency. Either creditors or debtors may declare this state. After proper documentation has been submitted to the courts, the judge rules on whether the business faces definitive insolvency. If the judge confirms the declaration, further action is taken to ascertain whether the insolvency was fraudulent or negligent. This determination is significant because if transactions prior to the declaration of insolvency are found to be fraudulent, they may be declared void. Generally, if it is clear that a transaction occurred only to defraud the creditor, it is void. Any debtor found guilty of fraudulent or negligent insolvency is also subject to criminal procedures.

Specific Types of Relief Available

Before a debtor files for one specific type of relief, the clerk of courts must give the debtor written notice of the other types of relief available. This requirement helps to ensure that the debtor has full information about the bankruptcy process.

Under the Bankruptcy Abuse Prevention and Consumer Protection Act of 2005, an individual may not be considered a debtor under any chapter unless within 180 days prior to filing, he or she receives credit counseling from a nonprofit budget and credit counseling agency.[6] If the individual does not fulfill the credit counseling requirement, the bankruptcy court will dismiss the bankruptcy petition—even if the individual faces immediate home foreclosure, as in the Case Nugget, or wage garnishment.[7]

Moreover, the 2005 bankruptcy reforms attempt to prevent "repeat filers" from filing one bankruptcy claim after another. Under BAPCPA, if an individual was a debtor in a bankruptcy case that was dismissed within 180 days of the current case, the individual is generally not eligible to be a debtor under Chapters 7, 11, or 13.[8] However, if the previous bankruptcy was completed rather than dismissed, the individual is generally permitted

[6] BAPCPA, sec. 109(h).

[7] Barbara L. Jones, "Bankruptcy Clerks, Practitioners Are Catching Their Breath following Filing Rush," *Minnesota Lawyer,* December 26, 2005.

[8] BAPCPA, sec. 109(f).

to file for bankruptcy again. If a party completes a Chapter 7 bankruptcy, the party is not permitted to seek a Chapter 7 bankruptcy again for eight years.

In the following sections we discuss the main types of relief available, including Chapter 7, 11, 12, and 13 bankruptcies.

CHAPTER 7: LIQUIDATION PROCEEDINGS

The most familiar type of bankruptcy proceeding is liquidation, which is sometimes called *straight bankruptcy.* **Liquidation** occurs when a debtor turns over all assets to a **trustee,** an individual who takes over administration of the debtor's estate. Trustees are usually attorneys in private practice who specialize in bankruptcy law. Every Chapter 7 proceeding has a trustee who sells the nonexempt assets and distributes the proceeds of the sale among the creditors. Liquidation provides an organized method of selling the debtor's property to generate cash to pay creditors.

Case Nugget — Bankruptcy and Credit Counseling

In re Dixon
Bankruptcy Appellate Panel of Eighth Circuit
2006 WL 355332

The debtor filed his bankruptcy case on November 10, 2005. His house was scheduled for foreclosure on November 10, 2005, at noon. With his petition, he requested a waiver of the prefiling debt counseling requirement under the Bankruptcy Abuse Prevention and Consumer Protection Act of 2005. In his waiver request, he stated that he did not contact an attorney to determine how to stop the foreclosure until approximately 6:30 p.m. on November 9, 2005. While the debtor was advised that he needed to complete credit counseling prior to filing his petition, the credit counseling agency told him it would be two weeks before the agency could offer debt counseling via phone and 24 hours before it could provide counseling via Internet. Because the debtor did not have a computer and thus did not have Internet access, he argued that it was impossible for him to receive credit counseling prior to filing. However, if he did not file for bankruptcy, his house would be subject to foreclosure.

Under BAPCPA, the bankruptcy court may waive the debt counseling requirement if exigent circumstances merit such a waiver. Here, the bankruptcy court concluded that the debtor's description did not constitute "exigent circumstances." In coming to this conclusion, the bankruptcy court was particularly influenced by the Missouri state law requiring 20 days' notice before foreclosure can occur. Thus, the fact that the debtor apparently waited 19 days to pursue a bankruptcy remedy was enough to convince the court to dismiss the debtor's bankruptcy petition.

Who is defined as a debtor for liquidation purposes? Under Chapter 7 liquidation proceedings, individuals, partnerships, and corporations are considered debtors. Railroads, insurance companies, banks, savings and loan associations, industrial banks, credit unions, and health maintenance organizations are not eligible for Chapter 7 relief.

What are the liquidation proceedings?

Petition filing. As is the case with most bankruptcies, liquidation begins when the petition is filed. Under Chapter 7, liquidation may be voluntary or involuntary; thus, a voluntary or involuntary petition is filed. The person filing the petition is also responsible for paying filing fees.

Voluntary liquidation petition. When the debtor decides to file for bankruptcy, he or she files a voluntary petition. The debtor must state that he or she understands the other types of bankruptcy relief available and chooses liquidation. Once the petition is filed, all the debtor's prepetition assets form the **bankruptcy estate.** Assets that the debtor gains after filing the petition are generally not part of the bankruptcy estate unless they fall under an exemption.

A debtor does not have to be insolvent, or completely unable to pay, to file for bankruptcy under Chapter 7. Instead, the debtor must be able to demonstrate that he or she owes money to someone. When the debtor files the liquidation petition, he or she must also submit extensive information regarding his or her financial affairs under oath. It is a crime to conceal assets or supply false information regarding the debtor's financial affairs. Exhibit 32-3 shows a listing of the 10 schedules the debtor is responsible for filing under Chapter 7.

Exhibit 32-3 Required Schedules for Liquidation

Under Chapter 7, the debtor is required to list:
Schedule A: All real property
Schedule B: All personal property
Schedule C: Property in A & B that is exempt
Schedule D: Secured creditors and their addresses
Schedule E: Unsecured priority claims
Schedule F: Unsecured nonpriority claims
Schedule G: Executory contracts and expired leases
Schedule H: List of co-debtors
Schedule I: Statement of current income of debtor
Schedule J: Statement of current expenditures

Involuntary liquidation petition. If a debtor isn't paying debts as they come due, creditors can attempt to force the debtor into bankruptcy by filing an involuntary petition under Chapter 7. By filing the petition, the creditors attempt to force the debtor to surrender his or her assets so that the proceeds from the sale of the assets may be distributed among the creditors. Remember, a debtor could be a corporation; thus, creditors could force a corporation into bankruptcy.

What exactly is needed to force a debtor into bankruptcy? If the debtor has 12 or more creditors, 3 or more creditors who have unsecured claims that total $12,300 must sign the petition for involuntary bankruptcy. However, if the debtor has fewer than 12 creditors, a single creditor with a claim of $12,300 or more can file the petition for involuntary bankruptcy. If the judge believes that creditors are using involuntary liquidation proceedings frivolously, the court may force the creditors to pay the attorney costs, fees of the debtor, and even punitive damages.

Not everyone can be forced into bankruptcy through Chapter 7. Farmers, ranchers, and nonprofit organizations are examples of debtors that cannot be forced into liquidation. Also, debtors that are ineligible to voluntarily file for Chapter 7 bankruptcy (railroads, insurance companies, banks, savings and loan associations, credit unions, and health maintenance organizations) are also excluded from forced bankruptcy.

Dismissal of petition. A bankruptcy judge may dismiss a voluntary or involuntary bankruptcy petition. Under BAPCPA, a bankruptcy judge may dismiss a petition "for cause." One cause for dismissal is failure of the *means test.* If an individual's debt is primarily consumer debt and if the individual's income is above the median income in his or her state,[9] the court may presume that the individual is abusing the bankruptcy provisions.[10] However, the individual may continue with the petition under the presumption.

Automatic stay. Once a petition, voluntary or involuntary, is filed, the code provides for an **automatic stay,** or moratorium, for almost all creditor litigation against the debtor. During the stay, creditors cannot bring or continue legal action against the debtor or his property. For example, creditors cannot attempt to repossess property during bankruptcy proceedings. Moreover, if a creditor received a judgment against a debtor prior to the bankruptcy filing, the creditor may not enforce the judgment.

There are some exceptions to the stay. First, under BAPCPA, if the debtor was a debtor in a bankruptcy case that was dismissed within a year of the current bankruptcy case filing,

[9] The court would take the debtor's current monthly income and multiply this number by 12. If the total is less than the median family income in the state, no one may file a motion to dismiss the bankruptcy petition; BAPCPA, sec. 707(b)(2).

[10] BAPCPA, sec. 707(b).

the stay automatically terminates 30 days after the current filing.[11] Second, legal actions to determine paternity or to collect child support or alimony payments are not subject to the stay. Third, the court may exclude secured creditors from the stay if they petition the court to show that they do not have "adequate protection" under the stay. Remember, secured creditors have an interest in property; they are therefore concerned that they will lose their interest through the stay. To provide protection for these creditors, the courts may force the debtor to make payments to these secured creditors during the stay.

If a creditor is aware of the stay and continues to engage in legal action against the debtor, the code provides that the debtor may recover damages, costs, attorney fees, and even possibly punitive damages. Again, Congress is providing protection to the debtor.

Order of relief. After a bankruptcy petition has been filed, the next step is for the court to determine whether an order of relief is granted. An **order of relief** means that bankruptcy relief is ordered; that is, the bankruptcy proceedings can continue. If the filing of the voluntary petition is proper, the petition automatically becomes an order of relief. Similarly, if a debtor does not object to an involuntary bankruptcy, the order of relief is automatic.

Should the debtor challenge the involuntary petition for bankruptcy, a hearing will be held. At the hearing, the judge generally will grant the order of relief for involuntary bankruptcy if one of two conditions occurs:

1. The debtor isn't paying debts as they become due.
2. The custodian took possession of almost all of the debtor's property within 120 days before filing the petition.

After the court enters the order of relief, a U.S. trustee, a government official appointed by the attorney general, selects an interim trustee. A *trustee* is the person responsible for collecting the debtor's available assets and liquidating the property into cash for the creditors. The interim trustee is responsible for organizing the creditors' meeting.

Creditors' meeting. Between 20 and 40 days after the order of relief has been granted, the interim trustee calls a **creditors' meeting**—a meeting of all the creditors listed in the Chapter 7 required schedules for liquidation. While the debtor and the interim trustee also attend this meeting, the bankruptcy judge does not attend.

If the debtor fails to appear at the meeting, the court may refuse to grant the bankruptcy. Why is the debtor's attendance so important? The principal purpose of the creditors' meeting is to enable the creditors and trustee to examine the debtor under oath regarding her financial affairs. The debtor's filing of the Chapter 7 required schedules does not necessarily provide enough information. Creditors want to know more about the way the debtor is handling her assets and property. Moreover, they want to ensure that the debtor is not concealing property. Not only does the trustee ask the debtor questions regarding her financial status, but the trustee also ensures that the debtor is aware of the other forms of bankruptcy relief as well as the consequences of filing for bankruptcy.

Another important purpose of the creditors' meeting is the election of a permanent trustee. The interim trustee might become the permanent trustee, or the creditors might elect a different one. The creditors elect the trustee because the trustee generally represents the creditors.

The trustee. The general duty of the trustee is to collect the debtor's available assets (i.e., the debtor's prefiling assets) and to liquidate the property to cash that will be distributed among the creditors. Thus, the trustee takes possession of the debtor's property and has it appraised. Moreover, the trustee examines the debtor's records and might even temporarily take over the debtor's business. If someone else holds the debtor's property, the trustee has the power to require the person to return that property. Next, the trustee separates the exempt

[11] BAPCPA, sec. 362(c)(3).

property from the nonexempt property and sells the nonexempt property. (We will discuss the distinction between these two types of property shortly.) The trustee is required to keep careful records of the property and the sale of the assets during the entire liquidation process.

In addition to selling the debtor's property, the trustee has a variety of powers that assist him in fulfilling his duties. First, the trustee has the power to sue and be sued. He can initiate collection actions but must also defend against creditor actions. He has the right to assume or reject executory contracts. Moreover, he has the right to obtain credit. Finally, the trustee has the power to void certain liens against the debtor's property. For example, a debtor's ability to exempt property is hindered by any liens against such possessions. Consequently, the trustee is permitted to void these liens.

Exempt property. A debtor is not required to give up all of her property through liquidation—only the nonexempt property. As previously stated, the trustee sorts the exempt property from the nonexempt property. How does the trustee make this distinction? The exemptions are stated in the Bankruptcy Code and are adjusted every three years based on the consumer price Index.

There are federal exemptions as well as state exemptions. States, through legislation, can and have opted out of the federal exemptions to give debtors the option for state exemptions only. However, in some states, a debtor may choose whether to make state or federal exemptions; the debtor cannot make some state exemptions and some federal exemptions. Under BAPCPA, if a debtor purchased a home less than 1,215 days prior to filing for bankruptcy, the debtor's homestead exemption is limited to $125,000. Exhibit 32-4 lists the federal exemptions. In addition to having the exemptions in Exhibit 32-4, a debtor is entitled to 100 percent of Social Security benefits, veteran's benefits, and civil service retirement benefits.

Why did Congress create such exemptions for property? Suppose that a debtor was forced to sell all of his property through liquidation. Remember, one purpose of bankruptcy is to provide a debtor with a fresh start. If a debtor were forced to sell *all* of his property, he would likely fall right back into debt again. Thus, the exemptions are for items considered necessary to earning a living.

One of these exemptions was recently added—retirement funds in an individual retirement account (IRA). Case 32-2 provides the Supreme Court's reasoning for why funds in an IRA are exempt.

Exhibit 32-4
Federal Bankruptcy Exemptions

1. Up to $15,000 for residence
2. Interest in a motor vehicle (not necessarily an automobile) up to $2,400
3. Interest, up to $400 for a particular item, in personal and household goods and furnishings, clothing, appliances, books, animals, crops, and musical instruments (aggregate total of all items limited to $8,000)
4. Interest in jewelry up to $1,000
5. $800 of any property the debtor chooses (functions as a "wild-card" exemption)
6. Tools of trade and professional books up to $1,500.
7. Any unmatured life insurance contract owned by the debtor
8. Professionally prescribed health aids
9. Interest in any other property up to $800, plus any unused part of the homestead exemption up to $7,500
10. The right to receive certain personal injury awards up to $15,000.
11. Retirement funds in an IRA or SEP.

CASE 32-2 ROUSEY v. JACOWAY

UNITED STATES SUPREME COURT
544 U.S. 320 (2005)

When Richard and Betty Jo Rousey stopped working at Northrup Grumman Corp., Northrup Grumman required them to take lump-sum distributions from their employer-sponsored pension plans. The Rouseys deposited the lump sums into two IRAs, one in each of their names. Several years after forming the IRAs, the Rouseys filed a joint Chapter 7 bankruptcy petition and listed their IRAs as exempt. The trustee objected to the claim that the IRAs were exempt, and the bankruptcy court agreed with the trustee. On appeal, the Bankruptcy Appellate Panel (BAP) agreed that IRAs were not exempt. Appellate courts across the country disagreed on the issue, so the Supreme Court granted certiorari.

JUSTICE THOMAS: The question in this case is whether debtors can exempt assets in their Individual Retirement Accounts (IRAs) from the bankruptcy estate pursuant to Section 522(d)(10)(E). This exemption provides that a debtor may withdraw from the bankruptcy estate his "right to receive– (E) a payment under a stock bonus, pension, profitsharing, annuity, or similar plan or contract on account of illness, disability, death, age, or length of service, to the extent reasonably necessary for the support of the debtor and any dependent of the debtor. . . ."

Under the terms of the statute, the Rouseys' right to receive payment under their IRAs must meet three requirements to be exempted under this provision: (1) the right to receive payment must be from "a stock bonus, pension, profitsharing, annuity, or similar plan or contract" and (2) the right to receive payment must be "on account of illness, disability, death, age, or length of service."

A

We turn first to the requirement that the payment be "on account of illness, disability, death, age, or length of service." "[O]n account of" in §522(d)(10)(E) requires that the right to receive payment be "because of" illness, disability, death, age, or length of service.

[Trustee] argues that the Rouseys' right to receive payment from their IRAs is not "because of" these listed factors. In particular, she asserts that the Rouseys can withdraw funds from their IRAs for any reason at all, so long as they are willing to pay a 10 percent penalty. Thus, [Trustee] maintains that there is no causal connection between the Rouseys' right to payment and age (or any other factor), because their IRAs provide a right to payment on demand.

We disagree. The statutes governing IRAs persuade us that the Rouseys' right to payment from IRAs is causally connected to their age. The Rouseys have a nonforfeitable right to the balance held in those accounts. That right is restricted by a 10 percent tax penalty that applies to withdrawals from IRAs made before the accountholder turns 59. Contrary to [trustee]'s contention, this tax penalty is substantial. It therefore limits the Rouseys' right to "payment" of the balance of their IRAs. And because this condition is removed when the accountholder turns age 59, the Rouseys' right to the balance of their IRAs is a right to payment "on account of" age. Accordingly, we conclude that the Rouseys' IRAs provide a right to payment on account of age.

B

In addition to requiring that the IRAs provide a right to payment "on account of" age . . . , 11 U.S.C. §522(d)(10)(E) also requires the Rouseys' IRAs to be "stock bonus, pension, profitsharing, annuity, or similar plan[s] or contract[s]." The issue is whether the Rouseys' IRAs are "similar plan[s] or contract[s]" within the meaning of §522(d)(10)(E). To be "similar," an IRA must be like, though not identical to, the specific plans or contracts listed in §522(d)(10)(E), and consequently must share characteristics common to the listed plans or contracts.

The common feature of all of these plans is that they provide income that substitutes for wages earned as salary or hourly compensation. This understanding of the plans' similarities comports with the other types of payments that a debtor may exempt under §522(d)(10)—all of which concern income that substitutes for wages.

Several considerations convince us that the income the Rouseys will derive from their IRAs is likewise income that substitutes for wages. First, the minimum distribution requirements require distribution to begin at the latest in the calendar year after the year in which the accountholder turns 70. Thus, accountholders must begin to withdraw funds when they are likely to

[CONTINUED]

be retired and lack wage income. Second, the Internal Revenue Code defers taxation of money held in accounts qualifying as IRAs until the year in which it is distributed, treating it as income only in such years. This tax treatment further encourages accountholders to wait until retirement to withdraw the funds: The later withdrawal occurs, the longer the taxes on the amounts are deferred. Third, absent the applicability of other exceptions discussed above, withdrawals before age 59 are subject to a tax penalty, restricting preretirement access to the funds. Finally, to ensure that the beneficiary uses the IRA in his retirement years, an accountholder's failure to take the requisite minimum distributions results in a 50-percent tax penalty on funds improperly remaining in the account. All of these features show that IRA income substitutes for wages lost upon retirement and distinguish IRAs from typical savings accounts.

***

In sum, the Rouseys' IRAs fulfill both of §522(d)(10)(E)'s requirements at issue here—they confer a right to receive payment on account of age and they are similar plans or contracts to those enumerated in §522(d)(10)(E).

REVERSED AND REMANDED.

CRITICAL THINKING

Return to the considerations enumerated in the next to last paragraph of this case. Justice Thomas determines that these considerations all move toward the conclusion that the income the Rouseys will derive from their IRAs is income that substitutes for wages. What alternative interpretations of those considerations would lead us to believe that the considerations do not lead to that conclusion?

ETHICAL DECISION MAKING

We can certainly understand the interests advanced by the decision made by the Court in this case. But what stakeholders are potentially harmed by this decision?

A debtor must file a list of the property that it claims is exempt. Under the Bankruptcy Code and the Bankruptcy Rules, creditors may file objections to the claimed exemptions. If a debtor improperly lists property as exempt and a creditor does not timely file an objection, the debtor will likely be permitted to claim the property as exempt.

Preferential payments. Because a major purpose of the Bankruptcy Code is to prevent debtors from making payments to one creditor and thus treating that creditor preferentially, the trustee has the power to recover **preferential payments,** or payments made by an insolvent debtor that give preferential treatment to one creditor over another. If the debtor made any payments within 90 days of the bankruptcy filing, the trustee can examine these payments as preferential payments. The trustee does not have to demonstrate the debtor's past insolvency; the debtor is assumed to be insolvent for 90 days prior to the bankruptcy. For a payment to be considered preferential, the trustee must show that the transfer gave the creditor more money than the creditor would have received through bankruptcy proceedings. Thus, other creditors are disadvantaged by the debtor's preferential payment.

If the preferred creditor is an insider, such as a relative or partner, the trustee has the power to recover payments made within two years before filing for bankruptcy. However, in such cases, the trustee must demonstrate the debtor's insolvency rather than assume insolvency. In contrast, the trustee may not recover preferential payments made for alimony or child support.

Suppose that your company has $5,000 in its checking account, but no other assets. You (i.e., your company) owe $4,000 to a credit union, $3,000 to your landlord, and $3,500 to the construction company that remodeled your offices a year ago. You pay the construction company $3,500, which leaves $1,500 for your $7,000 debt to your landlord and the credit union. A week later, you file for bankruptcy, and you have just $1,500 that will be applied to your debt to your landlord and credit union. Your landlord and credit union would have received more money through the bankruptcy proceedings if you had not paid the full amount to the construction company; thus, your $3,500 payment is a preferential payment that can be recovered from the construction company to be distributed more evenly among the creditors.

Fraudulent transfers. A trustee can recover preferential payments because these payments are not fair to creditors. Similarly, a trustee can void **fraudulent transfers** of property. These transfers can be actually or constructively fraudulent. An actual fraudulent transfer would be made with intent to defraud creditors. Generally, there is no direct evidence of intent to defraud (e.g., an e-mail written by a debtor who states that he is transferring assets to hide them). Rather, a trustee would establish intent through circumstantial evidence.

Similarly, if a debtor transfers property for an amount significantly lower than its fair market value, he or she may have engaged in a fraudulent transfer. Suppose that you are unable to pay your debts and are preparing to file for bankruptcy. You decide to sell your $50,000 boat to your business partner for $50. The trustee of your case could recover the boat if the sale occurred within two years of your filing for bankruptcy. Furthermore, you could be subject to criminal penalties for your attempt to hide your assets. By punishing debtors who attempt to hide their assets, the Bankruptcy Code provides protection for creditors.

Suppose that, instead of selling your boat to your business partner, you sold your boat to a creditor. Because you are making a payment to a creditor, the trustee would analyze this payment as a preferential payment (assessing how the other creditors would be harmed by this payment) rather than a fraudulent transfer (assessing the reasonableness of consideration for the transfer).

Creditors' claims. Within 90 days of the creditors' meeting, all creditors (except secured creditors) must file a proof of claim with the bankruptcy court clerk to receive a portion of the debtor's estate. This proof of claim lists the creditor's name and address and the amount of the debt owed to the creditor. If the creditor fails to file such a claim, the creditor may not receive a portion of the debt. However, the fact that the claim was filed does not mean that the creditor will automatically receive a portion of the proceeds from the sale of the debtor's assets. The trustee must permit the claim to be allowed, and there are numerous defenses to creditors' claims.

When the trustee is sorting and examining the property, the trustee must determine whether a creditor has a secured interest in the debtor's property. If a secured interest exists, the creditor has first claim to the property. The debtor may decide to surrender the property to the creditor to satisfy the debt. Alternatively, the creditor may foreclose on the property and use the proceeds of the sale to reduce the debt owed to the creditor. However, the secured party is secured only to the value of the collateral.

Distribution of property to creditors: priority claims. As suggested in the previous paragraph, all creditors do not have equal claims to the proceeds of the sale. Secured parties have priority over all unsecured parties in receiving portions of the proceeds of the liquidation. Thus, secured parties are paid first. But which unsecured parties are paid next? The code establishes classes of priority claims. One class must be completely paid before anyone in another class receives any payment. If there are insufficient funds to fully pay all the

global context

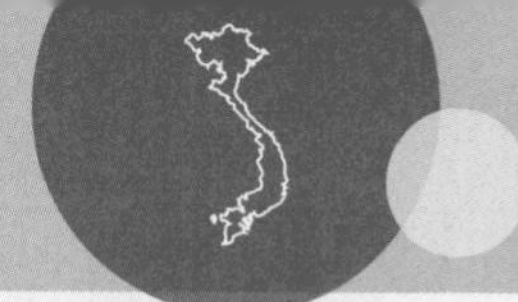

Bankruptcy in Vietnam

As in most countries, Vietnamese bankruptcy cases begin with an adjudication phase in the country's economic court. Here, the court either issues a plan for reorganization or declares insolvency. If insolvency is declared, the case is handed to the Judgment Enforcement Office, which is responsible for assigning an enforcement officer and a Property Realization Committee. While the officer supervises, the committee attends to the seizure and sale of the bankrupt party's assets.

Once the assets have been recovered, they are distributed in a particular hierarchy. All expenses incurred after bankruptcy was affirmed are reimbursed first. The recovery is then used to pay employee salaries, followed by outstanding taxes and, finally, individual creditor claims. The distribution is not definitive, however, as creditors do retain the right to appeal any decisions to the Department of Justice.

creditors in one class, one class is paid proportionately and the lower classes get nothing. The classes of priority claims among unsecured creditors are shown in Exhibit 32-5.

Thus, based on the different classes of unsecured creditors, when Steeltech Manufacturing, Inc., went bankrupt in 1999, the company's former employees were unable to collect over $250,000 in back wages for weeks they worked without pay. The debtor has no control over which creditors are paid.

If there is any remaining money after the proceeds are distributed to creditors, the remaining money is returned to the debtor. If there is not enough money to cover all the debts, most of the remaining debts are discharged.

Discharge. If a debtor has honestly dealt with her creditors during bankruptcy proceedings, the debtor is likely eligible for a discharge of her remaining debts. A **discharge** is a written federal court order signed by a bankruptcy judge stating that the debtor is immune from creditor actions to collect debts. When a debt is discharged, the debtor is essentially no longer responsible for the debt.

When is a discharge of debt appropriate? First, discharge of debt under Chapter 7 is available only to individuals, not partnerships or corporations. Second, discharge of debts

Exhibit 32-5
Classes of Priority Claims among Unsecured Creditors

Class 1	Any unpaid domestic support obligations (alimony or child support).
Class 2	Court costs, trustee fees, attorney fees, and other administrative expenses associated with the bankruptcy.
Class 3	Unsecured claims in involuntary bankruptcy that arise through the debtor's ordinary business expenses from the date of filing the petition to the date of the appointment of the trustee.
Class 4	Unsecured claims for unpaid wages, salaries, and commissions (up to $10,000 per individual) earned within 180 days of the filing of the petition.
Class 5	Unsecured claims for contributions to employee retirement plans (up to $10,000 per employee).
Class 6	Unsecured claims by farmers and fishers (up to $4,000) against grain operators of grain storage facilities or fish storage or processing facilities.
Class 7	Claims for deposits given to the debtor in connection with property or services never given.
Class 8	Certain taxes and penalties due to government units.
Class 9	Claims in bankruptcies related to federal depository institutions.
Class 10	Unsecured claims for personal injuries and deaths caused by debtor's operation of motor vehicle under influence of alcohol or drugs.

Exhibit 32-6 Nondischargeable Debts under the Bankruptcy Code

1. Claims for back taxes or government fines within three years of filing for bankruptcy.
2. Claims for liabilities against the debtor for his or her obtaining money or property under false pretenses, false representation, or fraud.
3. Claims by creditors who weren't listed on the schedule and did not have notification of the bankruptcy proceedings.
4. Claims based on fraud, embezzlement, and larceny by the debtor while she or he was acting in a fiduciary relationship.
5. Alimony, child support, and some property settlements.
6. Claims of willful or malicious conduct by the debtor that caused injury to another person or property.
7. Specific student loans, unless payment of the loans imposes undue hardship on the debtor.
8. Judgments against a debtor for claims resulting from the debtor's drinking and driving.
9. Debts not discharged in previous bankruptcies.
10. Claims for money borrowed to pay a tax to the United States that would be nondischargeable.
11. Cash advances beyond $1,500 on a credit card.

is a privilege, not a right. A judge determines which debts are dischargeable. If the debtor has received a previous discharge of debt within eight years of the current filing for bankruptcy, the judge will likely refuse a new discharge of debt.

Exceptions to discharge. Generally, most debts are discharged unless there are objections to the discharge or the debts are ineligible for discharge. If a major goal for bankruptcy law is to give debtors a fresh start, why are some debts nondischargeable? Some of the debts that are not dischargeable are debts to those who are in a weak bargaining position with the debtor. For example, child support and alimony payments are nondischargeable. Children and ex-spouses often depend on payments; consequently, the court will not permit the discharge of these debts. Exhibit 32-6 lists the debts that are nondischargeable as established by the Bankruptcy Code.

Case 32-3 provides an example of the court's consideration of whether a debt should be discharged. In this case, the debtor was found guilty of malpractice, and the debt was therefore dischargeable.

CASE 32-3

MARGARET KAWAAUHAU ET VIR, PETITIONERS, v. PAUL W. GEIGER

UNITED STATES SUPREME COURT
523 U.S. 57, 118 S. CT. 974 (1998)

In January 1983, Margaret Kawaauhau was treated by Dr. Paul Geiger for a foot injury. After examining Kawaauhau, Geiger prescribed oral penicillin to her despite his knowledge that intravenous penicillin would be more effective in fighting a potential infection. Geiger testified that he prescribed the oral penicillin because he knew that Kawaauhau was concerned about costs. Geiger then left town and placed Kawaauhau in the care of another physician, who transferred Kawaauhau to an infectious disease specialist. When Geiger returned, he canceled the transfer to the specialist and stopped Kawaauhau's antibiotic treatment. However, Kawaauhau's infection continued, and three days later, her leg was amputated below the knee.

Kawaauhau sued Geiger for malpractice and received a jury award for $355,000. Geiger, who did not carry malpractice insurance, moved to Missouri and filed for bankruptcy. Kawaauhau requested that the court refuse to discharge the malpractice judgment because the judgment was for a "willful and malicious injury" and was thus exempt from discharge. The bankruptcy court, finding that Geiger's treatment fell far below the standard of care, ruled that the debt was nondischargeable. The district court affirmed the ruling. The Eighth Circuit reversed the district court's decision, holding that malpractice was conduct that was negligent or reckless rather than intentional. Kawaauhau appealed.

JUSTICE GINSBURG: Section 523(a)(6) of the Bankruptcy Code provides:

> (a) A discharge . . . does not discharge an individual debtor from any debt
>
> . . . (6) for willful and malicious injury by the debtor to another entity or to the property of another entity.

The Kawaauhaus urge that the malpractice award fits within this exception because Dr. Geiger intentionally rendered inadequate medical care to Margaret Kawaauhau that necessarily led to her injury. According to the Kawaauhaus, Geiger deliberately chose less effective treatment because he wanted to cut costs, all the while knowing that he was providing substandard care. Such conduct, the Kawaauhaus assert, meets the "willful and malicious" specification of § 523(a)(6).

We confront this pivotal question concerning the scope of the "willful and malicious injury" exception: Does § 523(a)(6)'s compass cover acts, done intentionally that cause injury (as the Kawaauhaus urge), or only acts done with the actual intent to cause injury (as the Eighth Circuit ruled)? The words of the statute strongly support the Eighth Circuit's reading.

The word "willful" in (a)(6) modifies the word "injury," indicating that nondischargeability takes a deliberate or intentional *injury,* not merely a deliberate or intentional *act* that leads to injury. Had Congress meant to exempt debts resulting from unintentionally inflicted injuries, it might have described instead "willful acts that cause injury." Moreover, as the Eighth Circuit observed, the (a)(6) formulation triggers in the lawyer's mind the category "intentional torts," as distinguished from negligent or reckless torts. Intentional torts generally require that the actor intend "the *consequences* of an act," not simply "the act itself."

The Kawaauhaus' more encompassing interpretation could place within the excepted category a wide range of situations in which an act is intentional, but injury is unintended, *i.e.,* neither desired nor in fact anticipated by the debtor. Every traffic accident stemming from an initial intentional act—for example, intentionally rotating the wheel of an automobile to make a left-hand turn without first checking oncoming traffic—could fit the description.

Furthermore, "we are hesitant to adopt an interpretation of a congressional enactment which renders superfluous another portion of that same law." Reading § 523(a)(6) as the Kawaauhaus urge would obviate the need for § 523(a)(9), which specifically exempts debts "for death or personal injury caused by the debtor's operation of a motor vehicle if such operation was unlawful because the debtor was intoxicated from using alcohol, a drug, or another substance." 11 U.S.C. § 523(a)(9)

The Kawaauhaus heavily rely on *Tinker* v. *Colwell,* 193 U.S. 473, 48 L. Ed. 754, 24 S. Ct. 505 (1904), which presented this question: Does an award of damages for "criminal conversation" survive bankruptcy under the 1898 Bankruptcy Act's exception from discharge for judgments in civil actions for "'willful and malicious injuries to the person or property of another'"? The *Tinker* Court held such an award a nondischargeable debt. The Kawaauhaus feature certain statements in the *Tinker* opinion, in particular: "[An] act is willful . . . in the sense that it is intentional and voluntary" even if performed "without any particular malice," *id.,* at 485; an act that "necessarily causes injury and is done intentionally, may be said to be done willfully and maliciously, so as to come within the [bankruptcy discharge] exception," *id.,* at 487. *Tinker* placed criminal conversation solidly within the traditional intentional tort category, and we so confine its holding. That decision, we clarify, provides no warrant for departure from the current statutory instruction that, to be nondischargeable, the judgment debt must be "for willful and malicious *injury.*"

Finally, the Kawaauhaus maintain that, as a policy matter, malpractice judgments should be excepted from discharge, at least when the debtor acted recklessly or carried no malpractice insurance. Congress, of course, may so decide. But unless and until Congress makes such a decision, we must follow the current direction § 523(a)(6) provides.

We hold that debts arising from recklessly or negligently inflicted injuries do not fall within the compass of § 523(a)(6). For the reasons stated, the judgment of the Court of Appeals for the Eighth Circuit is affirmed.

AFFIRMED.

CRITICAL THINKING

The judge uses two primary analogies, traffic accidents and the conclusion. Do these two analogies possess relevant similarities and lack relevant differences as compared to the case at hand? Do these analogies provide valuable insights that warrant the judge's conclusion?

ETHICAL DECISION MAKING

What are the consequences of this decision for the parties involved as well as other individuals who might bring similar cases? Who is benefiting from the ruling in this case?

Objections to discharge. If a debt is not classified as a nondischargeable debt, the debt is presumably permitted to be discharged, pending the judge's approval. However, creditors or the trustee may object to discharge of debts. The objection process begins when a creditor or trustee files a complaint with the court. Any complaint must be filed within 60 days of the creditors' meeting. Once the complaint is filed, the court holds a hearing regarding the complaint. At the hearing, the court determines whether the debtor has engaged in any behavior that bars a discharge. The following behavior may cause the court to not discharge the debt:

1. The debtor has concealed or destroyed property in an attempt to defraud the creditors.
2. The debtor has concealed or destroyed financial records.
3. The debtor fails to account for a loss of assets.

Basically, if a debtor engages in dishonest behavior, the court will likely refuse to discharge the debts. Moreover, the court may sanction the debtor with a fine up to $5,000 and/or a prison sentence of up to five years. However, if the debtor has behaved honestly, the court will generally ignore the objection and grant the discharge.

Under BAPCPA, Congress added additional reasons for denying discharge. First, if the debtor fails to complete a course in personal finance management, the court may deny a discharge. Second, if there is a proceeding against the debtor for a felony charge for (1) a securities law violation, (2) a RICO civil penalty, or (3) a personal injury or death caused by the debtor's criminal or tortuous act, the court may deny a discharge.

Revocation of discharge. While a debt might be discharged, the discharge is not necessarily permanent. If the trustee or a creditor discovers that the debtor has acted fraudulently or dishonestly during the bankruptcy proceedings, the court may revoke the discharge within one year. The revocation of discharge allows the creditors to bring action against the debtor.

Reaffirmation of debt. Sometimes a debtor wishes to repay a debt even though the debt could be discharged. Why might the debtor wish to repay the debt? The debtor might owe money to a family member or a longtime business associate. To maintain a good relationship with these people, a debtor might choose to repay the debt instead of having the debt discharged. This repayment can occur through a **reaffirmation agreement,** an agreement in which the debtor agrees to pay the debt even though it could be discharged.

Unfortunately, creditors may attempt to pressure a debtor into reaffirming the debt. Congress was worried that debtors were unwisely surrendering their ability to discharge their debts by making reaffirmation agreements. Thus, Congress created the following extensive rules so that a decision for reaffirmation of debt cannot be an impulsive one:

1. The reaffirmation agreement must be made before the debt is discharged.
2. The debtor must be able to cancel the agreement, and the agreement must contain explicit information regarding the time frame in which the debtor may cancel the agreement.
3. The agreement should contain a statement notifying the creditor that the law does not require the agreement.
4. The agreement must be filed with the bankruptcy court. Typically, the debtor's attorney files a form along with the agreement stating that the debtor is voluntarily entering the agreement and the agreement will not result in hardship to the debtor. Unless the attorney files this form, court approval for the agreement is needed.

CHAPTER 11: REORGANIZATIONS

The largest bankruptcy in U.S. history was the 2002 WorldCom bankruptcy filing. As shown in Exhibit 32-7, WorldCom had over $103 billion in assets at the time of filing. Both WorldCom and United Airlines filed under Chapter 11, which allows the creditors and debtor to create a plan to reorganize the debtor's financial affairs under the supervision of the bankruptcy court instead of liquidating the assets. Generally, the creditors and debtor agree that part of the debt will be discharged while the other part is or will be paid. Creditors generally agree to these plans because they believe that the value of the operating business is greater than the value of the business broken up and sold in pieces.

Who is eligible for chapter 11 reorganization? Corporate debtors most frequently use Chapter 11 reorganization because they are permitted to remain in business. However, the debtor does not have to be a business entity to use reorganization; the debtor can be an individual unrelated to business. Stockbrokers, commodities brokers, banks, and savings and loan companies are not permitted to file under Chapter 11.

What are the reorganization proceedings? Most of the Chapter 11 reorganization procedures are similar to Chapter 7 liquidation procedures. Like liquidation, reorganization

Exhibit 32-7
Largest Bankruptcy Filings

COMPANY	FILING DATE	ASSETS PREBANKRUPTCY
WorldCom, Inc.	2002	$103,914,000,000
Enron Corp.	2001	$ 63,392,000,000
Conseco, Inc.	2002	$ 61,392,000,000
Texaco, Inc.	1987	$ 35,892,000,000
Refco Inc.	2005	$ 33,333,172,000
Global Crossing Ltd.	2002	$ 30,185,000,000
PG&E	2001	$ 29,770,000,000
Calpine Corporation	2005	$ 27,216,088,000
UAL Corp. (United)	2002	$ 25,197,000,000
Delta Air Lines, Inc.	2005	$ 21,801,000,000

Source: "The 10 Largest Bankruptcies 1980–Present," BankruptcyData.com (New Generation Research, Inc., Boston, MA), www.bankruptcydata.com/Research/10_LargestBankruptcies.htm.

may be voluntary, as with United Airlines, or involuntary. The reorganization process begins with the filing of the reorganization petition.

When the petition is filed, an automatic stay prohibits legal action against the debtor during the reorganization process. The debtor is required to file a list of creditors. Next, the order of relief is granted, and the court appoints a trustee, who appoints a creditors' committee of unsecured creditors. Because there may be hundreds of creditors, the creditors' committee is supposed to represent the interests of the range of creditors. The Bankruptcy Code contemplates seven creditors on the committee. The members of the creditors' committee have a fiduciary duty to the other creditors, and under BAPCPA, the creditors' committee must provide the other creditors with access to information.

The debtor may continue to operate the business as a debtor in possession (DIP). However, if the court feels that the debtor has mismanaged the business, the court may ask the trustee to operate the business.

Generally, the trustee is responsible for developing the reorganization plan to handle the creditors' claims. The *reorganization plan* is a contract between a debtor and his or her creditors. The goal of the plan is to rehabilitate the debtor while preserving the assets for the creditors. Reorganization plans usually state three things:

1. The classes of claims and interests in the debtor's property.
2. The treatment for each class of creditors.
3. A description of the means for execution of the agreement.

A debtor has an exclusive right to file a plan within the first 120 days of the case. If the debtor files a plan within this time period, no one else may file a plan within the first 180 days after filing. This time period allows the debtor time to persuade the creditors to accept the plan. The bankruptcy court may extend these exclusive periods. However, BAPCPA limits extensions of these time periods to 18 months and 20 months, respectively.

Once the plan has been developed, the creditors must vote to accept the plan. For the plan to be accepted, two-thirds of the creditors of each class of creditors must vote to approve it. If the plan is approved, it will go before the court for confirmation. The court may decide to reject the plan if it is not in the best interests of the creditors. When the court confirms a plan, the debts not under the reorganization plan are discharged.

Case 32-4 provides an example of the court's consideration of whether to confirm a reorganization plan. Exhibit 32-8 provides another example of a reorganization plan.

Collective bargaining agreements and reorganization. Through reorganization, a debtor can reject some contracts. In the early 1980s, legal scholars were concerned that debtors could use reorganization as a tool to avoid collective bargaining agreements. This issue became a serious concern when the Supreme Court held, in *National Labor Relations Board v. Bildisco & Bildisco,* that collective bargaining agreements are "executory contracts" and thus subject to rejection. In other words, a debtor was not required to engage in collective bargaining before rejecting part of the collective bargaining agreement through reorganization. However, in the opinion, the judge stated that rejection is not permitted unless the reorganization procedures would benefit through the rejection.

After the Supreme Court decision was handed down in 1984, Congress amended the code to prevent debtors from misusing Chapter 11 to reject collective bargaining agreements. The amendments set forth procedures under which the collective bargaining agreements can be rejected or modified. For instance, the code provides that a collective bargaining agreement can be rejected only if the debtor has first presented to the employees' representative the proposed changes to the collective bargaining agreement and the employees reject the changes without good cause. Furthermore, the debtor's financial situation under Chapter 11 must clearly benefit by the rejection of the collective bargaining agreement.

CASE 32-4 UNITED STATES v. THOMAS MILTON HAAS & BERNICE ELIZABETH HAAS, DEBTORS, NO. 97-6823

U.S. COURT OF APPEALS FOR THE ELEVENTH CIRCUIT
162 F.3D 1087 (1998)

Thomas Haas was a sole practitioner attorney. His wife, Betsy Haas, was employed full-time in her husband's law office as a clerical assistant. The Haases did not pay taxes over a period of years. In 1991, on the evening before the day their home was to be involuntarily sold, they filed for Chapter 11 reorganization.

The Haases owed $617,000 for income taxes and $68,000 for employment taxes. Almost this entire amount was secured by a federal tax lien. At the time they filed the petition, the Haases had $259,000 in assets. While the bankruptcy proceedings were pending, the Haases were to pay $1,651 a month into an account that would be applied to the secured claims. By October 16, 1995, this account held $64,000. An additional $7,600 was collected in a separate account. Thus, there was now $71,600 plus $259,000 in assets to satisfy the Haases' debts. The Haases submitted a reorganization plan, and the district court affirmed the plan. The IRS objected to the plan, arguing that the plan reclassified the tax debts and was not proposed in good faith.

JUDGE MORAN: There are, generally speaking, three types of claims in bankruptcy: (1) secured claims, (2) priority unsecured claims, and (3) general (non-priority) unsecured claims. Section 506(a) of the Bankruptcy Code, 11 U.S.C. § 506(a) (1993), provides that claims secured by liens on property of the bankruptcy estate are secured claims only to the extent of the value of the collateral, here $259,000, and any amount in excess of that is an unsecured claim. Employment taxes are, however, priority claims. Those claims are non-dischargeable, and a plan can be confirmed only if it provides for full payment over a period not exceeding six years. In addition, the plan must be feasible, and proposed in good faith.

The plan adopted by the bankruptcy court . . . provided that the $68,000 employment tax liability be paid in full from the $71,600 in the two special accounts. It provided further, however, that it be treated as a secured claim, thus reducing the amount of income taxes treated as a secured claim from $259,000 in estate assets to $191,000. The balance of the income tax liability is treated as an unsecured claim. The secured claims are to be paid from Thomas Haas' income as an attorney over a 30-year period, with interest at 8%, in monthly installments of $1,345.72. The unsecured IRS claims of $500,000 are to be paid at $500 per quarter over five years, an approximately 2% return without interest.

[T]he plan itself provides for only nominal recovery of unsecured tax claims. By treating the trust fund tax debt as a secured claim, rather than as a priority unsecured claim, the plan reduces the recovery by the IRS by $68,000. By ignoring the priority status of the trust fund tax claim the plan has, in effect, adjusted the priority of the claim, and this it cannot do. If we adopted the debtors' approach in this case we would essentially be ruling that when a creditor takes a lien to secure debt which Congress has classified as priority, the creditor has forfeited the protection Congress has specifically assigned to that debt to the extent the debt exceeds the value of the property subject to the security interest. Thus, to the extent the debt is under-secured, the creditor receives less protection than Congress intended. The plan, therefore, cannot be confirmed.

The IRS also claims that the plan is not feasible and was not proposed in good faith. It notes that the plan contemplates that a 68-year-old attorney will continue in the active practice of law for another 30 years, and it contends that such a plan does not offer "a reasonable assurance of success." Perhaps a bankruptcy court can entertain a somewhat greater risk of plan failure if, as here, the creditor, in the event of plan failure, has the protection of a pre-petition security interest. That protection, however, does not make a plan feasible if it does not, by its own terms, have a reasonable assurance of success. The plan itself must offer a reasonable prospect of success and be workable. As the bankruptcy court itself recognized, Thomas Haas "cannot be expected to practice law on a full-time basis for another 30 years." That alone dooms the plan as infeasible. With a recognition of the trust fund tax claim as a priority unsecured claim, the likelihood that no plan can provide a reasonable assurance of success substantially increases.

The decision of the district court confirming the plan is REVERSED and we REMAND for further consideration in light of this opinion.

REVERSED AND REMANDED.

[CONTINUED]

CRITICAL THINKING

Identify the reasoning that the judge used in the conclusion. Is this conclusion logically attained from the reasons you identified? Which of these reasons provide poor support for the conclusion, and how could they be better?

ETHICAL DECISION MAKING

Suppose you are Judge Moran. What purpose do you have in coming to your conclusion? Accordingly, what values do you share with the IRS that support your decision in favor of the IRS?

In November 2004, facing $1.8 billion of debt, Donald Trump's casino company, Trump Hotels and Casino Resorts, filed for Chapter 11 bankruptcy. Trump's company argued that because of its debt, it was unable to maintain and renovate its casinos. The Chapter 11 bankruptcy plan was *prepackaged*, or agreed on before filing, and reduced the company's debt to $1.25 billion. The interest rate on the debt was reduced from 15 to 8 percent. Thus, Trump Hotels gained access to cash through $102 million in reduced interest payments, new financing, and an increased line of credit. This cash was used to renovate hotel rooms and repair the casino floor in one of the casinos. The company emerged from bankruptcy in May 2005.

This 2005 reorganization was the second time that Trump Hotels and Casino Resorts took advantage of bankruptcy laws to restructure its debt. In 1992, Trump Hotels and Casino Resorts filed for Chapter 11 bankruptcy with $1 billion in debt.

Exhibit 32-8
Should Donald Trump Be Fired?

CHAPTER 13: INDIVIDUAL REPAYMENT PLANS

Chapter 13, "Adjustments of Debts for Individuals," permits individuals to pay their debts to creditors in installment plans under the supervision of the court. Repayment plans may seem similar to reorganization. Any debtor who files under Chapter 13 could also have filed under Chapter 11. However, Chapter 13 repayment plans are usually simpler and less expensive. By statute, these plans last between 36 and 60 months.

Who is defined as a debtor for a chapter 13 repayment plan? Only individuals are permitted to file under Chapter 13; partnerships and corporations are not eligible. Individuals must have a regular income and must owe less than $307,675 for fixed unsecured debts or $922,975 for fixed secured debts.

What are the repayment proceedings?

Filing the petition. As with the other forms of bankruptcy relief, the repayment process begins only when the debtor files the petition. However, repayment is distinct from other types of relief because repayment is voluntary only. A debtor cannot be forced into a repayment plan.

In the petition, the debtor states that he is unable to pay his debts. The debtor might request an extension of time to pay the debt or ask that the total amount of debt be reduced.

global context

An Alternative to Bankruptcy in Thailand

The function of bankruptcy law in Thailand is similar to that of American bankruptcy law. The law seeks to terminate the business undertakings of a failing operation, collect all assets, and compensate the creditors through redistribution of those assets. Thailand's law applies to businesses, citizens, and any person who "earns his living" within the borders of the country. Thus, foreign businesses and businesspersons operating in Thailand can petition for bankruptcy.

Thai law also offers businesses an alternative to filing for bankruptcy, which is similar to Chapter 11 bankruptcy in U.S. law. The alternative procedure is called *composition,* and its function is distinct from bankruptcy. Composition procedures allow debtors to remain in business while settling their outstanding obligations. Before the court will approve composition procedures, however, debtors must submit a clear and reliable repayment plan. Additionally, the objections of creditors are also to be considered. Nonetheless, acceptance of this alternative is quite plausible, especially in a developing country seeking to stimulate growth.

Alternatively, the debtor might request a combination of those options. As in liquidation proceedings, the debtor commonly files various schedules listing the creditors as well as the debtor's assets. Furthermore, an automatic stay on litigation against the debtor is granted when the debtor files the petition. However, one of the benefits of Chapter 13 is that this stay applies to creditors' attempts to collect from co-debtors.

Creditors' meeting and the repayment plan proceedings. After the debtor files the petition, the court calls a creditors' meeting. At this meeting, the debtor submits a plan of payment for her debts. This plan is not required to provide for the full payment of all claims. However, the plan must treat all same-class creditors equally, and the plan for repayment must not exceed a three-year period, unless the court approves otherwise.

Unlike the case with other chapters, creditors do not vote to approve a Chapter 13 plan; if the court approves of the plan, the plan is accepted. The court holds a hearing to determine whether to confirm the plan. Unsecured creditors may object to the plan at the hearing. However, the court can overrule these objections if all of the debtor's projected disposable income is used to make payments. If the court believes that the plan was created in good faith, the plan is accepted.

However, if the plan modifies a creditor's secured claim while proposing that the debtor keep the property securing the claim, the creditor may oppose the proposed plan. Court approval of an opposed plan that changes a secured claim is called a "cram down." After BAPCPA, it is harder for debtors to make changes to secured claims over the objections of creditors.

After the court approves the plan, the court then appoints a trustee to carry out the repayment plan. Every Chapter 13 case has a trustee. The debtor makes monthly payments to the trustee based on his or her disposable income. The trustee then disburses payments to the creditors. Moreover, as payment for services, the trustee receives a percentage of funds distributed to creditors.

Thirty days after the debtor files the plan, the debtor must begin making payments. The trustee must ensure that the debtor is making the payments. If the debtor fails to make payments, the court may decide to transfer the case to a liquidation bankruptcy or to refuse to grant the repayment plan

Suppose that you, a debtor, must make 12 more repayment installments to meet the terms of the repayment agreement. Suddenly you lose your job. What will happen? At any time before all payments are made in a repayment plan, the debtor, creditors, or trustee may request modification of the plan. If there are any objections to the modification, the court must hold a hearing. Thus, you and your creditors might modify the agreement such that your installments will be divided in half until you find a steady job.

Discharge of debts under repayment proceedings. After a debtor makes all payments under a repayment plan, the remaining debts are discharged. However, even if all payments are not made by the expiration of the plan, the court might discharge some of the debts if the debtor has experienced a severe hardship.

Like liquidation, some debts, such as alimony and child support debts, are not dischargeable. However, some debts that are dischargeable under Chapter 13 are not dischargeable under Chapter 7.

CHAPTER 12: FAMILY-FARMER PLANS

Chapter 12 provides for adjustment of debts of family farmers. Chapter 12 was added to the code in the midst of large numbers of farmers with severe debt in the 1980s. Many farmers had borrowed large amounts of money to increase their production; however, during that time there was a surplus of farm products. Consequently, many farmers faced serious financial problems. Congress addressed these problems with Chapter 12.

Who is eligible for the chapter 12 family-farmer plan? Not all farmers are eligible for Chapter 12 relief. A family farmer under Chapter 12 must have regular annual income, and the farmer's gross income must be at least 50 percent farm-dependent. Moreover, 80 percent of the debt must be farm-related. Finally, the total debt must be under $1.5 million.

What are the family-farm relief proceedings? Congress modeled Chapter 12 after Chapter 13 relief. The procedure begins when the farmer files a Chapter 12 petition. Automatic stay is granted to protect the farmer from legal action. Within 90 days of the filing, the farmer must file a plan. A trustee is appointed to oversee the financial affairs and is permitted to sell unnecessary assets. The court holds a hearing to rule on the proposed plan. Unsecured creditors are entitled to at least liquidation value of the debt owed to them. Once the farmer fulfills his or her adjustment plan, the farmer will likely receive a discharge from his or her debts and retain possession of the farm.

Exhibit 32-9 provides a summary of the types of bankruptcy relief available.

Exhibit 32-9 Summary of Bankruptcy Relief

	ELIGIBLE	PROCEDURE
Chapter 7	Individuals, partnerships, and corporations.	A debtor turns over all assets to a trustee, who then sells the nonexempt assets and distributes the proceeds of the sale to the creditors.
Chapter 11	Typically, corporate debtors; can be individuals.	The creditors and debtor create a plan to reorganize the debtor's financial affairs under the supervision of the bankruptcy court.
Chapter 12	Family farmer with regular annual income, gross income at least 50% farm-dependent, 80% of debt farm-related, total debt under $1.5 million.	Debtor is family farmer who works with creditors to adjust and discharge debt.
Chapter 13	Individuals exclusively; regular income, owe less than $250,000 for fixed unsecured debts or $750,000 for fixed secured debts.	Individuals pay their debts to creditors in installment plans under the supervision of the court.

CASE OPENER WRAP-UP

United Airlines

As part of the Chapter 11 reorganization plan, United was permitted to drop its four pension plans that covered 120,000 current and retired United workers. Consequently, employees lost thousands of dollars from their pensions each year. In February 2006, United Airlines emerged from Chapter 11 bankruptcy. United's legal bill for its 38-month restructuring totaled approximately $100 million.[12]

United Airlines wasn't the only airline to file for bankruptcy after September 11. In September 2005, both Delta and Northwest filed for bankruptcy. Notably, both airlines filed before BAPCPA went into effect.

[12] "United's Bankruptcy Tab: $335 Million-Plus in Fees," *USA Today,* March 16, 2006.

Summary

The Bankruptcy Act and Its Goals

Purpose:

1. To provide debtors with an opportunity to achieve a fresh financial start.
2. To offer protection to creditors.

Attributes of Bankruptcy Cases

1. Procedural rules set forth in Bankruptcy Rules
2. Cases filed in federal district courts and referred to bankruptcy judges,
3. Bankruptcy judges appointed and serve 14-year terms.
4. Bankruptcy appeals go to the district court judge.

Bankruptcy Proceedings

1. A filing of petition for bankruptcy.
2. Court grants an automatic stay for creditor actions against the debtor's estate.
3. Court determines whether an order of relief should be granted.
4. The creditors meet with the debtor.
5. A payment plan is created and approved, usually by the creditors and the court.
6. Debts remaining after the plan is carried out are usually discharged.

Specific Types of Relief Available

Chapter 7: Sale of nonexempt assets and the distribution of money to the creditors.

Chapter 11: Reorganization of the debtor's financial affairs under supervision of the bankruptcy court.

Chapter 12: Adjustment of family farmers' debts.

Chapter 13: Adjustment of individuals' debts.

Point / Counterpoint

Under the Bankruptcy Abuse Prevention and Consumer Protection Act of 2005, individual debtors must now complete a credit counseling requirement before filing under Chapter 7.

Is the Credit Counseling Requirement Helpful to Consumers?	
Yes	**No**
Congress's intent in including the consumer counseling requirement was to provide consumers with more information. Whether the counseling takes place in person, over the telephone, or over the Internet, the consumer gains a better understanding of her debt. Generally, the consumer explains how the debt developed. A credit counselor reviews the consumer's monthly income, expenses, liabilities, and assets. The consumer reviews options for dealing with debt; not every case needs to proceed through bankruptcy. The prefiling counseling requirement succeeds in giving consumers more power by understanding their options. This requirement is helpful to consumers.	The credit counseling requirement does not provide real information to consumers. Under BAPCPA, the credit counselors must charge a "reasonable fee" for their service. Generally, consumers have been paying $50 for the service, which is a significant amount to a person filing for bankruptcy. Because the debtor is required to complete the counseling prior to filing, the debtor may be persuaded to partake in a debt management plan. The counseling agency frequently receives part of the debts repaid in the debt management plan. The debtor may not be in a position to properly evaluate the debt management plan in relation to the bankruptcy options. Thus, the requirement is not helpful to consumers.

Questions & Problems

1. How does bankruptcy law benefit debtors and creditors?
2. Under what circumstances would Chapter 11 be used rather than Chapter 7?
3. Hall-Mark supplied electronic parts to Peter Lee. On September 23, 1992, a check that Lee had given Hall-Mark for $100,000 on September 11, 1992, was dishonored by the bank. Hall-Mark continued supplying parts to Lee, so Lee gave the company a cashier's check for $100,000 on September 25, 1992. After receiving the cashier's check, Hall-Mark supplied no more parts.

   On December 24, 1992, Lee filed a voluntary petition for bankruptcy, and the trustee attempted to have the $100,000 check to Hall-Mark set aside as a preferential payment. What were the arguments of Lee and the trustee? With whom do you believe the court would agree? [*In re Lee,* 179 B.R. 149 (1993).]
4. The U.S. trustee sought dismissal of the Chapter 7 proceeding of debtor Irma Estrada Rubio under Section 707(b) of the Bankruptcy Code as a substantial abuse of the provisions of Chapter 7. The trustee contended that if Rubio eliminated or reduced her repayment of a loan from her retirement plan and her payment of virtually all her

daughter's college expenses, she would have the ability to repay a substantial portion of her unsecured debts. Her "ability to pay," the trustee argued, constituted a substantial abuse of Chapter 7 and warranted dismissal. Rubio argued that such expenses are reasonable and necessary, that she is seeking relief under Chapter 7 in good faith, and that dismissal is therefore inappropriate. Would the granting of relief to Rubio constitute a substantial abuse of the provisions of Chapter 7? [*In re Irma Estrada Rubio, Debtor,* 249 B.R. 689, 2000 WL 807637.]

5. In September 1995, AT&T mailed Mercer an offer to open a credit card account. Mercer completed, signed, and returned her acceptance. Mercer provided AT&T an income figure of $24,500, a Social Security number, a date of birth, a home and business phone number, and a maiden name. AT&T then conducted a further review of Mercer's ability to service a credit line of $3,000 and then sent her a card and a cardmember agreement on November 10, 1995.

Mercer then used the account to obtain 14 cash advances from ATMs, some in casinos. By early December, she had exceeded her credit limit by $186.82, and AT&T barred her from further use of the account. In all, Mercer carried seven credit cards between March and December 1995.

Mercer filed a petition for bankruptcy relief under Chapter 7 of the Bankruptcy Code. AT&T challenged the dischargeability of the debt. The bankruptcy court concluded that the debt was dischargeable. The court determined that Mercer did not make any representations to AT&T regarding her creditworthiness. Because she had made no representations, AT&T could not meet the reliance requirement to challenge dischargeability. The district court affirmed the bankruptcy court's decision. Why do you think the appellate court should have upheld or reversed the district court's ruling? [*In the Matter of Constance P. Mercer,* 211 F.3d 214 (2000).]

6. Gergely, an obstetrician, performed an amniocentesis on Jordan Lee-Brenner's mother during her pregnancy. As a result of problems with the procedure, he was blinded in one eye. After his birth, and through his guardian, Lee-Brenner brought an action against Gergely, claiming that Gergely had misrepresented the need for amniocentesis and had performed it negligently. Lee-Brenner received an award for $780,282, which he failed to collect prior to Gergely's filing a Chapter 7 bankruptcy petition.

Lee-Brenner moved to have the judgment set aside as a nondischargeable debt. The bankruptcy court dismissed his petition, so he appealed. On what grounds could he argue that the debt should not have been discharged? Do you think his argument was successful before the appellate court? [*In re Gergely,* 110 F.3d 1448 (9th Cir 1997).]

7. First Jersey Securities, Inc., filed a petition for Chapter 11 bankruptcy after the Securities and Exchange Commission (SEC) obtained a court order against the firm to repay $75 million in illegal proceeds. On the same day that its petition was filed, First Jersey transferred $600,000 in assets to its attorneys, the law firm RSW, to pay for previous and future legal services. The trustee and SEC both challenged the transfer of the assets to the debtor's lawyers. The bankruptcy court and district court upheld the transfer. The trustee and SEC appealed. Why do you believe the circuit court either upheld or overturned the district court's ruling? [*In re First Jersey Securities, Inc.,* 180 F.3d 504 (3rd Cir. 1999).]

8. Florida Mining (FM) regularly sold concrete to A.W., a construction company. A.W. bounced a check to FM on March 5 to cover February deliveries, but it made good on the check on March 10. On May 3, A.W. filed for bankruptcy. The "trustee filed a complaint in the bankruptcy court seeking to void the March 10 payment as a preferential transfer." Do you think this behavior qualifies as a preferential transfer? Why or why not? [*A.W. & Associates, Inc. v. Florida Mining and Materials,* 1998 WL 115771 (11th Cir.) or 136 F.3d 1439 (11th Cir. 1998).]

9. Woodcock graduated from law school and finished his MBA in 1983. His student loans came due nine months later. Because he was a part-time student until 1990, he requested that payment be deferred, which the lender incorrectly approved. Since he was not in a degree program, payment should not have been deferred under the terms of the loan. Woodcock filed for bankruptcy in 1992, more than seven years after the loans first became due. Hence, that debt would be discharged unless there was an "applicable suspension of the repayment period." Do you feel this mistaken extension is an "applicable suspension"? Should his student loans be discharged through filing for bankruptcy? [*Woodcock v. Chemical Bank,* 144 F.3d 1340 (10th Cir. 1998).]

10. On August 2, 2000, Sheldon B. Toibb filed a voluntary petition for relief under Chapter 7 of the Bankruptcy Code, disclosing assets that included stock in an electric power company. When he discovered that the stock had substantial value, he decided to avoid its liquidation by moving to convert his Chapter 7 case to one under Chapter 11's reorganization provisions. After the bankruptcy court granted his motion and he filed his reorganization plan, the court dismissed his petition, finding that he did not qualify for relief under Chapter 11 because he was not engaged in an ongoing business. The district court and the court of appeals affirmed. Why do you believe the U.S. Supreme Court reversed or affirmed the lower court's ruling? [*In re Sheldon Baruch Toibb, Petitioner,* 501 U.S. 157, 111 S. Ct. 2197.]

11. Debtors Bill Brandon Beard and Peggy Jane Beard came up with a plan that permitted them to remit payments directly to an unsecured creditor, without having to transfer the funds to that creditor through the bankruptcy trustee. The two lower courts recognized that by granting the debtors the right to make these direct remittances and thus to bypass the standing trustee, the debtors would thereby avoid having to pay certain statutory fees that the standing trustee would normally receive in the course of administering the Chapter 12 bankruptcy estate.

The bankruptcy court approved the plan, as did the district court. The trustee appealed. Why should the appellate court affirm or overturn the lower court decision? [*In re Bill Brandon Beard and Peggy Jane Beard,* 45 F.3d 113 (6th Cir. 1985).]

Looking for more review material?

The Online Learning Center at **www.mhhe.com/kubasek1e** contains this chapter's "Assignment on the Internet" and also a list of URLs for more information entitled "On the Internet." Find both of them in the Student Center portion of the OLC, along with quizzes and other helpful materials.

Agency Formation and Duties

CASE OPENER

National Farmers Union Insurance and an Independent Contractor

Elmer Oestman was an insurance agent for National Farmers Union Insurance Company. The company had a contract providing that the "local agent, acting solely as an independent contractor, is hereby authorized to solicit and submit written applications for insurance policies and other contracts of insurer strictly in accordance with the instructions and direction of insurer." The contract specifically stated that "[n]othing contained herein shall be construed as creating the relationship of employer and employee between the local agent and insurer." Oestman was commissioned through the insurer, filed his own taxes as a self-employed individual, set his own and his staff's working hours, had sole discretion in hiring and firing his staff, bore all expenses in selling insurance, and provided his own transportation and office equipment. When his employment was terminated, Oestman sued the insurance company, claiming a violation of the Age Discrimination in Employment Act of 1967.

1. Based on the agreement between Oestman and the insurance company, do you think Oestman is justified in filing a lawsuit against the insurance company for firing him? Why?
2. What rights does Oestman have as an independent contractor? How would these rights differ if he were an employee of the insurance company?

The Wrap-Up at the end of the chapter will answer these questions.

CHAPTER 33

Learning Objectives

After reading this chapter, you will be able to answer the following questions:

1 What is agency law?
2 How is an agency relationship created?
3 What are the different types of agency?
4 What are the different types of agency relationships?
5 What are the duties of the agent?
6 What are the duties of the principal?

In the above scenario, it is important to determine whether Oestman is an employee or an independent contractor of the insurance company because different legal obligations arise, depending on the nature of the relationship. One of the most important relationships in the business world is the *agency relationship,* in which the employee may be an agent of the employer, having the ability, among others, to bind that employer legally. Agency relationships are crucial to running large businesses because the use of agents allows corporations to enter into contracts and therefore conduct business in multiple locations simultaneously. This chapter explores the nature and creation of the agency relationship, as well as the legal obligations that the parties take on when they form such a relationship.

Introduction to Agency Law

Agency is generally defined as a relationship between a principal and an agent. In an **agency relationship,** the agent is authorized to act for and on behalf of the principal, who hires the agent to represent him or her. The Restatement of Agency defines **agency** as "the fiduciary relation that results from the manifestation of consent by one person to another that the other shall act in his behalf and subject to his control, and consent by the other so to act."[1] (A *fiduciary* is a person who has a duty to act primarily for another person's benefit. A lawyer, for example, is a fiduciary for his or her client. We discuss fiduciaries in greater depth later in this chapter.)

Agency law is primarily state law. Thus, while there are similarities among the laws governing agency relationships, they may vary somewhat from state to state. For example, at least 27 states have enacted statutes governing the behavior of sports agents. Twenty-three of those states impose civil penalties or damages on the agent for violations of the athlete agent statutes. Twenty-four states (California and Florida, e.g.) have established criminal penalties for sports agents who violate the state statute. In contrast, only five states have criminalized violations of the statute by the athletes themselves.

Agency law is especially important for modern firms doing business in foreign countries. More and more companies are expanding their commercial ventures to overseas markets. While foreign countries offer fresh markets and eager consumers, American companies often run into legal difficulties in other countries. These difficulties may arise from a language barrier or simply a lack of knowledge about local laws. To avoid such problems, many companies hire agents familiar with local laws, customs, and customers to help them function smoothly in foreign markets.

Creation of the Agency Relationship

Agency relationships are consensual relationships formed by informal oral agreements or formal written contracts. However, an agency relationship exists only when the principal takes action to ask another individual to act on behalf of the principal.

When can an agency relationship be created? First, an agency relationship can be created only for a lawful purpose, in the same way that a contract cannot have an illegal purpose. Thus, a principal could not hire an agent to kill someone on behalf of the principal.[2] Second, almost anyone can act as an agent. A contract made by an agent is viewed as a contract between the principal and a third party. Therefore, a person can serve as an

[1] Restatement (Second) of Agency, sec. 1(1). The Restatement is a valuable reference that is well respected in the legal profession. The Restatement is frequently cited by judges as well as attorneys and scholars in making legal arguments. The Restatement provides a summary of agency law.

[2] Restatement (Second) of Agency, sec.19.

global context

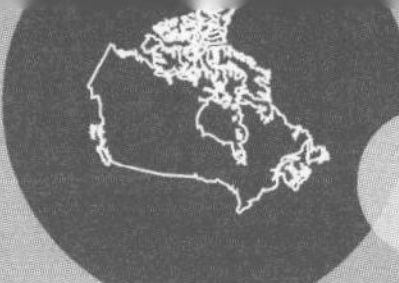

Agents in Canada

Taking notice of the increasing number of companies employing foreign agents, the Canadian government published guidelines for ensuring the legality of the agency contract. The first recommendation of the government is to clearly define the scope of the agent's authority.

While the precautions outlined by the Canadian government may cause some companies to reconsider hiring a foreign agent, managers should nevertheless give serious consideration to the idea. A foreign agent's familiarity with local laws and customs can be an invaluable asset in a company's expansion efforts.

agent regardless of age or competency.[3] However, if an individual does not have contractual capacity, the individual could not hire an agent to make contracts on his or her behalf. For example, because a minor cannot legally enter into contracts, most states do not allow minors to hire agents.

As long as these two criteria are met, agency relationships can be created based on any of the following four forms of authority:

1. By expressed agency, or agency by agreement.
2. By implied authority.
3. By apparent agency, or agency by estoppel.
4. By ratification.

The Case Nugget discusses the importance of apparent authority.

EXPRESSED AGENCY (AGENCY BY AGREEMENT)

When parties form an agency relationship by making a written or oral agreement, the agency is known as **expressed agency**, or agency by agreement. Expressed agency is the most common type of agency. As specified in the expressed agreement, the agent has the authority to contract on behalf of the principal. While a contract is not necessary, if an agency agreement is formed through a contract, the contract must meet all the elements of a contract discussed in Chapter 13. If a principal agrees to hire no other agent for a period of time or until a particular job is done, the principal and agent have entered into an exclusive agency contract.

One legal document that establishes agency relationships is a *power of attorney,* a document that gives an agent authority to sign legal documents on behalf of the principal. Powers of attorney can be classified in several ways. First, the power of attorney can be general or specific. For example, with a general power of attorney, a principal gives an agent broad authority to sign legal documents on behalf of the principal. In contrast, with a specific power of attorney, a principal gives authority to an agent only for the specific areas or purposes listed in the agreement.

Powers of attorney are often given for business and health care purposes. In the health care instance, a principal gives power of attorney to an agent so that the agent can make decisions about the principal's medical care in case the principal cannot make those decisions. Given that a principal must have the ability to enter into contracts to enter into an agency relationship, a principal may not enact a power of attorney after becoming incompetent. Therefore, a principal may preemptively enact a durable power of attorney.

[3] Restatement (Second) of Agency, sec. 21.

Case Nugget Apparent Authority and Agency

Steven A. B. Hannington, Appellant, v. Trustees of the University of Pennsylvania and Dr. Mark Bernstein, Appellees
Superior Court of Pennsylvania
2002 Pa. Super 314; 809 A.2d 406; 2002 Pa. Super. LEXIS 2873

Steven Hannington, a doctoral candidate at the University of Pennsylvania, was expelled for outstanding tuition fees, which he claimed had been waived in exchange for organizing a two-day conference on behalf of the university's Energy Management and Policy Program. Hannington filed suit against the university for breach of contract, and the university countersued for the outstanding tuition, fees, and interest. Before the case went to trial, Hannington and the university negotiated a settlement through their attorneys. Hannington's attorney notified the court that an agreement had been reached, and he filed an "Order to Settle, End, and Discontinue." One month later, Hannington obtained new counsel and filed a motion to restore the case to the trial list, claiming that his previous attorney had exceeded the scope of his authority by settling the case without his express authority. Hannington's motion was denied by the trial court, and he appealed.

The appellate court affirmed the trial court's decision, citing the doctrine of apparent authority for three reasons. First, the university was innocent and free from fault. Second, Hannington's attorney notified the university in a letter that Hannington had approved of the attached settlement release. Third, the negotiations took place over a six-month period, during which Hannington "had clothed his lawyer with the authority to communicate with the University on his behalf. Therefore, it was reasonable for the University and its lawyer to believe that Appellant had expressly authorized the settlement agreement." The court ruled that, regardless of Hannington's claims regarding the conduct of his attorney, the settlement was enforceable. If Hannington's attorney had not exceeded the scope of his authority, the settlement would be enforceable on its own. If Hannington's attorney had exceeded the scope of his authority, the doctrine of apparent authority would be applicable, giving the university the right to rely on the representation of Hannington's attorney to enter into a binding contract.

A *durable power of attorney* is a written document, created by a principal, expressing his or her wishes for an agent's authority not to be affected by the principal's subsequent incapacity. Alternatively, a durable power of attorney might become active only after a principal becomes incapacitated in any matter. Because the agreement is entered into before incapacitation, a durable power of attorney is legally binding after the principal becomes incapacitated. The Case Nugget examines the boundaries of the durable power of attorney.

It is important to note a few additional points. First, the Restatement states, "[A]n agency relation exists only if there has been a manifestation by the principle to the agent that the agent may act on his account, and consent by the agent so to act."[4] Therefore, in addition to the above criteria, there needs to be an agreement by the principal to have the

[4] Restatement (Second) of Agency, sec. 15.

Case Nugget Durable Power of Attorney

Penny Garrison et al. v. The Superior Court of Los Angeles et al.
132 Cal. App. 4th 253 (2005)

On Ella Needham's request, her daughter, Penny Garrison, was designated Needham's attorney through a durable power of attorney. After the execution of the durable power of attorney, Needham was admitted to a residential care facility. As part of the admissions process, Garrison, acting under the durable power of attorney, executed two arbitration agreements. Subsequent to Needham's death, Garrison and Needham's other daughters sought to sue the residential care facility for a number of concerns the family had regarding the care their mother received. The residential care facility sought to enforce the two arbitration agreements. However, the family contended that the arbitration agreements were unenforceable because Garrison could not legally enter into the agreements.

The durable power of attorney between Needham and Garrison gave Garrison power in two main areas. First, the durable power of attorney gave Garrison the authority to make all health care decisions for Needham according to what Garrison believed was in Needham's best interest. Second, the durable power of attorney gave Garrison the authority to make decisions relating to Needham's personal care, including, but not limited to, determining where she lived. Therefore, Garrison was legally in charge of picking the residential care facility, and she had the power to enter into agreements regarding Needham's care.

Nowhere in any of the enumerated legal powers did the durable power of attorney state that Garrison could not enter into arbitration clauses. Moreover, the arbitration clauses were optional to the original contract, and they allowed for a 30-day period during which Garrison could cancel the arbitration clause. Given the lack of coercion, and the fact that Garrison did have the legal authority to enter into the agreements, the parties were required to submit their claims to arbitration. The durable power of attorney was legal and enforceable, and the agent, Garrison, could not cancel the legal agreement into which she entered.

person act as an agent and by the agent to act for the principal. As noted below, this agreement can be reached in several different ways.

Second, agency agreements usually do not need to be in writing. However, there are two important exceptions. First, agency agreements need to be in writing whenever an agreement is reached for an agent to enter into a contract that the statute of frauds requires to be in writing. For example, Janet wants Phil to act as her agent. She grants him the power to enter into contracts. The statute of frauds, or, more specifically, the equal dignities rule, mandates that the type of contracts Phil is allowed to enter into must be in writing. Therefore, Phil's agreement with Janet must also be in writing. Also, whenever an agent is given power of attorney (discussed below), the agreement must be in writing.

Third, an important point relates to a specific type of agent known as a *gratuitous agent.* A gratuitous agent is one who acts without consideration; that is, he or she is not paid for his or her services. Gratuitous agents function much like regular agents, with a few specific exceptions, noted later in this chapter. The following sections discuss the forms of agency formation.

global context

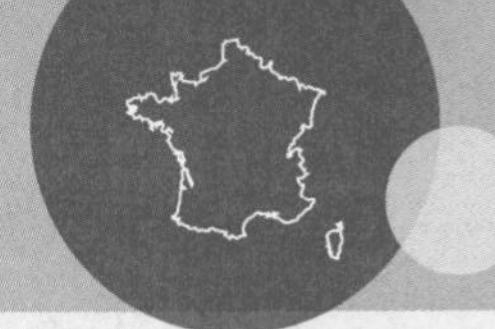

Formation of Power of Attorney under Civil Law in France

In the United States and other common law jurisdictions, granting power of attorney authorizes the agent to "conduct a series of transactions" under instruction from the principal. Specifying that the agent's power is limited to a series of transactions makes power of attorney in common law distinctly different from that provided by civil law. Power of attorney in civil law authorizes the agent to do "everything and anything which the principal himself could do." Under French Civil Code, the common law definition would actually be classified, for example, as portraying a special agent.

France recognizes the danger in granting unlimited power to the agent. Therefore, in 1988, France amended its Civil Code to say that power of attorney will refer only to acts of management and not those of disposition (or transference of property). Consequently, before signing a contract, the principal must carefully specify every type of disposition transaction that the agent may potentially engage in.

It is interesting to note that despite the danger associated with the broad definition in current civil law, Germany maintains that power of attorney authorizes the agent to do "everything and anything."

AGENCY BY IMPLIED AUTHORITY

In some cases, an agency relationship is not created by an express agreement but, rather, is implied by the conduct of the parties. The circumstances of a situation determine the extent of an agent's ability to conduct business on behalf of the principal. However, the implied authority cannot conflict with any express authority. Case 33-1 provides an example of the court's consideration of implied authority.

CASE 33-1 GRANITE PROPERTIES v. GRANITE INVESTMENT COMPANY ET AL.

APPELLATE COURT OF ILLINOIS, FIRST DISTRICT, FOURTH DIVISION
220 ILL. APP. 3D 711 (1991)

In 1988, Granite Properties and Granite Investment entered into an agreement involving a loan. According to that agreement, the parties conceded to submit any dispute to binding arbitration. In May 1989, Granite Properties filed a petition to compel arbitration of a dispute with Granite Investment. Granite Investment agreed to submit the dispute to arbitration and participate in the arbitration.

In late December, Granite Investment received a notice of hearing scheduled for January 2, 1990, on a petition to confirm arbitration filed by Granite Properties. James Green, general partner of Granite Investment, took the notice of hearing to his lawyer's office. Although his lawyer, Rex Carr, was out of town, Green left the notice with Carr's secretary, who later gave the notice to an associate, Staci M. Yandle, at the law firm. Without discussing the matter with Green or Carr, Yandle filed a general appearance on behalf of Granite Investment, and she signed the appearance "SMY Rex Carr." Later, the court confirmed the arbitration award for Granite Properties and restrained Granite Investment from prosecuting their claim. Granite Investment appealed the confirmation of the arbitration award on the basis that Yandle did not have the authority to enter the general appearance on their behalf.

JUDGE JIGANTI: The issue on appeal is whether attorney Yandle had the authority to file a general appearance on behalf of the defendants, thereby submitting them to the personal jurisdiction of the court. The law of principal and agent is generally applicable to the relationship between a client and an attorney. An agent's authority may be actual or apparent, actual being either express or implied. Apparent authority arises when a principal, through words or conduct, creates a reasonable impression the agent has authority to perform a certain act. Implied authority, on the other hand, is defined as "actual authority circumstantially proved" and is regarded as authority implied from the facts and circumstances. The party alleging an agency relationship must prove it by a preponderance of the evidence.

In the case at bar, defendant Green received a copy of the plaintiff's motion to confirm arbitration and a notice a hearing had been scheduled for January 2, 1990. He took the documents to the law office of Rex Carr, an attorney with whom Green had a longstanding relationship. Green admitted in his deposition he knew Carr was on vacation and "might have or might not have" known Carr was not expected to return until after the date scheduled for the hearing. Although he left no instructions other than asking to talk to Carr if Carr called the office, Green admitted he "would assume" he wanted the hearing postponed until Carr's return. Green took no other action regarding the matter. Sometime after January 2, 1990, when Green learned Carr's associate, Staci M. Yandle, was "handling it" or "did something on it," Green said nothing and did not discuss the matter with Yandle. The record shows that during this same time frame, Yandle signed a document filed by the defendants in their Madison County action. We believe the facts and circumstances of this cause are sufficient to establish at the time she filed the general appearance in this cause, Yandle had implied authority to act on behalf of the defendants.

AFFIRMED.

CRITICAL THINKING

Suppose the judge in this case could have asked the parties to supply particular pieces of missing information that would have improved her ability to make a ruling. What specific missing information would the judge most need to have?

How does the nature of this case lend itself especially well to concerns related to the ambiguity of language? What words or phrases contained in the decision are particularly ambiguous, and what different interpretations might be plausible? What effect does this have on the reasoning?

ETHICAL DECISION MAKING

What guidelines did Yandle follow in making her decision? In other words, what set of guidelines can people like Yandle follow to make more ethical business decisions?

What is the purpose of this decision? What ethical end does this ruling appear to pursue? Does it fit especially well with any particular ethical theory(s)? Why or why not?

How might a less traditional standard for ethical decision making, such as an ethics-of-care standard, view this decision? Is proper respect and concern for human relationships demonstrated, and is the ability of the relevant parties to fulfill responsibilities to one another protected?

APPARENT AGENCY (AGENCY BY ESTOPPEL)

Suppose a principal leads a third party to believe another individual serves as his or her agent; however, the principal has made no agreement with the so-called agent. Does an agency relationship exist? Yes, because by his or her conduct, the principal has created **apparent agency**, or **agency by estoppel**. According to the principal's conduct, the agent has apparent authority to act; thus, the principal is estopped, or prevented, from denying the individual is an agent.[5] When a third party relies on the principal's conduct and makes an agreement with an apparent agent, the principal must uphold any agreements made by the agent. If the principal attempts to deny an agency relationship existed, the third party must demonstrate that he or she reasonably believed, based on the principal's conduct, that an agency relationship existed. The court will consider the principal's conduct in determining whether an agency relationship existed.

Suppose a salesman enters the office of a third party claiming he represents a company that wants to do business. If the salesman is really not an agent for the company and provided no evidence of a link with the company, the company will not be held responsible under apparent agency because the third party had no interaction with the company, the principal. The third party had no reason to believe that an agency relationship existed, other than the agent's words. However, if the president of the company suggests to the third party that the salesman is a representative of the company, the president's conduct suggests that the salesman is an agent. Thus, the company would have to uphold any agreement the third party made with the apparent agent. In Case 33-2, pay close attention to how the court focuses on the principal's actions in this agency issue.

[5] Restatement (Second) of Agency, sec. 8B.

CASE 33-2 THOMAS & LINDA GENOVESE v. THERESA BERGERON

COURT OF APPEALS OF SOUTH CAROLINA
327 S.C. 567 (1997)

From October 1988 to December 1993, Theresa Bergeron paid $1,300 a month according to a yearly lease to rent a residence on Hilton Head Island from Thomas and Linda Genovese. Throughout the period Bergeron rented from the Genoveses, Doris Warner managed the property. In December 1993, Bergeron told Warner she had been offered employment in New York and Bergeron wanted to either terminate the lease she had with the Genoveses or sublease the property. Warner told Bergeron the landlords did not want her to sublease the property and the landlords were considering selling the property. Warner then told Bergeron she could vacate the premises and Bergeron should put her wish to terminate the lease in writing along with the fact she was vacating the premises.

In January 1994, when Bergeron was moving out, Warner inspected the property and told Bergeron she had to pay $1,360 for damages to the property. Because Bergeron's security deposit covered only $1,000 of the damages, Bergeron wrote a check to the Genoveses for $360.

The Genoveses, the landlords, brought a suit against Theresa Bergeron to recover unpaid rent and property damages. Bergeron argued there was evidence suggesting Warner had the apparent authority to release her from the lease. The trial court ruled in favor of the Genoveses, and Bergeron appealed.

JUDGE GOOLSBY: Apparent authority to do a particular act "is created as to a third person by written or spoken words or any other conduct of the principal which, reasonably interpreted, causes the third person to believe the principal consents to have the act done on his behalf by the person purporting to act for him." Muller v. Myrtle Beach Golf and Yacht Club, 303 S.C. 137, 142, 399 S.E. 2d 430, 433 (Ct. App. 1990) (citing RESTATEMENT (SECOND) OF AGENCY § 27 (1958)). The principal must either intend to cause the third person to believe the agent is authorized to act for him, or he should realize his conduct is likely to create such belief.

It is undisputed Warner was the landlords' agent. At issue, then, is the extent of Warner's agency. Genovese testified he gave Warner broad authority to manage the property. For instance, as the rental property manager for the landlords throughout the five-year period during which the tenant occupied the property, Warner managed the lease, received rent payments, and ordered necessary repairs to the property. Warner also prepared the rental agreements between the landlords and the tenant for their signing and negotiated the terms with the tenants. The landlords always dealt with the tenant through Warner and there were no contacts between the landlords and the tenant except through Warner.

When the tenant requested in writing whether she could terminate the lease or be allowed to sublet the property, Warner told the tenant the landlords were thinking about selling the property, and the landlords did not want the tenant to sublease it, so the tenant could vacate the property. The landlords did not communicate their opposition to this arrangement between the tenant and Warner until they filed this lawsuit.

Viewing the evidence in the light most favorable to the tenant, as we are required to do, we find there is some evidence in the record for a jury to conclude, under the doctrine of apparent authority, the conduct of the landlords in clothing Warner with so much authority to manage the property would allow a reasonably prudent person in the tenant's position to believe Warner had the authority to release the tenant from her obligations under the lease. See Rickborn v. Liberty Life Ins. Co., 321 S.C. 291, 468 S.E. 2d 292 (1996) (under the doctrine of apparent authority, a principal is bound by the acts of its agent when it has placed the agent in such a position persons of ordinary prudence, reasonably knowledgeable with business usages and customs, are led to believe the agent has certain authority and they in turn deal with the agent based on that assumption); Fernander v. Thigpen, 278 S.C. 140, 293 S.E. 2d 424 (1982) (agency may be implied or inferred and may be shown directly or circumstantially by the conduct of the purported agent exhibiting a pretense of authority with the knowledge of the alleged principal).

REVERSED.

CRITICAL THINKING

Suggest alternative meanings for any ambiguous phrases; explain how these ambiguities might have changed the judge's conclusion.

Is any important information missing from this decision that might further clarify the nature of the relationships between the concerned parties? How could more information in this area change the acceptability of the judge's reasoning?

ETHICAL DECISION MAKING

Identify values that characterize each side's argument. How would a different set of values change how each side made its decisions?

Does this ruling appear to follow a coherent ethical guideline? If so, what form does that guideline take? Who are the stakeholders in this situation? Are they awarded proper consideration under the selected ethical guideline?

AGENCY BY RATIFICATION

Suppose Fred is driving home and sees a car with a "For Sale" sign in the window. He stops to look at the car because his friend wants to buy a used car. He's amazed at the price and quality of the car, so he tells the owner his friend wants to buy the car. The owner claims another individual is coming to probably buy the car in an hour. So, to ensure that his friend gets this car, Fred signs a contract to purchase the car, but he notes on the contract that he is an agent of his friend. Because he is not an agent for his friend, the friend is not required to uphold the contract.

However, if Fred's friend agrees to purchase the car, the friend has accepted him as the agent for the contract. Fred's friend is now bound by the contract, and Fred cannot be held liable for misrepresenting himself as the agent. This type of agency relationship is *agency by ratification.* As suggested in the example above, there are two requirements for agency by ratification:

1. An individual must misrepresent himself or herself as an agent for another party.
2. The principal accepts or ratifies the unauthorized act.

For ratification to be effective, two additional requirements must be met:

1. The principal must have complete knowledge of all material facts regarding the contract.
2. The principal must ratify the entirety of the agent's act. (The principal cannot accept certain parts and reject other parts of the agent's act.)

Exhibit 33-1 summarizes the various ways that agency relationships are created.

Agency Relationships

There are generally three types of business relationships to which agency laws are relevant: the principal-agent relationship, the employer-employee relationship, and the employer–independent contractor relationship. We discuss all three in the following sections.

PRINCIPAL-AGENT RELATIONSHIP

The *principal-agent relationship* typically exists when an employer hires an employee to enter into contracts on behalf of the employer. This relationship is the most basic type of agency relationship. For example, suppose a salesclerk at Abercrombie & Fitch sells Amanda a shirt. The clerk is acting on behalf of the owner; consequently, any sales made by the salesclerk are binding on the owner of Abercrombie & Fitch. Similarly, think of all the advertisements seen on television in which a professional athlete speaks on behalf of a product. The athlete usually hires an agent to find and make agreements on behalf of the athlete to promote products.

EMPLOYER-EMPLOYEE RELATIONSHIP

Whenever an employer hires an employee to perform some sort of physical service, the parties have created an *employer-employee relationship.* The employee is subject to the

Exhibit 33-1
Creation of Agency Relationships

Expressed agency	Formed by making a written or oral agreement
Agency by implied authority	Formed by implication through the conduct of the parties
Agency by estoppel	Formed when a principal leads a third party to believe that another individual serves as his or her agent but the principal had made no agreement with the so-called agent
Agency by ratification	Exists when an individual misrepresents himself or herself as an agent for another party and the principal accepts or ratifies the unauthorized act

Exhibit 33-2 Types of Agency Relationships and Their Significance

RELATIONSHIP	HOW TO IDENTIFY	SIGNIFICANT FOR WHAT ISSUES?
Principle-agent	Parties have *agreed* that agent will have power to bind principal in contract.	Contract law
Employer-employee	Employer has right to *control* conduct of employees.	Tort law, tax law, wage law, discrimination law, copyright law
Employer–independent contractor	Employer has *no control* over details of conduct of independent contractor.	Tort law, tax law, wage law, discrimination law, copyright law

control of the employer.[6] Generally, all employees are considered to be agents of the employer. Even employees not legally authorized to enter into contracts binding their employer, or to interact with third parties, are considered agents. While all employees are agents, the reverse is not true. That is, not all agents are employees.

EMPLOYER–INDEPENDENT CONTRACTOR RELATIONSHIP

Employers often hire *independent contractors,* persons who are not employees, to conduct certain tasks. The Restatement of Agency defines an independent contractor as "a person who contracts with another to do something for him but who is not controlled by the other nor subject to the other's right to control with respect to his physical conduct in the performance of the undertaking."[7] For example, building contractors, doctors, stockbrokers, and lawyers are types of independent contractors. Furthermore, building contractors, doctors, stockbrokers, and lawyers are agents, while not employees. However, not all independent contractors are agents. Independent contractors cannot enter into contracts on behalf of the principal unless authorized to do so by the principal.

Exhibit 33-2 summarizes the various types of agency relationships and their significance.

Employee or independent contractor? The question of whether a worker is an employee or an independent contractor has important implications in terms of workers' compensation, workplace safety, and unemployment statutes. The employer-employee relationship is subject to the workers' compensation, workplace safety, employment discrimination, and unemployment statutes, while the employer–independent contractor relationship is not. Furthermore, as will be discussed in the following chapter, employers are generally liable in tort for the actions of their employees, while they are generally not liable for the actions of independent contractors.

When courts are deciding whether a worker is an employee or an independent contractor, perhaps the most important consideration they make is to determine how much control the employer exerts over the agent.[8] If the employer has substantial control over day-to-day operations of the worker, the worker is generally considered an employee.

Similar to the courts, the IRS also needs to make assessments regarding who is an employee and who is an independent contractor. The IRS outlined 20 different criteria for

[6] Restatement (Second) of Agency, sec. 2.

[7] Restatement (Second) of Agency, sec. 2.

[8] Restatement (Second) of Agency, sec. 2(3).

global context

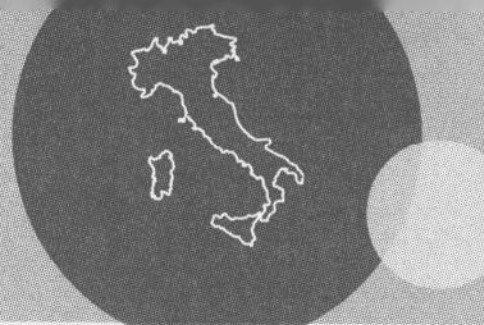

Formation of Agency in Italian Law

The Italian legal system has created an agency relationship resulting in unique powers for the agent. This relationship, though not formally recognized by the Italian Civil Code, is commonplace in business practices and has been upheld in a number of court cases.

The formation of the agency relationship begins much like the formation of agency in the United States. The principal and the agent enter into a contract under which the agent agrees to the principal's stipulations. This contract requires that the agent maintain the principal's property; in this sense the Italian law diverges from U.S. law. Under Italian law, the agent then becomes legal owner of the property on signing the contract. As a result, the agent possesses the legal power to transfer or contract the property without the consent of the principal. Such autonomous powers are not granted to agents in the United States, who must maintain communication and receive permission from principals unless otherwise specified.

The extended freedom of the agent under the Italian Civil Code results in considerably lengthy and detailed contracts between agents and principals. Both parties are looking to protect their own interests.

its auditors to consider in determining whether someone is an independent contractor. In 1997, the IRS, under advisement of the court, changed its criteria to focus on one element: how much control the employer exerts over the agent. The IRS needs to determine when people are employees and when they are independent contractors because of different tax liabilities employers face. The IRS examines situations in which an employer claims that a person is an independent contractor to ensure that the employer is not simply trying to lower his or her tax burden. When the IRS determines that someone who is claimed to be an independent contractor is really an employee, the employer becomes liable for all applicable taxes, such as Social Security and unemployment taxes.

While the degree of control an employer maintains is the central factor courts look at in determining whether a person is an employee or an independent contractor, it is by no means the only factor examined. Exhibit 33-3 lists the additional criteria the court considers in deciding whether a worker is an employee or an independent contractor. These criteria were established in the Restatement of Agency.[9]

Case 33-3 provides an illustration of the court's consideration of these criteria when determining whether a worker is an employee or an independent contractor.

The classification as an employee or independent contractor is also important in determining who owns the output of a work project. According to the Copyright Act of 1976,[10] when an employee completes work at the request of the employer, the product is considered a "work for hire." When a work for hire is completed by employees, according to the act, the employer owns the copyright. Conversely, an independent contractor normally maintains ownership of copyrights for his or her work product. Only by an agreement of both parties that a specific work is a work for hire may an employer gain copyright ownership of the work of an independent contractor.

Duties of the Agent and the Principal

An agency relationship is a fiduciary relationship of trust, confidence, and good faith. Thus, the formation of an agency relationship results in the creation of certain duties that the principal and agent owe each other. These duties are established in the agency agreement and are implied by the law. We discuss them in the following sections.

[9] Restatement (Second) of Agency, sec. 220.

[10] 17 U.S.C. §§ 101–810.

Exhibit 33-3 Independent Contractor or Employee?

CRITERIA	EMPLOYEE	INDEPENDENT CONTRACTOR
Does the worker engage in a distinct occupation or an independently established business?	No	Yes
Is the work done under the employer's supervision, or does a specialist without supervision complete the work?	Employer supervision	Specialist without supervision
Does the employer supply the tools?	Yes	No
What skill is required for the occupation?	No specialized skill	Great degree of skill
What is the length of time for which the worker is employed?	Long time	Varies
Is the worker a regular part of the business of the employer?	Yes	No
How is the worker paid?	Regular payments according to time	When the job is completed

CASE 33-3 CYNTHIA WALKER v. JOHN A. LAHOSKI ET AL.

COURT OF APPEALS OF OHIO, NINTH APPELLATE DISTRICT, SUMMIT COUNTY
1999 OHIO APP. LEXIS 3435 (1999)

In 1995, Cynthia Walker contracted with Genny's Home Health Care (Genny's) to find her employment as a home health-care worker. Genny's placed home health-care workers with customers in need of home health care. Ben Lahoski contacted Genny's to obtain twenty-four-hour home health care for his wife, Ann. Walker and another worker were assigned to provide home health care for Lahoski. Each worker would stay at the Lahoski's for either forty-eight or seventy-two hours, at which time the workers would switch. In September 1995, while Walker was mopping the floor in the Lahoski home, the mop handle knocked a cast iron clock off the wall. Walker was hit on the head by the clock, and she suffered a sprain of the neck and contusions on her face, scalp, and neck. Walker filed a claim with the Ohio Bureau of Workers' Compensation, naming Ben and Ann Lahoski as her employers. The Ohio Bureau refused Walker's claim by arguing the Lahoskis were not Walker's employers.

Walker filed a claim in court against the Lahoskis for denying her workers' compensation. The trial court granted summary judgment to the Lahoskis. Walker appealed.

JUDGE BAIRD: To prevail in her workers' compensation claim, Ms. Walker would have to establish she was an employee of Ben and Ann Lahoski at the time her injury occurred. The trial court's denial of her claim is based on its finding she was not their employee, but an independent contractor.

Appellees in this matter argue Walker was an independent contractor. In support of their position they point out there was no contract between Walker and the Lahoskis, the Lahoskis did not pay Walker but paid the agency, and Walker's contract with the agency specifically stated she was an independent contractor.

Courts have distinguished an employee from an independent contractor by resolving two key questions. The first is whether the "employer" controls the "manner or means" by which the work is done or if the "employer" is interested only in the results to be achieved. In the first case, the worker would be an employee while in the second case the worker would be an independent contractor.

The second question is how the worker is paid. If the worker is paid on an hourly basis, this tends to indicate the worker was an employee, while payment by the job tends to indicate the worker was an independent contractor. Thus, the overriding consideration for the fact-finder in these cases is who has the right to control the manner or means of the work performed.

[CONTINUED]

In the instant case, Walker signed a contract in which she acknowledged she was an independent contractor relative to Genny's and she would be an independent contractor relative to the customer, absent agreement by the customer she could be considered the customer's employee. However, such a contract provision is not necessarily controlling. The trial court must look to the substance of the relationship, not merely to a label attached to the relationship.

Appellees also assert when Walker and her coworker Peggy J. Seifert began to work for Ben Lahoski, Mr. Lahoski only briefly gave the women a tour of the house, then left it to them to perform their work as they saw fit. However, Cynthia Walker has testified otherwise, asserting Ben Lahoski was actively involved in directing her work for Mrs. Lahoski. In considering whether summary judgment was appropriate in this case, we must resolve the conflict in testimony in favor of the nonmoving party, Ms. Walker. Furthermore, the factual determination to be made in this case is who had the right to exercise control over the manner or means of the work performed.

[T]he "right to control" is agreeably the key factor in making the determination of whether an individual is an independent contractor or an employee. . . .

In the instant case, appellees merely assert "it is clear that Ben Lahoski did not reserve the right to control the manner or means of Appellant's work[.]" In point of fact, it is not clear Mr. Lahoski did not exercise such control. The statements of the two workers conflict on this point. Furthermore, even if Ben Lahoski did not exercise right to control, there is sufficient evidence to indicate he had the right to exercise that control.

The record below contains disputed facts and several indicia of employee status, such as hourly payment, control of hours worked, and control over the manner or means the work was performed. Appellees failed to meet their burden to show there was no genuine issue of material fact and reasonable minds could only decide favorably for the appellees. Thus, the trial court erred in granting summary judgment in favor of the defendants.

REVERSED.

CRITICAL THINKING

Clearly, all relevant information regarding the agreement is critical to the judge's conclusion. What other, missing information might be reason for the judge to form a different conclusion?

Do you see this reversal as related to an assumed preference in regard to the assignment of responsibility? What perspective on this issue does the judge seem to take? How does this affect the reasoning process and the conclusion reached?

ETHICAL DECISION MAKING

The court in this case argued that the law-governing agency in this particular fact pattern is unclear enough that the lower court should not grant a summary judgment. But Walker and Seifert worked for the Lahoskis. Are there values that employers in a position like that of the Lahoskis' should act on in their relationship with those who work for them? Should these values push employers toward going beyond what they are required to do by law?

PRINCIPAL'S DUTIES TO THE AGENT

When a principal contractually agrees that another person can make agreements on his or her behalf, the principal owes certain duties to the agent. If these duties are not fulfilled, the principal has violated the agent's rights. Consequently, the agent can bring a suit against the principal. If the agent is successful in bringing a suit against the principal, the agent is entitled to contract or tort remedies. Furthermore, if the principal has failed to meet duties owed to the agent, the agent can refuse to act on behalf of the principal until the failure is remedied.

Duty of compensation. The principal has a **duty to compensate** the agent for services provided unless the parties have agreed that the agent will act gratuitously. The agency contract will usually specify the type and amount of compensation as well as the time at which the compensation will be given to the agent. Thus, if a person were to hire an attorney to represent her, she has a duty to pay that attorney, her agent. If there is no agreement on the amount the principal will compensate the agent, the courts suggest that compensation should be calculated according to the customary fee in the situation.[11] The Case Nugget examines which individuals are responsible under the duty to compensate.

Case Nugget Duty to Compensate

Ralph T. Leonard et al. v. Jerry D. McMorris et al.
320 F.3d 1116 (2003)

NationsWay was one of the largest privately held trucking companies in the United States, with 3,200 employees operating in 43 different states. In 1999, NationsWay filed for Chapter 11 bankruptcy and terminated most of its employees. Ralph Leonard, and a number of the other employees who were terminated, sued Jerry McMorris and other NationsWay executives, arguing that the executives were personally liable for unpaid wages of the workers at the time of termination. Plaintiffs sought to enforce the executives' duty to compensate arising from the employer-employee relationship.

The defendants argued that they could not be held personally liable for agreements made between the employees and the corporation. While the case was beginning to proceed, NationsWay continued with its bankruptcy filings. As part of the Chapter 11 agreement, the former employees were to receive approximately $3 million in unpaid wages. However, the plaintiffs wanted additional amounts covering accrued vacation pay, sick-leave pay, holiday pay, and other nonwage compensation, as well as a 50 percent penalty and attorney fees.

In deciding the case, the court addressed the question of "[w]hether officers of a corporation are individually liable for the wages of the corporation's former employees under the Colorado Wage Claim Act." The court concluded, "[U]nder Colorado's Wage Claim Act, the officers and agents of a corporation are *not* jointly and severally liable for payment of employee wages and other compensation the corporation owes to its employees under the employment contract and the Colorado Wage Claim Act." Although there is a duty to compensate for the corporation, the executives who were the defendants were not individually liable to the former employees for the unpaid wages.

Duty of reimbursement and indemnification. The principal has a **duty of reimbursement and indemnification** to the agent. If an agent makes authorized expenditures in the course of working on behalf of the principal, the principal has a duty to reimburse

[11] Restatement (Second) of Agency, sec. 443.

the agent for that amount of money.[12] Thus, if an agent takes a trip on behalf of the principal, the principal must have authorized this trip if the agent is to be reimbursed by the principal.

Similarly, the principal has the duty to indemnify or reimburse the agent for any losses the agent incurs while working within the scope of authority on the principal's behalf.[13] For example, suppose an agent makes an agreement with a third party on behalf of the principal and the principal fails to uphold the agreement. The third party could sue the agent for damages because of the failure to uphold the agreement. The principal has a duty to indemnify the agent for the losses the third party regained.

Duty of cooperation. The principal also owes a *duty of cooperation* to the agent. Therefore, the principal must assist the agent in the performance of his or her duties. Furthermore, the principal can do nothing to interfere with the reasonable conduct of an agent. For example, suppose Suzy hired someone to sell her car for her. Suzy must be willing to let the agent show her car to interested buyers.

Duty to provide safe working conditions. The principal has a *duty to provide safe working conditions* for its agent. This includes the equipment, premises, and other working conditions. If the principal is aware of unsafe working conditions, the principal has a duty to warn the agent of the potential danger and make the necessary repairs. Federal and state statutes, such as the Occupational Safety and Health Act (OSHA), set specific standards for the working environment. When employers violate these standards, the employer may be subject to fines.

AGENT'S DUTIES TO THE PRINCIPAL

When an agent agrees to act on behalf of a principal, the agent owes certain duties to the principal. Because the agent makes agreements on behalf of the principal, the agent is in a position to potentially harm the principal. Say, for example, an agent makes numerous contracts the principal could not possibly carry out all at once. Because the agent has the power to make agreements on behalf of the principal, it is likely the third parties would sue the principal for not carrying out the agreements. Thus, because the agent can harm the principal, the agent is a fiduciary, a person in a position of trust and confidence, and as such owes certain duties to the principal. If the agent breaches these duties, the principal can sue the agent, and the principal may be entitled to a variety of contract and tort remedies beyond those stated in the contract.

Duty of loyalty. Courts suggest that the **duty of loyalty** is perhaps the most important duty an agent owes to a principal. Because the agency relationship is a fiduciary relationship (i.e., a relationship of trust), the agent has a responsibility to act in the interest of the principal.[14] There are a number of ways the agent owes a duty of loyalty to the principal, including avoiding conflicts of interest and protecting the principal's confidentiality.

An agent can represent and act on behalf of only one principal in an agreement. An agent cannot represent both the principal and a third party (who would then become another principal if represented by the same agent) in an agreement because there could be a conflict of interest. In addition to representing and acting on behalf of only one principal in an agreement, the agent also has a duty to notify the principal of any offers from third parties. For example, suppose Tony has hired a real estate agent to make land purchases for him. A

[12] Restatement (Second) of Agency, sec. 438.

[13] Restatement (Second) of Agency, secs. 438 and 439.

[14] Restatement (Second) of Agency, sec. 401.

e-commerce AND THE LAW

E-mail and Agency

How does the widespread use of e-mail affect agency law? Is e-mail communication a suitable means for conducting business relations? Agents have a duty to withhold any confidential information about the principal they represent. Thus, agents who communicate with the principal as well as third parties must be very cautious about making sure e-mail communication is secure.

third party notifies the real estate agent that some of his property will soon be going up for sale, and the third party wants to know whether Tony, the principal, would be interested in buying the property. The real estate agent cannot decide to buy that property for himself or herself until (1) the real estate agent has communicated the offer to Tony and (2) Tony has considered and rejected the offer.

The duty of loyalty also requires that the agent keep confidential any information about the principal during the course of agency, as well as after the agency relationship is terminated. The agent cannot disclose or misuse any information received during or after the agency relationship with the principal.

Duty of notification. Not only does the agent have to communicate offers from third parties, but the agent must also communicate any information the agent thinks could be important to the principal. This duty is known as the **duty of notification.**[15] For example, if a third party has made an agreement through an agent with a principal and the third party has failed to meet the agreement, the agent must notify the principal of this information in a timely manner. It is critical for an agent to inform the principal of all relevant information because the law typically assumes that the principal is aware of all information revealed to the agent, regardless of whether the agent shares all of this information with the principal. In Case 33-4 pay special attention to the duties of the agent to the principal.

[15] Restatement (Second) of Agency, sec. 381.

CASE 33-4

SIERRA PACIFIC INDUSTRIES v. JOSEPH H. CARTER

COURT OF APPEAL OF CALIFORNIA
104 CAL. APP. 3D 579 (1980)

Joseph H. Carter, a licensed California real estate broker, was hired by Sierra Pacific Industries to sell a ten-acre parcel of land for an asking price of $85,000, of which Sierra Pacific would receive $80,000 and Carter, $5,000. Carter showed the Willow Creek property to several prospective buyers; however, he eventually sold the property for $85,000 to his daughter and son-in-law, Debbie and David Benson, and retained the $5,000 commission without informing Sierra Pacific of his relationship to the buyers of the land. Sierra Pacific brought a claim of fraud against Carter. At trial, the jury ruled in favor of Carter; however, Sierra Pacific moved for a new trial, and the motion was granted. Carter appealed.

JUDGE RHODES: An agent bears a fiduciary relationship to his or her principal which requires, among other things, disclosure of all information in the agent's possession relevant to the subject matter of the agency. An agent may not compete with the principal, nor may he or she act as agent for another whose interests conflict with those of the principal.

In the context of an agreement to sell land on another's behalf, the general duties inherent in every agency become more specific. A real estate agent must refrain from dual representation in a sale transaction unless he or she obtains the consent of both principals after full disclosure. This means under most circumstances if the agent is related to the buyer in a way which suggests a reasonable possibility the agent him or herself could indirectly be acquiring an interest in the subject property, the relationship is a "material fact" which must be disclosed.

There is no question Carter concealed information material to this transaction from his principal, Sierra Pacific. He claims he was exempted from the disclosure requirement, however, on the basis of a so-called "net listing." Under a net-listing agreement the seller agrees to take a fixed sum of money for his property and the broker is entitled to all additional sums as his commission. It is true under this type of arrangement a broker may not be obligated to disclose any relationship he has to the buyer. The exception, however, has no applicability to the undisputed facts present here.

It, thus, is evident Carter owed a duty of disclosure to his principal, Sierra Pacific. It is equally evident the duty was breached. Given duty and breach, a minimum of $5,000 in damages to Sierra Pacific flows automatically. Apart from any actual and proximately caused loss on the price it received for its property, Sierra Pacific was entitled to recover the commission it paid to Carter. ". . . [A] real estate broker must act in good faith in the discharge of his duties as agent. . . . [By] misconduct, breach of conduct [sic] or willful disregard, in a material respect, of an obligation imposed upon him by the law of agency, he may forfeit his right to compensation." (Baird v. Madsen (1943) 57 Cal.App. 2d 465 at p. 475-476 [134 P. 2d 885].)

We thus are led to the inescapable conclusion Carter is liable to Sierra Pacific as a matter of law for a minimum of $5,000 and the jury's verdict to the contrary was in error.

AFFIRMED, in favor of Sierra Pacific.

CRITICAL THINKING

Why do you think the jury concluded the opposite of Judge Rhodes's conclusion? Where does the jury's argument falter, according to Judge Rhodes?

Removed to the level of abstraction, how could you define the issue being considered here? What opposing opinions are in conflict? Does the judge's decision rely on a stance in such a debate, and, if so, is his argument strong enough to support his position?

ETHICAL DECISION MAKING

Judge Rhodes believed that Carter "concealed information material to this transaction from his principal, Sierra Pacific." What set of guidelines could Carter have followed in making a more ethical decision? What guidelines does the judge appear to be following in reaching his decision? Are they ethically superior to those chosen by Carter? Why or why not?

Duty of performance. The agent owes the *duty of performance* to the principal. This duty is twofold. First, the agent must perform the duties as specified in the agency agreement. For example, suppose an insurance agent contacts Bethany about purchasing a car insurance policy. Bethany agrees to purchase the policy, but for some reason, the agent never obtains the policy for her. Bethany discovers the insurance agent's mistake when she gets into a car accident. The insurance agent did not meet the duty of performance. Consequently, Bethany could bring a claim against the insurance agent.

Second, the agent must perform the specified duties with reasonable skill and care. The agent is expected to provide the same standards of skill, care, and professionalism as the reasonable person in the same situation would provide. For example, when an attorney advertises that he is a specialist in certain types of law, this lawyer will be held to the reasonable standard of care in that specialty of law.[16] A gratuitous agent cannot be found liable for a breach of contract for failure to perform because no contract exists between the principal and agent. However, if a gratuitous agent begins to act as an agent and the principal affirms the relationship, a duty to perform arises insofar as the agent has begun a specific task for the principal.

Duty of obedience. Under the *duty of obedience,* the agent must follow the lawful instruction and direction of the principal.[17] Thus, if the agent makes an unauthorized agreement, the agent has failed to meet the duty of obedience. However, if the principal gives unlawful or unethical instructions, the agent is not required to behave in accordance with those instructions. For example, let's say a principal tells an agent to sell a basketball autographed by Michael Jordan; however, the agent knows that the principal forged the signature on the basketball. The agent is not required to obey the instructions of the principal.

Duty of accounting. Under the *duty of accounting,* the agent must keep an accurate account of the transactions of money and property made on behalf of the principal.[18] If the principal requests to see this accounting, the agent has a duty to provide the principal with the accounting. Part of this duty of accounting is the duty of the agent to keep separate accounts for the principal's funds and the agent's funds. The agent cannot allow the funds to "mix."

In Case 33-5, the plaintiffs allege that an insurance agent had a duty to advise them as a customer. However, the court determined that the agent's duty is to the principal, not the customer of the principal.

[16] Restatement (Second) of Agency, sec. 379.

[17] Restatement (Second) of Agency, secs. 383 and 385.

[18] Restatement (Second) of Agency, sec. 382.

CASE 33-5 GLORIA & TYRONE HARTS v. FARMERS INSURANCE EXCHANGE & GREGORY PIETRZAK

SUPREME COURT OF MICHIGAN
461 MICH. 1 (1999)

In early 1993, Gloria Harts was involved in an automobile accident with an uninsured vehicle. Mrs. Harts was injured, and her six-year-old son was killed. Mrs. Harts was driving a Chevrolet Cavalier covered by a policy that did not include optional uninsured motorist coverage. The Harts filed suit against Mr. Pietrzak, an employee of Farmers Insurance Exchange, for negligence for selling them an inadequate insurance policy. They also filed suit against Farmers Insurance Exchange for negligently supervising Mr. Pietrzak. The trial court granted summary judgment in favor of the defendants, and the court of appeals affirmed.

JUDGE TAYLOR: [The plaintiffs] ask this Court to determine a licensed insurance agent has a duty to offer advice or counsel concerning uninsured motorist coverage. In considering this question of duty and its potential expansion, it is appropriate to first look at the common-law duties inherent in an insurer-agent-insured relationship and then to consider the extent to which this relationship has been affected by certain Michigan statutes relevant to the establishment of an agent's duty.

It is uncontested, indeed it is essential to the cause of action pleaded by plaintiffs, Mr. Pietrzak was Farmers' agent. As such, under the common law, he had a duty to comply with the various fiduciary obligations he owed to Farmers and to act for its benefit. Moreover, because he was Farmers' agent, he had no common-law duty to advise plaintiffs. This general common-law rule is no doubt premised, at least in part, on the nature of the relationship of the parties. Specifically, the relationship between the insurer and insured is a contractual one. The relationship between the insurer and its agent is controlled by the principles of agency.

Sound policy reasons also support the general rule insurance agents have no duty to advise the insured regarding the adequacy of insurance coverage. For instance, in Nelson v Davidson, the Wisconsin Supreme Court noted a contrary rule (1) "would remove any burden from the insured to take care of his or her own financial needs and expectations in entering the marketplace and choosing from the competitive products available," (2) could result in liability for a failure to advise a client "of every possible insurance option, or even an arguably better package of insurance offered by a competitor," and (3) could provide an insured with an opportunity to self-insure "after the loss by merely asserting they would have bought the additional coverage had it been offered."

Thus, under the common law, an insurance agent whose principal is the insurance company owes no duty to advise a potential insured about any coverage. Such an agent's job is to merely present the product of his principal and take such orders as can be secured from those who want to purchase the coverage offered.

AFFIRMED.

CRITICAL THINKING

Evaluate the quality of the judge's reasoning in terms of the analogy used. Are there enough similarities to make a reasonable comparison between the two cases?

Do you think all necessary reasons to support the judge's conclusion are explained? For instance, what is the justification for the preference of preserving the principal-agent relationship over more basic principles of the protection of human safety? Is it complete? Valid? How might this affect the acceptability of the conclusion?

ETHICAL DECISION MAKING

At what point do you think an agent can recommend the best product for the customer, yet still fulfill his duties to the principal? What criterion might guide this decision? What sort of value preferences are implied in this decision? Are these the most desirable preferences to hold in considering such a case? Where would different ethical theories stand on this issue?

Rights and Remedies

PRINCIPAL'S RIGHTS AND REMEDIES AGAINST THE AGENT

Because the agency relationship generally *is* a contractual relationship, a principal has available contract remedies, discussed in depth in Chapter 20, for breach of fiduciary

global context

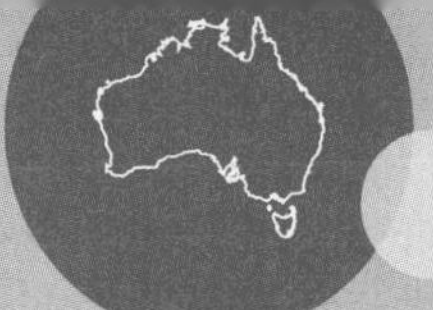

Duties of the Agent in Australia

Agents in Australia and the United States share many of the same duties to the principal. Some of these shared duties include following the principal's instructions, exercising reasonable care and skill, and not divulging or concealing confidential information.

While similarities between the two countries exist, agents in Australia have a unique duty. When performing services, the agent is obligated to "act personally" on behalf of the principal. For example, suppose an agent is hired to sell apartments owned by the principal. The agent turns around and hires an individual to sell the apartments for him. According to the law in Australia, the agent cannot receive commission from the sale.

The basis for such a law is quite logical. The agent was hired to exercise personal skills, such as availability, in the absence of the principal. When no personal skill is demonstrated, the agent shall not be granted any compensation or reward. Specifying that duties must be performed personally may seem like an obvious and unnecessary stipulation, but this specificity is important in protecting the interests of the principal.

duties. In addition, a principal may utilize tort remedies for an agent's misrepresentations, negligence, or other business failings causing damage to the principal. Furthermore, when an agent breaches his or her fiduciary duties, the principal has the right to terminate the agency relationship. While numerous possible remedies are available to the principal, the three main remedies are constructive trust, avoidance, and indemnification.

Constructive trust. Agency relationships exist primarily for the benefit of the principal. Therefore, principals are the legal owners of anything an agent may come to possess through the employment or agency relationship. Accordingly, when an agent through deceit or other means retains profits or goods obtained through the employment or agency relationship, which by law belong to the principal, the agent has breached his or her fiduciary duties. For example, Joy is an agent of Sarah's selling real estate. Joy sells a piece of property for $2,000 more than Sarah anticipated. Joy then keeps the extra $2,000 and reports the sale at the price Sarah anticipated. By law the profits belong to Sarah, and Joy has breached her fiduciary duties by keeping the money.

Also, an agent may not use the agency relationship to obtain goods or property for himself or herself when the principal desired to obtain the same goods or property. In an agency relationship, the principal always has right of first refusal. That is, before an agent may use the relationship for a personal acquisition, the principal has the opportunity to buy whatever goods or property are in question. Returning to Sarah and Joy, if Joy were to buy a piece of land she knew Sarah wished to purchase, she again would have breached her fiduciary duties to Sarah.

When an agent illegally benefits from the agency relationship, the principal may enact a constructive trust on the profits, goods, or property in question. A **constructive trust** is an equitable trust imposed on one who wrongfully obtains or holds legal right to property he or she should not possess. When a principal enacts a constructive trust, the court rules that the agent is merely holding the property or goods in trust for the principal, granting the principal legal right or possession.

Avoidance. When an agency relationship exists through a contract and the agent breaches the agreement or his fiduciary duties, the principal may use her right of avoidance. *Avoidance* allows a principal to nullify any contract the agent negotiated. Which, if any, contracts are voided is at the discretion of the principal.

Indemnification. Agents enter into contracts with third parties on behalf of the principal. If the third party believes that the agent is acting with actual or apparent authority, she may sue the principal for any breach of contract. However, when the breach was caused by the agent's negligence, the principal has a right to *indemnification.* That is, when sued by a third party, a principal may sue his agent to recover the amount assessed to the third party if the breach of contract is the agent's fault. For example, Ricardo is a principal employing Mercedes as his agent. Mercedes enters into a contract with Christina. Ricardo cannot possibly fulfill the contract with Christina, and Mercedes had the relevant information to determine Ricardo's inability to fulfill the contract. Christina sues Ricardo for breach of contract and recovers damages. Ricardo, under indemnification, is entitled to sue Mercedes to recover what he had to pay to Christina as damages.

In addition to recovering for negligence, a principal can recover if an agent fails to follow the principal's instructions. For example, Ricardo tells Mercedes not to take any more orders for widgets, which Ricardo produces. While Ricardo is out of town, Mercedes takes an order for 1,000 widgets. When Christina sues Ricardo for breach of contract, he can recover damages from Mercedes because she did not follow Ricardo's instructions. Courts have had difficulty in determining when a principal gives limiting instructions and when he merely gives advice. Going against advice does not impose liability on an agent, but violating limiting instructions does. For a principal to avoid a potential lawsuit from a third party, he should notify the third party whenever a relationship with an agent ceases or limiting instructions are given.

AGENT'S RIGHTS AND REMEDIES AGAINST THE PRINCIPAL

While agency relationships are intended to benefit the principal, the agent is not without rights and remedies. Whenever a duty is imposed on the principal, a corresponding right exists for the agent. Agents have available tort and contract remedies, in addition to the right to demand for an accounting.

Tort and contract remedies. Agents, much like principals, have certain tort and contract remedies available for situations in which a principal violates an agency agreement. These remedies are the same as standard tort and contract remedies, discussed in Chapters 8 and 20, respectively.

Demand for an accounting. When an agent feels she is not being properly compensated, especially when working on commission, the agent may *demand an accounting.* When an agent demands an accounting, she may withhold further performance of her duties until the principal supplies appropriate accounting data. For example, Hal is a used-car salesman working for Not a Lemon Car Dealers. When Hal receives his pay, he believes he has been shorted the appropriate amount he made on commission. Hal can request that Not a Lemon obtain an auditor to perform an audit and determine whether he was in fact paid the proper amount for his sales.

Specific performance. When a contract exists and a principal agrees to certain conditions, but fails to perform, under contract remedies the agent may seek court assistance in forcing the principal to perform the contract as stipulated. However, when the agency relationship is not contractual or the contract is for personal services, an agent does not have the right to seek specific performance. In noncontractual relationships, an agent may recover for services rendered, and/or future damages, but the agent may not force the principal to fulfill the specific contractual agreements or even to continue to employ the agent.

Exhibit 33-4 summarizes the duties that attach to an agency relationship.

PRINCIPAL TO AGENT	AGENT TO PRINCIPAL
Duty of compensation	Duty of loyalty
Duty of reimbursement and indemnification	Duty of performance
Duty of cooperation	Duty of notification
Duty to provide safe working conditions	Duty of obedience
	Duty of accounting

Exhibit 33-4
Summary of Duties in an Agency Relationship

CASE OPENER WRAP-UP

National Farmers Union Insurance Company

The issue in the case described at the opening of this chapter is whether Elmer Oestman is an employee or an independent contractor for National Farmers Union Insurance Company. The trial court found Oestman was an independent contractor, and since the Age Discrimination in Employment Act (ADEA) of 1967 relates only to employer-employee relationships, Oestman had no cause of action under ADEA.

Oestman appealed. The appellate court affirmed the trial court's decision. Oestman had no cause of action under ADEA, given the nature of his and the company's independent contractor relationship.

Oestman put himself through a lot of unnecessary trouble in pursuing this lawsuit. Almost all the evidence suggests that Oestman was an independent contractor, not an employee as he thought. If Oestman had a greater knowledge of the kinds of agency relationships, he could have saved himself large amounts of time and money.

Summary

Introduction to Agency Law

Agency: The relationship between a principal and an agent.

Agent: One authorized to act for and on behalf of a principal.

Principal: One who hires an agent to represent him or her.

Fiduciary: One with a duty to act primarily for another person's benefit.

Creation of the Agency Relationship

Expressed agency: Agency formed by making a written or oral agreement.

Power of attorney: Document giving an agent authority to sign legal documents on behalf of the principal.

Durable power of attorney: Power of attorney intended to continue to be effective or to take effect after the principal has become incapacitated.

Agency by implied authority: Agency formed by implication through the conduct of the parties.

Agency by estoppel: Agency formed when a principal leads a third party to believe that another individual serves as his or her agent but the principal had made no agreement with the so-called agent.

Agency by ratification: Agency that exists when an individual misrepresents himself or herself as an agent for another party and the principal accepts or ratifies the unauthorized act.

Agency Relationships	An *agency relationship* is a fiduciary relationship (a relationship of trust) in which an agent acts on behalf of the principal. A *principal-agent relationship* exists when an employer hires an employee to enter into contracts on behalf of the employer. An *employer-employee relationship* exists when an employer hires an employee to perform some sort of physical service. An *employer–independent contractor relationship* exists when an employer hires persons, other than employees, to conduct certain tasks.
Duties of the Agent and the Principal	*Principal:* • Duty of compensation • Duty of reimbursement and indemnification • Duty of cooperation • Duty of safe working conditions *Agent:* • Duty of loyalty • Duty of performance • Duty of notification • Duty of obedience • Duty of accounting
Rights and Remedies	*Principal:* • Constructive trust • Avoidance • Indemnification *Agent:* • Tort and contract remedies • Demand for an accounting • Specific performance

Point / Counterpoint

Should an Agent Fulfill the Duty of Loyalty Even When She or He Knows a Product Is Faulty but No Laws Have Been Broken?	
Yes	**No**
The agent should be loyal to the principal under all legal circumstances. According to the duty of loyalty, the relationship between the agent and the principal is a fiduciary relationship and the agent is obligated to act in the best interest of his or her principal.	The agent should not remain loyal to the principal when she or he knows the product is faulty, even if no laws are being broken. A moral rule is a moral rule. If we were to allow people to obey or disobey such rules as they saw fit, then the rule is not a guide to moral

Additionally, the agent can act only on behalf of one party in an agreement. The agent cannot be obligated to advise the consumer while acting on behalf of his or her principal because a conflict of interest would arise, meaning the best interests of the consumer are not necessarily the same interests as those of the principal.

Also, it is the responsibility of the consumer, not the agent, to become fully informed about the risks and potential problems with a product *before* purchasing the product. Consumers are able to quickly access product consumer reviews on the Internet, study frequently asked questions on company Web sites, and perform easy Internet searches for potential problems before purchasing the product. Just as it is the responsibility of the voter to become informed before elections, it is also the responsibility of the consumer to become informed about manufacturing processes, company history, and consumer feedback before making a purchase.

The responsibility of the agent is to his or her principal, no one else. Consumers are responsible for their own choices.

behavior but just a way for people to justify what they were going to do anyway. Moral rules exist as guidelines to protect people from manipulative businesspersons who are willing to bend and stretch laws to pinch pennies and increase profit, even to the detriment of the people. Agents do not need to reveal to consumers that they secretly think a competitor's product is better; in fact, agents do not need to reveal their opinion at all. However, when an employee knows, for example, that a new computer he is selling will break within one month of the expiration of the computer's warrantee, he should feel obligated to inform the consumer.

This transparency is not a matter of revealing trade secrets or secret recipes. Agents should simply provide sufficient information to allow for a careful decision to be made in a healthy, competitive business atmosphere. "Protecting" one's employer under the guise of a duty of loyalty does not excuse an agent from fulfilling his or her moral obligations to honestly and fully inform consumers.

Questions & Problems

1. Who can serve as an agent or a principal?
2. What are the similarities and differences between the types of agency relationships?
3. Why is it important to determine whether a worker is an independent contractor or an employee?
4. How is apparent agency, or agency by estoppel, different from expressed agency?
5. What are the principal's duties to the agent?
6. What are the agent's duties to the principal?
7. Calvin and Audrey Bones entered into a listing agreement with Agri Affiliates to sell ranch land. The agreement provided that Agri Affiliates, as broker, was to receive a commission of 6 percent for services provided "upon the Broker finding a purchaser who is ready, willing and able to complete the purchase as proposed by the Owner." The listing agreement allowed that the current tenants could purchase the land at the asking price and Agri Affiliates would receive a 1 percent commission. The current tenant of the property, Lydic Brothers, had been notified that the property was for sale, and Lydic was contacted numerous times about its desire to purchase the land. Dean Keller made an offer for the property at the full list price. The broker handling the deal had no further contact with Lydic after receiving Keller's offer. The Boneses signed the purchase agreement signed by Keller and inquired whether Lydic Brothers had any interest in the property, to which the broker replied that Lydic did not. The next morning, Lydic called the Boneses to inquire about the property. At that time,

Lydic was informed that a purchase agreement for the full listing price had already been signed. Lydic then informed the Boneses that it would purchase the property at the same price. The Boneses sought to get out of the contract with Keller, but Keller refused. Because Agri did not sell to the willing Lydic Brothers, the Boneses would not pay the full 6 percent commission, offering instead the 1 percent Agri would have made had Lydic Brothers purchased the land. Agri Affiliates brought action for the payment of the 6 percent commission under the listing agreement. The Boneses' answer alleged several defenses, including breach of fiduciary duty. Both parties filed motions for summary judgment. The district court ruled in favor of Agri, and the Boneses appealed. Did Agri breach its fiduciary duties by selling to Keller? Why? [*Agri Affiliates, Inc. v. Bones,* 265 Neb. 798 (2003).]

8. R. Edwin Powell was CEO and president of CAIRE, Inc., in addition to being a minority shareholder in Holdings, owning 11.9 percent of the company. In 1996, a group of investors decided to acquire Holdings and CAIRE. They formed MVE Investors, LLC. MVE purchased the shares of three retiring Holdings shareholders as part of a recapitalization of the company. MVE paid the retiring shareholders $125.456 per share, and became its primary owner. Powell did not sell his stock at this time and remained CAIRE's CEO and president. In response to CAIRE's financial setbacks, David O'Halloran, Holdings' CEO and president, met with Powell on January 23, 1997, to fire Powell. While the two men agreed on a number of provisions in Powell's severance package, they disagreed on the terms for the disposition of Powell's stock. Powell testified that O'Halloran agreed, on behalf of Holdings, to buy Powell's stock at the same price the retiring shareholders had been paid at the recapitalization. O'Halloran maintained he did not promise Powell that Holdings would buy Powell's stock. But O'Halloran conceded that at the meeting he gave Powell a detailed chart showing the number of shares Powell owned and how much money Powell would receive if those shares were sold or redeemed at the same price the retiring shareholders had received. O'Halloran also admitted he wrote a letter terminating Powell's employment if he chose not to resign. In the letter, O'Halloran expressed Holdings' intent to buy Powell's stock in the same manner as it had bought the retiring shareholders' stock. Holdings fired O'Halloran from his position as CEO and president. Powell brought action against Holdings, claiming, among other things, that Holdings had contracted to buy back his shares and then breached that contract. The district court found that Holdings had contracted to buy Powell's stock and breached the contract. The district court awarded Powell the amount Powell would have received had he sold his nonpledged stock for $125.456 per share. Holdings appealed, claiming that O'Halloran did not have authority to agree on its behalf to buy Powell's stock, the district court's finding that O'Halloran and Powell entered into a contract was contrary to the evidence, and any agreement was not the parties' final expression, is void for lack of consideration, and is against public policy. As an agent of Holdings, did O'Halloran enter into a contract on Holdings' behalf? Why? [*Powell v. MVE Holdings, Inc.,* 626 N.W.2d 451 (2001).]

9. Ward Manufacturing, Inc., decided to construct a casting facility on its property located in Blossburg, Pennsylvania. Ward entered into a written contract with Welliver-McGuire, Inc. Under the terms of the contract, Welliver agreed to indemnify Ward for any and all claims for bodily injury and property damage arising out of the performance of the work identified in the contract. Welliver assumed control, possession, and responsibility over the construction site throughout the project. Ward did, however, maintain an on-site representative to act as liaison and monitor the status of the project. Ward also had a safety representative on-site periodically to inspect the work site. Jonathon Olin worked as a carpenter for Welliver. Olin, while engaged in surveying activities on the Ward construction site, fell into an unbarricaded excavation pit allegedly covered with water and mud. As a result of the fall, Olin purportedly suffered severe injuries. Since the date of the accident, Olin had received total disability workers' compensation benefits from Welliver. Olin brought suit against Ward for negligence. Ward argued that Olin, through Welliver, was an independent contractor and that Ward therefore was not liable to Olin for damages. Furthermore, Ward argued that Welliver, and not Ward, was in charge of the site. Ward then moved for summary judgment. Was Ward successful in its motion for summary judgment? Why? [*Olin v. George E. Logue, Inc.,* 119 F. Supp. 2d 464 (2000).]

10. H&R Block's tax filing services allow customers to obtain faster tax refunds than would otherwise occur by simply mailing the return to the Internal Revenue Service. For customers who want to obtain a faster refund, H&R Block arranges bank loans with a third-party bank in the amount of the customer's refund through its "Rapid Action Loan" (RAL) program. H&R Block transmits the loan application to the bank for the customer. H&R Block then files the refund electronically with the IRS, and the IRS is informed to send the customer's tax refund check directly to the bank. The service allows customers to obtain the amount of their refund in a loan within a few days rather than waiting approximately two weeks for the IRS to send the actual refunds that are electronically filed. The cost of an RAL is described in the loan materials as a "finance charge" of the lender bank. For each RAL that it arranges between the taxpayer and the bank, H&R Block benefits financially in at least one way, and up to as many as three ways. First, for every RAL referred to a lending bank, H&R Block receives a "license fee." Second, through its subsidiary, H&R Block Financial, H&R Block purchases about one-half of the RALs from the lender banks. Finally, H&R Block has arranged with Sears, Roebuck & Company for H&R Block to receive 15 percent of the check-cashing fee Sears charges for cashing loan checks. H&R Block encourages RAL customers to cash their RAL checks at Sears. None of these three arrangements are disclosed to H&R Block customers. Plaintiffs in the class action claim focused on H&R Block's failure to disclose the various ways it might have benefited from the RAL program. They labeled these various benefits illegal "kickbacks" and asserted that the kickbacks were in violation of the fiduciary obligations H&R Block owed to its customers as a result of an agency relationship. H&R Block filed a motion to dismiss, which was granted by the trial court. Plaintiffs appealed. Did H&R Block violate a fiduciary duty through its failure to disclose its relationship with the banks involved? Why? [*Green v. H&R Block, Inc.,* 355 Md. 488 (1999).]

11. Ford Motor Company is the defendant in several product liability suits pending in the circuit court of Greene County. In each case, Ford raised a defense of improper venue and moved to transfer the case to a county where venue was proper. Venue in Missouri is determined by statute, which requires that actions be filed where the cause of action occurred or where the corporation has an office or agent conducting regular business. The cause of action was not in Greene County, and Ford does not have an office in Greene County. However, Ford Motor Credit Company, Ford's wholly-owned subsidiary, does maintain an office in Greene County. Ford Credit has its own offices and directors. It also has its own articles of incorporation and is organized under the laws of Delaware. Its principal place of business is Dearborn, Michigan. Ford Credit is in the business of purchasing retail contracts and leases of automobiles entered into by the dealer and its retail and commercial customers. Ford Credit also participates in commercial lending, including providing automobile wholesale inventory financing and capital, revolving, and mortgage loans to Ford and non-Ford dealers. A consumer is not required to finance a Ford Motor Company vehicle through Ford Credit. A consumer may choose to finance a vehicle through a bank or other credit service that may offer similar products and services. The manufacturer is not a party at any time to the retail installment contract or to lease agreements. Interest and principal payments from consumers and dealers are received by Ford Credit and not held in trust for Ford Motor Company. Ford Motor Company and Ford Credit are not parties to any agreement restricting or conditioning Ford Credit's ability to finance a customer's purchase of a vehicle or a dealer's inventory purchases. Is Ford Credit an agent of Ford Motor Company? Why? [*State ex rel. Ford Motor Co. v. Bacon,* 63 S.W.3d 641 (2002).]

12. In 1983, William and Carolyn Coldwell purchased an insurance policy that did not provide uninsured-motorist (UM) coverage. Mr. Coldwell was the only person named on the policy. Four years later, the insurance company offered UM coverage for the first time, at an additional premium. Mrs. Coldwell checked a box stating "I do not want [UM coverage] included in my policy" on her uninsured-motorist acceptance/rejection form, signed the form, and mailed it in. The insurance company removed UM coverage from the Coldwells' policy. In 1995, the Coldwells were in a major traffic accident with an uninsured motorist, who was faulted for the accident. The Coldwells eventually filed a complaint for a declaratory judgment on the issue of UM coverage with the insurance company, arguing that Mrs. Coldwell lacked the authority to enter into an agency relationship with the insurance company. How do you think the court decided? [*Coldwell v. Allstate Insurance Co.*, 1999 Ohio App. LEXIS 2758 (Ohio Ct. App. 1999).]

13. John Ray Lawrence, an employee of H.W. Campbell Construction Company, was killed when his head was crushed in the "pinch point" area of a crane. Coastal Marine Services of Texas, Inc., owned the crane, and Campbell employees were using it on Coastal's property when the accident occurred. Campbell took custody of the crane and began continued occupation of Coastal's property. Campbell was an independent contractor of Coastal, and no written contract existed between the two companies. Coastal employees were not directing or supervising Campbell's work on the project, nor were they on the job site when the accident occurred. Lawrence's surviving family and estate sued Campbell and Coastal, alleging, among other things, negligence. During the trial Coastal asserted that the Lawrences had presented no evidence that Coastal retained the right to control Campbell's work, a prerequisite for finding Coastal liable under a premises liability theory. The trial court agreed and submitted an instruction precluding a finding of negligence based on the manner in which Coastal controlled the premises. The jury found no negligence on Coastal's part. At trial, in response to a series of hypothetical questions, Campbell employees testified they would have complied with any instructions from Coastal about the movement of the crane if Coastal had given such instructions. Based on the Campbell employees' testimony, the court of appeals reversed the trial court's judgment, concluding that the testimony created a fact issue about Coastal's right to control the crane. Coastal appealed. What duties did Coastal owe Campbell as an independent contractor? How did the court rule on appeal? [*Coastal Marine Serv., Inc. v. Lawrence,* 988 S.W.2d 223 (1999).]

14. Sidney Carlson and Loren Wright worked for Everen Securities, Inc., where early on both signed a training agreement through which they agreed not to solicit Everen customers for 30 days after leaving Everen employment. Sometime in 1996, Carlson and Wright decided to resign from Everen and work for A.G. Edwards. Before leaving Everen, Carlson and Wright made photocopies of documents containing customer account information in order to contact the customers regarding their move to A.G.

Edwards. Carlson and Wright resigned and began working for A.G. Edwards. On their resignation, they immediately began soliciting the business of their former Everen customers. That same day, an Everen officer searched the office and recovered only 100 of Everen's 2,800 client files. Everen filed a complaint in state court alleging, among other things, breach of fiduciary duty by Carlson and Wright and aiding and abetting breach of fiduciary duty by A.G. Edwards. A hearing for a temporary restraining order (TRO) was held, through which Everen sought to bar Carlson and Wright from soliciting Everen customers for 30 days in accordance with the training agreement. Carlson and Wright, however, had entered into the agreement with a predecessor of Everen (Blunt, Ellis & Loewi). Because the agreement made no mention of the rights of successors and assignees of the original company, the court denied the TRO as to customer solicitation. The court partially granted the TRO, ordering the defendants to return all customer account information taken by Carlson and Wright until or unless the defendants received written authorization from the customers allowing the defendants to retain such information. Everen's claims were subsequently arbitrated. The defendants appealed the trial court's decision to confirm the arbitration award of $1,131,000 plus fees in favor of Everen. Did Carlson and Wright violate their duty of loyalty as part of their fiduciary duties to Everen? [*Everen Secs. v. A.G. Edwards & Sons,* 308 Ill. App. 3d 268 (1999).]

15. Nu-Look Design, Inc., operated as a residential home improvement company. During calendar years 1996, 1997, and 1998, Ronald A. Stark not only was Nu-Look's sole shareholder and president but also managed the company. He solicited business, performed necessary bookkeeping, otherwise handled finances, and hired and supervised workers. Rather than pay Stark a salary or wages, Nu-Look distributed its net income during 1996, 1997, and 1998 to him "as Mr. Stark's needs arose." Nu-Look reported on its tax returns in 1996, 1997, and 1998 net incomes of $10,866.14, $14,216.37, and $7,103.60, respectively. Stark, in turn, reported the very same amounts as nonpassive income on his 1996, 1997, and 1998 tax returns. On June 8, 2001, the IRS issued to Nu-Look a "Notice of Determination Concerning Worker Classification." The notice advised that the IRS had classified an individual at Nu-Look as an employee for purposes of federal employment taxes and such taxes "could" be assessed for calendar years 1996, 1997, and 1998. Nu-Look challenged this determination by filing a petition for redetermination in the United States Tax Court, disputing the propriety of the determination that Stark was an employee, and also sought relief from that determination. The tax court found that Stark performed more than minor services for Nu-Look and he had received remuneration for those services. As a result, the court held that Stark was an employee of Nu-Look and that Nu-Look was not entitled to relief. Nu-Look appealed. Does Stark meet the requirements for an employee? Should Nu-Look be liable for a tax assessed under the assumption Stark is an employee? [*Nu-Look Design, Inc. v. Commission of Internal Revenue,* 356 F.3d 290 (2004).]

Looking for more review material?

The Online Learning Center at **www.mhhe.com/kubasek1e** contains this chapter's "Assignment on the Internet" and also a list of URLs for more information entitled "On the Internet." Find both of them in the Student Center portion of the OLC, along with quizzes and other helpful materials.

Liability to Third Parties and Termination

CASE OPENER

The Liability of the Principal?

Toward the end of 1995, Paradise Magazine, Inc., submitted a proposal for a printing agreement to Dimension Graphics Inc., requesting Dimension to print *Paradise Magazine.* The president of Dimension contacted Paradise Magazine and informed the company he had no desire to engage in business with Paradise.

Acting as agents for Paradise, Ted Liebowitz and Bruce Jacobson represented themselves to Dimension as representatives for Worldwide Communications. The terms of the proposed agreement mailed to Dimension used the name "Worldwide Communications." In accordance with the resulting contract, over 100,000 copies of *Paradise Magazine* were printed and delivered in September 1996.

Dimension billed Worldwide for the printing but was not paid. Dimension filed suit against Worldwide for payment. As a result of its legal action, Dimension learned that Paradise conducts business as Worldwide Communications and that the principal in the contract was Paradise.

Dimension thereafter filed for summary judgment against Paradise Magazine, Inc. The trial court determined that the defendant, Paradise, was acting as an undisclosed principal. However, Dimension filed suit against the agents Liebowitz and Jacobson, alleging they were agents for a partially disclosed principal. If the classification of the principal was partially disclosed, Dimension could file suit against the principal, and the agents could still be held liable for their actions. The importance of the designation of what kind of principal the agents were should be better understood after reading this chapter.

1. If you were an agent for the principal Paradise Magazine, what would you have done differently from Liebowitz and Jacobson to avoid litigation?
2. As a business manager for Dimension, who could you sue for damages—the principal, the agents, or both?

The Wrap-Up at the end of the chapter will answer these questions.

CHAPTER 34

Learning Objectives

After reading this chapter, you will be able to answer the following questions:

1. What are the different types of authority of the agent?
2. Do the principal and the agent have any contractual liability? How so?
3. How does tort liability apply to the agency relationship?
4. How can an agency relationship be terminated?

Authority of the Agent: The Link to the Principal's Liability

In the previous chapter, we discussed how an agency relationship and its resulting authority could be created. That chapter introduced the important concepts of (1) expressed agency, or agency by agreement; (2) implied agency; and (3) agency by estoppel. Each of these avenues for creating agency includes a form of authority that attaches to that type of agency.

EXPRESS AUTHORITY

In an express agency relationship, the agent has **express authority** which is often referred to as *actual authority*. The principal has explicitly instructed the agent to do something. Therefore, if the principal requests that her agent sell her house for $100,000, the agent has explicit authority to sell the house for that amount. Express authority is binding in the sense that it gives the agent the power to make transactions and agreements with third parties. Because an agent with express authority has specific goals he or she is to achieve, the agent is also granted the use of other means, beyond the express agreement, reasonably necessary to achieve the desired goal.[1]

When express authority is granted for an agent to enter into a contract legally required to be in writing, most states require that the grant of authority also be in writing. This requirement is known as the **equal dignity rule.** When an agency agreement fails to adhere to the equal dignity rule, the subsequent contracts are typically considered to be voidable by the principal. This rule is based on the statute of frauds.

There are two key exceptions to the equal dignity rule. The first pertains to executive officers. When the executive officer is conducting business in the usual course of her job, she need not obtain written approval from the corporation for every decision she makes. The second exception is rooted in common sense. The equal dignity rule does not apply to the agent when the agent is working in the direct presence of the principal.

There is also a special type of express agent authority known as a **power of attorney.** The power of attorney is a specific form of express authority, usually in writing, granting an agent specific powers. There are two basic types of power of attorney: special and general. A **special power of attorney** grants the agent express authority over specifically outlined acts. In contrast, a **general power of attorney** allows the agent to conduct all business for the principal. While powers of attorney tend to terminate on the principal's death or incapacitation, a **durable power of attorney** specifies that the agent's authority is intended to continue beyond the principal's incapacitation.

IMPLIED AUTHORITY

In an implied agency relationship, the agent has **implied authority;** that is, the relationship is inferred from the conduct of the parties. Consequently, the authority of the agent is implied on the basis of words and actions of the principal to the agent.[2] An agent's implied authority is derived from an agent's express authority and consists of what is reasonably necessary for carrying out the agent's grant of express authority.

One way an agent may have implied authority is through custom. Therefore, it is important that third parties familiarize themselves with the trade. Furthermore, if an agent

[1] Restatement (Second) of Agency, sec. 35.

[2] Restatement (Second) of Agency, sec. 33.

must make an agreement or transaction to carry out the transaction he or she has agreed to perform for the agent, we can generally infer the presence of the authority.

For example, suppose one agrees to serve as a manager for a store. The contract probably does not expressly give authority for every decision the manager might need to make. However, the manager has implied authority to make agreements and transactions that customarily go along with the manager's position.

Another example of implied authority revolves around anyone, such as a purchasing agent, who ordinarily is the person who everyone in the industry expects to make contracts for particular inputs. For someone to act as if the purchasing agent lacks authority to make such commitments on behalf of the firm would be to act contrary to the expected lines of authority.

APPARENT AUTHORITY AND ESTOPPEL

As the previous chapter explained, apparent agency exists when a third party reasonably believes, on the basis of a *principal's* actions, that an agency relationship exists between the principal and another individual. Thus, if the third party reasonably believes the agent has authority to represent the principal, the principal must uphold any agreements made with the agent who has apparent authority.[3] The principal is prevented (estopped) from acting as if the agent had no such authority.

Contractual Liability of the Principal and Agent

In addition to identifying the type of authority an agent has, courts must identify a few other factors when making decisions about an agency relationship's liability to third parties. First, the court must determine the classification of the principal. Second, the court must decide whether the principal authorized the actions of the agent.

CLASSIFICATION OF THE PRINCIPAL

Classifications are made from the perspective of the third party. In other words, the extent of the third party's knowledge about the principal determines the classification of the principal.

What are potential ethical issues arising from questions about the authority of a particular agent? The law of agency places special weight on the viewpoint of the agency relationship from the perspective of the third party (neither the agent nor the principal). But who are the other stakeholders in a managerial decision who might be affected by the assignment of a particular form of authority?

When a principal is classified as a **disclosed principal**, the third party is aware that the agent is making an agreement on behalf of a principal and the third party also knows the identity of the principal. In contrast, if a third party is aware that an agent is making an agreement on behalf of a principal but the third party is unaware of the identity of the principal, the principal is classified as a **partially disclosed principal** or an **unidentified principal.** Finally, if a third party does not know an agent is acting on behalf of a principal, the principal is classified as an **undisclosed principal.** Remember, the classification of the principal is important because it is an important factor in determining the liability of the principal.[4]

[3] Restatement (Second) of Agency, secs. 27 and 159.

[4] Restatement (Second) of Agency, sec. 4.

In the Dimension and Paradise Magazine dilemma, the first issue the appellate court needed to address was the classification of the principal. Determining whether the trial court mistakenly labeled Paradise as an undisclosed principal was vital for a resolution. As discussed in the previous section, if the third party has no idea that the agent is acting on behalf of a principal at the time of the transaction, the principal is an undisclosed principal.

On the other hand, if the third party knows that the agent is acting on behalf of a principal but does not know the identity of the principal, the principal is a partially disclosed principal. Based on this distinction, the appellate court determined that the principal was a partially disclosed principal because Dimension knew the agents Liebowitz and Jacobson were acting on behalf of a principal even though Dimension did not know the principal was Paradise. There was no point during the transaction when Dimension thought the agents were acting on their own behalf; therefore, Paradise could not be considered an undisclosed principal.

AUTHORIZED ACTS

When an agent acts within the scope of her authority on behalf of a disclosed or partially disclosed principal, the agent is not liable for the acts of the principal.[5] The principal is liable only if the agent has some kind of authority to act on the principal's behalf. With a disclosed principal, the agent is not liable because he or she is not a party to the transaction.

Yet if the principal is partially disclosed, the agent can be held liable herself because the courts generally treat the agent as a party to the contract. As a party to the contract, the agent may be found liable to the third party for contractual nonperformance.[6] Whether disclosed or partially disclosed, apart from any liability the agent might have, the principal is liable for the agreements made with the third party.

When the agent acts within her authority on behalf of an undisclosed principal, the law will likely hold the agent liable for the agreement. Remember, with an undisclosed principal, the third party is not aware of the existence of the principal. Thus, in the eyes of the third party, the agent is the only possible person who could be liable. Yet, if the agent is liable to the third party, then the undisclosed principal is liable to the agent. However, there are certain situations in which the agent is the only party liable for the contract. These situations are:

1. The contract expressly excludes the principal from the contract. In that the principal was not a party to the contract, he or she has no liability to the agent.
2. The principal is not liable to the agent if the agent enters into a contract that is a negotiable instrument. The Uniform Commercial Code (UCC) governs negotiable instruments and states that other parties, that is, principals, cannot be liable for negotiable instruments if their name is not on the instrument or if the agent's signature does not indicate that it was made in a representative capacity.[7]
3. The third party enters into a contract with the agent such that the performance of the agent is required. In this case, the third party may reject the performance of the principal. For example, if the agent is a photographer and he enters into a contract for his principal without disclosing this fact, the third party may reject the principal's attempt to fulfill the contract by taking the third party's picture.

[5] Restatement (Second) of Agency, sec. 320.

[6] Restatement (Second) of Agency, sec. 321.

[7] UCC § 3-402(b)(2).

4. If the principal or agent knows a third party would not enter into a contract with the principal if the principal's identity were disclosed but the agent enters into a contract with the third party anyway, the agent will be the only party liable should the third party rescind the contract.

In situations in which a principal was undisclosed, a judgment for a third party against an agent, when the third party comes to know of the undisclosed principal's identity, releases the principal from liability.[8] Also, a judgment against a previously undisclosed principal frees the agent from liability.[9]

Determining the classification of Paradise Magazine, Inc., was important because the liabilities of the agents and the principal were different under each classification of the principal. As a partially disclosed principal, the agents and the principal are considered parties to the contract, and each may be liable separately from the other.

Because Paradise was classified as a partially disclosed principal, both the principal, Paradise, and the agents, Liebowitz and Jacobson, have separate liability and can each be sued by the third party, Dimension.

Exhibit 34-1 summarizes contractual liability to third parties for authorized acts of the agent.

Case 34-1 illustrates the importance of the court's consideration of the classification of the principal and its impact on the potential liability associated with this agency relationship.

Exhibit 34-1 Summary of Contractual Liability to Third Parties for Agent and Principal for Authorized Agent Acts

CLASSIFICATION OF PRINCIPAL	AGENT LIABILITY?	PRINCIPAL LIABILITY?
Disclosed	No	Yes
Partially disclosed	Possibly	Yes
Undisclosed	Yes	Yes

[8] Restatement (Second) of Agency, sec. 210.

[9] Restatement (Second) of Agency, sec. 337.

CASE 34-1 THE HEIBY OIL COMPANY v. GALEN V. PENCE ET AL.

COURT OF APPEALS OF OHIO, THIRD APPELLATE DISTRICT, AUGLAIZE COUNTY

1999 OHIO APP. LEXIS 2523 (1999)

The Corner Station, a service station located in the village of Waynesfield, Ohio, is owned and operated by Waynesfield Equipment. The Corner Station made purchases of gasoline from The Heiby Oil Company, a gasoline vendor. When the Corner Station's account with The Heiby Oil Company was overdue, Heiby filed suit to recover the money owed. At the trial court, Heiby attempted to hold Galen Pence and others—officers, directors, and shareholders of Waynesfield Equipment—personally liable for the debt. The trial court granted summary judgment to Pence. Heiby appealed, arguing it was unclear whether Pence contracted with Heiby on behalf of a disclosed principal.

JUDGE HADLEY: [Heiby] asserts a genuine issue of material fact remains to be litigated, specifically the issue of whether [Pence] contracted with [Heiby] on behalf of a disclosed principal, and whether [Heiby] was aware of that agency relationship. For the following reasons, we agree.

It is axiomatic that in order to avoid personal liability, an agent must disclose to the party with whom the agent is dealing (1) the agency relationship, and (2) the identity of the principal. Where an agent acts for a disclosed principal, in the name of such principal, and within the scope of authority, such agent is ordinarily not liable on the contracts the agent makes. Further, an agent avoids personal liability by conducting himself or herself with third parties in such a way those persons are aware they are dealing with the principal, not the agent individually. An agent's authority to act on behalf of its principal may be either actual or apparent. Actual authority, sometimes called real authority, may be expressed or implied.

In the case before us, the trial court held no genuine issue of material fact remains to be litigated as to whether [Heiby] had contracted with a disclosed principal, and whether [Heiby] was aware of that agency relationship. Specifically, the trial court found most conclusive the following evidence. First, many of the purchases of gasoline from Appellant were paid by checks drawn on an account entitled "Waynesfield Corner Station." Second, the Corner Station credit card sales slips which were given to Appellant bear the imprint "WFD Equip[.] Co[.] Inc."

We agree with the trial court that the foregoing evidence tends to show Appellant had contracted with a disclosed principal, and Appellant was aware of that agency relationship. However, a thorough review of the record also reveals evidence to the contrary. For example, David James, Vice-President of Heiby Oil Company, states in his affidavit neither Lynn Pence, Jill Pence, Galen Pence, or Alberta Pence had ever signed checks in a corporate capacity. The record also reveals six checks drawn on an account entitled "Waynesfield Corner Station" signed in an individual capacity by either Alberta Pence or Jill Pence. David James also states in his affidavit had the company known that the Corner Station was owned by Waynesfield Equipment, personal guarantees would have been procured against [Pence].

For the foregoing reasons, we find a genuine issue of material fact remains to be litigated as to whether [Pence] contracted with [Heiby] on behalf of a disclosed principal, and whether [Heiby] was aware of that agency relationship. Therefore, the trial court erred in granting summary judgment in favor of [Pence].

REVERSED.

CRITICAL THINKING

The court in *Heiby Oil* possesses conflicting evidence. Which pieces of evidence are in conflict? Is the court necessarily saying that the plaintiff lacks a strong argument?

ETHICAL DECISION MAKING

Consider the various stakeholders of Waynesfield Equipment. If you were a manager working for this firm, what could you have done to prevent negative impacts on the stakeholders? Using ethical reasoning, try to make an argument that justifies preventing those negative impacts *and* an argument that justifies not preventing those negative impacts.

UNAUTHORIZED ACTS

If an agent has no authority to act on behalf of a principal but the agent still enters into a contract with a third party, the principal, regardless of the classification, is not bound to the contract unless the principal ratifies the agreement.

When the agent exceeds his authority to act on behalf of the principal, the agent will likely be personally liable to the third party. Yet, when the third party is aware that the agent does not represent the principal, the law does not hold the agent liable for the agreement. In almost all other cases in which the agent claims to have authority to contract on behalf

global context

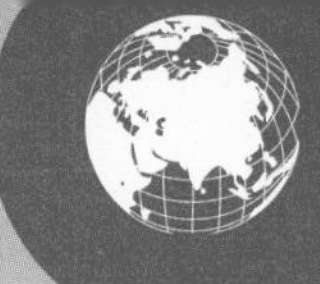

Liability of the Principal to the Third Party in Civil Law Countries

Sometimes, a third party enters into a transaction with an agent without realizing a principal is involved until after the transaction. In this case, civil law favors the protection of the principal by not allowing the third party to bring suit against him or her; the third party may sue only the agent. Civil law jurisdictions adopting this principle believe that the third party must be responsible for evaluating the trustworthiness of those with whom he does business.

In common law countries, the principal is responsible for judging the agent. The principal bears the risk that a third party may be harmed in the event of the agent's insolvency. Consequently, common law jurisdictions extend to the third party the right to sue either the agent or the principal when the involvement of a principal has not been disclosed.

of the principal, the law holds the agent liable to the third party. If an agent enters into a contract knowingly misrepresenting his alleged authority, the agent is liable to the third party in a tort action.

Agents who go beyond their authority when the principal is disclosed or partially disclosed are liable for a breach of implied warranty, not for a breach of contract. The agent cannot be found liable for breach of contract because the agent is never an intended party to the contract, even when exceeding his or her authority. The agent can breach the implied warranty intentionally, through a knowing misrepresentation, or unintentionally, through a good-faith mistake such as simply misjudging his or her authority. In either case, the agent is liable if the third party acted relying on the agent's alleged status.

Exhibit 34-2 summarizes the contractual liability of principals and agents to third parties for unauthorized acts of the agent.

Exhibit 34-2 Summary of Contractual Liability of Principal and Agent to Third Parties for Unauthorized Acts of the Agent

THIRD-PARTY BELIEF	AGENT LIABILITY?	PRINCIPAL LIABILITY?
Believes the agent has authority	Yes	No
Believes that the agent is mistaken about her authority	No	No

Tort Liability and the Agency Relationship

If an agent commits a tort that injures a third party, the agent is personally liable for his or her actions, regardless of both the classification of the principal and the liability of the principal.[10] The principal may also be held liable for the agent's actions. This liability can arise from authorized or unauthorized acts. Furthermore, tortious liability of the principal can be established directly or indirectly. Finally, if an agent is an employee and the principal/employer controls the employee's behavior, the principal can be found liable. The next section introduces these methods of establishing tortious liability.

PRINCIPAL'S TORTIOUS CONDUCT

The law holds a principal directly responsible for his own tortious conduct under two conditions. First, if the principal directs the agent to commit a tort, the principal is liable for

[10] Restatement (Second) of Agency, sec. 343.

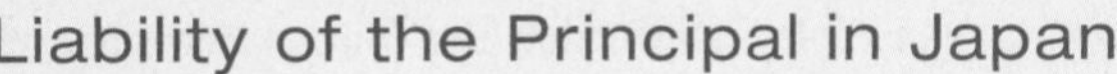

Liability of the Principal in Japan

In Japan, the laws binding the principal are rigid. For instance, under certain circumstances, the principal may be held liable for the actions of the agent even if the agent exceeds the boundaries of authority. For the principal to be liable, the boundary of authority must be indecipherable to an outsider. Additionally, the principal must have contributed to the *appearance* of authority. If such circumstances exist, the principal is bound to the actions performed by the agent, including actions involving a third party.

The precedent-setting case for this statute involved a suit brought against the Tokyo District Court. The district court was being held liable for a transaction made by a group of court employees. The group, working under the name of "Welfare Department," had an office in the courthouse. After the department failed to pay for new stationery it had purchased, the stationery company sued the district court. The company claimed that because of the Welfare Department's location, it assumed the group was an agent of the court. The supreme court found in favor of the printing company and ordered the district court to satisfy the owed payment. Justification for the ruling was that the district court had created an appearance of authority and therefore was bound to the department's actions.

any damages caused by this tort. The principal is authorizing the agent's unlawful behavior; thus, the principal is held responsible.[11] Similarly, the principal is liable for an agent's tortious act if the principal, although not condoning the agent's conduct, ratifies the agent's action knowing the agent acted illegally.[12]

Second, if the principal fails to provide proper instruments or tools or gives inadequate instructions to the agent concerning the necessity to employ competent agents, the law then holds the principal liable to a third party for negligence. Under this provision of liability, a principal is liable for his or her negligent hiring of an agent. Thus, a principal must use proper care in selecting an agent for a job. This doctrine of negligent hiring has been used when an agent commits a tort against a customer, who often argues that the principal is liable because he or she should have taken more care in hiring the agent.

Respondeat superior. The doctrine of **respondeat superior** (a Latin phrase meaning "let the superior speak") is used in the context of the principal/employer–agent/employee relationship. The principal/employer holds **vicarious liability** (i.e., liability assigned without fault) for any harm caused by the agent/employee during the time the agent/employee is working for the principal. In other words, the principal/employer is liable not because he or she was personally at fault but because he or she negligently hired an agent.

The rationale behind this doctrine is that employers should be held liable for employees who commit torts because the employer is furthering his or her business through the work of the employee. If the employer is benefiting by the work of the employee, the employer should also be responsible for the harms caused by the employee.

Therefore, when a third party is injured through the negligence of an employee during the course of the employee's work, the third party can sue either the employee or the employer.[13] To establish employer liability, the third party must establish that the wrongful act occurred within the scope of the employment. The courts consider the following elements in determining whether an act has occurred within the course and scope of employment:[14]

1. Did the employer authorize the employee's act?
2. Did the act occur within the time and space limits of employment?

[11] Restatement (Second) of Agency, sec. 212.

[12] Restatement (Second) of Agency, sec. 218.

[13] Restatement (Second) of Agency, secs. 216 and 219.

[14] Restatement (Second) of Agency, sec. 229.

3. Was the act performed, at least in part, on behalf of the employer?
4. To what extent were the employer's interests advanced by the act?
5. To what extent were the private interests of the employee involved?
6. Did the employer provide the means (i.e., tools) by which the act occurred?
7. Did the employee use force that was not expected by the employer?
8. Did the employer know that the act would involve the commission of a serious crime?

For example, if an employee is a delivery driver and negligently injures a third party while making deliveries on behalf of the employer, both the employee and the employer will be held liable.

Now suppose that the delivery driver is using the company vehicle when he stops at a drive-through at a fast-food restaurant to get some coffee. Could the employer be liable to a third party for an accident involving the delivery driver? If an agent makes a substantial departure from the course of the employer's business, the employer is not liable.

Courts often refer to a substantial departure as a "frolic of his own." However, if the deviation from the employer's business is *not* substantial, the employer can still be held liable. In Case 34-2, the court considers the scope of the employment relationship.

CASE 34-2 IGLESIA CRISTIANA LA CASA DEL SENOR, INC., ETC. v. L.M.

COURT OF APPEAL OF FLORIDA, THIRD DISTRICT
783 SO. 2D 353 (2001)

L.M. sued Ali Pacheco, the former pastor of Iglesia Cristiana La Casa Del Senor, Inc. (the Church), as well as the Church, alleging Pacheco had sexually assaulted her in July 1991 when she was a minor. The allegation of sexual assault formed the basis of L.M.'s claims against the Church based on respondeat superior. When the criminal act occurred, L.M. was sixteen years old.

Before the criminal act took place, Pacheco visited L.M.'s residence twice when L.M. had been left home alone. On another occasion, Pacheco visited L.M. at her school. L.M. told her mother about Pacheco's visit, but did not advise anyone from the Church.

According to L.M., on July 8, 1991, Pacheco called her at work and invited her to lunch to discuss her parents' marital problems. L.M. accepted, and Pacheco picked her up from work. L.M. noticed a sandwich and soft drink in the car. Pacheco drove to a Marriott Hotel. L.M. testified Pacheco led her to a room he had rented, and told her not to worry because she would finally be cured. He then proceeded to sexually assault her. Pacheco testified L.M. consented to having sex.

According to him, their meeting was prearranged. They had discussed the matter and had in fact been to the Marriot Hotel on the previous day intending to have sexual relations, but had decided against it. Pacheco testified he knew what he was doing was wrong, but explained it was a great temptation in his life.

The jury returned a verdict in L.M.'s favor, finding the Church liable for Pacheco's criminal act on the grounds of respondeat superior. *The Church appealed.*

PER CURIAM: Under the doctrine of respondeat superior, an employer cannot be held liable for the tortious or criminal acts of an employee, unless the acts were committed during the course of the employment and to further a purpose or interest, however excessive or misguided, of the employer. An employee's conduct is within the scope of his employment, where (1) the conduct is of the kind he was employed to perform, (2) the conduct occurs substantially within the time and space limits authorized or required by the work to be performed, and (3) the conduct is activated at least in part by a purpose to serve the master. An exception may exist where the tort-feasor was assisted in accomplishing the tort by virtue of the employer/employee relationship.

In this case, the sexual assault did not occur on Church property, and the record does not support a finding Pacheco's criminal act against L.M. constituted the kind of conduct he was employed to perform, or he was in any way motivated by his desire to serve the Church. On the contrary, the record establishes Pacheco's purpose in arranging the meeting that day was to satisfy his personal interests, not to further the Church's objectives. Regardless of the stated reason for the meeting between Pacheco and L.M., it is undisputed no counseling occurred on the day of the crime. While Pacheco may have had access to L.M. because of his position as the Church pastor, whom L.M. and her family had become friends with over time, he was not engaging in authorized acts or serving the interests of the Church during the time he tried to seduce her or on the day he raped her. The sexual assault was an independent, self-serving act by Pacheco; an act he knew was wrong to commit and the Church would surely have tried to prevent had it known of his plans.

We agree with the Church that Pacheco's sexual assault of L.M. did not occur within the scope of his employment. Accordingly, we find, as a matter of law, the Church cannot be held vicariously liable for Pacheco's criminal act.

Therefore, we reverse the trial court's final judgment and remand with instructions to enter judgment in favor of Appellant.

REVERSED AND REMANDED.

CRITICAL THINKING

Assume that L.M.'s account of the crime is true. Examine the exception to the "scope of employment" criteria mentioned by the judge. How could the plaintiff make an argument, using that exception, that Pacheco's conduct was within the scope of his employment?

ETHICAL DECISION MAKING

The judge in this case outlines a doctrine for determining the liability of an employer for the actions of employees. What value preference is highlighted by that doctrine?

If the third party is able to establish employee negligence such that the employer is liable, the employer has the right to recover from the employee any damages he paid to the third party as a result of the employee's negligence. The right to recover damages is referred to as the *right of indemnification.* However, if the employee is innocent of negligence, the employer is also free of liability.

Intentional torts and *respondeat superior.* The agent is liable for any torts he or she commits. In the same way the principal is responsible for the negligent acts of the employee under the doctrine of *respondeat superior,* the principal may be liable for any intentional torts of the employee. Furthermore, an employer may be responsible for any tortious acts of the employee if the employer knew or should have known that the employee had a tendency to commit a tortious act. Hence, a principal may be liable for negligent hiring if he or she fails to do a background check to learn about the tendencies of potential employees.

For example, the principal of an employee with a criminal background may be held liable for tortious acts committed by his or her hired agent even though the employee may not recognize the wrongfulness of his act. Therefore, employers will most likely purchase liability insurance in case particular employees engage in tortious activities.

AGENT MISREPRESENTATION

If an agent misrepresents himself or herself to a third party, the principal may be tortiously liable for the agent's misrepresentation. Unlike tort liability, which is based on whether the agent/employee was acting in the scope of employment, *misrepresentation liability* depends on whether the principal authorized the agent's act. If the principal authorizes the agent to engage in an act and the agent misrepresents herself intentionally or unintentionally, the principal is always tortiously liable to someone who relied on the agent's misrepresentation.

If an agent has misrepresented herself, the third party has two options:

1. The third party can cancel the contract with the principal and be compensated for any money lost.
2. The third party can affirm the contract and sue the principal to recover damages.

Principal's Liability and the Independent Contractor

As we discussed in the previous chapter, an independent contractor is not an employee of the individual who hires him or her to do work. The individual doing the hiring does not control the details of the independent contractor's performance. Consequently, an individual who hires an independent contractor cannot be held liable for the independent contractor's tortious actions under the doctrine of *respondeat superior.*

Suppose that while working on the outside of the building he is renovating, an independent contractor accidentally injures an innocent bystander when he drops a pile of bricks on the bystander. The owner of the building is not liable for the innocent bystander's injuries; the independent contractor is liable.[15]

If, however, the independent contractor engages in extremely hazardous activities, such as blasting operations, for the principal, the principal will be responsible for any damages by the independent contractor. Certain activities are held strictly liable because of their inherently dangerous nature. Thus, an employer cannot escape the strict liability associated with those hazardous activities simply by hiring an independent contractor to complete the activities. In addition, the employer cannot escape liability for an independent contractor's tort if the employer directs the contractor to commit the tort.

The Case Nugget demonstrates the role of tort principles in establishing the liability of those who employ independent contractors to engage in inherently dangerous activities.

Crime and Agency Relationships

If an agent commits a crime, clearly the agent is liable for the crime. If the agent commits the crime in the scope of employment for a principal without the authorization of the principal, the principal is not liable for the agent's crime. Remember, one of the elements of establishing that a crime has been committed is establishing the element of *intent.* If a principal is unaware of or had no intent for the agent to commit a crime, there is no rationale

[15] Restatement (Second) of Agency, sec. 250.

Case Nugget — Liability When Hiring Independent Contractors

Larry S. Lawrence v. Bainbridge Apartments et al.
Court of Appeals of Missouri, Western District
957 S.W.2d 400 (1997)

In 1989, Smart Way Janitorial offered a bid to Larry Lawrence to wash the windows of Bainbridge Apartments. In May 1989, when Larry went to look at the apartments, he was told that Bainbridge wanted the windows washed from outside the building so that the residents would not be disturbed. The Bainbridge property consisted of six buildings: two seven-story buildings and four four-story buildings. Even though Lawrence could not create a safety line for washing the outside of the windows of the four-story buildings, the building manager insisted that Lawrence wash the windows from the outside. When Lawrence started washing the windows from the outside, he fell from one of the shorter buildings and suffered injuries. He brought a suit against Bainbridge Apartments, arguing that Bainbridge was negligent based on the "inherently dangerous–activity" exception to the doctrine that landowners are not vicariously liable for injuries caused by the negligence of an independent contractor or his employees.

The trial court ruled that because Lawrence had recovered workers' compensation benefits, the injury was not covered by the inherently dangerous–activity exception. The trial court granted summary judgment to Bainbridge; however, when Lawrence appealed, the decision was reversed and remanded because the court of appeals ruled that Lawrence was not a covered employee entitled to workers' compensation benefits. At the trial court, Bainbridge moved for and was granted summary judgment. Lawrence appealed.

The court argued that in establishing the rule of liability in this case, it would look to which party can best avoid the harm and manage the risk of loss of the inherently dangerous activity in question. An independent contractor who knows he will not be compensated by the landowner for his injuries has a strong incentive to take additional care and avoid neglect in performing his duties. This encourages him to demand additional safety measures and compensation before he agrees to undertake an inherently dangerous activity. The independent contractor is free to bargain and negotiate without restraint with the landowner. An independent contractor holds himself out as an expert who is uniquely qualified and skilled to bid for and perform the acts in question. As an expert, he is in a better position to understand the risks and costs involved in a particular job, and he may demand sufficient remuneration and safety measures to cover what he believes the attendant risks to be. In return for his bargained-for price, he accepts the allocation of the risk. The court held that an injured independent contractor, although uninsured, cannot recover under the inherently dangerous–activity exception.

for the principal's criminal liability. The only time the principal can be liable for the crimes of an agent is when the principal has authorized the criminal act.

Termination of the Agency Relationship

There are multiple ways to end an agency relationship. The parties may act to terminate the relationship. Alternatively, some agencies terminate automatically by the lapse of time, fulfillment of purpose, or operation of law. If the agency relationship has ended, the agent no longer has authority to make agreements on behalf of the principal. However, the agent's apparent authority continues until the principal notifies third parties that the agency relationship has ended. What terminates the agency relationship?

Notice of the termination of an agency relationship can be given in two general forms: actual or constructive. **Actual notice** of termination is given when third parties are directly informed, orally or in writing, that an agency agreement has terminated.[16] Actual notice must be given to third parties who have had business interactions with the agent. Also, when the agent's authority was granted in writing, actual notice must also be given in writing. Parties not directly related to an agency agreement may receive **constructive notice**, which is how notice of the termination of an agency agreement is generally announced.[17] Constructive notice is most frequently delivered through publication in a generally circulating newspaper for the area where the agency agreement existed.

This issue of termination of the agency is especially important for global commerce. Recall from the previous chapter that the Canadian government has issued special managerial guidelines for using agents in Canada. When parties are forming a contract of agency in a foreign jurisdiction, it is extremely important that the parties include the conditions of termination within the contract.

Termination of an agency involving persons from separate jurisdictions often results in complicated legal battles over compensation and liability. For example, principals must be aware of local labor laws because these laws can create agents' compensation and pension rights that are unknown to the principal. Local legal counsel should be especially knowledgeable about the provisions surrounding termination of agency in the particular jurisdiction and be able to help managers avoid unnecessary legal battles.

For example, if a manager has business transactions in one of the European Union countries and wants to terminate an agency relationship, she would want to have access to knowledge about the intricacies of Chapter IV of the Agency Relationship Law, which focuses on termination. After the termination of an agency contract in those countries, the agent receives help from the law in collecting damages. Released agents receive compensation if they have brought the principal new customers from whom the principal continues to profit, if the agent is unable to otherwise recover costs incurred through the performance of the contract, or if the agent dies.

Under certain circumstances however, the law in European Union countries prohibits the agent's receiving compensation. For instance, if the principal has terminated the contract due to the incapacity of the agent, the principal is not obligated to dispense compensation. Also, compensation is not payable if the agent terminates the contract or assigns rights and duties under the agency contract to another person.

Case 34-3 highlights the importance of understanding how an agency relationship is terminated. The consequences of not knowing this critical area of agency law can be disastrous.

TERMINATION BY ACTS OF PARTIES

The agency relationship can be terminated following certain acts. Several possibilities are discussed in the following sections.

Lapse of time. If an agency agreement specifies that the agency relationship will exist for a certain amount of time, the relationship will end when the amount of time expires.[18]

[16] Restatement (Second) of Agency, sec. 136(2).

[17] Restatement (Second) of Agency, sec. 136(3).

[18] Restatement (Second) of Agency, sec. 105.

CASE 34-3 ANGELA & RAUL RUIZ v. FORTUNE INSURANCE COMPANY

COURT OF APPEAL OF FLORIDA, THIRD DISTRICT
677 SO. 2D 1336 (1996)

In September 1990, Angela and Raul Ruiz purchased a homeowner's insurance policy for their mobile home from Fortune Insurance Company through Bates Hernandez Associates, an insurance broker. Bates secured the insurance through Fortune's agent, Biscayne Underwriting Management. In November 1990, Fortune terminated its agency relationship with Biscayne. In July 1991, Fortune notified its customers it had terminated its agency relationship with Biscayne; consequently, Fortune sent the Ruizes a notice their homeowner's insurance would not be renewed.

However, in August 1991, even though the Ruizes' insurance policy had expired, Bates sent a renewal notice to the Ruizes. The Ruizes paid Bates $450 to renew their insurance policies with Fortune. Bates sent this money to Biscayne, which accepted the money. In August 1992, the Ruizes' mobile home was damaged by a hurricane. When the Ruizes reported the loss to Fortune, they were told they had no current insurance policy with Fortune. Thus, the Ruizes filed suit against Fortune. In a summary judgment, the trial court ruled for Fortune. The Ruizes appealed.

OPINION PER CURIAM: Although the Ruizes contended below they never received Fortune's notice of cancellation, Fortune produced below a copy of the notice of cancellation and proof it mailed the same to the Ruizes. The law is clear that an insurer's proof of mailing of a notice of cancellation to the insured prevails as a matter of law over the insured's denial as to its receipt.

Fortune's actual notice of cancellation to the Ruizes was legally sufficient and binding, whether the Ruizes read or understood the import of such notice. Any lack of understanding of this written notice on the part of the Ruizes only placed a duty upon them to make further inquiry of their broker, agent and/or insurer.

We further reject the Ruizes' argument on appeal that Fortune is estopped from disclaiming coverage where Biscayne accepted the Ruizes' renewal premium after Fortune's termination of its agency relationship with Biscayne. There is no evidence that Fortune engaged in any conduct or action which would reasonably lead the Ruizes to believe Biscayne had continuing actual or apparent authority to collect such premiums on behalf of Fortune.

AFFIRMED.

CRITICAL THINKING

The judge seems to think that Fortune fulfilled its obligation to the Ruizes by mailing them a notice of cancellation. Why do you think the Ruizes were confused about the cancellation? How could the plaintiffs argue that they were not properly made aware that their insurance had been canceled?

ETHICAL DECISION MAKING

Explain what you think the ethical obligations were for every party in this case: Fortune, Bates Hernandez Associates, Biscayne Underwriting Management, and the Ruizes.

For example, an agency agreement might state that the agency relationship will begin on September 1 and end on September 30. While the agent and principal can agree to continue the agency relationship through October, they will have to make a new agreement. The agent's express authority ends when the relationship ends; thus, it is the responsibility of the principal to notify third parties that the former agent no longer has the ability to act on the principal's behalf.

Fulfillment of purpose. Suppose a homeowner enters into an agreement with a real estate agent to sell his house. Once an agent succeeds in selling the house, the agent no longer has the authority to act on the seller's behalf. The agent has fulfilled the purpose of the agency relationship.[19]

Occurrence of a specific event. Depending on the purpose of the agency relationship, the relationship could be terminated on the occurrence of a specific event. For example, John employs Claire as an agent to sell his house. Once the sale is final, the agency relationship would terminate.

Mutual agreement by the parties. Remember, agency is a consensual agreement between two parties. Consequently, if the two parties mutually decide they do not wish to continue in the agency relationship, they can cancel the agreement and therefore terminate the agency relationship.

Revocation of authority. At any time, a principal can revoke an agent's authority.[20] Again, the basis of agency law is consensual agreement. If the principal does not want the agent to act on his behalf, the principal can revoke the agent's authority. However, the principal's revocation might constitute a breach of contract with the agent. Therefore, the principal could be liable for damages due to the breach of contract with the agent.[21] If the agent has somehow breached the fiduciary duty to the principal, the principal can revoke the agent's authority without being liable for damages to the agent.

Renunciation by the agent. In the same way that a principal terminates an agency relationship by revoking authority, the agent can terminate the agency relationship by renouncing the authority given to the agent. Again, the agent can be liable for breach of contract if the agency agreement has stated a specific amount of time the agency relationship is to exist.

Agency coupled with an interest. An **agency coupled with an interest** is a special kind of agency relationship. Unlike regular agency agreements, an agency coupled with an interest is created for the agent's benefit, not for the principal's. Given that the agent is the one who benefits, an agency coupled with an interest is also known as *power given as security.* Because the agency arrangement is created to benefit the agent, the principal may not terminate the relationship. Rather, the agency relationship is terminated when an event occurs that discharges the principal's obligation.

[19] Restatement (Second) of Agency, sec. 106.

[20] Restatement (Second) of Agency, sec. 119.

[21] Restatement (Second) of Agency, sec. 118.

global context

Death of a Principal in Mexico

Like the United States, Mexico recognizes the death of the principal as a termination of agency. However, Mexico does not see the death of the principal as an immediate end to the agent's obligations. Mexican law requires that an agent continue to manage the affairs of his agency after the principal's death. The agent is required to continue management only until the principal's heirs can assume the responsibilities of the deceased.

This provision (agents must wait for the heirs before relinquishing their obligations) results in agents in Mexico being bound to their deceased principals for years as heirs find continual excuses to avoid managerial duties. On the insistence of disgruntled agents, Mexico extended the agents' power in such cases. They can now request that a judge stipulate a period of time within which the heirs must take charge of the property. This change in Mexican law has given relief to agents who otherwise may have been burdened with a deceased principal's affairs for an inappropriate amount of time.

TERMINATION BY OPERATION OF LAW

Certain events lead to automatic termination of the agency relationship. These events may involve a situation in which the agent is unable to fulfill his task or one for which the principal would not desire to continue with the performance. In addition, automatic termination may occur when further pursuit of the agency relationship's objectives would be illegal. These events are discussed in the following sections.

Death. If either the principal or the agent dies, the agency relationship is automatically terminated. Even if one party is unaware of the other party's death, the agency relationship no longer exists. Suppose an agent has authority to buy antiques on behalf of a principal. However, without the agent knowing it, the principal dies, but the agent continues to purchase items on behalf of the principal. Those transactions are not binding on the principal's estate because as soon as the principal dies, the agent's authority to act is gone.

Insanity. If a principal or agent becomes insane, the agency relationship is finished. Some states have modified this law so that unless the person has been adjudicated insane, the agency contract still exists.

Bankruptcy. If the principal or agent files a bankruptcy petition, the agency relationship is generally no longer in existence. If the agent is filing for bankruptcy and the agent's credit is important to the agency relationship, the relationship will end. However, if the agent's financial history is not relevant to the agency relationship, the agency may continue. Insolvency, which is defined as the inability to pay debts or the condition of liabilities outweighing assets, does not necessarily result in the termination of the agency relationship.[22]

Changed circumstances. If there is an unusual change in circumstances that leads the agent to believe that the principal's instructions do not apply, the agency relationship terminates.[23] For example, suppose Smith contracts someone to act as her agent to sell a painting she found in her great-aunt's attic. Smith authorizes the agent to sell the painting for $5,000. However, in the course of showing the painting to several buyers, the agent

[22] Restatement (Second) of Agency, sec. 113.

[23] Restatement (Second) of Agency, sec. 109.

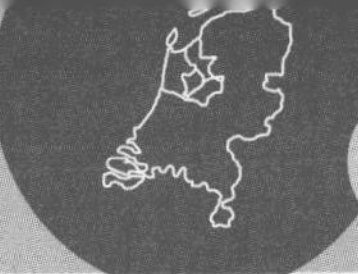

Termination in the Netherlands

After a relationship of agency ends in the Netherlands, the law offers several means for the agent to collect compensation. First, the agent is entitled to compensation if his or her duties are concluded within a "reasonable" time after termination. Second, compensation is due if the agent received the orders for a certain action before the termination of the contract.

Third—the most interesting triggering event for mandatory compensation of agents—the agent is entitled to "goodwill compensation" in certain situations. The three situations are (1) the agent brought the principal new customers; (2) the agent brought new agreements with clients who are still profitable to the principal; and (3) such payment is financially reasonable for the principal (i.e., the relationship is not being terminated due to bankruptcy).

The existence of any of these situations enables the agent to collect goodwill compensation after the termination of the contract. The agent must file for such compensation within five years of termination. Also, there is a ceiling on the amount the agent may receive from the courts. The goodwill compensation may not exceed the equivalent of the agent's average yearly salary.

learns the painting is a Van Gogh original. Thus, because the painting is worth much more than $5,000, the agent should infer that the principal does not want the original agency to continue.

Change in law. When a new law is passed subsequent to the formation of an agency agreement that makes the commission of the agency agreement illegal, the agency agreement is terminated. For example, Tyler hires Ryan to paint her house green. Then, after Ryan was hired, the city council passes a law making it illegal to paint one's house green. The new law automatically terminates the agency agreement.

Impossibility. Suppose that while in the process of attempting to sell the painting in our earlier example, there is a fire in Smith's house and the painting is destroyed. Because it is impossible for the agent to sell the painting, it is impossible for the agency relationship to continue.[24]

Additionally, if the agent loses qualifications needed to perform duties for the principal, the agency relationship ends because of impossibility. For example, Jackson hires a lawyer to serve as his agent. However, the lawyer has unfortunately engaged in a series of illegal actions and is disbarred. Because the lawyer can no longer fulfill the functions Jackson has authorized him to perform, the agency relationship is terminated.

Disloyalty of agent. An agency agreement is terminated whenever the agent, unknown to the principal, acquires interest against the principal's interest. The agency agreement is also terminated if the agent breaches the duty of loyalty he or she has to the principal.[25] For example, Mary is an attorney representing Lola in her suit against a pharmaceutical company. If the pharmaceutical company offers Mary a job and she accepts, the agency agreement would terminate because Mary has acquired an interest opposed to Lola's interests.

War. Imagine a principal who has an agent in Iran who is authorized to make business dealings on the principal's behalf.[26] If the United States goes to war with Iran, this agency relationship would no longer be in existence because there would be no way to enforce the rights of the parties.

[24] Restatement (Second) of Agency, sec. 124.

[25] Restatement (Second) of Agency, sec. 112.

[26] Restatement (Second) of Agency, sec. 115.

Electronic Contracts in Singapore

Many legislatures have found it necessary to add or create certain laws in response to technology. Singapore, for instance, addressed the growing use of electronic contracts with new legislation in 1997. Because of the possibility of e-mail and electronic fraud, certain risks are associated with forming electronic contracts. The new legislation attempts to combat those risks and specifies the consequences of such fraud.

The fourth section of this legislation pertains to the formation of agency contracts. Agency contracts made electronically will be valid and enforceable if the principal or a principal's designated agent sent the contract. As for contracts made between third parties, certain circumstances must exist for the third party to make the assumption that the electronic record is that of the principal.

Either the third party follows a procedure of clarification previously agreed on by the principal or he or she sees the message originated from an agent who has been endorsed by the principal. Under either of these circumstances, the third party is legally allowed to assume that the electronic message originated with the principal.

If an agent in Singapore sends an electronic record not approved by the principal, the third party has the right to act as a result of that message. In the event such actions result in injuries or damages to the third party, the principal is responsible under law. The principal cannot claim that he or she was unaware of the agent's actions. While there may have been no actual awareness, Singapore does not recognize the lack of awareness as a defense.

Singapore's new legislation intends to protect third parties from the poor judgment of principals by creating this direct link between them. Making the principal answerable and liable to the third party increases the pressure to employ reliable agents.

CASE OPENER WRAP-UP

Dimension

The appellate court found against the principal Paradise. Because the classification of the principal was determined by the appellate court to be a partially disclosed principal, the court's ruling does not remove liability from the agents Liebowitz and Jacobson. The appellate court therefore determined that the trial court mistakenly ruled in favor of Paradise. Thus, the decision was reversed, and the case was remanded for further proceedings. If Paradise better understood the liability issues related to agency relationships, it may have avoided the time and costs associated with the court processes by overseeing the operations of its agents.

Summary

Authority of the Agent: The Link to the Principal's Liability

Express authority: The principal has explicitly instructed the agent to do something.

Implied authority: The relationship is inferred from the conduct of the parties.

Apparent authority and estoppel: Apparent agency exists when a third party reasonably believes on the basis of a principal's actions that an agency relationship exists between the principal and another individual.

Contractual Liability of the Principal and Agent

Classification of the principal: Must be classified as either disclosed, partially disclosed, or undisclosed.

Authorized acts: These are acts within the scope of the agent's authority.

Unauthorized acts: These are acts that go beyond the scope of the agent's authority.

Tort Liability and the Agency Relationship	*Principal's tortious conduct:* The law holds a principal directly responsible for his or her own tortious conduct under two conditions: (1) The principal directs the agent to commit a tortious act, and (2) the principal fails to provide proper instruments, tools, or adequate instructions. *Agent misrepresentation:* If an agent misrepresents himself or herself to a third party, the principal may be tortiously liable for the agent's misrepresentation. *Respondeat superior:* The principal/employer is liable, not because he or she was personally at fault but because he or she negligently hired an agent.
Principal's Liability and the Independent Contractor	An individual who hires an independent contractor cannot be held liable for the independent contractor's tortious actions under the doctrine of *respondeat superior* unless the contractor engages in hazardous activities.
Crime and Agency Relationships	If an agent commits a crime, clearly the agent is liable for the crime.
Termination of the Agency Relationship	*Termination by acts of parties:* This may occur by lapse of time, fulfillment of purpose, occurrence of a specific event, mutual agreement by the parties, revocation of authority, or renunciation by the agent. *Termination by operation of law:* The agency relationship may be terminated automatically due to death, insanity, bankruptcy, changed circumstances, change in law, impossibility, disloyalty of agent, or war.

Point / Counterpoint

Should the Principal/Employer Be Indirectly Liable for the Actions of the Agent/Employee under the Doctrine of *Respondeat Superior?*

Yes	No
The employer should be held responsible for the actions of the employee while the employee is working for the employer. The employer gains from the benefits of the employee's work. Hence, there is a certain symmetry in requiring that the employer also accept the fruits of the negative behavior of the employee. In short, the benefit the employer experiences from the employee are paid for in part by the risk the employer must assume for the possible negligence of that same employee. When a company hires an employee for a position for which he or she is not competent, the company should be punished for any harm the agent causes while acting in his or her hired position. The agent would not be in a position to cause	The employer should not be held responsible for the actions of an employee while the employee is working for the employer. Employees make daily choices using basic human judgment. These employees are hired and trusted for their competence. If an employee makes a poor decision, he or she needs to be held individually responsible. Without a model of individual responsibility, individual workers need never fear the full consequences of their actions. The employees always know their parent companies will be forced to "take care of them" under the doctrine of *respondeat superior.* With the knowledge that their employers will be held somewhat accountable, employees do not necessarily exercise the same amount of caution as they would if they were held personally accountable for every decision they make.

harm had the company not negligently hired him or her in the first place. For example, if a pizza company hires a person with a marred driving record as a pizza delivery driver, the pizza company should be held accountable for any harm caused by that pizza driver while at work delivering pizza.

Harm should be compensated, and the employer is usually in a much more secure financial position than is the employee to provide that compensation.

Consider the example of the pizza delivery driver. The delivery driver injures a third party while delivering pizzas for her company, perhaps because she accidentally drove through a red traffic signal. Though delivering a pizza for her employer, it is the pizza delivery driver, not the pizza company, who ran a red light and injured a pedestrian. Individuals should be held accountable for individual choices. The parent companies need to be held responsible only for decisions that the parent companies make directly.

Questions & Problems

1. What are the different types of authority an agent might have, and why is it important to identify the type of an agent's authority?
2. Explain the difference between the various classifications of a principal.
3. Explain when a principal is or is not contractually liable for agreements made by an agent.
4. When might a principal be liable for torts committed by an agent?
5. Explain how the doctrine of *respondeat superior* affects agency relationships.
6. What terminates an agency relationship?
7. Land Transport employed Oscar Gonzalez to operate a Land Transport tractor-trailer rig. One day while working, Robert Nichols and Gonzalez were driving west on Route 9 toward Brewer, Maine. Gonzalez tried several times to pass Nichols in no-passing zones. Angered by Gonzalez's driving, Nichols made an obscene gesture to Gonzalez on two occasions. Thereafter, Gonzalez began to tailgate Nichols for several miles and continued to try to pass him. The two trucks then stopped at a traffic light. Nichols saw Gonzalez get out of his cab, and Nichols did the same. On approaching Gonzalez, Nichols attacked Gonzalez with a rubber-coated chain-linked cable. Nichols then grabbed Gonzalez, and they fell to the ground. During the scuffle, Gonzalez got up, brandished a knife, and stabbed Nichols. Nichols sued Gonzalez and Land Transport for the injuries he suffered. Land Transport moved for summary judgment. Was Land Transport successful with its motion for summary judgment? Why? [*Nichols v. Land Transport Corp.*, 103 F. Supp. 2d 25 (1999).]
8. Eleanor Schock discovered that her late father's attorney, Pat Nero, had embezzled from the estate of her father, Miller, including the sum of $23,331.72 in Miller's savings account at Old Stone Bank. At the time Nero withdrew the funds, Old Stone was being run under the conservatorship of the Resolution Trust Corporation (RTC), the FDIC's statutory predecessor. As holder of her father's estate's claims, Schock sued the FDIC, as receiver for Old Stone, for breach of contract, alleging that the bank permitted an unauthorized signatory (Nero) to withdraw funds on deposit in the Miller savings account. The FDIC-receiver argued that the bank had paid Nero, a fiduciary

who was authorized to receive the money in the account, in good faith and should not be held liable because Nero misappropriated the money. Schock argued that Nero's apparent authority to withdraw the money as Miller's agent ended by operation of law when Miller died. In response, the FDIC-receiver argued that apparent agency terminates only when a third party has notice of the termination. Schock offered evidence that the bank had actual notice Miller had died when it permitted the Nero savings account withdrawal. Schock's evidence included a bank employee's statement that the bank had in place a procedure for checking the obituaries in the local paper to see whether bank clients had died, as well as the fact that an obituary for Miller appeared in that paper. Was Schock successful at trial? Did the publication of an obituary constitute actual notice? [*Shock v. United States,* 254 F.3d 1 (2001).]

9. Water, Waste, & Land, Inc., is a land development and engineering company doing business under the name "Westec." Donald Lanham and Larry Clark were managers and also members of Preferred Income Investors (PII), LLC. PII is a limited liability company. Clark contacted Westec about the possibility of hiring Westec to perform engineering work in connection with a development project. In the course of preliminary discussions, Clark gave his business card to representatives of Westec. The business card included Lanham's address, which was also the address listed as PII's principal office and place of business. While PII's name was not on the business card, the letters "PII" appeared above the address on the card. However, there was no indication as to what the acronym meant or that PII was a limited liability company. Although Westec never received a signed contract, it did receive verbal authorization from Clark to begin work. Westec completed the engineering work and sent a bill for $9,183.40 to Lanham. No payments were made on the bill. Westec filed a claim against Clark and Lanham individually as well as against PII. At trial, PII admitted liability for the amount claimed by Westec. Accordingly, the court dismissed Clark from the suit, concluding he could not be held personally liable, and entered judgment in the amount of $9,183 against Lanham and PII. Lanham appealed. On appeal, was Lanham found liable for the amount due to Westec? Why? [*Water, Waste, & Land v. Lanham,* 955 P.2d 997 (1998).]

10. Brian Olander became a State Farm insurance agent in 1981. In August 1996, Olander was charged with murder after a violent altercation with a neighboring landowner. When Olander refused to take a leave of absence until the criminal charges were resolved, State Farm terminated his agency agreement and assigned other agents to serve the State Farm policyholders previously served by Olander's agency. In 1999, Olander brought suit against State Farm, alleging wrongful termination of the agency agreement. The district court granted State Farm's motion for summary judgment, concluding that Section III. A of the written State Farm Agent's Agreement unambiguously made the parties' contractual relationship terminable at will. On appeal, a divided panel of this court reversed. State Farm appealed. The issue on appeal may be quickly summarized. If the agreement was terminable at will by either party, then Olander has no wrongful termination claim, and his related claims were properly dismissed. Was the agency agreement one that could be terminated by either party? What duties did State Farm owe Olander when it terminated its agency agreement? [*Olander v. State Farm Mutual Automobile Ins. Co.,* 317 F.3d 807 (2003).]

11. Reyes Alvarez brought an action against Grazyna Ziolo for injuries sustained as a result of a motor vehicle accident in which Ziolo struck Alvarez's vehicle from behind while Alvarez waited at a traffic light. Ziolo was acting within the scope of her employment with the New Haven *Register* at the time of the accident. Alvarez and

Ziolo, through their insurance carrier, the Progressive Insurance Company, agreed to submit the claim to arbitration. The parties settled with the arbitrator. Although Alvarez's counsel submitted a satisfaction for payment of the award, Progressive rejected the satisfaction, insisting instead that Alvarez sign a "full release of all claims and demands." After executing the release, Alvarez sued the Register, claiming that the Register is vicariously liable under the doctrine of *respondeat superior* for the alleged negligent acts of its employee, Ziolo. The Register asserted that Alvarez's claim was barred because, in settling with Ziolo, Alvarez had discharged the Register from any vicarious liability. Alvarez denied the allegations, and the Register moved for summary judgment. Alvarez argued, at the time of settlement with Progressive, that he had never intended to release the Register from liability by signing the release and he had fully intended to pursue a claim against the Register. The trial court rendered summary judgment for the Register, concluding the release executed in favor of Ziolo operated, as a matter of law, to release the Register. Alvarez appealed. Is Alvarez entitled to recovery from the Register? Why? [*Alvarez v. New Haven Register, Inc.*, 249 Conn. 709 (1999).]

12. James Gravens, a gas station owner, purchased insurance covering his gas station from Bendix Insurance Agency. This policy's limit was $20,000. During the night of July 31, 1993, Gravens's service station was burgled, and he suffered a loss of over $20,000 from the theft. Gravens hired an attorney to assist him in pursuing a claim against the insurance company. He did not discuss with the attorney the amount for which he was willing to settle, nor did he give the attorney the authority to settle the claim without his consent. Nevertheless, the attorney accepted an offer from the insurance company to settle the claim for $18,000. The insurance company sent a draft of the settlement to Gravens's attorney along with a release form. Gravens immediately rejected the draft and refused to sign the form, which was then returned to the insurance company. Gravens's attorney withdrew from representation, and Gravens hired a new attorney and filed the case. The insurance company asserted that it had already satisfied its end of the deal by agreeing to pay the $18,000. Who won? Why? [*Gravens v. Auto-Owners' Insurance Company,* 666 N.E.2d 964 (1996).]

13. In 1989, William Petrovich's employer, the Chicago Federation of Musicians, provided health care coverage to all of its employees by enrolling them all in Share Health Plan of Illinois. Share is an HMO and pays only for medical care that is obtained within its network of physicians. To qualify for benefits, a Share member must select a primary care physician, who will provide that member's overall care and authorize referrals when necessary. Share gives its members a list of participating physicians from which to choose. Inga Petrovich, William's wife, selected Dr. Marie Kowalski from Share's list, and began seeing Kowalski as her primary care physician.

In September 1990, Mrs. Petrovich saw Kowalski because she was experiencing persistent pain in her mouth, tongue, throat, and face. She also complained of a foul mucus in her mouth. Kowalski referred her to Dr. Friedman, an ear, nose, and throat specialist who had a contract with Share. When Friedman ordered that an MRI be done, Kowalski refused and instead sent a copy of an old MRI. In June 1991, after Mrs. Petrovich had made multiple visits to both doctors, Friedman found cancerous growths in Mrs. Petrovich's mouth. He performed surgery to remove the cancer later that month.

Petrovich subsequently sued Share for medical malpractice. The complaint alleges that both Kowalski and Friedman were negligent in failing to diagnose Inga Petrovich's cancer in a timely manner and that Share is vicariously liable for their negligence. Share filed a motion for summary judgment, arguing that it cannot be held liable for the negligence of Kowalski or Friedman because they were acting as independent contractors, not as Share's agents. How should the court decide? What reasons should it give? [*Petrovich v. Share Health Plan of Illinois,* 719 N.E.2d 756 (1999).]

14. Solo Sales is a company that acts as an agent for various manufacturers of industrial equipment and helps them sell their products to other companies. Solo was the agent for North America OMCG in December 1994, and it negotiated a deal between the company and Dorco. North America OMCG was reluctant to sell the three machines requested by Dorco because of the significant amount of money involved and the possibility that the machines would not perform to Dorco's standards. Solo worked out an arrangement in which North America OMCG sold one machine to Dorco and leased a second machine with the option to return it to the defendant if Dorco so desired. Dorco also had the option of purchasing the second machine and a third machine, both at discounted prices.

The lease on the second machine lasted through March 1996. In December 1995, however, North America OMCG terminated its agency relationship with Solo Sales. In April 1996, Dorco purchased the second machine, which it had been leasing. In January 1997, Dorco purchased the third machine contemplated in the agreement. North America OMCG paid Solo Sales its commission for the sale of the first machine and for the lease of the second machine through December 1995, but it refused to pay Solo any commission for the lease payments or the sales of machines that occurred after December 1995.

Solo Sales sued, seeking to recover commissions for the remaining lease period and for the sales of the second and third machines. How do you think the court decided, and why? [*Solo Sales, Inc. v. North America OMCG, Inc.* 702 N.E.2d 652 (1998).]

15. Sam and Ruth Saliba purchased a warehouse occupied by the R.B. Dunning Company, an industrial supply wholesaler. The R.B. Dunning Company had been the building's only tenant and had rented the building from its former owner without a written lease. John Dunning was the company's sole officer and was responsible for the management and operation of the business. Dunning met with the Salibas and agreed on the terms of rent. In these negotiations, Dunning did not make clear the fact of his agency.

The R.B. Dunning Company occupied the building for approximately four years without any serious problems. One time, Dunning had been late paying the rent. On this occasion, he assured the Salibas that he "would personally take care of the rent if anything happens." However, once the company's business faltered, it failed to pay rent for about nine months before vacating the building.

The Salibas sued Dunning personally, seeking $14,800 in unpaid rent. Did the court find Dunning to be either an undisclosed principal or a partially disclosed principal and therefore find him personally liable for the unpaid rent? Why or why not? [*Estate of Saliba v. Dunning,* 682 A.2d 224 (Me. 1996).]

16. Lisa was 19 years old and pregnant when she had to seek treatment at Memorial Hospital's emergency room. The initial examining physician ordered an ultrasound for Lisa. Bruce Wayne Tripoli, the ultrasound technician, administered the examination. A third party was not present during the ultrasound.

Tripoli asked the plaintiff if she would like to know the sex of the baby. When she said yes, Tripoli falsely explained that to determine the sex he would have to scan "much further down." Then Tripoli inappropriately touched the plaintiff. Believing that contact in that private area was part of the examination, Lisa did not stop Tripoli. After describing Tripoli's behavior to her regular obstetrician, Lisa discovered that the behavior was not necessary and was inappropriate. Lisa then brought suit against Tripoli and the hospital, among others. The issue was whether Tripoli committed the sexual assault within the scope of his employment, thereby rendering the hospital "vicariously liable." For the type of liability the plaintiff was seeking, the employment situation must create a foreseeable risk that the employee might commit an offense. Was the hospital liable? [*Lisa M. v. Henry Mayo Memorial Hospital,* 907 P. 2d 358 (Supreme Court of California 1995).]

Looking for more review material?

The Online Learning Center at **www.mhhe.com/kubasek1e** contains this chapter's "Assignment on the Internet" and also a list of URLs for more information, entitled "On the Internet." Find both of them in the Student Center portion of the OLC, along with quizzes and other helpful materials.

Forms of Business Organizations

CASE OPENER

The McDonald's Franchise Agreement

The McDonald's Corporation operates numerous fast-food restaurants worldwide, organizing many of them as franchises. One McDonald's franchise was sold to the Robertson family in 1971. The Robertsons operated their franchise restaurant in Jacksonville, Florida, for many years with few problems. The McDonald's Corporation later notified them, however, that the franchise had been violating part of the license agreement. After repeated incidents, McDonald's Corporation (the franchisor) demanded termination of the franchise.

1. Did McDonald's lawfully revoke the Robertsons' franchise?
2. What are some potential problems that a franchisor and a franchisee might experience in their relationship?

The Wrap-Up at the end of the chapter will answer these questions.

Learning Objectives

After reading this chapter, you will be able to answer the following questions:

1. What are the major forms of business organizations?
2. What are the differences among the different forms of business organizations?
3. What are the specialized forms of business organizations?

CHAPTER 35

Suppose that you get an idea to produce a novel product. You think that production of this new product could lead to enormous profits. But what is the best way to produce this product? Should you produce it yourself by creating your own business? Do you have enough money to create your own business? What are the legal ramifications for you if your business is not successful? What legal responsibilities do you have with respect to your business?

Maybe you share your idea for this new product with your best friend, who suggests that the two of you become partners in the production and sale of this product. What are the benefits associated with forming a partnership? What are the disadvantages? Are there other forms of businesses that you should consider?

Deciding what form of business to create is one of the most important decisions a business makes. The extent of liability, as well as the extent of the control the owner will have over the business, is dependent on the form of the business. However, the business world is not static, and businesses can, and do, change form over time. Accordingly, this chapter is relevant not only to new businesses but also to already existing businesses. The first section in this chapter introduces the major types of business organizations, describing how these forms are both created and ended. The second section considers several types of business organizations that are less well known, but important nevertheless.

Major Forms of Business Organizations

SOLE PROPRIETORSHIP

If you decide to go into business on your own, you are creating a **sole proprietorship,** a business organization in which you, as the **sole proprietor,** are in sole control of the management and the profits. Thus, if you wanted to open a lawn-mowing business or a sewing shop, you would likely be creating a sole proprietorship.

Why might an entrepreneur choose to create a sole proprietorship over other business organizations? First, a sole proprietorship requires very few legal formalities. Thus, one advantage of the sole proprietorship is the ease of creating such a business. Second, a sole proprietor has complete control of the management of the business. Consequently, the sole proprietor has great freedom to hire employees, determine business hours, and expand or change the nature of the business. Finally, the sole proprietor keeps all the profits from the business. These profits are taxed as the personal income of the sole proprietor.

However, sole proprietorships have disadvantages, too. Suppose you are the sole proprietor of a restaurant in which someone is injured. This customer sues your business. You are personally liable for any losses or any of the obligations associated with the business. Consequently, if you accrue large debts because of your business, you might have to sell your home to cover those debts. Moreover, because the sole proprietorship is not considered a separate legal entity, you, as the owner and sole proprietor, can be personally sued. Sole proprietorships are terminated, however, when the sole proprietor dies.

Not only are you personally liable for any debts of the business, but the funding for your business is limited to your personal funds as well as loans you might be able to obtain. Thus, sole proprietorships often struggle in the initial stages of business because of large start-up costs in relation to the profits they make.

Sole proprietorships are by far the most popular form of business organization in the United States. Exhibit 35-1 summarizes their advantages and disadvantages. As the Global Context box illustrates, they are popular in Germany, too, although Germans call them "sole traders."

An alternative form of business organization that retains many of the advantages of the sole proprietorship but that addresses the funding drawback in part is the partnership.

ADVANTAGES	DISADVANTAGES
1. Creation is easy.	1. Personal liability for all losses.
2. Proprietor is in total control of management.	2. Funding limited to personal funds and loans.
3. Proprietor keeps all profits.	

Exhibit 35-1 Summary of Advantages and Disadvantages of the Sole Proprietorship

global context

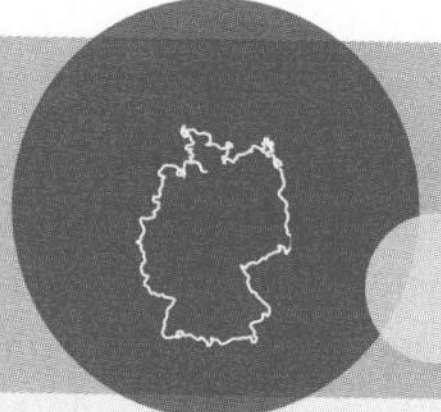

Sole Traders in Germany

Germany's equivalent to the United States' sole proprietor is the sole trader. Sole traders are not recognized as a separate business organization. Under German law, they are categorized as limited companies. The definition of a sole trader is quite broad. It includes "anyone carrying out business under his or her own name." Sole traders can employ a staff but may not have partners or shareholders. The German definition of a sole trader is further broken down by the distinction between major and minor traders.

Major traders are those operating a large-scale organization. Because the organizations are large, major traders must register their companies. If a sole trader is involved in manufacturing goods, trading with securities, or buying and selling large quantities of goods, registering would be necessary.

Minor traders are not permitted to register their organizations. If a minor trader wishes to elevate his or her status to that of a major trader, he or she submits company records to the registrar. The registrar must be satisfied that elements such as the number of employees and the amount of bank credit are large enough. While being elevated to a major trader does mean being governed by more extensive regulations, for many organizations it also presents opportunities for growth and expansion.

A final interesting point about sole traders is the difficulty Germany has had with the literal interpretation of the definition. Because the definition states that a sole trader must be operating under his or her own name, companies at one time had to change names when the sole trader sold his company. Changing names presented a problem to those who wished to keep the name because of its familiarity to clientele. Eventually, a stipulation was added to German law that permitted the "trading name" to be included in the sale of the company.

PARTNERSHIP

Suppose you and your best friend from college decide to create a business in which you plan to buy and sell used books and compact discs through the Internet. You both agree that you will share control of the Internet business and will split the profits equally. According to the Uniform Partnership Act, you have created a **partnership**, a voluntary association between two or more persons who co-own a business for profit. Except in a few cases, a partnership is not considered a separate legal entity and is dissolved when a partner dies. The Uniform Partnership Act (UPA) governs partnerships in most states in the absence of an express agreement.

What are the advantages associated with creating a partnership? First, the creation of a partnership is easy. The partners, who are each considered an agent of the partnership, are generally not required to create an official or even written agreement to create the partnership. Second, because the partnership is in most cases not considered a separate legal entity, the income from the business is taxed as individual income for each partner. Because the income is taxed as personal income, the partners can deduct the business losses.

Exhibit 35-2 Summary of Advantages and Disadvantages of Partnerships

ADVANTAGES	DISADVANTAGES
1. Creation is easy. 2. Income of business is personal income. 3. Business losses can be deducted from taxes.	1. Personal liability for all losses, including those of another partner (in most cases).

While there are certain advantages to creating a partnership, there are also disadvantages associated with partnerships. Most importantly, the partners are personally liable for the debts of the partnership. For instance, suppose you are in a partnership with your best friend, who embezzles $50,000 through your partnership. Because of the partnership, you would likely be held personally liable for the debts of the partnership. In other words, you would likely be responsible for the $50,000. Exhibit 35-2 summarizes the advantages and disadvantages of partnerships.

There are several types of partnerships: general partnerships, limited partnerships, and limited liability partnerships. A **general partnership** consists of an agreement that the partners will divide the profits (usually equally) and management responsibilities and share unlimited personal liability for the partnership's debts. Thus, in our Internet business example, you and your best friend would form a general partnership by agreeing to share the management responsibilities and profits as well as assuming unlimited personal liability.

Now, imagine that your parents want to invest in your Internet business. Suppose that they want to share in the profits associated with the business but they do not want to share in the management responsibilities or assume personal liability for the debts of the partnership. Your parents can join your business as limited partners, and your partnership would become a limited partnership. A **limited partnership (LP)** is an agreement between at least one general partner and at least one limited partner. The general partners, you and your best friend, assume unlimited personal liability for the debts of the partnership. However, your parents, the limited partners, assume no liability for the partnership beyond the capital they have invested in the business. Moreover, the limited partners do not have any part in the management of the company. However, limited partners pay taxes on their share of the business profit.

If a limited partner dies, the limited partnership is usually unaffected. If a general partner dies, however, the limited partnership is usually dissolved.

The limited partnership must meet certain requirements that are not expected of general partnerships. First, the limited partnership must use the word *limited* in its title. Second, to create a limited partnership, the parties must file a certificate of partnership with a state office. If the certificate of partnership is incorrectly filed, or simply not filed at all, the courts will rule that a general partnership exists. Consequently, all parties will be held personally liable for all the debts of the partnership.

Now suppose that you are an attorney and a partner in a law firm with 30 other partners. Suppose further that one of your partners is sued because he was negligent in his duties as an attorney. This partner has unlimited liability because of professional malpractice. But will you and the other partners at the firm be held liable for this partner's malpractice?

If you and your fellow partners have created a **limited liability partnership (LLP)**, a different form of partnership than the LP, all of the partners assume liability for one partner's professional malpractice to the extent of the partnership's assets. Thus, the limited liability partnership is distinguishable from other forms of partnerships because the partners' liability for professional malpractice is limited to the partnership. If one partner in an LLP is guilty of malpractice, the other partners' personal assets cannot be taken. Therefore, professionals who do business together commonly use the LLP. It is the extra protection awarded partners in an LLP that makes the LLP a *separate* form of partnership from a limited partnership. Limited partnerships are not the same as limited liability partnerships.

LLPs are fairly new; in 1991, Texas was the first state to enact a statute permitting the creation of LLPs. Almost all states now have similar statutes. Like the limited partnership, the LLP has several special requirements. First, the business name must include "Limited Liability Partnership" or an abbreviation of the phrase. Second, the parties must file a form with the secretary of the state to create the LLP.

The LLP is not considered a separate legal entity. Each partner pays taxes on his or her share of the income of the business.

An alternative form of business organization, the corporation, separates business ownership from business control.

CORPORATION

When you hear the word *business,* you probably think about businesses such as Wal-Mart, Kmart, McDonald's, and Nike. Perhaps the most dominant form of business organization is the **corporation,** a legal entity formed by issuing stock to investors, who are the owners of the corporation. The investor-owners are called **shareholders.** These shareholders elect a board of directors, which is responsible for managing the business. The board of directors, in turn, hires officers to run the day-to-day business.

The corporation is considered a separate legal entity; thus, the corporation can be sued. None of the other forms of business we have discussed are considered separate legal entities. How does a corporation become a separate legal entity? It must be created according to state law. Chapter 38 discusses the laws governing the creation and functioning of the corporation.

What are the consequences of a corporation's status as a separate legal entity? First, while the corporation can be held liable, shareholders cannot be held personally liable for the debts of the corporation. Their liability is usually limited to the amount they have invested. Second, the corporation is not dissolved when the shareholders die. Third, the corporation must pay taxes on its profits. In addition, the shareholders must pay taxes on the dividends they receive from the corporation.

One way that a corporation can avoid this double taxation is by forming an **S corporation,** a business organization formed under federal tax law that is considered a corporation yet is taxed like a partnership as long as it follows certain regulations. For example, the S corporation cannot have more than 75 shareholders. Any income of the corporation is taxed when it is distributed to the shareholders, who must report the income on their personal income tax forms. S corporations are always formed under federal law. S corporations cannot be formed under state law, whereas other forms of corporations are created under state law.

Exhibit 35-3 summarizes the advantages and disadvantages of the corporate form of business.

LIMITED LIABILITY COMPANY

An alternative form of business organization, the limited liability company, offers tax and liability advantages similar to those of an S corporation. The **limited liability company**

Exhibit 35-3 Advantages and Disadvantages of Forming a Corporation

ADVANTAGES	DISADVANTAGES
1. Limited liability for shareholders.	1. Corporate income taxed twice.
2. Ease of raising capital by issuing stock.	2. Formalities required in establishing and maintaining corporate form.
3. Profits taxed as income to the shareholders, not the partners.	

e-commerce AND THE LAW

Economics

Although shareholders are not personally liable for corporate debts, shareholders still bear the risk of loss should the company's stock decrease in value. However, shareholders are entitled to share in the corporation's profits. Corporations pay shareholders *dividends,* which is the amount of corporate profits minus the amount the company chooses to keep as retained earnings. A corporation can invest these retained earnings in the hope of generating larger profits. As a corporation becomes larger and more profitable, the stock value will likely increase, creating capital gains for shareholders. Hence, shareholders receive wealth from corporations in the form of dividends and capital gains. When investors expect dividends and capital gains to increase, investors are more willing to purchase a corporation's stock. However, expectations can also adversely affect corporate stock. If investors expect that a company will perform poorly, shareholders are more likely to sell their stock in the corporation and prospective investors are less willing to purchase the available stock, thereby decreasing demand for a corporation's stock while increasing the supply of stock. Consequently, the corporation's stock price would decrease.

Source: Bradley Schiller, *The Economy Today* (New York: McGraw-Hill/Irwin, 2006), pp. 678–681.

(LLC) is similar to the limited liability partnership, but the LLP is different because it was created for professionals who are in business together. The LLC has the limited liability of a corporation yet is taxed like a partnership. The owners of the LLC, the **members,** pay personal income taxes on the shares they report.

To get a better sense of the meaning of an LLC, imagine that you want to create a software firm. Your roommate's father is excited by your idea and offers to provide financial advice that you need to operate the proposed firm effectively. In return, you agree that he will have a 4 percent ownership interest in your software firm. You then organize your start-up firm as an LLC by filing the needed articles of organization with the state.

What requirements must a business meet to be considered a limited liability company? First, the company must file a form with a state agency. Second, the company name must include "Limited Liability Company" or an abbreviation of those words.

The LLC is very similar to the S corporation, but there is no limitation on the number of shareholders permitted in an LLC.

Exhibit 35-4 provides a comparison of alternative forms of business organization.

Specialized Forms of Business Organizations

In addition to the more traditional forms of business organizations mentioned above, the following specialized forms of business organizations have become increasingly important: cooperatives, joint stock companies, business trusts, syndicates, joint ventures, and franchises.

global context

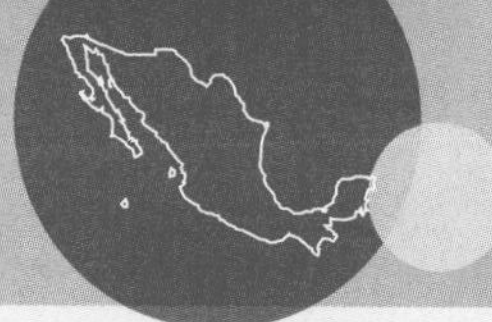

Limited Liability Companies in Mexico

A limited liability company in Mexico is "an association of individuals who are exempt from individual responsibility to third parties, yet who own the stock separately from the owner."

Limited liability companies are identifiable to the public because the company name must be followed by the phrase "Sociedad de Responsibilidad Limitada." Without this phrase, it is assumed that a partnership exists.

The important distinguishing factor in the business sense is that the members are an entity separate from the owners. Members, referred to as *share/stockholders,* invest capital into the company. There may be anywhere from 2 to 25 shareholders.

While members do not have any individual responsibility, collectively they must give their consent before they can sell shares to new members. No matter how many members there are, the decision must be unanimous, but the number of votes each member has corresponds to the number of shares he owns. Generally, members have one vote for every 100-peso share.

The Mexican limited liability company is derived from the model in Germany, where such companies are enormously popular. Mexico adopted the model in hopes of encouraging smaller companies. The country felt that the limited responsibilities of shareholders would attract more investors to small companies.

COOPERATIVE

A **cooperative** is an organization formed by individuals to market products. The cooperative is a business organization in which the members usually pool their resources together to gain some kind of advantage in the market. For instance, farmers might pool certain crops together to ensure that they get a high market price for their crops. Usually, members

Exhibit 35-4 Comparison of Alternative Forms of Business Organizations

	SOLE PROPRIETORSHIP	GENERAL PARTNERSHIP	LIMITED PARTNERSHIP	CORPORATION
Legal Position	Not a separate legal entity.	Not a separate legal entity in most states.	A separate legal entity.	A separate legal entity.
Control Considerations	Sole proprietor has total control.	Each partner is entitled to equal control.	Each partner is entitled to equal control.	Separation of ownership and control.
Liability	Sole proprietor has unlimited personal liability.	Each partner has unlimited personal liability for partnership debts.	Each partner has liability limited to his or her capital contribution.	Liability limited to loss of capital contribution.
Lifetime	Limited to life of proprietor.	Limited by life of partners.	Limited to life of general partners.	Can have unlimited life.
Taxation	Profits are taxed directly as income to the sole proprietor.	Profits are taxed as income for partners.	Profits are taxed as income for partners.	Profits are taxed as income to the corporation and as income to the partners in the form of dividends.
Transferability of Ownership Interest	Nontransferable.	Nontransferable.	Nontransferable.	Generally unlimited transfer.

Exploring Forms of Business Organization on the Internet

If you are considering starting a business, the Internet can provide much information to help you decide which form of business you should create. This format for acquiring information about which form of business is optimal should improve the quality of decisions about this crucial step in operating a business. For example, at Business Tools, http://smallbiz.findlaw.com/book, you can read more about sole proprietorships, partnerships, and corporations. Furthermore, using the Internet, you can learn about the laws that affect the forms of business within your specific state. For example, at Texas Business Forms, www.sos.state.tx.us/corp/forms.shtml, you can read about and actually retrieve the forms required to create various business types in Texas. Thus, the Internet can ease the difficulties associated with creating a business by increasing the information available to you about forms of business organization.

of the cooperative receive dividends in proportion to how many times per year they engage in business with the cooperative.

Cooperatives may be incorporated or unincorporated. Unincorporated cooperatives are treated like partnerships, meaning that the members share joint liability for the cooperative's actions. Members of incorporated cooperatives, on the other hand, enjoy limited liability just as do the shareholders of a corporation.

JOINT STOCK COMPANY

A **joint stock company** is a partnership agreement in which company members hold transferable shares while all the goods of the company are held in the names of the partners. Thus, the joint stock company is a mixture of a corporation and a partnership. As with the corporation, the members who hold shares of stock own the joint stock company. As with the partnership, the shareholders have personal liability, and in most cases the company is not a separate legal entity. The joint stock company is formed by agreement rather than statute.

BUSINESS TRUST

A **business trust** is a business organization governed by a group of **trustees,** who operate the trust for the **beneficiaries.** A written trust agreement establishes the duties and powers of the trustees and the interests of the beneficiaries.

As with a corporation, the trustees and beneficiaries enjoy limited liability, and in most states business trusts are taxed like corporations.

SYNDICATE

An investment group that comes together for the explicit purpose of financing a specific large project is a **syndicate.** Syndicates are often used in the purchase of professional sports teams. The syndicate is quite useful in the sense that it can raise large amounts of money in a small amount of time. Syndicates are usually considered a type of joint venture, and thus they are almost always governed by partnership law.

JOINT VENTURE

A **joint venture** is a relationship between two or more persons or corporations created for a specific business undertaking. This relationship may entail financing, producing, and

global context

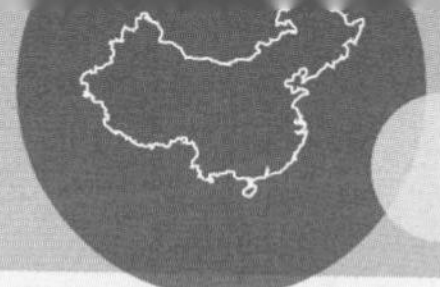

Types of Business Organizations in China

Before one can understand business organizations in China, the concept of legal persons must be explained. This concept is at the root of all Chinese business law. The Civil Code of China defines a legal person in the following way: "An organization which possesses civil legal capacity for civil acts and which, according to the law, independently enjoys civil rights and assumes civil obligations." The definition then goes on to describe two types of legal persons.

The first type is the *enterprise legal person.* An enterprise legal person is any enterprise that is privately, collectively, or state-owned. Before an organization is considered an enterprise, the local registrar must approve it. Approval depends on the satisfaction of four criteria: (1) existence of an outlined organizational structure, (2) an organization title, (3) articles governing the structure, and (4) the necessary funds and property. A foreign-owned or foreign joint venture may also acquire enterprise legal person status by applying for approval and registration.

The second type of legal persons is *other legal persons.* These include government agencies, institutions, and associations. Government agencies need not apply for registration because they are given legal person status on their establishment. In certain situations, other institutions and associations are subject to approval and registration. The criteria they must meet before acquiring legal person status are identical to those for enterprises. In October 1998, the State Council specified which situations required registration for these institutions and associations.

selling goods, securities, and commodities. Participants in the joint venture usually share the profits and losses of the joint venture equally.

Joint ventures can be agreements between small businesses as well as agreements between very large businesses. For example, General Motors and Toyota have entered into a joint venture to create the Saturn line of cars. Generally, joint ventures are taxed like partnerships. In fact, from a legal standpoint, partnerships and joint ventures are virtually the same. Thus, courts frequently apply partnership law to joint ventures. Joint ventures differ from partnerships, however, because a joint venture is usually created for making and selling a single product while a partnership creates an ongoing full business. Once all the single products are sold, the joint venture is usually terminated. The members, however, can determine when the joint venture will end.

Despite the similarities, there are several minor differences between partnerships and joint ventures in the eyes of the law. First, if one of the members of a joint venture dies, the joint venture is not automatically terminated. Second, the members of a joint venture have less authority than general partners because members of a joint venture are not agents of the other members.

The parties who compose a joint venture usually share equal management of the task for which they have come together. They, however, can make an agreement to give one party greater management responsibilities. Furthermore, the parties usually both assume liability for the project. Each party can be held responsible for the liability of the other party in the joint venture.

Like a partnership, a joint venture may be formed without drawing up a formal agreement. Case 35-1 illustrates how the courts determine whether a joint venture exists. What facts does the judge rely on to determine whether a joint venture existed between Yurko and Huisel, Fitchie, and Vincent?

CASE 35-1

JUDY FITCHIE v. RICK YURKO
ILLINOIS COURT OF APPEALS
570 N.E.2D 892 (1991)

Rick Yurko frequently visited Phyllis Huisel's coffee shop. While visiting the shop, Yurko regularly purchased Illinois state lottery tickets from Huisel. In February 1990, Yurko purchased $100 worth of $1 scratch off Fortune Hunt lottery tickets. Yurko had Huisel, Judy Fitchie (one of Huisel's employees), and Frances Vincent (another customer) help him scratch-off his tickets. Yurko stated that if they helped him scratch off the tickets, they would be his partners and share in the winnings.

Eventually, Judy uncovered a winning ticket that gave the owner a chance to compete for a $100,000 prize. The owner of the ticket was supposed to fill out his or her name and address and send in the ticket to the lottery commission to enter a drawing to win a spot on the lottery television show. Yurko suggested that Phyllis fill out the back of the ticket, but Phyllis did not want to appear on television. Yurko stated that he would appear on television, and Phyllis, Judy, Frances, and Yurko agreed that Yurko would be their representative. Yurko wrote "F.J.P. Rick Yurko" on the back of the lottery ticket and said that they would be partners.

The ticket was chosen for one of the spots on the television show. When Yurko appeared on the show, he won $100,000. However, Yurko claimed the $100,000 for himself. Phyllis, Judy, and Frances sued Yurko to recover their share of the award. The trial court ruled that Phyllis, Judy, and Frances were partners or joint venturers and thus entitled to shares of the $100,000. Yurko appealed.

JUSTICE BOWMAN: The evidence indicates that the arrangement between Yurko, Phyllis, Judy, and Frances constituted a joint venture. A joint venture is essentially a partnership carried on for a single enterprise.

A joint venture is an association of two or more persons to carry out a single enterprise for profit. Whether a joint venture exists is a question of the intent of the parties. The elements to be considered in determining the parties' intent are: an agreement to carry on an enterprise; a demonstration of intent by the parties to be joint venturers; a joint interest, as reflected in the contribution of property, finances, effort, skill, or knowledge by each party; a measure of proprietorship or joint control over the enterprise; and a provision for sharing of profits and losses. A formal agreement is not essential to establish a joint venture. Rather, the existence of a joint venture may be inferred from facts and circumstances demonstrating that the parties, in fact, undertook a joint enterprise.

The parties entered into an agreement and showed their intent to be joint venturers when they started playing the lottery together. Yurko invited the women, both verbally and by placing tickets in from of them, to play the lottery with him. Yurko told them that if they would help him scratch tickets they would be his partners and would share in any prize winnings. They expressed agreement with Yurko's proposal when they began scratching off the tickets.

Both Judy and Frances uncovered tickets that were good for small cash prizes or more tickets. None of the players tried to claim any of those prizes as their own. Rather, the tickets were turned in for more tickets, and the players kept on scratching. After the winning ticket was revealed, there was discussion amongst all the parties as to who would appear on the television show. Together, not individually, they decided that Yurko would be the one to go. Yurko impliedly acknowledged a joint effort when he printed the women's initials right alongside his own name on the back of the winning ticket, again amidst talk that he and the women were partners.

A joint interest in the effort to win the lottery is also found in the evidence. It is undisputed that Yurko paid for the tickets. Frances and Judy expended their time and energy and put forth effort to scratch their tickets. While Phyllis's part in this is not altogether clear, Phyllis scratched off a couple tickets, and it is evident the other parties considered her part of the enterprise.

Finally, with regard to provision for sharing of profits, Yurko told the women they would share in anything that was won if they helped scratch the tickets. Yurko also wrote the women's initials next to his own on the line provided on the lottery ticket for the ticket holder's

[CONTINUED]

name. This evidence proves that the joint venturers planned to share equally in any lottery prize ultimately won. We acknowledge the informality of the arrangement between Yurko and the women. Nonetheless, the parties should be bound by the terms of their agreement to jointly carry out an enterprise for profit.

AFFIRMED.

CRITICAL THINKING

What facts does the judge rely on most when reasoning that the parties entered a joint venture? Do you agree with the judge's conclusion? Why or why not?

What are the most persuasive reasons that Yurko could have provided to convince the court that the plaintiffs were not engaged in a joint venture with him? Are there elements of the facts that the court underemphasized when it reached its decision? The process of critical thinking requires that we ask critical questions about whatever reasoning we encounter, even if, as in this case, the reasoning appears very convincing.

ETHICAL DECISION MAKING

Place yourself in Yurko's position. What values would you promote in his situation? Consider the primary stakeholders in the situation. Are there ethical problems with Yurko's actions, or is he justified is claiming the winnings all to himself? Were the other involved parties acting in an ethically appropriate manner? Why or why not?

FRANCHISE

When you go into McDonald's to eat lunch, what type of business are you patronizing? You are likely eating at a **franchise**, a business that exists because of an arrangement between the **franchisor**, an owner of a trade name or trademark, and the **franchisee**, a person who sells goods or services under the trade name or trademark.

What are the advantages and disadvantages for the franchisor and the franchisee? Exhibits 35-5 and 35-6 summarize these advantages and disadvantages. First, the franchisee enjoys the franchisor's help in opening the franchise. Second, think about how many times you have driven through a strange town and felt relieved when you saw a Burger King. Even though you may have never been to that town before and did not know who controlled that particular business, you know Burger King. Before you walk into the restaurant, you know

Exhibit 35-5
Advantages and Disadvantages to the Franchisee of Starting a Franchise

ADVANTAGES	DISADVANTAGES
1. Help from the franchisor in starting the franchise.	1. Must meet the franchisor's standards or risk losing the franchise.
2. Instant recognition due to the franchisor's strong trademark or trade name.	2. Has little to no creative control over the business.
3. Benefits from the franchisor's worldwide advertising.	

Exhibit 35-6 Advantages and Disadvantages to the Franchisor of Starting a Franchise

ADVANTAGES	DISADVANTAGES
1. Low risk in starting a franchise.	1. Has little control over the franchise.
2. Increased income from franchises.	2. Can become liable for the franchise if it exerts too much control.

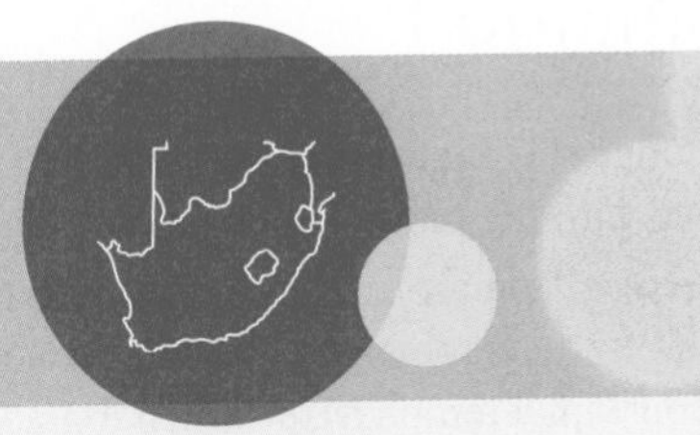

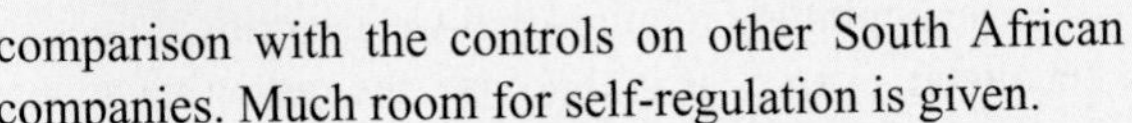

global context

Types of Business Organizations in South Africa

Due to the increasing number of foreign companies and investors engaging in South African business, the government now recognizes a unique type of business organization called the *external company.* An external company is defined as a foreign company operating through a branch in South Africa. External companies are broken down into four types: close corporations, partnerships, trading trusts, and international joint ventures.

The first of these types, the close corporation, is designed to suit small businesses. The members, who cannot exceed 10, have limited liability in much the same way as shareholders in a corporation. The regulations for close corporations are quite flexible in comparison with the controls on other South African companies. Much room for self-regulation is given.

Partnerships in South Africa may contain no more than 20 partners, except in the case of partnerships in certain professions (attorneys or accountants, e.g.). As in the United States, partnerships are not considered separate legal entities under South African law. While no specific statutory law governing partnerships in South Africa exists, contract law governs relations among partners.

Trading trusts allow greater flexibility to both foreign and domestic parties than any other trading relationship. External companies classified as trading trusts enjoy tax benefits, but the trustees who manage business property still enjoy limited liability.

Finally, international joint ventures are governed by common law regulations very similar to American law.

almost exactly what will be on its menu. Thus, on the one hand, the franchisee benefits from the franchisor's strong trade name or trademark. Moreover, the franchisee benefits from the franchisor's worldwide advertising of the trade name or trademark. The franchisor, on the other hand, benefits from this business arrangement because it does not take a large risk in creating the franchise yet it can greatly benefit from the agreement because of the income it receives from the franchisee.

Generally, franchises fall into one of three categories. McDonald's and Burger King are examples of chain-style business operations. In a **chain-style business operation,** the franchise operates under the franchisor's business name and is required to follow the franchisor's standards and methods of business operation.

The second category of franchises is the distributorship. **Distributorships** are franchises in which the franchisor manufactures a product and licenses a dealer to sell the product in an exclusive territory. A car dealership is an example of a distributorship.

Finally, the third category of franchises is the manufacturing arrangement. In a **manufacturing arrangement,** the franchisor provides the franchisee with the formula or necessary ingredient to manufacture a product. The franchisee then manufactures the product and sells it according to the franchisor's standards. Exhibit 35-7 contains a description of

Exhibit 35-7 Types of Franchises

FRANCHISE TYPE	DESCRIPTION
Chain-style business operation	Franchisor helps franchisee set up a business run under the franchisor's business name according to the franchisor's usual methods and standards.
Distributorship	Franchisor licenses franchisee to sell the franchisor's product in a specific area.
Manufacturing arrangement	Franchisor provides the franchisee with the technical knowledge to manufacture the franchisor's product.

Exhibit 35-8 The Top 10 Global Franchises, 2005

1. Subway
2. Curves
3. Quizno's Franchise Co.
4. Kumon Math & Reading Centers
5. KFC Corp.
6. The UPS Store
7. RE/MAX Int'l. Inc.
8. Domino's Pizza LLC
9. Jani-King
10. GNC Franchising Inc.

Source: Ranked by *Entrepreneur Magazine* based on financial strength and stability, growth rate, and size of the system; www.entrepreneur.com/franzone/listings/fran500/0,5831,,00.html.

the various types of franchises. Exhibit 35-8 provides a sense of just how important franchises are for the market economy.

Look at Case 35-2 to see how the supreme court of Arkansas determined whether a franchise agreement existed between Mary Kay Cosmetics and Janet Isbell.

CASE 35-2 MARY KAY, INC., A/K/A MARY KAY COSMETICS, INC. v. JANET ISBELL

SUPREME COURT OF ARKANSAS

338 ARK. 556; 999 S.W. 2D 669; 1999 ARK. LEXIS 443

In 1980, Janet Isbell signed an agreement to become a beauty consultant for Mary Kay. This agreement established that she would sell products to customers at home demonstration parties, but she was prohibited from selling the products in retail establishments. In September 1981, Isbell signed her first agreement to become a unit sales director. She signed her second agreement in July 1991. In addition to serving as a beauty consultant, Isbell recruited beauty consultants. She earned compensation in the form of commission on her sales as well as on the sales of the consultants she recruited. In 1994, she rented a space in a shopping mall to serve as a training center. In April 1994, Mary Kay's legal coordinator contacted Isbell, stating that the store space was not to be used to sell Mary Kay products. According to the agreement, Isbell's office could not look like a Mary Kay store. Furthermore, Isbell was told to cease all photo sessions of potential customers and to stop advertising "glamour tips."

In September 1995, the Vice President of sales development notified Isbell that Mary Kay was terminating its agreements with Isbell. Isbell filed suit against Mary Kay, claiming that she was a franchise under Arkansas' Franchise Practices Act. She argued that Mary Kay violated the Franchise Practices Act by refusing to comply with the FPA provisions for termination of a franchise. In August 1997, the trial court granted summary judgment to Isbell, but it did not explain why Isbell's relationships with Mary Kay could be considered a franchise. The trial court ruled as a matter of law that Mary Kay's termination of Isbell had violated the Act, and a jury awarded Isbell $110,583.33.

JUDGE GLAZE: The threshold issue to be decided is whether the Arkansas Franchise Practices Act applies, because if it does, Isbell would be entitled to the designation of franchisee and permitted to invoke the protections and benefits of that Act.

To determine whether the Arkansas Franchise Practices Act applies to this case depends upon our interpretation and construction of the pertinent provisions of the Act. In this view, we turn first to Ark. Code Ann. §4-72-202 (1) (Supp. 1997), which in relevant part defines "franchise" to mean the following:

> [A] written or oral agreement for a definite or indefinite period, in which a person grants to another a license to use a trade name, trademark, service mark, or related characteristic within an exclusive or nonexclusive territory, or to sell or distribute goods or services within an exclusive or nonexclusive territory, at wholesale, retail, by lease agreement, or otherwise.

While the Act's definition of franchise is helpful, that definition alone is not dispositive of the issue as to whether Isbell, under the parties' agreement, is or is not a franchisee. The answer, however, can be found in §§ 4-72-203 and 4-72-202 (6) of the Act. Section 4-72-203 clearly provides the Act applies only to a franchise that contemplates or requires the franchise to establish or maintain a place of business in the state. Next, § 4-72-202 (6) defines "place of business" under the Act as meaning "a fixed geographical location at which the franchisee [1] displays for sale and sells the franchisor's goods or [2] offers for sale and sells the franchisor's services."

We first should note that Isbell concedes that, as a sales director, her agreements with Mary Kay provided that she could not display for sale or sell Mary Kay products from an office, whether that office was located in her home or her training center. In fact, Isbell testified that she never displayed or sold Mary Kay products from her training center, and to have done so would have been a violation of her agreement with Mary Kay.

While conceding that the parties' agreements never contemplated that Isbell would or could sell the franchisor's goods from a fixed location, she argues no such prohibition prevented her from selling Mary Kay services from her home or training center. Specifically, Isbell suggests the facial makeovers and "Glamour Shots" photo sessions that were a part of Mary Kay's demonstration and training program constituted services that the parties contemplated could be sold by Isbell from her center.

Mary Kay's Director's Guide, which was made a part of the parties' agreements, very clearly provided that a sales director's office, albeit it her home or training center, could only be used to interview potential recruits and hold unit meetings and other training events. The Guide further provided that the office or center should not give the appearance of a cosmetic studio, facial salon or retail establishment, or give the appearance of being a "Mary Kay" store. Thus, nowhere in the parties' Guide or agreements can it be fairly said that the parties ever contemplated that Isbell could use her office or center as a fixed location to display or sell Mary Kay products or services.

Even if we could agree with Isbell's contention that she was not prohibited from selling (or was otherwise authorized to sell) Mary Kay services, her argument must fail for another reason. Isbell simply never showed she sold Mary Kay services. She claims that because her contract requires her to provide motivational, counseling, and training services, such services should be considered part of the sale and commission when the product is actually sold. Isbell offered no proof as to what part of the commission, if any, was attributable to services. Neither Isbell nor Mary Kay was shown to have received any separate compensation for services provided to potential customers, but, to the contrary, evidence was presented showing these services, like the photographs taken at makeover sessions, were provided at cost with only the photographer receiving payment.

Finally, Isbell argues that her home constituted a place of business under the Act because as a consultant she occasionally displayed and sold products there. This argument, however, is not supported by the parties' agreement, since it never contemplated a fixed location for the display and sale of products. As previously stated, a Mary Kay consultant's location for selling products is her home or those of her potential customers.

In sum, we conclude that the agreements between Janet Isbell and Mary Kay did not contemplate the establishment of a fixed place of business as that term is defined in Ark. Code Ann. § 4-72-202 (6). As such, the business relationship entered into by Isbell and Mary Kay was not a franchise within the protection of the Arkansas Franchise Practices Act, and the court below erred in so holding.

REVERSED AND DISMISSED.

CRITICAL THINKING

Outline the judge's reasoning in this case. What evidence does he use to support this reasoning?

What missing information would you call for when considering the facts of this case?

Would you interpret the Arkansas Franchise Practices Act and how it applies to the facts of the case differently than Judge Glaze does? Why or why not?

ETHICAL DECISION MAKING

Consider the WPH framework. What values is Isabel promoting? What values are in conflict? Was the court fair in assessing her actions in light of these values?

Franchise law. Because franchisors are usually larger than franchisees and have more resources, they often have the upper hand in franchise relationships. Federal and state laws, however, have been established to protect the franchisee in the franchise relationship.

A franchise is a contractual relationship between the franchisor and the franchisee. Thus, contract law, and the Uniform Commercial Code in particular, applies to the franchise relationship. If the terms of the contract are not met, either side can sue for breach of contract. For example, in *Ford Motor Co. v. Lyons,*[1] Lyons sued Ford for breach of its dealer franchise obligations. In the franchise agreement, Ford had agreed to send factory representatives to the dealership, as well as offer Lyons assistance with his business. However, Ford failed to perform its duties. Lyons sued, bringing forth evidence that Ford had intentionally failed to perform its contractual duties because one of the other dealership franchises was jealous of the dealership territory Ford had given to Lyons as part of the franchise agreement.

In addition, several laws that are more specific have been established to govern the franchise relationship. For example, the Federal Trade Commission has a franchise rule requiring franchisors to present prospective franchisees with material facts necessary for the franchisee to make an informed decision about entering a franchise relationship. Moreover, the Automobile Dealers' Franchise Act of 1965 prohibits car dealership franchisors from terminating franchise relationships in bad faith. Thus, for example, DaimlerChrysler could not terminate its franchise relationship with a dealer because the dealer failed to meet impossible standards. Finally, the Petroleum Marketing Practices Act of 1979 outlines the reasons for which a franchisor may terminate a gas station franchise. Franchises must also be aware of federal antitrust laws. Antitrust laws prohibit specific forms of anticompetitive behavior and might be applicable to franchises. Federal antitrust laws are discussed in more depth in Chapter 47.

Many states have adopted additional laws to protect franchisees. Fifteen states, for example, require that franchisors provide prospective franchisees with a host of information about the franchise relationship before the agreement can be signed. What ethical standards do you think these 15 states are promoting in their decision to mandate franchise protections?

[1] 405 N.W.2d 354 (Wis. Ct. App. 1987).

Creation of the franchise. In the franchise relationship, the parties make a **franchise agreement** regarding various factors: the payment to the franchisor, the location of the franchise, the restrictions the franchisee must follow, and the method of termination of the franchise.

First, the franchise agreement usually states that the franchisee pays a large sum to the franchisor for use of the trade name or trademark. Moreover, the agreement determines what percentage of the income from the sales of the goods will go to the franchisor.

Second, the agreement usually determines where the franchise will be located. If the franchise requires a building, the agreement will specify who will pay for buying or renting the building. Similarly, if the building must be constructed, the agreement will state who is responsible for the costs of the construction of the building.

Third, the franchisor usually includes in the agreement certain business practices that are forbidden and other business standards that must be met. For example, the franchisor might require that the business meet specific levels of cleanliness. Moreover, the franchisor can set certain sales quotas as well as requirements for record keeping of the franchisee. The franchisor can require that the franchisee purchase certain supplies from the franchisor at a set price, but the franchisor cannot attempt to establish the price at which the franchisee must sell the goods.

The disagreement in the opening scenario for this chapter arose because of these second and third factors in franchise agreements. First, McDonald's offered the Robertsons a new franchise to be located a block from the existing franchise. McDonald's purchased the property, agreed to income guarantees, and planned to give the Robertsons the new franchise in exchange for the existing franchise, which McDonald's would thereafter close. Negotiations between McDonald's and the Robertsons, however, were unsuccessful; the Robertsons continually refused the offer. Second, because many McDonald's restaurants are owned by franchisees, McDonald's has established a "McDonald's System," which promotes business practices enhancing the quality of food and services at each restaurant. McDonald's also has quality, safety, and cleanliness (QSC) standards for each of its franchises. The Robertsons' franchise agreement stipulated that McDonald's could inspect the Robertsons' restaurant at any reasonable time.

Although the franchisor has the legal authority to ensure that the franchisee maintains the quality of goods and services associated with the franchise, the franchisor must be cautious. If it exercises too much authority in the day-to-day affairs of the business, the franchisor could be held liable for the torts of the franchisee's employees.

Termination of the franchise. The franchise agreement establishes how the franchise will be terminated. The franchise is usually established for a trial period, such as a year. If the franchisee does not meet the requirements established in the franchise agreement, the franchisor can terminate the franchise agreement, but the franchisor must give the franchisee sufficient notice of the termination. Furthermore, the termination usually must have cause. Much of the litigation associated with franchises regards wrongful termination of a franchise. The typical agreement gives the franchisor broad authority to terminate a franchise. In recent years, however, many states have been giving the franchisee greater termination protection.

The courts usually rely heavily on the written franchise agreement when determining whether a franchise was wrongfully terminated. Look at Case 35-3, which illustrates the importance of the written franchise agreement.

CASE 35-3 COUSINS SUBS SYSTEMS, INC. v. MICHAEL R. MCKINNEY

U.S. DISTRICT COURT FOR THE EASTERN DISTRICT OF WISCONSIN
59 F. SUPP. 2D 816 (1999)

Cousins Subs Systems entered into an agreement with Michael McKinney, a Minnesota businessman who owned a company that operates a chain of gas stations, for McKinney to operate several Cousins submarine sandwich shops.

The sub shops were to be placed in the gas stations. In April 1998, McKinney became disillusioned with the agreement and terminated the agreement. McKinney claimed Cousins guaranteed him annual sales at each of [his] franchises ranging from $250,000 to $500,000. Furthermore, McKinney argued Cousins promised to provide advertising for the franchises. McKinney also claimed Cousins guaranteed it would provide assistance in recruiting other franchises. Finally, McKinney argued Cousins enforced unrealistically high prices of subs. McKinney alleges he terminated the agreement because Cousins failed to uphold these promises.

In June 1998, Cousins filed suit against McKinney for wrongfully terminating the agreement with Cousins. Later in 1998, McKinney filed a counterclaim against Cousins. Cousins filed a motion to dismiss the counterclaim.

JUDGE ADELMAN: McKinney first contends that Cousins violated Minn. Stat. § 80C.13, subd. 2, which provides:

> No person may offer or sell a franchise in this state by means of any written or oral communication which includes an untrue statement of a material fact or which omits to state a material fact necessary in order to make the statements made, in light of the circumstances under which they were made, not misleading.

McKinney does not clearly delineate his theory as to how this statute was violated. He appears to assert that Cousins violated this statute by making untrue oral representations to him about how much money he would make and about how much advertising and recruitment assistance it would provide. The main problem with this claim and, for that matter, with all of McKinney's claims is that the oral promises allegedly made by Cousins are directly contradicted by the written terms of the agreements that he signed and attached as exhibits to his pleadings. Where the allegations of a complaint are inconsistent with the terms of a written contract attached as an exhibit, the terms of the contract prevail over the averments differing therefrom. Unfortunately for McKinney, every oral representation that he alleges was made by Cousins is inconsistent with the written contracts he signed or the written circular he received.

McKinney alleges first that Cousins . . . orally guaranteed that annual sales at McKinney's franchises would be between $250,000 and $500,000, and that this level of sales was not realized. However, the Area Development Agreement states that McKinney "has not received any warranty or guaranty, express or implied, as to the potential volume, profits, or success of the business venture." The Franchise Agreement contains virtually identical language. Thus, McKinney's claim of guaranteed profits is directly contradicted by the written contracts. McKinney also claims that Cousins promised to provide "advertising . . . in excess of the amount paid by McKinney," and that Cousins failed to do so. But the Uniform Franchise Offering Circular states that "Cousins is not obligated to spend any specific amounts on advertising in the area where a particular franchisee is located. . . ." Thus, this claim too is directly contradicted by the written language of an exhibit. McKinney next alleges that Cousins "expressly guaranteed and promised to provide extensive assistance in recruitment of other franchisees in the development area," but that such assistance was not forthcoming. The Area Development Agreement, however, states, with respect to the recruitment issue, "AREA DEVELOPER shall be responsible for advertising for, recruiting and screening prospects for SHOPS within the Exclusive Area." Thus, every single oral promise that McKinney asserts was made by Cousins is inconsistent with the documents appended to his complaint. Under Seventh Circuit case law the language of the exhibits prevails.

McKinney's claims are further undermined by other language in the agreements. The area development and franchise agreements each contain integration clauses which expressly disavow any promises not included in the written agreements between the parties. The Area Development Agreement, for example, states that "this Agreement . . . constitutes the entire agreement of the parties, and there are no other oral or written understandings or agreements . . . relating to the subject matter of this agreement."

McKinney cannot prevail on his claim under the Minnesota statute unless, in offering him a franchise, Cousins made an untrue statement of material fact. Cousins offered the franchises to McKinney through the written franchise documents, not through the alleged oral promises that are inconsistent with the exhibits. And the written documents do not contain untrue statements of material fact or omissions of material facts, nor does McKinney claim that they do. Therefore, McKinney's claim that the Minnesota Franchise Act was violated fails.

In sum, McKinney is an experienced businessman who made a deal which turned out to be less favorable than he anticipated. McKinney expressly acknowledged in detailed written agreements negotiated with the assistance of counsel that his purchase of a franchise was not a risk-free endeavor. He now makes allegations that are directly contrary to the agreements he signed. For the reasons stated, his claim under the Minnesota statute fails.

DISMISSED.

CRITICAL THINKING

What are the primary facts of this case? How would you word the issue of the case in your own words?

Judge Adelman repeatedly states that the written terms of the contract between Cousins and McKinney are inconsistent with any alleged oral agreements that they made. Do you agree that written contracts should overrule oral agreements in most instances? Why or why not?

ETHICAL DECISION MAKING

The court ruled in favor of Cousins. Who are the primary stakeholders affected by the court's ruling for Cousins?

The decisions of a court have implications for business ethics. While Chapter 2 distinguishes between what the law requires of a manager and what ethics requires, the relationship between the law and ethics is reciprocal. While ethical judgments lie behind various laws, it is also the case that law has impacts on business ethics. For example, in this case, the court's decision is reminding us that business ethics must pay attention to the various stakeholders who feel the impacts of any business agreement.

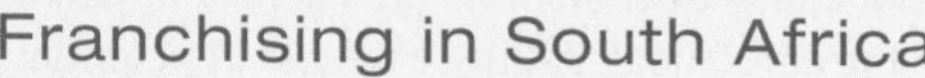

global context

Franchising in South Africa

Franchises are growing in popularity in South Africa. As Western and European franchises make their way into the economy, eager businesspersons sign on with these chains.

For a person aspiring to start a new business, having the support of a major franchise is a definite advantage. But because franchises are relatively new in South Africa, many of these eager individuals are uneducated and uninformed about the legal technicalities of this type of business organization.

For instance, franchise agreements almost always include clauses forbidding the franchisee from starting a similar business in the same area for a certain time after he or she has stopped using the franchise name. Without the proper guidance, a franchisee may discover he or she has entered into a contract with restrictive clauses.

Until those in the business community become better acquainted with the nature of franchises, the Franchise Association of Southern Africa (FASA) has created a code of ethics. Most of the clauses within the code are intended to protect the franchisee, which the FASA sees as the disadvantaged party. One example of protection is a clause requiring that franchises include both a disclosure document and a franchise agreement for the prospective manager. The franchise agreement must state that the information in the disclosure document is "true and accurate and that no material information has been withheld." Such provisions are necessary to avoid the exploitation of these new franchisee managers.

In the United States, where franchises have been growing for years, the FASA's code of ethics may appear cursory. We take for granted, however, that this form of business organization is widely familiar in the United States. For more information about the FASA and its code of ethics, check out FASA's Web site: www.fasa.co.za/newsite/about.htm.

CASE OPENER WRAP-UP

McDonald's

The Robertsons' McDonald's franchise failed two food safety audits. Consequently, the McDonald's Corporation sent the Robertsons a Notice of Default, stating that it would terminate the franchise if the Robertsons did not meet the QSC standards before a third audit was completed. The franchisor indicated in the Notice of Default that the unannounced audit would occur sometime after July. McDonald's completed the third audit; the franchisee again failed the food safety audit. Thereafter, McDonald's terminated the franchise. Under the provisions in the franchise agreement, McDonald's Corporation took possession of the franchise.

As a franchisor, McDonald's Corporation is permitted to establish certain standards for franchisees. With regard to the Robertsons' restaurant, McDonald's established standards for cleanliness and also negotiated plans for moving and building a new franchise. Although the Robertsons declined the offer for the new restaurant, the Robertsons' franchise failed three food and safety audits. In accordance with the provisions in the license agreement, McDonald's lawfully terminated the franchise. The Robertsons claimed that McDonald's revoked the franchise rights not because of food safety violations but because McDonald's wanted to move the franchise to a nearby location that would be more profitable. The food safety inspections were used only to justify McDonald's hidden agenda, or so the Robertsons claimed. However, the court of appeals agreed with the district court's ruling that any ulterior motives of McDonald's were irrelevant to the fact that the Robertsons violated the franchise license agreement. Thus, McDonald's was well within its legal rights to terminate the franchise agreement with the Robertsons.

Disagreements regarding standards and relocations of franchises are two examples of what could potentially go wrong with a franchising agreement. A third example of potential problems between franchisors and franchisees is disagreement over the termination of a franchise. All three of these potential problems exist in the McDonald's case described in the opening scenario. Both parties probably would have benefited from a greater understanding of the responsibilities of the franchisor and franchisee.

Summary

Major Forms of Business Organizations

Sole proprietorship: The owner has total control and unlimited personal liability, and profits are taxed directly as income to the sole proprietor.

General partnership: For most purposes, the partnership is not a legal entity, and each partner has equal control and unlimited liability, with profits that are taxed as income for partners.

Limited partnership: Limited partnerships are similar to general partnerships, except that limited partners' liability is limited to the extent of their capital contributions.

Corporation: A corporation is a separate legal entity wherein the owners' liability is limited to the amount of their contributions and the profits are taxed as income to the corporation.

Specialized Forms of Business Organizations

The specialized forms are cooperatives, joint stock companies, syndicates, business trusts, joint ventures, and franchises.

Point / Counterpoint

Should a New Restaurateur Open a New Location of a Restaurant Franchise Rather Than Become a Sole Proprietor?

Yes	No
A businessperson new to the restaurant business should open a restaurant as part of an existing franchise rather than begin an individual restaurant as a sole proprietor. A new restaurateur encounters substantial risks when opening a business as a sole proprietor. Sole proprietors have unlimited personal liability, meaning they are held solely accountable for the finances in their businesses. For example, a sole proprietor often needs to provide her house as collateral to obtain a small business loan.	A new restaurateur should open a new restaurant as a sole proprietor rather than a franchisee. A businessperson new to the restaurant business has greater potential for long-term success as a sole proprietor than as a franchisee. The main appeal of a franchise is less personal risk and liability at the start of the business. However, with careful research and expert advice, sole proprietors can obtain low-risk, longer-term loans that are unlikely to jeopardize their personal assets. Additionally, sole proprietors always hold the option of later adding a full business

Additionally, a restaurant sole proprietor can be held personally liable for injury in her restaurant. This personal liability means the restaurant owner could be personally sued for employee or customer injury. One main advantage of becoming a franchisee is that the franchisee usually is not held solely liable for an injury.

One primary concern should be that the businessperson is *new* to the restaurant business. The franchisee encounters limited financial risk. Additionally, a franchisor can fulfill the vital role of supervision and provide crucial guidance to a new businessperson. Because restaurant franchises are already successful, the new franchisee has a clear idea of business practices that have been proved successful by the franchisor.

Further, most franchisors offer new franchisees a clear outline of forbidden practices that would endanger the new franchise as well as minimum standards (cleanliness, service) that will assist the new franchise. Sole proprietors must experience a "trial-and-error" time period as they learn which business practices should be implemented. The franchisor's assistance eliminates the trial-and-error time period sole proprietors must experience because the franchisee is informed of and warned not to repeat past errors.

partner or a limited partner. Franchisees, however, usually do not retain that right after entering business with the franchisor. To decrease liability, sole proprietors can implement additional safety measures.

One major disadvantage of opening a new franchise is that the new franchise must pay the franchisor a percentage of profits for the duration the new franchise exists. For a sole proprietor, after debts are repaid, all profits are kept in the business for improvements and personal income.

Franchises are extremely restrictive in creativity. A sole proprietor is truly her own boss. A sole proprietor can change the "look" of her restaurant at any time.

Sole proprietors can determine how many and which hours they would like to be in operation. Sole proprietors can also decide whether to hire a manager or manage their restaurants directly. Additionally, sole proprietors can decide how many and what kind of individuals they would like to employ at their restaurants. Franchisees often face restrictions and limitations regarding size, hours, management, and employment practices.

Perhaps most important, a sole proprietor retains flexibility if the economy changes, which it frequently does. If need be, a sole proprietor can simply uproot the restaurant and move to a different location. Further, a sole proprietor can change her restaurant's menu and appearance if the customer constituency in her area changes.

Questions & Problems

1. What is the distinction between a general partnership and a limited partnership?
2. Explain why a cooperative could not claim to be a syndicate.
3. Suppose you were asked to review and assess a franchise agreement. What responsibilities would you expect to be included in that agreement?
4. Heating & Air Specialists, Inc. (A/C), was interested in becoming a dealer of Lennox equipment and supplies. The parties signed a dealer agreement stating that either party could terminate the agreement with or without cause. A/C originally operated only one location but later became interested in expanding the franchise. A/C was given verbal authorization to sell Lennox equipment at a new location in Tulsa on a temporary basis. After A/C began to operate in Tulsa, other Lennox dealers in the area began to complain. Lennox subsequently decided to terminate A/C's franchise at the Tulsa location. Lennox testified that its decision to terminate the Tulsa franchise was a result of A/C's failure to keep its accounts current. After A/C continued to default on its payments, Lennox notified A/C that the entire franchise would be terminated. A/C filed suit against Lennox for unlawfully terminating the franchise. Lennox

counterclaimed for the payments due. How do you think the court resolved this conflict? [*Heating & Air Specialists, Inc. v. Jones,* 180 F.3d 923 (1999).]

5. Lapinee Trade, Inc., entered into an oral agreement with Boon Rawd Brewery and began importing and distributing Singha beer in 1982. The beer was originally not well established in the American market, and Lapinee spent sufficient resources building a market for the beer. After successfully selling the beer in California, Lapinee obtained authorization from Boon Rawd to begin expanding into Arizona, Nevada, Washington, Texas, Minnesota, and Illinois. Though Boon Rawd and Lapinee originally enjoyed a good business relationship, the relationship began to deteriorate in the late 80s. In 1987, Boon Rawd terminated Lapinee as a distributor. No reasons for the termination were provided. Lapinee challenged the termination in the district court. The district court found that Boon Rawd had wrongfully terminated the distributorship agreement with Lapinee. The court held that it was the custom and practice in the beer industry to terminate distributorships only for a good cause. The court also stated, "Lapinee put great time and money into developing an American market for Singha beer and used its best efforts to build the market and sell Singha, and the distributorship was taken from it before it could reap any substantial benefit from its investment." Boon Rawd appealed the decision, stating that the termination was a result of Lapinee's failure to maintain clear business records. Do you think the court of appeals affirmed the earlier court's decision? Why or why not? [*Lapinee Trade v. Boon Rawd Brewery Account,* 91 F.3d 909 (1996).]
6. Clow gave birth to a baby at Riverside County Hospital in October 1967. Due to complications with the birth, as well as the malpractice of one of the attending resident medical students, Clow's son developed cerebral palsy. Clow sued the hospital for malpractice; the two parties settled out of court for $944,109. The hospital in turn sued Loma Linda University, whose medical school faculty provided teaching services to the hospital and whose medical students were residents at the hospital. The trial court jury found that the county hospital and the university were engaged in a joint venture and hence the university was liable for 50 percent of the settlement costs. Do you think the appellate court agreed with the trial court's finding? Why or why not? [*County of Riverside v. Loma Linda University,* 118 Cal. App. 3d 300 (1981).]
7. In 1975, Vylene, the operator of a restaurant franchise, and Naugles, the franchisor, entered into a 10-year franchise agreement. The agreement stated that Vylene would be given the opportunity to extend the franchise after expiration of the initial 10-year term "on terms and conditions to be negotiated." Vylene failed to make timely payments on its franchise fees and rent. At the end of the 10-year agreement, Naugles presented Vylene with a proposal to extend the franchise agreement. Vylene rejected the offer, believing that the conditions of the proposal would make it impossible to operate at a profit. Vylene continued to operate the business and used Naugles's federally registered trademarks. Naugles opened a new restaurant located less than 2 miles from Vylene's location. Naugles offered similar food options but at a much lower price. As a result of the new restaurant, Vylene's business deteriorated. Vylene subsequently filed an action against Naugles in bankruptcy court for relief based on Naugles's refusal to negotiate the extension offer. Naugles filed counterclaims for trademark violations, unfair competition, and misappropriation of trade secrets. The bankruptcy court held that Naugles had breached the franchise agreement and the covenant of good faith and fair dealing by opening a nearby competing franchise. The district court reversed the decision, finding that Naugles did not wrongfully terminate

the franchise agreement. Vylene then brought the case to the court of appeals. How do you think the court decided? [*In re Vylene Enterprises, Inc.*, 90 F.3d 1472 (1996).]

8. Shell Oil Company and AZ Services, Inc., entered into a five-year contractual relationship to establish a petroleum franchise. Under the agreement, AZ Services, Inc. was required to use Shell's trademarks, brand name, service marks, and other Shell identifications. The agreement stated, "If Dealer fails to exercise the rights granted hereunder by failing . . . to maintain at Dealer's Station a representative amount of each grade of Shell branded motor fuel for resale to the public . . . Shell shall have grounds to terminate or not renew this Agreement." One year into the relationship, AZ Services, Inc removed all Shell trademarks and identifications from the property, stopped selling Shell products, and began to sell the products of one of Shell's competitors. AZ Services, Inc's franchise agreement was immediately terminated, and Shell filed an action under the Petroleum Marketing Practices Act to force AZ Services, Inc to terminate the franchise and to vacate the service station. Do you think Shell was successful? Why or why not? [*Shell Oil Co. v. AZ Services, Inc.*, 990 F. Supp. 1406 (1997).]
9. Joe Orosco, an employee of Sun-Maid Growers, Inc., lost his arm in an industrial accident with a raisin elevator in 1991. Sun-Maid was one of four members of a marketing cooperative called the Sun-Diamond Corporation. According to the cooperative agreement, Sun-Diamond was authorized to provide certain management services to Sun-Maid. Orosco sued Sun-Maid and Sun-Diamond, arguing that both corporations were liable because they were involved in a joint venture to design, manufacture, construct, repair, maintain, install, and test the processing line on which Orosco lost his arm. Were the two corporations involved in a joint venture? What additional facts would you want to know before forming your answer? If they were involved in a joint venture, should Sun-Diamond be held liable for Orosco's injuries? Why or why not? [*Orosco v. Sun-Diamond Corp.*, 51 Cal. App. 4th 1659 (1997).]
10. Milburn Pierce was the sole proprietor of the Pierce Painting Company, a painting contracting company with two employees in addition to Pierce. Pierce bought workers' compensation insurance for his business through the Louisiana Workers' Compensation Corporation, but in the written agreement he chose to exclude himself from the policy's coverage. In August 2002, Pierce was working on a job for Tom Fullilove Construction Company when he fell off a roof. Pierce broke his left wrist and left femur and incurred more than $30,000 in medical bills for his treatment and therapy. Pierce filed a compensation claim in September 2002, and Fullilove paid his medical bills. In October 2002, Fullilove sued Pierce for reimbursement of the compensation payments. The Office of Workers' Compensation found for Fullilove. Pierce appealed, arguing that a Louisiana statute provided that a "sole proprietor with respect to such sole proprietorship may by written agreement elect not to be covered" under workers' compensation insurance. Thus, Pierce argued, he had elected not to be covered with respect to his sole proprietorship, a separate legal entity. But with respect to Tom Fullilove Construction Company, Pierce argued that he never elected not to be covered. How do you think the appellate court ruled? Why? [*Pierce v. Tom Fullilove Constr. Co.*, 892 So. 2d 757 (2005).]
11. "YOU AND I" was a thoroughbred racehorse owned by a syndicate composed of 40 equal ownership shares. The syndicate agreement stated that if an acceptable offer was made to purchase the horse from the syndicate, each syndicate member had a "first right to purchase" under which he could sell his interest in the horse or buy the interests of the other syndicate members who had elected to sell their interests

in the horse. The syndicate agreement, however, required that if a syndicate member planned to exercise his first right to purchase, he had to notify the syndicate manager of his intent within 10 days of his receiving notification of the acceptable offer. In September 2003, Brereton Jones, a syndicate member and the syndicate manager, received an offer from Blooming Hills Farms to buy YOU AND I for $500,000. Jones sent a memo to all the syndicate members notifying them that Blooming Hills Farms had made the offer, that he believed the offer to be fair, and that he planned to sell his interest. Jones received word from 39 of the 40 syndicate members that they planned to sell their interest in YOU AND I. The following day, Never Tell Farm, a syndicate member, notified Jones that it planned to exercise its first right to purchase. Jones and Never Tell proceeded to negotiate over whether Never Tell would exercise its first right to purchase, and the 10-day window elapsed. When the negotiations fell through, Never Tell notified Jones of its intent to exercise its first right to purchase. Jones told Never Tell that it had not timely asserted its right and thus the horse had been sold to Blooming Hills Farms. Never Tell sued Jones, claiming that under the syndicate agreement it should have had the right to purchase the other syndicate members' interests in YOU AND I. With whom do you think the court sided in this case? Why? [*Never Tell Farm, LLC v. Airdrie Stud, Inc.,* 123 Fed. Appx. 194 (2005).]

12. Chic Miller operated a General Motors (GM) franchise car dealership. His written franchise agreement with GM stipulated that Miller had to maintain a floor-plan financing agreement with a lender to enable him to buy new cars from GM. Initially, Miller maintained a line of credit with a GM affiliate (GMAC), but he terminated the agreement because he felt that GMAC charged him an exorbitant interest rate. Miller was able to find another line of credit from Chase Manhattan Bank, but Chase withdrew its financing agreement with Miller after one year. Miller attempted to resume the agreement with GMAC, but GMAC refused. Miller alleged *ipse dixit* (an assertion without evidence) that GMAC discouraged other lenders from providing a line of credit to Miller. GM then notified Miller that it was terminating its franchise relationship with him because he failed to satisfy the financing stipulation of the written franchise agreement. Two months after receiving this notice from GM, Miller attempted to sell his franchise to Kenneth Crowley, the owner of another car dealership. GM rejected this sale, alleging that Miller no longer had a franchise to sell because GM had terminated the franchise agreement two months earlier. Miller sued GM for failing to help his franchise obtain floor-plan financing and for rejecting the sale of his franchise to Crowley. How do you think the court ruled in this case? What requirements must GM meet to lawfully terminate a franchise? Did GM meet those requirements? [*Chic Miller's Chevrolet, Inc. v. GMC,* 352 F. Supp. 2d 251 (2005).]

13. Margaret Miller operated an H&R Block tax preparation franchise for 15 years. She hired William Hehlen as an income tax return preparer for five years, from 1997 to 2001. Each year, Miller and Hehlen signed an employment agreement drawn up by H&R Block. The 2001 agreement was between Hehlen and "Margaret Miller, doing business as H&R Block," and included stipulations prohibiting Hehlen from reproducing confidential business information and from soliciting clients away from Miller's business. Hehlen maintained on his home computer a spreadsheet of customer names that he obtained from Miller. In April 2001, H&R Block terminated its franchise agreement with Miller, and Miller subsequently operated her business as a sole proprietorship under the name "MJM & Associates." Hehlen's employment with Miller ended after the 2001 tax season. In December 2001, Miller sent advertising postcards to clients referring to Hehlen as one of her associates. When Hehlen,

who went to work for another H&R Block office, learned of the postcards, he began telephoning the customers whose names he had obtained from Miller. Miller learned of the calls in February 2002 and filed a cease-and-desist action against Hehlen, arguing that Hehlen was violating his employment contract with Miller. Hehlen argued that his employment contract was with Miller's H&R Block franchise, which ceased to exist after April 2001. Do you think Hehlen's employment contract was signed with Miller's franchise or with Miller's sole proprietorship? If you think Hehlen's contract was with Miller's franchise, should Miller have the right to enforce the contract provisions after H&R Block terminated her franchise agreement? Why or why not? [*Miller v. Hehlen,* 104 P.3d 193 (2005).]

14. Harvey Pierce was a work-release inmate from the local county jail who worked at an Arby's franchise restaurant owned by Dennis Rasmussen, Inc. (DRI). One day in June 1999, Pierce walked off the job without permission and crossed the street to wait for his former girlfriend, Robin Kerl, and her fiancé, David Jones, in the parking lot of the Wal-Mart store where both Kerl and Jones worked. When Kerl and Jones exited the store, Pierce shot both of them in the head, killing Jones and seriously injuring and permanently disabling Kerl. Pierce then shot himself and died immediately. Kerl and Jones's estate sued Arby's and DRI for negligent supervision, hiring, and retention, arguing that Arby's, the franchisor, was vicariously liable for the negligence of DRI, the franchisee. Do you think Arby's should be vicariously liable for the negligence of its franchisee? Why or why not? [*Kerl v. DRI and Arby's, Inc.,* 682 N.W.2d 328 (2004).]

Looking for more review material?

The Online Learning Center at **www.mhhe.com/kubasek1e** contains this chapter's "Assignment on the Internet" and also a list of URLs for more information entitled "On the Internet." Find both of them in the Student Center portion of the OLC, along with quizzes and other helpful materials.

Partnerships: Nature, Formation, and Operation

CASE OPENER

Rockwell and a Potential Partnership

Seth Rockwell filed a motion against Eric Swenson to try to receive lost wages and reimbursement for expenses he had incurred while working as Swenson's employee. Swenson immediately moved for summary judgment because Rockwell was supposedly his partner, not his employee. If Rockwell was Swenson's partner, it was possible that he would not be able to retrieve lost funds.

The district court found that Rockwell was Swenson's employee and not his partner. Swenson appealed the decision, continuing to argue that Rockwell was a partner who only had the right to request an accounting of the corporation. Depending on the appellate court's decision, Rockwell would be awarded $41,580 in unpaid wages and $10,896.39 in nonreimbursed expenses. Additionally, a potential maritime lien would be imposed on Swenson.

1. Why would a potential partnership between Rockwell and Swenson have any influence on the outcome of this case?
2. What could Swenson have done to avoid this suit?

The Wrap-Up at the end of the chapter will answer these questions.

CHAPTER 36

Learning Objectives

After reading this chapter, you will be able to answer the following questions:

1. What is a partnership?
2. What are the different ways in which a partnership can be formed?
3. What are the rights of partners as they interact with each other?
4. Are all members of a partnership liable for interactions with third parties?

The Uniform Partnership Act (UPA) is the main statute governing partnership law. If there is no express partnership agreement, the UPA establishes the rules for the partnership.

This chapter discusses the creation and operation of the partnership, while the following chapter considers how partnerships are terminated as well as special types of partnerships. The first section of this chapter considers the nature of the partnership relationship. The second section explains how a partnership is created. The final section then explains how partnerships function.

Nature of the Partnership

What exactly is a partnership? According to UPA Section 6, a **partnership** is "an association of two or more persons to carry on as co-owners a business for profit." It is important that we analyze all four parts of this definition in order to determine its exact meaning and implications.

First, by "association," UPA means that the partnership is a voluntary and consensual relationship. Thus, no one could force someone else to enter into a partnership with him. Second, a partnership requires "two or more persons." UPA defines *persons* as "individuals, partnerships, corporations, and other associations." Therefore, almost any individual or group of people could serve as a partner, but these persons must have the legal capacity to be partners. For example, although minors can serve as partners, the resulting partnership agreement is voidable.

Third, in a partnership, the partners must "carry on as co-owners a business for profit." Here, a *business* is defined as any trade, occupation, or profession. "Carrying on" a business refers to making several transactions. Finally, UPA requires that the partners be "co-owners" of the business, meaning the partners must share the profits or losses of the business as well as share in the management of the business.

Fourth, the final element of the definition of partnership is that it be "for profit," meaning that the partners must be intending to make some kind of profit from the business.

To summarize, a partnership has the following characteristics:

- *Voluntary* and *consensual* relationship.
- Between two or more *individuals, partnerships, corporations,* or other forms of business organization.
- Who engage in *numerous business transactions* over a period of time.
- Intending *to make a profit.*
- And *share* the *profits* and *management* of the business.

When parties dispute whether a partnership relationship exists, the courts will look for those factors in the case. The relationship between Rockwell and Swenson in the opening scenario did not constitute a partnership because it did not meet the aforementioned criteria. The two men had never voluntarily or consensually entered into a partnership. There was no evidence that the profits or management duties were shared between the two men.

Probably the most important factor in determining whether a partnership exists is determining whether the profits from the business are shared. However, UPA has established several exceptions in which a sharing of profits does not constitute a partnership. For example, when an employer shares profits with an employee as payment for work, there is no partnership. Similarly, when a landlord accepts shares of profits for payment of

connecting to the core

Management

Partnerships: Will the Sum Be Greater?

Why would two individuals want to form a partnership agreement? Two separate parties may decide to form a partnership when they believe that the partnership will result in *synergy,* meaning that the combined efforts of both partners will likely be more profitable than the efforts of the individuals working separately. In other words, after accounting for all partnership-related expenses and taxes, the partnership would be earning more profit than a situation in which each individual engaged in a similar business without participating in a partnership. However, for future business managers, it is imperative to evaluate the likelihood that the "sum would be greater than the parts" when deciding whether to enter into a partnership agreement. Synergy is merely an ideal of partnership agreements, not a guaranteed outcome.

Source: Angelo Kinicki and Brian K. Williams, *Management: A Practical Introduction* (New York: McGraw-Hill/Irwin, 2006), p. 189.

rent, there is no partnership. If a party receives a share of profits for any of the following reasons, there is no partnership:

- Payment of a debt.
- Payment of an annuity to a widow or representative of a deceased partner.
- Payment from the sale of goodwill of a business or other property.
- Payment of interest on a loan.

Case 36-1 illustrates the court's analysis of whether a partnership relationship indeed exists.

CASE 36-1 MAX NORMAN v. MONTGOMERY WHOLESALE LUMBER

COURT OF CIVIL APPEALS OF ALABAMA
678 SO. 2D 1110, 1996 ALA. CIV. APP. LEXIS 3

When Michael Norman failed to pay for lumber purchased from Montgomery Wholesale Lumber, Montgomery Lumber sued Michael Norman as a proprietor of Norman Builders. After Montgomery Lumber filed the complaint against Michael Norman, he filed a notice for bankruptcy. Montgomery Lumber then amended its complaint to add Max Norman, Michael's father, and Barbara Norman, Michael's wife, because they were part of the partnership, Norman Builders. Michael Norman, however, argued he was the sole proprietor of Norman Builders. The trial court found Norman Builders was a partnership consisting of Michael, Max, and Barbara. Max Norman argues that the trial court erred in finding that Norman Builders was a partnership because each of the Normans testified that (1) there was no partnership; (2) there was no partnership agreement; and (3) neither Barbara nor Max shared in the profits, losses, or management of Norman Builders.

JUDGE MONROE:

Section 10-8-20, Ala. Code 1975, sets out the rules for determining whether a partnership exists. It reads:

> In determining whether a partnership exists, these rules shall apply:
>
> (1) Except as provided by Section 10-8-55, persons who are not partners as to each other are not partners as to third persons.
>
> (2) Joint tenancy, tenancy in common, tenancy by the entireties, joint property, partnership,

whether such co-owners do or do not share any profits made by the use of the property.

(3) The sharing of gross returns does not of itself establish a partnership, whether or not the persons sharing them have a joint or common right or interest in any property from which the returns are derived.

(4) The receipt by a person of a share of the profits of a business is prima facie evidence that he is a partner in the business, but no such inference shall be drawn if such profits were received in payment:

a. As a debt by installments or otherwise;
b. As wages of an employee or rent to a landlord;
c. As an annuity to a widow or representative of a deceased partner;
d. As interest or other payment on a loan, though the amount of payment varies with the profits of the business; or
e. As the consideration for the sale of the goodwill of a business or other property by installments or otherwise.

(5) An express agreement among the partners, or between business associates, that a person, who would otherwise be deemed a partner under this chapter, will not personally be liable for partnership obligations is not, in itself, evidence that such person is not a partner; provided, that such agreement shall not be effective as against third parties unless such person is a limited partner under the laws of Alabama governing limited partnerships.

In addition, the Supreme Court has held that there is no settled test for determining the existence of a partnership. "That determination is made by reviewing all the attendant circumstances, including the right to manage and control the business." The record shows that while some evidence presented to the trial court supports Max's contention that Norman Builders was not a partnership, other evidence is to the contrary. For example, Preston and Mary Watts, whose home was built by Norman Builders, testified that Max was present during negotiations for the building of their house, that Max was the person responsible at the building site when Michael was not there, and that Max negotiated with subcontractors and materialmen. John James, whose home also was built by Norman Builders, testified that Max supervised at the building site; that after James had trouble with Michael's not paying the bills, Max took on the role of negotiator for future work and took control of the money; that when Michael had surgery, Max had the sole responsibility as contractor; and that Max and Barbara both conducted business and signed contracts as Norman Builders. Other testimony showed that Max often paid the debts of Norman Builders and paid for equipment used by the business.

There is also some evidence that Max and Barbara, neither of whom was an employee of Norman Builders, shared in the profits of the business. For example, Barbara said that Norman Builders regularly put money in amounts up to $2,000, into her savings account. Norman Builders provided Barbara and Max with cellular telephones. Michael testified that Norman Builders bought the home for the benefit of Max and Barbara.

The judgment of the trial court is affirmed insofar as it holds that Norman Builders was a partnership and that Max Norman was a partner in the business.

AFFIRMED.

CRITICAL THINKING

What evidence led the court to hold that Max Norman was a partner in Norman Builders partnership?

ETHICAL DECISION MAKING

Notice that business ethics requires that we think beyond ourselves. Clearly Max Norman had a good personal reason not to be labeled a partner. It would have cost a large sum of money to be included as a partner in Norman Builders. But ethics represents an appeal to our better selves. Use the universalization test to explain why one should not attempt to avoid partnership responsibilities.

e-commerce AND THE LAW

Forms of Partnerships in the ICT Sector in Developing Countries

In the information and communication technology (ICT) sector of developing countries, businesses are using partnerships between local and multinational companies to create a support structure for the sector. Three forms of partnership are especially important: (1) industrial districts, (2) *keiretsu* (a group of businesses in which each individual business has a stake in the others), and (3) offshore partnerships.

Industrial districts are loosely structured collectives of small to medium-size firms located in a specific area. The firms are highly specialized in one or more phases of a production process. Industrial districts are coordinated through both personal relationships and market-like mechanisms. One purpose of industrial districts is to pool local competencies.

Keiretsus bring foreign ICT companies into a partnership, and they serve as "hubs." Local ICT ventures serve the hubs. *Keiretsus* add the strength of a competent hub, but, over time, this strength could make it less likely that local firms will develop strength of their own.

Offshore partnerships combine the strengths of firms that operate in developing countries and firms that operate in countries that are foreign to the developing countries, for example, firms in the United States. Firms in developing countries use offshore partnerships to gain international exposure and technological competence. Foreign firms use offshore partnerships to gain (1) access to competent yet low-cost workers and (2) the opportunity to enter developing markets.

Now that you know how the courts determine whether a partnership exists, what kind of legal status do partnerships have? Partnerships can be treated two different ways: as entities or as aggregates.

PARTNERSHIP AS A LEGAL ENTITY

In some respects, a partnership is treated as a **legal entity**, a person separate from the partnership. Thus, in some cases, the partnership has a life of its own.

First, a partnership is often considered a legal entity when it is sued or being sued. States determine when the partnership can or cannot be named in the suit. Second, under the doctrine of marshaling assets, assets are arranged in a certain order to pay for any outstanding debts. Partnership creditors have first priority in obtaining partnership assets, while individual personal creditors have first priority to the assets of the individual partners. Thus, the partnership assets are kept separate from the individual partner assets.

Third, the title to property may be put in the partnership name. Therefore, the partnership may own property that individual partners do not hold. If the partners want to sell the partnership property to another party, all partners must participate in the transaction of the partnership property. Finally, every partner is considered to be an agent to the partnership, and every partner has a fiduciary relationship with the other partners.

PARTNERSHIP AS A LEGAL AGGREGATE

While the partnership is sometimes considered a separate legal entity, there are other cases in which the partnership is considered a legal aggregate of the partners. For instance, the debts of the partnership eventually become the debts of the individual partners. Furthermore, the partnership is not taxed as a separate being; instead, the partners pay taxes on the income generated through the partnership. Moreover, because the partnership ceases to exist when one of the partners dies (unless otherwise established by the partnership agreement), the partnership is considered an aggregate of the individual partners.

global context

Partnerships in Chile

The case of *Henry Chauncey v. Republic of Chile,* 1901, presented an interesting point about jurisdiction in foreign business relations. Henry Chauncey and John Wheelwright, both American citizens, were partners in the firm of Alsop & Company, which transacted its business in Chile. The firm went into liquidation in 1875. Wheelwright was appointed liquidator. When Wheelwright died unexpectedly, Chauncey became the liquidator and was responsible for settling the firm's claims against the Republic of Chile. He wished to settle the claims with the U.S. Chile Claims Commission. But did the commission have jurisdiction over the case?

The commission was created in 1897 with the stated purpose of examining "[a]ll claims on the part of corporations, companies, or private individuals, citizens of the United States, upon the Government of Chile, arising out of acts committed against the persons or property of citizens of the United States." Chauncey argued that the claim of Alsop fell under this definition.

However, Chauncey was unaware of a fundamental distinction between partnerships in common and civil law countries. Civil law countries, such as Chile, recognize partnerships as a juridical person distinct from the members considered individually. Therefore, it is not the individual members—in this case, American citizens—who transact the business; rather, it is the legal entity—Alsop & Company. The partnership is a citizen of Chile, subject to its laws. Recall that the commission's jurisdiction includes claims made by U.S. *citizens.* Consequently, the U.S. commission did not have jurisdiction over the case. Chauncey needed to file his claims with Chile and abide by Chilean liquidation statutes.

Formation of the Partnership

While an explicit written agreement is not required to create a partnership, the partners are advised to create one. The written agreement ensures that the terms of the partnership will be upheld. For example, suppose that you and your partner orally agree that you will receive three-fourths of the profits because you are doing significantly more management tasks. However, when you distribute the funds, your partner sues you because you give him only one-fourth of the profits. Without a written partnership agreement, the courts will have a difficult time ruling in your favor. A written agreement that creates a partnership is called the **articles of partnership.**

What kind of information do the articles of partnership usually include? First, the partners' names, as well as the name of the partnership, should be listed on the document. Second, the agreement should address the duration of the partnership. The agreement could include the date or event that would take place such that the partnership agreement would expire. Alternatively, the agreement could specify that the term of the partnership is indefinite. Third, the agreement should state the division of profits as well as losses. Fourth, the articles of partnership should establish the division of management duties. Fifth, the agreement should state exactly what capital contributions will be made by each partner. Creating articles of partnership can prevent legal problems by explicitly establishing the terms of the partnership agreement.

PARTNERSHIP BY ESTOPPEL

In some cases, parties who are not named in partnership agreements can be considered partners. How? Suppose you create a partnership agreement with your best friend. When you interact with your first potential customer, you tell this customer that your parents are also partners in this business. On the basis of your parents' participation in the partnership, the customer decides to place an order to purchase certain goods from you. Your parents discover that you have reported that they are your partners, but they do not contact the customer to tell her that they are not your partners. When your business cannot afford to purchase these goods to sell them to the customer, the customer sues you as well as your parents. Because your parents were aware of the misrepresentation but did not correct it, they will be estopped from denying they are your partners. While they will not be able to claim the rights associated with being a partner (e.g., sharing the profits), in many states they could be held liable for the costs of the damages to the customer.

Most states recognize two situations in which a partnership by estoppel exists. First, as in the example above, if a third party is aware of a misrepresentation of partnership and consents to the misrepresentation, a partnership by estoppel is present. Second, if a nonpartner has represented himself or herself as a partner and a third party *reasonably relies* on this information to his or her detriment, the nonpartner can be held liable for the third party's damages.

Interactions between Partners

The operation of the partnership encompasses two types of interactions: interactions between the partners and interactions between the partnership and third parties. The partners have certain rights and duties within each type of interaction.

DUTIES OF PARTNERS TO ONE ANOTHER

Most of the duties that partners hold to one another involve a duty to be loyal. These include the fiduciary duty to the other partners, the duty of obedience, and the duty of care.

Perhaps the most important duty of the partners is their fiduciary duty. They must, in good faith, work for the benefit of the partnership. They should not take any kind of action that will undermine the partnership. Consequently, the partners must not engage in any business that competes with the partnership.

Partners must disclose any material facts affecting the business. If a partner derives some kind of benefit from the partnership without the consent of the other partners, he or she must notify the partners of this benefit. Case 36-2 considers how a partner's fiduciary duty conflicts with a partner's belief that another partner is behaving unethically.

CASE 36-2

COLETTE BOHATCH v. BUTLER & BINION
SUPREME COURT OF TEXAS
977 S.W.2D 543

Colette Bohatch became an associate in the Washington D.C. office of Butler & Binion in 1986. John McDonald and Richard Powers, both partners, were the only other attorneys in the office. After Bohatch was made a partner in February 1990, she became concerned that McDonald was overbilling Pennzoil, the main client of the office. Bohatch met with the firm's managing partner, Louis Paine, to report her concern regarding McDonald's overbilling. In July 1990, McDonald met with Bohatch to report that Pennzoil was dissatisfied with her work.

The next day, Bohatch relayed her concern to Paine, as well as two other members of the firm's management committee. Paine led an investigation of Bohatch's complaint and discussed the billed hours with the in-house counsel at Pennzoil, who concluded that the bills were reasonable. In August 1990, Paine met with Bohatch, telling her that there was no basis for her claims against McDonald and that she should look for work elsewhere. The firm refused Bohatch a year-end partnership distribution for 1990. Finally, in August 1991, Bohatch was given until November to vacate her office. She filed suit in October 1991, and the firm voted to expel her from the partnership three days later.

At trial, the jury ruled that the firm breached the partnership agreement and its fiduciary duty and awarded Bohatch $57,000 for past lost wages, $250,000 for past mental anguish, $4,000,000 total in punitive damages (this amount was apportioned against several defendants), and attorney's fees. Later, the trial court reduced the punitive damages to around $237,000. The court of appeals ruled that the firm's only duty to Bohatch was to not expel her in bad faith. When they found no evidence that the firm fired Bohatch for self-gain, they ruled that Bohatch could not recover for breach of fiduciary duty. The case was appealed to the Supreme Court.

JUDGE ENOCH: We have long recognized as a matter of common law that "the relationship between . . . partners . . . is fiduciary in character, and imposes upon all the participants the obligation of loyalty to the joint concern and of the utmost good faith, fairness, and honesty in their dealings with each other with respect to matters pertaining to the enterprise." Yet, partners have no obligation to remain partners; "at the heart of the partnership concept is the principle that partners may choose with whom they wish to be associated." The issue presented, one of first impression, is whether the fiduciary relationship between and among partners creates an exception to the at-will nature of partnerships; that is, in this case, whether it gives rise to a duty not to expel a partner who reports suspected overbilling by another partner.

While Bohatch's claim that she was expelled in an improper way is governed by the partnership agreement, her claim that she was expelled for an improper reason is not. Therefore, we look to the common law to find the principles governing Bohatch's claim that the firm breached a duty when it expelled her.

Courts in other states have held that a partnership may expel a partner for purely business reasons. Further, courts recognize that a law firm can expel a partner to protect relationships both within the firm and with clients. Finally, many courts have held that a partnership can expel a partner without breaching any duty in order to resolve a "fundamental schism."

The fiduciary duty that partners owe one another does not encompass a duty to remain partners or else answer in tort damages. Nonetheless, Bohatch and several distinguished legal scholars urge this Court to recognize that public policy requires a limited duty to remain partners—i.e., a partnership must retain a whistleblower partner. They argue that such an extension of a partner's fiduciary duty is necessary because permitting a law firm to retaliate against a partner who in good faith reports suspected overbilling would discourage compliance with rules of professional conduct and thereby hurt clients.

While this argument is not without some force, we must reject it. A partnership exists solely because the partners choose to place personal confidence and trust in one another. Just as a partner can be expelled, without a breach of any common law duty, over disagreements about firm policy or to resolve some other "fundamental schism," a partner can be expelled for accusing another partner of overbilling without subjecting the partnership to tort damages. Such charges, whether true or not, may have a profound effect on the personal confidence and trust essential to the partner relationship. Once such charges are made, partners may find it impossible to continue to work together to their mutual benefit and the benefit of their clients.

We are sensitive to the concern expressed by the dissenting Justices that "retaliation against a partner who tries in good faith to correct or report perceived misconduct virtually assures that others will not take these appropriate steps in the future." However, the dissenting Justices do not explain how the trust relationship necessary both for the firm's existence and for representing clients can survive such serious accusations by one partner against another. The threat of tort liability for expulsion would tend to force partners to remain in untenable circumstance—suspicious of and angry with each other—to their own detriment and that of their clients whose matters are neglected by lawyers distracted with intra-firm frictions.

We emphasize that our refusal to create an exception to the at-will nature of partnerships in no way obviates the ethical duties of lawyers. Such duties sometimes necessitate difficult decisions, as when a lawyer suspects overbilling by a colleague. The fact that the ethical duty to report may create an irreparable schism between partners neither excuses failure to report nor transforms expulsion as a means of resolving that schism into a tort.

We hold that the firm did not owe Bohatch a duty not to expel her for reporting suspected overbilling by another partner.

AFFIRMED.

[CONTINUED]

CRITICAL THINKING

Think about the judge's reasoning that led to the conclusion that the firm did not owe Bohatch a duty not to expel her for reporting suspected overbilling. Is there any additional information you would have liked to know to determine whether the firm should have been allowed to dismiss Bohatch?

ETHICAL DECISION MAKING

In this case, Bohatch made a decision about ethics when she chose to report what she suspected to be overbilling by a colleague. Do you think that Bohatch made a good ethical decision? Would you guess that Bohatch was guided by the Golden Rule, deontology, the universalization test, or some other method of ethical reasoning?

The second duty that the partners have to each other is the duty of obedience, to obey the partnership agreement. If they do not obey the agreement, they can be held liable for any losses that the partnership incurs.

The third duty the partners have is a duty of care to the other partners. Each partner must perform her management functions to the best of her abilities. If a partner makes an honest mistake in fulfilling her responsibilities to the partnership, she will not be held liable for the mistake.

RIGHTS OF THE PARTNERS IN THEIR INTERACTIONS WITH OTHER PARTNERS

According to the law, partners have certain rights regarding their interactions with other partners.

Right to share in management. Unless otherwise stated in the partnership agreement, all partners have a right to participate equally in the management of the partnership. Even if one partner has an unusually large proportion of the management duties, each partner will have one vote in determining how the partnership is managed.

While most decisions are made by majority vote, some decisions require agreement by all partners. For instance, if the partners are voting on whether to change some element of the partnership agreement, all partners must agree with the change. Other types of decisions that require a unanimous vote include a decision to admit new partners or to alter the nature of the firm's business.

Right to share in profits. Each partner is entitled to a share of the profits of the partnership. How big is each partner's share? If the partnership agreement does not establish a certain division of profits, all partners will share the profits equally. Similarly, partners must share in the losses of the partnership. Thus, if there is no statement of how the losses will be divided among the partners, the losses will be divided in a proportion identical to the sharing of the profits.

Right to compensation. Unless otherwise agreed, no partner will receive compensation for his or her participation in the business. In other words, the partner will not receive a salary regardless of the amount of time and effort he or she devotes to the business. Of course, the partners may agree to create salaries for certain partners, but no partner enters the partnership relationship with a right to compensation for his or her business activities. If a partner dies during the term of the partnership, the surviving partner is, however, entitled to compensation for services in closing the business affairs.

Property rights. Partners have three property rights associated with the partnership: (1) the right to participate in the management of the business (discussed earlier), (2) the right to specific partnership property, and (3) the right to her partnership interest. Here, we examine the latter two property rights.

First, partners own the partnership property as *tenants in property,* which means that the partners own the property as a group. Any property that is brought into or acquired by the partnership is considered property of the partnership. If property is in the name of an individual partner but was purchased with partnership funds, the property will be considered partnership property.

One way to determine whether specific property will be considered a partnership asset is to determine the relationship of the asset to the partnership. If the asset is closely related to the business of the partnership, it will likely be considered a partnership asset.

Each partner has the right to possess partnership property. However, a partner cannot use this property to pay a personal debt. Similarly, the partner cannot sell or use the property if the purpose is outside the partnership interest.

What happens to the partnership property if a partner dies? According to the **right of survivorship,** the rights in specific partnership property pass to the surviving partner(s). However, the surviving partners must account to the deceased partner's estate for the value of that partner's interest in the specific property.

Second, a partner has a right to an interest in the partnership. This interest, composed of a combination of the partner's share of the profits and a return of capital contributed by the partner, is part of the partner's personal property. If necessary, a partner can sell his or her interest in the partnership to a creditor. A partner's personal creditor cannot seize specific items of partnership property; however, the creditor can obtain a **charging order,** which entitles the creditor to the partner's profits. The charging order permits the partner to continue to act as a partner and engage in the partnership business; however, the creditor simply collects the partner's share of the profits.

Right to inspect books. Each partner has the right to receive full information regarding partnership matters. This right corresponds to the fiduciary duty of the partners to disclose any information affecting the partnership. Thus, partners must have access to all partnership books and records and be allowed to make copies of these records. Unless otherwise agreed, the records must be kept at the principal business office.

Right to an account. An **accounting** is a review and listing of all partnership assets and/or profit. The accounting typically lists the distribution of assets and profit to the partners. Each partner has a right to an accounting in four circumstances:

- Whenever the partnership agreement provides for an accounting.
- Whenever the copartners wrongfully exclude a partner from the partnership or from access to the books.
- Whenever any partner fails to disclose a profit or benefit from the partnership, thus breaching his or her fiduciary duty.
- Whenever circumstances render an accounting as "just and reasonable."

Interactions between Partners and Third Parties

Each partner can serve as an agent for the other partners as well as the partnership. Consequently, as long as the partner has authority to act, each partner's act in performing business duties as well as making agreements with third parties is binding for the partnership. If the partner has authority to act and the partnership is bound by the act, each partner has unlimited personal liability for the obligation.

ACTUAL AUTHORITY OF THE PARTNERS

According to UPA, general agency principles establish that partners have the authority to bind a partnership in an agreement. Consequently, if a partner, following normal business procedures, establishes an agreement in which he or she binds the partnership to the agreement, both the partner and the partnership are liable for the obligation in the agreement.

Suppose Brittany is a partner in a firm. While allegedly carrying on partnership business, she engages in a business transaction and binds the partnership to the agreement. Yet suppose Brittany really didn't have authority to bind the partnership to the agreement with the third party. In this case, both Brittany and the firm are liable for the obligation.

However, suppose that the third party was aware that Brittany did not have the authority to bind the partnership to the agreement. If the party is aware that the authority is absent, Brittany will be held liable for the obligation but the partnership will not be held liable.

IMPLIED AUTHORITY OF THE PARTNERS

Because of the nature of the partnership, partners generally have greater implied authority than do typical agents. The implied authority of partners is usually determined by the nature of the business. For instance, a partner typically has the implied authority to enter into agreements necessary to carry on partnership business. Thus, a partner would have the authority to purchase goods that were necessary to perpetuate the business. However, a partner does not have implied authority to sell any property without the consent of all other partners.

LIABILITY TO THIRD PARTIES

According to UPA, if a partnership is liable, each partner has unlimited personal liability. That is, all partners are **jointly liable** for the partnership's debts. Thus, if a party wants to bring a successful claim, the party must name all partners as defendants. Instead of naming every partner in a lawsuit, a party can simply name the partnership. If the party is successful at bringing his or her claim, each partner is liable for the judgment. If one partner pays the entire judgment, the other partners are required to indemnify, or reimburse, him or her.

If a partner commits a tort or a breach of trust, all partners are jointly and severally liable. **Joint and several liability** means that a third party can choose to sue the partners separately or all partners jointly in one action. Suppose William sues your partnership, which has four partners. William might name one of the partners in the first action. If the partner is found liable, William can sue all three other partners separately. However, if in the first claim the court ruled that the partnership was not liable in any form, William cannot bring a successful claim against a second partner on the issue of the partner's liability.

If William brings a successful claim against a partner, he can collect the judgment only on the assets of one partner. The partner is required to reimburse the partnership for the damages it pays to William. Case 36-3 considers how partners in a partnership can be held liable for the negligence of one partner.

CASE 36-3 ERIC JOHNSON & LORI JOHNSON v. ST. THERESE MEDICAL CENTER

APPELLATE COURT OF ILLINOIS, SECOND DISTRICT
296 ILL. APP. 3D 341; 694 N.E.2D 1088;
1998 ILL. APP. LEXIS 301

In November 1990, Eric and Lori Johnson brought their 22-month-old daughter, Erica, to St. Therese Medical Center, where she was treated and released by Dr. Bruce Sands. Dr. Sands was a partner of Northern Illinois Emergency Physicians, Ltd. Drs. Richard Keller, Michael Oster, Thomas Braniff, Rodney Haenschen, and Phillip Gillespie were the other partners in the partnership. The Johnsons filed suit against Dr. Sands and the partnership. They argued that Dr. Sands negligently caused the death of Erica and the partnership was liable because St. Therese acted on behalf of the partnership. A jury gave the Johnsons a $4 million award against Dr. Sands, St. Therese, and the partnership. Dr. Sands later filed for bankruptcy.

All of the partners were issued citations to discover the assets of the partnership. At the citation hearings, all of the partners (except Gillespie) admitted they were partners in the partnership at the time of the Johnson incident. In February 1997, the trial court judge ruled that the Johnsons could proceed against the general partners individually if they were partners at the time of the incident. Consequently, the plaintiffs started motions to withhold the wages of all partners. Various court proceedings ensued in which various partners argued they should not be held personally liable. Several partners were sentenced to time in jail because they refused to testify regarding their personal assets. In June 1997, the trial court ruled that the assets of Keller, Haenschen, and Braniff be turned over to the Johnsons.

JUSTICE McLAREN: We acknowledge that all partners are jointly and severally liable for everything chargeable to the partnership for the loss or injury of a third person due to any wrongful act or omission of any partner acting in the ordinary course of the business of the partnership. Further, "an unsatisfied judgment against a partnership in its firm name does not bar an action to enforce the individual liability of any partner." However, "[a] judgment entered against a partnership in its firm name is enforceable only against property of the partnership and does not constitute a lien upon real estate other than that held in the firm name." Therefore, where judgment is entered against a partnership, but not against the individual partners, the judgment may not be satisfied by the personal assets of the individual partners.

For example, in Cook, the Department of Revenue issued a notice of tax liability to a partnership. The Department of Revenue was unable to enforce the tax liability against the partnership because the Partnership had previously filed for bankruptcy. Therefore, the Department of Revenue attempted to enforce the partnership's tax liability against the plaintiff, a general partner. The partner received a copy and was aware of the contents of the notice of tax liability issued to the partnership. However, the Department of Revenue did not issue a notice of tax liability or a final assessment to the partner in his individual capacity. Thus, the trial court granted the partner's motion for summary judgment.

This court affirmed, stating that, because a partnership can own property, it is a separate entity from its partners. Because the Department of Revenue issued notice of tax liability and the final assessment to the partnership, and not to the partner individually, and, because the Department of Revenue did not join the partner, the partner did not have notice that he could be liable personally for the partnership's tax debt. Thus, this court reasoned that the partner was denied due process.

The case at bar is closely analogous to Cook. The plaintiffs in the instant case named the Partnership, but not the individual Partners, in their complaint. The plaintiffs served the Partnership, but not the individual Partners. In addition, the Partners in this case, just like the partner in Cook, were aware of the contents of the plaintiffs' complaint against the Partnership. However, because the Partners were not named defendants and were not served in their individual capacities, they were not put on notice that their personal assets were at risk. Further, the plaintiffs in this case are unable to collect from Sands because he has filed for bankruptcy protection. Finally, judgment was entered against the Partnership, but not the individual Partners. Thus, the Partners were not judgment debtors and were not subject to citations proceedings to the extent that the plaintiffs had any claim upon the Partners' individual assets. Accordingly, the trial court erred when it attempted to enforce the judgment against the Partners by ordering the turnover of the Partners' assets and holding the Partners in contempt.

The plaintiffs argue that the Partners are judgment debtors because the partnership name is on the judgment order. However, the plaintiffs fail to recognize that "[a] judgment entered against a partnership in its firm name is enforceable only against property of the partnership." Because nothing in the record indicates that the Partners held assets which belonged to the Partnership, their argument fails.

Next, the plaintiffs argue that the Partners are judgment debtors because they are jointly and severally liable for the debts of the Partnership. We do not dispute this statement. However, the plaintiffs ignore the fact that judgment was entered against the Partnership, and not the Partners as individuals. Thus, until a judgment is entered against the Partners individually, the plaintiffs cannot recover from the Partners' personal assets.

The plaintiffs also argue that section 2-411(b) of the Code of Civil Procedure permits the enforcement of liability in supplementary proceedings against an individual partner. Section 2-411(b) provides, "An unsatisfied judgment against a partnership in its firm name does not bar an action to enforce the individual liability of any partner." Although "action" is not defined, the plaintiffs assert that a supplementary proceeding to collect a judgment is an "action" within the meaning of section 5/2-411(b). We disagree.

Section 12-102 of the Code of Civil Procedure provides that "[a] judgment entered against a partnership in its firm name is enforceable only against property of the partnership and does not constitute a lien upon real estate other than that held in the firm name." Under the plaintiffs' interpretation of section 2-411(b), this section has no meaning. Under the plaintiffs' interpretation, a judgment against only a partnership is enforceable against the partners individually without a judgment being entered against the partners individually. Because the plaintiffs' interpretation of section 2-411(b) renders section 12-102 ineffective, it cannot be adopted by this court.

Next, the plaintiffs assert that "a judgment against a partnership, by definition, is a judgment against each partner." However, this court's decision in Cook clearly contradicts the plaintiffs' position. In Cook, we held that, although partners are liable for the debts of the partnership, to be able to collect from the partners the plaintiff must provide the partners with notice that they will be individually liable for the partnership's debt. Since the plaintiffs failed to provide such notice, their argument fails.

REVERSED.

CRITICAL THINKING

Part of the confusion in this case was based on the ambiguity in Section 2-411(b) of the Code of Civil Procedure. Can you identify the ambiguity and explain how different interpretations of the code lead to different conclusions?

ETHICAL DECISION MAKING

Suppose you were one of the partners in this case. If you were guided by duty ethics, would any of the details of the case described above be altered?

global context

Silent Partnerships in Germany

The original intent behind silent partnerships was for two people to be able to engage in a partnership without having to inform the third party. Recently, both civil and common law countries have been moving away from this idea of total anonymity. For example, France permits the silent partner to choose whether he or she wishes to disclose the relationship. Germany, however, has held to the original intent of silent partnerships.

Under German law, a contract is formed between the silent partner (usually the financier) and the proprietor of the business. In exchange for his or her investment, the silent partner receives a designated share of the profits. Enlisting a silent partner does not require registration, and the company should continue to operate under the proprietor's name.

Because business is conducted under the proprietor's name and because the partnership remains a secret to the third party, silent partners are not held personally liable for damages incurred in the course of business. This nonliability factor makes silent partnerships less widely used in Germany than other countries. Nevertheless, the nonliability allows for unique situations. For instance, a proprietor could enlist his or her child as a silent partner. The child collects assets while remaining anonymous and ineligible for any liability claims. Nonliability guards the interests of the silent partner.

In Germany, the benefits swing in favor of the silent partner. While the proprietor transacts all the business and the third party remains unaware of the existence of the partnership relationship, silent partners enjoy minimal responsibility and no risk of personal liability.

You may be initially surprised that the silent partnership arrangement is legal in Germany. But as a critical thinker you have a responsibility to rethink your reasoning. Can you create a list of reasons for why our own legal system should encourage silent partnerships?

LIABILITY OF INCOMING PARTNERS

When a partnership adds another partner, the new partner assumes limited liability for any obligations that occurred before the partner was added. The new partner cannot be held personally liable for these obligations, but the capital that the new partner adds can be used to pay off these obligations. Clearly, because an incoming partner assumes limited liability, the dates of agreements, as well as the date that the new partner was added, are extremely important.

The Revised Uniform Partnership Act

The majority of the states have adopted a revised version of the Uniform Partnership Act that is typically referred to as the Revised Uniform Partnership Act (RUPA). Just as the original Uniform Partnership Act governs partnerships in the absence of an express agreement, RUPA is an updated version that has significantly changed several of the laws that relate to partnerships. Since being approved in 1996, RUPA has been adopted in roughly half of the states. Since the other half of the states have not yet adopted RUPA, it is wise to determine whether the state in which the partnership was formed operates under UPA or RUPA. Although RUPA generally serves to expand UPA, there is some disagreement between UPA and RUPA about the rules of partnership.

CASE OPENER WRAP-UP

Rockwell/Swenson

The relationship between Seth Rockwell and Eric Swenson did not constitute a partnership because the two men had not both had the intent required by the then existing version of the Uniform Partnership Act that was required to form a partnership. Both men did not have the intent to enter into a voluntary or consensual partnership that would be required for Swenson's argument to win the case. Thus, the appellate court ruled in favor of Rockwell, awarding him $41,580 in unpaid wages and $10,869.39 the court determined to be due to him as an employee of Swenson.

If a partnership had been established between the two men, they would have been bound by the duties and rights of partners that are described in this chapter. Thus, the outcome of this case may have been quite different if there were a partnership. Rockwell would have been entitled to an accounting of the organization, but may not have been entitled to lost wages and lost reimbursement funds.

Summary

Nature of the Partnership

The Uniform Partnership Act defines a partnership as "an association of two or more persons to carry on as co-owners a business for profit."

An essential element in a partnership is the sharing of profits from the partnership.

Formation of the Partnership

A partnership is created by the articles of partnership, which should include the name of each partner and the partnership, the duration of the partnership, how profits will be divided, the division of management duties, and the contributions to be made by each partner.

Interactions between Partners

Each partner has specific duties, including:

- Duty to be loyal
- Duty of obedience
- Duty of care

Each partner has specific rights, including:

- Right to share in management
- Right to inspect books
- Right to compensation
- Rights to partnership property

Interactions between Partners and Third Parties

If a partnership has a liability, each partner has unlimited personal liability. All partners are jointly and severally liable for the commission of a tort by any partner.

There is only implied liability when purchases are made to perpetuate the partnership's business.

The Revised Uniform Partnership Act

RUPA is a revised version of UPA, and its use varies from state to state.

Point / Counterpoint

Should a Minor Be Allowed to Enter into a Business Partnership?

Yes

Individuals under the age of 18 should be allowed to enter into business partnerships. If an existing business decides that a business created by a minor is a desirable partner, the minor should be able to enter into that partnership on grounds of personal liberty.

Though the United States and other countries act as if adulthood occurs at an arbitrary point in time (age 18 in the United States), contemporary research argues differently. According to Richard Fabes and Carol Lynn Martin's book *Exploring Child Development,** the age 18 is just one year in a five-year phase called *late adolescence* or *early adulthood.* Levels of maturity and decision-making abilities vary greatly. Additionally, individuals over the age of 18, who are automatically given the ability to enter into contracts and partnerships, may not be as mature as many young adults a few years their junior.

One argument against allowing minors to enter into business partnerships is that they are not accustomed to making large decisions that affect the lives of other people. Young adults under the age of 18 already make several life-altering decisions. In most states, the age of consent for sexual intercourse is 16, while some states (Iowa, Missouri, and South Carolina) and other developed countries (Italy and Iceland) set the age of consent as low as 14. Young adults can decide before the age of 18 to become parents—a major life-altering decision.

Young adults under the age of 18 make constant decisions while operating potentially deadly motor vehicles because 16- and 17-year-old individuals are allowed to obtain a driver's license in most states. Young adults under the age of 18 can be tried as an adult in a criminal court and sentenced to life in prison. Young adults make daily decisions that already have real, adult, life-altering consequences, especially regarding criminal activity.

Essentially, if a minor has been smart and responsible enough to create a profitable business, a business so successful that it is found to be desirable as a partner to another business, she or he should be allowed to make the decision whether to enter into a partnership.

No

Any individual under the age of 18 should not be allowed to enter into a business partnership. Individuals under the age of 18 are considered juveniles in the eyes of the law, and they are treated differently in court.

According to UPA, a partnership can be valid only when the relationship between partners is *voluntary* and *consensual.* Juveniles in the United States are not allowed to consent to participating in several activities because they are rightfully considered immature and inexperienced. Juveniles cannot consent to participate in a sexual relationship (in some states), consent to marriage or prenuptial agreements, purchase or smoke cigarettes or other tobacco products, gamble, or purchase or consume alcohol. Because this country does not consider individuals under the age of 18 sufficiently mature and life-experienced to smoke, gamble, or drink, they should also be considered too immature to make the life-altering decision of entering into a business

A juvenile is a dependent of his or her parents. Parents decide how to invest their child's money, which schools their child should attend, and what time their child should be required home as curfew. Because parents play such a significant role in their child's life, juveniles are not accustomed to making large decisions.

Juveniles are supposed to be focused on expanding their minds and learning in school, not forming businesses and making money. It isn't fair to the juvenile partner to expect him or her to take an equal role in the management of the partnership when he or she is still devoting most of his or her time to growing, developing, and learning in high school.

*Informational Web site: http://wps.ablongman/ab_fabes_exploring_2/0,4768,225940-,00.html.

Questions & Problems

1. Explain each element of UPA's definition of a partnership.
2. Explain the need for partnership by estoppel.
3. What is the distinction between partnership as a legal entity and partnership as a legal aggregate?
4. Why do partners owe duties to other partners?
5. What is the relationship between the obligations of a general partner and those of a limited partner?
6. What are the possible problems with any single list of the legal liabilities of a partner?
7. Paul Berkowitz is the minority shareholder of several related corporations and partnerships. He brought suit to force the appellants, Astro Moving and Storage Co., Inc., to produce certain books and records. Astro was currently in the process of voting to remove Berkowitz from his position as officer and director of the business entities. Berkowitz argued that his partner status gave him the right to inspect the books. According to Berkowitz, Astro had made an offer to buy him out, and he wanted to access the books to determine the true value of his shares. Do you think Berkowitz had a right to inspect the books? How do you think the court decided? [*Berkowitz v. Astro Moving and Storage Co., Inc.,* 658 N.Y.S.2d 425 (1997).]
8. Ian M. Starr was a partner in the law firm Fordham & Starrett. After Starr's first year of employment, the firm's profits were divided evenly among all partners. During his second year with the firm, Starr's relationship with the other partners began to deteriorate, and he quit the firm on the last day of the year. Listing several negative factors relevant to Starr's performance, the firm paid him less than half an equal share. Starr brought an action to recover amounts to which he claimed he was entitled pursuant to the partnership agreement. He also claimed breach of fiduciary duty. Starr's former partners counterclaimed that Starr had violated his fiduciary duties to the partners and breached the partnership agreement. How do you think the court settled this conflict? [*Starr v. Fordham,* 648 N.E.2d 1261 (1995).]
9. The Vancouver Group is made up of five investors, Pietz, Wynne, Fordham, Indermuehle, and Smith. The group entered into a partnership with Robert Berry for the joint purchase of the Sundance Hotel and Casino. The group and Berry made an offer to purchase the hotel. Pietz agreed to supply $500,000 to the deal and post a $285,000 letter of credit. However, after receiving information that caused him to doubt Berry, Pietz withdrew his interests from the partnership. Berry threatened to sue Pietz for breach of contract, fraud, and tortious breach of the covenant of good faith. Pietz and Berry settled, and Pietz subsequently sued the group for the cost of the settlement. The trial court rejected Pietz's claim of breach of fiduciary duty. He appealed the decision. How do you think the court decided? Was there a breach of fiduciary duty? [*Pietz v. Indermuehle,* 949 P.2d 449 (1998).]
10. Kevin Smith brought an action against Brown & Jones, his former law partnership. Smith alleged breach of the covenant of good faith and fair dealing and breach of fiduciary duty. According to the partnership agreement, Smith had the right to resign as long as he gave proper notice. The agreement also stated that a withdrawing partner would be compensated for work he or she had completed prior to withdrawing. Smith was compensated for only two-thirds of his contributions to the firm. He brought

the suit to receive full compensation. How do you think the court decided? [*Smith v. Brown & Jones,* 633 N.Y.S.2d 436 (1995).]

11. Richard Hunley, Nada Tas, Joseph Tas, and Kenneth Brown all became general partners of Parham-Woodman between 1986 and 1987. In 1985, Citizens Bank of Massachusetts loaned Parham-Woodman $2 million for the construction of a new office facility. When Parham-Woodman stopped making payments on the loan, the bank sold the building and sued the firm and the partners to recover the debt not paid. The partners argued that they were not liable for the debt because they had joined the firm after the loan agreement was made. Do you agree with them? Why or why not? [*Citizens Bank of Massachusetts v. Parham-Woodman Medical Associates,* 874 F. Supp. 705 (1995).]

12. Phillip Heller was a partner of the Pillsbury, Madison & Sutro law firm. The relationship between Heller and the firm was not strong, as Heller's work performance was unsatisfactory. He billed 1,000 hours fewer than he had estimated that he would produce, and he did not establish strong working relationships. Heller signed the partnership agreement in 1992. The agreement authorized the Executive Committee to expel partners. After Heller submitted a derogatory and lewd article entitled "Why I Fired My Secretary," the committee met and terminated Heller's partnership. Heller challenged the authority of the committee to expel him, regardless of whether he had signed the partnership agreement. Do you think the court agreed with him? Why or why not? [*Heller v. Pillsbury, Madison & Sutro,* 58 Cal. Rptr. 2d 336 (1996).]

13. Dr. Citrin had an agreement with Dr. Mehta that the latter would work in Citrin's offices when he was on vacation. While Citrin was on vacation, Mehta saw one of Citrin's patients and misdiagnosed the problem. The patient died, and the relatives sued Citrin, claiming that Mehta was Citrin's partner. What would determine whether the partnership did or did not exist? [*Impastato v. De Girolamo,* 459 N.Y.S.2d 512 (1983).]

14. Bane was a partner in a law firm that had a retirement plan funded only by current income. Retired partners would receive pensions based on their preretirement income. Bane retired in 1985. The law firm had an unsuccessful merger with another law firm. When the new firm dissolved, there were no remaining monies to fund payments to Bane. Bane's suit claimed that mismanagement by the managing partners had cost him his retirement pension. Did the mismanagement occur and create liability on the part of the managing partners? [*Bane v. Ferguson,* 890 F.2d 11 (1989).]

Looking for more review material?

The Online Learning Center at **www.mhhe.com/kubasek1e** contains this chapter's "Assignment on the Internet" and also a list of URLs for more information entitled "On the Internet." Find both of them in the Student Center portion of the OLC, along with quizzes and other helpful materials.

Partnerships: Termination and Limited Partnerships

CASE OPENER

Partnership Problems of First Interstate Bank

Jerome Arndt was one of eleven plaintiffs in a suit against First Interstate Bank of Utah. In 1975, Spence Clark and Clark Financial Group began seeking investments in several limited partnerships in which Clark was the general partner. According to the partnership agreements, the sale of real property would result in the immediate dissolution and liquidation of the partnership. Clark controlled all the partnership accounts, while the bank maintained the accounts. Clark also created a Pooled Income Fund with the bank, which he used for the purpose of taking funds from dissolved partnerships to finance less prosperous endeavors. Because Clark diverted the money from the fund, the plaintiffs did not receive their full distributions from the sales.

Therefore, the plaintiffs brought suit against the bank, alleging that the bank negligently or knowingly allowed Clark to redirect partnership proceeds from the fund. The plaintiffs also claimed that they had been personally damaged because of the conduct of the defendants. The trial court ruled against the wishes of the plaintiffs. The plaintiffs then appealed the trial court's ruling.

At first glance this decision seems to violate our sense of justice. But after you have studied this chapter, when the characteristics of limited partnerships and the process of terminating partnerships will be clearer, you will appreciate the court's reasoning.

1. If you were in Clark's position, what ethical concerns would you have with diverting proceeds?
2. What aspects of the business form called *limited partnership* led the Court to decide as it did?

The Wrap-Up at the end of the chapter will answer these questions.

CHAPTER 37

Learning Objectives

After reading this chapter, you will be able to answer the following questions:

1. What are the steps involved in the termination of the partnership?
2. How is a limited partnership formed?
3. What are the rights and privileges of a limited partner as opposed to a general partner?

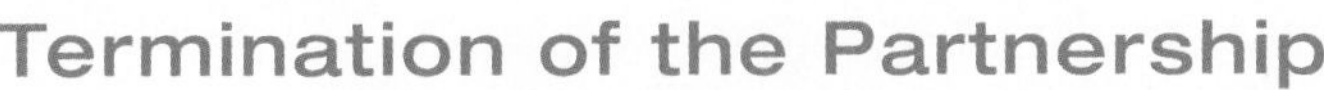

Termination of the Partnership

Before the termination of any partnership can be considered to be complete, a partnerships must experience what are referred to as the *dissolution stage* and the *winding-up stage.* The first of these stages, dissolution, is considered complete when any partner stops fulfilling the role of a partner to the business (by choice or default). The second stage, the winding-up stage, is complete by taking account of the assets of the partner who has left the partnership and redistributing them among the other partners. This process of forming and terminating the partnership is represented in Figure 37-1. The rest of this section explains the steps that must occur within the dissolution and winding-up stages for the termination of the partnership to be considered complete.

Dissolution of the Business

Section 29 of UPA defines **dissolution** as "the change in the relation of the partners caused by any partner's ceasing to be associated with the carrying on, as distinguished from the winding up"—the activity of completing unfinished partnership business, collecting and paying debts, collecting partnership assets, and taking inventory—"of the business." What might cause the dissolution of the partnership? The dissolution may occur by an act of the partners, an operation of the law, or an act of the court.

One significant issue in the case against First Interstate Bank of Utah was whether a dissolved partnership could bring suit prior to its having completed all unfinished

Figure 37-1 Forming and Dissolving a Partnership

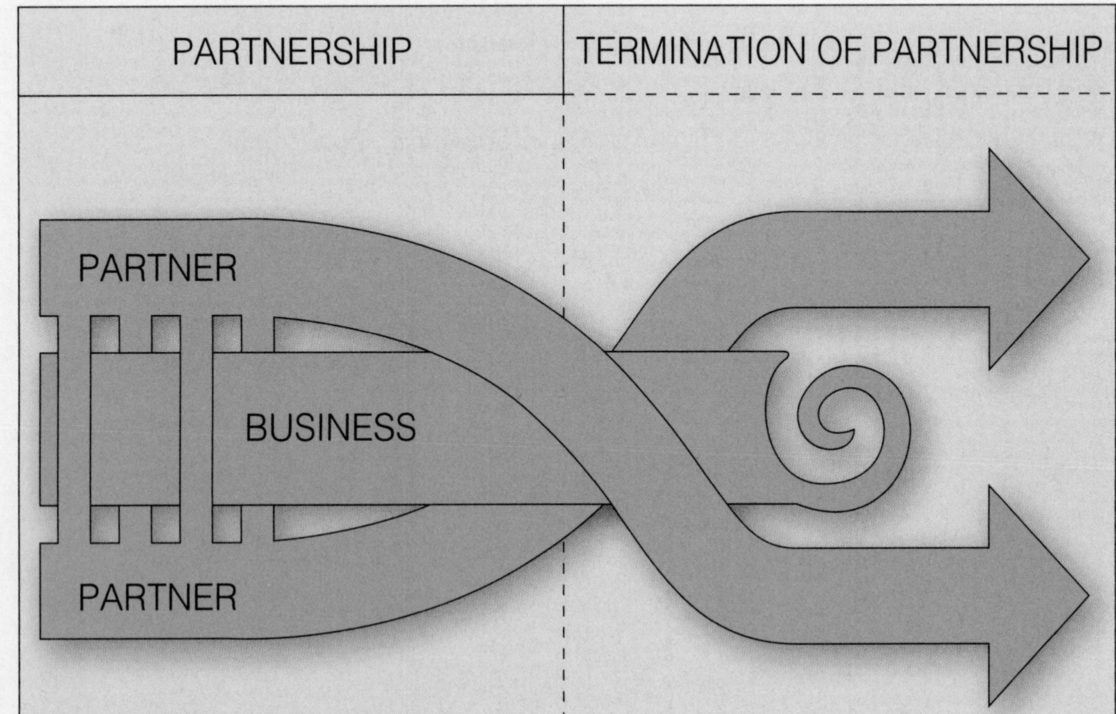

partnership business. Therefore, the court first looked at the definition of dissolution. First, the court referenced the definition of dissolution provided by UPA. Second, the court observed that dissolution is distinct from the winding up of the partnership, with dissolution occurring prior to winding up. Based on the partnership agreements, dissolution was to occur immediately after the sale of the partnership's real estate; thereafter, the partnership would be liquidated.

ACT OF PARTNERS

The partnership is a voluntary and consensual relationship, so the partners have the power to dissolve the relationship at almost any time. There are many reasons why an act of the partners might lead to the dissolution of the partnership. First, the partners may simply agree that the partnership will terminate at a certain time. For example, suppose that Lisa and Jason, two partners in a college preparation business, are graduating from college. They are both planning to accept jobs at other firms; consequently, neither thinks that she or he will be able to continue the college preparation business. Perhaps, when the college preparation business was created, the partners might have agreed to dissolve the partnership when one of them graduated from college.

Alternatively, once partners reach a certain objective, they might agree to dissolve the partnership. As an illustration, consider a partnership to sell homes in a housing development. Once all of those homes are sold, the partners may agree to dissolve the partnership.

Let's return to the college preparation–business example. Suppose the original agreement was that the partnership would be terminated when either partner graduates from college. However, suppose the business is either a flop or an enormous success. The partners can then agree to dissolve the partnership early or extend the terms of the partnership after graduation.

What are the circumstances in which a partnership can be **rightfully dissolved,** meaning that the partnership dissolution did not violate the partnership agreement? We have established two of these circumstances above (dissolution after meeting an established objective and dissolution at the end of the term stated in the partnership agreement). The following are also circumstances in which the partnership can be rightfully terminated:

1. *A partner withdraws from the partnership at will.* (A *partnership at will* is an agreement that does not specify the objective or duration of the partnership.)
2. *A partner withdraws in accordance with the partnership agreement.* The partnership agreement may establish specific reasons that a partner may withdraw.
3. *A partner is expelled from the partnership in accordance with the partnership agreement.* Suppose you are a partner in a law firm and you steal some type of property from the partnership. The partnership agreement will usually determine the cases in which a partner may be removed from the partnership, and theft is often one of the reasons for removal. Thus, your stealing would likely lead to your expulsion from the partnership.

If a partnership is rightfully dissolved, all partners can demand that the partnership be wound up and can participate in the winding up. Moreover, if the partners unanimously agree, they can continue the business using the partnership's name.

However, if a partner dissolves the partnership in violation of the partnership agreement, the partner can be held liable for **wrongful dissolution.** If a partner has wrongfully dissolved the partnership, that partner cannot require that the business be wound up. Furthermore, that partner can be held liable for damages to the remaining partners. The remaining partners can choose to continue the business under the partnership name or to wind up the business.

Case Nugget Partnership Dissolution

In re Leah Beth Woskob, Debtor; Alex Woskob; Helen Woskob; the Estate of Victor Woskob v. Leah Beth Woskob, Appellant
U.S. Court of Appeals for the Third Circuit
305 F.3d 177; 2002

In 1996, Leah Beth Woskob and Victor Woskob formed a partnership, the Legends Partnership, to construct, own, and operate the Legends, an apartment building. They were married at the time that the partnership was formed; however, they separated and filed for divorce the following year. During the divorce proceedings, Victor prevented Leah from receiving any of the partnership proceeds. Leah was granted a petition for special relief and awarded the exclusive right to manage and derive income from the partnership. Shortly thereafter, Victor filed for bankruptcy. Leah continued to file tax returns on behalf of the partnership, each of which listed Victor as a general partner. When Victor died in a car accident in 1999, Leah gave his estate notice that she was exercising her right to buy out Victor's interest in the partnership. Victor's estate sued, claiming that the partnership had been dissolved previously and requesting that someone be appointed to oversee the winding up of the partnership and a full accounting of the company's assets. When Leah filed for bankruptcy, the suits were moved to the bankruptcy court. The bankruptcy court ruled in favor of Leah, finding that the partnership had dissolved on Victor's death. Victor's estate appealed to the district court, which found that the partnership had dissolved two years before Victor's death, making Leah's attempt to buy out Victor's interest untimely. Leah appealed.

The task before the appeals court was to determine the timeliness of Leah's attempt to buy out Victor's interest in the partnership, which depended entirely on the date of the dissolution of the partnership. The court looked to the Uniform Partnership Act (UPA), which defined the dissolution of a partnership as "the change in the relation of the partners caused by any partner ceasing to be associated in the carrying on, as distinguished from the winding up, of the business." Victor's estate claimed that the dissolution of the partnership occurred at any one of three points, each at least 18 months prior to Victor's death. First, Victor excluded Leah from the partnership after they separated; second, Leah excluded Victor from the partnership after seeking special relief from the Court of Common Pleas; third, Victor filed for bankruptcy.

The appeals court found that the exclusions of Leah and Victor from the partnership were not, in and of themselves, grounds for automatic dissolution of the partnership. Rather, the exclusions could have provided a basis for dissolution, had either Leah or Victor sought judicial decree of the dissolution after the exclusions. In addition, bankruptcy in and of itself is not grounds for automatic dissolution of the partnership. If the nondebtor partner does not consent to continue the partnership with the debtor, bankruptcy may be grounds for dissolution. However, Leah continued to list Victor as a general partner on the tax returns she filed for the partnership, even after he filed for bankruptcy. Thus, the appeals court found that the partnership had not dissolved prior to Victor's death in 1999 and that Leah's attempt to buy out Victor's interest in the partnership was therefore timely.

OPERATION OF LAW

Several circumstances provided by law dissolve a partnership: if a partner dies, if a partner is adjudicated bankrupt, or if the partnership business engages in an activity that suddenly becomes illegal. For example, suppose Congress decides that cigarettes are illegal. If the partnership manufactures and sells cigarettes, the partnership would be automatically dissolved.

ACT OF THE COURT

A partner may make application to the court to dissolve the partnership for several reasons. First, a partnership can be dissolved when a partner is adjudicated insane. Second, if it becomes impractical to carry out the business of the partnership (e.g., if the continuation of the partnership will result in lost profits only), the court will likely dissolve the partnership. Third, if a partner is incapable of carrying out his or her duties as established by the partnership agreement, the court can dissolve the partnership.

Fourth, the court can dissolve the partnership for other circumstances. For instance, suppose that the partners in the college preparation business begin bitterly disagreeing about how the business should be managed. The disagreement is contrary to the cooperation necessary for a partnership to exist. In this instance, the court can dissolve the partnership.

Case 37-1 is one in which the court decided to dissolve a partnership. Exhibit 37-1 provides 13 reasons for dissolution of the partnership.

CASE 37-1

LIEM PHAN VU v. DAVIS HA ET AL.
SUPERIOR COURT OF CONNECTICUT
1997 CONN. SUPER. LEXIS 259

Liem Phan Vu and Davis Ha had an oral agreement to create a partnership to run a nail salon. They agreed that Ha would hold 60 percent of the partnership interest while Vu would hold 40 percent. They agreed to open a new salon. Vu was responsible for advertising as well as keeping the books and records for the salon. Ha was responsible for operating and managing the business. The salon opened in summer 1995, and the partnership ended in November 1995. In November, Vu presented Ha with a proposed agreement to make the partnership a limited liability company. Ha was unhappy with the agreement and changed the locks on the salon. Ha testified that he thought that Vu had taken items from the salon and was not sufficiently keeping records. Vu argued that Ha was excluding her from the business in violation of the partnership agreement. When the dispute went to trial, each party attempted to show that he or she had invested more in the partnership. Vu brought suit for fourteen claims of relief; however, she really wanted the partnership to be dissolved and her portion of the investment returned. After reviewing her claims, the court considered the dissolution of the partnership.

JUDGE D'ANDREA: The court has the power to dissolve a partnership by judicial decree, and may do so if it finds circumstances which would render a dissolution equitable. The court cannot imagine circumstances more compelling than exist in this case for such a finding. The parties have lost faith completely in each other; they each levy charges against the other for the failure of the business; one believes the other failed to keep proper records and to keep him apprised of the state of the finances; one claims physical exclusion from the business by the other and verbal attacks upon her.

Since the court cannot affix blame for the demise of the partnership on either party, and does not find that a breach of the partnership contract has been proven, the rights of the parties are generally governed by Connecticut General Statutes 34–76.

Accordingly, the court orders a dissolution of the partnership between the parties. Because the defendant Ha has continued in possession of the premises and continues to operate the business of the partnership, he is ordered to pay the plaintiff Vu the value of her interest in the partnership. No expert evidence was presented as to the value of the business, and the court can only be guided by the testimony of the defendant as to the value of the stock in trade. This figure is $2,000 and the plaintiff's interest in the partnership being forty percent, she is entitled to forty percent of that amount, or $800. The court also views the security deposit for the lease on the premises to be an asset of the business. That amount being $10,800, the plaintiff is entitled to forty percent thereof, or $4,320. Furthermore, the plaintiff shall not be responsible for the terms of the lease or for any existing obligation of the partnership.

Therefore, the court orders:

(1) A decree of dissolution of the partnership between the parties;

(2) That the defendant pay to the plaintiff the sum of $5,120 as the value of her interest in the partnership;

(3) That the defendant indemnify and hold the plaintiff harmless from any liability under the lease of the premises at 21 High Ridge Road, Stamford, and from all liabilities for the debts and obligations of the partnership.

Finding for the plaintiff.

CRITICAL THINKING

Review the court's reasoning in *Liem Phan Vu.* What evidence would the court have needed to refuse to dissolve the partnership despite the feuding between the partners? The court provides hints about what that evidence would be.

ETHICAL DECISION MAKING

The text discusses the dissolution of the partnership and explains how partners can be penalized if they attempt to leave the partnership wrongfully. What values are upheld by the court's protection of the partnership? In other words, if the court did not hold value *X,* the demise of the partnership would not be considered such a liability.

Exhibit 37-1
Summary of Reasons for Rightful Dissolution of the Partnership

1. The term established in the partnership agreement expires.
2. The partnership meets the established objective of the partnership.
3. A partner withdraws from the partnership at will.
4. A partner withdraws in accordance with the partnership agreement.
5. A partner is expelled from the partnership in accordance with the partnership agreement.
6. A partner dies.
7. A partner is adjudicated bankrupt.
8. The business of the partnership becomes illegal.
9. A partner is adjudicated insane.
10. A partner becomes incapable of performing the duties as established by the partnership agreement.
11. The business of the partnership can be carried on only at a loss of profits.
12. The disagreement between the partners is such that it undermines the nature of the partnership.
13. Other circumstances of the partnership necessitate the dissolution.

global context

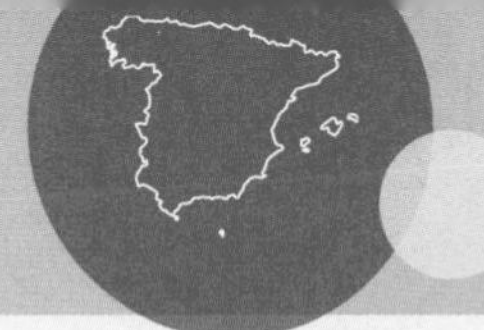

Termination of Partnerships in Spain

In Spain, there are four specific situations in which full dissolution is permitted (*full dissolution* simply means that the partnership ends without litigation or a waiting period): (1) if one partner dies, (2) if a partner is declared insane and unfit to manage the business, (3) if a partner is declared bankrupt, and (4) if a partner requests that the partnership be terminated.

In Spain there are other situations that call for provisional dissolution of the partnership. *Provisional dissolution* is followed by litigation to determine the legitimacy of the termination request. The six situations of provisional dissolution include (1) where a partner fails to comply with provisions of the contract, (2) where a partner unexplainably abandons the partnership and does not return on request, (3) where a partner fails to bring the capital he or she promised, (4) where a partner is accused of fraud or mismanagement, (5) where a partner exceeds the limits of his or her power, and (6) where a partner uses capital belonging to the partnership in his or her own name.

In any of these circumstances, the partnership is temporarily dissolved pending the outcome of litigation. During partial dissolution, the accused is excluded from all managerial responsibilities and profits. He or she is also excluded from any liability to business conducted during this time.

The stage of provisional dissolution prevents those unfairly accused of certain behaviors from losing position in the partnership. The process, however, can be a tedious and lengthy one whether the partial dissolution is moved to complete termination or the partnership resumes.

Consequences of Dissolution

If a partner intends to dissolve or withdraw from the partnership, the partner must give the other partners notice of this intent. When the partnership is dissolved, the partner no longer has actual authority to bind the partnership. However, if the partnership does not notify third parties of the dissolution, the partner can still have implied authority to bind the partnership. Suppose that Lisa, one of the partners in the college preparation business, intends to dissolve the partnership. However, Lisa has not yet notified Jason of her intent, and Jason makes an agreement to begin working with five new students to prepare them for college. Because Lisa has not yet given notice of her intent to dissolve, she is still liable for the agreement Jason has made.

To ensure that a dissolving partner does not create additional liability for the partnership, firms usually take active steps to notify third parties about the dissolution. Firms often place an advertisement in the newspaper to notify third parties, for example. However, firms must provide direct verbal or written notice to any third party that has provided credit to the partnership.

Read the Global Context box on Scotland. What ethical behavior does the Scottish law encourage that might not be encouraged under American law?

After the dissolution of the partnership, the partners' next step is either winding up the business or continuing the partnership or business after the dissolution. We'll discuss winding up the business first.

Winding Up the Business

Once a partnership is liquidated, the partners begin the process of **winding up,** the activity of completing unfinished partnership business, collecting and paying debts, collecting

global context

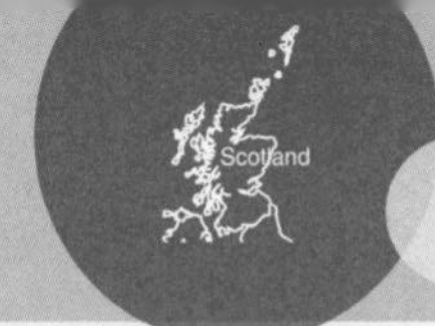

Effects of Dissolution in Scotland

In many countries, a partner's ability to bind the partnership immediately ceases on the termination of the partnership. In Scotland, however, a partner may engage in business transactions in the name of the partnership for an unlimited time provided the transactions are necessary to wind up the affairs of the former relationship. The intention behind this law is to prepare for any instances in which a partnership wishes to terminate quickly but may have pending business. The partners can go ahead and cease the relationship and then tie up any loose ends.

For example, a partnership waiting to collect profits from a certain venture can dissolve before the profits have been deposited. The Scottish law ensures that a bank is justified in accepting the signature of a partner wishing to deposit or withdraw money from a dissolved partnership's trust. The deposit and withdrawal are considered necessary in winding up the business of the partnership.

partnership assets, and taking inventory. During the winding up, the partners must still fulfill their fiduciary duty to one another, in the sense that they must disclose all information about the partnership assets. However, during the winding-up process, the partners can engage in business that competes with the partnership business. Case 37-2 examines a partner's fiduciary duty during the winding-up period of the termination of the partnership.

CASE 37-2 BILL L. TUCKER v. JOHN P. ELLBOGEN AND ELLBOGEN-TUCKER INTERESTS

COURT OF APPEALS OF COLORADO, DIVISION TWO
793 P.2D 592; 1989 COLO. APP. LEXIS 334; 13 BTR 1415 (1989)

In June 1981, Bill Tucker and John Ellbogen created a partnership with respect to certain oil and gas ventures. However, in November 1982, Ellbogen informed Tucker that the partnership was to be dissolved in December 1982. Tucker brought suit to ensure a final accounting of partnership assets, and Ellbogen counterclaimed, arguing that Tucker was liable for partnership debts. The trial court ruled that Ellbogen did not breach a fiduciary duty to Tucker during the winding up period. Tucker appealed.

JUDGE PLANK: Partners stand in a relationship of trust and confidence to each other and are bound by standards of good conduct and fair dealing. Each partner has the right to demand and expect from the other a full, fair, open, and honest disclosure of everything affecting their relationship.

Generally, a partnership dismantling proceeds through a three-step process: dissolution, winding up, and termination. A dissolution of a partnership does not terminate the relationship; rather, it continues until the winding up of the partnership affairs is completed. Upon the completion of winding up, the partnership is terminated.

In the absence of an agreement to the contrary, each partner is entitled to have equal rights in the management and conduct of the partnership business. However, partners may agree that one or more of them shall have exclusive control over the management of the partnership business.

Here, the agreement and the parties' conduct demonstrate that there was an agreement that Ellbogen was to be the managing partner.

Any partner ordinarily has the right to participate in the winding up process. Additionally, any partner has the right to a formal accounting as to partnership affairs whenever circumstances render it just and reasonable.

Here, the record reveals that in late November 1982, Ellbogen announced that effective December 31, 1982, all partnership activities would cease, that the office space and furnishings held in the partnership name would thereafter be held in Ellbogen's name, and that Tucker was to leave the premises and have nothing further to do with the partnership.

On January 13, 1983, Tucker's accountants sent Ellbogen a letter to arrange for the partnership to be wound up. Ellbogen did not answer this letter, and this action resulted.

When the trial court declared the partnership wound up on December 2, 1987, five years had passed since the dissolution of the partnership. During this time, over $200,000 in interest had accrued on a loan that the partnership had guaranteed. The trial court determined that Tucker would be responsible for 25 percent of the loan plus interest. This was error.

After the dissolution of a partnership, each partner continues to have a fiduciary duty to the other partner until the partnership assets have been divided and the liabilities have been satisfied.

Here, Tucker was excluded from the partnership business after December 31, 1982. Thus, we conclude it was Ellbogen's duty, as managing partner, to wind up the partnership. The winding up partner has the duty to wind up expeditiously so as not to cause waste.

During the five-year period which it took to wind up the partnership, Ellbogen did not give a final accounting to Tucker, allowed oil and gas leases to expire, and did not take any steps to resolve the bank debt. Furthermore, Ellbogen testified that he did nothing to resolve the bank debt because he was waiting to see what happened in the trial court case. We expressly reject this justification for delay asserted by Ellbogen since we conclude Ellbogen had the affirmative duty to wind up the partnership affairs as expeditiously as possible.

As a result of Ellbogen's actions, when the trial court declared the partnership wound up, substantial liabilities existed.

We conclude, as a matter of law, that a five-year period to wind up this partnership is unreasonable, and that Ellbogen's failure to act in a more efficacious manner was a breach of his fiduciary duty to Tucker. Thus, the matter must be remanded to the trial court for a new accounting and to determine what a "reasonable" time would have been for Ellbogen to wind up the partnership. The losses and or profits are to be valued as of that date, and they are to be divided between the partners according to the allocation which we have affirmed. The liabilities that have accrued after that date are to be the sole responsibility of Ellbogen.

REVERSED.

CRITICAL THINKING

Based on the given evidence, do you agree with the court's reasoning? What were some of the weaknesses in Tucker's argument?

ETHICAL DECISION MAKING

Who are the primary stakeholders in this decision? Did the court pay appropriate attention to the interests of these various people?

Who can demand that the winding-up process begin? As we stated earlier, if a partnership has been rightfully dissolved, any partner can demand that the winding-up stage begin. However, if a partner wrongfully dissolves a partnership, that partner has no right to demand a winding up. In Case 37-3, the court considers a demand for an accounting in the winding-up phase.

CASE 37-3 ROBERT M. TAFOYA v. DEE S. PERKINS, NO. 95CA0408

COURT OF APPEALS OF COLORADO, DIVISION FOUR
932 P.2D 836; 1996 COLO. APP. LEXIS 206;
20 BTR 1115

Robert Tafoya and Dee Perkins, brother and sister, entered into a partnership with Dee's husband, Eugene Perkins. Eugene Perkins bought an apartment complex in 1977; however, he did not want to manage it. Eugene Perkins held the title of the land in his name and contributed all necessary capital. Dee Perkins was to keep the books and assist in the management of the complex. Finally, Robert Tafoya was to live at, manage, and maintain the apartment complex. In 1979, the apartment complex was sold. The partnership took back a 10-year promissory note with a balloon payment due in 1989.

Ten years later, when the balloon payment was due, Eugene Perkins purchased the apartments again at a foreclosure sale. In December 1989, Eugene Perkins issued a Notice of Termination of Partnership because of losses associated with the partnership. At the same time, Robert Tafoya ceased being associated with the partnership. In July 1990, Eugene Perkins died. The trial court ruled that Perkins' death as well as Tafoya's separation from the partnership was sufficient to dissolve the partnership. Dee Perkins continued to manage the property until January 1994, when she sold the property for a profit. Tafoya filed his complaint before the sale of the property, arguing that Perkins had breached her fiduciary duty. Tafoya requested an accounting of the partnership's assets. The trial court found no breach of fiduciary duty yet concluded that Tafoya was entitled to an accounting and awarded him a share of the proceeds from the apartment complex sale. Dee Perkins appealed, arguing that Tafoya's claim was barred by a statute of limitations.

JUDGE DAVIDSON: Section 7-60-129, C.R.S (1986 Repl. Vol. 3A) of the Uniform Partnership Law (the Act) provides that:

> The dissolution of any partnership is the change in relation of the partners caused by any partner ceasing to be associated in the carrying on as distinguished from the winding up of the business.

Under this section, when a partner withdraws from the business, the partnership is dissolved as to that party. However, the remaining partners may elect to continue operating as a partnership.

Section 7-60-143, C.R.S. (1986 Repl. Vol. 3A) of the Act states as follows:

> The right to an account of his interest shall accrue to any partner or his legal representative, as against the winding up partners, the surviving partners, or the person or partnership continuing the business at the date of dissolution, in the absence of any agreement to the contrary.

Courts have reached varying conclusions, depending on the circumstances, about when a statute of limitations begins to run on a claim seeking an accounting. However, §§ 7-60-129 and 7-60-143, taken together, provide that, absent an agreement to the contrary, at least in the circumstances of a withdrawing partner seeking an accounting against any partners winding up or continuing the business, the cause of action accrues on the date the withdrawing partner ceases to be associated with the business, resulting in dissolution of the partnership. Hence, regardless of the legal effect of

[CONTINUED]

the husband's notice of termination or his later death, once plaintiff himself ceased to be associated with the partnership, not only did this dissolve any still-existing partnership, it also caused the statute of limitations to begin to run on his own claim for an accounting against plaintiff.

The Act does not set forth or specify the applicable statute of limitations. Nor does any statute of limitations specifically address an action for partnership accounting. We therefore conclude that the applicable statute of limitations is § 13-80-102(1)(i), C.R.S. (1987 Repl. Vol 6A), which sets forth a two-year "catch-all" period of limitations for "all other actions of every kind for which no other period of limitation is provided."

We do not agree with plaintiff's suggestion that, because the action is one to "recover . . . an unliquidated, determinable amount of money due" him, the appropriate statute of limitations for this action is six years under § 13-80-103.5. Because the amount due from the accounting was not capable of ascertainment by reference to the partnership agreement or by a simple computation derived from the agreement, that statute does not apply.

The trial court found that plaintiff ceased to be associated with the partnership in 1989, causing a dissolution of the then-existing partnership. That finding is not challenged on appeal. Plaintiff did not file his complaint until January of 1994. As a result, his claim for an accounting is not timely because it falls outside the two-year period of limitation in § 13-80-102(1)(i).

REVERSED.

CRITICAL THINKING

How do you react to the evidence in this case? Does it strike you as being seriously incomplete? What additional information would you have liked to have were you asked to decide this case?

ETHICAL DECISION MAKING

What were the primary values upheld by the court in its decision? If you were the judge reviewing the case, which values would motivate your decision?

Once all the partnership assets are gathered, the assets are distributed to the partners or any creditors that the partnership might have. If the partnership has been successful (i.e., has very little or no debt), the order of the distribution of assets is not too important. However, when the dissolved partnership has many creditors, the order of the distribution of the assets is immensely important. UPA establishes that when a partnership has debt, the distribution of liquidated assets must take the following order:

1. Payment to creditors of the partnership.
2. Payment of refunds or loans to partners for loans made to the firm.
3. Payment of partners for the capital they invested.
4. Payment of profits distributed to partners on the basis of the partnership agreement.

If the partners' liabilities for the partnership are greater than their liquidated assets, the partners are liable for the losses. Each partner must contribute his or her share of the losses to pay the creditors. If one partner is unable to contribute his or her share and another partner covers the first partner's unpaid share, the second partner has a right of contribution against the partner who did not pay.

connecting to the core

Accounting

Allocating Income among Partners

Most partnership agreements specify how profits will be divided among the partners. As you should remember from your accounting class, there are three common methods for dividing income or loss. First, a stated ratio basis provides each partner with a proportion of the total income or loss, based on agreement among the partners on the specific ratios. Second, the capital balances method divides income among partners on the basis of individual capital contributions. Hence, if partner A contributes two-thirds of the total capital and partner B contributes the other one-third, partner A would receive two-thirds of the income and partner B would receive one-third of the total income. Third, the services, capital, and stated ratio method allocates income or loss on the basis of differences in service and capital contributions.

This third method of allocating income and loss provides salary allowances for differences in service contributions and interest allowances for differences in capital contributions while including a stated ratio for any remaining income or loss. For example, the partnership agreement for partner A and partner B might allocate salary allowances of $45,000 and $20,000, respectively, based on higher service levels for partner A. In addition, the partnership agreement might specify that each partner receives an interest allowance of 10 percent of each partner's beginning-year capital balance. Furthermore, any remaining income or loss would be divided equally between the partners. Assuming partner A had a beginning-year capital balance of $20,000 and partner B had $10,000, and assuming the partnership generated $100,000 net income, the accounting under the services, capital, and stated ratio would be as follows: Partner A would receive $63,000 [$45,000 of salary allowance plus $2,000 interest allowance (10 percent of capital balance of $20,000) plus $16,000 (half the remaining balance)]; partner B would receive $37,000 [$20,000 of salary allowance plus $1,000 interest allowance (10 percent of capital balance of $10,000) plus $16,000 (half the remaining balance)]. However, as mentioned in this chapter, when the partnership agreement does not specify the allocation of income and losses, courts will generally divide profits and losses equally among the partners.

In the opening case involving the First Interstate Bank of Utah, the court examined the definition of winding up following the discussion of dissolution. Because UPA does not provide a definition for winding up, the court examined the Revised Business Corporation Act (RBCA) for guidance. This act states that a dissolved corporation may not engage in any activities other than those involved with the winding-up process and the liquidation of its business but the corporation does continue its existence. Included in the winding-up process is the collection of the partnership's assets and the disposition of its properties that will not be distributed to the shareholders.

As mentioned earlier, the process of winding up involves the completion of business activities. Under RBCA, a corporation's dissolution does not "prevent commencement of a proceeding by or against the corporation in its corporate name" (Section 16-10a-1405). Thus, the court determined that the partnership still exists as a legal entity with the ability to sue and be sued during the winding-up stage.

CONTINUING THE PARTNERSHIP AFTER DISSOLUTION

After a partnership is dissolved, the remaining partners have several options. One option is to continue the partnership after dissolution. What happens to the noncontinuing partner? Regardless of why the partner is noncontinuing, this partner must receive his or her interest in the partnership. For example, if a noncontinuing partner holds 20 percent of the partnership in which the assets are valued at $10,000, this partner must receive $2,000 after dissolution.

Case Nugget Continuing Partnership after Dissolution

Sanfurd G. Bluestein and Sylvia Krugman, Plaintiffs, v. Robert Olden, Defendant
U.S. District Court for the Southern District of New York
2004 U.S. Dist. LEXIS 3631

In 1978, Bluestein, Krugman, and Olden formed a partnership, the principal asset of which is a building located in New York City. For 26 years, Olden operated Olden Camera and Lens Company, Inc., in part of the building. Olden Camera itself had been in the building for more than 60 years. In 2001, the plaintiffs sent a letter to Olden to terminate the partnership in accordance with the terms of the partnership agreement. After the letter was sent, the partnership continued to operate in dissolution. The partners agreed to sell the building, but they could not agree on whom to sell to and how much to charge. Olden offered $9 million for the plaintiff's combined interest in the partnership, but he added that the plaintiffs must release any claims against him and his business, as well as any claims to profits from the partnership for 2002–2003. A competing offer from a third party contained no requirements and offered $15,400,000 for the building, but it provided for a reduction of the purchase price by $200,000 if Olden's business remained in the building.

The plaintiffs filed an order to show cause, requesting "1) the appointment of plaintiff Bluestein as Liquidating and/or Winding Up Partner of the general partnership; 2) a direction that Olden cooperate in the liquidation of the assets of the partnership; and 3) enjoining Olden from entering into any new leases or renewing any leases for space in the building." Because the partnership was terminated in accordance with the partnership agreement, the court ruled that Olden could not prevent maximization of the partnership's assets. Bluestein was appointed the liquidating partner and given sole authority to liquidate the partnership's assets and divide the proceeds after paying the partnership's debts. Olden was ordered to cooperate in the liquidation of the assets and enjoined from entering into or renewing any leases or agreements affecting the partnership's building in New York City. The court retained jurisdiction to ensure that the partners complied with its orders.

Perhaps the best way that partners can preserve a partnership business is through a *continuation agreement.* This agreement states that continuing partners can keep partnership property and carry on the partnership business, particularly in cases when a partner dies.

Limited Partnerships

Chapter 35 introduced limited partnerships. Limited partnerships, also known as *special partnerships,* originated in Europe more than 500 years ago and have existed in the United States for nearly 200 years. Limited partnerships are attractive to potential investors because of the limited liability as well as the tax advantages associated with this form of business.

Recall that the **limited partnership** is an agreement between at least one general partner and at least one limited partner. The general partner has management responsibility for the partnership and assumes unlimited personal liability for the debts of the partnership. In

global context

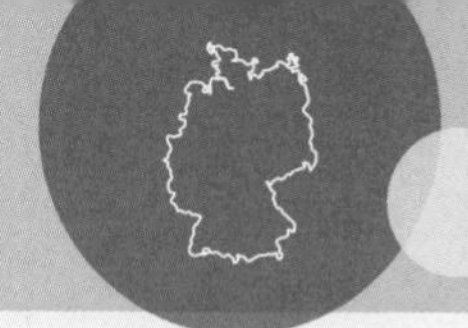

Dissolution of Partnership in Germany

In Germany, if a partner wishes to leave a partnership, he must give notice of his intention to do so at least six months before the end of the business year. On receiving notification, the other partners may begin placing bids for the purchase of the leaving partner's shares. The shares do not become officially available until the end of the business year.

If the remaining partners wish to continue the partnership after one leaves, declares bankruptcy, or dies, this possibility must be provided for in the contract agreement to terminate the partnership. The remaining partners may also opt to fully dissolve the relationship. Under this option, they become liquidators. As liquidators, the partners' duties include concluding all current business transactions, converting all assets to money, and paying all creditors. These duties are hopefully to be fulfilled within eight months. All claims against the partnerships are dismissed five years after termination.

contrast, the limited partner assumes no liability for the partnership beyond the capital he or she invested in the business.

Functioning as the equivalent of RUPA, the Revised Uniform Limited Partnership Act (RULPA) is the law governing limited partnerships. Like all law, RULPA is not static; it changes as lawmakers revise it to handle new issues that arise and to better achieve social goals. RULPA was originally drafted in 1976, revised in 1985, and revised again in 2001. About one-fourth of the states have adopted the 1976 version of RULPA, and about three-fourths have adopted the 1985 version. Only a handful of states have adopted the 2001 version. Louisiana is the only state not to have adopted any version of RULPA.

FORMATION OF THE LIMITED PARTNERSHIP

How is the limited partnership created? In contrast to the often-informal partnership agreements described in the previous chapter, the formation of a limited partnership must follow very specific statutory requirements. The general and limited partners must sign a **certificate of limited partnership** and file this certificate with the secretary of state. If the partners do not correctly fill out or do not file this certificate, the partners will not receive limited liability.

RIGHTS AND LIABILITIES OF THE LIMITED PARTNERS AND THE GENERAL PARTNERS

Limited partners generally have all the rights given to partners in general partnerships, as discussed in the previous chapter. Thus, the limited partner (as well as the general partner) has the right to share in the profits of the business. Furthermore, the limited partner has the right to an account of the partnership. Moreover, if the general partner wants to add a partner to the partnership, the general partner must have the consent of all partners in the limited partnership. Finally, an additional right of limited partners is that they often recover their investment before general partners.

However, the limited partner has a few special rights under RULPA. For example, if a general partner fails to bring a suit on behalf of the limited partnership, the limited partner can bring the suit.

What about the duties and liabilities of the partnership? While there are not many distinctions between the rights of the general partner and those of the limited partner, there are numerous distinctions in the duties and liabilities of each partner.

For instance, the general partner has unlimited personal liability for the debts of the partnership. This broad liability is in contrast to the limited partner's limited liability, which

e-commerce AND THE LAW

How the Internet Assists Business Owners Who Use Limited Partnerships

The Internet is making it easier for business owners to engage in business as limited partnerships. For example, at the Michigan Corporation Division page www.michigan.gov/cis/0,1607,7-154-10557_12901-25254--,00.html, you can download a certificate of limited partnership.

Additionally, the Internet provides partnerships with an easy opportunity to advertise to the public when there is a change in the partnership. For example, when a partnership is in the dissolution stage, it must notify third parties of the dissolution of the partnership. Thus, the partnership can simply post information on the Internet explaining the dissolution. You can see a sample partnership dissolution notice at http://smallbusiness.findlaw.com/business-forms-contracts/be28_8_1.html.

is restricted to the amount of capital the partner has invested in the business. Thus, if you enter into a limited partnership by contributing $10,000 to the partnership, as a limited partner you cannot be held liable for more than $10,000.

A limited partner's limited personal liability depends on the partner's maintaining three conditions:

1. The limited partner has complied in good faith with the requirement that a certificate of limited partnership is filed.
2. The limited partner does not participate in the control of the business.
3. The limited partner's surname is not part of the partnership name.

If any of these conditions are violated, the limited partner surrenders his or her limited liability. For example, the general partner typically has exclusive control and management of the limited partnership. In contrast, the limited partner does not share in this control of the partnership. If he or she does share in the management of the company, the courts will likely rule that the partner has forfeited his or her limited liability. Exhibit 37-2 distinguishes several aspects of general partners and limited partners.

DISSOLUTION OF THE LIMITED PARTNERSHIP

Dissolution of the limited partnership is very similar to dissolution of the general partnership. The limited partner has no right or power to dissolve the partnership. While the death or bankruptcy of the limited partner rarely dissolves the partnership, the death of the general partner usually dissolves the partnership (unless the agreement specifies otherwise). According to RULPA, a limited partnership can be dissolved for the following reasons:

1. The expiration of the term established in the certificate of limited partnership.
2. The completion of the objective established in the certificate.

Exhibit 37-2
Comparison of General Partners and Limited Partners

	GENERAL PARTNER	LIMITED PARTNER
Control of Business	Has *all* rights associated with controlling the business	Has *no* right to participate in the management and control of the business
Liability	Has unlimited personal liability for all partnership debts	Has liability limited to the amount of capital the partner has contributed to the business
Agency of Partnership	Acts as an agent of the partnership	Is not an agent of the partnership

connecting to the core

Accounting

Separate Accounts and Dissolution

Because ownership in a partnership is divided among the partners, each partner is entitled to a separate account. In other words, each partner has a separate capital account, withdrawal account, and portion of income earned or losses incurred, divided in accordance with the partnership agreement. Capital accounts include assets and liabilities that individual partners have invested. For instance, when entering a partnership, a partner may contribute cash and real property (both of which are assets), while also contributing a note payable, or bank loan (liability). Were a partnership to dissolve, these separate accounts could be used to determine how much profit each partner should receive or how much each partner is liable for losses.

Source: K. Larson, J. Wild, and B. Chiappetta, *Principles of Financial Accounting* (New York: McGraw-Hill/Irwin, 2005), p. 471.

3. The unanimous written consent of all partners (limited and general).
4. The withdrawal of the general partner (unless the certificate establishes that other general partners will continue).
5. An act of the court.

If the limited partnership is dissolved, the limited partnership's assets are distributed in the same format as described earlier in this chapter (i.e., payment to third-party creditors, payment to partners who have loaned the partnership money, payment to the partners according to their investments in the partnership, and payment to the partners on the basis of their shares of the profits).

Limited Liability Companies

Limited partnerships are a form of business that have been around for a number of years, but there is a relatively new form of business referred to as a *limited liability company (LLC)*. An LLC is similar to a limited partnership insofar as each member has limited liability dependent on the investment he makes, while still receiving the tax breaks that are often afforded to those in a partnership. Similar to the limited partnership, the LLC is created based on an agreement between members. Each member also gets a say in the management of the company, whereas in a limited partnership only the general partners get to make management decisions.

However, because LLCs are new, the Uniform Limited Liability Company Act that has been drafted to govern them has not been accepted by many states. Until a uniform system is adopted, one should check the laws with regard to LLCs in each state to ensure that the liabilities, as well as rights and duties, of a company established in one state continue to apply when conducting business outside that state.

CASE OPENER WRAP-UP

First Interstate Bank

Spence Clark was the general partner of several limited partnerships maintained by the First Interstate Bank of Utah. As the general partner, Clark was in charge of all partnership accounts. As we've discussed, terminating a partnership involves two steps: dissolution of the partnership according to the terms set forth in the partnership agreement and winding up the business. In this case, the terms of the agreement involved the "immediate dissolution and liquidation of the partnership" when the real property was sold.

As limited partners, the plaintiffs in this case could not prevent the loss of funds that Clark had been diverting through the bank. As the appellate court ruled, since this case involved a limited partnership, the general partner had the ability to make all managerial decisions. Choosing to invest in other potentially more profitable businesses is qualified as a managerial decision. Hence, there was no reason to hold the bank liable for allowing Clark to divert funds.

Summary

Termination of the Partnership Termination begins when a partnership dissolves. Once the partnership has been dissolved and the assets have been liquidated and distributed, the partnership has been terminated.

Dissolution of the Business *Dissolution* refers to the ceasing of a partnership. Acts of partners, the operation of the law, and acts of the court can serve to rightfully dissolve a partnership.

Consequences of Dissolution A partner who wishes to dissolve or withdraw from the partnership must give notice of his intent. Third parties are usually contacted promptly about a dissolving partner to prevent the creation of additional liability for the partnership.

Winding Up the Business *Winding up* is the activity of completing unfinished partnership business, collecting and paying debts, collecting partnership assets, and taking inventory.

Limited Partnerships The limited partnership involves an agreement between at least one general partner and at least one limited partner. This partnership permits investors to share in the profits of a partnership, yet it limits these limited partners' liability to the amount they invest in the business.

Limited Liability Companies An LLC is formed by an agreement between members, and each member has limited liability dependent on the investment he makes, while still receiving the tax breaks that are often afforded to those in a partnership. In addition, each member also gets a say in the management of the company.

Point / Counterpoint

Should a Partnership Be Allowed to Expel a Partner on the Basis of Illegal Personal Conduct Unrelated to the Terms of the Partnership Agreement?

Yes	No
A partnership should be able to expel a partner on the basis of illegal personal conduct even when the illegal conduct isn't specified in the partnership agreement. It would be nearly impossible to create a partnership agreement that dictated every possible situation	If a partner participates in an illegal activity unrelated to the partnership agreement, the partnership should not be allowed to expel the individual based on his or her involvement in the illegal activity. The partners had the opportunity when formulating the partnership agreement to include a stipulation

that would allow for dissolution of the partnership. Individuals are always expected to conduct themselves within the bounds of national, state, and local laws. Any illegal behavior should have implications for the partnership as an ongoing business enterprise.

A partner's personal behavior affects the entire partnership and associated business in many different ways. A partner's behavior outside the business atmosphere can damage the reputation of the company. For example, if one partner of a five-partner law firm is arrested for smoking marijuana, clients would associate this marijuana-smoking partner with the entire firm. Clients may first begin to question the single partner's priorities and ethical beliefs: If he participates in this illegal activity, in which other illegal activities does he partake? Does he keep faulty books? Will I be overcharged?

Next, clients (his clients and the other attorneys' clients) begin to question the firm as a whole for allowing a man who partakes in illegal activities to remain a partner in the firm. Do all the attorneys participate in illegal activities?

While a partner may suffer personal legal consequences for his actions, the whole partnership suffers when one partner makes a poor personal choice. Therefore, the partnership should be able to decide the consequences.

for the dissolution of the partnership if a partner engaged in illegal activity.

If the agreement did not specify the relevant illegal activities, an individual is not aware of the potential impact of her actions on her status as a partner. Had she known the possible consequences regarding her participation in the partnership, she might have acted differently. However, because the restrictions were not articulated in the partnership agreement, she cannot be expected to abide by restrictions that were not stated in the first place.

The logic behind dissolving the partnership based on an unrelated activity is faulty. Is it logical to revoke an individual's driver's license because she looked at pornography in a state where such an activity is illegal? Additionally, an individual can make a poor personal choice and still be capable of performing her expected duties. A rule allowing partnerships to expel a partner based on unrelated illegal activity could be easily abused. Partnerships that want to expel a partner for other reasons (inconvenience, additional profit, etc.) could easily say she participated in illegal activity and expel her from the partnership based on that reason alone. A partner should not be expelled from partnerships because she participates in unrelated criminal activity. The partner already suffers personal legal consequences and should not experience additional penalties for an activity that has no impact on the partnership.

Questions & Problems

1. What stages must occur for the termination of a partnership to be complete?
2. Name at least five circumstances that can dissolve a partnership.
3. What rights does a partner who wrongfully dissolves a partnership retain?
4. Why is the partnership's debt particularly important in the winding-up stage?
5. What are the advantages of being a limited partner rather than a general partner?
6. As a limited partner, a business associate of yours feels confident of limited liability. What error might he be making?
7. Jones and Hardy entered into an oral partnership agreement. They planned to develop and lease certain areas of land. Together, they formed the Bloomington Knolls Association. Jones and Hardy began to experience financial problems, and they brought in a third partner, Jackson, to arrange for additional financing for the project. Jones subsequently dissolved the partnership and requested that he be given a portion of the

land as his share of partnership assets. Jackson and Hardy did not honor his request, and Jones never received any assets of the partnership. Jones moved for an accounting and winding up of partnership affairs and brought the case to court. The district court entered judgment against Hardy and Jackson, jointly and severally, for an amount representative of Jones's interest in the partnership. Jackson and Hardy appealed the district court's decision. How do you think the court decided? [*MacKay v. Hardy,* 896 P.2d 626 (1995).]

8. Attorneys Schrempp, Salerno, and Gross formed a partnership. The partnership agreement stated that a withdrawing partner must forfeit "his interest in all work in process, clients of the partnership, client files, and papers, books, and records relating to Partnership clients." The partnership of Schrempp, Salerno, and Gross worked with another partnership, Byam & Byam, on a personal injury case involving Jones. The firms agreed to split any profits from the case evenly. Gross left the firm, but the partners agreed that he should continue to work on the case. After the parties in the Jones case settled, Gross refused to share the attorney fees with the partners. Gross also took another file with him when he left, and he also refused to share the fees from that case with his former partners. Schrempp, Salerno, and Gross brought the case to court. Do you think the court decided in favor of Schrempp, Salerno, and Gross. Did Gross have a fiduciary duty to share the attorney fees with his former partners? [*Schrempp and Salerno v. Gross,* 529 N.W.2d 764 (1995).]

9. Cider Mills, a limited partnership, was continued after the dissolution date for purposes of winding up. The partnership had entered into a contract for the sale of land three months prior to its dissolution date. The property was sold after the dissolution date. The parties disagreed as to the order in which payments would be made following the dissolution of the partnership. The limited partners argued that they should share in the profits from the sale. The court determined that the order of payment should be creditors, limited partners, general partners. Anthony Pappas, a limited partner, objected to the court's decision regarding the distribution of partnership assets. Do you think the court's decision was reversed on appeal? Why or why not. [*Pappas v. Arfaras,* 20 F. Supp. 2d 372 (1998).]

10. Stephen Wainger is a former partner of the law firm, Glasser & Glasser. According to the partnership agreement, a withdrawing partner is entitled to compensation for "any undivided profits of the firm with respect to uncollected fees which were fully earned by the firm prior to the effective date of his withdrawal, but which fees are received by the firm subsequent to such date." Prior to leaving the firm, Wainger worked on several asbestos compensation cases. After he left the partnership, the cases were settled and the firm received significant profits. Wainger argued that he should be compensated for his work despite the fact that he left the firm prior to the settlement of the cases. Do you agree? The trial court found that Wainger was entitled only to fees that had been fully earned at the time of his withdrawal. How do you think the court decided the case on appeal? [*Wainger v. Glasser & Glasser,* 462 S.E.2d 62 (1995).]

11. Richard H. Pettingell and Joseph A. Regan withdrew as partners from the Boston law firm of Morrison, Mahoney, & Miller. They brought an action to receive funds that they believed were due to them for voluntarily withdrawing from the firm. Pettingell and Regan left the partnership to establish a new, competing firm. The partnership agreement states that if a partner voluntarily withdraws from the firm and "engages in any activities which are in competition with the then-current activities of the firm, he shall forfeit all of the benefits" that would be received if the employee were to voluntarily withdraw. There was no evidence to indicate that the establishment of the new firm had seriously affected the original firm. Pettingell and Regan disagreed with the forfeiture provision of the partnership agreement. How do you think the court decided? [*Pettingell v. Morrison, Mahoney, & Miller,* 687 N.E.2d 1237 (1997).]

12. Kanawha Trace Development Partners (KTDP) was a limited partnership formed to develop a condominium project. The initial limited partners, Rawn and Thornton, each owned a 25 percent interest in the partnership. William B. Sloan Companies entered into a contract with KTDP to do construction work on the condominiums. KTDP subsequently filed for bankruptcy and did not pay Sloan for the construction work. Sloan successfully sued the partnership, but he also brought an action to impose personal liability on Thornton. According to Sloan, Thornton actively participated in the control of the business. Was Thornton's alleged active participation enough to make him personally liable for KTDP's debts? Why or why not? [*Sloan v. Thornton,* 457 S.E.2d 60 (1995).]
13. Astroline Company, a limited partnership, is in the investment business. Astroline heard of an opportunity to purchase the license to a television station, and the company developed a second limited partnership, Astroline Communications Company, to purchase the station. Astroline provided the funding for Astroline Communications Company but remained a limited partner of the company. Astroline Communications Company began to experience financial problems and filed for bankruptcy. Do you think the court found Astroline Company, as a limited partner, liable for Astroline Communications Company's debts? Why or why not? [*In re Astroline Communications Company Limited Partnership,* 188 BR 98 (1995).]
14. Mige Associates, a limited partnership, owned an apartment building. The building could have been developed into a housing cooperative. The projected profits for such a conversion were significant. The conversion required the signed agreement of one of Mige's general partners, Jon Meadow. Meadow's decision to sign the agreement was contingent on the promise that he receive more money from the deal than the other partners. After his request was denied, Meadow refused to sign the agreement. Two of the limited partners, Drucker and Schaffer, filed suit against Meadow. They claimed that he had breached his fiduciary responsibility to the general and limited partners of Mige Associates. The trial court found in favor of Meadow. How do you think the case was decided on appeal? Did the economic benefits of the conversion create a fiduciary obligation for Meadow to sign the agreement? [*Drucker v. Mige Associates,* 639 N.Y.S.2d 365 (1996).]
15. After the dissolution of a partnership formed to develop the Four Seasons Resort, TSA International Limited brought an action against Shimizu Corporation, alleging breach of fiduciary duty. TSA had approached Shimizu in 1986 with plans for developing the hotel. The two companies formed a partnership, and they began to make plans for several golf and hotel developments. The loans TSA and Shimizu had taken out soon became delinquent. The partners met to negotiate the payment of the hotel and golf course loans. At the request of Shimizu, the agreements were drafted in Japanese. TSA subsequently filed a complaint asserting, among other things, breach of fiduciary duty. When reaching the agreements, Shimizu had discouraged TSA from hiring its own accountants or legal counsel because of "the long-term relationship of trust between Shimizu and TSA." TSA also alleged that Shimizu arranged the agreement so that substantial tax advantages would be obtained. The circuit court found in favor of Shimizu. How do you think the case was decided on appeal? Did Shimizu breach its fiduciary duty? [*TSA Intern. Ltd. v. Shimizu Corp.,* 990 P.2d 713 (1999).]

16. The Silver Queen Limited Partnership consisted of four limited partners. The partnership bought the Silver Queen Motel from the Fabry Partnership. After two years, the limited partnership defaulted on a note it had acquired to enable the purchase of the motel. Fabry took over the motel and sued the individual limited partners for the amount owed. Fabry's argument was that the limited partnership was improperly formed in that registration occurred after the purchase of the motel. Will the limited partners receive the protection from liability that they seek? [*Fabry Partnership v. Christensen,* 794 P.2d 719 (Sup. Ct. Nev. 1990).]

17. Sims and Gilroy entered into negotiations for the construction of an office building. They established the limited partnership Gilroy, Sims & Associates, Ltd., with other interested investors. Sims and Gilroy served as general partners, and Green and Murphy served as limited partners. In reference to their title as limited partners, the partnership agreement stated, "The reference to them as Limited Partners shall not be taken to imply that they are not in fact liable as general partners." Green and Murphy took part in the day-to-day business operations of the partnership. The partnership obtained a loan of $11,500,000 in return for a promissory note executed by the partnership. The firm stopped making payments and defaulted on the loan. American National Insurance Co. filed an action to recover the money due. Green and Murphy argued that they cannot be held liable because they were limited partners. Do you agree with them? Why or why not? [*American National Insurance Co. v. Gilroy, Sims & Associates, Ltd.,* 874 F. Supp. 971 (1995).]

18. North Port Golf Associates (NPGA) is a limited partnership involved in real estate and golf course development. NPGA contacted the Palmer Course Design Company (PCDC) and the Arnold Palmer Golf Management Company (APGMC) to design and manage two championship golf courses. As part of the agreement, NPGA was prohibited from using Arnold Palmer's name to promote any other business. A disclaimer was placed on the official investment summary brochure of NPGA stating, "As described herein, golf course design and management services will be provided to the partnership by PCDC and APGMC, respectively. Neither of these companies, nor Arnold Palmer, is affiliated with the partnership or general partners." PCDC completed the design of the golf course, but APGMC terminated its contract after NPGA refused to pay. After the failure of the project, NPGA alleged that Arnold Palmer, APGMC, and PCDC were partners by estoppel and were partially responsible for the interests of the limited partnership. Do you think the court agreed with NPGA? Why or why not? [*Binkley v. Palmer,* 10 S.W.3d 166 (Mo. App. 1999).]

19. Elizabeth Evans established the Nashayte Associates Limited Partnership. Evans owned 70 acres of land, and she conveyed the property to the partnership. Along with Evans, the general partners included her four children, John Wagley, Elizabeth Danforth, Melinda Geddes, and Galen Beale. After Evans died, Danforth, Geddes, and Beale wanted to sell the property. The partnership agreement stated, "In the event more than one person is a General Partner, the rights and powers of the General Partners shall be exercised in such manner as all General Partners may agree in writing." Wagley did not want to sell the property, and he argued that the partnership agreement, which was signed by all parties, required unanimity. The trial court found in favor of Danforth, Geddes, and Beale. Wagley appealed the decision. Did each of the general partners have to agree to the sale of the property? Why or why not? [*Wagley v. Danforth,* 702 N.E.2d 822 (1998).]

20. Northampton fulfilled a contract obligation by installing a sewer system on land owned by Horne-Lang, a limited partnership with 18 limited partners. Horne-Lang

was unable to pay for the work. Northampton claimed that the 18 partners were actually general partners and were personally liable for the contract. What facts would have led the court to hold that the limited partners were indeed liable to Northampton? [*Northampton Valley Constructors, Inc. v. Horne-Lang Associates,* 456 A.2d 1077 (1983).]

Looking for more review material?

The Online Learning Center at **www.mhhe.com/kubasek1e** contains this chapter's "Assignment on the Internet" and also a list of URLs for more information, entitled "On the Internet." Find both of them in the Student Center portion of the OLC, along with quizzes and other helpful materials.

Corporations: Formation and Financing

CASE OPENER

The Formation of Goodyear Tire & Rubber Company

The Goodyear Tire & Rubber Company is the world's largest tire manufacturer, generating net sales of almost $20 billion in 2006. Named after Charles Goodyear, the broke inventor of vulcanized rubber, Goodyear Tire incorporated in 1898, largely through the efforts of promoters and subscribers. As a corporation, Goodyear Tire is an "artificial person," a status with legal ramifications for both the corporate entity and its owners.

1. What are the legal implications of Goodyear's status as a corporation?
2. How do corporations form? What factors should be considered by a businessperson interested in forming a corporation?

The Wrap-Up at the end of the chapter will answer these questions.

CHAPTER 38

Learning Objectives

After reading this chapter, you will be able to answer the following questions:

1. What are the characteristics of corporations?
2. What are the powers granted to corporations by the states?
3. How are corporations classified?
4. How are corporations formed?
5. What are some potential problems with the formation of corporations?
6. How do corporations get funding?

This chapter explains the steps necessary to establish a corporate entity. Although state law generally governs corporations and each state has its own corporate regulatory statutes, the Revised Model Business Corporation Act (RMBCA) is the basis of most state statutes. More than 25 states have adopted at least part of RMBCA. This chapter refers to specific RMBCA guidelines, but remember that not all states follow these guidelines.

The first section of the chapter examines characteristics of corporations. The chapter then explains corporations' powers. The third section describes different classifications of corporations. Next, the chapter explains the process of corporate formation. The fifth section considers problems associated with corporate formation, and the final section explains corporate financing.

Characteristics of Corporations

How are corporations different from other forms of business organization? We addressed some of their characteristics in Chapter 35. Let's now take a closer look.

LEGAL ENTITY

In American law, corporations are legal entities. In other words, corporations exist separately from their shareholders. Thus, corporations can sue or be sued by others.

RIGHTS AS A PERSON AND A CITIZEN

Courts consider corporations to be "legal persons." Thus, in most cases, corporations, like natural persons, have certain rights according to the Bill of Rights. Specifically, the Fifth and Fourteenth Amendments state that government cannot deprive any "person" of life, liberty, or property without due process. Courts have held that corporations are "persons" in this case and thus have a right to due process. Furthermore, courts consider corporations to be persons with respect to the Fourth Amendment. Hence, the Fourth Amendment protects corporations from unreasonable searches and seizures. Finally, courts consider corporations to be persons that have free speech rights protected by the First Amendment. As Chapter 5 explained, however, the First Amendment protects corporate commercial speech to a lesser degree than corporate political speech.

CREATURE OF THE STATE

State incorporation statutes establish the requirements for corporate formation. Each individual corporation's charter creates a contract between that corporation and the state.

LIMITED LIABILITY

Because corporations are legal entities separate from their shareholders, corporations assume liability for corporate actions. Shareholders' liability, therefore, is limited to their investment in the corporation. For example, in 1977 Big O Tire Dealers sued Goodyear Tire & Rubber Company. Big O Tire accused Goodyear of copying its Bigfoot trademark on new tires. The court agreed and awarded Big O Tire several million dollars in damages. The Goodyear corporation, and not individual Goodyear shareholders, paid the damages. Although payment of damages to Big O Tire may have reduced the dividends shareholders received, the court did not hold the shareholders individually liable for any portion of the award.

FREE TRANSFERABILITY OF CORPORATE SHARES

Generally, shareholders can freely transfer their corporate shares. For example, shareholders can sell their shares or give them to charity.

connecting to the core

Finance

The separation of ownership and management in corporations raises a very important issue, namely, whether managers act in the interests of shareholders. Although shareholders own a corporation, a board of directors is responsible for hiring managers who will pursue the interests of shareholders. Remember from your finance class that there are several reasons that managers generally act in shareholders' interests. First, a corporation's financial performance may directly affect managers' compensation, in the sense that managers may have stock options whereby they can purchase company stock at a discounted price. Hence, these options become more attractive to managers when their company's stock increases in value. A second reason that managers generally act in the interests of shareholders relates to promotional opportunities for managers. As a general rule, managers who meet shareholders' goals will be better prospects for upper-management positions. A third reason is that stockholders control a corporation by electing a board of directors, which hires and fires managers. If managers (or even a CEO) are unsuccessful in meeting shareholders' goals, the shareholders may elect to oust the underachieving managers. Although there may be periods when management's goals do not align with shareholders' goals, managers generally act in shareholders' interests.

Source: S. Ross, R. W. Westerfield, and B. D. Jordan, *Fundamentals of Corporate Finance* (New York: McGraw-Hill/Irwin, 2006), pp. 12–13.

PERPETUAL EXISTENCE

The life of a corporation does not end when the lives of its constituents end. If shareholders die, corporations do not dissolve. Similarly, if corporate directors or officers withdraw or die, the corporation continues to exist. In some cases, the **articles of incorporation,** a document a corporation files with the state explaining its organization, may include a restriction on the duration of the corporation. Otherwise, in most states, corporations continue to exist indefinitely.

A small number of states, however, set a maximum length of existence for corporations. After the maximum duration expires, corporations must formally renew their corporate existence.

CENTRALIZED MANAGEMENT

Unless the articles of incorporation specify otherwise, shareholders do not participate in corporate management. Instead, shareholders elect a board of directors. The board in turn selects officers to manage the day-to-day business of the corporation.

CORPORATE TAXATION

Because corporations are separate legal entities, government taxes their income directly (S corporations are an exception; this chapter discusses them, and their tax advantages, in more detail later). Corporations must pay federal and state taxes on their income.

Corporations, however, have control over their income. Corporations can distribute their income to shareholders in the form of **dividends,** although they do not receive tax deductions for distributing these dividends. When corporations distribute income to shareholders, the shareholders pay taxes on that income. In that the corporation pays income taxes and the shareholders are also paying taxes on their dividends, the dividends are subjected to double taxation, thus creating a disadvantage for corporations. Alternatively, corporations can keep profits, or **retained earnings,** to reinvest. Corporations' investment of retained earnings can lead to higher stock prices, thus benefiting shareholders when they sell their stock.

Exhibit 38-1 Summary of Characteristics of Corporations

1. Separate legal entity.
2. Status as "legal person" and "citizen."
3. Creature of the state.
4. Limited liability of shareholders.
5. Free transferability of corporate shares.
6. Perpetual existence.
7. Centralized management separate from owners.
8. Unique taxation method.
9. Corporate liability for torts and crimes of agents.

LIABILITY FOR OFFICERS AND EMPLOYEES

Because the relationship between corporations and their directors, officers, and employees is an agency relationship, corporations are liable for torts and crimes committed by their agents during the scope of their employment. Courts refer to this liability as the doctrine of *respondeat superior* (Latin for "let the master answer"). Although in the past courts were reluctant to impose criminal liability on corporations, prosecutions today are much more common. Chapter 7, "Crime and the Business Community," discusses corporate sentencing guidelines and punishment.

Exhibit 38-1 presents a summary of nine characteristics of corporations.

Corporate Powers

Because corporations are creatures of the state, they have only those powers states grant them. States give powers to corporations through state incorporation statutes and through each corporation's articles of incorporation.

EXPRESS AND IMPLIED POWERS

State incorporation statutes typically grant the following express powers to corporations: the power to perpetual existence; the power to sue and be sued in the corporation's name; the power to acquire property; the power to make contracts and borrow money; the power to lend money; the power to make charitable donations; and the power to establish rules for managing the corporation. Additionally, corporations may take whatever actions are necessary to execute these express powers. Thus, corporations have implied powers. Generally, the statement of corporate purpose in each corporation's articles of incorporation gives each corporation its implied powers.

ULTRA VIRES ACT

If corporations act beyond their express and implied powers, the act is called an *ultra vires* (Latin for "beyond powers") act. Corporations commit *ultra vires* acts most frequently when they create contracts outside the scope of their powers.

Today, most state incorporation statutes permit businesses to incorporate for any lawful purpose, and thus most articles of corporation do not limit corporate powers. Hence, the doctrine of *ultra vires* is much less significant today than it was in the past because very few corporate acts qualify as *ultra vires.*

Historically, courts have ruled that *ultra vires* acts are null and void. More recently, however, courts have permitted corporations to use the *ultra vires* defense if neither party to the contract has performed the terms of the contract. Yet courts uphold *ultra vires* contracts if one of the parties has executed her or his part of the contract.

For example, suppose a timber corporation's articles of incorporation specified that the corporation's purpose was to harvest and sell timber. Suppose further that the directors of the corporation entered into an *ultra vires* contract with a machinery company to purchase machines to mine coal on the corporation's cleared land. As long as the machinery company has not delivered the machinery to the timber corporation, courts will hold the contract null and void. If, however, the machinery company has delivered the machinery to the timber corporation, courts will uphold the *ultra vires* contract and require that the timber corporation fulfill the terms of the contract. Can you see which party, by upholding the *ultra vires* contract in this situation, the court is trying to protect?

If a corporation commits an *ultra vires* act, RMBCA provides several remedies:

1. Shareholders may sue to prohibit the corporation from fulfilling the *ultra vires* contract.
2. The corporation or shareholders may sue corporate directors or officers for the damages caused by the *ultra vires* act.
3. The state attorney general can have the corporation dissolved or prevent the corporation from fulfilling the *ultra vires* contract.

In Case 38-1, the California appellate court considered whether a corporation's political contribution constituted an *ultra vires* act.

CASE 38-1

GIULIO MARSILI ET AL. v. PACIFIC GAS AND ELECTRIC COMPANY ET AL.

COURT OF APPEAL OF CALIFORNIA, FIRST APPELLATE DISTRICT
51 CAL. APP. 3D 313 (1975)

Giulio Marsili and three other defendants brought suit against Pacific Gas and Electric Company (PGE), challenging a $10,000 contribution that Pacific Gas made to Citizens for San Francisco. Citizens for San Francisco advocated the defeat of Proposition T, a proposal to prohibit construction of any building taller than 72 feet high in San Francisco without the approval of voters. Marsili argued that the contribution was an ultra vires *act; consequently, the $10,000 should be returned to the corporation. The trial court ruled in favor of Pacific Gas. Marsili appealed.*

JUDGE KANE: Appellants contend that the contribution in question was *ultra vires* "because neither PGE's articles of incorporation nor the laws of this state permit PGE to make political donations. . . ." We disagree.

By definition adopted by appellants themselves, "*ultra vires*" refers to an act which is beyond the powers conferred upon a corporation by its charter or by the laws of the state of incorporation.

The parties are in agreement that the powers conferred upon a corporation include both express powers, granted by charter or statute, and implied powers to do acts reasonably necessary to carry out the express powers. In California, the express powers which a corporation enjoys include the power to "do any acts incidental to the transaction of its business . . . or expedient for the attainment of its corporate purposes."

The articles of PGE are manifestly consistent with this statutory imprimatur [mark of approval]. Thus, for example, they authorize all activities and endeavors incidental or useful to the manufacturing, buying, selling and distributing of gas and electric power, including the construction of buildings and other facilities convenient to the achievement of its corporate purposes, and the performance of "all things whatsoever that shall be necessary or proper for the full and complete execution of the purposes for which . . . [the] corporation is formed, and for the exercise and enjoyment of all its powers and franchises."

In addition to the exercise of such express powers, the generally recognized rule is that the management of a corporation, "in the absence of express restrictions, has discretionary authority to enter into contracts and transactions which may be deemed reasonably incidental to its business purposes." In short, "a corporation has authority to do what will legitimately tend to effectuate . . . [its] express purposes and objects. . . ." California is in accord with this general rule also: "Whatever transactions are fairly incidental or auxiliary to the main business of the corporation and necessary or expedient in the protection, care and management of its property may be undertaken by the corporation and be within the scope of its incorporated powers."

No restriction appears in the articles of PGE which would limit the authority of its board of directors to act upon initiative or referendum proposals affecting the affairs of the company or to engage in activities related to any other legislative or political matter in which the corporation has a legitimate concern. Furthermore, there are no statutory prohibitions in California which preclude a corporation from participating in any type of political activity. In these circumstances, the contribution by PGE to Citizens for San Francisco was proper if it can fairly be said to fall within the express or implied powers of the corporation.

The crux of the controversy at bench, therefore, is whether a contribution toward the defeat of a local ballot proposition can ever be said to be convenient or expedient to the achievement of legitimate corporate purposes. Appellants take the flat position that in the absence of express statutory authority corporate political contributions are illegal. This contention cannot be sustained. We believe that where, as here, the board of directors reasonably concludes that the adoption of a ballot proposition would have a direct, adverse effect upon the business of the corporation; the board of directors has abundant statutory and charter authority to oppose it.

AFFIRMED.

CRITICAL THINKING

Are there possible rival causes for why Pacific Gas contributed money to Citizens for San Francisco? How does the presence of the various causes influence your evaluation of the reasoning?

ETHICAL DECISION MAKING

While the court affirmed that PGE acted within the scope of its implied powers in contributing $10,000 to oppose Proposition T, do you think a kind of harm has been done to certain individuals? Who are the primary stakeholders at risk? Is the harm justified in this situation? Use the WPH framework from Chapter 2 to support your answer.

Classification of Corporations

Corporations can be classified as public or private; profit or nonprofit; domestic, foreign, or alien; publicly held or closely held; as an S corporation; or as a professional organization.

PUBLIC OR PRIVATE

A **public corporation** is a corporation created by government to help administer law. Thus, public corporations often have specific government duties to fulfill. The Federal Deposit Insurance Corporation (FDIC) is an example of a public corporation. Conversely, private persons create **private corporations** for private purposes. Private corporations do not have government duties.

PROFIT OR NONPROFIT

Most corporations are **for-profit corporations.** Thus, their objective is to operate for profit. Shareholders seeking to make a profit purchase the stock these corporations issue. This profit can take two forms. First, shareholders receive dividends from the corporation. Second, the market price of the stock can increase. Shareholders can then sell their stock at a higher price than the purchase price of the stock.

Nonprofit corporations may earn profits, but they do not distribute these profits to shareholders. In fact, nonprofit corporations do not have shareholders. More importantly, nonprofit corporations' objective is not to earn profit. They do not issue stock. Instead, nonprofit corporations provide services to their members (not shareholders). These corporations reinvest most of their profits in the business. Churches and charitable organizations are examples of nonprofit corporations.

DOMESTIC, FOREIGN, AND ALIEN CORPORATIONS

Every corporation is incorporated in a particular state. A corporation is a **domestic corporation** in the state in which it is incorporated. Many corporations, however, do businesses in more than one state. A corporation that does business in states other than the state in which it is incorporated must obtain a certificate of authority in each state in which it does business. A corporation is a **foreign corporation** in states in which it conducts business but is not incorporated. For example, the McDonald's Corporation is incorporated in Delaware but does business in all 50 states. Thus, McDonald's is a domestic corporation in Delaware and a foreign corporation in the other 49 states.

An **alien corporation** is a business incorporated in another country. Thus, if an American corporation wants to do business in Canada or Mexico, it is an alien corporation in those countries.

PUBLICLY HELD OR CLOSELY HELD

The stock of **publicly held corporations** is available to the public. Thus, if you wanted to invest in a corporation, you could purchase stock in a publicly held corporation. Most publicly held corporations have many shareholders, and managers of these corporations usually do not own large percentages of the corporation's stock. Shareholders wishing to sell their shares do not face many transfer restrictions.

In contrast, **closely held corporations** (also called *close, family,* or *privately held corporations*) generally do not offer stock to the general public. Shareholders are usually family members and friends who are often active in the business. Controlling shareholders typically manage closely held corporations. Because closely held corporations are often family businesses, they often maintain restrictions on the transfer of shares to prevent outsiders from obtaining control of the business. Although they account for only a small fraction of corporate assets and revenues, most U.S. corporations are closely held corporations. In fact, about 50 percent of all U.S. corporations are S corporations.

SUBCHAPTER S CORPORATION

Chapter 35 introduced **S corporations** (named after the subchapter of the Internal Revenue Code that provides for them), a particular type of closely held corporation. Government taxes S corporations differently from other corporations. Government taxes most corporations twice on their income: Corporations must pay income tax, and shareholders must pay taxes on dividends they receive. S corporations, however, enjoy the tax status of partnerships. Thus, shareholders of S corporations report their income from the corporation as personal income.

In addition to the avoidance of double taxation, S Corporations offer two more important tax advantages. First, shareholders in an S Corporation are allowed to deduct corporate losses from their personal income, ultimately lowering how much the shareholders have to pay in taxes. Second, depending on a shareholder's income, choosing to be an S corporation can result in the corporation's paying lower taxes. When the shareholder is part of a lower tax bracket than the bracket used for regular (that is, non-S) corporations, the entirety of the corporation's income is taxed at the shareholder's lower tax bracket. The lower tax bracket applies because of the relationship between the corporation and the personal income of the shareholders. The second advantage applies even if dividends are retained and not distributed.

To be classified as an S corporation, a corporation must meet certain requirements. First, it cannot have more than 100 shareholders. Second, only individuals, trusts, and (in certain circumstances) corporations can be shareholders (partnerships cannot be shareholders). Third, S corporations can issue only one class of shares, although not all shares must have identical voting rights. Fourth, all S corporations must be domestic corporations. Finally, no shareholder of an S corporation can be a nonresident alien.

PROFESSIONAL CORPORATIONS

If a group of dentists, doctors, or other professionals wants to practice as a corporation, all 50 states permit them to incorporate. Because of the nature of professional work, however, courts sometimes alter the liability associated with these corporations. For example, courts often impose personal liability on doctors in professional corporations for medical malpractice performed under their oversight.

Formation of the Corporation

The creation of a corporation involves two parts: general organizational activities and legal activities necessary for incorporation.

ORGANIZING AND PROMOTING THE CORPORATION

Two groups of important players are responsible for the organization of the corporation: promoters and subscribers. **Promoters** begin the corporate creation and organization process by arranging for necessary capital, financing, and licenses. Promoters raise capital for the infant corporation by making **subscription agreements** with **subscribers** (investors) in which the subscribers agree to purchase stock in the new corporation.

Promoters. Promoters have other organizational responsibilities besides making subscription agreements. For example, promoters prepare the corporation's incorporation papers. Promoters can also enter into contracts as needed to establish the new corporation. For example, promoters can purchase or lease buildings for the corporation. Frank Seiberling was the promoter who founded the Goodyear Tire & Rubber Company. In 1898, Seiberling purchased Goodyear's first plant in Akron, Ohio, with $3,500 borrowed from his brother-in-law. Seiberling also established Goodyear workers' hourly wages between 13 and 25 cents.

When problems with preincorporation contracts arise, courts generally hold promoters liable and rule that these contracts do not bind infant corporations. Courts usually hold that promoters are not agents of the infant corporation because promoters cannot serve as agents for a principal (the new corporation) that does not yet exist.

Once incorporated, however, corporations can accept or reject preincorporation agreements. Even so, if a corporation accepts a preincorporation agreement, courts usually still hold promoters liable for the contract.

In two cases, however, promoters are not personally liable for preincorporation contracts. A promoter can include a clause in the contract stating that the corporation's adoption of the contract terminates her liability. Alternatively, the corporation, the promoter, and the third party involved in the contract can enter into a novation. A **novation** occurs when parties to a contract agree to substitute a third party for one of the original two parties in the original contract, thus terminating the rights under the old contract.

In Case 38-2, the Colorado appellate court considered whether a promoter was liable for a preincorporation contract.

CASE 38-2 COOPERS & LYBRAND v. GARRY J. FOX

COURT OF APPEALS OF COLORADO, DIVISION FOUR
758 P.2D 683 (1988)

In November 1981, Garry Fox met with a representative of Coopers, a national accounting firm, to request a tax opinion and other accounting services. Fox told Coopers he was acting on behalf of G. Fox and Partners, Inc., a corporation he was in the process of forming. Coopers knew the corporation did not yet exist and accepted the agreement. G. Fox and Partners, Inc., incorporated in December 1981. When Coopers finished its work, it billed Fox $10,827. Neither Fox nor his corporation paid the bill. Coopers sued Fox personally, arguing that he was liable because he was the promoter. The trial court found that no agreement obligated Fox individually to pay the fee and found in favor of Fox. Coopers appealed.

JUDGE KELLY: As a preliminary matter, we reject Fox's argument that he was acting only as an agent for the future corporation. One cannot act as the agent of a nonexistent principal.

On the contrary, the uncontroverted facts place Fox squarely within the definition of a promoter. A promoter is one who, alone or with others, undertakes to form a corporation and to procure for it the rights, instrumentalities, and capital to enable it to conduct business.

When Fox first approached Coopers, he was in the process of forming G. Fox and Partners, Inc. He engaged Coopers' services for the future corporation's benefit. In addition, though not dispositive on the issue of his status as a promoter, Fox became the president, a director, and the principal shareholder of the corporation, which he funded, only nominally, with a $100 contribution. Under these circumstances, Fox cannot deny his role as a promoter.

Coopers asserts that the trial court erred in finding that Fox was under no obligation to pay Coopers' fee in the absence of an agreement that he would be personally liable. We agree.

As a general rule, promoters are personally liable for the contracts they make, though made on behalf of a corporation to be formed. The well-recognized exception to the general rule of promoter liability is that if the contracting party knows the corporation is not in existence but nevertheless agrees to look solely to the corporation and not to the promoter for payment, then the promoter incurs no personal liability. In the absence of an express agreement, the existence of an agreement to release the promoter from liability may be shown by circumstances making it reasonably certain that the parties intended to and did enter into the agreement.

Here, the trial court found there was no agreement, either express or implied, regarding Fox's liability. Thus, in the absence of an agreement releasing him from liability, Fox is liable.

Coopers also contends that the trial court erred in ruling, in effect, that Coopers had the burden of proving any agreement regarding Fox's personal liability for payment of the fee. We agree.

Release of the promoter depends on the intent of the parties. As the proponent of an alleged agreement to release the promoter from liability, the promoter has the burden of proving the release agreement.

Fox seeks to bring himself within the exception to the general rule of promoter liability. However, as the proponent of the exception, he must bear the burden of proving the existence of the alleged agreement releasing him from liability. The trial court found that there was no agreement regarding Fox's liability. Thus, Fox failed to sustain his burden of proof, and the trial court erred in granting judgment in his favor.

It is undisputed that the defendant, Garry J. Fox, engaged Coopers' services, that G. Fox and Partners, Inc., was not in existence at that time, that Coopers performed the work, and that the fee was reasonable. The only dispute, as the trial court found, is whether Garry Fox is liable for payment of the fee. We conclude that Fox is liable, as a matter of law, under the doctrine of promoter liability.

REVERSED.

CRITICAL THINKING

What is the court's reasoning in this case? Given that reasoning, what could Garry Fox have done differently, if anything, to avoid liability?

ETHICAL DECISION MAKING

The doctrine of promoter liability, like most other doctrines in business law, has ethical roots. Legal doctrines are trying to advance our achievement of particular values or, in the language of the WPH model, purposes. Try to discover the value emphasis underlying adherence to the doctrine of promoter liability.

Subscribers. Subscribers make offers to purchase stock in a corporation in the incorporation process. A subscriber becomes a shareholder once the corporation incorporates or accepts his purchase offer, whichever occurs first.

Courts interpret subscription agreements in two ways. In some states, courts see subscription agreements as continuing offers to buy stock in the corporation. Thus, in these situations, subscribers may revoke their offer at any time. In other states, courts view subscription agreements as contracts among various subscribers. These contracts cannot be revoked unless all subscribers consent. RMBCA states that subscribers cannot revoke subscription agreements for six months unless the agreements provide otherwise or unless all subscribers consent.

SELECTING A STATE FOR INCORPORATION

Next, an infant corporation must select a state in which to incorporate. Each state has different laws governing the incorporation process and different corporate tax rates. Other factors corporations consider when selecting a state for incorporation include the following:

- How much flexibility does the state grant to corporate management?
- What rights do state statutes give to shareholders?
- What restrictions does the state place on the distribution of dividends?
- Does the state offer any kind of protection against takeovers?

Although most corporations incorporate in the state in which they are located and do most of their business, more than half of all publicly held corporations, including more than half of the Fortune 500 companies, are incorporated in Delaware. Decades ago, Delaware law offered extremely low corporate tax rates and granted more extensive rights to management in the event of a takeover than other states. Thus, in the 1940s and 1950s, many corporations changed their state of incorporation to Delaware. Since then, other states have made their corporate laws more attractive to corporations. Many corporations remain incorporated in Delaware, however, because Delaware courts are highly experienced in issues surrounding corporate law.

Closely held corporations and professional corporations, however, almost always incorporate in the state in which most of their stockholders live.

Although a corporation can incorporate in only one state, it can file a certificate of authority to do business in other states. Some states fine corporations that fail to obtain a certificate of authority before conducting business in the state. Other states fine directors and officers of these corporations directly and hold them personally liable for contracts made in the state.

Once a corporation chooses a state for incorporation, it can begin the formal legal process of incorporation.

Legal Process of Incorporation

SELECTION OF CORPORATE NAME

All state incorporation statutes require that corporations indicate in the name of the corporation that the business is incorporated. Every corporation must attach *Corporation, Company, Limited,* or *Incorporated,* or an abbreviation of one of these terms, to the end of its business name. Additionally, corporations must distinguish their names from the names of all other domestic or foreign corporations licensed to do business within the state. This requirement protects third parties from confusion about similar names. Once the corporation has chosen a name, this name is subject to the approval of the state.

INCORPORATORS

An **incorporator** is an individual who applies to the state for incorporation on behalf of a corporation. RMBCA requires only one incorporator to incorporate a business, although it permits more. Although promoters frequently serve as incorporators, RMBCA does not require that incorporators be promoters or subscribers. In fact, RMBCA does not require that incorporators have an interest in the company. Generally, incorporators' only duty is to sign the articles of incorporation.

ARTICLES OF INCORPORATION

One of the most important elements of the corporate formation process is the *articles of incorporation,* a document providing basic information about the corporation. According to RMBCA, a corporation's articles of incorporation must include (1) the name of the corporation, (2) the address of the registered office, (3) the name of the registered agent (i.e., the specific person who receives legal documents on behalf of the corporation), and (4) the names and addresses of the incorporators.

Many articles of incorporation include several additional elements. For example, many articles include a clause describing the nature and purpose of the corporation. This statement of purpose grants the corporation power to engage in certain business activities.

global context

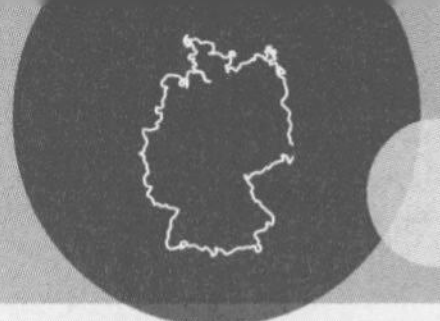

Corporate Structure in Germany

German law establishes three tiers of corporate power. The board is the lowest tier, management makes up the second tier, and the supervisory board is the top tier. The supervisory board is similar to a board of directors in an American corporation. The supervisors must approve managers' actions, including appointments, distribution of profits, and actions that affect the corporation's capital. Without the consent of the supervisors, managers are nearly powerless.

Managers enjoy considerable power, however, when dealing with third parties. As representatives of the corporation, managers can act on their own discretion. Supervisors cannot limit managerial powers with respect to third parties. Because supervisors cede considerable control of the corporation to managers in these situations, supervisors have the power to appoint managers who they feel will be reliable.

Although the board makes up the lowest tier of corporate power, it exercises considerable influence. Shareholders elect the board, a group of at least three members that acts as a mediator between shareholders and management. Because both managers and supervisors understand the importance of shareholders' interests, they listen to the board's recommendations.

Many articles also describe the corporate capital structure. For example, they authorize the corporation to issue a certain number of shares of stock.

The incorporators must execute and sign the articles of incorporation and file the document with the secretary of state, including the required filing fee, to legally form the corporation. Once the incorporators file the document, it governs the corporation. Next, the secretary of state usually issues a **certificate of incorporation,** a document certifying that the corporation is incorporated in the state and is authorized to conduct business.

FIRST ORGANIZATIONAL MEETING

After the secretary of state issues the certificate of incorporation, the shareholders meet to elect the corporate board of directors, pass corporate bylaws, and carry out other corporate business. In some cases, however, shareholders name the board of directors before the first organizational meeting and list the board members in the articles of incorporation. In these situations, the directors usually run the meeting.

At the first organizational meeting, shareholders adopt a set of corporate **bylaws,** or rules and regulations that govern the corporation's internal management. The articles of incorporation determine who has the power to amend the corporate bylaws after the first organizational meeting: shareholders, directors, or both.

Shareholders may also handle other corporate business at the first organizational meeting. For example, they may authorize the corporation to issue shares of stock and approve preincorporation contracts that promoters have made in the name of the corporation.

Potential Problems with Formation of the Corporation

Most businesses incorporate to enjoy limited liability or the perpetual existence of the corporation. Shareholders enjoy these benefits, however, only if the promoters and incorporator formally and correctly incorporate the business. If the incorporator or promoters make an error or omission during the incorporation process, courts may rule that the organization is not a corporation. In this case, the organization is a **defective corporation.** Shareholders may be personally liable for a defective corporation's actions.

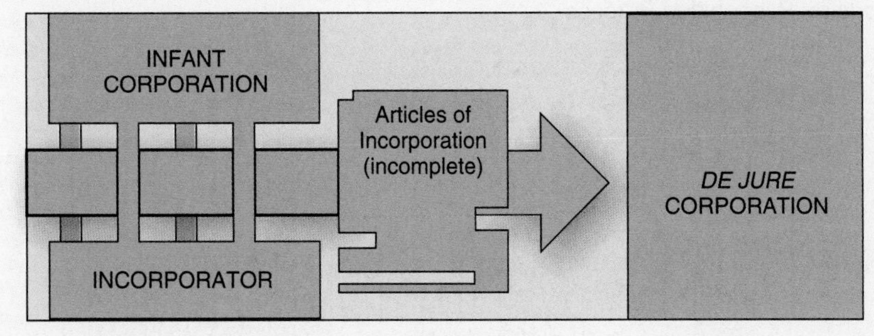

Figure 38-1
De Jure Corporation Formation

RESPONSES TO DEFECTIVE INCORPORATION

Suppose an incorporator incorrectly indicates the address of the corporate office in the articles of incorporation. Does the corporation still exist? Depending on the seriousness of the error, courts may disregard an error in the articles of incorporation by recognizing the corporation as a *de jure* or *de facto* corporation.

***De Jure* corporations.** A ***de jure* corporation** (literally, "a corporation from law," or a lawful corporation) has met the substantial elements of the incorporation process. A corporation that has received its certificate of incorporation has met the mandatory statutory provisions and is thus a *de jure* corporation. Courts usually hold that corporations that make minor errors in the incorporation process still enjoy *de jure* corporate status. Figure 38-1 illustrates the process for creating a *de jure* corporation.

Thus, even if the incorporator wrote the incorrect address of the corporate office in the articles of incorporation, courts would not revoke the corporation's limited liability. No party can question a *de jure* corporation's status as a corporate entity in court.

***De Facto* corporation.** Suppose, however, that the incorporator makes a more serious mistake or omission. For example, suppose the incorporator did not file the articles of incorporation with the secretary of state. In this case, courts may recognize the corporation as a ***de facto* corporation** (literally, "a corporation from the fact," or a corporation in fact). A *de facto* corporation has not substantially met the requirements of the state incorporation statute, but courts recognize it as a corporation for most purposes to avoid unfairness to third parties who believed it was properly incorporated. *De facto* corporations, regardless of whether the state has a general corporation statute, must meet the following requirements:

- The promoters, subscribers, and incorporator made a good faith attempt to comply with this incorporation statute.
- The organization has already conducted business as a corporation.

The process for recognizing a corporation as a *de facto* corporation is represented in Figure 38-2.

Only the state can challenge a *de facto* corporation's existence as a corporate entity in a suit called an action of *quo warranto* (Latin for "by what right").

Corporation by estoppel. Defective corporations cannot escape corporate entity status due to mistakes or omissions in their incorporation procedures. For example, suppose a corporation's articles of incorporation do not include the name of its registered agent. Suppose further that the corporation's directors, managers, and shareholders are unaware of the mistake. If the corporation conducts business with a third party who later sues for breach

Figure 38–2 *De Facto* Corporation Recognition Process

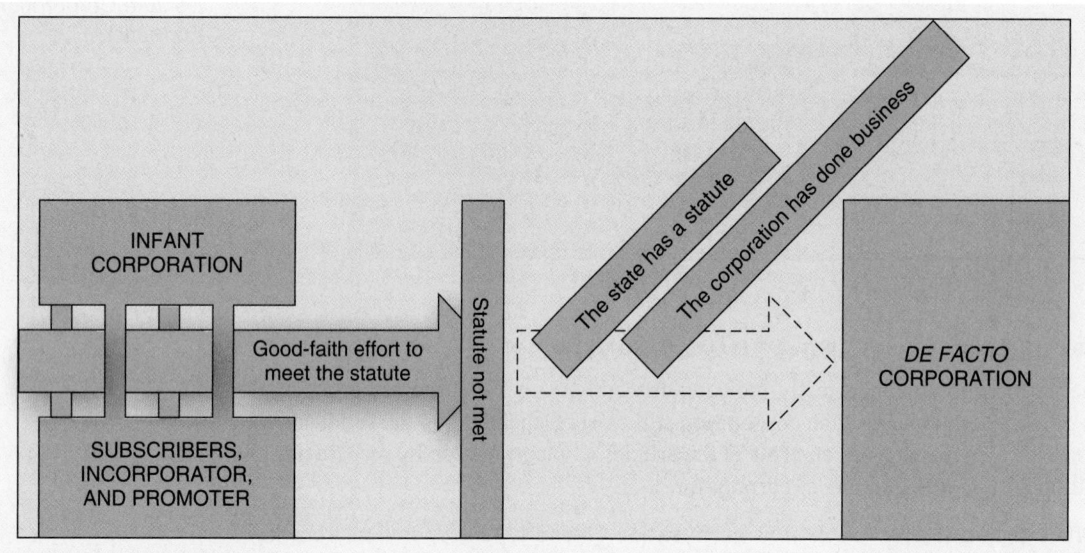

Case Nugget De Facto Incorporation

Pharmaceutical Sales and Consulting Corporation v. J.W.S. Delavaux Co.
District Court of New Jersey
59 F. Supp. 2d 398 (1999)

The plaintiff sued the defendant, alleging that the defendant failed to pay commissions due and owing to the plaintiff pursuant to a sales agreement between the parties. The sales agreement was signed by the plaintiff's president and on behalf of the plaintiff. The plaintiff had indicated that it was a corporation, but the defendant later discovered that the plaintiff was not a registered corporation. On learning that the plaintiff was not a corporation, the defendant filed its motion to dismiss the plaintiff's complaint.

The court denied the defendant's motion. The plaintiff maintained that the court should afford it *de facto* corporate status. The court disagreed and found that the plaintiff could not rely on the doctrine of *de facto* incorporation to demonstrate that it could sue the defendant for breach of the parties' agreement because the plaintiff had not made a bona fide attempt to incorporate before the plaintiff entered into the agreement with the defendant.

The defendant further maintained in this connection that the plaintiff's lack of corporate status as of the date of the parties' contract rendered the agreement invalid and unenforceable. The defendant relied on the absence of several documents that, in its view, were essential to any claim that PSCC had attained status as a *de facto* corporation.

of contract, the corporation cannot claim that it is not a corporate entity to escape liability. In such cases, courts hold that the corporation is a **corporation by estoppel;** thus, courts *estop* (bar) the corporation from denying its corporate status. Although a court ruling of corporation by estoppel prevents the business from denying corporate status, it does not remedy the error or grant the business corporate status for conducting future business.

If a corporation makes a significant error in the incorporation process and is not a *de jure* or *de facto* corporation, and corporation by estoppel does not apply to the situation, courts usually deny the organization corporate entity status. Thus, the organization does not enjoy limited shareholder liability.

Piercing the corporate veil. In some cases, courts will deny limited liability to a corporation that would normally have *de jure* or *de facto* status because shareholders have used the corporation to engage in illegal or wrongful acts. Shareholders attempt to hide behind the "corporate veil" of limited liability to protect themselves from personal liability. In these cases, courts *pierce the corporate veil,* or impose personal liability on shareholders. Shareholders of closely held and parent-subsidiary corporations frequently mix personal and corporate interests such that no separate corporate identity exists. Thus, courts often pierce the corporate veil of these corporations. Courts are likely to pierce the corporate veil when:

- A corporation lacked adequate capital when it initially formed.
- A corporation did not follow statutory mandates regarding corporate business.
- Shareholders' personal interests and corporate interests are commingled such that the corporation has no separate identity.
- Shareholders attempt to commit fraud through a corporation.

For example, corporations must keep corporate funds and records separate from shareholder funds and records. If a corporation does not carefully maintain these separate records, courts may pierce the corporate veil and impose personal liability on shareholders, as Case 38-3 illustrates.

CASE 38-3 J-MART JEWELRY OUTLETS, INC. v. STANDARD DESIGN

COURT OF APPEALS OF GEORGIA
218 GA. APP. 459 (1995)

Jim Halter, the major shareholder of J-Mart Jewelry Outlets, Inc., and several other corporations, was aware that J-Mart was in financial trouble. Before J-Mart went out of business, Halter paid off his personal credit cards using corporate funds. Halter also paid the corporation $1 for a corporate car purchased with corporation funding. Four of J-Mart's creditors brought suit against Halter in an attempt to recover corporate funds. The trial court jury pierced the corporate veil to hold Halter personally responsible for the debts. Halter appealed.

JUDGE BLACKBURN: The concept of piercing the corporate veil is applied in Georgia to remedy injustices which arise where a party has over extended his privilege in the use of a corporate entity in order to defeat justice, perpetrate fraud or to evade contractual or tort responsibility. Because the cardinal rule of corporate law is that a corporation possesses a legal existence separate and apart from that of its officers and shareholders, the mere operation of corporate business does not render one personally liable for corporate acts. Sole ownership of a corporation by one person or another corporation is not a factor, and neither is the fact that the sole owner uses and controls it to promote his ends. There must be evidence of abuse of the corporate form. Plaintiff must show that the defendant disregarded the separateness of legal entities by commingling on an interchangeable or joint basis or confusing the otherwise separate properties, records or control.

In deciding this enumeration of error, we are confronted with two maxims that sometimes conflict. On the one hand, we are mindful that great caution should be exercised by the court in disregarding the corporate entity. On the other, it is axiomatic that "when litigated, the issue of 'piercing the corporate veil' is for the jury[,]" unless there is no evidence sufficient to justify disregarding the corporate form. Our examination of the trial transcript convinces us that there is evidence in this case rising to such level.

Halter knew as early as late April but not later than June 1991 that J-Mart would have to cease operations as a result of its financial difficulties. There was direct evidence that the $6,902.87 balance on Halter's American Express personal account was paid by J-Mart on December 23, 1991, eight days before it ceased doing business. The check was marked "PAYMENT IN FULL: JIM'S PERSONAL[,]" indicating that a material question of fact existed as to whether Halter used corporate funds to pay a personal debt. The evidence also established that J-Mart, with knowledge that it would soon cease doing business, purchased a new Cadillac for Halter's use. It thereafter made three payments on the vehicle before transferring it to Halter for $1 and allowing him to assume the remaining payments, indicating the presence of further questions of material fact relative to a de facto unauthorized payment for Halter's personal benefit. In light of the evidence presented, the trial court properly denied the motion for a directed verdict upon the claim of Halter's personal liability for violation of the corporate form.

Evidence raising material questions of fact as to Halter's possible abuse of the corporate form were thus properly before the jury. On appeal, we construe all the evidence most strongly in support of the verdict, for that is what we must presume the jury did; and if there is evidence to sustain the verdict, we cannot disturb it. So viewing the evidence, we conclude that the jury's verdict was proper and must stand.

AFFIRMED.

CRITICAL THINKING

Given what you know of the facts of the case, is there any information Halter could have provided that would lead you to believe that he was not responsible for the debts? What would this information be?

ETHICAL DECISION MAKING

Describe the ethical conflict Halter was facing. For what purpose, or value, was he acting? Had Halter followed the Golden Rule, would he have chosen to act in the way he did? Given this information, what could have been done to convince Halter to refrain from using corporate funds to pay off his personal credit cards?

Corporate Financing

Corporations, like other businesses, need a source of funding. Corporations most commonly obtain financing by issuing and selling corporate securities: **debt securities** (bonds), which represent loans to a corporation, and **equity securities** (stocks), which represent ownership in a corporation.

DEBT SECURITIES

Debt securities, or bonds, represent loans to a corporation from another party. Bonds are usually long-term loans on which the corporation promises to pay interest. Bonds frequently list a maturity date on which the corporation must repay the face amount of the loan. Before the maturity date, however, corporations usually pay bond holders fixed-dollar interest payments on a scheduled basis. Hence, bonds are sometimes called *fixed-income securities.*

Corporations can issue the following types of bonds:

- *Unsecured bonds (debentures):* No assets support corporations' obligation to repay the face value of unsecured bonds.
- *Secured bonds (mortgage bonds):* Specific property supports corporations' obligation to repay secured bonds.
- *Income bonds:* A corporation pays interest on income bonds in proportion to its earnings.
- *Convertible bonds:* Convertible bonds allow shareholders to exchange their bonds for shares of company stock.
- *Callable bonds:* Callable bonds permit corporations to call in and repay the bonds at specific times.

EQUITY SECURITIES

Stocks and bonds are not identical. While bond owners have loaned money to a corporation, stock owners actually own part of a corporation. Thus, while bond owners have no voice in corporate management, stockholders own part of a corporation, so they have a voice in its control. Not all corporations issue bonds, but all corporations issue stock. Common stock and preferred stock are the two major types of stock.

Preferred stock. Owners of **preferred stock,** or *preferred shares,* enjoy preferences with respect to assets and dividends. Corporations often have several classes of preferred shares. Preferred stock shares many characteristics with bonds. For example, preferred stock owners usually receive a percentage of dividends associated with the face value of their preferred stock. Furthermore, corporations pay dividends to owners of preferred stock before they pay owners of common stock. Some corporations limit preferred stock owners' voting rights.

Many corporations have more than one type of preferred stock. For example, *cumulative preferred stock* requires that if a corporation cannot pay the required dividends in a given year, it must pay those dividends in the next year before it pays any common stock dividends. *Convertible preferred stock* allows its owner to convert her shares into common stock at any time. *Redeemable preferred stock* (also called *callable preferred stock*) permits the issuing corporation to buy back the shares from shareholders in certain circumstances. *Participating preferred stock* entitles its owner to both preferred stock dividends and, after the corporation has paid common stock dividends, additional dividends.

Common stock. Owners of **common stock,** or *common shares,* own a portion of a corporation but do not enjoy any preferences. A common stock owner is entitled to a portion of the corporation's dividends in proportion to the number of shares of common stock he owns. Common stock owners also have the right to vote in corporate elections. Each share is usually worth one vote in corporate elections. Thus, if you own 20,000 common shares of a corporation, you have 20,000 votes. In some cases, however, most notably the

global context

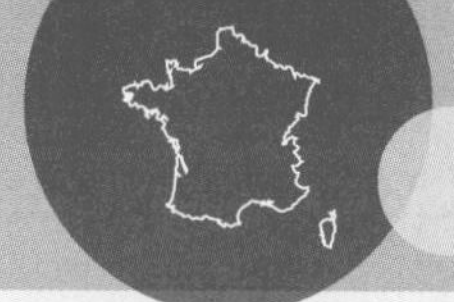

Company Law in France

French law categorizes companies into two types: Societe Anonymes (SA) or Societe Responsabilite Limitee (SARL). Several factors determine a company's category, including its relationship to shareholders, its management hierarchy, and the extent of its liabilities.

SA companies offer shares to the public. An SA company must have at least seven shareholders. SARL companies, on the other hand, sell shares exclusively to company members. They must have at least 2 but no more than 50 shareholders. Their shares are nonnegotiable and freely transferable among company members.

The managerial structure of SA companies differs from SARL companies' managerial structure. One managing director, together with as many as 14 subordinate directors, runs SA companies, and at least one of the directors must be a shareholder. SARL companies, in contrast, allow nonmembers to serve as managers. SARL companies generally have one or two managers. French law also requires that all SA companies appoint an independent auditor to verify the legality of their accounts. The auditor must report to the French government any irregularities she or he suspects to be criminal in nature. French law does not require that SARL companies appoint an auditor.

Member liability is closely related to the managerial structure of SA and SARL companies. Members of SARL companies are liable only to the extent of their contributions to the company. If the manager of a SARL company makes a transaction with a third party, all members are liable for the manager's action, regardless of whether she is a member of the company. Liability to third parties does not rest on all members in SA companies. Rather, in most cases the managing director is liable for damages caused by his actions, regardless of whether he benefited personally.

election of the board of directors, corporations use a method called *cumulative voting* to increase the influence of shareholders who own a small number of shares. The next chapter discusses cumulative voting in more detail.

Common stock owners have the lowest priority when a corporation distributes dividends. Creditors and preferred stock owners receive dividends first. Once a corporation pays these groups, however, common stock owners have a claim to the remainder of the corporate earnings.

CASE OPENER WRAP-UP

Goodyear

The actions of promoter Frank Seiberling were instrumental in forming the Goodyear Tire & Rubber Company. He purchased the first plant, organized Goodyear's finances, and completed the incorporation process. Since his contributions in 1898, Goodyear has developed into a multibillion-dollar corporation. Its corporate status allows Goodyear to enjoy perpetual existence; to sue and be sued; to acquire property; to make contracts; to borrow and lend money; to make charitable donations; and to establish rules for managing the corporation. Moreover, Goodyear's shareholders enjoy limited liability.

Summary

Characteristics of Corporations

Legal entity.

Rights as person and citizen.

Creature of the state.

Limited liability of shareholders.

Unrestricted transferability of corporate shares.

Perpetual existence.

Centralized management.

Corporate taxation.

Liability for corporate agents.

Corporate Powers

Corporations have both express and implied powers.

An *ultra vires* act is a corporate action beyond the scope of the corporation's authority.

Classification of Corporations

Public/private.

For profit/nonprofit.

Domestic/foreign/alien.

Publicly held/closely held.

S corporations.

Professional corporations.

Formation of the Corporation

Promoters organize corporate formation.

Subscribers offer to purchase stock in corporations in the formation process.

A state is selected for incorporation.

Legal Process of Incorporation

Selection of corporate name.

Drafting and filing articles of incorporation.

First organizational meeting.

Potential Problems with Formation of the Corporation

Remedies for defective incorporation:

- *De jure* corporations
- *De facto* corporations
- Corporations by estoppel
- Piercing the corporate veil

Corporate Financing

Debt securities

Equity securities:

- Preferred stock
- Common stock

Point / Counterpoint

Should Corporations Be Allowed the Status of "Legal Personhood" and Be Given Full Protection under the Bill of Rights as Persons?

Yes

On May 10, 1886, in the case of *Santa Clara County v. the Southern Pacific Railroad Company,* the Supreme Court clearly decided that "other corporations" deserved "equal protection of the laws," specifically the Fourteenth Amendment.

Several reasons support the position that corporations should be considered legal persons. A corporation is created by and is composed of natural persons. Actions on the corporation directly affect these natural persons associated with the corporation. The rights of the creators and shareholders cannot be violated, and violating the rights of the corporation indirectly violates the rights of the persons who created and are part of the corporation. Further, additional limitations should not be placed on a group of people simply because they have combined their efforts and formed a corporation.

Logical limitations are in place to restrict corporations' existence as "persons." Corporations cannot become official citizens and cannot vote. Even though the political system affects the corporation, the natural citizens involved with the corporation are expected to vote with the corporation's best interest in mind.

Finally, corporations deserve the same rights as natural persons because corporations fulfill the same obligations as natural persons as an entity separate from the natural persons associated with the corporation. For example, corporations pay government taxes on profits; the shareholders also pay taxes.

No

The Bill of Rights, including the Fourteenth Amendment, was created at a time when corporations clearly existed in the United States. However, a stipulation to include corporations *as a separate entity* was not included in the Bill of Rights. Clearly, the creators of the Bill of Rights were aware that corporations existed at the time. The corporations were not mentioned to have rights *independent of the natural persons associated with the corporations,* so the Bill of Rights was not designed to protect corporations as "legal persons."

Further, classifying corporations as "legal persons" and allowing them protection under the Bill of Rights, though advantageous for corporate interests, is harmful to human interests. For example, corporate money speaks much louder than one person's letter when influencing politicians.

If corporations are given rights as a natural person, the individuals making decisions behind the corporation are not held accountable to the larger world community. The corporation is punished for a poor decision rather than the individual who used poor judgment. When the corporation is punished rather than the individual who made the decision, the individual may not feel much, if any, of the consequences of his or her action.

Also, corporations should not be considered legal persons and protected as such because corporations do not face the same restrictions as a natural person. A natural person's life must end; however, a corporation is allowed perpetual existence.

Lastly, corporations do not face the same potential consequences as natural persons. A corporation cannot be sent to jail for its actions. A corporation cannot be rehabilitated and changed to become a profitable member of society if it breaks the law.

Questions & Problems

1. Name at least three characteristics that distinguish corporations from other forms of business organization.
2. How is an *ultra vires* act related to a corporation's powers?
3. How can one corporation be a domestic, foreign, and alien corporation at the same time?
4. Why might a corporation's status as a *de jure* corporation not guarantee that its shareholders are immune to personal liability?
5. Compare and contrast common stock and preferred stock.
6. Evaluate the following statement: "Promoters of a new corporation are not as important as subscribers."
7. Air India ordered 15,000 square meters of blue carpet from Pennsylvania Woven Carpet Mills (PWCM). Air India paid for the merchandise but never received it. Because PWCM was insolvent, Air India brought an action against its sole shareholder, president, and chief executive officer, Frank Pisano, to recover the funds. Pisano claimed that after the PWCM facility shut down, he lost all control of the facility and its contents. Air India alleged that Pisano falsely represented that the goods would be shipped on payment. Air India contended that he forwarded his own interests when neglecting to ship the carpet. Do you think the court was willing to pierce the corporate veil and hold Pisano personally responsible? Why or why not? [*Air India v. Pennsylvania Woven Carpet Mills, Inc.*, 978 F. Supp. 500 (1997).]
8. The Metacon Gun Club operated an outdoor shooting range adjacent to a river, a golf course, a riding stable, several private homes, and a state park. The Simsbury-Avon Preservation Society, a corporation composed of homeowners who live adjacent to the gun club, sued Metacon, alleging that the discharge of chromium, lead, lead shot, lead bullets, ammunition fragments, and ammunition wadding had contaminated groundwater. The members of the society depended on water resources in the vicinity of the gun club. Metacon argued that the society was not a corporation at the time it filed the suit because the state returned its paperwork several days later due to a missing address. Thus, Metacon argued, the society was not a legal entity and did not have standing to sue. How do you think the court ruled in this case? Why? [*Simsbury-Avon Pres. Soc'y, L.L.C. v. Metacon Gun Club, Inc.*, 2005 U.S. Dist. LEXIS 11699 (2005).]
9. Arthur Chesterton was the largest shareholder of the A.W. Chesterton Company, a family-owned S corporation. Frustrated by the difficulty of selling his shares, Chesterton planned to transfer a portion of his stock in the company to two shell corporations. Chesterton's proposed transfer, however, jeopardized the company's subchapter S status. According to its articles of organization, A.W. Chesterton Company had a right of first refusal if a shareholder seeks to transfer his or her shares to an individual outside the family. The company was suffering financial difficulties, however, and it was unable to purchase Chesterton's shares. The company nevertheless sued to enjoin Chesterton from transferring his stock out of the family. The district court held that the transfer violated Chesterton's fiduciary duty to the company. Chesterton appealed the court's decision. How do you think the appellate court ruled in this case? Why? [*A.W. Chesterton Company, Inc. v. Chesterton,* 128 F.3d 1 (1997).]
10. Attorney Nicholas Kepple, the president of M&K Realty, drew up a contract for the sale of a parcel of land (Lot 5) from Howard Engelsen to M&K. To establish a

purchase price for the sale, Engelsen had Lot 5 appraised. The appraisers based their appraisal of Lot 5 on several facts that Kepple and Engelsen learned were incorrect after they signed the contract. These facts included the total acreage of Lot 5 and whether Lot 5 could be divided into two separate lots without the need for a subdivision approval from the planning and zoning commissioner. After learning that these facts were in error, Kepple saw that the original purchase price was well below the market price for Lot 5, and he attempted to complete the sale for the original purchase price. Engelsen informed Kepple that he would not complete the sale of Lot 5 because M&K had never legally formed as a corporation under the state incorporation statutes and thus lacked the capacity to enter the contract in the first place. Do you think the court agreed with Engelsen's argument? Why or why not? [*BRJM LLC v. Output Systems, Inc., et al.,* 2005 Conn. Super. LEXIS 1699 (2005).]

11. The state of North Carolina suspended the corporate charter of Clary, Martin, McMullen & Associates, Inc., after the architectural firm failed to pay state franchise taxes. Before the state suspended CMMA's charter, Moodye Clary, CMMA's president and marketing director, negotiated an agreement with the Charles E. Torrence Company to provide graphic services for CMMA. Clary was unaware of the suspension of CMMA's charter during the negotiations with Torrence. When CMMA was unable to pay Torrence's bill, Torrence brought an action to recover payment from CMMA and from Clary individually. Do you think the court found Clary, as an officer of the corporation, personally liable? Why or why not? [*Charles A. Torrence Co. v. Clary,* 464 S.E.2d 502 (1995).]

12. Viola Scheutrum was killed when her car collided with a runaway horse on the highway. A police officer at the scene noted that there were at least eight horses running free on the highway. The horses escaped from the corral at the Sea Horse Ranch, Inc. The fence posts bordering the corral were old, weather-worn, bug-infested, and rotting. The horses had broken free from the corral on several previous occasions. Al Shipley, the president of Sea Horse Ranch, was aware of the inadequate condition of the fence. The state charged Sea Horse Ranch and Shipley with involuntary manslaughter. Do you think the court held Sea Horse Ranch, as a corporation, and Shipley, its president, criminally liable? Why or why not? [*Sea Horse Ranch, Inc. v. Superior Court of San Mateo County,* 30 Cal. Rptr. 2d 681 (1994).]

13. Michael Russell, a child, suffered injuries while under the care of physicians employed by Pediatric Neurosurgery (PN), P.C. Christine Russell, Michael's mother, filed a medical negligence action against the two physicians and PN. She claimed that the physicians' negligence worsened her son's condition and that according to the doctrine of *respondeat superior,* PN was liable for the acts and omissions of its employees. PN filed a motion to dismiss the charges, claiming that it was not liable for the negligence of its employee-shareholders. How do you think the court decided this case? Do you think the court should hold PN liable for the negligence of its employee physicians? Why or why not? [*Russell v. Pediatric Neurosurgery, P.C.,* 2000 Colo. App. LEXIS 3 (2000).]

14. Dorothy Oakley, a shareholder of and apartment owner in Longview Owners, Inc., a cooperative housing corporation in New York, wanted to sell her apartment. Several other shareholders recently had a few rooms in the housing corporation appraised, and the board of directors refused to approve any apartment sales for prices more than 10 percent below the appraised value of the apartment. The board of directors did not notify the shareholders of this resolution and did not give the shareholders an opportunity to vote on the issue. The Longview board of directors refused to approve the sale of Oakley's apartment because the proposed price was below the minimum price for the apartments. Oakley challenged the board's decision, arguing that it had exceeded its authority in refusing to approve the sale. Do you think the board's resolution was an *ultra vires* act? How do you think the court ruled? Why? [*Oakley v. Longview Owners, Inc.,* 628 N.Y.S.2d 468 (1995).]

15. Kathleen Eckhardt responded to an advertisement for Charter Hospital of Albuquerque, Inc., and attended a workshop given by Charter's counseling service. She met with Courtney Cook, an employee of Charter, and Cook referred Eckhardt to William McGregor. Though Charter had given only temporary privileges to McGregor, he maintained an office in Charter's counseling center, received support from Charter employees, and used Charter business cards. Eckhardt alleged that while she was under McGregor's care, he assaulted her. Eckhardt filed a civil action against Charter Hospital of Albuquerque, Inc., William McGregor, and Courtney Cook. The trial court awarded Eckhardt damages against Charter, McGregor, and Cook. The court found against Charter for negligent misrepresentation and negligent selection and supervision of McGregor. Charter appealed the trial court's decision, arguing that McGregor, not Charter, provided the services Eckhardt received. How do you think the appellate court decided the case? Why? Do you think the court should hold Charter liable for McGregor's actions? Why or why not? [*Eckhardt v. Charter Hosp. of Albuquerque, Inc.*, 953 P.2d 722 (1998).]

16. The Sunview Corporation had four directors, Demos and Stella Yiannatsis and John and Costas Stephanis. Demos, John, and Costas were the sole shareholders of Sunview. They agreed that if any of the three died, the corporation would have the first right to purchase the shares of the deceased shareholder. Costas died, and his executor offered to sell his stock to the corporation according to the shareholder agreement. The directors rejected the offer. The next day Stella bought the shares. John sued Stella, claiming she had exercised an opportunity reserved for the corporation. Did Stella fail to fulfill her responsibilities to the corporation? Why or why not? [*Yiannatsis v. Stephanis,* 653 A.2d 275 (1995).]

17. Citicorp, the owner of both Diners Club and Carte Blanche, merged the two credit card firms into one firm, giving Diners Club the dominant voice. Diners Club then ceased Carte Blanche's long-standing assistance to Carte Blanche Singapore (CBS). CBS sued Diners Club, claiming that it owed CBS a duty to continue providing services. CBS argued that because Carte Blanche and Diners Club were essentially the same firm, the court should pierce the corporate veil and hold Diners Club responsible for Carte Blanche's failure to provide services to CBS. How do you think the court ruled in this case? Why? [*Carte Blanche (Singapore) v. Diners Club International,* 2 F.3d 24 (1993).]

Looking for more review material?

The Online Learning Center at **www.mhhe.com/kubasek1e** contains this chapter's "Assignment on the Internet" and also a list of URLs for more information, entitled "On the Internet." Find both of them in the Student Center portion of the OLC, along with quizzes and other helpful materials.

Corporations: Directors, Officers, and Shareholders

CASE OPENER

Roles of Directors, Officers, and Shareholders of Hi-Way and Ken Corp.

In 1994, James and Thomas Marcuccilli, the dominant and controlling shareholders, officers, and directors of Hi-Way Drive-In Theatre, Inc., et al. (Hi-Way) and Ken Corporation (Ken Corp.) sold 18.73 acres of land to Lowe's and Kite Development for $200,000. James and Thomas Marcuccilli then proceeded to tell Elizabeth Marcuccilli et al. (the minority shareholders) about the $200,000. The two men did, however, withhold information from the minority shareholders about the overall transaction terms, which would have resulted in additional compensation to all shareholders.

Since 1994, the minority shareholders filed complaints against Hi-Way and Ken Corp. for what the suit alleged to be "failures to disclose [that] amounted to a breach of fiduciary duty." The shareholders sought both declaratory relief and damages by attempting to bring both derivative and direct suits against Hi-Way and Ken Corp.

1. If you were a minority shareholder in Ken Corp., would you think that James and Thomas Marcuccilli breached their fiduciary duty to disclose?
2. What rights do minority shareholders have within a corporation? What responsibilities does the majority shareholder have to the minority shareholders?

The Wrap-up at the end of the chapter will answer these questions.

CHAPTER 39

Learning Objectives

After reading this chapter, you will be able to answer the following questions:

1. Why is it important to regulate the interactions among directors, officers, and shareholders within a corporation?
2. What is the role of a director, an officer, and a shareholder?
3. What are the duties of directors, officers, and shareholders?
4. In what ways can a director, officer, and shareholder be held liable?
5. What are the rights of directors, officers, and shareholders?

As the opening scenario demonstrates, there are many groups of individuals with various priorities and agendas within a corporation. Not surprisingly, these priorities and agendas often come into conflict. To ensure that individuals, corporations, and the public achieve equitable outcomes to conflicts within corporations, statutory laws have been designed that delegate particular roles, duties, and rights to each group of individuals within corporations.

The statutory law governing corporations has a lengthy and dynamic history. In 1946, the American Bar Association (ABA) drafted the first version of the Model Business Corporation Act (MBCA). As with almost all new laws, MBCA met with varying degrees of success. Hence, over time, legislatures have molded and remolded the act in attempts to achieve certain objectives. The ABA amended the act numerous times since 1946, and more than 25 states adopted at least part of MBCA.

When the law changes, however, it often changes at an uneven pace. A sudden reformation sometimes interrupts a trend of incremental change. Thus, for example, after nearly 40 years of small revisions, the ABA discontinued its process of revising MBCA and drafted the Revised Model Business Corporation Act (RMBCA) in 1984. More than half of the states have adopted all or part of RMBCA. Thus, in most states, RMBCA governs corporations today. This chapter explains the duties and rights set forth in RMBCA and by common law.

Importance of Regulating Interactions among Directors, Officers, and Shareholders within a Corporation

The three major groups of individuals within a corporation are *directors, officers,* and *shareholders.* All three groups have different interests, and in many situations the interests of one group conflict with the interests of another. Statutory law provides rules to ensure that the directors, officers, and shareholders within a corporation work together to the benefit of all involved.

Although directors and officers play different roles within the corporation, they share the same goal. Both directors and officers attempt to ensure that their institution survives and that they keep their jobs. Shareholders, on the other hand, have a different agenda. Their goal is to raise the value of the company's stock.

These different agendas can lead to conflict within corporations. If a corporation has an opportunity to make a decision that will raise the value of its stock quickly, shareholders will push the directors and officers to make this decision. But if the directors and officers believe that the decision might jeopardize their jobs, they will resist the pressure of the shareholders. To resolve these conflicts, the law gives legal duties and rights to different groups within the corporation.

Roles of Directors, Officers, and Shareholders

Before discussing the duties and rights of each position within the corporation, it is important to understand the specific roles that directors, officers, and shareholders play. The rights and duties of each group of individuals are dependent on these roles.

DIRECTORS' ROLES

Directors play a vital role within every corporation. When a corporation faces an important decision, the board of directors meets to decide what course of action the corporation will take. Although directors enjoy considerable power within the organization, no one director wields a large amount of power by himself or herself. If one director wants the company to move in a certain direction, he or she must solicit the approval of other directors on the board before the company will begin to move in that direction.

Elections. Typically, shareholders use a majority vote to elect directors. The only exception is during incorporation. Because there are no shareholders in the beginning, either the incorporators appoint board members or the corporate articles name the board members. This first board then serves until the first shareholder meeting, at which the shareholders elect a new board. The corporate articles or bylaws specify the number of corporate directors. In the past, the minimum number of directors required was three, but today many states allow fewer. In fact, if a corporation has fewer than 50 shareholders, Section 7.32 of RMBCA allows companies to eliminate the board of directors altogether. This change in the minimum number of directors illustrates how practicality interests can stimulate change in the law. The benefits of the corporate form of business organization have drawn an enormous number of businesses, and especially small businesses, to incorporate in recent years. The requirement of at least three directors, however, burdened small corporations that did not generate sufficient business to warrant three directors. Hence, legislatures in many states eased or removed the three-director requirement.

Interestingly, almost anyone can become a director. The legal requirements for director qualification are incredibly lax. In most states, directors are not even required to own stock in the corporation. In some cases, however, statutory law and corporate bylaws require not only ownership but also a minimum age.

Directors typically serve for one year, but most state statutes allow for longer terms if the terms of the various directors are staggered. These terms can be terminated and the directors can be removed from their positions *for cause*—for failing to perform a required duty. Directors who are removed for cause, however, can ask the courts to review the legality of the removal. Although removal is typically a result of shareholder action, in some cases directors are given the power to remove other directors for cause. Only a few states allow removal of directors without cause, and only if shareholders reserve that right at the time of the election.

Meetings and voting. A minimum number of directors, or a quorum, must be present at each directors' meeting for decisions made at the meeting to be valid. Quorum requirements are different in each state, but most states leave the decision up to the corporation itself. Because a quorum is required at each meeting, directors are notified whenever special meetings are called. Directors vote in person, and each director has one vote. While ordinary decisions require a majority vote, more important decisions sometimes require a two-thirds vote.

Although directors' meetings are usually held in a central location, Section 8.20 of RMBCA permits directors' meetings to be held via telephone conferences.

Directors as managers. Although directors meet to vote on major decisions about the corporation, they are also responsible for many day-to-day managerial activities of the company. The directors appoint, supervise, and remove corporate officers as they see fit, and they declare and pay corporate dividends to shareholders. They are also responsible for making financial decisions and authorizing corporate policy decisions. Some directors are also officers or employees of the corporation; these directors are known as *inside directors*. Directors who are not officers or employees of the corporation are called *outside directors*. Outside directors are further divided into two groups: *affiliated directors* and *unaffiliated directors*. Affiliated directors have business contacts with the corporation, while unaffiliated directors do not.

Because the day-to-day tasks of a corporation can be overwhelming for a small board of directors that has larger issues to address, directors often appoint an executive committee to handle day-to-day responsibilities.

OFFICERS' ROLES

Officers are executive managers that the board of directors hires to run the organization. While directors are in charge of major policy decisions, officers run the day-to-day business of the corporation. Accordingly, their decisions influence the corporation immensely. Officers act as agents of the corporation, and thus the rules of agency apply to their work. (Refer to Chapter 32 for the rules of agency.)

Qualifications required of officers are set forth in the corporate articles and bylaws of each corporation, but in most cases an individual may serve as both a director and an officer. Many corporations find it beneficial to include an officer on their board of directors so that the board can stay in touch with the day-to-day operations of the company.

SHAREHOLDERS' ROLES

Shareholders own the firm. As soon as an individual purchases the stock of a particular corporation, she becomes an owner of the corporation. While she is not legally recognized as an owner of corporate property, she has an *equitable,* or ownership, interest in the company. Shareholders are not directly responsible for the daily management of the corporation, but they elect the directors who are responsible for that management.

Power of shareholders. The articles of incorporation established within each corporation and general incorporation law in each state grant shareholders certain powers within the institution. Because shareholders must approve major corporate decisions, they are in some sense empowered to make major decisions for the corporation.

Their most influential power, however, is the power to elect and remove the board of directors. The board of directors is responsible for making crucial policy decisions for the corporation, and the shareholders have the power to decide who these directors will be.

Shareholders also have the power to propose ideas for the corporation. If a shareholder feels that he has a worthwhile idea for the company, he can include his proposal in the *proxy materials* sent out to the shareholders before their annual meeting. The Securities and Exchange Commission (SEC) has established that any shareholder who owns more than $1,000 worth of stock in the corporation can submit proposals to be included in proxy materials.

Meetings. Typically, shareholders meet once a year, but in emergencies they can meet more often. The board of directors, shareholders who own at least 10 percent of the corporation's outstanding shares, and others authorized in the articles of incorporation may call a special shareholder meeting. Before each meeting, each shareholder receives notice of the time and place of the meeting. If the meeting is a special meeting, the purpose of the meeting is also included in the notice.

Like directors' meetings, shareholder meetings require a quorum. Generally, a quorum of shareholders exists when shareholders holding more than 50 percent of the outstanding shares are present. Once a quorum is present, a majority vote of the shares represented at the meeting is required to pass resolutions. Occasionally, however, articles of incorporation include supermajority provisions, which state that more than a majority is needed to pass major corporate proposals, such as corporate merger or dissolution.

Because shareholders cannot always attend shareholder meetings, they can authorize a third party to attend the meeting and vote in their place. This authorization is called a *proxy.* Under Section 7.22(c) of RMBCA, proxies last for 11 months and can be withdrawn at any time unless specifically designed to be irrevocable.

An individual shareholder can also enter a voting trust in which she transfers her share titles to a trustee in exchange for a *voting trust certificate.* The trustee is then responsible for voting for those shares. These trusts can prescribe how the trustee should vote, or they can allow the trustee to use his discretion. The shareholder, however, retains all other shareholder rights (discussed below).

Alternatively, before a shareholder meeting, shareholders can sign a *shareholder voting agreement* in which they agree to vote together in a certain manner. These agreements are usually legally enforceable.

Voting. Like directors, each shareholder is entitled to one vote per share in most instances. Corporations practice unique voting processes, however, that alter the influence of each shareholder's votes. These voting processes are especially important for minority shareholders within a corporation. One voting process required in most states, called *cumulative voting,* ensures that minority shareholders have a voice in electing the board of directors. The cumulative-voting process divides shareholders into majority and minority shareholders, and each group has a certain number of votes to cast in the election. The number of votes is determined by multiplying the number of shares the group owns by the number of open director positions. If a company is electing eight directors and the minority shareholders own 2,000 shares, the minority shareholders get 16,000 votes to cast in the election. If the majority shareholders in the same corporation own 8,000 shares, they get 64,000 votes.

Although in the example above it may seem that the minority shareholders have little influence in the election, the cumulative-voting process permits them to vote at least one director onto the board because they can cast all of their votes for one candidate. If the majority shareholders wish to elect all eight directors from their nominees, each nominee must receive more than 16,000 votes in order to beat the 16,000 votes of the minority nominee. But because the majority shareholders have only 64,000 votes to cast in the election, they cannot cast more than 16,000 votes for eight candidates (16,000 × 8 = 128,000). Thus, if the minority shareholders cast all of their 16,000 votes for one candidate, they guarantee that candidate's election.

Cumulative voting is more egalitarian than simple majority voting because it ensures that every voice within the corporation is heard. Without cumulative voting, the majority shareholders could monopolize control of the company and disregard the interests of the minority shareholders. The cumulative voting process, however, forces the corporation to listen to and consider the needs of everyone within the corporation—not just those with the most power. Cumulative voting, however, is not guaranteed in RMBCA; rather, it occurs only if the corporation's articles of incorporation provide for it. Exhibit 39-1 provides an overview of the respective roles of directors, officers, and shareholders.

Exhibit 39-1 Summary of the Roles of Directors, Officers, and Shareholders

POSITION	ROLES
Directors	Vote on important corporate decisions
	Appoint and supervise officers
	Declare and pay corporate dividends
	Manage the corporation
Officers	Run the day-to-day business of the firm
	Are agents of the corporation
Shareholders	Elect a board of directors
	Approve major decisions of the board

global context

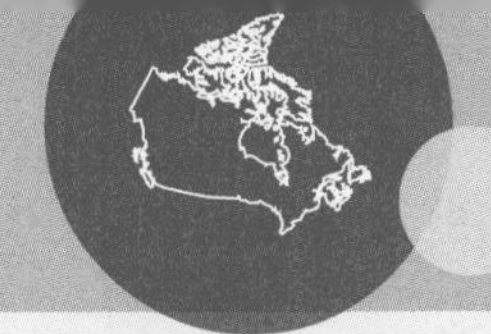

Board of Directors in Canada

Individuals who sit on the board of directors for Canadian corporations are classified as either inside or outside directors. Though definitions vary, *inside directors* are generally persons currently employed by the corporation. Thus, in addition to their other corporate duties, inside directors must also perform the duties of a board member.

Outside directors are typically defined as former or retired employees or employees of parent, controlling, or subsidiary companies. These individuals often have other jobs as lawyers, financial executives, or bank managers. According to the Canada Business Corporation Act, outside directors must be Canadian citizens.

Generally, both inside and outside directors serve on the board for fewer than five years. Occasionally, inside directors remain on the board after retirement and become outside directors. Many corporations have mandatory retirement ages for directors. Additionally, corporations reserve the right to demand early retirement at any time if a board member violates corporate policies.

Duties of Directors, Officers, and Shareholders

Because all individuals within a corporation depend on one another, the law requires that directors, officers, and shareholders perform certain duties within the business. In other words, individuals within the corporation have legal responsibilities to the corporation. Within legal discourse, these duties to the corporation are called *fiduciary duties.* Because individuals play different roles within the corporation, the fiduciary duties of individuals depend on whether they are directors, officers, or shareholders.

DUTIES OF DIRECTORS AND OFFICERS

Because the owners of the corporation, the shareholders, have little input in the day-to-day operations of the corporation, they trust the directors and officers to run the company to the best of their ability. Thus, directors and officers have duties to the shareholders and to the corporation. The two primary fiduciary duties of directors and officers are the duty of care and the duty of loyalty.

Duty of care. Directors and officers have a fiduciary *duty of care,* meaning that they must exercise *due care* when making decisions for the corporation. The phrase *due care* is ambiguous and various courts have interpreted it differently over time. In general, however, acting with due care requires that one exercise the care that an ordinary prudent person would exercise in the management of her own assets. In other words, if a person is acting with due care, she is acting in good faith and in a manner that she feels is in the best interest of the company.

Because directors and officers have a duty to act in the best interest of the company, they must supervise employees who work for the corporation to a reasonable extent. They also have a duty to attend director and corporate business meetings. Most important, however, directors and officers have a fiduciary duty to make informed and reasonable business decisions.

The directors and officers of Enron failed in their duty of care with regard to their shareholders by not acting in the best interest of the company. The directors and officers continued to advocate that employees invest in the employee stock-sharing options, even though it appears the directors and officers knew the stock was drastically overpriced.

e-commerce AND THE LAW

When a B2B Company Cooks the Books

When a business student thinks about companies that "cook the books," it is not surprising that companies such as Enron, Tyco, and Adelphia come to mind. Issues related to duty of care for officers and directors are expressed in questions such as, "Why did the officers and directors of the company fail to realize accountants were cooking company books? Were any officers or directors involved in the fraud?"

Students may have to revise their images of corrupt companies by adding business-to-business (B2B) e-commerce companies to their Enron-Tyco-Adelphia list. They may have to ask, "Why did the officers and directors of an *e-commerce business* fail to realize accountants were cooking company books? Were any officers or directors involved in the fraud?"

PurchasePro is one example of an e-commerce company that allegedly engaged in "overstating revenues, engaging in aggressive accounting practices and mismanaging corporate assets." Basically, the company manipulated its financial records to make it look far more successful than it really was. PurchasePro, which provided a business-to-business software company that gave companies access to an online marketplace, went bankrupt in September 2002.

Federal prosecutors charged company officers and directors with conspiracy, securities fraud, and obstruction of justice. Two senior officers, Jeffrey R. Anderson and Scott H. Miller, pleaded guilty to federal crimes in 2003. Their behavior was similar to that of officers of other, more well-known companies that have cooked the books—they had secret side deals with purchasers that gave the appearance of sales that did not really exist; they misrepresented the company's financial health so that investors could not make informed decisions; and, when news of alleged fraud surfaced, the officers used their energy to shred incriminating documents.

Furthermore, the directors and officers failed in their duty of care regarding oversight. The directors and officers either did not pay enough attention to see the collapse of their stock coming or purposely kept the information secret. Either way, the directors and officers at Enron breached their fiduciary duty of care and therefore are liable to their shareholders, many of whom were employees of Enron.

Directors and officers are expected to stay abreast of all important corporate matters. In other words, they must obtain information about business transactions, review contracts, read reports, and attend presentations. After all, if directors and officers are uninformed, they cannot make decisions that are in the best interest of the company. Because some directors are too busy to stay informed on every subject, RMBCA allows directors to make decisions based on information gathered by other employees. Interestingly, however, most corporations do not allow directors' decisions to be based on secondhand information.

The decisions that corporate directors and officers make must not only be informed, however, but also be reasonable. If a director or officer is taken to court for breaching his duty of care by making an unreasonable decision, the court typically inquires whether the decision had any rational business purpose. In other words, the courts ask whether there was good reason to think that the decision *could* have helped the company.

Part of the duty of care a director or officer owes a corporation, as was previously stated, is to act in the corporation's best interest. Therefore, when the corporation is doing something the director or officer does not think is in its best interest, it is up to her to voice her dissent. It is unusual for a dissenting director to be held personally liable for decisions made by the corporation that entail mismanagement. Accordingly, when a director or officer disagrees with a proposed action, it is part of her duty to voice this disagreement to the other directors or officers.

Case Nugget Duty of Care

In re Caremark Int'l
698 A.2d 959 (1996)

Caremark, a corporation headquartered in Illinois, provided patient care and managed health care services. The corporation was indicted by a grand jury for paying a doctor to distribute a drug produced by the corporation and for making inappropriate referral payments to a doctor. Several Caremark shareholders filed a derivative suit (discussed later in this chapter in the section entitled "Shareholder's Derivative Suit") alleging that Caremark's directors breached their fiduciary duty of care to the corporation by allowing situations to develop that exposed the corporation to enormous legal liability.

The Court of Chancery of Delaware ruled:

> [C]ompliance with a director's duty of care can never appropriately be judicially determined by reference to the content of the board decision that leads to a corporate loss, apart from consideration of the good faith or rationality of the process employed. That is, whether a judge or jury considering the matter after the fact, believes a decision substantively wrong, or degrees of wrong extending through "stupid" to "egregious" or "irrational," provides no ground for director liability, so long as the court determines that the process employed was either rational or employed in a good faith effort to advance corporate interests. To employ a different rule—one that permitted an "objective" evaluation of the decision—would expose directors to substantive second guessing by ill-equipped judges or juries, which would, in the long-run, be injurious to investor interests.

Duty of loyalty. Because directors and officers have great decision-making freedom, they have the power to make business decisions that will benefit themselves while harming the company. Thus, to protect shareholders, directors and officers have a fiduciary *duty of loyalty.* In other words, they have a fiduciary duty to put the corporation's interest above their own when making business decisions.

When directors or officers violate their duty of loyalty, they are **self-dealing.** There are two types of self-dealing in which a director or officer can engage. The first form of self-dealing, called *business self-dealing,* occurs when a director or officer makes decisions that benefit other companies with which he has a relationship. The second form of self-dealing, called *personal self-dealing,* occurs when a director or officer makes business decisions that benefit her personally. When Enron directors and officers advocated that employees buy more Enron stock so that the directors and officers would make more money, they engaged in self-dealing in breach of their fiduciary duty of loyalty.

In many situations, when a director or officer is self-dealing, he forces the corporation into unfair business deals. Directors and officers can also breach their fiduciary duty of loyalty, however, by *preventing* corporate opportunity. This breach usually happens when directors or officers own other companies that compete with their corporation without the consent of the board of directors or the shareholders. If a director or officer uses corporate assets to start another business, goes into the same line of business, or uses her position in the company to develop a new business that the company might have pursued, she is preventing corporate opportunity and can be held liable for violating her fiduciary duty of loyalty.

A director or officer convicted of breaching her duty of loyalty is required to cede to the corporation all the profits she earned as a result of the breach. The corporation need not have been able to earn those profits in the absence of the breach. The goal of the rule is to create incentives to discourage breaches of the duty of loyalty by taking from the director or officer all the profits that she made.

Case Nugget Duty of Loyalty

Patrick v. Allen
355 F. Supp. 2d 704 (2005)

RPO, a privately traded corporation, rented land to a private golf course, of which several of RPO's directors were members. The directors charged the golf course enough rent to cover only the property taxes on the land. Patrick, a shareholder of RPO, brought a suit against the directors of RPO, alleging that RPO's directors breached their fiduciary duty of loyalty to the corporation by failing to maximize the value of the corporation for shareholders. The directors argued that they were exempt from liability under the business judgment rule. (The business judgment rule is covered in the section entitled "Liabilities of Directors, Officers, and Shareholders.")

The U.S. District Court for the Southern District of New York ruled against the RPO's directors, holding:

> The business judgment rule will not protect a decision that was the product of fraud, self-dealing, or bad faith. Directors may benefit from the rule only if they possess a disinterested independence and do not stand in a dual relation which prevents an unprejudicial exercise of judgment. It is black-letter, settled law that when a corporate director or officer has an interest in a decision, the business judgment rule does not apply. . . . A director is considered interested in a transaction if the director stands to receive a direct financial benefit from the transaction which is different from the benefit to shareholders generally. . . . The duty of loyalty requires a director to subordinate his own personal interests to the interest of the corporation.

The fiduciary duties of care and loyalty are rooted in ethics. Without these legal duties, directors and officers could pursue their own interests at the expense of others. Through these fiduciary duties, however, the law requires that directors and officers consider the interests of others. Think back to Chapter 2 and the different ethical guidelines used to make ethical decisions. Which ethical guideline is the legal system using when it delegates fiduciary duties?

Duty to disclose conflict of interest. Because there are many times when individual directors and officers may personally benefit from decisions made by the board of directors, the directors and officers have a fiduciary duty to fully disclose conflicts of interest that arise in corporate transactions. Moreover, if the board of directors addresses an issue that might personally benefit a particular director, the director is not only required to disclose the self-interest but also to abstain from voting on that issue. Note that decisions can be made that will personally benefit one director or officer as long as (1) there is full disclosure of the interest and (2) the disinterested board members and/or disinterested shareholders approve it.

DUTIES OF SHAREHOLDERS

Although shareholders typically have few legal duties, in rare instances majority shareholders have fiduciary duties to the corporation and to minority shareholders. In some

Exhibit 39-2 Summary of the Duties of Directors, Officers, and Shareholders

POSITION	DUTIES
Directors	Duty of care Duty of loyalty Duty to disclose a conflict of interest Duty to apply best judgment
Officers	Duty of care Duty of loyalty Duty to disclose a conflict of interest
Shareholders	Duty to minority shareholders

corporations, the majority shareholder owns such a significant portion of the corporation's stock that he essentially controls the firm. When that individual sells his shares, the control of the company shifts to another individual. Thus, the majority shareholder in this situation has a fiduciary duty to act with care and loyalty when selling his shares. In closely held corporations, a breach of this fiduciary duty is known as *oppressive conduct.*

More than half of U.S. publicly traded corporations are incorporated in Delaware. Thus, when Delaware courts rule on the duties of majority shareholders to minority shareholders, for example, the courts' rulings have a far-reaching impact. In Case 39-1, brought before the supreme court of Delaware, minority shareholders sued the majority shareholder within their corporation for violating its fiduciary duties.

The respective duties of directors, officers, and shareholders are summarized in Exhibit 39-2.

CASE 39-1 FRIEDA H. RABKIN v. PHILIP A. HUNT CHEMICAL CORP.

SUPREME COURT OF DELAWARE
498 A. 2D 1099 (1985)

On March 1, 1983, Olin Corporation bought 63.4 percent of the outstanding shares of Hunt Chemical Corporation from Turner and Newall Industries, Inc., at $25 per share, which moved Olin into the position of majority shareholder. Before Turner and Newall Industries sold the shares to Olin, they insisted that Olin agree to pay $25 per share if Olin acquired the remaining Hunt stock within one year. On July 5, 1984, Hunt merged into Olin by buying out the remaining stock for $20 a share. The minority shareholders of Hunt then filed a suit against Olin that challenged the Olin-Hunt merger on the grounds that the price offered was grossly inadequate because Olin unfairly manipulated the timing of the merger to avoid the one year commitment, and that specific language in Olin's Schedule 13D, filed when it purchased the Hunt stock, constituted a price commitment by which Olin failed to abide, contrary to its fiduciary obligations to the minority shareholders. The trial judge dismissed the complaint on grounds that the only remedy legally available to the minority shareholders was an appraisal. The plaintiffs then sought and were denied leave to amend their complaints. They appealed.

JUDGE MOORE: The plaintiffs have charged that the merger does not meet the entire fairness standard required. They offer specific acts of unfair dealing constituting breaches of fiduciary duties which, if true, may have substantially affected the offering price. These allegations, unrelated to judgmental factors of valuation, should survive a motion to dismiss.

Olin's alleged attitude toward the minority, at least as it appears on the face of the complaints and their proposed amendments, coupled with the apparent absence of any meaningful negotiations as to price, all raise unanswered questions about the undiminished duty of loyalty to Hunt.

In our opinion, the facts alleged by the plaintiffs regarding Olin's avoidance of the one-year commitment support a claim of unfair dealing sufficient to defeat dismissal at this stage of the proceedings. At the very least, the facts alleged import a form of overreaching, and in the context of entire fairness they deserve more considered analysis than can be accorded them on a motion to dismiss.

REVERSED.

CRITICAL THINKING

What reasons does the court give for its conclusion? Are you persuaded by those reasons?

ETHICAL DECISION MAKING

Clearly, the court explicitly emphasizes a particular value in its ruling. What is this value? The court's emphasis of this particular value makes it difficult for the court to emphasize other values. Which value(s) does this ruling de-emphasize?

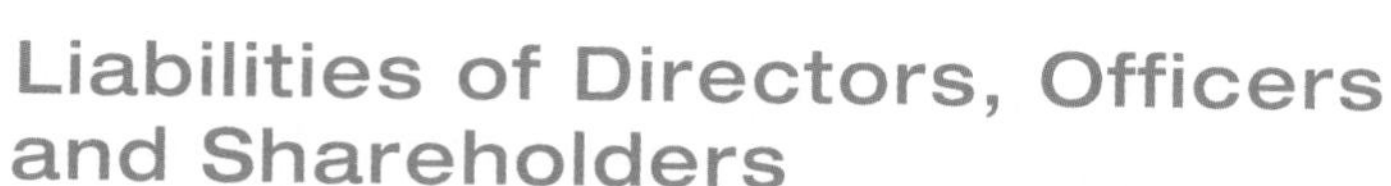

Liabilities of Directors, Officers, and Shareholders

Because almost all individuals within a corporation have legal fiduciary duties to the corporation, almost all individuals within the firm can be held liable for harming the business by violating these duties. There are, however, certain instances where directors, officers, and shareholders cannot be held liable for harming the business.

LIABILITY OF DIRECTORS AND OFFICERS

Directors and officers are held liable for many of the same actions because they have nearly identical fiduciary duties to the corporation. A shareholder can sue them if the shareholder feels that they have caused harm to the business by violating their fiduciary duties. In fact, directors and officers can be held liable for the torts and crimes of their employees. There are some situations, however, in which they are not liable for the harm they have caused the business.

Liability for torts and crimes. Although the corporations themselves are liable for the torts and crimes of their directors and officers, directors and officers can also be held personally responsible for their own torts and crimes. They can even be held personally responsible for the torts and crimes of other employees within the organization when they have failed to adequately supervise the employees' behavior.

According to the responsible person doctrine, a court may find a corporate officer criminally liable regardless of the extent to which the officer took part in the criminal activity. Even if the officer knew nothing about the criminal activity, the officer can still be held criminally liable if the court determines that a responsible person would have known about and could have prevented the illegal activity.

Corporate directors and officers may also be held liable for wrongful personal transactions involving company stock. Directors and officers who use inside information to trade the corporation's stock for a profit can be held liable for breaching their fiduciary duty to the shareholders from whom they purchase or to whom they sell the stock.

Case Nugget The Responsible Person Doctrine

United States v. Park
421 U.S. 658 (1975)

Defendant Park was the president of Acme Markets, a national food chain corporation. After several inspections of Acme's Philadelphia warehouse, FDA officials sent Park a memo indicating the unsanitary conditions at the warehouse. Park knew that the corporate officials in charge of the Philadelphia warehouse also ran Acme's Baltimore warehouse. After an FDA inspection of the Baltimore warehouse found similar unsanitary conditions, the FDA brought suit against Acme and against Park personally.

Park argued that he was not personally involved with the violations and therefore should not be held responsible for the violations. The U.S. Supreme Court, however, concluded that the offense was committed by everyone who had "a responsible share in the furtherance of the transaction which the [FDA] statute outlaws. . . . [T]hose corporate agents vested with the responsibility, and power commensurate with that responsibility, to devise whatever measures are necessary to ensure compliance with the [law] bear a 'responsible relationship' to, or have a 'responsible share' in, violations."

Business judgment rule. Although directors and officers are expected to make decisions that are in the best interest of the corporation, they are not expected to make perfect decisions all the time. Many directors and officers make decisions that inadvertently harm the corporation. Although shareholders may want to hold their directors and officers liable for these decisions, the *business judgment rule* does not allow them to do so. This rule claims that directors and officers are not liable for decisions that harm the corporation if

Case Nugget The Business Judgment Rule

Auerbach v. Bennett
393 N.E.2d 994 (1979)

An internal audit of the GTE Corporation suggested that the corporation's management had paid more than $11 million in bribes and kickbacks both in the United States and abroad over a four-year period. Auerbach, a GTE shareholder, immediately initiated a shareholder derivative action (discussed in the section entitled "Shareholder's Derivative Suit") against GTE's directors.

The Court of Appeals of New York, however, held that the business judgment rule exempted the GTE directors from liability for their poor business decisions. The court held:

> [The business judgment doctrine] bars judicial inquiry into actions of corporation directors taken in good faith and in the exercise of honest judgment in the lawful and legitimate furtherance of corporate purposes. Questions of policy of management, expediency of contracts or action, adequacy of consideration, lawful appropriation of corporate funds to advance corporate interests, are left solely to their honest and unselfish decision, for their powers therein are without limitation and free from restraint, and the exercise of them for the common and general interests of the corporation may not be questioned, although the results show that what they did was unwise or inexpedient.

they were acting in good faith at the time of the decision. In other words, if there was reason to believe that the decision was a good decision at the time, the directors and officers are not liable for the resulting harm.

Although the business judgment rule is not a statute, it is common law recognized by almost every court in the country. The rule is practical because it grants directors the freedom to work without constant fear of personal liability. The business judgment rule also encourages individuals to serve as directors by removing the threat of personal liability for inadvertent mistakes. Case 39-2 illustrates how the courts interpret and apply the business judgment rule.

CASE 39-2

STATE OF WISCONSIN INVESTMENT BOARD v. WILLIAM BARTLETT

COURT OF CHANCERY OF DELAWARE, NEW CASTLE C.A. NO. 17727 (2000)

The State of Wisconsin Investment Board (SWIB) owned 11.5 percent of the outstanding shares of common stock in the pharmaceutical company Medco Research, Inc. In 1996, Medco began searching for a merger partner. In a proxy statement on January 5, 2000, Medco recommended that shareholders vote for a merger between Medco and King Pharmaceuticals, Inc. On January 11, 2000, SWIB filed a request for injunctive relief on the grounds that the board of directors breached their fiduciary duties of care, loyalty, and disclosure in negotiating the merger. SWIB argued that the majority of Medco's directors were self-interested, and that no reasonably prudent businessperson of sound judgment would have negotiated the merger as Medco had negotiated. SWIB alleged that Medco failed to disclose all information material to the shareholders, did not adequately inform themselves of all information available about the merger, and failed to adequately supervise a self-interested director. Medco refutes all claims.

JUDGE STEELE: Unless this presumption [that a board of directors acted with care, loyalty, and in good faith] is sufficiently rebutted, raising a reasonable doubt about self-interest or independence, the Court must defer to the discretion of the board and acknowledge that their decisions are entitled to the protection of the business judgment rule.

In order to require application of the entire fairness standard, the plaintiff has to show that a majority of directors has a financial interest in the transaction or a motive to entrench themselves in office through the merger. Plaintiff's allegations of self-interest do not meet the threshold necessary to rebut the presumption of the business judgment rule.

The plaintiff's allegations do not demonstrate that the Medco board failed to inform itself of all material facts concerning the proposed merger with King. I conclude that Medco's board met its duty of care in proceeding with the King merger. Despite the material disputes of fact, I am confident that Medco's board adequately informed themselves of all material information necessary to execute the merger agreement.

I cannot, on the basis of these allegations, find that the board either willfully left itself uninformed in order to serve its "self-interest" or failed to act in "good faith and in the honest belief that the merger was in the best interests of the company." It is equally apparent to me that the board sufficiently complied with the "good-faith" standard set forth by this Court in Aronson. I have also been led to conclude that the directors were acting to benefit the economic interest of the shareholders.

Plaintiff's request for preliminary injunction is hereby denied with respect to the shareholder vote and denied with respect to the merger.

Judgment for defendant.

[CONTINUED]

CRITICAL THINKING

What words or phrases in the court's argument are ambiguous? Why are these ambiguous words important?

ETHICAL DECISION MAKING

Suppose you were on the board of directors in this case. The universalization test guides your ethical decisions. Would you have made a different decision?

LIABILITY OF SHAREHOLDERS

The main liability that shareholders face is liability for the debts of the corporation. Because shareholders are the owners of the corporation, they are liable to the extent of their investment when the company loses money. There are rare instances, however, in which shareholders are personally liable.

For instance, in some cases, individuals sign stock subscription agreements before incorporation. Once an individual signs a stock subscription agreement, she is contractually obligated to purchase shares in the corporation. For **par-value shares,** or shares that have a fixed face value noted on the stock certificate, the shareholder must pay the corporation at least the par value of the stock. For **no-par shares,** or shares without a par value, the shareholder must pay the corporation the fair market value of the shares. The shareholder is personally liable for breach of contract if she does not buy shares.

Alternatively, a shareholder can be held personally responsible if he receives **watered stock.** Watered stock is stock issued to individuals below its fair market value. When watered stock is issued to shareholders, the shareholder is individually liable for paying the difference between the price he paid for the shares and the stated corporate value of the shares.

A shareholder can also be held personally liable for receiving illegal dividends. A **dividend** is a distribution of corporate profits or income ordered by the directors and paid to the shareholders in proportion to their respective shares in the corporation. State statutes mandate that corporations pay dividends from only certain funds. Additionally, dividends are always illegal if they are paid when the corporation is insolvent or if they cause the corporation to become insolvent. If a shareholder knew that a dividend was illegal when she received it, she is personally liable and must return the funds to the corporation.

Rights of Directors, Officers, and Shareholders

Along with their specific roles and duties, directors, officers, and shareholders have specific rights within the corporation. Because shareholders are in a position of limited decision-making power, they have rights that allow them to participate within the corporation. Directors and officers also have specific rights that allow them to perform their duties within the corporation to the best of their abilities.

DIRECTORS' RIGHTS

The unique responsibilities of corporate directors call for unique rights. Directors have four major rights within a corporation: rights of compensation, participation, inspection, and indemnification.

global context

Assigned Directors in Japan

A common corporate practice in Japan is for multiple corporations, banks, and companies to form hierarchical conglomerates known as *keiretsus.* There are two types of *keiretsus.* The first is a horizontal *keiretsu,* in which a powerful bank acts as the unifying agent under which several large corporations come together. With the exception of the bank, power is shared equally among the members. The second type is a vertical *keiretsu.* In contrast to horizontal *keiretsus,* vertical *keiretsus* are hierarchically ordered with an unequal distribution of power. Large corporations often control several hundred subordinate companies.

Power distribution within *keiretsus* plays a key role in determining the board of directors. Usually the main bank or parent corporation assigns its own executives to serve on the boards of the less powerful companies. The prosperity of these companies is important to the main banks and parent corporations. The assigned directors act as overseers, consultants, and mentors. They want to promote simultaneously the interests of the parent corporation and the growth of the subordinate ones. Thus, the subordinate companies do not view the assignment of directors as a sign of mistrust. To the Japanese the logic is patent: If the success of the *keiretsu* and the success of each company are reciprocal, all parties should work together to achieve the collective goal.

All corporate directors have a right to compensation for their work, and different corporations grant compensation in different ways. Most directors hold other managerial positions within their companies and receive their compensation through those positions. Another common avenue for compensating directors is paying them nominal sums as honorariums for their contributions to the company. In some corporations, directors can determine their own compensation.

Because directors are required to make informed business decisions, they have the rights of participation and inspection. In other words, they have the right to get involved in and understand every aspect of the business. A corporate director has the right to be notified of all meetings and has access to all books and records.

Finally, because directors are in positions of great legal vulnerability, they have the right to indemnification. In other words, they have the right to reimbursement for any legal fees incurred in lawsuits against them.

OFFICERS' RIGHTS

Because corporate officers are technically employees of the corporation, their rights are defined by employment contracts drawn up by the board of directors or the incorporators. They are in a contractual relationship with the corporation, and if they are removed from their positions in violation of the terms of the contract, the corporation may be liable for breach of contract.

SHAREHOLDERS' RIGHTS

Although shareholders' most powerful right is the right to vote at shareholders' meetings, they also possess many other rights.

Stock certificates. Some corporations issue **stock certificates** to shareholders as proof of ownership in the corporation. Each certificate includes the corporation's name and the number of shares represented by the certificate. A sample stock certificate is shown in Figure 39-1. A shareholder's ownership in the corporation, however, does not depend on his possession of the physical stock certificate. For example, if the certificate is destroyed in a fire, the shareholder's ownership in the corporation is not destroyed. The

Figure 39-1
Example of a Stock Certificate

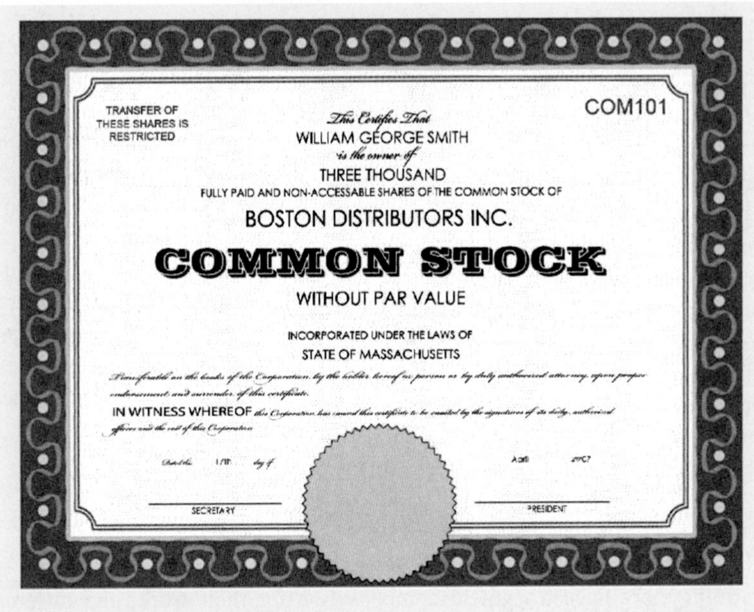

shareholder can request a reissued certificate from the corporation, although he may be required to guarantee payment to the corporation if the original certificate should reappear at a later date.

In most states, however, shares may be *uncertificated,* meaning that the corporation will not issue physical stock certificates. In these states, shareholders usually have a right to receive a letter from the corporation including the information typically included on the face of a stock certificate.

Preemptive rights. Under common law, shareholders have *preemptive rights.* Preemptive rights give preference to shareholders to purchase shares of a new issue of stock. Each shareholder receives preference in proportion to the percentage of stock she already owns.

For example, suppose that a shareholder owns 1,500 shares in a corporation with 5,000 outstanding shares. She owns 30 percent of the corporation's outstanding stock. But suppose that the corporation decides to issue an additional 10,000 shares. If the corporation does not grant preemptive rights, her relative control of the corporation will fall because she now owns 1,500 of the corporation's 15,000 outstanding shares, or 10 percent of its stock. But if the corporation does reserve preemptive rights, and the shareholder elects to purchase 3,000 shares of the newly issued stock, then she owns 4,500 shares of the corporation's 15,000 outstanding shares (30 percent). Thus, with preemptive rights, she can maintain her proportionate control of the corporation. This example is illustrated in Figure 39-2.

In most states, a corporation's bylaws can negate preemptive rights, so the corporation determines whether to grant preemptive rights. Preemptive rights are especially important for individuals who own stock in close corporations due to the relatively small number of issued shares. If a close corporation issues additional shares, an individual shareholder may lose proportional control over the firm if he does not buy newly issued shares. But if preemptive rights exist within the corporation, all shareholders receive **stock warrants,** which they can redeem for a certain number of shares at a specified price within a given time period. Like shares of stock, stock warrants are often traded publicly on securities exchanges.

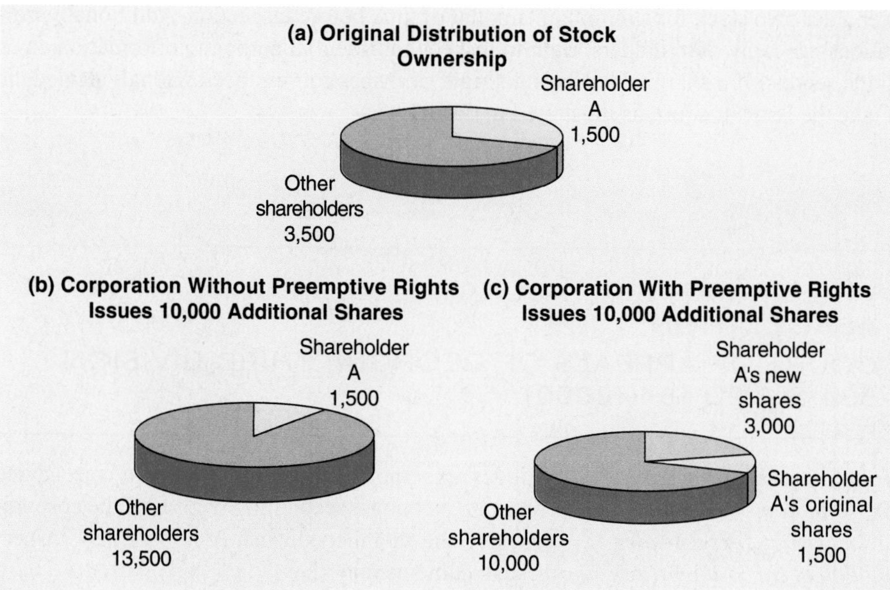

Figure 39-2
Preemptive Rights

connecting to the core

Financial Accounting

Remember from your accounting class that there are two primary reasons for declaration of stock dividends. First, directors are said to use stock dividends to keep the market price of the stock affordable. If a corporation is making profits and fails to pay out cash dividends, the price of the stock could rise so high that investors might be discouraged from purchasing the stock. Not every successful company, of course, sees a high stock price as a problem. In 2005, Berkshire Hathaway, for example, had not declared a dividend since 1967, and its price was roughly $75,000 per share.

Second, declaring stock dividends provides evidence of management's confidence that the company is doing well and will continue to do so.

Source: Larson, Wild, and Chiappetta, *Principles of Financial Accounting*, 17th ed. (New York: McGraw-Hill, 2005), p. 507.

Dividends. If directors fail to declare and distribute dividends, shareholders have the right to take legal action to force the directors to declare the dividends. In many cases, however, directors have good reason to hold dividends for a limited amount of time to finance major undertakings such as research or expansion. Thus, shareholders must show that the directors are acting unreasonably and abusing their discretion in withholding the dividend.

Inspection rights. All shareholders have the right to inspection in both statutory and common law. A shareholder can, moreover, appoint an agent to conduct the inspection on her behalf. To prevent abuse, however, this right has many limitations. Shareholders can inspect records and books only if they ask in advance and have a *proper purpose.* Many states have other statutory limitations to this right. For example, some states allow only shareholders with a minimum number of shares to inspect. Other states require that the shareholder own stock for a minimum amount of time before inspection. Additionally, corporations can deny shareholders' right to inspect confidential corporate information, such as trade secrets. If a shareholder feels his right of inspection has been wrongly denied, he can take the issue to court, as illustrated in Case 39-3.

CASE 39-3 PHILLIP PARKER v. CLARY LAKES RECREATION ASSOCIATION, INC.

COURT OF APPEALS OF GEORGIA, THIRD DIVISION
534 S.E.2D 154 (2000)

Phillip Parker was a member of Clary Lakes Recreation Association (CLRA), a nonprofit homeowners association. In 1997, he filed a suit against CLRA alleging mismanagement and violation of corporate bylaws. During the lawsuit proceedings, Parker sent a written request to CLRA to "inspect all accounting and/or corporate records of CLRA for the purpose of determining the performance of management and the condition of the corporation." These documents included records of all asset accounts, invoices and billing statements, profit and loss statements, tax returns, corporate meeting minutes, and membership lists. CLRA refused the request. Parker then applied to the Superior Court under OCGA § 14-3-1604 for an order directing CLRA to produce the documents. The judge denied Parker's request for all documents except the minutes from certain meetings. Parker appealed.

JUDGE RUFFIN: OCGA § 14-3-1602 divides corporate records into two categories. The first includes articles of incorporation, by-laws, minutes of meetings, and corporate resolutions. These records are accessible to any member who makes a written request at least five business days in advance. The second category includes excerpts of minutes of certain specialized corporate meetings, accounting records of the corporation, and the membership list. Members may inspect these documents only if:

1. The demand is made in good faith and for a proper purpose.
2. The member describes the purpose.
3. The records are directly connected with this purpose.
4. The records are to be used only for that purpose.

Because virtually all of the documents Parker sought fell into the second category, he had to show that he wanted them for a "proper purpose." The trial judge found that Parker did not sufficiently demonstrate proper purpose. We have held that a trial court's findings with respect to whether an applicant has shown a "proper purpose" to compel production of corporate documents must stand unless it is clearly erroneous. After reviewing the record, including the transcript of the hearing, we cannot say that the trial judge's findings are clearly erroneous.

AFFIRMED.

CRITICAL THINKING

What additional information could help you determine whether you agree or disagree with the court's ruling?

ETHICAL DECISION MAKING

Under the WPH process of ethical decision making, who are the stakeholders associated with the court's ruling?

Share transfer. The law generally permits property owners to transfer their property to another person, and, in most cases, stock is considered transferable property. In closely held corporations, however, transfer of stock is usually restricted so that shareholders can choose the corporation's other shareholders. Thus, shareholders in close corporations enjoy the corporate equivalent of the right of *delectus personae.* (Recall from Chapter 35 that the right of *delectus personae* allows partners to choose the individuals with whom they will go into business.) Restrictions on stock transferability must be included on the face of the stock certificate.

One method of restricting stock transferability is called the **right of first refusal.** If a corporation establishes this right in its bylaws, the corporation or its shareholders have the right to purchase any shares of stock offered for resale by a shareholder within a specified period of time.

Corporate dissolution. Shareholders have the right to petition the court to dissolve their corporation if they feel the company cannot continue to operate profitably. According to Section 14.30 of RMBCA, if a corporation engages in any of the following behaviors, shareholders have a legal right to initiate dissolution.

1. Directors are deadlocked in managerial decisions and harming the corporation.
2. Directors are acting in illegal, oppressive, or fraudulent ways.
3. Assets are being wasted or used improperly.
4. Shareholders are deadlocked and cannot elect directors.

Once dissolution has taken place and the corporation has settled its debts with its creditors, shareholders have a right to receive the remaining assets of the company in proportion to the number of shares they own.

Shareholder's derivative suit. One of the shareholder's most important rights is the right to a derivative suit. If corporate directors fail to sue when the corporation has been harmed by an individual, another corporation, or a director, individual shareholders can file a **shareholder's derivative suit** on behalf of the corporation. To be able to file a shareholder's derivative suit in most jurisdictions, a shareholder must have held stock at the time of the alleged wrongdoing. Before filing the suit, the shareholder must file a complaint with the board of directors. If nothing is done in response to the complaint, the shareholder can proceed with the suit. Enron shareholders have brought shareholder's derivative suits against various directors and officers from Enron. Case 39-4 concerns a derivative suit filed by a plaintiff who did not go to the board of directors before filing.

Derivative suits are important when shareholders believe that directors of the corporation are harming the corporation. It seems highly unlikely that directors will sue themselves for damages they caused in these cases. Thus, the shareholder's derivative suit is important to hold the directors accountable for their behavior. Because the shareholder files this suit on behalf of the corporation, all damages recovered are given to the corporation, not the individual shareholder.

Shareholder's direct suit. In addition to their right to bring suit on behalf of the corporation, shareholders can also bring a direct suit against the corporation. In a *shareholder's direct suit,* the shareholder alleges that she has suffered damages caused by the corporation. Several examples of shareholder's direct suits have already been discussed. For example, shareholders can bring a direct suit if the board of directors is improperly withholding dividends or if a shareholder is wrongly denied his right to inspect corporate records. If a court awards damages as a result of a shareholder's direct suit, the damages go to the shareholder personally.

CASE 39-4 MARQUIT v. DOBSON

U.S. DISTRICT COURT FOR THE SOUTHERN DISTRICT OF NEW YORK

U.S. DIST. FED. SEC. L. REP. (CCH) P90, 734 (1999)

Marquit filed a complaint that the management of three closed-end mutual funds in which she owned stock (The Central European Equity Fund, The Spain Fund, and The New Germany Fund) breached their fiduciary duties to their shareholders by trading stock at discounted rates. By trading at these reduced rates, Marquit alleged that they were able to ensure large numbers of outstanding shares, which led to large managerial fees. The defendants moved to dismiss these complaints on the grounds that the plaintiff's complaints were derivative and she failed to seek action from the board of directors before filing her complaint.

JUDGE MARTIN: Because plaintiff's claims are derivative, they must be pled in accordance with FRCP 23.1. Rule 23.1 requires plaintiff to first seek action from the board of directors or to show that such a request would be futile. In this case, plaintiff did not seek action from the funds' boards before instituting these actions, and she has not pled that such a request would be futile.

Nor does it appear from the face of any of the complaints that a demand would be futile. Under Maryland law, a shareholder demand would not be futile if the fund had at least two disinterested directors.

The New Germany Fund and The Spain Fund both have more than two disinterested directors who have no association with any other fund managed by Deutsche Bank. While the Central European Equity Fund has no director who does not serve on the board of at least one other fund managed by Deutsche Bank, more than two of these serve only on one other board and there is no allegation that their compensation is so substantial that it would have an impact on their independence. It is doubtful that the mere fact that a director serves on the board of two funds would be sufficient to compel the conclusion that he was not disinterested.

DISMISSED.

CRITICAL THINKING

What reasons did the court offer to support its conclusion? What do you think about the quality of those reasons?

ETHICAL DECISION MAKING

Recall the WPH framework. Suppose that your decision is guided by the Golden Rule. Why is application of the Golden Rule more complex than it may seem at first glance? CLUE: Are humans so similar that what one person would want to happen in a particular situation is identical to what every other person would want to happen?

Exhibit 39-3
Summary of the Rights of Directors, Officers, and Shareholders

POSITION	RIGHT
Directors	Right to compensation Right to participation Right to inspection Right to indemnification
Officers	Rights determined in employment contract
Shareholders	Stock certificates Preemptive rights Right to dividends Right to transfer shares Inspection rights Right to corporate dissolution Right to file a derivative suit Right to file a direct suit

If more than one shareholder has suffered damages caused by the same act of the corporation, the shareholders may bring a class action suit against the corporation. A *class action suit* is a suit that is brought by one shareholder on behalf of a group of shareholders and is aimed at recovering damages for the entire group.

Exhibit 39-3 lists the respective rights of directors, officer, and shareholders.

CASE OPENER WRAP-UP

Hi-Way and Ken Corp.

As shareholders in Ken Corp., the plaintiffs did have a right to bring suit against the two corporations for potential losses. To prove that James and Thomas Marcuccilli had breached their fiduciary duty, Elizabeth Marcuccilli et al. had to prove that the two men had failed to act in good faith in accordance with the statute. Although there is a great deal of ambiguity in determining what it means to act in good faith, the appellate court determined that the burden to prove that the men did not act in good faith fell to the plaintiffs. Thus, unless the plaintiff's could prove that the directors had acted in bad faith, it did not matter to the court whether they brought a direct or derivative action against the corporations. According to the court, the plaintiffs failed to meet their burden.

The plaintiffs may have been able to demonstrate that James and Thomas did not act in good faith, had they shown that the two men were engaging in personal self-dealing. To do so, the plaintiffs would have had to show that the financial losses they incurred were the result of intentional actions taken by the directors for personal gain.

Summary

Quorum
A corporate directors meeting is valid only when a minimum number of directors is present at the meeting; that minimum number is called a quorum.

Proxy materials
Proxy materials are often sent out to the shareholders before their annual meeting; these proxy materials detail shareholders' ideas for the company.

Proxy
A proxy provides authorization for a third party to vote in place of a shareholder at the shareholders' meeting.

Voting trust
A voting trust is an agreement between a stockholder and a trustee in which the stockholder transfers his or her legal share titles to the trustee, who is then responsible for voting for those shares.

Fiduciary duties
Fiduciary duties are those legal duties to a corporation that individuals within the corporation have. The following are the primary fiduciary duties:

Duty of care: Directors and officers must act in good faith and in a manner that they feel is in accordance with the best interests of the company.

Duty of loyalty: Directors and officers must put the corporation's interest above their own in business decisions. When a director or officer acts in a manner that violates this duty of loyalty, it is called self-dealing.

Duty to disclose conflict of interest: Directors and officers must fully disclose conflicts of interest that arise in corporate transactions.

Business judgment rule
The business judgment rule provides that directors and officers are not liable for decisions that harmed the corporation if they were acting in good faith at the time of the decision.

Watered stock
When stock is issued to individuals at a value below the fair market value, that stock is termed watered stock.

Par-value shares
Par-value shares have a fixed face value noted on the stock certificate.

No-par shares
Those stock shares without a par value are called no-par shares.

Stock subscription agreement
A stock subscription agreement contractually obliges an individual to buy shares in a corporation.

Preemptive rights
On occasion preferential or preemptive rights are given to shareholders to purchase shares of a new issue of stock. This preference is given in proportion to the percentage of stock that the shareholder already owns.

Dividend
Dividends are distributions of corporate profits or income ordered by the directors and paid to the shareholders in proportion to their respective shares in the corporation.

Right of first refusal
The right of first refusal given to existing shareholders to purchase any shares of stock offered for resale by a shareholder within a specified period of time.

Inspection rights
Inspection rights protect shareholder interests by giving them the right to inspect the corporation's books and records after asking in advance to inspect and having a proper purpose.

Stock warrants
Stock warrants are vouchers issued to shareholders entitling them to a given number of shares at a specified price.

Shareholder's derivative suit
A shareholder's derivative suit is filed by a shareholder of a corporation when corporate directors fail to sue in a situation where the corporation has been harmed by an individual or another corporation. Before the suit can be filed, the shareholder must file a complaint with the board of directors; the shareholder can proceed with the suit only if nothing is done in response to the complaint.

Point / Counterpoint

Should Both Majority and Minority Shareholders Have a Fiduciary Duty to Sell Their Shares in Ownership of the Corporation "with Care"?

Yes

Both majority and minority shareholders should sell their shares in ownership of the corporation "with care." Majority and minority shareholders have the potential to benefit from a successful corporation. Thus, all shareholders are obligated to practice care when selling shares of the corporation.

Majority shareholders need to act with care in selling their shares because one purchase of a majority shareholder's stock could give the new majority shareholder sufficient power to dismantle the corporation. However, the minority shareholders also have an obligation to be aware of the changes in stock sales and ownership. In some corporations, a potential shareholder could easily obtain enough minority-shareholder stock to become the majority shareholder—and potentially harm or dismantle the corporation.

Minority shareholders have a responsibility to sell their shares with care because their decision to sell shares (and to whom they sell their shares) influences a wide range of people. Other shareholders, directors, officers, employees, customers, associated businesses and corporations, and the outside community are all affected by a shareholder's decision to sell his shares in a corporation. All of these people trust and rely on the shareholders to keep their interests in mind when making decisions. If a minority shareholder sells his stock to a person who wishes to make a large personal profit through dismantling the corporation, everyone will be hurt. The future of a corporation depends on everyone associated with the corporation, from the smallest shareholder to the largest consumer, and from the majority shareholder to the newest employee.

No

While majority shareholders obviously need to act with care when selling their shares of a corporation, minority shareholders do not.

Minority shareholders are significantly less influential than the majority shareholder in a corporation. When a majority shareholder sells her shares of the corporation, the replacement shareholder has the ability to immediately enact significant changes in the corporation. If the majority shareholder owns a significant portion of the shares of the corporation, the new majority shareholder could even choose to dismantle the corporation. However, when a minority shareholder sells her stock, the new shareholder does not have the power to immediately dismantle the corporation or enact drastic changes without the support of other shareholders. The exception, of course, would occur if the minority shareholder sold her shares to the majority shareholder.

Minority shareholders also are not as heavily invested in the corporation. The majority shareholder holds the potential to benefit significantly more than the minority shareholders. Hence, the care taken by the majority shareholder should be proportionally greater than the care taken by minority shareholders. Because minority shareholders are not as heavily invested in the corporation, their burden and obligation to the corporation should also be less than those of the majority shareholder. Minority shareholders should not be obligated to take as much care or invest as much time when selling their shares.

Questions & Problems

1. Explain the primary duties of officers and directors.
2. Explain the primary duties of shareholders.
3. What is the business judgment rule?
4. XL America, Inc., acquired Intercargo Corporation for $12 a share on May 7, 1999. Before this date, several stockholders of Intercargo requested an injunction against the merger. The court denied this request, and the stockholders amended their complaints. The stockholders sued the directors of Intercargo for breach of fiduciary duty in connection with the merger. They alleged that the directors failed to ensure that the Intercargo stockholders would receive the highest value reasonably attainable and thus did not live up to their duties. They also alleged that the directors failed to disclose material information to the Intercargo stockholders that bore on the stockholders' decision of whether to approve the merger. What do you think the court decided in this case? What facts would the stockholders have to present to convince the judge that the directors had in fact breached their fiduciary duties? [*McMillan v. Intercargo Corporation,* C. A. No. 16963 (2000).]
5. Atlantic PBS, Inc., sued John Long, a former corporate officer, for breaching his fiduciary duties. Atlantic alleged that Long diverted business to another company he owned while still employed at Atlantic. Atlantic sold and installed insulation for commercial and residential buildings. In 1987, while still employed for Atlantic, Long became a 50 percent stockholder in another construction company, R.J. Loughton, Inc. Long left Atlantic later in 1987, but before he left, Long tried to persuade several Atlantic employees to join him at R.J. He also used his contacts at Atlantic to divert business to his new company. As a result of losing its customers, Atlantic suffered financial losses. Atlantic claimed that Long breached his fiduciary duty of loyalty to the company. Do you agree? Why or why not? [*Long v. Atlantic PBS, Inc.,* 681 A.2d 249 (1996).]
6. Sharon Dowell and P&A Irrigation, Inc., sued Steven Bitner for breaches of fiduciary duty owed to Dowell and P&A. Bitner, Dowell's former partner, left P&A to start a competing company. Bitner served as an officer, director, and employee of P&A prior to his departure. After he left P&A, Bitner entered into a contract with a competing supplier and solicited an employee of P&A to join the new business. Bitner established Central Illinois Irrigation on March 20, 1989. He stopped working for P&A on March 18, 1989, and his activities with respect to Central prior to that date were limited to planning and formation. Bitner subsequently contacted customers and notified them that P&A no longer employed him. He explained to the customers that he had started his own business and would appreciate their patronage. Do you think Bitner breached his fiduciary duty to P&A? Why or why not? [*Dowell v. Bitner,* 652 N.E.2d 1372 (1995).]
7. Performance Nutrition, Inc. (PNI), developed, marketed, and sold nutritional supplements. In 1996, Kennedy Capital Management, a major stockholder of PNI, organized an election of the board of directors to put in new management. Anthony Roth, a member of the board of directors, took over as the CEO of PNI. PNI faced financial difficulties, and Naturade, PNI's primary vendor, was interested in buying the company. Roth and officials at Naturade began negotiations, and Naturade assured Roth that a position would be created for him if the takeover was successful. According

to the plan, PNI would file for bankruptcy, and Naturade would purchase its assets. Roth did not share the plan with any other shareholders or members of the board of directors. Although Naturade's offer was unreasonably low, Roth did not make any efforts to sell PNI's assets to any company other than Naturade. Before PNI filed for bankruptcy in 1997, Roth signed a letter of intent to sell PNI's assets to Naturade. Despite the obvious conflict of interest, Roth never included other PNI directors in the decision making. Do you think Roth breached his fiduciary duties to the company? Why or why not? [*In re Performance Nutrition, Inc.,* 239 B.R. 93 (1999).]

8. Boston Children's Heart Foundation (BCHF) is a nonprofit corporation organized for the purposes of conducting medical research and providing medical services to patients at Boston Children's Hospital. Nadal-Ginard was the president and a member of the board of directors of BCHF. He also served as an investigator for the Howard Hughes Medical Institute (HHMI), where he was paid a substantial salary and was involved in similar research. Nadal-Ginard did not disclose his employment with HHMI to the other members of the board of directors. He determined his own salary with BCHF, established a severance benefit plan, and used BCHF funds for personal expenses. After learning that Nadal-Ginard was a salaried employee of HHMI, BCHF filed suit claiming that Nadal-Ginard breached his fiduciary duties to the corporation. The district court agreed with BCHF and awarded damages. Nadal-Ginard appealed the court's decision, arguing that he did not breach his fiduciary duty and that no conflict of interest existed. Do you think the court affirmed the district court's decision? Why or why not? [*Boston Children's Heart Foundation, Inc. v. Bernardo Nadal-Ginard,* 73 F.3d 429 (1996).]

9. Rooney Enterprises, Inc., operates a cemetery. After receiving payments on preened and perpetual-care burial contracts, the corporation failed to make deposits into the appropriate accounts. Paul Rooney, the president of Rooney Enterprises, was criminally convicted for the corporation's failure to make the deposits. Rooney argued that the trial court erred in convicting him for the corporation's actions. No evidence was presented to suggest that Rooney's duties included an accounting responsibility or direct corporate responsibility for withholding or depositing funds. How do you think the responsible person doctrine applies to this case? Was the trial court correct in finding Rooney criminally responsible for the corporation's actions? Why or why not? [*Rooney v. Commonwealth of Virginia,* 500 S.E.2d 830 (1998).]

10. The Oakland Raiders filed suit against the National Football League. The Raiders claimed that NFL management's wrongful control of the NFL entities resulted in a breach of fiduciary duty and adverse treatment of the Raiders. As part of its investigation, the Raiders wanted to inspect the corporate documents of National Football League Properties, Inc. (NFLP). Each of the 30 NFL teams is an equal shareholder of NFLP and has a licensing agreement with it. NFLP acknowledged that the Raiders club was a shareholder but refused to produce certain documents. According to NFLP, the Raiders did not have the right to inspect corporate documents protected by the attorney-client privilege. The court found that, as a member, director, and shareholder of NFLP, the Raiders had the right to examine privileged documents. NFLP challenged the court's decision. How do you think the court of appeals decided? Should the NFLP be compelled to produce the privileged documents? Why or why not? [*National Football League Properties, Inc. v. The Superior Court of Santa Clara County,* 65 Cal. App. 4th 100 (1998).]

11. Left Hand Ditch Company is a nonprofit corporation designed to provide water to shareholders in Boulder County. The shareholders use the water for irrigation,

domestic, industrial, and commercial purposes. Left Hand requires that the shareholders pay yearly payments to provide for funding and maintenance. David and Joan S. Hill own 33 shares of Left Hand stock. The Hills requested to examine a shareholder list. In their letter of request, the Hills explained that they wanted to inspect the list to sell or rent their shares, to better understand what may happen to Left Hand in the future, and to better communicate with other shareholders. Left Hand's board of directors denied the Hills' request, stating that the personal stock holdings were confidential. The Hills filed suit to compel the release of Left Hand's stockholder list. The trial court held that the shareholders were not entitled to inspect the ditch company's shareholder list. The court of appeals reversed the decision and held that the shareholders could inspect the ditch company's shareholder list. The case was then appealed to the supreme court of Colorado. How do you think the court decided? [*Left Hand Ditch Company v. David G. Hill,* 933 P.2d 1 (1997).]

12. Amalgamated Bank, a shareholder of UICI, a Delaware corporation, asked to inspect UICI's books and records to determine whether UICI's directors breached their fiduciary duties or otherwise harmed shareholders by acting illegally. Amalgamated also wanted to determine whether sufficient evidence existed to bring a shareholder action suit against UICI's directors, who had done business with the corporation and had profited handsomely. UICI denied Amalgamated's request for three reasons. First, the statute of limitations for bringing suit against the corporation had expired. Second, some of the meeting minutes requested by Amalgamated did not directly concern the transactions in question. Third, UICI wanted to require that Amalgamated maintain the confidentiality of the information it reviewed. The bank brought suit against UICI, alleging that it ought to be able to review the documents in question because it provided a proper purpose in its letter of request. How do you think the court ruled in this case? Why? [*Amalgamated Bank v. UICI,* 2005 Del. Ch. LEXIS 82 (2005).]

13. Rick Schussel, a director of New Dance Group (NDG) Studio, Inc., made undocumented and unapproved loans to NDG and charged the corporation exorbitant interest rates. To pay back the alleged loans, NDG was forced to mortgage its building. Moreover, Schussel and his family lived in NDG's building and used an NDG automobile for personal use without compensating the corporation. The attorney general brought a suit on behalf of NDG's shareholders to recover the damages Schussel caused and to remove Schussel from NDG's board of directors. Schussel moved to dismiss the suit because the suit was not filed in a timely manner. With whom do you think the court sided in this case? Why? [*Spitzer v. Schussel,* 792 N.Y.S.2d 798 (2005).]

14. Eugene Gagliardi founded TriFoods, Inc. In 1993, he was removed as chairman of the board and his employment with TriFoods was terminated. After Gagliardi left the company, the business of the company deteriorated significantly. Gagliardi owns 13 percent of the company's common stock. He filed a shareholder's derivative suit alleging that the board was liable to the plaintiff and other shareholders for its mismanagement of TriFoods. Though many of the decisions of the board were unsuccessful, the court was unable to determine that the board of directors made any decisions that were not in good faith. Do you think the court found in favor of Gagliardi? Why or why not? How does the business judgment rule apply? [*Gagliardi v. TriFoods International, Inc.,* 683 A.2d 1049 (1996).]

15. In August 1988, Sheldon H. Solow entered into a 10-year lease with PPI Enterprises, and in September 1991 PPI Enterprises breached the lease. Solow found out that the directors of PPI Enterprises entered into many unfavorable financial transactions, including a breach of the lease, that were designed to benefit PPI Enterprises' ultimate

parent, Polly Peck International. These unfavorable financial transactions eventually led to bankruptcy, and Solow could not obtain damages for breach of the lease. Solow brought suit against the directors of PPI Enterprises for breach of the fiduciary duties of care and loyalty. The district court dismissed the suit on grounds that Solow lacked standing to assert claims for breach of fiduciary duty as creditor. Solow appealed on the grounds that the district court erred in holding that he, as an outside creditor, lacked standing to sue PPI Enterprises' officers for breach of fiduciary duties. How do you think the court of appeals decided? Who has a right to file suit against directors for breaching fiduciary duties? [*Solow v. Stone,* 163 F.3d 151 (1998).]

Looking for more review material?

The Online Learning Center at **www.mhhe.com/kubasek1e** contains this chapter's "Assignment on the Internet" and also a list of URLs for more information, entitled "On the Internet." Find both of them in the Student Center portion of the OLC, along with quizzes and other helpful materials.

Corporations: Mergers, Consolidations, Terminations

CASE OPENER

The Merger between Chrysler and Daimler-Benz

When automotive manufacturing giants Chrysler and Daimler-Benz announced their plan to merge in 1998, numerous business law questions emerged. Which corporation's board would govern the new corporation? What would happen to Chrysler stock and Daimler-Benz stock? The merger created the world's fifth-largest automaker, behind General Motors, Ford, Toyota, and Volkswagen. How would antitrust laws affect the legality of the merger? The enormous size of the merger proposal created concern among various interests.

1. If you were a leader in the planned merger, what are some issues you should anticipate? Think about this question from the perspective of shareholders, federal regulatory agencies, and the general public.
2. What methods would you implement to ease these three groups' concerns?

The Wrap-Up at the end of the chapter will answer these questions.

CHAPTER 40

Learning Objectives

After reading this chapter, you will be able to answer the following questions:

1. What are mergers and consolidations?
2. What are the procedures for mergers and consolidations?
3. What are asset purchases?
4. What are stock purchases?
5. How can the nature of takeovers be described?
6. In what ways could the termination of mergers and consolidations occur?

Introduction to Mergers and Consolidations

Although many people believe that mergers and consolidations are synonymous, they are in fact two legally distinct procedures. Nevertheless, in both mergers and consolidations, corporations, shareholders, and creditors have the same rights and liabilities.

MERGERS

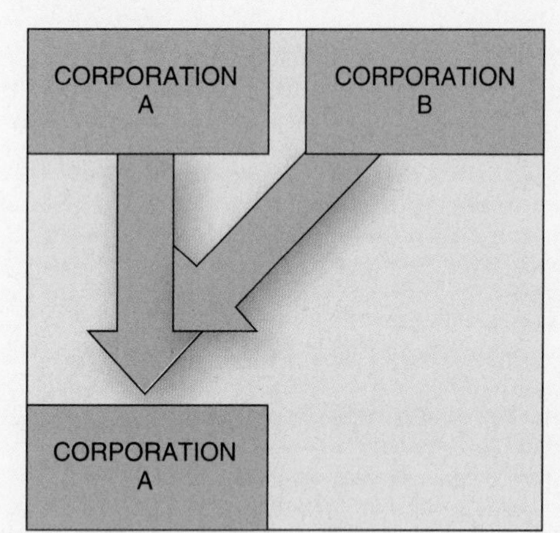

Figure 40-1 Merger

A *merger* occurs when a legal contract combines two or more corporations such that only one of the corporations continues to exist. A useful way to understand a merger is to think of one corporation absorbing another corporation (called an *absorbed corporation* or a *disappearing corporation*), yielding a single *surviving corporation,* as Figure 40-1 illustrates.

The surviving entity remains a single corporation, but it changes in several ways after the merger. First, its shareholders must amend its articles of incorporation according to the specific conditions of the merger. Second, the surviving corporation becomes liable for all debts and obligations of the absorbed corporation.

The surviving corporation also grows from the merger because it obtains the absorbed corporation's property and assets. Additionally, it acquires the absorbed corporation's rights, powers, and privileges. This acquisition can be complicated if the absorbed company had a legal right to sue third parties. The surviving corporation's right to sue for debt and damages on behalf of the absorbed corporation is called a **chose in action** (*chose* is French for "thing"). Although a few states do not allow corporations to transfer their rights, powers, and privileges in a merger, most states agree that if a corporation had a right to sue third parties before a merger, then the surviving corporation retains that right.

The union of Daimler-Benz and Chrysler was a merger because it resulted in a single corporation that took the names of the former corporations. The surviving corporation holds all the liabilities and assets each firm possessed prior to the merger.

CONSOLIDATIONS

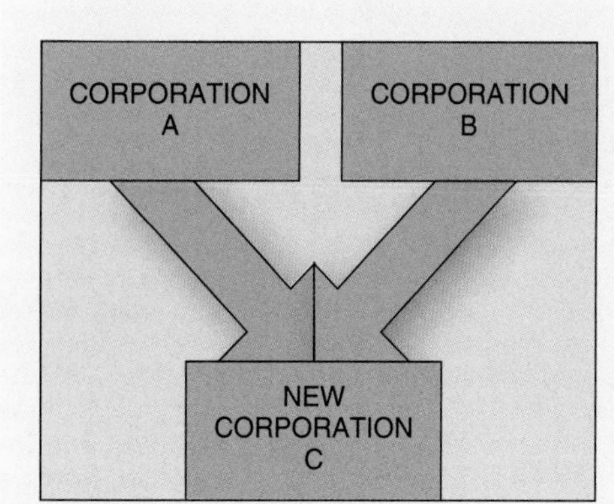

Figure 40-2 Consolidation

Like mergers, *consolidations* legally combine two or more corporations. In a consolidation, however, neither of the original corporations continues to exist legally. Rather, they form an entirely new corporation with its own legal status, as Figure 40-2 illustrates.

Because the new corporation has independent legal status, the articles of incorporation of the original companies are void. The shareholders of the new corporation create new articles of incorporation, called *articles of consolidation,* according to the details of the consolidation.

Consolidated entities assume the liabilities, debts, and obligations of the original corporations. The new corporation also acquires the original corporations' property and assets. Finally, the consolidated corporation takes on the rights, privileges, and powers of the original companies.

connecting to the core

Organizational Behavior

The law teaches us about the legalities that occur when there is a consolidation, but we must recognize that when a consolidation occurs, there are going to be changes in the day-to-day operations of the companies involved. Once employees even hear rumors of a consolidation, there may be pockets of resistance to the resulting change. For a merger or consolidation to go smoothly, the key players involved in the transaction need to remember what they learned in their organizational behavior classes about resistance to change because how key managers and employees respond to the changes brought about by the consolidation will play a key role in whether the new company thrives. Remember that a number of the reasons people resist change are fear of the unknown, insecurity, a belief that there are no reasons for the change, and a lack of good information. Therefore, managers may reduce the disruptions caused by the consolidation by letting employees know (1) how the change will benefit the employees being asked to change and (2) how the change is compatible with existing values of those who are going to be forced to change. To the extent possible, employees whose duties may change as a result of the consolidation should be given as much information as possible as soon as possible, be given the necessary support to make changes in operating procedures, and be given the opportunity to participate in decisions about how changes are to be implemented.

Source: Schermerhorn et al., *Organizational Behavior,* 6th ed. (New York: John Wiley & Sons, 1997).

Today, consolidations are very rare. As Section 11.01 of RMBCA reads, "In modern corporate practice consolidation transactions are obsolete since it is nearly always advantageous for one of the parties in the transaction to be the surviving corporation."

Procedures for Mergers and Consolidations

Whether corporations combine through merger or consolidation, the procedures governing the transition are identical.

State statutes govern mergers and consolidations. In most states, corporations can merge or consolidate with either domestic (in-state) or foreign (out-of-state) corporations. Because acquisitions between domestic corporations are very different from acquisitions between corporations from different states, different laws govern acquisitions between domestic corporations and acquisitions between foreign corporations. Although these laws vary across states, several requirements apply universally:

1. The boards of directors of all involved corporations must approve the merger or consolidation plan.
2. The shareholders of all involved corporations must approve the plan by a vote at a shareholder meeting. Most states require the approval of two-thirds of the outstanding shares of voting stock. If, however, a merger increases the number of the surviving corporation's shares by no more than 20 percent, most states do not require the approval of the surviving corporation's shareholders.
3. The involved corporations must submit the merger or consolidation plan to the secretary of state.
4. After reviewing the plan to ensure that the corporations have satisfied all legal requirements, the secretary of state issues a certificate to grant approval for the merger or consolidation.

global context

Merger Control in France

The aim of merger control statutes in France is not to discourage mergers but to ensure that the combination of businesses does not impede competition. The creation of the Commission for Competition helps foster this goal. The commission, composed of members of the Council of State, magistrates of the administrative or judicial order, and several part-time reporters, is available to offer advice to businesses seeking to merge. The French government, specifically the minister for the economy, also uses the commission as a resource when determining whether a proposed merger will benefit the French economy or whether the resulting concentration of power will decrease competition. After learning of a proposed merger, the minister has three months to issue an opinion. During this period, the minister employs the expertise of the commission. If the commission decides that a proposed merger exceeds reasonable concentration of power, the minister for the economy must intervene with an injunctive option depending on the particular circumstances of the merger. The minister can (1) enjoin the companies from completing the merger, (2) alter the merger's value, (3) make provisions to ensure higher degrees of competition in the market, or (4) arrange compensatory contributions to social or economic welfare if the merger will necessarily reduce competition.

In addition, the surviving or consolidated corporation issues shares or otherwise compensates shareholders of the corporation that no longer exists.

After much discussion, shareholders from Chrysler and Daimler-Benz agreed to a number of conditions for the planned merger. For example, they agreed that Daimler-Benz shareholders could exchange each of their shares for one share of DaimlerChrysler stock and that Chrysler shareholders could exchange each of their shares for .55 share of DaimlerChrysler stock.

Because Daimler-Benz and Chrysler competed in very different markets, federal trade regulators quickly determined that the merger did not violate federal antitrust laws. Other mergers, however, often present antitrust issues and thus require the approval of federal regulators. The 2000 merger between media giants AOL and Time Warner, for example, required the approval of federal trade regulators. In December 2000, approximately a year after the companies first announced the proposed merger, the Federal Trade Commission (FTC) unanimously approved the merger because the new company pledged to protect consumers' choice of services offered by competitors.

Following the FTC's decision, the Federal Communications Commission (FCC) approved the merger in early January, imposing similar conditions on the new company to promote a competitive Internet services market. For example, the FCC required that AOL Time Warner work with EarthLink, an Internet service provider (ISP) and AOL's biggest competitor, as well as with Microsoft and Juno. The FCC also demanded that AOL Time Warner allow subscribers to use its software (i.e., instant messaging) to communicate with subscribers of other ISPs. (Can you see what values the FCC is trying to advance and who it is trying to protect in placing these conditions on the AOL Time Warner merger?) Thus, federal regulators often impose conditions on mergers between competitors to promote competitive markets.

THE RIGHTS OF SHAREHOLDERS

When shareholders invest in corporations, they expect the board of directors to handle daily business issues. They also expect, however, to vote on exceptional matters, including mergers, consolidations, changes in partners, sales or leases of the corporation, and exchanges of assets. Because shareholders have a vested interest in the survival and prosperity of the corporation, these matters are of great significance to them. Thus, the merger and consolidation procedures require shareholder approval. In Case 40-1, the Delaware Supreme Court examined whether a shareholder vote in favor of a merger was legitimate.

CASE 40-1 SMITH v. VAN GORKOM
SUPREME COURT OF DELAWARE
488 A.2D 858 (1985)

Jerome Van Gorkom was a director at Trans Union, a Delaware-based business that leased railcars. He believed the company was in serious financial trouble and that a merger with another company was the best option for Trans Union. Knowing the board of directors and the shareholders were reluctant to negotiate a merger, Van Gorkom investigated the possibility of a merger privately. He sought out Marmon Group, Inc., and asked if it was interested in acquiring Trans Union. Marmon affirmed its interest and created a merger proposal.

Van Gorkom was confident that the deal would save Trans Union from termination, but when he submitted the proposal, Trans Union's board of directors rejected it. The board suggested several amendments to the proposal and made it clear that it would approve the merger only if the proposal included those amendments. Trans Union's stockholders agreed with the board's demands.

Marmon was unwilling to accommodate the changes. To avoid losing the merger deal, Van Gorkom assured the board and stockholders that Marmon would add the amendments to the agreement, even though he knew Marmon would never include them. Thus, the board of directors and shareholders voted to accept an agreement that did not exist.

The shareholders brought a class action suit against Trans Union's board, accusing the members of making an uninformed decision. The Court of Chancery of Delaware ruled that the board acted in an informed manner. Trans Union's shareholders appealed.

JUDGE HORSEY: The Court of Chancery concluded from the evidence that the Board of Directors' approval of the merger proposal fell within the protection of the business judgment rule [see Chapter 38]. The Court found that the Board had given sufficient time and attention to the transaction, since the directors had considered the proposal on three different occasions, on September 20, and on October 8, 1980, and finally on January 26, 1981. On that basis, the Court reasoned that the Board had acquired, over the four-month period, sufficient information to reach an informed business judgment. . . .

Under Delaware law, the business judgment rule is the offspring of the fundamental principle that the business and affairs of a Delaware corporation are managed by or under its board of directors. In carrying out their managerial roles, directors are charged with an unyielding fiduciary duty to the corporation and its shareholders. The business judgment rule exists to protect and promote the full and free exercise of the managerial power granted to Delaware directors. The rule itself "is a presumption that in making a business decision, the directors of a corporation acted on an informed basis, in good faith and in the honest belief that the action taken was in the best interests of the company." Thus, the party attacking a board decision as uninformed must rebut the presumption that its business judgment was an informed one.

We find that Trans Union's stockholders were not fully informed of all facts material to their vote on the merger and that the Trial Court's ruling to the contrary is clearly erroneous. We list the material deficiencies in the proxy materials:

1. The fact that the Board had no reasonably adequate information indicative of the intrinsic value of the Company, other than a concededly depressed market price, was, without question, material to the shareholders voting on the merger.

   Accordingly, the Board's lack of valuation information should have been disclosed. What the Board failed to disclose to its stockholders was that the Board had not made any study of the intrinsic or inherent worth of the Company; nor had the Board even discussed the inherent value of the Company prior to approving the merger on September 20, or at either of the subsequent meetings on October 8 or January 26.
2. We find misleading the Board's references to the "substantial" premium offered. The Board gave as their primary reason in support of the merger the "substantial premium" shareholders would receive. But the Board did not disclose its failure to assess the premium offered in terms of other relevant valuation techniques, thereby rendering questionable its determination as to the substantiality of

the premium over an admittedly depressed stock market price.

3. We find the Board's recital in the Supplemental Proxy of certain events preceding the September 20 meeting to be incomplete and misleading. It is beyond dispute that a reasonable stockholder would have considered material the fact that Van Gorkom suggested the $55 price.

   Although by January 26, the directors knew the basis of the $55 figure, they did not disclose that Van Gorkom chose the $55 price because that figure would enable [Marmon] to both finance the purchase of Trans Union through a leveraged buy out and, within five years, substantially repay the loan out of the cash flow generated by the Company's operations. . . .

4. The Board's Supplemental Proxy Statement, mailed on or after January 27, added significant new matter, material to the proposal to be voted on February 10, which was not contained in the Original Proxy Statement. Some of this new matter was information which had only been disclosed to the Board on January 26; much was information known or reasonably available before January 21 but not revealed in the Original Proxy Statement. Yet, the stockholders were not informed of these facts. Included in the "new" matter first disclosed in the Supplemental Proxy Statement were the following:

(a) The fact that prior to September 20, 1980, no Board member or member of Senior Management knew that Van Gorkom had discussed a possible merger;

(b) The fact that the sale price of $55 per share had been suggested initially by Van Gorkom;

(c) The fact that the Board had not sought an independent fairness opinion;

(d) The fact that several members of Senior Management had indicated concern at the September 20 Senior Management meeting that the $55 per share price was inadequate and had stated that a higher price should and could be obtained; and

(e) The fact that Romans had advised the Board at its meeting on September 20 that he and his department had prepared a study which indicated that the Company had a value in the range of $55 to $65 per share, and that he could not advise the Board that the $55 per share offer which was made was unfair.

The burden must fall on defendants who claim ratification based on shareholder vote to establish that the shareholder approval resulted from a fully informed electorate. On the record before us, it is clear that the Board failed to meet that burden.

We hold, therefore, that the Trial Court committed reversible error in applying the business judgment rule in favor of the director defendants in this case.

REVERSED.

CRITICAL THINKING

What are the primary facts of this case? What additional facts, were they provided, would better enable you to evaluate the judge's reasoning?

What do you think about the quality of the evidence offered in support of the court's conclusion? Does this evidence persuade you? If not, what evidence would persuade you?

ETHICAL DECISION MAKING

Van Gorkom truly believed that the merger was in the best interest of the company. Suppose you were in Van Gorkom's position. If your decision was guided by the Golden Rule, would you have behaved differently than Van Gorkom?

global context

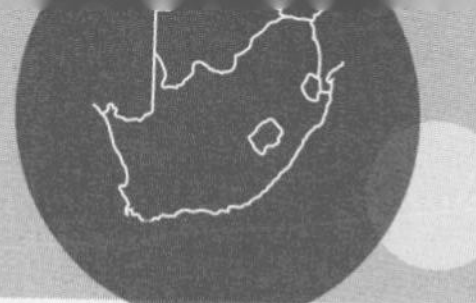

Merger Control in South Africa

South Africa, like many other countries, takes measures to secure a competitive but fair environment for mergers. Specifically, the Companies Act and the rules of the Johannesburg Stock Exchange control mergers. The Companies Act provides protection for minority shareholders. For instance, shareholders cannot approve a merger unless 90 percent of all shareholders vote to accept the offer. Additionally, minority shareholders have access to South African courts and may employ them when disputes arise. The Companies Act also establishes a panel to inquire about mergers or takeovers.

The Johannesburg Stock Exchange has established rules that govern the treatment of shareholders in mergers and takeovers. For example, if a change of corporate control takes place outside the stock exchange, the initiator of the merger must extend the offer to the shareholders and disclose all pertinent information to shareholders within a reasonable amount of time.

SHORT-FORM MERGERS

Although most mergers require shareholder approval, short-form mergers do not. A **short-form merger**, or a **parent-subsidiary merger**, occurs when a parent corporation merges with a subsidiary corporation. The procedure for short-form mergers, detailed in section 11.04 of RMBCA, is simpler than the procedure for mergers between unrelated corporations because short-form mergers can occur without shareholder approval.

Short-form mergers have other requirements, however. The parent corporation must own at least 90 percent of the outstanding shares of each class of the subsidiary's stock. If the proposed short-form merger satisfies this condition, the board of directors of the parent corporation can vote to approve the merger plan. The board must also submit the plan to the subsidiary's shareholders, even though they do not have veto power. Finally, the state must approve the merger proposition.

Although short-form mergers are legal, to protect shareholders from directors, courts often require that directors seek and adhere to shareholders' opinions.

APPRAISAL RIGHTS

The law protects shareholders as a group from corporations, but it also protects individual shareholders from one another. Suppose that although an overwhelming majority of shareholders vote to approve a merger, a single shareholder dissents. In this situation, the law does not force the dissenting shareholder to become a shareholder in a corporation different from the one in which she originally invested. Thus, the law permits dissenting shareholders to exercise their appraisal rights. An **appraisal right** is a dissenting shareholder's right to have his or her shares appraised and to receive monetary compensation from the corporation for their value.

Strict procedures govern appraisal rights. Before a shareholder vote, dissenting shareholders must submit a notification of dissent. By conveying their disapproval before the vote, the dissenting shareholders may sway other shareholders to reconsider their decision. If, however, the shareholder vote approves the transaction, the dissenting shareholders must issue another statement demanding adequate compensation for their shares.

The corporation must then present the dissenting shareholders with a document stating the value of their shares. Shareholders and corporations often clash when determining the value of these shares. Generally, however, they use the value of the shares on the day before the shareholder vote. The language of the law is of little help; it ambiguously calls for the "fair value of shares" (RMBCA 13.01). If the dissenting shareholders and the corporation cannot reach an agreement, courts intervene to establish the shares' value, as Case 40-2 illustrates.

CASE 40-2 CHARLAND v. COUNTRY VIEW GOLF CLUB, INC.

SUPREME COURT OF RHODE ISLAND
588 A.2D 609 (1991)

Gilbert Charland owned fifteen percent of the shares of the Country View Golf Club. Believing that the club's management was engaged in illegal activities, Charland petitioned for the dissolution of the corporation. The other shareholders, some of whom Charland suspected had been involved in the illegalities, did not want the corporation to be dissolved. The remaining shareholders enacted the section of Rhode Island's corporate code that allows shareholders to avoid dissolution by purchasing the dissenter's shares at "a price equal to their fair value . . . as of the close of the business on the day on which the petition for dissolution was filed."

Charland and the golf course's management bickered over the fair value of the shares. Eventually, they hired an outside appraiser to determine the shares' value. The appraiser concluded that Charland's shares were subject to a "minority discount." A minority discount means that the value of the shares is lower because they constitute only a minority of the total shares, and thus their owner lacks decision-making power.

Charland believed the discounted price was unfair. He claimed that it punished him, for if the dissolution were successful, he would be entitled to the same amount per share as all the other shareholders, regardless of how many shares he owned. Thus, by giving him the discounted value, the court would have rewarded the suspect ownership.

The district court ruled that the discounted value should stand. The appeals court, however, reversed the decision. The golf club appealed.

JUSTICE KELLEHER: We shall consider only one issue: whether Charland received fair value for his shares.

Three separate issues must be resolved in determining fair value. The first issue is whether this court should apply a minority discount to Charland's shares. The second issue is whether this court should apply a discount for lack of marketability. The third issue is whether any discount was, in fact, applied to Charland's shares with the result that Charland received less than the fair value.

A minority discount has been described as a second-stage adjustment for valuing minority shares. That is, after a minority shareholder's stock is initially discounted for the minority percentage owned, the pro rata [Latin for "in proportion"; refers to the amount the corporation must pay Charland based on the fractional share of his ownership] value is determined. Then, an additional discount is applied to the pro rata value because the minority shareholder lacks corporate decision-making power. This second calculation is called a minority discount.

The issue of whether to apply a minority discount in a situation in which a corporation elects to buy out a shareholder who has filed for dissolution has never been resolved by this court. In fact, few jurisdictions have decided this question.

Most courts that have considered this question have agreed that no minority discount should be applied when a corporation elects to buy out the shareholder who petitions for dissolution of the corporation.

Brown v. Allied Corrugated Box Co. is an often-cited case in this area of law. In *Brown* a minority shareholder in a closely held corporation initiated an action for involuntary dissolution. The majority shareholder asked to purchase the minority shareholder's stock. The two parties could not reach an agreement regarding the value of the minority shares. A commission comprising three appraisers valued the shares, and two of the three commissioners (majority commissioners) devalued the shares for their noncontrolling status.

On appeal the court reversed the judgment confirming the report of the majority commissioners. The court conceded that if the shares were placed on the open market, their minority status would substantially decrease their value. The court, however, went on to note that this devaluation has little validity when the shares are to be purchased by the corporation. When a corporation elects to buy out the shares of a dissenting shareholder, the fact that the shares are noncontrolling is irrelevant.

In addition, the court in *Brown* observed that had the plaintiffs proved their case and had the corporation been dissolved, each shareholder would have been entitled to the same amount per share. There would be no consideration given to whether the shares were controlling or noncontrolling. Furthermore an unscrupulous controlling shareholder could avoid a proportionate distribution under dissolution by buying out the shares, and the very misconduct and unfairness that incited the minority shareholders to seek dissolution could be used to oppress them further.

We agree with the rationale of *Brown* and hereby adopt the rule that in circumstances in which a corporation elects to buy out a shareholder's stock, we shall not discount the shares solely because of their minority status.

A second and more difficult issue to resolve is whether a lack of marketability discount should be applied to Charland's shares. This discount is separate from and bears no relation to a minority discount. The courts that have addressed this question are divided.

[W]e believe . . . a lack of marketability discount is inapposite when a corporation elects to buy out a shareholder who has filed for dissolution of a corporation. As a recent law review article noted:

> In dissolution cases, strong reasons support the use of pro rata value without a discount. A minority shareholder seeking dissolution claims that majority shareholders have engaged in some unfair, possibly tortious, action. If the minority shareholder succeeds in having the company dissolved, all shareholders will receive their pro rata share of the assets, with no account given to the minority [or illiquidity] status of their shares. Minority shareholders should not receive less than this value if, instead of fighting the dissolution action, the majority decides to seek appraisal of minority shares in order to buy out the minority and reduce corporate discord.

We therefore today adopt the rule of not applying a discount for lack of marketability.

We therefore remand this case to the Superior Court to determine the fair value of Charland's shares as of September 4, 1984, without applying a discount for either minority status or lack of marketability of his shares in Country View in conformity with the rules set forth herein.

REMANDED.

CRITICAL THINKING

Justice Kelleher's reasoning relies heavily on an analogy between the case at hand and *Brown v. Allied Corrugated Box Co.* Do you find this analogy to be persuasive? If *Brown v. Allied Corrugated Box Co.* never happened, what reasons do you think the court would use to support its conclusion?

ETHICAL DECISION MAKING

Think about the WPH process of ethical decision making. Which stakeholders are particularly affected by the court's ruling? Why?

Procedures for appraisal rights. The procedures governing appraisal rights are extensive. If the dissenting shareholders hope to receive compensation, they must follow the procedures accurately.

Dissenting shareholders who properly exercise their appraisal rights experience changes in their legal status as shareholders and in corresponding rights, depending on the jurisdiction. In some states, the law strips dissenting shareholders of their rights, including the right to vote and receive dividends. Shareholders who lose their legal status, however, retain the right to sue based on evidence of illegal conduct associated with the merger or consolidation. Some states that revoke dissenting shareholders' legal status reinstate their status during the appraisal process. Thus, shareholders can withdraw from the appraisal process, contingent on corporate approval. Other jurisdictions do not reinstate status until after the appraisal is finished.

The issue of legal status and rights arises only if dissenting shareholders properly invoke their appraisal rights. If dissenting shareholders do not properly invoke these rights, courts force them to comply with the decision of the majority of the corporations' shareholders. If you were to operate within the WPH framework, would you find these procedures adequate, restrictive, or overly simplistic?

Exhibit 40-1 summarizes the core concepts of corporation mergers.

Exhibit 40-1
Review of Mergers and Consolidations

- A merger occurs when a legal contract combines two or more corporations such that only one corporation continues to exist.
- A consolidation occurs when a legal contract combines two or more corporations, resulting in an entirely new corporation.
- The procedures governing mergers and consolidations are identical:
    1. The boards of directors of all involved corporations must approve the plan.
    2. Shareholders of all involved corporations must approve the plan.
    3. The corporations must submit the plan to the secretary of state.
    4. The state issues certification indicating its approval of the merger or consolidation.
- Short-form mergers do not require shareholder approval, but they can occur only when a parent company absorbs a subsidiary company.
- An appraisal right is a dissenting shareholder's right to have her or his shares appraised and to receive monetary compensation from the corporation for that value.

Purchase of Assets

In addition to engaging in mergers and consolidations, corporations can extend their business operations by purchasing all or a substantial amount of another corporation's assets. *Assets* include intangible items (such as goodwill, a company name, and a company logo) and tangible items (such as buildings and other property). When an asset purchase occurs, the acquiring corporation (the one purchasing the assets) assumes ownership and control over tangible and intangible assets of the selling corporation.

The selling corporation needs the approval of both its board of directors and its shareholders before it can sell its assets. Shareholders of the acquired corporation who disagree with the transfer can demand appraisal rights in most states. Whether the acquiring corporation needs shareholder approval depends on the extent to which the merger alters the corporation's business position. Asset purchases normally do not change a corporation's legal status; thus, acquiring corporations do not usually need shareholder approval.

Although asset purchases seem similar to mergers and consolidations, they are significantly different because a corporation that purchases the assets of another corporation does not acquire its liabilities. In contrast, mergers and consolidations transfer all obligations.

In three circumstances, however, the acquiring corporation does assume the liabilities of the selling corporation. First, the contract governing the purchase may expressly or impliedly state that the acquiring corporation takes on the selling companies' liabilities in addition to its assets.

Second, although the two corporations may intend the transaction to be a purchase of assets, it may fall within the legal framework of a merger or consolidation. Thus, the acquiring corporation receives both the assets and liabilities of the selling corporation.

Third, the purchaser does not avoid the selling corporation's liabilities if the corporations execute the sale under fraudulent circumstances. The U.S. Department of Justice and the Federal Trade Commission have stringent guidelines to ensure that the directors and shareholders of the acquired corporation have not used the asset sale to escape payment of obligations or pending lawsuits. These guidelines make it difficult, and sometimes impossible, for corporations to acquire other corporations through asset purchases. Thus, a corporation seeking to extend its business by purchasing another corporation's assets must be familiar with these guidelines to ensure that the sale is legal.

Some states and courts recognize a fourth circumstance in which acquiring corporations assume the liabilities of selling corporations. If the acquiring corporation continues one of the selling corporation's product lines, the acquiring corporation becomes liable for defects in those products.

Exhibit 40-2 summarizes the fundamental principles of asset purchases.

Exhibit 40-2 Review of Asset Purchases

- When one corporation purchases the assets of another, the purchaser assumes control over the tangible and intangible assets of the acquired corporation.
- The purchasing corporation does not, however, acquire the liabilities of the purchased corporation.

Purchase of Stock

Besides engaging in mergers, consolidations, and asset purchases, corporations can extend their operations by purchasing another corporation's stock. As with asset purchases, an acquiring corporation, or *aggressor,* can buy any or all of another corporation's voting shares. Through such a stock purchase, the purchasing corporation gains control of the selling corporation in a corporate takeover.

The Nature of Takeovers

During the 1980s, not only did the number of corporate takeovers increase, so too did the number of hostile takeovers. **Hostile takeovers** are takeovers to which the management of the target corporation objects. When a hostile takeover succeeds, the target corporation's management frequently compares the transition to a full-scale invasion characterized by layoffs and dramatic changes in company policy.

In the 1980s, corporations afraid of a hostile takeover concealed financial difficulties so as not to appear vulnerable to other corporations. Thus, they maintained a strong profile within the business community while their directors secretly sought a way out of their financial troubles.

TYPES OF TAKEOVERS

To initiate a stock purchase, the aggressor must appeal directly to the shareholders of the corporation it hopes to buy, known as the *target corporation.* The aggressor can offer several types of deals to the target shareholders. It can make a **tender offer,** in which it offers target shareholders a price above the current market value of the stock. Aggressors, however, often require that they receive a certain number of shares within a certain time frame.

global context

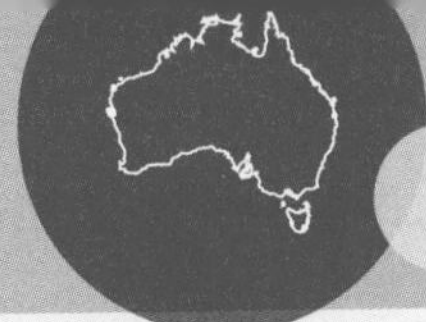

Mergers and Takeovers in Australia

The Foreign Investment Review Board (FIRB) oversees foreign takeovers and mergers of Australian businesses. The board bases its approval on the extent to which a takeover will help the Australian economy. The Department of the Treasury has legitimized the approval process by creating criteria to establish whether a particular takeover will benefit the economy.

Two methods dominate takeovers in Australia: formal takeovers and on-market offers. A *formal takeover* begins when the shareholder director of the Australian corporation sends shareholders a list of information about the potential foreign investor. Next, the investor sends details of the offer to the shareholders so that they have enough information to recommend or reject the takeover. After reviewing the information, the shareholders vote on the takeover and pass their decision along to the initiating corporation.

In an *on-market offer,* the foreign investor appoints a firm listed on the stock exchange to buy shares in the Australian corporation at a specified price during a stipulated time period. Because the firm must complete this transaction in cash, the formal takeover is more popular among foreigners wishing to acquire an Australian company.

Alternatively, the aggressor may make an exchange tender offer. In an **exchange tender offer,** the aggressor offers to exchange target shareholders' current stock for stock in the aggressor's corporation. The aggressor may also make a **cash tender offer** to the target shareholders in which it pays them cash for their stock.

Other types of takeovers are more covert than these tender offers. For example, a **beachhead acquisition** occurs when an aggressor gradually accumulates the target company's shares. (The accumulated bloc of shares is analogous to a beachhead, an initial area of control from which the aggressor can launch later attacks.)

After acquiring a substantial number of the target corporation's shares, the aggressor initiates a proxy fight by fighting for control over target shareholders' proxies. (Chapter 39 discusses proxies in more detail.) Because the holder of a proxy has the right to vote at shareholder meetings, if an aggressor can control a majority of proxies, it can outvote the other shareholders. The aggressor can then use the proxies it controls to elect a board of directors that supports the acquisition.

Before an aggressor can gain control of the target corporation through proxies, it needs a key piece of information: a list of target shareholders. Although resistant target corporations often wish to conceal this information, federal securities law requires that target corporations assist aggressors in some ways. Thus, to avoid lengthy and expensive lawsuits, target corporations often provide a list of shareholders voluntarily. Providing the list does not guarantee that the aggressor will succeed, especially because federal regulations protect the target corporation. For instance, federal regulations permit management of target companies to use corporate funds to educate shareholders on the disadvantages of a takeover.

Those seeking to acquire corporations have developed tactics to overcome the law's rules encouraging cooperation from target corporations. Because contacting each individual target shareholder is expensive, aggressors often try to win the favor of a few institutional investors that own a large bloc of shares. If an aggressor can obtain the proxies of these investors, it can win control of the target corporation.

RESPONSE TO TAKEOVERS

Once an aggressor has presented its offer to the target corporation's shareholders, the target corporation's board of directors must inform shareholders of all facts pertinent to shareholders' votes. After reviewing these material facts, the directors vote to accept or reject the offer and advise shareholders accordingly.

If the directors conclude that a takeover is not in the company's best interest, the company may employ many methods of resistance. One common method is a **self-tender offer**, in which the target corporation offers to buy its shareholders' stock. If the shareholders accept the offer, the target corporation maintains control of the business.

Alternatively, target corporations may defend themselves using leveraged buyouts. A **leveraged buyout (LBO)** occurs when a group within a corporation (usually management) buys all outstanding corporate stock held by the public. Thus, the group gains control over corporate operations by "going private," or becoming a privately held corporation.

LBOs are usually high-risk endeavors, however, because the target corporation must borrow money to purchase the outstanding stock. It may have to borrow money from an investment bank or issue corporate bonds.

Illustrative jargon describes many methods of resistance to corporate takeovers. Exhibit 40-3 decodes the language of takeover defenses. In Case 40-3, the Georgia court of appeals considers the legality of a "golden parachute."

Exhibit 40-3
The Language of Takeovers

Crown jewel	A corporation sells its most valuable asset, or "crown jewel," thereby making a takeover less attractive for aggressors.
Golden parachute	When an aggressor acquires a target corporation, it usually fires the target corporation's managers or asks them to retire. Anticipating takeover, the target corporation's management often establishes lavish termination and retirement benefits. Then, when the aggressor forces them to jump from the corporation's plane (figuratively, of course), their "parachutes" are lined with gold.
Greenmail	Aggressors using greenmail tactics are like blackmailers in the sense that they slowly accumulate shares of the target corporation. If the target corporation wishes to remain in control of the company, the aggressors charge it exorbitant prices for the shares.
Lobster trap	A target corporation forbids holders of convertible securities—corporate bonds or stocks that can be converted into common shares—from exchanging their securities into common shares if the conversion results in the owner holding more than 10 percent of the voting shares of stock. This defense prevents aggressors from targeting shareholders with large blocs of voting stock. It is similar to a lobster trap, which traps large lobsters but lets little ones escape.
Pac-Man	In the video game, Pac-Man swallows other characters. In business, a target corporation may defend against takeover by trying to "swallow" an aggressor in a takeover bid of its own.
Poison pill	A target corporation issues shares that can be redeemed for cash if a takeover occurs. This defense makes a takeover unattractive or impossible for aggressors.
Scorched earth	Target corporations make their businesses as barren, useless, and unattractive as a piece of scorched earth by selling off assets or taking out large loans.
Shark repellent	Target corporations often see aggressors as sharks seeking to destroy them. They attempt to repel sharks by amending their articles of incorporation to render takeovers more difficult.
White knight	Just as a white knight rescues those in distress, so, too, can a third party rescue a target corporation from a takeover. A target corporation solicits the "white knight" to make a more favorable offer to target shareholders.

CASE 40-3 ROYAL CROWN COMPANIES, INC. v. MCMAHON

COURT OF APPEALS OF GEORGIA
183 GA. APP. 543 (1987)

McMahon was the president of Arby's Inc., a subsidiary of Royal Crown Companies, Inc. It appeared that another corporation was positioning itself to buy Royal Crown. To reassure its top managers, Royal Crown enacted agreements stipulating that management would receive severance pay in the event of termination of employment or resignation after change of corporate control. McMahon resigned after the aggressor bought Royal Crown, but he did not receive his severance pay. He sued the corporation, and the trial court found in his favor. Royal Crown appealed.

JUDGE POPE: Royal Crown seeks to distinguish the agreement under consideration from the typical severance agreement because it is a special type of contract, which is commonly referred to as a "golden parachute." We are unpersuaded by Royal Crown's attempt, largely without legal support, to defeat this otherwise enforceable severance agreement simply because it is contingent upon a change in corporate control. The term "golden parachute" is not by itself legally significant. A severance contract by any other name would be just as enforceable.

Royal Crown argues that golden parachute agreements, in general, bear the taint of a conflict of interest in favor of the management beneficiaries to the detriment of the shareholders. We find no such conflict here. Plaintiff was not a member of the board of directors which approved this agreement. Moreover, the agreement was offered for the express purpose of protecting the shareholders by inducing the continued employment of plaintiff during a time of uncertainty when he might otherwise have been distracted by concerns for his own financial security to seek employment elsewhere.

Neither is the agreement void for failure of consideration. In the case at hand, plaintiff's employment was terminable at will and he was under no obligation to continue. The agreement was offered for the express purpose of inducing plaintiff to remain in his position during merger negotiations. Continued performance under a terminable-at-will contract furnishes sufficient consideration for the promise of additional severance pay. "We therefore reject any argument by the [employer] that any contract for severance pay is void as being without consideration."

AFFIRMED.

CRITICAL THINKING

Is there any missing information you would ask for when considering the facts of this case? If you were to argue to reverse the trial court's decision, what reasons would you offer? In your opinion, which of these reasons is the most persuasive? Do you find the court's reasons to affirm the trial court's decision to be equally persuasive?

ETHICAL DECISION MAKING

Think about the WPH process of ethical decision making. What is the purpose of the court's decision? In other words, which value is upheld? What value is in conflict with the reasoning of the court?

- When an aggressor purchases a substantial amount of the stock of a target corporation, the aggressor gains control of that corporation.
- The nature of these takeovers can be hostile.
- An aggressor can present the target corporation's stockholders with a tender offer, an exchange tender offer, or a cash tender offer. It can also acquire a target corporation through a beachhead acquisition or a leveraged buyout.
- A target corporation can defend against a takeover offer with a self-tender request.

Exhibit 40-4
Review of Stock Purchases

Federal securities laws and state statutes promote fair acquisitions by strictly regulating the stock purchase process. If a target corporation suspects that a takeover attempt violates federal law, it can petition for an injunction. Courts are likely to grant an injunction if the acquisition gives the aggressor unfair market power.

Exhibit 40-4 provides a review of stock purchases.

Response to Termination

The "death" of a corporation occurs in two phases: *dissolution,* the legal termination of the corporation, and *liquidation,* the process by which the board of directors converts the corporation's assets into cash and distributes them among the corporation's creditors and shareholders.

DISSOLUTION

Dissolution may be voluntary or involuntary, depending on who initiates and compels the dissolution. *Voluntary dissolution* occurs when the directors or shareholders trigger the dissolution procedures. The directors can initiate the proposal and submit it to the shareholders for a vote, or the shareholders can begin dissolution procedures. Either way, for dissolution to be successful, shareholders must unanimously vote for the proposal.

Regardless of whether the directors or shareholders initiate dissolution procedures, the corporation must follow specific procedures. First, the directors must file articles of dissolution with the secretary of state. These articles must include the company name, the date of dissolution, and the method of authorization of dissolution. Next, the directors must notify the shareholders. If shareholders or creditors have claims against the corporation, they must make them known within a stipulated time frame. Although the corporation establishes the time frame, the period must extend at least 120 days after the date of dissolution.

In an *involuntary dissolution,* the state forces the corporation to close. The state can initiate dissolution procedures, or individual shareholders can petition the state to order dissolution if they believe sufficient reason exists to terminate business operations. In some states, an individual shareholder of a closely held corporation can dissolve the corporation at will or after an event specified in the articles of incorporation occurs.

The secretary of state can compel involuntary dissolution for five reasons (RMBCA 14.20):

1. The corporation failed to pay taxes within 60 days of the due date.
2. The corporation failed to submit its annual report to the secretary of state within 60 days of the due date.
3. The corporation did not have a registered agent or office in the state for 60 days or more.
4. The corporation failed to notify the secretary of state within 60 days that its registered agent or registered office had changed.
5. The corporation's duration as specified in its articles of incorporation has expired.

In addition, courts can force involuntary dissolution for three reasons (RMBCA 14.30):

1. The corporation obtained its articles of incorporation fraudulently.
2. The directors have abused their power (*ultra vires* acts).
3. The corporation is insolvent.

Courts can also enforce involuntary dissolution if gridlock over an issue persists among the directors. Before ordering dissolution, however, courts usually urge shareholders to attempt to resolve the differences. If shareholders are unsuccessful, courts consider the extent to which the deadlock will result in irreversible damage to the corporation. If the disagreement will likely cause significant damage, courts will order the corporation to dissolve.

LIQUIDATION

The liquidation phase of termination begins once dissolution has occurred. In cases of voluntary dissolution, liquidation duties fall on the board of directors. The members of the board also become trustees of the corporate assets. As trustees, board members hold title to the corporation's property and become personally liable for breaches of fiduciary trustee duties.

Due to the heavy responsibilities trustees bear, some board members do not want to act as trustees. In other situations, shareholders do not want to entrust directors with the distribution of corporate assets. In these situations, the objecting party can petition the court to appoint a receiver not affiliated with the corporation to take over liquidation duties.

In cases of involuntary dissolution, courts automatically appoint a receiver to handle liquidation duties. Like the law in general, the law governing corporate terminations is dynamic; it changes in response to a host of external factors. Hence, although a company is legally terminated after it completes dissolution and liquidation, the law's view of the extent of the company's posttermination responsibilities has changed over time in response to scientific and technological developments. In the past, a corporation's liabilities dissolved when the corporation dissolved. Recently, however, scientists have discovered that companies' actions can have environmental effects that do not appear until many years later. Thus, stimulated by these scientific developments, courts have held that dissolved corporations remain responsible for their liabilities.

Case 40-4 arose out of an instance in which a party claims to have liquidated assets and thus is trying to avoid liability for environmental damage. However, at the heart of the case is this issue: Did Rock Island Line liquidate its assets? When reading the case, pay attention to how the court determines whether a liquidation occurred.

CASE 40-4 MAYTAG CORPORATION v. NAVISTAR INTERNATIONAL TRANSPORTATION CO. ET AL.

U.S. COURT OF APPEALS FOR THE SEVENTH CIRCUIT
219 F.3D 587 (2000)

The Rock Island Line, losing about $40 million annually, abandoned its railroad operations as part of a bankruptcy under § 77 of the Bankruptcy Act of 1898. Free of its cash sinkhole, the Rock Island retired its debts and emerged from bankruptcy as the Chicago Pacific Corporation, a holding company with more than $350 million in liquid assets, substantial operating loss carryovers, and a portfolio of miscellaneous business ventures. Chicago Pacific merged into Maytag Corporation, manufacturer of refrigerators, ranges, and other appliances.

One of Chicago Pacific's assets when the bankruptcy wrapped up was the Iowa Transfer Railway, which owned a railyard in Rock Island, Illinois, near the Sylvan Slough, a tributary of the Mississippi River. Four months out of bankruptcy, Chicago Pacific sold the Iowa Transfer to Heartland Rail Corporation, which leased the yard and other operating assets to Iowa Interstate Railroad. Iowa Interstate has operated that business ever since. In 1993 the Coast Guard concluded that petroleum is leaking from the railyard into the Sylvan Slough. Heartland and Iowa Interstate are cleaning up the premises and adjacent land, an expensive endeavor. Two of their neighbors, Navistar International Transportation Corp. and the Burlington Northern & Santa Fe Railway, blame Heartland and Iowa Interstate for pollution. They have sued under the Oil Pollution Act of 1990, demanding Heartland and Iowa Interstate contribute toward their own cleanup costs. Heartland, Iowa Interstate, Navistar, and Burlington Northern all believe that much of the oil seeped into the land while the Rock Island Line was operating the yard. All four have added Maytag (as Chicago Pacific's successor) as a third-party defendant. Maytag asserts, because the Rock Island was "liquidated" rather than "reorganized," Maytag did not inherit any of the Rock Island's debts. The district court agreed, and the other parties appealed.

JUDGE EASTERBROOK: Debts do not pass to those who buy assets (unless contracts provide for this transfer), though shareholders may be liable up to the amount of a net distribution when a corporation dissolves, and federal law does not displace the norm that corporate liability ends with the corporation's existence. Section 113(a)(1) of the Comprehensive Environmental Response, Compensation, and Liability Act (cercla), 42 U.S.C. § 9613(a)(1), permits a person who has paid for a cleanup to obtain contribution "from any other person who is liable or potentially liable under section 107(a)"; § 107(a)(2) in turn allows recovery from "any person who *at the time of disposal* of any hazardous substance owned or operated any facility at which such hazardous substances were disposed of" (emphasis added). A buyer or distributee of a polluter's assets does not qualify under this language. Even when state law makes the buyer of assets that constitute an ongoing business liable as a successor, it does not impose liability on firms that purchase assets unrelated to those that created the deferred liability.

The Northern District addressed the second of Maytag's arguments, concluded that the Rock Island Line had been liquidated rather than reorganized, and enjoined prosecution of the action against Maytag. According to the Northern District, "the Rock Island abandoned and liquidated its rail business more than three years prior to the consummation order. The only assets it retained were non-rail related, and which were used to create [Chicago Pacific] in an effort to maximize the ability to satisfy the claims of the Rock Island's creditors. . . . Therefore, we . . . [hold] that the Rock Island was liquidated, eliminating any entity which might be sued, regardless of when the claim arose."

The underpinning of this passage, and of the district court's conclusion, is that abandonment of the rail business is the same thing as corporate liquidation. But that is untenable. Corporations change lines of business frequently without liquidating. If Maytag tomorrow were to abjure the washing-machine business to concentrate on refrigerators and microwave ovens, it would not have "liquidated" and would remain liable for debts (including deferred environmental liabilities) associated with its whole line of appliances.

Just so with the Rock Island. During bankruptcy the Rock Island quit the railroad business but retained substantial assets. The corporate entity was renamed "Chicago Pacific Corporation" at the close of the bankruptcy, and Chicago Pacific avowedly was a continuation of the original firm, rather than (say) the buyer or distributee of the Rock Island's assets. How else could Chicago Pacific have retained the Rock Island's substantial operating loss carryforwards? Tax attributes cannot be sold or given away; only the company that generated the losses may use them. When the bankruptcy wrapped up, accumulated tax losses were a major asset of the estate. It would have been folly to throw them away, as a liquidation would have done. And there is substantial reason to doubt that § 77 of the old Bankruptcy Act even allowed liquidations; certainly they could not be accomplished under that name.

Liquidation in or out of bankruptcy means the end of a corporation's existence. Liquidation may occur without closing down a line of business: a firm may sell its assets as a going concern, then distribute the proceeds to its creditors (and, if a surplus remains, to its equity holders) and dissolve. Likewise abandonment may occur without liquidation. Many a firm in bankruptcy has a positive cash flow from current operations but is unable to meet its debts—perhaps because it has made promises to creditors that prove excessive in retrospect, perhaps because one line of business has gone sour. Such debtors withdraw from the losing line of business (by selling it *en bloc,* selling it piecemeal, or abandoning it utterly) and

[CONTINUED]

restructure their debt, emerging with bright prospects in their remaining endeavors. That classic reorganization is exactly what Rock Island the corporation did, retaining its profitable activities and transmuting into Chicago Pacific Corporation (and then Maytag), even though the Rock Island Line is defunct.

On remand the district court must consider whether Maytag, as the continuation of the Rock Island, is entitled to protection under the injunction issued in 1984.

REVERSED AND REMANDED.

CRITICAL THINKING

What were Judge Easterbrook's reasons for arguing that a liquidation did not occur? Given what you have just learned about liquidations, do you agree?

ETHICAL DECISION MAKING

Even if the court ruled that a liquidation had occurred, should Maytag be held liable for any environmental damage caused by Rock Island Line? Why?

Exhibit 40-5
Review of Termination

- Dissolution is the legal death of a corporation.
- Voluntary dissolution occurs when an entity within the corporation initiates corporate termination procedures.
- Involuntary dissolution occurs when the state orders a company to terminate.
- Liquidation is the distribution of corporate assets among creditors and shareholders.
- A trustee carries out the liquidation and can be either a director or a court-appointed receiver.

A review of termination of a corporation is provided in Exhibit 40-5.

CASE OPENER WRAP-UP

DaimlerChrysler

The $36 billion merger between Chrysler and Daimler-Benz carried many risks. Past mergers between large automobile manufacturers had not been successful. Moreover, the two companies involved in the merger had starkly different products and management styles.

But the directors of Chrysler and Daimler-Benz negotiated terms agreeable to shareholders of both companies. Daimler-Benz shareholders would own a majority of the new company's shares. The new company, incorporated in Germany, would have headquarters in Detroit, Michigan, and Stuttgart, Germany. Shareholders also agreed that, at least initially, Robert Eaton, Chrysler's chief executive, and Jurgen Schrempp, Daimler-Benz's chief executive, would jointly run the new company.

Summary

Introduction to Mergers and Consolidations

Merger: A legal contract combining two or more corporations such that only one of the corporations continues to exist.

Consolidation: A legal contract combining two or more corporations, resulting in an entirely new corporation.

Procedures for Mergers and Consolidations

1. Boards of directors of all involved corporations must approve the plan.
2. Shareholders must approve the plan through a vote at a shareholder meeting.
3. The corporations must submit their plan to the secretary of state.
4. The state reviews the plan and grants an approval certificate.

Short-form merger: The parent corporation merges with a subsidiary corporation. Short-form mergers do not require shareholder approval.

Rights of shareholders: Shareholders vote only on exceptional matters regarding the corporation.

Appraisal right: An appraisal right is the shareholder's right to have his or her shares appraised and to receive monetary compensation for their value.

Purchase of Assets

One corporation can extend its business operations by purchasing the assets of another company.

Purchase of Stock

An acquiring corporation can take control of another corporation by purchasing a substantial amount of its voting stock.

The Nature of Takeovers

A corporation can expand its size and operations by purchasing the stock of another firm.

A *hostile takeover* is a takeover to which the management of the target corporation objects.

Types of takeovers:

1. Tender offers
2. Exchange offers
3. Cash tender offers
4. Beachhead acquisitions

Response to Termination

Response to takeovers: Directors declare whether they accept or reject the offer. If they object to the offer, they can engage in methods of resistance.

Dissolution is the legal death of a corporation.

In *liquidation,* a corporation sells all of its assets and distributes them to repay its outstanding debts.

Point / Counterpoint

Is the Beachhead Acquisition Takeover Method Superior to the Tender Offer Takeover Method?

Yes

The best type of corporate takeover is easily a beachhead acquisition. First, an aggressor becomes gradually involved in the operations of a target company when preparing for a beachhead acquisition. In tender offers, the aggressor just buys out key shareholders at market value and forces the company to sell. Though tender offers are sometimes faster than beachhead acquisitions, the advantages of the beachhead acquisition far outweigh the speed of the tender offer. For example, gradually becoming involved in the company lessens suspicions of and increases trust in the aggressor. Dealing with fewer initial suspicions gives the aggressor time to gain support from within the company.

Second, taking over from "inside" the corporation, rather than just buying out the company directly, allows the aggressor to appear unified with part of the target company. The rest of the target company is less likely to resist a takeover if part of the company has already unified with the aggressor.

Further, inside support shows the public that the aggressor is strong. Additionally, inside support shows that after the takeover is complete, the acquisition of the target company will likely be smooth.

Some shareholders have a high personal investment in the target company. Hence, these shareholders would be extremely resistant to simply selling off their shares and allowing the aggressor to do as it pleases to the company. The shareholders would like to remain involved in their "pet" company. These shareholders, however, may be more willing to vote *with* the aggressor if they feel their interests will continue to be protected.

No

The beachhead acquisition is the most hostile takeover method and is inferior to the tender offer method.

The beachhead acquisition is excessively hostile. In performing the beachhead acquisition, aggressors "sneak" into the company and manipulate shareholders. Rather than being up front about intentions, aggressors try to convince shareholders that the aggressor company has the shareholders' best interests at heart.

Even after the takeover, the target company morale may be damaged due to the methods used in the beachhead acquisition. As a result, the aggressor company could be left with poor worker-management-shareholder relations in the remaining company.

Additionally, the hostile appearance of the beachhead acquisition may cause a strong defense against the aggressor company. The shareholders in the target company would be fighting a sneaky, "mean" company to protect their "pet" company. It is highly unfortunate for the aggressor if the target company fears the aggressor because the fear will make the process of taking over the target company lengthier and much more difficult overall.

The tender offer method is superior because buying out shareholders is often easier than convincing shareholders to change their opinion in support of a competitor. Quite frankly, people are persuaded by cold, hard cash. Cash-for-stock and stock-for-stock options are tangible and immediate. Promises-for-votes arrangements are intangible and not guaranteed. Money and stock are much more appealing because they are much more secure. Hence, the tender offer takeover is superior to the beachhead acquisition method.

Questions & Problems

1. What are the primary differences between mergers and consolidations?
2. Distinguish the various types of takeovers.
3. In 1993, Continental Brands, a small manufacturer of industrial adhesives, faced significant financial struggles. Not only was Continental substantially in debt, but defects with its products plagued the company. Continental was also responsible for the existence of hazardous waste it stored at one of its facilities. TACC International, Inc., agreed to invest in Continental. TACC combined its manufacturing operations with Continental's operations, and in 1993 TACC distributed an announcement stating, "TACC International Corporation . . . is pleased to announce the acquisition of the Continental Brands Corporation. . . . All key Continental personnel have joined TACC International to insure continuity and continued growth." National Gypsum Company (NGC) and L&W Supply Corp., suppliers of building materials to the construction industry, filed actions against Continental and TACC, alleging that Continental was directly liable for damage caused by its defective adhesive products and that TACC was liable as Continental's successor. How do you think the court decided this case? Do you think it should hold TACC liable? Why or why not? [*National Gypsum Company v. Continental Brands Corp.,* 895 F. Supp. 328 (1995).]
4. Hilton Hotels Corporation announced a $55 per share tender offer for the stock of ITT. When Hilton announced plans for a proxy contest at ITT's 1997 annual meeting, ITT formally rejected Hilton's tender offer and began to sell some of its assets. Hilton learned that ITT was not planning on conducting its annual meeting, and it sought an injunction to compel ITT to conduct the meeting. The court, however, denied Hilton's motion. Intent on avoiding Hilton's purchase effort, ITT announced a "Comprehensive Plan" to split ITT into three new entities. The members of ITT's board of directors would be the directors of the new ITT entities. ITT planned to implement the Comprehensive Plan without obtaining shareholder approval. ITT argued that its Comprehensive Plan was a more attractive option than Hilton's tender offer. Do you think the court allowed ITT to complete its plan? Why or why not? [*Hilton Hotels Corporation v. ITT Corporation,* 978 F. Supp. 1342 (1997).]
5. In January 2003, Motorola began a hostile tender offer to obtain the 26 percent of Next Level Communications, Inc., that it did not own. It offered Next Level shareholders $1.04 per share. After Next Level shareholders petitioned to stop the takeover, Motorola increased its offer to $1.18 per share. After four months, Motorola had acquired 88 percent of Next Level's outstanding stock. It then converted some of its preferred stock into common stock, increasing its common stock ownership of Next Level to more than 90 percent. Motorola then initiated a short-form merger with Next Level, cashing out Next Level's minority shareholders. One of these shareholders, Nick Gilliland, sued Next Level and Motorola for breach of their fiduciary duty to disclose information about Next Level's financial condition to Next Level minority shareholders. Gilliland argued that minority shareholders needed this information to decide whether to accept Motorola's cash-out offer or to exercise their appraisal rights. Motorola and Next Level argued that they sent minority shareholders information about Next Level's financial situation when Motorola made its initial tender offer. Moreover, they argued that the notice of the short-form merger they sent to minority shareholders met statutory requirements. Do you think the court sided with the corporations or with the minority shareholders in this case? Why?

If you think the court sided with the shareholders, what remedies do you think should be available to them? [*Gilliland v. Motorola, Inc.,* 873 A.2d 305 (2005).]

6. Two brothers, Alex and John, served as directors of Atlas Corporation, a closely held corporation. Alex was responsible for financial matters, and John handled the company's day-to-day operations. The relationship between the two brothers began to deteriorate in 1995. On several occasions, Alex used his position as majority shareholder to overrule the board's decisions. The conflict culminated when John learned that Alex had made decisions contrary to the majority and without informing John. The following morning, John found out that Alex no longer intended that John be president of Atlas. Alex subsequently offered John a position as a consultant. John refused and filed a complaint seeking judicial dissolution. He argued that Alex, as majority shareholder, "froze him out" of the corporation. Do you agree with John? Why or why not? [*Kiriakides v. Atlas Food Systems & Services, Inc.,* 2000 S.C. App. LEXIS 32 (2000).]
7. Greatland Directional Drilling voluntarily dissolved as a corporation and received a certificate of dissolution on October 19, 1993. Anadrill, a division of Schlumberger Technology Corporation, acquired Greatland's assets and assumed Greatland's corporate interest and liabilities. A faulty drill bit rack injured Timothy Gossman, an employee of Anadrill, while he was working at a storage facility formerly owned by Greatland. In 1984, one of Greatland's employees incorrectly modified the rack, forgetting to remount a device designed to prevent drill bits from rolling off the rack. Gossman sued Greatland for negligence. Anadrill argued to dismiss the claim because Greatland had dissolved. The superior court agreed with Anadrill, holding that, as a dissolved corporation, it could not hold Greatland liable. Do you agree with the court's decision? How do you think the appellate court decided the case on appeal? [*Gossman v. Greatland Directional Drilling, Inc.,* 973 P.2d 93 (1999).]
8. Gary and Debra Grinaker each owned 50 percent of the stock of Photo Express, Inc. In 1993, the couple filed for divorce. During the divorce proceedings, Gary changed the locks to Photo Express and restricted Debra's access to the business and its records. On one occasion, he threatened to throw her in jail if she entered Photo Express without his permission. Gary also claimed to own more than 50 percent of the stock of Photo Express, and he attempted to take control of the company. Debra requested that the trial court appoint a receiver to run the business during the divorce proceedings. The trial court granted Debra's request. In 1995, the trial court ordered the receiver to return Photo Express's assets to Gary. The court later awarded Gary all of Photo Express's stock. The court approved the receiver's final accounting and ordered Gary to pay $39,494.47 in receiver's fees and expenses. Gary, asserting that the trial court abused its discretion in ordering the appointment of a receiver, appealed the court's order. Do you think that the trial court's appointment of a receiver to run Photo Express during the divorce proceedings was appropriate? Why or why not? [*Grinaker v. Grinaker,* 553 N.W.2d 200 (1996).]
9. The directors of Lone Star Steakhouse & Saloon, Inc., set up a corporate provision that granted them significant retirement benefits if another company took over Lone Star and installed new directors. The corporate provision, however, held that the directors were not entitled to these golden-parachute benefits if they approved the new directors. The California Public Employees' Retirement System (CalPERS), a Lone Star shareholder, challenged the golden-parachute provision, arguing that it granted the existing directors undue voting power in director elections. Moreover, CalPERS argued that the golden-parachute provision discouraged potentially beneficial takeovers because the

provision made it costly for potential aggressors to alter Lone Star's management. Lone Star argued that the provision was a legitimate defense to hostile takeovers. With whom do you think the court sided in this case? Why? [*Cal. Pub. Emples. Ret. Sys. v. Coulter,* 2005 Del. Ch. LEXIS 54 (2005).]

10. In 1989, the Woodricks listed their home for sale with Jack Burke Real Estate, Inc. Burke, a corporation that conducted business under the name of Fox & Lazo Realtors, provided the Woodricks with a brochure stating the policies of Fox & Lazo. The brochure stated that all buyers would be prequalified to determine whether they would be able to obtain a mortgage commitment. The Woodricks subsequently entered into a contract to sell their home to Christine Clark. Clark, however, was unable to obtain a mortgage, and, as a result, the Woodricks were unable to close on the purchase of their new home. The Woodricks brought suit against Burke and Fox & Lazo in 1990. In 1993, Burke and Fox & Lazo entered into an asset purchase agreement whereby Fox & Lazo agreed to purchase Burke's assets and accounts payable. Following the closing of the agreement, Burke dissolved. The Woodricks named Fox & Lazo in their suit, but Fox & Lazo contended that it was not responsible for Burke's previous actions. How do you think the court ruled in this case? Why? Do you think the court should hold Fox & Lazo liable for Burke's debts? Why or why not? [*Woodrick v. Burke,* 703 A.2d 306 (1997).]

Looking for more review material?

The Online Learning Center at **www.mhhe.com/kubasek1e** contains this chapter's "Assignment on the Internet" and also a list of URLs for more information, entitled "On the Internet." Find both of them in the Student Center portion of the OLC, along with quizzes and other helpful materials.

Corporations: Securities and Investor Protection

CASE OPENER

The Martha Stewart Case

On December 27, 2001, Martha Stewart's stockbroker, Peter Bacanovic, informed Stewart that two of his clients, Samuel Waksal, CEO of the biopharmaceutical company ImClone, and Waksal's daughter, had just sold all of their ImClone stock. Waksal secretly knew that the FDA was about to reject Erbitux, a key cancer drug ImClone had developed. Stewart did not know about the impending FDA rejection of Erbitux, and information about Waksal's sale of ImClone's stock was not available to the public. After receiving the information about Waksal's transaction, Stewart instructed her broker to sell all of her shares of ImClone stock. The following day, the FDA announced its rejection of Erbitux, and ImClone's stock price plummeted 16 percent. Stewart's timely trade allowed her to avoid a $45,673 loss.

Eighteen months later, the Securities and Exchange Commission (SEC) filed charges against Stewart and her broker for illegal insider trading and securities fraud.[1]

1. Do you think Stewart violated federal securities law? Why or why not?
2. Do you think Stewart's broker violated federal securities law? Why or why not?

The Wrap-Up at the end of the chapter will answer these questions.

Learning Objectives

After reading this chapter, you will be able to answer the following questions:

1. What is a security?
2. What requirements are imposed by the Securities Act of 1933?

[1] www.sec.gov/news/press/2003-69.htm.

CHAPTER 41

3 How does the Securities Exchange Act of 1934 regulate the trading of securities?

4 How are investment companies regulated?

5 How do states regulate securities?

Companies frequently need to raise money to expand. One way they raise money is by issuing securities. For example, corporations issue corporate **securities**—stocks and bonds—to raise capital for corporate expansion.

But a security is simply a piece of paper; it has no intrinsic value. Consequently, without securities regulations, corporations could easily commit fraud by issuing large numbers of securities and then refusing to repay them. Thus, the government heavily regulates securities issuance and trading.

Securities regulation is a relatively recent body of law. Before the Great Depression, government did not regulate securities, and fraudulent transactions occurred frequently. After the stock market crash in 1929, Congress passed several laws to regulate securities markets.

This chapter begins by defining a security. It then examines federal securities regulations. Finally, the chapter briefly discusses state securities regulation.

What Is a Security?

Physically, a security is merely a piece of paper. But when investors buy securities, they are not buying a piece of paper. They are buying what the paper represents. The value of the security is based on what the paper represents.

Earlier, we loosely defined securities as stocks and bonds. To be more precise, securities include stocks, bonds, debentures, and warrants. Furthermore, certain items mentioned in securities acts, such as interests in oil and gas rights, are securities. In some cases, courts have even defined cosmetics, vacuum cleaners, and cemetery lots as securities. Finally, investment contracts, contracts in which individuals invest money with the expectation of making a profit, are securities. How can so many different things be securities?

The Securities Act of 1933 offers a complicated definition of *security,* and as a result, courts have struggled when determining whether a particular instrument is a security. In an effort to provide a framework for analysis, the U.S. Supreme Court stated in the 1985 case *Landreth Timber Co. v. Landreth* that courts should presumptively treat as a security any financial instrument designated as a note, stock, bond, or other instrument named in the 1933 act.

If, however, the instrument in question does not have the characteristics of an instrument specifically named in the 1933 act, the courts apply a three-part test. In the 1946 case *SEC v. W.J. Howey Co.,*[2] the U.S. Supreme Court defined a security as an (1) investment in a common enterprise with the (2) reasonable expectation of profit gained (3) primarily or substantially from others' efforts. Anything that meets these three criteria is subject to security law.

Case 41-1 illustrates how courts apply the Howey test.

[2] 328 U.S. 293, 66 S. Ct. 1100 (1946).

CASE 41-1 SECURITIES AND EXCHANGE COMMISSION v. LIFE PARTNERS, INC.

U.S. DISTRICT COURT FOR THE DISTRICT OF COLUMBIA
898 F. SUPP. 14 (1995)

Life Partners, Inc. ("LPI") facilitated the sale of life insurance policies of full blown AIDS victims to investors at discount prices. While the life insurance policies are sold to investors, the insurance policy is in the name of LPI. When the policy holder dies, the investors recover the face value of the policy. This arrangement allegedly benefited both the investors and the AIDS victims, who, when they sold their life insurance policies, received much needed money to cover their medical costs associated with their illness. This process of selling life insurance policies of terminally ill patients is known as "viatical settlements." The SEC argues that LPI was essentially creating securities by repackaging some of the insurance policies. Consequently, the SEC brought suit against LPI for nonregistration under the 1933 Act.

JUDGE LAMBERTH: The Court must decide whether the products offered by defendants qualify as investment contracts under section 2(1) of the Securities Act. An investment contract is

> a contract, transaction or scheme whereby a person invests his money [1] in a common enterprise and [2] is led to expect profits [3] solely from the efforts of the promoter or a third party.

SEC v. W.J. Howey Co., 328 U.S. 293, 298-99, 90 L. Ed. 1244, 66 S. Ct. 1100 (1946). [T]he Court will concentrate on the three prongs of the Howey test.

1. Common Enterprise.
Courts have identified types of commonality in a quest to bring meaning and uniformity to this prong of the Howey test. . . . Horizontal commonality exists through LPI's sale of fractional interests in the death benefit due under a single policy. The fortunes of each investor are tied to that of the other investors in that policy, with proceeds to be divided on a pro rata basis. . . . Defendants line up several investors for each settlement. The returns on each settlement are divided solely among the investors in that settlement.

Both types of vertical commonality are also present in this case. The investors' fortunes are tied to those of the promoter since LPI takes title to the policies. From the perspective of both the insurance company and the insured, LPI is the new owner and beneficiary of the life insurance policies. Investors are dependent upon LPI to protect their interests, and their interests would be greatly affected by LPI's dissolution or insolvency. Such risks are sufficient to meet the test for vertical commonality. LPI investments constitute a "common enterprise" under Howey.

2. Expectation of Profits.
The Supreme Court has defined "expected profits" for purposes of securities law as an investor's anticipation of profits either through capital appreciation resulting from development of the initial investment, or participation in earnings resulting from use of investors' funds. An instrument is likely to meet this prong of the Howey test when the purchaser's motivation is to receive a return on the investment rather than to use or consume the item.

The undisputed evidence in this case indicates that investors in viatical settlements are concerned with gaining a return on their investment. . . . Although the face value of the insurance policy is fixed, the return on investment varies based on the ability, or inability, of the terminally ill to outlast LPI's life expectancy estimates. The return is also based on LPI's ability to translate that estimate into a valuation of the policy. What results is the prospect of a fluctuating return tied to the performance of an entity rather than a fixed or market based return. Investors' return qualifies as profit under Howey.

3. Derived from the Efforts of Others.
It is clear from LPI's promotional materials that it offers diligence and expertise in discovering and evaluating the legal status of an insurance policy and the insured's medical condition before offering it for investment. After the investment is made, LPI offers continued services of a more ministerial nature: it periodically checks on whether the insured is alive; submits claims for death benefits to the insurance companies; accepts this payment; and computes and distributes pro-rata shares of benefits to investors.

[T]he pre-investment work by LPI . . . is undeniably essential to the overall success of the investment. More importantly, defendants' post-investment efforts are critical since LPI, not the investor, has the contractual relationship with the insurance company. The investors are dependent on LPI because they lack any contractual rights vis-à-vis the insurance company and are strangers to both the insurance company and the other investors who bought interests in the same policy.

The Court concludes that investors who purchase viatical settlements through LPI anticipate their profits to be derived principally from the efforts of others.

4. Conclusion.

The Court concludes that LPI's basic policy is an investment contract that is subject to federal securities law.

Judgment in favor of plaintiff.

CRITICAL THINKING

Why might the ambiguity in the definition of a security be a problem in securities regulation?

ETHICAL DECISION MAKING

You probably have a good idea of the ethical theory you agree with most. Under that ethical theory, what is your opinion of the business LPI?

Securities Regulation

Congress passed two crucial acts regulating securities transactions. The Securities Act of 1933[3] regulates how companies issue corporate securities, while the Securities Exchange Act of 1934[4] oversees the purchase and sale of securities. Both acts attempt to provide greater stability to securities transaction. First, the acts mandate that investors have access to certain information when deciding whether to buy or sell securities. Second, the acts strive to curb fraudulent securities transactions.

THE SECURITIES AND EXCHANGE COMMISSION

Perhaps the most significant component of the 1934 act was the creation of the Securities and Exchange Commission (SEC), an independent agency whose function is to administer federal securities laws. The SEC is headed by five individuals appointed by the president. These five individuals serve fixed five-year terms.

The SEC has a number of responsibilities. First, it is responsible for the enforcement of securities laws. Thus, in response to an allegation of violation of securities law, the SEC investigates and, if necessary, initiates an enforcement action against the violator. Enforcement actions often include penalties or injunctive remedies. If the violation is severe enough to warrant criminal prosecution, however, the Fraud Section of the Criminal Division of the Department of Justice will prosecute the alleged violator.

[3] 15 U.S.C. §§ 77a–77aa.

[4] 15 U.S.C. §§ 78a–78mm.

global context

Sweden's Securities Market

The Swedes divide securities into bonds and shares. Individuals invest in either the bond market or the stock market. Companies issue bonds to boost funds from sources outside their shareholders. Bondholders have a right to a fixed rate of interest regardless of whether the company earns a profit. Bondholders do not, however, have a right to take part in company decision making.

Companies issue shares to increase their equity capital. Unlike bond interest payments, shareholders' returns vary with the company's profits. Because shareholders' interests are closely tied to the success of the company, shareholders have a voice within the company. Generally, this voice comes in the form of a vote at general meetings.

Regulation of the stock and bond markets in Sweden is unique because Sweden has no equivalent of the SEC. Instead, banks themselves oversee the issuance of shares and bonds.

Second, the SEC interprets the securities acts and adopts rules to achieve the purposes of the acts. Thus, the SEC passes securities transaction regulations that have the force of law.

Third, the SEC regulates the activities of securities brokers, dealers, and advisers. All securities dealers and brokers must register with the SEC.

Fourth, the SEC regulates the trade of securities on securities exchanges. As you read about securities regulations in this chapter, remember that the SEC is responsible for their administration and enforcement.

Exhibit 41-1
The Expansion of SEC Powers in the 1990s

Securities Enforcement Remedies and Penny Stock Reform Act of 1990

Permits the SEC to:

- Issue a cease-and-desist order against a violator of any federal securities law.
- Seek civil money penalties against any violators.
- Create rules to require that brokers and dealers provide information concerning prices and risk associated with the penny-stock market.

Market Reform Act of 1990

Allows the SEC to suspend securities trading if prices vary excessively in a short time period.

Securities Acts Amendments of 1990

Permit the SEC to seek punishment of violators of foreign securities laws.

National Securities Markets Improvement Act of 1996

Permits the SEC to exempt persons, securities, and transactions from securities regulations.

Sarbanes-Oxley Act of 2002

- Increases corporate disclosure requirements.
- Penalizes violators of securities laws more heavily.
- Holds corporate executives responsible for errors in corporate reports filed with the SEC.
- Requires earlier filing of financial and stock transaction reports.
- Creates and establishes SEC oversight over the Public Company Accounting Oversight Board to regulate public accounting firms.

global context

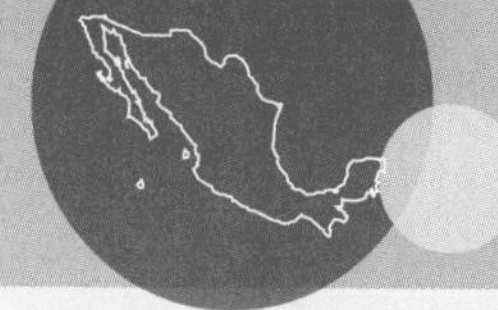

Mexican Securities Market

Established in 1907, the Mexican Stock Exchange, or the Bolsa Mexicana de Valones SA de CV (MSE), is a private sector corporation owned and operated by authorized brokerage dealers. Each dealer owns a share of stock in the MSE. The exchange requires that dealers complete all transactions on a cash basis and settle them within a 48-hour period.

The National Security Commission (CNV), governed by the Mexican Securities Law (MSL), regulates public offerings and securities trading. The 11-member CNV board of governors has the power to approve all applicants for listing on the MSE. These governors determine whether to accept applicants based on operating history and management and asset criteria. The board of governors also has the power to investigate possible infractions of MSL, suspend trading of certain securities, and intervene in management brokerage firms when necessary.

CNV's most demanding function is the regulation of public offerings. As defined by the boards, public offerings are made "through means of mass communication or to an 'unspecified' person in order to subscribe, sell, or acquire securities." Regulation of public offerings is limited to some extent because existing laws do not permit non-Mexican entities to issue securities. Existing laws do not, however, limit investments in securities outside Mexico by Mexican individuals or companies.

Other countries have bodies that serve similar functions to those of the SEC. In Singapore, for example, the government controls securities markets through the Securities Industry Council. The council is an advisory board to the minister of finance, who, based on the council's advice, issues guidelines for exchanges, mergers, and trading. Exhibit 41-1 illustrates how the powers of the SEC were enhanced during the 1990s.

The Securities Act of 1933

Congress passed the Securities Act of 1933 in reaction to the mistrust of securities transactions before the Great Depression. Thus, a function of the act was to legitimize security transactions by requiring the registration of securities offered to the public. Through the registration process, investors have more information to make better-informed decisions about their securities purchases.

Section 5 of the 1933 act mandates that any corporation, partnership, association, or individual that offers the sale of securities to the public through the use of mails or through any facility of interstate commerce is required to register that security unless it qualifies for an exemption (discussed later in this section). Any issuer of securities must file a written registration statement and a prospectus with the SEC.

REGISTRATION STATEMENT

Although the SEC requires different types of companies to complete slightly different registration forms, the SEC requires certain elements from all companies. The registration statement generally contains (1) a description of the securities offered for sale, (2) an explanation of how proceeds from the sale of the securities will be used, (3) a description of the registrant's business and properties, (4) information about the management of the company, (5) a description of any pending lawsuits in which the registrant is involved, and (6) financial statements certified by an independent public accountant.

Caution: Although the SEC requires the registration of securities, the SEC does not "approve" these securities. In other words, the SEC does not make any judgment about the worth of securities; it simply enforces the requirement that issuers provide certain information to potential buyers.

PROSPECTUS

Along with filing a registration statement, issuers of securities must also file a prospectus with the SEC. A **prospectus** is a written document that contains most of the same information as the registration statement. The prospectus is different from the registration statement, however, because it is an advertising tool that issuers distribute to potential investors who rely on the prospectus to help decide whether they should buy the securities.

The SEC requires, but cannot guarantee, the accuracy of facts stated in the registration statement and prospectus. If an issuer makes a false or misleading statement in a registration statement, the issuer can be subject to criminal or civil penalties. These penalties are discussed later in the chapter.

connecting to the core

Economics

Market Failure: Asymmetrical Information

Economics teaches that when certain conditions are met, markets allocate goods and services efficiently among individuals in society. But when those necessary conditions are not present, the result is often what economists call a *market failure*—a failure of the market to produce efficient results.

For example, for markets to work well, buyers and sellers must have access to the same information about the goods being sold. Suppose you need to buy a used car but you lack the ability to distinguish between dependable used cars and "lemons" (i.e., cars prone to breaking down). Your local used-car dealer, however, knows exactly what is wrong with each car on his lot. Of course, he is probably not going to tell you the problems with the car you are thinking about buying; if he did, you might not buy it. So he tells you how great the car is, and you buy it. A week later, the car breaks down—you bought a lemon.

Economists call this problem *asymmetrical information.* It leads to a market failure because it results in inefficient transactions that would not have taken place if both the buyer and the seller had access to the same information. You wouldn't have bought the car if you had known it was a lemon.

The asymmetrical information problem is present in unregulated securities markets. When investors purchase corporate securities, they lack knowledge about the securities' risks and potential rewards. But the companies issuing the securities know very well the risks and rewards the securities offer. In this situation, investors are unable to make efficient decisions about which securities to purchase, and the result is a market failure.

The Securities Act of 1933 attempts to remedy the asymmetrical information problem in the securities market. The act requires that all securities issuers disclose certain information to investors in the form of a prospectus. As a result, investors can appraise the value of the securities for themselves and make better investment choices.

Source: George A. Akerlof, "The Market for 'Lemons': Quality Uncertainty and the Market Mechanism," *Quarterly Journal of Economics.* 84 (1970), p. 488.

PERIODS OF THE FILING PROCESS

The filing process consists of three periods: prefiling, waiting, and posteffective.

Prefiling period. The prefiling period begins when an issuer begins to think about issuing securities, and it ends when the issuer files the registration statement and prospectus with the SEC. Before filing a registration statement and prospectus with the SEC, an issuer cannot make any offers to sell securities. The issuer can, however, negotiate with *underwriters,* investment banking firms that purchase securities from the issuing corporation with the intent of selling them to brokerage houses, which then sell them to the public.

Because they cannot offer to sell securities during the prefiling period, issuers, officers, directors, and underwriters usually try to avoid generating publicity about possibly issuing securities because the SEC may construe such publicity as an attempt to condition the market to generate interest in the securities. In fact, the SEC could consider speeches or press releases mentioning the potential issuance of securities to be an offer. The issuing firm is permitted, however, to publish a notice about the prospective offering, including the name of the issuer as well as a description of the potential securities, but the notice may not include the name of the underwriter.

Waiting period. Once an issuer files a registration statement and prospectus, the waiting period begins. During this period, the SEC reviews the information filed by the issuing firm. Issuers must wait 20 days after the filing date to sell their securities. During the waiting period, issuers may make oral offers to sell the securities and may distribute a **red-herring prospectus**—a prospectus with a warning written in red print at the top of the page warning investors that the registration has been filed with the SEC but not yet been approved. Moreover, the issuer may publish a **tombstone advertisement,** a brief ad with a format similar to that of a tombstone.

Posteffective period. The posteffective period begins when the SEC declares the registration statement effective, and it ends when the issuer sells all securities offered or withdraws them from sale. During this time, investors may buy and sell the securities, but purchasers must receive a final prospectus, a version of the prospectus the buyer must receive at the point of sale. If an issuer does not send the purchaser a final prospectus, the issuer has violated the 1933 Securities Act.

SPECIAL REGISTRATION PROVISIONS

Amendments to the 1933 act stipulate more relaxed registration requirements for companies that have consistently satisfied applicable registration requirements. For example, shelf registrations permit certain qualified issuers to register securities that they will sell "off the shelf" on a delayed or continuous basis in the future. SEC Rule 415 requires that corporations using shelf registrations keep information in the original registration accurate and up to date.

EXEMPTIONS UNDER THE 1933 ACT

Although these complex registration requirements are standard for most securities, they do not apply to all securities in all situations. Some securities are exempt because of the nature of the securities themselves—*exempt securities*—and others are exempt when exchanged in certain ways—*exempt transactions.*

Exempt securities. The 1933 act provides that certain securities are exempt from the registration procedures described above. These securities are *unregistered unrestricted securities,* and they include:

1. Securities issued by governments, including municipal, state, and federal governments.
2. Securities issued by nonprofit issuers, such as religious institutions or charitable organizations.
3. Securities issued by financial institutions supervised by banking associations.
4. Securities issued as a result of corporation reorganization in which one security is exchanged for another security.
5. Stock dividends and stock splits.

6. Insurance or annuity contracts issued by insurance companies.
7. Securities issued by federally regulated carriers (i.e., railways).
8. Short-term notes with a maturity date that does not exceed nine months.
9. Securities sold before July 27, 1933.
10. An issuer's offer of up to $5 million in securities in a 12-month period.

Although the last exemption permits the issuer to avoid the complex registration requirements of full registration, Regulation A[5] nevertheless requires that the issuer file certain reports with the SEC. For example, the issuer must file a notice of issue and an offering circular and provide the offering circular to investors before sale of the securities. Even with these requirements, however, the registration process under Regulation A is much less burdensome than the full registration process. For example, Regulation A permits issuers to "test the waters" for interest in their securities before preparing the offering circular, selling any securities, or gaining the commitment of interested buyers.

Exempt transactions. If a security does not fall under one of the exempt categories described above, an issuer can nevertheless avoid registering the security by making certain exempt transactions. These securities are *unregistered restricted securities.* Issuers might want to avoid the registration process because it can be costly, complicated, and time-consuming. Exempt transactions offer an opportunity to save time and money. Consequently, many issuers sell securities through exempt transactions.

Although these transactions are exempt from registration, issuers must still provide investors with information about the securities, such as annual reports and financial statements.

Exempt transactions include limited offers, intrastate issues, and resales of securities.

Limited offers. Certain securities transactions, limited offers, are exempt from the registration process because they either involve small amounts of money or are offered only to sophisticated investors. The investors who participate in limited offers generally do not need the protection afforded by the registration process.

The SEC's Regulation D[6] enumerates three exemptions for limited offers (Rules 504, 505, and 506). Section 4(6) of the 1933 act contains an additional limited-offer exemption.

Private Placement Exemption (Rule 506). Issuers who make private offerings of securities are exempt from the registration process. These issuers, however, cannot advertise these private offerings to the general public. This exemption, usually referred to as the *private placement exemption,* allows firms to issue an unlimited number of securities to an unlimited number of accredited investors. Consequently, firms can easily raise large amounts of capital. Firms may not, however, issue to more than 35 unaccredited investors.

The SEC defines an **accredited investor** as:[7]

1. Any natural person who has a net worth of at least $1 million.
2. Any natural person whose annual income has been at least $200,000 for the two previous years and expects to make at least $200,000 in the current year.
3. Any corporation or partnership with total assets in excess of $5 million.

[5] 17 C.F.R. §§ 230.251–230.263.
[6] www.law.uc.edu/CCL/33ActRls/regD.html.
[7] SEC Rule 501.

4. Insiders of the issuers, such as executive officers or directors.
5. Registered investment companies, colleges and universities, banks, and insurance companies.

The SEC assumes that accredited investors are better able to evaluate the financial risk associated with buying securities. Consequently, government protection in the form of required registration is less imperative.

The SEC also requires that firms selling to unaccredited investors under Rule 506 believe that these investors have expertise regarding securities trading. The firms must believe that the investors, or their representatives, have the reasonable ability to evaluate the financial risk associated with purchasing securities. If a firm privately offers any unaccredited investor the opportunity to purchase securities, all investors must receive the basic information contained in the registration statement (i.e., information about the issuing company and the securities). If no unaccredited investors are involved, however, the issuer does not have to disclose any information. While firms do not have to register these exempt securities with the SEC, they must notify the SEC of any sales made under the exemption.

The private placement exemption is one of the easiest ways for firms to raise capital. Instead of making a public offering, firms can simply make a private offering to investors capable of ascertaining the risk associated with buying securities. The firms cannot, however, advertise the securities to the general public.

Rule 505. Rule 505 is very similar to Rule 506, but it has two important differences. First, according to Rule 505, a firm's private offerings may not exceed $5 million in a 12-month period, while under Rule 506, a firm may issue an unlimited number of securities. Second, according to Rule 506, if a firm issues securities to unaccredited investors, it must believe that they have the knowledge to evaluate the risk associated with the security. In contrast, under Rule 505, firms need not believe that investors have the reasonable ability to evaluate the risk of purchasing securities.

Rule 504. *Noninvestment firms*—firms that do not engage primarily in the buying and selling of securities—that offer no more than $1 million in securities over a 12-month period are exempt from registration. An unlimited number of both accredited and nonaccredited investors may purchase these securities; however, the firms must notify the SEC of their securities sales. Issuers need not disclose any information to investors.

Section 4(6). If a firm offers securities only to accredited investors for an amount less than $5 million, the issuer is exempt from registration. An unlimited number of accredited investors may participate in the transactions, but no unaccredited investors may buy these securities. Firms may not advertise these securities to the public. Issuers do not have to disclose any information to investors, but they must notify the SEC of any sales under this exemption. Moreover, investors who want to resell these securities must register them with the SEC.

Intrastate issues. Under Section 3 of the 1933 act, any security offered or sold to a permanent resident of the single state where the issuer of the security resides and does business is exempt. Thus, local businesses can rely on local investors to raise an unlimited amount of capital without registration.

Courts and the SEC have interpreted this exemption very narrowly. Issuers must do at least 80 percent of their business within the state, receive at least 80 percent of their profits within the state, have at least 80 percent of their assets within the state, plan to use at least 80 percent of the profits within the state, and have their main offices in the state.

During the period of sale and for at least nine months after the period of sale, buyers of these securities under the intrastate exemption may not resell them to nonresidents. Issuers must take precautions against interstate resales.

Resales. The 1933 Securities Act created an exemption for "transactions by any person other than an issuer, underwriter, or dealer." Because another section of the act exempts dealers and brokers, only issuers and underwriters are not exempt from registering resales of securities.

Consequently, the average investor does not have to register securities when he or she wants to sell. If the investor acquired them through sales under Rule 505, 506, or Section 4(6) (e.g., intrastate issues and limited offers), they are **restricted securities.** If an investor wants to resell a restricted security, she must register the securities unless she follows Rule 144 or Rule 144a.

Rule 144. Under Rule 144, any person wanting to resell a restricted security is exempt from registration if certain criteria are met. First, the public must have access to adequate current information about the issuer. Second, the person selling the restricted security must have owned the security for at least two years. Third, the seller must sell the restricted securities in limited amounts in unsolicited broker transactions. Fourth, the seller must notify the SEC of the sale.

If a seller is not an affiliate of the issuer and has owned the securities for three years, he or she may sell the securities in unlimited amounts and is not subject to any of the criteria under Rule 144 for an exemption. An *affiliate* is a person who controls, is controlled by, or is in common control with the issuer. The 1933 act restricts sales by affiliates much more than sales by nonaffiliates. If an affiliate sells restricted or nonrestricted securities, he must meet all but one of the criteria to be exempt from registration. The affiliate does not need to hold a nonrestricted security for two years before reselling.

VIOLATIONS AND LIABILITY

If the SEC uncovers a potential violation of the 1933 act, it can (1) take administrative action, (2) take injunctive action, or (3) recommend criminal prosecution. If the SEC takes administrative action, it conducts a formal investigation of the potential violation by calling relevant witnesses to testify or produce evidence. If, through this investigation, the SEC uncovers evidence of a violation, the SEC may order an administrative proceeding before an administrative law judge, who can impose sanctions and even revoke a security's registration.

Usually the SEC takes injunctive action when it believes that a defendant is likely to continue to violate the law. Thus, the SEC may seek an injunction to prevent issuers from advertising securities by mail. In the Martha Stewart case at the beginning of the chapter, the SEC sought an injunction prohibiting Stewart and her broker from violating securities laws and limiting her activities as an officer of a public company.

Finally, if the SEC recommends criminal action, the Department of Justice prosecutes criminal charges against violators. Criminal penalties include a fine up to $10,000, imprisonment for up to five years, or both.

How might an issuing company violate the 1933 Securities Act? First, a company violates the act if it intentionally misleads investors by omitting or falsifying information on a registration statement or prospectus. Second, if a company is negligent in discovering a fraudulent statement, it can be liable. Third, an issuing company violates the act if it sells securities before the effective date of the registration statement.

Issuers charged with a violation of the 1933 act can raise several defenses. A company charged with the first or second violation described above may claim that the omitted or false statement was immaterial to the sale of the security. Similarly, if the issuer can prove that the plaintiff was aware of the omission or false statement when she bought the security, the defendant can avoid liability.

Any defendant except the issuer can assert the **due diligence** defense. This defense requires that the defendant demonstrate that she investigated the registration statement and had reasonable grounds to believe that the registration statement was accurate and had no omission of material facts.

If a defendant sold securities before the effective date of registration, however, she will almost certainly be liable because the 1933 act provides no defenses for this violation.

If an investor purchased securities and suffered damages as a result of an issuer's false or misleading statement, the investor is entitled to bring a civil suit to recover his losses. The burden of proof falls on the investor to demonstrate this incomplete or inaccurate disclosure of facts. Case 41-2 illustrates an investor's attempt to recover damages based on the omission of allegedly material facts from the prospectus and registration statement.

CASE 41-2

STEVEN KLEIN, WARREN BRANDWINE v. GENERAL NUTRITION COMPANIES, INC.

U.S. COURT OF APPEALS FOR THE THIRD CIRCUIT
186 F.3D 338 (1999)

Steven Klein and Warren Brandwine purchased shares of General Nutrition Companies (GNC) common stock between February and May 1996. During this time period, GNC sold over 1.5 million shares in public offering, realizing proceeds of over $33 million. However, at the end of May 1996, GNC announced that its store sales would be 3–6% lower than the previous quarter. Consequently, the price of GNC stock fell from around $21.50 to $14.00. Klein and Brandwine asserted that GNC violated several securities regulations by failing to disclose material facts in their prospectus. They argued that GNC's failure to disclose this information led to an artificially inflated stock price for the offering of securities. Consequently, Klein and Brandwine brought suit against GNC under Sections 11 and 12(a)(2) of the Securities Act, which creates a private cause of action when a registration statement or prospectus omits a material fact that is required to make the other statements not misleading. The District Court dismissed the case, and Klein and Brandwine appealed.

CIRCUIT JUDGE HARLINGTON WOOD, JR.: Appellants contend that the defendants fail[ed] to disclose in the prospectus (1) a loss of third-party advertising support; (2) a worldwide shortage of deodorized distillate, a raw material used to produce Vitamin E; and (3) the fact that GNC's new store openings would siphon business from existing stores. Both [Section 11] § 77k and [Section 12(a)(2)] § 77l(a)(2) require that an undisclosed fact be material at the time of offering in order for liability to attach. As this court has noted, "an omitted fact is material if there is a substantial likelihood that a reasonable [investor] would consider it important in deciding how to [act]." . . . A determination of "materiality" takes into account considerations as to the certainty of the information, its availability in the public domain, and the need for the information in light of cautionary statements being made. As our analysis will show, the three alleged nondisclosures in the present case are immaterial as a matter of law.

[A]ppellants assert that at the time of the public offering, defendants knew that advertising support from several third-party diet product manufacturers, including Cybergenics, was declining from the prior year. As support, appellants point to a portion of the complaint which alleges that in January 1996, GNC officials contacted senior executives at Cybergenics with respect to "concern about [Cybergenics'] lack of sales and its potential impact on Cybergenics' financial stability and ability to continue to provide GNC with free advertising support." This allegation addresses only "concern" and a "potential impact" on advertising support. "Where an event is contingent or speculative in nature, it is difficult to ascertain whether the reasonable investor would have considered the omitted information significant at the time." Shapiro, 964 F.2d at 283. Additionally, the complaint clearly states that "in January 1996, Cybergenics started a second wave advertising program for Quicktrim, that also provided free advertising support for GNC." According to the amended complaint, it was not until March 1996, a month after the public offering, that Cybergenics suspended or substantially reduced its advertising support for GNC.

Vitamin E is an important ingredient in many vitamin supplements marketed by GNC. The prospectus stated that GNC maintained multiple sources of all raw materials. Appellants contend that this statement was materially false and misleading because it failed to disclose the existence of a worldwide shortage of deodorized distillate, a material used to produce vitamin E. The complaint alleges that by the second quarter of 1995, worldwide demand for vitamin E was exceeding supply and that, after the public offering, in February 1996, GNC informed its franchisees that the shortage was adversely affecting its ability to meet the demand for certain products containing vitamin E. Significantly, the complaint does not allege that the vitamin E shortage was private, internal GNC information. In fact, the complaint asserts that at all relevant times, the market for GNC stock was an efficient market which "promptly digested current information regarding GNC from all publicly-available sources and reflected such information in GNC's stock price." Federal securities laws do not require a company to state the obvious. Furthermore, not only was the vitamin E shortage public knowledge, it was expected to be temporary as one of the two principal suppliers of deodorized distillate was in the process of building a new plant to increase its vitamin E production.

Appellants further allege that the prospectus failed to disclose that, at the time of the public offering, same store sales were being adversely affected by the opening of new stores in close proximity to existing locations. The prospectus stated that GNC planned to open 350 new stores each year through 1999. We conclude that the prospectus adequately cautioned investors that GNC's expansion plans might not be achieved and that, even if achieved, expansion might not be profitable. The prospectus clearly stated that the profitability of the expansion depended in part on obtaining suitable sites for the new stores. This warning defeats appellants' claims with respect to this issue. All of the alleged omissions are immaterial as a matter of law.

AFFIRMED in favor of defendant.

CRITICAL THINKING

This case is based on omitted information. An important skill in critical thinking is to determine whether the omitted information is important. Klein and Brandwine feel the omitted information is important, while the court does not. With whom do you agree and why?

ETHICAL DECISION MAKING

What stakeholders benefit from the court's decision? Using your favorite ethical perspectives, do you think that these stakeholders deserved the benefits they derived from the court's decision? Why?

The Securities Exchange Act of 1934

While the 1933 Securities Act regulates the issuance of securities, the 1934 Securities Exchange Act regulates the subsequent trading (resale) of securities, chiefly through the required registration of securities exchanges, brokers, dealers, and national securities associations. Moreover, the act requires that certain issuers file periodic reports with the SEC. The 1934 act also permits the SEC to monitor securities markets for fraud and market manipulation.

SECTION 10(B) AND RULE 10B-5

One of the most important sections of the 1934 act is Section 10(b), which prohibits the use of manipulative and deceptive devices to bypass SEC rules. Within this section, Subsection 5 prohibits fraud associated with the purchase or sale of all securities. Thus, even though securities may be exempt from registration, they are still subject to Rule 10b-5:

> It shall be unlawful for any person, directly or indirectly, by use of any means or instrumentality of interstate commerce or of the mails, or of any facility of any national securities exchange,
>
> a) to employ any device, scheme, or artifice to defraud,
>
> b) to make any untrue statement of a material fact or to omit to state a material fact necessary in order to make the statements made, in light of circumstances under which they were made, not misleading, or
>
> c) to engage in any act, practice, or course of business that operates or would operate as a fraud or deceit upon any person, in connection with the purchase or sale of any security.

Both Section 10(b) and Rule 10b-5 play an important role in preventing insider trading.

INSIDER TRADING

When a company employee or executive uses material inside information to make a profit, she or he is engaging in *insider trading.* Insider trading is illegal because it gives the violator an important advantage over the general public and shareholders.

Section 10(b) and Rule 10b-5 define *insiders* as corporate officers, directors, employees, lawyers, consultants, accountants, majority shareholders, or any other individuals who receive private information regarding the trading of securities.

A company employee or executive who has inside information may be liable depending on whether the information is material. If there is a material omission or misrepresentation during a securities transaction, the individual has violated Section 10(b) and Rule 10b-5. If the omission or misrepresentation is not material, however, the individual is not liable. Examples of material information include the following:

1. A change in the status of litigation against the company.
2. A change in dividends.
3. A contract for the sale of corporate assets or for the purchase of assets.
4. A new product, process, or discovery.
5. A significant change in the financial status of the company.

According to the SEC, an individual with material inside information should either refrain from using the information or disclose the information to the other parties involved in the transaction.[8] Case 41-3 is a classic example of how courts address insider trading.

[8] *Matter of Cady, Roberts & Co.*, 40 SEC 907 (1961).

CASE 41-3 SECURITIES AND EXCHANGE COMMISSION v. TEXAS GULF SULPHUR CO.

U.S. COURT OF APPEALS FOR THE SECOND CIRCUIT 401 F.2D 833 (1968)

In June 1963, Texas Gulf Sulphur acquired the option to buy land in Timmons, Ontario. A preliminary drilling in November 1963 suggested that the land held great amounts of copper and zinc. This information was supposed to be kept secret; not even officers and executives at TGS were supposed to know about the results of the drilling. TGS acquired the land and resumed drilling in March 1964. During the time from November 1963 to March 1964, certain directors, officers, and employees of TGS received "tips" and purchased TGS stock or options to buy shares at a fixed price. When drilling began in November 1963, these people had owned 1135 shares of TGS stock and possessed no calls; thereafter they owned a total of 8235 shares and possessed 12,300 calls.

In April 1964, when rumors of a major mineral find appeared in newspapers, TGS responded by claiming that the rumors of a major find did not have factual basis. However, a few days later, TSG confirmed that the strike was expected to yield many million tons of ore. In between the days that TGS claimed the rumors were false and later confirmed the rumors, two defendants, Clayton and Crawford, ordered a combined total of 500 shares of TGS stock. The SEC brought suit against TGS and 13 of its directors, officers, and employees for violation of Section 10(b) of the Exchange Act and SEC Rule 10(b)-5, seeking an injunction to prevent TGS from publishing misleading press releases and requesting rescission of TGS's purchases and stock options. The district court dismissed the charges against all defendants but Clayton and Crawford, and the SEC appealed.

JUDGE WATERMAN: Rule 10b-5 was promulgated pursuant to the grant of authority given the SEC by Congress in Section 10(b) of the Securities Exchange Act of 1934 (15 U.S.C. § 78j(b)). By that Act Congress purposed to prevent inequitable and unfair practices and to insure fairness in securities transactions generally, whether conducted face-to-face, over the counter, or on exchanges. The Act and the Rule apply to the transactions here, all of which were consummated on exchanges. Whether predicated on traditional fiduciary concepts, the Rule is based in policy on the justifiable expectation of the securities marketplace that all investors trading on impersonal exchanges have relatively equal access to material information. The essence of the Rule is that anyone who, trading for his own account in the securities of a corporation has "access, directly or indirectly, to information intended to be available only for a corporate purpose and not for the personal benefit of anyone" may not take "advantage of such information knowing it is unavailable to those with whom he is dealing," i.e., the investing public. Insiders, as directors or management officers are, of course, by this Rule, precluded from so unfairly dealing, but the Rule is also applicable to one possessing the information who may not be strictly termed an "insider" within the meaning of Sec.16(b) of the Act. Thus, anyone in possession of material inside information must either disclose it to the investing public, or, if he is disabled from disclosing it in order to protect a corporate confidence, or he chooses not to do so, must abstain from trading in or recommending the securities concerned while such inside information remains undisclosed.

. . . As we stated in List v. Fashion Park, Inc., 340 F.2d 457, 462, "The basic test of materiality . . . is whether a reasonable man would attach importance . . . in determining his choice of action in the transaction in question." This, of course, encompasses any fact ". . . which in reasonable and objective contemplation might affect the value of the corporation's stock or securities. . . ." Such a fact is a material fact and must be effectively disclosed to the investing public prior to the commencement of insider trading in the corporation's securities. Thus, material facts include not only information disclosing the earnings and distributions of a company but also those facts which affect the probable future of the company and those which may affect the desire of investors to buy, sell, or hold the company's securities.

In each case, then, whether facts are material within Rule 10b-5 when the facts relate to a particular event and are undisclosed by those persons who are knowledgeable thereof will depend at any given time upon a balancing of both the indicated probability that the event will occur and the anticipated magnitude of the event in light of the totality of the company activity.

The core of Rule 10b-5 is the implementation of the Congressional purpose that all investors should have equal access to the rewards of participation in securities transactions. It was the intent of Congress that all members of the investing public should be subject to identical market risks—which market risks include, of course, the risk that one's evaluative capacity or one's capital available to put at risk may exceed another's capacity or capital. The insiders here were not trading on an equal footing with the outside investors. They alone were in a position to evaluate the probability and magnitude of what seemed from the outset to be a major ore strike; they alone could invest safely, secure in the expectation that the price of TGS stock would rise substantially in the event such a major strike should materialize, but would decline little, if at all, in the event of failure, for the public, ignorant at the outset of the favorable probabilities would likewise be unaware of the unproductive exploration, and the additional exploration costs would not significantly affect TGS market prices. Such inequities based upon unequal access to knowledge should not be shrugged off as inevitable in our way of life, or, in view of the congressional concern in the area, remain uncorrected.

We hold, therefore, that all transactions in TGS stock or calls by individuals apprised of the drilling results were made in violation of Rule 10b-5.

REVERSED in favor of plaintiff.

CRITICAL THINKING

Again, omitted information is the concern of this case. Can you make a distinction between the omitted information here and that in the last case?

ETHICAL DECISION MAKING

What values are being emphasized by the prohibition on insider trading?

THE PRIVATE SECURITIES LITIGATION REFORM ACT OF 1995

Although Rule 10b-5 was designed to encourage disclosure of accurate information, one of its unintended side effects was the deterrence of forecasts. Shareholders who purchased stock in corporations with high earnings forecasts often brought suit against the corporations' directors if actual corporate earnings fell short of forecasted earnings, alleging that the directors violated Rule 10b-5 by disclosing misleading financial information.

Congress attempted to remedy this problematic side effect by passing the *Private Securities Litigation Reform Act of 1995 (PSLRA)*. Among other things, the act provides a "safe harbor" from liability for publicly held issuers who make financial forecasts as long as the forecasts are "accompanied by meaningful cautionary statements identifying important factors that could cause actual results to differ materially from those in the forward-looking statement."[9]

Innovative shareholders attempted to subvert PSLRA by suing corporate directors in state courts. Congress responded to these efforts by passing the *Securities Litigation Uniform Standards Act of 1998.* This act strictly limits shareholders' ability to bring class action suits against nationally traded corporations.

[9] 15 U.S.C. § 77z-2 (2005).

OUTSIDERS AND INSIDER TRADING

Not only may insiders be liable for omitting or misrepresenting material information, but certain "outsiders" may also be liable through two theories: *misappropriation theory* and the *tipper/tippee theory.* Consider whether Martha Stewart is liable under either theory.

Misappropriation theory. In addition to being a theory of tort (see Chapter 6), misappropriation can establish liability for insider trading. *Misappropriation theory* holds that if an individual wrongfully acquires (misappropriates) and uses inside information for trading for her personal gain, she is liable for insider trading. Because she wrongfully acquires inside information, she is essentially stealing information to use for her benefit.

Because it expands the SEC's power, application of misappropriation theory to insider trading has not gone uncontested. Case 41-4 was the first case in which the SEC convinced the courts to apply misappropriation theory to Rule 10b-5. Over 10 years later, in *United States v. O'Hagan,*[10] the U.S. Supreme Court conclusively established that misappropriation theory is applicable to Rule 10b-5.

[10] 117 S. Ct. 2199 (1997).

CASE 41-4

UNITED STATES OF AMERICA v. DAVID CARPENTER

U.S. COURT OF APPEALS FOR THE SECOND CIRCUIT 791 F.2D 1024 (1985)

In 1981, R. Foster Winans was a Wall Street Journal *reporter and a writer of the "Heard on the Street" column. Winans was aware of the* Wall Street Journal's *policy that all news material gained by employees in the course of their employment was confidential. However, Winans and Carpenter, a news clerk at the WSJ, participated in a scheme with Felis and Brant, both stockbrokers. Winans agreed to provide the stockbrokers Felis and Brant with securities-related information that was about to be printed in the "Head on the Street" column. Using this information, Felis and Brant would buy or sell the relevant securities. Carpenter served as a messenger between Winans and the stockbrokers. The net profit on the use of the information for securities trading was $690,000. Felis' brokerage firm noticed a correlation between the "Head on the Street" column and the trading in Felis' account. Although Felis denied the connection, he began making plans to cover up the trading. Soon, the SEC began an investigation. Later, Winans and Carpenter revealed the entire scheme to the SEC. The SEC brought suit under 10(b) of the Securities Exchange Act of 1934, arguing that the securities information had been misappropriated. The district court found Winans and Felis guilty of misappropriation under 10(b), and Carpenter was convicted for aiding and abetting the commission of securities fraud. They appealed.*

JUDGE PIERCE: In broadly proscribing "deceptive" practices in connection with the purchase or sale of securities pursuant to section 10(b) of the Securities Exchange Act of 1934, Congress left to the courts the difficult task of interpreting legislatively defined but broadly stated principles insofar as they apply in particular cases. This case requires us to decide principally whether a newspaper reporter, a former newspaper clerk, and a stockholder, acting in concert, criminally violated federal securities laws by misappropriating material, nonpublic information in the form of the timing and content of the *Wall Street Journal*'s confidential schedule of columns of acknowledged influence in the securities market, in contravention of the established policy of the newspaper, for their own profit in connection with the purchase and sale of securities.

It is clear that defendant Winans, as an employee of the *Wall Street Journal,* breached a duty of confidentiality to his employer by misappropriating from the *Journal* confidential prepublication information, regarding the timing and content of certain newspaper columns, about which he learned in the course of his employment. We are presented with the question of whether that unlawful conduct may serve as the predicate for the securities fraud charges herein.

[T]he misappropriation theory more broadly proscribes the conversion by "insiders" or others of material non-public information in connection with the purchase or sale of securities. It is precisely such conversion that serves as the predicate for the convictions herein. [W]e think that the application of the misappropriation theory herein promotes the purposes and policies underlying section 10(b) and Rule 10b-5. In construing the Rule's meaning, we must begin with its language. The Rule prohibits "any person," acting "directly or indirectly," from employing "any device, scheme or artifice to defraud." It equally prohibits "any act, practice, or course of business which operates as a fraud or deceit upon any person." This repeated use of the word "any" evidences Congress' intention to draft the Rule broadly.

The legislative intent of the 1934 Act is similarly broad-reaching. As this Court has noted in applying the misappropriation theory, "the antifraud provision was intended to be broad in scope, encompassing all 'manipulative and deceptive practices which have been demonstrated to fulfill no useful function.'" We perceive nothing "useful" about defendants' scheme.

In construing Congressional intent, we also find persuasive Congress' recent statements accompanying the Insider Trading Sanctions Act of 1984, relating to the purposes and scope of the 1934 Act and its antifraud provisions. Congress noted that the intent of the 1934 Act was to condemn all manipulative or deceptive trading "whether the information about a corporation or its securities originates from inside or outside the corporation." Congress apparently has sought to proscribe trading on material, nonpublic information obtained not through skill but through a variety of "deceptive" practices, unlawful acts which we term "misappropriation."

The information misappropriated here was the *Journal*'s own confidential schedule of forthcoming publications. It was the advance knowledge of the timing and content of these publications, upon which appellants, acting secretively, reasonably expected to and did realize profits in securities transactions. Since section 10(b) has been found to proscribe fraudulent trading by insiders or outsiders, such conduct constituted fraud and deceit, as it would had Winans stolen material nonpublic information from traditional corporate insiders or quasi-insiders.

Nor is there any doubt that this "fraud and deceit" was perpetrated "upon any person" under section 10(b) and Rule 10b-5. It is sufficient that the fraud was committed upon Winans' employer.

We can deduce reasonably that those who purchased or sold securities without the misappropriated information would not have purchased or sold, at least at the transaction prices, had they had the benefit of that information. Certainly the protection of investors is the major purpose of section 10(b) and Rule 10b-5.

Thus, because of his duty of confidentiality to the *Journal,* defendant Winans—and Felis and Carpenter, who knowingly participated with him—had a corollary duty, which they breached, under section 10(b) and Rule 10b-5, to abstain from trading in securities on the basis of the misappropriated information or to do so only upon making adequate disclosure to those with whom they traded.

AFFIRMED in favor of plaintiffs.

CRITICAL THINKING

Does the court provide you with enough evidence to feel confident about its decision? If not, what other information would you need? Do you agree with the court's interpretation of congressional intent? Why or why not?

ETHICAL DECISION MAKING

How might the application of the universalization test have prevented Winans's action?

Tipper/Tippee theory. The *tipper/tippee theory* holds that any individual who acquires material inside information as a result of an insider's breach of duty has engaged in insider trading. This individual, one who has received a "tip" from an insider, is called a **tippee.** The insider who gives the inside "tip" is called the **tipper.**

Suppose Jerry (the tipper) gives material inside information to Elaine (the tippee). Jerry is liable because he is passing on inside information. Furthermore, Elaine is liable if she makes trading decisions based on information that she should know is not public. Jerry is liable for any profits made by Elaine. Now, suppose Elaine passes the tip on to George. Elaine is now a tipper, and George is a tippee. Both Elaine and Jerry are liable for the profits made by George. George is liable for the profits of his transactions if he knew or should have known that the material information was not public.

SECTION 16(B)

Under Section 16(a) of the 1934 act, certain large stockholders, executive officers, and directors are considered **statutory insiders.** All statutory insiders must file a report detailing their ownership and trading of the corporation's securities.

To prevent statutory insiders from using inside information for their personal gain, Section 16(b) of the 1934 act requires that statutory insiders return all **short-swing profits,** or profits made from the sale of company stock within any six-month period by a statutory insider, to the company. Even if the insider did not use the inside information to make the transaction, all short-swing profits belong to the corporation. Section 16(b) imposes strict liability on statutory insiders who earn short-swing profits. In other words, violators cannot use lack of intent or lack of knowledge as a defense. Certain transactions, however, such as bankruptcy proceedings, are exempt from Section 16(b). Case 41-5 illustrates the elements considered when a statutory insider is charged with failing to return short-swing profits to a company.

CASE 41-5

JOHN LITZLER v. CC INVESTMENTS, L.D.C.
U.S. DISTRICT COURT, S.D. NEW YORK
411 F. SUPP. 2D 41, 2006, US DIST. LEXIX 2698 (2006)

Data Race, a small company based in Texas, needed capital to market a new product. It separately presented a preliminary term sheet to Citadel Limited Partnership, Capital Ventures International ("CVI"), and Castle Creek Partners, LLC ("CC"), without revealing the identity of potential investors to each other. After Citadel indicated interest, Data Race arranged for a due diligence session for all three potential investors at its headquarters.

Follow-up conference calls after the due diligence were arranged by Data Race, sometimes with all of the potential investors, other times with individual investors. Each investor engaged independent counsel to advise them on the transaction, and it was the policy of some or all of the investors to keep their due diligence evaluations and trading strategies to themselves. Each potential investor, based on its own due diligence analysis and advice from its own counsel, made an independent decision to invest in the Data Race stock. The investors appointed Citadel's attorney to act for all of the investors in negotiating an agreement with Data Race's attorneys.

The first batch of securities, valued at $5 million, closed on November 12, 1997, with a conditional purchase of an additional $3 million of convertible preferred stock planned for January 1998. Each holder had the right individually to convert the preferred stock at either a fixed or floating conversion price. After

February 11, 1998, each investor sent notices at various times to Data Race to convert different amounts of its respective shares of the stock. Citadel frequently sold and made delivery the same day by converting preferred stock and then delivering the common stock. The price of Data Race's common stock during the conversions affected by the investors declined from $5 per share on November 12, 1997 to $0.625 on July 13, 1998. By July 17, 1998, all of the convertible preferred stock had been converted. Citadel, CVI, and CC all agreed not to purchase shares in the second batch of securities.

In 1999, approximately a year after the conversions had been completed, a Data Race shareholder commenced an action under section 16(b) of the Securities Exchange Act of 1934 to recover short-swing profits realized by Citadel, CVI, and CC. It alleged that Citadel, together with CC and CVI—three separate hedge funds—acted as a group under section 13(d)(3) of the Securities Exchange Act of 1934 (hereinafter "SEA"), and thus "any profit realized by" them "from any purchase and sale" of equity securities in Data Race are "recoverable" by Data Race under section 16(b) of the SEA.

Citadel—the only Defendants remaining following settlements between Plaintiff and the other Defendants—moved to dismiss upon summary judgment. They argue that Plaintiff has failed to prove that Citadel acted with others as a group under section 13(d)(3), and thus were not liable to Plaintiff for profits under section 16(b), and that there are no triable issues.

HELLERSTEIN, J.: Section 16(b) of the Securities Exchange Act of 1934 makes "recoverable by the issuer" "any profit realized by" "a beneficial owner" from "any purchase and sale . . . of an equity of [the] issuer." To state a claim under section 16(b), Plaintiff must show: "(1) a purchase and (2) a sale of securities (3) by . . . a shareholder who owns more than ten percent of any class of the issuer's securities (4) within a six-month period." The shareholder must be a 10% beneficial owner before the short-swing transaction.

It is undisputed that Citadel could have owned, beneficially and of record, no more than 8.5% percent of Data Race's securities without taking into consideration the conversion caps, and no more that 4.99% taking into consideration the conversion caps. Plaintiff argues that the 10% required by section 16(b) is met because [Citadel, CVI, and CC] were a "group," and together they owned more than 10%.

Section 13(d)(3) of the Securities Exchange Act of 1934 considers a group of investors to be a single "owner" for the purposes of section 16(b) "[w]hen two or more persons act as a partnership, limited partnership, syndicate, or other group for the purpose of acquiring, holding, or disposing of securities of an issuer." To establish the existence of such a group, there must be evidence of an agreement. The parties need only have "combined to further a common objective with regard to one of those activities," that is, acquiring, holding, or disposing of securities. General allegations of parallel investments by institutional investors do not suffice to plead a "group."

Plaintiff argues that Citadel formed a group with the other Defendants in their acquisitions of Data Race's convertible preferred stock in the private placement. Plaintiff points out that they acted through a common lawyer. Plaintiff also argues that the group activity was apparent in the decisions of each investor to convert its preferred shares into common stock, and the decisions of each investor not to purchase shares in the second [batch]. There is no evidence of communications among the parties following the closing of the first [batch]. Although there is no other fact of concerted activity to which Plaintiff cites, Plaintiff argues nevertheless that the coordinated activities of purchase entitle him to argue his case to the jury. I hold to the contrary.

In this transaction, the three groups of investors—Citadel, CC, and CVI—were each represented by separate counsel, and made their decisions separately, based on their own, separate investment considerations. They appointed one of their lawyers to negotiate on behalf of the three, in response to the suggestions of Data Race's lawyers, and because the circumstances of a private placement require a single set of documents equally affecting all investors. The common lawyer took instructions from his own client and, through the other two lawyers, from their clients. It is not substantially disputed that Data Race did not consider the three as a group. Careless drafting referring to [the common lawyer] as "investors' counsel" and all of the investors as his "clients" are not significant evidence of Data Race's view. The Securities Purchase Agreement required each of the investors to agree that each alone could not acquire or convert to hold more than 5% of Data Race's securities, and Data Race did not make any disclosures of a group that would have been required if Data Race had believed that the investors were, in fact, a group. Each of the three investors made their own decisions when and how to convert their preferred shares to common stock, and sell those shares, at different market prices, at different times, and under different conditions. It is undisputed that neither Citadel, nor the other two investors, were interested in purchasing a controlling block of Data Race's securities, or otherwise exercising control of Data Race.

The SEC has acknowledged the "sound business considerations such as cost savings" that generally lead to "cooperative activity characteristic of an institutional placement." More than such cooperative activity has to be alleged and proved to show that the investors were motivated by "a desire to affect control," or by some other indicia of concerted activity. These concerns are embodied in the exception to Rule 13d-5(b)(1), whereby certain investors (registered broker dealers, registered investment companies, etc.) are deemed not to have acted as a group as long as the purchase was in the "ordinary course of each [investor's] business" and "[t]here is no agreement among, or between any [investors] . . . except for the purpose of facilitating the specific purchase involved."

Plaintiff shows nothing more than the use of a lead draftsman, at the behest of Data Race, by the investors. All other activities and decisions, including due diligence, the decision to purchase, and the decision to sell, were done individually. And no group activity is even alleged to have occurred thereafter. For the reasons stated, Defendant's motion for summary judgment is granted.

Defendant's motion for summary judgment GRANTED.

CRITICAL THINKING

What activities did the plaintiff need to prove Citadel engaged in to convince the judge that a crime had been committed? Why did the judge conclude that those activities had not taken place? Are you convinced by the judge's reasoning?

ETHICAL DECISION MAKING

Identify the value preference that supports the law discussed in this case. What value preferences would encourage a person to break this law? Why?

PROXY SOLICITATIONS

A **proxy** is a writing signed by a shareholder that authorizes the individual named in the writing to exercise the shareholder's votes (corresponding to his shares of stock) at a shareholders' meeting. Corporate managers often contact shareholders to request that they give a certain manager authority to vote on their behalf in an upcoming meeting. This process of obtaining authority to vote on behalf of a shareholder is called **proxy solicitation.** Because the proxy solicitation process is potentially susceptible to fraud, the SEC regulates the proxy solicitation process.

Section 14(a) states that an issuer making proxy solicitations must also furnish a written proxy statement to shareholders. This statement must disclose to the shareholder all facts pertinent to the voting that will occur in the meeting.

VIOLATIONS OF THE 1934 ACT

The 1934 act authorizes both civil and criminal penalties. If an individual engages in insider trading, a violation of Section 10(b) or Rule 10b-5, she has committed a criminal offense punishable with a fine up to $1 million, a prison sentence up to 10 years, or both.

If a defendant did not know of the rule she violated, she cannot be imprisoned. If a partnership or corporation engages in insider trading, it is subject to fines up to $2.5 million.

Both the SEC and private parties can bring civil actions against violators of the 1934 act. The SEC investigates alleged violations under the 1934 act. In the process of this investigation, the SEC can enter into consent orders with defendants or seek injunctions to stop certain actions by defendants.

Perhaps the most useful tool the SEC has for punishing those engaging in insider trading is the *Insider Trading Sanctions Act of 1984,* which permits the SEC to sue any individual who violates the 1934 act or who helps another person to engage in insider trading in violation of that act. If the SEC succeeds in demonstrating its claim, courts may assess a civil penalty up to triple the profits gained or losses avoided by the defendant.

Congress expanded the SEC's authority to punish violators of the 1934 act when it passed the *Insider Trading and Securities Fraud Enforcement Act of 1988.* This act subjects more individuals to civil liability for insider trading and grants the SEC power to award **bounty payments** (government rewards for acts beneficial to the public) to insider-trading whistle-blowers.

Private parties may also sue violators of the 1934 act. A private party may seek rescission of a contract to buy securities or may recover damages based on the violator's profits. If the court rules that an individual is liable for violations of the 1934 act, he can seek contribution from others, such as accountants or lawyers, who shared responsibility for the violation.

Regulation of Investment Companies

In the past century, smaller investors have become important players in securities markets. Investment companies facilitate their involvement in securities markets by purchasing a large, diverse portfolio of securities and managing it on behalf of small investor-owners. However, because small investors often lack the resources and ability to adequately supervise investment companies, they can be subject to fraud and exploitation.

To prevent exploitation of small investors, Congress passed the *Investment Company Act of 1940,* providing for SEC regulation of investment companies. Congress later expanded the SEC's power to regulate investment companies under the *Investment Company Act Amendments of 1970* and the *National Securities Markets Improvement Act of 1996.*

The *Investment Company Act* defines an *investment company* as any entity (1) that is engaged primarily in the business of investing, reinvesting, or trading in securities or (2) that is engaged in such business and in which more than 40 percent of the company's assets are investment securities. The act excludes a number of institutions, however, including banks, insurance companies, savings and loans, and finance companies.

The act requires that all investment companies file a notification of registration with the SEC. Additionally, they must file annual reports with the SEC and hold all securities in the custody of a bank or member of the stock exchange. The act prohibits investment companies from purchasing securities on the margin (borrowing money to purchase securities), selling short (selling securities that the company does not yet own), and participating in joint trading accounts.

State Securities Laws

Not only must issuers obey federal securities regulations, but they are also subject to state securities laws, often referred to as **blue-sky laws.** These laws regulate the offering and sale of purely intrastate securities. Hence, although certain securities are exempt from federal securities regulation, they may be subject to state securities laws.

e-commerce AND THE LAW

Marketing Securities on the Internet

Perhaps one of the most important and exciting developments in securities regulations is the explosion of the securities market on the Internet. The Web permits companies to sell securities in an online initial public offering (IPO), thereby avoiding the expensive filing requirements of a traditional IPO. For example, some Web sites allow customers to buy and sell securities online. This technology, however, presents a greater opportunity for fraud because anyone can create a Web site. Several cases of securities fraud have occurred simply because a company has offered "free stock" over the Internet. The SEC has issued cease-and-desist orders against companies that illegally offered free stock on their Web sites because they had not registered their stocks with the SEC.

Another type of online fraud, called "pumping and dumping," occurs when an owner of a particular stock tells other investors about the virtues of the stock, artificially increasing demand for the stock and pumping up its price, only to sell (dump) it for a quick profit. Unregulated message boards on the Internet permit pumping and dumping on a fast and efficient basis. In response to the increasing use of this method of stock price manipulation, the SEC has pursued harsher and more frequent prosecution of individuals who engage in pumping and dumping online.

The Web also provides potential investors with access to enormous amounts of information about securities. For example, the SEC maintains the Electronic Data Gathering, Analysis, and Retrieval (EDGAR) database to help investors access information about IPOs and other documents filed with the SEC. Visit www.sec.gov/edgar.shtml to learn more about EDGAR.

SEC regulations apply to online advertising and securities transactions. When a company delivers a paperless prospectus, it is subject to the following rules:

1. The company must provide timely and adequate notice of the delivery of information.
2. The company must use an easily accessible communication system such as the Internet.
3. The company must create evidence of the delivery of information.

Many state securities laws serve functions similar to those of federal securities laws. For example, many states have laws requiring registration of securities issued within the state and requiring disclosure of certain information. Moreover, state laws regulate securities brokers and dealers. Although the purposes of state and federal securities regulations overlap, the specific regulations differ. Consequently, to encourage greater coordination between federal and state securities laws, most states have adopted the Uniform Securities Act.

CASE OPENER WRAP-UP

Martha Stewart

Although the SEC sought to charge Martha Stewart with illegal insider trading, a grand jury did not indict Stewart on that charge. The grand jury did, however, indict Stewart and her broker on nine criminal charges, including securities fraud, obstruction of justice, and conspiracy. Stewart pled not guilty to all charges.

The district court threw out the securities fraud charge on grounds that "no reasonable jury could find it to be accurate." A week later, however, a jury convicted her of the four remaining counts against her, all of which related to her statements to SEC investigators in their investigation of her sale of ImClone stock. The jury sentenced her to five months in a minimum-security prison. A federal appellate court upheld her sentence.[11]

[11] 433 F.3d 273.

Summary

What Is a Security?

As defined by the Howey test, a security is an investment in a common enterprise with the reasonable expectation of profit gained predominantly from others' efforts.

Securities Regulation

The Securities and Exchange Commission (SEC) was created in 1934 to enforce securities laws, interpret provisions of securities acts, and regulate the trade of securities as well as the activities of securities brokers, dealers, and advisers.

The Securities Act of 1933

Registration statement: Document containing a description of the securities offered for sale, an explanation of how proceeds from the sale will be used, a description of the registrant's business and properties, information about the management of the company, a description of any pending lawsuits, and certified financial statements.

Prospectus: Written document that is similar to the registration statement and used as a selling tool for potential investors.

Periods of the filing process:

1. Prefiling period
2. Waiting period
3. Posteffective period

Exempt transactions:

1. *Limited offers* involve small amounts of money or are offered only to sophisticated investors. There are four possible exemptions:
   - *Private placement exemption:* Exempts private offerings of securities.
   - *Rule 505:* States that private offerings may not exceed $5 million in a 12-month period and firms do not have to believe that investors have a reasonable ability to evaluate risk.
   - *Rule 504:* Exempts noninvestment firms that offer no more than $1 million in securities in a 12-month period.
   - *Section 4(6):* Exempts securities offered only to accredited investors for an amount less than $5 million.
2. *Intrastate issues* exempt local investors in local businesses.
3. *Resales* exempt transactions by any person other than an issuer, underwriter, or dealer.

Restricted securities are securities acquired under Rule 505, Rule 506, or Section 4(6) that must be registered for resale unless the investor follows Rule 144 or Rule 144(a).

Violations may result in:

1. Administrative action
2. Injunctive action
3. Criminal prosecution

The Securities Exchange Act of 1934

Section 10(b): Regulation that prohibits the use of manipulative and deceptive devices to bypass SEC rules.

Insider trading: Trading in which a company employee or executive uses material inside information to make a profit.

Misappropriation theory: Theory that an individual who wrongly acquires and uses inside information for profit is liable for insider trading.

Tipper/tippee theory: Theory that an individual who receives material inside information as a result of an insider's breach of duty is guilty of insider trading.

Statutory insiders: Certain stockholders, executive officers, and directors who must file a report detailing their ownership and trading of the corporation's securities.

Short-swing profits: Profits made from the sale of company stock within any six-month period to a statutory insider; by Section 16(b), these must be returned to the company.

Proxy: Document that authorizes an individual to vote the shareholder's share of stocks at a shareholder's meeting.

Proxy solicitation: Process of obtaining the authority to vote on behalf of a shareholder.

Violations may result in:

1. Criminal penalties.
2. Civil penalties.
3. Suits against those involved in insider trading under the Insider Trading Sanctions Act of 1984.

State Securities Laws *Blue-sky laws* regulate the offering and sale of securities within the state only.

Point / Counterpoint

Should the Government Increase Regulation of Securities Markets?

No

The government currently overregulates securities markets.

Government regulation is inefficient and perpetually behind the times. For example, some securities do not provide investors with dividends or bond payments until several years after their issue date. The nature of these securities renders investors susceptible to fraud, yet they might not discover the fraud until several years later, at a point when the trail is cold and government is impotent to remedy the situation. In another infamous example, a 15-year-old in New Jersey used Internet chat rooms to "pump and dump" securities. He was able to make off with over $800,000 before the SEC discovered what he had done.

Left unregulated, securities markets will provide an efficient level of information and will punish those who commit securities fraud. Intelligent investors will refuse to purchase securities about which they have insufficient information and hence push companies that provide insufficient information out of the market. Alternatively,

Yes

The government currently underregulates securities markets.

A common and not unfounded perception of securities markets is that small investors frequently lose everything while big investors and insiders win big. Consider, for example, the corporate accounting scandals of the early 2000s. Insiders made off with millions of dollars, while many small investors lost their retirement savings. Unless the government does more to level the playing field, these scandals will continue to occur.

Markets produce efficient results only when certain conditions exist. As the Connecting to the Core box in this chapter points out, securities markets are plagued by asymmetrical information: Investors almost always know less about securities than do issuers. If left unremedied, asymmetrical information leaves investors susceptible to many forms of securities fraud.

Even if government is unable to catch every perpetrator of securities fraud, its ability to catch high-profile perpetrators and punish them heavily still serves as an effective deterrent to other potential violators. For example, the wide publicity of the Martha Stewart case, if companies themselves refuse to provide information about securities they issue, investors will demand information from other sources. This investor demand will encourage development of markets providing information about securities. Indeed, these information markets already exist in the form of publications (e.g., *The Wall Street Journal* and *The Financial Times*) and professional services (e.g., stockbrokers and financial advisers).

Moreover, as the chapter pointed out, the five leaders of the SEC are unelected. As a result, they are insulated from democratic pressure to regulate securities markets in a manner consistent with voters' goals. Thus, even if more government regulation were desirable in theory, in practice the SEC is ill-equipped to provide it.

explained at the outset of this chapter, sent a strong message to investors that the SEC will punish outsiders who use even small pieces of inside information for personal gain.

Moreover, the unelected nature of SEC board members allows the president to appoint individuals with tremendous expertise. Perhaps Congress lacks the institutional competence to regulate complex securities markets efficiently, but experts who have spent their careers working with securities are more likely to be able to regulate effectively.

Government regulation of securities markets will never be perfect, but the appropriate comparison is not between government regulation and perfect regulation but between government regulation and available alternatives.

Questions & Problems

1. What was the stimulus for the creation of securities regulation? State the purposes of the two main federal securities laws.
2. What is the function of the SEC?
3. Explain the process of registering securities.
4. Why are certain securities transactions exempt from the registration process?
5. Why is it illegal to use inside information in making securities transactions?
6. How does the misappropriation theory apply to insider trading?
7. Alleging security fraud and breach of promissory notes under Section 10(b) of the federal Securities Exchange Act of 1934, plaintiff Dale LeBrun filed suit against the defendants, Kuswa, BK Enterprises, and Tomorrow, Inc., LeBrun was a vendor/supplier for Tomorrow Inc., a company that needed more capital to continue production of its products. LeBrun and his family and friends agreed to lend approximately $105,000 to Tomorrow Inc. For each of the six lenders, Kuswa drafted a document entitled an "Agreement to Borrow Monies." The terms required that Kuswa repay the loan within 12 months and pay interest quarterly based on sales or pay 100 percent of the initial amount borrowed. The plaintiffs continued to communicate with Kuswa through mail, but Kuswa did not make full payments on the loans within the specified year. The plaintiffs argued that, under the federal Securities Exchange Act, the loans not repaid by the defendants were promissory notes that had matured a year ago. The defendants claimed that the promissory notes in question were not securities under the definition provided in the federal Securities Exchange Act and therefore no federal jurisdiction existed. How do you think the court decided? [*Lebrun v. Kuswa,* 24 F. Supp. 2d 641 (1998).]
8. Magma Power Company brought a suit against Dow Chemical Co. under Section 16(b) of the Securities Exchange Act of 1934. Dow owned at least 10 percent of Magma common stock and was the largest minority shareholder. In a 1995 merger, Magma became a wholly owned subsidiary of California Energy. The merger eliminated all minority shareholders, and the terms of the merger required that Magma

compensate Dow for its prior minority interest. Instead of going forward with the compensation, Magma held that Dow, a statutory insider, had earned short-swing profits by trading in Magma stock. Dow's first transaction occurred on September 12, 1994. Dow sold 857,143 shares of Magma stock to Garantia banking at the market price. Three weeks later, Dow reacquired the same amount of shares from Garantia at the market price. More than six months later, Dow engaged in another trade. Magma argued that, on these last two occasions, Dow's transactions constituted sales, and therefore Magma alleged that Dow earned short-swing profits. The district court denied Magma's motion and found in favor of Dow. How do you think the court decided on appeal? Why? [*Magma Power Company v. The Dow Chemical Company,* 136 F.3d 316 (2nd Cir. 1998).]

9. Charles Zandford was a securities broker when he convinced William Wood to invest money with him that he would "conservatively" invest. The account would be for Wood and his daughter. Zandford sold shares of the Woods' mutual fund for his own benefit, and Zandford wrote checks to himself from the Woods' account. Zandford generated the money in the Woods' account by selling securities. Zandford was convicted of 13 counts of wire fraud for the loss of $419,255 belonging to the Woods. The SEC subsequently filed a civil action against Zandford to prevent him from violating securities laws and to recover the gains Zandford made on the Woods' account. Securities laws do not cover all types of fraud; rather, the laws cover only fraud that is sufficiently connected to a securities transaction. That is, the laws cover fraud that occurred "in the offer or sale of any securities." The district court granted summary judgment for the SEC. Zandford appealed the decision. Did the court of appeals affirm or reverse Zandford's civil conviction? Why? [*Securities and Exchange Commission v. Charles Zandford,* 238 F.3d 559 (2001).]

10. Edward Downe was hired by his close friend, Fred Sullivan, to serve as the director of Kidde, Inc. As a director of Kidde, Downe was kept informed of all financial developments. In the spring of 1987, rumors spread that Kidde was a target for takeover. Sullivan and his board of directors met with two companies, Hanson Trust PLC and Kohlberg Kravis Roberts, to discuss potential buyouts. On August 5, Sullivan announced that Kidde would accept the buyout offer by Hanson Trust PLC. As a result of the merger, Kidde stock increased from a price of $34 dollars in June to a price of $66 dollars on August 6. During the months prior to the merger, Downe and his close friend, Thomas Warde, purchased warrants to buy Kidde shares. For example, after speaking with Sullivan on June 28, Downe called Warde and the two invested over $500,000 in Kidde. Downe and Warde continued to add to their investments as Downe became more informed of the merger. The Securities and Exchange Commission filed a complaint against Warde and Downe, accusing them of insider trading, a violation of Section 10(b) of the 1934 act. Warde and Downe insisted that their decisions to invest were based on "market savvy, rumor, and public information alone." The U.S. district court found Warde in violation of the Securities and Exchange Act of 1934. How do you think the court decided on appeal? [*SEC v. Warde,* 151 F.3d 42 (1998).]

11. Plaintiff Robert Taylor founded the Better Life Club. Membership cost $39 per year and included a subscription to his newsletter, discounts on seminars, and opportunities to participate in certain "wealth building projects." As a means of raising funds for advertising, Taylor developed the Advertising Club. Members paid money to the club and received a signed note from Taylor promising to repay double the original amount invested within 60 or 90 days. The SEC investigated Taylor and found him in violation of the registration provision of the Securities Act of 1933. Taylor did not register the notes because he did not believe that they qualified as securities. The SEC argued that

the notes were investment contracts and therefore securities under the 1933 registration provision. Do you think Taylor's notes were securities under the 1933 act? Why or why not? [*SEC v. Better Life Club of America,* 995 F. Supp. 167 (1998).]

12. Atul Bhagat was an employee of Nvidia Corporation. Nvidia successfully competed for a multimillion-dollar contract to develop the X-Box video game console for Microsoft. Nvidia's CEO sent a companywide e-mail announcing that Nvidia had won the contract. The next morning, Nvidia's CEO sent several follow-up e-mails instructing Nvidia employees to keep the information about the contract confidential and prohibiting them from buying any Nvidia stock for several days. Later that morning, Bhagat purchased a large quantity of Nvidia stock. Four days later, after Nvidia publicly announced the contract with Microsoft, Bhagat sold his stock in the company for a substantial profit. When the SEC brought criminal charges against him for insider trading, Bhagat claimed he had not read the e-mails from Nvidia's CEO prior to making his purchases; thus, he had no insider information when he made his purchase. How do you think the court ruled? Why? [*United States v. Bhagat,* 2006 WL 288129 (2006).]
13. The CFTC challenged the activities of Edward Collins and his brother Thomas Collins. Thomas and Edward operated Lake States Commodities, Inc. The CFTC found that the brothers were intentionally misrepresenting information to commodities investors. Edward solicited customers to invest money in commodities. Though the customers believed their money was being invested in commodities, it was actually being placed in an unregistered commodity pool. Thomas was primarily responsible for the scheme and executed all trades. In 1994, the scheme fell through and many investors lost most of their money. Thomas disappeared, and Edward has had no involvement in commodity futures trading since 1994. The CFTC brought an action against Edward Collins. Do you think this action was appropriate under Section 4b of the CEA? Why or why not? [*CFTC v. Collins,* 1997 U.S. Dist. LEXIS 1597 (1997).]
14. Vencor was a long-term health care provider that derived a large portion of its revenue from Medicare. When President Clinton proposed the Balanced Budget Act of 1997, many in the health care sector were alarmed because the act significantly changed aspects of Medicare. In July 1997, during the time the act was being considered, an internal Vencor memo detailed the act's potential impact on the company. However, the external communications made by Vencor were that earnings and returns would rise, making some stock analysts recommend Vencor as a "buy." Vencor did, in its literature, indicate that the effects of the budget act were unable to be assessed at that time and said that there was no guarantee that the act would not have an adverse effect. In October 1997, Vencor lowered its estimates of earnings due to analysis of the budget act, and Vencor's stock price fell from $42⅜ to $30. Several investors filed a class action lawsuit against Vencor, alleging that Vencor made misleading and false statements about the company's position to raise its stock price. The investors alleged that Vencor had analyzed the budget act's impact as early as April 1997 and also that Vencor's executive vice president had made statements in June 1997 acknowledging that the industry would fall on hard times because of cutbacks in Medicare. As well, between July and September 1997 Vencor executives divested themselves of $9.5 million in stock holdings. One executive of Vencor received more than $3 million in profits from his sales, which aroused curiosity in the financial media. The district court granted summary judgment for Vencor, and the court of appeals concluded that the investors had not stated a claim. However, the court of appeals agreed to a rehearing en banc. During the rehearing, Vencor maintained that its public statements about the budget act were not actionable because these statements were "soft information"

protected by nondisclosure. The court of appeals was deeply divided in its decision. What reasons would the court give to overturn its decision? What reasons would the court give in support of its original decision? [*A. Carl Hedwig et al. v. Vencor, Inc., et al.,* 2001 U.S. App. LEXIS 11236, 2001 FED App. 0179P (2001).]

15. Begun in 1997, Unique Financial Concepts offered the sale of foreign currency options that promised large returns on small investments. Unique advertised its services heavily, raising more than $6.5 million from investors. Until August 1998, Unique's information packet for investors indicated that investments would be pooled together, that gains would be distributed proportionally, and that Unique had sole discretion over the investments. These statements were removed after August 1998. The SEC was granted an injunction against Unique in October 1998 after it appeared that Unique was acting fraudulently. Only 38 percent of the investors' money was actually sent to the clearinghouses that would provide return on the investments. About $2.5 million of the investors' money went to payroll, the executives of Unique, and personal and business expenses; $1.2 million went to advertising; and just over half a million dollars was distributed to new investors. In its appeal, Unique argued that it was not subject to securities laws because its investments were not securities. From the Howey test, both sides agreed that the first prong was met, but there was disagreement over the other two prongs. Unique argued that despite its original investment packet, the company did not actually operate as the investment packet advertised, and Unique noted the fact that it had pulled the statements from its literature. Unique argued that it had maintained separate individual accounts, rather than pooling investments, and that investors had made all key strategic decisions. Were Unique's arguments accepted by the court of appeals? Why or why not? [*Securities and Exchange Commission v. Unique Financial Concepts, Inc., et al.,* 196 F.3d 1195 (1999).]

16. Westinghouse Electric Corporation, like many corporations in the 1980s, experienced large losses on its real estate investments. Investors brought a class action lawsuit against Westinghouse for their losses, alleging securities fraud. Several issues were raised at trial, but the district court dismissed all the investors' claims. One issue plaintiffs raised was that the underwriters of a public offering of Westinghouse stock, who solicited the plaintiffs to buy the stock, were liable to the plaintiffs for misrepresentation of material fact. The court of appeals examined the district court's decision, including the dismissal of the claim that the underwriters "offered or sold" Westinghouse securities. For an individual to be considered a seller, precedent offers three stipulations. First, the individual's participation in the transaction must substantially cause its occurrence. Second, he or she must receive consideration in exchange for the sale. Third, the individual must be "motivated by a desire to confer a direct or indirect benefit on someone other than the person advised." Could the investors have a legitimate claim against the underwriters based on the criteria for a seller? [*In re Westinghouse Securities Litigation,* 90 F.3d 696 (1996).]

Looking for more review material?

The Online Learning Center at **www.mhhe.com/kubasek1e** contains this chapter's "Assignment on the Internet" and also a list of URLs for more information, entitled "On the Internet." Find both of them in the Student Center portion of the OLC, along with quizzes and other helpful materials.

Employment and Labor Law

CASE OPENER

Madison and Save Right Pharmacy

For the last five years, Madison has worked 20 hours per week at Save Right Pharmacy. She has always been a reliable and efficient employee. When her mother became seriously ill, Madison decided to take some time off under the Family and Medical Leave Act (FMLA) to care for her. Madison notified Save Right Pharmacy that she planned to take up to 12 weeks off to care for her mother. Save Right Pharmacy denied Madison's request. When Madison left work anyway, Save Right Pharmacy terminated her employment. Madison then applied for unemployment compensation so that she would have income to live on while caring for her mother. Madison also applied, under COBRA, for continued insurance coverage through her former employer, even though she no longer worked there. If you were the CEO of Save Right Pharmacy, how would you handle the employment situation with Madison? By the end of this chapter, you should be able to answer all of the following questions:

1. Is Madison eligible for time off from work under the FMLA?
2. May Save Right Pharmacy legally terminate Madison's employment?
3. Given that Madison was fired by Save Right Pharmacy, is she eligible to collect unemployment compensation?
4. May Madison continue her insurance coverage through Save Right Pharmacy even though she has been fired from her job?

The Wrap-Up at the end of the chapter will answer these questions.

CHAPTER 42

Learning Objectives

After reading this chapter, you will be able to answer the following questions:

1. What are wage and hour laws?
2. What are the rights of employees and obligations of employers under the Family and Medical Leave Act?
3. What is FUTA?
4. What are the rules regarding workers' compensation?
5. What is COBRA?
6. What is ERISA?
7. What is OSHA?
8. What does it mean to be an "at-will" employee?
9. What are the rights of employees and obligations of employers with regard to privacy in the workplace?

Introduction to Labor and Employment Law

The employment relationship is a contractual relationship between the employer and employee: The employer agrees to pay the employee a certain amount of money in exchange for the employee's agreement to render specific services. Early in our history, the employer and employee were free to determine all the conditions of their employment relationship. What this meant, up until the early to middle portion of the 20th century, was that workers had virtually no rights. If a worker was injured on the job, he or she could be fired. There were no safety standards. Workers often toiled in unspeakable conditions.

> At the turn of the century, the average workweek was twelve hours a day and six days a week. Coal miners were suffering and dying in appallingly large numbers from both accident and the environment in which they worked. Poor and immigrant children often worked alongside their parents, kids as young as seven or eight working twelve hours a day—for low wages that poor families needed mainly for food. . . . At the turn of the century in the United States there was no income tax, and no social security, unemployment insurance or public housing for the aged or disabled. Families were obliged to take care of their aged and their handicapped, and grandmothers babysat the children of their sons and daughters.[1]

Today, both the federal and state governments impose a number of conditions on the employment relationship. This chapter explains many of the laws that created those constraints on the employer's ability to determine terms and conditions of employment and termination. The first half of this chapter covers wages, benefits, health and safety standards, and employee rights, including the right to privacy. Exhibit 42-1 lists several major areas of state and federal laws that are covered in the first half of this chapter. The second half of this chapter covers labor unions.

[1] World History—Ancient History to the 21st Century, "The United States to 1910: Life at the Turn of the Century," www.fsmitha.com/h2/ch03.htm.

Exhibit 42-1 Selected Laws Affecting Working Conditions in the U.S.

Wage and hour laws	Federal and state laws that impose minimum wage and hour requirements for employees.
Family and Medical Leave Act (FMLA)	Federal act requiring that employers establish a policy that provides all eligible employees with up to 12 weeks of leave during any 12-month period for several family-related occurrences (e.g., birth of a child or to care for a sick spouse).
Unemployment compensation	State system, created by the Federal Unemployment Tax Act (FUTA), that provides unemployment compensation to qualified employees who lose their jobs.
Workers' compensation laws	State laws that provide for financial compensation to employees or their dependents when the covered employee is injured on the job.
Consolidated Omnibus Budget Reconciliation Act (COBRA)	Federal law that ensures that when employees lose their jobs or have their hours reduced to a level at which they would not be eligible to receive medical, dental, or optical benefits from their employer, the employees will be able to continue receiving benefits under the employer's policy for up to 18 months by paying the premiums for the policy.

(Continued)

Employee Retirement Income Security Act (ERISA)	Federal law that sets minimum standards for most voluntarily established pension and health plans in private industry to provide protection for individuals in these plans.
The Occupational Safety and Health Act of 1970 (OSHA)	Federal law that established the Occupational Safety and Health Administration, the agency responsible for setting safety standards under the act, as well as enforcing the act through inspections and the levying of fines against violators.
Employment-at-will doctrine and wrongful discharge	Under the employment-at-will doctrine, the employer can fire the employee for any reason at all. The three exceptions to the doctrine are *implied contract, violations of public policy,* and *implied covenant of good faith and fair dealing.* In states that have adopted any of these three exceptions, employees may be able to sue for wrongful discharge.
Employee privacy	Privacy issues are of increasing importance in the workplace. Privacy policies should cover matters such as employer surveillance policies, control of and access to medical and personnel records, drug testing, and e-mail policies.

Fair Labor Standards Act

Employers may not unilaterally determine how much to pay employees or how many hours to require them to work. Federal minimum wage and hour laws must be followed. The Fair Labor Standards Act[2] (FLSA) covers all employers engaged in interstate commerce or the production of goods for interstate commerce.

FLSA requires that a minimum wage of a specified amount be paid to all employees in covered industries. The specified amount is periodically raised by Congress to compensate for increases in the cost of living caused by inflation. The most recent increase took effect on May 26, 2007. The federal minimum wage increased from $5.15 to $5.85 per hour during the summer of 2007. By the summer of 2009, the federal minimum wage will be $7.25. This is the first increase in almost 10 years.

FLSA mandates that employees who work more than 40 hours in a week be paid no less than one and one half times their regular wage for all the hours beyond 40 that they work during a given week. Four categories of employees are excluded:

- Executives
- Administrative employees
- Professional employees
- Outside salespersons

FLSA requires that employees earn at least a minimum amount of income and spend a certain amount of time engaged in specified activities before they can fall into any of those exempted categories. If employers try to evade the overtime rule, their employees may sue. Taco Bell recently felt the full impact of FLSA when several groups of its employees brought class action suits against the restaurant chain because the company allegedly shaved hours off the employee time cards to avoid paying employees overtime. One of the suits was settled by Taco Bell for $13 million.[3] More

[2] 29 U.S.C. §§201–260.

[3] "Taco Bell Loses Second Big Back-Pay Case as Ore. Jury Affirms Time-Card Tampering Charge," *Nation's Restaurant News,* March 26, 2001, p. 3.

recently, a class action lawsuit was brought against Wal-Mart by 187,000 employees who worked at Wal-Mart from 1998 through May 2006. Wal-Mart was ordered to pay $78 million for violating Pennsylvania state labor laws by forcing employees to work through rest breaks and off the clock.[4]

In contrast to many European countries, the United Kingdom is like the United States in having no laws requiring that employers give paid or even unpaid holidays. Interestingly, the United States, unlike most European nations, does not mandate any minimum amount of annual vacation time for employees.

global context

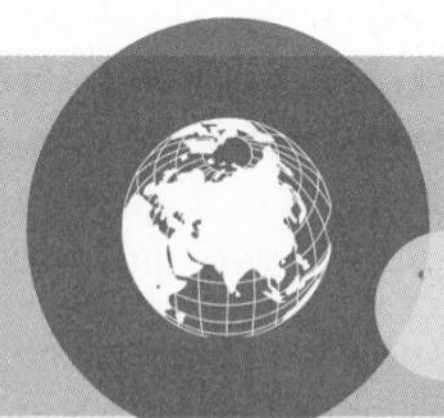

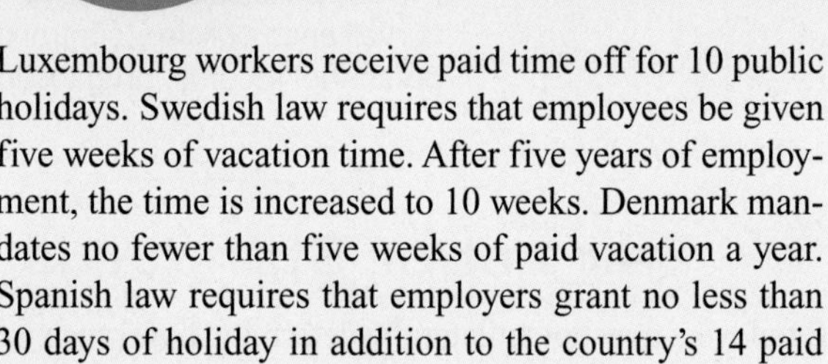

Paid Vacations in Other Countries

In Ireland, the Holiday Act of 1973 guarantees every worker, regardless of how long he or she has been with a company, three weeks of paid vacation time and nine additional days off for public holidays. Luxembourg also has tremendous holiday benefits. Regardless of the employee's age, he or she is given 25 days of holiday, 12 of which must be taken in succession. Additionally, Luxembourg workers receive paid time off for 10 public holidays. Swedish law requires that employees be given five weeks of vacation time. After five years of employment, the time is increased to 10 weeks. Denmark mandates no fewer than five weeks of paid vacation a year. Spanish law requires that employers grant no less than 30 days of holiday in addition to the country's 14 paid public ones.

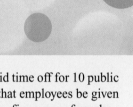

Family and Medical Leave Act

When the Family and Medical Leave Act (FMLA) went into effect in 1993, it was hailed by its supporters as a "breakthrough" in American law and feared by its opponents as an unwieldy encumbrance on business. FMLA covers all public employers, as well as private employers with 50 or more employees. It guarantees all eligible employees (those who have worked at least 25 hours a week for each of 12 months prior to the leave) up to 12 weeks of *unpaid* leave during any 12-month period for any of the following family-related occurrences:

- The birth of a child.
- The adoption of a child.
- The placement of a foster child in the employee's care.
- The care of a seriously ill spouse, parent, or child.
- A serious health condition that renders the employee unable to perform any of the essential functions of his or her job.

Remember Madison from the scenario at the beginning of the chapter? She worked for Save Right Pharmacy for five years, but worked only 20 hours per week. As such, under FMLA she would not be eligible to take leave to care for her mother.

[4] "Jury Orders Pa. Walmart to Pay $78 Million," http://cbs3.com/topstories/local_story_286145532.html, October 13, 2006.

The birth of a child is a fairly straightforward reason for a person to take leave under FMLA, but what about someone who claims he has a "serious health condition"? What exactly constitutes a serious health condition under FMLA? Case 42-1 discusses whether the flu can be a serious health condition.

CASE 42-1 KIMBERLY MILLER, PLAINTIFF-APPELLEE, v. AT&T CORPORATION, A FOREIGN CORPORATION, DEFENDANT-APPELLANT

U.S. COURT OF APPEALS, FOURTH CIRCUIT
250 F.3D 820 (2000)

Plaintiff Kimberly Miller worked for Defendant AT&T, and had accumulated so many absences that under the company's attendance policy, she would be terminated if she had any more unexcused absences. Absences covered by FMLA are not unexcused absences.

Miller began to feel sick while at work on December 26, 1999. She completed her shift that day but was too sick to work the next day. On December 28, she went to an urgent care center, where the doctor diagnosed her as being severely dehydrated and suffering from the flu.

On December 31, Miller telephoned the urgent care center and asked for a work-excuse slip for January 1, explaining that she was feeling better but needed an additional day off work. The urgent care center granted this request.

Upon returning to work, Miller filed for FMLA leave for the days she missed. Because it did not consider the flu to be a serious health condition, the company denied her request. The denial made her absence unexcused, and she was consequently terminated. Miller sued her employer for unlawfully denying her benefits under the Family and Medical Leave Act (FMLA). The United States District granted the employee's motion for partial summary judgment as to liability, and thereafter awarded back pay and attorneys' fees. The employer appealed.

CIRCUIT JUDGE WILKINS: . . . AT & T contends that it did not violate the FMLA because the illness for which Miller sought FMLA leave—an episode of the flu—was not a serious health condition as defined by the Act and implementing regulations; that if Miller's flu was a serious health condition under the applicable regulations, those regulations are contrary to congressional intent and are therefore invalid. . . .

The FMLA entitles an eligible employee to as many as 12 weeks of unpaid leave per year for "a serious health condition that makes the employee unable to perform the functions of the position of such employee." The Act defines "serious health condition" as an illness, injury, impairment, or physical or mental condition that involves—

(A) inpatient care in a hospital, hospice, or residential medical care facility; or

(B) continuing treatment by a health care provider.

Thus, as is relevant here, an eligible employee is entitled to FMLA leave for an illness that incapacitates the employee from working and for which the employee receives "continuing treatment," a term the FMLA does not define. The FMLA grants the Secretary of Labor authority to promulgate regulations implementing the Act. Pursuant to this authority, the Secretary promulgated the following regulation: A serious health condition involving continuing treatment by a health care provider includes . . . :

(i) A period of incapacity (i.e., inability to work) of more than three consecutive calendar days . . . that also involves:

(A) Treatment two or more times by a health care provider . . . ; or

(B) Treatment by a health care provider on at least one occasion which results in a regimen of continuing treatment under the supervision of the health care provider.

The FMLA allows an employer to require that a request for leave for an employee's serious health condition be supported by a certification from the employee's health care provider. Among other things, the employer may require that the certification include "appropriate medical facts" regarding the condition. If the employer doubts the validity of a certification, it may require the employee to obtain a second opinion at the employer's expense. In the event of a conflict between the two opinions, the employer may require the employee to obtain a third opinion, again at the employer's expense. The opinion of the third health care provider is binding on both parties. . . .

We turn first to AT & T's contention that Miller's flu was not a "serious health condition" under the Act and regulations. First, AT & T contends that Miller cannot satisfy the regulatory criteria for a serious health condition because she did not receive "treatment" on two or more occasions. Failing this, AT & T argues that even if Miller qualified for FMLA leave under the regulatory criteria for "continuing treatment," the regulations specifically exclude the flu from FMLA coverage.

We begin with AT & T's contention that Miller did not receive treatment from Dr. Sommerville on two or more occasions. AT & T asserts that Miller's second visit to Dr. Sommerville—during which he conducted a physical examination and drew blood—did not constitute "treatment" because Dr. Sommerville simply evaluated Miller's condition. However, this assertion is contradicted by the regulations, which define "treatment" to include "examinations to determine if a serious health condition exists and evaluations of the condition." Under this definition, Miller's second visit to Dr. Sommerville clearly constituted "treatment."

AT & T next argues that even if Miller satisfies the regulatory criteria for a "serious health condition," the regulations nevertheless specifically exclude the flu and other minor illnesses from coverage under the FMLA. AT & T points to the following regulatory language: Ordinarily, unless complications arise, the common cold, the flu, ear aches, upset stomach, minor ulcers, headaches other than migraine, routine dental or orthodontia problems, periodontal disease, etc., are examples of conditions that do not meet the definition of a serious health condition and do not qualify for FMLA leave. According to AT & T, this regulation establishes that absent complications, the flu is never a serious health condition even if the regulatory test is satisfied. We disagree. In light of our conclusion that § 825.114(c) does not preclude FMLA coverage of an episode of the flu when the regulatory definition of a serious health condition is satisfied, we need not decide whether Miller suffered from any complications.

There is unquestionably some tension between subsection (a), setting forth objective criteria for determining whether a serious health condition exists, and subsection (c), which states that certain enumerated conditions "ordinarily" are not serious health conditions. Indeed, that tension is evidenced by Miller's illness. Miller was incapacitated for more than three consecutive calendar days and received treatment two or more times; thus, she satisfied the regulatory definition of a serious health condition under subsection (a). But, the condition from which Miller suffered—the flu—is one of those listed as being "ordinarily" not subject to coverage under the FMLA. AT & T urges us to resolve this tension by holding that subsection (c) essentially excepts the enumerated ailments from FMLA coverage even when an individual suffering from one of those ailments satisfies the regulatory criteria of subsection (a).

. . . Complications, per se, need not be present to qualify as a serious health condition if the regulatory . . . tests are otherwise met. The regulations reflect the view that, ordinarily, conditions like the common cold and flu (etc.) would not be expected to meet the regulatory tests, not that such conditions could not routinely qualify under FMLA where the tests are, in fact, met in particular cases.

[W]e nevertheless conclude that § 825.114(c) is properly interpreted as indicating merely that common ailments such as the flu normally will not qualify for FMLA leave because they generally will not satisfy the regulatory criteria for a serious health condition.

Whenever possible, this court must reconcile apparently conflicting provisions. That is not difficult to do here. 29 C.F.R. § 825.114(c) provides that "ordinarily" the flu will not qualify as a serious health condition. Presumably, this is because the flu (and the other conditions listed in the regulation) ordinarily will not meet the objective criteria for a serious health condition, inasmuch as such an illness normally does not result in an inability to work for three or more consecutive calendar days or does not require continuing treatment by a health care provider. Section 825.114(c) simply does not automatically exclude the flu from coverage under the FMLA. Rather, the provision is best read as clarifying that some common illnesses will not ordinarily meet the regulatory criteria and thus will not be covered under the FMLA.

AFFIRMED in favor of the plaintiff.

CRITICAL THINKING

Explain the reasoning that the court provides to support its decision. If it were your job to criticize the reasoning, what would you identify as its most significant weaknesses?

ETHICAL DECISION MAKING

The court in this case made an exception to the rule written in FMLA that the flu, while generally considered too mild to be considered a serious health condition, can sometimes be serious enough to cross into a more severe bracket of medical illness. What ethical decision-making tools are prevalent beneath this interpretation of severity of the flu? In other words, what value preference lies at the heart of the justification to allow the flu, in certain extreme situations, to be considered a severe illness?

FMLA is a highly complex piece of legislation, containing six titles divided into 26 sections and regulations, designed to guide the implementation of the act, that are eight times longer than the statute itself! Consequently, many employers were still not in full compliance with the act a year after it became effective.

To exercise one's rights under FMLA, an employee whose need for a leave is foreseeable must advise the employer of that need at least 30 days prior to the anticipated date on which the leave needs to begin or as soon as practicable. A typical foreseeable leave would be one for the birth of a child. If the leave is unforeseeable, notice must be given as soon as practicable. "As soon as practicable" is defined as within one or two business days from when the need for the leave becomes known.

FMLA, however, does not provide a clear definition of exactly what type of notice is necessary. At a minimum, the employee must inform the employer of why the employee needs the leave and, if possible, the length of time needed. FMLA does not have to be specifically mentioned in the request.

When their FMLA leaves terminate, employees must be restored to the same position or one that involves substantially equivalent skills, effort, responsibility, and authority. In some cases an employee may not be able to return to work at the end of the 12-week period. In such situations, the employer has no responsibility to hold the position open for the employee any longer.

While FMLA does not require that leave be paid, the employer must continue health insurance benefits during the leave period. The employer may also require that an employee substitute paid time off for unpaid leave. For example, an employee who has 4 weeks of accrued sick leave and 2 weeks of vacation and wishes to take a 12-week leave for the birth of a new baby may be required to take the paid vacation and sick leave plus 6 weeks of unpaid leave.

REMEDIES FOR VIOLATIONS OF FMLA

If an employer fails to comply with FMLA, the plaintiff may recover damages for unpaid wages or salary, lost benefits, denied compensation, and actual monetary losses up to an amount equivalent to the employee's wages for 12 weeks, as well as attorney fees and court costs. If the plaintiff can prove bad faith on the part of the employer, double damages may be awarded. An employee may also be entitled to reinstatement or promotion. Although most awards under FMLA have not been extremely large, the size of the awards is beginning to grow. One of the larger awards was made in 1996. A California worker was demoted, and then fired, for taking time off from work for surgery for a brain tumor. He sued and was awarded $313,000.[5] In 1999, a state trooper was denied time off to care

[5] *Lawyer's Weekly* 6 (1996) p. 973.

for his pregnant wife, and subsequently his daughter, when his wife became ill during and after the pregnancy. He was awarded $375,000.[6] Many employment law specialists are now seeing FMLA as an act that employers must carefully follow.

Unemployment Compensation

While FMLA in some cases helps employees retain their jobs, what happens if they lose their jobs? The Federal Unemployment Tax Act (FUTA),[7] passed in 1935, created a state system to provide unemployment compensation to qualified employees who lose their jobs. Under this law, employers pay taxes to the states, which deposit the money into the federal government's Unemployment Insurance Fund. Each state has an account from which it can access the money in the fund in accordance with the rules the state establishes for eligibility. States have different minimum standards for qualifying for unemployment compensation, although almost all states require that the applicant did not voluntarily quit or get fired for cause. Remember Madison from the beginning of the chapter? Madison stopped going to work despite the fact that Save Right Pharmacy had denied her request for leave to care for her sick mother. Because Madison did not qualify to take leave under FMLA and she simply stopped coming to work, Save Right Pharmacy was legally within its rights to fire Madison. Whether Madison was fired or voluntarily quit her job, she would not be entitled to collect unemployment compensation in most states.

In the majority of states, benefit funding is based solely on a tax imposed on employers, with only three states requiring minimal employee contributions.[8] The amount of the benefit may also vary. As of January 1, 2001, the average weekly unemployment benefit as a percentage of the average weekly wage ranged from a low of 22 percent in California to a high of 50 percent in Hawaii. The percentage of unemployed individuals in the state receiving benefits ranged from 17 percent in New Hampshire to 67 percent in Massachusetts.[9]

Workers' Compensation Laws

Unlike many other laws affecting the employment relationship, workers' compensation legislation is purely state law. Our coverage of this topic must therefore be rather generalized. Prudent businesspeople will familiarize themselves with the workers' compensation statutes of the states within which their companies operate.

Workers' compensation laws ensure that covered workers who are injured on the job can receive financial compensation through an administrative procedure, rather than having to sue their employer. For administrative convenience, most states exclude certain types of businesses and small firms from coverage. Some states also allow businesses that have sufficient resources to be self-insured, rather than participating in the state program.

BENEFITS UNDER STATE WORKERS' COMPENSATION

To recover workers' compensation benefits, the injured party must demonstrate that:

1. He or she is an employee.
2. Both the employer and the employee are covered by the state workers' compensation program.
3. The injury occurred on the job.

[6] *Knussman v. State of Maryland et al.*, 65 F. Supp. 353 (1999).

[7] 26 U.S.C. §§ 3301–3310.

[8] U.S. Department of Labor, http://workforcesecurity.doleta.gov/unemploy/uifactsheet.asp.

[9] AFL-CIO, "Workers' Compensation and Unemployment Insurance under State Laws," Publication No. 01143-05-R-15, January 1, 2001.

Whether the injury occurred on the job is sometimes an issue when an employee files a claim. As a general rule, this requirement means that the accident leading to the injury must have taken place during the time and within the scope of the claimant's employment. Using what is commonly called the *premises rule,* if an employee is on company property, the courts generally find that the employee was on the job.

If an employee is forced to travel for work and the employee is injured on a business trip, many states will find that the employee is entitled to compensation for reasonable injuries suffered while on the trip. For example, a New York typist was required to travel to Canada to transcribe depositions, and she fell while showering in her hotel. She filed a successful workers' compensation claim.

An employee who is injured on the job must notify the employer of the injury and file a workers' compensation claim with the state workers' compensation board within a specified time (usually 30 to 60 days). The board will then conduct an investigation to verify the claim and determine the appropriate benefits. If the employer does not contest the claim, the employee will receive the benefits mandated by state law. If the employer contests the claim, there will be a hearing before the state workers' compensation board. If the claim is denied, most states provide some form of appeals process within the agency, followed by a provision for appeal to the courts.

The amounts and types of benefits recoverable under workers' compensation are specified by each state's relevant statutes. Most statutes cover medical, hospital, and rehabilitation expenses. Compensation under state statutes also generally includes payment for lost wages. When employees become disabled as a result of their injury, most states have a schedule that determines the amount of compensation for the disability, as well as compensation schedules for loss of body parts.

HISTORICAL BASIS FOR WORKERS' COMPENSATION

Workers' compensation laws came about as a result of the abuses injured employees often suffered on the job. Prior to workers' compensation, an injured employee's only recourse was to sue the employer for negligence. The traditional defenses against negligence were often successful, and employees who sued usually lost their cases. The three defenses used successfully against employees, prior to workers' compensation laws, are:

- **Contributory negligence** (meaning the employee was partially at fault).
- **Assumption of the risk** (meaning that the employee chose to work for the employer and thus assumed any risk of injury).
- The **fellow servant rule** (meaning that the injury was caused by a fellow worker's negligence, and therefore the fellow servant, not the employer, should be responsible).

With the passage of state workers' compensation laws, in return for being able to recover for injuries incurred on the job, the employee gives up the right to bring any negligence claims against the employer for injuries resulting from the on-the-job injury. In one notable example, a Texas state judge threw out a \$12.7 million jury award against Exxon in a wrongful death suit because the victim's family had accepted \$15,000 from a workers' compensation claim 22 years prior. This example demonstrates one way in which workers' compensation laws can be seen as "insurance" against large jury awards against businesses. The one exception to this is that an employee who is injured by a piece of defective machinery retains the option of bringing a product liability action against the manufacturer of the machinery (i.e., *not* against the employer). But what happens if the employer orders the employee to engage in an act that could be very harmful to the employee? Is that employee limited to compensation available under workers' compensation? Case 42-2 was decided by the New Mexico Supreme Court on that very issue.

CASE 42-2 DELGADO v. PHELPS DODGE CHINO, INC.
SUPREME COURT OF NEW MEXICO
34 P.3D 1148 (2001)

Reynaldo Delgado died following an explosion that occurred at a smelting plant in Deming, New Mexico, after a supervisor ordered him to perform a task that, according to Petitioner, was virtually certain to kill or cause him serious bodily injury. Respondents allegedly chose to subject Delgado to this risk despite their knowledge that he would suffer serious injury or death as a result. Delgado's widow brought a number of tort claims against Phelps Dodge and the individual supervisors who allegedly caused Delgado's death. The trial court dismissed the case on the grounds that the Workers' Compensation Act provides the exclusive remedy for Delgado's death, and that Respondents therefore enjoy immunity from tort liability. The Court of Appeals upheld that ruling in a memorandum opinion. We granted certiorari to determine whether Respondents' behavior falls within the Act's exclusivity provisions.

JUDGE GENE E. FRANCHINI: In the summer of 1998, thirty-three-year-old Reynaldo Delgado resided in Deming, New Mexico, with his wife, Petitioner Michelle Delgado, and two minor children. Mr. Delgado had been working at the Phelps Dodge smelting plant in Hurley, New Mexico, for two years. The smelting plant distills copper ore from unusable rock, called "slag," by superheating unprocessed rock to a temperature in excess of 2,000 degrees Fahrenheit. During the process, the ore rises to the top, where it is harvested, while the slag sinks to the bottom of the furnace where it drains through a valve called a "skim hole." From there, the slag passes down a chute into a fifteen-foot-tall iron cauldron called a "ladle," located in a tunnel below the furnace. Ordinarily, when the ladle reaches three-quarters of its thirty-five-ton capacity, workers use a "mudgun" to plug the skim hole with clay, thus stopping the flow of molten slag and permitting a specially designed truck, called a "kress-haul," to enter the tunnel and lift and remove the ladle.

On the night of June 30, Delgado's shorthanded work crew, under the supervision of Mike Burkett and Charlie White, was being pressured to work harder in order to compensate for the loss of production and revenue incurred after a recent ten day shut down. Suddenly, the crew experienced an especially dangerous emergency situation known as a "runaway." The ladle had reached three-quarters of its capacity but the flowing slag could not be stopped because the mudgun was inoperable and manual efforts to close the skim hole had failed. To compound the situation, the consistency of the slag caused it to flow at a faster rate than ever, thus resulting in the worst runaway condition that many of the workers on the site had ever experienced. Respondents could have shut down the furnace, thereby allowing the safe removal of the ladle of slag. However, in order to avoid economic loss, Respondents chose instead to order Delgado, who had never operated a kress-haul under runaway conditions, to attempt to remove the ladle alone, with the molten slag still pouring over its fifteen-foot brim. In doing so, Respondents knew or should have known that Delgado would die or suffer great bodily harm.

When Delgado entered the tunnel, he saw that the ladle was overflowing and radioed White to inform him that he was neither qualified nor able to perform the removal. White insisted. In response to Delgado's renewed protest and request for help, White again insisted that Delgado proceed alone. Shortly after Delgado entered the tunnel, the lights shorted out and black smoke poured from the mouth of the tunnel. Delgado's co-workers watched as he emerged from the smoke-filled tunnel, fully engulfed in flames. He collapsed before co-workers could douse the flames with a water hose. "Why did they send me in there?" Delgado asked co-workers, "I told them I couldn't do it. They made me do it anyway. Charlie sent me in." Delgado had suffered third-degree burns over his entire body and died three weeks later in an Arizona hospital.

When a worker suffers an accidental injury and a number of other preconditions are satisfied, the Act provides a scheme of compensation that affords profound benefits to both workers and employers. The injured worker receives compensation quickly, without having to endure the rigors of litigation or prove fault on behalf of the employer. The employer, in exchange, is assured that a worker accidentally injured, even by the employer's own negligence, will be limited to compensation under the Act and may not pursue the unpredictable damages available outside its boundaries. The Act represents the "result of a bargain struck between employers and employees. In return for the loss of a common law tort claim for accidents arising out of the scope of employment, [the Act] ensures that workers are provided some compensation.

. . . [T]he Act limits its scope to accidents, barring both compensation and exclusivity when the worker sustains a non-accidental injury. Because the basis for limiting exclusivity depends on the non-accidental character of the injury, Professor Larson argues:

> [T]he common-law liability of the employer cannot, under the almost unanimous rule, be stretched to include accidental injuries caused by the gross, wanton, willful, deliberate, intentional, reckless, culpable or malicious negligence, breach of statute, or other misconduct of the employer short of a conscious and deliberate intent directed to the purpose of inflicting an injury.

We hold that when an employer intentionally inflicts or willfully causes a worker to suffer an injury that would otherwise be exclusively compensable under the Act that employer may not enjoy the benefits of exclusivity, and the injured worker may sue in tort.

REVERSED AND REMANDED in favor of plaintiff.

CRITICAL THINKING

What are the key words in determining whether an injury falls under the Workers' Compensation Act? Is it clear when anyone acts intentionally? What factors would cause a court to see an act by a defendant as having "intentionally or willfully caused" a worker's injury?

ETHICAL DECISION MAKING

It is clear that the widow and children of Delgado are important stakeholders in whatever decision the court makes in this case. Similarly, Phelps Dodge is obviously an important stakeholder in the result. But ethical decisions require consideration of stakeholders who are often invisible at first glance. Who are other relevant stakeholders in this particular decision about coverage of the Workers' Compensation Act?

EMPLOYER AND EMPLOYEE ADVANTAGES AND DISADVANTAGES OF WORKERS' COMPENSATION

It should be clear from this section that workers' compensation laws offer both advantages and disadvantages to employers and employees. The employees benefit because with very little effort, they receive an almost certain recovery when injured, although the amount they receive is substantially less than they would have recovered in a successful negligence case against their employers. Employers, however, do have to pay into the workers' compensation fund every year, regardless of whether any of their employees are injured. The benefit for businesses is the knowledge that their employee injury costs are fixed and thus they do not have to worry about having to pay a huge negligence award to an injured employee.

connecting to the core

Personal Taxation

While the compensation one receives from workers' compensation is often criticized as not being adequate to completely compensate the injured victim, something you learned about in your personal taxation course makes the awards slightly better than they might at first appear to be. Even though the payments are in part intended to compensate for a loss of future income, Congress decided to specifically exempt workers' compensation benefits from inclusion in gross income, and therefore the recipient need not pay tax on these benefits.*

* William Hoffman, Jr., et al., *Individual Income Taxes 2006* (Thomson, 2006), pp. 5–12.

Consolidated Omnibus Budget Reconciliation Act of 1985

The Consolidated Omnibus Budget Reconciliation Act (COBRA) ensures that employees who lose their jobs or have their hours reduced to a level at which they are no longer eligible to receive medical, dental, or optical benefits can pay to continue receiving benefits for themselves and their dependents under the employer's policy. The employee must pay the premiums for the policy, plus up to a 2 percent administration fee, to maintain the coverage for up to 18 months, or 29 months for a disabled worker. This is often quite expensive. An employee has 60 days after coverage would ordinarily terminate to decide whether to maintain the coverage.

This obligation does *not* arise under either of two conditions:

1. The employee is fired for gross misconduct.
2. The employer decides to eliminate benefits for all current employees.

Madison, from our opening scenario, has applied under COBRA to retain her insurance benefits even though she no longer works for Save Right Pharmacy. If it is determined that Madison's conduct in failing to show up at her job is "gross misconduct," her insurance benefits may be terminated. In most cases, however, when an employee voluntarily quits his or her job, or even is fired (but not for gross misconduct), insurance benefits may be continued (though the *employee* must pay the full cost of the insurance).

Employers who fail to comply with the law may be required to pay up to 10 percent of the annual cost of the group plan or $500,000, whichever is less.

Employee Retirement Income Security Act of 1974

The Employee Retirement Income Security Act (ERISA) is "a federal law that sets minimum standards for most voluntarily established pension and health plans in private industry to provide protection for individuals in these plans."[10] Under ERISA, employers must provide participants with all the following:

1. Plan information (i.e., features and funding).
2. Assurances of the fiduciary responsibility of those in charge of managing and controlling the plan assets.

[10] Department of Labor, Employee Retirement Income Security Act, www.dol.gov/dol/topic/health-plans/erisa.htm.

3. A grievance and appeals process for participants to get benefits from their plans.
4. The right to sue for benefits and breaches of fiduciary duty.[11]

Employers are required to provide to employees, free of charge, a Summary Plan Description (SPD), which provides information as to how the plan operates, the benefits under the plan, how to apply for such benefits, when such benefits vest, and when benefits may be paid out.

ERISA has been amended several times. Some of the most important amendments are COBRA (discussed earlier in this chapter) and HIPAA (Health Insurance Portability and Accountability Act), "which provides important new protections for working Americans and their families who have preexisting medical conditions or might otherwise suffer discrimination in health coverage based on factors that relate to an individual's health."[12] ERISA does not apply to health plans for government employees, employees of churches, or plans that are maintained to comply with disability, workers' compensation, or unemployment laws.

Occupational Safety and Health Act of 1970

The federal government regulates workplace safety primarily through the Occupational Safety and Health Act (OSHA), which requires that every employer "furnish to each of his employees . . . employment . . . free from recognized hazards that are likely to cause death or serious physical harm." The Occupational Safety and Health Administration (abbreviated OSHA, the same as the act) is the agency that is responsible for promulgating workplace safety standards, inspecting facilities to ensure compliance with the standards, and bringing enforcement actions against the violators. In addition, the agency undertakes educational programs for employers and employees.

Employers are required to comply with the standards established under OSHA. Under the law, employers must prominently display in the workplace either the federal or a state OSHA poster to provide their employees with information on their safety and health rights. Employers with 11 or more employees (20 percent of the establishments OSHA covers) must keep records of work-related injuries and illnesses. Workplaces in low-hazard industries such as retail, service, finance, insurance, and real estate are exempt from record-keeping requirements.

PENALTIES UNDER OSHA

If OSHA inspectors find violations in the workplace, they may issue citations. Penalties for violations may range from $0 to $70,000 per violation, depending on the likelihood that the violation would lead to serious injury to an employee. Penalties may be reduced if an employer has a small number of employees, has demonstrated good faith, or has few or no previous violations. If a willful violation results in the death of a worker, criminal penalties may be imposed.

[11] Ibid.

[12] Ibid.

Case Nugget Occupational Safety and Health Act (OSHA)

Irving v. United States
162 F.3d 154 (1998)

In 1979, Somersworth Shoe Company operated a manufacturing plan in New Hampshire. That year, a Somersworth Shoe employee, Gail Irving, was stamping innersoles using a marker machine. She went behind her workbench to obtain materials from the die rack. While there, she dropped her glove. When she bent to retrieve the glove, her hair was drawn into the vacuum created by the high-speed rotation of a drive shaft that was delivering power to a nearby "die-out" machine. Irving was very seriously injured. Irving sued and after nearly two decades of litigation, won a $1 million judgment. The United States appealed.

At issue was the OSHA Inspection Manual and whether OSHA inspectors were required to inspect every machine in a facility or whether they could use their discretion in deciding what to inspect. OSHA's purpose is to provide for a satisfactory standard of safety, not to guarantee absolute safety. The United States demonstrated that permitting OSHA inspectors discretion was grounded in OSHA's policies; therefore, OSHA was not negligent and the award was reversed.

Employment-at-Will Doctrine and Wrongful Termination

Unless an employee belongs to a union or has an employment contract with his or her employer, the employment relationship is governed by the **employment-at-will doctrine**. This doctrine provides that a contract of employment for an indeterminate period of time may be terminated at will by either party, at any time, and for any reason.

The traditional employment-at-will doctrine has been restricted over the past few decades. The major restrictions on the doctrine have come from civil rights legislation (discussed in Chapter 42). States, however, have also created a number of exceptions to this doctrine. If an employee has been discharged for a reason that falls under one of the exceptions to the employment-at-will doctrine, the employee can bring a lawsuit against the employer for wrongful discharge.

The exceptions to at-will employment fall into three primary categories:

1. Implied contract.
2. Violations of public policy.
3. Implied covenant of good faith and fair dealing.

Not all states accept all of these exceptions. The most common exception today seems to be the **implied-contract exception**. An implied contract may arise from statements made by the employer in an employment handbook or in materials advertising the position. Below is an example of a typical implied-contract issue:

1. The company's employment handbook contains the steps for progressive discipline leading to discharge.
2. The handbooks makes no mention of the words *employment-at-will.*
3. The employee relies on that handbook.

If the employer does not follow the policies set forth in its own handbook, an employee discharged by that employer may sue the employer for wrongful discharge.

The second most common exception to at-will employment is the **public policy exception**, which prohibits employers from firing employees engaged in activities that further the public interest. Protected activities vary somewhat from state to state. These activities include, but are not limited to, serving on jury duty, doing military service, filing for or testifying at hearings for workers' compensation claims, and whistle-blowing. An employer may not fire an employee for engaging in these activities.

The least accepted exception to at-will employment is the **implied covenant of good faith and fair dealing exception**. This exception is premised on the assumption that every employment contract contains an implicit understanding that the parties will deal fairly with one another. Because there is no clear agreement on what constitutes fair treatment of an employee, most states do not use this exception.

Employee Privacy in the Workplace

With the rapid expansion of technology, new issues related to workplace privacy have evolved. Technology has stimulated the growth of such issues in a number of ways. On the one hand, technology has given employers new ways to gather information about employees. On the other hand, new technologies have provided more temptations for employees to be "off the job" at work, thus creating a stimulus for more employer monitoring.

For example, surveys have shown that 90 percent of employees with Internet access at work look at non-work-related Web sites at least once a day,[13] 90 percent receive non-work-related e-mail,[14] and 84 percent send non-work-related e-mail.[15] Given such statistics, it is understandable that employers would want to monitor what employees are doing when they are supposed to be on the job. Some employers go too far. For example, some are monitoring their employees' keystrokes, looking for words such as *union* and *strike*.[16] Issues related to monitoring illustrate the clash between employees' right to privacy and employers' right to control what happens in the workplace. Once employers monitor employees and discover wrongdoing, the issue of employers' right to fire at will becomes relevant.

For example, in a recent court case, *Michael A. Smyth v. The Pillsbury Company*,[17] a Pennsylvania court ruled on the issue of whether an employer's invasion of an employee's privacy rights could provide a basis for an employee's abusive-discharge case. The employee, Smyth, alleged that his employer, the Pillsbury Company, violated his privacy rights by reading his e-mail and then illegally fired him based on the content of some of his messages. In particular, Smyth had transmitted a message to his supervisor in which he expressed his opinion about the company's sales management team. He threatened to "kill the backstabbing bastards." He also referred to an upcoming company holiday party as the "Jim Jones Koolaid affair."[18]

The court granted the Pillsbury Company's motion to dismiss, ruling that Smyth did not have a reasonable expectation of privacy in e-mail communications he made voluntarily over the company e-mail system. The court was unimpressed with Smyth's assertion that management had repeatedly assured employees that it would not intercept e-mail messages. Ultimately, the court ruled that the employer's right to prevent inappropriate, unprofessional, and possibly illegal comments over its e-mail system outweigh an employee's privacy rights.

[13] Dyland Loeb McClain, "I'll Be Right with You, Boss, as Soon as I Finish My Shopping," *New York Times*, January 10, 2001, p. G-1.

[14] Ibid.

[15] Ibid.

[16] Stephen Lesavich, "Keystroke Spies: Conflicting Rights," *National Law Journal*, May 22, 2000, p. A23.

[17] 914 F. Supp. 97 (1996).

[18] Jim Jones is the cult leader whose followers committed mass suicide by drinking a poisoned drink in Jonestown, Guyana, in 1978.

ELECTRONIC MONITORING AND COMMUNICATION

Business owners need to understand the extent to which they can monitor employees' telephone conversations, read their e-mail, and listen to their voice mail. Questions related to such monitoring primarily involve the common law tort of invasion of privacy and two federal statutes: the Omnibus Crime Control and Safe Streets Act of 1968,[19] as amended by the Electronic Communications Privacy Act (ECPA) of 1986.[20]

Under the first statute, employers cannot listen to the private telephone conversations of employees or disclose the contents of these conversations. They may, however, ban personal calls and monitor calls for compliance, as long as they discontinue listening to any conversation once they determine it is personal. Violators may be subject to fines of up to $10,000. Under ECPA, employees' privacy rights were extended to electronic forms of communication including e-mail and cellular phones. ECPA outlaws the intentional interception of electronic communications and the intentional disclosure or use of the information obtained through such interception.

In recognition of the fact that employers may sometimes need to monitor employee conversations for the purpose of improving employee performance or to protect employees from harassing calls, ECPA includes a "business-extension exemption" that allows employers to monitor employee telephone conversations in the ordinary course of their employment. This exception is subject to the constraint that the employer cannot continue to listen to conversations after it becomes apparent that they are personal. Also, monitoring is allowed when employees give their prior consent.

The key question in cases involving employer monitoring and interception of employee communications via e-mail, telephone, or voice mail is whether the employee had a **reasonable expectation of privacy** with respect to the communication in question. From a rights perspective, the ECPA protects individuals' communications against government surveillance conducted without a court order, from third parties without legitimate authorization to access the messages, and from the carriers of the messages, such as Internet service providers. It provides little privacy protection to employees with respect to their communications conducted on the equipment owned by their employer.

As Case 42-3 illustrates, a carefully drafted policy can be very helpful in establishing the extent to which employees have a reasonable expectation of privacy in the workplace.

[19] 18 U.S.C. § 2210 et seq.
[20] 18 U.S.C. §§ 2510–2521.

CASE 42-3

UNITED STATES OF AMERICA, PLAINTIFF-APPELLEE, v. ERIC NEIL ANGEVINE, DEFENDANT-APPELLANT

TENTH CIRCUIT COURT OF APPEALS 281 F.3D 1130 (2002)

The defendant was a professor at Oklahoma State University, where pursuant to his employment, the University provided him an office computer. The computer was networked with other University computers and linked to the Internet. Professor Angevine used this computer to download over 3,000 pornographic images of young boys. After viewing the images and printing some of them, he deleted the pornographic files.

Oklahoma Police Department obtained a search warrant to look for child pornography on his University computer. Although the professor attempted to erase the pornographic files, a computer expert used special technology to retrieve the data that had remained latent in the computer's memory.

After police arrested the defendant, he submitted a motion to suppress the pornographic images seized from the University computer. The district court held the computer-use policies and procedures at Oklahoma State University prevented Professor Angevine from having a legitimate expectation of privacy in the data on the seized University computer. The defendant appealed the denial of the motion.

CIRCUIT JUDGE BRORBY: . . . Oklahoma State University has a computer policy that explains appropriate computer use, warns employees about the consequences of misuse, and describes how officials administer and monitor the University computer network. . . .

. . . "Determining whether a legitimate . . . expectation of privacy exists . . . involves two inquiries. First, the defendant must show a subjective expectation of privacy in the area searched, and second, that expectation must be one that society is prepared to recognize as reasonable." . . .

We address employees' expectations of privacy in the workplace on a case-by-case basis. . . . Additional factors we consider include: "(1) the employee's relationship to the item seized; (2) whether the item was in the immediate control of the employee when it was seized; and (3) whether the employee took actions to maintain his privacy in the item."

. . . Oklahoma State University policies and procedures prevent its employees from reasonably expecting privacy in data downloaded from the Internet onto University computers. The University computer-use policy reserved the right to randomly audit Internet use and to monitor specific individuals suspected of misusing University computers. The policy explicitly cautions computer users that information flowing through the University network is not confidential either in transit or in storage on a University computer. Under this policy, reasonable Oklahoma State University computer users should have been aware network administrators and others were free to view data downloaded from the Internet. The policy also explicitly warned employees legal action would result from violations of federal law. Furthermore, the University displayed a splash screen warning of "criminal penalties" for misuse and of the University's right to conduct inspections to protect business-related concerns. These office practices and procedures should have warned reasonable employees not to access child pornography with University computers.

Professor Angevine's relationship to the University computer also does not suggest a reasonable expectation of privacy. " 'Although ownership of the item [s] seized is not determinative, it is an important consideration in determining the existence and extent of a defendant's Fourth Amendment interests.' " . . . The University explicitly reserved ownership of not only its computer hardware, but also the data stored within. Professor Angevine does not dispute Oklahoma State University owned the computer and the pornographic data he stored on it. Because the computer was issued to Professor Angevine only for work related purposes, his relationship to the University computer was incident to his employment. Reasonable people in Professor Angevine's employment context would expect University computer policies to constrain their expectations of privacy in the use of University-owned computers. . . .

Finally, Professor Angevine did not take actions consistent with maintaining private access to the seized pornography. We are reluctant to find a reasonable expectation of privacy where the circumstances reveal a careless effort to maintain a privacy interest. . . . Professor Angevine downloaded child pornography through a monitored University computer network. University policy clearly warned computer users such data is "fairly easy to access" by third parties. The policy explained network administrators actively audit network transmissions for such misuse. While Professor Angevine did attempt to erase the child pornography, the University computer policy warned system administrators kept file logs recording when and by whom files were deleted. Moreover, given his transmission of the pornographic data through a monitored University network, deleting the files alone was not sufficient to establish a reasonable expectation of privacy.

Denial of motion affirmed in favor of prosecution.

CRITICAL THINKING

What lesson can employers learn from studying the judge's reasoning in this case?

[CONTINUED]

ETHICAL DECISION MAKING

What values are in conflict in this case? Explain how the judge might have come to a different conclusion if he had placed primary importance on a different value.

As Case 42-3 clearly illustrates, when it comes to establishing whether employees had a reasonable expectation of privacy, employers are in the strongest position if they have a clear policy establishing that there is no reasonable expectation of privacy. Employment law experts advise that having a clear employee privacy policy that employees sign will minimize the likelihood of being sued by employees for invasion of privacy. These policies should also be spelled out in the employee handbook, as well as explained to employees. At a minimum, employer privacy policies should cover the following issues:

1. Employer monitoring of telephone conversations.
2. Employer surveillance policies.
3. Employee access to medical and personnel records.
4. Drug testing policies.
5. Lie detector policies.
6. Ownership of computers and all issues unique to the electronic workplace.

Case Nugget — Lie Detector Tests

Polkey v. Transtrecs Corp.
404 F.3d 1264 (11th Cir. 2005)

Polkey was a supervisor in the mailroom at Pensacola Naval Air Station. The mailroom was run by a company called Transtrecs. After discovering that some mail had been tampered with, Polkey reported it to her supervisor. Transtrecs asked all six employees, including Polkey, to take a lie detector (i.e., polygraph) test. The employee most suspected was tested first, and the lie detector test indicated that he might have been the one who tampered with the mail. Polkey and the remaining employees then refused to take the lie detector test. Transtrecs fired Polkey. She sued for violation of the Employee Polygraph Protection Act (EPPA). The district court granted summary judgment for Polkey. Transtrecs appealed.

On appeal, the district court's judgment was affirmed. The court held that Transtrecs violated EPPA by requesting and even suggesting that the employees take a polygraph test. Transtrecs argued that it was exempted because of national security, but the appellate court said that this applies only to the government. Transtrecs was merely a contractor for the government. Transtrecs also argued that it was exempt because the polygraph was part of an ongoing investigation of Polkey and that she was under suspicion. For this exemption to apply, an employer must have an articulable basis in fact to indicate that the employee was involved in or responsible for an economic loss. Transtrecs could make no such showing. Polkey prevailed.

Employer Monitoring of Computer Usage

According to the 2005 Electronic Monitoring & Surveillance Survey by the American Management Association and the ePolicy Institute, 76% of employers monitor Web site connections of employees. 80% of surveyed employers inform employees that content, keystrokes, and time spent online is monitored, 82% inform employees that their computer files are stored and reviewed, 86% advise of e-mail monitoring, and 89% apprise employees that their Web usage is tracked. It is important to recognize that employers do have valid reasons for monitoring in certain instances. For example, employers have to be concerned about electronic evidence relating to litigation, intellectual property and trade secret misappropriation and dissemination through electronic means, electronic and online defamatory content, and true worker productivity. As a result, not only do employers monitor their employees, 84% have set up policies governing personal e-mail use, 81% have rules addressing personal Internet use, 42% have policies regarding personal IM use, 34% have rules with respect to the operation of personal Web sites on employer time, 23% have policies about postings on corporate blogs, and 20% have guidelines regarding operation of personal blogs on employer time.*

* Employer Monitoring: It's a Small World After All, http://www.usatoday.com/tech/columnist/ericjsinrod/2005-06-01-employer-monitoring_x.htm.

DRUG TESTING IN THE WORKPLACE

Because of their potential liability for actions of their employees, employers have increasingly become interested in testing employees for the use of illegal drugs. For companies receiving federal financial assistance or having federal government contracts worth over $25,000, the Drug-Free Workplace Act requires that the employers develop an antidrug policy for employees, provide drug-free awareness programs for them, and warn them of penalties for violating the company's drug-free policies.

Private employers engaged in drug testing are not limited by the U.S. Constitution as are public employers, but they still need to be aware of state statutory and constitutional limits on drug testing. In most states, private companies have virtually unfettered discretion to test employees for drug usage. One exception is California, as its state constitution includes an explicit right to privacy that applies to the actions of private businesses.[21] Seven additional states have enacted legislation that places at least some restrictions on drug testing in the workplace: Montana, Iowa, Vermont, Rhode Island, Minnesota, Maine, and Connecticut.[22] In addition to state limits on drug testing, some collective bargaining agreements may restrict the employer's ability to test for drugs or may provide specific testing procedures that must be followed.

Labor Law

Many people would argue that the laws that improved workers' conditions most significantly were not any of those previously discussed but, rather, were the laws that gave employees the right to organize and bargain collectively over wages and terms and conditions of employment. During the Great Depression, workers were first given the right to organize, and since that time unionization rates have varied significantly. During the post-World War II period, over one-third of American workers were organized. Yet by 2005, only 12.5 percent of workers were unionized.[23]

[21] Lectic Law Library, "Drug Testing in the Workplace," ACLU Briefing Paper No. 5, www.lectlaw.com/files/emp02.htm.

[22] Ibid.

[23] Bureau of Labor Statistics, www.bls.gov/news.release/union2.nr0.htm.

Not all occupations are equally organized, with the main base of unions being in the industrial sector. Unions, however, are increasingly organizing professionals and those in the service industry. Today, nearly 4 in 10 government workers belong to a union, and protective service workers, a group that includes police and firefighters, had the highest unionization rate of all occupations during 2005: 37 percent.[24]

Labor-management relations in the United States today are governed by three major pieces of legislation:

1. The Wagner Act of 1935.
2. The Taft-Hartley Act of 1947.
3. The Landrum-Griffin Act of 1959.

The Taft-Hartley Act amended the Wagner Act, and they are jointly referred to as the *National Labor Relations Act (NLRA)*.

THE WAGNER ACT OF 1935

The first major piece of federal legislation adopted explicitly to encourage the formation of labor unions and provide for **collective bargaining** between employers and unions as a means of obtaining the peaceful settlement of labor disputes was the Wagner Act. Collective bargaining "consists of negotiations between an employer and a group of employees so as to determine the conditions of employment."[25] The key sections of the Wagner Act are:

1. Section 7, which provides, " Employees shall have the right to self-organization, to join, form or assist labor organizations, to bargain collectively through representatives of their own choosing, and to engage in concerted activities for the purpose of collective bargaining or other mutual aid and protection."
2. Section 8(a), which specifies the actions that are prohibited as employer unfair labor practices (see Exhibit 42-2).

The Wagner Act also created an administrative agency, the *National Labor Relations Board (NLRB),* to interpret and enforce the NLRA. Finally, it provides for judicial review in designated federal courts of appeal.

Exhibit 42-2
Employer Unfair Labor Practices

NLRA SECTION	EMPLOYER UNFAIR PRACTICE
8(a)1	Interference with employees' Section 7 rights
8(a)2	Employer-dominated unions
8(a)3	Discrimination by employers in hiring, firing, and other employment matters because of union activity
8(a)4	Retaliation against an employee who testifies or makes charges before the National Labor Relations Board
8(a)5	Failure to engage in good-faith collective bargaining with duly certified unions

[24] Ibid.
[25] Legal Information Institute, www.law.cornell.edu/topics/collective_bargaining.html.

THE TAFT-HARTLEY ACT OF 1947

The 12 years between passage of the Wagner Act and that of the Taft-Hartley Act saw a huge growth in unionization, which resulted in an increase in workers' power. Public perception of this trend led to the passage of the **Taft-Hartley Act,** also known as the *Labor-Management Relations Act,* which was designed to curtail some of the powers the unions had acquired under the Wagner Act. Just as Section 8(a) designated certain employer actions as unfair, Section 8(b) of the Taft-Hartley Act designated certain union actions as unfair. (See Exhibit 42-3.)

THE LANDRUM-GRIFFIN ACT OF 1959

The **Landrum-Griffin Act** primarily governs the internal operations of labor unions. This act, which was a response to evidence of certain undesirable internal labor union practices, requires certain financial disclosures by unions and establishes civil and criminal penalties for financial abuses by union officials. "Labor's Bill of Rights," contained in the act, protects employees from their own unions. The rights established by the Landrum-Griffin Act are summarized in Exhibit 42-4.

THE NATIONAL LABOR RELATIONS BOARD

The **National Labor Relations Board (NLRB)** is the administrative agency that interprets and enforces the **National Labor Relations Act (NLRA).** The NLRB's three primary functions are to:

1. Monitor the conduct of the employer and the union during an election to determine whether workers want to be represented by a union.
2. Prevent and remedy unfair labor practices by employers or unions.
3. Establish rules interpreting the act.

The NLRB has jurisdiction over all employees *except* those who work in federal, state, and local government and those covered by the Railway Labor Act (employees in the transportation industry); independent contractors; agricultural workers; household domestics; persons employed by a spouse or parent; and supervisors, managerial employees, and confidential employees.

Exhibit 42-3
Union Unfair Labor Practices

NLRA SECTION	UNION UNFAIR PRACTICE
8(b)1	Restraining or coercing employees' exercise of their Section 7 rights
8(b)2	Forcing the employer to discriminate against employees on the basis of union or antiunion activity
8(b)3	Failing to engage in good-faith collective bargaining with the employer
8(b)4	Striking, picketing, and engaging in secondary boycotts for illegal purposes
8(b)5	Charging excessive union dues or initiation fees in a union shop
8(b)6	Featherbedding (charging employers for services not performed)
8(b)7	Picketing to obtain recognition or to force collective bargaining under certain circumstances

Exhibit 42-4
Employee Rights under the Landrum-Griffin Act

SECTION OF LANDRUM-GRIFFIN	RIGHT GUARANTEED TO EMPLOYEES
101(a)1	*Equal rights:* Every union member has an equal right to nominate candidates, vote in elections, and attend and fully participate in membership meetings, subject to the organization's reasonable constitution and bylaws.
101(a)2	*Freedom of speech and assembly:* Members have the right to meet freely with one another at any time and to express any views about the labor organization, candidates for office, or business affairs at organization meetings, subject to reasonable rules pertinent to conduct of meetings.
101(a)3	*Dues, initiation fees, and assessments:* Increases in local union dues, initiation fees, or assessments must be voted on by a majority of the members through secret ballot.
101(a)4	*Protection of right to sue:* Labor organizations cannot prohibit members from bringing any legal actions, including those against the organization. Organizations may require that members first exhaust reasonable hearing procedures established by the organization.
101(a)5	*Safeguards against improper discipline:* No member may be fined or otherwise disciplined except for nonpayment of dues without being (1) served with written notice of specific charges, (2) given a reasonable time to prepare a defense, and (3) afforded a full and fair hearing.

The stimulus for forming a union is typically employee dissatisfaction with some policy of or treatment by their employer. This discontent stimulates contact with a national union representing other employees engaged in the same type of work. As an illustration, those who work for a rubber manufacturing firm would naturally enough contact officials of the United Rubber, Cork, Linoleum & Plastic Workers of America (URW) to investigate formation of a union. The URW would then authorize a representative to meet with interested employees to explain what unionization would do for them.

Should the workers be attracted to the idea of unionization, the union representative would then assist the employees in an organizational campaign designed to persuade a majority of the workers to accept the union as their exclusive representative. Once a majority of workers sign authorization cards indicating an interest in being represented by the union, they present the cards to the employer. The employer then decides whether to formally recognize the new local union.

If the employer refuses, the union organizers can petition the NLRB for a representation election. Within seven days of the NLRB's ordering an election, the employer must file with the NLRB's regional director a list of the names and addresses of all employees eligible to vote. This list, known as the *Excelsior list* (after the case that created it), is then made available to the union or union organizers by the regional director. If at least 30 percent of the employees in an appropriate bargaining unit demonstrate their interest by their signatures on an authorization card, an election is scheduled.

The NLRB will supervise the election, and if the union receives a majority of the votes in the secret-ballot election, the union will be certified as the bargaining representative. Regardless of the outcome of the election, there cannot be another election for one year. Nor can there be an election during the term of a collective bargaining agreement, unless either the union is defunct or there is such a division in the ranks of the union that it is unable or unwilling to represent the employees.

During the course of the organizing campaign, certain activities of both employers and employees are prohibited by the NLRA and by rules of conduct developed by the NLRB. The constraints on employers' behavior under the NLRA are found primarily in Section 8(a)1, which prohibits interference in employees' exercise of their Section 7 rights. If an employer engages in prohibited activity during the organizing campaign, the NLRB may set aside the results of an election and order a new election. In an extreme case where the employer's conduct was so egregious as to make it impossible to hold a fair election, and the union had previously collected authorization cards signed by a majority of the employees, the NLRB may order the employer to bargain with the union without a new election.

Employers should be sure their speech and conduct during an organizing campaign do not rise to the level of coercion, restraint, or interference. Employers may express views, arguments, or opinions as long as they do not contain any threats of reprisals or promises of benefits. However, employers cannot make express threats, such as saying wages will be cut in half if the union wins the election. Likewise, employers cannot give the employees new benefits once an election has been ordered. Also, captive-audience speeches (situations where the employees have no choice but to listen to the speech) are prohibited within 24 hours of an election.

Finally, employers may prohibit union solicitation and the distribution of literature during work time. However, during non-work time, such as lunch and coffee breaks, employers may prohibit organizing activity on company property *only* if there are legitimate safety or efficiency reasons for doing so and the restraint is not manifestly intended to thwart organizing efforts. The burden of proof is on the employer to demonstrate these safety or efficiency concerns. Case 42-4 demonstrates the kind of behavior that is likely to be found to be an unfair labor practice during an organizing campaign.

CASE 42-4

FRAZIER INDUSTRIAL COMPANY, INC., PETITIONER, v. NATIONAL LABOR RELATIONS BOARD, RESPONDENT

U.S. COURT OF APPEALS, DISTRICT OF COLUMBIA CIRCUIT
213 F.3D 750, 164 L.R.R.M. (BNA) 2516 (2000)

John Ramirez was one of the welders hired during the start up phase of Defendant Frazier Industrial Company's Pocatello, Idaho, plant. After working at the plant for a month, he began asking employees to attend organizational meetings and sign union authorization cards. Every day, before and after work and while on break, he spoke with workers. He spoke repeatedly to those who were noncommittal, but immediately stopped trying to recruit anyone who expressed opposition to the union.

From April through June, supervisors attempted to find out why employees were interested in unionizing, and in response to suggestions that the union might negotiate better pay and benefits for the workers, one supervisor said that "before the company went union they would either hire non-union or shut the plant down." Supervisors continually reminded them that the company had a policy prohibiting the discussion of unions on the job, and asked the workers whether the organizers were harassing them.

In June of 1996, Ramirez was discharged, allegedly because his behavior was affecting productivity and other employees were complaining that he was harassing them about the union.

He filed an unfair labor practice charge. At his hearing, the Administrative Law Judge (ALJ) found that the company violated § 8(a)(1) by threatening to discharge employees who engage in union activities, coercively interrogating employees about their union activities and sympathies, threatening employees that it would close the plant if employees chose union representation, and maintaining and enforcing a rule prohibiting union talk while permitting other non-work discussions. The Board also adopted the judge's findings that the company violated § 8(a)(1) and (a)(3) by discharging Ramirez because of his union activity, and ordered reinstatement and back pay. The NLRB adopted the ALJ's findings. The company appealed.

CIRCUIT JUDGE ROGERS: Section 8(a)(1) and (3) of the Act makes it an unfair labor practice for an employer "to interfere with, restrain or coerce employees in the exercise of the rights guaranteed" by the Act, and "by discrimination in regard to hire or tenure of employment or any term or condition of employment to encourage or discourage membership in any labor organization." To establish a causal nexus between adverse employment decisions and an employee's union affiliation, the complaining party must first show that protected activity "was a 'motivating factor'" in the adverse employment decision, and then the employer may show that it would have made the adverse decision even had the employee not engaged in the protected activity.

To establish an employer's discriminatory motive, the Board may "consider[ ] such factors as the employer's knowledge of the employee's union activities, the employer's hostility toward the union, and the timing of the employer's action." In addition, evidence that an employer has violated § 8(a)(1) of the Act can support an inference of anti-union animus. The court will affirm the findings of the Board unless they are "unsupported by substantial evidence in the record considered as a whole," or unless the Board "acted arbitrarily or otherwise erred in applying established law to the facts."

The company maintains that, even if Ramirez's actions constituted protected activities, its termination of Ramirez's employment was lawful because it would have discharged him in the absence of protected conduct for his insubordination and dishonesty. We hold that there is substantial evidence in the record to support the Board's conclusions that Ramirez's conduct was protected union activity under the Act, that the company violated the Act by discharging Ramirez for engaging in such protected union activity, and that the company's other proffered reasons for termination of Ramirez's employment—insubordination and dishonesty—are insufficient to meet its burden.

In support of its contention that Ramirez's conduct was not protected by the Act because he was engaged in repeated harassment of fellow employees during work time resulting in frequent interruptions of work, the company relies on [a case], which held that "an employee who disrupts other employees during working hours is not engaged in a protected activity even though he is discussing union business." Similarly, Board precedent states that "activity that would otherwise be protected may lose that protection if the means by which that activity is conducted are sufficiently abusive or threatening." Under such precedent, the company contends, the fact that Ramirez was attempting to organize the company's work force is immaterial because he had no legitimate protected interest in repeatedly approaching and harassing his co-workers while they were trying to work. Although this interpretation of evidence may be reasonable, the Board's finding to the contrary was supported by substantial evidence in the record.

The Board found that Ramirez's activities were protected because "it is clear that . . . all of Ramirez' work time solicitations were brief and did not involve any obvious disruption in production." Adding that "there is no evidence that employees whom Ramirez solicited more than once ever even told him that he was interfering with their work or that further solicitations would have that effect," the Board found that although Ramirez tenaciously solicited employees to sign cards, attend the union's meetings, or meet individually with a union organizer, he did not pursue such matters with employees over their expressed objections. On the

[CONTINUED]

contrary, the Board found that "his persistence, in the main, resulted in those instances where he received tepid or inconclusive responses from the employees with whom he spoke." The Board thus concluded that Ramirez's conduct, while persistent, did not rise "to the level of unprotected harassment."

Judgment of NLRB affirmed.

CRITICAL THINKING

From the court's reasoning, what kind of behavior would Ramirez have had to engage in before the court would have decided against the NLRB decision?

ETHICAL DECISION MAKING

A central value in a market economy is consumer sovereignty. In other words, the marketplace is assumed to have as its primary purpose to please consumers. Considering the effects of unionization, is consumer sovereignty enhanced by a decision such as the one in this case, or is the court suggesting that another value is even more important?

While Case 42-4 illustrates an employer unfair labor practice, remember that employees may also engage in unfair labor practices during an organizing campaign.

THE COLLECTIVE BARGAINING PROCESS

Once the union has been certified, union and management must begin to bargain in good faith about wages, hours, and other terms and conditions of work. Note that the NLRB can order the parties only to bargain in good faith; it cannot order them to reach an agreement with respect to any contract term.

Both the employer and the bargaining unit representative are required by the NLRA to bargain collectively in good faith with respect to wages, hours, and other terms and conditions of employment. This means they must:

1. Meet at reasonable times and confer in good faith.
2. Sign a written agreement if one is reached.
3. When intent on terminating or modifying an existing contract, give 60 days' notice to the other party, with an offer to confer over proposals, and give 30 days' notice to the federal or state mediation services in the event of a pending dispute over the new agreement.
4. Neither strike nor engage in a lockout during the 60-day notice.

An employer who fails to bargain in good faith is committing an unfair labor practice under Section 8(a)5. Employers violate this section not only by disregarding proper procedural standards but also by refusing to even discuss an issue. Other acts of the employer that constitute unfair labor practices in the collective bargaining process include failing to provide the union with the information it needs to represent employees in the collective bargaining process or taking a unilateral action with respect to bargaining items during the term of a collective bargaining agreement.

If a union refuses to bargain in good faith, it violates Section 8(b)3. Such violations are not typical, however, because the union is trying to obtain benefits for its employees and ordinarily wants to quickly get a contract that benefits its members. The most common violation by a union is insisting on bargaining for clauses that fall outside the scope of mandatory bargaining. Of course, it is not always clear whether an item falls within that scope. For example, in a dispute with Ford Motor Company, the union argued that the prices charged by the outside caterer Ford had hired to provide food for workers in the plant's cafeteria should be subject to collective bargaining. Ford argued that it had no control over prices charged by a third party and so it should not be forced to bargain over this issue. The Supreme Court, however, found that under its contract with the supplier, Ford retained the right to review and control food services and prices and, therefore, that Ford should be required to bargain over what the NLRB had found to be an important aspect of the working conditions of the Ford employees.[26]

Case Nugget Collective Bargaining

Freightliner, LLC v. Teamsters Local 305 2004 WL 2075028, D. Ore., 2004

Thomas was a forklift operator for Freightliner. He was involved in an accident, and the company ordered a drug test. After the test indicated a high level of THC, Thomas admitted using marijuana. In fact, Thomas had a prescription for marijuana to relieve pain in his knees. He did not, however, use marijuana during work hours. Freightliner fired Thomas, and he filed a grievance, pursuant to his union's collective bargaining agreement. The arbitrator ordered that Thomas be reinstated because he was not under the influence while working and he had received the marijuana legally through prescription under Oregon's Medical Marijuana Act. Freightliner appealed to the federal courts.

The federal trial court held that an arbitrator must show manifest disregard for the law in order for the award to be overturned. In this case, the plain language of the collective bargaining agreement established the drug policy. Moreover, because Thomas's THC level was 70 times the amount allowed, he was legally under the influence. The fact that the collective bargaining agreement did not take into account Oregon's Medical Marijuana Act does not affect the outcome. The employer's motion to overturn the arbitrator's award was granted.

STRIKES, PICKETING, AND BOYCOTTS

Three other activities that employers may have to confront are strikes, picketing, and boycotts. The NLRA offers management guidance as to how to respond to these activities.

A **strike** is a temporary, concerted withdrawal of labor. It is the most powerful weapon used by employees to secure recognition and improve their working conditions, but it is also potentially the most dangerous to use. An illustration of the use of a strike to

[26] *Ford Motor Company v. NLRB,* 441 U.S. 488 (1979).

attempt to obtain better pay was the 2001 strike by Delta Air Lines' Comair pilots. After an eight-week work stoppage and a loss to parent company Delta Air Lines of $1.5 to $2 million per day, an agreement was reached.

A refusal to deal with, purchase goods from, or work for a business is a **boycott.** Like a strike, it is a technique for prohibiting a company from carrying on its business so that it will accede to union demands. **Primary boycotts,** which are boycotts against an employer with whom the union is directly engaged in a labor dispute, are lawful. However, **secondary boycotts** are illegal. A secondary boycott occurs when unionized employees have a labor dispute with their employer and boycott another employer to force it to cease doing business with their employer.

Individuals who place themselves outside an employer's place of business for the purpose of informing passers-by of the fact(s) of a labor dispute are engaged in **picketing.** Picketing may occur as part of a strike or independently. If picketing is done by off-duty employees without a strike, employees may continue to work and get paid while still getting their message across.

The various forms of picketing are entitled to different amounts of legal protection. Picketing designed to truthfully inform the public of a labor dispute between an employer and the employees is called **informational picketing** and is protected. However, if the picketing prevents deliveries or services to the employer, the protection is lost. This form of picketing in which service to the employer is cut off is called **signal picketing** and is unprotected behavior.

CASE OPENER WRAP-UP

Madison and Save Right Pharmacy

At the beginning of this chapter, you were asked what you would do if you were the CEO of Save Right Pharmacy and were confronted with the situation involving Madison. By now you should be able to answer all the questions asked at the beginning of the chapter.

Madison had worked for Save Right Pharmacy for five years, but she worked only 20 hours per week. As such, under FMLA, she would not be eligible to take leave to care for her mother. Under FMLA, an employee must work a minimum of 25 hours per week.

Madison stopped going to work despite the fact that Save Right Pharmacy denied her request for leave to care for her sick mother. Because Madison did not qualify to take leave under FMLA and she simply stopped coming to work, Save Right Pharmacy was legally within its rights to fire Madison. Moreover, whether Madison was fired or voluntarily quit her job, she would not be entitled to collect unemployment compensation in most states.

If it is determined that Madison's conduct in failing to show up at her job is "gross misconduct," her insurance benefits may be terminated. In most cases, however, when an employee voluntarily quits his or her job, or even is fired (but not for gross misconduct), insurance benefits may be continued (though the *employee* must pay the full cost of the insurance). These are basic issues that every employer and employee should be familiar with. Knowledge of employment issues benefits both the employer and the employee.

Summary

Introduction to Labor and Employment Law	Both the federal and state governments impose a number of conditions on the employment relationship. The purpose of this chapter was to explain many of the laws that created those constraints on the employer's ability to determine terms and conditions of employment and termination. The first half of this chapter covered wages, benefits, health and safety standards, and employee rights, including the right to privacy. The second half of this chapter covered labor unions.
Fair Labor Standards Act	Employers must follow federal minimum wage and hour laws. FLSA covers all employers engaged in interstate commerce or the production of goods for interstate commerce and requires that a "minimum wage" of a specified amount be paid to all employees in covered industries. The specified amount is periodically raised by Congress to compensate for increases in the cost of living caused by inflation. The most recent increase took effect on September 1, 1997, when the minimum wage rose to $5.15 per hour. There has been no increase in the federal minimum wage since that time.
Family and Medical Leave Act	Requires certain employers to establish a policy that provides all eligible employees with up to 12 weeks of leave during any 12-month period for several family-related occurrences (e.g., birth of a child, to care for sick spouse, etc.)
Unemployment Compensation	The Federal Unemployment Tax Act (FUTA) created a state system that provides unemployment compensation to qualified employees who lose their jobs.
Workers' Compensation Laws	State laws that provide financial compensation to employees or their dependents when the covered employee is injured on the job.
Consolidated Omnibus Budget Reconciliation Act	COBRA ensures that when employees lose their jobs or have their hours reduced to a level at which they would not be eligible to receive medical, dental, or optical benefits from their employer, the employees will be able to continue receiving benefits under the employer's policy for up to 18 months by paying the premiums for the policy.
Employee Retirement Income Security Act	ERISA is a federal law that sets minimum standards for most voluntarily established pension and health plans in private industry to provide protection for individuals in these plans.
Occupational Safety and Health Act of 1970	The Occupational Safety and Health Administration is responsible for setting safety standards under OSHA, as well as enforcing the act through inspections and the levying of fines against violators.
Employment-at-Will Doctrine and Wrongful Termination	Under the employment-at-will doctrine, the employer can fire the employee for any reason at all. The three exceptions to the doctrine are *implied contract, violations of public policy,* and *implied covenant of good faith and fair dealing.* In states that have adopted any of these three exceptions, employees may be able to sue for wrongful discharge.
Employee Privacy in the Workplace	Privacy issues are of increasing importance in the workplace. Privacy policies should cover matters such as employer surveillance policies, control of and access to medical and personnel records, drug testing, and e-mail policies. *Omnibus Crime Control and Safe Streets Act of 1968:* Employers cannot listen to the private telephone conversations of employees or disclose the contents of these conversations. They may, however, ban personal calls and monitor calls for compliance as long as they discontinue listening to any conversation once they determine it is personal. Violators may be subject to fines of up to $10,000.

Electronic Communications Privacy Act (ECPA) of 1986: Under ECPA, employees' privacy rights were extended to electronic forms of communication including e-mail and cellular phones. ECPA outlaws the intentional interception of electronic communications and the intentional disclosure or use of the information obtained through such interception.

Labor Law

The Wagner Act of 1935: The Wagner Act was the first major piece of federal legislation adopted explicitly to encourage the formation of labor unions and provide for *collective bargaining* between employers and unions as a means of obtaining the peaceful settlement of labor disputes.

Collective bargaining: Collective bargaining consists of negotiations between an employer and a group of employees to determine the conditions of employment.

National Labor Relations Board (NLRB): The Wagner Act created the NLRB, an administrative agency, to interpret and enforce the National Labor Relations Act (NLRA) and to provide for judicial review in designated federal courts of appeal.

The Taft-Hartley Act of 1947: Also known as the *Labor-Management Relations Act,* the Taft-Hartley Act is designed to curtail some of the powers the unions had acquired under the Wagner Act. Just as Section 8(a) designated certain employer actions as unfair, Section 8(b) of the Taft-Hartley Act designated certain union actions as unfair.

The Landrum-Griffin Act of 1959: The Landrum-Griffin Act primarily governs the internal operations of labor unions. It requires certain financial disclosures by unions and establishes civil and criminal penalties for financial abuses by union officials. "Labor's Bill of Rights," contained in the act, protects employees from their own unions.

Point / Counterpoint

The federal minimum wage was recently raised, the first increase since 1997.

Do You Believe It Was Time for an Increase?	
Yes	**No**
A recent poll indicated that 83 percent of the American public support raising the federal minimum wage to $7.15.* There is strong bipartisan support for raising the federal minimum wage. The purchasing power of the current federal minimum wage has significantly declined since 1997. Hard-working Americans deserve a living wage. Everyone benefits when the lowest-paid Americans have more spending power. *"Poll: Maximum Support for Raising the Minimum: Most Americans Now Live in States That Have Raised the Wage Floor," April 16, 2006, www.pewtrusts.org/ideas/ideas_item.cfm?content_item_id=33.	An increase in the federal minimum wage would hurt business owners and lower their profit margin. Business owners may pass the increased cost on to consumers. Many states have already passed laws requiring that employers pay a state minimum wage that is higher than the federal minimum wage. We should let each state decide what it wants to do based on the cost of living in that state.

Questions & Problems

1. What is the current amount of the federal minimum wage? When was the last time the federal minimum wage was increased?
2. What is required for an employee to be eligible for benefits under the Family and Medical Leave Act (FMLA)?
3. If an employee voluntarily quits his job, may the employee collect unemployment compensation? What if the employee is fired?
4. May an employee who is injured on the job collect workers' compensation and also sue the employer for negligence?
5. List and explain the exceptions to the employment-at-will doctrine.
6. What is the purpose of COBRA?
7. Safeway operates a bread-baking facility in Denver, Colorado. Safeway periodically holds company-sponsored outdoor barbecues for its employees, and it purchased a gas grill equipped with a 20-pound propane tank for the barbecues. To ensure that the grill had sufficient gas for the barbecues, Safeway purchased a 40-pound tank. The larger tanks have a warning label stating that they should not be used with a grill ordinarily equipped with a 20-pound tank. Safeway planned to hold an employee barbecue on July 17, 1998. The plant superintendent, Edward Boone, instructed the plant engineer, Jerry Lewis, to set up the grill for the barbecue. On being informed that the grill was not adequately cooking the meat, the plant manager, Jim Kirk, again summoned Lewis. Lewis and the day-shift maintenance foreman, Fred Lake, attempted to improve the flow of gas to the grill by checking the regulator and repositioning the tank. While Lewis and Lake were working on the grill, fuel escaped and a "ball of fire" erupted. Lewis suffered severe burns to his hand and Lake's facial hair was singed. After an investigation, an OSHA inspector issued a citation to Safeway. Safeway appealed the decision. Was this a workplace safety violation? Why or why not? [*Safeway, Inc. v. Occupational Safety & Health Rev. Comm.*, 382 F.3d 1189 (10th Cir. 2004).]
8. Baxter Pharmacy paid its pharmacists a salary but no overtime pay. Under the Fair Labor Standards Act (FLSA), employers must pay employees overtime for hours worked in excess of 40 hours per week. Baxter Pharmacy believes that the pharmacists are exempt under FLSA because they are "professionals." The pharmacists disagree. Is being a professional an exemption from the requirement to pay overtime under FLSA? Are pharmacists professionals? How do you think the court ruled? [*De Jesus-Rentas v. Baxter Pharmacy Services Corp.*, 400 F.3d 72 (1st Cir. 2005).]
9. Antonucci worked as a dental assistant. She was stuck in the thumb with an instrument twice during a period of two months. Antonucci claimed that she feared for her health and safety. She quit her job and applied for unemployment compensation. Did Antonucci have "good cause" to quit her job? Should Antonucci be permitted to collect unemployment compensation? How do you think this matter was decided by the court? [*Antonucci v. State of Florida,* 793 So.2d 1116 (Fla. Dist. Ct. App. 2001).]
10. Meadows worked as an assistant manager at a Dollar General store. While she was ringing up an order for a customer, he became verbally abusive. After she finished ringing up the sale, the customer threw the bag, containing a can of motor oil, at Meadows, hitting her in the eye. Meadows suffered a detached retina. The trial court awarded Meadows permanent partial disability under workers' compensation for her injury. Dollar General appealed the decision, arguing that the injury did not occur in the "course

of employment." Do you believe that Meadows's injury occurred during the course of her employment? Why or why not? Was the trial court correct in granting her permanent partial disability, or did the appeals court overturn that decision? [*Dollar General Corp. v. Meadows,* 63 P.3d 548 (2002 WL 31991909, Okla. Ct. Civ. App. 2002).]

11. Guess worked on the assembly line at Sharp Manufacturing Company of America. While working one day, a co-worker cut his hand. The co-worker's blood got on Guess's hand. Guess testified that she had cuts on her hand and had just gotten a manicure. Guess became hysterical because she believed her co-worker to be gay and thought he had AIDS because he "looked and acted gay." Guess was later diagnosed with posttraumatic stress disorder. She applied for workers' compensation, and it was granted based on her mental injury. Sharp Manufacturing appealed the decision, arguing that Guess had been tested for HIV five times and that all results had been negative. How do you think the appellate court should rule? [*Guess v. Sharp Manufacturing Co. of America,* 114 S.W.3d 480 (Tenn. Sup. Ct. 2003).]

12. Solomon worked as an at-will employee (truck driver) for Mission Petroleum Carriers. Truck drivers are required by the company to take random drug tests. Solomon tested positive for marijuana and was terminated. He claimed that the company did not use reasonable care in administering the drug test because he was given an unsealed container in which to provide his urine sample. When Solomon applied for other truck-driving jobs, Mission Petroleum Carriers informed the companies that Solomon had been fired for failing a drug test. Solomon sued Mission Petroleum Carriers, and the jury awarded him a total of $900,000. Mission Petroleum Carriers appealed the decision. The issue before the appellate court was whether an employer that collects a urine specimen under (federal) Department of Transportation regulations has a duty to conduct the drug test with reasonable care. How did the appellate court decide? Was the company required to use reasonable care in administering the urine test? And may an at-will employee be fired based on information that is gathered in a careless manner? [*Mission Petroleum Carriers, Inc. v. Solomon,* 46 Tex. Sup. J. 649 (Tex. Sup. Ct. 2003).]

13. Metro is a Minnesota corporation that sells office furniture. From 1997 through February 24, 2000, Starr worked for Metro. During that time, Metro had an established employee welfare benefit plan as required by ERISA. Masanz was the plan's designated administrator, and she was responsible for providing employees with notice of their rights to continue coverage under COBRA. Starr was enrolled in the plan, under which he received medical and dental coverage for himself and his minor daughter, Cotton. Metro terminated Starr on February 24, 2000. Metro asserts that on March 3, 2000, Masanz mailed to Starr's last known address a COBRA notice that described Starr's election rights for continuation of coverage under COBRA. Starr asserts that neither he nor his daughter received the notice. Consequently, they never made any election to continue their benefits under the plan. Metro terminated Starr's and Cotton's coverage under the plan in June 2000. In August 2000, Cotton's appendix ruptured. She had surgery and later experienced complications associated with her ruptured appendix. The medical expenses associated with Cotton's appendectomy and complications totaled $116,187.86. Starr sued Metro and filed a motion for summary judgment, asking the court to declare that he and his daughter were covered under COBRA. How should the court decide? State the reasoning for your decision. [*Starr v. Metro Systems,* 2004 U.S. Dist. LEXIS 15744 (Minn. 2004).]

14. Cynthia Anderson worked for the city of Columbus, Georgia, answering telephone calls from citizens. Anderson knew that calls from citizens were recorded, but she was unaware that, due to a glitch, the telephone system continued to record her statements through her headset after a call was terminated. Anderson made disparaging remarks about the city manager's office, and her employment was terminated. Anderson sued the city, alleging that it had no right to record her private conversations with co-workers, which were unrelated to city business. Who should prevail? Why? [*Anderson v. City of Columbus, Georgia,* 2005 U.S. Dist. LEXIS 12612 (Ga. 2005).]

15. Several engineering department employees at the Reading Hospital and Medical Center discovered that they were being secretly tape-recorded by the hospital. In particular, a meeting between the employees and a labor-management consultant was recorded. The employees contend that the complaints made to the consultant were going to be reported to the hospital by the consultant; however, the names of the employees making the complaints were to be kept confidential. After a tape recorder was discovered in a locker, the employees brought a lawsuit against the hospital, alleging violation of their privacy. Did the hospital employees have a "reasonable expectation of privacy" in their conversation with the labor-management consultant? May the hospital secretly tape-record the employees? Why or why not? [*Care et al. v. Reading Hosp. & Med. Ctr., Inv.,* 2004 U.S. Dist. LEXIS 5485 (E.D. Pa. 2004).]

Looking for more review material?

The Online Learning Center at **www.mhhe.com/kubasek1e** contains this chapter's "Assignment on the Internet" and also a list of URLs for more information, entitled "On the Internet." Find both of them in the Student Center portion of the OLC, along with quizzes and other helpful materials.

Employment Discrimination

CASE OPENER

Brad Gets Fired from "So Clean!"

Brad has worked in the marketing department of "So Clean!" for the last five years. So Clean is a company that produces household cleaners. Brad is an excellent employee and was recently promoted. Shortly after his promotion, Brad decided to reveal publicly that he is a homosexual. His family and most of his co-workers have been very supportive.

Soon after his promotion and announcement that he is gay, Brad began having problems with his female boss, Jennifer. She began asking Brad questions about his personal life. At first it was small things, such as asking Brad if he was a smoker (he is, though only outside the workplace). Jennifer then began asking Brad very personal questions about his sexuality and told him she did not like weak men. The final straw for Brad occurred when Jennifer announced that she would "cure" his homosexuality and told him to come home with her that night after work or be fired. Jennifer was careful that there were never any witnesses around when she asked Brad personal questions or propositioned him.

Brad refused Jennifer's advances and was fired. He filed an administrative complaint with the Equal Employment Opportunity Commission (EEOC), alleging wrongful termination, retaliation, sexual harassment, and sexual discrimination. Jennifer's response was that she fired Brad because of "creative" differences about how to run the marketing department and because he is a smoker. Jennifer has denied Brad's accusations about sexual discrimination and harassment.

1. May an employer fire an employee because that employee is gay?
2. May an employer fire an employee because the employee smokes outside the workplace?
3. May a man file a claim of sexual discrimination? Sexual harassment?
4. What rights does an employee have in the workplace?
5. What defenses does an employer have to allegations of discrimination?

The Wrap-Up at the end of the chapter will answer these questions.

CHAPTER 43

Learning Objectives

After you have studied this chapter, you will be able to answer the following questions:

1. When may an employee be legally fired?
2. What are the federal laws governing employment situations?
3. What are the legal requirements for a charge of sex discrimination?
4. What is the difference between discrimination based on disparate treatment and discrimination based on disparate impact?
5. What are the legal requirements for a charge of sexual harassment?
6. What is Title VII, and what are the employers' defenses to a charge under Title VII?
7. What are the legal requirements for a charge of age discrimination?
8. What are the legal requirements for a charge of pregnancy discrimination?
9. What is the Equal Pay Act?
10. May employers discriminate against smokers?

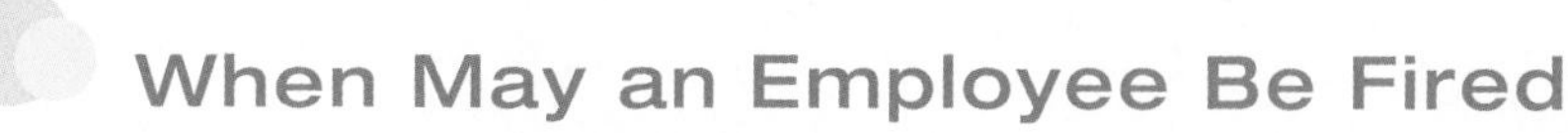

When May an Employee Be Fired?

During the 18th and 19th centuries in the United States, employees had no protection in the workplace. An employee who was injured could be fired. In fact, an employer could fire a worker for no reason at all. This concept came to be known as *at-will employment.*[1] At-will employment applied in all states with no exceptions until 1959.[2]

Today, any employee who is not employed under a contract or a collective bargaining agreement[3] is considered to be an at-will employee. This means that the employee may quit at any time for any reason or no reason at all, with no required notice to the employer.[4] Similarly, an employer may fire the employee at any time, with no notice, for almost any reason. For example, your employer could decide he doesn't like the color of your shirt and fire you on the spot! The exception to the at-will rule is that an employer may not fire an employee for an illegal reason. What is an illegal reason? Broadly, any termination based on a violation of a state statute, state constitution, federal law, U.S. Constitution, or public policy is illegal. (An in-depth discussion of at-will employment can be found in Chapter 42.) Exceptions to at-will employment have also been found through breaches of implied contracts with employees on the basis of employee handbooks.[5]

Case Nugget At-Will Employment

Brown v. Sabre, Inc.
173 S.W.3d 581 (Tx. Ct. App. 2005)

Brown was an employee of Sabre. After Sabre was sold to EDS, Brown and 4,000 other at-will employees had a choice of moving to EDS or quitting. Brown moved to EDS. Under Sabre's vacation policy, vacation days were earned one year and taken the next year. Brown and others were told that EDS would honor its vacation policy, but then it changed the policy. Brown received pay for half his vacation days but lost the value of the other half of his vacation days. He sued for breach of contract.

The district court rejected Brown's claim, so he appealed. The appellate court affirmed the decision of the district court, holding that any modification of an employee's at-will employment status must be an express, rather than an implied, agreement and that it must be clear and specific. Statements in employee handbooks and policy manuals are general guidelines and do not create implied contracts. Given the disclaimer in the employee handbook, the employer had the right to amend, modify, or terminate the policy at any time.

[1] See *Toussaint v. Blue Cross & Blue Shield of Mich.*, 408 Mich. 579, 600, 292 N.W.2d 880, 885 (1980) (for an extended discussion on the at-will rule).

[2] BambooWeb Dictionary, www.bambooweb.com/articles/a/t/At-Will_Employment.html. The first judicial exception to the at-will rule was created in *Peterman v. Intl. Bhd. of Teamsters, Chauffeurs, Warehousemen, and Helpers of Am., Local 396,* 174 Cal. App. 2d 184, 344 P.2d 44 (1959).

[3] Union employees are covered by collective bargaining agreements.

[4] Most employees do give an employer notice before leaving a job as a matter of professional courtesy. Such action, however, is not required under the law.

[5] "Some challenges and exceptions to at-will employment include: breach of implied contracts through employee handbooks, public policy violations, reliance on an offer of employment, and intentional infliction of emotional distress" (Legal Database, www.legal-database.net/at-will.htm).

Federal Laws Governing Employers

Employees are protected in the workplace by a number of both federal and state laws. Federal laws apply to everyone in the United States. Federal law may be described as a "minimum" level of protection for all workers. State laws may give employees more, but not less, protection than federal laws. Exhibit 43-1 is an overview of some of the most important federal employment discrimination laws.

Civil Rights Act—Title VII

During the 1960 presidential election, candidate John F. Kennedy (JFK) proposed that the United States pass national civil rights legislation. After winning the presidency, JFK began work with Congress on just such legislation. On November 22, 1962, JFK was assassinated. His vice president, Lyndon B. Johnson (LBJ), became president and saw JFK's quest for national civil rights legislation through to completion. The Civil Rights Act of 1964 (CRA) was signed by LBJ and became federal law, assuring everyone in the nation of certain basic rights. The act is divided into sections, called *titles*. Title VII deals with discrimination in employment.

Title VII prohibits employers from hiring, firing, or otherwise discriminating in terms and conditions of employment and prohibits segregating employees in a manner that would affect their employment opportunities on the basis of their race, color, religion, sex, or national origin. There are two ways to prove discrimination under Title VII—disparate treatment and disparate impact.

Exhibit 43-1
Federal Discrimination Laws

FEDERAL LEGISLATION	PURPOSE
The Civil Rights Act of 1964 (CRA)—Title VII (as amended by the Civil Rights Act of 1991)	Protects employees against discrimination based on race, color, religion, national origin, and sex. Also prohibits harassment based on the same protected categories.
Pregnancy Discrimination Act of 1987 (PDA)	Amended Title VII of the CRA to expand the definition of sex discrimination to include discrimination based on pregnancy.
Age Discrimination in Employment Act of 1967 (ADEA)	Prohibits employers from refusing to hire, discharging, or discriminating in terms and conditions of employment on the basis of an employee's or applicant's being age 40 or older.
Americans with Disabilities Act (ADA)	Prohibits discrimination against employees and job applicants with disabilities.
Equal Pay Act of 1963 (EPA)	Prohibits an employer from paying workers of one gender less than the wages paid to employees of the opposite gender for work that requires equal skill, effort, and responsibility.

Title VII of the Civil Rights Act applies to employers who have 15 or more employees for 20 consecutive weeks within one year and who are engaged in a business that affects commerce. The U.S. government, corporations owned by the government, agencies of the District of Columbia, Indian tribes, private clubs, unions, and employment agencies are also covered by Title VII.

PROVING DISPARATE-TREATMENT DISCRIMINATION UNDER TITLE VII

In order to sue for disparate treatment under Title VII, the plaintiff must be a member of a protected class as listed in the act. In other words, the employee must have been discriminated against based on race, color, national origin, religion, or sex (i.e., gender). If the employee has been hired, fired, denied a promotion, and so on, based on membership in that protected class, this is a form of intentional discrimination and qualifies the employee to sue for disparate-treatment discrimination. Proving disparate-treatment discrimination in employment under Title VII is a three-step process:

1. Plaintiff (the employee) must demonstrate a prima facie case of discrimination.
2. Defendant (the employer) must articulate a legitimate, nondiscriminatory business reason for the action.
3. Plaintiff (the employee) must show that the reason given by the defendant (the employer) is a mere pretext.

To illustrate more clearly, let's break down each step. First, the plaintiff-employee has the burden of proving a prima facie case of discrimination. *Prima facie* is Latin for "at first view"[6] and means that the evidence is sufficient to raise a presumption that discrimination occurred. In the chapter opening scenario between Brad and Jennifer, Brad has alleged that Jennifer discriminated against him. Brad's prima facie case may be summed up as follows: Brad was a good employee for five years. After being promoted and transferred to Jennifer's department, Jennifer began treating him differently than she did the females in the department. Jennifer told Brad that she did not like "weak males," asked him to come home with her (he refused), and eventually fired him. This is likely sufficient to satisfy the prima facie requirement.

Once Brad (the employee) has set forth his prima facie case (step 1), the burden shifts to Jennifer and So Clean (the employer) to articulate a legitimate, nondiscriminatory reason for firing Brad (step 2). Jennifer and So Clean could meet this burden by arguing that Brad was not fired based on his sex (because he is a male) but rather because of his "creative" differences with Jennifer in the marketing department (remember, Brad has no contract, therefore he is an at-will employee).

Once Jennifer and So Clean (the employer) set forth their nondiscriminatory reason for terminating Brad (the employee), the burden shifts back to Brad one last time. Brad must demonstrate that the employer's given reason for terminating him was a mere pretext (step 3). This last step requires that Brad show that "despite his qualifications," he was fired.[7]

After all the evidence has been presented, the trier of fact (a jury in most cases)[8] must decide whether discrimination has occurred. The burden of proof in a civil case is preponderance of the evidence (i.e., more likely than not). If the jury finds in favor of the plaintiff-employee, damages must be assessed. Damages under Title VII include up to two years of back pay, compensatory damages, punitive damages (limited in some cases), attorney fees,

[6] Lectic Law Library, www.lectlaw.com/def2/p078.htm.

[7] *McDonnell Douglas v. Green,* 411 U.S. 792, 802 (1973).

[8] In a bench trial, the judge becomes the trier of fact as no jury is impaneled. A discrimination case could also be decided by a judge on motion for summary judgment.

court costs, court orders (including reinstatement), and remedial seniority. If the jury finds in favor of the defendant-employer, the plaintiff-employee receives nothing.

PROVING DISPARATE-IMPACT DISCRIMINATION UNDER TITLE VII

Disparate-impact cases are sometimes called *unintentional-discrimination cases*. While it is very difficult to prove disparate treatment, it is even more difficult to prove disparate impact. Disparate-impact cases arise when a plaintiff attempts to establish that while an employer's policy or practice appears to apply to everyone equally, its actual effect is that it disproportionately limits employment opportunities for a protected class.

The plaintiff proves a case based on disparate impact by first establishing statistically that the rule disproportionately restricts employment opportunities for a protected class. The burden of proof then shifts to the defendant, who can avoid liability by demonstrating that the practice or policy is a business necessity. The plaintiff, at this point, can still recover by proving that the "necessity" was promulgated as a pretext for discrimination.

The initial steps for proving a prima facie case of disparate impact were set forth in *Griggs v. Duke Power Co.*[9] In that case, the employer-defendant required all applicants to have a high school diploma and a successful score on a professionally recognized intelligence test for all jobs except laborer. The stated purpose of these criteria was to upgrade the quality of the workforce.

The plaintiff statistically demonstrated the discriminatory impact by showing that 34 percent of the white males in the state had high school diplomas, whereas only 12 percent of the black males did, and by introducing evidence from an EEOC study showing that 58 percent of the whites, compared to 6 percent of the blacks, had passed tests similar to the one given by the defendant. Because the defendant could not demonstrate any business-related justification for either employment policy, the plaintiff was successful. Requiring a high IQ or high school or college diploma may be necessary for some jobs but not for all jobs at Duke Power.

SEXUAL HARASSMENT UNDER TITLE VII

Harassment is a relatively new basis for discrimination. It first developed in the context of discrimination based on sex, and it evolved to become applicable to other protected classes. The definition of sexual harassment stated in the Equal Employment Opportunity Commission (EEOC) guidelines and accepted by the U.S. Supreme Court is "unwelcome sexual advances, requests for sexual favors, and other verbal or physical conduct of a sexual nature" that implicitly or explicitly makes submission a term or condition of employment; makes employment decisions related to the individual dependent on submission to or rejection of such conduct; or has the purpose or effect of creating an intimidating, hostile, or offensive work environment. Did the actions of Jennifer create a sexually hostile environment for Brad?

Two distinct forms of sexual harassment are recognized. The first, and generally easiest to prove, is *quid pro quo,* which occurs when a supervisor makes a sexual demand on someone of the opposite sex and this demand is reasonably perceived as a term or condition of employment. The basis for this rule is that the supervisor would not make similar demands on someone of the same sex. In the opening scenario, Jennifer demanded that Brad come home with her so that she could "cure" his homosexuality. When Brad refused, Jennifer fired him. Brad has a cause of action for quid pro quo sexual harassment.

The second form of sexual harassment involves the creation of a hostile work environment. Case 43-1 demonstrates the standard used by the U.S. Supreme Court to determine whether an employer's conduct has created a hostile work environment.

[9] *Griggs v. Duke Power*, 401 U.S. 424 (1971).

CASE 43-1 TERESA HARRIS v. FORKLIFT SYSTEMS, INC.
UNITED STATES SUPREME COURT
510 U.S.17, 114 S. CT. 367 (1994)

During her tenure as a manager at defendant Forklift Systems, Inc., plaintiff Harris was repeatedly insulted by defendant's president because of her gender and subjected to sexual innuendos. In front of other employees, the president frequently told Harris, "You're just a woman, what do you know?" He sometimes asked Harris and other female employees to remove coins from his pockets and made suggestive comments about their clothes. He suggested to Harris in front of others that they negotiate her salary at the Holiday Inn. He said that he would stop when Harris complained, but he continued behaving in the same manner, so Harris quit. She then filed an action against the defendant for creating an abusive work environment based on her gender.

The district court found in favor of the defendant, holding that some of the comments were offensive to the plaintiff, but were not so serious as to severely affect Harris' psychological well-being or interfere with her work performance. The court of appeals affirmed. Plaintiff Harris appealed to the U.S. Supreme Court.

JUSTICE O'CONNOR: As we made clear in *Meritor Savings Bank* v. *Vinson,* this language [of Title VII] "is not limited to 'economic' or 'tangible' discrimination. The phrase 'terms, conditions, or privileges of employment' evinces a congressional intent 'to strike at the entire spectrum of disparate treatment of men and women' in employment," which includes requiring people to work in a discriminatorily hostile or abusive environment. When the workplace is permeated with "discriminatory intimidation, ridicule, and insult," that is "sufficiently severe or pervasive to alter the conditions of the victim's employment and create an abusive working environment."

This standard, which we reaffirm today, takes a middle path between making actionable any conduct that is merely offensive and requiring the conduct to cause a tangible psychological injury. As we pointed out in *Meritor,* "mere utterance of an . . . epithet which engenders offensive feelings in an employee," does not sufficiently affect conditions of employment to implicate Title VII. . . . Likewise, if the victim does not subjectively perceive the environment to be abusive, the conduct has not actually altered the conditions of the victim's employment, and there is no Title VII violation.

But Title VII comes into play before the harassing conduct leads to a nervous breakdown. A discriminatorily abusive work environment, even one that does not seriously affect employees' psychological well-being, can and often will detract from employees' job performance, discourage employees from remaining on the job, or keep them from advancing in their careers. Moreover, even without regard to these tangible effects, the very fact that the discriminatory conduct was so severe or pervasive that it created a work environment abusive to employees because of their race, gender, religion, or national origin offends Title VII's broad rule of workplace equality. The appalling conduct alleged in *Meritor,* and the reference in that case to environments "so heavily polluted with discrimination as to destroy completely the emotional and psychological stability of minority group workers," merely present some especially egregious examples of harassment. They do not mark the boundary of what is actionable.

. . . Certainly Title VII bars conduct that would seriously affect a reasonable person's psychological well-being, but the statute is not limited to such conduct. So long as the environment would reasonably be perceived, and is perceived, as hostile or abusive, there is no need for it also to be psychologically injurious.

This is not, and by its nature cannot be, a mathematically precise test. But we can say that whether an environment is "hostile" or "abusive" can be determined only by looking at all the circumstances. These may include the frequency of the discriminatory conduct; its severity; whether it is physically threatening or humiliating, or a mere offensive utterance; and whether it unreasonably interferes with an employee's work performance. The effect on the employee's psychological well being is, of course, relevant to determining whether the plaintiff actually found the environment abusive. But while psychological harm, like any other relevant factor, may be taken into account, no single factor is required.

REVERSED AND REMANDED
in favor of plaintiff.

CRITICAL THINKING

Identify the Court's reasons. Do you think these reasons were sufficient to overturn the previous ruling? Why or why not?

ETHICAL DECISION MAKING

Imagine that Justice O'Connor is operating under a duty-based system of ethics. What duty is she advocating in terms of employer-employee relationships? Would this ruling serve well as a universal standard?

Sexual harassment cases were not filed in large numbers immediately after Title VII's passage, with only 10,532 sexual harassment cases filed with the EEOC or state and local agencies in the year ending on October 1, 1992. Then the number of claims increased steadily until 1995, when 15,549 cases were filed. Since 1995, the number of claims has steadily declined, with only 12,025 complaints in fiscal year 2006.[10] While the likelihood of being sued for sexual harassment is not great, once a business is sued, its reputation may be tarnished and payment of damages is a real possibility. It is therefore critically important that businesspersons be able to recognize sexual harassment and prevent its occurrence in the workplace. As a business owner or manager, how would you prevent sexual harassment claims? According to one bar association article:

> There are four essential steps that managers can take to protect their businesses from being involved in sexual harassment litigation. They are: (1) implement a policy against sexual harassment; (2) require supervisory training; (3) provide a mechanism for receiving complaints; and (4) create a method for conducting prompt and thorough investigations.[11]

Under California state law, managers are required to undergo training to prevent sexual harassment in the workplace.

Harassment in cyberspace. Unfortunately, new forms of technology have provided new opportunities for harassment. Consider, for example, the possibilities for online harassment. A New Jersey appellate court has ruled that employers have a duty to remedy online harassment when they have notice that employees are engaged in a pattern of retaliatory harassment using a work-related online forum.[12] Airline pilot Tammy Blakey sued her former employer, Continental Airlines, for sexual harassment, and part of her claim focused on retaliatory harassment that took place on an electronic bulletin board, the "Crew Members Forum." In particular, Blakey's fellow pilots posted information on the bulletin board that suggested that Blakey was a poor pilot and a "feminazi" and that, by filing a sexual harassment lawsuit, she was using the legal system "to get a quick buck."[13]

[10] U.S. EEOC, "Sexual Harassment Charges: EEOC & FEPAs Combined: FY 1992–FY 2000," January 18, 2001, www.eeoc.gov/stats/harass.html (May 1, 2001); and U.S. EEOC, "Sexual Harassment Charges: EEOC & FEPAs Combined: FY 1997–FY 2006," January 31, 2007.

[11] Laura Smith, "Avoiding Sexual Harassment Lawsuits," www.dcba.org/brief/profresp/0299.htm.

[12] *Blakey v. Continental Airlines,* 751 A. 2d 538 (N.J. 2000).

[13] *Blakey v. Continental Airlines, Inc.,* 2000 WL 703018.

In ruling on the bulletin board issue, the court stated that although an electronic bulletin board did not have a physical location within an airport terminal, hangar, or aircraft, it might nonetheless have been so closely related to the workplace environment and beneficial to the employer that continuation of harassment on the forum should be regarded as part of the workplace.

This case shows that, in some situations, employers have a duty to monitor their employees' use of e-mail and the Internet. They cannot allow harassment, including retaliatory harassment on an online bulletin board. Employers can reduce their liability exposure by conducting sexual harassment training and outlining clear workplace policies that prohibit harassing behavior, including behavior that takes place in cyberspace.

Same-sex harassment—the supreme court speaks. Initially, same-sex harassment was not covered by Title VII. By 1997, however, the courts were split on the issue. This issue was resolved in 1998 (see Case 43-2).

CASE 43-2 ONCALE v. SUNDOWNER OFFSHORE SERVICES, INC.

UNITED STATES SUPREME COURT
523 U.S. 75, 118 S. CT. 998 (1998)

On several occasions, the employee was forcibly subjected to sex-related, humiliating actions against him by fellow employees in the presence of the rest of the oil-platform crew. He was also physically assaulted in a sexual manner and was threatened with rape. When his complaints to supervisory personnel produced no remedial action, the employee filed a complaint against his employer, alleging that he was discriminated against in his employment because of his sex.

The district court granted the employer's motion for summary judgment, which the appellate court affirmed, holding that the employee, who was a male, had no cause of action under Title VII for harassment by male co-workers. On certiorari, the Court held that nothing in Title VII necessarily barred a claim of discrimination because of sex merely because the plaintiff and the defendant, or the person charged with acting on behalf of the defendant, were of the same sex. In reversing the judgment, the Court concluded that sex discrimination consisting of same-sex sexual harassment is actionable under Title VII. The Court reversed the appellate court's order and remanded the case for further proceedings.

JUSTICE SCALIA: This case presents the question whether workplace harassment can violate Title VII's prohibition against "discrimination . . . because of . . . sex," *42 U.S.C. § 2000e-2*(a)(1), when the harasser and the harassed employee are of the same sex.

Title VII of the Civil Rights Act of 1964 provides, in relevant part, that "it shall be an unlawful employment practice for an employer . . . to discriminate against any individual with respect to his compensation, terms, conditions, or privileges of employment, because of such individual's race, color, religion, sex, or national origin." We have held that this not only covers "terms" and "conditions" in the narrow contractual sense, but "evinces a congressional intent to strike at the entire spectrum of disparate treatment of men and women in employment."

"When the workplace is permeated with discriminatory intimidation, ridicule, and insult that is sufficiently severe or pervasive to alter the conditions of the victim's employment and create an abusive working environment, Title VII is violated." *Harris v. Forklift Systems, Inc., 510 U.S. 17, 21, 126 L. Ed. 2d 295, 114 S. Ct. 367 (1993)*

Title VII's prohibition of discrimination "because of . . . sex" protects men as well as women . . . and in the related context of racial discrimination in the workplace we have rejected any conclusive presumption that an employer will not discriminate against members of his own race. "Because of the many facets of human motivation, it would be unwise to presume as a matter of law that human beings of one definable group will not discriminate against other members of that group."

If our precedents leave any doubt on the question, we hold today that nothing in Title VII necessarily bars a claim of discrimination "because of . . . sex" merely because the plaintiff and the defendant (or the person charged with acting on behalf of the defendant) are of the same sex.

We see no justification in the statutory language or our precedents for a categorical rule excluding same-sex harassment claims from the coverage of Title VII. As some courts have observed, male-on-male sexual harassment in the workplace was assuredly not the principal evil Congress was concerned with when it enacted Title VII. But statutory prohibitions often go beyond the principal evil to cover reasonably comparable evils, and it is ultimately the provisions of our laws rather than the principal concerns of our legislators by which we are governed. Title VII prohibits "discrimination . . . because of . . . sex" in the "terms" or "conditions" of employment. Our holding that this includes sexual harassment must extend to sexual harassment of any kind that meets the statutory requirements.

Courts and juries have found the inference of discrimination easy to draw in most male-female sexual harassment situations, because the challenged conduct typically involves explicit or implicit proposals of sexual activity; it is reasonable to assume those proposals would not have been made to someone of the same sex. The same chain of inference would be available to a plaintiff alleging same-sex harassment, if there were credible evidence that the harasser was homosexual. But harassing conduct need not be motivated by sexual desire to support an inference of discrimination on the basis of sex. A trier of fact might reasonably find such discrimination, for example, if a female victim is harassed in such sex-specific and derogatory terms by another woman as to make it clear that the harasser is motivated by general hostility to the presence of women in the workplace. A same-sex harassment plaintiff may also, of course, offer direct comparative evidence about how the alleged harasser treated members of both sexes in a mixed-sex workplace. Whatever evidentiary route the plaintiff chooses to follow, he or she must always prove that the conduct at issue was not merely tinged with offensive sexual connotations, but actually constituted "*discrimination* . . . because of . . . sex."

Because we conclude that sex discrimination consisting of same-sex sexual harassment is actionable under Title VII, the judgment of the Court of Appeals for the Fifth Circuit is reversed, and the case is remanded for further proceedings consistent with this opinion.

REVERSED AND REMANDED in favor of plaintiff.

CRITICAL THINKING

What assumptions would the Court have had to make for it to rule against the plaintiff in this case? Did the reasoning explicitly reject these assumptions?

ETHICAL DECISION MAKING

What stakeholders are affected by this decision? In answering the question, push yourself to go beyond the direct and obvious stakeholders.

Harassment by nonemployees under Title VII. Employers may be held liable for harassment of their employees by nonemployees under very limited circumstances. If an employer knows that a customer repeatedly harasses an employee yet the employer does nothing to remedy the situation, the employer may be liable. For example, in *Lockhard v. Pizza Hut, Inc.*,[14] the franchise was held liable for the harassment of a waitress by two male customers because no steps had been taken to prevent the harassment.

HARASSMENT OF OTHER PROTECTED CLASSES UNDER TITLE VII

Hostile-environment cases have also been used in cases of discrimination based on religion and race. For example, in a 1986 case, *Snell v. Suffolk County,*[15] Hispanic and black corrections workers demonstrated that a hostile work environment existed by proving that they had been subjected to continuing verbal abuse and racial harassment by co-workers and that the county sheriff's department had done nothing to prevent the abuse. The white employees had continually used racial epithets and posted racially offensive materials on bulletin boards, such as a picture of a black man with a noose around his neck, cartoons favorably portraying the Ku Klux Klan, and a "black officers' study guide," consisting of children's puzzles. White officers once dressed a Hispanic inmate in a straw hat, sheet, and sign that said "spic." Such activities were found by the court to constitute a hostile work environment.

PREGNANCY DISCRIMINATION ACT OF 1987—AN AMENDMENT TO TITLE VII

In 1987, Title VII was amended by the Pregnancy Discrimination Act (PDA). This law expanded the definition of discrimination based on gender to include discrimination based on pregnancy. "Discrimination on the basis of pregnancy, childbirth or related medical conditions constitutes unlawful sex discrimination under Title VII."[16] Under the act, temporary disability caused by pregnancy must be treated the same as any other temporary disability.

DEFENSES TO CLAIMS UNDER TITLE VII

As a business owner or manager, how would you respond if one of your employees filed a lawsuit under Title VII? Are there any legal exceptions for discriminating against a protected class? The answer, surprising to many business owners and managers, is yes. The three most important defenses available to defendants in Title VII cases are the bona fide occupational qualification, merit, and seniority system defenses. These defenses are raised by the defendant after the plaintiff has established a prima facie case of discrimination based on either disparate treatment or disparate impact. They would obviously not be applicable to a claim based on harassment.

The bona fide occupational qualification defense. The bona fide occupational qualification (BFOQ) defense allows an employer to discriminate in hiring on the basis of sex, religion, or national origin (but not race or color) when doing so is necessary for the performance of the job. Necessity must be based on actual qualifications, not stereotypes about one group's abilities. For example, being a male cannot be a BFOQ for a job because it is a dirty job, although there may be a valid requirement that an applicant be able to lift a certain amount of weight if such lifting is a part of the job. Conversely, being a female may be a BFOQ for modeling female clothing. An employer would not be required or expected to hire a male for such a job. Employer arguments about inconvenience to the employer,

[14] 162 F.3d 1062 (10th Cir. 1998).

[15] *Snell v. Suffolk County,* 782 F.2d 1094 (1986).

[16] EEOC, "Facts about Pregnancy Discrimination," www.eeoc.gov/facts/fs-preg.html.

such as having to provide two sets of restroom facilities, have not been persuasive in the courts. Nor have customer preferences to be served by a particular gender or nationality. The only exception to customer preference is sexual privacy (e.g., female restroom attendants in the women's restroom and male attendants in the men's room).[17]

The merit defense. The merit defense is usually raised when hiring or promotion decisions are partially based on test scores. Professionally developed ability tests that are not designed, intended, or used to discriminate may be used. While these tests may have an adverse impact on a class, as long as they are manifestly related to job performance, they do not violate the act. Since 1978, the "Uniform Guidelines on Employee Selection Procedures" (UGESP) have guided government agencies charged with enforcing civil rights, and they provide guidance to employers and other interested persons about when ability tests are valid and job-related. Under these guidelines, tests must be validated in accordance with standards established by the American Psychological Association.

Three types of validation are acceptable: (1) *criterion-related validity,* which is the statistical relationship between test scores and objective criteria of job performance; (2) *content validity,* which isolates some skill used on the job and directly tests that skill; and (3) *construct validity,* wherein a psychological trait needed to perform the job is measured. A test that required a word processor to use a computer would be content-valid. A test of patience for a teacher would be construct-valid.

The seniority system defense. A bona fide seniority system is a legal defense under Title VII. Even though a seniority system, in which employees are given preferential treatment based on their length of service, may perpetuate past discrimination, such systems are considered bona fide and are thus not illegal if (1) the system applies equally to all persons; (2) the seniority units follow industry practices; (3) the seniority system did not have its genesis in discrimination; and (4) the system is maintained free of any illegal discriminatory purpose.

REMEDIES UNDER TITLE VII

A plaintiff may seek both equitable and legal remedies for violations of Title VII. Courts have ordered parties to engage in diverse activities ranging from publicizing their commitment to minority hiring to establishing special training programs for minorities. A successful plaintiff may recover back pay for up to two years from the time of the discriminatory act. *Back pay* is the difference between the amount of money the plaintiff earned since the discriminatory act and the amount of money she would have earned had the discriminatory act never occurred. For example, if one year before the case came to trial the defendant refused a promotion to a plaintiff on the basis of her sex, and the job for which she was rejected paid $1,000 more per month, she would be entitled to recover back pay in the amount of $1,000 per month multiplied by 12 months. (If the salary increased at regular increments, these are also included.) The same basic calculations are used when plaintiffs are not hired because of discrimination. Such plaintiffs are entitled to the back wages that they would have received minus any actual earnings during that time. Defendants may also exclude wages for any period during which the plaintiff would have been unable to work.

A plaintiff who was not hired for a job because of a Title VII violation may also receive remedial seniority dating back to the time when the plaintiff was discriminated against; compensatory damages, including those for pain and suffering; and in some cases, punitive

[17] *In The Matter of the Accusation of the Department of Fair Employment and Housing v. San Luis Obispo Coastal Unified School District, Respondent; Marlene Anne Mendes, Complainant,* Case No. E95-96 L-0725-00s, 98-14 (October 7, 1998). See www.dfeh.ca.gov/PrecedentialD/1998-14.html.

damages. In cases based on discrimination other than race, however, punitive damages are capped at $300,000 for employers of more than 500 employees; $100,000 for firms with 101 to 200 employees; and $50,000 for firms with 100 or fewer employees. An employer will not be held vicariously liable for punitive damages as long as it made "good-faith efforts" to comply with federal law.

Attorney fees may be awarded to a successful plaintiff in Title VII cases. They are typically denied only when special circumstances would render the award unjust. If it is determined that the plaintiff's action was frivolous, unreasonable, or without foundation, the courts may award attorney's fees to the prevailing defendant. For more information on Title VII, visit the EEOC Web site at www.eeoc.gov.

PROCEDURE FOR FILING A CLAIM UNDER TITLE VII

Filing a claim under Title VII is much more complicated than simply filing a lawsuit. Failure to follow the proper procedures within the strict time framework may result in a plaintiff's losing his or her right to file a lawsuit under Title VII.

Filing a charge with the EEOC. The first step in initiating a Title VII action is the aggrieved party's filing of a charge with the state Equal Employment Opportunity Commission or, if no such agency exists, the federal EEOC. A *charge* is a sworn statement that states the name of the charging party, the name(s) of the defendant(s), and the nature of the discriminatory act. In states that do *not* have state EEOCs, the aggrieved party must file the charge with the federal EEOC within 180 days of the alleged discriminatory act. In states that *do* have such agencies, the charge must be filed either with the federal EEOC within 180 days of the discriminatory act or with the appropriate state agency within the time limits prescribed by local law, which cannot be less than 180 days. If initially filed with the local agency, the charge must be filed with the federal EEOC within 300 days of the discriminatory act or within 60 days of receipt of notice that the state agency has disposed of the matter, whichever comes first.

EEOC conciliation attempts. Within 10 days of receiving the charge, the EEOC must notify the alleged violator of the charge. Then the EEOC investigates the matter to determine whether there is "reasonable cause" to believe that a violation has occurred. If the EEOC does find such reasonable cause, it attempts to eliminate the discriminatory practice through conciliation, that is, by trying to negotiate a settlement between the two parties. If unsuccessful, the EEOC *may* file suit against the alleged discriminator in federal district court. Failure to file suit does not necessarily mean that the EEOC does not think the plaintiff does not have a valid claim; it may be that the EEOC simply feels that it is not the type of claim the commission wishes to use its limited resources to pursue.

The EEOC right-to-sue letter. If the EEOC decides not to sue, it notifies the plaintiff of his or her right to file an action and issues the plaintiff a *right-to-sue letter,* which is not intended to be anything other than a statement that the plaintiff has followed the proper initial procedures and therefore may file a lawsuit. The plaintiff must have this letter in order to file a private action. The letter may be requested at any time after 180 days have elapsed since the filing of the charge. As long as the requisite time period has passed, the EEOC will issue the right-to-sue letter regardless of whether or not the EEOC members find a reasonable basis to believe that the defendant engaged in discriminatory behavior. In reality, due to the number of complaints, the EEOC and state EEOCs routinely issue right-to-sue letters without filing a lawsuit on the aggrieved party's behalf. Once an employee receives a right-to-sue letter, he or she is free to hire an attorney and file a lawsuit against the employer.

Age Discrimination in Employment Act of 1967

The Age Discrimination in Employment Act of 1967 (ADEA) was enacted to prohibit employers from refusing to hire, discharging, or discriminating in terms and conditions of employment against employees or applicants age 40 or older. The language describing the prohibited conduct is virtually the same as that of Title VII, except that age is the prohibited basis for discrimination. ADEA applies to employers having 20 or more employees. It also applies to employment agencies and to unions that have at least 25 members or that operate a hiring hall. As a consequence of the Supreme Court ruling in *Kimel v. Florida Board of Regents,*[18] ADEA does not apply to state employers.

It is important that business owners and managers understand ADEA because the number of claims under this act have increased, perhaps in response to a weakening economy since early 2000 and the aging of the baby-boomer generation. In 1999, approximately 1,400 age discrimination claims were filed under ADEA. Conversely, in 2001, 17,405 age discrimination claims were filed.

PROVING AGE DISCRIMINATION UNDER ADEA

Remember, ADEA does not protect *all* individuals from discrimination based on age but protects only those age 40 or over. Thus, an employer can refuse to promote an employee under 40 because he or she is too old or too young. Once a person is in the protected class, discrimination under ADEA may be proved in the same ways that discrimination is proved under Title VII: by the plaintiff's showing disparate treatment or disparate impact.

Termination is the most common cause of ADEA cases. To prove a prima facie case of age discrimination involving a termination, the plaintiff must establish facts sufficient to create a reasonable inference that age was a determining factor in the termination. The plaintiff raises this inference by showing that he or she:

- Belongs to the statutorily protected class (those age 40 or older).
- Was qualified for the position held.
- Was terminated under circumstances giving rise to an inference of discrimination.

The plaintiff need not prove replacement by someone outside the protected class.[19]

Once the plaintiff sets forth the facts that give rise to an inference of discrimination, the burden of proof shifts to the defendant to prove there was a legitimate, nondiscriminatory reason for the discharge. If the employer meets this standard, the plaintiff may recover only if he or she can show by a preponderance of the evidence that the employer's alleged legitimate reason is a pretext for discrimination. Case 43-3 demonstrates how some employers will use a pretext for discriminating against older employees.

[18] 120 S. Ct. 631 (2000).

[19] *O'Conner v. Consolidated Caterers Corp.*, 517 U.S. 308, 116 S. Ct. 1307 (1996).

CASE 43-3 JAMES v. SEARS, ROEBUCK & CO.

UNITED STATES COURT OF APPEALS FOR THE TENTH CIRCUIT
21 F.3D 989, 1994 U.S. APP. LEXIS 7073 (1994)

The facts before the jury presented either an ill-conceived and poorly executed corporate efficiency move or a deliberate corporate attempt to reduce payroll costs by replacing experienced and well-paid workers forty years of age or older with lesser experienced and lower paid, younger workers. The jury decided it was the latter and rendered judgment in favor of Plaintiffs.

JUDGE BRORBY: Sears decided to cut costs in its service centers. Sears transferred some of the clerical functions formerly performed at its Ogden, Utah, service center to a larger center in Salt Lake City, Utah, even though at the time the Ogden center was the more profitable of the two centers. Sears then eliminated the jobs of the two oldest full-time clerical employees of its Ogden service center. One of those terminated service center employees is a plaintiff in this suit. Sears did not allow the service center plaintiff to transfer to the Salt Lake center where her former work had been transferred. Sears then hired predominately younger, part-time employees to work in the Ogden and Salt Lake service centers.

Simultaneous with the service center cuts, Sears offered the employees in its Ogden retail store and service center a buy-out. Five of the Plaintiffs worked at the retail store. Under the buy-out, employees leaving Sears' employment would receive a week of severance pay for each year they worked for Sears, with a cap of twenty-six weeks. The purpose of the buy-out was to provide the cut service center employees "comparable jobs" in the retail store. However, the turnover at the Ogden and Salt Lake City service centers was so high the cut service center employees could have been easily reabsorbed within three months.

A form of the buy-out called early retirement was offered to employees fifty years of age or older. As offered by Sears, Plaintiffs accepting early retirement lost thirty-five per cent of their accrued pension because they were under sixty-two years of age. Further, plaintiffs between ages fifty and fifty-four had to wait until reaching age fifty-five before their pension payments could begin.

Sears pressured Plaintiffs to accept the buy-out/early retirement in order to achieve its predetermined quota for older employees leaving. Sears' internal document shows it planned on thirteen older, full-time employees leaving under the buy-out. There were twenty full-time employees under the age of forty who were eligible for the buy-out. Sears did not plan for any of the eligible younger employees to accept.

Sears obtained the acceptances of the five retail store Plaintiffs by conduct that constituted their constructive discharge. Sears' treatment of Plaintiffs included negative job reviews and threatening them with transfers to less desirable and lower paying positions if they did not accept the buy-out/early retirement. Sears' internal document shows that the retail store was not being reorganized and none of the retail employees were to be moved or lose their jobs as a result of the changes in the service centers or the buy-out.

The Age Discrimination in Employment Act ("ADEA") provides it is unlawful for any employer "to fail or refuse to hire or to discharge any individual . . . because of such individual's age." *29 U.S.C. 623* (a)(1). The protected class under the ADEA includes individuals "who are at least 40 years of age."

Plaintiffs had the burden of establishing age discrimination by a preponderance of the evidence. The often repeated elements of a prima facie case of age discrimination are met when an employee shows "(1) [employee] was within the protected age group, (2) [employee] was doing satisfactory work, (3) [employee] was discharged, and (4) [employee's] position was filled by a younger person." Once the employee establishes these elements, the employer can offer evidence to show it was motivated by a legitimate nondiscriminatory reason for the challenged action. The employee need not prove the employer's justifications were false, id., or "that age was the sole motivating factor in the employment decision." Instead, the employee must show age was also a reason for the employer's decision, and "age was the factor that made a difference."

The evidence demonstrated Sears forced the retail Plaintiffs to accept the buy-out or early retirement in several ways. During the months before the offer, two Plaintiffs working as salespersons were singled out among similarly situated employees and pressured about quotas in a way younger employees were not. Although they were top sellers, they were threatened, pressured and systematically "written up" over quotas even though the quotas were almost never met by other salespersons. Sears then used these reviews as a pretext for telling those two salespersons Plaintiffs they would be fired or transferred to lower paying positions if they did not accept. Sears threatened to move the remaining three retail store Plaintiffs from their current jobs into high pressure sales jobs involving unreachable quotas for the sales of maintenance agreements. The record viewed in the light most favorable to Plaintiffs as prevailing parties supports the jury verdict.

REVERSED in favor of plaintiffs.

CRITICAL THINKING

The one-sided nature of this case makes it difficult to see how unclear causation often is. But to help you see exactly that potential lack of clarity, suppose this case had been tried without any of the internal documents from Sears. Under those conditions, how would the behavior of Sears be more difficult to attribute to age discrimination?

ETHICAL DECISION MAKING

The laws in this chapter are stimulated by what particular value preference? Would it be possible to argue in any fashion that Sears shares this value preference?

DEFENSES UNDER ADEA

As under Title VII, decisions premised on the operation of a bona fide seniority system are not unlawfully discriminatory despite any discriminatory impact. Likewise, employment decisions may also be based on "reasonable factors other than age." Another defense available in both Title VII and ADA cases is the bona fide occupational qualification (BFOQ) defense. To succeed with this defense, the defendant must establish that he or she must hire employees of only a certain age to safely and efficiently operate the business in question. The courts generally scrutinize very carefully any attempt to demonstrate that age is a BFOQ.

One example of an employer's successful use of this defense is provided by *Hodgson v. Greyhound Lines, Inc.,*[20] a case in which the employer refused to hire applicants age 35 or older. Greyhound demonstrated that its safest drivers were those between the ages of 50 and 55, with 16 to 20 years of experience driving for Greyhound. Greyhound argued that this combination of age and experience could never be reached by those who were hired at age 35 or older. Therefore, in order to ensure the safest drivers, Greyhound should be allowed to hire only applicants younger than 35. In this case, the court accepted the employer's rationale.

Even if none of the foregoing defenses are available to the employer, termination of an older employee may be legal because of the *executive exemption.* Under this exemption, an individual may be mandatorily retired after age 65 if two conditions are met:

- He or she has been employed as a bona fide executive for at least two years immediately before retirement.
- On retirement, he or she is entitled to nonforfeitable annual retirement benefits of at least $44,000.

[20] 499 F.2d 859 (7th Cir. 1974).

Remember, however, that federal laws are a minimum level of protection. If a state wishes, it may pass laws granting employees in its state more rights than those under federal law.

Americans with Disabilities Act

The goal of the Americans with Disabilities Act (ADA) is preventing employers from discriminating against employees and applicants with disabilities. ADA attempts to attain this objective by requiring that employers make reasonable accommodations to the known physical or mental disabilities of an otherwise qualified person with a disability unless the necessary accommodation would impose an undue burden on the employer's business.

> When the ADA was before Congress, some members predicted a flood of lawsuits that would bankrupt or at least overburden business. . . . Studies have shown, however, that businesses have adapted to the ADA much more easily—and inexpensively—than the doomsayers predicted. . . . Law Professor Peter Blanck of the University of Iowa has studied business compliance with the ADA, including Sears Roebuck and many other large businesses, and found that compliance was often as easy as raising or lowering a desk, installing a ramp, or modifying a dress code. Another survey found that three-quarters of all changes cost less than $100. Moreover, the predicted flood of lawsuits proved to be imaginary. Almost 90 percent of the cases brought before the Equal Employment Opportunity Commission are thrown out. And only about 650 lawsuits were filed in the ADA's first five years—a small number compared to 6 million businesses, 666,000 public and private employers, and 80,000 units of state and local governments that must comply. The American Bar Association recently conducted a survey and learned that, of the cases that actually go to court, 98 percent are decided in favor of the defendants, usually businesses.[21]

WHO IS PROTECTED UNDER ADA?

A disabled individual, for purposes of ADA, is defined as a person who meets one of the following criteria:

- Has a physical or mental impairment that substantially limits one or more of the major life activities of such individual.
- Has a record of such impairment.
- Is regarded as having such an impairment.

Employers often find it difficult to know how ADA applies to those who have mental disabilities. From 1992 to1998, emotional/psychiatric impairment claims were 12 percent of all claims.[22] Psychiatric disorders constituted about 9 percent of the ADA lawsuits brought by the EEOC to court in 1998.[23] Typical accommodations for those with mental disabilities include providing a private office, flexible work schedule, restructured job, or time off for treatment. Despite the years' experience we have had in defining covered individuals, the issue of whether someone is a disabled person under the act is still frequently litigated. In Case 43-4, the U.S. Supreme Court tried to give greater guidance on this issue.

[21] The Center for an Accessible Society, "Disability Issues Information for Journalists," www.accessiblesociety.org/topics/ada.

[22] National Council on Disability, "Equal Employment Opportunity Commission—Promises to Keep: A Decade of Federal Enforcement of the Americans with Disabilities Act," June 27, 2000, www.ncd.gov/newsroom/publications/promises_3.htm/#6 (May 1, 2001).

[23] Sheryl J. Powers and Carolyn L. Wheeler, "Docket of Americans with Disabilities Act (ADA) Litigation," September 30, 1998, www.eeoc.gov/docs/ada-98.html (May 1, 2001).

CASE 43-4 TOYOTA MOTOR MANUFACTURING, KENTUCKY, INC., PETITIONER, v. ELLA WILLIAMS

UNITED STATES SUPREME COURT
534 U.S. 184 (2002)

Plaintiff-Respondent Williams developed carpel tunnel syndrome while working at defendant-petitioner's auto assembly plant. She was put on light duty work for a while, but then the duties of her work team changed, and she once again began having symptoms. There was a dispute over whether she asked to be reasonably accommodated by being put into a different job, but she did start missing more work due to her condition, and was fired for poor attendance. She filed a complaint with the EEOC, and filed suit after receiving her right to sue letter. The petitioner granted summary judgment to Toyota.

JUSTICE O'CONNOR: We conclude that the Court of Appeals did not apply the proper standard in making this determination because it analyzed only a limited class of manual tasks and failed to ask whether respondent's impairments prevented or restricted her from performing tasks that are of central importance to most people's daily lives. . . .

IV

The Court of Appeals' analysis of respondent's claimed disability suggested that in order to prove a substantial limitation in the major life activity of performing manual tasks, a "plaintiff must show that her manual disability involves a 'class' of manual activities," and that those activities "affec[t] the ability to perform tasks at work." Both of these ideas lack support. . . .

While the Court of Appeals in this case addressed the different major life activity of performing manual tasks, its analysis circumvented Sutton by focusing on respondent's inability to perform manual tasks associated only with her job. This was error. When addressing the major life activity of performing manual tasks, the central inquiry must be whether the claimant is unable to perform the variety of tasks central to most people's daily lives, not whether the claimant is unable to perform the tasks associated with her specific job. Otherwise, Sutton's restriction on claims of disability based on a substantial limitation in working will be rendered meaningless because an inability to perform a specific job always can be recast as an inability to perform a "class" of tasks associated with that specific job.

There is also no support in the Act, our previous opinions, or the regulations for the Court of Appeals' idea that the question of whether an impairment constitutes a disability is to be answered only by analyzing the effect of the impairment in the workplace. . . .

Even more critically, the manual tasks unique to any particular job are not necessarily important parts of most people's lives. As a result, occupation-specific tasks may have only limited relevance to the manual task inquiry. In this case, "repetitive work with hands and arms extended at or above shoulder levels for extended periods of time," the manual task on which the Court of Appeals relied, is not an important part of most people's daily lives. The court, therefore, should not have considered respondent's inability to do such manual work in her specialized assembly line job as sufficient proof that she was substantially limited in performing manual tasks.

At the same time, the Court of Appeals appears to have disregarded the very type of evidence that it should have focused upon. It treated as irrelevant "[t]he fact that [respondent] can . . . ten[d] to her personal hygiene [and] carr[y] out personal or household chores." . . . Yet household chores, bathing, and brushing one's teeth are among the types of manual tasks of central importance to people's daily lives, and should have been part of the assessment of whether respondent was substantially limited in performing manual tasks.

The District Court noted that at the time respondent sought an accommodation from petitioner, she admitted that she was able to do the manual tasks required by her original two jobs. . . . In addition, according to respondent's deposition testimony, even after her condition worsened, she could still brush her teeth, wash her face, bathe, tend her flower garden, fix breakfast, do laundry, and pick up around the house. App. 32-34. The record also indicates that her medical conditions caused her to avoid sweeping, to quit dancing, to occasionally seek help dressing, and to reduce how often she plays with her children, gardens, and drives long distances. . . . But these changes in her life did not amount to such severe restrictions in the activities that are of central importance to most people's daily lives that they establish a manual-task disability as a matter of law. On this record, it was therefore inappropriate for the Court of Appeals to grant partial summary judgment to respondent on the issue whether she was substantially limited in performing manual tasks, and its decision to do so must be reversed.

Summary judgment for plaintiff reversed.

CRITICAL THINKING

How does the ambiguity of "manual disability" play a central role in the disagreement between the courts in this case?

ETHICAL DECISION MAKING

What values must be balanced in deciding cases of this type under ADA?

ENFORCEMENT PROCEDURES UNDER ADA

ADA is enforced by the EEOC in the same way that Title VII is enforced. To bring a successful claim under ADA, the plaintiff must show that he or she meets all of the following:

- Had a disability.
- Was otherwise qualified for the job.
- Was excluded from the job solely because of that disability.

Under ADA, the plaintiff may file a charge with the appropriate state agency or with the EEOC within 180 days of the discriminatory act. If a charge has been filed with the state agency, an EEOC charge must be filed within 300 days of the discrimination or within 30 days of receiving notice of the termination of state proceedings, whichever comes first. The charge must identify the defendant and specify the nature of the discriminatory act. On receipt of a charge, the EEOC must notify the accused and attempt to conciliate the matter. If conciliation fails, the EEOC may then bring a civil action against the violator.

REMEDIES FOR VIOLATIONS OF ADA

Remedies for ADA violations are similar to those available under Title VII. A successful plaintiff may recover reinstatement, back pay, and injunctive relief. In cases of intentional discrimination, limited compensatory and punitive damages are also available. An employer who has repeatedly violated the act may be subject to fines of up to $100,000.

Case Nugget Americans with Disabilities Act

Chevron USA, Inc. v. Echazabal
536 U.S. 73 (2002)

Echazabal worked at Chevron's oil refinery in El Segundo, California, in 1972. He was a contract worker who was employed by various maintenance contractors. During most of his work at Chevron, he worked in the coker unit. In 1992, Echazabal applied to work directly for Chevron at the same coker unit location. Chevron denied him employment after a preemployment physical examination showed that he had hepatitis C, indicating that exposure to solvents and chemicals present in the coker unit could damage his liver. Echazabal continued working in the same job for various maintenance contractors, and Chevron made no effort to have him removed. In 1995, Echazabal again applied for a job working directly with Chevron in the coker unit. This time, Chevron not only refused to hire him but asked that Echazabal be immediately removed from the refinery or placed in a position that eliminated his exposure to solvents and chemicals.

Echazabal sued under the Americans with Disabilities Act (ADA), claiming that Chevron's failure to permit him to work in the coker unit was discrimination. Chevron argued that it did not have to permit him to work because of the "direct threat defense," that is, that working in the coker unit would be a direct threat to Echazabal's health. Echazabal argued that the direct threat defense would apply only if he was a direct threat to others, but not to himself. The Ninth Circuit Court of Appeals agreed with Echazabal, but the U.S. Supreme Court reversed, stating that the direct threat defense is allowable when based on a "reasonable medical judgment and/or the best available objective evidence" and on an expressly "individualized assessment of the individual's present ability to safely perform the essential functions of the job." In other words, Echazabal could be denied employment because it presented a threat to his own health.

Equal Pay Act of 1963

When the Equal Pay Act (EPA) was passed, the average wages of women were less than 60 percent of those of men. The primary purpose of the law was to eliminate situations where women, working alongside men or replacing men, would be paid lower wages for doing substantially the same job. The EPA prohibits any employer from discriminating within any "establishment . . . between employees on the basis of sex by paying wages to employees in such establishment at a rate less than the rate at which he pays wages to employees of the opposite sex . . . for equal work on jobs the performance of which requires equal skill, effort, and responsibility, and which are performed under similar working conditions, except where payment is made pursuant to (i) a seniority system; (ii) a merit system; (iii) a system which measures earnings by quantity or quality of production; or (iv) differential based on any factor other than sex."[24]

[24] 29 U.S.C.A. § 206(d)1.

DEFINING *EQUAL WORK* UNDER EPA

The burden of proof in an EPA claim is on the plaintiff to show that the defendant-employer pays unequal wages to men and women for doing equal work at the same establishment. The courts have interpreted *equal* to mean substantially the same in terms of all four factors listed in the act:

- Skill
- Effort
- Responsibility
- Working conditions

The factors are looked at individually. If one job requires greater effort, whereas the other requires greater responsibility, and the other two factors are exactly the same, the jobs are not equal. Thus, a sophisticated employer could vary at least one duty and then pay men and women different wages or salaries. However, to warrant different pay, the differences must be real and not just some minor change added to make the jobs appear different.

The legal standard is that the jobs must be "substantially similar," not perfectly equal. A good illustration of this is the 2002 case of *Hunt v. Nebraska Public Power District.*[25] Lynda Hunt had been a clerk for 17 years in the district office, where she had various clerical duties. The office also employed two other clerks, a district supervisor, a district superintendent, and an office manager. When the district supervisor retired, Lynda Hunt was asked to take on most of his duties, in addition to her old duties, and was told she would receive a pay raise and title change. The former supervisor was earning $3,138 per month when he retired, compared to Hunt's $1,739, which did not change. The duties Hunt took on after her supervisor retired included training, disciplining, and evaluating the performance of other employees, although the actual performance forms were filled out by the remaining office manager. Other office employees testified that after the old supervisor retired, Hunt assumed the retiree's tasks and "ran the office." Hunt prevailed at trial. On appeal, the court found that the minor differences between what Hunt did and what the male supervisor had done were not significant enough to overturn the jury's finding that the jobs were substantially similar.[26]

THE IMPACT OF EXTRA DUTIES UNDER EPA

Another way to attempt to legitimize pay inequities is to give members of one sex additional duties. The courts scrutinize these duties very closely, and require that:

- The extra duties are *actually performed* by those receiving the extra pay.
- The extra duties *regularly* constitute a *significant* portion of the employee's job.
- The extra duties are *substantial,* as opposed to inconsequential.
- The extra duties are commensurate with the pay differential.
- The extra duties are available on a nondiscriminatory basis.

The courts will also make sure that different, comparable additional duties are not imposed on the parties not receiving the additional pay.

[25] 282 F.3d 1021 (8th Cir. 2002)

[26] Ibid.

connecting to the core

Personal Taxation

If a claimant is successful in proving a violation of the Equal Pay Act and receives a significant back-pay award, are these damages taxable? You may recall from your tax class that these damages are indeed taxable as ordinary income because they do not involve physical personal injury.

Source: William Hoffman, Jr., et al., *Individual Income Taxes 2006,* (Thomson, 2006), pp. 6–11.

DEFENSES UNDER EPA

As a business owner or manager, what happens if you are accused of violating EPA? There are four defenses available to the employer:

- A bona fide seniority system.
- A bona fide merit system.
- A pay system based on quality or quantity of output.
- Factors other than sex.

Seniority, merit, and productivity-based wage systems must be enacted in good faith and must be applied to both men and women. At a minimum, employers should have written documentation of these policies. They should also be sure these policies are enforced. In one case, a former employee alleged she was discriminated against because men of the same ability and ranking were consistently given higher merit raises. The employee won, despite the fact that the employer had a written merit system, because she was able to demonstrate that the merit policy was not enforced. By not considering attendance records and positions within the salary grade when giving raises, the employer had violated its own merit-raise policy.[27]

Proving that a factor other than sex resulted in the pay differential often presents great problems. The greater availability of females and their willingness to work for lower wages do *not* constitute factors other than sex. Training programs often fall into this category. A training program that requires that trainees rotate through jobs that are normally paid lower wages will be upheld as long as it is a bona fide training program and not a sham for paying members of one sex higher wages for doing the same job.

REMEDIES FOR VIOLATIONS OF EPA

Plaintiffs may recover back pay in the amount of the difference between what they make and what is paid to members of the opposite sex, plus attorney fees. If the employer was not acting in good faith in paying the discriminatory wage rates, the court will also award the plaintiff damages in an additional amount equal to the back pay.

Discrimination Based on Sexual Orientation—Actionable?

There is currently no federal legislation that prohibits discrimination based on sexual orientation. What does exist are individual state laws that prohibit such discrimination. Discrimination against sexual orientation and gender identity is prohibited in the District of Columbia,

[27] *Ryduchowski v. Port Authority,* 203 F.3d 135 (2d Cir. 2000).

California, Minnesota, New Mexico, and Rhode Island.[28] An additional 10 states prohibit discrimination based solely on sexual orientation. Those states are Connecticut, Hawaii, Maryland, Massachusetts, Nevada, New Hampshire, New Jersey, New York, Vermont, and Wisconsin.[29] Another 11 states have either executive orders, administrative orders, or personnel regulations prohibiting discrimination against public employees based on sexual orientation and/or gender identity.[30]

When the issue is narrowed to relationship recognition (i.e., marriage licenses, civil unions, and spousal rights for unmarried couples), the number of states recognizing such rights becomes much smaller. The only state to issue marriage licenses is Massachusetts.[31] One state, Vermont, permits civil unions that include state-level spousal rights for same-sex couples within the state.[32] Three states provide some spousallike rights to unmarried couples: Hawaii, Maine, and New Jersey. Finally, only one state, California, has a statewide law that provides almost all the state-level spousal rights to unmarried couples.[33]

What do these laws mean to Brad, the employee in our opening scenario? It depends on where Brad lives. If Brad lives in Texas, and he is fired for being gay, he has absolutely no legal rights and cannot sue his employer. Conversely, if Brad lives in California (or one of the above-mentioned states), Brad may sue Jennifer and So Clean, his employer, for discrimination based on sexual orientation. In California and a handful of states, discriminating in terms of employment (i.e., failure to hire, firing, failure to promote) based on a person's sexual orientation is prohibited.

[28] "Human Rights Campaign: Statewide Anti-Discrimination Laws & Policies," www.hrc.org.

[29] Ibid.

[30] Ibid.

[31] "Human Rights Campaign: Relationship Recognition in the U.S.," www.hrc.org (retrieved November 27, 2004).

[32] Ibid.

[33] Ibid.

Case Nugget Sexual Orientation Discrimination

Hope v. California Youth Authority
134 Cal. App. 4th 577 (2005)

Hope got a job as a cook at California Youth Authority (CYA). Not long after he began working there, his supervisors starting calling him derogatory names based on his sexual orientation. Moreover, all cooks, including Hope, were entitled to have "wards" (those incarcerated at the facility) give them substantial assistance with their jobs. Hope was stripped of his wards and forced to work alone. One of Hope's supervisors would take trash and throw it into the areas that Hope had just cleaned. When wards at the facility got physically dangerous toward Hope, he would fill out reports and turn them in to his supervisor. The supervisor would tear up the reports in front of the wards. Hope sued the CYA under California's Fair Employment and Housing Act (FEHA) for discrimination based on sexual orientation, retaliation, and harassment. A jury awarded Hope almost $2 million in damages. CYA appealed.

The appellate court concluded that substantial evidence supported the jury's determinations that Hope was subjected to harassment because of his sexual orientation, the harassment was sufficiently severe or pervasive, Hope's superiors either knew or should have known about the harassment and its cause, and Hope's supervisor did not take immediate and corrective action to stop the harassment.

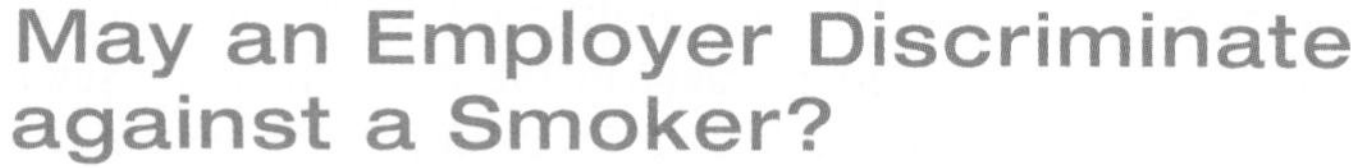

May an Employer Discriminate against a Smoker?

In the opening scenario, Jennifer discovered that Brad was a smoker. Later, she fired him. One of Jennifer's given reasons for terminating Brad's employment was that he was a smoker. May Jennifer and So Clean legally fire an employee for smoking outside the workplace? The answer is, "It depends!"

A recent trend has been for employers to consider a potential-employee's lifestyle when deciding whether to hire that person. Employers argue that smokers have higher health care costs and miss more work, lowering productivity.

> The Centers for Disease Control and Prevention estimated that $75 billion is spent annually on medical expenses attributed to smoking. Businesses lose $82 billion in lost productivity from smokers. And smokers take about 6.5 more sick days a year than nonsmokers. About one in five Americans—or 46 million people—smoke.[34]

As a result, some companies either won't hire smokers or are threatening to fire current employees who will not or are unable to quit smoking. In 2005, Michigan-based Weyco, Inc., announced that it would terminate all workers who did not stop smoking.[35] Many states have passed laws preventing companies from engaging in such action.

> Michigan, with 1.9 million smokers and one of the highest cigarette taxes in the nation, has no "smoker's rights law" found in 29 other states, so there isn't much that employees can do. Weyco terminated four of its employees this month after they refused to submit to a smoking breath test in light of the company's new policy that bans tobacco use among its 200 employees during work and even when they are off the clock. "We are saying people can smoke if they choose to smoke. That's their choice," said Gary Climes, Weyco's chief financial officer. "But they just can't work for us."[36]

If Brad lives in Michigan, Jennifer and So Clean may legally terminate him for smoking outside the workplace. Conversely, if Brad works in any of the 29 states with "smoker's rights laws," he could not be legally terminated for smoking outside the workplace. Finally, employers should be aware that giving breaks on health care plans to employees who are nonsmokers could be in violation of "smoker's rights law."

Employment Discrimination Internationally

With many American firms having operations overseas, the question of the extent to which the U.S. laws prohibiting discrimination apply in foreign countries naturally arises. The Civil Rights Act of 1991 extended the protections of Title VII and ADA to U.S. citizens working abroad for American employers. Amendments to ADEA in 1984 had already extended that act's protection in a similar manner. The provisions of these acts also apply to foreign corporations controlled by a U.S. employer.

It is not always easy to determine whether a multinational corporation will be considered "American" enough to be covered by U.S. antidiscrimination laws. According to guidelines issued by the EEOC in October 1993, the EEOC will first consider where the

[34] "Workers Fume as Firms Ban Smoking at Home," www.detnews.com/2005/business/0501/27/A01-71823.htm.

[35] Ibid.

[36] Ibid.

global context

Legal Discrimination against Women in Saudi Arabia

In Saudi Arabia, not only are women not entitled to pay equal to that of men, but there are actual legal statutes sanctioning discrimination against women in both public and private situations. Women, who are not even allowed to drive, constitute only 5 percent of Saudi Arabia's workforce. This number may not be surprising considering the limited labor opportunities for women. The law severely limits the industries in which women can be employed. Women are forbidden to receive business licenses if they may have to interact with males or government officials. If a woman is fortunate enough to find a job, it will probably be in education or health care. Some women can be found in various retail businesses or the banking industry.

Despite its difficulties, finding a job may be easy in comparison to the discrimination Saudi Arabian women will face at work. For instance, all places of employment are segregated by sex. The only way women can be in contact with a man is by telephone or electronic exchange. Many women complain of sexual and physical abuse while on the job. These complaints come from women at all levels in the workforce, from sweatshops to hospitals. And their situation is made worse because they have basically no legal redress. The courts have unreasonably strict evidentiary rules for harassment and discrimination cases. These rules, as well as the social shame that would arise from trying to challenge a man in public, deter women from seeking a legal solution to discriminatory treatment.

company is incorporated. If the company is not incorporated, the EEOC will evaluate factors such as the company's principal place of business, the nationality of the controlling shareholders, and the nationality and location of management. No one factor is considered determinative, and the greater the number of factors linking the employer to the United States, the more likely the employer is to be considered "American."

To determine whether a foreign corporation is controlled by an American employer, the EEOC will again look at a broad range of factors. Some such factors include the interrelation of operations, common management, centralized labor relations, and common ownership or financial control over the two entities. A corporation that is clearly a foreign corporation and not controlled by an American entity is not subject to U.S. equal employment laws.

CASE OPENER WRAP-UP

Brad versus So Clean and Jennifer

At the beginning of this chapter, you were confronted with the situation between Brad and Jennifer. By now you should be able to answer all the questions presented to you.

In many states, an employee can legally be fired based on sexual orientation. Discrimination in this area is based solely on state law. There is no federal protection against discrimination based on being gay. Similarly, firing an employee for smoking (including off the job) is also a state law issue. In Michigan, for example, such a firing would be legal. Many states are now passing laws preventing employers from firing those who smoke outside the workplace.

Brad is an at-will employee, but that does not mean that he can be fired for an illegal (i.e., discriminatory) reason. Laws protecting employees against sex discrimination and sexual harassment are just as applicable to men as they are to women. Anyone who is treated in a discriminatory way "based on sex" may sue under the appropriate state or federal antidiscrimination laws. Most, though not all states, have their own state laws against discrimination and harassment. States may give more protection than federal laws but not less protection. There are still a few states that have no state laws against discrimination (one such state is Georgia).

These are basic issues that every employer and employee should be familiar with. Remember, knowledge is power. The more you know, the better off you and your business will be.

Summary

When May an Employee Be Fired?

At-will employment means that any employee who is not employed under a contract or a collective bargaining agreement may quit at any time for any reason or no reason at all, with no required notice to the employer. Moreover, the employer may fire the employee at any time, with no notice, for almost any reason.

Federal Laws Governing Employers

Federal employment laws provide a minimum level of protection for employees. The states may give employees more rights, but not less rights, than they have under federal law.

Civil Rights Act —Title VII

Title VII of CRA (1964, as amended by the Civil Rights Act of 1991) protects employees against discrimination based on race, color, religion, national origin, and sex. It also prohibits harassment based on the same protected categories. Defenses to a charge of discrimination under Title VII include *merit, seniority,* and *bona fide occupational qualification (BFOC).*

Disparate treatment: If the employee has been hired, fired, denied a promotion, and so on, based on membership in a protected class under Title VII, this is a form of intentional discrimination and qualifies the employee to sue for disparate-treatment discrimination.

Disparate impact: Disparate-impact cases arise when a plaintiff attempts to establish that while an employer's policy or practice appears to apply to everyone equally, its actual effect is that it disproportionately limits employment opportunities for a protected class.

Sexual harassment: Sexual harassment includes unwelcome sexual advances, requests for sexual favors, and other verbal or physical conduct of a sexual nature that implicitly or explicitly makes submission a term or condition of employment; makes employment decisions related to the individual dependent on submission to or rejection of such conduct; or has the purpose or effect of creating an intimidating, hostile, or offensive work environment. Two recognized forms are *hostile-environment* and *quid pro quo* harassment.

Pregnancy Discrimination Act of 1987: PDA amended Title VII of CRA to expand the definition of sex discrimination to include discrimination based on pregnancy.

Age Discrimination in Employment Act of 1967

ADEA prohibits employers from refusing to hire, discharging, or discriminating in terms and conditions of employment on the basis of an employee's or applicant's being age 40 or older.

Americans with Disabilities Act

ADA prohibits discrimination against employees and job applicants with disabilities.

Equal Pay Act of 1963

EPA prohibits an employer from paying workers of one gender less than the wages paid to employees of the opposite gender for work that requires equal skill, effort, and responsibility.

Discrimination Based on Sexual Orientation—Actionable?	In many states, an employee can legally be fired based on sexual orientation. Discrimination in this area is based solely on state law. There is no federal protection against discrimination based on sexual orientation.
May an Employer Discriminate against a Smoker?	In many states, an employer may fire or refuse to hire an employee who smokes, even outside the workplace. Approximately 29 states, however, have "smokers' rights" laws that prohibit such employment action.
Employment Discrimination Internationally	The Civil Rights Act of 1991 extended the protections of Title VII and ADA to U.S. citizens working abroad for American employers. The provisions of these acts also apply to foreign corporations controlled by a U.S. employer.

Point / Counterpoint

Should Employers Be Permitted to Fire Employees for Activities, Such as Smoking, That They Do Outside Working Hours?

Yes	No
The Centers for Disease Control and Prevention estimated that $75 billion is spent annually on medical expenses attributed to smoking. Businesses lose $82 billion in lost productivity from smokers. Smokers take about 6.5 more sick days a year than nonsmokers.	Employers should have no say in what employees do outside the workplace. Forcing employees to take tests to reveal whether they are smokers is an invasion of the employees' privacy. Many employees are addicted to cigarettes and would unfairly lose badly needed employment if unable to quit smoking.

Questions & Problems

1. Name five statutes that prohibit discrimination in employment.
2. How is *equal work* defined under the Equal Pay Act?
3. Why is a disparate-impact case more difficult to establish than a disparate-treatment case?
4. Does Title VII apply to same-sex harassment?
5. Whom does the Age Discrimination in Employment Act protect?
6. List the protected classes under the Civil Rights Act of 1964 (as amended in 1991).
7. Machinchick worked for PB Power for six years. He received excellent reviews. Two years after beginning work, he was promoted to vice president. Four years after his promotion, Machinchick got a new supervisor and the company adopted a new management approach. The new supervisor, Knowlton, stated his plan to "hand-pick employees whose mindset resides in the 21st Century." On April 7, 2002, Knowlton sent an e-mail in which he stated that he wanted to "strategically hire some younger engineers and designers." Two days later, Knowlton sent an e-mail to the Human

Resources Department criticizing Machinchick's performance. A short time later, Machinchick, age 63, was fired. He was told to turn over his client base to Betz, age 42. Machinchick sued PB Power, alleging it had violated the Age Discrimination in Employment Act. The trial court granted motion for summary judgment in favor of PB Power. Machinchick appealed. How should the appellate court decide? Has Machinchick shown enough evidence of age discrimination to warrant allowing the case to be heard by a jury? Explain your decision. [*Machinchick v. PB Power, Inc.*, 398 F.3d 345 (5th Cir. 2005).]

8. Jermer worked as an engineer at Siemens Energy & Automation, Inc. After complaints about air quality at the facility, Siemens had its insurance company do some testing. The results were inconclusive. The following year, after additional complaints by employees, Jermer asked the company to install certain types of filters. Jermer's supervisor, Kroeger, rejected the idea. Shortly after, Kroeger was told he needed to fire one of the four engineers in his department. Kroeger recommended firing Jermer. After that recommendation, but before Jermer was told, Jermer made a complaint to the company's ethics hotline about the air quality. The claim was investigated and thrown out. Jermer was fired. He sued, alleging that he was fired for being a whistle-blower (i.e., for complaining about the air quality). The trial court granted motion for summary judgment for the company, and Jermer appealed. Did Jermer state a proper claim for retaliatory termination (i.e., because he was a whistle-blower)? What do you think the appellate court decided? [*Jermer v. Siemens Energy & Automation, Inc.*, 395 F.3d 655 (6th Cir. 2005).]

9. Jennifer Erickson was employed by Bartell Drug Company. Jennifer sued Bartell Drug Company because its insurance plan failed to provide coverage for prescription contraceptives. She alleged that this was a form of sex discrimination under Title VII and a violation of the Pregnancy Discrimination Act. Her employer defended by arguing that its failure to provide coverage for prescription contraceptives did not violate Title VII or the PDA because contraceptives were voluntary, were preventive, and did not treat or prevent an illness or disease and because control of one's fertility was not pregnancy, childbirth, or a related medical condition under PDA. If you were the court, how would you decide? Is failure to provide insurance coverage of prescription contraceptives a form of sex discrimination? Or pregnancy discrimination? Both? Neither? Explain the reasons for your answer. [*Erickson v. Bartell Drug Co.*, 141 F. Supp. 2d 1266 (U.S. Dist. Ct., Wash., 2001).]

10. Patricia Corley and Joseph Smith were employed by the Detroit Board of Education to work in its adult education program. Corley was employed part-time as a counselor, and Smith was her supervisor. During the course of their employment, Corley and Smith became romantically involved in a relationship that lasted three or four years. The relationship ended when Smith started dating another employee, Barbara Finch. Corley alleged that after Smith and Finch became involved, Smith repeatedly threatened her with adverse employment action if she said or did anything that interfered with his relationship with Finch. Corley also alleged that Finch taunted, embarrassed, and humiliated her by causing her workstation to be moved and by engaging in "catty" conversations with others that were about her and intended to be overheard by her. According to Corley, the alleged harassment culminated when she was discharged at the conclusion of the 1995–1996 school year. Does Corley have a claim for sexual harassment? Explain your reasoning. [*Corley v. Detroit Bd. of Ed.*, 470 Mich. 274 (Mich. Sup. Ct. 2004).]

11. Danilo Peralta began working for Avondale Industries in 1990 as an outside machinist in the ship-building department. On July 30, 2001, he sustained "severe personal injury"

when his supervisor struck him with a metal chair. Peralta was unable to work and was placed on temporary total disability. Peralta attempted to return to work on August 1, 2002, and October 1, 2002, but could not be medically cleared. Peralta was found to be permanently disabled by an administrative law judge in a longshoremen's proceeding. Avondale fired Peralta on February 4, 2003, for failure to return from a leave of absence. Peralta then sued Avondale, alleging violation of the Americans with Disabilities Act. In his deposition, Peralta explained that his knee injury is his only claimed disability. He explained that he is able to walk, although not for long. He does not use crutches or a wheelchair, although he does use a velcro-type wrap brace. Peralta is able to feed himself, bathe, dress, cook, carry small items, and drive a car, although his knee bothers him when he drives. He admitted that he drives for himself and his parents notwithstanding that his medication blurs his vision and makes him dizzy. Peralta repeatedly identified his inability to work as the only major life activity that he is now unable to do as a result of his impairment, that is, his injured knee. Does Peralta have a claim for disability under ADA? Explain your reasoning. [*Peralta v. Avondale Industries,* 2004 U.S. Dist. LEXIS 22640 (16 Am. Disabilities Cas (BNA) 889; 2004).]

12. Christina Hackett sued her former employer, Clifton Gunderson, L.L.C. (CG), for CG's decision to terminate her while she was on maternity leave. Hackett alleges that the termination constituted unlawful pregnancy discrimination in violation of the Pregnancy Discrimination Act. Hackett became pregnant with her second child a few months after she started working for CG, and in the fall she announced her pregnancy. According to Hackett, her supervisor questioned her several times during her pregnancy about whether she would return to work after the birth of her second child, each time showing skepticism when she announced her intent to return to work after taking maternity leave. Her supervisor also allegedly expressed concern about Hackett's ability to handle two children and a job and about the impact Hackett's pregnancy might have on the team. Hackett continued to work until the birth of her daughter, when she began a 12-week FMLA maternity leave. She was scheduled to return to work on July 1; however, on June 27, Hackett was informed that her office was being consolidated into another office and, as a result, she was being terminated. Hackett provided the court with a prima facie case of discrimination. CG argued that Hackett's job was eliminated due to downsizing (i.e., not her pregnancy). Does Hackett have enough evidence to show that CG's business justification is a mere pretext? Why or why not? If you were the judge, would you grant summary judgment for CG and throw out the case? Or would you let Hackett proceed to a trial on the merits? [*Hackett v. Clifton Gunderson, L.L.C.,* 2004 U.S. Dist. LEXIS 21919 (N.D. Ill. 2004).

13. Barie Hamilton worked as a retail store manager for Bally of Switzerland. She claimed that she was sexually harassed by her female supervisor and that she was fired and given negative references because she filed a complaint about the supervisor's behavior. The employer claimed that the employee was fired because her store was losing money. Hamilton alleged that her supervisor's behavior included telling her that the supervisor was gay, inviting Hamilton for drinks after work, complimenting her appearance, and touching her breast on one occasion. Bally alleges that Hamilton was fired after a worldwide reorganization of the company. The question before the court is whether Hamilton has pled sufficient facts to constitute hostile-environment sexual harassment? What do you think the court decided? Why? [*Hamilton v. Bally of Switzerland,* 2005 U.S. Dist. LEXIS 9319 (S.D.N.Y. 2005).]

14. Following separate lawsuits by female prisoners in Michigan and by the Civil Rights Division of the U.S. Department of Justice, both of which alleged rampant sexual abuse of female prisoners in Michigan, the Michigan Department of Corrections (MDOC) barred males from working in certain positions at its female prisons. Specifically, the MDOC designated approximately 250 correctional officer and residential unit officer positions in housing units at female prisons as "female only." A group of MDOC employees, both males and females, sued the MDOC, alleging that the MDOC's plan violated Title VII of the Civil Rights Act of 1964. The issue before the court was whether gender was a bona fide occupational qualification for the positions in question. How do you think the court should rule? Why? [*Everson v. Michigan Dept. of Corrections,* 391 F.3d 737 (6th Cir. 2004).]

15. Anthony Romeo was an openly gay student at Seton Hall, a Catholic university. He claimed that he elected to attend Seton Hall in part because of its published antidiscrimination policy. In 2003, he applied to the Seton Hall University Department of Student Affairs for provisional recognition of a gay and lesbian student organization. Dr. Laura Wankel, vice president of Student Affairs at Seton Hall, responded to Romeo's application in a letter, stating in pertinent part: "I am informing you that your application for provisional recognition has been denied. No organization based solely upon sexual orientation may receive formal University recognition." Wankel went on to say that "the Division of Student Affairs remains prepared to work with gay and lesbian students to meet their needs. I am committed to working collaboratively with you and other students in fostering a positive, safe and caring community." Wankel then made a modest proposal giving the group some rights. The proposal, however, was not satisfactory to the students, and Romeo filed his complaint alleging violations of New Jersey's Law against Discrimination. He also cited Seton Hall's nondiscrimination policy: "No person may be denied employment or related benefits or admission to the University or to any of its programs or activities, either academic or nonacademic, curricular or extracurricular, because of race, color, religion, age, national origin, gender, sexual orientation, handicap and disability, or veteran's status." How should the court rule? May a Catholic university prevent recognition of a gay and lesbian student organization? Does the university's nondiscrimination policy make a difference? Why or why not? [*Romeo v. Seton Hall University,* 2005 N.J. Super. LEXIS 197 (N.J. Sup. Ct. 2005).]

Looking for more review material?

The Online Learning Center at **www.mhhe.com/kubasek1e** contains this chapter's "Assignment on the Internet" and also a list of URLs for more information, entitled "On the Internet." Find both of them in the Student Center portion of the OLC, along with quizzes and other helpful materials.

Administrative Law

CASE OPENER

Does the EPA Have an Obligation to Regulate Automobile Emissions?

On October 20, 1999, a group of 19 private organizations filed a rule-making petition asking the Environmental Protection Agency (EPA) to regulate "greenhouse gas emissions from new motor vehicles" under the Clean Air Act.[1] The petitioners cited the fact that 1998 was the "warmest year on record," that greenhouse gas emissions have significantly accelerated climate change, and that carbon dioxide is the most important man-made contribution to climate change. Fifteen months after the petition was filed, the EPA requested public comment on the issues. Then, on September 8, 2003, the EPA entered an order denying the rule-making petition, citing two reasons: (1) The Clean Air Act does not authorize the EPA to issue mandatory regulations to address global climate change; and (2) even if the agency had authority, it would be unwise to do so at this time. The case, *Massachusetts v. EPA,* eventually worked its way up to the U.S. Supreme Court, which had to decide whether the EPA was improperly failing to regulate carbon dioxide gas in automobile exhaust as a climate-changing pollutant.

1. What is rule making, and how does it work?
2. What, if any, limits are there on an agency's authority to regulate?
3. When may the courts review an agency decision?

The Wrap-Up at the end of the chapter will answer these questions.

[1] *Massachusetts v. EPA,* 127 S.Ct. 1438 (2007).

CHAPTER 44

Learning Objectives

After you have studied this chapter, you will be able to answer the following questions:

1. What is administrative law?
2. What is an administrative agency?
3. What types of powers do administrative agencies have?
4. How and why are administrative agencies created?
5. What is the difference between an executive agency and an independent agency?
6. What is the Administrative Procedures Act?
7. What is the *Federal Register?*
8. Describe the differences between formal and informal rule making.
9. What is hybrid rule making?
10. What are the limits on agency power?

Introduction to Administrative Law

WHAT IS ADMINISTRATIVE LAW?

As a business owner or manager, you will need to be aware of regulations that will affect your business. In addition to learning about laws passed by Congress, you will also need to know about rules passed by administrative agencies. **Administrative law** consists of the substantive and procedural rules created by **administrative agencies** (government bodies of the city, county, state, or federal government) involving applications, licenses, permits, available information, hearings, appeals, and decision making.

An administrative agency is generally defined as any body created by the legislative branch (e.g., Congress, a state legislature, or a city council) to carry out specific duties. Agencies have three types of power: *legislative, judicial,* and *executive.* They may make rules for an entire industry, adjudicate individual cases, and investigate corporate misconduct. Because legislative, judicial, and executive powers have traditionally been placed in separate branches of government by the Constitution, the role of administrative agencies has led some to refer to agencies as the unofficial **"fourth branch of government."** Although there is a semblance of truth to that characterization, administrative agencies are not in fact another branch, primarily because all their authority is simply delegated to them and they remain under the control of the three traditional branches of government.

The first federal administrative agency, the **Interstate Commerce Commission (ICC),** was created by Congress near the end of the 19th century. Congress felt that the anticompetitive conduct of railroads could best be controlled by a regulatory body. The ICC no longer exists as a separate agency,[2] but for over 100 years the ICC regulated passenger and freight transportation. Following the crash of the stock market and the Great Depression of the 1930s, Congress saw a need for additional agencies that could assist in guiding market decisions in the public interest. Since then, numerous agencies have been created whenever Congress believed there was an area that required more intense regulation than Congress could provide. In fact, after the Enron scandal there was talk that Congress might create a new agency to regulate the accounting industry. To date, no such agency has materialized.

WHY AND HOW ARE AGENCIES CREATED?

When Congress sees a problem that it believes needs regulation, it may create an administrative agency to deal with that problem. The idea is that the agency can be staffed with people who have special expertise in the area the agency is regulating and therefore are capable of knowing what types of regulations are necessary to protect the citizens in that area. Agencies typically act more swiftly than Congress in creating and enacting new laws. Today, administrative agencies actually create more rules than Congress and the courts combined.

Administrative agencies are created by Congress through passage of **enabling legislation,** which is a statute that specifies the name, functions, and specific powers of the administrative agency. The enabling statutes grant agencies broad powers for the purpose of serving the "public interest, convenience, and necessity." These broad powers include rule making, investigation, and adjudication.

Rule making. Enabling statutes permit administrative agencies to issue rules that control individual and business behavior. These rules are, in effect, laws. If an individual or business fails to comply with agency rules, there are often civil, as well as criminal, penalties. Agencies may enact three types of rules: procedural, interpretive, and legislative.

[2] The functions of the ICC were transferred to the Transportation Department by Congress as part of a cost-saving measure.

Procedural rules are rules regarding the internal operations of an agency. *Interpretive rules* are rules that explain how the agency views the meaning of the statutes for which the agency has administrative responsibility. Finally, *legislative rules* are policy expressions that have the effect of law. The various rule-making processes will be discussed later in this chapter.

Investigation. Enabling statutes grant executive power to agencies to investigate potential violations of rules or statutes. Many times, companies cooperate with agencies and voluntarily furnish information. Other times, however, agencies must use their investigative powers, defined in their enabling legislation, to gather information. Such powers typically include the power to issue a **subpoena** (i.e., an order to appear at a particular time and place and provide testimony) and a **subpoena *duces tecum*** (i.e., an order to appear and bring specified documents). Case 44-1 demonstrates the broad powers given to agencies to investigate willful violations of agency rules.

CASE 44-1 | LAKELAND ENTERPRISES OF RHINELANDER, INC. v. CHAO

SEVENTH CIRCUIT COURT OF APPEALS
402 F.3D 739 (7TH CIR. 2005)

Lakeland is a northern Wisconsin sewer and water contractor. In August 2002 the company was engaged in an excavation project to install sewer and water lines on a public street in the Mill Creek Industrial Park development in Marshfield, Wisconsin. The citation at issue here arose from an August 28 impromptu inspection conducted by Chad Greenwood, an OSHA compliance officer who was driving by the industrial park project and noticed the excavation in progress. Greenwood parked his car, walked past some traffic cones blocking street traffic from the site, and observed Lakeland employee Ron Krueger excavating a trench with a backhoe. Greenwood also observed another Lakeland employee, Tony Noth, working at the bottom of the trench. The trench contained neither a ladder nor a trench box, a device used to prop up the walls and prevent collapse.

Greenwood began videotaping the scene, at which point Jim Gust, the project superintendent, asked him to step back and informed him that the road was closed. Greenwood explained that he was an OSHA compliance officer and indicated the nature of the inspection. While Gust and Greenwood were speaking, Noth began climbing up one of the walls of the trench. Greenwood observed loose dirt falling back into the trench, apparently unsettled by Noth's feet as he scaled the slope. Krueger later admitted that he knew Noth was not supposed to be working in the trench and that he failed to remove him. After Noth climbed out of the trench, Krueger told him he should not have been working in the trench without a trench box. Krueger then resumed the excavation. . . . The slope of the trench walls concerned Greenwood. Sloping is "a method of protecting employees from cave-ins by excavating to form sides of an excavation that are inclined away from the excavation so as to prevent cave-ins." 29 C.F.R. § 1926.650(b). Eyeballing the trench, Greenwood believed the walls were too steep and there was a fair chance they could collapse. Greenwood measured the slope of the trench walls. . . . Greenwood also took soil samples. . . .

Based on the soil samples and Greenwood's measurements of both the soil quality and the trench dimensions, OSHA's office in Madison, Wisconsin, issued three citations to Lakeland, including the citation at issue on this review—willfully permitting an employee to work in a trench without adequate protection (inadequately sloped trench walls). . . .

CIRCUIT JUDGE SYKES: Lakeland argues that Greenwood's warrantless inspection violated the Fourth Amendment and that the evidence seized in the inspection should have been suppressed. The

ALJ [Administrative Law Judge] denied Lakeland's suppression motion, concluding that Lakeland had no right of privacy on a jobsite on a public roadway and that the excavation site was covered by the "open fields" doctrine. The ALJ also found waiver because Lakeland did not object to the inspection and ask for a warrant at the scene . . . the ALJ correctly concluded that any Fourth Amendment objection was waived because Lakeland did not object to Greenwood's inspection and request a warrant at the scene. . . . The evidence indicates that although Gust initially told Greenwood that the road was closed, when Greenwood identified himself as an OSHA compliance officer and announced the reason for his presence, Lakeland employees acquiesced and cooperated in the inspection. Although perhaps more properly characterized as consent rather than waiver, the ALJ's conclusion that Lakeland waived any Fourth Amendment objection to the inspection is consistent with case law in this circuit.

CRITICAL THINKING

What are the key facts responsible for Judge Sykes's opinion? What facts would have needed to be different for Judge Sykes to have overturned the ALJ?

ETHICAL DECISION MAKING

This case is typical in that it rests on certain value preferences. Do you believe that the value preferences of the judges shape which facts they tend to weight heavily in a case?

Adjudication. Enabling statutes delegate judicial power to agencies to settle or adjudicate individual disputes that an agency may have with businesses or individuals. After investigation, the agency will hold an administrative hearing before an **administrative law judge (ALJ).** The ALJ will try to convince the parties to reach a settlement via a **consent order** but also has the authority to render a binding decision (**order**) after a hearing (administrative law matters are heard only by the ALJ, as there is no right to a jury trial in administrative agencies). An appeal to the full commission or the head of an agency may then be filed. That decision may then be appealed to the circuit court of appeals. If there are no appeals, the ALJ's initial order becomes the final order. Decisions of the ALJ are typically upheld.

Example of an administrative problem. The EPA administrator, using the congressional mandate under the Clean Air Act, sets forth rules governing the amount of certain hazardous air pollutants that may be emitted into the atmosphere. Using these standards, another branch of the EPA sends investigators to inspect a plant suspected of violating the act. If the inspector finds a violation and the EPA imposes a penalty, the plant operator will most likely contest the imposition of the fine, and a hearing will be held before an ALJ employed in another division of the EPA. If the matter is not settled at the hearing, the ALJ will preside over another hearing and render a binding order. That order may be appealed within the agency and finally to the federal court. The courts, however, typically defer to the expertise of the agency and the associated ALJ. In other words, most orders by an ALJ are upheld.

Case Nugget Appeal of Administrative Decision

Murphy et al. v. New Milford Zoning Commission et al.
402 F.3d 342 (2005)

The Murphys own a single-family home located on a cul-de-sac lined with six other single-family homes. The Murphys had been hosting Sunday afternoon prayer group meetings since 1994 and claimed that because of Robert Murphy's severe illness their home was the only acceptable location to host such meetings. The number of people who attended the meetings varied, ranging from as few as 10 to perhaps as many as 60 participants. In August 2000, New Milford's zoning office and the New Milford Zoning Commission received complaints from the Murphys' neighbors regarding the prayer meetings. Neighbors complained of large numbers of cars traveling to and from the Murphys' home, of these cars parking in the street and causing access problems, and of excessive noise when meeting attendees departed. In response, the Zoning Commission directed the zoning enforcement officer (ZEO) to investigate. The ZEO presented her findings to the Zoning Commission, which in turn issued an opinion concluding that the weekly, sizable prayer meetings were not a customary accessory use in a single-family residential area. Based on this opinion, on November 29, 2000, the ZEO sent the Murphys an informal letter advising them that their meetings violated zoning regulations. Two days later the Murphys sued New Milford, alleging numerous constitutional and statutory claims. Thereafter, on December 19, 2000, the ZEO issued a formal cease-and-desist order charging the Murphys with violating New Milford's single-family zoning regulations. The Murphys did not appeal the cease-and-desist order to the Zoning Board of Appeals, where they could have sought a variance from the zoning regulations. (A *variance* is authority granted to a property owner to use his property in a manner forbidden by the zoning regulations.) The court held that the Murphys had prematurely commenced their lawsuit. Until the variance and appeals process was exhausted and a final, definitive decision from local zoning authorities was rendered, the dispute remained a matter of unique local import, over which the court lacked jurisdiction.

Different Types of Administrative Agencies

Agencies are classified as either executive or independent. The administrative head of an **executive agency** is appointed by the president with the advice and consent of the U.S. Senate. Executive-agency heads may be discharged by the president at any time, for any reason. When a new president is elected, he or she will typically place his or her appointees in charge of executive agencies. These agencies are generally located within the executive branch, under one of the cabinet-level departments. Hence, executive agencies are referred to as *cabinet-level agencies.* Examples of traditional executive agencies are the Federal Aviation Agency (FAA), located within the Department of Transportation, and the Food and Drug Administration (FDA), located within the Department of Health and Human Services.

Independent agencies are governed by a board of commissioners, one of whom is the chair. The president appoints the commissioners of independent agencies with the advice

Exhibit 44-1 Major Administrative Agencies

INDEPENDENT AGENCIES	EXECUTIVE AGENCIES
Commodity Futures Trading Commission (CFTC)	Federal Deposit Insurance Corporation (FDIC)
Consumer Product Safety Commission (CPSC)	General Services Administration (GSA)
Equal Employment Opportunity Commission (EEOC)	International Development Corporation Agency (IDCA)
Federal Communications Commission (FCC)	National Aeronautics and Space Administration (NASA)
Federal Trade Commission (FTC)	National Science Foundation (NSF)
Interstate Commerce Commission (ICC)	Occupational Safety and Health Administration (OSHA)
National Labor Relations Board (NLRB)	Office of Personnel Management (OPM)
Nuclear Regulatory Commission (NRC)	Small Business Administration (SBA)
Securities and Exchange Commission (SEC)	Veterans Administration (VA)

and consent of the Senate, but these commissioners serve fixed terms and cannot be removed except for cause. No more than a simple majority of an independent agency can be members of any single political party (e.g., if the board consists of seven members, no more than four may be from the same political party). Serving fixed terms is said to make the commissioners less accountable to the will of the executive (thus the term *independent* agency). These agencies are generally not located within any department. Examples of independent agencies are the Federal Trade Commission (FTC), the Securities and Exchange Commission (SEC), and the Federal Communications Commission (FCC).

Another difference between these two types of agencies is the scope of their regulatory authority. Executive agencies tend to have responsibility for making rules covering a broad spectrum of industries and activities. Independent agencies, often called *commissions,* tend to have more narrow authority over many facets of a particular industry, focusing on such activities as rate making and licensing. Executive agencies have a tendency to focus more on *social regulation,* whereas independent agencies are more often focused on what we refer to as primarily *economic regulation.* Exhibit 44-1 provides a summary of the major administrative agencies.

Some agencies do not fall clearly into one classification or the other. These agencies are typically referred to as **hybrid agencies**. Created as one type of agency, the body may share characteristics of the other. The EPA, for example, was created as an independent agency, not located within any department of the executive branch. Yet it is headed by a single administrator who serves at the whim of the president. During the early 1990s, in fact, there were discussions of the need to transform the EPA into a cabinet-level executive agency. (These initiatives did not get beyond the discussion stage.) Another example is the "independent" Federal Energy Regulation Commission (FERC), which has the typical structure of an independent agency yet is located within the Department of Energy.

How Are Agencies Run?

In 1946 Congress passed the **Administrative Procedures Act (APA)** as a major limitation on how agencies are run. Prior to passage of APA, agencies could decide on their own how to make rules, conduct investigations, and hold hearings and trials. Under APA, there are very specific guidelines on rule making by agencies. The two most common types of rule making are informal and formal; each is discussed below. A third type of rule making, known as *hybrid,* will also be discussed. There are also a few exemptions that will be discussed.

INFORMAL RULE MAKING

The primary type of rule making used by administrative agencies is **informal rule making,** or **notice-and-comment rule making.** Informal rule making applies in all situations where the agency's enabling legislation or other congressional directives do not require another form. An agency initiates informal rule making by publishing the proposed rule in the *Federal Register,* along with an explanation of the legal authority for issuing the rule and a description of how the public can participate in the rule-making process.

Exhibit 44-2 Stages of Informal Rule Making

1. **Agency drafts a rule in consultation with interested parties.**
2. **Proposed rule is published in the *Federal Register.***
3. **Interested parties can file written comments on the written draft within a 30-day period from publication in the *Federal Register.***
4. **Final draft of the rule is published in the *Federal Register* 30 days before it takes effect. A statement of its purpose and cost-benefit analysis must accompany its publication.**
5. **Agency receives feedback from interested parties during the 30-day period and makes a decision on whether the final draft should be rewritten. If not, it becomes law.**

Following this publication, opportunity is provided for all interested parties to submit written comments. These comments may contain data, arguments, or other information a person believes might influence the agency in its decision making. Although the agency is not required to hold hearings, it has the discretion to receive oral testimony if it wishes to do so. While the agency is not required to respond to all comments it receives, it is required to respond to comments that significantly concern the proposed rule. After considering the comments, the agency may alter the rule. It publishes the final rule, with a statement of its basis and purpose, in the *Federal Register.* This publication also includes the date on which the rule becomes effective, which must be at least 30 days after publication. Exhibit 44-2 summarizes this process.

Informal rule making is most often used because it is more efficient for the agency in terms of time and cost. No formal public hearing is required, and no formal record need be established. Some people believe that informal rule making is unfair because parties who are interested in the proposed rule have no idea what types of evidence the agency has received from other sources with respect to that rule. Thus, if the agency is relying on what one party might perceive as flawed or biased data, that party has no way to challenge that data.

FORMAL RULE MAKING

The APA requires **formal rule making** when an enabling statute or other legislation requires that all regulations or rules be enacted by an agency as part of a formal hearing process that includes a complete transcript. This procedure is initiated in the same manner as is informal rule making, beginning with publication of a notice of proposed rule making by the agency in the *Federal Register.*

The second step in formal rule making is a public hearing at which witnesses give testimony on the pros and cons of the proposed rule and are subject to cross-examination. An official transcript of the hearing is kept. Based on information received at the hearing, the agency makes and publishes formal findings. On the basis of these findings, an agency may or may not promulgate a regulation. If a regulation is adopted, the final rule is published in the *Federal Register.* Because of the expense and time involved in obtaining a formal transcript and record, most enabling statutes do not require a formal rule-making procedure when promulgating regulations. If a statute is drafted in a manner that is at all ambiguous with respect to the type of rule making required, the court will *not* interpret the law as requiring formal rule making.

Case Nugget Formal Rule Making

Alexis Perez v. John Ashcroft
236 F. Supp. 2d 899 (2002)

Perez, a native and citizen of Venezuela, had been a member of El Buen Pastor since November 1996. Beginning in December 1996 he had worked as that congregation's music director, a full-time paid position. Under the law, a limited number of visas are available to an immigrant who, among other things, seeks to enter the United States to work for an organization in a professional capacity in a religious vocation or occupation. The Immigration and Naturalization Service (INS) denied Perez's visa application based on his lack of religious training. Perez argued that the INS adopted the requirement of religious training in violation of the Administrative Procedures Act (APA), because it is a substantive rule adopted without the use of notice and comment or other formal rule-making procedures. Perez argued that he met all the requirements specified by APA and INS regulations and, further, that the INS regulations contained no mention of a formal-religious-training requirement. INS countered that its imposition of the formal-training requirement—and its denial of Perez's visa request because he lacked that training—simply represented a reasonable interpretation of the INS regulations and that Perez's visa application was properly denied because he had no such training. There is no dispute that INS did not engage in any sort of formal rule-making process before adopting the requirement of formal religious training. The INS argued that the formal-training requirement was simply an interpretation of their regulations—more specifically, of the definition of "religious occupation"—and that therefore no formal rule making was necessary. The court disagreed. All substantive rules adopted by an agency, that is, rules that create law, must be implemented through formal rule-making procedures.

HYBRID RULE MAKING

After agencies began regularly making rules in accordance with the appropriate procedures, the flaws of each type of rule making became increasingly apparent. In response to these problems, a form of hybrid rule making became acceptable to the courts and legislature. Hybrid rule making is an attempt to combine the best features of both formal and informal rule making. The starting point, publication in the *Federal Register,* is the same. Publication is followed by the opportunity for submission of written comments, and then there is an informal public hearing with a more restricted opportunity for cross-examination than that in formal rule making. The publication of the final rule is done in the same manner as it is for other forms of rule making.

EXEMPTED RULE MAKING

The APA contains an exemption from rule making that allows an agency to decide whether public participation will be allowed. Exemptions include rule-making proceedings with regard to "military or foreign affairs" and "agency management or personnel." Exemptions are also granted for rule-making proceedings relating to "public property, loans, grants, benefits or contracts" of an agency. Military and foreign affairs often need speed and secrecy, which are incompatible with public notice and hearings. Other exemptions are becoming more difficult to justify in the eyes of the courts unless they meet one of the exemptions of the *Freedom of Information Act* (discussed later in this chapter).

Also exempted from the rule-making procedures are interpretive rules and general policy statements. An **interpretive rule** is a rule that does not create any new rights or duties but is merely a detailed statement of the agency's interpretation of an existing law. Interpretive rules are generally very detailed, step-by-step statements of what actions a party is to take to be considered in compliance with an existing law. Case 44-2 demonstrates the courts' deference to reasonable agency interpretations of arguably unclear statutes.

CASE 44-2 NATIONAL CABLE & TELECOMMUNICATIONS ASSN. v. GULF POWER CO.

UNITED STATES SUPREME COURT
122 S. CT. 782 (SUP. CT. 2002)

The Pole Attachments Act . . . requires the Federal Communications Commission (FCC) to set reasonable rates that can be charged by owners of utility poles, such as telephone and electric poles, for certain attachments to their poles. Under [the Act] a "pole attachment" includes "any attachment by a cable television system or provider of telecommunications service" to a utility pole. Some pole-owning utilities challenged, in various Federal Courts of Appeals, an FCC order that interpreted the Act to cover attachments that provided commingled cable television and high-speed Internet services and to cover attachments by wireless telecommunications providers. . . . The United States Court of Appeals for the Eleventh Circuit, in reversing the FCC on both points, held that (1) attachments for commingled services were not covered by either of the Act's two specific rate formulas . . . and (2) attachments for wireless communications were excluded from the Act by negative implication, where 224(a)(1) defined a "utility" as the owner of a pole that was used for wire communications. . . .

JUSTICE KENNEDY: (1) The FCC's assertion of jurisdiction under the Act to regulate rates charged for attachments that provided commingled cable television and high-speed Internet access was reasonable and, therefore, entitled to deference, because the term "any attachment by a cable television system" in 224(a)(4) covered at least those attachments that provided cable television service.

(2) The FCC's assertion of jurisdiction under the Act to regulate rates charged for attachments by wireless telecommunications providers was reasonable and, therefore, entitled to deference, because the term "any attachment by a . . . provider of telecommunications service" covered at least those that provided telecommunications. . . .

The attachments at issue in this suit—ones which provide commingled cable and Internet service and ones which provide wireless telecommunications—fall within the heartland of the Act. The agency's decision, therefore, to assert jurisdiction over these attachments is reasonable and entitled to our deference. The judgment of the Court of Appeals for the Eleventh Circuit is reversed, and the cases are remanded for further proceedings consistent with this opinion.

It is so ordered.

CRITICAL THINKING

Why is the concept of deference less helpful than it seems at first glance? In other words, does not any habit of deference also have its limits?

ETHICAL DECISION MAKING

What values are advanced by a doctrine of deference in this case? What values are downplayed when courts uphold the doctrine of deference?

Case Nugget Agency Interpretation of Statutes

Warner-Lambert Company v. United States
425 F.3d 1381 (2005)

Warner-Lambert imports and sells lozenges in packages under the name "Halls Defense Vitamin C Supplement Drops." The drops are composed primarily of sugar and glucose syrup, which together constitute more than 95 percent of each drop. Vitamin C constitutes just under 2 percent of each drop, with the remaining small percentage consisting of citric acid, flavors, and color. The Customs Service reclassified imported Vitamin C Supplement Drops from their previous duty-free status as medicaments to dutiable status as sugar confectionery. As a result, the drops were subject to a duty of 6.1 percent. Warner-Lambert sued in the Court of International Trade. On appeal, the Customs Service reclassification was upheld. In a six-page detailed letter ruling, Customs explained the reasons for its action, including that its prior classification of the drops was "based upon the belief that Vitamin C imparted therapeutic or prophylactic character to the merchandise" but that "additional research indicates that Vitamin C has not been shown in the U.S. to have substances which imbue it with therapeutic or prophylactic properties or uses." The Court of International Trade held that Customs justifiably concluded that although the merchandise "may possess medical properties, it is being marketed as much for its flavor as for its medicinal value. Thus, it cannot be said that this merchandise is suitable only for medical purposes." The drops are marketed to provide users with their requirement of Vitamin C, not to prevent or cure disease. If a statute is ambiguous and if the implementing agency's construction is reasonable, the federal courts must accept the agency's construction of the statute, even if the agency's reading differs from what the court believes is the best statutory interpretation.

Policy statements are general statements about directions in which any agency intends to proceed with respect to its rule-making or enforcement activities. Again, these statements have no binding impact on anyone; they do not directly affect anyone's legal rights or responsibilities.

A final exemption occurs when public notice and comment procedures are "impracticable, unnecessary, or contrary to the public interest." This exemption is used most commonly either when the issue is so trivial that there would probably be very little, if any, public input, or when the nature of the rule necessitates immediate action. Whenever an agency chooses to use this exception, it must make a "good-cause" finding and include in its publication of the final rule a statement explaining why there was no public participation in the process.

REGULATED NEGOTIATION

The exceedingly high number of challenges to regulations, as well as a growing belief that structured bargaining among competing interest groups might be the most efficient way to develop rules, has stimulated interest in a number of agencies in a relatively new form of rule making, often referred to as **reg-neg.** Each concerned interest group and the agency itself sends a representative to bargaining sessions led by a mediator. After the parties achieve a consensus, that agreement is forwarded to the agency.

The agency is then expected to publish the compromise as a proposed rule in the *Federal Register* and follow through with the appropriate rule-making procedures. The agency, however, is not bound to do so. If it does not agree with the proposal the group negotiated, the agency is free to try and promulgate a completely different rule or a modification of the one obtained through the negotiation. The reasoning behind reg-neg is similar to that supporting the increased use of mediation. If the parties can sit down and try to work out a compromise solution together, that solution is much more likely to be accepted than one handed down by some authority. The parties who hammered out the agreement now have a stake in making it work because they helped to create it.

Admittedly, reg-neg is not possible in all situations. If there is an unmanageably large group of interests that would have to be represented, if any possible compromise would have to result from one group's backing away from a fundamental principle, or if two groups feel so antagonistic toward each other that they would be unable to rationally sit down and talk, reg-neg would probably not even be worth trying.

PROBLEMS ASSOCIATED WITH RULE MAKING

Agency employees are not subject to the same political pressures as legislators, but they are also not unbiased. Often the people with the necessary expertise to regulate specific areas come from the industry they are now going to be regulating. There is some concern that it will be difficult for regulators to ignore their past ties to industry and pass regulations that are in the public interest, especially when the regulations would increase costs to the industry or are opposed by the industry for other reasons. When people are discussing an agency in which they perceive this problem as existing, they will often refer to the agency as being a "captured" agency. The counterargument is that those who have been deeply involved in an industry know it best.

Regulators must be sensitive to the role the economy plays in the public's willingness to accept or support certain regulations. When the economy is flourishing and unemployment is low, there is much greater acceptance of regulations. When unemployment is high, people are much more reluctant to accept regulations that they believe might cause some workers to lose their jobs and/or cause the prices of products to rise.

OTHER ADMINISTRATIVE ACTIVITIES

Agencies perform a variety of less well known but equally important tasks. These include advising, conducting research, issuing permits, and managing property. One of the most common ways individuals come into contact with agencies occurs when an agency advises businesses and individuals as to whether the agency considers an activity legal or illegal. Agencies also conduct studies of industry and markets. For example, the FTC, OSHA, and FDA conduct studies to determine, respectively, the level of economic concentration, safety in the workplace, and safety of drugs. Also, agencies provide information to the general public on various matters through hotlines, publications, and seminars. Agencies also devote much of their time to issuing licenses or permits. The EPA, for example, helps protect the environment by requiring certain environmentally sound activities before granting permits. Local agencies are responsible for issuing liquor licenses and cabaret (dancing) permits to local bars and restaurants. Finally, agencies often are responsible for managing government property.

Case 44-3 illustrates limitations on an agency's use of its powers to issue, and in this case revoke, the license of a real estate broker.

CASE 44-3 DEARBORN v. REAL ESTATE AGENCY
SUPREME COURT OF OREGON
53 P.3D 436 (OR. SUP. CT. 2002)

A 16-year-old male runaway was detained by police on drug charges. The youth reported that he had used drugs provided by the broker at the broker's apartment. The youth also reported that the broker had engaged in sexual acts while the youth was present and had shown the youth pictures of naked men. The police obtained a warrant and went into the broker's apartment. There they found the broker with a man, who told police that the broker had picked him up for the purpose of having sex with him and that the broker had obtained drugs for the man. The broker pleaded guilty to drug charges. The real estate commissioner revoked the broker's real estate license. . . .

JUSTICE J. GILLETTE: The Commissioner explained in his order that he was concerned that broker would "indiscriminately seek sexual liaisons with strangers, who could be juveniles, and entice them with drugs." . . . The Commissioner also suggested that a broker who abuses cocaine and methamphetamine might convert money held in trust for clients to support his or her habit. . . . To be entitled to discipline a licensee, the Commissioner first must be able to show that one or more acts of a licensee violated one or more subsections of ORS 696.301 (1995). Whether this licensee—broker—has committed acts that violate those subsections is a question concerning the meaning and scope of those subsections. Such an inquiry is a matter of statutory construction . . . we conclude . . . that the reference in subsection (31) to "any act or conduct . . . which constitutes or demonstrates bad faith, incompetence or untrustworthiness, or dishonest, fraudulent or improper dealing," is a reference to conduct that is substantially related to the broker's trustworthiness, competence, honesty, or good faith to engage in real estate activity. . . . As the Commissioner acknowledges in his order, however, there is "no evidence" that broker's criminal activities arose out of broker's "use of his position as a real estate licensee."

. . . [T]he Commissioner's right to discipline must arise out of something that a licensee *has done,* not out of something that a licensee *might do.* So far as this record discloses, none of broker's criminal acts had anything to do with his real estate activities. None involved clients, real estate, or money entrusted to broker. Without such a nexus, the Commissioner could not permissibly conclude that broker had violated ORS 696.301(26) (1995). We hold, in short, that the Commissioner erred in concluding that broker's drug possession convictions were "substantially related" to broker's real estate activities. . . .

REVERSED.

CRITICAL THINKING

The court in this case is seeking a nexus between the criminal acts and the responsibilities of a real estate broker. What additional facts, had they existed, would have provided the link between the responsibilities of a real estate broker and the specific crimes in this case?

ETHICAL DECISION MAKING

What is the central value conflict in this case? What value was the real estate commissioner trying to uphold by his decision?

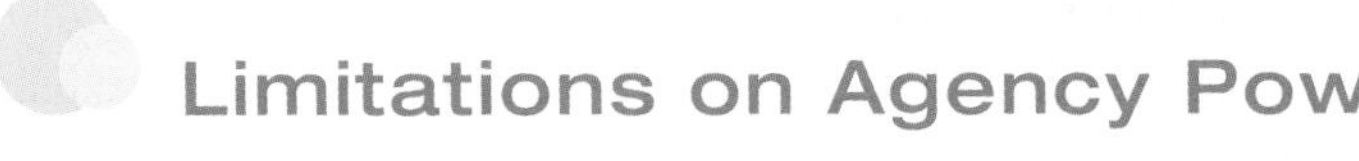

Limitations on Agency Powers

There are four basic limits on agency power: political, statutory, judicial, and informational. The hope is that these limitations will keep the agencies and their thousands of employees from abusing their discretion.

POLITICAL LIMITATIONS

As discussed earlier in this chapter, the president appoints the administrative heads of all executive agencies with the advice and consent of the Senate. If the president is unhappy with the head of such an agency, that person may be fired at any time for any (or no) reason. As such, executive agencies are particularly accountable to the executive branch. Moreover, the political slant (liberal/conservative) of the agency is significantly influenced by the president.

Congress also has significant control over agencies, as the Senate must approve presidential nominees for them to become the administrative heads of agencies. Moreover, Congress has control over the budgets of all agencies. If Congress decides that a particular agency is not performing as it wishes, that agency's budget may be cut or even defunded. Just prior to the Enron crisis, Congress, after being heavily lobbied by the accounting industry, threatened to defund the Securities and Exchange Commission (SEC). In effect, Congress did not like the SEC's proposal that stock options be charged as expenses. Arthur Levitt, then head of the SEC, heard the warning loud and clear and decided to walk away from his firmly held position. In later interviews, Levitt said it was his biggest regret as head of the SEC.[3]

STATUTORY LIMITATIONS

Congress has the power to create, or dissolve, an agency. If Congress is unhappy with an agency, it may amend the agency's enabling legislation and limit the agency's power. Moreover, in 1996 legislation was signed into law that gives Congress 60 days to review proposed agency rules. Congress may override those rules before they become effective. In addition, APA (passed by Congress in 1946) sets forth guidelines that all agencies must follow when engaged in rule making.

JUDICIAL LIMITATIONS

An individual or business that believes itself harmed by an administrative rule may challenge that rule in federal court once all administrative procedures are exhausted.[4] This is probably the biggest constraint on agency power. If a rule is subjected to judicial review, the court will consider the following:

1. *The facts of the case:* Courts typically defer to an agency's fact finding. The facts must be supported by **substantial evidence.**
2. *The agency's interpretation of the rule:* Once again, the courts typically defer to the expertise of the agency and uphold the agency's interpretation of the rule.
3. *The scope of the agency's authority:* Has the agency exceeded the authority granted it by its enabling legislation?

[3] PBS video, *Bigger Than Enron—How Greed and Politics Undercut America's Watchdogs* (1999).

[4] In a few situations, a court may not review an agency action. These include situations involving politically sensitive issues and those in which the agency's enabling legislation prohibits judicial review.

INFORMATIONAL LIMITATIONS

Agency power is limited by the Freedom of Information Act, the Government in Sunshine Act, and the Privacy Act of 1974.

Freedom of Information Act. The **Freedom of Information Act (FOIA)**, passed in 1966, requires that federal agencies publish in the *Federal Register* places where the public can get information from the agency. The act requires similar publication of proposed rules and policy statements. It requires that the agencies make such items as staff manuals and interpretations of policies available for copying to individuals, on request. Finally, all federal government agencies must publish records electronically.

Any individual or business may make an FOIA request to a federal government agency. Information may be obtained regarding how the agency gets and spends its money. Statistics and/or information collected by the agency on a given topic is also available. Perhaps most important, citizens are entitled to any records that the government has about them. For example, you could contact the Internal Revenue Service (IRS) and request all information that it has collected about you. FOIA does not apply to Congress, the federal courts, the executive staff of the White House, state or local governments, and private businesses. Exemptions to FOIA include, but are not limited to, national security, internal agency matters (e.g., personnel issues), criminal investigations, financial institutions, and an individual's private life.

Government in sunshine act. The Government in Sunshine Act requires that agency business meetings be open to the public if the agency is headed by a collegiate body. A *collegiate body* consists of two or more persons, the majority of whom are appointed by the president with the advice and consent of the Senate. This open-meeting requirement applies only when a quorum is present. The law also requires that agencies keep records of closed meetings.

Privacy act. Under the Privacy Act of 1974, a federal agency may not disclose information about an individual to other agencies or organizations without that individual's written consent.

Federal and State Administrative Agencies

Currently more than 100 federal agencies are in operation, as well as countless state agencies. Often, when there is a federal agency, there will also be comparable state agencies to which the federal agency will delegate much of its work. For example, the most important federal agency affecting environmental matters is the Environmental Protection Agency. Every state has a state environmental protection agency to which the federal EPA delegates primary authority for enforcing environmental protection laws. However, if at any time the state agency fails to enforce these laws, the federal EPA will step in to enforce them.

CASE OPENER WRAP-UP

EPA

At the beginning of this chapter, you will recall that 19 private organizations had petitioned the EPA to require that it regulate carbon dioxide from automobile emissions. After holding hearings and requesting comments from the public, the EPA refused authority to regulate. The matter was appealed and eventually worked its way up to the U.S. Supreme Court. The Bush White House filed an *amicus curie* (i.e., "friend of the court") brief arguing that the

EPA was attempting to get the automobile industry to voluntarily reduce emissions. The Alliance of Automobile Manufacturers came to the EPA's defense, arguing that the EPA, as well as the states, had no authority to regulate automobile emissions.

In a 5-4 decision, the U.S. Supreme Court disagreed, holding that the Clean Air Act authorizes the EPA to regulate greenhouse gas emissions from new motor vehicles in the event that the EPA forms a "judgment" that such admissions contribute to climate change. Moreover, the Court held that the Clean Air Act's definition of *air pollutant* includes carbon dioxide. As a result of the Court's decision, many are now calling for national standards on emissions from automobiles.[5]

[5] Kelpie Wilson, "Supreme Court Deals Win for Environment," www.alternet.org/story/50330 (April 9, 2007).

Summary

Introduction to Administrative Law

Administrative law consists of the substantive and procedural rules created by administrative agencies (government bodies of the city, county, state, or federal government) involving applications, licenses, permits, available information, hearings, appeals, and decision making.

An *administrative agency* is generally defined as any body created by the legislative branch (e.g., Congress, a state legislature, or a city council) to carry out specific duties.

Administrative agencies are created by Congress through passage of *enabling legislation,* which is a statute that specifies the name, functions, and specific powers of the administrative agency. The enabling statutes grant agencies broad powers for the purpose of serving the "public interest, convenience, and necessity."

Administrative law judge: An Administrative Law Judge (ALJ) presides over an administrative hearing. The ALJ may attempt to get the parties to settle, but has the power to issue a binding decision.

Different Types of Administrative Agencies

Executive agency: The administrative head of an executive agency is appointed by the president with the advice and consent of the U.S. Senate. Executive-agency heads may be discharged by the president at any time, for any reason. Executive agencies are generally located within the executive branch, under one of the cabinet-level departments (and thus are referred to as *cabinet-level agencies*). Examples are the Federal Aviation Agency (FAA) and the Food and Drug Administration (FDA).

Independent agency: Independent agencies are governed by a board of commissioners. The president appoints the commissioners with the advice and consent of the Senate. Commissioners serve fixed terms and cannot be removed except for cause. No more than a simple majority of an independent agency can be members of any single political party.

Hybrid agency: Some agencies do not fall clearly into one classification or the other. These agencies are typically referred to as *hybrid agencies.* Created as one type of agency, the body may share characteristics of the other. The EPA, for example, was created as an independent agency, not located within any department of the executive branch.

How Are Agencies Run?

In 1946 Congress passed the *Administrative Procedures Act (APA)* as a major limitation on how agencies are run. Under APA, there are very specific guidelines on rule making by agencies:

- *Informal rule making:* Under APA, the proposed rule is published in the *Federal Register,* and there is opportunity for public comment.

- *Formal rule making:* Formal rule making requires that all rules be enacted by an agency as part of a formal hearing process that includes a complete transcript. It begins with publication of a notice of proposed rule making by the agency in the *Federal Register.* Next, there is a public hearing at which witnesses give testimony on the pros and cons of the proposed rule and are subject to cross-examination. The agency makes and publishes formal findings. If a regulation is adopted, the final rule is published in the *Federal Register.*
- *Hybrid rule making:* Hybrid rule making is an attempt to combine the best features of formal and informal rule making. The starting point is publication in the *Federal Register,* followed by the opportunity for submission of written comments, and then an informal public hearing with a more restricted opportunity for cross-examination than in formal rule making.
- *Exempted rule making:* The APA contains an exemption from rule making that allows an agency to decide whether public participation will be allowed. Exemptions include rule-making proceedings with regard to "military or foreign affairs," "agency management or personnel," and "public property, loans, grants, benefits or contracts" of an agency.

Interpretive rules: Interpretive rules are rules that do not create any new rights or duties, but are merely a detailed statement of the agency's interpretation of an existing law. They are generally very detailed, step-by-step statements of what actions a party is to take to be considered in compliance with an existing law.

Reg-neg: Each concerned interest group and the agency itself sends a representative to bargaining sessions led by a mediator. If the parties achieve a consensus, that agreement is forwarded to the agency. The agency is then expected to publish the compromise as a proposed rule in the *Federal Register* and follow through with the appropriate rule-making procedures. If the agency does not agree with the proposal the group negotiated, the agency is free to try and promulgate a completely different rule or a modification of the one obtained through the negotiation.

Limitations on Agency Powers

There are four basic limits on agency power: political, statutory, judicial, and informational.

Freedom of Information Act: FOIA, passed in 1966, requires that federal agencies publish in the *Federal Register* places where the public can get information from the agencies. Any individual or business may make a FOIA request to a federal government agency. Information may be obtained regarding how the agency gets and spends its money; statistics and/or information collected by the agency on a given topic is available; and citizens are entitled to any records that the government has about them. Exemptions to FOIA include, but are not limited to, national security, internal agency matters (e.g., personnel issues), criminal investigations, financial institutions, and an individual's private life.

Government in Sunshine Act: This act requires that agency business meetings be open to the public if the agency is headed by a collegiate body (i.e., two or more persons, the majority of whom are appointed by the president with the advice and consent of the Senate).The law also requires that agencies keep records of closed meetings.

Privacy Act: Under the Privacy Act, a federal agency may not disclose information about an individual to other agencies or organizations without that individual's written consent.

Federal and State Administrative Agencies

An administrative agency is generally defined as any body created by the legislative branch (e.g., Congress, a state legislature, or a city council) to carry out specific duties.

Point / Counterpoint

Do Agencies Have Too Much Power?	
Yes	**No**
The U.S. government is founded on separation of powers. That is why we have three branches of government: executive, legislative, and judicial. Giving administrative agencies all three powers—executive, legislative, and judicial—gives administrative agencies power to do anything they wish with virtually no oversight. Agencies hire people who formerly worked in industry. As such, these people often view regulation skeptically, yet these are the same people who will run the agency.	Administrative agencies came into existence because Congress, as well as state and local governments, did not have the expertise, time, or resources to deal with specialized problems such as air pollution, securities regulation, and banking administration. Without administrative agencies, these problems would not be addressed. An agency employs professionals with expertise and experience in the area the agency regulates. These people understand the industry and the ways in which it needs to be regulated.

Questions & Problems

1. How are federal agencies created?

2. Why are agencies created?

3. What are the three main powers given to agencies?

4. List the three categories of agencies.

5. Describe the adjudication process of agencies.

6. Describe the various types of rule making.

7. Morales, a native and citizen of Mexico, was arrested in 1994 for entering the United States without inspection. He was released and served with a mail-out order to show cause why he should not be sent back to Mexico. Eventually, a removal hearing was scheduled, and Morales was notified via certified mail of the time and place of the hearing. When Morales failed to attend the hearing, he was ordered removed in absentia. The INS apprehended and removed Morales from the United States in 1998. He attempted to reenter illegally in January 2001—this time using a false border-crossing card. He was apprehended at the port of entry, and was expeditiously removed. Undaunted, Morales reentered the United States undetected the following day. Sometime between his 1998 and 2001 removals, Morales married a United States citizen. In March 2001, Morales' wife filed an I-130 alien relative petition based on his marriage to a United States citizen. When Morales and his wife met with the INS in January 2003, an immigration officer served them with a denial of the I-130 petition and a notice of intent to reinstate Morales' removal order. The case came before a three-judge panel, which held that the regulation authorizing immigration officers to issue reinstatement orders is invalid and Morales' removal order could only be reinstated by an immigration judge. Until 1997, removal orders could only be reinstated by immigration judges (i.e. not immigration officers). In 1997, the Attorney General changed the applicable regulation to delegate this authority, in most cases, to immigration officers. Does the Attorney General have the authority to change an INS regulation? Why or why not? [*Raul Morales-Izuierdo v. Alberto R. Gonzales, Attorney General,* 2007 U.S. App. LEXIS 10865 (9th Cir. 2007)].

8. In 1986, Congress passed the Honey Act, which, under the supervision of the Secretary of Agriculture, administers the program mandated by Congress. The Honey Board consists of seven honey producers, two honey handlers, two honey importers, and one officer, director or employee of a national honey marketing cooperative. The Honey Board's goal is to increase the demand for honey. To achieve this goal, the Honey Board promotes honey as a desirable product. To that end, the Honey Board initiates budgets, marketing ideas, and program ideas. The Honey Board is funded through mandatory assessments paid by honey producers and honey importers. The United States Department of Agriculture (USDA) acts as supervisor to the Honey Board during the development of promotion, research, education, and information activities. The USDA retains final approval authority over every assessment dollar spent by the Board. On September 28, 2001, the American Honey Producers brought an administrative petition contending that the Honey Act as written and applied violated their First Amendment rights. Plaintiffs sought exemption from the assessments and a refund of previously paid assessments. Does the Honey Act violate the First Amendment rights of the honey producers? Why or why not? [*American Honey Producers Association, Inc. v. The United States Department of Agriculture,* 2007 U.S. Dist. LEXIS 37310 (Eastern Dist. CA 2007)]

9. The Internal Revenue Service (IRS) made assessments against the taxpayer for, and notified him of its intent to file a levy to collect, the trust fund portion of employment taxes a company the taxpayer owned had failed to collect. The taxpayer requested and received an administrative hearing. He did not dispute his tax liability but requested to enter into a payment plan. A settlement officer met with the taxpayer to consider, but recommended against accepting the taxpayer's proposal. The appeals officer issued a notice of determination sustaining the IRS collection in full. The taxpayer then sued. Is the taxpayer entitled to a hearing on the merits before a trial court? Why or why not? [*David A. Tilley v. United States of America,* 2004 U.S. Dist. LEXIS 7792 (U.S. Dist.Ct., Eastern District PA, 2004)].

10. Invention Submission Corporation (ISC) brought a lawsuit under the Administrative Procedures Act against James Rogan in his official capacity as undersecretary of commerce for intellectual property and director of the U.S. Patent and Trademark Office (PTO). The PTO started an advertising campaign to warn inventors about invention promotion scams. After a reporter saw the advertisement, he contacted the PTO about a testimonial given in the advertisement. The reporter followed up with a story identifying ISC as the scam promoter. ISC contends that PTO's advertising campaign was both false and unauthorized, targeting ISC in order to penalize it and put it out of business. It argues that the Inventors' Rights Act of 1999 granted the PTO only limited authority to create a forum to publish complaints and responses to them and that the PTO's 2002 advertising campaign directed at ISC went beyond this stated authorization. Therefore, it asserts that the campaign was an illegal agency action and exceeded any statutory authority conferred on the PTO. Was the advertising campaign an illegal agency action? Should the court review PTO's actions? Why or why not? [*Invention Submission Corporation v. Rogan,* 357 F.3d 452 (4th Cir. 2004).]

11. Six conservation organizations filed a petition in Thurston County Superior Court asking that court to hold, pursuant to a provision in the Administrative Procedures Act, that the Washington Forest Practices Board, the Washington Department of Ecology, and the Washington Department of Natural Resources (agencies) "failed to promulgate forest practice rules that advanced the environmental protection purposes and policies of the Forest Practices Act of 1974." The agencies countered by arguing that a formal petition for rule making must precede any petition for judicial review. Must an interest group exhaust administrative remedies before suing in a state or federal court? Why or why not? [*Northwest Ecosystem Alliance v. Washington Forest Practices Board,* 66 P.3d 614 (2003).]

12. Babington and other taxpayers sued both identified and unidentified employees of the Internal Revenue Service (IRS) for alleged violations of federal law. Under the appropriate statutes, a taxpayer who seeks redress because the IRS or its employees allegedly acted in violation of federal law must first file an administrative claim. A civil lawsuit in federal court is barred until such filing occurs. In the case of Babington and other taxpayers, all the administrative claims were to be sent "in writing to the Area Director, Attn: Compliance Technical Support Manager of the area in which the taxpayer currently resides." The taxpayers improperly sent their administrative claims to an agency office in Jacksonville, Florida, and not to the area director for compliance in Atlanta, Georgia. Have the taxpayers exhausted their administrative remedies? Assuming that an IRS employee (improperly) directed the taxpayers to send their administrative claim to the Jacksonville office, have the taxpayers exhausted their administrative remedies? Should the court assert jurisdiction and hear the claim? [*Babington et al. v. Everson et al.,* 2005 U.S. Dist. LEXIS 17571 (Fla. Dist. Ct. 2005).]

13. On January 21, 2003, Robbins filed an application for site plan approval to construct an asphalt plant within the town limits of Hillsborough. Robbins had entered into a contract to purchase the property prior to submitting his application for site plan review and subsequently purchased the property. At the time he filed his application, an asphalt plant was a permitted use in a general industrial (GI) district subject to a site plan review. The property on which the asphalt plant was to be constructed was zoned GI. In reliance on the zoning ordinance in effect at the time of his application, Robbins spent approximately $100,000 to engineer and submit a site plan to comply with the conditional-use requirements set forth in the ordinance and to prepare for the required public hearings before the Town of Hillsborough Board of Commissioners. Three public hearings were held. The board received evidence but reached no decision. At the close of the third hearing, the board scheduled a fourth hearing. Prior to the fourth hearing, the board amended the zoning ordinance to temporarily suspend review, consideration, and issuance of permits for manufacturing processes. Robbins's fourth hearing was canceled. Eventually, the suspension became a moratorium on permits until the end of the year. Robbins filed a complaint in Orange County Superior Court, alleging that he was entitled to rely on the language of the zoning ordinance in effect at the time he applied for the permit; that the board violated the law by failing to give notice of a public hearing or hold a public hearing prior to its decision to extend the moratorium; and that the defendant's decision to permanently prohibit asphalt plants was arbitrary and capricious. How should the court decide? Explain your answer. [*Robbins v. Town of Hillsborough,* 625 S.E.2d 813 (N.C. Ct. App. 2006).]

14. Tommy Robinson, a 60-year-old black male employee of the Food Safety and Inspection Service (FSIS), a division of the U.S. Department of Agriculture, alleged that the department discriminated against him on account of his age, sex, and race, in violation of Title VII of the Civil Rights Act of 1964, when it refused to promote him to the position of customer safety officer. The district court concluded that the complaint failed to state a claim for relief and dismissed it because Robinson failed to contact an equal employment opportunity (EEO) counselor and complain about the alleged discrimination. Federal sector employees, such as Robinson, who believe that they have been subject to discrimination, must initiate contact with an EEO counselor within 45 days of the effective date of the personnel action. An agency, however, "shall extend the 45-day time limit in paragraph (a)(1) of this section when the individual shows that . . . he or she did not know and reasonably should not have known that the discriminatory matter or personnel action occurred." In an attempt to get around the limitations bar, Robinson made two arguments: First, he says that he did not learn of the unlawful discrimination until November 15, 2001; and second, he says that he did not learn that the person who obtained the position was white until sometime after he filed his grievance with the union on October 16, 2001. Robinson failed to make either argument to the district court. On appeal, he argued that the court of appeals should extend the 45-day time limit. How did the court of appeals rule? Why? [*Robinson v. Jojanns, Secretary of Agriculture,* 2005 U.S. App. LEXIS 19561 (11th Cir. Ct. App. 2005).]

15. Harvey is a producer and handler of organic blueberries and other crops, an organic inspector employed by USDA-accredited certifiers, and a consumer of organic foods. He alleged that multiple provisions of the National Organic Program Final Rule were inconsistent with the Organic Foods Production Act of 1990 (OFPA). The OFPA is a law passed by Congress to set national standards for organic food. The rule is the secretary of agriculture's interpretation of the law, set forth as a regulation. Harvey alleged that the portions of the rule that permitted synthetic substances to be used in organic foods was inconsistent with the law as set forth in OFPA, which states that no synthetic ingredients may be added during processing or handling. Moreover, the rule allowed dairy animals classified as "organic" to be fed 80 percent organic food for 9 months prior to their sale, while the OFPA standard is 100 percent organic food for 12 months. Must agency interpretations of a statute be consistent with congressional intent? How should the court rule? [*Arthur Harvey v. Ann Veneman, Secretary of Agriculture,* 396 F.3d 28 (1st Cir. Ct. App. 2005).]

Looking for more review material?

The Online Learning Center at **www.mhhe.com/kubasek1e** contains this chapter's "Assignment on the Internet" and also a list of URLs for more information, entitled "On the Internet." Find both of them in the Student Center portion of the OLC, along with quizzes and other helpful materials.

Consumer Law

CASE OPENER

The Firestone Recall

On August 9, 2000, Bridgestone/Firestone Inc. announced a recall of 14.4 million tires, including all 15-inch Firestone ATX, ATX II, and 15-inch Wilderness AT tires used by Ford Motor Company on its popular SUVs. This announcement came 10 years after the first suit was filed against these companies for defective tires. Secrecy and protective orders within the courts kept this information hush-hush for 10 years until a local news station in Houston, Texas, got word in 1999 that Ford was replacing tires on Explorers in Saudi Arabia through what it called a "customer notification enhancement action." In response, the National Highway Traffic Safety Administration opened an investigation of the cases associated with these tires.[1]

In the original recall press release, Ford and Firestone claimed that they had each just been made aware of the safety problem and were consequently recalling the tires. However, some have argued that Ford and Firestone knew about the safety problems with the tires as much as 10 years earlier but did not inform the National Highway Traffic Safety Administration of the potential danger.

1. Suppose you were a member of Congress when this case emerged. What action would you take to ensure that situations such as this would not occur again?
2. Suppose you were the manager of Ford or Firestone. Would you have handled the situation differently, and if so, why?

The Wrap-Up at the end of the chapter will answer these questions.

[1] Terril Yue Jones, "Cause of Tire Failures Still a Matter of Dispute," *Los Angeles Times,* October 22, 2000, p. C1.

CHAPTER 45

Learning Objectives

After reading this chapter, you will be able to answer the following questions:

1. What is the purpose of the Federal Trade Commission Act?
2. How does the Federal Trade Commission determine what constitutes deceptive advertising?
3. What is the purpose of labeling and packaging laws?
4. What are the different methods of sales?
5. What are the different acts that provide credit protection?
6. What are the different acts that help ensure consumer health and safety?

Consumers buy products and services from sellers every day. In some instances, however, consumers do not have as much power in the transaction as the seller. As we see in the Firestone case, the seller had more knowledge about the product or service, how it was made, and pricing strategies than did the consumers. Because Congress has recognized the opportunities for sellers to take advantage of buyers in this way, it has created laws that regulate transactions between consumers and sellers. A **consumer law** is a statute or administrative rule serving to protect consumer interests.

Various state and federal consumer laws protect consumers from unfair trade practices of sellers as well as unsafe products. Although the laws differ among the states, many of the state laws provide consumer protection exceeding that guaranteed by federal law. This chapter explores a range of consumer laws concerning deceptive advertising, product labeling, sales procedures, health and product safety, and consumer credit. But first, it discusses a federal agency that is one of the most important creators and enforcers of consumer protection laws—the Federal Trade Commission.

The Federal Trade Commission

Congress created the Federal Trade Commission (FTC) through the Federal Trade Commission Act of 1914.[2] The purpose of the act was to prevent fraud, deception, and unfair business practices. The FTC has responsibility for carrying out the act.

The FTC is an independent federal agency with five commissioners appointed by the president and confirmed by the Senate. Each commissioner serves a seven-year term. The president chooses one commissioner to serve as chair of the FTC.

How does the FTC meet its goal of protecting consumers? The FTC helps to protect consumers through two methods: (1) consumer education and (2) legal action. First, the FTC creates campaigns to educate consumers about laws that protect them. Second, the FTC educates businesses to help them comply voluntarily with consumer laws. For example, the FTC creates **industry guides,** interpretations of consumer laws, to encourage businesses to stop unlawful behavior. When businesses follow the FTC guidelines, they can cut potentially steep costs associated with violating consumer laws.

HOW THE FTC BRINGS AN ACTION

The FTC receives a variety of complaints about businesses from consumer groups and individuals. When consumers file a complaint with the FTC, they trigger a chain of events leading to an FTC action against the violator. The FTC typically begins a nonpublic investigation of the company.

If, after its investigation, the FTC believes that a company violated the law, the FTC sends a complaint to the alleged violator. At that time, the FTC may settle the complaint through a consent order with the company. A **consent order** is a statement in which the company agrees to stop the disputed behavior but does not admit it broke the law. Should the company violate the consent order, it will usually be forced to pay a fine.

If the company refuses to enter into a consent agreement, the FTC may then decide to issue a formal administrative complaint. The issuing of this complaint leads to a hearing before an administrative law judge. If the judge decides that the company has violated the law, the FTC issues a **cease-and-desist order,** requiring that the company stop the illegal behavior. However, the company may appeal this decision to the five commissioners. If the commissioners uphold the ruling, the company may appeal to the U.S. court of appeals and, finally, to the Supreme Court. Figure 45-1 presents a visual description of the process that an FTC action can follow.

[2] 15 U.S.C. §§ 41–58.

Figure 45-1 FTC Complaint Process

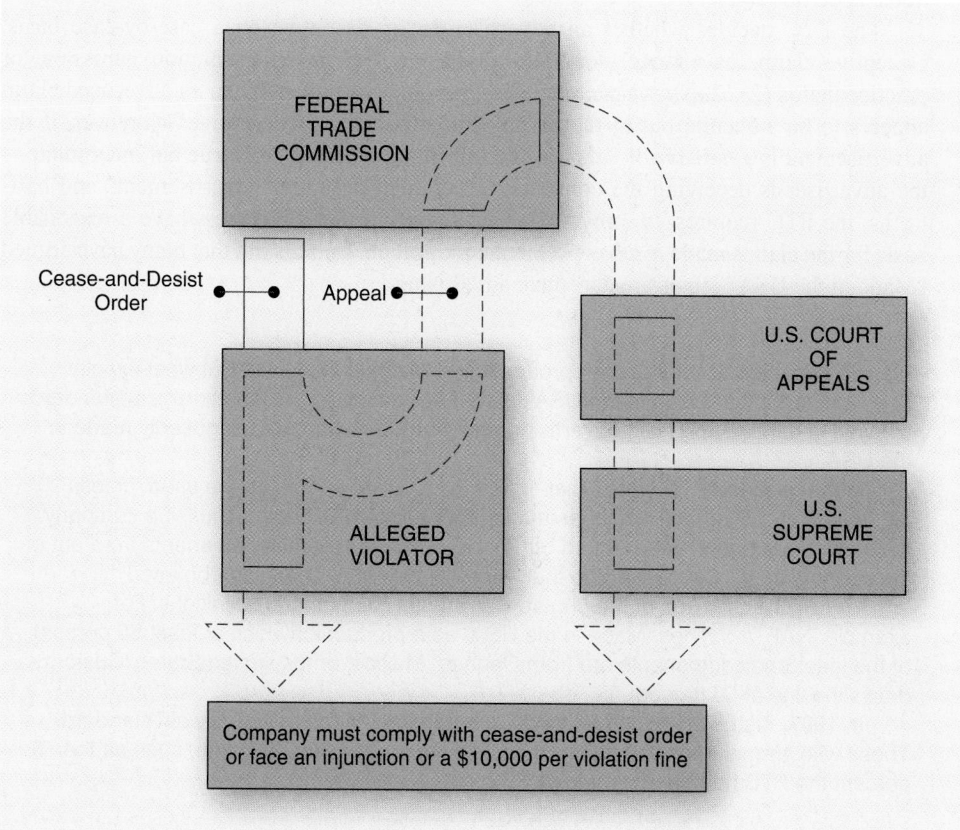

If the courts uphold the FTC's decision, the company must follow the cease-and-desist order. If the company violates the order, the FTC can seek an injunction against the company or fine the company up to $10,000 per violation.

TRADE REGULATION RULES

Bringing an action may be effective in protecting consumers from the activities of one company, but how can the FTC protect consumers if most companies within one industry are using the same unfair or deceptive practices? Bringing actions against all of these companies would be costly and time-consuming.

An alternative method of addressing these practices is through trade regulation rules. If the FTC finds that deception is pervasive in an industry, the FTC can recommend rule making. An administrative rule has the effect of law. Furthermore, the FTC can bring legal action against those who violate FTC rules.

Deceptive Advertising

Section 5 of the Federal Trade Commission Act prohibits deceptive and unfair acts in commercial settings, including consumer purchases. This section of the chapter specifically analyzes **deceptive advertising,** in other words, those advertising claims that mislead or could mislead a reasonable consumer. **Puffing,** the use of generalities and clear exaggerations, is permissible.

The FTC decides whether an advertisement is deceptive on a case-by-case basis. Deceptive claims have three elements:[3] (1) a *material* misrepresentation, omission, or practice that is (2) *likely to mislead* a (3) *reasonable* consumer. When an advertised claim appears to be authentic but in fact is not, the advertising is deceptive. Moreover, if the advertisement is a **half-truth**—that is, the information presented is true but incomplete—the advertiser is deceiving the consumer. To combat deceptive advertisements and half-truths, the FTC requires **ad substantiation,** requiring that advertisers have a reasonable basis for the claims made in advertisements. Exhibit 45-1 points out that many have argued "Made in the USA" labels are deceptive advertising.

Exhibit 45-1
"Made in the USA" Labels and the FTC

Many companies boast that their products are "Made in the USA." But what exactly does it mean to be "Made in the USA"? The FTC is charged with setting forth standards to avoid deception and false advertising about products that are supposedly made in the USA.

In the past, the FTC stated that "Made in the USA" should not be used "unless all, or virtually all, of the components and labor are of U.S. origin." Thus, if a company assembled a product in the United States but shipped in some components from out of the country, the FTC would argue that "Made in the USA" should not be used.

The FTC's definition of the phrase was stricter than others' definitions. For example, NAFTA defines "Made in the USA" as a product for which at least 55 percent of the labor and components are from Canada, Mexico, or the United States. Customs draws the line at 50 percent.

In 1997, the FTC decided to continue enforcing the "all or virtually all" standard. Those with strong union ties had argued against any weaker definition, such as the 75 percent the FTC had been debating.

Source: Federal Trade Commission, FTC Consumer Report, "Complying with the Made in the USA Standard," www.ftc.gov/bcp/conline/pubs/buspubs/madeusa.shtm.

An illustration of an FTC claim of deceptive advertising involved Body Wise International, Inc.'s "AG-Immune" Dietary Supplement. In 1995, Body Wise was prohibited from using false or unsubstantiated claims while advertising *any* of its products as part of its settlement with the FTC for using deceptive advertising to market a different dietary supplement. Body Wise then entered into a contract with Dr. Stoff to market AG-Immune. Stoff was paid royalties on every bottle of AG-Immune that Body Wise sold. However, no connection between Body Wise and Stoff was ever admitted in any of the advertisements for the product.

The FTC then alleged that Body Wise violated the 1995 order with its advertisements for AG-Immune. According to the FTC, Body Wise advertised that AG-Immune was able to "prevent or treat numerous diseases or conditions, including cancer, HIV/AIDS, heart disease, chronic fatigue syndrome, and asthma" and that scientific research supported the claims. Body Wise also allegedly claimed that AG-Immune improved the immune system's "ability to prevent or treat the aforementioned and many other diseases and conditions."[4] The FTC also argued that Stoff falsely claimed that the advertisements were supported by scientific data and that he was in a professional position to assess the efficacy of AG-Immune.

[3] FTC's 1983 Policy Statement on Deception.

[4] Federal Trade Commission, "Body Wise International to Pay over $3.5 Million to Settle Federal and State Deceptive Advertising Charges for 'AG-Immune' Dietary Supplement," www.ftc.gov/opa/2005/01/bodywise.htm (January 18, 2005).

Body Wise and Stoff both agreed to settle with the FTC out of court. Both parties were responsible for paying hefty fines to the FTC for their deceptive advertisements. The main thrust of the FTC's argument was related to the fact that no scientific data existed to back Body Wise's claims regarding AG-Immune.

The existence of deceptive advertisements is not enough alone to prove damages for recovery when individual civil suits are filed. For example, in *Oliveira v. Amoco Oil Co.,*[5] a class action suit was brought against Amoco for deceptive advertisements. Amoco made many claims over a seven-year period about the superiority of its premium gasoline. However, according to the plaintiffs, no scientific evidence supported Amoco's claims. The plaintiffs then argued that the advertisements created a higher demand for Amoco gas, creating artificially high gas prices that hurt consumers regardless of specific reliance on the advertisements. The court rejected this argument, ruling that a "market theory" of causation is not enough to establish damages in an individual case. Moreover, reliance on the advertisements is a crucial element in establishing liability. Case 45-1 provides an example of the FTC's consideration of the elements of deceptive advertising.

[5] 201 Ill. 2d 134 (2002).

CASE 45-1

KRAFT INC. v. FEDERAL TRADE COMMISSION
U.S. COURT OF APPEALS FOR THE SEVENTH CIRCUIT
970 F.2D 311 (1992)

Individually wrapped cheese slices generally come in two varieties: process cheese slices and imitation slices. Process cheese slices have at least 51 percent natural cheese, whereas imitation slices have little or no cheese. Kraft Singles, which are process cheese food slices, began losing market share to imitation slices. In response, Kraft initiated the "Five Ounces of Milk" campaign to inform consumers Kraft singles are made from 5 ounces of milk and are thus more nutritious and more expensive than imitation slices. This campaign ran through two major ads, the "Skimp" ad and the "Class Picture" ad, which explicitly addressed the calcium in Kraft Singles.

The "Skimp" ad consisted of a mother describing how she could not skimp on her daughter by buying imitation cheese slices. She states, "Imitation slices use hardly any milk. Kraft has five ounces per slice. Five ounces. So her little bones get the calcium they need to grow." In the "Class Picture" ad, the announcer reports that "a government study says that half the school kids in America don't get all the calcium recommended for growing kids. That's why Kraft Singles are important. Kraft is made from five ounces of milk per slice. So they're concentrated with calcium."

In response to these ads, the FTC filed a complaint against Kraft, arguing the "Five Ounces" campaign was deceptive advertising. Although Kraft uses five ounces of milk while making each Single, approximately 30 percent of the calcium contained in the milk is lost during processing. Moreover, most of the imitation slices contain the same amount of calcium as Kraft Singles. Thus, the FTC argued Kraft made two deceptive claims: (1) a Kraft Single contains the same amount of calcium as five ounces of milk (the "milk equivalency" claim); and (2) a Kraft Single contains more calcium than imitation cheese slices (the "imitation superiority" claim).

The administrative law judge ruled both the Skimp and Class Picture ads implicitly made the milk equivalency claim and the imitation superiority claim. Consequently, he ordered Kraft to cease and desist from making those claims about cheese slices. Kraft appealed, and the full Commission upheld most of the judge's decision, except in ruling the Class Picture ad did not make the imitation superiority claim. The FTC Commission then extended the cease and desist order to apply to any Kraft cheese items. Kraft appealed.

JUDGE FLAUM: [A]n advertisement is deceptive under the [FTC] Act if it is likely to mislead consumers, acting reasonably under the circumstances, in a material respect. . . . In implementing this standard, the Commission examines the overall net impression of an ad and engages in a three-part inquiry: (1) what claims are conveyed in the ad; (2) are those claims false or misleading; and (3) are those claims material to prospective consumers. . . .

I.

In determining what claims are conveyed by a challenged advertisement, the Commission relies on two sources of information: its own viewing of the ad and extrinsic evidence. Its practice is to view the ad first and, if it is unable on its own to determine with confidence what claims are conveyed in a challenged ad, to turn to extrinsic evidence. The most convincing extrinsic evidence is a survey "of what consumers thought upon reading the advertisement in question," but the Commission also relies on other forms of extrinsic evidence including consumer testimony, expert opinion, and copy tests of ads.

Kraft has no quarrel with this approach when it comes to determining whether an ad conveys express claims, but contends the FTC should be required, as a matter of law, to rely on extrinsic evidence rather than its own subjective analysis in all cases involving allegedly implied claims. The basis for this argument is implied claims, by definition, are not self-evident from the face of an ad. This, combined with the fact consumer perceptions are shaped by a host of external variables—including their social and educational backgrounds, the environment in which they view the ad, and prior experiences with the product advertised—makes review of implied claims by a five-member commission inherently unreliable. The Commissioners, Kraft argues, are simply incapable of determining what implicit messages consumers are likely to perceive in an ad.

Kraft's case rests on the faulty premise implied claims are inescapably subjective and unpredictable. The Commission does not have license to go on a fishing expedition to pin liability on advertisers for barely imaginable claims falling at the end of this spectrum. However, when confronted with claims that are implied, yet conspicuous, extrinsic evidence is unnecessary because common sense and administrative experience provide the Commission with adequate tools to makes its findings. The implied claims Kraft made are reasonably clear from the face of the advertisements, and hence the Commission was not required to utilize consumer surveys in reaching its decision.

I.B.

. . . Kraft asserts the literal truth of the Class Picture ads—they are made from five ounces of milk and they *do* have a high concentration of calcium—makes it illogical to render a finding of consumer deception. The difficulty with this argument is even literally true statements can have misleading implications. Here, the average consumer is not likely to know much of the calcium in five ounces of milk (30 percent) is lost in processing, which leaves consumers with a misleading impression about calcium content. The critical fact is not reasonable consumers might believe a 3/4 ounce slice of cheese actually contains five ounces of milk, but reasonable consumers might believe a 3/4 ounce slice actually contains the calcium in five ounces of milk.

I.C.

Kraft next asserts the milk equivalency and imitation superiority claims, even if made, are not material to consumers. A claim is considered material if it "involves information important to consumers and, hence, likely to affect their choice of, or conduct regarding a product."

In determining the milk equivalency claim was material to consumers, the FTC cited Kraft surveys showing 71 percent of respondents rated calcium content an extremely or very important factor in their decision to buy Kraft Singles, and 52 percent of female, and 40 percent of all respondents, reported significant personal concerns about adequate calcium consumption. The FTC further noted the ads were targeted to female homemakers with children and the 60 milligram difference between the calcium contained in five ounces of milk and that contained in a Kraft Single would make up for most of the RDA calcium deficiency shown in girls aged 9–11.

Significantly, the FTC found further evidence of materiality in Kraft's conduct: despite repeated warnings, Kraft persisted in running the challenged ads. Before the ads even ran, ABC television raised a red flag when it asked Kraft to substantiate the milk and calcium claims in the ads. Kraft's ad agency also warned Kraft in a legal memorandum to substantiate the claims before running the ads. Moreover, in October 1985, a consumer group warned Kraft it believed the Skimp ads were potentially deceptive. Nonetheless, a high-level Kraft executive recommended the ad copy remain unaltered because the "Singles business is growing for the first time in four years due in large part to the copy." Finally, the FTC and the California Attorney General's Office independently notified the company in early 1986 investigations had been initiated to determine whether the ads conveyed the milk equivalency claims. Notwithstanding these warnings, Kraft continued to run the ads and even rejected proposed alternatives that would have allayed concerns over their deceptive nature. From this, the FTC inferred—we believe, reasonably—that Kraft thought the challenged milk equivalency claim induced consumers to purchase Singles and hence the claim was material to consumers.

ENFORCED.

CRITICAL THINKING

What are the primary facts of this case? Is there any missing information you would call for to better enable you to evaluate the court's reasoning? What evidence does the court use to support its decision? Are you persuaded by this evidence?

ETHICAL DECISION MAKING

Do you think Kraft's advertising was ethical given the facts of the case? Review the WPH process of ethical decision making in Chapter 1. What value did the court highlight in its decision?

Case 45-1 illustrates the importance of understanding specific consumer protection laws. Future business managers need to understand what kinds of advertising claims are permissible in our legal environment. To simplify this understanding for consumers and business owners, the FTC has classified certain types of deceptive or unfair advertising practices and created specific rules defining and prohibiting violations of these rules. The next section will examine these classifications.

BAIT-AND-SWITCH ADVERTISING

When sellers advertise a low price for an item generally unavailable to the consumer and then push the consumer to buy a more expensive item, they are engaging in **bait-and-switch advertising.** The low advertised price "baits" the consumer. Then the salesperson "switches" the consumer to a higher-priced item. In 1968 the FTC prohibited bait-and-switch advertising.

According to the FTC's "Guides against Bait Advertising," a seller can engage in bait-and-switch advertising in several ways. For instance, the seller might advertise a low price but have too little of the advertised good in stock or might discourage employees from selling the advertised item. These bait-and-switch advertising techniques violate FTC rules.

Case Nugget Bait-and-Switch Advertising

Paula E. Rossman, individually and for all others similarly situated v. Fleet Bank (R.I.) National Association et al.
U.S. Court of Appeals for the Third Circuit
280 F.3d 384 (2002)

In 1999, Paula Rossman received a credit card offer from Fleet Bank, advertising the "Fleet Platinum MasterCard" with a low annual percentage rate and no annual fee. A few months after Rossman's account was opened, Fleet imposed an annual fee. Fleet sent a letter to Rossman stating that a $35 annual fee would be charged to her account annually on the anniversary of her account's opening; however, a second letter notified Rossman that the annual fee would be charged to her account within months. Rossman sued Fleet, claiming that Fleet had violated the disclosure requirements of the Truth in Lending Act (TILA) and engaged in a bait-and-switch advertising scheme. The district court dismissed Rossman's TILA claim for failing to state a claim on which relief could be granted. Rossman appealed to the Third Circuit Court of Appeals.

The appeals court applied a two-part test to determine whether Fleet's statement that the card had no annual fee was lawful. "First, it must have disclosed all of the information required by the statute. And second, it must have been true—i.e., an accurate representation of the legal obligations of the parties at that time—when the relevant solicitation was mailed." Rossman claimed that Fleet was required to disclose all fees that were currently imposed, as well as any fees that may be imposed later. Rossman also claimed that Fleet's disclosure was misleading by suggesting that there would never be an annual fee. Additionally, Rossman claimed that Fleet engaged in a bait-and-switch scheme, using the "no annual fee" provision to lure consumers into a contract when Fleet had no intention of honoring said provision.

Fleet argued that it was not required to disclose any future fees that may be imposed, but only those that currently existed. Fleet also turned to a clause in the solicitation disclosure insert that it "reserve[d] the right to change the benefit features associated with your Card at any time." The court found that Fleet's disclosure, as placed and worded, did not adequately link itself to the no-annual-fee provision. Thus, if the annual fee was permitted to be changed within the first annual term of the agreement, then the court found that the statement "no annual fee" was an inadequate disclosure.

Turning its attention to Rossman's claim that Fleet had engaged in a bait-and-switch advertising scheme, the court did not see Fleet's behavior as resembling the classic bait-and-switch design. Ordinarily, consumers are baited with certain terms, but the switch for less enticing products or terms is made before the consumer enters into an agreement or contract. Rather, the court found Fleet's behavior to be even more egregious because Fleet actually bound the consumer in a contract before making the switch to charge an annual fee. Thus, Fleet had violated the provisions of TILA. The appeals court reversed the district court's ruling and remanded for proceedings.

FTC ACTIONS AGAINST DECEPTIVE ADVERTISING

If the FTC takes action against a company and proves the advertising is deceptive, the FTC may issue a cease-and-desist order. To go a step beyond cease-and-desist orders, the FTC may also issue **multiple-product orders.** A multiple-product order is a form of cease-and-desist order issued by the FTC applying not only to the product that was the subject of the action but also to other products produced by the same firm. Alternatively,

connecting to the core

Economics

As you read in this chapter about the FTC's role in regulating advertising, think about how the FTC is fulfilling a government function discussed in your economics class: attempting to prevent one kind of market failure. Remember from your economics class that economists assume that markets exist in an almost perfect form. For a market to be perfect, certain conditions have to exist. When those conditions fail to exist, the government might act to correct the failure. For example, economists often assume that buyers must have perfect information about the products they are buying for the market to achieve optimal results. We recognize that sellers would often provide faulty information or conceal information if doing so would help them sell their products. Thus, the FTC , with its regulation of advertising, tries to prevent the problem of imperfect information, thereby improving the functioning of the market.

Source: David C. Colander, *Economics,* 6th ed. (New York: McGraw-Hill, 2006), pp. 432–434.

the FTC may require that the company engage in **corrective advertising** (or counteradvertising), running advertisements in which the company explicitly states that the formerly advertised claims were untrue.

The rationale for corrective advertising is that consumers who saw the previous ads will see the new ads; the new ads will then correct the deceptive advertising. In a commission decision regarding the deceptive advertising of Doan's Pills, Commissioner Sheila Anthony described the characteristics of a situation requiring corrective advertising:

> Requiring the dissemination of a truthful message to counteract beliefs created or reinforced by a respondent's deceptive message is an appropriate method of restoring the *status quo ante* and denying a respondent the ability to continue to profit from its deception. . . . Corrective advertising is an appropriate remedy if (1) the challenged ads have substantially created or reinforced a misbelief; and (2) the misbelief is likely to linger into the future.[6]

However, some companies—and even one of the commissioners of the FTC—argued that corrective advertising is a form of compelled speech and thus violates the First Amendment right to engage in free speech.

TELEMARKETING AND ELECTRONIC ADVERTISING

Consumer law, like all law, is dynamic, and technology is often a driving force of change in consumer law. Although technological developments provide consumers with a host of benefits, these developments are often prone to abuses not covered by existing consumer law. For example, telephones and fax machines facilitate fast and inexpensive communication around the world, but telemarketers can use these technologies to deceive consumers and invade their privacy. Hence, lawmakers have passed new laws to address these issues.

Two major acts regulate advertising by telephone and fax, the Telephone Consumer Protection Act (TCPA) of 1991 and the Telemarketing and Consumer Fraud and Abuse Prevention Act of 1994.[7] TCPA, which the Federal Communications Commission agency enforces, forbids phone solicitation using an automatic telephone dialing system or a prerecorded voice. TCPA also makes it illegal to transmit advertisements via fax unless the recipient agrees to the fax transmission. TCPA allows for consumers to obtain a private right to legal action. In other words, the act gives consumers the right to recover for their losses. If a telemarketer violates TCPA, the consumer can recover either monetary losses

[6] FTC Press Release, "Doan's Pills Must Run Corrective Advertising: FTC Ads Claiming Doan's Is Superior in Treating Back Pain Were Unsubstantiated," May 27, 1999.

[7] 47 U.S.C. § 227.

global context

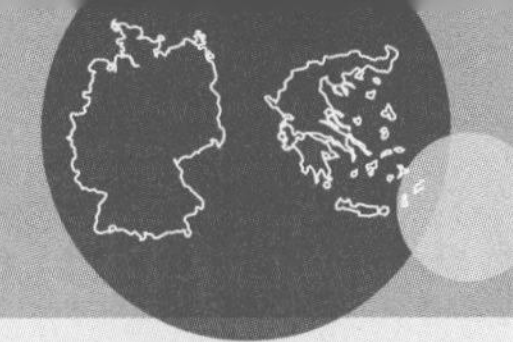

Regulating the Psychological Aspects of Advertisements

The governments of Germany and Greece believe that consumers need protection from the potentially dangerous psychological effects of advertisements. Germany, in particular, has strict advertising regulations.

Specifically, ads that exert a "moral pressure" to purchase a product or service are outlawed in Germany. Urging the consumer to act out of gratitude, decency, or compassion might create this pressure. This regulation is applied stringently when there is no logical connection between the emotional appeal and the function of the product being promoted. For example, an advertisement that insinuated "good mothers" buy brand X peanut butter would be prohibited. Additionally, the German law prohibits marketers from using persons of authority to solicit business. For example, a marketer cannot ask the supervisor of a company to recommend a product to employees because the employees would feel obligated to purchase it.

The laws protecting consumers from the dangers of advertising in Greece vary from the German laws. If an ad "causes fear" by use of partially untrue statements, it is considered unlawful in Greece. In some instances, the use of true statements to evoke fear in the consumer is considered illegal.

or $500 per violation. However, if the telemarketer willfully violated the act, the court can decide to triple the amount owed to the consumer.

Sometimes laws are ineffective in achieving their goals, however, so legislatures draft new laws to supplement existing law. Thus, even though the goals of consumer laws may not change, specific rules and provisions do. For example, despite the protection of TCPA, consumers still lost an estimated $40 billion in telemarketing fraud after the act went into effect.

To give consumers more protection against deceptive and abusive telemarketing practices, Congress enacted the Telemarketing and Consumer Fraud and Abuse Prevention Act of 1994.[8] Through this act Congress asked the FTC to define "deceptive and abusive" telemarketing practices and required that the FTC create and enforce rules governing telemarketing that would prohibit such practices. Consequently, the FTC created the Telemarketing Sales Rule of 1995,[9] which requires that telemarketers (1) identify the call as a sales call; (2) identify the product name and seller; (3) tell the total cost of goods being sold; (4) notify the listener or reader of whether the sale is nonrefundable; and (5) remove the consumer's name from the potential contact list if the consumer so requests.

Moreover, the FTC established that certain telemarketing behaviors are abusive, such as using profane or obscene language toward a customer and calling a person who has requested previously to be taken off the particular seller's calling list. Additionally, if the telemarketer calls a residence before 8 a.m. or after 9 p.m., the telemarketer is engaging in abusive behavior. If a telemarketer violates the rule, the FTC or the state attorney general may bring an action against the telemarketer. If the action is successful, the telemarketer can face fines up to $10,000 per violation.

While reviewing and amending the Telemarketing Sales Rule in 2002, the FTC created a "Do Not Call" registry. The FTC states the purpose of the Do Not Call registry as giving consumers a choice regarding telemarketing calls. The registry makes it illegal for telemarketers to call any number that has been registered for more than 31 days. The registration lasts for five years, and can be completed online through the FTC's Web site. Both the FTC and the Federal Communications Commission (FCC) are responsible for maintaining the list, with help from local state law enforcement officials.

The Global Context box discusses different restrictions placed on advertisements in other countries.

[8] 15 U.S.C. §§ 6101–6108.
[9] 16 C.F.R. § 310.

e-commerce AND THE LAW

Consumers on the Net

Every year, e-commerce becomes more and more popular. In 2006, 52 million individuals shopped online, and this was up from 35 million in 2005. These consumers are likely to encounter some type of problem through e-commerce. Perhaps they will respond to an unsolicited e-mail claiming that the consumer can quickly earn money. Or perhaps they will win their bid on an item through an Internet auction but will never receive the product.

Consumers can be defrauded on the Internet in numerous ways. The anonymity associated with Internet use makes it easier for sellers to engage in deceptive business practices.

Source: Cap, Gemini, Ernst, & Young, "Global Online Retailing" (report), www.capgemini.de/sews/studien/retaking.html; and FTC, "Unsolicited Commercial E-mail," statement before the Subcommittee on Telecommunications, Trade, and Consumer Protection of the Committee on Commerce, U.S. House of Representatives, November 3, 1999.

TOBACCO ADVERTISING

The tobacco industry's advertising is regulated through two acts: the Public Health Cigarette Smoking Act[10] of 1970 and the Smokeless Tobacco Health Education Act[11] of 1986. The Public Health Cigarette Smoking Act prohibits radio and television cigarette advertisements, and the Smokeless Tobacco Act imposes the same restrictions for smokeless tobacco ads.

Labeling and Packaging Laws

When consumers examine a product to decide whether to buy it, the label often influences the decision to purchase. For example, many of us have purchased food because the label said the food was "low fat." Unfortunately, manufacturers can include or omit information on labels that mislead consumers.

Consequently, federal and state governments have passed laws that regulate product labeling. These laws generally require that the manufacturer provide accurate, understandable information on the label. Furthermore, if the product is potentially harmful, the manufacturer must make the consumer aware of this harm.

Several federal laws regulate product labeling. The Wool Products Labeling Act of 1939[12] requires accurate labeling of wool products. Similarly, the Fur Products Labeling Act of 1951[13] requires the accurate labeling of fur products. The Flammable Fabrics Act of 1953[14] made it illegal to produce or distribute clothing "so highly flammable as to be dangerous when worn." The Fair Packaging and Labeling Act of 1966[15] requires that products carry labels that identify the product and provide specific information about the contents, such as the quantity of the contents and the size of a serving, if the number of servings is stated. Moreover, under this act, food product labels must show the nutritional content of the product. Similarly, the Nutrition Labeling and Education Act of 1990[16] requires that standard nutrition information (i.e., calories and fat) be provided on food labels. Additionally, this act defines the words *fresh* and *low fat.* In 1994 the

[10] 15 U.S.C. § 1331.
[11] 15 U.S.C. §§ 4401–4408.
[12] 15 U.S.C. §§ 1331–1341.
[13] 15 U.S.C. § 69.
[14] 15 U.S.C. § 1191.
[15] 15 U.S.C. §§ 1451 et seq.
[16] 21 U.S.C. § 343-1.

global context

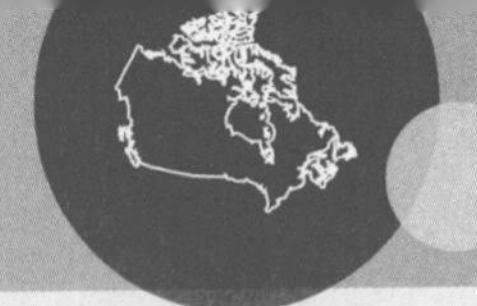

Respecting Languages of the Consumer

U.S. consumers often purchase products that are labeled or give directions in various languages, such as Spanish and French. The United States does not require that other publications, such as billboards, restaurant menus, or television advertisements, be multilingual. However, these requirements do exist in France and Canada.

During the early 1970s, French consumers voiced concern about foreign imports. Most of those products were labeled in languages other than French, so it became difficult to read directions or determine the content and function of a product. The government responded by passing a law in 1975 that regulated the labels and advertising of imported goods. The law mandated that French and English had to be the languages used for product labels, instructions, and all forms of advertising.

Canada passed a similar decree concerning the use of the French language. The Consumer Packaging and Labeling Act of Canada requires that all goods be labeled in both French and English.

While France and Canada were legislating the inclusion of both languages, Quebec legislated the exclusion of English. The Charter of the French Language, drafted by the Quebec government, requires that all public signs and advertisements be solely in French. If a product is produced and sold in Quebec, its packaging and product instructions are also to be in French alone.

FTC issued a statement saying it would apply these label restrictions to food advertising to prevent deceptive advertising. Thus, not only do sellers need to be concerned about the use of *high, low,* and *light* on labels, but they are also required to use these words in particular ways in advertisements.

The goal of these laws is to provide consumers with specific information about product content. However, Congress has passed several laws that require information about the potential harms associated with a product. For example, the Federal Hazardous Substances Act of 1960 requires that all items containing dangerous substances carry warning labels.

Canada's cigarette labeling requirements are even more stringent than the U.S. requirements. In Canada, approximately 40 percent of cigarette packaging must be devoted to health warnings.[17] The Canadian Bureau of Tobacco Control, however, has proposed a new rule requiring that manufacturers dedicate 50 percent of cigarette packages to such warnings, which would include explicit pictures and images of mouth cancer or other severe diseases caused by cigarette use.[18]

Sales

The FTC and other government agencies have the power to regulate sales. For example, the Federal Reserve Board of Governors has the power to govern credit provisions related to sales contracts through its Regulation Z.[19] The FTC has created rules that govern specific types of sales in which the consumer is in a more vulnerable position compared to a consumer who walks into a traditional retail setting. This section examines FTC regulation of three of these uncommonly vulnerable commercial settings: door-to-door, telephone, and mail-order sales.

[17] Tobacco Products Control Regulations, SOR/89-21.

[18] Action on Smoking and Health Press Release, "Majority of Canadians Want Larger Warnings on Cigarette Packages," October 2000.

[19] 12 C.F.R. § 226.

DOOR-TO-DOOR SALES

Imagine that you hear a knock at your door, open it, and discover a salesperson for an Internet provider. The person who knocked knows that you have just purchased a computer and are interested in learning about the Internet. The salesperson explains the price of various programs by which you can become familiar with the Internet. You listen, but decide that you would like to get additional information from an alternative provider. However, the salesperson is extremely pushy; to get the salesperson out of your house, you decide to purchase one of his plans.

In most door-to-door sales, the consumer does not have a chance to compare products and services to find the best service for his or her money. In addition, many consumers find it difficult to escape the salesperson in their home. It is much easier to walk out of a store. Because the consumer is in a particularly vulnerable position in a door-to-door sale, the FTC has created special rules for such sales.

The FTC created the Cooling-Off Rule, giving consumers three days to cancel purchases they make from salespeople who come to their homes. Moreover, the salesperson must notify the consumer, both verbally and in writing, that the sales transaction may be canceled. The FTC rule also requires that the consumer be notified in writing in the same language in which the oral negotiations were conducted, so as to avoid unscrupulous businesses from taking advantage of non-English speakers.

The following case provides an example of the kinds of pressures that the FTC is trying to offset: Consolidated Promotions offered consumers a free gift for setting up a meeting in their home to discuss Consolidated products. This in-home meeting was in fact a sales pitch for Consolidated's photography packages, which included film and discounted photo processing. These packages cost from $1,200 to $2,500. When Consolidated Promotions refused to cancel some of the consumers' contracts, the FTC approved a complaint and referred it to the Department of Justice. The FTC alleged that the company violated the Cooling-Off Rule by "1) failing to honor valid cancellation notices; 2) misrepresenting consumers' rights to cancel their contracts; and 3) failing to inform each buyer orally of his or her right to cancel their order."[20] The FTC proposed that Consolidated Promotions enter into a consent decree whereby Consolidated would be required to send notice to all customers who bought a photography package after July 1, 1996, giving them an opportunity to cancel their contracts.

TELEPHONE AND MAIL-ORDER SALES

Most consumers have purchased at least one item from a catalog. Unfortunately, telephone and mail-order purchases trigger more complaints than traditional retail or door-to-door sales. Suppose the office manager of a small accounting firm ordered five new chairs for the office through a catalog. The writing in the catalog indicated that the chairs would arrive within two weeks. The office manager called in the chair order, but six weeks later he had heard nothing from the company. What rights does he have in this situation?

The FTC originally addressed problems with mail-order sales through the 1975 Mail-Order Rule.[21] The Mail or Telephone Order Merchandise Rule of 1993 amended the 1975 Mail-Order Rule to extend protections to consumers who purchase goods over phone lines, including through computers and fax machines.

[20] Federal Trade Commission Press Release, "FTC Settlement Protects Door-to-Door Sales Consumers," May 2, 2000.

[21] 16 C.F.R. §§ 435.1–435.2.

The rule established three key guidelines. First, sellers must ship items within the time promised. If they do not specify a time, the seller is limited to 30 days from receipt of the order. Second, if the seller cannot ship the item within the promised time, the seller must notify the customer in writing and offer an opportunity to cancel. Third, if a customer decides to cancel the order, the seller must refund the customer's money within a specified period of time.

Unsolicited merchandise. When a consumer goes to her mailbox only to discover that a company has sent her a book, must she pay for the book? Anyone who receives unsolicited merchandise may treat the item as a gift. She may keep or dispose of it without any obligation to the sender. In accordance with the Postal Reorganization Act of 1970,[22] any unsolicited merchandise sent by mail is free to be used by the recipient as he or she sees fit with no obligation by the recipient to the sender.

FTC REGULATION OF SALES IN SPECIFIC INDUSTRIES

In certain industries, sellers have extensive opportunities to take advantage of customers. Thus, the FTC—and in some cases, Congress—creates special rules for certain sales practices specific to certain industries.

Used-car sales. Consumers who purchase a used car often have very little information about the car's history. For instance, they do not know whether the car has been in an accident or whether there are any serious problems that are just not visible.

To protect used-car buyers, Congress passed the Odometer Act of 1973, which protects against odometer fraud in used-car sales. The FTC extended its protection through the 1984 Used Motor Vehicle Registration Rule.[23] Under this rule, a dealer must attach a buyer's guide label to any used car he or she is attempting to sell. The label must state that the car is being sold "as is." This label is a warning to the customer that the seller is not guaranteeing anything at all about the performance of the car. Furthermore, the label must include a suggestion that the buyer obtain an inspection for the used car before any decision to purchase.

Consumer protections against fraud in used-car sales vary widely from state to state. During the 1960s and 1970s there was widespread pressure to reform our legislative system to protect consumers from fraud; many states responded more favorably to that pressure than did others. All states enacted the Uniform Commercial Code (UCC), but in each case the UCC was enacted with significant variations. The difference between states was also heightened in that each state had unique, nonuniform consumer protection statutes. Consequently, the consumer protection laws against used-car fraud (also known as "lemon laws") vary from state to state. Some states provide minimum protection, while others states, such as Minnesota, presume that one unsuccessful effort to repair a used car demonstrates nonrepairability. Minnesota's laws also extend statutory protection to potential buyers of returned vehicles by banning resale of automobiles returned because of major safety defects.[24]

Funeral home services. Consumers who must purchase goods and services for a funeral and burial are often vulnerable for several reasons. The consumer is usually preoccupied with his or her loss of a relative or friend and is unlikely to "comparison shop." Additionally, grieving consumers can be more readily persuaded to purchase

[22] 16 C.F.R. § 256.

[23] 16 C.F.R. §§ 455.1–455.5.

[24] David A. Rice, "Product Quality Laws and the Economics of Federalism," *Boston University Law Review* 65 (1985), p. 1.

global context

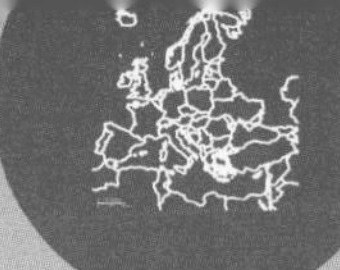

EU Consumer Law

The Overbooking Regulation is a regulation designed to compensate tourists and business travelers with airline reservations who are denied access to a flight because the airline overbooked the flight. In general, the compensation provided by the EU regulation is more favorable than that which a consumer would receive at the national level. In other words, the European Union provides more consumer protection than would be provided in the individual European countries.

After a consumer gets shut out of an overbooked flight, he or she has the right to receive reimbursement for the full ticket price or get a seat on a rerouted flight at the earliest time or a later date. Regardless of the choice, the consumer must receive monetary compensation of a predesignated amount as soon as access to the flight has been denied. The compensation amount cannot exceed the price of the ticket. Due to the inconvenience caused by delayed travel plans, the airline is required to provide the conveniences of complimentary phone, fax, meals, and hotel accommodations.

unnecessary, expensive items for this last tribute to their loved ones. To prevent funeral homes from taking advantage of these customers, the FTC created the 1984 Funeral Rule and revised it in 1994. The rule requires that those who operate funeral homes provide customers itemized price information about funeral goods and services. Furthermore, funeral homes may not misrepresent legal or cemetery requirements or require that the customer buy certain funeral goods and services as a condition for receiving other funeral goods and services.

Real estate sales. Because real estate purchases are probably one of the largest purchases a consumer will make, Congress passed several acts requiring that sellers disclose certain information about the property. First, the Interstate Land Sales Full Disclosure Act,[25] passed in 1968, requires disclosure of information to consumers so that they can make informed decisions about real estate purchases. Under this act, anyone planning to sell or lease 100 or more lots of unimproved land through a common promotional plan must file an initial statement of record with the Department of Housing and Urban Development's (HUD's) Office of Interstate Land Sales Registration. Before the developer can offer land for sale, HUD must approve the initial statement

Congress provided more protection for those purchasing homes in the Real Estate Settlement Procedures Act of 1974[26] and its 1976 amendments. This act requires the disclosure of information regarding mortgage loans to the buyer. For example, the lender must give the buyer an estimate of costs for finalizing the real estate purchase.

Online sales. With the ever-expanding reach of the Internet, there has been an increase in business-to-consumer (B2C) sales transactions. Anyone with an Internet connection can make purchases from his or her favorite stores, from Barnes & Noble to Macy's. Most existing consumer protection laws were developed to protect consumers in their interactions with businesses face-to-face. Hence, protecting consumers online requires new approaches. Although not a specific industry, the Internet facilitates such a huge volume of commerce that additional focused protective legislation is needed.

Despite the difficulty of prosecuting online fraud, the FTC has brought a number of enforcement actions against online businesses. The federal statutes already in existence

[25] 15 U.S.C. §§ 1701–1720.

[26] 12 U.S.C. §§ 2601–2617.

prohibiting wire fraud apply to online transactions. In addition, several states have begun to amend statutes to explicitly protect online consumers.

Credit Protection

The widespread use of credit to purchase goods and services means consumer credit protection has become increasingly important. This section explores three key federal laws regulating the credit industry to protect consumers: the Truth-in-Lending Act, the Fair Credit Reporting Act, and the Fair Debt Collection Practices Act.

THE TRUTH-IN-LENDING ACT

One of the earliest, most significant statutes regulating credit is Title I of the Consumer Credit Protection Act (CCPA), referred to as the *Truth-in-Lending Act (TILA)*.[27] The purpose of the act is to require that sellers disclose the terms of the credit or loan to help consumers compare a variety of credit lines or loans. More important, consumers must be able to understand this disclosure of terms. TILA is administered, in part, by the Federal Reserve Board through the previously mentioned Regulation Z.

Suppose your business extends credit to customers. Are your credit lines through your business subject to TILA? First, TILA applies to consumer loans only. Second, TILA applies to those who lend money or arrange for credit through the ordinary course of business. Third, the credit or loan must be in the amount of $25,000 or less, unless the loan is secured by a mortgage on real estate. Fourth, the creditor must be making the loan to a natural person, not a legal entity. Fifth, the credit or loan must be subject to a finance charge or must have repayments of more than four installments.

All creditors subject to TILA must disclose the finance charge and the annual percentage rate of the credit or loan. This information must be disclosed in a meaningful way, which prevents creditors from burying the information in a large paragraph unrelated to the credit terms.

Consider the following example: In May 1999 a jury heard *Carlisle v. Whirlpool Financial National Bank.*[28] According to the case facts, Gulf Coast Electric's salespeople traveled door-to-door, selling satellite dishes through financing. The price of the satellite dish was $1,100. However, consumers could purchase this disk for approximately $200 in stores. The consumers argued that the salespeople hid the number of payments the buyers would have to pay, thereby violating TILA. The jury found in favor of the customers and awarded them $581 million.

Types of loans under TILA. TILA includes three categories of loans: open-end credit, closed-end credit, and credit card applications and solicitations. Each category has specific disclosure requirements. For example, an *open-end credit line* permits repeated transactions and assesses a finance charge on unpaid balances. A creditor of an open-end credit line is required to disclose information in periodic statements. In contrast, a *closed-end credit line* is one for a loan given for a specific amount of time. The creditor of a closed-end credit line must disclose the total amount financed and the number, amount, and due dates of payments. Finally, credit card applications and solicitations must include the APR, annual fees, and the grace period for paying without a finance charge.

[27] 15 U.S.C. §§ 1601–1693r.

[28] No. 97-068 (Cir. Ct., Hale Co., Ala).

Unauthorized charges and disputes. TILA establishes certain consumer protection rules regarding unauthorized charges to credit cards. If your credit card is stolen and someone makes unauthorized purchases on your account, your liability for those charges cannot exceed $50 per card if prompt notification of the theft is made to the credit card company. If you notify the credit card company before unauthorized charges are made, you cannot be held liable for any of the charges. Similarly, if a credit card company sends you an unsolicited card in the mail and the card is stolen, you cannot be held liable for any of the charges.

TILA offers another protection to consumers who unknowingly purchase damaged goods using a credit card. If three requirements are met, the consumer will not be obligated to pay for the good. First, the consumer must purchase the item near her home (i.e., the business is in the same state as the consumer's home or within 100 miles of the home). Second, the item must cost more than $50. Third, the consumer must make a good-faith effort to resolve the dispute, such as asking the store for a refund. If these requirements are met, the credit card company cannot bill the consumer for the damaged item.

Consumer leasing act. In 1988 the Consumer Leasing Act (CLA)[29] amended TILA to provide greater protection for people leasing automobiles and other goods. CLA applies to those who lease goods as part of their regular business. For CLA to apply, the lease must be for a minimum of four months and the price must not exceed $25,000. Under CLA, and its controlling regulation, Regulation M,[30] anyone leasing goods must disclose up front, in writing, all the material terms and conditions of the lease.

Equal credit opportunity act. In the 1970s, a woman old enough to have children would have had difficulty securing credit because creditors believed that married women with children would be less likely to pay their debts. In response to this discrimination, Congress passed the Equal Credit Opportunity Act (ECOA)[31] as a 1974 amendment to TILA. This amendment makes it illegal for creditors to deny credit to individuals on the basis of race, religion, national origin, color, sex, marital status, or age. When determining the creditworthiness of a credit applicant, the creditor cannot use information about the applicant's marital status, nor can the creditor require that a spouse co-sign the application. Finally, the act prohibits creditors from denying credit on the basis of whether the applicant receives public assistance benefits.

THE FAIR CREDIT REPORTING ACT

If you own a credit card, you also have a credit report. If you apply for a new credit card or a loan, the creditor will check your credit history to make a judgment about your creditworthiness by examining a copy of your credit report. This report contains information about your financial transactions, such as payments on credit, debt collection, and other financial information the creditor needs to know about if entering a business transaction with you.

Because credit bureaus influence consumers' ability to make purchases and secure loans, Congress passed the Fair Credit Reporting Act (FCRA)[32] of 1970 to ensure accurate credit reporting. FCRA regulates the issuance of credit reports for limited business purposes, such as a determination of credit or insurance eligibility, employment, and licensing. If a credit bureau issues a consumer credit report for a reason not specified by FCRA, it may be held liable for damages and additional fines. Furthermore, anyone who uses a credit report for purposes other than those specified in the act may be held liable for damages.

[29] 15 U.S.C. §§ 1667–1667e.

[30] 12 C.F.R. Part 213.

[31] 15 U.S.C. §1691–1691f.

[32] 15 U.S.C. § 1681–1681t.

Case Nugget Equal Credit Opportunity Act

Alvin Ricciardi, Appellant, v. Ameriquest Mortgage Company
U.S. Court of Appeals for the Third Circuit
164 Fed. Appx. 221; 2006

Alvin Ricciardi bought a home in May 2001, took out a home equity loan, and then applied for a loan to refinance the two mortgages through Ameriquest. Ricciardi closed the loan in September 2002, at which point he received the "Borrower's Acknowledgment of Final Loan Terms." The acknowledgment stated the terms of the loan that Ricciardi had originally requested, as well as the final terms of the loan. Ricciardi signed all the documents presented during the closing. Eight months later, Ricciardi filed suit against Ameriquest for violating the Equal Credit Opportunity Act, the Truth in Lending Act, and the Pennsylvania Unfair Trade Practices Act and Consumer Protection Law. The district court granted summary judgment regarding Ricciardi's ECOA claim, finding for Ameriquest. At a later nonjury trial, the court ruled in favor of Ameriquest on all counts of Ricciardi's claim as well as Ameriquest's counterclaim. Ricciardi appealed.

Ricciardi's appeal put forth three arguments. First, Ricciardi argued that the district court erred in granting summary judgment in favor of Ameriquest on his ECOA claim because Ameriquest failed to provide notice of its counteroffer before the closing of the loan. Second, Ricciardi argued that the district court erred in its adverse credibility finding. Third, Ricciardi argued that Ameriquest violated TILA by overcharging him for insurance and thereby gave him the right to rescind the loan. The appeals court rejected each of Ricciardi's arguments, affirming the ruling of the district court.

The appeals court addressed each of Ricciardi's arguments in turn. First, TILA requires that a creditor respond to an applicant within 30 days of receipt of a completed loan application. Ameriquest did respond to Ricciardi within 30 days. Contrary to Ricciardi's claim, Ameriquest was not required to respond in the form of a counteroffer. Additionally, there is no requirement that a counteroffer be received before the closing of the loan. Thus, Ricciardi's argument was without merit. Second, the appeals court found that the district court had not erred in its adverse credibility finding. Ricciardi contradicted himself numerous times on the record, in addition to committing fraud by misrepresenting his occupation and income on the loan application to Ameriquest. Third, the appeals court found that Ricciardi had not presented sufficient evidence to substantiate his claim that Ameriquest had overcharged him for insurance. In Pennsylvania, state-mandated insurance rates are published in the *Rate Manual.* The rates decrease if the property is being refinanced and was previously insured. Ricciardi failed to show that the property was previously insured; thus, the district court correctly found that there was no evidence that Ameriquest had overcharged Ricciardi.

In Case 45-2, a husband and wife sued banks that offered them preapproved credit cards but then rejected their applications. The couple argued that by rejecting the applications for the preapproved credit cards, the banks ultimately obtained their credit reports under false pretenses under FCRA.

CASE 45-2 RICHARD D. KENNEDY AND SALLY S. KENNEDY v. CHASE MANHATTAN BANK, USA, N.A., ET AL.

U.S. COURT OF APPEALS FOR THE FIFTH CIRCUIT
369 F.3D 833 (2004)

Richard and Sally Kennedy received pre-qualified offers for credit card accounts from Chase Manhattan and Bank of America (BOA). Based on the representations made by the banks the Kennedys believed they were pre-approved for credit, and they accepted the offers by returning the applications. The banks, however, obtained consumer credit reports from Experian and Transunion and notified the Kennedys, based upon the information in these reports, the banks would not open credit card accounts for the Kennedys.

Each pre-approved offer provides, in part, that the offered credit may not be extended if, after the consumer responds to the offer, the bank determines the consumer does not meet the criteria used to select the consumer for the offer or any "applicable criteria bearing on creditworthiness."

The Kennedys contended the banks violated section 1681q of the Fair Credit Reporting Act by obtaining information under the Act under false pretenses. Sally Kennedy contended the offer of credit evidenced the fact she satisfied Chase Manhattan's credit criteria and Chase Manhattan violated the Act by not extending this credit to her after it obtained her credit report without her knowledge. She argued this constituted obtaining the credit report under false pretenses.

The banks filed for summary judgment, and the district court granted all of the motions. The Kennedys appealed.

JUDGE PRADO: In their complaint, the Kennedys specifically complained the banks violated section 1681q of the Act by obtaining their credit information under false pretenses. Section 1681q provides a cause of action for obtaining credit information under false pretenses. To prove this claim, the Kennedys were required to show the banks had an impermissible purpose in obtaining the credit report; that is, the banks lacked a permissible purpose. "Permissible purposes" for obtaining consumer reports are set out in section 1681b of the Act. That section provides, in relevant part, a consumer credit report may be furnished in connection with a credit transaction not initiated by the consumer if the applicable transaction consists of a firm offer of credit, or the consumer authorizes the report.

The Kennedys' complaint and the attached pre-approved credit mailings, however, show the banks obtained the Kennedys' credit reports for a permissible purpose. The complaint alleged: the Kennedys received pre-qualified offers for credit card accounts, the Kennedys accepted the offers by returning the applications, the banks obtained credit reports, and the banks notified the Kennedys they would not open credit card accounts for them.

Indeed, the pre-approved certificates notified the Kennedys the offered credit might not be extended if, after the Kennedys responded to the offers, the banks determined the Kennedys did not meet the criteria used to select them for the offers and any other applicable criteria bearing on credit worthiness. Thus, the banks fully apprised the Kennedys the banks would review their credit history prior to determining whether the banks would extend the offered credit. The Kennedys signed the pre-approved certificates, agreed to the terms of the offers, and authorized the banks to access their credit information.

Thus, the complaint and the pre-approved certificates show the banks did not obtain the Kennedys' credit information under false pretenses. Instead, the banks pre-screened customers for firm offers of credit, and then post-screened accepted offers to determine eligibility based on credit worthiness. Consequently, the complaint failed to state a claim under section 1681q.

AFFIRMED.

[CONTINUED]

CRITICAL THINKING

What are the issue and conclusion of this case? Explain how rival causes affect this case. Considering the information available to you, what do you think is the most likely cause leading to the bank's obtaining the Kennedys' credit information?

ETHICAL DECISION MAKING

Who are the primary stakeholders affected by the facts in this case? How would it affect the quality of the decision making if judges were to simply forget about some of these stakeholders?

Case 45-2 illustrates one application of the Fair Credit Reporting Act. FCRA establishes other duties for credit reporting. For example, the credit bureau cannot report obsolete information. (General credit information is considered obsolete after seven years.) However, a bankruptcy will be reported for 10 years. Also, any time a credit applicant is denied credit, the applicant has a right to the name and address of the credit bureau that reported the information. Finally, FCRA imposes a duty on the reporting agency to ensure its information is as accurate as possible. Consequently, if a consumer reports an error in his or her credit report, the credit bureau is required to investigate the error and make the corrections in the report, if necessary.

THE FAIR DEBT COLLECTION PRACTICES ACT

Suppose a consumer owes $3,000 on his credit card and has not been able to make monthly payments for the past six months. The credit card company will likely refer the case to a collection agency, which will notify the consumer in an attempt to get him to pay the debt. The collection agency then may start calling the consumer regularly to discuss the debt. Next, the agency might start contacting the consumer's acquaintances, telling them about the debt in an effort to pressure the consumer into paying the debt.

This type of debt-collecting behavior is prohibited by the Fair Debt Collection Practices Act (FDCPA).[33] This act applies only to debt collectors who regularly attempt to collect debts on behalf of others. The following collection behaviors are expressly prohibited by FDCPA:

1. Contacting a debtor at work if the debtor's employer objects.
2. Contacting a debtor who has notified the collection agency that he or she wants no contact with the agency.
3. Contacting the debtor before 8 a.m. or after 9 p.m.
4. Contacting third parties about the debt (exceptions: contacting the debtor's parents, spouse, or financial adviser).
5. Using obscene or threatening language when communicating with the debtor.
6. Misrepresenting the collection agency as a lawyer or a police officer.

The act states that these restrictions apply to "debt collectors." Case 45-3 considers whether lawyers fall under the definition of *debt collector*.

[33] 15 U.S.C. § 1692.

CASE 45-3 GEORGE W. HEINTZ ET AL. v. DARLENE JENKINS
UNITED STATES SUPREME COURT
514 U.S. 291, 115 S. CT. 1489 (1995)

Darlene Jenkins borrowed money from Gainer Bank to purchase a car. The loan required Jenkins keep an insurance policy on the car. Jenkins had an insurance policy but she let the insurance expire. The bank took out an insurance policy to cover the car. Next, she defaulted on her loan. Gainer Bank sued Jenkins to recover the money for the loan. George Heintz, a lawyer for the law firm representing Gainer Bank, sent a letter to Jenkins' lawyer. This letter indicated the amount Jenkins owed the bank and included $4,173 for the insurance. In response, Jenkins brought a Fair Debt Collection Practices Act suit against Heintz. She argued Heintz was misrepresenting the amount Jenkins owed because the insurance policy was not only protecting her car against "loss or damage" but also against her failure to repay the bank's loan. The District Court dismissed the suit, ruling the FDCPA does not apply to lawyers engaging in litigation. The Court of Appeals disagreed and reversed.

JUSTICE BREYER: The issue before us is whether the term "debt collector" in the Fair Debt Collection Practices Act applies to a lawyer who "regularly," *through litigation,* tries to collect consumer debts.

The Fair Debt Collection Practices Act prohibits "debt collector[s]" from making false or misleading representations and from engaging in various abusive and unfair practices. . . . The Act's definition of the term "debt collector" includes a person "who regularly collects or attempts to collect, directly or indirectly, debts owed [to] . . . another."

There are two rather strong reasons for believing the Act applies to the litigating activities of lawyers. *First,* the Act defines the "debt collector[s]" to whom it applies as including those who "regularly collect or attempt to collect, directly or indirectly, [consumer] debts owed or due or asserted to be owed or due another." In ordinary English, a lawyer who regularly tries to obtain payment of consumer debts through legal proceedings is a lawyer who regularly "attempts" to "collect" those consumer debts.

Second, in 1977, Congress enacted an earlier version of this statute, which contained an express exemption for lawyers. That exemption said the term "debt collector" did not include "any attorney-at-law collecting a debt as an attorney on behalf of and in the name of a client." In 1986, however, Congress repealed this exemption in its entirety, without creating a narrower, litigation-related, exemption to fill the void. Without more, then, one would think Congress intended lawyers be subject to the Act whenever they meet the general "debt collector" definition.

Heintz argues we should nonetheless read the statute as containing an implied exemption for those debt-collecting activities of lawyers that consist of litigating (including, he assumes, settlement efforts). He relies primarily on three arguments.

First, Heintz argues many of the Act's requirements, if applied directly to litigating activities, will create harmfully anomalous results Congress simply could not have intended. We address this argument in light of the fact, when Congress first wrote the Act's substantive provisions, it had for the most part exempted litigating attorneys from the Act's coverage; when Congress later repealed the attorney exemption, it did not revisit the wording of these substantive provisions; and, for these reasons, some awkwardness is understandable. Particularly when read in this light, we find Heintz's argument unconvincing.

Second, Heintz points to a statement of Congressman Frank Annunzio, one of the sponsors of the 1986 amendment that removed from the Act the language creating a blanket exemption for lawyers. Representative Annunzio stated, despite the exemption's removal, the Act still would not apply to lawyers' litigating activities. Representative Annunzio said the Act

> regulates debt collection, not the practice of law. Congress repealed the attorney exemption to the act, not because of attorney[s'] conduct in the courtroom, but because of their conduct in the backroom. Only collection activities, not legal activities, are covered by the act. . . . The act applies to attorneys when they are collecting debts, not when they are performing tasks of a legal nature. . . . The act only regulates the conduct of debt collectors, it does not prevent creditors, through their attorneys, from pursuing any legal remedies available to them.

This statement, however, does not persuade us.

For one thing, the plain language of the Act itself says nothing about retaining the exemption in respect to litigation. The line the statement seeks to draw between "legal" activities and "debt collection" activities was not necessarily apparent to those who debated the legislation, for litigating, at first blush, seems simply one way of collecting a debt. For another thing, when Congress considered the Act, other Congressmen expressed fear repeal would limit lawyers' "ability to contact third parties in order to facilitate settlements" and "could very easily interfere with a client's right to pursue judicial remedies." They proposed alternative language designed to keep litigation activities outside the Act's scope, but that language was not enacted. *Ibid.* Further, Congressman Annunzio made his statement not during the legislative process, but *after* the statute became law. It therefore is not a statement upon which other legislators might have relied in voting for or against the Act, but it simply represents the views of one informed person on an issue about which others may (or may not) have thought differently.

Finally, Heintz points to a "Commentary" on the Act by the FTC's staff. It says:

> Attorneys or law firms that engage in traditional debt collection activities (sending dunning letters, making collection calls to consumers) are covered by the [Act], but *those whose practice is limited to legal activities are not covered.*

We cannot give conclusive weight to this statement. The Commentary of which this statement is a part says it "is not binding on the Commission or the public." More importantly, we find nothing either in the Act or elsewhere indicating Congress intended to authorize the FTC to create this exception from the Act's coverage—an exception that, for the reasons we have set forth above, falls outside the range of reasonable interpretations of the Act's express language.

For these reasons, we agree with the Seventh Circuit that the Act applies to attorneys who "regularly" engage in consumer-debt-collection activity, even when that activity consists of litigation.

AFFIRMED.

CRITICAL THINKING

What ambiguity is central to this case? Do you agree with the way the Court interpreted the ambiguous word or phrase? Can you think of an alternative reasonable definition?

ETHICAL DECISION MAKING

Who are the primary stakeholders affected by the court's ruling? Does the Supreme Court have a stronger ethical obligation to protect the interests of some stakeholders over others? Explain.

Again, Case 45-3 illustrates only one example of an FDCPA violation. A debt collector could also be in violation of FDCPA if she did not send written notice to the debtor within five days of initial contact. This notice must include the amount of the debt as well as the name of the creditor. If a debt collector violates FDCPA, the collector is liable for actual damages, attorney fees, and other fines up to $1,000.

THE CREDIT CARD FRAUD ACT

Credit card fraud is a serious problem in the United States, costing consumers millions of dollars per year. Accordingly, Congress passed the Credit Card Fraud Act of 1984[34] to

[34] 18 U.S.C. § 1029(a)(1-4).

close existing loopholes in federal laws that allowed credit card fraud to be pervasive. The Credit Card Fraud Act states that it is unlawful to (1) possess an unauthorized credit card; (2) counterfeit or alter a credit card; (3) use account numbers of another's credit card to perpetuate fraud; or (4) use a credit card obtained from a third party with his or her consent, even if the third party conspires to report the card as stolen. The act also increases the penalty for committing credit card fraud.

THE FAIR CREDIT BILLING ACT

Did your credit card company fail to extend your credit when it informed you that your credit would be extended? Were you ever charged for merchandise you did not purchase or receive? Were you ever charged twice for one purchase? If so, you have been the victim of a credit billing error. The Fair Credit Billing Act (FCBA) of 1986[35] was created to handle such billing errors as those previously listed, as well as many others.

FCBA, enforced by the FTC, creates procedures consumers are to follow in filing complaints when billing errors occur. FCBA also requires that creditors explain to the consumer and FTC why the error occurred and promptly fix any billing errors. When a complaint is filed, the creditor may not try to collect on the disputed amount, or take any action against the consumer, until the complaint is answered.

THE FAIR AND ACCURATE CREDIT TRANSACTIONS ACT

The Fair and Accurate Credit Transactions Act (FACTA) of 2003[36] was passed in response to the growing number of identity theft cases. If someone thinks she is a victim of identity theft, she may contact the FTC and an alert will be placed in her credit files. The credit files then serve as a national fraud alert system to better enable authorities to catch those who are stealing identities.

Several other requirements created by the act protect consumers. First, major credit reporting agencies are now required to provide consumers with a free copy of their credit reports every 12 months. Second, receipts from credit card purchases are now to list an abbreviated version of the card number, so as to protect consumer accounts. Third, financial institutions must work with the FTC to "red-flag" suspicious transactions that might be a sign of identity theft. Fourth, assistance will be provided to victims of identity theft to help them rebuild their credit. Fifth, victims of identity theft may report fraud directly to creditors to protect their credit ratings.

Consumer Health and Safety

The legislation and rules we have examined regulate the advertising, labeling, and sale of products. Now we turn to legislation regarding product safety. This legislation is directly related to the Firestone-Ford investigation. The purpose of such regulations is to ensure that companies like Firestone and Ford produce safe products for consumers who do not have all the information. The two main federal statutes that address product safety are the Federal Food, Drug, and Cosmetic Act and the Consumer Product Safety Act.

THE FEDERAL FOOD, DRUG, AND COSMETIC ACT

In 1906 Congress created the first federal legislation regulating food and drugs, the Pure Food and Drugs Act. Subsequently, Congress amended the Pure Food and Drugs Act when

[35] 15 U.S.C. § 1601.

[36] Pub. L. No. 108-159, 117 Stat. 1952.

it created the Federal Food, Drug, and Cosmetic Act (FFDCA)[37] in 1938 to protect consumers against misbranded or adulterated food, drugs, medical devices, or cosmetics. The U.S. Food and Drug Administration (FDA), the agency responsible for administering FFDCA, creates standards to regulate food and drugs, thus protecting consumers. Specifically, the FDA must ensure that food, drugs, cosmetics, and medical devices meet specific safety standards.

Under FFDCA, the FDA must follow a set of procedures to determine whether a drug is safe to enter the market. Recently, the Supreme Court ruled on the issue of whether the FDA has the authority to regulate tobacco (see Case 45-4). According to the FDA, it (1) has authority to regulate drugs and (2) considers nicotine a drug.

[37] 21 U.S.C. §§ 301–393.

CASE 45-4 FOOD AND DRUG ADMINISTRATION ET AL. v. BROWN & WILLIAMSON TOBACCO CORPORATION ET AL.

UNITED STATES SUPREME COURT
120 S. CT. 1291 (2000)

Before 1995, the FDA consistently stated it did not have the power to regulate tobacco. However, in 1995, the FDA established nicotine is a "drug" and cigarettes and smokeless tobacco are "devices" for administering the drug. The FFDCA grants the FDA authority to regulate drugs and devices. Consequently, in August 1995, the FDA published a proposed rule restricting the sale of cigarettes and smokeless tobacco to children. This rule was designed to reduce the attractiveness and availability of tobacco to young people. In August 1996, the agency issued the final rule with restrictions on sale, promotion, and labeling of tobacco products, directed at behaviors marketed to kids. Examples of these restrictions include the following: prohibiting tobacco manufacturers from distributing promotional items bearing the manufacturer's brand name as well as outdoor advertising within 1000 feet of a school or playground.

A group of tobacco manufacturers, retailers, and advertisers filed suit against the FDA, arguing it did not have authority to regulate tobacco products and the advertising restrictions were not permissible under the Constitution. The district court ruled the FFDCA authorizes the FDA to regulate tobacco products and the labeling requirements were permitted. The Fourth Circuit Court of Appeals reversed, finding Congress did not give the FDA jurisdiction to regulate tobacco products.

JUSTICE O'CONNOR: The FDA's assertion of jurisdiction to regulate tobacco products is founded on its conclusions nicotine is a "drug" and cigarettes and smokeless tobacco are "drug delivery devices."

Because this case involves an administrative agency's construction of a statute it administers, our analysis is governed by Chevron U.S.A. Inc. v. Natural Resources Defense Council, Inc., 467 U.S. 837 (1984). Under Chevron, a reviewing court must first ask "whether Congress has directly spoken to the precise question at issue." If Congress has done so, the inquiry is at an end; the court "must give effect to the unambiguously expressed intent of Congress." But if Congress has not specifically addressed the question, a reviewing court must respect the agency's construction of the statute so long as it is permissible.

A

. . . Considering the FFDCA as a whole, it is clear Congress intended to exclude tobacco products from the FDA's jurisdiction. A fundamental precept of the FFDCA is any product regulated by the FDA—but not banned—must be safe for its intended use. Various provisions of the Act make clear this refers to the safety of using the product to obtain its intended effects, not the public health ramifications of alternative administrative actions by the FDA. That is, the FDA must determine there is a reasonable assurance the product's therapeutic benefits outweigh the risk of harm to the consumer. According to this standard, the FDA has concluded, although tobacco products might be effective in delivering certain pharmacological effects, they are "unsafe" and "dangerous" when used for these purposes. Consequently, if tobacco products were within the FDA's jurisdiction, the Act would require the FDA to remove them from the market entirely. But a ban would contradict Congress' clear intent as expressed in its more recent, tobacco-specific legislation. The inescapable conclusion is there is no room for tobacco products within the FFDCA's regulatory scheme. If they cannot be used safely for any therapeutic purpose, and yet they cannot be banned, they simply do not fit.

B

In determining whether Congress has spoken directly to the FDA's authority to regulate tobacco, we must also consider in greater detail the tobacco-specific legislation Congress has enacted over the past 35 years. Congress has enacted six separate pieces of legislation since 1965 addressing the problem of tobacco use and human health. . . .

Taken together, these actions by Congress over the past 35 years preclude an interpretation of the FFDCA that grants the FDA jurisdiction to regulate tobacco products. We do not rely on Congress' failure to act—its consideration and rejection of bills that would have given the FDA this authority—in reaching this conclusion. To the contrary, Congress has enacted several statutes addressing the particular subject of tobacco and health, creating a distinct regulatory scheme for cigarettes and smokeless tobacco. In doing so, Congress has been aware of tobacco's health hazards and its pharmacological effects. It has also enacted this legislation against the background of the FDA repeatedly and consistently asserting it lacks jurisdiction under the FFDCA to regulate tobacco products as customarily marketed. Further, Congress has persistently acted to preclude a meaningful role for any administrative agency in making policy on the subject of tobacco and health. Moreover, the substance of Congress' regulatory scheme is, in an important respect, incompatible with FDA jurisdiction. Although the supervision of product labeling to protect consumer health is a substantial component of the FDA's regulation of drugs and devices, the FCLAA and the CSTHEA explicitly prohibit any federal agency from imposing any health-related labeling requirements on cigarettes or smokeless tobacco products.

Under these circumstances, it is clear Congress' tobacco-specific legislation has effectively ratified the FDA's previous position it lacks jurisdiction to regulate tobacco. Congress has affirmatively acted to address the issue of tobacco and health, relying on the representations of the FDA it had no authority to regulate tobacco. It has created a distinct scheme to regulate the sale of tobacco products, focused on labeling and advertising, and premised on the belief the FDA lacks such jurisdiction under the FFDCA. As a result, Congress' tobacco-specific statutes preclude the FDA from regulating tobacco products as customarily marketed.

By no means do we question the seriousness of the problem the FDA has sought to address. The agency has amply demonstrated tobacco use, particularly among children and adolescents, poses perhaps the single most significant threat to public health in the United States. Nonetheless, no matter how "important, conspicuous, and controversial" the issue, and regardless of how likely the public is to hold the Executive Branch politically accountable, an administrative agency's power to regulate in the public interest must always be grounded in a valid grant of authority from Congress. And "in our anxiety to effectuate the congressional purpose of protecting the public, we must take care not to extend the scope of the statute beyond the point where Congress indicated it would stop." Reading the FFDCA as a whole, as well as in conjunction with Congress' subsequent tobacco-specific legislation, it is plain Congress has not given the FDA the authority it seeks to exercise here. For these reasons, the judgment of the Court of Appeals for the Fourth Circuit is

AFFIRMED.

DISSENT BY JUSTICE BREYER: with whom Justice Stevens, Justice Souter, and Justice Ginsburg join, dissenting.

The Food and Drug Administration (FDA) has the authority to regulate "articles (other than food) intended to affect the structure or any function of the body. . . ." Unlike the majority, I believe tobacco products fit within this statutory language.

In its own interpretation, the majority nowhere denies the following two salient points. First, tobacco products (including cigarettes) fall within the scope of this statutory definition, read literally. . . . Second, the statute's basic purpose—the protection of public health—supports the inclusion of cigarettes within its scope.

Despite the FFDCA's literal language and general purpose (both of which support the FDA's finding that cigarettes come within its statutory authority), the majority nonetheless reads the statute as excluding tobacco products for two basic reasons. . . . In my view, neither of these propositions is valid. The FFDCA does not significantly limit the FDA's remedial alternatives. And the later statutes do not tell the FDA it cannot exercise jurisdiction, but simply leave FDA jurisdictional law where Congress found it.

In short, I believe the most important indicia of statutory meaning—language and purpose—along with the FFDCA's legislative history (described briefly in Part I) are sufficient to establish the FDA has authority to regulate tobacco. The statute-specific arguments against jurisdiction the tobacco companies and the majority rely upon (discussed in Part II) are based on erroneous assumptions and, thus, do not defeat the jurisdiction-supporting thrust of the FFDCA's language and purpose. The inferences the majority draws from later legislative history are not persuasive, since one can just as easily infer from the later laws Congress did not intend to affect the FDA's tobacco-related authority at all. And the fact the FDA changed its mind about the scope of its own jurisdiction is legally insignificant because the agency's reasons for changing course are fully justified. Finally, as I explain in Part V, the degree of accountability that likely will attach to the FDA's action in this case should alleviate any concern Congress, rather than an administrative agency, ought to make this important regulatory decision.

[T]he Court today holds a regulatory statute aimed at unsafe drugs and devices does not authorize regulation of a drug (nicotine) and a device (a cigarette) the Court itself finds unsafe. Far more than most, this particular drug and device risks the life-threatening harms administrative regulation seeks to rectify. The majority's conclusion is counter-intuitive. And, for the reasons set forth, I believe the law does not require it.

CRITICAL THINKING

The first reason the majority offers for its conclusion that the FDA does not have authority to regulate tobacco is that the regulation of tobacco does not "fit" with the FDA's scheme for evaluating drugs. Consequently, the FDA would be forced to ban tobacco. What evidence does the court offer for this reason? Are you persuaded by the evidence?

ETHICAL DECISION MAKING

Consider both the majority and the dissenting opinions. Who are the primary stakeholders affected by the decision that the FDA cannot regulate tobacco?

Case 45-4 demonstrates the significant influence the FDA has over the lives and health of American citizens. It also illustrates the problems with some of its regulation devices. The Food and Drug Administration Modernization Act of 1997 amended FFDCA to help improve the regulation process, particularly for drugs and medical devices. For example, the 1997 act reauthorized a drug program that cut the time required for a drug review from 30 months to 15 months. The act also increased patient access to experimental drugs and accelerated the review of important new medications.

THE CONSUMER PRODUCT SAFETY ACT

In the Consumer Product Safety Act of 1972 Congress created the Consumer Product Safety Commission (CPSC) and directed it to "protect the public against unreasonable risks of injuries and deaths associated with consumer products."[38]

The CPSC protects the public from injuries associated with consumer products in several ways. First, the CPSC issues and enforces mandatory standards regarding product safety. Similarly, the commission works with industries to develop voluntary product standards. If the CPSC cannot establish a standard that would adequately protect the public, it can ban consumer products from the market. In addition, the CPSC can administer existing product safety legislation. Examples of such legislation include the Child Protection and Toy Safety Act of 1969[39] and the Federal Hazardous Substance Act of 1960.[40]

Second, the CPSC can arrange for a recall of products. Although the CPSC has the authority to issue product recalls on its own, usually the CPSC works with companies that are voluntarily issuing recalls for dangerous products. For example, in August 2006, both Dell and Apple issued voluntary recalls, with the help of the CPSC, for lithium ion batteries sold in their laptops. Both companies received several separate complaints about their batteries overheating, and thus the CPSC aided the companies in the battery recall.

Third, the commission conducts research regarding potentially hazardous products. The National Highway Traffic Safety Administration (NHTSA) is similar to the CPSC in that it, too, conducts investigations about the safety of potentially hazardous products. The NHTSA, however, focuses primarily on motor vehicles. The NHTSA was the agency that investigated the Ford-Firestone case to determine exactly what was causing the tire blowouts in Ford Explorers.

Fourth, the CPSC educates consumers about product safety. One important way the CPSC offers this education is through the National Injury Information Clearinghouse.

This section examined two of the most significant laws governing the safety of consumer products. Exhibit 45-2 lists six additional consumer product safety laws.

Exhibit 45-2 Other Consumer Protection Laws

STATUTE	PURPOSE
Pure Food and Drugs Act of 1906 (amended by the Federal Food, Drug, and Cosmetic Act)	Forbids the adulteration and mislabeling of food and drugs
Meat Inspection Act of 1906 Wholesome Meat Act of 1967	Provides for meat inspection Amended the Meat Inspection Act to promulgate standards for animal slaughter for meat
Flammable Fabrics Act of 1953	Prohibits the sale of highly flammable clothing
Child Protection and Toy Safety Act of 1969	Requires childproof devices and toy labeling
Toy Safety Act of 1984	Permits the Consumer Product Safety Commission to recall toys and other articles used by children
Drug-Price Competition and Patent-Term Restoration Act of 1984	Simplifies the Food and Drug Administration's process of approving generic drugs

[38] 15 U.S.C. § 2051.

[39] Amendments to 15 U.S.C. §§ 1261, 1262, and 1274.

[40] 15 U.S.C. §§ 1261–1277.

CASE OPENER WRAP-UP

Firestone

By 2000, the National Highway Traffic Safety Administration placed the number of deaths in the United States associated with Firestone tires at 119. The rising number of deaths and the huge press associated with this case eventually led Congress to pass an auto safety bill that would raise fines and criminal penalties for firms that deceive regulators about safety.

As the press received word of the possible deception associated with these companies, the public began to respond unfavorably to both corporations. To counteract this public dissatisfaction, Ford launched an advertising campaign that featured its CEO apologizing to the public for any and all safety problems occurring as a result of the defective tires. Future business managers need to be aware of their legal and ethical obligations to consumers, as well as all the other stakeholders affected by their market decisions.

Summary

The Federal Trade Commission

How the FTC brings an action:

1. FTC conducts an investigation.
2. FTC sends a complaint to the violator.
3. FTC and the violator settle the complaint through a consent agreement.
4. If the company refuses to enter the consent agreement, the FTC may issue a formal administrative complaint, which leads to an administrative hearing.
5. If the company has violated the law, the FTC issues a cease-and-desist order.

If the company violates the order, the FTC can seek an injunction against the company or fine the company up to $10,000 per violation.

Deceptive Advertising

Bait-and-switch advertising: Advertising a low price to "bait" the consumer into the store only so that the salesperson can "switch" the consumer to another, higher-priced item.

FTC actions against deceptive advertising:

- *Cease-and-desist actions*: Court orders requiring that firms stop their current advertising behavior.
- *Multiple-product orders:* Court orders requiring that firms stop current advertisements on numerous products, as opposed to one specified product.
- *Corrective advertising:* Advertisements in which the company explicitly states that the formerly advertised claims were untrue.

Telemarketing and electronic advertising:

- *1991 Telephone Consumer Protection Act:* Telemarketers cannot use an automatic telephone dialing system or a prerecorded voice.
- *Telemarketing and Consumer Fraud and Abuse Prevention Act of 1994:* This act created certain requirements regarding when and how telemarketers may make calls.
- *Federal Do Not Call registry:* Telemarketers cannot call consumers who have voluntarily placed their phone numbers on the federal Do Not Call list.

Tobacco advertising: Cigarette and smokeless-tobacco advertising is restricted.

Labeling and Packaging Laws	Federal and state governments have passed laws requiring that manufacturers provide accurate, understandable information on labels. Furthermore, if a product is potentially harmful, the manufacturer must make the consumer aware of this harm.
Sales	*Door-to-door sales:* The *Cooling-Off Rule* gives consumers three days to cancel purchases they make from salespeople who come to their homes. *Telephone and mail-order sales:* The *Mail or Telephone Order Merchandise Rule of 1993* extends protections to those who purchase over the phone or by fax. *Unsolicited merchandise:* The consumer is allowed to treat any such unsolicited merchandise as a gift. Thus, she is free to keep or return the merchandise as she wishes. *FTC regulation of specific industries:* **1.** Used-car sales **2.** Funeral home services **3.** Real estate sales **4.** Online sales
Credit Protection	The *Truth-In-Lending Act* requires that sellers disclose the terms of the credit or loan to facilitate the consumer's comparison of a variety of credit lines or loans. The *Fair Credit Reporting Act* ensures accurate credit reporting. The *Fair Debt Collection Practices Act* regulates the actions of debt collectors that regularly attempt to collect debts on behalf of others. The *Credit Card Fraud Act* closes loopholes in federal laws to further punish people who commit credit card fraud. The *Fair Credit Billing Act* seeks to rectify problems and abuses associated with credit billing errors. The *Fair and Accurate Credit Transactions Act* takes affirmative actions to control and prosecute identity theft.
Consumer Health and Safety	The *Federal Food, Drug, and Cosmetic Act* protects consumers against misbranded or adulterated food, drugs, medical devices, or cosmetics. The *Consumer Product Safety Act* created the Consumer Product Safety Commission (CPSC) to "protect the public against unreasonable risks of injuries and deaths associated with consumer products."

Point / Counterpoint

Should Firms Be Prevented from Concealing Valuable Product Information from Consumers?

Yes	No
Consumer protection legislation should protect consumers against sellers who wish to sell goods and services under cover of deception. The great benefit of markets is that they satisfy consumers. But a consumer cannot be sovereign when he is asked to purchase a tainted version of the good he thought he was buying. When firms conceal information that they well know would affect the likelihood of a sale, they are encouraging a culture of mistrust. They are saying by their behavior that it is appropriate business behavior to deceive in the interest of encouraging an exchange.	The best way to protect consumers is by placing responsibility on them to ask the right questions. They and only they know what they are seeking from a good or service. No regulatory agency understands why consumers are purchasing a particular product. To try to protect consumers against any and all possible harm is to treat them as if they were infants, incapable of watching out for themselves. A business firm should not be required to mention every attribute possessed by a product just to satisfy some utopian goal of full disclosure.

Questions & Problems

1. What is the goal of the FTC, and how does it achieve its goal? What are some pieces of legislation that enable the FTC to achieve its goal?
2. What are the elements of a deceptive advertisement, and how does the FTC prove an ad is deceptive?
3. What are the main provisions of the Truth-in-Lending Act, and how does it aid consumers?
4. Until 2002, the City of Bethlehem contractually retained the private law firm of Portnoff Law Associates (PLA), Ltd., to collect payment for overdue water and sewer obligations. The city notified PLA of delinquent water and sewer assessments, and PLA then contacted homeowners in attempts to collect on those claims. On February 20, 2002, the city notified PLA of a delinquent water service obligation of Bridget and Michael Piper in the amount of $252.71. PLA sent numerous letters, some on its letterhead and some on the city's letterhead, as well as made a number of telephone calls to the Piper residence in an effort to secure payment of the delinquent water service fees. PLA has never disputed that the letters it sent to Mr. and Mrs. Piper failed to include the debt verification language required by Section 1692(g) of FDCPA. PLA has likewise never disputed that its letters did not state they were sent by a debt collector, the debt collector was attempting to collect a debt, and any information obtained by PLA would be used for that purpose, as required by Section 1692(e)(11) of FDCPA. Bridget Piper filed suit against PLA and two of its attorneys in the U.S. District Court for the Eastern District of Pennsylvania. The complaint alleged that PLA's attempts to collect payment of water and sewer bills owed to the city violated FDCPA. The complaint alleged that PLA violated this statute by failing to include statutory disclosures required for communications sent to consumers, by falsely representing or implying that the letters were from an attorney, and by collecting and attempting to collect fees not permitted by the agreement creating the debt or by law. Were the Pipers successful in their suit against PLA? Why? [*Piper v. Portnoff Law Assocs.,* 396 F.3d 227 (2005).]
5. On March 7, 2001, the United States District Court for the Eastern District of Virginia, after finding that H&R Block willfully and maliciously engaged in a false and misleading advertising campaign aimed at preventing Liberty Tax Service and 13 of its franchisees from competing for customers, entered a permanent nationwide injunction against H&R Block requiring, among other things, that its advertisements "clearly and prominently" disclose whether an advertised product is actually a loan. On October 10, 2001, and January 10, 2002, Liberty filed two separate civil contempt motions alleging that H&R Block was in violation of the district court's injunction because its "Instant Money" advertisements used much smaller type and less apparent color print for the term *loan* than for terms such as *refund, check today,* and *instant money.* Liberty further alleged that H&R Block's advertisements failed to "clearly and prominently" disclose whether an advertised product was a loan because the loan disclosures contained therein were placed in areas that increased the likelihood they would go unnoticed and consequently unread. Liberty argued that the injunction's "clearly and prominently" language required that H&R Block's loan disclosures be presented in a manner that made them immediately noticeable to consumers. The district court ruled in favor of H&R Block because the reasonable person reading the H&R Block ads would be able to tell that

the "Instant Money" campaign actually referred to loans taken out against an expected refund. Liberty appealed. Was Liberty successful on appeal? Why? [*JTH Tax, Inc. v. H&R Block E. Tax Servs.*, 359 F.3d 699 (2004).]

6. Brenda Laramore receives federal assistance pursuant to Section Eight of the United States Housing Act. "Section [Eight] is a federal program designed to assist the elderly, low income, and disabled pay rent for privately owned housing." The assistance generally comes in the form of a voucher the recipient can use to pay a portion of his or her rent. On October 21, 2002, Laramore telephoned Ritchie, the company responsible for managing the apartment in question, to request an application for a lease. The woman who took the call initially told Laramore the apartment was available to rent. After Laramore informed her she intended to use a Section 8 Voucher to pay a portion of the rent, however, the woman told Laramore the apartment was not available to persons using Section 8 vouchers. On February 21, 2003, Laramore filed suit, claiming that Ritchie violated ECOA by denying her a rental application because she receives public assistance. Ritchie moved to dismiss the complaint on the ground that a rental application is not a credit transaction under ECOA. The district court agreed with Ritchie and dismissed the suit. Laramore appealed. Did Ritchie violate ECOA? Should ECOA apply to rental applications? [*Laramore v. Ritchie Realty Mgmt. Co.*, 397 F.3d 544 (2005).]

7. In August 1999, United Artists contracted with ABF, a company in the business of distributing advertisements by fax, to send a one-page advertisement for discount movie ticket packages. The following month, ABF transmitted the advertisement to about 90,000 fax machines in the Phoenix area. United Artists received $12,080 through the ad, and paid ABF $3,375 for its services. ESI is the only recipient that complained to United Artists about receiving the advertisement. After ESI received the faxed advertisement, it filed a complaint, alleging violation of the Telephone Consumer Protection Act (TCPA), which makes it unlawful for persons within the United States to, among other things, "use any telephone facsimile machine, computer, or other device to send an unsolicited advertisement to a telephone facsimile machine." ESI requested statutory damages of $500 per violation with possible trebling (tripling) of those damages, and injunctive relief. ESI sought to represent a class consisting of "all persons and entities who received on a telephone facsimile machine" the particular advertisement sent by ABF for United Artists. United Artists objected to the class certification, arguing, among other things, that a class action suit could lead to liability against United Artists disproportionate to the harm caused. ESI offered to waive the statutory minimum recovery of $500 per violation and to reduce damages to $90 or, alternatively, to modify and reduce the number of the class. The trial court denied ESI's motion for certification of the class. ESI appealed the trial court's ruling. Should United Artists be required to pay for sending out its one-page fax? If you were on the court, how would you rule? Why? [*ESI Ergonomic Solutions, LLC v. UA Theatre Circuit, Inc.*, 50 P.3d 844 (2002).]

8. American Collections Enterprise, Inc. (ACEI), is a debt collector that contracted with Capital One in 2001 to provide debt collection services. Under the terms of the collection agreement, Capital One assigned delinquent accounts to ACEI for collection, and ACEI collected these debts on a contingent-fee basis. Pooja Goswami owed approximately $900 on her Capital One credit card and failed to pay. Capital One referred that debt to ACEI for collection on March 20, 2001, and ACEI pursued Goswami's delinquent account. It sent a collection notice letter to Goswami on December 7, 2001. A second form letter was sent on January 25, 2002, more than

180 days after the debt had been referred to ACEI. The second letter was sent to Goswami in an envelope that bore a half-inch-thick blue bar across the entire envelope that contained the words "Priority Letter" in white. ACEI admitted that the markings on the envelope had been developed to entice debtors to open the letter. The letter itself contained a second blue bar and "Priority Letter" marking as a header. After receiving the letter, Goswami filed a complaint alleging violation of FDCPA, in particular 15 U.S.C. Sections 1692f(8) and 1692e(10). Goswami complained that the markings on the envelope violate Section 1692f(8), which prohibits any markings on debt collection letter envelopes besides the name and address of the sender and the addressee. She further complained that the contents of the letter were deceptive, in violation of Section 1692e(10). ACEI moved for summary judgment, arguing that neutral or benign expressions on an envelope, such as "priority letter," that in no way indicate it is a collection letter, are not banned by FDCPA. The district court agreed, granted the defendant's summary judgment motion, and dismissed the case. Goswami appealed. Are the markings on the envelope and letter misleading and a violation of FDCPA? Why? [*Goswami v. Am. Collections Enter.,* 377 F.3d 488 (2004).]

9. Mary Grendahl's daughter Sarah became engaged to marry Lavon Phillips and moved in with him. Mary Grendahl became suspicious that Phillips was not telling the truth about his past. She did some preliminary investigation herself before she contacted Kevin Fitzgerald, a family friend who worked for McDowell, a private investigation agency. She asked Fitzgerald to do a "background check" on Phillips. Fitzgerald began his search by obtaining Phillips's Social Security number from a computer database and used it to request that Econ Control furnish a finder's report on Phillips. According to the president of Econ Control, a finder's report could be obtained without authorization of the person who was the subject of the report because the finder's report contained no information on credit history or creditworthiness, whereas a credit report requires authorization from the subject. Fitzgerald met with Mary Grendahl and gave her the results of his investigation, including the finder's report. Phillips brought suit against Mary Grendahl, McDowell Agency, and Econ Control, alleging, "Defendants willfully and maliciously obtained Plaintiff's credit report for impermissible and illegal purposes in violation of the Fair Credit Reporting Act." Phillips appended to his complaint a "Credit History" on himself, which, among other things, showed that Sherlock Information (the trade name of Econ Control) had requested a credit history on him. Phillips and the defendants filed cross-motions for summary judgment. The district court ruled in favor of the defendants, and Phillips appealed. Did the court find that Grendahl and the other defendants violated the Fair Credit Reporting Act through their investigation? Why? [*Phillips v. Grendahl,* 312 F.3d 357 (2002).]

10. Aroma Housewares Co. is a California corporation that distributes electric kitchen appliances. Aroma distributed between 30,000 and 40,000 juice extractors in the United States. The juicers employed a rapidly spinning metal grater, whose sharp teeth pulverized fruits and vegetables that were inserted through a plastic chute. Aroma began receiving consumer reports of failed juicers. Exploding juicers, the reports claimed, "[threw] with great violence pieces of the clear plastic cover and shreds of the razor-sharp separator screen as far as eight feet." One consumer called the juicer "an unsafe and dangerous machine which exploded in [his] face." A flying blade sliced the hand of another. And one injured woman was taken by ambulance to the hospital, where she stayed overnight, and she sustained permanent damage to her fingers, hand, and arm. In all, Aroma received complaints from 23 consumers. Aroma tested the juicers but was unable to replicate the malfunctions. It reported none of this to the Consumer Product Safety Commission. But some of the consumers did. Alerted to the problems, the commission asked the company to report what it knew about the dangers posed by its juicers. Aroma disclosed the consumer complaints, as well as the results of its own tests. A few months later, Aroma and the commission jointly announced that the juicers were being recalled. The United States subsequently sued Aroma, alleging that the company had violated the reporting requirements of the Consumer Product Safety Act. The district court granted partial summary judgment for the United States. Aroma appealed. Did Aroma violate CPSA? Should Aroma have reported the defective juicers even though it could not replicate the malfunctions? [*U.S. v. Mirama Enters.*, 387 F.3d 983 (2004).]

11. Seven plaintiffs brought suit against Boise Cascade for deceptive advertising. Boise Cascade produced a composite wood siding from 1960 to 1984. All seven of the plaintiffs live in homes covered in Boise Cascade's composite siding. Only two of the seven plaintiffs are original owners of their homes. The plaintiffs allege that Boise Cascade's composite siding was defective and Boise Cascade deceptively advertised the composite siding. The complaint also claims Boise Cascade fraudulently and deceptively failed to disclose that its siding "performed poorly in the field," with a "high rate of failure," was sensitive to moisture, and required "highly particularized maintenance." None of the plaintiffs actually received any representations regarding the siding from Boise Cascade. The circuit court granted Boise Cascade summary judgment, finding the claimed damages were not proximately caused by the alleged deceptive advertising as there was no evidence of reliance on the advertisements. Plaintiffs appealed. The appellate court reversed, holding that the circuit court erred by requiring privity, "some sort of direct contact between the plaintiffs and the representations made by Boise Cascade." According to the appellate court, consumers are afforded broad protection by prohibiting any deception or false promise. The appellate court further held that the circuit court erred in its conclusion there was no proximate causation. The court held that reliance on deceptive advertisements can be proved by the fact that a market for a good existed. Boise Cascade appealed. How did the court ultimately rule on appeal? Why? [*Shannon v. Boise Cascade Corp.*, 208 Ill. 2d 517 (2004).]
12. Fairbanks Capital Corp. acquired 12,800 allegedly delinquent high-interest mortgages from ContiMortgage, including one owed by Chad and Frances Schlosser. Identifying itself as a debt collector, Fairbanks sent the Schlossers a letter asserting their debt was in default. Fairbanks was mistaken; the Schlossers were not in default. The Schlossers tried to inform Fairbanks they were not in default, and Fairbanks tried to foreclose. The foreclosure was eventually stopped. The Schlossers then filed suit, claiming Fairbanks's letter failed to notify them of their right to contest the debt, as required by the Fair Debt Collection Practices Act. The district court concluded, because the debt was not actually in default when Fairbanks acquired it, that Fairbanks was not a debt collector within the meaning of FDCPA. The court granted Fairbanks's motion to dismiss, and the Schlossers appealed. How did the court rule on appeal? Why? [*Schlosser v. Fairbanks Capital Corp.*, 323 F.3d 534 (2003).]

Looking for more review material?

The Online Learning Center at **www.mhhe.com/kubasek1e** contains this chapter's "Assignment on the Internet" and also a list of URLs for more information, entitled "On the Internet." Find both of them in the Student Center portion of the OLC, along with quizzes and other helpful materials.

Environmental Law

CASE OPENER

Rogers Corporation's Hazardous Waste Debacle

Rogers Corporation is a Massachusetts company that manufactures foam products in Connecticut. During the production process, hazardous wastes are created by oil dripping from the machinery. Rogers Corporation allowed these wastes to collect in an area on the floor underneath the machine and then pumped the oil into drums. The oil in these drums was sampled to determine whether excessive levels of polychlorinated biphenyls (PCBs) were present. PCBs are persistent toxic pollutants that are regulated under environmental laws because of their effects on humans and wildlife. From 1988 through 1992, concentrations of PCBs in the drums were less than 50 parts per million (ppm), an amount that is in full compliance with the law.

In April 1993, another sample of the drums indicated the presence of PCBs of between 50 and 170 ppm, an amount in excess of federal standards. The testing company informed Rogers Corporation of this violation in June 1993, and Rogers shipped the wastes off-site in a manner required by the law. Later, in December 1993, the Connecticut Department of Environmental Protection inspected the premises. A sample from the area underneath the machinery was taken, where Rogers Corporation allowed the waste to pool before putting it into drums. This sample was found to have PCB concentrations of 170 ppm, with samples of drums indicating the presence of PCBs at a level of 70 ppm. Additionally, more samples from the testing company indicated that the storage area had PCB concentrations of 110 to 140 ppm. The company cleaned the floor storage area on March 15, 1994.

1. Given this information, do you think the company was in violation of the law?
2. Given that Rogers Corporation was aware of exceeding PCB limitations as early as April 1993, should managers in the company have proceeded more quickly to clean up the area?

The Wrap-Up at the end of the chapter will answer these questions.

CHAPTER 46

Learning Objectives

After reading this chapter, you will be able to answer the following questions:

1. What are the alternative ways to protect the environment?
2. What are the responsibilities of the Environmental Protection Agency?
3. How does this country regulate air quality?
4. How does this country regulate water quality?
5. How does this country regulate waste?
6. How does this country regulate toxic substances?

The law is not a fixed set of statutes and rules; rather, it changes over time in response to many factors. One principal cause of change in the law is our understanding of the world around us. As we learn more about the effects of certain actions, lawmakers alter old laws and adopt new laws to temper the harmful effects of those actions. For example, as recently as 30 years ago, the behavior of the management of the Rogers Corporation was not only typical but lawful. Early laws attempted to protect a few aspects of the environment, but lawmakers did not enact most of our current environmental regulations until after 1970. Prior to that time, we viewed evidence of pollution, such as black smoke billowing in the air, as a sign of a productive economy. Today, we recognize the harm that can result from some of the by-products of production, and we alter the law to limit those potentially hazardous consequences.

This chapter begins with an examination of the alternative ways we can protect our environment, followed by an introduction to the primary agency responsible for protecting the environment. The bulk of the chapter then provides an overview of some of the major environmental laws. The chapter concludes with a brief discussion of international environmental law.

Alternative Means of Protecting the Environment

TORT LAW

Tort law is the oldest, and many argue the least effective, means of protecting the environment. Remember from Chapter 8 that a tort is an injury to one's person or property. Pollution causes injury to individuals and their property, so it is only logical that when people first started recognizing that pollution was causing them harm, they turned to tort law.

Nuisance. The initial tort theory used was **nuisance.** A nuisance arises when one person uses his or her property in a manner that unreasonably interferes with another's use and enjoyment of his or her land. Thus, when a plant is emitting particulates that fall on a person's property, defacing the house and making it difficult for family members to breathe, the homeowner would sue the plant's operator for nuisance. Traditionally, in an action for nuisance, the remedy being sought would be an injunction to stop the plant from emitting the particulates into the air. This remedy was ordinarily granted when the nuisance could be proved, making nuisance appear to be an effective way to eliminate pollution. Case 46-1, however, set a precedent that limited the effectiveness of nuisance as a means of controlling pollution.

CASE 46-1

BOOMER v. ATLANTIC CEMENT COMPANY
NEW YORK STATE COURT OF APPEALS
257 N.E.2D 870 (1970)

Every day considerable amounts of dirt and smoke were emitted into the air by a cement plant operated by defendant Atlantic Cement Company. The plaintiffs, Boomer and other property owners located close to the plant, brought a nuisance action against the defendant, seeking an injunction. The trial court ruled in favor of the defendant, finding a nuisance, but denying plaintiffs the injunction they sought. The plaintiffs appealed to the intermediate appellate court, and the judgment of the trial court was affirmed in favor of the defendant. Plaintiffs then appealed to the state's highest appellate court.

JUDGE BERGAN: . . . The cement making operations of defendant have been found by the Court at Special Term to have damaged the nearby properties of plaintiffs in these two actions. That court accordingly found defendant maintained a nuisance and this has been affirmed at the Appellate Division. The total damage to plaintiffs' properties is, however, relatively small in comparison with the value of defendant's operation and with the consequences of the injunction which plaintiffs seek.

The ground for the denial of injunction, notwithstanding the finding both that there is a nuisance and that plaintiffs have been damaged substantially, is the large disparity in economic consequences of the nuisance and of the injunction.

[T]o grant the injunction unless defendant pays plaintiffs such permanent damages as may be fixed by the court seems to do justice between the contending parties. All of the attributions of economic loss to the properties on which plaintiffs' complaints are based will have been redressed.

It seems reasonable to think that the risk of being required to pay permanent damages to injured property owners by cement plant owners would itself be a reasonably effective spur to research for improved techniques to minimize nuisance.

The damage base here suggested is consistent with the general rule in those nuisance cases where damages are allowed. "Where a nuisance is of such a permanent and unabatable character that a single recovery can be had, including the whole damage past and future resulting therefrom, there can be but one recovery." It has been said that permanent damages are allowed where the loss recoverable would obviously be small compared with the cost of removal of the nuisance.

Thus it seems fair to both sides to grant permanent damages to plaintiffs which will terminate this private litigation.

REVERSED in favor of the plaintiff.

CRITICAL THINKING

What are the primary facts in *Boomer v. Atlantic Cement Company?* Which missing facts in the case, were they provided, would better enable you to evaluate the judge's reasoning?

ETHICAL DECISION MAKING

If this court operated under an ethics-of-care philosophy, would its decision have been different? If so, how? If not, why not?

The plaintiffs technically "won" the case because the plaintiffs were granted a greater remedy than the lower courts had provided. They were awarded permanent damages, and if the defendant failed to pay within a set period of time, they would receive an injunction. However, damages were not what the plaintiffs wanted; they wanted the traditional remedy of elimination of the nuisance through an injunction.

Thus, by establishing the rule that the court would compare the harms that would result from the injunction to the benefits to be attained from the injunction, the court essentially kept nuisance law from becoming an effective means for controlling pollution. Some argue that part of the reason for the court's decision was the judge's inability to understand the true costs of the pollution. Nonetheless, courts today rarely award injunctions against pollution.

Nuisance actions are still used to fight pollution. However, their role is limited to providing a way for victims of pollution to receive compensation for their loss. The availability of these actions may also serve as a deterrent.

Negligence. Negligence is another tort theory that can be used to protect the environment. To use this theory, plaintiffs must establish the elements of negligence as described in Chapter 9: duty, breach of duty, causation, and damage. Negligence would most often be used in either (1) a case where a defendant's polluting behavior harmed a plaintiff or (2) a situation in which a defendant's product contained a toxic chemical and the use of that product hurt the plaintiff. An illustration of the first kind of situation is a case in which the defendant improperly stored hazardous waste in metal barrels on his property. The barrels leaked, and the waste seeped out into the soil and into the groundwater, eventually contaminating the plaintiff's well water and injuring the plaintiff. The plaintiff might bring a negligence action.

Negligence actions involving hazardous materials are often difficult for plaintiffs to win because of the difficulty in proving causation. Because many of the hazardous pollutants' effects do not show up for a significant length of time after exposure, it is difficult to link the harm to the defendant.

Another problem with negligence is that the defendant can often raise the defenses of contributory or comparative negligence, as well as assumption of the risk, thereby limiting the defendant's potential liability. Finally, like nuisance, negligence is reactive. Prevention of the pollution itself would be a preferable approach.

Trespass. **Trespass,** discussed in Chapter 8, may also be used. Trespass occurs when someone goes onto another's property without the owner's permission or places something on someone else's property without the owner's permission. For example, if a company decided to dispose of some hazardous chemicals by throwing them into a stream that flowed through the company's property and into a small lake on your land, the company would be engaging in a trespass, because it is intentionally putting the chemicals into a stream that will carry them directly onto your property. Again, this tort alone cannot prevent pollution, but it can be used to provide compensation for those whose property was harmed by such activities.

GOVERNMENT SUBSIDIES

Government subsidies are another approach to preventing pollution. Under a subsidy system, the government gives firms tax credits, low-interest loans, and/or grants if they install pollution control devices or change their production methods to reduce harmful emissions. Of course, because the subsidies rarely cover the entire cost of the new technology, the firm may still be at a slight competitive disadvantage when others in the industry make no such investment. Sometimes, however, firms find that the installation of the new technology ultimately provides them with a competitive advantage because it makes their operations more efficient and reduces their energy costs.

MARKETABLE DISCHARGE PERMITS

Marketable discharge permits are seen as a way to regulate pollution more efficiently. Under such a system, the government determines how much of a given pollutant should be emitted during a year. It then issues the requisite number of permits and prohibits any emissions without a permit. Firms that can reduce their emissions at a lower cost will do so and then sell their unused permits to firms for which reducing emissions would be extremely costly or "bank" them for use in the future. Each successive year the government can issue fewer permits, thereby reducing the level of pollution.

The most well known use of such a system is the United States' Acid Rain Trading Program that began in 1991. That year, the Environmental Protection Agency (EPA) issued 150,010 permits to electric generating plants, with each permit allowing its holder to emit 1 ton of sulfur dioxide (a precursor to acid rain). By the year 2005, the number of permits issued annually had been reduced to 125,000.

At least initially, the program has been deemed a success. By 1995, the 100 largest sulfur dioxide–emitting plants were showing a 50 percent reduction from 1980 emission levels. In the year 2000, sulfur dioxide emissions were 2 million tons (29 percent) below the allowable level for 1999.

connecting to the core

MARKET FAILURE: EXTERNALITIES

You may recall from your economics class a discussion of market failures that might help explain the need for a variety of approaches to promote more environmentally sound business practices. For instance, we presume that people tend to seek their own personal welfare at the expense of others' welfare. Similarly, we presume that firms, by design, seek to maximize their own welfare at society's expense. Unfortunately, environmentally sound practices are generally not advantageous to profit-maximizing firms, in the sense that firms often reduce costs by engaging in behavior that more heavily pollutes the environment. Many firms typically do not take external costs into consideration when making decisions, as these are costs incurred by society. The external costs could be in the form of a greater likelihood of disease, reduced life spans, or other damages as a result of pollution, but these costs do not affect a firm's revenues or expenses. For instance, if a power plant can produce energy most profitably by burning coal while not using other expensive technologies that would reduce the harmful emissions, the plant has an incentive to continue operating without the use of emissions-reducing resources. Because the market fails to consider these social costs, in the sense that most firms do not consider external costs when making production decisions, other approaches are needed to encourage more "green-friendly" business practices, including many of the approaches discussed in this chapter.

Source: Bradley R. Schiller, *The Economy Today* (New York: McGraw-Hill/Irwin, 2006), pp. 602–603.

GREEN TAXES

An idea that is more popular in European nations but is gaining interest in the United States is the imposition of green taxes. *Green taxes* involve the taxation of environmentally harmful activities. The money from the taxes can be used to fund environmental projects, and the imposition of the taxes should make environmentally harmful activities more costly, thereby discouraging consumers and firms from engaging in these activities. For example, when a province in Canada imposed a $.10 tax on each alcoholic beverage sold in a nonrefillable container, there was a dramatic shift among beer drinkers from nonrefillable containers to more environmentally friendly reusable bottles.

Green taxes, along with other economic instruments that can be used to protect the environment, are consistent with international environmental law's principle of "polluter and user pay." The ultimate goal of this approach is to phase out environmentally harmful action through the imposition of a tax. One problem with this approach, however, is that if such taxes become the sole source of government revenue, revenue may decrease when the environmentally harmful action ceases.

DIRECT REGULATION

The primary approach to protecting the environment since 1970 has been direct regulation, establishing a comprehensive set of regulations to protect the environment. These regulations set specific limits on the amount of pollutants that can be discharged, and they subject violators to fines and in some cases prison terms. While we take these laws for granted, we have to remember that not all countries' regulatory systems are so complete. For example, both Nicaragua and Colombia have passed statutes mandating the compilation of their scattered environmental norms into a cohesive set of environmental laws; no such compilations are as yet in existence.

Most of the early environmental regulations in the United States were *technology forcing,* meaning that they were based primarily on health considerations, with the assumption that once standards have been established, the industries will be forced to develop the technology to meet the standards. In some cases, this approach was highly successful, and impressive technological gains were made. In other cases, the necessary technology was not developed, and we were unable to meet our goals.

Other standards are *technology-driven* standards, meaning they are set to achieve the greatest possible improvements while taking into account the existing levels of technology. These standards are easier to meet, but some argue that the result is that our environment is not as clean as it could be.

Environmental regulations are enforced primarily by administrative agencies through administrative proceedings. In some cases, however, either agencies or citizens groups are forced to resort to the court system to enforce the laws. The degree of vigor with which the environmental regulations are enforced often depends on how committed the president is to vigorous enforcement, because the heads of the agencies charged with enforcing our environmental regulations are appointed by the president.

The Environmental Protection Agency

Environmental law, like other areas of administrative law, consists primarily of regulations passed by a federal agency operating under the direction of Congress. For the past 30 years the primary agency responsible for passage and enforcement of these regulations has been the Environmental Protection Agency (EPA).

Eighteen thousand people are employed in EPA headquarters program offices, 10 regional offices, and 17 labs across the country. EPA employs a highly educated, technically trained staff, more than half of whom are engineers, scientists, and environmental protection specialists. A large number of employees are legal, public affairs, financial, and computer specialists.

The EPA was significantly reorganized under the Clinton administration, in an attempt to get the agency to act in a more integrated manner. In October 1993 then-administrator Carol Browner established, under the Office of Enforcement and Compliance Assurance (OECA), an Office of Compliance, which has as its primary focus "providing industry with coherent information about compliance requirements." The office is divided into groups of regulators who focus on separate sectors of the economy: energy and transportation, agriculture, and manufacturing. Browner also created the Office of Regulatory Enforcement, also under the OECA, which was established to take on the tough responsibility of deciding which polluters would be taken to court.

One area of special concern to business managers, especially since 1990, has been the EPA's use of criminal sanctions, including incarceration, to enforce environmental laws. The cases are not actually tried by the EPA but are passed on by the EPA to the Justice Department with a recommendation for prosecution.

The agency's criminal enforcement program was established in 1982. In 1988, the EPA was given full law enforcement authority, and with the 1990 Pollution Prosecution Act, the agency's criminal enforcement program was further expanded. This program has successfully prosecuted significant violations of all major environmental statutes, including data fraud cases (e.g., private laboratories submitting false environmental data to state and federal environmental agencies); unlawful hazardous waste dumping that resulted in serious injuries and death; oil spills that caused significant damage to waterways, wetlands, and beaches; international smuggling of CFC refrigerants that damage the ozone layer and increase skin cancer risk; and illegal handling of hazardous substances such as pesticides and asbestos that exposed children, the poor, and other especially vulnerable groups to potentially serious illness.

According to EPA press releases, since 1990, there has been an almost nonstop annual increase in the number of successful criminal prosecutions. According to the agency, EPA enforcement actions concluded in fiscal year (FY) 2004 will reduce a projected 1 billion pounds of pollution and require cleanups estimated to total a record $4.8 billion—significant increases from the previous year. The agency also claims that almost every other annual measure of its enforcement and compliance activity—such as the number of inspections (up 11 percent from FY 2003) and investigations (up 32 percent from FY 2003)—surpassed or kept pace with previous years. These statistics, the agency suggests, indicate continued progress in deterring violations of the nation's environmental laws and reflect an emphasis on environmental benefits and compliance.

Environmental law, like all American law, is dynamic. Because we live and do business in a constantly changing world, lawmakers are always trying to devise new ways to protect the environment without overly burdening businesses. The policy statements that govern EPA enforcement activities reflect the dynamic nature of environmental law.

Two policy statements currently guide the EPA in its enforcement activities. Under the first, issued in 1994, agents are to look for "significant environmental harm" and "culpable conduct." The meaning of the first criterion is obvious. Factors considered under the second criterion include a "history of repeated violations," "concealment of misconduct," "falsification of required records," "tampering with monitoring or control equipment," and "failing to obtain required licenses or permits." From this policy, it is clear that the EPA intends to focus on the worst violators.

The second policy, the "Final Policy on Penalty Reductions," issued in 1995, encourages firms to engage in environmental self-auditing. When a firm demonstrates that it undertook a voluntary self-audit, discovered a violation as a consequence, and then moved to correct the problem, the EPA will seek to reduce the penalty for the violation. This policy rewards firms that engage in self-auditing and come into compliance with the law. Of course, the failure of a firm to move to correct any violation it discovers makes the firm a candidate for criminal prosecution. See Exhibit 46-1 for a checklist managers can use to ensure that they have a successful environmental auditing program.

Despite the glowing reports from the EPA, however, there have been some signs of potential problems in EPA enforcement during the past few years. On February 27, 2002, Eric Schaeffer, who had been director of the Office of Regulatory Enforcement for the previous five years and an employee in the department for the previous 12, resigned out of frustration over the difficulty of fighting a White House that "seems determined to weaken the rules we are trying to enforce." One of the biggest projects the enforcement office had been working on over the previous 15 months had been actions against nine huge power plants that had been unlawfully pumping over 7 million tons of harmful emissions into the air every year.

The agency had reached settlement agreements with two of the violators and was close to having agreements with several others that would have significantly improved the quality of the air, when the White House chose to put a moratorium on enforcing the law. The moratorium was supposed to last 90 days, but it stretched to nine months. The agency lost its momentum as the violators decided they could safely walk away from the negotiating table as well as the agreements that had been reached but not yet signed. At this point, the director decided that he had to leave. His departure was also stimulated by the president's decision to cut the number of staff positions in the civil enforcement division by 200, a move that Schaeffer felt was going to make it much more difficult for the enforcement division to do its job.

Exhibit 46-1
Checklist for a Successful Auditing Program

- Is senior management supportive of the auditing program?
- Is senior management willing to make changes to remedy problems discovered in the audit?
- Will we have an independent environmental auditor?
- Will the environmental auditor be well trained and have a well-trained staff that is large enough to fulfill its duties?
- Does our auditing program have specific objectives, a broad-enough scope, and sufficient resources to implement the program?
- Will the audit team use a process that collects, analyzes, interprets, and documents information sufficient to achieve audit objectives?
- Will audits be conducted frequently enough to make the program useful?
- Is there a procedure for the prompt preparation of candid and clear written reports of the audit findings, corrective actions, and schedules for implementing necessary corrections?
- Will we be able to verify the accuracy and thoroughness of the audits?

The National Environmental Policy Act

The **National Environmental Policy Act (NEPA)** was one of the first major environmental laws enacted by the United States. It serves two primary functions: It requires that agencies take into account the environmental consequences of their actions, and it established an advisory body called the *Council on Environmental Quality (CEQ)*. The CEQ prepares a report on the state of the environment every year, advises the president about environmental issues, and works with the agencies to help them prepare environmental impact statements.

ENVIRONMENTAL IMPACT STATEMENTS

NEPA requires agencies to take environmental consequences into account in their decision-making process by mandating that an environmental impact statement (EIS) must be filed for (1) every federal legislative proposal or agency action (2) that is major, requiring a substantial commitment of resources and (3) would have a significant impact on the quality of the human environment. A substantial number of such statements are filed every year, over which a significant amount of litigation results. Not surprisingly, there is much litigation over whether an EIS is even necessary, with the key element of dispute being whether the potential environmental consequence will have a *significant* impact on the environment.

The U.S. Supreme Court, in Case 46-2, clarified when certain potential consequences constituted a significant impact on the environment, such that an EIS is required.

CASE 46-2 DEPARTMENT OF TRANSPORTATION v. PUBLIC CITIZEN

UNITED STATES SUPREME COURT
124 S. CT. 2204 (2004)

When the Federal Motor Carrier Safety Administration (FMCSA) prepared new regulations to allow Mexican trucking companies into the United States, the agency decided to perform an Environmental Assessment (EA) instead of an Environmental Impact Study (EIS). The former is used when impacts on the environment of the proposed activity or regulations are deemed to be insignificant, whereas the latter is required if the new regulations are likely to have a significant impact on the environment. Public Citizen, a watchdog group, challenged the decision not to perform an EIS, arguing that FMCSA should have considered the significant environment impact of the increased number of trucks that would be admitted into the United States. The district court sided with FMCSA because it had control over only the passage of regulations and not over the trucks admitted.

JUSTICE THOMAS: In this case, we confront the question whether the National Environmental Policy Act of 1969 (NEPA), and the Clean Air Act (CAA) require the Federal Motor Carrier Safety Administration (FMCSA) to evaluate the environmental effects of cross-border operations of Mexican-domiciled motor carriers, where FMCSA's promulgation of certain regulations would allow such cross-border operations to occur. Because FMCSA lacks discretion to prevent these cross-border operations, we conclude that these statutes impose no such requirement on FMCSA.

FMCSA's decision not to prepare an Environmental Impact Statement (EIS) can be set aside only upon a showing that it was "arbitrary, capricious, an abuse of discretion, or otherwise not in accordance with law." Respondents criticize the EA's failure to take into account the various environmental effects caused by the increase in cross-border operations of Mexican motor carriers.

Under NEPA, an agency is required to provide an EIS only if it will be undertaking a "major Federal action," which "significantly affects the quality of the human environment." Thus, the relevant question is whether the increase in cross-border operations of Mexican motor carriers, with the correlative release of emissions by Mexican trucks, is an "effect" of FMCSA's issuance of the Application and Safety Monitoring Rules; if not, FMCSA's failure to address these effects in its EA did not violate NEPA, and so FMCSA's issuance of a finding of no significant impact cannot be arbitrary and capricious.

Respondents have only one complaint with respect to the EA: It did not take into account the environmental effects of increased cross-border operations of Mexican motor carriers. Respondents' argument that FMCSA was required to consider these effects is simple. FMCSA is barred from expending any funds to process or review any applications by Mexican motor carriers until FMCSA implemented a variety of specific application and safety-monitoring requirements for Mexican carriers. This expenditure bar makes it impossible for any Mexican motor carrier to receive authorization to operate within the United States until FMCSA issued the regulations challenged here. The promulgation of the regulations, the argument goes, would "cause" the entry of Mexican trucks (and hence also cause any emissions such trucks would produce), and the entry of the trucks is "reasonably foreseeable." Thus, the argument concludes, FMCSA must take these emissions into account in its EA when evaluating whether to produce an EIS.

Respondents' argument, however, overlooks a critical feature of this case: FMCSA has no ability to countermand the President's lifting of the moratorium or otherwise categorically to exclude Mexican motor carriers from operating within the United States. Under FMCSA's entirely reasonable reading of this provision, it must certify *any* motor carrier that can show that it is willing and able to comply with the various substantive requirements for safety and financial responsibility contained in DOT regulations; only the moratorium prevented it from doing so for Mexican motor carriers before 2001. Thus, upon the lifting of the moratorium, if FMCSA refused to authorize a Mexican motor carrier for cross-border services, where the Mexican motor carrier was willing and able to comply with the various substantive safety and financial responsibilities rules, it would violate the law.

We hold that where an agency has no ability to prevent a certain effect due to its limited statutory authority over the relevant actions, the agency cannot be considered a legally relevant "cause" of the effect. Hence, under NEPA regulations, the agency need not consider these effects in its EA when determining whether its action is a "major Federal action." Because the President, not FMCSA, could authorize (or not authorize) cross-border operations from Mexican motor carriers, and because FMCSA has no discretion to prevent the entry of Mexican trucks, its EA did not need to consider the environmental effects arising from the entry.

FMCSA did not violate NEPA regulations when it did not consider the environmental effect of the increase in cross-border operations of Mexican motor carriers in its EA. Nor did FMCSA act improperly by not performing, pursuant to the CAA and relevant regulations, a full conformity review analysis for its proposed regulations. We therefore reject respondents' challenge to the procedures used in promulgating these regulations. Accordingly, the judgment of the Court of Appeals is reversed, and the case is remanded for further proceedings consistent with this opinion.

REVERSED AND REMANDED.

CRITICAL THINKING

What is the reasoning Justice Thomas uses to support his argument?

Is the evidence used to support the decision in this case reliable and abundant?

ETHICAL DECISION MAKING

Given the consequentialist theory of ethics, do you think the outcome of this case will yield the greatest amount of good for the greatest amount of people? If Justice Thomas were a consequentialist, would considering the potential long-term negative effects this decision could have on the environment be enough to change his mind?

When an activity meets the previously discussed threshold requirements, an EIS must be filed that contains a detailed statement of:

1. The environmental impact of the proposed action.
2. Any adverse environmental effects that cannot be avoided should the proposal be implemented.
3. Alternatives to the proposed action.
4. The relationship between local short-term uses of the human environment and the maintenance and enhancement of long-term productivity.
5. Any irreversible and irretrievable commitments of resources that would be involved in the proposed activity should it be implemented.

While many applaud the EIS process because it forces the agencies to take into account the environmental consequences of their behavior, and because sometimes agencies change their proposals and end up following an alternative course of behavior that has fewer negative consequences, others are unhappy with the process. Some are concerned about how much time it takes to prepare an adequate statement. Others are bothered because they see the EIS requirement as "toothless"; even if the process shows that the action has significant harmful consequences and an alternative would be more benign, the agency is not required to alter its plans. All the courts can do is force agencies to prepare EISs that adequately describe the consequences and the alternatives. Despite these criticisms, many other countries have followed the United States' lead and implemented similar procedures designed to reveal in advance potential environmental consequences.

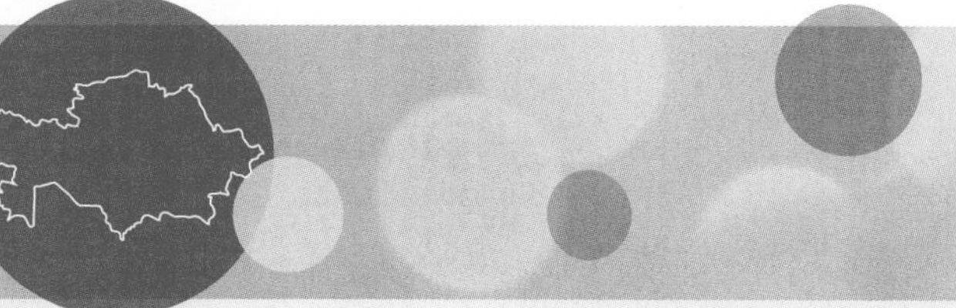

global context

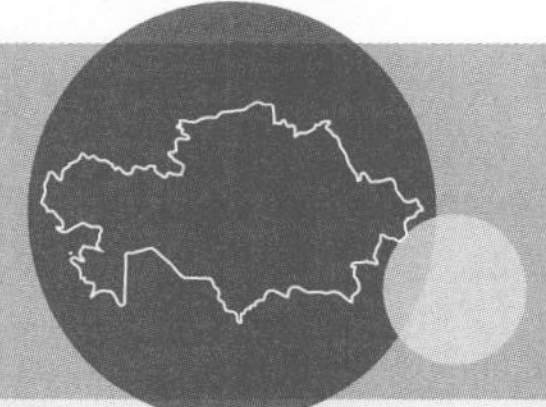

EIA (Environmental Impact Assessment) in Kazakhstan

The EIA includes (1) determination of the types and levels of impact that the proposed activity would have on the environment, (2) prognosis of probable environmental changes should the project be implemented, (3) development of measures for protection of the environment in the process of implementation of the project, and (4) elaboration of requirements for environmental protection in the project. It must be prepared with a consideration of the local environmental situation and of alternatives to the proposed activity, including that of no action. Forecasts of social and economic development of the region are also included. Documentation about the proposed project, along with the EIA, is then submitted for a State EE.

A State EE is required for almost everything, including (1) proposals of projects, contracts, and international treaties that may affect the environment, (2) drafts of laws and other legal documents that, if adopted, are likely to affect the environment, (3) documents that control the monitoring of environmental requirements during the operation of economic activity, and (4) documents supporting application for licenses and certificates for the use of natural resources. It does not matter whether the activity is being undertaken by a public or private entity. Before any legal, organizational, or entrepreneurial decisions that might affect the environment are made, there must be a positive State EE opinion. The purpose of this opinion is to determine whether the proposed activity conforms to the standards of quality of environmental laws, thereby preventing eventual negative effects of human activity on the environment.

Regulating Air Quality

This section and the next three provide an overview of how U.S. laws protect various aspects of our environment. As Exhibit 46-2 reveals, there are far too many environmental laws for us to describe in detail, so we will focus on those that have the most significant impact on our environment. We begin by examining how we protect the air.

Air quality is better today than it was in 1970, as Figure 46-1 illustrates, yet over 160 million tons of harmful pollutants are still pumped into the atmosphere every year. While the overall air quality is better, concentrations of some regulated pollutants have gotten higher over the last 10 years. Approximately 121 million people in the United States live in areas where the air is unhealthy because it contains excessive concentrations of at least one of six major conventional air pollutants: carbon monoxide, nitrogen oxide, sulfur dioxide, lead, ozone, and suspended particulates. Exhibit 46-3 illustrates some of the most common problems caused by these pollutants, frequently referred to as *criteria pollutants.* National air quality standards established under the Clean Air Act provide the primary basis for regulating criteria pollutants.

Exhibit 46-2
Major Environmental Laws

LAW	PURPOSE
Clean Water Act	Protect and improve the quality of surface water and preserve existing wetlands
Safe Drinking Water Act	Set drinking water standards to ensure that the water we drink does not contain contaminants that can harm human health
Marine Protection, Research, and Sanctuaries Act	Regulate dumping of materials into the ocean
Clean Air Act	Protect and improve the quality of the air through the National Ambient Air Quality Standards, mobile-source performance standards, and new-source performance standards
Resource Conservation and Recovery Act (RCRA)	Provide cradle-to-grave regulation of hazardous waste and provide guidelines for states for regulation of nonhazardous waste
Underground Storage Tank Act	Regulate underground storage tanks to prevent and respond to leaks
Comprehensive Environmental Response, Compensation and Liability Act (CERCLA/Superfund Act)	Provide a program to respond to and ensure cleanup of contaminated sites
Federal Insecticide, Fungicide and Rodenticide Act (FIFRA)	Regulate the labeling and use of pesticides
Toxic Substances Control Act	Regulate the use of chemicals
Noise Control Act of 1972	Require that EPA establish maximum noise standards based on a best-achievable-technology standard
Oil Pollution Act of 1990	Establish liability for cleanup of navigable waters after oil spills and set tanker standards
Endangered Species Act	Protect species that are in danger of becoming extinct

NATIONAL AMBIENT AIR QUALITY STANDARDS

The **Clean Air Act (CAA),** with all of its amendments, now runs over 700 pages; the regulations implementing this act are even longer, so this chapter can provide only a basic overview of the most significant aspects of this law. The centerpiece of our statutory scheme for regulating air quality is the National Ambient Air Quality Standards (NAAQS), established by the administrator of the EPA for each of the conventional, or criteria, pollutants identified in the previous paragraph.

The administrator must set both primary and secondary standards, with *primary standards* being those necessary to protect the public health, including an adequate margin of safety, and *secondary standards* being the more stringent limits that will protect the public welfare (crops, building, and animals) from any known or anticipated adverse effect associated with the pollutant.

Exhibit 46-3
Conventional Air Pollutants: Their Associated Health Problems and Sources

POLLUTANT	ASSOCIATED HEALTH PROBLEMS	MAIN HUMAN SOURCES
Carbon monoxide	Angina, impaired vision, lack of alertness, loss of coordination, and damage to the central nervous system of offspring of those having long-term prenatal exposure Contributes to the greenhouse effect and the formation of ozone	Automobile emissions, wood stoves, incinerators
Lead	Neurological system and kidney damage Inhibits photosynthesis and respiration in plants	Emissions from leaded gasoline, paints, leaded pipes
Nitrogen oxides	Lung and respiratory-tract damage Contributes to depletion of the ozone layer, to acid deposition, and to smog	Motor vehicle emissions, power plant and other industrial plant emissions
Ozone	Eye irritation, increased nasal congestion, asthma, reduction of lung functions, possible damage to lung tissue, and reduced resistance to infection Harms vegetation by inhibiting photosynthesis and increasing susceptibility to disease and drought	Formed when nitrogen oxides react with oxygen in the presence of sunlight, especially in the presence of hydrocarbons
Particulate matter	Reduced resistance to infection; eye, ear, and throat irritation Reduces visibility	Steel mills, power plants, cotton gins, smelters, cement plants, diesel engines, grain elevators, demolition sites, industrial roadwork, construction, wood-burning stoves, and fireplaces
Sulfur dioxide	Lung and respiratory-tract damage Contributes to the creation of acid deposition	Burning of sulfur-containing fuel, especially coal-burning electric generating plants

Every five years the administrator must review the scientific evidence to determine whether new discoveries have shown that standards need to be changed. When evidence demonstrates that current standards are no longer adequate, the EPA must then establish a new standard consistent with the evidence. The administrator of the EPA retains the authority to establish new primary and secondary standards if, at any time, scientific evidence indicates that the present standards are inadequate or if evidence indicates that some currently unregulated pollutant requires regulation.

While the EPA is required to review the NAAQS every five years, proposed changes in standards are almost always controversial. The most recent controversy was generated by the agency's issuance of new standards for both particulate matter and ozone. These standards were challenged in two cases that were ultimately heard together by the Supreme Court. In that consolidated case (see Case 46-3), the Court was asked to address two important issues: (1) whether the delegation of authority to the EPA to establish the standards was an unconstitutional delegation of legislative power and (2) whether the administrator was required to consider the cost of implementation when establishing NAAQS.

CASE 46-3 CHRISTINE TODD WHITMAN, ADMINISTRATOR OF ENVIRONMENTAL PROTECTION AGENCY, ET AL. v. AMERICAN TRUCKING ASSOCIATIONS, INC., ET AL.

UNITED STATES SUPREME COURT
531 U.S. 457 (2001)

In 1997, the Administrator revised the NAAQS for ozone and particulate matter. Some states and private companies, challenging these standards, filed petitions for review in the United States Court of Appeals for the District of Columbia Circuit Court. The Court of Appeals, in ordering a remand of the cases to the EPA for further consideration, concluded that (1) 109(b)(1), as interpreted by the EPA Administrator, delegated legislative power to the Administrator in contravention of Article I, §1 of the Federal Constitution; and (2) the EPA was not permitted to consider the cost of implementing a NAAQS in setting the initial standard. The EPA appealed to the U.S. Supreme Court.

JUSTICE SCALIA: . . . In *Lead Industries Assn, Inc. v. EPA,* the District of Columbia Circuit Court held that "economic considerations [may] play no part in the promulgation of ambient air quality standards under Section 109 of the CAA." In the present cases, the court adhered to that holding, as it had done on many other occasions. . . . Respondents argue that these decisions are incorrect. We disagree. . . .

Section 109(b)(1) instructs the EPA to set primary ambient air quality standards the attainment and maintenance of which . . . are requisite to protect the public health" with "an adequate margin of safety." Were it not for the hundreds of pages of briefing respondents have submitted on the issue, one would have thought it fairly clear that this text does not permit the EPA to consider costs in setting the standards. The language, as one scholar has noted, "is absolute." . . . The EPA "based on" the information about health effects contained in the technical "criteria" documents compiled under §108(a)(2), is to identify the maximum airborne concentration of a pollutant that the public health can tolerate, decrease the concentration to provide an "adequate" margin of safety, and set the standard at that level. Nowhere are the costs of achieving such a standard made part of the initial calculation.

Against this most natural of readings, respondents make a lengthy, spirited, but ultimately unsuccessful attack. They begin with the object of §109(b)(1)'s focus, the "public health." When the term first appeared in federal clean air legislation . . . its ordinary meaning was "the health of the community." . . . Respondents argue, however, that §109(b)(1), as added by the Clean Air Amendments of 1970 (1970 Act), . . . meant to use the term's secondary meaning: "the ways and means of conserving the health of the members of a community, as by preventive medicine, organized care of the sick, etc." Words that can have more than one meaning are given content, however, by their surroundings, and in the context of §109(b)(1) this second definition makes no sense. Congress could not have meant to instruct the Administrator to set NAAQS at a level "requisite to protect" "the art and science dealing with the protection and improvement of community health." . . . We therefore revert to the primary definition of the term: the health of the public.

To summarize our holdings in these unusually complex cases: (1) The EPA may not consider implementation costs in setting primary and secondary NAAQS under §109(b) of the CAA. (2) Section 109(b)(1) does not delegate legislative power to the EPA in contravention of Art. 1, §1 of the Constitution.

REVERSED IN PART AND AFFIRMED IN PART.

CRITICAL THINKING

Which significant ambiguities are present in the reasoning? How would different definitions of these ambiguities change the validity of Justice Scalia's reasons?

ETHICAL DECISION MAKING

What primary stakeholder's interest could this decision be seen as protecting?

CAA provides an interesting mix of state and federal responsibilities. Once the administrator of the EPA, a federal official, establishes the NAAQS, each state has nine months to draft a state implementation plan (SIP). This plan must address the means by which the state is going to ensure that the pollutants in the air within its boundaries will meet the primary NAAQS within three years of their establishment and secondary standards within a reasonable time.

States did not meet the original NAAQS within the time frames specified by Congress. When Congress passed the 1990 Clean Air Act amendments, it addressed these so-called nonattainment areas. These areas are classified in five categories ranging from "marginal" to "extreme," based on how far out of compliance they are. New deadlines for meeting the primary standard for ozone were set ranging from 5 to 20 years. Nonattainment areas were also required to establish or upgrade vehicle inspection and maintenance programs, as well as follow additional guidelines, depending on their classification.

In addition to establishing the NAAQS, the EPA administrator also establishes (1) national, uniform emission standards for new motor vehicles and (2) new-source performance standards, emission standards for new stationary sources of air pollution and major expansions of existing stationary sources. The new-source performance standards are to reflect the best available control technology, as limited by the costs of compliance.

TOXIC OR HAZARDOUS AIR POLLUTANTS

Not all air pollutants are regulated by the NAAQS. Some air pollutants are much more hazardous than the six criteria pollutants for which we have NAAQS. These more hazardous pollutants pose a significant risk to human health when they are emitted into the atmosphere in even tiny amounts. They are likely to cause an increase in mortality or in serious, irreversible illness, and they are regulated by the 1990 Air Toxics Program of the CAA amendments of 1990.

To protect the public from the effects of these pollutants, Congress identified 189 hazardous air pollutants, including asbestos, benzene, beryllium, coke oven emissions, mercury, and vinyl chloride. Industries emitting these pollutants were ordered to phase in the use of pollution control equipment for these pollutants that meets the maximum achievable control technology (MACT) standard. The EPA publishes guidelines as to what equipment meets this standard.

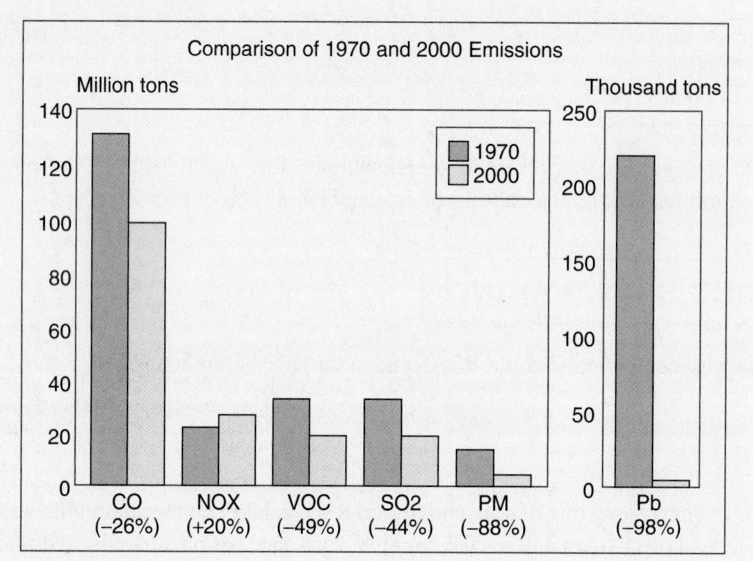

FIGURE 46-1
Criteria Pollutant Emissions

Source: AIR Trends 2000 Summary, http://www.epa.gov/oar/aqtrnd00/ (last updated February 8, 2002).

ENFORCEMENT OF THE CLEAN AIR ACT

The Clean Air Act can be enforced by both the federal EPA and the state environmental agency. The act also authorizes citizens to file civil actions to enforce the act. Violations of emission limits under the act can result in civil penalties of up to $25,000 per day. Violations of other aspects of the act, such as record-keeping violations, can result in fines of up to $5,000 per day.

Parties that knowingly violate the act can be subject to criminal fines of up to $1 million per day. Corporate officers are also potentially subject to imprisonment for up to two years for violating certain provisions of the act.

Regulating Water Quality

The second major aspect of the environment that is protected is water. Two major laws protect our water quality: the Federal Water Pollution Control Act and the Safe Drinking Water Act. The first protects the quality of water in navigable waterways, while the second protects the quality of the water we drink.

CLEAN WATER ACT

The 1972 amendments to the **Federal Water Pollution Control Act (FWPCA),** commonly known as the **Clean Water Act (CWA),** provide the foundation for our system of regulating the waters of the U.S. today. These amendments established two goals: (1) "fishable" and "swimmable" waters by 1983 and (2) the total elimination of pollutant discharges into navigable waters by 1985. Under this technology-forcing statute, these goals were to be achieved through a system of permits and effluent discharge limitations. While the country did not meet the goals, our waterways today are significantly cleaner than they were in 1972, and their quality continues to improve.

Point-source effluent limitations. Point-source effluent limitations are the primary tool for improving water quality. *Point sources* are distinct places from which pollutants can be discharged into water. Examples of point sources include factories, refineries, and sewage treatment facilities. *Effluents* are discharges from a specific source. *Effluent limitations,* therefore, are the maximum amounts of pollutants that can be discharged from a source within a given time period.

The act created the National Pollutant Discharge Elimination System (NPDES), which requires that every point source that discharges pollutants obtain a discharge permit from the EPA or from the state if the state has an EPA-approved plan. The permits specify the types and amounts of effluent discharges allowed, based on the type of technology available for that type of source.

Most sources today must use the best-available control technology (BACT). All new sources must meet this standard, but some existing facilities are allowed to meet a slightly lower standard, best-practicable control technology (BPCT). The discharger is responsible for monitoring all discharges; administrative, civil, or criminal penalties may be issued for discharges occurring either without a permit or in amounts in excess of those stated in the permit.

Enforcement of the act is left primarily to the states, although the federal government still retains the authority to engage in monitoring, inspection, and enforcement. Negligent violation of the act can result in fines of up to $25,000 a day, whereas violating the act with the knowledge that you are placing another person in imminent danger can result in a criminal fine of up to $250,000 for an individual and $1 million for an organization. Any individual knowingly endangering someone while violating the act may also face up to 15 years in prison.

SAFE DRINKING WATER ACT

The **Safe Drinking Water Act (SDWA)** was originally passed in 1974 and was amended in 1989 and again in 1996. Originally, the EPA was required to establish standards for drinking water supplied by a public water supply system. A *public water supply system* is defined by the SDWA as a water supply system that has at least 15 service connections or serves 25 or more persons.

The EPA was initially required to establish two levels of drinking-water standards for potential drinking-water contaminants. Primary standards were to protect human health, and secondary standards were to protect the aesthetic quality of drinking water. When the act was amended in 1986, the EPA had not established standards for all drinking-water contaminants for which it was supposed to set standards. Its mandate was modified to require that the agency establish maximum contaminant-level goals (MCLGs) and maximum contaminant levels (MCLs) for any drinking-water contaminant that could have an adverse effect on human health. MCLGs are nonenforceable health goals that are set at the level at which there would be absolutely no adverse health effects. MCLs are enforceable standards that are set as close as possible to the MCLGs, taking into account available technology and costs of treatment.

Current SDWA standards can be found on the Internet. Under the "right to know" provision of the 1996 Safe Drinking Water Act amendments, drinking-water suppliers must provide every household with annual reports detailing the water contaminants in their drinking water and the health problems the contaminants may cause.

Regulating Hazardous Waste

Everyone wants to enjoy the benefits of modern technology. Unfortunately, when many of the products we enjoy today are made, hazardous by-products are also created. The potential health risks from these by-products include a plethora of cancers, respiratory ailments, skin diseases, and birth defects. Environmental risks include not only pollution of the air and water but also unexpected explosions and soil contamination.

Two primary acts focus on hazardous waste: the Resource Conservation and Recovery Act and the Comprehensive Environmental Response, Compensation and Liability Act of 1980. The first focuses on the best way to treat and dispose of hazardous waste. The second focuses on situations in which hazardous waste was not properly treated after it was produced and has subsequently caused problems. As you read about these acts, try to figure out with which act or acts the Rogers Corporation needed to be in compliance.

RESOURCE CONSERVATION AND RECOVERY ACT

The **Resource Conservation and Recovery Act (RCRA)** regulates both hazardous and nonhazardous waste, but its primary purpose is controlling hazardous waste. The act does not explicitly attempt to reduce the amount of hazardous waste that is created but, instead, tries to ensure that the waste is safely handled from its creation through its disposal. Some people argue that making the generators pay the full costs of the safe treatment, storage, transportation, and disposal of hazardous waste will provide the financial incentive for them to generate less waste.

The manifest program. The central mechanism for the safe handling of hazardous waste is the manifest program. A waste may be considered hazardous, and thus be regulated under the manifest program, in one of three ways. First, it may be listed by the EPA as a hazardous waste. Second, the generator may choose to designate the waste as hazardous. Third, it may be "garbage, refuse, or sludge or any other waste material that has any of four defining characteristics: corrosivity, ignitability, reactivity, or toxicity."

Under the manifest program, generators of hazardous waste must maintain records called **manifests** for all hazardous waste they produce. These manifests list the amount and type of waste produced, how it is to be transported, and how it will ultimately be disposed of. The method of disposal must be in accordance with other provisions of RCRA, which specify how certain kinds of wastes must be treated and disposed of. For example, some wastes must receive chemical treatment to reduce toxicity or stabilize them before they can be disposed of in a landfill.

When the waste is transported to a landfill, the transporter must have received a license under the act. When the transporter picks up the waste, he or she signs the manifest, certifying that he or she is transporting it in the manner required by law. The owner of the disposal site must be certified under the act and must sign the respective section of the manifest, certifying that the waste has been properly disposed of. He or she then returns the manifest to the creator of the waste. The purpose of such manifests is to provide a record of the location and amount of all hazardous wastes at all times and to ensure that such waste will be properly transported and disposed of.

RCRA amendments of 1984 and 1986. Congress amended RCRA twice. The primary effect of the amendments was to make advanced treatment, recycling, incineration, and other forms of hazardous waste treatment the primary means of disposing of hazardous waste. Landfills are viewed as a last resort, and some wastes were banned from landfill disposal after 1988.

e-commerce AND THE LAW

RetroBox Models How to Dispose of E-Waste

According to *Waste Age,* Americans throw away approximately 2 million tons of electronic products every year. This trash includes millions of computers and cell phones. Within the waste stream, e-waste is one of the fastest-growing sectors. E-waste is a problem because it often includes lead and other harmful toxins.

Some businesses have responded to companies with e-waste by offering handling services. One example is a company called RetroBox, which is headquartered in Columbus, Ohio. RetroBox works with companies that want to get rid of e-waste in environmentally friendly, efficient ways. RetroBox picks up e-waste and takes it to a processing center. At the processing center, RetroBox carefully removes information from hard drives to protect customers' security. It refurbishes computers and other electronic equipment when possible. RetroBox then takes care to dispose of the remaining trash by taking it to appropriate recycling centers for glass and plastic and to smelters that melt and reuse metals.

Although the federal government has yet to pass legislation aimed specifically at e-waste processing, 40 states have passed laws that place restrictions on how companies must handle e-waste. Consequently, businesses like RetroBox are likely to become even more important in the years ahead.

Nonhazardous solid waste. Managing nonhazardous solid waste has always been a responsibility of the states. Congress had no desire to bring management of such waste under the direct responsibility of the federal government. Hence, the federal role under RCRA has been limited primarily to setting national standards for municipal solid waste landfills (those not accepting hazardous waste) and providing technical and financial assistance to the states. The law also requires that each state have a solid waste management plan that must include provisions for encouraging resource conservation or recovery.

Enforcement of RCRA. The EPA enforces RCRA. However, if a state sets up its own program for managing hazardous waste that is at least as stringent as the federal program, the EPA gives the state the first opportunity to prosecute violators.

If the state fails to prosecute a violator within 30 days, the EPA will then enforce the state's requirements. The EPA may issue informal warnings, seek temporary or permanent injunctions, seek criminal penalties of up to $50,000 per day of violation and/or civil penalties of up to $25,000 per violation, or impose other penalties that the EPA administrator finds appropriate.

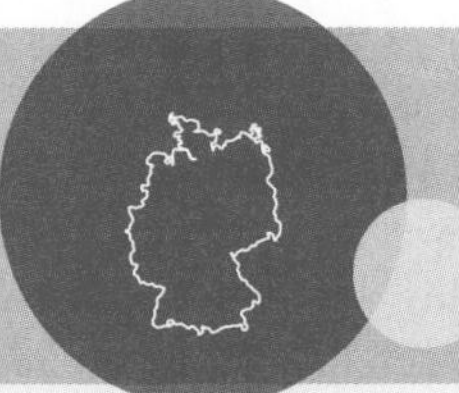

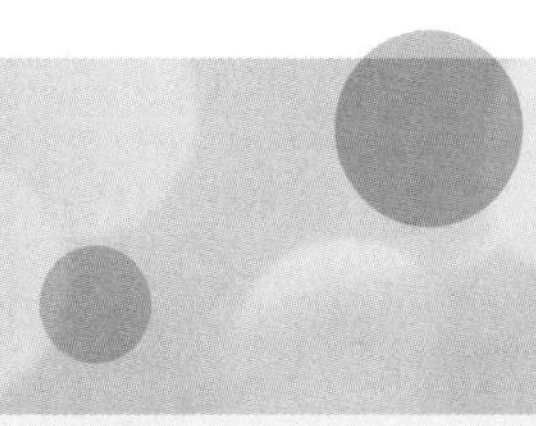

global context

Take-Back Law in Germany

Germany has found one effective way to help alleviate problems with trash: a packaging law that requires that manufacturers be responsible for their product's packaging. German manufacturers must take back packing materials such as crates, drums, boxes, and shrink wrap. They may not dispose of these items in the public waste disposal system. The legislation also requires that retailers take back packaging materials, such as cartons and antitheft devices placed on such products as CDs.

COMPREHENSIVE ENVIRONMENTAL RESPONSE, COMPENSATION AND LIABILITY ACT OF 1980, AS AMENDED BY THE SUPERFUND AMENDMENT AND REAUTHORIZATION ACT OF 1986

Prior to the enactment of RCRA, firms were not careful about where they dumped their waste. Consequently, there were thousands of sites across the country that were contaminated by a wide variety of toxic substances, and the federal government had no authority to do anything about those sites. In 1980, however, Congress passed the **Comprehensive Environmental Response, Compensation and Liability Act (CERCLA),** which contained a scheme to both (1) clean up existing hazardous sites and (2) respond to hazardous material spills.

Under CERCLA, ultimate liability for cleanup of land contaminated by waste is placed on so-called potentially responsible parties (PRPs). PRPs include (1) present owners or operators of a facility where hazardous materials are stored, (2) owners or operators at the time the waste was deposited there, (3) generators of the hazardous waste that was dumped at the site, and (4) those who transported hazardous waste to the site. When the PRPs are easily identifiable and solvent, the EPA can simply order them to clean up the site.

More commonly, however, the PRPs are unknown, insolvent, no longer in existence, or simply unwilling to pay. To handle such circumstances, CERCLA created the *Superfund,* a pool of money funded primarily by taxes on corporations in industries that create significant amounts of hazardous waste. The money in the Superfund is used by the EPA or state and local governments to pay for cleaning hazardous waste disposal sites under these circumstances. After completing a cleanup, the EPA tries to find the PRPs and collect the costs of the cleanup, thereby replenishing the fund. The fund can also be used to pay for immediate responses to spills of hazardous waste other than oil spills.

Case Nugget — Is There a Threshold for Liability for PRPs?

Kalamazoo River Study Group v. Menasha Corp.
228 F.3d 648 (6th Cir. 2000)

When there are multiple PRPs who have contributed to a site, the court will allocate liability among the parties in accordance with how much each contributed to the site. And in the Kalamazoo River Study Group case, the court determined that there was no threshold level of contribution that must be met in order for a PRP to be liable. In that case, in which a number of polluters were sued for their contamination of the Kalamazoo River, the district court initially held that the pollution of two paper mills did not reach the "threshold of significance standard" for contributing pollutants and therefore they would not have to contribute to the costs of the cleanup. The court of appeals, however, overruled the lower court, finding that there was no threshold level for liability and that the district court could "properly consider the causal link between each defendant's waste and the resulting environmental harm, along with other relevant equitable factors, in allocating response costs."

There are two kinds of action under CERCLA. The first is a *removal action,* which occurs when there is a spill or an immediate danger to human health or the environment posed by a hazardous waste site. Action is necessary to provide immediate protection, not to

connecting to the core

Cost-Benefit Analysis: How Much Should We Pollute?

As you probably learned in your economics class, evaluating the costs and benefits of various standards of clean air and clean water could be useful in making rational decisions about what those standards should be. For instance, most people would agree that they prefer clean air and clean water, but at what costs? What are the opportunity costs related to making decisions that promote a cleaner environment? Are we willing to devote limited resources to clean the environment, even if those resources cannot be used for other purposes, such as providing homes for the poor, establishing parks, or improving public transportation systems? The more resources we devote to one cause, the fewer resources we can use for other purposes. You might have also learned about the concept of optimality in your economics class. In this context, we could discuss the optimal rate of pollution as the point at which the marginal benefit of pollution-reducing methods equals the marginal cost of pollution-reducing methods. In other words, some economists would argue that we should control pollution to this optimal point, where a dollar spent on cleaning the environment or preventing pollution equals a dollar benefit to society. However, if we spent a dollar on pollution controls and generated less than a dollar of social benefit, according to proponents of the optimal rate of pollution method, we should reduce the amount we are spending on pollution controls until the marginal benefit of pollution control equals the marginal cost.

Source: Bradley R. Schiller, *The Economy Today* (New York: McGraw-Hill/Irwin, 2006), p. 610.

provide a permanent solution. Removal actions are limited to 12 months' cleanup time and a maximum of $2 million in costs. A typical removal action might occur where a neighbor notices that there are drums sitting on an abandoned dumpsite and leaking some sort of corrosive material. The EPA would come in and remove the leaking drums. The soil would still need to be cleaned and other hazardous materials removed, but once the leaking drums have been removed, the immediate danger is gone and the removal action complete.

The other type of action is a *remedial action.* Under CERCLA, the EPA developed a hazard ranking system by which it evaluates sites containing hazardous waste on a 12-point scale. The sites that have the highest rankings (i.e., are the most contaminated) are placed on the National Priorities List (NPL).

Once a site is on the NPL, it may be selected by the EPA for remediation, a formal and complex process beginning with a detailed assessment of the situation to determine the best way to proceed with the cleanup and including the opportunity for public participation. Sites are then remediated, or cleaned up, in accordance with the plan. The PRPs may be brought in at any time during the process. Obviously, the EPA would prefer to bring them in earlier so that the PRPs can directly fund the cleanups, but, again, money from the Superfund is generally used to at least begin the process, and then the PRPs are sued to recover the Superfund expenditures.

Of course, recovering funds is not always easy, but the EPA has been successful in recovering cleanup funds in a number of cases. However, the agency has not been as successful in replenishing the fund as Congress had hoped. Consequently, funding for the Superfund was increased by the Superfund Amendment and Reauthorization Act of 1986 (SARA) to $8.5 billion, generated primarily by taxes on petroleum, chemical feedstocks, imported chemical derivatives, and a new "environmental tax" on corporations. SARA also provided more stringent cleanup requirements.

In 1995, however, the tax for the Superfund expired and has not been reinstated. Because the Superfund is no longer funded by polluter and industry dollars, the completion of Superfund cleanups has decreased. However, new sites continue to be discovered and sites continue to be cleaned up, just at a slower pace.

Regulating Toxic Substances

Some toxic substances are found not in waste but as part of products we use every day. The two primary acts for regulating these substances are the Toxic Substances Control Act and the Federal Insecticide, Fungicide, and Rodenticide Act.

TOXIC SUBSTANCES CONTROL ACT

The **Toxic Substances Control Act (TSCA)** regulates under the act any chemicals or mixtures whose manufacture, processing, distribution, use, or disposal may present an unreasonable risk of harm to human health or the environment. The act's primary role is to establish the procedures that must be followed whenever a new chemical is about to be introduced into the market. Under TSCA, every manufacturer of a new chemical must submit a premanufacturing notice (PMN) or Section Five Notice, to the EPA at least 90 days before the first use of the substance in commerce. The PMN must give a significant amount of information, including the chemical name, identity, and molecular structure; trade names or synonyms; and by-products related to its manufacture. The most important information contained in the notice, however, is the test data related to the impact of the new chemical on human health and the environment.

After receiving the PMN, the EPA decides whether the substance presents an unreasonable risk to health or whether further testing is required to establish the substance's safety. When the risk of harm is unacceptable, manufacture of the product is not allowed. If more testing is required, a manufacturer of the product must wait until the tests have been satisfactorily completed. If there is no unreasonable risk or need for further testing, manufacturing may begin as proposed.

FEDERAL INSECTICIDE, FUNGICIDE, AND RODENTICIDE ACT

Not all potentially toxic substances are regulated primarily under TSCA. *Pesticides,* defined as substances manufactured to prevent, destroy, repel, or mitigate any pest or to be used as a plant regulator or a defoliant, are instead regulated under the **Federal Insecticide, Fungicide, and Rodenticide Act (FIFRA).** Pesticides perform a wide range of functions, from killing insects that would transmit disease or destroy crops to killing pests that simply cause us discomfort.

Yet pesticides have harmful side effects. Pesticides may harm species that were not their intended target. Pesticides that do not degrade quickly enough may be consumed when the crops on which they were used are eaten, potentially harming the consumer's health. A pesticide may seep into the ground and contaminate the groundwater aquifer or get washed into a stream and contaminate marine life and animals that drink from that stream. Once a pesticide gets into the food chain, it may do inestimable harm.

Under FIFRA, a registration system controls pesticide use. Before a pesticide can be sold in the United States, it must be registered and properly labeled. A pesticide will be registered when the following three criteria are met: (1) The pesticide's composition warrants the claims made for it; (2) its label complies with the act; and (3) data provided by the manufacturer demonstrate that the pesticide can perform its intended function, in accordance with commonly accepted practice, without presenting unreasonable risks to human health or the environment. A pesticide meeting these three criteria is given general-use registration, and it may be sold without any limits anywhere in the United States.

If the pesticide cannot meet the third criteria unless some restriction is placed on it, it may be given restricted-use registration, meaning that it can be sold only with the restriction that prevents it from causing an unreasonable risk to human health or the environment. Common restrictions include allowing it to be applied by only a certified applicator (someone who has passed a test indicating specialized knowledge of pesticide application) or to be sold for use only during certain seasons or in certain quantities.

As of 1999, approximately 20,000 pesticides had been registered with the EPA's Office of Pesticide Programs. While not common, sometimes the EPA discovers evidence that a registered pesticide may pose a previously unknown risk to health or the environment. In such a situation, the agency will institute proceedings to cancel the pesticide's registration.

Pesticide tolerances in food. FIFRA is not the only law to regulate pesticide use. The EPA sets allowable levels of pesticide residues on foods sold in this country. Under the 1996 Food Quality Protection Act, the EPA was required to establish a single, health-based standard for residues. For a level of residue to be acceptable, it must be such that the EPA can conclude with reasonable certainty that no harm will result from aggregate exposure to each pesticide from dietary and other sources. When a pesticide is registered under FIFRA, tolerance levels for its residues will be established.

International Environmental Considerations

The United States is justifiably proud of its system of environmental regulations. Many countries have looked to our laws as models when establishing their systems of environmental regulations. However, a recent study of 142 countries found that the United States was not first in terms of environmental health; the United States was 51st. The top five countries were Finland, Norway, Sweden, Canada, and Switzerland. The five worst were Haiti, Iraq, North Korea, Kuwait, and the Emirates.

The study took into account 68 variables to determine environmental sustainability, that is, the likely environmental quality of life over the next generation. Some of the variables included a country's approach to water and air pollution, how corrupt the government is, and how seriously it takes global climate change. The authors of the study said that no nation was on a clear path to sustainability. The purpose of the study, they said, was to help countries become more rigorous in their environmental decision making.

Regardless of how the United States is ranked in any particular study of environmental factors, most Americans realize that because environmental problems do not recognize boundaries, there is a real need for international cooperation on environmental issues. For countries whose landmasses are located next to each other, the interdependence on environmental matters is obvious, but because of air and water patterns, our interdependence on nations across the globe is just as real. For example, because of the prevailing wind patterns, air pollutants emitted anywhere between 30 and 60 degrees north of the equator may ultimately end up in either China or the United States because both countries are located within those latitudes. The migration of animals and plants can likewise spread pollutants. If DDT gets into our water, migrating fish ingest it. Birds eat the contaminated fish and pass through another country during their winter migration. If they die in that other country, that pollutant from the United States may now enter the food chain in that country.

The United States can play a role in establishing global environmental policies in a number of ways, primarily through sharing research we have done on pollution prevention and cleanup with other nations, making economic aid to foreign countries contingent on compliance with environmental standards, and negotiating and signing environmental treaties.

Exhibit 46-4
Environmental Treaties and Their Purposes

TREATY	PURPOSE
Montreal Protocol	Significantly reduce (and in some countries ban) the use of ozone-depleting air pollutants, namely chlorofluorocarbons and halons.
Eastern Pacific Ocean Tuna Fishing Agreement (1983)	Help regulate the harvest of tuna by granting international licenses to those who wish to catch tuna within 200 miles of the coasts of the signatories to the treaty (the United States and several Latin American countries). Fees are collected and distributed to the member nations based on the poundage of fish taken within the respective nations' coastal limits.
Stockholm Convention on Persistent Organic Pollutants	Require signatory countries to ban or severely restrict the use of nine of the most harmful persistent organic pesticides and work toward the ultimate goal of a total ban on their use.
Marine Pollution Prevention Protocol (MARPOL)	Require signatory nations to adopt laws to "prevent, reduce and control" any significant pollution of the marine environment.
Convention on International Trade in Endangered Species (CITES)	Prohibit international trade of endangered plants and animals.
Convention on Regulation of Antarctic Mineral Resource Activity	Regulate exploitation of mineral resources in Antarctica.
Treaty for Amazonian Cooperation	Balance economic growth and environmental protection (an agreement among eight countries with territories in the Amazon).

The last method is perhaps the most prevalent, but in recent years it has been one of the most controversial. Treaties are written agreements by nations to resolve a particular problem in an agreed-on manner. The most effective treaties spell out consequences for failure to live up to the terms of the treaty. Different nations give different parts of their government the authority to enter into treaties. In the United States, treaties are negotiated by a representative of the executive branch and must be ratified by two-thirds of the Senate. Implementation of most environmental treaties generally requires passage of federal legislation that accomplishes the objectives of the treaties.

Treaties may be bilateral, between just two countries, or multilateral, involving a large number of nations. Often multilateral treaties are negotiated by nations, but then they do not come into force until signed and ratified by a specified number of countries. Exhibit 46-4 lists some of the more important environmental treaties and their purposes.

The most controversial environmental treaty today is the Kyoto Agreement. This treaty has attempted to find a way to limit the amount of so-called *greenhouse gases,* gases that most scientists believe contribute to the problem of global warming. In 1997, in Kyoto, Japan, representatives of 150 countries met to create a treaty that would commit developed nations to bringing down their emissions to certain levels by specific dates. The parties to the convention agreed that developed countries would have a legally binding commitment to reduce their collective emissions of six greenhouse gases by at least 5 percent compared to 1990 levels by 2008–2012. Sweden, Central and Eastern Europe, and the European Union would reduce emissions by 8 percent. The United States, Canada, Hungary, Japan, and Poland would reduce emissions by 6 percent, whereas Russia, New Zealand, and the Ukraine would be expected to stabilize their emissions. Some countries, such as Norway, Australia, and Iceland could increase their emissions. Each country would agree to make "demonstrable progress" by 2005, and meet the agreed-on emission targets by 2008–2012.

The protocol was opened for signatures on March 16, 1998, and enters into force when ratified by 55 parties to the convention. When President Bush announced that the United States was withdrawing from the protocol, many believed the treaty would never go into effect. However, near the end of 2004, the final signature needed to activate the treaty was obtained when Russia signed the protocol.

CASE OPENER WRAP-UP

Rogers Corporation

Rogers Corporation was indeed found to be in violation of the law. Specifically, Rogers Corporation had violated Section 15 of TSCA and a section of the Code of the Federal Regulations by failing to clean up a hazardous area in a timely manner. A trial in front of the administrative law judges (ALJs) of the EPA resulted in a civil penalty of $281,400, which was later affirmed by the Environmental Appeals Board.

After reading this chapter, you should have a sense of the importance of understanding and following environmental regulations. Violations of environmental laws can result in jail time for not only the violators but also the owners, as well as hefty fines. Regarding your response to question 2 in the opening scenario, if you answered that Rogers Corporation did not need to clean up the area sooner, you should now realize that by taking such action they might have escaped liability, regardless of whether the law required them to do so. Even if we do not take these regulations into account, perhaps Rogers Corporation *should have* cleaned up the area to protect the health of the workers.

Summary

Alternative Means of Protecting the Environment

Tort law:

- *Nuisance* is unreasonable interference with another's enjoyment and use of his or her land.
- A *negligence* action involves establishing the elements of duty, breach of duty, causation, and damage.
- *Trespass* occurs when someone places something on someone's property without the owner's permission.

Government subsidies approach: Government pays polluters to reduce their emissions.

Emissions charges approach: Polluters are charged a flat fee on every unit of the pollutant they discharge.

Marketable discharge permits: Government issues a set number of permits for pollutant discharges; companies are free to sell the permits among themselves.

Green taxes: Government imposes taxes on activities that are environmentally harmful.

Direct regulation: Government regulates pollution. This is the primary approach used today.

The Environmental Protection Agency

The EPA, created in 1970, is the largest federal agency and has a mandate to address issues of pollution in the areas of air, water, solid waste, pesticides, radiation, and toxic substances. The Office of Enforcement and Compliance Assurance has been particularly successful in ensuring that companies that break environmental laws are prosecuted by the Department of Justice.

The National Environmental Policy Act

Implementing the National Environmental Policy Act: The act requires the preparation of an environmental impact statement (EIS).

- *Threshold consideration:* The activity must be federal, be major, and have a significant impact on the human environment.
- *Content of the EIS:*
    - Environmental impact of proposed action.
    - Adverse environmental effects of action.
    - Alternatives to action.
    - Relationship between the local short-term uses of the human environment and the maintenance and enhancement of long-term productivity.
    - Any irreversible commitments of resources.
- *Effectiveness of the EIS:* Has the EIS changed the quality of environmental decision making or merely the process?

Regulating Air Quality

National Ambient Air Quality Standards:

Carbon monoxide
Particulate matter
Ozone
Sulfur dioxide
Nitrogen dioxide
Lead

Primary standards: Levels necessary to protect public health.

Secondary standards: Levels necessary to protect public welfare.

Toxic air pollutants: 189 pollutants that cause serious consequences even in small amounts.

Maximum achievable control technology (MACT): Standard that must be met by industry pollution control equipment.

Acid Rain Control Program: Program that allows auctioning of sulfur dioxide permits to reduce total emissions in the most efficient way possible.

Regulating Water Quality

Federal Water Pollution Control Act:

Fishable and swimmable waters.

Total elimination of pollutant discharges into navigable waters.

Point-source effluent limitations: Maximum allowable amounts of pollutants that can be discharged from a source within a given time period.

Safe Drinking Water Act:

The act sets standards for drinking water supplied by a public water supplier.

"Right to know" provisions mean utilities must provide annual reports detailing water contaminants and harm they may possibly cause.

Regulating Hazardous Waste

Resource Conservation and Recovery Act:

Manifest program: Provides "cradle-to-grave" regulation of hazardous waste by requiring that every generator of hazardous waste maintain records on the waste.

RCRA amendments of 1984 and 1986: Made landfills a last resort for the disposal of many types of waste.

Enforcement of RCRA: Enforced by the EPA. States can set up their own programs, but EPA retains ultimate authority to investigate and fine violators.

Comprehensive Environmental Response, Compensation and Liability Act of 1980 (CERCLA), as Amended by the Superfund Amendment and Reauthorization Act of 1986:

Money in the Superfund is used for toxic waste cleanup.

EPA may sue to recover costs.

So far, the Superfund has not been able to recoup its cleanup costs.

Regulating Toxic Substances

Toxic Substances Control Act:

Toxic substance: Any chemical or mixture whose manufacture, processing, distribution, use, or disposal may present an unreasonable risk of harm to human health or the environment.

Premanufacturing notice: Notification given to the EPA at least 90 days before the first use of a chemical; contains information on the risk posed by the chemical.

Federal Insecticide, Fungicide, and Rodenticide Act:

Registration of pesticides is required for use and selling.

- *General use:* There are no restrictions.
- *Restricted use:* Pesticide must be used in a specific manner in order not to pose an unreasonable risk.

Registration lasts five years.

Federal Food, Drug, and Cosmetic Act:

Allows EPA to establish permissible levels of pesticide residues in food.

International Environmental Considerations

Because environmental problems know no boundaries, there is a need for international cooperation over environmental matters.

The United States primarily plays a role in establishing global environmental policies by sharing research we have done on pollution prevention and cleanup with other nations; making economic aid to foreign countries contingent on compliance with environmental standards; and negotiating and signing environmental treaties.

Point / Counterpoint

Should the EPA Play the Primary Role in Enforcing Environmental Regulation?

As you are thinking about each argument, you may want to ask yourself which ambiguous word (or phrase) is crucial to both arguments, and how different definitions of that word affect the strength of each argument.

No	Yes
The EPA should not be a primary instrument in enforcing environmental regulation. EPA officials are appointed, not elected. Thus, they lack the political accountability necessary to make legitimate decisions about environmental regulation. For example, if EPA officials strike an unpopular or ineffective balance between environmental protection and economic development, citizens cannot vote those officials out of office. An institution less insulated from popular sovereignty would be better suited to make these important decisions. Those who champion the importance of the EPA's role often point out EPA officials' expertise (especially relative to Congress) in environmental regulation. But expertise isn't everything; incentives matter, too. Without political accountability, EPA officials lack strong incentives to vigorously enforce environmental regulation. Tort law solves this problem. When a factory's pollution infringes the rights of individuals downwind or downstream, tort law promises those individuals pecuniary restitution if they vigorously pursue their cases in court.	The EPA should be the foremost instrument in enforcing environmental regulation. Although the EPA lacks the political accountability of the elected branches of government, it is not entirely insulated from the popular will. The president of the United States appoints the administrator, the EPA's top-ranking official. If the EPA's enforcement of environmental regulation becomes sufficiently ineffective or unpopular, the appointment of the next administrator will be an important issue in the next election. Moreover, what the EPA lacks in political accountability it makes up for in expertise. More than half of the EPA's 18,000 employees are scientists or engineers. Even the most educated congressperson could master only a fraction of the EPA's knowledge. This specialization renders the EPA well suited to be the primary enforcer of environmental regulation. Those who argue that tort law should be the primary instrument in enforcing environmental regulation overlook the constitutional requirement of *standing* (see Chapter 3). Article III of the Constitution requires that, for federal courts to hear a case, the plaintiff must have sustained an injury. Yet many violations of environmental regulations produce no measurable injury. For example, a factory that spews pollutants into the air may not result in a measurable injury to anyone. Thus, tort law is impotent to redress many violations of environmental regulations.

Questions & Problems

1. Explain the common law methods of resolving pollution problems, and evaluate their effectiveness.
2. List the elements that must be contained in an environmental impact statement.
3. Explain the structure of the Clean Air Act, describing how each of the primary segments of the act contributes to the act's overall goal of improving air quality.
4. Explain the relationship between the Clean Water Act and the Safe Drinking Water Act.
5. What is erroneous about the argument that we no longer need the Superfund because the Resource Conservation and Recovery Act now ensures that all waste is properly disposed of.
6. How would an understanding of the concept of externalities help a person to understand why we need legislation to protect the environment?
7. L. A. Moore bought property from Texaco in 1955 that was adjacent to his own property. On his death in 1976, the property went to his son, Tommy Moore. Both Tommy and his father knew that Texaco had housed on the land some barrels that had been

used for oil storage. These barrels were removed in 1954. The younger Moore sued Texaco when he discovered in 1997 that soil and groundwater on the property were contaminated. Moore sued for several different claims, including nuisance, for which he claimed that Texaco owed him damages and abatement. The nuisance claim was both a public and a private nuisance claim. The district court denied both of Moore's nuisance claims, and the court of appeals affirmed. Identify possible reasons that would allow for a denial of the nuisance claims. [*Moore v. Texaco, Inc.*, 244 F.3d 1229 (2001).]

8. In 1985, the EPA began a civil action against Sugarhouse Realty, Inc. (SRI), under CERCLA to recover the costs of cleaning up hazardous materials on several sites owned by SRI. A court decree required that the hazardous materials be removed by February 1986 or a penalty of more than $1 million would be assessed. SRI failed to meet this deadline, so in 1991 the court had a sufficient amount of SRI's assets liquidated to cover the costs of the cleanup. Meanwhile, Ultimate Sportsbar, Inc. (USI), had leased property in 1990 from SRI with the intention of building an outdoor restaurant and bar. However, SRI was having financial trouble, including liens on its assets, and filed for bankruptcy in 1993 when it began falling behind on mortgage payments. USI's lease was terminated during bankruptcy litigation. The original lease had a clause stating that if the lease was terminated, a fee of $100,000 would be paid by SRI to USI. SRI never paid this fee. USI brought suit against the United States, alleging that the government had effected a taking of its property for two reasons. First, USI argued that a taking occurred because the United States was a party in the bankruptcy proceedings. Second, USI argued that a taking occurred because the EPA's move to recover cleanup costs drove SRI to bankruptcy. The United States moved to dismiss the claims. Do you think the court granted the United States' motion? Why or why not? [*Ultimate Sportsbar, Inc. v. The United States,* 48 Fed. Cl. 450 (2001).]

9. From the 1950s to 1968, an unpermitted waste disposal site was operated in Crosby, Texas. Several companies dumped chemical and oil-based wastes at this site. In 1980, the EPA took soil samples that indicated the presence of many hazardous materials, such as lead, cadmium, chromium, mercury, and benzene. In 1988, the EPA put up a fence around the contaminated area, and in 1989 it accepted bids to clean up the area. In April 1990, a bid was accepted, and the contractor began surveying on-site in August 1990. In September 1990, the area was prepared for construction by widening a road and placing office trailers on-site. A notice to proceed with on-site work filed with the state of Texas was effective October 10, 1990. Cleanup was completed in January 1995 and cost more than $125 million.

From 1996 to 1998, the EPA used alternative dispute resolution methods to negotiate with potentially responsible parties for reimbursement under CERCLA. During negotiations, one of the items determined by the parties was that the statute of limitations would end on October 1, 1996. However, the negotiations were unsuccessful, and the government brought suit against the companies in 1998. The defendants filed for summary judgment, stating that the six-year statute of limitations had expired because the government had started work on the site prior to October 1, 1990. The defendants argued that on-site construction for remediation began in 1988 when the EPA erected the fence. The government argued that the actions before October 1, 1990, were preconstruction actions and actions related to removal rather than the remedial action. Do you think the court granted the defendants' motion for summary judgment? Why or why not? [*United States of America et al. v. Atlantic Richfield et al.*, 2001 U.S. Dist. LEXIS 2161 (2001).]

10. Several railroad companies operated in Columbus, Ohio, in the 1800s. Sometime during their operation, a box filled with creosote and benzene was buried near a railroad depot. Subsequently, the railroad companies' successor, American Premier Underwriters (APU), Inc., received over $5 million for the land from the City of Columbus when the city exercised eminent domain in 1973. In October 1989, the Franklin County Convention Facilities Authority (CFA) became interested in the land and performed environmental assessments to determine the quality of the property. After the testing, CFA subleased the property from the city with the intention of building a facility on it. In October 1990, a contractor was digging to create a storm sewer line when he split open the creosote- and benzene-filled box. A strong odor was emitted, and an environmental consultant was immediately notified and came to the property. The Ohio EPA was also notified, and later CFA notified the city. The remedial action chosen by CFA was to remove and transport the contamination materials. A contractor performed the action, for which CFA paid. During the remedial action, it was discovered that the creosote had migrated 45 feet and surrounded a sewer line. The appropriate barrier was erected. CFA then commenced an action against APU to recover the costs of the cleanup under CERCLA. Although CFA is not a state, CFA could still recover under CERCLA if its cleanup was performed in a manner consistent with the National Oil and Hazardous Substances Pollution Contingency Plan. The district court found that CFA had performed a CERCLA-quality cleanup, found APU to be the only responsible party, and assessed 100 percent of the cleanup costs to APU. APU appealed the decision on many counts, but particularly the finding that CFA was not a potentially responsible party. How do you think the court of appeals ruled on the issue of whether CFA was a potentially responsible party? [*Franklin County Convention Facilities Authority v. American Premier Underwriters, Inc., et al.*, 240 F.3d 534 (2001).]

11. The Buckey Reclamation Landfill was declared a Superfund sight in 1983, and Consolidation Coal was found liable for its cleanup expenses. Under CERCLA, Consolidation Coal sought a declaration of liability and equitable allocation of expense cost to Nevill Chemical for admittedly dumping 472,000 gallons of waste sludge into the landfill in the late 1970s. The chemical company appealed the lower court's decision that under CERCLA it was liable for a portion of the cleanup costs, arguing that the wasteful sludge caused no harm. Was Nevill Chemical successful in removing its liability from the Superfund cleanup? Why was Nevill Chemical, or why was it not, successful? [*United States v. Consolidation Coal Co.*, 345 F.3d 409 (2003).]
12. The Hudson Riverkeeper Fund, Inc., and the Village of Hastings-on-Hudson sued Atlantic Richfield Company (ARCO) under RCRA for contamination of the Hudson River that allegedly occurred from a site taken over by ARCO. The site was used by Anaconda Wire & Cable Company from 1919 to 1975 for the manufacture of copper wire and cable, a process that uses PCBs. In 1981 Anaconda was merged into ARCO, and ARCO assumed all of Anaconda's liabilities. In court, ARCO argued that the plaintiffs claim under RCRA was preempted by TSCA because PCBs are not hazardous wastes and thus RCRA contaminations are preempted by the specific PCB sections in TSCA. Do you think the court agreed with ARCO on the issue of TSCA preemption? Why or why not? [*Hudson Riverkeeper Fund, Inc. and Village of Hastings-on-Hudson v. Atlantic Richfield Company,* 2001 U.S. Dist. LEXIS 4061 (2001).]
13. The environmental group Bluewater Network sought review of the EPA's emission standards for snowmobiles under the Clean Air Act and NAAQ standards. The proposed regulations of carbon monoxide (CO), hydrocarbons (HC), and nitrogen oxides (NOx) required that snowmobile engines meet progressively more stringent emission standards in three successive phases. However, Bluewater argued that the

standards were excessively lenient. Further, Bluewater disagreed with the EPA's ruling that pollution prevention technologies could not be applied to all new snowmobiles by 2012. Arguing in the opposite direction, the International Snowmobile Manufacturers Association (ISMA) challenged the EPA's authority to implement the regulations of CO, HC, and NOx. Did the EPA exceed its authority in regulating CO, HC, and NOx emissions from snowmobiles? Or did the EPA not go far enough in the creation of stringent emission standards? [*Bluewater Network v. EPA,* 370 F.3d 1 (2004).]

Looking for more review material?

The Online Learning Center at **www.mhhe.com/kubasek1e** contains this chapter's "Assignment on the Internet" and also a list of URLs for more information, entitled "On the Internet." Find both of them in the Student Center portion of the OLC, along with quizzes and other helpful materials.

Antitrust Law

CASE OPENER

The NCAA and Restrictions on Participation in Tournaments

The National Collegiate Athletic Association (NCAA) is a voluntary organization guiding collegiate athletics. The NCAA creates rules governing student athletes, including Division I men's basketball. In men's basketball, the schools are divided up in conferences. Then the teams play other teams in their conference, as well as have the option to schedule a number of games with schools outside the conference. However, the NCAA has set rules outlining how many and what kind of games a school may play in a single season.

Each year, there are also a number of tournaments available to the schools. Some of these tournaments are considered "certified." In certified tournaments, schools play a number of teams in numerous games, typically early in the season. Believing the better schools were abusing these tournaments, the NCAA created regulations to limit schools' involvement in these tournaments in order to promote competition at the tournaments. The NCAA's new regulation, 98-92, increases the number of games any school can play in one season to 28. Then 98-92 states that participation in a certified event constitutes one game toward the maximum number of games a team may play. However, schools may participate only in one certified event per season and no more than two in a four-year period.

Feeling cheated by the new rule, certified tournament promoters decided to take action. The promoters accused the NCAA of antitrust actions, specifically related to the Two in Four Rule (referencing the number of certified tournaments in which a school may participate) of 98-92. The promoters claimed that the rule limited the business they could do and harmed their profits by not allowing them to schedule certified tournaments where the best schools would all compete. As such, the promoters claimed that the Two in Four Rule was a violation of the Sherman Antitrust Act, and they sought an injunction under the Clayton Act.[1]

[1] *Worldwide Basketball & Sports Tours, Inc. v. NCAA*, 388 F.3d 955 (2004).

CHAPTER 47

1. Suppose you were a board member for the NCAA. If you opposed the claims against your organization, what values would be guiding your views?
2. In addition to proving that a company holds monopoly power, what else must a court prove to find a monopoly guilty of abusing its market power?

The Wrap-Up at the end of the chapter will answer these questions.

Learning Objectives

After reading this chapter, you will be able to answer the following questions:

1. What is the rationale for antitrust law?
2. What is the Sherman Act?
3. What is explored in Section 1 of the Sherman Act?
4. What is explored in Section 2 of the Sherman Act?
5. What is the Clayton Act?
6. What is the Federal Trade Commission Act?

The purpose of this chapter is to introduce you to antitrust law. First, we consider the history of and rationale for antitrust law. What exactly is antitrust law, and why do we need it? Second, we consider the major statutes regarding antitrust law. These statutes prohibit certain anticompetitive behaviors, but the courts have taken a large role in specifying how the statutes are to be enforced. As you read this chapter, think about how the NCAA case is related to the various antitrust issues and concerns.

History of and Rationale for Antitrust Law

THE NEED FOR REGULATION

A **trust** is a business arrangement in which stock owners appoint beneficiaries and place their securities with trustees, who manage the company and pay a share of their earnings to the stockholders. A trust is similar to a corporation in many ways; the beneficiaries of a trust are not responsible for any debt. However, a trust and a corporation are different entities and should be treated as such.

In the 1870s and 1880s, companies such as Standard Oil used trusts in an attempt to drive out their competition. For example, Standard Oil traded a trustee stock in the company for stock certificates. The trustee then made business decisions that altered prices in such a way that other corporations could not operate effectively. Standard Oil had, through the trustee, created a monopoly. In an attempt to fight such anticompetitive behavior, antitrust law was created.

Common law actions against the restraints to trade (i.e., the trusts' anticompetitive behavior) were not strong enough to stop such anticompetitive behavior. In 1887 Congress passed the Interstate Commerce Act,[2] which created the Interstate Commerce Committee, intended to regulate railroads to fight anticompetitive business behavior. Then Senator John Sherman, who was respected for his financial opinion, and others created a bill that would prohibit unfair practices and provide an action against companies that engaged in such behavior. In 1890, this bill was enacted as the Sherman Act.[3] Because the regulations were aimed at trusts engaging in anticompetitive behavior, the regulations were called *antitrust* laws.

Despite the Sherman Act, business abuses continued, and concern about antitrust policies heightened during the presidential election of 1912. As a result of this election, Congress created the Clayton Act[4] and Federal Trade Commission Act[5] in 1914.

RATIONALE FOR ANTITRUST LAWS

Before the Sherman Act was passed, several scholars argued that the prohibition of the behavior of the trusts was wrong. They argued that such behavior was natural and a result of competition. If the large trusts were successful, it was because they deserved to be successful. In contrast, others argued that the monopolies were successful through unfair business practices; they did not have to compete with others because of these practices. Consequently, monopolies were not natural occurrences and needed to be regulated.

The debate about the need and purpose of antitrust law has not been quashed; in fact, Microsoft has been the target of several antitrust suits, renewing the debate and

[2] 49 U.S.C. §§ 501–526.
[3] 15 U.S.C. §§ 1–7.
[4] 15 U.S.C. §§ 12–26a.
[5] 15 U.S.C. §§ 45–48a.

controversy over the purpose of antitrust law. Arguments regarding the purpose of antitrust law can generally be classified under one of two categories: traditional antitrust theories and Chicago School theories.

Traditional antitrust theories. Traditional antitrust theorists argue that a few, powerful sellers should not dominate the economy. They argue that accumulation of economic power leads to an accumulation of political power; politicians simply would not be able to ignore such economic power and would be "bought" by this power. Thus, not only do monopolies cause economic damage, but they also cause political disadvantages. Consequently, traditional antitrust theorists want many buyers and sellers in the market; they want to foster real competition.

Traditional antitrust theorists believe that efficiency is an important goal of antitrust law but is not the only goal or even the most important goal. As you will see, this idea is clearly in conflict with the Chicago School theories.

Chicago school theories. Chicago school theorists argue that the central, and perhaps only, purpose of antitrust law is to encourage economic **efficiency**, that is, getting the most output from the least input. Unless efficiency is the sole criterion for antitrust policy, consumers will be harmed. These scholars are not persuaded by the traditional antitrust argument that concentration of economic power leads to undesirable social and political consequences.

If a company held great economic power, Chicago School theorists would determine how the company's power affected efficiency. If the concentrated power led to efficiency, Chicago theorists believe the company should be left alone. Overall, Chicago theorists tend to be more lenient regarding the enforcement of antitrust laws.

RECENT REGULATORY ATTITUDES

From the early 1960s to the early 1970s, the courts embraced a traditional antitrust theory. The courts displayed a preference for decentralizing economic power over economic efficiency. For example, the courts ruled that certain market practices were per se illegal. However, in the 1970s, the courts' preference changed; efficiency was given greater weight. In a landmark case in 1977, the Supreme Court stated that antitrust laws "were enacted for the 'protection of competition, not competitors.'"[6]

During the Reagan administration, courts and administrative agencies practiced a restricted antitrust policy; in other words, the courts and agencies permitted questionable business actions in the name of competition and efficiency. These courts and administrators gave much weight to Chicago School thought. However, in the 1990s, the courts and agencies have become more expansive in bringing more claims against companies for antitrust violations.

Some scholars, who would be more aligned with Chicago School thought, argue that antitrust law is outdated and thus damages the market. Some go so far as to argue that all antitrust laws should be repealed.[7] Opponents argue that antitrust laws need to be even more strictly enforced because large corporations are gaining too much power. They argue that the Sherman Act's strength is its flexibility and adaptability. Are proponents of traditional antitrust policies or proponents of the Chicago School more likely to find that the NCAA violated antitrust laws?

[6] *Brunswick Corp. v. Pueblo Bowl-O-Mat., Inc.*, 429 U.S. 477 (1977).

[7] See D. T. Armentano, "It's Time to Reexamine Antitrust Legislation," *CATO: This Just In*, November 13, 1997, www.cato.org/dailys/11-13-97.html; D. T. Armentano, "Myths of Antirust Progress," *Regulation*, www.cato.org/pubs/regulation/reg20n2a.html.

global context

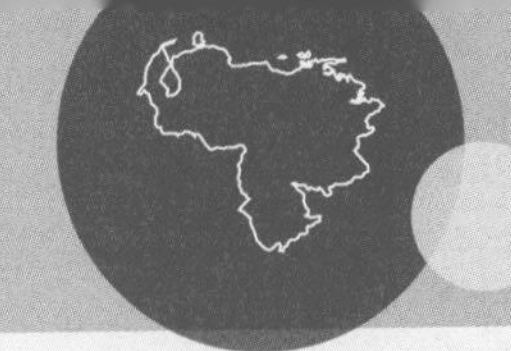

The Struggle for Fair Competition in Venezuela

Venezuela is an example of a country that recognizes the need for antitrust laws but struggles to effectively enact them. In 1974, Venezuela passed a law regulating economic liberty and consumer protection. It has been revised several times since. The bill, based on Spanish antitrust laws, clearly states its goals and provisions.

The clarity of the law is undermined, however, by several problems. First of all, due to the lack of scholarship on antitrust laws in the country, most judges are untrained in the subject. This lack of training results in poor interpretation and enforcement of the law. This particular problem is not confined to less advanced countries. The United States has had similar trouble with judges uneducated in economics.

Another major setback for the Venezuelan law is that the state is given the power to exempt any enterprise from the bill without satisfying specific criteria. Major companies regularly circumvent the law because of their financial ties to the government.

Finally, Venezuelan antitrust is ineffective at obtaining its goal of protecting the "right to economic liberty." This right was suspended in 1939 and remains suspended today. As a consequence, the bill's goal and the economic practices it wishes to implement are only theoretical. Venezuela's situation illustrates the importance of a compatible political and economic environment to prevent unfair competitive business practices.

EXEMPTIONS FROM ANTITRUST LAW

Before we start to examine the specific antitrust laws, note that certain groups and activities are exempt from antitrust regulation. These groups are listed in Exhibit 47-1. They are exempted either through federal statute or case law.

Exhibit 47-1
Groups and Activities Exempt from Antitrust Law

GROUP OR ACTIVITY	BASIS FOR EXEMPTION
Agricultural groups and activities and fisheries	Section 6 of the Clayton Act permits farmers to belong to cooperatives that legally set prices. In accordance with the Fisheries Cooperative Marketing Act of 1976, individuals in the fishing industry can cooperate for purposes of catching and preparing fish for market. Both farmers and fishers may set prices, as long as they do not prevent competition in their markets.
Professional baseball	The Supreme Court ruled in *Federal Baseball Club of Baltimore, Inc. v. National League of Professional Baseball Clubs* that baseball was a sport, not a trade. Furthermore, the Court ruled that baseball did not involve interstate commerce. Thus, baseball was not subject to antitrust laws. However, the case has since been amended by the Curt Flood Act of 1998, which allows players to sue team owners for anticompetitive violations if owners work together to drive certain players out of the sport or to keep wages down. Regardless, no other professional sport has been explicitly exempted.

(continued)

Labor union activities	Section 6 of the Clayton Act permits labor unions to organize and bargain without violating antitrust law. Section 20 of the Clayton Act also allows unions to legally strike, as long as they do not organize with any nonunion groups.
Export activities	The Webb-Pomerene Trade Act of 1918 exempted the formation of selling cooperatives as long as this activity does not significantly enhance or depress prices in the United States. The Webb-Pomerene Trade Act was expanded by the Export Trading Company Act of 1982, which allows the DOJ to certify export-trading companies as qualified. Certified companies cannot be subjected to antitrust claims in the area of certification.
Insurance	When insurance businesses are subject to state antitrust regulation, the McCarran-Ferguson Act exempts the insurance businesses from federal antitrust law.
Regulated industries (utilities, airlines, banking, etc.)	These industries have been regulated in the public interest. The regulatory bodies have the authority to approve behaviors that might otherwise violate antitrust law.
Oil marketing	According to the Interstate Oil Compact of 1935, states can set their own quotas regarding the amount of oil to be sold in interstate commerce.
Research cooperation among businesses	The Small Business Act of 1958 allows small businesses to legally engage in cooperative research. The National Cooperative Research Act of 1984, later amended by the National Cooperative Research and Production Act of 1993, allows competitors to cooperate as joint ventures to develop new products, services, or production methods.

The Sherman Act

As we described earlier, the Sherman Act (or Sherman Antitrust Act) attempts to stop trusts from unfairly restricting market competition. The main thrust of the Sherman Act is contained in Sections 1 and 2. Section 1 of the Sherman Act states:

> Every contract, combination in the form of trust or otherwise, or conspiracy, in restraint of trade or commerce among the several States, or with foreign nations, is declared to be illegal. Every person who shall make any contract or engage in any combination or conspiracy hereby declared to be illegal shall be deemed guilty of a felony, and, on conviction thereof, shall be punished by fine not exceeding $10,000,000 if a corporation, or, if any other person, $350,000, or by imprisonment not exceeding three years, or by both said punishments.

Section 2 of the Sherman Act states:

> Every person who shall monopolize, or attempt to monopolize, or combine or conspire with any other person or persons, to monopolize any part of the trade or commerce among the several States, or with foreign nations, shall be deemed guilty of a felony, and, on conviction thereof, shall be punished by fine not exceeding $10,000,000 if a corporation, or, if any other person, $350,000, or by imprisonment not exceeding three years.

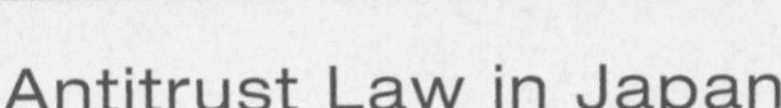

global context

Antitrust Law in Japan

Prior to World War II the Japanese economy was dominated by monopolies, or *zaibatsu.* These huge enterprises controlled their respective markets. Around 1947 however, Japan began adopting antitrust laws similar to those of the United States.

The core of Japan's laws prohibits three particular practices. The first is the prohibition of private monopolization. This section, modeled after the Sherman Act, forbids businesses to set unreasonably low prices, places limits on large enterprise shareholding, and regulates mergers. In addition to these regulations, the law also deems cartels illegal if they "restrain competition substantially contrary to public interest." Cartels may try to restrain competition by fixing prices or limiting production. The Japanese law does permit depression and rationalization cartels.

The law concludes by banning "unfair" business practices. Obviously this description is riddled with ambiguity, but there are some practices generally considered unfair. Some examples of these are a refusal to deal, abuse of bargaining power, and unreasonable interference in consumer affairs.

Despite the implementation of these antitrust laws, new conglomerate businesses called *keiretsus* have sprung up in Japan. The *keiretsu* resembles an oligopoly or an enterprise that dominates a market with few competitors. Many in Japan support the huge enterprises and continue to believe they are the most efficient way to conduct business.

As you can see, the sections themselves are quite short. Congress did not specify which specific behaviors were prohibited under the Sherman Act. Instead, it left this task to the courts. The courts have interpreted these sections to prohibit efforts by competitors to fix prices, restrict output, and exclude rival companies.

JURISDICTION OF THE SHERMAN ACT

The Sherman Act applies to business practices that restrain trade or commerce "among the several States, or with foreign nations." Congress passed the Sherman Act through its authority to regulate interstate commerce. (Recall the discussion of the commerce clause in Chapter 5. Therefore, to violate the Sherman Act, a business action must have directly interfered with the flow of goods in commerce. Alternatively, the action must have had an "effect on commerce." The Sherman Act also applies to foreign companies that conduct business that affects U.S. commerce.

The certified tournament promoters argue that the NCAA regulations affected commerce by preventing the best teams, from different states, from all participating in the same tournament. Having the best teams in one tournament would sell more tickets, and the regulations prohibiting the best teams from competing therefore interfere with commerce. Do the tournament promoters have a valid antitrust claim?

SECTION 1 OF THE SHERMAN ACT

To constitute a violation of Section 1 of the Sherman Act, a business act or practice must have three characteristics. The act must be (1) a combination, contract, or conspiracy (i.e., an agreement between two parties), (2) an *unreasonable* restraint on trade, and (3) a restraint that affects interstate commerce. The rationale for this violation is that consumers will be harmed if companies are permitted to combine their market power. For example, two companies who make agreements to raise prices and restrict their output harm consumers by making them pay more for a good, simply because of the two firms' unfair agreement.

However, not all agreements between firms harm consumers. Some firms enter into agreements through which they engage in joint research. This research leads to reduced costs for both firms and thus helps consumers. While the language of Section 1 states that "every contract . . . is illegal," the courts have interpreted this comment to apply to agreements that *unreasonably* restrain trade. How does a court determine whether an agreement is an unreasonable restraint on trade?

Rule-of-reason analysis and per se violations. The Supreme Court has developed two different approaches to evaluating the reasonableness of a restraint on trade. First, the court has established the **rule-of-reason analysis,** an inquiry into the competitive effects of a company's behavior to determine whether the benefits of the behavior outweigh the harm of the anticompetitive behavior. If the court finds that certain social benefits or positive effects on competition outweigh the harm, the court will rule that the behavior was not a violation. Specifically, when engaging in rule-of-reason analysis, the court considers the following: (1) the nature and purpose of the restraint on trade, (2) the scope of the restraint, (3) the effect of the restraint on business and competition, and (4) the intent of the restraint.

However, certain business practices will always hurt consumers. These practices are called **per se violations.** To establish a per se violation, a plaintiff would simply have to prove that the prohibited conduct occurred. The defendant can offer no justification for the behavior; he or she can argue only that the behavior did not occur. Per se violations are useful in the sense that they give businesses an unambiguous guide to acceptable and unacceptable business practices. In summary, when the court establishes per se violations, it figuratively draws a line in the sand. If a company engages in behavior on the wrong side of the line, the behavior is a violation.

Both approaches have been criticized. Some scholars argue that the per se violations are too rigid, prohibiting some cases of pro-competitive behavior. Others argue that the rule-of-reason analysis is too expensive and time-consuming.

Recently, the courts have been moving away from the per se standard. At least one restraint of trade that was previously judged a per se violation is now being judged by rule-of-reason analysis. Additionally, another standard for assessing restraints of trade has emerged as an amalgamation of rule-of-reason analysis and per se violation. This new standard, called the **"quick-look" standard,** permits the defendant to offer justification for his per se violation. If the defendant can offer justification, the court then engages in rule-of-reason analysis.

While these three standards (i.e., rule of reason, per se, and quick look) are available to the courts, it is not always clear when a certain standard should be used. In *California Dental Association v. Federal Trade Commission,*[8] the Supreme Court clarified the reasons for choosing the quick-look standard over the rule of reason. However, the Court later suggested there might even be another standard—a "less quick look"—to guide analysis. In conclusion, while these standards seem quite distinct, the lines between them are actually somewhat thin.

Courts apply these standards to two types of restraints of trade: horizontal and vertical restraints. We now consider these specific restraints.

Horizontal restraints of trade. When two competitors in the same market make an agreement to restrain trade, this agreement is called a **horizontal restraint of trade.** For example, two competitors make an agreement to raise the prices on their shoe lines. Types of agreements classified as horizontal restraints of trade are price fixing, horizontal division of markets, group boycotts, trade associations, and joint ventures. Some of these restraints are per se violations.

[8] 119 S. Ct. 1604 (1999).

Price fixing. When two or more competitors agree to set prices for a product or service, they are engaging in **price fixing.** Why is price fixing harmful? Such agreements simply cut out competition among companies; thus, the consumer will likely pay higher prices for goods. In *United States v. Socony-Vacuum Oil Co.,*[9] the Supreme Court ruled that any kind of horizontal price fixing is a per se violation of the Sherman Act. In this case, Justice Douglas compared free market competition and competitive pricing to the central nervous system of the economy. Justice Douglas then argued that anticompetitive actions are like diseases that attack the body's central nervous system.

Price fixing may consist of raising, lowering, fixing, or stabilizing the price of a good or service. For example, two companies might agree to set a minimum or maximum price for a certain product. Recently, two convenience-store chains filed suit against five tobacco companies, arguing that these companies met regularly to artificially inflate cigarette prices as they began the process of settling health claims against the companies.[10] In order to win their suit, however, the convenience stores must be able to prove that an agreement to fix prices existed.

A form of price fixing is **bid rigging,** an agreement among firms not to bid against one another or to submit a certain level of bid. Suppose you are accepting bids from companies that wish to perform construction work for you. You note that all the competitors submit identical bids. Alternatively, there is an unexplainable significant price difference between the winning bid and all the other bids. Your bids may have been affected by bid rigging. In the 1980s, the Department of Justice (DOJ) uncovered a bid-rigging scheme in the dairy industry. The industry was rigging its bids to supply milk and dairy products to the public school systems in Florida. As a result of its investigation, the DOJ issued almost $70 million in criminal fines against corporations and individuals for their role in the dairy bid-rigging scheme.[11]

Horizontal division of markets. Suppose two shoe companies agreed to not compete with each other in California, Washington, Florida, and Georgia. They agreed that company 1 would sell shoes only in California and Washington while company 2 would sell shoes in Florida and Georgia. In another agreement, company 1 agrees to sell only men's shoes, while company 2 agrees to sell only women's shoes in Ohio, Michigan, and Pennsylvania. These agreements would be examples of a **horizontal division of market,** an agreement between two or more competitors to divide markets among themselves by geography, customers, or products. The courts have held these divisions to be per se violations of Section 1 because they serve only to eliminate competition. Each division becomes a little monopoly.

Group boycotts. When two or more competitors agree to refuse to deal with a certain person or company, the sellers are engaging in a **group boycott,** or **refusal to deal.** For example, two competing sellers may refuse to sell their products to a certain customer. Alternatively, two competing buyers may refuse to buy from certain sellers. The Supreme Court has ruled that these boycotts are per se illegal if the boycotting competitors intend to harm competition with their boycott. For example, if the competitors are boycotting to drive out a competitor, they have committed a per se violation of Section 1. However, if they are boycotting to increase efficiency or for political reasons, their actions are legal.

[9] 310 U.S. 150 (1940).

[10] "Convenience Stores Level Price-Fixing Charges against Big Tobacco," *Antitrust Litigation Reporter* 7 (May 2000), p. 13.

[11] U.S. Department of Justice, "Antitrust Enforcement and the Consumer."

Vertical restraints of trade. When two parties at different levels in the manufacturing and distribution process make an agreement that restrains trade, they have made a **vertical restraint against trade.** For example, if a manufacturer and a retailer make an agreement that restricts trade, it is likely a vertical restraint. However, if two manufacturers make an agreement, it is a horizontal restraint. Examples of vertical restraints include resale-price maintenance and territorial and customer restrictions.

Territorial and customer restrictions. If a manufacturer limits the territory in which a retailer may sell the manufacturer's product, the manufacturer has created a territorial restriction. Similarly, a manufacturer may mandate that a retailer can sell products only to certain customers. The manufacturer may have legitimate reasons for these territorial and customer restrictions (also called *vertical restraints on distribution* or *nonprice vertical restraints*). Some scholars argue that these restrictions can increase economic efficiency and increase competition. For example, territorial restrictions permit a manufacturer to cut costs by focusing advertising in smaller areas. However, when a manufacturer forces a retailer to agree to these restrictions on territory or resale, the manufacturer may be committing a Section 1 violation.

Historically, the courts assessed territorial restrictions and customer restrictions as per se violations;[12] however, in the landmark case presented in Case 47-1, the Supreme Court changed the standard from per se to rule-of-reason analysis.

[12] *United States v. Arnold, Schwinn & Co.*, 388 U.S. 365 (1967).

CASE 47-1

CONTINENTAL T.V., INC. v. GTE SYLVANIA INC.
UNITED STATES SUPREME COURT
433 U.S. 36 (1977)

When GTE Sylvania discovered it was losing market share to other television manufacturers, it developed a franchise plan that limited the number of retailers selling its product in each area. Moreover, it established the location in each area where the stores could be located. Sylvania required that each franchise sell only Sylvania products.

Sylvania became unhappy with its sales in San Francisco, so it established another location that would be in competition with the existing franchise, Continental T.V. Continental was upset by GTE's action, so it canceled a large order of televisions and ordered a competing brand. Sylvania terminated Continental's franchise and sued for money owed. Continental filed a cross-claim, arguing Sylvania had violated Section 1 of the Sherman Act by restricting the location of retailers that could sell its product. The district court ruled in favor of Continental, while the court of appeals reversed the decision in favor of Sylvania. Continental appealed.

JUSTICE POWELL: The [Schwinn] Court articulated the following "bright line" per se rule of illegality for vertical restrictions: "Under the Sherman Act, it is unreasonable without more for a manufacturer to seek to restrict and confine areas or persons with whom an article may be traded after the manufacturer has parted with dominion over it." But the Court expressly stated the rule of reason governs when "the manufacturer retains title, dominion, and risk with respect to the product and the position and function of the dealer in question are, in fact, indistinguishable from those of an agent or salesman of the manufacturer."

In essence, the issue before us is whether Schwinn's per se rule can be justified under the demanding standards of Northern Pac. R. Co. The Court's refusal to endorse a per se rule in White Motor Co. was based on its uncertainty as to whether vertical restrictions satisfied those standards. Addressing this question for the first time, the Court stated:

> We need to know more than we do about the actual impact of these arrangements on competition to decide whether they have such a "pernicious effect on competition and lack . . . any redeeming virtue" (Northern Pac. R. Co. v. United States, supra, p. 5) and therefore should be classified as per se violations of the Sherman Act. 372 U.S., at 263.

Only four years later the Court in Schwinn announced its sweeping per se rule without even a reference to Northern Pac. R. Co. and with no explanation of its sudden change in position.

The market impact of vertical restrictions is complex because of their potential for a simultaneous reduction of intrabrand competition and stimulation of interbrand competition. . . . Vertical restrictions reduce intrabrand competition by limiting the number of sellers of a particular product competing for the business of a given group of buyers. . . . Vertical restrictions promote interbrand competition by allowing the manufacturer to achieve certain efficiencies in the distribution of his products. These "redeeming virtues" are implicit in every decision sustaining vertical restrictions under the rule of reason. Economists have identified a number of ways in which manufacturers can use such restrictions to compete more effectively against other manufacturers.

Economists also have argued manufacturers have an economic interest in maintaining as much intrabrand competition as is consistent with the efficient distribution of their products. Although the view that the manufacturer's interest necessarily corresponds with that of the public is not universally shared, even the leading critic of vertical restrictions concedes Schwinn's distinction between sale and nonsale transactions is essentially unrelated to any relevant economic impact.

We conclude the distinction drawn in Schwinn between sale and nonsale transactions is not sufficient to justify the application of a per se rule in one situation and a rule of reason in the other. The question remains whether the per se rule stated in Schwinn should be expanded to include nonsale transactions or abandoned in favor of a return to the rule of reason. We have found no persuasive support for expanding the per se rule. As noted above, the Schwinn Court recognized the undesirability of "prohibit[ing] all vertical restrictions of territory and all franchising. . . ." And even Continental does not urge us to hold all such restrictions are per se illegal.

Accordingly, we conclude the per se rule stated in Schwinn must be overruled. In so holding we do not foreclose the possibility that particular applications of vertical restrictions might justify per se prohibition under Northern Pac. R. Co. But we do make clear that departure from the rule-of-reason standard must be based upon demonstrable economic effect rather than—as in Schwinn—upon formalistic line drawing.

In sum, we conclude the appropriate decision is to return to the rule of reason that governed vertical restrictions prior to Schwinn. When anticompetitive effects are shown to result from particular vertical restrictions they can be adequately policed under the rule of reason, the standard traditionally applied for the majority of anticompetitive practices challenged under 1 of the Act. Accordingly, the decision of the Court of Appeals is

AFFIRMED.

CRITICAL THINKING

The Court in this case overturned the previous decision made by the Supreme Court in the *Schwinn* case. Why did the Court decided to overrule the *Schwinn* decision? Do you agree with the Court's overruling?

ETHICAL DECISION MAKING

Suppose you were a business manager at GTE Sylvania who wished to open a store near the Continental store. If you were guided by the universalization test, would your actions have been different? Why?

Resale-price maintenance agreements. Suppose a manufacturer sells products to a retailer. The manufacturer and retailer enter into an agreement in which the retailer sets a specific price for the resale of the products. This agreement is called a **resale-price maintenance agreement,** or *vertical price fixing.* One party may legally suggest a resale price; however, when an agreement exists that requires this resale price, the courts have traditionally held such agreements as per se violations of Section 1 of the Sherman Act. Recently, however, in Case 47-2, the Supreme Court overruled an earlier Supreme Court decision that made resale-price maintenance agreements per se violations. (Notice that the holding in this case is similar to the holding in *Continental T.V. v. GTE Sylvania.*)

CASE 47-2 STATE OIL COMPANY, PETITIONER, v. BARKAT U. KHAN AND KHAN & ASSOCIATES, INC.

UNITED STATES SUPREME COURT
522 U.S. 3 (1997)

Barkat Khan leased and operated a gas station and convenience store owned by State Oil. Khan got the station's gasoline supply from State Oil, who created a suggested retail price for the gas. Khan had to pay 3.25 cents less than the suggested retail price per gallon. Khan could charge any amount in the resale of the gasoline; however, if Khan charged a price higher than the suggested retail price, he had to pay State Oil the difference.

Khan fell behind in lease payments, and State Oil notified Khan they intended to terminate the agreement. State Oil found someone else to run the station in place of Khan; however, this new person was not subject to the gasoline price rule. Consequently, Khan argued State Oil violated Section 1 of the Sherman Act by engaging in price fixing. The district court entered summary judgment for State Oil, ruling Khan did not demonstrate antitrust injury. The Court of Appeals reversed, finding State Oil's pricing scheme was a per se antitrust violation under Albrecht v. Herald Co., 390 US 145 (1968). While the Court of Appeals opined Albrecht was "unsound when decided," it felt constrained to follow the decision. The Supreme Court granted certiorari.

JUSTICE O'CONNOR: Albrecht . . . involved a newspaper publisher who had granted exclusive territories to independent carriers subject to their adherence to a maximum price on resale of the newspapers to the public. Influenced by its decisions in Socony-Vacuum and Schwinn, the Court concluded it was per se unlawful for the publisher to fix the maximum resale price of its newspapers.

Nine years later, in Continental T.V., Inc. v. GTE Sylvania Inc., 433 U.S. 36, 53 (1977), the Court overruled Schwinn, thereby rejecting application of a per se rule in the context of vertical nonprice restrictions. The Court concluded, because "departure from the rule-of-reason standard must be based upon demonstrable economic effect rather than—as in Schwinn—upon formalistic line drawing," the appropriate course would be "to return to the rule of reason that governed vertical restrictions prior to Schwinn."

Subsequent decisions of the Court, however, have hinted the analytical underpinnings of Albrecht were substantially weakened by GTE Sylvania. We noted in Maricopa County vertical restraints are generally more defensible than horizontal restraints.

B

Thus, our reconsideration of Albrecht's continuing validity is informed by several of our decisions, as well as a considerable body of scholarship discussing the effects of vertical restraints. Our analysis is also guided by our general view that the primary purpose of the antitrust laws is to protect interbrand competition. "Low prices," we have explained, "benefit consumers regardless of how those prices are set, and so long as they are above predatory levels, they do not threaten competition." Our interpretation of the Sherman Act also incorporates the notion that condemnation of practices resulting in lower prices to consumers is "especially costly" because "cutting prices in order to increase business often is the very essence of competition."

So informed, we find it difficult to maintain vertically-imposed maximum prices could harm consumers or competition to the extent necessary to justify their per se invalidation. . . . We recognize the Albrecht decision presented a number of theoretical justifications for a per se rule against vertical maximum price fixing. But criticism of those premises abounds.

Albrecht reflected the Court's fear that maximum price fixing could be used to disguise arrangements to fix minimum prices, which remain illegal per se. Although we have acknowledged the possibility that maximum pricing might mask minimum pricing, we believe that such conduct—as with the other concerns articulated in Albrecht—can be appropriately recognized and punished under the rule of reason.

Not only are the potential injuries cited in Albrecht less serious than the Court imagined, the per se rule established therein could in fact exacerbate problems related to the unrestrained exercise of market power by monopolist-dealers. Indeed, both courts and antitrust scholars have noted that Albrecht's rule may actually harm consumers and manufacturers.

After reconsidering Albrecht's rationale and the substantial criticism the decision has received, however, we conclude there is insufficient economic justification for per se invalidation of vertical maximum price fixing. That is so not only because it is difficult to accept the assumptions underlying Albrecht, but also because Albrecht has little or no relevance to ongoing enforcement of the Sherman Act.

C

As we have explained, the term "restraint of trade," as used in § 1, also "invokes the common law itself, and not merely the static content the common law had assigned to the term in 1890." Accordingly, this Court has reconsidered its decisions construing the Sherman Act when the theoretical underpinnings of those decisions are called into serious question.

Although we do not "lightly assume that the economic realities underlying earlier decisions have changed, or that earlier judicial perceptions of those realities were in error," we have noted "different sorts of agreements" may amount to restraints of trade "in varying times and circumstances," and "it would make no sense to create out of the single term 'restraint of trade' a chronologically schizoid statute, in which a 'rule of reason' evolves with new circumstances and new wisdom, but a line of per se illegality remains forever fixed where it was."

Although the rule of Albrecht has been in effect for some time, the inquiry we must undertake requires considering " 'the effect of the antitrust laws upon vertical distributional restraints in the American economy today.' " As the Court noted in ARCO, there has not been another case since Albrecht in which this Court has "confronted an unadulterated vertical, maximum-price-fixing arrangement." Now that we confront Albrecht directly, we find its conceptual foundations gravely weakened.

VACATED AND REMANDED.

CRITICAL THINKING

What reasons did the Court offer to support its conclusion that *Albrecht* should be overturned? Are you persuaded by those reasons?

ETHICAL DECISION MAKING

According to the WPH process of ethical decision making, who are the relevant stakeholders affected by this decision?

e-commerce AND THE LAW

Web Sites as Antitrust Violations

Antitrust law and the Internet have recently begun clashing in several ways. For example, numerous companies are joining with their competitors to buy and sell goods over the Internet. For example, the three largest automobile makers—Ford, General Motors, and DaimlerChrysler—are planning to create a Web site together. Government officials are concerned that Web sites may provide ample opportunity for competitors to share market information in ways that will harm consumers and other competitors. For example, if a seller does not have access to this information on the Internet, will the seller be excluded from certain exchanges? Federal officials have not offered clear guidelines about acceptable business Web exchanges.

Another example of the clash between antitrust law and the Internet is a recent DOJ investigation of eBay, the online auction site. Other auction sites argue that eBay is maintaining a monopoly by refusing to permit rival auction sites to scan eBay prices for price comparisons. However, eBay argues that it has a protected property right in the information; intellectual property owners are usually free from antitrust liability. However, even if the court rules that eBay has a property right in the price information, the DOJ could decide that access to comparative information is necessary for competition.

These examples demonstrate that the application of antitrust laws to businesses' use of the Internet is far from perfect.

SECTION 2 OF THE SHERMAN ACT

According to economic theory, companies with monopoly power use their economic power to limit production and raise prices, thus harming the consumer. Section 2 of the Sherman Act was designed to prohibit the unfair use of monopoly power.

Monopolization. The language of Section 2 may appear to prohibit *all* monopolies; however, the courts have interpreted this section to prohibit *conduct that monopolizes.* What is the distinction? The courts permit a monopoly to exist; however, if a company *monopolizes*—that is, it (1) possesses market power and (2) unfairly achieved this market power or uses this market power for abuse—the court will rule that this company has violated the Sherman Act. The plaintiff in a monopolization case must demonstrate both elements of monopolizing.

Monopoly power. **Monopoly or Market power** is the ability to control price and drive competitors out of the market. How do the courts determine whether a company has market power? Generally, the courts consider the company's **market share,** a firm's fractional share of the relevant market. If a company enjoys 70 percent of the relevant market, the court usually holds that the firm has monopoly power. If, however, the market share is less than 70 percent, it is questionable whether the court will consider the company to hold market power.

Before a court can determine a company's market share, the court must first identify the company's *relevant market.* The way the court defines the relevant market is immensely important in determining whether a company is monopolizing. When the court identifies the relevant market, it considers two markets: product and geographic markets. A **product market** is a market in which all products identical to or substitutes for the company's product are sold. Suppose a company is accused of monopolizing the coffee market. In its consideration of the product market, the court would identify all coffee produced by other firms. Furthermore, the court would consider tea sales because tea is considered a substitute for coffee.

The second market a court considers while identifying the relevant market is the **geographic market,** which is the area in which the company competes with others in the relevant product market. The plaintiff usually stipulates the geographic market as local, regional, or national. For example, if the company's products are sold throughout the United States, the geographic market would be the United States market.

Case 47-3 provides an illustration of the court's consideration of the requirement that the plaintiff establish the relevant market.

CASE 47-3 PEPSICO, INC., PLAINTIFF, v. THE COCA-COLA COMPANY, DEFENDANT

U.S. COURT OF APPEALS FOR THE SECOND CIRCUIT
315 F.3D 101 (2002)

Coca-Cola and PepsiCo, in addition to selling their famous beverages in bottles and cans, sell fountain syrup to numerous customers, including large restaurant chains, movie theater chains, and other "on-premise" accounts. PepsiCo and Coca-Cola bid for agreements to supply fountain syrup and negotiate a price directly with the customer and then pay a fee to a distributor to deliver the product. Historically, PepsiCo delivered fountain syrup primarily through bottler distributors; Coca-Cola delivered fountain syrup through bottler distributors as well as IFDs, who can offer customers one-stop shopping for all of their restaurant supplies. In the late 1990s, PepsiCo decided it wanted to start delivering fountain syrup via IFDs, but when it sought to do so, Coca-Cola began to enforce the so-called "loyalty" or "conflict of interest" policy contained in its agreements with IFDs, which provides distributors who supply customers with Coca-Cola may not "handle the soft drink products of [PepsiCo]." IFDs who breach the loyalty policy risk termination by Coca-Cola. As the district court observed, "a distributor subject to the loyalty policy can supply all its customers with either Pepsi or Coke, not both. Because distributors are given an all or nothing choice, a customer of a distributor subject to Coca-Cola's loyalty policy who wants Pepsi will have to go elsewhere to get it."

PepsiCo filed an antitrust complaint alleging the loyalty provisions constituted an illegal monopolization and attempted monopolization under Section 2 of the Sherman Act. The district court granted Coca-Cola's motion for summary judgment. PepsiCo appealed.

PER CURIAM:

II. Section 2 of the Sherman Act

As noted by the district court, in order to state a claim for monopolization under Section 2 of the Sherman Act, a plaintiff must establish "(1) the possession of monopoly power in the relevant market and (2) the willful acquisition or maintenance of that power as distinguished from growth or development as a consequence of a superior product, business acumen, or historic accident." To state an attempted monopolization claim, a plaintiff must establish "(1) the defendant has engaged in predatory or anti-competitive conduct with (2) a specific intent to monopolize and (3) a dangerous probability of achieving monopoly power."

A. The Relevant Market

As an initial matter, it is necessary to define the relevant product and geographic market Coca-Cola is alleged to be monopolizing. The parties do not dispute the relevant geographic market is the United States. A relevant product market consists of "products that have reasonable interchangeability for the purposes for which they are produced—price, use and qualities considered." Products will be considered to be reasonably interchangeable if consumers treat them as "acceptable substitutes."

In its complaint, PepsiCo defined the relevant market as the "market for fountain-dispensed soft drinks distributed through [IFDs] throughout the United States." PepsiCo sought to narrow this market definition on summary judgment by confining it to customers with certain characteristics, specifically "large restaurant chain accounts that are not 'heavily franchised' with low fountain 'volume per outlet.'" The district court rejected this definition on the grounds 1) it was not substantiated by the evidence; and 2) it was not supported by the practical indicia enunciated in Brown Shoe.

Reviewing the evidence submitted on summary judgment, the district court held fountain syrup delivered by bottler distributors was an "acceptable substitute" for fountain syrup delivered by IFDs—and thus had to be included in the relevant product market—because none of the numerous customers who were deposed or submitted affidavits for the summary judgment motion said the availability of delivery via IFDs was determinative of its choice of fountain syrup. Tellingly, in PepsiCo's own survey of 99 major customers, the availability of one-stop-shopping IFDs was ranked 35 out of 38 in importance among various factors they considered in choosing a fountain syrup.

The district court also rejected PepsiCo's argument the relevant market should be confined to certain customers, an argument the district court characterized as "PepsiCo['s attempt] to define the elements of the relevant market to suit its desire for high Coca-Cola market share, rather than letting the market define itself." The district court found, although the affidavits and exhibits submitted on the summary judgment motion showed many customers have a preference for receiving fountain syrup through IFDs because of the advantages provided by one-stop-shopping, these customers did not constitute a discrete group, but rather were included in various groups of fountain syrup customers. Indeed, franchisees, a group PepsiCo sought to exclude from the market definition, purchased 63 percent of the Coca-Cola fountain syrup delivered by IFDs. Identical types of customers expressed preferences for either IFDs or bottler distributors, and most customers stated method of delivery was simply one of several non-determinative factors they considered in deciding which fountain syrup to stock. We agree with the district court PepsiCo failed to provide evidentiary support for its market definition restricted by distributor and customer.

AFFIRMED.

CRITICAL THINKING

What is there about the idea of a "market" that makes it ambiguous? Why can we not all agree about what the relevant market is for antitrust purposes?

ETHICAL DECISION MAKING

Using the universalization principle, would you prefer to have markets defined broadly or narrowly? Think about who benefits and who loses from these alternatives.

In summary, when determining whether a company holds monopoly power, the court first identifies the relevant market, which includes the product and geographic market. After the court identifies the relevant market, it determines the company's market share. If the market share is greater than or equal to 70 percent, the court will likely rule that the company in question has monopoly power. Given the geographic market requirement, it is possible for a firm that operates nationally to operate in separate, distinct markets. As such, a national firm might have a monopoly in one of the geographic markets but not in others.

Case Nugget Intent to Monopolize

Covad Communications Co. et al. v. BellSouth Corp. et al. 299 F.3d 1272 (2002)

Covad supplies its customers with high-speed DSL Internet service, which works through existing phone lines. BellSouth, the regional telephone service provider, also provides DSL service. Covad contracted with BellSouth to have access to BellSouth's phone lines so that Covad could supply its customers with Internet access. Covad sued BellSouth under Section 2 of the Sherman Act, alleging that BellSouth failed to live up to its agreement, thereby helping to further BellSouth's monopolistic control over phone and Internet service in the region and costing Covad its customers. The district court dismissed Covad's claims, and Covad appealed.

Covad alleged that BellSouth's behavior indicated an attempt to monopolize, in violation of the Sherman Act. Attempts to monopolize involve "(1) anticompetitive or exclusionary conduct; (2) with specific intent to monopolize; and (3) a dangerous probability of achieving monopoly power."

To prove its claim, Covad argued that BellSouth denied Covad access to an "essential facility," the phone lines, and that this constituted exclusionary conduct given the nature of phone and Internet service. If BellSouth, the inheritor of the local phone monopoly created with the rest of the "Baby Bells" in the 1983 breakup of AT&T, does not grant competitors access to the phone lines, the only way any company could compete would be to install a completely new grid of phone lines. Given the enormity of the costs associated with re-creating a phone grid, denying access to the existing phone grid constitutes exclusionary and anticompetitive conduct with the intent to monopolize. Without access to existing phone lines, almost no companies could enter the market, thus creating a significant barrier to entry.

Ultimately, the court of appeals determined that sufficient evidence existed to find that BellSouth acted with the intent to monopolize. The court reversed the district court's decision to dismiss and remanded the case.

The intent requirement. After the court determines that a company has monopoly power, it next considers the company's intent. A firm that holds monopoly power is not necessarily violating Section 2. This firm might have legitimately earned dominance in the market. For example, this firm might be manufacturing a high-quality product, or its managers may have made very wise business decisions. However, if the firm *intends* to monopolize or engages in anticompetitive activity in an attempt to maintain its monopoly power, the firm has violated Section 2. Courts look at the specific behavior of the company to determine its intent.

Part of the certified tournament promoters' claims against the NCAA is that the regulation's stated intent, promoting greater competition by limiting the unfair advantage of the better schools, is a sham. Rather, the promoters claim, the NCAA is concerned with limiting the amount of money outside promoters can make based on their

global context

German Antitrust Law

German antitrust law includes the prohibition of market domination and the practices associated with this domination. A single company is considered to be unfairly dominating if it commands one-third or more of a market (except if its annual sales do not exceed DM250 million). Two or three combined companies cannot command half or greater of the market (except if the total annual sales are less than DM100 million). Finally, four to five companies are prohibited from controlling two-thirds or more of a market (unless the annual sales never exceed DM100 million).

More significant than these antitrust provisions is an aspect of the law permitting relative market domination. *Relative market domination* occurs when a company operates only in respect to customers or suppliers who lack alternatives to the dominating product or service. A German federal court upheld this section in an important case involving a sporting goods store. The court found that the store could be dependent on Rossignol skis despite the fact that the market share was only 8 percent. Without Rossignol, the court declared, the store could not be considered competitive.

tournaments. Given the intent, as characterized by the tournament promoters, it would appear the NCAA established a monopoly, because the regulations are a manifestation of an intent to monopolize. If so, the NCAA violated the Sherman Act.

Attempts to monopolize. Suppose a company does not currently hold market power; however, this company starts to use certain business practices in the hope it will gain a greater share of the market and make more profit. If this company intended these practices to (1) exclude competitors and (2) allow the company to gain monopoly power, the courts would consider these practices as **attempts to monopolize.** However, another important element of an attempt to monopolize is the probability of success. Only those practices that have a dangerous probability of success constitute an attempt to monopolize. For example, suppose a company that recently introduced a new soft drink attempted to monopolize the soft-drink industry. Because it is unlikely this company could monopolize an industry largely dominated by Coke and Pepsi, the company would likely not be found guilty of an attempt to monopolize.

Exhibit 47-2 describes a case against U.S. Tobacco for attempting to monopolize.

Companies may use various different practices in attempts to monopolize. For example, they may steal another company's trade secrets. Alternatively, they might engage in predatory pricing. When a company prices one product below normal cost until competitors are eliminated and then sharply increases the price, the company is practicing **predatory pricing.**

Exhibit 47-2 Tobacco Companies and Attempts to Monopolize

In April 2000, a jury decided in *Conwood Co. v. U.S. Tobacco Co.*[*] that U.S. Tobacco, a manufacturer that controlled almost 80 percent of the smokeless-tobacco market, used illegal means in an attempt to monopolize the industry. These practices included removing Conwood's display racks from stores and paying under-the-table cash rebates to retailers. The jury ruled that U.S. Tobacco had to pay Conwood $350 million in damages; however, these damages are trebled under federal antitrust law. Consequently, U.S. Tobacco must pay $1.05 billion. U.S. Tobacco appealed, and the court affirmed the lower court's ruling.[†]

[*] No. 5:98cv 108-R (W.D. Ky., Mar. 28, 2000).
[†] 290 F.3d 768 (200 2).

Case Nugget Predatory Pricing

Spirit Airlines, Inc. v. Northwest Airlines, Inc.
2005 U.S. App. LEXIS 29338 (2005)

Spirit Airlines was based out of Detroit and focused its business toward "leisure or low-price-sensitive" passengers. Spirit's main flights were direct flights from Detroit to Boston and Philadelphia. Northwest Airlines, which uses Detroit as one of its main hubs, also flies direct flights from Detroit to Boston and Philadelphia. In addition, Northwest controls 64 of the 86 gates at Detroit's airport. When Spirit began selling tickets at costs far lower than those of Northwest, Northwest drastically lowered its prices and increased the number of seats available from Detroit to both Boston and Philadelphia, in addition to preventing Spirit from using any gate owned by Northwest. Spirit sued Northwest under Section 2 of the Sherman Antitrust Act, alleging predatory pricing and other predatory tactics. The district court granted summary judgment in favor of Northwest, and Spirit appealed.

At trial, Northwest alleged that it never operated below cost and therefore did not engage in predatory pricing. The district court agreed with Northwest's assertion. Furthermore, Northwest argued that the proper market included all passengers passing through Detroit to Boston or Philadelphia, not just those with direct flights. In addition, Northwest claimed that its lower price was due to a competitive response, as market logic would predict, to the entering of another firm (Spirit) into the market.

In response, Spirit argued that Northwest intentionally lowered its prices and increased capacity on the specific routes Detroit to Boston and Philadelphia. Spirit used as evidence an article an executive at Northwestern wrote and published specifically explaining that the best way to drive out competition from an upstart is to undercut in price and increase seats to ensure no potential customers are turned away. Further evidence of Northwest's predatory behavior included the fact that Northwest increased its prices on both Detroit to Boston and Detroit to Philadelphia once Spirit canceled these routes, thus regaining its monopoly on flights to these two cities out of Detroit.

The appellate court, in reconsidering the evidence from the trial, determined there was sufficient evidence for a fact finder to determine that Northwest did engage in predatory pricing. The court writes,

> In sum, even if the jury were to find that Northwest's prices exceeded an appropriate measure of average variable costs, the jury must also consider the market structure in this controversy to determine if Northwest's deep price discounts in response to Spirit's entry and the accompanying expansion of its capacity on these routes injured competition by causing Spirit's departure from this market and allowing Northwest to recoup its losses and to enjoy monopoly power as a result.

The appellate court reversed and remanded the lower court's decision.

Exemption for states. Some firms that monopolize are permitted to exist. Section 2 of the Sherman Act does not apply to states; consequently, the state may create monopolies. Case 47-4 illustrates the state's right to create monopolies.

CASE 47-4 NEO GEN SCREENING, INC., PLAINTIFF, APPELLANT, v. NEW ENGLAND NEWBORN SCREENING PROGRAM

U.S. COURT OF APPEALS FOR THE FIRST CIRCUIT
187 F.3D 24 (1999)

Neo Gen Screening, a private, for-profit corporation, sells the service of medical screening of newborn children. According to Massachusetts law, newborns must be screened for certain diseases. Neo Gen sells hospitals in various states screening services; however, Neo Gen could not sell the services in Massachusetts because the Massachusetts Department of Health had a statewide screening program run by the New England Newborn Screening Program (NENSP) through the University of Massachusetts (UMASS). When Neo Gen attempted to sell its services (which were almost ½ the cost of NENSP's service) in Massachusetts, the Department of Health issued new regulations essentially requiring a newborn to be screened through NENSP. The screening program was at one time a unit of the Department of Health. Neo Gen filed suit against the NENSP and UMASS for monopolizing and attempting to create a monopoly for screening services. The District Court dismissed the suit under the Eleventh Amendment, arguing NENSP and UMASS were arms of the state and thus immune from lawsuit.

CIRCUIT JUDGE BOUDIN: The difficulty for Neo Gen is it is clearly established the Sherman Act does not itself apply to state action. In Parker v. Brown, 317 U.S. 341, 350-51 (1943), the Supreme Court determined Congress had not meant to require states to comply with the Sherman Act. Accordingly, a state is free to regulate, or act on its own behalf, in ways that are anti-competitive and would not be permitted to a private individual. Id. This doctrine is so well settled that its rationale and underpinnings are scarcely worth discussing.

No doubt the emergency regulations create an effective monopoly for the University of Massachusetts in conducting the screening of Massachusetts newborns. By regulation, the blood must be made available to the Department, and the Department has chosen to contract with the University to do the testing. Although a hospital could also choose to engage Neo Gen, no hospital is likely to pay twice for the same service. But a regulation or purchase of services made by the state is classic state action immunized from the Sherman Act.

Neo Gen mistakenly attempts to distinguish Parker v. Brown and the long line of cases that have followed it by arguing the Massachusetts legislature did not "clearly articulate" a purpose to supplant competition with monopoly. . . . Neo Gen argues the Massachusetts legislature did not expressly approve or authorize the kind of regulation or contract involved in this case; but we have rejected a "clear articulation" test as applied to the state's executive branch, at least where a full-fledged department is concerned. Given the Commonwealth statutes that authorize testing, there is nothing extraordinary or unforeseeable about the Department of Public Health's regulation requiring testing or its decision to do the testing itself or through a chosen instrument.

It may be, as Neo Gen charges, the defendants' actions reflect a cozy arrangement that gives newborns inferior screening at higher cost and that everyone—except possibly the Screening Program—would be better off if hospitals could contract competitively for screening services, just as they procure drugs, bandages, and other resources. The state, in turn, says its contract provides for extra research and follow-up that Neo Gen fails to provide; such cross-subsidy arguments are traditional defenses for monopoly but not invariably without merit. At bottom, this is a policy matter to be resolved by the Commonwealth.

AFFIRMED.

CRITICAL THINKING

Identify the court's conclusion. Now identify the reasons for the conclusion. Is there any information missing from the facts of this case that would help you determine the worth of this conclusion? (*Clue:* Think about the court's willingness to consider economic efficiency in so many other cases in this chapter.)

[CONTINUED]

ETHICAL DECISION MAKING

Think back to the WPH process of ethical decision making. Who are the primary stakeholders affected by the court's ruling?

Exhibit 47-3 provides a summary of the relationship between Section 1 and Section 2 of the Sherman Act.

Exhibit 47-3 Integration of Section 1 and Section 2 of the Sherman Act

1. The number of parties involved in Section 1 and Section 2 violations differs. To violate Section 1, two parties must be involved. However, one party can violate Section 2.

   Explanation: Section 1 prohibits contracts, combinations, and conspiracies that restrict trade. Two parties must be involved in a combination or conspiracy. Thus, a violation of Section 1 requires the actions of two parties. In contrast, one company can monopolize or attempt to monopolize. Thus, a violation of Section 2 requires only one party.
2. Both sections prohibit unfair business behavior. However, you would demonstrate this unfair business behavior in different ways under the respective sections.

   Explanation: To demonstrate a violation of Section 2, you would show that a company is using its monopoly power to affect prices. In contrast, under Section 1, you would show that a company made an agreement with another party to somehow restrict trade.

The Clayton Act

During the 1912 presidential election, antitrust law was a dominant issue for the candidates. The Supreme Court had recently ruled that only those restraints on trade that were unreasonable under rule-of-reason analysis were subject to the Sherman Act. Candidate Woodrow Wilson argued that rule-of-reason analysis was not specific enough for businesspeople; he asserted that the government needed to establish specific business practices that were antitrust violations. Wilson was elected, and Congress soon enacted the Clayton Act in 1914.

The Clayton Act identifies the following four business practices not covered under the Sherman Act:

1. Price discrimination (Section 2 of the Clayton Act).
2. Exclusionary practices (Section 3).
3. Mergers (Section 7).
4. Interlocking directorates (Section 8).

These practices are considered illegal when they significantly harm competition. We will now examine these specific business practices.

SECTION 2: PRICE DISCRIMINATION

Section 2 of the Clayton Act (as amended by the Robinson-Patman Act in 1936) prohibits price discrimination by sellers. A seller engages in **price discrimination** when it sells the same goods to competing buyers for different prices. Sellers may use price discrimination to bring about monopoly power.

To demonstrate a violation of Section 2 of the Clayton Act, a plaintiff must show two basic elements. First, the seller that engaged in price discrimination must be involved in interstate commerce. Second, the seller's price discrimination must have substantially lessened competition or tended to create a monopoly.

Specifically, Section 2(a) of the act prohibits discrimination in price by sellers between two buyers of a commodity of like grade and quality. Offers to sell are not violations of this section. For example, suppose a manufacturer agrees to sell 100 pairs of jeans to a retailer for $25 per pair. However, the manufacturer offers to sell another retailer 100 pairs of jeans for $20 per pair. If he did not make the sale to the second retailer, he has not violated Section 2(a).

Suppose for a moment that the manufacturer did make the sale to the second retailer. However, the jeans he sold to the second retailer were of lower quality; they had slight defects in their manufacturing. If he can demonstrate a physical difference between the jeans he sold to the two retailers, he has not violated Section 2(a).

There are several reasons why a seller might legitimately engage in price discrimination. For example, the production costs associated with the products sold to the first buyer might be lower than the production costs for the products sold to the second buyer. If a seller can justify the price difference through cost difference, the seller has not violated Section 2 of the Clayton Act. Moreover, if a seller engages in price discrimination to compete in good faith with another seller's low price, the seller is not guilty of violating the Clayton Act. This defense to price discrimination is called the **meeting-the-competition defense.**

SECTION 3: EXCLUSIONARY PRACTICES

The Clayton Act spells out a large number of forbidden exclusionary practices that violate the objectives of a market economy. Section 3 of the Clayton Act provides the general basis for defining these methods of unfair competition. For instance, courts have interpreted Section 3 as prohibiting exclusive-dealing contracts and tying agreements.

If an exclusive-dealing contract or tying agreement involves services or intangibles, Section 3 does not apply to that contract. Instead, Section 3 applies only to the lease or sale of commodities. Services and intangibles in exclusive-dealing contracts or tying agreements may be tried under the Sherman Act.

Exclusive dealing. An **exclusive-dealing contract** is an agreement in which a seller requires that a buyer buy products supplied only by that seller. This agreement prohibits a buyer from buying the seller's competitor's products. If this agreement lessens competition or tends to create a monopoly, the agreement is in violation of Section 3 of the Clayton Act.

Perhaps the most well known case that considered exclusive-dealing contracts is *Standard Oil v. United States.*[13] Standard Oil, the largest gasoline seller at the time of the case, created exclusive-dealing contracts with independent stations. Approximately half of Standard Oil's sales came from these independent stations. Six of Standard Oil's largest competitors created their own exclusive-dealing contracts. Standard Oil and its six largest competitors, through their exclusive-dealing contracts, accounted for 65 percent of the market. The court ruled that although exclusive-dealing agreements could have positive competitive effects, the exclusive-dealing contracts in this case gave Standard Oil 7 percent of the total gas sales in the area ($58 million). Furthermore, the

[13] 37 U.S. 293 (1949).

exclusive-dealing contracts created a situation where competitors could not freely enter into the market. Consequently, the Supreme Court ruled that these exclusive-dealing contracts were illegal under Section 3.

Consider the following case: Blockbuster Video entered into an exclusive agreement to market a Barbra Streisand concert video with an additional song not included in other versions of the video.[14] ERI Max Entertainment sued, arguing that the exclusive agreement was a violation of antitrust law. The court ruled that although Blockbuster controls a large proportion of the video market, the exclusive agreement did not cause injury to competition, particularly because the exclusive-dealing agreement applied to one song on one tape.

Tying arrangements. When a seller agrees to sell a product, the tying product, to a buyer on the condition that the buyer will also purchase another product, the tied product, the seller has created a **tying arrangement.** The sale of one product is tied to the sale of another product. For example, suppose a manufacturer agrees to sell men's shoes to a retailer as long as the retailer also buys women's shoes to resell.

Like exclusive-dealing contracts, tying arrangements are not necessarily illegal. In evaluating the legality under Section 3, courts ask the following questions:

1. Are the products being tied clearly separate?
2. What is the purpose of the tying agreement?
3. Does the seller tying the products hold market power?

If the tying arrangement leads to competitive harm, the court will likely find the arrangement to be illegal.

Remember, tying arrangements apply only to commodities; therefore, arrangements tying services must be tried under the Sherman Act. For example, a plaintiff brought a suit against a funeral home for violating Section 3 of the Clayton Act by tying funeral services to the purchase of a casket.[15] The court stated that for the case to be tried under the Clayton Act, both the funeral services and the casket must be a good.

SECTION 7: MERGERS

Section 7 prohibits anticompetitive mergers or acquisitions. We define **merger** as the acquisition of one company by another. Specifically, the text of the section prohibits one person or company from owning or acquiring stocks or assets in another corporation when the effect would be to lessen competition.

Given the importance placed on competition, many merger cases also focus on market concentration. Markets are considered concentrated when a few firms in the relevant market enjoy large market shares.

We restrict mergers through Section 7 because we want to ensure that competition can thrive in the market; some mergers are likely to inhibit competition because these mergers may permit companies to form monopolies. For example, suppose you are competing with another major company to sell laptop computers. Instead of trying to compete with this company, you create an offer to acquire the company. You think once you acquire the company, you will be able to increase your prices to increase your profit. Who else will compete with you?

[14] *ERI Max Entertainment Inc. d/b/a Vidi-O v. Streisand et al.*, No. 95-615-Appeal (RI Sup. Ct., March 17, 1997).

[15] *Chatelain et al. v. Mothe Funeral Homes Inc., et al.*, E.D. La., July 1, 1998.

Case Nugget Mergers

South Austin Coalition Community Council et al. v. SBC Communications, Inc.
274 F.3d 1168 (2001)

Private parties sued to block SBC and Ameritech's merger. Under the proposed plan, Ameritech would be merged into SBC, both of which are Baby Bells created during the breakup of AT&T in 1983. The parties that sued SBC were trying to stop the merger on antitrust grounds, claiming that the merger would violate Section 7 of the Clayton Act because the merger precluded potential competition between the parties. The plaintiffs argued that were SBC and Ameritech not to merge, each would entered the other's core markets and created extra competition to consumers' benefit. The district court ruled in favor of SBC, and the plaintiffs appealed.

The thrust of the antitrust argument was a focus on the loss of future competition, not an immediate decrease in existing competition. However, this main focus is flawed. Section 7 of the Clayton Act specifically creates an exception for common carriers that do not directly compete. SBC and Ameritech are common carriers, with primary business in different cities, and thus they do not directly compete. The court stated, "The last clause of [the relevant portion of Section 7] allows 'such common carrier' to 'extend' its lines by merger, provided 'there is no substantial competition between the company extending its lines and the company whose stock, property, or an interest therein is so acquired.'"

The court stated that to allow "potential competition" to constitute "substantial competition" under Section 7 of the Clayton Act would be the same as negating the exception. Furthermore, we do not know whether the two companies would compete in the future, and the expansion of cell phone service as competition to land-line service minimizes any potential negative impact of the merger. As such, the court affirmed the lower court's decision in favor of SBC.

There are three types of mergers: horizontal, vertical, and conglomerate. Exhibit 47-4 is a list of some of the major U.S. mergers. The classification of type of merger depends on the relationship between the acquirer and the acquired company. However, of the three types of mergers, the Department of Justice and the courts are most likely to challenge horizontal mergers.

Horizontal mergers. A merger between two or more companies producing the same or similar products is a **horizontal merger.** Because these firms are at the same competitive level, a horizontal merger usually eliminates a competitor from the market. Historically, if a horizontal merger led to undue concentration in the market (i.e., a relatively large market share), the merger was likely to be presumed illegal. Exhibit 47-5 is an example of a horizontal merger.

However, in the 1970s, courts became more willing to consider certain economic factors. The FTC and DOJ created guidelines to assess the legality of mergers. Not only would the courts look at the market share of the resulting firm, but they would also look at the degree of concentration in the market. The FTC and DOJ use an index system to determine the level of concentration in the market. If the market is concentrated (i.e., a small number of companies control a large portion of the market), the FTC and DOJ

Exhibit 47-4
Some of the Top U.S. Mergers

COMPANIES	DATE	AMOUNT (BILLIONS)
America Online acquired Time Warner	1/2000	$165
MCI acquired Sprint	10/1999	115
Exxon acquired Mobil	11/1999	81
Glaxo Wellcome acquired SmithKline Beecham	12/2000	74
Travelers Group acquired Citicorp	4/1998	72.6
SBC Communications acquired Ameritech	5/1998	72.4
Bell Atlantic acquired GTE Corp.	7/1998	70
AT&T acquired Tele-Communications Inc.	6/1998	69
NationsBank acquired Bank America	4/1998	61
Procter & Gamble acquired Gillette	10/2005	57
British Petroleum acquired Amoco Corp.	8/1998	55
AT&T acquired Media One	6/2000	44
WorldCom acquired MCI	10/1997	37
Sprint acquired Nextel	12/2004	35
Hewlett-Packard acquired Compaq	9/2001	25

Exhibit 47-5
Example of Horizontal Merger

In June 2000, the FTC sought an injunction to block Kroger Co.'s acquisition of 74 Winn-Dixie supermarkets in Texas and Oklahoma.* Approximately half of the stores were in Fort Worth, where Kroger and Winn-Dixie were in strong competition. The proposed merger would have given Kroger 33 percent of all supermarket sales. The FTC argued that the merger was a violation of Section 7 of the Clayton Act because the merger would substantially reduce competition. By the end of June 2000 the district court found that the injunction sought by the FTC would be in the public interest.† Thus, Kroger and Winn-Dixie were prohibited from taking any further steps toward a merger.

*FTC press release, "FTC to Seek Injunction to Block Kroger Co. Purchase of Winn-Dixie Supermarkets in Texas and Oklahoma," June 2, 2000.

†*FTC v. Kroger et al.*, Civil Action No. 3-00CV1196-R (N.D. Texas).

will probably challenge the merger. (Remember, the goal is to preserve competition.) However, the FTC and DOJ consider a variety of other factors: the financial condition of the acquired and acquiring firm, barriers to entry in the industry, and the economic efficiency associated with the merger. Moreover, the courts might look at the history of the acquiring firm. Has this firm acquired smaller companies in the past? Is the company aggressive? The courts will also attempt to predict the success of the resulting firm from the merger.

Case 47-5 provides an illustration of courts' willingness to consider, even if they are not always persuaded by, efficiency arguments rather than simply presuming a horizontal merger is illegal.

CASE 47-5 FEDERAL TRADE COMMISSION, PLAINTIFF-APPELLANT, v. H.J. HEINZ CO. AND MILNOT HOLDING CORP., DEFENDANTS-APPELLEES

U.S. COURT OF APPEALS FOR THE DISTRICT OF COLUMBIA CIRCUIT
246 F.3D 708 (2001)

The baby food market is dominated by three firms, Gerber Products Company, Heinz and Beech-Nut. Gerber, the industry leader, enjoys a 65 per cent market share while Heinz and Beech-Nut come in second and third, with a 17.4 per cent and a 15.4 per cent share respectively. Gerber enjoys unparalleled brand recognition with a brand loyalty greater than any other product sold in the United States. Gerber's products are found in over 90 per cent of all American supermarkets.

By contrast, Heinz is sold in approximately 40 per cent of all supermarkets. Despite its second-place domestic market share, Heinz is the largest producer of baby food in the world with $1 billion in sales worldwide. Heinz lacks Gerber's brand recognition; it markets itself as a "value brand" with a shelf price several cents below Gerber's.

Beech-Nut has a market share (15.4%) comparable to that of Heinz (17.4%). Beech-Nut maintains price parity with Gerber, selling at about one penny less. It markets its product as a premium brand. Consumers generally view its product as comparable in quality to Gerber's.

Heinz and Beech-Nut proposed a merger. Under the terms of their merger agreement, Heinz would acquire 100 per cent of Beech-Nut's voting securities for $185 million. The Federal Trade Commission filed an administrative complaint against Heinz and Beech-Nut, charging the proposed merger violates section 7 of the Clayton Act. The court concluded it was "more probable than not consummation of the Heinz/Beech-Nut merger will actually increase competition in jarred baby food in the United States." The FTC appealed and sought injunctive relief.

CIRCUIT JUDGE HENDERSON: Section 7 of the Clayton Act prohibits acquisitions, including mergers, "where in any line of commerce or in any activity affecting commerce in any section of the country, the effect of such acquisition may be substantially to lessen competition, or to tend to create a monopoly." Merger enforcement, like other areas of antitrust, is directed at market power. The Congress has empowered the FTC, inter alia, to weed out those mergers whose effect "may be substantially to lessen competition" from those that enhance competition.

In *United States v. Baker Hughes Inc.*, we explained the analytical approach by which the government establishes a section 7 violation. First the government must show the merger would produce "a firm controlling an undue percentage share of the relevant market, and [would] result in a significant increase in the concentration of firms in that market." Such a showing establishes a "presumption" the merger will substantially lessen competition. To rebut the presumption, the defendants must produce evidence that "shows the market-share statistics [give] an inaccurate account of the [merger's] probable effects on competition" in the relevant market.

The appellees . . . attempt to rebut the FTC's prima facie showing [by] their contention the anticompetitive effects of the merger will be offset by efficiencies resulting from the union of the two companies, efficiencies which they assert will be used to compete more effectively against Gerber. It is true a merger's primary benefit to the economy is its potential to generate efficiencies.

Although the Supreme Court has not sanctioned the use of the efficiencies defense in a section 7 case, the trend among lower courts is to recognize the defense.

Nevertheless, the high market concentration levels present in this case require, in rebuttal, proof of extraordinary efficiencies, which the appellees failed to supply.

In support of its conclusion post-merger efficiencies will outweigh the merger's anticompetitive effects, the district court found the consolidation of baby food production in Heinz's under-utilized Pittsburgh plant "will achieve substantial cost savings in salaries and operating costs." The court also credited the appellees' promise of improved product quality as a result of recipe consolidation. The only cost reduction the court quantified as a percentage of pre-merger costs, however, was the so-called "variable conversion cost": the cost of processing the volume of baby food now processed by Beech-Nut. The court accepted the appellees' claim this cost would be reduced by 43% if the Beech-Nut production were shifted to Heinz's plant, a reduction the appellees' expert characterized as "extraordinary."

The district court's analysis falls short of the findings necessary for a successful efficiencies defense in the circumstances of this case. We mention only three of the most important deficiencies here. First, "variable conversion cost" is only a percentage of the total variable manufacturing cost. A large percentage reduction in only a small portion of the company's overall variable manufacturing cost does not necessarily translate into a significant cost advantage to the merger.

Second, the percentage reduction in *Beech-Nut's* cost is still not the relevant figure. After the merger, the two entities will be combined, and to determine whether the merged entity will be a significantly more efficient competitor, cost reductions must be measured across the new entity's combined production—not just across the pre-merger output of Beech-Nut.

Finally, and as the district court recognized, the asserted efficiencies must be "merger-specific" to be cognizable as a defense. That is, they must be efficiencies that cannot be achieved by either company alone because, if they can, the merger's asserted benefits can be achieved without the concomitant loss of a competitor. Yet the district court never explained why Heinz could not achieve the kind of efficiencies urged without merger. The question is how much Heinz would have to spend to make its product equivalent to the Beech-Nut product and hence whether Heinz could achieve the efficiencies of merger without eliminating Beech-Nut as a competitor. The district court, however, undertook no inquiry in this regard. In short, the district court failed to make the kind of factual determinations necessary to render the appellees' efficiency defense sufficiently concrete to offset the FTC's prima facie showing.

We conclude the FTC has raised serious and substantial questions. We also conclude the public equities weigh in favor of preliminary injunctive relief and therefore that a preliminary injunction would be in the public interest.

REVERSED.

CRITICAL THINKING

One of the core ideas in critical thinking is the insistence on the idea that reasons matter. Is there anything about the reasoning in this case that might suggest to you that the court had its conclusion in mind from the start and that the reasons are more an afterthought than a basis for the formation of the conclusion?

ETHICAL DECISION MAKING

Are there any stakeholders in this decision who from your perspective did not get adequate attention in the decision by the court?

Vertical mergers. When one company at one level of the manufacturing-distribution system acquires a company at another level of the system, this merger is called a **vertical merger.** For example, when a manufacturer acquires a retailer, they have engaged in a vertical merger.

Unlike horizontal mergers, vertical mergers do not lead to concentration in the market. However, vertical mergers can cause other harm to competition. Most important, a vertical merger may permit one firm to foreclose competition. For example, suppose you manufacture shoes, and you decide to acquire a retail outlet for your shoes. First, you have foreclosed competition among those who were trying to purchase your products for resale. Second, when you sell the shoes through your retail outlet, you will likely not carry other brands of shoes. Thus, you have affected competition for the resale of your shoes.

Generally, courts have been most concerned with the foreclosure element associated with vertical mergers. However, the courts usually also examine the history of vertical mergers in the industry as well as by the acquiring company. If the merger does not harm competition, courts will usually permit merger.

Conglomerate mergers. When a company merges with another company that is not a competitor or a buyer or seller to the company, this merger is called a **conglomerate merger**. The two companies that are merging are unrelated in their respective businesses.

Conglomerate mergers exist in three basic forms. The first is *product extension,* which exists when a firm merges with another firm producing a related product. The purpose behind a product-extension merger is to enable the acquiring company to obtain the production of the related product and add it to the acquiring company's production of the current product. For example, if one automobile manufacturer acquires another automobile manufacturer, that would be an example of a product-extension conglomerate merger. The second type of conglomerate merger is *market extension.* Market-extension conglomerate mergers involve a firm attempting to extend the market for one of its current products by merging with a firm already active in the target market. A market-extension conglomerate merger can be seen when a company that makes air fresheners attempts to extend its product line by purchasing a company that produces fragrant candles. The third type of conglomerate merger is a *diversification merger.* Diversification mergers occur when the acquiring firm desires to spread into new markets where it currently does not have a product. The acquiring firm will merge with another firm and continue to produce the other firm's product in the target market. An example of a diversification merger is a real estate firm's acquisition of a telephone service provider.

Why might conglomerate mergers be violations of the Clayton Act? Suppose a company is planning to move into a certain industry; however, the company makes an acquisition to ease its way into the market. Instead of creating another competitor in the market (and thus benefiting consumers), the original company simply acquired its way into the market. In sum, conglomerate mergers may not encourage competitors to enter the market. Why would a company enter a new market when it can simply rely on the acquired company to carry the original company into the new market?

SECTION 8: INTERLOCKING DIRECTORATES

Section 8 of the Clayton Act prohibits a person from becoming a director in two or more corporations if any of the corporations (1) have capital and profits totaling more than $13.8 million or (2) are or were competitors. However, a person can serve as a director for two firms that are vertically related.

Why does Section 8 prohibit a person from serving as a director in two competing companies? If the same person exerts control over two different companies, it is possible the person will engage in some kind of anticompetitive behavior in an attempt to increase profits for both companies. This prohibition is a preventive measure; instead of waiting until anticompetitive behavior occurs, Section 8 takes steps to ensure that the behavior does not occur at all.

The Federal Trade Commission Act

When Congress passed the Clayton Act, it also passed the Federal Trade Commission Act. This act prohibits unfair and deceptive methods of competition. Therefore, any anticompetitive behavior not prohibited by the Sherman Act or the Clayton Act is illegal under the Federal Trade Commission Act.

The broad language of the Federal Trade Commission Act permits the Federal Trade Commission to investigate and bring antitrust claims. For example, in May 2000, the FTC settled charges against the five largest compact-disc distributors. In the early 1990s, popular CDs were typically priced at $9.99 because of a price war among competing retailers. However, in 1995–1996, in an attempt to end the price war, the distributors adopted policies in which they required that retailers advertise popular CDs at prices at or above the distributors' set price. Consequently, CD prices increased. The FTC estimated that consumers paid approximately $480 million because of the distributors' requirement.

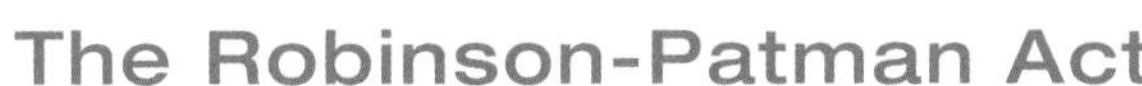

The Robinson-Patman Act

As originally written, the Clayton Act did not apply to buyers. Therefore, in an effort to limit buyers' power, as well as sellers', Congress adopted the Robinson-Patman Act in 1936. The Robinson-Patman Act amended Section 2 of the Clayton Act by further prohibiting price discrimination in interstate commerce, this time targeting buyers. Now, neither buyers nor sellers may engage in price discrimination. Similar to Section 2 of the Clayton Act, whenever price discrimination lessens competition or creates a monopoly, the guilty party will be subject to civil liability.

Much like the Clayton Act, when price differentials can be justified as legitimate, they do not constitute illegal practices. For example, a buyer who solicits an unreasonably low price on a product while offering the seller a portion of the profits is engaging in illegal behavior if the low price leads to a noncompetitive environment. However, if the seller offered the same price to other buyers, competition would not be affected and the activity would not be illegal.

The Robinson-Patman Act identifies three specific types of injuries. **Primary-line injuries** occur when preferential treatment is given to a competitor. **Secondary-line injuries** are those created when preferential price treatment is granted to specific buyers. Most often, large buyers are given preferential treatment at the cost of small buyers. That is, large buyers are given discounts that are subsidized by charging small buyers a higher rate. Finally, **tertiary-line injuries** exist when someone who is given an illegally low price passes his or her savings on to his or her customers. For example, Jim is a seller who supplies Erin with coats at a discounted price. Erin then sells her coats at a lower price, pulling in more business. Erin's extra business comes from Jack, who also sells coats but was not given a discount on his order of coats. The business Jack lost because of the discount Erin received and passed on to customers is a tertiary-line injury.

Enforcement of Antitrust Laws

Antitrust laws are enforced in both the public and the private sectors. The Department of Justice and the Federal Trade Commission enforce antitrust laws in the public sector. Any

connecting to the core

Corporate Taxation and Accounting

As you may know from your accounting or corporate taxation course, accounting can get complicated when you have to pay a fine for violating a federal statute, such as the Sherman Antitrust Act. According to generally accepted accounting principles, the fine and other expenses related to the violation must be recorded as expenses when calculating the firm's financial accounting income, or book income, but may not be deducted as an expense for tax purposes. Thus, the accountant must file a reconciliation schedule to account for the differences between its book income and tax income.

Source: Anderson et al., *Federal Taxation 2006* (Prentice Hall, 2006), pp. 3-38–3-39.

individual who has been injured by an illegal business practice may bring a private suit against the business.

PUBLIC ENFORCEMENT

Some violations of the Sherman Act are criminal acts; thus, the Antitrust Division of the DOJ can bring criminal or civil actions against violators. If a corporation commits a crime under the Sherman Act, the corporation could face a $10 million fine for each offense. Furthermore, officers and employees who are convicted under the Sherman Act face a maximum fine of $350,000 and/or jail time of up to three years.

No violations of the Clayton Act are crimes, so the DOJ or the FTC can bring a civil action against violators under the Clayton Act. Part of the DOJ's power to bring civil suits includes the ability to request divestiture or dissolution. Divestiture occurs when the DOJ requests that the court force a company to give up part of its operation procedures. For example, a court could order a firm that sells all of its products out of stores it owns to sell off the stores or allow other firms' products to be sold in the stores. The FTC has sole authority for investigating and making claims against those who violate the Federal Trade Commission Act. When either the DOJ or the FTC makes a civil claim against a potential violator, the parties may decide to settle the case by entering into a **consent decree,** an agreement that binds the violating party to cease his or her illegal behavior.

PRIVATE ENFORCEMENT

Congress wanted to encourage private parties to stop anticompetitive behavior. Thus, if a party is harmed by a company's anticompetitive behavior, the party can bring a private suit under the Sherman Act or the Clayton Act. If the party successfully demonstrates its antitrust claim, the party is entitled to attorney fees and damages. More important, the Sherman Act entitles the party to receive treble damages (triple the amount of damages awarded). Treble damages serve as an incentive for private parties to bring suits; thus, treble damages also serve as an incentive for companies to ensure that they do not commit violations under the Sherman or Clayton Act. Private parties are responsible for almost all the antitrust claims brought to court in recent years, such as the suit against the NCAA mentioned at the start of this chapter.

e-commerce AND THE LAW

Microsoft's Monopoly

In 1998 Microsoft Corporation was charged with violating Sections 1 and 2 of the Sherman Act. According to the plaintiff, Microsoft possessed a "dominant, persistent, and increasing share of the relevant market." Microsoft's share of the market for Intel-compatible PCs was over 95 percent. To maintain its monopoly power, Microsoft convinced developers to concentrate on producing Windows-specific platforms. As a result, Microsoft's competition was unable to reach its full potential because the available technologies did not exist. Microsoft also bundled its browser, Internet Explorer, with its operating system. This action was a result of Microsoft's desire to combat competition from rival browser, Netscape Navigator. The plaintiff, the U.S. DOJ, argued that Microsoft violated Section 2 of the Sherman Act by engaging in exclusionary, anticompetitive, and predatory acts to maintain a monopoly. The court ruled in favor of the plaintiff, which contended that Microsoft had violated Sections 1 and 2 of the Sherman Act by tying its browser to its operating system and attempting to monopolize the Web browser market.

CASE OPENER WRAP-UP

NCAA

In the opening case to this chapter, the tournament promoters filed a claim that the Two in Four Rule was a violation of antitrust laws under the Sherman Antitrust Act and sought an injunction under the Clayton Act. The district court held that allowing schools to participate in only one certified event per season and no more than two in a four-year period had clear economic impact on tournament promoters and skills. According to the ruling provided by the court, although the stated intent was to promote fair competition, the regulations still provided an unreasonable restraint on trade. Therefore, the district court found in favor of the tournament promoters.

The case was, however, appealed. The appellate court found that the tournament promoters could recover lost funds if they demonstrated, under the rule-of-reason test, that the regulation in question created significant restraints on commerce in the *relevant* markets. Thus, in addition to showing the same evidence of economic strain that they had shown to the district court, the promoters had to provide evidence of restraint on *specific* product and geographic markets.

After the tournament promoters made their case, the appellate court found that they had failed to establish what the relevant product and geographic markets were. Based on the appellate court's decision, the promoters could not recover funds under Section 1 of the Sherman Act. A court cannot say an act is anticompetitive without a relevant market to consider.

Summary

History of and Rationale for Antitrust Law

Regulation of business activity is necessary when firms violate certain principles of fairness that result in harm to consumers.

The Sherman Act

The Sherman Act applies to business practices that restrain trade or commerce "among the several States, or with foreign nations." Congress passed the Sherman Act through its authority to regulate interstate commerce. Therefore, to violate the Sherman Act, a business act must have directly interfered with the flow of goods in commerce. Alternatively, the act must have had an "effect on commerce."

Section 1 of the Sherman Act: To constitute a violation of Section 1 of the Sherman Act, a business act or practice must have three characteristics. The act must be: (1) a combination, contract, or conspiracy (i.e., an agreement between two parties), (2) an *unreasonable* restraint on trade, and (3) a restraint that affects interstate commerce. The rationale for this violation is consumers will be harmed if companies are permitted to join their market power.

Horizontal restraints of trade: When two competitors in the same market make an agreement to restrain trade, this agreement is called a horizontal restraint of trade.

Price fixing: When two or more competitors agree to set prices for a product or service, they are engaging in price fixing. These agreements simply cut out competition among companies; thus, the consumer will likely pay higher prices for goods.

Horizontal divisions of markets are agreements between two or more competitors to divide markets by geography, customers, or products among themselves. The courts have held these divisions to be *per se* violations of Section 1 because they serve only to eliminate competition.

Group boycotts occur when two or more competitors agree to refuse to deal with a certain person or company; these are also per se illegal.

Vertical restraints of trade: When two parties at different levels in the manufacturing and distribution process make an agreement that restrains trade, they have made a vertical restraint against trade.

Section 2 of the Sherman Act: According to economic theory, companies with monopoly power would use their economic power to limit production and raise prices, thus harming the consumer. Section 2 of the Sherman Act was designed to prohibit the unfair use of monopoly power.

Monopolization: The courts permit a monopoly to exist; however, if a company *monopolizes,* i.e., it (1) possesses market power, and (2) unfairly achieved this market power or uses this market power for abuse, the court will rule this company has violated the Sherman Act.

Attempt to monopolize: If a company intends its behavior to (1) exclude competitors and (2) allow the company to gain monopoly power, the courts would consider these practices as attempts to monopolize.

The Clayton Act

Section 2, Price discrimination: Section 2 of the Clayton Act (as amended by the Robinson-Patman Act in 1936) prohibits price discrimination by sellers. A seller engages in price discrimination when it sells the same goods to competing buyers for different prices.

Section 3, Exclusionary practices: Section 3 prohibits a number of activities that restrict the vigorous competition needed to protect consumers. For example, it prohibits exclusive dealing and tying arrangements.

Section 7, Mergers: Anti-competitive mergers and acquisitions are prohibited by Section 7.

1. *Horizontal merger:* A merger between two or more companies producing the same or similar products is a horizontal merger. Because these firms are at the same competitive level, a horizontal merger usually eliminates a competitor from the market.

2. *Vertical mergers:* When one company at one level of the manufacturing-distribution system acquires a company at another level of the system, this merger is called a vertical merger.
3. *Conglomerate mergers:* When a company merges with another company that is not a competitor or a buyer or seller to the company, this merger is called a conglomerate merger. The two companies who are merging are unrelated in their respective businesses.

The Federal Trade Commission Act This act prohibits unfair and deceptive methods of competition. Therefore, any anticompetitive behavior not prohibited by the Sherman Act or the Clayton Act is illegal under the Federal Trade Commission Act.

The Robinson-Patman Act As originally written, the Clayton Act did not apply to buyers. Therefore, in an effort to limit buyers' power, as well as sellers', Congress adopted the Robinson-Patman Act in 1936.

Point / Counterpoint

Should Government Control Monopolies Aggressively?

No	Yes
The government currently exercises too much control over large businesses when they are successful in forming monopolies. Large businesses are unfairly discriminated against solely because they are successful. Government regulation is largely not necessary—natural market competition will provide sufficient product options for the consumer. In the market, the firms that satisfy consumer desires to the greatest extent will flourish. A company goes out of business because its product isn't good enough for the consumer. Why force the most powerful company with the best product to leave 30 percent of the relevant market to companies with worse products? Section 2 of the Sherman Act is designed to prohibit all "conduct that monopolizes." The main problem with this legislation is the focus on *intent.* According to Section 2, a monopoly is sometimes allowed to exist when formed naturally and without anticompetitive behavior. However, if a company is discovered to have the *intent* to form a monopoly, the company can be declared in violation of Section 2. Companies should not be prevented from filling consumer need because they have the best product, best advertising, and best investments. They should be rewarded for spurring continued economic growth, not restricted and prevented from expanding their business.	The government currently ignores much serious social harm caused when large firms form monopolies. Current laws do not prevent large companies from forming monopolies. In fact, some monopolies are allowed to continue even after they are discovered as and labeled "monopolies." Section 2 of the Sherman Act was written in highly ambiguous language, and the act is subject to interpretation by the courts. Section 2 was designed to limit only unfair use of monopoly power, or "conduct that monopolizes," not to prevent monopolies completely. Additionally, a company violates Section 2, and therefore can be penalized, only when it *intends* to participate in anticompetitive behavior. However, intent has little to do with the consequences of possessing a monopoly of a specific market. The mere existence of a monopoly, whether gained through "fair" or "unfair" means, is still detrimental to the consumer. The consumer needs the benefits of competition among competing firms whether a monopoly exists or not. When a monopoly exists, the single powerful company is able to overcharge for its product because the company does not have competition. Additionally, society suffers when a company obtains a monopoly because competition among companies for consumer demand forces companies to continue improving their products to keep consumers purchasing their products. When a monopoly exists, the single company's product is the only, and therefore best, option available, so demand continues even when product development stagnates. Competing ideas create better products, better music, better food, and a better standard of living.

Questions & Problems

1. What is a rule-of-reason analysis, and what is its purpose in the courts? What are the four things the courts consider when engaging in a rule-of-reason analysis?
2. What business practices can be considered illegal as a result of the Clayton Act, which Congress passed in 1914?
3. In what ways can horizontal and vertical mergers be harmful to competition?
4. How can antitrust laws be enforced, and who is responsible for enforcing them?
5. To administer its prescription drug benefits, Blue Cross set up a "closed" network of pharmacies, providing greater insurance coverage to the subscribers who use network pharmacies. In exchange for inclusion in the network, and therefore increased volume of drug sales, the network pharmacies typically agree to provide drugs at lower prices, resulting in lower costs to the insurer. Blue Cross Selected PharmaCare to manage its closed network, which included CVS pharmacies and most independent pharmacies in Rhode Island. Not all Blue Cross customers are covered by plans that effectively restrict them to closed-network pharmacies. Two-thirds to three-fourths of Blue Cross's customers are restricted to closed networks under its plans. Unhappy with losing the opportunity to serve many Blue Cross customers on competitive terms, Stop & Shop and Walgreens brought action against Blue Cross, PharmaCare, and CVS, charging violations of federal and state antitrust laws. The pretrial report by the plaintiffs' expert witness, Dr. Bruce Stangle, claimed that the closed network would maintain control of 85 percent of the relevant market. Stangle claimed the relevant market was all people who have reimbursed prescriptions. Does the closed network constitute an anticompetitive action? If you were a judge hearing this case, what test or tests would you use in making your decision? [*Stop & Shop Supermarket Co. v. Blue Cross & Blue Shield,* 373 F.3d 57 (2004).]
6. The Senior PGA Tour cosponsors professional golf tournaments for players over the age of 50. The rules and regulations of the tour specify the requirements for player eligibility. According to the rules, a player who qualifies to play in a tour event may not enter a nontour tournament scheduled on the same date. A player can submit a written request for an exception, and the tour commissioner has discretionary authority to grant a tour member two releases annually. The rules allow the commissioner to deny the request if it can be determined that the exemption "would cause the Tour to be in violation of a contractual commitment to a tournament or would otherwise significantly or unreasonably harm the Tour and such tournament." The tour receives funding for its tournaments through both local and title sponsors. Harry Toscano challenged the tour's regulations governing player participation in non-PGA events. Toscano alleges that individual officers and directors of the tour and various sponsors of the tour's golf tournaments conspired to restrain trade in senior professional golf in violation of Section 1 of the Sherman Act. Do you agree? How do you think the court decided? [*Toscano v. PGA Tour, Inc.,* 70 F. Supp. 2d (1999).]
7. A star high school soccer player, Rhiannon Tanaka, was heavily recruited by the athletic programs of a number of universities, including the University of Southern California (USC), which belongs to the Pacific-10 Conference. Tanaka quickly became dissatisfied with the state of USC's women's soccer program and the quality of her USC education. In the spring, she received permission from USC to communicate with other schools about transferring to their programs. She decided to transfer to UCLA, another Pac-10 member institution. USC opposed Tanaka's transfer to UCLA,

however, and sought sanctions against her pursuant to Pac-10 Rule C 8-3-b, which governs intraconference transfer. The rule prevents students who transfer from one Pac-10 school to another from participating in athletics their first year, and they must also lose another year of collegiate athletic eligibility. Tanaka filed suit, asserting a claim under the Clayton Act predicated on a violation of Section 1 of the Sherman Act. The district court dismissed with prejudice. The court held that the Pac-10 transfer rule was beyond the reach of the Sherman Act because the transfer rule was not unreasonable under the rule of reason. Tanaka appealed. Is the Pac-10 regulation so unreasonable as to constitute an antitrust violation? Why? [*Tanaka v. University of S. Cal.*, 252 F.3d 1059 (2001).]

8. The Chicago Skyway toll bridge is a 7.8-mile-long high-speed, limited-access highway that joins the Indiana Tollway with the rest of Interstate 90 at the Illinois-Indiana border. The skyway is one of two interstate routes that connect Chicago's Dan Ryan Expressway (Interstate 90/94) to the Indiana Tollway. On several occasions (14 times) the city has raised the toll rates in order to pay the skyway's maintenance and operating costs and to make the skyway "a self-sufficient enterprise." As a result, the current toll rate schedule ($2, or 25.6 cents per mile for most automobiles) is higher than the rate for other highways in the area. The city sold skyway bonds to help pay for refinancing for the skyway. The excess $52 million raised from the bond sale was used to fund other city transportation improvements. As with past bond sales, the bonds are to be repaid solely from revenues the skyway generates through tolls and concessions. Two individuals brought an antitrust suit against the city, arguing that the city had a monopoly on high-speed expressways connecting Chicago and Indiana. Moreover, the city was abusing its monopoly by charging tolls higher than actual operating costs. The city filed a motion to dismiss the action, which the district judge granted. Endsley and Graham now appeal. Are Chicago's actions in violation of the Sherman Antitrust Act? Why? [*Endsley v. City of Chicago,* 230 F.3d 276 (2000).]

9. Intel manufactures high-performance computer microprocessors. The microprocessors are sold to various original equipment manufacturers (OEMs). Intergraph Corporation is an OEM of Intel and develops, makes, and sells computer workstations. From 1987 to 1993, Intergraph used Clipper microprocessors in its computer workstations. Intergraph owns the Clipper technology and patents. Intergraph discontinued the use of Clipper microprocessors in 1993 and switched to Intel microprocessors. Intel labeled Intergraph a "strategic customer" and provided Intergraph with several special benefits. Intergraph subsequently charged several Intel OEM customers with infringement of the Clipper patents. Intel wished to obtain licenses to the Clipper patents, and Intel and Intergraph began negotiations. The negotiations failed, and Intergraph sued Intel for infringement of the Clipper patents. As a result of the deteriorated relationship, Intel stopped providing Intergraph with strategic-customer benefits. Intergraph charged Intel with violating Sections 1 and 2 of the Sherman Act. The district court held that Intel was a monopolist and found in favor of Intergraph. The decision mandated that Intel supply Intergraph with all Intel product information. Intel appealed the decision, arguing that its response was a typical commercial response to Intergraph's suit, not an antitrust violation. Intergraph contended that, without the services and benefits from Intel, it would be unable to compete. Do you think the court agreed with Intergraph? Was Intel in violation of Sections 1 and 2 of the Sherman Act? [*Intergraph Corp. v. Intel Corp.*, 195 F.3d 1346 (1999).]

10. Maurice Clarett, a former running back for Ohio State University and a Big Ten Freshman of the Year, wanted to enter the NFL draft. However, Clarett was precluded under the NFL's current rules governing draft eligibility. Clarett was a season shy of the three necessary to qualify under the draft's eligibility rules. The NFL's collective bargaining group and the NFL Players Association, which is the players' union, agreed on the most recent version of the eligibility requirement. The eligibility requirement is intended to promote college attendance and has existed almost as long as the NFL. Clarett filed suit, alleging that the NFL's draft eligibility rules are an unreasonable restraint of trade in violation of Section 1 of the Sherman Act, 15 U.S.C. Section 1, and Section 4 of the Clayton Act, 15 U.S.C. Section 15. Clarett sought summary judgment on the merits of his antitrust claim. The NFL asserted that Clarett lacked "antitrust standing" and, as a matter of law, the eligibility rules were immune from antitrust attack by virtue of the nonstatutory labor exemption. The district court granted summary judgment in favor of Clarett and ordered him eligible to enter that year's draft. The NFL appealed. How did the court rule on appeal? Why? [*Clarett v. NFL,* 369 F.3d 124 (2004).]

11. Southwestern Bell enjoyed a legal monopoly over the pay-phone market in the state of Oklahoma. Eventually, the Oklahoma legislature decided to move from monopoly to competition in this market. In response, Southwestern Bell undertook an intentional campaign to make entry into the Oklahoma pay-phone market more difficult by attempting to secure every possible pay-phone location through long-term contracts between Southwestern Bell and the location owners. Southwestern Bell's anticompetitive actions were highly successful. Although its competitors offered better commissions to location owners and better phones at cheaper rates to customers, at the end of the second year of competition Southwestern Bell retained more than 87 percent of the market, with no single competitor above 2.4 percent. Nine independent pay-phone service providers filed suit against Southwestern Bell, claiming violations of federal and state antitrust laws. The plaintiffs argued that the relevant market was the provision of pay-phone facilities and services to location owners. Southwestern Bell argued that the product market should be evaluated from the viewpoint of the end user of the phone services and should therefore include both pay phones and cell phones, which Southwestern Bell argued were reasonably interchangeable at the end-user level. If you were a judge hearing this case, how would you define the relevant product market? Based on your definition, which party would win the suit? [*Telecor Communs., Inc. v. Southwestern Bell Tel. Co.,* 305 F.3d 1124 (2002).]
12. Dr. Alga Morales-Villalobos, an anesthesiologist, brought antitrust claims under Section 1 of the Sherman Antitrust Act against her former employers, the overlapping directors of an anesthesiology group and the only two hospitals in Arecibo. After arranging an exclusive-dealing contract between their organization and the hospitals on behalf of all parties, the group eventually fired Morales-Villalobos and prevented her from working at either hospital. No patient complaints were ever filed against Morales-Villalobos. Despite doctors' requesting her services in private surgery, the group would not let Morales-Villalobos work in the hospitals. She alleged that the exclusive-dealing arrangement between the hospitals and the group prevented her from competing to offer her services. She also alleged that the defendants engaged in a group boycott to exclude her from the anesthesiology group and subsequently denied her certification to practice at those hospitals. Was Morales-Villalobos successful with her antitrust claim? Why? [*Morales-Villalobos v. Garcia-Llorens,* 316 F.3d 51 (2003).]
13. 3M, which manufactures Scotch tape for home and office use, dominated the U.S. transparent-tape market with a market share above 90 percent until the early 1990s.

LePage's sold a variety of office products including "second-brand" and private-label transparent tape, that is, tape sold under the retailer's name rather than under the name of the manufacturer. By 1992, LePage's had 88 percent of the private-label tape sales in the United States, which represented but a small portion of the transparent-tape market. LePage's brought an antitrust action asserting that 3M used its monopoly over its Scotch tape brand to gain a competitive advantage in the private-label tape portion of the transparent-tape market in the United States through the use of 3M's multitiered "bundled rebate" structure, which offered higher rebates when customers purchased products in a number of 3M's different product lines. LePage's also alleged that 3M offered to some of LePage's customers large lump-sum cash payments, promotional allowances, and other cash incentives to encourage them to enter into exclusive-dealing arrangements with 3M. If you were an executive for LePage's, which sections of the various antitrust laws would you think 3M violated? Are your claims likely to prevail in court? [*LePage's, Inc. v. 3M,* 324 F.3d 141 (2003).]

Looking for more review material?

The Online Learning Center at **www.mhhe.com/kubasek1e** contains this chapter's "Assignment on the Internet" and also a list of URLs for more information, entitled "On the Internet." Find both of them in the Student Center portion of the OLC, along with quizzes and other helpful materials.

The Nature of Property, Personal Property, and Bailments

CASE OPENER

Prisoners and Personal Property

Warner Melvin, a prisoner at a U.S. penitentiary, was required to move to a new cell. Melvin was able to move most of his belongings to his new cell before his work shift. A few items remained in his old cell: a pair of Adidas shoes, some electronic equipment, and some food. Melvin hid the property and asked the guard to deadlock the cell. The guard, Richard, looked in the cell and determined it was empty. He did not lock the cell.

When Melvin returned from work, he noticed that his property was missing. There are conflicting claims as to whether Richard knowingly allowed the other prisoners to take Melvin's property, but it is known that the cell was not locked. Melvin argued that Richard was a bailee and Richard was responsible for the lost property. Clearly the relationship between a prisoner and a prison guard is unique and different from more standard relationships, such as the relationship between a boarder and an innkeeper. However, whether this difference was strong enough to diminish any duty owed by Richard to Melvin was the question the court confronted.

Although it is often difficult for prisoners to bring litigation, several cases across the country illustrate that the loss of their personal property is not uncommon. In *Sellers v. United States,* a frequently cited case, the prison restricted the amount of personal items inmates could keep in their cells. Pursuant to the restriction, the prison authorities took from Sellers an oil painting of his wife, 41 law books, an almanac, and other personal items. Sellers' items were subsequently lost. The Seventh Circuit held that once a prisoner establishes a bailment relationship and loss of property, the government is liable for conversion.[1]

[1] Source: *Melvin v. United States,* 963 F. Supp. 1052 (1997); *Sellers v. United States,* 1996 U.S. App. LEXIS 24353. For other cases involving prisoners and lost property, see *Moore v. United States,* 1996 U.S. Dist. LEXIS 16900; *Jungerman v. City of Raytown,* 925 S.W.2d 202 (1996); *Bacote v. Ohio Dept. of Rehabilitation and Correction,* 578 N.E.2d 565 (1988).

CHAPTER 48

1. Do you think a bailment relationship existed between Richard and Melvin?
2. Pretend that Melvin was a guest at a hotel. The hotel manager asked Melvin to move to another room. Melvin was able to transfer most of his belongings to the new room, but he then had to rush to an appointment. He requested that the front-desk attendant lock his old room. Do you think this scenario is easier to resolve? Why or why not?

The Wrap-Up at the end of the chapter will answer these questions.

Learning Objectives

After reading this chapter, you will be able to answer the following questions:

1 What are the classifications of property?

2 How is personal property transferred?

3 What are the rights and responsibilities of parties to a bailment?

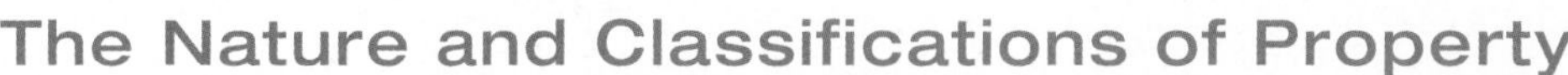

The Nature and Classifications of Property

When people hear the word *property,* they generally think of physical objects: land, houses, cars. However, this pattern of thought reflects an incomplete understanding of the concept of property. Property is a set of rights and interests in relation to others with reference to a tangible or intangible object. The essence of the concept of property is that the state provides the mechanism to allow the owner to exclude others. A less technical way to think about property is that it is anything you can own.

Those with great amounts of property have an especially significant amount of power. Because possessing property facilitates the acquisition of even more property, the identification of those who possess a disproportionate amount of property provides insight into the dynamics of influence and authority in our society.

Property is generally categorized into two basic categories, real property and personal property. *Real property,* land and anything permanently attached to the land, is the focus of the next chapter. In this chapter, we will examine the laws governing *personal property,* which is generally defined as property that is not attached to the land, or movable property. Sometimes property is initially movable but then becomes attached to the land. In such a situation, the property is called a *fixture.* Fixtures are treated like real property, and so they are discussed in the next chapter.

Personal Property

All property that is not land or not permanently affixed to land is **personal property.** Personal property may be either tangible or intangible. *Tangible property* is property that can be identified by the senses. It is property that you can see or touch. Tangible property includes items such as furniture, cars, and other goods.

Intangible property includes such items as bank accounts, stocks, and insurance policies. Because most intangibles (with the exception of some of those classified as intellectual property and discussed in Chapter 12) are evidenced by writings, most of the following discussion applies to both tangible and intangible property. The primary issues that arise in conjunction with personal property involve (1) the means of acquiring ownership of the property and (2) the rights and duties arising out of a bailment. Both are discussed in this chapter in detail.

VOLUNTARY TRANSFER OF PROPERTY

Voluntary transfer, as a result of either a purchase or a gift, is the most common means by which property is acquired. Ownership of property is referred to as *title,* and title to property passes when the parties so intend. When transfer of the property is by purchase, the acquiring party gives some consideration to the seller in exchange for title to the property. Such a transfer of ownership usually requires no formalities, but in a few cases changes of ownership must be registered with a government agency. Sales of motor vehicles, watercraft, and airplanes are among the primary transfers requiring registration. To transfer such property, a certificate of title must be signed by the seller, taken to the appropriate government agency, and then reissued in the name of the new owner.

Gifts are another voluntary means of transferring ownership. They differ from purchases in that there is no consideration given for a gift. As you know from your previous reading, a promise to make a gift is therefore unenforceable. Once properly made, however, a gift is irrevocable.

global context

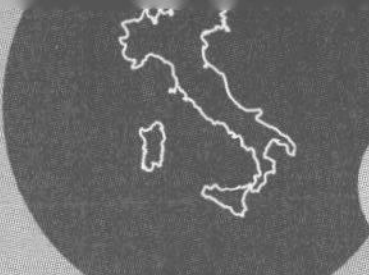

Distinctions in Italian Property Law

In Italian law, there is a significant distinction between physical possession and a mental intention to possess. The term to describe the latter is *usucapione.* Instances of *usucapione* are characterized by persons having legal possession equivalent to that of the owner but only for a certain length of time.

Before a transition from legal possession to full ownership can occur, several requirements must be satisfied. These requirements differ depending on whether the property is classified as immovable or movable. For immovable property, the potential owner must possess the property for no less than 20 years. Movables require a 10-year period of possession. These periods of possession must be uninterrupted. If possession of the property is lost, the individual has one year to regain it before having to start the term of possession over.

Understanding the distinction between immovable and movable property is thus important to determining the required length of possession prior to ownership. Immovable property includes anything attached to the ground, such as trees, buildings, homes, and arenas. Movables, therefore, include any property not attached to the ground. Movables are further divided into those that require registration and those that do not. Registration is necessary for the transference, sale, or termination of certain movable property.

connecting to the core

Marketing

Levels of Consumer Involvement in Voluntary Transfers of Property

In your marketing class, you may have discussed the varying levels of consumer involvement in purchasing decisions, or decisions as to whether a consumer wants to acquire title to property. These levels of consumer involvement are sometimes labeled routine problem solving, limited problem solving, and extended problem solving. *Routine problem solving* refers to purchasing decisions in which consumers have the lowest level of involvement, in the sense that consumers spend very little time examining alternative brands, evaluating differentiating characteristics, or seeking the advice of others to make their purchases. Routine problem solving would likely involve the purchasing of products such as toothpaste, deodorant, and household cleaners.

Limited problem solving refers to purchasing decisions in which consumers spend more time researching several alternatives and may perhaps rely on external sources for more information. Examples include a consumer's purchasing a toaster, choosing a restaurant for dinner, or buying a CD. Finally, *extended problem solving* refers to high-involvement purchasing decisions in which consumers spend much time comparing, researching, and seeking advice from other sources before making a decision. Examples include a consumer's purchasing a car, computer, or high-end audio system. These distinctions in consumer involvement may be useful for marketers in the sense that for low-involvement purchases, companies could place a greater emphasis on maintaining product quality and reassuring consumers that they made the right choice. In contrast, companies might continuously provide additional product information and introduce new evaluative criteria that distinguish their products in high-involvement purchasing decisions, as the companies realize consumers are constantly evaluating alternatives before they buy. Notice that the kinds of purchases for which the law requires more formalities for acquiring title tend to be those that fall into the high-involvement category.

Source: Roger A. Kerin et al., *Marketing* (New York: McGraw-Hill/Irwin, 2006), pp. 124–125.

e-commerce AND THE LAW

E-Businesses and Their Customers Benefit from New Labeling and Shipping Options

Within the past few years, the boom in e-commerce has inspired improvements in Internet postal technology. Now, e-businesses can use Internet postal technology to print labels and pay for shipping postage using accounts such as PayPal accounts.

For a small business that operates through eBay, for instance, this means the business can operate more efficiently. Prior to improvements in Internet postal technology, it was likely that a small business would print mailing labels by hand and make multiple trips to the post office. Now, it is possible for small businesses to print out labels and arrange for pickups from carriers.*

An additional benefit to both buyers and sellers is that they can track packages. Claims that the postal service "lost" a package are now less likely. Consequently, small businesses save money by not having to replace the package contents. Litigation over lost packages should go down, too. Or at least the new technology will help plaintiffs determine what went wrong in the shipping process and which party was negligent.

*Beth Cox, "The Online Auction Site's New Integrated Labeling and Shipping Payment Options Can Improve Sellers' Operations—But They Are Not without Hitches," ecommerce.internet.com, March 25, 2004 (retrieved July 29, 2005).

Three elements are necessary for a valid gift. First, there must be a *delivery* of the gift. Delivery may be actual, which is the physical presentation of the gift itself, or constructive, which entails the delivery of an item that gives access to the gift or represents it, such as the handing over of the keys to a car. Second, the delivery must be made with *donative intent* to make an immediate gift. The donor makes the delivery with the purpose of turning over ownership at the time of delivery. Third, there must be *acceptance,* a willingness of the donee to take the gift from the donor. Usually, acceptance is not a problem, although a donee may not want to accept a gift because of a desire to not feel obligated to the donor or because of a concern that ownership of the gift may impose some unwanted legal liability.

The gifts we have been discussing so far have been what are called *inter vivos* gifts, gifts that are made by a person during his or her lifetime. Another type of gift that can be made is a gift *causa mortis.* A *gift causa mortis* is a gift that is made in contemplation of one's immediate death. It can be revoked any time before the death of the donor, and it is automatically revoked if the donor recovers.

Litigation over gifts *causa mortis* often arises because the three elements of delivery, donative intent, and acceptance still have to occur before the gift is complete and that means before the death of the donor. Case 48-1 illustrates how difficult it can sometimes be to determine whether in fact all the elements of a gift *causa mortis* have been met.

CASE 48-1

MARGARET ANN COLEY, APPELLANT, v. MARGIE WALKER, AS ADMINISTRATRIX OF THE ESTATE OF WILLODEAN DUKE CRAY

COURT OF CIVIL APPEALS OF ALABAMA
680 SO.2D 352 (1998)

In December 1992, 69-year-old Willodean Duke Cray was taken to a hospital emergency room. She had suffered a major heart attack and would have to undergo open-heart surgery. When told that she could not wear her rings to surgery, she asked her niece, the defendant, Margaret Ann Coley, to keep them for her. On the way to surgery, in the presence of her minister, Paul Ingram, Cray asked Margaret Ann if she had the rings and told

Margaret Ann that she wanted her to keep them if she died in surgery.

Cray died in surgery. Cray's sister, Margie Walker, and another niece were appointed as co-administratrices of her estate. In administering the estate, they filed a petition asking that Margaret Ann be required to return to the estate the rings that Cray had previously given to Margaret Ann.

The lower court found that the donor did not make a valid gift causa mortis of rings. The defendant-donee appealed.

JUDGE MONROE: The trial court entered its judgment finding that Cray had not met the requirements of a gift causa mortis of the rings to Margaret Ann. The trial court specifically found that Cray had surrendered possession of the rings to Margaret Ann; that Cray had intended that Margaret Ann become the owner of the rings if Cray did not survive surgery; and that Cray intended ownership to pass only upon her death. However, the trial court further found that Margaret Ann had not proven that, at the time Cray gave possession of the rings to Margaret Ann or at the time she verbally communicated her intent regarding the rings, Cray believed her death to be imminent. Margaret Ann appeals.

Margaret Ann contends that the trial court erred in finding that the elements of a gift causa mortis had not been met. She argues that the trial court misinterpreted the requirement that the gift be made in immediate apprehension of death.

There is no recent Alabama case law regarding gifts causa mortis. However, our Supreme Court has established the following guidelines for such gifts:

> A gift causa mortis is a gift of personal property made in the immediate apprehension of death, subject to the conditions, express or implied, that if the donor should not die, as expected, or if the donee should die first, or if the donor should revoke the gift before death, the gift should be void; or a gift made "in expectation" of death, then imminent, and upon the essential condition that the property shall belong fully to the donee, in case the donor dies, as anticipated, leaving the donee surviving him, and the gift is not in the meantime revoked, but not otherwise. It is essential to the validity of a gift causa mortis that the property be delivered to the donee, either actually or constructively.

In this case the donor had a realistic fear of impending imminent peril. The record reveals that, when Cray verbally communicated to Margaret Ann and the minister her intent that Margaret Ann keep the rings if Cray died during surgery, Cray knew that she was about to undergo open heart surgery and that there was a serious risk of death. Furthermore, although the appellate court did not have to determine whether the gifts were made with the "immediate apprehension of death," in two cases with facts similar to the present case, the court found that the conveyances were valid gifts causa mortis. See *Smith v. Eshelman* (where the donor made the gift as he was about to undergo an operation); and *Benson v. Jefferson Mortgage Co* (where the donor had been sick for quite some time with heart disease when he made the gift).

We find the testimony by Margaret Ann and the minister to be sufficient proof that the gift of the rings was made "in immediate apprehension of death" to support a finding of a valid gift causa mortis.

JUDGMENT REVERSED in favor of defendant.

CRITICAL THINKING

What ambiguity did the court have to decide to render a decision in this case? How did the court resolve this ambiguity in this case?

ETHICAL DECISION MAKING

What ethical norm is being followed by the decision in this case?

You should remember from the chapter on contracts that sometimes a contract is drafted so that one person's obligations under a contract do not arise until the happening of a certain event. These contracts are called *conditional contracts.* Gifts can also be conditional. Case 48-2 illustrates how courts tend to handle one of the most common conditional gifts, the engagement ring.

CASE 48-2 | HEINMAN v. PARRISH, APPELLANT SUPREME COURT OF KANSAS (1997)

Plaintiff Heinman purchased an engagement ring in August 1994 for $9,033. Plaintiff terminated the engagement in October 1995. Defendant Parrish refused to return the ring, and so the plaintiff filed this case against his former fiancée to recover engagement ring. The District ordered ring returned to plaintiff, and the defendant appealed.

CHIEF JUSTICE MCFARLAND: The issue before us concerns the ownership of an engagement ring after the engagement was terminated.

The issues may be summarized as follows. Was the engagement ring a conditional gift given in contemplation of marriage? If this question is answered affirmatively, then, upon termination of the engagement, should ownership of the ring be determined on a fault or no-fault basis?

Defendant Parrish argues that the gift of an engagement ring should be gauged by the same standards as for any other inter vivos gift, and that, once delivery and acceptance have occurred, the gift is irrevocable. She contends Kansas does not recognize conditional gifts.

Plaintiff Heinman argues that an engagement ring is inherently a conditional gift, as it is given in contemplation of marriage. If the wedding does not occur, the ring should be returned to its donor.

While there is a paucity of Kansas law on gifts in contemplation of marriage in general, and engagement rings in particular, courts in many other states have wrestled with the issues arising therefrom.

In the absence of a contrary expression of intent, it is logical that engagement rings should be considered, by their very nature, conditional gifts given in contemplation of marriage. Once it is established the ring is an engagement ring, it is a conditional gift.

Other types of property may be shown to be conditional gifts given in contemplation of marriage, but such a classification would require specific evidence of such intent as opposed to just showing the ring was an engagement ring given in contemplation of marriage.

In the action herein, the parties stipulated that the object in dispute is an engagement ring given in contemplation of marriage. We conclude the district court correctly held that it was a conditional gift. . . .

Generally, with regard to who is entitled to the engagement ring once the engagement has been broken, courts have taken two divergent paths. One rule states that when an engagement has been unjustifiably broken by the donor, the donor shall not recover the ring. However, if the engagement is broken by mutual agreement or, unjustifiably by the donee, the ring should be returned to the donor. This is the fault-based line of cases. The other rule (the so-called "modern trend") holds that as an engagement ring is an inherently conditional gift, once the engagement has been broken the ring should be returned to the donor. Thus, the question of who broke the engagement and why, or who was "at fault," is irrelevant. This is the no-fault line of cases.

After careful consideration, we conclude the no-fault line of cases is persuasive. What is fault or the unjustifiable calling off of an engagement? By way of illustration, should courts be asked to determine which of the following grounds for breaking an engagement is fault or justified? (1) The parties have nothing in common; (2) one party cannot stand prospective in-laws; (3) a minor child of one of the parties is hostile to and will not accept the other party; (4) an adult child of one of the parties will not accept the other party; (5) the parties' pets do not get along; (6) a party was too hasty in proposing or accepting the proposal; (7) the engagement was a rebound situation which is now regretted; (8) one party has untidy habits that irritate the other; or (9) the parties have religious differences. The list could be endless. . . .

The engagement period is one where each party should be free to reexamine his or her commitment to the other and be sure he or she desires the commitment of marriage to the other. . . . Litigating fault for a broken engagement would do little but intensify the hurt feelings and delay the parties' being able to get on with their lives.

We conclude that fault is ordinarily not relevant to the question of who should have ownership and possession of an engagement ring after the engagement is broken. Ordinarily, the ring should be returned to the donor, regardless of fault. . . . We recognize there may be "extremely gross and rare situations" where fault might be appropriately considered. No such rare situation has been suggested to be involved herein. The district court did not err in awarding the ring to Jerod after concluding fault was irrelevant.

AFFIRMED in favor of plaintiff.

CRITICAL THINKING

Do you agree with the outcome of this case? Why or why not?

ETHICAL DECISION MAKING

What role do you think the public disclosure rule played in influencing either the plaintiff's or the defendant's behavior in this case?

INVOLUNTARY TRANSFERS OF PERSONAL PROPERTY

Involuntary transfers of ownership occur when property has been abandoned, lost, or mislaid. The finder of such property *may* acquire ownership rights to such property through possession.

Property that the original owner has discarded is *abandoned* property. Anyone finding such property becomes its owner by possessing it. Recall the opening scenario. Assume that Richard, the prison guard, believed that Melvin had moved all of his property to the new cell. While cleaning out the cell, Richard came across the shoes, food, and electronic equipment. Does he now possess the property? The court did not address this hypothetical, but it illustrates, as does Case 48-3, that it is not always easy to determine whether property has in fact been abandoned.

CASE 48-3

PAUL LONG, INDIANA STATE PIPE TRADES ASSOCIATION AND UNITED ASSOCIATION LOCAL v. DILLING MECHANICAL CONTRACTORS, INC.

COURT OF APPEALS OF INDIANA
705 N.E.2D 102 (1999)

Plaintiff Dilling maintained an office building in Logansport, Indiana. Outside of the office building was a lidded dumpster in which Dilling deposited trash. This dumpster, which Dilling leased for its exclusive use, stood on Dilling's property and was located about two feet from a public sidewalk. The rear of the dumpster abutted the building, and Dilling had constructed a wall slightly taller than the dumpster around the two sides of the dumpster. There was no wall in front of the dumpster, which remained open to public access. A waste management firm, pursuant to a contract with Dilling, was assigned to dispose of materials placed in the dumpster.

Since February of 1995, Long had been employed by the Association as a labor organizer. Long was seeking to organize Dilling's employees for union membership. In the early morning of August 24, 1995, Long went to Dilling's Logansport property and removed five or six filled plastic trash bags from the dumpster. Long took these trash bags hoping they would contain records revealing the names and phone numbers of Dilling employees, with whom Long wished to discuss collective bargaining. Long took these trash bags to a hotel room, where he rummaged though the bags' contents. Long then re-bagged the trash and deposited it in the hotel's trash receptacle.

Plaintiff Dilling Mechanical Contractors sued the labor organizer and his union to recover damages for a number of property offenses, including theft and receiving stolen property, stemming from labor organizer's actions in removing trash from employer's dumpster in an attempt to find names and phone numbers of employees.

The Circuit Court of Appeals granted summary judgment in favor of the plaintiff employer. The unions and labor organizer appealed.

MATTINGLY, JUDGE: Although numerous issues were raised on appeal, we find one issue dispositive: Whether the bags of trash Long took from Dilling's dumpster were abandoned property.

I. Abandonment

The Defendants argue that the trash in Dilling's dumpster was abandoned property. State property law guides our analysis of the abandonment issue. . . .

"Abandonment has been defined as the relinquishment of property to which a person is entitled, with no purpose of again claiming it, and without concern as to who may subsequently take possession. . . ." To constitute an abandonment of property, there must be a concurrence of the intention to abandon and an actual relinquishment. "An intention to abandon property . . . may be inferred as a fact from the surrounding circumstances, and it can be shown by acts and conduct clearly inconsistent with any intention to retain and continue the use or ownership of the property." Abandonment of property divests the owner of his ownership, so as to bar him from further claim to it. Except that he, like anyone else, may appropriate it once it is abandoned if it has not already been appropriated by someone else. . . .

Under [our existing] standard, Dilling abandoned its trash. Dilling placed filled trash bags in an unlocked dumpster for a waste disposal firm's disposition. Generally, one relinquishes personalty when he voluntarily makes it available for someone else's disposition.

In addition, there is a widely held and longstanding doctrine that personalty discarded as waste is considered abandoned. ("Abandoned property is property the owner has thrown away.") The abandonment of property is the relinquishment of all title, possession or claim to or of it—a virtual intentional throwing away of it. Dilling claims that it did not abandon the contents of the trash bags taken by Long. Instead, it claims that it, as the generator of the trash, "retains ownership of the contents of the garbage until such time as the contracted carrier has exercised custody and control over those contents."

. . . [A previous] decision addressed the question of who owned the trash once it was picked up by the hauler. It did not address the question presented in our case, that being whether an owner may abandon trash before the contracted carrier picks it up.

. . . We answer that question in the affirmative and conclude that, if a generator of trash wishes to retain ownership or control of that trash, then it must take affirmative steps to do so. Although Dilling claimed that the trash bags taken by Long contained Dilling's sensitive and confidential company documents, it took no steps to protect those documents from abandonment. Those documents were neither shredded, nor placed in locked containers nor in an area which was not readily accessible to others. When trash, whether it be documents or other discarded material, is placed in trash bags, and those trash bags are placed in an unlocked dumpster on the curtilage and readily accessible to others, that trash has been abandoned. In that context, trash is trash. As noted [previously] "[i]t has often been said that if you do not want others to know what you drink, don't put empties in the trash."

II. The Effect of Abandonment

As a result of Dilling's abandonment of its trash, its property rights were not abrogated by Long's taking of the bags. Consequently, there can be no showing that Long committed theft, receiving stolen property, [or other property offenses]. In order to establish liability under any of these offenses as alleged, Dilling was required to show that it had a property right in the trash bags. Dilling cannot make this showing because it abandoned and, therefore, did not own the trash.

The trial court erred when it entered summary judgment in Dilling's favor. Further, as Dilling cannot recover on any of the legal theories it advances, the trial court erred in refusing to grant the Defendants' summary judgment on Dilling's other claims. We therefore hold that Defendants' "Motion to Dismiss and/or for Summary Judgment" should have been granted.

REVERSED in favor of defendant.

CRITICAL THINKING

Explain why the court ruled in favor of the defendant.

ETHICAL DECISION MAKING

While Long had the legal right to take the property, would any ethical principle suggest that he should not have taken it?

Lost property is property that the true owner has unknowingly or accidentally dropped or left somewhere. He or she has no way of knowing how to retrieve it. In most states, the finder of lost property has title to the lost good against all except the true owner.

Mislaid property differs from lost property in that the owner has intentionally placed the property somewhere but has forgotten its location. The person who owns the realty on which the mislaid property was placed has the right to hold the mislaid property. The reason is that it is likely that the true owner will return to the realty looking for the mislaid property.

In some states, the law requires that before becoming the owner of lost or mislaid property, a finder must place an ad in the paper that will give the true owner notice that the property has been found and/or must leave the property with the police for a statutorily established reasonable period of time.

Bailment

A **bailment** of personal property is a relationship that arises when one party, the *bailor,* transfers possession of personalty to another, the *bailee,* to be used by the bailee in an agreed-on manner for an agreed-on time period.

The most common illustration of a bailment occurs when a woman leaves her coat in a coat-check room. She hands her coat to the clerk and is given a ticket identifying the object of the bailment so that it can be reclaimed.

The bailment may be gratuitous or for consideration and may be to benefit the bailor, the bailee, or both. Determining who benefits from the bailment is important for determining the standard of care owed by the bailee. If the bailment is intended to benefit only the bailor, the bailee is liable for damage to the property caused by the bailee's gross negligence. An example of such a bailment would occur when a person agrees to keep a friend's houseplants for a week for no compensation while the friend is gone on a business trip.

If the bailment is solely for the bailee's benefit, the bailee is responsible for harm to the property caused by even the slightest lack of due care on the part of the bailee. An illustration of this type of bailment would occur if Jim borrowed his roommate's bike to go to the library.

Finally, if the bailment is for the mutual benefit of bailee and bailor, the bailee is liable for harm to the bailed property arising out of the bailee's ordinary or gross negligence. If the property is harmed by an unpreventable "act of God," there is no liability on the part of the bailee under any circumstances. Despite the existence of these general rules, the parties to a bailment contract can limit or expand the liability of the bailee by contract. Also, conspicuous signs have been held sufficient to limit liability. For example, a health club may have lockers with a huge sign saying, "Rent a lock for a locker for $1.00. Health Club not responsible for items stolen from unlocked lockers." If a person leaves their jacket in an unlocked locker, the health club will not be liable.

RIGHTS AND DUTIES OF THE BAILOR

The bailor has certain rights and duties in the bailment relationship. Some of these rights and duties may change depending on whom the relationship primarily benefits and whether the bailment is gratuitous. This section highlights some of these important rights and duties.

In general, the bailor has the right to expect the bailee to (1) take reasonable care of the bailed property, repairing and maintaining it as necessary; (2) use the bailed property only as stipulated in the bailment agreement; (3) not alter the bailed property in any unauthorized manner; and (4) return the bailed property in good condition at the end of the bailment.

The bailor has two fundamental duties. One is the duty of compensation and reimbursement. This duty requires that the bailor provide the bailee with any agreed-on compensation for the bailment. Obviously, this aspect of the bailment has no application in a gratuitous bailment. However, in all bailments, the bailor must reimburse the bailee for any necessary costs incurred by the bailee in keeping and maintaining the bailed property, unless the bailment contract provides otherwise.

The bailor's other duty is to provide the bailee with property that is free from hidden defects that could harm the bailee. If the bailment is for the mutual benefit of both parties, the bailor must warn the bailee of any known defects or any that could have been discovered through reasonable investigation. If, however, the bailment is solely for the benefit of the bailee, the standard is slightly lower, and the bailor must warn of only known defects. If the bailor fails to live up to this duty, he may be sued for negligence by the bailee or any reasonably foreseeable third party who is injured as a result of the defect.

RIGHTS AND DUTIES OF THE BAILEE

The rights of the bailee generally complement the duties of the bailor, and the duties of the bailee complement the rights of the bailor. As with the bailor's rights and duties, those of the bailee also vary depending on the purpose of the bailment.

Foremost among the bailee's rights is the right to possess the bailed property during the term of the bailment. If anyone steals the bailed property from the bailee, he or she may take legal action to recover the bailed property and may even seek compensation for the loss of the property or damage to it.

The bailee has the right to use the property consistent with the terms and purpose of the bailment. For example, if you are borrowing your friend's car while yours is being repaired, driving to work and to the grocery store would be consistent with the bailment.

However, if you own an auto repair shop and you have possession of Smith's car to repair it, you cannot use the car to go on a date.

The bailee, unless the bailment is gratuitous, has the right to be compensated in accordance with the terms of the bailment. Regardless of the type of bailment, he or she has the right to be reimbursed for expenses that were necessary to maintain the bailed property.

If the bailee is to receive compensation for the bailment, the bailee may retain possession of the bailed property until payment is made. In most states, when the bailor refuses to provide the agreed-on compensation to the bailee, the bailee may ultimately sell the property after proper notice and a hearing. To enforce this right to sell the property, the bailee is given a *bailee's lien,* or a possessory lien on the property. Then, when it is sold, the proceeds are first used to pay the bailee and to cover the costs of the sale. The remaining proceeds go to the bailor.

In the opening scenario, Melvin argued that he entered into an implied bailment relationship with Richard. Although Melvin did not explicitly ask Richard to watch his property, he argued that Richard should have known that his request was made because his property was still in the cell. As the bailee, Richard became responsible for exercising a reasonable duty of care of Melvin's personal property.

Case Nugget Ziva Jewelry, Inc. v. Car Wash Headquarters, Inc.

Supreme Court of Alabama
897 So. 2d 1011; 2004 Ala. LEXIS 238

A bailee can be liable only for the property he knows he possesses. In this case, Smith left his car and his keys with a car-wash employee. A case full of jewelry was locked in the trunk, but Smith did not tell any of the car-wash employees that it was in the trunk. Smith watched the car go through the car-wash tunnel and watched the employees dry the vehicle. As he was standing at the counter waiting to pay the cashier, he saw the employee wave a flag, indicating that his car was ready to be driven away. Smith then saw the employee walk away from his vehicle. While Smith was still at the counter, someone jumped into Smith's vehicle and sped off the car-wash premises. The police were called, and Smith's car was recovered 15 minutes later. The car was not damaged, but the jewelry, valued at $851,935, was missing from the trunk and never recovered.

Smith sued for negligent failure to safeguard the jewelry, but the trial court granted the defendant a summary judgment on the grounds that a bailment for the jewelry had never been established. The Supreme Court of Alabama affirmed on grounds that a bailee is not liable for the loss of the contents of a bailed vehicle when the bailee did not have actual or implied knowledge of the contents of the vehicle. In this case, there was no evidence that the car wash knew or should have reasonably foreseen or expected that it was taking responsibility for over $850,000 worth of jewelry when it accepted Smith's vehicle for the purpose of washing it.

DOCUMENTS RELATED TO BAILMENTS

Bailment agreements. Bailments may be either express or implied. When a bailment is express, there is no need for a written agreement unless the statute of frauds applies to the bailment. As you should recall from Chapter 18, the statute of frauds requires a writing for any contract that cannot be performed within a year, so any bailment relationship that will last more than a year requires a writing to be enforceable. It is probably a good idea to put all bailments in writing, especially when the property involved is valuable. If the agreement is in writing, there will be far fewer disputes over each party's responsibilities and rights.

Documents of title. When a bailment is for the purpose of transportation or storage of goods, certain **documents of title,** governed by Article VII of the Uniform Commercial Code, may be issued in conjunction with the bailment. The UCC defines a document of title as one that "must purport to be issued by or addressed to a bailee and purport to cover goods in the bailee's possession which are either identified or are fungible portions of an identified mass."

The three types of documents of title governing bailments are bills of lading, warehouse receipts, and delivery orders. A **bill of lading** is a document issued by a person engaged in the business of transporting goods that verifies receipt of the goods for shipment. A **warehouse receipt** is a receipt issued by one who is engaged in the business of storing goods for compensation. A *delivery order* is a written order to deliver goods directed to a party who, in the ordinary course of business, issues warehouse receipts or bills of lading.

Negotiability of documents of title. As you should recall from Chapter 26, if an instrument contains the word *bearer* or the phrase *to the order of,* it is negotiable. Thus, if a document of title specifies that the goods are to be delivered to the bearer or to the order of a named person, the person who possesses that document of title is entitled to receive, hold, and dispose of the goods it covers. Further, a good-faith purchaser of such a document of title may actually have greater rights to the document and goods than the transferor had or had the right to convey.

SPECIAL BAILMENTS

Certain bailments impose additional obligations on the bailee. These bailments will be discussed in detail in the following sections.

Common carriers. Common carriers are licensed to provide transportation services to the public, as opposed to private carriers, which provide transportation services to a select group. Common carriers are subject to regulation by agencies and may be limited in the scope of services they provide by geographic region or type of goods they carry, but as long as a party seeking their services does not ask them to make any deliveries outside the scope of their ordinary course of business, the common carrier cannot refuse to provide the service.

When a common carrier accepts a package for transport, a mutual-benefit bailment is created. But because the bailee is a common carrier, he or she is held to a higher standard of care. He or she is held to a standard of strict liability in protecting the bailed property. In other words, the common carrier is absolutely liable for any harm done to the property, even if there was no negligence on the part of the common carrier.

The only situations where the common carrier will not be liable for harm to the bailed property are those in which the injury was caused by an act of God, an act of a public enemy, an act of the shipper, or the inherent nature of the good. These exceptions are interpreted narrowly. For example, the common carrier is still liable when the harm to the property was caused by an accident or by intentional acts of a third party. Thus, if the bailed property is stolen from the common-carrier truck that was transporting it, or if the truck gets into an accident and the contents are damaged as a result, the trucking firm is liable.

connecting to the core

Management and Marketing

Choosing a Carrier

As you may know from a management or marketing course, there are five primary modes of transporting products or personal property: railroads, motor carriers, air carriers, pipelines, and water carriers. To determine which mode of transportation best suits a product's delivery, individuals or business owners may employ six criteria: consideration for the cost of transportation, the time or speed of the shipment, capability of the mode to deliver a certain kind of product, dependability in the sense that business owners can rely on the carrier to avoid loss and damage of the goods, accessibility of the routes of the carrier, and frequency or scheduling of deliveries. With regard to relative advantages and disadvantages among the three most common modes, railroads provide a less expensive mode of transportation, fully capable of transporting most kinds of goods. However, railroads can be slower than truck trailers or air carriers, but trucks and air carriers are more expensive modes. Trucks also provide the convenience of direct delivery from the pickup site to the delivery site, but they must comply with weight and size restrictions. Air carriers, although the fastest mode, have limited capabilities in addition to high costs, but air carriers transport goods without much risk of damage. The aforementioned criteria could be useful to individuals or business owners when selecting a common carrier to transport products or personal property. Fortunately for individuals relying on common carriers, the common carriers are liable for any damage to individuals' goods.

Roger A. Kerin et al., *Marketing* (New York: McGraw-Hill/Irwin, 2006), pp. 432–434.

However, if the fragile glass property being shipped gets broken because it was improperly crated by the owner, or if a tornado picks up the truck and drops it, demolishing the truck and its contents in the process, the common carrier will not be liable. Case 48-4 provides an illustration of a situation in which the court imposed liability on the common carrier.

CASE 48-4

MISSOURI PACIFIC RAILWAY CO., APPELLANT, v. ELMORE & STAHL

UNITED STATES SUPREME COURT 377 U.S. 134 (1964)

The Plaintiff, a fruit shipper, contracted with the defendant, a common carrier, to transport 640 crates of honeydew melons from Rio Grande City, Texas, to Chicago, Illinois. When the melons arrived, they were spoiled. The plaintiff filed an action to recover damages for the defective condition in which the goods were delivered.

The jury found that the melons were in good condition when turned over to the shipper, but arrived at their destination in a damaged condition. They found no evidence of negligence on the part of any of the carriers. They also found that there was not a preponderance of evidence that the condition of the melons was solely due to an "inherent vice" at the time the goods were delivered to the shipper.

JUSTICE STEWART: The question presented in this case is whether a common carrier which has exercised reasonable care and has complied with the instructions of the shipper, is nonetheless liable to the shipper for spoilage in transit of an interstate shipment of perishable commodities, when the carrier fails to prove that the cause of the spoilage was the natural tendency of the commodities to deteriorate. . . .

. . . [A] carrier, though not an absolute insurer, is liable for damage to goods transported by it unless it can show that the damage was caused by "(a) the act of God; (b) the public enemy; (c) the act of the shipper himself; (d) public authority; (e) or the inherent vice or nature of the goods."

. . . [I]n an action to recover from a carrier for damage to a shipment, the shipper establishes his prima facie case when he shows delivery in good condition, arrival in damaged condition, and the amount of damages. Thereupon, the burden of proof is upon the carrier to show both that it was free from negligence and that the damage to the cargo was due to one of the excepted causes relieving the carrier of liability. . . .

. . . It is apparent that the jury was unable to determine the cause of the damage to the melons. . . . But the jury refused to find that the carrier had borne its burden of establishing that the damaged condition of the melons was due solely to "inherent vice," as defined in the instruction of the trial judge—including "the inherent nature of the commodity which will cause it to deteriorate with a lapse of time. . . ."

The general rule of carrier liability is based upon the sound premise that the carrier has peculiarly within its knowledge "[a]ll the facts and circumstances upon which (it) may rely to relieve (it) of (its) duty. In consequence, the law casts upon (it) the burden of the loss which (it) cannot explain or, explaining, bring within the exceptional case in which (it) is relieved from liability." We are not persuaded that the carrier lacks adequate means to inform itself of the condition of goods at the time it receives them from the shipper, and it cannot be doubted that while the carrier has possession, it is the only one in a position to acquire the knowledge of what actually damaged a shipment entrusted to its care.

AFFIRMED in favor of plaintiff.

CRITICAL THINKING

Explain why the court ruled in favor of the plaintiff in this case?
What ethical norm is advanced by the decision in this case? Why?

ETHICAL DECISION MAKING

One of the most important values in American law is personal responsibility. How does this decision reflect the importance of that value?

Sometimes a party will transport property using two or more connecting carriers. In such cases, a *through bill of lading* is used, which lists all carriers. Under this document, the shipper can recover from the original carrier or any of the connecting carriers. However, there is a presumption that the last carrier received the property in good condition.

Innkeepers' liability. At common law, innkeepers, as well as anyone else who provided lodging to others, were held to the same strict-liability standard of care for their guests' property as were common carriers. However, today this standard applies only to those who are regularly in the business of making lodging available to the public. The standard also applies only to guests, or travelers, as opposed to lodgers, who are defined as permanent residents of the facility.

Some states further allow innkeepers to avoid strict liability for their guests' personal property by providing them with a safe in which they may keep their valuables. Guests must be clearly notified of the existence of the safe and the limitation on the innkeeper's liability in the event that the guests fail to take advantage of the safe. Under some statutes, failure to use the safe will merely limit the innkeeper's liability; under others, it will relieve the innkeeper from liability other than that caused by his or her ordinary negligence.

Case Nugget Innkeepers' Liability

GNOC Corp. v. Powers
2006 WL 560687 (Super. Ct., N.J., 2006)

New Jersey's State Innkeeper's Act is a law that protects hotels from being liable for losses to their guests, as Powers unfortunately discovered. He was gambling in town and staying at a Hilton Hotel. While Powers was asleep one night, the hotel issued a second key to his room to an unknown person, who allegedly entered Power's room and stole over $75,000 in cash winnings and chips. Powers sued, claiming negligence by the hotel. The trial court ruled in favor of the Hilton Hotel, and Powers appealed. The appeals court affirmed, holding that under New Jersey law, a hotel could not be held liable for the loss of valuables that could have been deposited in the hotel safe. Both the cash and the chips fell into the category of such valuables.

Generally, the innkeeper does not have any responsibility for a guest's automobile. However, if the innkeeper provides parking facilities, then a bailment exists and the innkeeper is held to the standard of reasonable care.

CASE OPENER WRAP-UP

Prisoners and Personal Property

The court determined that a bailment relationship existed between Melvin and Richard. Further, the court explained that the relationship between an inmate and a prison official is more substantial than that between a boarder and his host. Inmates do not pay prison officials to safeguard their personal belongings; thus, the relationship cannot constitute a bailment for hire. However, the restrictions on an inmate's property and his or her ability to control access to the property are imposed for the benefit of prison officials of the United States and for the protection of inmates. Although Melvin did not tell Richard that there was property in his cell, Richard did not suggest any other reason as to why Melvin would desire to have his cell locked other than to secure his property. Once Richard agreed to lock the cell, he had the duty, as a bailee, to act with reasonable care. The court took the majority position in holding that the personal property of inmates is protected.

Summary

The Nature and Classifications of Property

Property is a set of rights in relation to a tangible object, the most significant of which is probably the right to exclude others.

Property can be divided into three categories:

Real property: Land and anything permanently attached to it.

Personal property: Tangible movable objects and intangible objects.

Intellectual property: Property that is primarily the result of one's mental rather than physical creativity.

Personal Property Personal property can be transferred voluntarily through a gift or sale. It may also be transferred involuntarily if it is lost or mislaid.

Bailment A bailment is a special relationship in which one party, the *bailor,* transfers possession of personalty to another, the *bailee,* to be used by the bailee in an agreed-on manner for an agreed-on time period.

Point / Counterpoint

What Constitutes "Possession" of Personal Property?

Barry Bonds, the San Francisco Giants slugger, stepped up to the plate in the first inning with 72 home runs for the season. With the bases empty and a full count, Bonds connected with a slow knuckleball, sending it over the right-field wall and into the baseball glove of a fan named Alex Popov. Before Popov could establish secure possession of the ball, however, a crowd of fans mobbed him, jarring the ball loose. Patrick Hayashi, a nearby fan who was not part of the crowd that mobbed Popov, picked up the ball on the ground nearby. Popov sued Hayashi for the property rights to the ball.

Should Popov Win?	
Yes	**No**
Popov asserted as much control over the ball as the nature of the situation permitted. If the unruly mob of fans had not descended on him as he caught the ball and jarred it loose, he likely would have been able to exercise complete and secure control over it. The court should be wary of establishing a rule that sanctions mob rule in the stands. A ruling for Hayashi would signal to fans everywhere that a ball is fair game as long as no one exercises complete control over it. As a result, fans would have a strong incentive to assault other fans right before they could gain possession of a ball. This form of competition is not socially beneficial. Hence, the court should establish a clear rule that interference from other fans cannot deprive the original possessor of his property rights in the ball. Allowing Popov to bring suit against the mob that jarred the ball loose from his glove is unsatisfactory for several reasons. First, it is impossible for Popov to show that but for the actions of the mob, he would have established complete control over the ball.	The standard rule in property law is that an individual must demonstrate full control over an object before he is deemed to have possession of that object. Popov did not have complete possession of the ball before it came loose. If the ball had been jarred loose because Popov collided with an inanimate wall, he could not argue that he had possession of the ball. This case is no different, because Hayashi did not cause the ball to fall out of Popov's glove. A ruling for Hayashi would not tend to encourage physical fighting for the ball because Hayashi was an innocent bystander, not a part of the mob that attacked Popov. The law should not allow those who use force to take baseballs from other fans to profit from their force. But if the ball comes loose before any fan establishes certain possession of it, any other fan who did not intentionally cause the ball to come loose may capture the rights to the ball by gaining possession of it. A ruling for Hayashi does not leave Popov without a remedy. He is free to bring suit against the fans

And second, because the mob was quite large, it is impossible to determine which fans were acting maliciously and which fans were inadvertently pulled into the mix. Hence, even though Hayashi is not guilty of any wrongdoing himself, he should not be able to profit from the wrongdoing of others.

who mobbed him and caused the ball to come loose from his glove. If he can demonstrate that they deprived him of control over the ball, he can recover the value of the ball from them. That result is the most fair because the unruly fans were the wrongdoers in this case, not Hayashi.

Questions & Problems

1. Explain which type of property each of the following is:
   - **a.** A tree
   - **b.** Lumber
   - **c.** A car
   - **d.** A built-in oven
2. What are the three essential elements of a gift?
3. What is the difference between a gift *causa mortis* and an *inter vivos* gift?
4. What is a conditional gift?
5. How is lost property different from mislaid property, and why is that distinction important?
6. What is the relationship between the rights of the bailee and the duties of the bailor?
7. Orson Cornia and Dennis Weston entered into an agreement with James Wilcox for the "total care" of approximately 500 cattle for one year. The agreement defined *total care* as "salt, water, range feed, and trailing of the cattle." Wilcox was not responsible for vaccinations, medicine, or trucking. Cornia and Weston delivered 478 cows to Wilcox. When Cornia and Weston returned for their cattle, 107 of their cows and 177 of their expected calves were not returned. The cattle that were returned were in poor health. Cornia and Weston brought suit against Wilcox for breach of the pasture agreement. Do you think the bailee, Wilcox, was held responsible for the damages? Why or why not? [*Cornia v. Wilcox,* 898 P.2d 1379 (1995).]
8. Ellen Brin filed an action against Roger Stutzman to recover several articles of personal property. Brin and Stutzman had previously been involved in a relationship, but the relationship had since been completely terminated. Brin demanded that Stutzman return several pieces of personal property, including a computer and a treadmill. The trial record indicated that Brin transferred the computer to Stutzman "on the condition that [Stutzman] would eventually marry her, as this was her perception." In her testimony, Brin indicated that she had lent the treadmill to Stutzman for his personal use. Brin claims that the computer and treadmill were not intended as gifts. Do you think the court agreed? Should the property be returned to Brin? Why or why not? [*Brin v. Stutzman,* 951 P.3d 291 (1998).]
9. Winston Hutton entered into a rental agreement for a storage space with Public Storage Management, Inc., a self-storage facility. He was given his own lock for his storage space, and the rental agreement stated that Public Storage Management did not have the lock or combination to his space. Hutton was also not required to provide Public Storage Management with a list of the items being stored. After certain items

of Hutton's property were lost, he argued that Public Storage Management should be liable. Hutton believed that the relationship constituted a bailment. Do you think the court agreed with Hutton? Did Hutton transfer possession of his personal property to Public Storage Management? [*Hutton v. Public Storage Management, Inc.,* 676 N.Y.S.2d 886 (1998).]

10. Packaging Etc. arranges for the packaging and delivery of items. Judy Hayes gave $340 to Packaging Etc. to be sent to her daughter via Federal Express. When her daughter did not receive the package, Hayes contacted Federal Express. Packaging Etc. had not sent the package to Federal Express. Hayes demanded that Packaging Etc. return the property, but it failed to do so. Packaging Etc. noted that the Federal Express packaging used by Hayes clearly prohibits the sending of cash through Federal Express. However, a Packaging Etc. employee advised Hayes to use the envelope for the shipment. Do you think the court ordered that the lost bailment property be returned to Hayes? [*Hayes v. Reani,* 44 Va. Cir. 464 (1998).]
11. Linda Koehler brought an action against her former husband, Gary Koehler, to retrieve certain items of personal property. During their courtship, Linda provided Gary with very generous gifts, including a valuable watch, an automobile, a bike, and a kayak. After deciding to marry, Linda paid the down payment on a new home. Though Gary made no financial contributions, both Gary and Linda were listed as joint tenants. After 11 months of marriage, Linda and Gary filed for divorce. Linda argued that most of the purchases she made, including the items purchased for Gary prior to their marriage, should be returned to her. Gary argued that the items in question were gifts. Do you agree? How do you think the court decided? [*Koehler v. Koehler,* 697 N.Y.S.2d 478 (1999).]
12. Harry and Cheryl Nadjarian were invited by Caesars Tahoe to attend a New Year's Eve gala and were provided with a complimentary room. The Nadjarians checked into the hotel and placed their personal property in their room. When they returned to their room, the Nadjarians discovered that it was occupied by another guest. They contacted the hotel manager, and they were moved to another room. Hotel personnel promised to deliver the Nadjarians' personal property to their new room, but only a ski bag and a sweater were delivered. The lost items included clothing and other items of considerable value. The Nadjarians sued Caesars to recover the value of the lost property. The district court granted summary judgment in favor of Caesars. Do you agree with this decision? Was Caesars a bailee of the Nadjarians' property? How do you think the court decided? [*Nadjarian v. Desert Palace, Inc.,* 898 P.2d 1291 (1995).]
13. Sherman Hawkins is an inmate at Montana State Prison. Hawkins escaped from prison on July 12, 1997. After his escape, the prison officials placed Hawkins's personal property in a box and removed it from his cell. Two days later, Hawkins was caught and returned to the prison. Though he requested the return of his personal property, prison officials allowed him to retain only his legal papers and legal materials. Hawkins was informed that his property was considered abandoned and would be destroyed. The property included a television, a stereo, a word processor, glasses, and books. Hawkins argued that his personal property was not abandoned. Because he was returned to the prison within two days and the prison officials had retained possession of his personal property, Hawkins believed that the property should have been returned. Do you think the court agreed with him? Was the property abandoned? [*Hawkins v. Mahoney,* 990 P.2d 776 (1999).]
14. Dole Fresh Fruit Company and Delaware Cold Storage (DCS), Inc., entered into a contract for cold-storage services. Under the terms of the contract, DCS was to

cold-store Dole's pears from February 1, 1994, to July 31, 1994. DCS was provided with specific instructions detailing the required temperature of the cold room and was directed to contact Dole with any problems resulting from the storage. DCS had trouble keeping the room to the specified temperature, and the pears began to ripen prematurely. Many of the stored pears began to rot and were removed from storage. Dole blamed DCS for the condition of the pears and filed a complaint against DCS for negligent bailment. DCS claimed that the pears were already damaged when they arrived at the facility. How do you think the court decided? [*Dole Fresh Fruit Company v. Delaware Cold Storage, Inc.*, 961 F. Supp. 676 (1997).]

15. In Florida, the owner of an automobile is liable for another's negligent misuse of the vehicle. Marsha Pabon rented a minivan from InterAmerican Car Rental. She listed Phillips as the authorized driver. Phillips was using the minivan to take his tennis team to an out-of-town tournament. He allowed an unauthorized driver, Moore, to drive the minivan. Moore fell asleep while driving, and the minivan rolled off the road. One of the passengers, McCloud, was killed in the accident. Was Pabon, as a bailee of InterAmerican, responsible for McCloud's death? Why or why not? [*Pabon v. InterAmerican Car Rental, Inc.*, 715 So. 2d 1148 (1998).]

16. Jeff Lewis filed a negligence action against Lawless Homes, Inc., to recover damages sustained when his backhoe was damaged while in Lawless Homes' possession. Lewis had been using the backhoe on a Lawless Homes construction site. The backhoe was 10 years old but in good working condition. Lewis was planning on returning to work the following day and left the backhoe on the sight. Lawless Homes called him the next morning requesting his permission to use the backhoe. Lewis gave permission but requested that the backhoe not be used for digging. When Lewis arrived on the site, the backhoe had been seriously damaged. He argued that a bailment existed, and that Lawless Homes should pay him damages for ruining the property. Do you agree? Was this relationship a bailment? [*Lewis v. Lawless Homes, Inc.*, 984 S.W.2d 583 (1999).]

17. First Chicago Bank sold a number of used storage cabinets to a secondhand furniture dealer. He sold some of these cabinets to Strayer, who gave one of them, a locked one without a key, to his friend Michael. Six weeks later, Michael was moving the cabinet and it fell over, causing the lock to break. Inside the cabinet were several certificates of deposit, many made payable to bearer, worth about $666,687,948.85. Michael called the FBI, who took possession of the certificates. Michael filed an action to have the court determine ownership of the certificates. In whose favor did the court rule, Michael's or First Chicago Bank's? Why? [*Michael v. First Chicago Corporation*, 487 N.E.2d 403 (1986).]

Looking for more review material?

The Online Learning Center at **www.mhhe.com/kubasek1e** contains this chapter's "Assignment on the Internet" and also a list of URLs for more information, entitled "On the Internet." Find both of them in the Student Center portion of the OLC, along with quizzes and other helpful materials.

Real Property

CASE OPENER

Economic Redevelopment in Poletown

General Motors wished to expand its facility but was unable to acquire the land it needed, so it approached the Detroit Economic Development Corporation with a request that the commission use its power of eminent domain to acquire a large parcel of land on which members of the plaintiff organization, Poletown Neighborhood Council, resided and had small businesses. Once the commission had acquired the land, it would be conveyed to General Motors for its plant expansion. The justification for the use of eminent domain in the case would be that the acquisition and transfer of the property would create jobs for the economically depressed area.

The plaintiffs, who did not want their community destroyed, sued the city and the development council on the grounds that they were attempting to abuse their power of eminent domain to take private property for a private use.

1. Can business managers ask the city to buy real property for them when the owners do not wish to sell it?
2. What would determine whether the government can legally take the property for the corporation?

The Wrap-Up at the end of the chapter will answer these questions.

CHAPTER 49

Learning Objectives

After reading this chapter, you will be able to answer the following questions:

1. What are the interests in real property that one can hold?
2. How is real property voluntarily transferred?
3. How is real property involuntarily transferred?
4. How is the use of property restricted?

Ownership of real property seems to be one of the goals of most Americans. In this chapter we examine the nature of real property, the types of interests one can own in real property, and how those interests can be transferred. As the opening scenario implies, transfers can be either voluntary or involuntary.

The Nature of Real Property

Real property, commonly referred to as *realty,* is land and everything permanently attached to it. The type of ownership interest a person has in a piece of property determines his or her rights to the property. In the next section, the various types of interests a person may have will be described in detail. These interests may be conveyed or transferred under legal guidelines for property rights. Most transfers of property are voluntary. However, for the benefit of the public, and to protect public health, safety, and welfare, the government may require involuntary transfers of property.

The definition of real property as land and items permanently attached to it seems straightforward, but the application of that definition is not always as easy as it sounds. Many disputes over whether an item is real or personal property have revolved around whether the item really is permanently attached. The courts have generally held that a given item is attached if its removal would hinder the functioning of the structure. Because removing built-in appliances would damage a building, these are held to be part of the real property; a freestanding appliance would be personal property. Also, in certain cases where an item is not permanently attached but is essential to the use of the building, the courts have ruled the item to be part of the real property.

FIXTURES

A *fixture* is an item that was originally a piece of personal property but became part of the realty after it was permanently attached to the real property in question. For example, if a tenant installs a built-in dishwasher in the property he is renting, the dishwasher becomes part of the real property. When he leaves, the tenant may not take the dishwasher with him. However, there are two exceptions to this rule.

The first exception arises when there is an agreement between the parties in question that specific features will be treated as personal property. This agreement must be in writing if it is to be enforced.

The second exception is for personal property that is attached to realty for the use of a business renting the property. Such items are known as *trade fixtures* and are treated as personal property based on the presumption that neither party intends such fixtures to become a permanent part of the realty. For example, if a businessperson rents a storefront for a barbershop and installs barber chairs, these chairs are trade fixtures. If the businessperson relocates, he will need the chairs at a new location, and the next tenant will have her own needs.

This exception did not hold true, however, in a case in an Arizona state appellate court. Two air service businesses, Air Commerce Center, LLP, and Airport Properties, held interest in public land at Scottsdale Municipal Airport. Airport Properties had built air service–related improvements that it believed were trade fixtures. However, the court found that the improvements were the property of the city: The interest the companies held in the improvements was only a possessory interest. The improvements made by businesses to land leased from the city were declared to be the property of the city. Thus, if there is any concern on the part of the tenant about how improvements will be treated, it is best to get an agreement in writing if the tenant wishes to retain possession of material used in improving the property.

EXTENT OF OWNERSHIP

The landowner's rights to property go beyond simply the surface of the land. The airspace above the land, extending to the atmosphere, is also part of the legal concept of real property. Rights to airspace generally do not generate much controversy, but occasionally disputes arise that involve aircraft flying "too low" over individuals' property. Alternatively, a tree's branches may hang over into the airspace of the property next door, and the owner of that airspace may want to cut the overhanging branch.

In dense, commercial urban areas, airspace may actually be an asset. Owners of two commercial buildings might want to build an overhead walkway adjoining their buildings across a parking lot that you own. They will have to pay you handsomely for the right to build in your airspace.

In addition to having airspace rights, the owner of real property also has *water rights,* the legal ability to use water flowing across or underneath the property. However, these rights are somewhat restricted; one cannot deprive the landowners downstream from the use of the water by diverting the water elsewhere.

Figure 49-1 Extent of Rights

Finally, ownership of real property extends to *mineral rights;* these rights involve the land below the surface. The landowner has the legal ability to dig or mine the materials from the earth, and he may sell or give these rights to another person. Ownership of these *subsurface rights* includes the right to enter onto the property to remove the underground materials. These rights are illustrated in Figure 49-1.

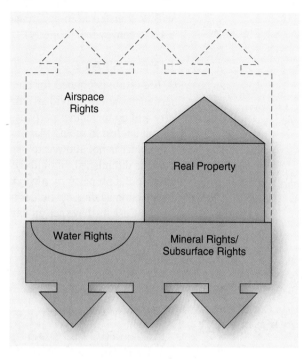

Interests in Real Property

There are a number of different types of interests in land, ranging from temporary to permanent to future. The duration of one's ownership interest and the power one has over using the land depend on the type of *estate* one is said to hold. The following sections describe these interests in detail.

FEE SIMPLE ABSOLUTE

A **fee simple absolute** is the most complete estate a person may have. Exclusive rights to ownership and possession of the land belong to the person who has a fee simple absolute. It is this type of estate to which most people refer when they speak of "buying" a house or piece of land. A fee-simple-absolute interest is passed to the owner's heirs when the owner of such an estate dies. What most people expect when they buy a home is a fee-simple-absolute interest in the property.

CONDITIONAL ESTATE

The owner of a **conditional estate** possesses the same interest as the owner of a fee simple absolute, only this interest is subject to a condition. Should a certain required event fail to occur, or should a specific prohibited event occur, the interest would be terminated.

For example, Todd may be given property rights to a Victorian house on the condition that he is to preserve it in its original form. If he violates this condition by turning the house into a piano showroom or a beer hall, the house either will revert to the original owner or will be transferred in accordance with the terms of the deed (the *deed* is the instrument used to convey real property).

LIFE ESTATE

A **life estate** is granted for the lifetime of an individual; the right to possess the property terminates at the individual's death. On the death of the holder of the life estate, the property will go to another party as designated by the original grantor. Thus, this future owner has an interest in seeing that the life tenant does not *waste* the property; in other words, the life holder is not allowed to neglect or abuse the property in such a way that the property value is diminished. Should the life tenant fail to make necessary repairs, or should he or she use the property in ways damaging to its future value, the future holder could bring legal action against the holder of the life estate to recover damages for waste.

In Case 49-1 we see an example of the type of behavior that the courts have found to constitute waste.

CASE 49-1 SAULS v. CROSBY

DISTRICT COURT OF APPEALS OF FLORIDA 258 SO. 2D 326 (1972)

Annie Sauls, the defendant-appellant, conveyed a future interest in certain property to plaintiff-appellees Dan and Bertha Crosby, and reserved a life estate in the property. She attempted to cut timber on the property to sell, and the holders of the future interest sought to enjoin her from doing so. The district court held that defendant Sauls was not entitled to cut timber and keep the proceeds for herself. She appealed the lower court's ruling.

JUDGE RAWLS: On the 9th day of October 1968, appellant conveyed to appellees certain lands situated in Hamilton County, Florida, with the following reservation set forth in said conveyance: "The Grantor herein, reserves a life estate in said property." By this appeal appellant now contends that the trial court erred in denying her, as a life tenant, the right to cut merchantable timber and enjoy the proceeds.

The English common law, which was transplanted on this continent, holds that it is waste for an ordinary life tenant to cut timber upon his estate when the sole purpose is to clear the woodlands. American courts today as a general rule recognize that an ordinary life tenant may cut timber and not be liable for waste if he uses the timber for fuel; for repairing fences and buildings on the estate; for fitting the land for cultivation; or for use as pasture if the inheritance is not damaged and the acts are conformable to good husbandry; and for thinning or other purposes which are necessary for the enjoyment of the estate and are in conformity with good husbandry.

In this jurisdiction a tenant for life or a person vested with an ordinary life estate is entitled to the use and enjoyment of his estate during its existence. The only restriction on the life tenant's use and enjoyment is that he not permanently diminish or change the value of the future estate of the remainderman. This limitation places on the "ordinary life tenant" the responsibility for all waste of whatever character.

An instrument creating a life tenancy may absolve the tenant of responsibility for waste by stating that the life tenant has the power to consume or that the life tenant is without impeachment for waste. Thus, there is a sharp distinction in the rights of an ordinary life tenant or life tenant without impeachment for waste or life tenant who has the power to consume.

[CONTINUED]

An ordinary life tenant has no right to cut the timber from an estate for purely commercial reasons and so to do is tortious conduct for which the remainderman may sue immediately.

In the case before us, the trial court was concerned with the rights of an ordinary life tenant and correctly concluded that appellant does not have the right to cut merchantable timber from the land involved in this suit unless the proceeds of such cutting and sale are held in trust for the use and benefit of the remaindermen. . . .

AFFIRMED in favor of plaintiff.

CRITICAL THINKING

What fact could you add to this case that would change the outcome?

ETHICAL DECISION MAKING

In rendering his decision, the judge gave primary weight to the interests of which stakeholders?

FUTURE INTEREST

The plaintiffs in the foregoing case held a future interest in the estate in question. A **future interest** is a person's present right to property ownership and possession in the future. Such an interest usually exists in conjunction with a life estate or a conditional estate. For example, Joe owns a life estate in Oak Hills Apartments, and on his death, the property will pass to Sarah with fee-simple-absolute rights. Sarah, in this case, holds a future interest in Oak Hills Apartments, and if Joe allows the buildings to deteriorate from neglect, Sarah may sue Joe to enjoin him from engaging in waste of the property.

LEASEHOLD ESTATES

The interest of a **leasehold** differs from the interests previously described in that the holder of such an estate has a possessory interest but not an ownership interest. This interest is transferred by a contract known as a *lease.* Both the owner of the property (the lessor, or landlord) and the tenant (the lessee) sign the lease. The contract generally specifies the property to be leased, the amount of the rent payments and when they are due, the duration of the leasehold, and any special rights or duties of either party. A leasehold gives the lessee, or tenant, exclusive rights to the use and possession of the land, including the right to exclude the property owner under most circumstances, for the term specified by the lease.

The tenant's and landlord's rights and obligations may vary according to the lease, but some states have statutes requiring that landlords keep the property in good condition for the tenant's use, giving the tenant the right to withhold rent payments should the landlord fail to maintain the premises. However, should the tenant fail to make the agreed-on payments without such grounds, the landlord may evict the tenant. The landlord is not allowed to enter the property, except in an emergency or when the tenant has given permission to enter to make repairs. Near the end of the leasehold, the landlord may enter with notice to the tenant for the purpose of showing the property to a potential tenant.

global context

Property Interests in Vietnam

In the United States, we take for granted the right to go out and purchase a piece of property if we have the money to do so. Property is not so freely available and transferable in all nations. Vietnam's new constitution, written in 1992, provides guidelines for the allocation, transfer, and sale of private property. However, the constitution still asserts that the people, or the state, own all the land. Thus, if individuals or private enterprises want to use land, they must pay tax on it as a form of rent. Those who agree to pay the tax on the land are granted a "use of right" which entitles them to extended use. The use of right also gives the renter the freedom to transfer the property. Technically, the property is not being transferred, but rather the right to use the property.

Transference of property can occur only with the approval of a state official. The official ensures that the new owner intends to use the land for the original, state-approved purpose. Moreover, the new owner can never be given a longer term of right or more extensive rights over the land than the original owner had. Finally, the state official determines the price the property will be transferred for. The government has specified certain prices depending on how the land is used. Considering the involvement of the state in such property transactions, the extent to which the Vietnamese enjoy private property rights is undermined.

Subleasing of the property by the tenant to another party is permissible unless specifically prohibited by the lease. However, the initial tenant is liable throughout the entire term of the lease for payment of the rent to the landlord.

Leases are discussed in greater detail in Chapter 50, "Landlord-Tenant Law."

NONPOSSESSORY ESTATES

While most people think of interests in land as being possessory in nature, some estates do not include the right to possess the property. Such interests include easements, profits, and licenses.

Easements and profits. Easements and profits are similar in that they are neither ownership nor possessory interests, and they are subject to similar rules, but they are not exactly the same. An **easement** is an irrevocable right to use some part of another's land for a specific purpose without taking anything from it. A **profit** is the right to go onto someone's land and take part of the land or a product of it away from the land. For example, if Bill has the right to drive his car across Jenny's property to get to his property, he has an easement, but if he has the right to go onto her property and remove the topsoil he needs from it for his landscaping business, he has a profit.

Easements and profits may be appurtenant or in gross. An easement or profit is *appurtenant* when it runs with land adjacent to the property on which it exists. In the previous example, if Bill's property is adjacent to Jenny's, he has an easement (or profit) appurtenant, which can be used only by Bill. Similarly, the easement can be transferred only in conjunction with the transfer of Bill's property.

Easements or profits *in gross* are those that are not dependent on owning property adjacent to the land on which the nonpossessory interest exists. An example of an easement in gross is an easement that the gas company has to run gas lines across one's property.

Easements or profits can be transferred in multiple ways: by express agreement, inheritance, necessity, implication, or prescription. Transfer by *express agreement* occurs when the landowner expressly grants the agreed-on use of the land to the holder of the easement. For example, a farmer may have been expressly granted an easement to run a ditch across part of his neighbor's property to drain a field. This easement should be recorded in the county office that keeps property records or described on the deed to the land to protect the holder of the easement if the property is sold. If the transfer of the interest is to be by *inheritance,* its terms are simply incorporated into one's will.

An *easement by prescription* is created by state law when certain conditions are met. In most states, if one openly uses a portion of another's property for a statutory period of time (usually 25 years), an easement arises by law.

If a piece of property is divided and one portion is landlocked as a result, an *easement by necessity* is created. For purposes of entrance to and exit from the land, the owner of the landlocked parcel has an easement to cross the other portion.

If the land that benefits from the easement or profit is sold, the nonpossessory interest goes with the property. Thus, if Bill sold his land to Sonny, Sonny would also receive the easement across Jenny's property. Similarly, if Jenny sold her property, the new owner would have the burden of Bill's easement as long as it had been properly recorded. Of course, just as easements and profits can be created, they can also be terminated, with the most common method of termination being by agreement. The easement holder may simply deed the easement back to the property owner. If the easement arose by necessity, and the necessity no longer exists, the easement would terminate.

An easement by implication is said to exist when an apparent and continuous use existed on the servient tenement before the conveyance of that land and the easement is reasonably necessary for the enjoyment of the dominant tenement.

License. A **license** is a right to use another's property that is both temporary and revocable. For example, when a person purchases a theater ticket, he or she has the right to a specific use of the property for a limited time, subject to good behavior. No property interest goes to the license holder.

Co-ownership

An interest in real property may be owned by a single individual or corporation. An interest may also be held by two or more persons. When more than one person possesses the same property rights, **co-ownership** exists. The type of co-ownership, like the type of individual interest above, determines the ownership rights to the property.

While having multiple forms of co-ownership may seem confusing, consider whether having these options is a better system than that in Japan, where there is only one form of co-ownership, which the Japanese call *joint ownership.* Under the Japanese system, the joint owners share expenses proportionate with their ownership interest. To alter the property, all owners must agree, whereas less important decisions require a majority interest. Any joint owner may sue to have the property partitioned at any time.

TENANCY IN COMMON

Tenancy in common is the type of co-ownership that occurs most often. Each co-owner has the right to sell his or her interest without the consent of the other owners, may own an unequal share of the property, and may have a creditor attach his or her interest. The heirs of a tenant in common receive the property interest on the tenant's death.

JOINT TENANCY

Joint tenants, like tenants in common, may sell their shares without the consent of the other owners, as well as have their interest attached by creditors. However, joint tenants all own equal shares of the property, and on the death of one tenant, the property is divided equally among the surviving joint owners.

TENANCY BY THE ENTIRETY

Tenancy by the entirety describes co-ownership by married couples: One owner cannot sell his or her interest without the other's consent, and creditors of one owner cannot attach the property. If one owner dies, the surviving spouse assumes full ownership. If the owners divorce, the interest becomes that of tenancy in common.

In each of the three types of co-ownership, all tenants have the equal right to occupy all the property. Besides this shared characteristic, other characteristics are listed in Exhibit 49-1.

Exhibit 49-1
Joint Ownership

TYPE OF OWNERSHIP	POSSIBLE DIVISION OF OWNERSHIP	RIGHTS OF OWNERS' CREDITORS	OWNERSHIP OF PROPERTY UPON DEATH OF AN OWNER
Tenancy in Common	Shares can be equal or unequal.	Creditors can attach any owner's interest.	Deceased owner's share is transferred to heirs.
Joint Tenancy	Shares are equal.	Creditors can attach any owner's interest.	Deceased owner's share is divided among other joint tenants.
Tenancy by the Entirety	Shares are equal.	Owner's creditors cannot attach interest.	Deceased owner's share goes to surviving spouse.

CONDOMINIUMS AND COOPERATIVES

Over the past 20 years, two types of joint ownership have become increasingly popular. One of these is the *condominium* interest. The holder of this type of interest has exclusive ownership rights of a "unit" within the condominium and shares tenancy in common with the other condominium owners over the land, buildings, and improvements of the "common areas" of the development. The architecture and use of common areas is regulated by a condominium association, which has the power to levy assessments against the unit owners for the maintenance of the common areas. This association is directed by a document known as a *Declaration of Covenants, Conditions and Restrictions* (called *CC&Rs),* which is filed when the condominium is formed. This document contains instructions for the architecture and use of the common areas, as well as for the condominium association and assessments.

This form of ownership often causes conflicts, such as the one we see in Case 49-2, a case in California.

The second type of joint ownership is often involved in ownership of apartments. This type of interest is known as a *cooperative.* In a cooperative, the investor resident is a shareholder in the corporation owning the apartment buildings; he or she will receive a permanent lease on one unit of the facility on acquiring stock. All the unit owners are governed by a board of directors, usually elected from among the unit owners to manage the property and establish rules for the owners. If a member violates these rules, the cooperative may evict the member and repurchase the evicted member's unit. In many cooperatives, one of the rules is that before an apartment can be sold, the board must approve of the buyer, a rule that sometimes makes it difficult for owners to sell their apartments.

CASE 49-2

NATORE A. NAHRSTEDT v. LAKESIDE VILLAGE CONDOMINIUM ASSOCIATION, INC., ET AL., AND RESPONDENTS

SUPREME COURT OF CALIFORNIA
8 CAL. 4TH 361, 878 P.2D 1275 (1994)

Plaintiff Natore Nahrstedt purchased a Lakeside Village Condominium that was governed by CC&Rs containing a restriction against keeping cats, dogs, and other animals in the condominium development. The plaintiff moved in with three cats. When the Association learned of the cats' presence, it demanded their removal and assessed fines against the plaintiff for each successive month that she remained in violation of the pet restriction.

The plaintiff filed a lawsuit against the Association, its officers, and two of its employees, asking the trial court to: invalidate the assessments; enjoin future assessments; award damages for violation of her privacy when the Association "peered" into her condominium unit; and declare the pet restriction "unreasonable" as applied to indoor cats (such as hers) that are not allowed free run of the project's common areas. She asserted that the restriction was "unreasonable" as applied to her because she kept her three cats indoors and because her cats were "noiseless" and "created no nuisance." She also claimed that she was unaware of the restriction when she moved in.

The Association counterclaimed for enforcement of fines that it had imposed, and argued that she was aware of the restrictions when she moved in.

Agreeing with the premise underlying the plaintiff's complaint, the Court of Appeals concluded that the homeowners association could enforce the restriction only upon proof that plaintiff's cats would be likely to interfere with the right of other homeowners "to the peaceful and quiet enjoyment of their property" and enjoined the enforcement of the restriction. However, the Court denied her other causes of action.

The plaintiff then appealed to the State Supreme Court.

JUSTICE KENNARD: [T]he issue before us is not whether in the abstract pets can have a beneficial effect on humans. Rather, the narrow issue here is whether a pet restriction that is contained in the recorded declaration of a condominium complex is enforceable against the challenge of a homeowner. The Legislature has required that courts enforce the covenants, conditions and restrictions contained in the recorded declaration of a common interest development "unless unreasonable."

Because a stable and predictable living environment is crucial to the success of condominiums and other common interest residential developments, and because recorded use restrictions are a primary means of ensuring this stability and predictability, the Legislature has afforded such restrictions a presumption of validity and has required of challengers that they demonstrate the restriction's "unreasonableness" by the deferential standard applicable to equitable servitudes.

Under this standard established by the Legislature, enforcement of a restriction does not depend upon the conduct of a particular condominium owner. Rather, the restriction must be uniformly enforced in the condominium development to which it was intended to apply unless the plaintiff owner can show that the burdens it imposes on affected properties so substantially outweigh the benefits of the restriction that it should not be enforced against any owner.

Restrictions on property use are not the only characteristic of common interest ownership. Ordinarily, such ownership also entails mandatory membership in an owners association, which, through an elected board of directors, is empowered to enforce any use restrictions contained in the project's declaration or master deed and to enact new rules governing the use and occupancy of property within the project.

. . . [O]wners associations "can be a powerful force for good or for ill" in their members' lives. Therefore, anyone who buys a unit in a common interest development with knowledge of its owners association's discretionary power accepts "the risk that the power may be used in a way that benefits the commonality but harms the individual." Generally, courts will uphold decisions made by the governing board of an owners association so long as they represent good faith efforts to further the purposes of the common interest development, are consistent with the development's governing documents, and comply with public policy. Thus, subordination of individual property rights to the collective judgment of the owners association together with restrictions on the use of real property comprise the chief attributes of owning property in a common interest development.

Of course, when an association determines that a unit owner has violated a use restriction, the association must do so in good faith, not in an arbitrary or capricious manner, and its enforcement procedures must be fair and applied uniformly, in reliance on the CC&R's.

As we have explained, when, as here, a restriction is contained in the declaration of the common interest development and is recorded with the county recorder, the restriction is presumed to be reasonable and will be enforced uniformly against all residents of the common interest development unless the restriction is arbitrary, imposes burdens on the use of lands it affects that substantially outweigh the restriction's benefits to the development's residents, or violates a fundamental public policy.

We conclude, as a matter of law, that the recorded pet restriction of the Lakeside Village condominium development prohibiting cats or dogs but allowing some other pets is not arbitrary, but is rationally related to health, sanitation and noise concerns legitimately held by residents of a high-density condominium project such as Lakeside Village, which includes 530 units in 12 separate 3-story buildings.

. . . [as to the privacy claim, there is no case law that provides] any support for the position that the recognized scope of autonomy privacy encompasses the right to keep pets: courts that have considered condominium pet restrictions have uniformly upheld them.

Affirmed, in favor of Defendant.

CRITICAL THINKING

The outcome in this case turned on the interpretation of an ambiguous phrase: "unless unreasonable." How did the court of appeals and the state supreme court differ in interpreting that phrase? Explain which interpretation you agree with and why.

ETHICAL DECISION MAKING

How would the public disclosure test affect the decision of the members of the association to enforce this restriction against the plaintiff?

Voluntary Transfer of Real Property

LEGAL REQUIREMENTS

The owner's ability to transfer real property is part of the value of property. Any or all of the owner's property may generally be transferred to anyone for any price or no price, as the owner desires.

However, to effectuate such a transfer, certain legal procedures must be followed. These procedures are *execution, delivery, acceptance,* and *recording,* with the last requirement required to protect the recipient of the property. These procedures are illustrated in Figure 49-2. Such a conveyance is presumed to be the conveyance of a fee simple absolute, unless the contrary is stated.

Figure 49-2 Steps in a Voluntary Transfer

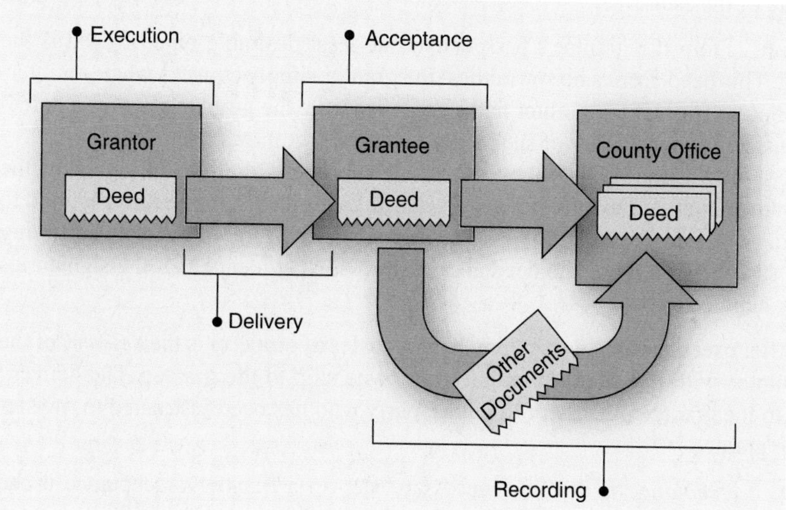

Execution. Transfer of property is initiated by the *execution* (or preparation and signing) of the deed, which is the instrument of conveyance. To be properly drafted, a deed must contain the following:

1. Identification of the grantor (the person conveying the property) and the grantee (the person receiving the property).
2. An expression of the grantor's intent to convey the property.
3. A legally sufficient description of the property, including its physical boundaries and any easements.
4. Any warranties or promises made by the grantor in conjunction with the conveyance.

General warranty deed. There are different types of deeds that may be used to transfer property voluntarily. The most commonly used deed is a **general warranty deed.** This type of deed is preferred by grantees because it contains certain warranties or promises by the grantor. Although such covenants may vary slightly from state to state, they generally include the following:

1. A promise that the grantor owns the interest that he or she is conveying.
2. A promise that the grantor has the right to convey the property.
3. A promise that there are no mortgages or liens against the property that are not stated in the deed.
4. A promise that the grantee will not be disturbed by anyone who has a better claim to title of the property and a promise to defend the grantee's title against such claims or to reimburse the grantee for any money spent in the defense and/or settlement of such claims.
5. The promise that the grantor will provide the grantee with any additional documents that the grantee needs to perfect his or her title to the property.

Special warranty deed. A grantor may not necessarily feel comfortable making all those warranties and may instead execute a *special warranty deed.* In making this type of transfer, the only promise the grantor is making is that he or she has not done anything to lessen the value of the estate.

Quitclaim deed. From the grantee's perspective, the least desirable type of deed is the *quitclaim* deed. This deed carries no warranties; the grantor simply conveys whatever interests he or she holds. Thus, if the grantor had a defective title, the grantee receives a defective title. Because of the insecurity of such a deed, very few grantees would accept it.

Whichever type of deed is chosen, once it has been properly drafted and signed by the grantor and grantee, it is said to have been *executed.* In many states, the deed is required to be witnessed or notarized. *Notarization* is the witness by an official of the state certifying that she or he saw the signing of the deed and was provided evidence that the signatories were who they claimed to be.

Delivery. After execution, the next step in legal transfer of property is the *delivery* of the deed to the grantee with the intent of transferring ownership to the grantee. The delivery may be made to the grantee directly or to a third party who has been instructed to transfer the deed to the grantee.

Acceptance. *Acceptance* is the final necessary step in a transfer. Acceptance is the grantee's expression of intent to possess the property, and it is assumed if the grantee retains possession of the deed.

Recording. **Recording** is not a required step for transfer of ownership. However, recording is so important to the subsequent rights of the grantee that it should be a part of every process of conveyance. Recording is achieved by filing the deed, with any other related documents, such as mortgages, with the appropriate county office, thus giving the world official notice of the transfer. Depending on the state, this office may be the county clerk's office or the county recorder's office. The significance of recording the transfer is demonstrated by the laws in many states giving ownership (in the case of two deeds allegedly conveying the same piece of realty) to the person whose deed was recorded first.

SALES TRANSACTIONS

The foregoing steps are necessary for the legal transfer of ownership of property. Transfer of real property is usually a little more complicated, however. In this section we will discuss the stages of a transfer of real estate resulting from the sale of the property.

Negotiation of a sales contract. Real property is generally transferred as a result of a sale. The owner is transferring his property in exchange for money. Generally, a person seeking to sell real property will contact a real estate agent, or broker. A broker is licensed by the state in which he or she is operating and is familiar with the real estate laws, as well as available properties. The agent generally is responsible for advertising the property, showing it to potential buyers, and guiding the seller through the formalities of the transfer. When a seller hires a broker, the broker works for the seller and receives a commission from the sale of the property.

In most states, a broker cannot act as an agent for both buyer and seller unless both parties consent. Given the differing interests of both the buyer and the seller, it would be difficult for a broker to really be an agent for both parties, or a dual agent. In some states, when the buyer does not have a broker or lawyer as a representative in the transaction, the seller's broker may handle all the necessary paperwork, but the buyer must sign a statement that acknowledges that he or she knows that the broker is working exclusively for the seller.

Traditionally, only the seller used a broker, but we are increasingly seeing the use of buyer's brokers. Buyer's brokers will be looking out for the buyer's interests in the transaction and will save the buyer time, as the broker can do much of the preliminary searching for property that the buyer would have otherwise done alone. The buyer's broker makes money by splitting the commission that the seller's agent was to receive.

Once the buyer finds a property she is interested in, she will make a written offer to purchase the property under specified conditions and will put up *earnest money.* Earnest money is designed to establish the seriousness of the offer. If the seller accepts the contract, the money will apply toward the purchase price of the property. If the buyer changes her mind before the seller accepts the offer, the earnest money is forfeited. If the seller does not accept the offer, the money is returned. In the case of General Motors' attempt to purchase land from residents of Poletown, because the residents did not accept General Motors' offer, they would not have been able to retain any earnest money that the company might have put up to buy the property.

The offer will contain a time limit within which the seller must accept the offer. Failure to accept within the time is considered a rejection. As with any contract, the seller may make a counteroffer at a different price or under different conditions.

Once the offer is accepted, a sales contract is drawn up in accordance with the terms of the offer. The contract will generally include a description of the property, the names and addresses of the parties, the purchase price, the type of deed, and who will bear the risk of loss if the property is destroyed before the sale has been completed.

The contract generally requires that the buyer put a deposit on the property in an account maintained by a neutral third party where the money can be held until all the necessary preliminary steps to the transfer can be made. This account is called an *escrow account.* The money from the escrow account, which is typically 10 percent of the purchase price, will be turned over to the seller at the *closing,* when the transfer is completed.

Seller's duty to disclose. One of the issues that often arises during the process of negotiating the sales contract is the extent to which the seller has a duty to disclose known defects to the buyer. The traditional rule was *caveat emptor,* or "Let the buyer beware." What this rule meant in terms of ordinary real estate transactions was that the seller had no obligation to tell the buyer about any problems. Can you tell which value is being replaced in the move from a doctrine of *caveat emptor* to a standard based more on reasonableness?

Today, most states impose a duty on the seller to warn the buyer about any defects he knows about that (1) the reasonable buyer would not be able to discover through a thorough examination of the property and (2) materially affect the value of the property. If the seller fails to disclose such a defect, and the buyer discovers it only after the sales transaction has been completed, the buyer can then sue the seller for fraud or misrepresentation.

If the house is a new home, most states provide that an implied warranty of habitability automatically arises out of the transaction. This warranty, comparable to the implied warranty of merchantability, provides that the seller guarantees that everything in the house is in reasonable working order and is of sound construction. For example, if you purchased a new home during the winter, and as soon as the weather got warm, you turned on the air conditioning but it did not run, you could sue the seller for breach of the implied warranty of habitability if he refused to fix the defective air conditioner.

Title examination. One of the things going on while the money is in escrow is the title examination. A title company or representative of the buyer or seller will search the county records to make sure that the seller in fact has legal title to the property, that there are no liens on the property, and that there are no restrictions on the property of which the buyer is not aware. A title that is free of such defects is called a **marketable title.**

If, during the course of the title search, a material defect is found that has not been disclosed in the sales contract, the seller is considered to have breached the contract. The buyer would then be able to file an action to rescind the contract, obtain damages, or get an order for specific performance with a reduction in price based on the loss in value caused by the defect. For example, a dispute arose between Sun International and Greenlands Realty during a title examination. Sun was attempting to purchase property from Greenlands but sought to void the sale, claiming that Greenlands did not possess marketable title to the property because a different, and then-defunct, realty company held part of the title. When the dispute went to court, a judge granted a motion for summary judgment in Greenlands' favor, determining that the defunct company had conveyed all its title in the property and therefore Greenlands did possess marketable title.

A title search may not reveal every single defect in the title, however, so most buyers purchase (or have the seller purchase for them) title insurance. Title insurance protects the buyer from losses resulting in a defect against the title. The title insurance company will represent the buyer in legal actions resulting from any title defects.

Financing. Most buyers do not have the cash in the bank to purchase property, so most sales contracts are conditional contracts, being conditioned on the buyer's being able to obtain financing within a certain period of time. Financing is obtained by going to a financial institution and obtaining a loan to pay for the property, in exchange for which the lender receives a security interest in the property, called a *mortgage.* While the payments are being made to the mortgagor, or lender, either the mortgagor or a third party will hold the title to the property. If the payments are not made, the property can be sold and the mortgagor will receive enough money from the proceeds of the sale to cover the loan and the expenses of the sale. If any funds are left over from the sale, they will be returned to the buyer.

Closing. Once the financing has been obtained, the meeting at which the transfer of title actually takes place is held. This is where the delivery and acceptance occur. The seller signs over the deed, and the buyer gives the seller a check for the amount due. The mortgage on the property, if one was necessary, is executed at this time. Following the closing, the deed and mortgage are recorded, as explained previously.

Involuntary Transfer of Real Property

The transfer of the owner's interest in real property is not always voluntary. Transfer of property may also take place without the owner's knowledge and even, in some cases, against his or her will, by either adverse possession or condemnation.

ADVERSE POSSESSION

Adverse possession describes the actions of a person who takes ownership of property by treating a piece of real property as his or her own, without protest or permission from the owner. Most states have established statutes determining a length of time after which such a possessor receives the ownership interest in the property. The exact lengths of time vary from state to state, but such adverse possession must be *actual* (the person lives on or uses the land as an owner would), *open* (not secretive), and *notorious* (without the owner's permission). In some states, the adverse possessor must have performed certain acts such as the payment of real estate taxes. In other states, such possession must have taken place "under color of title"; in other words, the adverse possessor was operating under the assumption that he or she actually held the title to the land.

Case 49-3 illustrates how difficult it sometimes is to determine whether or not the party really is entitled to the land by adverse possession.

CASE 49-3 JUNG KEE KIM v. DOUVAL CORPORATION, D/B/A WASH FAIR

SUPREME COURT OF VIRGINIA
2000 WL 429446 (2000)

Plaintiff Kim purchased property identified as Parcel 4-A in 1994. The property was adjacent to parcel 4-E. Defendant Douval Corporation had operated a car wash, Wash Fair, on Parcel 4-E since 1961, under leases with various owners of Parcel 4-E. M. Bond managed the car wash from 1962 until 1977, when he and his wife purchased all the shares of the Defendant Douval Corporation.

Since 1962, a portion of Parcel 4-A had been used by the car wash. In 1996, Jung attempted to license the use of this portion of his property to the defendant. When the defendant refused, Plaintiff Kim brought an action to eject the car wash from his property. The defendant corporation that owned car wash counterclaimed, alleging adverse possession of the strip of property in question.

The jury returned a verdict in favor of the plaintiff, and awarded damages, but the Circuit Court granted the corporation's motion to set aside judgment and entered judgment for corporation. Kim appealed.

JUSTICE KINSER: The parties agree that the disputed property is a triangular-shaped tract bounded on one side by the property line between Parcels 4-A and 4-E, and on the other side by a concrete curb situated on Parcel 4-A. The curb has been in place since at least 1962, but the record does not disclose precisely when, or by whom, it was erected.

According to Mr. Bond, Wash Fair has used the disputed property since 1962. Initially, it utilized the triangular strip of Parcel 4-A as a "driveway" for cars entering and departing the car wash. Wash Fair also erected a sign pole that abutted the concrete curb and placed asphalt on the disputed area over to the curb.

In 1969, Wash Fair installed outside lighting at the car wash by placing poles and concrete bases on the disputed property along the curb. In order to lay the electrical conduit for those lights, the asphalt had to be dug up. After the installation of the lights was completed, Wash Fair paved the disputed area with asphalt again. During the ensuing years, Wash Fair asphalted the area on several more occasions. It also erected a fence at the rear of the disputed property in 1969 and replaced the fence in 1982 or 1983. Finally, Wash Fair painted the concrete curb at least twice each year and placed planters in the disputed area in 1990.

Jung testified that Wash Fair installed vacuums on the disputed property approximately six or seven months after he purchased Parcel 4-A in 1983. Jung did not give Wash Fair permission to install the vacuums, nor did Wash Fair request permission from him to do so. Jung also testified that he "didn't mind" Wash Fair's using part of his property because Wash Fair needed it. Jung likewise did not object when Wash Fair paved the disputed property with new asphalt because the asphalt benefited his property.

Mr. Bond admitted that Wash Fair used the disputed property even though he knew it was not part of Parcel 4-E. However, he asserted that no one instructed Wash Fair not to use or make improvements on the triangular strip of Parcel 4-A over to the curb. Mr. Bond further testified that Wash Fair never received permission from any of the owners of Parcel 4-A to occupy and use the disputed portion of that parcel.

However, Kim, through his attorney, offered Douval a license agreement to use the disputed strip of Parcel 4-A in 1995. According to the attorney, Mr. Bond claimed at that time that he did not know about the encroachment on Parcel 4-A and asserted that he "had built entirely on the Wash Fair property."

Kim established his claim for ejectment by introducing evidence to prove his chain of title for Parcel 4-A and his damages resulting from Douval's actions. Kim also testified that he asked Douval to remove the vacuums from the disputed strip of Parcel 4-A and that it refused to do so.

"To establish title to real property by adverse possession, a claimant must prove actual, hostile, exclusive, visible, and continuous possession, under a claim of right, for the statutory period of 15 years." The claimant bears the burden of proving the elements of adverse possession by clear and convincing evidence.

Kim acknowledges that Douval's possession of the disputed strip of Parcel 4-A has been open and notorious. However, he argues that there is a conflict in the evidence and the reasonable inferences that can be drawn from the evidence with regard to the question whether Douval's possession was "hostile" under a claim of right. In fact, the circuit court noted in its letter opinion that this issue was the only genuinely disputed one at trial.

It is well-established that a claimant's possession is "hostile" if it is under "a claim of right and adverse to the right of the true owner." The phrase "claim of right," when used in the context of adverse possession, refers to the intent of a claimant to use land as the claimant's own to the exclusion of all others. The existence of a claim of right does not depend on the claimant having any actual title or right to the property. However, "[w]here the original entry on another's land was by agreement or permission, possession regardless of its duration presumptively continues as it began, in the absence of an explicit disclaimer."

As Kim notes, the record does not indicate the circumstances under which Wash Fair's possession of the disputed strip of Parcel 4-A began. Wash Fair commenced operating the car wash in 1961. Mr. Bond testified that Wash Fair was using the disputed property in 1962.

However, we do not know whether, at that time, Wash Fair's landlord, who owned Parcel 4-E, obtained permission from the owner of Parcel 4-A for Wash Fair to utilize the disputed property. Although Mr. Bond began managing Wash Fair in 1962 and testified that he had no knowledge of any agreement between Wash Fair's landlord and the owner of Parcel 4-A with regard to Wash Fair's use of the disputed property, he and Mrs. Bond did not become Wash Fair's landlord until 1984 when they purchased Parcel 4-E. Thus, he would not have been a party to any such agreement prior to 1984. Mr. Bond admitted that some of the previous owners are deceased and that he therefore could not confer with them about whether any such agreement existed before he and Mrs. Bond became Wash Fair's landlord.

In contrast, we know that Jung, a prior owner of Parcel 4-A, did not give Wash Fair permission to install the vacuums on the disputed strip of property in 1983, shortly after he purchased Parcel 4-A. Also, Kim asked Douval to remove those vacuums in 1995, but Douval refused to do so.

Douval argues that its actual occupation, use, and improvement of the disputed property as if it were in fact an owner establishes that its possession was under a claim of right. We agree that a claim of right can be inferred from unequivocal conduct that is inconsistent with any other reasonable inference. However, whether the conduct relied upon is sufficient to establish a claim of right is generally a question for the jury.

Upon reviewing the evidence in the light most favorable to Kim, we conclude that conflicting inferences can be drawn from the evidence with regard to the questions whether Wash Fair began its possession and use of the disputed property under a claim of right, or with the permission of the owner of Parcel 4-A; whether, if Wash Fair's possession started with permission from the owner of Parcel 4-A, the possession later changed to one under a claim of right; and whether any possession by Wash Fair under a claim of right has continued for the requisite 15-year statutory period. The jury resolved the conflicting inferences in favor of Kim, and the inferences "necessarily underlying the conclusion reflected in the verdict are reasonably deducible from the evidence." Thus, we conclude that the circuit court erred in setting aside the jury verdict.

REVERSED in favor the plaintiff.

CRITICAL THINKING

What evidence, which was not available to the court, would have been helpful to it in its decision making?

ETHICAL DECISION MAKING

There is a conflict between two values presented by this case. Which value did the judge further by his decision, and which received less consideration?

The laws of adverse possession in this country are very similar to the law in Japan, where adverse possession of property for 20 years leads to a transfer of ownership as long as the possessor began possession with a nonnegligent good-faith belief that he or she had legal title to the property.

CONDEMNATION

Condemnation is the legal process by which a transfer of property is made against the protest of the property owner. As you will remember from earlier sections in Chapter 5 discussing the taking clause of the Fifth Amendment, the government has a constitutional right to take private property for the use of the public, upon providing the owner fair compensation. This right may be exercised at any government level, and it sometimes is exercised on behalf of a private company operating to benefit the public. For example, in the Poletown case, a private business argued that the creation of new jobs was essential to the economic future of the area, and reducing unemployment through job creation took precedence over the residents' individual property rights.

When the government decides to exercise its power of eminent domain, it will first make an offer to purchase the property for what it believes is the fair market value. If the owner either does not want to sell or feels the price is too low, the government will initiate a condemnation proceeding, and the court will determine whether the government body bringing the action has a valid claim that the taking is for a legitimate public purpose. If the court determines that, in fact, the taking of the property will benefit the public interest, the court will then determine the fair market value of the property. This price will be paid to the owner, and the property will be transferred to the government.

It is sometimes difficult to determine whether the exercise of eminent domain is actually for the public's benefit when the property will be conveyed by the government to another private individual. In the opening scenario describing the Poletown case, we see that a private corporation will clearly benefit from the government's taking of the property of the residents of the Poletown community. Could this benefit be described as being for a public use? Since the 1980s, businesses increasingly have been appealing to cities to use their power of eminent domain to assist the businesses in acquiring land that the owners did not want to sell. As this transference of property from one private individual to another is for the alleged public use of economic development, an increasing number of state supreme courts began to address the issue of whether economic development was a public use under the constraints of the Fifth Amendment. Some state supreme courts found that job creation and expansion of the tax base did constitute public use, while other courts found that they did not constitute public use. The U.S. Supreme Court finally settled the issue—at least for the present time—in the 5-4 decision presented in Case 49-4. As you read this case, ask yourself whether there are any significant differences between the facts in *Poletown* and those in Case 49-4.

CASE 49-4

KELO v. CITY OF NEW LONDON
UNITED STATES SUPREME COURT
126 S. CT. 326 (2005)

The city of New London approved an integrated development plan designed "to create in excess of 1,000 jobs, to increase tax and other revenues, and to revitalize an economically distressed city, including its downtown and waterfront areas." Using its development agent, the city purchased most of the property it needed for the project from willing sellers. A few property owners refused to sell, and so the city initiated condemnation proceedings to take their property. The property owners argued that the taking of their properties would violate the "public use" restriction in the Fifth Amendment's Takings Clause. The trial court granted a permanent restraining order prohibiting the taking of some of the properties, but allowing the taking of others. The Connecticut Supreme Court affirmed in part and reversed in part, upholding all of the proposed takings. The United States Supreme Court agreed to hear the property owners' appeal.

JUSTICE STEVENS: . . . On the one hand, it has long been accepted that the sovereign may not take the property of *A* for the sole purpose of transferring it to another private party *B,* even though *A* is paid just compensation. On the other hand, it is equally clear that a State may transfer property from one private party to another if future "use by the public" is the purpose of the taking. . . . Neither of these propositions, however, determines the disposition of this case.

As for the first proposition, the City would no doubt be forbidden from taking petitioners' land for the purpose of conferring a private benefit on a particular private party. . . . Nor would the City be allowed to take property under the mere pretext of a public purpose, when its actual purpose was to bestow a private benefit. The takings before us, however, would be executed pursuant to a "carefully considered" development plan. The trial judge and all the members of the Supreme Court of Connecticut agreed that there was no evidence of an illegitimate purpose in this case. Therefore, the City's development plan was not adopted "to benefit a particular class of identifiable individuals."

. . . On the other hand, this is not a case in which the City is planning to open the condemned land—at least not in its entirety—to use by the general public. Nor will the private lessees of the land in any sense be required to operate like common carriers, making their services available to all comers. But although such a projected use would be sufficient to satisfy the public use requirement, this "Court long ago rejected any literal requirement that condemned property be put into use for the general public."

The disposition of this case therefore turns on the question whether the City's development plan serves a "public purpose." Without exception, our cases have defined that concept broadly, reflecting our longstanding policy of deference to legislative judgments in this field. In *Berman v. Parker* (1954), this Court upheld a redevelopment plan targeting a blighted area of Washington, D.C., in which most of the housing for the area's 5,000 inhabitants was beyond repair. Under the plan, the area would be condemned and part of it utilized for the construction of streets, schools, and other public facilities. The remainder of the land would be leased or sold to private parties for the purpose of redevelopment, including the construction of low-cost housing. The owner of a department store located in the area challenged the condemnation, pointing out that his store was not itself blighted and arguing that the creation of a "better balanced, more attractive community" was not a valid public use. Justice Douglas refused to evaluate this claim in isolation, deferring instead to the legislative and agency judgment that the area "must be planned as a whole" for the plan to be successful. The Court explained that "community redevelopment programs need not, by force of the Constitution, be on a piecemeal basis—lot by lot, building by building." The public use underlying the taking was unequivocally affirmed. . . .

In *Hawaii Housing Authority v. Midkiff,* the Court considered a Hawaii statute whereby fee title was taken from lessors and transferred to lessees in order to reduce the concentration of land ownership. We unanimously upheld the statute and rejected the Ninth Circuit's view that it was "a naked attempt on the part of the state of Hawaii to take the property of A and transfer it to B solely for B's private use and benefit." Reaffirming *Berman's* deferential approach to legislative judgments in this field, we concluded that the State's purpose of eliminating the "social and economic evils of a land oligopoly" qualified as a valid public use. . . . [I]t is only the taking's purpose, and not its mechanics," that matters in determining public use.

. . . For more than a century, our public use jurisprudence has wisely eschewed rigid formulas and intrusive scrutiny in favor of affording legislatures broad latitude in determining what public needs justify the use of the takings power.

Those who govern the City were not confronted with the need to remove blight in the Fort Trumbull area, but their determination that the area was sufficiently distressed to justify a program of economic rejuvenation is entitled to our deference. The City has carefully formulated an economic development plan that it believes will provide appreciable benefits to the community, including—but by no means limited to—new jobs and increased tax revenue. As with other exercises in urban planning and development, the City is endeavoring to coordinate a variety of commercial, residential, and recreational uses of land, with the hope that they will form a whole greater than the sum of its parts. To effectuate this plan, the City has invoked a state statute that specifically authorizes the use of eminent domain to promote economic development. Given the comprehensive character of the plan, the thorough deliberation that preceded its adoption, and the limited scope of our review, it is appropriate for us, as it was in *Berman,* to resolve the challenges of the individual owners, not on a piecemeal basis, but rather in light of the entire plan. Because that plan unquestionably serves a public purpose, the takings challenged here satisfy the public use requirement of the Fifth Amendment.

To avoid this result, petitioners urge us to adopt a new bright-line rule that economic development does not qualify as a public use. Putting aside the unpersuasive suggestion that the City's plan will provide only purely economic benefits, neither precedent nor logic supports petitioners' proposal. Promoting economic development is a traditional and long accepted function of government. There is, moreover, no principled way of distinguishing economic development from the other public purposes that we have recognized. . . . Clearly, there is no basis for exempting economic development from our traditionally broad understanding of public purpose.

Petitioners contend that using eminent domain for economic development impermissibly blurs the boundary between public and private takings. Again, our cases foreclose this objection. [T]he government's pursuit of a public purpose will often benefit individual private parties. For example, in *Midkiff,* the forced transfer of property conferred a direct and significant benefit on those lessees who were previously unable to purchase their homes. . . . Our rejection of that contention has particular relevance to the instant case: "The public end may be as well or better served through an agency of private enterprise than through a department of government—or so the Congress might conclude. We cannot say that public ownership is the sole method of promoting the public purposes of community redevelopment projects."

It is further argued that without a bright-line rule nothing would stop a city from transferring citizen *A*'s property to citizen *B* for the sole reason that citizen *B* will put the property to a more productive use and thus pay more taxes. Such a one-to-one transfer of property, executed outside the confines of an integrated development plan, is not presented in this case. While such an unusual exercise of government power would certainly raise a suspicion that a private purpose was afoot, the hypothetical cases posited by petitioners can be confronted if and when they arise. They do not warrant the crafting of an artificial restriction on the concept of public use.

Alternatively, petitioners maintain that for takings of this kind we should require a "reasonable certainty" that the expected public benefits will actually accrue. Such a rule, however, would represent an even greater departure from our precedent. "When the legislature's purpose is legitimate and its means are not irrational, our cases make clear that empirical debates over the wisdom of takings—no less than debates over the wisdom of other kinds of socioeconomic legislation—are not to be carried out in the federal courts." . . . The disadvantages of a heightened form of review are especially pronounced in this type of case. Orderly implementation of a comprehensive redevelopment plan obviously requires that the legal rights of all interested parties be established before new construction can be commenced. A constitutional rule that required postponement of the judicial approval of every condemnation until the likelihood of success of the plan had been assured would unquestionably impose a significant impediment to the successful consummation of many such plans.

Just as we decline to second-guess the City's considered judgments about the efficacy of its development plan, we also decline to second-guess the City's determinations as to what lands it needs to acquire in order to effectuate the project. . . . Once the question of the public purpose has been decided, the amount and character of land to be taken for the project and the need for a particular tract to complete the integrated plan rests in the discretion of the legislative branch.

. . . We emphasize that nothing in our opinion precludes any State from placing further restrictions on its exercise of the takings power. Indeed, many States already impose "public use" requirements that are stricter than the federal baseline. Some of these requirements have been established as a matter of state constitutional law, while others are expressed in state eminent domain statutes that carefully limit the grounds upon which takings may be exercised. As the submissions of the parties and their *amici* make clear, the necessity and wisdom of using eminent domain to promote economic development are certainly matters of legitimate public debate. This Court's authority, however, extends only to determining whether the City's proposed condemnations are for a "public use" within the meaning of the Fifth Amendment to the Federal Constitution.

AFFIRMED in favor of respondent City of New London.

JUSTICE O'CONNOR, WITH WHOM THE CHIEF JUSTICE, JUSTICE SCALIA, AND JUSTICE THOMAS JOIN, DISSENTING: Over two centuries ago, just after the Bill of Rights was ratified, Justice Chase wrote: "An ACT of the Legislature (for I cannot call it a law) contrary to the great first principles of the social compact, cannot be considered a rightful exercise of legislative authority. . . . A few instances will suffice to explain what I mean. . . . [A] law that takes property from A. and gives it to B: It is against all reason and justice, for a people to entrust a Legislature with SUCH powers; and, therefore, it cannot be presumed that they have done it." . . .

Today the Court abandons this long-held, basic limitation on government power. Under the banner of economic development, all private property is now vulnerable to being taken and transferred to another private owner, so long as it might be upgraded—*i.e.,* given to an owner who will use it in a way that the legislature deems more beneficial to the public—in the process. To reason, as the Court does, that the incidental public benefits resulting from the subsequent ordinary use of private property render economic development takings "for public use" is to wash out any distinction between private and public use of property—and thereby effectively to delete the words "for public use" from the Takings Clause of the Fifth Amendment. Accordingly I respectfully dissent.

. . . [W]e have read the Fifth Amendment's language to impose two distinct conditions on the exercise of eminent domain: "the taking must be for a 'public use' and 'just compensation' must be paid to the owner." . . . These two limitations serve to protect "the security of Property," . . . Together they ensure stable property ownership by providing safeguards against excessive, unpredictable, or unfair use of the government's eminent domain power—particularly against those owners who, for whatever reasons, may be unable to protect themselves in the political process against the majority's will.

While the Takings Clause presupposes that government can take private property without the owner's consent, the just compensation requirement spreads the cost of condemnations and thus "prevents the public from loading upon one individual more than his just share of the burdens of government." . . . The public use requirement, in turn, imposes a more basic limitation, circumscribing the very scope of the eminent domain power: Government may compel an individual to forfeit her property for the *public's* use, but not for the benefit of another private person. This requirement promotes fairness as well as security. . . .

Where is the line between "public" and "private" property use? We give considerable deference to legislatures' determinations about what governmental activities will advantage the public. But were the political branches the sole arbiters of the public-private distinction, the Public Use Clause would amount to little more than hortatory fluff. An external, judicial check on how the public use requirement is interpreted, however limited, is necessary if this constraint on government power is to retain any meaning. . . . But "public ownership" and "use-by-the-public" are sometimes too constricting and impractical ways to define the scope of the Public Use Clause. Thus we have allowed that, in certain circumstances and to meet certain exigencies, takings that serve a public purpose also satisfy the Constitution even if the property is destined for subsequent private use. . . .

The Court's holdings in *Berman* and *Midkiff* were true to the principle underlying the Public Use Clause. In both those cases, the extraordinary, precondemnation use of the targeted property inflicted affirmative harm on society—in *Berman* through blight resulting from extreme poverty and in *Midkiff* through oligopoly resulting from extreme wealth. And in both cases, the relevant legislative body had found that eliminating the existing property use was necessary to remedy the harm. Thus a public purpose was realized when the harmful use was eliminated. Because each taking *directly* achieved a public benefit, it did not matter that the property was turned over to private use. Here, in contrast, New London does not claim that Susette Kelo's and Wilhelmina Dery's well-maintained homes are the source of any social harm. . . .

In moving away from our decisions sanctioning the condemnation of harmful property use, the Court today significantly expands the meaning of public use. It holds that the sovereign may take private property currently put to ordinary private use, and give it over for new, ordinary private use, so long as the new use is predicted to generate some secondary benefit for the public—such as increased tax revenue, more jobs, maybe even aesthetic pleasure. But nearly any lawful use of real private property can be said to generate some incidental benefit to the public. Thus, if predicted (or even guaranteed) positive side-effects are enough to render transfer from one private party to another constitutional, then the words "for public use" do not realistically exclude *any* takings, and thus do not exert any constraint on the eminent domain power.

CRITICAL THINKING

When you examine the reasoning in both the majority and the dissenting opinions, you can see that a significant conflict between the opinions exists because of the ambiguity of a key term. Identify this term, and explain how its interpretation affects the reasoning. How do you think the courts should define the term?

ETHICAL DECISION MAKING

Who are the primary stakeholders involved in this case? How are they affected by the ruling? What are the implications of this ruling in terms of the distinction between public and private property? Further, this case highlights an important value conflict. Can you explain how certain values would lead one to support the majority opinion, whereas different values would lead to support for the dissenting opinion? How might holding a different value determine how one predicts the implications of this ruling?

Whereas the *Kelo* and *Poletown* cases involve government attempts to take property from individuals to sell to companies, sometimes governments seek to take the property of one company for use by another company. For instance, in June 2000, Costco, a large retail chain, wanted to expand its warehouse in Lancaster, California. Afraid of losing the large store, which threatened to move if it could not expand, the city considered using its eminent domain powers to acquire an adjacent 99 Cents Only store so that Costco could obtain the property. This example demonstrates that even businesses may be at risk of losing their property to larger, more powerful businesses.

The state courts had been split fairly evenly between those who supported a more narrow view of public use and those recognizing a broader view, so many people were surprised at the fact that this ruling generated a rare outcry from a number of congresspersons. Within a week of the decision, some members of Congress were drafting a bill attempting to limit the use of eminent domain for economic development purposes, while others were criticizing the proposed legislation as an unconstitutional attempt to interfere with the Supreme Court's exercise of its proper role.

The response to the *Kelo* decision was widespread. President Bush issued an executive order limiting the taking of private property by the federal government to "situations in which the taking is for public use, with just compensation, and for the purpose of benefiting the general public, and not merely for the purpose of advancing the economic interest of private parties to be given ownership or use of the property taken." During the year and a half after *Kelo,* 30 state legislatures enacted statutes limiting the use of eminent domain. Additionally, in 2006, nine states passed ballot measures restricting the definition of public use for purposes of eminent domain. Thus, it appears that the ultimate impact of the *Kelo* decision will be the opposite of what that decision held; by statute, a much more restrictive definition of public use will govern government takings.

Restrictions on Land Use

No one is allowed to use the land in a *completely* unrestricted manner. As previously indicated, the doctrine of waste prohibits some uses and abuses of land. There are other such restrictions, both voluntary and involuntary.

RESTRICTIVE COVENANTS

Restrictive covenants, that is, promises to use or not to use one's land in particular ways, may be voluntarily entered into by property owners. These covenants, which are generally included in the deeds, are binding on the owners as long as the covenants are for lawful acts. For example, a restrictive covenant not to construct only single-story dwelling houses on property would be lawful and enforceable, whereas a covenant never to convey property to a woman would be unlawful and thus unenforceable.

The covenants that restrict the activities of the owner of the land must be related to the land. In other words, a restriction that the land never be used for hog farming is related to the land, whereas a restriction that the owner of the land always ride a bicycle to work is not, and therefore only the first restriction would be valid. Finally, the successors to the original makers of the covenant must have notice of the covenant.

The most common use of restrictive covenants today is in planned urban developments sometimes called *planned communities.* When a developer builds a planned community, each deed contains a promise on the part of the grantee to abide by the rules of the community that have been established initially by the developer, as well as those that may be established by a homeowners' association that will consist of representatives of the future homeowners. Many people who move into these developments subsequently become unhappy because the restrictions imposed on the owners can be substantial. Others like planned communities because the restrictions help to ensure that the properties within the community maintain their value. As a general rule, courts will uphold these restrictive covenants.

ZONING

Zoning, government restriction of property use, is a legitimate exercise of the state's police power. Zoning allows for the orderly growth and development of a community and protects the health, safety, and welfare of its citizens. Zoning commonly restricts the type of use to which land may be put, such as residential, commercial, industrial, or agricultural. Zoning laws may also regulate land use in geographic areas based on such factors as the intensity (single or multifamily dwellings), the size, or the placement of buildings.

When new zoning ordinances are enacted by a community, there is generally a public hearing on the proposed change in zoning. Often, the community allows a *nonconforming use* of a particular property when the zoning of an area changes. This exception to the zoning law occurs when the property in question was being used for a purpose not allowed under the new zoning statutes but, because of the prior use, the owner is allowed to continue using the property in the nonconforming manner.

A landowner who wishes to use her or his land in a manner prohibited by zoning laws may seek a variance from the appropriate government unit, usually a zoning board or a planning commission. A *variance* is permission to use a piece of land in a manner prohibited by the zoning laws. Variances are generally granted to prevent undue hardship.

Sometimes, those negatively affected by a zoning law challenge that ordinance. Zoning is allowed under the police power, the power of the state to regulate to protect the health, safety, and welfare of the public. To be a valid exercise of such power, the zoning ordinance must not be arbitrary or unreasonable. An ordinance is unreasonable if (1) it

connecting to the core

Economics

Eminent Domain and Market Forces

Markets depend on voluntary transactions to allocate resources efficiently. Individuals are willing to buy goods as long as they get more benefit out of the goods than the price they pay for them. Similarly, individuals are willing to sell goods as long as the price they receive is higher than the benefit they would get from keeping the goods. Thus, voluntary transactions benefit the buyer and seller because they are both better off after making the exchange.

Economists call the difference between the price a buyer was willing to pay for a good and the price she actually pays for it her *consumer surplus.* Similarly, the difference between the price at which a seller was willing to sell a good and the price at which she actually sold it is her *producer surplus.* Consumer surplus and producer surplus are measures of how much better off market transactions make people. As long as individuals make transactions voluntarily, they enjoy a producer or consumer surplus.

Government's eminent domain power, however, distorts market forces by allowing involuntary transfers of property, as long as government uses the property for "public benefit." If government forces a private property owner to sell her property, we know she is worse off as a result of the transaction. (After all, if the transaction makes her better off, she would have voluntarily agreed to sell her property.) Hence, her producer surplus is negative. If the taking is to yield a net public benefit, it must produce public benefits large enough to offset her negative producer surplus.

But when government uses its eminent domain power to transfer private property from one individual to another, it distorts the market in another way, too. When a business receives property to use for economic development from the government for less than it would have had to pay the owner, it is effectively receiving a subsidy from the government. *Subsidies* are government payments to producers. When government subsidizes some firms' land purchases, those firms can produce their products at a lower cost and earn higher economic profits than firms that did not receive the government subsidy.

Economics can't tell government whether it should exercise its eminent domain power to take private property from one individual and give it to another. Economics can, however, tell government about the costs that result when it distorts market forces.

Source: David C. Colander, *Microeconomics,* 4th ed. (McGraw-Hill, 2001).

Case Nugget — Restrictive Covenants

Country Club Dist. Homes Assn. v. Country Club Christian Church
Missouri Court of Appeals
118 S.W.3d 185 (Mo. Ct. App. 2003)

All the property in the Hampstead Gardens Subdivision was covered by a restrictive covenant providing that "none of said lots shall be improved, used nor occupied for other than private residence purposes." The Country Club Christian Church owned three lots adjacent to the lot on which its church was located. It decided that it wanted to turn these lots into parking lots, but the Country Club District Homeowners Association sued to enforce the restrictive covenant and obtain a permanent injunction prohibiting the church from violating the agreement and turning the property into parking lots. The trial court upheld the agreement and granted the injunction. The appellate court affirmed the lower court's ruling, stating that the terms of a restrictive covenant will not be enforced only in a case where a defendant can prove that (1) there has been a radical change in conditions since the covenant was entered into, (2) as a result of the change, enforcement of the restrictions will work an undue hardship on the defendant, and (3) continuing enforcement of the restriction provides no substantial benefit to the plaintiff. Given this standard, it is fairly easy to see why most restrictive covenants are upheld.

encroaches on the private property rights of landowners without a substantial relationship to a legitimate government purpose, or (2) there is no reasonable relationship between the ends to be obtained and the means used to attain those ends. An unreasonable ordinance is one that encroaches on private property rights either without a substantial benefit to public health, safety, or welfare or without a reasonable relationship between the government's purpose in the ordinance and the means the government uses to obtain its purpose.

Because zoning is intended to regulate property, not to take it, it is unreasonable for a zoning ordinance to destroy the economic value of a piece of property. In an instance where this occurs, the zoning is considered a constructive taking of the property, and the owner of the property is entitled to fair compensation. Frequently, an owner will challenge zoning regulations on such grounds. However, such a challenge is usually unsuccessful.

OTHER STATUTORY RESTRICTIONS ON LAND USE

Another instance, besides zoning, of government restriction of property is the passing in some states of historic preservation statutes: owners of buildings with historical importance are subject to certain restrictions on the use and maintenance of such buildings. The property owner is usually required by such statutes to keep the building in good repair. Also, if the owner wishes to alter the building's facade, his or her plans must be approved before any modifications are made.

Any instance of the government's use of its police power to restrict private use of property by individuals may be challenged on constitutional grounds. In Case 49-5, the Court clarified and toughened the requirement for government planners to produce specific justifications when they issue building permits on the condition that a party renders part of the property for public use. This is a type of regulation that is being increasingly challenged.

CASE 49-5

DOLAN v. CITY OF TIGARD
UNITED STATES SUPREME COURT
114 S. CT. 2309 (1994)

When Dolan applied for a permit from the City of Tigard to expand her store and pave her parking lot, the city conditioned granting her permit on her dedication of a portion of her property for (1) a public greenway to minimize flooding that would otherwise be likely to result from her construction and (2) a pedestrian/bicycle pathway to decrease congestion in the business district.

Dolan appealed the decision of the planning commission to the Land Use Board of Appeals, which found that the land dedication requirements were reasonably related to her proposed construction, and therefore did not constitute a taking. The State Court of Appeals and State Supreme Court both affirmed the decision in favor of the city. Dolan appealed to the United States Supreme Court.

JUSTICE REHNQUIST: One of the principal purposes of the Takings Clause is "to bar Government from forcing some people alone to bear public burdens which, in all fairness and justice, should be borne by the public as a whole." Without question, had the city simply required petitioner to dedicate a strip of land along Fanno Creek for public use, rather than conditioning the grant of her permit to redevelop her property on such a dedication, a taking would have occurred. Such public access would deprive petitioner of the right to exclude others, "one of the most essential sticks in the bundle of rights that are commonly characterized as property."

On the other side of the ledger, the authority of state and local governments to engage in land use planning has been sustained against constitutional challenge. . . . A land use regulation does not effect a taking if it "substantially advance[s] legitimate state interests" and does not "den[y] an owner economically viable use of his land."

Petitioner contends that the city has forced her to choose between the building permit and her right under the Fifth Amendment to just compensation for the public easements. Petitioner does not quarrel with the city's authority to exact some forms of dedication as a condition for the grant of a building permit, but challenges the showing made by the city to justify these exactions. She argues that the city has identified "no special benefits" conferred on her, and has not identified any "special quantifiable burdens" created by her new store that would justify the particular dedications required from her which are not required from the public at large.

In evaluating petitioner's claim, we must first determine whether the "essential nexus" exists between the "legitimate state interest" and the permit condition exacted by the city. If we find that a nexus exists, we must then decide the required degree of connection between the exactions and the projected impact of the proposed development.

Undoubtedly, the prevention of flooding along Fanno Creek and the reduction of traffic congestion in the Central Business District qualify as the type of legitimate public purposes we have upheld. It seems equally obvious that a nexus exists between preventing flooding along Fanno Creek and limiting development within the creek's 100-year floodplain. Petitioner proposes to double the size of her retail store and to pave her now-gravel parking lot, thereby expanding the impervious surface on the property and increasing the amount of stormwater run-off into Fanno Creek.

The same may be said for the city's attempt to reduce traffic congestion by providing for alternative means of transportation. In theory, a pedestrian/bicycle pathway provides a useful alternative means of transportation for workers and shoppers: "Pedestrians and bicyclists occupying dedicated spaces for walking and/or bicycling . . . remove potential vehicles from streets, resulting in an overall improvement in total transportation system flow."

The second part of our analysis requires us to determine whether the degree of the exactions demanded by the city's permit conditions bear the required relationship to the projected impact of petitioner's proposed development.

"The distinction, therefore, which must be made between an appropriate exercise of the police power and an improper exercise of eminent domain is whether the requirement has some reasonable relationship or nexus to the use to which the property is being made or is merely being used as an excuse for taking property simply because at that particular moment the landowner is asking the city for some license or permit."

We think a term such as "rough proportionality" best encapsulates what we hold to be the requirement of the Fifth Amendment. No precise mathematical calculation is required, but the city must make some sort of individualized determination that the required dedication is related both in nature and extent to the impact of the proposed development.

It is axiomatic that increasing the amount of impervious surface will increase the quantity and rate of stormwater flow from petitioner's property. The city has never said why a public greenway, as opposed to a private one, was required in the interest of flood control. We conclude that the findings upon which the city relies do not show the required reasonable relationship between the floodplain easement and the petitioner's proposed new building.

With respect to the pedestrian/bicycle pathway, we have no doubt that the city was correct in finding that the larger retail sales facility proposed by petitioner will increase traffic on the streets of the Central Business District. Dedications for streets, sidewalks, and other public ways are generally reasonable exactions to avoid excessive congestion from a proposed property use. But on the records before us, the city has not met its burden of demonstrating that the additional number of vehicle and bicycle trips generated by the petitioner's development reasonably relate to the city's requirement for a dedication of the pedestrian/bicycle pathway easement.

As Justice Peterson of the Supreme Court of Oregon explained in his dissenting opinion, however, "The findings of fact that the bicycle pathway system '*could* offset some of the traffic demand' is a far cry from a finding that the bicycle pathway system *will,* or is *likely to,* offset some of the traffic demand."

Cities have long engaged in the commendable task of land use planning, made necessary by increasing urbanization particularly in metropolitan areas such as Portland. The city's goals of reducing flooding hazards and traffic congestion, and providing for public greenways, are laudable, but there are outer limits to how this may be done. "A strong public desire to improve the public condition [will not] warrant achieving the desire by a shorter cut than the constitutional way of paying for the change."

REVERSED AND REMANDED in favor of the plaintiff.

[CONTINUED]

CRITICAL THINKING

What additional evidence could the city have presented at the trial that might have led to a more favorable decision for it?

ETHICAL DECISION MAKING

Which stakeholders' interests were given primary weight by the judge, and which stakeholders' interests were given less weight?

The struggle over when a government restriction of the use of environmentally sensitive land is a taking has been one of the most contentious issues since the late 20th century. No doubt, it will continue to be a major source of controversy well into the 21st century.

CASE OPENER WRAP-UP

Poletown

In the end, the Economic Redevelopment Committee exercised its right of eminent domain and acquired the property in Poletown for General Motors. While the plaintiffs argued that whatever incidental benefit may accrue to the public, assembling land to General Motors' specifications for conveyance to General Motors for its uncontrolled use in profit making is really a taking for private use and not a public use because General Motors is the primary beneficiary of the condemnation, the Michigan State Supreme Court disagreed. The court stated, "The determination of what constitutes a public purpose is primarily a legislative function, subject to review by the courts when abused, and the determination of the legislative body of that matter should not be reversed except in instances where such determination is palpable and manifestly arbitrary and incorrect."

The court further found that the legislature had determined that taking the land to create an industrial site that would be used to alleviate and prevent conditions of unemployment and fiscal distress met a public need and serves an essential public purpose. Thus the taking was constitutional.

Interestingly, during the spring of 2005, just a few months prior to the *Kelo* decision, the Michigan Supreme Court had a chance to reconsider its reasoning in Poletown and, in the case of *Wayne v. Hathcock,* overruled that decision. The court stated that "Poletown's conception of a public use—that of 'alleviating unemployment and revitalizing the economic base of the community' has no support in the Court's eminent domain jurisprudence." The persuasiveness of *Hathcock,* however, was rapidly overshadowed by the U.S. Supreme Court's decision in *Kelo.*

Clearly, the question of what constitutes public use is not one that is easily answered. While it appears from the high court's most recent pronouncement that public use is going to be interpreted broadly enough to include takings for economic redevelopment, even when those takings involve some private benefit from the transfer of property from one private entity to another, these transfers are much more likely to be upheld when the transfer is part of a well-conceived plan for development, and not just an individual transfer, as was the case in Poletown. And, as noted earlier in this chapter, in response to this decision, many states are now passing statutes to tighten the circumstances under which state governments may use their power of eminent domain.

global context

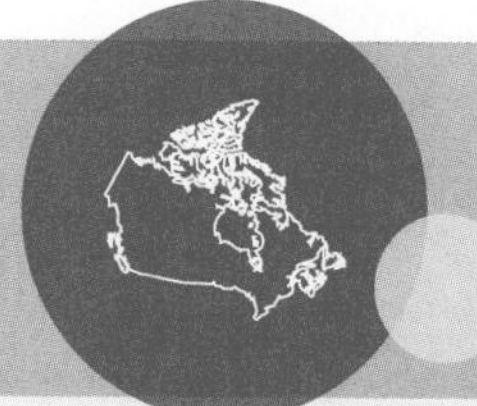

Citizen Property Rights in Canada

Environmentally concerned citizens in Canada are demanding that a new type of property rights be recognized: citizen property rights. Advocates are seeking to have rights over the use of *citizen property,* which is defined as "property rights sought or claimed by ordinary citizens, either as individuals or as groups, permitting them to ameliorate current and future negative effects of current resource use." In other words, people concerned with private and state owners polluting and abusing the environment want to protect themselves and their children from the harmful implications of others' irresponsible behavior. Thus, advocates of citizen property rights do not want to increase government control but, rather, want to redistribute rights more equally between owners and citizens. For example, if a chemical plant is polluting the reservoirs of a local fishery, the fishery should have as much right to decide what happens in that river as the chemical plant.

Obviously though, the solution is not as simple as a quick redistribution of rights. A method of damage assessment must be established, which would be problematic because environmental damage has numerous direct and indirect consequences that are not easily measurable. Other questions to consider include who would be responsible for making the assessment and who would determine and impose the penalties? In addition, one must consider the inevitable opposition such reforms would yield. While these obstacles have prevented citizen property rights from manifesting thus far, the issue is unlikely to simply disappear. It represents a unique democratic dilemma in which the rights of private citizens must be weighed against the pubic good.

Summary

The Nature of Real Property

Property is land and anything permanently affixed to the land.

Interests in Real Property

Fee simple absolute: Right to possess for life and devise to heirs on death; the most all-encompassing interest.

Conditional estate: Interest comparable to a fee simple absolute, except that the interest will terminate on the happening or nonhappening of a specified condition.

Leasehold estate: Right to possess property for an agreed-on period of time.

Easement: Irrevocable right to use a portion of someone else's land for a specified purpose.

License: Right to temporarily use another's property.

Co-ownership

The traditional forms of co-ownership are:

Tenancy in common: Equal or unequal shares may be held that can be attached by creditors and pass on to heirs at death.

Joint tenancy: Equal shares are held by all owners, and on death shares are divided among other owners.

Tenancy by the entirety: Available to married couples only, shares are equal and pass to the spouse on death.

Two newer forms of co-ownership are:

Condominium ownership: Owner acquires title to a "unit" within a building, along with an undivided interest in the land, buildings, and improvements of the common areas of the development.

Cooperative ownership: Investor resident acquires stock in the corporation owning the facility and receives a permanent lease on one unit of the facility.

Voluntary Transfer of Real Property

For a transfer to be legal, the transferor must follow the steps of *execution, delivery, acceptance,* and, to protect the recipient of the property, *recording.*

Involuntary Transfer of Real Property

There are two forms of involuntary transfers:

Adverse possession: When a person openly treats realty as his or her own, without protest or permission from the real owner, for a statutorily established period of time, ownership is automatically vested in that person.

Condemnation: The government acquires the ownership of private property for a public use for just compensation over the protest of the owner of the property.

Restrictions on Land Use

Restrictive covenants: Promises to use or not to use land in particular ways.

Zoning: The restriction of the use of property to allow for the orderly growth and development of a community and to protect the health, safety, and welfare of its citizens.

Point / Counterpoint

Should Legislatures Be Able to Use the Power of Eminent Domain to Take Private Property from One Individual and Give It to Another Private Entity in the Name of "Public Use"?

The argument against this use of eminent domain favors reliance on the market economy to promote efficient use of property; the argument for this use of eminent domain favors reliance on democracy. What assumptions does each argument make in its reliance on these underlying institutions?

No	Yes
The Fifth Amendment reads: "nor shall private property be taken for public use, without just compensation." This text suggests that government cannot use eminent domain unless the condemned property is available for use by the public. If, as in *Poletown,* the condemned property is transferred to a private corporation, the public cannot use it. Hence, this use of eminent domain does not comport with the plain meaning of the constitutional text.	Arguments emanating from constitutional text do not clearly support the position that eminent domain must yield property for use by the public. The text prohibits taking of private property for public use "without just compensation," but it says nothing about the taking of private property for *private* use. Thus, a literal reading of the constitutional text does not prohibit the use of eminent domain in question.

Even if the constitutional text allows this use of eminent domain, the Constitution does not hold corporations accountable for their promises to create jobs and generate tax revenues. If a corporation promises 6,500 jobs and $10 million in tax revenue to a local municipality in exchange for an advantageous piece of property, and only 3,000 jobs and $800,000 in tax revenue materialize, the corporation suffers no consequences. Thus, corporations have a perverse incentive to overstate the number of jobs and amount of tax revenue they are likely to create. As a result, legislatures are more likely to use eminent domain in cases where, had they known the actual state of affairs, they would not have used it.

A third strong argument against this use of eminent domain focuses on the alternative to eminent domain. If the private property in question is so desirable to a corporation, American society has established a market mechanism by which the corporation can purchase the property directly from the private owner. If the private owner is unwilling to give up her property for the price offered by the corporation, the outcome is not necessarily bad. Indeed, economists would say the result is efficient because the property ends up where it is most highly valued: in the private owner's hands.

Moreover, even if the use of eminent domain in question creates perverse incentives for corporations to make unrealistic promises, the best solution is not a blanket ban on the practice. Rather, the best solution is the solution we use in almost every other area of government: popular sovereignty. If citizens oppose the use of eminent domain to condemn private property and transfer that property to another private entity, they have recourse in the ballot box: They can vote for candidates for local legislature who share their views. Many economic policies are unwise, but they are nevertheless not unconstitutional. As Justice Oliver Wendell Holmes famously wrote, the Constitution "does not enact Mr. Herbert Spencer's Social Statics." (Spencer's Social Statics was a popular economic theory during Holmes's time.) Along the same lines, Justice Scalia once remarked that "[a] law can be both economic folly and constitutional."

Finally, the argument that society ought to use markets instead of eminent domain ignores the possibility of *positive externalities*—positive effects that accrue to third parties when two individuals engage in a market transaction. If the sale of private property to corporations is likely to produce positive externalities in the form of additional jobs and increased tax revenue, legislatures may want to compel more of these sales through the use of eminent domain.

Questions & Problems

1. Explain what a fixture is and when it is not treated as a part of the real property to which it is attached.
2. Explain the five possessory interests in land.
3. List the primary characteristics of three forms of joint ownership.
4. List the steps of the voluntary transfer of ownership of real property.
5. Explain how a piece of property could be involuntarily transferred.
6. Pandick leased building space from NationsBank in the Huntersville Business Park. NationsBank also loaned Pandick money to refurbish the office. Pandick entered into a separate agreement with Capital Associates to lease office furniture, equipment, air conditioners, and computers for its business. The room and rooftop air conditioners were installed to protect the computers. After being in business for a short time, Pandick filed for bankruptcy and abandoned the property located in the business park to its creditors. NationsBank allowed Capital Associates to remove all of its equipment and furnishings from the premises except for several rooftop heating and air-conditioning units and five room air-conditioning units. NationsBank argued that the air-conditioning units were fixtures. Capital Associates claimed ownership of the air-conditioning units, arguing that they were trade fixtures. Why do you believe the

court agreed or disagreed with Capital Associates? [*NationsBank of N.C. v. Capital Associates Intern.,* 916 F. Supp. 549 (1996).]

7. Outdoor Systems Advertising (OSA), Inc., previously occupied a building owned by Jefferson Properties. When OSA vacated the building, it left behind two billboards located on the roof and east wall of the building. OSA notified Jefferson Properties of its ownership of the billboards and requested that the advertisements attached to the billboard structures be removed. The trial court held that the panel boards, the exterior portion of the billboards, belonged to OSA and that the billboard structure, which was attached to the building, was part of Jefferson Properties realty. On appeal, OSA argued that both the panel boards and the billboard structure were trade fixtures. Jefferson Properties maintained that the billboard structures were fixtures and should remain affixed to the property. How do you think the court resolved this conflict? Were the billboard structures trade fixtures? [*Outdoor Systems Advertising, Inc. v. John J. Korth,* 1999 Mich. App. LEXIS 316.]
8. Malcom Fox and his brother Harvey Fox owned an enclosed portion of land. The entire parcel of land had previously been divided into six portions, and the Foxes' portion was not adjacent to any roads. To access the highway, the Foxes had to pass through others' land. The Foxes rarely stayed on their property, but they frequently rented it to hunters. The other landowners objected to the Foxes' and hunters' use of roads leading to the highway, and one owner erected a locked fence to prevent the Foxes and hunters from using the road. The Foxes argued for an easement allowing the use of the road. How do you think the court decided? Was this an easement by necessity? [*Daniel v. Fox,* 917 S.E.2d 106 (1996).]
9. After they were married, Helen and Burr Dietz purchased real property as tenants by entirety. Helen subsequently moved out, and the parties agreed that, if they were to become divorced, they would share the proceeds of the sale of their property. Helen and Burr divorced, and their tenancy by the entirety was converted into a tenancy in common. Burr continued to live in the residence, and Helen brought an action for the partition or sale of the property. She sought to receive half of the proceeds of the sale and rent for the period that she did not live on the property. The trial court determined that the property could not be partitioned and therefore directed the parties to sell the property and divide the proceeds accordingly. Burr did not want to sell the property and appealed the court's decision. How do you think the case was decided on appeal? [*Deitz v. Deitz,* 664 N.Y.S.2d 868 (1997).]
10. Willard W. Smith had owned a salvage yard since 1980. In 1984 the county enacted a zoning ordinance requiring a permit for salvage yards. Because the operation of Smith's yard predated the 1984 ordinance, he was not subjected to the permit requirement. A relevant regulation stated, "Any salvage yard which was licensed prior to June 12, 1988 may continue to be operated and maintained in accordance with the statutes and regulations in effect at the time the yard was initially licensed." In 1992, Smith sold the yard to Poole. Poole continued to use the property as a salvage yard. The use and operation of the property did not change. After Poole failed to apply for a permit, the circuit court found that the previous lawful, nonconforming use of the property was terminated when Smith sold the land to Poole. Poole appealed the court's decision. Do you think he was successful? Why or why not? [*Poole v. Berkeley County Planning Com'n,* 488 S.E.2d 349 (1997).]
11. The Hatherleigh existed as a multiunit apartment building for over 80 years. A 1966 ordinance zoned the area on which the Hatherleigh was located for only one- and two-family dwellings. Because the building contained five apartment units, it did not

conform to the 1966 ordinance. However, due to the fact that the building had previously been in existence, the Hatherleigh's use of the building became a legally established nonconforming use. The building was subject to another ordinance prohibiting the conversion of nonconforming buildings. The Hatherleigh subsequently remodeled its interior to make three additional apartment units. The Metropolitan Development Commission brought an action against Ragucci, the owner of the Hatherleigh, alleging that his building was in violation of the zoning ordinance. Ragucci argued a legally established nonconforming use. The trial court found in favor of the commission. On appeal, the court entered judgment in favor of Ragucci. The case was then appealed to the state supreme court. How do you think it was decided? [*Ragucci v. Metropolitan Development Commission* 702 N.E.2d 677 (1998).]

12. Rick Smith purchased several lots of land. He intended to place manufactured homes on the lots. Smith was issued building permits for the placement of the manufactured homes. After he had completed the placement on one of the lots, a new city ordinance prohibiting the placement of manufactured homes on certain areas of land was passed. The ordinance was passed in response to significant tornado damage that other manufactured homes had experienced. Smith argued that because he was issued the permits before the new ordinance, he should be allowed to complete the placement of manufactured homes on the lots. How do you think the court handled this zoning conflict? Should the lots be controlled by the earlier ordinance, which permitted the placement of manufactured homes? Why or why not? [*Smith v. City of Arkadelphia,* 984 S.W.2d 392 (1999).]

Looking for more review material?

The Online Learning Center at **www.mhhe.com/kubasek1e** contains this chapter's "Assignment on the Internet" and also a list of URLs for more information entitled "On the Internet." Find both of them in the Student Center portion of the OLC, along with quizzes and other helpful materials.

Landlord-Tenant Law

CASE OPENER

Landlord Liability for Tom Wenzel

Aaron Sikora was attending a party at a friend's rented condominium when the attached deck collapsed. Sikora was injured by the collapse and sued the landlord, Tom Wenzel; the contractor who built the deck; and the design company. His suit was based on negligence, and he asked the court to impose joint and several liability on all the defendants. During the trial, it was revealed that the deck had not been approved by the city of Fairborn, Ohio, but that the city issued the developer (and then-owner) a certificate of occupancy nonetheless. The developer then sold the property to Wenzel. Neither Sikora nor Wenzel argued that Wenzel had any knowledge about any defects in the deck. The trial court granted summary judgment in favor of Wenzel because he lacked any notice of a defect.

The appeals court, however, reversed the trial court's decision. The appeals court found Wenzel strictly liable under a landlord liability precedent in another case. Wenzel appealed to the Ohio Supreme Court.

1. In this chapter you will learn more about the important area of landlord liability. Do you think the Ohio Supreme Court should have reversed or affirmed the appellate court decision? Why?
2. Sikora did not sue the city even though the city granted a certificate of occupation without further inspection of the modified premises. Could Sikora have sued the city? Why or why not?

The Wrap-Up at the end of the chapter will answer these questions.

CHAPTER 50

Learning Objectives

After reading this chapter, you will be able to answer the following questions:

1 How is the landlord-tenant relationship created?

2 What are the rights and duties of the landlord and tenant?

3 What are landlords' liabilities for injuries on the premises?

4 How are interests in leased property transferred?

5 How are leases terminated?

Suppose you are a manager for a new business. One of your responsibilities is to secure office space for the business. You meet with the business owner to talk about whether you should rent or purchase the office space. If you rent the office space, you will enter into a contractual agreement with the owner such that you will be responsible for paying a specific amount of money for a specific period of time to have temporary possession of a certain space. While this agreement will name a specific piece of property (i.e., provide the street address of the property), the lease is typically an agreement for use of some structure on the property. If you will potentially be renting housing or office space for your business, you should be aware of the laws that govern the landlord-tenant relationship.

A clear understanding of the language used in the landlord-tenant relationship is essential. The owner of the property is called the **landlord** or the **lessor.** In contrast, the **lessee,** or the **tenant,** is the party who assumes temporary ownership of the property. The property in question is called the **leasehold estate.** The actual agreement between the landlord and the tenant is called the **lease.**

In the landlord-tenant relationship, the landlord grants the tenant the temporary, exclusive right to occupy and use a specific space for a specific amount of time. In turn, the tenant is obligated to pay rent to the landlord, who retains the title to the land. This entire relationship is usually established in a contractual agreement.

The landlord-tenant relationship has become more complex in recent years. In 1972, the National Conference of Commissioners on Uniform State Laws created the Uniform Residential Landlord and Tenant Act (URLTA), an act that created more uniformity among the state laws governing the landlord-tenant relationship.

The first part of this chapter explains how the landlord-tenant relationship is created. The next section explains the rights and responsibilities associated with the landlord-tenant relationship. The third section focuses on liability associated with injuries that occurred on rental premises. The fourth section considers how landlords and tenants can transfer their interests in the rental property. The final section explains the ways a lease can be terminated.

Creation of the Landlord-Tenant Relationship

How is the landlord-tenant relationship established? It is usually established by an oral or written contract. Generally, if the lease exceeds one year, it must be in writing. A landlord-tenant relationship requires the following elements: (1) the names of the tenant(s) and landlord, (2) an express or implied intent to create a landlord-tenant relationship, (3) a description of the property, (4) the specific length of the lease, and (5) the amount of rent to be paid to the landlord.

The most distinguishing factor of the landlord-tenant relationship is the tenant's right to exclusive possession of the property named in the lease. If the landlord retains control of and access to the property, the relationship is likely not a landlord-tenant relationship because the tenant does not have an exclusive right to possession of the property.

TYPES OF LEASES

There are four categories of leases that can be created: definite term, period tenancy, tenancy at will, and tenancy at sufferance. Why should you understand the differences between these categories of leases? These categories are distinguishable by the duration of the agreement specified or unspecified in the lease. Some of these categories allow the landlord or tenant to terminate a lease at specific times, while other categories would consider termination before the end of the term as a breach. As a future business manager, you

Case Nugget Do Americans Have a Constitutional Guarantee of Access to Housing of a Particular Quality?

Lindsey v. Normet
405 U.S. 56 (1972)

When reading about landlord-tenant law, it is important to understand the larger context of legal rules with regard to housing. In *Lindsey v. Normet,* tenants challenged Oregon's judicial procedure for eviction on constitutional grounds. Part of their challenge to the statute relied on their assumption that the "need for decent shelter" and the "right to retain peaceful possession of one's home" are fundamental interests. They argued that the state should have to demonstrate a superior or compelling interest before infringing on these interests.

The U.S. Supreme Court disagreed, stating:

> We do not denigrate the importance of decent, safe, and sanitary housing. But the Constitution does not provide judicial remedies for every social and economic ill. We are unable to perceive . . . any constitutional guarantee of access to dwellings of a particular quality. . . . Absent constitutional mandate, the assurance of adequate housing and the definition of landlord-tenant relationships are legislative, not judicial functions.

need to be aware of the distinctions in the types of leases so that you are aware of what kind of lease will and will not permit you to terminate the agreement.

First, a **definite-term** lease, also known as a *term for years,* automatically expires at the end of the specified term. The landlord is not required to give any notification of termination. Thus, a lease that states that the tenant has temporary possession of the property from August 1, 2000, to July 31, 2001, is an example of a definite-term lease. Second, a **periodic-tenancy** lease is created for a recurring term, such as month to month. The periodic-tenancy lease is distinct from the definite-term lease because the periodic-tenancy lease is for an indefinite time period. While either the landlord or the tenant can terminate during the recurring period, each party is required to give the other party sufficient notice. Third, parties to a **tenancy-at-will** lease may terminate the lease at any time. Fourth, if a tenant fails to leave the property after the termination of the lease, a **tenancy-at-sufferance** lease is created. The landlord may choose either to permit the tenant to remain on the property or to demand repossession of the property.

FAIR HOUSING ACT

When deciding to create a landlord-tenant relationship, the landlord has much freedom in deciding whether to accept someone as a tenant. If the individual has a history of not paying rent or severely damaging the premises, the landlord does not have to enter into an agreement with this person. However, under the Fair Housing Act, the landlord may not discriminate against a prospective tenant with regard to race, color, sex, religion, national origin, or familial status. Thus, if a landlord denies a rental application because of the tenant's religion (or other protected class), the prospective tenant can bring a suit against the landlord. Case 50-1 considers whether certain rules for an apartment complex violated the Fair Housing Act.

global context

Leases in French Law

Leases in France are governed by the Civil Code. Leases are under the code's jurisdiction because they engender personal contractual rights rather than property rights. The Civil Code places the rights of the tenant above the rights of the renter. Tenants are also given considerable freedom to engage in various agreements without the landlord's involvement or consent. If the lease is not renewed, the tenant has the right to collect compensation. The tenants' sovereignty, however, is a personal right. The landlord still maintains the property rights. The tenant is merely acting as his or her agent.

There are two special leases that transfer property rights to the tenant. The first is an *emphyteusis,* in which the tenant is going to be involved in extensive work on the property for anywhere between 18 and 99 years. During this period, the property rights of the land are given to the tenant, who pays a small rent fee in return. The second type of lease is a *construction lease.* It is similar to an *emphyteusis* in the sense that the tenant receives property rights for working on the land. Specifically, the tenant in a construction lease will be building and maintaining structures. If either of these leases are entered into, the property rights are ceded to the tenant for the period specified in the agreement.

CASE 50-1 | FAIR HOUSING CONGRESS v. CHARLES WEBER

U.S. DISTRICT COURT FOR THE CENTRAL DISTRICT OF CALIFORNIA
993 F. SUPP. 1286 (1997)

Maureen Tabon and her son, Eric Tabon, filed a complaint against Charles Weber because they alleged that he, as general owner of the Vista De Anza apartment complex, was violating the Fair Housing Act of California. Weber was the supervisor to Mary Russell and Douglas Russell, who served as the managers of the apartment complex. All tenants who lived in the apartment complex had to sign a copy of the building and pool rules. For example, Rule 4 on the list of rules stated "Children will not be allowed to play or run around inside the building area at any time because of disturbance to other tenants or damage to building property. Bikes, carriages, strollers, tricycles, wagons, etc. must be kept inside apartments or in garage area and not left outside." Because various other rules limited the activities of children in the complex, Tabon argued that the landlord was discriminating against families with children in violation of the Fair Housing Act.

JUDGE BAIRD: The Fair Housing Act, 42 U.S.C. §§3604, prohibits discrimination on the basis of familial status, including discrimination against families with children. Under §804(c), it is unlawful to "make, print, or publish, or cause to be made, printed or published any notice, statement, or advertisement, with respect to the sale or rental of a dwelling that indicates any preference, limitation, or discrimination based on . . . familial status, . . . or an intention to make any such preference, limitation, or discrimination." Under HUD regulations, which are entitled to considerable judicial deference, this subsection applies to both written and oral statements.

The standard for determining whether a given statement violates §804(c) is whether the statement suggests a preference to the ordinary reader or listener. No discriminatory intent is required.

The first sentence of Rule 8 . . . is a facially discriminatory restriction on the use of apartment facilities by tenant children, which in turn discriminates against tenants with children on the basis of their familial status (a group of persons living together without children are not subject to the first sentence of Rule 8). It is not disputed that Rule 8 was promulgated and enforced by defendants. On this basis, plaintiffs seek summary adjudication that Rule 8 violates §804(c).

Plaintiffs cite Blomgren v. Ogle, 850 F. Supp. 1427 (E.D. Wash. 1993) in support of their motion. In Blomgren, the Washington district court held that a written apartment rule stating "no children (other than visiting) or pets allowed in the apartments" violated § 804(c) as a matter of law, although the plaintiff tenant testified that she had never seen the rule, and defendants testified the rule was never enforced. The Blomgren court granted summary adjudication in favor of the plaintiff on the §804(c) issue, holding that "a violation occurs . . . when the communication implies an obvious discriminatory preference. Alternatively, intent to discriminate also need not be proved to establish violation where the ordinary reasonable reader infers the particular discriminatory preference."

Defendants seek to distinguish this case from Blomgren because neither sentence of Rule 8 is an outright ban on children. However, the Blomgren court made clear that "discriminatory preference," not an outright ban, is the basis for an §804(c) violation. Defendants also argue that Blomgren supports the lawfulness of Rule 8, insofar as rules restricting children's play and requiring that bicycles and other wheeled items be kept out of halls, also present in the Blomgren lease, were not held to violate §804(c). At most, however, this would save only the second sentence of Rule 8.

Plaintiffs also cite HUD v. Paradise Gardens, Fair Housing - Fair Lending P25,037 at 25,391 (HUD ALJ 1992), an HUD administrative law decision finding that community rules which facially discriminated against families with children in access to community facilities violate §804(c). In Paradise Gardens, restrictions were placed on children's use of the swimming pool which did not apply to other residents.

While Rule 8 is not an outright ban on children as tenants, the rationale of Blomgren and Paradise Gardens applies to its first sentence. The first sentence of Rule 8 is clearly a "limitation" on the use by children tenants of the apartment facilities, and an ordinary reader of the first sentence of Rule 8 could not reasonably interpret it otherwise. The first sentence of Rule 8 restricts children's play activities as such, even when those activities do not violate Rule 4 (banning loud and/or dangerous behavior) or "annoy or disturb other tenants or create a nuisance in any way." Defendants have presented no admissible evidence of any nondiscriminatory alternative interpretation, other than Ms. Tabon's subjective impression of the rule as vague and open to interpretation. Nor have defendants provided statutory or caselaw authority for their contention that so long as plaintiffs were not actually discouraged from renting the apartment, there was no violation of §804(c). Therefore, under Ragin, Jancik, Blomgren, and Paradise Gardens, supra, summary adjudication is GRANTED in favor of plaintiffs that the first sentence of Rule 8 violates §804(c).

However, the second sentence of Rule 8 is not facially discriminatory, and plaintiffs have not demonstrated that the second sentence of Rule 8 "indicates any preference, limitation, or discrimination based on . . . familial status," as prohibited by §804(c), especially given Rule 7, which prohibits all tenants from leaving any objects inside the pool or building area at any time. An ordinary reader would not infer an anti-children preference from a requirement that all tenants keep the sidewalks and building areas clear. Therefore, summary adjudication in favor of plaintiffs that the second sentence of Rule 8 violates §804(c) is DENIED.

SUMMARY JUDGMENT in favor of the plaintiff, in part.

CRITICAL THINKING

Outline the reasoning the court used to support its two rulings. How strong are the reasons and forms of evidence used to support the conclusions?

Are there significant ambiguities in this case that you think compromise the strength of the court's reasoning? How would you interpret these ambiguities?

ETHICAL DECISION MAKING

How might the landlord have designed the policies so as to be nondiscriminatory but to accomplish the goals the landlord desired?

Case Nugget **What Test Applies under the Fair Housing Act When a Mentally Impaired Tenant Seeks a Reasonable Accommodation?**

Douglas v. Kriegsfeld Corporation
884 A.2d 1109 (2005)

In *Douglas v. Kriegsfeld,* a tenant (Douglas) with a mood disorder asked for "reasonable accommodation" under the Fair Housing Act. In particular, she wanted time and assistance in cleaning her apartment before the landlord could succeed in an action for possession. The landlord wanted to consider the impact Douglas's unclean apartment had on other tenants. Although the trial court was willing to consider this factor, the appellate court clarified that the test for establishing a reasonable-accommodation defense focuses on the landlord-tenant relationship, not on the impact one tenant has on other tenants. In particular, the court said:

> To establish a reasonable accommodation defense under the Fair Housing Act, the tenant must demonstrate that (1) she suffered from a "handicap" (or "disability"), (2) the landlord knew or should have known of the disability, (3) an accommodation of the disability may be necessary to afford the tenant an equal opportunity to use and enjoy her apartment, (4) the tenant has requested a reasonable accommodation, and (5) the landlord refused to grant a reasonable accommodation.

The court emphasized that each case should be judged on its unique facts, and it remanded the case to the lower court for consideration according to the test it had outlined.

Rights and Duties of the Landlord and the Tenant

Both the landlord and the tenant gain certain rights and responsibilities when creating a lease. Each duty corresponds with a right. If the landlord has a duty to perform *X,* the tenant has the right to *X.* As a future business manager, you could be either a landlord or a tenant; thus, it is important to understand what your responsibilities and rights would be as each party to the lease. These duties and rights can be classified under four main areas: possession, use, maintenance, and rent.

POSSESSION OF THE PREMISES

One of the few obligations that the landlord has to the tenant is to give the tenant possession of the premises. What exactly does *possession* mean? In the majority of states, the landlord is required to give the tenant physical possession of the premises. Suppose that you are supposed to move into your new office space tomorrow. Unfortunately, the previous tenant has refused to leave the premises. In the majority of states, the landlord is required to remove the previous tenant or break the agreement with the new tenant.

In contrast, in a minority of states, the landlord is required to simply provide legal possession of the premises. In other words, in the same situation where the previous tenant has refused to leave the premises, the tenant is responsible for asserting her legal right to the premises and thus removing the previous tenant.

If, however, the tenant does not receive possession of the premises because of an act of the landlord, the landlord will be held liable. The tenant can bring an action for possession against the landlord.

Because the landlord has the duty to provide the tenant with possession of the premises, the tenant has the right to possession of the premises according to the terms of the lease. An element of the tenant's right to possess the premises is the right to quietly enjoy the premises. One of the most important promises that a landlord makes in a lease is the **covenant of quiet enjoyment,** a promise that the tenant has the right to quietly enjoy the land. What exactly does this mean? The landlord promises that he or she will not interfere with the tenant's use and enjoyment of the property. If the landlord does interfere, the tenant can sue the landlord for breach of this covenant. In Case 50-2, a New York city court explores the covenant of quiet enjoyment.

CASE 50-2

JANET I. BENITEZ v. SEBASTIANO RESTIFO
CITY COURT OF NEW YORK, YONKERS
167 MISC. 2D 967; 641 N.Y.S.2D 523; 1996 N.Y. MISC. LEXIS 106 (1996)

Janet I. Benitez was a tenant in a basement apartment in New York, and Sebastiano Restifo was her landlord. On August 10, 1995, a large amount of water fell through the ceiling in Benitez's apartment, causing severe damage to much of Benitez's property (e.g., carpet, a bed, clothing, etc.). Benitez replaced the carpet, mattress, bureau, and some clothing. The source of the water was from a third floor apartment rented by Mrs. Alamar, who had previously caused flooding in Benitez's apartment. According to Restifo, Mrs. Alamar was a "problem tenant" who would intentionally fill up her kitchen sink so that the water would overflow onto the kitchen floor and eventually flood Benitez's apartment. Restifo was aware that Alamar was responsible for the floods in Benitez's apartment but did not take steps to have Alamar evicted. Benitez brought suit to recover money based on a breach of covenant of quiet enjoyment.

JUDGE DICKERSON: In this case the plaintiff seeks to recover monies expended in replacing her personal property (carpet, furniture, bedding and clothing), all of which suffered water damage. In this case the water came from a third floor apartment in which a tenant intentionally allowed water to overflow onto her kitchen floor.

Based upon a review of the facts the court finds that plaintiff has asserted the following causes of action: (1) breach of the covenant of quiet enjoyment and (2) breach of the warranty of habitability as set forth in Real Property Law §235-b.

Breach of Covenant of Quiet Enjoyment

Implicit in the lease agreement between the landlord and tenant was a covenant of quiet enjoyment which "is an agreement on the part of the landlord that for the period of the term of the lease the tenant shall not be disturbed in his quiet enjoyment of the leased premises" (2 Rasch, New York Landlord and Tenant—Summary Proceedings 27.1 [3d ed]).

The breach of a covenant of quiet enjoyment requires actual or constructive eviction (2 Rasch, *op. cit.,* §28.1, 28.21). Constructive eviction arises when the landlord interferes with the tenant's possession of the premises to such an extent that the tenant is deprived of its beneficial enjoyment.

In this case it was the landlord's inaction and unwillingness to evict the third floor tenant, Mrs. Alamar, which directly led to the most recent flooding of the plaintiff's apartment. By failing to act, the defendant condoned and impliedly authorized Mrs. Alamar to leave the water running in her apartment, causing damage to plaintiff's apartment below (74 NY Jur 2d, Landlord and Tenant, §259-260, 265; *Brauer v Kaufman,* 72 Misc 2d 718, 721 [1972] ["It may well be that if a landlord by deliberate and affirmative action invites, encourages or permits lessees to engage in illegal and immoral conduct on the premises . . . result(s) in an endangerment to the life, health or safety of the other (tenants) . . . It should be on knowledge or upon a reckless disregard of the facts"]).

The defendant breached the covenant of quiet enjoyment in the lease agreement and is liable for all appropriate damages flowing therefrom.

JUDGMENT in favor of plaintiff.

CRITICAL THINKING

What would be the ramifications of not having a covenant of quiet enjoyment?

ETHICAL DECISION MAKING

How could the landlord have used the WPH framework to avoid this lawsuit?

EVICTION

Generally, interference with a tenant's quiet enjoyment of property is usually in the form of an eviction. Suppose that you find that your landlord has changed the lock on your apartment and refuses to give you a new key for your apartment. The landlord has evicted you from the premises and has thus interfered with your use and possession of the property. When a landlord physically prevents you from entering the leased premises, this eviction is known as an **actual eviction.**

An actual eviction may be full or partial. If a landlord physically prevents you from entering any part of the premises, it is a **full eviction.** However, if the landlord prevents you from entering a part of the premises, it is a **partial eviction.** For example, if you are renting an office building and the landlord changes the locks on certain offices in the building, you have been partially evicted. In both partial and full evictions, the tenant is released from the obligation to pay rent. Furthermore, the tenant can sue for damages or bring a suit against the landlord for breach of contract.

Although a landlord might not actively prevent a tenant from using and enjoying the property, a landlord might wrongfully perform or fail to perform certain acts that cause a substantial injury to the tenant's use and enjoyment of the property. If the premises become unsuitable for use because of the landlord's wrongful or omitted act, a **constructive eviction** has occurred. For example, suppose your heater in your office space breaks. For a constructive eviction to occur, you must have notified the landlord of the problem. You notify your landlord, who then refuses to repair your heat. Clearly, in the winter, the premises are unsuitable for use without heat. Consequently, you would be permitted to abandon the premises and terminate the lease. However, you must abandon the premises within a reasonable amount of time. If a constructive eviction occurs, the tenant may bring a suit to recover damages or to attempt to move back onto the property. Considering the effects eviction can have on a tenant, what duties do you think the landlord should exercise in regard to eviction? Think about these questions when reading Case 50-3, which provides an example of a constructive eviction.

e-commerce AND THE LAW

Housing Court Judge for Sale on eBay

When Joanne Schoenberg did not like the way a housing judge in New York City handled her landlord-tenant dispute, she vented her frustrations through the world of e-commerce. How? She offered the judge, Jerald R. Klein, for sale on eBay. She advertised free worldwide shipping as part of the deal.

Technically, Schoenberg offered for sale an audiocassette of the proceedings, rather than the judge himself. She did, however, post the judge's picture and a list of her grievances against him. Judge Klein had evicted her from her apartment.

Schoenberg viewed her ad as art and as a way to voice her opinion. She also viewed certain aspects of the ad as parody or comedy. For instance, she tried to sell the judge under the category "sporting goods, archery, arrows, and shafts." Schoenberg points out that *shafts* has more than one meaning. (She once worked as a comedy writer.) Judge Klein was not amused. He raised many concerns, but most of them related to eBay's flawed filters, which he believes should have prevented the ad from running in the first place.

Before eBay pulled the ad, the high bid for Judge Klein (or, technically, the audiotape) was $127.50.

CASE 50-3

PROCTOR ET AL. v. FRAME ET AL.
STATE OF OHIO, AKRON MUNICIPAL COURT, SUMMIT COUNTY
90 OHIO MISC. 2D 11; 695 N.E.2D 357; 1998 OHIO MISC. LEXIS 3 (1998)

On November 6, 1996, Mr. Frame showed Mr. and Mrs. Proctor a rental property. The Proctors gave Frame a security deposit of $260 along with a welfare voucher for $400. Although the utilities in the rental unit were not working at that time, the Proctors moved their belongings into the unit. Mrs. Proctor attempted to have the utilities turned on, but the electric company refused to turn on those utilities without a copy of the lease for the rental unit. The Proctors attempted to contact Frame to get a copy of the lease, which had been promised to them on November 7. While Mr. and Mrs. Proctor spent a few nights at the rental unit, their children could not move into the unit because of the cold temperature. The Proctors simply could not inhabit their rental unit. When they met with Frame on November 30, he refused to give the Proctors a copy of the lease until he received their rent payment for December.

On December 2, Frame posted a three-day eviction notice and had the locks on the unit changed. Consequently, the Proctors could not remove their belongings from the rental unit. A few days later, some of the Proctors' belongings were found on the curb. On December 4, Frame accepted a security deposit to rent the same premises to another individual.

JUDGE MOORE: The court finds from the evidence that the parties did enter into a binding legal contract on November 6 for rental of the premises in question. Defendant failed to give to plaintiffs, at any time, the original or a copy of the lease agreement with the information required by R.C. 5321.18. As a result, the plaintiffs were precluded from having any utilities turned on in their unit. Even though their personal effects had been moved into the apartment, they could not use any appliances or even move their children into the apartment. The court finds the reasonable rental value of the apartment to be zero.

The plaintiffs accuse defendant of taking or otherwise disposing of their belongings. Plaintiffs were unable to produce any evidence that the defendant actually disposed of their property. It is clear that he had access to and control of the rental unit in that he admitted changing the locks to the doors immediately after the November 30th meeting when the Proctors announced their intention to move out. There were no eyewitnesses, however, to defendant's having placed any of plaintiffs' items on the curb or to his otherwise disposing of the personal property. Assuming plaintiffs were able to prove defendant had disposed of their property, the evidence presented as to damages was woefully inadequate to meet the burden of proof required by law. Mrs. Proctor struggled to come up with values of most of the items listed as having been lost, and at one point on cross-examination, conceded that she was "pulling numbers from the air."

There is little question, however, that defendant's actions in failing to provide plaintiffs with the lease was knowing and intentional. This is supported by the fact that he asked for December's rent as a precondition to providing plaintiffs with that to which they had a legal right. R.C. 5301.11; *Glyco v. Schultz* (1972), 35 Ohio Misc. 25, 62 Ohio Op. 2d 459, 289 N.E.2d 919. The court finds from the evidence that defendant knew or should have known that plaintiffs would be unable to inhabit the premises without a copy of the lease. Unquestionably, he had actual knowledge of this fact on November 30. His failure to provide plaintiffs with a copy of the lease was violative of Ohio law and constituted constructive eviction from the premises. R.C. 5321.04(A)(4); *Nye v. Schuler* (1959), 110 Ohio App. 443, 13 Ohio Op. 2d 208, 165 N.E.2d 16; *Keener v. Ewert* (1979), 67 Ohio App. 2d 17, 21 Ohio Op. 3d 336, 425 N.E.2d 914.

Further, the defendant acted in bad faith in changing the locks on the doors prior to the expiration of the three-day notice he posted. Credible testimony was given that defendant posted the three-day notice and that the next day changed the locks on the door, preventing the plaintiffs from obtaining their belongings. The court finds this action on the part of the defendant to have been willful and malicious. The practices by the defendant of accepting rent monies and then making himself unavailable to tenants by giving fictitious or nonworking phone numbers was as questionable as his implying the corporate status of the so-called company "Services Inc.," which he conceded at trial is not a corporation. Accordingly, plaintiffs are entitled to compensatory damages in the amount of $460 and punitive damages in the amount of $5,000, plus court costs.

JUDGMENT in favor of plaintiff.

CRITICAL THINKING

What do you think would be appropriate proof that the landlord had removed the tenants' possessions to the curb?

ETHICAL DECISION MAKING

Did the Proctors have any obligation to research Frame more thoroughly? Why or why not?

USE OF THE PREMISES

Generally, the landlord is not responsible for ensuring that the leased premises are tenantable. Why? Historically, the land was the more important element being leased. Some states have modified this rule to make the landlord more responsible for the dwellings on the property.

This rule has particularly been modified in the creation of residential leases. Most states have imposed an **implied warranty of habitability** of the premises, a requirement that the premises be fit for ordinary residential purposes. These states have recognized that most people currently enter into lease agreements because they are looking for shelter. Consequently, the dwelling, not the land, is the more important element of the lease.

Tenant use of the premises. How may the tenant use the premises? A landlord and tenant may make an agreement to limit the uses of the premises. Obviously, if they agree that the premises will be used for certain purposes only, the tenant has a duty to abide by that agreement. If there is no agreement that limits the tenant's use of the property, the tenant may use the premises in any manner as long as the use is legal and does not impose substantial injury to the premises. However, the tenant must not use the premises in a way that creates a nuisance for the surrounding tenants.

During the tenant's use of the leased property, the tenant has a duty not to commit waste. Any tenant conduct that causes permanent and substantial injury to the landlord's property is considered **waste.** For example, if a tenant cuts down several trees in the yard of the rental property without the landlord's permission, the tenant has committed waste.

Who is responsible for damages associated with use of the apartment? It depends. The tenant is not responsible for the ordinary wear and tear on the apartment. Thus, if the carpet in the rental unit becomes worn, the tenant is not responsible for replacing the carpet. If the tenant intentionally or negligently damages the apartment, however, the tenant will be responsible for paying for the damage. Consequently, if you have a party in your apartment and the guests spill drinks all over the carpet such that the carpet is permanently stained, you will likely be responsible for replacing the carpet.

Case 50-4 considers whether tobacco residue left inside an apartment constitutes ordinary wear and tear.

CASE 50-4

NANCY MCCORMICK v. ROBERT MORAN, SMALL CLAIMS #5176

JEFFERSON COUNTY CITY COURT OF WATERTOWN
699 N.Y.S.2D 273 (1999)

Nancy McCormick entered into a written lease with Robert Moran for an apartment for the period 7/13/98 to 7/12/99. McCormick brought suit against Moran to get a refund of McCormick's $375.00 security deposit. Moran responded by arguing that McCormick should pay $455.64 for the costs of the general cleaning of the apartment done after McCormick moved out. McCormick argued that such cleaning was unnecessary because she left the apartment in a better condition than when she moved in on 7/13/98. Moran argues that the extensive cleaning was necessary to remove the smoke residue from McCormick's heavy smoking.

JUDGE HARBERSON: The defendant's request for the cost to clean the floors, walls, windows, woodwork and carpets must be based on a showing such a clean-up was for conditions beyond ordinary "wear and tear" during reasonable use of the premises by the tenant. The landlord has the burden to prove such clean-up was for conditions caused by other than ordinary wear and tear due to reasonable use of the apartment by the tenant or a violation of the lease terms.

The landlord testified that the basic reason such an extensive cleaning was required was due to the excessive smoking by the tenants leaving a smelly residue of tobacco smoke throughout the leasehold on the walls, woodwork, carpets and other surfaces.

The lease provides at B (2) "Tenant shall use reasonable care to keep the premises in such condition as to prevent health and sanitation problems from arising." Paragraph 3 states "the $375.00 security deposit . . . may be used . . . at the time premises vacated by tenant toward reimbursement . . . for charges for cleaning not performed prior to vacating. . . ."

In PBN Associates v. Xerox Corp., the Court acknowledged a cause of action for breaking "provisions" of a lease. In this case the Court finds the plaintiff had agreed to "use reasonable care to keep the premises in such condition as to prevent health . . . problems from arising" (paragraph B [2]). The Court finds that the plaintiff's conduct of excessive smoking while in the house caused the tobacco smoke residue to collect on various surfaces of the house creating an offensive odor and a potential health risk that may arise to others who may use the premises.

There is no question that the dangers of such a situation to health due to particulate matter on surfaces left by smoke from tobacco has been recognized by the State. . . . The expression of the State's concern in this area of public health is found in Public Health Law section 1399 - P(2) which allows hotel or motel operators "to implement a smoking policy for rooms rented to guests" and, if such a policy is adopted "shall post a notice . . . as to the availability . . . of rooms in which no smoking is allowed." Section 1399 - q(1) provides that Article 13 -E does not apply, however, "to private residences."

The Court finds that while Article 13 -E does not apply to private residences, the landlord could have specifically prohibited smoking in the leased premises as part of the lease contract for the obvious health reasons outlined above. Notwithstanding the failure to specifically prohibit tobacco smoking by the plaintiff in the lease, this omission did not relieve the tenant from the obligation assumed under the lease to use reasonable care to keep the premises in such a condition as "to prevent health . . . problems from arising" (para. B[2]). The Court finds that the tenant failed to use such "reasonable care" while smoking tobacco to prevent such indoor air pollution from tobacco smoke to occur in violation of this lease term and must reimburse the plaintiff for the cost to remedy the problems since the tenant failed to do so before leaving.

The defendant is awarded as provided at paragraph 3 of the lease "reimbursement for the charges for cleaning not performed prior to vacating" the house in the amount of $455.64 to remove the tobacco smoke residue on the various surfaces of the house.

In addition the Court finds that ordinary wear and tear should not leave a leasehold in a condition that violates the warranty of habitability. When the use of tobacco by a tenant causes such a pervasive coating of tobacco smoke residue on a leasehold's surfaces, this condition results in more than ordinary wear and tear to the premises because the residue must be removed to make the rooms habitable for the protection of the health of the next tenants—a condition which if it were not corrected would be "detrimental to their life, health or safety" possibly subjecting the landlord to a violation of the warranty of habitability under Section 235 - b of the Real Property Law.

The plaintiff's petition for refund of the security deposit is denied because the defendant's counterclaim damages exceed the amount remaining. The defendant is awarded $455.64 for the cost to clean the house of tobacco smoke residue. The plaintiff is entitled to an off-set for the $375.00 security deposit.

JUDGMENT in favor of defendant.

CRITICAL THINKING

There are several ambiguous phrases in this case, including "reasonable care," "health and sanitation problems," and "ordinary wear and tear." What do you think the implied definitions of these phrases are, given the context that the court uses them in? Would you define these phrases differently? How would various definitions change the validity of the court's conclusion? No evidence was provided that previous tenants of the residence did not contribute to the tobacco residue. Could there be rival causes for the presence of the residue? Can you tell from the facts provided?

ETHICAL DECISION MAKING

Suppose McCormick held the ethical theory of consequentialism. Would her decision to smoke in the apartment have been the same? Why or why not?

Exhibit 50-1
Examples of Duties and Corresponding Rights of Landlord and Tenant

DUTY	CORRESPONDING RIGHT
1. Landlord duty to put tenant in possession	**1.** Tenant's right to retain possession
2. Landlord duty of covenant of quiet enjoyment	**2.** Tenant's right to quiet enjoyment of the property
3. Tenant duty not to commit waste	**3.** Landlord right to reimbursement for tenant's waste

Suppose that you, as a tenant, want to put wallpaper in three rooms in the office space you are renting. Are you permitted to paint or wallpaper rooms in rental property? Alternatively, perhaps you want to construct a wall to divide one large room into two offices. Is construction of this wall permitted? In most states, tenants cannot make **alterations,** changes that affect the condition of the premises, without the landlord's consent. In a minority of states, tenants can make alterations as long as the alterations are necessary for the use of the property and do not reduce the value of the property.

Perhaps you want to install shelves in the offices in your rental space. Depending on the courts, you may or may not be permitted to remove these shelves later without paying for damages. Once the shelves become attached to the property, they are considered fixtures. In some states, fixtures may not be removed because they are considered the landlord's property.

The duties and rights of landlords and tenants are numerous; Exhibit 50-1 provides a summary of some of them.

MAINTENANCE OF THE PREMISES

Landlords must ensure that the premises meet certain safety and health codes. Earlier in the chapter, we discussed the implied warranty of habitability. In most states, if a landlord leases residential property, the landlord is responsible for ensuring that the property is habitable. Part of this responsibility is making certain repairs to the premises. The implied warranty of habitability generally ensures that the landlord is responsible for repairs to major defects in the rental property. For example, if there is a hole in the wall that interferes with the electricity in the rental unit, the landlord would be responsible for repairing the hole.

Moreover, the landlord is generally responsible for ensuring that the premises meet certain statutory requirements. For example, the city ordinances might have specific standards for building structures or wiring and plumbing within the premises. Thus, the landlord would be responsible for making repairs to rental units that do not meet these standards (assuming that tenant damage did not lead to the need for those repairs). For instance, a city health and safety law might require the installation of a fire hose and sprinkler system in all office buildings. The landlord would be required to pay for this change.

If you are the landlord of an office building or apartment complex, you would be responsible for repairs to **common areas,** areas such as yards, lobbies, elevators, stairs, and hallways that are used by all tenants. Thus, if certain steps in a stairway are in need of repair, you are responsible for the repairs.

The responsibility for repairs to a property in a long-term lease is a little more complicated. Suppose that you plan to rent an office space to a tenant for 10 years. Generally, when creating the lease, the parties determine who will be responsible for repairs to the rental unit. Typically, in long-term leases, the tenant is responsible for more of the repairs to the rental property. However, the tenant will usually not be required to pay for major repairs.

Pretend that you are leasing an apartment. What can you do if your landlord fails to maintain the leased property by making certain repairs? If the repairs breach the warranty of habitability or constitute constructive eviction, you have the option of terminating the lease. If you want to retain possession of the apartment, you have several options available.

First, you can withhold a rent payment. This withholding is usually justified by the landlord's breach of the implied warranty of habitability. If the tenant wishes to withhold a rent payment, he or she must usually place a specific amount of the rent due in an escrow account, an account held by an escrow agent such as the court. The funds will remain in this account until the landlord makes the repairs. However, the tenant cannot withhold all the rent; instead, the tenant can withhold only an amount associated with the defect.

Second, you might be able to have the repairs made and deduct the costs of the repairs from the rent due to your landlord. Several states have created repair-and-deduct statutes. However, the repair-and-deduct option may not be the best choice because some statutes restrict the amount of deductible rent. Furthermore, repair-and-deduct options are often restricted to essential services, such as gas, water, and electric services. However, before you attempt to repair and deduct, you must have notified the landlord, who must then refuse to make the repairs.

Third, you can sue the landlord for damages. You can attempt to recover damages associated with the landlord's breach of the implied warranty of habitability.

Case Nugget How Does the Theory of Negligence Per Se Apply to Landlords?

Gradjelick v. Hance
646 N.W.2d 225 (2002)

Plaintiff Gradjelick was injured during a fire in the dwelling he rented from the Hance family. The fire was caused in part by careless smoking in another apartment, but it was allegedly exacerbated by the landlord's failure to maintain the premises. In particular, the tenant alleged that the landlord had violated several sections of the Uniform Building Code (UBC).

The court articulated the test for how the theory of negligence per se applies to landlords who allegedly violate the UBC. The court said:

> [A] landlord is not negligent per se for code violations unless the following four elements are present:
>
> (1) the landlord or owner knew or should have known of the Code violation;
> (2) the landlord or owner failed to take reasonable steps to remedy the violation;
> (3) the injury suffered was the kind the Code was meant to prevent; and
> (4) the violation was the proximate cause of the injury or damage.

RENT

Rent can be defined as the compensation paid to the landlord for the tenant's right to possession and exclusive use of the premises. The tenant has a duty to pay rent to the landlord.

global context

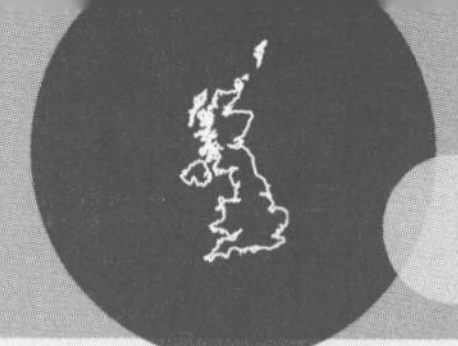

Landlord-Tenant Relations in Britain

In 1965, the British Parliament ratified the immensely popular Rent Act. Parliament hoped this bill would remedy the severe decline in hospitable relations between landlords and tenants. This end was intended to be accomplished by introducing rent regulation, abolishing rent control, and expanding both tenant and landlord protections. Despite the Rent Act's initial popularity, the undesirable consequences of it cooled the enthusiasm.

One of these consequences was the strengthening of business-oriented landlords' position. While the act's provisions appeared to be universally applicable, business-oriented landlords discovered and abused loopholes. For example, rental agreements were supposed to be registered with the rent officers to ensure the agreements' legitimacy. However, if an agreement was called a "rental purchase" or a "deferred purchase," it was not subject to the officer oversight. Such agreements were seen as business sales. Without officer oversight, abuse of rent regulation and landlord obligation statutes was easier. Business-oriented landlords also had the sympathy of prominent banks, building societies, real estate agents, and lawyers. With these resources, large, prosperous landlords could circumvent the Rent Act, while smaller landlords, who might not be as likely to abuse the statutes in the first place, got all the authorities' attention. The situation in Britain illustrates that there are competing interests not only between landlords and tenants but also between various types of landlords.

Rent can be paid in various forms, such as money or services to the landlord. The lease usually specifies the form of the rent as well as the payment schedule.

How much rent should be paid to the landlord? In some cases, the landlord has much freedom in determining how much rent should be charged. However, in other cases, the government establishes rent ceilings.

When the lease is initially created, the landlord typically asks the tenant to pay a security deposit, usually in the amount of one month's rent. This security deposit ensures that the tenant will fulfill the duties of the lease agreement.

At the expiration of the lease, the landlord is required to return to the tenant the security deposit minus any costs for damages caused by the tenant. If the landlord retains any portion of the security deposit, the landlord must provide the tenant with a list of the damages. Each state usually determines the amount of time that the landlord has to return the security deposit to the tenant. If the landlord exceeds this deadline, the tenant can recover the deposit, plus attorney fees. Recently, a court ruled that a landlord would have to pay a tenant $7,000 (security deposit plus attorney fees) because the landlord exceeded the deposit return deadline.

If a tenant fails to pay rent when it is due, the landlord may charge a late fee. This fee may not be excessive and must be related to the amount of rent past due. Thus, if you are two days late in paying a rent amount of $350, the landlord could not charge you $350 as a late fee. If the landlord wishes to terminate the lease because of a late payment, the landlord is generally required to give the tenant notice of the termination proceedings.

Once a lease has been signed, the landlord cannot increase the price of the rent, unless there is a **rent escalation clause** included in the lease. This clause permits the landlord to increase the rent in association with increases in costs of living, property taxes, or the tenant's commercial business. A rent escalation clause would typically be found in a long-term lease.

Suppose you are a landlord, and you discover that one of your tenants has refused to pay rent. What are your options? First, you may sue the tenant to collect the unpaid rent. Second, depending on what state you live in, you might have the option of a **landlord's lien,** the right to some or all of the tenant's personal property. You would be required to initiate court proceedings so that the sheriff would seize the tenant's property. This property is often considered as security for the unpaid rent.

What can a landlord do if the tenant has vacated the premises and fails to pay rent? The tenant is responsible for paying rent to the landlord until the expiration of the lease. The landlord could choose to simply let the premises stand vacant until the expiration of the lease. Thus, the tenant would be responsible for the entire amount of rent.

Some states are requiring that landlords make a reasonable attempt to lease the property to another party. The tenant is liable for the unpaid rent for the time that it would reasonably take the landlord to find a new tenant. If a reasonable attempt to find a new tenant is made but the attempt is unsuccessful, the tenant remains responsible for the entire amount of the unpaid rent.

Liability for Injuries on the Premises

Suppose you own a building and you rent the ground floor of the building to a tenant who uses the space as a restaurant. One night, while you are watching the news, you see a story that a woman was critically injured by a large piece of ice that fell off your building. The woman was leaving the restaurant on the ground floor of your building. Will you be held responsible for the woman's injuries? Will the tenant?

These questions are tricky. Liability for injuries generally depends on who is in control of the area in which the injury occurred. The courts use the standard of reasonable care in deciding these cases. The person who is in control of the area must take the same precautions for safety that the reasonable person would take.

LANDLORD'S LIABILITY

When will the landlord be liable for injuries on the premises? Generally, the landlord is responsible for injuries that occur in common areas, such as elevators, hallways, and stairwells. For example, if you are a landlord for an apartment complex and an injury occurs in the elevator, you can be held responsible for the injury. The landlord is expected to inspect and repair the common areas.

Moreover, the landlord can be held responsible for injuries when he or she has a responsibility to make repairs to the premises yet wrongfully or negligently makes those repairs. Generally, the landlord has a certain amount of time to make the repairs. Thus, if a visitor to the restaurant described in the example above was injured by falling plaster from the ceiling and the landlord had assumed the responsibility for repairs to the premises, the landlord could be responsible for the visitor's injuries. However, the landlord's liability depends on the tenant's notification of need for repair.

If an injury occurs on the premises because of a condition that the landlord knew or should have known about, the landlord can be held responsible for the injury. Furthermore, if the landlord is aware of a dangerous condition but does not make the tenant aware of the condition or hides the condition from the tenant, the landlord will be responsible for the injury. Thus, if a landlord is aware that several beams within an office space are in need of repair but does not disclose this information to the tenant when signing the lease, the landlord would likely be liable if the tenant was injured by a falling beam. Remember that in the Sikora case at the beginning of the chapter, landlord liability was an important issue.

If premises are used for commercial purposes, the landlord has a responsibility to ensure that the premises are in reasonably good condition before the tenant takes control of the property. However, the tenant is responsible for maintaining the premises. If injuries occur because the tenant was negligent in keeping the premises in good condition, the landlord will not be held responsible.

global context

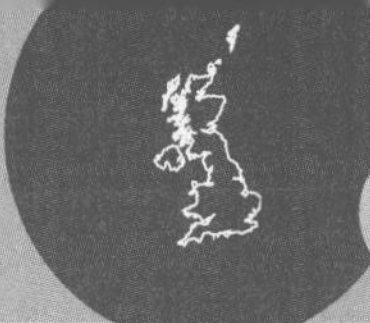

Landlord Liability in England

Landlords are not significantly restrained by common law in terms of their liability to the tenant at the time of letting. Landlords can be held liable if the lease is violated or if they are responsible for negligence or nuisance. The 1906 case of *Cavalier v. Pope* is the current precedent for the principle that the landlord owes no duty outside the contract with the tenant. For a landlord to be held liable due to negligence, he or she must have created the disputed defect. For instance, if a tenant were to injure himself on a standard feature of the rented property, the landlord could not be found guilty of negligence for letting a dangerous apartment because she did not actually create the disputed defect. The builder created the defect. Another way a landlord may be held liable is if he or she lets property without disclosing an obvious nuisance. However, if the court feels the nuisance was not apparent, the landlord is cleared of liability. Because these statutes favor protection of the landlords, tenants need to be especially wary of any defects or nuisances on the property before signing a lease

Who is liable when a customer in a ground-floor restaurant is injured while the restaurant is being robbed? The landlord could *potentially* be held liable for the injuries. How? Courts consider several factors when determining whether a landlord should be held responsible for injuries due to crimes of third parties. The most important factor that courts consider is the foreseeability of the crime. If the crime is foreseeable and the landlord does not attempt to prevent the crime, he or she could be liable. How many times has the restaurant been robbed? Is the neighborhood surrounding the restaurant infamous for its high crime rates? Case 50-5 considers the landlord's liability for an alleged crime and resulting damages to a rental unit by a third party.

CASE 50-5

KAREN JENKINS v. TONI BOYCE
STATE OF OHIO, AKRON MUNICIPAL COURT, SUMMIT COUNTY
94 OHIO MISC. 2D 98 (1998)

Karen Jenkins entered into a lease to rent an apartment to Toni Boyce. Boyce was to pay Jenkins $635 per month for rent and paid $635 as a security deposit. When Boyce fell behind in her rent payments, Jenkins began eviction proceedings in May 1998. On July 4, 1998, Jenkins accepted $439 for rent and agreed not to evict Boyce for thirty days. However, on July 9, 1998, the court ordered Boyce to leave the premises by July 20. Boyce moved her four children and herself to a shelter on July 14, but she left most of her personal property in the apartment because she had nowhere to move the property. Boyce did not inform Jenkins that she was leaving, and she placed the apartment keys in the mailbox.

Jenkins testified that she was in the premises on July 7 and saw minor damage at that time. However, when she returned to the premises on July 15, she discovered severe damage to the apartment. There were holes in the walls, severe damage to the countertops and cabinets, and ketchup and mustard smeared all over the walls and carpet. There was no sign of forced entry to the apartment. While Boyce admitted that some of the minor damage to the apartment was her responsibility, she denied responsibility for the severe damage and argued that vandals were responsible. She argues that she should not be held responsible for the damage because she had left the premises and turned in the keys. Jenkins argued that Boyce should be held responsible for the damage because she was still a tenant and therefore responsible for all damages according to the lease agreement.

JUDGE STORMER: Paragraph 3 of the agreement reads: "Tenant has examined and knows the condition of said premises and has received the same in good order and repair and will surrender pocession [*sic*] of said premises in like condition as reasonable and careful use will permit."

Paragraph 8 of the agreement reads in part: "The tenant will be charged for all damages done to the renta [*sic*] unit during their tenancy."

Chapter 5321 of the Ohio Revised Code codifies the Landlord and Tenant Act of 1974, spelling out the rights and obligations of residential landlords and tenants.

Specific to this case, R.C. 5321.05(A)(6) explains the duty that a tenant owes to the landlord regarding damages to the property:

> (A) A tenant who is a party to a rental agreement shall do all of the following:
>
> (6) Personally refrain and forbid any other person who is on the premises with his permission from intentionally or negligently destroying, defacing, damaging, or removing any fixture, appliance, or other part of the premises[.]

R.C. 5321.05(A)(6) establishes the liability of a tenant for the negligent acts of permitted guests. It does not address the criminal acts of unpermitted persons upon the property, nor do any cases that have interpreted the statute. Thus, this is a case of first impression. Two cases are helpful, however.

In Ohio Cas. Ins. Co. v. Wills (1985), 29 Ohio App. 3d 219, the landlord and insurance company sought to hold the tenant liable for damages caused by the negligent acts of a permitted guest: The court considered R.C. 5321.05(A)(6), stating that interpretation of the statute should achieve a reasonable balance between the rights of the landlord and tenant. The court noted:

> To require a tenant to predict and prevent a guest from acting carelessly would place the onerous burden of constant and personal supervision on a tenant. The legislature could not have intended to impose such an unrealistic burden on a tenant. Id.

Upon similar facts in Allstate Ins. Co. v. Dorsey (1988), the Ninth District cited Wills with approval for the proposition that a tenant must at least be cognizant of a third party's presence and of his intentions or actions to be liable under R.C. 5321.05(A)(6). The court also held that while the parties may include provisions in a lease agreement that are not codified in R.C. Chapter 5321, according to R.C. 5321.06, they may not include ones which are prohibited by or inconsistent with any of the statutes. Therefore, any provision which makes a tenant liable for all damages caused by an unidentified third party's carelessness or vandalism is unenforceable under R.C. 5321.06.

In this case, landlord Jenkins claims that Boyce either intentionally caused the damage herself or had some of her adult friends do it for her. The court finds that Jenkins has not proven these allegations. Therefore, Jenkins's only claim for Boyce's liability is that under R.C. 5321.05(A)(6), Boyce should be held liable for damages resulting from the criminal acts of trespassers. To require a tenant to prevent the criminal actions of those who are not guests would impose a much greater burden on the tenant than that which was rejected in Wills and Dorsey. Such a burden of strict liability upon the tenant is unreasonable and is not contemplated by R.C. 5321.05(A)(6).

Jenkins also claims that Boyce was still a tenant when the damages occurred because she had not formally surrendered her keys and informed Jenkins that she was leaving. Plaintiff argues that Boyce still has an obligation under Section 8 of the lease agreement for all damages to the premises. As a tenant, Boyce is responsible for all damages arising as a result of her own negligence under R.C. 5321.05(A)(6).

Any act on the part of the landlord that amounts to an eviction makes a formal surrender of the premises unnecessary. Because the formal eviction had begun and the moveout date was less than a week away, Boyce's vacation of the property and leaving of the keys in the mail box operate as the required surrender of the premises, terminating any rights or obligations that she or Jenkins had under the lease agreement.

The court holds that R.C. 5321.05(A)(6) does not permit a tenant's liability for damages resulting from criminal acts of trespassers. Lease provisions attempting to impose such tenant liability are unenforceable as contradictory to law. If Boyce had been a tenant at the time the vandalism occurred, she would not be liable for the damages under R.C. 5321.05(A)(6). Even if Boyce were negligent in leaving her keys in the mailbox, it would be unreasonable to hold her responsible when unrelated criminal trespassers were the cause in fact of the damages.

Jenkins has failed to prove that Boyce caused the damages or that she had a duty to prevent the damage that resulted from the criminal acts of others. However, Jenkins is entitled to restitution for the damages to which Boyce has admitted. According to the testimony

[CONTINUED]

of both parties, it appears that there was some other nonmalicious damage to the apartment, beyond normal wear and tear, the extent of which cannot be proven exactly due to the substantial nature of the subsequent damage. The court finds that Jenkins is entitled to keep the security deposit, but judgment is entered in favor of the defendant at plaintiff's costs.

JUDGMENT in favor of plaintiff, in part.

CRITICAL THINKING

The court draws analogies between this case and two previous cases. Do you find these analogies to be strong? How do the rulings of the two previous cases play into the court's reasoning?

ETHICAL DECISION MAKING

How might the use of the WPH framework have avoided this whole situation?

The landlord may attempt to escape liability for all injuries occurring on rental property by inserting an exculpatory clause in the lease. An *exculpatory clause* usually states that the landlord is not responsible for any injuries or damages occurring on the leased property, even injuries caused by the landlord's negligence. This clause does not permit the landlord to escape liability for injuries caused by the landlord's failure to meet laws establishing the landlord's responsibilities.

Some courts have considered exculpatory clauses as unenforceable because the clauses violate public policy. Other courts enforce the clauses. Generally, the courts look unfavorably at the clauses and will not enforce the clauses when injuries occur due to the landlord's negligence.

TENANT'S LIABILITY

The tenant has a responsibility to keep the premises in which he or she is in control in a reasonably safe condition. For example, the tenant who runs the restaurant would be responsible for the injuries of a customer who slipped and fell on a wet floor inside the restaurant. However, if the customer slipped and fell after entering a room that said "Employees Only," the tenant would not be responsible. The tenant is responsible only for those areas in which the customer is reasonably expected to go. Is the tenant in the Sikora case at the beginning of the chapter responsible for Sikora's injuries? Why or why not?

Transferring Interests of Leased Property

Unless prohibited by the lease agreement, both the landlord and the tenant may transfer their respective interests in the property.

LANDLORD TRANSFER OF INTEREST

Because the landlord is the owner of the leasehold estate, he or she can transfer that property. While the landlord can transfer ownership of the property to someone else, the lease is still legally binding. In other words, if you are renting an office space and the landlord sells the title to the lease property, the new owner could not force you to move out of your office space. The new owner becomes your landlord until your lease agreement expires.

Once a landlord provides possession of a property to a tenant, the landlord has the right to receive rent and other benefits for the property. The landlord can transfer this right to receive rent.

TENANT TRANSFER OF INTEREST

A tenant can transfer his or her interest in the leased property in two ways: assignments and subleases. Suppose you decide that you want to rent an office space to open your own business and you sign a lease that will begin next month. Unfortunately, you later discover that you don't have enough money to start your business at this time. You are still a party to the lease agreement, but you now have no use for the office space. However, your friend is interested in renting office space. You could transfer your entire interest in the leased property to your friend. A transfer of a tenant's entire interest in the leased property is an **assignment.**

Usually, a lease requires that the landlord must consent to a tenant's assignment of her interest in the lease. Why would the lease contain such a requirement? The requirement for a landlord's consent to an assignment is protection for the landlord. Perhaps the assignee, the person to whom the lease interests have been transferred, has a history of severely damaging property that he has previously rented. Consequently, if the tenant tries to assign the lease without the landlord's consent, the landlord may terminate the lease agreement. However, if the landlord knowingly accepts rent from the assignee, the landlord essentially waives the consent requirement.

Let's return to the example described above. Suppose that you make an assignment of your interest in the office space to your friend. Your friend acquires all your rights under the lease. However, your friend fails to make the rent payment for the first month. Who can be held liable for that rent? You can be. The assignment requires that your friend pay the rent, but it does not relieve you of your responsibility to pay the rent. You will have to pay the rent, but you have a right to be reimbursed by your friend. Thus, both you and your friend, the assignee, are liable to the landlord for failure to pay rent.

How is a sublease different from an assignment? Suppose that you are currently renting an office space but you decide to take a job that is three states away. Your lease for the office space ends in six months. You can try to find someone to sublease the office space for the six months. A **sublease** is a transfer of less than all the interest in a leased property. In essence, a sublease creates a landlord-tenant relationship between the original tenant and the sublessee. If you decided to sublease the office space to someone (with the consent of the landlord), this person would not have any legal obligations to the landlord. Instead, the legal obligations are to you, the tenant to the lease. Thus, if your sublessee does not pay rent, the landlord can hold you responsible for the rent payment.

Termination of the Lease

Generally, at the end of the term of a lease, the lease is terminated. The tenant returns possession of the premises to the landlord unless there is an option for renewal in the lease. The tenant must leave the premises.

Connecting to the core

Accounting

Leases on Balance Sheets

Prior to November 1976, companies could enter into lease agreements without disclosing these agreements on their balance sheets. However, the Financial Accounting Standards Board (FASB) in 1976 began requiring that companies report certain financial leases on their balance sheets. The rationale for this ruling was that companies' balance sheets looked better when these companies had leases but did not report them. In other words, companies could have multiple lease obligations but appear to have fewer liabilities by omitting these leases on their balance sheets. Therefore, the FASB requires that companies report leases that meet one or more of the following four criteria:

- The lessee becomes the property owner by the end of the term of lease.
- The lessee can purchase the property below fair market value at the end of the leasing term.
- The leasing term constitutes 75 percent or more of the expected life of the property.
- At the beginning of the leasing term the present value of lease payments exceeds 90 percent of the property's fair market value.

When a company enters a lease agreement that meets one or more of these criteria, the lease is considered a capital lease and must be reported on a balance sheet. Future business managers should know whether particular lease agreements meet one or more of the four criteria of a *capital lease,* as the kinds of leases could affect how companies report their liabilities on their balance sheets.

Source: S. Ross, R. W. Westerfield, and B. D. Jordan, *Fundamentals of Corporate Finance* (New York: McGraw-Hill/Irwin, 2006), pp. 829–831.

Other than expiration of the term of the lease, there are several other ways in which a lease can be terminated. Remember that in almost all of these cases, the termination of the lease agreement relieves the tenant from the obligation of rent.

BREACH OF CONDITION BY LANDLORD

As we discussed earlier, when a landlord interferes with a tenant's use and enjoyment of the property, the landlord has breached the covenant of quiet enjoyment. This interference usually takes place in the form of an eviction. One possible reaction to the eviction is that the tenant can choose to terminate the lease agreement.

FORFEITURE

Similarly, suppose that either the tenant or the landlord fails to perform a condition stated in the lease. That party's breach is referred to as **forfeiture** because the party is forfeiting his or her interest in the premises. For instance, if a tenant fails to pay rent by the date specified by the lease agreement, the tenant could be considered as forfeiting her interest in the property. Because forfeiture is quite severe, the courts generally do not favor upholding forfeiture.

DESTRUCTION OF THE PREMISES

If a fire or other disaster has destroyed the subject matter of the lease, most states allow termination of the lease. The tenant is released from paying rent. If the landlord had not been able to do something to prevent the disaster, the landlord is generally not expected to restore and repair the premises.

SURRENDER

Suppose that you get a job offer to manage a business in California. You have to move, but you have one month left on your lease agreement for your apartment in Ohio. You speak with your landlord, who agrees to end the lease agreement early. You are surrendering, or returning, your interest in the premises, and the landlord is agreeing to accept the return of the interest. Thus, **surrender** is a mutual agreement between a landlord and a tenant. The landlord accepts the tenant's offer to surrender the interest in the premises. Generally, a surrender of property must be in writing.

ABANDONMENT

If a tenant moves out of leased premises before the end of the term, has no intent to return, and has defaulted on rent payments, the tenant is essentially making an offer of surrender to the landlord. This tenant behavior is called **abandonment.** If the landlord accepts the property, the tenant is usually relieved of the rent obligation, and the lease is terminated.

CASE OPENER WRAP-UP

Landlord Liability

The Ohio Supreme Court reversed the appellate court decision, holding that Wenzel was not liable for Sikora's injuries. The court noted that "most courts refuse to impose strict liability in the context of landlord liability . . . for defective conditions, recognizing the need for some kind of notice element prior to the imposition of liability." Because Wenzel neither knew nor should have known about the deck defects, he is not liable for Sikora's injuries. Is this the outcome you predicted? Based on the information presented in this chapter, do you think the court made the right decision? Note that any action against the city would have been barred by immunity. Ordinarily, government officials cannot be sued.

Summary

Creation of the Landlord-Tenant Relationship

Landlord: Owner of the property, also known as a *lessor.*
Tenant: Party who assumes temporary ownership of the property, also called the *lessee.*
Leasehold estate: The property in question.
Lease: Actual agreement between the landlord and the tenant.
Types of leases:

1. *Definite term:* Automatically expires at the end of a given term.
2. *Periodic tenancy:* Created for a recurring term.
3. *Tenancy at will:* Termination may occur at any time.
4. *Tenancy at sufferance:* Tenant fails to leave the property after the termination of the lease.

Fair Housing Act: Prohibits landlords from discriminating on the basis of race, color, sex, religion, national origin, or familial status.

Rights and Duties of the Landlord and the Tenant

Possession and use of the premises:

Covenant of quiet enjoyment: Promise that the tenant has the right to quietly enjoy the land.

Eviction:

1. *Actual eviction:* Landlord physically prevents tenant from entering premises; can be full (prohibited from all parts) or partial (prohibited from some parts).
2. *Constructive eviction:* Premises become unsuitable for use due to landlord.

Use of the premises:

Implied Warranty of Habitability: Requirement that the premises be fit for ordinary residential purposes.

Tenant use of the premises:

Waste: Tenant conduct that causes permanent and substantial injury to the landlord's property.

Alterations: Changes that affect the condition of the premises; generally cannot be made without the landlord's consent.

Maintenance of the premises:

Common areas: Areas used by all tenants for which the landlord is responsible.

Options when repairs are not done:

1. Terminate the lease.
2. Withhold rent payment.
3. Repair and deduct costs.
4. Sue landlord.

Rent: Defined as compensation paid to the landlord for the tenant's exclusive use of and right to possess the premises. Landlords may charge a late fee, but it must be related to the amount of rent past due.

Rent escalation clause: Clause included in the lease that allows the landlord to increase the rent for increases in cost of living, property taxes, or the tenant's commercial business.

Landlord's lien: Landlord's right to some or all of the tenant's property when rent is unpaid.

Liability for Injuries on the Premises

Landlord liability: Landlord can be held liable for injuries sustained in common areas and for injuries that occurred outside common areas due to repairs the landlord should have made. The landlord has the responsibility to ensure that the premises are in reasonably good condition before the tenant takes control. The foreseeability of a crime is also a factor in liability.

Tenant's liability: Tenant must keep premises in a reasonably safe condition but is responsible only for those areas where the customer can be reasonably expected to go.

Transferring Interests of Leased Property

Landlord transfer of interest: Landlord may transfer property and the new owner becomes the landlord until the tenant's lease expires.

Tenant transfer of interest:

Assignment: Transfer of tenant's entire interest in the leased property.

Sublease: Transfer of less than all of the tenant's interest in a leased property.

Termination of the Lease

Termination may occur in the following instances:

1. *Breach of condition by landlord:* Landlord interferes with tenant's use and enjoyment of premises.
2. *Forfeiture:* Tenant or landlord fails to perform conditions specified in the lease.
3. *Destruction of the premises:* Fire or other disaster destroys the premises.
4. *Surrender:* Mutual agreement between landlord and tenant.
5. *Abandonment:* Tenant moves out of leased premises before the end of the term.

Point / Counterpoint

Should State Legislatures Be Sensitive to the Unique Needs of Mobile-Home Owner-Tenants Who Face the Possibility of Eviction?[1]

Yes

Individuals who own a mobile home but rent a lot from a park owner are called *mobile home owner-tenants.* Mobile-home owner-tenants are in a landlord-tenant relationship with the park owner because they rent a lot, or "pad." Such landlord-tenant relationships are hybrid relationships—somewhere between owning and renting.

Currently, state laws vary with regard to the extent to which mobile-home owner-tenants are treated more like apartment renters or more like traditional homeowners. The extent to which mobile-home owner-tenants are treated like traditional homeowners is especially important when the landlord wants to evict the tenant for nonpayment of rent.

In some states, legislation treats mobile-home owner-tenants more like renters than owners. This is important because, unlike the case with an apartment dweller, when a mobile-home owner-tenant is evicted, the mobile-home owner-tenant must move both herself and her home.

Many people assume that mobile homes are easy to move. In reality, mobile homes are not very mobile. It is often difficult and expensive to move these homes. It is not as if a mobile-home owner can hitch the home to a vehicle and drive off. Often, mobile homes are designed to stay put once they are set down on a pad.

When a traditional homeowner gets behind on payments, this owner typically stays in the home 12 to 18 months before the lender can remove the owner from the home. Not so with the mobile-home owner-tenant. Park owners in some states can use eviction procedures that lock mobile-home owners out of their homes in less than a month!

State legislatures should protect the sanctity of the American home for mobile-home owner-tenants by changing laws to respond to the unique needs created by hybrid relationships.

No

Individuals are free to enter into contracts with owners to rent property. The right to rent comes with responsibilities, especially the responsibility of paying for rented space. When mobile-home owner-tenants fail to pay their rent, they become undesirable tenants, and landlords have every right to evict them. Landlords who evict tenants are preserving their investment.

Sometimes, state legislatures get involved in matters related to landlord-tenant relationships. They should get involved to address chronic, rather than temporary, problems.

Problems related to mobile-home owner-tenants are typically temporary problems. It is not a public policy issue when tenants cannot pay their bills. Issues between landlords and mobile-home owner-tenants are best resolved on a case-by-case basis.

If state legislatures do respond to the unique needs created by hybrid relationships, they should respond with an eye toward protecting owners. Owners provide an important contribution to society. They make it possible for good tenants to create stable homes. If state legislatures take any action at all, it should be to create incentives for park owners to enter into long-term relationships with good tenants, not with tenants who violate the fundamental terms of their contracts.

[1] This point/counterpoint is based primarily on information from J. Royce Fichtner, "The Iowa Mobile Home Park Landlord-Tenant Relationship: Present Eviction Procedures and Needed Reforms," 53 *Drake Law Review* 181 (Fall 2004). The "no" argument also relies on information from Paul Sullivan, "Security of Tenure for the Residential Tenant: An Analysis and Recommendations," 21 *Vermont Law Review* 1015 (1997).

Questions & Problems

1. What is the most distinguishing element of a landlord-tenant relationship?
2. What is a connection between the covenant of quiet enjoyment and eviction?
3. As a tenant, what are the remedies available to you if the landlord breaches the implied warranty of habitability?
4. When can a tenant be held liable for injuries that occur on the premises of a leased property?
5. Explain the distinction between assignment and sublease.
6. What is the difference between surrender and abandonment in the termination of a lease?
7. Michael Harper and his wife rented their home from Osborn Coleman. Harper noticed that the brackets holding the air-conditioning unit to his home were loose. He attempted to move the air-conditioning unit, but when he touched the bracket, he was electrocuted and injured. Harper sued Coleman, alleging that the defective air-conditioning unit had been negligently or wantonly installed. Coleman testified that he had allowed a previous tenant to install the air-conditioning unit in exchange for a rent payment. There was no evidence to indicate that the tenant who installed the unit was a licensed electrician, and Coleman did not have the unit inspected. Coleman argued that he was unaware of the defects in the air-conditioning unit. The trial court found in favor of Coleman, but Harper appealed the decision. Do you think the decision was upheld? Why or why not? [*Ex Parte Coleman,* 705 So. 2d 392 (Ala. 1997).]
8. Stanley Jancik owned and rented apartments in a large housing complex. Though the apartments contained only one bedroom, they were large enough to house more than one person, and people of all ages, including children, lived in the housing complex. Jancik placed an advertisement in the newspaper stating that a "mature person" was preferred. When Jancik was contacted by potential tenants, he explained that he did not want any teenagers and that he was looking only for middle-aged tenants without children. He also inquired about the race of the potential tenants. Jancik was sued for violating a provision of the Fair Housing act that makes discrimination based on "race, color, religion, sex, handicap, familial status, or national origin" unlawful. Do you think that his actions were unlawful? Why or why not? [*Jancik v. Department of Housing & Urban Development,* 44 F.3d 553 (7th Cir. 1995).]
9. John McNamara was interested in leasing space from the Wilmington Mall Realty Corp. for the development of a custom jewelry store. He signed a five-year lease for the store and renovated the space at his own expense. An aerobic studio was subsequently located in the space next to McNamara's store. McNamara was informed that the studio would be soundproofed, but immediately after the studio opened, McNamara began to complain that the music from the studio could be heard in his store. The studio installed insulation, but McNamara still argued that the noise was disrupting his business. McNamara informed Wilmington that he would withhold rent until the matter was resolved. More insulation was installed, but McNamara still did not pay rent and eventually abandoned the space. He sued Wilmington based on theories of constructive eviction and breach of the covenant of quiet enjoyment. Wilmington countersued for the unpaid rent. The trial court found in favor of McNamara and awarded him $110,000 in damages. Wilmington appealed the decision. How do you

think this conflict was resolved? [*McNamara v. Wilmington Mall Realty Corp.*, 466 S.E.2d 324 (N.C. App. 1996).]

10. Although his lease expired on December 31, Kevin Schill continued to live in his rented apartment. He had previously written a letter to the apartment management stating that the apartment "has severe water leaks and severe water damage." A.G. Spanos Development, Inc., the owner of the apartments, brought an action against Schill for nonpayment of the rent. Schill filed a counterclaim against Spanos, alleging that his property was damaged by the water leaks. The damages had occurred after the December 31 expiration. Because Schill had previously complained about the problem, A.G. Spanos argued that Schill voluntarily remained in the apartment notwithstanding his knowledge of the water leaks and, therefore, was responsible for any property damages. Do you think the courts agreed with Spanos? Why or why not? [*Schill v. A.G. Spanos Development, Inc.*, 457 S.E.2d 204 (Ga. App. 1995).]

11. Defendants John and Terry Hoffius advertised for rent a piece of residential property. The ad was answered by Kristal McCready and Keith Kerr. After learning that McCready and Kerr were unmarried, the defendants refused to rent the property to them. Another unmarried couple, Rose Baiz and Peter Perusse, were also prevented from renting the property. The couples argued that they were unfairly discriminated against because of their marital status. The defendants argued that they were motivated by a strong religious belief that unmarried couples should not live together. Do you think that this is a reasonable reason for refusing to rent the property? Why or why not? [*McCready v. Hoffius,* 586 N.W.2d 723 (Mich. 1998).]

12. Shortly after moving into their apartment, Michael Paxton and Mary Lowder notified the apartment manager that the plumbing and wiring needed to be repaired. The manager made minor repairs, but Paxton and Lowder were unsatisfied with the results. Paxton and Lowder complained that the refrigerator was inoperable, the sinks were leaking, the bathroom walls were decaying, and the carpet was deteriorated. They contacted the Health Department with their concerns. The day after the landlord received notice of the complaint, Paxton and Lowder were served with an eviction notice. When they refused to leave the apartment, the landlord brought an action against them to vacate the apartment. Paxton and Lowder counterclaimed, alleging that the eviction was retaliatory. Did the landlord's actions constitute a retaliatory eviction? How do you think the court decided? [*Bldg. Monitoring Systems, Inc. v. Paxton,* 905 P.2d 1215 (Utah 1995).]

13. Tenants renting from the New York City Housing Authority (NYCHA) had paid their rent on time for approximately seven years. However, in January 1997, petitioners began to withhold rent due to several problems, including a leak in a plumbing waste pipe. The tenants asked the NYCHA to fix the unsanitary conditions in their apartment. Despite promises to fix the plumbing, inspections revealed that the plumbing was not satisfactorily repaired. In January 1998, an inspector determined that the pipe had been replaced but that a moisture problem still existed. In response to the condition of the apartments, the tenants continued to withhold rent. The NYCHA brought administrative charges against the tenants for "chronic rent delinquency." Do you think that the NYCHA breached a warranty of habitability? Did the tenants have a right to withhold rent? [*In the matter of Geraldine Law et al. v. Franco,* 690 N.Y.S.2d 893 (1999).]

14. St. George International, Inc., leased office space to the law firm Murges, Bowman & Corday (MBC). Both Bowman and Corday left the firm to establish a new practice at a different location. Murges, who was unable to satisfy MBC's lease requirements by himself, vacated the leased premises. St. George terminated the lease for nonpayment

of rent and filed suit for breach of contract against MBC. Under the Illinois code, "[A] landlord or his or her agent shall take reasonable measures to mitigate the damages recoverable against a defaulting lessee." However, the lease signed by MBC and St. George explicitly stated that "in the event of the termination of this lease by Landlord . . . Landlord shall be entitled to recover from Tenant all Monthly Base Rent and Operating Expense Adjustments accrued and unpaid for the period up to and including such termination date." After MBC abandoned the property, St. George sued the law firm for damages under the lease. St. George originally was awarded damages of $171,553, but the decision was later reversed. How do you think the case was decided on appeal? [*St. George Chicago, Inc. v. Murges & Associates, Ltd.,* 695 N.E.2d 503 (Ill. App. 1998).]

15. Ana Cordero is raising three grandchildren: Jessica (age 16), Veronica (12), and Raymond (10). Her son, the children's father, is in jail. Jessica and Veronica had the same mother, and she is now deceased. Raymond's mother abandoned him. Cordero has been raising her grandchildren since they were infants or toddlers. Veronica has cerebral palsy. A landlord-tenant dispute arose between Cordero and Totaram (the landlord) when Cordero stopped paying the rent. Cordero asked the court for more time to vacate the property, as she needed more time to find a suitable home. By contrast, the landlord claimed that the nonpayment of rent was creating an economic hardship. Cordero had already been given ample time to find a suitable home. Does the judge have the discretion to extend the stay of eviction, given that Cordero is caring for a disabled child? What result? [*Totaram v. Cordero,* 2003 N.Y. Slip Op. 50663(U) (N.Y.City Civ. Ct.), available at 2003 WL 1904081.]

16. Escobar, a college student, sustained injuries when he fell from a fourth-story window of the Mark Tower residence hall at the University of Southern California (USC). Before he fell, he had been sleeping on a bed that was placed against a window in Mark Tower. Escobar's friends had taken him to this residence hall so that he could sleep off the effects of excessive alcohol consumption. USC sought to have the lawsuit dismissed because the fall was caused by Escobar's gross consumption of alcohol. Escobar contested USC's claim, alleging that his fall was caused by a dangerous condition in the residence hall. Specifically, when the university redesigned rooms in 1996, it created a dangerous condition by removing permanently affixed desks, which had prevented beds from being placed against the window. The university should have considered what its redesign would do to furniture arrangement and how new arrangements might place students at risk. What result? Will Escobar get to go forward with his claim? [*Escobar v. University of Southern California,* No. B166522, Los Angeles Sup. Ct., No. BC259972, available at 2004 WL 2094602.]

Looking for more review material?

The Online Learning Center at **www.mhhe.com/kubasek1e** contains this chapter's "Assignment on the Internet" and also a list of URLs for more information, entitled "On the Internet." Find both of them in the Student Center portion of the OLC, along with quizzes and other helpful materials.

Insurance Law

CASE OPENER

Nationwide Life Insurance

On August 6, 1996, Robert Altman purchased a life insurance policy worth $200,000 from Nationwide Life Insurance Company. He made all the necessary payments before passing away on February 11, 1998. The sole beneficiary to the policy was his wife, Karon Altman, and she began motions to collect on this policy on February 18, 1998. However, Nationwide began an investigation of the policy, claiming that Mr. Altman had made misrepresentations on the policy that rendered it void. Ms. Altman took Nationwide to court to receive the insurance money owed to her. As you will learn in this chapter, the insurance policy had an incontestability clause that did not allow misrepresentations to void a policy after two years of the effective date of the policy. At issue in the trial was whether or not Nationwide had begun to investigate misrepresentations prior to the two-year deadline.

1. From the information given above, who appears to have more ground for judgment in their favor at the trial?
2. Assuming Mr. Altman did commit fraud, how did his actions harm others?

The Wrap-Up at the end of the chapter will answer these questions.

CHAPTER 51

Learning Objectives

After reading this chapter, you will be able to answer the following questions:

1. What is the nature of the insurance relationship?
2. What does the insurance contract include?
3. How is an insurance policy canceled?
4. What are the obligations of the insurer and insured?
5. What is the insurer's defense for nonpayment?
6. What are the types of insurance available to consumers?

This chapter will help readers become familiar with basic terminology and principles of insurance law. **Insurance** is defined as a contract in which the insured party makes payments to the insurer in exchange for the insurer's promise to make payment or transfer goods to another party (either the insured party or a beneficiary) in the event of injury or destruction to the insured party's property or life. Thus, if an individual was interested in buying life insurance, that person would pay a certain amount of money to the insurance company in exchange for its promise to pay a specified amount of money to a designated beneficiary (e.g., a spouse) in the event of death.

The insurance industry is one of the most pervasive industries in society: Millions of dollars are spent on private insurance, while the government spends similarly large amounts on social insurance. While numerous types of insurance exist today, the first type of insurance was marine insurance. Merchants who engaged in trade across the sea created marine insurance to protect against the hazards of their trade. Next, property insurance evolved, largely in the form of fire insurance. Typical kinds of modern insurance include life, automobile, and homeowner's insurance.

This chapter will help you understand the role of insurance in the context of business. We first provide definitions of important concepts in insurance law. Then we carefully examine the insurance contract. Finally, we consider the different types of insurance available.

The Nature of the Insurance Relationship

Before readers begin to learn about insurance law, they need to have a clear understanding of the following terms: insured party, premium, insurer, beneficiary, and policy. First, the **insured party** is the party who makes a payment, a **premium**, in exchange for a payment in the event of damage or injury to property or person. The **insurer**, sometimes called the **underwriter**, is the party who receives the payments from the insured party and makes the payment to the **beneficiary**, the person who receives the insurance proceeds, in the event of injury or damage. In most insurance policies (except life insurance policies), the beneficiary and the owner are the same person. These parties express their agreement for insurance in a document called a **policy**.

RISK

The most important element of the insurance agreement is **risk**, a potential loss. In our society, we try to identify potential risks and manage these risks by transferring and distributing the risks. Through the insurance agreement, the insured party *transfers* its risk of loss of property or life to the insurance company. The insurance company distributes this risk among a large group of persons who share the same risk. Consequently, if the loss does occur, one party is not forced to bear the entire weight of the loss.

For example, there is a risk that your house might burn down. Many other people face the risk of their houses burning down. Consequently, when you purchase insurance to protect against fire, you pay a premium to the insurance company. This premium is small relative to the amount of money you would receive if your house burned down, because the insurance company has distributed the risk of fire among all the individuals who purchased the insurance. This transfer and distribution of risk is known as **risk management.**

To summarize, we have introduced the parties to the insurance policy as well as the concepts of premiums and risk. What can be insured? Who can create an insurance policy? The next section will answer these questions.

global context

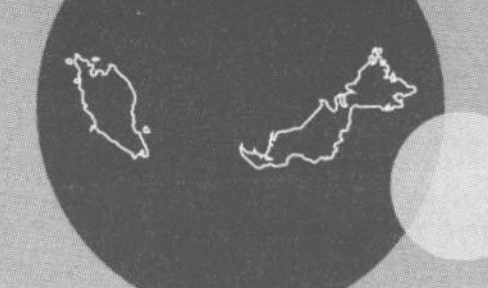

Insurance in Malaysia

In Malaysia, as in most countries, the possession of insurable interest is a prerequisite for collecting on a life insurance policy. In most instances, Malaysian insurance policies are void if there is no insurable interest at the time of the loss. However, exceptions to this rule do exist. For instance, if at the time the policy is affected, the insured has a spouse, child, or other dependent under a designated age, the policy cannot be declared void. This exception also holds true for any employees or wholly dependent individuals. Thus, for the collection of life insurance in Malaysia, underage dependents cancel out the insurable-interest requirement. Preventing the insurance policy from being declared void on these grounds is contingent on accurate disclosure of personal information at the creation of the contract. If a dependent's age is not stated, the policy is invalid. This Malaysian law may seem harsh, but warnings against full disclosure are made obvious to all those who are signing policies.

INSURABLE INTEREST

A person who has an interest in property or life has an **insurable interest** in this property or life. This interest must translate into an economic interest; the person must suffer an economic loss if there were damage or harm to the person or property. Only individuals who have insurable interests in person or property can enter into a valid insurance agreement.

Exhibit 51-1 Examples of Interesting Insurance Cases

Bruce Springsteen's mouth—$6 million
Dolly Parton's breasts—$600,000
Guitar player Keith Richards's right index finger—$1.6 million
Pitcher Kevin Brown's right arm—$67.5 million
Dancer Michael Flatley's legs—$40 million
British stripper Frankie Jackeman's penis—$1.6 million

Source: *Time,* December 20,1999, p. 32.

The insurable interest can exist in either a person or property. For example, a person or company can take out an insurance policy on someone whom that person or company expects to benefit from during his or her continued life. Microsoft Corporation could take out a life insurance policy on Bill Gates's life because the corporation would likely suffer an economic loss if he were to die. If the insurable interest is in a life, the interest must exist at the time the policy is obtained. In contrast, an individual has an insurable interest in property when that person derives a financial benefit from the continued use of the property. However, if the insurable interest is in property, the interest must exist *at the time of the loss.* If a person has an interest in property when the insurance was obtained but the interest did not exist at the time of the damage, that person cannot collect the beneficiary payment on the insurance.

Many things can be and have been insured. Exhibit 51-1 contains just a few dramatic illustrations.

How exactly is the insurance agreement created? What kinds of restrictions are placed on the creation and execution of the insurance agreement? The next section will examine these questions.

The Insurance Contract

Many of the elements of contract law that you learned in Chapters 13 to 16, such as offer, acceptance, and consideration, are relevant to the creation of an insurance contract.

APPLICATION FOR INSURANCE

The process of creating an insurance relationship usually begins when the party with the insured interest makes an offer to purchase insurance by completing and sending in an insurance company application. Based on the information described in the application, the insurance company evaluates the risk and determines whether to accept or reject the offer.

Applicants have a duty to reveal all significant information regarding the risk associated with the insurance policy. If the applicant makes a misleading or misrepresentative material statement and the insurance company relies on this false statement, the insurance company can void the contract. The insurance company must demonstrate two elements to void the contract: (1) The misrepresentation was material, and (2) the company's knowledge of this misrepresentation would have resulted in the rejection of the offer. Case 51-1 considers what constitutes misrepresentation on an insurance application.

CASE 51-1 C. STAN DERBIDGE v. MUTUAL PROTECTIVE INSURANCE COMPANY

COURT OF APPEALS OF UTAH
963 P.2D 788 (1998)

In June 1989, Esma Seymour met with a Mutual Protective Insurance Company (MPIC) representative to apply for insurance. MPIC asked various questions regarding Seymour's health history in the application such as whether Seymour had received medical advice or treatment, taken any medications, or consulted with any doctors over the last five years for conditions such as high blood pressure or organic mental disorders or diseases. Seymour responded that she had received treatment for high blood pressure but not for organic mental disorders. Seymour and the representative signed the application, and Seymour paid a premium of $910.

Six months after MPIC issued a long-term care policy to Seymour, she submitted a claim that she required care in a nursing facility due to Alzheimer's disease. When investigating her claim, MPIC discovered that since November 1985, Seymour's doctor had diagnosed Seymour as suffering from memory impairment. She was hospitalized in November 1985 because her memory problems interfered with her taking her high blood pressure medication. Seymour's medical records indicated that in January 1988, her doctor concluded that organic brain syndrome was probable.

MPIC rescinded Seymour's insurance policy in February 1990, arguing that Seymour had misrepresented material facts in her application. In 1993, Seymour brought suit for breach of contract. She argued that she had no knowledge of the memory-impairment diagnosis. Thus, she claimed that any misstatements in her application were innocent and consequently did not constitute misrepresentation. Her doctor reported that he never discussed Alzheimer's disease with her until June 1989, after she had applied for the insurance. MPIC requested summary judgment, arguing that Seymour's statements in her application were misrepresentations even if she did not then know they were false. The trial court granted summary judgment, ruling that the statements were material and relied upon by MPIC. During the course of this case, Seymour died; her son, Stan Derbidge, carried on the lawsuit as executor of her estate.

JUDGE ORME:

"Misrepresentation" under Section 31A-21-105(2)

[Under Utah statute], an insurer may rescind a policy if any one of these three provisions is met: (1) the insurer relies on a material misrepresentation made by the applicant; (2) the insurer relies on a misrepresentation that was made by the applicant with the intent to deceive; or (3) the applicant's misrepresentation contributes to the loss. However, while the insurer must show only one of these three provisions has been met, under each alternative a threshold requirement is that the applicant have [*sic*] made a "misrepresentation." . . .

In Berger v. Minnesota Mut. Life Ins. Co., 723 P.2d 388 (Utah 1986), the Utah Supreme Court noted that Utah's misrepresentation statute is similar or identical to the statutes of, inter alia, Colorado, Idaho, Illinois, and Oklahoma. All of these states require something more than an innocent misstatement before an insurer can rescind an insurance policy based on misrepresentations in an application. . . .

As explained in Long v. United Benefit Life Ins. Co., 29 Utah 2d 204, 507 P.2d 375 (1973), general principles of Utah insurance law support the view that something more than an applicant's innocent misstatement is required before an insurer can rescind a policy on the ground of misrepresentation. In Long, Justice Crockett explained the rationale for permitting an insurer, under certain circumstances, to rescind an insurance policy:

> The insurance company should be able to reject insurance if in its investigation, or in the medical examination, it is found that there exists some sound reason, *known to the applicant* but not to the insurance company, why [the applicant] was not insurable. . . . E.g., if the insured had a fatal disease, or some affliction which would make him uninsurable, and which fact was concealed from the insurance company, or where there has been any kind of fraud or deception practiced which would make the insurance contract void or voidable. 507 P.2d at 380.

Thus, the policy justification for permitting rescission centers on the applicant's knowledge of an undisclosed condition, i.e., the insurer is entitled to know what the applicant knows, but cannot reasonably expect to know more by relying only on the applicant. . . .

Finally, construing section 31A-21-105(2) to require something more than an innocent misstatement would be consistent with our statutory obligation to "effect the objects of the statutes and to promote justice." Accordingly, we note that the Utah Insurance Code specifically provides that one of the purposes of the Code is to "ensure that . . . claimants . . . are treated fairly and equitably." Moreover, "the primary purpose of . . . adopting [misrepresentation statutes] is to protect the insured or the insured's beneficiary." Statutes pertaining to representations in insurance contracts "are to be liberally construed against the insurer and in favor of the insured."

Fairness dictates that an insured should not be penalized for misstatements that the insured had no idea were inaccurate. Concluding that an innocent misstatement constitutes a "misrepresentation" that justifies rescission of an insurance policy would, we believe, contravene our statutory mandate of ensuring that "claimants . . . are treated fairly and equitably."

In addition to our concern for unfairness to insureds, we must also be sensitive to the "unacceptable consequences" of MPIC's construction of the statute, with an eye to achieving the best result in practical application. Construing "misrepresentation" to embrace innocent misstatements would lead to the disquieting consequence of potentially large numbers of good-faith insurance applicants having their policies rescinded because they suffer from undiagnosed and/or unmanifested pre-existing conditions. As powerfully stated by the Knysak court,

> we are dying the minute we are born. Kidneys, hearts, intestines, livers, and backs may be in a terrible condition unbeknownst to anyone. In the past few decades, we have discovered through advances in medicine that people are predisposed to having certain diseases or defects because of their genes. A person could have congenital heart problems, a predisposition towards diabetes, cancer, lupus, Huntington's disease, schizophrenia, and even alcoholism, all of which would materially affect the acceptance of the risk assumed by the insurer. Arthur Ashe and "Magic" Johnson contracted AIDS that went undetected for some time. People in power plants are just now dying 20 years after exposure to asbestos. Many diseases and mental and physical defects do not manifest themselves for years. Yet, when the disease or defective organ comes to light after the application for insurance, the insured may suddenly discover that his safety net does not exist.

652 N.E.2d at 837. It would not accord with fairness or the Insurance Code's purposes to pull the safety net from beneath an insured who makes an innocent misstatement in an application. . . .

For all of the foregoing reasons, we believe the statute contemplates at least some level of knowledge or awareness of a misstatement to make it a misrepresentation. We need not say precisely what the level is in this case, for viewing the facts in the light most favorable to plaintiff, as we must, Ms. Seymour made the misstatements about not having an organic mental condition, and not being hospitalized or treated for any reason other than the blood-pressure condition she disclosed, in complete innocence. If the fact finder ultimately believes plaintiff's version of the facts, then Ms. Seymour, in making her innocent misstatements, made no "misrepresentations" under section 31A-21-105(2).

REVERSED AND REMANDED in favor of plaintiff.

[CONTINUED]

CRITICAL THINKING

What sorts of evidence could strengthen or weaken the reasoning provided by the judge?

ETHICAL DECISION MAKING

The doctor did not inform Seymour of her mental condition until nearly four years after problems began occurring. Under the WPH framework, did the doctor make the ethical choice?

Effective date. How does the insurance company accept the insurance agreement? Generally, the acceptance occurs when the insurance company communicates to the insured party its intent to accept the agreement. The date that the insurance policy becomes effective, the **effective date,** is extremely important. What happens if someone sends in an insurance application and is injured in an accident two days later? Who is responsible for the losses associated with the accident? In some cases, the insurance coverage does not begin until the company sends a formal letter to the insured party. In other cases, the insurance may begin as soon as the insured party signs the application. Let's look a little more closely at the effective date.

Suppose Ashley meets with an insurance agent to create an insurance policy. If Ashley pays a premium, signs the insurance application, and gives the application to the insurance agent, she will be covered. The insurance agent will likely write a **binder,** an agreement that gives temporary insurance until the company decides to accept or reject the insurance application.

In contrast, suppose Ashley makes an agreement with the insurance company that the policy will be issued at some later date. The insurance will not become effective until Ashley receives the insurance policy. Therefore, if she had some kind of accident, the insurance would not cover the losses.

Suppose Ashley receives an insurance application in the mail. She sends in this insurance application along with a premium. She does not hear anything from the insurance company. Suddenly she suffers a loss that could potentially be covered under the insurance policy. The insurance company delayed in acting on Ashley's application. Is the insurance company responsible? Generally, insurance companies are not responsible for losses because they delayed in acting on an application. However, if the insurance company keeps the premium for an unreasonable amount of time and does not contact the potentially insured party, the insurance company may be held liable for the losses.

Case 51-2 provides an example of the court's consideration of when an insurance policy is considered effective. While this particular case considers whether a renewal of an insurance contract is effective, it demonstrates how complicated cases that consider the effective date of the policy can be.

CASE 51-2 EQUITY FIRE & CASUALTY COMPANY v. LAURENCE TRAVER

SUPREME COURT OF ARKANSAS
330 ARK. 102 (1997)

Laurence Traver received a notice with a due date of renewal of his auto insurance as March 9, 1994, and an expiration date of March 14, 1994. Traver's payment was postmarked March 12, 1994, and later postmarked again on March 21, 1994. Equity received the payment and reinstated the insurance policy on March 22, 1994.

Traver was involved in an automobile accidence on March 19, 1994. The other party to the accident filed a claim with his own insurance carrier, who then filed a suit against Traver, who filed an action against his insurance carrier, Equity. Equity refused to cover the accident because they argued that Traver's policy was not effective on the date of the accident and had lapsed on March 14, 1994.

The trial court ruled in favor of Traver, finding that the mailing of the premium before March 14, 1994, was an effective renewal of the policy.

JUDGE ARNOLD: There is no Arkansas case directly addressing this issue. In Kempner v. Cohn, we recognized the mailbox rule for the acceptance of a contract. Once an offer has been made, a contract is completed when the acceptance is mailed if the acceptance is made in a reasonable amount of time. If a letter of withdrawal is mailed, before the mailing of the acceptance, it is effective only if the party to whom the offer was made receives the withdrawal before making the acceptance.

Despite the fact that this case was decided in the 1800s, there are few cases following it which expound upon this theory. The Kempner decision has been followed as a routine matter of contract theory, with the proviso that parties are free to dictate the terms of offers and acceptances as they deem necessary.

In the case before us, the policy language requires actual receipt of a premium payment prior to the expiration date of the policy to constitute acceptance of a renewal offer. The actual renewal notice gave the due date as a date five days before the expiration date. It does not contain the language requiring actual receipt of the premium payment; it instructs the insured to pay the amount listed as due in order to renew the policy.

In Mississippi Insurance Underwriting Association v. Maenza, 413 So. 2d 1384 (Miss. 1982), the Mississippi Supreme Court examined a situation closely analogous to the case at bar. A property and casualty policy renewal notice/offer was sent to the insured with an expiration date of September 10, 1979. The insured mailed payment on September 8, 1979, but it was not received by the insurer until September 11, 1979. A hurricane destroyed the insured's property on September 11, 1979. The insurer accepted the payment, but claimed the policy had lapsed because payment was not received on or before the due date. The insurer then treated the payment as an application for new coverage and issued a policy with the effective date of September 14, 1979.

The insured brought a claim before the Mississippi Insurance Commission, and it rendered a ruling that the renewal was effective when the premium payment was deposited in the United States mail, as long as it was deposited in time to reach the insurer on or before the expiration date. The insurance commission determined that neither party was to blame for a delay within the postal service; however, the insurer was the party that should bear the imputed burden because it adopted the postal service as its agent when allowing premiums to be transported via mail. 413 So. 2d at 1386.

The Mississippi Supreme Court affirmed the findings of the insurance commission. Specifically, that court held that the insurer's renewal notice is an offer that is accepted by the offeree/insured sending premium payments. The insurer in this instance required that payment be received before acceptance became effective; the Mississippi court rejected this notion because there was no clear language to suggest that acceptance was not effective until receipt. However, the court went on to conclude that in circumstances where an insurer invites premiums to be forwarded through the mail, it adopts the postal service as its agent and deposit of a payment with that agent constitutes acceptance of coverage. According to the Mississippi court, adopting the postal service as an agent imputed any negligence on their behalf to the insurer despite any contract language to the contrary; therefore contract language requiring receipt before acceptance was valid does not render the mailbox acceptance rule inapplicable. Id. at 1388.

In Maenza, the Mississippi court based the finding that the insurer invited the use of the postal service on several factors. First of all, the renewal notice itself indicated that payment could be made via mail, and the insurer utilized the mail to send the renewal notice. The insurer's office was over 100 miles from most of its insureds, so personal delivery would have been impractical. There are two other important factors to note in the Maenza decision. First, the payment was deposited with the postal service prior to the expiration date, in apt time to reach the insurer in a timely manner. Second, upon receipt of the payment it deemed late, the insurer made no attempt to refund the money, but caused a new policy to come into effect with a gap in the coverage.

In the case before us, Equity did have written language requiring receipt of the payment in order for acceptance to be effective; however, that language was in the policy and not on the actual renewal notice. Equity utilized the postal service as a carrier for its offer and expected to receive the acceptance via the mail. Traver mailed the premium payment in a timely manner where, absent negligence or mistake by the postal service, it had ample time to reach Equity prior to the termination date. Upon receipt of Traver's check, Equity did not refuse the payment, yet accepted it as an application for a new policy.

Based upon the facts of this case, it is our determination that Traver's placing the renewal premium in the mail in a timely manner constituted acceptance of Equity's renewal offer. Due to the peculiar factual scenario provided here, this holding is limited to the particular facts and circumstances of this case. We do not institute an absolute rule of applying the "mailbox rule" to all renewal premium payments, nor do we hold that parties are not free to dictate the terms of acceptance of offers. The facts before us present a unique situation where Traver was not afforded notice through the actual offer that receipt of payment was required before acceptance was effective. Given the fact that there was no fraud or negligence on behalf of Traver and the fact that Traver placed the payment in the mail with ample time for it to reach Equity prior to the expiration of the offer, we hold that in this instance there was a manifest acceptance of the renewal offer. Therefore, Traver's policy did not lapse, and it was effective beginning on March 14, 1984.

AFFIRMED in favor of defendant.

CRITICAL THINKING

Judge Arnold states that "the facts before us present a unique situation." What are these facts? In what regard do they make the situation unique?

ETHICAL DECISION MAKING

Which party seems to be benefiting from the court's decision in this case? Who, in the business world, is similarly likely to benefit? If the insurance company were acting under the public disclosure test, would it have behaved differently?

IMPORTANT ELEMENTS OF THE INSURANCE CONTRACT

Generally, the insurance company fashions the insurance contract. However, most states require that certain insurance contracts contain certain clauses. Why? These states recognize that the insurance companies are usually in a power position compared to the position of the insured because the insurance company determines what will or will not be included in the insurance contract. The state-mandated clauses serve to give the insured a little more power. Even if a contract does not include a state-mandated clause but *should* have included such a clause, the courts will hold that the contract did include the clause.

This section will describe several state-mandated clauses as well as other important clauses that might be included in an insurance contract.

While reading about these clauses, readers will likely encounter language that is specific to insurance law. Perhaps readers will have difficulty understanding this language. The courts, recognizing that the average person does not understand insurance law terms, usually interprets any ambiguous words or phrases or confusing clauses in favor of the insured. The insurance company, as the creator of the insurance contract, has an opportunity to be extremely explicit in the creation of the agreement. Therefore, if the company creates a confusing policy, the courts will find in favor of the insured. In Case 51-3, the court considers the definition of *accident* in an insurance policy. The plaintiff in this case argues that *accident* is ambiguous while the defendant disagrees.

CASE 51-3 EILEEN NYGAARD v. STATE FARM INSURANCE COMPANY

COURT OF APPEALS OF MINNESOTA
591 N.W.2D 738 (1999)

On February 27, 1995, Eileen Nygaard's daughter committed suicide by driving her car into an 18-wheel tractor-trailer driven by Lonnie Odegard. Before she committed suicide she wrote letters in which she indicated her intent to kill herself to her parents and best friend. As a result of the crash, Odegard developed problems that needed surgery and was forced to miss work. Odegard's insurance company brought suit against Nygaard's insurance company, State Farm, to cover the damages from the collision. Eileen Nygaard joined Odegard's insurance company in the suit to force State Farm to pay for the damages from the collision. State Farm refused to cover the damages because of an "accident" provision in the insurance policy. State Farm argued that Nygaard's daughter had an intent to commit suicide by driving into Odegard's truck; consequently, the collision was not an "accident" as defined by the policy, which stated: "We will:

1. pay damage which an insured becomes legally liable to pay because of: bodily injury to others, and damage to or destruction of property including loss of its use, caused by accident and resulting from ownership, maintenance or use of your car; . . ."

The district court granted summary judgment for State Farm without any explanation. Nygaard appealed.

JUDGE ANDERSON:

Issue

Does the deceased's suicide qualify as an "accident" for the purpose of motor-vehicle third-party coverage?

Analysis

The result here rests on the interpretation and application of respondent's insurance policy issued to the decedent. "An insurance policy provision is to be interpreted according to both its plain, ordinary meaning and what a reasonable person in the position of the insured would have understood it to mean." . . . Unambiguous language in an insurance policy must be accorded its plain and ordinary meaning. Finally, a court "must not create an ambiguity where none exists in order to afford coverage to the insured."

The decedent's policy is unambiguous. The policy provides coverage for an "accident." The supreme court has defined "accident" to have a generally understood meaning: "an accident is simply a happening that is unexpected and unintended." If the collision in this case were unexpected or unintended, then coverage exists, and if not, then coverage is barred.

Appellant argues that Odegard's perspective is controlling, and, because the collision was "unexpected" from that perspective, coverage should exist. But such a conclusion overlooks the rulings of the supreme court in McIntosh.

The McIntosh court confronted a policy similar to our present case which also provided coverage only for an "accident." In addition, the policy question in McIntosh featured an intentional act that caused injury. The insured was injured by a disgruntled former boyfriend who shot her in the head during a car chase. The insured claimed both first-party no-fault coverage and uninsured motorist benefits because the boyfriend lacked automobile insurance.

The court explained that the case rested on whose perspective defines "accident." The court noted that the "term 'accident' takes its meaning form the context in which it is used." In the first-party no-fault context, the term "accident" is considered from the point of view of the victim. The court reached this result because no-fault benefit eligibility depends "exclusively on the injured victim and whether she has been hurt under circumstances arising from the use of a motor vehicle."

The court ruled an "accident" is viewed from the perspective of the tortfeasor in the context of uninsured-underinsured coverage. The court so concluded by first noting that liability focuses on the conduct of the uninsured motorist because compensation under an insured's policy rests on proving that the uninsured is liable. Ruling that uninsured motorist coverage is not first-party in nature, the court explained that "uninsured motorist coverage is not no-fault coverage; fault on the part of the uninsured motorist must be proven under tort law."

The court's uninsured/underinsured analysis is persuasive in the present case, because the third-party liability benefits that appellant claims must also be proven under tort law. Appellant pursues indemnity for the decedent's act. Such indemnity rests on the decedent's tort liability for Odegard's injuries.

Moreover, as cited by the McIntosh court, the committee comment to section 2 of the Uniform Motor Vehicle Accident Reparations Act (UMVARA) notes that the term "accident" as applied to the obligation to maintain security for tort liability, refers to events which are "accidents" from the point of view of the person causing harm.

Thus, liability to a third party for the first party's acts naturally focuses on the actions of the tortfeasor, which in this case is the decedent.

Next, we move to decide whether coverage exists under the decedent's policy. Appellant concedes that the decedent intentionally collided with Odegard to commit suicide. Because the collision was neither unexpected nor unintended from the decedent's perspective, it was not an accident. As a result, coverage is not afforded by this court under State Farm's policy.

Yet, appellant argues that because the decedent did not intend to injure Odegard, the intentional act exclusion is not applicable. But our case is distinguishable from such [argument] because the decedent's subjective intent is irrelevant. This case does not depend on an intent to injure, but instead focuses on whether the collision qualifies as an "accident" under the policy.

Decision

The district court did not err in denying coverage. The decedent's intentional act of suicide does not constitute an "accident" for purposes of third-party liability insurance coverage.

AFFIRMED in favor of defendant.

CRITICAL THINKING

One of the three judges in this case dissented from the majority opinion presented above. Judge Amundson found that State Farm should cover the costs of Odegard's injuries. Of the reasons given above for rendering the majority decision, explain which one you think Amundson disagreed with to find in favor of the plaintiff.

ETHICAL DECISION MAKING

Whom did State Farm's stance hurt? Whom did the court's decision help?

global context

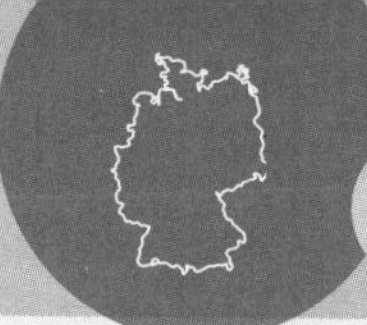

Insurance in Germany

German manufacturing businesses often obtain insurance that covers the risk of product liability. The policies have generally been straightforward, but as the manufacturers expand their businesses internationally, insurance has become more complicated.

German manufacturers distributing their products outside the country's borders are concerned with how and to what extent product liability risk can be insured. For these businesses the question arises as to the location of their insurer. Manufacturers could decide to seek insurance through a German insurance company, regardless of where their products are shipped. This is beneficial because a close, and even personal, relationship can be established with the insurer. However, coverage by a native company may be a problem considering the significant differences in the product liability statutes of various markets. German insurers may not take into consideration differences in foreign markets. For example, insurance companies in the United States generally award larger compensations for product liability cases than do German insurers. Thus, it can be advantageous for manufacturers to seek coverage according to their markets. This option would mean that in addition to having a German insurance company, the manufacturers would also have an insurance company in Spain, Japan, America, or wherever else they sent their goods. Obviously, complications may arise from having several different insurance companies in several different countries. Thus far, it is unclear what option is more advantageous, and each manufacturer's situation should be considered before settling on an option.

Incontestability clause. The incontestability clause is an example of a state-mandated clause. This clause states that after an insurance policy has existed for a specified period of time (usually two years), the insurance company cannot contest any statements made in the insurance application. This clause prohibits the insurer from delaying payment to the insured who files a claim because the insurer decides to investigate the insurance application for potential fraud. Thus, once the insurance policy becomes incontestable, the insurance company cannot claim that the policy does not exist because of the insured's misrepresentation on the application. This type of clause was described in the opening scenario regarding Robert Altman's insurance policy.

Antilapse clause. Suppose you accidentally forget to pay the premium for your insurance. Is the insurance policy lapsed and no longer effective? Some statutes require that insurance companies include antilapse clauses in the insurance contract. These clauses are typically included in life insurance policies. An **antilapse clause** usually states that the insured has a grace period, typically 30 days, in which to make an overdue payment. During this grace period, the insurance is effective. If the insured fails to make a payment in those 30 days, the insurer may not necessarily cancel the insurance policy. Thus, the antilapse clause provides protection for the insured. If a payment is slightly late, the insurance company cannot simply cancel the policy.

Appraisal clause. Suppose that some of your property that is insured for $50,000 is damaged in a fire. The insurance company evaluates the damage and determines that you have suffered a loss of $10,000. You believe that your loss is around $25,000. If you and the insurance company cannot come to an agreement regarding the amount of the loss, you can demand an appraisal under an appraisal clause. Both you and the insurance company will select a disinterested appraiser. Each appraiser will evaluate the loss and state the actual value and loss of each item. If the appraisers fail to agree on the loss, they will typically submit their different appraisals to an umpire who will resolve the differences. Thus, the appraisal clause serves as a method of resolving a dispute over the amount of loss.

Coinsurance clause. Those who wish to insure their property, particularly from fire damage, realize that they typically do not face total loss of the property. Consequently, they do not insure their property for its full value. For example, if you purchased fire insurance for your business, you might insure 40 percent of the total value of your property because you believe that your property would not be severely destroyed because of the extensive sprinkler system in your building. However, the insurance company wants you to insure more of your total property value because it makes greater profits at higher levels of insurance. Because the insurance company has an incentive for creating policies for greater percentages of the value of the property, the insurance company will often include a coinsurance clause in the insurance contract.

The coinsurance clause states that if the insured covers her property at a certain percentage, the insurance company will cover any loss up to this stated percentage. Usually, companies set this percentage at 80 percent of the full value of the property. However, if the insured covers the property at a value less than 80 percent, the insured will be responsible for covering some of the loss. Because the insured will be held responsible, the insured is considered a coinsurer.

Exhibit 51-2 Sample Coinsurance Calculation

$$\frac{\text{Upper limit of insurance}}{80\% \text{ of full property value}} = (\text{recovery }\%)(\text{amount of loss})$$

Recovery amount

$$\frac{\$100,000}{(.80)(\$200,000)} = .625 \times \$50,000 = \$31,250$$

For example, suppose you insure your $200,000 property for $100,000. Your property is damaged, and you suffer a loss of $50,000. Under the coinsurance clause, the insurance company uses the formula in Exhibit 51-2 to determine how much it will cover of the $50,000 loss.

Thus, in this case, the insurance company would pay $31,250 toward the loss, while you would be responsible for the remaining $18,750.

Some states have prohibited the inclusion of coinsurance clauses in insurance contracts. Other states, however, have permitted these clauses if the insurance company either explicitly makes the insured aware of the clause or reduces the premium that the insured must pay.

Other-insurance or multiple-insurance clauses. Suppose you purchase insurance policies from three different companies to protect your business from fire. These policies cover the same risk (i.e., fire damage) and benefit the same party (i.e., you). The building is valued at $100,000, but the insurance policies combine to provide $150,000 worth of coverage. You have overinsured the property and could potentially profit from the damage to your property.

In order to discourage individuals from overinsuring property, most insurance companies include an *other-insurance* or *multiple-insurance* clause that essentially voids or reduces coverage when other insurance policies cover the same risk and benefit the same individual. The most common way to reduce insurance coverage through an other-insurance clause is through the use of pro rata liability. The insurer is liable for a prorated portion of the liability for the loss.

Arbitration clause. Some insurance contracts include clauses that force both the insurer and the insured to submit any dispute over liability that they might encounter to an arbitrator. Such a clause serves to swiftly settle disputes between the insured and the insurer.

Canceling the Insurance Policy

Suppose an insured party decides to discontinue an insurance policy. The insured party may cancel an insurance policy at any time by simply stopping paying the premiums. Moreover, a person might contact his insurance company to tell it he wants to cancel the policy. What happens if the insurer does not want to continue your insurance policy? When is the insurer allowed to cancel the policy?

The insurer may cancel a policy only in certain instances. However, before an insurance company can cancel a policy, the company must give the insured advance notice of the cancellation. This advance notice is usually required by statute and typically notifies the insured that he or she is entitled to a grace period before the policy is canceled. Furthermore, the insured may be entitled to a refund of premium payments.

Exactly when is an insurer permitted to cancel a policy? As discussed earlier, an insurer can cancel a policy if the insured misrepresented a material fact on the insurance application. Furthermore, if the insured fails to pay the premiums after a certain period of time, the insurance company may cancel the policy. Specific types of insurance may be canceled under specific circumstances. For example, car insurance may be canceled if the insured loses her license because of a driving violation. State statutes usually establish when an insurance policy may be canceled.

Case Nugget — When May an Insurer Rescind a Marine Insurance Policy?

Cigna Property and Cas. Ins. Co. v. Polaris Pictures Corp.
159 F.3d 412 (1998)

Cigna sought to rescind a marine insurance contract based on Polaris's failure to disclose material facts in the insurance application. In particular, Cigna claimed that Polaris was in fact the alter ego of Rex K. DeGeorge, a Beverly Hills attorney with a history of "bad luck" resulting in successful claims against a variety of insurance companies.

In particular, Cigna discovered that DeGeorge had in the past lost three yachts under suspicious circumstances, plus a variety of other property from luggage to cars. He had also in the past claimed that he was disabled by a bipolar personality disorder and sought payouts under an insurance policy. In all of these cases, DeGeorge threatened litigation if the insurer involved in each claim did not settle the claim.

Cigna challenged Polaris/DeGeorge with regard to a claim about a fourth yacht, which it had insured. Cigna sought to rescind the marine insurance contract because, among other things, Polaris/DeGeorge had not disclosed his loss history. The court agreed with Cigna and allowed the rescission. The court said:

> Whether or not asked, an applicant for a marine insurance policy is bound to reveal every fact within his knowledge that is material to the risk. An insurer may rescind an insurance contract "if it can show either intentional misrepresentation of a fact, regardless of materiality, or nondisclosure of a fact material to the risk, regardless of intent." This principle, known as *uberrimae fidei* exists under both California insurance law, and federal admiralty law.

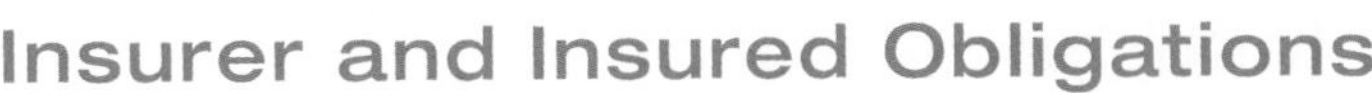

Insurer and Insured Obligations

As parties to the insurance contract, both the insurer and the insured have certain obligations that each party must fulfill. If either party does not meet its obligation, the other party can usually sue for breach of contract.

INSURER DUTY TO DEFEND THE INSURED

The insurer has a duty to defend the insured from claims for which the insured is liable. For example, suppose a driver (person 1) runs a stop sign and crashes into another driver (person 2). Person 2 files a claim with her insurance company, which then files a claim against person 1's insurance company. Person 1's insurance company has a duty to defend person 1. To begin the defense process, the insured must first notify the insurer. Next, the insurer must provide an attorney to defend the insured, and the insurer is responsible for the attorney costs as well as any litigation costs. If the insurer does not provide an attorney, the insurer has breached the contract.

INSURED DUTY TO PAY SUMS OWED BY THE INSURED

Let's return to the stop-sign accident. If person 1 is liable to person 2 for any damages to person 2's vehicle, the insurer has a duty to pay the damages owed to person 2. These damages are compensatory damages.

Most of the claims for damages for third parties are settled through negotiation between the insurance company and the third party. However, if the claim cannot be settled, the dispute will go to court.

INSURED DUTY TO DISCLOSE INFORMATION

As we stated earlier, the insured has a duty to disclose all material information on the application. Thus, the insured must fully answer any questions truthfully.

INSURED DUTY TO COOPERATE WITH THE INSURER

We have already discussed the insurer's duty to defend the insured. However, for the insurer to meet its duty to defend, the insured must provide the insurer with information regarding the incident that led to the claim. Let's return to the stop-sign accident. Suppose that after person 1 runs the stop sign, he refuses to discuss the accident with his insurance company. If the insurance company does not have enough information about the accident, it cannot defend person 1. Consequently, person 1 has a duty to cooperate with the insurer.

This duty extends into certain elements that lead to a trial. For example, individuals who are insured might be asked to provide the insurance company with a deposition. Moreover, insured individuals might be asked to testify at the trial.

The Insurer's Defenses for Nonpayment

If the insured fails to fulfill either its duty to provide all material information on the insurance contract or its duty to cooperate with the insurer, the insurer may argue that the insured has breached the contract; consequently, the insurer is not required to pay on a claim. The insurer may also use several other defenses for nonpayment of an insurance claim.

First, the insurer can argue that the insured did not have an insurable interest. Thus, the insurance contract is void; the insurer is not required to pay. Second, the insurer can claim that the insured engaged in some type of illegal activity that permits the insurer to cancel the insurance policy. For example, suppose a person intentionally sets fire to her business to receive the insurance benefits. The insurance company, assuming it can provide evidence that the fire was intentionally set, can claim that the insured's behavior is a defense against payment of the claim.

Types of Insurance

There are several ways to categorize insurance policies. First, is the policy an individual or group insurance policy? If the insured party is the party purchasing the insurance, this type of insurance is **individual insurance.** In contrast, if a party who is neither the insured party nor the insurer (e.g., an employer) purchases the insurance, the insurance is considered **group insurance.**

Second, is the insurance personal or commercial? Generally, if a policy covers an individual's life or health, the insurance is **personal insurance.** However, if the insurance covers some type of business risk, the insurance is commonly called **commercial insurance.** Examples of commercial insurance include title, contractor, and fidelity insurance.

Third, is the insurance property or casualty insurance? If the policy is to protect property from loss or damage, the insurance is **property insurance.** Examples of property insurance include fire, theft, homeowner's, and marine insurance. If, however, the primary purpose of the insurance is to protect a person or property from accidental injury, the insurance is **casualty insurance.** Examples of casualty insurance include workers' compensation, health, machine, and auto insurance.

In this section, we will look more closely at several specific types of insurance that are particularly important for businesspeople. While the types of insurance are similar, certain principles apply to certain types of insurance. Consequently, you need to be aware of the distinctions of the types of insurance. Exhibit 51-3 presents a summary of various types of insurance for readers who want a quick overview.

LIABILITY INSURANCE

Liability insurance is perhaps one of the most important types of insurance you will need to be concerned with as a businessperson. You would purchase **liability insurance** to protect your business from tort liability to third parties. For example, suppose a customer is injured while doing business at a particular office. The business is probably now liable to the customer for her injuries. If the business does not have liability insurance, it could suffer severe losses if the customer chooses to sue for damages. Thus, liability insurance helps to prevent these severe business losses.

First, a business manager should purchase a policy that protects against a broad range of risks, a **commercial general liability policy** (previously known as a *comprehensive general liability policy*). When purchasing the policy, a businessperson can decide what exactly will be covered under the policy. A commercial general liability policy generally provides protection for the insured for bodily injury as well as property injury to third parties. Thus, the policy can protect against personal injury suits by customers as well as suits involving disputes with competitors over intellectual property.

The commercial general liability policy, however, is subject to several exclusions. The insurance policy will state which exclusions apply specifically to your policy. First, the policy does not provide protection for intentional acts. For example, if an individual shoves a customer down a flight of steps, the liability policy will not protect the individual from a suit filed by this customer. Because it is expected that shoving the customer down the

EXHIBIT 51-3 Summary of Various Types of Insurance

Casualty insurance: Covers accidental injury to persons and property.
Group insurance: One insurance policy is issued to an entity, such as an employer or union, to provide coverage for the individual members of a group, such as all employees or union members.
Health insurance: Protects the insured from losses caused by specific types of illnesses and related expenses.
Liability insurance: Protects the insured against liability.

- *Contractors' liability insurance:* Protects contractors against liability for injuries that might occur while completing a job (excluding injuries to employees).
- *Garage liability:* Protects the garage owner from liability to persons who are injured by the operation of the garage.
- *Product liability insurance:* Protects the producer or manufacturer of a good from loss due to damages paid to people who are injured using the good.
- *Professional liability:* Protects members of specific professions from liability associated with their professional acts.

Life Insurance: Provides a specific sum of money on the death of the insured.
Property Insurance: Protects against destruction or loss of property.

- *Burglary and theft.*
- *Fire insurance:* Protects property from loss or damage from fire.
- *Insurance against property by damage caused by riot, strike, or other civil commotion.*
- *Livestock:* Protects owner of livestock from loss due to injury or death of the livestock.
- *Water, weather, and natural forces insurance:* Flood insurance, water damage, weather insurance (such as tornado, cyclone, hurricane, and rain), hail insurance, lightning insurance, etc.

Risks associated with a specific device, location, or activity: Airplane insurance, automobile insurance, boiler and machinery insurance, bridge insurance, builder's risk, elevator insurance, homeowner's insurance, jewelers' block policy, marine insurance, sprinkler leakage insurance, transportation insurance.
Unemployment insurance and disability insurance: Protects the insured when he or she is unable to earn money due to inability to find or perform work.

stairs will cause injury, the insurance company will not cover the loss. Second, the policy does not protect against certain types of environmental liability. If the company has been intentionally discharging pollutants into a river and is later sued, the liability policy will not apply. However, if the discharge was "sudden and accidental," the policy will apply.

Depending on what type of business a person manages, he or she might want to consider several other forms of insurance. First, if the business is a manufacturing company, the owner might wish to purchase **product liability insurance.** We discussed product liability in Chapter 10. As readers may recall, a customer might be injured through the use of a product. A manufacturing company might be liable for a customer's injuries. Suppose that 500 customers are injured while using the product. The liability has severely increased!

Case Nugget What Is the Purpose of No-Fault Insurance?

Greenspan v. Allstate Ins. Co.
937 F. Supp. 288 (S.D.N.Y. 1996)

Under New York's no-fault insurance law, the New York Comprehensive Motor Vehicle Insurance Reparations Act, victims of motor vehicle accidents may be reimbursed by an insurance carrier for medical expenses. Typically, victims assign their right to receive no-fault benefits to their health care provider, who then seeks payment from the insurer.

In the *Greenspan* case, the plaintiffs were health care providers in New York State who submitted claims to Allstate Insurance Company under no-fault policies it had issued to persons the plaintiffs had treated. The plaintiffs claimed that Allstate had engaged in a variety of practices designed to deny or delay reimbursement for properly submitted and documented claims for medically necessary services.

The court stated, "The purpose of no-fault insurance law [is] to institute an inexpensive, efficient method of compensating accident victims." If Allstate had erected barriers to reimbursement, this would cause harm to the public interest in an inexpensive, efficient compensation system. Here, the court ultimately ruled in favor of Allstate because it found there had been no injury to the public interest.

Product liability insurance may help cover the cost of recalling and replacing the products. Second, professionals are likely to want to purchase **professional insurance,** which protects professionals from suits by third parties who claim negligent job performance.

Third, if a person has employees, he or she will likely need a **workers' compensation policy,** which provides payments to employees who are injured through an employment-related accident. The employer is required by statute to pay benefits to injured workers, and the insurance policy can cover the required payments.

FIRE INSURANCE

Fire insurance protects property from any damage caused by fire. However, there are some limits to this protection. First, owners cannot have started the fire with the intent of causing damage to their property. Second, the insurance company typically makes a distinction between **friendly fire,** a fire contained in a place where it is intended to burn (e.g., a fireplace), and **hostile fire,** a fire that occurs in a place where it was not intended to burn (e.g., an electric outlet). Most policies provide protection for hostile fires but not for friendly fires. Thus, if business property is damaged by smoke from a fireplace in the office, fire insurance will likely not cover the damage.

MARINE INSURANCE

The first type of insurance created was **marine insurance,** which protected against loss of ship and cargo from "perils of the sea." Marine insurance continues to be important for businesspeople. For example, marine insurance is particularly important for companies that drill oil and carry the oil overseas. Similarly, businesses in the Great Lakes area might transport goods across the lakes.

When a person applies for marine insurance, he or she is required to disclose all material information about the vessel that might affect its seaworthiness. The applicant also

e-commerce AND THE LAW

Internet Liability Protection

As courts and legislatures decide the legal rules that will govern e-commerce, insurance companies are revising the products they offer businesses that engage in e-commerce. One new form of insurance is Internet liability protection.

Internet liability protection protects companies against copyright and trade infringement–related claims. It also protects companies against additional e-commerce risks, including claims that allege plagiarism via the Internet, failure to protect confidential information gathered online, and failure to stop a computer virus. Typically, Internet liability protection does not cover claims related to patents or trade secrets, which are more expensive than other intellectual property claims.

Insurance companies that offer Internet liability protection are likely to assist their customers by engaging in interactions designed to prevent claims. For instance, one insurance company, Chubb, offers a handbook with a checklist that allows customers to rethink some of their Internet and Web site practices. A company that follows the checklist is likely to take a look at its Web site's links, for instance. Doing so may help the company decide whether its linking techniques leave it vulnerable to litigation. Through this form of interaction, insurance companies also get to know their clients better, thereby helping the companies determine which forms of protection their clients need.

agrees that the vessel can withstand the normal wear and tear of water travel. Additionally, at application time, the applicant needs to determine where the vessel will be traveling. If a person is traveling on the ocean, he or she needs an **ocean marine** policy. However, if travel will take place on inland waterways, such as lakes, rivers, and canals, the person needs an **inland marine** policy. Applicants also need to decide for what period of time the insurance will apply. A person might choose insurance that applies for a specific time period, such as 30 days. Alternatively, a person can specify in the agreement that the insurance will last as long as the marine trip will last.

LIFE INSURANCE

Life insurance is important in the business context because a business might want to take out a life insurance policy on a key employee. Suppose Bill Gates had been severely disabled or killed within the first few years that Microsoft exploded in the technology market. Would Microsoft have been able to become so successful without Bill Gates?

Life insurance offers protection by providing a payment on the death of the person whose life is insured. You can choose among several different types of life insurance. First, **whole-life insurance** provides protection for the entire life of the insured. The owner of the life insurance policy pays a premium in exchange for the protection on the death of the insured. However, whole-life insurance policies are distinctive because they have a cash-surrender value. In other words, if you decide to cancel the policy, you will receive a certain amount of cash back. This value increases as more premiums are paid. This cash-surrender value also permits the owner of the policy to borrow money from the insurance company at a favorable interest rate.

Second, **term-life insurance** provides coverage for a specified term (e.g., six months, one year, ten years). The premiums for term-life insurance are usually smaller than the premiums for whole-life insurance. However, the beneficiary is paid only if the person whose life is insured dies within the term specified by the insurance contract. Therefore,

global context

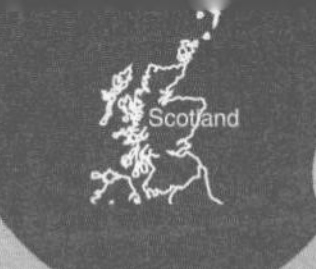

Marine Insurance in Scotland

In 1906, Scotland added the Marine Insurance Act to its mercantile law. The act legitimized the finer points of insurance contracts related to "marine adventure." Marine insurance policies cover most items involved in marine activities, including ships under construction, ships being used on the sea, goods transported by sea, or liability to third parties in the event of difficulties while at sea.

Marine insurance policies tend to be demanding in detail. For example, before an insurance provider will sign a marine insurance policy, it requires that the value of the item to be insured be agreed on and specified in the contract. This value is nonnegotiable after the signing. Thus, if a business wishes to insure a ship under construction, it can insure it only for its value as an incomplete vessel. The value specified in the contract is definite, regardless of the passage of time or a change in the nature of the item. The conclusiveness of the value means that the hypothetical business above would have to cancel the policy that states the value of the incomplete ship once the ship is finished. Otherwise, the insurance policy would not cover the true value of the completed ship. This stipulation is just one of many contained within marine insurance. For inconclusive reasons, this type of insurance is one of the most complicated in Scotland.

the insurance company may never have to make a payment to the beneficiary. Moreover, term-life insurance is distinct from whole-life insurance because there is usually no cash-surrender value or loan opportunities associated with term-life insurance.

Term-life insurance policies are also distinct because they usually have a guaranteed renewability clause, which permits the owner to renew the policy without regard for the health of the person whose life is insured. Instead of renewing the policy, the owner might also choose to convert the policy to another type of life insurance policy.

While there are other variations of whole-life and term-life insurance, this discussion of types of life insurance policies introduced you to the basic kinds of policies available. What types of situations are excluded from payment under a life insurance policy? Generally, insurance companies do not pay if the person whose life was insured died through suicide, war, or execution by the state. Almost any other type of death is covered under a life insurance policy.

Let's look at a few of the major legal issues associated with life insurance. One of the most frequent problems associated with life insurance policies is misrepresentation on the insurance application. An individual applying for insurance might make some type of misrepresentation about his or her health that might impact the insurance company's willingness to offer the insurance policy. For example, if you have cancer when you apply for insurance and do not make the insurance company aware of your disease, your insurance policy will likely be void. However, if you are unaware that you have a disease when you apply for insurance, the insurance company cannot void your insurance policy.

One frequent form of misrepresentation is the applicant's age. Generally, the older the applicant is, the higher the premiums are. Thus, if you apply for an insurance policy as a 30-year-old, your premium will be significantly smaller than it would be if you applied as a 40-year-old. Misrepresentation of age, however, is not cause for the cancelation of your policy. Instead, the insurance company will lower its payment to the beneficiary to reflect the payment of premiums appropriate for the correct age.

Case Nugget: Will States Protect the Terminally Ill from Being Taken Advantage Of?

Life Partners, Inc. v. Miller
420 F. Supp. 2d 452 (2006)

A terminally ill woman, "Jane Doe," asked the state of Virginia to protect her from the unscrupulous act of a Texas investment company, Life Partners, Inc., which had paid her $29,900 on a life insurance policy worth $115,000. By state law, the Virginia Viatical Settlements Act, the minimum Jane Doe should have received was $69,000.

Life Partners, Inc., challenged Virginia's law as unconstitutional under the commerce clause. Life Partners, Inc., was unsuccessful in making this challenge. In defending Virginia's statute, the judge pointed out that the law does not discriminate against interstate commerce. Its effect on interstate commerce is only incidental. Additionally, the court determined that the law is an appropriate use of the state's police powers. The state is allowed to protect dying Virginians who want to sell their life insurance. The court said: "It is obvious to the court that a terminally-ill person . . . is in a particularly vulnerable position and could easily fall prey to sharp business practices and fraud."

CASE OPENER WRAP-UP

Karon Altman

This case is slightly more complicated than indicated in the opening scenario. Mr. Altman's life insurance policy actually had two clauses regarding misrepresentation. The first clause was the state-mandated clause on incontestability, reading as follows: "[A]fter this policy has been in force during the lifetime of the insured for two years from the policy date, we will not contest it for any reason except nonpayment of premiums." However, Mr. Altman did not live to see the end of the two-year deadline, and Nationwide contended that this meant it could contest the application indefinitely. The judge pointed out that Nationwide had included a clause of its own in the policy that was not dependent on the insured party's remaining alive for the two years; this clause required only two years to pass before precluding challenge to the application. Because Nationwide had not legally indicated its intent to deny Ms. Altman the benefits of the policy until November 12, 1998, Nationwide missed its own two-year deadline. Judgment was for Ms. Altman in the amount of $200,000.

How does the conclusion of this case fit with your predictions above? The verdict in this case rested heavily on legal maneuvers. For instance, although Nationwide ignored Ms. Altman's claim for benefits, it did not formally deny her the benefits until after the two-year deadline, causing the judge to rule that Nationwide had surpassed the deadline for a misrepresentation challenge. If Nationwide had formally indicated its intent to revoke the benefits before August 6, 1998, perhaps this case would have turned out differently.

If Mr. Altman did commit fraud, his actions harm other life insurance customers. When Nationwide pays benefits to customers who have committed fraud, it is likely the company passes these costs along to all customers by raising premiums.

Summary

The Nature of the Insurance Relationship

Insured party: Party who pays a premium in exchange for payment in the event of damage or injury.

Premium: Payment on policy.

Insurer: Party who receives premiums from insured party.

Beneficiary: Person who receives insurance proceeds.

Policy: Document that expresses agreement between the insured party, beneficiary, and insurer.

Risk:

1. Potential loss
2. Transfer and distribute

Insurable interest:

1. Property interest must exist at time of loss.
2. Life interest must exist at time policy is obtained.

The Insurance Contract

Application for insurance:

Effective date: Date that policy becomes effective.

Binder: Gives temporary insurance until a decision to accept or reject application is made.

Important elements of the contract:

1. *Incontestability clause:* Ensures insurance company cannot contest statements made in an insurance application after a certain period of time.
2. *Antilapse clause:* Grace period for insured to pay premium.
3. *Appraisal clause:* Insured party and insurer select disinterested appraiser for second opinion on damages.
4. *Coinsurance clause:* If insured party covers property at a certain percentage, the insurance company will cover any loss up to this stated percentage.
5. *Other-insurance or multiple-insurance clause:* Voids or reduces insurance to ensure that property or people are not overinsured.
6. *Arbitration clause:* Disputes must be submitted to an arbitrator.

Canceling the Insurance Policy

While either the insurer or the insured may cancel the insurance policy at specific times, the insurer is very limited as to when it may cancel the policy. If either party breaches its duties as established in the insurance policy, the other party has some type of remedy.

Insurer and Insured Obligations

Insurer duty to defend insured: Insurer must defend insured party from claims for which the insured party is liable

Insurer duty to pay sums owed by the insured: Insurer must pay damages to third party.

Insured duty to disclose material information on application: Insured party must fully and truthfully answer questions.

Insured duty to cooperate with the insurer: Insured party must discuss claims with insurer to be defended.

The Insurer's Defenses for Nonpayment

Insurer has a multitude of defenses, including breach of contract, lack of insurable interest, and illegal activity.

Types of Insurance

Individual insurance: Insured party is party purchasing insurance.

Group insurance: Party who is neither the insured party nor the insurer purchases the insurance.

Personal insurance: Covers individual's life or health.

Commercial insurance: Covers business interests.

Property insurance: Protects property from loss or damage.

Casualty insurance: Protects person or property from accidental injury.

Liability:

- *Commercial general liability policy:* Protects a business against a broad range of risks.
- *Product liability insurance:* Covers the cost of recalling and replacing products.
- *Professional insurance:* Protects professionals from suits by third parties who claim that the professional was negligent in job performance.
- *Workers' compensation policy:* Payments to employees who are injured through a work-related accident.

Fire:

- *Friendly fire:* Contained in a place where fire is intended to burn; generally not covered.
- *Hostile fire:* Fire occurs in place not intended to burn.
- *Marine:*
  - *Ocean marine:* Protects oceangoing vessels against loss of ship and cargo due to perils of the sea.
  - *Inland marine:* Protects inland-waterway-traveling ships from loss of ship and cargo due to perils of the sea.

Life:

- *Whole-life insurance:* Protection for entire life of the insured.
- *Term-life insurance:* Provides coverage for a specified term; beneficiary paid only if insured party dies during this term.

Point / Counterpoint

Should Private Insurance Companies Be Quick to Pay Homeowners Whose Property Is Damaged or Destroyed by a Natural Disaster, Such as Hurricane Katrina?	
Yes	**No**
When a natural disaster such as Hurricane Katrina strikes, homeowners count on private insurance companies to pay them quickly for the damage caused by the disaster Quick payment is necessary for a variety of reasons. First, homeowners are eager to rebuild and get on with their lives. Insurance companies can help this process happen quickly when they pay legitimate claims. Second, homeowners are entitled to quick settlements, as they have often paid premiums	When a natural disaster such as Hurricane Katrina strikes, private insurance companies must be careful to make payouts consistent with the terms of the insurance policies they have issued. Hasty decision making could yield mistakes in settling claims. The last thing an insurance company will want is to have to take back a payment it has granted

for years—they are simply cashing in on the coverage they have purchased. Third, insurance companies should realize they have much more knowledge than their clients about the types of coverage their clients need. Insurance companies should err on the side of granting rather than denying claims.

For example, Paul and Julie Leonard's home was damaged by Hurricane Katrina. The first floor of their Pascagoula, Mississippi, home received 5 feet of water during the hurricane. They spent $30,000 of their own money after the hurricane because their insurance company denied their claim. The Leonards thought they were insured. It turned out they were not insured for flood damage. The Leonards believed their insurance agent misled them by selling them a hurricane policy, which they assumed protected them when a hurricane caused a flood.

If the insurance company had paid the Leonards quickly, the family could have moved on with their lives. They would have also felt goodwill toward their insurance company. Now, they, and many other homeowners, feel distrustful of the companies they have relied on for years.*

too quickly, based on erroneous decision making.

For example, after Hurricane Katrina, many private insurance companies refused to pay homeowners' claims. The insurance companies believed that much of the damage from the hurricane was caused by flooding, and most homeowners did not have flood insurance. Instead, they had insurance to cover damage caused by wind.

Although homeowners argued that the flooding was caused by wind, insurance companies waited for courts to rule. To date, it appears that courts are ruling in favor of insurance companies. That is good news for insurance companies and the economy as a whole. A spokesman for the Property Casualty Insurers Association of America has stated, "A healthy insurance market is absolutely key to a rejuvenated economy [on the Gulf Coast]."†

*This side of the debate relies on facts from Michael Kunzelman, "Trial Begins over Katrina Insurance Payments," *St. Louis Post-Dispatch,* July 16, 2006, p. C2.

†Michael Kunzelman, "Insurance Company Wins Case on Katrina: Won't Have to Pay for Water Damage," *New Jersey Record,* August 16, 2006, p.A06.

Questions & Problems

1. Why do states often require that insurance contracts include certain clauses?

2. When may the insurer cancel the insurance policy?

3. Why are liability policies important for businesses?

4. On February 10, 1987, Anthony Fioretti applied for life insurance with Massachusetts General Life Insurance Company. The benefactor of the $1,947,111 policy was his brother, Vincent Fioretti. Anthony had previously applied for life insurance with another company, but his application was denied because of his HIV status. On the MassGen application Anthony misrepresented his birth date and pertinent medical information. The application required a blood test, and Anthony arranged for someone else to be blood-tested under his name. Anthony was also required to submit a "Statement of Good Health," stating that he was in good health and had not previously been denied life insurance by another company. After Anthony returned the Statement of Good Health, MassGen approved his application. On February 28, 1989, Anthony died at his home in Florida. His death certificate indicated that the cause of death was AIDS. Vincent Fioretti filed a claim with MassGen to receive the benefits of Anthony's life insurance policy. MassGen argued that Anthony's fraudulent behavior and misrepresentation relieved it of the policy obligations. Vincent Fioretti argued that under the incontestability clause MassGen was required to honor his claim. How do you think the U.S. court of appeals decided? [*Fioretti v. Massachusetts General Life Insurance Company,* 53 F.3d 1228 (1995).]

5. Gail Riggins worked 42 miles from home, and for several years she operated a car pool with her co-workers. The riders each gave Riggins $17 per week for gas and expenses. On February 18, 1992, Riggins decided that she would work a late shift and arranged for one of the riders, Larry Ramsey, to drive the van. To compensate Ramsey for driving, Riggins agreed to collect only $12 from him that week. During the trip, Ramsey collided with Sheila Markham's car, killing both drivers and injuring the eight other riders in the van. Ramsey's insurer, Meridian Mutual Insurance Co., provided coverage for accidents involving Ramsey's permitted use of another's automobile. However, Meridian denied liability in this instance based on a policy provision that excluded coverage for damages incurred during "the use of a vehicle when used to carry persons or property for a fee." Do you think the court found this provision to be applicable to the car pool? Why or why not? [*Meridian Mutual Insurance Co. v. Auto-Owners Insurance Company,* 698 N.E.2d 770 (1998).]
6. Defendant Jean D'Alessandro's car broke down on the highway. She left her car in the breakdown lane, and a state police officer offered her assistance. The officer parked his car behind D'Alessandro's and waited with her for a tow truck to arrive. An uninsured motorist subsequently struck the officer's car, and both the officer and D'Alessandro were injured. D'Alessandro filed a claim with her parent's insurance company, General Accident. The policy provided uninsured-motorist coverage for her parents and any family member residing in the house of the insured. D'Alessandro's vehicle was uninsured, and a stipulation in the policy stated that General Accident would not provide coverage for injuries sustained by any person "while occupying or when struck by, any motor vehicle owned by you or any family member which is not insured for this coverage under this policy." The policy defined "occupying" as "in, upon, getting in, on, out, or off." Because of this provision, General Accident refused to cover D'Alessandro's accident. The superior court of Rhode Island granted summary judgment in favor of General Accident. D'Alessandro appealed the decision to the supreme court of Rhode Island. Do you think the court affirmed the earlier decision? [*General Accident Insurance Company of America v. Jean D'Alessandro,* 671 A.2d 1233 (1996).]
7. While driving her motorcycle on a four-lane street, Henault was struck by a car. The force of the impact knocked her off her motorcycle and into a lane of oncoming traffic. Shortly after being thrown into the lane, Henault was struck by an uninsured truck driver. She received compensation from the insurer of the car that struck her motorcycle, but it did not cover the full amount of her claimed damages. Henault filed a personal injury claim with her insurance agency, Mid-Century. Though Henault's truck was insured by Mid-Century, her motorcycle was uninsured. The policy included an owned-vehicle exclusion provision stating that injury sustained while occupying a vehicle not covered by the policy would not be covered. *Occupying* was defined by the policy as "in, on, getting into or out of" one's vehicle. On this basis, Mid-Century denied coverage to Henault because she was occupying her uninsured motorcycle at the time of the accident. The court of appeals found that the owned-vehicle exclusion did not apply because Henault was not occupying the motorcycle at the time of her accident. The case was appealed to the Washington Supreme Court. Do you think the court affirmed or reversed the earlier decision? [*Mid-Century Ins. Co. v. Henault,* 128 Wash. 2d 207 (1995).]

8. Heniser and his wife purchased a vacation home in Michigan. After they divorced, Heniser remained in possession of the property but did not inhabit the home. When a fire destroyed his property, Heniser filed an insurance claim with Frankenmuth Mutual Insurance Company, the insurer of the property. Frankenmuth denied coverage based on a stipulation in the policy that stated that the building must be occupied in order to be covered by the policy. Frankenmuth terminated the policy and returned the unearned premium to Heniser. Heniser argued that the destruction of property should be covered by homeowner's insurance. An earlier court found that the destruction of the building was not within the scope of the policy. Do you think the court affirmed this decision? Why or why not? [*Heniser v. Frankenmuth Mutual Insurance,* 534 N.W.2d 502 (1995).]
9. Hatcher Autoplex employed Patricia Moore. As an employee, she was provided with a "demonstrator vehicle." She used the company car as her primary means of transportation. Moore was not required to sign any contract that would prevent other family members from driving the car. On New Year's Eve she allowed her teenage daughter Stacy to use the car to go to a party. Moore instructed Stacy to go straight to the party and not to give anyone a ride. Stacy did not follow her mother's instructions, and on the way home from the party she and two of her passengers were injured in a one-car accident. The Moores filed claims with their insurance company, Tennessee Farmers Mutual, and with Hatcher Autoplex's insurance company, Universal Underwriters. The insurance companies argued that Stacy's use of the car was not within the scope of permission granted by Moore. The insurers concluded that the accident was excluded from coverage. How do you think the court decided? [*Tennessee Farmers Mutual Insurance Company v. Moore,* 958 S.W.2d 759 (1997).]
10. Grange Mutual Casualty Company provided fire insurance for DeMoonie. The policy stated in an occupancy clause that the insured was required to be currently residing in the insured house. DeMoonie had left her property vacant for more than 30 days when a fire substantially damaged her home. The fire was intentionally set, and Grange believed that DeMoonie was responsible for starting the fire. Because of the possibility of arson and DeMoonie's failure to occupy the insured house, Grange denied coverage. DeMoonie challenged Grange's decision, and the court found that she was entitled to insurance benefits. Grange appealed the decision. Do you think the court reversed or affirmed the decision of the earlier court? [*Grange Mutual Casualty Company v. DeMoonie,* 227 Ga. App. 812 (1997).]
11. After the terrorist attacks on the World Trade Center on September 11, 2001, owners and lessees of World Trade Center properties brought claims against a number of insurance companies, asking those insurance companies to defend them in litigation brought by the families of those who died in the attacks and the many people injured on September 11, 2001. Issues arose as to which owners and lessees were insured under documents that existed as of September 11, 2001. The issue was important because insurance companies must defend those who are insured. Five entities that leased World Trade Center properties formed a group, the World Trade Center Properties (WTCP), which had obtained binders from Zurich American Insurance Company. WTCP brought an action against Zurich, asking the court to clarify Zurich's obligations to defend WTCP, and the Port Authority, which owned and operated the World Trade Center properties (and had leased them to WTCP). Zurich filed an action raising the same issues and added to the litigation certain excess carriers, insurance companies obligated to provide coverage in excess of Zurich's coverage. What result? [*In re September 11th Liability Ins. Coverage Cases,* 333 F. Supp. 2d 111 (S.D.N.Y. 2004).]

12. Approximately 90 plaintiffs sued the Roman Catholic Diocese of Orange (the church), alleging they were victims of sexual abuse by certain priests. The church's liability insurers, including Travelers Casualty & Surety Company, asked an appellate court to vacate a written order by a judge assigned to settle the case. The settling judge's order attempted to determine the settlement value of the claims, place limits on the insurers' ability to refuse to cover the settlement, and provide evidence of the insurers' bad faith. The insurers believed the settling judge went beyond his authority and misunderstood his role as a mediator. By contrast, the settling judge thought the insurers were trying to stymie the settlement process, and his order reflected that belief. Did the settling judge's order exceed his authority? [*Travelers Cas. and Sur. Co. v. Superior Court,* 126 Cal. App. 4th 1131, 24 Cal. Rptr. 3d 751 (2005).]

Looking for more review material?

The Online Learning Center at **www.mhhe.com/kubasek1e** contains this chapter's "Assignment on the Internet" and also a list of URLs for more information, entitled "On the Internet." Find both of them in the Student Center portion of the OLC, along with quizzes and other helpful materials.

Wills and Trusts

CASE OPENER

The Battle of the Billionaires

Many Americans can take an educated guess at which men and women are the richest businesspersons in America. Businessmen such as Bill Gates of Microsoft and Larry Ellison of Oracle Corporation are in the news as their riches rise and fall. In 2000, Larry Ellison was in the news because he had surpassed Gates in terms of high-tech wealth. In particular, the value of Ellison's fortune in Oracle stock had surpassed Gates's fortune in Microsoft stock. In terms of stock holdings in their own companies, Ellison was winning the battle.[1] By 2003, however, Gates had regained his lead. Gates's net worth was listed at $46 billion, while Ellison's net worth was listed at $18 billion.[2]

Ellison and Gates are both wealthy, but they are strikingly different. One writer describes Bill Gates as "a geek who likes golf and bridge, and wears sensible sweaters,"[3] while Larry Ellison "flies Russian MiG-29 fighter jets over San Jose, chases women and wears black turtleneck sweaters."[4] No matter their differences, they share the need to figure out what to do with their assets, especially how to create a lasting legacy.

Gates and Ellison are not alone. Even ordinary Americans are becoming millionaires at an increasing rate. According to an article in *Bank Investment Marketing,*[5] the number of "millionaires next door" keeps growing. By 2003, 3.5 million households will own more than $1 million in investable assets. The consequences of increasing wealth vary widely.

[1] "Gates Slips to No. 2 in Tech Wealth," www.elcom.co.uk/nes/General-00000484.htm (December 30, 2000).

[2] www.forbes.com/finance/lists/54/2003/LIR.jhtml?passListId=54&passYear=2003&passListType=Person&uniqueId=JKEX&datatype=Person.

[3] "Feud Samurai Versus Nerd," *The Guardian,* December 19, 2000.

[4] Ibid.

[5] John Scroggin, "Rich, but Not Idle: Incentive-Based Estate Planning Involves Providing Opportunity, but Not Lifestyle, to Family Members," *Bank Investment Marketing,* February 1, 1999.

CHAPTER 52

Some new millionaires complain they are suffering from "sudden wealth syndrome,"[6] which means they feel confused and have problems as a consequence of their wealth, while others such as Gates and Ellison appear quite content with their riches.

1. What decisions are Gates and Ellison making regarding their assets while they are alive?
2. What decisions do we all make regarding our deaths, regardless of whether we are millionaires or billionaires?

The Wrap-Up at the end of the chapter will answer these questions.

Learning Objectives

After reading this chapter, you will be able to answer the following questions:

1 How does one engage in estate planning?

2 What legal issues relate to wills?

3 How are trusts used as estate planning tools?

4 What end-of-life decisions are important from a legal perspective?

5 How does international law protect wills?

[6] Peter Carbonara, "Heal the Rich!" *Money,* May 2000, pp. 109, 110.

This chapter focuses on what happens to an individual's property during his or her life and especially after life. Some people think carefully about how they want their property to be distributed; others die without expressing their wishes. State law protects the wishes individuals have outlined. Additionally, state law provides guidance for what to do with a person's property if the person did not express his or her wishes. Generally, then, this chapter focuses on state law regarding estate planning.

In particular, this chapter presents information about a wide range of topics, including a general discussion of estate planning, an overview of how to create a will, an outline of how individuals use trusts as estate planning tools, a summary of decisions individuals make at the end of life (i.e., what to do with their body), and an explanation of how wills are protected worldwide. This information helps individuals make informed decisions about what to do with their assets.

Estate Planning

Estate planning is the process by which an individual decides what to do with his or her real and personal property during and after life. Estate planning also encourages individuals to make decisions about issues that frequently arise at the end of life, such as what to do with a person's organs and body after death.

THE UNIFORM PROBATE CODE

Laws that govern issues related to estate planning vary from state to state. As in other areas of law that this book covers, the National Conference of Commissioners on Uniform State Laws has developed uniform laws that make recommendations about what legal rules should govern a particular topic. One example of a uniform law that provides guidance in the area of estate planning is the **Uniform Probate Code,** which covers a wide range of topics, from wills to gifts to life insurance.

TOOLS OF ESTATE PLANNING

This chapter highlights wills and trusts because these are the most important tools of estate planning. A **will** is a legal document that outlines how a person wants his or her property distributed on death. As the Global Context box explains, a **trust** allows a person to transfer property to another person, and this property is used for the benefit of a third person.

WHY INDIVIDUALS ENGAGE IN ESTATE PLANNING

Individuals engage in estate planning for a variety of reasons. Some people want to make sure they provide for their family financially after their death. Others want to arrange their property in ways that reduce taxes so that the family can preserve its wealth. Another purpose of estate planning is to promote family harmony. In other words, families fight less about assets after a loved one dies if that loved one expressed his or her wishes clearly. Finally, for nontraditional family arrangements, such as gay or lesbian couples or an unmarried heterosexual couple, careful estate planning can provide benefits that resemble those provided by marriage.[7] For example, careful estate planning can ensure that a surviving member of a nontraditional couple can stay in the home the couple established during their life together.

[7] For a complete discussion of estate planning for nontraditional couples, see Erica Bell, "Special Issues in Estate Planning for Non-Marital Couples and Nontraditional Families," *Practicing Law Institute/Estate* 283 (1999), p. 859.

global context

Religion and Family Wealth in India

In the United States, we have developed certain legal constructs that allow families to pass assets from generation to generation in ways that help families accomplish particular goals, such as reducing taxes and making sure family assets are not mismanaged. One such construct is known as a *trust.* A trust allows a person to transfer property to another person, and this property is used for the benefit of a third person. This legal construct is consistent with our culture, which emphasizes freedom and individual decision making.

In countries such as India, legal constructs exist that are similar to trusts. However, whereas European civil law provides the underpinnings of trusts, in countries such as India religion provides the underpinnings of legal constructs that determine how families can pass wealth from generation to generation. India has a large Islamic population. Under the religious law of Islam, families can use what is known as a family *waqf* as a tool to manage family wealth.* The family *waqf* resembles a trust, although the beneficiary of a family *waqf* must have a religious, pious, or charitable purpose.

Some legal scholars have suggested that although *waqfs* and trusts are similar, the religious roots of the *waqf* have made this construct less flexible and responsive to change over time than the trust, with its secular roots.

* For additional information about the *waqf,* see Jeffrey A. Schoenblum, "The Role of Legal Doctrine in the Decline of the Islamic Waqf: A Comparison with the Trust," *Vanderbilt Journal of Transnational L.* 32 (1999), p.1191.

Recently, courts have started to respond to issues that arise in nontraditional families. One form of nontraditional family is a family in which a surviving member of an unmarried heterosexual couple wants to conceive a child using a deceased partner's sperm. In Case 52-1, the court decides whether frozen sperm is "property" that can be distributed under a settlement agreement. As you read the case, ask yourself whether the case might have had a different outcome if William Everett Kane, Sr., had not been clear about his wishes regarding the use of his sperm.

CASE 52-1 DEBORAH ELLEN HECHT v. WILLIAM EVERETT KANE, JR.

COURT OF APPEALS, SECOND DISTRICT, CALIFORNIA

59 CAL. RPTR. 2D 222 (1996)

For several years, William Everett Kane Jr. and Katherine Kane, the adult children of William Everett Kane, tried to prevent Deborah Ellen Hecht (Hecht) from conceiving a child using their deceased father's sperm. The decedent had deposited fifteen vials of sperm in a cryobank facility before he committed suicide. He signed several forms and letters that made it clear that he intended the sperm for the use of Deborah Ellen Hecht. Decedent's adult children challenged Kane Sr.'s will. The parties settled this lawsuit and signed a global settlement as to the disposition of the estate's assets. The settlement allowed Hecht twenty percent of the estate's assets. Shortly after this settlement, Hecht went to the cryobank to claim the sperm vials so she could use them to become pregnant with the decedent's child. The executor of the will blocked the release of the sperm, and several court challenges followed. The executor believed the vials of the decedent's sperm were "assets" of the estate subject to the global settlement. Hecht disagreed.

In 1994, a probate judge decided that Hecht should receive twenty percent of the sperm as "assets" of the estate under the property settlement. She used three of the fifteen vials in her attempt to conceive a child and was unsuccessful. Because she was then forty years old and her chances of conceiving were dropping each year, she sought immediate release of the other vials so her doctors could continue to help her conceive a child. The decedent's children contested her claim for the remaining vials. In the present case, the judge is asked to decide whether to enforce the global settlement, which would mean that the remaining vials should be distributed to William Everett Kane Sr.'s adult children rather than to Hecht.

ASSOCIATE JUSTICE JOHNSON: [T]he genetic material involved here is a unique form of "property." It is not subject to division through an agreement among the decedent's potential beneficiaries which is inconsistent with decedent's manifest intent about its disposition. A man's sperm or a woman's ova or a couple's embryos are not the same as a quarter of land, a cache of cash, or a favorite limousine. Rules appropriate to the disposition of the latter are not necessarily appropriate for the former. If we are to honor decedent's intent as expressed in several written documents, his sperm can only be used by and thus only has value to one person, the petitioner in this case. . . .

From decedent's clear expressions of intent, it is apparent he created these vials of sperm for one purpose, to produce a child with this woman. Not to produce a child with any other specific woman or with an anonymous female. Not to produce a descendant with any other genetic makeup than would result from a combination of his sperm and this woman's ovum. Even Hecht lacks the legal entitlement to give, sell, or otherwise dispose of decedent's sperm. She and she alone can use it. Even she cannot allow its use by others, if the law is to honor the decedent's clearly expressed intent. Thus, in a very real sense, to the extent this sperm is "property" it is only "property" for that one person. As such it is not an "asset" of the estate subject to allocation, in whole or in part, to any other person, whether through agreement or otherwise.

. . . [T]he decedent's right to procreate with whom he chooses cannot be defeated by some contract which third persons—including his chosen donee—construct and sign. . . . The only way for the law to ensure the decedent's [fundamental interest is not used as an item for negotiation and trade among the claimants for the decedent's estate] is to remove it from the negotiating table. And, the only way to remove it from the table is to refuse to enforce any contract term which purports to impair realization of the decedent's intent his sperm be used to produce a child with the woman he wanted to bear that child.

. . . [Hecht is entitled] to the sperm of a particular donor, the man she had loved and lived with for five years . . . [Hecht's] petition is granted. Let a peremptory writ issue directing the probate court to order the administrator to release the remaining vials of decedent's sperm to petitioner upon her request.

REVERSED.

CRITICAL THINKING

The judge compares sperm to other assets, including land, cash, and a limousine. Why does the judge compare sperm to these other items?

ETHICAL DECISION MAKING

In deciding that sperm is not an asset that can be divided like other property, the judge is showing a preference for which value that underlies ethical decision making: freedom, security, justice, or efficiency? Explain.

Legal Issues Related to Wills

In an ideal world, every person would write a legally valid will that clearly expresses the person's wishes about how his or her property should be distributed after death. Unfortunately, many people die without wills. In our rushed society, many people do not take the time to consult a lawyer about a will. Also, some people do not want to spend the money to seek legal advice about a will. Finally, a reality of life is that many people procrastinate. They simply might die before getting around to writing a will.

INTESTACY STATUTES

If a person dies without a will, state laws outline how the person's property will be distributed. The state laws that outline how a person's property will be distributed if he or she dies without a will are called **intestacy statutes.** When a person dies without a will, we say the person died **intestate.** Intestacy statutes address issues such as the rights of a surviving spouse. Surprisingly, state laws vary regarding the amount a surviving spouse inherits when a spouse dies intestate. The surviving spouse usually splits real and personal property with children of the marriage, children not of the marriage (e.g., children from the deceased's previous marriage), and the deceased's parents. For instance, if a person dies intestate in the state of California, the surviving spouse generally receives half the intestate's real and personal property if the intestate is survived by children of the marriage, children not of the marriage, or parents. In Oregon, the surviving spouse generally receives *all* real and personal property, unless the intestate is survived by children not of the marriage, in which case the surviving spouse receives half the intestate's real and personal property.

REQUIREMENTS FOR A LEGALLY VALID WILL

Individuals should create legally valid wills so that their own wishes control what happens to their property. Otherwise, the wishes of a state legislature will control, and legislators may or may not place the same importance on the roles of particular family members in a person's life. A person who writes a will is called a **testator.**

A will is generally valid if it meets four requirements. Exhibit 52-1 summarizes these requirements. First, the testator must have **testamentary capacity.** Testamentary capacity means the person must be old enough to write a will (age 18 in most states) and be of sound mind. Courts decide whether a person is of sound mind by considering whether the testator knows the extent of his or her property, understands traditions regarding who should get the property (even though the testator does not have to follow tradition), knows he or she is making a will, and is not delusional. Second, a will usually must be in **writing.** Almost always, a will must be in writing to be valid. (Exhibit 52-2 provides a list of special kinds of wills.) One exception is that a person may make a verbal will as he or she is about to die. The writing may take a variety of forms, but usually a will is typewritten on regular paper. It is possible, however, for a legally valid will to be written in handwriting on a pillowcase! Third, the person writing the will must **sign** the will. Usually, a person signs his or her name at the end of the will and signs or initials each page to make sure no one adds or omits a page after the testator dies.

Exhibit 52-1 Requirements for a Legally Valid Will

- Testamentary capacity
- Writing
- Testator's signature
- Attestation

Exhibit 52-2
Special Kinds of Wills

Oral will: Will that testator declares verbally during his or her last illness, in front of witnesses, who later write the person's wishes.

Holographic will: Will that testator writes and signs in his or her own handwriting. Usually, states do not require witnesses because when the entire will is in handwriting there is less chance of fraud or forgery.

Mutual will: Will that two or more testators execute in which they leave property to each other as long as the survivor agrees that when he or she dies, the remaining property will be distributed according to a plan created by all testators.

Fourth, witnesses must **attest** to the will. A witness must witness the signing of the will and then sign as a witness at the end of the document. A person who will receive property under a will, a **beneficiary,** cannot be a witness. Also, witnesses must be of sound mind.

GROUNDS FOR CONTESTING A WILL

When a person with *standing* (an interest in a will, such as that of a potential beneficiary) has doubts about whether a particular will is legally valid, he or she may contest the will. Usually, wills are contested in two circumstances. First, a person contests a will if he or she believes that the will does not meet the four criteria the preceding section outlined. For instance, a person might doubt whether the testator wrote the will when he or she was of sound mind. Another possibility is that it was not signed or witnessed properly.

Second, a person contests a will if he or she believes that although the will is technically valid, the testator was a victim of **fraud** or **undue influence.** Fraud occurs when the testator relied on false statements when he or she made a will. Undue influence occurs when the testator wrote a will under circumstances in which a person the testator trusted took advantage of the testator's weak physical or emotional condition to persuade the testator to write the will in a particular way. Case 52-2 illustrates both circumstances. Children of a decedent are contesting a will, claiming that the testator lacked testamentary capacity to write a will. The children also claim that the testator was unduly influenced by her brother to disinherit them.

CASE 52-2

IN RE THE ESTATE OF LEANORA DIAZ
SUPREME COURT OF GEORGIA
1999 WL 1049245

On October 8, 1996, Leanora Diaz served her husband, Ralph Diaz, with divorce papers. The following weekend, Diaz's children, appellants Brian Diaz, Donna Diaz Crandall, Dawn Diaz Williams and Denise Diaz Leto, visited their mother at her home and tried to convince her to seek medical attention for perceived physical and mental problems. She refused. The Diaz children then called county deputies to assist them in having their mother involuntarily committed. Diaz spoke with the deputies, called her brother James O'Brien in Florida, then agreed to go to the hospital. She was diagnosed with mild clinical depression due to family discord and impending divorce, then was released.

Soon after, Leanora Diaz cut off all communication with her children because they were "Judases" for forcing her to go to the hospital. She stated that she might forgive them, but she would never forget what they had done. In February 1997, Diaz was hospitalized and diagnosed with cancer. While in the hospital, Diaz asked O'Brien to have her divorce attorney draw up a power of attorney and will. On February 18, 1997, Diaz executed a power of attorney giving O'Brien authority over her business affairs and a will leaving her personal effects to O'Brien and all other property to her grandchildren. On February 27, 1997, Diaz executed a codicil expressly stating that after much reflection and due to recent events, her husband and children were to take nothing under the will. Leanora Diaz died on April 3, 1997. After her death, the children challenged the will and codicil, alleging that Diaz did not possess the necessary testamentary capacity at the time the will and codicil were executed and that these documents were not executed of her own free will. In this case, Georgia's highest court considers issues related to both testamentary capacity and undue influence.

JUSTICE HUNSTEIN: Appellants contend Diaz did not possess the necessary testamentary capacity to execute a will because she was suffering from cancer and disease and related delusions at the time she executed the 1997 will and codicil. The right to make a will is a valuable one, and a stringent standard must be met to deprive a person of this right. Accordingly, a testator will be upheld not to possess the mental capacity to make a will based upon delusion behavior only if the testator suffers from an insane delusion, that is a delusion having no foundation in fact and that springs from a diseased condition of the mind.

A review of the record demonstrates that the evidence is insufficient to make a clear and convincing showing that Diaz lacked the mental capacity to dispose of her property at the time she executed her February 1997 will and codicil. During the bench trial, Diaz's doctor testified that he saw no evidence of delusions during her illness and she was coherent at each of his daily visits during the time she executed the will and codicil. He also testified that Diaz told him she was estranged from her husband and children and they were to be told nothing about her diagnosis and could have no part in her treatment. The witnesses to the signing of the will and codicil stated Diaz was coherent at all times while the will and codicil were being read to her, that she appeared to understand the meaning of their contents, and she did not appear to be delusional or overly medicated. Appellants' allegations of arguably irrational behavior at times other than when the will and codicil were executed do not controvert the positive testimony of her medical doctor and the subscribing witnesses that at the time the will and codicil were executed Diaz seemed to understand the effect of the will and codicil, was capable of recognizing the property she possessed and the persons related to her, and was capable of making a rational disposition of her property. The record clearly supports the probate court's finding that Diaz possessed the necessary testamentary capacity at the time the will and codicil were executed.

Appellants also contend the will and codicil are invalid because O'Brien exerted undue influence over Diaz at the time of their execution. Appellants argue that because O'Brien lived with Diaz from February 1997 until her death, he precluded appellants from talking to or visiting with Diaz, and refused to provide them with information about Diaz's physical health. There is sufficient evidence of undue influence. Undue influence upon the testator will be found to exist only if such influence deprives the testator of her free agency and substitutes the will of another person for her own at the time the will is executed. Evidence showing nothing more than an opportunity to influence and a substantial benefit under the will does not establish the exercise of undue influence. Because Diaz was in the final states of cancer, there naturally was some evidence that her physical and mental health deteriorated from October 1996 until her death in April 1997. The record is devoid, however, of any evidence that at the time Diaz executed her 1997 will and codicil she did not act of her own free will. To the contrary, the subscribing witnesses testified that Diaz voluntarily signed the will and codicil after they were read to her in their entirety and that she was talkative and polite at the time. Appellants themselves testified that Diaz was a strong-willed woman whose will was not easily overridden, that as early as October 1996 Diaz refused to discuss her physical condition with them, and after the attempted involuntary committal she independently cut off virtually all communication with them. Thus, the evidence shows at most an opportunity for O'Brien to exert undue influence over Diaz and not the requisite clear and convincing evidence that the will and codicil were the result of O'Brien's undue influence. Appellants' suspicions of undue influence cannot be allowed to supplant direct evidence on the issue.

AFFIRMED.

[CONTINUED]

CRITICAL THINKING

In Chapter 1, you learned of the importance of a particular set of facts in determining the outcome of a case. If you were the children of Leanora Diaz, what one fact would you want to change to make this case have a different outcome?

ETHICAL DECISION MAKING

Which values clash in this case? In other words, the judge prefers one value or ethical norm, while the children prefer another. Describe the clash between the judge and the children in terms of values.

Case Nugget — Should Courts Affirm the Influence of a Wife?

Cook v. Huff
274 Ga. 186, 552 S.E.2d 83 (2001)

Can a wife ever have undue influence over a husband? Yes! In *Cook v. Huff,* a couple had been married for 53 years when the husband executed a new will. He had just come home from a six-month hospital stay after having a stroke. A few months after the husband executed the new will, he died. The wife was the primary beneficiary of a substantial portion of the estate.

A dispute arose when three children from the husband's former marriage challenged the new will, asserting that the wife had asserted undue influence. A jury agreed with the children from the former marriage. The jury considered the husband's age, poor health, and the fact that the wife had attempted to alienate her husband from the children of the prior marriage. Additionally, the wife had actively encouraged the husband to create the new will and was present when it was executed. An appellate court affirmed the jury's decision, indicating that sometimes a wife can have undue influence over her spouse.

A dissenting judge disagreed, affirming the influence of a wife. The dissenting judge quoted the 1849 Georgia case, *Potts v. House:* "If a wife [by her virtues] has gained such an ascendancy over her husband, and so rivaled his affections that her good pleasure is a law to him, such an influence can never be a reason for impeaching a will made in her favor, even to the exclusion of the residue of his family."

CHANGING A WILL

Wills are **ambulatory,** which means testators can change them. It is not uncommon for people to change their wills several times during their life. People change their wills through **codicils,** which are separate documents with new provisions that outline changes to the will. Testators must go through the same procedures to make a valid codicil as those followed in making the original will. For instance, testators must sign the codicil in front of witnesses. After a person writes a codicil, it is read with the will as a unit that expresses the testator's wishes.

Case 52-3 illustrates problems that arise when a testator tries to change a will without the assistance of a lawyer. The case involves Charles Kuralt, the journalist known for his CBS show *On the Road.*

REVOKING A WILL

In Case 52-3, Kuralt could have clarified his intent regarding property for Shannon by clearly **revoking** or canceling the formal will he executed in May 1997. He could have revoked the 1997 will by physically destroying it. Then he could have executed a new will that made it clear he had revoked the 1997 will. Instead, he initiated sham sales of property so that his wife would not find out about his secret intimate companion.

CASE 52-3

IN RE THE ESTATE OF CHARLES KURALT, DECEASED

SUPREME COURT OF MONTANA
981 P.2D 771 (1999)

This case arose when Charles Kuralt died, leaving behind both a wife and a secret intimate companion, with whom he had a close personal relationship for nearly thirty years. Mr. Kuralt was hospitalized on June 18, 1997, after he became suddenly ill. He died on July 4, 1997. After his death, his wife, Petie, filed proof of authority to probate certain property in Montana. Petie did not know about her husband's secret intimate companion until Patricia Elizabeth Shannon (Shannon) filed a petition for ancillary probate of will, claiming a letter Kuralt wrote on June 18, 1997, and mailed to her constituted a valid holographic will with regard to the Montana property.

At issue in the case is the language in the letter dated June 18, 1997. Mr. Kuralt had taken three actions prior to June 19, 1997, to clarify what he wanted to happen to his property upon his death. On May 3, 1989, he executed a holographic will in which he bequeathed certain Montana property to Shannon. On May 4, 1997, Kuralt executed a formal will in which he devised all his property to his wife, Petie. On April 9, 1997, Mr. Kuralt deeded his interest to certain land in Montana to Shannon. He transferred a twenty-acre parcel of land with a cabin along the Big Hole River to Shannon through a sham sale; he disguised the transaction to look like a sale even though he gave Shannon the $80,000 needed to buy the parcel. Shannon and Kuralt agreed to the "sale" of an additional ninety acres along the Black Hole River. The sale was to be consummated in September 1997. Unfortunately for Shannon, Mr. Kuralt became ill and died prior to the transaction.

Here is what the June 18, 1997 letter said:

Dear Pat—
Something is terribly wrong with me and they can't figure out what. After cat-scans and a variety of cardiograms, they agree it's not lung cancer or heart trouble or blood clot. So they're putting me in the hospital today to concentrate on infectious diseases. I am getting worse, barely able to get out of bed, but still have high hopes for recovery . . . if only I can get a diagnosis! Curiouser and curiouser! I'll keep you informed. I'll have the lawyer visit the hospital to be sure you inherit the rest of the place in MT if it comes to that.

I send love to you & [your youngest daughter,] Shannon. Hope things are better there!

Love,
C.

Shannon sought to probate this letter dated June 18, 1997, as a valid holographic codicil to Mr. Kuralt's formal 1994 will. She did so because she wanted to make sure she got the ninety acres of Montana property she believed Mr. Kuralt wanted her to have.

A district court in Madison County, Montana, ruled that the estate should be granted a summary judgment regarding the June 18 letter. The district court rejected Shannon's claim that the letter was a valid holographic codicil and Shannon appealed. In the following case, the highest court of Montana decides whether the lower court was correct in granting the estate a summary judgment. If the lower court erred, Shannon will be allowed to present evidence in a trial of Kuralt's intent regarding who should get the Montana property.

JUSTICE W. WILLIAM LEAPHART: We disagree with the Estate's position that Shannon's extrinsic evidence is "immaterial" to the question of testamentary intent, and is merely "an insubstantial attempt to manufacture a material issue of fact." Rather, we agree with Shannon that the District Court improperly resolved contested issues of material fact when it found, in support of its conclusion that the letter "clearly contemplates a separate testamentary instrument not yet in existence," that: The extrinsic evidence—none of which is contested—confirms this conclusion. Petitioner herself testified during her deposition and at trial that the decedent intended to "sell"—not "will"—the Montana property to her in the fall of 1998 [*sic*]. While the extrinsic evidence substantiates a close and personal relationship between Petitioner and the decedent extending over twenty-nine years, during which she and her children were apparently entirely housed, supported, educated, and temporarily set up in business by the decedent, those facts are not sufficient to create a testamentary intent which the language of the letter clearly refutes.

When drawing all reasonable inference in favor of Shannon, as the party opposed to summary judgment, we conclude that the extrinsic evidence raises a genuine issue of material fact as to whether Mr. Kuralt intended to gift, rather than sell, the remaining ninety acres of his Madison County property to Shannon. The plain language of the letter of June 18, 1997, indicates, as Shannon points out, that Mr. Kuralt desired that Shannon "inherit" all of his property along the Big Hole River. While other language in the letter—"I'll have the lawyer visit the hospital . . . if it comes to that"—might suggest, as the Estate argues and as the District Court concluded, that Mr. Kuralt was contemplating a separate testamentary instrument not yet in existence, it is far from certain that this is the result Mr. Kuralt intended by the letter.

At the very least, when reading the language of the letter in light of the extrinsic evidence showing the couple's future plans to consummate the transfer of the remaining ninety acres vis-à-vis a mock "sale," there arises a question of material fact as to whether Mr. Kuralt intended, given the state of serious illness, that the very letter of June 18, 1997, effect a posthumous disposition of his ninety acres of Madison County. Nor are the parties merely arguing different interpretations of the facts here; we have, in this case, a fundamental disagreement as to a genuine material fact which would be better reconciled by trial.

. . . We hold that, because there is a genuine issue of material fact, the District Court erred in granting judgment as a matter of law. Accordingly, we reverse the court's grant of summary judgment and remand, for trial, the factual question of whether, in light of the extrinsic evidence, Mr. Kuralt intended the letter of June 18, 1997, to effect a testamentary disposition of the ninety acres in Madison County to Shannon.

REVERSED AND REMANDED.

CRITICAL THINKING

As a critical thinker, you want to be able to identify strengths as well as weaknesses in arguments. What is particularly good about this court's reasoning in deciding in favor of Shannon?

ETHICAL DECISION MAKING

Compare the universalization and the Golden Rule guidelines as they apply to the facts of this case. Which guideline best supports Petie Kuralt's perspective on what should happen to her husband's assets?

e-commerce AND THE LAW

Do You Need a Will in a Hurry?

If you need a will in a hurry, what better way to create one than to do one yourself with help from forms available on the Internet? One advertisement on the Web says: "Save Time and Money!! Why go to an attorney when you can make your own Will and Trust? These are easy-to-use documents that you can individually customize for your specific needs."*

Is it true? Should you avoid the time, energy, and money it takes to have a lawyer prepare a will or trust when you can write your own using forms available on the Internet?

The best answer is, "It depends." For some people, creating a will using an easy-to-use form available on the Internet is better than not having a will at all. However, the risks of making mistakes by using such forms are high. The risks of using these forms come in two varieties. First, it is risky to use the forms if your family structure is complicated. For instance, if you have a family with the standard grandparents, parents, children, and grandchildren, all of whom get along and treat one another fairly, perhaps the forms will work for you. If, however, the parents are separated or divorced, grandmother has a secret lover, and grandfather wants to disinherit unruly grandchildren, you will probably need to consult a lawyer. Second, it is risky to use the forms if family property is complicated. For example, if your family has standard assets, such as a handful of heirlooms, one large house, few investments, and little accumulated wealth, perhaps the forms will work for you. In contrast, if your family has accumulated so much wealth that estate taxes are a concern or if the family needs to create one or more trusts, you need to consult an attorney.

The primary reason you should be cautious about using forms available on the Internet is that the law of trusts and estates has its own special language and you might not know enough about legal terms to write a will or trust that expresses your wishes. Do you know the difference between personal property and tangible property? (*Personal property* is all property other than real property, while *tangible property* is any real or personal property that can be possessed physically.) Between distribution *per stirpes* and distribution *per capita*? (Distribution *per stirpes* means distributing an estate by class or representation, while distribution *per capita* means distributing an estate by the individual.) Between a devise and a behest? (A *devise* is a gift of real property by will, while a *behest* is a gift of personal property.) When you consult a lawyer, he or she will know legal terminology and have a good understanding of the law of your particular state.

* www.easylegalforms.com.

SETTLEMENT OF AN ESTATE

When someone dies, a **personal representative** chosen by the testator collects the testator's property, pays debts and taxes, and makes sure the remainder of the estate is distributed. He or she makes sure **gifts** of real and personal property go to the correct *beneficiaries,* persons who inherit under a will. The process of settling an estate is known as **probate.**

Some property a person owns does not become part of the estate. Property that is not part of the probate estate is called **nonprobate property.** The most important forms of nonprobate property are life insurance with named beneficiaries, pension plan distributions, and property held in certain kinds of trusts, which are described in the next section.

Trusts as Estate Planning Tools

HOW AND WHY INDIVIDUALS CREATE TRUSTS

A person who creates a trust is called a **settlor.** A settlor delivers and transfers legal title to property to another person, called a **trustee,** who holds the property and uses it for the benefit of a third person. This third person is called the *beneficiary.* Trusts are usually created through formal, written documents.

Case Nugget **Tortious Interference with the Expectancy of Inheritance or Gift**

Vickie Lynn Marshall (aka Anna Nicole Smith) v. E. Pierce Marshall
253 B.R. 550, 36 Bankr. Ct. Dec. 254 (2000)

Debtor Vickie Lynn Marshall, also known as Anna Nicole Smith, was the surviving widow of the richest man in Texas, J. Howard Marshall II. E. Pierce Marshall, J. Howard's son from a prior marriage, contended that J. Howard died penniless.

In one of many proceedings between Vickie Lynn Marshall and E. Pierce Marshall, a bankruptcy court decided that Pierce had tortiously interfered with Vickie's expectancy of an *inter vivos* gift that J. Howard instructed his attorneys to arrange.

J. Howard had repeatedly told Vickie that she would receive half of what he owned, and he instructed his tax and estate planning experts, Sorensen and Hunter, to create a trust that would give Vickie half of what he owned. Pierce, however, fired Sorensen and conspired with Hunter to make sure he did not follow J. Howard's instructions.

Vickie won the case because she was able to show "(1) the existence of an expectancy; (2) a reasonable certainty that the expectancy would have been realized, but for the interference; (3) intentional interference with that expectancy; (4) tortious conduct involved with the interference; and (5) damages."

Trusts usually have two components: income and the trust corpus. The trust corpus is the property held in trust, while the income is generated by the trust through interest or appreciation. Often, income is paid to an **income beneficiary**, who may or may not have access to the trust corpus. When the trust is terminated, a designated person called a **remainderman** gets the trust corpus.

Individuals create trusts for a variety of reasons. Sometimes, a person creates a trust because he or she wants to protect another person. A settlor can even create a trust to protect an animal. For instance, a person can create a trust to provide for her or his beloved pet. Settlors also create trusts to prevent individuals from getting access to certain assets. For instance, the Wrigley family, known for its chewing gum, placed Wrigley Company stock in trusts and made family members income beneficiaries, not owners of the stock itself.[8] The significance of these legal actions is that when Wrigley family members marry and later divorce, the outsider who married a Wrigley family member cannot get Wrigley Company stock because it is "separately owned" property that cannot be divided on divorce. A final reason settlors create trusts is to avoid paying taxes. For instance, a person might create a charitable trust to avoid paying federal estate tax.

BASIC KINDS OF TRUSTS

Two basic kinds of trusts exist. The most common kind of trust is the **express trust.** Express trusts are trusts the settlor creates either while he or she is alive (**living trusts**) or by will (**testamentary trusts**). Usually, express trusts are written and called trust **instruments** or **agreements.**

[8] For more information about the expert estate planning related to the Wrigley family, see Darryl Van Duch, "Double Wrigley Trouble," *The National Law Journal,* May 31, 1999, p. A01.

Totten trust: Trust created when a person creates a bank deposit and deposits her money in her own name as trustee for another person.

Charitable trust: Trust created for the benefit of the general public. Charitable trusts are usually created for religious, charitable, or educational purposes.

Spendthrift trust: Trust created to protect the beneficiary from reckless spending. This trust provides funds to maintain a person who spends recklessly and makes sure that person cannot sell his interest or allow creditors to get it.

Exhibit 52-3
Special Kinds of Trusts

A second kind of trust is the **implied trust.** Implied trusts are also called *involuntary trusts* because courts, rather than settlors, create them. Courts create implied trusts in two situations. The first occurs when an express trust fails and the court can imply a trust from certain behavior. For instance, if a person pays for property and names a different person on the title, a court can infer that the person intended to create a trust. This kind of trust is a **resulting trust.** The second situation occurs when the law steps in to protect someone from fraud or other wrongdoing. Courts create **constructive trusts** to hold property in trust for its rightful owner. For instance, a court can place assets of a partnership in a constructive trust if it discovers that one partner is engaging in fraudulent or unconscionable conduct that might negatively affect the interests of another partner.

Many people who acquire a considerable amount of wealth worry about what that wealth will do to their families. They often create special kinds of trusts, for instance those described in Exhibit 52-3. They wonder: Will my family members start to fight over the family business? If I give my children money and assets, will they end up lacking character? Will my children be reluctant to work hard if I give them too much? One new kind of trust is a **family incentive trust.** This kind of trust responds to concerns raised by wealthy businesspersons, such as Bill Gates and Larry Ellison, who worry about what their wealth might do to their families. With a family incentive trust, the person who designs the trust can create incentives for certain behavior. For instance, the trust can pay "awards" to family members who make significant contributions in certain fields, such as education, science, law, or medicine. The trust can also pay a sum of money to descendants who obtain graduate degrees. By creating family incentive trusts, wealthy individuals can promote the kind of behavior that matters to them.

HOW TRUSTS ARE TERMINATED

A settlor is not allowed to revoke a trust unless he or she reserves a right to revoke the trust. Usually, a trust includes a provision that specifies the date on which the trust will terminate. Alternatively, the trust document states that the trust will terminate when an event happens, such as when the remainderman reaches a certain age. For instance, Diana, princess of Wales, created a trust that ends when Princes William and Harry reach the age of 30.

End-of-Life Decisions

ADVANCE DIRECTIVES

In 1990, in *Cruzan v. Director, Missouri Department of Health,*[9] the U.S. Supreme Court made a decision that indicated that a person has a constitutionally protected right under the Fourteenth Amendment to refuse life-sustaining medical procedures. Since that time,

[9] 497 U.S. 261 (1990).

states have clarified the nature and extent of this liberty interest by clarifying common and statutory law related to a patient's **right to die.** The right to die refers to a person's right to place limits on other people's efforts to prolong life. A person can express his or her wishes regarding these limits through **advance directives.** The term *advance directive* covers a variety of legal instruments a person can use to express his or her wishes about efforts to prolong life. The most frequently used advance directives are the living will, health care proxy, and durable power of attorney. Individuals who are gravely ill may use one or more of these instruments to express their wishes.

Nearly every state has enacted statutes that allow people to express their wishes regarding the extent of medical treatment they want if an accident or illness prevents them from participating in making medical decisions. The document that allows them to express their wishes is called a **living will.** Usually, a person who writes a living will does so because he wants to make sure that he dies a natural death and that his death is not prolonged through medical or surgical treatment. A person who writes a living will must make sure that his living will complies with the legal requirements of his particular state. The Internet assignment at the end of the chapter provides direction about how to find the particular requirements of your state.

Some states have passed laws that allow an agent to make medical decisions for a principal who is unable to participate in medical decisions. The document that outlines this principal-agent relationship is called a **health care proxy.** Some states outline instead a **durable power of attorney,** which is similar to a health care proxy. A durable power of attorney is a written document executed when the principal is in good mental health that allows an agent to make medical decisions for the principal at some later date when the principal can no longer make decisions. For example, a patient in the early stages of Alzheimer's disease could execute a durable power of attorney that allows another person, such as a spouse, to make medical decisions once that patient is no longer able to do so.

Case Nugget The Terry Schiavo Case

In re Guardianship of Schiavo
851 So. 2d 182, 186-187 (Fla. 2d DCA 2003) ("Schiavo IV")

In April 2005, Terry Schiavo died, 15 years after she had a heart attack and lapsed into a vegetative state. After a seven-year legal battle between her husband, Michael Schiavo, and her parents, Robert and Mary Schindler, a court granted permission to terminate life support. In the Schiavo case, life support was a feeding tube. The Schiavo case was the longest-running, most politically charged right-to-die battle in recent U.S. history.

The case is significant because it demonstrates what happens when a person fails to express her wishes with regard to end-of-life decisions. As a judge in one of many Schiavo cases stated: "It may be unfortunate that when families cannot agree, the best forum we can offer for this private, personal decision is a public courtroom and the best decision-maker we can provide is a judge with no prior knowledge of the ward, but the law currently provides no better solution that adequately protects the interests of promoting the value of life."

The judge's words in Schiavo IV make clear the extent to which, in the absence of an advance directive, judges are likely to view themselves as protectors of life. It is in everyone's best interests to write down the circumstances in which they do and do not want protection.

global context

Organ Donation in Japan

In 1997, Japan for the first time accepted the definition of brain death and passed a nationwide Organ Transplant Law. This change in law is significant because the concept of brain death allows doctors to harvest organs even though a person's heart and lungs might still be functioning. Prior to 1997, death in Japan was official only when the heart stopped beating.

Currently, the waiting list for organ transplants in Japan is long because of an organ shortage. Many Japanese patients receive transplants in the United States, United Kingdom, and other countries. Some people are concerned that the unwillingness of the Japanese to donate organs creates an unfair situation in which Japan burdens individuals in other countries by taking organs without adding organs to the pool of organs available for transplant.*

Although the law has changed in Japan, it is unlikely that the Japanese will be quick to favor organ donation. Doctors will declare brain death, but the Japanese law allows families to veto this diagnosis. It is likely that many families will reject the diagnosis because of different cultural norms regarding bodies and death. In Japan, many view death as a process, not a specific point in time. Also, religious traditions in Japan shape attitudes toward brain death. Many believe that respect for the dead ensures the welfare of the living. Additionally, some cultural traditions require that a corpse be buried intact. Some religious beliefs assert that the spirit of the deceased will be content only if there is no violence to the body. Organ removal is one form of violence to the body. Perhaps most important, for the Japanese, the mind and body are one. And no matter what the 1997 law says, it is the heart, not the brain, that controls the body.

* For additional information on this topic, see Samantha Weyrauch, "Acceptance of Whole-Brain Death Criteria for Determination of Death: A Comparative Analysis of the United States and Japan," *University of California Los Angeles Pacific Basin Law Journal* 17 (1999), p. 91.

ANATOMICAL GIFTS

The Uniform Anatomical Gifts Act (UAGA) has been adopted by every state in the United States. This law provides that any individual age 18 or older may give all or any part of his or her body to a donee on death. These donations are **anatomical gifts.** Individuals may donate parts of their body or their whole body to a hospital, physician, surgeon, medical or dental school, college or university, organ bank, or any person they specify who needs a transplant.

The UAGA has made it possible for thousands of people to receive organ transplants. In the United States, surgeons use a brain-death standard rather than a heart-lung standard to determine death. The brain-death standard allows surgeons to make use of organs such as the heart, lungs, liver, and kidney. You will see in the Global Context box that cultural and religious beliefs about the body affect individual and familial decisions about what to do with organs on death.

A person may express his or her wishes regarding organ donation in more than one way. A person may donate organs by expressing this gift through language in a will. Also, a person may sign a document such as an **organ donor card** that expresses his or her desire to donate organs or tissue. Sometimes donors register with a national donor registry, such as the Living Bank. In some states, the administrative agency that registers motor vehicles creates and maintains a program that allows people to make anatomical gifts when they receive a driver's license. It is common for a person's driver's license to identify the person as an organ donor. Finally, adult members of a person's family sometimes make decisions related to anatomical gifts.

CHOICES ABOUT THE BODY AFTER DEATH

When a person dies, someone has to decide what to do with the body. The best scenario occurs when the decedent made his or her wishes about the body clear. Sometimes people have clearly outlined wishes regarding whether the family should cremate their remains, what kind of funeral service they should have, and whether the body should be buried or be donated to a hospital or university for scientific study.

If the decedent did not make his or her wishes clear, sometimes families have disputes about who should decide what happens to the decedent's body. In Case 52-4, you will see how a family dispute could have been avoided if the decedent had made her wishes known. The case also makes clear why it is especially important for people to make their wishes known if they are separated, rather than divorced.

CASE 52-4

DEBORAH M. ANDREWS v. WILLIAM T. MCGOWAN
DISTRICT COURT OF APPEALS OF FLORIDA, FIFTH DISTRICT
739 SO. 2D 132 (1999)

This case arose when Evelyn McGowan died on July 12, 1996, without including a provision in her will that outlined what she wanted to happen to her remains. A conflict arose between Evelyn McGowan's daughter, Deborah Andrews, and Deborah's father, William T. McGowan. At the time of Evelyn McGowan's death, she had been separated for approximately three years after forty years of marriage. Evelyn and William McGowan lived separately, and a court had issued a final judgment of separate maintenance in 1993. This order required William to maintain existing health insurance for Evelyn and to pay her monthly support.

Evelyn's will named her daughter Deborah personal representative. When Evelyn died, Deborah notified her father that Woodlawn Memorial Park, Inc., would be handling funeral arrangements and that Woodlawn requested a written authorization from William for cremation since no final judgment of dissolution of marriage had been entered. William indicated that he would cooperate. Deborah signed a contract with Woodlawn for cremation and Woodlawn took custody of Evelyn's body.

Later that day, David McGowan, Deborah's brother, contacted her and demanded that he and his father, William, have a private viewing, or "she would be sorry." Deborah advised that there would be no private viewing. William McGowan then made arrangements through Levitt Weinstein Memorial Chapels, Inc., to pick up Evelyn's body from Woodlawn for funeral and cremation services in South Florida, where he lived. Pursuant to William's written authorization, Levitt Weinstein took possession of Evelyn's body and subsequently arranged a funeral service and viewing at Levitt Weinstein's West Palm Beach Facility. The service was held on July 15, 1996. Deborah Andrews and her husband were invited to attend but did not do so.

The next day, Deborah and another brother, John McGowan, traveled to Levitt Weinstein's facility and demanded to view their mother's body. On July 17, 1996, Deborah filed a petition for return of decedent's remains and for injunctive relief. On July 19, 1996, a court ordered Levitt Weinstein to deliver cremated remains to Deborah.

Deborah Andrews then filed a lawsuit against both funeral homes alleging tortious interference with lawful rights of burial, conversion, intentional infliction of emotional distress, civil conspiracy, fraud and deceit, and negligence. She sued in her capacity as personal representative and next of kin. The funeral homes filed a motion to dismiss. Judge Conrad granted motions to dismiss filed by both Woodlawn and Levitt Weinstein, ruling that section 470.002(18) *Florida Statutes* (1996) *controls, and that William McGowan had the right to determine burial and disposition of Evelyn's remains. This appeal considers whether the Florida statute applies and whether Judge Conrad interpreted it correctly. Levitt Weinstein is not mentioned in the following appeal because it was in bankruptcy at the time of the appeal.*

JUDGE COBB: There are no material issues of disputed fact present here. Rather, there is a dispute as to the applicable law. The appellants recognize that the general rule is that in the absence of testamentary direction to the contrary, a surviving spouse, followed by next of kin, has the lawful right to possession of the body of the deceased for burial or other lawful position. The question presented concerns the effect, if any, of a separation decree on the surviving spouse's right to determine the disposition of the decedent spouse's remains. The appellants assert an absence of Florida law on point and rely on out-of-state case law in support of their position that a separation decree divests the surviving spouse of the right to determine disposition. Woodlawn counters that out-of-state case law is irrelevant because section 470.002(18) *Florida Statutes* governs and gives the surviving spouse the power of disposition. It provides: (18) "Legally authorized person" means, in the priority listed, the decedent, when written *inter vivos* authorizations and directions are provided by the decedent, the surviving spouse, son or daughter who is 18 years of age or older, parent, brother or sister 18 years of age or over, grandchild who is 18 years of age or older, or grandparent or any person in the next degree of kinship. . . .

. . . Woodlawn argues that this subsection creates a priority of rights regime for disposition of human remains (which is consistent with the Florida case law previously set out) and that Evelyn's remains were accordingly subject to disposition by her surviving spouse. Appellants challenge the application of the statute, arguing initially that its applicability was not timely raised but that, even if it was, the statute is simply part of the regulatory scheme for funeral homes and in no way was intended to decide, among survivors, the legal right to dispose of the remains of another.

. . . While there is some logic to this assertion, an equally if not more compelling case could be made that *section* 470.002(18) was designed as much to give guidance to funeral home operators by clearly delineating the priority of those persons who are legally authorized to make funeral arrangements for a deceased person. The instant dispute would seem to be a classic case for utilization of such a statute which provides clear and simple guidance to the funeral home operator. . . . *Section* 470.002(18) was designed to establish a priority of rights, and the appellants' contention that judicially separated spouses should be treated differently in this regard than other spouses is more properly taken up with the legislature, which can determine whether public policy warrants differing treatment. . . .

. . . Under Florida statutory law, William McGowan, as lawful husband of the decedent, was the legally authorized person to direct the disposition of the decedent's remains. Thus, as a matter of law, Woodlawn is not liable to the appellants in tort.

AFFIRMED.

CRITICAL THINKING

When you evaluate a judge's reasoning, one useful tool is to consider whether the judge has oversimplified a case. Notice how Judge Cobb made the decision easy. How has the judge oversimplified the case?

ETHICAL DECISION MAKING

Does the judge in this case make a decision that is consistent with the universalization guideline? In other words, who benefits from this decision? Is society in general better off than it would have been if the judge had made a different ruling? Explain.

International Protection for Wills

In 1973, official delegates of 42 countries met in Washington, D.C., to adopt "The Convention Providing for a Uniform Law on the Form of an International Will."[10] The convention was sponsored by the International Institute for the Unification of Private Law

[10] J. Rodney Johnson, "Annual Survey of Virginia Law: Wills, Trusts, and Estates," *University of Richmond Law Review* 29 (1995), pp. 1175, 1190.

(UNIDROIT). UNIDROIT is an independent intergovernmental organization that prepares uniform private laws that strive to promote harmony and unity in private law worldwide.

Those who signed the 1973 convention for uniform law agreed to accept wills of other signatories for probate, as to matters of form, if such wills are executed with the provisions of the convention. In 1991, the U.S. Senate gave its advice and consent to the ratification of the convention. Congress is working on the legislation necessary to implement the uniform law. In order for an American's will to be recognized by other signatory countries, that American's state legislature must have enacted implementing legislation. Currently, states are enacting such legislation.

Readers can find the complete text of the Uniform International Wills Act in Part 10 of the Uniform Probate Code. This uniform legislation ensures that wills that meet the key requirements for a legally valid will (described earlier in the chapter) will be accepted by other countries that signed the 1973 convention. Wills must be written, witnessed, and signed.

CASE OPENER WRAP-UP

Billionaire

If the battle of the billionaires is described in terms of charitable giving, Bill Gates is clearly winning. The Bill and Melinda Gates Foundation is the largest private medical research charity in the world, with an endowment of $29.1 billion.[11] The Bill and Melinda Gates Foundation funds research to develop vaccines for diseases, including HIV/AIDS, malaria, and tuberculosis. Its primary focus is on global health. The foundation strives to ensure that people in developing countries enjoy an equal chance for good health.[12]

Apparently, Ellison is not trying to compete in a battle over giving wealth away. Unlike Gates, Ellison does not follow the philosophy of Andrew Carnegie, who stated that "the man who dies rich dies in disgrace."[13] Gates has cited Carnegie as his chief inspiration. Carnegie gave away $324 million of his $500 million fortune to charity before he died in 1919.[14] The world will be watching to see what people like Gates, Ellison, and the "millionaires next door" do with their assets in life and after life.

Although many of us would enjoy the opportunity to consider how to use our vast riches to improve the world, our questions are more basic. We wonder whether we will need a will, whether some of our property should be held in trust, and, depending on what we have, who should get family heirlooms when we die. No matter how much money we have, we or someone else makes a decision regarding what happens to our body after death. Our body goes somewhere, whether to a potter's grave or to a shrine our loved ones or we create to honor our legacy.

[11] www.gatesfoundation.org/MediaCenter/FactSheet/default.htm.

[12] Ibid.

[13] "Bill Gates' Charity Becomes Second Largest in the World," www.ippf.org.uk/newsinfo/archive/9908/42.htm (December 30, 2000).

[14] Ibid.

Summary

Estate Planning

Estate planning: The process by which an individual decides what to do with his or her real and personal property during and after life.

The *Uniform Probate Code* guides states in developing laws related to estate planning. Two important estate planning tools are:

- *Will:* A legal document that outlines how a person wants his or her property distributed on death.
- *Trust:* Allows a person to transfer property to another person, and this property is used for the benefit of a third person.

Individuals engage in estate planning:

- To *provide for their family* financially after their death.
- To *reduce taxes* and preserve wealth.
- To promote family *harmony.*
- To allow individuals in *nontraditional family relationships* to gain benefits of traditional family relationships.

Legal Issues Related to Wills

Intestacy statutes: Outline how a person's property will be distributed if he or she dies without a will.

To have a legally valid will, a person must have:

- *Testamentary capacity,* which means the person must be old enough to write a will, and must be of sound mind.
- A document in *writing,* which usually means a typed, written statement.
- A *signature,* which includes initials on each page.
- Witnesses, who *attest* to the will.

Grounds for contesting a will: The most common grounds for contesting a will are that a person believes the will fails to meet legal requirements and that a person believes that although the will is legally valid, the testator was a victim of fraud or undue influence.

Changing a will: Individuals are allowed to change wills by writing *codicils.*

Revoking a will: The most common way to revoke a will is to destroy it.

Settlement of an estate: A personal representative settles an estate through a process known as *probate.*

Trusts as Estate Planning Tools

How individuals create trusts: Trusts are created when a settlor delivers and transfers legal title to property to another person, called a *trustee,* who holds the property and uses it for the benefit of a third person. Trusts can be express or implied.

Individuals create trusts for a variety of reasons, but usually to protect another person. Basic kinds of trusts include:

- *Express trusts:* Created when a settlor is alive or through a will.
- *Implied trusts:* Created by courts.

Trusts are terminated through a clause in the trust itself, which indicates the date on which the trust will be terminated.

End-of-Life Decisions

Advance directives: Individuals can express their wishes regarding medical treatment at the end of life by using advance directives. Advance directives include:

- *Living wills:* Allow individuals to express their wishes regarding the extent of medical treatment if they are in an accident or suffer from a life-threatening illness.
- *Health care proxies or durable powers of attorney:* Allow a person to make medical decisions for someone else.

Anatomical gifts: Allow individuals to donate all or any part of their body to a donee on death. *Choices about your body after death* should be made prior to death.

International Protection for Wills

The *Uniform International Wills Act* protects wills written in other countries, as long as the wills follow a particular format. This act is part of the Uniform Probate Code.

Point / Counterpoint

As a Society, Should We Be Concerned about the Extent to Which Doctors Are Using Feeding Tubes on Seriously Ill Patients with Limited Cognitive Function?*

Yes

Today, doctors are overusing feeding tubes on seriously ill patients. Often, doctors use feeding tubes at the request of family members. It is important to educate Americans about the extent to which feeding tubes truly benefit patients in terms of how long they live or whether they maintain a particular quality of life.

Families in situations that ask them to decide whether to use a feeding tube on a loved one often make the decision based on an incorrect assumption. They assume that a relatively safe procedure that provides nutrition to the patient will help the patient recover from illness.

Studies in recent years have suggested that feeding tubes provide few benefits to patients, especially patients with dementia. Only rarely do patients and/or their families report improvement in nutrition, physical function, cognitive function, mood, pain, or quality of life. In fact, with regard to comfort, it is not uncommon for patients with feeding tubes to be restrained, either physically or via sedating drugs, so that they will not pull the feeding tube out.

Ongoing medical care for patients who will never recover and never regain their cognitive function is expensive. One reason patients or their surrogate decision makers seek feeding tubes is because a third party (such as an insurer) is usually paying for it. We should

No

Under current law, patients are allowed to forgo artificial nutrition and hydration by making their wishes clear or by designating a surrogate decision maker to make the decision when necessary. It is possible the law could change. Legally, we could require that doctors ask some patients to comply with a *duty* to refuse feeding tubes. If this happens, vulnerable patients may become victims of abuse.

The bottom line is that, even if a person is terminally ill and lacks cognitive function, families generally do not want to hasten a loved one's death. They want to know they did everything possible to keep their loved one alive.

People who argue that doctors are overusing feeding tubes on some seriously ill patients disregard the sanctity of human life. In addition, they disregard the symbolic value of nourishment. Even if a scientist can tell us feeding tubes do not benefit some patients, it is still important for families to engage in behavior that shows a desire to keep a loved one alive. Decisions families make near the end of a loved one's life have a profound effect on their grieving process. Anyone who argues against feeding tubes denies that reality.

More practically, doctors and medical facilities have a duty to provide care to their patients, including use of feeding tubes. If, as a society, we start asking be concerned about the extent to which doctors are using feeding tubes. If doctors would discuss the issue with patients in a nonsentimental way, perhaps patients and their surrogate decision makers would make wiser decisions.

questions about which patients "deserve" resources near the end of life, we start on a path that may lead to even more egregious decisions about the extent to which a life deserves protection.

*Information from David Orentlicher and Christopher Callahan, "Feeding Tubes, Slippery Slopes, and Physician-Assisted Suicide," *The Journal of Legal Medicine* 25 (2004), p. 389.

Questions & Problems

1. Identify and describe the two most important estate planning tools.
2. What are intestacy statutes, and why are they important?
3. Describe two scenarios that are likely to lead someone to contest a will.
4. What is the difference between a living will and a health care proxy?
5. What is the Uniform International Wills Act? Why is it important?
6. Look through the chapter and find two examples of situations in which advances in technology and/or medical science have led to legal challenges that fall under the topic of wills and trusts.
7. Alvin Miller died, leaving Lavern and Alliene Cannon, his longtime friends and neighbors, as the sole beneficiaries of his estate. His niece, Rita Hodges, contested the will, alleging that she had an oral contract with Moore whereby he would make her a beneficiary of his will in return for her moving into his house and taking care of him. What theory did she use to contest the will? Was she successful? [*Hodges v. Cannon,* 5 S.W.3d 89 (1999).]
8. Dorothy Wehrheim, now deceased, signed a will on July 23, 2002. She relied on the assistance of Rebecca Fierle, a geriatric care manager, who helped her arrange her personal affairs. This will named Golden Pond Assisted Living Facility as the primary beneficiary. It also named Fierle as Dorothy Wehrheim's personal representative. Wehrheim lived at this assisted living facility in 2002, and she died in the facility. After Wehrheim's death, her three children, Gary, Albert, and Debra, contested the 2002 will on the grounds of undue influence and lack of testamentary capacity. Three prior wills had not included the children as beneficiaries. Do the Wehrheim children have standing to challenge the will and ask that the state's intestacy statute be invoked? [*Wehrheim v. Golden Pond Assisted Living Facility,* 905 So. 2d 1002, 2005 WL 1537488 (Fla. App. 5 Dist. 2005).]
9. Warren Brown died in June 1997. On June 27, Candice Mathis, Brown's grandniece, admitted her copy of Warren Brown's will into probate. Her copy was complete, while the will in Warren Brown's papers at the time of his death was missing page 4, which reflected signatures. Several witnesses testified that Warren Brown viewed Candice as a daughter. He was devoted to her and on several occasions made it clear that he wanted nearly all his property to go to Candice "because she was just like his daughter." Joe Brown, Warren Brown's brother, sought to be the administrator of his brother's estate. Witnesses testified that Joe Brown did not have much of a relationship with Warren until the last two years of his life. Evidence also revealed the

possibility that Joe Brown might have had something to do with the missing page 4 of the executed will. What result? [*In re Estate of Warren Glenn Brown,* 1999 WL 802718 (1999).]

10. In 1988, Walter E. Havighurst created a trust before he died that had as its mission "to promote and fund educational projects through the Miami University International Center, Oxford, Ohio, for building cross-cultural understanding between the peoples of the United States of America and the Union of Soviet Socialist Republics." Heirs to the testator's estate filed an action, asking the court to declare that this charitable trust failed after the political, economic, and social conditions of the USSR changed, making Soviet-American relations a less compelling subject for study because the USSR no longer existed. They wanted the trust property to become part of the residual estate and pass to heirs. Did the court protect the trust? [*State v. Montgomery,* 1999 WL 694945 (1999).]

11. When John Muller died, he created a charitable trust to preserve a group of historic homes in Charleston, South Carolina. At the time of his death in 1984, the properties were in a state of disrepair. The Trustee fully restored the exterior of the properties, created 27 separate apartments in the group of nine properties, and rented them. Beneficiaries of Muller's estate filed an action asking the court to consider whether Muller had created a "charitable trust" when the properties were not open to the public. How do you think the court ruled? [*Evangelical Lutheran Charities Society of Charleston, South Carolina, v. South Carolina National Bank,* 495 S.E.2d 199 (1998).]

12. Frances Kelly, wife of Michael Kelly, held a health care proxy for her husband that allowed her to make medical decisions as his health declined. He suffered from non-Hodgkin's lymphoma and died at age 42. Mr. Kelly's doctor, Dr. Michael Vasconcelles, urged Mrs. Kelly to allow Brigham & Women's Hospital, where Michael Kelly had been treated, to perform a limited autopsy to study his lungs and liver. Mrs. Kelly was reluctant to allow a limited autopsy because she thought it was too intrusive. Dr. Vasconcelles informed Mrs. Kelly that a trained pathologist would perform the autopsy procedure. He gestured with his hands that the incision would be around 4 inches in length. Mrs. Kelly consented. Later, the funeral director informed Mrs. Kelly that the incision was not small. Mrs. Kelly had the funeral director take photos of the incision. Although Mrs. Kelly and the hospital disagreed about the length of the incision, it was clear the incision was at least 10 inches long. Mrs. Kelly sued the hospital, alleging tortious interference with a dead body, negligent and intentional infliction of emotional distress, and intentional misrepresentation. What result? [*Kelly v. Brigham & Women's Hospital,* 1998 WL 512983 (1998).]

13. Celia Blackman, age 88, had designated her grandson, Brent Ribnick, as her health care proxy in the event that she could not make her own determinations and decisions about her health care. Ribnick sought the court's help because he wanted to oppose any further intubation of his grandmother. Blackman made the decision that she no longer wanted to be intubated, although it was not clear that she understood whether she would die or survive following disintubation. Various parties influenced Blackman and Ribnick, including the hospital staff. The hospital wanted Blackman to have surgery to prolong her life, even though she weighed approximately 50 pounds, could barely see, and could not hear. What result? [*Blackman v. New York City Health and Hospitals Corporation,* 660 N.Y.S.2d 643 (1997).]

14. Robert Lee Wright, Jr., died on July 30, 1994. His parents described his death as "prolonged, painful and tragic." Wright suffered from AIDS. He went to the hospital, where he had a heart attack after a blood transfusion, was resuscitated from this cardiac arrest, and then died 10 days later. Of those 10 days, he was in a coma for two and then after that he was capable of moaning and calling out for his mother. He had executed a living will in February 1993. He had also made his mother his agent in making medical decisions for him at the end of life. Wright's parents sued health care providers for wrongfully prolonging their son's life. What result? [*Wright v. The Johns Hopkins Health Systems Corporation,* 728 A.2d 166 (1999).]

15. After Cynthia Shealey's 11-year-old son died at George H. Lanier Memorial Hospital following an asthma attack, a nurse asked Shealey whether she would be willing to donate her son's corneas to the Alabama Eye Bank so that they could be transplanted. Shealey told the nurse that it did not matter to her. Paul Cau from the Eye Bank came to the hospital and removed the corneas after the nurse said that the mother had granted consent via telephone. The father, Steven Andrews, arrived at the hospital and refused to sign the consent form. It was unclear whether the corneas had already been removed when Andrews arrived at the hospital. The parents sued the hospital, certain employees of the hospital, the Eye Bank, and Cau, alleging that the defendants acted negligently and outrageously in harvesting their son's corneas for organ donation. What result? [*Andrews v. Alabama Eye Bank,* 272 So. 2d 62 (1999).]

16. Jessie Peterson died in 1998. She was 102 years old. Her children disagreed about what to do with her body. Four of the children wanted her to be buried with their father in Solway, Minnesota. Two other children wanted her to be buried with her son from her first marriage, whose remains were in Bemidji, Minnesota. Peterson had made her wishes clear. She wanted her body to be donated to science and then her remains to be cremated and given to her daughter, Carole Carr. A problem arose when the medical center she donated her body to rejected her body. Over the years, Peterson had changed her mind about burial. Four of the children argued that there was no proof she wanted to be buried in Bemidji with her son from her first marriage. Carr said that Peterson had told her during the last few years that she wanted to be buried with her son. Peterson had revoked burial plans that placed her in Solway. Where should her body be buried? [*Peterson v. Carr,* 1999 WL 1048618 (1999).]

Looking for more review material?

The Online Learning Center at **www.mhhe.com/kubasek1e** contains this chapter's "Assignment on the Internet" and also a list of URLs for more information, entitled "On the Internet." Find both of them in the Student Center portion of the OLC, along with quizzes and other helpful materials.

Appendix A

THE CONSTITUTION OF THE UNITED STATES OF AMERICA

Preamble

We the People of the United States, in Order to form a more perfect Union, establish Justice, insure domestic Tranquility, provide for the common defense, promote the general Welfare, and secure the Blessings of Liberty to ourselves and our Posterity, do ordain and establish this Constitution for the United States of America.

Article I

Section 1 All legislative Powers herein granted shall be vested in a Congress of the United States, which shall consist of a Senate and House of Representatives.

Section 2 The House of Representatives shall be composed of Members chosen every second Year by the People of the several States, and the Electors in each State shall have the Qualifications requisite for Electors of the most numerous Branch of the State Legislature.

No Person shall be a Representative who shall not have attained to the age of twenty five Years, and been seven Years a Citizen of the United States, and who shall not, when elected, be an Inhabitant of that State in which he shall be chosen.

Representatives and direct Taxes shall be apportioned among the several States which may be included within this Union, according to their respective Numbers, which shall be determined by adding to the whole Number of free Persons, including those bound to Service for a Term of Years, and excluding Indians not taxed, three fifths of all other Persons.[1] The actual Enumeration shall be made within three Years after the first Meeting of the Congress of the United States, and within every subsequent Term of ten Years, in such Manner as they shall by Law direct. The Number of Representatives shall not exceed one for every thirty Thousand, but each State shall have at Least one Representative, and until such enumeration shall be made, the State of New Hampshire shall be entitled to choose three, Massachusetts eight, Rhode-Island and Providence Plantations one, Connecticut five, New York six, New Jersey four, Pennsylvania eight, Delaware one, Maryland six, Virginia ten, North Carolina five, South Carolina five, and Georgia three.

When vacancies happen in the Representation from any State, the Executive Authority thereof shall issue Writs of Election to fill such Vacancies.

The House of Representatives shall chuse their Speaker and other Officers; and shall have the sole Power of Impeachment.

Section 3 The Senate of the United States shall be composed of two Senators from each State, chosen by the Legislature thereof,[2] for six Years; and each Senator shall have one Vote.

Immediately after they shall be assembled in Consequence of the first Election, they shall be divided as equally as may be into three Classes. The Seats of the Senators of the first Class shall be vacated at the Expiration of the second Year, of the second Class at the Expiration of the fourth Year, and of the third Class at the Expiration of the sixth Year, so that one third may be chosen every second Year; and if Vacancies happen by Resignation, or otherwise, during the Recess of the Legislature of any State, the Executive thereof may make temporary Appointments until the next Meeting of the Legislature, which shall then fill such Vacancies.[3]

No Person shall be a Senator who shall not have attained to the Age of thirty Years, and been nine Years a Citizen of the United States, and who shall not, when elected, be an Inhabitant of that State for which he shall be chosen.

The Vice President of the United States shall be President of the Senate, but shall have no Vote, unless they be equally divided.

The Senate shall chuse their other Officers, and also a President pro tempore, in the Absence of the Vice President, or when he shall exercise the Office of President of the United States.

[1] Changed by the Fourteenth Amendment.

[2] Changed by the Seventeenth Amendment.

[3] Changed by the Seventeenth Amendment.

The Senate shall have the sole Power to try all Impeachments. When sitting for that Purpose, they shall be on Oath or Affirmation. When the President of the United States is tried, the Chief Justice shall preside: And no Person shall be convicted without the Concurrence of two thirds of the Members present.

Judgment in Cases of Impeachment shall not extend further than to removal from Office, and disqualification to hold and enjoy any Office of honor, Trust or Profit under the United States: but the Party convicted shall nevertheless be liable and subject to Indictment, Trial, Judgment and Punishment, according to Law.

Section 4 The Times, Places and Manner of holding Elections for Senators and Representatives, shall be prescribed in each State by the Legislature thereof; but the Congress may at any time by Law make or alter such Regulations, except as to the Places of chusing Senators.

The Congress shall assemble at least once in every Year, and such Meeting shall be on the first Monday in December, unless they shall by Law appoint a different Day.[4]

Section 5 Each House shall be the Judge of the Elections, Returns and Qualifications of its own Members, and a Majority of each shall constitute a Quorum to do Business; but a smaller Number may adjourn from day to day, and may be authorized to compel the Attendance of absent Members, in such Manner, and under such Penalties as each House may provide.

Each House may determine the Rules of its Proceedings, punish its Members for disorderly Behaviour, and with the Concurrence of two thirds, expel a Member.

Each House shall keep a Journal of its Proceedings, and from time to time publish the same, excepting such Parts as may in their Judgment require Secrecy; and the Yeas and Nays of the Members of either House on any question shall, at the Desire of one fifth of those Present, be entered on the Journal.

Neither House, during the Session of Congress, shall, without the Consent of the other, adjourn for more than three days, nor to any other Place than that in which the two Houses shall be sitting.

Section 6 The Senators and Representatives shall receive a Compensation for their Services, to be ascertained by Law, and paid out of the Treasury of the United States. They shall in all Cases, except Treason, Felony and Breach of the Peace, be privileged from Arrest during their Attendance at the Session of their respective Houses, and in going to and returning from the same; and for any Speech or Debate in either House, they shall not be questioned in any other Place.

No Senator or Representative shall, during the Time for which he was elected, be appointed to any civil Office under the Authority of the United States, which shall have been created, or the Emoluments whereof shall have been encreased during such time; and no Person holding any Office under the United States, shall be a Member of either House during his Continuance in Office.

Section 7 All Bills for raising Revenue shall originate in the House of Representatives; but the Senate may propose or concur with Amendments as on other Bills.

Every Bill which shall have passed the House of Representatives and the Senate, shall, before it becomes a Law, be presented to the President of the United States; If he approves he shall sign it, but if not he shall return it, with his Objections to that House in which it shall have originated, who shall enter the Objections at large on their Journal, and proceed to reconsider it. If after such Reconsideration two thirds of that House shall agree to pass the Bill, it shall be sent, together with the Objections, to the other House, by which it shall likewise be reconsidered, and if approved by two thirds of that House, it shall become a Law. But in all such Cases the Votes of both Houses shall be determined by Yeas and Nays, and the Names of the Persons voting for and against the Bill shall be entered on the Journal of each House respectively. If any Bill shall not be returned by the President within ten Days (Sundays excepted) after it shall have been presented to him, the Same shall be a Law, in like Manner as if he had signed it, unless the Congress by their Adjournment prevent its Return, in which Case it shall not be a Law.

Every Order, Resolution, or Vote to which the Concurrence of the Senate and House of Representatives may be necessary (except on a question of Adjournment) shall be presented to the President of the United States; and before the Same shall take Effect, shall be approved by him, or being disapproved by him, shall be repassed by two thirds of the Senate and House of Representatives, according to the Rules and Limitations prescribed in the Case of a Bill.

Section 8 The Congress shall have Power To lay and collect Taxes, Duties, Imposts and Excises, to pay the Debts and provide for the common Defence and

[4] Changed by the Twentieth Amendment.

general Welfare of the United States; but all Duties, Imposts and Excises shall be uniform throughout the United States.

To borrow Money on the credit of the United States;

To regulate Commerce with foreign Nations, and among the several States, and with the Indian Tribes;

To establish an uniform Rule of Naturalization, and uniform Laws on the subject of Bankruptcies throughout the United States;

To coin Money, regulate the Value thereof, and of foreign Coin, and fix the Standard of Weights and Measures;

To provide for the Punishment of counterfeiting the Securities and current Coin of the United States;

To establish Post Offices and post Roads;

To promote the Progress of Science and useful Arts, by securing for limited Times to Authors and Inventors the exclusive Right to their respective Writings and Discoveries;

To constitute Tribunals inferior to the supreme Court;

To define and punish Piracies and Felonies committed on the high Seas, and Offences against the Law of Nations;

To declare War, grant Letters of Marque and Reprisal, and make Rules concerning Captures on Land and Water;

To raise and support Armies, but no Appropriation of Money to that Use shall be for a longer Term than two Years;

To provide and maintain a Navy;

To make Rules for the Government and Regulation of the land and naval Forces;

To provide for calling forth the Militia to execute the Laws of the Union, suppress Insurrections and repel Invasions;

To provide for organizing, arming, and disciplining, the Militia, and for governing such Part of them as may be employed in the Service of the United States, reserving to the States respectively, the Appointment of the Officers, and the Authority of training the Militia according to the discipline prescribed by Congress;

To exercise exclusive Legislation in all Cases whatsoever, over such District (not exceeding ten Miles square) as may, by Cession of particular States, and the Acceptance of Congress, become the Seat of the Government of the United States, and to exercise like Authority over all Places purchased by the Consent of the Legislature of the State in which the Same shall be, for the Erection of Forts, Magazines, Arsenals, dock-Yards, and other needful Buildings;—And

To make all Laws which shall be necessary and proper for carrying into Execution the foregoing Powers, and all other Powers vested by this Constitution in the Government of the United States, or in any Department or Officer thereof.

Section 9 The Migration or Importation of such Persons as any of the States now existing shall think proper to admit, shall not be prohibited by the Congress prior to the Year one thousand eight hundred and eight, but a Tax or duty may be imposed on such Importation, not exceeding ten dollars for each Person.

The Privilege of the Writ of Habeas Corpus shall not be suspended, unless when in Cases of Rebellion or Invasion the public Safety may require it.

No Bill of Attainder or ex post facto Law shall be passed.

No Capitation, or other direct, Tax shall be laid, unless in Proportion to the Census of Enumeration herein before directed to be taken.[5]

No Tax or Duty shall be laid on Articles exported from any State.

No Preference shall be given by any Regulation of Commerce or Revenue to the Ports of one State over those of another: nor shall Vessels bound to, or from, one State, be obliged to enter, clear, or pay Duties in another.

No Money shall be drawn from the Treasury, but in Consequence of Appropriations made by Law; and a regular Statement and Account of the Receipts and Expenditures of all public Money shall be published from time to time.

No Title of Nobility shall be granted by the United States: And no Person holding any Office of Profit or Trust under them, shall, without the Consent of the Congress, accept of any present, Emolument, Office, or Title, of any kind whatever, from any King, Prince, or foreign State.

Section 10 No State shall enter into any Treaty, Alliance, or Confederation; grant Letters of Marque and Reprisal; coin Money; emit Bills of Credit; make any Thing but gold and silver coin a Tender in Payment of Debts; pass any Bill of Attainder, ex post facto Law, or Law impairing the Obligation of Contracts, or grant any Title of Nobility.

No State shall, without the Consent of the Congress, lay any Imposts or Duties on Imports or Exports,

[5] Changed by the Sixteenth Amendment.

except what may be absolutely necessary for executing its inspection Laws: and the net Produce of all Duties and Imposts, laid by any State on Imports or Exports, shall be for the Use of the Treasury of the United States; and all such Laws shall be subject to the Revision and Controul of the Congress.

No State shall, without the consent of Congress, lay any Duty of Tonnage, keep Troops, or Ships of War in time of Peace, enter into any Agreement or Compact with another State, or with a foreign Power, or engage in War, unless actually invaded, or in such imminent Danger as will not admit of delay.

Article II

Section 1 The executive Power shall be vested in a President of the United States of America. He shall hold his Office during the Term of four Years, and, together with the Vice President, chosen for the same Term, be elected, as follows

Each state shall appoint, in such Manner as the Legislature thereof may direct, a Number of Electors, equal to the whole Number of Senators and Representatives to which the State may be entitled in Congress: but no Senator or Representative, or Person holding an Office of Trust or Profit under the United States, shall be appointed an Elector.

The Electors shall meet in their respective States, and vote by Ballot for two Persons, of whom one at least shall not be an inhabitant of the same State with themselves. And they shall make a List of all the Persons voted for, and of the Number of Votes for each; which List they shall sign and certify, and transmit sealed to the Seat of the Government of the United States, directed to the President of the Senate. The President of the Senate shall, in the Presence of the Senate and House of Representatives, open all the Certificates, and the Votes shall then be counted. The Person having the greatest Number of Votes shall be the President, if such Number be a Majority of the whole Number of Electors appointed; and if there be more than one who have such Majority, and have an equal Number of Votes, then the House of Representatives shall immediately chuse by Ballot one of them for President; and if no Person have a Majority, then from the five highest on the List the said House shall in like Manner chuse the President. But in chusing the President, the Votes shall be taken by States, the Representation from each State having one Vote; A quorum for this purpose shall consist of a Member or Members from two thirds of the States, and a Majority of all the States shall be necessary to a Choice. In every Case, after the Choice of the President, the Person having the greatest Number of Votes of the Electors shall be the Vice President. But if there should remain two or more who have equal Votes, the Senate shall chuse from them by Ballot the Vice President.[6]

The Congress may determine the Time of chusing the Electors, and the Day on which they shall give their Votes; which Day shall be the same throughout the United States.

No Person except a natural born Citizen, or a Citizen of the United States, at the time of the Adoption of this Constitution, shall be eligible to the Office of President; neither shall any Person be eligible to that Office who shall not have attained to the Age of thirty five Years, and been fourteen Years a Resident within the United States.

In Case of the Removal of the President from Office, or of his Death, Resignation, or Inability to discharge the Powers and Duties of the said Office, the Same shall devolve on the Vice President, and the Congress may by Law provide for the Case of Removal, Death, Resignation or Inability, both of the President and Vice President, declaring what Officer shall then act as President, and such Officer shall act accordingly, until the Disability be removed, or a President shall be elected.[7]

The President shall, at stated Times, receive for his Services, a Compensation, which shall neither be encreased nor diminished during the Period for which he shall have been elected, and he shall not receive within that Period any other Emolument from the United States, or any of them.

Before he enter on the Execution of his Office, he shall take the following Oath or Affirmation:—"I do solemnly swear (or affirm) that I will faithfully execute the Office of President of the United States, and will to the best of my Ability, preserve, protect, and defend the Constitution of the United States."

Section 2 The President shall be Commander in Chief of the Army and Navy of the United States, and of the Militia of the several States, when called into the actual Service of the United States; he may require the Opinion, in writing, of the principal Officer in each of the executive Departments, upon any Subject relating to the Duties of their respective Offices, and he shall have Power to grant Reprieves and Pardons for Offences against the United States, except in Cases of Impeachment.

[6] Changed by the Twelfth Amendment.

[7] Changed by the Twenty-fifth Amendment.

He shall have Power, by and with the Advice and Consent of the Senate, to make Treaties, provided two thirds of the Senators present concur; and he shall nominate, and by and with the Advice and Consent of the Senate, shall appoint Ambassadors, other public Ministers and Consuls, Judges of the supreme Court, and all other Officers of the United States, whose Appointments are not herein otherwise provided for, and which shall be established by Law; but the Congress may by Law vest the Appointment of such inferior Officers, as they think proper, in the President alone, in the Courts of Law, or in the Heads of Departments.

The President shall have Power to fill up all Vacancies that may happen during the Recess of the Senate, by granting Commissions which shall expire at the End of their next Session.

Section 3 He shall from time to time give to the Congress Information of the State of the Union, and recommend to their Consideration such Measures as he shall judge necessary and expedient; he may, on extraordinary Occasions, convene both Houses, or either of them, and in Case of Disagreement between them, with Respect to the Time of Adjournment, he may adjourn them to such Time as he shall think proper; he shall receive Ambassadors and other public Ministers; he shall take Care that the Laws be faithfully executed, and shall Commission all the Officers of the United States.

Section 4 The President, Vice President and all civil Officers of the United States, shall be removed from Office on Impeachment for, and Conviction of, Treason, Bribery, or other high Crimes and Misdemeanors.

Article III

Section 1 The judicial Power of the United States, shall be vested in one supreme Court, and in such inferior Courts as the Congress may from time to time ordain and establish. The Judges, both of the supreme and inferior Courts, shall hold their Offices during good Behaviour, and shall, at stated Times, receive for their Services, a Compensation, which shall not be diminished during their Continuance in Office.

Section 2 The judicial Power shall extend to all Cases, in Law and Equity, arising under this Constitution, the Laws of the United States, and Treaties made, or which shall be made, under their Authority;—to all Cases affecting Ambassadors, other public Ministers and Consuls;—to all Cases of admiralty and maritime Jurisdiction;—to Controversies to which the United States shall be a party;—to Controversies between two or more States;—between a State and Citizens of another State;[8]—between Citizens of different States;—between Citizens of the same State claiming Lands under Grants of different States, and between a State, or the Citizens thereof, and foreign States, Citizens or Subjects.

In all Cases affecting Ambassadors, other public Ministers and Consuls, and those in which a State shall be Party, the supreme Court shall have original Jurisdiction. In all the other Cases before mentioned, the supreme Court shall have appellate Jurisdiction, both as to Law and Fact, with such Exceptions, and under such Regulations as the Congress shall make.

The Trial of all Crimes, except in Cases of Impeachment, shall be by Jury: and such Trial shall be held in the State where the said Crimes shall have been committed; but when not committed within any State, the Trial shall be at such Place or Places as the Congress may by Law have directed.

Section 3 Treason against the United States, shall consist only in levying War against them, or in adhering to their Enemies, giving them Aid and Comfort. No Person shall be convicted of Treason unless on the Testimony of two Witnesses to the same overt Act, or on Confession in open Court.

The Congress shall have Power to declare the Punishment of Treason, but no Attainder of Treason shall work Corruption of Blood, or Forfeiture except during the Life of the Person attainted.

Article IV

Section 1 Full Faith and Credit shall be given in each State to the public Acts, Records, and judicial Proceedings of every other State. And the Congress may by general Laws prescribe the Manner in which such Acts, Records and Proceedings shall be proved, and the Effect thereof.

Section 2 The Citizens of each State shall be entitled to all Privileges and Immunities of Citizens in the several States.

A Person charged in any State with Treason, Felony, or other Crime, who shall flee from Justice, and be found in another State, shall on Demand of the executive Authority of the State from which he fled, be delivered up, to be removed to the State having Jurisdiction of the Crime.

No Person held to Service or Labour in one State, under the Laws thereof, escaping into another, shall,

[8] Changed by the Eleventh Amendment.

in Consequence of any Law or Regulation therein, be discharged from such Service or Labour, but shall be delivered up on Claim of the Party to whom such Service or Labour may be due.[9]

Section 3 New States may be admitted by the Congress into this Union; but no new State shall be formed or erected within the Jurisdiction of any other State; nor any State be formed by the Junction of two or more States, or Parts of States, without the Consent of the Legislatures of the States concerned as well as of the Congress.

The Congress shall have Power to dispose of and make all needful Rules and Regulations respecting the Territory or other Property belonging to the United States; and nothing in this Constitution shall be so construed as to Prejudice any Claims of the United States, or of any particular State.

Section 4 The United States shall guarantee to every State in this Union a Republican Form of Government, and shall protect each of them against Invasion; and on Application of the Legislature, or of the Executive (when the Legislature cannot be convened) against domestic Violence.

Article V

The Congress, whenever two thirds of both Houses shall deem it necessary, shall propose Amendments to this Constitution, or, on the Application of the Legislatures of two thirds of the several States, shall call a Convention for proposing Amendments, which, in either Case, shall be valid to all Intents and Purposes, as Part of this Constitution, when ratified by the legislatures of three fourths of the several States, or by Conventions in three fourths thereof, as the one or the other Mode of Ratification may be proposed by the Congress; Provided that no Amendment which may be made prior to the Year One thousand eight hundred and eight shall in any Manner affect the first and fourth Clauses in the Ninth Section of the first Article; and that no State, without its Consent, shall be deprived of its equal Suffrage in the Senate.

Article VI

All Debts contracted and Engagements entered into, before the Adoption of this Constitution, shall be as valid against the United States under this Constitution, as under the Confederation.

The Constitution, and the Laws of the United States which shall be made in Pursuance thereof; and all Treaties made, or which shall be made, under the Authority of the United States, shall be the supreme Law of the Land; and the Judges in every State shall be bound thereby, any Thing in the Constitution or Laws of any State to the Contrary notwithstanding.

The Senators and Representatives before mentioned, and the Members of the several State Legislatures, and all executive and judicial Officers, both of the United States and of the several States, shall be bound by Oath or Affirmation, to support this Constitution; but no religious Test shall ever be required as a Qualification to any Office or public Trust under the United States.

Article VII

The Ratification of the Conventions of nine States, shall be sufficient for the Establishment of this Constitution between the States so ratifying the Same.

Done in Convention by the Unanimous Consent of the States present the Seventeenth Day of September in the Year of our Lord one thousand seven hundred and eighty seven and of the Independance of the United States of America the Twelfth. In witness whereof We have hereunto subscribed our Names.

Amendments

[The first 10 amendments are known as the "Bill of Rights."]

Amendment I (Ratified 1791) Congress shall make no law respecting an establishment of religion, or prohibiting the free exercise thereof; or abridging the freedom of speech, or of the press; or the right of the people peaceably to assemble, and to petition the Government for a redress of grievances.

Amendment 2 (Ratified 1791) A well regulated Militia, being necessary to the security of a free State, the right of the people to keep and bear Arms, shall not be infringed.

Amendment 3 (Ratified 1791) No Soldier shall, in time of peace be quartered in any house, without the consent of the Owner, nor in time of war, but in a manner to be prescribed by law.

[9] Changed by the Thirteenth Amendment.

Amendment 4 (Ratified 1791) The right of the people to be secure in their persons, houses, papers, and effects, against unreasonable searches and seizures, shall not be violated, and no Warrants shall issue, but upon probable cause, supported by Oath or affirmation, and particularly describing the place to be searched, and the persons or things to be seized.

Amendment 5 (Ratified 1791) No person shall be held to answer for a capital, or otherwise infamous crime, unless on a presentment or indictment of a Grand Jury, except in cases arising in the land or naval forces, or in the Militia, when in actual service in time of War or public danger; nor shall any person be subject for the same offence to be twice put in jeopardy of life or limb; nor shall be compelled in any criminal case to be a witness against himself, nor be deprived of life, liberty, or property, without due process of law; nor shall private property be taken for public use, without just compensation.

Amendment 6 (Ratified 1791) In all criminal prosecutions, the accused shall enjoy the right to a speedy and public trial, by an impartial jury of the State and district wherein the crime shall have been committed, which district shall have been previously ascertained by law, and to be informed of the nature and cause of the accusation; to be confronted with the witnesses against him; to have compulsory process for obtaining Witnesses in his favor, and to have assistance of counsel for his defence.

Amendment 7 (Ratified 1791) In Suits at common law, where the value in controversy shall exceed twenty dollars, the right of trial by jury shall be preserved, and no fact tried by a jury, shall be otherwise re-examined in any Court of the United States, than according to the rules of the common law.

Amendment 8 (Ratified 1791) Excessive bail shall not be required, nor excessive fines imposed, nor cruel and unusual punishments inflicted.

Amendment 9 (Ratified 1791) The enumeration in the Constitution, of certain rights, shall not be construed to deny or disparage others retained by the people.

Amendment 10 (Ratified 1791) The powers not delegated to the United States by the Constitution, nor prohibited by it to the States, are reserved to the States respectively, or to the people.

Amendment 11 (Ratified 1795) The Judicial power of the United States shall not be construed to extend to any suit in law or equity, commenced or prosecuted against one of the United States by Citizens of another State, or by Citizens or Subjects of any Foreign State.

Amendment 12 (Ratified 1804) The Electors shall meet in their respective states, and vote by ballot for President and Vice-President, one of whom, at least, shall not be an inhabitant of the same state with themselves; they shall name in their ballots the person voted for as President, and in distinct ballots the person voted for as Vice-President, and they shall make distinct lists of all persons voted for as President, and of all persons voted for as Vice-President, and of the number of votes for each, which lists they shall sign and certify, and transmit sealed to the seat of the government of the United States, directed to the President of the Senate;—The President of the Senate shall, in the presence of the Senate and House of Representatives, open all the certificates and the votes shall then be counted;—The person having the greatest number of votes for President, shall be the President, if such number be a majority of the whole number of Electors appointed; and if no person have such majority, then from the persons having the highest numbers not exceeding three on the list of those voted for as President, the House of Representatives shall choose immediately, by ballot, the President. But in choosing the President, the votes shall be taken by states, the representation from each state having one vote; a quorum for this purpose shall consist of a member or members from two-thirds of the states, and a majority of all the states shall be necessary to a choice. And if the House of Representatives shall not choose a President whenever the right of choice shall devolve upon them, before the fourth day of March next following, then the Vice-President shall act as president, as in the case of the death or other constitutional disability of the President.[10]—The person having the greatest number of votes as Vice-President, shall be the Vice-President, if such number be a majority of the whole number of Electors appointed, and if no person have a majority, then from the two highest numbers on the list,

[10] Changed by the Twentieth Amendment.

the Senate shall choose the Vice-President; a quorum for the purpose shall consist of two-thirds of the whole number of Senators, and a majority of the whole number shall be necessary to a choice. But no person constitutionally ineligible to the office of President shall be eligible to that of Vice-President of the United States.

Amendment 13 (Ratified 1865) Section 1 Neither slavery nor involuntary servitude, except as a punishment for crime whereof the party shall have been duly convicted, shall exist within the United States, or any place subject to their jurisdiction.

Section 2 Congress shall have power to enforce this article by appropriate legislation.

Amendment 14 (Ratified 1868) Section 1 All persons born or naturalized in the United States, and subject to the jurisdiction thereof, are citizens of the United States and of the State wherein they reside. No State shall make or enforce any law which shall abridge the privileges or immunities of citizens of the United States; nor shall any State deprive any person of life, liberty, or property, without due process of law; nor deny to any person within its jurisdiction the equal protection of the laws.

Section 2 Representatives shall be apportioned among the several States according to their respective numbers, counting the whole number of persons in each State, excluding Indians not taxed. But when the right to vote at any election for the choice of electors for President and Vice President of the United States, Representatives in Congress, the Executive and Judicial officers of a State, or the members of the Legislature thereof, is denied to any of the male inhabitants of such State, being twenty-one[11] years of age, and citizens of the United States, or in any way abridged except for participation in rebellion, or other crime, the basis of representation therein shall be reduced in the proportion which the number of such male citizens shall bear to the whole number of male citizens twenty-one years of age in such State.

Section 3 No person shall be a Senator or Representative in Congress, or elector of President and Vice President, or hold any office, civil or military, under the United States, or under any State, who, having previously taken an oath, as a member of Congress, or as an officer of the United States, or as a member of any State legislature, or as an executive or judicial officer of any State, to support the Constitution of the United States, shall have engaged in insurrection or rebellion against the same, or given aid or comfort to the enemies thereof. But Congress may by a vote of two-thirds of each House, remove such disability.

Section 4 The validity of the public debt of the United States, authorized by law, including debts incurred for payment of pensions and bounties for services in suppressing insurrection or rebellion, shall not be questioned. But neither the United States nor any State shall assume or pay any debt or obligation incurred in aid of insurrection or rebellion against the United States, or any claim for the loss or emancipation of any slave; but all such debts, obligations and claims shall be held illegal and void.

Section 5 The Congress shall have power to enforce, by appropriate legislation, the provisions of this article.

Amendment 15 (Ratified 1870) Section 1 The right of citizens of the United States to vote shall not be denied or abridged by the United States or by any State on account of race, color, or previous condition of servitude.

Section 2 The Congress shall have power to enforce this article by appropriate legislation.

Amendment 16 (Ratified 1913) The Congress shall have power to lay and collect taxes on incomes, from whatever source derived, without apportionment among the several States, and without regard to any census or enumeration.

Amendment 17 (Ratified 1913) The Senate of the United States shall be composed of two Senators from each State, elected by the people thereof, for six years; and each Senator shall have one vote. The electors in each State shall have the qualifications requisite for electors of the most numerous branch of the State legislatures.

When vacancies happen in the representation of any State in the Senate, the executive authority of such State shall issue writs of election to fill such vacancies: *Provided,* That the legislature of any State may empower the executive thereof to make temporary appointments until the people fill the vacancies by election as the legislature may direct.

This amendment shall not be so construed as to affect the election or term of any Senator chosen before it becomes valid as part of the Constitution.

[11] Changed by the Twenty-sixth Amendment.

Amendment 18 (Ratified 1919; Repealed 1933) Section 1 After one year from the ratification of this article the manufacture, sale, or transportation of intoxicating liquors within, the importation thereof into, or the exportation thereof from the United States and all territory subject to the jurisdiction thereof for beverage purposes is hereby prohibited.

Section 2 The Congress and the several States shall have concurrent power to enforce this article by appropriate legislation.

Section 3 This article shall be inoperative unless it shall have been ratified as an amendment to the Constitution by the legislatures of the several States, as provided in the Constitution, within seven years from the date of the submission hereof to the States by the Congress.[12]

Amendment 19 (Ratified 1920) The right of citizens of the United States to vote shall not be denied or abridged by the United States or by any State on account of sex.

Congress shall have power to enforce this article by appropriate legislation.

Amendment 20 (Ratified 1933) Section 1 The terms of the President and Vice President shall end at noon on the 20th day of January, and the terms of Senators and Representatives at noon on the 3d day of January, of the years in which such terms would have ended if this article had not been ratified; and the terms of their successors shall then begin.

Section 2 The Congress shall assemble at least once in every year, and such meeting shall begin at noon on the 3d day of January, unless they shall by law appoint a different day.

Section 3 If, at the time fixed for the beginning of the term of the President, the President elect shall have died, the Vice President elect shall become President. If a President shall not have been chosen before the time fixed for the beginning of his term, or if the President elect shall have failed to qualify, then the Vice President elect shall act as President until a President shall have qualified; and the Congress may by law provide for the case wherein neither a President elect nor a Vice President elect shall have qualified, declaring who shall then act as President, or the manner in which one who is to act shall be selected, and such person shall act accordingly until a President or Vice President shall have qualified.

Section 4 The Congress may by law provide for the case of the death of any of the persons from whom the House of Representatives may choose a President whenever the right of choice shall have devolved upon them, and for the case of the death of any of the persons from whom the Senate may choose a Vice President whenever the right of choice shall have devolved upon them.

Section 5 Sections 1 and 2 shall take effect on the 15th day of October following the ratification of this article.

Section 6 This article shall be inoperative unless it shall have been ratified as an amendment to the Constitution by the legislatures of three-fourths of the several States within seven years from the date of its submission.

Amendment 21 (Ratified 1933) Section 1 The eighteenth article of amendment to the Constitution of the United States is hereby repealed.

Section 2 The transportation or importation into any State, Territory, or possession of the United States for delivery or use therein of intoxicating liquors, in violation of the laws thereof, is hereby prohibited.

Section 3 This article shall be inoperative unless it shall have been ratified as an amendment to the Constitution by conventions in the several States, as provided in the Constitution, within seven years from the date of the submission hereof to the States by the Congress.

Amendment 22 (Ratified 1951) Section 1 No person shall be elected to the office of the President more than twice, and no person who has held the office of President, or acted as President, for more than two years of a term to which some other person was elected President shall be elected to the office of the President more than once. But this Article shall not apply to any person holding the office of President when this Article was proposed by the Congress, and shall not prevent any person who may be holding the office of President, or acting as President, during the term within which this Article becomes operative from holding the office of President or acting as President during the remainder of such term.

[12] Repealed by the Twenty-first Amendment.

Section 2 This Article shall be inoperative unless it shall have been ratified as an amendment to the Constitution by the legislatures of three-fourths of the several States within seven years from the date of its submission to the States by the Congress.

Amendment 23 (Ratified 1961) Section 1 The District constituting the seat of Government of the United States shall appoint in such manner as the Congress may direct:

A number of electors of President and Vice President equal to the whole number of Senators and Representatives in Congress to which the District would be entitled if it were a State, but in no event more than the least populous State; they shall be in addition to those appointed by the States, but they shall be considered, for the purposes of the election of President and Vice President, to be electors appointed by a State; and they shall meet in the District and perform such duties as provided by the twelfth article of amendment.

Section 2 The Congress shall have power to enforce this article by appropriate legislation.

Amendment 24 (Ratified 1964) Section 1 The right of citizens of the United States to vote in any primary or other election for President or Vice President, for electors for President or Vice President, or for Senator or Representative in Congress, shall not be denied or abridged by the United States or any State by reason of failure to pay any poll tax or other tax.

Section 2 The Congress shall have power to enforce this article by appropriate legislation.

Amendment 25 (Ratified 1967) Section 1 In case of the removal of the President from office or of his death or resignation, the Vice President shall become President.

Section 2 Whenever there is a vacancy in the office of the Vice President, the President shall nominate a Vice President who shall take office upon confirmation by a majority vote of both Houses of Congress.

Section 3 Whenever the President transmits to the President pro tempore of the Senate and the Speaker of the House of Representatives his written declaration that he is unable to discharge the powers and duties of his office, and until he transmits to them a written declaration to the contrary, such powers and duties shall be discharged by the Vice President as Acting President.

Section 4 Whenever the Vice President and a majority of either the principal officers of the executive departments or of such other body as Congress may by law provide, transmit to the President pro tempore of the Senate and the Speaker of the House of Representatives their written declaration that the President is unable to discharge the powers and duties of his office, the Vice President shall immediately assume the powers and duties of the office as Acting President.

Thereafter, when the President transmits to the President pro tempore of the Senate and the Speaker of the House of Representatives his written declaration that no inability exists, he shall resume the powers and duties of his office unless the Vice President and a majority of either the principal officers of the executive department or of such other body as Congress may by law provide, transmit within four days to the President pro tempore of the Senate and the Speaker of the House of Representatives their written declaration that the President is unable to discharge the powers and duties of his office. Thereupon Congress shall decide the issue, assembling within forty-eight hours for that purpose if not in session. If the Congress, within twenty-one days after receipt of the latter written declaration, or, if Congress is not in session, within twenty-one days after Congress is required to assemble, determines by two-thirds vote of both Houses that the President is unable to discharge the powers and duties of his office, the Vice President shall continue to discharge the same as Acting President; otherwise, the President shall resume the powers and duties of his office.

Amendment 26 (Ratified 1971) Section 1 The right of citizens of the United States, who are eighteen years of age or older, to vote shall not be denied or abridged by the United States or by any State on account of age.

Section 2 The Congress shall have power to enforce this article by appropriate legislation.

Amendment 27 (Ratified 1992) No law, varying the compensation for the services of the Senators and Representatives, shall take effect, until an election of Representatives shall have intervened.

Appendix B

UNIFORM COMMERCIAL CODE

Article 2–Sales

Part 1: Short Title, General Construction and Subject Matter

§ 2–101. Short Title. This Article shall be known and may be cited as Uniform Commercial Code—Sales.

§ 2–102. Scope; Certain Security and Other Transactions Excluded from This Article. Unless the context otherwise requires, this Article applies to transactions in goods; it does not apply to any transaction which although in the form of an unconditional contract to sell or present sale is intended to operate only as a security transaction nor does this Article impair or repeal any statute regulating sales to consumers, farmers or other specified classes of buyers.

§ 2–103. Definitions and Index of Definitions.

(1) In this Article unless the context otherwise requires
- **(a)** "Buyer" means a person who buys or contracts to buy goods.
- **(b)** "Good faith" in the case of a merchant means honesty in fact and the observance of reasonable commercial standards of fair dealing in the trade.
- **(c)** "Receipt" of goods means taking physical possession of them.
- **(d)** "Seller" means a person who sells or contracts to sell goods.

(2) Other definitions applying to this Article or to specified Parts thereof, and the sections in which they appear are:

"Acceptance"	Section 2–606.
"Banker's credit"	Section 2–325.
"Between merchants"	Section 2–104.
"Cancellation"	Section 2–106(4).
"Commercial unit"	Section 2–105.
"Confirmed credit"	Section 2–325.
"Conforming to contract"	Section 2–106.
"Contract for sale"	Section 2–106.
"Cover"	Section 2–712.
"Entrusting"	Section 2–403.
"Financing agency"	Section 2–104.
"Future goods"	Section 2–105.
"Goods"	Section 2–105.
"Identification"	Section 2–501.
"Installment contract"	Section 2–612.
"Letter of Credit"	Section 2–325.
"Lot"	Section 2–105.
"Merchant"	Section 2–104.
"Overseas"	Section 2–323.
"Person in position of seller"	Section 2–707.
"Present sale"	Section 2–106.
"Sale"	Section 2–106.
"Sale on approval"	Section 2–326.
"Sale or return"	Section 2–326.
"Termination"	Section 2–106.

(3) The following definitions in other Articles apply to this Article:

"Check"	Section 3–104.
"Consignee"	Section 7–102.
"Consignor"	Section 7–102.
"Consumer goods"	Section 9–109.
"Dishonor"	Section 3–502.
"Draft"	Section 3–104.

(4) In addition Article 1 contains general definitions and principles of construction and interpretation applicable throughout this Article.

As amended in 1994.

See Appendix XI for material relating to changes made in text in 1994.

§ 2–104. Definitions: "Merchant"; "Between Merchants"; "Financing Agency".

(1) "Merchant" means a person who deals in goods of the kind or otherwise by his occupation holds himself out as having knowledge or skill peculiar to the practices or goods involved in the transaction or to whom such knowledge or skill may be attributed by his employment of an agent or broker or other intermediary who by his occupation holds himself out as having such knowledge or skill.

(2) "Financing agency" means a bank, finance company or other person who in the ordinary course of business makes advances against goods or documents of title or who by arrangement with either the seller or the buyer intervenes in ordinary course to make or collect payment due or claimed under the contract for sale, as by purchasing or paying the seller's draft or making advances against it or by merely taking it for collection whether or not documents of title accompany the draft. "Financing agency" includes also a bank or other person who similarly intervenes between persons who are in the position of seller and buyer in respect to the goods (Section 2–707).

(3) "Between merchants" means in any transaction with respect to which both parties are chargeable with the knowledge or skill of merchants.

§ 2–105. Definitions: "Transferability"; "Goods"; "Future" Goods; "Lot"; "Commercial Unit".

(1) "Goods" means all things (including specially manufactured goods) which are movable at the time of identification to the contract for sale other than the money in which the price is to be paid, investment securities (Article 8) and things in action. "Goods" also includes the unborn young of animals and growing crops and other identified things attached to realty as described in the section on goods to be severed from realty (Section 2–107).

(2) Goods must be both existing and identified before any interest in them can pass. Goods which are not both existing and identified are "future" goods. A purported present sale of future goods or of any interest therein operates as a contract to sell.

(3) There may be a sale of a part interest in existing identified goods.

(4) An undivided share in an identified bulk of fungible goods is sufficiently identified to be sold although the quantity of the bulk is not determined. Any agreed proportion of such a bulk or any quantity thereof agreed upon by number, weight or other measure may to the extent of the seller's interest in the bulk be sold to the buyer who then becomes an owner in common.

(5) "Lot" means a parcel or a single article which is the subject matter of a separate sale or delivery, whether or not it is sufficient to perform the contract.

(6) "Commercial unit" means such a unit of goods as by commercial usage is a single whole for purposes of sale and division of which materially impairs its character or value on the market or in use. A commercial unit may be a single article (as a machine) or a set of articles (as a suite of furniture or an assortment of sizes) or a quantity (as a bale, gross, or carload) or any other unit treated in use or in the relevant market as a single whole.

§ 2–106. Definitions: "Contract"; "Agreement"; "Contract for Sales"; "Sale"; "Present Sale"; "Conforming" to Contract; "Termination"; "Cancellation".

(1) In this Article unless the context otherwise requires "contract" and "agreement" are limited to those relating to the present or future sale of goods. "Contract for sale" includes both a present sale of goods and a contract to sell goods at a future time. A "sale" consists in the passing of title from the seller to the buyer for a price (Section 2–401). A "present sale" means a sale which is accomplished by the making of the contract.

(2) Goods or conduct including any part of a performance are "conforming" or conform to the contract when they are in accordance with the obligations under the contract.

(3) "Termination" occurs when either party pursuant to a power created by agreement or law puts an end to the contract otherwise than for its breach. On "termination" all obligations which are still executory on both sides are discharged but any right based on prior breach or performance survives.

(4) "Cancellation" occurs when either party puts an end to the contract for breach by the other and its effect is the same as that of "termination" except that the cancelling party also retains any remedy for breach of the whole contract or any unperformed balance.

§ 2–107. Goods to Be Severed from Realty: Recording.

(1) A contract for the sale of minerals or the like (including oil and gas) or a structure or its materials to be removed from realty is a contract for the sale of goods within this Article if they are to be severed by the seller but until severance a purported present sale thereof which is not effective as a transfer of an interest in land is effective only as a contract to sell.

(2) A contract for the sale apart from the land of growing crops or other things attached to realty and capable of severance without material harm thereto but not described in subsection (1) or of timber to be cut is a contract for the sale of goods within this Article whether the subject matter is to be severed by the buyer or by the seller even though it forms part of the realty at the time of contracting, and the parties can by identification effect a present sale before severance.

(3) The provisions of this section are subject to any third party rights provided by the law relating to realty records, and the contract for sale may be executed and recorded as a document transferring an interest in land and shall then constitute notice to third parties of the buyer's rights under the contract for sale. As amended in 1972.

Part 2: Form, Formation and Readjustment Of Contract

§ 2–201. Formal Requirements; Statute of Frauds.

(1) Except as otherwise provided in this section a contract for the sale of goods for the price of $500 or more is not enforceable by way of action or defense unless there is some writing sufficient to indicate that a contract for sale has been made between the parties and signed by the party against whom enforcement is sought or by his authorized agent or broker. A writing is not insufficient because it omits or incorrectly states a term agreed upon but the contract is not enforceable under this paragraph beyond the quantity of goods shown in such writing.

(2) Between merchants if within a reasonable time a writing in confirmation of the contract and sufficient against the sender is received and the party receiving it has reason to know its contents, it satisfies the requirements of subsection (1) against such party unless written notice of objection to its contents is given within 10 days after it is received.

(3) A contract which does not satisfy the requirements of subsection (1) but which is valid in other respects is enforceable

(a) if the goods are to be specially manufactured for the buyer and are not suitable for sale to others in the ordinary course of the seller's business and the seller, before notice of repudiation is received and under circumstances which reasonably indicate that the goods are for the buyer, has made either a substantial beginning of their manufacture or commitments for their procurement; or

(b) if the party against whom enforcement is sought admits in his pleading, testimony or otherwise in court that a contract for sale was made, but the contract is not enforceable under this provision beyond the quantity of goods admitted; or

(c) with respect to goods for which payment has been made and accepted or which have been received and accepted (Section 2–606).

§ 2–202. Final Written Expression: Parol or Extrinsic Evidence. Terms with respect to which the confirmatory memoranda of the parties agree or which are otherwise set forth in a writing intended by the parties as a final expression of their agreement with respect to such terms as are included therein may not be contradicted by evidence of any prior agreement or of a contemporaneous oral agreement but may be explained or supplemented

(a) by course of dealing or usage of trade (Section 1–205) or by course of performance (Section 2–208); and

(b) by evidence of consistent additional terms unless the court finds the writing to have been intended also as a complete and exclusive statement of the terms of the agreement.

§ 2–203. Seals Inoperative. The affixing of a seal to a writing evidencing a contract for sale or an offer to buy or sell goods does not constitute the writing a sealed instrument and the law with respect to sealed instruments does not apply to such a contract or offer.

§ 2–204. Formation in General.

(1) A contract for sale of goods may be made in any manner sufficient to show agreement, including conduct by both parties which recognizes the existence of such a contract.

(2) An agreement sufficient to constitute a contract for sale may be found even though the moment of its making is undetermined.

(3) Even though one or more terms are left open a contract for sale does not fail for indefiniteness if the parties have intended to make a contract and there is a reasonably certain basis for giving an appropriate remedy.

§ 2–205. Firm Offers. An offer by a merchant to buy or sell goods in a signed writing which by its terms gives assurance that it will be held open is not revocable, for lack of consideration, during the time stated or if no time is stated for a reasonable time, but in no event may such period of irrevocability exceed three months; but any such term of assurance on a form supplied by the offeree must be separately signed by the offeror.

§ 2–206. Offer and Acceptance in Formation of Contract.

(1) Unless otherwise unambiguously indicated by the language or circumstances
  (a) an offer to make a contract shall be construed as inviting acceptance in any manner and by any medium reasonable in the circumstances;
  (b) an order or other offer to buy goods for prompt or current shipment shall be construed as inviting acceptance either by a prompt promise to ship or by the prompt or current shipment of conforming or non-conforming goods, but such a shipment of non-conforming goods does not constitute an acceptance if the seller seasonably notifies the buyer that the shipment is offered only as an accommodation to the buyer.

(2) Where the beginning of a requested performance is a reasonable mode of acceptance an offeror who is not notified of acceptance within a reasonable time may treat the offer as having lapsed before acceptance.

§ 2–207. Additional Terms in Acceptance or Confirmation.

(1) A definite and seasonable expression of acceptance or a written confirmation which is sent within a reasonable time operates as an acceptance even though it states terms additional to or different from those offered or agreed upon, unless acceptance is expressly made conditional on assent to the additional or different terms.

(2) The additional terms are to be construed as proposals for addition to the contract. Between merchants such terms become part of the contract unless:
  (a) the offer expressly limits acceptance to the terms of the offer;
  (b) they materially alter it; or
  (c) notification of objection to them has already been given or is given within a reasonable time after notice of them is received.

(3) Conduct by both parties which recognizes the existence of a contract is sufficient to establish a contract for sale although the writings of the parties do not otherwise establish a contract. In such case the terms of the particular contract consist of those terms on which the writings of the parties agree, together with any supplementary terms incorporated under any other provisions of this Act.

§ 2–208. Course of Performance or Practical Construction.

(1) Where the contract for sale involves repeated occasions for performance by either party with knowledge of the nature of the performance and opportunity for objection to it by the other, any course of performance accepted or acquiesced in without objection shall be relevant to determine the meaning of the agreement.

(2) The express terms of the agreement and any such course of performance, as well as any course of dealing and usage of trade, shall be construed whenever reasonable as consistent with each other; but when such construction is unreasonable, express terms shall control course of performance and course of performance shall control both course of dealing and usage of trade (Section 1-205).

(3) Subject to the provisions of the next section on modification and waiver, such course of performance shall be relevant to show a waiver or modification of any term inconsistent with such course of performance.

§ 2–209. Modification, Rescission and Waiver.

(1) An agreement modifying a contract within this Article needs no consideration to be binding.

(2) A signed agreement which excludes modification or rescission except by a signed writing cannot be otherwise modified or rescinded, but except as between merchants such a requirement on a form supplied by the merchant must be separately signed by the other party.

(3) The requirements of the statute of frauds section of this Article (Section 2–201) must be satisfied if the contract as modified is within its provisions.

(4) Although an attempt at modification or rescission does not satisfy the requirements of subsection (2) or (3) it can operate as a waiver.

(5) A party who has made a waiver affecting an executory portion of the contract may retract the waiver by reasonable notification received by the other party that strict performance will be required of any term waived, unless the retraction would be unjust in view of a material change of position in reliance on the waiver.

§ 2–210. Delegation of Performance; Assignment of Rights.

(1) A party may perform his duty through a delegate unless otherwise agreed or unless the other party has a substantial interest in having his original promisor perform or control the acts required by the contract. No delegation of performance relieves the party delegating of any duty to perform or any liability for breach.

(2) Unless otherwise agreed all rights of either seller or buyer can be assigned except where the assignment would materially change the duty of the other party, or increase materially the burden or risk imposed on him by his contract, or impair materially his chance of obtaining return performance. A right to damages for breach of the whole contract or a right arising out of the assignor's due performance of his entire obligation can be assigned despite agreement otherwise.

(3) Unless the circumstances indicate the contrary a prohibition of assignment of "the contract" is to be construed as barring only the delegation to the assignee of the assignor's performance.

(4) An assignment of "the contract" or of "all my rights under the contract" or an assignment in similar general terms is an assignment of rights and unless the language or the circumstances (as in an assignment for security) indicate the contrary, it is a delegation of performance of the duties of the assignor and its acceptance by the assignee constitutes a promise by him to perform those duties. This promise is enforceable by either the assignor or the other party to the original contract.

(5) The other party may treat any assignment which delegates performance as creating reasonable grounds for insecurity and may without prejudice to his rights against the assignor demand assurances from the assignee (Section 2–609).

Part 3: General Obligation and Construction of Contract

§ 2–301. General Obligations of Parties. The obligation of the seller is to transfer and deliver and that of the buyer is to accept and pay in accordance with the contract.

§ 2–302. Unconscionable Contract or Clause.

(1) If the court as a matter of law finds the contract or any clause of the contract to have been unconscionable at the time it was made the court may refuse to enforce the contract, or it may enforce the remainder of the contract without the unconscionable clause, or it may so limit the application of any unconscionable clause as to avoid any unconscionable result.

(2) When it is claimed or appears to the court that the contract or any clause thereof may be unconscionable the parties shall be afforded a reasonable opportunity to present evidence as to its commercial setting, purpose and effect to aid the court in making the determination.

§ 2–303. Allocation or Division of Risks. Where this Article allocates a risk or a burden as between the parties "unless otherwise agreed", the agreement may not only shift the allocation but may also divide the risk or burden.

§ 2–304. Price Payable in Money, Goods, Realty, or Otherwise.

(1) The price can be made payable in money or otherwise. If it is payable in whole or in part in goods each party is a seller of the goods which he is to transfer.

(2) Even though all or part of the price is payable in an interest in realty the transfer of the goods and the seller's obligations with reference to them are subject to this Article, but not the transfer of the interest in realty or the transferor's obligations in connection therewith.

§ 2–305. Open Price Term.

(1) The parties if they so intend can conclude a contract for sale even though the price is not settled. In such a case the price is a reasonable price at the time for delivery if
- **(a)** nothing is said as to price; or
- **(b)** the price is left to be agreed by the parties and they fail to agree; or
- **(c)** the price is to be fixed in terms of some agreed market or other standard as set or recorded by a third person or agency and it is not so set or recorded.

(2) A price to be fixed by the seller or by the buyer means a price for him to fix in good faith.

(3) When a price left to be fixed otherwise than by agreement of the parties fails to be fixed through fault of one party the other may at his option treat the contract as cancelled or himself fix a reasonable price.

(4) Where, however, the parties intend not to be bound unless the price be fixed or agreed and it is not fixed or agreed there is no contract. In such a case the buyer must return any goods already received or if unable so to do must pay their reasonable value at the time of delivery and the seller must return any portion of the price paid on account.

§ 2–306. Output, Requirements and Exclusive Dealings.

(1) A term which measures the quantity by the output of the seller or the requirements of the buyer means such actual output or requirements as may occur in good faith, except that no quantity unreasonably disproportionate to any stated estimate or in the absence of a stated estimate to any normal or otherwise comparable prior output or requirements may be tendered or demanded.

(2) A lawful agreement by either the seller or the buyer for exclusive dealing in the kind of goods concerned imposes unless otherwise agreed an obligation by the seller to use best efforts to supply the goods and by the buyer to use best efforts to promote their sale.

§ 2–307. Delivery in Single Lot or Several Lots. Unless otherwise agreed all goods called for by a contract for sale must be tendered in a single delivery and payment is due only on such tender but where the circumstances give either party the right to make or demand delivery in lots the price if it can be apportioned may be demanded for each lot.

§ 2–308. Absence of Specified Place for Delivery. Unless otherwise agreed

(a) the place for delivery of goods is the seller's place of business or if he has none his residence; but

(b) in a contract for sale of identified goods which to the knowledge of the parties at the time of contracting are in some other place, that place is the place for their delivery; and

(c) documents of title may be delivered through customary banking channels.

§ 2–309. Absence of Specific Time Provisions; Notice of Termination.

(1) The time for shipment or delivery or any other action under a contract if not provided in this Article or agreed upon shall be a reasonable time.

(2) Where the contract provides for successive performances but is indefinite in duration it is valid for a reasonable time but unless otherwise agreed may be terminated at any time by either party.

(3) Termination of a contract by one party except on the happening of an agreed event requires that reasonable notification be received by the other party and an agreement dispensing with notification is invalid if its operation would be unconscionable.

§ 2–310. Open Time for Payment or Running of Credit; Authority to Ship Under Reservation. Unless otherwise agreed

(a) payment is due at the time and place at which the buyer is to receive the goods even though the place of shipment is the place of delivery; and

(b) if the seller is authorized to send the goods he may ship them under reservation, and may tender the documents of title, but the buyer may inspect the goods after their arrival before payment is due unless such inspection is inconsistent with the terms of the contract (Section 2–513); and

(c) if delivery is authorized and made by way of documents of title otherwise than by subsection (b) then payment is due at the time and place at which the buyer is to receive the documents regardless of where the goods are to be received; and

(d) where the seller is required or authorized to ship the goods on credit the credit period runs from the time of shipment but postdating the invoice or delaying its dispatch will correspondingly delay the starting of the credit period.

§ 2–311. Options and Cooperation Respecting Performance.

(1) An agreement for sale which is otherwise sufficiently definite (subsection (3) of Section 2–204) to be a contract is not made invalid by the fact that it leaves particulars of performance to be specified by one of the parties. Any such specification must be made in good faith and within limits set by commercial reasonableness.

(2) Unless otherwise agreed specifications relating to assortment of the goods are at the buyer's option and except as otherwise provided in subsections (1)(c) and (3) of Section 2–319 specifications or arrangements relating to shipment are at the seller's option.

(3) Where such specification would materially affect the other party's performance but is not seasonably made or where one party's cooperation is necessary to the agreed performance of the other but is not seasonably forthcoming, the other party in addition to all other remedies
   (a) is excused for any resulting delay in his own performance; and
   (b) may also either proceed to perform in any reasonable manner or after the time for a material part of his own performance treat the failure to specify or to cooperate as a breach by failure to deliver or accept the goods.

§ 2–312. Warranty of Title and Against Infringement; Buyer's Obligation Against Infringement.

(1) Subject to subsection (2) there is in a contract for sale a warranty by the seller that
   (a) the title conveyed shall be good, and its transfer rightful; and
   (b) the goods shall be delivered free from any security interest or other lien or encumbrance of which the buyer at the time of contracting has no knowledge.

(2) A warranty under subsection (1) will be excluded or modified only by specific language or by circumstances which give the buyer reason to know that the person selling does not claim title in himself or that he is purporting to sell only such right or title as he or a third person may have.

(3) Unless otherwise agreed a seller who is a merchant regularly dealing in goods of the kind warrants that the goods shall be delivered free of the rightful claim of any third person by way of infringement or the like but a buyer who furnishes specifications to the seller must hold the seller harmless against any such claim which arises out of compliance with the specifications.

§ 2–313. Express Warranties by Affirmation, Promise, Description, Sample.

(1) Express warranties by the seller are created as follows:
   (a) Any affirmation of fact or promise made by the seller to the buyer which relates to the goods and becomes part of the basis of the bargain creates an express warranty that the goods shall conform to the affirmation or promise.
   (b) Any description of the goods which is made part of the basis of the bargain creates an express warranty that the goods shall conform to the description.
   (c) Any sample or model which is made part of the basis of the bargain creates an express warranty that the whole of the goods shall conform to the sample or model.

(2) It is not necessary to the creation of an express warranty that the seller use formal words such as "warrant" or "guarantee" or that he have a specific intention to make a warranty, but an affirmation merely of the value of the goods or a statement purporting to be merely the seller's opinion or commendation of the goods does not create a warranty.

§ 2–314. Implied Warranty: Merchantability; Usage of Trade.

(1) Unless excluded or modified (Section 2–316), a warranty that the goods shall be merchantable is implied in a contract for their sale if the seller is a merchant with respect to goods of that kind. Under this section the serving for value of food or drink to be consumed either on the premises or elsewhere is a sale.

(2) Goods to be merchantable must be at least such as
   (a) pass without objection in the trade under the contract description; and
   (b) in the case of fungible goods, are of fair average quality within the description; and
   (c) are fit for the ordinary purposes for which such goods are used; and
   (d) run, within the variations permitted by the agreement, of even kind, quality and quantity within each unit and among all units involved; and
   (e) are adequately contained, packaged, and labeled as the agreement may require; and
   (f) conform to the promise or affirmations of fact made on the container or label if any.

(3) Unless excluded or modified (Section 2–316) other implied warranties may arise from course of dealing or usage of trade.

§ 2–315. Implied Warranty: Fitness for Particular Purpose. Where the seller at the time of contracting has reason to know any particular purpose for which the goods are required and that the buyer is relying on the seller's skill or judgment to select or furnish suitable goods, there is unless excluded or modified under the next section an implied warranty that the goods shall be fit for such purpose.

§ 2–316. Exclusion or Modification of Warranties.

(1) Words or conduct relevant to the creation of an express warranty and words or conduct tending to negate or limit warranty shall be construed wherever reasonable as consistent with each other; but subject to the provisions of this Article on parol or extrinsic evidence (Section 2–202) negation or limitation is inoperative to the extent that such construction is unreasonable.

(2) Subject to subsection (3), to exclude or modify the implied warranty of merchantability or any part of it the language must mention merchantability and in case of a writing must be conspicuous, and to exclude or modify any implied warranty of fitness the exclusion must be by a writing and conspicuous. Language to exclude all implied warranties of fitness is sufficient if it states, for example, that "There are no warranties which extend beyond the description on the face hereof."

(3) Notwithstanding subsection (2)

  (a) unless the circumstances indicate otherwise, all implied warranties are excluded by expressions like "as is", "with all faults" or other language which in common understanding calls the buyer's attention to the exclusion of warranties and makes plain that there is no implied warranty; and

  (b) when the buyer before entering into the contract has examined the goods or the sample or model as fully as he desired or has refused to examine the goods there is no implied warranty with regard to defects which an examination ought in the circumstances to have revealed to him; and

  (c) an implied warranty can also be excluded or modified by course of dealing or course of performance or usage of trade.

(4) Remedies for breach of warranty can be limited in accordance with the provisions of this Article on liquidation or limitation of damages and on contractual modification of remedy (Sections 2–718 and 2–719).

§ 2–317. Cumulation and Conflict of Warranties Express or Implied. Warranties whether express or implied shall be construed as consistent with each other and as cumulative, but if such construction is unreasonable the intention of the parties shall determine which warranty is dominant. In ascertaining that intention the following rules apply:

(a) Exact or technical specifications displace an inconsistent sample or model or general language of description.

(b) A sample from an existing bulk displaces inconsistent general language of description.

(c) Express warranties displace inconsistent implied warranties other than an implied warranty of fitness for a particular purpose.

§ 2–318. Third Party Beneficiaries of Warranties Express or Implied. Note: *If this Act is introduced in the Congress of the United States this section should be omitted. (States to select one alternative.)*

Alternative A

A seller's warranty whether express or implied extends to any natural person who is in the family or household of his buyer or who is a guest in his home if it is reasonable to expect that such person may use, consume or be affected by the goods and who is injured in person by breach of the warranty. A seller may not exclude or limit the operation of this section.

Alternative B

A seller's warranty whether express or implied extends to any natural person who may reasonably be expected to use, consume or be affected by the goods and who is injured in person by breach of the warranty. A seller may not exclude or limit the operation of this section.

Alternative C

A seller's warranty whether express or implied extends to any person who may reasonably be expected to use, consume or be affected by the goods and who is injured by breach of the warranty. A seller may not exclude or limit the operation of this section with respect to injury to the person of an individual to whom the warranty extends.

As amended in 1966.

§ 2–319. F.O.B. and F.A.S. Terms.

(1) Unless otherwise agreed the term F.O.B. (which means "free on board") at a named place, even though used only in connection with the stated price, is a delivery term under which

  (a) when the term is F.O.B. the place of shipment, the seller must at that place ship the goods in the manner provided in this Article (Section 2–504) and bear the expense and risk of putting them into the possession of the carrier; or

  (b) when the term is F.O.B. the place of destination, the seller must at his own expense and risk transport the goods to that place and there tender delivery of them in the manner provided in this Article (Section 2–503);

(c) when under either (a) or (b) the term is also F.O.B. vessel, car or other vehicle, the seller must in addition at his own expense and risk load the goods on board. If the term is F.O.B. vessel the buyer must name the vessel and in an appropriate case the seller must comply with the provisions of this Article on the form of bill of lading (Section 2–323).

(2) Unless otherwise agreed the term F.A.S. vessel (which means "free alongside") at a named port, even though used only in connection with the stated price, is a delivery term under which the seller must

(a) at his own expense and risk deliver the goods alongside the vessel in the manner usual in that port or on a dock designated and provided by the buyer; and

(b) obtain and tender a receipt for the goods in exchange for which the carrier is under a duty to issue a bill of lading.

(3) Unless otherwise agreed in any case falling within subsection (1)(a) or (c) or subsection (2) the buyer must seasonably give any needed instructions for making delivery, including when the term is F.A.S. or F.O.B. the loading berth of the vessel and in an appropriate case its name and sailing date. The seller may treat the failure of needed instructions as a failure of cooperation under this Article (Section 2–311). He may also at his option move the goods in any reasonable manner preparatory to delivery or shipment.

(4) Under the term F.O.B. vessel or F.A.S. unless otherwise agreed the buyer must make payment against tender of the required documents and the seller may not tender nor the buyer demand delivery of the goods in substitution for the documents.

§ 2–320. C.I.F. and C. & F. Terms.

(1) The term C.I.F. means that the price includes in a lump sum the cost of the goods and the insurance and freight to the named destination. The term C. & F. or C.F. means that the price so includes cost and freight to the named destination.

(2) Unless otherwise agreed and even though used only in connection with the stated price and destination, the term C.I.F. destination or its equivalent requires the seller at his own expense and risk to

(a) put the goods into the possession of a carrier at the port for shipment and obtain a negotiable bill or bills of lading covering the entire transportation to the named destination; and

(b) load the goods and obtain a receipt from the carrier (which may be contained in the bill of lading) showing that the freight has been paid or provided for; and

(c) obtain a policy or certificate of insurance, including any war risk insurance, of a kind and on terms then current at the port of shipment in the usual amount, in the currency of the contract, shown to cover the same goods covered by the bill of lading and providing for payment of loss to the order of the buyer or for the account of whom it may concern; but the seller may add to the price the amount of the premium for any such war risk insurance; and

(d) prepare an invoice of the goods and procure any other documents required to effect shipment or to comply with the contract; and

(e) forward and tender with commercial promptness all the documents in due form and with any indorsement necessary to perfect the buyer's rights.

(3) Unless otherwise agreed the term C. & F. or its equivalent has the same effect and imposes upon the seller the same obligations and risks as a C.I.F. term except the obligation as to insurance.

(4) Under the term C.I.F. or C. & F. unless otherwise agreed the buyer must make payment against tender of the required documents and the seller may not tender nor the buyer demand delivery of the goods in substitution for the documents.

§ 2–321. C.I.F. or C. & F.: "Net Landed Weights"; "Payment on Arrival"; Warranty of Condition on Arrival. Under a contract containing a term C.I.F. or C. & F.

(1) Where the price is based on or is to be adjusted according to "net landed weights", "delivered weights", "out turn" quantity or quality or the like, unless otherwise agreed the seller must reasonably estimate the price. The payment due on tender of the documents called for by the contract is the amount so estimated, but after final adjustment of the price a settlement must be made with commercial promptness.

(2) An agreement described in subsection (1) or any warranty of quality or condition of the goods on arrival places upon the seller the risk of ordinary deterioration, shrinkage and the like in transportation but has no effect on the place or time of identification to the contract for sale or delivery or on the passing of the risk of loss.

(3) Unless otherwise agreed where the contract provides for payment on or after arrival of the goods the seller must before payment allow such preliminary inspection as is feasible; but if the goods are lost delivery of the documents and payment are due when the goods should have arrived.

§ 2–322. Delivery "Ex-Ship".

(1) Unless otherwise agreed a term for delivery of goods "ex-ship" (which means from the carrying vessel) or in equivalent language is not restricted to a particular ship and requires delivery from a ship which has reached a place at the named port of destination where goods of the kind are usually discharged.

(2) Under such a term unless otherwise agreed

(a) the seller must discharge all liens arising out of the carriage and furnish the buyer with a direction which puts the carrier under a duty to deliver the goods; and

(b) the risk of loss does not pass to the buyer until the goods leave the ship's tackle or are otherwise properly unloaded.

§ 2–323. Form of Bill of Lading Required in Overseas Shipment; "Overseas".

(1) Where the contract contemplates overseas shipment and contains a term C.I.F. or C. & F. or F.O.B. vessel, the seller unless otherwise agreed must obtain a negotiable bill of lading stating that the goods have been loaded in board or, in the case of a term C.I.F. or C. & F., received for shipment.

(2) Where in a case within subsection (1) a bill of lading has been issued in a set of parts, unless otherwise agreed if the documents are not to be sent from abroad the buyer may demand tender of the full set; otherwise only one part of the bill of lading need be tendered. Even if the agreement expressly requires a full set

(a) due tender of a single part is acceptable within the provisions of this Article on cure of improper delivery (subsection (1) of Section 2–508); and

(b) even though the full set is demanded, if the documents are sent from abroad the person tendering an incomplete set may nevertheless require payment upon furnishing an indemnity which the buyer in good faith deems adequate.

(3) A shipment by water or by air or a contract contemplating such shipment is "overseas" insofar as by usage of trade or agreement it is subject to the commercial, financing or shipping practices characteristic of international deep water commerce.

§ 2–324. "No Arrival, No Sale" Term. Under a term "no arrival, no sale" or terms of like meaning, unless otherwise agreed,

(a) the seller must properly ship conforming goods and if they arrive by any means he must tender them on arrival but he assumes no obligation that the goods will arrive unless he has caused the non-arrival; and

(b) where without fault of the seller the goods are in part lost or have so deteriorated as no longer to conform to the contract or arrive after the contract time, the buyer may proceed as if there had been casualty to identified goods (Section 2–613).

§ 2–325. "Letter of Credit" Term; "Confirmed Credit".

(1) Failure of the buyer seasonably to furnish an agreed letter of credit is a breach of the contract for sale.

(2) The delivery to seller of a proper letter of credit suspends the buyer's obligation to pay. If the letter of credit is dishonored, the seller may on seasonable notification to the buyer require payment directly from him.

(3) Unless otherwise agreed the term "letter of credit" or "banker's credit" in a contract for sale means an irrevocable credit issued by a financing agency of good repute and, where the shipment is overseas, of good international repute. The term "confirmed credit" means that the credit must also carry the direct obligation of such an agency which does business in the seller's financial market.

§ 2–326. Sale on Approval and Sale or Return; Consignment Sales and Rights of Creditors.

(1) Unless otherwise agreed, if delivered goods may be returned by the buyer even though they conform to the contract, the transaction is

(a) a "sale on approval" if the goods are delivered primarily for use, and

(b) a "sale or return" if the goods are delivered primarily for resale.

(2) Except as provided in subsection (3), goods held on approval are not subject to the claims of the buyer's creditors until acceptance; goods held on sale or return are subject to such claims while in the buyer's possession.

(3) Where goods are delivered to a person for sale and such person maintains a place of business at which he deals in goods of the kind involved, under a name other than the name of the person making delivery, then with respect to claims of creditors of the person conducting the business the goods are deemed to be on sale or return. The provisions of this subsection are applicable even though an agreement purports to reserve title to the person making delivery until payment or resale or uses such words as "on consignment" or "on memorandum". However, this subsection is not applicable if the person making delivery

- **(a)** complies with an applicable law providing for a consignor's interest or the like to be evidenced by a sign, or
- **(b)** establishes that the person conducting the business is generally known by his creditors to be substantially engaged in selling the goods of others, or
- **(c)** complies with the filing provisions of the Article on Secured Transactions (Article 9).

(4) Any "or return" term of a contract for sale is to be treated as a separate contract for sale within the statute of frauds section of this Article (Section 2–201) and as contradicting the sale aspect of the contract within the provisions of this Article on parol or extrinsic evidence (Section 2–202).

§ 2–327. Special Incidents of Sale on Approval and Sale or Return.

(1) Under a sale on approval unless otherwise agreed

- **(a)** although the goods are identified to the contract the risk of loss and the title do not pass to the buyer until acceptance; and
- **(b)** use of the goods consistent with the purpose of trial is not acceptance but failure seasonably to notify the seller of election to return the goods is acceptance, and if the goods conform to the contract acceptance of any part is acceptance of the whole; and
- **(c)** after due notification of election to return, the return is at the seller's risk and expense but a merchant buyer must follow any reasonable instructions.

(2) Under a sale or return unless otherwise agreed

- **(a)** the option to return extends to the whole or any commercial unit of the goods while in substantially their original condition, but must be exercised seasonably; and
- **(b)** the return is at the buyer's risk and expense.

§ 2–328. Sale by Auction.

(1) In a sale by auction if goods are put up in lots each lot is the subject of a separate sale.

(2) A sale by auction is complete when the auctioneer so announces by the fall of the hammer or in other customary manner. Where a bid is made while the hammer is falling in acceptance of a prior bid the auctioneer may in his discretion reopen the bidding or declare the goods sold under the bid on which the hammer was falling.

(3) Such a sale is with reserve unless the goods are in explicit terms put up without reserve. In an auction with reserve the auctioneer may withdraw the goods at any time until he announces completion of the sale. In an auction without reserve, after the auctioneer calls for bids on an article or lot, that article or lot cannot be withdrawn unless no bid is made within a reasonable time. In either case a bidder may retract his bid until the auctioneer's announcement of completion of the sale, but a bidder's retraction does not revive any previous bid.

(4) If the auctioneer knowingly receives a bid on the seller's behalf or the seller makes or procures such a bid, and notice has not been given that liberty for such bidding is reserved, the buyer may at his option avoid the sale or take the goods at the price of the last good faith bid prior to the completion of the sale. This subsection shall not apply to any bid at a forced sale.

Part 4: Title, Creditors and Good Faith Purchasers

§ 2–401. Passing of Title; Reservation for Security; Limited Application of This Section. Each provision of this Article with regard to the rights, obligations and remedies of the seller, the buyer, purchasers or other third parties applies irrespective of title to the goods except where the provision refers to such title. Insofar as situations are not covered by the other provisions of this Article and matters concerning title become material the following rules apply:

(1) Title to goods cannot pass under a contract for sale prior to their identification to the contract (Section 2–501), and unless otherwise explicitly agreed the buyer acquires by their identification a special property as limited by this Act. Any retention or reservation by the seller of the title (property) in goods shipped or delivered to the buyer is limited in effect to a reservation of a security interest. Subject to these provisions and to the provisions of the Article on Secured Transactions (Article 9), title to goods passes from the seller to the buyer in any manner and on any conditions explicitly agreed on by the parties.

(2) Unless otherwise explicitly agreed title passes to the buyer at the time and place at which the seller completes his performance with reference to the physical delivery of the goods, despite any reservation of a security interest and even though a document of title is to be delivered at a different time or place; and in particular and despite any reservation of a security interest by the bill of lading

(a) if the contract requires or authorizes the seller to send the goods to the buyer but does not require him to deliver them at destination, title passes to the buyer at the time and place of shipment; but

(b) if the contract requires delivery at destination, title passes on tender there.

(3) Unless otherwise explicitly agreed where delivery is to be made without moving the goods,

(a) if the seller is to deliver a document of title, title passes at the time when and the place where he delivers such documents; or

(b) if the goods are at the time of contracting already identified and no documents are to be delivered, title passes at the time and place of contracting.

(4) A rejection or other refusal by the buyer to receive or retain the goods, whether or not justified, or a justified revocation of acceptance revests title to the goods in the seller. Such revesting occurs by operation of law and is not a "sale".

§ 2–402. Rights of Seller's Creditors Against Sold Goods.

(1) Except as provided in subsections (2) and (3), rights of unsecured creditors of the seller with respect to goods which have been identified to a contract for sale are subject to the buyer's rights to recover the goods under this Article (Sections 2–502 and 2–716).

(2) A creditor of the seller may treat a sale or an identification of goods to a contract for sale as void if as against him a retention of possession by the seller is fraudulent under any rule of law of the state where the goods are situated, except that retention of possession in good faith and current course of trade by a merchant-seller for a commercially reasonable time after a sale or identification is not fraudulent.

(3) Nothing in this Article shall be deemed to impair the rights of creditors of the seller

(a) under the provisions of the Article on Secured Transactions (Article 9); or

(b) where identification to the contract or delivery is made not in current course of trade but in satisfaction of or as security for a pre-existing claim for money, security or the like and is made under circumstances which under any rule of law of the state where the goods are situated would apart from this Article constitute the transaction a fraudulent transfer or voidable preference.

§ 2–403. Power to Transfer; Good Faith Purchase of Goods; "Entrusting".

(1) A purchaser of goods acquires all title which his transferor had or had power to transfer except that a purchaser of a limited interest acquires rights only to the extent of the interest purchased. A person with voidable title has power to transfer a good title to a good faith purchaser for value. When goods have been delivered under a transaction of purchase the purchaser has such power even though

(a) the transferor was deceived as to the identity of the purchaser, or

(b) the delivery was in exchange for a check which is later dishonored, or

(c) it was agreed that the transaction was to be a "cash sale", or

(d) the delivery was procured through fraud punishable as larcenous under the criminal law.

(2) Any entrusting of possession of goods to a merchant who deals in goods of that kind gives him power to transfer all rights of the entruster to a buyer in ordinary course of business.

(3) "Entrusting" includes any delivery and any acquiescence in retention of possession regardless of any condition expressed between the parties to the delivery or acquiescence and regardless of whether the procurement of the entrusting or the

possessor's disposition of the goods have been such as to be larcenous under the criminal law.

[*Publisher's Editorial Note: If a state adopts the repealer of Article 6—Bulk Transfers (Alternative A), subsec. (4) should read as follows:*]

(4) The rights of other purchasers of goods and of lien creditors are governed by the Articles on Secured Transactions (Article 9) and Documents of Title (Article 7).

[*Publisher's Editorial Note: If a state adopts Revised Article 6—Bulk Sales (Alternative B), subsec. (4) should read as follows:*]

(4) The rights of other purchasers of goods and of lien creditors are governed by the Articles on Secured Transactions (Article 9), Bulk Sales (Article 6) and Documents of Title (Article 7).

As amended in 1988.

For material relating to the changes made in text in 1988, see section 3 of Alternative A (Repealer of Article 6—Bulk Transfers) and Conforming Amendment to Section 2–403 following end of Alternative B (Revised Article 6—Bulk Sales).

Part 5: Performance

§ 2–501. Insurable Interest in Goods; Manner of Identification of Goods.

(1) The buyer obtains a special property and an insurable interest in goods by identification of existing goods as goods to which the contract refers even though the goods so identified are non-conforming and he has an option to return or reject them. Such identification can be made at any time and in any manner explicitly agreed to by the parties. In the absence of explicit agreement identification occurs

(a) when the contract is made if it is for the sale of goods already existing and identified;

(b) if the contract is for the sale of future goods other than those described in paragraph (c), when goods are shipped, marked or otherwise designated by the seller as goods to which the contract refers;

(c) when the crops are planted or otherwise become growing crops or the young are conceived if the contract is for the sale of unborn young to be born within twelve months after contracting or for the sale of crops to be harvested within twelve months or the next normal harvest season after contracting whichever is longer.

(2) The seller retains an insurable interest in goods so long as title to or any security interest in the goods remains in him and where the identification is by the seller alone he may until default or insolvency or notification to the buyer that the identification is final substitute other goods for those identified.

(3) Nothing in this section impairs any insurable interest recognized under any other statute or rule of law.

§ 2–502. Buyer's Right to Goods on Seller's Insolvency.

(1) Subject to subsection (2) and even though the goods have not been shipped a buyer who has paid a part or all of the price of goods in which he has a special property under the provisions of the immediately preceding section may on making and keeping good a tender of any unpaid portion of their price recover them from the seller if the seller becomes insolvent within ten days after receipt of the first installment on their price.

(2) If the identification creating his special property has been made by the buyer he acquires the right to recover the goods only if they conform to the contract for sale.

§ 2–503. Manner of Seller's Tender of Delivery.

(1) Tender of delivery requires that the seller put and hold conforming goods at the buyer's disposition and give the buyer any notification reasonably necessary to enable him to take delivery. The manner, time and place for tender are determined by the agreement and this Article, and in particular

(a) tender must be at a reasonable hour, and if it is of goods they must be kept available for the period reasonably necessary to enable the buyer to take possession; but

(b) unless otherwise agreed the buyer must furnish facilities reasonably suited to the receipt of the goods.

(2) Where the case is within the next section respecting shipment tender requires that the seller comply with its provisions.

(3) Where the seller is required to deliver at a particular destination tender requires that he comply with subsection (1) and also in any appropriate case tender documents as described in subsections (4) and (5) of this section.

(4) Where goods are in the possession of a bailee and are to be delivered without being moved

(a) tender requires that the seller either tender a negotiable document of title covering such goods or procure acknowledgment by the bailee of the buyer's right to possession of the goods; but
(b) tender to the buyer of a non-negotiable document of title or of a written direction to the bailee to deliver is sufficient tender unless the buyer seasonably objects, and receipt by the bailee of notification of the buyer's rights fixes those rights as against the bailee and all third persons; but risk of loss of the goods and of any failure by the bailee to honor the non-negotiable document of title or to obey the direction remains on the seller until the buyer has had a reasonable time to present the document or direction, and a refusal by the bailee to honor the document or to obey the direction defeats the tender.

(5) Where the contract requires the seller to deliver documents
(a) he must tender all such documents in correct form, except as provided in this Article with respect to bills of lading in a set (subsection (2) of Section 2–323); and
(b) tender through customary banking channels is sufficient and dishonor of a draft accompanying the documents constitutes non-acceptance or rejection.

§ 2–504. Shipment by Seller. Where the seller is required or authorized to send the goods to the buyer and the contract does not require him to deliver them at a particular destination, then unless otherwise agreed he must

(a) put the goods in the possession of such a carrier and make such a contract for their transportation as may be reasonable having regard to the nature of the goods and other circumstances of the case; and
(b) obtain and promptly deliver or tender in due form any document necessary to enable the buyer to obtain possession of the goods or otherwise required by the agreement or by usage of trade; and
(c) promptly notify the buyer of the shipment.

Failure to notify the buyer under paragraph (c) or to make a proper contract under paragraph (a) is a ground for rejection only if material delay or loss ensues.

§ 2–505. Seller's Shipment Under Reservation.

(1) Where the seller has identified goods to the contract by or before shipment:
(a) his procurement of a negotiable bill of lading to his own order or otherwise reserves in him a security interest in the goods. His procurement of the bill to the order of a financing agency or of the buyer indicates in addition only the seller's expectation of transferring that interest to the person named.
(b) a non-negotiable bill of lading to himself or his nominee reserves possession of the goods as security but except in a case of conditional delivery (subsection (2) of Section 2–507) a non-negotiable bill of lading naming the buyer as consignee reserves no security interest even though the seller retains possession of the bill of lading.

(2) When shipment by the seller with reservation of a security interest is in violation of the contract for sale it constitutes an improper contract for transportation within the preceding section but impairs neither the rights given to the buyer by shipment and identification of the goods to the contract nor the seller's powers as a holder of a negotiable document.

§ 2–506. Rights of Financing Agency.

(1) A financing agency by paying or purchasing for value a draft which relates to a shipment of goods acquires to the extent of the payment or purchase and in addition to its own rights under the draft and any document of title securing it any rights of the shipper in the goods including the right to stop delivery and the shipper's right to have the draft honored by the buyer.

(2) The right to reimbursement of a financing agency which has in good faith honored or purchased the draft under commitment to or authority from the buyer is not impaired by subsequent discovery of defects with reference to any relevant document which was apparently regular on its face.

§ 2–507. Effect of Seller's Tender; Delivery on Condition.

(1) Tender of delivery is a condition to the buyer's duty to accept the goods and, unless otherwise agreed, to his duty to pay for them. Tender entitles the seller to

acceptance of the goods and to payment according to the contract.

(2) Where payment is due and demanded on the delivery to the buyer of goods or documents of title, his right as against the seller to retain or dispose of them is conditional upon his making the payment due.

§ 2–508. Cure by Seller of Improper Tender or Delivery; Replacement.

(1) Where any tender or delivery by the seller is rejected because non-conforming and the time for performance has not yet expired, the seller may seasonably notify the buyer of his intention to cure and may then within the contract time make a conforming delivery.

(2) Where the buyer rejects a non-conforming tender which the seller had reasonable grounds to believe would be acceptable with or without money allowance the seller may if he seasonably notifies the buyer have a further reasonable time to substitute a conforming tender.

§ 2–509. Risk of Loss in the Absence of Breach.

(1) Where the contract requires or authorizes the seller to ship the goods by carrier
  (a) if it does not require him to deliver them at a particular destination, the risk of loss passes to the buyer when the goods are duly delivered to the carrier even though the shipment is under reservation (Section 2–505); but
  (b) if it does require him to deliver them at a particular destination and the goods are there duly tendered while in the possession of the carrier, the risk of loss passes to the buyer when the goods are there duly so tendered as to enable the buyer to take delivery.

(2) Where the goods are held by a bailee to be delivered without being moved, the risk of loss passes to the buyer
  (a) on his receipt of a negotiable document of title covering the goods; or
  (b) on acknowledgment by the bailee of the buyer's right to possession of the goods; or
  (c) after his receipt of a non-negotiable document of title or other written direction to deliver, as provided in subsection (4)(b) of Section 2–503.

(3) In any case not within subsection (1) or (2), the risk of loss passes to the buyer on his receipt of the goods if the seller is a merchant; otherwise the risk passes to the buyer on tender of delivery.

(4) The provisions of this section are subject to contrary agreement of the parties and to the provisions of this Article on sale on approval (Section 2–327) and on effect of breach on risk of loss (Section 2–510).

§ 2–510. Effect of Breach on Risk of Loss.

(1) Where a tender or delivery of goods so fails to conform to the contract as to give a right of rejection the risk of their loss remains on the seller until cure or acceptance.

(2) Where the buyer rightfully revokes acceptance he may to the extent of any deficiency in his effective insurance coverage treat the risk of loss as having rested on the seller from the beginning.

(3) Where the buyer as to conforming goods already identified to the contract for sale repudiates or is otherwise in breach before risk of their loss has passed to him, the seller may to the extent of any deficiency in his effective insurance coverage treat the risk of loss as resting on the buyer for a commercially reasonable time.

§ 2–511. Tender of Payment by Buyer; Payment by Check.

(1) Unless otherwise agreed tender of payment is a condition to the seller's duty to tender and complete any delivery.

(2) Tender of payment is sufficient when made by any means or in any manner current in the ordinary course of business unless the seller demands payment in legal tender and gives any extension of time reasonably necessary to procure it.

(3) Subject to the provisions of this Act on the effect of an instrument on an obligation (Section 3-310), payment by check is conditional and is defeated as between the parties by dishonor of the check on due presentment.

As amended in 1994.

See Appendix XI for material relating to changes made in text in 1994.

§ 2–512. Payment by Buyer Before Inspection. *1995 Amendments to text indicated by strikeout and underline*

(1) Where the contract requires payment before inspection non-conformity of the goods does not excuse the buyer from so making payment unless

(a) the non-conformity appears without inspection; or
(b) despite tender of the required documents the circumstances would justify injunction against honor under this Act (Section 5-109(b)).
(2) Payment pursuant to subsection (1) does not constitute an acceptance of goods or impair the buyer's right to inspect or any of his remedies.

As amended in 1995.

See Appendix XIV for material relating to changes made in text in 1995.

§ 2–513. Buyer's Right to Inspection of Goods.

(1) Unless otherwise agreed and subject to subsection (3), where goods are tendered or delivered or identified to the contract for sale, the buyer has a right before payment or acceptance to inspect them at any reasonable place and time and in any reasonable manner. When the seller is required or authorized to send the goods to the buyer, the inspection may be after their arrival.
(2) Expenses of inspection must be borne by the buyer but may be recovered from the seller if the goods do not conform and are rejected.
(3) Unless otherwise agreed and subject to the provisions of this Article on C.I.F. contracts (subsection (3) of Section 2–321), the buyer is not entitled to inspect the goods before payment of the price when the contract provides
(a) for delivery "C.O.D." or on other like terms; or
(b) for payment against documents of title, except where such payment is due only after the goods are to become available for inspection.
(4) A place or method of inspection fixed by the parties is presumed to be exclusive but unless otherwise expressly agreed it does not postpone identification or shift the place for delivery or for passing the risk of loss. If compliance becomes impossible, inspection shall be as provided in this section unless the place or method fixed was clearly intended as an indispensable condition failure of which avoids the contract.

§ 2–514. When Documents Deliverable on Acceptance; When on Payment. Unless otherwise agreed documents against which a draft is drawn are to be delivered to the drawee on acceptance of the draft if it is payable more than three days after presentment; otherwise, only on payment.

§ 2–515. Preserving Evidence of Goods in Dispute. In furtherance of the adjustment of any claim or dispute

(a) either party on reasonable notification to the other and for the purpose of ascertaining the facts and preserving evidence has the right to inspect, test and sample the goods including such of them as may be in the possession or control of the other; and
(b) the parties may agree to a third party inspection or survey to determine the conformity or condition of the goods and may agree that the findings shall be binding upon them in any subsequent litigation or adjustment.

Part 6: Breach, Repudiation and Excuse

§ 2–601. Buyer's Rights on Improper Delivery. Subject to the provisions of this Article on breach in installment contracts (Section 2–612) and unless otherwise agreed under the sections on contractual limitations of remedy (Sections 2–718 and 2–719), if the goods or the tender of delivery fail in any respect to conform to the contract, the buyer may

(a) reject the whole; or
(b) accept the whole; or
(c) accept any commercial unit or units and reject the rest.

§ 2–602. Manner and Effect of Rightful Rejection.

(1) Rejection of goods must be within a reasonable time after their delivery or tender. It is ineffective unless the buyer seasonably notifies the seller.
(2) Subject to the provisions of the two following sections on rejected goods (Sections 2–603 and 2–604),
(a) after rejection any exercise of ownership by the buyer with respect to any commercial unit is wrongful as against the seller; and
(b) if the buyer has before rejection taken physical possession of goods in which he does not have a security interest under the provisions of this Article (subsection (3) of Section 2–711), he is under a duty after rejection to hold them with reasonable care at the seller's disposition for a time sufficient to permit the seller to remove them; but
(c) the buyer has no further obligations with regard to goods rightfully rejected.
(3) The seller's rights with respect to goods wrongfully rejected are governed by the provisions of this Article on Seller's remedies in general (Section 2–703).

§ 2–603. Merchant Buyer's Duties as to Rightfully Rejected Goods.

(1) Subject to any security interest in the buyer (subsection (3) of Section 2–711), when the seller has no agent or place of business at the market of rejection a merchant buyer is under a duty after rejection of goods in his possession or control to follow any reasonable instructions received from the seller with respect to the goods and in the absence of such instructions to make reasonable efforts to sell them for the seller's account if they are perishable or threaten to decline in value speedily. Instructions are not reasonable if on demand indemnity for expenses is not forthcoming.

(2) When the buyer sells goods under subsection (1), he is entitled to reimbursement from the seller or out of the proceeds for reasonable expenses of caring for and selling them, and if the expenses include no selling commission then to such commission as is usual in the trade or if there is none to a reasonable sum not exceeding ten per cent on the gross proceeds.

(3) In complying with this section the buyer is held only to good faith and good faith conduct hereunder is neither acceptance nor conversion nor the basis of an action for damages.

§ 2–604. Buyer's Options as to Salvage of Rightfully Rejected Goods. Subject to the provisions of the immediately preceding section on perishables if the seller gives no instructions within a reasonable time after notification of rejection the buyer may store the rejected goods for the seller's account or reship them to him or resell them for the seller's account with reimbursement as provided in the preceding section. Such action is not acceptance or conversion.

§ 2–605. Waiver of Buyer's Objections by Failure to Particularize.

(1) The buyer's failure to state in connection with rejection a particular defect which is ascertainable by reasonable inspection precludes him from relying on the unstated defect to justify rejection or to establish breach
- **(a)** where the seller could have cured it if stated seasonably; or
- **(b)** between merchants when the seller has after rejection made a request in writing for a full and final written statement of all defects on which the buyer proposes to rely.

(2) Payment against documents made without reservation of rights precludes recovery of the payment for defects apparent on the face of the documents.

§ 2–606. What Constitutes Acceptance of Goods.

(1) Acceptance of goods occurs when the buyer
- **(a)** after a reasonable opportunity to inspect the goods signifies to the seller that the goods are conforming or that he will take or retain them in spite of their non-conformity; or
- **(b)** fails to make an effective rejection (subsection (1) of Section 2–602), but such acceptance does not occur until the buyer has had a reasonable opportunity to inspect them; or
- **(c)** does any act inconsistent with the seller's ownership; but if such act is wrongful as against the seller it is an acceptance only if ratified by him.

(2) Acceptance of a part of any commercial unit is acceptance of that entire unit.

§ 2–607. Effect of Acceptance; Notice of Breach; Burden of Establishing Breach After Acceptance; Notice of Claim or Litigation to Person Answerable Over.

(1) The buyer must pay at the contract rate for any goods accepted.

(2) Acceptance of goods by the buyer precludes rejection of the goods accepted and if made with knowledge of a non-conformity cannot be revoked because of it unless the acceptance was on the reasonable assumption that the non-conformity would be seasonably cured but acceptance does not of itself impair any other remedy provided by this Article for non-conformity.

(3) Where a tender has been accepted
- **(a)** the buyer must within a reasonable time after he discovers or should have discovered any breach notify the seller of breach or be barred from any remedy; and
- **(b)** if the claim is one for infringement or the like (subsection (3) of Section 2–312) and the buyer is sued as a result of such a breach he must so notify the seller within a reasonable time after he receives notice of the litigation or be barred from any remedy over for liability established by the litigation.

(4) The burden is on the buyer to establish any breach with respect to the goods accepted.

(5) Where the buyer is sued for breach of a warranty or other obligation for which his seller is answerable over
  (a) he may give his seller written notice of the litigation. If the notice states that the seller may come in and defend and that if the seller does not do so he will be bound in any action against him by his buyer by any determination of fact common to the two litigations, then unless the seller after seasonable receipt of the notice does come in and defend he is so bound.
  (b) if the claim is one for infringement or the like (subsection (3) of Section 2–312) the original seller may demand in writing that his buyer turn over to him control of the litigation including settlement or else be barred from any remedy over and if he also agrees to bear all expense and to satisfy any adverse judgment, then unless the buyer after seasonable receipt of the demand does turn over control the buyer is so barred.
(6) The provisions of subsections (3), (4) and (5) apply to any obligation of a buyer to hold the seller harmless against infringement or the like (subsection (3) of Section 2–312).

§ 2–608. Revocation of Acceptance in Whole or in Part.

(1) The buyer may revoke his acceptance of a lot or commercial unit whose non-conformity substantially impairs its value to him if he has accepted it
  (a) on the reasonable assumption that its non-conformity would be cured and it has not been seasonably cured; or
  (b) without discovery of such non-conformity if his acceptance was reasonably induced either by the difficulty of discovery before acceptance or by the seller's assurances.
(2) Revocation of acceptance must occur within a reasonable time after the buyer discovers or should have discovered the ground for it and before any substantial change in condition of the goods which is not caused by their own defects. It is not effective until the buyer notifies the seller of it.
(3) A buyer who so revokes has the same rights and duties with regard to the goods involved as if he had rejected them.

§ 2–609. Right to Adequate Assurance of Performance.

(1) A contract for sale imposes an obligation on each party that the other's expectation of receiving due performance will not be impaired. When reasonable grounds for insecurity arise with respect to the performance of either party the other may in writing demand adequate assurance of due performance and until he receives such assurance may if commercially reasonable suspend any performance for which he has not already received the agreed return.
(2) Between merchants the reasonableness of grounds for insecurity and the adequacy of any assurance offered shall be determined according to commercial standards.
(3) Acceptance of any improper delivery or payment does not prejudice the aggrieved party's right to demand adequate assurance of future performance.
(4) After receipt of a justified demand failure to provide within a reasonable time not exceeding thirty days such assurance of due performance as is adequate under the circumstances of the particular case is a repudiation of the contract.

§ 2–610. Anticipatory Repudiation. When either party repudiates the contract with respect to a performance not yet due the loss of which will substantially impair the value of the contract to the other, the aggrieved party may

  (a) for a commercially reasonable time await performance by the repudiating party; or
  (b) resort to any remedy for breach (Section 2–703 or Section 2–711), even though he has notified the repudiating party that he would await the latter's performance and has urged retraction; and
  (c) in either case suspend his own performance or proceed in accordance with the provisions of this Article on the seller's right to identify goods to the contract notwithstanding breach or to salvage unfinished goods (Section 2–704).

§ 2–611. Retraction of Anticipatory Repudiation.

(1) Until the repudiating party's next performance is due he can retract his repudiation unless the aggrieved party has since the repudiation cancelled or materially changed his position or otherwise indicated that he considers the repudiation final.
(2) Retraction may be by any method which clearly indicates to the aggrieved party that the repudiating party intends to perform, but must include any assurance justifiably demanded under the provisions of this Article (Section 2–609).
(3) Retraction reinstates the repudiating party's rights under the contract with due excuse and allowance to

the aggrieved party for any delay occasioned by the repudiation.

§ 2–612. "Installment Contract"; Breach.

(1) An "installment contract" is one which requires or authorizes the delivery of goods in separate lots to be separately accepted, even though the contract contains a clause "each delivery is a separate contract" or its equivalent.

(2) The buyer may reject any installment which is non-conforming if the non-conformity substantially impairs the value of that installment and cannot be cured or if the non-conformity is a defect in the required documents; but if the non-conformity does not fall within subsection (3) and the seller gives adequate assurance of its cure the buyer must accept that installment.

(3) Whenever non-conformity or default with respect to one or more installments substantially impairs the value of the whole contract there is a breach of the whole. But the aggrieved party reinstates the contract if he accepts a non-conforming installment without seasonably notifying of cancellation or if he brings an action with respect only to past installments or demands performance as to future installments.

§ 2–613. Casualty to Identified Goods. Where the contract requires for its performance goods identified when the contract is made, and the goods suffer casualty without fault of either party before the risk of loss passes to the buyer, or in a proper case under a "no arrival, no sale" term (Section 2–324) then

(a) if the loss is total the contract is avoided; and

(b) if the loss is partial or the goods have so deteriorated as no longer to conform to the contract the buyer may nevertheless demand inspection and at his option either treat the contract as avoided or accept the goods with due allowance from the contract price for the deterioration or the deficiency in quantity but without further right against the seller.

§ 2–614. Substituted Performance.

(1) Where without fault of either party the agreed berthing, loading, or unloading facilities fail or an agreed type of carrier becomes unavailable or the agreed manner of delivery otherwise becomes commercially impracticable but a commercially reasonable substitute is available, such substitute performance must be tendered and accepted.

(2) If the agreed means or manner of payment fails because of domestic or foreign governmental regulation, the seller may withhold or stop delivery unless the buyer provides a means or manner of payment which is commercially a substantial equivalent. If delivery has already been taken, payment by the means or in the manner provided by the regulation discharges the buyer's obligation unless the regulation is discriminatory, oppressive or predatory.

§ 2–615. Excuse by Failure of Presupposed Conditions. Except so far as a seller may have assumed a greater obligation and subject to the preceding section on substituted performance:

(a) Delay in delivery or non-delivery in whole or in part by a seller who complies with paragraphs (b) and (c) is not a breach of his duty under a contract for sale if performance as agreed has been made impracticable by the occurrence of a contingency the non-occurrence of which was a basic assumption on which the contract was made or by compliance in good faith with any applicable foreign or domestic governmental regulation or order whether or not it later proves to be invalid.

(b) Where the causes mentioned in paragraph (a) affect only a part of the seller's capacity to perform, he must allocate production and deliveries among his customers but may at his option include regular customers not then under contract as well as his own requirements for further manufacture. He may so allocate in any manner which is fair and reasonable.

(c) The seller must notify the buyer seasonably that there will be delay or non-delivery and, when allocation is required under paragraph (b), of the estimated quota thus made available for the buyer.

§ 2–616. Procedure on Notice Claiming Excuse.

(1) Where the buyer receives notification of a material or indefinite delay or an allocation justified under the preceding section he may by written notification to the seller as to any delivery concerned, and where the prospective deficiency substantially impairs the value of the whole contract under the provisions of this Article relating to breach of installment contracts (Section 2–612), then also as to the whole,

(a) terminate and thereby discharge any unexecuted portion of the contract; or

(b) modify the contract by agreeing to take his available quota in substitution.

(2) If after receipt of such notification from the seller the buyer fails so to modify the contract within a reasonable time not exceeding thirty days the contract lapses with respect to any deliveries affected.

(3) The provisions of this section may not be negated by agreement except in so far as the seller has assumed a greater obligation under the preceding section.

Part 7: Remedies

§ 2–701. Remedies for Breach of Collateral Contracts Not Impaired. Remedies for breach of any obligation or promise collateral or ancillary to a contract for sale are not impaired by the provisions of this Article.

§ 2–702. Seller's Remedies on Discovery of Buyer's Insolvency.

(1) Where the seller discovers the buyer to be insolvent he may refuse delivery except for cash including payment for all goods theretofore delivered under the contract, and stop delivery under this Article (Section 2–705).

(2) Where the seller discovers that the buyer has received goods on credit while insolvent he may reclaim the goods upon demand made within ten days after the receipt, but if misrepresentation of solvency has been made to the particular seller in writing within three months before delivery the ten day limitation does not apply. Except as provided in this subsection the seller may not base a right to reclaim goods on the buyer's fraudulent or innocent misrepresentation of solvency or of intent to pay.

(3) The seller's right to reclaim under subsection (2) is subject to the rights of a buyer in ordinary course or other good faith purchaser under this Article (Section 2–403). Successful reclamation of goods excludes all other remedies with respect to them.

As amended in 1966.

§ 2–703. Seller's Remedies in General. Where the buyer wrongfully rejects or revokes acceptance of goods or fails to make a payment due on or before delivery or repudiates with respect to a part or the whole, then with respect to any goods directly affected and, if the breach is of the whole contract (Section 2–612), then also with respect to the whole undelivered balance, the aggrieved seller may

(a) withhold delivery of such goods;

(b) stop delivery by any bailee as hereafter provided (Section 2–705);

(c) proceed under the next section respecting goods still unidentified to the contract;

(d) resell and recover damages as hereafter provided (Section 2–706);

(e) recover damages for non-acceptance (Section 2–708) or in a proper case the price (Section 2–709);

(f) cancel.

§ 2–704. Seller's Right to Identify Goods to the Contract Notwithstanding Breach or to Salvage Unfinished Goods.

(1) An aggrieved seller under the preceding section may

(a) identify to the contract conforming goods not already identified if at the time he learned of the breach they are in his possession or control;

(b) treat as the subject of resale goods which have demonstrably been intended for the particular contract even though those goods are unfinished.

(2) Where the goods are unfinished an aggrieved seller may in the exercise of reasonable commercial judgment for the purposes of avoiding loss and of effective realization either complete the manufacture and wholly identify the goods to the contract or cease manufacture and resell for scrap or salvage value or proceed in any other reasonable manner.

§ 2–705. Seller's Stoppage of Delivery in Transit or Otherwise.

(1) The seller may stop delivery of goods in the possession of a carrier or other bailee when he discovers the buyer to be insolvent (Section 2–702) and may stop delivery of carload, truckload, planeload or larger shipments of express or freight when the buyer repudiates or fails to make a payment due before delivery or if for any other reason the seller has a right to withhold or reclaim the goods.

(2) As against such buyer the seller may stop delivery until

(a) receipt of the goods by the buyer; or

(b) acknowledgment to the buyer by any bailee of the goods except a carrier that the bailee holds the goods for the buyer; or

(c) such acknowledgment to the buyer by a carrier by reshipment or as warehouseman; or

(d) negotiation to the buyer of any negotiable document of title covering the goods.

(3) (a) To stop delivery the seller must so notify as to enable the bailee by reasonable diligence to prevent delivery of the goods.

(b) After such notification the bailee must hold and deliver the goods according to the directions of the seller but the seller is liable to the bailee for any ensuing charges or damages.

(c) If a negotiable document of title has been issued for goods the bailee is not obliged to obey a notification to stop until surrender of the document.

(d) A carrier who has issued a non-negotiable bill of lading is not obliged to obey a notification to stop received from a person other than the consignor.

§ 2–706. Seller's Resale Including Contract for Resale.

(1) Under the conditions stated in Section 2–703 on seller's remedies, the seller may resell the goods concerned or the undelivered balance thereof. Where the resale is made in good faith and in a commercially reasonable manner the seller may recover the difference between the resale price and the contract price together with any incidental damages allowed under the provisions of this Article (Section 2–710), but less expenses saved in consequence of the buyer's breach.

(2) Except as otherwise provided in subsection (3) or unless otherwise agreed resale may be at public or private sale including sale by way of one or more contracts to sell or of identification to an existing contract of the seller. Sale may be as a unit or in parcels and at any time and place and on any terms but every aspect of the sale including the method, manner, time, place and terms must be commercially reasonable. The resale must be reasonably identified as referring to the broken contract, but it is not necessary that the goods be in existence or that any or all of them have been identified to the contract before the breach.

(3) Where the resale is at private sale the seller must give the buyer reasonable notification of his intention to resell.

(4) Where the resale is at public sale

(a) only identified goods can be sold except where there is a recognized market for a public sale of futures in goods of the kind; and

(b) it must be made at a usual place or market for public sale if one is reasonably available and except in the case of goods which are perishable or threaten to decline in value speedily the seller must give the buyer reasonable notice of the time and place of the resale; and

(c) if the goods are not to be within the view of those attending the sale the notification of sale must state the place where the goods are located and provide for their reasonable inspection by prospective bidders; and

(d) the seller may buy.

(5) A purchaser who buys in good faith at a resale takes the goods free of any rights of the original buyer even though the seller fails to comply with one or more of the requirements of this section.

(6) The seller is not accountable to the buyer for any profit made on any resale. A person in the position of a seller (Section 2–707) or a buyer who has rightfully rejected or justifiably revoked acceptance must account for any excess over the amount of his security interest, as hereinafter defined (subsection (3) of Section 2–711).

§ 2–707. "Person in the Position of a Seller".

(1) A "person in the position of a seller" includes as against a principal an agent who has paid or become responsible for the price of goods on behalf of his principal or anyone who otherwise holds a security interest or other right in goods similar to that of a seller.

(2) A person in the position of a seller may as provided in this Article withhold or stop delivery (Section 2–705) and resell (Section 2–706) and recover incidental damages (Section 2–710).

§ 2–708. Seller's Damages for Non-acceptance or Repudiation.

(1) Subject to subsection (2) and to the provisions of this Article with respect to proof of market price (Section 2–723), the measure of damages for non-acceptance or repudiation by the buyer is the difference between the market price at the time and place for tender and the unpaid contract price together with any incidental damages provided in this Article (Section 2–710), but less expenses saved in consequence of the buyer's breach.

(2) If the measure of damages provided in subsection (1) is inadequate to put the seller in as good a position as performance would have done then the measure

of damages is the profit (including reasonable overhead) which the seller would have made from full performance by the buyer, together with any incidental damages provided in this Article (Section 2–710), due allowance for costs reasonably incurred and due credit for payments or proceeds of resale.

§ 2–709. Action for the Price.

(1) When the buyer fails to pay the price as it becomes due the seller may recover, together with any incidental damages under the next section, the price
 (a) of goods accepted or of conforming goods lost or damaged within a commercially reasonable time after risk of their loss has passed to the buyer; and
 (b) of goods identified to the contract if the seller is unable after reasonable effort to resell them at a reasonable price or the circumstances reasonably indicate that such effort will be unavailing.

(2) Where the seller sues for the price he must hold for the buyer any goods which have been identified to the contract and are still in his control except that if resale becomes possible he may resell them at any time prior to the collection of the judgment. The net proceeds of any such resale must be credited to the buyer and payment of the judgment entitles him to any goods not resold.

(3) After the buyer has wrongfully rejected or revoked acceptance of the goods or has failed to make a payment due or has repudiated (Section 2–610), a seller who is held not entitled to the price under this section shall nevertheless be awarded damages for non-acceptance under the preceding section.

§ 2–710. Seller's Incidental Damages. Incidental damages to an aggrieved seller include any commercially reasonable charges, expenses or commissions incurred in stopping delivery, in the transportation, care and custody of goods after the buyer's breach, in connection with return or resale of the goods or otherwise resulting from the breach.

§ 2–711. Buyer's Remedies in General; Buyer's Security Interest in Rejected Goods.

(1) Where the seller fails to make delivery or repudiates or the buyer rightfully rejects or justifiably revokes acceptance then with respect to any goods involved, and with respect to the whole if the breach goes to the whole contract (Section 2–612), the buyer may cancel and whether or not he has done so may in addition to recovering so much of the price as has been paid
 (a) "cover" and have damages under the next section as to all the goods affected whether or not they have been identified to the contract; or
 (b) recover damages for non-delivery as provided in this Article (Section 2–713).

(2) Where the seller fails to deliver or repudiates the buyer may also
 (a) if the goods have been identified recover them as provided in this Article (Section 2–502); or
 (b) in a proper case obtain specific performance or replevy the goods as provided in this Article (Section 2–716).

(3) On rightful rejection or justifiable revocation of acceptance a buyer has a security interest in goods in his possession or control for any payments made on their price and any expenses reasonably incurred in their inspection, receipt, transportation, care and custody and may hold such goods and resell them in like manner as an aggrieved seller (Section 2–706).

§ 2–712. "Cover"; Buyer's Procurement of Substitute Goods.

(1) After a breach within the preceding section the buyer may "cover" by making in good faith and without unreasonable delay any reasonable purchase of or contract to purchase goods in substitution for those due from the seller.

(2) The buyer may recover from the seller as damages the difference between the cost of cover and the contract price together with any incidental or consequential damages as hereinafter defined (Section 2–715), but less expenses saved in consequence of the seller's breach.

(3) Failure of the buyer to effect cover within this section does not bar him from any other remedy.

§ 2–713. Buyer's Damages for Non-delivery or Repudiation.

(1) Subject to the provisions of this Article with respect to proof of market price (Section 2–723), the measure of damages for non-delivery or repudiation by the seller is the difference between the market price at the time when the buyer learned of the breach and the contract price together with any incidental and consequential damages provided in this Article (Section 2–715), but less expenses saved in consequence of the seller's breach.

(2) Market price is to be determined as of the place for tender or, in cases of rejection after arrival or revocation of acceptance, as of the place of arrival.

§ 2–714. Buyer's Damages for Breach in Regard to Accepted Goods.

(1) Where the buyer has accepted goods and given notification (subsection (3) of Section 2–607) he may recover as damages for any non-conformity of tender the loss resulting in the ordinary course of events from the seller's breach as determined in any manner which is reasonable.

(2) The measure of damages for breach of warranty is the difference at the time and place of acceptance between the value of the goods accepted and the value they would have had if they had been as warranted, unless special circumstances show proximate damages of a different amount.

(3) In a proper case any incidental and consequential damages under the next section may also be recovered.

§ 2–715. Buyer's Incidental and Consequential Damages.

(1) Incidental damages resulting from the seller's breach include expenses reasonably incurred in inspection, receipt, transportation and care and custody of goods rightfully rejected, any commercially reasonable charges, expenses or commissions in connection with effecting cover and any other reasonable expense incident to the delay or other breach.

(2) Consequential damages resulting from the seller's breach include

(a) any loss resulting from general or particular requirements and needs of which the seller at the time of contracting had reason to know and which could not reasonably be prevented by cover or otherwise; and

(b) injury to person or property proximately resulting from any breach of warranty.

§ 2–716. Buyer's Right to Specific Performance or Replevin.

(1) Specific performance may be decreed where the goods are unique or in other proper circumstances.

(2) The decree for specific performance may include such terms and conditions as to payment of the price, damages, or other relief as the court may deem just.

(3) The buyer has a right of replevin for goods identified to the contract if after reasonable effort he is unable to effect cover for such goods or the circumstances reasonably indicate that such effort will be unavailing or if the goods have been shipped under reservation and satisfaction of the security interest in them has been made or tendered.

§ 2–717. Deduction of Damages from the Price. The buyer on notifying the seller of his intention to do so may deduct all or any part of the damages resulting from any breach of the contract from any part of the price still due under the same contract.

§ 2–718. Liquidation or Limitation of Damages; Deposits.

(1) Damages for breach by either party may be liquidated in the agreement but only at an amount which is reasonable in the light of the anticipated or actual harm caused by the breach, the difficulties of proof of loss, and the inconvenience or nonfeasibility of otherwise obtaining an adequate remedy. A term fixing unreasonably large liquidated damages is void as a penalty.

(2) Where the seller justifiably withholds delivery of goods because of the buyer's breach, the buyer is entitled to restitution of any amount by which the sum of his payments exceeds

(a) the amount to which the seller is entitled by virtue of terms liquidating the seller's damages in accordance with subsection (1), or

(b) in the absence of such terms, twenty per cent of the value of the total performance for which the buyer is obligated under the contract or $500, whichever is smaller.

(3) The buyer's right to restitution under subsection (2) is subject to offset to the extent that the seller establishes

(a) a right to recover damages under the provisions of this Article other than subsection (1), and

(b) the amount or value of any benefits received by the buyer directly or indirectly by reason of the contract.

(4) Where a seller has received payment in goods their reasonable value or the proceeds of their resale shall be treated as payments for the purposes of subsection (2); but if the seller has notice of the buyer's breach before reselling goods received in part performance, his resale is subject to the conditions laid down in this Article on resale by an aggrieved seller (Section 2–706).

§ 2–719. Contractual Modification or Limitation of Remedy.

(1) Subject to the provisions of subsections (2) and (3) of this section and of the preceding section on liquidation and limitation of damages,

(a) the agreement may provide for remedies in addition to or in substitution for those provided in this Article and may limit or alter the measure of damages recoverable under this Article, as by limiting the buyer's remedies to return of the goods and repayment of the price or to repair and replacement of non-conforming goods or parts; and

(b) resort to a remedy as provided is optional unless the remedy is expressly agreed to be exclusive, in which case it is the sole remedy.

(2) Where circumstances cause an exclusive or limited remedy to fail of its essential purpose, remedy may be had as provided in this Act.

(3) Consequential damages may be limited or excluded unless the limitation or exclusion is unconscionable. Limitation of consequential damages for injury to the person in the case of consumer goods is prima facie unconscionable but limitation of damages where the loss is commercial is not.

§ 2–720. Effect of "Cancellation" or "Rescission" on Claims for Antecedent Breach. Unless the contrary intention clearly appears, expressions of "cancellation" or "rescission" of the contract or the like shall not be construed as a renunciation or discharge of any claim in damages for an antecedent breach.

§ 2–721. Remedies for Fraud. Remedies for material misrepresentation or fraud include all remedies available under this Article for non-fraudulent breach. Neither rescission or a claim for rescission of the contract for sale nor rejection or return of the goods shall bar or be deemed inconsistent with a claim for damages or other remedy.

§ 2–722. Who Can Sue Third Parties for Injury to Goods. Where a third party so deals with goods which have been identified to a contract for sale as to cause actionable injury to a party to that contract

(a) a right of action against the third party is in either party to the contract for sale who has title to or a security interest or a special property or an insurable interest in the goods; and if the goods have been destroyed or converted a right of action is also in the party who either bore the risk of loss under the contract for sale or has since the injury assumed that risk as against the other;

(b) if at the time of the injury the party plaintiff did not bear the risk of loss as against the other party to the contract for sale and there is no arrangement between them for disposition of the recovery, his suit or settlement is, subject to his own interest, as a fiduciary for the other party to the contract;

(c) either party may with the consent of the other sue for the benefit of whom it may concern.

§ 2–723. Proof of Market Price: Time and Place.

(1) If an action based on anticipatory repudiation comes to trial before the time for performance with respect to some or all of the goods, any damages based on market price (Section 2–708 or Section 2–713) shall be determined according to the price of such goods prevailing at the time when the aggrieved party learned of the repudiation.

(2) If evidence of a price prevailing at the times or places described in this Article is not readily available the price prevailing within any reasonable time before or after the time described or at any other place which in commercial judgment or under usage of trade would serve as a reasonable substitute for the one described may be used, making any proper allowance for the cost of transporting the goods to or from such other place.

(3) Evidence of a relevant price prevailing at a time or place other than the one described in this Article offered by one party is not admissible unless and until he has given the other party such notice as the court finds sufficient to prevent unfair surprise.

§ 2–724. Admissibility of Market Quotations. Whenever the prevailing price or value of any goods regularly bought and sold in any established commodity market is in issue, reports in official publications or trade journals or in newspapers or periodicals of general circulation published as the reports of such market shall be admissible in evidence. The circumstances of the preparation of such a report may be shown to affect its weight but not its admissibility.

§ 2–725. Statute of Limitations in Contracts for Sale.

(1) An action for breach of any contract for sale must be commenced within four years after the cause of action has accrued. By the original agreement the parties may reduce the period of limitation to not less than one year but may not extend it.

(2) A cause of action accrues when the breach occurs, regardless of the aggrieved party's lack of knowledge of the breach. A breach of warranty occurs when tender of delivery is made, except that where a warranty explicitly extends to future performance of the goods and discovery of the breach must await the time of such performance the cause of action accrues when the breach is or should have been discovered.

(3) Where an action commenced within the time limited by subsection (1) is so terminated as to leave available a remedy by another action for the same breach such other action may be commenced after the expiration of the time limited and within six months after the termination of the first action unless the termination resulted from voluntary discontinuance or from dismissal for failure or neglect to prosecute.

(4) This section does not alter the law on tolling of the statute of limitations nor does it apply to causes of action which have accrued before this Act becomes effective.

Article 2A: Leases

Part 1: General Provisions

§ 2A–101. Short Title. This Article shall be known and may be cited as the Uniform Commercial Code—Leases.

See Appendix VI [following Amendment 24 therein] for material relating to changes in the Official Comment to conform to the 1990 amendments to various sections of Article 2A.

§ 2A–102. Scope. This Article applies to any transaction, regardless of form, that creates a lease.

§ 2A–103. Definitions and Index of Definitions.

(1) In this Article unless the context otherwise requires:

(a) "Buyer in ordinary course of business" means a person who in good faith and without knowledge that the sale to him [or her] is in violation of the ownership rights or security interest or leasehold interest of a third party in the goods buys in ordinary course from a person in the business of selling goods of that kind but does not include a pawnbroker. "Buying" may be for cash or by exchange of other property or on secured or unsecured credit and includes receiving goods or documents of title under a preexisting contract for sale but does not include a transfer in bulk or as security for or in total or partial satisfaction of a money debt.

(b) "Cancellation" occurs when either party puts an end to the lease contract for default by the other party.

(c) "Commercial unit" means such a unit of goods as by commercial usage is a single whole for purposes of lease and division of which materially impairs its character or value on the market or in use. A commercial unit may be a single article, as a machine, or a set of articles, as a suite of furniture or a line of machinery, or a quantity, as a gross or carload, or any other unit treated in use or in the relevant market as a single whole.

(d) "Conforming" goods or performance under a lease contract means goods or performance that are in accordance with the obligations under the lease contract.

(e) "Consumer lease" means a lease that a lessor regularly engaged in the business of leasing or selling makes to a lessee who is an individual and who takes under the lease primarily for a personal, family, or household purpose [, if the total payments to be made under the lease contract, excluding payments for options to renew or buy, do not exceed $________].

(f) "Fault" means wrongful act, omission, breach, or default.

(g) "Finance lease" means a lease with respect to which:

(i) the lessor does not select, manufacture, or supply the goods;

(ii) the lessor acquires the goods or the right to possession and use of the goods in connection with the lease; and

(iii) one of the following occurs:

(A) the lessee receives a copy of the contract by which the lessor acquired the goods or the right to possession and use of the goods before signing the lease contract;

(B) the lessee's approval of the contract by which the lessor acquired the goods or the right to possession and use of the goods is a condition to effectiveness of the lease contract;

(C) the lessee, before signing the lease contract, receives an accurate and complete statement designating the promises and warranties, and any disclaimers of warranties, limitations or modifications of remedies, or liquidated damages, including those of a third party, such as the manufacturer of the goods, provided to the lessor by the person supplying the goods in connection with or as part of the contract by which the lessor acquired the goods or the right to possession and use of the goods; or

(D) if the lease is not a consumer lease, the lessor, before the lessee signs the lease contract, informs the lessee in writing (a) of the identity of the person supplying the goods to the lessor, unless the lessee has selected that person and directed the lessor to acquire the goods or the right to possession and use of the goods from that person, (b) that the lessee is entitled under this Article to the promises and warranties, including those of any third party, provided to the lessor by the person supplying the goods in connection with or as part of the contract by which the lessor acquired the goods or the right to possession and use of the goods, and (c) that the lessee may communicate with the person supplying the goods to the lessor and receive an accurate and complete statement of those promises and warranties, including any disclaimers and limitations of them or of remedies.

(h) "Goods" means all things that are movable at the time of identification to the lease contract, or are fixtures (Section 2A–309), but the term does not include money, documents, instruments, accounts, chattel paper, general intangibles, or minerals or the like, including oil and gas, before extraction. The term also includes the unborn young of animals.

(i) "Installment lease contract" means a lease contract that authorizes or requires the delivery of goods in separate lots to be separately accepted, even though the lease contract contains a clause "each delivery is a separate lease" or its equivalent.

(j) "Lease" means a transfer of the right to possession and use of goods for a term in return for consideration, but a sale, including a sale on approval or a sale or return, or retention or creation of a security interest is not a lease. Unless the context clearly indicates otherwise, the term includes a sublease.

(k) "Lease agreement" means the bargain, with respect to the lease, of the lessor and the lessee in fact as found in their language or by implication from other circumstances including course of dealing or usage of trade or course of performance as provided in this Article. Unless the context clearly indicates otherwise, the term includes a sublease agreement.

(l) "Lease contract" means the total legal obligation that results from the lease agreement as affected by this Article and any other applicable rules of law. Unless the context clearly indicates otherwise, the term includes a sublease contract.

(m) "Leasehold interest" means the interest of the lessor or the lessee under a lease contract.

(n) "Lessee" means a person who acquires the right to possession and use of goods under a lease. Unless the context clearly indicates otherwise, the term includes a sublessee.

(o) "Lessee in ordinary course of business" means a person who in good faith and without knowledge that the lease to him [or her] is in violation of the ownership rights or security interest or leasehold interest of a third party in the goods, leases in ordinary course from a person in the business of selling or leasing goods of that kind but does not include a pawnbroker. "Leasing" may be for cash or by exchange of other property or on secured or unsecured credit and includes receiving goods or documents of title under a preexisting lease contract but does not include a transfer in bulk or as security for or in total or partial satisfaction of a money debt.

(p) "Lessor" means a person who transfers the right to possession and use of goods under a lease. Unless the context clearly indicates otherwise, the term includes a sublessor.

(q) "Lessor's residual interest" means the lessor's interest in the goods after expiration, termination, or cancellation of the lease contract.

(r) "Lien" means a charge against or interest in goods to secure payment of a debt or performance of an obligation, but the term does not include a security interest.

(s) "Lot" means a parcel or a single article that is the subject matter of a separate lease or delivery, whether or not it is sufficient to perform the lease contract.

(t) "Merchant lessee" means a lessee that is a merchant with respect to goods of the kind subject to the lease.

(u) "Present value" means the amount as of a date certain of one or more sums payable in the future, discounted to the date certain. The discount is determined by the interest rate specified by the parties if the rate was not manifestly unreasonable at the time the transaction was entered into; otherwise, the discount is determined by a commercially reasonable rate that takes into account the facts and circumstances of each case at the time the transaction was entered into.

(v) "Purchase" includes taking by sale, lease, mortgage, security interest, pledge, gift, or any other voluntary transaction creating an interest in goods.

(w) "Sublease" means a lease of goods the right to possession and use of which was acquired by the lessor as a lessee under an existing lease.

(x) "Supplier" means a person from whom a lessor buys or leases goods to be leased under a finance lease.

(y) "Supply contract" means a contract under which a lessor buys or leases goods to be leased.

(z) "Termination" occurs when either party pursuant to a power created by agreement or law puts an end to the lease contract otherwise than for default.

(2) Other definitions applying to this Article and the sections in which they appear are:

"Accessions"	Section 2A–310(1).
"Construction mortgage"	Section 2A–309(1) (d).
"Encumbrance"	Section 2A–309(1) (e).
"Fixtures"	Section 2A–309(1) (a).
"Fixture filing"	Section 2A–309(1) (b).
"Purchase money lease"	Section 2A–309(1) (c).

(3) The following definitions in other Articles apply to this Article:

"Account"	Section 9–106.
"Between merchants"	Section 2–104(3).
"Buyer"	Section 2–103(1) (a).
"Chattel paper"	Section 9–105(1) (b).
"Consumer goods"	Section 9–109(1).
"Document"	Section 9–105(1) (f).
"Entrusting"	Section 2–403(3).
"General intangibles"	Section 9–106.
"Good faith"	Section 2–103(1) (b).
"Instrument"	Section 9–105(1) (i).
"Merchant"	Section 2–104(1).
"Mortgage"	Section 9–105(1) (j).
"Pursuant to commitment"	Section 9–105(1) (k).
"Receipt"	Section 2–103(1) (c).
"Sale"	Section 2–106(1).
"Sale on approval"	Section 2–326.
"Sale or return"	Section 2–326.
"Seller"	Section 2–103(1) (d).

(4) In addition Article 1 contains general definitions and principles of construction and interpretation applicable throughout this Article.

As amended in 1990.

§ 2A–104. Leases Subject to Other Law.

(1) A lease, although subject to this Article, is also subject to any applicable:

(a) certificate of title statute of this State: (list any certificate of title statutes covering automobiles, trailers, mobile homes, boats, farm tractors, and the like);

(b) certificate of title statute of another jurisdiction (Section 2A–105); or

(c) consumer protection statute of this State, or final consumer protection decision of a court of this State existing on the effective date of this Article.

(2) In case of conflict between this Article, other than Sections 2A–105, 2A–304(3), and 2A–305(3), and a statute or decision referred to in subsection (1), the statute or decision controls.

(3) Failure to comply with an applicable law has only the effect specified therein.

As amended in 1990.

§ 2A–105. Territorial Application of Article to Goods Covered by Certificate of Title. Subject to the provisions of Sections 2A–304(3) and 2A–305(3), with respect to goods covered by a certificate of title issued under a statute of this State or of another jurisdiction, compliance and the effect of compliance or noncompliance with a certificate of title statute are governed by the law (including the conflict of laws rules) of the jurisdiction issuing the certificate until the earlier of (a) surrender of the certificate, or (b) four months after the goods are removed from that jurisdiction and thereafter until a new certificate of title is issued by another jurisdiction.

§ 2A–106. Limitation on Power of Parties to Consumer Lease to Choose Applicable Law and Judicial Forum.

(1) If the law chosen by the parties to a consumer lease is that of a jurisdiction other than a jurisdiction in which the lessee resides at the time the lease agreement becomes enforceable or within 30 days thereafter or in which the goods are to be used, the choice is not enforceable.

(2) If the judicial forum chosen by the parties to a consumer lease is a forum that would not otherwise have jurisdiction over the lessee, the choice is not enforceable.

§ 2A–107. Waiver or Renunciation of Claim or Right After Default. Any claim or right arising out of an alleged default or breach of warranty may be discharged in whole or in part without consideration by a written waiver or renunciation signed and delivered by the aggrieved party.

§ 2A–108. Unconscionability.

(1) If the court as a matter of law finds a lease contract or any clause of a lease contract to have been unconscionable at the time it was made the court may refuse to enforce the lease contract, or it may enforce the remainder of the lease contract without the unconscionable clause, or it may so limit the application of any unconscionable clause as to avoid any unconscionable result.

(2) With respect to a consumer lease, if the court as a matter of law finds that a lease contract or any clause of a lease contract has been induced by unconscionable conduct or that unconscionable conduct has occurred in the collection of a claim arising from a lease contract, the court may grant appropriate relief.

(3) Before making a finding of unconscionability under subsection (1) or (2), the court, on its own motion or that of a party, shall afford the parties a reasonable opportunity to present evidence as to the setting, purpose, and effect of the lease contract or clause thereof, or of the conduct.

(4) In an action in which the lessee claims unconscionability with respect to a consumer lease:

- **(a)** If the court finds unconscionability under subsection (1) or (2), the court shall award reasonable attorney's fees to the lessee.
- **(b)** If the court does not find unconscionability and the lessee claiming unconscionability has brought or maintained an action he [or she] knew to be groundless, the court shall award reasonable attorney's fees to the party against whom the claim is made.
- **(c)** In determining attorney's fees, the amount of the recovery on behalf of the claimant under subsections (1) and (2) is not controlling.

§ 2A–109. Option to Accelerate at Will.

(1) A term providing that one party or his [or her] successor in interest may accelerate payment or performance or require collateral or additional collateral "at will" or "when he [or she] deems himself [or herself] insecure" or in words of similar import must be construed to mean that he [or she] has power to do so only if he [or she] in good faith believes that the prospect of payment or performance is impaired.

(2) With respect to a consumer lease, the burden of establishing good faith under subsection (1) is on the party who exercised the power; otherwise the burden of establishing lack of good faith is on the party against whom the power has been exercised.

Part 2: Formation and Construction of Lease Contract

§ 2A–201. Statute of Frauds.

(1) A lease contract is not enforceable by way of action or defense unless:

- **(a)** the total payments to be made under the lease contract, excluding payments for options to renew or buy, are less than $1,000; or

(b) there is a writing, signed by the party against whom enforcement is sought or by that party's authorized agent, sufficient to indicate that a lease contract has been made between the parties and to describe the goods leased and the lease term.

(2) Any description of leased goods or of the lease term is sufficient and satisfies subsection (1) (b), whether or not it is specific, if it reasonably identifies what is described.

(3) A writing is not insufficient because it omits or incorrectly states a term agreed upon, but the lease contract is not enforceable under subsection (1) (b) beyond the lease term and the quantity of goods shown in the writing.

(4) A lease contract that does not satisfy the requirements of subsection (1), but which is valid in other respects, is enforceable:

(a) if the goods are to be specially manufactured or obtained for the lessee and are not suitable for lease or sale to others in the ordinary course of the lessor's business, and the lessor, before notice of repudiation is received and under circumstances that reasonably indicate that the goods are for the lessee, has made either a substantial beginning of their manufacture or commitments for their procurement;

(b) if the party against whom enforcement is sought admits in that party's pleading, testimony or otherwise in court that a lease contract was made, but the lease contract is not enforceable under this provision beyond the quantity of goods admitted; or

(c) with respect to goods that have been received and accepted by the lessee.

(5) The lease term under a lease contract referred to in subsection (4) is:

(a) if there is a writing signed by the party against whom enforcement is sought or by that party's authorized agent specifying the lease term, the term so specified;

(b) if the party against whom enforcement is sought admits in that party's pleading, testimony, or otherwise in court a lease term, the term so admitted; or

(c) a reasonable lease term.

§ 2A–202. Final Written Expression: Parol or Extrinsic Evidence. Terms with respect to which the confirmatory memoranda of the parties agree or which are otherwise set forth in a writing intended by the parties as a final expression of their agreement with respect to such terms as are included therein may not be contradicted by evidence of any prior agreement or of a contemporaneous oral agreement but may be explained or supplemented:

(a) by course of dealing or usage of trade or by course of performance; and

(b) by evidence of consistent additional terms unless the court finds the writing to have been intended also as a complete and exclusive statement of the terms of the agreement.

§ 2A–203. Seals Inoperative. The affixing of a seal to a writing evidencing a lease contract or an offer to enter into a lease contract does not render the writing a sealed instrument and the law with respect to sealed instruments does not apply to the lease contract or offer.

§ 2A–204. Formation in General.

(1) A lease contract may be made in any manner sufficient to show agreement, including conduct by both parties which recognizes the existence of a lease contract.

(2) An agreement sufficient to constitute a lease contract may be found although the moment of its making is undetermined.

(3) Although one or more terms are left open, a lease contract does not fail for indefiniteness if the parties have intended to make a lease contract and there is a reasonably certain basis for giving an appropriate remedy.

§ 2A–205. Firm Offers. An offer by a merchant to lease goods to or from another person in a signed writing that by its terms gives assurance it will be held open is not revocable, for lack of consideration, during the time stated or, if no time is stated, for a reasonable time, but in no event may the period of irrevocability exceed 3 months. Any such term of assurance on a form supplied by the offeree must be separately signed by the offeror.

§ 2A–206. Offer and Acceptance in Formation of Lease Contract.

(1) Unless otherwise unambiguously indicated by the language or circumstances, an offer to make a lease contract must be construed as inviting acceptance in any manner and by any medium reasonable in the circumstances.

(2) If the beginning of a requested performance is a reasonable mode of acceptance, an offeror who is

not notified of acceptance within a reasonable time may treat the offer as having lapsed before acceptance.

§ 2A–207. Course of Performance or Practical Construction.

(1) If a lease contract involves repeated occasions for performance by either party with knowledge of the nature of the performance and opportunity for objection to it by the other, any course of performance accepted or acquiesced in without objection is relevant to determine the meaning of the lease agreement.

(2) The express terms of a lease agreement and any course of performance, as well as any course of dealing and usage of trade, must be construed whenever reasonable as consistent with each other; but if that construction is unreasonable, express terms control course of performance, course of performance controls both course of dealing and usage of trade, and course of dealing controls usage of trade.

(3) Subject to the provisions of Section 2A–208 on modification and waiver, course of performance is relevant to show a waiver or modification of any term inconsistent with the course of performance.

§ 2A–208. Modification, Rescission and Waiver.

(1) An agreement modifying a lease contract needs no consideration to be binding.

(2) A signed lease agreement that excludes modification or rescission except by a signed writing may not be otherwise modified or rescinded, but, except as between merchants, such a requirement on a form supplied by a merchant must be separately signed by the other party.

(3) Although an attempt at modification or rescission does not satisfy the requirements of subsection (2), it may operate as a waiver.

(4) A party who has made a waiver affecting an executory portion of a lease contract may retract the waiver by reasonable notification received by the other party that strict performance will be required of any term waived, unless the retraction would be unjust in view of a material change of position in reliance on the waiver.

§ 2A–209. Lessee Under Finance Lease as Beneficiary of Supply Contract.

(1) The benefit of a supplier's promises to the lessor under the supply contract and of all warranties, whether express or implied, including those of any third party provided in connection with or as part of the supply contract, extends to the lessee to the extent of the lessee's leasehold interest under a finance lease related to the supply contract, but is subject to the terms of the warranty and of the supply contract and all defenses or claims arising therefrom.

(2) The extension of the benefit of a supplier's promises and of warranties to the lessee (Section 2A–209(1)) does not: (i) modify the rights and obligations of the parties to the supply contract, whether arising therefrom or otherwise, or (ii) impose any duty or liability under the supply contract on the lessee.

(3) Any modification or rescission of the supply contract by the supplier and the lessor is effective between the supplier and the lessee unless, before the modification or rescission, the supplier has received notice that the lessee has entered into a finance lease related to the supply contract. If the modification or rescission is effective between the supplier and the lessee, the lessor is deemed to have assumed, in addition to the obligations of the lessor to the lessee under the lease contract, promises of the supplier to the lessor and warranties that were so modified or rescinded as they existed and were available to the lessee before modification or rescission.

(4) In addition to the extension of the benefit of the supplier's promises and of warranties to the lessee under subsection (1), the lessee retains all rights that the lessee may have against the supplier which arise from an agreement between the lessee and the supplier or under other law.

As amended in 1990.

§ 2A–210. Express Warranties.

(1) Express warranties by the lessor are created as follows:

- **(a)** Any affirmation of fact or promise made by the lessor to the lessee which relates to the goods and becomes part of the basis of the bargain creates an express warranty that the goods will conform to the affirmation or promise.
- **(b)** Any description of the goods which is made part of the basis of the bargain creates an express warranty that the goods will conform to the description.
- **(c)** Any sample or model that is made part of the basis of the bargain creates an express warranty that the whole of the goods will conform to the sample or model.

(2) It is not necessary to the creation of an express warranty that the lessor use formal words, such as "warrant" or "guarantee," or that the lessor have a specific intention to make a warranty, but an affirmation merely of the value of the goods or a statement purporting to be merely the lessor's opinion or commendation of the goods does not create a warranty.

§ 2A–211. Warranties Against Interference and Against Infringement; Lessee's Obligation Against Infringement.

(1) There is in a lease contract a warranty that for the lease term no person holds a claim to or interest in the goods that arose from an act or omission of the lessor, other than a claim by way of infringement or the like, which will interfere with the lessee's enjoyment of its leasehold interest.
(2) Except in a finance lease there is in a lease contract by a lessor who is a merchant regularly dealing in goods of the kind a warranty that the goods are delivered free of the rightful claim of any person by way of infringement or the like.
(3) A lessee who furnishes specifications to a lessor or a supplier shall hold the lessor and the supplier harmless against any claim by way of infringement or the like that arises out of compliance with the specifications.

§ 2A–212. Implied Warranty of Merchantability.

(1) Except in a finance lease, a warranty that the goods will be merchantable is implied in a lease contract if the lessor is a merchant with respect to goods of that kind.
(2) Goods to be merchantable must be at least such as
  (a) pass without objection in the trade under the description in the lease agreement;
  (b) in the case of fungible goods, are of fair average quality within the description;
  (c) are fit for the ordinary purposes for which goods of that type are used;
  (d) run, within the variation permitted by the lease agreement, of even kind, quality, and quantity within each unit and among all units involved;
  (e) are adequately contained, packaged, and labeled as the lease agreement may require; and
  (f) conform to any promises or affirmations of fact made on the container or label.
(3) Other implied warranties may arise from course of dealing or usage of trade.

§ 2A–213. Implied Warranty of Fitness for Particular Purpose. Except in a finance lease, if the lessor at the time the lease contract is made has reason to know of any particular purpose for which the goods are required and that the lessee is relying on the lessor's skill or judgment to select or furnish suitable goods, there is in the lease contract an implied warranty that the goods will be fit for that purpose.

§ 2A–214. Exclusion or Modification of Warranties.

(1) Words or conduct relevant to the creation of an express warranty and words or conduct tending to negate or limit a warranty must be construed wherever reasonable as consistent with each other; but, subject to the provisions of Section 2A–202 on parol or extrinsic evidence, negation or limitation is inoperative to the extent that the construction is unreasonable.
(2) Subject to subsection (3), to exclude or modify the implied warranty of merchantability or any part of it the language must mention "merchantability", be by a writing, and be conspicuous. Subject to sub-section (3), to exclude or modify any implied warranty of fitness the exclusion must be by a writing and be conspicuous. Language to exclude all implied warranties of fitness is sufficient if it is in writing, is conspicuous and states, for example, "There is no warranty that the goods will be fit for a particular purpose".
(3) Notwithstanding subsection (2), but subject to subsection (4),
  (a) unless the circumstances indicate otherwise, all implied warranties are excluded by expressions like "as is," or "with all faults," or by other language that in common understanding calls the lessee's attention to the exclusion of warranties and makes plain that there is no implied warranty, if in writing and conspicuous;
  (b) if the lessee before entering into the lease contract has examined the goods or the sample or model as fully as desired or has refused to examine the goods, there is no implied warranty with regard to defects that an examination ought in the circumstances to have revealed; and
  (c) an implied warranty may also be excluded or modified by course of dealing, course of performance, or usage of trade.
(4) To exclude or modify a warranty against interference or against infringement (Section 2A–211) or any part of it, the language must be specific, be by a writing, and be conspicuous, unless the

circumstances, including course of performance, course of dealing, or usage of trade, give the lessee reason to know that the goods are being leased subject to a claim or interest of any person.

§ 2A–215. Cumulation and Conflict of Warranties Express or Implied. Warranties, whether express or implied, must be construed as consistent with each other and as cumulative, but if that construction is unreasonable, the intention of the parties determines which warranty is dominant. In ascertaining that intention the following rules apply:

(a) Exact or technical specifications displace an inconsistent sample or model or general language of description.

(b) A sample from an existing bulk displaces inconsistent general language of description.

(c) Express warranties displace inconsistent implied warranties other than an implied warranty of fitness for a particular purpose.

§ 2A–216. Third Party Beneficiaries of Express and Implied Warranties.

ALTERNATIVE A

A warranty to or for the benefit of a lessee under this Article, whether express or implied, extends to any natural person who is in the family or household of the lessee or who is a guest in the lessee's home if it is reasonable to expect that such person may use, consume, or be affected by the goods and who is injured in person by breach of the warranty. This section does not displace principles of law and equity that extend a warranty to or for the benefit of a lessee to other persons. The operation of this section may not be excluded, modified, or limited, but an exclusion, modification, or limitation of the warranty, including any with respect to rights and remedies, effective against the lessee is also effective against any beneficiary designated under this section.

ALTERNATIVE B

A warranty to or for the benefit of a lessee under this Article, whether express or implied, extends to any natural person who may reasonably be expected to use, consume, or be affected by the goods and who is injured in person by breach of the warranty. This section does not displace principles of law and equity that extend a warranty to or for the benefit of a lessee to other persons. The operation of this section may not be excluded, modified, or limited, but an exclusion, modification, or limitation of the warranty, including any with respect to rights and remedies, effective against the lessee is also effective against the beneficiary designated under this section.

ALTERNATIVE C

A warranty to or for the benefit of a lessee under this Article, whether express or implied, extends to any person who may reasonably be expected to use, consume, or be affected by the goods and who is injured by breach of the warranty. The operation of this section may not be excluded, modified, or limited with respect to injury to the person of an individual to whom the warranty extends, but an exclusion, modification, or limitation of the warranty, including any with respect to rights and remedies, effective against the lessee is also effective against the beneficiary designated under this section.

§ 2A–217. Identification. Identification of goods as goods to which a lease contract refers may be made at any time and in any manner explicitly agreed to by the parties. In the absence of explicit agreement, identification occurs:

(a) when the lease contract is made if the lease contract is for a lease of goods that are existing and identified;

(b) when the goods are shipped, marked, or otherwise designated by the lessor as goods to which the lease contract refers, if the lease contract is for a lease of goods that are not existing and identified; or

(c) when the young are conceived, if the lease contract is for a lease of unborn young of animals.

§ 2A–218. Insurance and Proceeds.

(1) A lessee obtains an insurable interest when existing goods are identified to the lease contract even though the goods identified are nonconforming and the lessee has an option to reject them.

(2) If a lessee has an insurable interest only by reason of the lessor's identification of the goods, the lessor, until default or insolvency or notification to the lessee that identification is final, may substitute other goods for those identified.

(3) Notwithstanding a lessee's insurable interest under subsections (1) and (2), the lessor retains an insurable interest until an option to buy has been exercised by the lessee and risk of loss has passed to the lessee.

(4) Nothing in this section impairs any insurable interest recognized under any other statute or rule of law.

(5) The parties by agreement may determine that one or more parties have an obligation to obtain and pay for insurance covering the goods and by agreement may determine the beneficiary of the proceeds of the insurance.

§ 2A–219. Risk of Loss.

(1) Except in the case of a finance lease, risk of loss is retained by the lessor and does not pass to the lessee. In the case of a finance lease, risk of loss passes to the lessee.

(2) Subject to the provisions of this Article on the effect of default on risk of loss (Section 2A–220), if risk of loss is to pass to the lessee and the time of passage is not stated, the following rules apply:

(a) If the lease contract requires or authorizes the goods to be shipped by carrier

(i) and it does not require delivery at a particular destination, the risk of loss passes to the lessee when the goods are duly delivered to the carrier; but

(ii) if it does require delivery at a particular destination and the goods are there duly tendered while in the possession of the carrier, the risk of loss passes to the lessee when the goods are there duly so tendered as to enable the lessee to take delivery.

(b) If the goods are held by a bailee to be delivered without being moved, the risk of loss passes to the lessee on acknowledgment by the bailee of the lessee's right to possession of the goods.

(c) In any case not within subsection (a) or (b), the risk of loss passes to the lessee on the lessee's receipt of the goods if the lessor, or, in the case of a finance lease, the supplier, is a merchant; otherwise the risk passes to the lessee on tender of delivery.

§ 2A–220. Effect of Default on Risk of Loss.

(1) Where risk of loss is to pass to the lessee and the time of passage is not stated:

(a) If a tender or delivery of goods so fails to conform to the lease contract as to give a right of rejection, the risk of their loss remains with the lessor, or, in the case of a finance lease, the supplier, until cure or acceptance.

(b) If the lessee rightfully revokes acceptance, he [or she], to the extent of any deficiency in his [or her] effective insurance coverage, may treat the risk of loss as having remained with the lessor from the beginning.

(2) Whether or not risk of loss is to pass to the lessee, if the lessee as to conforming goods already identified to a lease contract repudiates or is otherwise in default under the lease contract, the lessor, or, in the case of a finance lease, the supplier, to the extent of any deficiency in his [or her] effective insurance coverage may treat the risk of loss as resting on the lessee for a commercially reasonable time.

§ 2A–221. Casualty to Identified Goods. If a lease contract requires goods identified when the lease contract is made, and the goods suffer casualty without fault of the lessee, the lessor or the supplier before delivery, or the goods suffer casualty before risk of loss passes to the lessee pursuant to the lease agreement or Section 2A–219, then:

(a) if the loss is total, the lease contract is avoided; and

(b) if the loss is partial or the goods have so deteriorated as to no longer conform to the lease contract, the lessee may nevertheless demand inspection and at his [or her] option either treat the lease contract as avoided or, except in a finance lease that is not a consumer lease, accept the goods with due allowance from the rent payable for the balance of the lease term for the deterioration or the deficiency in quantity but without further right against the lessor.

Part 3: Effect of Lease Contract

§ 2A–301. Enforceability of Lease Contract. Except as otherwise provided in this Article, a lease contract is effective and enforceable according to its terms between the parties, against purchasers of the goods and against creditors of the parties.

§ 2A–302. Title to and Possession of Goods. Except as otherwise provided in this Article, each provision of this Article applies whether the lessor or a third party has title to the goods, and whether the lessor, the lessee, or a third party has possession of the goods, notwithstanding any statute or rule of law that possession or the absence of possession is fraudulent.

§ 2A–303. Alienability of Party's Interest Under Lease Contract or of Lessor's Residual Interest in Goods; Delegation of Performance; Transfer of Rights.

(1) As used in this section, "creation of a security interest" includes the sale of a lease contract that is subject to Article 9, Secured Transactions, by reason of Section 9–102(1) (b).

(2) Except as provided in subsections (3) and (4), a provision in a lease agreement which (i) prohibits the voluntary or involuntary transfer, including a transfer by sale, sublease, creation or enforcement of a security interest, or attachment, levy, or other judicial process, of an interest of a party under the lease contract or of the lessor's residual interest in the goods, or (ii) makes such a transfer an event of default, gives rise to the rights and remedies provided in subsection (5), but a transfer that is prohibited or is an event of default under the lease agreement is otherwise effective.

(3) A provision in a lease agreement which (i) prohibits the creation or enforcement of a security interest in an interest of a party under the lease contract or in the lessor's residual interest in the goods, or (ii) makes such a transfer an event of default, is not enforceable unless, and then only to the extent that, there is an actual transfer by the lessee of the lessee's right of possession or use of the goods in violation of the provision or an actual delegation of a material performance of either party to the lease contract in violation of the provision. Neither the granting nor the enforcement of a security interest in (i) the lessor's interest under the lease contract or (ii) the lessor's residual interest in the goods is a transfer that materially impairs the prospect of obtaining return performance by, materially changes the duty of, or materially increases the burden or risk imposed on, the lessee within the purview of subsection (5) unless, and then only to the extent that, there is an actual delegation of a material performance of the lessor.

(4) A provision in a lease agreement which (i) prohibits a transfer of a right to damages for default with respect to the whole lease contract or of a right to payment arising out of the transferor's due performance of the transferor's entire obligation, or (ii) makes such a transfer an event of default, is not enforceable, and such a transfer is not a transfer that materially impairs the prospect of obtaining return performance by, materially changes the duty of, or materially increases the burden or risk imposed on, the other party to the lease contract within the purview of subsection (5).

(5) Subject to subsections (3) and (4):

(a) if a transfer is made which is made an event of default under a lease agreement, the party to the lease contract not making the transfer, unless that party waives the default or otherwise agrees, has the rights and remedies described in Section 2A–501(2);

(b) if paragraph (a) is not applicable and if a transfer is made that (i) is prohibited under a lease agreement or (ii) materially impairs the prospect of obtaining return performance by, materially changes the duty of, or materially increases the burden or risk imposed on, the other party to the lease contract, unless the party not making the transfer agrees at any time to the transfer in the lease contract or otherwise, then, except as limited by contract, (i) the transferor is liable to the party not making the transfer for damages caused by the transfer to the extent that the damages could not reasonably be prevented by the party not making the transfer and (ii) a court having jurisdiction may grant other appropriate relief, including cancellation of the lease contract or an injunction against the transfer.

(6) A transfer of "the lease" or of "all my rights under the lease", or a transfer in similar general terms, is a transfer of rights and, unless the language or the circumstances, as in a transfer for security, indicate the contrary, the transfer is a delegation of duties by the transferor to the transferee. Acceptance by the transferee constitutes a promise by the transferee to perform those duties. The promise is enforceable by either the transferor or the other party to the lease contract.

(7) Unless otherwise agreed by the lessor and the lessee, a delegation of performance does not relieve the transferor as against the other party of any duty to perform or of any liability for default.

(8) In a consumer lease, to prohibit the transfer of an interest of a party under the lease contract or to make a transfer an event of default, the language must be specific, by a writing, and conspicuous.

As amended in 1990.

§ 2A–304. Subsequent Lease of Goods by Lessor.

(1) Subject to Section 2A–303, a subsequent lessee from a lessor of goods under an existing lease contract obtains, to the extent of the leasehold interest transferred, the leasehold interest in the goods that the lessor had or had power to transfer, and except as provided in subsection (2) and Section 2A–527(4), takes subject to the existing lease contract. A lessor with voidable title has power to transfer a good leasehold interest to a good faith subsequent lessee for value, but only to the extent set forth in the preceding sentence. If goods have been delivered under a transaction of purchase, the lessor has that power even though:

- **(a)** the lessor's transferor was deceived as to the identity of the lessor;
- **(b)** the delivery was in exchange for a check which is later dishonored;
- **(c)** it was agreed that the transaction was to be a "cash sale"; or
- **(d)** the delivery was procured through fraud punishable as larcenous under the criminal law.

(2) A subsequent lessee in the ordinary course of business from a lessor who is a merchant dealing in goods of that kind to whom the goods were entrusted by the existing lessee of that lessor before the interest of the subsequent lessee became enforceable against that lessor obtains, to the extent of the leasehold interest transferred, all of that lessor's and the existing lessee's rights to the goods, and takes free of the existing lease contract.

(3) A subsequent lessee from the lessor of goods that are subject to an existing lease contract and are covered by a certificate of title issued under a statute of this State or of another jurisdiction takes no greater rights than those provided both by this section and by the certificate of title statute.

As amended in 1990.

§ 2A–305. Sale or Sublease of Goods by Lessee.

(1) Subject to the provisions of Section 2A–303, a buyer or sublessee from the lessee of goods under an existing lease contract obtains, to the extent of the interest transferred, the leasehold interest in the goods that the lessee had or had power to transfer, and except as provided in subsection (2) and Section 2A–511(4), takes subject to the existing lease contract. A lessee with a voidable leasehold interest has power to transfer a good leasehold interest to a good faith buyer for value or a good faith sublessee for value, but only to the extent set forth in the preceding sentence. When goods have been delivered under a transaction of lease the lessee has that power even though:

- **(a)** the lessor was deceived as to the identity of the lessee;
- **(b)** the delivery was in exchange for a check which is later dishonored; or
- **(c)** the delivery was procured through fraud punishable as larcenous under the criminal law.

(2) A buyer in the ordinary course of business or a sublessee in the ordinary course of business from a lessee who is a merchant dealing in goods of that kind to whom the goods were entrusted by the lessor obtains, to the extent of the interest transferred, all of the lessor's and lessee's rights to the goods, and takes free of the existing lease contract.

(3) A buyer or sublessee from the lessee of goods that are subject to an existing lease contract and are covered by a certificate of title issued under a statute of this State or of another jurisdiction takes no greater rights than those provided both by this section and by the certificate of title statute.

§ 2A–306. Priority of Certain Liens Arising by Operation of Law. If a person in the ordinary course of his [or her] business furnishes services or materials with respect to goods subject to a lease contract, a lien upon those goods in the possession of that person given by statute or rule of law for those materials or services takes priority over any interest of the lessor or lessee under the lease contract or this Article unless the lien is created by statute and the statute provides otherwise or unless the lien is created by rule of law and the rule of law provides otherwise.

§ 2A–307. Priority of Liens Arising by Attachment or Levy on, Security Interests in, and Other Claims to Goods.

(1) Except as otherwise provided in Section 2A–306, a creditor of a lessee takes subject to the lease contract.

(2) Except as otherwise provided in subsections (3) and (4) and in Sections 2A–306 and 2A–308, a creditor of a lessor takes subject to the lease contract unless:

- **(a)** the creditor holds a lien that attached to the goods before the lease contract became enforceable;
- **(b)** the creditor holds a security interest in the goods and the lessee did not give value and receive delivery of the goods without knowledge of the security interest; or
- **(c)** the creditor holds a security interest in the goods which was perfected (Section 9–303) before the lease contract became enforceable.

(3) A lessee in the ordinary course of business takes the leasehold interest free of a security interest in the goods created by the lessor even though the security interest is perfected (Section 9–303) and the lessee knows of its existence.

(4) A lessee other than a lessee in the ordinary course of business takes the leasehold interest free of a security interest to the extent that it secures future advances made after the secured party acquires knowledge of the lease or more than 45 days after the lease contract becomes enforceable, whichever first occurs, unless the future advances are made pursuant to a commitment entered into without knowledge of the lease and before the expiration of the 45-day period.

As amended in 1990.

§ 2A–308. Special Rights of Creditors.

(1) A creditor of a lessor in possession of goods subject to a lease contract may treat the lease contract as void if as against the creditor retention of possession by the lessor is fraudulent under any statute or rule of law, but retention of possession in good faith and current course of trade by the lessor for a commercially reasonable time after the lease contract becomes enforceable is not fraudulent.

(2) Nothing in this Article impairs the rights of creditors of a lessor if the lease contract (a) becomes enforceable, not in current course of trade but in satisfaction of or as security for a preexisting claim for money, security, or the like, and (b) is made under circumstances which under any statute or rule of law apart from this Article would constitute the transaction a fraudulent transfer or voidable preference.

(3) A creditor of a seller may treat a sale or an identification of goods to a contract for sale as void if as against the creditor retention of possession by the seller is fraudulent under any statute or rule of law, but retention of possession of the goods pursuant to a lease contract entered into by the seller as lessee and the buyer as lessor in connection with the sale or identification of the goods is not fraudulent if the buyer bought for value and in good faith.

§ 2A–309. Lessor's and Lessee's Rights When Goods Become Fixtures.

(1) In this section:

(a) goods are "fixtures" when they become so related to particular real estate that an interest in them arises under real estate law;

(b) a "fixture filing" is the filing, in the office where a mortgage on the real estate would be filed or recorded, of a financing statement covering goods that are or are to become fixtures and conforming to the requirements of Section 9–402(5);

(c) a lease is a "purchase money lease" unless the lessee has possession or use of the goods or the right to possession or use of the goods before the lease agreement is enforceable;

(d) a mortgage is a "construction mortgage" to the extent it secures an obligation incurred for the construction of an improvement on land including the acquisition cost of the land, if the recorded writing so indicates; and

(e) "encumbrance" includes real estate mortgages and other liens on real estate and all other rights in real estate that are not ownership interests.

(2) Under this Article a lease may be of goods that are fixtures or may continue in goods that become fixtures, but no lease exists under this Article of ordinary building materials incorporated into an improvement on land.

(3) This Article does not prevent creation of a lease of fixtures pursuant to real estate law.

(4) The perfected interest of a lessor of fixtures has priority over a conflicting interest of an encumbrancer or owner of the real estate if:

(a) the lease is a purchase money lease, the conflicting interest of the encumbrancer or owner arises before the goods become fixtures, the interest of the lessor is perfected by a fixture filing before the goods become fixtures or within ten days thereafter, and the lessee has an interest of record in the real estate or is in possession of the real estate; or

(b) the interest of the lessor is perfected by a fixture filing before the interest of the encumbrancer or owner is of record, the lessor's interest has priority over any conflicting interest of a predecessor in title of the encumbrancer or owner, and the lessee has an interest of record in the real estate or is in possession of the real estate.

(5) The interest of a lessor of fixtures, whether or not perfected, has priority over the conflicting interest of an encumbrancer or owner of the real estate if:

(a) the fixtures are readily removable factory or office machines, readily removable equipment that is not primarily used or leased for use in the operation of the real estate, or readily removable replacements of domestic appliances that are goods subject to a consumer lease, and before the goods become fixtures the lease contract is enforceable; or

(b) the conflicting interest is a lien on the real estate obtained by legal or equitable proceedings after the lease contract is enforceable; or

(c) the encumbrancer or owner has consented in writing to the lease or has disclaimed an interest in the goods as fixtures; or

(d) the lessee has a right to remove the goods as against the encumbrancer or owner. If the lessee's right to remove terminates, the priority of the interest of the lessor continues for a reasonable time.

(6) Notwithstanding subsection (4) (a) but otherwise subject to subsections (4) and (5), the interest of a lessor of fixtures, including the lessor's residual interest, is subordinate to the conflicting interest of an encumbrancer of the real estate under a construction mortgage recorded before the goods become fixtures if the goods become fixtures before the completion of the construction. To the extent given to refinance a construction mortgage, the conflicting interest of an encumbrancer of the real estate under a mortgage has this priority to the same extent as the encumbrancer of the real estate under the construction mortgage.

(7) In cases not within the preceding subsections, priority between the interest of a lessor of fixtures, including the lessor's residual interest, and the conflicting interest of an encumbrancer or owner of the real estate who is not the lessee is determined by the priority rules governing conflicting interests in real estate.

(8) If the interest of a lessor of fixtures, including the lessor's residual interest, has priority over all conflicting interests of all owners and encumbrancers of the real estate, the lessor or the lessee may (i) on default, expiration, termination, or cancellation of the lease agreement but subject to the agreement and this Article, or (ii) if necessary to enforce other rights and remedies of the lessor or lessee under this Article, remove the goods from the real estate, free and clear of all conflicting interests of all owners and encumbrancers of the real estate, but the lessor or lessee must reimburse any encumbrancer or owner of the real estate who is not the lessee and who has not otherwise agreed for the cost of repair of any physical injury, but not for any diminution in value of the real estate caused by the absence of the goods removed or by any necessity of replacing them. A person entitled to reimbursement may refuse permission to remove until the party seeking removal gives adequate security for the performance of this obligation.

(9) Even though the lease agreement does not create a security interest, the interest of a lessor of fixtures, including the lessor's residual interest, is perfected by filing a financing statement as a fixture filing for leased goods that are or are to become fixtures in accordance with the relevant provisions of the Article on Secured Transactions (Article 9).

As amended in 1990.

§ 2A–310. Lessor's and Lessee's Rights When Goods Become Accessions.

(1) Goods are "accessions" when they are installed in or affixed to other goods.

(2) The interest of a lessor or a lessee under a lease contract entered into before the goods became accessions is superior to all interests in the whole except as stated in subsection (4).

(3) The interest of a lessor or a lessee under a lease contract entered into at the time or after the goods became accessions is superior to all subsequently acquired interests in the whole except as stated in subsection (4) but is subordinate to interests in the whole existing at the time the lease contract was made unless the holders of such interests in the whole have in writing consented to the lease or disclaimed an interest in the goods as part of the whole.

(4) The interest of a lessor or a lessee under a lease contract described in subsection (2) or (3) is subordinate to the interest of

(a) a buyer in the ordinary course of business or a lessee in the ordinary course of business of any interest in the whole acquired after the goods became accessions; or

(b) a creditor with a security interest in the whole perfected before the lease contract was made to the extent that the creditor makes subsequent advances without knowledge of the lease contract.

(5) When under subsections (2) or (3) and (4) a lessor or a lessee of accessions holds an interest that is superior to all interests in the whole, the lessor or the lessee may (a) on default, expiration, termination, or cancellation of the lease contract by the other party but subject to the provisions of the lease contract and this Article, or (b) if necessary to enforce his [or her] other rights and remedies under this Article, remove the goods from the whole, free and clear of all interests in the whole, but he [or she] must reimburse any holder of an interest in the whole who is not the lessee and who has not otherwise agreed for the cost of repair of any physical injury but not for any diminution in value of the whole caused by the absence of the goods removed or by any necessity for replacing them. A person entitled to reimbursement may refuse permission to remove until the party seeking removal gives adequate security for the performance of this obligation.

§ 2A–311. Priority Subject to Subordination. Nothing in this Article prevents subordination by agreement by any person entitled to priority.

As added in 1990.

Part 4: Performance of Lease Contract: Repudiated, Substituted and Excused

§ 2A–401. Insecurity: Adequate Assurance of Performance.

(1) A lease contract imposes an obligation on each party that the other's expectation of receiving due performance will not be impaired.
(2) If reasonable grounds for insecurity arise with respect to the performance of either party, the insecure party may demand in writing adequate assurance of due performance. Until the insecure party receives that assurance, if commercially reasonable the insecure party may suspend any performance for which he [or she] has not already received the agreed return.
(3) A repudiation of the lease contract occurs if assurance of due performance adequate under the circumstances of the particular case is not provided to the insecure party within a reasonable time, not to exceed 30 days after receipt of a demand by the other party.
(4) Between merchants, the reasonableness of grounds for insecurity and the adequacy of any assurance offered must be determined according to commercial standards.
(5) Acceptance of any nonconforming delivery or payment does not prejudice the aggrieved party's right to demand adequate assurance of future performance.

§ 2A–402. Anticipatory Repudiation. If either party repudiates a lease contract with respect to a performance not yet due under the lease contract, the loss of which performance will substantially impair the value of the lease contract to the other, the aggrieved party may:

(a) for a commercially reasonable time, await retraction of repudiation and performance by the repudiating party;
(b) make demand pursuant to Section 2A–401 and await assurance of future performance adequate under the circumstances of the particular case; or
(c) resort to any right or remedy upon default under the lease contract or this Article, even though the aggrieved party has notified the repudiating party that the aggrieved party would await the repudiating party's performance and assurance and has urged retraction. In addition, whether or not the aggrieved party is pursuing one of the foregoing remedies, the aggrieved party may suspend performance or, if the aggrieved party is the lessor, proceed in accordance with the provisions of this Article on the lessor's right to identify goods to the lease contract notwithstanding default or to salvage unfinished goods (Section 2A–524).

§ 2A–403. Retraction of Anticipatory Repudiation.

(1) Until the repudiating party's next performance is due, the repudiating party can retract the repudiation unless, since the repudiation, the aggrieved party has cancelled the lease contract or materially changed the aggrieved party's position or otherwise indicated that the aggrieved party considers the repudiation final.
(2) Retraction may be by any method that clearly indicates to the aggrieved party that the repudiating party intends to perform under the lease contract and includes any assurance demanded under Section 2A–401.
(3) Retraction reinstates a repudiating party's rights under a lease contract with due excuse and allowance to the aggrieved party for any delay occasioned by the repudiation.

§ 2A–404. Substituted Performance.

(1) If without fault of the lessee, the lessor and the supplier, the agreed berthing, loading, or unloading facilities fail or the agreed type of carrier becomes unavailable or the agreed manner of delivery otherwise becomes commercially impracticable, but a commercially reasonable substitute is available, the substitute performance must be tendered and accepted.

(2) If the agreed means or manner of payment fails because of domestic or foreign governmental regulation:

(a) the lessor may withhold or stop delivery or cause the supplier to withhold or stop delivery unless the lessee provides a means or manner of payment that is commercially a substantial equivalent; and

(b) if delivery has already been taken, payment by the means or in the manner provided by the regulation discharges the lessee's obligation unless the regulation is discriminatory, oppressive, or predatory.

§ 2A–405. Excused Performance. Subject to Section 2A–404 on substituted performance, the following rules apply:

(a) Delay in delivery or nondelivery in whole or in part by a lessor or a supplier who complies with paragraphs (b) and (c) is not a default under the lease contract if performance as agreed has been made impracticable by the occurrence of a contingency the nonoccurrence of which was a basic assumption on which the lease contract was made or by compliance in good faith with any applicable foreign or domestic governmental regulation or order, whether or not the regulation or order later proves to be invalid.

(b) If the causes mentioned in paragraph (a) affect only part of the lessor's or the supplier's capacity to perform, he [or she] shall allocate production and deliveries among his [or her] customers but at his [or her] option may include regular customers not then under contract for sale or lease as well as his [or her] own requirements for further manufacture. He [or she] may so allocate in any manner that is fair and reasonable.

(c) The lessor seasonably shall notify the lessee and in the case of a finance lease the supplier seasonably shall notify the lessor and the lessee, if known, that there will be delay or nondelivery and, if allocation is required under paragraph (b), of the estimated quota thus made available for the lessee.

§ 2A–406. Procedure on Excused Performance.

(1) If the lessee receives notification of a material or indefinite delay or an allocation justified under Section 2A–405, the lessee may by written notification to the lessor as to any goods involved, and with respect to all of the goods if under an installment lease contract the value of the whole lease contract is substantially impaired (Section 2A–510):

(a) terminate the lease contract (Section 2A–505(2)); or

(b) except in a finance lease that is not a consumer lease, modify the lease contract by accepting the available quota in substitution, with due allowance from the rent payable for the balance of the lease term for the deficiency but without further right against the lessor.

(2) If, after receipt of a notification from the lessor under Section 2A–405, the lessee fails so to modify the lease agreement within a reasonable time not exceeding 30 days, the lease contract lapses with respect to any deliveries affected.

§ 2A–407. Irrevocable Promises: Finance Leases.

(1) In the case of a finance lease that is not a consumer lease the lessee's promises under the lease contract become irrevocable and independent upon the lessee's acceptance of the goods.

(2) A promise that has become irrevocable and independent under subsection (1):

(a) is effective and enforceable between the parties, and by or against third parties including assignees of the parties; and

(b) is not subject to cancellation, termination, modification, repudiation, excuse, or substitution without the consent of the party to whom the promise runs.

(3) This section does not affect the validity under any other law of a covenant in any lease contract making the lessee's promises irrevocable and independent upon the lessee's acceptance of the goods.

As amended in 1990.

Part 5: Default

§ 2A–501. Default: Procedure.

(1) Whether the lessor or the lessee is in default under a lease contract is determined by the lease agreement and this Article.

(2) If the lessor or the lessee is in default under the lease contract, the party seeking enforcement has rights and remedies as provided in this Article and, except as limited by this Article, as provided in the lease agreement.
(3) If the lessor or the lessee is in default under the lease contract, the party seeking enforcement may reduce the party's claim to judgment, or otherwise enforce the lease contract by self-help or any available judicial procedure or nonjudicial procedure, including administrative proceeding, arbitration, or the like, in accordance with this Article.
(4) Except as otherwise provided in Section 1–106(1) or this Article or the lease agreement, the rights and remedies referred to in subsections (2) and (3) are cumulative.
(5) If the lease agreement covers both real property and goods, the party seeking enforcement may proceed under this Part as to the goods, or under other applicable law as to both the real property and the goods in accordance with that party's rights and remedies in respect of the real property, in which case this Part does not apply.

As amended in 1990.

§ 2A–502. Notice After Default. Except as otherwise provided in this Article or the lease agreement, the lessor or lessee in default under the lease contract is not entitled to notice of default or notice of enforcement from the other party to the lease agreement.

§ 2A–503. Modification or Impairment of Rights and Remedies.

(1) Except as otherwise provided in this Article, the lease agreement may include rights and remedies for default in addition to or in substitution for those provided in this Article and may limit or alter the measure of damages recoverable under this Article.
(2) Resort to a remedy provided under this Article or in the lease agreement is optional unless the remedy is expressly agreed to be exclusive. If circumstances cause an exclusive or limited remedy to fail of its essential purpose, or provision for an exclusive remedy is unconscionable, remedy may be had as provided in this Article.
(3) Consequential damages may be liquidated under Section 2A–504, or may otherwise be limited, altered, or excluded unless the limitation, alteration, or exclusion is unconscionable. Limitation, alteration, or exclusion of consequential damages for injury to the person in the case of consumer goods is prima facie unconscionable but limitation, alteration, or exclusion of damages where the loss is commercial is not prima facie unconscionable.
(4) Rights and remedies on default by the lessor or the lessee with respect to any obligation or promise collateral or ancillary to the lease contract are not impaired by this Article.

As amended in 1990.

§ 2A–504. Liquidation of Damages.

(1) Damages payable by either party for default, or any other act or omission, including indemnity for loss or diminution of anticipated tax benefits or loss or damage to lessor's residual interest, may be liquidated in the lease agreement but only at an amount or by a formula that is reasonable in light of the then anticipated harm caused by the default or other act or omission.
(2) If the lease agreement provides for liquidation of damages, and such provision does not comply with subsection (1), or such provision is an exclusive or limited remedy that circumstances cause to fail of its essential purpose, remedy may be had as provided in this Article.
(3) If the lessor justifiably withholds or stops delivery of goods because of the lessee's default or insolvency (Section 2A–525 or 2A–526), the lessee is entitled to restitution of any amount by which the sum of his [or her] payments exceeds:
    (a) the amount to which the lessor is entitled by virtue of terms liquidating the lessor's damages in accordance with subsection (1); or
    (b) in the absence of those terms, 20 percent of the then present value of the total rent the lessee was obligated to pay for the balance of the lease term, or, in the case of a consumer lease, the lesser of such amount or $500.
(4) A lessee's right to restitution under subsection (3) is subject to offset to the extent the lessor establishes:
    (a) a right to recover damages under the provisions of this Article other than subsection (1); and
    (b) the amount or value of any benefits received by the lessee directly or indirectly by reason of the lease contract.

§ 2A–505. Cancellation and Termination and Effect of Cancellation, Termination, Rescission, or Fraud on Rights and Remedies.

(1) On cancellation of the lease contract, all obligations that are still executory on both sides are discharged, but any right based on prior default or performance

survives, and the cancelling party also retains any remedy for default of the whole lease contract or any unperformed balance.

(2) On termination of the lease contract, all obligations that are still executory on both sides are discharged but any right based on prior default or performance survives.

(3) Unless the contrary intention clearly appears, expressions of "cancellation," "rescission," or the like of the lease contract may not be construed as a renunciation or discharge of any claim in damages for an antecedent default.

(4) Rights and remedies for material misrepresentation or fraud include all rights and remedies available under this Article for default.

(5) Neither rescission nor a claim for rescission of the lease contract nor rejection or return of the goods may bar or be deemed inconsistent with a claim for damages or other right or remedy.

§ 2A–506. Statute of Limitations.

(1) An action for default under a lease contract, including breach of warranty or indemnity, must be commenced within 4 years after the cause of action accrued. By the original lease contract the parties may reduce the period of limitation to not less than one year.

(2) A cause of action for default accrues when the act or omission on which the default or breach of warranty is based is or should have been discovered by the aggrieved party, or when the default occurs, whichever is later. A cause of action for indemnity accrues when the act or omission on which the claim for indemnity is based is or should have been discovered by the indemnified party, whichever is later.

(3) If an action commenced within the time limited by subsection (1) is so terminated as to leave available a remedy by another action for the same default or breach of warranty or indemnity, the other action may be commenced after the expiration of the time limited and within 6 months after the termination of the first action unless the termination resulted from voluntary discontinuance or from dismissal for failure or neglect to prosecute.

(4) This section does not alter the law on tolling of the statute of limitations nor does it apply to causes of action that have accrued before this Article becomes effective.

§ 2A–507. Proof of Market Rent: Time and Place.

(1) Damages based on market rent (Section 2A–519 or 2A–528) are determined according to the rent for the use of the goods concerned for a lease term identical to the remaining lease term of the original lease agreement and prevailing at the times specified in Sections 2A–519 and 2A–528.

(2) If evidence of rent for the use of the goods concerned for a lease term identical to the remaining lease term of the original lease agreement and prevailing at the times or places described in this Article is not readily available, the rent prevailing within any reasonable time before or after the time described or at any other place or for a different lease term which in commercial judgment or under usage of trade would serve as a reasonable substitute for the one described may be used, making any proper allowance for the difference, including the cost of transporting the goods to or from the other place.

(3) Evidence of a relevant rent prevailing at a time or place or for a lease term other than the one described in this Article offered by one party is not admissible unless and until he [or she] has given the other party notice the court finds sufficient to prevent unfair surprise.

(4) If the prevailing rent or value of any goods regularly leased in any established market is in issue, reports in official publications or trade journals or in newspapers or periodicals of general circulation published as the reports of that market are admissible in evidence. The circumstances of the preparation of the report may be shown to affect its weight but not its admissibility.

As amended in 1990.

§ 2A–508. Lessee's Remedies.

(1) If a lessor fails to deliver the goods in conformity to the lease contract (Section 2A–509) or repudiates the lease contract (Section 2A–402), or a lessee rightfully rejects the goods (Section 2A–509) or justifiably revokes acceptance of the goods (Section 2A–517), then with respect to any goods involved, and with respect to all of the goods if under an installment lease contract the value of the whole lease contract is substantially impaired (Section 2A–510), the lessor is in default under the lease contract and the lessee may:

(a) cancel the lease contract (Section 2A–505(1));

(b) recover so much of the rent and security as has been paid and is just under the circumstances;

(c) cover and recover damages as to all goods affected whether or not they have been identified to the lease contract (Sections 2A–518 and 2A–520), or recover damages for nondelivery (Sections 2A–519 and 2A–520);

(d) exercise any other rights or pursue any other remedies provided in the lease contract.

(2) If a lessor fails to deliver the goods in conformity to the lease contract or repudiates the lease contract, the lessee may also:

(a) if the goods have been identified, recover them (Section 2A–522); or

(b) in a proper case, obtain specific performance or replevy the goods (Section 2A–521).

(3) If a lessor is otherwise in default under a lease contract, the lessee may exercise the rights and pursue the remedies provided in the lease contract, which may include a right to cancel the lease, and in Section 2A–519(3).

(4) If a lessor has breached a warranty, whether express or implied, the lessee may recover damages (Section 2A–519(4)).

(5) On rightful rejection or justifiable revocation of acceptance, a lessee has a security interest in goods in the lessee's possession or control for any rent and security that has been paid and any expenses reasonably incurred in their inspection, receipt, transportation, and care and custody and may hold those goods and dispose of them in good faith and in a commercially reasonable manner, subject to Section 2A–527(5).

(6) Subject to the provisions of Section 2A–407, a lessee, on notifying the lessor of the lessee's intention to do so, may deduct all or any part of the damages resulting from any default under the lease contract from any part of the rent still due under the same lease contract.

As amended in 1990.

§ 2A–509. Lessee's Rights on Improper Delivery; Rightful Rejection.

(1) Subject to the provisions of Section 2A–510 on default in installment lease contracts, if the goods or the tender or delivery fail in any respect to conform to the lease contract, the lessee may reject or accept the goods or accept any commercial unit or units and reject the rest of the goods.

(2) Rejection of goods is ineffective unless it is within a reasonable time after tender or delivery of the goods and the lessee seasonably notifies the lessor.

§ 2A–510. Installment Lease Contracts: Rejection and Default.

(1) Under an installment lease contract a lessee may reject any delivery that is nonconforming if the nonconformity substantially impairs the value of that delivery and cannot be cured or the nonconformity is a defect in the required documents; but if the nonconformity does not fall within subsection (2) and the lessor or the supplier gives adequate assurance of its cure, the lessee must accept that delivery.

(2) Whenever nonconformity or default with respect to one or more deliveries substantially impairs the value of the installment lease contract as a whole there is a default with respect to the whole. But, the aggrieved party reinstates the installment lease contract as a whole if the aggrieved party accepts a nonconforming delivery without seasonably notifying of cancellation or brings an action with respect only to past deliveries or demands performance as to future deliveries.

§ 2A–511. Merchant Lessee's Duties as to Rightfully Rejected Goods.

(1) Subject to any security interest of a lessee (Section 2A–508(5)), if a lessor or a supplier has no agent or place of business at the market of rejection, a merchant lessee, after rejection of goods in his [or her] possession or control, shall follow any reasonable instructions received from the lessor or the supplier with respect to the goods. In the absence of those instructions, a merchant lessee shall make reasonable efforts to sell, lease, or otherwise dispose of the goods for the lessor's account if they threaten to decline in value speedily. Instructions are not reasonable if on demand indemnity for expenses is not forthcoming.

(2) If a merchant lessee (subsection (1)) or any other lessee (Section 2A–512) disposes of goods, he [or she] is entitled to reimbursement either from the lessor or the supplier or out of the proceeds for reasonable expenses of caring for and disposing of the goods and, if the expenses include no disposition commission, to such commission as is usual in the trade, or if there is none, to a reasonable sum not exceeding 10 percent of the gross proceeds.

(3) In complying with this section or Section 2A–512, the lessee is held only to good faith. Good faith conduct hereunder is neither acceptance or conversion nor the basis of an action for damages.

(4) A purchaser who purchases in good faith from a lessee pursuant to this section or Section 2A–512 takes the goods free of any rights of the lessor and the supplier even though the lessee fails to comply with one or more of the requirements of this Article.

§ 2A–512. Lessee's Duties as to Rightfully Rejected Goods.

(1) Except as otherwise provided with respect to goods that threaten to decline in value speedily (Section 2A–511) and subject to any security interest of a lessee (Section 2A–508(5)):

(a) the lessee, after rejection of goods in the lessee's possession, shall hold them with reasonable care at the lessor's or the supplier's disposition for a reasonable time after the lessee's seasonable notification of rejection;

(b) if the lessor or the supplier gives no instructions within a reasonable time after notification of rejection, the lessee may store the rejected goods for the lessor's or the supplier's account or ship them to the lessor or the supplier or dispose of them for the lessor's or the supplier's account with reimbursement in the manner provided in Section 2A–511; but

(c) the lessee has no further obligations with regard to goods rightfully rejected.

(2) Action by the lessee pursuant to subsection (1) is not acceptance or conversion.

§ 2A–513. Cure by Lessor of Improper Tender or Delivery; Replacement.

(1) If any tender or delivery by the lessor or the supplier is rejected because nonconforming and the time for performance has not yet expired, the lessor or the supplier may seasonably notify the lessee of the lessor's or the supplier's intention to cure and may then make a conforming delivery within the time provided in the lease contract.

(2) If the lessee rejects a nonconforming tender that the lessor or the supplier had reasonable grounds to believe would be acceptable with or without money allowance, the lessor or the supplier may have a further reasonable time to substitute a conforming tender if he [or she] seasonably notifies the lessee.

§ 2A–514. Waiver of Lessee's Objections.

(1) In rejecting goods, a lessee's failure to state a particular defect that is ascertainable by reasonable inspection precludes the lessee from relying on the defect to justify rejection or to establish default:

(a) if, stated seasonably, the lessor or the supplier could have cured it (Section 2A–513); or

(b) between merchants if the lessor or the supplier after rejection has made a request in writing for a full and final written statement of all defects on which the lessee proposes to rely.

(2) A lessee's failure to reserve rights when paying rent or other consideration against documents precludes recovery of the payment for defects apparent on the face of the documents.

§ 2A–515. Acceptance of Goods.

(1) Acceptance of goods occurs after the lessee has had a reasonable opportunity to inspect the goods and

(a) the lessee signifies or acts with respect to the goods in a manner that signifies to the lessor or the supplier that the goods are conforming or that the lessee will take or retain them in spite of their nonconformity; or

(b) the lessee fails to make an effective rejection of the goods (Section 2A–509(2)).

(2) Acceptance of a part of any commercial unit is acceptance of that entire unit.

§ 2A–516. Effect of Acceptance of Goods; Notice of Default; Burden of Establishing Default After Acceptance; Notice of Claim or Litigation to Person Answerable Over.

(1) A lessee must pay rent for any goods accepted in accordance with the lease contract, with due allowance for goods rightfully rejected or not delivered.

(2) A lessee's acceptance of goods precludes rejection of the goods accepted. In the case of a finance lease, if made with knowledge of a nonconformity, acceptance cannot be revoked because of it. In any other case, if made with knowledge of a nonconformity, acceptance cannot be revoked because of it unless the acceptance was on the reasonable assumption that the nonconformity would be seasonably cured. Acceptance does not of itself impair any other remedy provided by this Article or the lease agreement for nonconformity.

(3) If a tender has been accepted:

(a) within a reasonable time after the lessee discovers or should have discovered any default, the lessee shall notify the lessor and the supplier, if any, or be barred from any remedy against the party not notified;

(b) except in the case of a consumer lease, within a reasonable time after the lessee receives notice of litigation for infringement or the like (Section 2A–211) the lessee shall notify the lessor or be barred from any remedy over for liability established by the litigation; and

(c) the burden is on the lessee to establish any default.

(4) If a lessee is sued for breach of a warranty or other obligation for which a lessor or a supplier is answerable over the following apply:

(a) The lessee may give the lessor or the supplier, or both, written notice of the litigation. If the notice states that the person notified may come in and defend and that if the person notified does not do so that person will be bound in any action against that person by the lessee by any determination of fact common to the two litigations, then unless the person notified after seasonable receipt of the notice does come in and defend that person is so bound.

(b) The lessor or the supplier may demand in writing that the lessee turn over control of the litigation including settlement if the claim is one for infringement or the like (Section 2A–211) or else be barred from any remedy over. If the demand states that the lessor or the supplier agrees to bear all expense and to satisfy any adverse judgment, then unless the lessee after seasonable receipt of the demand does turn over control the lessee is so barred.

(5) Subsections (3) and (4) apply to any obligation of a lessee to hold the lessor or the supplier harmless against infringement or the like (Section 2A–211).

As amended in 1990.

§ 2A–517. Revocation of Acceptance of Goods.

(1) A lessee may revoke acceptance of a lot or commercial unit whose nonconformity substantially impairs its value to the lessee if the lessee has accepted it:

(a) except in the case of a finance lease, on the reasonable assumption that its nonconformity would be cured and it has not been seasonably cured; or

(b) without discovery of the nonconformity if the lessee's acceptance was reasonably induced either by the lessor's assurances or, except in the case of a finance lease, by the difficulty of discovery before acceptance.

(2) Except in the case of a finance lease that is not a consumer lease, a lessee may revoke acceptance of a lot or commercial unit if the lessor defaults under the lease contract and the default substantially impairs the value of that lot or commercial unit to the lessee.

(3) If the lease agreement so provides, the lessee may revoke acceptance of a lot or commercial unit because of other defaults by the lessor.

(4) Revocation of acceptance must occur within a reasonable time after the lessee discovers or should have discovered the ground for it and before any substantial change in condition of the goods which is not caused by the nonconformity. Revocation is not effective until the lessee notifies the lessor.

(5) A lessee who so revokes has the same rights and duties with regard to the goods involved as if the lessee had rejected them.

As amended in 1990.

§ 2A–518. Cover; Substitute Goods.

(1) After a default by a lessor under the lease contract of the type described in Section 2A–508(1) , or, if agreed, after other default by the lessor, the lessee may cover by making any purchase or lease of or contract to purchase or lease goods in substitution for those due from the lessor.

(2) Except as otherwise provided with respect to damages liquidated in the lease agreement (Section 2A–504) or otherwise determined pursuant to agreement of the parties (Sections 1–102(3) and 2A–503), if a lessee's cover is by a lease agreement substantially similar to the original lease agreement and the new lease agreement is made in good faith and in a commercially reasonable manner, the lessee may recover from the lessor as damages (i) the present value, as of the date of the commencement of the term of the new lease agreement, of the rent under the new lease agreement applicable to that period of the new lease term which is comparable to the then remaining term of the original lease agreement minus the present value as of the same date of the total rent for the then remaining lease term of the original lease agreement, and (ii) any incidental or consequential damages, less expenses saved in consequence of the lessor's default.

(3) If a lessee's cover is by lease agreement that for any reason does not qualify for treatment under subsection (2), or is by purchase or otherwise, the lessee may recover from the lessor as if the lessee had elected not to cover and Section 2A–519 governs.

As amended in 1990.

§ 2A–519. Lessee's Damages for Nondelivery, Repudiation, Default, and Breach of Warranty in Regard to Accepted Goods.

(1) Except as otherwise provided with respect to damages liquidated in the lease agreement (Section 2A–504) or otherwise determined pursuant to agreement of the parties (Sections 1–102(3) and 2A–503), if a lessee elects not to cover or a lessee elects to cover and the cover is by lease agreement that for any reason does not qualify for treatment under Section 2A–518(2), or is by purchase or otherwise, the measure of damages for nondelivery or repudiation by the lessor or for rejection or revocation of acceptance by the lessee is the present value, as of the date of the default, of the then market rent minus the present value as of the same date of the original rent, computed for the remaining lease term of the original lease agreement, together with incidental and consequential damages, less expenses saved in consequence of the lessor's default.

(2) Market rent is to be determined as of the place for tender or, in cases of rejection after arrival or revocation of acceptance, as of the place of arrival.

(3) Except as otherwise agreed, if the lessee has accepted goods and given notification (Section 2A–516(3)), the measure of damages for nonconforming tender or delivery or other default by a lessor is the loss resulting in the ordinary course of events from the lessor's default as determined in any manner that is reasonable together with incidental and consequential damages, less expenses saved in consequence of the lessor's default.

(4) Except as otherwise agreed, the measure of damages for breach of warranty is the present value at the time and place of acceptance of the difference between the value of the use of the goods accepted and the value if they had been as warranted for the lease term, unless special circumstances show proximate damages of a different amount, together with incidental and consequential damages, less expenses saved in consequence of the lessor's default or breach of warranty.

As amended in 1990.

§ 2A–520. Lessee's Incidental and Consequential Damages.

(1) Incidental damages resulting from a lessor's default include expenses reasonably incurred in inspection, receipt, transportation, and care and custody of goods rightfully rejected or goods the acceptance of which is justifiably revoked, any commercially reasonable charges, expenses or commissions in connection with effecting cover, and any other reasonable expense incident to the default.

(2) Consequential damages resulting from a lessor's default include:

(a) any loss resulting from general or particular requirements and needs of which the lessor at the time of contracting had reason to know and which could not reasonably be prevented by cover or otherwise; and

(b) injury to person or property proximately resulting from any breach of warranty.

§ 2A–521. Lessee's Right to Specific Performance or Replevin.

(1) Specific performance may be decreed if the goods are unique or in other proper circumstances.

(2) A decree for specific performance may include any terms and conditions as to payment of the rent, damages, or other relief that the court deems just.

(3) A lessee has a right of replevin, detinue, sequestration, claim and delivery, or the like for goods identified to the lease contract if after reasonable effort the lessee is unable to effect cover for those goods or the circumstances reasonably indicate that the effort will be unavailing.

§ 2A–522. Lessee's Right to Goods on Lessor's Insolvency.

(1) Subject to subsection (2) and even though the goods have not been shipped, a lessee who has paid a part or all of the rent and security for goods identified to a lease contract (Section 2A–217) on making and keeping good a tender of any unpaid portion of the rent and security due under the lease contract may recover the goods identified from the lessor if the lessor becomes insolvent within 10 days after receipt of the first installment of rent and security.

(2) A lessee acquires the right to recover goods identified to a lease contract only if they conform to the lease contract.

§ 2A–523. Lessor's Remedies.

(1) If a lessee wrongfully rejects or revokes acceptance of goods or fails to make a payment when due or repudiates with respect to a part or the whole, then, with respect to any goods involved, and with respect to all of the goods if under an installment lease contract the value of the whole lease contract is substantially impaired (Section 2A–510), the lessee is in default under the lease contract and the lessor may:

(a) cancel the lease contract (Section 2A–505(1));

(b) proceed respecting goods not identified to the lease contract (Section 2A–524);

(c) withhold delivery of the goods and take possession of goods previously delivered (Section 2A–525);

(d) stop delivery of the goods by any bailee (Section 2A–526);

(e) dispose of the goods and recover damages (Section 2A–527), or retain the goods and recover damages (Section 2A–528), or in a proper case recover rent (Section 2A–529);

(f) exercise any other rights or pursue any other remedies provided in the lease contract.

(2) If a lessor does not fully exercise a right or obtain a remedy to which the lessor is entitled under subsection (1), the lessor may recover the loss resulting in the ordinary course of events from the lessee's default as determined in any reasonable manner, together with incidental damages, less expenses saved in consequence of the lessee's default.

(3) If a lessee is otherwise in default under a lease contract, the lessor may exercise the rights and pursue the remedies provided in the lease contract, which may include a right to cancel the lease. In addition, unless otherwise provided in the lease contract:

(a) if the default substantially impairs the value of the lease contract to the lessor, the lessor may exercise the rights and pursue the remedies provided in subsections (1) or (2); or

(b) if the default does not substantially impair the value of the lease contract to the lessor, the lessor may recover as provided in subsection (2).

As amended in 1990.

§ 2A–524. Lessor's Right to Identify Goods to Lease Contract.

(1) After default by the lessee under the lease contract of the type described in Section 2A–523(1) or 2A–523(3) (a) or, if agreed, after other default by the lessee, the lessor may:

(a) identify to the lease contract conforming goods not already identified if at the time the lessor learned of the default they were in the lessor's or the supplier's possession or control; and

(b) dispose of goods (Section 2A–527(1)) that demonstrably have been intended for the particular lease contract even though those goods are unfinished.

(2) If the goods are unfinished, in the exercise of reasonable commercial judgment for the purposes of avoiding loss and of effective realization, an aggrieved lessor or the supplier may either complete manufacture and wholly identify the goods to the lease contract or cease manufacture and lease, sell, or otherwise dispose of the goods for scrap or salvage value or proceed in any other reasonable manner.

As amended in 1990.

§ 2A–525. Lessor's Right to Possession of Goods.

(1) If a lessor discovers the lessee to be insolvent, the lessor may refuse to deliver the goods.

(2) After a default by the lessee under the lease contract of the type described in Section 2A–523(1) or 2A–523(3) (a) or, if agreed, after other default by the lessee, the lessor has the right to take possession of the goods. If the lease contract so provides, the lessor may require the lessee to assemble the goods and make them available to the lessor at a place to be designated by the lessor which is reasonably convenient to both parties. Without removal, the lessor may render unusable any goods employed in trade or business, and may dispose of goods on the lessee's premises (Section 2A–527).

(3) The lessor may proceed under subsection (2) without judicial process if it can be done without breach of the peace or the lessor may proceed by action.

As amended in 1990.

§ 2A–526. Lessor's Stoppage of Delivery in Transit or Otherwise.

(1) A lessor may stop delivery of goods in the possession of a carrier or other bailee if the lessor discovers the lessee to be insolvent and may stop delivery of carload, truckload, planeload, or larger shipments of express or freight if the lessee repudiates or fails to make a payment due before delivery, whether for rent, security or otherwise under the lease contract, or for any other reason the lessor has a right to withhold or take possession of the goods.

(2) In pursuing its remedies under subsection (1), the lessor may stop delivery until

(a) receipt of the goods by the lessee;
(b) acknowledgment to the lessee by any bailee of the goods, except a carrier, that the bailee holds the goods for the lessee; or
(c) such an acknowledgment to the lessee by a carrier via reshipment or as warehouseman.

(3) **(a)** To stop delivery, a lessor shall so notify as to enable the bailee by reasonable diligence to prevent delivery of the goods.
(b) After notification, the bailee shall hold and deliver the goods according to the directions of the lessor, but the lessor is liable to the bailee for any ensuing charges or damages.
(c) A carrier who has issued a nonnegotiable bill of lading is not obliged to obey a notification to stop received from a person other than the consignor.

§ 2A–527. Lessor's Rights to Dispose of Goods.

(1) After a default by a lessee under the lease contract of the type described in Section 2A–523(1) or 2A–523(3) (a) or after the lessor refuses to deliver or takes possession of goods (Section 2A–525 or 2A–526), or, if agreed, after other default by a lessee, the lessor may dispose of the goods concerned or the undelivered balance thereof by lease, sale, or otherwise.

(2) Except as otherwise provided with respect to damages liquidated in the lease agreement (Section 2A–504) or otherwise determined pursuant to agreement of the parties (Sections 1–102(3) and 2A–503), if the disposition is by lease agreement substantially similar to the original lease agreement and the new lease agreement is made in good faith and in a commercially reasonable manner, the lessor may recover from the lessee as damages (i) accrued and unpaid rent as of the date of the commencement of the term of the new lease agreement, (ii) the present value, as of the same date, of the total rent for the then remaining lease term of the original lease agreement minus the present value, as of the same date, of the rent under the new lease agreement applicable to that period of the new lease term which is comparable to the then remaining term of the original lease agreement, and (iii) any incidental damages allowed under Section 2A–530, less expenses saved in consequence of the lessee's default.

(3) If the lessor's disposition is by lease agreement that for any reason does not qualify for treatment under subsection (2), or is by sale or otherwise, the lessor may recover from the lessee as if the lessor had elected not to dispose of the goods and Section 2A–528 governs.

(4) A subsequent buyer or lessee who buys or leases from the lessor in good faith for value as a result of a disposition under this section takes the goods free of the original lease contract and any rights of the original lessee even though the lessor fails to comply with one or more of the requirements of this Article.

(5) The lessor is not accountable to the lessee for any profit made on any disposition. A lessee who has rightfully rejected or justifiably revoked acceptance shall account to the lessor for any excess over the amount of the lessee's security interest (Section 2A–508(5)).

As amended in 1990.

§ 2A–528. Lessor's Damages for Nonacceptance, Failure to Pay, Repudiation, or Other Default.

(1) Except as otherwise provided with respect to damages liquidated in the lease agreement (Section 2A–504) or otherwise determined pursuant to agreement of the parties (Sections 1–102(3) and 2A–503), if a lessor elects to retain the goods or a lessor elects to dispose of the goods and the disposition is by lease agreement that for any reason does not qualify for treatment under Section 2A–527(2), or is by sale or otherwise, the lessor may recover from the lessee as damages for a default of the type described in Section 2A–523(1) or 2A–523(3) (a), or, if agreed, for other default of the lessee, (i) accrued and unpaid rent as of the date of default if the lessee has never taken possession of the goods, or, if the lessee has taken possession of the goods, as of the date the lessor repossesses the goods or an earlier date on which the lessee makes a tender of the goods to the lessor, (ii) the present value as of the date determined under clause (i) of the total rent for the then remaining lease term of the original lease agreement minus the present value as of the same date of the market rent at the place where the goods are located computed for the same lease term, and (iii) any incidental damages allowed under Section 2A–530, less expenses saved in consequence of the lessee's default.

(2) If the measure of damages provided in subsection (1) is inadequate to put a lessor in as good a position as performance would have, the measure of damages is the present value of the profit, including reasonable overhead, the lessor would have made from full performance by the lessee, together with any incidental damages allowed under Section 2A–530, due allowance for costs reasonably incurred and due credit for payments or proceeds of disposition.

As amended in 1990.

§ 2A–529. Lessor's Action for the Rent.

(1) After default by the lessee under the lease contract of the type described in Section 2A–523(1) or 2A–523(3) (a) or, if agreed, after other default by the lessee, if the lessor complies with subsection (2), the lessor may recover from the lessee as damages:

(a) for goods accepted by the lessee and not repossessed by or tendered to the lessor, and for conforming goods lost or damaged within a commercially reasonable time after risk of loss passes to the lessee (Section 2A–219), (i) accrued and unpaid rent as of the date of entry of judgment in favor of the lessor, (ii) the present value as of the same date of the rent for the then remaining lease term of the lease agreement, and (iii) any incidental damages allowed under Section 2A–530, less expenses saved in consequence of the lessee's default; and

(b) for goods identified to the lease contract if the lessor is unable after reasonable effort to dispose of them at a reasonable price or the circumstances reasonably indicate that effort will be unavailing, (i) accrued and unpaid rent as of the date of entry of judgment in favor of the lessor, (ii) the present value as of the same date of the rent for the then remaining lease term of the lease agreement, and (iii) any incidental damages allowed under Section 2A–530, less expenses saved in consequence of the lessee's default.

(2) Except as provided in subsection (3), the lessor shall hold for the lessee for the remaining lease term of the lease agreement any goods that have been identified to the lease contract and are in the lessor's control.

(3) The lessor may dispose of the goods at any time before collection of the judgment for damages obtained pursuant to subsection (1). If the disposition is before the end of the remaining lease term of the lease agreement, the lessor's recovery against the lessee for damages is governed by Section 2A–527 or Section 2A–528, and the lessor will cause an appropriate credit to be provided against a judgment for damages to the extent that the amount of the judgment exceeds the recovery available pursuant to Section 2A–527 or 2A–528.

(4) Payment of the judgment for damages obtained pursuant to subsection (1) entitles the lessee to the use and possession of the goods not then disposed of for the remaining lease term of and in accordance with the lease agreement.

(5) After default by the lessee under the lease contract of the type described in Section 2A–523(1) or Section 2A–523(3) (a) or, if agreed, after other default by the lessee, a lessor who is held not entitled to rent under this section must nevertheless be awarded damages for nonacceptance under Section 2A–527 or Section 2A–528.

As amended in 1990.

§ 2A–530. Lessor's Incidental Damages. Incidental damages to an aggrieved lessor include any commercially reasonable charges, expenses, or commissions incurred in stopping delivery, in the transportation, care and custody of goods after the lessee's default, in connection with return or disposition of the goods, or otherwise resulting from the default.

§ 2A–531. Standing to Sue Third Parties for Injury to Goods.

(1) If a third party so deals with goods that have been identified to a lease contract as to cause actionable injury to a party to the lease contract (a) the lessor has a right of action against the third party, and (b) the lessee also has a right of action against the third party if the lessee:

(i) has a security interest in the goods;

(ii) has an insurable interest in the goods; or

(iii) bears the risk of loss under the lease contract or has since the injury assumed that risk as against the lessor and the goods have been converted or destroyed.

(2) If at the time of the injury the party plaintiff did not bear the risk of loss as against the other party to the lease contract and there is no arrangement between them for disposition of the recovery, his [or her] suit or settlement, subject to his [or her] own interest, is as a fiduciary for the other party to the lease contract.

(3) Either party with the consent of the other may sue for the benefit of whom it may concern.

§ 2A–532. Lessor's Rights to Residual Interest. In addition to any other recovery permitted by this Article or other law, the lessor may recover from the lessee an amount that will fully compensate the lessor for any loss of or damage to the lessor's residual interest in the goods caused by the default of the lessee.

As added in 1990.

Article 3–Negotiable Instruments

Part 1: General Provisions and Definitions

§ 3–101. Short Title. This Article may be cited as Uniform Commercial Code—Negotiable Instruments.

§ 3–102. Subject Matter.

(a) This Article applies to negotiable instruments. It does not apply to money, to payment orders governed by Article 4A, or to securities governed by Article 8.

(b) If there is conflict between this Article and Article 4 or 9, Articles 4 and 9 govern.

(c) Regulations of the Board of Governors of the Federal Reserve System and operating circulars of the Federal Reserve Banks supersede any inconsistent provision of this Article to the extent of the inconsistency.

§ 3–103. Definitions.

(a) In this Article:

(1) "Acceptor" means a drawee who has accepted a draft.

(2) "Consumer account" means an account established by an individual primarily for personal, family, or household purposes.

(3) "Consumer transaction" means a transaction in which an individual incurs an obligation primarily for personal, family, or household purposes.

(4) "Drawee" means a person ordered in a draft to make payment.

(5) "Drawer" means a person who signs or is identified in a draft as a person ordering payment.

(6) ["Good faith" means honesty in fact and the observance of reasonable commercial standards of fair dealing.]

(7) "Maker" means a person who signs or is identified in a note as a person undertaking to pay.

(8) "Order" means a written instruction to pay money signed by the person giving the instruction. The instruction may be addressed to any person, including the person giving the instruction, or to one or more persons jointly or in the alternative but not in succession. An authorization to pay is not an order unless the person authorized to pay is also instructed to pay.

(9) "Ordinary care" in the case of a person engaged in business means observance of reasonable commercial standards, prevailing in the area in which the person is located, with respect to the business in which the person is engaged. In the case of a bank that takes an instrument for processing for collection or payment by automated means, reasonable commercial standards do not require the bank to examine the instrument if the failure to examine does not violate the bank's prescribed procedures and the bank's procedures do not vary unreasonably from general banking usage not disapproved by this Article or Article 4.

(10) "Party" means a party to an instrument.

(11) "Principal obligor," with respect to an instrument, means the accommodated party or any other party to the instrument against whom a secondary obligor has recourse under this article.

(12) "Promise" means a written undertaking to pay money signed by the person undertaking to pay. An acknowledgment of an obligation by the obligor is not a promise unless the obligor also undertakes to pay the obligation.

(13) "Prove" with respect to a fact means to meet the burden of establishing the fact (Section 1–201(8)).

(14) ["Record" means information that is inscribed on a tangible medium or that is stored in an electroinic or other medium and is retrieveable in perceivable form.]

(15) "Remitter" means a person who purchases an instrument from its issuer if the instrument is payable to an identified person other than the purchaser.

(16) "Remotely-created consumer item" means an item drawn on a consumer account, which is not created by the payor bank and does not bear a handwritten signature purporting to be the signature of the drawer.

(17) "Secondary obligor," with respect to an instrument, means (a) an indorser or an accommodation party, (b) a drawer having the obligation described in Section 3–414(d), or (c) any other party to the instrument that has recourse against another party to the instrument pursuant to Section 3–116(b).

(b) Other definitions applying to this Article and the sections in which they appear are:

"Acceptance"	Section 3–409
"Accommodated party"	Section 3–419
"Accommodation party"	Section 3–419
"Account"	Section 4–104
"Alteration"	Section 3–407
"Anomalous indorsement"	Section 3–205
"Blank indorsement"	Section 3–205
"Cashier's check"	Section 3–104
"Certificate of deposit"	Section 3–104
"Certified check"	Section 3–409
"Check"	Section 3–104
"Consideration"	Section 3–303
"Draft"	Section 3–104
"Holder in due course"	Section 3–302
"Incomplete instrument"	Section 3–115
"Indorsement"	Section 3–204
"Indorser"	Section 3–204
"Instrument"	Section 3–104
"Issue"	Section 3–105
"Issuer"	Section 3–105
"Negotiable instrument"	Section 3–104
"Negotiation"	Section 3–201
"Note"	Section 3–104
"Payable at a definite time"	Section 3–108
"Payable on demand"	Section 3–108
"Payable to bearer"	Section 3–109
"Payable to order"	Section 3–109
"Payment"	Section 3–602
"Person entitled to enforce"	Section 3–301
"Presentment"	Section 3–501
"Reacquisition"	Section 3–207
"Special indorsement"	Section 3–205
"Teller's check"	Section 3–104
"Transfer of instrument"	Section 3–203
"Traveler's check"	Section 3–104
"Value"	Section 3–303

(c) The following definitions in other Articles apply to this Article:

"Banking day"	Section 4–104
"Clearing house"	Section 4–104
"Collecting bank"	Section 4–105
"Depositary bank"	Section 4–105
"Documentary draft"	Section 4–104
"Intermediary bank"	Section 4–105
"Item"	Section 4–104
"Payor bank"	Section 4–105
"Suspends payments"	Section 4–104

(d) In addition, Article 1 contains general definitions and principles of construction and interpretation applicable throughout this Article.

Legislative Note. A jurisdiction that enacts this statute that has not yet enacted the revised version of UCC Article 1 should add to Section 3–103 the definition of "good faith" that appears in the official version of Section 1–201(b)(20) and the definition of "record" that appears in the official version of Section 1–201(b)(31). Sections 3–103(a)(6) and (14) are reserved for that purpose. A jurisdiction that already has adopted or simultaneously adopts the revised Article 1 should not add those definitions, but should leave those numbers "reserved." If jurisdictions follow the numbering suggested here, the subsections will have the same numbering in all jurisdictions that have adopted these amendments (whether they have or have not adopted the revised version of UCC Article 1).

§ 3–104. Negotiable Instrument.

(a) Except as provided in subsections (c) and (d), "negotiable instrument" means an unconditional promise or order to pay a fixed amount of money, with or without interest or other charges described in the promise or order, if it:

(1) is payable to bearer or to order at the time it is issued or first comes into possession of a holder;

(2) is payable on demand or at a definite time; and

(3) does not state any other undertaking or instruction by the person promising or ordering payment to do any act in addition to the payment of money, but the promise or order may contain (i) an undertaking or power to give, maintain, or protect collateral to secure payment, (ii) an authorization or power to the holder to confess judgment or realize on or dispose of collateral, or (iii) a waiver of the benefit of any law intended for the advantage or protection of an obligor.

(b) "Instrument" means a negotiable instrument.

(c) An order that meets all of the requirements of subsection (a), except paragraph (1), and otherwise falls within the definition of "check" in subsection (f) is a negotiable instrument and a check.

(d) A promise or order other than a check is not an instrument if, at the time it is issued or first comes into possession of a holder, it contains a conspicuous statement, however expressed, to the effect that the promise or order is not negotiable or is not an instrument governed by this Article.

(e) An instrument is a "note" if it is a promise and is a "draft" if it is an order. If an instrument falls within the definition of both "note" and "draft," a person entitled to enforce the instrument may treat it as either.

(f) "Check" means (i) a draft, other than a documentary draft, payable on demand and drawn on a bank or (ii) a cashier's check or teller's check. An instrument may be a check even though it is described on its face by another term, such as "money order."

(g) "Cashier's check" means a draft with respect to which the drawer and drawee are the same bank or branches of the same bank.

(h) "Teller's check" means a draft drawn by a bank (i) on another bank, or (ii) payable at or through a bank.

(i) "Traveler's check" means an instrument that (i) is payable on demand, (ii) is drawn on or payable at or through a bank, (iii) is designated by the term "traveler's check" or by a substantially similar term, and (iv) requires, as a condition to payment, a countersignature by a person whose specimen signature appears on the instrument.

(j) "Certificate of deposit" means an instrument containing an acknowledgment by a bank that a sum of money has been received by the bank and a promise by the bank to repay the sum of money. A certificate of deposit is a note of the bank.

§ 3–105. Issue of Instrument.

(a) "Issue" means the first delivery of an instrument by the maker or drawer, whether to a holder or nonholder, for the purpose of giving rights on the instrument to any person.

(b) An unissued instrument, or an unissued incomplete instrument that is completed, is binding on the maker or drawer, but nonissuance is a defense. An instrument that is conditionally issued or is issued for a special purpose is binding on the maker or drawer, but failure of the condition or special purpose to be fulfilled is a defense.

(c) "Issuer" applies to issued and unissued instruments and means a maker or drawer of an instrument.

§ 3–106. Unconditional Promise or Order.

(a) Except as provided in this section, for the purposes of Section 3–104(a), a promise or order is unconditional unless it states (i) an express condition to payment, (ii) that the promise or order is subject to or governed by another record, or (iii) that rights or obligations with respect to the promise or order are stated in another record. A reference to another record does not of itself make the promise or order conditional.

(b) A promise or order is not made conditional (i) by a reference to another record for a statement of rights with respect to collateral, prepayment, or acceleration, or (ii) because payment is limited to resort to a particular fund or source.

(c) If a promise or order requires, as a condition to payment, a countersignature by a person whose specimen signature appears on the promise or order, the condition does not make the promise or order conditional for the purposes of Section 3–104(a). If the person whose specimen signature appears on an instrument fails to countersign the instrument, the failure to countersign is a defense to the obligation of the issuer, but the failure does not prevent a transferee of the instrument from becoming a holder of the instrument.

(d) If a promise or order at the time it is issued or first comes into possession of a holder contains a statement, required by applicable statutory or administrative law, to the effect that the rights of a holder or transferee are subject to claims or defenses that the issuer could assert against the original payee, the promise or order is not thereby made conditional for the purposes of Section 3–104(a); but if the promise or order is an instrument, there cannot be a holder in due course of the instrument.

§ 3–107. Instrument Payable in Foreign Money. Unless the instrument otherwise provides, an instrument that states the amount payable in foreign money may be paid in the foreign money or in an equivalent amount in dollars calculated by using the current bank offered spot rate at the place of payment for the purchase of dollars on the day on which the instrument is paid.

§ 3–108. Payable on Demand or at Definite Time.

(a) A promise or order is "payable on demand" if it (i) states that it is payable on demand or at sight, or otherwise indicates that it is payable at the will of the holder, or (ii) does not state any time of payment.

(b) A promise or order is "payable at a definite time" if it is payable on elapse of a definite period of time after sight or acceptance or at a fixed date or dates or at a time or times readily ascertainable at the time the promise or order is issued, subject to rights of (i) prepayment, (ii) acceleration, (iii) extension at the option of the holder, or (iv) extension to a further definite time at the option of the maker or acceptor or automatically upon or after a specified act or event.

(c) If an instrument, payable at a fixed date, is also payable upon demand made before the fixed date, the instrument is payable on demand until the fixed date and, if demand for payment is not made before that date, becomes payable at a definite time on the fixed date.

§ 3–109. Payable to Bearer or to Order.

(a) A promise or order is payable to bearer if it:

(1) states that it is payable to bearer or to the order of bearer or otherwise indicates that the person in possession of the promise or order is entitled to payment;

(2) does not state a payee; or

(3) states that it is payable to or to the order of cash or otherwise indicates that it is not payable to an identified person.

(b) A promise or order that is not payable to bearer is payable to order if it is payable (i) to the order of an identified person or (ii) to an identified person or order. A promise or order that is payable to order is payable to the identified person.

(c) An instrument payable to bearer may become payable to an identified person if it is specially indorsed pursuant to Section 3–205(a). An instrument payable to an identified person may become payable to bearer if it is indorsed in blank pursuant to Section 3–205(b).

§ 3–110. Identification of Person to Whom Instrument Is Payable.

(a) The person to whom an instrument is initially payable is determined by the intent of the person, whether or not authorized, signing as, or in the name or behalf of, the issuer of the instrument. The instrument is payable to the person intended by the signer even if that person is identified in the instrument by a name or other identification that is not that of the intended person. If more than one person signs in the name or behalf of the issuer of an instrument and all the signers do not intend the same person as payee, the instrument is payable to any person intended by one or more of the signers.

(b) If the signature of the issuer of an instrument is made by automated means, such as a check writing machine, the payee of the instrument is determined by the intent of the person who supplied the name or identification of the payee, whether or not authorized to do so.

(c) A person to whom an instrument is payable may be identified in any way, including by name, identifying number, office, or account number. For the purpose of determining the holder of an instrument, the following rules apply:

(1) If an instrument is payable to an account and the account is identified only by number, the instrument is payable to the person to whom the account is payable. If an instrument is payable to an account identified by number and by the name of a person, the instrument is payable to the named person, whether or not that person is the owner of the account identified by number.

(2) If an instrument is payable to:

(i) a trust, an estate, or a person described as trustee or representative of a trust or estate, the instrument is payable to the trustee, the representative, or a successor of either, whether or not the beneficiary or estate is also named;

(ii) a person described as agent or similar representative of a named or identified person, the instrument is payable to the represented person, the representative, or a successor of the representative;

(iii) a fund or organization that is not a legal entity, the instrument is payable to a representative of the members of the fund or organization; or

(iv) an office or to a person described as holding an office, the instrument is payable to the named person, the incumbent of the office, or a successor to the incumbent.

(d) If an instrument is payable to two or more persons alternatively, it is payable to any of them and may be negotiated, discharged, or enforced by any or all of them in possession of the instrument. If an instrument is payable to two or more persons not alternatively, it is payable to all of them and may be negotiated, discharged, or enforced only by all of them. If an instrument payable to two or more persons is ambiguous as to whether it is payable to the persons alternatively, the instrument is payable to the persons alternatively.

§ 3–111. Place of Payment. Except as otherwise provided for items in Article 4, an instrument is payable at the place of payment stated in the instrument. If no place of payment is stated, an instrument is payable at the address of the drawee or maker stated in the instrument. If no address is stated, the place of payment is the place of business of the drawee or maker. If a drawee or maker has more than one place of business, the place of payment is any place of business of the drawee or maker chosen by the person entitled to enforce the instrument. If the drawee or maker has no place of business, the place of payment is the residence of the drawee or maker.

§ 3–112. Interest.

(a) Unless otherwise provided in the instrument, (i) an instrument is not payable with interest, and (ii) interest on an interest bearing instrument is payable from the date of the instrument.

(b) Interest may be stated in an instrument as a fixed or variable amount of money or it may be expressed as a fixed or variable rate or rates. The amount or rate of interest may be stated or described in the instrument in any manner and may require reference to information not contained in the instrument. If an instrument provides for interest, but the amount of interest payable cannot be ascertained from the description, interest is payable at the judgment rate in effect at the place of payment of the instrument and at the time interest first accrues.

§ 3–113. Date of Instrument.

(a) An instrument may be antedated or postdated. The date stated determines the time of payment if the instrument is payable at a fixed period after date. Except as provided in Section 4–401(c), an instrument payable on demand is not payable before the date of the instrument.

(b) If an instrument is undated, its date is the date of its issue or, in the case of an unissued instrument, the date it first comes into possession of a holder.

§ 3–114. Contradictory Terms of Instrument. If an instrument contains contradictory terms, typewritten terms prevail over printed terms, handwritten terms prevail over both, and words prevail over numbers.

§ 3–115. Incomplete Instrument.

(a) "Incomplete instrument" means a signed writing, whether or not issued by the signer, the contents of which show at the time of signing that it is incomplete but that the signer intended it to be completed by the addition of words or numbers.

(b) Subject to subsection (c), if an incomplete instrument is an instrument under Section 3–104, it may be enforced according to its terms if it is not completed, or according to its terms as augmented by completion. If an incomplete instrument is not an instrument under Section 3–104, but, after completion, the requirements of Section 3–104 are met, the instrument may be enforced according to its terms as augmented by completion.

(c) If words or numbers are added to an incomplete instrument without authority of the signer, there is an alteration of the incomplete instrument under Section 3–407.

(d) The burden of establishing that words or numbers were added to an incomplete instrument without authority of the signer is on the person asserting the lack of authority.

§ 3–116. Joint and Several Liability; Contribution.

(a) Except as otherwise provided in the instrument, two or more persons who have the same liability on an instrument as makers, drawers, acceptors, indorsers who indorse as joint payees, or anomalous indorsers are jointly and severally liable in the capacity in which they sign.

(b) Except as provided in Section 3–419(f) or by agreement of the affected parties, a party having joint and several liability who pays the instrument is entitled to receive from any party having the same joint and several liability contribution in accordance with applicable law.

§ 3–117. Other Agreements Affecting Instrument. Subject to applicable law regarding exclusion of proof of contemporaneous or previous agreements, the obligation of a party to an instrument to pay the instrument may be modified, supplemented, or nullified by a separate agreement of the obligor and a person entitled to enforce the instrument, if the instrument is issued or the obligation is incurred in reliance on the agreement or as part of the same transaction giving rise to the agreement. To the extent an obligation is modified, supplemented, or nullified by an agreement under this section, the agreement is a defense to the obligation.

§ 3–118. Statute of Limitations.

(a) Except as provided in subsection (e), an action to enforce the obligation of a party to pay a note payable at a definite time must be commenced within six years after the due date or dates stated in the note or, if a due date is accelerated, within six years after the accelerated due date.

(b) Except as provided in subsection (d) or (e), if demand for payment is made to the maker of a note payable on demand, an action to enforce the obligation of a party to pay the note must be commenced within six years after the demand. If no demand for payment is made to the maker, an action to enforce the note is barred if neither principal nor interest on the note has been paid for a continuous period of 10 years.

(c) Except as provided in subsection (d), an action to enforce the obligation of a party to an unaccepted draft to pay the draft must be commenced within three years after dishonor of the draft or 10 years after the date of the draft, whichever period expires first.

(d) An action to enforce the obligation of the acceptor of a certified check or the issuer of a teller's check, cashier's check, or traveler's check must be commenced within three years after demand for payment is made to the acceptor or issuer, as the case may be.

(e) An action to enforce the obligation of a party to a certificate of deposit to pay the instrument must be commenced within six years after demand for payment is made to the maker, but if the instrument states a due date and the maker is not required to pay before that date, the six-year period begins when a demand for payment is in effect and the due date has passed.

(f) An action to enforce the obligation of a party to pay an accepted draft, other than a certified check, must be commenced (i) within six years after the due date or dates stated in the draft or acceptance if the obligation of the acceptor is payable at a definite time, or (ii) within six years after the date of the acceptance if the obligation of the acceptor is payable on demand.

(g) Unless governed by other law regarding claims for indemnity or contribution, an action (i) for conversion of an instrument, for money had and received, or like action based on conversion, (ii) for breach of warranty, or (iii) to enforce an obligation, duty, or right arising under this Article and not governed by this section must be commenced within three years after the [cause of action] accrues.

§ 3–119. Notice of Right to Defend Action. In an action for breach of an obligation for which a third person is answerable over pursuant to this Article or Article 4, the defendant may give the third person notice of the litigation in a record, and the person notified may then give similar notice to any other person who is answerable over. If the notice states (i) that the person notified may come in and defend and (ii) that failure to do so will bind the person notified in an action later brought by the person giving the notice as to any determination of fact common to the two litigations, the person notified is so bound unless after seasonable receipt of the notice the person notified does come in and defend.

Part 2: Negotiation, Transfer, and Indorsement

§ 3–201. Negotiation.

(a) "Negotiation" means a transfer of possession, whether voluntary or involuntary, of an instrument by a person other than the issuer to a person who thereby becomes its holder.

(b) Except for negotiation by a remitter, if an instrument is payable to an identified person, negotiation requires transfer of possession of the instrument and its indorsement by the holder. If an instrument is payable to bearer, it may be negotiated by transfer of possession alone.

§ 3–202. Negotiation Subject to Rescission.

(a) Negotiation is effective even if obtained (i) from an infant, a corporation exceeding its powers, or a person without capacity, (ii) by fraud, duress, or mistake, or (iii) in breach of duty or as part of an illegal transaction.

(b) To the extent permitted by other law, negotiation may be rescinded or may be subject to other remedies, but those remedies may not be asserted against a subsequent holder in due course or a person paying the instrument in good faith and without knowledge of facts that are a basis for rescission or other remedy.

§ 3–203. Transfer of Instrument; Rights Acquired by Transfer.

(a) An instrument is transferred when it is delivered by a person other than its issuer for the purpose of giving to the person receiving delivery the right to enforce the instrument.

(b) Transfer of an instrument, whether or not the transfer is a negotiation, vests in the transferee any right of the transferor to enforce the instrument, including any right as a holder in due course, but the transferee cannot acquire rights of a holder in due course by a transfer, directly or indirectly, from a holder in due course if the transferee engaged in fraud or illegality affecting the instrument.

(c) Unless otherwise agreed, if an instrument is transferred for value and the transferee does not become a holder because of lack of indorsement by the transferor, the transferee has a specifically enforceable right to the unqualified indorsement of the transferor, but negotiation of the instrument does not occur until the indorsement is made.

(d) If a transferor purports to transfer less than the entire instrument, negotiation of the instrument does not occur. The transferee obtains no rights under this Article and has only the rights of a partial assignee.

§ 3–204. Indorsement.

(a) "Indorsement" means a signature, other than that of a signer as maker, drawer, or acceptor, that alone or accompanied by other words is made on an instrument for the purpose of (i) negotiating the instrument, (ii) restricting payment of the instrument, or (iii) incurring indorser's liability on the instrument, but regardless of the intent of the signer, a signature and its accompanying words is an indorsement unless the accompanying words, terms of the instrument, place of the signature, or other circumstances unambiguously indicate that the signature was made for a purpose other than indorsement. For the purpose of determining whether a signature is made on an instrument, a paper affixed to the instrument is a part of the instrument.

(b) "Indorser" means a person who makes an indorsement.

(c) For the purpose of determining whether the transferee of an instrument is a holder, an indorsement that transfers a security interest in the instrument is effective as an unqualified indorsement of the instrument.

(d) If an instrument is payable to a holder under a name that is not the name of the holder, indorsement may be made by the holder in the name stated in the instrument or in the holder's name or both, but signature in both names may be required by a person paying or taking the instrument for value or collection.

§ 3–205. Special Indorsement; Blank Indorsement; Anomalous Indorsement.

(a) If an indorsement is made by the holder of an instrument, whether payable to an identified person or payable to bearer, and the indorsement identifies a person to whom it makes the instrument payable, it is a "special indorsement." When specially indorsed, an instrument becomes payable to the identified person and may be negotiated only by the indorsement of that person. The principles stated in Section 3–110 apply to special indorsements.

(b) If an indorsement is made by the holder of an instrument and it is not a special indorsement, it is a "blank indorsement." When indorsed in blank, an instrument becomes payable to bearer and may be negotiated by transfer of possession alone until specially indorsed.

(c) The holder may convert a blank indorsement that consists only of a signature into a special indorsement by writing, above the signature of the indorser, words identifying the person to whom the instrument is made payable.

(d) "Anomalous indorsement" means an indorsement made by a person who is not the holder of the instrument. An anomalous indorsement does not affect the manner in which the instrument may be negotiated.

§ 3–206. Restrictive Indorsement.

(a) An indorsement limiting payment to a particular person or otherwise prohibiting further transfer or negotiation of the instrument is not effective to prevent further transfer or negotiation of the instrument.

(b) An indorsement stating a condition to the right of the indorsee to receive payment does not affect the right of the indorsee to enforce the instrument. A person paying the instrument or taking it for value or collection may disregard the condition, and the rights and liabilities of that person are not affected by whether the condition has been fulfilled.

(c) If an instrument bears an indorsement (i) described in Section 4–201(b), or (ii) in blank or to a particular bank using the words "for deposit," "for collection," or other words indicating a purpose of having the instrument collected by a bank for the indorser or for a particular account, the following rules apply:

- **(1)** A person, other than a bank, who purchases the instrument when so indorsed converts the instrument unless the amount paid for the instrument is received by the indorser or applied consistently with the indorsement.
- **(2)** A depositary bank that purchases the instrument or takes it for collection when so indorsed converts the instrument unless the amount paid by the bank with respect to the instrument is received by the indorser or applied consistently with the indorsement.
- **(3)** A payor bank that is also the depositary bank or that takes the instrument for immediate payment over the counter from a person other than a collecting bank converts the instrument unless the proceeds of the instrument are received by the indorser or applied consistently with the indorsement.
- **(4)** Except as otherwise provided in paragraph (3), a payor bank or intermediary bank may disregard the indorsement and is not liable if the proceeds of the instrument are not received by the indorser or applied consistently with the indorsement.

(d) Except for an indorsement covered by subsection (c), if an instrument bears an indorsement using words to the effect that payment is to be made to the indorsee as agent, trustee, or other fiduciary for the benefit of the indorser or another person, the following rules apply:

- **(1)** Unless there is notice of breach of fiduciary duty as provided in Section 3–307, a person who purchases the instrument from the indorsee or takes the instrument from the indorsee for collection or payment may pay the proceeds of payment or the value given for the instrument to the indorsee without regard to whether the indorsee violates a fiduciary duty to the indorser.
- **(2)** A subsequent transferee of the instrument or person who pays the instrument is neither given notice nor otherwise affected by the restriction in the indorsement unless the transferee or payor knows that the fiduciary dealt with the instrument or its proceeds in breach of fiduciary duty.

(e) The presence on an instrument of an indorsement to which this section applies does not prevent a purchaser of the instrument from becoming a holder in due course of the instrument unless the purchaser is a converter under subsection (c) or has notice or knowledge of breach of fiduciary duty as stated in subsection (d).

(f) In an action to enforce the obligation of a party to pay the instrument, the obligor has a defense if payment would violate an indorsement to which this section applies and the payment is not permitted by this section.

§ 3–207. Reacquisition. Reacquisition of an instrument occurs if it is transferred to a former holder, by negotiation or otherwise. A former holder who reacquires the instrument may cancel indorsements made after the reacquirer first became a holder of the instrument. If the cancellation causes the instrument to be payable to the reacquirer or to bearer, the reacquirer may negotiate the instrument. An indorser whose indorsement is canceled is discharged, and the discharge is effective against any subsequent holder.

Part 3: Enforcement of Instruments

§ 3–301. Person Entitled to Enforce Instrument. "Person entitled to enforce" an instrument means (i) the holder of the instrument, (ii) a nonholder in possession of the instrument who has the rights of a holder, or (iii) a person not in possession of the instrument who is entitled to enforce the instrument pursuant to Section 3–309 or 3–418(d). A person may be a person entitled to enforce the instrument even though the person is not the owner of the instrument or is in wrongful possession of the instrument.

§ 3–302. Holder in Due Course.

(a) Subject to subsection (c) and Section 3–106(d), "holder in due course" means the holder of an instrument if:

- **(1)** the instrument when issued or negotiated to the holder does not bear such apparent evidence of forgery or alteration or is not otherwise so irregular or incomplete as to call into question its authenticity; and
- **(2)** the holder took the instrument (i) for value, (ii) in good faith, (iii) without notice that the instrument is overdue or has been dishonored

or that there is an uncured default with respect to payment of another instrument issued as part of the same series, (iv) without notice that the instrument contains an unauthorized signature or has been altered, (v) without notice of any claim to the instrument described in Section 3–306, and (vi) without notice that any party has a defense or claim in recoupment described in Section 3–305(a).

(b) Notice of discharge of a party, other than discharge in an insolvency proceeding, is not notice of a defense under subsection (a), but discharge is effective against a person who became a holder in due course with notice of the discharge. Public filing or recording of a document does not of itself constitute notice of a defense, claim in recoupment, or claim to the instrument.

(c) Except to the extent a transferor or predecessor in interest has rights as a holder in due course, a person does not acquire rights of a holder in due course of an instrument taken (i) by legal process or by purchase in an execution, bankruptcy, or creditor's sale or similar proceeding, (ii) by purchase as part of a bulk transaction not in ordinary course of business of the transferor, or (iii) as the successor in interest to an estate or other organization.

(d) If, under Section 3–303(a)(1), the promise of performance that is the consideration for an instrument has been partially performed, the holder may assert rights as a holder in due course of the instrument only to the fraction of the amount payable under the instrument equal to the value of the partial performance divided by the value of the promised performance.

(e) If (i) the person entitled to enforce an instrument has only a security interest in the instrument and (ii) the person obliged to pay the instrument has a defense, claim in recoupment, or claim to the instrument that may be asserted against the person who granted the security interest, the person entitled to enforce the instrument may assert rights as a holder in due course only to an amount payable under the instrument which, at the time of enforcement of the instrument, does not exceed the amount of the unpaid obligation secured.

(f) To be effective, notice must be received at a time and in a manner that gives a reasonable opportunity to act on it.

(g) This section is subject to any law limiting status as a holder in due course in particular classes of transactions.

§ 3–303. Value and Consideration.

(a) An instrument is issued or transferred for value if:

(1) the instrument is issued or transferred for a promise of performance, to the extent the promise has been performed;

(2) the transferee acquires a security interest or other lien in the instrument other than a lien obtained by judicial proceeding;

(3) the instrument is issued or transferred as payment of, or as security for, an antecedent claim against any person, whether or not the claim is due;

(4) the instrument is issued or transferred in exchange for a negotiable instrument; or

(5) the instrument is issued or transferred in exchange for the incurring of an irrevocable obligation to a third party by the person taking the instrument.

(b) "Consideration" means any consideration sufficient to support a simple contract. The drawer or maker of an instrument has a defense if the instrument is issued without consideration. If an instrument is issued for a promise of performance, the issuer has a defense to the extent performance of the promise is due and the promise has not been performed. If an instrument is issued for value as stated in subsection (a), the instrument is also issued for consideration.

§ 3–304. Overdue Instrument.

(a) An instrument payable on demand becomes overdue at the earliest of the following times:

(1) on the day after the day demand for payment is duly made;

(2) if the instrument is a check, 90 days after its date; or

(3) if the instrument is not a check, when the instrument has been outstanding for a period of time after its date which is unreasonably long under the circumstances of the particular case in light of the nature of the instrument and usage of the trade.

(b) With respect to an instrument payable at a definite time the following rules apply:

(1) If the principal is payable in installments and a due date has not been accelerated, the instrument becomes overdue upon default under the instrument for nonpayment of an installment, and the instrument remains overdue until the default is cured.

(2) If the principal is not payable in installments and the due date has not been accelerated, the instrument becomes overdue on the day after the due date.
(3) If a due date with respect to principal has been accelerated, the instrument becomes overdue on the day after the accelerated due date.

(c) Unless the due date of principal has been accelerated, an instrument does not become overdue if there is default in payment of interest but no default in payment of principal.

§ 3–305. Defenses and Claims in Recoupment; Claims in Consumer Transactions.

(a) Except as otherwise provided in this section, the right to enforce the obligation of a party to pay an instrument is subject to the following:

(1) a defense of the obligor based on (i) infancy of the obligor to the extent it is a defense to a simple contract, (ii) duress, lack of legal capacity, or illegality of the transaction which, under other law, nullifies the obligation of the obligor, (iii) fraud that induced the obligor to sign the instrument with neither knowledge nor reasonable opportunity to learn of its character or its essential terms, or (iv) discharge of the obligor in insolvency proceedings;

(2) a defense of the obligor stated in another section of this Article or a defense of the obligor that would be available if the person entitled to enforce the instrument were enforcing a right to payment under a simple contract; and

(3) a claim in recoupment of the obligor against the original payee of the instrument if the claim arose from the transaction that gave rise to the instrument; but the claim of the obligor may be asserted against a transferee of the instrument only to reduce the amount owing on the instrument at the time the action is brought.

(b) The right of a holder in due course to enforce the obligation of a party to pay the instrument is subject to defenses of the obligor stated in subsection (a)(1), but is not subject to defenses of the obligor stated in subsection (a)(2) or claims in recoupment stated in subsection (a)(3) against a person other than the holder.

(c) Except as stated in subsection (d), in an action to enforce the obligation of a party to pay the instrument, the obligor may not assert against the person entitled to enforce the instrument a defense, claim in recoupment, or claim to the instrument (Section 3–306) of another person, but the other person's claim to the instrument may be asserted by the obligor if the other person is joined in the action and personally asserts the claim against the person entitled to enforce the instrument. An obligor is not obliged to pay the instrument if the person seeking enforcement of the instrument does not have rights of a holder in due course and the obligor proves that the instrument is a lost or stolen instrument.

(d) In an action to enforce the obligation of an accommodation party to pay an instrument, the accommodation party may assert against the person entitled to enforce the instrument any defense or claim in recoupment under subsection (a) that the accommodated party could assert against the person entitled to enforce the instrument, except the defenses of discharge in insolvency proceedings, infancy, and lack of legal capacity.

(e) In a consumer transaction, if law other than this article requires that an instrument include a statement to the effect that the rights of a holder or transferee are subject to a claim or defense that the issuer could assert against the original payee, and the instrument does not include such a statement:

(1) the instrument has the same effect as if the instrument included such a statement;

(2) the issuer may assert against the holder or transferee all claims and defenses that would have been available if the instrument included such a statement; and

(3) the extent to which claims may be asserted against the holder or transferee is determined as if the instrument included such a statement.

(f) This section is subject to law other than this article that establishes a different rule for consumer transactions.

Legislative Note: If a consumer protection law in this state addresses the same issue as subsection (g), it should be examined for consistency with subsection (g) and, if inconsistent, should be amended.

§ 3–306. Claims to an Instrument. A person taking an instrument, other than a person having rights of a holder in due course, is subject to a claim of a property or possessory right in the instrument or its proceeds, including a claim to rescind a negotiation and to recover the instrument or its proceeds. A person having rights of a holder in due course takes free of the claim to the instrument.

§ 3–307. Notice of Breach of Fiduciary Duty.

(a) In this section:
  (1) "Fiduciary" means an agent, trustee, partner, corporate officer or director, or other representative owing a fiduciary duty with respect to an instrument.
  (2) "Represented person" means the principal, beneficiary, partnership, corporation, or other person to whom the duty stated in paragraph (1) is owed.

(b) If (i) an instrument is taken from a fiduciary for payment or collection or for value, (ii) the taker has knowledge of the fiduciary status of the fiduciary, and (iii) the represented person makes a claim to the instrument or its proceeds on the basis that the transaction of the fiduciary is a breach of fiduciary duty, the following rules apply:
  (1) Notice of breach of fiduciary duty by the fiduciary is notice of the claim of the represented person.
  (2) In the case of an instrument payable to the represented person or the fiduciary as such, the taker has notice of the breach of fiduciary duty if the instrument is (i) taken in payment of or as security for a debt known by the taker to be the personal debt of the fiduciary, (ii) taken in a transaction known by the taker to be for the personal benefit of the fiduciary, or (iii) deposited to an account other than an account of the fiduciary, as such, or an account of the represented person.
  (3) If an instrument is issued by the represented person or the fiduciary as such, and made payable to the fiduciary personally, the taker does not have notice of the breach of fiduciary duty unless the taker knows of the breach of fiduciary duty.
  (4) If an instrument is issued by the represented person or the fiduciary as such, to the taker as payee, the taker has notice of the breach of fiduciary duty if the instrument is (i) taken in payment of or as security for a debt known by the taker to be the personal debt of the fiduciary, (ii) taken in a transaction known by the taker to be for the personal benefit of the fiduciary, or (iii) deposited to an account other than an account of the fiduciary, as such, or an account of the represented person.

§ 3–308. Proof of Signatures and Status as Holder in Due Course.

(a) In an action with respect to an instrument, the authenticity of, and authority to make, each signature on the instrument is admitted unless specifically denied in the pleadings. If the validity of a signature is denied in the pleadings, the burden of establishing validity is on the person claiming validity, but the signature is presumed to be authentic and authorized unless the action is to enforce the liability of the purported signer and the signer is dead or incompetent at the time of trial of the issue of validity of the signature. If an action to enforce the instrument is brought against a person as the undisclosed principal of a person who signed the instrument as a party to the instrument, the plaintiff has the burden of establishing that the defendant is liable on the instrument as a represented person under Section 3–402(a).

(b) If the validity of signatures is admitted or proved and there is compliance with subsection (a), a plaintiff producing the instrument is entitled to payment if the plaintiff proves entitlement to enforce the instrument under Section 3–301, unless the defendant proves a defense or claim in recoupment. If a defense or claim in recoupment is proved, the right to payment of the plaintiff is subject to the defense or claim, except to the extent the plaintiff proves that the plaintiff has rights of a holder in due course which are not subject to the defense or claim.

§ 3–309. Enforcement of Lost, Destroyed, or Stolen Instrument.

(a) A person not in possession of an instrument is entitled to enforce the instrument if:
  (1) the person seeking to enforce the instrument:
    (i) was entitled to enforce the instrument when loss of possession occurred; or
    (ii) has directly or indirectly acquired ownership of the instrument from a person who was entitled to enforce the instrument when loss of possession occurred;
  (2) the loss of possession was not the result of a transfer by the person or a lawful seizure; and
  (3) the person cannot reasonably obtain possession of the instrument because the instrument

was destroyed, its whereabouts cannot be determined, or it is in the wrongful possession of an unknown person or a person that cannot be found or is not amenable to service of process.

(b) A person seeking enforcement of an instrument under subsection (a) must prove the terms of the instrument and the person's right to enforce the instrument. If that proof is made, Section 3–308 applies to the case as if the person seeking enforcement had produced the instrument. The court may not enter judgment in favor of the person seeking enforcement unless it finds that the person required to pay the instrument is adequately protected against loss that might occur by reason of a claim by another person to enforce the instrument. Adequate protection may be provided by any reasonable means.

§ 3–310. Effect of Instrument on Obligation for Which Taken.

(a) Unless otherwise agreed, if a certified check, cashier's check, or teller's check is taken for an obligation, the obligation is discharged to the same extent discharge would result if an amount of money equal to the amount of the instrument were taken in payment of the obligation. Discharge of the obligation does not affect any liability that the obligor may have as an indorser of the instrument.

(b) Unless otherwise agreed and except as provided in subsection (a), if a note or an uncertified check is taken for an obligation, the obligation is suspended to the same extent the obligation would be discharged if an amount of money equal to the amount of the instrument were taken, and the following rules apply:

(1) In the case of an uncertified check, suspension of the obligation continues until dishonor of the check or until it is paid or certified. Payment or certification of the check results in discharge of the obligation to the extent of the amount of the check.

(2) In the case of a note, suspension of the obligation continues until dishonor of the note or until it is paid. Payment of the note results in discharge of the obligation to the extent of the payment.

(3) Except as provided in paragraph (4), if the check or note is dishonored and the obligee of the obligation for which the instrument was taken is the person entitled to enforce the instrument, the obligee may enforce either the instrument or the obligation. In the case of an instrument of a third person which is negotiated to the obligee by the obligor, discharge of the obligor on the instrument also discharges the obligation.

(4) If the person entitled to enforce the instrument taken for an obligation is a person other than the obligee, the obligee may not enforce the obligation to the extent the obligation is suspended. If the obligee is the person entitled to enforce the instrument but no longer has possession of it because it was lost, stolen, or destroyed, the obligation may not be enforced to the extent of the amount payable on the instrument, and to that extent the obligee's rights against the obligor are limited to enforcement of the instrument.

(c) If an instrument other than one described in subsection (a) or (b) is taken for an obligation, the effect is (i) that stated in subsection (a) if the instrument is one on which a bank is liable as maker or acceptor, or (ii) that stated in subsection (b) in any other case.

§ 3–311. Accord and Satisfaction by Use of Instrument.

(a) If a person against whom a claim is asserted proves that (i) that person in good faith tendered an instrument to the claimant as full satisfaction of the claim, (ii) the amount of the claim was unliquidated or subject to a bona fide dispute, and (iii) the claimant obtained payment of the instrument, the following subsections apply.

(b) Unless subsection (c) applies, the claim is discharged if the person against whom the claim is asserted proves that the instrument or an accompanying written communication contained a conspicuous statement to the effect that the instrument was tendered as full satisfaction of the claim.

(c) Subject to subsection (d), a claim is not discharged under subsection (b) if either of the following applies:

(1) The claimant, if an organization, proves that (i) within a reasonable time before the tender, the claimant sent a conspicuous statement to the person against whom the claim is asserted that communications concerning disputed debts, including an instrument tendered as full satisfaction of a debt, are to be sent to a designated person, office, or place, and (ii) the instrument or accompanying communication was not received by that designated person, office, or place.

(2) The claimant, whether or not an organization, proves that within 90 days after payment of the instrument, the claimant tendered repayment of the amount of the instrument to the person against whom the claim is asserted. This paragraph does not apply if the claimant is an organization that sent a statement complying with paragraph (1)(i).

(d) A claim is discharged if the person against whom the claim is asserted proves that within a reasonable time before collection of the instrument was initiated, the claimant, or an agent of the claimant having direct responsibility with respect to the disputed obligation, knew that the instrument was tendered in full satisfaction of the claim.

§ 3–312. Lost, Destroyed, or Stolen Cashier's Check, Teller's Check, or Certified Check.

(a) In this section:

(1) "Check" means a cashier's check, teller's check, or certified check.

(2) "Claimant" means a person who claims the right to receive the amount of a cashier's check, teller's check, or certified check that was lost, destroyed, or stolen.

(3) "Declaration of loss" means a statement, made in a record under penalty of perjury, to the effect that (i) the declarer lost possession of a check, (ii) the declarer is the drawer or payee of the check, in the case of a certified check, or the remitter or payee of the check, in the case of a cashier's check or teller's check, (iii) the loss of possession was not the result of a transfer by the declarer or a lawful seizure, and (iv) the declarer cannot reasonably obtain possession of the check because the check was destroyed, its whereabouts cannot be determined, or it is in the wrongful possession of an unknown person or a person that cannot be found or is not amenable to service of process.

(4) "Obligated bank" means the issuer of a cashier's check or teller's check or the acceptor of a certified check.

(b) A claimant may assert a claim to the amount of a check by a communication to the obligated bank describing the check with reasonable certainty and requesting payment of the amount of the check, if (i) the claimant is the drawer or payee of a certified check or the remitter or payee of a cashier's check or teller's check, (ii) the communication contains or is accompanied by a declaration of loss of the claimant with respect to the check, (iii) the communication is received at a time and in a manner affording the bank a reasonable time to act on it before the check is paid, and (iv) the claimant provides reasonable identification if requested by the obligated bank. Delivery of a declaration of loss is a warranty of the truth of the statements made in the declaration. If a claim is asserted in compliance with this subsection, the following rules apply:

(1) The claim becomes enforceable at the later of (i) the time the claim is asserted, or (ii) the 90th day following the date of the check, in the case of a cashier's check or teller's check, or the 90th day following the date of the acceptance, in the case of a certified check.

(2) Until the claim becomes enforceable, it has no legal effect and the obligated bank may pay the check or, in the case of a teller's check, may permit the drawee to pay the check. Payment to a person entitled to enforce the check discharges all liability of the obligated bank with respect to the check.

(3) If the claim becomes enforceable before the check is presented for payment, the obligated bank is not obliged to pay the check.

(4) When the claim becomes enforceable, the obligated bank becomes obliged to pay the amount of the check to the claimant if payment of the check has not been made to a person entitled to enforce the check. Subject to Section 4–302(a)(1), payment to the claimant discharges all liability of the obligated bank with respect to the check.

(c) If the obligated bank pays the amount of a check to a claimant under subsection (b)(4) and the check is presented for payment by a person having rights of a holder in due course, the claimant is obliged to (i) refund the payment to the obligated bank if the check is paid, or (ii) pay the amount of the check to the person having rights of a holder in due course if the check is dishonored.

(d) If a claimant has the right to assert a claim under subsection (b) and is also a person entitled to enforce a cashier's check, teller's check, or certified check which is lost, destroyed, or stolen, the claimant may assert rights with respect to the check either under this section or Section 3–309.

Part 4: Liability of Parties

§ 3–401. Signature.

(a) A person is not liable on an instrument unless (i) the person signed the instrument, or (ii) the person is represented by an agent or representative who signed the instrument and the signature is binding on the represented person under Section 3–402.

(b) A signature may be made (i) manually or by means of a device or machine, and (ii) by the use of any name, including a trade or assumed name, or by a word, mark, or symbol executed or adopted by a person with present intention to authenticate a writing.

§ 3–402. Signature by Representative.

(a) If a person acting, or purporting to act, as a representative signs an instrument by signing either the name of the represented person or the name of the signer, the represented person is bound by the signature to the same extent the represented person would be bound if the signature were on a simple contract. If the represented person is bound, the signature of the representative is the "authorized signature of the represented person" and the represented person is liable on the instrument, whether or not identified in the instrument.

(b) If a representative signs the name of the representative to an instrument and the signature is an authorized signature of the represented person, the following rules apply:

(1) If the form of the signature shows unambiguously that the signature is made on behalf of the represented person who is identified in the instrument, the representative is not liable on the instrument.

(2) Subject to subsection (c), if (i) the form of the signature does not show unambiguously that the signature is made in a representative capacity or (ii) the represented person is not identified in the instrument, the representative is liable on the instrument to a holder in due course that took the instrument without notice that the representative was not intended to be liable on the instrument. With respect to any other person, the representative is liable on the instrument unless the representative proves that the original parties did not intend the representative to be liable on the instrument.

(c) If a representative signs the name of the representative as drawer of a check without indication of the representative status and the check is payable from an account of the represented person who is identified on the check, the signer is not liable on the check if the signature is an authorized signature of the represented person.

§ 3–403. Unauthorized Signature.

(a) Unless otherwise provided in this Article or Article 4, an unauthorized signature is ineffective except as the signature of the unauthorized signer in favor of a person who in good faith pays the instrument or takes it for value. An unauthorized signature may be ratified for all purposes of this Article.

(b) If the signature of more than one person is required to constitute the authorized signature of an organization, the signature of the organization is unauthorized if one of the required signatures is lacking.

(c) The civil or criminal liability of a person who makes an unauthorized signature is not affected by any provision of this Article which makes the unauthorized signature effective for the purposes of this Article.

§ 3–404. Impostors; Fictitious Payees.

(a) If an impostor, by use of the mails or otherwise, induces the issuer of an instrument to issue the instrument to the impostor, or to a person acting in concert with the impostor, by impersonating the payee of the instrument or a person authorized to act for the payee, an indorsement of the instrument by any person in the name of the payee is effective as the indorsement of the payee in favor of a person who, in good faith, pays the instrument or takes it for value or for collection.

(b) If (i) a person whose intent determines to whom an instrument is payable (Section 3–110(a) or (b)) does not intend the person identified as payee to have any interest in the instrument, or (ii) the person identified as payee of an instrument is a fictitious person, the following rules apply until the instrument is negotiated by special indorsement:

(1) Any person in possession of the instrument is its holder.

(2) An indorsement by any person in the name of the payee stated in the instrument is effective as the indorsement of the payee in favor of a person who, in good faith, pays the instrument or takes it for value or for collection.

(c) Under subsection (a) or (b), an indorsement is made in the name of a payee if (i) it is made in a name substantially similar to that of the payee or (ii) the instrument, whether or not indorsed, is deposited in a depositary bank to an account in a name substantially similar to that of the payee.

(d) With respect to an instrument to which subsection (a) or (b) applies, if a person paying the instrument or taking it for value or for collection fails to exercise ordinary care in paying or taking the instrument and that failure substantially contributes to loss resulting from payment of the instrument, the person bearing the loss may recover from the person failing to exercise ordinary care to the extent the failure to exercise ordinary care contributed to the loss.

§ 3–405. Employer's Responsibility for Fraudulent Indorsement by Employee.

(a) In this section:

(1) "Employee" includes an independent contractor and employee of an independent contractor retained by the employer.

(2) "Fraudulent indorsement" means (i) in the case of an instrument payable to the employer, a forged indorsement purporting to be that of the employer, or (ii) in the case of an instrument with respect to which the employer is the issuer, a forged indorsement purporting to be that of the person identified as payee.

(3) "Responsibility" with respect to instruments means authority (i) to sign or indorse instruments on behalf of the employer, (ii) to process instruments received by the employer for bookkeeping purposes, for deposit to an account, or for other disposition, (iii) to prepare or process instruments for issue in the name of the employer, (iv) to supply information determining the names or addresses of payees of instruments to be issued in the name of the employer, (v) to control the disposition of instruments to be issued in the name of the employer, or (vi) to act otherwise with respect to instruments in a responsible capacity. "Responsibility" does not include authority that merely allows an employee to have access to instruments or blank or incomplete instrument forms that are being stored or transported or are part of incoming or outgoing mail, or similar access.

(b) For the purpose of determining the rights and liabilities of a person who, in good faith, pays an instrument or takes it for value or for collection, if an employer entrusted an employee with responsibility with respect to the instrument and the employee or a person acting in concert with the employee makes a fraudulent indorsement of the instrument, the indorsement is effective as the indorsement of the person to whom the instrument is payable if it is made in the name of that person. If the person paying the instrument or taking it for value or for collection fails to exercise ordinary care in paying or taking the instrument and that failure substantially contributes to loss resulting from the fraud, the person bearing the loss may recover from the person failing to exercise ordinary care to the extent the failure to exercise ordinary care contributed to the loss.

(c) Under subsection (b), an indorsement is made in the name of the person to whom an instrument is payable if (i) it is made in a name substantially similar to the name of that person or (ii) the instrument, whether or not indorsed, is deposited in a depositary bank to an account in a name substantially similar to the name of that person.

§ 3–406. Negligence Contributing to Forged Signature or Alteration of Instrument.

(a) A person whose failure to exercise ordinary care substantially contributes to an alteration of an instrument or to the making of a forged signature on an instrument is precluded from asserting the alteration or the forgery against a person who, in good faith, pays the instrument or takes it for value or for collection.

(b) Under subsection (a), if the person asserting the preclusion fails to exercise ordinary care in paying or taking the instrument and that failure substantially contributes to loss, the loss is allocated between the person precluded and the person asserting the preclusion according to the extent to which the failure of each to exercise ordinary care contributed to the loss.

(c) Under subsection (a), the burden of proving failure to exercise ordinary care is on the person asserting the preclusion. Under subsection (b), the burden of proving failure to exercise ordinary care is on the person precluded.

§ 3–407. Alteration.

(a) "Alteration" means (i) an unauthorized change in an instrument that purports to modify in any respect the obligation of a party, or (ii) an unauthorized addition of words or numbers or other change to an incomplete instrument relating to the obligation of a party.

(b) Except as provided in subsection (c), an alteration fraudulently made discharges a party whose obligation is affected by the alteration unless that party assents or is precluded from asserting the alteration. No other alteration discharges a party, and the instrument may be enforced according to its original terms.

(c) A payor bank or drawee paying a fraudulently altered instrument or a person taking it for value, in good faith and without notice of the alteration, may enforce rights with respect to the instrument (i) according to its original terms, or (ii) in the case of an incomplete instrument altered by unauthorized completion, according to its terms as completed.

§ 3–408. Drawee Not Liable on Unaccepted Draft. A check or other draft does not of itself operate as an assignment of funds in the hands of the drawee available for its payment, and the drawee is not liable on the instrument until the drawee accepts it.

§ 3–409. Acceptance of Draft; Certified Check.

(a) "Acceptance" means the drawee's signed agreement to pay a draft as presented. It must be written on the draft and may consist of the drawee's signature alone. Acceptance may be made at any time and becomes effective when notification pursuant to instructions is given or the accepted draft is delivered for the purpose of giving rights on the acceptance to any person.

(b) A draft may be accepted although it has not been signed by the drawer, is otherwise incomplete, is overdue, or has been dishonored.

(c) If a draft is payable at a fixed period after sight and the acceptor fails to date the acceptance, the holder may complete the acceptance by supplying a date in good faith.

(d) "Certified check" means a check accepted by the bank on which it is drawn. Acceptance may be made as stated in subsection (a) or by a writing on the check which indicates that the check is certified. The drawee of a check has no obligation to certify the check, and refusal to certify is not dishonor of the check.

§ 3–410. Acceptance Varying Draft.

(a) If the terms of a drawee's acceptance vary from the terms of the draft as presented, the holder may refuse the acceptance and treat the draft as dishonored. In that case, the drawee may cancel the acceptance.

(b) The terms of a draft are not varied by an acceptance to pay at a particular bank or place in the United States, unless the acceptance states that the draft is to be paid only at that bank or place.

(c) If the holder assents to an acceptance varying the terms of a draft, the obligation of each drawer and indorser that does not expressly assent to the acceptance is discharged.

§ 3–411. Refusal to Pay Cashier's Checks, Teller's Checks, and Certified Checks.

(a) In this section, "obligated bank" means the acceptor of a certified check or the issuer of a cashier's check or teller's check bought from the issuer.

(b) If the obligated bank wrongfully (i) refuses to pay a cashier's check or certified check, (ii) stops payment of a teller's check, or (iii) refuses to pay a dishonored teller's check, the person asserting the right to enforce the check is entitled to compensation for expenses and loss of interest resulting from the nonpayment and may recover consequential damages if the obligated bank refuses to pay after receiving notice of particular circumstances giving rise to the damages.

(c) Expenses or consequential damages under subsection (b) are not recoverable if the refusal of the obligated bank to pay occurs because (i) the bank suspends payments, (ii) the obligated bank asserts a claim or defense of the bank that it has reasonable grounds to believe is available against the person entitled to enforce the instrument, (iii) the obligated bank has a reasonable doubt whether the person demanding payment is the person entitled to enforce the instrument, or (iv) payment is prohibited by law.

§ 3–412. Obligation of Issuer of Note or Cashier's Check. The issuer of a note or cashier's check or other draft drawn on the drawer is obliged to pay the instrument (i) according to its terms at the time it was issued or, if not issued, at the time it first came into possession of a holder, or (ii) if the issuer signed an incomplete instrument, according to its terms when completed, to the extent stated in Sections 3–115 and 3–407. The obligation is owed to a person entitled to enforce the instrument or to an indorser who paid the instrument under Section 3–415.

§ 3–413. Obligation of Acceptor.

(a) The acceptor of a draft is obliged to pay the draft (i) according to its terms at the time it was accepted, even though the acceptance states that the draft is payable "as originally drawn" or equivalent terms, (ii) if the acceptance varies the terms of the draft, according to the terms of the draft as varied, or (iii) if the acceptance is of a draft that is an incomplete instrument, according to its terms when completed, to the extent stated in Sections 3–115 and 3–407. The obligation is owed to a person entitled to enforce the draft or to the drawer or an indorser who paid the draft under Section 3–414 or 3–415.

(b) If the certification of a check or other acceptance of a draft states the amount certified or accepted, the obligation of the acceptor is that amount. If (i) the certification or acceptance does not state an amount, (ii) the amount of the instrument is subsequently raised, and (iii) the instrument is then negotiated to a holder in due course, the obligation of the acceptor is the amount of the instrument at the time it was taken by the holder in due course.

§ 3–414. Obligation of Drawer.

(a) This section does not apply to cashier's checks or other drafts drawn on the drawer.

(b) If an unaccepted draft is dishonored, the drawer is obliged to pay the draft (i) according to its terms at the time it was issued or, if not issued, at the time it first came into possession of a holder, or (ii) if the drawer signed an incomplete instrument, according to its terms when completed, to the extent stated in Sections 3–115 and 3–407. The obligation is owed to a person entitled to enforce the draft or to an indorser who paid the draft under Section 3–415.

(c) If a draft is accepted by a bank, the drawer is discharged, regardless of when or by whom acceptance was obtained.

(d) If a draft is accepted and the acceptor is not a bank, the obligation of the drawer to pay the draft if the draft is dishonored by the acceptor is the same as the obligation of an indorser under Section 3–415(a) and (c).

(e) If a draft states that it is drawn "without recourse" or otherwise disclaims liability of the drawer to pay the draft, the drawer is not liable under subsection (b) to pay the draft if the draft is not a check. A disclaimer of the liability stated in subsection (b) is not effective if the draft is a check.

(f) If (i) a check is not presented for payment or given to a depositary bank for collection within 30 days after its date, (ii) the drawee suspends payments after expiration of the 30–day period without paying the check, and (iii) because of the suspension of payments, the drawer is deprived of funds maintained with the drawee to cover payment of the check, the drawer to the extent deprived of funds may discharge its obligation to pay the check by assigning to the person entitled to enforce the check the rights of the drawer against the drawee with respect to the funds.

§ 3–415. Obligation of Indorser.

(a) Subject to subsections (b), (c), (d), (e) and to Section 3–419(d), if an instrument is dishonored, an indorser is obliged to pay the amount due on the instrument (i) according to the terms of the instrument at the time it was indorsed, or (ii) if the indorser indorsed an incomplete instrument, according to its terms when completed, to the extent stated in Sections 3–115 and 3–407. The obligation of the indorser is owed to a person entitled to enforce the instrument or to a subsequent indorser who paid the instrument under this section.

(b) If an indorsement states that it is made "without recourse" or otherwise disclaims liability of the indorser, the indorser is not liable under subsection (a) to pay the instrument.

(c) If notice of dishonor of an instrument is required by Section 3–503 and notice of dishonor complying with that section is not given to an indorser, the liability of the indorser under subsection (a) is discharged.

(d) If a draft is accepted by a bank after an indorsement is made, the liability of the indorser under subsection (a) is discharged.

(e) If an indorser of a check is liable under subsection (a) and the check is not presented for payment, or given to a depositary bank for collection, within 30 days after the day the indorsement was made, the liability of the indorser under subsection (a) is discharged.

§ 3–416. Transfer Warranties.

(a) A person who transfers an instrument for consideration warrants to the transferee and, if the transfer is by indorsement, to any subsequent transferee that:

(1) the warrantor is a person entitled to enforce the instrument;

(2) all signatures on the instrument are authentic and authorized;

(3) the instrument has not been altered;

(4) the instrument is not subject to a defense or claim in recoupment of any party which can be asserted against the warrantor;

(5) the warrantor has no knowledge of any insolvency proceeding commenced with respect to the maker or acceptor or, in the case of an unaccepted draft, the drawer; and

(6) with respect to a remotely-created consumer item, that the person on whose account the item is drawn authorized the issuance of the item in the amount for which the item is drawn.

(b) A person to whom the warranties under subsection (a) are made and who took the instrument in good faith may recover from the warrantor as damages for breach of warranty an amount equal to the loss suffered as a result of the breach, but not more than the amount of the instrument plus expenses and loss of interest incurred as a result of the breach.

(c) The warranties stated in subsection (a) cannot be disclaimed with respect to checks. Unless notice of a claim for breach of warranty is given to the warrantor within 30 days after the claimant has reason to know of the breach and the identity of the warrantor, the liability of the warrantor under subsection (b) is discharged to the extent of any loss caused by the delay in giving notice of the claim.

(d) A [cause of action] for breach of warranty under this section accrues when the claimant has reason to know of the breach.

§ 3–417. Presentment Warranties.

(a) If an unaccepted draft is presented to the drawee for payment or acceptance and the drawee pays or accepts the draft, (i) the person obtaining payment or acceptance, at the time of presentment, and (ii) a previous transferor of the draft, at the time of transfer, warrant to the drawee making payment or accepting the draft in good faith that:

(1) the warrantor is, or was, at the time the warrantor transferred the draft, a person entitled to enforce the draft or authorized to obtain payment or acceptance of the draft on behalf of a person entitled to enforce the draft;

(2) the draft has not been altered;

(3) the warrantor has no knowledge that the signature of the drawer of the draft is unauthorized; and

(4) with respect to any remotely-created consumer item, that the person on whose account the item is drawn authorized the issuance of the item in the amount for which the item is drawn.

(b) A drawee making payment may recover from any warrantor damages for breach of warranty equal to the amount paid by the drawee less the amount the drawee received or is entitled to receive from the drawer because of the payment. In addition, the drawee is entitled to compensation for expenses and loss of interest resulting from the breach. The right of the drawee to recover damages under this subsection is not affected by any failure of the drawee to exercise ordinary care in making payment. If the drawee accepts the draft, breach of warranty is a defense to the obligation of the acceptor. If the acceptor makes payment with respect to the draft, the acceptor is entitled to recover from any warrantor for breach of warranty the amounts stated in this subsection.

(c) If a drawee asserts a claim for breach of warranty under subsection (a) based on an unauthorized indorsement of the draft or an alteration of the draft, the warrantor may defend by proving that the indorsement is effective under Section 3–404 or 3–405 or the drawer is precluded under Section 3–406 or 4–406 from asserting against the drawee the unauthorized indorsement or alteration.

(d) If (i) a dishonored draft is presented for payment to the drawer or an indorser or (ii) any other instrument is presented for payment to a party obliged to pay the instrument, and (iii) payment is received, the following rules apply:

(1) The person obtaining payment and a prior transferor of the instrument warrant to the person making payment in good faith that the warrantor is, or was, at the time the warrantor transferred the instrument, a person entitled to enforce the instrument or authorized to obtain payment on behalf of a person entitled to enforce the instrument.

(2) The person making payment may recover from any warrantor for breach of warranty an amount equal to the amount paid plus expenses and loss of interest resulting from the breach.

(e) The warranties stated in subsections (a) and (d) cannot be disclaimed with respect to checks. Unless notice of a claim for breach of warranty is given to the warrantor within 30 days after the claimant has reason to know of the breach and the identity of the warrantor, the liability of the warrantor under subsection (b) or (d) is discharged to the extent of any loss caused by the delay in giving notice of the claim.

(f) A [cause of action] for breach of warranty under this section accrues when the claimant has reason to know of the breach.

§ 3–418. Payment or Acceptance by Mistake.

(a) Except as provided in subsection (c), if the drawee of a draft pays or accepts the draft and the drawee acted on the mistaken belief that (i) payment of the draft had not been stopped pursuant to Section 4–403 or (ii) the signature of the drawer of the draft was authorized, the drawee may recover the amount of the draft from the person to whom or for whose benefit payment was made or, in the case of acceptance, may revoke the acceptance. Rights of the drawee under this subsection are not affected by failure of the drawee to exercise ordinary care in paying or accepting the draft.

(b) Except as provided in subsection (c), if an instrument has been paid or accepted by mistake and the case is not covered by subsection (a), the person paying or accepting may, to the extent permitted by the law governing mistake and restitution, (i) recover the payment from the person to whom or for whose benefit payment was made or (ii) in the case of acceptance, may revoke the acceptance.

(c) The remedies provided by subsection (a) or (b) may not be asserted against a person who took the instrument in good faith and for value or who in good faith changed position in reliance on the payment or acceptance. This subsection does not limit remedies provided by Section 3–417 or 4–407.

(d) Notwithstanding Section 4–215, if an instrument is paid or accepted by mistake and the payor or acceptor recovers payment or revokes acceptance under subsection (a) or (b), the instrument is deemed not to have been paid or accepted and is treated as dishonored, and the person from whom payment is recovered has rights as a person entitled to enforce the dishonored instrument.

§ 3–419. Instruments Signed for Accommodation.

(a) If an instrument is issued for value given for the benefit of a party to the instrument ("accommodated party") and another party to the instrument ("accommodation party") signs the instrument for the purpose of incurring liability on the instrument without being a direct beneficiary of the value given for the instrument, the instrument is signed by the accommodation party "for accommodation."

(b) An accommodation party may sign the instrument as maker, drawer, acceptor, or indorser and, subject to subsection (d), is obliged to pay the instrument in the capacity in which the accommodation party signs. The obligation of an accommodation party may be enforced notwithstanding any statute of frauds and whether or not the accommodation party receives consideration for the accommodation.

(c) A person signing an instrument is presumed to be an accommodation party and there is notice that the instrument is signed for accommodation if the signature is an anomalous indorsement or is accompanied by words indicating that the signer is acting as surety or guarantor with respect to the obligation of another party to the instrument. Except as provided in Section 3–605, the obligation of an accommodation party to pay the instrument is not affected by the fact that the person enforcing the obligation had notice when the instrument was taken by that person that the accommodation party signed the instrument for accommodation.

(d) If the signature of a party to an instrument is accompanied by words indicating unambiguously that the party is guaranteeing collection rather than payment of the obligation of another party to the instrument, the signer is obliged to pay the amount due on the instrument to a person entitled to enforce the instrument only if (i) execution of judgment against the other party has been returned unsatisfied, (ii) the other party is insolvent or in an insolvency proceeding, (iii) the other party cannot be served with process, or (iv) it is otherwise apparent that payment cannot be obtained from the other party.

(e) If the signature of a party to an instrument is accompanied by words indicating that the party guarantees payment or the signer signs the instrument as an accommodation party in some other manner that does not unambiguously indicate an intention to guarantee collection rather than payment, the signer is obliged to pay the amount due on the instrument to a person entitled to enforce the instrument in the same circumstances as the accommodated party would be obliged, without prior resort to the accommodated party by the person entitled to enforce the instrument.

(f) An accommodation party who pays the instrument is entitled to reimbursement from the accommodated party and is entitled to enforce the instrument against the accommodated party. In proper circumstances, an accommodation party may obtain relief that requires the accommodated party to perform its obligations on the instrument. An accommodated party that pays the instrument has no right of recourse against, and is not entitled to contribution from, an accommodation party.

§ 3–420. Conversion of Instrument.

(a) The law applicable to conversion of personal property applies to instruments. An instrument is also converted if it is taken by transfer, other than a negotiation, from a person not entitled to enforce the instrument or a bank makes or obtains payment with respect to the instrument for a person not entitled to enforce the instrument or receive payment. An action for conversion of an instrument may not be brought by (i) the issuer or acceptor of the instrument or (ii) a payee or indorsee who did not receive delivery of the instrument either directly or through delivery to an agent or a co-payee.

(b) In an action under subsection (a), the measure of liability is presumed to be the amount payable on the instrument, but recovery may not exceed the amount of the plaintiff's interest in the instrument.

(c) A representative, other than a depositary bank, who has in good faith dealt with an instrument or its proceeds on behalf of one who was not the person entitled to enforce the instrument is not liable in conversion to that person beyond the amount of any proceeds that it has not paid out.

Part 5: Dishonor

§ 3–501. Presentment.

(a) "Presentment" means a demand made by or on behalf of a person entitled to enforce an instrument (i) to pay the instrument made to the drawee or a party obliged to pay the instrument or, in the case of a note or accepted draft payable at a bank, to the bank, or (ii) to accept a draft made to the drawee.

(b) The following rules are subject to Article 4, agreement of the parties, and clearing-house rules and the like:

(1) Presentment may be made at the place of payment of the instrument and must be made at the place of payment if the instrument is payable at a bank in the United States; may be made by any commercially reasonable means, including an oral, written, or electronic communication; is effective when the demand for payment or acceptance is received by the person to whom presentment is made; and is effective if made to any one of two or more makers, acceptors, drawees, or other payors.

(2) Upon demand of the person to whom presentment is made, the person making presentment must (i) exhibit the instrument, (ii) give reasonable identification and, if presentment is made on behalf of another person, reasonable evidence of authority to do so, and (iii) sign a receipt on the instrument for any payment made or surrender the instrument if full payment is made.

(3) Without dishonoring the instrument, the party to whom presentment is made may (i) return the instrument for lack of a necessary indorsement, or (ii) refuse payment or acceptance for failure of the presentment to comply with the terms of the instrument, an agreement of the parties, or other applicable law or rule.

(4) The party to whom presentment is made may treat presentment as occurring on the next business day after the day of presentment if the party to whom presentment is made has established a cut-off hour not earlier than 2 p.m. for the receipt and processing of instruments presented for payment or acceptance and presentment is made after the cut-off hour.

§ 3–502. Dishonor.

(a) Dishonor of a note is governed by the following rules:

(1) If the note is payable on demand, the note is dishonored if presentment is duly made to the maker and the note is not paid on the day of presentment.

(2) If the note is not payable on demand and is payable at or through a bank or the terms of the note require presentment, the note is dishonored if presentment is duly made and the note is not paid on the day it becomes payable or the day of presentment, whichever is later.

(3) If the note is not payable on demand and paragraph (2) does not apply, the note is dishonored if it is not paid on the day it becomes payable.

(b) Dishonor of an unaccepted draft other than a documentary draft is governed by the following rules:

(1) If a check is duly presented for payment to the payor bank otherwise than for immediate payment over the counter, the check is dishonored if the payor bank makes timely return of the check or sends timely notice of dishonor or nonpayment under Section 4–301 or 4–302, or becomes accountable for the amount of the check under Section 4–302.

(2) If a draft is payable on demand and paragraph (1) does not apply, the draft is dishonored if presentment for payment is duly made to the drawee and the draft is not paid on the day of presentment.

(3) If a draft is payable on a date stated in the draft, the draft is dishonored if (i) presentment for payment is duly made to the drawee and payment is not made on the day the draft becomes payable or the day of presentment, whichever is later, or (ii) presentment for acceptance is duly made before the day the draft becomes payable and the draft is not accepted on the day of presentment.

(4) If a draft is payable on elapse of a period of time after sight or acceptance, the draft is dishonored if presentment for acceptance is duly made and the draft is not accepted on the day of presentment.

(c) Dishonor of an unaccepted documentary draft occurs according to the rules stated in subsection (b)(2), (3), and (4), except that payment or acceptance may be delayed without dishonor until no later than the close of the third business day of the drawee following the day on which payment or acceptance is required by those paragraphs.

(d) Dishonor of an accepted draft is governed by the following rules:

(1) If the draft is payable on demand, the draft is dishonored if presentment for payment is duly made to the acceptor and the draft is not paid on the day of presentment.

(2) If the draft is not payable on demand, the draft is dishonored if presentment for payment is duly made to the acceptor and payment is not made on the day it becomes payable or the day of presentment, whichever is later.

(e) In any case in which presentment is otherwise required for dishonor under this section and presentment is excused under Section 3–504, dishonor occurs without presentment if the instrument is not duly accepted or paid.

(f) If a draft is dishonored because timely acceptance of the draft was not made and the person entitled to demand acceptance consents to a late acceptance, from the time of acceptance the draft is treated as never having been dishonored.

§ 3–503. Notice of Dishonor.

(a) The obligation of an indorser stated in Section 3–415(a) and the obligation of a drawer stated in Section 3–414(d) may not be enforced unless (i) the indorser or drawer is given notice of dishonor of the instrument complying with this section or (ii) notice of dishonor is excused under Section 3–504(b).

(b) Notice of dishonor may be given by any person; may be given by any commercially reasonable means, including an oral, written, or electronic communication; and is sufficient if it reasonably identifies the instrument and indicates that the instrument has been dishonored or has not been paid or accepted. Return of an instrument given to a bank for collection is sufficient notice of dishonor.

(c) Subject to Section 3–504(c), with respect to an instrument taken for collection by a collecting bank, notice of dishonor must be given (i) by the bank before midnight of the next banking day following the banking day on which the bank receives notice of dishonor of the instrument, or (ii) by any other person within 30 days following the day on which the person receives notice of dishonor. With respect to any other instrument, notice of dishonor must be given within 30 days following the day on which dishonor occurs.

§ 3–504. Excused Presentment and Notice of Dishonor.

(a) Presentment for payment or acceptance of an instrument is excused if (i) the person entitled to present the instrument cannot with reasonable diligence make presentment, (ii) the maker or acceptor has repudiated an obligation to pay the instrument or is dead or in insolvency proceedings, (iii) by the terms of the instrument presentment is not necessary to enforce the obligation of indorsers or the drawer, (iv) the drawer or indorser whose obligation is being enforced has waived presentment or otherwise has no reason to expect or right to require that the instrument be paid or accepted, or (v) the drawer instructed the drawee not to pay or accept the draft or the drawee was not obligated to the drawer to pay the draft.

(b) Notice of dishonor is excused if (i) by the terms of the instrument notice of dishonor is not necessary to enforce the obligation of a party to pay the instrument, or (ii) the party whose obligation is being enforced waived notice of dishonor. A waiver of presentment is also a waiver of notice of dishonor.

(c) Delay in giving notice of dishonor is excused if the delay was caused by circumstances beyond the control of the person giving the notice and the person giving the notice exercised reasonable diligence after the cause of the delay ceased to operate.

§ 3–505. Evidence of Dishonor.

(a) The following are admissible as evidence and create a presumption of dishonor and of any notice of dishonor stated:

(1) a document regular in form as provided in subsection (b) which purports to be a protest;

(2) a purported stamp or writing of the drawee, payor bank, or presenting bank on or accompanying the instrument stating that acceptance or payment has been refused unless reasons for the refusal are stated and the reasons are not consistent with dishonor;

(3) a book or record of the drawee, payor bank, or collecting bank, kept in the usual course of business which shows dishonor, even if there is no evidence of who made the entry.

(b) A protest is a certificate of dishonor made by a United States consul or vice consul, or a notary public or other person authorized to administer oaths by the law of the place where dishonor occurs. It may be made upon information satisfactory to that person. The protest must identify the instrument and certify either that presentment has been made or, if not made, the reason why it was not made, and that the instrument has been dishonored by nonacceptance or nonpayment. The protest may also certify that notice of dishonor has been given to some or all parties.

Part 6: Discharge and Payment

§ 3–601. Discharge and Effect of Discharge.

(a) The obligation of a party to pay the instrument is discharged as stated in this Article or by an act or agreement with the party which would discharge an obligation to pay money under a simple contract.

(b) Discharge of the obligation of a party is not effective against a person acquiring rights of a holder in due course of the instrument without notice of the discharge.

§ 3–602. Payment.

(a) Subject to subsection (e), an instrument is paid to the extent payment is made by or on behalf of a party obliged to pay the instrument, and to a person entitled to enforce the instrument.

(b) Subject to subsection (e), a note is paid to the extent payment is made by or on behalf of a party obliged to pay the note to a person that formerly was entitled to enforce the note only if at the time of the payment the party obliged to pay has not received adequate notification that the note has been transferred and that payment is to be made to the transferee. A notification is adequate only if it is signed by the transferor or the transferee; reasonably identifies the transferred note; and provides an address at which payments subsequently are to be made. Upon request, a transferee shall seasonably furnish reasonable proof that the note has been transferred. Unless the transferee complies with the request, a payment to the person that formerly was entitled to enforce the note is effective for purposes of subsection (c) even if the party obliged to pay the note has received a notification under this paragraph.

(c) Subject to subsection (e), to the extent of a payment under subsections (a) and (b), the obligation of the party obliged to pay the instrument is discharged even though payment is made with knowledge of a claim to the instrument under Section 3–306 by another person.

(d) Subject to subsection (e), a transferee, or any party that has acquired rights in the instrument directly or indirectly from a transferee, including any such party that has rights as a holder in due course, is deemed to have notice of any payment that is made under subsection (b) after the date that the note is transferred to the transferee but before the party obliged to pay the note receives adequate notification of the transfer.

(e) The obligation of a party to pay the instrument is not discharged under subsections (a) through (d) if:

(1) a claim to the instrument under Section 3–306 is enforceable against the party receiving payment and (i) payment is made with knowledge by the payor that payment is prohibited by injunction or similar process of a court of competent jurisdiction, or (ii) in the case of an instrument other than a cashier's check, teller's check, or certified check, the party making payment accepted, from the person having a claim to the instrument, indemnity against loss resulting from refusal to pay the person entitled to enforce the instrument; or

(2) the person making payment knows that the instrument is a stolen instrument and pays a person it knows is in wrongful possession of the instrument.

(f) As used in this section, "signed," with respect to a record that is not a writing, includes the attachment to or logical association with the record of an electronic symbol, sound, or process with the present intent to adopt or accept the record.

§ 3–603. Tender of Payment.

(a) If tender of payment of an obligation to pay an instrument is made to a person entitled to enforce the instrument, the effect of tender is governed by principles of law applicable to tender of payment under a simple contract.

(b) If tender of payment of an obligation to pay an instrument is made to a person entitled to enforce the instrument and the tender is refused, there is discharge, to the extent of the amount of the tender, of the obligation of an indorser or accommodation party having a right of recourse with respect to the obligation to which the tender relates.

(c) If tender of payment of an amount due on an instrument is made to a person entitled to enforce the instrument, the obligation of the obligor to pay interest after the due date on the amount tendered is discharged. If presentment is required with respect to an instrument and the obligor is able and ready to pay on the due date at every place of payment stated in the instrument, the obligor is deemed to have made tender of payment on the due date to the person entitled to enforce the instrument.

§ 3–604. Discharge by Cancellation or Renunciation.

(a) A person entitled to enforce an instrument, with or without consideration, may discharge the obligation of a party to pay the instrument (i) by an intentional voluntary act, such as surrender of the instrument to the party, destruction, mutilation, or cancellation of the instrument, cancellation or striking out of the partyís signature, or the addition of words to the instrument indicating discharge, or (ii) by agreeing not to sue or otherwise renouncing rights against the party by a signed record.

(b) Cancellation or striking out of an indorsement pursuant to subsection (a) does not affect the status and rights of a party derived from the indorsement.

(c) In this section, "signed," with respect to a record that is not a writing, includes the attachment to or logical association with the record of an electronic symbol, sound, or process with the present intent to adopt or accept the record.

§ 3–605. Discharge of Secondary Obligors.

(a) If a person entitled to enforce an instrument releases the obligation of a principal obligor in whole or in part, and another party to the instrument is a secondary obligor with respect to the obligation of that principal obligor, the following rules apply:

(1) Any obligations of the principal obligor to the secondary obligor with respect to any previous payment by the secondary obligor are not affected. Unless the terms of the release preserve the secondary obligor's recourse, the principal obligor is discharged, to the extent of the release, from any other duties to the secondary obligor under this article.

(2) Unless the terms of the release provide that the person entitled to enforce the instrument retains the right to enforce the instrument against the secondary obligor, the secondary obligor is discharged to the same extent as the principal obligor from any unperformed portion of its obligation on the instrument. If the instrument is a check and the obligation of the secondary obligor is based on an indorsement of the check, the secondary obligor is discharged without regard to the language or circumstances of the discharge or other release.

(3) If the secondary obligor is not discharged under paragraph (2), the secondary obligor is discharged to the extent of the value of the consideration for the release, and to the extent that the release would otherwise cause the secondary obligor a loss.

(b) If a person entitled to enforce an instrument grants a principal obligor an extension of the time at which one or more payments are due on the instrument and another party to the instrument is a secondary obligor with respect to the obligation of that principal obligor, the following rules apply:

(1) Any obligations of the principal obligor to the secondary obligor with respect to any previous payment by the secondary obligor are not affected. Unless the terms of the extension preserve the secondary obligor's recourse, the extension correspondingly extends the time for performance of any other duties owed to the secondary obligor by the principal obligor under this article.

(2) The secondary obligor is discharged to the extent that the extension would otherwise cause the secondary obligor a loss.

(3) To the extent that the secondary obligor is not discharged under paragraph (2), the secondary obligor may perform its obligations to a person entitled to enforce the instrument as if the time for payment had not been extended or, unless the terms of the extension provide that the person entitled to enforce the instrument retains the right to enforce the instrument against the secondary obligor as if the time for payment had not been extended, treat the time for performance of its obligations as having been extended correspondingly.

(c) If a person entitled to enforce an instrument agrees, with or without consideration, to a modification of the obligation of a principal obligor other than a complete or partial release or an extension of the due date and another party to the instrument is a secondary obligor with respect to the obligation of that principal obligor, the following rules apply:

(1) Any obligations of the principal obligor to the secondary obligor with respect to any previous payment by the secondary obligor are not affected. The modification correspondingly modifies any other duties owed to the secondary obligor by the principal obligor under this article.

(2) The secondary obligor is discharged from any unperformed portion of its obligation to the extent that the modification would otherwise cause the secondary obligor a loss.

(3) To the extent that the secondary obligor is not discharged under paragraph (2), the secondary obligor may satisfy its obligation on the instrument as if the modification had not occurred, or treat its obligation on the instrument as having been modified correspondingly.

(d) If the obligation of a principal obligor is secured by an interest in collateral, another party to the instrument is a secondary obligor with respect to that obligation, and a person entitled to enforce the instrument impairs the value of the interest in collateral, the obligation of the secondary obligor is discharged to the extent of the impairment. The value of an interest in collateral is impaired to the extent the value of the interest is reduced to an amount less than the amount of the recourse of the secondary obligor, or the reduction in value of the interest causes an increase in the amount by which the amount of the recourse exceeds the value of the interest. For purposes of this subsection, impairing the value of an interest in collateral includes failure to obtain or maintain perfection or recordation of the interest in collateral, release of collateral without substitution of collateral of equal value or equivalent reduction of the underlying obligation, failure to perform a duty to preserve the value of collateral owed, under Article 9 or other law, to a debtor or other person secondarily liable, and failure to comply with applicable law in disposing of or otherwise enforcing the interest in collateral.

(e) A secondary obligor is not discharged under subsections (a)(3), (b), (c), or (d) unless the person entitled to enforce the instrument knows that the person is a secondary obligor or has notice under Section 3–419(c) that the instrument was signed for accommodation.

(f) A secondary obligor is not discharged under this section if the secondary obligor consents to the event or conduct that is the basis of the discharge, or the instrument or a separate agreement of the party provides for waiver of discharge under this section specifically or by general language indicating that parties waive defenses based on suretyship or impairment of collateral. Unless the circumstances indicate otherwise, consent by the principal obligor to an act that would lead to a discharge under this section constitutes consent to that act by the secondary obligor if the secondary obligor controls the principal obligor or deals with the person entitled to enforce the instrument on behalf of the principal obligor.

(g) A release or extension preserves a secondary obligorís recourse if the terms of the release or extension provide that:

(1) the person entitled to enforce the instrument retains the right to enforce the instrument against the secondary obligor; and

(2) the recourse of the secondary obligor continues as if the release or extension had not been granted.

(h) Except as otherwise provided in subsection (i), a secondary obligor asserting discharge under this section has the burden of persuasion both with respect to the occurrence of the acts alleged to harm the secondary obligor and loss or prejudice caused by those acts.

(i) If the secondary obligor demonstrates prejudice caused by an impairment of its recourse, and the circumstances of the case indicate that the amount of loss is not reasonably susceptible of calculation or requires proof of facts that are not ascertainable, it is presumed that the act impairing recourse caused a loss or impairment equal to the liability of the secondary obligor on the instrument. In that event, the burden of persuasion as to any lesser amount of the loss is on the person entitled to enforce the instrument.

Appendix C

TITLE VII OF THE CIVIL RIGHTS ACT OF 1964

The U.S. Equal Employment Opportunity Commission

An Act

To enforce the constitutional right to vote, to confer jurisdiction upon the district courts of the United States to provide injunctive relief against discrimination in public accommodations, to authorize the attorney General to institute suits to protect constitutional rights in public facilities and public education, to extend the Commission on Civil Rights, to prevent discrimination in federally assisted programs, to establish a Commission on Equal Employment Opportunity, and for other purposes. Be it enacted by the Senate and House of Representatives of the United States of America in Congress assembled, That this Act may be cited as the "Civil Rights Act of 1964".

***

DEFINITIONS

SEC. 2000e. *[Section 701]*

For the purposes of this subchapter-

(a) The term "person" includes one or more individuals, governments, governmental agencies, political subdivisions, labor unions, partnerships, associations, corporations, legal representatives, mutual companies, joint stock companies, trusts, unincorporated organizations, trustees, trustees in cases under title 11 *[bankruptcy]*, or receivers.

(b) The term "employer" means a person engaged in an industry affecting commerce who has fifteen or more employees for each working day in each of twenty or more calendar weeks in the current or preceding calendar year, and any agent of such a person, but such term does not include (1) the United States, a corporation wholly owned by the Government of the United States, an Indian tribe, or any department or agency of the District of Columbia subject by statute to procedures of the competitive service (as defined in section 2102 of title 5 *[of the United States Code]*), or (2) a bona fide private membership club (other than a labor organization) which is exempt from taxation under section 501(c) of title 26 *[the Internal Revenue Code of 1954]*, except that during the first year after March 24, 1972 *[the date of enactment of the Equal Employment Opportunity Act of 1972]*, persons having fewer than twenty five employees (and their agents) shall not be considered employers.

(c) The term "employment agency" means any person regularly undertaking with or without compensation to procure employees for an employer or to procure for employees opportunities to work for an employer and includes an agent of such a person.

(d) The term "labor organization" means a labor organization engaged in an industry affecting commerce, and any agent of such an organization, and includes any organization of any kind, any agency, or employee representation committee, group, association, or plan so engaged in which employees participate and which exists for the purpose, in whole or in part, of dealing with employers concerning grievances, labor disputes, wages, rates of pay, hours, or other terms or conditions of employment, and any conference, general committee, joint or system board, or joint council so engaged which is subordinate to a national or international labor organization.

(e) A labor organization shall be deemed to be engaged in an industry affecting commerce if (1) it maintains or operates a hiring hall or hiring office which procures employees for an employer or procures for employees opportunities to work for an employer, or (2) the number of its members (or, where it is a labor organization composed of other labor organizations or their representatives, if the aggregate number of the members of such other labor organization) is (A) twenty five or more during the first year after March 24, 1972 *[the date of enactment of the Equal Employment Opportunity Act of 1972]*, or (B) fifteen or more thereafter, and such labor organization-

(1) is the certified representative of employees under the provisions of the National Labor Relations Act, as amended *[29 U.S.C. 151 et seq.]*, or the Railway Labor Act, as amended *[45 U.S.C. 151 et seq.]*;

(2) although not certified, is a national or international labor organization or a local labor organization recognized or acting as the representative of employees

of an employer or employers engaged in an industry affecting commerce; or

(3) has chartered a local labor organization or subsidiary body which is representing or actively seeking to represent employees of employers within the meaning of paragraph (1) or (2); or

(4) has been chartered by a labor organization representing or actively seeking to represent employees within the meaning of paragraph (1) or (2) as the local or subordinate body through which such employees may enjoy membership or become affiliated with such labor organization; or

(5) is a conference, general committee, joint or system board, or joint council subordinate to a national or international labor organization, which includes a labor organization engaged in an industry affecting commerce within the meaning of any of the preceding paragraphs of this subsection.

(f) The term "employee" means an individual employed by an employer, except that the term "employee" shall not include any person elected to public office in any State or political subdivision of any State by the qualified voters thereof, or any person chosen by such officer to be on such officer's personal staff, or an appointee on the policy making level or an immediate adviser with respect to the exercise of the constitutional or legal powers of the office. The exemption set forth in the preceding sentence shall not include employees subject to the civil service laws of a State government, governmental agency or political subdivision. **With respect to employment in a foreign country, such term includes an individual who is a citizen of the United States.**

(g) The term "commerce" means trade, traffic, commerce, transportation, transmission, or communication among the several States; or between a State and any place outside thereof; or within the District of Columbia, or a possession of the United States; or between points in the same State but through a point outside thereof.

(h) The term "industry affecting commerce" means any activity, business, or industry in commerce or in which a labor dispute would hinder or obstruct commerce or the free flow of commerce and includes any activity or industry "affecting commerce" within the meaning of the Labor Management Reporting and Disclosure Act of 1959 *[29 U.S.C. 401 et seq.]*, and further includes any governmental industry, business, or activity.

(i) The term "State" includes a State of the United States, the District of Columbia, Puerto Rico, the Virgin Islands, American Samoa, Guam, Wake Island, the Canal Zone, and Outer Continental Shelf lands defined in the Outer Continental Shelf Lands Act *[43 U.S.C. 1331 et seq.]*.

(j) The term "religion" includes all aspects of religious observance and practice, as well as belief, unless an employer demonstrates that he is unable to reasonably accommodate to an employee's or prospective employee's religious observance or practice without undue hardship on the conduct of the employer's business.

(k) The terms "because of sex" or "on the basis of sex" include, but are not limited to, because of or on the basis of pregnancy, childbirth, or related medical conditions; and women affected by pregnancy, childbirth, or related medical conditions shall be treated the same for all employment related purposes, including receipt of benefits under fringe benefit programs, as other persons not so affected but similar in their ability or inability to work, and nothing in section 2000e-2(h) of this title *[section 703(h)]* shall be interpreted to permit otherwise. This subsection shall not require an employer to pay for health insurance benefits for abortion, except where the life of the mother would be endangered if the fetus were carried to term, or except where medical complications have arisen from an abortion: Provided, That nothing herein shall preclude an employer from providing abortion benefits or otherwise affect bargaining agreements in regard to abortion.

(l) The term "complaining party" means the Commission, the Attorney General, or a person who may bring an action or proceeding under this subchapter.

(m) The term "demonstrates" means meets the burdens of production and persuasion.

(n) The term "respondent" means an employer, employment agency, labor organization, joint labor management committee controlling apprenticeship or other training or retraining program, including an on the job training program, or Federal entity subject to section 2000e-16 of this title.

EXEMPTION

SEC. 2000e-1. *[Section 702]*

(a) This subchapter shall not apply to an employer with respect to the employment of aliens outside any State, or to a religious corporation, association, educational institution, or society with respect to the employment of individuals of a particular religion to perform work connected with the carrying on by such corporation, association, educational institution, or society of its activities.

(b) It shall not be unlawful under section 2000e-2 or 2000e-3 of this title *[section 703 or 704]* for an employer (or a corporation controlled by an employer), labor organization, employment agency, or joint labor management committee controlling apprenticeship or other training or retraining (including on the job training programs) to take any action otherwise prohibited by such section, with respect to an employee in a workplace in a foreign country if compliance with such section would cause such employer (or such corporation), such organization, such agency, or such committee to violate the law of the foreign country in which such workplace is located.

(c) (1) If an employer controls a corporation whose place of incorporation is a foreign country, any practice prohibited by section 2000e-2 or 2000e-3 of this title *[section 703 or 704]* engaged in by such corporation shall be presumed to be engaged in by such employer.

(2) Sections 2000e-2 and 2000e-3 of this title *[sections 703 and 704]* shall not apply with respect to the foreign operations of an employer that is a foreign person not controlled by an American employer.

(3) For purposes of this subsection, the determination of whether an employer controls a corporation shall be based on-

(A) the interrelation of operations;

(B) the common management;

(C) the centralized control of labor relations; and

(D) the common ownership or financial control, of the employer and the corporation.

UNLAWFUL EMPLOYMENT PRACTICES

SEC. 2000e-2. *[Section 703]*

(a) It shall be an unlawful employment practice for an employer-

(1) to fail or refuse to hire or to discharge any individual, or otherwise to discriminate against any individual with respect to his compensation, terms, conditions, or privileges of employment, because of such individual's race, color, religion, sex, or national origin; or

(2) to limit, segregate, or classify his employees or applicants for employment in any way which would deprive or tend to deprive any individual of employment opportunities or otherwise adversely affect his status as an employee, because of such individual's race, color, religion, sex, or national origin.

(b) It shall be an unlawful employment practice for an employment agency to fail or refuse to refer for employment, or otherwise to discriminate against, any individual because of his race, color, religion, sex, or national origin, or to classify or refer for employment any individual on the basis of his race, color, religion, sex, or national origin.

(c) It shall be an unlawful employment practice for a labor organization-

(1) to exclude or to expel from its membership, or otherwise to discriminate against, any individual because of his race, color, religion, sex, or national origin;

(2) to limit, segregate, or classify its membership or applicants for membership, or to classify or fail or refuse to refer for employment any individual, in any way which would deprive or tend to deprive any individual of employment opportunities, or would limit such employment opportunities or otherwise adversely affect his status as an employee or as an applicant for employment, because of such individual's race, color, religion, sex, or national origin; or

(3) to cause or attempt to cause an employer to discriminate against an individual in violation of this section.

(d) It shall be an unlawful employment practice for any employer, labor organization, or joint labor management committee controlling apprenticeship or other training or retraining, including on the job training programs to discriminate against any individual because of his race, color, religion, sex, or national origin in admission to, or employment in, any program established to provide apprenticeship or other training.

(e) Notwithstanding any other provision of this subchapter, (1) it shall not be an unlawful employment practice for an employer to hire and employ employees, for an employment agency to classify, or refer for employment any individual, for a labor organization to classify its membership or to classify or refer for employment any individual, or for an employer, labor organization, or joint labor management committee controlling apprenticeship or other training or retraining programs to admit or employ any individual in any such program, on the basis of his religion, sex, or national origin in those certain instances where religion, sex, or national origin is a bona fide occupational qualification reasonably necessary to the normal operation of that particular business or enterprise, and (2) it shall not be an unlawful employment practice for a school, college, university, or other educational institution or institution of learning to hire and employ employees of a particular religion if such school, college, university, or other educational institution or institution of learning is, in whole or in substantial part, owned, supported, controlled, or managed by a particular religion or by a particular religious corporation, association, or society, or if the curriculum of such school, college, university, or other educational institution or institution of learning is directed toward the propagation of a particular religion.

(f) As used in this subchapter, the phrase "unlawful employment practice" shall not be deemed to include any action or measure taken by an employer, labor organization, joint labor management committee, or employment agency with respect to an individual who is a member of the Communist Party of the United States or of any other organization required to register as a Communist action or Communist front organization by final order of the Subversive Activities Control Board pursuant to the Subversive Activities Control Act of 1950 *[50 U.S.C. 781 et seq.]*.

(g) Notwithstanding any other provision of this subchapter, it shall not be an unlawful employment practice for an employer to fail or refuse to hire and employ any individual for any position, for an employer to discharge any individual from any position, or for an employment agency to fail or refuse to refer any individual for employment in any position, or for a labor organization to fail or refuse to refer any individual for employment in any position, if-

(1) the occupancy of such position, or access to the premises in or upon which any part of the duties of such position is performed or is to be performed, is subject to any requirement imposed in the interest of the national security of the United States under any security program in effect pursuant to or administered under any statute of the United States or any Executive order of the President; and

(2) such individual has not fulfilled or has ceased to fulfill that requirement.

(h) Notwithstanding any other provision of this subchapter, it shall not be an unlawful employment practice for an employer to apply different standards of compensation, or different terms, conditions, or privileges of employment pursuant to a bona fide seniority or merit system, or a system which measures earnings by quantity or quality of production or to employees who work in different locations, provided that such differences are not the result of an intention to discriminate because of race, color, religion, sex, or national origin, nor shall it be an unlawful employment practice for an employer to give and to act upon the results of any professionally developed ability test provided that such test, its administration or action upon the results is not designed, intended or used to discriminate because of race, color, religion, sex or national origin. It shall not be an unlawful employment practice under this subchapter for any employer to differentiate upon the basis of sex in determining the amount of the wages or compensation paid or to be paid to employees of such employer if such differentiation is authorized by the provisions of section 206(d) of title 29 *[section 6(d) of the Fair Labor Standards Act of 1938, as amended]*.

(i) Nothing contained in this subchapter shall apply to any business or enterprise on or near an Indian reservation with respect to any publicly announced employment practice of such business or enterprise under which a preferential treatment is given to any individual because he is an Indian living on or near a reservation.

(j) Nothing contained in this subchapter shall be interpreted to require any employer, employment agency, labor organization, or joint labor management committee subject to this subchapter to grant preferential treatment to any individual or to any group because of the race, color, religion, sex, or national origin of such individual or group on account of an imbalance which may exist with respect to the total number or percentage of persons of any race, color, religion, sex, or national origin employed by any employer, referred or classified for employment by any employment agency or labor organization, admitted to membership or classified by any labor organization, or admitted to, or employed in, any apprenticeship or other training program, in comparison with the total number or percentage of persons of such race, color, religion, sex, or national origin in any community, State, section, or other area, or in the available work force in any community, State, section, or other area.

(k) (1) (A) An unlawful employment practice based on disparate impact is established under this title only if-

(i) a complaining party demonstrates that a respondent uses a particular employment practice that causes a disparate impact on the basis of race, color, religion, sex, or national origin and the respondent fails to demonstrate that the challenged practice is job related for the position in question and consistent with business necessity; or

(ii) the complaining party makes the demonstration described in subparagraph (C) with respect to an alternative employment practice and the

respondent refuses to adopt such alternative employment practice.

(B) (i) With respect to demonstrating that a particular employment practice causes a disparate impact as described in subparagraph (A)(i), the complaining party shall demonstrate that each particular challenged employment practice causes a disparate impact, except that if the complaining party can demonstrate to the court that the elements of a respondent's decision making process are not capable of separation for analysis, the decision making process may be analyzed as one employment practice.

(ii) If the respondent demonstrates that a specific employment practice does not cause the disparate impact, the respondent shall not be required to demonstrate that such practice is required by business necessity.

(C) The demonstration referred to by subparagraph (A)(ii) shall be in accordance with the law as it existed on June 4, 1989, with respect to the concept of "alternative employment practice".

(2) A demonstration that an employment practice is required by business necessity may not be used as a defense against a claim of intentional discrimination under this title.

(3) Notwithstanding any other provision of this title, a rule barring the employment of an individual who currently and knowingly uses or possesses a controlled substance, as defined in schedules I and II of section 102(6) of the Controlled Substances Act (21 U.S.C. 802(6)), other than the use or possession of a drug taken under the supervision of a licensed health care professional, or any other use or possession authorized by the Controlled Substances Act *[21 U.S.C. 801 et seq.]* or any other provision of Federal law, shall be considered an unlawful employment practice under this title only if such rule is adopted or applied with an intent to discriminate because of race, color, religion, sex, or national origin.

(l) It shall be an unlawful employment practice for a respondent, in connection with the selection or referral of applicants or candidates for employment or promotion, to adjust the scores of, use different cutoff scores for, or otherwise alter the results of, employment related tests on the basis of race, color, religion, sex, or national origin.

(m) Except as otherwise provided in this title, an unlawful employment practice is established when the complaining party demonstrates that race, color, religion, sex, or national origin was a motivating factor for any employment practice, even though other factors also motivated the practice.

(n) (1) (A) Notwithstanding any other provision of law, and except as provided in paragraph (2), an employment practice that implements and is within the scope of a litigated or consent judgment or order that resolves a claim of employment discrimination under the Constitution or Federal civil rights laws may not be challenged under the circumstances described in subparagraph (B).

(B) A practice described in subparagraph (A) may not be challenged in a claim under the Constitution or Federal civil rights laws-

(i) by a person who, prior to the entry of the judgment or order described in subparagraph (A), had-

(I) actual notice of the proposed judgment or order sufficient to apprise such person that such judgment or order might adversely affect the interests and legal rights of such person and that an opportunity was available to present objections to such judgment or order by a future date certain; and

(II) a reasonable opportunity to present objections to such judgment or order; or

(ii) by a person whose interests were adequately represented by another person who had previously challenged the judgment or order on the same legal grounds and with a similar factual situation, unless there has been an intervening change in law or fact.

(2) Nothing in this subsection shall be construed to-

(A) alter the standards for intervention under rule 24 of the Federal Rules of Civil Procedure or apply to the rights of parties who have successfully intervened pursuant to such rule in the proceeding in which the parties intervened;

(B) apply to the rights of parties to the action in which a litigated or consent judgment or order was entered, or of members of a class represented or sought to be represented in such action, or of members of a group on whose behalf relief was sought in such action by the Federal Government;

(C) prevent challenges to a litigated or consent judgment or order on the ground that such judgment or order was obtained through collusion or fraud, or is transparently invalid or was entered by a court lacking subject matter jurisdiction; or

(D) authorize or permit the denial to any person of the due process of law required by the Constitution.

(3) Any action not precluded under this subsection that challenges an employment consent judgment or order described in paragraph (1) shall be brought in the court, and if possible before the judge, that entered such judgment or order. Nothing in this subsection shall preclude a transfer of such action pursuant to section 1404 of title 28, United States Code.

OTHER UNLAWFUL EMPLOYMENT PRACTICES

SEC. 2000e-3. *[Section 704]*

(a) It shall be an unlawful employment practice for an employer to discriminate against any of his employees or applicants for employment, for an employment agency, or joint labor management committee controlling apprenticeship or other training or retraining, including on the job training programs, to discriminate against any individual, or for a labor organization to discriminate against any member thereof or applicant for membership, because he has opposed any practice made an unlawful employment practice by this subchapter, or because he has made a charge, testified, assisted, or participated in any manner in an investigation, proceeding, or hearing under this subchapter.

(b) It shall be an unlawful employment practice for an employer, labor organization, employment agency, or joint labor management committee controlling apprenticeship or other training or retraining, including on the job training programs, to print or publish or cause to be printed or published any notice or advertisement relating to employment by such an employer or membership in or any classification or referral for employment by such a labor organization, or relating to any classification or referral for employment by such an employment agency, or relating to admission to, or employment in, any program established to provide apprenticeship or other training by such a joint labor management committee, indicating any preference, limitation, specification, or discrimination, based on race, color, religion, sex, or national origin, except that such a notice or advertisement may indicate a preference, limitation, specification, or discrimination based on religion, sex, or national origin when religion, sex, or national origin is a bona fide occupational qualification for employment.

EQUAL EMPLOYMENT OPPORTUNITY COMMISSION

SEC. 2000e-4. *[Section 705]*

(a) There is hereby created a Commission to be known as the Equal Employment Opportunity Commission, which shall be composed of five members, not more than three of whom shall be members of the same political party. Members of the Commission shall be appointed by the President by and with the advice and consent of the Senate for a term of five years. Any individual chosen to fill a vacancy shall be appointed only for the unexpired term of the member whom he shall succeed, and all members of the Commission shall continue to serve until their successors are appointed and qualified, except that no such member of the Commission shall continue to serve (1) for more than sixty days when the Congress is in session unless a nomination to fill such vacancy shall have been submitted to the Senate, or (2) after the adjournment sine die of the session of the Senate in which such nomination was submitted. The President shall designate one member to serve as Chairman of the Commission, and one member to serve as Vice Chairman. The Chairman shall be responsible on behalf of the Commission for the administrative operations of the Commission, and, except as provided in subsection (b) of this section, shall appoint, in accordance with the provisions of title 5 *[United States Code]* governing appointments in the competitive service, such officers, agents, attorneys, administrative law judges *[hearing examiners]*, and employees as he deems necessary to assist it in the performance of its functions and to fix their compensation in accordance with the provisions of chapter 51 and subchapter III of chapter 53 of title 5 *[United States Code]*, relating to classification and General Schedule pay rates: Provided, That assignment, removal, and compensation of administrative law judges *[hearing examiners]* shall be in accordance with sections 3105, 3344, 5372, and 7521 of title 5 *[United States Code]*.

(b) (1) There shall be a General Counsel of the Commission appointed by the President, by and with the advice and consent of the Senate, for a term of four years. The General Counsel shall have responsibility for the conduct of litigation as provided in sections 2000e-5 and 2000e-6 of this title *[sections 706 and 707]*. The General Counsel shall have such other duties as the Commission may prescribe or as may be provided by law and shall concur with the Chairman of the Commission on the appointment and supervision of regional attorneys. The General Counsel of the Commission on the effective date of this Act shall continue in such position and perform the functions specified in this subsection until a successor is appointed and qualified.

(2) Attorneys appointed under this section may, at the direction of the Commission, appear for and represent the Commission in any case in court, provided that the Attorney General shall conduct all litigation to which the Commission is a party in the Supreme Court pursuant to this subchapter.

(c) A vacancy in the Commission shall not impair the right of the remaining members to exercise all the powers of the Commission and three members thereof shall constitute a quorum.

(d) The Commission shall have an official seal which shall be judicially noticed.

(e) The Commission shall at the close of each fiscal year report to the Congress and to the President concerning the action it has taken *[the names, salaries, and duties of all individuals in its employ]* and the moneys it has disbursed. It shall make such further reports on the cause of and means of eliminating discrimination and such recommendations for further legislation as may appear desirable.

(f) The principal office of the Commission shall be in or near the District of Columbia, but it may meet or exercise any or all its powers at any other place. The Commission may establish such regional or State offices as it deems necessary to accomplish the purpose of this subchapter.

(g) The Commission shall have power-

(1) to cooperate with and, with their consent, utilize regional, State, local, and other agencies, both public and private, and individuals;

(2) to pay to witnesses whose depositions are taken or who are summoned before the Commission or any of its agents the same witness and mileage fees as are paid to witnesses in the courts of the United States;

(3) to furnish to persons subject to this subchapter such technical assistance as they may request to further their compliance with this subchapter or an order issued thereunder;

(4) upon the request of (i) any employer, whose employees or some of them, or (ii) any labor organization, whose members or some of them, refuse or threaten to refuse to cooperate in effectuating the provisions of this subchapter, to assist in such effectuation by conciliation or such other remedial action as is provided by this subchapter;

(5) to make such technical studies as are appropriate to effectuate the purposes and policies of this subchapter and to make the results of such studies available to the public;

(6) to intervene in a civil action brought under section 2000e-5 of this title *[section 706]* by an aggrieved party against a respondent other than a government, governmental agency or political subdivision.

(h) **(1)** The Commission shall, in any of its educational or promotional activities, cooperate with other departments and agencies in the performance of such educational and promotional activities.

(2) In exercising its powers under this title, the Commission shall carry out educational and outreach activities (including dissemination of information in languages other than English) targeted to-

(A) individuals who historically have been victims of employment discrimination and have not been equitably served by the Commission; and

(B) individuals on whose behalf the Commission has authority to enforce any other law prohibiting employment discrimination, concerning rights and obligations under this title or such law, as the case may be.

(i) All officers, agents, attorneys, and employees of the Commission shall be subject to the provisions of section 7324 of title 5 *[section 9 of the Act of August 2, 1939, as amended (the Hatch Act)],* notwithstanding any exemption contained in such section.

(j) (1) The Commission shall establish a Technical Assistance Training Institute, through which the Commission shall provide technical assistance and training regarding the laws and regulations enforced by the Commission.

(2) An employer or other entity covered under this title shall not be excused from compliance with the requirements of this title because of any failure to receive technical assistance under this subsection.

(3) There are authorized to be appropriated to carry out this subsection such sums as may be necessary for fiscal year 1992.

ENFORCEMENT PROVISIONS

SEC. 2000e-5. *[Section 706]*

(a) The Commission is empowered, as hereinafter provided, to prevent any person from engaging in any unlawful employment practice as set forth in section 2000e-2 or 2000e-3 of this title *[section 703 or 704].*

(b) Whenever a charge is filed by or on behalf of a person claiming to be aggrieved, or by a member of the Commission, alleging that an employer, employment agency, labor organization, or joint labor management committee controlling apprenticeship or other training or retraining, including on the job training programs, has engaged in an unlawful employment practice, the Commission shall serve a notice of the charge (including the date, place and circumstances of the alleged unlawful employment practice) on such employer, employment agency, labor organization, or joint labor management committee (hereinafter referred to as the "respondent") within ten days, and shall make an investigation thereof. Charges shall be in writing under oath or affirmation and shall contain such information and be in such form as the Commission requires. Charges shall not be made public by the Commission. If the Commission determines after such investigation that there is not reasonable cause to believe that the charge is true, it shall dismiss the charge and promptly notify the person claiming to be aggrieved and the respondent of its action. In determining whether reasonable cause exists, the Commission shall accord substantial weight to final findings and orders made by State or local authorities in proceedings commenced under State or local law pursuant to the requirements of subsections (c) and (d) of this section. If the Commission determines after such investigation that there is reasonable cause to believe that the charge is true, the Commission shall endeavor to eliminate any such alleged unlawful employment practice by informal methods of conference, conciliation, and persuasion. Nothing said or done during and as a part of such informal endeavors may be made public by the Commission, its officers or employees, or used as evidence in a subsequent proceeding without the written consent of the persons concerned. Any person who makes public information in violation of this subsection shall be fined not more than $1,000 or imprisoned for not more than one year, or both. The Commission shall make its determination on reasonable cause as promptly as possible and, so far as practicable, not later than one hundred and twenty days from the filing of the charge or, where applicable under subsection (c) or (d) of this section, from the date upon which the Commission is authorized to take action with respect to the charge.

(c) In the case of an alleged unlawful employment practice occurring in a State, or political subdivision of a State, which has a State or local law prohibiting the unlawful employment practice alleged and establishing or authorizing a State or local authority to grant or seek relief from such practice or to institute criminal proceedings with respect thereto upon receiving notice thereof, no charge may be filed under subsection (a) of this section by the person aggrieved before the expiration of sixty days after proceedings have been commenced under the State or local law, unless such proceedings have been earlier terminated, provided that such sixty day period shall be extended to one hundred and twenty days during the first year after the effective date of such State or local law. If any requirement for the commencement of such proceedings is imposed by a State or local authority other than a requirement of the filing of a written and signed statement of the facts upon which the proceeding is based, the proceeding shall be deemed to have been commenced for the purposes of this subsection at the time such statement is sent by registered mail to the appropriate State or local authority.

(d) In the case of any charge filed by a member of the Commission alleging an unlawful employment practice occurring in a State or political subdivision of a State which has a State or local law prohibiting the practice alleged and establishing or authorizing a State or local authority to grant or seek relief from such practice or to institute criminal proceedings with respect thereto upon receiving notice thereof, the Commission shall, before taking any action with respect to such charge, notify the appropriate State or local officials and, upon request, afford them a reasonable time, but not less than sixty days (provided that such sixty day period shall be extended to one hundred and twenty days during the first year after the effective day of such State or local law), unless a shorter period is requested, to act under such State or local law to remedy the practice alleged.

(e) **(1)** A charge under this section shall be filed within one hundred and eighty days after the alleged unlawful employment practice occurred and notice of the charge (including the date, place and circumstances of the alleged unlawful employment practice) shall be served upon the person against whom such charge is made within ten days thereafter, except that in a case of an unlawful employment practice with respect to which the person aggrieved has initially instituted proceedings with a State or local agency with authority to grant or seek relief from such practice or to institute criminal proceedings with respect thereto upon receiving notice thereof, such charge shall be filed by or on behalf of the person aggrieved within three hundred days after the alleged unlawful employment practice occurred, or within thirty days after receiving notice that the State or local agency has terminated the proceedings under the

State or local law, whichever is earlier, and a copy of such charge shall be filed by the Commission with the State or local agency.

(2) For purposes of this section, an unlawful employment practice occurs, with respect to a seniority system that has been adopted for an intentionally discriminatory purpose in violation of this title (whether or not that discriminatory purpose is apparent on the face of the seniority provision), when the seniority system is adopted, when an individual becomes subject to the seniority system, or when a person aggrieved is injured by the application of the seniority system or provision of the system.

(f) (1) If within thirty days after a charge is filed with the Commission or within thirty days after expiration of any period of reference under subsection (c) or (d) of this section, the Commission has been unable to secure from the respondent a conciliation agreement acceptable to the Commission, the Commission may bring a civil action against any respondent not a government, governmental agency, or political subdivision named in the charge. In the case of a respondent which is a government, governmental agency, or political subdivision, if the Commission has been unable to secure from the respondent a conciliation agreement acceptable to the Commission, the Commission shall take no further action and shall refer the case to the Attorney General who may bring a civil action against such respondent in the appropriate United States district court. The person or persons aggrieved shall have the right to intervene in a civil action brought by the Commission or the Attorney General in a case involving a government, governmental agency, or political subdivision. If a charge filed with the Commission pursuant to subsection (b) of this section, is dismissed by the Commission, or if within one hundred and eighty days from the filing of such charge or the expiration of any period of reference under subsection (c) or (d) of this section, whichever is later, the Commission has not filed a civil action under this section or the Attorney General has not filed a civil action in a case involving a government, governmental agency, or political subdivision, or the Commission has not entered into a conciliation agreement to which the person aggrieved is a party, the Commission, or the Attorney General in a case involving a government, governmental agency, or political subdivision, shall so notify the person aggrieved and within ninety days after the giving of such notice a civil action may be brought against the respondent named in the charge (A) by the person claiming to be aggrieved or (B) if such charge was filed by a member of the Commission, by any person whom the charge alleges was aggrieved by the alleged unlawful employment practice. Upon application by the complainant and in such circumstances as the court may deem just, the court may appoint an attorney for such complainant and may authorize the commencement of the action without the payment of fees, costs, or security. Upon timely application, the court may, in its discretion, permit the Commission, or the Attorney General in a case involving a government, governmental agency, or political subdivision, to intervene in such civil action upon certification that the case is of general public importance. Upon request, the court may, in its discretion, stay further proceedings for not more than sixty days pending the termination of State or local proceedings described in subsection (c) or (d) of this section or further efforts of the Commission to obtain voluntary compliance.

(2) Whenever a charge is filed with the Commission and the Commission concludes on the basis of a preliminary investigation that prompt judicial action is necessary to carry out the purposes of this Act, the Commission, or the Attorney General in a case involving a government, governmental agency, or political subdivision, may bring an action for appropriate temporary or preliminary relief pending final disposition of such charge. Any temporary restraining order or other order granting preliminary or temporary relief shall be issued in accordance with rule 65 of the Federal Rules of Civil Procedure. It shall be the duty of a court having jurisdiction over proceedings under this section to assign cases for hearing at the earliest practicable date and to cause such cases to be in every way expedited.

(3) Each United States district court and each United States court of a place subject to the jurisdiction of the United States shall have jurisdiction of actions brought under this subchapter. Such an action may be brought in any judicial district in the State in which the unlawful employment practice is alleged to have been committed, in the judicial district in which the employment records relevant to such practice are maintained and administered, or in the judicial district in which the aggrieved person would have worked but for the alleged unlawful employment practice, but if the respondent is not found within any such district, such an action may be brought within the judicial district in which the respondent has his principal office. For purposes of sections 1404 and 1406 of title 28 *[of the United States Code],* the judicial district in which the respondent has his principal office

shall in all cases be considered a district in which the action might have been brought.

(4) It shall be the duty of the chief judge of the district (or in his absence, the acting chief judge) in which the case is pending immediately to designate a judge in such district to hear and determine the case. In the event that no judge in the district is available to hear and determine the case, the chief judge of the district, or the acting chief judge, as the case may be, shall certify this fact to the chief judge of the circuit (or in his absence, the acting chief judge) who shall then designate a district or circuit judge of the circuit to hear and determine the case.

(5) It shall be the duty of the judge designated pursuant to this subsection to assign the case for hearing at the earliest practicable date and to cause the case to be in every way expedited. If such judge has not scheduled the case for trial within one hundred and twenty days after issue has been joined, that judge may appoint a master pursuant to rule 53 of the Federal Rules of Civil Procedure.

(g) **(1)** If the court finds that the respondent has intentionally engaged in or is intentionally engaging in an unlawful employment practice charged in the complaint, the court may enjoin the respondent from engaging in such unlawful employment practice, and order such affirmative action as may be appropriate, which may include, but is not limited to, reinstatement or hiring of employees, with or without back pay (payable by the employer, employment agency, or labor organization, as the case may be, responsible for the unlawful employment practice), or any other equitable relief as the court deems appropriate. Back pay liability shall not accrue from a date more than two years prior to the filing of a charge with the Commission. Interim earnings or amounts earnable with reasonable diligence by the person or persons discriminated against shall operate to reduce the back pay otherwise allowable.

(2) (A) No order of the court shall require the admission or reinstatement of an individual as a member of a union, or the hiring, reinstatement, or promotion of an individual as an employee, or the payment to him of any back pay, if such individual was refused admission, suspended, or expelled, or was refused employment or advancement or was suspended or discharged for any reason other than discrimination on account of race, color, religion, sex, or national origin or in violation of section 2000e-3(a) of this title *[section 704(a)]*.

(B) On a claim in which an individual proves a violation under section 2000e-2(m) of this title *[section 703(m)]* and a respondent demonstrates that the respondent would have taken the same action in the absence of the impermissible motivating factor, the court-

(i) may grant declaratory relief, injunctive relief (except as provided in clause (ii)), and attorney's fees and costs demonstrated to be directly attributable only to the pursuit of a claim under section 2000e-2(m) of this title *[section 703(m)]*; and

(ii) shall not award damages or issue an order requiring any admission, reinstatement, hiring, promotion, or payment, described in subparagraph (A).

(h) The provisions of chapter 6 of title 29 *[the Act entitled "An Act to amend the Judicial Code and to define and limit the jurisdiction of courts sitting in equity, and for other purposes," approved March 23, 1932 (29 U.S.C. 105-115)]* shall not apply with respect to civil actions brought under this section.

(i) In any case in which an employer, employment agency, or labor organization fails to comply with an order of a court issued in a civil action brought under this section, the Commission may commence proceedings to compel compliance with such order.

(j) Any civil action brought under this section and any proceedings brought under subsection (i) of this section shall be subject to appeal as provided in sections 1291 and 1292, title 28 *[United States Code]*.

(k) In any action or proceeding under this subchapter the court, in its discretion, may allow the prevailing party, other than the Commission or the United States, a reasonable attorney's fee **(including expert fees)** as part of the costs, and the Commission and the United States shall be liable for costs the same as a private person.

CIVIL ACTIONS BY THE ATTORNEY GENERAL

SEC. 2000e-6. *[Section 707]*

(a) Whenever the Attorney General has reasonable cause to believe that any person or group of persons is engaged in a pattern or practice of resistance to the full enjoyment of any of the rights secured by this subchapter, and that the pattern or practice is of such a nature and is intended to deny the full exercise of the rights herein described, the Attorney General may bring a civil action in the appropriate district court of the United States by filing with it a complaint (1) signed by him (or in his absence the Acting Attorney General), (2) setting forth facts pertaining to such pattern or practice, and (3) requesting such relief, including an application for a permanent or temporary injunction, restraining order or other order against the person or persons responsible for such pattern or practice, as he deems necessary to insure the full enjoyment of the rights herein described.

(b) The district courts of the United States shall have and shall exercise jurisdiction of proceedings instituted pursuant to this section, and in any such proceeding the Attorney General may file with the clerk of such court a request that a court of three judges be convened to hear and determine the case. Such request by the Attorney General shall be accompanied by a certificate that, in his opinion, the case is of general public importance. A copy of the certificate and request for a three judge court shall be immediately furnished by such clerk to the chief judge of the circuit (or in his absence, the presiding circuit judge of the circuit) in which the case is pending. Upon receipt of such request it shall be the duty of the chief judge of the circuit or the presiding circuit judge, as the case may be, to designate immediately three judges in such circuit, of whom at least one shall be a circuit judge and another of whom shall be a district judge of the court in which the proceeding was instituted, to hear and determine such case, and it shall be the duty of the judges so designated to assign the case for hearing at the earliest practicable date, to participate in the hearing and determination thereof, and to cause the case to be in every way expedited. An appeal from the final judgment of such court will lie to the Supreme Court.

In the event the Attorney General fails to file such a request in any such proceeding, it shall be the duty of the chief judge of the district (or in his absence, the acting chief judge) in which the case is pending immediately to designate a judge in such district to hear and determine the case. In the event that no judge in the district is available to hear and determine the case, the chief judge of the district, or the acting chief judge, as the case may be, shall certify this fact to the chief judge of the circuit (or in his absence, the acting chief judge) who shall then designate a district or circuit judge of the circuit to hear and determine the case.

It shall be the duty of the judge designated pursuant to this section to assign the case for hearing at the earliest practicable date and to cause the case to be in every way expedited.

(c) Effective two years after March 24, 1972 *[the date of enactment of the Equal Employment Opportunity Act of 1972]*, the functions of the Attorney General under this section shall be transferred to the Commission, together with such personnel, property, records, and unexpended balances of appropriations, allocations, and other funds employed, used, held, available, or to be made available in connection with such functions unless the President submits, and neither House of Congress vetoes, a reorganization plan pursuant to chapter 9 of title 5 *[United States Code]*, inconsistent with the provisions of this subsection. The Commission shall carry out such functions in accordance with subsections (d) and (e) of this section.

(d) Upon the transfer of functions provided for in subsection (c) of this section, in all suits commenced pursuant to this section prior to the date of such transfer, proceedings shall continue without abatement, all court orders and decrees shall remain in effect, and the Commission shall be substituted as a party for the United States of America, the Attorney General, or the Acting Attorney General, as appropriate.

(e) Subsequent to March 24, 1972 *[the date of enactment of the Equal Employment Opportunity Act of 1972]*, the Commission shall have authority to investigate and act on a charge of a pattern or practice of discrimination, whether filed by or on behalf of a person claiming to be aggrieved or by a member of the Commission. All such actions shall be conducted in accordance with the procedures set forth in section 2000e-5 of this title *[section 706]*.

EFFECT ON STATE LAWS

SEC. 2000e-7. *[Section 708]*

Nothing in this subchapter shall be deemed to exempt or relieve any person from any liability, duty, penalty, or punishment provided by any present or future law of any State or political subdivision of a State, other than any such law which purports to require or permit the doing of any act which would be an unlawful employment practice under this subchapter.

INVESTIGATIONS, INSPECTIONS, RECORDS, STATE AGENCIES

SEC. 2000e-8. *[Section 709]*

(a) In connection with any investigation of a charge filed under section 2000e-5 of this title *[section 706]*, the Commission or its designated representative shall at all reasonable times have access to, for the purposes of examination, and the right to copy any evidence of any person being investigated or proceeded against that relates to unlawful employment practices covered by this subchapter and is relevant to the charge under investigation.

(b) The Commission may cooperate with State and local agencies charged with the administration of State fair employment practices laws and, with the consent of such agencies, may, for the purpose of carrying out its functions and duties under this subchapter and within the limitation of funds appropriated specifically for such purpose, engage in and contribute to the cost of research and other projects of mutual interest undertaken by such agencies, and utilize the services of such agencies and their employees, and, notwithstanding any other provision of law, pay by advance or reimbursement such agencies and their employees for services rendered to assist the Commission in carrying out this subchapter. In furtherance of such cooperative efforts, the Commission may enter into written agreements with such State or local agencies and such agreements may include provisions under which the Commission shall refrain from processing a charge in any cases or class of cases specified in such agreements or under which the Commission shall relieve any person or class of persons in such State or locality from requirements imposed under this section. The Commission shall rescind any such agreement whenever it determines that the agreement no longer serves the interest of effective enforcement of this subchapter.

(c) Every employer, employment agency, and labor organization subject to this subchapter shall (1) make and keep such records relevant to the determinations of whether unlawful employment practices have been or are being committed, (2) preserve such records for such periods, and (3) make such reports therefrom as the Commission shall prescribe by regulation or order, after public hearing, as reasonable, necessary, or appropriate for the enforcement of this subchapter or the regulations or orders thereunder. The Commission shall, by regulation, require each employer, labor organization, and joint labor management committee subject to this subchapter which controls an apprenticeship or other training program to maintain such records as are reasonably necessary to carry out the purposes of this subchapter, including, but not limited to, a list of applicants who wish to participate in such program, including the chronological order in which applications were received, and to furnish to the Commission upon request, a detailed description of the manner in which persons are selected to participate in the apprenticeship or other training program. Any employer, employment agency, labor organization, or joint labor management committee which believes that the application to it of any regulation or order issued under this section would result in undue hardship may apply to the Commission for an exemption from the application of such regulation or order, and, if such application for an exemption is denied, bring a civil action in the United States district court for the district where such records are kept. If the Commission or the court, as the case may be, finds that the application of the regulation or order to the employer, employment agency, or labor organization in question would impose an undue hardship, the Commission or the court, as the case may be, may grant appropriate relief. If any person required to comply with the provisions of this subsection fails or refuses to do so, the United States district court for the district in which such person is found, resides, or transacts business, shall, upon application of the Commission, or the Attorney General in a case involving a government, governmental agency or political subdivision, have jurisdiction to issue to such person an order requiring him to comply.

(d) In prescribing requirements pursuant to subsection (c) of this section, the Commission shall consult with other interested State and Federal agencies and shall endeavor to coordinate its requirements with those adopted by such agencies. The Commission shall furnish upon request and without cost to any State or local agency charged with the administration of a fair employment practice law information obtained pursuant to subsection (c) of this section from any employer, employment agency, labor organization, or joint labor management committee subject to the jurisdiction of such agency. Such information shall be furnished on condition that it not be made public by the recipient agency prior to the institution of a proceeding under State or local law involving such information. If this condition is violated by a recipient agency, the Commission may decline to honor subsequent requests pursuant to this subsection.

(e) It shall be unlawful for any officer or employee of the Commission to make public in any manner whatever any information obtained by the Commission pursuant to its authority under this section prior to the institution of any proceeding under this subchapter involving such information. Any officer or employee of the Commission who shall make public in any manner whatever any information in violation of this subsection shall be guilty, of a misdemeanor and upon conviction thereof, shall be fined not more than $1,000, or imprisoned not more than one year.

INVESTIGATORY POWERS

SEC. 2000e-9. *[Section 710]*

For the purpose of all hearings and investigations conducted by the Commission or its duly authorized agents or agencies, section 161 of title 29 *[section 11 of the National Labor Relations Act]* shall apply.

POSTING OF NOTICES; PENALTIES

SEC. 2000e-10. *[Section 711]*

(a) Every employer, employment agency, and labor organization, as the case may be, shall post and keep posted in conspicuous places upon its premises where notices to employees, applicants for employment, and members are customarily posted a notice to be prepared or approved by the Commission setting forth excerpts, from or, summaries of, the pertinent provisions of this subchapter and information pertinent to the filing of a complaint.

(b) A willful violation of this section shall be punishable by a fine of not more than $100 for each separate offense.

VETERANS' SPECIAL RIGHTS OR PREFERENCE

SEC. 2000e-11. *[Section 712]*

Nothing contained in this subchapter shall be construed to repeal or modify any Federal, State, territorial, or local law creating special rights or preference for veterans.

RULES AND REGULATIONS

SEC. 2000e-12. *[Section 713]*

(a) The Commission shall have authority from time to time to issue, amend, or rescind suitable procedural regulations to carry out the provisions of this subchapter. Regulations issued under this section shall be in conformity with the standards and limitations of subchapter II of chapter 5 of title 5 *[the Administrative Procedure Act]*.

(b) In any action or proceeding based on any alleged unlawful employment practice, no person shall be subject to any liability or punishment for or on account of (1) the commission by such person of an unlawful employment practice if he pleads and proves that the act or omission complained of was in good faith, in conformity with, and in reliance on any written interpretation or opinion of the Commission, or (2) the failure of such person to publish and file any information required by any provision of this subchapter if he pleads and proves that he failed to publish and file such information in good faith, in conformity with the instructions of the Commission issued under this subchapter regarding the filing of such information. Such a defense, if established, shall be a bar to the action or proceeding, notwithstanding that (A) after such act or omission, such interpretation or opinion is modified or rescinded or is determined by judicial authority to be invalid or of no legal effect, or (B) after publishing or filing the description and annual reports, such publication or filing is determined by judicial authority not to be in conformity with the requirements of this subchapter.

FORCIBLY RESISTING THE COMMISSION OR ITS REPRESENTATIVES

SEC. 2000e-13. *[Section 714]*

The provisions of sections 111 and 1114, title 18 *[United States Code],* shall apply to officers, agents, and employees of the Commission in the performance of their official duties. Notwithstanding the provisions of sections 111 and 1114 of title 18 *[United States Code],* whoever in violation of the provisions of section 1114 of such title kills a person while engaged in or on account of the performance of his official functions under this Act shall be punished by imprisonment for any term of years or for life.

TRANSFER OF AUTHORITY

[Administration of the duties of the Equal Employment Opportunity Coordinating Council was transferred to the Equal Employment Opportunity Commission effective July 1, 1978, under the President's Reorganization Plan of 1978.]

EQUAL EMPLOYMENT OPPORTUNITY COORDINATING COUNCIL

SEC. 2000e-14. *[Section 715]*

[There shall be established an Equal Employment Opportunity Coordinating Council (hereinafter referred to in this section as the Council) composed of the

Secretary of Labor, the Chairman of the Equal Employment Opportunity Commission, the Attorney General, the Chairman of the United States Civil Service Commission, and the Chairman of the United States Civil Rights Commission, or their respective delegates.]

The Equal Employment Opportunity Commission *[Council]* shall have the responsibility for developing and implementing agreements, policies and practices designed to maximize effort, promote efficiency, and eliminate conflict, competition, duplication and inconsistency among the operations, functions and jurisdictions of the various departments, agencies and branches of the Federal Government responsible for the implementation and enforcement of equal employment opportunity legislation, orders, and policies. On or before October 1 *[July 1]* of each year, the Equal Employment Opportunity Commission *[Council]* shall transmit to the President and to the Congress a report of its activities, together with such recommendations for legislative or administrative changes as it concludes are desirable to further promote the purposes of this section.

EFFECTIVE DATE

SEC. 2000e-15. *[Section 716]*

[(a) This title shall become effective one year after the date of its enactment.

(b) Notwithstanding subsection (a), sections of this title other than sections 703, 704, 706, and 707 shall become effective immediately.

(c)] The President shall, as soon as feasible after July 2, 1964 *[the enactment of this title]*, convene one or more conferences for the purpose of enabling the leaders of groups whose members will be affected by this subchapter to become familiar with the rights afforded and obligations imposed by its provisions, and for the purpose of making plans which will result in the fair and effective administration of this subchapter when all of its provisions become effective. The President shall invite the participation in such conference or conferences of (1) the members of the President's Committee on Equal Employment Opportunity, (2) the members of the Commission on Civil Rights, (3) representatives of State and local agencies engaged in furthering equal employment opportunity, (4) representatives of private agencies engaged in furthering equal employment opportunity, and (5) representatives of employers, labor organizations, and employment agencies who will be subject to this subchapter.

TRANSFER OF AUTHORITY

[Enforcement of Section 717 was transferred to the Equal Employment Opportunity Commission from the Civil Service Commission (Office of Personnel Management) effective January 1, 1979 under the President's Reorganization Plan No. 1 of 1978.]

EMPLOYMENT BY FEDERAL GOVERNMENT

SEC. 2000e-16. *[Section 717]*

(a) All personnel actions affecting employees or applicants for employment (except with regard to aliens employed outside the limits of the United States) in military departments as defined in section 102 of title 5 *[United States Code]*, in executive agencies *[other than the General Accounting Office]* as defined in section 105 of title 5 *[United States Code]* (including employees and applicants for employment who are paid from nonappropriated funds), in the United States Postal Service and the Postal Rate Commission, in those units of the Government of the District of Columbia having positions in the competitive service, and in those units of the legislative and judicial branches of the Federal Government having positions in the competitive service, and in the Library of Congress shall be made free from any discrimination based on race, color, religion, sex, or national origin.

(b) Except as otherwise provided in this subsection, the Equal Employment Opportunity Commission *[Civil Service Commission]* shall have authority to enforce the provisions of subsection (a) of this section through appropriate remedies, including reinstatement or hiring of employees with or without back pay, as will effectuate the policies of this section, and shall issue such rules, regulations, orders and instructions as it deems necessary and appropriate to carry out its responsibilities under this section. The Equal Employment Opportunity Commission *[Civil Service Commission]* shall-

(1) be responsible for the annual review and approval of a national and regional equal employment opportunity plan which each department and agency and each appropriate unit referred to in subsection (a) of this section shall submit in order to maintain an affirmative program of equal employment opportunity for all such employees and applicants for employment;

(2) be responsible for the review and evaluation of the operation of all agency equal employment opportunity programs, periodically obtaining and publishing (on at least a semiannual basis) progress reports from each such department, agency, or unit; and

(3) consult with and solicit the recommendations of interested individuals, groups, and organizations relating to equal employment opportunity.

The head of each such department, agency, or unit shall comply with such rules, regulations, orders, and instructions which shall include a provision that an employee or applicant for employment shall be notified of any final action taken on any complaint of discrimination filed by him thereunder. The plan submitted by each department, agency, and unit shall include, but not be limited to-

(1) provision for the establishment of training and education programs designed to provide a maximum opportunity for employees to advance so as to perform at their highest potential; and

(2) a description of the qualifications in terms of training and experience relating to equal employment opportunity for the principal and operating officials of each such department, agency, or unit responsible for carrying out the equal employment opportunity program and of the allocation of personnel and resources proposed by such department, agency, or unit to carry out its equal employment opportunity program.

With respect to employment in the Library of Congress, authorities granted in this subsection to the Equal Employment Opportunity Commission *[Civil Service Commission]* shall be exercised by the Librarian of Congress.

(c) Within **90 days** of receipt of notice of final action taken by a department, agency, or unit referred to in subsection (a) of this section, or by the Equal Employment Opportunity Commission *[Civil Service Commission]* upon an appeal from a decision or order of such department, agency, or unit on a complaint of discrimination based on race, color, religion, sex or national origin, brought pursuant to subsection (a) of this section, Executive Order 11478 or any succeeding Executive orders, or after one hundred and eighty days from the filing of the initial charge with the department, agency, or unit or with the Equal Employment Opportunity Commission *[Civil Service Commission]* on appeal from a decision or order of such department, agency, or unit until such time as final action may be taken by a department, agency, or unit, an employee or applicant for employment, if aggrieved by the final disposition of his complaint, or by the failure to take final action on his complaint, may file a civil action as provided in section 2000e-5 of this title *[section 706],* in which civil action the head of the department, agency, or unit, as appropriate, shall be the defendant.

(d) The provisions of section 2000e-5(f) through (k) of this title *[section 706(f) through (k)],* as applicable, shall govern civil actions brought hereunder, **and the same interest to compensate for delay in payment shall be available as in cases involving nonpublic parties.**

(e) Nothing contained in this Act shall relieve any Government agency or official of its or his primary responsibility to assure nondiscrimination in employment as required by the Constitution and statutes or of its or his responsibilities under Executive Order 11478 relating to equal employment opportunity in the Federal Government.

SPECIAL PROVISIONS WITH RESPECT TO DENIAL, TERMINATION, AND SUSPENSION OF GOVERNMENT CONTRACTS

SEC. 2000e-17. *[Section 718]*

No Government contract, or portion thereof, with any employer, shall be denied, withheld, terminated, or suspended, by any agency or officer of the United States under any equal employment opportunity law or order, where such employer has an affirmative action plan which has previously been accepted by the Government for the same facility within the past twelve months without first according such employer full hearing and adjudication under the provisions of section 554 of title 5 *[United States Code],* and the following pertinent sections: Provided, That if such employer has deviated substantially from such previously agreed to affirmative action plan, this section shall not apply: Provided further, That for the purposes of this section an affirmative action plan shall be deemed to have been accepted by the Government at the time the appropriate compliance agency has accepted such plan unless within forty five days thereafter the Office of Federal Contract Compliance has disapproved such plan.

Appendix D

THE CIVIL RIGHTS ACT OF 1991

The U.S. Equal Employment Opportunity Commission.

TITLE I - FEDERAL CIVIL RIGHTS REMEDIES

PROHIBITION AGAINST ALL RACIAL DISCRIMINATION IN THE MAKING AND ENFORCEMENT OF CONTRACTS

SEC. 101

Section 1977 of the Revised Statutes (42 U.S.C. 1981) is amended-

(1) by inserting "(a)" before "All persons within"; and

(2) by adding at the end the following new subsections:

"(b) For purposes of this section, the term 'make and enforce contracts' includes the making, performance, modification, and termination of contracts, and the enjoyment of all benefits, privileges, terms, and conditions of the contractual relationship.

"(c) The rights protected by this section are protected against impairment by nongovernmental discrimination and impairment under color of State law."

DAMAGES IN CASES OF INTENTIONAL DISCRIMINATION

SEC. 102

The Revised Statutes are amended by inserting after section 1977 (42 U.S.C. 1981) the following new section: "SEC. 1977A. DAMAGES IN CASES OF INTENTIONAL DISCRIMINATION IN EMPLOYMENT. *[42 U.S.C. 1981a]*

"(a) Right of Recovery. -

"(1) Civil Rights. - In an action brought by a complaining party under section 706 or 717 of the Civil Rights Act of 1964 (42 U.S.C. 2000e-5) against a respondent who engaged in unlawful intentional discrimination (not an employment practice that is unlawful because of its disparate impact) prohibited under section 703, 704, or 717 of the Act (42 U.S.C. 2000e-2 or 2000e-3), and provided that the complaining party cannot recover under section 1977 of the Revised Statutes (42 U.S.C. 1981), the complaining party may recover compensatory and punitive damages as allowed in subsection (b), in addition to any relief authorized by section 706(g) of the Civil Rights Act of 1964, from the respondent.

"(2) Disability. - In an action brought by a complaining party under the powers, remedies, and procedures set forth in section 706 or 717 of the Civil Rights Act of 1964 (as provided in section 107(a) of the Americans with Disabilities Act of 1990 (42 U.S.C. 12117 (a)), and section 505(a)(1) of the Rehabilitation Act of 1973 (29 U.S.C. 794a(a)(1)), respectively) against a respondent who engaged in unlawful intentional discrimination (not an employment practice that is unlawful because of its disparate impact) under section 501 of the Rehabilitation Act of 1973 (29 U.S.C. 791) and the regulations implementing section 501, or who violated the requirements of section 501 of the Act or the regulations implementing section 501 concerning the provision of a reasonable accommodation, or section 102 of the Americans with Disabilities Act of 1990 (42 U.S.C. 12112), or committed a violation of section 102(b)(5) of the Act, against an individual, the complaining party may recover compensatory and punitive damages as allowed in subsection (b), in addition to any relief authorized by section 706(g) of the Civil Rights Act of 1964, from the respondent.

"(3) Reasonable Accommodation and Good Faith Effort. - In cases where a discriminatory practice involves the provision of a reasonable accommodation pursuant to section 102(b)(5) of the Americans with Disabilities Act of 1990 or regulations implementing section 501 of the Rehabilitation Act of 1973, damages may not be awarded under this section where the covered entity demonstrates good faith efforts, in consultation with the person with the disability who has informed the covered entity that accommodation is needed, to identify and make a reasonable accommodation that would provide such individual with an equally effective opportunity and would not cause an undue hardship on the operation of the business.

"(b) Compensatory and Punitive Damages. -

"(1) Determination of punitive damages. - A complaining party may recover punitive damages under this section against a respondent (other than a government, government agency or political subdivision) if the complaining party demonstrates that the respondent engaged in a discriminatory practice or discriminatory practices with malice or with reckless indifference to the federally protected rights of an aggrieved individual.

"(2) Exclusions from compensatory damages. - Compensatory damages awarded under this section shall not include back pay, interest on back pay, or any other type of relief authorized under section 706(g) of the Civil Rights Act of 1964.

"(3) Limitations. - The sum of the amount of compensatory damages awarded under this section for future pecuniary losses, emotional pain, suffering, inconvenience, mental anguish, loss of enjoyment of life, and other nonpecuniary losses, and the amount of punitive damages awarded under this section, shall not exceed, for each complaining party -

"(A) in the case of a respondent who has more than 14 and fewer than 101 employees in each of 20 or more calendar weeks in the current or preceding calendar year, $50,000;

"(B) in the case of a respondent who has more than 100 and fewer than 201 employees in each of 20 or more calendar weeks in the current or preceding calendar year, $100,000; and

"(C) in the case of a respondent who has more than 200 and fewer than 501 employees in each of 20 or more calendar weeks in the current or preceding calendar year, $200,000; and

"(D) in the case of a respondent who has more than 500 employees in each of 20 or more calendar weeks in the current or preceding calendar year, $300,000.

"(4) Construction. - Nothing in this section shall be construed to limit the scope of, or the relief available under, section 1977 of the Revised Statutes (42 U.S.C. 1981).

"(c) Jury Trial. - If a complaining party seeks compensatory or punitive damages under this section -

"(1) any party may demand a trial by jury; and

"(2) the court shall not inform the jury of the limitations described in subsection (b)(3).

"(d) Definitions. - As used in this section:

"(1) Complaining party. - The term 'complaining party' means -

"(A) in the case of a person seeking to bring an action under subsection (a)(1), the Equal Employment Opportunity Commission, the Attorney General, or a person who may bring an action or proceeding under title VII of the Civil Rights Act of 1964 (42 U.S.C. 2000e et seq.); or

"(B) in the case of a person seeking to bring an action under subsection (a)(2), the Equal Employment Opportunity Commission, the Attorney General, a person who may bring an action or proceeding under section 505(a)(1) of the Rehabilitation Act of 1973 (29 U.S.C. 794a(a)(1)), or a person who may bring an action or proceeding under title I of the Americans with Disabilities Act of 1990 (42 U.S.C. 12101 et seq.).

"(2) Discriminatory practice. - The term 'discriminatory practice' means the discrimination described in paragraph (1), or the discrimination or the violation described in paragraph (2), of subsection (a).

ATTORNEY'S FEES

[This section amends section 722 of the Revised Statutes (42 U.S.C. 1988) by adding a reference to section 102 of the Civil Rights Act of 1991 to the list of civil rights actions in which reasonable attorney's fees may be awarded to the prevailing party, other than the United States.]

SEC. 103

The last sentence of section 722 of the Revised Statutes (42 U.S.C. 1988) is amended by inserting ",1977A" after "1977".

DEFINITIONS

SEC. 104

[This section amends section 701 of the Civil Rights Act of 1964 (42 U.S.C. 2000e) by adding the following new subsections: (l) "complaining party," (m) "demonstrates," and (n) "respondent".]

BURDEN OF PROOF IN DISPARATE IMPACT CASES

SEC. 105

(a) *[This subsection amends section 703 of the Civil Rights Act of 1964 (42 U.S.C. 2000e-2) by adding a new subsection (k), on the burden of proof in disparate impact cases.]*

(b) No statements other than the interpretive memorandum appearing at Vol. 137 Congressional Record S 15276 (daily ed. Oct. 25, 1991) shall be considered legislative history of, or relied upon in any way as legislative history in construing or applying, any provision of this Act that relates to Wards Cove - Business necessity/cumulation/alternative business practice. *[42 U.S.C. 1981 note]*

PROHIBITION AGAINST DISCRIMINATORY USE OF TEST SCORES

SEC. 106

[This section amends section 703 of the Civil Rights Act of 1964 (42 U.S.C. 2000e-2) by adding a new subsection (l), on the prohibition against discriminatory use of test scores.]

CLARIFYING PROHIBITION AGAINST IMPERMISSIBLE CONSIDERATION OF RACE, COLOR, RELIGION, SEX, OR NATIONAL ORIGIN IN EMPLOYMENT PRACTICES

SEC. 107

(a) In general. *[This subsection amends section 703 of the Civil Rights Act of 1964 (42 U.S.C. 2000e-2) by adding a new subsection (m), clarifying the prohibition against consideration of race, color, religion, sex, or national origin in employment practices.]*

(b) Enforcement provisions. *[This subsection amends section 706(g) of the Civil Rights Act of 1964 (42 U.S.C. 2000e-5(g)) by renumbering existing subsection (g), and adding at the end a new subparagraph (B) to provide a limitation on available relief in "mixed motive" cases (where the employer demonstrates it would have made the same decision in the absence of discrimination).]*

FACILITATING PROMPT AND ORDERLY RESOLUTION OF CHALLENGES TO EMPLOYMENT PRACTICES IMPLEMENTING LITIGATED OR CONSENT JUDGMENTS OR ORDERS

SEC. 108

[This section amends section 703 of the Civil Rights Act of 1964 (42 U.S.C. 2000e-2) by adding a new subsection (n), on the resolution of challenges to employment practices implementing litigated or consent judgments or orders.]

PROTECTION OF EXTRATERRITORIAL EMPLOYMENT

SEC. 109

(a) Definition of Employee. *[This subsection amends the definition of "employee" in section 701(f) of the Civil Rights Act of 1964 (42 U.S.C. 2000e(f)) and section 101(4) of the Americans with Disabilities Act of 1990 (42 U.S.C. 12111(4)) by adding a sentence to the end of each definition to include U.S. citizens employed abroad within the laws' protections.]*

(b) Exemption. *[This subsection amends section 702 of the Civil Rights Act of 1964 (42 U.S.C. 2000e-1) by adding new subsections (b) (on compliance with the statute if violative of foreign law) and (c) (on the control of a corporation incorporated in a foreign country). This subsection similarly amends section 102 of the Americans with Disabilities Act of 1990 (42 U.S.C. 12112) by relettering the existing subsections and adding a new subsection (c) "Covered Entities in Foreign Countries."]*

(c) Application of Amendments. - The amendments made by this section shall not apply with respect to conduct occurring before the date of the enactment of this Act. *[42 U.S.C. 2000e note]*

TECHNICAL ASSISTANCE TRAINING INSTITUTE

SEC. 110

(a) Technical Assistance. *[This subsection amends section 705 of the Civil Rights Act of 1964 (42 U.S.C. 2000e-4) by adding a new subsection (j), establishing the Technical Assistance Training Institute.]*
(b) Effective Date. - The amendment made by this section shall take effect on the date of enactment of this Act. *[42 U.S.C. 2000e-4 note]*

EDUCATION AND OUTREACH

SEC. 111

[This section amends section 705(h) of the Civil Rights Act of 1964 (42 U.S.C. 2000e-4(h)) by renumbering the existing subsection and adding at the end a paragraph requiring the EEOC to engage in certain educational and outreach activities.]

EXPANSION OF RIGHT TO CHALLENGE DISCRIMINATORY SENIORITY SYSTEMS

SEC. 112

[This section amends section 706(e) of the Civil Rights Act of 1964 (42 U.S.C. 2000e-5(e)) by renumbering the subsection and adding at the end a paragraph to expand the right of claimants to challenge discriminatory seniority systems.]

AUTHORIZING AWARD OF EXPERT FEES

SEC. 113

(a) Revised Statutes. - Section 722 of the Revised Statutes is amended-

(1) by designating the first and second sentences as subsections (a) and (b), respectively, and indenting accordingly; and

(2) by adding at the end the following new subsection:

"(c) In awarding an attorney's fee under subsection (b) in any action or proceeding to enforce a provision of section 1977 or 1977A of the Revised Statutes, the court, in its discretion, may include expert fees as part of the attorney's fee." *[42 U.S.C. 1988]*

(b) Civil Rights Act of 1964. *[This section amends section 706(k) of the Civil Rights Act of 1964 (42 U.S.C. 2000e-5(k)) to provide for recovery of expert fees as part of an attorney's fees award.]*

PROVIDING FOR INTEREST AND EXTENDING THE STATUTE OF LIMITATIONS IN ACTIONS AGAINST THE FEDERAL GOVERNMENT

SEC. 114

[This section amends section 717 of the Civil Rights Act of 1964 (42 U.S.C. 2000e-16) by extending the time for federal employees or applicants to file a civil action from 30 to 90 days (from receipt of notice of final action taken by a department, agency or unit), and allowing federal employees or applicants the same interest to compensate for delay in payments as is available in cases involving nonpublic parties.]

NOTICE OF LIMITATIONS PERIOD UNDER THE AGE DISCRIMINATION IN EMPLOYMENT ACT OF 1967

SEC. 115

[This section amends section 7(e) of the Age Discrimination in Employment Act of 1967 (ADEA) (29 U.S.C. 626(e)) by eliminating the two- and three-year statute of limitations and making ADEA suit-filing requirements the same as those under Title VII, and requiring the EEOC to provide notice to charging parties upon termination of the proceedings.]

LAWFUL, COURT-ORDERED REMEDIES, AFFIRMATIVE ACTION, AND CONCILIATION AGREEMENTS NOT AFFECTED

SEC. 116 *[42 U.S.C. 1981 note]*

Nothing in the amendments made by this title shall be construed to affect court-ordered remedies, affirmative action, or conciliation agreements, that are in accordance with the law.

COVERAGE OF HOUSE OF REPRESENTATIVES AND THE AGENCIES OF THE LEGISLATIVE BRANCH

SEC. 117

(a) Coverage of the House of Representatives. *[This subsection extends the rights and protections of Title VII of the Civil Rights Act of 1964, as amended, to employees of the U.S. House of Representatives. Procedures for processing discrimination complaints are handled internally by the House, not by the EEOC.] [2 U.S.C. 60l]*

(b) Instrumentalities of Congress. *[This subsection extends the rights and protections of the Civil Rights Act of 1991 and Title VII of the Civil Rights Act of 1964, as amended, to "Instrumentalities of Congress," which are defined to include: the Architect of the Capitol, the Congressional Budget Office, the General Accounting Office, the Government Printing Office, the Office of Technology Assessment, and the United States Botanic Garden. Each agency is to establish its own remedies and procedures for enforcement.]*

ALTERNATIVE MEANS OF DISPUTE RESOLUTION

SEC. 118 *[42 U.S.C. 1981 note]*

Where appropriate and to the extent authorized by law, the use of alternative means of dispute resolution, including settlement negotiations, conciliation, facilitation, mediation, fact finding, minitrials, and arbitration, is encouraged to resolve disputes arising under the Acts or provisions of Federal law amended by this title.

TITLE II - GLASS CEILING

[This title sets up a "Glass Ceiling Commission" to focus attention on, and complete a study relating to, the existence of artificial barriers to the advancement of women and minorities in the workplace, and to make recommendations for overcoming such barriers. The Commission is to be composed of 21 members, with the Secretary of Labor serving as the Chairperson of the Commission. This title does not directly impose any responsibilities or obligations on the EEOC except to provide information and technical assistance as requested by the new Commission.] [42 U.S.C. 2000e note]

TITLE III - GOVERNMENT EMPLOYEE RIGHTS

GOVERNMENT EMPLOYEE RIGHTS ACT OF 1991

SEC. 301 *[2 U.S.C. 1201]*

(a) Short title. - This title may be cited as the "Government Employee Rights Act of 1991".

(b) Purpose. - The purpose of this title is to provide procedures to protect the right of Senate and other government employees, with respect to their public employment, to be free of discrimination on the basis of race, color, religion, sex, national origin, age, or disability.

(c) Definitions. - For purposes of this title:

(1) Senate employee. - The term "Senate employee" or "employee" means -

(A) any employee whose pay is disbursed by the Secretary of the Senate;

(B) any employee of the Architect of the Capitol who is assigned to the Senate Restaurants or to the Superintendent of the Senate Office Buildings;

(C) any applicant for a position that will last 90 days or more and that is to be occupied by an individual described in subparagraph (A) or (B); or

(D) any individual who was formerly an employee described in subparagraph (A) or (B) and whose claim of a violation arises out of the individual's Senate employment.

(2) Head of employing office. - The term "head of employing office" means the individual who has final authority to appoint, hire, discharge, and set the terms, conditions or privileges of the Senate employment of an employee.

(3) Violation. - The term "violation" means a practice that violates section 302 of this title.

DISCRIMINATORY PRACTICES PROHIBITED

SEC. 302 *[2 U.S.C. 1202]*

[Sections 320 and 321 (which protect Presidential appointees and previously exempt state employees who may file complaints of discrimination with EEOC under

this title) refer to the rights, protections and remedies of this section and section 307(h).]

All personnel actions affecting employees of the Senate shall be made free from any discrimination based on -

(1) race, color, religion, sex, or national origin, within the meaning of section 717 of the Civil Rights Act of 1964 (42 U.S.C. 2000e-16);

(2) age, within the meaning of section 15 of the Age Discrimination in Employment Act of 1967 (29 U.S.C. 633a); or

(3) handicap or disability, within the meaning of section 501 of the Rehabilitation Act of 1973 (29 U.S.C. 791) and sections 102–104 of the Americans with Disabilities Act of 1990 (42 U.S.C. 12112-14).

[SECTIONS 303 THROUGH 306: Section 303 (2 U.S.C. 1203) establishes the Office of Senate Fair Employment Practices, which will administer the procedures set forth in sections 304 through 307. Section 304 (2 U.S.C. 1204) outlines the four-step procedure described in Sections 305 through 309 for consideration of alleged violations. Section 305 (2 U.S.C. 1205) describes the Step I counseling procedures. Section 306 (2 U.S.C. 1206) describes the Step II mediation process. Section 307 (2 U.S.C. 1207), described fully below, sets forth the formal complaint and hearing procedures.]

STEP III: FORMAL COMPLAINT AND HEARING

SEC. 307 *[2 U.S.C. 1207]*

[SECTION 307, SUBSECTIONS (a) THROUGH (g), AND (i): Subsections (a) through (g), and (i) of Section 307 describe the process from the formal complaint through the hearing stage.]

[Sections 320 and 321 (which protect Presidential appointees and previously exempt state employees who may file complaints of discrimination with EEOC under this title) refer to the rights, protections and remedies of section 302 and the following subsection.]

(h) Remedies. - If the hearing board determines that a violation has occurred, it shall order such remedies as would be appropriate if awarded under section 706 (g) and (k) of the Civil Rights Act of 1964 (42 U.S.C. 2000e-5 (g) and (k)), and may also order the award of such compensatory damages as would be appropriate if awarded under section 1977 and section 1977A (a) and (b)(2) of the Revised Statutes (42 U.S.C. 1981 and 1981A (a) and (b)(2)). In the case of a determination that a violation based on age has occurred, the hearing board shall order such remedies as would be appropriate if awarded under section 15(c) of the Age Discrimination in Employment Act of 1967 (29 U.S.C. 633a(c)). Any order requiring the payment of money must be approved by a Senate resolution reported by the Committee on Rules and Administration. The hearing board shall have no authority to award punitive damages.

[SECTIONS 308 THROUGH 313: Section 308 (2 U.S.C. 1208) describes the procedures by which a Senate employee or head of an employing office may request a review by the Select Committee on Ethics of a decision issued under Section 307. Section 309 (2 U.S.C. 1209) describes the circumstances under which a Senate employee or Member of the Senate may petition for a review by the United States Court of Appeals for the Federal Circuit. Section 310 (2 U.S.C. 1210) describes the procedures by which a complaint may be resolved. Section 311 (2 U.S.C. 1211) enumerates reimbursable costs of attending hearings. Section 312 (2 U.S.C. 1212) prohibits intimidation or reprisal against any employee because of the exercise of a right under this title. Section 313 (2 U.S.C. 1213) outlines confidentiality requirements for counseling, mediation, hearings, final decisions, and records.]

EXERCISE OF RULEMAKING POWER

SEC. 314 *[2 U.S.C. 1214]*

The provisions of this title, except for sections 309, 320, 321, and 322, are enacted by the Senate as an exercise of the rulemaking power of the Senate, with full recognition of the right of the Senate to change its rules, in the same manner, and to the same extent, as in the case of any other rule of the Senate. Notwithstanding any other provision of law, except as provided in section 309, enforcement and adjudication with respect to the discriminatory practices prohibited by section 302, and arising out of Senate employment, shall be within the exclusive jurisdiction of the United States Senate.

TECHNICAL AND CONFORMING AMENDMENTS

SEC. 315

[This section makes technical and conforming amendments to section 509 of the Americans with Disabilities

Act of 1990 (ADA) (42 U.S.C. 12209) with respect to Senate employees.]

[SECTIONS 316 THROUGH 319: Section 316 (2 U.S.C. 1215) states that the consideration of political affiliation, domicile, and political compatibility with the employing office in an employment decision shall not be considered a violation of this title. Section 317 (2 U.S.C. 1216) states that a Senate employee may not commence a judicial proceeding to redress a prohibited discriminatory practice, except as provided in this title. Sec. 318 (2 U.S.C. 1217) expresses the Senate's view that legislation should be enacted to provide the same or comparable rights and remedies as are provided under this title to Congressional employees lacking such rights and remedies. Section 319 (2 U.S.C. 1218) reaffirms the Senate's commitment to Rule XLII of the Standing Rules of the Senate.]

COVERAGE OF PRESIDENTIAL APPOINTEES

SEC. 320 *[2 U.S.C. 1219]*

(a) In General. -

(1) Application. - The rights, protections, and remedies provided pursuant to section 302 and 307(h) of this title shall apply with respect to employment of Presidential appointees.

(2) Enforcement by administrative action. - Any Presidential appointee may file a complaint alleging a violation, not later than 180 days after the occurrence of the alleged violation, with the Equal Employment Opportunity Commission, or such other entity as is designated by the President by Executive Order, which, in accordance with the principles and procedures set forth in sections 554 through 557 of title 5, United States Code, shall determine whether a violation has occurred and shall set forth its determination in a final order. If the Equal Employment Opportunity Commission, or such other entity as is designated by the President pursuant to this section, determines that a violation has occurred, the final order shall also provide for appropriate relief.

(3) Judicial review. -

(A) In general. - Any party aggrieved by a final order under paragraph (2) may petition for review by the United States Court of Appeals for the Federal Circuit.

(B) Law applicable. - Chapter 158 of title 28, United States Code, shall apply to a review under this section except that the Equal Employment Opportunity Commission or such other entity as the President may designate under paragraph (2) shall be an "agency" as that term is used in chapter 158 of title 28, United States Code.

(C) Standard of review. - To the extent necessary to decision and when presented, the reviewing court shall decide all relevant questions of law and interpret constitutional and statutory provisions. The court shall set aside a final order under paragraph (2) if it is determined that the order was -

(i) arbitrary, capricious, an abuse of discretion, or otherwise not consistent with law;

(ii) not made consistent with required procedures; or

(iii) unsupported by substantial evidence.

In making the foregoing determinations, the court shall review the whole record or those parts of it cited by a party, and due account shall be taken of the rule of prejudicial error.

(D) Attorney's fees. - If the presidential appointee is the prevailing party in a proceeding under this section, attorney's fees may be allowed by the court in accordance with the standards prescribed under section 706(k) of the Civil Rights Act of 1964 (42 U.S.C. 2000e-5(k)).

(b) Presidential appointee. - For purposes of this section, the term "Presidential appointee" means any officer or employee, or an applicant seeking to become an officer or employee, in any unit of the Executive Branch, including the Executive Office of the President, whether appointed by the President or by any other appointing authority in the Executive Branch, who is not already entitled to bring an action under any of the statutes referred to in section 302 but does not include any individual -

(1) whose appointment is made by and with the advice and consent of the Senate;

(2) who is appointed to an advisory committee, as defined in section 3(2) of the Federal Advisory Committee Act (5 U.S.C. App.); or

(3) who is a member of the uniformed services.

COVERAGE OF PREVIOUSLY EXEMPT STATE EMPLOYEES

SEC. 321 *[2 U.S.C. 1220]*

(a) Application. - The rights, protections, and remedies provided pursuant to section 302 and 307(h) of this title shall apply with respect to employment of any individual chosen or appointed, by a person elected to public office in any State or political subdivision of any State by the qualified voters thereof -

(1) to be a member of the elected official's personal staff;

(2) to serve the elected official on the policymaking level; or

(3) to serve the elected official as an immediate advisor with respect to the exercise of the constitutional or legal powers of the office.

(b) Enforcement by administrative action. -

(1) In general. - Any individual referred to in subsection (a) may file a complaint alleging a violation, not later than 180 days after the occurrence of the alleged violation, with the Equal Employment Opportunity Commission, which, in accordance with the principles and procedures set forth in sections 554 through 557 of title 5, United States Code, shall determine whether a violation has occurred and shall set forth its determination in a final order. If the Equal Employment Opportunity Commission determines that a violation has occurred, the final order shall also provide for appropriate relief.

(2) Referral to state and local authorities. -

(A) Application. - Section 706(d) of the Civil Rights Act of 1964 (42 U.S.C. 2000e-5(d)) shall apply with respect to any proceeding under this section.

(B) Definition. - For purposes of the application described in subparagraph (A), the term "any charge filed by a member of the Commission alleging an unlawful employment practice" means a complaint filed under this section.

(c) Judicial review. - Any party aggrieved by a final order under subsection (b) may obtain a review of such order under chapter 158 of title 28, United States Code. For the purpose of this review, the Equal Employment Opportunity Commission shall be an "agency" as that term is used in chapter 158 of title 28, United States Code.

(d) Standard of review. - To the extent necessary to decision and when presented, the reviewing court shall decide all relevant questions of law and interpret constitutional and statutory provisions. The court shall set aside a final order under subsection (b) if it is determined that the order was -

(1) arbitrary, capricious, an abuse of discretion, or otherwise not consistent with law;

(2) not made consistent with required procedures; or

(3) unsupported by substantial evidence.

In making the foregoing determinations, the court shall review the whole record or those parts of it cited by a party, and due account shall be taken of the rule of prejudicial error.

(e) Attorney's fees. - If the individual referred to in subsection (a) is the prevailing party in a proceeding under this subsection, attorney's fees may be allowed by the court in accordance with the standards prescribed under section 706(k) of the Civil Rights Act of 1964 (42 U.S.C. 2000e-5(k)).

SEVERABILITY

SEC. 322 *[2 U.S.C. 1221]*

Notwithstanding section 401 of this Act, if any provision of section 309 or 320(a)(3) is invalidated, both sections 309 and 320(a)(3) shall have no force and effect.

PAYMENTS BY THE PRESIDENT OR A MEMBER OF THE SENATE

SEC. 323 *[2 U.S.C. 1222]*

The President or a Member of the Senate shall reimburse the appropriate Federal account for any payment made on his or her behalf out of such account for a violation committed under the provisions of this title by the President or Member of the Senate not later than 60 days after the payment is made.

REPORTS OF SENATE COMMITTEES

SEC. 324 *[2 U.S.C. 1223]*

(a) Each report accompanying a bill or joint resolution of a public character reported by any committee of the Senate (except the Committee on Appropriations and the Committee on the Budget) shall contain a listing of the provisions of the bill or joint resolution that apply to Congress and an evaluation of the impact of such provisions on Congress.

(b) The provisions of this section are enacted by the Senate as an exercise of the rulemaking power of the Senate, with full recognition of the right of the Senate to change its rules, in the same manner, and to the same extent, as in the case of any other rule of the Senate.

INTERVENTION AND EXPEDITED REVIEW OF CERTAIN APPEALS

SEC. 325 *[2 U.S.C. 1224]*

(a) Intervention. - Because of the constitutional issues that may be raised by section 309 and section 320, any Member of the Senate may intervene as a matter of right in any proceeding under section 309 for the sole purpose of determining the constitutionality of such section.

(b) Threshold Matter. - In any proceeding under section 309 or section320, the United States Court of Appeals for the Federal Circuit shall determine any issue presented concerning the constitutionality of such section as a threshold matter.

(c) Appeal. -

(1) In general. - An appeal may be taken directly to the Supreme Court of the United States from any interlocutory or final judgment, decree, or order issued by the United States Court of Appeals for the Federal Circuit ruling upon the constitutionality of section 309 or 320.

(2) Jurisdiction. - The Supreme Court shall, if it has not previously ruled on the question, accept jurisdiction over the appeal referred to in paragraph (1), advance the appeal on the docket and expedite the appeal to the greatest extent possible.

TITLE IV - GENERAL PROVISIONS

SEVERABILITY

SEC. 401 *[42 U.S.C. 1981 NOTE]*

If any provision of this Act, or an amendment made by this Act, or the application of such provision to any person or circumstances is held to be invalid, the remainder of this Act and the amendments made by this Act, and the application of such provision to other persons and circumstances, shall not be affected.

EFFECTIVE DATE

SEC. 402 *[42 U.S.C. 1981 NOTE]*

(a) In General. - Except as otherwise specifically provided, this Act and the amendments made by this Act shall take effect upon enactment.

(b) Certain Disparate Impact Cases. Notwithstanding any other provision of this Act, nothing in this Act shall apply to any disparate impact case for which a complaint was filed before March 1, 1975, and for which an initial decision was rendered after October 30, 1983.

Approved November 21, 1991.

Glossary

A

abuse of process The malicious and deliberate misuse or perversion of regularly issued court process.

abandonment When a tenant moves out of a leased premises and discontinues making rent payments.

absolute privilege An absolute special right, immunity, permission, or benefit given to an individual to make any statement, right or false, about someone without being held liable for defamation for any false statements made, regardless of intent or knowledge of the falsity of the claim.

absolutism Any set of ethics that is based on rules. These rules are considered moral regardless of perspective or dilemma.

acceptance A key element of a contract consisting of one party, the offeree, agreeing to the terms of the offer in the contract made by the other party, the offeror.

acceptor A person (drawee) who accepts and signs a draft to agree to pay the draft when it is presented.

accommodation party A party who signs an instrument to provide credit for another party that has also signed the instrument.

accord and satisfaction In a contract, when one of the parties wishes to substitute a different performance for his or her original duty under the contract; the promise to perform the new duty is called the accord, and the actual performance of that new duty is called the satisfaction.

accountant-client privilege The right of an accountant to not reveal any information given in confidence by a client. The privilege is not granted by every state, nor by the federal government.

accounting A review and listing of all partnership assets and/or profit.

accredited investor A private investor who is allowed to accept private securities offerings under certain specific guidelines set by the SEC.

act utilitarianism The method of ethics where all of the possible outcomes of a decision are weighed. This principle states that the outcome that creates the most happiness is the one that should be chosen.

actual cause The determination that the defendant's breach of duty resulted directly in the plaintiff's injury.

actual eviction When a landlord physically prevents a lessee from entering the leased premises.

actual notice Notice given about the termination of an agency relationship when third parties are directly informed.

actual malice A statement that is made or materials that are published with knowledge that the information was false or with reckless disregard of whether it was false.

actus reus Latin words for "guilty act." It refers to a wrongful behavior that is associated with the physical act of a declared crime.

ad substantiation An FTC standard requiring that advertisements have reasonable basis for the claims made in the ad.

adhesion contract A contract rescinded on the grounds of unconscionability and the absence of one party's free will to enter a contract.

administrative agency Generally defined as any body created by the legislative branch (e.g., Congress, a state legislature, or a city council) to carry out specific duties.

administrative law The collection of rules and decisions made by administrative agencies to fill in the particular details missing from constitutions and statutes.

administrative law judge (ALJ) Presides over an administrative hearing; may attempt to get the parties to settle, but has the power to issue a binding decision.

Administrative Procedures Act (APA) Created as a major limitation on how agencies are run; contains very specific guidelines on rule making by agencies.

admission A statement made in court, under oath, or at some stage during a legal proceeding, where a party against whom charges have been brought admits an oral contract existed, even though the contract was required to be in writing.

advance directives A variety of legal instruments a person can use to express his or her wishes without efforts to prolong life.

adversarial negotiation Negotiation where each party seeks to maximize its own gain.

adverse possession A means of involuntarily transferring property whereby a person acquires ownership of property by treating a piece of real property as his or her own, without protest or permission from the owner.

affiliate A business enterprise that is directly or indirectly owned and controlled by another enterprise.

affirm A term used to refer to an appellate court's accepting a lower court's judgment in a case that has been appealed.

affirmative defense A defendant's response to a plaintiff's claim in which a defendant takes the offense and responds to the allegations by attacking the plaintiff's legal right to bring the action rather than attacking the fact of the claim or making excuses for unlawful behavior. Some of the most common defenses include expiration of the statute of limitation, mistake of fact, intoxication, insanity, duress, and entrapment.

after-acquired property Property acquired by the debtor after the security arrangement is made.

Age Discrimination in Employment Act of 1967 (ADEA) Federal law that prohibits employers from refusing to hire, discharging, or discriminating in terms and conditions of employment on the basis of an employee's or applicant's being age 40 or older.

agency "Fiduciary relation that results from the manifestation of consent by one person to another that the other shall act in his behalf and subject to his control, and consent by the other so to act." *The Restatement of Agency*

agency by estoppel An agency relationship created by operation of law when one party, by his actions, causes a third party to believe someone is his agent when that person actually has no authority; also called **apparent agency.**

agency coupled with an interest An agency relationship created for the benefit of the agent, not the principal.

agency relationship The association between one party and an agent who acts on behalf of that party.

agent A party who has the authority to act on behalf of and bind another party.

agreement One of the four elements necessary for a contract; consists of an offer made by one party, the offeror, and the acceptance of the offer by another party, the offeree.

alien corporation A business incorporated in a foreign country.

allonge Accompanying a negotiable instrument, an allonge provides room for an endorsement if such room is not available on the negotiable instrument.

alterations Changes that affect the condition of the premises.

alternative dispute resolution (ADR) The resolution of legal problems through other methods besides litigation.

ambulatory The ability to be changed by a testator.

Americans with Disabilities Act (ADA) Federal law that prohibits discrimination against employees and job applicants with disabilities.

anatomical gifts Parts of an individual's body that the individual wishes to donate to a hospital, university, organ bank, etc.

answer The response of the defendant to the plaintiff's complaint.

antidumping duties Special tariffs imposed on imported goods in order to offset illegal dumping.

antilapse clause States that the insured has a grace period in which to make an overdue payment.

apparent agency An agency relationship created by operation of law when one party, by his actions, causes a third party to believe someone is his agent when that person actually has no authority; also called **agency by estoppel.**

appeal The act or fact of challenging the decision of a trial court after final judgment or other legal ruling by taking the matter to the appropriate appellate court, and in some cases to the U.S. Supreme Court, in an attempt to reverse the decision.

appraisal right A dissenting shareholder's right to have his or her shares appraised and to receive monetary compensation from the corporation for their value.

appropriation for commercial gain A privacy tort that occurs when someone uses a person's name, likeness, voice, identity, or other identifying characteristics for commercial gain without that person's permission.

arbitration A type of alternative dispute resolution wherein disputes are submitted for resolution to private nonofficial persons selected in a manner provided by law or the agreement of the parties.

arraignment The first appearance in court by the defendant in which he or she is advised of the pending charges, the right to counsel, and the right to trial by jury and to plea to the charge.

arrest The action of the police, or person acting under the law, to seize, hold, or take an individual into custody.

arson Crime of setting fire to another's property.

articles of incorporation A document a corporation files with the state, explaining its organization.

articles of partnership The written agreement that creates a partnership.

artisan's lien A claim on personal property to satisfy a person's debt related to the property.

assault A civil wrong that occurs when one person intentionally and voluntarily places another in fear or apprehension of an immediate or offensive physical harm. Assault does not require an actual contact.

assignee In a contract, the party who receives the rights of another party to collect what was contractually agreed upon in the first contract.

assignment (1) A transfer of a tenant's entire interest in the leased property.

assignment (2) When a party to a contract (an assignor) transfers his or her rights to a contract to a third party (an assignee); i.e., the assignor gives to an assignee the right to collect what was contractually agreed upon in the first contract.

assignor In a contract, the party who transfers his or her rights to a contract to a third party (an assignee), giving the assignee the right to collect what was contractually agreed upon in the first contract.

assumption of the risk (defense) A defense whereby the defendant must prove that the plaintiff voluntarily assumed the risk the defendant caused.

attachment The point at which the creditor becomes the secured party who has a security interest in the collateral.

attempt to monopolize An intention to gain market by excluding competitors and thereby gain monopoly power.

automated teller machines Machines connected to banking computers allowing customers to conduct transactions without having to enter their bank.

automatic stay After bankruptcy has been filed, the automatic stay acts as a shield to prevent creditors from taking further action against the debtor or his or her property.

B

bail A thing of value such as a money bail bond or any other form of property that is given to the court to temporarily allow a person's release from jail and to ensure his or her appearance in court.

bailment of personal property A relationship that arises when one party, the bailer, gives possession of personal property to another, the bailee, for an agreed-upon time period, with an agreed-upon compensation, if any, and the bailee's treatment of the property to be agreed upon in advance.

bait-and-switch advertising When a seller advertises a low-priced item, generally unavailable to the consumer, then pushes the consumer to buy a more expensive item.

Bankruptcy Abuse Prevention and Consumer Protection Act of 2005 A renovation in the system of bankruptcy to address: increased numbers of bankruptcy filings, significant losses associated with bankruptcy filings, loopholes and incentives that allowed for abuse, and the financial ability of debtors.

bankruptcy estate The assets that are collected from a debtor in the event that he or she files for bankruptcy.

battery A civil wrong that occurs when one person intentionally and voluntarily brings about a nonconsented harmful or offensive contact with a person or to something closely associated with him/her. Battery requires an actual contact.

beachhead acquisition When an aggressor gradually accumulates the target company's shares.

bearer instrument An instrument payable to cash or whomever is in possession of the instrument.

bench trial Refers to trial before a judge in which the defendant has waived his/her right to a jury trial and the judgment is decided by means of a judge rather than a jury.

beneficiaries Those who can expect to benefit from a relationship.

beneficiary The person who receives, or will receive, the proceeds from an insurance policy or a will.

bid rigging An agreement among firms to not bid against one another or to submit a certain level of bid.

bilateral contract A promise exchanged for a promise.

bilateral trade agreements An international agreement between two states relating to trade between them.

bill of lading A document issued by a person engaged in the business of transporting goods that verifies receipt of the goods for shipment.

binder An agreement that gives temporary insurance until the company decides to accept or reject the insurance application.

binding arbitration clause A provision in a contract mandating that all disputes arising under the contract must be settled by arbitration.

blank endorsement A payee's or last endorsee's signature on a negotiable instrument.

blank qualified endorsement The mode of endorsement wherein the name of the payee or beneficiary of the instrument is not mentioned so as to make it freely transferable on delivery, and the words recourse limit the liability of the endorser.

blue-sky laws Laws that regulate the offering and sale of purely intrastate securities.

booking A procedure during which the name of the defendant, after he/she was arrested, is recorded in the investigating agency or police department's records.

bounty payments Government rewards for acts beneficial to the public.

boycott A refusal to deal with, purchase goods from, or work for a business.

bribery A corrupt and illegal activity in which a person offers or receives money, services, or soliciting of any thing of value in order to gain an illicit advantage.

brief A brief or factum is a written legal document that is presented to a court arguing why the party to the case should prevail.

burden of proof The duty of the plaintiff or prosecution to establish a claim or allegation by admissible evidence and to prove that the defendant committed all the essential elements of the crime to the jury's or court's satisfaction beyond any reasonable doubt, in order to convict the defendant.

burglary When someone unlawfully enters a building with intention to commit a felony or theft.

business ethics The use of ethics and ethical principles to solve business dilemmas.

business law The enforceable rules of conduct that govern the actions of buyers and sellers in market exchanges.

business trust A business organization governed by a group of trustees, who in turn operate the trust for beneficiaries.

buyer in the ordinary course of business A person who routinely buys goods in good faith from a person who routinely sells these goods.

bylaws Rules or regulations that govern a corporation's internal management.

C

capacity The legal ability to enter into a binding contract.

case law The collection of legal interpretations made by judges; they are considered to be law unless otherwise revoked by a statutory law. (Also known as **common law.**)

case or controversy A term used in the United States Constitution to describe the structure and the requirement of conflicting claims of individuals that could be brought before a federal court for resolution. It is also referred to as a justifiable controversy that is required to consist of an actual dispute between parties over their legal rights that remain in conflict at the time the case is presented and must be a proper matter for judicial determination.

cash tender offer Where cash is paid for current shareholders' stocks.

cashier's check A check produced in which both drawer and drawee are the same bank.

casualty insurance Insurance that protects a party from accidental injury.

categorical imperative The principle that an act is ethical when we would wish for all people to act according to its dictates.

cease-and-desist order An FTC order requiring that a company stop its illegal behavior.

certificate of deposit A document whereby a bank promises to pay a payee a certain amount of money at a future time.

certificate of incorporation A document certifying that the corporation is incorporated in the state and is authorized to conduct business.

certificate of limited partnership A document signed upon the formation of a limited partnership and filed with the secretary of state.

certified check Any check accepted by the bank from which the funds are drawn.

chain-style business operation A type of franchise where the franchise operates under the franchisor's business name and is required to follow the franchisor's standards and methods of business operation.

charging order The entitling of a creditor to a partner's profits.

chattel paper A writing that indicates both monetary obligations and security interest in specific goods.

check A special draft ordering that a bank (the drawee) pay a specified sum of money to the drawer.

choice-of-law clause A contractual clause wherein the parties choose the law of a certain state to apply to the interpretation of the contract or in the event of a dispute.

chose in action The surviving corporation's right to sue for debt and damages on behalf of the absorbed corporation.

Circuit Court of Appeal A court that hears appeals from the district courts located within its circuit, as well as appeals from decisions of federal administrative agencies. Also called Federal District Court of Appeal.

civil law Those laws that govern the rights and responsibilities either between persons or between persons and their government.

closely held corporation A corporation that does not sell stock to the general public.

closing The meeting at which the transfer of title actually takes place. It is the meeting at which the seller signs over the deed, and the buyer gives the seller a check for the amount due.

codicil The document by which a testator changes his or her will.

collateral The property that is subject to the secured interest.

collecting bank Any bank, with the exception of the payor bank, that handles a check during the check collection.

collective bargaining The process whereby workers organize collectively and bargain with employers regarding the workplace.

commerce clause Clause 3 of Article I, Section 8 of the United States Constitution authorizes and empowers the United States Congress "To regulate Commerce with foreign Nations, and among the several States, and with the Indian Tribes."

commercial general liability policy A policy that generally provides protection for the insured for bodily injury as well as property injury to third parties.

commercial insurance Insurance that covers some type of business risk.

commercial reasonableness Reasonable commercial standards of fair dealing, required of merchants in addition to honesty in fact.

commercial speech Speech made by business about commercial matters such as sale of goods and services is protected by the First Amendment.

common areas Areas that are used by all tenants.

common-carrier delivery contract A type of contract in which purchased goods are delivered to the buyer via an independent contractor, such as a trucking line.

common carriers Carriers that are licensed to provide transportation services to the public.

common law See **case law.**

common stock A portion of the shares of a corporation that do not include any preference.

communication In a contract, an offer made to the offeree or the offeree's agent.

comparative law The study of the legal systems of different states.

compensatory damages Money awarded to the plaintiff according to the amount of actual damage or harm to property, lost wages or profits, pain and suffering, medical expenses, disability, etc.

complaint A formal written document that begins a civil lawsuit, which contains the plaintiff's list of allegations against the defendant, along with the damages the plaintiff.

complete performance When all aspects of the parties' duties under the contract are carried out perfectly.

computer crime Crime committed using a computer.

concealment The active hiding of the truth about a material fact.

concurrent condition In a contract, when each party's performance is conditioned on the performance of the other, occurring only when the parties are required to perform for each other simultaneously.

condemnation The legal process by which a transfer of property is made against the protest of the property owner.

condition precedent The first thing that must occur when an entire contract is conditioned upon that something first occurring.

condition subsequent In a contract, a future event that terminates the obligations of the parties when it occurs.

conditional contract A contract that becomes enforceable only upon the happening or termination of a specified condition.

conditional endorsement An endorsement whereby payment can be made only upon fulfillment of a predecided condition, e.g., painting one's house.

conditional estate Gives the holder the same interest as that of a fee simple absolute, only this interest is subject to a condition.

conditional privilege A special right, immunity, permission, or benefit given to an individual to make any statement, right or false, about someone without being held liable for defamation for any false statements made without actual malice.

conditional sales contract Type of contract in which the sale itself is contingent on approval: either a sale-on-approval contract or a sale-or-return contract.

conforming goods Goods that conform to contract specifications.

conglomerate merger When a company merges with another company that is not a competitor or a buyer or seller to the company.

consent decree An agreement that binds the violating party to cease his or her illegal behavior.

consent order A statement where a company agrees to stop disputed behavior, but does not admit it broke the law.

consequential damages In a contract, foreseeable damages that arise due to special facts and circumstances arising outside the contract itself; damages must be within the contemplation of the parties at the time the breach occurs.

consequentialism The ethical theory based on consequences. It states that in considering what action is ethical, the only thing that matters is its consequences.

consideration The bargain for exchange; what each party gets in exchange for his/her promise under the contract.

Consolidated Omnibus Budget Reconciliation Act (COBRA) Federal law that ensures that when employees lose their jobs or have their hours reduced to a level at which they would not be eligible to receive medical, dental, or optical benefits from their employer, the employees will be able to continue receiving benefits under the employer's policy for up to 18 months by paying the premiums for the policy.

constitutional law The general limits and powers of a government as interpreted from its written constitution.

constructive eviction When a property has become unsuitable for use due to the unlivable quality of the property.

constructive notice The manner in which notice of agency termination is announced.

constructive trust (1) An implied trust where a party is named to hold the trust for its rightful owner.

constructive trust (2) An equitable trust imposed on one who wrongfully obtains or holds legal right to property he or she should not possess.

consumer good A good used or bought for use primarily for personal, family, or household purposes.

consumer lease A lease that has a value of $25,000 or less and exists between a lessor regularly engaged in the business of leasing or selling and a lessee who leases the goods primarily for a personal, family, or household purpose.

contract A promise or set of promises for the breach of which the law gives a remedy or the performance of which the law in some way recognizes a duty.

contract clause The clause that prohibits the government from unreasonably interfering with an existing contract.

contract under seal A contract that has a seal to make it legal.

contractual capacity The legal ability to enter into a binding agreement.

contributory negligence A defense to negligence whereby the defendant can escape all liability by proving that the plaintiff failed to act in such a way as to protect him or herself from an unreasonable risk of harm, and that negligent behavior contributed in any way to the plaintiff's accident.

Convention on the International Sale of Goods An international agreement applicable to transactions involving the commercial sale of goods.

conversion The permanent interference with another's use and enjoyment of his or her personal property.

co-ownership When multiple individuals possess ownership interests in a property.

cooperative An organization formed by individuals to market new products. Individuals in a cooperative pool their resources together to gain an advantage in the market.

copyright The protection of a creative work that has been placed in a fixed form.

corporation A legal entity formed by issuing stock to investors, who are the owners of the corporation.

corporation by estoppel A corporation that has conducted business with a third party and thereby cannot deny its status as a corporation.

corrective advertising (counteradvertising) Running advertisements in which the company explicitly states that the formerly advertised claims were untrue.

cost-benefit analysis An economic school of jurisprudence where all costs and benefits to a law are given monetary values. Those laws with the highest ratio of benefits to costs are then preferable to those with lesser ratios.

counterclaim A claim by the defendant against the plaintiff that is filed along with the defendant's answer.

counteroffer An offer made by an offeree to the offeror relating to the same matter as the original offer and proposing a substituted bargain differing from that proposed by the original offer.

countervailing duties Special tariffs imposed on subsidized goods in order to offset the beneficial effect of an illegal subsidy.

course of dealing Previous commercial transactions between the same parties.

course of performance The history of dealings between the parties in the particular contract at issue.

court of appellate jurisdiction (appellate court) A higher court usually consisting of more than one judge, which reviews the decisions and results of a lower court (either a trial court or a lower-level appellate court) when a losing party files for an appeal. Appellate courts do not hold trials but may request additional oral and written arguments from each party. Appellate courts issue written decisions, which collectively constitute case law or the common law.

covenant of quiet enjoyment A promise that the tenant has the right to quietly enjoy the land.

covenants not to compete Agreement not to compete for a party for a set period of time.

cover A buyer's right to substitute goods for those due under the sales or lease agreement when the seller provides nonconforming goods.

creditor An entity to which a debtor owes money.

creditor beneficiary A third party who benefits from a contract where the promisor agrees to pay the promisee's debt.

creditor's meeting A meeting of all the creditors listed in the Chapter 7 required schedule for liquidation.

criminal fraud A crime or an offense encompassing a variety of means by which an individual intentionally uses some sort of misrepresentation to gain an advantage over another person.

criminal law A classification of law involving the rights and responsibilities an individual has with respect to the public as a whole.

criteria air pollutant One of the six air pollutants that are subject to the National Ambient Air Quality Standards under the Clean Air Act.

critical thinking skills The ability to understand the structure and worth of an argument by evaluating the facts, issue, reasons, and conclusion of that argument.

cross-licensing A contractual arrangement between two or more parties who own intellectual property under which each party grants to the other a license of specified intellectual property.

cure The breaching party's right to provide conforming goods when nonconforming goods were initially delivered; subject to a reasonable time test.

customary international law A general and consistent practice by states accepted as binding law.

customs union A free trade area with the additional feature of a common external tariff on products originating from outside the union.

cyber terrorist A hacker whose intention is the exploitation of a target computer or network to create a serious impact, such as the crippling of a communications network or the sabotage of a business or organization, which may have an impact on millions of citizens if the terrorist's attack is successful.

cyberlaw A classification of law regulating business activities that are conducted online.

D

de facto corporation A corporation that has not met the requirements of the state incorporation statutes.

de jure corporation A corporation that has received its certificate of incorporation.

debt securities Securities that represent loans to a company.

debtor An entity that owes money to another entity.

deceptive advertising The practice of advertising using claims that mislead or could mislead a reasonable consumer.

defamation A false statement or actions of another that harm the reputation or character of an individual, business, product, group, government, or nation.

default Failure to make payments on a loan.

default judgment Judgment for the plaintiff when the defendant fails to respond to the complaint.

defective corporation A corporation in which an error or omission has been made during its incorporation process.

defendant The person, party, or entity against whom a civil or criminal lawsuit is filed in a court of law.

definite and certain terms Requirement under common law that calls for the clearly defined terms of a contract to include all material terms.

definite term lease A lease that expires at the end of a specified term.

delegatee The third party who although not part of the original contract yet is transferred duties from one of the parties (a delegator).

delegation Occurs when a party to a contract (a delegator) transfers his or her duty to perform to a third party who is not part of the original contract (a delegatee).

delegator Party in a contract who transfers his or her duties to perform to a third party who is not a part of the original contract (a delegatee).

demand instrument A type of draft where the payee can demand payment at any time from a holder.

deontology The ethical theory that states that an action can be determined ethical regardless of its consequences.

depositary bank The first bank that receives a check for payment.

depositions A pretrial sworn and recorded testimony of a witness that is acquired out of court with no judge present.

design defect When all products of a particular design are defective and dangerous.

digital cash Money stored electronically in place of physical currency.

direct deposit The process, preauthorized by a customer, allowing funds to be received into or paid from the customer's bank account(s).

directed verdict A ruling by the judge after the plaintiff has put forward his or her case, but before any evidence was put forward by the defendant, in favor of the defendant because the plaintiff has failed to put forward the minimum amount of evidence necessary to establish his or her claim.

discharge A written federal court order signed by a bankruptcy judge stating that the debtor is immune from creditor actions to collect debt, i.e., a release from liability.

disclosed principal Making a third party aware that the agent is making an agreement on behalf of a principal, where the third party knows the identity of the principal.

discovery The pretrial phase in a lawsuit during which each party requests relevant documents and other evidence from the other side in an attempt to "discover" pertinent facts and to avoid any surprises in the courtroom during the trial. Discovery tools include requests for admissions, interrogatories, depositions, requests for inspection, and document production requests.

dishonored Payment that has been refused despite a holder's presenting an instrument in a timely and proper manner.

dishonored instrument An instrument that a party has refused to pay.

disparagement A business tort that a statement is intentionally used to defame a business product or service.

disparate impact Arises when an employee attempts to establish that, while an employer's policy or practice appears to apply to everyone equally, its actual effect is that it disproportionately limits employment opportunities for a protected class.

disparate treatment If an employee has been hired, fired, denied a promotion, etc. based on membership in that protected class, this is a form of intentional discrimination; proving disparate treatment is a three step process: (1) the employee must demonstrate a prima facie case of discrimination; (2) the employer must articulate a legitimate, nondiscriminatory business reason for the action; and (3) the employee must show that the reason given by the employer is a mere pretext.

dispute settlement understanding An agreement that is part of the WTO system whereby recognized governments of WTO member states may bring an action alleging a violation of the GATT by other member states.

dissolution The change in the relation of the partners caused by any partner's ceasing to be associated with the activity of completing unfinished partnership business, collecting and paying debts, collecting partnership assets, and taking inventory.

distributor A merchant who purchases goods from a seller for resale in a foreign market.

distributorship A type of franchise where the franchisor manufactures a product and licenses a dealer to sell the product in an exclusive territory.

district court A trial court in the federal system.

dividend A distribution of corporate profits or income ordered by the directors and paid to the shareholders.

document of title A transport document that, when appropriately made out, entitles the bearer to claim the goods from the carrier.

domestic corporation A corporation lying within the borders of some state.

donee beneficiary Third party who benefits from a contract where a promisor agrees to give a gift to the third party.

dormant commerce clause Refers to the negative implications of the commerce clause of the United States Constitution on states. The power given to the United States Congress to enact legislation that affects interstate commerce implies a negative converse and restriction that prohibit a state from passing legislation that improperly burdens interstate commerce.

draft An instrument validating an order by a *drawer* to a *drawee* to pay a payee.

dram shop acts Regulations that allow bartenders to be held liable for injuries caused by individuals who become intoxicated in their bar.

drawee The party who must obey an order. In the context of banking, the drawee is the bank that must pay the funds ordered by a customer's check.

drawer The party who writes an order, or the person who writes a check.

due diligence defense When a defendant argues that he or she applied the appropriate degree of attention, care or research expected of a party in a given situation and had reasonable grounds to believe that certain facts and statements were accurate and had no omission of material facts.

due process clause A clause in the Fifth Amendment of the United States Constitution providing that the government cannot deprive an individual of life, liberty, or property without a fair and just hearing.

durable power of attorney Specifies that an agent's authority is intended to continue beyond the principal's incapacitation.

duress Any unlawful act or threat exercised upon a person whereby he/she is forced to enter into an agreement or to perform some other act against his/her will.

duty The standard of care a defendant must meet so as to not subject a person in the position of the plaintiff to an unreasonable risk of harm.

duty of loyalty The expectation that an agent will act in the interest of the principal.

duty of notification The expectation that an agent will inform the principal of his or her actions as agent to that principal.

duty to compensate Required payment to an agent for his or her services.

E

e-money Electronic, nonphysical forms of currency.

easement An irrevocable right to use some part of another's land for a specific purpose, without taking anything from it.

easement by prescription Created by state law when certain conditions are met, most frequently by openly using a portion of another's property for a statutory period of time (usually 25 years).

effective date The date that insurance takes effect.

efficiency Getting the most output from the least input.

Electronic Communications Privacy Act (ECPA) of 1986 Federal law that extended employees' privacy rights to electronic forms of communication including e-mail and cellular phones. ECPA outlaws the intentional interception of electronic communications and the intentional disclosure or use of the information obtained through such interception.

electronic fund transfer (EFT) Any funds transmitted by an electronic terminal, telephone, or computer.

embezzlement A wrongful conversion of another's funds or property by one who is lawfully in possession of those funds or that property.

Employee Retirement Income Security Act (ERISA) Federal law that sets minimum standards for most voluntarily established pension and health plans in private industry to provide protection for individuals in these plans.

employment-at-will standard Permits either the employer or employee to terminate the employment relationship at any time.

enabling legislation A statute that specifies the name, functions, and specific powers of the administrative agency; and grants the agency broad powers for the purpose of serving the "public interest, convenience, and necessity."

endorsee The person receiving an endorsement.

endorsement for deposit/ collection only The most common type of endorsement, providing that the instrument can only be deposited into an account.

endorsement to prohibit further endorsement An endorsement allowing increased protection to the endorsee.

endorser One who issues an endorsement.

English rule States the first assignee to give notice of assignment to the obligor is the party with rights to the contract.

entrapment A relatively common defense that claims the defendant would not have committed the crime or broken the law if not induced or tricked by law enforcement officials.

entrustment The transfer of goods to a merchant who ordinarily deals in that type of goods, who may subsequently sell them to a good-faith third-party purchaser who acquires then good title to the goods.

environmental impact statement A document containing a detailed statement of

1. The environmental impact of the proposed action
2. Any adverse environmental effects that cannot be avoided should the proposal be implemented
3. Alternatives to the proposed action
4. The relationship between local short-term uses of the human environment and the maintenance and enhancement of long-term productivity
5. Any irreversible and irretrievable commitments of resources that would be involved in the proposed activity should it be implemented

that must be filed whenever there is a major, federal activity that may have a significant impact on the environment.

equal dignity rule Requires contracts that would normally fall under a statute and require a writing if negotiated by the principal to be in writing even if negotiated by an agent.

Equal Pay Act of 1963 (EPA) Prohibits an employer from paying workers of one gender less than the wages paid to employees of the opposite gender for work that requires equal skill, effort, and responsibility.

Equal Protection Clause A clause in the Fourteenth Amendment of the United States Constitution that prevents states from denying "the equal protection of the laws" to any citizen. This clause implies that all citizens are created equal.

equity securities Securities that represent ownership in a corporation.

Establishment Clause One of two provisions in the First Amendment of the United States Constitution that protect citizens' freedom of religion. It prohibits (1) the establishment of a national religion by Congress and (2) the preference of one religion over another or of religion over nonreligious philosophies in general.

estate planning The process whereby an individual decides what to do with his or her real and personal property during and after life.

ethical dilemma A question about how one should behave that requires one to reflect about the advantages and disadvantages of the optional choices for various stakeholders.

ethical guideline A simple tool to help determine whether an action is moral.

ethical relativism The ethical theory that denies the existence of an ultimate ethical system. According to this theory, a decision must be determined ethical on the basis of its own context.

ethics The study and practice of decisions about what is good or right.

ethics of care The ethical theory that places its emphasis on human interaction. According to this theory, what makes a decision ethical is how well it builds and promotes human relationships.

European Union A customs union consisting of an association of states with a basis in international law formed for the purpose of forging closer ties among the peoples of Europe.

exchange tender offer In a takeover, the aggressor offers to exchange the target shareholders' current stock for stock in the aggressor's corporation.

exclusive-dealing contract An agreement where a seller requires that a buyer buy products supplied only by that seller.

exculpatory clause A clause in a contract that basically frees one party (usually the drafter of the agreement) from all liability arising out of performance of that contract, generally based on factors such as consumer ignorance or a great deal of unexplained fine print, that serve to deprive the less powerful party of a meaningful choice.

executive agency The administrative head of an executive agency is appointed by the president with the advice and consent of the U.S. Senate and may be discharged by the president at any time, for any reason. Executive agencies are generally located within the executive branch, under one of the cabinet-level departments (and thus are referred to as *cabinet-level agencies*). Examples are the Federal Aviation Agency (FAA) and the Food and Drug Administration (FDA).

executed When all of the terms of the contract have been fully performed.

executive order Dictates that have the force of law, but are issued by a Governor or the President.

executory A contract in which not all of the terms have been fully performed.

exemplary damages Monetary damages and can include compensatory, punitive, nominal, and liquidated damages.

exempted rule making The APA contains an exemption from rule making that allows an agency to decide whether public participation will be allowed. Exemptions include rule-making proceedings with regard to "military or foreign affairs," "agency management or personnel," and "public property, loans, grants, benefits or contracts" of an agency.

express condition A condition specifically and explicitly stated in the contract and usually preceded by words such as *conditioned on, if, provided that,* or *when.*

express contract A contract in which all the terms are clearly set forth in either written or spoken words.

express trust A trust created either while the settlor is alive or by will.

express warranty Any description of a good's physical nature or its use, either in general or specific circumstances, that becomes part of the contract.

expressed agency An agency created in written or oral agreement.

extortion (blackmail) A criminal offense that occurs when a person obtains money, property, and/or services from another by wrongfully threatening or inflicting harm to his person, property, or reputation.

F

failure to provide adequate warnings A defect whereby the product is not labeled to indicate that it can be dangerous.

fair-use doctrine The lawful use of a limited, noncommercial portion of another's work for purposes of criticism, comment, news reporting, teaching, scholarship, or research.

Fair Labor Standards Act (FLSA) Requires that a minimum wage of a specified amount be paid to all employees in covered industries; mandates that employees who work more than 40 hours in a week be paid no less than 1½ times their regular wage for all the hours beyond 40 that they work during a given week.

False Claims Act An act that allows employees to sue employers on behalf of the federal government for fraud against the government. The employee retains a share of the recovery as a reward for his/her efforts.

false imprisonment Unlawful restraint of another against the person's will.

false light A privacy tort that occurs when highly offensive information is published about an individual that is not valid or places the person in a false light.

false pretense Materially false representations of an existing fact, with knowledge of the falsity of the representations, with the intention to defraud.

Family and Medical Leave Act (FMLA) Federal act requiring that employers establish a policy that provides all eligible employees with up to 12 weeks of leave during any 12-month period for several family-related occurrences (e.g., birth of a child or a sick spouse).

family incentive trust Trusts designed to take effect upon the completion of specified behavior.

federal preemption A principle asserting the supremacy of the federal over the state legislation over the same subject matter.

Federal Register An agency initiates informal rule making by publishing the proposed rule in the *Federal Register*, along with an explanation of the legal authority for issuing the rule and a description of how the public can participate in the rule-making process.

Federal Unemployment Tax Act (FUTA) Passed in 1935 to created a state system to provide unemployment compensation to qualified employees who lose their jobs.

federalism A system of government where power is divided between a central authority and constituent political units.

fee simple absolute The most comprehensive ownership interest, which gives exclusive rights to ownership and possession of the land to the holder.

fellow servant rule Outdated defense that prohibited an employee from suing an employer for negligence if the employee's injury was caused by another employee.

felony A serious crime, such as murder, rape, or robbery, which is punishable by imprisonment for more than one year or death.

fictitious payees (rule) A UCC rule governing the liability of companies and their endorsed checks. A fictitious payee is someone having no right to payment. Any check made out to a fictitious payee and endorsed must be honored and is not considered a forgery.

finance lease Lease in which the lessor does not select, manufacture, or supply the goods, but acquires title to the goods or the right to their possession and use in connection with the terms of the lease.

financing statement Lists the names and addresses of all those parties involved, a description of the collateral, and the signature of the debtor.

fire insurance Protects property from losses caused by any damages by fire.

firm offer An offer made in writing and giving assurances that it will be irrevocable for a period of time not longer than three months despite a lack of consideration for the irrevocability.

first appearance The initial appearance of an arrested individual before a judge, who determines whether or not there was probable cause for the arrest. If the judge ascertains that probable cause did not exist, the individual is freed.

first assignment in time rule States the first party granted the assignment is the party correctly entitled to the contractual right.

fixture An item that was originally a piece of personal property, but becomes part of the realty after it is permanently attached to the real property in question.

food disparagement A tort that provides ranchers and farmers a cause of action when someone spreads false information about the safety of a food product.

for-profit corporation A corporation whose objects are to make a profit.

foreign corporation A corporation that conducts business in a state but is not incorporated.

Foreign Corrupt Practices Act A U.S. federal statute prohibiting U.S. companies from offering or paying bribes to foreign government officials, political parties, and candidates for office for the purpose of obtaining or retaining business.

foreign sales representative An agent who distributes, represents, or sells goods on behalf of a foreign seller, usually in return for the payment of a commission.

forfeiture A party's forfeiting his or her interest in the premises.

forgery A criminal falsification by imitating, impersonating, or altering a real document with the intent to deceive or defraud.

formal contract A contract that must have a special form or must be created in a specific manner.

formal rule making Under APA, all rules must be enacted by an agency as part of a formal hearing process that includes a complete transcript, begins with publication of a notice of proposed rule making by the agency in the *Federal Register,* followed by a public hearing at which witnesses give testimony on the pros and cons of the proposed rule and are subject to cross-examination. The agency makes and publishes formal findings. If a regulation is adopted, the final rule is published in the *Federal Register.*

Forum selection agreement A contractual clause wherein the parties choose the location where disputes between them will be resolved.

franchise A business form that exists because of an arrangement between an owner of a trade name or trademark, and a person who sells goods or services under the trade name or trademark.

franchise agreement A contract whereby a company (known as the franchisor) grants permission (a license) to another entity (known as a franchisee) to utilize the franchisor's name, trademark, or copyright in the operation of a business and associated sale of goods in return for payment.

franchisee The seller of goods or services under a trade name or trademark in a franchise.

franchisor Owner of the trade name or trademark in a franchise.

fraud An intentional deception that causes harm to another. As a basis for contesting a will, this occurs when the testator relied on false statements when he or she made a will.

fraud in the factum When a party signs a negotiable instrument without knowing that it is a negotiable instrument.

fraudulent misrepresentation Occurs when the representation is made with intent to facilitate personal gain and with the knowledge that it is false.

fraudulent transfers A transfer made with intent to defraud creditors or made for an amount significantly lower than its fair market value within two years of filing for bankruptcy.

free exercise clause One of two clauses in the First Amendment of the United States Constitution. It states that government (state and federal) cannot make a law "prohibiting the free exercise" of religion. This clause is interpreted to include absolute freedom to believe and freedom to act that may face state restriction.

free trade agreement An international agreement between two or more states wherein tariffs and other trade barriers are reduced and gradually eliminated.

Freedom of Information Act (FOIA) Passed in 1966, requires that federal agencies publish in the *Federal Register* places where the public can get information from the agencies. Any individual or business may make an FOIA request to a federal government agency. Information may be obtained regarding how the agency gets and spends its money; statistics and/or information collected by the agency on a given topic are available; and citizens are entitled to any records that the government has about them. Exemptions to FOIA include, but are not limited to, national security, internal agency matters (e.g., personnel issues), criminal investigations, financial institutions, and an individual's private life.

friendly fire A fire contained in a place where it is intended to burn.

full eviction When a landlord physically prevents a lessee from entering the leased premises.

full faith and credit clause The clause of the United States Constitution (Article IV, Section 1) that addresses the duty that the various states must recognize, respect, and enforce public records, legislative acts, and judicial decisions of the other states within the United States.

future interest A person's present right to property ownership and possession in the future.

G

garnishment order An order that satisfies a debt by seizing a debtor's property that is being held by a third party.

General Agreement on Tariffs and Trade A comprehensive multilateral trading system designed to achieve distortion-free international trade through the minimization of tariffs and removal of artificial barriers.

general partnership An agreement that the partners who own a business will divide profits, management responsibility, and share unlimited personal liability for the business.

general personal jurisdiction A doctrine permitting adjudication of any claims against a defendant regardless of whether the claim has anything to do with the forum.

general power of attorney Allows the agent to conduct all business for the principal.

general warranty deed A deed containing a covenant whereby the seller agrees to protect the buyer against being dispossessed because of any adverse claim against the land.

geographic market An area in which a company competes with others in the relevant product market.

gift causa mortis A gift that is made in contemplation of one's immediate death.

Golden Rule The idea that we should act in the way that we would like others to act toward us.

good faith Honesty in fact.

good Samaritan statute A statute that exempts from liability a person, such as a physician passer-by, who voluntarily renders aid to an injured person but who negligently, but not unreasonably negligently, causes injury while rendering the aid.

good title Title acquired from someone who already owns the goods free and clear.

goods All physically existing things that are movable at the time of identification to the contract for sale.

goods-in-bailment contract Type of contract in which the purchased goods are in some kind of storage under the control of a third party, such as a warehouseman.

Government in Sunshine Act Requires that agency business meetings be open to the public if the agency is headed by a collegiate body (i.e., two or more persons, the majority of whom are appointed by the president with the advice and consent of the Senate); the law also requires that agencies keep records of closed meetings.

green taxes Taxes imposed on environmentally harmful activities.

gross negligence Acting with extreme reckless disregard for the property or life of another person.

group boycott When two or more competitors agree to refuse to deal with a certain person or company.

group insurance A policy purchased by neither the insured party nor the insurer.

guaranty Similar to a suretyship, but this type of contract ensures that the third party is secondarily liable for the debt to be paid.

H

hacker A person who illegally accesses or enters another person's or company's computer system to obtain information or to steal money.

Hague evidence convention A multilateral convention establishing procedures for transnational discovery between private persons in different states.

half-truth Information presented to be true, but which is not complete.

health care proxy An agent commissioned to make medical decisions for a principal who is unable to participate in medical decisions.

historical school/tradition A school of jurisprudence where traditions are used as the model for future laws and behavior.

holder A party in possession of a negotiable instrument.

holders in due course An individual who acquires a negotiable instrument in good faith.

homestead exemption An exemption allowing a debtor to retain all or a portion of the family home so that the family will retain some form of shelter when he is declared bankrupt.

horizontal division of market An agreement between two or more competitors to divide markets among themselves by geography, customers, or products.

horizontal merger Merger between two or more competitors producing the same or similar products.

horizontal restraint of trade When two competitors in the same market make an agreement to restrain trade.

hostile fire A fire that occurs in a place where it was not intended to burn.

hostile takeover A takeover where the management of the target corporation objects.

hybrid agencies Some agencies do not fall clearly into one classification or the other. These agencies are typically referred to as *hybrid agencies.* Created as one type of agency, the body may share characteristics of the other. The EPA, for example, was created as an independent agency, not located within any department of the executive branch.

hybrid rule making An attempt to combine the best features of formal and informal rule making; the starting point is publication in the *Federal Register,* followed by the opportunity for submission of written comments, and then an informal public hearing with a more restricted opportunity for cross-examination than in formal rule making.

I

identification with the vulnerable A school of jurisprudence where fairness is sought. Particular attention is therefore paid to the poor, the ill, and the elderly.

illusory promise Not consideration at all; when a party appears to commit, but really has not committed to anything.

implied authority The relationship that is inferred from the conduct of the parties.

implied covenant of good faith and fair dealing exception An exception to the employment at-will doctrine that imposes a duty on the employer to treat employees fairly with respect to termination.

implied conditions Those that are not specifically and explicitly stated, but which are inferred from the nature and language of the contract.

implied contract A contract that arises not from words of agreement but rather from the conduct of the parties.

implied-contract exception An exception to the employment at-will doctrine that arises when the employer has taken steps to make it appear as if the employee has a contract to not be fired unless certain conditions occur. An employee handbook or statements of the employer can create the implied contract.

implied trust Trusts created by courts when (1) an express trust fails and the court can imply a trust from certain behavior and (2) the law steps in to protect someone from fraud or other wrongdoing.

implied warranty of fitness for a particular purpose An assurance inferred in a UCC sale that when a seller or lessor knows or has reason to know why the buyer or lessee is purchasing or leasing the goods in question, then the buyer or lessee is relying on him or her to make the selection and has an enforceable warranty if such assurance is false.

implied warranty of habitability A requirement that the premises be fit for ordinary residential purposes.

implied warranty of merchantability An assurance inferred in every sale, unless clearly disclaimed, that merchantable goods will conform to a reasonable performance expectation; the purchaser must have purchased or leased the good from a merchant.

implied warranty of trade usage An assurance created in the context of a UCC sale, dependent on the circumstances, that can be created through a well-accepted course of dealing or trade usage.

imposter rule If one obtains a negotiable instrument by impersonating another, and endorses it with the impersonated party's signature, the loss falls on the drawer of the instrument.

in pari delicto In equal fault.

***in personam* jurisdiction (jurisdiction in personam)** Also called **personal jurisdiction.** The power of a court to require a party (usually the defendant) or a witness to come before the court. The court must have personal jurisdiction to enforce its judgments or orders against a party. *In personam* jurisdiction extends only to the state's borders in the state court system and across the court's geographic district in the federal system.

***in rem* jurisdiction** The power of a court over property or a status of an out-of-state defendant located within the court's jurisdiction area.

incidental beneficiary One who unintentionally gains a benefit from a contract between other parties.

incorporator An individual who applies for incorporation on behalf of a corporation.

independent agencies Governed by a board of commissioners; the President appoints the commissioners with the advice and consent of the Senate; commissioners serve fixed terms and cannot be removed except for cause; no more than a simple majority of an independent agency can be members of any single political party.

indictment Finding by the grand jury that there is evidence to charge the defendant and bring him to trial.

individual insurance A policy where the insured party is an individual.

industry guides Interpretations of consumer laws to encourage businesses to stop unlawful behavior.

infant A person who is not legally an adult is considered to be an infant under the law. The legal definition of entering adulthood usually varies between ages 15–21. However, reaching the age of 18 makes a child a legal adult in most the U.S. localities. Those who have not reached adulthood typically are considered to lack the mental capabilities of an adult, and thus infancy can be used as a partial defense to defuse the guilty mind requirement of a crime.

informal contracts Contracts that require no formalities.

informal rule making A proposed APA rule, published in the *Federal Register* available for public comment.

information Finding by a magistrate that there is enough evidence to charge the defendant and bring him to trial.

informational picketing Picketing designed to truthfully inform the public of a labor dispute between an employer and the employees.

injunction An order either forcing a party to do something or prohibiting the party from doing something.

inland marine policy A policy that protects against loss of ship and cargo from "perils of the sea" when a ship is traveling on inland waterways.

innkeepers Entities that are regularly in the business of making lodging available to the public.

innocent misrepresentation Results from a false statement about a fact material to an agreement that the person making the statement believed to be true, when the person who made the false statement had no knowledge of the falsity of the claim.

insanity An affirmative defense claiming that the defendant had a severe mental illness extant at the time the crime was committed that substantially impaired the defendant's capacity to understand and appreciate the moral wrongfulness of the act.

insider trading Illegal buying or selling of a corporation's stock or other securities by corporate insiders such as officers and directors in breach of a fiduciary duty or other relationship of trust and confidence, while in possession of material, nonpublic information about the security.

insolvent debtor A debtor who cannot pay debts in a timely fashion.

instruments Writings that serve as evidence of rights to payment of money.

insurable interest A party who has interest in property or life.

insurance A contract in which the insured party makes payments to the insurer in exchange for the insurer's promise to make payment or transfer goods to another party in the event of injury or destruction to the insured party's property or life.

insured party The party who makes a payment in exchange for payment in the event of damage or injury to property or person.

insurer The party who receives payments from the insured party and makes the payment to the beneficiary.

integrated contracts Written contracts intended to be the complete and final representation of the parties' agreement.

intellectual property Intangible property that is the product of one's mind and not one's hands.

intended beneficiary Third party to a contract whom the contracting parties intended to benefit directly from their contact.

intent The intended purpose or goal of an action, especially in a contract.

intentional inflection of emotional distress The defendant intentionally engages in extreme conduct designed to cause the plaintiff emotional distress.

intentional interference with contract Intentionally taking an action that will cause a person to breach a contract that he has with another.

intentional misrepresentation In a contract, when the party making the misrepresentation either knows or believes that the factual claim is false, or he or she knows that there is no basis for the assertion, and scienter is clear.

intentional tort A civil wrong resulting from an intentional act committed upon a person, property, or economic interest of another. Intentional torts include: assault, battery, conversion, false imprisonment, intentional infliction of emotional distress, trespass to land, and trespass to chattels.

inter vivos gift A gift that is made by a person during his or her lifetime.

intermediary bank Any bank that is not a payor or depository bank that transfers a check during the check collection process.

intermediate scrutiny A standard of review under which the law must be necessary to achieve a substantial, or important, governmental interest, and it must be narrowly tailored to that interest.

international agreement A written agreement between two or more states governed by international law and relating to an international subject matter.

International Labor Organization An international organization operating under the principle that "labor should not be regarded merely as a commodity or article of commerce" implemented through the drafting of declarations and conventions.

international law Laws governing the conduct of states and international organizations and their relations with one another and natural and juridical persons.

interpretive rules Rules that do not create any new rights or duties, but are merely a detailed statement of the agency's interpretation of an existing law. They are generally very detailed, step-by-step statements of what actions a party is to take to be considered in compliance with an existing law.

interrogatories Also called requests for further information. A formal set of written questions to a party to a lawsuit asked by the opposing party as part of the pretrial discovery process in order to clarify matters of evidence and help to determine in advance what facts will be presented at any trial in the case. These questions are required to be answered in writing under oath or under penalty of perjury within a specified time.

Interstate Commerce Commission (ICC) The first federal administrative agency; created to regulate the anticompetitive conduct of railroads.

intestacy statutes Statutes that outline how a person's property will be handled if that person dies without a will.

intestate The state of dying without a will.

intrusion on an individual's affairs or seclusion A physical, electronic, or mechanical intrusion that occurs for the purpose of invading someone else's solitude, seclusion, or personal affairs when he or she has the right to expect privacy. The legal wrong occurs at the time of the intrusion; no publication is necessary.

involuntary intoxication Intoxication is involuntary if the defendant took the intoxicant without awareness of its likely effect or mistook its identity, or if the intoxicant was taken under force.

involuntary intoxication defense An affirmative defense claming that the defendant took the intoxicant without awareness of its likely effect, mistook its identity, or the intoxicant was taken under force.

Islamic law A legal system based upon the fundamental tenet that law is derived from and interpreted in harmony with Shari'a (God's law) and the Koran.

J

joint and several liability In this arrangement of liability, a third party has the ability to sue the partners separately or all partners jointly in one action.

joint stock company A partnership agreement whereby company members hold transferable shares while all the goods of the company are held in the names of the partners.

joint tenancy A form of co-ownership in which owners may sell their shares without the consent of the other owners and have their interest attached by creditors. However, joint tenants all own equal shares of the property, and upon the death of one tenant, the property is divided equally among the surviving joint owners.

joint tenants Parties who hold property in joint tenancy.

joint venture An association between two or more parties wherein the parties share profits and management responsibilities with respect to a specific project.

jointly liable Shared liability for the partnership's debts.

judicial lien Legal action taken by a creditor to satisfy his debt through property of the debtor.

judicial review The power of a court to review legislative and executive actions such as a law or an official act of a government employee or agent to determine whether they are constitutional.

jurisdiction The power of a court to hear cases and resolve disputes.

justifiable use of force Use of force is necessary to prevent imminent death or great bodily harm to ones' self or to another or to prevent the imminent commission of a forcible felony.

L

lack of genuine assent A defense to the agreement of a contract in which one party claims the offeror secured the agreement through improper means, such as duress, fraud, undue influence, or misrepresentation.

landlord Owner of the property being leased.

landlord's lien The right to some or all of the tenant's personal property.

Landrum-Griffin Act Primarily governs the internal operations of labor unions; requires certain financial disclosures by unions, and establishes civil and criminal penalties for financial abuses by union officials; includes "Labor's Bill of Rights," to protect employees from their own unions.

larceny Unlawful taking, attempting to take, carrying, leading, or riding away of another person's property with intent to deprive the rightful owner of property permanently.

last-clear-chance doctrine Doctrine used by the plaintiff when the defendant establishes contributory negligence. If the plaintiff can establish that the defendant had the last opportunity to avoid the accident, the plaintiff may still recover, despite being contributorilly negligent.

lease "A transfer of the right to possession and use of goods for a term in return for consideration." (UCC Section 2A-103(j))

leasehold interest A possessory interest, but not an ownership interest transferred by contract.

leasehold estate The leased property.

legal assent A promise to buy or sell that the courts will require the parties to obey.

legal positivism The school of jurisprudence that insists that because society requires authority, a legal and authoritarian hierarchy should exist. When a law is made, therefore, obedience is expected because authority created it.

legal realism The school of jurisprudence that dictates that context must be considered as well as law. Context includes factors such as economic conditions and social conditions.

lessee A person who acquires the right to possession and use of goods under a lease.

lessor A person who transfers the right to possession and use of goods under a lease.

letter of credit A binding document that a buyer can request from his bank to guarantee that the payment for goods will be made to the seller.

leveraged buyout Strategy involving the acquisition of another company using a significant amount of borrowed money (bonds or loans).

lex mercatoria The "law of merchants" as defined by customs or trade usages developed by merchants to facilitate business transactions.

liability insurance Insurance that protects a business from tort liability to third parties.

liability without fault (strict liability) A legal term that imposes responsibility for damages regardless of the existence of negligence.

license The right to temporarily use another's property.

licensing agreement A contract whereby one company (known as the licensor) grants permission to a company (known as the licensee) to utilize the licensor's intellectual property in return for payment.

lien A claim to property.

life estate Grants the holder the right to possess the property until death.

Limited liability company Similar to a limited liability partnership, but the LLC is taxed like a partnership, where the members pay personal income taxes.

limited liability partnership In this type of partnership all partners assume liability for one partner's professional malpractice to the extent of the partnership's assets.

limited partnership An agreement between general partners and limited partners in a company where the general partners assume all liability for the company, and where the limited partners assume no responsibility beyond their originally invested capital.

liquidated damages Damages identified as a term of the contract before a breach of contract occurs.

liquidated debt When there is no dispute between the parties about the fact that money is owed and the amount of money owed.

liquidation When a debtor turns over all assets to a trustee.

living will The document that allows someone to express his or her advance directives.

long-arm statute A statute that enables a court to obtain jurisdiction against an out-of-state defendant as long as the defendant has sufficient minimum contacts within the state such as committing a tort or doing business in the state.

M

mailbox rule An acceptance is valid when it is placed in the mailbox, whereas a revocation is effective only when received by the offeree; in some jurisdictions the mailbox rule has been expanded to faxes.

maker A person promising to pay a set sum to the holder of a promissory note or certificate of deposit.

malicious prosecution (action for) Action brought against a defendant who is responsible for the institution of a criminal proceeding against the plaintiff without probable cause, who was subsequently exonerated, for the sole purpose of causing problems for the plaintiff.

malpractice actions An action filed against a professional person for failure to act in accordance with prevailing professional standards.

manifests Document that records possession of hazardous waste from inception to disposal.

manufacturing agreement A type of franchise where the franchisor provides the franchisee with the formula or necessary ingredient to manufacture a product.

manufacturing defect When an individual product has a defect making it more dangerous than other, identical products.

marine insurance Protects against loss of ships and cargo from the "perils of the sea."

market share A firm's fractional share of the relevant market.

marketable title Title for property to which the seller in fact has legal title, and against which there are no liens or restrictions of which the buyer is not aware.

material breach A substantial breach of a significant term or terms of a contract that excuses the nonbreaching party from further performance under the contract and gives the nonbreaching party the right to recover damages.

material terms Those terms that would allow a court to determine what the damages would be in the event that one of the parties was to breach the contract, including the subject matter, quantity, price, quality, and parties.

mechanic's lien A claim against real property to satisfy a debt incurred to make improvements to that real property.

med-arb A type of dispute resolution process where both parties start out in mediation and, if successful, agree to arbitration.

mediation A type of intensive negotiation where parties select a neutral party to help facilitate communication and suggest ways for the parties to solve their dispute.

meeting-the-competition defense A defense to the Clayton Act where one firm engages in price discrimination to compete in good faith with another seller's low price.

members Owners of a limited liability company.

mens rea Latin words for "guilty mind." It refers to the mental state accompanying the wrongful behavior.

merchant "A person who deals in goods of the kind, or otherwise by his occupation holds himself out as having knowledge or skill peculiar to the practices or goods involved in the transaction, or to whom such knowledge or skill may be attributed by his employment of an agent or broker or other intermediary who, by his occupation, holds himself out as having such knowledge or skill." (UCC Section 2-104(1))

merger The acquisition of one company by another.

merger clause A clause parties include in a written agreement within the statute of frauds that states the written agreement accurately reflects the final, complete version of the agreement.

minitrial A type of conflict resolution where lawyers present each side to a neutral adviser who offers an opinion as to what the verdict would be if it were a trial. This decision is not binding.

Miranda rights The rights that are given to an arrested individual by a law enforcement agent before he/she is asked questions relating to the commission of a crime.

mirror-image rule The terms of the acceptance must mirror the terms of the offer; if the terms of the acceptance do not mirror the terms of the offer, then no contract is formed; instead, the attempted acceptance is a counteroffer.

misappropriation theory A theory of insider trading that holds that if an individual wrongfully acquires (misappropriates) and uses inside information for trading for his or her personal gain, that person is liable for insider trading.

misdemeanor A crime that is less serious than a felony and that is punishable by fine and/or imprisonment for less than one year.

misrepresentation An untruthful assertion by one of the parties about a material fact.

mistake An erroneous belief about the facts of the contract at the time the contract is concluded, when legal assent is absent.

mistake of fact A mistake that is not caused by the neglect of a legal duty by the person committing the mistake but rather consists of an unconscious ignorance of a past or present material event or circumstance.

mistake-of-fact defense An affirmative defense that tries to prove a defendant made an honest and reasonable mistake that negates the "guilty mind" element of a crime.

mixed sale A contract that combines a good(s) with a service(s).

mock trial A contrived or imitation trial with a jury consisting of volunteers that attorneys preparing for a real trial might use to test theories or experiment with arguments to try to predict the outcome of the real trial.

model law See **uniform law.**

modified comparative negligence defense A defense accepted in some states whereby the defendant is not liable for the percentage of harm that he/she can prove can be attributed to the plaintiff's own negligence if the plaintiff's own negligence is responsible for less than 50 percent of the plaintiff's harm; if the defendant establishes that the plaintiff's own negligence caused more than 50 percent of the plaintiff's harm, the defendant has no liability.

modify When an appellate court grants an alternative remedy in a case when the court finds that the decision of the lower court was correct, but the remedy was not.

monetary damages Money claimed by or ordered paid to a party to compensate for injury or loss caused by the wrong of the opposite party.

money order A way to transfer funds between two parties. A money order is a signed document indicating that funds are to be paid from the drawee to the drawer.

monopoly or market power The ability to control price and drive competitors out of the market.

motion An application by a party to a judge or a court in a civil case requesting an order in favor of the applicant.

motion for judgment on the pleadings A request by a party to a judge or a court, after pleadings have been entered in a civil case, to issue a judgment.

motion for summary judgment A request by either party in a civil litigation to promptly and expeditiously dispose of a case without a trial. Any evidence or information that would be admissible at trial under the rules of evidence such as affidavits, interrogatories, depositions, and admissions may be considered on a motion for summary judgment. A court may hold oral arguments or decide the motion on the basis of the parties' briefs and supporting documentation alone.

motion to dismiss or demurrer A request to a judge or a court in a civil case by the defendant to dismiss the case because even if all the allegations are true, the plaintiff is not entitled to any legal relief.

movability The quality of a negotiable instrument that ensures it is mobile and available.

multilateral trade agreement An international agreement between three or more states relating to trade between them.

multiple-product orders A form of cease-and-desist order issued by the FTC that applies not only to a specified product, but also to others produced by the same firm.

mutual mistake The result of an error by both parties about a material fact, i.e., one that is important in the context of a particular contract.

N

National Labor Relations Board (NLRB) Created by the Wagner Act to interpret and enforce the National Labor Relations Act (NLRA).

national treatment A principle of law prohibiting states from regulating, taxing, or otherwise treating imported products any differently than domestically produced products.

natural law A school of jurisprudence that recognizes the existence of higher law, or law that is morally superior to human laws.

necessity defense The defendant was acting to prevent imminent harm, and there was no legal alternative to the action he took.

negligence Behavior that creates an unreasonable risk of harm to others.

negligence per se Allows a judge or jury to infer duty and breach of duty from the fact that a defendant violated a criminal statute that was designed to prevent the type of harm that the defendant incurred.

negligent misrepresentation In a contract, when one party makes a statement of material fact that he/she thinks is true, but is negligent in making the assertion; also results when the party making the statement would have known the truth about the fact had he/she used reasonable care to discover or reveal the fact.

negligent tort A civil wrong that occurs when the defendant fails to act and thereby subjects other people to an unreasonable risk of harm. In other words, the defendant is careless, to someone else's detriment. It is usually used to achieve compensation for accidents and injuries.

negotiable instrument An acceptable medium to exchange value from one person to another.

negotiation (1) A bargaining process in which disputing parties interact informally to attempt to resolve their dispute.

negotiation (2) Transferring the rights to a negotiable instrument from one party to another.

New York Convention An international agreement governing the use of arbitration as a method of resolving private international disputes.

no-par shares Shares without par value.

nolo contendere A plea in which the defendant does not admit guilt, but agrees not to contest the charges.

nominal damages Monetary damages awarded to a plaintiff in a very small amount, typically $1 to $5, which serve to signify that the plaintiff has been wronged by the defendant.

nondisclosure A failure to provide pertinent information about a projected contract.

nonprobate property Property that is not part of the probate estate.

nonprofit corporation An organization incorporated under state laws and approved by both the state's Secretary of State and its taxing authority as operating for educational, charitable, social, religious, civic or humanitarian purposes.

nontariff barrier Any impediment to international trade other than tariffs.

normal trade relations A principle of law requiring states to treat like goods coming from other states on an equal basis.

North American Free Trade Agreement An international agreement between the United States, Canada, and Mexico wherein tariffs and other trade barriers are reduced and gradually eliminated.

note A promise by the maker of the note to pay the payee of the note.

notice-and-comment rule making See **informal rule making.**

novation In a contract, when the parties to the agreement wish to replace one of the parties with a third party; the original duties remain the same under the contract, but one party is discharged and the third party now takes that original party's place.

nuisance The use by one person of his or her property in a manner that unreasonably interferes with another's use and enjoyment of his or her land.

objective impossibility of performance In a contract, when it is in fact not possible to lawfully carry out one's contractual obligations.

obligees Contractual parties who agreed to receive something from the other party.

obligors Contractual parties who agreed to do something for the other party.

ocean marine policy A policy that protects against loss of ship and cargo from "perils of the sea" when a ship is traveling on the ocean.

Occupational Safety and Health Act of 1970 (OSHA) Federal law that established the Occupational Safety and Health Administration, the agency responsible for setting safety standards under the act, as well as enforcing the act through inspections and the levying of fines against violators.

offer A key element of a contract consisting of the terms and conditions set by one party, the offeror, and presented to another party, the offeree.

Omnibus Crime Control and Safe Streets Act of 1968 Federal statute banning employers from listening to the private telephone conversations of employees or disclosing the contents of these conversations. Employers may, however, ban personal calls and monitor calls for compliance, as long as they discontinue listening to any conversation once they determine it is personal.

option contract An agreement whereby the offeree gives the offeror a piece of consideration in exchange for the offeror's agreement to hold the offer open for the specified period of time.

order An order to appear and bring specified documents.

order instrument An instrument payable to a specific, named payee.

order of relief An order that bankruptcy proceedings can continue.

organ donor card A document that expresses a party's wishes to donate organs or tissue.

output contract An agreement whereby the seller guarantees to sell everything he/she produces to one buyer and no quantity is stated; valid under the Uniform Commercial Code (UCC), but not under common law.

overdraft A bank's action to pay an amount specified on a check, without there being sufficient funds in its customer's account.

P

par-value shares Shares that have a fixed face value noted on the stock certificate.
parol evidence rule A common law rule specifically addressing the admissibility of oral evidence as it relates to written contracts; states that oral evidence of an agreement made prior to or contemporaneously with the written agreement is inadmissible when the parties intend for a written agreement to be the complete and final version of their agreement.
partial eviction When a landlord prevents a tenant from entering part of the leased premises.
partial performance When portions of an agreement have been fulfilled by one or both parties absent of an agreement in writing; partial performance can prove that an oral contract exists between two parties.
partially disclosed principal Making a third party aware that the agent is making an agreement on behalf of a principal, but the third party is unaware of the identity of the principal.
partnership A voluntary association between two or more people who co-own a business for profit.
past consideration Work done in the past, by definition, has already been performed. As such, nothing has been given in exchange, and the court will not enforce the promise.
patent Protects a product, process, invention, or machine, or a plant produced by asexual reproduction.
payee The party that receives the benefit of an order (check, etc.).
payor bank The bank responsible for disbursing the funds indicated on a check.
per se violations Those where the very existence of a condition carries with it liability, as opposed to actions violative of a rule of reason.
peremptory challenge The right of the plaintiff and the defendant in jury selection in a jury trial to reject a certain number of potential jurors who appear to have an unfavorable bias, without stating a reason.
perfect tender rule Requirement that the seller deliver the goods in conformity with the contract, down to the last detail.
perfection The series of legal steps a secured party takes to protect its right in the collateral from the other creditors who wish to have their debt returned through the same collateral.
periodic tenancy A lease created for a recurring term.
personal defenses A defense to liability not applicable to holders.
personal insurance A policy that covers an individual's health or life.
personal jurisdiction The power of the court over the persons appearing before it.
personal property Any property that is not land or permanently affixed to the land.
personal representative The person chosen by the testator to collect the testator's property, pay the debt and taxes, and make sure the remainder of the estate gets distributed.
personal service When an officer of the court hands legal documents such as a summons and complaint to the defendant.
petit jury A group to six or twelve citizens who are summoned to and sworn by the court to hear evidence presented by both sides and render a verdict in a trial.
petty offense A minor crime that is punishable by a small fine and/or imprisonment for less than six months in prison.
picketing When individuals place themselves outside an employer's place of business for the purpose of informing passers-by of the facts of a labor dispute.
plain-meaning rule When interpreting words in a contract, these should be given their ordinary meaning.
plaintiff The person or party who initiates a lawsuit (also known as an action) before a court by filing a complaint with the clerk of the court against the defendant(s); also known as a claimant or a complainant.
plea bargain An agreement in which the prosecutor agrees to reduce charges, drop charges, or recommend a certain sentence if the defendant pleads guilty. Plea bargaining benefits both parties: the defendant gets a lesser sentence and the prosecution saves time and resources by not trying the case.
pledge The transfer of the collateral to the secured party.
point-of-sale system An EFT system allowing consumers to directly transfer funds from a banking account to a merchant.
police power Retained power of the state to pass laws to protect health, safety, and welfare of citizens.
policy statements General statements about directions in which any agency intends to proceed with respect to its rulemaking or enforcement activities, having no binding impact on anyone.
policy The insurance document signed by the insured party and the insurer.
political speech Speech that is used to support political candidates or referenda. Political speech is given a high level of protection by the First Amendment as compared to other types of speech.
posteffective period Begins when the SEC declares the registration statement effective and ends when the issuer sells all securities offered or withdraws them from sale.
posttrial motions A request filed after a trial is over by either party to the trial court. A motion for new trial, a

motion for judgment notwithstanding the verdict (JNOV), or a motion to amend or nullify the judgment are types of posttrial motions.

power of attorney A specific form of express authority, granting an agent specific powers.

precedent A tool used by judges to make rulings on cases based on key similarities to previous cases.

predatory pricing When a company prices one product below normal cost until competitors are eliminated and then sharply increases the price.

preexisting duty A promise to do something that one is already obligated to do; is not considered valid consideration.

preferential payments Payments made by an insolvent debtor that give preferential treatment to one creditor over another.

preferred stock Stock that enjoys preferences with respect to assets and dividends.

prefiling period Begins when an issuer begins to think about issuing securities and ends when the issuer files the registration statement and prospectus with the SEC.

Pregnancy Discrimination Act of 1987 (PDA) Amended Title VII of the Civil Rights Act of 1964 (CRA) to expand the definition of sex discrimination to include discrimination based on pregnancy.

prejudicial error of law An error of law that was so significant that it affects the outcome of the case.

premium An insurance payment.

prenuptial agreement An agreement two parties enter into before marriage that clearly states the ownership rights each party enjoys in the other party's property; to be enforceable, prenuptial agreements must be in writing.

presentment Making a demand for the drawee to pay.

presentment warranty A warranty covering the parties accepting instrument for payment. These are created to ensure the accepting or paying parties are paying the proper party.

pretrial An event that includes consultation with attorneys, pleadings, the discovery process, and the pretrial conference.

price discrimination Selling the same goods to different buyers at different prices.

price fixing When two or more competitors agree to set prices for a product or service.

prima facie Latin for "at first view"; means that the evidence is sufficient to raise a presumption that a wrong occurred.

primarily liable The party who must pay the amount designated on an instrument when it is presented for payment.

primary boycott A boycott against an employer with whom the union is directly engaged in a labor dispute.

primary-line injuries Injury to competitors of a seller who offers a discriminatory price.

principal The party that an agent's authority can bind or act on behalf of.

principle of rights The principle that judges the morality of a decision on the basis of how it affects the rights of all those involved.

Privacy Act Under the Privacy Act, a federal agency may not disclose information about an individual to other agencies or organizations without that individual's written consent.

privacy tort A wrongful act or damage to an individual due to invasion of privacy for which a civil action can be brought. Four distinct torts to protect the individual's right to keep certain things out of the public view, even if they are true, are: false light, public disclosure of private facts, appropriation for commercial gain, and intrusion on an individual's affairs or seclusion.

private corporation Corporations that do not have government duties.

private law Involves suits between private individuals or groups.

private nuisance A nuisance that affects only a single or very limited number of individuals.

private placement exemption When private offerings of securities are exempt from the registration process normally required by the SEC because the offerings are being made to private accredited investors and cannot be advertised to the general public.

private trial An ADR method where a referee is selected and paid by the disputing parties to offer a legally binding judgment in a dispute.

privileges and immunities clause Clause that requires the state to grant citizens of other states the same legal benefits that it grants its own citizens.

privity of contract The relationship that exists between parties to a contract.

probable cause Refers to the essential elements and standards by which a lawful officer may make a valid arrest, conduct a personal or property search, or obtain a warrant.

probate The process of settling an estate.

problem-solving negotiation Negotiation where the parties seek to achieve joint gain.

procedural due process The steps a government must take before depriving a person of his or her life, liberty, or property.

procedural unconscionability The unconscionability that derives from the process of making a contract.

proceeds What is exchanged for a debtor's sold collateral.

product liability insurance Insurance that protects a company from liability in the event that its customers suffer injury.

product market A market in which all products identical to or substitutes for a company's product are sold.

professional insurance Insurance that protects professionals from suits by third parties who claim negligent job performance.

profit The right to go onto someone's land and take part of the land or a product of it away from the land.

promisee In a third-party beneficiary contract, the party to the contract who owes something to the promisor in exchange for the promise made to the third-party beneficiary.

promisor In a third-party beneficiary contract, the party to the contract who made the promise that benefits the third party.

promissory estoppel Legal enforcement of an otherwise unenforceable contract due to a party's detrimental reliance upon the contract.

promoters Those who begin the corporate creation and organization process.

property insurance Insurance that protects property from loss or damages.

prospectus An advertising tool that is a written document containing a description of a security and other financial information regarding the company offering the security; contains most of the same information as the registration statement.

proximate cause The extent to which, as a matter of policy, a defendant may be held liable for the consequences of his/her actions; in the majority of states, proximate cause requires that the defendant and the type of injury suffered by the defendant were foreseeable at the time of the accident. In the minority of states, proximate cause exists if the defendant's actions led to the plaintiff's harm.

proxy A writing signed by a shareholder that authorizes the individual named in the writing to exercise the shareholder's votes (corresponding to his or her shares of stock) at a shareholders' meeting.

proxy solicitation The process of obtaining authority to vote on behalf of shareholders.

public corporation A corporation created by government to help administer law.

public disclosure of private facts A privacy tort that occurs when a person publishes a highly offensive private fact, such as information about one's sex life or failure to pay debts, about someone who did not waive his or her right to privacy.

public disclosure test The ethical guideline that urges us to consider how others may view our actions when making a decision.

public figure privilege A special right, immunity, or permission given to people to make any statement about public figures, typically politicians and entertainers, without being held liable for defamation for any false statements made about them.

public law Involves suits between private individuals or groups and their governments.

public policy exception An exception to the employment at-will doctrine that prohibits the employee for being fired for doing something that is consistent with furthering public policy.

publicly held corporation A corporation available to the public.

puffing The use of generalities and clear exaggerations.

punitive damages A compensation that is awarded to a plaintiff beyond the actual harms or damages to punish the defendant and deter such conduct in the future.

purchase-money security interest A security interest formed when a debtor uses borrowed money from the secured party to buy the collateral.

pure comparative negligence defense A defense accepted in some states whereby the defendant is not liable for the percentage of harm that he/she can prove can be attributed to the plaintiff's own negligence.

Q

qualified endorsement An endorsement that does not bind the endorser to the negotiable instrument in the event that the creator does not honor that instrument.

quantitative restrictions Limitations upon imported goods imposed on the basis of number of units, weight, or value.

quasi-contracts A court-imposed contractual obligation to prevent unjust enrichment.

quasi *in rem* jurisdiction or attachment jurisdiction A type of jurisdiction exercised by a court over an out-of-state defendant's property within the jurisdictional boundaries of the court. It applies to personal suits against the defendant, where the property is not the source of the conflict but is sought as compensation by the plaintiff.

"quick-look" standard Allows a defendant in a restraint of trade case to offer justification for his or her per se violation.

quitclaim deed A deed that carries no warranties; the grantor simply conveys whatever interests he or she holds.

R

ratify Approve an unauthorized agent's signature on an instrument.

rational-basis test The lowest standard of review; it requires that the law is designed to protect a legitimate state interest and is rationally related to that interest.

reaffirmation agreement An agreement where the debtor agrees to pay a debt even though it could have been discharged.

real defense A defense to liability able to be universally applied.

reasonable person standard A measurement of the way members of society expect an individual to act in a given situation.

recognizances When a party acknowledges in court that he or she will perform some specified act or pay.

recording Filing the deed, with any other related documents, such as mortgages, with the appropriate county office, thereby giving official notice of the transfer to all interested parties.

red herring prospectus A prospectus with a warning written in red print at the top of the page telling investors that the registration has been filed with the SEC but not yet approved.

refusal to deal See **group boycott.**

reg-neg Each concerned interest group and the agency itself send a representative to bargaining sessions led by a mediator; if the parties achieve a consensus, that agreement is forwarded to the agency and the agency is then expected to publish the compromise as a proposed rule in the *Federal Register* and follow through with the appropriate rule-making procedures. If the agency does not agree with the proposal the group negotiated, the agency is free to try to promulgate a completely different rule or a modification of the one obtained through the negotiation.

registration statement A description of the securities offered for sale, including an explanation of how proceeds from the sale of the securities will be used, a description of the registrant's business and properties, information about the management of the company, a description of any pending lawsuits in which the registrant is involved, and financial statements certified by an independent public accountant.

rejection In a contract, when an offeree does not accept the offer or terms of a contract, thereby terminating the contract.

relative permanence The quality of a negotiable instrument that ensures its longevity.

remand The act of an appellate court that decides an error was committed that may have affected the outcome of a case and that therefore the case must be returned to the trial court for a new trial or for limited hearing on a specified subject matter.

rent The compensation paid to the landlord for the tenant's right to possession and exclusive use of the premises.

rent escalation clause A clause permitting the landlord to increase the rent in association with increases in costs of living, property taxes, or the tenant's commercial business.

requests to produce documents In a lawsuit, the right of a party to examine and copy the opposing party's papers that are relevant to the case. A legal request may be made and the categories of the documents must be stated to allow the other party to know what documents he/she must produce.

requirement contract An agreement whereby the buyer agrees to purchase all his/her goods from one seller and no quantity is stated in the contract; is valid under Uniform Commercial Code (UCC), but not under common law.

reply Response of the plaintiff to the defendant's counterclaim.

res ipsa loquitur A doctrine that allows the judge or jury to infer that, more likely than not, the defendant's negligence was the cause of the plaintiff's harm, when there is no direct evidence of the defendant's lack of due care.

resale-price maintenance agreement An agreement through which a manufacturer and retailer set a specific price for the resale of products.

rescind To cancel a contract,

rescission The termination of a contract.

respondeat superior The principle by which liability is held by the principal.

restatement of the law Summaries of common law rules in a particular area of the law. Restatements do not carry the weight of law, but can be used to guide interpretations of particular cases.

restitution Restoration of anything to the one to whom it properly belongs.

restricted securities Securities that have limited transferability and are usually issued in a private placement.

restrictive covenants Promises to use or not to use one's land in particular ways.

restrictive endorsement Endorsements aimed to limit the transferability of the instrument or control the manner of payment under the instrument.

retained earnings Profits that a corporation keeps.

reverses When an appellate court decision overturns the judgment of a lower court, concluding that the lower court was incorrect and cannot be allowed to stand.

revocation In a contract, when an offeror takes back the initial offer and annuls the opportunity for the offeree to accept the offer.

RICO Act Stands for Racketeer Influenced and Corrupt Organizations Act, a United States law that provides for extended penalties for criminal acts performed as part of an ongoing criminal organization.

right of first refusal A method of restricting stock transferability whereby a corporation or its shareholders have the right to purchase any shares of stock offered for resale by a shareholder within a specified time frame.

right of survivorship The right that specific partnership property will pass on to the surviving partner(s).

right to die Refers to a person's right to place limits on other people's efforts to prolong that person's life.

rightfully dissolved A dissolution of a partnership that does not violate its partnership agreement.

ripeness The readiness of a case for a decision to be made. The goal is to prevent premature litigation for a dispute that is insufficiently developed. A claim is not ripe for litigation if it rests upon contingent future events that may not occur as anticipated, or indeed may not occur at all.

risk A potential loss.

risk management The transfer and distribution of risk.

robbery Taking or attempting to take personal property of a person by force or threat of force or violence and/or by putting the victim in fear.

rule-of-reason analysis An inquiry into the competitive effects of a company's behavior to determine whether the benefits of the behavior outweigh the harm of the anticompetitive behavior, considering the following: (1) the nature and purpose of the restraint on trade, (2) the scope of the restraint, (3) the effect of the restraint on business and competition, and (4) the intent of the restraint.

rule utilitarianism A subset of utilitarianism that proposes a number of rules for determining generally what creates the most happiness.

S

S corporation A corporation that enjoys the tax status of a partnership.

Sabbath laws Laws that require certain activities to be prohibited on the Sabbath.

sale The passing of title from the seller to the buyer for a price.

sale-on-approval contract The seller allows the buyer to take possession of the goods before deciding whether to complete the contract by making the purchase.

sale-or-return contract The buyer and seller agree that the buyer may return the goods at a later time.

Sarbanes-Oxley Act An act that criminalizes specific nonaudit services when provided by a registered accounting firm to an audit client. Also increases the punishment for a number of white collar offenses. Also known as the Public Company Accounting Reform and Investor Protection Act of 2002.

scienter Deliberately or knowingly.

search warrant A court order that authorizes law enforcement agents to search for or seize items specifically described in the warrant.

secondarily liable The party that must pay the amount designated on an instrument should the primarily liable party default.

secondary boycotts Occurs when unionized employees have a labor dispute with their employer and boycott another employer to force it to cease doing business with their employer.

secondary-line injuries Injuries created when preferential treatment is granted to specific buyers.

secured interest "Interest in personal property or fixtures which secures payment or performance" to a creditor. (UCC §1-201(37))

secured party The party who holds the interest in the secured property.

secured transaction Transaction in which the payment of a debt is guaranteed by personal property owned by the debtor.

security Any financial instrument designated as a note, stock, bond, or other instrument named in the Securities Act of 1933.

security agreement The arrangement where the debtor gives the secured interest to the secured party.

self-dealing When directors or officers violate their duty of loyalty.

self-tender offer When a target corporation offers to buy its shareholders' stock to resist a takeover.

service of process The procedure by which a court delivers copies of the statement of claim or other legal documents such as a summons, complaint, or subpoena to the defendant.

settler A person who creates a trust.

sexual harassment Unwelcome sexual advances, requests for sexual favors, and other verbal or physical conduct of a sexual nature that implicitly or explicitly makes submission a term or condition of employment; makes employment decisions related to the individual dependent on submission to or rejection of such conduct; or has the purpose or effect of creating an intimidating, hostile, or offensive work environment. There are two kinds of sexual harassment: hostile environment and *quid pro quo.*

shadow jury Also called mock jury. Jury selection firms set up mock trials by recruiting individuals who are demographically matched to the real jury to listen to attorneys' arguments and witnesses' testimony before presenting their case to the actual jury.

shareholders Investors in a corporation who, in turn, own the corporation.

shareholder's derivative suit The ability of a shareholder to file a lawsuit on behalf of the corporation.

shelter principle The principal dictating that when an item is transferred, the transferee acquires all of the rights the transferor had to the item.

short-form merger (parent-subsidiary merger) When a parent corporation merges with a subsidiary corporation.

short-swing profits Profits made from the sale of company stock within any six-month period by a statutory insider.

signal picketing An unprotected form of picketing in which services and/or deliveries to the employer are cut off.

signature liability Liability attributed because of a party's signature on an instrument.

simple delivery contract Type of contract in which purchased goods are transferred to the buyer from the seller at either the time of the sale or sometime later by the seller's delivery.

situational ethics A branch of ethical relativism that urges us to envision ourselves in the shoes of others, yet allows us to judge the decisions of others.

slander of quality A business tort occurs when false statements criticize a business product or service and result in a loss of sales.

slander of title A business tort occurs when false published statements are related to the ownership of the business property.

smart card Similar to a check or ATM card, a smart card is a way to electronically transfer funds. Smart cards use computer chips to store information on a card, where check and ATM cards use magnetic strips.

social responsibility of business The expectations that a community places on the actions of firms inside that community's borders.

Socialist law A legal system based upon the premise that the rights of society as a whole outweigh the rights of the individual.

sole proprietor The single person at the head of a sole proprietorship.

sole proprietorship A business in which one person (sole proprietor) is in control of the management and profits.

special damages Consequential damages.

special endorsement An endorser's signature accompanying the name of the endorsee.

special power of attorney Grants the agent express authority over specifically outlined acts.

special qualified endorsement An endorsement containing an item that somehow limits the enforceability of the check, such as the term *without recourse (which means the endorser will not be liable).*

special warranty deed A deed that the seller warrants against defects in title since he/she has had possession of the property, but not before that time.

specific performance An order of the court ordering a person to do something.

specific personal jurisdiction A doctrine permitting adjudication of claims arising from or relating to the defendant's activities in the forum.

stakeholders The groups of people affected by a firm's decisions.

stale check A check that is not presented to a bank within six months of its date.

standing The legal right of a party or an individual to bring a lawsuit by demonstrating to the court sufficient connection to and harm from the law or action challenged. In other words, the plaintiff has to demonstrate that the plaintiff is harmed or will be harmed. Otherwise, the court will dismiss the case, ruling that the plaintiff "lacks standing" to bring the suit.

stare decisis "Standing by the decision." A principle stating that rulings made in higher courts are binding precedent for lower courts.

statute of frauds State-level legislation that addresses the enforceability of contracts that fail to meet the requirements set forth in the statute; serves to protect promisors from poorly considered oral contracts by requiring certain contracts to be in writing.

statutory insiders Certain large stockholders, executive officers, and directors that are determined to be insiders according to the Securities Exchange Act of 1934.

statutory law The assortment of rules and regulations put forth by legislatures.

stock certificates Proof of ownership of a corporation.

stock warrants A type of security issued by a corporation (usually together with a bond or preferred stock) that gives the holder the right to purchase a certain amount of common stock at a stated price.

stop-payment order An order by a drawer to its drawee bank not to pay an issued check.

stored-value card Plastic cards that carry a customer's information, allowing EFTs to be made.

strict-liability offenses Offense for which no mens rea is required.

strict liability tort A civil wrong that occurs when the defendant takes an action that is inherently dangerous, and cannot ever be undertaken safely, no matter what precautions the defendant takes. In such situations a defendant is liable for plaintiff's damages without any requirement that the plaintiff prove that the defendant was negligent.

strict scrutiny The most exacting standard of review used by the court in determining the constitutionality of a statute; requires a compelling government interest and the least restrictive means of attaining that objective.

strike A temporary, concerted withdrawal of labor.

subject-matter jurisdiction The power of a court over the type of case presented to it.

subjective impossibility of performance In a contract, when it would be very difficult for a party to carry out his or her contractual obligations.

sublease A transfer of less than all of the interest of a lease to a lease property.

submission agreement A contract that a specific conflict will be resolved in arbitration.

subpoena An order to appear at a particular time and place and provide testimony.

subpoena duces tecum An order to appear and bring specified documents.

subscribers Investors who agree to purchase stock in a new corporation.

subscription agreements An agreement between those raising capital for a new corporation and investors, who agree to purchase stock in the new corporation.

subsidy A financial contribution by a government that confers a benefit upon a specific industry or enterprise.

substantial impairment A concept used to modify the perfect tender rule in cases of the buyer revoking acceptance of goods; and an installment contract if the buyer/lessee rejects an installment of a particular item.

substantial performance Occurs when nearly all of the terms of an agreement have been met, there has been an honest effort to complete all terms, and there has been no willful departure from the terms of the agreement.

substantive due process The requirement that laws depriving an individual of life, liberty, or property be fair and not arbitrary.

substantive unconscionability A finding that a contract's terms are so one-sided, unjust, or overly harsh that the contract should not be enforced.

summary jury trial An abbreviated trial that leads to a nonbinding jury verdict.

summons A legal document that is issued by a court and addressed to a defendant to notify him or her of the lawsuit and how and when to respond to the complaint. A summons may be used in both civil and criminal proceedings.

supremacy clause Article VI, Paragraph 2 of the United States Constitution, which states that the United States Constitution and all laws and treaties of the United States constitute the supreme law of the land. This means any state or local law that directly conflicts with the U.S. Constitution or federal laws or treaties is void.

suretyship A contract between a creditor and a third party who agrees to pay another person's debt.

surrender A mutual agreement between a landlord and tenant where a lessee returns his or her interest in the premises to the landlord.

syndicate An investment group that comes together for the explicit purpose of financing a specific large project.

T

Taft-Hartley Act Also known as the Labor-Management Relations Act, was designed to curtail some of the powers the unions had acquired under the Wagner Act by designating certain union actions as unfair.

takings clause (just compensation clause) A clause in the Fifth Amendment of the United States Constitution requiring that when government uses its power to take private property for public use, it must pay the owner just compensation, or fair market value, for his/her property.

tariff A tax levied on imported goods.

teller's check A check in which the drawer and drawee are separate banks.

tenancy at sufferance A tenant who was lawfully in possession of a leased property remains in possession of that property unlawfully after the lease ends because the person with the power to evict him failed to do so.

tenancy at will A lease that may be terminated at any time.

tenancy by the entirety Available to married couples only. Co-ownership shares are equal and pass to the spouse upon death.

tenancy in common Co-ownership interest in which each tenant has the right to sell his or her interest without the consent of the other owners, may own an unequal share of the property, and may have a creditor attach his or her interest.

tenant Person who assumes the temporary legal right to possess the property.

tender An offer of a party in a contract to be ready, willing and able to perform a duty outlined in that contract.

tender of delivery Requirement that the seller/lessor have and hold conforming goods at the disposal of the buyer/lessee and give the buyer/lessee reasonable notification to enable him or her to take delivery.

tender offer The offering to shareholders of a price above their stock's current market value.

term-life insurance Life insurance that provides coverage for a specified term.

termination In a contract, when an offer can no longer be accepted as part of a binding agreement, or when an offeree no longer has the power to form a legally binding contract by accepting the offer; an offer can terminate in one of five ways: revocation by the offeror; rejection by the offeree; death or incapacity of offeror; destruction or subsequent illegality of subject matter of the offer; or lapse of time or failure of other condition stated in the offer.

termination statement An amendment to a financing statement that states that a debtor has no obligation to the secured party.

tertiary-line injuries When someone who is given an illegally low price passes his or her savings to the customers.

testamentary capacity The minimum age required to write a legal will and be of sound mind.

testator A person who writes a will.

testamentary trusts An express trust created by a will.

third-party beneficiary Created when two parties enter into a contract with the effect of benefiting a third party.

time instrument A type of draft allowing the payee to collect payment only at a specific time in the future.

tippee One who receives confidential information from an insider.

tipper An insider who gives inside information to someone.

tipper/tippee theory A theory of insider trading that holds that any individual who acquires material inside information as a result of an insider's breach of duty has engaged in insider trading. The individual who has received a tip from an insider is called a tippee; the insider who gives the inside tip is called the tipper.

Title VII of The Civil Rights Act of 1964 (CRA) (as amended by the Civil Rights Act of 1991) Federal law that protects employees against discrimination based on race, color, religion, national origin, and sex. Also prohibits harassment based on the same protected categories.

tombstone advertisement Print advertisement announcing a forthcoming sale of securities with a layout and format similar to a tombstone.

tort A violation of another person's rights or a civil wrongdoing that does not arise out of a contract or statute. Torts are most commonly classified as intentional, negligent, or strict liability torts.

tort feasor A person who commits an intentional or through-negligence tort that causes a harm or loss for which a civil remedy may be sought.

trade dress The overall appearance and image of a product.

trade libel A business tort that occurs when false published-in-printed-form statements are criticisms of a business product or service that resulted in a loss of sales.

trade secret A process, product, method of operation, or compilation of information that gives a businessperson an advantage over his or her competitors.

trademark A distinctive mark, word, design, picture, or arrangement used by a seller in conjunction with a product and tending to cause the consumer to identify the product with the producer.

trademark dilution The use of "distinctive" or "famous" trademarks, such as McDonald's, in such a manner as to diminish the value of the mark.

transfer warrant A warranty created by a party who transfers a negotiable instrument regarding the instrument and the transfer.

traveler's check An order that is payable on demand, is drawn on or through a bank, is designated by "traveler's check," and requires a countersignature. A traveler's check contains a copy of the customer's signature and requires a countersignature for verification.

treaty A binding agreement between two states or international organizations.

trespass to personality The temporary interference with another's use or enjoyment of his or her personal property.

trespass to realty A tort that occurs when someone goes on another's property without permission, or places something on another's property without permission.

trial An event in which parties to a dispute present evidence in court, before a judge or a jury, in order to achieve a resolution to their dispute.

trial court (court of original jurisdiction) Also called court of first instance; a court in which most civil or criminal cases start when they first enter the legal system. In these courts, the parties present evidence and call witnesses to testify. Trial courts are referred to as courts of common pleas or county courts in state court systems and district courts in the federal system.

trust A business arrangement in which stock owners appoint beneficiaries and place their securities with trustees, who manage the company and pay a share of their earnings to the stockholders.

trust endorsement An endorsement that allows the endorser rights of a holder by virtue of the trust endorsement.

trustee In bankruptcy proceeding, an individual who takes over administration of debtor's estate.

trustees Those who operate a trust for beneficiaries in a business trust.

tying arrangement When the sale of one product is tied to the sale of another.

unconscionability When one party has so much more bargaining power than another party that he or she dictates the terms of an agreement and eliminates the other party's free will.

underwriter The party who receives the payments from the insured party and makes the payment to the beneficiary.

undisclosed principal When a third party does not know an agent is acting on behalf of a principal.

undue influence When one party has taken advantage of his or her dominant position in a relationship to unduly persuade the other party and when the persuasive efforts of the dominant party have interfered with the ability of the other party to make his or her own decision.

unemployment compensation State system, created by the Federal Unemployment Tax Act (FUTA), that provides unemployment compensation to qualified employees who lose their jobs.

unenforceable When a law prohibits a court from enforcing the terms of a contract.

unfair competition Competing with another for the sole purpose of driving that other out of business and not to make a profit.

unfortunate accident An incident that simply could not be avoided, even with reasonable care.

unidentified principal A principal whose relationship with the agent has not been made known.

Uniform Commercial Code (UCC) A statutory source of contract law in the United States applicable to transactions involving the sale of goods. Code was created in 1952 and adopted by all 50 states, the District of Columbia, and Virgin Islands; may be modified by each state to reflect the wishes of the state legislature.

uniform law Laws created to account for the variability of laws among states. These laws serve to standardize the otherwise different interstate laws (also called **model law**).

unilateral contract A promise exchanged for an act.

unilateral mistake The result of an error by one party about a material fact, i.e., one that is important in the context of a particular contract.

United Nations Convention on Contracts for the International Sale of Goods (CISG) The legal structure for international sales, including business-to-business sales contracts.

universalization test The ethical guideline that urges us to consider, before we do an action, what the world would be like if everyone acted in this way.

unliquidated debt When the parties either dispute the fact that any money is owed or agree that some money is owed but dispute the amount.

unqualified opinion letter Letter issued by an auditor when the financial statements presented are free of material misstatements and are in accordance with GAAP.

unprotected speech Although the First Amendment gives the right to free speech, limited types of speech are not protected by the First Amendment including hate speech, insulting or fighting words, defamation, or speech that harms the reputation of another.

usage of trade Any practice that members of an industry expect to be part of their dealings.

usury Charging an exorbitant or unlawful rate of interest.

utilitarianism The ethical principle that urges individuals to act in a way the creates the most happiness for the largest number of people.

V

valid An enforceable contract that includes all four elements of a contract: an offer and agreement, consideration, contractual capacity, and a legal object.

values Positive abstractions that capture our sense of what is good and desirable.

venue (1) The place where a hearing takes place. Its geographic location is determined by each state's statutes and based on where the parties live or where the event occurred or the alleged wrong was committed.

venue (2) A legal doctrine relating to the selection of a court with subject-matter and personal jurisdiction that is the most appropriate geographical location for the resolution of the dispute.

vertical merger When a company at one level of the manufacturing-distribution system acquires a company at another level of the system.

vertical restraint against trade When two parties at different levels in the manufacturing-distribution system make an agreement that restrains trade.

vest The maturing of rights such that a party can legally act upon the rights.

vicarious liability The liability or responsibility of a person, a party, or an organization for damages caused by another. It is most commonly used in relation to employment, where the employer is vicariously held liable for the damages caused by its employees.

virtue ethics The ethical system concerned with the development of character traits. This system proposes that a decision is ethical when it promotes positive character traits like honesty, courage, or fairness.

virus A computer program that rearranges, damages, destroys, or replaces computer data.

void Contract that is not valid because its object is illegal or it has some defect that is too serious.

void title Not true title; as when someone knowingly or unknowingly purchases stolen goods.

voidable When one or both parties has the ability to either withdraw from a contract or enforce it.

voidable title Occurs in situations where the contract between the original parties would be void but the goods have already been sold to a third party.

voir dire Process of questioning potential jurors to ensure that the jury will be made up of nonbiased individuals.

W

waiting period The period after an issuer files a registration statement and prospectus with the Securities and Exchange Commission requesting to offer a security and before the offer is approved by the SEC, which is a minimum of 20 days.

Wagner Act The first major piece of federal legislation adopted explicitly to encourage the formation of labor unions and provide for collective bargaining between employers and unions as a means of obtaining the peaceful settlement of labor disputes.

warehouse receipt A receipt issued by one who is engaged in the business of storing goods for compensation.

warranties Assurances, either express or implied, by one party that the other party can rely on its representations of fact.

warranties of title An assurance inferred in every UCC sales transaction that the seller has good and valid title to the goods and has the right to transfer title free and clear of any liens, judgments, or infringements of intellectual property rights of which the buyer does not have knowledge.

warranty A binding promise regarding a product in the event that the product does not meet the manufacturer's or seller's promises.

warranty liable Liability attributed when the transfer of an instrument breaches a warranty associated with an instrument.

waste Permanent and substantial injury to the landlord's property.

watered stock Stock issued to individuals below its fair market value.

white-collar crime Crimes performed by white-collar employees.

whole-life insurance Life insurance that provides protection for the entire life of the insured.

will A legal document that outlines how a person wants his or her property distributed upon death.

winding up The act of completing unfinished partnership business.

workers' compensation laws State laws that provide for financial compensation to employees or their dependents when the covered employee is injured on the job.

workers' compensation policy Provides payment to employees who are injured through an employment-related accident.

working papers The various documents used and developed during an audit, including notes, calculations, copies, memorandums, and other papers constituting the accountant's work product.

World Trade Organization An international organization facilitating international cooperation in opening markets and providing a forum for future trade negotiations and the settlement of international trade disputes.

WPH process of ethical decision making A set of ethical guidelines that urges us to consider: whom the action affects, the purpose of an action, and how we view its morality (whether by utilitarian ethics, deontology, etc).

writ of certiorari A decision by the Supreme Court to hear an appeal and order the lower court to send to the Supreme Court the record of the appealed case.

writ of execution A court order authorizing a local law officer to seize and sell any of the debtor's real or personal nonexempt property within the court's geographic jurisdiction to enforce a judgment awarded by the court.

writing A type of documentation showing contractual intent that can satisfy the statute of frauds requirement.

wrongful civil proceedings A civil action brought against a person with no justifiable basis for the action.

wrongful dissolution A dissolution of a partnership in violation of its partnership agreement.

Z

Zoning Restrictions placed by the government on the use of property to allow for the orderly growth and development of a community and to protect the health, safety, and welfare of its citizens.

Name Index

K

L

M

N

O

P

Q

R

S

T

W

Y

Subject Index

A

B

C

D

E

F

H

J

K

L

M

N

S

T